Violano Virtuoso
F.H. ROBINSON

# ENCYCLOPEDIA

*of*

# Automatic Musical Instruments

by

**Q. DAVID BOWERS**

Cylinder Music Boxes
Disc Music Boxes
Piano Players and Player Pianos
Coin-Operated Pianos
Orchestrions
Photoplayers
Organettes
Fairground Organs
Calliopes
and other self-playing instruments
mainly of the 1750-1940 era

---

Including a
Dictionary of Automatic Musical Instrument Terms

Published by THE VESTAL PRESS / VESTAL, NEW YORK 13850 U.S.A.

*Library of Congress Card Catalogue Number: 78-187497*
*International Standard Book Number (ISBN): 0-911572-08-2*



*Other books by Q. David Bowers:*

*Coins and Collectors*
*Early American Car Advertisements*
*Guidebook of Automatic Musical Instruments, Vol. I and II*
*Put Another Nickel In*
*U.S. Half Cents 1793-1857*



*Correspondence relating to the editorial content and information contained in this book may be addressed to: Q. David Bowers; Post Office Box 1669; Beverly Hills, California 90210. European correspondents may write to: Q. David Bowers; c/o Mekanisk Musik Museum; Vesterbrogade 150; Copenhagen, Denmark.*

*The picture for the dust jacket and for the frontispiece was done by artist Ted Robinson of Vestal, New York, especially for this book. It is adapted from an early Mills Novelty Company advertising drawing.*

*To:*
*Mary, Wynn, and Lee at home*
*and Claes in Denmark*

*. . . for enthusiasm and encouragement*

# THOSE WHO HELPED


Although specific acknowledgements are given throughout the text, the author thanks the following persons for help in various ways — ranging from supplying a single picture or piece of historical data to contributing an editorial section of this book:

"Doc" Abrams, Dan Adams, Frank Adams, William Allen, Roy Arrington, Automatic Musical Instrument Collectors Association (AMICA).

Joseph Bacigalupi, Giovanni Bacigalupo, Els Baets, Richard Baker, Gene Ballard, Nelson Barden, A.E. Barham, Carl Barker, Charles Barnes, Mr. Barny, Donald D. Barr, Leo F. Bartels, W.J. Bassil, Baud Frères, Adolf Baude, Emil Baude, E. Bayly, Melvin Beardsley, Herbert Becke, Ted Behymer, Walter Bellm, Leo Benson, Rice Berkshire, D.R. Berryman, Tom B'hend, George Bidden, Robert and Virginia Billings, Etienne Blyelle, Hendrik Bocken, Vince Bond, Karl Bormann, Ruth G. Bornand, Terry Borne, Sen. Charles Bovey, Van Allen Bradley, David Bright, Morris Bristol, Arthur Bronson, Gustav Bruder, Otto Bruder, Leon Bryan, Noël Burndahl, Arthur Bursens, E.C. Byass.

John E. Cann, Otto Carlsen, James Carroll, Donald Carter, Ken Caswell, W.G. Chamberlain, John E.T. Clark, Murray Clark, Dr. George and Susie Coade, Eric V. Cockayne, Jerry and Sylvia Cohen, Jocko Conlon, J. Lawrence Cook, Orville Cooper, G.T. Cushing.

J.C. Daggs, Warren Dale, Jacob DeBence, Max Deffner, Demusa, James DeRoin, Eugene DeRoy, Max Donath, Jerry Doring.

Paul Eakins, James Elfers, H. Epton.

Clarence and Marguerite Fabel, Fair Organ Preservation Society, Dr. John Field, Dr. Howard and Helen Fitch, G. Flynn, Rita Ford, Amos Fowler, Carl Frei, Jr., Harold Freiheit, Ed Freyer, Claes O. Friberg, Gert B. Friberg, Frederick Fried, Lt. Col. Jackson Fritz, From Music Boxes to Street Organs Museum.

Kenneth C. German, Mr. and Mrs. Robert W. Gibson, Michael Gilbert, J.J. Gillet, Larry Givens, Sam Gordon, John Gourley, Lewis Graham, Frank S. Greenacre, Roger Gregg, Leonard Grymonprez, Oscar Grymonprez, Guesthouse of the Sun (Gasthaus Sonne), Murtogh D. Guinness.

Spencer Hagan, Leslie Hagwood, Ben M. Hall, M.A. Hall, Bernard F. Hallenberg, Roy Haning, Keith Harding, C.H. Hart, Terry Hathaway, Paul Haug, Ed Hayden, Douglas Heffer, Tom Herrick, Douglas Hickling, C.E. Hine, Hobbies Magazine, Judge Roy O. Hofheinz, Clay Holbrook, Frank Holland, Robert Horn, Richard Howe, Günther Hupfeld.

Albert Imhof.

Ellsworth Johnson, Robert Johnson, Alex Jordan, David L. Junchen, Carl Jung.

P.M. Keast, W. Keating, Lloyd G. Kelley, Donald G. Kemp, Les King, Osborne Klavestad, Kring van Draaiorgelvrienden, Heinz Kuhn, Steve Kukich.

Lyndesay G. Langwill, Steve Lanick, Milt Larsen, Oskar Lensch, Stephen M. Leonard, Alan Lightcap, Lincoln Center of the Performing Arts, Edwin A. Link, Mr. and Mrs. Gordon Lipe, Jesse Lippincott, Jr., Arthur List, Jr., Little Falls Felt Shoe Co., Mel Locher, Richard Lokemoen, A. Lomas.

Donald MacDonald, Jr., G.W. MacKinnon, James Mangan, Marken Collection, Lyle Martin, A.B. Mason, John Maxwell, H.B. McClaran, McGraw-Hill Publishing Co., Wallace McPeak, Lannon F. Mead, Mekanisk Musik Museum, Tom Merkx, Dr. Byron Merrick, George Messig, A. Middleton, James Miller, Dr. Robert Miller, Arthur Mills, Michael Montgomery, Max Morath, Roger Morrison, Musical Box Society of Great Britain, Musical Box Society International, Musical Wonder House.

Leonard Nadel, Mildred Neaman, Milo Nellis, J.B. Nethercutt, Netherlands Film Museum, Nordisk Pressefoto.

Ralph and Elaine Obenchain, Arthur W.J.G. Ord-Hume, Drs. Robert and Edith Owen.

Marg Paape, Duke Parish, Pavilion Amusement Park, Gijs Perlee, Stan Peters, Howard Philipps, Alan R. Pier, Wyatte Pittman, Player Piano Group, Carlo Polidori, Harold Powell, James Prendergast, Arthur Prinsen, Edwin Pugsley.

Q-R-S Music Rolls, Inc.

Benjamin G. Rand, Arthur Reblitz, Kenneth Redfern, A.E. Reed, Victor Reina, Frank Rider, Ripley Collection, Eduard Robbins, Richard Robbins, Don Robertson, David Robinson, P.S. Robinson, Dr. David Rockola, Harvey and Marion Roehl, Dr. Joseph Roesch, Willy Rombach, Dr. Benoit Roose, Louis Rosa, Christopher Ross, Royal American Shows, Hughes Ryder.

Gary Sage, Arthur Sanders, David Saul, Peter Schaeble, Richard Schlaich, E. Jan Schoondergang, Otto Schulz, William Scolnik, N. Marshall Seeburg, Ivan and Joan Shapiro, Bernard Shirar, Inger Sihm, Richard C. Simonton, William Singleton, Charles Smallwood, Thomas Sprague, Andy "Swede" Subwick, Al Svoboda.

W.J. Teunisse, Carl Thomsen, Ramsi P. Tick, Daniel Tillmanns.

Universal Studios, Colin P. Upchurch.

A. Valente, Frits van Butsele, H.E. Van der Boom, Jan L.M. van Dinteren, Van Hyfte Piano Co., Alain Vian, August Von Kleist (son of Eugene DeKleist), C.H. von Lehndorff.

E.F. Walcker & Cie., Raymond Wallace, Mr. and Mrs. John Watson, Graham Webb, Kathy Weber, Carl M. Welte, Edwin Welte, Neal White, Stewart Whitlock, Brian Williams, Heinrich Wolf, Harold Woodworth, Oswald Wurdeman, Farny Wurlitzer.

Louis Zaharakos, Edward Zelinsky, Dr. Helmut Zeraschi.

The following persons, also listed above, contributed text material in the categories indicated: Tom B'hend (American Photo Player Co.), John E. Cann (Regina Music Box Co.), Claes O. Friberg (Hupfeld; portable hand-cranked barrel organs; general historical); Larry Givens ("How to Care for Your Collection"), Leonard Grymonprez (Th. Mortier), Ben M. Hall (Welte Mignon reproducing piano), David L. Junchen (music roll arranging and perforating), Arthur W.J.G. Ord-Hume ("London in the 'Nineties;" general permission to use his writings in the automatic musical instrument field; permission to use information from "The Music Box," journal of the Musical Box Society of Great Britain), Arthur Reblitz (Link Piano Co.; Marquette Piano Co.; roll making), Richard C. Simonton (M. Welte & Söhne), Graham Webb (general permission to use his many writings in the field of cylinder and disc music boxes), Brian Williams (Q-R-S Music Rolls, Inc.).

Otto G. Carlsen and Eugene DeRoy, both now deceased, helped in many ways. Otto Carlsen provided much of what now comprises the author's collection of original catalogues and literature. Eugene DeRoy (see Symphonia Music Roll Co. section of this book) also provided many original catalogues, and accompanied the author on many trips seeking information in Europe. Both Otto G. Carlsen and Eugene DeRoy provided help in many other ways as well. They would have enjoyed reading this book.

Claes O. Friberg of Copenhagen, Denmark, founder of the Mekanisk Musik Museum (of which the author is also a co-owner and director), provided valuable assistance with historical information concerning many of the European firms whose products are described in this book. Claes' help with many portions of the manuscript, his many days and miles of travel in search of information, and his enthusiasm and friendship during the years in which this book was being prepared cannot be measured in words.

Larry Givens, author ("Rebuilding the Player Piano" and "Re-Enacting the Artist") and historian in the field of automatic musical instruments, proofread this book and helped with many technical details.

Terry Hathaway, a friend and business associate of the author, helped with much information in this book, particularly on the subjects of acoustics and mechanics.

Jan L.M. van Dinteren of Geleen, Holland, collector and enthusiast in the field of fairground organs, provided assistance with historical information concerning many organ builders.

To "whose who helped" in so many ways, the author expresses his appreciation. Without you the book would not have been written.

———Q. David Bowers

# TABLE OF CONTENTS


CYLINDER MUSIC BOXES ........ 15 to 96

Cylinder music boxes; automata; musical novelties; musical clocks and watches; related items.

DISC MUSIC BOXES ........ 97 to 252

Disc-type music boxes; disc-operated pianos; related instruments: Harmonia 107; Kalliope 108-111; Komet 112; Lochmann "Original" 113-117; Mermod Frères disc boxes and related instruments including Stella, Mira, Sirion, New Century 118-128; Polyhymnia; Monopol 129-131; Orphenion 132-133; F.G. Otto & Sons instruments including Capital, Criterion, Olympia, Pianette 134-143; Polyphon 144-169; Regina 170-212; Symphonion 213-236; Troubadour 237; Zimmermann instruments: Fortuna, Adler 238-242; Britannia 243; Imperial 243; Perfection 243; Saxonia 244; Libellion 244; Imperator 244-245; Miscellaneous types 104 and 246-247; "London in the 'Nineties," by Arthur W.J.G. Ord-Hume, 249-251.

PLAYER PIANOS ........ 253 to 270

Piano players; player pianos; related items.

REPRODUCING PIANOS ........ 271 to 342

Reproducing pianos; expression pianos: Ampico 277-292; Artecho 293; Artrio-Angelus 294; Duo-Art 295-310; Hupfeld 311-316; Philipps 317; Recordo 318; Welte-Mignon 319-338; Miscellaneous types 339-341.

COIN-OPERATED PIANOS; ORCHESTRIONS ........ 343 to 736

Coin-operated pianos; orchestrions; violin players; mechanical pianos; mechanical zithers; photoplayers; related instruments: Mechanical zithers 356-359; Mechanical dulcimers 360-361; Mechanical pianos and orchestrions 362-366; American Photo Player Co. 367-381; American Piano Player Co. 382; Auto-Electric Piano Co. 383; Automatic Orchestra Co. 384; Barbieri 385; Hegeler & Ehlers 385; Berry-Wood 386-387; Blessing 388-389; Chicago Electric 390; Dienst 391-394; Pierre Eich 395-396; Electrova 397; Encore Banjo 398-418; Etzold & Popitz 419; Frati 420-423; Harwood 424; Heilbrunn 425-426; Heizmann 427; Hofmann & Czerny (Continental Musikwerke) 428-429; Holzweissig 429; Hupfeld 430-462; Imhof & Mukle 463-479; Kaufmann 480; Link 481-487; Lochmann Original 488; Paul Lösche 489-493; Lyon & Healy 494-496; Marquette (Cremona) 497-505; Mills Novelty Co. 506-526; National 527; Nelson-Wiggen 528-532; Neue Leipziger Musikwerke 533; Saxon Orchestrion Manufactory 533; Niagara 534; North Tonawanda Musical Instrument Works 535-541; Operators Piano Co. (Coinola and Reproduco) 542-551; Peerless 552-562; Philipps 563-579; Piano Player Mfg. Co. 580-581; Pianotist 582; Popper 583-593; Regina 594-596; Resotone Grand 597; Seeburg 598-619; Standard 620; Symphonia (Eugene DeRoy) 621-623; Symphonion 624; Gebr. Weber 625-631; Welte 632-654; Weser 655; Wildbredt 655; Western Electric 656-660; Wurlitzer 661-702; Miscellaneous instruments, supplies, accessories 703-713; "Music Rolls and Their Makers," by David L. Junchen, 714-721; "How to Care for Your Collection," by Larry Givens, 730-736.

ORGANETTES; PLAYER ORGANS ........ 737 to 800

Organettes; player reed organs; player pipe organs: Organettes 746-776; Aeolian player reed organs 777-780; Wilcox & White player reed organs 781-782; Miscellaneous player reed organs 783; Organ clocks 784; Barrel-operated chamber organs 785-786; Estey player pipe organs 787 and 799; Electromagnetic Orchestra 787; Aeolian player pipe organs 788-790; Aeolian-Hammond player electronic organ 791; Welte Philharmonic Organ 792-798; Wurlitzer player pipe organs 799; Walcker player pipe organs 800; Kimball player pipe organs 800.

FAIRGROUND ORGANS ........ 801 to 944

Fairground organs; dance organs; portable hand-cranked barrel organs; street organs; calliopes; related instruments: Portable hand-cranked barrel organs 805-812; Artizan 813-814; Berni 815-817; Böcker (Boecker) 818-822; Bruder 823-832; Bursens 833-837; Calliopes (Tangley, National, etc.) 838-844; Cocchi 845; Decap 846-847; Dutch street organs 848-849; Duwyn 850; Frati 851-854; Carl Frei 855; Gaudin 856; Gavioli 857-868; Armitage Herschell 869-873; Hooghuys 874; Koenigsberg 875; Limonaire 876-883; Mangels 884; Marenghi 885-889; Molinari 890-891; Mortier 892-905; Muzzio 896; Niagara 907-908; North Tonawanda Musical Instrument Works 909-913; Parker 914-919; Ruth 920-922; Verbeeck 923; Wellershaus 924-926; Welte 927-928; Wrede 929; Richter 929; Wurlitzer 930-944.

DICTIONARY OF AUTOMATIC MUSICAL INSTRUMENT TERMS ........ 945 to 981

BIBLIOGRAPHY ........ 982

INDEX ........ 983 to 1008

The author and his two sons, Lee and Wynn, listen to a Mason & Hamlin Model B Ampico reproducing piano.

## PREFACE

What makes an old-time automatic musical instrument interesting? Interesting to hear? Interesting to own? For some, a music box "brings back the Good Old Days." And yet, few of us can remember when coin pianos, reproducing pianos, and other instruments of the 'twenties were in their height of popularity, even fewer can remember the golden age of music boxes, and none can remember the original use of instruments of an earlier era.

It may be the elusive, never-to-be-recaptured feeling of an earlier era – an era that, somehow, seems to be wistfully carefree and nostalgic – that makes such instruments fascinating today. The sound produced by a carefully restored instrument is the *exact sound* that our ancestors heard and enjoyed. Advancing technology, the grim reaper of so many things, has not marred the automatic instruments of an earlier era. One can listen to an old phonograph record or view an old film and comment, perhaps silently, that today's technology, if in use then, could have produced better products. Not so with automatic musical instruments. There is no since-obsoleted medium between you today and the "performer" of years ago. The performer is here today – and plays for you undiminished, with nothing lost and with nothing changed, just as in years past. The performance that delights you today may have delighted *in exactly the same way* Napoleon, Queen Victoria, the King of Siam, a San Francisco theatregoer, or a Paris streetwalker years ago. The emotions of another time, another place – the entertainment of another era comes to life unaltered and undimmed today.

The following paragraphs are included to transmit, at least in part, some of the enthusiasm I developed for automatic musical instruments. "How did it all begin?" is a question often asked. It is answered here:

My first encounter with a music box came in 1957 when I was a student at the Pennsylvania State University. Always interested in antiques and old things in general and in rare coins in particular (buying and selling rare coins paid my way through college and, since, has "subsidized" my interest in automatic musical instruments and their history) I was a frequent visitor to central Pennsylvania antique shops.

During one of these excursions I stopped to see a dealer who had a few old coins for sale. While there I was fascinated by a large console-type music box. Bearing the *Regina* trademark it could play metal tune discs and phonograph records with equal ease. In retrospect I believe it was a Style 240, but it may have been a different model. Tempted, I played the Regina several times. But other considerations intervened, and I left the music box behind.

My first purchase of a music box happened in the summer of 1960. By that time I had graduated from Penn State and had moved to Binghamton, New York, with my newlywed wife, Mary. My business was rare coins, an enterprise that had expanded greatly since college days. My hobbies were varied and included, among other things, a representative collection of presidential autograph letters and a group of old lithographs, primarily Currier & Ives.

It was a warm summer day in July when I ventured into an antique show held in Johnson City, New York's Endicott-Johnson auditorium. At one of the exhibit spaces I spied a rather plain-looking music box and, near it, a stack of gleaming metal discs separated by old newspaper sheets. I asked the age of the music box and was told that it was made in 1889, the patent date on the music discs, and that it was "very rare." A few minutes later, and after some half-hearted negotiation (I really wanted to own that box!) to unsuccessfully reduce the price asked, I was the proud owner. Later that day I played each of the discs through. None of the tunes was recognizable to me at the time. I picked a lilting tune, *The Last Rose of Summer*, as my favorite – and kept it in playing position on the box. In the years since 1960 I've come to recognize and like hundreds of obscure and long-forgotten tunes encountered in my experiences with automatic instruments. Anyone who wonders where an old-time radio show like *Stop the Music* ever found its unguessable tunes has only to look through a stack of old music box discs or piano rolls!

The little Regina music box, an 11" model, fascinated Mary and me. Soon presidential autographs and prints were forgotten, and the search for more music boxes was on!

Within the next few weeks I visited dozens of different antique shops. At first I expected to have my pick of many different music boxes. At the time Currier & Ives prints were fairly plentiful in shops, as were other items in which I had a collecting interest. I was very surprised to receive such replies from antique dealers as "I haven't seen one of those in years," and "I'd like to buy some music boxes, too. If you find some, let me know!" In short, none could be found.

A few weeks later I received a telephone call from Gobel Ziemer, a well-known antique dealer in Owego, New York. He had, he said, "something he wanted me to see." We lost no time in driving the twenty or so miles from Binghamton to Owego. There we were confronted with a truly beautiful cylinder music box. Although I didn't know it at the time, the box was made by Mermod Frères of St. Croix, Switzerland. The most unusual feature of the instrument was a little plate marked "Jacot's Patented Safety Check, 1886," which bobbed up and down as the instrument played. Fearful that what seemed to be the world's only available music box would slip away, I hastened to pay Mr. Ziemer's price. Today, this same box is a prized piece in the collection of Jerry and Sylvia Cohen (I traded it to them several years later). I see it on occasional visits to the Cohen home, and always look wistfully at it!

Up to autumn 1960 I thought that the world of automatic music consisted of an 11" Regina music box and a beautiful Swiss box with interchangeable cylinders. Then, on a trip to my parents' home near Harrisburg, Pennsylvania, my father told me of a "self-playing piano" he had seen at Wray's Music Company in the nearby town of Lemoyne. We all hurried to see it. Bearing the name *Automatic Musical Company*, it played whenever a nickel was dropped in its beckoning slot. Before even one tune finished playing I knew that I must have the piano. Soon I was the proud new owner.

The coin-operated piano whetted my appetite for more instruments of that nature. There was something really fascinating about the large cases, the unfamiliar and wonderful mechanisms, and the ornate appearance of these old-time music makers that gave them a charm I never before had experienced with any other items in the field of antiques. Incidentally, this charm and the thrill of seeing and hearing a restored but previously-silent-for-years instrument is still with me today – despite having seen and heard countless instruments since then.

Someone, I don't remember who, gave me the name and address of Mrs. Ruth Bornand. She was, they said, a dealer in all sorts of music boxes and other things. From Mrs. Bornand I acquired a Mills Violano-Virtuoso violin-player. Purchased as unrestored, it didn't play even a squeak. But it looked beautiful and I knew that with some restoration (something I didn't have the slightest knowledge of at the time!) it would be just like new someday. For the moment the most important thing was to own it as I had never heard of such a wonderful instrument before!

In 1961 my collection consisted of the 11" Regina music box, the Mermod box with three interchangeable cylinders in a light golden oak cabinet, a little Edison phonograph, the Automatic Musical Company coin piano, and the newly-acquired Violano-Virtuoso.

About this time, Miss Roz Spallone, a neighbor and a feature editor for the Binghamton *Evening Press* learned of my hobby and wrote an illustrated "human interest" article about it. At the time I had visions of receiving dozens of calls from Binghamton residents who had music boxes to offer me but days went by and, sadly, no such thing happened!

Also about this time Dave Greacen, a local businessman, asked me if I knew Harvey and Marion Roehl of nearby Vestal. "They have a fabulous collection of the things you are interested in," Dave said.

I wasted no time in contacting Harvey. I was rewarded immediately with an invitation to visit. There in the Roehl home I saw a virtual treasure trove of music boxes, nickelodeon pianos, large and wonderful instruments that Harvey called *orchestrions,* and other pieces — including a Wurlitzer merry-go-round organ and two pianos which played just like human pianists.

I asked Harvey and Marion if they knew where I could learn more about player pianos and orchestrions. Harvey showed me the work he was doing on his *Player Piano Treasury* book and said that, when published, it would have a lot of information. At that time he had no idea that it would go into many printings and sell thousands and thousands of copies!

In *Player Piano Treasury* Harvey Roehl pictures himself standing among instruments. The illustration is captioned: "This group of rare, early 44-note pianos represents, in spite of their deplorable condition, the sort of 'find' that all collectors dream of making! They were located in 1957 in a barn in downtown Providence, Rhode Island, by the writer who lost no time in acquiring them. There were 45 in all, and they formed the basis of the Roehl piano collection — many were sold and swapped for other machines, and some were kept. A few years later quite a number had been restored to their original condition by various owners . . . In the thirty or so years of storage in an unheated, unattended, and often damp barn, they became badly deteriorated, but not so much that many hours of work by a number of people weren't gladly spent in an effort to hear them once again!"

I inquired if Harvey had any instruments for sale. He offered me an Electrova 44-note cabinet piano from the Rhode Island hoard — a group which, by that time, had been reduced to just several extra instruments available for sale or trade. Further, Harvey and his wife Marion offered to show me all about restoring it if I cared to spend a few evenings in their workshop. I accepted. Soon I knew quite a bit of basic information about just what made various old-time instruments work.

The spark of enthusiasm ignited by my beginning collection of several instruments was fanned into a flame by seeing and hearing the Roehl instruments and learning of the interesting stories that went with them.

In various pursuits of business and hobbies I have always had an insatiable appetite for historical information. However, I soon learned that there was a big difference between finding information on other types of antiques and finding information about automatic musical instruments. The musical instrument references were so hard to find that, after several years of searching, I owned less than a single bookshelf full!

It was to make available the information that I had so much trouble in finding, information mostly available only on a loan basis from the proud catalogue owners, that I wrote *Put Another Nickel In* in 1965 and, in 1967, *A Guidebook of Automatic Musical Instruments* — the forerunner of the present volume.

The spark ignited in 1960 burns brighter than ever. Just before this book went to press I learned (via Günther Hupfeld, son of Ludwig Hupfeld) of the one-time existence of the Violina Orchestra, an automatic orchestra which incorporated a piano, three real violins, and other effects — all operated by a perforated paper music roll. And, as luck would have it, an actual specimen of one of these previously-unknown instruments turned up a few weeks later! My excitement was no less than the interest of eleven years earlier when I acquired my first Regina music box.

The desire to learn more about the history of automatic musical instruments has led me to travel hundreds of thousands of miles, including dozens of trips to Europe, during the past decade. Once, two days were spent on a long trip to view a previously-unseen Wurlitzer catalogue. That was a lucky trip. Others resulted in dead ends.

But the rewards were there. I often contemplate how fortunate I was to make the acquaintance of Eugene DeRoy, Stewart Whitlock, and others, now dead, who helped me with research in the 1960's. I used to visit Mr. DeRoy, who lived in Belgium, with a new list of dozens of questions each time! His answers, based upon his personal dealings with most of the automatic musical instrument makers in Europe, were graciously, carefully, and patiently provided. Gustav Bruder, one of the most brilliant men the field has ever seen, likewise answered seemingly-interminable questions about the days of another era. From these persons, hundreds of facts — information that would otherwise be lost to history or, perhaps even worse, incorrectly reconstructed — are in this book for your reading today. What a pity it is that we could not have interviewed the brothers Mermod, Gustave Brachhausen, the Nicole and Lecoultre partners, and other luminaries of years past.

Many others who live today — Farny Wurlitzer, Edwin A. Link, Howard Philipps, Günther Hupfeld, Benjamin Rand, are but a few of the people — provided first-hand experiences, data, clarification of mysteries, and help in many, many ways. This is, in a real sense, their book — for they and their predecessors made it all possible. What, for instance, would have happened if Farny Wurlitzer, then a young man of 19 years age, hadn't visited the Leipzig Trade Fair in 1902? Young Farny was thrilled with the orchestrions he saw — and set about importing them to America, a step which, with others, made Wurlitzer pre-eminent in the field during the early 20th century.

Automatic musical instruments, unlike many other objects from the past, don't just "stand there." They are ever-willing to perform with the flick of a switch or lever, the cranking of a handle, or the drop of a coin in a slot. As do most collectors, I feel that instruments are meant to be *enjoyed.* The instruments in my house are played and enjoyed often. It is not difficult to relate to the enjoyment that they provided others years ago. The Regina disc-changer spent most of its earlier life in a Connecticut mansion. The Hupfeld Super Pan Orchestra entertained thousands of visitors to a Holland restaurant from the 1920's to the 1960's. The Ampico reproducing piano was originally sold to a home in Bethlehem, Pennsylvania. The Hupfeld Phonoliszt-Violina saw use in a theatre in Sweden. What good times they must have seen (make that *they must have caused*) years ago!

In this book you will read about the influence that a Welte orchestrion, a self-playing orchestra, had on Mme. Adelina Patti, one of the foremost divas of the late 19th century. Miss Patti, who lived in a castle and who had every material comfort, considered the Welte to be her favorite possession. You'll read about Paderewski, Gershwin, and other immortals of the keyboard – and how their very personalities were captured by the ingenious mechanisms of the reproducing piano. You'll read about a calliope that was so powerful that it could be heard over ten miles away; and you'll read of musical watches that play so softly that you have to hold them up to your ear to appreciate the delicate melodies. You'll learn of Queen Victoria's successful 1851 concert, a command performance featuring automatic musical instruments made by the Kaufmann family. You'll learn of the concert that almost, but not quite, occurred when King Edward VII, inquisitive about the curious Mills self-playing violin, directed that one be brought before him.

Zulu-Kaffir music anyone? No problem if you have an Ariston organette! Lead your own orchestra and you don't even know the first thing about music? Simple, get an Aeolian Orchestrelle! You want the finest music for your hotel (or restaurant or, yes, your "sporting club")? Then buy a Wurlitzer PianOrchestra. Or a Hupfeld Helios. Or a Seeburg or Coinola.

I have tried to be factual throughout the book, and the author's opinions and conjectures, when stated, are clearly identified as such. However, with many other fields available for by-the-numbers and 1001-footnotes-type historical research, it seems to me that the history of automatic musical instruments should be treated otherwise. To be sure, the facts and figures are there (you can learn how many centimeters high, wide and deep a given Polyphon music box measures; you can learn precisely how many Wurlitzer Style LX orchestrions were made, etc.) – but I have included (and have identified as such) a generous serving of the romance that was once used to sell these instruments. Strip away the romance and you have the body – a bare skeleton of dictionary-type facts that you might refer to once in a while. I have included the skeleton but, equally important in my estimation, I have not overlooked the personality and charm of the instruments – in the hope that the combination of statistics, historical data, original advertising, and romance will impart to you the pleasure I have had visiting where the instruments were made, examining instruments and listening to them perform, and writing this book. It is my hope that you will *use* this volume and will refer to it often.

To me, automatic musical instruments have brought a fullness of life and appreciation of the past that would be impossible to duplicate in any other field. When I visited Waldkirch, North Tonawanda, and a hundred and one other places I did it for *you.* In that spirit, here is the *Encyclopedia of Automatic Musical Instruments.*

–––Q. David Bowers
Beverly Hills, California
March 1, 1972

### The Reason Why

In 1887, Edward Bellamy, in *Looking Backward,* wrote: "If we could have devised an arrangement for providing everybody with music in their homes, perfect in quality, unlimited in quantity, suited to every mood, and beginning and ceasing at will, we should have considered the limit of human felicity already attained."

Could Josef Hofmann, the immortal pianist, have heard the answer to Bellamy's dream when he wrote twenty years later of the Welte-Mignon, a piano which reproduced perfectly a recorded (on paper music rolls) artist's performance: "The incomparable Welte-Mignon Art Piano has opened an eventful future before the musical world. Henceforth the piano player will be on a level with the productive artist in regard to the imperishability of his work, since he will live for all time in his work. What a loss it means to us not to have had the Welte-Mignon long ago! But what a blessing it will prove to future generations!"

Would Bellamy have shared Johann Strauss' admiration for orchestrions (automatic orchestras) produced by Ludwig Hupfeld of Leipzig? Strauss noted that he was ". . . greatly delighted by the music of your Helios Orchestrions. Being myself a musician I was eager to hear what the sounding effect would be, and I must confess that nothing is missing from the music, whether it be euphony, fullness of tone, rhythm or accentuation. . ."

As impressive as they were in their day, such automatic musical instruments are now largely unknown to the public. Their era ended during the 1930's. Now, some forty years later, they are curiosities; museum pieces. Capable of playing *serious* music? Hardly, one might say. For isn't today's technology ever so much better? Could it be that our ancestors had something *better* than we have? Quite possibly. In fact, yes.

A few years ago the author received a letter from an official of a European government. The writer of the letter had learned of our interest in automatic musical instruments and was desirous of learning more about the field. What prompted his interest in these old-time devices? In his own words: "I recently visited Holland during a weekend trip and heard the great Hupfeld orchestrion in 's Hertogenbosch. I never dreamed such instruments existed!" Another letter, received just before this book went to press, was from one of Japan's leading industrialists – a gentleman who manufactures high fidelity components and who presumably is as up-to-date as it is possible to be on the subject of reproduced sound. It seems that he heard a Welte-Mignon reproducing piano on a trip to the United States. That the instrument, owned by a collector and carefully restored to its condition when new (c.1912), impressed him is an understatement. "Where have such instruments been all my life?" he asked. "Where can I buy one? Why aren't they being made today?"

Automatic musical instruments aren't a necessity of life; they are a *pleasure* of life. Those comparatively few instruments which survive today are appreciated for the curiosity, happiness, and other emotions they arouse in their listeners. Years ago the same instruments and their brethren were appreciated for the same reasons.

### The 19th Century and Earlier

Automatic or self-playing musical instruments date back to antiquity. Pipe organs which played simple tunes by means of a program arranged by placing pins in a pattern on a revolving barrel were used in ancient times. Records, usually incomplete so far as details of the mechanisms are concerned, tell of automatic flute-players, mechanical birds, and similar lifelike automata used in Europe during the 1500-1800 era. Such devices, however, were the playthings of royalty. The ordinary citizen had little chance of ever hearing one and an even slimmer chance of owning such an instrument or automaton. Music for the masses awaited the end of that period.

During the late 18th century workshops devoted to the manufacturing of self-playing instruments were established in several localities, especially in Switzerland and in the Black Forest section of Germany. By the early 1800's the Swiss, long famous for their watches, were producing music boxes which played melodies on a tuned steel music comb. The music was arranged on a brass cylinder by means of tiny protruding pins. Turned out by dozens of different artisans working in as many different workshops, these instruments were exported to France, England, and other countries where they found a ready market. Fine examples of these early Swiss boxes originally sold for the equivalent of just a few dollars. By 1880 the Swiss music box industry accounted for a sizable percentage of that country's exports. Instruments were made in price ranges from a dollar or so up to elegant furniture-styled music boxes which sold for the equivalent of $5000 or more. The Swiss music box industry, active as it was, sharply diminished a decade later when the disc-type music box, a German innovation, captured the market.

At the same time the Swiss music box industry was in its infancy, a thriving business of building organ clocks – clocks which played melodies by means of organ pipes – was growing in the Black Forest. The popularity of these clocks spread worldwide. By the 1820's the Blessing family was operating a school to train craftsmen in the art of building organ clocks and related instruments. By the 1830's dozens of different workshops were turning out these musical products. The success of the organ clocks generated dreams of larger instruments – instruments that represented not just the sound of a flute (as did the organ clocks) but the sound of an *entire orchestra.* To be sure, a few such automatic orchestras, or orchestrions as they came to be known, had been built earlier – but not on a regular commercial production basis. By 1850, Blessing, Imhof, Welte, and several other makers saw a brilliant future awaiting them – and, in the meantime, had all the orders they could handle.

As the years went by, other types of automatic musical instruments became popular. By the 1890's, large factories, mostly in Germany and Switzerland, were busy producing automatic pianos, orchestrions, music boxes, fairground organs, and other items. In America tiny hand-cranked reed organs were made by the hundreds of thousands. Music was available for the masses. For under $10 one could buy a disc music box and a selection of the latest tunes to go with it, a small reed organ, or any one of many different automatic instruments produced for the home. Commercial establishments – hotels, beer halls, dancing pavilions, amusement parks, and other places – were candidates for self-playing pianos, loudly-voiced fairground organs, orchestrions, and other larger instruments, most of which cost from a few hundred dollars to several thousand dollars. Costlier yet were large orchestrions, many of which sold for $5000 to $10,000 or more, made by Welte and Imhof & Mukle. Staggering as these prices may seem today (these figures are the equivalent of paying perhaps $50,000 to $100,000 in terms of today's purchasing power), Welte nonetheless published a roster showing that many crowned heads of Europe and a goodly number of dukes, barons, and, in America in particular, businessmen, willingly parted with the needed sums.

### The 20th Century

The automatic musical instrument industry constantly changed. The charming and often exquisitely-wrought Swiss cylinder music boxes of the mid-19th century were obsolete by 1900. The disc-type music box, first produced in Germany and later produced in the United States and Switzerland as well, captured the market. By World War I the disc-type box became an anachronism – as it was replaced by still newer and seemingly more interesting products.

Music for the home was provided by the push-up piano player, a cabinet-style device that was operated by pushing its felt-covered mechanical "fingers" up to a nearby piano keyboard and pumping the device's foot pedals. During the 1900-1905 years, thousands of these piano players were sold, mostly for about $250 each. The appeal of taking a paper music roll, putting it on the device, and magically producing a veritable concert was a strong one. Once the demand was created for the push-up player, its successor, the player piano (with all of the mechanisms built into the piano case) almost sold itself. The "concert in your home" appeal was irresistible, and millions of player pianos were sold all over the world.

Early in the 20th century, the Welte firm introduced the Welte-Mignon, a piano which not only played the musical notes perforated on a music roll but which played with artistic expression as well. By means of special recording apparatus the very personality of a pianist – his performance with all of its tonal shadings and subtleties – was captured for posterity. The success of this instrument, called the reproducing piano, was immediate. Welte soon had competition in the field. By the 1920's virtually every famous keyboard artist had committed his playing to the rolls made by Welte, Ampico, or Duo-Art – the three leading reproducing piano systems.

The early 20th century saw great advances in the building of other types of automatic pianos. Nickel-in-the-slot electric pianos were first made in America in 1898. By 1905, Wurlitzer, Peerless, and several other makers were selling them as fast as they came off the production lines. By 1910 over a dozen large firms were actively producing a wide range of instruments from abbreviated 44-note cabinet pianos to orchestrions which imitated a six- or eight-piece band. In Germany the industry was even greater. From the factories of Hupfeld, Popper, Philipps, and others came a fantastic array of instruments. In 1909, Ludwig Hupfeld announced the sale of the first Helios V, an instrument which contained over 1000 pipes, which represented an orchestra of 120 musicians, and which was priced at $12,000. Soon the Phonoliszt-Violina (an automatic violin player) and the Pan (a sophisticated orchestrion which was said to be able to perfectly imitate a symphony orchestra) were being sold in quantity. Ever eager to innovate, the German makers introduced devices which changed rolls automatically, colorful scenic effects for piano and orchestrion fronts, and other ingenious things which helped to sell an ever-increasing number of instruments.

Meanwhile, music on the circus midway was being provided by wonderfully ornate fairground organs made by Bruder, Wurlitzer, Gavioli, and other firms. These instruments, voiced loudly in imitation of a military band, had a charm all their own.

Motion pictures drew millions of patrons into nickelodeon theatres each week. To accompany the action on the silent screen a new type of instrument, the photoplayer, was developed. Essentially, photoplayers were orchestrions built into low cabinets to fit in the orchestra pit under the screen. Thousands of photoplayers were sold in America for prices mostly in the $3000 to $6000 range.

### The End of an Era

By the late 1920's the automatic musical instrument field had developed a wonderful technology. Automatic violin players, orchestrions, reproducing pianos, pipe organs with roll-playing attachments, and other self-playing instruments had achieved veritable perfection. Clearly, music in the home and in public places had reached a high level. At the flick of a switch Paderewski himself played in your living room. Or a half dozen of the world's great organists performed at your command. Or, in a hotel lobby or ballroom an unseen orchestra, its soul captured in the perforations of a music roll, filled the air with a majestic concert. Only one thing was missing to complete this perfect picture: enough customers to buy the instruments.

What happened? No one thing caused the demise of the automatic musical instrument business. Disc-type music boxes fell victim to the popularity of the phonograph. World War I severely curtailed the production of large orchestrions in Europe. When the war ended, economic hard times restricted the number of customers who were willing to pay thousands of dollars for large instruments. In America, Prohibition closed taverns, at least officially. The speakeasies of the 1920's were customers for small types of automatic pianos, not large ones. Sound movies replaced silent films in the late 1920's, thus ending the market for photoplayers. Although the phonograph co-existed with the player piano and the reproducing piano in the 1920's, the radio did not. Those once in the piano industry credit the radio as the factor in the great reduction of automatic piano sales which began in 1926-1927. Likewise, the use of radio programs in public places ended the market for coin pianos (automatic phonographs, or "juke boxes" as they are called, were not produced in large quantities until the early 1930's – so had little effect on the coin piano field). By 1929 there wasn't much left of the automatic musical instrument business. What little remained fell victim to the economic depression in America and Europe.

Within a few years the thousands of technicians, parts suppliers, and others so essential to the industry had turned to other fields. The factories were converted to other uses. The momentum, once lost, was never regained.

Today, when one considers the scientific and technological advances in our everyday life, one cannot help but feel certain that things will be even still more advanced forty or fifty years from now. One can only surmise that the builders of automatic musical instruments had similar thoughts in the 1920's. What would the reproducing piano or orchestrion of the 1970's or 1980's be like? Inconceivably wonderful, no doubt. It didn't work out that way. If the instrument makers of years ago could have foretold the future, would they have been happy? In a way, perhaps – as it might have been satisfying to know that one was living in the industry's ultimate era; its highest point. But in a way it would have been disappointing to realize that the end was near. "What a blessing [the reproducing piano] will prove to future generations" noted Hofmann in 1907. The "future generations," alas, were to forget their musical endowment.

### Instruments Today

Today the automatic musical instruments of generations past are again being appreciated – for their history, for their curiosity value, for their music.

Many of the instruments described in the following pages are known only by their catalogue descriptions; no actual examples have survived the ravages of time. Others, fortunately, are still with us. If you are interested in learning about the several non-profit organizations whose members are dedicated to the preservation of these instruments and their history, request the "Collectors' Organizations List" and send a self-addressed stamped envelope to the Vestal Press.

# AUTOMATIC MUSICAL INSTRUMENTS — Periods of Greatest Popularity

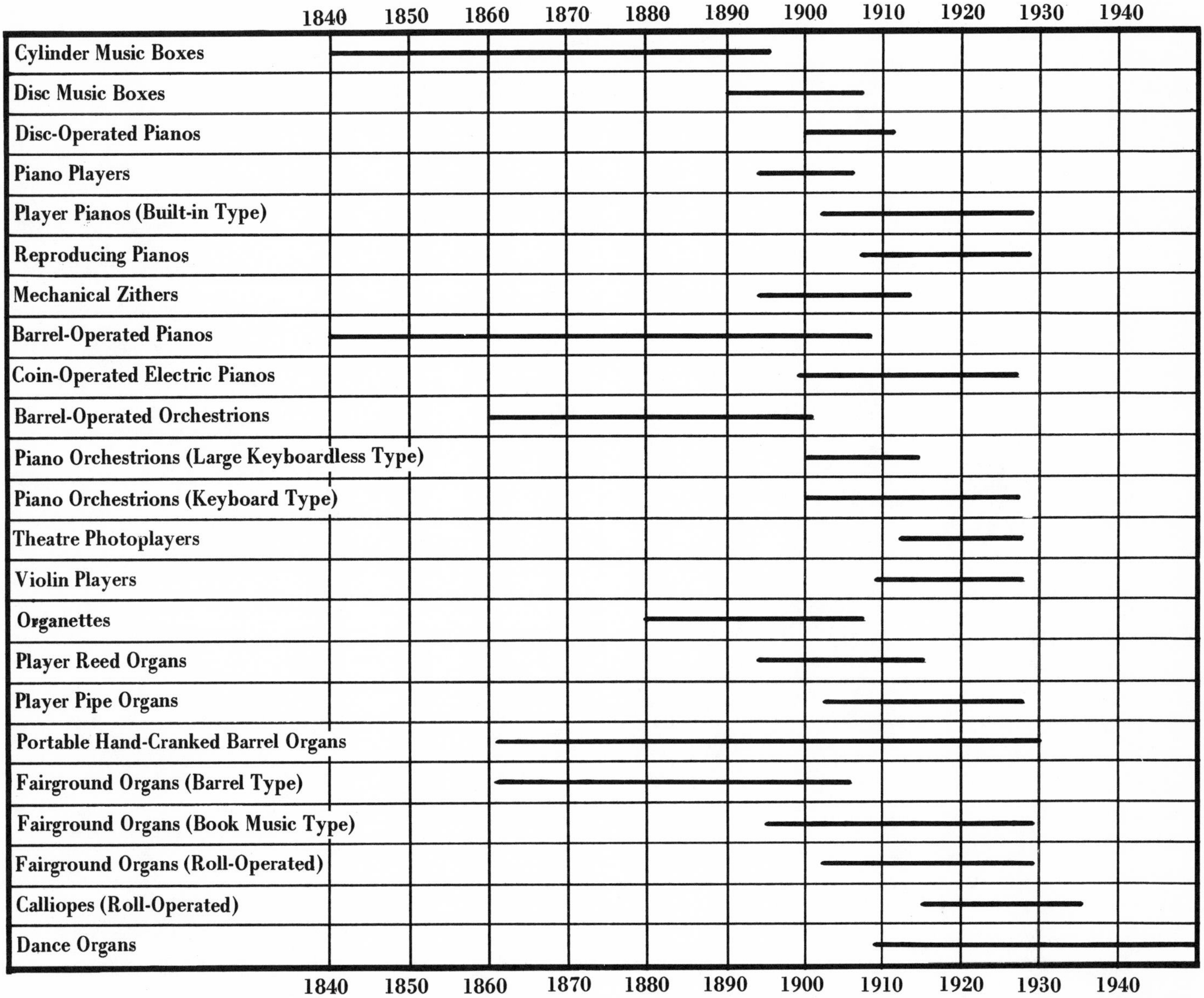


Notes: The spans shown are the periods of *greatest* popularity of the various automatic musical instrument types. In most instances instruments were made in smaller quantities before and after the year spans indicated. The above spans consider instruments on a worldwide basis. If individual countries were to be considered, there would be some differences. For instance, the reproducing piano market was very active in Europe nearly a decade before comparable activity occurred in the United States. Large keyboardless piano orchestrions sold well in Belgium and Holland during the 1920's, well after the market for such instruments ended in most other parts of the world. Some automatic instruments — player pianos, portable hand-cranked barrel organs, fairground organs, and dance organs are examples — are still being made today, but the quantities produced are far less than they were during the periods of greatest popularity as indicated above.

## LEADING MANUFACTURERS
### of Automatic Musical Instruments

We list several leading manufacturers for each category given above. If a firm was dominant in Europe, the name is followed by a †. Corresponding American firms are indicated by an *.

CYLINDER MUSIC BOXES: L'Epee (France); in Switzerland: Abrahams, Baker-Troll, Mermod†, Nicole, Paillard†, and many others.

DISC MUSIC BOXES: Kalliope, Monopol, Polyphon†, Symphonion†, Regina*.

DISC-OPERATED PIANOS: Lochmann†, Polyphon†, Regina (sold Polyphon instruments), Symphonion.

PIANO PLAYERS: Aeolian*, Melville Clark, Hupfeld†, Wilcox & White.

PLAYER PIANOS (built-in type): Aeolian*, Autopiano, Hupfeld†, hundreds of other brand names.

REPRODUCING PIANOS: Ampico*, Duo-Art*, Hupfeld, Welte†, Welte (Licensee)*.

MECHANICAL ZITHERS: Chordephon†, Triola.

BARREL-OPERATED PIANOS: Many different makers; no dominant firm.

COIN-OPERATED ELECTRIC PIANOS: Hupfeld†, Seeburg*, Wurlitzer*.

BARREL-OPERATED ORCHESTRIONS: Imhof & Mukle, Welte†, other Black Forest (Germany) area makers.

PIANO ORCHESTRIONS (Large Keyboardless Type): Hupfeld†, Imhof & Mukle, Philipps, Popper, Weber, Welte.

PIANO ORCHESTRIONS (Keyboard Type): Hupfeld†, Operators Piano Co., Philipps†, Popper, Seeburg*, Wurlitzer*.

THEATRE PHOTOPLAYERS: American Photo Player Co.*, Seeburg*, Wurlitzer*.

VIOLIN PLAYERS: Hupfeld†, Mills Novelty Co.*

ORGANETTES: Many different manufacturers.

PLAYER REED ORGANS: Aeolian*†, Spaethe, Wilcox & White.

PLAYER PIPE ORGANS: Aeolian*†, Welte*† (both firms active in Europe and America)

PORTABLE HAND-CRANKED BARREL ORGANS: Many different manufacturers.

FAIRGROUND ORGANS (Barrel Type): Bruder, Frati†, Gavioli†, Limonaire, Ruth.

FAIRGROUND ORGANS (Book Music Type): Bruder†, Gavioli†, Limonaire, Ruth.

FAIRGROUND ORGANS (Roll-Operated): Bruder†, Wurlitzer*.

CALLIOPES (Roll-Operated): National, Tangley*.

DANCE ORGANS: Bursens, Mortier†, Decap†.

# CYLINDER MUSIC BOXES

Cylinder Music Boxes
Musical Novelties
Automata

Characteristics of the Cylinder Box

The term "cylinder music box," or musi*cal* box (the preferred term in Europe), may be defined as a self-playing musical instrument, usually actuated by winding a spring, which plays one or more tunes by plucking the tuned teeth in a steel music comb with metal pins arranged in the form of a musical composition on a revolving metal cylinder.

The various components of the cylinder music box are attached to a common foundation or bedplate of brass (early instruments) or iron. The bedplate with its mechanisms is housed in a case or cabinet of wood. The case acts as a sounding board and amplifies the tone.

Important parts of the cylinder music box are:

(1) The Comb: The musical comb consists of a series of tuned teeth or prongs which when plucked by the pins in the cylinder cause the desired notes to play. Very early combs are not really combs at all but are individual teeth, each of which is affixed to a common bedplate with its own metal screw. Later combs made during the closing years of the 18th century and during the first two or three decades of the 19th century often have several (groups of four or five are common) teeth made as a unit and, when several such groups are affixed to a bedplate together, are called sectional combs. After the 1820 - 1830 period most music combs were made as a single unit. This format was continued until the production of larger types of cylinder instruments ceased during the early 20th century. Some later boxes, particularly large ones, were made with single-unit combs in groups for special effects: sublime harmonie, forte-piano, etc., as will be noted later in the text.

Music combs are made of steel. The temper of the metal was varied to produce desired effects. Soft steel combs produce a mellow tone, extremely hard steel a harsh or strident tone. The pitch of a tooth in the music comb is dependent upon the number of vibrations it makes per second.

In his book, "Mechanical Musical Instruments," Dr. Alexander Buchner discusses some principles relating to comb tuning and construction:

"The sound mechanism in these musical boxes was the steel comb with teeth of different length, each representing a certain note. The comb had to have as many teeth as there were notes in the piece to be played by the musical box. The tuning of these teeth was an empirical business; the lower notes called for longer teeth, but for the very lowest they had to fix small lead weights [resonators] to the end of the teeth, slowing down the oscillation and producing a deeper note than corresponded to the length of the tooth.

"Today we know that the teeth of the comb are governed by the laws of cross-oscillating bars, which means that the rate of oscillation depends more or less on the length of the teeth and the material they are made from, in direct relation to the length and the square root of the modulus of elasticity. On the other hand it is in the opposite relation to the square of the length and the root of the specific weight. For this reason the breadth of the teeth, for example, had no effect on the note sounded.

"Nevertheless it seems that there is no fixed law governing the relation between the height or depth of the tone and the strength or length of the teeth. If the tooth was weaker toward the bedplate end, it gave a lower note than if it was weaker towards the tip. It was possible to reduce the rate at which the teeth had to be lengthened partly because of the law of acoustics by which a bar (in this case the tooth) when reduced by half its length gives out a note two octaves higher and not, as do strings, only one octave higher; and partly by the lead resonators placed beneath the tip of the longest teeth. Therefore the teeth of a comb are not of such differing lengths as the strings on a stringed instrument."

As a general rule most music boxes made before the mass-marketing years of the 1870's and 1880's have softly-toned musical combs which have smaller and more finely-shaped teeth than their descendants.

Beginning in the 1870's and continuing until the end of the cylinder music box era the emphasis shifted to such non-musical considerations as the total number of airs or tunes on a cylinder, the loudness or volume, and the appearance of the instrument. The finely-spaced combs of an earlier era gave way to widely-spaced combs which permitted a cylinder to play eight, ten, or even more tunes, instead of the two to six found on earlier instruments. The softly-toned combs were replaced by harder steel combs which sacrificed sweetness and musical quality for sheer volume of sound.

The typical cylinder music box of 1900, with its raspy tone, simply arranged music, and cheap case, was but a musical shadow of the fine cylinder boxes of decades earlier.

A tooth in a music comb, particularly a large bass tooth, will continue to vibrate for many seconds after it has been plucked. If a cylinder pin comes into contact with a tooth which is still vibrating from a previous pin, a raspy or buzzing sound will be the outcome. This problem was solved in two ways. Often a music comb has two or more teeth tuned to the same note. If a note is to be sounded twice in quick succession it can be first sounded on one tooth and then on the other. The combs in disc music boxes, which are constructed similarly to those in cylinder boxes, used this method extensively – but it was used in cylinder instruments as well. However, the main solution to the repetition problem was to affix a tiny muting device called a damper to all but the shortest treble teeth. Early movements utilize a small piece of feather quill which is attached to the underside of each tooth. The cylinder pin, approaching the tooth from the underside, would come into contact with the quill damper first and would lightly push the quill against the still-vibrating tooth an instant before it was plucked again.

The quill damper was subject to wearing out quickly. The solution was found when the steel spring damper was devised about 1815. The spring damper fit into a tiny hole in the underside of the tooth and was secured there by a tapered metal pin. The spring, formed in a graceful curve which ended just beneath the tooth tip, effectively silenced the tooth when it was pressed against the tooth by a cylinder pin.

(2) The Cylinder. The cylinder consists of a hollow sleeve in which are inserted tiny metal pins. As the cylinder revolves these pins come into contact with the teeth in the music comb and cause the desired notes to be played.

The forerunner of the cylinder was the platform or disc movement. On the surface of a flat disc small pins were arranged in order. Separate steel teeth, arranged in a fanlike pattern around the periphery of the disc, played in the desired order as the tips of their teeth came into contact with the vertical pins. This type of movement, used mainly in the late 18th century for musical watches and snuffboxes, was suitable only for the simplest melodies. A great amount of energy was needed to drive this type of movement, and a high ratio of mechanical noise to musical sound was the result.

Arthur W.J.G. Ord-Hume, historian of the musical box, credits David Lecoultre, of Brassus, Switzerland, with the invention of the cylinder in its most familiar form: "[Lecoultre] applied the brass cylinder, already known in the manufacture of bell-playing carillon clocks for some years, to the musical box. He sought to make the cylinder play music from musical steel teeth arranged parallel to each other (as compared with the fan arrangement hitherto used in disc-type miniature movements and the laminated teeth arranged in a vertical 'stack' and driven by a studded spring barrel). The musical box now emerged in a form which we can recognize today.

"The thin-walled brass tube or cylinder was set with steel pins. This was turned with a fusee-wound spring motor at one end; and the power absorbed through a train of wheels ending in a governor at the other . . ."

The cylinder was programmed with a number of different tunes, ranging from two to over a dozen. After a tune is played, a cam or snail gear pushes the cylinder to the side ever so slightly, thus bringing a new arrangement of pins into the playing position. The number of tunes on a cylinder is dependent upon the care with which the cylinder pins are aligned and the spacing of the teeth tips. Widely-spaced tips, such as those commonly found on late 19th century boxes, permitted many tunes to be programmed on the cylinder.

The number of tunes on a cylinder is no gauge of an instrument's quality. By way of example, it takes about the same amount of effort to pin a cylinder to play four tunes on a musical comb of 120 teeth (such as would be the case for a fine early overture box with closely-spaced teeth) as it does to pin a cylinder to play twelve tunes on 40 teeth. The former box would be considered to be by far the more desirable of the two, but the latter would have more "promotional value" to the uninitiated buyer who wrongly believes that the more tunes, the better the box. It is precisely this situation that led to the deterioration of cylinder box quality in the late 19th century.

Cylinders were prepared by hand until the invention of the cylinder pricking or marking machine in the late 19th century. Arthur W.J.G. Ord-Hume describes the use of this instrument and the pinning of cylinders:

"The machine, at least in one form, consisted of a type of keyboard having one key for each note that could be played on the musical box comb. The brass cylinder was first of all scribed on the machine to represent the spacing between the points of the teeth. Then, in the first tune position, the cylinder would be rotated while the transcriber marked the music from the keys on to the cylinder. This job required an extremely high degree of both engineering and musical skill.

"When the cylinder pricker had finished with the cylinder, its surface was covered with small dents or marks. If a mistake was made he would scratch a tiny line through the incorrect mark, indicating that it must not be drilled.

"The pricked cylinder or barrel would then pass on to the piercer whose job was to drill a small hole through the thin brass shell at every prick mark. The piercer passed the cylinder on to the pinner who would insert a tiny wire pin into each hole. This job was often undertaken by women and even by young children. The pin wire for this was specially prepared on a pin lathe which notched the wire every quarter of an inch or so. This enabled the wire to be broken off easily after insertion, as well as providing a tapered end to push into the hole."

The cylinder was then filled with a combination of pitch, powdered stone, and other substances which were heated to the consistency of molasses. The cylinder, partially filled with this gooey mass, was then turned slowly on a lathe until the interior had cooled and hardened, leaving a hole through the cylinder suitable for inserting the shaft.

The cylinder was then taken to another lathe on which it was rotated at high speed as a grinding wheel moved back and forth to trim the pins to an even length.

Then a justifier, a specially trained craftsman, adjusted the pins individually to their correct positions so that all of the notes of the chords sounded at once, so that there were no wrong notes, and so on.

As a final step, cylinders on more expensive boxes were carefully polished, a task requiring great skill so as not to disturb the alignment of the pins. Some cylinders – Mermod Frères instruments of the 1880's and 1890's are examples – were brightly nickel plated. The cylinder was then ready for use in the music box. If the cylinder was destined for use in an interchangeable type of box, a serial number corresponding to the program card was stamped on one end and special flanges were attached for the changing mechanism.

(3) The Bedplate. The bedplate is the foundation for the music box mechanism. Early types were made of brass and were often highly polished. Later types were made of cast iron with a lined or textured upper surface which helped disguise any small irregularities in the casting. These later bedplates were often painted with a silver or gold finish.

The richness and resonance of a music box is directly related to the amount of mass that is set in motion by the vibrating music tooth. Around 1900 Paul Lochmann, the Regina Music Box Company, and several other makers found that by making the bedplate (in this instance, for disc boxes) as small as possible in relation to the music comb, a much greater degree of richness could be obtained. This acoustical discovery came too late for use in large cylinder instruments. However, it is generally conceded by collectors today that the finest tone is found in cylinder music boxes in which the bedplate serves its minimum function to support the comb, cylinder, and spring. Many large instruments with huge bedplates and with multiple springs, drum and orchestra attachments, and other accessories have a very weak tonal power as a large mass of metal must be set into vibration before the tone is transmitted to the music box case itself – which then acts as an amplifier and sounding board.

On many types of music boxes the maker's initials or

name can be found punched into the bedplate. The comb and the governor are other locations for such identification.

(4) Other Components: The mechanisms vary from one type of cylinder music box to another, but most contain these components: Power is provided by one or two (in the case of very large boxes) spring motors which are wound by a key, a lever, or a winding handle. The power from the spring motor is transmitted to the cylinder by a gear train. Connected to the cylinder by a series of gears is the governor which is usually in the form of a fan. Air resistance provides an effective way of regulating the speed. Some boxes have a separate speed regulator which utilizes friction to adjust the tempo. Other mechanisms provide for either changing the tune or repeating the previous one, as desired, for changing cylinders (on interchangeable cylinder instruments), for stopping and starting the box, etc.

(5) Music Box Cases: Early musical box movements were usually incorporated into watch or clock cases, into snuffboxes, or other items in which the musical movement played a secondary role. Beginning about 1810, music boxes achieved great popularity as a featured entertainment item on their own.

Most music boxes made from about 1810 through the 1860's are in rather plain cases, usually without ornamentation of any kind. Beginning in the 1860's the cabinetmaker's art joined that of the music box craftsman, and the result was a series of elaborate cases with decorative inlay, scalloped sides, ornate handles and fittings, and other frills. Custom instruments were made in the form of writing desks, ladies' cabinets, and other articles of furniture.

Most music boxes, even the smaller ones, of the 1870's and 1880's, were decorated with inlaid designs. These were nearly always on the top of the music box lid, slightly less often on the front, rarely on the ends, and almost never on the back. Most inlay work consisted of striping the edges of boxes with light-colored woods and applying a decorative scene, often of a musical theme, on the cover. More ornate cases were ornamented with inlaid brass, mother-of-pearl, polished stone mosaics, tooled silver, and other touches of elegance. It would be nice at this point to say that these very ornate boxes represented the zenith of the music box development, but such is not the case. The cabinets of the 1870's and 1880's, even the most expensive ones, usually contained musical movements of just average quality so far as craftsmanship and musical tone are concerned. However, the brightly polished mechanisms, the impressive-appearing large cylinders, the added percussion instruments, and other visual attractions make these instruments highly desired today for reasons of Victorian elegance if not for music!

## A Chronology of the Swiss Music Box

The birthplace of the cylinder music box was in the western part of Switzerland near the French border. The earliest musical movements related to the cylinder box were made as part of watches and clocks, the main industry in that part of Switzerland during the late 18th century.

During the 1790 - 1820 period the cylinder music box industry developed as an independent entity. The city of Geneva and the town of St. Croix were the two principal centers, but Neuchatel, Chaux de Fonds, LeLocle, Brassus, and other towns in the canton of Vaud each had from one to several makers. Until Paillard established a production-line factory in St. Croix in 1875 the business of music box making was a "cottage industry." Individual craftsmen would work in their homes, often isolated from the outside world by the deep snows of winter, and would build many examples of a particular part. One worker might build dozens of music box cases, another would assemble governor mechanisms, another would arrange musical compositions for use on cylinders, and so on. These various parts would then be taken to the main "factory," often a modest building no larger than a small home of today, and assembled.

Further to the south, in Geneva particularly, the factory system was more formally followed, and many components were made on the premises of Bremond, Baker, and others of that city. Even so, many parts were brought in from outside sources.

From the beginning the cylinder music box was identified as being synonymous with Switzerland. In later years some factories in France (such as the L'Epee works in St. Suzanne, c.1830 - 1914), Germany, Austria, Czechoslovakia, and elsewhere were established, but the production was small in relation to the output of the Swiss firms.

In the 1830 - 1860 period many fine musical movements were produced. Usually housed in simple rectangular cases, these music boxes were made for their musical qualities rather than their appearance. Most were of the key-wind type and played several tunes, usually overtures or operatic airs, on finely-made and closely-spaced music combs. Instruments of Nicole Frères, Lecoultre, Ducommun Girod, and their contemporaries of this era are highly desired by collectors today.

The 1860 - 1870 decade saw the appearance of a large number of ornately inlaid and decorated music box cases. The international expositions of 1851 and 1862, both of which awarded prizes for elaborately designed furniture, art objects, vehicles, implements, and other things, set the stage for the decorative era of music boxes.

The 1870 - 1890 era was one of great elegance. As noted earlier, some wonderfully ornate custom cases were built during this time. Even smaller instruments usually displayed elaborate inlay and other decorations. Such innovations as the orchestra box, the organ box, boxes with birds, the revolver box, and others, all of which are prime collectors' items today, reached their ascendancy during this period. Leading makers of these large instruments included Paillard, Bremond, Allard, Baker - Troll, and Greiner.

The 1890 - 1914 era marked the end of the age of large cylinder instruments. The disc-type of music box as made by Polyphon, Symphonion, Regina, and others drove the cylinder instruments from the marketplace. Some fine large cylinder instruments were made in the early 1890's, notably by Mermod Frères, but by 1900 the industry was, for all practical purposes, dead. Cheap small musical movements were made by B.H. Abrahams, by L'Epee, and by others until World War I, but production was small compared to former years. Except for small novelty movements, World War I ended what was left of the cylinder music box industry.

Since World War I musical movements have been made by Thorens, Reuge, and other Swiss firms and, more recently, by manufacturers in Japan. These instruments are mainly novelties and have cylinders measuring from about an inch to six inches in length.

———————

## TYPES AND MECHANICAL VARIETIES of CYLINDER MUSIC BOXES AND MOVEMENTS

An explanation of terms relating to various types of cylinder music boxes.

### Long Playing Cylinder Boxes

The playing time of certain boxes was lengthened by increasing the size of the spring barrel or by providing an instrument with two or four separate spring barrels, all geared together. L.G. Jaccard, writing in "Hobbies Magazine," noted:

"The 'Longue Marche' music box appeared about 1876. It was so called because of the longer duration of its playing time. This was obtained by adding a wheel, large or small (according to the time desired), between the spring barrel and the cylinder pinion. The music box with this arrangement could play one or two hours or even longer.

"The double spring barrel was the forerunner of the Longue Marche and had already doubled the playing time of the old style music box. There formerly had been double springs in orchestra boxes, but these were arranged with one in front of and the other in back of the cylinder pinion, and although this doubled the spring power, the playing time remained the same as for a single barrel box. As many as four spring barrels were found in some music boxes.

"Another type of Longue Marche was produced by placing two or three springs in the same barrel and a time wheel; this arrangement, because of the extreme pressure on the pinion, was not practical, and the cogs also showed a tendency to bend because of the small diameter of the barrel.

"There were also made Longue Marche types with two large spring barrels and a time wheel of large diameter which meshed with a double pinion. The second pinion meshed with the cylinder wheel placed in this particular type, at the left end of the cylinder.

"Still another kind of Longue Marche used on the interchangeable cylinders existed. This one consisted of two spring barrels on the same shaft, one meshing with a pinion whose shaft had a time wheel with an inner gearing. The inner gearing meshed with a pinion and a driving wheel attached to the escapement. The motor was independent of the cylinder, which was placed on two bridges and connected with the driving wheel by means of a short pin fastened at its left and fitted in a groove in the driving wheel.

"The first type of interchangeable cylinder box made did not have independent spring motors and the spring had to be held in check by a special apparatus when the cylinders were changed. Each cylinder had its own pinion meshing with the spring barrel. These cylinders were clumsy to handle and eventually led to the independent spring motor."

### Revolver Boxes

Revolver boxes have three, four, five, or more cylinders fastened to common end plates and grouped around a central shaft. After the tunes on one cylinder have been heard, the cylinder can be changed by revolving the mechanism and bringing another cylinder into the comb position. See accompanying illustration page.

### "Plerodienique" Music Boxes

L.G. Jaccard, music box historian, wrote that "It may be considered the most perfect of long tune music boxes ever made and is capable of playing, without interruption, one tune of six revolutions. The chief characteristic of this piece is that tunes of unequal length can be played on the six revolutions." See accompanying illustration page for more details.

### Duplex Cylinder Music Boxes

This type of box features two cylinders, one behind the other, synchronized with each other and driven by a common spring. Made in limited numbers, mainly during the 1880's and 1890's. See accompanying illustration page for more information.

### Interchangeable Cylinder Music Boxes

About 1850 one of the most important cylinder music box innovations was devised – the interchangeable cylinder box, or "rechange" box as it was originally designated. Instead of having one fixed cylinder, the interchangeable box could have any number of extra cylinders. These were usually stored in a drawer built into the bottom of the music box, in a drawer in a matching table, or in a separate case or cabinet.

Early rechange boxes of the 1850 - 1880 period had custom-fitted cylinders. The interchangeable cylinders were adjusted at the factory to fit one particular box and no other (unless modifications in alignment were made). While some firms continued this custom-fitting until the demise of this box type in the 1890's, other firms, notably Mermod Frȇres, produced instruments in which the cylinders were universally interchangeable with other boxes of the same design type.

Unusual variations of the interchangeable cylinder box include the Alexandra and L'Universelle, as illustrated and described on an accompanying page.

### Helicoidal and "Semi-Helicoidal" Boxes

The helicoidal box features one or more cylinders with the pins arranged on a continuous spiral. The shifting from one tune to another, and the attendant necessary pause, is eliminated as the cylinder is screw-fed and slowly and continuously moves to the side in synchronization with the pins. Such an arrangement was ideal for playing long overtures, operatic airs, and other selections without interruption. The helicoidal principle, in common use on barrel operated orchestrions and organs of the 19th century, was a rare feature in cylinder music boxes, and only a few were ever made.

Related to the helicoidal box is the "semi-helicoidal" (a term coined by Murtogh Guinness) cylinder box. The pins on this type are arranged at a 90-degree angle to the music comb as in a regular cylinder box, except that in the normally-blank space reserved for shifting the cylinder, the pins are arranged diagonally so as to correspond precisely with the position of the cylinder during the moment of shifting. Such a semi-helicoidal box shifts in the normal fashion at the end of each revolution but keeps playing during the shifting. Two semi-helicoidal boxes seen by the author each were equipped with two types of cylinders: One cylinder type is of the semi-helicoidal format and has a special cut-out or bypass device at the end of the cylinder. This bypasses the "stop" lever and permits the box to keep playing through the end of one revolution and on through succeeding revolutions until the end of the tune – even though the box may be set in the stop position. The other type of cylinder lacks this bypass device and has the cylinder pinned in the normal way, with a blank space at the end of each tune. This second type of cylinder stops in the normal manner after each revolution.

### Telescoping Cylinder Boxes

In "Musical Boxes, a History and an Appreciation," the late John E.T. Clark wrote of a box of this type: "In the 1862 Exhibition, Messrs. Paillard, of St. Croix, showed a very large and elaborate musical box with a greatly improved system for changing the cylinders. This was the largest and most ambitious musical box yet seen in this country [England]. It had six interchangeable cylinders and they were telescopic, so that they expanded while the tune was playing, and the cylinder revolved six times nonstop in playing one tune. The present writer has had this instrument through his hands. One cylinder had on it the overture to 'Barber of Seville;' the other, Weber's 'Invitation to the Valse.' There were two combs of equal length, and the cylinders extended were 20" long." (This was an early version of the plerodienique box – Ed.)

### Mandoline Boxes

The mandoline cylinder box has a brilliant and distinctive sound. The music combs have from several to seven or eight teeth tuned to the same musical note. The pins are arranged so that each note is plucked several times in rapid succession, using a different tooth for each repetition. The result is a bright and pleasing mandolin-like sound that has made this type of instrument a favorite with collectors today.

### Forte-piano Cylinder Boxes (Piano-forte)

Forte-piano, or piano-forte, boxes have two separate musical combs. One comb is considerably longer than the other and is voiced loudly (forte). The smaller comb is voiced softly (piano). This type of movement usually has a cylinder pinned so that the two combs play in an alternating fashion, thus giving remarkable expression to the music. When both combs play at once, the result is a double forte or especially loud tone. Forte-piano boxes were introduced circa 1840 and were popular for many years thereafter, although production was limited in comparison to standard comb types. Fine forte-piano instruments were made by Nicole Frères, Baker - Troll, Paillard, and others.

### Early Drum and Bell Boxes

Beginning shortly before 1850, tuned bells and a drum were added to certain musical movements. Early drum and bell boxes, such as those made by Nicole Frères, had the saucer-type bells, often a dozen or more in number, nested closely together and mounted out of sight beneath the bedplate. Certain of these instruments were equipped also with a small drum. The bells and drum effect on early boxes was subsidiary to the music played by the regular music comb and served as a cheerful accompaniment to the melody.

Boxes of this early type are usually referred to as "hidden bell boxes" by collectors today. The musical movements of such early bell boxes are, for the most part, of high quality.

### Late Drum and Bell Boxes
### Orchestra Boxes

It was soon learned that having the bells in view added to the popular appeal of a music box. Most bell boxes of the 1870's and later have the bells in full view, usually mounted behind the cylinder and struck with metal hammers.

The bell box was the forerunner of the orchestra box. The next innovation was the organ attachment. The organ section consists of a small harmonium or reed organ, usually of seventeen reeds, but occasionally with up to three dozen or more. A crankshaft connected to a driving gear powers a small leather-covered bellows assembly which provides the wind pressure to operate the reeds. The reeds are actuated by a series of metal keys usually located at the center of the cylinder, with a regular music comb to each side. The music is pinned on the cylinders by extended staple-like pins which provide for sustaining the notes. Most organ sections play continuously as there is no on-off lever. However, a number of more expensive instruments were originally provided with organ sections that can be turned on or off as desired. A much rarer type of organ attachment is that with real pipes. These pipes are usually of the flute type and are built into the bottom of the music box beneath the bedplate and out of view. Such flute pipe instruments are highly desired today.

The tonal balance of the reed organ section must be just right, or the sweet sound of the music combs will be overpowered and the instrument will sound more like a small reed organ than a music box! Originally, most such boxes did sound like reed organs. Today many collectors achieve a more pleasing tonal balance by dampening the organ section with a heavy cloth baffle.

Orchestra boxes feature one or more music combs, a set of bells, a snare drum, a wood drum (sometimes called castanets or wood block), and occasionally a triangle or gong. Many have reed organ sections as well. Most orchestra boxes are of the interchangeable cylinder type and were made during the 1870 - 1890 era when spectacular - appearing instruments with ornate cases were in vogue.

### "Pièce à Oiseau" Boxes

Certain types of large boxes feature a tiny mechanical bird (or "oiseau" in French) in a small glass-fronted display cabinet, usually at the front of the music box case. A small set of pipes provides a fanciful chirping or twittering sound as the bird flits about and moves its wings. Such instruments are more prized for their novelty appearance than for their musical value today. Early "pièces à oiseau" are of considerably better workmanship than later ones and are prized by collectors of automata.

### "Polytype" Boxes

The "Polytype" cylinder box, as described by L.G. Jaccard, features several different types of musical arrangements on the same cylinder. On one turn it could play in the sublime harmonie style, on another turn a mandolin-style arrangement, and on another revolution, another style. The large number of teeth, many tuned to the same musical note, found on the comb of a box of this type made such variations possible.

### Sublime Harmonie Cylinder Boxes

The sublime harmonie box uses two, three, or more combs of equal scale, each tuned alike (or with a slight intentional dissonance to introduce a celeste), and provides a louder volume of music without introducing harshness. During the 1870's and in later years many variations were made. The Mermod Frēres pages of this book describe many of these – such as "Sublime Harmonie Piccolo" (sublime harmonie combs plus a higher-pitched piccolo or treble comb), "Forte Piccolo" (loud tone, mostly in the upper octaves), and so on.

### Other Cylinder Box Variations and Attachments

The "Harp Eolienne" box is similar in appearance to the forte-piano box, but has the short comb voiced more loudly than the short comb in a forte-piano box; thus its main use is for accompaniment purposes, rather than for expression. Some late types of cylinder boxes have the tip of every other tooth removed; the "dummy" tooth is thought to have been intended as a sympathetic resonator for the tooth next to it – in order to provide a richer tone. The "safety check" device, mainly found on expensive instruments made after 1880, is attached to the music box cylinder. If the cylinder speeds up to an unusual speed, the safety check locks the cylinder in place and prevents a disastrous high-speed "run" and the consequent broken teeth thereby caused. The "tune indicator" device is a circular dial or, more frequently, a pointer and curved scale which shows which tune on the cylinder is playing. The "tune selector," or "tune skipper" (as Mermod Frēres designated it), permits the cylinder to be advanced to any desired tune, skipping over intermediate tunes without playing them. Tune selectors were used only on certain types of late boxes. A "zither" or "mandolin" (not to be confused with the mandoline type of music box comb arrangement) is a simple clamp holder with a rolled tube of stiff tissue paper affixed to its underside. When brought into contact with the music comb the result is a plinking mandolin-like or banjo effect.

### Tune Cards

Most cylinder music boxes were originally equipped with tune cards which listed the musical program. In the intervening years many such cards have been lost, giving the present-day music box owner his own "name that tune" quiz! The unknown is interesting, and guessing the tunes is often cited as one of the appeals of owning an early box.

From the early 19th century until about 1870, most tune cards were of a single color, usually white with a black, blue, or sepia border. The tunes were written in by hand, usually in flowing script. Depending upon where the music boxes were to be marketed, the tune titles were in French, English, German, or whatever. If made for general sale the titles were in French, the native tongue of the area of Switzerland in which most music boxes were made.

The 1870's and 1880's saw many types of ornate tune cards, including some which were hand engraved on silver plaques. Interchangeable cylinder boxes had tune cards listing the program for each cylinder originally ordered for the box. If the number of tunes was too large for convenient listing, a program book was provided. These program books usually were in the form of several or more tune cards bound together loosely within two covers.

After 1880 tune sheets or program cards took the form of colorful lithographs with blank lines (for the writing in of the program by hand) bordered by scenes of childhood days, of Swiss landscapes, castles, and other motifs. Some listed the names of famous musicians – Beethoven, Mozart, et al – on Grecian columns. As many different manufacturers of music boxes apparently ordered their tune cards from the same source, the cards are, for the most part, standard and bear no maker's name or notation referring to the box on which it was used. This information was written in by hand. Often a title was given to the instrument, "Bells in Vue," "Voix Celeste," or something similar. The tunes were then listed in order and numbered below the title.

Some very late music boxes of the cheaply-made variety have typewritten tune cards or, in the instance of certain B.H. Abrahams boxes, completely pre-printed programs.

### Aids for the Collector

To assist the collector and historian there are several excellent books available on the subject of cylinder music boxes. The "Cylinder Musical Box Handbook," by Graham Webb (Faber and Faber, Ltd., London, 1968) and "Collecting Music Boxes and How to Repair Them," by Arthur W.J.G. Ord-Hume (George Allen & Unwin, Ltd., London, 1967), both give excellent histories of cylinder boxes and information concerning their care and restoration. "Musical Boxes, a History and an Appreciation," by John E.T. Clark (George Allen & Unwin, Ltd., London, third edition, 1961) gives many personal experiences of the author in the music box field and is a source of useful historical information.

The Musical Box Society International and the Musical Box Society of Great Britain are both non-profit organizations devoted to the preservation and history of these and related automatic instruments.

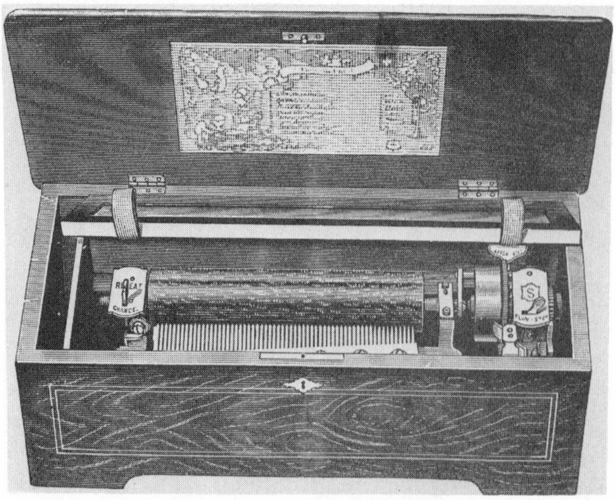

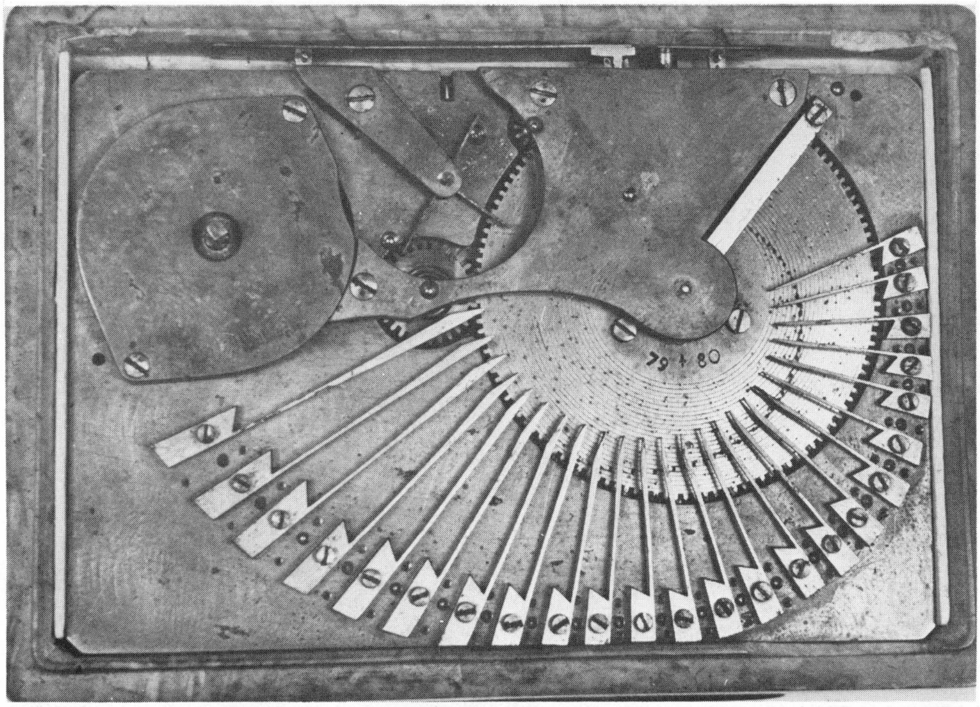

Left: Musical movement from musical snuff box of the late 18th century. The 2-tune musical unit is located in the bottom. The tunes are played by raising or lowering the disc which is pinned on both sides. The comb is a single toothed fan-shaped unit. This type of movement is called a platform or turntable movement by collectors today. The snuff box measures 3" wide by 2" deep. (Collection of Clarence W. Fabel)

Right: Early 19th century musical movement for use in a clock base. Inverted V-shaped comb; fusee drive on the spring barrel. The cylinder measures 9" long. (Collection of Clarence W. Fabel)

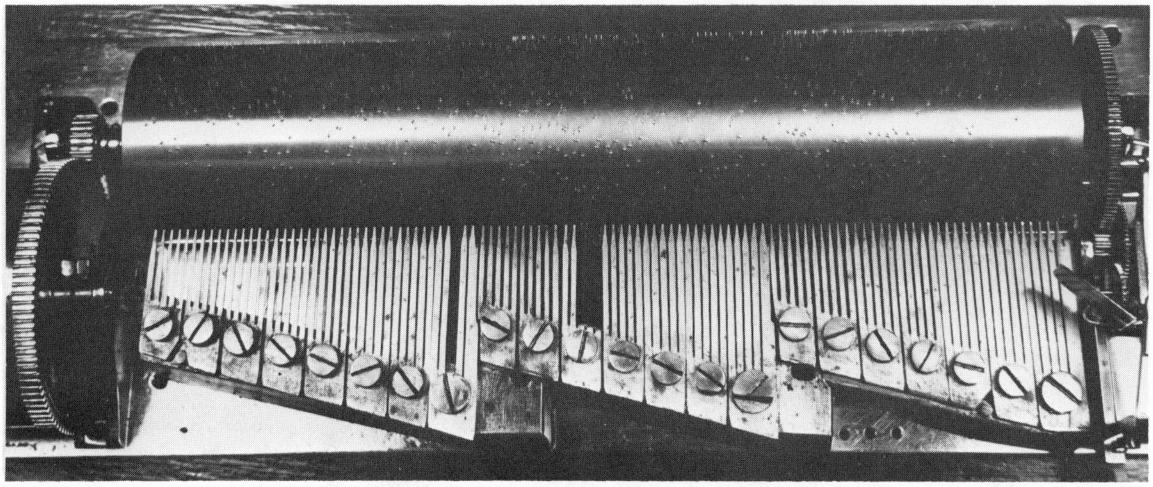

Above: Musical unit for clock base. Unmarked, but attributed to David LeCoultre, circa 1820. Staggered comb, sectional comb units, with each small comb unit having five teeth. The cylinder measures 7 1/2" long. (Collection of Clarence W. Fabel)

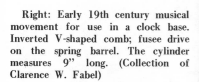

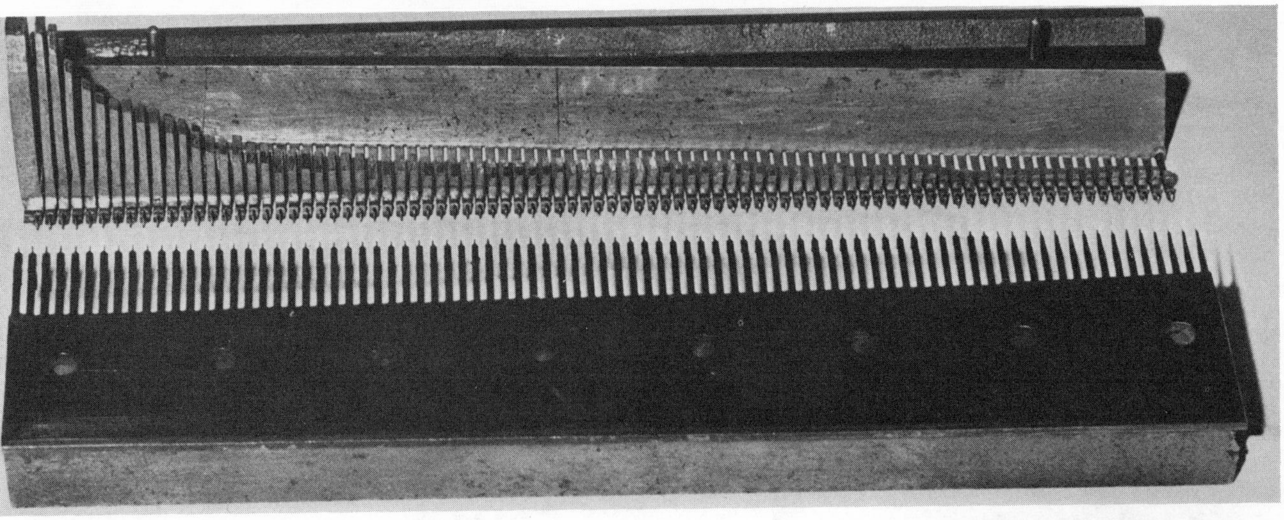

VIEWS OF TWO MUSIC COMBS: The upper comb is shown upside down. The bass notes on the left side have lead resonators attached. These weights reduce the frequency of vibration of the individual teeth thereby causing them to sound lower notes. The two guide pins near the top of the comb permit accurate alignment with the bedplate. The lower comb is in the regular position with the upper surface shown. The eight holes accommodate the screws which fasten the comb to the bedplate.

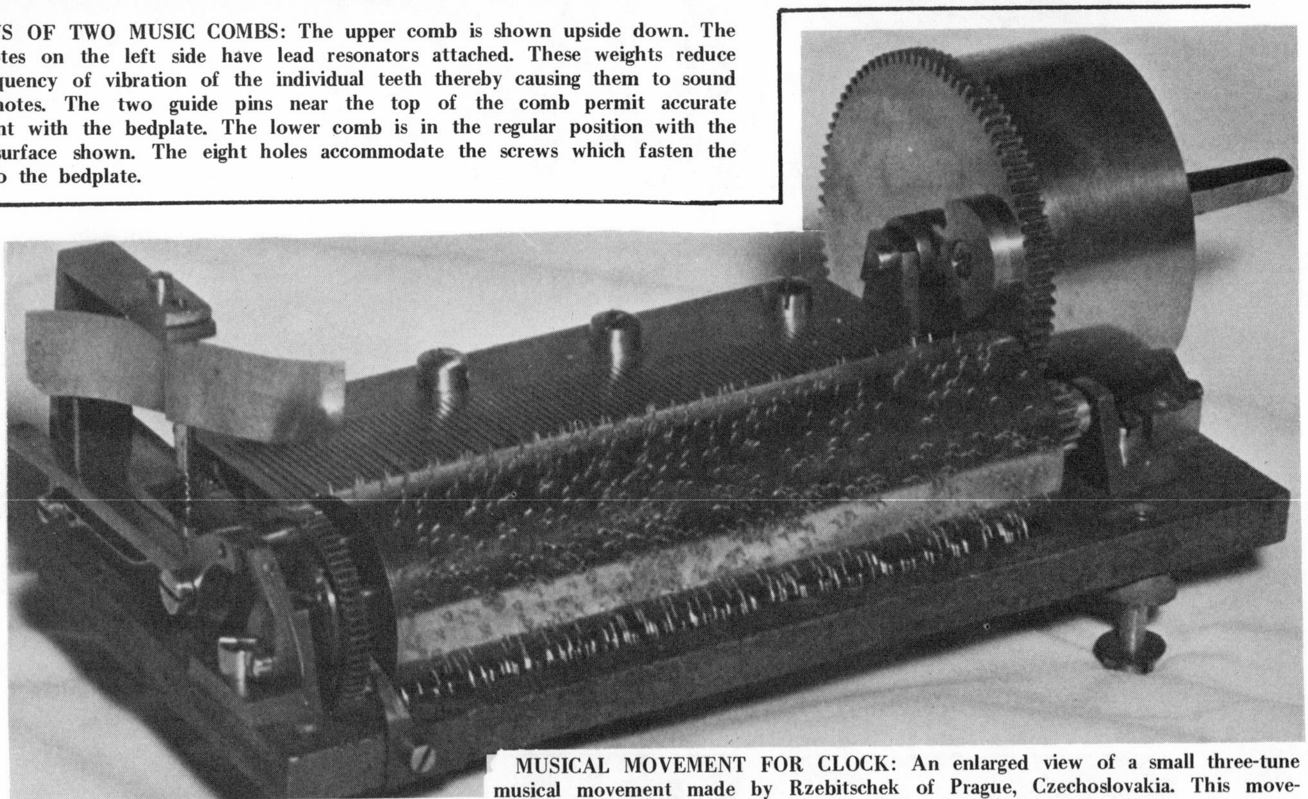

MUSICAL MOVEMENT FOR CLOCK: An enlarged view of a small three-tune musical movement made by Rzebitschek of Prague, Czechoslovakia. This movement, one of three discovered in unused condition and still in the original wrappings by Graham Webb in 1968, was originally intended for use in a musical clock. The horizontal lever at the left end of the mechanism starts the music playing.

MUSIC TO GAMBLE BY: To the left is shown a 10-tune Swiss musical movement in a "Puck" model slot machine manufactured by Caille Brothers of Detroit, Michigan, circa 1910. From about 1895 until World War I many musical movements, including some fine ones by Bremond and other leading Swiss makers, were imported into the U.S.A. by Mills, Caille, and others for use in gambling devices. Such music played whether or not the player won or lost at the game of chance and, hence, made slot machines legal in certain areas.

## —Music Box Inlay Art—

Music boxes, particularly those of the 1870 - 1890 era, were often inlaid on the top of the lid, sometimes the front, and rarer, on the ends. Inlay work on expensive or custom made boxes was often quite elaborate. In addition to colored woods, mother-of-pearl and brass were utilized. At the lower left of this page is a Nicole Frères box with the lid inlaid in tooled brass or boullé design. More often, designs featured a musical motif. Mandolins and flutes were especially popular in this regard. Lyres, lutes, sheet music scrolls, aeolian harps, violins, trumpets, military drums, and other musical instruments were styled in colored wood. Among non-musical inlay items we find birds and flowers were popular as were sprays and garlands of flora. Rarer are implements such as garden tools (see second picture below this caption), carpenters' tools, crests and coats of arms, owners' initials and monograms, scenes (of Egypt, ancient ruins, cityscapes, etc.), and made-to-order designs. On the simple side are rhomboids, curlicues, and other geometric or quasi-geometric ornaments. In addition to the inlaid design, many boxes feature inlaid striping of tulipwood or other light woods. These together with matched veneer edges serve to frame the central design.

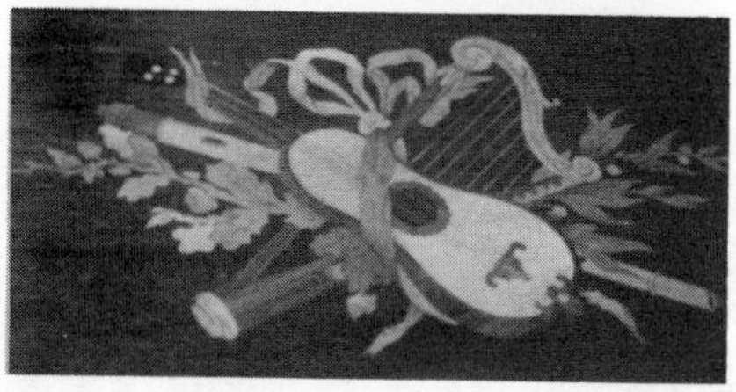

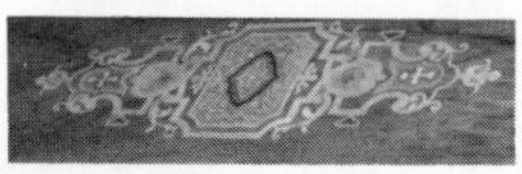

## TYPES OF BELL STRIKERS

Bells were a popular addition to music boxes, particularly in the 1880's and 1890's. Bell strikers took many forms and ranged from simple metal knobs to ornately enameled or painted butterflies and birds. Some Swiss boxes had automaton bell strikers, usually Oriental or African figures. Others had animated monkeys. Some variations are shown on this page.

This Swiss orchestra box has bell strikers in the form of tiny honeybees — a popular type of striker. The bells are chased or engraved with designs, a feature of more expensive instruments. The bells in most bell boxes and orchestra boxes can be disconnected by a lever provided for that purpose.

Three figures, an African, an Oriental (or Mandarin, as they were sometimes called in music box catalogues), and another African, each have two beaters. Music boxes with moving animated figures are quite scarce.

Three gaily-colored butterflies strike the bells in this B.H.A. music box from the 1890's.

Colorful dragonflies are the bell strikers in this box, also from the 1890's.

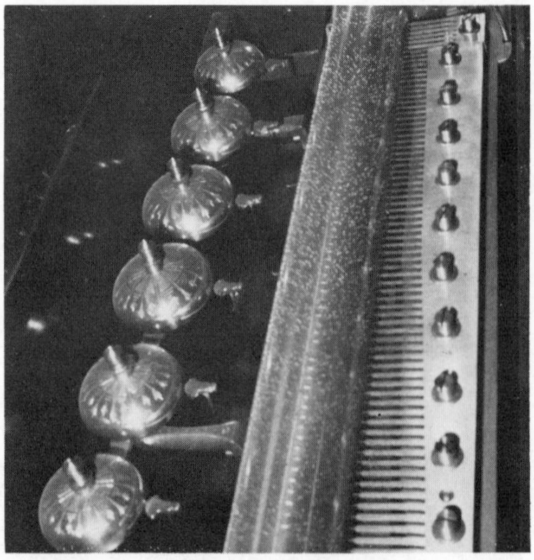

Hammers or wedges used as bell strikers. Note that the bells are engraved. A finer type of bell box dating from the 1880's.

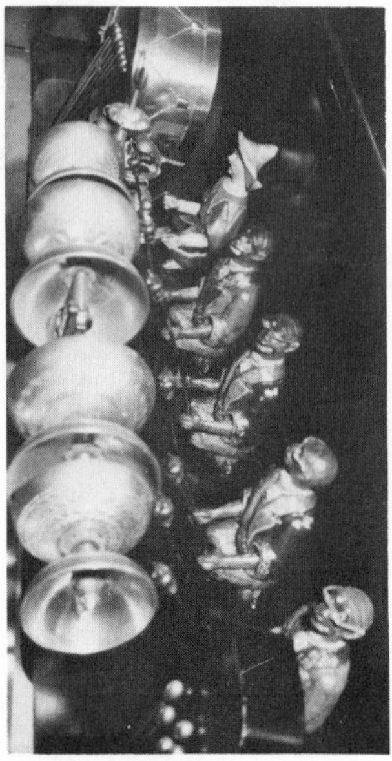

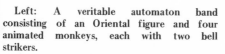

Above: Simple knob-type beaters. These and honeybee strikers are the types most often seen in bell boxes.

Left: A veritable automaton band consisting of an Oriental figure and four animated monkeys, each with two bell strikers.

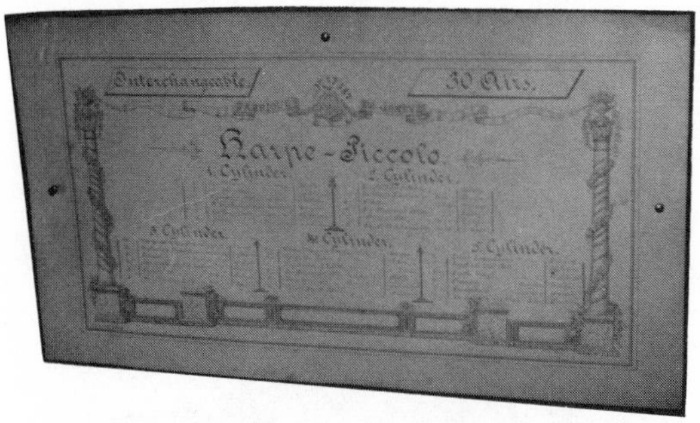


"Harpe - Piccolo" tune card from Bremond box. Lists the program for five cylinders.

"Flutes Celestial Voices" tune sheet for late 19th century box sold in England. An example of a meaningless tune card title – the box had no flutes or other pipes. Celestial voices?

Colorfully lithographed "Tambour et Timbres" (drum and bells) tune card from late 19th century Swiss box.

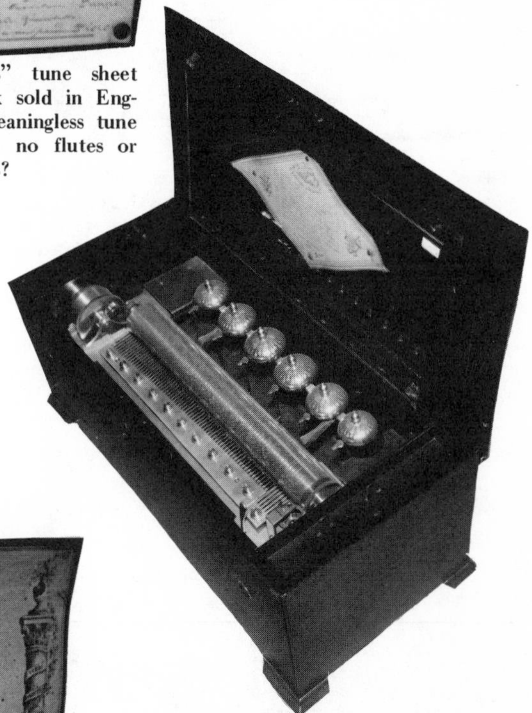

This Bremond bell box has a rhomboidal tune sheet, an unusual shape. From the 1880's.

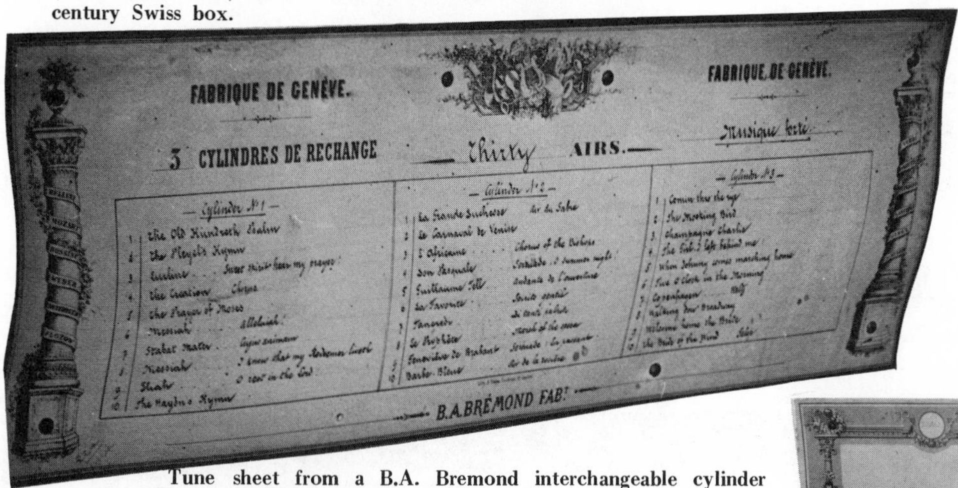


Tune sheet from a B.A. Bremond interchangeable cylinder box once owned by the Mellon family of Pittsburgh. The program for three cylinders is listed.

Ornately framed "Mandoline Piccolo" tune card from an interchangeable box with four cylinders. From the 1880's.

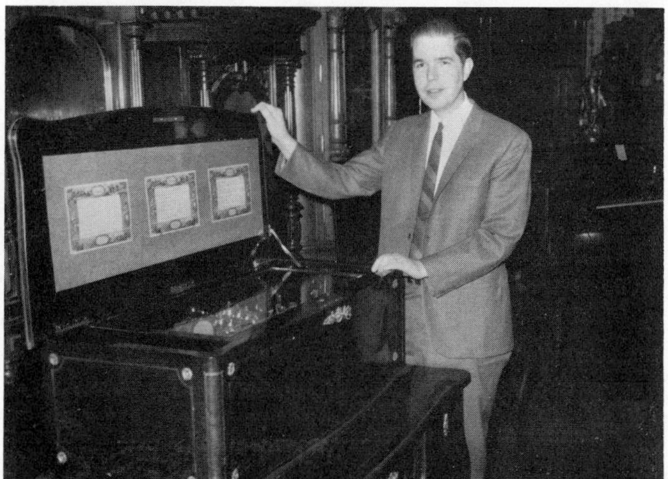

The author in 1969 with a large Allard orchestra box. Three separate tune cards list the program on each of the three cylinders with the box.

Paillard, Vaucher Fils (P.V.F.) program card from the 1880's. "Timbres en Vue" (bells in view).

The double spring barrel of this orchestra box gives it an exceptionally long playing time. Several other interesting features are visible: Directly to the right of the spring is the governor with the tempo control (adjusted by a knurled knob) on top. Behind the tempo control and near the back of the box is the safety check rod. Should the cylinder speed up, the heavy knob on one end will cause the rod to fly out and hit the transverse stop — thus halting the movement. At the lower right of the illustration is the tune indicator with its pointer. In the right background is the snare drum with eight beaters.

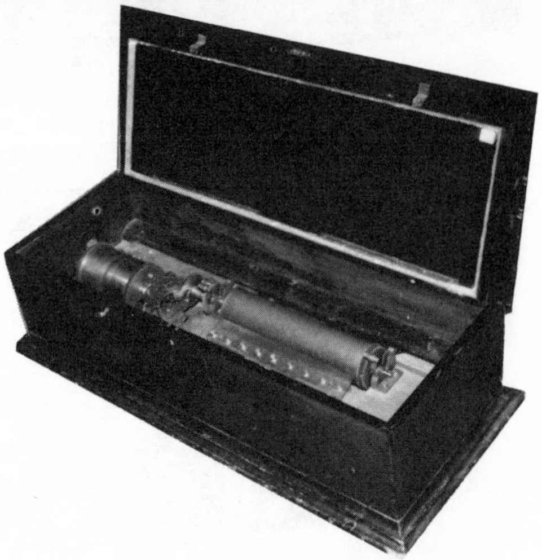

—Some Major Spring Types—

Above Right: The large double spring barrel on this Nicole Frères overture box gives it extended playing time. Boxes of this type, with a finely-spaced comb, feature a program of overtures or operatic selections. With a playing time of a half hour or more (when the box was new and the spring at its maximum strength) such an instrument provided home entertainment in Victorian times.

Left: The two massive spring barrels of this huge box are mounted one in front of the other and drive the central shaft. The result is increased power, not increased playing time. This particular box has a large reed organ section which requires additional power to drive the wind bellows.

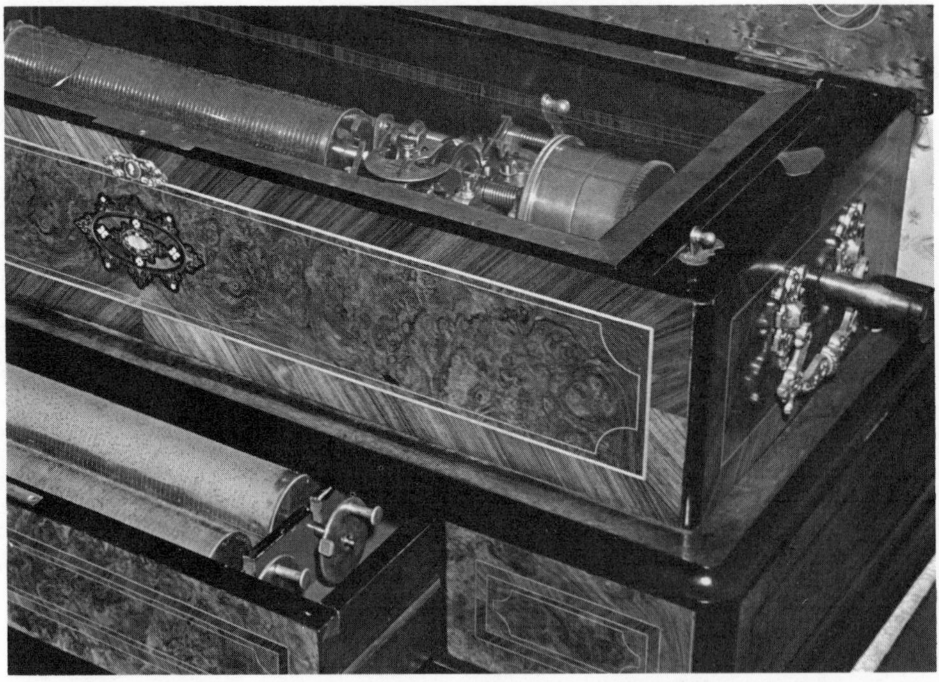

Music box with double spring barrel at the right-hand side of the instrument. (Dan Adams collection)

## ZITHER ATTACHMENTS

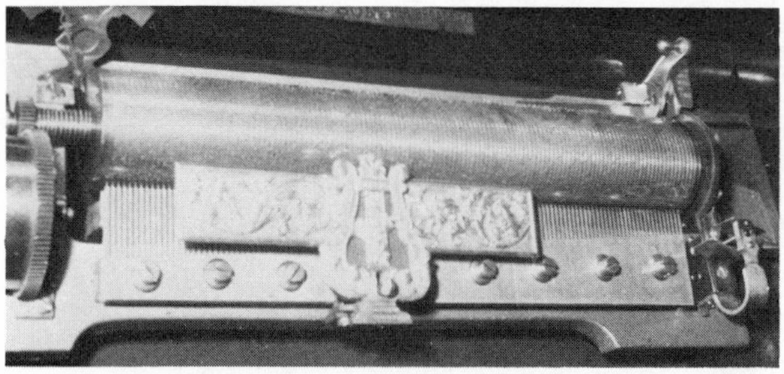

Mermod Frères box from the 1880's. The ornate zither attachment covers slightly more than half of the comb. A small lever at the base of the lyre design permits the zither attachment to be raised and lowered.

This large tubular-style zither attachment covers the entire music comb. This is a plain-appearing attachment; most zither attachments are ornate.

The zither attachment on this orchestra box is so large that it completely obscures the music comb teeth from view — and covers the "combs" used to operate the percussion effects (separate combs at the left and right) as well!

This large Allard orchestra box has two separate zither attachments, one for each of the music combs to each side of the center organ keys. The levers in front of the organ keys permit the organ reeds to be turned on or off — an unusual feature.

## ORGAN COMBS

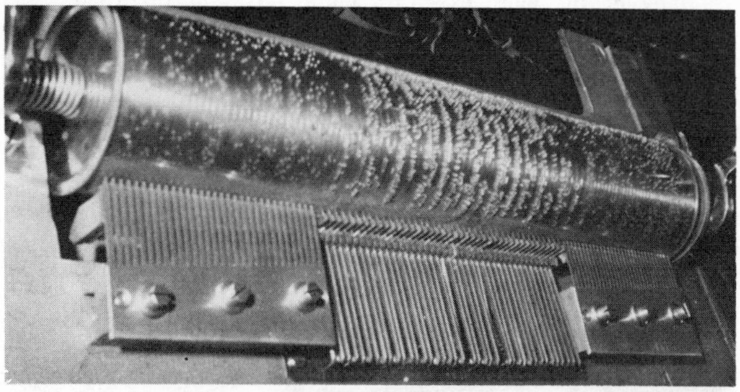

Organ "comb" or set of key levers between two music combs on a large Swiss box from the 1880's. The organ section is particularly large in this model.

A Paillard orchestra box of the 1880's with a 19-note organ section.

## EARLY AND LATE TOOTH SPACING

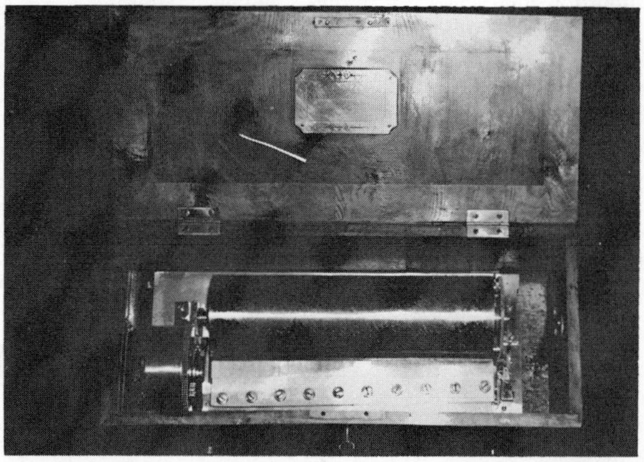

A basic difference between the tooth spacing of an early box in comparison to a later one is shown here. The top box is a finely crafted key-wind music box with a closely-spaced music comb containing 251 teeth. The box was made circa 1840 - 1850 and plays four overtures. (George Bidden photograph).

The bottom instrument is from the late 1880's and although the comb measures 14 inches wide, there are fewer than 60 musical teeth (plus teeth to operate the bells and drum)! The very wide spacing of the teeth permits a program of twelve tunes.

## —Storing Interchangeable Cylinders—

Many of the more expensive music boxes of the 1870 - 1895 era were made with interchangeable cylinders. Earlier models were made to fit a particular instrument and no other. Later cylinders were, in many cases, standardized. For instance, one could purchase an "Ideal Sublime Harmonie" music box from Mermod Frères and order additional cylinders for this standard type at a later date.

Extra cylinders are usually stored in the base of the music box or in a drawer in the table upon which the music box sits. For a large group of cylinders a chest of drawers serves well. Some makers furnished additional cabinents for this purpose. Others made decorative roll storage facilities in the form of tea carts or benches, usually with wheels to permit moving it closer to the music box to change cylinders.

Above: The former owner of this Paillard box really enjoyed it, for he purchased three cases full of cylinders! The music box itself is shown at the left foreground; the plain wood storage cases are above and to the right. Some makers produced cylinder cases with inlay and decoration to match the parent music box.

Right: A typical Swiss cylinder box with a single drawer full of cylinders. This was the most standard format. In some models the front panel of the drawer hinges forward and the cylinders slide out on a rack, making access to the cylinders, particularly those toward the back of the drawer, easier.

"Ideal Sublime Harmonie" music box by Mermod Frères of St. Croix, Switzerland, circa 1895. The particular instrument above has thirteen cylinders, each with six tunes — for a total program of seventy eight different melodies. Note that the music box itself has a drawer in its base. That usually sufficed for most buyers. Only occasionally was a matching chest with many extra cylinders purchased. Mermod Frères cylinder boxes of the 1890's, usually of oak wood but occasionally of mahogany, were extremely popular in America and were sold in large numbers.

Swiss cylinder box with two drawers in its matching table. Most music box tables are of the one-drawer style. This one is unusual.

This large Allard orchestra box has three drawers for cylinder storage. The cylinders are mounted lengthwise in the drawer, rather than in the usual crosswise fashion.

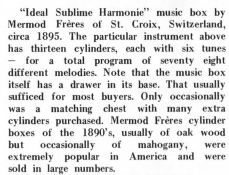

—Revolver Boxes—

The handling of extra cylinders in an interchangeable cylinder type of box was a task requiring steadiness of hand, precise alignment, a goodly amount of strength (especially in the case of larger boxes), and a great amount of care.

On August 2, 1870, Amedee Paillard, member of the well-known Paillard music box family in St. Croix, Switzerland, was granted U.S. Patent No. 105,972 for what collectors know today as the revolver box. This type of box has three, four, or more cylinders affixed to common end plates which turn about a center shaft. Each cylinder can be brought into playing position by means of a ratcheted lever which turns the entire group. As each cylinder is brought before the music comb the mechanism clicks or locks into place. While in place each cylinder will play several tunes, six or eight for example, shifting to the side slightly at the end of each tune — just like a regular cylinder box. When a new cylinder program is desired the group of cylinders can be rotated until the desired new cylinder is in the playing position.

The revolver box thus provides a multi-cylinder program of tunes without the necessity of having to lift cylinders in and out of the box each time a new cylinder is to be heard. Unfortunately for posterity, revolver boxes were strictly limited-production items. Although they were produced by Paillard, Baker - Troll, Nicole Frères, Cuendet, and possibly other makers as well, the total number produced was small. The appeal of revolver boxes lies not in their musical excellence, for the musical quality is just average for the period, but in the unique-appearing mechanism. For this reason a revolver box is a highlight in a collection today.

The number of cylinders used in revolver boxes varied. The author has seen examples with 3, 4, 5, and 6 cylinders, and possibly larger formats were made as well. Many revolver boxes featured zither attachments. A few had reed organ comb sections.

Changing the cylinders could be accomplished in any one of several ways, depending upon the model. A ship's wheel-like device, a ratcheted lever, and a knurled knob were three of the methods employed.

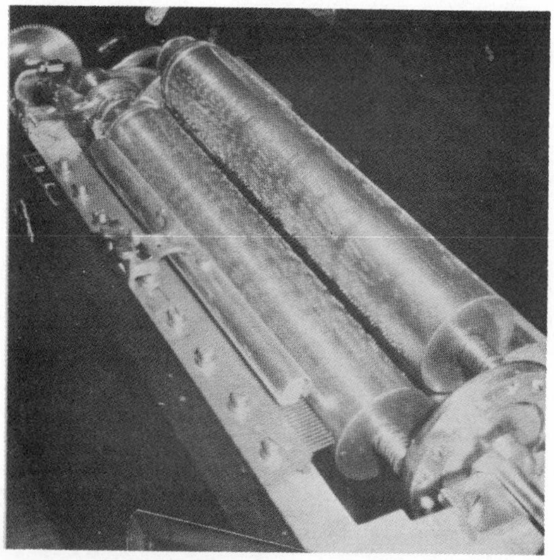

Revolver box attributed to Nicole Frères. Four cylinders each play six tunes. The end plates and other mechanisms of the revolver box are all hand-machined brass. (Collection of Bellm's Cars & Music of Yesterday; Sarasota, Fla.)

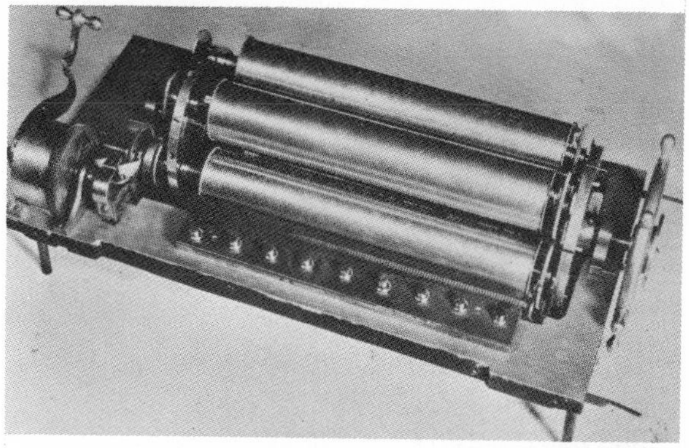

Revolver music box mechanism with five cylinders, each playing eight tunes. Note the ship's wheel turning device at the right end just beyond the bedplate. (George Bidden photograph)

Revolver music box mechanism made by Baker-Troll of Geneva, circa 1890. Three cylinders play eight tunes each. Such revolver boxes are extremely rare today. (George Bidden photograph)

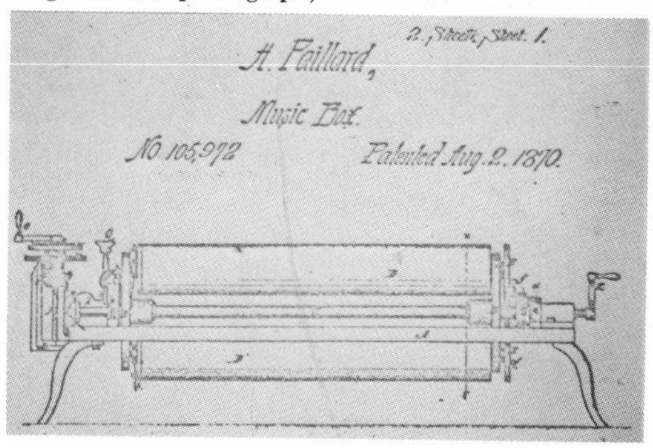


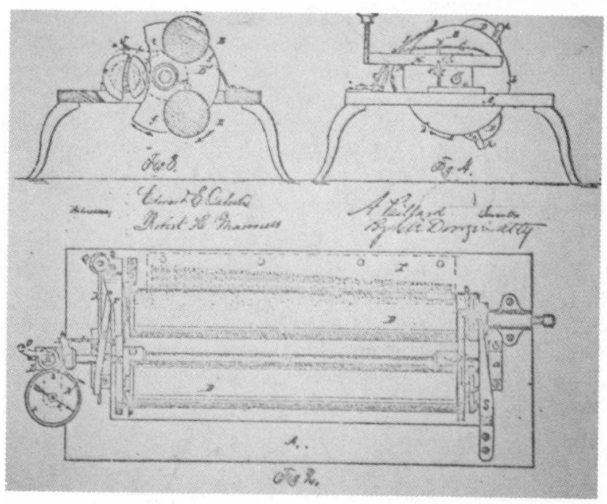

Patent drawings for the revolver box per U.S. Patent No. 105,972 granted to Amedee Paillard of St. Croix, Switzerland, on August 2, 1870.

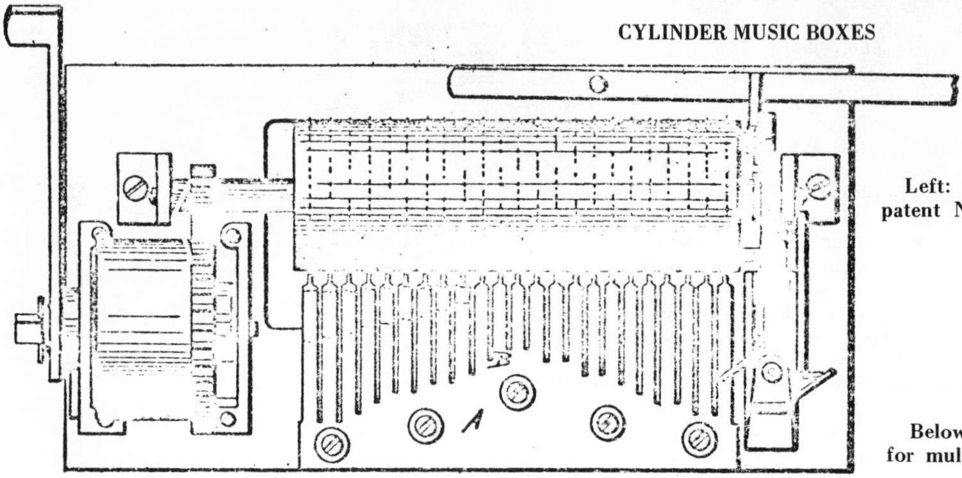

—Two Paillard Comb Patents—

Left: The Paillard and Recordon-Sulliger U.S. patent No. 369,258 for V-shaped or pyramidal comb.

Below: Charles Paillard's U.S. patent No. 161,055 for multiple "sublime harmonie" combs.

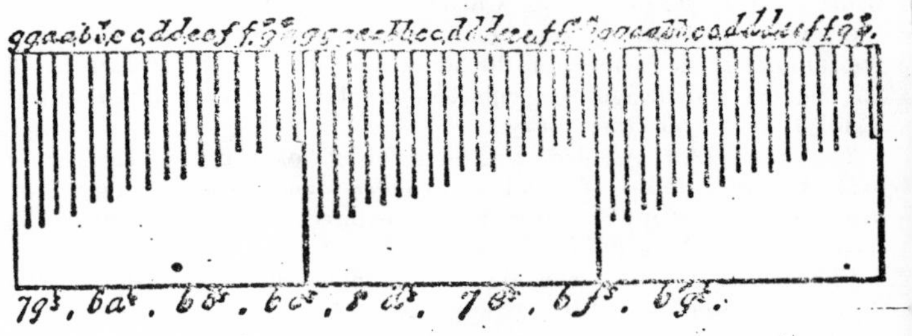

The problem of increasing the loudness of a music box without producing a rasping or strident tone was a perplexing one, and several solutions were proposed over the years. On August 30, 1887, Charles Paillard and Louis Recordon-Sulliger, both of St. Croix, Switzerland, were granted a patent on a V-shaped comb as shown above. One of the patent claims, "a comb for musical boxes, having teeth decreasing in length from the ends of the comb toward the middle," was hardly new, having been used a century earlier for musical movements (see the "Early Music Combs" page of this book). But, like so many inventions in the musical field, the earlier one was not patented – and in 1887 Paillard's "new" idea was considered patentable.

The tonal concept is similar to that of the sublime harmonie idea: "Heretofore the musical boxes known as 'sublime harmony' [sic] boxes have been constructed with two or more combs so tuned and arranged that teeth of the same pitch or having a slight dissonance were provided in the several combs, whereby a greater volume of the same tone could be produced without having the sound waves interfere with each other.

"The object of my invention is to provide a comb with two or more teeth of the same pitch or having a slight dissonance, the teeth being separated sufficiently to prevent interference of sound. The invention consists of a comb in which the teeth decrease in length and increase in pitch from the ends to the middle. . ."

Earlier, on March 23, 1875, Charles Paillard secured a patent on the sublime harmonie comb arrangement, as illustrated at the upper right of this page. The sublime harmonie comb, also not a new concept at the time, was extensively used in late 19th century cylinder boxes and, later, in disc music boxes – particularly those of the Symphonion make.

Paillard's patent application claims these advantages for this type of comb:

"Prior to my invention, so far as known to me, musical boxes were furnished with but one comb, and but a feeble and metallic sound was obtained, while, if more volume of sound was desired, larger and more numerous prongs or vibrators were used, thus diminishing the pitch and lengthening the duration of the vibration, the effect of which was to cause interference of the vibrations or sound waves, and destroy the harmony and produce discord. . .

"My invention is designed to remedy these imperfections and consists in combining, with a revolving music cylinder, two or more combs, the similar notes of which are of similar pitch or nearly so. . . In tuning the teeth of the music combs of the same tone I introduce a very slight dissonance, and the fact of this dissonance, and the teeth of the same pitch being separated, produces a more powerful and harmonious sound. . . If the object of the box is to produce a more powerful and harmonious tone than that of other musical boxes, it is only necessary to let the same air be played completely by two or more combs; but if I wish to produce the different shades of musical expression, such as the 'pianos,' the 'crescendos,' the 'fortes,' the 'decrescendos,' etc., I let one or more combs play at a time, according to the effect I wish to produce . . .

"I am aware of musical boxes having two combs, one large and the other smaller. [Paillard refers here to the forte-piano type of movement – Ed.] The teeth of the latter comb are weakened considerably in order to play the soft parts; but only two shades of expression can be introduced – the fortes and the pianos – and in a very different way from that observed in my invention where none of the combs are weakened, and where the expression is obtained by the use of one or more teeth of the same sound in the different combs.

"I am also aware that in many large musical boxes the comb is made in two sections, one section containing the high, and the other the low, notes, thus in reality forming but one scale. . ."

The preceding Paillard patent is a good example why patent records must be taken with a grain of salt. Other examples abound in musical patent files: the U.S. patent No. 1,028,496 granted to H. K. Sandell on June 4, 1912, for his "new" symmetrical piano, a concept identical to that used by Polyphon over a decade earlier, is another excellent example of undeserved credit.

The author interviewed a gentleman who had been associated with the musical instrument business in America in the early 20th century, a man whose firm was the assignee of many patents. Some of the patents would have been invalid if someone with a sense of history had seriously challenged them at the time. "We patented everything possible, knowing in some instances that our fellow American competitors [who, unlike the author of these comments, did not trade with Germany] would not be aware of German developments and would not know that the ideas were not new. When the patents reached litigation, as they often did, we usually won, but sometimes we lost. In the meantime the thought of legal action kept many of our competitors from using the same ideas." We refrain from comment at this point, except to note that patent files (and we've been through the U.S., English, and German ones) aren't always a reliable source of information!

NICOLE FRÈRES
–Cylinder Music Boxes–

Nicole Frères of Geneva made fine quality cylinder boxes during the mid 19th century. Three examples are shown on this page.

At top left is a lever-wind long-comb box of the forte-piano style. The short comb plays soft music (piano); the long comb, loud music (forte).

The inset illustration at the upper right is Nicole box No. 28,959, a key-wind instrument which plays eight tunes from a 13" cylinder.

At the lower right is a fine key-wind Nicole box of the "fat cylinder" type playing six tunes, all overtures. Boxes of this general type are known as "key-wind overture boxes" by collectors today. They are much desired for their elaborate musical arrangements played on closely-spaced fine-toothed combs. The music is soft. On some cylinders the revolution may take a minute or longer. The key is detachable. When not in use the left side of the box hinges upward and the key is stored in the recess or slot thus created.

Mrs. Rita Ford provided the description of this interesting box: a ship captain's desk that plays delicate music...

In this music box, a circa 1875 adaptation of a ship captain's desk, is found a combination of the furniture maker's and music box maker's art. The cabinet was made in England, perhaps by the firm of Edwards & Roberts, renowned for for their work with inlays. Overall measurements are 33" wide by 24" deep by 56" high, with the lid in the open position. The cabinet is of rosewood with inlaid stripes on the edges. In place of the usual motif of flowers or musical instruments on the lid and front, the artistic cabinet maker inlaid scenes of ancient Egypt.

The musical movement is not signed, but it bears strong characteristics of B.A. Bremond. The instrument is of the interchangeable cylinder type and has six tunes on each of six cylinders. The maker created an innovation in handling of the cylinders: instead of lifting out through the top, the cylinders are pulled out the right-hand side. Safety locks prevent damage to the music comb or cylinder during the changing period. Instructions are engraved on a brass plate.

## SOME FINE CYLINDER BOXES

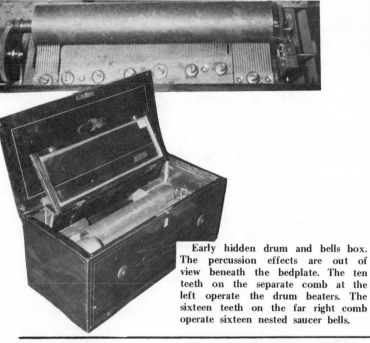

Early hidden drum and bells box. The percussion effects are out of view beneath the bedplate. The ten teeth on the separate comb at the left operate the drum beaters. The sixteen teeth on the far right comb operate sixteen nested saucer bells.

Hidden drum and bells box manufactured circa 1850 - 1860 by Henri Capt of Geneva, Switzerland. Note the ornate serpentine case and similarly shaped glass cover — unusual features for a cylinder box. Capt boxes are considered to be of exceptionally fine quality. (George Bidden photograph)

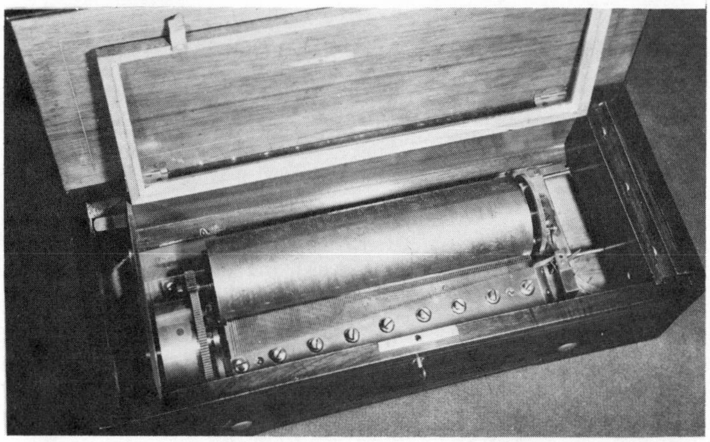

4-overture key-wind box made by Frederick William Ducommun-Girod of Geneva. The cylinder is 14" long and 3" in diameter. (Mrs. Ruth Bornand photograph)

Forte-piano music comb from an early Swiss box formerly in the Shackleton Collection. Notice the two separate combs. The longer one is voiced loudly; the smaller, softly. Such a comb arrangement makes possible beautiful expression effects. (Roy Haning and Neal White photograph)

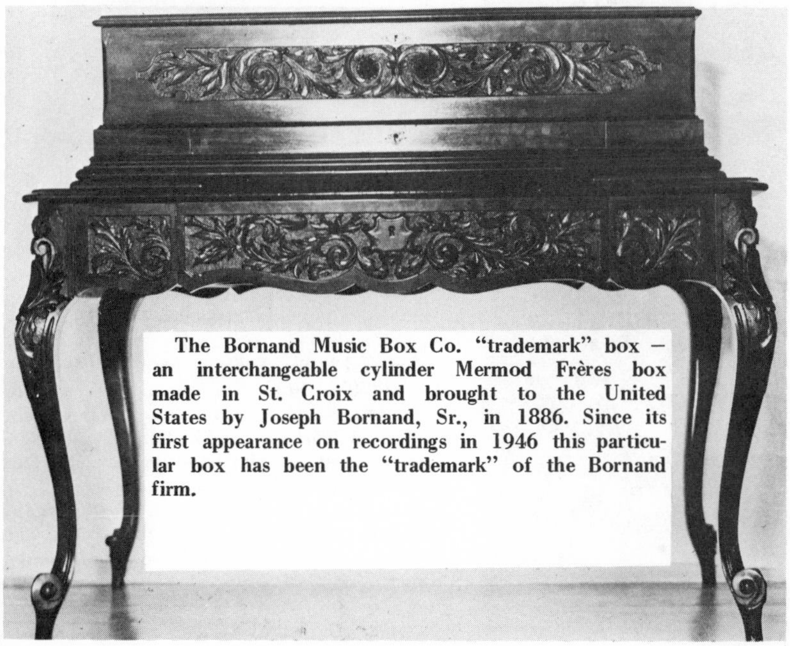

The Bornand Music Box Co. "trademark" box — an interchangeable cylinder Mermod Frères box made in St. Croix and brought to the United States by Joseph Bornand, Sr., in 1886. Since its first appearance on recordings in 1946 this particular box has been the "trademark" of the Bornand firm.

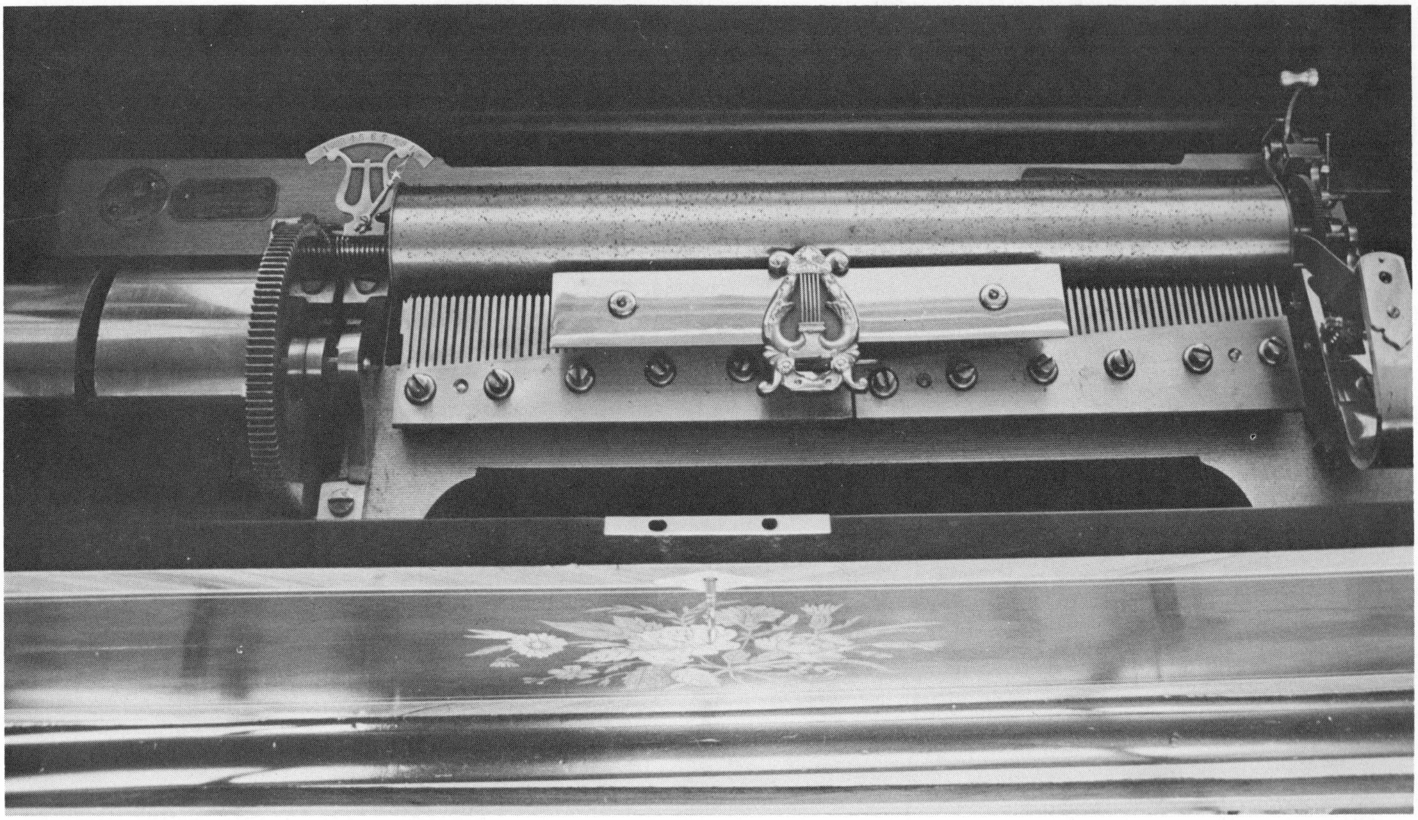

—Two Paillard Boxes—

Above: Paillard 10-tune single cylinder "Sublime Harmonie Longue Marche." The "Longue Marche" spring arrangement permits very long playing time on one winding. The nickel plated cylinder of the box is 18 1/4" long and is 3" in diameter. Overall dimensions of the box are 38" wide by 15" high (lid open), by 11" deep. Made circa 1881 by Paillard of St. Croix, Switzerland. The Paillard firm is still active in St. Croix and in the former music box factories fine Bolex cameras and other precision devices are built today.

(Above instrument from the collection of Robert W. Gibson)

Left: 12-tune Paillard orchestra box of the 1880's. Note the organ keys at the right foreground and the corresponding part of the cylinder, a combination of pins and staples, used to play the organ part. The tune indicator shows that tune No. 2 is now playing. Some of the most ornate orchestra boxes made during the 1870's and 1880's were by the Paillard firm. (Roy Haning and Neal White photograph)

Paillard orchestra box of the 1870's in an ornate case with serpentine front and sides, burled walnut finish with extensive inlay, and with a built-in writing desk. Five drawers provide storage for the interchangeable cylinders. Music boxes in ornate cabinets such as this originally cost several thousand dollars each and were made on special order.

Drum and bells box from the late 1880's or early 1890's. The movement is mounted vertically. The box is equipped with two front doors instead of the usual hinged lid. (Harold Freiheit collection; Graham Webb photograph)

A very unusual type of bell box with the bells and a dancing doll mounted in a display window at the front of the instrument. The box is of the interchangeable-cylinder type and has a matching table. From the 1870's or early 1880's. (Collection of J.B. Nethercutt)

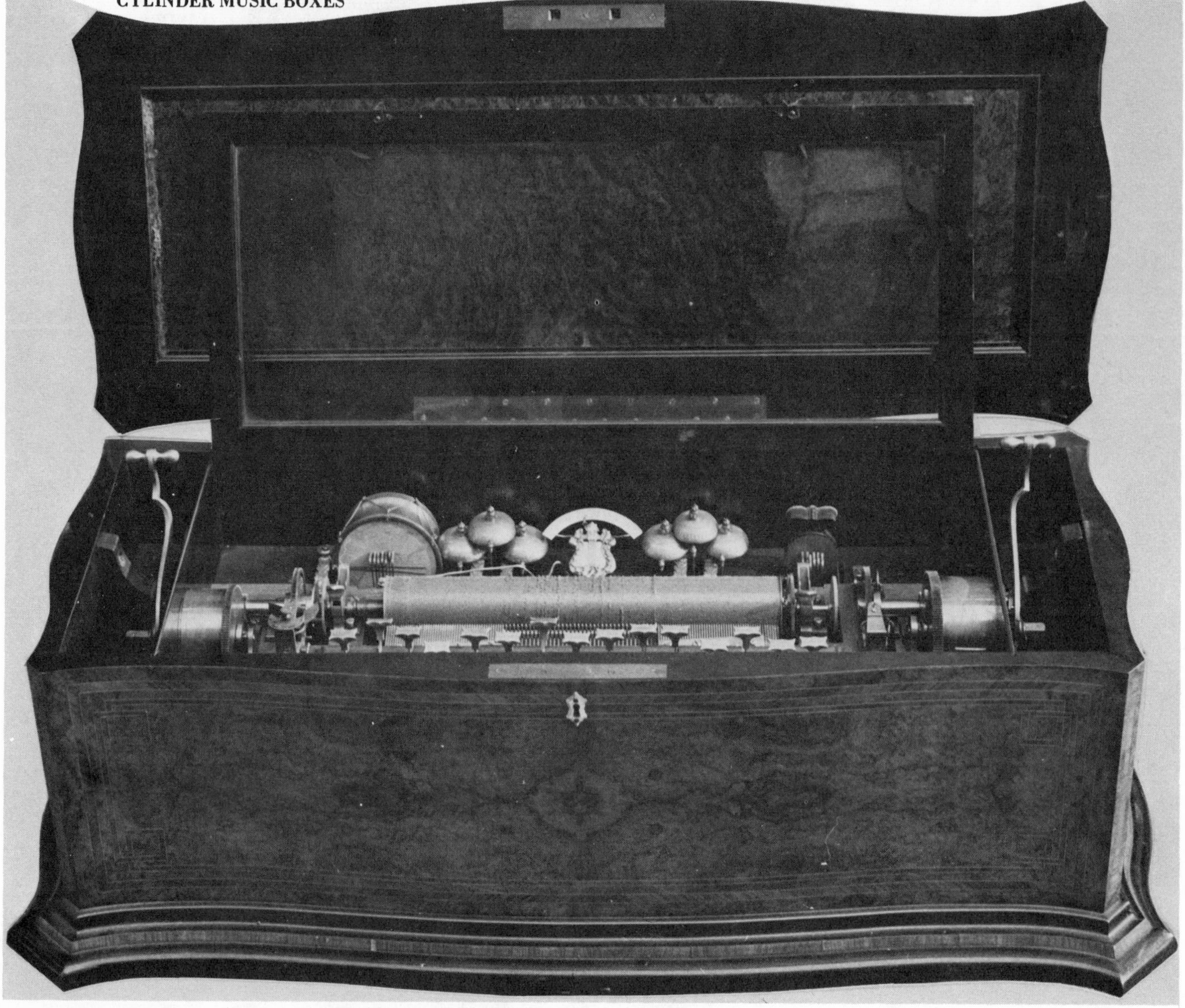

This large Swiss cylinder box dates from the late 19th century. The instrument has a matching table (not shown above). The music is provided by a treble or soprano comb of 42 teeth, a bass comb of 36 teeth, a 38-reed organ section, six bells, a drum with seven beaters, and a wood block (which provides the sound of castanets).

The box is of the interchangeable cylinder type and has eight cylinders with it. Each cylinder measures 17" in length and is pinned with six selections.

There are two large spring barrels, one at each end (an unusual feature; usually the springs are at the same end). (Description and photograph courtesy of Rita Ford)

CYLINDER MUSIC BOXES

Two unusual cylinder boxes: The top instrument is marked "Perin-Shopard" on the tune sheet and "Nicole Frères" on the mechanism. The keyboard is used to play the organ section, either separately or in accompaniment to the program pinned on the cylinder. The lower instrument is an interchangeable cylinder box in the shape of a building. It bears the portico label: "Importers; Alex M. Hays & Co.; Maiden Lane, New York." (Murtogh D. Guinness Collection)

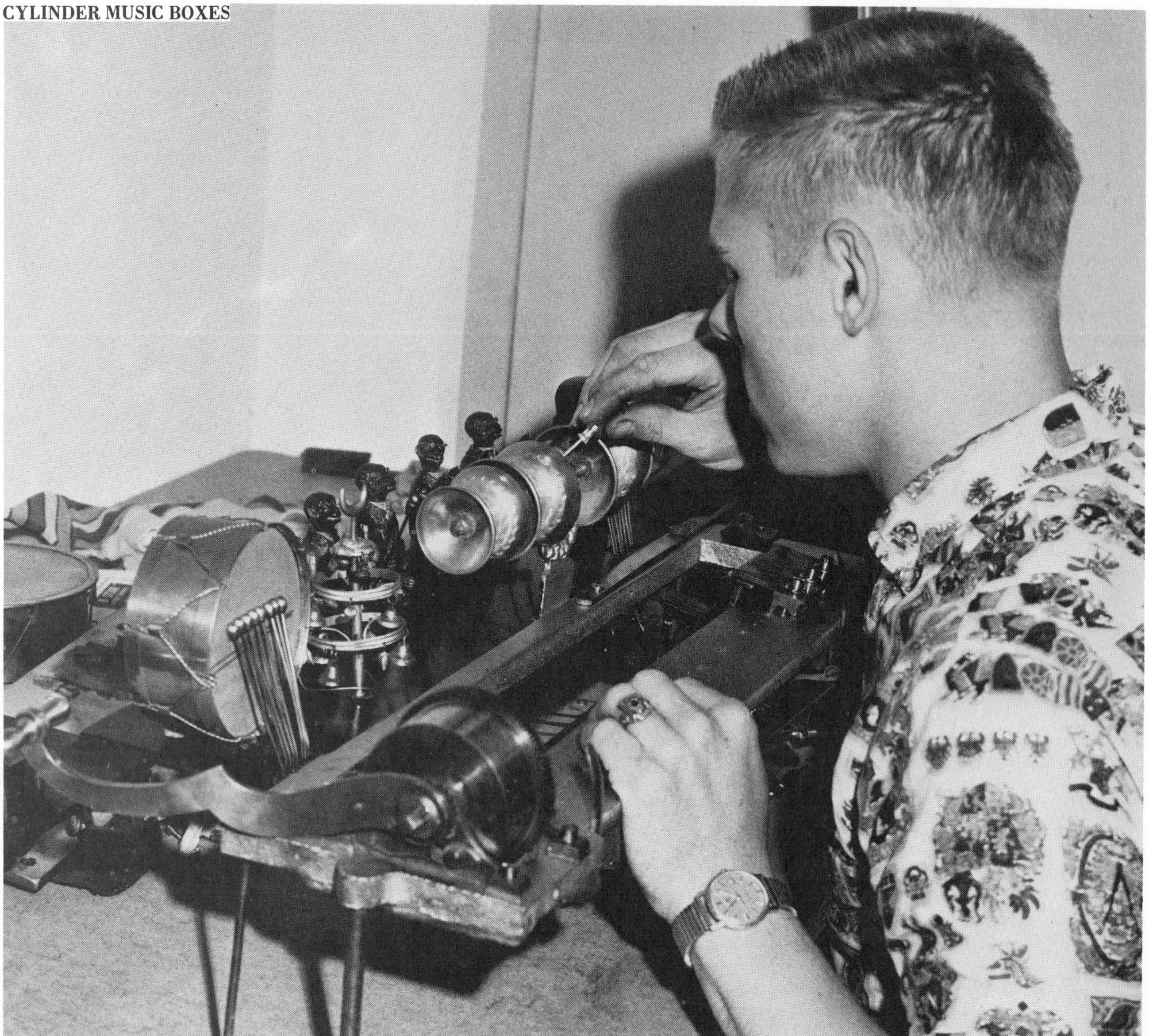

—Music Box Restoration—

Above: Noël Burndahl puts the final regulating touches on a large orchestra music box. Note the bell strikers in the form of monkeys. The tree-like bell-laden device to the right of the drum is a cymbalstern.

Left: The late Adrian V. Bornand, factory-trained in the repair of music boxes, is shown working on an orchestral music box mechanism. Mr. Bornand passed away at the age of 49, leaving a wife, Mrs. Ruth Bornand, and two daughters who carry on the family tradition of music boxes at the Bornand Music Box Company in Pelham, New York.

The repair of music boxes is exacting work requiring great skill and patience. Restoration by a fine craftsman can make a Swiss cylinder box look and play like it did when it was new.

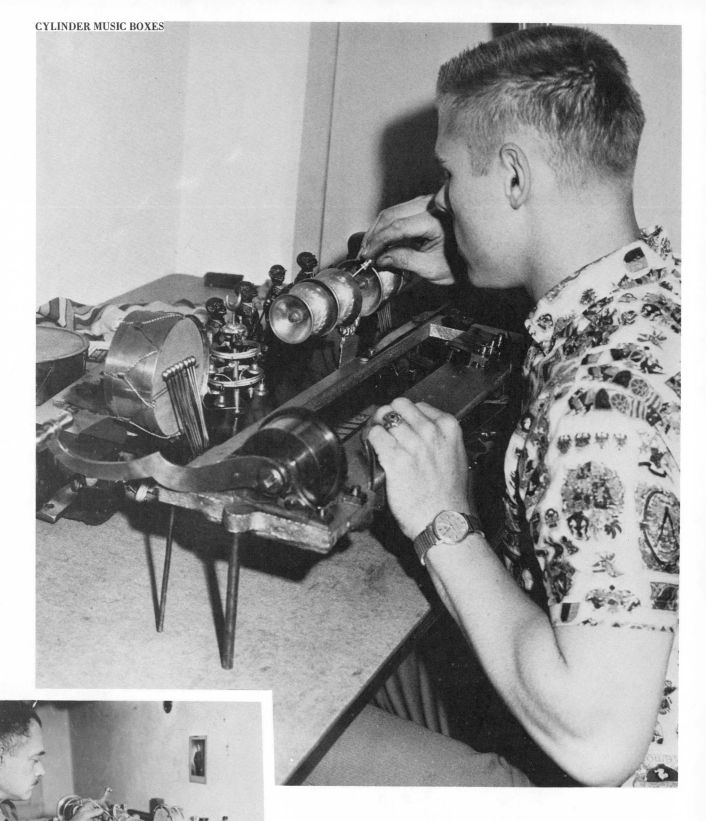

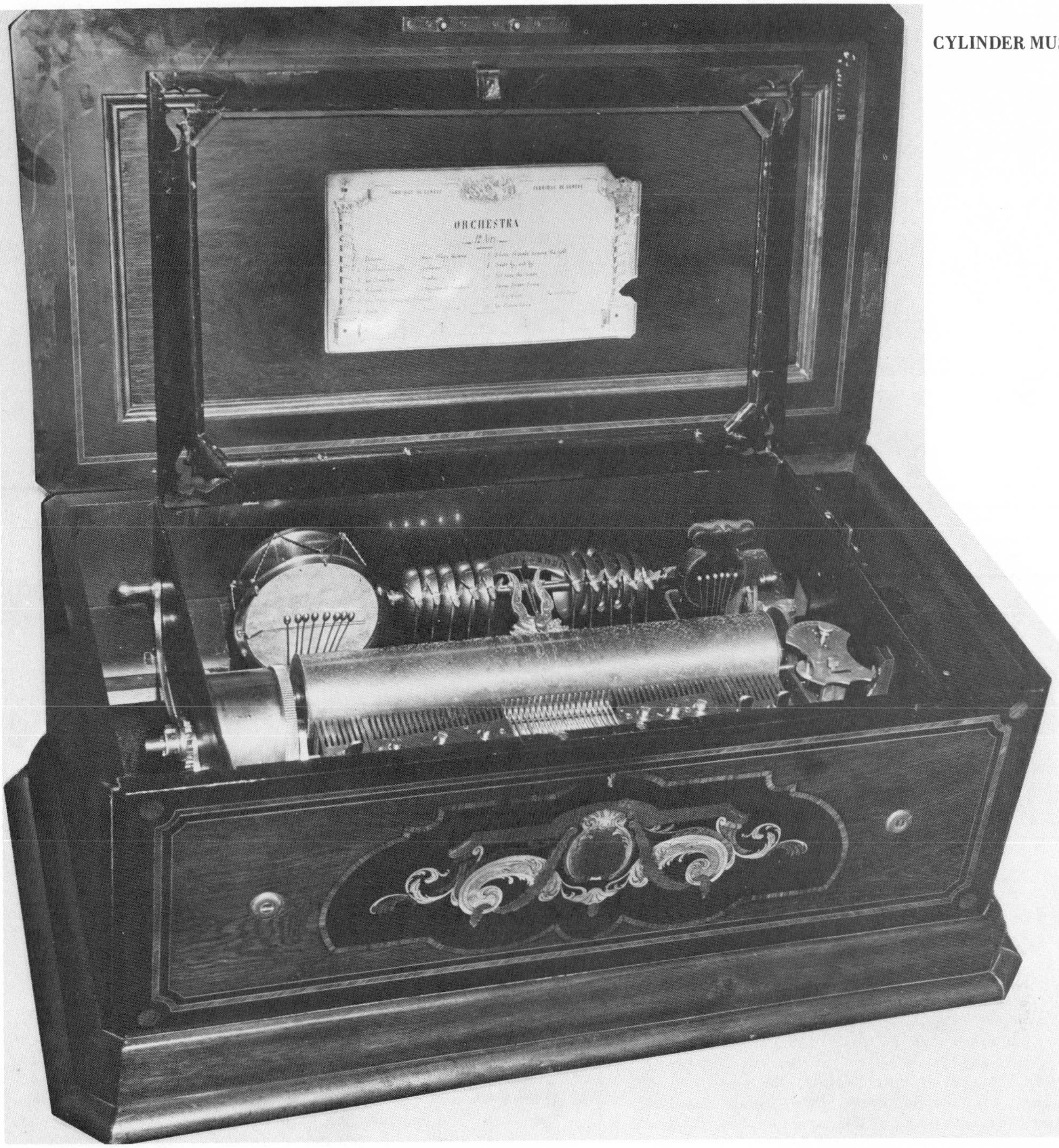


Above: An orchestra box of the general type made during the late 1870's through the early 1890's. From left to right behind the cylinder are seen a snare drum with eight beaters, ten bells (mounted in an unusual nested vertical position) with the tune indicator in the center, and, to the far right, a wood drum (often called "wood block" or "castanets"). At the front center of the cylinder are the keys for operating the reed organ attachment. In certain expensive orchestra boxes the reed organ section could be disconnected by a lever, however this was the exception. The percussion effects nearly always could be disconnected in this manner. As many different manufacturers ordered drums, organ reeds, and other components from common suppliers and as most makers did not sign their instruments it is often difficult to attribute later boxes to specific makers today. Sometimes, however, initials or trademarks are found on the music comb, governor, or bedplate. These can often be identified by checking references such as "Collecting Music Boxes and How to Repair Them" by Arthur W.J.G. Ord-Hume or "The Cylinder Musical Box Handbook" by Graham Webb.

Right: Musical movement of a cylinder box by Allard of Geneva, Switzerland. Note that the layout, with the exception of the bells, is similar to the instrument shown at the top of the page.

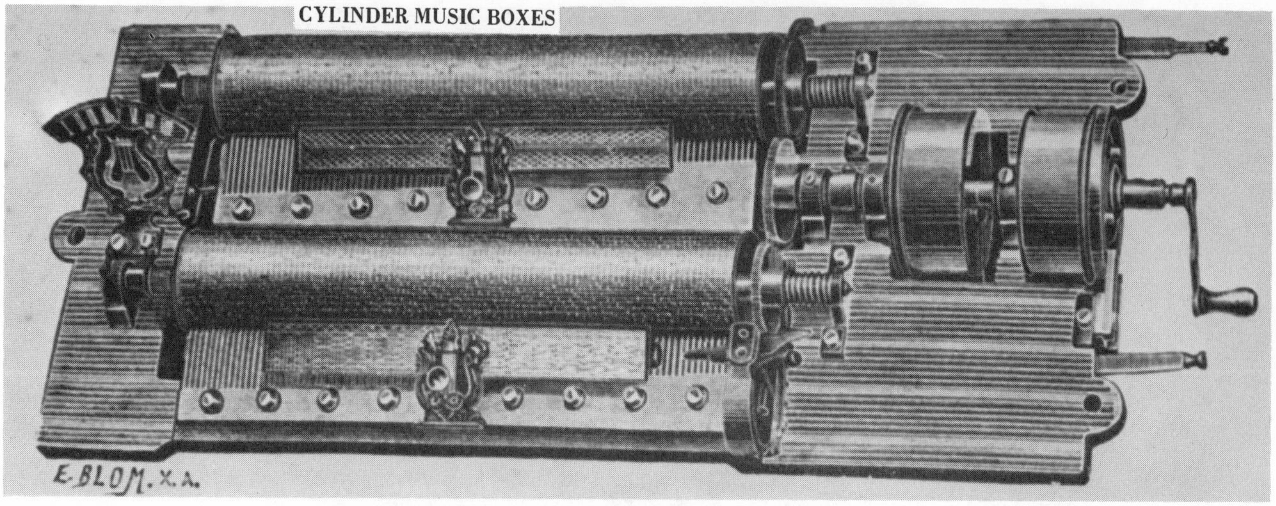

Duplex music box (from an 1895 catalogue).

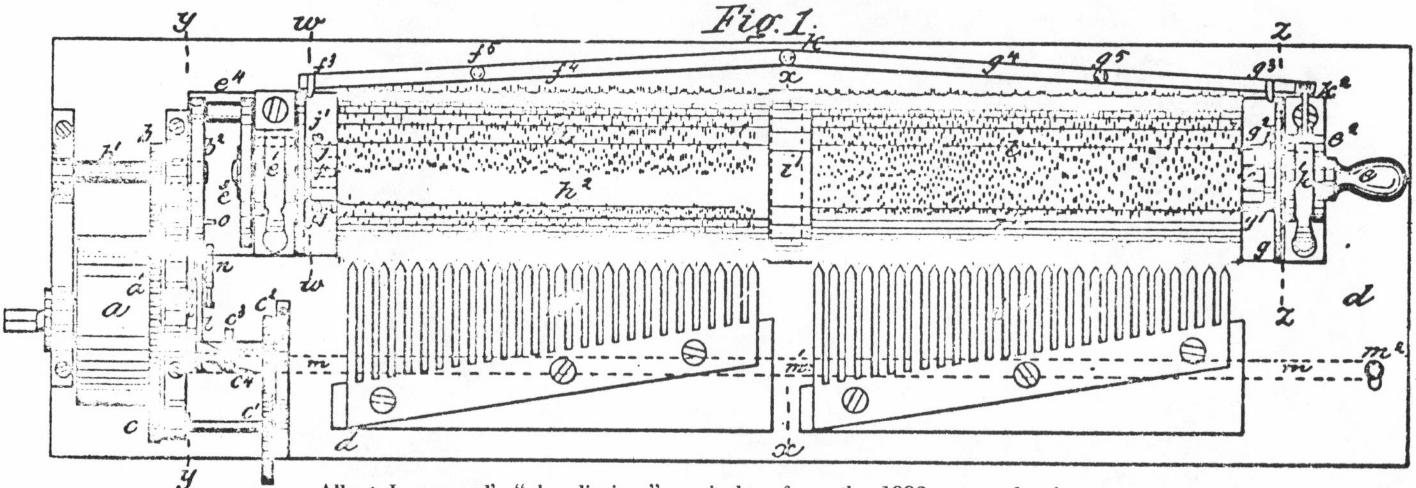


Albert Jeanrenaud's "plerodienique" music box from the 1882 patent drawing.

—Duplex and Plerodienique Boxes—

The duplex cylinder box, patented by Alfred Junod in the 1880's, consists of two cylinders, each of the same length and number of tunes, mounted one in front of the other. The two cylinders are synchronized by being geared together, as the top illustration shows. A single governor provides the speed control. As both cylinders play simultaneously, there is no tonal or musical arrangement advantage that this type of box possesses over a single cylinder box with the same total cylinder length. The top illustration on this page is from an 1895 catalogue which notes that the instrument can be purchased in two formats, each with cylinders measuring 31 cm. long. One type has eight tunes and the other has the teeth spaced a greater distance apart and plays ten tunes.

Apart from its novelty appearance, the duplex cylinder box offered little advantage to the purchaser. Probably for this reason only a few were manufactured.

The plerodienique type of box, as it is called by collectors today, was invented in the 1880's by Albert Jeanrenaud of St. Croix, Switzerland. U.S. Patent No. 266,826 was granted on October 31, 1882, and was assigned to M.J. Paillard & Co. of New York. The cylinders in the plerodienique box are placed end-to-end on the same shaft. As one plays, the other shifts laterally and changes tunes — with a continuous musical performance being the result. Jeanrenaud's patent application states the advantages succinctly:

"In ordinary music boxes there is an intermission at the end of each revolution of the cylinder, on account of the longitudinal blank space on the cylinder, necessary to permit it, without injury to the pins or teeth, to be moved by the tune-changer to bring another set of pins into action opposite the points of the keys. Thus such instruments can play only short selections.

"It has been attempted [by others] to remedy this by arranging the pins on the cylinder spirally, and imparting to the same a gradual longitudinal movement corresponding to the spiral arrangement of the pins as it is rotated in front of the keys. [Editor's note: This arrangement, called the "helicoidal" system, was used infrequently on cylinder boxes. It was, however, commonly used on barrel-type orchestrions.] This was impractical as a complex mechanism would be required to bring the cylinder away from the teeth in order to return the cylinder to the starting position.

"Now, my improvements in musical boxes are such that pieces of music which require two or more revolutions of the pin-studded cylinder may be rendered with perfect continuity in a practical manner. They consist of:

"First, in arranging two similar pin-studded cylinders of the ordinary construction end-to-end on the one driving shaft, opposite the teeth in the music comb, each cylinder being provided with an independent tune-changing device, and the blank longitudinal spaces on the cylinder arranged in different planes, so when the blank space of one cylinder is opposite its comb of teeth and its tune-changer is actuating it the pins of the other cylinder are moving over the other comb of teeth. Thus the music is without intermission when the two cylinders are alternately moving longitudinally to bring a new section of pins in front of their respective teeth. . ."

As a result, operatic selections and other pieces of music of extended length could be performed without abbreviating the musical score. As with many inventions, the plerodienique was not a new concept. Earlier a virtually identical system was employed by Welte in the construction of orchestrions.

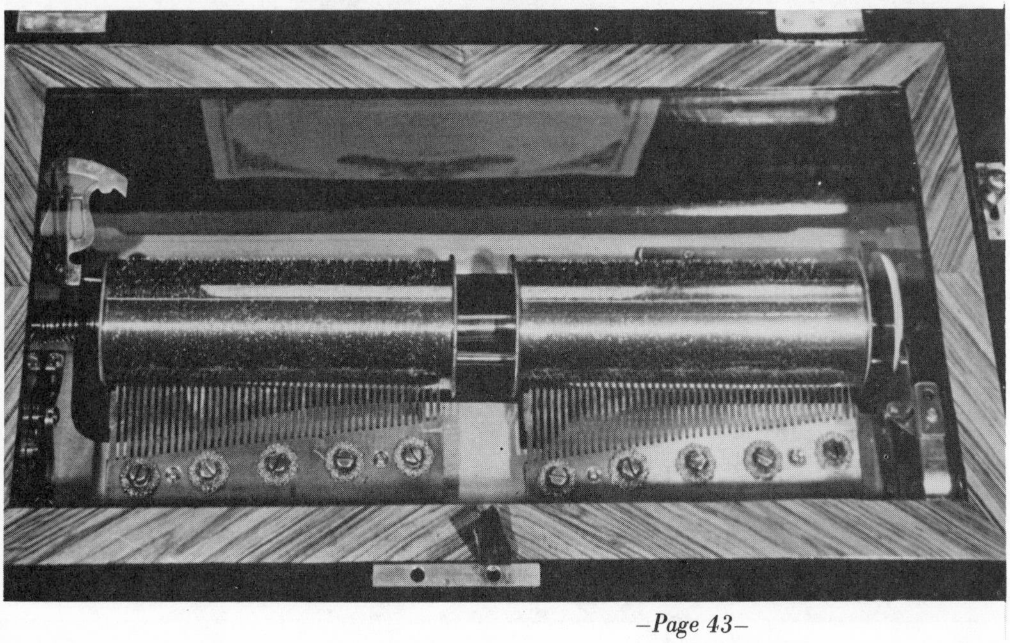

—Duplex Boxes—

Two varieties of duplex cylinder boxes from the Murtogh D. Guinness Collection are shown on this page.

Above is a Paillard box which features two cylinders and two combs. Both cylinders play at the same time.

To the left is a "lateral duplex" box with two cylinders fitted on a common shaft. Both cylinders play at the same time.

Both instruments are c.1890-1895.

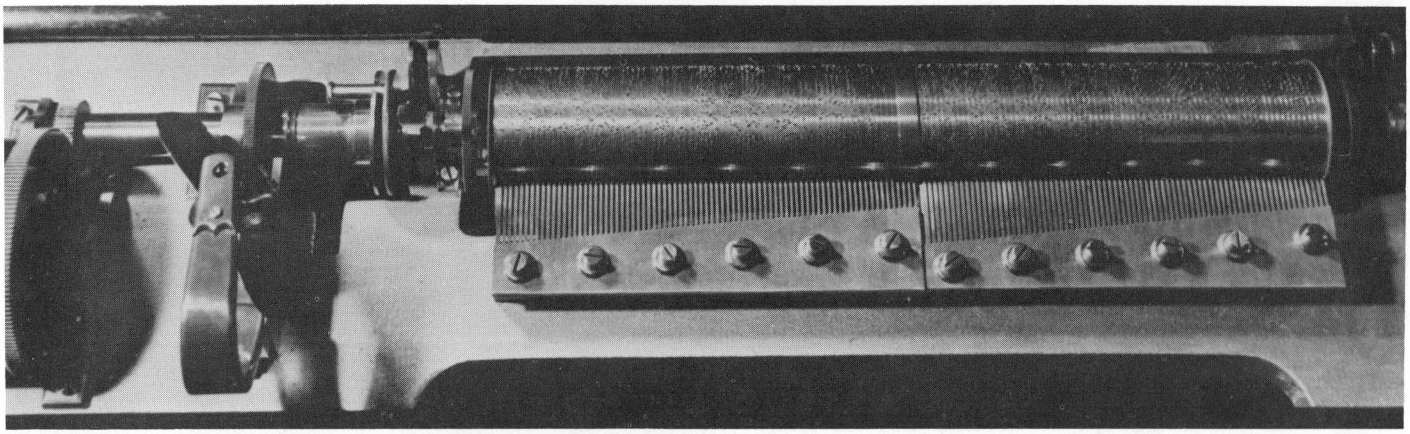

Above and left: Plerodienique or "telescopic" box by Paillard. The cylinders are separate and have tune changers at each end. First, one cylinder changes, and then the other changes; a continuous performance is the result. Although boxes of similar concept were made as early as the 1860's (see the introductory text in this cylinder music box section), most duplex cylinder boxes known today are by Paillard and date from the late 1880's or early 1890's.

Below: A beautifully-made piano-forte box made by Nicole Frères. Note the fine spacing of the teeth and the seemingly countless pins on the cylinder.

(Instruments pictured on this page are from the Murtogh D. Guinness Collection)

Semi-helicoidal orchestra box by Allard & Cie. of Geneva. (Murtogh D. Guinness Collection)

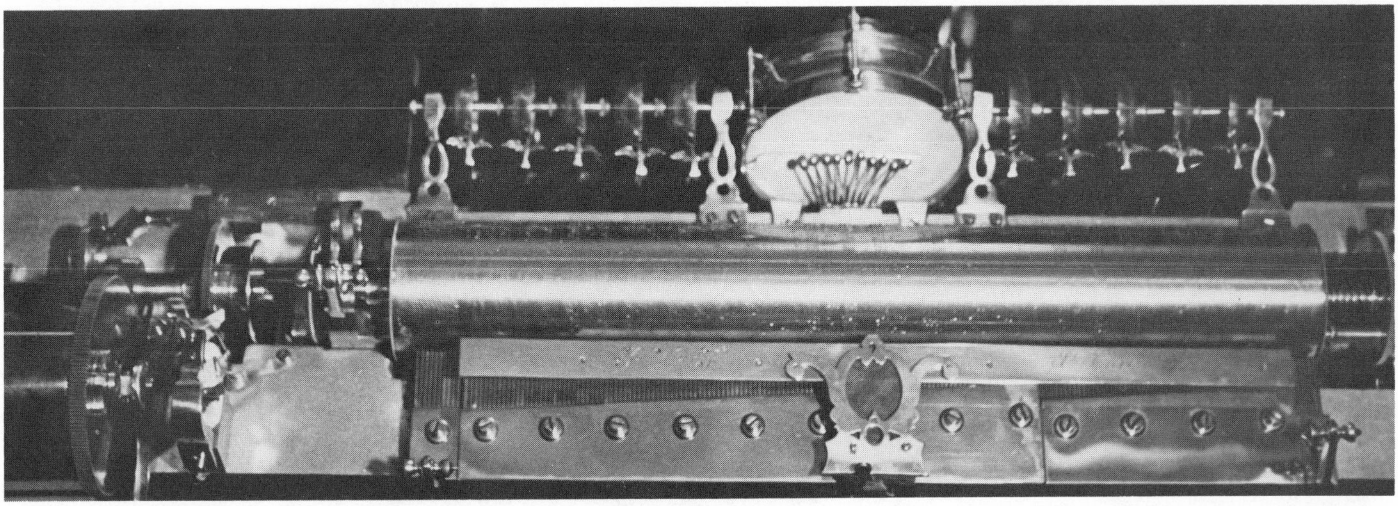

Completely helicoidal box by Paillard. Cylinder shifts continuously as the music plays. (Murtogh D. Guinness Collection)

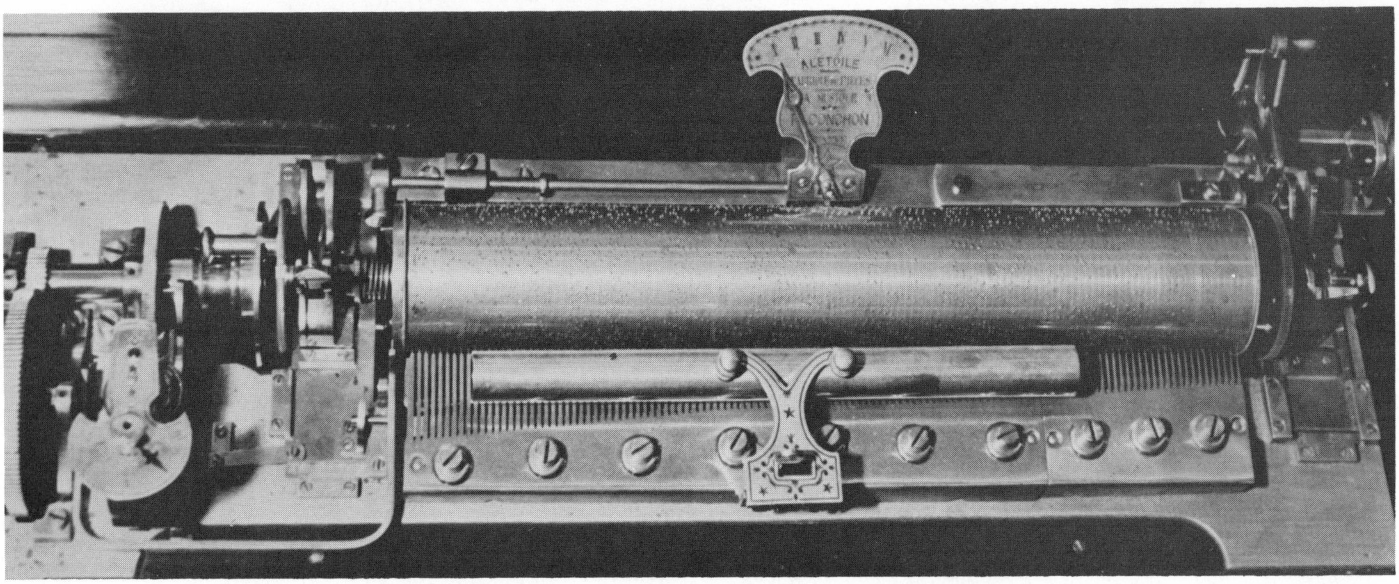

Semi-helicoidal box by Conchon. (Murtogh D. Guinness Collection)

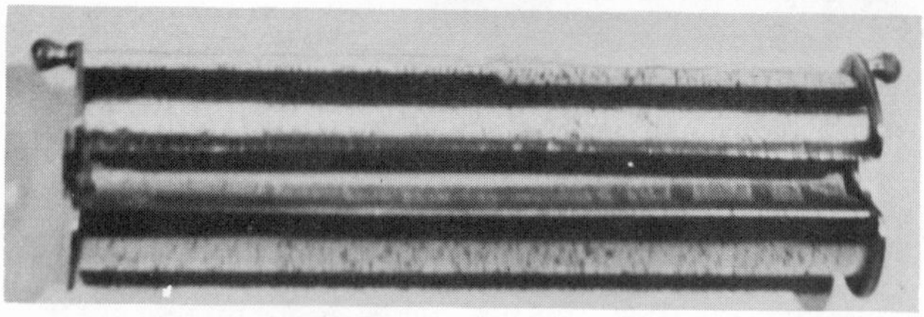

**Above: Paillard No. 601, an unusual instrument with large grooves in each of the interchangeable cylinders. A hinged bar locks the cylinder in place. (Murtogh D. Guinness Collection). Paillard made many different types of unusual cylinder boxes during the 1880's and 1890's. Other interesting products included duplex and plerodienique boxes.**

**Below: Original instruction sheet for Paillard 601 and 602. (Courtesy of Keith Harding)**

# PAILLARD'S MUSICAL BOXES.

STYLES No 601 & 602.

## Instructions for changing the Cylinders.

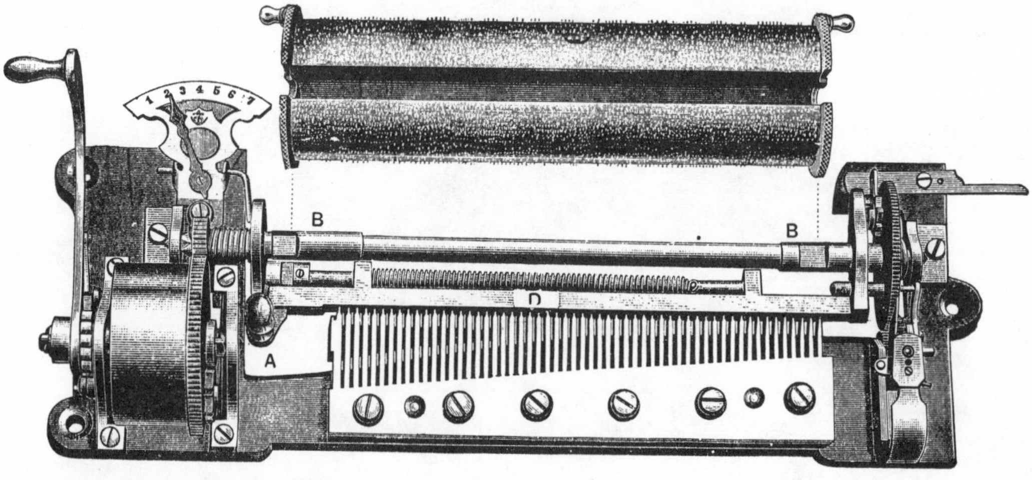


To take out the Cylinder, push the knob A to the left, at the same time pressing downward until it catches; then withdraw the Cylinder.

To insert another Cylinder, slide it in and over the slots B B, pressing it toward the comb, and lift knob A, which will push the Cylinder in place. The box will not start unless these instructions are properly followed.

It is important that no attempt should be made either to take out or insert a Cylinder before the tune is finished, when the bar D rests in front of the comb.

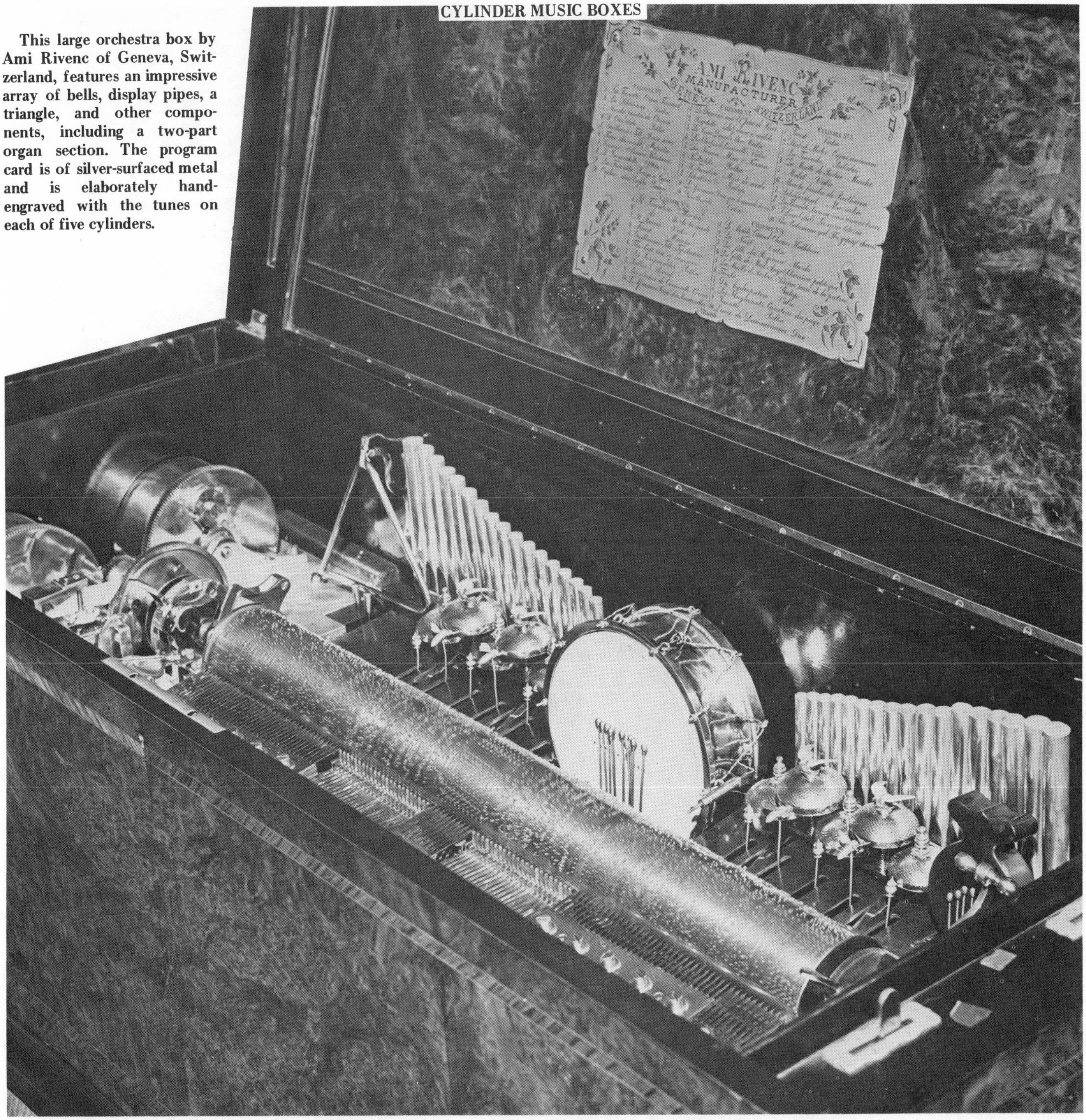

**This large orchestra box by Ami Rivenc of Geneva, Switzerland, features an impressive array of bells, display pipes, a triangle, and other components, including a two-part organ section. The program card is of silver-surfaced metal and is elaborately hand-engraved with the tunes on each of five cylinders.**

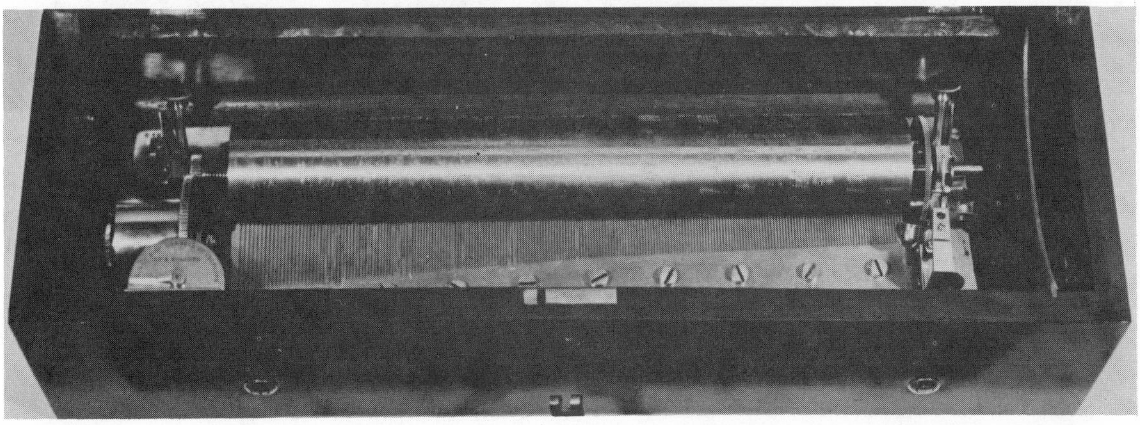

**An unusual long and short pin piano-forte box. The piano-forte effect is accomplished by using long pins in the cylinder for louder passages (the longer pins lift the teeth in the comb higher and cause them to play with greater volume) and short pins for softer passages. Marked "Kapt" – for Henri Kapt (or Capt; he used both spellings) of Geneva, Switzerland. (Murtogh D. Guinness Collection)**

The movement from an unusual "music box" which has no music combs at all! The music is provided by a large organ section comprised of a harmonium or reed organ (note pallet valves for this section at the left foreground) plus wooden flute pipes (visible behind the bells). Accompaniment is provided by bells, a wood block, and a snare drum. Such instruments are called "organ boxes." (Courtesy of Baud Frères; L'Auberson, Switzerland)

Desk model Nicole Frères music box with ten 19" cylinders, each cylinder with four overtures. Custom made circa 1880. Writing desk / music box combinations were popular in the last half of the 19th century, and most leading music box makers produced them on special order. (Mrs. Ruth Bornand photograph)

Music box made in 1878 for Czar Nicholas II of Russia. The musical movement is in an ornate ebony cabinet with ormolu trim and three signed Sevres porcelain plaques. With ten interchangeable 24"-long cylinders. Maker not identified, but attributed to Paillard. (Mrs. Ruth Bornand photograph)

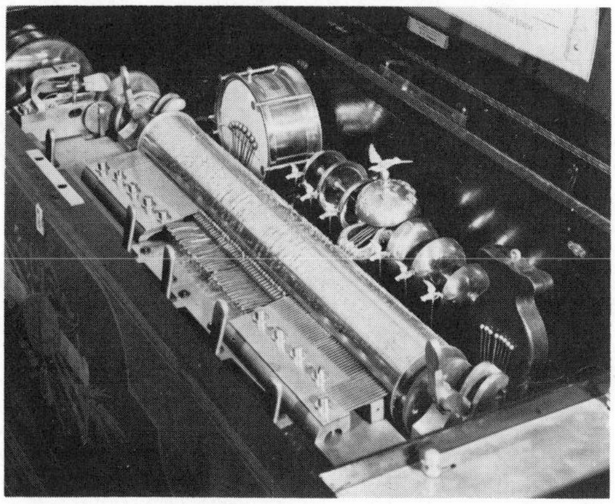

Orchestra box by B.A. Bremond. With beautiful matching base and table containing twelve interchangeable cylinders. Instrumentation consists of music combs, reed organ, flute pipes, bells, drum, and wood block. Each cylinder is 19" long and has eight melodies programmed on it. Manufactured in Geneva, Switzerland, in 1886. (Mrs. Ruth Bornand photograph)

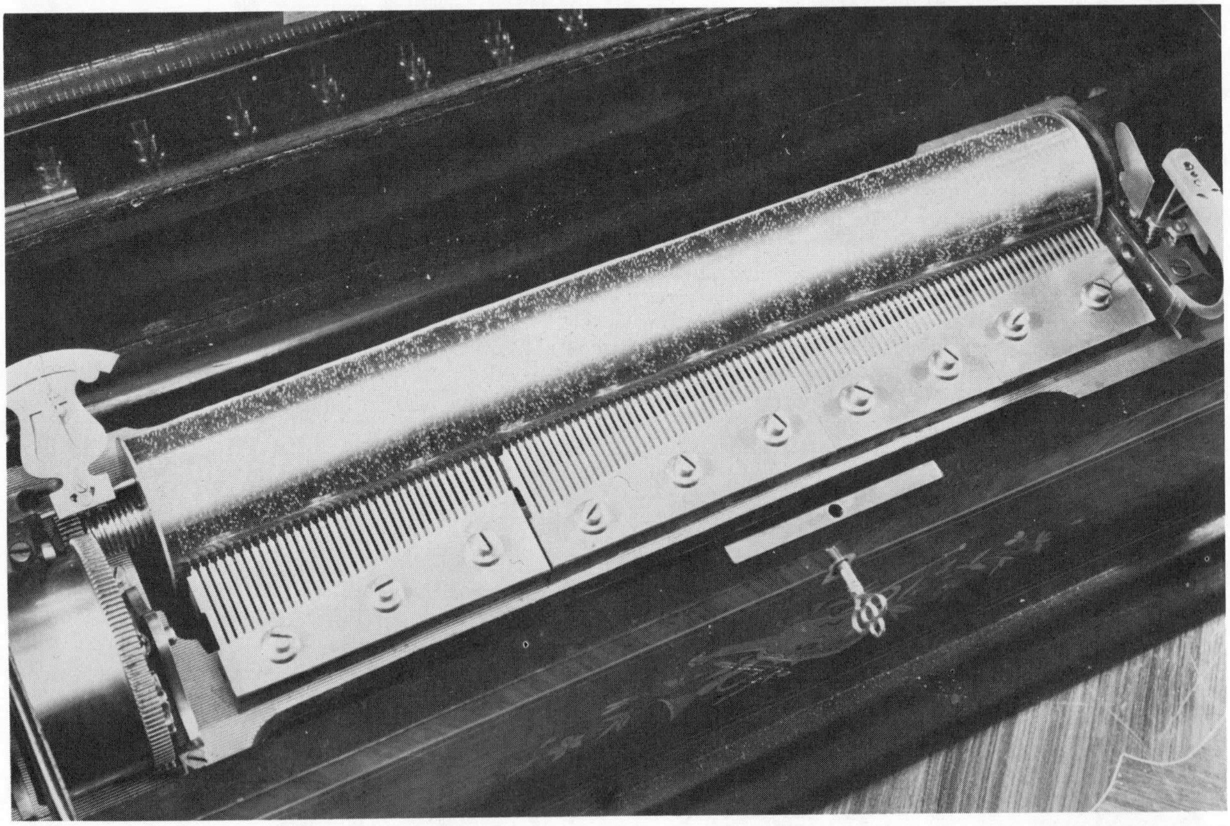

Dating from the 1880's, this Swiss music box bears the title "Quatour Expression Piccolo" on the tune sheet. The 17½" cylinder plays eight tunes on four music combs comprising 122 teeth.

The case is richly veneered in rosewood with holly banding and tulipwood borders. The lid displays a recessed panel with an elaborate inlaid design of musical instruments in multicolored woods; the front of the case has a similar but not identical design.

The two larger combs on the left (each 5 3/16" long with 37 teeth) constitute the sublime harmonie type format. The third comb to the right (3 5/16" long with 24 teeth) is pinned with bright melody arrangements. The fourth comb to the right (3 5/16" long with 24 teeth) is the "piccolo" comb and carries a bright accompaniment. (Collection of Drs. Robert and Edith Owen)

—Music Boxes at an Exhibition—

This photograph, taken in 1893 at the World's Columbian Exposition in Chicago, shows the exhibit of Mermod Frères of St. Croix, Switzerland. Featured in the exhibit are many ornate instruments of the "Ideal" and "Peerless" trademarks. Sponsored by Jacot & Son of New York City, the exhibit has several signs which read "Jacot's Ideal Musical Boxes Play Any Number of Tunes." Note the many cylinders hanging from the backdrop.

Mermod Frères music boxes were the most popular type of quality music box (as opposed to small musical movements used in souvenirs, novelties, etc.) sold in the United States in the late 19th century. Distribution was by means of music stores, department stores, and jewelry firms in most metropolitan areas. While no figures are available, it is apparent that the instruments were sold by the thousands, if not by the tens of thousands. Priced from about $50 for a small (but high quality) box to over $1000 for one of the elaborate models, the Mermod Frères instruments met with great success. The brilliant tone, considered by many enthusiasts to be among the finest of the later instruments (as compared to the early, softly-voiced overture boxes), combined with a musical program containing many American favorite tunes helped to a large degree.

Many of the Mermod Frères cylinder boxes of the late 1880's and the 1890's were made of light golden oak, a wood finish popular on the American market, but a format used by few other Swiss cylinder box makers.

What appears to be a lightly decorated solid plaque directly above the cylinders in the above photograph is an artist's retouching. The plaque was really a large and boldly lettered sign which read, in part, "MERMOD FRÈRES - Ste. CROIX, SWITZERLAND." The above illustration is from a history of the Columbian Exposition. Perhaps it was considered desirable to downplay advertising of foreign music box makers in 1894, the year the book was prepared. At that time the American music box industry, spearheaded by Regina, was beginning. We learned of this "censorship" by seeing a part of the same scene reproduced, complete with the bold sign, in a Mermod Frères catalogue.

When the market for cylinder music boxes faded in the late 1890's, Mermod Frères entered the disc music box market. The firm produced the Mira (also called "Empress") and Stella boxes, two of the finest instrument types ever made — from a tonal quality viewpoint. At the same time the firm engaged in the manufacture of pocket watches and other timepieces.

# INTERCHANGEABLE CYLINDER MUSICAL BOXES.

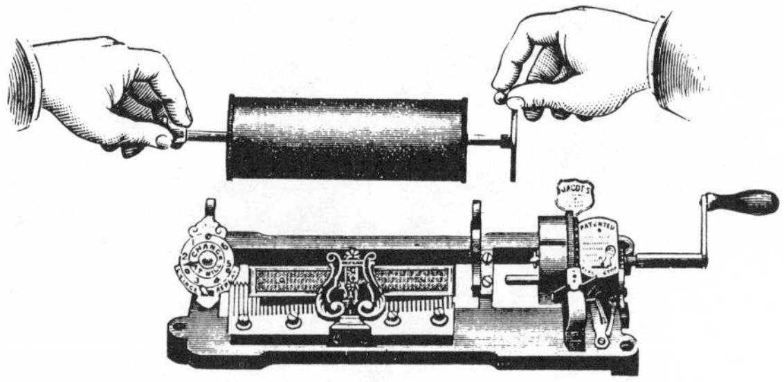

MOVEMENT OF THE PEERLESS FORTE-PICCOLO.

## PEERLESS FORTE-PICCOLO.

Inlaid rosewood case, nickel movement, wound with a crank and playing 8 to 10 minutes with one winding, tune indicator, tune skipper, and safety check.

Each.
No. 366, 6 tunes, 7½-inch cylinder, case 20 x 9½ x 7 inches.............$50.00
" 367, extra cylinder of 6 tunes for above............................ 11.25

## PEERLESS FORTE-PICCOLO,

WITH ZITHER.

Each.
No. 370, 6 tunes, 9-inch cylinder, case 22 x 9 x 7 inches.................$75.00
" 371, extra cylinder of 6 tunes for above........................... 18.75

## PEERLESS FORTE-PICCOLO.

Nickel movement, wound with a crank, and playing 8 to 10 minutes with one winding, tune indicator, tune skipper and safety check. The case is of American manufacture, with paneled cover, and guaranteed never to warp or split.

Each
No. 368, 6 tunes, 7½-inch cylinder, oak or mahogany case, 22 x 12½ x 8½ inches.............................................$60.00
" 367, extra cylinders of 6 tunes for above......................... 11.25
" 372, 6 tunes, 9-inch cylinder, zither attachment, oak or mahogany cases, 24½ x 13½ x 8½ inches................................ 87.50
" 371, extra cylinder of 6 tunes for above........................... 18.75

## PEERLESS FORTE-PICCOLO.

Oak or mahogany case, with drawer to hold three cylinders.

Each.
No. 369, 6 tunes, 7½-inch cylinder, case 23 x 13½ x 11 inches............$75.00
" 367, extra cylinder of 6 tunes for above........................... 11.25
" 374, 6 tunes, 9-inch cylinder, zither attachment, case 25½ x 14½ x 11 inches............................................100.00
" 371, extra cylinder of six tunes for above.......................... 18.75

**MERMOD FRÈRES**

**Founded in 1816 (some sources say 1815), the firm described itself as being "horologists and makers of musical movements." It was during the last half of the 19th century that the firm became the largest Swiss maker of large music boxes.**

**During the 1880 - 1900 period the firm of Mermod Frères (Mermod Brothers) was composed of Gustave Alfred Mermod, Louis Philippe Mermod, and Leon Marcel Mermod. While other firms, notably Paillard and Bremond in Switzerland and L'Epee in France, made music boxes in large quantities, none of these firms adopted mass-production techniques to the extent that Mermod Frères did.**

**The interchangeable cylinder boxes made by this firm were not only interchangeable on the same box, they were interchangeable with other boxes of the same style as well. This was a sharp departure from the practice of most other makers who fitted and adjusted cylinders so that they would fit one particular box and no other.**

Nos. 366 and 370.

No. 372.

No. 374.

With coupled mainspring, tune indicator, tune skipper, moderator (for fast or slow), nickel movement, cylinders of extra large diameter, safety check, playing 18 to 20 minutes with one winding, in cases of American manufacture, guaranteed never to warp or split.

## IDEAL EXCELSIOR,

WITH ZITHER.

Each.
No. 395, 6 tunes, 9-inch cylinder, oak or mahogany case, 24 x 11 x 8 inches.$112.50
" 396, extra cylinder of 6 tunes for above........................... 22.50
" 397, case to hold four 9-inch cylinders............................ 6.25

## IDEAL GUITARE,

WITH ZITHER.

Each.
No. 410, 6 tunes, 11-inch cylinder, oak or mahogany case, 29 x 13 x 9 ins..$145.00
" 411, extra cylinder of 6 tunes for above........................... 26.25

## IDEAL PICCOLO,

WITH ZITHER.

Each.
No. 412, 6 tunes, 11-inch cylinder, oak or mahogany case, 29 x 13 x 9 ins.$145.00
" 413, extra cylinder of 6 tunes for above........................... 28.75

## IDEAL SUBLIME HARMONIE,

WITH ZITHER.

Each.
No. 414, 6 tunes, 11-inch cylinder, oak or mahogany case, 29 x 13 x 9 ins..$157.50
" 415, extra cylinder of 6 tunes for above........................... 31.25

## IDEAL SOPRANO,

WITH ZITHER.

Each.
No. 416, 6 tunes, 14½-inch cylinder, oak or mahogany case, 32 x 13 x 9 ins.$205.00
" 417, extra cylinder of 6 tunes for above........................... 40.00

## CYLINDER BOXES.

These are handsomely polished of oak or cherry to match above cases.

Each.
No. 403, case to hold four 11-inch cylinders........................... $6.25
" 418, case to hold four 14½-inch cylinders........................... 7.50

## IDEAL GUITARE,

WITH ZITHER.

Each.
No. 421, 6 tunes, 11-inch cylinder, oak or mahogany case, 30½ x 14½ x 11 inches.............................................$162.50
" 411, extra cylinder of 6 tunes for above........................... 26.25

## IDEAL PICCOLO,

WITH ZITHER.

Each.
No. 423, 6 tunes, 11-inch cylinder, oak or mahogany case, 30½ x 14½ x 11 inches.............................................$162.50
" 413, extra cylinder of 6 tunes for above........................... 28.75

## IDEAL SUBLIME HARMONIE,

WITH ZITHER.

Each.
No. 425, 6 tunes, 11-inch cylinder, oak or mahogany case, 30½ x 14½ x 11 inches.............................................$175.00
" 415, extra cylinder of 6 tunes for above........................... 31.25

## IDEAL SOPRANO,

WITH ZITHER.

Each.
No. 431, 6 tunes, 14½-inch cylinder, oak or mahogany case, 34 x 15½ x 11 inches.............................................$225.00
" 417, extra cylinder of 6 tunes for above........................... 40.00

## CYLINDER BOXES.

These are handsomely polished, of oak or cherry, to match above cases.

Each.
No. 403, case to hold four 11-inch cylinders...........................$6.25
" 418, " " 14½ " " ........................... 7.50

**Mermod Frères Cylinder Music Boxes**

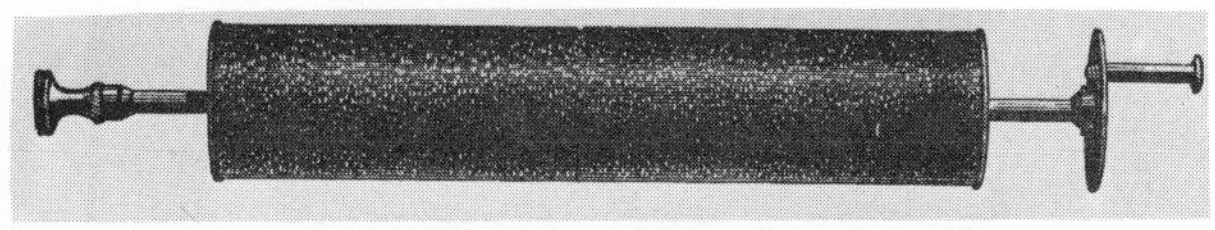

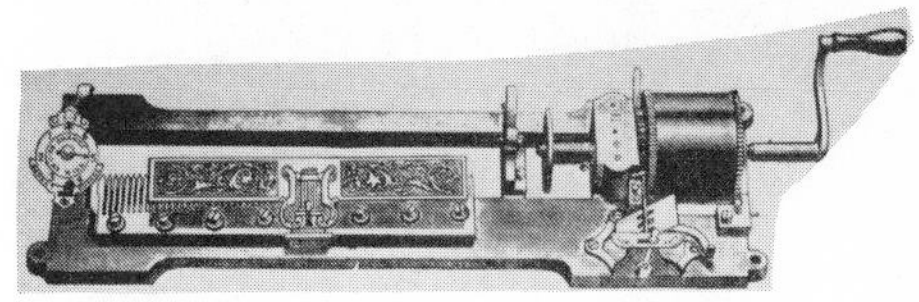

MOVEMENT OF IDEAL MUSICAL BOX.

Nos. 395, 410, 412, 414 and 416.

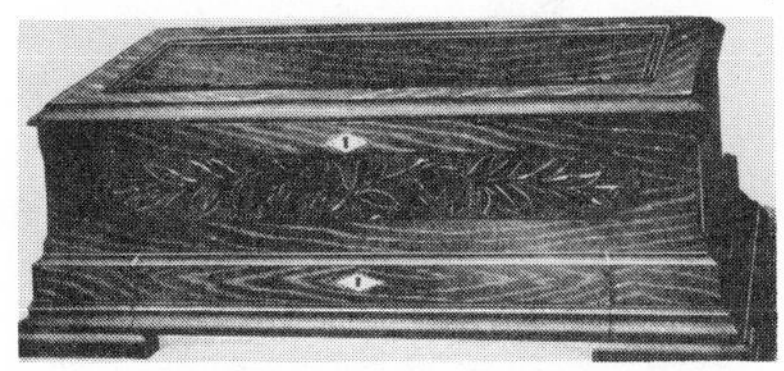

Nos. 421, 423, 425 and 431.

**(Mermod Frères, cont'd)**

**Mermod Frères' main sales area seems to have been America. The firm's catalogues noted that the cases were "of American manufacture." Examination of extant instruments today indicates that most, if not all, of the carved oak cabinets and carved mahogany cabinets of the same designs were of American origin. The uncarved but elaborately inlaid styles of the 1880's appear to have been made in Europe. Certain rare Mermod Frères movements exist in nearly square cases of the same general appearance as those used by Regina, F.G. Otto, and the Symphonion Manufacturing Company – all of New Jersey.**

**In his book, "Collecting Music Boxes and How to Repair Them," Arthur W.J.G. Ord-Hume notes that "the firm was noted for remarkably ingeniously constructed musical boxes and the music on their cylinder machines was always set up in a most brilliant form." The music was brilliant and rich without the raspiness that characterized certain other "brilliant" boxes of the 1890's. For this reason the instruments of Mermod Frères are considered to be first class by collectors today.**

**The 1895 Mermod Frères catalogue preface tells of the various types of music boxes made by the firm and gives other details:**

**"In every age the ennobling and elevating power of music has made itself felt and appreciated. From the savage to the most highly cultivated, none are exempt from its charms; indeed, so important a place does it occupy as an accomplishment, that no education is complete without it. But how much time and money must be sacrificed before a person becomes proficient in playing the piano or other instruments in an acceptable manner? In this busy age comparatively few are willing to devote the time necessary to do this.**

SOLID MAHOGANY CASE.

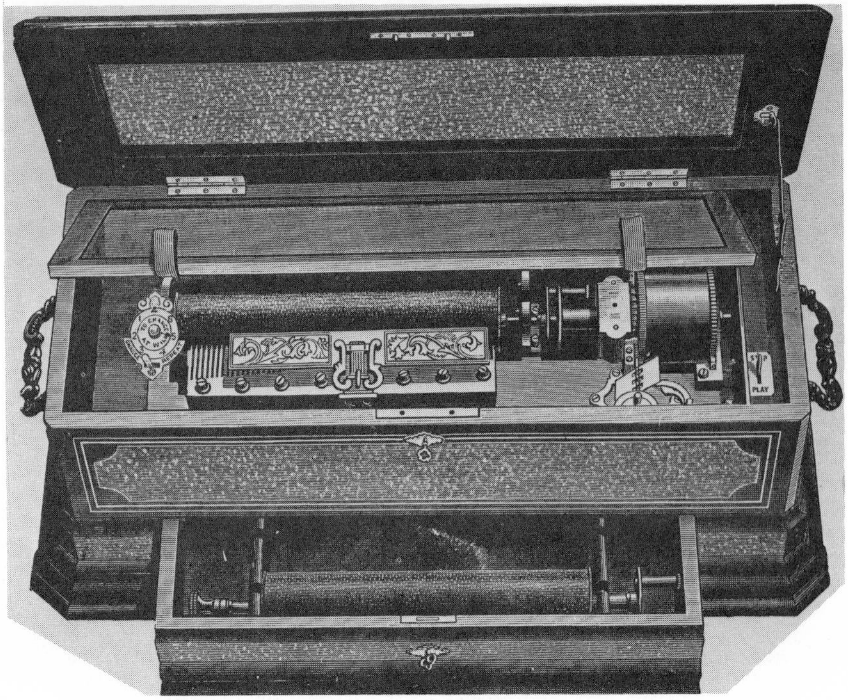

INLAID MAHOGANY CASE.

## IDEAL GUITARE,

WITH ZITHER.

| | Each. |
|---|---|
| No. 420, 6 tunes, 11-inch cylinder, inlaid mahogany case, 31 x 16 x 11 inches | $197.50 |
| " 420¼, 6 tunes, 11-inch cylinder, mahogany case, 31 x 16 x 11 inches | 197.50 |
| " 420½, 6 tunes, 11-inch cylinder, oak case, 31 x 16 x 11 inches | 185.00 |
| " 411, extra cylinder of 6 tunes for above | 26.25 |

## IDEAL PICCOLO,

WITH ZITHER.

| | Each. |
|---|---|
| No. 422, 6 tunes, 11-inch cylinder, inlaid mahogany case, 31 x 16 x 11 inches | $197.50 |
| " 422¼, 6 tunes, 11-inch cylinder, mahogany case, 31 x 16 x 11 inches | 197.50 |
| " 422½, 6 tunes, 11-inch cylinder, oak case, 31 x 16 x 11 inches | 185.00 |
| " 413, extra cylinder of 6 tunes for above | 28.75 |

## IDEAL SUBLIME HARMONIE,

WITH ZITHER.

| | Each. |
|---|---|
| No. 424, 6 tunes, 11-inch cylinder, inlaid mahogany case, 31 x 16 x 11 inches | $210.00 |
| " 424¼, 6 tunes, 11-inch cylinder, mahogany case, 31 x 16 x 11 inches | 210.00 |
| " 424½, 6 tunes, 11-inch cylinder, oak case, 31 x 16 x 11 inches | 197.50 |
| " 415, extra cylinder of 6 tunes for above | 31.25 |

## IDEAL SOPRANO,

WITH ZITHER.

| | Each. |
|---|---|
| No. 430, 6 tunes, 14½-inch cylinder, inlaid mahogany case, 34x16x11 inches | $257.50 |
| " 430¼, 6 tunes, 14½-inch cylinder, mahogany case, 34 x 16 x 11 inches | 257.50 |
| " 430½, 6 tunes, 14½-inch cylinder, oak case, 34 x 16 x 11 inches | 245.00 |
| " 417, extra cylinder of 6 tunes for above | 40.00 |

## IDEAL SUBLIME HARMONIE PICCOLO,

WITH ZITHER.

| | Each. |
|---|---|
| No. 435, 6 tunes, 18-inch cylinder, inlaid mahogany case, 40 x 18 x 12 inches | $362.50 |
| " 435¼, 6 tunes, 18-inch cylinder, solid mahogany case, 40 x 18 x 12 inches | 362.50 |
| " 435½, 6 tunes, 18-inch cylinder, oak case, 40 x 18 x 12 inches | 350.00 |
| " 436, extra cylinder of 6 tunes for above | 55.00 |
| " 437, case to hold four 18 inch cylinders | 8.75 |

**(Mermod Frères, cont'd)**

**"To obviate the difficulty, men of genius have labored for years to produce an instrument that will furnish refined music for the home without the necessity of years of study in its use.**

**"Among the many devices which have come to light, none fills better the purpose, nor gives more satisfactory results, than the Ideal Music Box, such as is now sold by us. Everyone hearing for the first time these instruments, and especially those of a higher grade, marvels at the power, sweetness of tone, purity and perfection with which they reproduce the most complicated music. In fact, we can confidently say that no money spent for the gratification of musical taste will be better invested than in one of these delightful instruments.**

**"Our stock of musical boxes is not limited to the varieties contained in this catalogue, but embraces other styles and sizes, which can be examined upon visiting our establishment, known to be the headquarters in the line of musical boxes.**

**"We solicit orders with the assurance that we can give to all purchasers the satisfaction that they may expect from a reliable firm and one which possesses the largest stock in the world to choose from.**

**"All orders received by mail are promptly and carefully attended to, and satisfaction is guaranteed to persons who, being not yet familiar with music boxes, leave to us the selection of the best box for the amount invested.**

**"In presenting this catalogue we wish to call particular attention to the fact that the old style musical boxes with a limited number of tunes have been superseded by a new creation, an instrument for which any number of tunes can be obtained by means of interchangeable cylinders of six tunes each, which play in rotation or repeat at will. These cylinders for the different styles and sizes all play six tunes each, but vary from 7 1/2" to 25" in length and from 2" to 3 1/2" in diameter.**

**"The length of a tune depends upon the diameter of the cylinder, while the volume of tone and number of variations depend upon its length, as the longer the comb or keyboard is the greater number of keys (teeth) it contains.**

The following style combines with the deep tone of the Sublime Harmonie orchestral effects produced by bells, drum and castanets, which can be applied separately, altogether or suppressed, playing 18 to 20 minutes with one winding, and has coupled mainsprings, tune indicator, tune skipper, moderator (for fast or slow), nickel movement, cylinders of extra large diameter and safety check. The case is of American manufacture, with carved front, and guaranteed never to warp or split. The drawer will hold three cylinders.

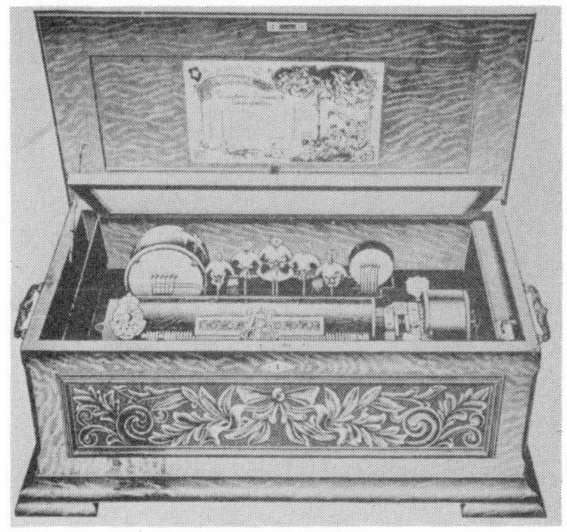

No. 500½.

## IDEAL SUBLIME HARMONIE, BELLS, DRUM AND CASTANETS,

WITH ZITHER.

| | Each. |
|---|---|
| No. 500¼, 6 tunes, 14½-inch cylinder, mahogany case 34 x 18 x 13 inches | $337.50 |
| " 500½, 6 tunes, 14½-inch cylinder, oak case 34 x 18 x 13 inches | 325.00 |
| " 501, extra cylinder of 6 tunes for above | 45.00 |
| " 418, case to hold four 14½-inch cylinders | 7.50 |

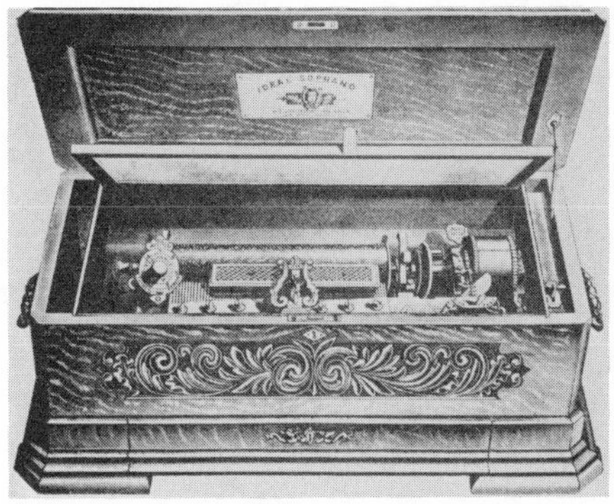

ANTIQUE OAK CASE.

## IDEAL SOPRANO,

WITH ZITHER.

| | Each. |
|---|---|
| No. 510¼, 6 tunes, 14½-inch cylinder, mahogany case, 38 x 19 x 13 inches | $387.50 |
| " 510½, 6 tunes, 14½-inch cylinder, oak case, 38 x 19 x 13 inches | 375.00 |
| " 511, extra cylinder of 6 tunes for above | 80.00 |
| " 512, case to hold three 14½-inch cylinders | 8.75 |

## IDEAL QUATUOR SOPRANO,

WITH ZITHER.

| | Each. |
|---|---|
| No. 440, 6 tunes, 20-inch cylinder, inlaid mahogany case, 42 x 19 x 13 inches | $650.00 |
| " 440¼, 6 tunes, 20 inch cylinder, solid mahogany case, 42 x 19 x 13 inches | 650.00 |
| " 440½, 6 tunes, 20-inch cylinder, oak case, 42 x 19 x 13 inches | 637.50 |
| " 441, extra cylinder of 6 tunes for above | 130.00 |
| " 442, case to hold three 20-inch cylinders | 10.00 |

OAK TABLE IN COMBINATION WITH IDEAL MUSICAL BOX.

## IDEAL SUBLIME HARMONIE PICCOLO,

WITH ZITHER.

| | Each. |
|---|---|
| No. 520¼, 6 tunes, 24½ inch cylinder, mahogany case, 49 x 20 x 14 inches | $787.50 |
| " 520½, 6 tunes, 24½-inch cylinder, oak case, 49 x 20 x 14 inches | 775.00 |
| " 521, extra cylinder of 6 tunes for above | 175.00 |

## IDEAL ORCHESTRAS.

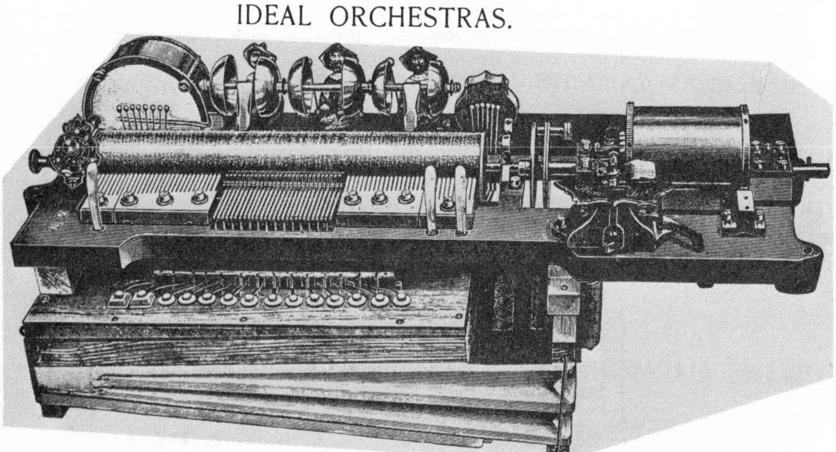

This style combines the tone of a music box with rich and mellow reed music (Celestial Voices), having a very deep bass and orchestral effects of Bells, Drum and Castanets.

Nos. 438 and 443.

# INTERCHANGEABLE CYLINDER MUSICAL BOXES.



IN MAHOGANY CABINETS.

a beautiful mahogany cabinet, the upper part of which contains the movement, and the lower a set of drawers to contain extra cylinders, while just under the movement are two small drawers for programme cards, etc. This cabinet is elaborately carved, beautifully polished and guaranteed not to warp or split. The dimensions are: Length, 42 inches; height, 48 inches; width, 18 inches.

## IDEAL SUBLIME HARMONIE PICCOLO,

WITH ZITHER.

PLAYING 30 TO 35 MINUTES.

| | Each. |
|---|---|
| No. 438, 6 tunes, 18-inch cylinder, 2½ inches in diameter, with cabinet and 7 drawers to hold 20 cylinders | $812.50 |
| " 436, extra cylinder of 6 tunes for above | 55.00 |

## IDEAL QUATUOR SOPRANO.

PLAYING 50 TO 60 MINUTES AND LONG TUNES.

| | Each. |
|---|---|
| No. 443, 6 tunes, 20-inch cylinder, 3½ inches in diameter, with cabinet and 6 drawers to hold 12 cylinders | $1,100.00 |
| " 441, extra cylinder of 6 tunes for above | 130.00 |

# SMALL MUSICAL BOXES.

WITH SPRING.

*Highly polished inlaid cases and mahogany cases with chromo covers.*

| | | | | | Each. |
|---|---|---|---|---|---|
| No. 26, | 2 tunes, | 1½-inch cylinder, | self-changing; | case 4¾ x 3 inches | $4.88 |
| " 28, | 2 " | 2 " | " " | " 5¼ x 3½ " | 5.50 |
| " 30, | 2 " | 2½ " | " " | " 5¼ x 3½ " | 6.88 |
| " 32, | 4 " | 2½ " | " " | " 5¼ x 3½ " | 8.75 |
| " 34, | 4 " | 3 " | " " | " 5¼ x 3½ " | 10.63 |
| " 36, | 6 " | 3 " | " " | " 5¼ x 3½ " | 11.88 |

## HARP-ZITHER ATTACHMENT.

*The Zither is a novel contrivance to produce the sound of a stringed instrument combined with the usual tone of the Music Box. It can be removed at will, and can be attached to any box, new or old.*

| | Each. |
|---|---|
| No. 64, Harp-Zither for Nos. 71, 72 and 76 | $2.50 |
| " 65, " " " 78 to 113 | 3.13 |

**(Mermod Frères, cont'd)**

**"Our interchangeable cylinder music boxes are divided into two groups: the Ideal and the Peerless.**

**"The Peerless is a low priced instrument with a single spring, while the Ideal contains two coupled mainsprings and all the latest improvements. Both these styles are made of the best material and with improved American machinery, which makes all parts of the same style absolutely interchangeable except the combs. All the cases except those of rosewood are of American manufacture, of thoroughly seasoned wood, hand carved, and finely finished. [Editor's note: While the machinery used to make the Mermod Frères boxes may have been made in America, the boxes themselves were made in Switzerland — except for certain of the wood exterior cases, as noted. Perhaps due to now-forgotten xenophobia, the Swiss origin of the boxes was nowhere mentioned in the Mermod literature distributed in this country.]**

**"Besides the cylinders regularly in stock for all our Ideal and Peerless boxes, cylinders which contain selections from the principal operas, the latest popular music, ballads, hymns, etc., we make to order cylinders playing any melodies that may be desired. Such cylinders can be had in two or three months' time.**

**"The tone of a music box depends upon the tuning of the comb or combs, and the way that the pins are arranged on the cylinder. The best results are obtained from music boxes having two combs, such as the Sublime Harmonie and the Soprano, etc., and each style is arranged to play different effects.**

**"PEERLESS FORTE-PICCOLO. This style produces new musical effects and has a loud, full tone with brilliant piccolo variations.**

**"IDEAL EXCELSIOR. The tone of this style is much better than that of the ordinary grade of music boxes, both stronger and deeper without being harsh.**

**"IDEAL GUITARE. The tone of this style is rather soft, and in combination with the zither is similar to that of a guitar or mandolin; it is produced by a number of keys of the same pitch playing in rapid succession, which give it a tremolo sound. We recommend it to all desiring a sweet toned instrument.**

**"IDEAL PICCOLO. This is similar in principle to the Guitare, but with a light tremolo and the addition of an octave of very high notes, introducing beautiful variations and imitating the piccolo flute, producing a brilliant effect.**

**"IDEAL SUBLIME HARMONIE. This style has two combs, each with bass and treble, which result in producing a much deeper and more mellow tone, fine effects of forte and piano and greater expression.**

**"IDEAL SOPRANO. This has all the qualities of the Sublime Harmonie, but the four parts, soprano, alto, tenor, and bass, are more evenly combined.**

**"IDEAL SUBLIME HARMONIE PICCOLO. This style has the deep tone of the Sublime Harmonie, and in addition, the beautiful variation of the Piccolo. The melody is more distinct in this than in the Soprano, as the treble and bass predominate.**

**"Improvements:**

**"Coupled Mainsprings. This improvement doubles the running time of a music box, and makes the Ideals play eighteen to sixty minutes with one winding, according to size.**

**"Tune Indicator. This is a dial with figures corresponding to those on the programme, and a hand controlled by the motion of the cylinder and pointing to the number of the tune playing.**

**"Tune Skipper. This is a mechanism by means of which the cylinder can be set at once on any tune desired without being obliged to listen to the intervening tune. It consists of a thumb-screw in the center of the tune indicator, which is turned until the hand of the indicator points to the tune desired.**

# LARGE MUSICAL BOXES.

*These boxes are operated by a powerful spring, and are wound with a crank at the right end of case. They have an inside glass cover, nickel-plated trimmings, locks, etc., and the movement is our improved model, playing 7 to 10 minutes with one winding.*

| | | | | |
|---|---|---|---|---|
| No. 71, | 6 tunes, | 3½-inch cylinder, | case 14 x 7 inches | $15.63 |
| " 72, | 6 " | 4½ " " | " 16 x 8 " | 21.25 |
| " 76, | 8 " | 5½ " " | " 17 x 9 " | 26.25 |
| " 78, | 10 " | 7½ " " | " 20 x 9½ " | 32.50 |

No. 78 with Safety Check.

*With imitation Rosewood case, tune indicator, safety check, and nickel-plated cylinder.*

| | | | | |
|---|---|---|---|---|
| No. 77, | 8 tunes, | 9-inch cylinder, | case 21½ x 10 inches | $40.00 |
| " 79, | 10 " | 9 " " | " 21½ x 10 " | 42.50 |
| " 82, | 12 " | 10 " " | " 22½ x 10 " | 45.00 |

*With inlaid Rosewood cover, tune indicator, tune skipper, safety check, and nickel-plated Cylinder.*

| | | | | |
|---|---|---|---|---|
| No. 111, | 10 tunes, | 11-inch cylinder, | case 24½ x 10½ inches | $56.25 |
| " 113, | 12 " | 13 " " | " 26½ x 10½ " | 65.00 |

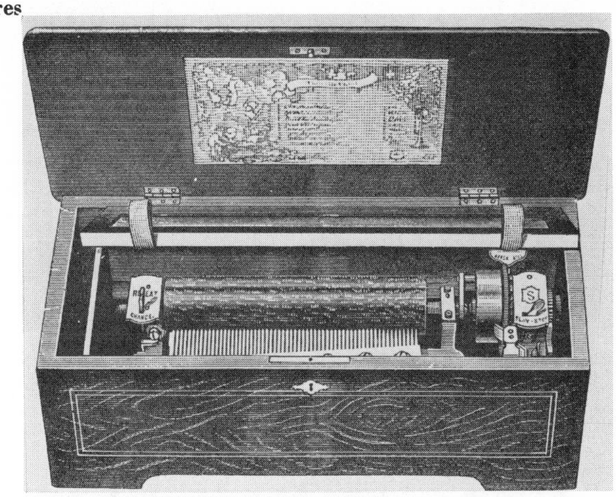

No. 77.

*With imitation Rosewood case.*

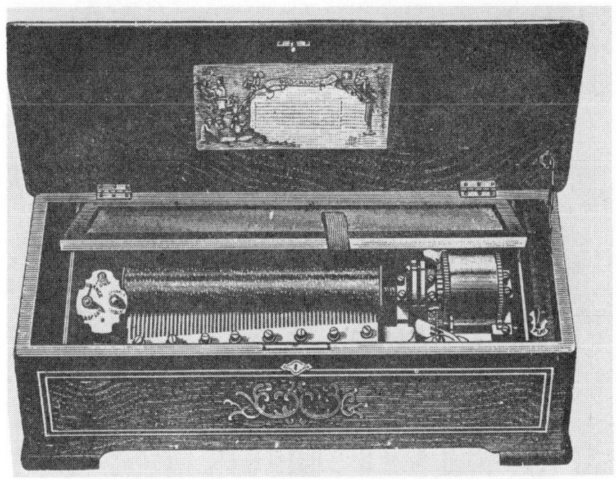

Nos. 115 and 116.

# LARGE MUSICAL BOXES.

PLAYING 18 TO 20 MINUTES.

*These Music Boxes are operated by two coupled mainsprings, wound with a crank at the right end of the case. They have an inside glass cover, nickel movement of our new model, and cylinders 2½ inches in diameter, giving longer tunes; also a tune indicator, tune skipper moderator (for fast or slow), and safety check.*

Nos. 115½ to 131½.

## INLAID ROSEWOOD CASES.

| | | | | Each. |
|---|---|---|---|---|
| No. 115, | 8 tunes, | 9-inch cylinder, | case 21 x 10½ x 7½ inches | $53.75 |
| " 116, | 10 " | 9 " " | " 21 x 10½ x 7½ " | 58.75 |

WITH ZITHER.

| | | | | Each. |
|---|---|---|---|---|
| No. 125, | 8 tunes, | 9 inch cylinder, | case 21 x 10½ x 7½ inches | $56.88 |
| " 126, | 10 " | 9 " " | " 21 x 10½ x 7½ " | 61.88 |

## ANTIQUE OAK CASES.

*With carved front, paneled cover and guaranteed never to warp or split.*

| | | | | Each. |
|---|---|---|---|---|
| No. 115½, | 8 tunes, | 9-inch cylinder, | case 21 x 10½ x 7½ inches | $60.00 |
| " 116½, | 10 " | 9 " " | " 21 x 10½ x 7½ " | 65.00 |
| " 117½, | 10 " | 11 " " | " 24 x 11 x 8 " | 72.50 |
| " 121½, | 12 " | 13 " " | " 28 x 11 x 8 " | 82.50 |

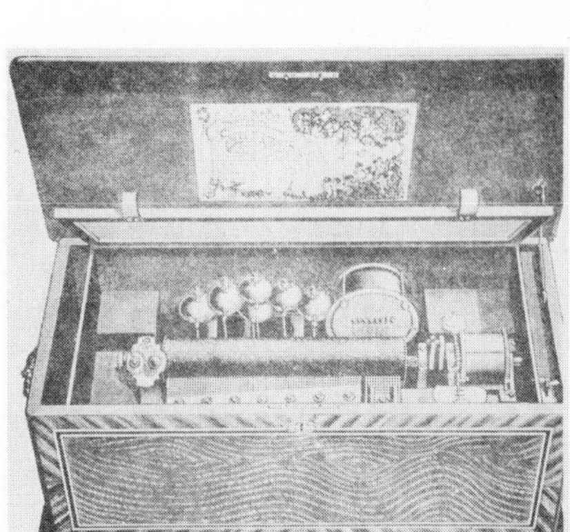

No. 160.

WITH ZITHER.

| | | | | Each. |
|---|---|---|---|---|
| No. 125½, | 8 tunes, | 9-inch cylinder, | case 21 x 10½ x 7½ inches | $63.13 |
| " 126½, | 10 " | 9 " " | " 21 x 10½ x 7½ " | 68.13 |
| " 127½, | 10 " | 11 " " | " 24 x 11 x 8 " | 75.63 |
| " 131½, | 12 " | 13 " " | " 28 x 11 x 8 " | 85.63 |

# LARGE MUSICAL BOXES.



*These styles in addition to the music produced by the comb have an accompaniment of Bells, Bells and Drum, and Bells, Drum and Castanets, any of which can be suppressed or used at will by means of a lever in the box.*

## BELLS.

*Imitation rosewood case, tune indicator, tune skipper and three bells.*

Each.

No. 135, 8 tunes, 5½-inch cylinder, case, 16 x 11 x 8½ inches........... $40.00

*Inlaid rosewood case, six bells, tune indicator, tune skipper, nickel movement and safety check.*

Each.

No. 137, 8 tunes, 9-inch cylinder, case 19 x 11 x 8½ inches.............. $77.50

*Rich rosewood case with moulding, nickel movement, six bells, coupled mainsprings, tune indicator, tune skipper, moderator (fast or slow), safety check and extra large cylinder.*

Each.

No. 140, 10 tunes, 11-inch cylinder, case 27 x 15 x 12 inches............$115.00

## BELLS AND DRUM.

*Same description as No. 140, with the addition of a Drum.*

Each.

No. 160, 8 tunes, 11-inch cylinder, case 27 x 15 x 12 inches.............$130.00

## BELLS, DRUM AND CASTANETS.

*Same description as No. 140 with the addition of Drum and Castanets.*

Each.

No. 182, 10 tunes, 13-inch cylinder, case 29 x 15 x 13 inches............$160.00

# MUSICAL BOXES WITH COIN ATTACHMENT.

These numbers are provided with a mechanism which starts them when a coin is dropped in the slot, and they require no other attention than to be wound up. They can be ordered with a penny or nickel attachment.

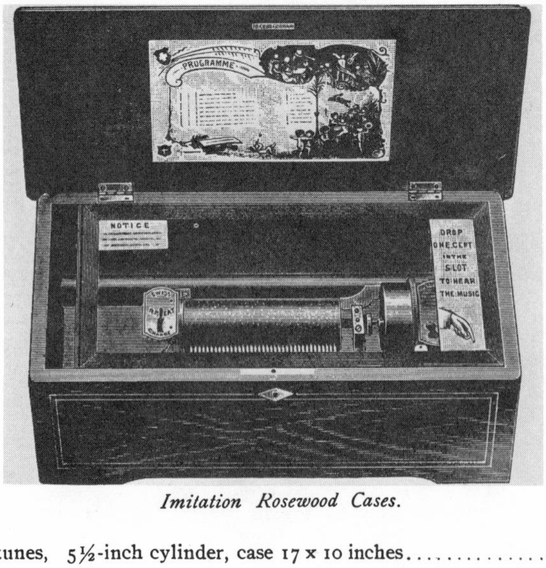


*Imitation Rosewood Cases.*

Each.

No. 76c, 8 tunes, 5½-inch cylinder, case 17 x 10 inches................$28.75
" 78c, 10 " 7½ " " safety check, case 20 x 9½ inches... 35.00
" 82c, 12 " 10 " " " " indicator, tune skipper, case 22½ x 10 inches........................................ 47.50

(Mermod Frères, cont'd)

"Harp Zither. The zither, or harp attachment, is an ingenious contrivance, consisting of a metal frame or holder sustaining a roll of paper which, when pressed on the comb or keyboard, gives the music box the tone of a stringed instrument. It can be removed at will by moving back a small lever and can be attached to any music box, new or old.

"Moderator. This consists of a mechanism adapted to the escapement or fan, by means of which the speed can be regulated at will and the music box made to run fast or slow. The Ideal moderator gives it the same speed whether fully wound or nearly run down.

"Safety Check. This is an invaluable improvement which prevents any music box provided with it from being damaged if anything gives away in its mechanism. It answers the same purpose as a brake in an elevator."

Among Mermod Frères boxes are to be found two of the most magnificent sounding cylinder instruments ever produced: No. 443, the Ideal Quatour Soprano, with a 20-inch cylinder and matching cabinet, and No. 520¼, the Ideal Sublime Harmonie Piccolo, with a 24 1/2" cylinder. Extra cylinders for the latter cost the staggering sum (in 1895) of $175.00 each!

The small music boxes with cylinders ranging from 1 1/2" to 3" in length were not serious musical instruments but were toys or novelties. Similar boxes were made by Thorens and other Swiss makers of the era and are still being produced by some firms today. Coin-operated Mermod Frères instruments were made in limited quantities and are rare today. In 1894 Charles H. Jacot, of Jacot & Son (American distributor for Mermod Frères), patented a coin mechanism for cylinder music boxes. The patent drawings (U.S. patent No. 518,720) depict a large console-style cylinder music box with a slanted glass window in the front.

A distinctive feature of Mermod Frères music boxes produced after the late 1880's was the Parachute Safety Check patented by Jacot in 1886. This device has a large shield-shaped plate which bobs up and down as the box plays.

During the late 1890's and early 1900's Mermod Frères produced an illustrious series of disc music boxes, the Stella, Mira, and Empress. The Miraphone, a Mira music box in combination with a disc phonograph, was similar in concept to the Reginaphone.

Mermod Frères ceased business, it is believed, sometime around the beginning of World War I. Advertisements of the firm c.1913 feature such diverse items as soap dispensers and phonographs.

Refer to the section on Mira and Stella music boxes (beginning on page 118) for more information about Mermod Frères.

# MUSICAL COIN MACHINE.

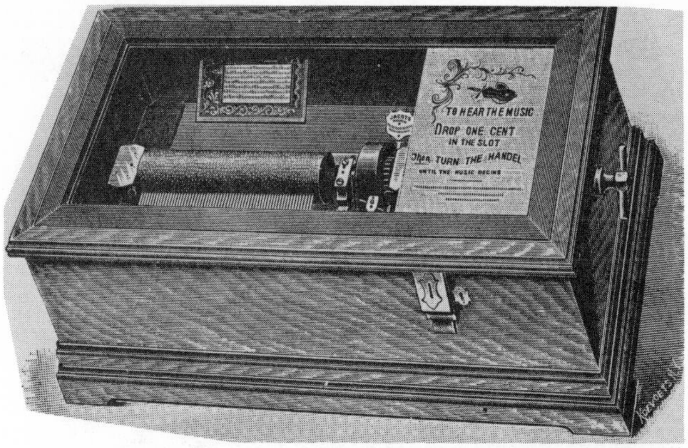


This number is a substantially built coin machine which does not require any attention, as the operation of starting it also winds it up after a coin is dropped in the slot.

The case is of quartered-oak, with a plate glass cover, and a drawer on the end into which the coins fall. Can be ordered either with a penny or nickel attachment.

No. 100, 8 tunes, case 25½ x 14 x 11 inches .......................... $75.00

# JACOT'S PATENT SAFETY CHECK.

MUSICAL BOXES are operated by one or several powerful springs, the speed being controlled and regulated by a series of wheels and pinions terminating in a fly-wheel. Now, if the fly-wheel be broken or removed, or any of the wheels get loose from the pinion when the spring is wound, the cylinder will revolve with lightning rapidity, causing the partial or complete ruin of the instrument, by bending and breaking the pins on the cylinder as well as the teeth of the comb.

In order to prevent this destructive "*run*" (which, as dealers well know, is constantly occurring), we have invented and patented an attachment, illustrated above, which will entirely prevent this accident by checking instantaneously the cylinder, whenever by any cause whatever the speed of the cylinder is unduly increased. The value of this attachment will be appreciated when it is known that more boxes are ruined by this accident than by wear and tear, or any other cause; to which fact we can testify by the number we receive for repairs.

Another important feature of this attachment, which will be appreciated by watchmakers, is that it can be used for checking the cylinder while the fly-wheel is removed for cleaning or repairing, thus saving the trouble of letting down the spring.

☞ To release the check after the fly-wheel is replaced, turn the latter a few times *backward*, and the check will fall of itself. ☜

# DIRECTIONS

# FOR OILING MUSIC BOXES.

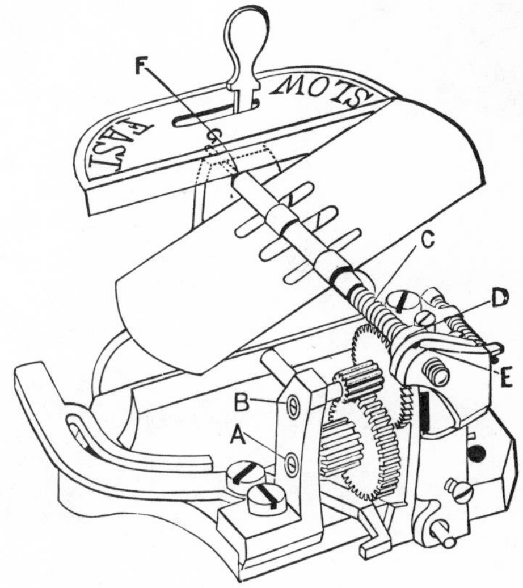


It is very important that the parts indicated as A, B, C, D, E and F be well oiled. One drop should be put at each of these points at least every three months, also on all bearings.

The cylinder pins should always be kept oiled, otherwise they will produce a disagreeable grating sound. To do this, take a thin piece of metal one or two inches wide (or the blade of a large table knife will do), oil it well, and pass it over the pins from one end of cylinder to the other while the box is playing, so that all the pins shall be oiled.

It is of great importance that the right kind of oil be used. We have devoted much time in experimenting with different kinds, and have one now that gives excellent results.

Watch and clock oil has not enough body.

**Credit note: Most of these Mermod Frères illustrations and catalogue prices are from a Mermod catalogue reprinted by Mrs. Ruth Bornand of the Bornand Music Box Co., Pelham, N.Y. Prices listed are what the instruments originally sold for circa 1895; not what the instruments are worth today.**

**An unusual variety of Ideal Piccolo box by Mermod Frères. The dampers are unlike those in normal cylinder boxes, nor do they resemble those in disc boxes. They "flip over" at the ends of the teeth. This novel idea was evidently tried for a short time and then was discontinued. The mechanisms were made in Mermod's St. Croix, Switzerland, factory. The case is American-made and is of quartered oak. (Collection of Murtogh D. Guinness)**

Musical stereopticon. Dating from the 1880's the musical movement in this stereopticon provides a musical accompaniment to the changing picture cards. As the cylinder movement plays, dolls pirouette. Such devices, made with coin slots or without, were popular entertainment devices during the late 19th century.

Made in Switzerland during the late 19th century, this showcase box was an attraction for many years at San Francisco's Cliff House. The box measures 3'7" wide by 3'2" high by 2' deep. Two cylinders each have six tunes.

Also made for public entertainment was this showcase box. Playing eight tunes on a long cylinder, the instrument has two large double springs for extended playing without the necessity for frequent winding. The five dolls twirl and dance as the music plays. This instrument probably dates from about 1890 - 1895.

Paillard music box in large ornate cabinet with glass on four sides. This instrument has a drum, six bells, wood block, organ section, and five dancing girls. Such musical cabinets were once popular in hotel lobbies, drawing rooms, and similar places. For commercial use a coin slot was often employed. They were mostly custom-made, with the cabinet by one manufacturer and the musical mechanism by another. (Lewis Graham photograph)

—"The Universal" Cylinder Box—

Made in the 1890's by Cuendet, the L'Universelle sought to provide a type of cylinder instrument for which additional cylinders could be purchased cheaply. To this aim, cylinders were made of one-tune length. This permitted less attention to be paid to alignment and accuracy and lent itself to mass production. The L'Universelle owner could keep up-to-date with the latest tunes just by visiting his music box dealer regularly.

The box is wound by a unique-appearing "ship's wheel" on the inside left-hand side of the case. Cylinders on the model illustrated are 7 1/2" long. A lever on the right-side panel permits quick changing of cylinders and locking them into place. The music is played on a steel music comb and three saucer bells. While great sales were undoubtedly expected of L'Universelle, they did not materialize for the box could not effectively compete with the cost and convenience of the ubiquitous disc boxes of the same era.

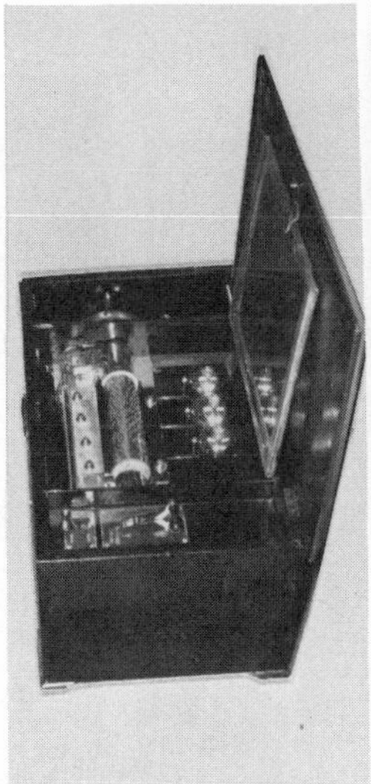

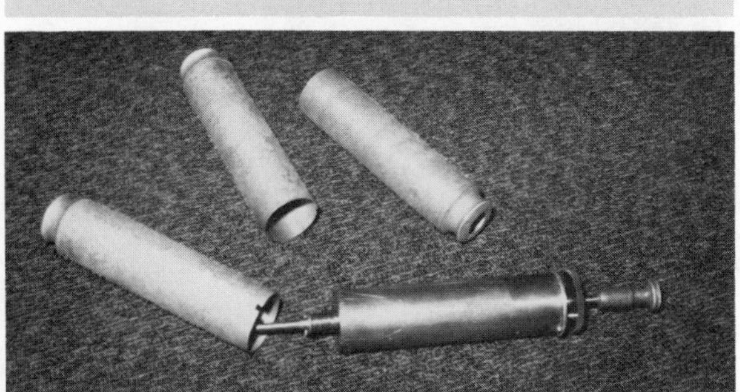

—The "Alexandra" Cylinder Box—

Invented by Alfred Junod, Jules Jaccard, and Paul Calame, the Alexandra made its appearance about 1890. The novel mechanism consists of a brass mandrel over which interchangeable hollow sleeves or cylinders may easily be fitted. The inventors intended to provide the multiple-tune extended-scale repertoire of a cylinder box in combination with the economy of a mass-produced lightweight new cylinder type which could be made much more cheaply than could the standard heavy wax-filled cylinder.

The Alexandra was made in several sizes, including a 6" cylinder and 10 1/8" cylinder format. A 6" cylinder type is illustrated here. Pylons at the sides provide storage for the cylinders (the 10 1/8" style has pylons at the rear of the case).

A search of patent records reveals that literally hundreds of music box innovations have been patented over the years. Two of the unusual ones, L'Universelle and the Alexandra, are shown on this page. While each was hardly a best seller, modest sales and production did occur. For each of these successful examples, dozens of other ideas were stillborn. The eclipse of the large cylinder box was final in the 1890's, and although L'Epee and others continued to produce medium-size instruments until World War I and novelty movements later, the era of the large ornate interchangeable cylinder box was dead.

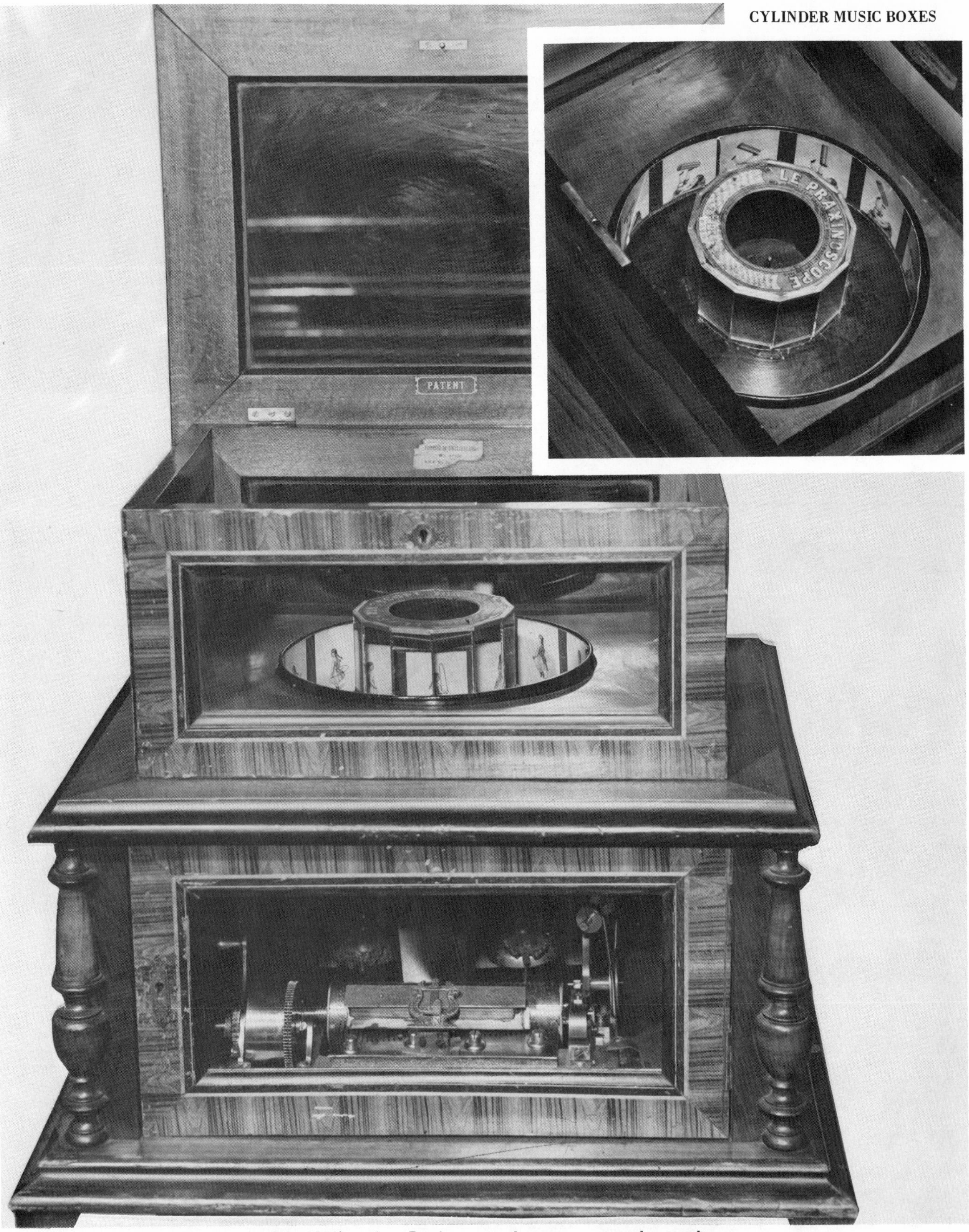


Introduced in the 1870's, the Praxinoscope became a popular parlor entertainment device. A forerunner of the motion picture, the device has twelve mirror facets mounted on a center carousel. As the carousel rotates, twelve pictures on a strip, each picture representing an action slightly different from the preceding one, are reflected and appear to move. The Praxinoscope was exhibited at the Paris Exposition in 1878 and, again, in 1889 at the Universal Exposition held in the same city. The above instrument is combined with a musical bell box (by B.H.A. of St. Croix, Switzerland). The Praxinoscope is driven by a pulley and belt connected to the music box mainspring. (Universal City collection; Hollywood, California)

## Music-automaton „Illusions".

No. 1705. 52 steel tongues, 3 chineses beating 6 bells, interchangeable barrels of music, 7½ × 2 inches, double spring, self-acting piece-marker. During the play a door openes itself and by electric light, which changes three times its colour, a ballet of about 100 dancers begins to performe. — Most effectful show. — Case of walnut highly finished and of best workman-hip. In case that this automaton shall be set in connection with an existing electric stream please mention this when ordering; the price will in this case 30 shillings less.

## „Fidelio" music automaton No. 50.

Self-acting, with changeable music-barrels, [illegible] inches long, each playing 6 tunes. The music swiss systeme is accompanied by five tuned bells which are played by two bowing chineses.

Highly finished walnut case with painted glass door.

Can also be had with construction to illuminate the interior during play. Very attractive.

Note: The Fidelio music boxes shown here incorporated Swiss movements and were made by the Fidelio Musikwerke A.G., of Berlin. The firm was active from the late 19th century until the 1930's, with its main business in the music box field being in the 1895-1910 years. (In later years phonographs, radios, etc. were handled.) Fidelio also produced "Illusions-Automat" instruments with disc music box movements.

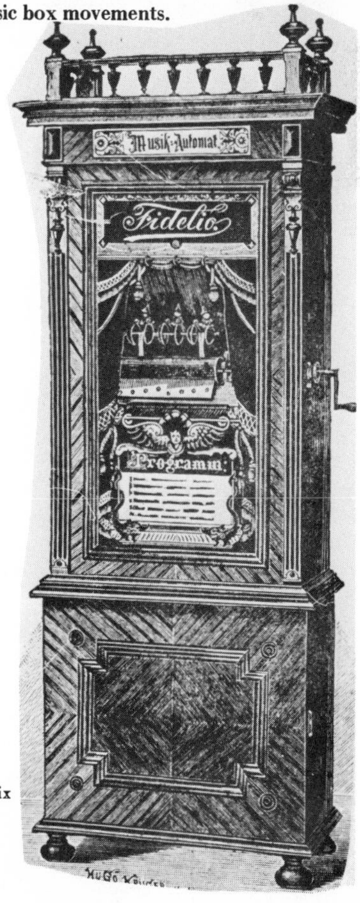


## Ideal Fidelio No. 80T.

Music-automaton, self-acting with changeable music-barrels each 11 inches long, playing six tunes accompanied by six tuned bells and one drum. The bells being played by three chineses. Highly finished walnut case with richly painted glass door and one aneroid barometer on top.

Can also be had with construction to illuminate the interior during play.

Very attractive.

## Ideal Fidelio music-automaton No. 60.

Sublime Harmony, self-acting with changeable music-barrels 11 inches long, each playing six tunes, accompanied by six tuned bells which are played by three bowing chineses.

Highly finished walnut case with painted glass door.

Can also be had with construction to illuminate the interior during play.

Very attractive.

—Inexpensive Music Boxes of the 1890's—

The advent of the disc-type music box in the late 1880's, and the immense popularity of the disc box in the 1890's, brought about a sharp decline in quality of the cylinder boxes made during that period. In place of the finely crafted cylinder music boxes of a decade earlier, the market in the 1890's was flooded by cheaply-built cylinder instruments made to compete on price alone. The quality was often dubious, and the addition of bells (usually three) was not done as a melodic accompaniment, but, as Graham Webb has written, "to cover a poor arrangement and indifferent tone, so that by the 1890's, movements with 6-inch cylinders and three bells playing ten tunes were making a hideous noise... These boxes, despite the poor sound, are quite popular today for their novelty value." Perhaps the leading maker of the novelty-type box of the 1890's was B.H. Abrahams of St. Croix, Switzerland. The quality, or absence of quality, of these instruments gave St. Croix a poor reputation in the trade in the late 1890's — an unfair situation as Mermod Frères, maker of some of the finest cylinder and disc boxes ever produced, was also located there.

Hallmarks of such boxes of the 1890's include the sparing use of inlay (decals were easier and cheaper to use!), indifferent tone, simple cases (often painted a solid color or with simulated wood grain), widely-spaced teeth in the music comb, a small winding spring, and a large number of tunes per box. Some boxes, in order to have a "large program," would have a tune sheet listing 16 tunes instead of 8 — with each tune occupying just half of a cylinder revolution. Paillard, also of St. Croix, well-known maker of quality boxes a decade earlier, produced a line of cheaply-made instruments in the 1890's.

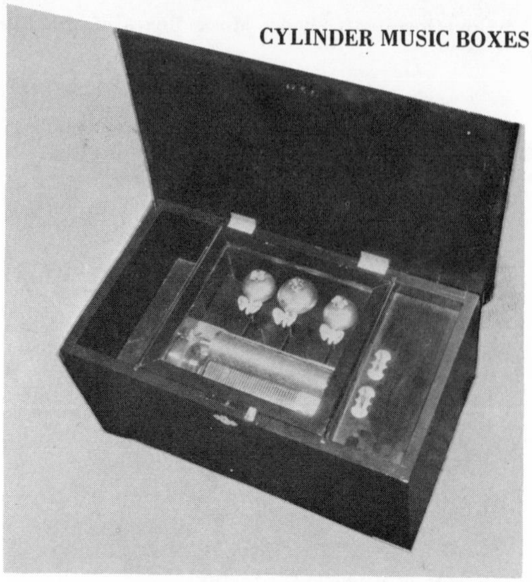

Typical Swiss 3-bell box of the 1890's. These boxes usually play eight tunes. The main market for these boxes was England. Few were sold in America.

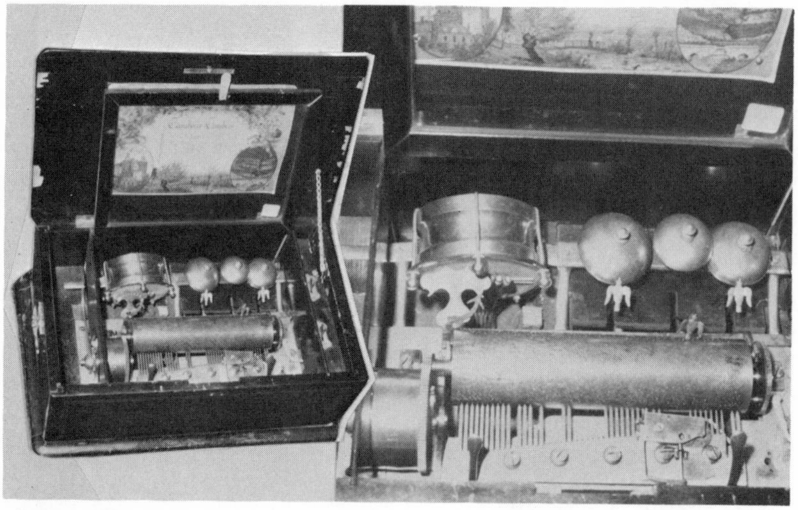

Medium-size orchestra box from the 1890's. This particular box, in rather poor condition with broken teeth, peeling veneer, and other problems, can be restored by someone with a lot of patience! Instruments in such condition are worth but a fraction of the price of perfect ones.

"The Victoria," a cylinder box with three bells in an upright walnut case. This particular style, which was also built with a clock on the top, is a B.H. Abrahams product and was marketed in England.

Large and rather impressive-appearing cylinder box from the 1890's. However, unlike its ancestors of a decade or two earlier, this instrument is on a rather wobbly table and is decorated with decals, rather than inlaid wood designs. Note the "zither attachment" above the comb. Graham Webb, in "The Cylinder Musical Box Handbook," notes: "This device was a roll of tissue paper in a metal holder which, when pushed on to the comb, dampened all or some of the teeth. At the time of its inception in the 1880's this effect was extremely popular, although music lovers will agree that it adds nothing to the quality of the sound."

Left: This drum and bells box is built into an unusual cabinet, the front of which folds down for use as a writing desk. Made by L'Epee of St. Suzanne, France — one of the few large producers of cylinder boxes outside of Switzerland. L'Epee products are usually unsigned. Many boxes of this firm can be recognized by the unusual shape of the tune indicator (see additional photo here of another L'Epee box with similar mechanisms), the shape of the bell rack, and other similarities.

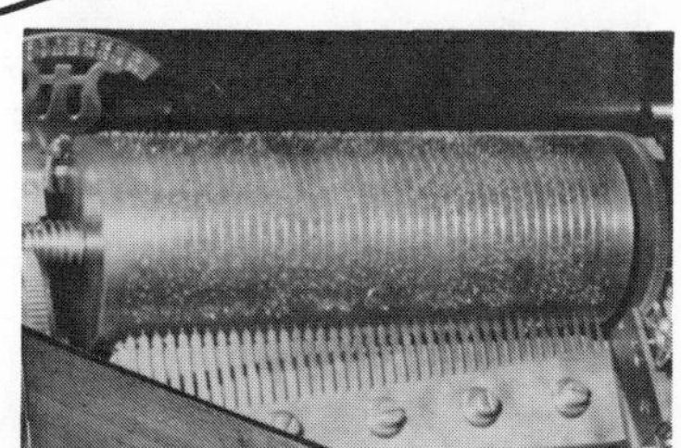

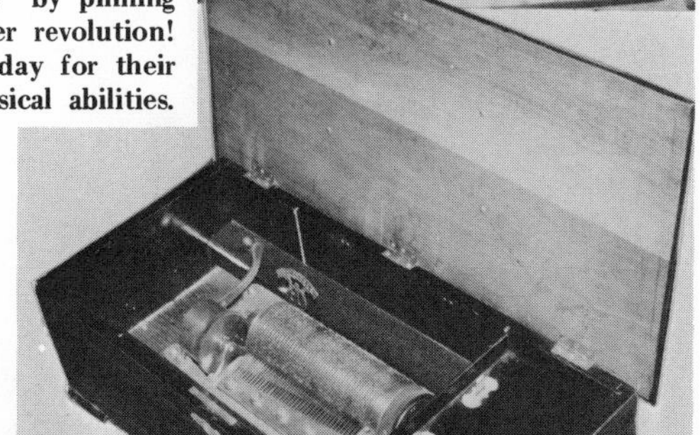

"20-tune" Swiss box from the 1890's. Each tune used half a cylinder revolution. One similar box had "30 tunes" by pinning each tune for 1/3 of a cylinder revolution! Such instruments are desired today for their novelty value, not for their musical abilities.

Coin-operated cylinder box from the 1890's. The space at the top is for a program card and operating instructions. Such a box found use on the counter of a tavern or store.

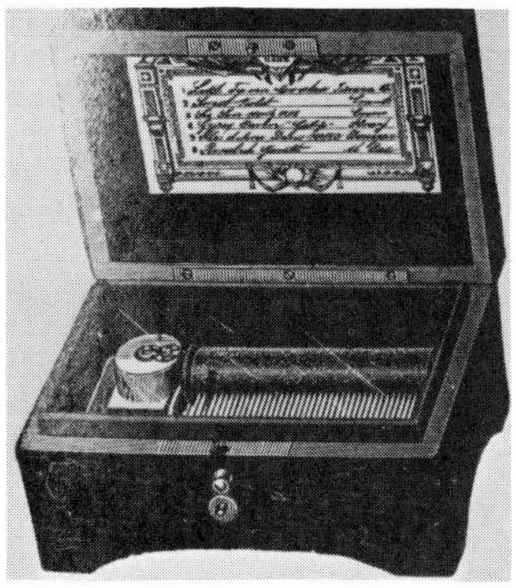

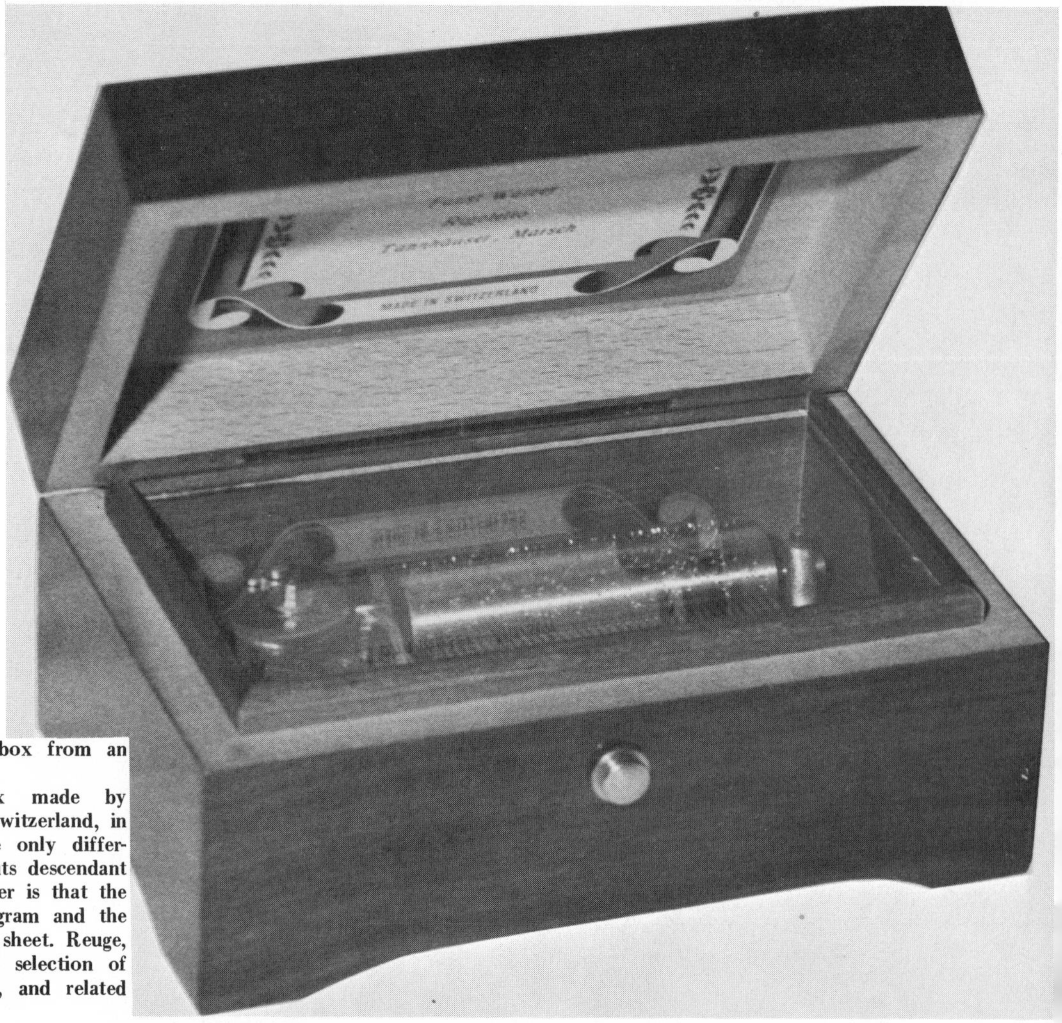



**Above:** A small Swiss music box from an 1895 catalogue.

**Right:** A Swiss music box made by Hermann Thorens of St. Croix, Switzerland, in modern times (1969). About the only difference between the 1895 one and its descendant of three quarters of a century later is that the early one has a hand-written program and the later one has a printed selection sheet. Reuge, also of St. Croix, makes a fine selection of small music boxes, singing birds, and related items today.

---

—Small Swiss Music Boxes—

The styles shown here were popular in 1895. Most were spring wound but some (Nos. 106 - 159 and 140 - 135 are examples) are of the manivelle or hand-cranked type.

For the past century such instruments have been popular sellers in jewelry stores, department stores, gift shops, and similar places. There are several dozen makers of small musical items in Switzerland today. Baud Frères, operators of an outstanding musical museum in L'Auberson, informed the author during a 1971 visit that the little L'Auberson village had four music box makers alone! In nearby St. Croix, famed years ago as the home of Paillard and Mermod Frères music boxes, the firms of Reuge and Thorens make thousands of small musical movements each year and ship them all over the world.

Nos. 106-159.

Nos. 140-135.

Nos. 101-102.

Nos. 79-89.

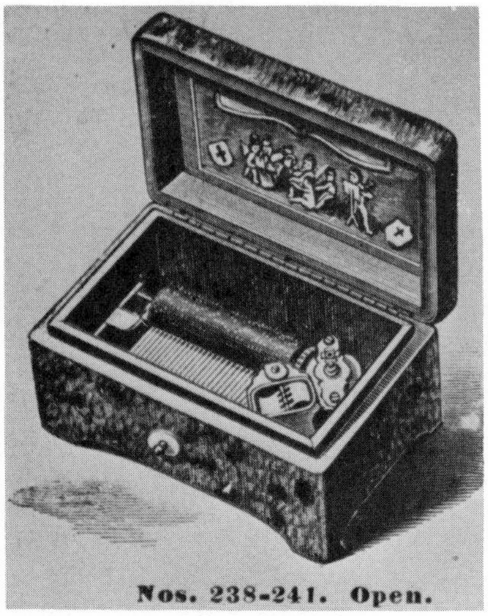

Nos. 238-241. Open.

Nos. 238-241. Closed.

## Tableaux mécaniques.

## Automatic pictures.

No. 1099. 41×52 cm (16 1/2 × 21").

No. 1105. 41×52 cm (16 1/2 ×21")

No. 1101. 40×32 cm (16×13").

No. 1103, 40×32 cm (16×13").

No. 1099. Laughing and crying children working 3 hours.
„ 1101. Gymnastic excercises by cats „ 3 „ 5 figures moving.
„ 1103. „ „ „ (with music) working 4 minutes 5 figures moving.
„ 1104. Picture without clock, gymnastic exercises by cats working 3 hours, 12 figures moving.
„ 1105. „ with „ „ „ „ „ 3 „ 12 „ „

No. 123a. 40 × 32 cm.

No. 34II. 40 × 32 cm.

No. 58.

No. 536. 46 × 46 × 29 cm.

No. 115. 40 × 32 cm.

No. 54. 40 × 32 cm.

No. 34II. Drunken man on pillar box mising with key the entrance door.
„ 54. Shoomaker's workroom.
„ 58. Cats dancing.
„ 115. Windmill. The miller dries to make wind.
„ 123a. Dog and cat dancing, accompanied by the clown.

### —Mechanical Pictures—

Mechanical pictures, made since the 1700's, were especially popular in the 1890's and early 1900's. The quality varied from ornate and artistic productions made in three dimensions with oil-painted mechanical rivers, people, etc., to simple printed pictures with moving cardboard cut-outs.

Many types featured a clock, usually a watch mounted on the back side of the painting, which appeared as part of the scene. The watch face appeared as a steeple clock or a clock in a windmill, hotel, town hall, or other building. With relatively few exceptions, the clock mechanisms were separate from the rest of the musical and mechanical movement and did not actuate it.

The musical movements usually were small Swiss or Austrian cylinder movements, usually of two or three tune programs. By means of a pull string or a key the music movement and the mechanism could be wound up. When a lever was pulled the scene moved and the music played.

Some types, especially those made in Austria around the turn of the 20th century, consisted of a painting incorporating a clock face into the scene, and a musical movement — without any mechanical figures. Such paintings were often in oil and were done on a copper or other metal sheet and were enclosed in an ornate gilded plaster frame.

## MUSICAL NOVELTIES

Beginning about 1870 cheap musical movements were fitted to a wide variety of household articles and souvenirs. Those illustrated on this page mostly date from the 1890 - 1910 period and include Swiss chalets (small souvenir types), a musical decanter (with movement in base; mechanism is actuated when the decanter is lifted), musical steins with movements in the bases, a musical sewing kit with a mechanical scene on the underside of the lid, a musical smoking stand, and musical jewel boxes. At the right is an 1895 advertisement for musical movements for novelty items. These range from 1-tune 28-tooth movements to 6-tune 50-tooth movements.

Other musical items of the Victorian era included chairs, footstools, trivets, kitchen utensils, Christmas tree stands, door knockers, lamps, humidors, cigarette cases, opera glasses, stereopticons, and photo albums.

Many of these general types of articles are still being made today, primarily in Switzerland and Japan.

**Musiques seules avec mouvement.** **Music works for photo-albums, work boxes**

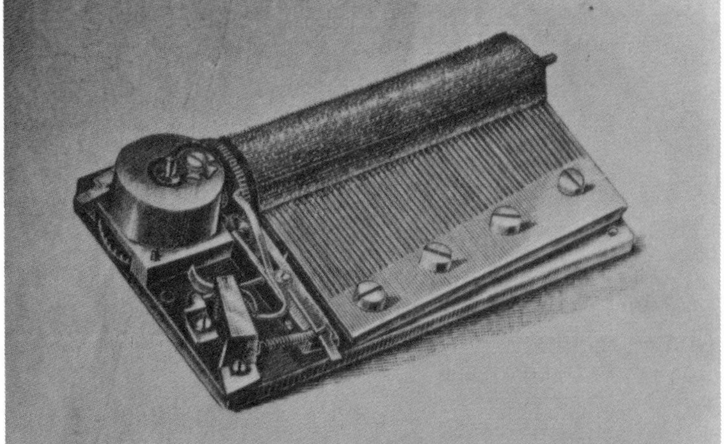

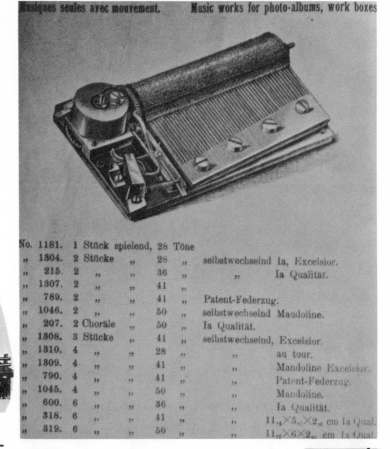

| | | | | | | |
|---|---|---|---|---|---|---|
| No. 1181. | 1 | Stück spielend, | | 28 | Töne | |
| " 1304. | 2 | Stücke | " | 28 | " | selbstwechselnd Ia, Excelsior. |
| " 215. | 2 | " | " | 36 | " | " Ia Qualität. |
| " 1307. | 2 | " | " | 41 | " | |
| " 789. | 2 | " | " | 41 | " | Patent-Federzug. |
| " 1046. | 2 | " | " | 50 | " | selbstwechselnd Mandoline. |
| " 207. | 2 | Choräle | " | 50 | " | Ia Qualität. |
| " 1308. | 3 | Stücke | " | 41 | " | selbstwechselnd, Excelsior. |
| " 1310. | 4 | " | " | 28 | " | " au tour. |
| " 1309. | 4 | " | " | 41 | " | " Mandoline Excelsior. |
| " 790. | 4 | " | " | 41 | " | " Patent-Federzug. |
| " 1045. | 4 | " | " | 50 | " | " Mandoline. |
| " 600. | 6 | " | " | 36 | " | " Ia Qualität. |
| " 318. | 6 | " | " | 41 | " | " 11,4×5,7×2,6 cm Ia Qual. |
| " 319. | 6 | " | " | 50 | " | " 11,8×6×2,6 cm Ia Qual. |

No. 489.
MUSICAL ALARM.

Nos. 485 to 488,
SWISS CHALETS.

No. 460.
MUSICAL DECANTER.

**Jewel and glove cases with music.**

No. 1071.

No. 1079

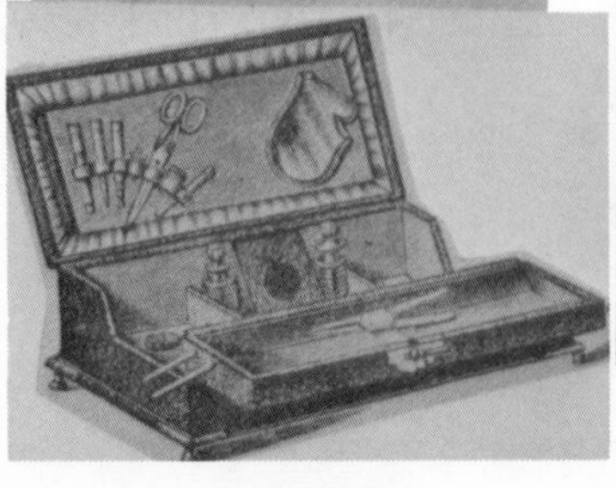

No. 1275.

### –High-Quality Musical Chalets–

During the 1880's and 1890's large Swiss chalets were made with elaborate musical movements. Paillard, Bremond, Baker - Troll, and other manufacturers supplied large cylinder boxes, drum and bell boxes, and, occasionally, full orchestra (with reed organ) boxes for use in these colorful chalets. These large chalets are not to be confused with the myriad of small pieces with cheap movements which have been made in Switzerland since the 19th century and which are still popular tourist souvenirs today.

Left: Large (43" wide) elaborately carved Swiss chalet music box which plays one of ten tunes when a coin is inserted. In addition to the regular cylinder music box mechanisms it contains dancing dolls, Oriental bell strikers, and drums. The mechanism is by Mermod Frères of St. Croix, Switzerland.

Right: Mrs. Hilaire Bornand Coy, daughter of Adrian V. and Ruth Bornand, is shown with a carved musical Swiss chalet liquor dispenser and humidor. The top opens to disclose a liquor tray and a set of matched glasses. The right side opens to reveal the humidor. In the base is an eight-tune cylinder mechanism.

Left: A large and finely made cylinder movement by B.A. Bremond of Geneva, Switzerland. The movement is shown mounted in the bottom of a large Swiss chalet, with the top part removed.

## —Musical Albums—

Many different varieties of musical albums were produced from about 1880 onward. These usually consist of a number of stiff cardboard pages suitable for the mounting of photographs. The back part of the album conceals a musical movement, usually of two tunes, which plays when the album is opened. Winding is by means of a key or a pull string.

These were sold as novelties and, as is the case with other similar novelties, the music produced was of secondary importance.

Above is shown a musical album with family photographs in place. The cylinder movement is visible at the right in the lower picture.

Below and to the left are typical musical album covers from a catalogue of the 1895 - 1900 era. The quality ranged from beautifully tooled leather to pressed cardboard.

# Musik-Albums.

Albums à musique. Photo-albums with music.

No. 745.

No. 1333.

No. 1616.

No. 1083.

No. 1332.

No. 1620.

—19th Century Automata—

Dating from the late 19th century and early 20th century these automata were popular parlor entertainers in the Victorian age. Most pieces illustrated on this page are variations of popular themes. The Surprised Cook (center right) was made in several forms. As the pot lid is lifted a "live" animal peers out! Guitarists, violinists, and mandolinists (directly right) were favorites. No music is actually made on the tiny instrument itself; as in other automata, the music comes from a tiny cylinder movement in the base of the figure.

The large center picture illustrates a rare automaton figure of an African queen. At the top of the pole a child acrobat performs.

(Most automaton illustrations courtesy of Lewis Graham and Mr. and Mrs. Gordon Lipe)

**Above:** The ladder-climbing acrobat was a favorite automaton subject of the 1870 - 1890 period. Made in various sizes and in various qualities (L'Ascenseur, circa 1875, is nearly two feet high and is a masterpiece of mechanical ingenuity, for example). Shown above is a medium-priced figure from the early 20th century. Typically, such figures ascend the ladder, perform a two-hand headstand, and then with appropriate hesitation slowly lift one hand for a one-hand stand. Then the figure goes down the ladder again, and the cycle begins anew. Elaborate models have cycles which take a minute or more.

**Left:** Two sorceresses. Each time the cover is lifted a new set of tiny balls, dice, or other objects appear on the table. A musical movement in the base provides a tuneful accompaniment to the magic show. The pieces illustrated are from the late 19th century. Sorcerers and sorceresses of similar concept are still being made in Switzerland today.

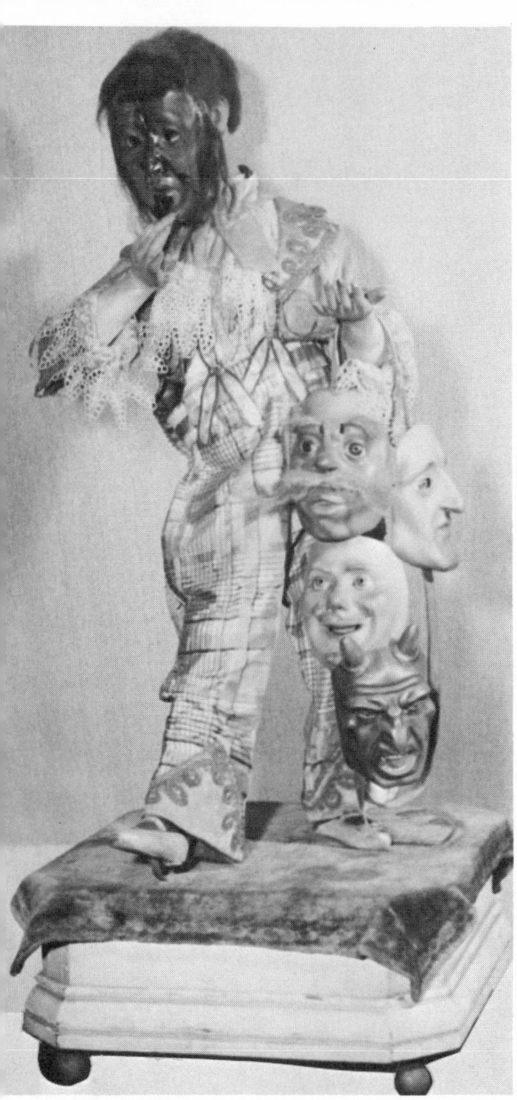

One of the cleverest automata ever constructed, this clown applies a mask to his face. The four masks in his left hand are automated and have moving eyes. Lewis Graham, owner of the Museum of Music Collection, considered this to be the finest of his several dozen automata.

Two mechanical dolls from the late 19th century. The girl at the left sips from a bowl of soup. The guitarist at the right is dressed as a jester. As he strums the instrument he moves his eyes, sticks out his tongue, and performs other gestures.

This attractive automaton girl puppeteer manipulates a marionette by strings. Combination mechanical figures such as this are rare. (Lewis Graham photograph)

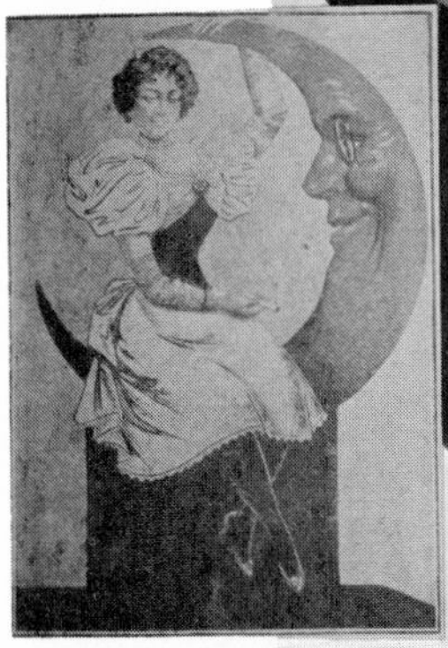

"Singing to the moon" was a favorite subject of the 1890's and early 1900's. The moon is of papier maché and has moving eyes and tongue. The large illustration above shows a guitarist serenading. The small inset illustration, circa 1904, is of a girl cigarette smoker. Mechanical smokers have interior bellows systems to blow the smoke and were made in many varieties.

In contrast to the usual spring motor wound automata, these miniature orchestra figures are of the manivelle or continuously hand-cranked type. Circa 1900 - 1910.

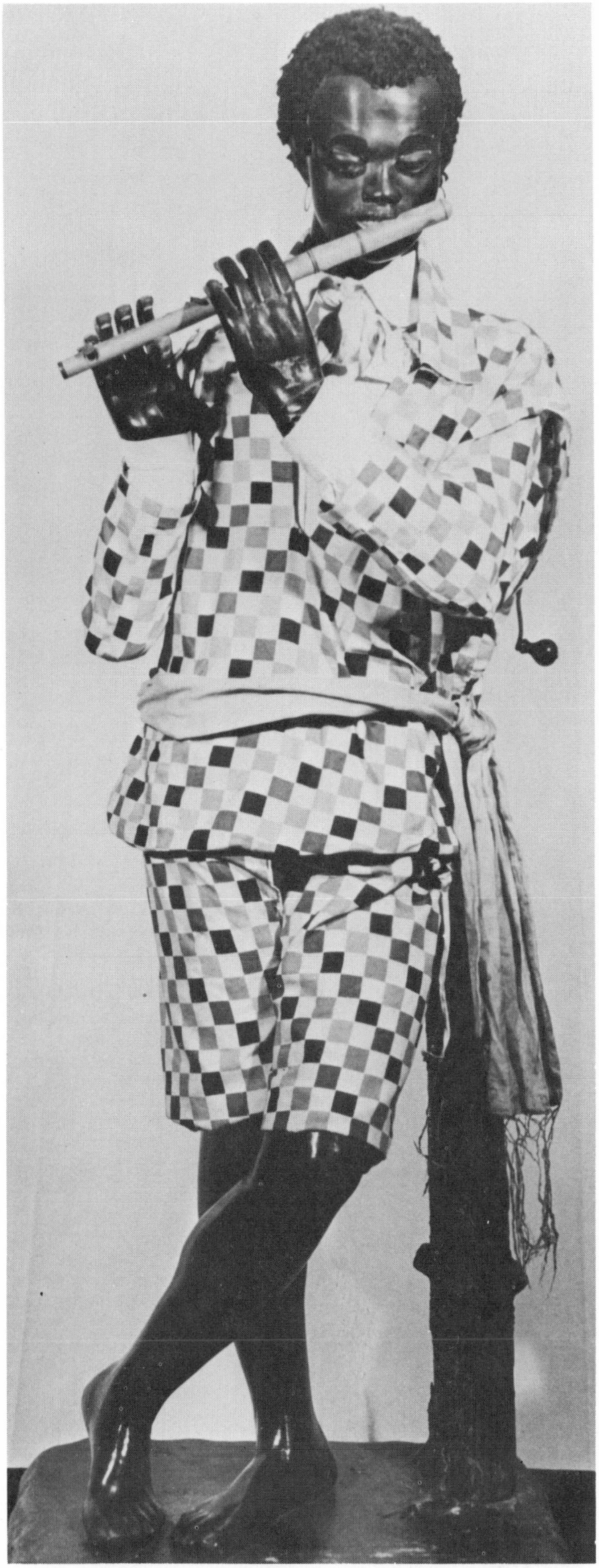

Above: Flute player, the size of a small child. The music is played by flute pipes operated from a pinned wooden cylinder. Such automata were once popular decorations in dining rooms, salons, and hotel lobbies in America and Europe. The mechanisms are of superb craftsmanship. (Murtogh Guinness Collection)

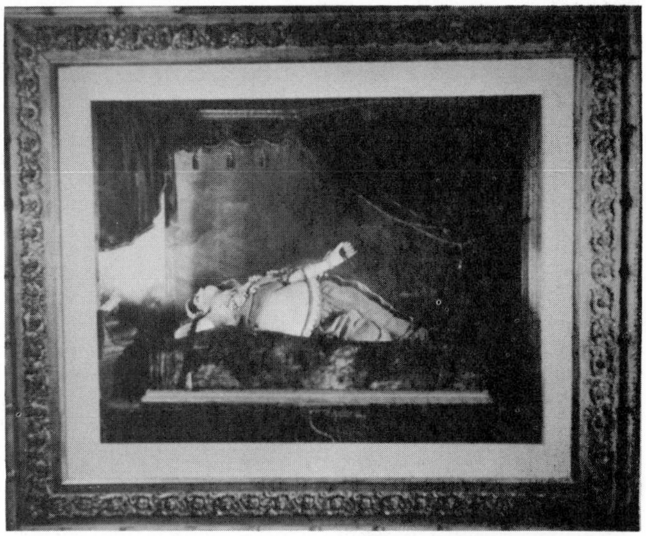

Above: Cleopatra shadow box. Her breasts heave, her eyes roll, and her eyelids open and close. One snake writhes at her feet. Another, an asp, moves in her hand and at one moment bites her breast! (Murtogh Guinness Collection)

Right: Bird trainer automaton. The bird sings; the head, mouth, and eyelids of the trainer move, and his arm raises the flute; the bird stops singing; a musical movement plays while the trainer fingers the flute. (Murtogh Guinness Collection)

Below: The mechanisms of a musical Christmas tree stand. Four small Swiss cylinder movements, wound from a common shaft, each play two or three Christmas melodies. 1-, 2-, and 3-cylinder models were made as well. Circa 1905.

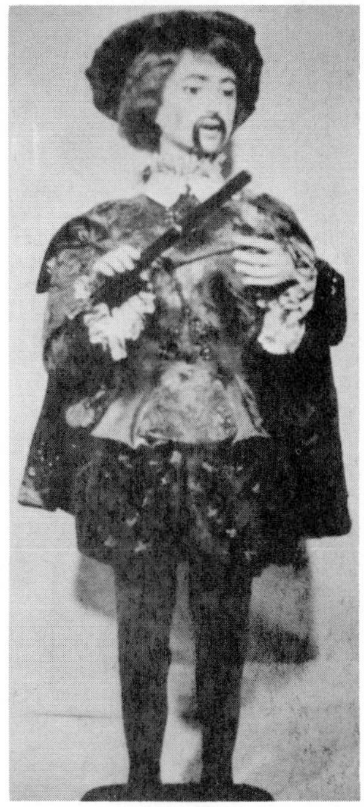

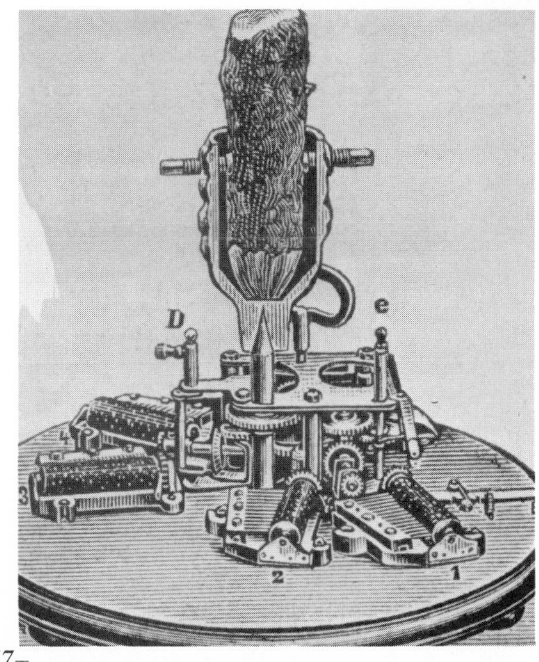

**No. 3. Advocat (Richter.)**

**Advocate (Judge).** Standing on the rostrum and giving his judgement by moving his head, eyes, lips and arms in a near-natural manner.

The movements appear almost lifelike, and the decor and wardrobe look elegant. This automaton is **most effective** and suitable for any business that wishes to use it for advertising purposes.

The text will be shown on a plaque attached to the rostrum. Height ca. 75 cm. **Price 175 Mk.**

**No. 4. Grosse trommelnde Bäre u. Hasen**

**Large Drumming Bears and Rabbits** with brown and white fur, beat a loud roll on the drum and growl, while moving the head, snout, feet, etc., in a very natural manner.

Bears, white or brown, ca. 80 cm. high, **Price 90 Mk.** Rabbits, white or grey, ca. 80 cm. high, **Price 100 Mk.**

(The mechanisms are most solidly and durably constructed.)

**No. 5. Automat-Kraftmesser „Herkules mit Musik".**

**Sicherer und leichter Broderwerb.**

Automatic Strength-Measurer **"Hercules with Music". Certain and easy for making a living.** This automaton has been accepted with considerable approval due to its originality so that in fairs and markets, restaurants and cafes, it is sure to bring in a good revenue because everybody is ready to risk 5 pfennig to test his strength, particularly since on doing so a beautiful musical piece will be heard. For **panoramas, museums, restaurants,** etc., the automatic strength-measure "Hercules" is a distinguished **capital investment** which pays for itself.

**Size:** 48 cm. high, 30 cm. wide and 26 cm. deep.

**Weight** about 10 kilos, so that it is easily transportable. The mechanism of the automatic action is very strong and of the most solid construction.

Further details including guarantees available upon request. **Price** including 5 musical pieces **66 Mk.**

"No. 6. Mech. singende Vogel"

**Mechanical Singing Birds** of all types and prices in cages or on flower bouquets, are in stock. However, as truly practical and effective show-pieces and money-makers the two following are especially recommended:

1. **Mechanical Singing Bird** (American Bluebird) with an exquisite loud nightingale-song, in pauses or warbling continuously, in a richly gilded cage with an imitation stone grotto decorated with flowers on which the bird sits. **Price 170 Mk.**
2. **Ditto with 2 Birds** with splendid loud songs, answering each other, stopping and then continuing, in a gilded cage. **Price 190 Mk.**

**These birds with a coin-slot on the base are available for 30 marks more.** Cages with 3 and 4 singing birds are also available on order.

I state again emphatically that these birds are the most practical show-pieces and money-makers and represent the most perfect and reliable inside and outside construction for traveling purposes, also that the birds have an exceptionally loud song that is most natural.

**"No. 7. Mech. singender Paradiesvogel"**

**Mechanical Singing Bird of Paradise.** As pictured above, lifesize (with its splendid original plumage) sitting on a rose tree and warbling a merry tune. Height about one meter; the bird itself is the size of a pigeon. **Price 275 Mk.**

Fabrik und Lager mechanisch-automatischer Schaustücke.

**No. 8. Mechanischer Pfau.**

**Mechanical Peacock** walks, turns its head and makes a fan with its tail. **Price 55 Mk.**

**No. 9. Grosser mechanischer Pfau,**

**Larger Mechanical Peacock.** Lifesize, a truly exemplary specimen. Height ca. 55 cm., with fan opened ca. 170 cm; with tail stretched out, the Peacock has a length of about 2 meters. He walks entirely like a live Peacock, turns his head from side to side, stands still, make a fan and screams. It is also available standing still on a pedestal. **Price 275 Mk.**

**No. 10. Mechanischer Vogel**

**Mechanical Bird** about the size of a pigeon, standing free on a little pedestal, with loud powerful song, besides moving head, beak and wings in a natural manner, made ready for traveling with a leather case fitted with handle and lock; extremely practical for travel. **Price 260 Mk.**

**No. 11. *Dosen-Colibris.***

**Hummingbird Snuffboxes particularly suited for special museums.**

No. 1 Snuffbox in imitation tortoise with a Japanese medallion from which a bird (little hummingbird) springs out and sings. The song, the movement of head, beak, wings, etc., are copied most realistically, so that these snuffboxes are considered the most effective mechanical works of art. **Price 250 Mk.**

Ditto cased in magnificently engraved silvered or gilt metal. **Price 300 Mk.**

These snuffboxes with 2 birds alternatively singing are **100 marks** more per box.

**Reparaturen werden gewissenhaft ausgeführt.**

# Lebensgrosse automatische Figuren.

Lifesize Automatic Figures.

(Mech. automatischer Neger No. 12.)

## No. 12. Automatischer Neger.

**Automatic Negro** blowing the flute (playing 4 pieces), sumptuously attired in velvet and silk, nodding his head while moving eyes and fingers in a natural manner.

Size ca. 1 meter 40 cm. (magnificent special piece). The sound is an exact flute tone, and the movements are absolutely natural. **Price 1150 Mk.**

## No. 13. Mech.-automatischer Trompeter

**Mechanical-automatic Trumpeter.** The trumpet is blown in a most natural manner, playing 4 popular songs or calls as desired, and the movements are copied in a life-like manner.

The costume is that of a 16th century cavalryman.

Size ca. 1 meter 40 cm. **Price 900 Mk.**

## No. 14. Mech.-automatischer Trommler

**Mechanical-automatic Drummer** beating out marches and twirling the drum sticks. These movements are most genuine. Costumed the same as the trumpeter.

Size ca. 1 meter 40 cm. **Price 750 Mk.**

## No. 15. Mech.-automatischer Trompeter

**Mechanical-Automatic Trumpeter,** the most perfect automaton that I furnish. Blows the trumpet or piston in a most natural manner, playing 4 popular songs, etc. Head, eyes, arms, fingers, etc., are moved most naturally and the trumpet is raised and lowered. Size ca. 1 meter 70 cm. **Price 1400 Mk.**

The sound of both automata is a very strong and full piston or trumpet tone, and the melodies as well as the costumes may be selected to your preference.

**—A Catalogue of Automata—**

**The illustrations on this and the following two pages are from a circa 1900 catalogue issued by Gustav Uhlig of Halle, Germany. The material in the borders at the top and bottom of the pages reads "Gustav Uhlig, Halle on the Salle, Province of Saxony, makes and stocks mechanical automatic show pieces. Repairs are carried out conscientiously."**

**This catalogue, loaned by Mr. Barny, translated by Paul Haug, and photographed by Dan Adams, appeared in Volume XVI of the Musical Box Society "Bulletin" and is reproduced here through the courtesy of Dr. and Mrs. Howard Fitch, editors of that publication.**

Fabrik und Lager mechanisch-automatischer Schaustücke.

## No. 16. „Zwischen-Act“

(grossartiges Effectstück.)

"Between Acts" (magnificent display piece). Clown sitting on a stool playing banjo and moving head, eyes, arms, hands and feet in an extremely original and natural manner. Splendidly attired in silk and satin. The clown falls asleep while he plays and lets the banjo fall. When a bell rings the first time, he starts, but falls asleep again. Now the bell sounds the second time, and the clown starts again and looks around, but again falls asleep. It is only when the bell rings the third time that he wakes completely, looks around in surprise as though nothing had happened, lifts his banjo and resumes playing. With music. Height ca. 75 cm. **Price 175 Mk.**

## No. 17. Mech. Kugelfangspieler

**Mechanical Bilboquet (Cup-and-Ball) Player.** A highly effective automaton ca. 75 cm. tall. Richly dressed in velvet and silk of the period of Franz I, with a very realistic posture. Throws the ball high and then catches it, while moving arms, head, eyes, lips, etc., in a natural manner. **Price 145 Mk.**

## No. 18. Zigeunerin das Tambourin spielend,

**Gypsy Woman Playing a Tambourine.** Exquisitely set up, and moving head, eyes and arms in a very natural manner. Size ca. 75 cm. **Price 175 Mk.**

## No. 19. Pariser Cocotte.

**Parisian Cocotte.** Sits on a park bench and flirts, moving head, eyes and arms most naturally, in addition to raising and lowering her lorgnette and fanning herself with the other arm. Splendidly and most fashionably dressed in silk. Height ca. 70 cm. **Price 200 Mk.**

Gustav Uhlig, Halle a. S., Provinz Sachsen.

## No. 20. Mechanisch-automatischer Vogelbezähmer

grossartiges effectvolles Kunstwerk.

**Mechanical-automatic Bird Trainer. A most magnificent and effective work of art.** The automaton, dressed in extraordinarily rich court fashion, plays the flute (playing in one cycle 4 pieces of music), correctly covering the individual openings with his fingers just as a human would do, moves the flute up and down correctly, nods head and moves eyes, lips, etc., most realistically. As soon as the flute stops, the bird sitting on the left hand of the automaton replies to the playing with a loud song in a joyful manner, turning its head and moving its beak naturally. Height ca. 1 meter 30 cm. **Price 675 Mk.**

## No. 21. Clown als Balanxeur

**Balancing Clown.** Balancing a ladder, chair, etc., on his nose and fanning himself with one hand while moving head, eyes and arms in a natural manner. Very elegantly attired in silk tricot. With music. Height ca. 1 meter. **Price 300 Mk.**

Reparaturen werden gewissenhaft ausgeführt.

Fabrik und Lager mechanisch-automatischer Schaustücke.

## No. 22. Mechanische Soubrette

**Mechanical Soubrette.** Plays the mandolin while moving head, arms, etc., in a natural manner. With music; most tastefully attired in satin and silk. Height ca. 75 cm. **Price 175 Mk.**

## No. 23. Mechanischer Clown

**Mechanical Clown.** Splendidly and most originally dressed in silk and satin. Plays the mandolin while making the most horrible grimaces; with music. Height ca. 75 cm. **Price 145 Mk.**

## No. 24. Clown als Hylophonist

**Clown as Hylophonist.** Stands in front of a small table and plays the hylophone (music from a musical movement substituted); the movements of the head, wig, eyes, tongue and arms are most originally and naturally reproduced; sumptuously dressed in silk. Height ca. 70 cm. **Price 200 Mk.**

Reparaturen werden gewissenhaft ausgeführt.

# Mechanische Raucher

**Mechanical Smokers** of the most varied kinds and various national costumes, such as Negro, Chinese, Mexican, Egyptian, Englishman, Turk, monkey, etc., unusually fine and elegant as well as original in their attire of satin and silk. Arms, head eyes, lips, etc., move naturally to bring cigar or cigarette to and from the mouth, inhaling and exhaling the smoke like a human. With music. Height ca. 75 cm.

## No. 25. Gentlemann.

**Gentleman.** A mechanical smoker most fashionably dressed in a red jacket, white vest, short silken breeches and long stockings. Places a cigarette in and out of the mouth, smoking naturally. Moves head, eyes, lips and arms, one arm moving a collapsible high hat to and fro. Height ca. 75 cm. **Price 150 Mk.**

## No. 26. Maler-Palette

**Painter's Palette** from which two heads with arms protrude, the lower one that of an old gentleman reading a newspaper, smoking and lifting his glasses from his nose now and then.

A clown above amuses himself with the one below and offers his blessings while moving his arms and wig and blowing away the smoke, so that the whole arrangement presents an extraordinarily astonishing impression. With music, Height ca. 80 cm. **Price 160 Mk.**

## No. 27. Affe.

**Monkey** smoking a cigarette, splendidly dressed in satin and silk (in Rococo fashion). Makes the most original grimaces, while moving head, eyes, lips and arms in a natural manner. One hand moves the cigarette to and from the lips while smoking, as the other hand waves a monocle back and forth. All movements are made in a most original and realistic manner. Height ca. 75 cm. **Price 145 Mk.**

## No. 28. Mech. Raucher (Neger)

**Mechanical Smoker (Negro),** free-standing on a pedestal smoking a cigarette. Moves head and arms, bringing the cigarette up and down. The movements are very natural. Height ca. 65 cm. **Price 60 Mk.**

## No. 29. Der Vollmond als Mode-Geck

**The Full Moon as a Fop.** Exceptionally original representation of someone in love. The eyes, eyelids, arms and cane move; a cigarette is raised and lowered, and smoke is inhaled and exhaled in a natural manner. Height ca. 75 cm. **Price 160 Mk.**

## No. 30. Desgleichen ein mechanisch. Raucher

Likewise a **Mechanical Smoker** made as a mogul stretched out on a costly divan, richly dressed in satin and silk set off with rich pearls. Smokes a water pipe that is in front of him, raising and lowering the mouthpiece and moving head, arms, mouth, eyes, etc., in a very natural manner. With music. Length ca. 75 cm. **Price 225 Mk.**

No 35.

## *No. 34. Clown den Mond*

**Clown Singing to the Moon,** most effectively made (as shown in the illustration). The clown plays the mandoline (music from a musical movement substituted), moving his head, tongue, arms, etc., naturally, while the moon laughs at him, rolling its eyes and distorting its mouth. Height ca. 60 cm. **Price 150 Mk.**

## *No. 35. Mechanische Fratze*

**Mechanical Caricature.** Eyes and mouth distort in a most original manner, and the mouth opens to show a frog inside moving back and forth, while an unusual figure sitting on the caricature tickles it with a peacock feather. With music, the whole very striking and effective. Height ca. 50 cm. **Price 140 Mk.**

## *No. 36. Japanese (Theetrinker)*

**Japanese (Tea Drinker).** Moves the cup to his mouth and puts it down with his right hand, rests a parasol on his shoulder with his left hand, turning it alternately to the right and to the left. Head, eyes, mouth, etc., move. The costume is elegantly made of silk with hand embroidery. With music. Height ca. 75 cm. **Price 175 Mk.**

## *No. 37. Japanesin mit Fächer*

**Japanese Girl with Fan.** Very effective as an individual exhibition piece, however it is a suitable companion to the tea drinker described above. Likewise twirls a parasol over the shoulder and with the other hand fans herself, head, eyes and arms moving naturally. Elegantly dressed in silk as above. Height ca. 75 cm. **Price 185 Mk.**

Neger No. 31.

**No. 31. Neger (billiger Raucher)**

**Negro (inexpensive Smoker)** sitting on a bale smoking a cigar and inhaling and exhaling the smoke. The figure is without movement, but appears otherwise very life-like and is durably and solidly constructed. Height ca. 50 cm. **Price 55 Mk.**

**No. 32. Reklame-Clown**

**Advertising Clown** sitting on a stool laughing at people and beckoning to them. Head, eyes, and tongue move naturally; feet and arms are moved in such a manner that he can be used for every kind of advertising. Height ca. 60 cm. **Price 55 Mk.**

***No. 33. Gr. mechanisches Tablean***

**Large Mechanical Picture.** Landscape 1 meter 5 cm. long and 80 cm. high in magnificently gilded frame. Has rising balloons, waterfall, mill, railroad and rocking ship, the whole marvelously inlaid with mother-of-pearl. **Price 375 Mk.**

**Other pictures with landscapes of all kinds from 350 to 500 Mk.**

## „Automaten mit Phonograph."

Clown mit Mond.

**No. 38. Trompeter.**

**Trumpeter** blows genuine bugle calls, raising and lowering the trumpet; head and arm move. In the pedestal of the trumpeter a phonograph is placed which produces the tunes loudly and clearly. Additional bugle calls are available and cost per extra cylinder **5 Mk.**

The figure is dressed most tastefully in old German riding apparel. Height ca. 50 cm. **Price 70 Mk.**

**No. 39. Clown mit Mandoline (Phonograph).**

**Clown with Mandolin (Phonograph).** Mechanical clown seated on a well playing a mandolin. From the clouds the moon suddenly appears and sings to his friend Pierrot, moving his mouth and eyes. After the song is ended, the clouds slide across the moon, and the clown looks up in surprise and starts playing again. The song of the moon comes from a phonograph placed in the well that operates automatically and is louder than a good gramophone. Cylinders with various melodies can be supplied at **5 Mk.** per extra cylinder.

Height of the entire most elegantly and originally constructed group is 60 cm. **Price 160 Mk.**

Negerknabe als Büste. Negermädchen als Büste.

***No. 40. Büste Negerknabe***

**Bust of a Negro Boy** playing the banjo, from time to time thumbing his nose and sticking out his tongue; head, eyes, tongue, arms and hands move naturally. Splendidly and originally dressed in silk. With music. Height ca. 56 cm. **Price 145 Mk.**

***No. 41 Büste Negermädchen***

**Bust of a Negro Girl** playing the lyre; head, eyes, arm, hand, etc., move naturally. Beautifully and originally dressed in silk, with music (excellently suited as a companion to the above). Height ca. 56 cm. **Price 145 Mk.**

***No. 42 Schwerttänzerin**

**Sword Dancer** dancing a ballet with sword held horizontally over her head, turning on the toes of one foot, swinging the other leg, and moving the entire torso naturally to the right and to the left. The figure is piquantly and marvelously dressed in tights and an airy costume. With music. Height over 90 cm. **Price 365 Mk.**

No. 44. Kammerzofe No. 43. Mech. Koch.

**No. 43. Mechanischer Koch.**

**Mechanical Chef.** A very effective piece, splendidly dressed in silk. Moves mouth, head, eyes and arms, and swallows correctly as a red wine bottle is raised and lowered in the right hand. The other hand carries a cooking pot with a cover that goes on and off. From the pot the head of a cat peeps out, sticks out its tongue and then disappears again. With music. Height ca. 75 cm. **Price 150 Mk.**

**No. 44. Mechanische Kammerzofe**

**Mechanical Chambermaid**, serving tea. Carries in one hand a serving tray on which are found a cup, a sugar bowl, and a cream pitcher. The other hand holds a tea pot from which at regular intervals she pours tea into the cup. Whenever her head is turned, there appear a frog in the cup, a mouse in the cream pitcher, and a bird in the sugar bowl. With music. Height ca. 75 cm. **Price 200 Mk.**

**Mechanical Automatic Snake Charmer.** This automaton, dressed in the rich clothing of the Indies, stands under a palm tree and subdues 4 snakes, which rise up and coil themselves around him in a natural manner, while he looks about proudly and moves head, eyes and mouth as though alive.

At the foot of the Indian sits a negro playing the flute (the music of a musical movement substitutes for this instrument) and moving eyes, head and arms. The group is most originally and effectively put together, and the movements of the figures as well as the snakes are true to life.

Height of the Indian is ca. 1 meter 10 cm. The base is an additional 30 cm.

**Price 600 Mk.**

***No. 46. Zauberin***

**Sorceress.** Stands behind a small table and conjures. On the table stand 2 large cups and 1 cube which she conjures and opens with her magic wand, lifting them alternately to show each time something different, such as a monkey's head, a child's head, or a clown's head, each moving naturally. The movements of the sorceress are most natural, and she is spendidly dressed in silk. With music. Height ca. 80 cm.

***No. 47. Zauberer*** Price 275 Mk.

**Magician.** Likewise standing behind a little table and conjuring 2 cups, which are alternately lifted from the table and under which the most varied objects are conjured forth and made to disappear. The actions are most natural, and the figure is grandly dressed and fitted out in silk. With music. Height ca. 80 cm. **275 Mk.**

*** No. 48. Clown als Frosch-Dresseur.***

**Clown as Frog Trainer.** A clown, most originally and authentically dressed in silk sits on a chair with his feet stretched out. On one leg sits a trained frog that produces his clever tricks in an original manner, while the clown mimics the frog and applauds, moving head, eyes, tongue and arms most naturally. With music. Height ca. 75 cm.

**Price 240 Mk.**

*** No. 49. Schönheit als Balanxeuse***

**Balancing Beauty** in Japanese style, holds in one hand supported on her body a long pole that revolves and supports a figure playing a violin, while fanning herself with a fan held in the other hand and moving head, etc., most naturally. Splendidly dressed in velvet and silk (trimmed with pearls). With music. Height of the figure ca. 80 cm. and with pole 1 meter 20 cm. **Price 250 Mk.**

*** No. 50 Clown als Balanxeur. ***

**Balancing Clown**, most originally dressed in silk as above and sitting on a chair. Holds in one hand a rod on which a rolling ball is balanced, directed by the other hand. Moves head, eyes, tongue, arms, etc., in the most natural manner. Height ca. 75 cm. **Price 240 Mk.**

**No. 51. Dame als Fensterklopfer.**

(Dame als Fensterklopfer.)

**Lady Window Tapper.** Attractive free-standing chromolithograph. Moves head, fan and arm. The lady taps at different periods of time on the window and then hides behind the fan. Everyone is involuntarily forced to look and stay to watch. Height 58 cm. **Price 36 Mk.**

**No. 52. Engländer auf Reisen.**

**Traveling Englishman.** Raises and lowers a travel guide with one hand and binoculars with the other, moving head, eyes, arms, etc., naturally. Height 95 cm. **Price 65 Mk.**

**No. 53. Matrose als Trinker**

**Drinking Sailor.** Raises and lowers a glass and fills it with natural movements of head, eyes, arms, etc. Height ca. 65 cm. **Price 60 Mk.**

**No. 54. Clown als Balanxeur.** Balancing Clown, 60-70 cm. high, with original natural movements. **Price 50-60 Mk.**

**No. 55. Mechanischer Knödelfresser.**

**Mechanical Dumpling Glutton.** Very suitable for organs or as a money-maker for carousels, panoramas, etc. A farmer, very originally characterized in a seated posture with a bowl of dumplings in his lap and fork in hand, merrily eating them and making faces. Height ca. 1 meter. **Price 100 Mk.**

**No. 56. Mechanischer Knödelfresser.**

**Mechanical Dumpling Glutton**, as above except only ca. 50 cm. high. **Price 55 Mk.**

**No. 57. Neger als Diener.**

**Negro Servant**, brushing a hat and moving head, eyes and arms, etc., very naturally. Height ca. 65 cm. **Price 55 Mk.**

**No. 59. Mech. Stiefelputzer**

**Mechanical Shoe Shiner** with very original movement of head, eyes and arms. Height ca. 55 cm. **Price 55 Mk.**

(Mechanisches Mühlenbild.)

**No. 58. Mech. Mühlenbild.**

**Mechanical Mill Picture,** with correctly-running clock and 6 moving figures; a very effective show-piece and a good value. Height ca. 52 cm., width 41 cm. Runs 9 hours. **Price 30 Mk.**

**No. 60. Mech. Strickerin.**

**Mechanical Knitter.** An old lady knitting, moving head, eyes, arms, etc., in a most original manner. Height ca. 50 cm. **Price 50 Mk.**

## Billigere Schau- und Cassen-Stücke

**Inexpensive show-pieces and money-makers, less elaborately made and fitted out – nevertheless durably constructed.**

**No. 62. Rheinlandschaft.**

**Rhine Landscape.** A very beautifully-arranged, effective mechanical picture with moving water, figures crossing a bridge, and smoke rising from a blacksmith's forge. The windmill also moves, as does the bell in the tower, which contains a correctly-running clock. The chimney sweep in the chimney and the waterwheel move, the smith hammers the turning wheel, and children rock on the wagon shaft. Height ca. 32 cm., width 41 cm. **Price 45 Mk.**

**No. 63. Mechanisches Tableau.**

**Mechanical Picture.** A beautiful landscape with moving figures of all kinds. The smith shoes the horse and talks to his child, a boy feeds the horse, the dog barks, the chickens eat, and in the background children see-saw and people go about their work. In the tower is a correctly-running clock with chimes that play continually. Height ca. 32 cm., width 41 cm.

Price **33 Mk**; without the clock and chimes **25 Mk.**

**No. 64. Mech. Clown (Geigenspieler).**

**Mechanical Clown (Violin Player).** Sits on a chair and plays the violin, moving head, eyes and arms and sticking out his tongue from time to time. The movements are most natural and original; the jointed feet are movable to any position. Height ca. 60 cm. **Price 65 Mk.**

**No. 65. Mech. Schuhmacher.**

**Mechanical Shoemaker.** The shoemaker patches a boot, moving head, mouth, eyes and arms appropriately. Height ca. 50 cm. **Price 66 Mk.**

**No. 66. Mech. Elephant**

**Mechanical Elephant** (free-standing chromolithograph). Moves head, eyes, and tail, while the monkey seated under the parasol moves arm and head. Runs for 8-10 hours. Height ca. 56 cm., width ca. 56 cm.

Price including a correctly-running clock **33 Mk.**, without clock **28 Mk.**

**No. 67. Mech. Weihnachtsmann.**

**Mechanical Santa Claus,** naturally and most originally constructed. The head, mouth, eyes and arms move appropriately, and the automaton has a pack with all kinds of toys, such as dolls, trumpets, beads, etc., hanging out, while from his pockets all sorts of dolls peep out. Height ca. 80 cm. **Price 75 Mk.**

## Achtung!

Attention! Permit me to bring to your attention particularly that my small automata are now to be found displayed in the largest museums, panoramas, waxworks, etc., and according to testimonials of my valued customers, they compare most effectively with the largest and most expensive show-pieces, due to their originality, elegance and precise operation, thus yielding the greatest effect.

The numbers marked *can be supplied with a coin slot (so that on depositing a specified coin the automaton begins to function and automatically turns itself off), which increases the price ca. 25 Marks.

All automata can be supplied if desired with different costumes.

### Bedingungen.

**Conditions.** For automata that are not in stock, three to four weeks should be allowed for delivery.

Half of the cost is to be sent with the order, and the other half is payable on delivery.

All orders will be promptly and most conscientiously filled.

**Reparaturen**

Repairs on mechanical-automatic apparatus of every kind will be promptly and inexpensively made in my workshop.

*Most respectfully,* **Gustav Uhlig.**

## Achtung!

**Attention!** *Permit me particularly to point out that I have most of the catalogued show-pieces and money-makers at all times ready-made in stock; for the others I must ask production time lasting 3 to 4 weeks.*

*All of the show-pieces I mention are designed so that* **the mechanism is of top quality**, *the movements are* **most natural and original**, *and the clothing is most* **authentically and elegantly** *contrived, and you can also be assured that even the* **least expensive and smallest of my listed show-pieces** *do not fail to be effective in their natural imitations.*

**Reparaturen werden gewissenhaft ausgeführt.**

**The automata illustrated on the preceding pages are examples of the hundreds of different varieties that were made during the 19th and early 20th centuries. When first sold, these were especially popular in England, France, and Germany – and most were marketed there.**

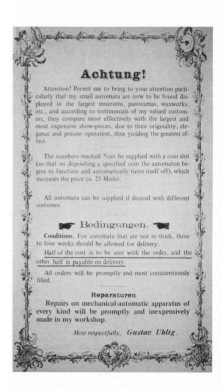

The monkey fisherman automaton vainly tries to catch a tiny mechanical fish in the pool. As he raises his pole the fish darts about in the water. Seeing the fish, the monkey lowers his hook – and the fish disappears.

A musical movement is in the base. This is a particularly elaborate example of a fine glass-domed automaton of the late 19th century. (Collection of Mr. and Mrs. Gordon Lipe)

The monkey sorcerer plays a late 19th century version of the shell game. A seemingly baffling array of dice and colored balls appear and disappear as the magician lifts the cups. A musical movement is in the base.

Such magicians were popular during the Victorian era. Fewer were made of these than of other kinds of automata as the now-you-see-it, now-you-don't mechanisms were expensive to make. Some types had Turks or fortune tellers for the figures.

Two domed musical tableaux in the collection of Mr. and Mrs. Jerry Cohen are shown flanking a Nicole Frères 4-tune key-wind overture box. Tableaux, or "domed pieces" as they are sometimes called by collectors, were especially popular during the 19th century, although their history dates from earlier times. Small musical movements made in Austria or Switzerland are usually in the base.

Two different tableaux with rocking ships. The one at the left awaits restoration of the "waves." Note the musical movement beneath the ship.

Tableau of a castle and bridge. When the mechanisms are actuated the music plays and a colorful little train crosses the bridge span. The castle is in the form of a watchtower and has an enamel-faced clock.

An unusual double-sided domed piece with a separate tableau on each side. One is of a castle with a drawbridge. A tiny figure moves about on the castle parapet. The other side features a ship on a stormy sea.

This tableau is especially large and measures 2'2" high. Water appears to be flowing from a lake and cascading over a large waterfall which tails into a gorge of rapids. On either side of the chasm are quaint and colorful old buildings. A suspension bridge spans the gorge. When the tableau is actuated the ship rides the rapids, a railroad train crosses the bridge, and a windmill on the right bank of the gorge turns its sails. The book "Automata," by Alfred Chapuis and Edmond Droz, notes that similar scenes were made as early as 1750 by Paris clockmakers.

Typical Austrian cylinder music box movement from a musical painting. Circa 1895.

Above: An exceptionally complex mechanical picture from the 19th century. Behind the glass front of the scene a panorama set about 1850 unfolds. A hot air balloon of the Montgolfier type drifts across the sky. In the foreground a fully rigged sailing ship rides out a storm on a wave-tossed sea. In the background are ancient buildings. High on the left-side hill are the ruins of an ancient castle.

The picture measures 1'2" high by 1'5" wide by 5" deep. The scenes are of painted papier maché and cardboard. The mechanisms are driven by cams, levers, and a system of cords and pulleys.

Most such three-dimensional scenes or tableaux were made one-at-a-time by artists. No two were alike, although certain themes such as stormy seas and moving trains were used frequently.

Above: A typical, although above average in artistic quality, oil-on-metal painting of the 1890's. The scene is of a lakeside village. In the background are ancient ruins surmounted, for some reason, by a prominent clock tower. The tower clock operates and is wound by the two holes at either side of the clock face. There are no mechanical figures or other animated effects. A music box is concealed in the back of the painting and plays at desired intervals. This is an unusual feature as most contemporary paintings had the clock and music box mechanisms independent of each other.

Right: Three-dimensional scene of a Mediterranean seashore. Figures dance in a pavilion while a small ship rocks to and fro in the waves.

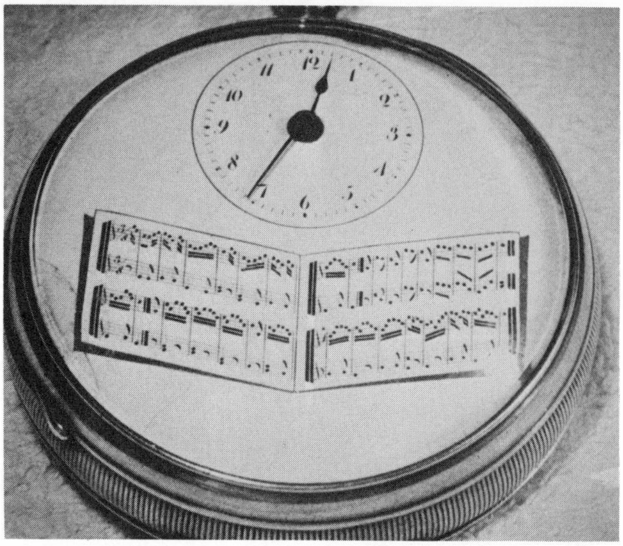

The faces of these two musical watches have musical motifs. A cheerful melody pinned on a tiny cylinder movement plays at intervals.

Mechanical or automaton watch (not musical). The two horsemen appear to strike bells on the hour and half hour. The actual sound is produced by a tiny gong within the watch. Scenes of blacksmiths striking anvils, cupids sharpening arrows, and, occasionally, pornographic (or "lubricious," as the old catalogues called them) subjects were used on watch and clock faces of the late 18th and early 19th centuries.

A fine cylinder movement in a pocket watch from the mid-19th century. Early types of watches had laminated combs (with teeth stacked one atop another vertically) or teeth arranged in a fan pattern. Never common, musical watches are prized collectors' items today.

Each of these tiny musical seals has a loop for suspension from a necklace or bracelet. Each contains a tiny musical movement which plays a simple tune.

(Most items pictured on this page are from the J.B. Nethercutt Collection)

Interior and exterior views of a 19th century pocket watch with a cylinder musical mechanism. The teeth in the musical comb are covered by the engraved plate.

The subject of musical clocks and watches is immense. Most makers of timepieces during the 18th and 19th centuries incorporated musical chimes or, less frequently, cylinder music box movements into some of their products. In this book we illustrate but a few examples. "Automata," a book by Alfred Chapuis and Edmond Droz, published in an English edition in 1958 by Editions Du Griffon, Neuchatel, Switzerland, treats the subject of musical and mechanical timepieces in detail. The interested reader is urged to refer to that source for additional information.

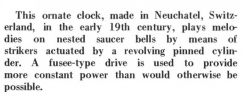

This ornate clock, made in Neuchatel, Switzerland, in the early 19th century, plays melodies on nested saucer bells by means of strikers actuated by a revolving pinned cylinder. A fusee-type drive is used to provide more constant power than would otherwise be possible.

A French ormolu clock from the last half of the 19th century. The base, which originally supported a glass dome, contains a musical movement.

## –Some 19th Century Musical Clocks–

Mantel clocks were made in hundreds of varieties during the 19th century. Those shown on this page are examples of clocks with cylinder music box movements. Some were cheap — the tiny alarm clock pictured directly below is one; others were expensive — the clocks with mechanical birds shown at the lower right of this page, for example.

Cheap metal-cased musical alarm clock of the 1890-1910 era.

Framed wall clocks with musical movements.

Viennese clock with automaton scene on top and music box in base; right, musical clock with animated scene.

Musical clocks with 3-dimensional tableaux.

French ormolu clocks with allegorical figures. The bottom of each contains a musical movement.

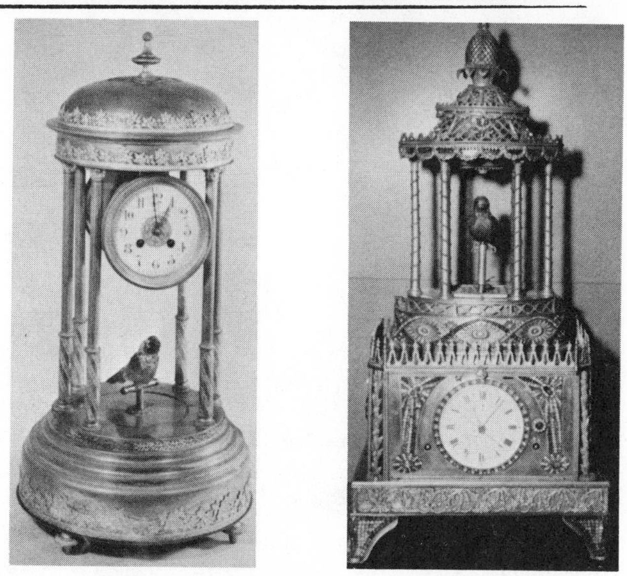

Clocks with animated birds — a rare type.

Musical bird box made by Charles Abram Bruguier of Geneva, Switzerland, circa 1825. The inner movement is shown to the right of the case. Early bird boxes such as this are much more intricate than the later types and contain perhaps ten times as many parts and often sing five or six different song verses. As the bird sings he turns from side to side, flaps his wings, moves his tail, turns his head, and opens and closes his beak. (George Bidden photograph)

Inexpensive bird boxes with much simpler movements are still being made in Switzerland today.

Left: Swiss bird box from about 1885. The case is of solid silver and is engraved and decorated with enamel in various colors.

Right: Swiss bird box of the type made circa 1885 - 1890. A watch is on the front of the case. The case is of solid silver and is enameled.

(George Bidden photographs)

An automaton figure built in a housing of bird box format. A music movement is within. The figure waves his baton and moves his leg as the music plays. (Rita Ford photograph)

## MECHANICAL SINGING BIRDS

The mechanical singing birds shown on this page are from a 1910 French catalogue. Similar birds have been made since the late 19th century and are still being made today, although not in as many varieties as previously. Generally, the boxes come in 1-bird, 2-bird, or 3-bird sizes, the larger ones being the more expensive and desirable.

The mechanisms consist of small bellows which operate a slide whistle or flute which gives a warbling sound. Bird chirps, not musical melodies, are produced — some in very realistic imitation of actual bird calls.

515

517 - 519

520

529

hand-cranked bird call

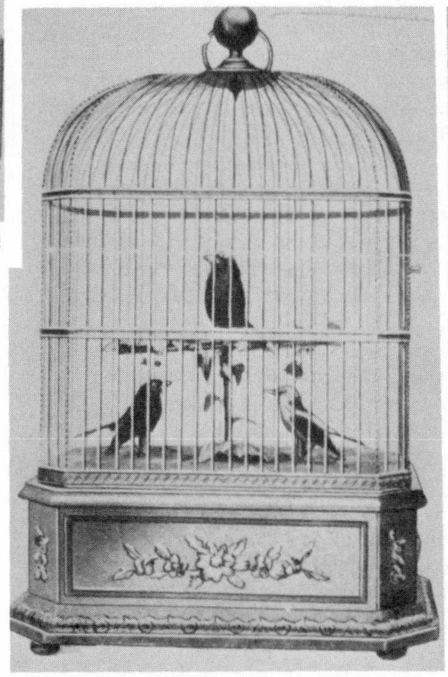

521

510

514

509 - 511

557

558

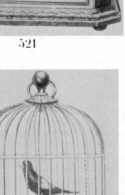

Above Right: Bonnie Tekstra holds a singing bird made in 1969 by Reuge & Co. of St. Croix, Switzerland. 1-, 2-, and 3-bird sizes are still made today.

## MUSICAL GAMBLING DEVICES

### In General

A wide variety of musical gambling devices once entertained the public in Europe, America, and elsewhere. These devices ranged from small dice shakers, roulette machines, mechanical race horses, and other table-top amusement devices to large upright slot machines weighing hundreds of pounds. All of these devices had one thing in common: they were gambling machines first and music machines second.

Warning: Laws concerning the possession of gambling equipment vary from place to place — particularly with respect to slot machines and other instruments which pay out monetary rewards.

Some authorities may take a lenient view. An item which appeared in the Los Angeles Herald Examiner of April 11, 1969, is an example:

"Police Must Return Old Slot Machine— San Diego (Associated Press). A Superior Court judge has ordered the return of a 1920's model slot machine, seized by police last February, to its owner. . .

"The slot machine, called an 'art object' by its owner, was taken from a local home by the police chief. Judge James L. Focht ruled that 'this machine is well over the hill in the antique line and is no more vicious in the home than an oil painting of a slot machine.' "

Other rulings have been different, and many fine collectors' items have been axed, dumped in lakes, and have met other fates at the hands of law enforcement agencies. Before purchasing or otherwise acquiring one of these we urge you to check the laws in your own area.

### Parlor Gambling Devices

During the late 19th century and early 20th century, small table-top size mechanical dice shakers, poker players, spinning race horses, and other gadgets were a popular form of home entertainment. Lacking coin slots and payoff mechanisms, these were played for "fun," or, if gambling was done, it was done on the side.

Some of these same devices were made in more costly models equipped with slots that took a coin, usually a cent or a nickel, and either paid off cash rewards or tokens. In some types of instruments there was no automatic payoff. A winner would notify the business proprietor and be paid in cash or merchandise. Such devices were especially popular in saloons where they were an ideal bar-top entertainment device.

The music mechanisms of these are tiny cylinder movements, usually of Swiss make. As musical instruments they are not of consequence; in fact, the movements are the same as those sold in cheap $1 to $5 musical toys of the period. However, these gambling devices are interesting to watch and to play with — and, as such, they are quite popular with collectors today.

### Musical Slot Machines

Beginning around the turn of the 20th century the Mills Novelty Company of Chicago (see Mills section of this book for further information on this concern), Caille Brothers of Detroit, and others added musical movements to slot machines. This was done in an attempt to circumvent state and local laws which prohibited slot machines as gambling devices. The logic of the manufacturers was that with the musical feature the slot machines were transformed into "musical entertainment devices" — thus, hopefully, making them legal for play in otherwise closed areas.

Mills produced a metal sign with the following wording. This sign was designed to be placed on top of a musical slot machine.

"THIS IS NOT A GAMING DEVICE. Any person desiring to gamble must not put any money in this machine. As a consideration for the use of this music machine and the music furnished, it is expressly agreed that all of the nickels which come out of the cup below must and shall be played back into the machine, thereby giving more music."

And here is what the ever-innovative minds at the Mills Novelty Company had to say about the efficacy of the sign — as printed in a Mills catalogue: "This sign is made entirely of metal with raised letters and is handsomely plated. It can be attached or detached in a moment's notice (Editorial comment: When the sheriff is knocking at the door???) — it is simply clamped to the coin detector. In many places this sign 'takes off the curse' and machines are allowed to be operated in places where without it operation would be entirely out of the question. We know of operators who have submitted this sign to chiefs of police, mayors, and judges, with the result that in many instances the machines were allowed to run."

Today musical slot machines are very scarce. Among extant antique slot machines (as a general rule, those with a large disc in front are considered to be "antique" — the later 3-reel "one armed bandit" types of later years are not, for the most part, classified as collectors' items) perhaps one in twenty has a music box in it.

In their early catalogues Mills and Caille, the largest manufacturers of slot machines at the time, listed their varous machines as being available with or without music as desired. Mills instruments equipped with music usually, but not always, had a plaque which read "Musical Cabinet" on the front.

The most popular of all musical slot machines (as evidenced by the numbers produced) was the Mills "Dewey." Other Mills machines which were optionally equipped with music included the Judge, Owl, 20th Century, Roulette, Cricket, and Big Six.

Mills had a problem with the "counterfeiting" of its machines. Other lesser-known makers produced their own machines using Mills names. Thus the Dewey was illicitly made by at least two other manufacturers. The problem became so intense that Mills devoted great space in its slot machine catalogues to the evils of buying sham Deweys and other Mills-named instruments. To be official, Mills noted, a Dewey or other seemingly Mills-made machine had to have the bright red Mills "owl" trademark.

The various Mills, Caille, etc. musical slot machines utilized Swiss cylinder box movements, usually with multiple tunes. Cylinders averaged from six to eight inches in length. On surviving machines we have seen music movements by Mermod Frères, Bremond, and several other prominent Swiss makers.

Usually the pushing of the crank on the front of the machine (the crank used to spin the front disc once a coin was deposited) also wound the music box (a slip clutch prevented overwinding) and started it playing. In some boxes the cylinder would revolve and play one tune — and then stop. Others had no stop provision. The box would play for as long as the winding impetus permitted — usually starting to play in the middle of one tune and ending somewhere in another tune.

Rarer than slot machines with cylinder music boxes are those with disc boxes. At least two different styles of slot machines — the "Numero Uno" is an example — used Regina disc music box movements. These were made only in small quantities — probably because the movements were more expensive to install and took up more room in the cabinet than did the Swiss cylinder types. As the intent was to make the machines "legal" and not to musically entertain the wagerers, musical quality made little difference. Collectors today usually have to completely rebuild the musical mechanisms of these instruments as they received hard use and little service attention.

### Musical Pianos

Covered in other sections of this book are the so-called "profit sharing player pianos" made or sold by Rockola, Nelson-Wiggen, Gray, Evans, and the Operators Piano Company. Basically, these are all cabinet style electric pianos, usually of a type that uses a standard 10-tune "A" roll. Built into each piano, usually at the top, is a three-reel (usually) slot machine of the type that shows lemons, cherries, oranges, etc.

Other pianos — the Mills Race Horse Piano, the Seeburg Grayhound, and the Western Electric Derby are examples — had no payoff slot. Gambling was encouraged "on the side."

The Mills description of the Race Horse Piano's ability to encourage customer betting is typical of the sales appeal used in advertising this general class of gambling piano:

"Six numbered horses line up at the miniature judges' stand and start off around the track. They disappear around the bend in the track only to appear a few seconds later dashing down the home stretch. It's thrilling — fascinating — keeps the crowd on their toes with excitement. They can't wait for the next race. They deposit nickel after nickel while the same piece is being played. A few seconds completes a race so the crowds can have ten to fifteen races while one piece of music is being played. Every time a nickel is deposited the horses start on another race, so this instrument may take in 50c or 75c while a single selection of music is being rendered.

"Friendly groups stand around trying to guess the winner each time. If their favorite doesn't win the first time, they are anxious for another race. They want to guess the winner, and they play it again and again. They not only drop nickel after nickel into the instrument, but also liberally settle their arguments with drinks, cigars, and other merchandise."

It is obvious from the above description that the musical feature of such instruments is strictly secondary in importance!

Technical note: Usually coin pianos have an accumulator device which registers the coins deposited and plays a tune for each. Several coins deposited at once result in several tunes being played in order. The gambling pianos have no accumulator device (or they have it, and it is blocked off). Additional coins activate the horses but do not register additional coin plays. At the end of a tune the piano shuts off. The next coin in the slot starts the music playing again.

Above: Caille "Eclipse" manufactured circa 1905 by Caille Brothers of Detroit, Michigan. Caille instruments were generally more ornate and had more cast nickel-plated metalwork than did the instruments of competitors.

Right: Mills "Dewey," probably the most popular musical gambling machine ever made. The name "Dewey" was used by several other makers as well, notably by Caille, causing Mills to refer to its products as the "Original Dewey." Admiral Dewey, the hero of Manila, is depicted in the lower center of the spinning wheel and also in a raised plaque just above the payoff cup. Mills "Dewey" slot machines were sold from about 1900 to after 1930 (they are listed in the 1931 catalogue) — an extraordinary span.

## New Century Detroit Machines.

Here is where you see the original machine, which exposes to the player's full **view the pay wheel**, in other words, this machine is made especially for the wise ones, inasmuch, to all appearances it is supposed to be impossible to plug or manipulate these machines in any way, for the reason that the Dial contains a hole for each color. The lucky color winning is designated and proved by the Plunder coming through the Color's hole in the Dial, and as the player sees this operation there can be no room for dispute.

For Operators, Saloons and Hotels there is positively not another machine on the market which to all appearances is as legitimate as the New Century Detroit, and as to the profits we cannot say too much. That is the part we prefer to leave to you, as we are confident that once you have the machine in operation for a month, you would never part with same.

The Cabinets are of quarter-sawed oak, piano finish, fancy panels. The metal work is heavily nickel-plated and of exquisite design, which makes the machine in every way attractive to human eyes as well as human hearts. It pays from 10c to $2.00. The Musical New Century has an attachment, which cannot be excelled by that in any of our competitors' machines. Remember that all our machines are covered clearly to you by guarantee. Not only in perfection as to material, but most important to you, **the profits.**

All these Machines can be had with or without Musical attachments

## Musical Black Cat.

The greatest money maker on the market to day. Winnings in full sight. Is handsomely made in every particular not one point having been overlooked to make it perfect in its construction in every way. The case is of quarter sawed oak. The musical box shows through the most perfect and artistic bronze panel ever placed on a Slot Machine. The construction of mechanism is perfect, simple and durable and like all other machines we handle, will remain in order, thus saving you time, money and annoyance.

The Black Cat has a positive register a flag showing up in top of coin detector on the color that has been played.

## The Musical Fox

**A Five-way** Automatic Slot-Machine that has made a record for itself. It positively cannot be manipulated or cheated in any manner. We have added our original flag system of registering every play, thus avoiding all disputes with reference to colors played, which often happened with the old style machines. We have added our new coin detector, which is conceded to be the handsomest and simplest ever put on a slot-machine. It positively cannot be manipulated. The musical movement is not a toy, but a sweet toned Swiss musical movement with automatic changing device.

## Our Musical Dewey

This machine is the same as our Improved Dewey with the addition of an elegant Swiss musical attachment as shown in cut, which is set in motion every time the machine is operated. The tunes change automatically. The machine can be played while the musical attachment is in operation thus losing no time waiting for the tune to be played. The musical attachment can be disconnected at will without interfering with the machine proper. This machine, like our Improved Dewey, is encased in an elegant quarter-sawed oak cabinet, old English oak finished, with artistically chased trimmings and coin top; and we have added an elegantly designed metal frame with glass front, through which musical movement can be seen. (See cut.) It pays all prizes in cash, from 10c. to $2.00. Height 5 feet 4 in., width 25½ in., depth 14 in., weight packed for shipping 240 lbs. We gurantee the machine

## The Musical Judge

This machine like the ORIGINAL JUDGE is so well known we will not take up the reader's time describing it, but we would warn all prospective purchasers to get the genuine from the originators. Some unscrupulous manufacturers have seen fit to copy our make of machines, a frank acknowledgment that our machines are superior to their own make. Do not be deceived. We guarantee all our machines, and if not satisfactory after 10 days' trial will refund your money less transportation charges. See discription of ORIGINAL JUDGE for description of the above. This machine is fitted with an elegant Swiss musical movement with automatic tune changing device. **It is not** a 6 inch toy as used by some of our competitors. All bets paid in nickels, 10c. to $1.00. Guaranteed for six months. Height 5¼ feet, width 22 inches, depth 12 inches, weight, packed for shipping, 225 lbs.

## The Musical Uno

A few reasons why it is superior to all other makes:

1. Because it is impossible to manipulate it.
2. It does not get out of order.
3. The coin detector is the handsomest and simplest ever made; every slot works independent of the other and is fitted with lock, enabling the owner to remove any spurious coin without opening the cabinet, and shows last two nickels played in each slot.
4. The mechanism of the machine proper is simplicity and durability personified; all small parts are stamped out of sheet steel and every hole in the entire machine is drilled by jigs, so in case of accidental breakage, parts can be replaced without the use of tools.
5. Every play is registered by a flag appearing in view directly above the dial corresponding with color or colors played and remaining in view until the machine is again operated.
6. The musical attachment is entirely original; we have the only machine in which the disc movement can be used. The music box is no toy but a sweet sounding, practical music box. The music box is entirely separate from the machine proper.
7. The machine can be operated with or without the musical attachment, or the music can be played without operating the machine proper, an advantage over all so called competitors.
8. Over a thousand different tunes can be played. Extra discs furnished at cost price.

Pays all bets in nickels, 10c. to $1.00. Height 5½ feet, width 22 inches, depth 12 inches, weight packed for shipping 225 pounds. Guaranteed for six months.

## Our Musical Puck

**Our Improved Musical Puck** is the same as our improved Puck with the addition of an elegantly toned Swiss musical movement, as shown in cut. This machine, like our other Puck machine, is too familiar to need any introduction, unless we repeat what we said before that it has been entirely rebuilt, and we have eliminated all the delicate and intricate parts and have added the new crank handle as shown in cut. We claim it is now one of the simplest machines on the market; paying all prizes in cash, from 10c. to $2.00. We will pay $1000 to the first person that will show us how to manipulate it, as we claim it cannot be cheated. Height, 5 feet 4 inches over all, width 25½ inches, depth 14 inches, weight packed for shipping 240 lbs. We guarantee the machine proper for 6 months.

## The Musical Cupid

**The acme of perfection in a five-slot machine.**

For beauty of design, symetrical outlines, simplicity and durability, this machine is destined to outlive all other five-slot automatic devices of this kind. It has only been on the market a short time but has become so popular some of our unscrupulous competitors have seen fit to try to copy it, but being one of the largest manufacturers in the business, we can undersell our competitors and give the people original ideas. This machine is fitted with one of our imported sweet toned musical movements. (**No toy music box**). The cabinet is quarter-sawed oak, piano finish, elegantly trimmed with artistically chased metal trimmings. All bets paid in nickels, 10c. to $1.00. Guaranteed for six months. Height 5¼ feet, width 22 inches, depth 12 inches, weight packed for shipping 250 pounds.

## The Musical Marquette

This machine is destined to become as popular as the man after whom it is named. This machine is built on the same lines as our other 5-slot machines, but we have added a new device which enables the owners to operate this machine where the regular money machines are prohibited, by using our split check system. The checks are bought at the counter and played into the machine and all winnings are paid in trade or cash, as the circumstances will allow. The machine can only be operated with the split checks, as no coin or other check, or slugs can be put in the machine. We have the only machine this system can be used on. 500 checks go with each machine, at an additional cost of $7.50. This machine is built with or without musical attachment. The cabinet is quarter-sawed oak, piano finish, and ornamented with artistically chased trimmings. Height 5¼ feet, width 22 inches, depth 12 inches, weight packed for shipping 200 pounds.

## The Musical Star

This is the same machine as our New Star with an elegantly toned Swiss musical movement attached. The tunes change automatically every time the machine is operated. This machine can be operated while the music is playing.

All prizes paid in cash from 10c to $1.00.

Height 5½ feet, width 22 in., depth 12 in., weight packed for shipping 225 lbs.

**Above left: The Musical Uno, a gambling machine usually made with a disc mechanism (see Regina section of this book) but illustrated here with a Swiss cylinder movement. "The musical attachment is entirely original; we have the only machine in which the disc movement can be used" notes the description.**

**Right: Small table-model musical roulette game, representative of many such small gambling devices which were equipped with musical movements, usually very small Swiss cylinder units.**

**Above: The instruments depicted above are mostly by Caille Brothers of Detroit. Caille instruments usually had larger and better-grade musical movements than did those of Mills. Note the reference (in The Musical Judge caption) "This machine is fitted with an elegant Swiss musical movement with automatic tune changing device. It is not a 6-inch toy as used by some of our competitors." "Judge" and "Dewey" were names also used by Mills.**

### The Judge....5 Way

An attractive five way machine which pays from 10 cents to $1 00. It is built on the principle of the Owl, but has in addition a register which shows colors played; this in itself is a great feature, as it settles all disputes instantly. This machine is imitated, and very poorly. Remember this when purchasing and do not allow a few dollars difference to influence you. The first day's play will make it up.

### The Judge Musical....5 Way

Is similar in every respect to the Judge regular, except that it has a high-grade musical attachment, so connected that a play on the machine starts the music and changes the tune automatically, thus giving you a tune with each play. The musical attachment is contained in an ornamental case at the bottom of the machine.

SHIPPING WEIGHT 600 LBS.
16 WAY

### Mills 20th Century Twins

Mills 20th Century Twins is the greatest twin machine ever built. It is made up of any cein combination of Nickel, Quarter, Half Dollar or Dollar Machines. It is two machines in one. Write for a special circular of this one.

### Mills Duplex Musical....Ten Way

Has musical cabinet, otherwise is exactly the same as the above in its appearance and construction. It has a high grade and large musical attachment, which plays a tune every time machine is put in operation. This renders the machine permissible in many towns, which otherwise would be closed tight.

Be sure and write for our prices and liberal method of shipping.

Mills Duplex Musical....Ten Way

SHIPPING WEIGHT 560 LBS.

### Mills Twins

12 WAY

Made up of any combination of Mills Chicago and Dewey Machines. Nickels or Quarters. Write for special circulars of these machines.

On the Square Musical

### On the Square...5 way

Built like the Owl, so that five persons can play at one time. Has nickel plated percentage wheel in front of dial showing no plugs. This is a great feature and is bound to get the play.

### On the Square Musical

Same as above, but with music box attachment. This device enables machine to be operated in many localities where they would not otherwise be allowed, as value is given for every coin in music.

Write for our price list. It will pay you to investigate.

**Write for fuller description of our machines, price, terms and explanation of our liberal proposition to give trial of the machine before purchase is completed. :: :: :: ::**

Chicago Musical....Six Way

Chicago.... With Trade Check Attachment
View of Inside

### The Chicago Machine

is in size, appearance and method of construction just like the Dewey. It is a six-way machine, paying prizes from 10 cents to $2.00, which makes it more attractive than any of the five-way machines, whose largest prize is $1.00. It has the latest improved coin detector, showing the last three coins played in each slot, also a register just below the detector showing which colors were played last. In addition, the Chicago has as its great feature, a nickel-plated ratchet percentage wheel in front of the dial. This has no plugs on it and makes the machine appear to be entirely fair. This makes the Chicago doubly valuable for operating purposes.

### The Chicago Musical

is the same machine as the Chicago, except that it has a high class Music Box attachment, which plays a tune every time the machine is operated. This feature will enable you to run the machine in many places where the ordinary style is not allowed.

The Dewey Musical...Six Way

### The Dewey...Six Way

The King of six-way automatic machines. Pays prizes from 10 cents to $2.00. Has coin detector and a color register showing colors last played. A handsome machine and one of the most popular of the "Mills" make. Write for our reduced prices.

### The Dewey Musical...Six Way

Is the same as the Dewey, except that it has a musical attachment, with eight to twelve tunes playing one for each nickel. This musical feature makes machines unobjectionable in many places where they are otherwise barred out. Remember this and write for our price list.

**Mills Musical Slot Machines: Shown on this page are some of the more popular Mills musical slot machines. Actually, Mills advertised that just about any model in the Mills line could be equipped with a music box attachment at extra cost — a measure designed to circumvent restrictive laws pertaining to slot machines — but those shown here were specifically advertised as having the musical feature. Refer to the Mills Novelty Company section of this book for more historical information on Mills and its other products, including gambling and arcade machines.**

**The Mills Novelty Company of Chicago, Illinois, and Caille Brothers of Detroit, Michigan, were the two leading makers of musical slot machines. While these instruments were used earlier and later, the main period of popularity was from about 1900 to 1920.**

### The Famous Mills "Owl"

The greatest and most popular 5 way machine ever made; pays from 10 cents to $1.00. No way yet found to beat this machine. Will always be in order.

This is the original "Owl" which is virtually the basis on which all other slot machines have been built. More concerns have "gone broke" trying to make a successful imitation of this machine than still remain in the business. There is only one "Owl" and this is it. Beware of imitations. There are a few left and the fact that we openly call your attention to the same is warrant for you to give the matter your earnest consideration. Every opportunity given intending purchasers to satisfy themselves of the "Owl's" merit by our three days' trial proposition.

### The Owl Musical....5 Way

Similar in every way to the regular "Owl" except that it has a high-grade musical attachment which plays a tune every time a nickel goes into machine. Frequently where the plain machines are not permitted, the musicals are not disturbed.

# DISC MUSIC BOXES

**Disc Music Boxes**
**Disc-Operated Pianos**
**and related instruments**

## Introduction to Disc Music Boxes

"A disc music box is best described as a wooden case enclosing a musical movement which employs projections or holes on an interchangeable revolving metal disc to play the melody. The projections or holes of the disc cause star wheels to turn, striking the tuned teeth of a metal comb or combs in sequence so as to cause a tune to be played. The discs are interchangeable so as to permit any amount of tunes to be played, limited only by the number of discs available. The discs from any one machine will play on any machine of the same make, size, and type of comb.

"The disc machine consists of two main assemblies: the bedplate assembly containing those parts which make the music from the disc, and the motor assembly which drives the disc." (From "The Disc Musical Box Handbook," by Graham Webb – with permission)

In 1882, Miguel Boom, a citizen of Haiti, patented in the United States a music box which played tunes from movable pegs set in a revolving disc. Boom's invention found no commercial application. In 1885 and 1886, Paul Lochmann and Ellis Parr patented several improvements in disc boxes. In 1886 the first interchangeable disc instrument was made. This box featured two combs, each mounted in a vertical position, above which was placed a stationary perforated cardboard disc, in the manner of a Herophon organette. The combs were turned by a spring-wound mechanism. Metal discs with projections on the underside which plucked stationary music combs were produced in 1887. In 1889 Paul Wendland (of the Symphonion Musikwerke) patented the star wheel, the basic device that was to be used in nearly every disc music box made in later years.

During the late 1880's, the Symphonion Musikwerke, located in Gohlis, a suburb of Leipzig, Germany, was the dominant and just about the only force in the beginning industry. By early 1888 Symphonion employed "120 hands in the factory, plus a number of girls who prepare the discs in their own homes," according to a contemporary account (see Symphonion section of this book). It is interesting to note that Symphonion, the first large firm in the music business, was also one of the last. Operations, although on a severely diminished scale, were carried on through the early 1920's.

Symphonion, under the direction of Paul Lochmann, expanded its product line so that by 1894 several dozen different styles were being produced. The product line ranged from tiny boxes which were used as children's toys to musical hall clocks to large upright coin-operated boxes designed for commercial use.

Shortly before 1890, the Polyphon Musikwerke was founded by Gustave Brachhausen and and Paul Riessner, Symphonion's foreman and one of Symphonion's engineers respectively. Polyphon went on to employ over 1000 people (compared to Symphonion's high of about 400 and Regina's 325) and become the world's largest maker of disc-type music boxes. Polyphon produced a large variety of instruments in many different disc sizes and case styles.

In September, 1892, Gustave Brachhausen went to America to establish a branch factory for Polyphon. With the financial backing of Knauth, Nachod & Kühne, Leipzig bankers, the Regina Music Box Company was incorporated in 1894. At first the firm sold music boxes imported from Polyphon. By the autumn of 1894 Regina was producing its own instruments in Rahway, New Jersey. The Regina Music Box Company became the dominant factor in the American market for disc-type boxes. About 100,000 instruments were sold from 1894 to 1921.

Polyphon, Regina, and Symphonion, the "big three" as they are sometimes referred to today, had perhaps 90% of the market. But there was still room for several dozen other makes of music boxes, some of superb quality, to achieve success. Paul Ehrlich, manufacturer of the Ariston disc-played organette and other mechanical instruments, produced a number of music boxes, including a cardboard disc model (produced in the late 1880's, this box used levers to pluck the comb teeth) and the Monopol series of conventional disc boxes. The Kalliope Musikwerke manufactured many fine boxes, including some of very large size, during the 1890's and early 1900's. J.H. Zimmermann made and sold the Adler and Fortuna boxes. Paul Lochmann, the founder of Symphonion, started a new business in 1901 and produced Lochmann "Original" disc boxes, instruments of exceptionally fine tonal quality. From the earliest years Leipzig was established as the center of the disc music box industry, a position it never relinquished.

The Swiss, leaders in the production of cylinder music boxes, saw their market for these instruments erode after disc boxes captured the public's fancy in the early 1890's. The louder volume of the disc box (due to the greater plucking force of the star wheel and disc system as compared to that of the relatively fragile pins on a cylinder), the available of cheap interchangeable discs, the lower prices of disc boxes, and the aggressive merchandising methods followed by the Leipzig manufacturers combined to make the cylinder music box obsolete in the marketplace by 1895. Most Swiss manufacturers ignored the disc box and thus went out of business. A notable exception was Mermod Frères of St. Croix. Mermod introduced the Stella and Mira boxes which were sold in large quantities, particularly in the late 1890's and early 1900's. Mermod also supplied disc music box components to other manufacturers.

The height of the disc music box market was the decade from 1895 to 1905. By the latter year the phonograph was dominant in the home entertainment market and the coin-operated piano had captured most of the commercial market. Disc music box makers diversified in an attempt to stay in business. Regina marketed a series of phonographs, as did Polyphon, Mermod, Kalliope, and Symphonion. The "big three" entered the coin piano market with the Polyphona, Symphoniola, and Reginapiano instruments, none of which ever achieved large sales. Other diversifications were tried. By 1920, Polyphon and Symphonion music boxes were being sold under the aegis of Paul Scheibe of the Symphonion Musikwerke in Gera, Germany. The Polyphon Musikwerke merged with Deutsche Grammophon in 1917 and went on to achieve success in the phonograph field. Regina manufactured its last music box in 1919, continued shipments until 1921, and underwent bankruptcy in 1922 (the business was reorganized, and it thrives today, but in different product lines). The other makers, one by one, went out of business, mostly before 1914. An exception was the St. Croix firm of Hermann Thorens. Producing small disc-type movements, mostly for use in novelties, this company still makes 4½" music boxes today. Discs made by Thorens in 1900 will fit on the latest models!

In the following section we present a listing of various types of disc music boxes. Also included are related items, music boxes which use cardboard strips and disc-operated pianos for instance. These disc-operated stringed instruments, while not "disc music boxes," are more closely related to the disc music box series than to pneumatically-operated pianos, so in instances in which disc music box makers (Lochmann, Polyphon, Regina, Symphonion) made them, we include these instruments in the present section.

———————

## TYPES AND MECHANICAL VARIETIES of DISC MUSIC BOXES AND MOVEMENTS

As a general introduction to the listings of music box models we give a description of some of the different types and varieties produced.

### Types of Discs

In the 1880's certain discs were made of pressed cardboard. By 1888 zinc became standard. It was soon learned that projections on zinc discs became brittle and broke off easily, so by about 1895 most manufacturers had switched to steel discs, although zinc discs for New Century, Olympia, Criterion, and a few other makes were still being sold around 1900.

Most discs were made with projections on the underside. These projections took many forms, including two projections bent downward to meet at the center (Symphonion), sturdy U-shaped projections made by bending the metal strip back up to touch the underside of the disc (Polyphon, Regina, Sirion, etc.), scoop-shaped (Capital "cuff," New Century), scoop-shaped with pointed ends (Mira, Thorens), dimple-like indentations (Polymnia), and simple downward-bent metal projections (early Symphonion). Other discs used on certain models of Harmonia, Komet, and Stella (to cite just three makes) were projectionless. This latter type of disc had several advantages, including cheap production cost, ease of handling, and compact storage.

In our descriptions of models we give the disc diameters as advertised in the original catalogues. Actually, the precise measurements are usually different. For example, Stella's "26-inch" size is really 25 11/16" in diameter, Regina's "27-inch" size is closer to 26 3/4" and so on. Polyphon never did decide whether its most popular disc size measured 15 1/2" or 15 3/4" in the English system; both specifications were used from time to time. This size of disc is interchangeable with Regina's 15 1/2" size, although Polyphon discs are usually of slightly larger diameter. As the precise diameter of a disc is determined by the amount of metal trimmed from the outer edge, variations in trimming caused size differences. Often a collection or "library" of discs of a particular type will show minor variations in this regard.

Types of Disc Drives: Most smaller disc sizes are of the center-drive type. To the side of the center spindle are one, two, or three positioning pins which serve to drive the disc. Sometimes (cf. Symphonion) the arrangement of the center pins indicates which discs are to be used in the various positions of a multiple-disc instrument. By pushing against the metal near the center of the disc, these pins drive the disc. Most types of discs which measure over 15" in diameter have an edge drive. The amount of energy needed to turn a large disc could not be imparted satisfactorily at the center. Symphonion center-drive discs of the 11- to 13-inch size often show bent or otherwise damaged metal at the drive holes; damage caused when the disc stuck and the center post continued to revolve. Operation of center-drive discs was somewhat jerky and erratic by comparison to edge-driven types. Due to problems encounted in this regard, Regina's largest center-driven model was the 11" disc type. The 12 1/4" type, made mainly for commercial use in which ease of maintenance was a factor, was created by using 11" disc arrangements on larger diameter discs with edge drive.

Most edge-driven discs are powered by a sprocket wheel which engages round (usually), rectangular, or rhomboidal (Adler and Fortuna) holes near the outer edge of the disc. This gives a excellent mechanical advantage and permits the disc to turn evenly and smoothly. A variation of the sprocket drive is found on certain instruments (some, but not all, 27 1/2" Symphonion boxes, for example) which have downward-pointing projections on the underside of the disc near the outer edge. These projections engage corresponding recesses in the drive wheel. Still another variation of the edge drive is found on certain discs of smaller sizes (Kalliope, Monopol, Symphonion, and Thorens are examples) which have toothed rims. These rim teeth directly engage a drive gear which makes contact at the disc's outer edge. This gear-drive system is very durable and originally found use in applications in which the music box received very hard use — in children's toys, in a small clock, or in a Christmas tree base, for instance.

Names on Discs: It was usual practice to put the name of the tune on each disc. Often the name of the music box, the disc type (Symphonion's "No. 30," for example), and patent numbers appeared also. Certain types of discs (Monopol, Celesta, Orphenion, late Regina, and late Symphonion are examples) are embellished with transfer designs featuring trademarks, allegorical scenes, etc. Early Regina steel discs were copper plated; these have a bright bronze color. Certain Monopol and Orphenion discs have the surfaces colored blue. Others, Sirion for example, have the trademark in another color. Discs produced by American makers are usually found with the tune title in English. Discs produced by German and Swiss makers are often found with German inscriptions or with multilingual titles: German, French, and English for example. The composer's name is usually given as is the character of the music — march, hymn, or whatever.

Ludicrous errors in spelling and attribution are not rare among disc titles. Frank Greenacre, British historian of the music box, has written that "Most disc box makers seem to have had enormous difficulty in finding the correct composers' names — even with well-known popular songs — and mirth-provoking errors are frequent. An instance is "Rule Britannia" (written by Dr. Thomas Arne; first performed in 1740) which Polyphon concedes to have been produced by L. Zampa, Symphonion to Handel, and Monopol to Leghorn!"

In his book, "Collecting Musical Boxes and How to Repair Them," Arthur W.J.G. Ord-Hume notes that certain Polyphon disc blanks were imprinted before they were perforated. If too many blanks were printed with a slow-selling title, the blanks were simply turned over and imprinted with a better-selling tune and then punched out with the latter melody on them. "Thus one sometimes comes across 11" Polyphon discs which have a different title on each side. A classic example is a disc which was to have been 'Nearer My God to Thee,' turned over and issued as 'Beer, Glorious Beer.' "

Sometimes the copyright of a music arrangement is to be found on a disc. An early projectionless 17 1/4" zinc Stella disc of "Trilby" bears the stamped notation "Copyrighted 1896 by Mermod Frères," and "She Wanted Something to Play With" bears the "Copyrighted 1897 by Mermod Frères" notice. These are just two of many such examples.

Most firms established a numbering system for discs. Thus discs of a certain size would be in the 2000 series, another size in the 3000 series, still another size in the 5000 series, and so on. When a new title was released it would be keyed to this system and would appear, for example, as 2043, 3043, and 5043. This simplified record keeping and inventory problems.

Each disc size provided a definite amount of playing time for the musical selection. The compositions were arranged (or "set up," as per the original terminology) to fit the time available. If the tune was too short, embellishments or perhaps an extra chorus would be added at the end. If the tune theme was very short (Symphonion's arrangement of "Gypsy Love Song" is an example) it would be played twice. If a tune was too long it would be abbreviated where the music box arranger saw fit; at a point that often disagreed with the composer's original intentions! A blank space was provided between the stopping and starting points. This space was usually of sufficient size so that precise alignment of the starting position on edge-drive instruments was not necessary. However, sometimes in an automatic changer box the discs would shift and become misaligned to the extent that the listener would receive, for instance, the last eighth of a song, then silence as the disc went by the stop and start space, and then the first seven-eighths of the tune! With few exceptions, the period of revolution was controlled by the gear drive mechanism and not by the disc. The center drive or edge drive was made to play the disc through for one revolution regardless of how the disc was aligned on the box. Certain other boxes (Mira and Stella boxes are examples) had the stop and start controlled by an edge indentation – so were not susceptible to misalignment.

Certain discs (several different Regina sizes, for example) were of the "continuous" variety and had no stop or start position. The end of the song arrangement was blended with the beginning. Such discs were "ideal for dancing," it was advertised. The music box on-off lever would be left in the "on" position and the disc would play over and over again. Such Regina discs were marked "Continuous."

Other markings on discs include an arrow used on many disc types to indicate the starting point and patent numbers pertaining to the basic music system (rather than to the arrangement of a particular tune). For example, most Regina discs bear the patent dates of December 17, 1889 and June 27, 1893. These bear no relationship whatsoever to the date that the music box was made. Regina, for instance, wasn't even incorporated until 1894! Most dealers are quite familiar with such statements as "I have a Regina music box made in 1889," as helpfully provided by the owner of an instrument who seeks knowledge of its value.

Interchangeability of Disc Types: Certain makes of discs are interchangeable with other brands. Regina and Polyphon discs are interchangeable in the 11" and 15 1/2" diameters. Certain Monopol and Symphonion disc sizes fit on instruments of either make. These and certain other instances are due to interrelationships between the companies which originally made the music boxes. Other music box discs can be interchanged if adaptations are made to the center or edge drive holes. In America the same basic comb types used on certain Regina boxes, particularly the 15 1/2" size, were also used on Criterion, Monarch, Olympia, Triumph, and even the uniquely-designed Capital "cuff" boxes. While Capital boxes have their own music system (see F.G. Otto & Sons pages in the following section), certain discs of the other American makers are interchangeable if adaptations are made, as noted.

## Types of Music Combs

Music combs for disc-type boxes were made in several different formats and combinations. Basic types are:

Single Comb: The single-comb music box is equipped with a music comb arranged with the treble teeth at the outside of the disc and the bass notes near the center spindle (the arrangement used in all types of disc boxes). The larger bass teeth require more energy to pluck and are used less often than treble teeth, so their position near the center was well suited to the slower speed (circumferential, not radial) of the disc at this point and the greater mechanical advantage. If the musical scale is particularly large the single comb may be in two or three sections, but the scale is continuous and all sections are on the same side of the star wheels. Most combs have the teeth in a continuously graduated scale increasing in size from treble to bass. Some combs have large bass teeth of a different scale from the treble and middle-range teeth. These overly large bass teeth (found in certain Mermod boxes, for example) give a rich foundation tone to the music.

The term "teeth" is used most often to describe the individual sound-producing tines in a music comb, but "reeds" and "tongues" are also found in music box literature. Occasionally the term "forte" or "loud" was used in the original sales literature to describe combs with teeth made of especially hard steel. Certain boxes (for example, Orphenions) could be ordered with "regular" or "forte" teeth in the music combs.

Double Comb: Double-comb or "duplex" comb boxes have two similarly-scaled combs, one on each side of the star wheels. As with single combs, the double combs are often made in two or three sections, particularly in the case of large boxes. Both combs are plucked at the same time by the same star wheel. The effect is to give an increased volume of sound. The percentage of increase ranges from hardly noticeable to perhaps 25% or more, depending on the particular instrument. The sound is not doubled (as originally advertised by Regina and others) in intensity. If one comb is tuned slightly higher or lower than the other, the result is a celeste or tremolo effect that gives a "three-dimensional quality" to the sound, as one historian put it. The richness and brilliancy of certain Kalliope, Mira, and Stella boxes (to cite just a few) is accounted for by this tuning method. Such tuning was not practiced consistently, however, and not all boxes of a given type are tuned in the same manner. In fact, some boxes, particularly ones of smaller diameters, were tuned only approximately when they were first made.

The terms "double (or duplex) comb" or "double combs," the last using the plural form, were used interchangeably in original music box catalogues.

Sublime Harmonie Comb: Certain music combs (examples are some models of Monopol, New Century, and Symphonion) were set up in the so-called "sublime harmonie" format. Two combs are diametrically opposed on each side of the center spindle. Each comb plays the same notes at the same time, as in a regular double-comb model, except that twice as many projections are needed on the disc to operate the two sets of star wheels, one for each comb. The intention of the makers of sublime harmonie combs was to separate two identically-tuned or closely-tuned combs so that the music from each would reinforce rather than destructively interfere with the other.

Other comb types: Certain types of rare music boxes (for example, Imperator and some New Century models) have four combs – two sets of duplex combs, one on each side of the center spindle. Boxes with bells and other accessories have "combs" (actually, these are not musical but are tooth-shaped actuating levers) which operate these devices.

Number of Teeth: The number of teeth in a particular box depends on whether the non-musical abbreviated teeth which end at the star wheel idler discs (these hold the disc surface above the star wheels) are counted. Sometimes original advertisement writers would count them, and other times they would not. Thus, for example, double-comb 15 1/2" Polyphon/Regina boxes are variously described as having 152, 154, or 156 teeth. At times Polyphon thoughtfully described this type as having "156(152) steel tongues" – meaning that there were 156 teeth in all, and of that number just 152 were musical. The number of teeth did sometimes actually vary. Certain boxes using the same type of disc were made with regular combs containing, say, 100 teeth or with combs having double-width bass comb teeth which resulted in a total tooth count of, say, 70.

Comb Attachments: Zither attachments were popular, especially in the 1900-1910 years. These contributed little, if anything, from a musical standpoint but were a popular sales feature. Felt-padded dampers to mute the volume were available on certain types of instruments also.

Miscellaneous: There are many exceptions to the standard types of comb features and arrangements, and many of these are noted in the descriptions of individual boxes which follow. The duplex comb type (used in certain Capital, Mira, and Stella boxes) which has one visible comb and one comb under the bedplate is an example. A discussion of the tonal aspects of music combs is found in the introduction to the cylinder music box section of this book. Disc boxes and cylinder boxes incorporate many similar features.

### Added Instruments

Many different music boxes were provided with bells. On certain small-diameter disc models the bells would be played from the comb position used for music notes. Sometimes a music comb would be on one side of the star wheels and, directly opposite a section of notes and using the same disc projections, would be a bell "comb" on the other side. Most larger disc-type music boxes had separate "bell combs" which were played from a specially-arranged group of projections located near the outer rim of the disc. These bell notes would often be added to a regular music arrangement (as found on smaller discs). For instance, the 22" Polyphon (with bells) uses 19 5/8" standard Polyphon arrangements with a series of disc projections added for bells. The diameter of the disc was increased by an appropriate amount.

Bells found in disc boxes are of three types: Saucer bells (cup-shaped) and bar-type or glockenspiel bells were the two most popular. The former bells have more overtones or harmonics. Steel bar-type bells are of nearly pure tone and sound for a longer period of time after they are struck. Regina used bells only on a special 15 1/2" instrument. Polyphon, Kalliope, Lochmann "Original," Symphonion, and most other German-made boxes made liberal use of bells, particularly in the larger disc sizes.

Tubular bells, the third type used by disc box makers, were used by Lochmann, Polyphon, Symphonion, and others, particularly in very large instruments. Use was infrequent, however, by comparison to saucer and bar-type bells.

An Adler/Fortuna box which uses a 26" disc is equipped with a triangle, snare drum, and a set of organ reeds. A certain Symphonion box has reeds, bells, drum, and triangle. Another Symphonion has a tuned comb and a set of piano strings. Other interesting varieties are discussed in the following pages.

### Multiple-Disc Music Boxes

Several different types of music boxes were provided with mechanisms which played two or three discs synchronously. The most famous of these is the Symphonion "Eroica," a 3-disc instrument which was made in large numbers during the 1890's and early 1900's. Discs (marked A, B, and C) were made in two styles: (1) three identical discs, each with exactly the same music arrangement, and (2) three discs, each of which differed very slightly in the musical arrangement. The Symphonion Manufacturing Company, the American branch of the Symphonion Musikwerke, produced a 3-disc instrument of different format from the Eroica.

Two-disc instruments were made by a variety of firms, including Symphonion, Lochmann (in the "Original" series), Zimmermann (Adler and Fortuna boxes), and Ehrlich (Monopol).

The only multiple-disc instrument ever produced in large quantities was the Symphonion Eroica.

### Disc-Changing Music Boxes

Automatic disc-changing music boxes were produced in many different formats. Regina, Polyphon, and Symphonion each made a number of styles. Regina disc-changing boxes were made by the thousands and are the most familiar examples today. Polyphon disc-changers were made in lesser numbers and are considerably rarer now. Symphonion made only a few such automatic instruments, and these are of extreme rarity. Symphonion also produced two automatic changers which differed from the usual vertical format of others. One was an instrument which held a stack of discs, played them, and then ejected them through a slot in the back of the box. The other held a stack of discs arranged horizontally. A desired disc was taken from the stack, moved sideways to the playing position, played, and then was put back again.

Detailed descriptions of automatic disc changers appear in the Polyphon, Regina, and Symphonion pages of this book.

### Disc-Shifting Music Boxes

In 1896 Alfred Keller and G. Bortmann patented a mechanism which permitted two tunes to be played on two revolutions of the same disc. During the first revolution the first tune would play. At the end of the first tune the center spindle of the music box would shift very slightly and bring a new set of disc projections for a second tune into the playing position. Mermod Frères of St. Croix, Switzerland, was the assignee of these and other patents relating to disc-shifting boxes, including a new type which could play from three to six tunes (patented in 1903; not used for commercial production, to the author's knowledge).

Sirion disc-shifting boxes in German-made cases and New Century disc-shifting instruments in European-made and American-made cabinets are sometimes encountered today. Each of these incorporates Mermod mechanisms.

### Power for Disc Boxes

Most types of disc boxes are powered by spring motors, usually of the tightly-wound steel band type, but occasionally using a spiral spring wound on a horizontal rod. These springs are wound by a removable crank handle. Most table-model boxes originally played for about ten minutes on a single winding. Large upright models intended for commercial use would play for 20 to 30 minutes or more. Due to the crystallization of the spring steel, music boxes found today will play for a shorter period of time.

Certain smaller boxes have no spring motors and are operated by continuously turning a small hand crank. Originally called "manivelles," this term is coming into use again with collectors. Manivelle boxes were made by many different manufacturers. Most used discs from about 4" to 9" in diameter.

Electric motors were available in certain large upright Symphonion music boxes intended for commercial use. Stella nd Mira console-type music boxes were available with electric rive also. The number of electrically-driven music boxes made of all types was very small.

### Disc Music Box Cabinets and Case Designs

Woods Used: In Europe most disc music boxes were made n walnut-veneered oak cabinets. Mahogany and oak finishes were used to a lesser extent. Some models were available in black or red painted cases. Smaller disc boxes were often made n painted cases with decal designs on the top. Mother-of-pearl, colored wood, and brass inlay was used on certain deluxe styles of table model music boxes. Larger boxes of the upright tyles were usually ornamented with turned posts, applied carvings, and other decorations.

In America most disc boxes were made with oak or mahogany finishes. Unlike the European straight-sawed oak inish, American boxes used quartered oak which displays cross-striping from the original growth rings in the wood. Walnut, Europe's most popular disc-box finish, was used only arely by American makers. After 1900, Regina offered the Rookwood finish which consisted of hand-painted cameo scenes on a mahogany background.

Ornately-carved cases were offered by European and American makers. Sometimes these carvings were the real thing. In other instances the "carvings" consisted of molded composition designs which were applied to the box surface or of "carvings" made by pressing a roller die against the wood.

Styling: Cabinet styles used by disc music box manufacturers were many, as the following pages will illustrate. Generally speaking, Leipzig-made boxes are fairly standard in concept. A comparison of various models of Symphonion and Polyphon instruments will show this clearly. About 1900, "modern style" cases were introduced by the Leipzig makers. These used fewer carvings and usually lacked the spooled top railing of their predecessors. "Modern" cases never achieved great popularity.

Unusual Cases: Musical movements were incorporated into a number of distinctive cabinets. Regina's Musical China Closet, Musical Desk, and Musical Library Table are self-explanatory. An unusual Monopol features an automaton gnome who beckons for the passerby to drop a coin in his cup or plate. If the wrong size of coin is deposited, the gnome shakes his head as if to say "So sorry!" When the correct coin is given, the gnome gestures his approval. The "Gambrinus" Symphonion features a statue of the legendary Flemish "beer king." Kalliope and Adler mechanisms, to mention just two of many, were incorporated into display cabinets which featured automaton jugglers, trapeze artists, and other attractions. Slot machines with disc movements; music boxes which vend gum, cigarettes, or candy; children's toys which incorporate musical movements; and other devices of a like nature (many of which were made by outside manufacturers who purchased the musical mechanisms from disc box makers and installed them in their own cabinets) attract attention when displayed as part of a collection today.

### Home Models and Coin-Operated Styles

In America, most upright (with the disc mounted in a vertical position) music boxes made during the 1890's and early 1900's were sold for commercial use. These were actuated by a coin slot. A cent played one tune; a nickel, either one or two tunes, depending upon the generosity of the establishment's proprietor. Table model boxes (with the disc mounted horizontally) were made primarily for home use. After about 1903 most American boxes, both table and upright models, were made for the home market.

In Germany music box sales followed a similar pattern, except that very few upright models were ever sold for home use, even in the post-1900 years. Certain types of German boxes (examples: Polyphon and Kalliope) were fitted with a tube in addition to the coin slot. The proprietor of a business establishment would drop a marble in the tube when he wanted to play music "on the house." When the proceeds from the coin box were divided between the music box route operator and the tavern owner, the marbles would be ignored. Such instruments are very rare today.

### Clocks with Disc Music Box Movements

Clocks incorporating disc-type music mechanisms were popular from the 1890's onward. By 1894 Symphonion and Polyphon each offered several models, most of which were incorporated into Lenzkirch hall clocks. Polyphon later introduced an immense clock which used the 24 1/2" movement.

Regina produced musical movements for clocks from 1894 until the closing years of the business. Some movements were built into Seth Thomas and other types of hall clocks and were marketed by Regina. Other movements were sold to clock makers who sold them under various names. The Regina Chime Clock, produced in several styles, is not a music box at all, but is a disc-operated clock chime movement. The Jacot Music Box Co. of New York City offered Stella and Mira movements in American-made hall clock cases.

Small disc mechanisms made by Symphonion, Thorens, and others were built into shelf-type clocks. Junghans, Germany's largest clockmaker, produced dozens of different clocks, many of which used Symphonion movements.

Top crests or galleries with clocks were offered by Polyphon, Regina, Symphonion, and others. Sometimes these were connected with the music movement and played the discs at regular intervals (Regina automatic changers with clocks are examples), but more often the clock attachment was independent of the music.

### Music Box / Phonograph Combinations

When it became evident in the early 1900's that the phonograph was taking over the sales position enjoyed by music boxes, several music box manufacturers produced combination instruments. Featuring a disc-type music box and a disc-type phonograph (usually), both of which were operated from the same spring, these two-in-one devices were sold with moderate success, mainly in America.

Lochmann "Original," Mira, Polyphon, Regina, and Symphonion boxes, and possibly others as well, were made with phonograph attachments. By far the best seller was the Reginaphone, which was made in many different styles.

As noted earlier, a number of music box makers went into the phonograph business. The "big three" makers, Polyphon, Symphonion, and Regina, each followed this route. Symphonion, which by 1920 incorporated the disc music box portion of Polyphon's business as well (Polyphon itself merged with Deutsche Grammophon in 1917 and concentrated on phonographs), sold small music boxes and phonographs in the 1920's. Regina offered its Princess and Corona phonographs.

### Disc-Operated Pianos

Closely allied to music boxes, but not music boxes in the strict sense as they do not use a tuned comb, are the disc-operated pianos. These instruments, made by Lochmann, Polyphon, Regina, and Symphonion, use a disc to actuate piano hammers which play tuned strings. Often such instruments, usually sold as "disc orchestrions," incorporate drums, bells, and other percussion effects. Some have pipes or reeds.

Miscellaneous

Because of their relationship to the music box manufacturers, we include Regina phonographs, Polyphon roll-operated and strip-operated pianos and orchestrions, and other products in this section.

Are the strip-operated Libellion, Roepke, and similar mus boxes more closely related to cylinder boxes or to disc boxes As an intermediate system (e.g., levers or star wheels) is use between the music strip and the tuned comb, we include the in this section.

**MISCELLANEOUS DISC MUSIC BOXES**

**We list a number of other disc music boxes, instruments not covered elsewhere in the text. Information is mainly from Arthur W.J.G. Ord-Hume's "Collecting Musical Boxes and How to Repair Them" and Graham Webb's "The Disc Musical Box Handbook." Information concerning the Monarch and Triumph music boxes (made by the American Music Box Company) is previously unpublished and was provided by Hughes Ryder, well-known music box historian.**

**CELESTE: Made by Heinrich Hermann of Bernau, Germany.**

**CHEVOB: 15 5/8" disc diameter. "Made by Chevob & Cie., formerly Baker-Troll." (Ord-Hume)**

**DIORAMA: Made by Kirsch & Co. (Germany).**

**Gloria box of the 18 1/2" disc size. Note that the combs are set at an angle on the bedplate. (Richard Baker Collection)**

**GLORIA: "Made by the Société Anonyme, Geneva, Switzerland. The Gloria was made in both upright and horizontal models and used discs and combs of the classic disc machine type . . . The firm later made the 'Polymnia' disc box." (Webb) Note: Certain Monopol boxes (made in Leipzig by Ehrlich) were also sold under the Gloria name.**

**MONARCH: Manufactured in Hoboken, New Jersey, by the American Music Box Company. A 15½" model uses discs numbered in the 2000 series and is compatible with Regina discs of similar size except that the drive systems are different. The American Music Box Company was capitalized for $150,000 in 1896. Emile L. Cuendet owned 50 shares (at $100 par each) and was president; Isaac Ingleson was treasurer. Emile L. Cuendet, a resident of St. Croix, Switzerland, came to America and was associated with the Jacot Music Box Company of New York City, American agents for Mermod Frères (and several other lines). F.J. Bernard was Cuendet's co-patentee for several inventions relating to music boxes. American Music Box Company also made Monarch music boxes. (Information courtesy of Hughes Ryder)**

**POLYMNIA: "Made by Société Anonyme, Geneva, Switzerland. The Polymnia was a later addition to the disc musical box range of this company. The machine used a type of projection which was made by raising the metal of the disc in the form of a dimple." (Webb)**

**TRIUMPH: Made by the American Music Box Company of Hoboken, New Jersey. 15½" disc size; discs numbered in the 4000 series. See information under preceding Monarch listing. (Information courtesy of Hughes Ryder)**

---

**–Some Features of Disc Boxes–**

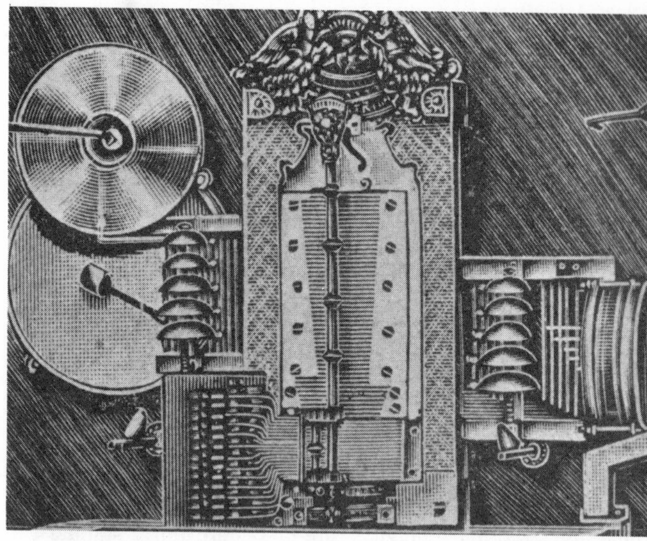

**This unusual Symphonion box has a duplex music comb, a set of reeds (lower left), a group of bells, a small drum, and a triangle.**

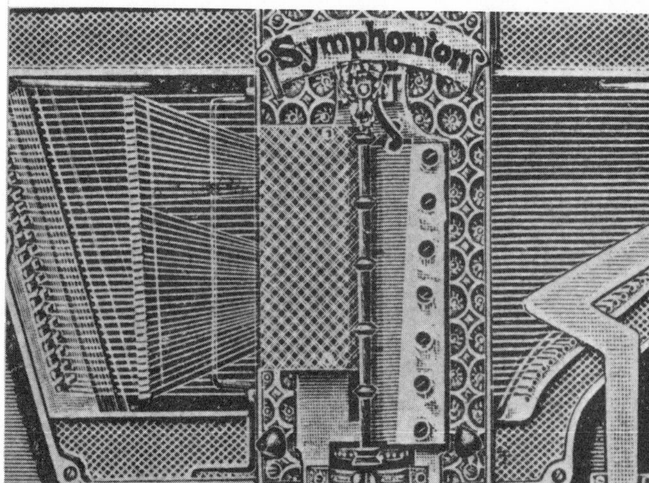


**Another unusual Symphonion, an instrument with a tuned music comb on the right side of the star wheels and a piano hammer mechanism (which plays tuned piano strings) on the other!**

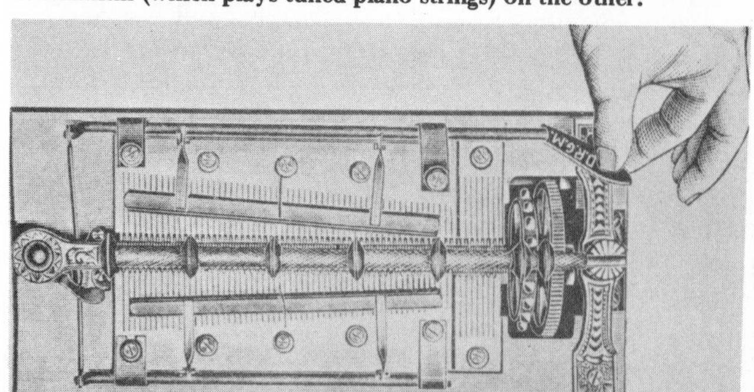

**Mandolin or zither effect on a double-comb music box. Such attachments were available for nearly every type of disc box made.**

## —Types of Disc Music Box Combs—

Small single comb on a Symphonion box. Most small-diameter disc boxes are of the single-comb type.

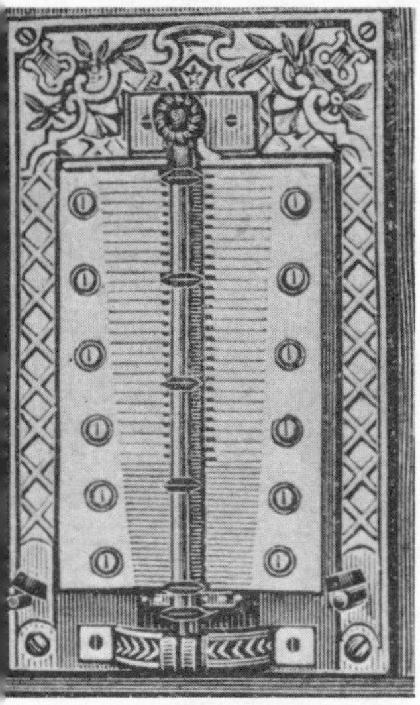

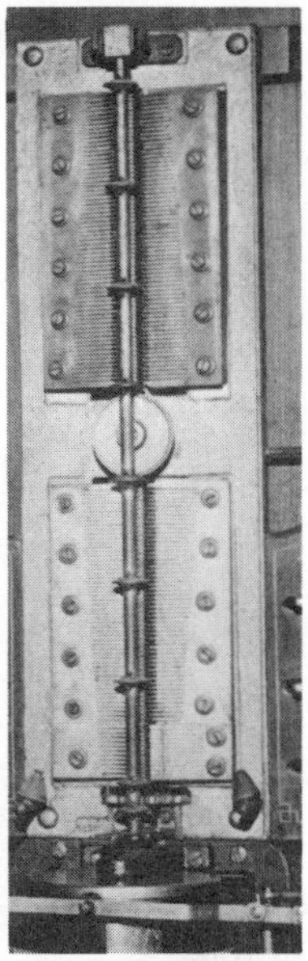

Above: Duplex comb of an upright Kalliope. Most disc boxes (of various makes) of greater than 15" disc size are of the duplex or double comb type.

Above right: Four combs of an Imperator box. Such comb arrangements are very rare.

Sublime harmonie comb arrangement as used on certain Symphonion (shown above), Monopol, and New Century boxes. The two combs are diametrically opposed on either side of the center spindle.

## —Types of Bells Used in Disc Boxes—

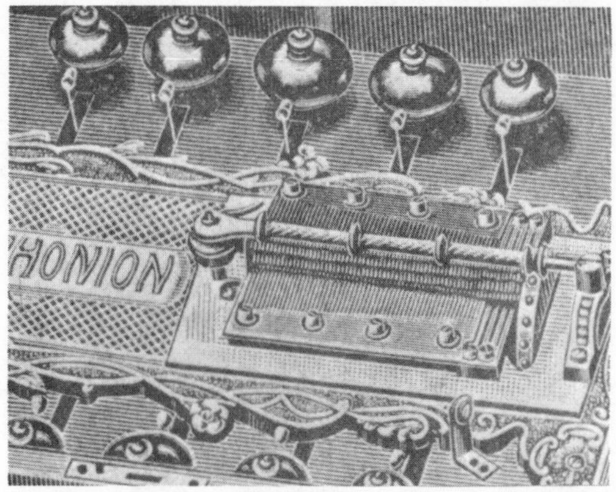

Saucer bells. Such bells were used on many different types of music boxes. Note the special bell "comb" next to the sprocket wheel at the right end of the music comb.

Bar-type bells. Popular, but used less frequently than saucer-type bells. These originally cost more than bells of the saucer type.

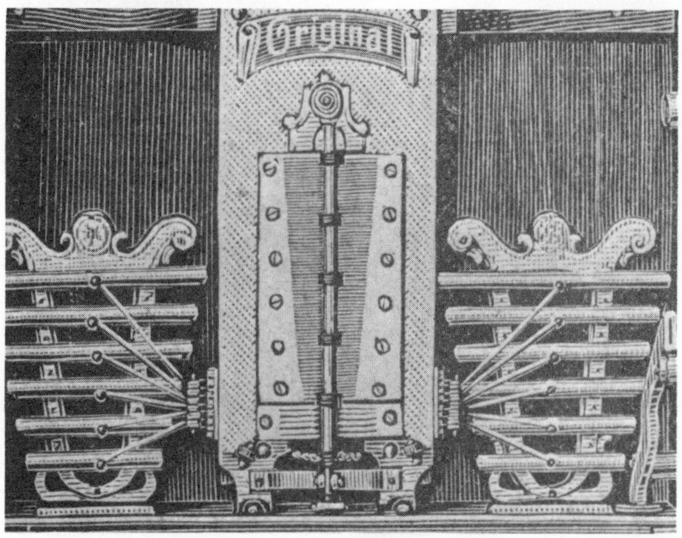


Tubular bells. Used infrequently.

## —Types of Drive Springs—

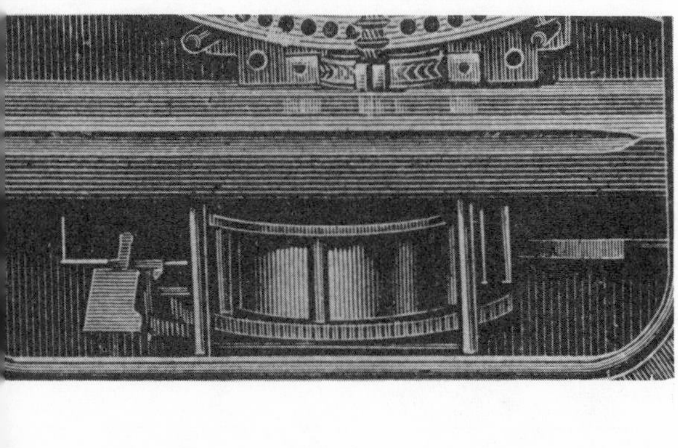

Left: The standard type of coiled spring as used in most types of disc music boxes.

Above: Spiral spring coiled around a center shaft. Introduced in the late 1890's and used infrequently.

**SOME DIFFERENT TYPES OF DISC PROJECTIONS**
**Enlarged 3 diameters.**

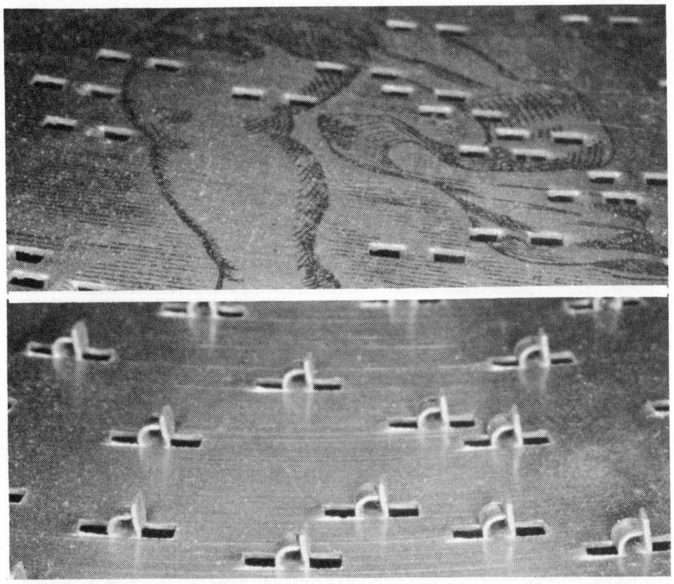

**Top and bottom of a Symphonion disc.**

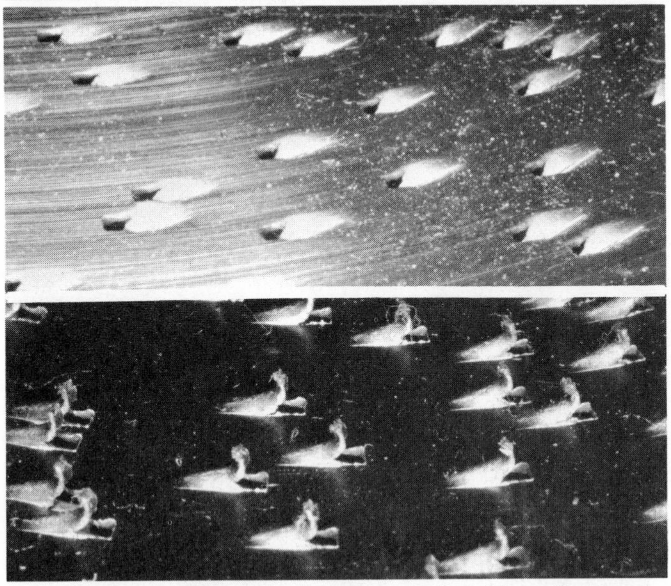

**Top and bottom of a Mira disc. Appears scoop-shaped from the top.**

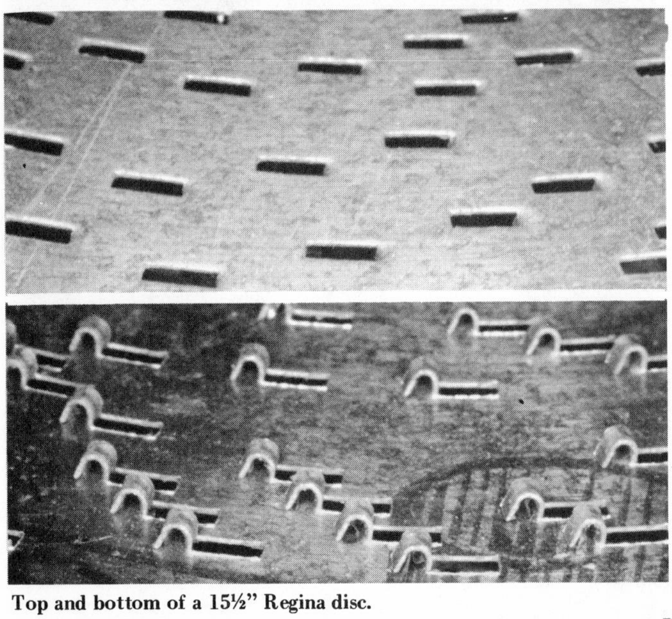

**Top and bottom of a 15½" Regina disc.**

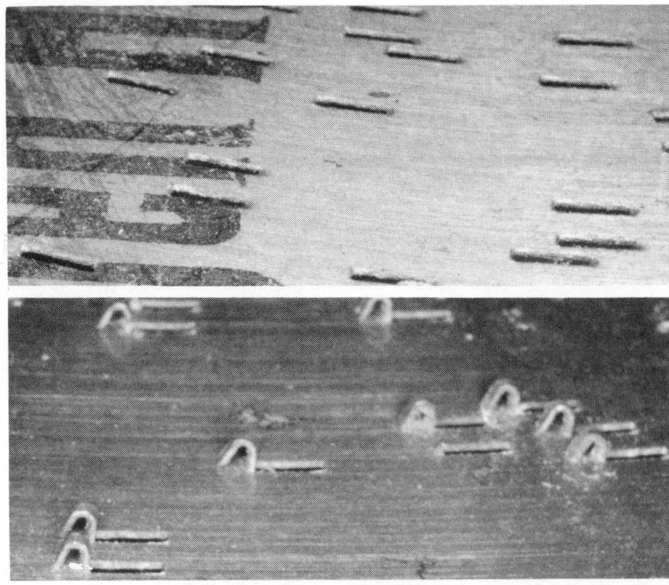

**Sirion disc (note narrowness of projections).**

**Inside view (right) and outside view (below) of the projections on a Capital "cuff."**

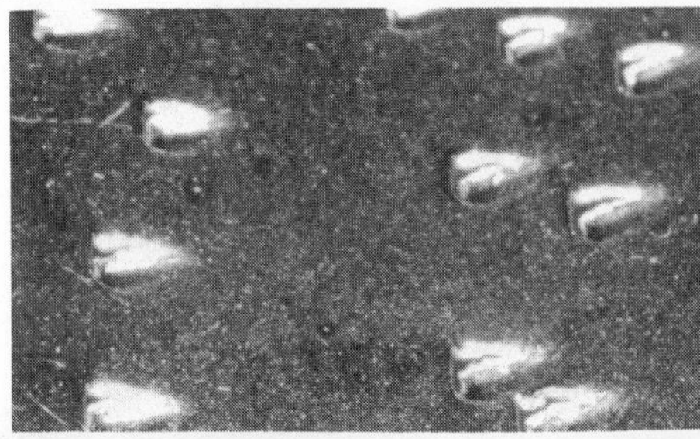

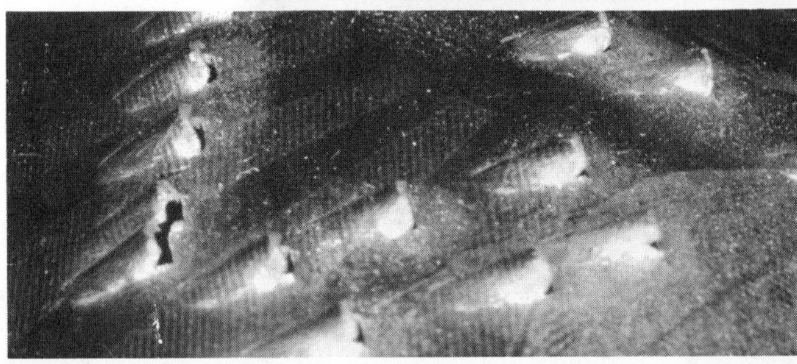

**Projections on the underside of a 4½" Thorens disc.**

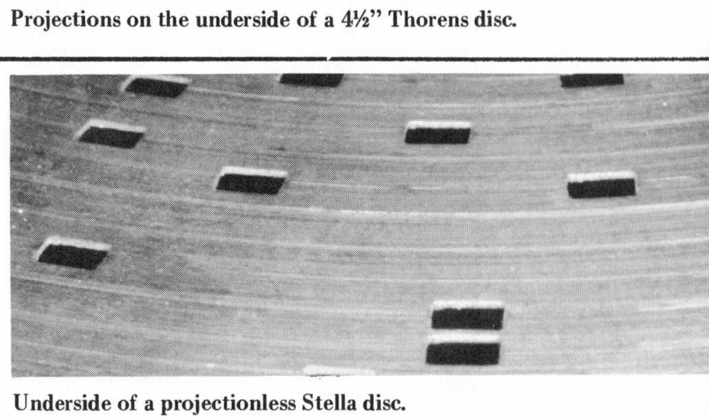

**Underside of a projectionless Stella disc.**

# Swiss Harmonia Musical Boxes

Having Tune Sheets WITHOUT PINS OR PROJECTIONS.

**305** Sublime Harmonie Piccolo,
78 NOTES.

PRICE - - - £8 10 0

Extra Tunes, 2/6 each.

Size, 25 × 20 × 11 ins. Tunes, 16½ ins. diameter.

**306** Sublime Harmonie Piccolo, Duplex,
156 NOTES.

PRICE - - - £10 10 0

Extra Tunes, 2/6 each.

Size 25 × 20 × 11 ins. Tunes 16½ ins. diameter.

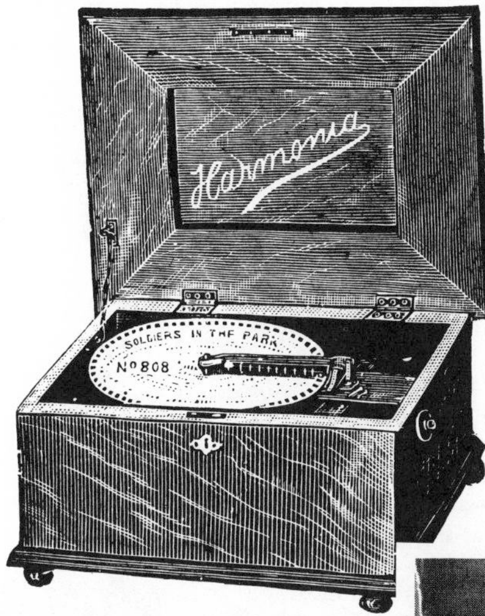


**Nos. 305 and 306.**

**HARMONIA DISC BOXES**

**Sold by Nicole Frères' London showrooms (at 21 Ely Place, Holborn Circus) in the early 1900's (and possibly by other agents as well), the Harmonia disc boxes were made in Switzerland. A projectionless disc similar to that employed by Stella music boxes (made by Mermod Frères of St. Croix, Switzerland) was used.**

**Harmonia styles shown on this page include 42-, 54-, 78-, 84-, and 156-note models, some with duplex combs and one with bells, which use discs of 10-inch and 16 1/2-inch diameters.**

**Never sold in large quantities, Harmonia boxes are quite scarce today.**

**Bedplate and comb of a Harmonia box. (Michael Gilbert Collection; Graham Webb photo [with permission from "The Disc Musical Box Handbook"])**

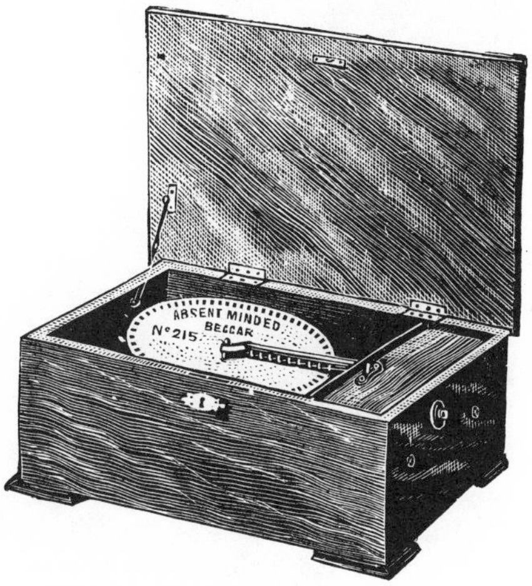


**No. 301.**

Size, 17 × 13 × 7 ins.

42 NOTES.

Price - - - £3 0 0

Tunes 10 ins. diameter.

Extra Tunes 1/6 each.

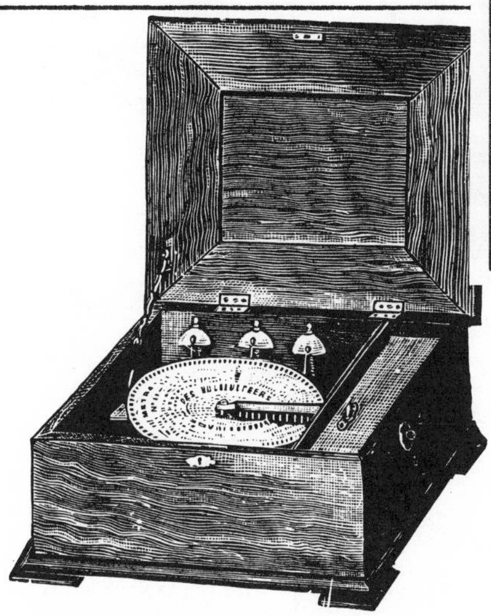

**No. 304. With Bells.**

Size, 18 × 18 × 8 ins.

42 NOTES.

Price - - - £4 7 6

Extra Tunes 1/6 each.

**302** "Harmonie" Piccolo,
54 NOTES.

**303** "Harmonie" Duplex,
84 NOTES,

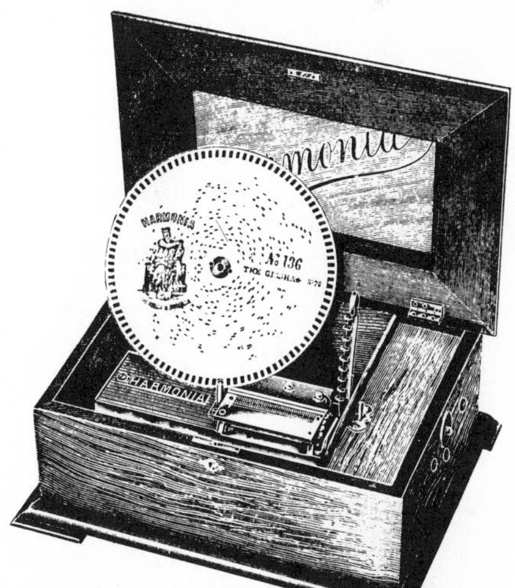


**Nos. 302 and 303.**

Price of 302 - £3 12 0

Size, 17 × 13 × 7 ins.

Price of 303 - £4 12 0

Size, 17 × 13 × 7 ins.

Tune 10 ins. diameter. Extra Tunes 1/6 each.

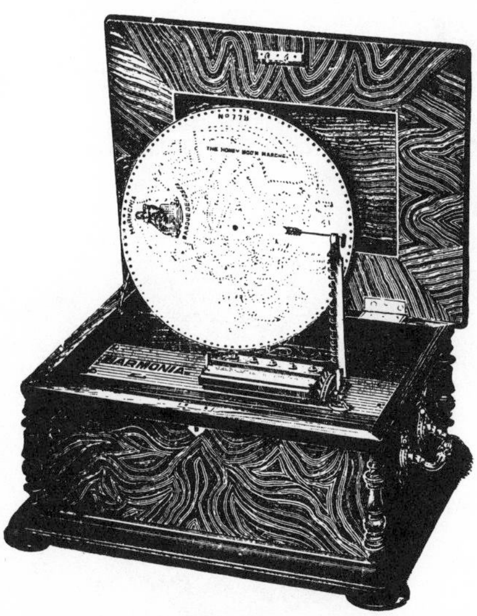


**Nos. 307 and 308.**

**307** Sublime Harmonie Piccolo,
78 NOTES.

PRICE - - - £10 10 0

Extra Tunes, 2/6 each.

Size, 27 × 22 × 12 ins. Tunes 16½ ins. diameter.

**308** Sublime Harmonie Piccolo Duplex.
156 NOTES.

PRICE - - - £12 15 0

Extra Tunes, 2/6 each.

Size, 27 × 22 × 12 ins. Tunes 16½ ins. diameter.

No. 308, with Long-running Movement.

PRICE - - - £14 0 0

## KALLIOPE
—Kalliope Musikwerke—
(Leipzig, Germany)

During the 1890's and early 1900's the Kalliope Musikwerke produced a large number of disc-type music boxes. Most were sold under the "Kalliope" name, but some were produced with "Calliope" spelling.

Kalliope disc boxes are of generally excellent tonal quality. Even the smaller models are brilliant and resonant without being harsh. Many smaller models were made with the center spindle serving also as a winding post. Numbers 26, 37, 40, etc. shown below are examples.

Bells were a popular addition to Kalliope boxes, and many instruments, even table models, were equipped with them. Although bells were offered in three varieties (saucer bells, bar-type bells, and tubular chimes), most instruments utilized the saucer type.

Kalliope music box mechanisms were sold to various novelty manufacturers who incorporated them into gambling machines, arcade exhibits (mechanical jugglers, dancers, etc.), and other devices. One novel instrument marketed by the Kalliope firm itself was the "Panorama." Made in several models, this box featured a diorama of racing horses.

In 1919 the Kalliope Musikwerke was merged into Menzenhauer & Schmidt (builder of the Guitarophone), a firm headed by Henry Langfelder. Menzenhauer & Schmidt's premises were at Rungestrasse 17 in Berlin. During the 1920's Kalliope phonographs were marketed by this firm. Earlier, some Kalliophon combination music box and phonograph instruments were made.

No. 60: 61 teeth. 40x38x19 cm. case. Uses 34 cm. discs. Sold for 80 Mk. in 1903. Extra discs cost 1.40 Mk. each. Zither for 60 or 60G cost 4 Mk.

Note: Most smaller Kalliope boxes use the center spindle as a winding post.

No. 60G: Similar specifications to 60, but with 10 bells. Sold for 106 Mk. Table model Kalliope boxes with bells were very popular, and many were sold.

The Kalliope Musikwerke in Leipzig, c.1906

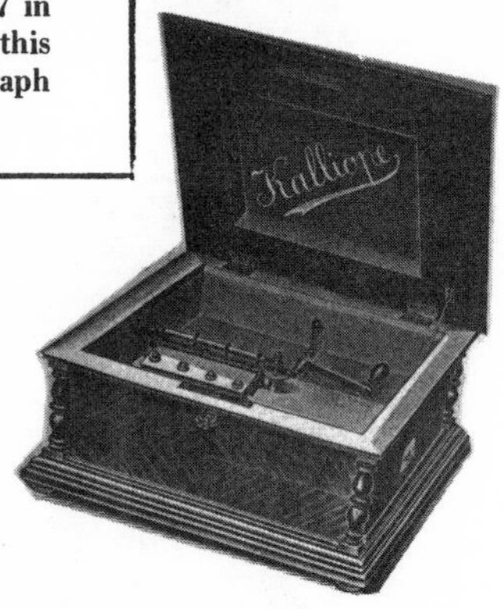


No. 62 (illustrated above): 61 teeth. 45.5x44x23 cm. case. Uses 34 cm. discs. Sold for 100 Mk. in 1903. "In deluxe walnut case."

No. 62G: As above, but with 10 bells. Sold for 126 Mk.

Note: Certain Kalliope instruments were sold under the "Calliope" name in France.

Circa 1900 case style for the following models. Not center-wound. No. 42: 42 teeth. 33x28x16 cm. case. Uses 25 cm. discs. Sold for 34 Mk. in 1903. Extra discs cost 0.80 each. No. 45: As above, but with glass inner lid. Cost 40 Mk. No. 107: 106 teeth in double comb. Larger case. Uses 45 cm. discs. Cost 160 Mk. Discs cost 2 Mk. Offered at "clearance prices" in 1904.

No. 26 (shown above): 26 teeth. 18x16x13 cm. case. Uses 14.5 cm. discs. Sold for 22 Mk. in 1903. Extra discs cost 0.32 Mk. Spring-wound.

No. 25: As above, but of the manivelle (hand-cranked) type. Sold for 11 Mk.

No. 37: 36 teeth. 24x21x16 cm. case. Uses 18 cm. discs. Cost 35 Mk. in 1903. Extra discs cost 0.50 Mk. each. Spring-wound. Illustrated above.

No. 36: As above, but of the manivelle type. 24x22x9 cm. case. Sold for 17.50 Mk.

No. 40G (shown above): 36 teeth, plus 4 bells. 25.5x23x16 cm. case. Uses 18 cm. discs. Cost 48 Mk. in 1903.

No. 40: As preceding, but without bells. Cost 37 Mk.

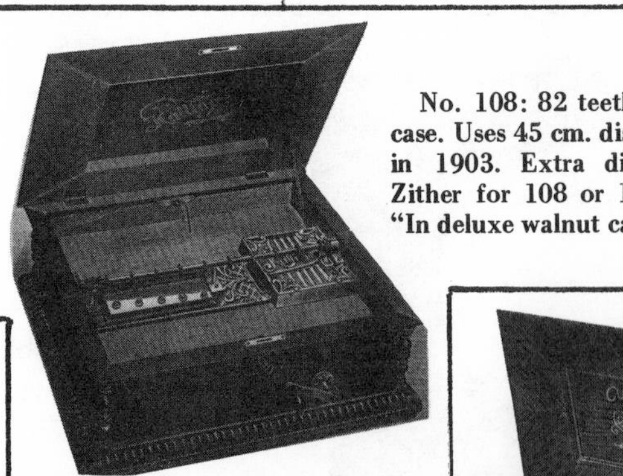

No. 108: 82 teeth. 64x55x25 cm. case. Uses 45 cm. discs. Cost 150 Mk. in 1903. Extra discs cost 2 Mk. Zither for 108 or 108G cost 5 Mk. "In deluxe walnut case."

No. 50: 49 teeth. 30x27x17 cm. case. Uses 23.5 cm. discs. Sold for 50 Mk. in 1903. Extra discs cost 0.80 Mk. each.

No. 50G: As above, but with 6 bells. Cost 67 Mk. Zither attachment for 50 or 50G cost 3 Mk.

No. 107: 82 teeth. 73x57x29 cm. case. Uses 45 cm. discs. Cost 200 Mk. in 1903.

No. 107D: With double comb containing 164 teeth; otherwise like No. 107. Cost 240 Mk.

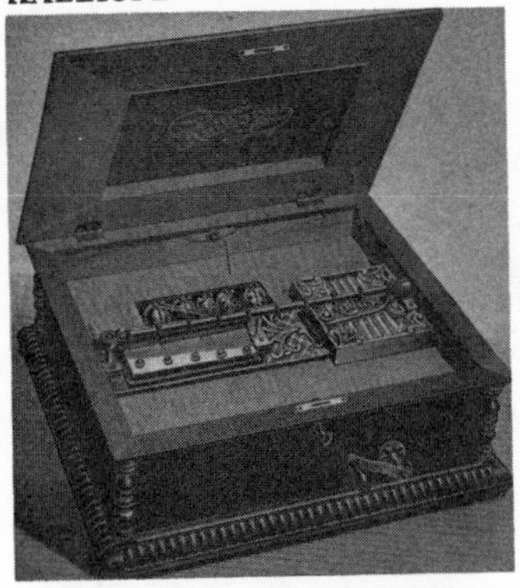

No. 108G: 82 teeth, plus 10 bells. 64x55x25 cm. case. Uses 45 cm. discs. Cost 176 Mk. in 1903. Extra discs cost 2 Mk. each.

No. 64: 61 teeth. 87.5x50.5x28 cm. case. Uses 34 cm. discs. Sold for 132 Mk. in 1903. Extra discs cost 1.40 Mk. each. "Inexpensive wall-hanging coin-operated music box. Can be set for 1 or 2 plays per coin."

No. 164J (shown above): 106 "extra-wide" teeth. 140x73x42 cm. case. Uses 45 cm. discs. Sold for 250 Mk. in 1903.

No. 164: Same, but in old-style case similar to No. 216. Sold for 250 Mk. Extra discs cost 2 Mk. each.

No. 216: 145 "extra-wide" teeth. 151x85x45 cm. case. Uses 58 cm. discs. Sold for 330 Mk. in 1903. Extra discs cost 4 Mk. each. Zither cost 15 Mk.

Kalliope

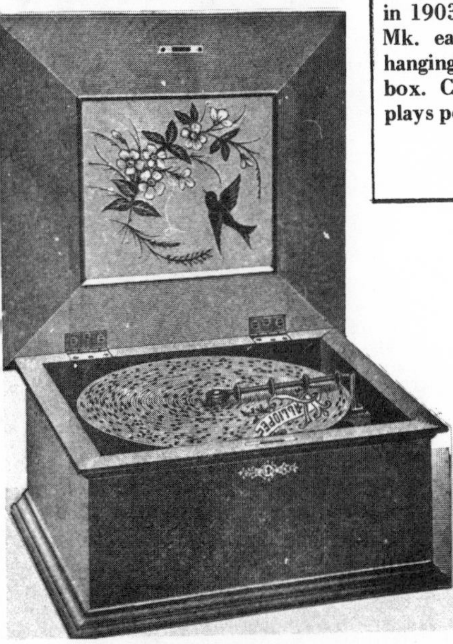

Early (c.1895) case style for: No. 61: 61 teeth. 45x41x24 cm. case. Uses 34 cm. discs. (61 cm. discs are in two series: "old series" and "new series" - these use the old.) No. 82: 82 teeth. 56x52x26 cm. case. Uses 45 cm. discs.

No. 62. Coin-operated model. 61 teeth. 94x48x31 cm. (38x19x12½") case in walnut. Uses 34 cm. old series discs. Above illustration is from an 1895 catalogue.

No. 83: Coin-operated model. 82 teeth. 103x60x36 cm. (41x24x14") case in walnut. Uses 45 cm. discs. 1895 illustration.

"Gloriosa" Christmas tree stands with Kalliope movements: No. N-II (shown above): Uses 18 cm. discs. 46x28x16 cm. case. Sold for 69 Mk. in 1903. No. N-II Automat. Same, but coin-operated. Cost 100 Mk. No. G/Gl. (shown near right): With bells. Uses 18 cm. discs. Sold for 88 Mk. No. G/Gl. Automat: Same, but coin-operated. Sold for 124 Mk. No. 50G (shown far right): With bells. Uses 23.5 cm. discs. Sold for 100 Mk. No. 50: Same, but without bells. Sold for 83 Mk. No. 53 and 53G: Same as 50 and 50G, but in cases resembling regular music boxes (more nearly square). Sold for 59 and 76 Mk. respectively.

—Kalliope Panorama—

Known as the Kalliope Panorama Automat, this case style features a colorful panorama of racing horses which run as the music plays. "Bets can be paid off with prizes of beer, cigarettes, etc." An interesting entertainment device for taverns. Made in the following models: No. 164P (P="Panorama"): 106 teeth. 140x73x42 cm. case. Uses 45 cm. discs. Sold for 320 Mk. in 1903. No. 216P: 145 "extra-wide" teeth. 151x85x45 cm. case. Uses 58 cm. discs. Sold for 390 Mk. No. 176P: 120 "extra-wide" teeth, plus 12 bells. 136x73x42 cm. case. Uses 52.5 cm. discs. Sold for 380 Mk. No. 176P in case for No. 201; cost 400 Mk. No. 176P in case for No. 176J; cost 380 Mk. No. 200P: 158 "extra-wide" teeth, plus 12 saucer bells. 150x80x43 cm. case. Uses 64.5 cm. discs. Sold for 460 Mk. No. 201P: Same but with bar-type or glockenspiel bells. Case measures 151x85x45 cm. and has top trim similar to No. 201. Cost 470 Mk.

Base cabinets for 164, 164P, 176, and 176P cost 72 Mk.; for 216, 216P, 200P, and 201P cost 92 Mk.

No. 176: 120 "extra-wide" teeth, plus 12 saucer bells. Painted-red or walnut case measures 136x73x42 cm. Uses 52.5 cm. discs. Cost 320 Mk. in 1903. Extra discs cost 2.80 Mk. each. "Available in slightly larger case for 340 Mk., or in modern case similar to No. 164J for 320 Mk."

No. 201: 158 "extra-wide" teeth, plus 12 bar-type bells. 151x85x45 cm. case. Uses 64.5 cm. discs. Cost 410 Mk. in 1903. Extra discs cost 5 Mk. each.

No. 200: As above, but with saucer bells. Cost 400 Mk.

Note: Prices and specifications of 176, 200, and 201 do not include base cabinets.

**KALLIOPE**

This large Kalliope music box stands 8'10" high and is 3' wide by 1'8" deep. It is coin-operated and uses discs which measure about 28 5/8" (72.5 cm.) in diameter. This is one of the largest discs found on a music box without bells. Apparently only a very few of this style were ever made.

No. 180 Musician Clown Automat: "Uses type 156 Kalliope discs." 220x80x68 cm. case. The clown's head disappears and reappears as the music plays. Kalliope mechanism is in the base. The clown is in a glass case at the top. Sold for 825 Mk. in 1900.

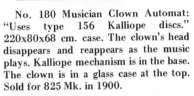

Clown-Kapelle ("comic orchestra") model: Uses 58 cm. Kalliope discs. Case measures 207x103x68 cm. Sold for 710 Mk. in 1900.

Right: Interior view of a Kalliope which uses 64.5 cm. discs. The twelve bells (the three far left ones are not shown here) are of the saucer type.

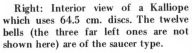

No. 164: 106 teeth. Walnut case with clock in the top. Sold as the "Komet Victoria" model. Uses projectionless discs. Popular c. 1895-1900.

## KOMET DISC MUSIC BOXES
### (Weissbach & Co.; Leipzig)

Made in Germany and embodying certain Swiss features, Komet music boxes were distributed on a limited basis during the 1890's and early 1900's. Table models and upright styles were made. Coin-operated Komet boxes were given the "Komet Victoria" name, indicating original use in England.

The trade mark of the Komet is a man blowing a horn. Instruments were made in a number of disc sizes, including 13-, 17-, 21 5/8-, and 33 1/2-inch diameters. Certain smaller sizes used flat discs without projections, an unusual feature used only on a few other types of music boxes (e.g., certain models by Lochmann ["Original" disc-operated pianos], Polyphon [certain disc pianos], Stella, and Harmonia).

Little is known about the Komet instruments today. Apparently few were sold originally – mostly in England and in Germany. Komet boxes of all disc diameters are very rare today. The aforementioned 33 1/2" Komet with bells was first reported to collectors in the Christmas 1964 issue of "The Music Box" in an article, "Giant Komet Appears," by Graham Webb.

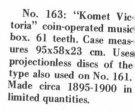

No. 163: "Komet Victoria" coin-operated music box. 61 teeth. Case measures 95x58x23 cm. Uses projectionless discs of the type also used on No. 161. Made circa 1895-1900 in limited quantities.

No. 161: 61 teeth in the music comb. Case measures 49x43x23 cm. Uses projectionless discs. Popular c.1895-1900.

No. 162: 106 teeth. Case measures 74x66x34 cm. Uses projectionless discs of the same type as used on No. 164. Illustration c.1895.

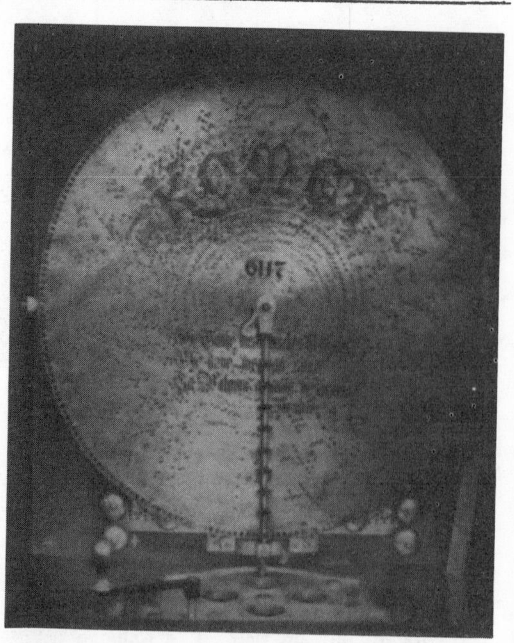

Huge Komet music box which uses 33 1/2" discs and has 198 teeth in the music comb, plus 14 bells with butterfly strikers (an unusual feature). The cabinet shown is not original. (Graham Webb photograph of an instrument owned by A.E. Barham)

## LOCHMANN "ORIGINAL" DISC MUSIC BOXES
### —Original Musikwerke Paul Lochmann G.m.b.H.
### (Leipzig and Zeulenroda, Germany)

Around 1901 Paul Lochmann, who earlier founded the Symphonion Musikwerke (first called the Lochmannscher Musikwerke A.G.) in Gohlis, Leipzig, formed a new company, the Original Musikwerke Paul Lochmann G.m.b.H. Facilities were maintained in Leipzig and in Zeulenroda (an industrial town near Zwickau, Germany).

During the 1901-1915 years Lochmann music boxes, sold under the Lochmann "Original" name (note: "Original" was nearly always in quotation marks in original advertising and on the instruments themselves), were marketed in many different styles. The instruments were generally of superb design from an acoustical viewpoint. A curved wooden bridge connected the bedplate to the sounding board (usually of spruce, a more resonant wood than the oak used by most other firms). A brilliant and rich tone resulted.

Other innovations: reinforced disc rims (made by folding over the metal), a side-to-side winding rod which made winding from either side possible, ball bearings in the winding crank hole, and other features were found on certain models. The springs on some boxes are undersized; apart from this, the mechanisms are superbly engineered.

Most large Lochmann "Original" boxes were equipped with bells, usually of the tubular or saucer bell type, but occasionally of the bar type (glockenspiel). Most Lochmann disc box types are illustrated on the following pages.

In addition to disc boxes, Lochmann made a series of "Original" Concert-Piano disc-played pianos. (Note: "Original" was often without quotation marks when used as part of the Concert-Piano name.) Some of these featured projectionless discs. As explained in the captions to follow, there is a strong resemblance between certain Lochmann disc pianos and disc pianos made by Polyphon. Lochmann's pianos were made in several sizes, including 25 1/2-, 28-, and 32-inch diameters (the same approximate diameters used by contemporary Polyphon instruments of the same genre).

Lochmann "Original" instruments were first produced after the turn of the 20th century — after the height of the market for the disc music box had passed. As a result Lochmann instruments, even the smaller sizes, are quite scarce today. This is a shame — for from a tonal viewpoint connoisseurs consider the Lochmann "Original" series to be among the finest disc music boxes ever made.

No. 48D: Duplex comb w/96 teeth. Uses 28 cm. discs. Case: 44x34x22 cm. Cost 100 Mk. Extra discs: @1.20 Mk. No. 48DZ: With zither. Cost 108 Mk.

No. 60: 60 teeth in music comb. Uses 39 cm. discs. Case measures 62x46x26 cm. Cost 108 Mk. Extra discs: @2 Mk. Also: 60Z (w/zither; 116 Mk.); 60D (w/120-tooth duplex comb; 140 Mk.); 60DZ (duplex comb w/zither; 150 Mk.).

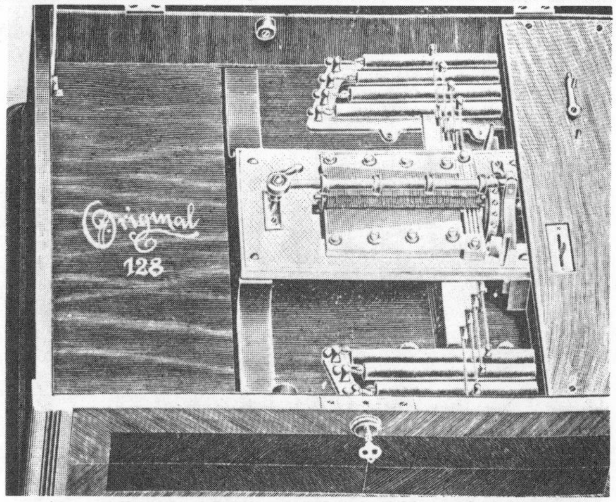


Above: Detail of Lochmann Original No. 128 showing the tubular bells arranged parallel to the bedplate and on either side. Note also the curved bridge which connects the end of the bedplate to the sounding board.

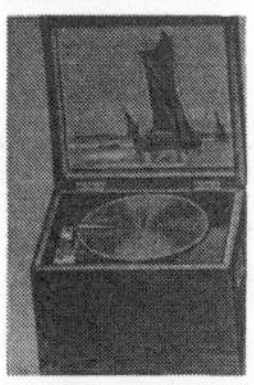

No. 20: 20 teeth in music comb. Uses 13 cm. discs. Case measures 20x16x14 cm. Disc spindle serves as winding post. Sold for 20 Mk. in 1904. Discs cost 0.30 Mk. each.

No. 30: 30 teeth in music comb. Uses 18 cm. discs. Case measures 26x20x18 cm. Disc spindle serves as winding post. Sold for 32 Mk. in 1904. Discs cost 0.50 Mk. each.

No. 40: 41 teeth. Uses 21 cm. discs. Case: 29x24x18 cm. Sold for 42 Mk. Extra discs cost 0.60 Mk. each. No. 40Z: As above, but with zither attachment.

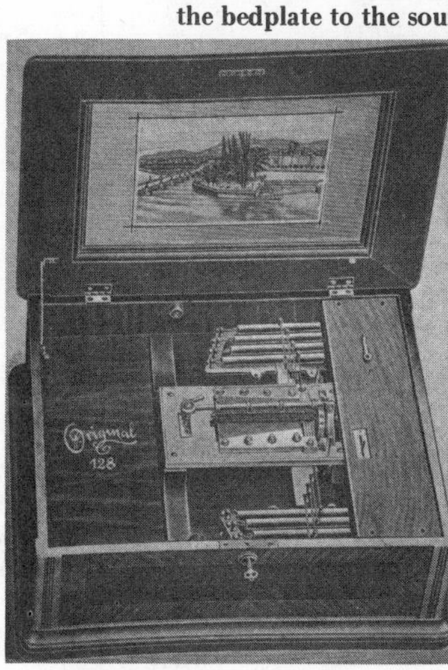

No. 128: Duplex comb with 120 teeth; 8 tubular bells (described by Lochmann as "clock chimes"). Uses 43 cm. discs. Case measures 68x54x28 cm. Cost 192 Mk. in 1904. Extra discs cost 2.20 Mk. each. No. 128Z: With zither. Cost 204 Mk.

No. 128HS: Cabinet model with "(H)angen" (hanging hooks for mounting on a wall) and "(S)tellen" (feet for placing on a counter or table top); hence "HS." Duplex comb with 120 teeth; 8 tubular bells. 120x64x36 cm. case. Uses 43 cm. discs. Cost 250 Mk. in walnut; 270 Mk. in mahogany. Discs: @ 2.20 Mk.

No. 50: 48 teeth in music comb. Uses 28 cm. discs. Case measures 33x30x18 cm. Sold for 64 Mk. in 1904. Extra discs cost 1.20 Mk. each. No. 50Z: With zither. Sold for 70 Mk.

No. 68: 60 teeth in music comb; 8 tubular bells. Uses 43 cm. discs. Case: 68x54x28 cm. Sold for 160 Mk. Extra discs cost 2.20 Mk. each. No. 68Z: With zither. Cost 172 Mk.

LOCHMANN "ORIGINAL"

No. 172: Duplex music comb with 160 teeth; 12 bells. Available with three types of bells: "Klangohren" (tubular chimes; illustrated right); "Glocken" (saucer bells); and "Klangplatten" (glockenspiel-type or bar bells) — all at the same cost. Uses 62 cm. discs (usually referred to the 24 3/8" size in the English system). Cost 380 Mk. in 1904. Extra discs cost 4 Mk. each. As of August, 1903, there were "about 450 different disc selections" available for this instrument.

A large double-disc version of No. 172 was made. This instrument, once owned by the author and now in the collection of Bellm's Cars & Music in Sarasota, Florida, is described by Graham Webb as being "in a large upright case, complete with a base containing two sets of slots for spare discs. The machine is some 5 feet long, and the movement is constructed by setting two upright bedplates end-to-end across the case with two spring barrels controlled by one governor in the center. The discs are viewed through two round 'portholes' in the front of the case."

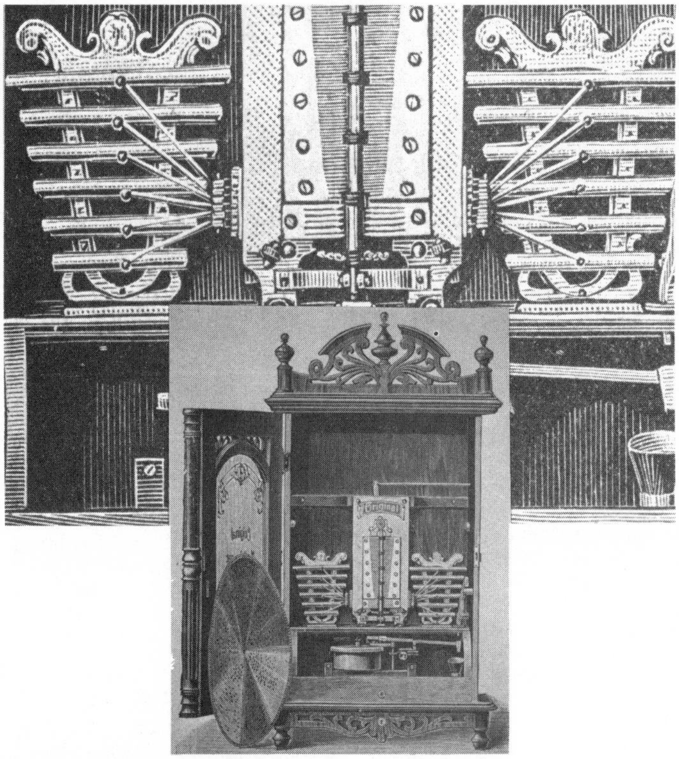

No. 172 with base cabinet. Lochmann offered separate base cabinets for No. 172: "measures 93x90x46 cm. [cabinet measurements; not including music box]. In walnut or oak, 100 Mk. In mahogany, 110 Mk." Cabinet for 128HS "measures 88x82,42 cm. In walnut or in oak, 80 Mk." It was the practice of Lochmann, Polyphon, Symphonion, and others to offer separate cabinets for most upright models.

No. 172L: In "(L)uxus" (deluxe) case with base cabinet built as an integral part. 262 cm. high. In oak or walnut, 560 Mk.; in mahogany, 590 Mk. Available with three types of bells: tubular bells, saucer bells, and bar-type bells.

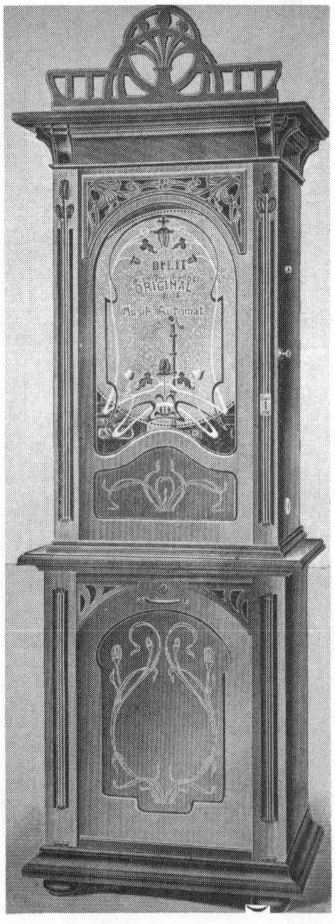

No. 172MW: (with "Weinrotes" [grape blossom and vine decorations]). 238 cm. high. "Ideal for taverns, hotels, etc." Mechanism is the same as No. 172. Usually made with tubular chimes, but available with bar bells or saucer bells. Sold for 440 Mk. in 1904.

No. 300: "Original Concert Automaton." Duplex music combs with 160 teeth; 12 bells (usually of the tubular type); cymbal; bass drum; snare drum; zither attachment. 279 cm. high (or without top crest, 243 cm.) by 115 cm. wide by 58 cm. deep. Uses 74 cm. discs. Sold for 900 Mk. in 1904. Extra discs cost 7 Mk. each.

Only a few No. 300 instruments were ever made.

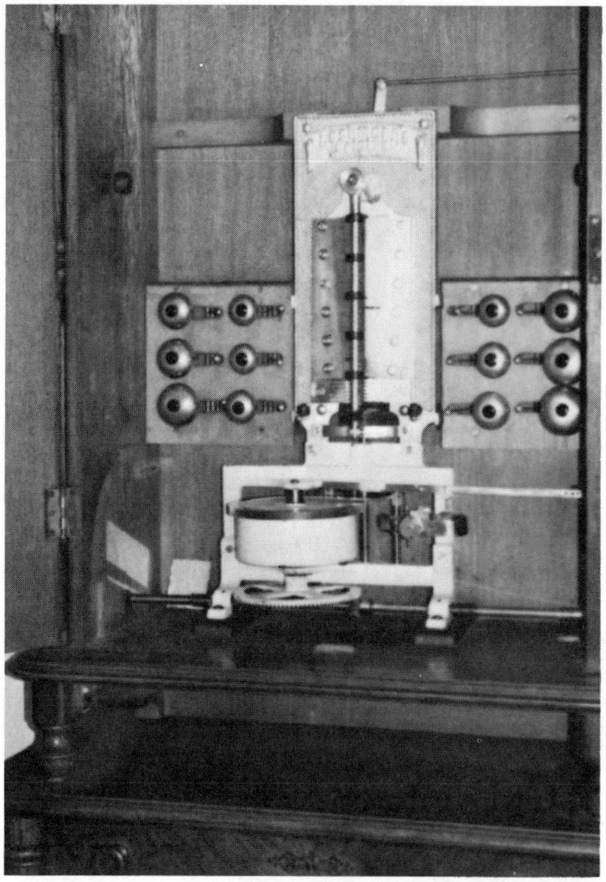

This attractive Lochmann "Original" music box is from the Leon Bryan collection. Using 62 cm. (24 3/8") diameter discs, the instrument plays a duplex music comb and twelve saucer bells. This model, No. 172, was one of Lochmann's best-selling coin-operated styles. As of August, 1903, some 450 different tunes were available for it. Catalogues listing available discs were printed in German and English. A No. 172 (with saucer bells) in the Mekanisk Musik Museum (Denmark) has a collection of Danish tunes, especially made by Lochmann for the Danish market, with it.

---

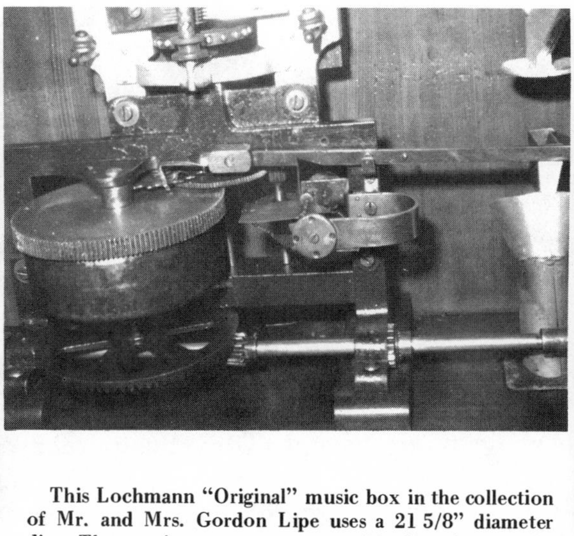

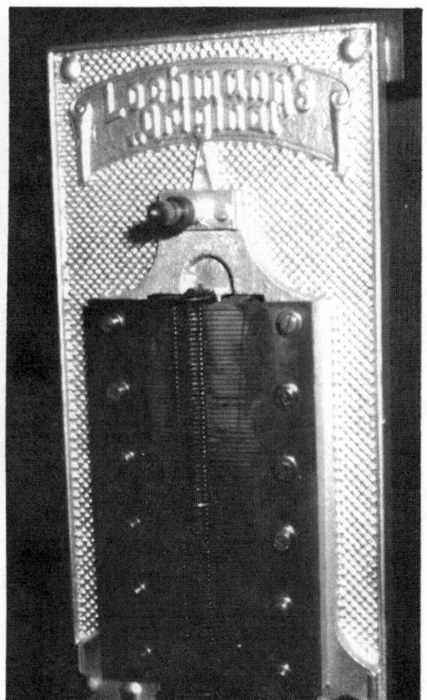


This Lochmann "Original" music box in the collection of Mr. and Mrs. Gordon Lipe uses a 21 5/8" diameter disc. The music arrangements on this disc size are the same as on the 24 3/8" size, except that the former size is without bells and is thus of smaller diameter.

Lochmann's "Original" Concert-Piano was made in several different formats. The instrument bears a startling resemblance to the Polyphon Concerto (and Regina Concerto): The Lochmann instrument uses an 81 cm. disc (about 32"); Polyphon, an 80 cm. disc. Both have 80 piano notes, 10 tubular bells, large and small drums, and cymbal. (The Polyphon has a triangle; the Lochmann does not). Both were usually built with tubular bells, but could be obtained with saucer bells instead.

Both have a symmetrical piano – a very unusual feature. The cabinet designs are similar in many ways, including the shape of the glass and the fretwork on the front doors, the number of corbels (5) on the top front molding, and the size.

Measurements of the Lochmann "Original" Concert-Piano are: 260x126x61 cm. The instrument was sold in two formats with two catalogue numbers: No. 350N "(N)ussbaum" (walnut) sold for 1250 Mk. in 1904; No. 350E "(E)iche" (oak) sold for 1300 Mk. Extra 81-cm. discs sold for 8 Mk. each. Export packing for tropical climates cost 150 Mk. extra.

The Lochmann "Original" Concert-Piano was built under the following German patents: 114,997; 147,440; 147,441; 189,688; 189,689; 193,327; 193,711; 194,403; and 199,512.

Above: Lochmann "Original" Concert-Piano No. 350. The most popular of several case styles which used the 81 cm. disc. As this type of instrument uses piano strings and has no music combs, it is a disc-operated piano, not a music box.

Left: Polyphon Concerto, shown here for comparison purposes. There are many similarities between this and Lochmann No. 350.

As of November, 1903, 150 different tunes were available on discs for No. 350.

Below: September, 1907, advertisement for Original Dance Automaton (coin-operated) No. 100. Described as having "complete percussion effects. A mechanical stringed instrument [with piano] with vibrating hammers. Uses discs without projections . . ."

Above: Lochmann "Original" Concert-Piano with Phonograph. Specifications are the same as No. 350, except that instrument has a phonograph attachment. Sold as No. 350 Sch. ("Sch." = abbreviation for "Schallplatten" or disc phonograph).

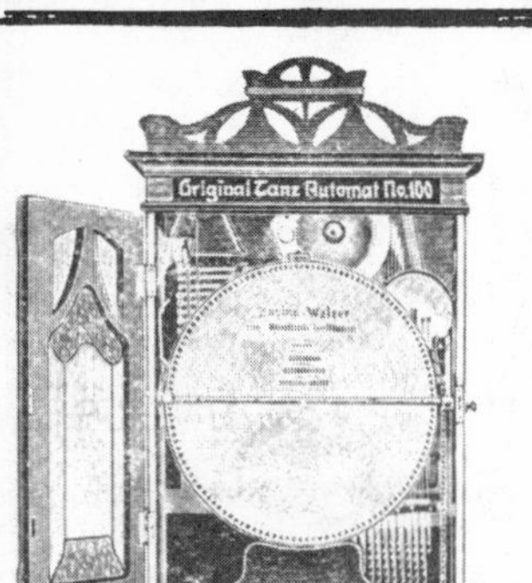


**Grossartige Original-Neuheit!**

**Original-Tanz-Automat Nr. 100**

**mit komplettem Schlagzeug.**

Mechanisches Saiten-Instrument mit vibrierenden Hämmern und runden Stahlnotenscheiben **ohne Zähne,**
**ganz besonders für Tanzmusik geeignet.**

Neue, ganz eigenartige Tongebung, sehr präzises Spiel, scharf ausgeprägter Rhythmus, weittragende Musik.
Hochelegante Diaphanieverglasung mit Messingfassung.

FI
940

**Original-Musikwerke Paul Lochmann G. m. b. H.**
**Leipzig,** Thomasgasse 4, III.

21.7.07

[968]

"Original" No. 200 disc-operated piano. The model shown at the left is from a 1904 advertisement; the model at the right is from a 1907 listing. The later model is equipped with a set of ten bells.

"Original" No. 250 disc-operated orchestrion. An early (c.1903-1904) case style is shown at the left; a 1907 style at the right. Note the differences in case design and in the placement of the cymbal.

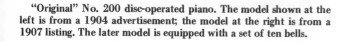

Concert-Original No. 300, disc-operated orchestrion as illustrated in a 1902 Lochmann advertisement. "An excellent substitute for an orchestrion!" the advertisement noted.

Original-Orchester-Piano No. 400. A 1906 advertisement noted: "Mechanical piano with vibrating hammers; uses round discs without projections. . . Finest forte and piano tonal shadings."

Original-Orchestrion No. 500 as shown in a 1906 advertisement. "Mechanical piano (83 notes) with vibrating hammers and complete percussion effects; uses round discs without projections. Our newest dance and concert instrument . . ."

## MIRA and STELLA BOXES
### —Mermod Frères—
### (St. Croix, Switzerland)

Mermod Frères, founded in 1816 and for many years one of Switzerland's premier makers of fine cylinder boxes, entered the disc music box field in the 1890's. The firm's principal products were the Stella, a music box which used discs without projections (patented by André Junod) which were acted upon by spring-loaded star wheels, and the Mira, a box with conventional projections on the discs. These were produced through at least 1909, by which year the firm had diversified into such fields as clocks (which Mermod had also made in earlier years) and, of all things, soap dispensers! Pathé phonographs were handled also, alone and in combination with a music box, the Miraphon (or Miraphone in the English-speaking markets).

Most Stella and Mira mechanisms were sold without cases. Distributors in England, America, France, and other countries imported the mechanical portion of the box and incorporated it into cabinets made in the country of destination. Thus there are no standard Stella or Mira models so far as universally-used case designs are concerned.

In 1896 G. Bortmann and Alfred Keller patented a disc-shifting mechanism whereby two tunes could be played on a single disc by playing the first tune on the first revolution and then shifting the disc spindle slightly to bring a new set of disc projections into contact with the comb and thus play a second tune on the second revolution. These disc-shifting boxes were sold under the New Century and Sirion names. Apparently Mermod Frères made only the mechanisms. In most instances the cabinets were provided by others. In 1903 Mermod Frères was assigned the patent to a disc-shifting mechanism which provided for 3 to 6 tunes to be played on a single disc. It is not known if any of this type were ever made.

In America, Mermod Frères products were sold through the Jacot Music Box Company of New York City. This firm (which was also closely allied with Paillard of St. Croix) issued several catalogues of Mermod disc boxes. Certain Stella boxes sold by Jacot were available with electric motor operation.

Stella and Mira boxes, originally made in large numbers, are available today in modest numbers in comparison to surviving instruments of the "big three," Polyphon, Regina, and Symphonion. The Mermod instruments are generally of superb tonal quality and are considered to be among the very finest disc-type music boxes ever made.

New Century boxes, made in several formats including disc-shifting models, are found in American-made and European-made cases and are very rare today. Sirion instruments, seen by the author only in disc-shifting styles and in German-built cases, are extremely rare.

Note: Refer to the cylinder music box section of this book for more information on Mermod Frères. The firm's extensive series of Ideal and Peerless boxes are described.

Note: Stella discs, first made of zinc and later made of steel, and Mira discs were made with English titles and also with tri-lingual titles (English, French, German).

# STELLA
## MUSIC BOXES
## JACOT MUSIC BOX CO.

SOLE AGENTS FOR
MERMOD FRÈRES,
STE CROIX SWITZERLAND.

39 UNION SQUARE, NEW YORK.

No. 63: Oak or mahogany case. Single comb. Uses 14" discs. Case measures 24x19½x12".

No. 84: Oak or mahogany case. Single comb. Uses 17¼" discs. Case measures 29x22x13" and contains a drawer that will hold 100 discs.

No. 80: (Original catalogue description follows:) Oak or mahogany case. With large spring motor, duplex comb, and a moderator to give the desired tempo. Case is 18" long by 17" wide by 11½" high. Uses a 9½" disc.

No. 126: Oak or mahogany case. Duplex comb. Uses 14" discs. Case measures 24x19½x12".

No. 40: Oak or mahogany case. Single comb. Uses 9½" discs. Case measures 15½x11x8½".

# STELLA MUSIC BOXES

No. 202: "Contains same musical movement as No. 200. For home use. Measures 6' high by 3' wide by 1'8" deep. Uses 26" discs." (actual disc measurement is 25 11/16")

No. 203: As preceding, but with coin slot for commercial use.

Both styles were available in oak or mahogany. Designated as the "Orchestral Grand."

No. 168: "Oak or mahogany case. With large spring motor, duplex combs, and a moderator to give the desired tempo. The case is 2'5" wide by 1'1" high by 1'10" deep and contains a drawer that will hold one hundred tune sheets. The tune sheet is of steel and is 17¼" in diameter." Designated as the Stella Grand model (as were other styles which use the 17¼" discs).

No. 150: "Stella Concert. Oak or mahogany case. With large spring motor, duplex combs, and a moderator to give the desired tempo. The case is 2'3" wide by 12½" high by 1'9" wide. Uses 15½" discs."

# STELLA

No. 200: "Mahogany or golden oak. The Stella Orchestral Grand has a remarkable volume of tone without being unpleasantly loud, as it retains the Stella tone; it is therefore particularly suitable for large parlors and halls. It has a powerful spring motor, two duplex combs, and a moderator to give the desired tempo. The cabinet is of artistic design, and the lower part contains a compartment for storing the tune sheets. Its dimensions are: 3'5" wide by 2'6" deep by 2'10" high. The tune sheet is of steel and is 26" in diameter." The Orchestral Grand was made in many different case styles. Those with electric motor drive were designated as the Electric Orchestral Grand.

No. 268: "Mahogany or golden oak cabinet. Mechanism of Stella No. 168 in handsome and artistic cabinet combining the box and stand. The lower part is subdivided by a number of vertical partitions, for greater convenience in storing the tune sheets. It is 2'6" wide by 3' high by 1'10" deep and is supplied with casters." Made in several different cabinet styles, the No. 268 was one of the most popular models. Uses 17¼" discs.

The Jacot Music Box Company showroom at 39 Union Square, New York City, c.1905. The three men on the right side are (left to right) C.H. Jacot, A.D. Jacot, and A.H. Jacot (manager). Among interesting things on display are a Mermod Frères disc-playing clock (left foreground), a long row of Stella and Mira console models (center), and a Miraphone (between A.D. and C.H. Jacot at the right). (Photograph courtesy of the Musical Box Society)

Mermod Frères display at the 1900 Paris Exhibition. Featured are Peerless cylinder boxes (see cylinder box section of this book for more information) and Stella disc boxes. Note the very ornate cases of some of the instruments. (Photograph courtesy of Mrs. Ruth Bornand)

Stella
Sweetest in Tone.
STELLA
Best in Quality.
A music box with a
PIANO TONE
Playing any number of tunes, with smooth metallic tune sheets. No pins or projections to break off. Write for catalogue.
JACOT & SON
39 Union Sq., New York.
Department P.


Advertisement for the Stella. The projectionless disc feature of Stella boxes is emphasized.

STELLA (Mermod Frères)

THE "STELLA" is a new music box containing desirable features which are found in no other disc music box. It is manufactured by Mermod Frères, at Ste. Croix, Switzerland, a firm established in 1816, and whose products have always obtained a high award in all the Expositions where they have been exhibited, to which fact the sixteen gold medals they have received will testify. Their factory is fully equipped with up-to-date machinery, partly of American manufacture; and this, together with the technical skill and inventive talent of Swiss workmen, has combined to create the wonderful "Stella" music box.

**Motor.** The "Stella" music box consists of a metal bed plate with a spring motor of very simple and substantial construction, and one or more steel combs, the teeth of which are acted upon and made to produce a beautiful musical tone by a circular metallic tune sheet without the objectionable pins or projections which are found in all the other makes of music boxes.

**Tune sheets.** The advantage of this tune sheet is obvious. As each perforation in the "Stella" tune sheet IS A NOTE, and is represented in other music boxes by a pin or projection, it is readily seen that, if from any cause the pins or projections break, these notes are gone forever and the music is imperfectly rendered. Another advantage of the Stella's style of tune sheet is its convenience in handling, and the small space it occupies in the drawer of the instrument or cabinet.

**Tone quality.** THE GREAT MERIT OF THE "STELLA" MUSIC BOX LIES IN ITS MUSICAL TONE. This quality of tone is distinctly its own, and is found in no other music box; in the duplex (double comb) styles particularly this quality is very remarkable, these instruments being noted for expression, harmony and volume of tone. It is this feature which has made the "Stella" so popular and a favorite among persons of refined musical taste.

**Length of tunes.** In the "Stella," as in all similar instruments, the length of a tune depends on the diameter of the tune sheet; but, owing to our system of tune sheets WITHOUT PINS, we can set the notes closer together and therefore have tunes twenty to twenty-five per cent. longer than on tune sheets of the same diameter containing pins. Our musical artists transpose all music to be reproduced by the "Stella" so as to obtain the very best results, musically, considering the compass of each style.

**Duplex combs.** Other music boxes may have two or more combs without improving the tone. It should be noted that the quality of tone in OUR DUPLEX SYSTEM comes from the fact that two steel keys are vibrated in unison for every note on the tune sheet, while only one key is vibrated in music boxes with one comb, or with two combs not set so as to be operated by the same star wheel, as in our instruments.

**Speed regulator.** By means of this important improvement we are able to reproduce nearly all songs or melodies of moderate length as originally written. If the tune is long, the music is set closely on the tune sheet, and the instrument is made to play slowly by moving the lever of the regulator toward "slow" on the indicator until the desired tempo is obtained. Our speed regulator is so constructed that the speed of the instrument is always constant, whether the mainspring is fully wound up or nearly run down.

Views of a Stella Grand music box. This particular cabinet style was the most popular of all Stella models. Unlike most other Stella instruments illustrated here, this console cabinet design was originated by Mermod in Switzerland. Instruments of this style were distributed worldwide. (Most other Stella styles shown here are in American-made cases).

DIRECTIONS FOR THE

STELLA MUSIC BOX.

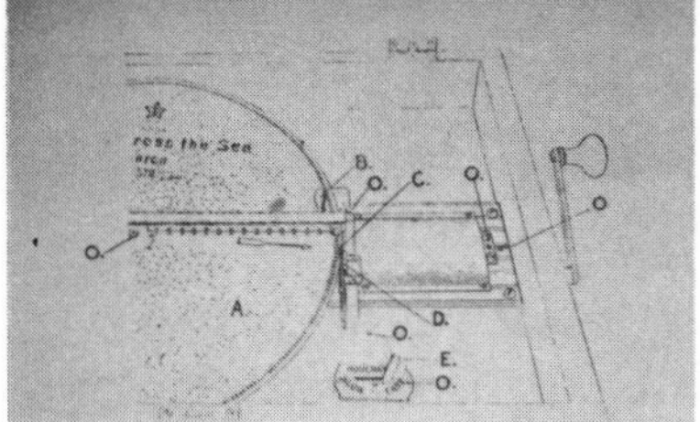


**Wind Up the Box Slowly** until the crank comes to a stop.

**To Set the Tune Sheet in Position,** open lever "B" and slide the tune sheet under horizontal rod until the center pin projects through the hole in the center of sheet, taking care that the catch "C" goes into the notch; then hold the tune sheet down with the left hand, seeing that the teeth of sprocket wheel project through the perforations at the edge, and close lever "B."

**To Start the Box,** move lever "D" to "Play."

**To Make It Run Slow,** move lever of moderator "E" toward slow until the required tempo is obtained.

CAUTION.

Do not remove the tune sheet before the end of the tune.

IMPORTANT.

The under side of tune sheets must be kept clean.

Put a drop of music box oil at all points marked "O" about once a month.

AFFIDAVIT.

Messrs. JACOT & SON,
39 Union Square, New York.

DEAR SIRS:—

The Stella tune sheet No. 246, "Angel's Serenade," which we send you with this Affidavit, has played from May 9th to July 20th, 1898, that is, more than fifty days, at a rate of about six hundred and fifty tunes per day, on a "Stella" music box of the 168-key style. It has therefore played more than 32,000 tunes (thirty-two thousand tunes), and as you can see its pivot hole, gearing, as well as notes, are absolutely intact and without appreciable wear.

Yours truly,
MERMOD FRÈRES.

STE. CROIX, Switzerland, Sept. 8, 1898.

Signed and sworn to before me at Ste. Croix, the 8th Sept., 1898.

AD. JACCARD,
*Notary.*

**We imagine that "Angel's Serenade" was never played in the Mermod Frères factory after the above test was completed!**

**17¼" Stella Grand in a decal-decorated mahogany cabinet identical to that used for the popular 18½" Mira instrument. (Mrs. Ruth Bornand photograph)**

**Credit note: Much of the information concerning Stella and Mira boxes presented here is from Mrs. Ruth Bornand, who has written that these instruments are "considered to be of exceptionally fine tonal quality and musical arrangement."**

Stella Orchestral Grand in a hand-carved case made of Central American mahogany. Measures 3'1½" wide by 2'9½" high by 2'6" deep. Custom-made for the family of Evelyn Nesbit Thaw. (Note: Evelyn was the center figure in the celebrated Thaw-White murder trial of 1907. Socialite Harry K. Thaw, Evelyn's new husband, shot noted architect Stanford White when the latter attempted to continue an earlier love affair with her.) (Music box illustration courtesy of Mrs. Ruth Bornand)

Below: Views of a 26" (actual disc measurement is 25 11/16") Stella Orchestral Grand (James Prendergast Collection). The mechanism was built around the turn of the century by Mermod Frères and was shipped to the Jacot Music Box Company in New York City. The cabinet is American-made. Beginning in the early 1890's, most Mermod imports into the United States consisted of the mechanisms of cylinder and disc boxes, not the cabinets. The cases, offered in standard styles as well as custom models, were usually of quartered oak or mahogany.

The owner of the instrument shown below describes it: "Star wheels are mounted individually on their own axles and spring up into the slots as the disc revolves. Two combs, each with 101 teeth, are positioned at right angles to one another so that one star wheel plucks two teeth simultaneously, one on each comb. The teeth of one comb are tuned slightly sharper or flatter than the corresponding teeth on the other, causing 'beats' which lend a pleasant throbbing effect to the music. The case measures 40¼" wide by 44¾" high by 21½" deep and is finished in quartered oak."

COMBINATION MUSIC BOX AND TALKING MACHINE.

$100.00 in Value for $70.00.

The two most popular instruments for home entertainment combined into one.

The "Miraphone" will find a place in every household, as it combines the variety obtained from talking machines with the sweet musical tones of the music box, appealing to the most varied taste for music and entertainment. When there is a division of opion which to purchase, a talking machine or music box, the "Miraphone" entirely fills the requirements.

Its fine mechanism is noiseless and will run seven 7-inch or four 10-inch or three 12-inch records with perfect regularity, and it is the equal of any sixty dollar talking machine. As a music box, it has comb or combs of the finest quality, producing remarkable sweetness of tone.

**Write for Catalogues of Mira tune sheets and Victor records.**

**The Miraphone, a disc music box and phonograph combination, was made in limited quantities c.1903-1910. In 1909 Mermod Frères noted in "Zeitschrift für Instrumentenbau," a German music trade publication, that "Miraphones are made particularly for the American market where such double-purpose instruments are very popular."**

**Miraphones were made in table model and console formats. Sales were limited, however, in comparison to the Reginaphone, a similar combination instrument.**

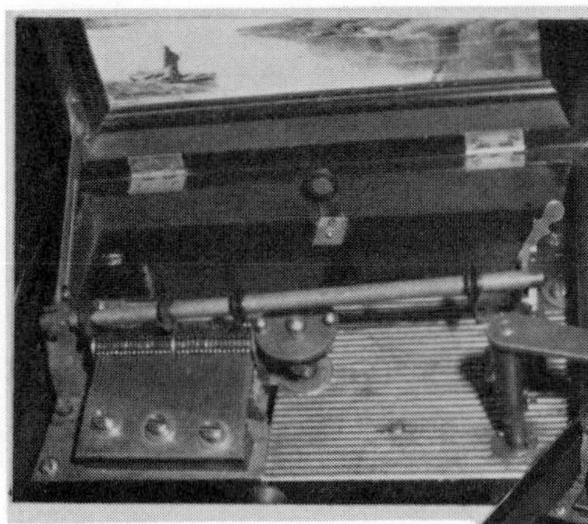

**A small single-comb Mira box from the 1900 era.**

**Small double-comb Mira table model music box which uses a 12" disc. Note that the idler arm, which fits completely across the disc, is hinged at the left side.**

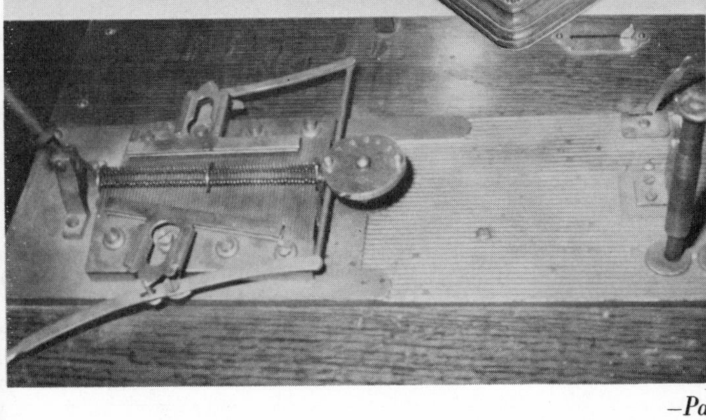

**Advertisement of Alfred Geater notes that Stella boxes "can be supplied in best English cabinet-made cases, plain or inlaid." Mermod Frères sold many musical movements to agents and manufacturers in Germany, France, England, and America. These outlets incorporated the mechanisms into their own styles of cabinets. As a result, there are no standard Stella or Mira case designs. Those sold in England are different from those sold in America. Those relatively few instruments sold in Germany (few were sold in that country due to the competition from Leipzig manufacturers) are in cases resembling contemporary Polyphon and Symphonion models.**

Right: 1904 advertisement for the Mira music box. Note that the advertisement translates "Mira" to "Marvelous." This particular Mira style was the most popular of all large Mira instruments, at least from the standpoint of those sold in the United States. Large quantities, probably over 1000 units, were sold. Those sold by Lyon & Healy (Chicago, Illinois) bore the Empress Concert Grand name but were otherwise identical.

These instruments have an exceedingly brilliant and full tone and are considered by collectors today to be one of the very finest types of music box ever made.

—Some Mermod Patents—

Right: 1897 patent awarded to Aristides H. Jacot (of Stapleton, N.Y.) and assigned to Mermod Frères of St. Croix. Basic patent for the device used on Stella and Mira boxes to hold the disc against the star wheels.

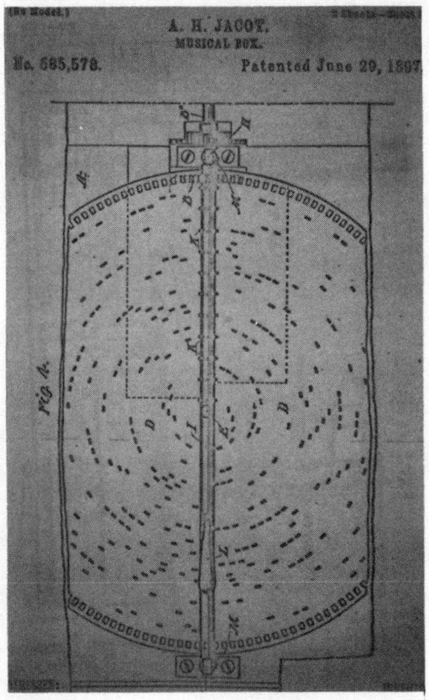


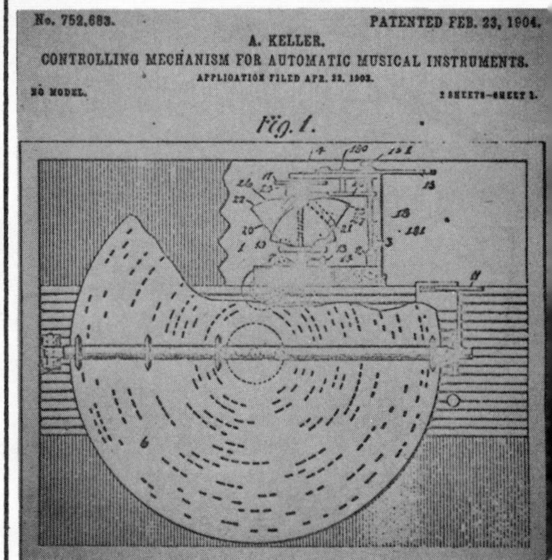


Above: Patent awarded to Alfred Keller (a German citizen who resided in St. Croix; co-patentee earlier of the disc-shifting box as used in Sirion instruments) and assigned to Mermod Frères; for a new type of speed governor. One of several Keller patents of this era. This type of governor was used on a number of late Mermod mechanisms, including disc-shifting types (see Sirion).

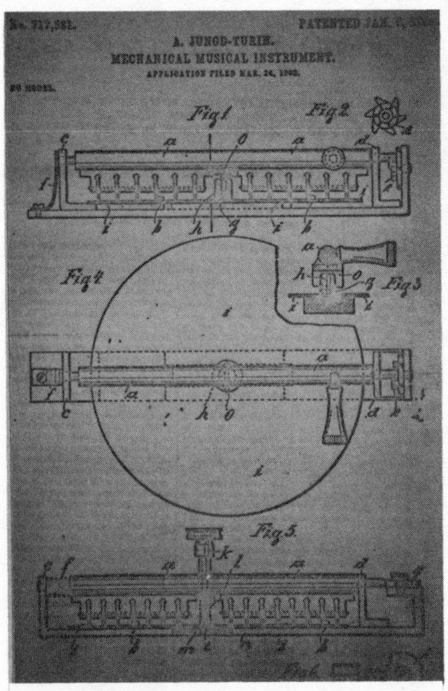


Left: Patent awarded to Arthur Junod-Turin (of St. Croix) and assigned to Mermod Frères. Mermod Frères produced disc-shifting mechanisms, mostly of the type as used on Sirion and New Century boxes — mechanisms with a shifting center spindle. The Junod-Turin patent pertains to a new device which relates to "a device for holding the discs [of music boxes], and has for its purpose to provide means for easily moving the axle around which the discs turn. The moving of the axle has the purpose that between the rows of perforations or pins of the discs further rows of such perforations or pins may be provided, which after moving the situation of the center of the discs by moving the axle around which they turn, engage with the star wheels or sounding tongues of the instrument, so that several music pieces can be played by means of one disc or that pieces can be played which are three or four times as long as the pieces which can be played in case the center of the music discs cannot be moved and the intermediate rows of pins or perforations are not provided." The former device, as used on Sirion and New Century boxes, shifted the center spindle. The Junod-Turin device provided for shifting of the disc assembly from above by shifting the entire idler wheel assembly. Note the six-pointed snail gear in the patent drawing (upper right). Evidently a disc which shifted three or four times (as described in the patent) or even six times (as indicated by the snail gear) was contemplated.

Right: the upper part of a console Mira music box showing an 18½" disc in playing position. The idler wheel assembly is fitted to a tilting crossbar which turns to clamp the disc securely between the idler wheels and the star wheels. Similar assemblies were used on most other styles of Mermod-made boxes, particularly Stella boxes and the larger Mira boxes, after about 1897-1898. Other instruments, including most smaller Mira styles, have conventional idler wheels (with the idler arm hinged at one end and with a locking device on the other) as used by Symphonion, Monopol, and certain other instruments.

Lower right: A similar instrument in a pin-striped cabinet. Sold by Lyon & Healy, Chicago musical instrument retailers, this box bears the Empress Concert Grand name. Empress, the house brand name of Lyon & Healy, was used on everything from music boxes to band organs.

Lower left: Another view of an 18½" Mira box. Note that the idler wheels have been turned 180 degrees to permit a disc to be inserted below them. Unlike Stella boxes, Mira instruments use discs with projections.

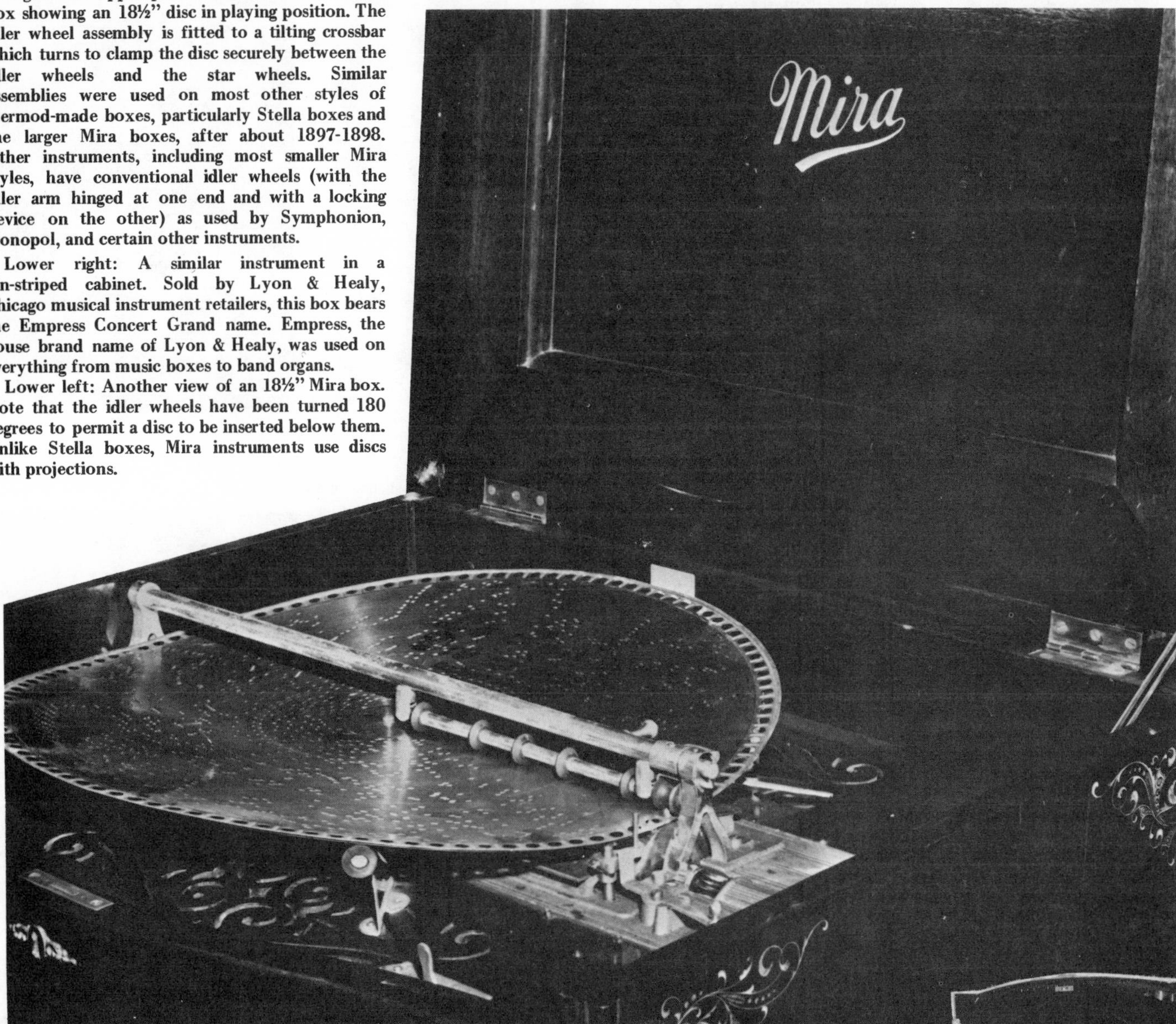


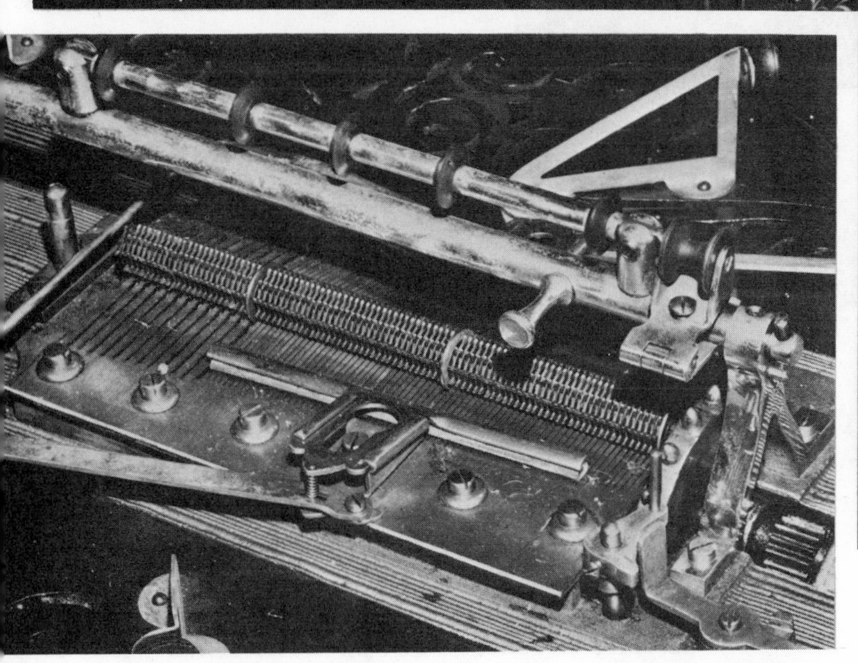

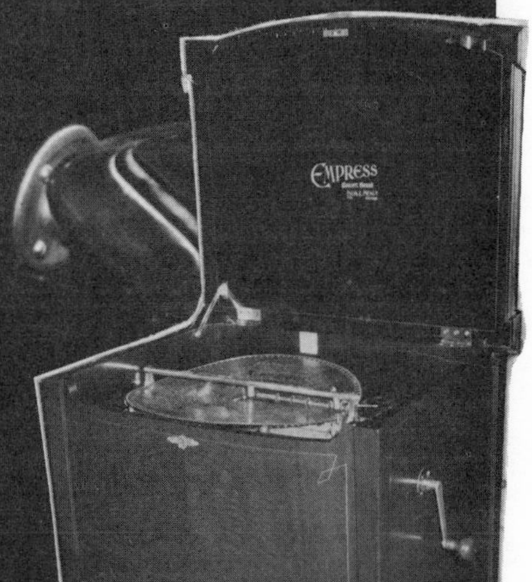

(1)

(2)

(3)

—Details of a Sirion Disc-Shifting Box—

This disc-shifting Sirion uses 22¾" discs, each of which has two tunes. During the first revolution the first melody plays. The center spindle then shifts slightly and plays the second tune from another set of disc projections. Our descriptions refer to the number by each picture: (1) The German-made (circa 1903) case measures 3' wide by 6'1" high by 1'8" deep. (2) Sirion name and radiant sun trademark as shown on a disc. (3) Center spindle in the upper position. (4) Center spindle has shifted downward to play the second tune. (5) Duplex music comb arrangement of the Sirion. Eight bass teeth are on each side of the top of the upper comb. (6) Alfred Keller's patented governor assembly (U.S. No. 752,683; Feb. 23, 1904; assigned to Mermod Frères). (7) "Made in Dresden" notation on a Sirion disc. (8) Alfred Keller's patented winding clutch assembly (U.S. No. 788,265; April 25, 1905; assigned to Mermod Frères). (9) Drive and governor assembly of the Sirion. Note the ornate top plate with its fretwork. The entire works were originally made with a highly polished surface.

(4)

(5)

(6)

(7)

(8)

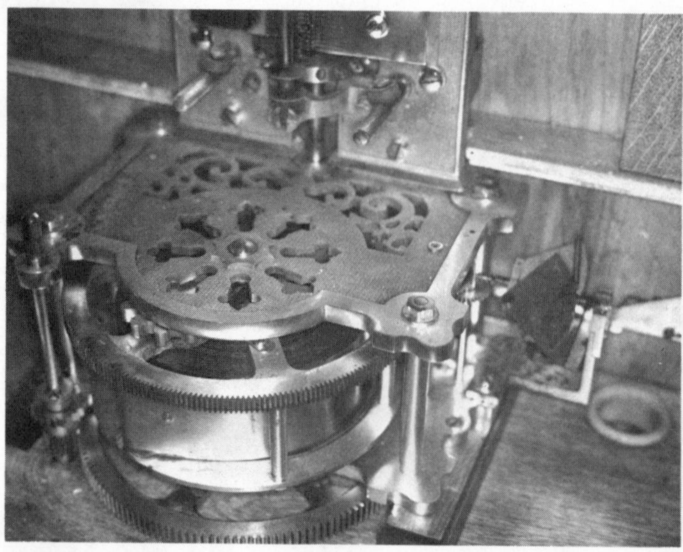

(9)

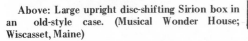

Above: Large upright disc-shifting Sirion box in an old-style case. (Musical Wonder House; Wiscasset, Maine)

Left: New Century disc box (not of the shifting type) in a tall American-made cabinet. The cabinet appears oversize in comparison to the disc diameter; this is typical of most upright New Century styles. (Wallace McPeak photograph)

New Century boxes were made in these comb configurations: (1) single comb; (2) double comb, regular arrangement [used on disc-shifting models]; (3) double comb, sublime harmonie arrangement; (4) 4 combs, 2 on each side of spindle [like Imperator].

American and European New Century boxes each have different case styles. The discs have scoop-shaped projections.

Etienne Blyelle is shown with a large upright European-case New Century box with four large music combs. (Arthur W.J.G. Ord-Hume photograph)

New Century disc-shifting box in an American-made case and with some American-made parts. The disc can be set to repeat the same tune or to play the first tune and then the second, via a "Repeat-Change" lever. Average playing time for a continuous 2-revolution performance is about 2 minutes, 45 seconds. The discs are of zinc, have scoop-shaped projections, and have the titles in English only (indicating they were made in America or were made specifically for the English-speaking market). Numbers are in the 6000 series. The above-pictured discs uses two revolutions to play the "Martha Overture." (J.B. Nethercutt Collection; photograph by Roger Morrison)

Left: Table model disc-shifting Sirion box. Uses a 19 1/4" disc.

Right: The Sirion, as advertised for sale by the New Polyphon Supply Co., Ltd., of London. "The latest automatic musical box. Novelty. The Sirion. Superseding all others. Two airs in place of one."

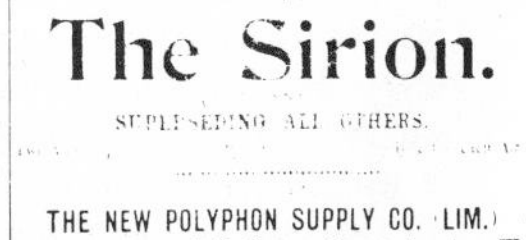

## MIRA AND STELLA (Mermod Frères)

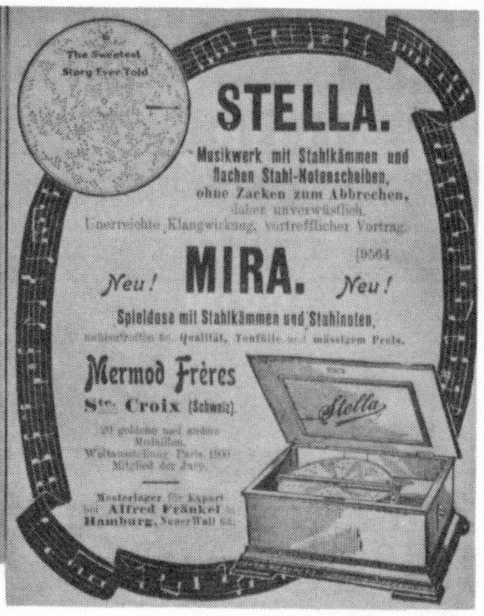


**Above left: 1902 advertisement for the Stella music box.**

**Above right: 1903 advertisement for the Stella music box. This advertisement was one of the first to mention the Mira disc box ("New! – MIRA. – New!"). The Mira trademark was registered in Germany by Mermod Frères on October 23, 1902.**

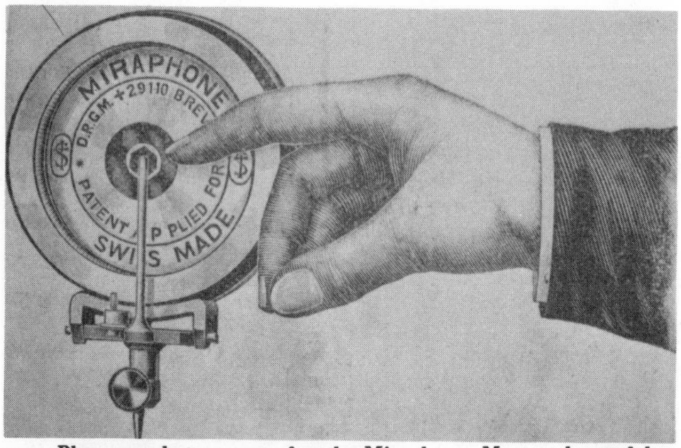


**Phonograph tone arm for the Miraphone. Most early models (and later models made for the American market) combined a Mira disc-type music box with a Miraphone phonograph. Later, phonographs (without music boxes) bearing the Miraphone name were sold, as were Pathé-trademarked phonographs.**

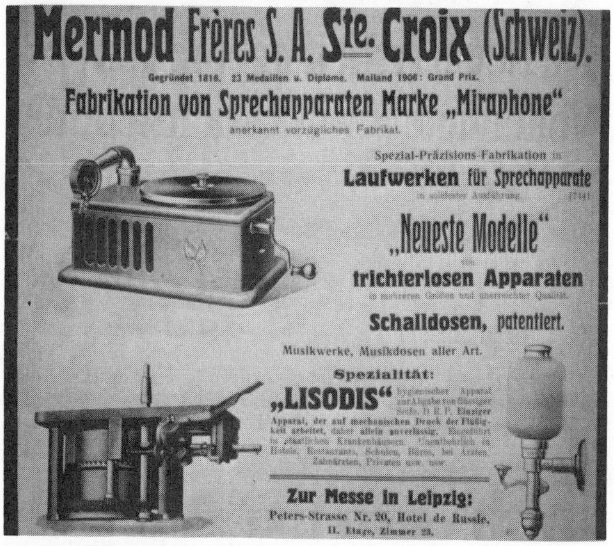


**1911 Mermod advertisement featuring the Miraphone phonograph (here spelled with an "e"; most German advertisements used the "Miraphon" spelling) which was available in inside-horn (illustrated) models and models with a large detachable outside horn; a spring mechanism suitable for use with a phonograph (Mermod supplied music box mechanisms and, later, phonograph mechanisms to many different manufacturers); and the "Lisodis" soap dispenser.**

## POLYHYMNIA MUSIC BOXES
### (Metall-Industrie Schönebeck A.G.)
### –Schönebeck, Germany–

**Polyhymnia music boxes, resembling the popular Polyphon music boxes in appearance and name, were sold by the Metall-Industrie Schönebeck around the turn of the 20th century. The illustrations shown below appeared in 1902.**

**1913 Mermod advertisement featuring spring-drive mechanisms for phonographs and disc-type music boxes. This was one of the last Mermod advertisements to appear. The firm evidently ceased business within the next year or two.**

## MONOPOL
### Leipziger Musikwerke (Paul Ehrlich & Co.)
### –Leipzig, Germany–

The Leipziger Musikwerke (later Paul Ehrlich & Co.), maker of a wide variety of musical items including the best-selling Ariston organette, produced the Monopol series of disc music boxes during the 1890's and early 1900's.

Although Monopol instruments were produced in sizes from 5 3/4" to 32", the most popular size seems to have been the 30-tooth 7 1/2" size which was widely used in toys and novelties. Most 7 1/2" movements were of the hand-cranked (not spring-wound) type.

Among larger Monopol boxes the 84-tooth and 100-tooth sizes, interchangeable with 11 3/4" and 13 5/8" Symphonion discs respectively, were very popular. The mechanisms of Monopol and Symphonion boxes, including the aforementioned two sizes, are identical in many instances. The sublime harmonie comb system is used in several sizes, including the 84- and 100-tooth types.

Among the more interesting Monopol products is an automaton in the form of a gnome which accepts coins of different denominations, but which plays music only when the correct value is deposited (see description on following page).

----------

**No. 33.**
The Tunes are placed upon the back.
Size 9½ × 8¼ × 4½ inches

**No. 30, 31 & 130**
Size 10¼ × 8¾ × 6 inches.

**Motor 'Bus.**

**No. 300.**
Size 9½ × 8 × 3¾ inches.

**No. 32.**
Size 11½ × 8¾ × 9¾ inches.

**Lithograph used to decorate the underside of the lid on a 7½" (19 cm.) Monopol box.**

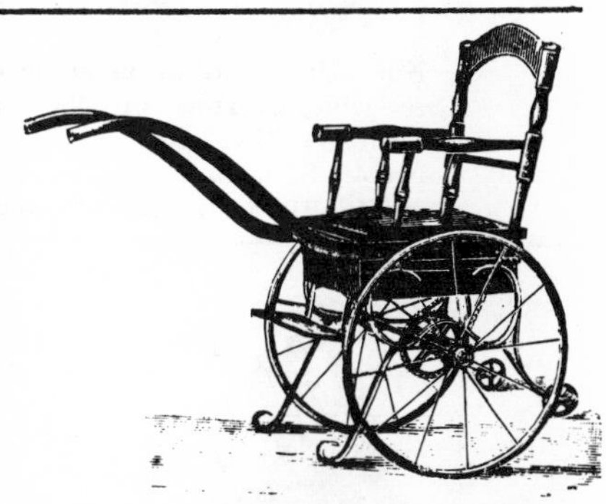

**Mail Cart.**

**No. 30P: "With puppet stage and mechanical figure." Hand-cranked (manivelle) type. No. 30D: Same as preceding, but without stage and figure. Also called "No. 300." No. 30S: Same as 30D, but self-playing (spring-wound) mechanism.**

**Details of a 7½" Monopol music box.**

**Lithograph used to decorate a 7½" Monopol box.**

**On this page are shown some of the many Monopol music box styles which use the 7½" disc. Most of these instruments were made as children's toys, not as serious musical instruments. Circa 1900-1905.**

# MONOPOL MUSICAL BOXES

## (30 Tongues).

No. 30, 31, 32, 33, 130, 300, Motor Car, Mail Cart, Piano, and Motor Bus Models

**Motor Car.**

Automatic Monopol No. 45Sch. Measures 19x17½x17¼ inches. 84 teeth in music comb. Uses Monopol or Symphonion discs. (Symphonion's No. 25 size)

Automatic Monopol No. 50Sch. Measures 20½x17½x17¼ inches. 100 teeth in music comb.

No. 42b: 50 teeth in music comb. Case with columns on the corners measures 41x37x25 cm.

No. 46: 84 teeth in music comb.

No. 51: 100 teeth in music comb.

Monopol No. 73: 84 teeth.

Monopol No. 71: 100 teeth.

This 5' high automaton features a gnome who indicates that a coin is to be dropped into his cup. If a coin of the wrong size is deposited, the gnome shakes his head, keeps the coin, and no music plays. Then when a coin of the right size is given, the gnome indicates his approval, and the music box plays. One of the cleverest coin-operated automata of the 1890-1900 period.

Monopol Style 396: Music box with rotating spindle for display of flowers, a Christmas tree, store window exhibits, etc. Base contains a Monopol music box mechanism with a very powerful long-running spring. Circa 1895.

Similar devices were made with Kalliope, Symphonion, and Polyphon music box movements. Refer to the Kalliope section of this book for more information.

No. 55a (above left): 84 teeth in music comb. Case measures 115x58x40 cm. (46x23x16"). Walnut with chromo picture on front.

No. 56b (above right): 100 teeth in music comb. Case measures 135x74.5x38 cm. (54x30x15"). Walnut with gold, green, and red chromo design on front. Clock at top of case.

No. 56a: Same as No. 56, but without clock.

No. 42a: 50 teeth in music comb. Polished black case with gold engraving. 36x32x22 cm.

No. 45: 84 teeth in music comb.

No. 50: 100 teeth in music comb.

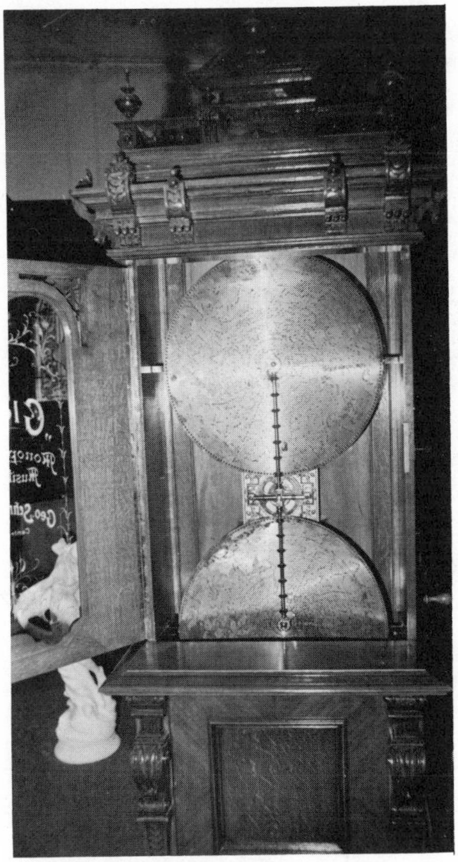

(1)

(2)

(3)

(4)

The Monopol "Gloria"
—an unusual double-disc box—

Sold by Geo. Schneider, Nachfolger (successors to Geo. Schneider) of Centralhalle, Leipzig, Germany, this large instrument is marked: "GLORIA" – MONOPOL MUSIK AUTOMAT.

The music box plays two 26 1/2" diameter discs at the same time. Both are driven from the same set of sprockets on the center drive wheel. The idler wheel arms are both hinged on the same horizontal shaft. To play the "Gloria," each disc must be carefully put in position, with the starting indicator arrow on the top disc pointing downward towards the center of the drive wheel and with the corresponding arrow on the bottom disc pointing upward towards the center. Upon deposit of a coin the box will begin to play. As both discs are driven from the same sprocket wheel, the discs themselves rotate in opposite directions – unlike most other types of double-disc boxes which have independent drive for each disc so that the discs turn in the same direction. The contra-rotating discs are startling when first seen in operation, particularly if the observer has been conditioned by watching discs of other types of instruments.

The specimen shown measures 8'7" high by 3'5" wide by 2'11" deep. The playing time for one selection is about 2 minutes, 15 seconds. Discs have projections similar to those on very large Polyphon, Regina, and Symphonion (but unlike those on small Symphonion) discs; the projections resemble the letter P lying on its back. Titles are in German, French, and English, and have 4-digit numbers such as No. 0671. (J.B. Nethercutt Collection; Roger Morrison photograph)

The photographs on this page are of: (1) The Monopol "Gloria" with the front door open and with both discs in the playing position. (2) Overall view of the instrument. The bottom, which is built with an appearance similar to a disc-storage cabinet, accommodates the lower playing disc. Extra discs must be stored elsewhere. (3) The music comb assembly with the top idler wheel bar tilted so as to permit a disc to be placed on the center spindle. Spindles are at each end of the ornate bedplate. Note the spruce sounding board and the curved bridges which transmit the sound from the bedplate. The "Gloria" is superb from a tonal viewpoint. (4) Another view of the comb assembly. The center drive disc has sprockets on the top of its outer rim. These sprockets engage corresponding round holes in the disc periphery and drive both discs simultaneously.

## ORPHENION
**—Bruno Rückert—**
**(Leipzig, Germany)**

**Orphenion disc boxes were produced by Bruno Rückert of Leipzig, Germany. Those illustrated here are from 1894, 1895, and 1897 catalogues. The firm's main period of activity seems to have been in the 1890's.**

**In 1900 Ludwig Hupfeld, a sales outlet for the Orphenion, held a clearance sale on Orphenion boxes, each of which was described as being "just like new." Instruments offered and the sale prices were: No. 118 (coin-operated) 139 Mk., discs 1 Mk. each; No. 106 (coin-operated) 324 Mk., discs 1 Mk. each; No. 92P (premium-vending) 124 Mk.; No. 120 (coin-operated) 191 Mk.; No.94F 138 Mk.; No. 93F 121 Mk., discs 1 Mk. each; No. 93 108 Mk.; No. 76 77 Mk.; No. 71 60 Mk.; No. 40F (hand-cranked "with dancing cats") 13 Mk.; No. 36 24 Mk. Hupfeld, who had listed Orphenions in earlier catalogues, did not offer them for sale after 1900.**

**The several Orphenion boxes examined by the author were well made and were of exceptionally fine tonal quality. Orphenion boxes, apparently never made in large numbers, are quite rare today.**

——————————

**No. 92: 90 teeth. Piccolo; fine walnut case; colored glass door.**

**No. 92F: The same, but with fortissimo (louder) music arrangement.**

**Case measures 113x65x36 cm. (45x26x14½").**

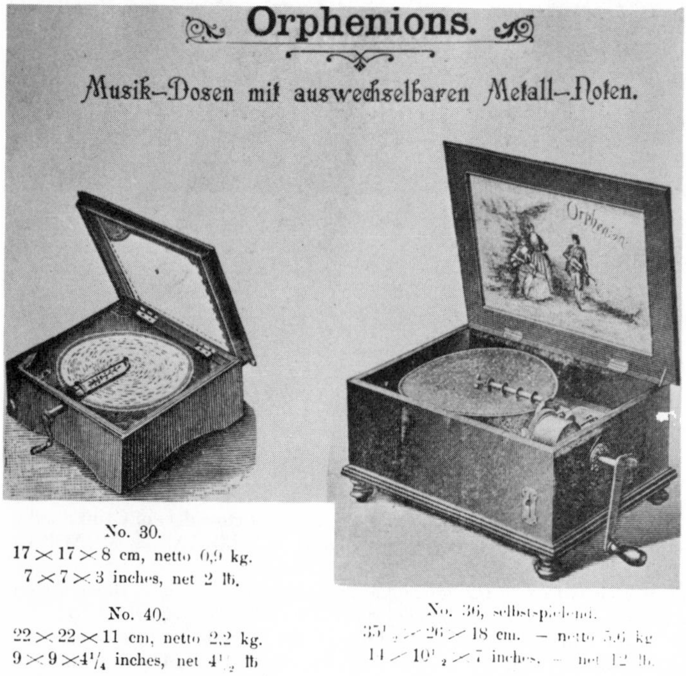

Orphenions.
Musik-Dosen mit auswechselbaren Metall-Noten.
Orphenion
No. 30.
17×17×8 cm, netto 0,9 kg.
7×7×3 inches, net 2 lb.
No. 40.
22×22×11 cm, netto 2,2 kg.
9×9×4¼ inches, net 4½ lb
No. 36, selbst-spielend.


**No. 30: 32 teeth in music comb. Hand-cranked (manivelle) type. Black polished case.**

**No. 40: 40 teeth in music comb. Hand-cranked type. Polished walnut case.**

**No. 36: 40 teeth in music comb. Spring-wound type. Walnut (veneer) case.**

**No. 72: 70 teeth. Walnut case with colored glass door. Case measures 114x58x31 cm. (45½x23x12½").**

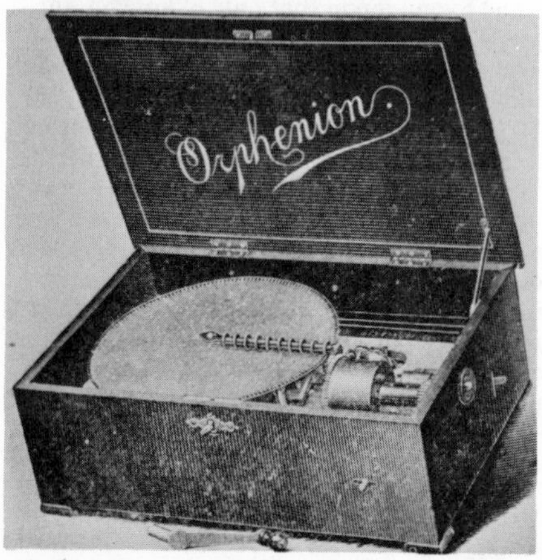


**No. 51: 50 teeth. 46x30x15 cm. case.**

**No. 71: 70 teeth. 55x37x18 cm. case.**

**No. 91: 90 teeth. 69x49x26 cm. case.**

**No. 91F: Same as 91, but with stronger (louder) teeth.**

**No. 93: 90 teeth. Case with corner posts.**

**No. 93F: Same as 93, but with stronger teeth.**

**No. 72P: 70 teeth. Walnut case with colored glass door. Premium-vending instrument dispenses tokens good in trade for beer at the bar. With clock in the top gallery. 114x58x31 cm. (45½x23x12½") case.**

**No. 92P: 90 teeth. Walnut case with colored glass door. Premium-vending. 113x65x36 cm. (45x26x14½") case.**

**No. 92FP: Same as 92P, but with stronger (louder) teeth.**

ORPHENION

No. 96 (shown at the right): Coin-operated musical cabinet, similar in styling to contemporary (c.1895) instruments by Polyphon and Symphonion. 90 teeth in music comb. Walnut case with painted glass door. Case measures 183x63x39 cm. (73x25x16 inches). Advertisements could be painted on the door instead of the "Musik Automat" lettering.

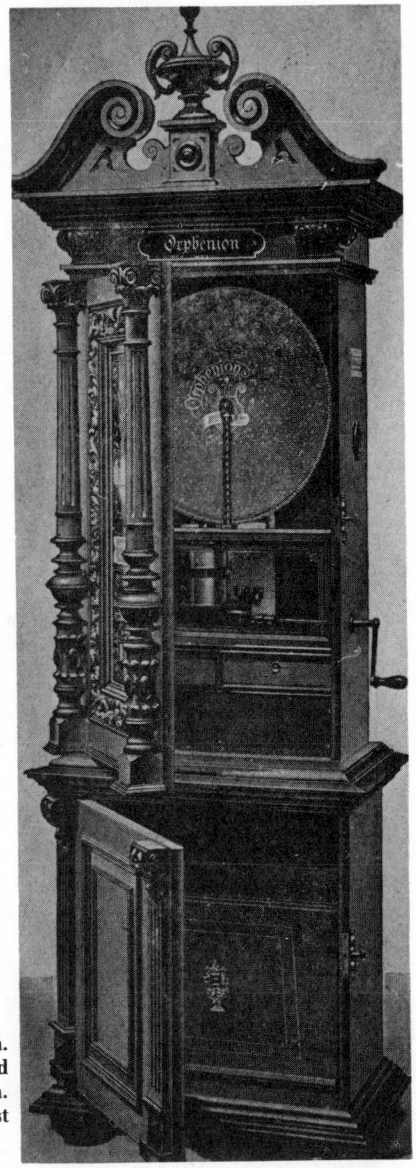


No. 106: (shown at the right): 100 teeth. Large double winding springs for extended playing time. Case measures 235x90x50 cm. (94x36x20 inches). "The tone is of the highest degree. Plays for twenty minutes."

Above, below, and below right: Views of a No. 71 Orphenion music box. Note that the spring barrel is exposed, as on a cylinder box. This format, an unusual one, was also used in certain Fortuna and Adler instruments.

## F.G. OTTO & SONS
### —Capital "Cuff" Boxes—
### —Criterion Disc Boxes—
### —Olympia Disc Boxes—
### —Pianette Disc Piano—

### Introduction and Credit

Nearly all of the following information is taken from an article, "The Capital Cuff Box," which appeared in Vol. XIII, No.2 issue of the Musical Box Society "Bulletin," and is used with the kind permission of the author, Mr. Hughes Ryder, and the Musical Box Society International.

### Early History of F.G. Otto & Sons

In 1875 Frederick G. Otto established the firm of F.G. Otto & Sons in Jersey City, New Jersey, as manufacturers of surgical instruments and electrical batteries. With his sons Edmund, Gustav, and Albert, Frederick Otto ran an eminently successful manufacturing business, employing over 60 people, with the original factory at 48 Sherman Avenue, which was later expanded to include the adjacent building at 50 Sherman Avenue.

The father and his sons lived not far from the factory in a fine home at 96 - 101 Sherman Place, in a prosperous residential area. It is here that two series of events merge. Gustave Brachhausen, a founder of the Regina Music Box Company, lived directly across the street from the Otto family in 1893 and 1894, the years when Brachhausen was setting up the Regina firm. It does not take much imagination to conjure up a scene in which Gustave Brachhausen is talking to Frederick Otto and his sons over a bottle of local brew or schnapps, and convincing the manufacturing company of the great future of disc music boxes in the United States. It is very easy to surmise that Brachhausen also told them not to copy his type of movement, but to work out a completely new design. With a well established factory, and with skilled machinists and metal working machines at their disposal, the production of music boxes could indeed be a potentially profitable diversification for F.G. Otto & Sons.

Employed by the Otto company as a pattern maker was Henry Langfelder, a resident of Jersey City, who had already invented a variety of mechanical items. During the fall and winter of 1893-4 Langfelder was put to work by the firm on this new project, and by February, 1894, had filed patent application No. 519,816, which was granted May 15, 1894, for a music box with a conical shaped note barrel, the original, rather crude cuff note-disc and comb mechanism. Langfelder assigned half the patent rights to F.G. Otto & Sons and reserved half for himself. The patent attorney for the Cuff Box was Briesen Knauth who also had handled the Regina patents for Brachhausen.

### The Capital Cuff Box

Langfelder's patent shows a fairly conventional spring barrel. In April of 1894, Gustav Otto himself patented a spring motor for music boxes based on a series of elliptical springs, commonly known as buggy or wagon springs. This patent, No. 525,717, shows the cuff note-disc in place, as well as his novel drive mechanism, which resembles in a most elementary fashion the fusee drive used on the earliest musical movements. The elliptical springs were fastened to a chain drive, which in turn ran to the drum of the main drive gear and thus provided the motive power. It is logical to assume that this was not an economical or practical power arrangement, for Capital boxes with this feature are much rarer than conventional spring barrel types today. Another type of Capital Cuff Box power source, likewise rare today, consisted of one or two spiral springs which were compressed on a wooden dowel which ran through their centers. As the spring pushed outward it provided motive power.

The head bookkeeper for F.G. Otto & Sons was Adolph Schaub. In the family business tradition of that time, his son Ferdinand had been brought into the business, and by 1894 had risen to the position of shop foreman. He, also, was put to work on the new project, and by the autumn of 1894 Ferdinand Schaub had patented a vastly improved cuff note-disc, or cuff, as it is familiarly known by collectors today. His patent, No. 532,290, was assigned to F.G. Otto & Sons and was the prototype for all the cuffs that were manufactured. The patent shows the note projection as being an S curve; in actual production this was not the case, and the note-punching machine

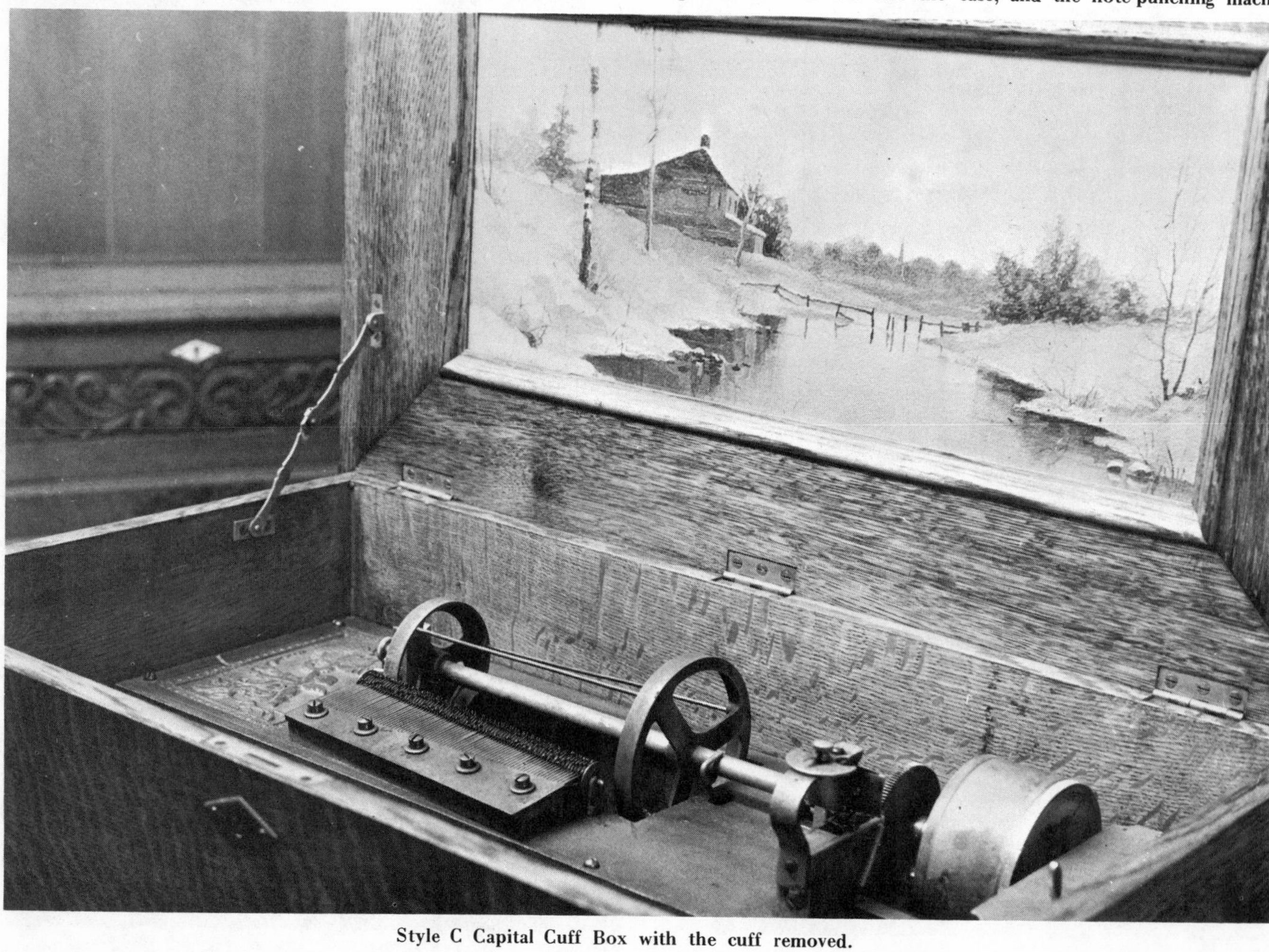

Style C Capital Cuff Box with the cuff removed.

produced projections that were really more elliptical than S-curved.

During this same year, Patrick Kennedy, of Brooklyn, N.Y., a machinist and designer for Otto, was designing the machine for punching out the cuffs, and we can safely assume that F.G. Otto & Sons was ready to turn out Capital Cuff Boxes in production by early 1895. This would indicate that the Capital was put on the market soon after the Regina Music Box.

The cuffs were made in three sizes, which fit the four main models made, since the large single-comb and large double-comb boxes took the same size cuff. The cuffs were made of steel, printed in blue, with the eagle emblem superimposed in bright gold on the deep blue background, a most striking color scheme.

The cases for the Capital Cuff movements were furnished in highly polished oak or mahogany. A case with a pressed-wood design was listed as Extra, and for the large model single- or double-comb movements a case combining pressed and carved wood with a stepped lid was available. The inside of the lid was usually fitted with a colorful rural winter scene, generally of a landscape sloping toward a brook, with a small home in the distance. The scene varied in some models. The picture used for Style O included the figure of a girl seated in a landscape. This was the economy model with a 44-tooth comb and was spring wound by a ratchet on the left, much in the manner of a Swiss music box.

The iron bedplate runs the length of the case, taking up about two thirds of the width, and is elevated by a wooden frame, thereby occupying about half the depth of the case. This arrangement provides a storage area for the spare cuffs directly in front of the movement, and by nesting them, a good many may be conveniently stored there. The exception to this arrangement is found in the Model F double-comb box, which has a split bedplate, with the start and stop lever, the spring barrel, and the governor on one section of the bedplate and the comb and damper assembly on the other section, which is depressed. This arrangement is necessary because the double comb has a common star wheel assembly and the cuff note-disc must play on the very top of the star wheels in the same manner as the Regina or Polyphon double-comb boxes, whereas in the single-comb Cuff Boxes, the note discs are at a 90-degree angle to the star wheels when playing. On the extreme left hand side of the bedplate of the large models C, D, E, and F, there is cast into the bedplate an emblem similar to a trademark, which is usually painted silver in contrast to the normal gold color of the bedplate itself. This combination, together with the deep royal blue of the cuffs, makes the appearance of the interior of the boxes most pleasing.

The spring barrel is wound by a crank at the right hand side of the box, using a counterclockwise motion. When the start lever is moved, the spring barrel casing, to which is affixed the main drive shaft, moves in a counterclockwise direction, driving the governor by means of a main gear on the drive shaft and at the same time turning the cuff, which is secured on a cuff frame-holder attached to the same drive shaft. The main shaft is very simply hinged at the right of the frame-holder so that upon the conclusion of a tune, one merely raises the shaft from the left, and when it is in an upright position, the cuff may be removed with a slight clockwise twist of the wrist. The cuff has a bayonet lock-slot which fits over a pin on the large end of the frame-holder, thus holding it in place. When putting on a new cuff, one simply slides it on the frame-holder and locks it on with a counterclockwise twist, and it is then ready to operate. The cuff rotates counterclockwise, with the projections on it turning the star wheels clockwise, and they in turn pluck the teeth of the comb.

The Capital damper assembly is fastened to the bedplate and is adjusted into the star wheel assembly. It remarkably resembles

Putting the cuff on a Capital box is an easy operation.

the Regina offset damper and functions in this manner: the side of the star wheel hits the offset portion of the damper, moving it laterally to damp an individual tooth, and then allows it to move off the tooth just prior to the tooth's being plucked by the upcoming star wheel's point.

Another interesting comparison can be made by matching a comb from a 15½" Regina box with the single comb of a Style C Capital box. The two are virtually identical!

There were good selections of tune-discs available for all sizes of Capital Cuff Boxes, and the arrangements were well set up, especially for the larger models. Due to the flare of the bass note section of the tune-disc, the musical balance is more normal than in most disc music, with its limited bass. The tonal qualities of models C, D, and E are pleasant and compare favorably with the single-comb 15½" Regina instruments. Double-comb Model F, with a total of 162 teeth, and with each star wheel plucking two teeth simultaneously, has a much richer tonal quality.

With the exception of the Model F double-comb box, all of the Cuff Boxes have two important safety-control features, one controlling the flywheel of the governor and the other locking the extreme left end of the main shaft in place while the box is in operation. The shorter of the two safety rods is activated by the start and stop lever which, when in stop position, moves a rod against the flywheel upon the conclusion of a tune, thus preventing any accidental starting of the mechanism while raising the drive shaft to put on a new tune-disc. The other safety rod, which is offset, runs from underneath the drive shaft at the right of the cuff to the shaft-holder at the extreme left of the cuff. Thus, when the main shaft is lowered into place for playing, it depresses this offset rod, whose extreme left end then goes through the left shaft-holder and locks the shaft in place, preventing it from lifting out of the shaft holder while playing.

The model F double-comb box has the safety-control rod controlling the flywheel of the governor as in the other models, but due to the offset portion, its bedplate does not have the longer safety-rod from the main shaft to the left shaft-holder; instead it has a manually-controlled lock-lever for the shaft.

With production of the Capital well underway in early 1895, the Ottos appointed the firm of M.J. Paillard, 680 Broadway, New York City, as sales agent. The fifty-year-old head of this firm, Alfred E. Paillard, had been engaged in selling Swiss music boxes for thirty-four years, and was no doubt not only pleased to be able to handle this brand-new disc machine, but was also in an admirable position to effect its maximum distribution. Research has proved that the Capital Cuff Box was manufactured through the year 1897, but the mists of time have covered any traces of the total number of these interesting boxes made and the final date of their manufacture.

### The Criterion Disc Box

For the firm of F.G. Otto & Sons, however, the Capital Cuff Boxes were just one phase in the production of music boxes, because after the Capital had gone on the market, the firm evidently felt that there was overwhelming evidence that the public preferred the more popular flat-disc box, such as the Regina, Polyphon, and Symphonion, and the F.G. Otto & Sons draftsmen and machinists were put to work again!

By February of 1895, Ferdinand Schaub had filed a patent application for a flat-disc music box with a center-wound spring barrel, in which the upper spring barrel arbor was the drive shaft for the disc to be played. This is the same principle as that used in smaller models of the German-made Kalliope music boxes, and the governor, with light-tension springs attached to the vanes of the flywheel, is not unlike that used on the Kalliope, Regina, and Polyphon. The center-wind design was never used by Otto, perhaps due to the possibility of an infringement on Kalliope's patent, but the firm went ahead and set up production of a new disc box, and by November of 1896 their new item, the Criterion Music Box, was on the market.

M.J. Paillard & Co. of New York was the sales agent for the Criterion Music Box also, and evidence shows that in the first five months of production between 80 and 100 Criterions monthly were passing through their hands alone, not taking in to account direct sales to others by the Otto company.

Criterions were cased in attractive boxes of oak or mahogany, most of them with pressed wood trim and carved side and front panels. Suitable matching stands were available, with storage space for discs under the stand.

Criterions were produced in three main sizes: 11 5/8", 15 3/4", and 20 1/2" diameters. Most were single comb machines, although in the larger sizes double combs were available. The tune discs were usually of zinc, on which the Criterion emblem and the name and number of the tune were printed in black ink. On the smaller model, some of the discs were a steel alloy, with a metallic gold lacquer applied in the style of the medium-sized Symphonion discs. The principal type produced was the table model, although in the 20 1/2" size a single-play upright model over six feet in height was available, with a tilting storage bin underneath the movement. Later, the company produced an automatic Criterion in the larger size, and attempted to go Regina one better by having a carriage holding 15 discs, as compared to the 12-disc carriage of the automatic Regina models.

Because of the Criterion's similarity to the Regina in so many features, the Otto firm was subjected to a patent infringement suit through their agent, M.J. Paillard & Co. This case, which was in the New York courts in 1896 and 1897, has been discussed earlier in the Musical Box Society "Bulletin," in a feature article by Mr. Arthur Sanders.

### The Olympia Disc Box

During the year 1898, F.G. Otto & Sons came out with a third line of music boxes, known as the Olympia, advertised as a Self-Playing Music Box, and cased in boxes similar to those of Criterion; in fact, some models were identical in appearance. The same type of zinc disc was used as for the Criterion, but of course the emblem printed on it was the new Olympia trademark, together with the name and number of the tune. The picture used on the inside of certain Olympia lids is identical to that used on the inside lid of some Capital Cuff Boxes.

The "Industrial Directory of New Jersey" shows that in 1899 F.G. Otto & Sons employed 64 people in the manufacture of music boxes. This was a goodly number, but far short of the number (over 300) employed by the Regina Music Box Company at the same time, indicating how far ahead Regina must have been in sales volume. Possibly during the year 1902, the manufacture of the Olympia was moved out of the main factory, for during that year the Olympia Musical Automaton Company was located at 107 Franklin Street, just around the corner from F.G. Otto, and Stephen F. Tritschler was listed as manager.

### The Pianette Disc Piano

With the early 1900's the era of marvelous new automatic musical instruments had arrived, and spurred on by the marketing of the Polyphon and Regina Concerto, tall automatic pianos with music arranged on large 32" metal discs, F.G. Otto & Sons prodded Ferdinand Schaub again. By November of 1904, Schaub had applied for a patent on an automatic piano operated by a punched metal disc, and this patent, No. 805,989, was granted in November of 1906. A separate company was formed, the Otto Manufacturing Company, with Edmund Otto, Gustav Otto, and Ferdinand Schaub as directors, and was located at 107 Franklin Street, the address of the Olympia Musical Automaton Co.

The Pianette, as the disc-operated Otto piano was called, was manufactured in several different case styles. A Pianette advertisement by Lyon & Healy, Chicago musical instrument retailers (see Lyon & Healy section of this book), featured a model of the Pianette and described it as, "an automatically adjusted self-playing piano, operated by a long-running spring motor contained in a metal barrel. . . The action is of metal and plays thirty nine notes; has a double row of hammers with dampers, permitting full expression to the rendition of each tune. The soundboard and frame are of the regular piano type. The instrument is 75" high, 35" wide, 17" deep, and weighs 420 pounds." The buyer's choice of mahogany or oak woods was offered.

### Epilogue and Comments

The Hughes Ryder history of the Otto Firm, quoted nearly in its entirety here, concludes with the note that by 1909 the Otto Manufacturing Company was back in the production of electrical goods and out of the music box business. One brother, Edmund Otto, was still making and repairing music boxes at 96 Sherman Place, the old family home.

Henry Langfelder, inventor of the cuff system, went back to Germany (his homeland) and, later, headed Menzenhauer & Schmidt, the firm which acquired the Kalliope Musikwerke in 1919. While in America, Langfelder helped market the Schmidt-made Guitarophone.

Today, the Capital Cuff Box, representing as it does a hybrid between the disc box and cylinder box, is a favorite with collectors.

# THE "CAPITAL"

# SELF-PLAYING MUSIC BOX

## With Interchangeable Steel Tune Cylinders.

*Manufactured and Patented by*

F. G. OTTO & SONS,

44 to 50 Sherman Ave., Jersey City, N. J.

PATENTED.

April 9, 1889. Nos. 401,187 and 401,188.
Dec. 17, 1889.
May 15, 1894.
June 12, 1894.
Jan. 8, 1895.

### Style O.

rice with one tune ........................................ $11.00
xtra tunes, each ........................................ 0.20

Furnished in Mahogany or Oak Case, highly polished.
44 Teeth in Comb.
Size of Box 12½x7½x6½ inches high.
Each instrument packed in substantial box for shipping.

### Style O, EXTRA.

rice with one tune ........................................ $13.00

The styles shown on this and the next several pages are powered by a vertically mounted spring barrel. An unusual, and probably not very popular, feature of the Capital sales catalogue was that "As tunes are furnished with this Box without charge, they must be accepted as selected by the Manufacturer. No tunes exchanged." (Original catalogue illustrations courtesy of Mrs. Ruth Bornand.)

### Style A.

Price with 8 tunes, Manufacturers' selection .................... $15.00
Extra tunes, each ........................................ 0 20

Furnished in Mahogany or Oak Case, highly polished.
44 Teeth in Comb.
Size of Case 14½x11½x7 inches high.
Each instrument packed in substantial box for shipping.

### Style A, EXTRA.

Price with 8 tunes, Manufacturers' selection .................... $17.50

# THE "CAPITAL" SELF-PLAYING MUSIC BOX

## Style B.

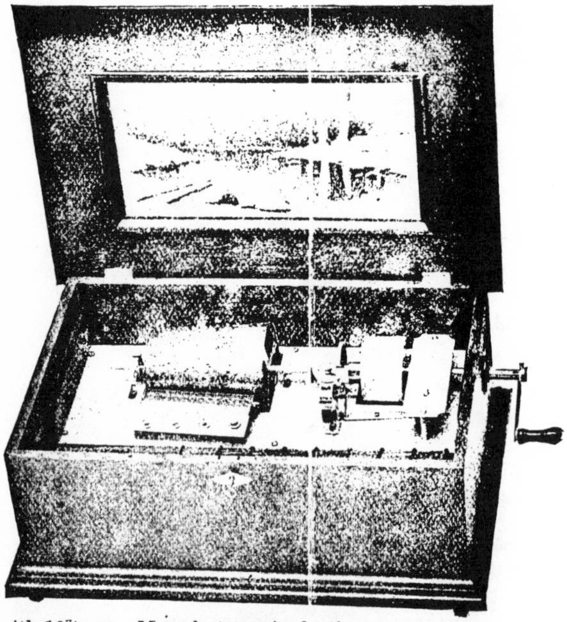

Price with 10 tunes, Manufacturers' selection .................. $28.00
Extra tunes, each .......................... 0.30

Furnished in Mahogany or Oak Case, highly polished.
58 Teeth in Comb.
Size of Case 21x14x8½ inches high.
Each Instrument packed in substantial box ready for shipping.

## Style B, EXTRA.

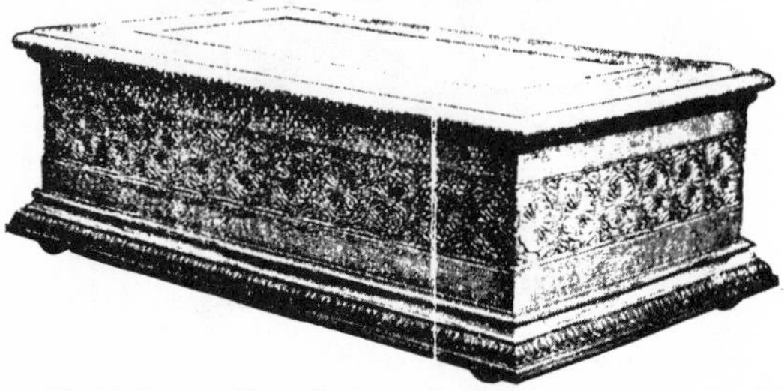

Price with 10 tunes, Manufacturers' selection ........ $32.00

## Capital Zither Attachment.

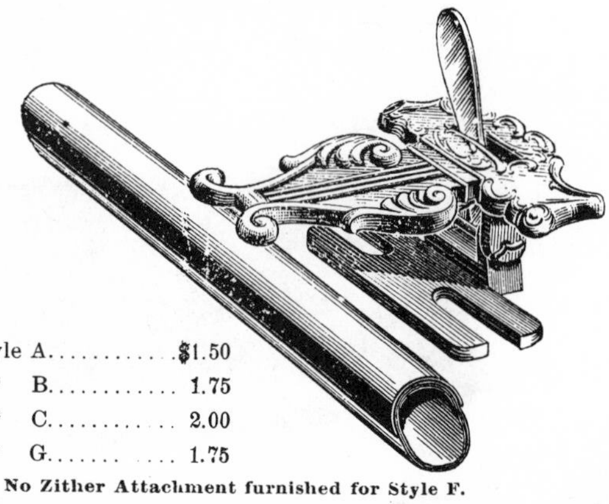

| | | |
|---|---|---|
| Price for Style | A | $1.50 |
| " " | B | 1.75 |
| " " | C | 2.00 |
| " " | G | 1.75 |

**No Zither Attachment furnished for Style F.**

## Style C.

Price with 12 tunes, Manufacturers' selection .................. $40.00
Extra tunes, each .......................... 0.40

Furnished in Mahogany or Oak Case, highly polished.
81 Teeth in Comb.
Size of Case 26½x17x9½ inches high.
Each Instrument packed in substantial Box ready for shipping.

## Style D.

Price .......................................... $49.00
Extra tunes, each .......................... 0.40
When arranged to play 2 tunes for 1 penny .................. 52 00

Furnished in Mahogany or Oak Case, highly polished.
81 Teeth in Comb.
Size of Case 26½x17x9½ inches high.

Style D is the same as style C but has an Automatic Penny Attachment, which is of excellent construction and very reliable.

**As TUNES are furnished with this Box without charge, they must be accepted as selected by the Manufacturer.**

NO TUNES EXCHANGED.

## STYLE C. EXTRA.

Price with 12 tunes, Manufacturers' selection .......................... $45.00

## Style E.

Price ........................................................... $52.00
Extra tunes, each ........................................................... 0.40

Is the same as style C with Nickel Attachment, so arranged that two tunes are played for one nickel.

## Style F. "Duplex."

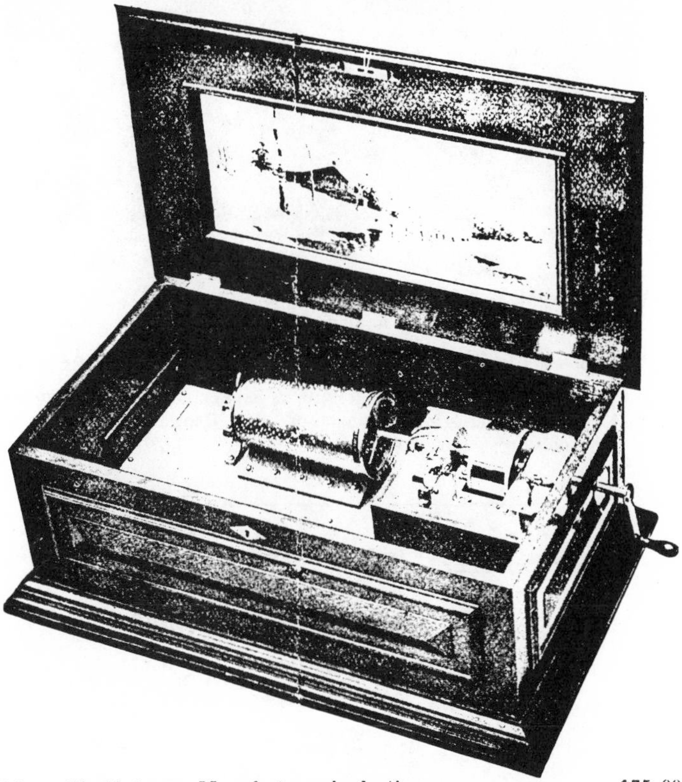

Price with 12 tunes, Manufacturers' selection ........................ $75.00
Extra tunes, each ........................................................... 0.40

Furnished in Mahogany or Oak Case, highly polished.
162 Teeth in Comb.
Size of Case 28x17x12 inches high.

This Instrument is so arranged that two Combs, each with 81 Teeth are operated by one set of Sprocket wheels.

The music this Instrument produces is as rich in tone and volume as that of any box existent.

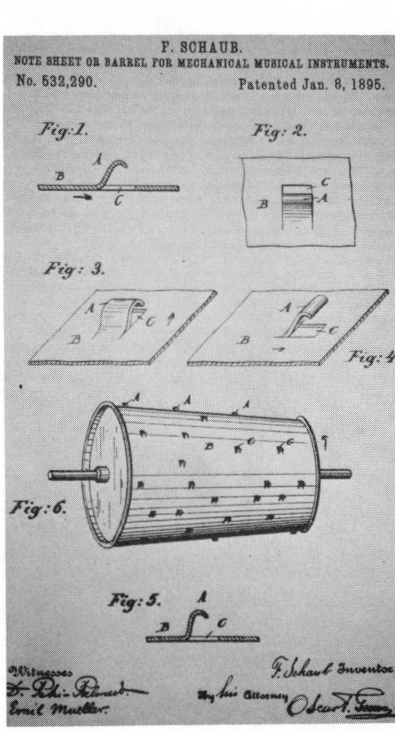


## Style G.

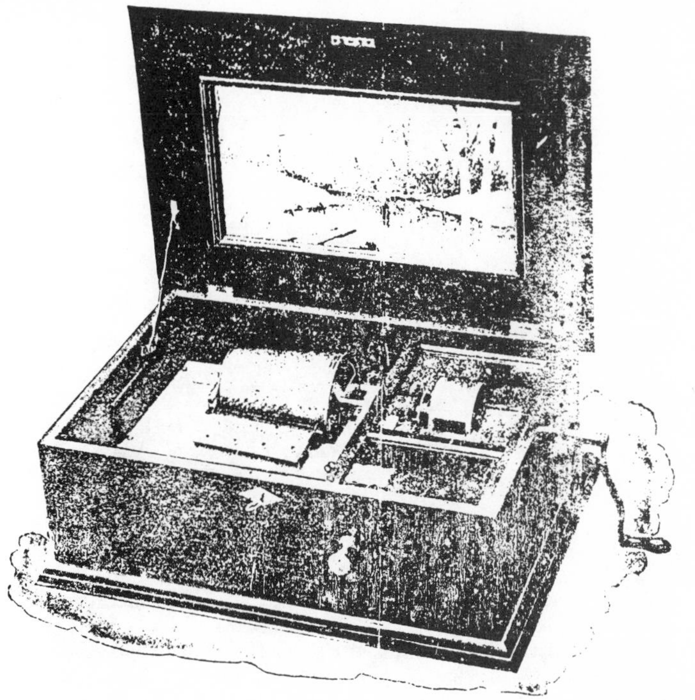

Price with 10 tunes, manufacturers' selection ........................ $37.00
Extra tunes, each ........................................................... 0.30

Furnished in Mahogany or Oak Case, highly polished.
58 Teeth in Comb.
Size of Case 21x14x8½ inches high.

This is the same as style B but has a Penny Attachment and is arranged to play two tunes for one cent. The Attachment is the same as in style D in principle and is very reliable.

## STYLE F. EXTRA.

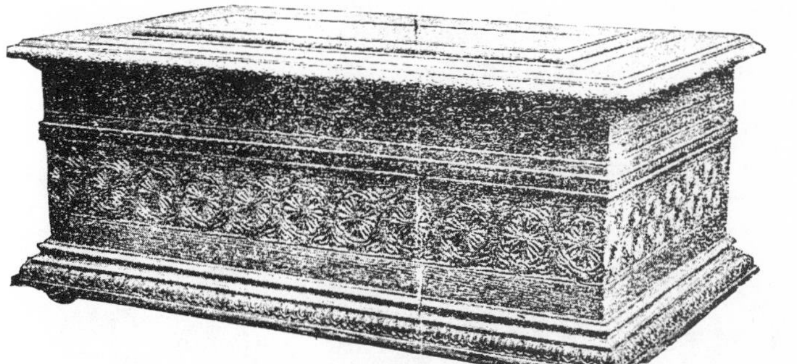

Price with 12 tunes, Manufacturers' selection ........................ $85.00

## STYLE F. SUPERFINE.

Price with 12 tunes, Manufacturer's selection ........................ $100.00

## DIRECTIONS FOR CAPITAL SELF PLAYING MUSIC BOX.

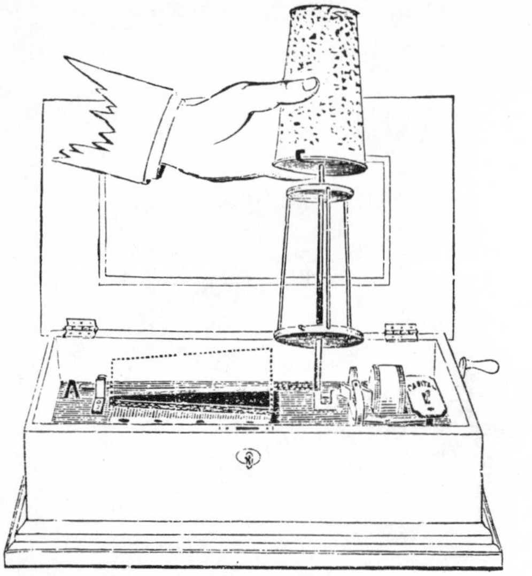


**To Wind,** turn the crank at right hand side of box toward you.

**To Start,** push the lever on the plate at right hand side from you until it cannot be pushed farther.

**To Repeat,** leave the lever in the position of start.

**To Stop,** draw the lever toward you.

**To Change the Tunes,** take the shaft of note holder with two fingers at A (see cut) and raise to an upright position as shown, then turn the note cylinder slightly to the left and raise it from the note holder. Take another cylinder, replace it on the holder so the bayonet lock falls over the pin on the large end of note holder, turn slightly to the right so the pin will be in the slot of the bayonet lock, then lower the note holder to a horizontal position, as shown by dotted line in cut, when it will be ready to play.

If the note Cylinders be placed carefully and ordinary care taken the Music Box will remain in good working order for many years.

**To Oil,** the only part that will ever need oil is the Governor or fly wheel shaft. To oil this use watch makers' oil and apply at the lower end of shaft, at the worm or screw, and at upper end of shaft.

If the Music Box is received in extremely cold weather, allow it to stand in a heated room an hour before playing the same.

**A Capital Cuff Box with a large number of cylinders. The interesting format of the Capital makes it a collectors' favorite today.**

Capital Cylinder Sizes

| Style | Cylinder dimensions (inches) |
|---|---|
| O, A | 4 1/4 x 3 3/8 x 2 1/4 |
| C, D, E, F | 7 3/4 x 4 1/4 x 3 1/4 |
| G, B | 5 1/2 x 4 1/4 x 3 1/2 |

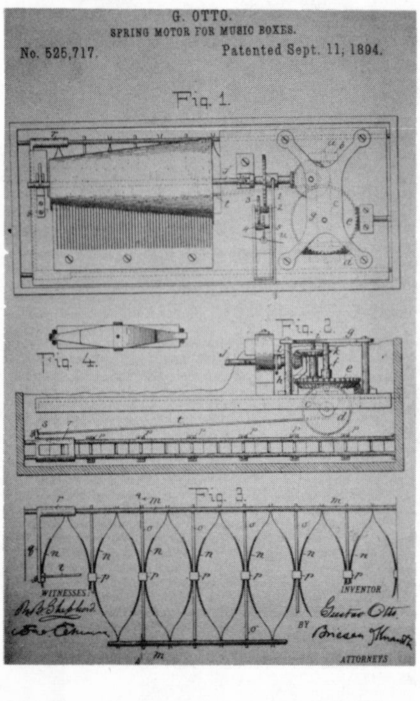


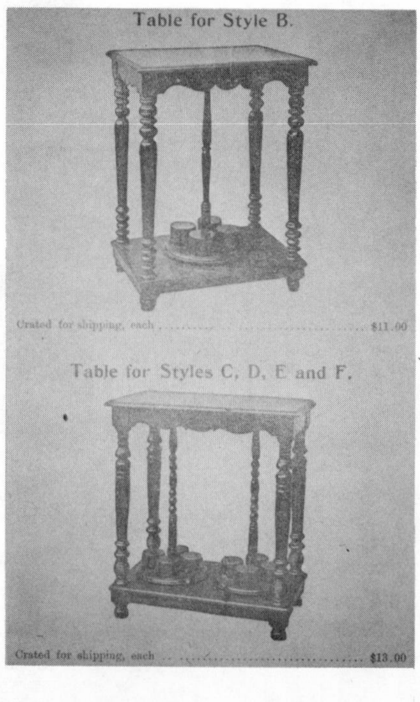

Table for Style B.
Crated for shipping, each .................... $11.00
Table for Styles C, D, E and F.
Crated for shipping, each .................... $13.00


## Style G with Table.

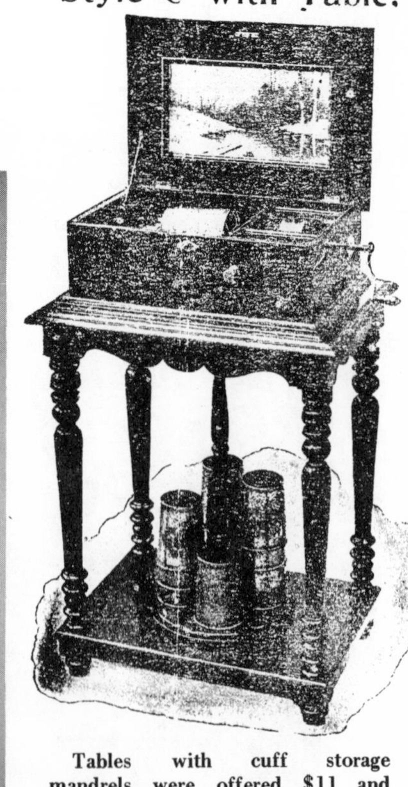

**Tables with cuff storage mandrels were offered $11 and $13 each.**

# THE CAPITAL MUSIC BOX.

## AMERICAN MANUFACTURE.

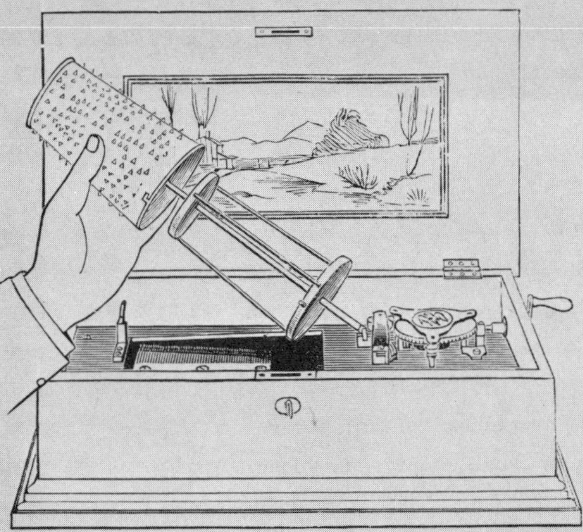

METHOD OF CHANGING TUNE CYLINDER.

STYLES A AND B.

**All Sizes are furnished in American Oak or Mahogany Cases.**

| | | | |
|---|---|---|---|
| Style A. | Size of Case 14½ x 11½ x 7 inches, 44 Notes in Comb, Plays about 18 Tunes to a Winding. . | Each | $ 32 00 |
| | Tune Cylinders for same.................................................. | " | 53 |
| Style B. | Size of Case 21 x 14 x 8½ inches, 58 Notes in Comb, Plays about 20 Tunes to a Winding. . | " | 69 00 |
| | Tune Cylinders for same.................................................. | " | 80 |

STYLE C.

| | | | |
|---|---|---|---|
| Style C. | Size of Case 26½ x 17 x 9½ inches, 81 Notes in Comb, Plays about 25 Tunes to a Winding. . | Each | $ 96 00 |
| | Tune Cylinders for same.................................................. | " | 1 12 |
| Style D. | Same as Style C, with Automatic Penny Drop Attachment.................... | " | 118 00 |
| | Tune Cylinders for same.................................................. | " | 1 12 |

NOTE.—PRINTED LIST OF AIRS FURNISHED ON APPLICATION.

**Capital Cuff Boxes from an 1895 catalogue of the Gordon Music Co. of New York City. Note that these particular models have a large horizontal spring winding gear at the right.**

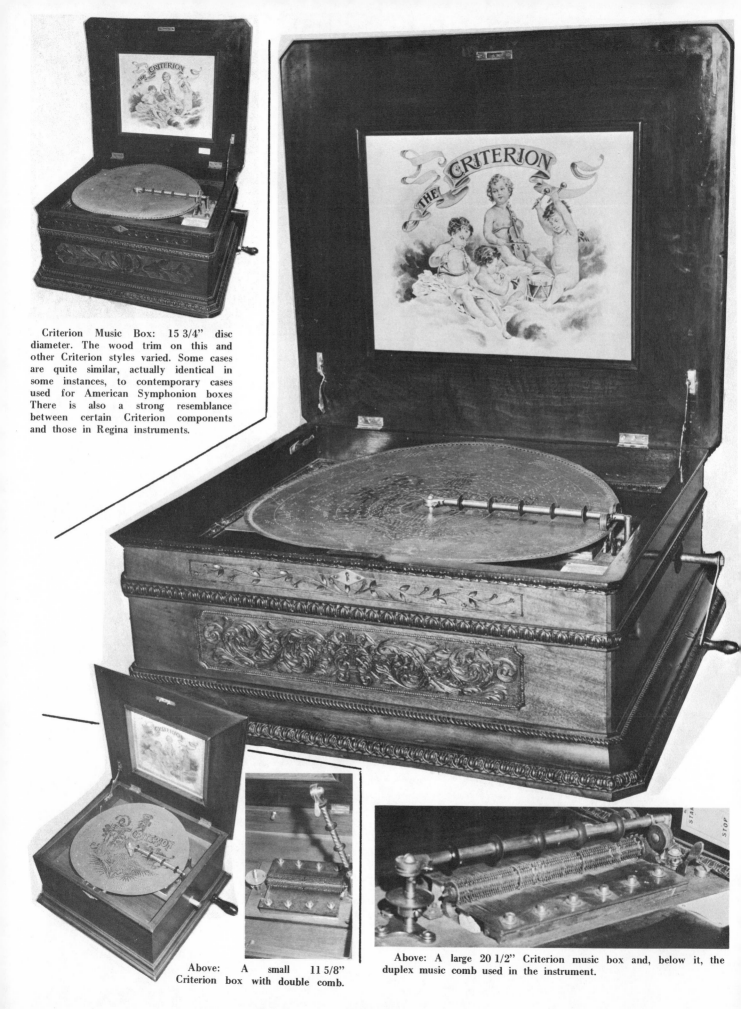

Criterion Music Box: 15 3/4" disc diameter. The wood trim on this and other Criterion styles varied. Some cases are quite similar, actually identical in some instances, to contemporary cases used for American Symphonion boxes There is also a strong resemblance between certain Criterion components and those in Regina instruments.

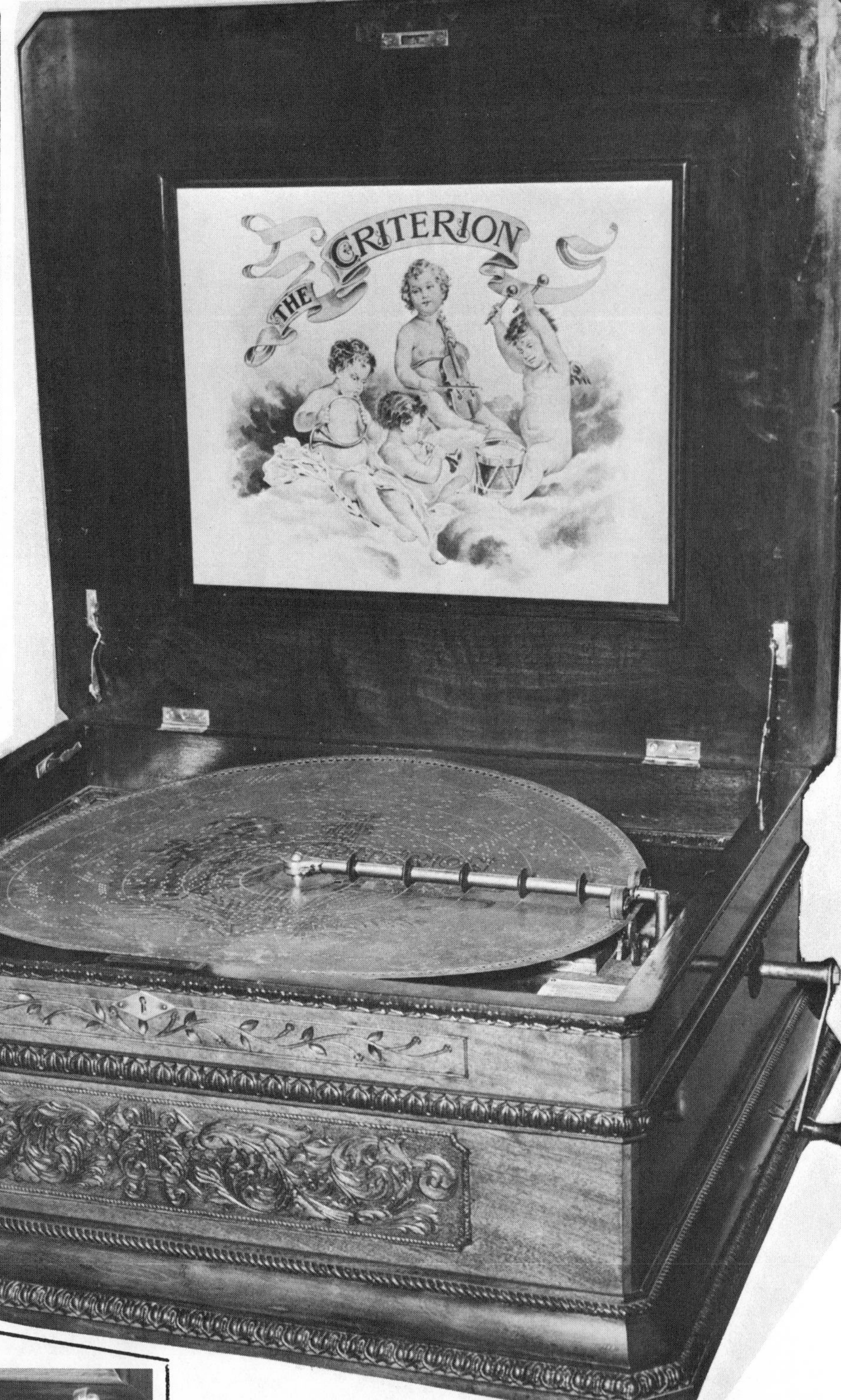

Above: A small 11 5/8" Criterion box with double comb.

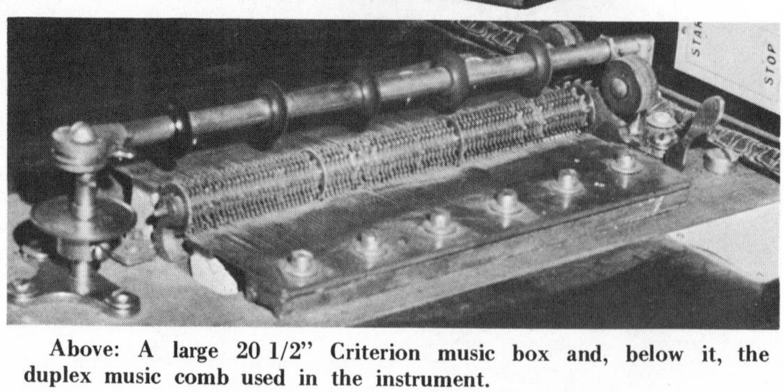

Above: A large 20 1/2" Criterion music box and, below it, the duplex music comb used in the instrument.

PLAYS OVER A THOUSAND TUNES
THE
OLYMPIA
SELF-PLAYING MUSIC BOX
The Olympia Self-Playing Music Box is the latest and most improved of all the Music Boxes with interchangeable Tune-Disks.
The Piano Cannot Produce the richness attained by the Olympia unless played by six or eight hands, and then the players must be experts—for Olympia disks are as much superior to all others in their correct and expressive rendering as the Olympia Music Box itself is superior to every other make in tone and simplicity of construction.
This Wonderful Richness of Tone you'll realize at once ; the durability you'll appreciate years from now, after inferior makes would have been worn out and useless. It doesn't have to be coaxed to play; any child can give the winding-crank a few turns—enough for a dozen tunes—30 minutes without re-winding. Disks are easily changed—they're practically indestructible.
Over 500 Tunes are ready now, and the latest music is constantly being added.
Charming Home Entertainments may be arranged without notice if an Olympia is in the parlor—Dancing, singing, instrumental renderings—Hymns and Church Music, too.
$6.00 and Upward.
Send for handsome illustrated Catalogue of Music Boxes at all prices and list of tunes.
Insist on an Olympia, there is none as good.
Sent on Trial On receipt of price, we will send the Olympia on ten days' trial. If you are not entirely satisfied, then you can return it and we will refund the money.
AGENTS WANTED.
Write to
OLYMPIA MUSIC BOX CO., 48-50 W. 4th St., New York, N.Y.
Or inquire of Dealers in Musical Instruments and Jewelers.

Above: Advertisement in Harper's Weekly, September 30, 1899, for the Olympia Music Box (originally used in an article, "Remember the Olympia," by Jesse Lippincott, Jr., in the Musical Box Society "Bulletin," Vol. XIII, No.6). Note that a headline in the advertisement says that the Olympia "plays over a thousand tunes," while the text of the advertisement notes that "Over 500 tunes are ready now." During the same era Sears & Roebuck offered 8 3/4-, 11 5/8-, and 15 3/4-inch disc models for sale.

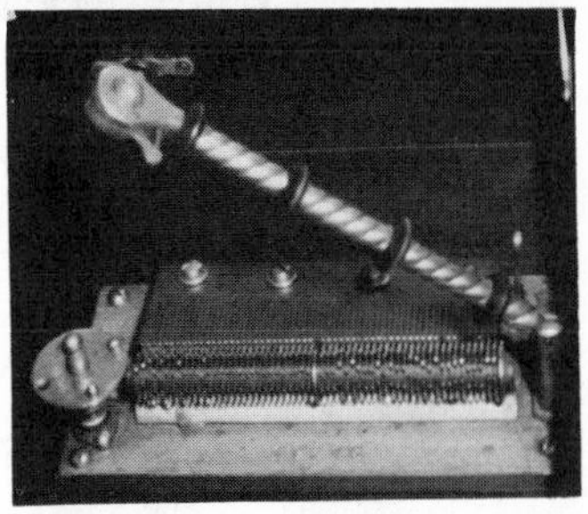

Olympia 11 5/8" disc movement (compatible with the same size of Criterion disc).

Olympia box on carved stand. (J.B. Nethercutt collection)

Olympia music box (lid not shown) with disc in the playing position.

THE OLYMPIA SELF-PLAYING MUSIC BOX
is the latest and most improved of all the Music Boxes with Interchangeable Tune-Disks.
Send for Handsome Illustrated Catalogue of Music Boxes at all prices, and list of tunes.
OVER 500 TUNES are ready, and the latest music is constantly being added.
Insist on an OLYMPIA There is no "Just as Good."
THE PIANO CANNOT PRODUCE the richness attained by the Olympia unless played by six or eight hands, and then the players must be experts. It is superior to every other make in tone and simplicity of construction. The durability you'll appreciate years from now, after inferior makes would have been worn out and useless. Disks are easily changed — they're practically indestructible.
CHARMING HOME ENTERTAINMENTS may be arranged without notice if an Olympia is in the parlor—Dancing, singing, instrumental renderings; Hymns and Church Music, too.
THIS ILLUSTRATION shows Style IV—polished mahogany or oak case—22x20x10 in. high. Price, including One Tune-Disk, $45.00. Extra Tunes, 60 Cents each. Sent on receipt of price.
SENT ON TRIAL. On receipt of $48.60 ($3.60 being for six extra tune-disks) we will send the Olympia on 10 days' trial. You can return it, and get your money back, if not entirely satisfied. Write to us.
F. G. OTTO & SONS, 41 Sherman Ave., JERSEY CITY, N. J.
Or from Dealers in Musical Instruments and Jewelers.

Right: Advertisement in The Youth's Companion, January 12, 1899, for the Olympia Music Box (originally used in the aforementioned Hughes Ryder article in the Musical Box Society "Bulletin"). The lid illustration is the same as that used on certain Capital Cuff Box models.

## POLYPHON MUSIC BOXES
### —And related instruments—
### (Polyphon Musikwerke; Leipzig, Germany)

The Polyphon Musikwerke (Music Works) was founded shortly before 1890 by Gustave Brachhausen and Paul Riessner, both of whom were formerly with the maker of Symphonion music boxes (Paul Lochmann).

The firm produced the "Polyphon" line of disc music boxes. By 1895 several dozen different models were being produced, ranging from small hand-held models to tall upright instruments which were eight feet or more high. Within the next few years Polyphon became the world's largest manufacturer of music boxes. At one time over 1,000 persons were employed at the factory in Wahren, a suburb of Leipzig, Germany.

The height of the Polyphon music box business was in the 1895-1905 era. During the 1900-1910 decade Polyphon diversified into several other fields, including phonographs, roll-operated mechanical (non-pneumatic) pianos, and a series of pneumatic pianos and orchestrions (some of which were designated as Polyphonas). The latest-dated Polyphon catalogue seen by the author was distributed in 1914. By that year the firm had discontinued its Polyphon Orchestrion series and had consolidated its listings to the Concerto I and II, the Polyphon 200, and about two dozen different types of disc music boxes, mostly of the table model format. For all practical purposes, the Polyphon music box business ended about 1914, although small numbers of music boxes were sold until at least 1920. During the 1920's and 1930's the firm, with its corporate structure revised, sold a wide variety of phonographs (including Brunwick instruments) as well as various items outside of the musical field.

### Polyphon Disc Boxes

Polyphon disc music boxes were made in a wide variety of types. The smallest used a 16.5 cm. (6½") diameter disc and was operated by turning a handle continuously. The largest popular style made in quantity was the 62.5 cm. (24½") disc type. Between these limits were dozens of different case styles and variations made in nearly a dozen different disc sizes. Some models were equipped with bells.

With a few exceptions, the table model styles were intended for home use. Many of these were produced in cases with ornately inlaid lids and with carvings or gilt engraved designs on the sides. The lid undersides of early table models were illustrated with sepia-toned engravings of fine quality. Later styles had multicolored lithographs, many of which depicted various landscape and city scenes.

Most Polyphon disc boxes were powered by flat coil springs. In the late 1890's a new spiral spring was introduced. While this never entirely supplanted the coil spring, the spiral spring did find use on many different models — including many of the larger coin-operated models.

Several different folding-top styles, Nos. 49C and 52 being examples, were produced for home use. These permitted large discs to be played on a small instrument as the lid of the case folded outward to provide support for the tune disc. The paucity of existing specimens today indicates that few of these folding-top models were originally made.

Many different upright Polyphon styles were made. Most of these were of 39.8 cm. (15¾") disc size or larger and were equipped with slots for coin operation. In the original Polyphon catalogues these were known as "Automata" as they operated automatically when a coin was inserted. The American term "automat" (coin-operated food dispenser) has a similar derivation. Some of these coin-operated models dispensed premiums in addition to playing a tune. Those that did so were designated with a "P" after the model number, as "Style No. 106P." The premiums or prizes vended included chocolate bars, gum, cigarettes, and brass tokens (which could be redeemed by the business establishment owner).

Other nomenclature: Certain models were equipped with bells. Bells were made in two forms: bar-type flat bells known as "Klangplatten" or orchestra bells. Instruments so equipped were designated with a "K" after the model number. These were very popular. The other form was the saucer-type of bell. Instruments with these bells, known as "Glocken," had a "G" after the model number. Complicating things is the fact that Polyphon was not consistent in using its own designations and sometimes the "G" or "K" was omitted. Thus, Style No. 6 always came equipped with bells of one type or another. Some catalogues list this model simply as "No.6" without reference to the bells, and others list it as "No.6K" or "No.6G," depending upon the type of bells. Polyphons equipped with a clock ("Uhr" in German) were designated with a "U" after the model number. Certain Polyphons could be ordered with a phonograph disc and outside brass horn attachment. This was the "Polygraphon" attachment and was designated by a "PG" after the model number — as in "No.43PG." Coin-operated models (Automata) of the Polygraphon were designated as "PGA" styles — as in "No.43PGA." Other nomenclature used sporadically by Polyphon included a suffix "S" (for ''schwarz" which means "black" in German) for certain models with an ebony finish — such as "No.45S." The same "S" suffix was also used for smaller models to indicate self-playing ("Selbstspielend" = self-playing or spring-wound) instruments, as opposed to hand-cranked ones. Thus "No.28SG" referred to a No.28 box which was self-playing (hence "S") and had bells ("G" for "Glocken."). Confusing, isn't it? The suffix "N" was sometimes used to designate a single comb model; "D," a duplex

or double comb — as in Nos. 42D and 42N. In other instances (rare) "N" was used to designate a box equipped with a spiral spring motor — such is in the disc changing model "No.1N." Other designations used from time to time were "M" (for Majolica door — on large upright models), "C" (for Chocolate vending), and capital and lower-case A, B, and C letters to note case style variations.

Automatic disc changers: The automatic disc changing apparatus was patented by Brachhausen in 1897. Soon thereafter Polyphon and Regina commenced production of several different styles incorporating this device. Polyphon disc changers were made in various disc sizes from 39.8 cm (15¾") to 62.5 cm. (24½"). With the exception of No.1N (24½" changer which uses 12 discs) all have a 10-disc capacity. Selections are made by sliding an indicator to the left or right until it points to the desired tune card. A coin in the slot will then cause the wanted melody to play. Unlike the Regina changers, most models of Polyphon changers do not advance automatically to the next tune in sequence. Subsequent coins deposited in the Polyphon will result in the same tune being played over again, unless the indicator is moved.

### Polyphon Clocks

Many different types of Polyphon musical clocks were made. With a few exceptions, these were produced by purchasing cases from a clock manufacturer (usually Lenzkirch) and installing Polyphon mechanisms in them. As Symphonion also ordered clock cases from Lenzkirch, some Polyphon and Symphonion musical clocks resemble each other quite closely in case styling. Polyphon clocks ranged in size from those using 28.1 cm. (11¼") disc to a monster clock described as follows by John E.T. Clark in his book, "Musical Boxes": "The second of these giant Polyphon clocks was even larger — and had open carving on the panel. The 8-day clock had a quarter-hour repetition and would play one tune on the hour, or the music could be started at will. This clock contained a Polyphon movement playing 24½" discs. Size of the case: 125 inches high by 45 inches wide by 25 inches deep. . ." For use in hotels and similar public places many of the Polyphon clocks were equipped with coin slots. Thus music could be heard at any time (in addition to the hourly concert which was automatic and free!) by dropping a coin in the aperture.

### Polyphon Orchestrions

During the first years of the 20th century several different varieties of Polyphon Orchestrions were produced. These use thick paper rolls and are mostly of three-tune length. Certain of these were sold in the United States under the Regina Sublima name. Instrumentation varied from a piano to a piano with the accompaniment of drum and trap effects. An unusual model, Polyphon Orchestrion No. 10, used an endless roll to play mandolin arrangements on a piano with three strings and three hammers for each playing note. Polyphon Orchestrions were available with either weight-driven or electric motor mechanisms. Although a wide variety of Polyphon Orchestrions was listed in contemporary catalogues and although one 1906 brochure noted that 600 specimens of the Polyphon Rossini (No.II Orchestrion) were sold, the instruments are of exceeding rarity today. By 1920 such instruments were severely obsolete for use in public places — and most were discarded.

A series of Walzen Orchestrions was produced in the late 1890's and early 1900's. These used cabinets similar to the roll-operated Polyphon Orchestrion series and had the music arranged on pinned wooden barrels, usually of eight tunes per barrel.

### Polyphon Pneumatic Pianos

Polyphon advertisements in German music trade papers of the 1908 - 1912 era indicate that the Polyphona series of pneumatic coin pianos was "pushed" heavily. These use thin paper rolls (as opposed to the very heavy almost cardboardlike rolls of the Polyphon Orchestrion series) similar in concept to those used on pneumatic pianos of Hupfeld, Philipps, and other contemporary manufacturers. In the collectors' field today little is known of the Polyphona coin pianos. Evidently they were produced only in limited quantities.

### Additional Comments

The "Big Three" in the world of disc music boxes were Polyphon, Regina, and Symphonion — probably in that order so far as quantities of instruments produced. In the early 1890's Polyphon provided the financial backing and the expertise which led to the founding of the Regina Music Box Company in New Jersey. Gustave Brachhausen came to America and personally founded the Regina firm. This accounts for many similarities between the products of the Regina and Polyphon firms. The first Regina products sold in America were music boxes imported from Polyphon and simply affixed with "Regina" labels. Such imported early instruments included a large number of 15½" Regina table model music boxes and a number of upright 15½" models in stylish cabinets. Later, Regina imported the Polyphon Concerto and some of the Polyphon Orchestrion instruments (these latter pieces were sold as the Regina Sublima — although, still later, the Sublima cases were made in the U.S.A. and just the interior parts imported). Regina and Polyphon discs are interchangeable in the 11", 15½", and 32" (Concerto) sizes.

As noted in the following information, the disc sizes given by Polyphon are just approximate and show variations even from one Polyphon catalogue to another! The same informality is still used today by collectors who are accustomed, for instance, to referring to the "27-inch Regina" discs when the actual size of the disc is a fraction less. The English translation sections of the Polyphon catalogues in the possession of the author refer to the 50 cm. disc as being of "20-inch" diameter. Actually, 50 cm. equals 19.68 inches, which is close to the standard terminology of 19 5/8" used by most collectors and dealers today. So, when actually measuring discs it is important to remember that Polyphon and other makers usually just approximated their measurements, and if you find one that differs just slightly from the published figure you haven't discovered a new disc size!

A zither was available at extra cost on most Polyphon models. This was a simple brass frame which pressed a tube of tissue paper against the comb in order to produce a harp-like sound.

Two well-known names in the musical field, Nicole Frères (their London branch) and Popper & Co. of Leipzig, were among the many distributors of Polyphon products. The Nicole Frères name in particular is often found on Polyphon boxes, especially those originally sold in England, and sometimes causes confusion among the uninitiated.

Music boxes marked "Euphonion" and some Troubadour boxes are sometimes found with cases and/or mechanisms identical to certain Polyphon styles. It is likely that Euphonion boxes, at least in certain sizes, were actually manufactured by Polyphon.

Taking Polyphon and Regina together, these firms probably accounted for 60% or more of all of the disc type music boxes ever manufactured. It is fortunate that the products of both firms were well-constructed, of attractive appearance, and generally of musical excellence. They are favorites with collectors today.

----------

### POLYPHON DISC SIZES

A late (1914) Polyphon catalogue lists the following different disc sizes in use at that time and the style numbers of the instruments on which the discs were used.

16.5 cm. Style Nos. 28, 28S, 35, 36.

20.7 cm. Style Nos. 29, 70G.

20.7 cm. Style Nos. 40, 41, 41R, 41CG, 71, 2041.

24.6 cm. Style Nos. 71G, 41G, 2041G.

24.3 cm. Style Nos. 46, 72, 2046, 46CG.

28.1 cm. Style Nos. 42, 42R, 42N, 42D, 57, 73, 100, 2042, 2042D.

36 cm. Style Nos. 42CG, 48, 73G.

39.8 cm. Style Nos. 43, 43B, 44, 44D, 2043, 2043D, 45, 45S, 50, 51, 62, 65, 103.

45 cm. Style No. 43BG.

50 cm. Style Nos. 47C, 104, 118, 4.

56 cm. Style Nos. 2, 3, 5, 6, 49.

62.5 cm. Style Nos. 52, 54, 105, 1N.

63 cm. Style Nos. 200, 200S.

71 cm. Style No. Polyphon Concerto II.

80 cm. Style No. Polyphon Concerto I.

Approximate English measurement equivalents (values as given in the English Polyphon catalogue):

16.5 cm. = 6½"
20.7 cm. = 8" to 8¼"
24.3 cm. = 9½"
24.6 cm. = 9¾"
28.1 cm. = 11¼"
36 cm. = 14½"
39.8 cm. = 15¾"
45 cm. = 17½"
50 cm. = 19 5/8"
56 cm. = 22½"
62.5 cm. = 24½"
63 cm. = 25¼"
71 cm. = 28"
80 cm. = 32"

Notes: 28.1 cm. (or 11¼" per the Polyphon conversion chart) is interchangeable with what is referred to as the 11-inch Regina; 39.8 cm. (or 15¾") Polyphon is interchangeable with 15½" Regina; 80 cm. (or 32") Polyphon is interchangeable with 32" Regina Concerto.

The commonly-used Polyphon discs (the most popular sizes) were those of 11¼", 15¾" (THE most popular), 19 5/8" (often referred to as 20" also), and 24½" diameters.

# Polyphon (15.5 cm. or 6 1/2" discs)

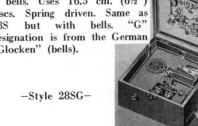

–Style 30 "Manivelle"–

30 teeth in music comb. Uses 16.5 cm. (6½") discs. Hand-cranked model in a metal case measuring 7" in diameter and 1½" thick. Made as a child's toy, few of these have survived – attesting to their one-time popularity with the younger set!

–Style 28–

Hand-cranked (without spring; must be steadily cranked) model. 30 teeth in comb. 16.5 cm. or 6½" discs.

–Style No.28S–

30 teeth. Uses 16.5 cm (6½") discs. Same as No.28 but with spring. "S" designation is from the German "selbstspielend" or "self-playing."

30 teeth in music comb plus 4 bells. Uses 16.5 cm. (6½") discs. Spring driven. Same as 28S but with bells. "G" designation is from the German "Glocken" (bells).

–Style 28SG–

–Style No.36–

30 teeth in music comb. Uses 16.5 cm. (6½") discs. In polished walnut case. Spring-wound. Underside of lid decorated with colorful lithograph. Case measurements: 7¼" by 7¼" by 4" deep.

No. 36.

–Style No. 35–

30 teeth in music comb. Uses 16.5 cm. (6½") discs. In black painted case with celluloid cover. Spring-wound. (From 1895 Polyphon catalogue)

(20.7 cm. or 8" discs)

–Style No.40–

41 teeth in music comb. Uses 20.7 cm. (8" to 8¼") discs. Hand-cranked model or "Manivelle." Walnut case with decal or transfer design on lid. Intended for use as a child's toy. 10¼" wide by 9" deep by 6¼" high (lid closed). (Circa 1895 description)

–Style No.40–
(1914)

Hand-cranked model (no spring). 41 teeth in comb. 20.7 cm. or 8" discs.

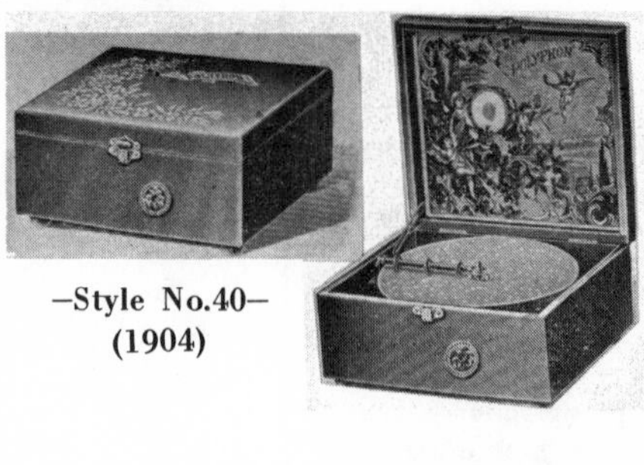


–Style No.40–
(1904)

(20.7 cm. or 8" discs)

–Style No.29–
(1914)

30 teeth in music comb plus 4 saucer bells (cup shaped). Spring wound via front lever. 20.7 cm. or 8" discs.

–Style No.41CG–

41 teeth in music comb plu 4 bells. Uses 20.7 cm. (8" to 8¼") discs.

Made in 30- and 41-not models; both use the same dis size.

–Style No.41C–

–Style No.41C–
(1904)

41 teeth in comb. Uses 20.7 cm. (8¼") discs. Spring wound.

(20.7 cm. or 8" discs)

–Style 41R–
20.7 cm. (8" to 8¼") discs. 41 teeth in comb. Serpentine case. Usually seen in walnut. Colorful lithograph on underside of lid.

–Style No.41–

–Style No.2041–
(1914)
41 teeth in comb. Winding lever in front. Uses 20.7 cm. or 8¼" discs.

The Gloriosa Christmas tree stand (see Kalliope section of this book) was available also with a 41-note Polyphon movement. This style was sold as Gloriosa No.N.

POLYPHON

(24.3 cm. or 9½" discs)

–Style No.2046–
(1914)
46 teeth in comb. Uses 24.3 cm. (9½") discs. In same case as used for 2041G.

–Style No.46CG–
46 teeth in music comb plus 6 bells. Uses 24.3 cm. (9½") discs.

–Style No.46C–
(1904)
46 teeth in music comb. Uses 24.3 cm. (or 24.5 as sometimes catalogued by Polyphon) discs (9½").

–Style No.46–
(1914)
46 teeth in comb. Uses 24.3 cm. or 9½" discs.

(24.6 cm. or 9¾" discs)

–Style No.41G–
(1914)
41 teeth in comb; 6 saucer bells. Bells may be shut off if desired. 24.6 cm. or 9¾" discs.

–Style No. 2041G–
(1914)
41 teeth in comb; 6 bells. Uses 24.6 cm. (9¾") discs. Same case as used for No.2046 also.

**POLYPHON**

(28.1 cm. or 11¼" discs)

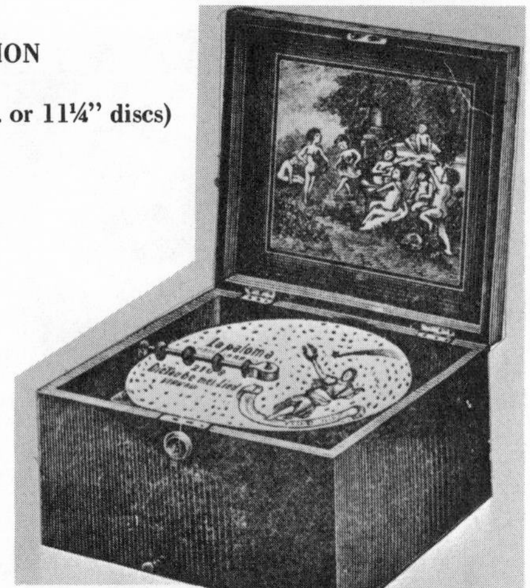

–Style No.42–

54 teeth in music comb. Uses 28.1 cm. (11¼") discs. Spring wound model. In walnut case. 13½" wide by 12" deep by 8" high (lid closed). Also Style No. 42a (same as Style 42, but in rosewood case instead of walnut). As described in the 1895 Polyphon catalogue.

–Style No. 46G–
(1914)

46 teeth; 8 saucer bells. Uses 28.1 cm. (11¼" discs). As with other Polyphon bell models the bells may be disconnected at will. The underlid lithographs are subject to wide variation on this and other late Polyphon models.

–Style 42 PG–
–Style 42 PGA–

Note: Styles with coin slots were known as PGA models. Thus a Style No. 42PG with coin slot would be designated as a 42PGA – the "A" being for "Automaton." The 1904 Polyphon catalogue listed Styles 42PG, 42PGA, 43 PG, 43PGA, 45 PG, 45PGA, 105PG, 105PGA, Polygraphon Concerto and Polygraphon Concerto Automaton. Undoubtedly many more models were made.

–Style No.42N–
(1914)

54 teeth in comb. Uses 28.1 cm. (11¼") discs. Usually seen in walnut cabinet with light inlay on the top lid. One of the most popular Polyphon styles, 42N (also known over the years by other numbers) was sold by the thousands.

–Style No.42C–
(1904)

54 teeth in music comb. Uses 28.1 cm (11¼") discs.

–Style No.42D–
(1914)

108 teeth in comb. Uses 28.1 cm. (11¼") discs. Duplex comb version of No.42N. "Two combs, therefore very powerful tone" noted the catalogue.

–Polyphon Chocolate Vendors–

An external attachment suitable for affixing to the left side of a music cabinet was sold for Polyphon and Symphonion boxes. This was suitable for Polyphon No.65. With the chocolate vendor, Style No.65 was known as No.65J; Style No.65a was known as No.65K. (See Symphonion section of this book for similar apparatus.)

–Style 42R–

28.1 cm. (11¼") discs. 56 teeth in comb. Serpentine case, usually in walnut, with banded veneer around lid.

–Style No.2042)–
(1914)

54 teeth in comb. Uses 28.1 cm. (11¼") discs. "Cabinet of satinwood, polished, and with real inlay, measures 15½" x 13¾" x 9½" (lid closed)."

–Style No.2042D–
(1914)

108 teeth in music comb. Uses 28.1 cm. (11¼") discs. Duplex comb version of No.2042. Actually, most 11¼" Polyphons were of the single comb variety; duplex models are scarce.

–Style No.59C–

54 teeth in music comb. Uses 28.1 cm. (11¼") discs. "Vends a roll of the best chocolate with each tune. In light oak cabinet. Inscription on the door can be furnished in English or in any other language desired." 34" high by 21" wide by 10" deep.

It appears that the model illustrated has two separate coin slots, one of which causes chocolates to be vended; the other, cigarettes.

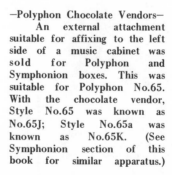

–Style 100 "Savoyard"–
108 teeth in music comb. Uses 28.1 cm. (11¼") discs. Note: Style 100 was also made with 39.8 cm. disc movement. Coin operated. "Figure of terra cotta in seven fast colors with moving arm turning handle while tune plays. Walnut case. Imitation flutes in front." Size, including figure: 63" high by 28" wide by 22" deep. This is the earlier style with smaller music box. See also later style, also known as No.100 "Savoyard."

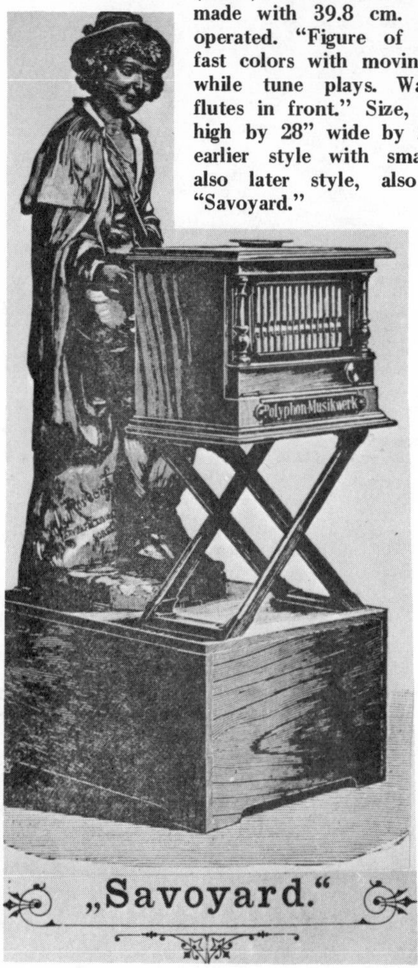

–Style No.57–
54 teeth in music comb. Uses 28.1 cm. (11¼") discs. Duplex comb model. In walnut case with lettering on glass for advertising purposes. 66" high by 21" wide by 13" deep.

Style 57M – The same as the preceding, except with colored majolica door.

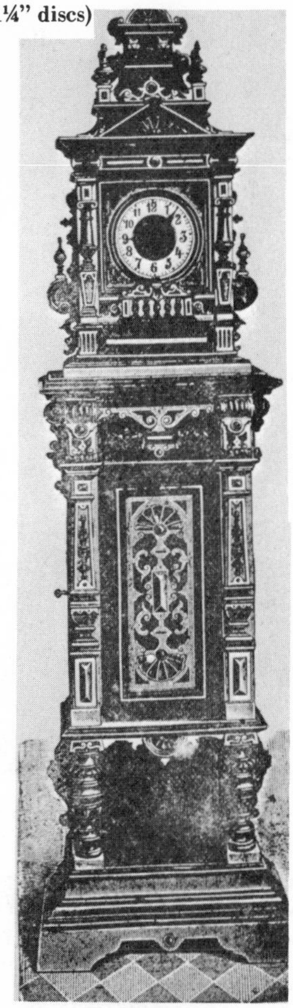

–Style No.63–
54 teeth in music comb. Uses 28.1 cm. (11¼") discs. "Highly polished and carved walnut (usually) or oak case. 13-day pendulum clock, striking on gong. Polyphon will play on the hour, or may be silenced if desired." "Grandmother's clock" size – 80" high by 21" wide by 13" deep. (Compare to Symphonion Style No. 25St. – a somewhat similar clock in a Lenzkirch case.) A petite and very beautiful instrument.

–Style No.64–
54 teeth in music comb. Uses 28.1 cm. (11¼") discs. Sometimes seen also with double comb mechanism (108 teeth), as is No.63. Walnut case with glass door. "14-day pendulum clock, striking on gong." The Polyphon plays hourly, or it may be silenced. 92" high by 24" wide by 15" deep. Sometimes also seen in oak wood.

Spiral spring as used in certain later Polyphons, mainly those of the 20th century.

Changing the disc on a 24½" upright Polyphon, Style 54. Changing the disc can be done in a few seconds' time. Care must be taken not to close the door while the idler arm (the arm that holds the disc against the star wheels) is in the down position or glass breakage will result! Also, care must be taken to place the disc in position carefully to avoid damage to the disc projections, the star wheels, or the music comb teeth.

(36 cm. or 14½" discs)

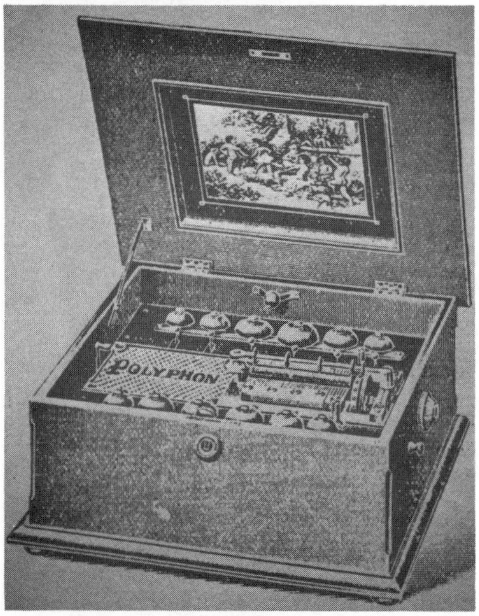

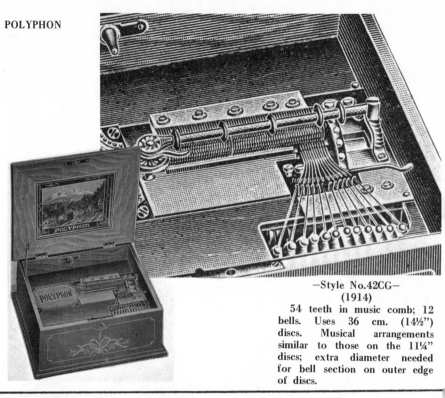

–Style 48–
36 cm. (14½") discs. 112 notes; 12 saucer bells. In walnut case with inlaid lid.

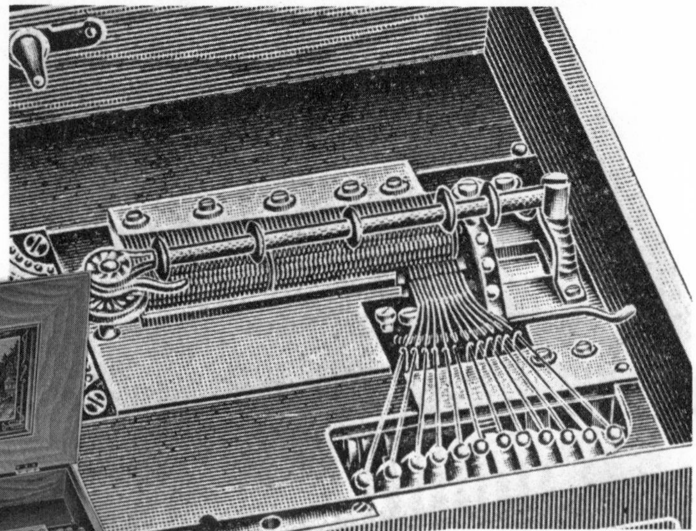

–Style No.42CG–
(1914)
54 teeth in music comb; 12 bells. Uses 36 cm. (14½") discs. Musical arrangements similar to those on the 11¼" discs; extra diameter needed for bell section on outer edge of discs.

(39.8 cm. or 15½" discs)

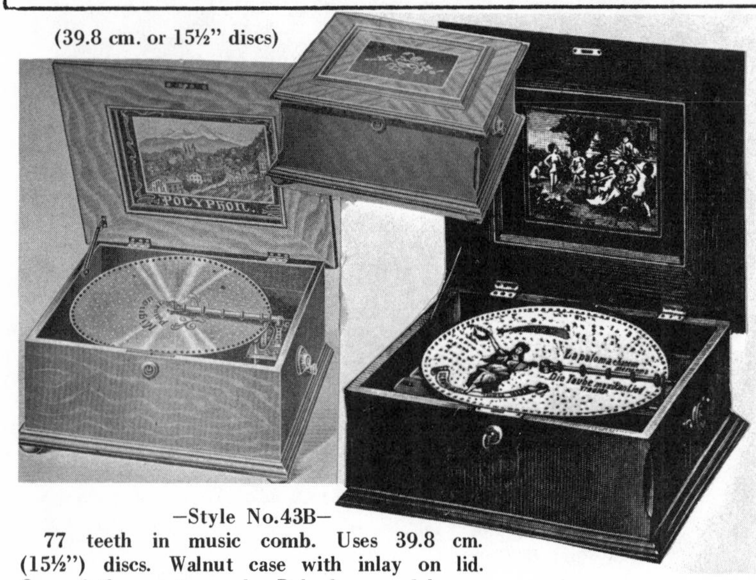


–Style No.43B–
77 teeth in music comb. Uses 39.8 cm. (15½") discs. Walnut case with inlay on lid. One of the most popular Polyphon models.

–Style No.43D–
154 teeth in music comb. Uses 39.8 cm. (15½") discs. Duplex comb model.

–Style No.43N–
View showing spiral spring mechanism as available on 43B and 43D (same as 43N but with duplex combs).

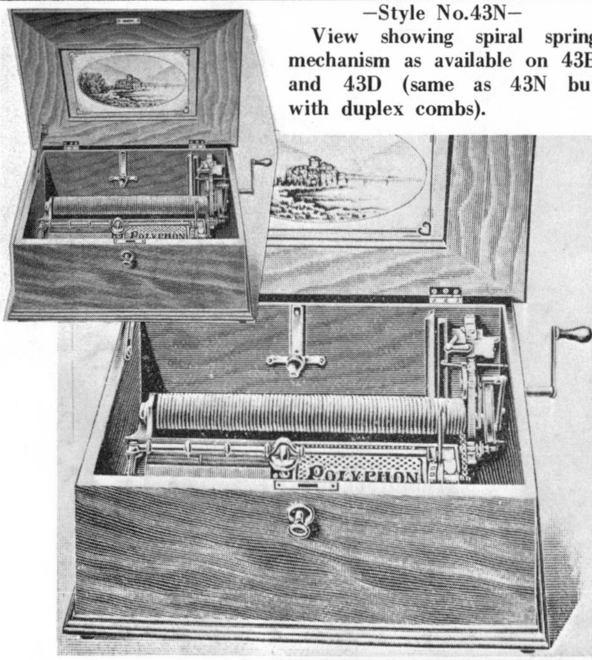

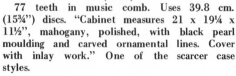

–Style 2043–
(1914)
77 teeth in music comb. Uses 39.8 cm. (15¾") discs. "Cabinet measures 21 x 19¼ x 11½", mahogany, polished, with black pearl moulding and carved ornamental lines. Cover with inlay work." One of the scarcer case styles.

–Style No.2043D–
(1914)
154 teeth in music comb. Uses 39.8 cm. (15¾") discs. Duplex comb model. Scarce case style; only a few were made with decoration as shown.

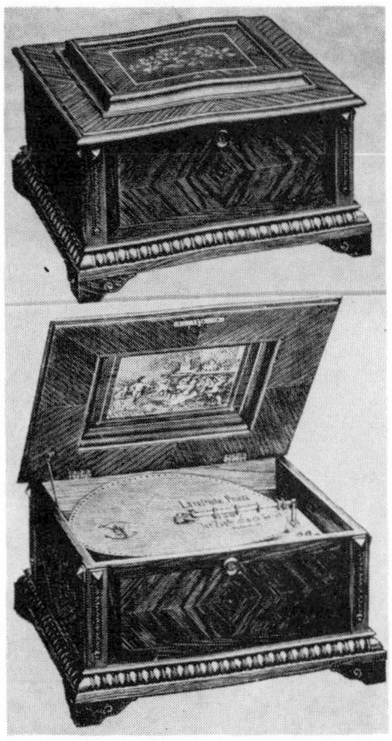

–Style 44D–
(1914)

154 teeth in music comb. Uses 39.8 cm. (15¾" discs). Duplex comb model. One of the more popular case styles. Polished walnut with inlay on lid.

–Style No.45–

154 teeth in music comb. Uses 39.8 cm. (15¾") discs. Duplex comb. Sometimes called the "Sublime Harmonie Piccolo" style in Polyphon literature. Style 45 is one of the most beautiful Polyphon table models made. The case is of walnut with elaborate carving and inlay. Some models have "POLYPHON" inlaid in brass letters on the underside of the lid. The discs of Style No.45 and other 39.8 cm. Polyphons are interchangeable with the 15½" Regina discs.

Style 45S: A variation of Style 45, but with finish in polished black wood with gilt decorations.



–Style No.45–

–Style 100 "Savoyard"–

77 musical notes. Uses 39.8 cm. (15¾") discs. A terra-cotta or a papier mache figure appears to be playing a Style No. 103 Polyphon box (in a special case). As the music box plays a crank connected to the figure's arm gives it a circular motion in the manner of an organ grinder. The coin slot is in the form of an alms dish at the top of the "organ." Several different case styles made. Total dimensions, including figure: 159 cm. high by 69 cm. wide by 55 cm. deep. A popular style made from the 1890's through the early 20th century.

–Style 45a–

156 (or 152 or 154) teeth in duplex combs. Uses 39.8 cm. (15½" or 15¾") discs. In ornate walnut case with raised decorations. Drawer at the bottom provides a storage area for discs. Early case style from the 1895 catalogue.

–Style No.45b–

156 (or 152 or 154) teeth in music comb. Uses 39.8 cm. (15½" or 15¾") discs. "In highly finished black polished case, richly engraved and gilded. Case with drawer at bottom to hold tunes." An early style made in the 1890's.

–Style No. 65–

78 teeth in music comb. Uses 39.8 (or 15½" or 15¾") discs. "Excelsior Piccolo" model. Coin operated. Walnut case. Colored terra cotta door. Designed for hanging on wall. 44" high by 25" wide by 13" deep.

Style 65a – As above, but with polished brass lyre in door; cloth panel behind lyre.

Both styles may be obtained with an 8-day clock mounted in the top gallery.

–Style No.61–

156 (or 152) teeth in comb. Uses 39.8 cm. (15½" or 15¾") discs. "Highly finished and carved case with antique glass door. 14-day pendulum clock, striking on gong. Every hour as the clock strikes, a lever is lifted and the Polyphon plays one tune. The music mechanism can be started at any time independent of the clock and can be put to 'silent' during night or absence." 104 inches high by 28 inches wide by 17 inches deep. Walnut (usually) or oak wood.



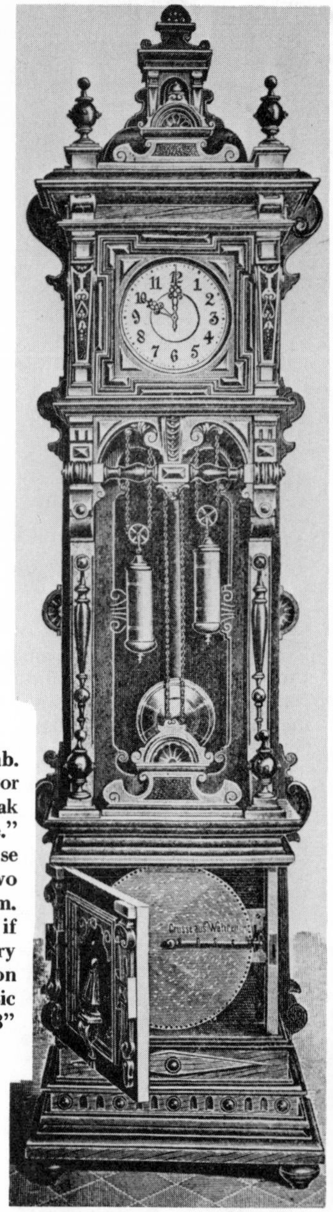

–Style No.62–

156 (or 152) teeth in comb. Uses 39.8 cm. (15½" or 15¾") discs. Walnut or oak case in "Renaissance Style." With open-fronted case permitting a view of the two weights and the pendulum. Provided with coin slot if desired. Plays a tune every hour, or it can be set on 'silent' to still the music mechanism. 110" high by 28" wide by 14" deep.

–Style No.60–

156 (or 152) teeth in music comb. Uses 39.8 cm. (15½" or 15¾") discs. "The Drawing Room Polyphon" – without coin operation. Walnut case with carved front. 76" high by 28" wide by 16" deep.

No.60A – The same, but with coin slot.

Typical music disc storage cabinets. These cabinets could be purchased separately and used with appropriate Polyphon, Symphonion, etc. boxes – either as a supporting base for the music box or as a separate cabinet.

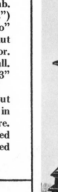

–Style No.48–

78 teeth in music comb. Uses 39.8 cm. (15½" or 15¾") discs; single comb model. Coin operated. Walnut case. Glass lid cover with red lettering on the underside. Coin slot at front.

Note: Later, Style No.48 was made using 36 cm. (14½") discs; the movement was provided with bells in addition to the music comb.

An early style from the 1890's.

–Style No.49–

156 teeth (or 152 or 154) in music comb. Uses 39.8 cm. (15½" or 15¾") discs. Duplex comb. "Automatic Polyphon, coin in slot. Solid walnut case, with drawer to hold tunes. Lid with red lettering on glass." 25" wide by 20½" deep by 13" high (lid closed). Made to take 10 centime pieces (for use in France), 1-penny pieces (England), 5-pfennig pieces (Germany), 1-cent pieces (U.S.A. via Regina), or any other coin desired.



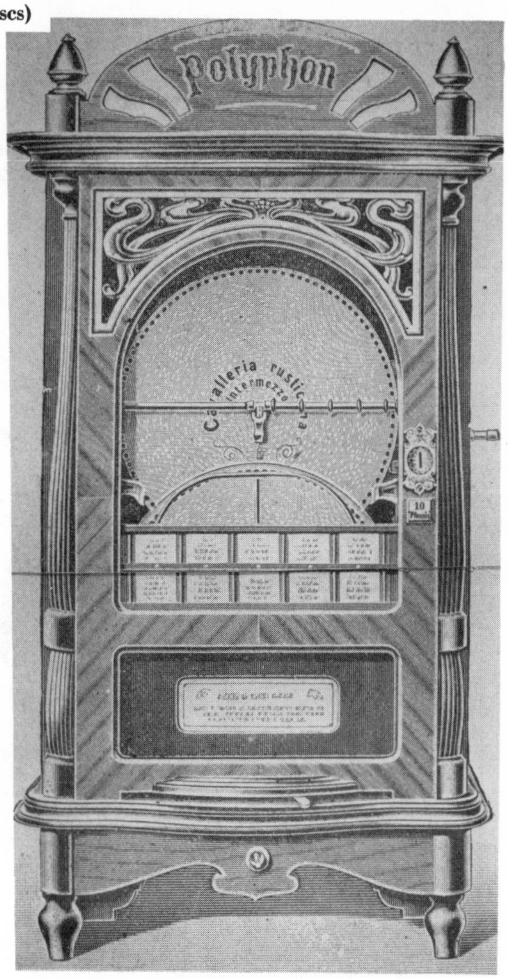


–Style 51–

154 teeth in music comb. Uses 39.8 cm. (15½ or 15¾") discs. Duplex comb model. Automatic disc changing style. Stores ten discs and changes them automatically. The desired tune is selected by means of a sliding pointer on the front of the case. Dimensions: 127 cm. high by 70 cm. wide by 43 cm. deep.

Unlike contemporary Regina changers, the Polyphon disc changing models were made only in limited quantities. Thus they are very rare today.

Note: This Style 51 instrument is entirely different from another earlier Style 51 which is an upright non-changer model.

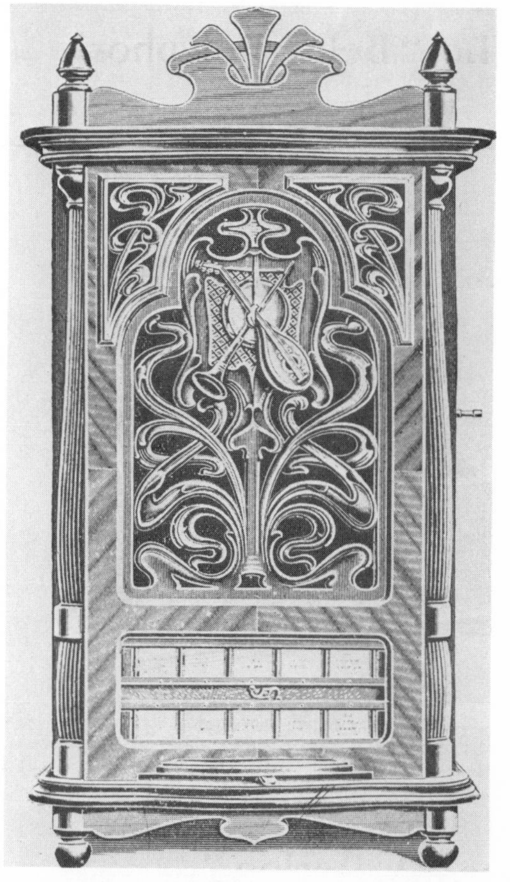

–Style 50–

39.8 cm. (15¾") discs. Automatic changer. "With 156 notes, walnut case, with artistically carved front panels and 'Self-changing Tune Device" for 10 tunes. By moving the little indicator underneath, the tune desired will play, then it goes back to its previous position. Extremely sweet in tone."

(39.8 cm. or 15¾" discs)

–Style No.51–
156 teeth (or 152 or 154) in music comb. Uses 39.8 cm. (15½" or 15¾") discs. Coin operated. Walnut case with majolica door with Polyphon design (or with personalized advertisement made to order). 68" high by 26" wide by 14" deep. A number of Styles 51, 52, 53, and 55 were sold in the United States by the Regina Music Box Company.

–Style No.52–
156 teeth (or 152 or 154) in music comb. Uses 39.8 cm. (15½" or 15¾") discs. Coin operated. "Walnut case with red lettering on white glass for advertising purposes." 68" high by 26" wide by 14" deep. Virtually identical to Style No. 51.

–Style No.53–
156 (or 152 or 154) teeth in music comb. Uses 39.8 cm. (15½" or 15¾") discs. Walnut case with polished brass lyre in door. Cloth panel behind lyre to permit sound escapement. 70" high by 26" wide by 14" deep. Similar to Style 55, but without advertising panel (No.53 has a solid panel.)

–Style 55–
156 (or 152 or 154) teet in music comb. Uses 39.8 cm (15½" or 15¾") discs. Walnu case with polished brass lyre i door. Cloth panel behind lyr to permit effective soun dispersion. With frosted glas lettered for advertisin (otherwise similar to No.53, 70" high by 26" wide by 14 deep.

–Style 103; 103U–
78 teeth in music comb. Uses 39.8 cm. (15¾") discs. Walnut wood. Several case design variations, especially with regard to the top gallery and the front columns. Coin operated model for use in public places.

Style 103U – The same as preceding but with clock mounted in the top gallery. (The "U" is from the German "Uhr" which means "clock" – Most different upright Polyphons were available with clocks; and in this format a U is placed after the regular model number).

Style 103P – Same style but with vending apparatus to dispense cigarettes, a small chocolate bar, or another item. The designation "P" (from the German "Pramien" or "prize" or "premium") was used on any of the various upright Polyphon models equipped with dispensing apparatus. Some models did not dispense merchandise but vended tokens which could be redeemed at the bar for beer, cigarettes, and other items.

**·LYPHON**
**(45 cm. or 17½" discs)**

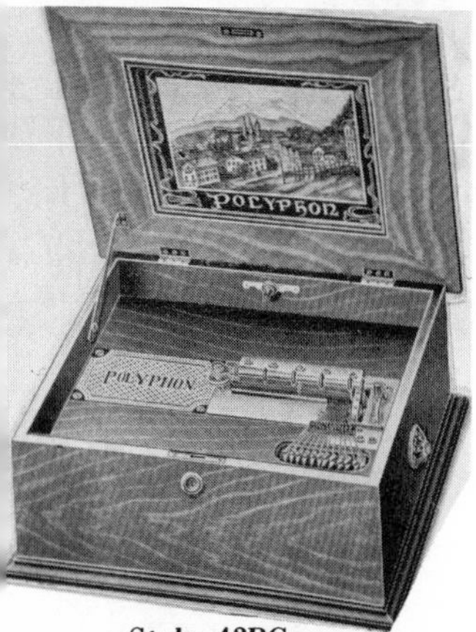


–Style 43BG–
77 teeth in music comb plus 2 bells. Uses 45 cm. (17½") iscs. Walnut case with inlay n lid. The music arrangements e similar to those found on 9.8 cm. (15½" or 15¾") iscs, but with extra diameter provide for the bell section.

**(50 cm. or 19 5/8" discs)**

**POLYPHON**

–Style No.47C–
(1914)
118 teeth in music comb. Uses 50 cm. (20" or 19 5/8" – catalogues vary in the description, however all discs are of the same size) discs. Walnut case with inlaid lid. Gilt lines on front. "The tone is powerful but sweet as a result of the very careful elaboration of the tune combs."

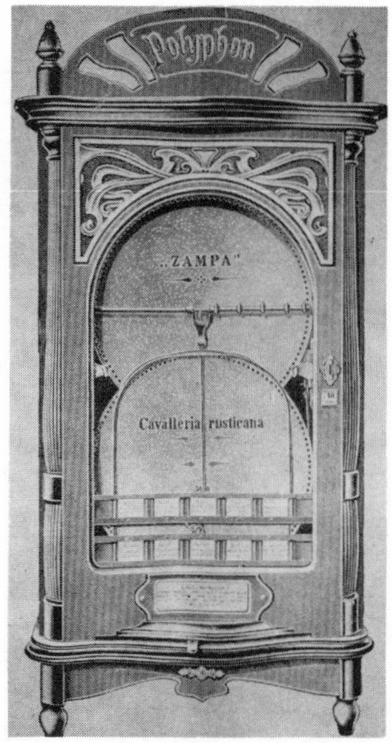


–Style 4–
118 notes in music comb. Uses 50 cm. (19 5/8" or 20") discs. Automatic disc changing model; stores ten discs and plays them automatically. The desired tune may be selected by means of an indicator on the front. Usually seen in walnut wood.

Style 4U – Style 4 with clock in top gallery.

---

–Styles 104; 104U; 104P–
118 teeth in music comb. Uses 50 cm. 19 5/8" or 20") discs. Upright model. Many ase design variations, particularly with respect o the top gallery and the front columns. Coin perated model especially popular for use in avern use. In England this was the most opular Polyphon style for use on pub ounters, and thousands served that purpose. sually seen in walnut wood, but occasionally een in oak.

By means of a lever the owner of the olyphon could set the instrument to play nce or twice per coin insertion. Most large pright Polyphon models had this option eature.

"Automaton" was the name given to all oin operated music boxes by the German nakers. Some have a single slot (on the right ide); others have two coin slots, one on each ide. Measurements: 4'3" high by 2'4" wide y 1'4" deep.

Style 104 was a very popular model and vas made from the 1890's until well into the 0th century.

Style 104U – Style 104 with clock in the op gallery.

Style 104P – Style 104 with vending nechanism.

104P

**(50 cm. or 19 5/8" discs)**

104

104U

**POLYPHON (50 cm. or 19 5/8" discs)**

This 50 cm. (19 5/8") Polyphon has inset panels of burled walnut and is built on top of a gracefully styled writing desk. It may have once seen use in the lobby of a fine hotel. (Lewis Graham photo)

**POLYPHON (56 cm. or 22½" discs)**

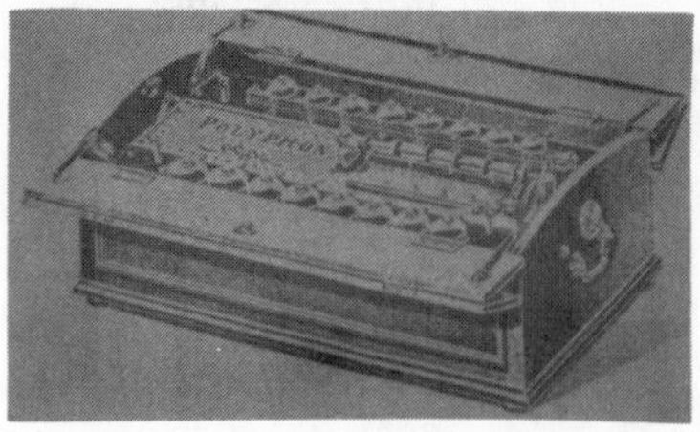

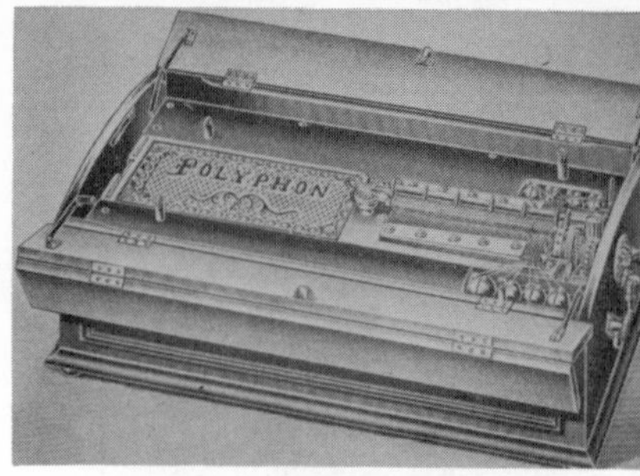

–Style No.49C–

118 notes in music comb plus 16 bells. Uses 56 cm. (22½") discs. Spiral spring. Rare "casket" or "folding top" style.

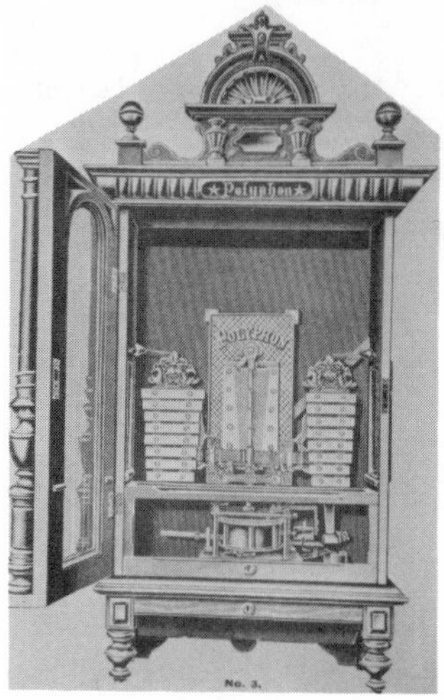

No. 3

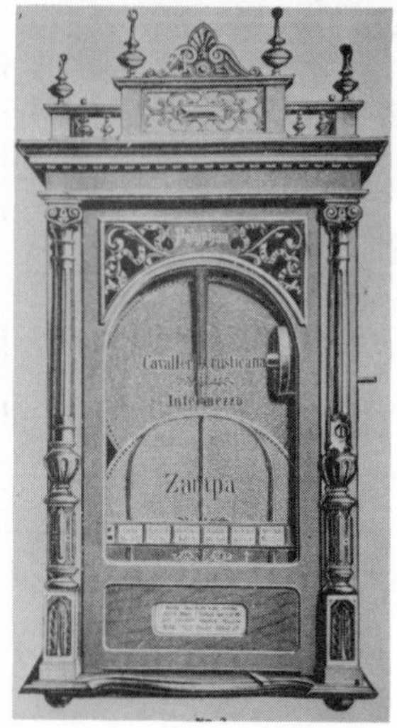

No. 2
Automatic disc-changing model.

**POLYPHON (56 cm. or 22½" discs)**

Styles 6, 6K, 6G

118 teeth in the music comb plus 16 bells (see below). Uses 56 cm. (22½") discs. Early models made with coil spring; later models with spiral spring. 4'10" high by 2'8" wide by 1'6" deep. Usually coin operated. Coin slot in the right side of the front door.

Style 6 – General name for this style, used in some Polyphon catalogues to cover both the 6K and 6G models.

Style 6K – Style 6 with bar-type bells (K from "Klangplatten" or orchestra bells).

Style 6G – Style 6 with saucer-type bells (G from "Glocken" or bells).

With clock: With clock attachment in the top gallery this model was known variously as 6U, 6KU, or 6GU.

Style 6P – With vending apparatus.

Style 6G

Style 6K

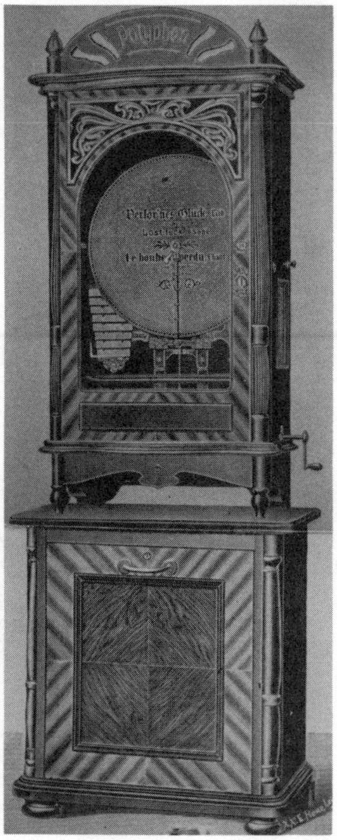


Bases for any instrument were available at extra cost. Two typical base cabinets are shown with Polyphon music boxes on them.

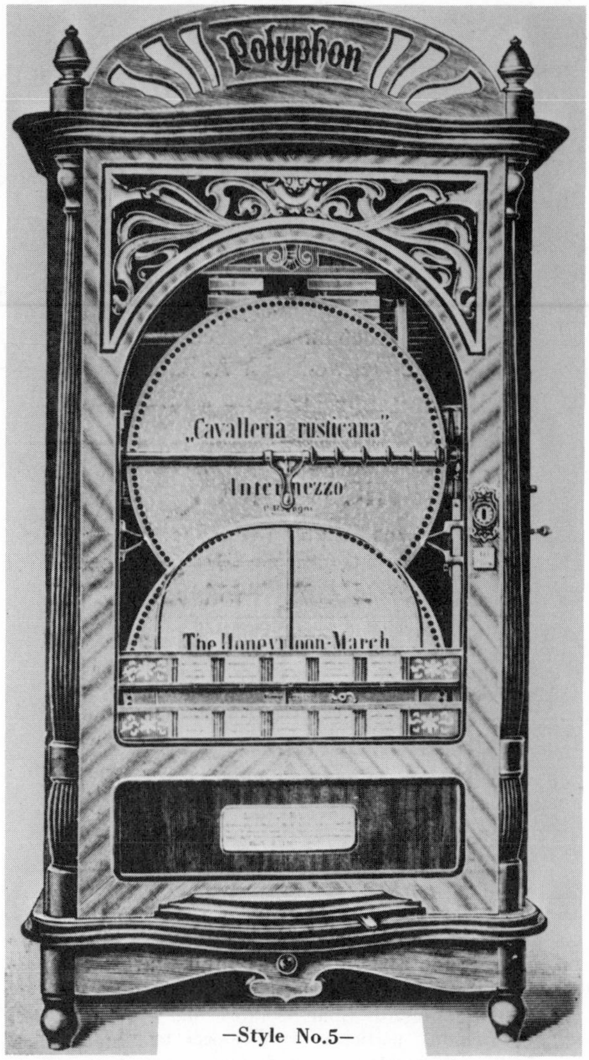


–Style No.5–

118 teeth in the music comb plus 16 bells. Uses 56 cm. (22½") discs. 5'6" high by 3' wide by 1'9" deep. Automatic disc changing model; stores ten different discs in bottom rack. Selection is made via a pointer index at the front. Point the indicator at the desired tune card, drop a coin in the slot, and the wanted melody is played.

(Disc-operated pianos)

–Style No.200–
(1914)

With 44 notes (on 88 piano strings), 12 tubular chimes, and mandolin attachment. Uses special 63 cm. (25¼") discs. "Elegant oak case on detachable stand. Door ornamented with fretwork and stained glass center piece, handsomely painted. Mechanical piano with vibrating hammers and interchangeable discs. Coil spring motor. 7'7" high by 2'10¼" wide by 1'4½" deep."

–Style 200S–
(1914)

With 44 piano notes (on 88 strings), 12 tubular chimes, mandolin attachment, large and small drum, and Chinese cymbal. Uses special 63 cm. (25¼") discs. Coil spring motor. 8' high by 2'10½" wide by 1'6½" deep. Made in limited quantities during the early 20th century. See illustration of Style 200S on another page.

Note: Lochmann (see Lochmann "Original" section of this book) made similar instruments which used projectionless discs.

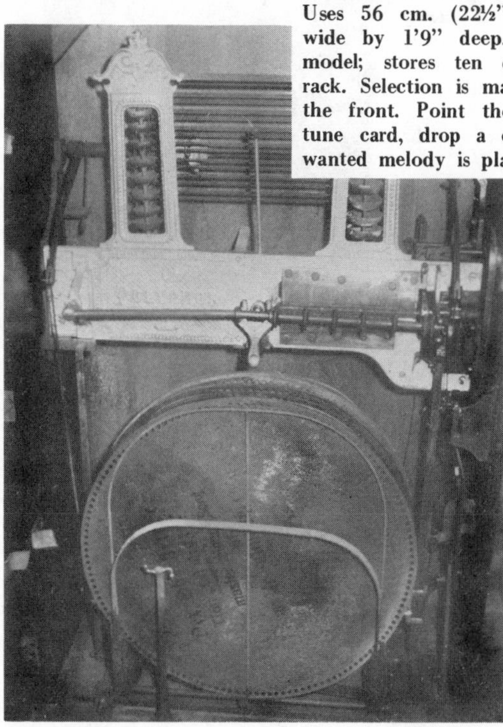


Two types of bells were available with Style 5; bar-type bells as shown above and saucer bells as shown to the left.

Style 5 was also known as Style 6 in certain Polyphon catalogues. A non-changer upright model with bells, also of the 56 cm. size, was known as Style 3.

(62.5 cm. or 24½" discs)

–Style Nos. 49C and 52–

View of exterior of case showing folding top in the closed position. Regina made music boxes of similar concept in 20¾" and 27" disc sizes.

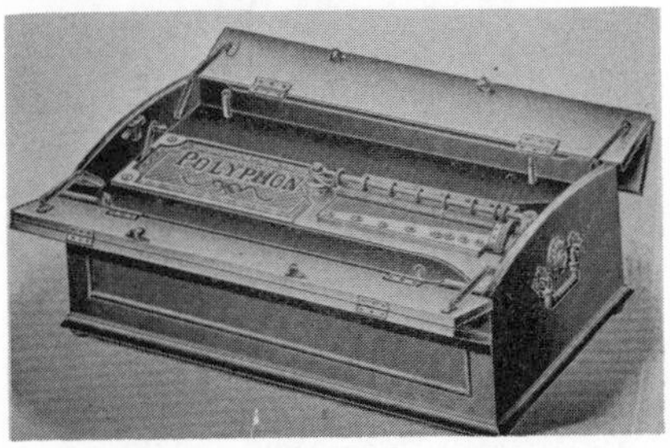


–Style No.52–

159 teeth in duplex combs. Uses 62.5 cm. (24½") discs. Usually seen in mahogany wood (as is 49C). Spiral spring drive. Rare; only a few of this style were made.

–Style No.105–

–Styles 105; 105U; 105P–

159 teeth in music comb. Uses 62.5 cm. (24½") discs. A very popular model made from the 1890's onward. Coin operated. Many case style variations, particular with respect to the top gallery and side column designs. Like Style 104 the Style 105 was very popular in England where it found use as a penny operated entertainer on pub counters. Usually seen in walnut wood, but made also in oak.

Measurements: 5' high by 2'8" wide by 1'6" deep.

Style 105U – Style 105 with clock in the top gallery.

Style 105P – Style 105 with vending apparatus.

Style 105PG – Style 105 "Polygraphon" – with external brass horn and phonograph disc playing attachment. The "PG" or Polygraphon attachment could also be obtained with Styles 42, 43, 45, 105, and the Concerto.

Style 105PGA – Style 105 "Polygraphon Automat" (coin-operated). The "A" suffix was occasionally used after "PG" to designate a coin-operated model (but was more often omitted and coin-operated models were simply designated with the "PG" suffix). Thus such references as Style 42PGA, Style 43PGA, etc. may be encountered.

–Style No.105–

Style 105S: With base.

–Style 54–

159 teeth in comb. Uses 62.5 cm. (24½") discs. "159 steel teeth, of extra large size and special construction, whereby an enormous loud and powerful tone is produced; no other mechanical instrument with steel tongues can reach the No. 54. The spring, which is of special construction, is visible below the music disc. The instrument when fully wound up plays for about 45 minutes. A coin in the slot will play the tune through once or twice as desired. The unexcelled music arrangement produces tone effects which never have been heard before in any musical automaton. The case is very solid and tasteful, carved in walnut, and is of the highest workmanship. This instrument can also be had without coin slot for drawing room purposes."

The No.54 was the most popular of all large Polyphon styles, and thousands were originally sold. Several case design variations were made, differing from each other mainly with respect to the top gallery and the front columns. A disc storage bin is in the bottom of the instrument and tilts outward for easy access.

–Style No.1N–

159 notes. Uses 62.5 cm. (24½") discs. Holds 12 discs and changes them automatically. The desired selection can be made by pointing the sliding indicator on the front to the appropriate tune card. Walnut wood. The largest of the Polyphon disc changing music boxes, the 1N was made from the 1890's through the first decade of the 20th century.

Dimensions: 241 cm. high by 101 cm. wide by 73 cm. deep.

(62.5 cm. or 24½" discs)

Views of two 24½" upright Polyphons showing two different spring sizes.

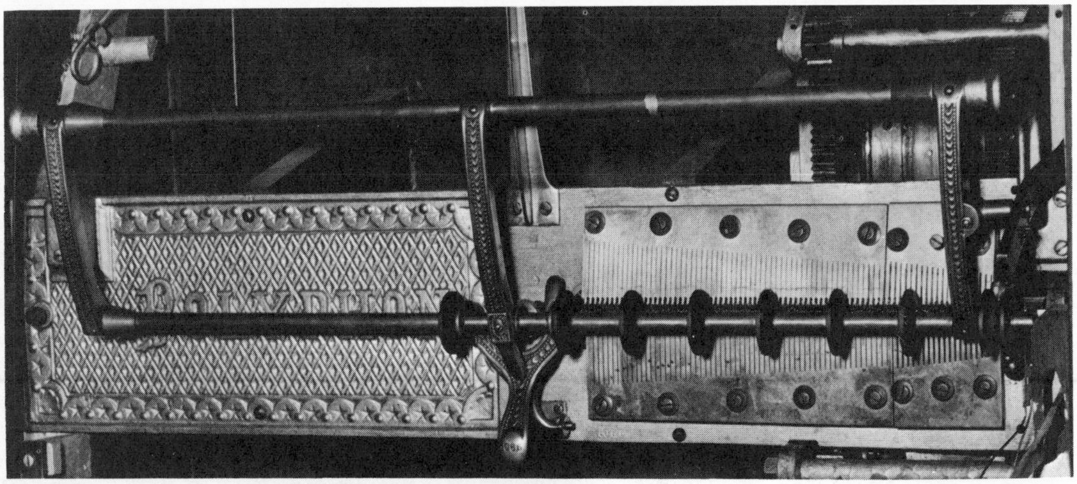

(62.5 cm. or 24½" discs)

Above is a view of the music combs and the idler bar from a Style 1N 24½" Polyphon automatic changer. Note the ornate cast bedplate. At the left is a view of the instrument with all of the discs in the storage rack. The changing action of the Polyphon 1N is rapid (although smaller Polyphon changers are slower) – perhaps twice the speed of a Regina disc changer.

(56 cm. or 22½" discs)

Above: The exterior and interior of a Polyphon Style No. 5K. The "K" represents "Klangplatten," the German word for "bar-type orchestra bells." A similar style but with saucer bells (cup-shaped, like a doorbell), known as "Glocken" in the German language is designated as Style No. 5G. In both instruments sixteen bells are played from a 22½" (56 cm.) diameter disc. The changer holds ten different discs, any one of which may be selected by moving a lever on the front of the instrument until a pointer is centered on the program card of the tune desired.

The author with a 24½" Style 1N Polyphon automatic changer. The front panels have been removed to permit a view of the interior.

### —Fanciful Polyphon Names—

Around the turn of the century Nicole Frères, Ltd., of 21 Ely Place, Holborn Circus, London, issued an illustrated catalogue of music boxes. Among the items offered for sale were a number of Polyphon models which were assigned names such as "Geneva," "Mikado," and "Geisha," "Diamond Jubilee," "Sandringham," "Osborne," etc.

As most names were either of English extraction (e.g., "Sandringham"), referred to Gilbert & Sullivan productions (e.g., "Mikado"), or were associated with English events (e.g., "Diamond Jubilee" — a reference to the 1897 celebration of Queen Victoria's 50 years on the throne), these names were evidently intended for the most part for use in England.

The names are listed herewith:

| | |
|---|---|
| "Infanta" | No. 28 (6 1/2" disc; manivelle type) |
| "London" | No. 28s (6 1/2" disc, spring-wound) |
| "Paris" | No. 40 (8 1/4" disc) |
| "Kleberg" | No. 41 (8 1/4" disc) |
| "Geneva" | No. 41b (8 1/4" disc) |
| "Havelock" | No. 42n (11 1/4" disc) |
| "Gordon" | No. 46 (9 5/8" discs) |
| "Khartoum" | No. 42d (11 1/4" disc) |
| "Royal" | No. 42b (11 1/4" disc) |
| "Eugene" | No. 43b (15 3/4" disc) |
| "Bell" | No. 48 (14 1/8" disc, bells type) |
| "Louis" | No. 44 (15 3/4" disc) |
| "Waterloo" | No. 44d (15 3/4" disc) |
| "Arthur" | No. 45 (15 3/4" disc) |
| "Athelstane" | No. 45b (15 3/4" disc) |
| "Navy" | No. 47 (19 5/8" disc) |
| "Drawing Room" | No. 50 (24 1/2" disc changer) |
| "Emerald" | No. 49 (22" disc, bells type) |
| "Carmen" | No. 52 (24 1/2" disc) |
| "Jubilee" | No. 103 (15 3/4" disc) |
| "Diamond Jubilee" | (15 3/4" disc; with clock) |
| "Sandringham" | No. 104 (19 5/8" disc) |
| "Osborne" | No. 104u (19 5/8" disc; with clock) |
| "Nicole" | No. 105 (24 1/2" disc) |
| "Kitchener" | No. 3 (22" disc; bells type) |
| "Hamilton" | No. 6 (22" disc; bells type) |
| "Raby" | No. 118 (19 5/8" disc) |
| "Holborn" | No. 51 (15 3/4" disc changer) |
| "Salisbury" | No. 4 (19 5/8" disc changer) |
| "Roberts" | No. 2 (22" disc; bells type) |
| "Gold Medal" | No. 1 (24 1/2" disc changer) |
| "Geisha" | No. 62 (15 3/4" disc; hall clock type) |
| "Mikado" | No. 54 (24 1/2" disc) |
| "Mikado Polyphon Clock" | No. 54u (24 1/2" disc; hall clock) |
| "Grand Musical Hall Clock" | (24 1/2" disc; hall clock) |

Notes: Tune sheet dimensions are approximate. The 15 3/4" disc is the same as the 15 1/2" disc described elsewhere.

The "Mikado" Polyphon Clock.
No. 54u.
For Halls, Banqueting Rooms, and Private Residences.
Plays over 20 minutes.
159 NOTES.
Richly Carved Walnut Cabinet.
Price, £62 10 0
THE ABOVE PRICES INCLUDE SIX TUNES.


"Mikado Polyphon Clock" No. 54u (24 1/2" disc; hall clock)

## Grand Musical Hall Clock

WITH "MIKADO" POLYPHON MOVEMENT.

159 Notes. Plays over twenty minutes.

Size, 120 × 45 × 25 ins.

### Eight-Day Clock

with very fine Quarter Repetition Gong.

At every hour the Clock will play one tune, but if desired the Music can also be started at any moment by means of a lever.

"Grand Musical Hall Clock"
(24 1/2" disc; hall clock)

–Polyphon 200S–

–Polyphon 200–

–Polyphon 200–

–Polyphon Orchestrion V–

POLYPHON

Polyphon Concerto No.2

–Polyphon Concerto No.2–

(Disc-operated pianos)

POLYPHON 200 – Made in several case designs. Used a special 63 cm. (25¼") disc without projections. 44-note piano plus 12 bells.

POLYPHON ORCHESTRION V – Roll operated; 44-notes. 3 tunes per roll. 227 cm. high by 88 cm. wide by 40 cm. deep. Note that the case is the same as used for one of the Polyphon 200 styles.

POLYPHON CONCERTO II – 65 piano notes, 10 bells, cymbal, two drums. A junior-size version of the Concerto I, this model uses its own 71 cm. (28") disc. "Spiral spring permits the instrument to play for ten minutes" noted a Polyphon catalogue. In walnut, "imitation walnut," or oak cabinet. Front decorated with opalescent glass.

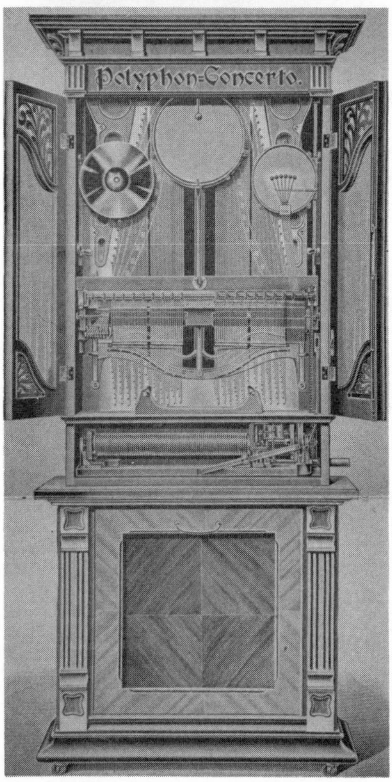


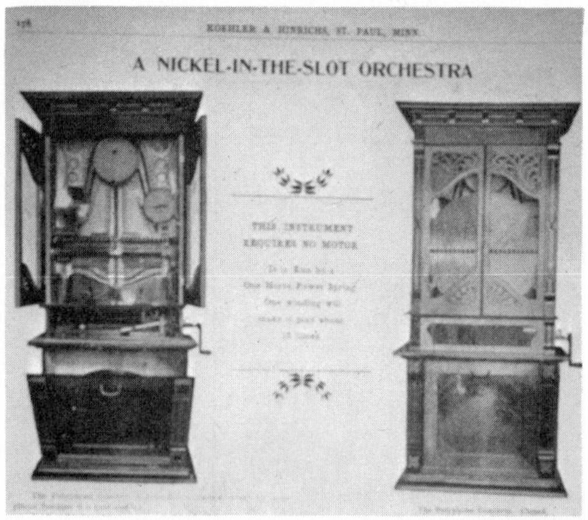

POLYPHON CONCERTO I – An orchestrion which uses an 80 cm. (32") steel disc. Made in several different case styles, including the basic style as shown to the left. This design was imported by Regina and sold as the "Polyphone Concerto" (as per the illustration directly above – from a U.S. tavern supply catalogue – the name "Polyphone," not Regina, is used) and, later, as the Regina Concerto. Spring motor or electric motor operation. To the right is a later and more elaborate case variation. Also sold as the Polygraphon Concerto – a model equipped with an external brass horn and a phonograph record turntable, in addition to the regular instrumentation of piano, tubular chimes, cymbal, and drums. Also made in a shorter version (without base cabinet).

Note: Regina used the "Polyphone" spelling in its advertisements

POLYPHON ORCHESTRION I – Several case styles as illustrated. 9'2" high; weight about 750 pounds. With electric motor or with 465-pound weight! 73-note roll, usually of 3 tunes per roll.

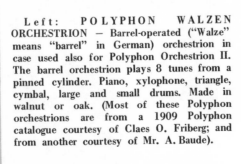

Left: POLYPHON WALZEN ORCHESTRION – Barrel-operated ("Walze" means "barrel" in German) orchestrion in case used also for Polyphon Orchestrion II. The barrel orchestrion plays 8 tunes from a pinned cylinder. Piano, xylophone, triangle, cymbal, large and small drums. Made in walnut or oak. (Most of these Polyphon orchestrions are from a 1909 Polyphon catalogue courtesy of Claes O. Friberg; and from another courtesy of Mr. A. Baude).

Right: POLYPHON ORCHESTRION II – Several case designs as shown. Also sold as the "Polyphon Rossini" Orchestrion. 73-note roll of 3 tunes per roll. Made with several different interior formats including: (1) Piano only; (2) Piano with mandolin effect; (3) Piano with drum and trap effects. 8'4" high. Weight driven or electric motor operation.

Certain models of the Polyphon Orchestrion were sold in America by Regina.

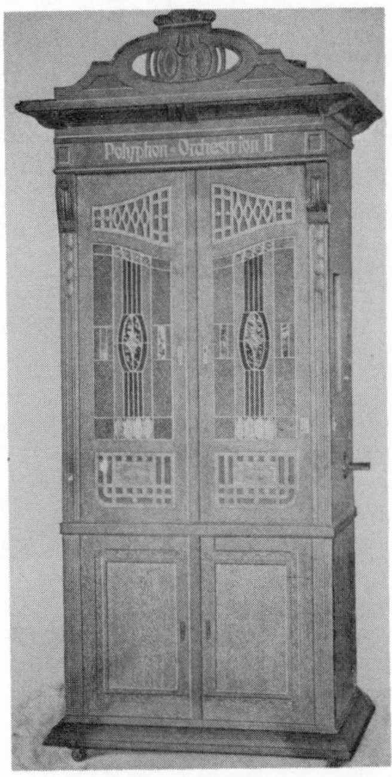

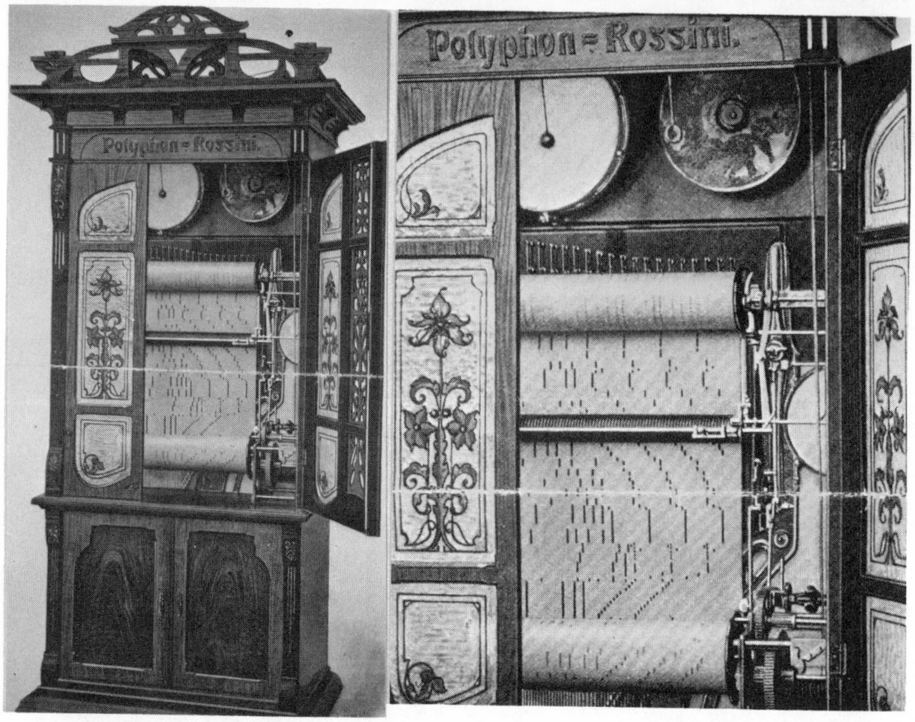


POLYPHON ROSSINI – Or Polyphon Orchestrion II. 73-note roll; piano and trap effects. "Over 600 instruments in use" noted a 1906 Polyphon catalogue! It is not known whether this figure refers to all Polyphon Orchestrions or just the Rossini model. As all Polyphon Orchestrions are exceedingly rare today, the 600 figure may have represented all models.

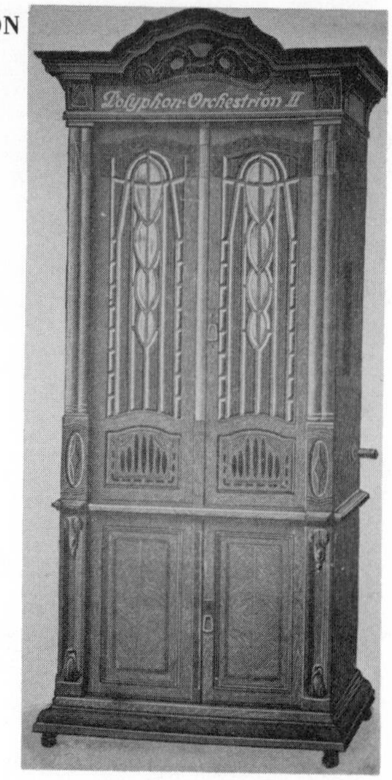


POLYPHON ORCHESTRION II – Case design variation. This particular model has attractive beveled glass mirrors on the front.

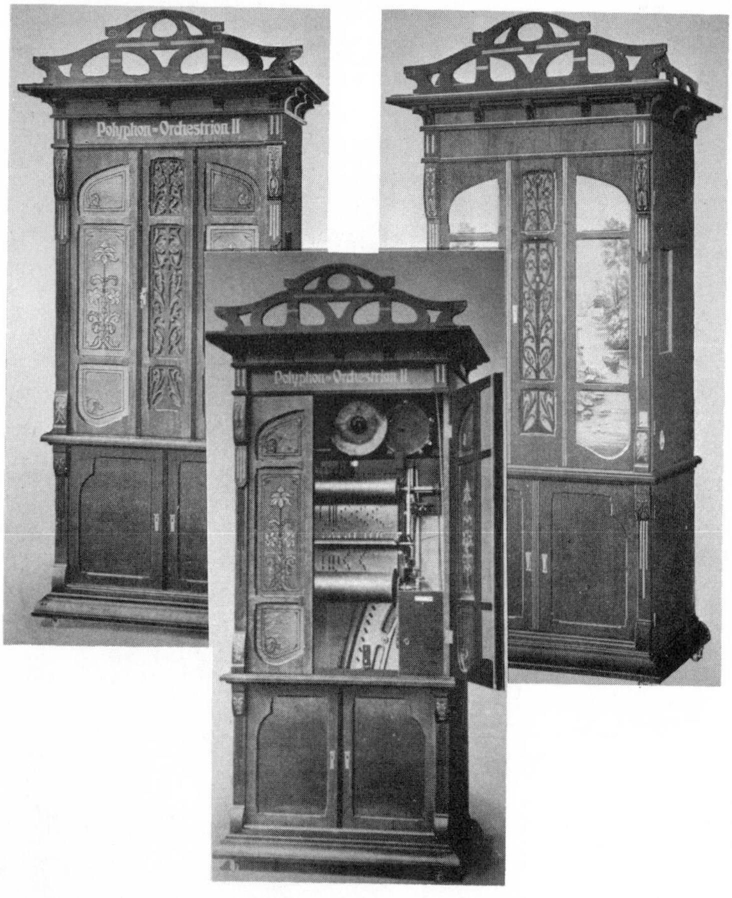


POLYPHON ORCHESTRION II – Additional case design variations. The II (or 2 – Arabic and Roman numeral designations were used interchangeably by Polyphon) was the most popular Polyphon Orchestrion model, and more case variations were made of this than of any other.

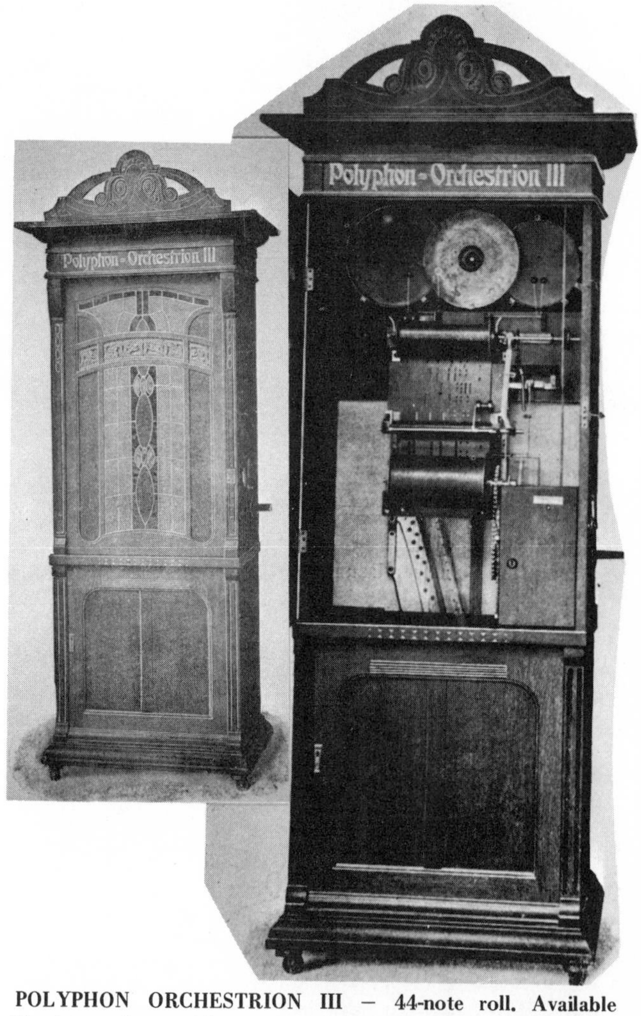


POLYPHON ORCHESTRION III – 44-note roll. Available with piano only or with two drums and cymbal (as shown). Several case styles made.

POLYPHON ORCHESTRION IV – 73-note roll of 3 tunes per roll. Piano and mandolin effect. Elaborate moving light effects on front. 260 cm. high.

POLYPHON ORCHESTRION No.10 – 43 piano notes (3 strings per note), bass drum, snare drum, cymbal, 10 tubular bells, mandolin effect. The use of a very wide roll and 3 strings per note (each string having a separate hammer) permitted elaborate mandolin arrangements as a fast repetition rate could be achieved (the use of 3 strings meant that it was not necessary to wait for a string to dampen before the same note could be sounded again). Used a special 4-tune endless roll. 260 cm. high by 150 cm. wide by 75 cm. deep. Available in several case styles including one with painted scenic panels (left), the "DeLuxe" style with beveled mirrors (upper right), and the "Standard" style shown at the right. Some models were equipped with saucer bells for 12 notes (see upper left illustration).

Typical Style PGA

Typical Style PG

–Polygraphon Models–

Above are shown two table model Polygraphon models, the one directly above being a PGA (the "A" is for "Automaton" as it is coin operated – note the coin drawer), and the one at the above right being a regular PG style.

The 1904 Polyphon catalogue listed Styles 42PG, 42PGA, 45PG, 45PGA, 105PG, 105PGA, and the Polygraphon Concerto. Undoubtedly many more models were made. To use the music box comb on table models as shown above the record turntable had to be removed. The Polygraphon models were an attempt to succeed in two markets – that of the music box and of the phonograph – much in the same vein as the Reginaphone, Miraphone, and other music box / phonograph combination units made by other manufacturers.

## POLYPHON COIN PIANOS (pneumatically operated)

Polyphona II

Polyphona VI

Polyphona II

Polyphona II and Harmonium-Polyphona

Polyphona IV

Polyphona I

Polyphona V

Polyphona II

Polyphon coin pianos (pneumatically-operated) c.1909-1910. Polyphona I contains piano, mandolin, xylophone, bells. Polyphona II: piano, mandolin. Polyphona IV: piano, mandolin, xylophone. Polyphona V ("Polyphona-Dux") piano which uses artists' rolls. Polyphona VI: ("Polyphona-Dux") piano which uses artists' rolls. "Harmonium-Polyphona" piano with 65-note harmonium section – uses the same case as Polyphona II.

## —Polyphon Musikwerke; Business Aspects and Sidelines—

The Polyphon business was financed by the sale of shares to the public and by the financial sponsorship of the Leipzig banking house of Knauth, Nachod & Kühne (the same firm which financed Polyphon's American branch, the Regina Music Box Company of Rahway, New Jersey). Polyphon's height of success came during the late 1890's and early 1900's when the firm's disc-type music boxes were at their height of popularity. During the 1897-1899 years Polyphon could barely keep pace with the fantastic demand for its products.

Shortly after 1900 Polyphon began to diversify into other fields. The Polymobil automobile and the Polygraph typewriter were the two most important non-musical products. Each of these produced a profit. Annual reports to stockholders were issued in April or May of each year. The 1910 report, excerpted here, is typical:

"Polyphon Musikwerke AG; 1910: During the last fiscal year there has been a profit of 380,912 Mk., which includes a payment of 200,000 Mk. on the account of the banking house of Knauth, Nachod & Kühne. Against this figure there are expenses amounting to 272,693 Mk., the writing off of 88,033 Mk., and the transfer of 20,186 Mk. to the stockholders' account . . . The statement, presented here by a new board of directors, shows the effect of prior years' business. The reorganization of the firm has taken a lot of time, and the sale of obsolete inventory [disc-type music boxes — Ed.] has resulted in very high losses. We would further recommend writing off the remainder of the old inventory now in stock. Also, some manufacturing activities of the past year were not profitable. The outstanding debts of prior years are even worse than we suspected earlier. Besides this, many of the purchases of recent years [music box parts] have meant a large loss for the firm.

"It is further noted that the sales of orchestrions and large automatic musical instruments have suffered due to the high taxes levied on entertainment and on automatic musical instruments; therefore very heavy write-offs were necessary. The sales of electric pianos have been much better, however — and this division is in good condition at the moment. The record and phonograph division should develop well in the future, but prices for the time being are very low due to competition. We can report a very surprising development concerning the Dux [successor to the Polymobil] Automobile Division. The four-cylinder cars of the company have had much success in the first part of the year. For example, at the Eisenach Race the Dux was praised and appreciated by many people. The Dux Division is in good condition at this time.

"The 5% bond loan mentioned in our previous report has been taken in the amount of 600,000 Mk.; and the market has valued these bonds (which were sold at par) at 103. Also, we must thank Knauth, Nachod & Kühne who have once again shown the kindness not to raise their interest rate and who have absorbed the very heavy losses incurred during our recent write-offs. [The banking firm apparently credited Polyphon's 200,000 Mk. payment back to the Polyphon firm, thus turning into a nominal profit what would have otherwise been a large loss — Ed.]

"Concerning the coming business year, the board of directors thinks the situation will be favorable, but still the adjustment of the old inventory will take much time and expense."

In 1917 a merger was effected with Deutsche Grammophon. Polyphon phonographs were made in large quantities throughout the 1920's and 1930's. The Polyphon trademark is still being used on phonographs today.

An imaginative Polyphon advertisement of 1908.

Another 1908 advertisement.

Two successful non-musical Polyphon products during the early 20th century were the Polymobil (later, the Dux) automobile and the Polygraph typewriter. The Polymobil and Dux were sold through automobile dealerships. Polygraph typewriters were sold through many outlets, including many Polyphon music box agents.

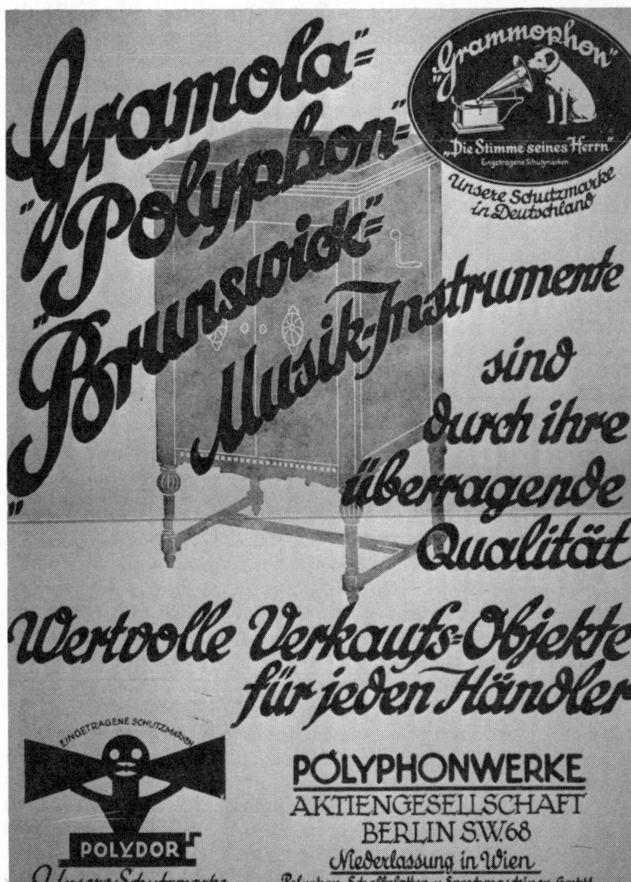


Polyphonwerke advertisement of February, 1930.

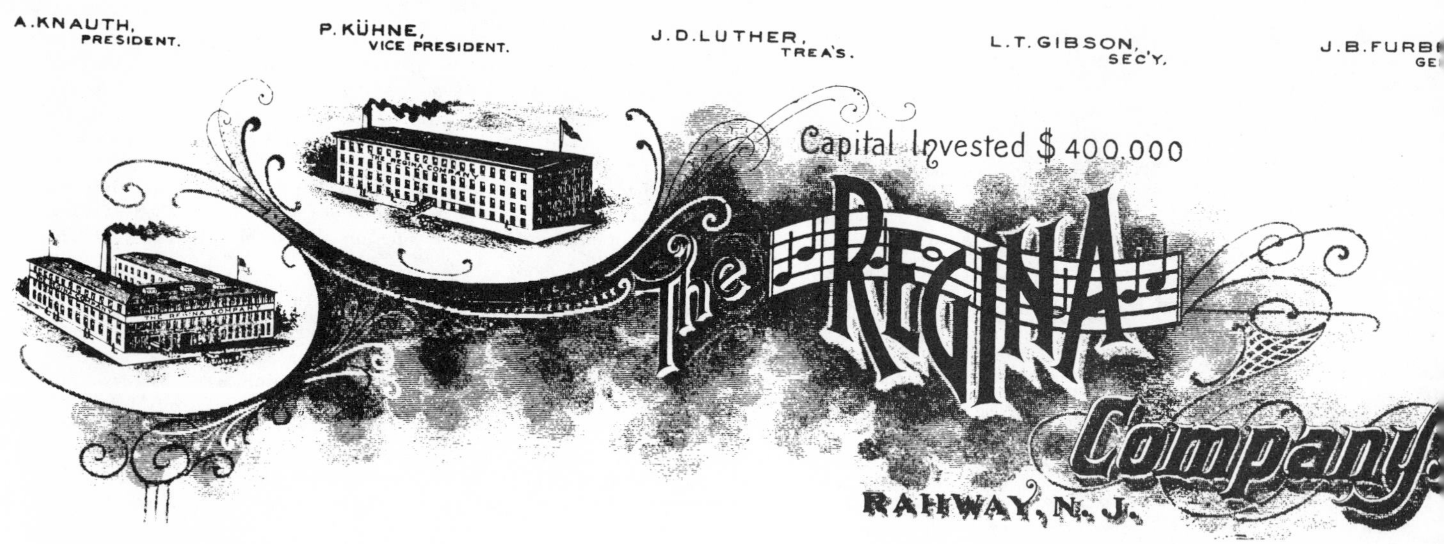


## THE REGINA MUSIC BOX COMPANY
### —Rahway, New Jersey—

#### Introductory Comments

To many Americans "Regina" is synonymous with the term "music box." With 80% to 90% of the American market for disc-type music boxes, Regina enjoyed the golden age of the disc instruments — an era which, for Regina, lasted from about 1894 to World War I, although instruments were shipped as late as 1921.

Regina instruments, adapted in most instances from those devised by Polyphon, offered simplicity of operation, ruggedness and durability, and a wide range of models to choose from. Nationwide advertising to the music trade and to the public created the necessary demand. As a result Regina sold about 100,000 instruments.

The following Regina section is the most comprehensive survey ever published concerning the famous New Jersey firm. The editor is indebted to John E. Cann, who granted permission to use the text of his "Regina, American Queen" article which appeared in the June, 1966 issue of the Musical Box Society "Bulletin." Written with the assistance of the Regina Corporation (whose present business in Rahway consists of making household appliances), the article provided much of the historical data used in the first several pages of this Regina section. The Regina Music Box Company manufacturing records and ledgers were acquired by the editor several years ago. Hundreds of hours were spent poring over data concerning the approximately 100,000 Regina music boxes, phonographs, and other items listed therein. These ledgers have made possible most of the production figures, specific model information, and other technical data presented in this book. Mention also must be made of Lloyd G. Kelley who acquired in 1939 much of the surviving equipment for disc-making from the Regina firm. During the next several decades Mr. Kelley produced new Regina discs for collectors desiring them.

Perhaps someday a definitive book will be written on the Regina Music Box Company. Of all firms which graced the American scene in the "good old days" few brought more happiness and enjoyment to Americans than did Regina via its music boxes.

—————

#### History of the Regina Music Box Company

(Adapted from "Regina, The American Queen," by John E. Cann):

"WANTED — Comb cutters, comb tuners, tune disc perforators, and wheel cutters. Apply at the Regina Music Box Company, 54 West Cherry Street, Rahway, New Jersey." It is doubtful if this want-ad ever appeared in the "Rahway Record," at least in those words, but if it had, it would not have been particularly unusual to anyone living in or around that northern New Jersey town during the "Gay Nineties." In 1892 a brand-new American industry had been born there, one that flourished for a decade as an early symbol of mass production, only to fall victim to a machine that had never been meant to compete with it. Before the death knell was sounded, however, its products were to find their way into thousands of homes, hotels, saloons, and ice cream parlors.

It seems rather strange that, in spite of the fact that America constituted a sizable market for music boxes, there was not a single manufacturer of them in this country until 1892. This was largely because of the degree of specialization, and the degree of painstaking, eye-straining labor needed. These instruments had borrowed much in principle from fine watch and clock movements, so who were better equipped to make them than the Swiss and Germans?

The story of the Regina Music Box Company has its beginnings in Germany. About 1889, Gustave Brachhausen, foreman of the Symphonion works in Leipzig, and Paul Riessner, an engineer in the same factory, left Symphonion and founded the Polyphon Musikwerke. Within a few years Polyphon became the world's largest manufacturer of disc-type music boxes.

Although the exact financial arrangements are not known today, Brachhausen evidently sensed that the American market furnished an ideal area for expansion, and with the backing of Polyphon he sailed to America in September, 1892. At the age of 35 Brachhausen established the Regina Music Box Company. The first premises were leased in Jersey City, New Jersey.

The 1892 and 1893 years were spent setting up the business and applying for American patents, many of which had Riessner as the co-patentee. By 1894 the new business had been formally incorporated as the Regina Music Box Company. The three major shareholders were Paul Riessner and Johannas J. Korner, both of Leipzig, and Gustave Brachhausen. Financing was by Knauth, Nachod & Kühne, bankers.

The first Regina instruments sold were 11" and 15½" disc boxes imported in their entirety from Polyphon, although the German origin was not mentioned at the time. Later, Regina imported the mechanical parts from Polyphon and installed them in American-built wood cases. By the mid-1890's most Regina boxes were entirely American-made, although certain components of certain instruments continued to be imported until well into the 1900's.

Regina's success was immediate. Within a year Brachhausen was shopping for a permanent location. It was found at 54 Cherry Street in Rahway, New Jersey — in a 25,000-square-foot building that had been occupied previously by a printing and publishing concern.

As the residents of Rahway listened to the tinkling strains of "The Blue Danube" and "Silent Night" issuing from the open windows of the Regina factory, Gustave Brachhausen journeyed to New York, Philadelphia, Chicago, and the western United States to set up a network of distributors. Department stores, music houses, jewelry stores, and other retailers were encouraged to handle the Regina line by offering them a discount which amounted to about 50% of the list price.

As orders poured in, Brachhausen contacted his acquaintances at the Polyphon and Symphonion factories in Germany. At least sixty German and Swiss music box technicians and specialists were brought to Rahway during the first few years.

The comb tuners sat side-by-side along a bench running the length of one room in the Regina factory. At one point Brachhausen became extremely annoyed by the constant chatter among the tuners. Thinking that less talk would result in more efficient work, he erected barriers between the men so that, in effect, each man worked in his own private cubicle. Or so Brachhausen planned. The talk diminished, but so did the tuning. The whole group walked out and refused to return until the barriers were taken down. With the barriers down and peace restored, the men and women at Regina set about making some of the best music boxes ever produced in this country.

In the preparation of new tune discs the most painstaking task was arranging the music to take optimum advantage of the wide frequency range of the combs, adding the right amount of trills and runs to compensate for the inability of the combs to sustain notes. Tunes would usually have to be edited as well, because, unlike a phonograph record, the disc makes just one revolution to complete a selection. Octave Felicien Chaillet had been superintendent of music for the elementary school system of Switzerland prior to being enticed to America by Regina. However, it was probably not this facet of his work experience that attracted Regina. More important was that Chaillet had arranged many tune discs for Symphonion. Soon Chaillet established himself as one of Regina's most highly paid and most highly regarded employees. He composed several selections, "set up" the arrangements of hundreds of other melodies, and, with the addition of arrangements obtained from Germany, produced over 2,000 different selections of the 15½" disc size and lesser numbers of the other disc types.

From the beginning, Regina music boxes were marketed extensively through distributors, although many direct sales were made to people who read Regina advertisements in popular magazines and took advantage of ordering by mail. Once each year Brachhausen took a trip across the United States to call on his distributors and to seek orders for the coming year.

Nearly all Regina music boxes were of standard designs, a situation which permitted the standardization of many parts and the employment of certain mass-production techniques. Many of the popular models were made in production "runs" of several dozen to several hundred or more instruments at a time. The instruments would then be stored in the Rahway factory and shipped over a period of a few months or years. When the inventory became low another production run was started.

Production-line techniques were applied to disc making as well. A hydraulic stamping machine was utilized to punch almost a dozen discs simultaneously from one master disc.

Various Regina models were identified chiefly by reference to the diameter of the tune discs which they accommodated, the smallest Regina-made disc being 8½" in diameter and the largest 32 inches across, the latter being for the 32" Concerto piano orchestrion. The 27" Regina was the largest instrument with music combs. The 27" box, popular in commercial establishments and in the homes of the wealthy, had combs encompassing over seven octaves. It played for about two minutes during a single revolution of the disc.

Most of the early German-made Symphonion and Polyphon music boxes were of coin-operated styles. The home market for instruments did not become large until around 1900. The coin-operated disc boxes were spring-wound, but the springs were massive enough so that many discs could be played through before the instrument had to be wound up again. A frequent complaint was that the same tune would play over and over every time a patron deposited a coin in the slot, until the owner had the time or inclination to change the disc. The automatic disc-changing music box was the next logical development.

The automatic disc-changing box was invented by Gustave Brachhausen who patented it in 1897. The first such instruments were constructed in the Regina factory during that year. By 1898 and 1899 they were being shipped by the hundreds to customers all over America. Made in the 15½", 20¾" and 27" models, the Regina automatics held a dozen discs on a special carriage in the base of the instrument. Tunes could be selected by means of a dial on the side of the box, or the mechanism could be set to play the discs in sequence. As most of Regina's larger models made during the early years were equipped with coin slots, the advent of the disc changer really spurred Regina sales.

With the advent of the automatic changer, Regina formed a service group which operated directly from Rahway. Company personnel installed and serviced the coin-operated boxes, periodically collecting the coins and putting new discs in the racks.

Between 1892 and 1921 some 100,000 music boxes were shipped by the Regina Music Box Company. Sales surpassed $2 million per year for a time. The original building was added to; then a building on the next block was acquired and used only for cabinet making. About 325 employees occupied the two buildings. At the same time the Symphonion Manufacturing Co. (American branch of the German firm) was operating a branch plant in New Jersey, as were F.G. Otto & Sons and one or two others. In spite of this competition, Regina held unquestioned lead among all the American manufacturers. All signs pointed to a long and prosperous future for the company.

The year 1901 saw a general business recession which affected Regina's sales to some degree. Sales were back to normal by the end of the year. In 1903, however, sales experienced a sharp plunge from which the company never fully recovered as a music box firm. The Rahway enterprise had been financed by a German bank which, seeing its investment in jeopardy, sent men to Rahway to assume control of the company. Gustave Brachhausen, whose genius and ambition had sparked Regina to its position of pre-eminence in the American music box field, stayed on, but only as a factory manager. This shake-up did not improve conditions as much as had been hoped. Nor did a new line of styles, the Regina Musical Desk and others, introduced in 1903-1904 help much either. What was wrong?

Some years before Brachhausen left Germany, young Thomas Alva Edison invented the phonograph. Ironically, Edison's laboratory was then in Menlo Park, New Jersey, barely five miles from Rahway. By the time Brachhausen came to America, Edison had moved his operations to West Orange, New Jersey, and was about to introduce his phonograph to the public. He visualized it as an office machine, and he had been rather insulted by the suggestions of some associates that it had a potential in the field of entertainment. He wanted no part of that! It is doubtful that, in the beginning, either Brachhausen or Edison foresaw the phonograph's threat to the music box business, but the inevitable happened. Edison was finally convinced that he should provide not only blank cylinders for dictating, but also pre-recorded entertainment. Once introduced to the phonograph the public clamored to buy the products of Edison and other early manufacturers. Crude and screechy as they were, the phonograph cylinders were sufficient to fire the dreams of men to the point of seemingly ridiculous predictions of a day when the sounds of an entire orchestra would be captured on wax. From then on, music boxes — grand as they were in both form and tonal quality — began to move upstairs . . . to a dark corner of the attic. The music box market, both in America and overseas, was on its way out.

Regina's first real attempt to cope with the worsening situation came in 1902, with a change in the corporate name to "The Regina Company" and the introduction of a hand-pumped pneumatic vacuum cleaner. It was so cumbersome that two people were required to operate it satisfactorily. Still, it meant diversification, and how else was the company to survive? Later, in 1909, an electric vacuum cleaner made its appearance. From just after 1900 until 1922, an assortment of products bore the Regina name, including player pianos, printing presses, copying presses, and a combination music box and phonograph in one cabinet — the Reginaphone. The last Regina music box was made in 1919. Shipments of music boxes continued until 1921. During the last several years Regina made a valiant but too-late attempt to enter the phonograph business in a large scale. Several different models of the Corona Talking Machine, the Princess Phonograph, and the Reginaphone (later styles which, while called "Reginaphone," did not have a music box but were phonograph only) were made, some by the hundreds. However, by that time the phonograph market was dominated by Victor, Edison, and Columbia — and Regina's effort met with failure. In 1922 The Regina Company was bankrupt.

Historical Postscript: If Gustave Brachhausen had been in a different frame of mind one day soon after the turn of the century, Regina's history might have been vastly different. Rahway had become a Mecca for every inventor or would-be-inventor of schemes to produce music mechanically. A certain Eldridge R. Johnson called on Brachhausen and

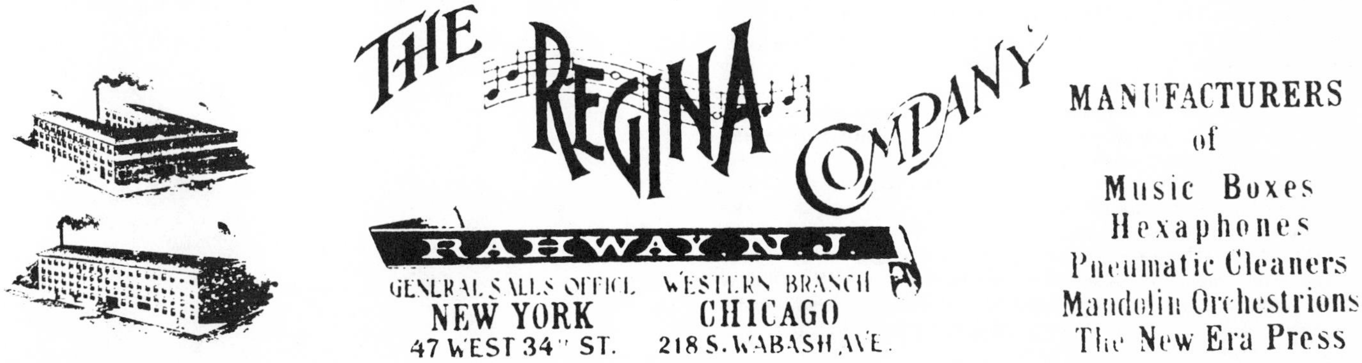

the principals of Regina and tried to interest them in the new lateral-cut phonograph disc. History is somewhat hazy on this point, but it would appear that Johnson tried to promote Emile Berliner's invention. It was a revolutionary approach, as the Edison machines used cylinders on which the grooves were cut vertically. Brachhausen listened briefly, scoffed at the idea, and sent the fellow on his way. Johnson next tried to sell the patent to Edison, but Edison decided to stick to his own methods, even though he could have bought the patent for about $12,000. Johnson went home to Camden, New Jersey, and founded the Victor Talking Machine Company. Sales in 1901, the first year, amounted to just $500. Four years later sales were $12,000,000. In 1921, the year that Regina shipped its last instruments, Victor sales were $51,000,000!

Regina Today: Regina has been back in business since 1924. Reorganized as the Regina Corporation, the firm has grown steadily to its present stature as one of the leading manufacturers of floor polishers and lightweight vacuum cleaners. A modern, 200,000-square-foot plant is occupied in Rahway. Unrelated as floor polishers are to music boxes, the present management is not unappreciative of the early groundwork done by Gustave Brachhausen. Mr. Lannon F. Mead, Regina's board chairman, acknowledges that some mass-production techniques used today trace their inception to the earlier music box business.

-----------

### Regina Instruments

The various Regina automatic musical instruments are delineated on the pages to follow, with the exception of Regina coin-operated pianos which are covered in a separate section of this book. Briefly, the Regina instruments produced were:

MUSIC BOXES: Initially, 11", 15½" and some smaller hand-cranked boxes were imported from Polyphon. These were sold under the Regina name. By the mid-1890's Regina produced nearly all of its instruments in their entirety in Rahway. Disc sizes made were: 8½, 11, 12¼, 15½, 20¾, and 27 inches. 11" and 12¼" disc instruments utilized the same size combs and featured discs with the same music arrangements; the only difference being that the 12¼" instruments had an outside edge drive, and this necessitated a larger diameter disc to accommodate the drive sprocket holes around the circumference of the disc. 15½" discs were made in two separate and non-compatible formats, one for regular instruments and another for instruments with bells. Only a few of the bell-playing type were ever made. 11" and 15½" Regina discs (15½" of the regular or non-bells type) are interchangeable with Polyphon discs of like diameters. The disc diameters given are those used in Regina advertisements and are not precise. For example, the so-called "27-inch" disc measures closer to 26¾ inches.

AUTOMATIC CHANGERS: Automatic disc-changing music boxes were made only in the 15½" (without bells), 20¾" and 27" diameters. In addition, the 32" Concerto, actually not a music box but, rather, a disc-operated piano, was made in changer form. All automatic changers hold 12 discs and change them automatically, with the exception of the 32" Concerto which holds 10 discs. Discs will play in sequence, or a desired tune may be selected by means of an index knob on the right side of the case.

COIN-OPERATED AND HOME MODELS: Generally, most Regina boxes of the 8½" to 15½" size were of the home model format. Most 20¾" and larger instruments were equipped with coin slots for commercial use. The majority of coin-operated models were made during the 1894-1903 years. Most later boxes were for home use.

REGINAPHONES: In the early 1900's Regina installed phonograph mechanisms (made by the American Graphophone Co. of Bridgeport, Conn., maker of the "Columbia" line) in certain music box styles. These instruments, which featured regular disc music box movements (with tuned music combs) and phonograph mechanisms as well, were sold under the "Reginaphone" name.

COIN PIANOS: These are detailed in a separate section of this book. Several different Regina instruments were sold — many under the "Reginapiano" name. The instruments were made by others and were sold by Regina. The Sublima series of pianos featured German-made mechanisms incorporated into Regina-built cases. These were very popular during the early 1900's.

PHONOGRAPHS: In addition to the previously-mentioned Reginaphones (music box / phonograph combinations), a number of phonograph-only Reginaphone instruments were made. Hexaphone phonographs were made mainly for commercial use and were equipped with coin slots. Corona Talking Machines and Princess Phonographs were made for the home market, mainly in the 1917-1920 years.

CONCERTO: The Concerto, made in regular and in automatic changer forms, uses a 32" disc and is a mechanical piano. We include it in the music box section of this book as it has been traditionally collected as such, but strictly speaking it is not a music box at all as it contains no music combs.

NOMENCLATURE: Regina nomenclature changed over the years. The term "Reginaphone" mainly was used to refer to music box/phonograph combinations, but early coin-operated phonographs (without music boxes) were sold under this name as were certain later phonographs for home use. The "Sublima" term was used to describe 20¾" disc music boxes and also to describe the Regina Sublima Piano. Model or style numbers changed over the years also, as noted in the following descriptions.

### Miscellaneous Notes

Regina was America's number one music box manufacturer. On a worldwide basis, Polyphon was larger. Perhaps Regina was second, with Symphonion being third. Or perhaps the order was Polyphon, Symphonion, and then Regina. The relative positions of Regina and Symphonion will never be known unless Symphonion data comes to light. These firms are collectively referred to as the "big three" by collectors today. As the preceding text notes, the three firms are closely related and have common historical roots — Brachhausen and Riessner having been associated at one time or another with each of the firms.

Regina instruments were mainly sold in the United States. Modest sales were achieved in Canada. A few instruments were sold in Europe, mainly in England in conjunction with Polyphon boxes.

The romance, history, and general excellence of Regina instruments have combined to make them collectors' favorites. Regina instruments, particularly those of the larger sizes, have been admired by many writers. Examples:

"Queen of them all [disc-changing music boxes], however, must certainly be the 27-inch Regina, with a quality of tone which is unsurpassed." ("The Disc Musical Box Handbook," by Graham Webb, page 37).

"The Regina was most probably the finest disc musical box ever produced, both in tone and musical arrangement. The standard of manufacture and case style was of the highest order, being the result of all the best of Polyphon and Symphonion, plus the Swiss musical knowledge of several generations." ("Collecting Musical Boxes," by Arthur W.J.G. Ord-Hume, page 47).

And another view, a comparison with Polyphon: "This [24½"] Polyphon was, without doubt, the best of its kind ever made. It rendered some of the classical music even better than the later and larger 27" Regina box . . . The Regina Company made the best quality disc music boxes from the start, and were continually improving upon them. Generally speaking, these were a much superior instrument, having the advantage of later improvements, but they never quite eclipsed the large [24½"] disc of the Polyphon, good as they undoubtedly were." ("Musical Boxes," by John E.T. Clark, page 104).

In America, more has been written about Regina instruments than has been written about other makes, simply because there are more Regina instruments around today and because of the interesting appearance of certain Regina models — the automatic changers and the Reginaphones, as examples.

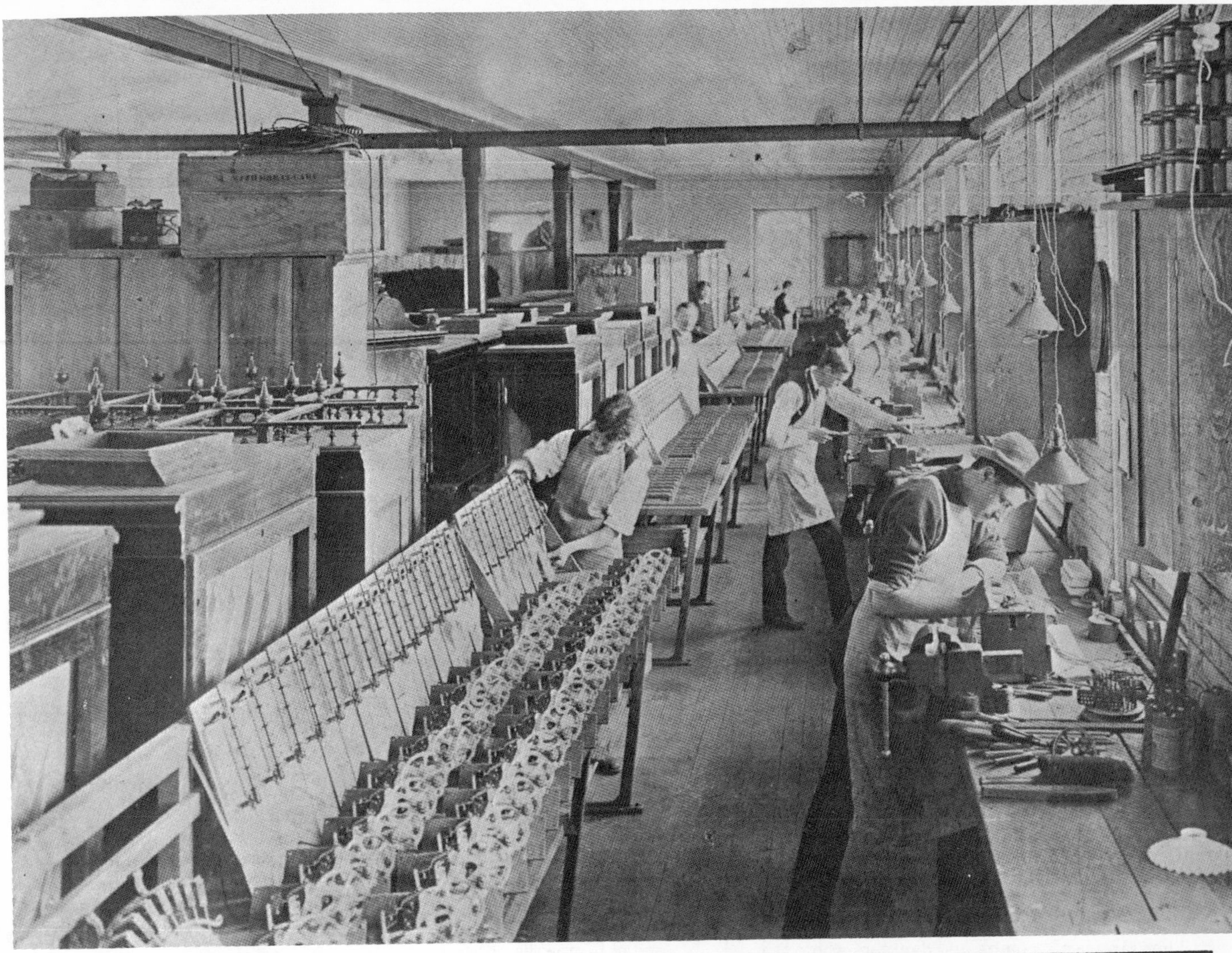

Above: Photograph taken at the Regina Music Box Company's Rahway, New Jersey, factory about 1900. To the left are about twenty of the 27" automatic disc changing boxes, some without top gallery and with piano sounding board and others with the ornate gallery and with the panel-type back door. On the benches in the foreground are many bedplates for 15½" table model boxes, many drive gears, and other mechanisms.

(Photographs on this page courtesy of Larry Givens)

Above: A wagon load of crated music boxes is on its way out the factory gate enroute to the railroad station. The stencils on the boxes proclaim that this group is headed for Lyon & Healy in Chicago.

Left: Busy workmen at the Regina factory.

# REGINA MECHANISM

IT is obviously impossible to give a complete detailed description of all the parts of the Regina within the limits of a catalogue, and yet a few words in reference to its construction may be found interesting.

**Motive Power**

The motive power of a Regina consists of a high-grade clockwork with a very powerful steel spring, the action being controlled by a reliable governor which keeps the music perfectly steady at all times. The power from the spring is transmitted to the tune disc by means of a driving wheel, with sprockets which mesh into holes near the circumference of the disc.

**Tempo Regulator**

A tempo regulator which is a part of the governor, enables the operator to play any selection, as fast or as slow as desired.

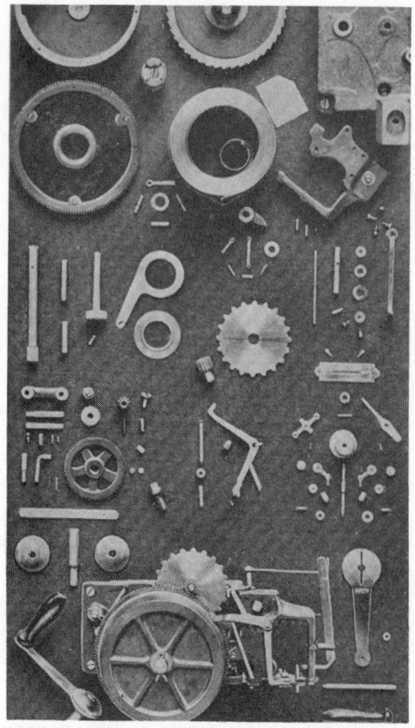

FIG. I.

*Simplicity and durability* are the virtues most needed in a motor and they are present in high degree in the Regina; in fact our spring motors have been brought to such a state of perfection that they have been known to remain in use for several years without oiling—although such neglect is not to be recommended. Regina motors are so well and favorably known in the trade that they have been used extensively by other manufacturers in various devices requiring spring motors.

Fig. I. shows all the parts of a Spring Motor and governor for Style No. 50 Regina Music Box.

**Star Wheels, Combs, and Dampers**

The star wheels, combs, and dampers when assembled and mounted form what is called the bedplate. This is the "heart" of the music box—its most important part.

When a tune disc is placed in the proper position and is made to revolve, the projections come in contact with the star wheels and in so doing each projection moves a star wheel forward one notch. The star wheels are placed in a row on a steel shaft and as each one moves forward it picks the corresponding steel tongue on the comb, thereby producing a musical vibration.

The comb is the most important and expensive part of the entire instrument, requiring in its manufacture fifty-two separate mechanical operations. (See Fig. III.)

Regina combs are made from the best imported English steel, and are specially tempered so as to produce the best tones and so that the tongues will be just elastic enough to permit them to vibrate without breaking. These combs are all tuned by skilled musicians, who have had long experience in this work. After they are tuned they are covered with the best Egyptian lacquer to prevent them from rusting, and are then carefully adjusted in position. This adjustment, as regards their position and the distance from the star wheels, must be accurate to the thousandth part of an inch; otherwise, the effect would be spoiled. Every comb is guaranteed to be absolutely correct in harmony and pitch, and any defective comb will be cheerfully replaced.

The vibrations of the tongues on the combs are hushed at the proper time by a complete set of German silver dampers, there being one damper for each star wheel and tongue. This set of dampers is a very important part of the instrument, without them the music would be spoiled, and the effect would be much the same as that obtained by playing a piano with one's foot constantly on the loud pedal. Regina dampers act automatically and positively, and will last as long as the instrument itself.

Fig. II. shows all of the parts of a complete bedplate for Style No. 50 Regina Music Box, including the star wheels, combs and dampers.

Especial attention is called to the finish of all Regina cases. This finish is of the highest grade, equal to the finish on the best piano, and all instruments are hand polished. Cases for nearly all styles are made both in carefully selected mahogany and quarter sawed oak, there being no difference in the price, except in a few instances.

Regina tune discs are made of steel, having a copper finish. They are interchangeable and practically indestructible. On the under side of each disc are hundreds of projections, each one of which represents a note of music.

FIG. II.

In the early days of the music box industry, when discs were made of zinc, these projections would sometimes break, but for many years we have used nothing but steel in the manufacture of discs, and now such a thing as a broken projection is unheard of. Each one of these projections will sustain a lateral weight of over twenty-five pounds.

Regina discs are made in six different sizes, ranging from eight inches to twenty-seven inches in diameter, and the complete list comprises over 2500 different selections.

New tunes are being added to the list every month, and the best of all new music may always be found on our lists almost as soon as the sheet music is published.

**The "Regina Mechanism" – from a circa 1910 Regina catalogue. In an era in which most automatic musical instrument companies concentrated on the "hard sell," Regina took the time to carefully explain, and in an accurate manner, how a music box was made and how the mechanisms worked.**

**The catalogue in which this appeared listed the following styles (in order as listed in the catalogue): 91, 20, 72, 172, 71, 171, 41, 42, 141, 142, 55, 155, 50, 150, 40, 140, 67, 43, 143, 26, 126, 39, 139, 44, 144, 45, 145, 35, and 33. Particularly emphasized were the Reginaphone music box and phonograph combination units.**

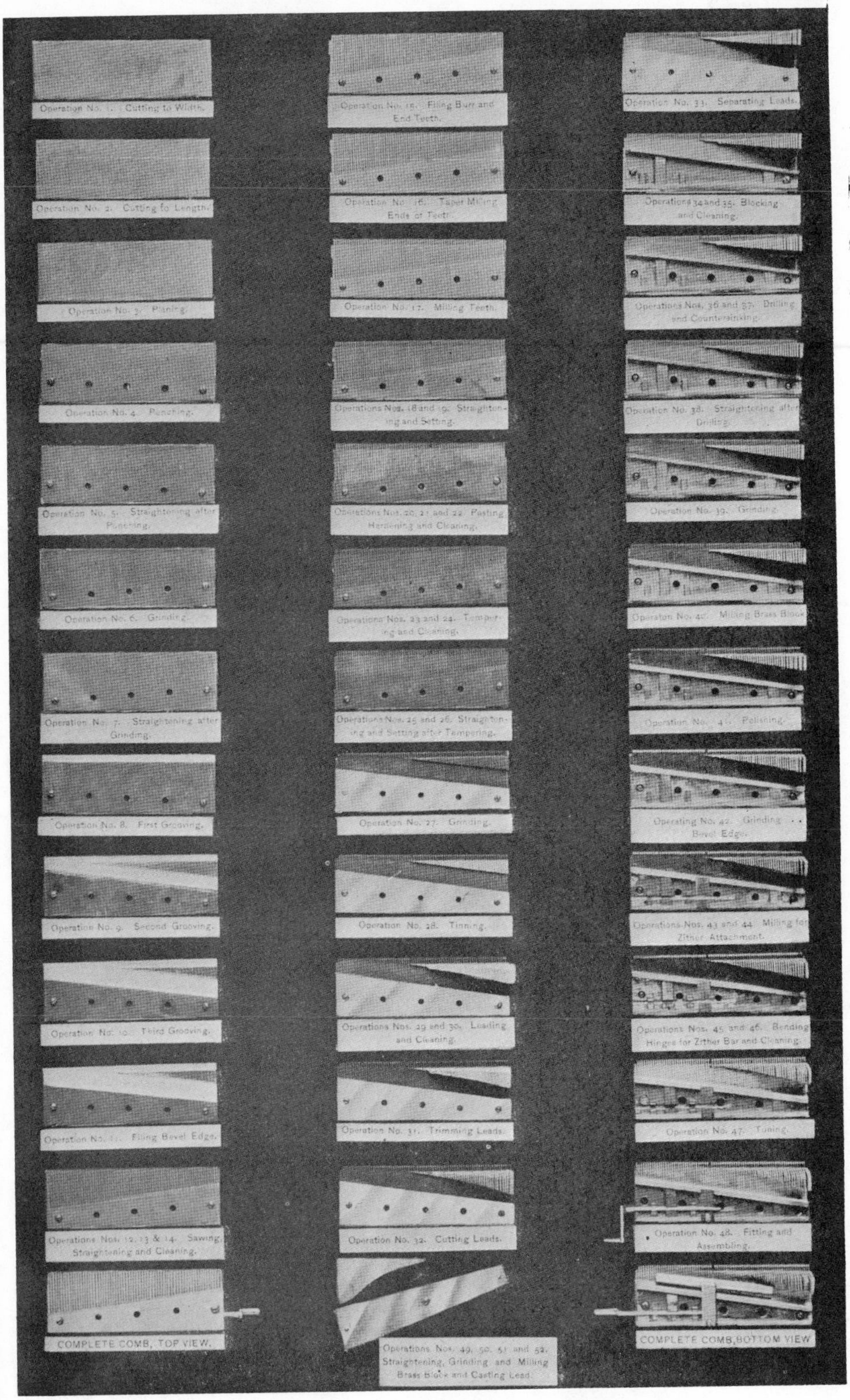


FIG. III.
This shows the Fifty-two separate mechanical operations required in the manufacture of one Regina Comb.

**Manufacturing a Music Comb: (From a c.1910 Regina catalogue). 1. Cutting steel blank to width; 2. Cutting to length; 3. Planing; 4. Punching holes for bedplate screws; 5. Straightening after punching; 6. Grinding; 7. Straightening; 8. First grooving; 9. Second grooving; 10. Third grooving; 11. Filing bevel edge; 12-14. Sawing, straightening, cleaning; 15. Filing burr and end teeth; 16. Taper milling ends of teeth; 17. Milling teeth; 18, 19. Straightening and setting; 20-22. Pasting, hardening, cleaning; 23, 24. Tempering and hardening; 25, 26. Straightening and setting; 27. Grinding; 28. Tinning; 29, 30. Leading (for resonators) and cleaning; 31. Trimming leads; 32. Cutting leads; 33. Separating leads; 34, 35. Blocking and cleaning; 36, 37. Drilling and countersinking; 38. Straightening; 39. Grinding; 40. Milling brass block; 41. Polishing; 42. Grinding bevel edge; 43, 44. Milling for zither attachment; 45, 46. Bending hinges for zither bar and cleaning; 47. Tuning; 48. Fitting and assembling; 49-52. Straightening, grinding, and milling brass block and casting lead.**

THE genius of masters
lives ever within it,
The melodies dear to the heart
and the past,
The songs that come tinkling
from grandmother's spinnet,
The tune that won public
approval the last.

The waltzes, the marches, gay
Parisian measures,
The minuet stately, the coon
rag-time song,
Now merry, now tender, now
measured sedately—
A river of music that pours
all day long.

The best works of Chopin,
Bizet and De Koven,
Strauss, Sousa and Verdi,
and ten thousand more,
Whose genius and mastership
long years have proven,
From out the **REGINA**
melodiously pour.

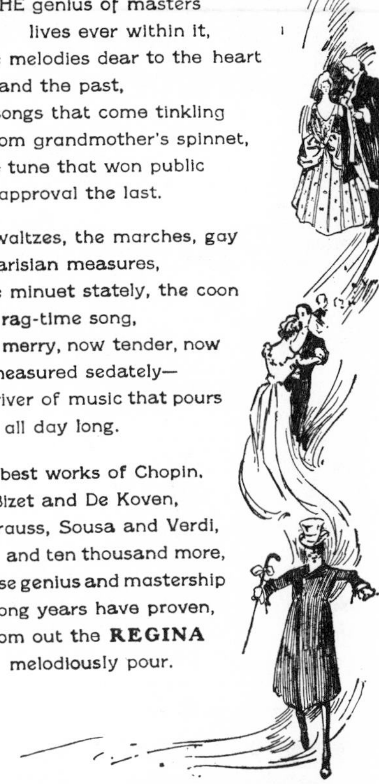

## *Regina Music Boxes.*

| | With 12 Tunes. | Fxtra Tune Sheets. |
|---|---|---|
| No. 1, - | $125.00 | $0.60 |
| " 2, - | 100.00 | .60 |
| " 3, - | 255.00 | .60 |
| " 4, - | 220.00 | 2.00 |
| " 6, - | 145.00 | 2.00 |
| " 10, - | 95.00 | .60 |
| " 11, - | 75.00 | .60 |
| " 11, Carved, | 70.00 | .60 |
| " 13, - | 50.00 | .60 |
| " 13, Carved, | 45.00 | .60 |
| " 16, - | 45.00 | .45 |
| " 17a, - | 50.00 | .45 |
| " 19, - | 40.00 | .40 |
| " 20, - | 29.00 | .40 |
| " 21, - | 10.00 | .25 |
| " 22, - | 17.00 | .25 |
| " 24, - | 175.00 | 1.50 |
| " 26, - | 115.00 | 1.50 |
| " 28, - | 140.00 | 1.50 |
| " 29, - | 38.00 | .45 |
| " 31, - | 275.00 | 1.50 |
| " 33, - | 350.00 | 2.00 |
| " 35, - | 175.00 | .60 |
| " 38, - | 275.00 | 1.50 |

**Above: From a c.1902 Regina catalogue.**

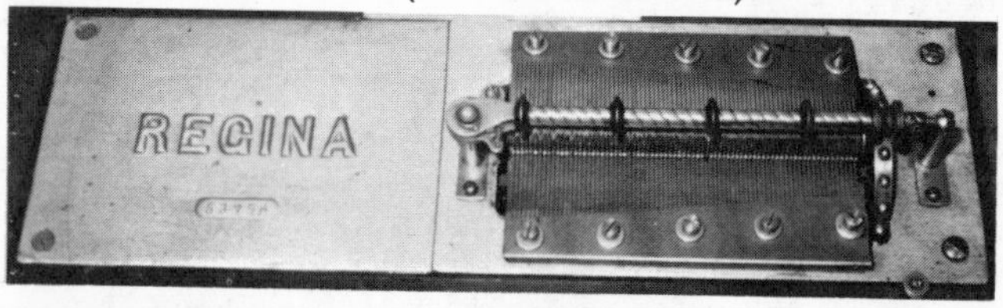

Two main types of bedplates were used on Regina instruments. The long bedplate (shown above) was used on all automatic changers, all Regina boxes made during the 1890's, and most Regina instruments of all types made up to the 1902-1904 years. The short bedplate (shown at the left) was used on most instruments made after the above-noted years – including most 7-digit serial number instruments (except changers) and most Reginaphones. The short bedplate shown here is part of a Reginaphone.

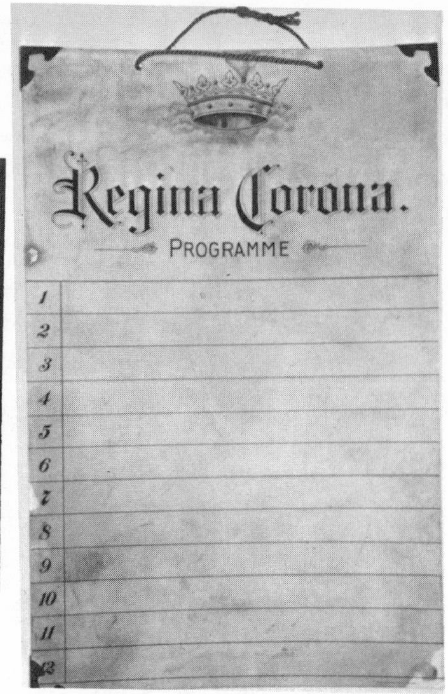


Above: Regina Corona (15½" disc changer) program card with spaces to be filled in for each of the tunes. Also shown is a portion of the right side of a Style 35 Corona. The small knob at the top is the tempo regulator. Below it is the stop-start-repeat lever. Next is the winding crank. At the bottom is the tune-selecting index knob.

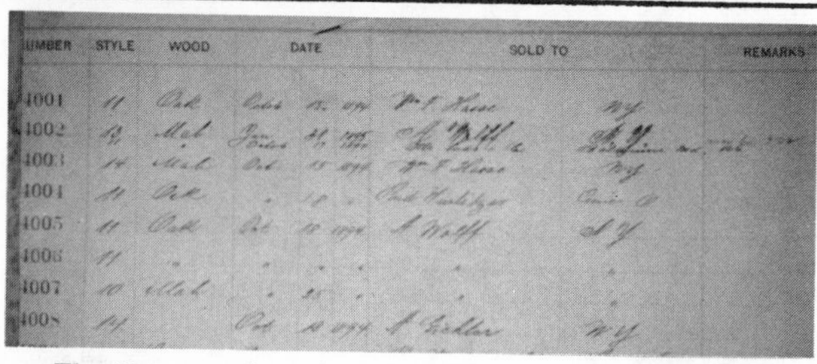


The first several entries in the Regina serial number ledgers. No. 4001, a Style 11 (15½" disc) box in oak, was shipped on October 15, 1894, to William F. Hasse of New York City. Shipments continued until the autumn of 1921. Approximately 100,000 instruments were sold during that span.

Right: Close-up view of the projections on the underside of a 20¾" Regina disc.

Types of Reginaphone horns: (1) Inside horn on Style 240. (2) Brass horn on Style 155. (3) Bright nickel horn on Style 150. (4) Painted horn on Style 142. (5) Wooden horn on Style 150.

1.

2.

3.

4.

5.

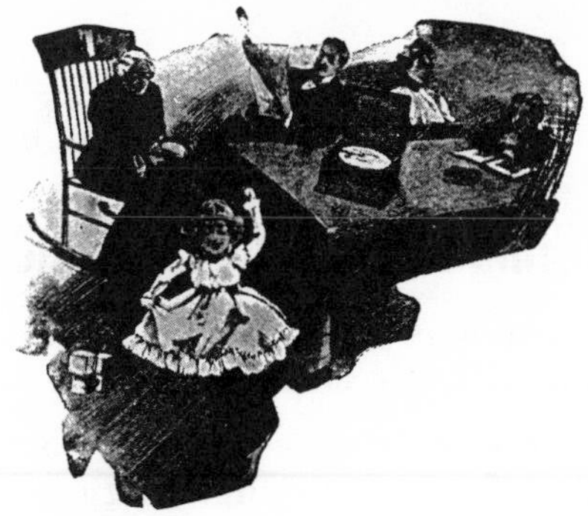

### –Regina Serial Numbers–

Regina serial numbers were assigned in advance to "runs" of a particular model. For instance, a group of 27" automatic changers, serial numbers 30001 to 30500, was started in 1898. However, shipping dates of these instruments range from 1898 to 1910! Also, it was the practice to occasionally assign a number to a bedplate and then not use the bedplate for five or ten years. This situation isn't common, but it does occur dozens of times throughout the tens of thousands of numbers listed in the Regina records – so it is worth mentioning here. This explains why a late style of instrument is sometimes found with an early serial number.

Thousands of numbers were skipped, particularly after the first few years, perhaps to keep the competition from learning that business was slow. So, the 82,000+ serial numbers in this list do not represent that many instruments.

Beginning in late 1904 a new serial system was adopted. A 7-digit number was used. The first digits consisted of the model number and the last digits represented the number of the individual instrument. For instance, Style 51 instruments whose manufacturing commenced after late 1904 were assigned numbers in the 5100000 series. The 239th specimen made after that date would be assigned serial number 5100239. These later numbers were often discontinuous and cannot be used as a guide to the total quantity made.

Instruments whose manufacturing commenced before late 1904 or early 1905 (depending upon the model) used the regular serial numbers in the 4001 to 86619 group surveyed below. As some of these instruments, although assigned their bedplate numbers earlier, were shipped after 1904 - 1905, some later dates appear in this list. Confusing, isn't it! However, some guide is probably better than none. The following list at least gives an approximation of the time period involved.

Note: We used the "000" figure in each thousand series, but in instances in which that number wasn't assigned we used the next higher number. For instance, the first number in the 73000 series is 73,233 – the numbers from 73,000 to 73,232 weren't used. The dates represent shipping dates.

Notes (recommended for the dedicated historian/collector only!): No serial numbers assigned in the 83000 or 84000 series. The first serial number, 4001, was shipped on October 15, 1894 to William F. Hasse of New York City. The instrument was a Style 11 in oak. The last serial number, 86619, also a Style 11, was shipped to C.J. Heppe & Son of Philadelphia, on July 16, 1907. This box, made of mahogany, was sold by Hesse under the "Universal" name.

In many instances two instruments were each assigned the same serial number. This was evidently done in error, for the records show that two listings had to be "squeezed in" – usually the second listing in tiny lettering above the first. Also, sometimes instruments were shipped as one style, returned to the factory, and the bedplate was used to make another style!

As noted earlier, certain numbers were never assigned. The following numbers represent major gaps in the serial sequence. In some instances there are a few, very few, numbers within the gap, but the total is small. For instance, no numbers were assigned from 65917 to 66000 inclusive, except the solitary number 65980. These major number omissions occurred: 31220-31500; 32728-33000; 37457-37481; 51917-52001; 54251-54275; 60881-60900; 63551-63568; 63735-63773; 63907-63975; 64813-64844; 65917-66000; 69276-69300; 69323-69335; 69511-69535; 69551-69561; 69581-69999; 70898-71000; 71051-71075; 71101-71125; 71151-71257; 71358-71501; 71585-71695; 71606-71624; 71687-72125; 72182-74000; 74024-75000; 78986-79000; 79037-79241; 79317-79817; 79853-79977; 80003-80009; 80028-80152; 80178-80310; 80347-80364; 80383-80582; 80611-80888; 80898-85000 (a huge gap, save for 15 scattered numbers); 85413-86615.

Note: The author has seen several Regina music boxes which have had the number omitted from the bedplate. Whether or not this was intentional is not known. Also, early Regina instruments imported from Polyphon have serial numbers that do not correspond with the Regina lists. These instances, however, are rare and are not apt to be encountered.

| | | | | | | | |
|---|---|---|---|---|---|---|---|
| 4001 | Shipped Oct. 15, 1894 | 26000 | ....January 19, 1898 | 48000 | ......April 30, 1901 | 70000 | ....January 13, 1904 |
| 5000 | ......January 3, 1895 | 27000 | ......April 27, 1898 | 49000 | ....January 31, 1902 | 71001 | ......April 30, 1906 |
| 6000 | ....... June 12, 1895 | 28000 | ....February 7, 1898 | 50000 | ...... June 17, 1902 | 72126 | ....February 4, 1907 |
| 7000 | ....September 5, 1895 | 29000 | .......July 26, 1898 | 51000 | ....February 8, 1902 | 73233 | ...... June 20, 1903 |
| 8000 | ......August 13, 1895 | 30001 | ....... April 5, 1898 | 52002 | .. December 31, 1902 | 74001 | ... December 8, 1906 |
| 9000 | .....October 26, 1895 | 31000 | .. December 21, 1899 | 53000 | ....January 14, 1904 | 75001 | ..... March 21, 1903 |
| 10000 | ..September 21, 1895 | 32000 | .......July 20, 1899 | 54000 | .. December 31, 1902 | 76000 | ....October 31, 1903 |
| 11000 | .. November 21, 1895 | 33001 | .. November 10, 1898 | 55000 | .. November 26, 1900 | 77000 | ...... March 5, 1904 |
| 12000 | ... December 7, 1895 | 34000 | .. December 18, 1898 | 56000 | ....January 30, 1901 | 78000 | ... December 2, 1904 |
| 13000 | ...February 10, 1896 | 35000 | .. December 28, 1899 | 57000 | ..September 23, 1901 | 79001 | ... December 1, 1904 |
| 14000 | ...February 29, 1896 | 36000 | ....October 16, 1899 | 58000 | .. November 11, 1901 | 80000 | .. November 15, 1905 |
| 15000 | .......May 15, 1896 | 37000 | ..... March 17, 1900 | 59000 | ...... June 25, 1903 | 81280 | ...... March 1, 1905 |
| 16000 | .. December 15, 1896 | 38000 | .....August 14, 1900 | 60000 | .......May 31, 1902 | 82343 | ........May 3, 1904 |
| 17000 | .. November 30, 1896 | 39000 | .......May 10, 1899 | 61000 | ... December 3, 1902 | 85001 | ....... June 3, 1903 |
| 18000 | ....October 22, 1896 | 40000 | ...... April 19, 1901 | 62000 | ....... June 6, 1902 | | |
| 19000 | ...February 26, 1897 | 41000 | ....February 1, 1900 | 63000 | .....October 9, 1902 | | |
| 20000 | ...February 13, 1897 | 42000 | .. December 14, 1898 | 64000 | ....October 13, 1906 | | |
| 21000 | .......May 12, 1897 | 43000 | ...... March 3, 1900 | 65000 | ........July 5, 1904 | | |
| 22000 | ... December 3, 1897 | 44000 | .....August 18, 1899 | 66001 | ....... June 6, 1902 | | |
| 23000 | .. November 16, 1897 | 45000 | ....October 12, 1900 | 67000 | ...September 7, 1906 | | |
| 24000 | ......August 6, 1897 | 46000 | .....August 16, 1899 | 68001 | .....August 13, 1903 | | |
| 25000 | .......May 23, 1898 | 47000 | ....October 10, 1899 | 69001 | ..... March 31, 1904 | | |

# The New Regina Corona

## The greatest achievement attained in the construction of Music Boxes

**The first and only Disk Music Box made which is provided with a mechanism that automatically changes its tune sheets**

**It overcomes the only objection ever raised against the Disk Music Box, namely, the necessity of changing the tune sheets**

**The instrument automatically changes its Tune Sheets . . . .**

plays any tune at will, and repeats it as often as desired. Without being touched, after once started, plays successively, by a continuous automatic motion, all the tunes of the repertoire, consisting of 12 disks, which are contained in the lower part of the case.

In brilliancy and volume of tone the **REGINA CORONA.**

**. . . Excels any Music Box . . .**

ever made; having two Large Steel Combs, tuned in chromatic scale, embracing over 7 octaves, the key, in arranging the music, can be changed repeatedly, and any piece can be faithfully rendered with all counter melodies that would be given it if played by an orchestra.

The **Steel** Tune Sheets for the **REGINA CORONA** are large enough to render it possible to play Songs, Dances, Operatic Airs, and parts of overtures complete, without having to cut out some of the finest movements as has heretofore been necessary in other boxes.

**THE REGINA CORONA** has a Long-running Clock Movement, which is interchangeable in all its parts, and with ordinary care will not get out of order.

**THE REGINA CORONA** is a great attraction everywhere. It is very suitable for Hotels and Summer Resorts, and will furnish delightful music to its hearers without requiring any attendance whatever.

**NEW MUSIC ISSUED EVERY WEEK.**

By means of a Piano Sounding Board, introduced in The Automatic Corona Nos. 34, 36 and 38, a volume of tone, heretofore unknown in music boxes, is obtained, which makes this style specially suitable for halls and ballrooms.

**"$30.00 PER MONTH FOR SIX MONTHS."**

Gents: Wayland, N. Y., June 8th.

Your favor of the 7th at hand and in reply will say to you that the instrument in the last six months has taken in about $30.00 per month. Besides this I had the instrument in my dining room every day during dinner and supper time and it has increased my bar trade from $3.00 to $6.00 per day. I can frankly say that I would not be without one.

Yours very truly, OTTO F. LIEDERS.

**"AVERAGE $25.00 PER MONTH."**

Gentlemen: Oneonta, N. Y., June 11th.

Your letter in regard to the music box received, and owing to the lack of time, it has been neglected. It has averaged $25.00 per month. It is an excellent entertainer and no doubt holds the people.

Respectfully, O. G. RICHMOND & CO.

**"RECEIPTS AVERAGE $3.00 PER DAY."**

Dear Sirs: Troy, N. Y., June 9th.

I received the music O. K. I find them nice and had no trouble in fitting them. I am pleased with the Corona that I purchased from you, it has earned on an average $3.00 per day and has been a great benefit to my bar, and furnished my house with music for which I was obliged to pay a musician $15.00 per week.

Yours respectfully, E. BARRY.

**Corona No. 34,** if so desired, can also be arranged to repeat the same tune, or to play two successive tunes for a nickel.

**Coronas Nos. 36 and 38,** aside from playing one tune for a coin, can only be changed to play two successive tunes, if desired.

**"IMMENSELY WELL PLEASED."**

Gentlemen: San Antonio, Tex., July 5th.

In reply to your favor inquiring "how we liked the Music Box." desire to say, we are immensely pleased with it and would not be without it for anything. We did not buy the box with the intention of making money out of it, but simply as an attraction to our place of business. The box, however, has made us on an average of $2.00 per day since we put it in. We intend to buy another "Reginia No. 34" as soon as we can dispose of the Criterion we have at our branch saloon.

Yours truly, BULL BROS.

**These advertisements for the Regina automatic disc changing music box appeared about 1901. The "We intend to buy another 'Regina No. 34' as soon as we can dispose of the Criterion we have at our branch saloon" letter shown at the left was a slap at a competitor — something quite unusual in Regina advertising.**

**Regina disc-changing music boxes were made in 15½" ("Corona"), 20¾" ("Sublima Corona"), and 27" ("Orchestral Corona") styles. In addition, a disc-changing piano orchestrion, the Concerto, was made in the 32" disc size.**

**In the 1890's Regina directed its advertising for large instruments to the restaurant owner, saloonkeeper, and other commercial operators. The emphasis later shifted to home use as coin operated music boxes became obsolete in commercial locations, having been supplanted by coin pianos. By 1908 nearly all large instruments sold were for home use (and did not have coin slots).**

THE Wedding of the Regina Music Box and the talking machine occurred about six years ago. This new family took the name of "Reginaphone" —a Reginaphone being a Regina and a talking machine combined in one instrument. The improvements made during six years have been very great, and today the Reginaphone is in a class by itself—the instrument *par excellence*—the queen of all home entertainers.

The Regina Music Box has its hosts of friends, and the talking machine has brought delight to thousands. Each instrument has its own advantages, and each its champions. Until recently it was impossible to buy these two entertainers in combination, but now if there is a division of opinion in any household as to the merits of music box or talking machine, the question is easily settled by the purchase of a Reginaphone.

The Reginaphone brings to the home everything that can be sung or spoken or played; it plays Regina discs and talking machine records with equal facility and the change from one to the other can be made in less than ten seconds; it will play more records with one winding and run more evenly than any other talking machine, because it has a better and stronger motor; it will play any talking machine disc record up to fourteen inches in diameter.

We invite comparison between the Reginaphone, *as a talking machine*—without considering its further advantage as a music box—with *any* other talking machine at *any* price. We also ask you to consider that this superior talking machine is an *attachment* to the Regina Music Box. The combination giving you entertainment that may be infinitely varied, song and speech, monologue and grand opera, interspersed with most delightful instrumental music from Regina discs. No mere talking machine or phonograph can give you the added delight of Regina Music. But the Reginaphone *does*.

The Reginaphone is made in various styles and each style costs just twenty-five dollars more than the *corresponding* style of Regina Music Box. For this additional sum we guarantee you as good a talking machine as one that costs you one hundred dollars or more, as good results as you can get on any talking machine at any price.

Each Reginaphone has a high-grade sound box, improved tapering arm, and large nickel-plated flower horn, and with each instrument we furnish 200 needles and twelve Regina discs. All sold under the Regina guarantee.

The talking machine attachments are all exactly the same on all Reginaphones described in this catalogue. The only differences are in the music box parts of the various styles.

**Would you be interested in exchanging your Regina for one of our new Reginaphones as per illustration? If so, please give us the serial number of your Regina which you will find on the bed-plate of the instrument.**

**THE REGINA COMPANY.**

218 Wabash Ave., CHICAGO, ILL. 47 West 34th St., N. Y. C.

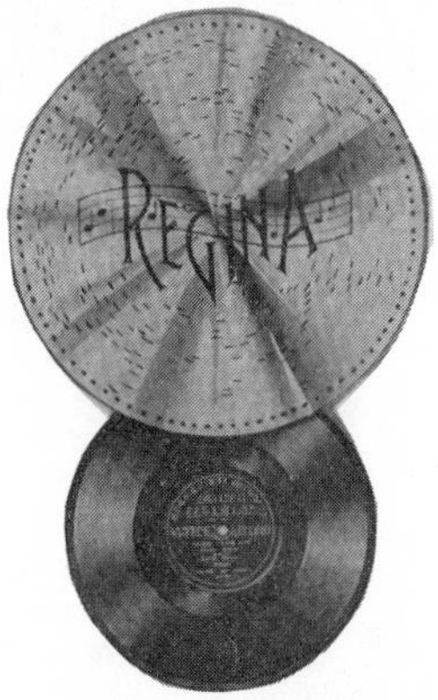

**When the popularity of the home phonograph became apparent shortly after 1900, Regina, although wary of the phonograph and skeptical of its worth (Regina advertisements usually mention phonographs in a condescending manner), decided to incorporate a phonograph attachment to several of its music box styles. A phonograph turntable was driven by placing it on a special mandrel or post connected to the music box spring. When not in use as a phonograph, the Reginaphone turntable was removed, and the instrument could then be operated as a normal music box. The phonograph tone arm was swung to the side and out of the way when discs were played. Certain compact models (Style 250, for example) had detachable phonograph arms.**

**Outside-horn models, the styles with "morning glory" type horns, were given 100-series style numbers. Thus a Style 50 music box equipped with an outside horn became a Style 150 Reginaphone. The phonograph horn was detachable to permit closing the music box lid (or to permit conveniently playing the instrument as a music box). Outside-type horns were made in several styles including lacquered brass, polished nickel, painted metal, and wood.**

**Inside-horn type Reginaphones were assigned 200-series numbers. Thus a Style 50 music box with a wooden horn built into the case (as per the picture directly above) was called a Style 250. 200-series models were popular in the mid-'teens.**

**Reginaphones were made with music boxes of 12¼, 15½, 20¾, and 27" disc sizes. The 15½" size was the most popular.**

**Certain Reginaphones were sold as "Columbia Grafonolas," and no mention was made of the Regina name.**

**The description at the left is from a Regina catalogue of 1908.**

**Similar music box and phonograph combinations were made by Polyphon, Mira, and other disc music box manufacturers. None of these other makes ever achieved the wide popularity that was given to the Reginaphone instruments.**

## —8½" Regina Music Boxes—

8½" disc instruments were the smallest Regina music boxes made. Style 21, a "manivelle" or hand-cranked model (without spring), sold for just $7 in 1896 and $10 in 1901 — and was the cheapest of all Regina boxes. Style 22, the cheapest spring-wound Regina, sold for $14 in 1896 and $17 in 1900. Style 23, the Musical Savings Bank, sold for $17.50 in 1896.

### Style 21

The hand-cranked Style 21 was popular from about 1895 to 1907. Most were sold in the 1899-1903 years. The lowest recorded serial number is 5100 for an instrument shipped on March 8, 1895. One of the best customers for the Style 21 was the Larkin Soap Company of Buffalo, New York (and other addresses).

Style 21 was made in large quantities. A run of instruments, serially numbered from 32501 to 32727 inclusive, included instruments that were shipped from 1902 to 1907. Another production run, No. 41501 to No. 41700, was mostly shipped in 1899 (although the numbers were later than those of the previously-mentioned run). Yet another run, assigned most (but not all) of the numbers from 49500 to 50000, was shipped from 1899 to 1902. The precise number of Style 21 instruments made will never be known as some were not assigned serial numbers at all. The same applies to Style 22.

### Style 22

Style 22 instruments were made by the thousands and were popular from about 1895 to 1906. The lowest serial number is 4241, assigned to an instrument shipped on January 31, 1895.

Production runs include 20 movements (without cases) shipped on August 19, 1895, to the W.F. Main Co. of Iowa City, Iowa; and the following complete Style 22 instruments as per their serial numbers: 11301 to 11400 (shipped in 1895); 27401 to 27500 (shipped in 1897 and 1898); 41701 to 43000 (shipped 1898-1900); 48001 to 48500 (this run included some Style 23's — shipped 1900-1901); 61001 to 62000 (also with some Style 20's and 23's — shipped 1900-1902); 66001 to 67000 (shipped 1902-1906, including many to Larkin Soap Co.); and 68027 to 68997 (included some Style 23's — shipped 1903-1905). In addition, scattered smaller runs were made from time to time. Some Style 22 instruments were made without serial numbers, so the total number manufactured will never be known.

### Style 23 — Musical Savings Bank

First sold in 1894 (earliest serial: 4201 shipped November 8, 1894), the Style 23 was popular until about 1906. Most were manufactured as part of Style 22 production runs, but a few separate runs of just Style 23's were made also (for instance, numbers 68001 to 68025 — shipped 1903-1906).

The front of most bore a notice which read: "Musical Savings Bank — You Pay - I Play." Upon receipt of a coin a tune was played. Although quite a few Style 23 instruments were originally made, they are quite rare today — probably as most were used by children and suffered a high attrition rate.

### Style 91

In later years styles 21, 22, and 23 were dropped from the Regina line, and Style 91 became the standard instrument which used the 8½" disc. The June 1, 1908, price list omits styles 21-23 and prices Style 91 at $25 (with extra discs at 25c each).

The catalogue description read: "No. 91. This instrument is the smallest Regina made. It will play about ten minutes with one winding. The comb has 41 steel tongues, and in this style the driving power is applied at the center of the disc. Tune discs 8 [sic] inches in diameter. Cases in oak or mahogany. Dimensions 14¾x11¾x8¾ inches."

Style 91's are serially numbered with seven digits. The lowest is 9100001; the highest, 9100414. Shipments were made from 1907 to 1915.

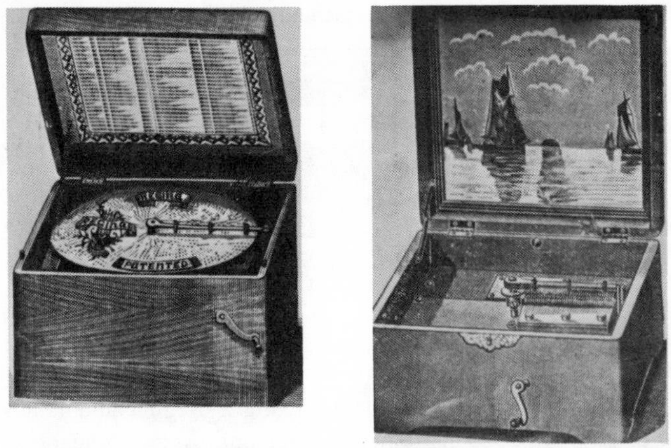

STYLE 21: Hand-cranked (without spring) style. Single comb with 41 teeth. Dimensions: 9¼x8¼x7". Made in oak or mahogany. Made with crank in front (as illustrated) or on the right side of the case. Several case style variations, all minor, two of which are shown above.

STYLE 22: Spring wound. Single comb with 41 teeth. Oak or mahogany cases or special Japanese lacquer case (as shown at above right). Dimensions: 12½x9½x7¾". Usually seen with post for winding crank located below the lower right of the music comb as illustrated above. Many Style 21 and 22 boxes were made without serial numbers. Others have the serial number on the bedplate.

STYLE 23 — MUSICAL SAVINGS BANK. 41 teeth, single comb. Made in two case sizes: 12¼x9½x7¼ inches and 17x12x6 inches. Available in oak (usually) or mahogany woods. With "Musical Savings Bank — You Pay — I Play" sign on the lower front. Like the Symphonion Musical Savings Bank (see Symphonion section of this book) the Style 23 was mainly used by children.

STYLE 91: Late style 8½" disc box shipped from the factory from 1907 to 1915. The Rudolph Wurlitzer Company was the best customer for the Style 91 and ordered dozens. Serially numbered with 7-digits (see accompanying text).

## —11" Regina Music Boxes—

Music boxes of the 11" disc size were made in two main styles: those with a single comb (of 56 teeth) were designated as Style 20; duplex comb models (with 112 teeth) were designated as Style 19.

Although 11" instruments were listed in Regina catalogues from the very beginning, only a minimal effort was made to advertise and promote this size. Perhaps the 11" models were too close in size to the 15½" styles to feature both sizes effectively at the same time. Whatever the reason, the quantities were small in comparison to instruments of the 15½" size.

11" Regina instruments, like Polyphon music boxes of the same disc diameter, have the music comb on the left side of the box — an unusual situation as most others have the comb on the right.

Most 11" discs are numbered in the 2000 series. In most instances the tunes were similar to those used on 12¼" discs with related numbers, except that 12¼" discs are in the 6000 series. For instance, the tune "Stephanie Gavotte," the first tune listed, is No. 2001 on an 11" disc and 6001 on a 12¼" disc.

### Style 19

11" Regina music boxes with duplex combs were designated as Style 19. A 1900 advertisement described the Style 19 as follows: "112 steel tongues. Dimensions 14 7/8 by 14 5/8 by 9 1/2 inches. Tune sheets, 11 inches in diameter. Case richly carved in walnut only." Most Style 19 instruments were carved and in walnut, but others were in oak or mahogany cases. Most cases were with machine-carved panels (as illustrated), but some were made in plain oak or mahogany cases.

The earliest Style 19 serial number is 20000, assigned to an instrument shipped on February 13, 1896. From about 1896 to 1904 many hundreds of Style 19's were made. After 1904 just nineteen Style 19's were made with 7-digit numbers, made in order from 1900001 to 1900019. The last of these was shipped in 1908.

The largest production run of Style 19 boxes bore serial numbers from 44650 to 45000 (not continuous) and consisted of carved models in walnut and mahogany woods. These were shipped from the factory from 1900 to 1902.

### Style 20

A general description of the Style 20 from the 1910 catalogue follows: — "No. 20. Uses 11-inch discs. In this instrument the comb has fifty-six steel tongues, and the harmonic range is, therefore, about 40 percent greater than in Style No. 91 [an 8½" instrument]. On account of the increased diameter of the tune disc, the surface area is almost double that of the 8½-inch disc, and the music can therefore be made much more complete than on the smaller size, where the tunes must be abridged. Style No. 20 plays about twelve minutes with one winding. Cases in oak or mahogany. Dimensions 15¼x14x9½ inches."

Style 20 sold for $29 in 1900; for $35 in 1908. Extra discs cost 40c each.

Although many different case variations were made, Regina music boxes which used the 11" disc and which had a single music comb were generally assigned the Style 20 designation. The lowest serial number is 4880, assigned to an instrument shipped on December 20, 1894.

Several large production runs of Style 20 instruments were made. Serial numbers 10001 to 11200 inclusive were assigned to Style 20 boxes shipped in 1895 and 1896. Serial numbers 40001 to 41000 inclusive were mainly for Style 20's, although some of styles 19, 29, and 30 were in the same number range. These were shipped from 1898 to 1900. Likewise, the following runs were mostly (but not all) Style 20's: 41191 to 41490; 60001 to 60799 (shipped 1900-1903); 67101 to 67500 (shipped 1903-1904); and 67801-67900 (shipped 1904-1906).

Some later instruments were assigned 7-digit numbers in the 2000000 series. Serial numbers from 2000001 to 2000162 represented 152 instruments (some numbers were not used) shipped from 1905 to 1913.

### Other 11" Instruments

Style 20a: Some duplex comb plain-case (not carved) 11" instruments were designated as Style 20a; others were designated as Style 19 (although Style 19 was a designation mainly used for carved instruments).

Musical Salesman: The Style 18 "Musical Salesman," similar to the type illustrated later among the 12¼" instruments, was also made in 11" and 15½" formats. These dispense a pack of gum upon receipt of a one-cent piece.

Musical Clocks: Several early Regina clocks, including some imported from Polyphon (using Lenzkirch cases), used 11" discs.

STYLE 19: With duplex music comb assembly; 112 teeth. Usually made with a carved case as illustrated, but sometimes in plain oak or mahogany. Carvings are applied to the main structure of the case.

No. 20. Single Comb.

STYLE 20: 11" Regina music box, table model with single comb of 56 teeth. (Some duplex comb models with 112 teeth were designated as Style 20a and are in similar cases). The case designs varied over the years. Note that the instrument at the right is wound by a lever on the front (instead of the usual crank). Most, however, were crank-wound — as per the others illustrated here. Early models had a scene of children at play. Later ones featured a "Queen of Music" scene. The very latest ones had "REGINA" on the underside of the lid (as per illustration at the lower right from a 1910 catalogue).

Note that the music comb is on the left side — an unusual feature.

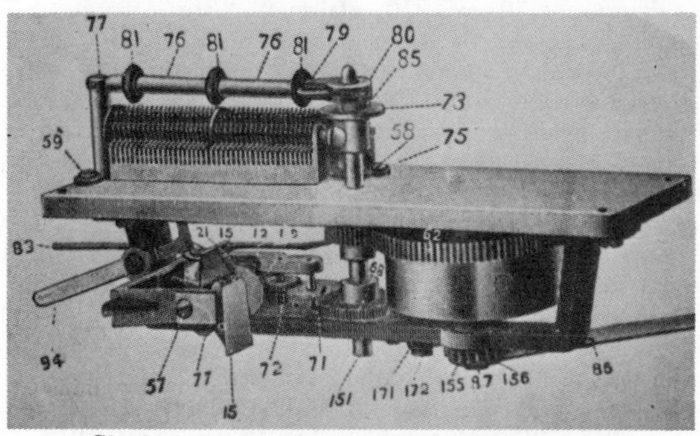


Clockwork (spring) mechanism of the Style 20.

## –12¼" Regina Music Boxes–

Although 12¼" boxes were made from the 1890's until well into the 'teens many fewer of this disc size were made than were produced of the other standard diameters. Despite the limited production, a number of different models were produced.

12¼" models that were most important in terms of original quantities produced were:

Table models: These were made in two popular styles, with coin operation and with an on-off lever (for home use). Single comb and duplex models were produced. Single models for home use were designated as Style 29; duplex models as Style 16. The coin operated versions of these styles were designated styles 30 and 17 respectively.

Coin-operated vertical models: Made for counter use in business establishments were styles 17a and 18. Each style was made in a number of case variations.

In addition to the above-mentioned 12¼" instruments, a number of Reginaphones, late-style home models in serpentine (with curved sides) cases, and other styles were made, but the numbers produced were small. Below we survey the various 12¼" instruments as listed in the Regina factory records.

### 12¼" Styles:

STYLE 16: Table model, duplex comb (112 teeth). This is the duplex comb version of Style 29. The lowest serial number surveyed is 28501, assigned to an instrument shipped on April 20, 1898. Style 16's were produced continuously over the years. A run numbered from 63797 to 63906 contained Style 16's and some Style 116's (the Reginaphone version of Style 16). The latest Style 16's made were with 7-digit numbers (1600001 to 1600149) and were shipped in 1906 and 1907.

STYLE 17: Table model, duplex comb. Coin operated version of Style 16. Earliest serial number: 28502, shipped on April 15, 1898.

STYLE 17a: Coin operated model with the disc mounted vertically. Made in several variations, including one with a gum-vending apparatus. Style 17a and Style 16 instruments, although differing from each other in appearance, were usually made in the same production runs. Serial numbers 62001 to 63634 were assigned to one such run; the instruments were shipped from 1900 to 1905. 17a instruments have duplex combs.

STYLE 18: This style number was given to vertical disc boxes with vending apparatus; most of which used 12¼" discs, but some of which used 11" or 15½" discs. The lowest serial number is 5977, assigned to an instrument shipped on February 18, 1895. As this is several years earlier than the initial shipping dates of other 12¼" models, this particular box was probably a 15½" style. Serial number runs of Style 18 boxes include 67001 to 67049 (shipped 1902-1903) and later 7-digit series models (1800000 series) of which about 160 instruments were shipped from 1909 to 1918. The location of the vending apparatus varied: some had the dispenser on the front; others on the right side of the instrument.

STYLE 29: Single-comb version of Style 16. 56 teeth. Lowest serial number: 29041 (an 1897 serial number which was assigned to an instrument that wasn't shipped until 1912!). The first regular shipment was of serial 40276 shipped on April 12, 1899. Production runs (which sometimes included Style 129 instruments as well) include: 60901 to 61000 (shipped in 1901-1902) and 67501 to 67799 (shipped in 1903 and 1904). Later instruments were given serial numbers in the 7-digit range, from 2900001 to 2900109, and were shipped from 1906 to 1913.

STYLE 30: Single-comb version of Style 17. Coin operated. Lowest serial number: 40277. These were often made in the same production runs with Style 20 (11" disc – but with same music comb) instruments.

STYLE 41: Duplex comb floor model with attached base cabinet. Regina's description (from 1910 catalogue): "Nos. 41 and 42. These instruments contain exactly the same mechanism as Nos. 71 and 72. In these styles there is a commodious cabinet underneath the instrument for holding Regina discs . . . Cases in oak or mahogany. Dimensions 40¾x18x16¼ inches." Initially produced around the turn of the century. Lowest serial number is 31779 (an 1897 number) assigned to an instrument that was shipped on July 3, 1903. Later, Style 41's were made in the 7-digit series from 4100001 to 4100053. Eighteen of these 7-digit boxes were made (some numbers were skipped), of which the American Graphophone Co. purchased four. The last Style 41 was shipped on December 6, 1913.

STYLE 42: Single-comb version of Style 41. Made in small quantities during the early 20th century. In the 7-digit series, six instruments were made and were numbered from 4200001 to 4200042 (some numbers were not used). Last instrument shipped on November 24, 1913.

STYLE 71: Duplex comb table model in curved or serpentine case. Regina's description (circa 1910): "This instrument is of the same size and has the same case as No. 72, but contains duplex combs with 112 steel tongues. One comb is a duplicate of the other, and two steel tongues are struck at the same instant by each star wheel, thus giving twice as much volume of sound as in No. 72. [Editor's note: this is not correct; the sound is increased, but not doubled or even nearly so.] No. 71 is also equipped with a new style banjo attachment operating on both combs, improved bedplate and sounding board similar to that in No. 50, and tempo regulator . . . Cases in oak or mahogany, curved front and sides." Serial numbers in the 7-digit series from 7100001 to 7100315 plus one anomalous late number, 7100654 (shipped in 1920). First shipped on January 12, 1907. Last shipped (except No. 7100654) in 1916.

STYLE 72: Single-comb version of Style 71. Regina noted (c.1910): "The discs on this instrument are driven by a sprocket wheel from the circumference, and the motor is similar to that used in our highest-priced instruments. By means of the outside drive a uniform speed is obtained. [Editor's note: The 12¼" discs are the same as the 11" discs, except that the latter are of larger diameter to accommodate the sprocket holes – the 11" discs are center driven.] No. 72 has a long running movement with a tempo regulator and banjo attachment and plays about fifteen minutes with one winding . . . On this style [and on most 7-digit serially numbered Reginas with short bedplates – Ed.] the bedplate is detachable, making it more convenient to oil the clockwork. Cases in oak or mahogany. Curved front and sides. Dimensions 16¾x15x10¾ inches." Serially numbered from 7200001 to 7200177. Shipped from 1907 to 1917.

STYLE 116: Reginaphone version of Style 16. Lowest serial number: 62637, assigned to a Style 116 shipped on April 5, 1905. Over 100 instruments produced in a production run (serials 63636 to 63791) that included some Style 16's as well. Later instruments were assigned 7-digit numbers from 1160001 to 1160138 and were shipped from 1905 to 1909.

STYLE 129: Reginaphone version of Style 29. Lowest serial number is 67092, an instrument originally made as a Style 29, but then converted to a Style 129. A production run of serial numbers 67911 to 67951 was mostly of Style 129; the instruments were shipped in 1905 and 1906. 7-digit models were made in later years; commencing with 1290101 (not 1290001) and continuing to 1290131. These few instruments were shipped from 1907 to 1909.

STYLE 141: Reginaphone version of Style 41. 58 made with 7-digit serial numbers in the 1410001 to 1410070 series. Shipped from 1908 to 1917.

STYLE 142: Reginaphone version of Style 42. 21 made with 7-digit serial numbers in the 1420001 to 1420039 series. Shipped from 1908 to 1916.

STYLE 171: Reginaphone version of Style 71. 124 made with 7-digit serial numbers in the 1710001 to 1710173 series. Shipped from 1907 to 1917.

STYLE 172: Reginaphone version of Style 72. Early serial No. 67930 was altered from a Style 129, but was not shipped until 1912. Most Style 172's were in the 7-digit series and were numbered from 1720001 to 1720159. Shipping dates: 1907-1916.

### Notes

A 1900 Regina price list offered the following 12¼" models: Style 16 $45.00; Style 17a $50.00; Style 29 $38.00.

The June 1, 1908 list offered these models: Style 72 $50.00; Style 71 $65.00; Style 42 $80.00; Style 41 $95.00; Style 172 $75.00; Style 171 $90.00; Style 142 $105.00; Style 141 $120.00.

It will be noted that $15 more was charged for duplex comb models than for single-comb styles. $25 more was charged for the phonograph attachment (on Reginaphones).

STYLES 17 and 30, 16 and 29. (The "7" instead of 17 is a typographical error). Table models of the 12¼" disc size. 17 and 16 are duplex comb models; 30 and 29 are single-comb models. 17 and 30 are for home use; 16 and 29 are coin operated. Cases in oak or mahogany.

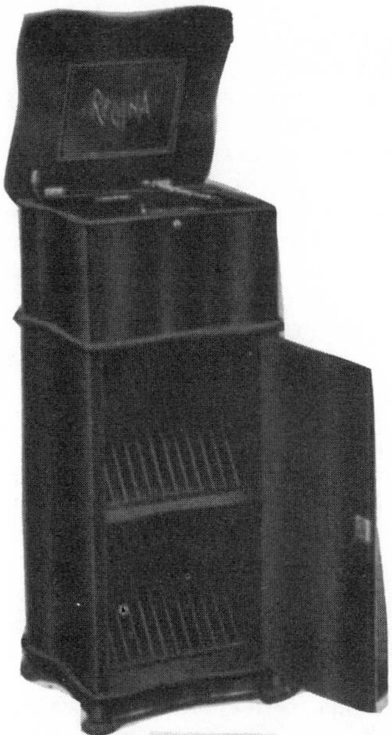
41 and 42

71 and 72

STYLES 41 and 42, 71 and 72. Curved case or serpentine models from Regina's 1910 catalogue. In later years the serpentine styles replaced the previous straight-sided models. Later models were also made with short bedplates.

STYLE 17a: Coin operated 12¼" Regina music box of vertical format. The cases of Style 17a, either of mahogany or oak, were exceptionally well made. The tonal quality was particularly brilliant also.

171 and 172

141 and 142

STYLES 171 and 172, 141 and 142. Reginaphone versions of styles 71, 72, 41, and 42. The phonograph attachment (which cost $25 extra) enabled the instrument to serve two functions: that of a music box and also of a phonograph. Horns were made in a variety of styles including painted metal, bright nickel (as illustrated), and wood.

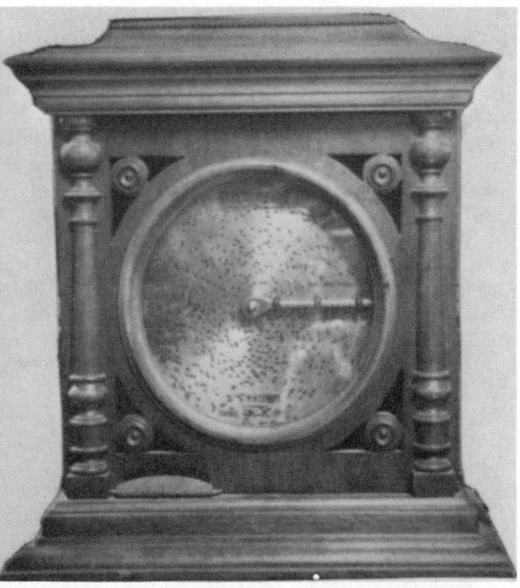
17a with gum vending apparatus at lower left.

Left: Two varieties of Style 17a, a coin operated model housed in a distinctive and ornate case. The one directly to the left has a gum-vending apparatus and dispenses a stick of gum as the music plays.

Right: Style 18. This same general case design was used with Regina mechanisms of the 11", 12¼", and 15½" sizes. Style 18 instruments were made in various configurations. Some had a sign on the top; others had a sign on the inside of the glass panel (as shown). Some had the vending apparatus on the right side of the case; others had the chute on the lower front. The Style 18 was billed as "A Musical Salesman – Regina Gum Vending Machine."

STYLE No. 18

## –15½" Regina Music Boxes–

Music boxes of the 15½" disc size were the mainstay of Regina's business. More 15½" instruments were made than were music boxes of all other disc sizes combined. More different styles of 15½" instruments were made than of any other disc size.

The first 15½" Regina music boxes sold were imported from the Polyphon Musikwerke. Later, mechanisms only were imported from Polyphon, and the cases were built in America. By 1895 the mechanisms and cases of most (but not all) were made by Regina. It is interesting to note that the 15½" size was also Polyphon's most popular. Regina and Polyphon discs are interchangeable in 11" and 15½" sizes.

While Regina catalogues nearly always noted that single-comb 15½" instruments had 78 teeth in the music comb and duplex models had 156 teeth, counting teeth in the actual music combs will produce a count of 76 and 152 respectively. There are, indeed, 78 teeth in each comb, but two of the teeth are abbreviated at the point at which the star wheel idler disc meets the comb, and thus these teeth are non-musical and non-functional. Polyphon, in its description of 15½" instruments, noted sometimes that the combs had, for instance, 152 teeth, other times that the combs had 156 teeth, and still other times wrote the description as: "156 (152) steel tongues."

The numbering system used by Regina for the 15½" discs was as follows. The first discs made by Regina (after importation from Polyphon stopped) commenced with 1001, "William Tell (Prayer)." When the 1999 number was reached the 2000 series could not be used as that had been set aside earlier for use with 12¼" diameter discs. So, the jump was made to 10001 and a new series commenced from that point. When the 10000 series was completed, numbering was continued in the 11000 series. One of the latest-numbered is "Shades of Night," – disc No. 11370. Another numbering series for the 15½" discs, the 3000 series, was used for "Continuous – specially suitable for dancing purposes" discs. These discs had no blank space at the starting position, and the end of the tune was musically arranged to merge with the beginning. Thus with the music box set for the "on" position the tune would play on, and on, and on! Only a few dozen different titles in the 3000 series were produced. The first was 3001, "Tuck Me to Sleep in My Old 'Tucky Home." Discs were usually sold for 60c each.

Note: Do not confuse the 15½" disc instruments discussed here with the special 15½" disc type used on the Style 216 and Style 217 music boxes with bells. See the "Regina 15½" (With Bells) Music Boxes" page for a discussion of these.

In the following paragraphs we discuss some of the many 15½" styles. The author would welcome correspondence from anyone having information concerning additional 15½" styles or interesting variations of standard styles. As many limited-production 15½" instruments were made, this is a fertile field for further research.

In the 1890's Regina followed the practice of using the same number for another style of instrument once the first-designated style had been discontinued. Hence, a Style 2 Regina may refer to a tall upright coin operated "Musical Automaton" of the mid-1890's or, later, an entirely different Style 2 grandfather's clock incorporating a 15½" automatic disc changer – as made circa 1900 - 1905. Likewise, Style 15 refers to an early coin operated instrument with the disc mounted vertically, or a later table model style with a horizontal disc. One type of Style 51 was sold as a coin operated instrument; another style 51 as a home model. What later became Style 50 was called Style 11a for a time before the designation was changed to 50. In addition to the Style-50-like 11a, there were other entirely-different-appearing 11a instruments made from time to time.

Actually, considering the tremendous number of instruments made by Regina and the proliferation of styles, the nomenclature is fairly straightforward. The examples cited in the preceding paragraph represent just a tiny percentage of the Regina output – and the style designations, for the most part, are consistently and logically presented in the various Regina catalogues.

It was usually the practice to give different style numbers to single and duplex comb models of the same basic instrument. It was also usual to give a separate style numbers to coin operated models.

When Reginaphones were introduced, an effort was made to number the instruments in a logical manner. While the entire system isn't known to the author, generally it was the practice to raise the basic model number by 100 for a Reginaphone with an outside horn and raise it by 200 for a model with an inside horn. Thus a Style 50 Regina with an outside horn was designated as a Style 150. The same style but with an inside horn was called a Style 250.

### Description of 15½" Models

STYLE 1: Used very early (serial number 4009, shipped October 16, 1894, for instance) to denote a hall clock style.

STYLE 1: Also used in the early years, circa 1894 - 1898, to designate a tall upright coin operated "Regina Musical Automaton" in a rectangular cabinet similar to contemporary Polyphon and Symphonion models (but not identical; Regina's cabinets were made in America). No. 1 was described as: "Duplex, 156 steel tongues. Long-running movement. Case in oak or mahogany. Dimensions 71½x23½x13½ inches." Another case style variation of No. 1 had dimensions of 6' high by 22½" wide by 1' deep. In 1896 Regina sold No. 1 for $120 wholesale (or $250 retail).

STYLE 2: Used in early years to designate the single-comb version of the "Regina Musical Automaton" (see Style 1). Lowest serial number: 5140, shipped on January 4, 1895.

STYLE 2: Used after 1900 to designate a very tall grandfather's clock which incorporated a 15½" automatic disc changing device with a storage capacity of 6 (instead of the usual 12) discs.

STYLE 3: A hall clock which incorporates a 15½" (or, rarely, an 11") Regina movement. Most clock cases were purchased from Seth Thomas. Regina added the musical mechanisms only. Made in a wide variety of clock case styles. Especially popular in the 1895 - 1905 years.

STYLE 9: Table model. Duplex combs. Most Style 9's were in cases covered with ornately carved paneling, similar in concept to the smaller Style 19 (11"). Made in walnut, oak, and mahogany woods, although some catalogues noted "case richly carved in walnut only."

STYLE 9: Table model. Duplex comb. (The duplex comb version of the Style 12). In a rather plain case as used also for Style 12. Only a few of these were made. Oak or mahogany woods.

STYLE 9: Used in very early years to designate a tall floor-standing cabinet model in an Egyptian-style furniture case with a brass railing around the top. Duplex musical movement. Dimensions: 4'10" high by 22½" wide by 13½" deep. The discs are stored in the base and are accessible through a hinged panel in the right side. The front top panel folds down to permit changing the disc. Wholesale price was $95; retail was $230 (in 1896).

STYLE 10: Table model. Duplex comb. Long-running movement. In especially ornate oak or mahogany cabinet with carved molding around the base, upper base, and lid, and with turned columns on the corners. Lowest serial number: 4007, assigned to an instrument shipped on October 25, 1894. "Style 10½" was the designation given to several models (No. 6892, shipped April 8, 1895, for instance).

STYLE 11: The most popular of all Regina music box styles, Style 11 was made by the thousands. Style 11 also has the distinction of being the first Regina instrument shipped from the factory. No. 4001, the first, was of oak wood and was shipped on October 15, 1894. Style 11 instruments were first advertised as having "long-running movements." A variety with a "regular movement" (not long-running) was designated as Style 11a in the early years. Early Style 11 and 11a instruments were made in a wide variety of minor case designs, all of the table model format. At least two cases incorporated a small drawer in the base which was suitable for storing extra discs. Style 11 was the mainstay of the Regina music box business during the 1890's and early 1900's. Style 11 instruments were often made in production runs with Style 15's (coin operated). Some Style 11 boxes (serial numbers 79001 to 79036, for instance) were designated as "Universal Boxes" and were shipped to C.J. Heppe & Son of Philadelphia, Pennsylvania. Possibly these were of distinctive design. Style 11 boxes manufactured after the autumn of 1904 were assigned 7-digit serial numbers (ranging from 1100001 to 1100142). Numbers 1000001 to 1000010 inclusive were "Universal Boxes" and were sent to C.J. Heppe & Son. The 1902 Regina catalogue priced the Style 11 at $75 retail, and a model designated as "Style 11, Carved" at $5 lower, or $70. Possibly the "carving" was actually pressed wood (a carving substitute that was popular at the time), and the production of "carved" models was cheaper than the making of "plain" ones with polished or highly finished surfaces. This is conjecture, however.

STYLE 11a: Late-type Style 11a instruments are of the type more familiarly known as Style 50. The 11a designation was used for a short time and then was changed to Style 50. These Style 11a (50) instruments were advertised as: "This corresponds with the catalogue description of our famous No. 11 except it has the new case as illustrated herewith." Early-type 11a instruments are discussed in the preceding paragraph.

STYLE 12: Table model. Single comb. Plain case. "Regular movement" (not long-running). Lowest serial number: 4103, a mahogany instrument shipped on November 12, 1894.

STYLE 12: Table model. Single comb. Carved case. Single-comb version of the popular Style 9 with carved case. Only a few Style 12's of this type were made.

STYLE 13: Table model. Single comb. "Regular movement." Single-comb version of the Style 11 (which is duplex). Lowest serial number: 4002. These were made by the thousands, often in the same production runs with Style 14 boxes. Examples of such large runs which contained mostly (but not all) Style 13 instruments are serial numbers 48501 to 49500 (shipped 1900 - 1903), 64000 to 64999 (shipped 1902 to 1904), and 69001 to 69580 (shipped from 1904 to 1906). Late Style 11's were given 7-digit serial numbers ranging from 1300001 to 1300169. These were shipped until 1913.

STYLE 14: Table model. Single comb. Equipped with coin slot for 1c or 5c operation. Lowest serial number: 4003, a mahogany instrument shipped on October 15, 1894. This model was exceedingly popular, especially in 1899 and 1900, and hundreds were made.

STYLE 14a: Same as preceding, but with duplex combs. These were first shipped in 1895, as were some models designated as "Style 14½."

STYLE 14 — MUSICAL SALESMAN: With disc in the vertical position. Somewhat similar in design to the 11-inch Style 18 "Musical Salesman." Equipped with gum-vending mechanism which dispenses gum through a chute at the front or at the right side (models differ). Coin operated, usually with a 1c piece.

STYLE 15: Used in very early years to designate a coin operated model with the disc mounted in a vertical position. These were made in two styles: one for placing on a base or a counter top, and the other for hanging on a wall.

STYLE 15: Table model. Duplex combs. Long-running movement. Coin operated (1c or 5c). "If ordered with nickel drop, unless otherwise stipulated, the tune will play twice for one coin." Cases in mahogany or oak. A coin operated version of the popular Style 11, the Style 15 was often made in production runs which included Style 11's also. Style 15 was extremely popular from about 1899 to 1903, and large quantities were made. After the autumn of 1904 only a few were manufactured. The factory archives record just 11 instruments made in the 7-digit 1500000 series. These were shipped as late as 1914.

STYLE 15: "Regina Gum Vending Machine." Duplex combs. Designed for counter top use in business establishments. Usually equipped with a 1c slot.

STYLE 35: Regina automatic disc changer. With on-off lever for home use. See separate page where these are discussed in detail.

STYLE 36: Regina automatic disc changer. Coin operated for use in commercial locations. See separate page where these are discussed in detail.

STYLE 40: Floor-standing home model with duplex combs. Regina noted (circa 1910): "All that has been said in reference to the musical qualities of No. 50 applies equally well to style No. 40 as the mechanism is exactly the same. The difference lies in the design of the case and in the fact that No. 40 contains a cabinet below the music box to hold the tune discs. This cabinet is most convenient, having patented double-acting doors and a capacity for holding one hundred and fifty 15½" discs. Made in oak and mahogany, also furnished when desired with the popular "Rookwood" finish. Dimensions 40x22x19 inches." Style 40 was also available in Vernis Martin finish or with the Marqueterie (inlaid wood designs) surface. The June 1, 1908, Regina list offered Style 40 boxes for $135 in oak or mahogany or $145 with the Rookwood (painted scenic panels) finish. The lowest serial number: 52113, assigned to an instrument shipped on December 20, 1902. A number were made in the 7-digit series with serial numbers from 4000001 to 4000300. The last Style 40 was shipped from the factory in 1915. Note: An anomalous (c.1896) serial number, No. 17353, was assigned to a Style 40 which was shipped on May 9, 1904. This represents the use of a left-over bedplate from earlier days.

STYLE 43: Floor-standing model made for home use. Duplex combs. Regina noted (circa 1910): "Style No. 43 also contains the famous No. 50 mechanism, and differs from No. 40 only in the style of the case which has swell front and sides. Its lines are similar to those of No. 50, and it is an artistic creation which has been greatly admired. When furnished without the talking machine attachment the tune disc compartment is made like that in Style 40 and will hold one hundred and fifty 15½" discs. . ." Dimensions 41x23½x20 inches. Only 23 Style 43's were made, including eight that were sold to the American Graphophone Company. 7-digit serial numbers from 4300001 to 4300038. First shipped on October 6, 1908.

STYLE 50: Table model. Duplex combs. Curved or serpentine case. Successor to Style 11a. Most Style 50's have short bedplates. Regina noted: "No. 50. This is the most popular instrument of the kind ever produced. It is the same size as Style 55, but is enclosed in a more handsome case, having swell front and sides. It differs from Style 55 in that it has a double or duplex comb with 156 steel tongues instead of 78. This means [a louder] tone over Style 55. In purchasing an instrument of this kind, its music-producing capacity is, of course, of the first importance. In Style 50 is offered an instrument having [a louder] musical volume than a single-comb instrument of the same size, and at a comparably slight additional expense. Style No. 50 has been one of the most popular instruments ever made by the Regina Company. It is known all over the world, and has been a standard with which other instruments have been compared. Style 50 is equipped with a banjo attachment operating on both combs, tempo regulator, and has the improved bedplate and sounding board. Tune discs, 15½" in diameter, long-running movement, playing about thirty minutes with one winding. Cases in oak or mahogany. Dimensions 22¼x20x13 inches." Sold by the thousands, the Style 50 was the successor to Style 11. Lowest serial number specifically assigned to a Style 50: 73418. (Note that Style 50 was earlier called Style 11a — see paragraph on Style 11a.) Most models shipped from 1905 to 1918 (the last date) were of the 7-digit series in the 5000001 to 5002551 serial number range. The American Graphophone Company of Bridgeport, Connecticut, was a good customer for Style 50 and ordered them in large lots. An anomalous serial number, No. 36395, (an 1899 serial number) was assigned to a Style 50 that was shipped on June 27, 1918! Evidently this bedplate was left over from earlier operations.

STYLE 51: Table model. Duplex combs. Coin operated. Advertised as: "Regina No. 51 — Duplex. This is a new style and is the successor to our well-known Style 15. Has improved bedplate and sounding board, also speed regulator, 156 steel tongues, tune sheets 15½" in diameter, long-running movement playing from twenty minutes to half an hour with one winding. Plays tunes once or twice as desired for each coin. Cases in quartered oak or mahogany. Dimensions 22x20x12 inches. Weight, packed, about 75 pounds. This instrument is a favorite with many coin machine operators. It pays well and is easily handled. One of these instruments taking in only five cents per day will pay 20% on the investment in one year. If it takes in $1 per day, it pays 400% on the investment." Note: Some Regina distributors (Koehler & Hinrichs of St. Paul, Minnesota, for example) featured the new Style 51 but illustrated it with a cut of the long-bedplate-type Style 15.) Generally, a Style 51 (coin operated version) may be identified as having: (1) a straight-sided case (not serpentine), (2) duplex combs, (3) short bedplate, and (4) a coin slot. However, there seems to have been some overlapping between the Style 15 and Style 51 nomenclature, and some short-bedplate instruments that should have been called Style 51 were shipped as Style 15's, and vice versa.

STYLE 51: Table model. Duplex combs. Not coin operated. Straight-sided case. Duplex comb version of Style 55 (see following description of No. 55). Advertised as: "Style 51 has a duplex set of combs, having 156 steel tongues, thus assuring good volume, with an extremely mellow and sweet tone. Regina's catalogue illustration shows a long-bedplate model, although it is probable that most Style 51's were of the short-bedplate variety. Style 51's (of both varieties — this and the one described in the preceding paragraph) were shipped by the hundreds, mainly in the 1900 - 1905 years. The lowest regular serial number assigned to a Style 51 was 30018, given to an instrument shipped on February 2, 1899. (Serial No. 18609, actually an 1896 number, was given to an instrument shipped on July 21, 1910 — but this represented a later use of a mechanism on hand from earlier days.) A number of Style 51's, including many coin operated ones, were shipped from 1906 to 1920 and had serial numbers in the 7-digit series; beginning with 5100001 and ending with 5100239.

STYLE 55: Table model. Single comb. Straight-sided case. Usually seen with "REGINA" and musical scale trademark on underside of lid; case with striped inlay on the front and (sometimes) top. Early Style 55's are of the long-bedplate type. Later models have short bedplates. Regina described the latter variety in the 1910 catalogue: "No. 55. Uses 15½" discs. Comb has seventy-eight steel tongues, giving an increase of 40% in harmonic range [over a 12¼" instrument]. There are several advantages in buying an instrument using 15½" discs, the first and important one being that because of the increased capacity of the comb with seventy-eight tongues the instrument has a much greater harmonic range, which makes it possible for the musicians to write music for the discs much more completely than is possible for the smaller sizes. Second, 15½" tune discs can be selected from a much larger repertoire than discs of smaller size; in fact, there are over 2000 different tunes of this size produced for Reginas. Style No. 55 also has improved bedplate and sounding board, tempo regulator, banjo attachment, and long-running clockwork which plays about thirty minutes with one winding. Cases in oak or mahogany. Dimensions 22x19¾x13¾ inches." Style 55's were shipped from the factory up to 1915. Later models have 7-digit serials from 5500001 to 5500146 inclusive.

STYLE 62: Library Table model — built in the form of a gracefully-styled small desk. Duplex combs. Short bedplate. The mechanisms are on the right side under the lid. On the left side are four slide-out drawers for disc storage, behind double doors. Small lion's heads are carved on all corners. First shipped in 1904, Style 62 instruments were short-lived. The last was shipped in 1906. Early models had regular 5-digit serials. Only three 7-digit (6200000 series) instruments were made. All Style 62 instruments were made in the Rookwood (painted scenes) finish.

STYLE 66: Rococo-style console model with open sliding disc storage beneath the box. Usually finished in Rookwood. Sold in limited numbers circa 1906.

STYLE 67: Cabinet model. Duplex combs. Short bedplate. Described by Regina as: "No. 67. A handsome parlor cabinet in 'Rookwood' finish, beautifully decorated. Contains swinging rack for tunes, and has all the advantages of Style 50; upright long-running movement with duplex combs and 156 tongues; improved bedplate, sounding board, and tempo regulator; double self-acting [when one door opens, the other opens also by means of a synchronized mechanism] doors; tune discs, 15½" in diameter. On account of its upright construction no talking machine attachment is furnished with this style. Dimensions: 52x23x13 inches." The lowest serial number: 79979, assigned to an instrument shipped on December 19, 1905. Later Style 67's were made in the 7-digit series commencing with 6700001 and continuing to 6700067. The last Style 67 was shipped in 1911. All were of the Rookwood finish.

STYLE 113: Reginaphone version of Style 13. Lowest serial number: 69026, assigned to an instrument shipped on September 3, 1904. Later models were made in the 7-digit series from 1130001 to 1130113 inclusive. The last instrument was shipped in 1910. Style 113's were usually made in the same production runs as Style 13's. With outside (detachable) horn.

STYLE 140: Reginaphone version of Style 40 (floor-standing cabinet model). 92 made with 7-digit numbers (1400001 to 1400163). Shipped from 1907 to 1915. The American Graphophone Company of Bridgeport, Connecticut, purchased several.

STYLE 143: Reginaphone version of Style 43 (floor-standing cabinet model). With detachable outside horn (as per all 100-series Reginaphones). 30 Style 143's were made in the 7-digit series (numbers 1430001 to 1430043 inclusive) and were shipped from 1908 to 1912.

STYLE 150: Reginaphone version of Style 50. About 1050 of these were made in the 7-digit series (numbers 1500001 to 1501108) and were shipped from 1905 to 1915. An extremely popular model.

STYLE 155: Reginaphone version of Style 55. Table model. Single comb. 45 instruments made in the 7-digit serial range (1550001 to 1550061); shipped from 1908 to 1914.

STYLE 240: Reginaphone console model in curved case. Lion's heads on the front corners. Duplex combs. Short bedplate. Inside horn (as have all 200-series Reginaphones). 356 instruments were made in the 7-digit series (serial numbers 2400001 to 2400458). Some were sent to the Columbia Phonograph Company; all traces of the Regina origin were concealed (even a special serial number plate was made) and the instruments were sold under the name of "Columbia Grafonola." Others were sent to Wurlitzer – and were without serial number plates and the customary "REGINA" lettering on the underside of the lid. Most Style 240's, however, were sold with Regina markings. Regina advertised the 240: "The Reginaphone Style 240. Many cultured people who find great delight in high class music hesitate to purchase a talking machine of the ordinary type because of their somewhat ungainly appearance. In most cases when such an instrument fails to please it is the horn especially which is criticized. In order to meet the demand for a combination instrument that will appeal to the eye as well as to the ear, we have designed the Style 240 Reginaphone. It is an instrument of the most modern type, intended for those particular people who want something better than the ordinary. We could not eliminate the horn, but we have made it of spruce – the most resonant of all woods – and have concealed it within the case, where it is out of sight, and is no longer an objectionable feature. We think that Style No. 240 Reginaphone is the most beautiful instrument that we have ever made. It is worthy of a place in the most exquisitely furnished drawing room. It has the great advantage of being two different instruments combined in one – an excellent talking machine of the latest type and the best music box ever made – the Regina. The same motive power operates both instruments, and the change from one style of music to another can be made in a few seconds. As a talking machine the Style 240 Reginaphone will play disc records of any size desired, with great brilliancy and purity of tone, the volume of which may be easily controlled by opening or closing the small sliding doors covering the horn. As a music box it has duplex combs with 156 steel tongues, mandolin attachment operating on both combs, tempo regulator, improved bedplate and sounding board, and uses tune discs 15½" in diameter. The case is of selected mahogany [or oak – ed.] highly finished and polished. The lower part of the cabinet is adapted to hold Regina discs and talking machine records. The outside dimensions are 48½x22¼x20 inches. To all those who wish the latest and best home entertainer, one that will appeal to every member of the family – let their tastes be what they may – the Style 240 Reginaphone is recommended without reserve."

STYLE 246: Reginaphone console model in rectangular cabinet. Duplex combs. Short bedplate. Built in a case similar to that used by many phonograph makers of the period. With inside horn and with a hinged "expression panel" in the top of the cabinet. A late model – shipped from 1915 to 1919. 190 Style 246 Reginaphones were made. 7-digit serial numbers range from 2460001 to 2460250.

STYLE 250. Reginaphone. Inside-horn version of styles 50 and 150. Table model. Duplex combs. Short bedplate. Serpentine case. 291 Style 250's were shipped from 1914 to 1920. Serial numbers are in the 7-digit series and range from 2500001 to 2500413.

STYLE 251: Reginaphone. Inside-horn version of Style 51. Table model. Duplex combs. Short bedplate. 53 Style 251's were shipped from 1915 to 1920. 7-digit serial numbers from 2510001 to 2510062.

STYLE 255: Reginaphone. Inside-horn version of styles 55 and 155. Table model. Single comb. 44 Style 255's were shipped from 1916 to 1920. 7-digit serial numbers from 2550001 to 2550052.

STYLE 335: "Musical China Closet." Equipped with the Regina 15½" automatic disc changer as used in Style 35 (hence the "35" part of the "Style 335" nomenclature). Shipped in 1905 and 1906. 11 were made and were serially numbered in the 7-digit series from 3350002 to 3350012. "Musical China Closet" was the name Regina used in the factory records to describe this style.

Regina Style 335, the "Musical China Closet." (Photograph courtesy of Mrs. Ruth Bornand)

## WOOD FINISHES USED BY REGINA

Most Regina instruments were made of either mahogany or oak. However, other woods and finish styles were used over the years. Rookwood (cameo or vignette scenes painted on wooden panels) was popular for certain models in the 1904-1906 years particularly. Marqueterie (or marquetry) or inlay was applied to certain styles which Regina sold as having "Marqueterie" finish. These, too, were mainly popular in the 1904-1906 years. Vernis Martin, a French finish, was likewise popular during the same time.

Other woods and surface finishes listed in the Regina factory records include walnut, maple, Japan (black lacquer with painted yellow and/or red motifs), cherry, gilt (gold-leafed), ebony, and striped mahogany.

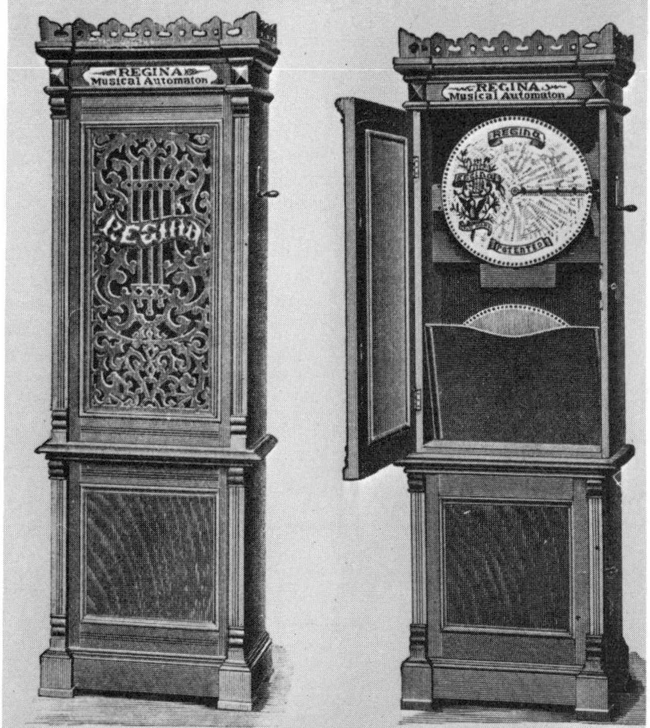
With Penny or Nickel Slot Attachment.

It is also made without Slot for Parlor use.

CLOSED. OPEN.

No. 1. Duplex, (2 Combs). 156 Steel Tongues.
PRICE, - - $250

No. 2. Single Comb. 78 Steel Tongues.
PRICE, - - - $200

Tune Sheets, 15½ inches Diameter, $1.30
Dimensions, 6 feet high, 22½ ins. wide, 12 ins. deep.

Regina No. 9.

DUPLEX.

CLOSED. OPEN.

156 Steel Tongues.

Dimensions, 4 feet 10 ins. high, 22½ ins. wide, 13½ ins. deep.

Regina, Nos. 1 and 2

No. 1, Duplex, 156 Steel Tongues; No. 2, Single Comb, 78 Ste
Tongues; Long-running Movement; Case in Oak or Mahogan
Dimensions, 71½ x 23½ x 13½ inches; Tune Sheets, 15½ inch
diameter.

—Very Early Styles—

The models shown on this page are very early styles from the 1890's. All were discontinued by 1900.

The No. 1 and No. 2 models were made in several different case styles, most of which were similar in concept to contemporary upright cabinet-style instruments made by Polyphon and Symphonion. Like the German makers, Regina referred to these coin operated models as "Musical Automatons."

The Style 9, the model in the classical-style case shown at the upper right, was sold in limited quantities circa 1896. Like styles 1 and 2, No. 9 could be purchased with or without coin slot.

Style 15, as shown at the right, was made in two styles: the illustrated type, suitable for use on a base cabinet or on the counter of a business establishment or other commercial location; and another style with a carved decoration at the bottom of the case, a style made for hanging on a wall.

As the accompanying text notes, all of these very early designations, styles 1, 2, 9, and 15, were used in later years to describe entirely different Regina models.

Style 15

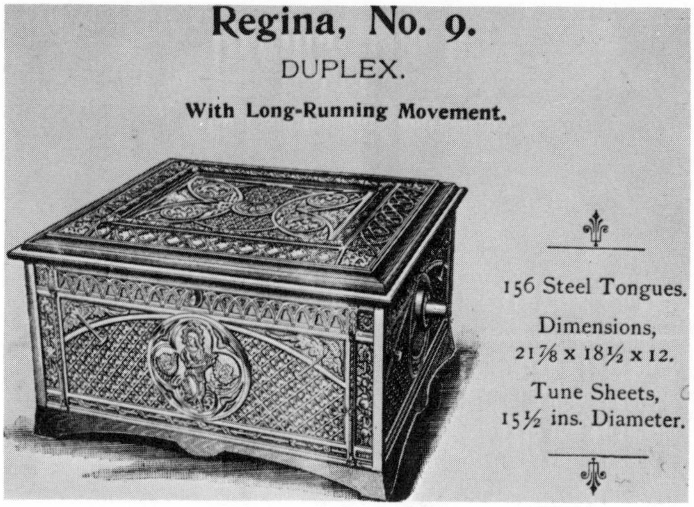

Regina, No. 9.
DUPLEX.
With Long-Running Movement.
156 Steel Tongues.
Dimensions,
21⅞ x 18½ x 12.
Tune Sheets,
15½ ins. Diameter.


Left: Regina Style 9, a duplex comb model in a carved (or, later, heavily lacquered pressed wood) case. Comparable in styling to the 11" Style 19 Regina. The case itself is not carved. The ornate panels are applied to a basic cabinet. Made in oak, mahogany, and walnut. See accompanying text for detailed descriptions of this and other Regina models illustrated on this page.

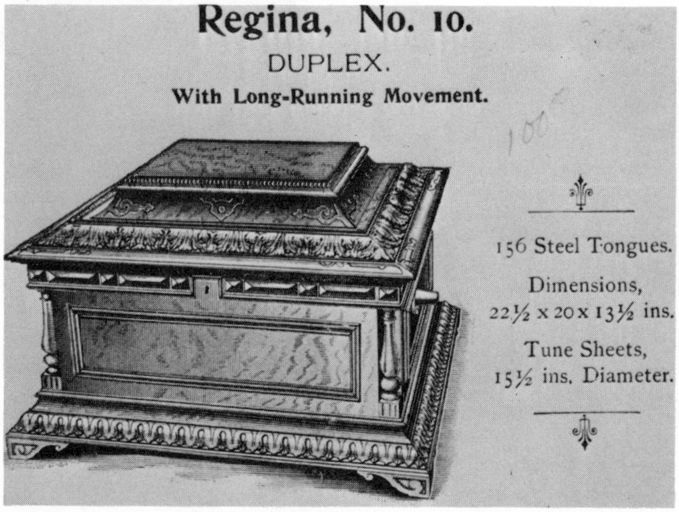

Regina, No. 10.
DUPLEX.
With Long-Running Movement.
156 Steel Tongues.
Dimensions,
22½ x 20 x 13½ ins.
Tune Sheets,
15½ ins. Diameter.


Above: Style 10. Duplex comb model in an especially ornate case.

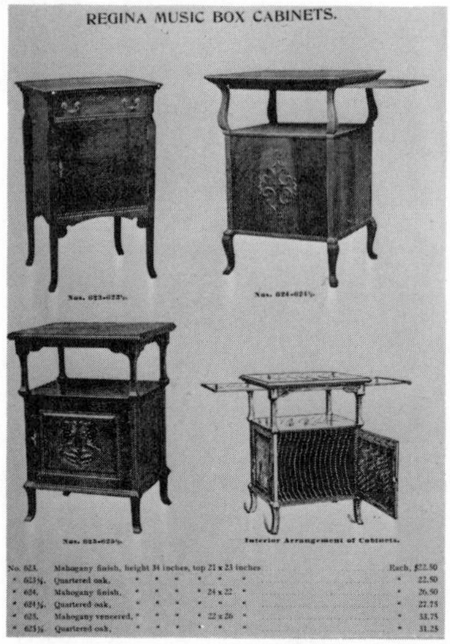

REGINA MUSIC BOX CABINETS.
Interior Arrangement of Cabinets.
No. 623. Mahogany finish, height 34 inches, top 21 x 23 inches Each, $22.50
" 623½. Quartered oak, " " " " " " " 22.50
" 624. Mahogany finish, " " " " 24 x 22 " " 26.50
" 624½. Quartered oak, " " " " " " " 27.75
" 625. Mahogany veneered, " " " " 22 x 26 " " 33.75
" 625½. Quartered oak, " " " " " " " 31.25


These matching cabinets were available in 1898 at prices ranging from $22.50 to $33.75. They were widely used with table models in homes and commercial establishments. A disc storage rack is in the base of each cabinet.

15½" Regina music box in a very heavily carved mahogany case. The base is similar to that of Style 10.

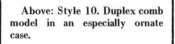

Regina No. 13,
Single Comb, With Regular Movement
78 Steel Tongues,
Dimensions,
21 x 19 x 10 inches
Tune Sheets,
Case in Mahogany and Oak.

Left: Style 13 Regina music box. Single comb version of Style 11. A very popular model, the Style 13 was produced in large quantities and in several different case style variations from 1894 until well into the 20th century. It filled the need for an inexpensive instrument which used the basic 15½" disc size. Plain case (as shown) models sold for $50 in 1902; "carved" (probably pressed wood) case models sold for $45.

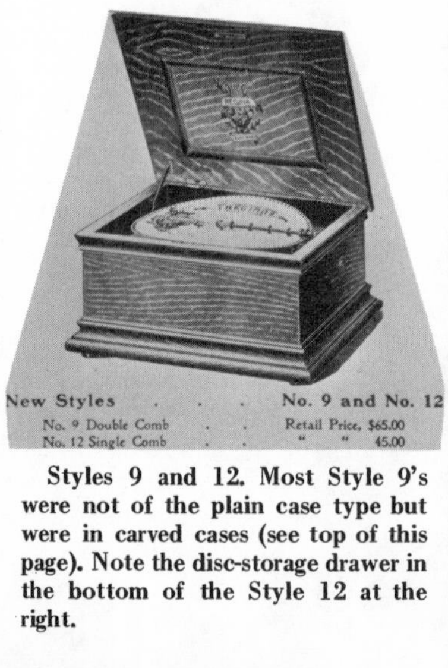

New Styles . . . No. 9 and No. 12
No. 9 Double Comb . . . Retail Price, $65.00
No. 12 Single Comb . . . " " 45.00


Styles 9 and 12. Most Style 9's were not of the plain case type but were in carved cases (see top of this page). Note the disc-storage drawer in the bottom of the Style 12 at the right.

## REGINA 15½" MUSIC BOXES

Style 11

Style 11a

Style 11a (later, Style 50)

Style 11

–Style 11–

Style 11 was the most popular of all Regina music boxes. First made in 1894, many thousands were shipped from then until the early years of the 20th century. Later, the Style 50 took the place of the Style 11 as Regina's best seller.

The 15½" disc size was Regina's most popular. The Style 11 instrument, equipped with duplex music combs and housed in a compact case, was the logical instrument for the average customer to purchase. Priced at about $75, the duplex-comb Style 11 was only $25 more than a single-comb Style 13 – and yet, so the Regina advertisements noted, it had "twice the musical volume of a single-comb instrument of the same size." While that statement was not true from an scientific viewpoint (the sound would increase on a logarithmic basis; this, coupled with some destructive interference caused by two almost-identically-pitched combs vibrating in unison, resulted in just a slight increase in volume), it was a good sales point – and many more double comb instruments were sold.

Style 11

## COIN OPERATED TABLE MODELS

Regina, No. 15.
LONG-RUNNING MOVEMENT.
WITH PENNY OR NICKEL COIN ATTACHMENT.
If ordered with Nickel Drop, unless otherwise stipulated, the tune will play twice for one coin.
Duplex, 156 Steel Tongues.
Dimensions, 22¾ x 20½ x 12½ inches.
Tune Sheets, 15½ ins. diameter.
Case in Mahogany or Oak.


Coin operated version of the Style 11. Extremely popular.

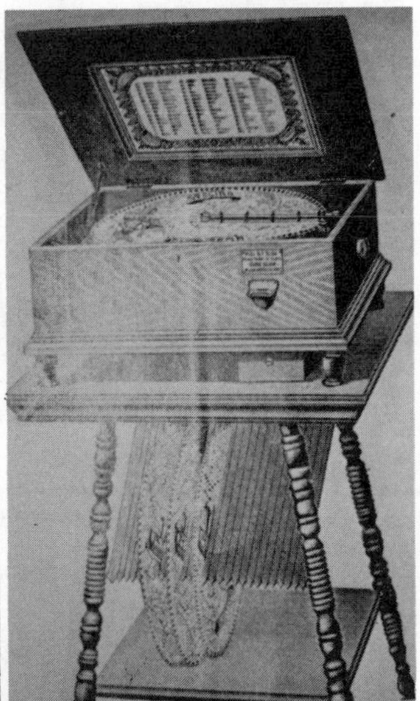

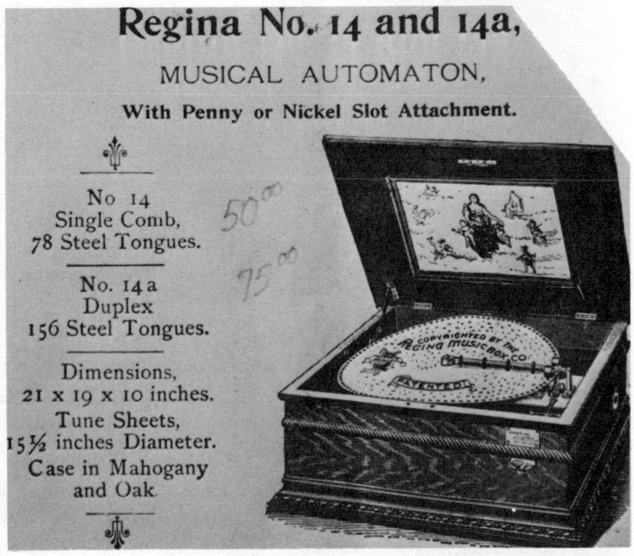

Regina No. 14 and 14a,
MUSICAL AUTOMATON,
With Penny or Nickel Slot Attachment.
No 14
Single Comb,
78 Steel Tongues.
50.00
No. 14 a
Duplex
156 Steel Tongues.
75.00
Dimensions,
21 x 19 x 10 inches.
Tune Sheets,
15½ inches Diameter.
Case in Mahogany and Oak.


Table model coin operated Regina music boxes – Style 14 (single comb) and 14a (double comb). As 14a and 15 were quite similar, the production of 14a instruments was curtailed in favor of Style 15. The Style 14 shown at the left is on a base stand.

REGINA No. 51–DUPLEX.
This is a new style, and is the successor to our well-known style No. 15. Has improved bedplate and sounding board, also speed regulator, 156 steel tongues, tune sheets 15½ inches diameter, long-running movement playing from twenty minutes to half an hour with one winding. Plays tunes once or twice as desired for each coin.
Cases in quartered oak or mahogany. Dimensions 22 x 20 x 12 inches.
Weight, packed, about 75 pounds.
This instrument is a favorite with many coin-machine operators. It pays well and is easily handled. One of these instruments taking in only FIVE CENTS a day will pay 20 per cent. on the investment in one year. If it takes in $1.00 per day, it pays 400 per cent. on the investment.


Left: Regina No. 51 – Duplex. A coin operated table model music box. "The successor to our well-known Style 15." The "Style 51" nomenclature was also used to describe a table model for use in the home (without coin slot) – as the accompanying text notes. The label on the underside of the lid reads: "REGINA, The First Music Box Manufactured in the United States. . ."

Right: Regina Gum Vending Machine. Upon receipt of a coin a stick of gum would appear in the chute at the lower left front of the case. Other styles had the chute on the right side (rather than the front) of the case. The pictured model uses a 15½" disc and may have been designated as a variety of Style 14. Similar instruments were made in 11" and 12¼" disc sizes.

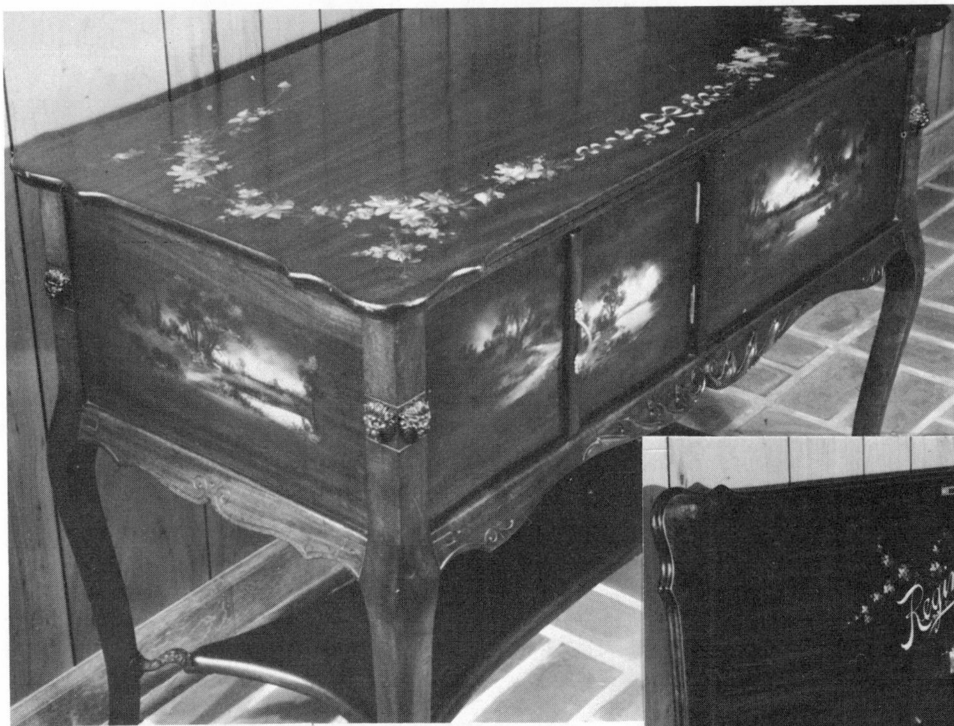

Left: Style 62, musical "Library Table," built in the form of an attractively-styled lady's desk. Rookwood finish with cameo scenes on the front and side panels; floral figures on top. Made with (as illustrated) or without bottom shelf. Dimensions: 40½" wide by 20" deep by 30¾" high (lid closed). The specimen illustrated is from the collection of Drs. Edith and Robert Owen, and bears serial number 78933. It was shipped from the Regina factory on October 6, 1905, to the Thiebes, Stierlin Music Co. of St. Louis, Missouri.

Style 67, a cabinet model with Rookwood finish. List price was $150 in 1908. One of the most beautiful of the later Regina styles.

Above left: Style 143 Reginaphone. Above right: Style 43. Floor-standing cabinet model with disc storage.

Style 40 (left). Style 140 Reginaphone (right).

Style 40, a console-type 15½" instrument popular during the 1902 - 1915 years, was available in several different finishes – including Rookwood (as shown at the left) and quartered oak (as shown at the right in a 1904 advertisement).

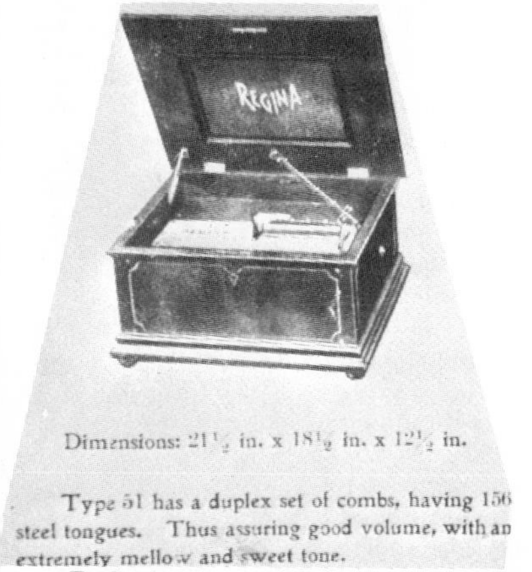

REGINA
Dimensions: 21½ in. x 18½ in. x 12½ in.
Type 51 has a duplex set of combs, having 156 steel tongues. Thus assuring good volume, with an extremely mellow and sweet tone.

Early home model Style 51 (double comb) and Style 55 (single comb) with long bedplate.

Style 55 (above left) single-comb music box and Style 155 (above right), the Reginaphone version of the same instrument. From Regina's 1910 catalogue.

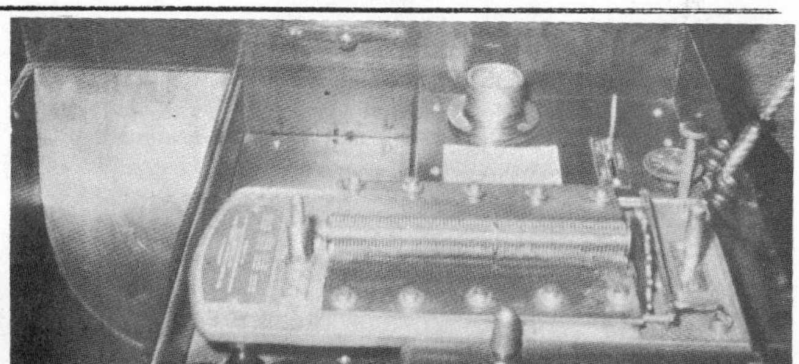

Style 250 Reginaphone with inside horn. (Note horn opening to the left of the bedplate). The phonograph arm was detached when music discs were played.

Styles 50 (left) and the Reginaphone version, Style 155 (above left). Style 50, a duplex-comb instrument in a curved or serpentine case, was a best-selling instrument during the early 1900's. It was the successor to the immensely popular Style 11 – a somewhat similar model but in a straight case and with a long bedplate.

Disc storage cabinets as pictured in Regina's 1910 catalogue. Of serpentine lines, these formed ideal bases for the popular Style 50 and other curved-case instruments.

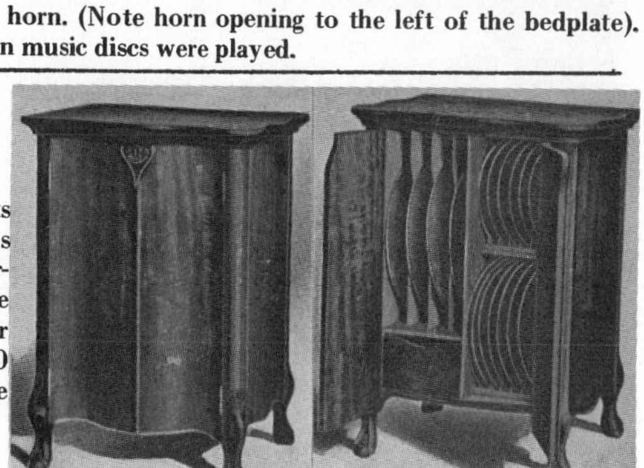

THE NEW REGINAPHONE

THE disc talking machine has hosts of friends. The Regina Music Box has brought delight to many thousands of homes. Some prefer the one, some the other, and often in the same family opinions are divided when a choice is being made between these two musical entertainers.

In the new REGINAPHONE, however, both instruments are combined in one—a new style high grade up-to-date disc talking machine and a Regina Music Box of the latest design—both instruments operated by the same powerful spring motor, which is of superior construction and will run longer with each winding than the ordinary automatic instruments.

The REGINAPHONE is an instrument of the most modern type, which will appeal to those particular people who want something better than the ordinary. It will play regular disc talking machine records, as well as Regina steel tune discs, thus providing entertainment that may be infinitely varied—in fact, its scope is almost unlimited. Grand opera selections, band music, songs, speeches and monologues, may be interspersed with most delightful instrumental music obtained from the Regina Music Box combs and discs.

No mere talking machine or phonograph can furnish the added delight of Regina music that the REGINAPHONE does. The change of music from one kind to another is easily accomplished and requires but a few seconds.

In the new REGINAPHONE the tone waves from the talking machine are projected upward from the interior of the case instead of being sent out through the front. Thus the sound is most evenly distributed and harshness of tone avoided.

Reginaphones are made by skilled workmen with the utmost care and precision. They are beautifully finished in selected oak and mahogany cases and are worthy of a place in the most exquisitely furnished drawing room. They are fully guaranteed.

MANUFACTURED BY

THE REGINA COMPANY

47 WEST 34th STREET, NEW YORK

218 SO. WABASH AVE., CHICAGO — Factory: RAHWAY, NEW JERSEY

—Style 246 Reginaphone—

The Style 246 Reginaphone was one of the latest Reginaphones to be introduced. First sold in 1915, some 190 instruments in all were shipped from then to 1920. The cabinet is rectangular and resembles many phonographs of the World War I era.

All styles of inside-horn Reginaphones generally have very excellent tonal quality. An effort was made to construct the cases along acoustic principles — with the result that the music box portion of the Reginaphone plays with exceptional brilliance.

The inside horn of the above-illustrated Style 246 begins at the base of the phonograph tone arm, continues within the cabinet, and then emerges on the left side of the instrument, facing upward just to the left of the bedplate.

Style 246 Reginaphone

—Style 240—

No. 240

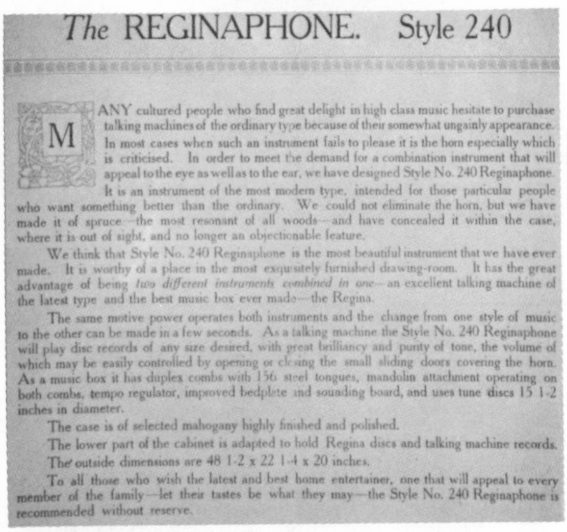

The REGINAPHONE. Style 240

MANY cultured people who find great delight in high class music hesitate to purchase talking machines of the ordinary type because of their somewhat ungainly appearance. In most cases when such an instrument fails to please it is the horn especially which is criticised. In order to meet the demand for a combination instrument that will appeal to the eye as well as to the ear, we have designed Style No. 240 Reginaphone.

It is an instrument of the most modern type, intended for those particular people who want something better than the ordinary. We could not eliminate the horn, but we have made it of spruce—the most resonant of all woods—and have concealed it within the case, where it is out of sight, and no longer an objectionable feature.

We think that Style No. 240 Reginaphone is the most beautiful instrument that we have ever made. It is worthy of a place in the most exquisitely furnished drawing-room. It has the great advantage of being *two different instruments combined in one*—an excellent talking machine of the latest type and the best music box ever made—the Regina.

The same motive power operates both instruments and the change from one style of music to the other can be made in a few seconds. As a talking machine the Style No. 240 Reginaphone will play disc records of any size desired, with great brilliancy and purity of tone, the volume of which may be easily controlled by opening or closing the small sliding doors covering the horn. As a music box it has duplex combs with 156 steel tongues, mandolin attachment operating on both combs, tempo regulator, improved bedplate and sounding board, and uses tune discs 15 1-2 inches in diameter.

The case is of selected mahogany highly finished and polished.

The lower part of the cabinet is adapted to hold Regina discs and talking machine records.

The outside dimensions are 48 1-2 x 22 1-4 x 20 inches.

To all those who wish the latest and best home entertainer, one that will appeal to every member of the family—let their tastes be what they may—the Style No. 240 Reginaphone is recommended without reserve.

**Style 240, billed as "the most beautiful instrument we have ever made," was the best seller among the 200-series (inside horn) Reginaphones.**

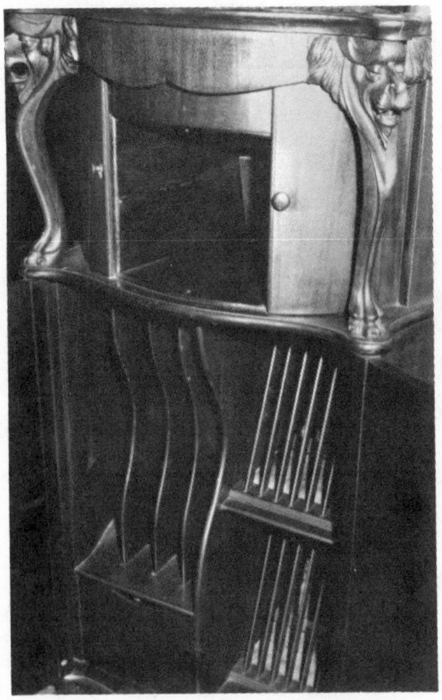

**View of the horn opening and the storage racks in a Style 240 Reginaphone.**

**"Columbia Grafonola" phonograph in the same case as used for Style 240.**

## –Regina Corona Style 35–
## (15½" changer)

The Regina Corona Style 35 was one of the most popular of all Regina changers. First introduced in 1899, this style was popular until 1910-1912, and some examples were shipped from the factory even after that date.

Style 35 and its coin-operated counterpart, Style 36, each contain music combs of the duplex style and are equipped with a 12-disc automatic changing device. "Parlor models," as the non-coin-operated styles are called today, are operated by a lever which can be set to play one tune and then stop, to repeat a given tune, or to play the discs in order. If set to the "on" position the discs will play one after the order in succession as, for example, disc number 5 followed by 6 then 7, 8, 9, 10, 11, 12, 11, 10, 9, 8, 7, 6, 5, 4, 3, 2, 1, 2, 3, and so on. When discs are played singly, the selection can be made by turning an index knob on the right side of the case.

Coin operated models (Style 36) play one tune upon receipt of a cent or nickel. When the next nickel is deposited, the next tune in succession is played – unless another tune is selected by the index knob. There is no accumulating mechanism; a coin must be deposited after each tune ends in order to hear the next tune.

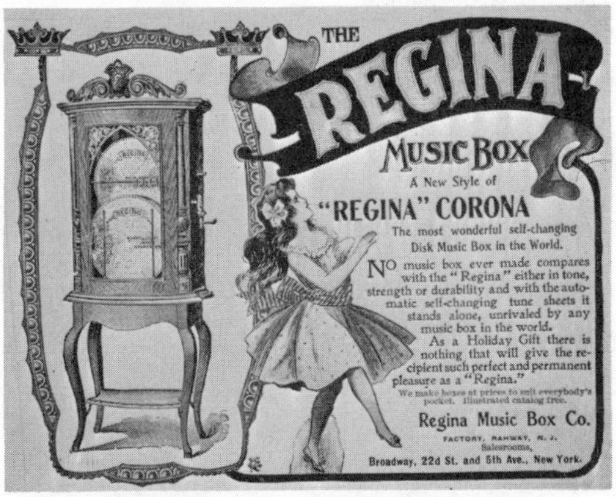


November, 1900 Regina advertisement depicting an early case design of the Style 35 Regina Corona.

1904 advertisement featuring a Style 35 with a clock in the top gallery.

### Regina Catalogue Description

The following description, taken from a c.1910 Regina catalogue, is typical of the advertising used to sell the Style 35:

"Regina Corona, No. 35 – This instrument contains the Regina automatic tune changing mechanism, so constructed that each tune contained in the carriage is lifted into position, played, and returned to its place automatically, without any attention on the part of the operator. It will play twelve tunes through twice in regular order with one winding, playing altogether about thirty minutes. It is almost human in its action. This instrument is especially suitable for use in the dining room, and has been a great favorite for that purpose. It is equipped with a tempo regulator and the Regina piano sounding board, which greatly strengthens and improves the tone. It also contains a drawer which will hold two dozen tune discs. [Referral is made here to the storage drawer in the bottom of the instrument, not the changer rack – Ed.] The discs contained in the carriage are easily changed, the only care necessary being to place them right side up. Any tune in the carriage can be selected and played at will and any particular tune may be repeated as often as desired. Style No. 35 contains double or duplex combs, having 156 steel tongues, improved banjo attachment operating on both combs, and uses 15½" discs. Cases in oak or mahogany. Dimensions are 66x26¼x22 inches.

"Style No. 35 may be equipped with a high-grade eight-day clock. When so equipped the clock is connected with the mechanism so that a different tune is played automatically every hour or every half hour. This is a pleasing improvement, as it is a very agreeable way to be reminded of the passing hours. The clock attachment is of the very best construction, made especially for this purpose.

"Style No. 35 can also be equipped with an art glass door. This art glass door is built up of small pieces of art glass set in lead, containing an appropriate design."

### Data Concerning Style 35

Style 35's were first shipped from the factory in 1899. The earliest serial number listed in the Regina records is No. 21859, an 1897-series number that was used on an instrument that wasn't shipped until May 24, 1905. This model, equipped with a top clock, evidently was made from an older bedplate that was made in 1897 but which was not used until several years later. Many Style 35 and Style 36 instruments seen today are from the tremendous production run (nearly 2000 instruments!) that commenced with No. 50,001 and continued to No. 51916. Instruments from this run were shipped from 1899 to 1905.

A number of Style 35's were equipped with a spring-wound 8-day clock or with an art glass front, or both. A June 1, 1908, Regina price list offered the Style 35 for $200. The clock attachment was $25 extra and the art glass door was $20 extra. These prices varied slightly over the years. The art glass door, while attractively made (with a "corona" [crown] motif), was not especially popular for, in the words of a Regina sales agent: "Part of the fascination of the Regina changer was being able to watch the discs change and the mechanisms operate. Most people preferred the clear glass front for this reason."

In keeping with Regina's policy, serial numbers assigned after the autumn of 1904 were of the 7-digit type. From 1906 to 1915 many 7-digit Style 35's were shipped. The 7-digit numbers assigned began with 3500001 and ended with 3500267.

As the accompanying illustrations show, there are several case style variations among Style 35 Regina Coronas. The usual type has a plain glass front, a door with spiral columns on each side, and a scallop-design top gallery or crest. Very early models have a differently designed top gallery with an oval cameo or cartouche in the center. These early models usually are found with spiral columns also, but some have columns of different design.

The Style 35 models equipped with the 8-day clock (made by Seth Thomas) have a larger and differently designed crest to accommodate the clock face.

### Style 36 (With Coin Mechanism)

The Style 36 instruments were made in two main formats. Many were of the rounded-front "parlor model" format as used for Style 35's, but were equipped with a coin slot for 1c or 5c coins. The main difference between this type, sold as "Regina Corona No. 36 – Round," and the Style 35 is the addition of a coin mechanism.

The type sold as "Regina Corona No. 36 – Flat" is of entirely different appearance. Made for heavy duty use in arcades, the Style 36 – Flat is equipped with heavy black cast iron legs. The front is flat and the top gallery is of a different design.

This style was sold as: "Regina Corona No. 36 – Flat. This style is very popular with slot machine operators. It has a piano sounding board, automatic tune changing device, and long-running movement, also speed regulator. Duplex combs with 156 steel tongues. Tune sheets 15½" in diameter. Cases oak or mahogany. Dimensions 68x25½x21 inches. Built very strong to withstand use in public places."

Style 36 instruments were built in the 50,000 series (as noted earlier) and also in the 7-digit series commencing with No. 3600001 and ending with 3600187. Shipments were made from about 1900 to 1920, with the greatest popularity being in the 1900 - 1907 years.

As Style 36 Regina Coronas were used in commercial locations most of the instruments were scrapped after their commercial usefulness ended. Hence, proportionately fewer Style 36's survive today than do Style 35's. The Style 35 music boxes were made for home use and often saved as a prized family possession.

—Regina 15½"— Automatic Changer

The 15½" automatic changer, introduced in 1899, was made in several case variations. At the upper right is the standard style with clear glass front and with spiral columns on the sides of the front door. At the upper left is an instrument with a clock top and an art glass front – both of which features were available as added-cost options. To the right is an early (1899) model with differently styled front columns and with a different top crest.

All of these were sold as the Regina Corona, Style 35, and were of the on-off lever (rather than coin slot) type. Those with coin slots were designated as Style 36.

Inside views of two Style 35 Regina Corona automatic changers. The top instrument, serial number 3500169 (shown on a wide metal plaque with curved top – the type of serial plaque used on 7-digit instruments produced after November, 1904), was shipped from the factory September 25, 1908. Note the "REGINA" transfer design on the back panel – as used on late instruments (early ones had a paper "Queen of Music" lithograph). The lower picture is of serial number 51379 which was shipped on January 10, 1903.

To complete the record we mention that the early Style 35, the one with the early style top gallery and with the non-spiral columns, shown on this page at left center is serial number 50009 and was shipped on December 28, 1899. This was one of the very first 15½" changers sold.

REGINA CORONA No. 36—FLAT.

This style is very popular with slot-machine operators. It has piano sounding board, automatic tune-changing device, and long-running movement, also speed regulator. Duplex combs with 156 steel tongues. Tune sheets 15½ inches in diameter. Cases oak or mahogany. Dimensions 68 x 25½ x 21 inches.
Built very strong to withstand use in public places.

REGINA CORONA No. 36—ROUND.

This instrument is very attractive in appearance. It has all of the special advantages of No. 34, such as piano sounding board and automatic tune-changing device, also speed regulator. It has two combs with 156 tongues, and takes tune sheets 15½ inches in diameter. It is 68 inches high, 25½ inches wide, and 21 inches deep. It is made with swell front. No coin-operated instrument has ever been made that can approach styles 34, 36, and 38 in musical quality or nickel-getting ability.

Style 36, the 15½" changer equipped with a coin slot, was available in two main styles: the flat front and the round front.

### —15½" Regina with 12 Bells— Styles 216 and 217 (and single-comb Style 215)

The styles 216 and 217 featured a duplex music comb system with welve bells, six on either side. While such instruments with bells were quite popular in Europe (Polyphon and Symphonion sold many, for xample), they failed to generate much interest with Regina's ustomers. Only a few were sold.

Style 216 and Style 217 are basically similar, except that 217 has a oin slot mechanism and was intended for commercial use. Regina ioted of Style 217: "These instruments are all fitted with coin ttachments. Unless otherwise instructed, we always adapt Style 217 or use with pennies."

These instruments do not take the standard 15½" Regina disc, but se a special 15½" disc with a section (near the outer rim) with music rranged for bells. The discs have "For Bell Instrument Only" and ictures of two bells in black ink near the bottom.

Regina advertised the instruments as follows: "Regina No. 217 [or :16] With Bells. An entirely new style, having an accompaniment of weet and clear-toned bells, tuned in harmony with the combs, and which are played in perfect time. This instrument will become very popular and must be heard to be appreciated. Made in oak and nahogany. Duplex combs with 124 steel tongues. Dimensions, :2x18¾x13¾ inches. Tune discs, 15½ inches diameter, specially rranged for bells."

Style 215 is listed as a "15½" Regina bell box with single comb." Apparently even fewer were made of 215 than of 216 and 217.

### Style 216

Style 216 instruments were shipped from the Regina factory from 1904 to 1906. In addition, many movements only (without cases) were shipped to the Yale Wonder Clock Company of Burlington, Vermont, in 1905 and 1907.

Serial numbers of Style 216 commence with 2160001 and end with 2160200. Distribution was as follows: 71 units with cases were made for general sale; 95 movements without cases were shipped to the Yale Wonder Clock Company. For details on the Yale firm, see the "Regina Gambling Machines" page in this Regina section.

### Style 217

Style 217 instruments, the same as Style 216 but with the addition of a 1c coin slot, were shipped from the Regina factory from 1905 to 1908. The first serial number used was 2170001 (which means Style 217, instrument number 0001); the last, 2170274. Some serial numbers were omitted. 71 Style 217's were made in all — the same number as made of the with-case Style 216's.

### Commentary

Some models have the bells covered with a heavy formed screen which hides the bells from view — something which must have done little to help the sales of this instrument.

Although most other manufacturers of disc music boxes produced many varieties of instruments with bells (and such instruments sold very well), Regina's only into the bell-equipped box field (although some Regina clocks had bells) was the Style 215-217 series. These instruments operated well and there seems to have been no technical reason for their discontinuance. Rather, Regina probably didn't like bells, perhaps because they override the softer tones of the music combs. Lacking a sales "push," these styles simply passed from the scene. Another factor may have been inventory problems involved in the stocking of two different and not interchangeable types of 15½" discs. Whatever the reason may have been, Regina gave the 215, 216, and 217 very little publicity or advertising.

———————

## REGINA No. 217 WITH BELLS.

An entirely new style, having an accompaniment of sweet and clear-toned bells, tuned in harmony with combs, and which are played in perfect time. This instrument will become very popular and must be heard to be appreciated. Made in oak and mahogany. Duplex combs with 124 steel tongues. Dimensions, 22 x 19¾ x 13¾ inches. Tune discs, 15½ inches diameter, specially arranged for bells.

## —20¾" Regina Music Boxes—

Regina music boxes of the 20¾" disc size were first made in 1897 and first shipped from the factory in 1898. Of the three largest Regina music box disc sizes — 15½", 20¾", and 27" — far fewer 20¾" models were made than were instruments of the other two sizes.

The 20¾" series, despite its brevity, contains some interesting models. Regina automatic disc-changing boxes of this size were made in four styles: 31, 32, 37, and 38. Although shipments continued for some years thereafter, the 20¾" changer type was manufactured only from late 1898 to 1904 inclusive. None with 7-digit serial numbers (indicating manufacture after late 1904) are listed in the Regina records. Regina 20¾" changers were not listed in Regina catalogues after 1906. The 20¾" size changer was probably redundant from a sales viewpoint. Customers who desired a small automatic changer were sold the 15½" size; those who wanted a larger and more impressive one were candidates for 27" models. Thus the 20¾" instruments were left with an uncertain market. The same may be said about the 20¾" table models.

Discs used on 20¾" boxes are numbered in the 5000 series.

The general scarcity of 20¾" instruments is unfortunate today. Collectors consider this size to be one of Regina's best. The tonal quality is generally very excellent — often better than that found on the larger 27" styles.

### Style 24

Style 24 was the designation assigned to the parlor model (not coin operated) large upright model. As with most other styles, this was designated as a "Regina Sublima" — not to be confused with the later Regina Sublima Piano of similar name.

The lowest serial number recorded is 21731, assigned to an instrument shipped on April 21, 1905. The lowest regular serial number (the preceding was an anomaly) is 29001, on an instrument shipped on August 31, 1898.

The Style 24 is similar to the Style 25, and both were usually made in the same production runs. Style 24 proved unpopular for the parlor use for which it was intended, and within a few years just the Style 25 was listed.

### Style 25

Style 25 is the same as Style 24, but with the addition of a coin slot. The lowest serial number recorded is 29003, assigned to an instrument shipped on April 26, 1898. Although Style 25 was deleted from Regina catalogues shortly after the turn of the 20th century, a very late model, serial number 250001, was shipped on December 19, 1919 — long after most others!

Style 24 and 25 were made in several case designs. Early models had three circles above the bottom rectangular panels. Later ones had the panels only.

### Style 26

Early type: The Style 26 designation was first given to the folding-top 20¾" music box made for parlor use (without coin slot). The lowest serial number assigned is 29060, for an instrument shipped on May 13, 1898. Called "folding top" (Regina's term), "casket style," or "accordion top" boxes by collectors today, these early Style 26 instruments are quite rare.

Late type: Following the discontinuation of the folding-top style, the Style 26 designation was assigned to represent the standard straight-sided parlor model music box of the 20¾" size. A 1910 Regina catalogue described this type: "No. 26. This instrument has the special advantages of the No. 50 [a 15½" size described in the same catalogue]; that is, the improved sounding board and tempo regulator, and at the same time uses a much larger disc, 20¾" in diameter. This allows nearly twice as much surface for arranging the music, and as the combs in the instrument have 130 steel tongues tuned in chromatic scale, there is about twice the harmonic range of the smaller instruments. The arrangement of the teeth on these combs is such that they can be made much wider and heavier than the teeth of duplex combs [Note: this is a meaningless statement as Style 26 has duplex combs — Ed.], and the result is a much richer tone than that of any of the other styles heretofore described. No. 26 has the improved banjo attachment operating on both combs, and a long-running clockwork playing about thirty minutes with one winding. Cases in oak or mahogany, with 'cupola' top through which the tone issues in full volume when the lid is closed. Dimensions 28½ x 23¾ x 13¼ inches." Late-type Style 26 instruments were made in several case variations. Not all had the ventilated or "cupola" top. Early models had long bedplates; later models, short ones. Late models were made in the 7-digit series and were numbered from 2600001 to 2600171. These were shipped from 1905 to 1916. The factory records also note that many Style 26 movements (without cases) were shipped in 1901 to the Equitable Manufacturing Company.

### Style 27

Early type: Style 27 was first used to designate the coin operat version of the early Style 26 with folding top. The lowest seri number, No. 29096, was assigned to an instrument shipped on Augu 16, 1898. Production of these was curtailed shortly after 1900.

Late type: Following the discontinuation of the folding-top styl the Style 27 designation was generally applied to the various styles coin operated table model boxes of the 20¾" size. These were made several case variations; some with ventilated or "cupola" lids and som with solid lids. Sometimes Style 27 was advertised and illustrated wi an engraving of a smaller 15½" model (see accompanying catalog illustrations), a situation which may be confusing to the collect today. Sold for use in commercial locations, Style 27 was offered a "Another new style. This is a magnificent instrument, sold at a popul price. Has improved bedplate and sounding board, also speed regulato Long-running movement, two large combs with 130 steel tongues tun in chromatic scale. Cases in quartered oak or mahogany. Dimensio 28½ x 23¼ x 13¼ inches." The first Style 27's of the late type ma were with long bedplates; later ones had short bedplates. Those ma after late 1904 had 7-digit serial numbers from 2700001 to 270008 The last Style 27 was shipped in 1914.

### Style 28

At the same time the folding-top Style 26 was being made, som regular table model 20¾" boxes were also being constructed. The were designated as Style 28. Following the discontinuation of the ear Style 26, the 26 number was applied to the type known as Style 28 although some Style 28's were so designated for a few years thereafte Perhaps these were in cases with ornate bottom molding and corn posts (as per illustration on accompanying page). The lowest seri number, No. 29075, was assigned to an instrument shipped o September 3, 1899. Some Style 28 instruments (serial No. 32307, f example) were called "combination" boxes in the Regina ledgers. Seri No. 32297 was made with a special "German case." Some Style 28 were made with a Vernis Martin finish.

### Style 31

Style 31 is modeled after its 27" counterpart, the Style 33. The cas were made in several different variations. The main ones are the ty with a carved dragon motif on the top door and with rounded corne to the base, and the second type with two decorative spandrels the upper corners of the top door. All types seen by the author we originally equipped with a decorative top gallery consisting of a railin with two finials, one at each corner. It is possible, even probable, th custom designs were made utilizing other configurations.

Equipped with an on-off lever, the Style 31 was made for home us An advertisement noted: "Style 31. For parlor use, long-runnin movement, two large combs, with 130 tongues, tuned in chromati scale, embracing over seven octaves, case in oak or mahogan dimensions 64x34x24 inches. Dimensions of tune sheets: 20¾ diameter."

The earliest Style 31 serial number is 45001; assigned to a instrument which was shipped on February 8, 1899. 45001 commence a large run of Style 31 and 32 (same as 31, but with coin slot) whic continued through No. 45828. This was followed by a run (using mos numbers from 45830 to 45986) of Style 37 and 38 instruments (se following).

Of the 31 and 32 styles, the coin operated Style 32 was the mor popular — as evidenced by a greater number made.

### Style 32

Style 32, the coin operated counterpart of Style 31, was popula from about 1899 to 1905. The earliest serial number assigned wa 45002 — for an instrument that was part of the large production ru described earlier. The Style 32 could be set to play each disc throug once or twice (when played twice the disc stays in position on th music combs and goes through two revolutions before being returned t the rack) for each coin. Or, it could be set to play two successive tune (rather than the same tune twice). A usual practice was to give one pla for a cent or two plays if the instrument was equipped with a nicke slot. The coin mechanisms are not accumulative, and a separate coi must be deposited each time.

The coin box on this and on the 27" changer styles is located unde the floor of the instrument and is accessible from the right side. Man coin boxes were equipped with two locks, each with a different key The owner of the restaurant would have one key and the coin machin route operator (who owned the instrument and placed it on location o a commission basis) would have another key. In this way the coin box the determiner of profits, could only be opened with both partie present!

### Style 37

First shipped in 1900, the Style 37 was built as an oversized copy of the highly successful Regina Corona Style 35 (15½"). The styling wasn't as graceful and perhaps for this reason the Style 37 was not a particularly good seller.

Regina advertised the Style 37 as follows: "Sublima Corona, No. 37. With piano sounding board. Automatic tune changing device. Long running movement. Two large combs, with 130 tongues, tuned in chromatic scale, embracing over 7 octaves. Dimensions of tune sheet: 20¾" diameter. Case in oak or mahogany. Dimensions 75x34x26 inches."

A very few of these were made with a clock in the top gallery. The earliest serial number (but not the first to leave the factory) recorded was 45813, an instrument shipped on August 5, 1902. Some later serial numbers were shipped in 1900 and 1901.

### Style 38

Style 38 was built in two configurations: the round-front style which was identical to the Style 37 except for the addition of a coin slot, and a flat-front style in a special case.

The Style 38 was introduced in 1900 and achieved its greatest popularity in the 1901 - 1905 years. The lowest serial number (but not the first instrument shipped) assigned was 45803.

The model similar to the Style 37 but with a coin slot was sold as the "No. 38 – Round."

The style sold as "No. 38 – Flat" was built in a distinctive case with a flat front. The factory records do not differentiate between the flat and round Style 38's, so it is not known how many of each were made. However, the great rarity of the flat front type today indicates that just a few must have been built.

Note: Several Regina advertisements show an illustration for the flat-front Regina Style 36, give a description of the Style 36 - Flat (the variety with iron legs – see description on another page), and then note: "Sublima Corona No. 38 – Flat. Design same as above." Whether flat-front Style 38's were made of the Style 36 design is not known; however it seems probable that they were not and that this type of listing was simply a space-saving expedient in advertising.

### Style 39

Style 39 instruments were made in curved or serpentine cases. The top was of the ventilated or "cupola" style. All had short bedplates. The lowest serial number assigned was 85285, for an instrument manufactured in 1904 and shipped on January 1, 1905. Those manufactured after late 1904 had 7-digit numbers in the 3900001 to 3900411 range, with the exception of one solitary instrument which bore No. 3900861. These late instruments were shipped from 1905 to 1917. The American Graphophone Company of Bridgeport, Connecticut, ordered many Style 39's in 1910.

### Style 44

Style 44 featured a 20¾" mechanism in a mission-style cabinet. It was advertised as: "Style 44 contains exactly the same mechanism as Style 39 but is combined with a convenient tune disc cabinet. This is a very beautiful and substantial instrument built on colonial lines and must be seen to be appreciated. The tone is rich and powerful. When furnished without the talking machine attachment the lower compartment is fitted as in Style 40 [a 15½" model] to hold about two hundred Regina discs. When sold as a Reginaphone [Style 144] we furnish a combination interior with a capacity of one hundred Regina discs and two hundred talking machine records. Made in mahogany only. Dimensions 43 x 36¼ x 25¼ inches."

The factory records list just ten of these instruments, serially numbered from 4400001 to 4400011 (No. 4400006 was not used). The first was shipped on October 6, 1908; the last, February 24, 1913. The June 1, 1908, Regina price list offered Style 44 at $200 and the Reginaphone version, Style 144, at $225.

### Style 61

Style 61, the Regina Musical Desk, was announced to the music industry in 1903. First shipments were made from the factory in the autumn of the same year. The lowest serial number assigned was 85007. Later Style 61's were given 7-digit numbers from 6100001 to 6100014 and were shipped as late as 1914. Examples were made in oak and mahogany. The left pedestal of the desk is a compartment for the storage of music discs. The music movement is on the right. The controls of most (but not all) are on the right vertical panel of the desk so that Style 61 may be operated without having to open the lid.

### Style 64

One Style 61 "Musical Desk," serial number 6100030, was designated as a Style 64 – made on special order. This instrument was shipped to Edward Riggin of Jersey City, N.J., on November 20, 1908.

### Style 126

Reginaphone version of Style 26 (table model with regular, not folding, top). 7-digit serial numbers were assigned in the 1260001 to 1260138 range to instruments shipped from 1907 to 1915.

### Style 139

Reginaphone version of Style 39. Serpentine case table model. 7-digit serial numbers were assigned in the 1390101 (sic) to 1390277 range to instruments shipped from 1907 to 1915. The American Graphophone Company bought several.

### Style 144

Reginaphone version of Style 44. Six instruments were shipped from 1908 to 1914 and were assigned serial numbers in the 1440001 to 1440007 range. Two Style 144's were purchased by the American Graphophone Co.

### Style 161

Reginaphone version of Style 61, the "Musical Desk." One specimen listed in the factory records; given a 7-digit 6100000 series number: No. 6100028, shipped on April 2, 1908, to Grinnell Brothers of Detroit, Michigan.

### Style 226

Reginaphone (with inside horn) version of styles 26 and 126. 39 instruments made, serially numbered from 2260001 to 2260141. Shipped from 1915 to 1919.

### Style 239

Reginaphone (with inside horn) version of styles 39 and 139. 95 instruments made, serially numbered from 2390001 to 2390124. Shipped from 1914 to 1921.

## REGINA INSTRUMENTS NOT DESCRIBED

The following Regina styles listed in the factory records are not illustrated or described in this book. Perhaps additional information will be located, permitting detailed information in a future edition.

The disc sizes used by these instruments are not known.

STYLE 60: Serial number 75137 shipped December 30, 1904. Others shipped in that era.

STYLE 63: Serial number 85227 shipped April 7, 1905. Others shipped in that era.

STYLE 64: Probably regularly made with 15½" discs; some with 20¾" discs. Serial number 85207, a Rookwood-finish instrument, was shipped on October 11, 1905. Others were shipped around this time also.

STYLE 306: Shipped from 1908 to 1913. Serial numbers from 3060001 to 3061426 with many skipped numbers. Just 26 instruments made.

STYLE 626: Serial number 36037 (an 1897 serial number!) shipped on June 12, 1918.

STYLE 700: Shipped from 1918 to 1920. Serial numbers from 7000001 to 7000406. Many numbers skipped. About 210 made. Probably a Reginaphone (phonograph-only) instrument.

STYLE 800: Shipped from 1917 to 1921. Serial numbers from 8000001 to 8000760. Many numbers skipped. Just 104 instruments made. Probably a phonograph-only Reginaphone.

STYLE 901: Shipped from 1919 to 1921. Serial numbers from 9010001 to 9010080. Some numbers skipped. Just 62 made. Probably a phonograph-only Reginaphone.

STYLE 932: Special disc music box model made for Sears & Roebuck. Serial numbers from 9320001 to 9320050. Some numbers skipped. 26 made. Consignment of 25 shipped on July 6, 1905 to Sears; consignment returned intact to Regina on July 31, 1906. One single instrument shipped on December 4, 1906, to Hoeffler Mfg. Co. of Milwaukee and kept by that firm.

STYLE 930: Special disc music box model made for Sears & Roebuck. Serial numbers from 9300001 to 9300100. Some numbers skipped. 51 made. Consignment of 50 shipped on July 6, 1905, to Sears; consignment returned intact to Regina on July 31, 1906. One single instrument shipped on December 4, 1906, to Hoeffler Mfg. Co. and kept.

STYLE 934: Special disc music box model made for Sears & Roebuck. Serial numbers from 9340001 to 9340030. Some numbers skipped. 14 made. Consignment of 13 shipped on July 6, 1905, to Sears; consignment returned intact to Regina on July 31, 1906. One single instrument shipped on December 4, 1906, to Hoeffler Mfg. Co. and kept.

STYLE 936: Special disc music box model made for Sears & Roebuck. Serial numbers from 9360001 to 9360042. Some numbers skipped. 21 made. Consignment of 19 shipped on July 6, 1905, to Sears; consignment returned intact to Regina on July 31, 1906. One instrument shipped on December 4, 1906, to Hoeffler Mfg. Co. and kept. One instrument shipped later to Sears, on April 12, 1907, and kept.

Kipp Brothers Special Orders: In 1905, Kipp Brothers of Indianapolis, Indiana, ordered some models, case designs unspecified, which were made on special order. The serial number ranges are given herewith. The first three digits apparently referred to the style numbers (such as 2020001 would have been for Style 202), but further descriptions are lacking. Perhaps some of these instruments still exist today. If so, the editor would welcome further information. "Style 202" (Editor's conjectural description, not Regina's): Serial numbers 2020001 to 2020005; "Style 209" 2090001 to 2090005; "Style 106" 1060001 to 1060004; "Style 103" 1030001 to 1030010; "Style 101" 1010001 to 1010014; "Style 206" 2060001 and 2060002; "Style 501" (apparently different from Style 501 as described in the Regina phonograph section of this book) 5010001 to 5010003.

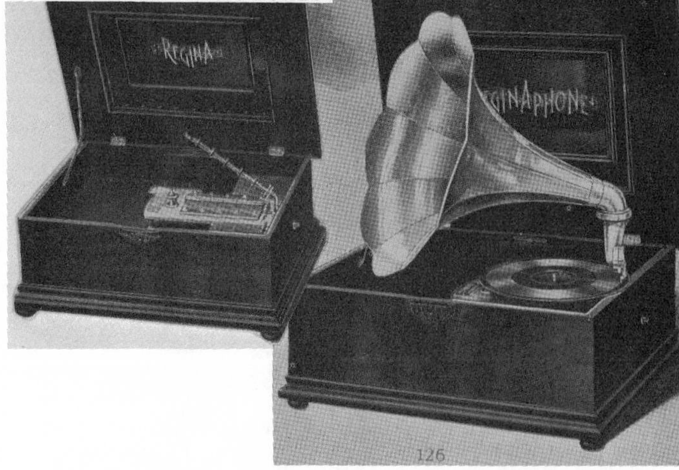


Late-model Style 26 (upper left) in regular case. Model illustrated has a short bedplate, although some had long bedplates. At the upper right is the Reginaphone version, Style 126.

Above and right: Style 39 in curved or serpentine case with "cupola" lid. Below: The Reginaphone version, Style 139.

Right: Styles 44 and 144 (Reginaphone). The same illustrations were used to describe Styles 45 and 145, the 27" versions in similar cabinets. Very few of these were made.

New Regina Sublima,
No. 25.
LONG-RUNNING MOVEMENT.
WITH COIN ATTACHMENT.
Two large Combs, with 130 Tongues, tuned in chromatic scale.
Dimensions of Tune Sheets, 20¾ ins. diameter.
Case in Oak or Mahogany.

Regina Sublima, Nos. 24 and 25

No. 24, for Parlor use; No. 25, with Slot Attachment; Long-running Movement; two large Combs, with 130 Tongues, tuned in chromatic scale; Case in Oak or Mahogany; Dimensions, 71 x 36 x 16 inches; Dimensions of Tune Sheets, 20¾ inches diameter.

**Above: Styles 24 (without coin slot, for parlor use) and 25 (with coin slot). Although other minor variations were made, the two main cabinet designs are those shown above. The one to the right is the earlier and has three circles above the bottom rectangular panels. Like many other 20¾" Regina styles, these were given the "Regina Sublima" name — not to be confused with the similarly-named Regina Sublima Piano of later years.**

**Style 25 was the more popular of the two and was used in commercial locations around the turn of the 20th century.**

Regina Sublima, Nos. 26 and 27

No. 26, for Parlor use; No. 27, with Slot Attachment; Long-running Movement; two large Combs, with 130 Tongues, tuned in chromatic scale; Case in Oak or Mahogany; Dimensions, 29 x 20½ x 11½ inches; Dimensions of Tune Sheets, 20¾ inches diameter.

**Early styles 26 and 27 with folding-top case. Similarly designed models were also made in the 27" format. These were manufactured during the late 1890's.**

REGINA, STYLE No. 27.

Another new style. This is a magnificent instrument, sold at a popular price. Has improved bedplate and sounding board, also speed regulator. Long-running movement, two large combs with 130 steel tongues tuned in chromatic scale. Cases in quartered oak or mahogany. Dimensions 28½ x 23½ x 13¾. Tune Sheets 20¾ inches diameter.

REGINA NO. 27. $120.00.

Another new style for 1904. This is a magnificent instrument, sold at a popular price. Has improved bedplate and sounding board, also speed regulator. Long-running movement, two large combs with 130 steel tongues tuned in chromatic scale.

Cases in quartered oak or mahogany. Dimensions 28¼x23¼x13¼. Tune sheets 20¾ inches in diameter.

**Late Style 27 instruments. The illustration above is correct (except that the coin slot is omitted). The illustration shown at the left is erroneous. An engraving of a 15½" Regina was used in error to describe No. 27, a 20¾" box.**

**Style 27 instruments are coin operated and were originally equipped with 1c or 5c slots. 5c models played the tune through twice for one coin.**

**Left: Style 61 Regina Musical Desk. Shown with the desk top in the raised position. The pedestal on the left side is for the storage of discs. The musical movement is on the right.**

**Serial No. 6100028, a special order model, was equipped with an outside horn and was a Reginaphone.**

Regina Sublima, No. 28

Long-running Movement; two large Combs, with 130 Tongues, tuned in chromatic scale; Case in Oak or Mahogany; Dimensions, 30 x 24¼ x 14¼ inches; Dimensions of Tune Sheets, 20¾ inches diameter.

**Style 28: An ornate long-bedplate 20¾" table model box first made in the late 1890's. These were made concurrently with early Style 26 (folding-top) boxes.**

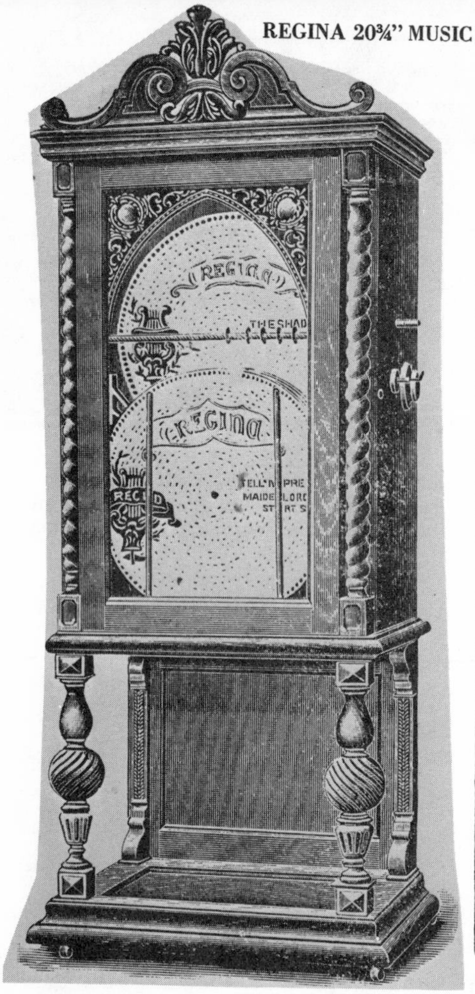
REGINA
THE SHAD
REGINA

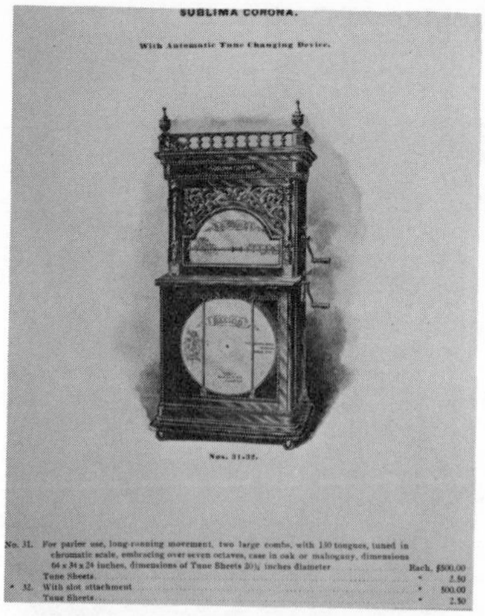
SUBLIMA CORONA.
With Automatic Tune Changing Device.
Nos. 31-32.
No. 31. For parlor use, long-running movement, two large combs, with 130 tongues, tuned in chromatic scale, embracing over seven octaves, case in oak or mahogany, dimensions 64 x 34 x 24 inches, dimensions of Tune Sheets 20¾ inches diameter Each, $500.00
Tune Sheets " 2.50
" 32. With slot attachment " 500.00
Tune Sheets " 2.50

Above and above right: Styles 31 and 32 Regina Sublima Corona, automatic disc-changing boxes which use the 20¾" discs. The styles of these are similar to their 27" disc counterparts, except that the proportions are slightly different. Style 31 instruments have the lever type on-off mechanism; Style 32's are coin operated.

REGINA

## Sublima Corona, No. 38.

**with Piano Sounding Board.**

AUTOMATIC TUNE CHANGING DEVICE.
WITH COIN ATTACHMENT. LONG-RUNNING MOVEMENT.

Two large Combs, with 130 Tongues,
tuned in chromatic scale, embracing over 7 octaves.
Case in Oak or Mahogany.
Dimensions, 78 x 32 x 24 inches.

No. 38, Flat.—Case with flat front, like cut.
No. 38, Round.—Case with round front.

REGINA

Sublima Corona, No. 37
with Piano Sounding Board.
AUTOMATIC TUNE-CHANGING DEVICE.
LONG-RUNNING MOVEMENT.
Two large Combs, with 130 Tongues, tuned in chromatic scale, embracing over 7 octaves. Dimension of Tune Sheet, 20¾ inches diameter. Case in Oak or Mahogany. Dimensions, 75 x 34 x 26 inches.

Style 37, round-front "parlor model" style. Built without (usually) or with clock attachment. This style was built only in limited numbers.

Above and right:
Filling the empty disc rack of a Style 31 with twelve 20¾" diameter tune sheets. Care must be taken to put each disc in the proper alignment (with the "Regina" name centered at the top) so that the disc will begin at the beginning of the tune and stop at the end.

## –27" REGINA MUSIC BOXES–
### General Information

The 27" disc size is the largest Regina music box (the 32" Concerto is not strictly a music box as it plays piano strings). This size was first marketed in 1896, a year that saw the introduction of vertical styles 4 and 5 and the folding-top styles 6 and 7. In the following year, 1897, the automatic disc changer made its appearance. The disc changer was sold as styles 8, 8a, 33, and 34. A decade later, styles 45 and 145, cabinet model 27" single-play instruments, the 145 with a phonograph attachment, made their appearance.

All 27" instruments have duplex music combs, each comb having 86 teeth, for a total of 172 (however, advertisements sometimes put the figure at 173 or 175). A zither attachment, called a "banjo" effect by Regina, was available at extra cost.

Regina 27" discs are numbered in the 4000 series. Hundreds of titles were produced.

———————

### –27" Orchestral Regina–
### Styles 4 and 5

These tall upright Regina instruments are of the single-disc (non-changer) type. Of vertical format, tall examples of the 4 and 5 measure close to 80" high and are thus the tallest regular Regina music box style (the Concerto, actually a piano, is taller).

Models without coin slot were first known as Style 4, and those with coin slot were designated as Style 5. Most of the upright Reginas made in this design were equipped with coin mechanisms. Very few Style 4's, a model designated for home use, were manufactured.

The Style 4 was introduced in 1896 and was sold through the early 1900's. The earliest serial number is 18520. The Style 5 was introduced in the same year. The earliest number is 21004.

Case style variations include several styles with disc storage bins that tilt outward to the front. One, shown near the center top of this page, has two large rectangular panels in the lower section. Although just two brass spandrels are shown in the catalogue illustration, this model usually has four. At the upper right of this page is a popular style which has the entire front (top and bottom sections) hinged as a single door. A storage compartment is in the base and can be reached by opening the entire front. At the lower right of this page is an unusual model with a crest-type gallery. Near the lower center is a model with a separate bin at the bottom (hinges outward from the front) and two doors at the top. Other models (not illustrated) are equipped with a door at the right side of the case for access to the disc bin or with a counterweighted (like a window sash) front panel. Woods used were mainly oak and mahogany, although a few walnut models were produced.

The large, imposing, and quite ornate Style 5 found ready acceptance in penny arcades, restaurants, and other public locations. These were made through the early 1900's and were popular until about 1905.

### –Regina 27" "Folding-Top"–
### Orchestral Regina, Nos. 6 and 7

Introduced in 1896, the folding-top or accordion-top (as collectors call them today; also "casket model" is sometimes used) Regina was designated as Style 6 if for home use, or Style 7 if equipped with a coin slot. These were made by the dozens and were mainly popular from 1896 to about 1900.

The earliest serial number for Style 6 is No. 21066; for Style 7, 21495. Similar-appearing instruments were made in the 20¾" disc size. Also, Polyphon of Leipzig, Germany, made instruments of similar concept.

Orchestral Regina, Nos. 4 and 5

Orchestral Regina, Nos. 6 and 7

No. 6, for Parlor use; No. 7, with Slot Attachment; Long-running Movement; two large single Combs; with 172 Tongues, tuned in chromatic scale, embracing over seven octaves; Case in Oak or Mahogany; Dimensions of Case, 34 x 20 x 12½ inches; Dimensions of Tune Sheets, 27 inches diameter.

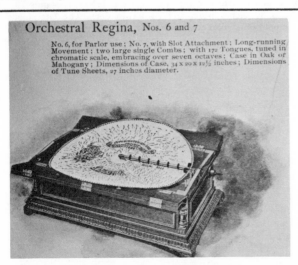

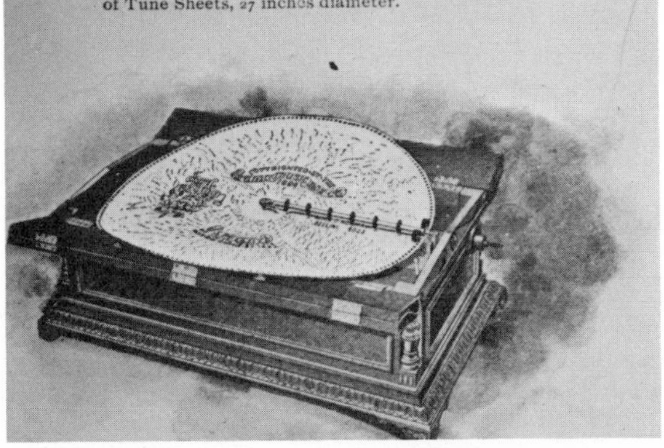

Style 45.

Style 145.

—Regina 27" – Style 45—

The Style 45, a mission-style cabinet containing a 27" disc mechanism, was listed in Regina catalogues as early as 1906. Apparently only a few were sold. The factory records note that the first instrument was shipped on December 19, 1910, and the last was shipped on December 28, 1913. Just ten instruments were made in the serial range from 4500001 to 4500012. It is possible that earlier instruments were made, possibly using bedplates assigned to folding-top or large upright 27" models and so listed in the factory records, but if this is so, there is no way of verifying it today unless a specimen comes to light with a serial number not in the series mentioned above.

—Regina 27" – Style 145 Reginaphone—

The Reginaphone version of the Style 45. The factory records note that but five pieces were made, all with serial numbers in the 14500001 to 14500006 range (one number was omitted). These were shipped from 1908 to 1913. One was sold to the American Graphophone Company of Bridgeport, Connecticut.

The June 1, 1908, Regina price list featured the Style 45 at $225.00 and the Style 145 at $250.00. The illustrations used were the same as used for the 20¾" models 44 and 144.

—Regina 27" Automatic Disc-Changing Music Box—

General Catalogue Description

The following description appeared about 1899 and covers the various styles of Regina changers then available:

"The Regina Music Boxes, the first manufactured in the United States, are in their various features fully protected by patents. They must not be confounded with the Swiss Music Boxes, as their working mechanisms are entirely different. The old-time cylinder, comprising a limited number of tunes, selected, not to the taste of the buyer, but to that of the manufacturer, is discarded, and interchangeable steel tune sheets, unlimited in number, are employed in their stead. The list of tunes is increased daily, and is already large and varied enough to meet the taste of every purchaser. The disagreeable noise occasioned in winding the ordinary box is entirely overcome in the Regina; a patented attachment renders it absolutely noiseless, and a safety crank prevents overwinding. The motive force of the Regina consists of an extremely solid but simple clockwork, and the steel tune discs, readily interchanged, are virtually indestructible. In the construction of the Regina, as the best available materials are used, and as all parts are absolutely interchangeable, an instrument of the highest standard is produced, which with reasonable care will last a lifetime. All cases, of elegant design and finish, are made of solid hardwood of American growth.

"The Orchestral Regina and the Regina Corona exceed not only in size, brilliancy, and volume of tone any Music Box ever made, but the latter is also the first and only disc instrument manufactured which automatically changes the tune sheets. The wonderful mechanism of the Regina Corona represents the greatest achievement yet attained in the construction of Music Boxes. It raises at will any desired tune disc from the receptacle in which they are contained, places and adjusts it automatically, and after having rendered it replaces it in its original position, continuing the operation until the entire repertoire is heard, or will repeat any tune ad libitum. The size of the tune sheets used for both the Orchestral Regina and the Regina Corona makes it possible to play songs, dances, operatic airs, and parts of overtures complete, with all the counter melodies, as if played by a complete orchestra."

Regina Catalogue Descriptions (c.1906) of Styles 33 and 34

"Regina Orchestral Corona, Style 33. This is the largest sized Regina and is the finest instrument of its kind that has ever been made. It has all the advantages of every other instrument [in the Regina line], and because of the very large discs and combs and the piano sounding board it has a volume and sweetness of tone to be compared only with the finest piano. Tune discs are 27" in diameter, or nearly twice the surface area of the next smaller size [20¾"]. On these large discs, very long and intricate compositions can be rendered in a most complete and satisfactory manner. The combs have 172 steel tongues tuned in chromatic scale, embracing over seven octaves. This instrument contains two very strong springs, each one-quarter horsepower. Any tune in the carriage can be selected and played at will, and any tune may be repeated as desired. The music of Style 33 is of such volume as to fill a large room or suite of rooms, and these instruments are to be found in some of the best homes in the country. Cases in oak or mahogany. Dimensions 66 x 37½ x 25 inches."

"Regina Orchestral Corona, No. 34 (with coin slot). This instrument has a piano sounding board, changes the discs automatically, and has a long-running movement. It has two large combs with 175 [sic] tongues, embracing over seven octaves. Tune sheets are 27" in diameter. The case is either mahogany or oak, highly polished. It stands 75 inches high, is 39 inches wide, and 24 inches deep. The largest and best instrument of its kind ever made."

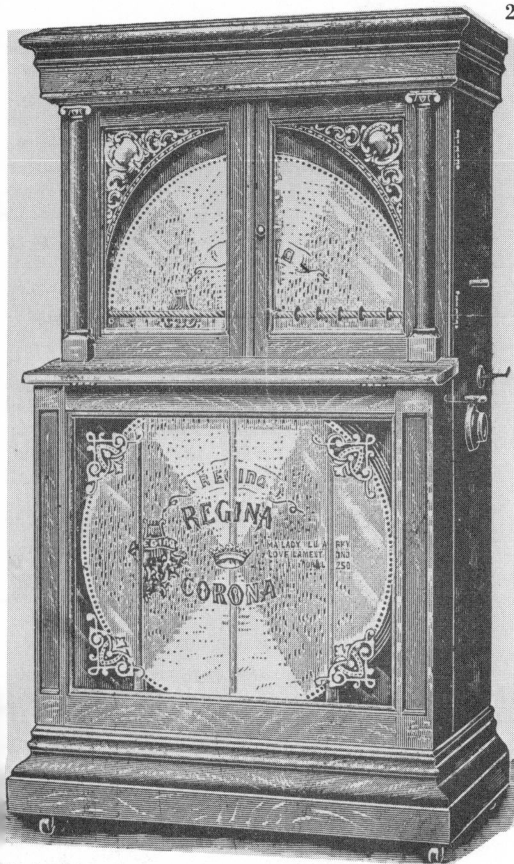

Style 34

Style 8

Style 34 with gallery.

Left: Style 34 (with coin slot). Above: Style 8 (with lever for stopping and starting). Upper right: Style 34 with top gallery. Center right: Style 33 or 34 with unusual gallery. Lower right: Style 33, late illustration from 1908 Regina catalogue. The beveled glass, as illustrated, was seldom actually used.

Style 33 or 34.

Late Style 33.

### –Regina 27" Automatic Disc-Changing Music Box– Orchestral Corona – Styles 8, 8a, 33, 34

The 27" Regina automatic disc changer is perhaps the best known of all Regina instruments today. The large disc size, the interesting changing mechanisms, and the relative ease with which a specimen may be acquired (aside from financial requirements!) have combined to keep the Orchestral Corona "in the news" with collectors.

These instruments were made in a wide range of case varieties. Basically, those with a four-panel hinged rear door (not unlike a house door in appearance) were designated as Style 8 if for home use (no coin slot) and 8a if equipped with a coin mechanism. Basically, those with a ribbed "piano sounding board" were designated as Orchestral Corona No. 33 if for home use; No. 34 if equipped with a coin slot. However, there was no absolute consistency in this regard, and 8 and 8a models manufactured in 1898 and 1899 were sold as 33 or 34 models if they were marketed in the early 1900's.

Earlier instruments are the most ornate of all and have a spooled railing or gallery across the top with a carved finial at each front corner. Some models have other types of architectural finials, a center scallop or a broken arch for example, but these are rare. Rare also are models with solid wood panels rather than clear glass at the bottom. One of the most popular varieties was the plain-top style with two upper front doors, each with a brass spandrel (the same spandrel, by the way, as used on the Link Self-Playing Xylophone – see Link section of this book). Some of these did have top galleries, as the illustration at the upper right shows. Models with a motif of carved dragons were made in two styles: the early (mostly 8 and 8a) type with the carving in one piece, and the later type (mostly 33) with the upper part divided into two doors.

While the "piano sounding board" feature made good advertising copy, it didn't necessarily relate to the tonal quality of 27" instruments. Collectors today find that 27" instruments are like fine old violins – some have a sweet and resonant tone and others do not – and the presence of a piano sounding board doesn't seem to make a difference.

Serial number information: The lowest serial number given to a 27" changer was No. 4533. This instrument, delivered on July 28, 1899, was made from a comb and bedplate assembly made in 1894 and not used until much later. The same happened with No. 4577, shipped also on July 28, 1899. The first 27" changer was No. 21674, delivered on March 12, 1897, but later returned to the factory (for unexplained reasons). The first large production run of 27" instruments had numbers from 30001 to 30500 inclusive (500 in all). Most of these were shipped in 1898 and 1899. Some were later shipped as 33 and 34 models. The first No. 33 regularly made as such was No. 46595, shipped on October 13, 1899. A large production run of 33 and 34 models was numbered from 65000 to 65916. These instruments were shipped from 1901 until 1908. Others were made from time to time, including some with earlier components (as No.6596, a Style 34 made with a c.1895 comb and bedplate).

—Anatomy of a Regina—
27" Automatic Changer
Style 8a (1898)

The Style 8a, a 27" Regina dis changer which holds twelve discs an plays the patron's choice upon receip of a nickel, was shipped from th Regina factory in Rahway, N.J., to th Rudolph Wurlitzer Co. in Cincinnati o October 29, 1898. This particular Styl 8a, which differs from the Style 8 b the addition of a coin mechanism, i in red mahogany wood.

Views of the interior of this Styl 8a, serial number 30094, appear o the following two pages.

The first 27" Regina changer t leave the factory was No. 21674 whic was shipped on March 12, 1897, bu which was later returned (for reason unspecified). The first regular produc tion run of 27" changers commence with No. 30001 and continued t 30500, five hundred instruments in all These were mostly shipped in 189 and 1899 and were sold as Styles and 8a. Some were shipped later an were sold as Style 34, the later desig nation for the 27" changer model.

With disc in the playing position.

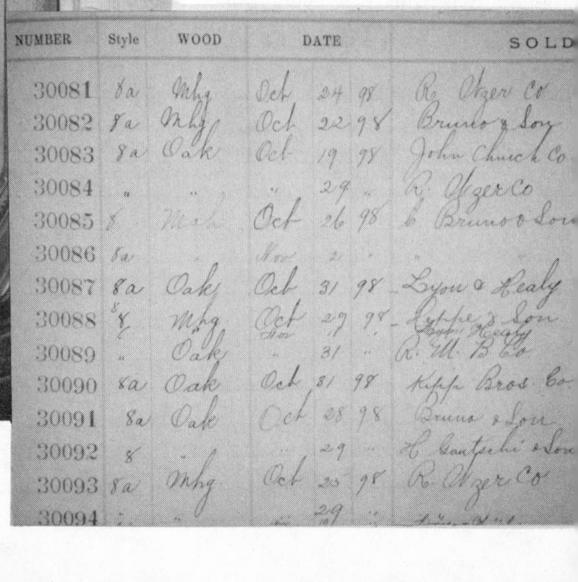

| NUMBER | Style | WOOD | DATE | | | SOLD |
|---|---|---|---|---|---|---|
| 30081 | 8a | Mhg | Oct | 24 | 98 | R. Wzer Co |
| 30082 | 8a | Mhg | Oct | 22 | 98 | Bruno & Son |
| 30083 | 8a | Oak | Oct | 19 | 98 | John Church Co |
| 30084 | " | " | " | 29 | " | R. Wzer Co |
| 30085 | 8 | Mah | Oct | 26 | 98 | C Bruno & Son |
| 30086 | 8a | " | Nov | 2 | " | " |
| 30087 | 8a | Oak | Oct | 31 | 98 | Lyon & Healy |
| 30088 | 8 | Mhg | Oct | 29 | 98 | Leppe & Son |
| 30089 | " | Oak | " | 31 | " | R. W. B. Co |
| 30090 | 8a | Oak | Oct | 31 | 98 | Kipp Bros Co |
| 30091 | 8a | Oak | Oct | 28 | 98 | Bruno & Son |
| 30092 | 8 | " | " | 29 | " | H. Gautschi & Son |
| 30093 | 8a | Mhg | Oct | 25 | 98 | R. Wzer Co |
| 30094 | " | " | [illegible] | 29 | " | [illegible] |

Right: Regina ledger showing that No. 30094 (the bottom listing) was shipped to the "R. Wzer Co." (Rudolph Wurlitzer Co.) on October 29, 1898.

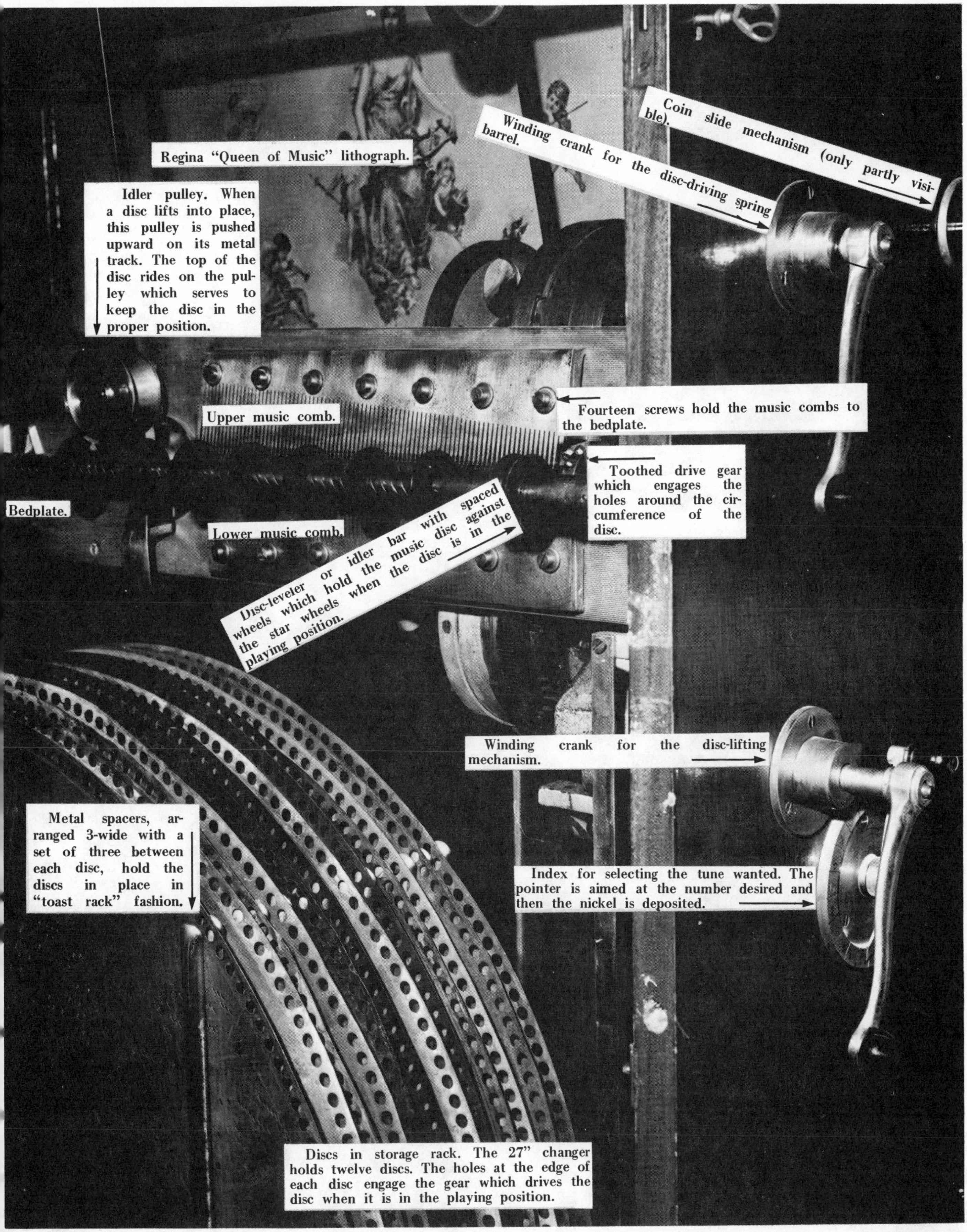

Regina "Queen of Music" lithograph.
Idler pulley. When a disc lifts into place, this pulley is pushed upward on its metal track. The top of the disc rides on the pulley which serves to keep the disc in the proper position.
Winding crank for the disc-driving spring barrel.
Coin slide mechanism (only partly visible).
Upper music comb.
Fourteen screws hold the music combs to the bedplate.
Toothed drive gear which engages the holes around the circumference of the disc.
Bedplate.
Lower music comb.
Disc-leveler or idler bar with spaced wheels which hold the music disc against the star wheels when the disc is in the playing position.
Winding crank for the disc-lifting mechanism.
Metal spacers, arranged 3-wide with a set of three between each disc, hold the discs in place in "toast rack" fashion.
Index for selecting the tune wanted. The pointer is aimed at the number desired and then the nickel is deposited.
Discs in storage rack. The 27" changer holds twelve discs. The holes at the edge of each disc engage the gear which drives the disc when it is in the playing position.

Interior view of the Style 8a Regina with the upper and lower front panels removed to permit a better view. Any one of twelve discs may be selected. When a nickel is put in the coin slide the desired disc is lifted into the playing position. The brass idler wheel, which rides along the top of the disc as it plays, keeps the face of the disc curved slightly inward – thus keeping the disc's inner surface tightly against the star wheel mechanism when it is held there by the black wheels.

Upper tune sheet or disc in the playing position.
End of coin slide.
Primary steel lifting strap or band which powers (by means of a pulley arrangement) the two straps which lift the disc into the playing position.
Spring barrel for driving the disc.
Pan which receives the nickel.
Lead resonators or tuning weights on the back of the music combs. The deepest bass notes have the largest resonators.
Coin trip mechanism.
Centering pin rod.
Bedplate.
Coin chute which leads to locked coin box under the floor of the instrument (and accessible from the outside).
Speed governor.
Spring barrel for operating the disc-lifting mechanism.
Lower disc — the rearmost tune sheet in the 12-disc storage rack.
Metal spacer to hold the disc in position, one of a set of three at the front and back of each disc.
Indexing mechanism for the tune selector. This can be operated by hand. When played without selecting, the indexing mechanism will play the discs through in order in the sequence of 1, 2, 3, 4, 5, 6, 7, 8, 9, 10, 11, 12, 11, 10, 9, 8, 7, 6, 5, 4, 3, 2, 1, 2, 3, and so on.

Rear view of the Style 8a Regina 27" automatic disc changer with a disc in the playing position. A hinged door, extending from the top to the bottom of the instrument, swings out to permit easy access for servicing from the rear.

### General Description

The Regina Concerto is a disc-operated instrument which plays tuned piano strings. As it contains no music combs it is not, strictly speaking, a "music box." However, as it is usually classified with Regina disc-operated instruments we include it in this music box section.

Measurements are approximately 8'6" high by 46½" wide by 2' deep. All specimens seen by the author have been in walnut or oak wood. The instrumentation consists of a piano with the strings arranged symmetrically. Certain notes have more than one set of strings and more than one hammer, in order to permit rapid repetition of that note. Otherwise a given note could not be sounded until the piano hammer lifted from sounding the previous note, went back into the rest position, and then came forward again – a process requiring an audibly-measurable amount of time. Other instrumentation consists of a set of tubular bells (on some, not all instruments), a cymbal, a small tenor drum, and a snare drum. To achieve the proper repetition the snare drum has six beaters.

The unit is operated by 32" diameter steel discs. Two main types exist: (1) the early style (without changer) imported in its entirety from the Polyphon Musikwerke and (2) the later style with the cabinet, changer, and certain other parts built in America by Regina.

### The Polyphon Concerto

The Polyphon Concerto (or "Polyphone" – most Regina advertisements anglicized the name by adding an "e") was imported by Regina from the Polyphon Musikwerke of Leipzig, Germany. Although Polyphon made several different Concerto-style instruments, apparently only the 32" diameter style was imported by Regina. These were imported in two formats. Most were of the tall floor-standing type as illustrated. A few were without base cabinet, were shorter in stature, and were intended for placement on a tavern counter.

In 1903 Regina advertised the Polyphon Concerto and made bold note that it was an imported instrument: "THE GREATEST SUCCESS OF THE YEAR – First Importation All Sold! – New Lot on the Way, and Orders Awaiting Their Arrival!. Testimonial: Gentlemen: The Concerto which I recently purchased from you is about the best investment I have ever made. It is not only profitable because of the money actually received from it, but it is an attraction which brings more patronage into my place of business. It gives absolutely no trouble and in that respect is much superior to electrically operated players which require current and electric motors. Yours truly, Henry Horstmann, 501 Washington Street, Hoboken, N.J., April 17, 1903."

This same advertisement goes on to describe the Concerto: "The Concerto plays on piano strings – also when desired on bells, cymbals, and drums. It plays for a nickel or can be operated with a key as desired. With a sample of this instrument you can sell to every up-to-date hotel, cafe, or restaurant in your city. Write for terms and territory to: Regina Music Box Company; 11 East 22nd St., New York City [Regina's early address]; or 259 Wabash Ave., Chicago."

Another contemporary view of the Polyphon Concerto is provided by a listing in the catalogue of Koehler & Hinrichs, bar and restaurant suppliers of St. Paul, Minnesota. Note the mention of the "Polyphone" name:

"A NICKEL-IN-THE-SLOT ORCHESTRA. This instrument requires no motor. It is run by a one horsepower spring. One winding will make it play about 15 times. The Polyphone Concerto is intended to furnish music for large places, because it is loud and big. It plays by dropping a nickel in the slot – either one or two tunes for a single coin. It plays piano, bells, cymbals, drums – all of them together or separately as desired. It works with tune sheets, 32 inches in diameter. It runs with a spring motor – no battery to get out of order. It is loud enough to be heard all over the largest concert hall, beer garden, hotel, cafe, club room, or dancing hall. It is 8½ feet high, 46½ inches wide, and 24½ inches deep. The illustration shows the Polyphone open. It shows the tune sheets in the cabinet below and shows the drums, cymbals, bells, and piano strings. The woodwork is highly finished and well designed, and it will be an attractive ornament to any place."

Most of this type of Polyphon Concerto were in walnut cabinets. It is not recorded how many of these early (non-changer) Polyphon Concertos were sold altogether by Regina. The Regina factory records note that about 300 Concerto instruments were sold in 1905 and 1906. These instruments were serially numbered from 1 to 449, with some numbers skipped. As many Polyphon Concertos were sold previous to 1905, this 300 figure is not a total. We are assuming that these instruments bearing numbers 1 through 449 are not the changer models, for the changer models have a separate listing in the records and are called "Automatic Concertos" and are serially numbered from 3001 to 3101 and from 3000001 to 3000216.

### Automatic Concerto – Style 300

Beginning in 1904 the Regina Automatic Concerto, known as the Style 300, was marketed. Basically this unit consists of an imported Polyphon piano and disc-playing mechanism combined with a Regina-made cabinet, automatic disc changing device, and accessory parts. Most were housed in oak cabinets. Oak, a wood used often by Regina, was seldom used by Polyphon (which preferred walnut).

The mechanism consists of the same basic instrumentation and components as the Polyphon Concerto, except that the Style 300 is equipped with an automatic changing device. The changer holds 10 discs (rather than the 12 that are standard on other Regina changer sizes).

When introduced, the Automatic Concerto was advertised thus: "HERE IS THE LATEST ADDITION TO THE REGINA FAMILY. This new instrument is the Automatic Regina Concerto. It is quite a buster for so young a baby – weighs 950 lbs., is 45 inches wide, 27 inches deep, and stands 8 feet 2 inches high in its stocking feet. Like most youngsters it has a loud voice. It plays on piano strings, bells, cymbals, and drums, all together or separately, as desired, and can be heard all over the largest concert hall, beer garden, hotel, cafe, clubroom, or dancing hall. Its mission is to furnish good music for large places, because it is loud and big, and yet, when so desired, its tones can be softened so that it is no louder than an ordinary piano.

"The Regina Concerto plays whenever a nickel is fed to it, and is guaranteed never to lose its appetite. Its tune discs are of steel, of course, and are 32 inches in diameter, and the power is furnished by a quadruple spring motor, the most powerful we have ever built. It will play either one or two tunes for a single coin, and can also be adjusted to play the same tune twice [on one coin], but the nicest thing about it is that it is automatic (like our Coronas), and requires practically no attention.

"The Regina Concerto has a repertoire of ten tunes, and these are automatically lifted into position, played, and returned to their place in the tune carriage, without any attention upon the part of the operator.

"This is a brief description of the latest and best nickel-in-the-slot machine. The Regina Concerto will attract customers to your place, and attract their nickels for music, to say nothing about their other patronage. There is no other instrument made as large as this, and which will do the same work. The woodwork is of oak, highly finished, and well designed.

"From inquiries already received we are almost sure to have orders within the next thirty days for all of these instruments that we can build during the next four months. Judging from our experience with the Polyphone Concerto, which was not automatic, but which was the prototype of the new Regina Concerto, the demand for this instrument will be very great. Get your order in early. First come, first served. The nimble nickel beats the slow dollar."

The first Regina Automatic Concerto, Style 300, was serial number 3001 and was shipped to the St. Louis Exposition in 1904. Regular shipments to customers commenced in the summer of that year. Serial numbers for the Style 300 are divided into two categories. Numbers 3001 to 3101 were produced until November, 1904, when the serial system was changed to the 7-digit style (all serial numbers for all Regina instruments were so changed). Beginning in November, 1904, the serial numbers commenced with 3000001 (which means: Style 300, instrument number 0001) and continued to 3000216.

Style 300 Regina Concertos were shipped from the factory from 1904 until 1917. 316 were made (1 serial number was omitted from the above-mentioned sequences). Some were equipped with electric motors instead of the customary quadruple spring motors.

### Commentary

Even though Automatic Concertos were shipped from the factory as late as 1917, the instrument was technologically obsolete by 1910. By that time spring-wound instruments were no competition in public places in comparison to the electrically-operated 44-note cabinet pianos, keyboard pianos, and larger orchestrions.

As few, if any, were used in private homes (if they were, more would have been saved) and as this type of instrument was obsolete at an early date, few survived past the 1920's. As a result, the Concerto is much rarer today in proportion to the original quantity produced than are Regina instruments made for home use.

---

Note: See the Lochmann "Original" music box section of this book for information concerning disc-operated pianos, including some that are similar to the Regina Concerto, made by that firm. Refer also to the Polyphon section for disc-piano information, including details concerning the Concerto.

Views of a Regina (Polyphon) Concerto. The two top illustrations appeared in a Regina advertisement of 1903. The illustration to the right is of a Concerto in the Svoboda Collection.

TESTIMONIAL.

Hoboken, N. J., April 17, 1903.

"REGINA MUSIC BOX CO.,
New York."

Gentlemen: The Concerto which I recently purchased from you is about the best investment I have ever made. It is not only profitable because of the money actually received from it, but it is an attraction which brings more patronage into my place of business. It gives absolutely no trouble and in that respect is much superior to electrically operated players which require current and electric motors. Yours truly,

Henry Horstmann,
501 Washington St."

---

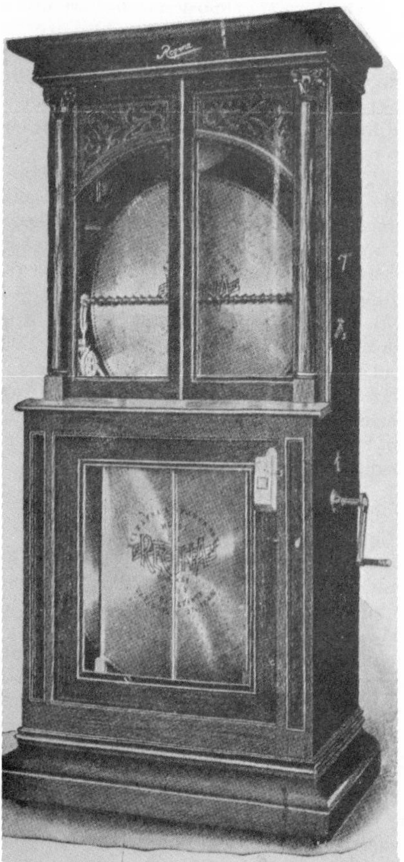

Regina Automatic Concerto. Closed.

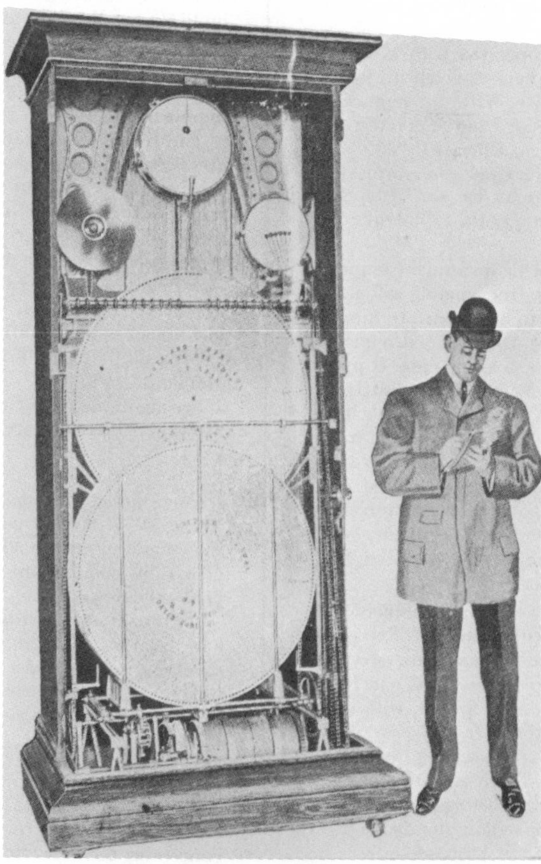

—Regina Concerto Disc-Operated Piano—
(Style 300) (32" diameter discs)

Left: Style 300 Regina Concerto as featured in a Regina advertisement for this model. The case and changer mechanism of this model were made in Rahway by Regina; the instrumental part and the upper disc mechanism were supplied by the Polyphon Musikwerke of Leipzig, Germany.

Disc-operated piano orchestrions, popular in Europe and made in various styles by several different German manufacturers, were of minor importance in the American market. The Pianette, a disc-operated piano made by F.G. Otto & Sons, and the Regina Concerto were the two main types sold in this country.

Polyphon made disc-operated pianos in a number of disc sizes (see Polyphon section of this book), but so far as is known the only size imported by Regina was the 32" diameter.

The Concerto, actually a piano and not a music box, is included in this music box section as it is disc-operated and is generally considered a "music box" by collectors. For information on roll-operated Reginapianos, Regina Sublimas, and other instruments please refer to the Regina coin piano section of this book.

Directly above: Empty cabinet that once housed an Automatic Cashier & Discount Machine. The other three pictures show the musical movement (Regina serial number 2160143 shipped on Nov. 1, 1907) and other details of another Automatic Cashier & Discount Machine.

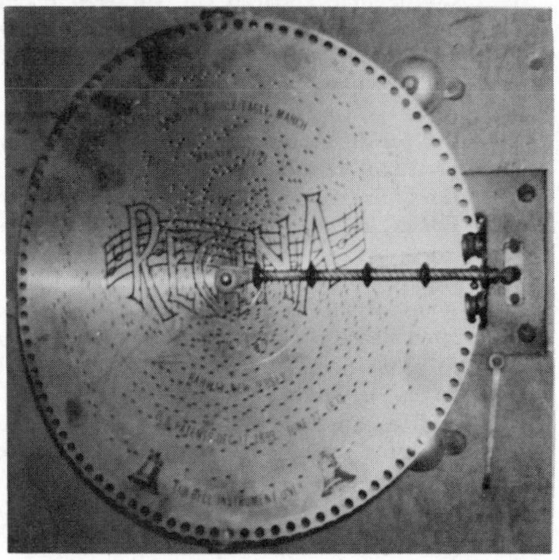


Above: Views of the Automatic Cashier & Discount Machine made by the Yale Wonder Clock Company of Burlington, Vermont. This particular type uses a Regina Style 216 movement with special 15½" discs which play duplex music combs and twelve bells. The discs are marked "For Bell Instrument Only."

Left: Partial view of a tall Musical Uno (top signholder not in picture). Incorporating a 15½" regular (without bells) Regina musical movement, the Musical Uno was made in at least three different cabinet styles.

### Sale of Musical Movements

The Regina factory records reveal the sale of hundreds of musical movements (without cases) to various firms. In 1895 dozens of Regina 8½" movements were shipped to the W.F. Main Company of Iowa City, Iowa. In 1901 many 20¾" movements were sent to the Equitable Manufacturing Company.

Beginning in 1901 and continuing through 1907 the Yale Wonder Clock Company of Burlington, Vermont, ordered movements by the hundreds! Many more movements were shipped to Regina's New York City sales outlet where they were presumably sold to manufacturers in the New York area.

While some of the Regina movements undoubtedly became a part of custom-built furniture pieces, the greatest number were used in gambling machines. The addition of a musical movement to a slot machine meant that the patron would be rewarded by hearing a tune, regardless of whether he won a jackpot or not. This "value received for money spent" made the machines legal in some areas in which regular slot machines were not allowed. While most such musical slot machines incorporated Swiss cylinder movements, at least several hundred were built with Regina disc mechanisms.

Among these disc-type musical machines two of the most interesting are the Musical Uno and the Automatic Cashier & Discount Machine.

### The Musical Uno

The Musical Uno incorporates a 15½" Regina duplex comb movement. The disc is mounted in a vertical position and is visible through a circular glass window in the front. The Musical Uno was made in at least three case design variations ranging from a small size measuring about 5' high to a 7' (approximately) instrument with space for an advertising sign at the top. The makers of the Musical Uno did not use Regina movements exclusively. One early advertisement shows a Musical Uno with the same circular window but with a Swiss cylinder movement within.

### The Yale Wonder Clock Company

Perhaps the most prolific user of Regina movements was the Yale Wonder Clock Company of Burlington, Vermont. Beginning in 1901 this firm ordered 15½" Regina duplex musical movements by the dozens. When the special 15½" movement with 12 bells (using a special disc) was introduced in 1904, the Yale Wonder Clock Company shifted its orders to movements of this type. In fact, this firm was the largest consumer of Style 216 movements. The factory records reveal that 71 Style 216's were made with cases and sold through normal outlets, but a greater number, some 95 movements, went to the Yale Wonder Clock Company!

One of the Yale Wonder Clock Company's products, the Automatic Cashier & Discount Machine, was a veritable entertainment center! At the top an album with ever-changing scenes (each measuring 7½x10") provided the viewer with portraits of famous personages, mountain scapes, views of tradesmen at work, and similar pictures. Some probably also featured advertisements. A gambling mechanism permitted payouts of varying amounts. While all of this was going on, the musical movement played tunes on the duplex music combs and twelve bells!

### Comments

While such disc music boxes are not, strictly speaking, "Regina" products, they are of sufficient similarity that they are included here. In Europe, Polyphon, Symphonion, Kalliope, Adler (Zimmermann), and others sold movements to makers of gambling machines. Disc music box movements in such devices are rare today, however.

(Credit note: Illustrations courtesy of Kenneth C. German and Don Robertson)

The Musical Uno

## —Regina Clocks—

Regina clocks were made in two main categories. The standard types used regular Regina musical movements of the 11" or 15½" disc size, usually of the duplex-comb format. Another category, the instruments sold as Regina Chime Clocks, did not have music boxes but were equipped with a series of tuned chimes.

### Clocks with Disc Music Box Movements

In the first year or two of its operation the Regina Music Box Company imported Polyphon clocks with 11" or 15½" movements and sold them under the Regina name. These clocks, made in Lenzkirch, Germany, and incorporating disc movements (usually with duplex combs) are illustrated in the Polyphon section of this book.

Among Regina-made clocks, the Style 3 was the most popular. This style, illustrated in two variations on an accompanying page, was made in the Regina factory by adding a standard 15½" Regina movement to a hall clock manufactured by Seth Thomas. A number of different Seth Thomas clock case styles were used over the years, resulting in a number of variations — some rather plain and others quite ornate — being produced. These clocks play automatically on the hour, or they can be played at any time in between by pressing a button on the side. At least one Style 3 was made with a coin slot. This particular clock was used for years in a hotel lobby in Providence, Rhode Island. On the hour it would play automatically. Anyone desiring to play it at another time had to deposit a one-cent piece!

Other disc-operated musical clocks were designated as Style 1 and Style 2. Serial No. 4009, an instrument shipped October 16, 1894, was designated as a "hall clock." Little else is known about this model.

After 1900 a Style 2 clock was produced. This huge (9'7" high) instrument incorporated a 15½" automatic disc-changing mechanism which played the six discs in its storage rack. This obviated the necessity of otherwise having to hear the same disc again and again. Only a few of these Style 2's were ever made.

Regina automatic disc-changing music boxes in the 15½" (Style 35) and 20¾" (Style 37) sizes were made with clocks in the top gallery. The clock attachment was purely secondary and was available as an optional extra for $25. Regina noted: "Style 35 may be equipped with a high-grade eight-day clock. When so equipped the clock is connected to the mechanism so that a different tune is played automatically every hour or every half hour. This is a pleasing improvement, as it is a very agreeable way to be reminded of the passing hours. The clock attachment is of the very best construction, made especially for this purpose."

All of the Regina clocks described in the foregoing paragraphs use regular 15½" (or, in the case of a few early models, 11") discs.

### Regina Chime Clocks

The Regina Chime Clock is not a music box. Rather, it is a clock in which the chiming bells (not a musical comb) are actuated by a disc — rather than a pinned cylinder (the usual practice). However, as Chime Clocks are collected as part of the Regina music box series, we include information about them here.

The musical mechanism consists of tuned bells, each with a resonator (tube) which gives the sound a "depth." The bell strikers are operated from two actions which superficially resemble music combs. Some bells have multiple strikers so that a given note can be repeated quickly (without having to wait for the striker to re-position itself). The music, two series of chimes and four musical tunes, is programmed on an easily-changeable 12 1/8" diameter steel disc.

The Regina factory records list the following Chime Clock models:

STYLE 80: Movements only (rather than cased clocks) appear to have been sold: 77 in all, mainly shipped to the Colonial Manufacturing Company, a clockmaker of Zeeland, Michigan. One movement went to Tiffany & Co. Serial numbers from 8000001 to 8000110. Shipped in 1905 and 1906.

STYLE 81: Regina Chime Clock in ranch-style case with open support columns. 58 made. Serial numbers from 8100001 to 8100081. Shipped from 1905 to 1917.

STYLE 82: 11 made. Serial numbers from 8200001 to 8200013. Shipped from 1906 to 1908.

STYLE 83: 12 made. Serial numbers from 8300001 to 8300018. Shipped from 1907 to 1912.

STYLE 84: 12 made. Serial numbers from 8400001 to 8400012. Shipped from 1906 to 1908. The first serial number went to Jordan Marsh & Co., well-known Boston department store.

STYLE 85: 11 made. Serial numbers from 8500001 to 8500020. Shipped from 1906 to 1909. Two went to John Wanamaker (department store) in Philadelphia. The Metropolitan Advertising Company of New York City purchased three.

STYLE 86: 5 made. Serial numbers from 8600001 to 8600011. Shipped from 1906 to 1908. The first went to John Wanamaker's New York store on March 3, 1906.

STYLE 87: 17 made. Serial numbers from 8700001 to 8700022. Shipped from 1906 to 1912.

### Regina Distributors

From 1894 to 1921, the range of years during which Regina shipped music boxes, sales were made to literally hundreds of different accounts. Anyone with a legitimate resale business could order directly from the factory. Sales are recorded to music stores, department and dry goods stores, novelty shops, jewelers, and other establishments in virtually every medium and large size city in America. In addition a relatively few instruments were shipped to foreign countries — mainly to Canada, but some to Cuba, and a number to Nicole Frères, Ltd. of London, Thibouville-Lamy of Paris, and other overseas musical sales agents. As it was difficult to compete in Europe with the European-made Polyphon and Symphonion instruments, only a few Reginas were ever sold there. An occasional instrument was shipped to the Polyphon Musikwerke in Leipzig, the sponsor of Regina, probably so that Polyphon could keep abreast of Regina's products.

The American Graphophone Company of Bridgeport, Connecticut, purchased many Regina music boxes in the 1905 - 1915 decade. Included in the Graphophone purchases were at least one of nearly every Reginaphone (combination music box and phonograph) model. Some of these were sold under the Graphophone label.

A complete listing of Regina sales outlets would fill a volume by itself. We give some of the more important ones. The premier Regina sellers were the Rudolph Wurlitzer Company and Regina's own New York City retail store. A brief but unsuccessful (all but one of the music boxes were returned unsold!) flirtation with that sales giant, Sears, Roebuck & Co., was a disappointment. Sears' arch-competitor Montgomery Ward sold a modest number of Regina instruments, mostly small table models, over the years.

Major Regina customers, 1894 - 1921: Arbuckle Brothers; Bruno & Son; John Church Company; Cocklin & Oyler; Cohen & Hughes; Continental Tobacco Co. (ordered mainly styles 11 and 15); Oliver Ditson & Company; Florodora Tag Company; H. Gautschi & Son (of Philadelphia; earlier this firm was one of America's leading importers of large Swiss musical movements); Gourlay, Winter & Leeming; Gimbel Brothers; Grinnell Brothers; John C. Haynes & Co.; Heeren Brothers & Co. (of Pittsburgh, Pa.; earlier, a main American outlet for the cylinder boxes of Mermod Frères of St. Croix, Switzerland); C.J. Heppe & Son (of Philadelphia; some Heppe-ordered boxes were marked "Universal Boxes" in the Regina ledgers — indicating they may have had special cases or special "Universal" markings); Hoeffler Manufacturing Company (of Milwaukee, Wisc.; an extremely active distributor for all types of mechanical musical instruments — including Wurlitzer and, later, Seeburg pianos); O.K. Houck Company; Jacot & Sons (New York City; the main U.S. sales agent for the cylinder and disc [Stella, Mira] boxes of Mermod Frères); J.W. Jenkins Sons Music House (several midwestern locations; later to become the main distributor for "Coinola" pianos); Kipp Brothers Company; Knight-Campbell Music Company; Ludden, Campbell, Smith & Co.; Lyon & Healy (Chicago's leading musical instrument retailer — a large volume purchaser from Regina); C.C. Mellor Company; Montgomery Ward; Murray, Blanchard, Young & Co. (Providence, R.I.; successors to the next-listed firm); Murray, Spink & Company; National Novelty Company; Nicole Frères, Ltd. (of London; later formed the Polyphon & Regina Music Box Co. there); August Pollmann (New York City; sales agent and importer for many types of musical instruments); Regina Music Box Company (company-owned outlets at Broadway and 17th St., New York; 215 [later, 259] Wabash Ave., Chicago); Sherman Clay & Co. (many Pacific Coast outlets; leading musical distributor for many types of instruments); Shryock, Johnson Manufacturing Company; Smith & Nixon Piano Company; Southern California Music Company; Jerome Thibouville-Lamy & Co. (Paris); Thiebes, Stierlin Music Co. (of St. Louis; also known as Thiebes Piano Co.); John Wanamaker (department stores in New York City and Philadelphia); Julius Wellner (of Philadelphia; an active music box seller and patentee during the 1890's and early 1900's; later a major outlet for J.P. Seeburg); Whaley, Royce & Company; A. Wolff (leading New York City sales agent for Regina in the 1890's, before Regina established its own showroom there); and Wulschner & Son.

The REGINA
Hall Clock
Music
Box
is one of the most attractive forms in which this famous music box appears. The clock is modelled after a handsome antique pattern and starts the music immediately after striking the full hour. The music box may be played at any time independently.
Write for our catalogue showing our full line, costing from $10 to $400—with lists of new music—free. Address Dept. (D).
Regina Music Box Co.
Regina Building, New York
or
259 Wabash Ave., Chicago


Left and right: Style 3 Regina Hall Clock. Style 3's were made in many different case variations. Most were made by installing Regina music box mechanisms in hall clocks made by Seth Thomas. Most used the 15½" discs; however a few were made with 11" movements.

Style 2 Hall Clock, an early 20th century clock which incorporates an automatic disc changer and which uses 15½" discs. The changer holds six discs.

This Style 2 is a very large instrument and stands 9'7" high. It was shipped from the Regina Music Box Company factory on April 29, 1905, and was sold to a Chicago buyer.

Regina No. 3.
MUSICAL AUTOMATON. DUPLEX.
With Hall Clock.
CLOSED.
PRICE, $400
OPEN.
The clock will start the music immediately after striking the full hour; can also played at any time, independently of the clock, by pressing a button on the side


Left: Early models of the Regina Style 3. Regina never made its own clocks. Rather, Regina mechanisms were installed in grandfather's clocks made by various clockmakers – usually Seth Thomas. Very early Regina clocks were imported from Polyphon and consisted of Polyphon 11" or 15½" movements in Lenzkirch clocks.

Right: Style 81 Regina Chime Clock. By means of a disc, tunes are played on a series of chimes. As this style contains no music combs it is not a music box in the strict sense of the term.

Several styles of Chime Clocks were made, as the accompanying text notes.

**Regina Chime Clock**
**Style No. 81**

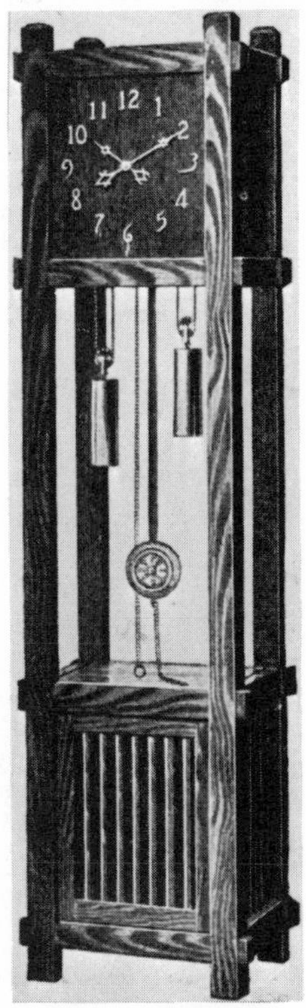

## Regina Phonographs

While the concern of this Regina section is music boxes, Regina phonographs are intertwined with Regina music box history – and for this reason we include a page about Regina phonographs here.

Regina phonographs were made in several styles: (1) The Automatic Reginaphone appeared early, was made in 1-cylinder and 6-cylinder models (with 2-minute cylinders), had an outside horn (or ear tubes), and was operated by a coin. (2) The Reginaphone, in its form most familiar to collectors today, is a music box and phonograph combination made in a wide variety of models – and as discussed elsewhere in this Regina section. (3) The Hexaphone, a coin operated phonograph which stored six cylinders (4-minute length) and permitted the patron to select the tune of his choice, was the most popular of all coin operated Regina phonographs. (4) The Corona Talking Machine – made in at least two styles (401 and 402) in the 'teens. (5) The Princess Talking Machine – the last Regina phonograph, sold until 1921.

## Production Data

The following brief information is given concerning Regina phonograph models.

STYLE 100 AUTOMATIC REGINAPHONE. Outside horn. Shipped 1905 to 1911. About 650 made. Serially numbered from 1000001 to 1000659.

STYLE 101 HEXAPHONE. Shipped 1909-1912. About 1400 made. Serially numbered from 1010001 to 1011423.

STYLE 102 HEXAPHONE. Shipped 1911-1915. About 2450 made. Serially numbered from 1020001 to 1022475. Factory notes: "No.1020275 – First machine with wooden horn." "No.1020523 – First machine with diamond point; also plunger on cam." "No.1021128 – First machine with large mandrel gears, wide winding wheel, balance wheels, and belt idler governor."

STYLE 103 HEXAPHONE. Shipped 1914-1921. Serially numbered from 1030001 to 1031642. Many made.

STYLE 104 HEXAPHONE. Shipped 1915-1921. 1606 made. Serially numbered from 1040001 to 1041677.

STYLE 401 CORONA TALKING MACHINE. Shipped 1915-1917. About 930 made. Serially numbered from 4010010 (sic) to 4010981.

STYLE 402 CORONA TALKING MACHINE. Shipped 1918-1919. 722 made. Every serial number from 4020001 to 4020722 was used.

STYLE 403 REGINAPHONE/PRINCESS. Serial Nos. 4030001 to 4030876 (about 850 made) were designated as "Style 403 Reginaphone" and were shipped 1919-1921. Serial Nos. 4031111 to 4031165 (54 made) were designated as "Style 403 Princess Phonograph" and were shipped 1920-1921.

STYLE 500 REGINAPHONE. Shipped 1917-1920. About 465 made. Serially numbered from 5000001 to 5000921.

STYLE 501 REGINAPHONE/PRINCESS. Serial Nos. 5010001 to 5010468 (about 360 made) were designated as "Style 501 Reginaphone" and were shipped 1919-1921. Serial Nos. 5011111 to 5011131 (13 made) were designated as "Style 501 Princess Phonograph" and were shipped in November and December, 1920.

STYLE 550 REGINAPHONE. Shipped 1918-1920. 1002 made. Serially numbered from 5500001 to 5501003 (except No.5501002).

STYLE 551 REGINAPHONE/PRINCESS. Serial Nos. 5510001 to 5510863 (about 575 made) were designated as "Style 551 Reginaphone" and were shipped 1919-1921. Serial Nos. 5511111 to 5511514 (about 270 made) were designated as "Style 551 Princess Phonograph" and were shipped 1920-1921.

Left: Early model "Reginaphone" cylinder phonograph which uses 2-minute cylinders. Equipped with either outside horn (horn shown here is not the original) or with ear tubes. (MBS "Bulletin" photo; Marken Collection)

STYLE 552 PRINCESS PHONOGRAPH. Just 12 made, serial numbers 5520001 to 5520012. All shipped on March 18, 1921.

STYLE 600 REGINAPHONE. Shipped 1918-1920. About 210 made. Serially numbered from 6000001 to 6000395; some numbers omitted.

STYLE 601 REGINAPHONE/PRINCESS. Serial Nos. 6010001 to 6010907 (about 875 made) were designated as "Style 601 Reginaphone" and were shipped 1919-1921. Serial Nos. 6011111 to 6011243 (about 125 made) were designated as "Style 601 Princess Phonograph" and were shipped in 1920.

STYLE 701 REGINAPHONE/PRINCESS. Serial Nos. 7010001 to 7010705 (about 690 made) were designated as "Style 701 Reginaphone" and were shipped 1919-1921. Serial Nos. 7011111 to 7011192 (about 70 made) were designated as "Style 701 Princess Phonograph" and were shipped in 1920-1921.

STYLE 800 REGINAPHONE. Shipped 1919-1921. 104 made. Serially numbered from 8000001 to 8000760.

STYLE 801 REGINAPHONE/PRINCESS. Serial Nos. 8010001 to 8000147 (128 made) were designated as "Style 801 Reginaphone" and were shipped 1920-1921. Serial Nos. 8011111 to 8011123 (13 made) were designated as "Style 801 Princess Phonograph" and were shipped in 1920-1921.

STYLE 803 REGINAPHONE. Factory records note: "Serial No. 8030001 shipped on September 22, 1921 per order No. B1883."

STYLE 825 REGINAPHONE/PRINCESS. Serial Nos. 8250001 to 8250190 (about 170 made) were designated as "Style 825 Reginaphone" and were shipped 1919-1921. Serial Nos. 8251111 to 8251118 (just 8 made) were designated as "Style 825 Princess Phonograph" and were shipped from November 1920 to January 1921.

STYLE 900 REGINAPHONE. Shipped 1918-1921. 60 made. Serially numbered from 9000001 to 9000064.

Views of a Regina Hexaphone six-selection phonograph. These were made in different case styles. The most common is shown here. Another style has a latticework over the horn opening. Most were originally equipped with a sign at the top (not shown here).

## SYMPHONION MUSIC BOXES
Leipzig, Germany

### History of Symphonion

In 1885 or 1886 Symphonion music boxes, the first practical interchangeable disc boxes to be marketed, were introduced. From then until the late 1920's the firm enjoyed a wide market for its products (although the business of the last decade consisted primarily of phonographs, not music boxes).

An interesting interview with Ellis Parr, an associate of Paul Lochmann (the prime mover of the Symphonion firm), appeared in the February 16, 1888, issue of the "Pall Mall Budget." We excerpt this article here as it gives an interesting commentary about the early years of the business:

### "Music by Mechanism"

"An interview with the inventor of the Symphonion:

"The old notion that we are not a nation of musicians is still widely prevalent, although the severe saying has been somewhat toned down. As we understand ourselves at present, we are at least endowed with a sense that makes us understand and appreciate good music. Anything, therefore, connected with vocal and instrumental music is deemed of interest, and the latest of inventions in the kingdom of 'sweet sound' is at this moment receiving considerable attention.

"This is the Symphonion, a development of the musical box, which is now being exhibited on the premises of Messrs. Ellis Parr & Co. at 16 Longlane, London, E.C. Mr. Parr, who has taken out a patent for the Symphonion, called at our office a day or two ago and furnished us with some interesting particulars concerning his invention.

" 'How is it,' Mr. Parr was asked, 'that in this age, when everybody plays some kind of instrument, there is still a demand for automatic musical instruments?'

" 'That question is easily answered,' said Mr. Parr. 'People like change, and if every human being were a good pianist the trade in musical boxes would be brisker than ever. People get tired of playing, or of hearing others play, with more or less perfection, and here they have, without any trouble, pleasant music faultlessly performed. And not only is there a demand, but there has been an increasing demand for musical boxes ever since they were improved, as of late years they have been, to produce really good music, and a variety of it. The only drawback has always been that a box only played a limited number of tunes, of which people naturally got tired, after hearing them again and again. Dealers have often said to me that if we could invent some means by which any tune might be played on a box, there would be an endless demand. And this want has now been supplied by the Symphonion, the mechanism of which is similar to that of the ordinary music box, but which, instead of the fixed barrel, contains a disc which is easily and quickly adjusted. If you want another tune you substitute another disc, and as we have an infinite variety of them there can no longer be any question of monotony.'

" 'But do not the discs make the Symphonion rather an expensive instrument if you wish to have a variety of tunes?'

" 'Not by any means. We have the instrument in different sizes, at prices ranging from 5 shillings to fifty guineas; the very small ones are, of course, more toys than anything else; but the discs cost at the most only about two shillings, which price you have to pay at least if you buy the same piece of music at any music seller's.'

" 'Which class of the public takes best to the Symphonion?'

" 'All classes alike; those who can afford it buy large and expensive instruments, and those who cannot are satisfied with the smaller. But both in London and in the country the sale is very good indeed, and we do a good business in exporting.'

" 'To what countries chiefly?'

" 'To the Australian colonies.'

" 'Then is your Symphonion made abroad too, and is it not somewhat unfair to employ foreign labor when so many are compelled to idleness in this country?'

" 'Yes, the Symphonion is made at Leipzig, where my co-patentee, a German gentleman, is at the head of our factory. Of course I should employ English labor, if such were possible, but as yet we have not the necessary skill in this country. It requires a long and thorough education before the work can be done, and the workers skilled in this particular handicraft are not to be found in England. We employ about 120 hands in the factory at Leipzig, besides a number of girls who prepare the discs in their own homes, but we shall require a much larger number before long, for as it is, the demand for the Symphonion is very great and is still increasing. I have only lately ordered 400 to be sent to me, and I find that the order cannot be executed sooner than March. As a curiosity it may perhaps interest you to know that Mr. Paul Lochmann, my German co-patentee, made precisely the same invention only a week after I made mine. I was on my way to Switzerland without knowing anything about him, when at the Leipzig Trade Fair I heard of his invention. At first I took action against him to prevent him from interfering with the sale in England, but eventually we became partners, and are now both trying to improve our instrument in every possible way, till it shall be quite perfect.'

" 'I suppose you could not reproduce any longer pieces of music on the Symphonion? For instance, parts of an oratorio or a whole quadrille?'

" 'Not with one disc, but with a series of discs without difficulty. There are, in every musical composition, intervals of longer or shorter duration, and as the changing of the discs requires only about one quarter of a minute, no objectionable break need occur. In dance music it is even easier, as between each part of, say, a quadrille, there is necessarily a pause. As the time can also be regulated on the Symphonion, there is not the slightest reason why the instrument should not be as successfully used in a ballroom as anywhere else.'

" 'But even supposing every other difficulty could be removed, would not the music be insufficient in volume to make it suitable as an accompaniment to dancing?'

" 'In a large public room, yes. In a private room of 50 ft. by 25 ft. it would be perfectly sufficient, owing to its clear, carrying tone, which, like the sound of the violin, is heard above far larger and more powerful instruments.' "

In his book, "Collecting Music Boxes and How to Repair Them," Arthur W.J.G. Ord-Hume relates that the first interchangeable disc music box was made by Paul Lochmann in 1886. The first instrument had two combs, each mounted in a vertical position, above which was placed a stationary perforated cardboard disc, in the manner of a Herophon or similar cardboard-disc reed organ. The combs were turned by a spring mechanism. Problems resulted, and this format was soon dropped. Metal discs with projections on the underside which plucked stationary music combs were a reality by 1887; by 1889, the star wheel system was in use. Thus by 1890 the disc type music box of the type that was to remain the standard for the next several decades was in use.

Lochmann, earlier a manufacturer of decorative automatic water fountains for home use, established the Symphonion Musikwerke in Gohlis, a suburb of Leipzig. The first Symphonion boxes were the short-lived cardboard variety. Judging from the above-printed 1888 interview, the standard type of metal-disc box was being made by 1888. As noted, by 1890 the Symphonion had reached what was to be its final stage of development.

Symphonion enjoyed an excellent business through the 1890's. By 1895 the product line contained several dozen different styles and variations ranging from small hand-cranked instruments to large upright coin-operated models. About the same time

Symphonion provided the financial and technical backing for the Symphonion Manufacturing Company, a subsidiary with manufacturing facilities in Bradley Beach, near Asbury Park, New Jersey, and sales offices in New York City.

Around the turn of the century the firm of Ludwig Hupfeld A.G., noted manufacturers of electric pianos and orchestrions, acquired an ownership interest in Symphonion. About this time Paul Lochmann apparently dissociated himself from the firm he had founded, and set up independent facilities for the manufacture of the "Original" (trademark) series of music boxes. "Original" was probably Lochmann's prideful way of recollecting his past importance in the industry. Indeed, the "Original" series of boxes, made around the turn of the century, are superbly built and feature many tonal improvements (particularly with regard to sounding board construction; a subject overlooked by many in the music box field) not found in contemporary instruments.

It has been reported in several references that the Symphonion Musikwerke went out of business shortly after 1900. The American branch of the firm did, indeed, pass from the scene about that time. However, the Leipzig factory continued in operation. Many are the advertisements for Symphonion products which appear in musical trade journals during the first decade of

the 20th century. Typical is the advertisement on page 694 of the April 1, 1909, issue of "Zeitschrift für Instrumentbau" – it features a large display ad for Symphonion, gives the address as the standard "Leipzig - Gohlis" listing, and notes that the firm has a large line of music boxes, phonographs, electric pianos (six different models), and pneumatic orchestrions to offer. Information concerning the 20th century operations of Symphonion, particularly after about 1914, is sketchy at best. The author would welcome correspondence from anyone with more information to offer.

The latest-dated Symphonion catalogue seen by the author is that dated 1911/1912. The business was continued in later years – at least until the late 1920's. In the 1920's the Symphonion Musikwerke was directed by Paul Scheibe and was located at Bärengasse 14/40, Gera, Reuss (Germany). Although Symphonion and Polyphon (sic) music boxes were sold in the 1920's, the business consisted mainly of phonographs.

### Types of Symphonion Music Boxes

Symphonion produced a simply staggering number of disc varieties. The reason for doing this is not clear, as many of them differ only slightly from others. Certainly, this lack of standardization must have presented quite a few problems with inventory handling and distribution.

The 4½" disc size was one of the smallest ever made by any manufacturer. It was used by Symphonion for novelty instruments (toys) and also as a movement built into the top of a small alarm clock. The largest Symphonion disc size encountered by the author was the mammoth 76 cm. (30 inches) type used on the gigantic Duplex Orchestrion. This latter instrument was not really a music box at all (it had no music combs) but was a disc-played piano orchestrion similar in concept to the Polyphon / Regina "Concerto" and other like instruments. The largest music box disc size was the No.162 disc as used on a large music box / orchestrion (with steel music combs in the music box portion) known by the same designation, No.192. This disc measures 75 cm. (29½") in diameter.

A number of the small and medium-size Symphonion boxes have their music combs arranged with one comb on each side of the center spindle. Arranging combs in this manner was known as the "sublime harmonie" format. A similar configuration was also used on certain contemporary Monopol music boxes, some of which were manufactured (possibly on a contractual basis) by Symphonion.

The multiple-disc instruments made by Symphonion are of special interest to collectors today. The most famous of these is the "Eroica." Made in several styles, including some in hall clock cases, the Eroica used three 14-inch diameter discs and played them simultaneously on six music combs. Two-disc models were made in table-top box format. These played two discs simultaneously. Perhaps the most impressive of the multiple-disc Symphonions were the huge (they used 64 cm. – 25¼" discs) instruments built into piano-like cabinets. These models featured either two or three discs arranged vertically side-by-side. Somewhat similar instruments were also made by the Symphonion Manufacturing Company (the subsidiary) in Bradley Beach, New Jersey. As were all American-made Symphonions, these latter were referred to as "Imperial" Symphonions.

Several varieties of Symphonion clocks were made. These ranged in size from the aforementioned 4½"-disc model to large upright styles with the 3-disc "Eroica" system. For the most part these were made by adding Symphonion musical mechanisms to clocks made in Lenzkirch. As Lenzkirch also supplied clocks to Polyphon, Monopol, and a few other makers, the products of these various firms are somewhat similar in outward appearance.

Three Symphonion disc changers.

When automatic disc changers come to mind today, one thinks first of Regina and Polyphon – whose products were well known and, at least in the case of Regina, were made in large quantities. However, it was Symphonion which produced an interesting array of different changing mechanisms – a variety unequalled by any other maker. Several large upright changers were made. These stored six or twelve discs, any one of which could be selected by using a crank at the front of the machine. Despite the fact that these upright models were made in several different styles and were listed in several different Symphonion catalogues over the years, they met with an indifferent reception in the marketplace – and relatively few were made.

Especially interesting, and of very limited production originally, are the No.120S and No.120V. The former stored a stack of eight discs and changed them by sliding them horizontally from the rack to the music comb. The operation was automatic, and the entire group of records would play through without any attention once the mechanism was started. The No.120V stored a group of up to 25 discs, played them one-at-a-time, and then ejected them through a slot in the back of the box. Perhaps the

SYMPHONION

scarring and scratching of surrounding furniture by the ejected discs was enough to make this model unpopular! In any event, few were produced.

Symphonion pioneered in the use of electric motors to operate disc music boxes. As early as 1900 the style No.192St.E appeared. It was basically a standard No.192St. Symphonion with electric motor drive. An accumulating device permitted up to 30 coins to be dropped in the coin slot at once — also an interesting innovation. Although most upright Symphonion boxes could be ordered with electric motors (in which case an "E" suffix was added to the style number), apparently only a few were made.

Other Symphonion products: Symphonion was very active in the phonograph market and produced a large number of styles. Most were of the disc record type. Early models were equipped with external horns; later ones with built-in horns. Symphoniola automatic pianos, foot-pumped models for home use and coin-operated models for commercial use, were made in several different styles. Pneumatically-operated piano orchestrions were produced in the 'teens and were sold with limited success.

Symphonion in America

During the late 1890's Symphonion maintained an American subsidiary, the Symphonion Manufacturing Company. Sales offices were established at 18 East 24th Street in New York City. Limited manufacturing facilities were set up in Bradley Beach, N.J. Products bore the "Symphonion Mfg. Co., New York" designation.

The trademark "Imperial Symphonion" appeared on the music discs. The "Imperial" designation differentiated the American-made discs from the German ones that the firm imported.

An 1898 Symphonion advertisement (reprinted in the MBS "Bulletin," Vol.XIV, No.4) noted: "The new American-made Symphonion is the first and only music box made with patented indestructible steel discs. It has patented flywheel, speed regulator, side dampers, double comb arrangement, and its parts are interchangeable. It requires but one winding to play 30 minutes, and is recognized among the leading dealers to be the standard 'up to date' music box. The Symphonion received the highest awards at Chicago, 1893, and Antwerp, 1894. Prices ranging from $4 to $300. Catalogue containing thousands of tunes to select from. For sale by all prominent dealers."

The smaller table model Imperial Symphonion boxes bear, in some instances, close resemblance to contemporary Regina instruments so far as the casework, trim, and some of the hardware are concerned. It is possible that some parts were purchased from Regina, or that Symphonion and Regina both purchased components from a common supplier.

The largest Imperial Symphonion instrument known to the author is a tall upright "Imperial Symphonion Orchestrion," an instrument with music combs, 12 bells, and which uses a 27 5/8" disc. The instrument is virtually identical to the German-made Symphonion Orchestrion No.118Gl. An unusual Imperial Symphonion instrument is the 3-disc instrument with the three discs arranged horizontally. This is somewhat similar in concept to the German-made "Pianoform" Style No.292PG. Many Imperial Symphonion instruments were made with German Symphonion movements.

The American firm ceased operations in the early 1900's. An advertisement in the May 24, 1902, issue of "Music Trades" noted that the firm had branches in Leipzig, Germany, and in St. Croix, Switzerland. The St. Croix reference is unexplained and is quite interesting!

Collecting Symphonion Music Boxes Today

In 1903 Symphonion stated that it was manufacturing instruments at the rate of about 5000 to 6000 per year and was making about 100,000 discs annually. With Polyphon and Regina, Symphonion was one of the "big three" disc music box makers. As a result, Symphonion music boxes are fairly plentiful today.

As might be expected, the main population of extant Symphonions is comprised of table models up to and including the 34.5 cm. (13 5/8") disc size. Among larger upright models those with 48.5 cm. (19 1/8") discs are sometimes seen; mainly those which were earlier used in English pubs in which market they competed with the similar 19 5/8" Polyphon. Still rarer are upright models using 64 cm. (25¼") discs. The other large Symphonion instruments are all extremely rare and, in some instances, not known to exist today.

Perhaps more than any other popular type of disc box, the difference between an "average" Symphonion box and a well-regulated one can be tremendous. For this reason attention to regulation of the star wheels, dampers, and other music comb accessories, not to mention tightness of the sounding board, is recommended. This can be done by any competent music box repairer and will pay real dividends in tonal quality.

—Symphonion Disc Sizes—

We give the diameter in inches, the diameter in centimeters, and the Disc Number (as used by Symphonion). Disc numbers varied over the years, thus accounting for several numbers for the same disc.

4½" — 11.5 cm. — Disc No. 20

5¾" — 14.5 cm. — Disc No. 28

6¼" — 16 cm. — Disc No. 32

7 11/16" — 19.5 cm. — Disc No. 10

8¼" — 21 cm. — Disc No. 2/2N

9½" — 24 cm. — Disc No. 4/4N

10" — 25.5 cm. — Disc No. 48

10 5/8" — 27 cm. — Disc No. 6/6N

11¾" — 30 cm. — Disc No. 25

13¼" — 33.5 cm. — Disc No. 60/120; 60

13 5/8" — 34.5 cm. — Disc No. 30

14" — 35.5 cm. — Disc No. 38 (sold in sets of 3 for the "Eroica").

14¾" — 37.5 cm. — Disc No. 121

15¾" (sometimes called "15½") — 40 cm. — Known as Disc No. 178/256; 178; and 178/257.

18¼" — 46 cm. — Disc No. 193

19 1/8" — 48.5 cm. — Disc No. 106

21¼" — 54 cm. — Disc No. 130; or, when ordered for the disc changer (different printing orientation on disc required), No. 100/102

25¼" — 64 cm. — Disc No. 192; or 143/192; or 292

27½" — 70 cm. — Disc No. 118

29½" — 75 cm. — Disc No. 162.

30" — 76 cm. — Disc No. 98

(Comment: Nearly two dozen disc sizes in all — what an inventory problem Symphonion must have had!)

SYMPHONION

(11.5 cm. or 4½" No. 20 discs)

The Gloriosa Christmas tree stand (see Kalliope section of this book) was available also with a Symphonion movement.

Two views of a small Symphonion musical clock. This variety, made in quantity around the 1900-1905 years, incorporates a mechanism which uses 11.5 cm. (4½") No. 20 discs. Discs of this size were available in center-drive and edge-drive (with a toothed rim which engaged a drive gear) models, and clocks were built with both types.

(11.5 cm. or 4½" No.20 discs)

–Style 20D–
–Style 20S–

–Style No.20JN–

–Style 20D–
11.5 cm. (4½") discs. 20 teeth in music comb. 16 cm. wide by 13 cm. deep by 10½ cm. high (lid closed). Hand cranked model (without spring). Case in satinwood. Uses No. 20 discs.

–Style 20S–
11.5 cm. (4½") discs. 20 teeth in music comb. Spring wound. Satinwood case. Uses No. 20 discs.

–Style No.20JN–
11.5 cm. (4½") discs. 20 teeth in music comb. Hand cranked model. Case in alder or walnut wood. Uses No. 20 discs.

(11.5 cm. or 4½" No.20 discs)

–Style 28S–

–Style No. 28SN–

–Style No. 28SR–

–Style 28S–
14.5 cm. (5¾") discs. 40 teeth in music comb. Jacaranda wood. "Symphonion Simplex" in ornate script on the lid of some models. 19½ cm. wide by 17½ cm. deep by 13 cm. high (lid closed). Uses No. 28 discs.

–Style No. 28SN–
14.5 cm. (5¾") discs. 40 teeth in music comb. Walnut wood. "N" in style number comes from "Nussbaum" – German for "walnut." Uses No. 28 discs.

–Style No. 28SR–
14.5 cm. (5¾") discs. 40 teeth in music comb. Redwood case. "R" in style number is from the German "Rotholz" – for "redwood." Uses No. 28 discs.

(14.5 cm. or 5¾" No.28 discs)

–Style No.28L–
Portable Box Organ
14.5 cm. (5¾") discs. 40 teeth in music comb. Hand cranked instrument called "Symphonion Box Organ, portable." With carrying strap; instrument in the style of an organ but with regular music box movement. 24 cm. high by 31½ cm. wide by 20 cm. deep. "Polished case with brass fittings. The box contains a shelf for the keeping of discs." Uses No.28 discs.

(14.5 cm. or 5¾" No.28 discs)

Details of No.28R (Monkey cyclist)

–Moving Figures with Music–
The following incorporate the mechanism of Symphonion No. 28S, a 40-note music box using No. 28 discs. The following animation effects and their style numbers were available in 1904:

No.28Ns: .................................. Dancing pigs
No.28N: .................................. Sleeping monkeys
No.28K: .................................. Dancing cats
No.28R: .................................. Monkey cyclist
No.28B .................................. Swinging cats

–No.28Ns (Dancing pigs)–

–No.28R (Monkey cyclist)–

–Style 28 (hand cranked)–

–Style 28–
14.5 cm. (5¾") discs. 40 teeth in music comb. In case decorated with decals or transfer designs; usually black finish to case and background. Hand cranked. Uses No. 28 discs.

–Style 28E–
14.5 cm. (5¾") discs. 40 teeth in music comb. Hand cranked type (without spring). 17 cm. square by 9 cm. high (lid closed). Uses No. 28 discs.

–Style 28JN–
14.5 cm. (5¾") discs. 40 teeth in music comb. Case in alder or walnut wood with decoration. Hand cranked. Uses No. 28 discs.

SYMPHONION (16 cm. or 6¼" No. 32 discs)

–Style No. 32–

16 cm. (6¼") discs. 32 teeth in music comb. 21 cm. wide by 19 cm. deep by 13 cm. high (lid closed). Winding lever on front (or right side). Uses No. 32 discs.

Variation: Style 32 – Available with 4 bells on special order. Uses No. 32 discs.

–Style No. 32P–

16 cm. (6¼") discs. 32 teeth in music comb. "P" in style number comes from "Palisander" ("rosewood" in German). Case in rosewood. Uses No. 32 discs.

Variation: Available with 4 bells on special order. Uses No. 32 discs.

Symphonion Styles 2N, 4N, 6N (three different disc sizes)

–Style Nos. 2N; 4N; 6N–

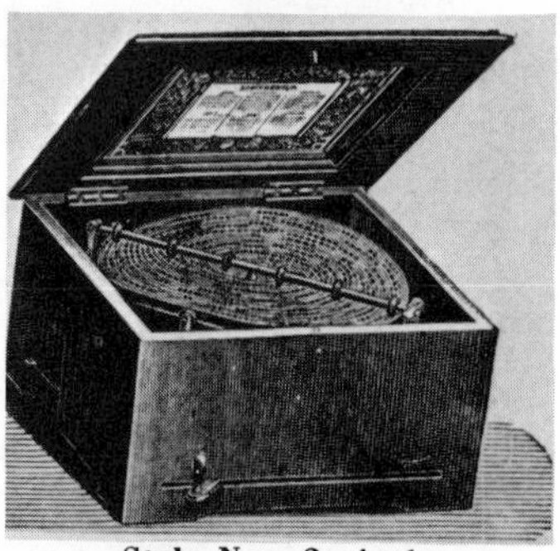

–Style Nos. 2; 4; 6–

–Style Nos. 2; 4; 6–

Usually listed together in a series of three in the Symphonion catalogues. These all used special discs.

No.2: 21 cm. (8¼") discs. 60 teeth in music comb. Black polished wood case with decal or transfer design on lid. Uses No. 2/2N discs.

No.4: 24 cm. (9½") discs. 72 teeth in music comb. Black polished wood case with decal or transfer design on lid. Uses No. 4/4N discs.

No.6: 27 cm. (10 5/8") discs. 84 teeth. Black polished wood case with decal or transfer design on lid. Uses No. 6/6N discs.

–Style Nos. 2N; 4N; 6N–

As Nos. 2, 4, and 6 above, but with case of natural walnut ("N" for "Nussbaum" – German for "walnut").

(19.5 cm. or 7 11/16" No.10 discs)

No.10

No.10

No.10N

No.10

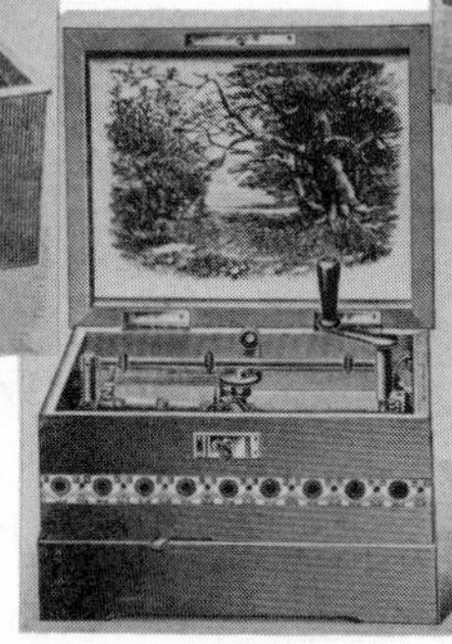

No.10NK

View of the saucer bells in No.10Gl.

No.10Gl

No.10Gl

19.5 cm. (7 11/16") discs. 41 notes. Case in Walnut with decoration. 28½ cm. wide by 24 cm. deep by 18½ cm. high. Note: Zither attachments were available for most Symphonions for a nominal charge. Uses No. 10 discs.

Variation: Available with 4 bells on special order.

SYMPHONION

(19.5 cm. or 7 11/16" No.10 discs)

—Symphonion No.10S—
Musical Savings Bank

19.5 cm. (7 11/16") discs. 41 teeth in music comb. "Smart, solid case of walnut or oak with brass decoration. The construction of this instrument is made in such a way as to set the movement into action and start the music by dropping a coin (of any weight or size) into the slot on the top of the case. The saving of one, two, or three pennies or cents, or even shillings and dollars, will reward the child by hearing a piece of music after the insertion of the coin." 45 cm. high by 29 cm. wide by 19 cm. deep (about 17¾" high). Weight: 5.8 kg. or about 13 pounds. Uses No. 10 discs.

(25.5 cm. or 10" No.48 discs)

No.48

No.48NJ

No.48E (ornate case)

—Style Nos. 48, 48K, 48Gl—

No.48: 25½ cm. (10") discs. 48 teeth in music comb. Walnut wood. Uses No. 48 discs.

No.48K: As above, but with 6 bar-type bells ("K" for "Klangplatten" — or orchestra bells). Uses No. 48 discs.

No.48Gl: As above, but with 6 saucer-type bells ("Gl" for "Glocken" or bells). Uses No. 48 discs.

48K

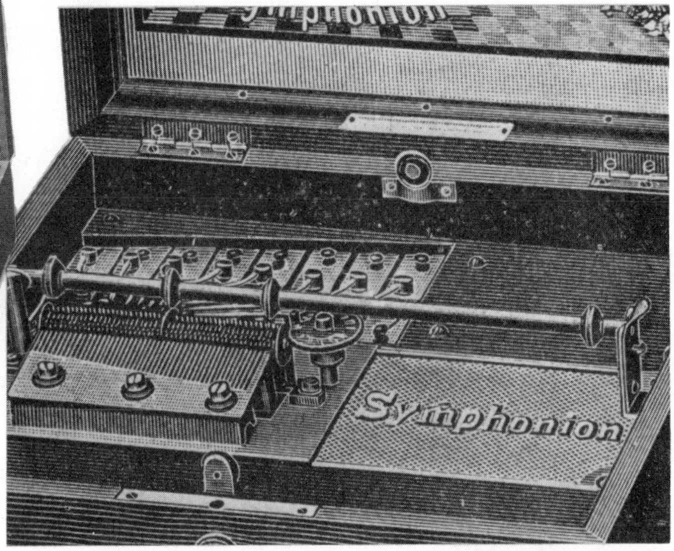


Close-up of 48K (or 48Kl, as it is sometimes known)

—Style Nos.12R; 25R—

12R: 19.5 cm. (7 11/16") discs. 41 teeth in music comb. Wall clock in combination with Symphonion music box movement. 100 cm. high by 37 cm. wide by 22 cm. deep. Uses No.10 discs.

25R: 30 cm. (11¾") discs. 84 teeth in two music combs; sublime harmonie arrangement. Can be coin operated if desired. "Remarkably rich walnut or oak case suitable for any drawing room. The clock with one winding runs a fortnight (14 days). First class Lenzkirch workmanship. Silver dial about 9 inches diameter. The clock, with gong movement, strikes every hour or every second hour [or every half hour], according to your desire, and sets the music box playing after striking the time. The mechanism can be stopped during the night, and the music can likewise be played independently of the clock. Style 25R, if desired, can be obtained with clear glass panel in place of bottom wood panel — at no extra charge." Measurements: 129 cm. high by 47 cm. wide by 32 cm. deep. Uses No. 25 discs.

—Style No. 48R—

Symphonion wall clock. 25.5 cm. (10") discs. 48 teeth in comb. 14-day pendulum clock in combination with Symphonion music movement. 121 cm. high by 52 cm. wide by 29 cm. deep. Uses No. 48 discs.

**SYMPHONION**
(30 cm. or 11¾" No.25 discs)

—Nos. 25N and 30N—

—Style 25N—

30 cm. (11¾") discs. 84 teeth in the sublime harmonie arrangement (two opposed combs). Case in walnut. Brass handles at ends. Uses No. 25 discs.

25A and 30A

—Style 25A—

30 cm. (11¾") discs. 84 teeth in two combs; sublime harmonie arrangement. Walnut cabinet with ornate corner posts, inlaid lid, brass handles on end; protective glass plate over music disc mechanism. 49 cm. wide by 38 cm. deep by 26 cm. high (lid closed). Uses No. 25 discs.

—Style 25C "Rococo"—

30 cm. (11¾") discs. 84 teeth. Two combs diametrically arranged in the format used for many medium size Symphonion boxes — the "sublime harmonie" arrangement. Very elaborately carved "Rococo" case. Uses No. 25 discs.

The disc storage cabinet shown above in combination with Style 25A could be obtained in different sizes for other Symphonions and Polyphons as well.

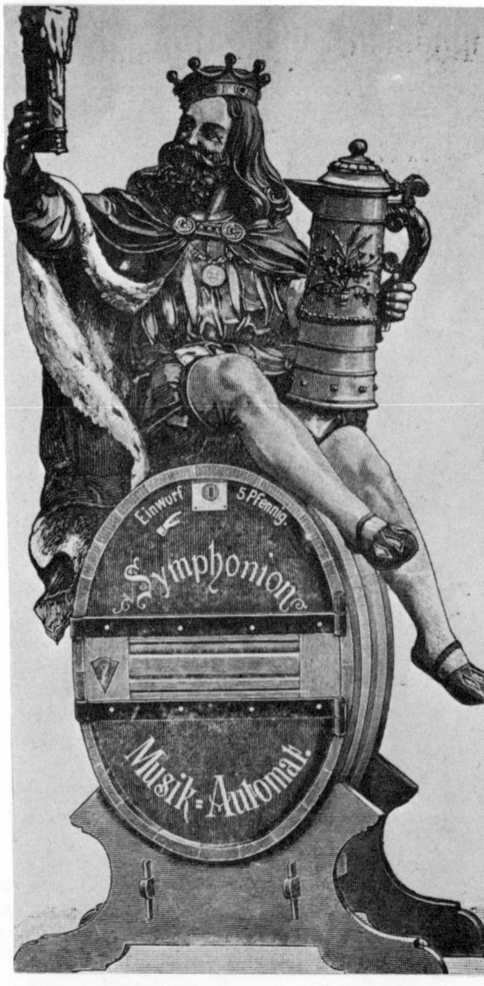


—Style No.25GS— "Gambrinus"

30 cm. (11¾") discs. 84 teeth in music combs; sublime harmonie arrangement. Music mechanism built into a clay figure of Gambrinus, the mythical Flemish king who reputedly invented beer. 105 cm. high by 60 cm. wide by 35 cm. deep. Recommended "For putting up on bars, etc." in the Symphonion catalogue.

—Style No.25St—

30 cm. (11¾") discs. 84 teeth in two combs in the sublime harmonie arrangement. "Symphonion Hall Clock, No.25St. (Ed. note: "St." is the abbreviation for "Standuhr" - or "standing clock" in German). Beautifully carved walnut case with first class Lenzkirch clock. Runs 14 days. Silver dial about 8 inches in diameter. The clock with gong movement strikes every hour or every second hour, according to order, and sets the musicwork running after striking fully. During the night the music works can be silenced. The music can be played independently of the clock." Note: The author has seen several Style No.25St. clocks which play music every half hour (rather than every second hour) if set to do so. Uses No.25 discs.

–Style No.33a–
"Lyra" Automaton

30 cm. (11¾") discs. 84 teeth in two music combs. Coin operated version of No.33b. "Automatic music box for hanging on the wall or standing. Solid, rich case in oak or walnut, with decorated glass panels and gold letters. This automaton can be supplied with a picture similar to that used on No.33b. Uses No.25 discs.

Variation: May be ordered with clock in top gallery."

–Style 33S–

30 cm. (11¾") discs. 84 teeth in two music combs; sublime harmonie style. "Black Forest chalet style case in light and dark colors. Of wonderful resonance. Can be attached to wall or stand." 98 cm. high by 45 cm. wide by 32 cm. deep. Uses No.25 discs.

Style No.33SA: As above, but with coin slot.

–Style No.1496–
Chocolate-Vending

30 cm. (11¾") discs. 84 teeth in two music combs; sublime harmonie arrangement. "Coin in the slot automatic Symphonion in walnut case; vends a roll of chocolate after playing a musical tune." 129 cm. high by 50 cm. wide by 37 cm. deep. Internal storage capacity of 36 rolls of chocolate. Uses No.25 discs.

–Symphonion Chocolate Vendors–

An external attachment suitable for affixing to the left side of a music cabinet was sold for Polyphon and Symphonion boxes. Recommended for Symphonion Styles 33 and 39, the addition of a vending apparatus changed the style numbers as follows:

No.33 with vendor= .................................No.33C
No.33a with vendor= ...............................No.33D
No.33b with vendor= ...............................No.33E
No.33a/b with vendor= ............................No.33F
No.39 with vendor= .................................No.39G
No.39S with vendor= ...............................No.39H

–Style No.33b "Lyra"–

30 cm. (11¾") discs. 84 teeth in two music combs arranged in the sublime harmonie style. "Splendid case, magnificently fitted out, in walnut or oak. With colored painting, artistically designed. Very suitable for families. The painting in very delicate colors (behind glass) is extremely effective, and a most valuable piece of furniture at the same time, so that, upon the whole, the possession of this music box serves two purposes. It forms a tasteful decoration." 100 cm. high by 48 cm. wide by 32 cm. deep. For hanging on the wall. Uses No.25 discs.

Style No.33a/b: Same as No.33a but with feet on the case – for standing upright on a table.

(30 cm. or 11¾" No.25 discs)

–Style No.1495–
Chocolate-Vending

30 cm. (11¾") discs. 84 teeth in two music combs; sublime harmonie arrangement. "Walnut case with illustration in front. Automatic Symphonion vends a roll of chocolate after playing the musical tune. 36 rolls of chocolate are given with each automaton." 75 cm. high by 59 cm. wide by 33 cm. deep. Uses No.25 discs.

–Style No. 25AE–
"Aeola"

30 cm. (11¾") discs. 84 teeth in two combs of the sublime harmonie arrangement. "Very elegant, smart walnut case with ornamental top piece and photo under glass on the front. Very handy and easy to carry from one place to another." 55 cm. high by 50 cm. wide by 38 cm. deep. The scene on the front is a lithograph, not a photograph as stated. Uses No.25 discs.

Style No. 25AT: Same as No.25AE, but with coin slot. Uses No.25 discs.

(33.5 cm. or 13¼" No.60/120 or No.60 discs) 

–Styles 60; 120–

Style 60: 33½ cm. (13¼") discs. 60 teeth in single comb. Walnut case with ornate molding. Uses No. 60/120 discs.

Variation (of No.60 only): Available with 8 bells on special order. Uses No. 60/120 discs.

Style 120: Duplex comb version, 120 teeth, of No. 60 (without bells). Uses No. 60/120 discs.

–Styles 60P; 120P–

Style 60P: 33½ cm. (13¼") discs. 60 teeth in single comb. Uses No. 60/120 discs.

Variation (of 60P only): Available with 8 bells on special order.

–Nos. 120W; 120WU–

No.120W: 33.5 cm. (13¼") discs. 120 notes in two combs. Coin operated. Made for hanging on the wall of a restaurant or other public place. Uses No. 60/120 discs.

No.120WU: Same as No. 120W but with clock ("U" for "Uhr" – "clock" in German) in top gallery. Measurements 115 cm. high by 64 cm. wide by 36 cm. deep. Available with feet for standing upright, on special order. Uses No. 60/120 discs.

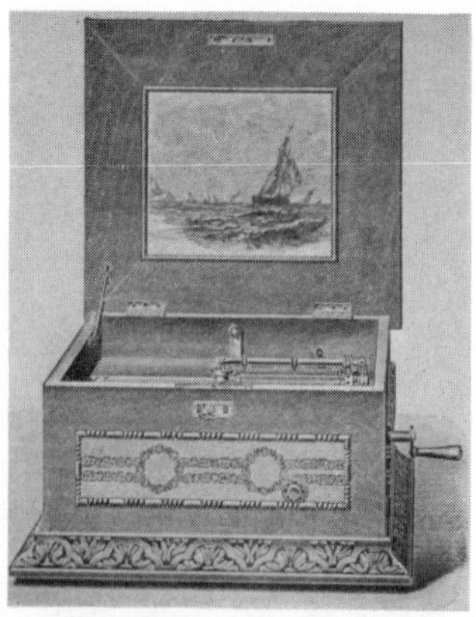

–Style No. 60NO; 120NO–

No.60NO: 33½ cm. (13¼") discs. 60 teeth in single comb. In ornate case with carvings and applied molding. Walnut. Uses No. 60/120 discs.

Variation (of 60NO only): Available with 8 bells on special order. Uses No. 60/120 discs.

No. 120NO: 120 teeth in duplex combs. Otherwise similar to 60NO (without bells). Uses No. 60/120 discs.

Bell Nomenclature Note:

Certain models with bells sometimes (but not always) had a suffix letter after the style number. "K" was the suffix for bar-type bells (Klangplatten); "Gl" was the suffix for saucer-type bells (Glocken). Thus 48K and 48Gl have these types of bells respectively. Likewise, No. 60 was available as 60K and 60Gl.

Zither Nomenclature Note:

Rarely a model with zither attachment would have a "Z" suffix. Thus No.10N with zither was sometimes known as No.10NZ.

(34.5 cm. or 13 5/8" No.30 discs)

25A and 30A

**–Style 30A–**

34.5 cm. (13 5/8") discs. 100 teeth in two combs; sublime harmonie arrangement. Walnut cabinet with ornate corner posts, inlaid lid, brass handles on ends, protective glass plate over music disc. 55 cm. wide by 45 cm. deep by 26 cm. high (lid closed). Uses No. 30 discs.

(See 25N on other page for illustration of this style)

**–Style 30N–**

34.5 cm. (13 5/8") discs. 100 teeth in two combs (sublime harmonie arrangement). Cabinet in walnut with brass handles at ends. Uses No. 30 discs.

**–Style No.37 "Haydn"–**

34.5 cm. (13 5/8") discs. 100 teeth in duplex combs. "Sublime Harmonie Piccolo. Wonderful, highly carved case in walnut (or oak). Disc storage area in bottom of case." 205 cm. high by 72 cm. wide by 43 cm. deep. Uses No.30 discs.

Style No.37B: With pane made up of circular art glass discs in center rectangle; or with advertising painted on back of glass.

Style No.37H: With carved wood panel in center.

**–Style No.36–**

34.5 cm. (13 5/8") discs. 100 teeth in duplex combs; sublime harmonie arrangement. Case in walnut or oak, carved wood panel on front. 160 cm. high by 60 cm. wide by 40 cm. deep. Disc storage area in bottom of case. Uses No.30 discs.

Style No.36B: Same as No.36 but with colored glass panel in center.

**–Style 39 "Meteor"–**

34.5 cm. (13 5/8") discs. 100 teeth in duplex combs; sublime harmonie arrangement. "Ornamental and stylish case in walnut for hanging on the wall. Instead of a glass panel this box can be had with a polished brass lyre in the door, cloth panel behind lyre, at the same price." 115 cm. high by 64 cm. wide by 36 cm. deep. Uses No.30 discs.

Style No.39a: As above, but with clock in top gallery.

Style No.39S: As No.39, but with feet for standing upright on a table.

Style 39 mounted on base cabinet.

Style No. 39a

(34.5 cm. or 13 5/8" No.30 discs)

–Style No.30St–

34.5 cm. (13 5/8") discs. 100 teeth in duplex combs, arranged in the sublime harmonie style. "Sublime Harmonie Piccolo. Grand walnut case, highly finished, with first class Lenzkirch clock. Runs 14 days. Silver dial about 9 inches in diameter. The clock with gong strikes every hour or every second hour and sets the music works running. During the night the music can be stopped. The music can be played independently of the clock." Available with colored art glass, with painted frosted glass (with allegorical scene), or with clear glass front in place of the carved panel. Clock also available in oak wood. 240 cm. high by 60 cm. wide by 36 cm. deep. Probably the most popular Symphonion grandfather's clock in terms of the numbers originally sold. Uses No.30 discs.

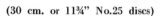

(30 cm. or 11¾" No.25 discs)

–Style No.37St–

30 cm. (11¾") discs. 84 teeth in music comb. "Symphonion Hall Clock, No.37St. Sublime Harmonie Piccolo, 100 teeth. Grand walnut or oak case, highly finished, the panel of the door being pierced. The back of this door is covered with gauze, thus enhancing the effect of the music. First rate Lenzkirch clock; runs a fortnight. Silver dial about 11" in diameter. The clock with gong movement strikes every hour or every second hour, according to order, and sets the music works running. During the night the music can be stopped. The music can be played independently of the clock. A disc storage compartment is inside the case." 270 cm. high by 71 cm. wide by 43 cm. deep. Uses No.30 discs.

**Illustration of a typical "sublime harmonie" two-comb movement as used in small and medium size Symphonions.**

**SYMPHONION**

**(34.5 cm. or 13 5/8" No.30 discs)**

**–Style No.34–**

**34.5 cm. (13 5/8") discs. 100 teeth in duplex combs; sublime harmonie arrangement. "Coin operated. Beautiful, highly ornamented case (sideboard form) in walnut or oak, with table top, very solid. Any inscription on glass or any other decoration can be applied in the center of the wood panel. Bottom part of the case serves as a disc storage area." 200 cm. high by 80 cm. wide by 50 cm. deep. Uses No.30 discs.**

**(35.5 cm. or 14" No.38 discs)**

**Three-Disc Symphonion**

**Right: One popular style of the "Eroica" or 3-Disc Symphonion case. To the left is a catalogue illustration; to the right is a photo (by Dan Adams) of the specimen in the Jerry Doring Collection. This type of case was more or less a standard item and was used also for style Nos. 36 and 37. As can be noted from the Polyphon section of this Encyclopedia, the Polyphon firm had similar (but not identical) cases for some of its models.**

View of three discs, arranged one above the other and overlapping as they play, in a 3-Disc Symphonion "Eroica" music box. The discs, which are numbered A, B, and C, each feature slightly different musical arrangements, although any one disc played by itself will give a creditable rendition of the melody. (Jerry Cohen Collection)

Note: A 2-Disc Symphonion was also made for use with pairs of No.38 discs. These 2-Disc models, made only in small quantities, were available in upright and table model styles. (2-Disc model not illustrated here)

### –Style 38 "Eroica"–
### 3-Disc Symphonion

35.5 cm. (14") discs; used in sets of three. Three separate music movements, each with 100 teeth (each movement consists of two 50-note combs in the sublime harmonie arrangement). Known as the "Three-disc Symphonion" by collectors today. The three discs, each identified by a letter (A, B, C) are played simultaneously. The intention was to provide an exceptional tonal volume and musical arrangement capacity. "The unexcelled capacity of modulation possessed by this instrument produces effects which never have been heard before in any mechanical music box. The case, either walnut or oak, is very solid and tasteful. Available with painted glass panel or with carved wood panel in front." Author's note: Actually, the intended volume of sound was not achieved as the bedplates of each of the three sets of combs are anchored to the side walls of the case – which tends to dampen the tone. Had they been mounted to the back of the case in the manner of a sounding board (as was done by Lochmann and some other makers) the desired brilliance would have been obtained. The 3-disc Symphonion is a collectors' favorite today because of the unusual feature of the multiple discs. Measurements: 205 cm. high by 72 cm. wide by 43 cm. deep. Uses 3-disc sets of No.38 discs.

No.38at: As above, but with coin slot.

No.38Bz: As No.38, but with art glass panel made up of pieces of colored circular glass.

No.38H: As No.38, but with wood panel on the front.

No.38R: As No.38, but with custom advertisement painted on glass on front.

### "Eroica" Discs

Discs for the 3-Disc Symphonion, or "Eroica," were numbered in the 8000 series, beginning with No.8001. Typical selections are: "Spinn! Spinn!" (No.8016); "O Tannenbaum" (No.8018); "Blue Danube" (No.8032); "Estudiantina Waltz" (No.8049); "Columbia, Gem of the Ocean" (No.8104); "Sidewalks of New York" (No.8121); and "The High School Cadets" (No.8161).

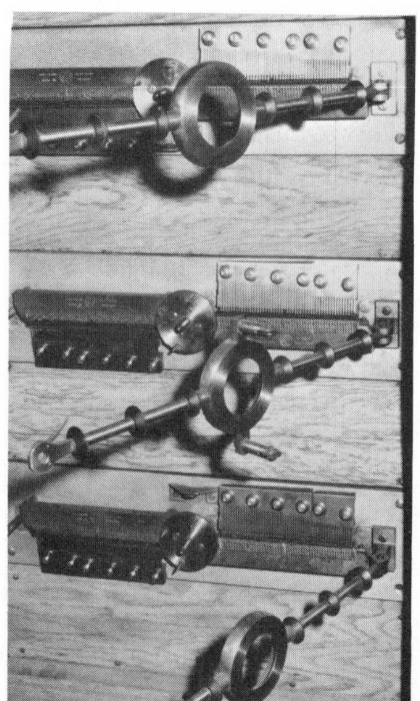

—No.38A "Eroica"—
3-Disc w/Hall Clock

35.5 cm. (14") discs used in sets of three. 300 teeth in 3 sets of two combs per set. Regular 3-Disc Symphonion movement built into a Lenzkirch hall clock. 275 cm. high by 72 cm. wide by 43 cm. deep. Uses 3-disc sets of No.38 discs.

—No.38B "Eroica"—
3-Disc w/Hall Clock

35.5 cm. (14") discs used in sets of three. 300 teeth in 3 sets of two combs per set (total: 6 combs). Regular 3-Disc Symphonion movement built into a Lenzkirch hall clock. 270 cm. high by 65 cm. wide by 43 cm. deep. "The case, wonderfully carved, can be delivered in oak or walnut and has a marvelous resonance. It is a grand piece of furniture for any drawing room." The 38B was sold in larger quantities than 38A, if surviving specimens are an indication. Uses 3-disc sets of No.38 discs.

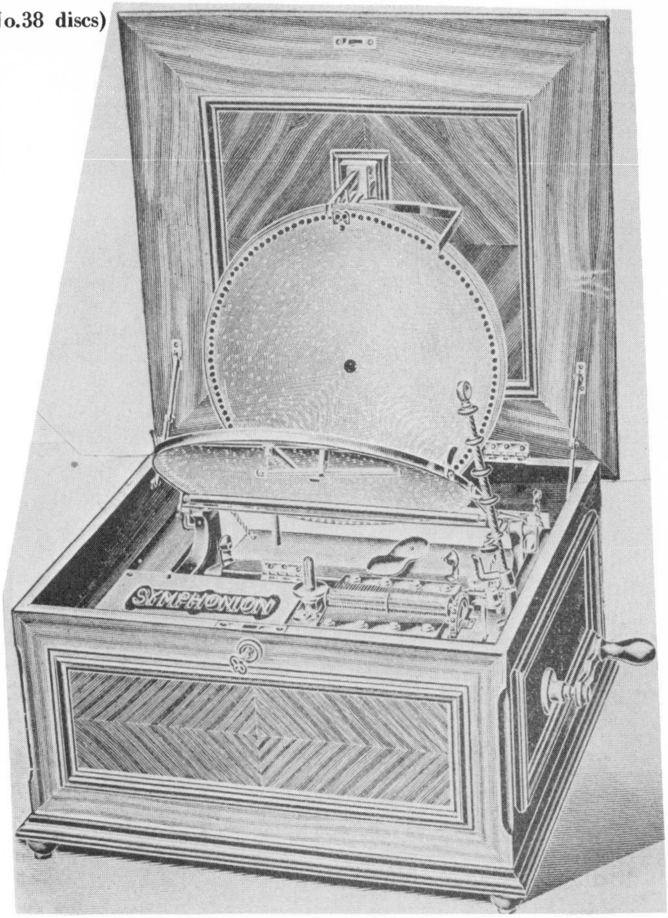


—Style No. 120V—

35.5 cm. (14") discs. "Einzig" model with an ingenious type of automatic disc changer. 25 discs (!) are stored in a rack above the music comb. One at a time the discs are played and then ejected through a slot in the back of the cabinet. A very rare model; only a few were made.

—Style 120S—

35.5 cm. (14") discs. "Einzig" model; stores eight discs and changes them automatically. 120 notes. Walnut case measuring about 60 cm. wide by 50 cm. deep by 34.5 cm. high (lid closed). Clear glass lid permits view of interior when lid is closed. A very rare model; only a few were made.

## SYMPHONION

(37.5 cm. or 14¾" No.121 discs)

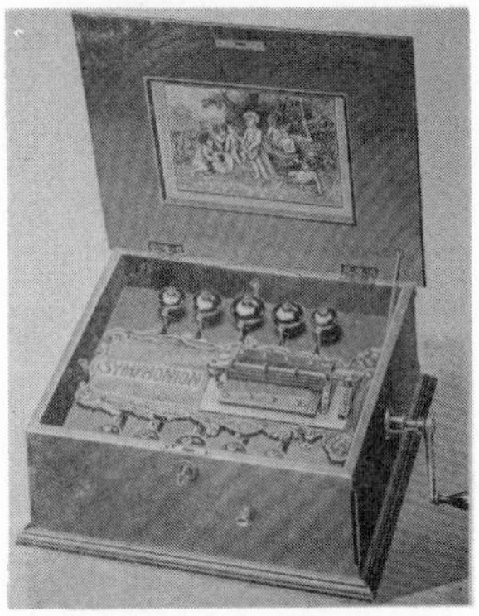


–No.121Gl (10 saucer bells)–
(horizontal arrangement of bells)

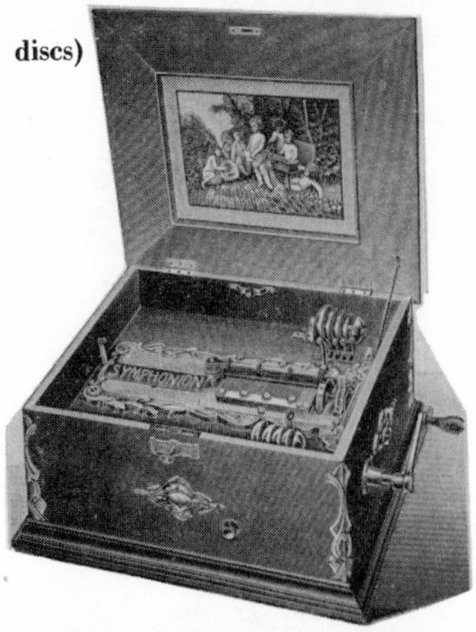


–No.121 Gl (10 saucer bells)–
(vertical arrangement of bells)

–Style 121Gl–

37½ cm. (14¾") discs. 120 in duplex combs plus separate comb section to operate 10 bells ("Gl" in designation is from "Glocken" – German for "bells"). 54 cm. wide by 48 cm. deep by 29 cm. high (lid closed). Uses No. 121 discs.

(40 cm. or 15¾" discs)

–Styles 178; 257–

No.178: 40 cm. (15¾") discs. 78 teeth in single comb. Uses No. 178/256. discs.

Variation: Available with 10 bells on special order. Uses No. 178/256 discs.

No.257: Duplex comb version of No. 178 (without bells); with 156 teeth in two combs. Uses No. 178/256 discs.

(46 cm. or 18¼" No.193 discs)

–Style No.92–

46 cm. (18¼") discs. 192 teeth in two music combs. Large upright style known as the "Monster Automaton No. 92." In cabinet 240 cm. high by 87 cm. wide by 57 cm. deep. Uses No.193 discs.

Variation: Same cabinet but with mechanism for No. 192 discs (192 notes also; but with larger diameter of 25¼")

(40 cm. or 15¾" discs)

–Styles 179; 256–

No.179: 40 cm. (15¾") discs. 78 teeth in single comb. Case in ornately carved walnut. Uses No. 178/256 discs.

Variation: Available with 10 bells on special order. Uses No. 178/256 discs.

No.256: 156 teeth in duplex combs. Otherwise similar to No. 179 (without bells). Uses No. 178/256 discs.

Note: The nomenclature concerning this particular disc size is confusing in the original Symphonion literature. At various times the same disc style (apparently; although the author would welcome clarification or information otherwise) was known as 78/156, 178/256, and, rarely, 179/259. Depending upon the catalogue the diameter is given as 38 cm., 39 cm., or 40 cm.!

Likewise, case descriptions are sometimes confusing. In several instances little regard was given to illustrating the precise case style of the style number in question. Apparently a "typical" Symphonion music box was a sufficient illustration for several different styles, some of which in actuality differed considerably from each other.

(48.5 cm. or 19 1/8" No.106 discs)

SYMPHONION

–Style No. 38B/106–
48.5 cm. (19 1/8") discs. 106 notes in two combs. Symphonion music movement in combination with a grandfather's clock. 270 cm. high by 65 cm. wide by 43 cm. deep. Uses No.106 discs.

–Style No. 106N–
48.5 cm. (19 1/8") discs. 106 teeth in duplex music comb. Walnut case. Many variations in cabinetry, particular with respect to the top gallery and the front posts. With wooden panel covering spring motor. Measurements: 122 cm. high by 66 cm. wide by 42 cm. deep. Uses No. 106 discs.

Variations: No.106NS is similar to 106N, except it has a clear glass plate over the spring barrel mechanism in the base – to permit a view of it. 106NU and 106NSU are equipped with clocks in the top gallery. All use No. 106 discs.

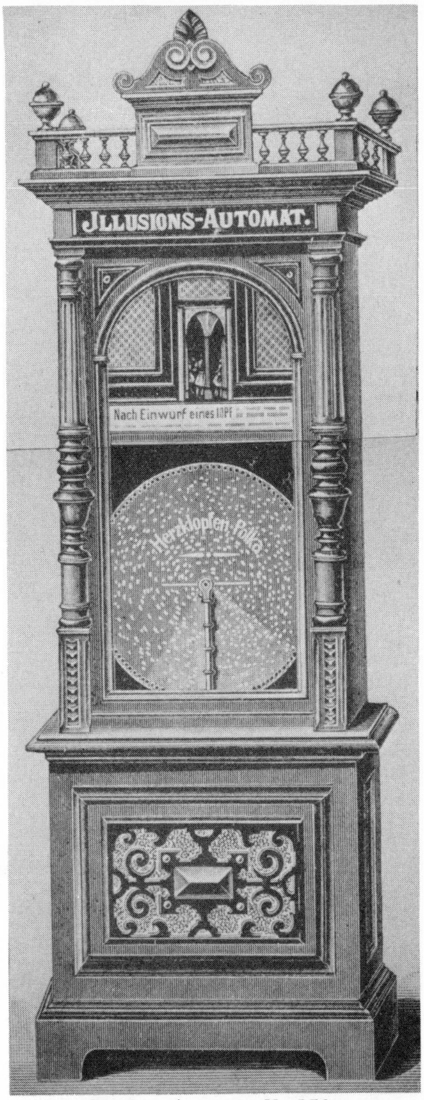


–Illusions-Automat No.150–
48.5 cm. (19 1/8") discs. With No. 106 Symphonion disc movement. Electrically operated. Top part has scene of ballet stage with many dancers. 215 cm. high by 72 cm. wide by 51 cm. deep. Uses No. 106 discs.

(54 cm. or 21¼" No.130 discs)

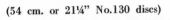

–Style 131–
(Mechanism of Style 130 built into Style 192 case).

–Style No. 130–
54 cm. (21¼") discs. 120 teeth in duplex music combs plus special section for 10 saucer bells (arranged as shown to the right; also in "nested" one-atop-another form). Upright style in walnut. Case variations occur, particularly with respect to the top gallery and the front columns. Coin-operated. Uses No. 130 discs.

–Style Nos. 130StE; 130E–
130E is similar to No. 130, but with power provided by an electric motor. 130StE is the same as 130E, except with a base cabinet for the storage of discs.

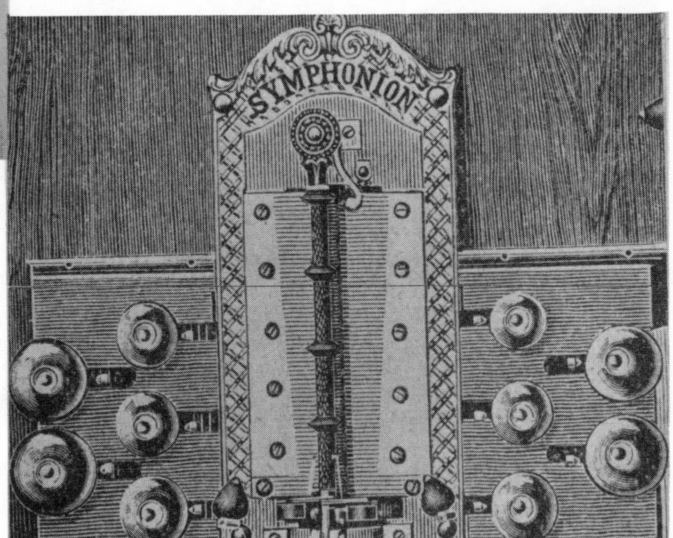

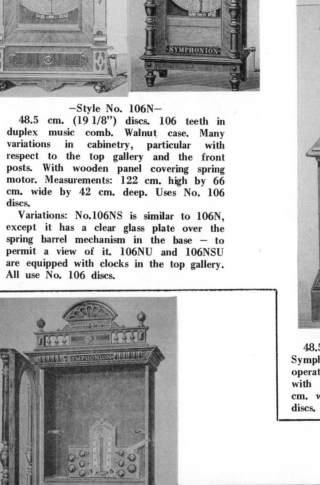

SYMPHONION

(54 cm. or 21¼" No.130 discs)

–Style 132–

54 cm. (21¼") discs. 120 teeth in duplex music combs; separate section for 10 saucer bells. Walnut wood of modernistic design; similar in concept to certain upright Polyphon boxes of the early 1900's. Coin operated. Uses No. 130 discs.

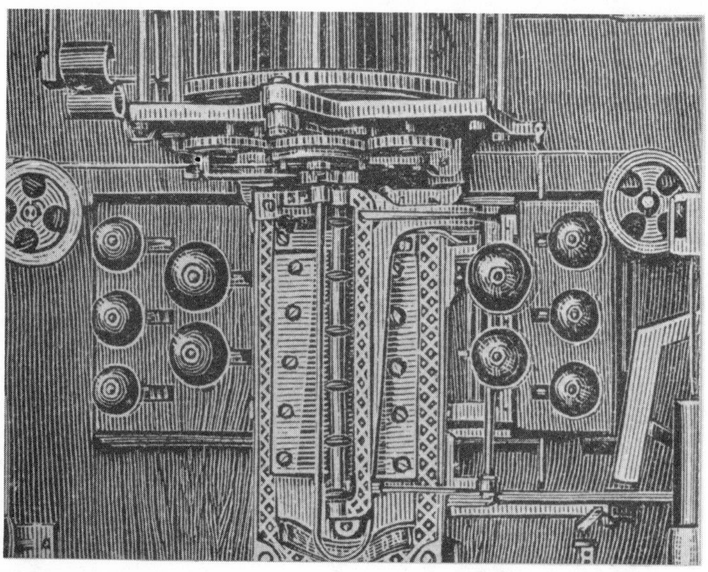

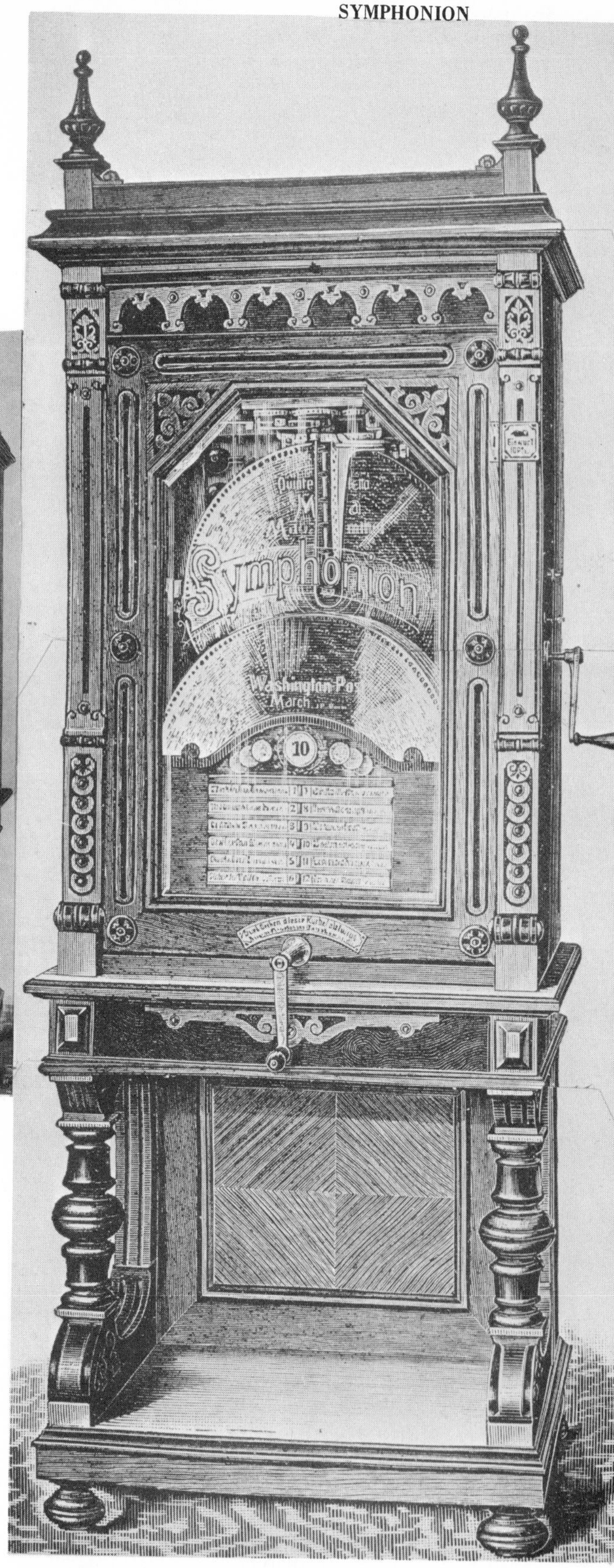


–Style No. 100–

54 cm. (21¼") discs. 120 musical notes plus ten saucer bells. Large upright automatic disc changer; holds twelve discs and changes them automatically. Selection made via a crank extending from the front of the case. Walnut case measuring 252 cm. high by 92 cm. wide by 73 cm. deep. A very large and impressive instrument but one which was sold only in small numbers. Few survive today. Uses No. 100/102 (Same as No. 130) discs.

SYMPHONION

(54 cm. or 21¼" No.130 discs)

–Style No.101–

54 cm. (21¼") discs. 120 notes; 10 saucer bells. Automatic disc changing model. Holds six discs and changes them automatically. Desired tunes are selected by turning a crank handle at the front. This actuates a spiral screw and moves the disc storage rack to the front or back. A small circular aperture above the program cards shows the number of the tune in the playing position. Dimensions of case: 153 cm. high by 87 cm. wide by 54 cm. deep. Cabinet bases with a disc storage bin could be purchased separately. Uses No. 100/102 (same as No.130) discs.

–Style No. 102–

54 cm. (21¼") discs. 120 musical notes plus 10 saucer bells. Automatic disc changing model. Holds six discs and changes them automatically. The same as No.101 but built in a modernistic walnut case measuring 163 cm. high by 91 cm. wide by 54 cm. deep. Case style similar to that used for certain contemporary upright Polyphon styles. Symphonion disc changers of any style are exceedingly rare today. Uses No. 100/102 (same as No. 130) discs.

(64 cm. or 25¼" No.192 discs)

–Nos. 192; 192W; etc.–

No.192: 64 cm. (25¼") discs. 192 teeth in duplex music combs. Large floor standing model with base cabinet. Measures 236 cm. high by 86 cm. wide by 52 cm. deep. In walnut wood. Uses No. 192 discs.

No.192W: As above, but without base cabinet. Measures 153 cm. high. Spring covered by wooden panel.

No.192WU: As above, but with clock in top gallery.

No.192 WS: As 192W, but with spring works behind clear glass panel.

No.192WSU: As 192WS, but with clock in top gallery.

Note: Certain smaller-disc upright styles were available built into the Style 192 case. Style 130 built into this case was known as Style 131. Style 142 models often utilized this case also.

–Style No. 192St–

64 cm. (25¼") discs. 192 teeth in two music combs. Tall cabinet style Symphonion in walnut case. "Discs play for about two minutes each; instrument operates for about 18 minutes on one winding" noted an early catalogue. 225 cm. high by 85 cm. wide by 50 cm. deep. Uses No. 192 discs.

–Style 192StE–

64 cm. (25¼") discs. 192 teeth in duplex combs. Similar to Style 192St, but operated by an electric motor. The "Electric Symphonion." 225 cm. high by 85 cm. wide by 50 cm. deep. Interior lighted by an electric lamp. Accumulator device registers up to 30 coins deposited in slot. Uses No.192 discs.

(64 cm. or 25¼" No.192 discs)

Views of Style 143 (above) and 143N (with base, as illustrated to the left). Actually, any upright Symphonion could be ordered with a base cabinet, some of which fit the styling exactly, others of which were "about right" in appearance.

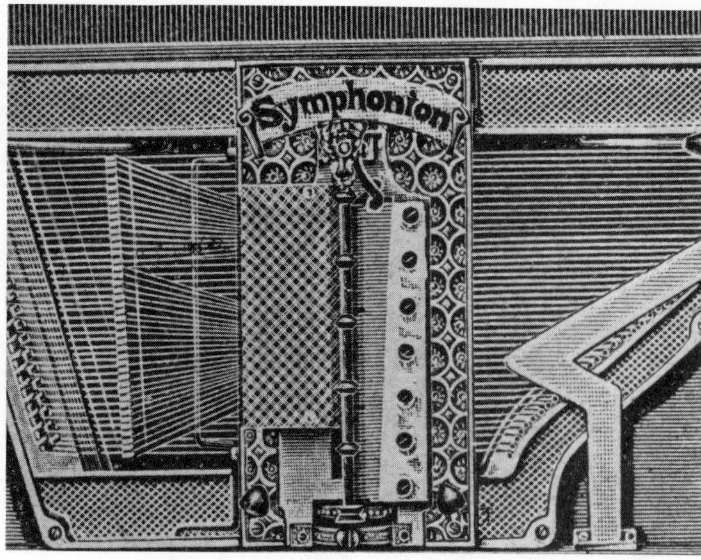


–Style 143–

64 cm. (25¼") discs. 96 teeth in music comb plus 42 piano notes (played on horizontal piano strings). In walnut cabinet measuring about 163 cm. high by 96 cm. wide by 48 cm. deep. Uses No. 192 discs.

No.143G: 96 teeth in music comb; 42 piano notes; 7 bells. Uses No. 192 discs.

No.143G.Schl: As above, but with "Schlagzeug" (drums and cymbal). Uses No. 192 discs.

No.143N: Base cabinet for use in combination with the above; of matching style – to be ordered separately.

---

–Style No. 292PG–

64 cm. (25¼") discs. Duplex model with two separate double combs and eight bells. Built into piano-like case. "P" = "Pianoform" (description of the case style); "G" = "Glocken" or bells. 158 cm. high by 160 cm. wide by 60 cm. deep. Uses pairs of No.292PG discs (same form as No.192).

Style No. 292P: Same as above, but without bells.

Variation: Instrument similar to above, but wider and with three discs.

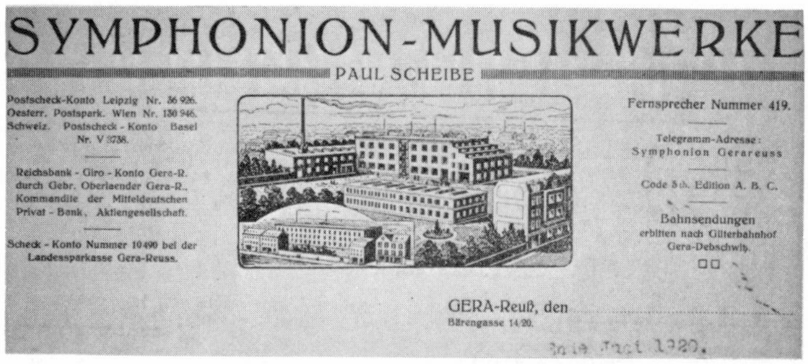

SYMPHONION-MUSIKWERKE

PAUL SCHEIBE

Postscheck-Konto Leipzig Nr. 36 926.
Oesterr. Postspark. Wien Nr. 130 946.
Schweiz. Postscheck-Konto Basel Nr. V 3738.

Reichsbank-Giro-Konto Gera-R. durch Gebr. Oberlaender Gera-R., Kommandite der Mitteldeutschen Privat-Bank, Aktiengesellschaft.

Scheck-Konto Nummer 10490 bei der Landessparkasse Gera-Reuss.

Fernsprecher Nummer 419.

Telegramm-Adresse: Symphonion Gerareuss

Code 5th. Edition A. B. C.

Bahnsendungen erbitten nach Güterbahnhof Gera-Debschwitz.

GERA-Reuß, den
Bärengasse 14/20.

Symphonion letterhead, June 1920.

View of the two large comb sections of Style 292PG. Almost identical instruments (from an external appearance viewpoint) were sold by the Symphonion Manufacturing Co. of New Jersey and New York. The above illustration is of a German-made model from a 1900 Symphonion catalogue.

(70 cm. or 27½" No.118 discs)

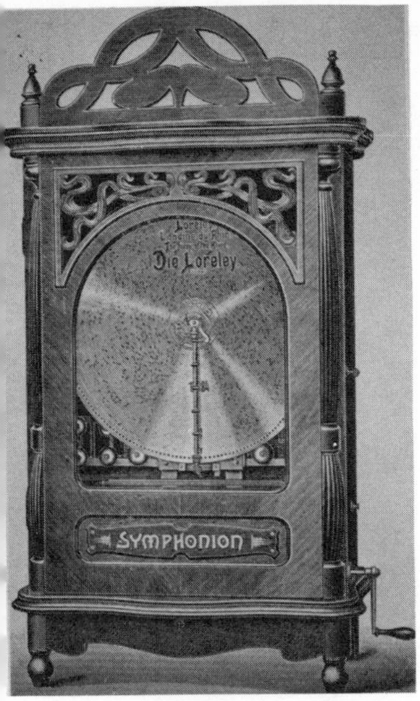


No.118W

–Nos. 118W; 118Gl–

No.118W: 70 cm. (27½") discs. 167 musical notes in comb plus 12 bells (saucer type). "In new style walnut case." 158 cm. high by 90 cm. wide by 53 cm. deep.

No.118Gl: 70 cm. (27½") discs. 118 notes. In large "Symphonion Orchestrion" case measuring 265 cm. high by 115 cm. wide by 63 cm. deep. Uses No.118 discs.

–Style 118Gl–
"Symphonion Orchestrion"

(75 cm. or 29½" No.162 discs)

–Style No. 162–

75 cm. (29½") discs. 120 musical teeth in duplex combs, 10 saucer bells, 26 organ reeds, large and small drums, cymbal. 263 cm. high by 92 cm. wide by 73 cm. deep. The "Symphonion Orchestrion" (one of several different types of instruments given that designation). Made in different case styles. Uses No. 162 discs.

(76 cm. or 30" No.98 discs)

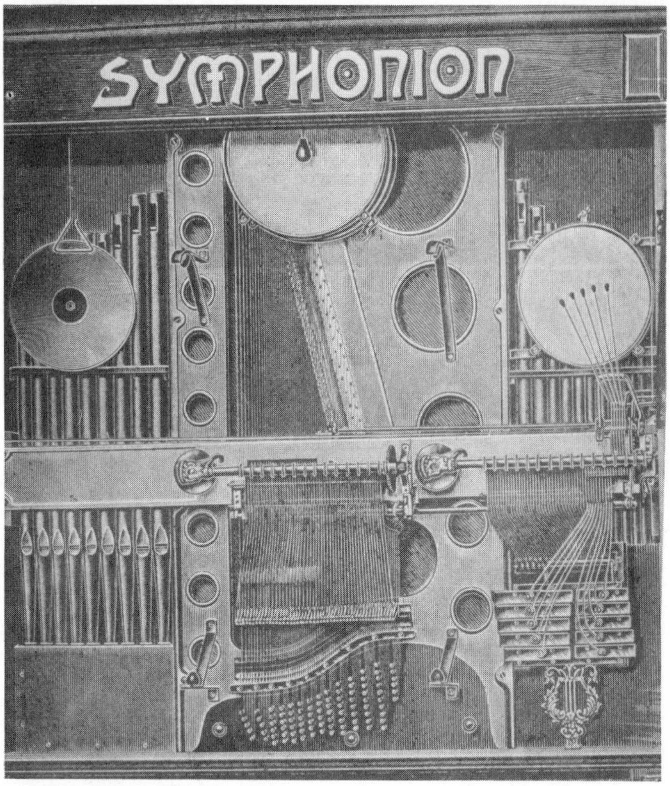

–Symphonion Duplex Orchestra–
–Style No.98–

76 cm. (30") discs. Piano orchestrion (no musical combs) with 52 piano notes (2 strings per note), 36 metal organ pipes, 10 bar-type bells, large and small drums, cymbal, and triangle. Uses two discs simultaneously, one overlapping the other. Long playing time of 3½ minutes per tune. Measurements: 260 cm. high by 150 cm. wide by 70 cm. deep. The Duplex Orchestra, which measures about 6' wide and over 10' high, is certainly one of the largest disc instruments ever manufactured. Introduced circa 1903, only a few were sold. Uses pairs of No.98 discs.

Style 98E: Same as Style No. 98 but with electric motor power instead of a winding crank. Uses pairs of No. 98 discs.

Details of some large upright Symphonion mechanisms. . .

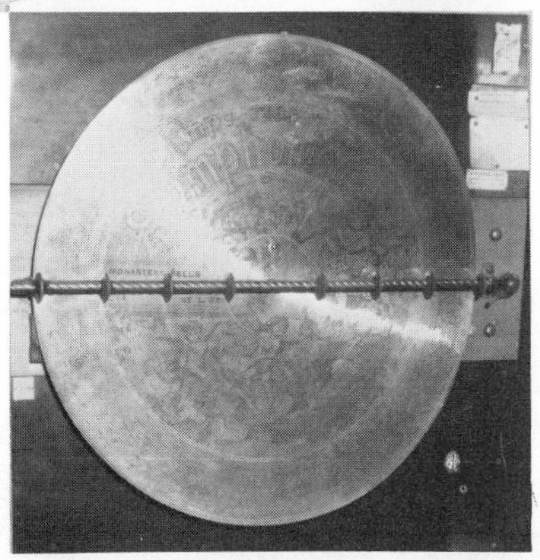

Style 106 American Symphonion (differs from the No.106 German). Uses 17 5/8" discs; the same disc that is used in sets of three on the 3-Disc American instrument shown on another page. Note that the cabinet styling is similar also.

This ornate Symphonion features an American-made cabinet with the musical mechanisms (using regular No.25 discs) and the lid picture made in Germany.

During the 1890's the American protective tariffs made it economically advisable to build music boxes in the United States; a situation which led to the founding of the Regina (by Polyphon) and Symphonion factories in New Jersey.

The three discs of the Imperial Symphonion.

The three bedplates, each with two "sublime harmonie" combs.

This 3-Disc Symphonion uses Imperial Symphonion No.106 discs measuring 17 5/8" in diameter (different from German No.106 discs). The three discs are arranged vertically in a side-by-side format. Each of the three discs — labeled A, B, and C — have slightly different embellishments. The result is a "stereo" effect when the instrument is heard while standing near the front.

Rear view: There are three separate motors, all wound from a common shaft. The five gears are interlocking and keep the three discs playing synchronously.

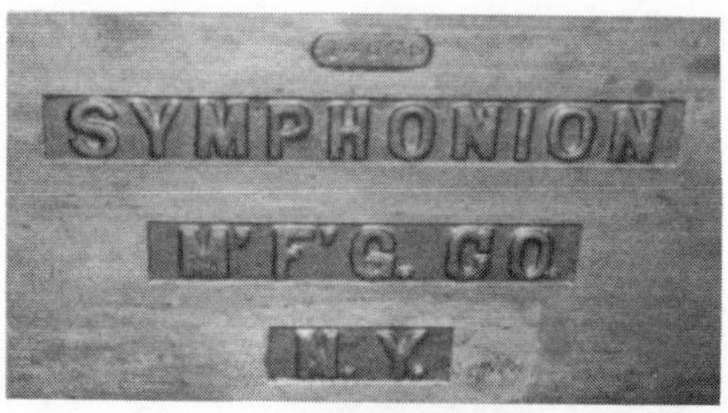


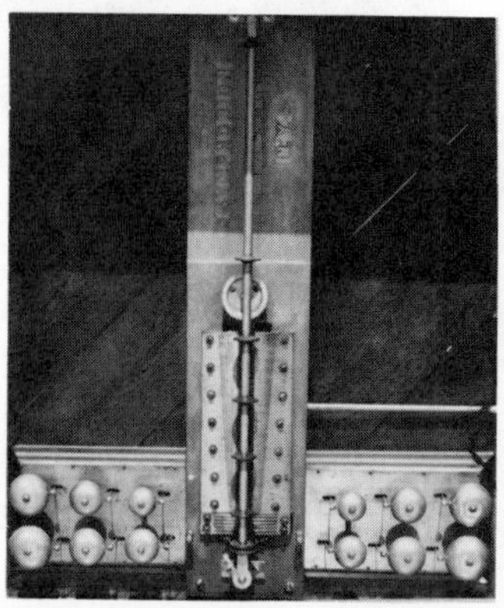

This large Symphonion Orchestrion uses 27 5/8" Imperial Symphonion discs or regular German-made discs (No.118) of the same diameter. The German instruments are driven by a series of dimples impressed into the edge of the disc; the American, by a toothed wheel which engages slots in the disc. To make the Imperial Symphonion disc compatible with the German, the American-made disc has dimples and slots alternately along the rim.

American Symphonion products are of three main types: (1) German-made music boxes bearing "Symphonion Mfg. Co." labels; (2) German-made movements in American-made cabinets; (3) American-made instruments.

## TROUBADOUR DISC BOXES
### B. Grosz & Co. (Leipzig)

Made in several sizes, Troubadour disc boxes were products of B. Grosz & Co. of Leipzig, Germany. Introduced in the 1890's, Troubadour instruments were sold through the early 1900's.

Arthur W.J.G. Ord-Hume relates (in his "London in the 'Nineties" article – see elsewhere in this book) that "towards the end of 1896, Martin Hirsch became the sole London agent for the Troubadour disc-playing music box made by B. Grosz & Co., Breitkopfstrasse 9, Reudnitz, Leipzig. Among the special features used as selling points were the 'larger comb (with additional teeth) and metal discs.' A repertoire of almost one hundred tunes was available initially, and the masters for each disc were said to have cost the manufacturers three pounds sterling each to make. Hirsch's showroom contained several models ranging from the largest (six feet high) to the small table models."

Troubadour disc boxes were sold in small numbers compared to the quantities marketed of Polyphon, Symphonion, and Regina disc instruments. Very few Troubadours survive today.

# Troubadour

No. 44B: 44 teeth in the music comb. Uses 22.5 cm. discs. Case measures 27x24x15 cm. and is of walnut with gold engraving. Cost 47 Mk. in 1904. No. 44L: In larger walnut case measuring 39x36x21 cm. Cost 55 Mk. Extra discs cost 0.58 Mk. each.

No. 56: 56 teeth in the music comb. Walnut case measures 39x36x21 and is the same as used for No. 44L. Uses 30 cm. discs. Cost 96 Mk. in 1904. Extra discs cost 1.44 Mk. each.

No. 30: 33 teeth in the music comb. Uses 18 cm. discs. Case measures 21½x19x15 cm. The center spindle of the music box also serves as a winding crank. The idler arm is hinged from the left side – an unusual feature. Sold for 25 Mk. in 1904. Extra discs cost 0.48 Mk. each.

Troubadour/Polyphon note: Certain Troubadour boxes contain Polyphon mechanisms and may have been manufactured by the Polyphon Musikwerke in Leipzig.

No. 79W; No. 79WD (Not illustrated)

No. 79W "Troubadour Wall Automaton" (coin-operated model made for hanging on a wall). "Made in the same cabinet as used for Symphonion No. 130 with the same top gallery as used on Symphonion No. 101" noted the original Troubadour catalogue description. However, the dimensions given for the cabinet of 79W (128x75x34 cm.) differ somewhat for those of Symphonion No. 130 (142x73x46 cm.), so the cabinets may have been similarly-styled rather than precisely identical. 79W uses 52 cm. discs. Sold for 240 Mk. in 1904. Extra discs cost 2.80 Mk. each.

No. 79WD: The same as the foregoing, but with duplex music comb assembly with 158 teeth. Sold for 300 Mk. in 1904. Uses the same type of 52 cm. discs.

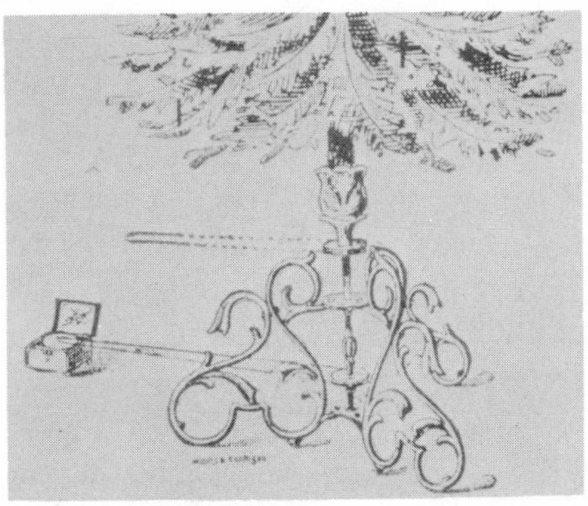

–Triumph/Troubadour Christmas Tree Stands–

Troubadour models 44B, 44L, and 56 could be modified for use with the Triumph series of Christmas tree stands by purchasing a drive mechanism which cost 9 Mk. Power from the rotating center spindle of the music box causes the Christmas tree stand to rotate. The music box and tree stand are connected by a pulley and belt assembly.

Triumph No. 1 cost 5 Mk. and was recommended for "middle-size Christmas trees." With this model the Troubadour styles 44B and 44L were used.

Triumph No. 2 cost 7.50 Mk. and was recommended for larger trees. Troubadour No. 56 was recommended for use with it.

Musical Christmas tree stands or attachments were made by a number of different German music box makers. Kalliope, Troubadour, Symphonion, Monopol, and other disc boxes were employed. Other stands used small cylinder movements.

## ADLER AND FORTUNA MUSIC BOXES
### Jules Heinrich Zimmermann
### (Leipzig, Germany)

Jules Heinrich Zimmermann (usually written as Jul. Heinr. Zimmermann in original advertisements) produced Adler and Fortuna music boxes. The Adler and Fortuna boxes are, for all practical purposes, identical — the only difference between the two being the name on the instrument (and cast into the bedplate). Although Zimmermann advertised that its factories were located in Moscow and St. Petersburg (now Leningrad), Russia, and Leipzig, Germany, the main center of activity was the latter location. Sales outlets were maintained in leading cities. A London showroom was maintained from the late 1890's until about 1905.

Nearly all Adler instruments and discs, and some of Fortuna as well, bear the Adler eagle ("Adler" = "eagle" in German) trademark.

A wide variety of instruments was produced during the late 1890's and early 20th century. These included hand-cranked novelty or toy boxes, spring-wound table models, and large upright coin-operated styles. Some of the latter were equipped with automaton figures such as trapeze artists or jugglers.

One of the most popular of the larger Adler/Fortuna styles was No. 370. This music box featured a 14-note reed organ, a snare drum, and a triangle, in addition to the music combs. More of these survive today (the term "more of these" is used reservedly — they are still quite rare!) than do examples of any other large coin-operated Adler/Fortuna style, indicating that No. 370 must have been very popular. A huge duplex version of this instrument, designated as No. 435, used two discs mounted vertically side-by-side. Only a few No. 435's were made.

Adler and Fortuna music boxes, despite the large number of cabinet styles and disc sizes originally made, are quite scarce today. Perhaps many instruments were sold in Russia and are unknown to western collectors today. The establishment of two branch factories in that country indicates this possibility.

No. 210: 33 teeth in music comb. Uses 18 cm. discs. Case measures 22½x19x13 cm. Manivelle (hand-cranked, not spring-wound) type. Sold for 11.25 Mk. in 1903. Extra discs cost 0.40 Mk. each. No. 210Z: Same, but with zither.

No. 215 (formerly No. 20): 40 teeth in music comb. Uses 21 cm. discs. Case measures 24½x23x14 cm. Manivelle type. Sold for 17.65 Mk. in 1903. Extra discs cost 0.50 each. No. 215Z: Same, but with zither. Sold for 19.90 Mk.

No. 220 (formerly No. 15): 33 teeth in music comb. Uses 18 cm. discs. Case measures 23-x19½x15½ cm. Spring-wound by front lever. Sold for 25.50 Mk. in 1903. No. 220Z: Same, but with zither. Sold for 27.60 Mk.

No. 225 (formerly No. 25): 40 teeth in music comb. Uses 21 cm. discs. Case measures 25x24x17 cm. Spring-wound by front lever. Sold for 34.50 Mk. in 1903. No. 225Z: Same, but with zither. Sold for 36.75 Mk.

No. 230 (formerly No. 120): 61 teeth in two music combs (30 and 31 teeth). Uses 26.5 cm. discs. Case measures 34x30x20 cm. Spring-wound by front lever. Sold for 58.50 Mk. in 1903. Extra discs cost 0.90 Mk. each. No. 230Z: Same, but with zither.

No. 235 (formerly No. 35): 50 teeth in music comb. Uses 28 cm. discs. Case measures 44x31½x20½ cm. Sold for 79.50 Mk. in 1903.

No. 240 (formerly No. 30): 50 teeth in music comb. Uses 28 cm. discs. Case measures 48x35½x20½ cm. Sold for 87 Mk. in 1903. No. 240Z: Same, but with zither. Sold for 90 Mk.

No. 245 (new model in 1900): 50 teeth in music comb. Uses 28 cm. discs. Case measures 48x35x24 cm. Walnut with inlay. Sold for 90 Mk. in 1903.

No. 250 (formerly No. 70): 77 teeth in music comb. Uses 37 cm. discs. Case measures 60x46x25 cm. Sold for 118.50 Mk. in 1903. Extra discs cost 1.60 Mk. each.

No. 255 (new model in 1900): 77 notes in music comb. Uses 37 cm. discs. Case measures 61x47x28 cm. Walnut with inlay. Sold for 122.25 Mk. in 1903. No. 255Z: Same, but with zither. Sold for 131.65 Mk.

No. 260 (formerly No. 40): 90 teeth in music comb. Uses 41 cm. discs. Case measures 64x50x29 cm. Sold for 160.50 Mk. in 1903. Extra discs cost 1.65 Mk. each. No. 260Z: Same, but with zither. Sold for 171 Mk.

Note: Nos. 230 and 235 were known as "Family Music Boxes;" Nos. 245, 250, 255, 260, and 265 as "Salon Music Boxes" in the original Adler catalogue.

No. 265 (new model in 1900): 90 teeth in music comb. Uses 41 cm. discs. Case measures 64x50x29 cm. Walnut with inlay. Sold for 165 Mk. in 1903. No. 265Z: Same, but with zither. Sold for 175.50 Mk.

No. 270 (formerly No. 41): 90 teeth in music comb. Uses 41 cm. discs. Case measures 65x54x31 cm. Case decorated with carvings. Sold for 198 Mk. in 1903. No. 270Z: Same, but with zither. Sold for 208.50 Mk.

No. 280 (new model in 1900): 108 teeth in music comb. Uses 47.5 cm. discs. Case measures 78x60x31 cm. Sold for 217.50 Mk. in 1903. No. 280Z: Same, but with zither. Sold for 228.75 Mk. Discs cost 2.25 Mk. each.

No. 300 (formerly No. 75): 77 teeth. "Elegant coin-operated model for wall hanging or for counter use." Uses 37 cm. discs. Case measures 100x57x33½ cm. Cost 159.75 Mk. in 1900. Extra discs cost 1.60 Mk. each. No. 300Z: Same, but with zither attachment. Sold for 169.15 Mk.

No. 310 (formerly No. 46): 90 teeth. Uses 41 cm. discs. Case measures 106½x67x38 cm. Sold for 168.75 Mk. in 1900. Extra discs sold for 1.65 Mk. each. No. 310Z: Same, but with zither. Sold for 179.25 Mk.

No. 320 (formerly No. 45): 90 teeth. Uses 41 cm. discs. Case measures 114½x62x35 cm. Sold for 187.50 Mk. in 1900. No. 320Z: Same, but with zither attachment. Sold for 198 Mk.

Adler and Fortuna instruments in the 300 series were designated as "Musik Automaten" (coin-operated music boxes), as "Music Automat No. 300." All 300-series instruments were equipped for coin operation. Cabinets were usually built of walnut.

No. 330 (formerly No. 115): 108 teeth. Uses 47.5 cm. discs. Case measures 147x70x49 cm. Sold for 216 Mk. in 1900. Discs cost 2.25 Mk. each. No. 330Z: Same, but with zither attachment. Sold for 227.25 Mk. One of the most popular Adler coin-operated models.

No. 365: 149 teeth. Uses 65.5 cm. discs. Measurements, including base: 236x89x50 cm. Sold for 360 Mk. in 1900 (includes base), or the base cabinet alone could be purchased for 67.50 Mk. No. 365Z: Same, but with zither. Sold for 375 Mk. Extra discs cost 3.90 Mk. each. "Recommended for use in large locations."

Nos. 360 and 360Z: As above, but without base cabinet. Deduct 67.50 Mk. from above prices.

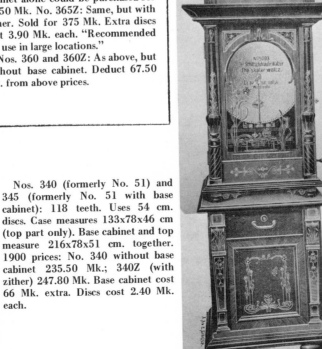

Nos. 340 (formerly No. 51) and 345 (formerly No. 51 with base cabinet): 118 teeth. Uses 54 cm. discs. Case measures 133x78x46 cm (top part only). Base cabinet and top measure 216x78x51 cm. together. 1900 prices: No. 340 without base cabinet 235.50 Mk.; 340Z (with zither) 247.80 Mk. Base cabinet cost 66 Mk. extra. Discs cost 2.40 Mk. each.

Nos. 350 (without base cabinet) and 355 (with cabinet): 118 teeth. Uses 54 cm. discs. Measurements, including base cabinet: 218x76x48 cm. 1900 prices: No. 350 244.50 Mk.; No. 350Z (with zither) 256.80 Mk.; No. 355 307.50 Mk.; No. 355Z (with zither) 319.80 Mk. Extra discs cost 2.40 Mk. each.

Note: Compare the general styling of Adler/Fortuna No. 350 with that of Polyphon No. 104 illustrated on another page.

No. 400 (formerly No. 95): "Upright Concert Automaton." 149 teeth. Uses 65.5 cm. discs. Case measures 298x96x57 cm. Sold for 675 Mk. in 1900. Extra discs cost 3.90 Mk. each. No. 400Z: Same, but with zither. Sold for 690 Mk.

In 1900 this model was the largest in the Adler/Fortuna series of regular music boxes (without orchestra effects).

Art Automaton No. 1: A clown applauds as a mechanical trapeze artist and gymnast perform. "Uses Adler music mechanism No. 330; 100 notes" (this differs from the No. 330 description which gives 108 notes — Ed.). Case measures 175x87x50 cm. (Note: "175" is the editor's estimate; the original specifications are given as "75x87x50 cm." — with the first figure being a typographical error.) Sold for 780 Mk. in 1900.

The Juggler, No. 204: A juggler performs with an aluminum ball. The large (110 cm. high) juggler is in a glass-walled case above the base. In the bottom compartment is "the mechanism of Adler No. 350; with 118 notes." Case measurements are 215x92x92 cm. Sold for 675 Mk. in 1900.

Similar automata were made with other types of disc mechanisms. Such instruments are extremely rare and are highly desired by collectors today.

Right: Views of Adler No. 330, a 47.5 cm. disc instrument. Most larger Adler instruments used double combs, although this was usually not mentioned in the catalogue (which reads, for example, "108 teeth in music comb").

Above and left: Views of a diminutive Adler box, No. 210Z, of the manivelle or hand-cranked type.

The underside of the lid and a metal plate in front of the star wheels are decorated with an eagle motif. Adler is the German word for eagle.

—Adler and Fortuna Discs—

Most, if not all, large-size Adler/Fortuna discs have the drive slots at the outer edge set at an angle. Some slots have rounded ends (see the illustration of a table model Fortuna in this section); others have straight ends (see the illustration of a No. 330 Adler directly above).

Discs for Adler/Fortuna models are in the following sizes. The letter designations (B, D, F, etc.) were used in Adler and Fortuna catalogues. Size B: (18 cm.); size D (21 cm.); size F (26.5 cm.); size H (28 cm.); size K (37 cm.), size M (41 cm.); size O (47.5 cm.), size R (54 cm.); size T (65.5 cm); size Z (66.5 cm.).

The following numbering system was used for tunes: Size B: 1000 series numbers; D: 2000 series; F: 12,000 series; H: 3000 series; K: 7000 series; M: 4000 series; O: 11,000 series; R: 5000 series; T: 8000 series; Z: 6000 series.

Thus the popular march, "Under the Double Eagle," appeared on discs numbered 1011 (for size B), 2011 (size D), 12011, and so on. A selection of over 500 tunes was available for most sizes.

Fortuna music box in the collection of Mrs. Ruth Bornand. This instrument uses a scarce type of disc numbered in the 9000 series. No. 9463, "The Wedding March," is shown. The diameter is approximately 11 inches.

This instrument is beautifully made. The bedplate is attached to a suspended spruce sounding board which results in an exceptionally rich tone. The case is of mahogany with fluted pilasters at the corners. The spring mechanism is beneath a clear glass panel. Measurements of the case are: 21" high (with lid open) by 20" wide by 15" deep.

Note the diagonally slotted drive holes at the edge. The instrument's specifications resemble those of No. 230 in some respects. No. 230 has a double comb with 61 teeth and uses a type F disc which measures 26.5 cm. Type F discs are numbered in the 12,000 series. The instrument pictured at the left has a notice (in German) which reads "Uses type F discs." However, the discs used are in the 9000, not the 12,000, series. A mystery!

Above: Fortuna No. 370.

Left: Fortuna No. 375 (the same as No. 370, but with base cabinet).

—The Fortuna Orchestrion—

No. 435: "The Fortuna Orchestrion." This large instrument uses two 66.5 cm. discs which are arranged side-by-side vertically and which play synchronously. Specifications of No. 435 are: 236 teeth, plus 14 harmonium reeds, triangle, and drum. Case measurements are 206x160x64 cm. In England the instrument sold for 70 pounds sterling (about $330 U.S. funds) in 1902. The above illustration was originally reproduced in "The Music Box," journal of the Musical Box Society of Great Britain.

—Adler/Fortuna Nos. 370 and 375—

No. 370: "The Marvel." 118 teeth in the music combs, plus 14 organ reeds, snare drum, and triangle. Uses 66.5 cm. discs. Sold for 390 Mk. in 1900. Extra discs cost 4.20 Mk. each.

No. 375: As preceding, but with matching base cabinet. Dimensions: 237x88x50 cm. (includes base). Sold for 457.50 Mk. in 1900. "The only instrument of its kind."

Arthur W.J.G. Ord-Hume, the owner of a Style 370, described it in an article in the Easter 1963 issue of "The Music Box" (used here with permission):

"The 26" Fortuna Orchestrion which I own is one of but a very few remaining in England. It has 118 broad-tooth twin combs of the same arrangement as the larger Polyphons, together with a 14-reed harmonium, a drum, and a triangle. The instrument is coin-operated and is driven by a large clockwork motor.

"The comb mechanism is plucked in the same manner as with other disc machines with this type of comb arrangement. One gantry of star wheels is employed, alternate wheels plucking the leading comb and the lower comb. The dampers are unusual in that the damper strip is pressed outward by the star wheel to dampen the tooth on the recessed end of the tooth which is square-cut in two steps . . .

"The way in which sustained notes are produced on the harmonium is interesting. The disc uses the normal type of projection. Each harmonium note is operated by two immediately adjacent levers coupled together and spring-loaded to shut the reed when the lifting force is removed. To sustain a note, the disc carries a double row of alternately-spaced projections. The first projection engages the first lever, sounding the reed. As the disc turns, the second projection engages the second lever as the first is released. The result is a slight tremolo effect to the music. Because the reeds are on either side of the center, the left hand seven notes are operated by linking levers.

"The coin mechanism is finely balanced so that the coin tray oscillates before the mechanism is fully released. This insures that the coin is lying flat in the tray; otherwise it cannot pass through the hinged bottom of the receiver. The coin is not released into the coin bux until the end of the disc is reached.

"The organ bellows are mounted to the left of the motor and are driven via a link to an eccentric protruding through the top of the top motor plate. A wind chest [reservoir] is affixed to the rear of the bellows and is sprung from the back of the cabinet. Any percussion effect or the organ section can be disengaged by appropriate levers. It takes 1 minute, 40 seconds to play a disc. The instrument has a superb tone."

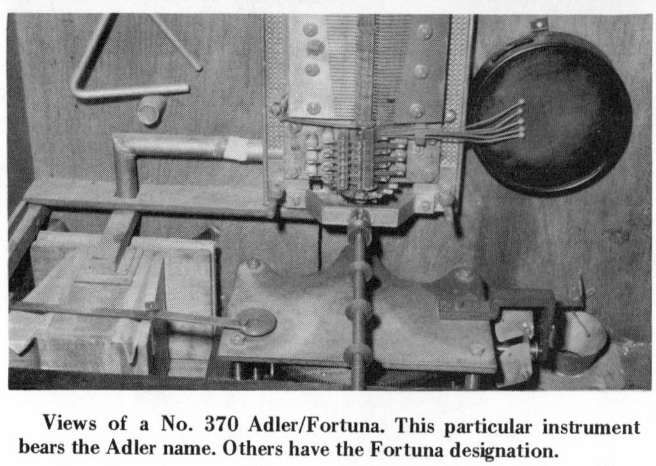

Views of a No. 370 Adler/Fortuna. This particular instrument bears the Adler name. Others have the Fortuna designation.

## BRITANNIA and IMPERIAL
—B.H. Abrahams—
(St. Croix, Switzerland)

B.H. Abrahams, well-known maker of cheap (quality and price) cylinder music boxes, produced the Britannia and Imperial series of disc boxes, beginning about 1898. Most of these were sold in England through the Star Silver Depot in London.

"The Britannia," an article by Frank S. Greenacre (cf. Vol.3, No. 6 of "The Music Box"), notes that Britannia disc sizes include 5-, 8 1/8-, 9- (same as 8 1/8" but with outside drive rather than center drive), 12-, and 25-inch types. Certain boxes up to and including the 12-inch size were also sold under the Imperial name, but are otherwise identical to Britannia models. Some of the table models are in cases that were multi-purpose and which resemble some of Abrahams' cylinder boxes. The Imperial shown at the bottom of the page is an example.

The tone of the Britannia/Imperial boxes is very loud. Collectors' comments about this are varied and range from "pleasing" and "a tone which many find preferable to a Polyphon (cf. Greenacre)" to "strident" and "harsh."

Left:Britannia No. 6, a large upright model. Note that Britannia is misspelled on the nameplate! Large Britannia instruments are very rare.

## PERFECTION
—Perfection Music Box Co.—
(Jersey City, N.J.)

The Perfection Music Box Company was formed in Jersey City, N.J., in 1897. Early in 1900 the firm moved to Newark. From 1898 to 1901 over two dozen people were employed.

The Perfection music box employed an unusual damper system. Instead of the usual metal damper assembly mounted beneath the combs, the Perfection used star wheels which were made of felt discs sandwiched between two thin star-shaped pieces of metal. The felt dampened the movement of the teeth effectively. However, the felt dampers wore out quickly, and replacing the felt discs was another thing entirely! Thus, the Perfection was impractical. As historian Hughes Ryder has said, the Perfection wasn't "perfection" at all!

(Information courtesy of Hughes Ryder; photographs taken by Q. David Bowers at the Musical Museum, Deansboro, N.Y.)

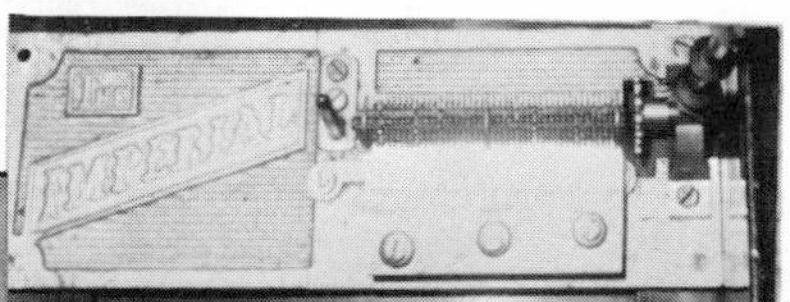

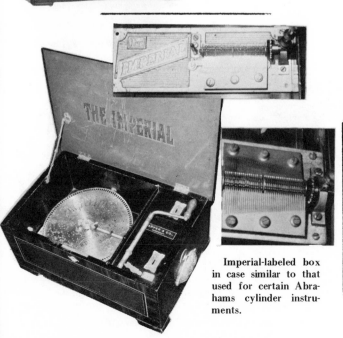

Imperial-labeled box in case similar to that used for certain Abrahams cylinder instruments.

The "Alexandra" model.

Britannia "smoking cabinet" model which uses a 9" disc. The duplex comb has 80 teeth. The clock ornament on top resembles that used on certain Abrahams cylinder boxes of the period. Many of the Abrahams instruments were labeled with initials only; as "B.H.A."

## IMPERATOR and LIBELLION
### –F.A. Richter & Co.–
### (Rudolstadt, Germany)

During the 1890's and early 1900's Friedrich Adolf Richter, whose address in 1895 was given as Rudolstadt, Germany, produced a series of music boxes. Disc-type boxes were sold under the Imperator name. These were made with excellent craftsmanship.

The Libellion, a music box played by folding cardboard music books, was patented in 1894 and 1895. These were made through the early 1900's.

F.A. Richter & Co. displayed its products at the 1900 Paris Exhibition. The medallic award obtained there was reproduced in etched glass on the front of certain Imperator boxes made after that date.

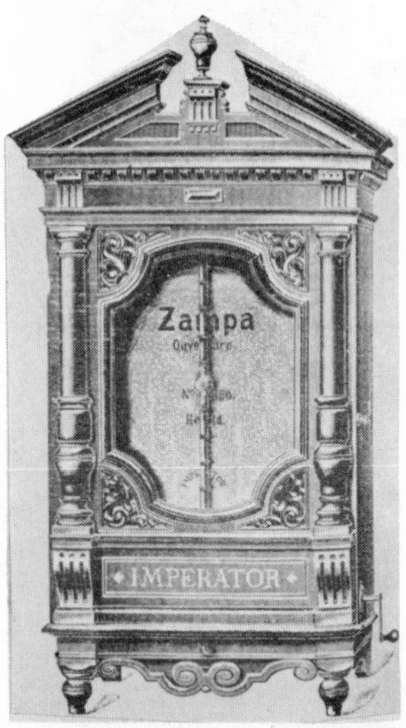


Above: Style 49 Imperator disc box with twelve bells. Note the unusual arrangement of the music combs. Made c.1905.

Left: A counter-top Imperator box of somewhat similar styling. An advertisement noted that Imperator boxes "are acknowledged to be of most excellent workmanship and of the richest tone; they can be had with hooks for fastening to the wall, or in the shape of stand-up boxes."

## SAXONIA
### Phönix Musikwerke
### (Leipzig, Germany)

Made by the Phönix Musikwerke (Schmidt & Co.) of Leipzig, well-known manufacturer of disc-operated organettes, the Saxonia music box shown below appeared in an 1895 catalogue. Coin-operated, the Saxonia was made for use on tavern counters and similar places.

Little is known of the Saxonia series of music boxes today. The Phönix firm (full corporate name: Leipziger Musikwerke Phönix Schmidt & Co.) was immensely successful with its many different models of organettes (see organette section of this book), and perhaps it concentrated its efforts in this direction. A 1909 trade exhibit of the company's products featured organettes and did not include disc-type music boxes.

**„Saxonia"-Musik-Automat.**

**zum Hängen und Stellen; auswechselbare Metallnoten.**

**Grösse.**
dimensions. size.
76 × 30 × 41 cm.
31½ × 12 × 16½ inch.

**Gewicht.**
poids. weig
netto 12,5 kg.
net 28 lb.

No. 347. **„Saxonia"-Automaton** with interchangeable discs, **42 steel tongues,** walnut

**To hang up or stand.**

The cheapest and nevertheless good toned automaton in existence.

The Libellion, a music box which uses folding cardboard music books. Described as "a steel-tongued parlor instrument with interchangeable sheets . . . Even the largest pieces of music can be reproduced in full." The example shown above uses a 9¾" wide music strip which passes through the instrument at the rate of about 4' lineal feet a minute. (Illustrations by Arthur W.J.G. Ord-Hume; instrument owned by Vince Bond)

Style 49 Imperator music box by F.A. Richter & Co. The trademark of the Imperator, a flaming torch, appears on medallions above the bells. The fine Richter workmanship is evident in the bell mechanism covers, the spruce sounding board (connected to the bedplate by a curved bridge), and other features. Note the unusual arrangement of the four music combs: two are above the center spindle and two are below. The coin slot mechanism is missing. The front door of the Style 49 is one piece and covers the top part as well as the bottom disc storage compartment.

## Miscellaneous Disc-Type Music Boxes

CELESTA: Made by Pietschmann & Sohn, Berlin, Germany, during the 1890's. Produced in several different models and disc sizes, including 11 1/2" and 19 5/8" diameters. The latter size is interchangeable with Polyphon discs of the same specification.

EUPHONIA: Certain Criterion music boxes (to which refer) were sold under this name.

EUPHONION: Certain Euphonion instruments (11", 15 3/4", and 19 5/8" disc sizes) known today are simply Polyphon boxes which were sold under the Euphonion name. Other Euphonion boxes use non-Polyphon types of discs, however.

GLORIOSA: Christmas tree stands with Symphonion, Kalliope, and other disc movements. Conceived by Eckardt of Stuttgart, Germany.

SUN: In the late 1890's Schrämli & Tschudin, the Sun Music Box Manufacturing Co., of Geneva, Switzerland, advertised a line of instruments which included disc-type music boxes. Also offered were orchestrions, cylinder music boxes, and other musical articles. Little is known of the Sun Music Box Manufacturing Company today. Whether the firm actually manufactured music boxes or whether it simply acted as an agent for other makers is unknown.

Celesta No. 10: 41 teeth. 26x22x16 cm. case. (Shown above).
Celesta No. 20 (not illustrated): 56 teeth. 37x34x22 cm. case.

### CELESTA

No. 37: 56 teeth. 94x48x31 cm. case. No. 35: Duplex-comb (112 teeth) model of No. 37. Coin-operated.

Celesta No. 25: 78 teeth. 58x47x23 cm.
Not illustrated: No. 20: 56 teeth. 37x34x22 cm. case. No. 23: 56 teeth. 41x37x25 cm. case.

No. 27: 78 teeth. 100x60x32 cm. case. Coin-operated. All Celesta illustrations shown here are from an 1895 catalogue.

Schrämli & Tschudin
..Sun" Music Box Manufacturing Co.
Fabrique de Pièces à Musique en tous genres
2. Rue des Pâquis 2. Genève, Suisse.
Boîtes à musique à Disques et à Cylindres interchangeables
Orchestrions
Phonographes-Suisses
Cylindres régistrés et vièrges
Panorama à musique avec Lumière éléctrique
Articles de fantaisie
Oiseaux chantants
Nouveautés, etc.
Garantie 1ère qualité.
Musical boxes with interchangeable Disks and Cylinders
Orchestrions
Swiss-Phonographs
Registered and unregistered Cylinders
Panoramas with Music and electric light
Musical Fancy Goods
Singing Birds
Novelties, etc.
Guaranteed 1st quality.
279

Jul. Berthold & Co. of Klingenthal, Germany, offered for sale equipment for the making of music discs and music rolls — "Music-perforating Machines."

Left: Advertisement for the Sun Music Box Manufacturing Company — Schrämli & Tschudin. The illustrated "Sun" music box is in a German case similar to contemporary (late 1890's) models by Polyphon.

## SMALL DISC BOXES
### —Thorens, Junghans, et al—

From the 1890's to the present time, Hermann Thorens (firm founded in 1846) of St. Croix, Switzerland, has made a series of small-size disc boxes. In recent years 4½" instruments have been made in large quantities. Diameters of earlier instruments include 3, 7 11/16, and 8 1/8 inches. Diameters varied over the years, with the result that, for example, the "4½-inch" size discs were made from about 4 3/8" to 4 5/8". All were gear-driven. The discs have a toothed edge.

Junghans, Germany's largest clockmaker, produced many clocks, novelties, and other devices which used small disc movements. A popular size measured 11.5 cm. (approximately) and was available in center-drive and edge-drive types. Some are interchangeable with Symphonion discs of like diameter. Helvetia small-size disc boxes were made in St. Croix and use discs measuring from about 4 to 8 inches in diameter. Edelweiss (Paillard; later Thorens) boxes were made mostly in small sizes, but some very large instruments using projectionless discs were also produced.

Silvanigra No. I: 30 teeth in music comb. Case in imitation mahogany. Uses 11.5 cm. center-drive discs. "About 440 different tunes available (c.1903)." Wound by front lever. Sold for 18 Mk. Many different case variations were made.

Silvanigra No. III: 36 teeth. 26x24x17 cm. case. Uses 20.5 cm. center-drive discs. "Over 140 tunes available." Cost 30 Mk.

No. 4915B (open)

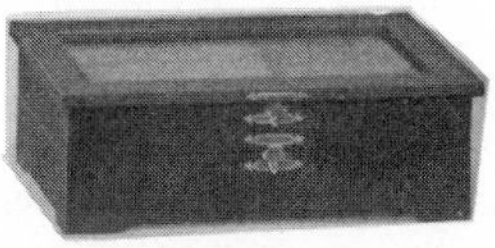

No. 4915B (closed)

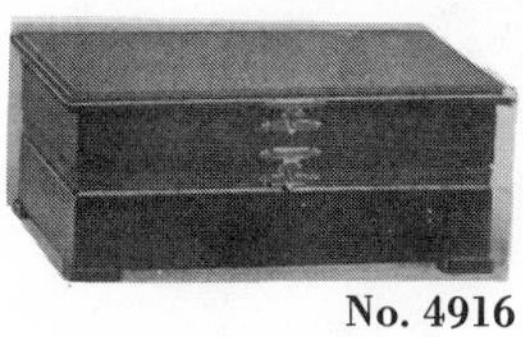

No. 4916

No. 4915B: Box for storing cigarettes, chocolate, etc. With compartment and glass lid. 29x19x9.5 cm. case. Uses 11.5 cm. gear-drive Junghans discs. (30-note size, same as 30-note Silvanigra discs, but with edge rather than center drive). Cost 16 Mk.

No. 4915N: Same, but in polished walnut case.

No. 4916N: Same (in walnut), but without glass lid. Cost 18 Mk.

A 1904 catalogue noted: "Your own advertisement or trade name put on any box if many are ordered." Such small-size movements were incorporated into many novelty items and were sold under dozens of different trade names.

## ORPHEUS
### Ludwig & Co.
### (Leipzig, Germany)

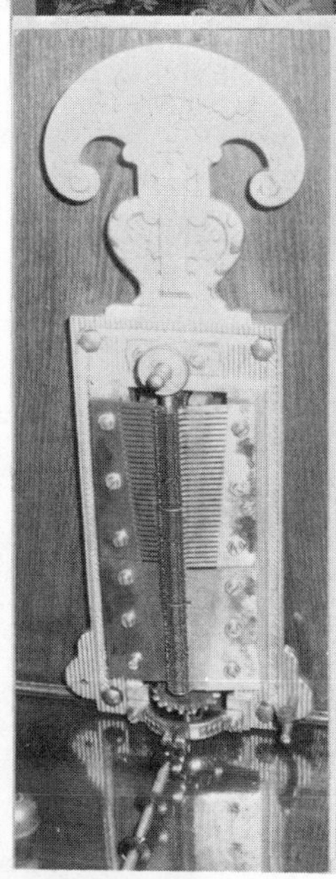

Made in several sizes, including 12" and 22 5/8", Orpheus disc boxes were produced in limited quantities around the turn of the century. A table model (illustrated at lower left) was described by Frank Greenacre in "The Music Box" (No. 6, Summer 1964): "The motor, which can be seen operating through an elaborately etched glass panel, is mounted beside the base plate and closely follows Swiss practice for a machine of this type. The spring itself is stamped with an unfamiliar complicated trademark and also the year 1899. Dampers, which act on the single mellow comb, are strange indeed. They are vaguely reminiscent of the Kalliope pattern in which a section of spring wire is pressed forward on to the tip of each tooth, except the ones at the extreme end of the treble registers . . . The artist who designed the lid lithograph (which is in glorious color) seems to have confused Orpheus with Father Neptune! The discs are musically arranged in a somewhat pleasant if somewhat overembellished manner and are rotated by square peripheral drive holes."

The larger example shown at the left uses a 22 5/8" disc (with square drive holes) and is in a cabinet measuring 4'9" high by 2'4" wide by 1'7" deep. The cabinet, of unembellished rectangular proportions, does not resemble contemporary German instruments. The front is ornamented with an ornate etched glass panel, as shown to the left.

Junghans No. 5008: Clock with 11.5 cm. gear-drive disc movement. Also made with center-drive style. Clock face and movement similar to that used on a small Symphonion model. Sold for 27 Mk. in 1904. "Gounod" model.

Junghans No. 4711: Clock with disc music box movement. Available in center-drive or gear-drive models. Known as the "Concordia" model. Sold for 29.20 Mk. Note: Most, if not all, Junghans mechanisms appear to be of Symphonion origin. The discs were made by the Symphonion Musikwerke also.

No. 4261 (with alarm) and No. 4262: The "Offenbach" model. 52 cm. high. Uses 11.5 cm. Junghans (nee Symphonion) discs. Sold for 40.40 Mk.

Note: Junghans, a clock maker, produced many different case styles over the years.

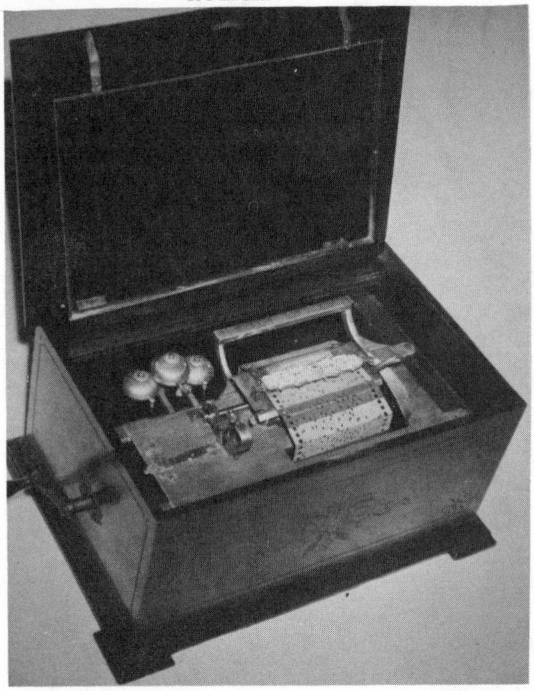

Left and below are photographs of a Roepke music box which plays folded cardboard strips. The instrument has three bells in addition to the music comb. Some of the music box parts resemble those used on contemporary (c.1890-1900) L'Epee instruments.

Roepke produced several models which employed this system. Table model instruments were produced of at least two strip sizes. Hall clocks with the Roepke music system were made, as were cabinet models driven by hot air engines.

In "Collecting Music Boxes and How to Repair Them" Arthur W.J.G. Ord-Hume has this listing: "Carl Albert Roepke; Glasshouse Street, Regent Road, Salford, Manchester, Lancs., [England]. Formerly from Berlin, Roepke patented in 1890 a method of plucking a musical box comb by means of a strip of moving cardboard or similar material. He manufactured the 'Orchestral Music Box' in England c.1895."

Music boxes played with paper strips or folding cardboard were produced by several makers. The Libellion (produced by Richter) is shown on another page.

UNIKON: Above is shown a Unikon, an instrument which has 41 playing teeth and which uses a 4 5/16" music strip. Arthur W.J.G. Ord-Hume describes the instrument: "The strip presses the 41 spring-loaded brass keys down . . . When a slit allows a key to lift, a lever pressed down in front of the tooth and wire damper acts on the front of the tip of the tooth. When the key is again depressed, the lever is tilted up and plucks the comb."

ARNO: The Arno music box, devised by Oliver H. Arno of Boston, Massachusetts, who was associated with the Massachusetts Organ Co. (see organette section of this book). Mr. Ord-Hume describes the Arno strip-played music box: "In essence the pneumatic organette system was modified so that the small bellows, instead of opening the valves to the reeds in the organette, were used to pluck the teeth on a musical comb. With little load on the controlling strip, paper rolls [or strips] of any length could be used. The case of the Arno box is slightly more than one foot square . . ."

# LONDON IN THE 'NINETIES

*by Arthur W.J.G. Ord-Hume*

*"London in the 'Nineties," a survey of mechanical music in the closing years of the XIXth century, was written by Arthur W.J.G. Ord-Hume for "The Music Box," journal of the Musical Box Society of Great Britain, and is used here with permission of the author. The spirit of the era is captured in a nostalgic manner. You are there – London in the 1890's:*

The last five years of the nineteenth century were indeed great ones for the mechanical music industry. The century had been one of tremendous achievement, of successful endeavors in almost every field.

From the primitive world of the time of King George III to the closing years of Queen Victoria's reign England had come a long, long way, perhaps far more than in any other similar period in history, before then or after. Factories were being equipped with "the electric light" so that workers need no longer strain their eyes in the flickering gas light (even so, many a church organist was unhappy at the thought of playing an organ with the new electromagnetic action, so uncertain was the electric supply). The steam engines which drove the wheels of our factories now also drove generators. One piano factory in North London actually installed a 10 horsepower steam engine solely for the production of electric light current - luxury indeed!

And in mechanical music, there had also been great strides. From the invention of the tuned steel comb, one hundred years had passed and now musical boxes could be found which performed remarkable and intricate music with a degree of perfection that was more than satisfactory. Mr. Ludwig Hupfeld in Leipzig, Germany, had just moved from the suburbs into a new factory closer to the center of that town where he was making pianos which played perforated paper roll music via a pneumatic action which was driven from an electric motor. Hupfeld's invention and perfection of this device preceded the American moves in this direction by a number of years. Hupfeld also made "electric orchestrephones" and the first of these to be seen in London was nightly entertaining the audiences at Maskelyne & Cook's magical performances at the Egyptian Hall in Piccadilly.

Musical boxes abounded and the amusement sideshow in Piccadilly, lit by the electric lights strung from the ceiling, was just one place where you could find a 24½" Polyphon surrounded by people. Street music, of course, was everywhere, the Italian barrel piano makers having settled in Clerkenwell where they produced many a colorful instrument on a handcart. Chiappa was making street organs and barrel harmoniums in Eyre Street Hill, Pasquale was producing street pianos and in many cafes and ale houses the "automatics" stood by the bar - the clockwork barrel pianos.

But what about the makers and agents who had their offices in London? Let's take them alphabetically. There was Barnett Henry Abrahams at 128 Houndsditch - the London warehouse of the Swiss B.H.A. firm which made both cylinder and disc music boxes including the Britannia and the Imperial. At 31, Aldermanbury was the warehouse of Ball, Beavon & Company. Karl Bender & Co. resided at 2a, Dysart Street, Finsbury. George Bendon & Co., a wholesaler, could be found at Nos. 36 and 37, Ely Place with additional premises at 1, Charterhouse Street. Beutner & Company specialized in organettes as well as musical boxes and they had a special line of these, including the Ariosa and Phoenix, at 65 and 66, Basinghall Street, their warehouse being at 5, 6, and 7, St. Georges Avenue. E. Camerer, Kuss & Co. were also agents, and they had their offices at 56, New Oxford Street and 2, Broad Street, Bloomsbury.

Thomas Dawkins & Company was located at 17, Charterhouse Street with their factory down among the Italian barrel piano makers at 49, Warner Street in Clerkenwell. Holding the Royal Warrant for the manufacture of musical instruments for Queen Victoria was Imhof & Mukle at 110, New Oxford Street. Across the Thames River at 17 and 18, Railway Approach, London Bridge, was King's Universal Supply Limited, a retailing firm.

Another retailer was Hermann Lange at 13 and 14, Camomile Street, E.C. Antoine Lateulere sold musical boxes at 19, Clerkenwell Road where he employed Swiss craftsmen in repair work. Mermod Frères had their London office at 81, Milton Street, E.C., and Mojon, Manger & Co. were at 26 and 27 Bartlett's Buildings. Alfred Muller retailed boxes at 23, Sloane Street, S.W. and Nicole Frères sold their cylinder boxes and also Polyphons at 21, Ely Place. C. Paillard & Co. had showrooms at 28, Berners Street off Oxford Street, having moved from 62, Holborn Viaduct in 1894. Silber & Fleming Limited could be found at 56½ to 62 and 71, Wood Street, E.C. and also 2, London Wall, E.C.

Jerome Thibouville-Lamy & Co. were established at 7, 9, and 10, Charterhouse Street. The firm of John Tritschler & Co. were at 85, Oxford Street (they did not move to 40, Great Russell Street until 1898), and Wales & McCulloch were at 20, Ludgate Hill and 56, Cheapside. Finally in this alphabetical listing Joseph Wallis & Son Limited were at 133 and 135, Euston Road.

Specialists in musical box repair work included Dawkins, Imhof & Mukle, Lateulere, Nicole Frères, Paillard, Joseph Fackler at 6, St. John's Square, and William Savage at 110, St. John Street until his death in 1897.

Nicole Frères, having taken over the remainder of their house at Ely Place as warerooms, stocked large numbers of Polyphons, the discs of some of these instruments being as cheap as 5d. each. They also had no fewer than 1,000 cylinder musical boxes in stock. To handle the Polyphon sales they formed a new company at the same address which was known as the Polyphon & Regina Music Box Company, which also undertook the repair and overhaul of these instruments.

Jacques Ullmann, partner with his brother Charles in the firm of Ch. and J. Ullmann of Paris and Ste. Croix, opened as a repairer and retailer at 9, Butler Street, Milton Street, E.C. and Alban Voigt, who stocked Symphonions, tackled all repair work at 14, Edmund Place. Voigt, incidentally, took over Paillard's interests when that firm closed its London office early in the present century.

Although this article purports to deal with the musical box in London, some account must be taken of the European environment in order to add, in some measure, the balance to the picture. London concerned itself only with selling the product in the best possible and most profitable manner; Leipzig had to meet the demand of the many agents and wholesalers who were establishing musical box trade in the metropolis.

Leipzig was indeed leading the world in mechanical music in the closing years of the nineteenth century. In 1898, more than 3,000 hands were employed in the trade. Instruments were constantly being invented, perfected, and improved upon. The products of Polyphon, Lochmann, the Adler and Euphonika firms were exported to most parts of the world. However, because of the high protective tariff levied on these goods by the United States, sales to that country were restricted and most of the principal firms began their own factories in America.

We can now see how the centre of the musical box industry had shifted from Switzerland, first to France, then across Europe to Berlin, Leipzig, and Austria. The Swiss naturally were most concerned about this loss of their trade and so, in an attempt to recoup some of their rights, several manufacturers formed themselves into a consortium. This was the Société Anonyme Fabriques Reunies founded in 1896. Their first offices were at 12, rue Binivard, Geneva, but they subsequently moved to 18, Quai de St. Jean. The group comprised the three firms of Rivenc, Langdorff, and Billon, and thus they could trace their beginnings back to 1838. A London office was opened to introduce their disc-playing musical box to the British market directly and without having to pay an agent's commission. This was the Gloria, available in both table and upright models. Several years later they brought out the Polymnia which was advertised as having "indestructible discs." The projections were in the form of dimples.

Towards the end of 1896, Martin Hirsch became the sole London agent for the Troubadour disc-playing musical box made by B. Grosz & Co., Breitkopfstrasse 9, Reudnitz, Leipzig. Among the special features used as selling points were the "larger comb (with additional teeth) and metal discs." A repertoire of almost one hundred tunes was available initially and the masters for each disc were said to have cost the manufacturers about three pounds sterling each to make. Hirsch's showroom contained several models ranging from the largest (six feet high) to the small table models.

Across Europe another of the seemingly endless legal wrangles concerning the disc musical box was taking place. Paul Ehrlich, in the newly adopted name of his company, the Leipziger Musikwerke, was claiming a monopoly in the use of star wheels for mechanical musical instruments. The case had come up in the summer of 1896 and Ehrlich had lost. He now appealed to the Court of Naumburg against the earlier decision. Considerable weight of objection to his appeal was lodged by the house of Lochmann (which denied to the Ehrlich factory all rights to forbid anybody to use star wheels as plectra for the tongues of musical boxes) and other Leipzig and Berlin factories. It was, in fact, claimed that other makers had been using star wheels much earlier than Ehrlich. The court subsequently dismissed the appeal. And still the export trade with Great Britain prospered. The houses of H. Peters and Popper & Co. were expanding their intercourse with wholesalers in this country.

Imhof & Mukle orchestrions could be seen, heard, and purchased at 110, New Oxford Street, but if you wanted an orchestrion to fit into a steamship, yacht, or convenient saloon, then you could direct your attention to the wares of Leopold Mukle at 92, Albany Street, Regents Park - only a hundred yards or so from the site of the old Colosseum where the Bevington Apollonicon used to perform in the 1840's and 1850's. Leopold Mukle made orchestrions which were driven by compressed air instead of by electricity or descending weights as were those in Oxford Street. The compressed air was supplied by the bellows and impinged upon an anemometer-type windmill. Orchestrions, incidentally, were more popular in France than in England at this time, although demand constantly was increasing here. Leopold Mukle's factory was at Furtwangen, Baden, where the work was superintended by Joseph Mukle.

Mr. Alban Voigt dealt primarily with stringed instruments at 14, Edmund Place, but he entered the musical box trade by stocking the Symphonion and carrying, certainly in 1898, the largest stock in London. Fortunately his premises escaped the disastrous fire of November 19, 1896, which laid waste several busy streets in Aldersgate.

The well-known wholesaler, Henry Klein, advertised widely to the trade and published numerous illustrated catalogues. He primarily stocked Polyphons and amusement machines. In the summer of 1897, he introduced larger models of the Amorette playing on 44 and 72 reeds and costing from five guineas upwards. The Amorette was made in sizes from 16 to 108 reeds and was the product of the famed Euphonika Musikwerke of Friedrich Listrasse 11, Leipzig. The company also produced a rather attractive and probably unique "orchestrion" or mechanical organ which was played by a perforated disc. The case resembled that of an upright Polyphon or Symphonion and contained 20 pewter organ pipes, a large drum, cymbal, and ten-note glockenspiel, all backed up by 48 tuned steel teeth on a comb. This instrument was introduced at the end of the 19th century and it seems as though few, if any, entered this country.

Gerald H. Murphy was showing the first piano fitted with an Angelus inner player. This had the roll-playing attachment fitted under the keyboard with the complete pneumatics located out o sight inside the piano case. The bellows protruded only nin inches out of the back of the piano case and the music ro could be watched as it played in a small housing to the right o the keyboard and below it.

But other pianos were available in London - electric ones an primarily the products of Ludwig Hupfeld A.G. These could b had with their own power supply so that they could b independent of the "electric light current." The supply was i the shape of wet-cell rechargable accumulators made by the Berli firm of Pfluger Accumulatoren-Werke A.G., one of several firm making such batteries.

Traveling into London, as your train slowed down into Broa Street (City) station, and provided that you were sitting wi your back to the engine, you could see the large moder premises taken over in July of 1897 by Ball, Beavon & Co Across the factory was written "Manufacturers & Importers o Musical Instruments, Wholesale Only." The firm had begun fort or fifty years previously as Ihlee & Horne, later becoming Ihle & Sankey. But for the previous eleven years it had been Bal Beavon & Co. at premises in Aldermanbury. But now the lon move had been completed to 5, Skinner Street, Bishopsgate Stree Without. On the four floors were all manner of goods an processes, one whole floor being devoted to stringed instrument The first elevator in London had probably been the "ascendin room" at the Colosseum; now they were becoming commonplac although that at B.B. & Co.'s was for goods, not people.

The Leipzig firm of Ludwig & Co. (Ludwig & Wild) wer seeking agents and representatives in London to sell their Orpheu disc musical box. The chief sales point of all these disc boxe seemed to concentrate not on portability or compactness, but t dwell on sheer bulk and hulk of the largest in the range. Th Orpheus, for example, included a model 86" high, 30" wide, 20 deep and playing 22 5/8" discs on a comb of 220 teeth.

All was not well in Leipzig, though. Although the undoubte center of the world's musical box manufacture (the total numbe of employees far exceeding that of the Swiss), petty squabble legal battles, manufacturing problems, labor problems, and, abov all, the activities of disreputable companies abounded. In 1897 steep rise in the price of steel threatened to reflect in the cos of musical boxes and their discs. In a manner strangely familia to our modern ears, the workers were urged to "back Leipzig and achieve more for their wages to help absorb the rising cost With cheap Bohemian labor from across the nearby borde Leipzig managed to weather that storm.

Back in London, a particularly fine summer's day turned ou to have a sting in its tail for one Italian organ grinder. H persisted in playing his street barrel organ outside the home o Parliament member Justin McCarthy, who chanced to be in hi sickbed at the time. The 'grinder was caught and awarded on month's hard labor for his efforts.

The firm of Paul Ehrlich had recently changed its name to th Leipzig Music Works and at their 57, Basinghall Street showroom could be seen yet another behemoth musical box - the 7 ft. hig Monopol "Excelsior." November of 1897 saw the incorporation a a limited liability company of the house of Nicole Frères.

Jules Heinrich Zimmermann took up the London agency fo the Symphonion; the Symphonion Company was not formed i London until 1900. Zimmermann was later to produce th Fortuna range of disc-playing musical boxes and also the Adle this last-mentioned being a particularly fine and well-mad machine.

With the introduction of the player reed organ and its grea popularity, George Whight took up the agency for the Aeolian a their 225, Regent Street showrooms and soon got themselve involved in a lawsuit with the music publisher, Mr. Boosey, wh alleged infringement of musical copyright in the selling of Aeolia rolls. "My Lady's Bower," "The Better Land," and "The Hol City" were the cause of the objection and judgment was foun for Boosey on a technical point. In September, 1899, th Orchestrelle Company bought Whight's business which had bee sorely depleted by the legal action. In the space of a few years the Orchestrelle Company was taken over by the America Aeolian Company, finally adopting the title itself in 1912.

Yet another copyright case beleagured Polyphon in 1898 whe the firm of Henry Litolff's Edition of Brunswick sued th manager of Polyphon for the unauthorized use of "March Lorraine," composed by Louis Ganne, a Frenchman. The case wa a particularly interesting one for several technical reasons regard ing the interpretation of the copyright laws, the Bernese Conven tion, and the involvement of a French musician's work. However it suffices here to say that the case went against Polyphon, and the court ordered that all discs, together with master plates, appliances for the production of the discs, etc. should be confiscated, whether in the hands of Polyphon or their agents anywhere in the world. So "Marche Lorraine" is a very rare disc on Polyphon, should anyone have it today! The decision of the Reiches Gerichts dismissed Polyphon's appeal against the verdict of the Royal District Court of Leipzig.

Back in London, the usual crop of large disc boxes were being displayed. Mr. Ernst Holzweissig opened his large warerooms in Newman Street and revealed a gigantic Symphonion on which he played Lohengrin's "Wedding Song." This vast model was mounted in a carved oak case and stood nine feet high. It included a set of bells and sold for thirty guineas. He also stocked the coin-operated Kalliope, which sold for about ten guineas, and the Adler as well as table models and Amorettes, musical chairs, decanters, and other fancy musical goods.

But for the largest disc musical box to be seen anywhere in London, one had to go to the showrooms of William Gerecke at 8 and 9, Goring Street, Houndsditch. Gerecke was agent for the Komet, and one model he showed was no less than eleven feet high and played discs almost 33 inches across.

The closing years of the 19th century were rich indeed for the numbers of mechanical musical instruments made. Although by this time the quality of the cylinder musical box and its market were deteriorating steadily in the face of competition from cheaper and, in some cases, better instruments, the demand was increasing at such a rate that the diminishing percentage was counteracted by the general rise in all areas of the market.

Although Nicole Frères and several other reputable makers refused to lower their standards and by that decision gradually lost their share of the market, many others moved with the times, and the factories of Paillard, Thorens, Karrer, and so on applied mass-production techniques to their assembly lines.

In the late 1880's and 1890's, the principal rival to the cylinder musical box had been the organette, some of which sold for but a few shillings. Now, with the invention and perfection of the disc musical box, the decline of the traditional [cylinder] musical box accelerated. The industry geared itself to disc boxes and, as we noted earlier in this story, a wide variety of extremely fine instruments was being produced.

Zimmermann was probably first to produce a "new generation" of disc boxes, absorbing all the best features of his contemporaries into his Fortuna range. He then formed a subsidiary company to produce the Adler (which used the same trademark as the Fortuna).

It fell to the Swiss to invent the projectionless musical box disc and a machine to play it. Mermod Frères introduced the Stella, the discs for which were absolutely smooth on both sides. It was possible to play the disc either way around and, as many present day collectors know, some interesting effects can be produced by playing your favorite disc upside down!

The Stella agency, first held by Geater, was looked after in London by Imhof & Mukle from 1898 onwards. It is a sad truth that most of these boxes, although by many standards better than Polyphon, Symphonion, and Regina, did not achieve the sales they deserved. Names became household words, and the names of the "big three" were known and respected. It was usually for their products and their products alone that customers asked.

The last years of the 19th century also saw the perfection of the pneumatic player action, first devised for harmoniums and organs, and later applied by E.S. Votey to the piano player and later still to the player piano.

The Chicago firm of Story & Clark had a London showroom, and in 1898 they introduced in England the Orpheus self-playing organ. Competition in this particular field was strong, for Geo. Whight was selling the Victolian, William Gerecke the Pneuma made in Germany by Kuhl & Klatt, and Robert Marples had the agency for Kimball player organs. All these were reed instruments and were generally inferior to the Wilcox & White "Symphony" being marketed by Murdoch's in London. The peak of perfection of these instruments came with the Aeolian Orchestrelle in 1899-1900.

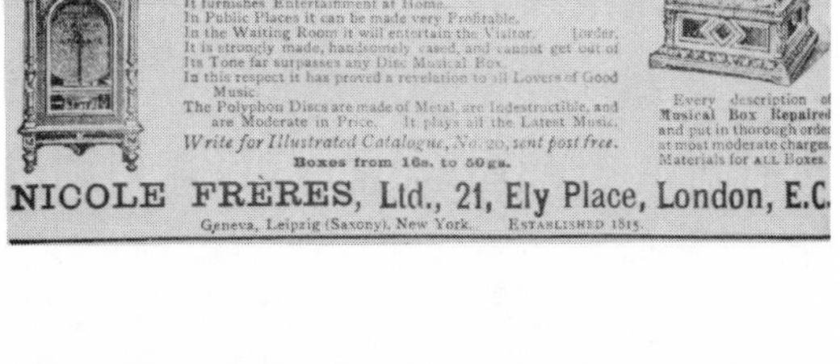


It was a far cry from these primitive pneumatic-action player harmoniums to the player organs of the next quarter century which was to see the arrival of the famed Mustel organ with roll-playing attachment, not to mention great pipe organs by such British makers as R. Spurden Rutt, Jardines, and others. Alas! no examples of these survive with player actions, having long since been "improved." But we are a long, long way ahead of ourselves at this point.

Today many people misspell the products of the house of Lochmann in Leipzig as "Symphonium" instead of "Symphonion." That this is no new foible is shown by the number of contemporary references in sales material to the instrument as "Symphonium."

The Symphonion Company opened its doors in 1900 in Ely Place, that stately row of mansions in Holborn built on the site of the famous palace of Ely Place. As well as stocking their own musical boxes, they sold phonographs, the Phoenix organette, and also did repairs to all types of musical boxes.

It was during 1901 that Paul Lochmann moved from Leipzig to Zeulenroda (Thuringen) in central Germany, setting up the Original Musikwerke Paul Lochmann GmbH. Here he put into production his new brainchild, the Lochmann Original series of disc-playing musical boxes. These were very fine pieces of work and, no doubt following on some of the acoustical teachings evidenced by the Regina, used the entire case as a resonator. He also made a piano orchestrion called the Original Konzert Piano. This was made in 1902.

In that same year, Schubbe & Company of Berlin, a firm which claimed to be the oldest factory in Germany engaged in manufacturing mechanical musical instruments, brought out their largest orchestrion organ made to special order for an eastern potentate.

The Sun was another disc musical box which was a "non starter" in the popularity polls. Made in Geneva by Schrämli & Tschudin, it was available in both table and upright models. The firm also advertised as manufacturers of orchestrion organs, but no instrument has so far come to light bearing their name and they may just have been agents for German makers. Orchestrions were, of course, also made in Switzerland, perhaps the largest manufacturers being Heller of Berne, the well-known musical box makers.

Disc musical boxes were "big business" throughout Europe and at least one firm set up in business to manufacture the machinery needed to stamp out discs. Julius Berthold of Klingenthal would not only make the stamping machinery and supply the blanks, but the firm would also contract to make discs for musical box makers who were perhaps too small to set up their own disc-making plant. Berthold's also produced music strips for book-playing instruments, organs, and the like.

The tremendous spread of business made this type of business venture a paying proposition and the subcontracting of component manufacture became fairly common. In the manufacture of orchestrion organs, for example, those worked by descending weights mostly used standardized components produced as sets by Karl Ganter of Furtwangen, Germany.

This vast industry sent its products far and wide and London was just one of many markets, London being the clearing house for the whole of the British Isles. But one product probably never came into Great Britain. This was the last great enterprise of the Symphonion Company in Leipzig — the 25" automatic disc changer. Made in 1902 as their answer to the similar models turned out by Polyphon and Regina, this giant instrument was made only in limited numbers.

The decline of the cylinder musical box continued during the ten to fifteen brief years of the boom in the disc musical box, but before the new century was but five years old, the musical box in all its forms was on a slippery slope. The great names closed their doors for the last time, the "for sale" signs went up, dealers either shut down (like Klein) or took on other lines such as the newfangled gramophone. The new century was filled with its own sounds which did not include those of the musical box. Germany shrugged its shoulders and applied all its talents to the improvement of the orchestrion. For London, however, attention was directed more toward player pianos than orchestrions. And the world as a whole was changing.

# PLAYER PIANOS

## Piano Players
## —and—
## Player Pianos

Introduction

In 1963, "Rebuilding the Player Piano," a how-to-do-it ook by Larry Givens, first appeared. As of this writing 1972), "Rebuilding the Player Piano" stands uncontested as he most popular book ever written on the subject of utomatic musical instruments. Tens of thousands of copies ave been distributed by the Vestal Press.

The introduction (by Harvey Roehl) to that book tells of he appeal of that once-omnipresent instrument:

"Time was in the United States when no home could really e considered complete without its player piano. From the arly years of the twentieth century to the closing days of the Roaring 'Twenties,' the player piano reigned supreme as the utstanding medium of home entertainment. Many were the arents who scrimped and saved so that their children might now of the finer things in life by having one of these arvelous instruments at their command.

"Of course, they were really family affairs. The old folks ould pedal away at 'Annie Laurie' and 'Silver Threads Among ne Gold' to their hearts' content – after the youngsters had heir turn at the 'William Tell Overture' and 'Paderewski's linuet.' Of course, the younger set probably preferred to pend their time with rolls like the 'Dill Pickles Rag' and Moonlight and Roses,' but only after they had absorbed their aily quota of culture would mother be likely to permit such undane listening!

"During World War I when, as in all periods of crisis, ntertainment of any variety was at a premium, the player iano neatly filled this bill by providing an easy means for afting into the air such tunes as 'Roses of Picardy,' 'My uddy,' and 'Goodbye Broadway, Hello France.' And players elped entertain the boys, too – one well-known battleship ad six of them on board! And when the boys came back, very player owner felt obliged to rush to his music store for ne latest release of 'How You Gonna Keep 'em Down on the arm – (after they've seen Paree).'

"In the homes of the wealthy, for they were the only eople who could afford their rather astronomical price tags, ere the reproducing pianos – the players capable of exact e-enactment of the performances of the great artists of the ay. At a time when the phonograph was barely capable of apturing and playing back squeaks and squawks, the eproducing piano was able to bring into the home magnificent erformances from an actual instrument, right there on the pot, exactly as the artist intended.

"With the tremendous advances in technology in recent ears, this situation has changed. Modern high-fidelity lectronic equipment has permitted every home to be a eritable music hall of the highest character. But for just plain un, coupled with the nostalgia which Americans in their eisure hours are so fond of seeking, the player piano is simply nequalled . . ."

History of the Player Piano

Although barrel-operated stringed instruments were known enturies earlier, the first roll-operated piano seems to have een conceived by Claude-Felix Seytre of Lyons, France, who atented in 1842 a piano-playing system which used a music neet made of stiff cardboard. Alexander Bain's 1848 English atent for a roll-operated piano describes a perforated roll of ormal thickness. In 1863 Fourneaux, a Frenchman, patented neumatically-operated player piano. Called the Pianista (a erm later used generically in France to describe other types of players), Fourneaux's instrument, unlike its predecessors, was made in commercial quantities and was sold with success. The Pianista was exhibited at the Centennial Exhibition in Philadelphia in 1876, and it caused much comment at the time.

Early devices were called piano players. They played upon the piano and were considered to be a separate device to be used with the piano. The "player piano" term came when the so-called "inner player," the piano which incorporated pneumatic devices within the piano case, was developed.

Push-up piano players were popular in the 1890's. Introduced in that decade, many different piano player makes were on the market by 1900. Wilcox & White of Meriden, Connecticut, Roth & Engelhardt (later, the Peerless Piano Player Company) of St. Johnsville, N.Y., the Farrand Organ Company of Detroit, Michigan, and others were heavy advertisers around the turn of the 20th century. The Cecilian, the brand of push-up piano player made by Farrand, was adopted by the public as a term used to describe general types of roll-operated pianos, including those by other makers. Later, the Pianola trademark would achieve that same distinction.

Credit for popularizing the piano player to its fullest goes to the Aeolian Company. By using multiple-page advertisements, Aeolian convinced magazine readers that its product, the Pianola, was almost as necessary as life itself! A 1902 Aeolian advertisement noted, in part: "The Pianola solves the problem of music in the home. Its production was the crowning achievement of musical activity in the century just closed. Within the home, where there is a Pianola, music reigns supreme, and every member of the household may be a performer . . . The Pianola is found to be a pleasure-giving instrument for all, both tyro and musician, enabling them to play on the piano with absolute correctness and with human feeling. More could not be asked of mortal ingenuity. Less never would have served to place the Pianola where it stands today – the greatest and most widely popular of musical inventions, the only practical solution of, and the Royal Road to, Music in the Home. The price of the Pianola is $250."

The same advertising theme was later used to sell thousands of Aeolian's Orchestrelle player reed organs and Duo-Art reproducing pianos.

Most early push-up piano players used 65-note rolls. In "Player Piano Treasury," the basic history of the player piano in America, Harvey Roehl relates that Melville Clark pioneered the introduction of the 88-note roll, the size later adopted (at a manufacturers' convention in Buffalo, N.Y., in 1908) as standard by the industry, in 1902.

Although inner-players or player pianos, as they came to be called universally, were made earlier (a Wilcox-White inner player piano and reed organ combination was made in 1892, for instance, and was sold commercially), the popularization of the piano with built-in mechanisms began shortly after 1900. By 1910 the old-style piano player was obsolete, although a number of manufacturers came out with 88-note push-up models and continued to sell them until about 1915.

From the early 1900's to 1930, approximately two million player pianos were made in America, according to an estimate provided by an Aeolian Company executive. The peak of popularity was in the early 1920's. Typical production figures quoted in "Player Piano Treasury" are: 1909, 34,495 player pianos; 1919, 166,091; 1921, 101,534; 1923, 170,549; 1925 143,831; 1927, 76,447; 1929, 17,336; 1931, 1,692; 1935,

418. In the year 1937 approximately 250 instruments were made. Since then, the player piano has enjoyed a revival – and as of the early 1970's, several thousand are made each year.

In the early 1900's most piano manufacturers viewed player pianos as a curiosity. Then, as Aeolian chalked up multimillion-dollar yearly sales and opened showrooms all over the world, the curiosity turned to interest, and then to participation. By 1915 most makers were producing a line of player pianos. By 1920 production of player models outstripped that of non-players.

Although Aeolian had most of the market, dozens of other piano manufacturers enjoyed success in the player piano field. Hundreds of different brands were sold – well-known nationally-distributed instruments as well as "stencil pianos" labeled with names of local piano merchants, department stores, and other retailers.

In Europe the market was equally active. Virtually every piano maker offered a series of player instruments. Pleyel of France and Hupfeld of Germany were among the best-selling makes. At one time 75% of the player pianos sold in Germany were products of the Ludwig Hupfeld firm!

Most American piano makers purchased the player actions from the Standard Pneumatic Action Company, the Auto Pneumatic Action Company, or another supplier of player mechanisms and installed them in various styles of instruments. Most popular by far was the regular 88-note upright style. Also sold were 65/88-note combination instruments, a type especially popular around 1910 when the 65-note rolls and 88-note rolls were both being sold. Foot-pumped player grand pianos were offered by a number of makers, but few were sold in comparison to upright models. Various player pianos with a built-in radio or phonograph were marketed, but not with great success.

88-note rolls were produced by dozens of different firms. The leading one, QRS, is very much in business today and currently offers a selection of over 1,000 different titles.

Player pianos, easily obtainable "for the taking away" in the 1950's, became scarcer in the 1960's as the demand for them increased. Today they still furnish an excellent way to enter the hobby. The principles learned by rebuilding a player piano are to a large degree applicable in the rebuilding of more sophisticated instruments – orchestrions and reproducing pianos, for instance. Player pianos are easy to use and are, as the advertisements used to say, "fun for the entire family."

**Push-up piano players were very popular around the turn of the 20th century. The Pianola, the Aeolian Company's entry in the field, was sold by multi-page color advertisements in popular American and European magazines.**

**In Europe, push-up piano players were sold by the tens of thousands by Ludwig Hupfeld and by Aeolian.**

**WHEREVER THERE IS A PIANO THERE SHOULD BE A PIANOLA**

THE PIANOLA multiplies the value of a piano, as it furnishes the medium by means of which any one, with or without technical knowledge, can play upon the piano practically any piece of music ever written for it. The musical classics of the great composers, the popular airs of the day, and both song and dance music are instantly available.

*It supplies technic*, the mechanical obstacle which has heretofore debarred the novice from musical expression, and which has been acquired only at the expense of unlimited application by the great musicians.

The sixty-five fingers of the Pianola strike the sixty-five keys of the piano by means of a pneumatic, according to the technic of the composition, the elasticity of the air producing a pliant, yielding, and remarkably sympathetic attack that is almost identical with that of the human fingers.

*Expression*, which alone crystallizes musical emotion, is entirely subject to the will of the performer. He may vary the touch, as a writer in the *Musical Courier* says,

"From the feathery touch of a Joseffy
to the lion's touch of Rubinstein."

In other words, the Pianola, through semi-automatic methods, makes possible an *individualized result.*

The fact that the Pianola has eliminated the technical requirements of the player while preserving his entire power of direction over expression, tempo, touch, and tone-coloring has excited the wonder of musical critics. It is significant that *the Pianola is the only piano-player which has ever been endorsed by musicians.*

It plays any piano. Any one can play it.

**PRICE, $250.00**

# PIANOLA *Points*

## *What it is, and what it will do*

THE PIANOLA is a piano-player. It is a long time since an invention has captured and charmed the public as the Pianola has done. It has piqued the imagination and stimulated the curiosity of *musician and layman alike.* Nothing is more amusing and naive than the surprise of the skeptical at its startling performances. It is hardly possible to believe until you hear. Piano-playing without an artist! How is it done? Well, in this case *hearing is believing.* Any one can hear it who will take the trouble to call; yes, and see it too. It is a small thing, an ornamental cabinet, beautifully proportioned, in oak or mahogany or ebony; you simply roll it up to the keyboard, and it is ready to play. There is a roll of paper to be inserted in sockets, and a pair of foot-treadles—levers which regulate degree of force and speed, as the player wills. Playing-directions appear upon the paper as the roll unwinds. The thing is complete. Every style of music—Beethoven, Mozart, Chopin, Liszt—available at a moment's notice; coon songs too, if you wish them; Sousa's marches, Herbert's and Sullivan's operas—everything your heart can desire.

To own a Pianola is to be independent of concert and opera, of musical seasons, of city opportunities, and of the whims of players and of the whole tribe of stumbling and helpless amateurs.

The point about the Pianola is that it is an instrument which gives *unending pleasure to young and old.* Everybody in the house can play it. Children become as familiar with good music as with nursery rhymes, and it interests them more. Every one who loves music should hear this wonderful instrument.

Visitors always welcome. Our instruments are gladly shown to the merely curious as well as to intending purchasers. If unable to call at our warerooms, write for Catalogue B, giving full description.

**The Aeolian Company**

18 West 23d Street
New York City

500 Fulton Street
Brooklyn, N. Y.

124 E. 4th Street
Cincinnati, O.

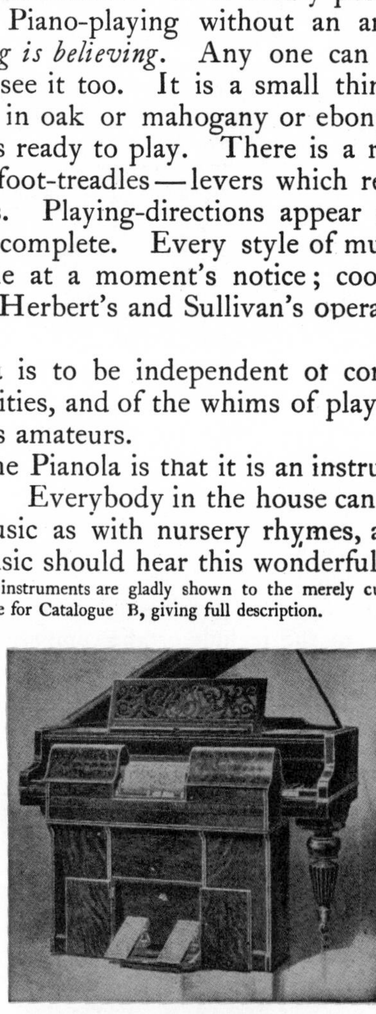

Pianola in use with grand piano
Price, $250

The Orchestrelle Co., London
The M. Steinert & Sons Co., Boston
C. J. Heppe & Son, Philadelphia
Lyon & Healy, Chicago
Wm. Knabe & Co., Washington
Wm. Knabe & Co., Baltimore
The B. Dreher's Sons Co., Cleveland
Kohler & Chase, San Francisco
Lauter Company, Newark
Grinnell Bros., Detroit
M. B. Wells Co., The Aeolian Music Co., Portland
L. E. N. Pratte & Co., Montreal
H. Tracy Balcom, Buffalo
Cluett & Sons, Albany
Cluett & Sons, Troy
C. C. Mellor Co., Pittsburg
J. W. Jenkins' Sons Music Co., Kansas City
Metropolitan Music Co., Minneapolis
W. J. Dyer & Bro., St. Paul
Whitney & Currier Co., Toledo
Denver Music Co., Denver
Walter D. Moses & Co., Richmond
Daynes Music Co., Salt Lake City

Fleming & Carnrick Press, New York

# PLAYER-PIANOS

During the last few years the self-playing piano, that is to say, the piano which is played by an automatic mechanism, has developed a wonderful popularity, and has had a great share in still further popularizing the pianoforte itself.

These mechanisms may be divided into the piano-player, which was the form in which they first became known, that is to say, a mechanism contained in a box more or less ornate, which is wheeled up to the piano, and which, with the aid of perforated rolls produces music of all kinds, ranging from popular dance music and songs to the highest kind of classical pieces. After that development, the next evolution has been the placing of the mechanism in the piano itself, in which case it forms what is known as the "player-piano." This form has practically superseded that of the separate mechanism which is only found in the second-hand trade and in remote districts.

What has been said of the pianoforte itself, with regard to the advisability of buying only instruments bearing the names of makers of repute and standing, will apply, of course, both to piano-players and player-pianos.

The manufacture of automatic instruments has now been brought to such perfection, and has been developed by some of our large manufacturers to such a point, that it is possible to obtain instruments at a moderate figure, which are reliable and will give good service, though what applies to the highest grades and highest priced pianos will also apply to the mechanical pianos; namely, that the purchaser must not expect the same artistic excellence in the lower priced instruments, as he has the right to expect in those that are higher priced, and therefore of higher grade.

The claims of the various manufacturers of these automatic pianos vary, for the reason that a great many inventions and improvements have been introduced by the various makers, some of which have great merit. Others, however, are merely what is called "talking points" and have no real or intrinsic value.

The mechanisms of these instruments vary greatly. Some are simple; others are very complicated. Some that are simple are also substantial, and so may be depended upon, as they possess durability.

Many instruments of this character differ in the manner in which the principle of the pneumatic action is applied.

At first the mechanism covered only forty-four notes of the piano; after that sixty-five note and eighty-eight note players appeared, the last-named operating the entire seven and a third octaves of the piano keyboard. This last named is now in general use.

At first the interior mechanism was applied almost exclusively to upright pianos, but in later years, after considerable experimenting, successful efforts have been made to incorporate it in grand pianos as well. A great many patents have been sought and granted for such incorporation.

We may say, therefore, that within a period of not much more than twenty years, the idea of a mechanically operated pianoforte has developed from a mechanism contained in an outside cabinet, playing only a part of the piano keyboard, to a grand piano which is also a player-piano in itself, in which the entire keyboard of eighty-eight notes is operated.

The development of these mechanical players has involved, on the part of the piano industry, an expenditure of vast sums of money in the way of experiments, and more particularly in the way of specially constructed machinery. Some of the best experts and men of the highest inventive genius have been engaged, and are still engaged, in developing and perfecting this form of instrument, which seems destined to be the popular form of piano in the future, especially as the fear of those who purchase such instruments, that if they get out of order it will be difficult to repair them, has been made groundless, owing to the increasing number of tuners, piano mechanics and others who are able to remedy any trouble that may arise.

The latest development in the world of mechanical players is an electric device which can be introduced by any competent tuner into any grand or upright piano which can then be made to play any of the standardized music rolls.

While in the earlier piano-players and even in the earlier player-pianos, much of the manner in which the piece was performed was restricted to what could be done with the music roll itself, of later years a number of excellent devices have been invented and successfully introduced for controlling the tempo and for introducing into a piece a number of effects and even *nuances*, so that the performance is not merely a mechanical one, but one whose effectiveness depends greatly upon the taste, and even musical

## PLAYER-PIANOS—Continued

knowledge, of the person operating the instrument. So it can be said with conviction that there are many player-pianos on the market to-day which give opportunity for artistic playing.

With this development of the instrument itself, there has been a corresponding development in the manner in which the music rolls themselves have been prepared. Some reproduce with startling accuracy the particular playing of particular artists of particular pieces, so that it is possible to-day, when the instrument is in the hands of a person of musical knowledge and taste, to almost reproduce exactly the rendition of standard works by individual artists of distinction.

That the player-piano, when properly handled, is a great aid to anyone desirous of acquiring a musical education cannot be controverted. It is easy to see how a young person, or even a child who desires to play a piece on the piano, can be greatly aided by playing the piece itself on the mechanical piano.

One distinct type of the player-piano is an instrument that is operated electrically; that is to say, all that is necessary for a performance of the music is to insert the music roll and turn on the electric current by shifting the power from a switch, or by dropping a coin in a slot in the piano case, from which many of the latter instruments have become known as "coin operated pianos" or "electric player-pianos."

Within the last year a movement was inaugurated for the physical development and commercial exploitation of the electrically driven player-piano. Fostered by THE MUSIC TRADES, this movement was brought to the attention of the allied electric light and power and electrical manufacturing interests, as united in the "National Electric Light Association" and, receiving the official endorsement of that body, became crystallized in an association known as "The National Electric Piano Makers."

The purpose of the new organization is to band the electrically driven player-piano manufacturers together to promote the interests of producers of an electrical-current-consuming device.

Much attention has been devoted by some of the manufacturers to these types of instruments, and during the past few years striking advances have been made in their construction.

While the expression in the case of an electric piano is not as thorough as that of a piano which is worked by the operator himself, still the musical effect produced by the better class of the electrically operated player-pianos is such that they have won considerable popularity for use in restaurants, cafés, seaside resorts, theatres and other public places.

Sometimes these electric pianos are equipped with other instruments, such as drums, cymbals and triangles, and have been piped to produce flute and violin effects, and have been put into theatres to take the place of human orchestras.

It would seem that the general tendency in the piano industry will be to continue to progress on the line of the automatic instrument, though it is not believed that these can be produced much more reasonably and sold at much more reasonable prices than those at which they are to-day offered the public.

All that has been said with regard to the care of the piano and that it should not be exposed to extremes of heat or cold, that it should not be exposed to dampness, and also should be kept free from dirt, will naturally apply with even greater force to a mechanical instrument, for the reason that the mechanism is more complicated.

To the people living in isolated localities, or in homes that are far from the city, these mechanical instruments have been a boon. They have not only cheered the homes, especially during the long winter nights, but they have introduced beautiful music, and even the works of great masters, where they had never been heard before.

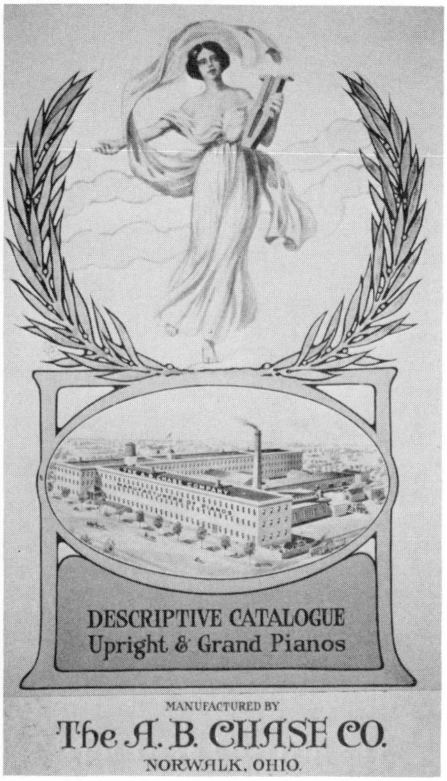

These early player pianos, manufactured in the early 1900's by the A.B. Chase Company, featured 65-note, 88-note, and 65/88-note combination models. Note the unusual position of the roll. Similarly-placed roll mechanisms were used by several other manufacturers, including Chickering and Hupfeld.

Gulbransen Trade Mark.

Above: "Easy to Play," the trademark of the Gulbransen player piano, was familiar to Americans during the 'teens and 'twenties. Today, Gulbransen player pianos, when rebuilt, are indeed easy to play due to a specially-designed valve system.

Right: Advertisement of Melville Clark. The Clark factory in DeKalb, Illinois, later became part of the Rudolph Wurlitzer enterprise. In the pre-Wurlitzer years Clark made many interesting instruments, including Apollo reproducing and expression pianos (in several varieties) and player pianos, including the novel 58-, 65-, 70-, 82-, and 88-note combination instrument shown at the right. An interesting upright Clark player piano embodied a disc phonograph.

58, 65, 70, 82, 88
NOTE
FIVE PLAYERS
IN ONE
The Apollo Grand Piano Player, Only One of Its Kind
The APOLLO PLAYER is the only player that gives access to all of the libraries of perforated music, irrespective of width or make, and the MELVILLE CLARK PIANO CO. is the only manufacturing establishment making an 88 NOTE PLAYER and cutting the music for it.
FOURTEEN other acknowledged points of superiority, including the transposing device found only in the MELVILLE CLARK player instruments and the spring motor enabling the re-rolling of music without pumping.
All of the new instruments are provided with a telescopic arrangement whereby 65 note music can be used. This feature makes the instrument the only one on the market playing all rolls, 58, 65 and 88 note music alike. With the new divided pedal railing either the treble or the bass may be modified at will.
IF YOU ARE NOT KEEPING PACE WITH APOLLO IMPROVEMENTS PERMIT US HELP YOU CATCH UP
THE MELVILLE CLARK PIANO COMPANY
STEINWAY HALL :: :: :: :: :: :: :: CHICAGO

PLAYER MECHANISM SHOWING FRONT VIEW OF TOP AND BOTTOM ACTIONS AND PLAYING LEVERS

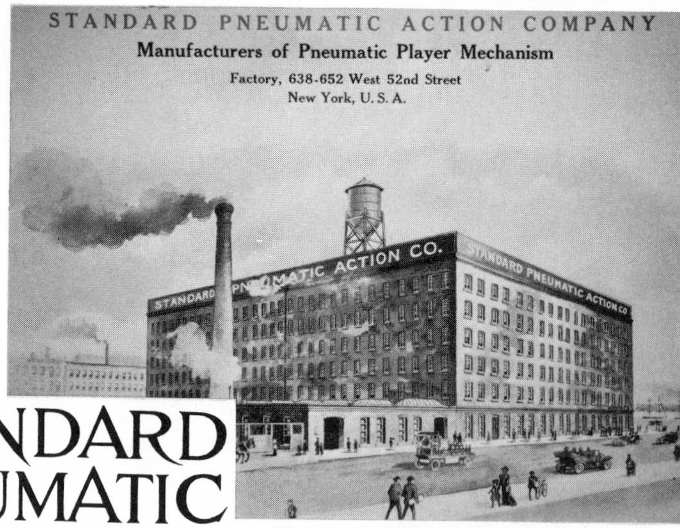


# STANDARD PNEUMATIC PLAYER ACTION

**The Standard Pneumatic Action was used in a large number of different player piano brands. The firm also made roll mechanisms for photoplayers (such as those used on Wurlitzer and American Photo Player Co. 88-note systems).**

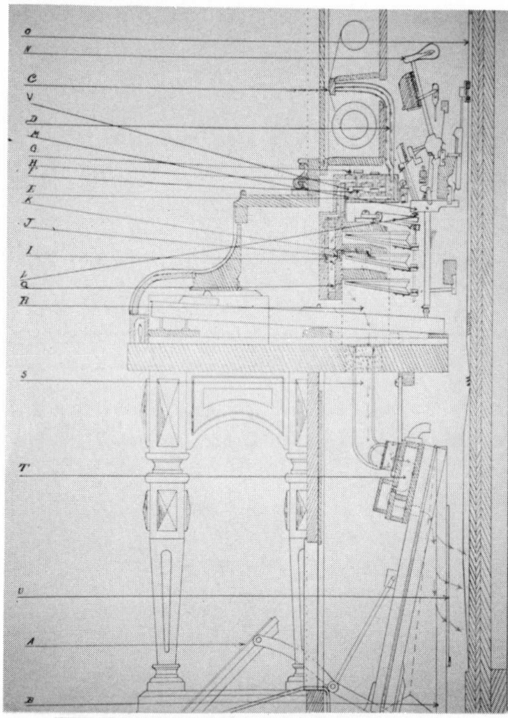

THE Red Arrows on Cut 5 indicate how the air is taken in. Pressure of the foot on the Treadles "A" causes the Feeders "B" to expand and thereby create a state of partial vacuum in the Bellows Chest "T" and Action Chest "Q". When a perforation in the paper registers with the corresponding hole in the Tracker Bar, air is taken in and carried down through the Metal Tubes "D" into the Primary Channels "E". It should be borne in mind that Valve Chambers "Q" and "T" are connected with the exhaust. Pressure of the air at "F" causes the Primary Pouches, or Diaphragms as they are sometimes called, to be expanded, thus forcing the Primary Valve Buttons "G" to open away from their upper seats and at the same time closing their lower or inside seats. This allows the air to be taken in again through the Primary outside inflation Channel "H," through which it is forced against the Secondary Pouch "I" or Diaphragm. This Pouch is in turn expanded and likewise causes the Secondary Valve "J" to be opened, which causes the air to be drawn from the Pneumatics "K". By the collapse of these Pneumatics, the Flexible Striking Finger "L", which rests under the Piano Wippen "M", is raised and this in turn causes the Piano Hammer "N" to strike against the Piano Strings "O".

When the Secondary Valve "J" is operated, causing the Striking Pneumatic "K" to close, the air is drawn through the Action Chest "Q," through the Wind Trunk "R", following down through the Rubber Tubing "S" into what is known as the Pump Channel "T" and from there into the Feeding Pumps or Feeders "B" and is exhausted through the Palate "U" on the outside of the Pump.

IT is universally conceded that the STANDARD PNEUMATIC ACTION COMPANY has reached its present eminent position—that of producing more Player Actions than any institution in the world, through turning out a product remarkable not only for its wonderful playing qualities but for simplicity and durability as well. There may be occasions, however, where through various causes, slight corrections and repairs become necessary and the instructions given herein, if carefully followed, should enable anyone, who is at all accustomed to the use of ordinary tools, to make the requisite repair.

The price-card upon this up-to-date player-piano conveys the impression that the instrument being offered is a modern Angelus piano. But the fact is that the price-card refers to an old style 58-note Angelus Cabinet Piano-Player (the kind you push up in front of an upright piano, as shown below), and not to the player-piano displayed in the window.

This strategem is practiced all over the country by Wrong Method dealers, who use for this purpose all other well-known cabinet players, such as Pianola, Apollo, Cecilian and Simplex.

*The Angelus Cabinet Player in this instance was twelve years old.*

The card on the player illustrated above is meant to give the impression that the present price of the instrument in the window is $212. As a matter of fact, it does not refer to the Pianola in the window, but to an old-style 65-note player in some out-of-the-way corner of the store. Note also that the card reads, "Reduced $212," and not, "Reduced to $212." Many Wrong Method dealers make constant use of this means of securing prospects.

*This is the Old Style Pianola referred to on the price card in the window.*

| PIANOLA PIANO NEW | | | |
|---|---|---|---|
| Original Price | - | - | $675 |
| Reduced | - | - | 212 |
| Price NOW | - | - | $463 |

This window illustrates a wily ensnarement used by certain dealers to induce owners of "silent" pianos to convert them into player-pianos. This card attracts piano owners who cannot play, for it seems a delightfully small expense for what is deemed a costly luxury. Upon inquiry they find that while the mere installation is only $40, the player action is probably $250 additional, and the cartage $10 besides. Sometimes the Wrong Method dealer actually installs a player-action in the hoodwinked purchaser's old piano before the whole story is told.

*A dealer who stoops to such methods to bring you into his store would hardly be a safe man with whom to deal.*

| | | | |
|---|---|---|---|
| Player Action | - | - | $250 |
| Installation | - | - | 40 |
| Cartages | - | - | 10 |
| TOTAL COST | | - | $300 |

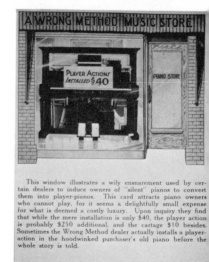

**Shenanigans in the piano business, especially the market for used instruments, are nothing new. If you think that the "Steinway grand — reduced — $1200" ad you've just read in the paper is a new way of selling, then read what "The Limelight" had to say about the "Wrong Method Music Store." This was back in 1915!**

"The Player Piano Finds a Voice." This pamphlet issued by the Standard Pneumatic Action Company features a disc phonograph system which conveniently fits into the upper left part of the piano case. Few such combinations were actually sold, however.

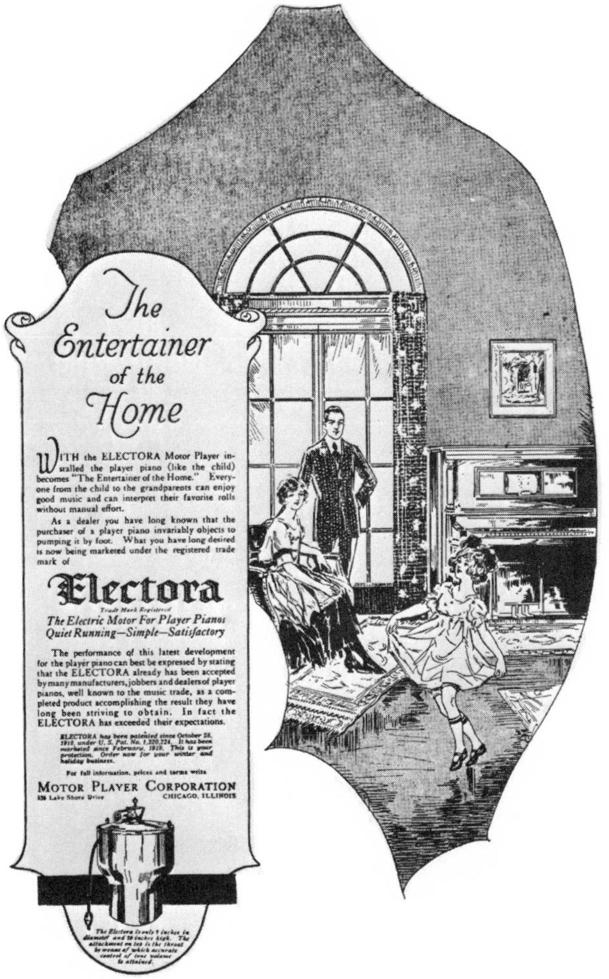


The Electora vacuum pump eliminated foot pumping. Note that the fine print of the advertisement refers to foot-pumping as "manual effort."

A related device, the Moto-Playo Bench, which incorporated a vacuum unit into a piano bench, achieved limited sales during the 1920's also.

The Weydig Piano Corporation offered its Radi-O-Player, a player piano which incorporated a radio. Such combination instruments, while fine in theory, did poorly in the marketplace.

# THE STORY AND CLARK PLAYER PIANO

This is an instrument for everyone who loves music, especially those who are musical, but are unable to play the ordinary piano. Anyone from a little child up to old age can operate it, so easily does it play. By a little study most beautiful effects can be obtained, and all thoughts of mechanical music are quickly eliminated.

Player Piano Open, Ready to Play Automatically

The Story & Clark Player Piano is the result of over twelve years of careful study and experimental work, and is today, in our judgment, as well as of hundreds of satisfied customers, perfect in every detail. It is somewhat different from the majority of so-called player pianos, in the fact that we build it in its entirety in our own shop. We do not purchase the player action in the open market and install it in one of our regular styles of pianos and call it our player piano, as is done in most instances, but it is built from the raw materials to completion by ourselves. Everyone must realize that a player piano will be used probably ten times as much as an ordinary piano, for *everybody can play it.* We therefore build a piano especially to withstand this extra usage. This is not customary, and is too vital a point to be overlooked when selecting a player piano. We have won and maintained a reputation for building pianos that endure. When we make a piano it has honor—brightness to the last particular—and our player pianos conform to the same rule. Throughout the entire instrument the greatest degree of simplicity consistent with practicability is sought for.

There are many exclusive features incorporated and utilized that have been perfected by years of work: In operation, a slide below the keys is pulled forward and the pumping pedals come from their hiding place; the slide in the music-swing is pushed back; the roll of music inserted; the cover over the levers is dropped down, and with a few strokes of the pedals perfect music, from the thunder of Wagner to the tune of the hour, is at the command of the operator. Reverse the operation and the pedals disappear, all mechanism of the player is hidden, and you have the usual piano except for the extreme beauty of case design, ready to play by hand, and one that the most fastidious musician will delight in.

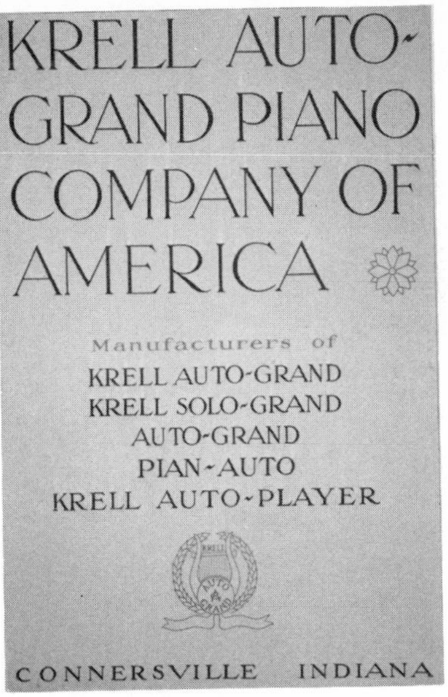

KRELL AUTO-GRAND PIANO COMPANY OF AMERICA

Manufacturers of

KRELL AUTO-GRAND
KRELL SOLO-GRAND
AUTO-GRAND
PIAN-AUTO
KRELL AUTO-PLAYER

CONNERSVILLE INDIANA

## KRELL PLAYER-PIANO

The truly marvelous tone-quality of the Krell Player-Piano, mellow, full-voiced, resonant throughout the scale, yet also truly reponsive to the mood and motif of the music, is always provocative of praise from appreciative musicians.

The Krell Player-Piano is first-of-all a magnificent piano. In every item of its construction lies the making of fine tone-quality. In the Krell Player-Piano is built a mechanically perfect pneumatic player mechanism manufactured in our own factories and installed exclusively in our pianos.

The Krell Player-Piano is sensitive to every impulse of the musician at the keyboard. All the beauties of musical phrasing and artistic interpretation are obtained at will through the pedaling. The pedal-action is unusually light and easy, and instantaneous in the control of accent and expression. Patented features of construction, to be found exclusively in our player-pianos, enable the novice to play as beautifully as would a thorough master of the difficult technique and art of the pianist.

The magnificent tones of the Krell Player-Piano are especially appreciated in the home of the true lover of music. Pleasant hours beguiled by the wondrous music of this noble instrument pass into years of constant satisfaction in the possession of a player so handsome, so serviceable and durable.

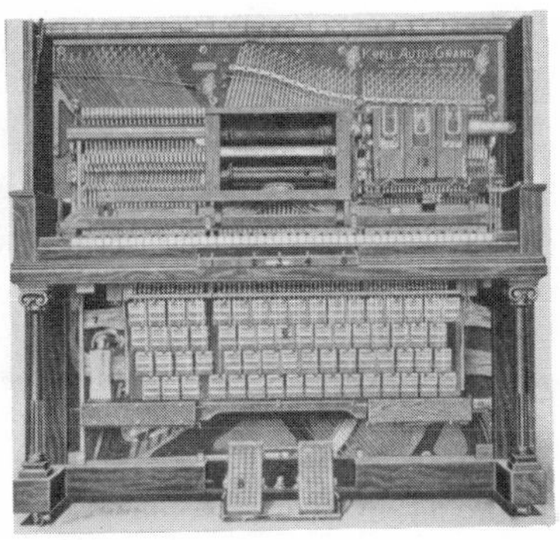

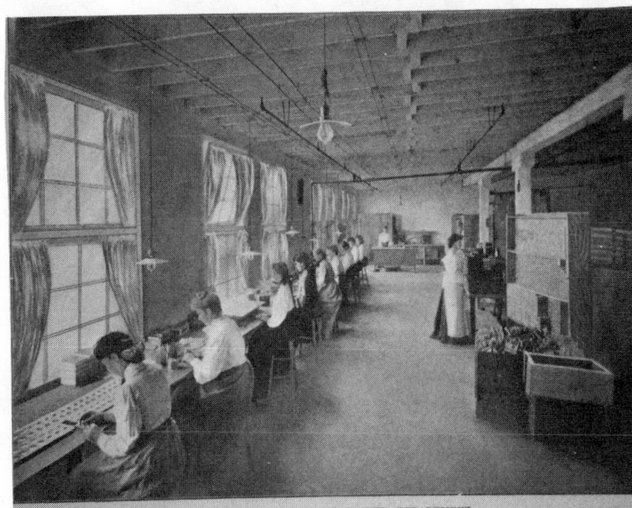

PNEUMATIC ROOM IN THE PLAYER DEPARTMENT

**Illustrations from a Krell player piano catalogue of the 'teens. The instrument with post lamps pictured at the far left is the first cousin to a "nickelodeon" piano, at least in appearance! Note what a fine job the photograph retoucher has done by adding lace curtains (indeed!) to the windows of the pneumatic room in the Krell factory! Below is shown the pneumatic system of a Krell piano. The pneumatics are of the unit type and are secured by two screws. A similar easy-to-service arrangement was used by Link and a few other manufacturers.**

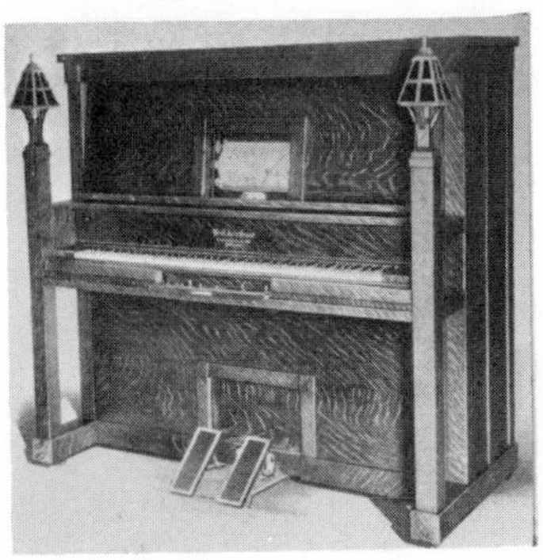

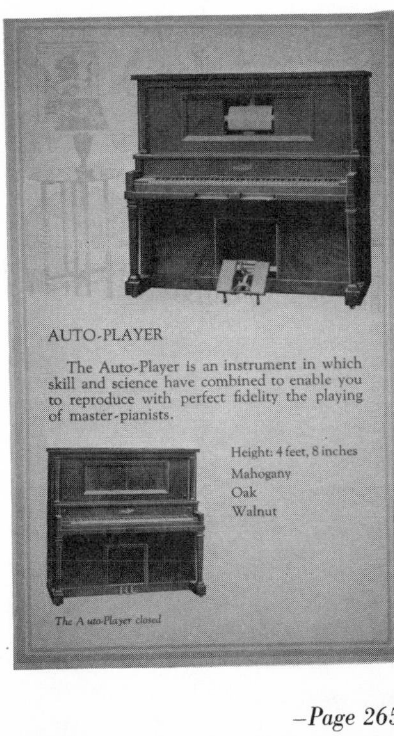

AUTO-PLAYER

The Auto-Player is an instrument in which skill and science have combined to enable you to reproduce with perfect fidelity the playing of master-pianists.

Height: 4 feet, 8 inches
Mahogany
Oak
Walnut

*The Auto-Player closed*

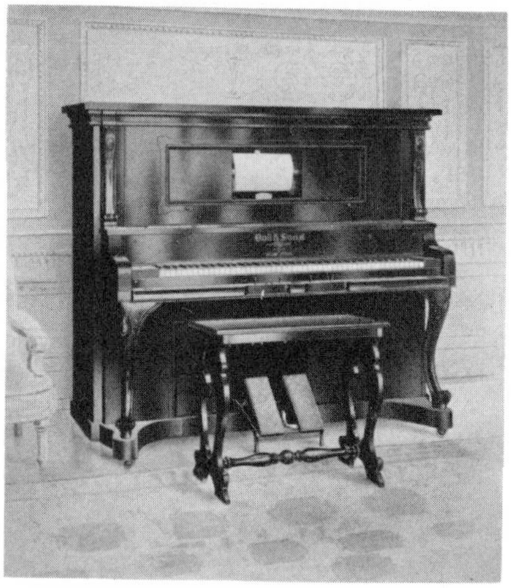

## The Doll & Sons' Player Piano and How to Play It.

SIMPLICITY is the keynote of the Doll & Sons' Player; you are not compelled to keep your eyes on a number of stops that confuse instead of helping you. Only four levers and two buttons—the two latter marked "S.B." and "S.T." respectively. These four levers and buttons are scientifically arranged in the front of the piano, so you have, at all times, the piano under control. Reading from left to right, the levers and buttons operate as follows: *loud pedal lever, soft bass button, soft treble button, soft pedal lever, tempo lever, re-wind lever.*

The re-wind lever is only used when wanting to rewind the roll of music when finished, or to attach a new roll. It has nothing to do with the time or expression, or the method of playing.

One of the most important features of the Doll & Sons' Player is the tempo lever—for this controls the changes in time. By the use of this lever you accelerate or retard, emphasize any chord or note by a quick, short turning to the left—play the music as you personally would interpret it—give it any phase or change of meaning that you wish. Hold between the index and second finger, and move back and forth. Almost at once you will learn the value of sound, learn to play with expression, and without any of the mechanical sound which would naturally result did you play a selection always in the same unchanging tempo. To start the music in its proper tempo, merely set the pointer to the name that corresponds with the time printed on the music-roll.

The bass and treble buttons on the Doll & Sons' Player make an advance as radical in the construction of piano-players as it is possible to conceive. Any selection may be played in the bass, and then reversed and played in the treble, for by pressing the bass button the melody is carried in the treble, while by using the treble button, the melody is given by the bass. The variations possible by this manipulation are practically limitless, and many selections can be given almost new readings—depending entirely on the whim of the performer.

In nearly every piano-player, the work of using the pedals has nothing to do with the expression of the music, the pumping merely providing air to operate; but with the Doll & Sons' Player a newer effect is possible. By the use of the pedals on the Doll & Sons' Player the performer can absolutely control the expression, depending entirely on whether he uses hard or soft work on the pedals. The advantages of this are manifest—the eyes and hands may be given over unrestricted to the reading of the music and the control of the levers and buttons. The mere pumping can control the expression. The best effect on the pedal is produced by an ankle movement, putting the feet well upon the pedals and resting more on the ball of the foot than on the heel, and working the pedals alternately. No great effort need be expended—a little knack makes the playing of the Doll & Sons' Player almost without exertion.

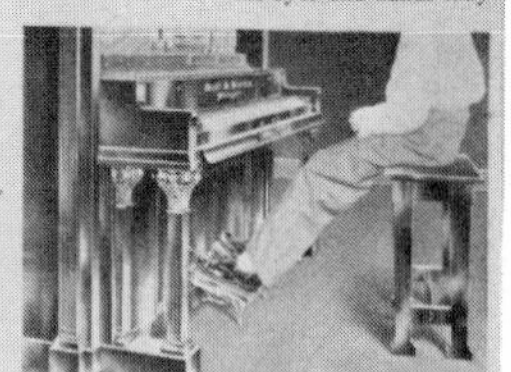

Always roll your music tightly when finished and keep the music from damp places or from near radiators. A dry place will preserve the rolls indefinitely. To place the roll in the piano, hold roll so that the name of the selection faces you, then put the pin on the left hand end of the roll in the sliding-pocket on the left side of the spool-shaped box. Put the winged pin end in the grooved socket on the right hand side, and throw the re-wind lever over to the left, which releases the take-up spool; then hitch the loop, on the end of the music, to the hook on the take-up spool. Now wind the music with your hand until you see the tempo-mark printed on the roll, then throw back the re-wind lever to its first position, and you are ready to play.

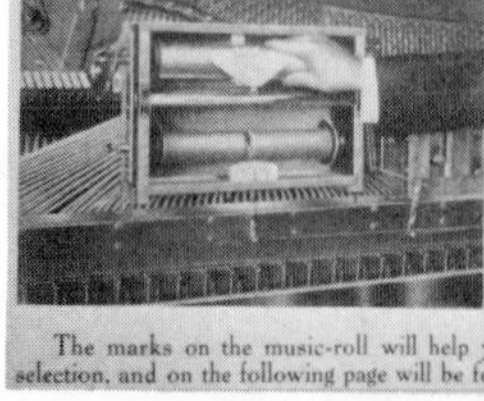

The indicator in front of the music spool box (illustrated on page 16) should be moved to correspond with the tempo marked on the music-roll. At the beginning of every music-roll the tempo is marked—merely move the indicator to correspond with that mark.

The marks on the music-roll will help you to a full understanding of the selection, and on the following page will be found a definition of all of the terms printed on the rolls. When a dotted blue line, for instance, starts at the right, or center, and then runs to the left, it means the music should gradually soften, and the soft lever and soft pedal should be used. When the line runs to the right, the music should grow louder. It is a mistake, though, to hold the loud

lever in one position when the line runs to the right—move the lever back and forth so some change of expression follows. The effect is not only better, but gives greater tone-color to your playing.

Remember that your own individuality plays a considerable part in the interpretation of the Doll & Sons' Player—that your own mood can really be reproduced in many of the classic selections. Familiarity with the levers and the terms shown on the music-rolls are all that is necessary—the operation is so easy that a child can play the Doll & Sons' Player, not only without fatigue, but without the least technical knowledge of music.

**Dynamic Marks**

| | |
|---|---|
| Very loud, | **FF** |
| Loud, | **F** |
| Moderately loud, | **MF** |
| Soft, | **P** |
| Very soft, | **PP** |
| Accented, | **SF or <** |
| Gradually louder, | **Cres** |
| Gradually softer, | **Dim** |

**Marks Indicating Change of Tempo**

| | |
|---|---|
| Gradually faster, | **Accel** |
| Gradually slower, | **Ritard** |
| Faster (more movement), | **Piu Mosso** |
| Slower (less movement), | **Meno Mosso** |
| Hold or pause, | 𝄐 |
| Resume the original tempo, | **Tempo** |

**Marks Indicating Tempo**

| | |
|---|---|
| The fastest tempo, | **Presto** |
| Fast, | **Allegro** |
| Moderately fast, | **Allegretto** |
| In moderate tempo, | **Moderato** |
| Rather slow, | **Andante** |
| A little slower than Andante, | **Andantino** |
| Very slow, | **Adagio** |
| The slowest tempo, | **Lento** |

**Marks Indicating Style**

| | |
|---|---|
| In broad style, generally very slow, | **Largo** |
| Majestic, | **Maestoso** |
| Lively and usually fast, | **Vivace** |
| Agitated, | **Agitato** |
| With movement, | **Con Moto** |
| With fury, | **Con Fuoco** |
| Animated, sometimes gradually faster, | **Animato** |

# Behning

## PLAYER PIANOS

### BEHNING QUALITY IS AN INHERITANCE

BEHNING Pianos and Player Pianos have always been made by a Behning. Created by an ancestor of the present Behning family, Behning quality is a product of the days when piano makers, unhampered by the spirit of commercialism, strove for artistic perfection with untiring and undivided zeal.

Proud of the Art of their ancestor, the present House of Behning has ever sought to maintain and enhance the quality standards that made the Behning one of the world's leading pianos.

Built into the Style 7 Player Piano are the ideals and experience gained by sixty years of high-grade piano making. Its quality is excelled by no other player, regardless of name or price.

Like all other Behning Player Pianos the Style 7 is Behning built from start to finish, including the player action which is of the approved single valve type.

It is equipped with every approved device required for the artistic expression of music, including the unique Behning Transposing Device.

Behning Player Pianos are famous for the remarkable flexibility of the pedal control. It is so sensitive to the foot pressure that the most delicate shadings may be produced without recourse to any other controlling device. No other make of player has this feature so perfectly developed.

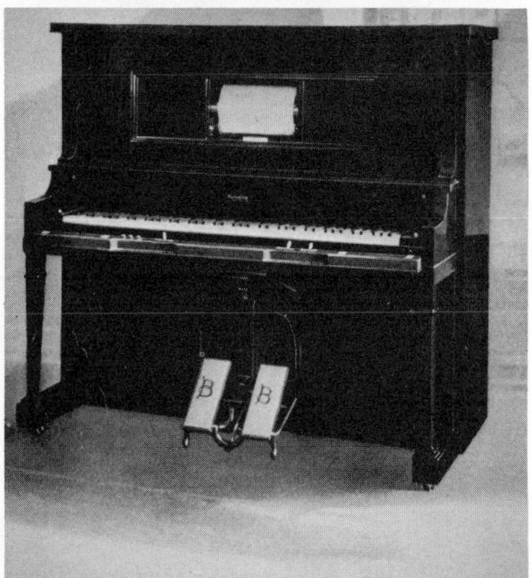

STYLE 7 PLAYER PIANO

Height, 4 feet 6½ inches
Depth, 2 feet 5 inches
Length, 5 feet 2½ inches

*Mahogany, Walnut and Oak—Polished or Art Finish*

# MARSHALL

## PLAYER-PIANOS

*BUILT TO MEET THE REQUIREMENTS OF THE GREAT MAJORITY OF PLAYER PURCHASERS*

The broad experience of the men behind the MARSHALL is assurance of the high quality of the product. Prices are right.

*Ask about the Agency.*

MARSHALL
J. P. SEEBURG, President
PIANO COMPANY

1508-1514 Dayton Street. CHICAGO

UNIVERSAL PIANO CO.

MANUFACTURERS OF

# UNIVERSAL

STRAIGHT 65-NOTE STRAIGHT 88-NOTE

## PLAYER PIANOS

FACTORY AND OFFICE

190-192 SOUTHERN BOULEVARD, NEW YORK

UNIVERSAL 88-NOTE PLAYER PIANO

INTERIOR CONSTRUCTION

UNIVERSAL 65-NOTE PLAYER PIANO

Open Player

UNIVERSAL 88-NOTE PLAYER PIANO

# FRENCH

## & SONS

## Artistic Pianos and Players

JESSE FRENCH & SONS PIANO CO.

NEW CASTLE, IND.

WRITE FOR CATALOG AND LIST OF TERRITORY YET OPEN

JESSE FRENCH
PIANOS and PLAYERS
are *STANDARD—HIGH-GRADE*

# Schaff Bros. Co.

## High Grade Pianos and Player-Pianos

Are noted for purity and power of tone, responsiveness to touch, and all around excellency. A moderate priced leader since 1868.

## Link & Son and Oliver PIANOS

for the dealer who is looking for something in a reliable piano at a moderate price, pianos that are real money makers.

SCHAFF BROS. CO.

CHICAGO, ILL. HUNTINGTON, IND.

# Bush & Lane Pianos

Bush & Lane Cecilian Player-Pianos
Victor Pianos
Victor Cecilian Player-Pianos

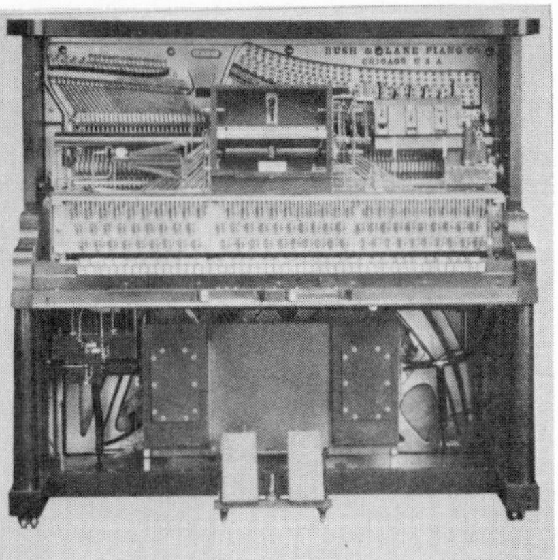

THE CECILIAN PLAYER MECHANISM
View of Bush & Lane Cecilian with front removed to show the principal working parts of the player action.

BUSH & LANE CECILIAN, STYLE 18

VICTOR CECILIAN, STYLE C

BUSH & LANE CECILIAN, STYLE 20

BUSH & LANE CECILIAN, STYLE 22

Starr—Style "H"

STYLE 20

Style R.P.
Davenport-Treacy Player Piano

Claes O. Friberg, of Copenhagen, Denmark, accompanies QRS roll No. 8854, the "Ivory Rag," on the piano. Claes, a personal friend of (and co-director of Denmark's Mekanisk Musik Museum with) the author, provided valuable assistance during the preparation of this book by gathering information about many of the European automatic musical instrument firms.

# REPRODUCING PIANOS

## Reproducing Pianos
## —and—
## Expression Pianos

# REPRODUCING PIANOS

*by David L. Saul*

## Introduction

Unique among mechanical musical instruments in many ways, the reproducing pianos deserve a large measure of distinction for the design refinements and sophisticated technology within their otherwise normal-appearing cases.

The really paramount feature of these remarkable instruments, however, is their music – phenomenally lifelike in character – which demands hearing to be fully appreciated. Once nearly forgotten by a generation reeling from the impact of mass entertainment media, reproducing pianos are now enjoying a vigorous rebirth of interest among collectors, historians, and music buffs. The virtuosity of such keyboard greats as Rachmaninoff, Paderewski, Hofmann, and a host of others once again is called forth to be heard on a growing number of meticulously restored instruments now carefully preserved in collections around the world.

The musical significance of the reproducing piano was succinctly stated by Josef Hofmann over a half century ago. Writing a testimonial for M. Welte & Sons he said: "The incomparable Welte Mignon art piano has opened an eventful future before the musical world. Henceforth the piano player will be on a level with the productive artist in regard to the imperishability of his work. What a loss it means to us not to have had [the reproducing piano] long ago! But what a blessing it will prove to future generations!" It seems incredible even in today's age of technological miracles that a great pianist's art could ever be adequately represented by perforations on a paper roll. Yet several decades ago this seemingly impossible task was accomplished with a remarkable degree of success. Virtually every great pianist of the 'teens and the 1920's not only recorded his playing for one or another of the competing brands of reproducing pianos, but he emphatically endorsed the recordings thus produced as exact replicas of his personal playing – perfect in every detail!

The actual degree of "perfection" thus achieved is even today subject to controversy. A growing consensus, however, tends to support the reproducer's claim to being a valid artistic medium, even if it doesn't unfailingly attain the soaring heights of absolute perfection heralded by the early advertisements. One of these ads, for example, insisted that the artist's personal touch was actually conveyed (presumably by phantom hands illustrated therein) to the keys of the piano!

The brand names of "Welte Mignon," "Duo-Art," and "Ampico" identified the products of the German firm of M. Welte & Sons (also with a factory in the U.S.A. and, later, a licensee of Welte mechanisms to over 100 brands of pianos), New York's Aeolian Corporation, and the American Piano Company, respectively.

Welte, Duo-Art, and Ampico – the "big three" – dominated most of the American market, although a number of others made less spectacular appearances. In Europe the Hupfeld "Dea," the Philipps "Duca," and several other types of reproducing pianos enjoyed success in the marketplace.

Each manufacturing firm installed its respective mechanism in a selected line of pianos either controlled by the firm or having more or less exclusive business arrangements for installations of this type. Practically every famous make of piano could be obtained in the 1920's with one or another of the reproducing mechanisms installed in it. Steinway pianos with Duo-Art mechanisms, Mason & Hamlin instruments with Ampico mechanisms, and Baldwin pianos with Welte (Licensee) mechanisms are just three of well over a hundred examples. Both upright and grand models were available in a wide variety of sizes and furniture styles. Some instruments, comparatively few in number, were housed in elaborate art cases or were made to order with other distinguishing features. These examples, rarer still today, are considered particularly desirable by collectors.

Far too expensive to achieve mass popularity (only the wealthy could afford the $1000 to $4000 price tag of a reproducing piano – twice to several times the cost of ordinary foot-pumped home player pianos), the reproducers nevertheless sold well in pre-depression times when prosperity abounded and there was little serious competition from other home entertainment media capable of producing realistic musical performances. In an era when sales of common foot-pumped players were counted in the millions, reproducing pianos were sold by the thousands.

Although generally well constructed, the reproducing system parts fell victim to the ravages of time more quickly than did the pianos in which they were installed. After decades of neglect these mechanisms ceased to work at all or, even worse, they played so erratically as to arouse contempt and disrespect. The pitiful sounds evoked by tired machinery frequently turned apathy to scorn and harm was done to the artistic reputation of this type of instrument. The distinction, so important, between the foot-pumped player piano and the soulful and artistic reproducing piano was forgotten and both types were equated to be something worthy of curiosity but not of serious musical ability.

Many reproducing pianos were stripped of their reproducing parts, thus reverting to the status of ordinary pianos. This unfortunate practice is on the decline now, but in recent decades countless numbers of really fine instruments have been impaired in this manner. To counter the damage some resourceful enthusiasts have managed to locate and re-install mechanisms in their former instruments. However, the fact remains that tons of priceless parts were carelessly discarded and are now permanently lost.

While collectors have acquired many fine examples of reproducing pianos, a number of instruments still remain undiscovered and turn up from time to time in private homes, storage warehouses, schools, and in other locations. In recent years the number of discoveries, particularly of the rarer and more desired types, has slowed to a trickle – portending a day, perhaps not too distant, when finding one of these will be an unusual event.

As of this writing, reproducing pianos, while scarce, are not exceedingly rare. The enthusiast with some patience can acquire a fine example from an instrument dealer, from another collector, or from another source.

### A Closer Look

Reproducing mechanisms were designed and built by competing companies, each with its own set of patents designed either to circumvent or improve upon the designs of others. As a result, none of the systems is compatible. Duo-Art rolls can be played only on a piano with the Duo-Art mechanism, Ampico rolls can be played only on Ampico pianos, and so on. Of course, this had the economic advantage of providing a captive market for the rolls designed for each. As a result, prices for rolls often were $2 to $4 each (Welte charged up to $20 for some performances!) in an era in which a dollar was worth a dollar.

All of the systems, although differing widely in mechanical design, are similar in concept and purpose. They also share the common principle of pneumatic operation with power supplied (except in rare cases) by some form of electrically driven vacuum pump. The reproducing piano, in whatever form, owes much of its mechanical heritage to the common foot-pumped player piano, although the reproducing piano should never be thought of as merely being a player piano with a few extra devices added. The reproducing piano incorporates, particularly in later models, a level of engineering refinement placing it in a class far removed from its mass produced cousin.

The technical feature most directly responsible for the reproducer's distinguished musical character is precise control of loudness or dynamics. Each type of mechanism utilizes some arrangement of automatic intensity or volume controls capable of extremely rapid action. These automatic controls respond to special "expression" perforations in the music roll – perforations coded in some methodical way to correspond to the loudness of each particular note, chord, or group of notes originally played by the recording artist. The aforementioned automatic controls, under direct influence of the music roll's expression perforations, cause the piano to play as loudly or softly, at any instant in time, as the artist did while making the recording. Some way of pneumatically partitioning the keyboard into separate bass and treble sections is also commonly used to divide the musical performance more or less evenly between two independent loudness controlling devices. The notes to be played appear in a conventional manner on the reproducing roll, much as they would on an ordinary player piano roll. The expression coding usually appears as a sprinkling of perforations along either edge. The recording of the pianist's pedaling is coded there also.

While no two pianos ever respond in exactly the same way, the intensities of successive notes are brought to relative levels in accordance with a pattern closely following the rise and fall of dynamics in the original performance, with results that are aesthetically pleasing. With operating vacuum stages and relative dynamic levels adjusted for best musical results, one might suppose that a performance obtained by playing a roll is not unlike the recording artist's actual "in person" performance.

Perhaps the most frequent criticism of reproducing pianos is aimed at their theoretical inability to accent (i.e., to make noticeably louder) one particular note among several struck simultaneously in the same section of the keyboard. This turns out to be of relatively little practical concern since human pianists find it very difficult to strike several notes at exactly the same time with different forces applied. With the fingers of one hand it is all but impossible. The problem is therefore largely academic. In the few cases that do arise, a trivially small displacement in time (as evidenced by a displacement of the perforation on the roll) allows the accented note to be struck at the proper intensity. The result is quite convincing and acceptable.

Pedaling has been another point of contention with some critics. Concern about this is not without justification in view of so-called "half pedaling" and other subtle effects sometimes employed by artists. Suffice it to say here that the roll makers were well aware of fine points such as this. Stimulated by intense competition, the respective companies took great pains to see that all available resources were utilized to achieve results that were musically proper. Although pedal mechanisms were not designed for half-pedaling, their action and timing were accurately predictable. The music roll editors quickly learned how to exploit these and other characteristics of reproducing mechanisms to obtain very subtle musical effects, thus turning out rolls that met with the enthusiastic approval of both the recording artists and the public.

Musicians, rather than technical personnel, were commonly employed as editors. One might suppose that the recording artists – who generally had to approve release of their performances – would have withheld any that were obviously deficient in pedaling or other musical qualities. The result is a legacy of rolls containing music nearly "too good to be true" (mistakes were also carefully removed by editing) while at the same time preserving the dynamics, phrasing, rubato, and many other musical qualities that make each pianist's playing uniquely his own.

### The Old and the Renewed

Ownership of a reproducing piano can be a rich and rewarding experience. A newcomer on the threshold of acquiring his first reproducing instrument, however, may immediately find himself in a bit of a dilemma when suddenly faced with the unique restoration problems of the reproducing mechanism. The chances of finding one of these in original condition and still playing well are essentially nil. Thus, the prospective buyer should consider an instrument as being either restored or unrestored – and if the restoration work is partial, or worse, incompetent, it is in the latter category value-wise.

Even with the best of care and housing a reproducing piano from the 1920's will have suffered deterioration of the cloth, leather, and rubber components due to normal ageing. This is to be expected. A well cared-for instrument may then be in "good restorable condition." Damage from mice, weather, termites, mixed drinks spilled into the mechanisms, etc. all produce different gradations of quality. As is the case with other types of automatic musical instruments, it takes a qualified person to tell, for example, which of two instruments – each ostensibly appearing the same – is worth twice as much as the other.

A choice of sorts may exist between purchasing an instrument already restored or acquiring one in unrestored condition and trying to have it rebuilt properly. There are certain advantages to both procedures, but the underlying objective is to assure oneself that a top-quality instrument capable of performing properly will result.

High standards of skill, workmanship, and quality of materials are mandatory in all types of automatic musical instrument restorations if top results are to be obtained. Few other instruments are so demanding of virtual perfection as are reproducing pianos. Finding a qualified technician – a really qualified one – may well be the most critical situation faced by the prospective owner.

Ability to refurbish ordinary player pianos – a skill that can be learned with rapidity by the beginning rebuilder – by no means qualifies the technician to rebuild reproducing piano mechanisms. Also, it is important to note that expertise with pianos in general – the abilities possessed by many piano tuners and maintenance men – are different from expertise with reproducing mechanisms.

The reproducing piano rebuilder must discipline himself to exceptionally high standards of airtightness and devote whatever effort may be required to achieve absolute uniformity among the scores of pneumatic devices that contribute to the proper operation of each individual piano key. In other words, if you're not an expert with reproducing systems, have the work done by someone who is!

The normal piano parts – hammers, action components, strings, the sounding board, etc. – all play vital roles in the musical quality of the instrument. The finest pneumatic rebuilding job possible will be lost if the piano itself is not of equal top quality. To this end the perfectionist will want to have whatever is necessary done to equate the piano to like-new condition. All of this, of course, is expensive – but the expenditure is worth it!

One of the most reliable procedures for finding a qualified rebuilder is to insist on hearing an instrument previously restored by that individual. Most reputable technicians (or proprietors of firms employing them or referring them) will be happy to cooperate. A person of limited musical background may wish to take along a musician in order to obtain a more accurate appraisal.

Likewise, caution is urged when purchasing a reproducing piano from someone – a private individual or piano dealer accustomed to regular pianos but not to reproducers – not familiar with reproducing pianos or their mechanisms. Comments such as "All it needs is to have a leak in the bellows fixed," or "My tuner replaced some of the tubing and it plays like new," have to be taken with a large grain of salt! The reproducing piano is a complex instrument and nothing short of a rebuilding by a competent and experienced technician will satisfy the perfectionist.

Even though the preceding several sentences may tend to sound cynical, there is no reason whatever for pessimism or hesitation when it comes to the ownership of a reproducing piano. Fully aware of facts and circumstances, the aspiring reproducing piano enthusiast can avoid situations that might otherwise mar a pleasant and rewarding acquaintance with an artistic medium whose musical legacy transcends the power of spoken or written words to describe.

### Some Particulars

Usually desiring to preserve a more or less conventional outward appearance, manufacturers of reproducing pianos were faced not only with the problem of concealing perhaps two hundred pounds of special parts, but also with installing the spoolbox – in which rolls are placed for playing – in a convenient location. Upright models presented no particular difficulties; it was a simple matter to follow the example of the ordinary player piano. As a result, these instruments resemble one another to such an extent that a fairly close inspection may be required to determine whether a supposed upright player piano might actually be a reproducer, or vice versa.

Reproducing grand pianos customarily employ either of two different spoolbox locations. Some manufacturers preferred to install a drawer underneath the keyboard (Welte Licensee and Ampico systems were installed this way). When a roll isn't being changed, a drawer of this type can remain inconspicuously hidden away underneath the keyboard even as the instrument plays.

Other manufacturers (Welte original and Duo-Art systems are typical) preferred to install the spoolbox in the upper front part of the piano above the keyboard. Since conventional grand pianos have very little available space at that particular location, special piano cases had to be built to accommodate such installations. As a result, reproducing grands which have spoolboxes of the built-in variety are lengthened to some extent to make room for the extra components. The overall length of such instruments may be increased by amounts ranging from several inches to nearly a foot, with a typical figure being about six inches. Persons accustomed to using length as a criterion for judging and evaluating grand pianos should make a mental note of any such extended piano casework.

Lengths of all grand pianos are customarily measured from the "small end," i.e., the part most distant from the keys, to the edge of the piano along the front of the keyboard. Grand pianos are sometimes classified according to their lengths and placed in any of three general categories of size. The shortest is the baby grand, which measures up to about five feet. The next larger size is the parlor grand which measures from about five feet to seven feet. Most pianos encountered are of the so-called parlor grand size. The concert grand, largest of all, is a minimum of seven feet; most grands actually used in concert stage performances are approximately nine feet long. All of these categories are subject to a certain flexibility in colloquial usage, and when describing a piano it is always best to give an exact measurement in feet and inches, in order to avoid any misunderstanding.

Reproducing grands frequently, but not always, have six legs instead of the usual three. The so-called double leg style serves a dual function in providing extra strength while at the same time doing a more effective job of concealing parts which may be attached to the instrument's underside. Attached in that position may be a drawer, a pneumatic stack, or both. Found in one form or another in all types of pneumatically operated pianos, the pneumatic stack is simply an assembly containing all of the mechanical parts which operate the various piano keys.

Since the age of a given piano is frequently of special interest to the collector, it is worthwhile to mention that most dealers, tuners, and piano technicians have access to a source from which this information can be readily obtained. The age of nearly any piano can be determined to the nearest year by looking up its serial number in "Pierce's Piano Atlas" (formerly known as "Michel's Piano Atlas"). The practice commonly followed in the piano industry was to assign serial numbers in the same order regardless of which instruments of a given brand contain reproducing mechanisms. Reproducing pianos consequently bear serial numbers of the same sequence as conventional pianos of the same particular brand name.

*David L. Saul, writer of much of the reproducing piano section of this Encyclopedia, is shown with an Ampico B grand in his home. With a graduate degree in Physics and a long term interest in reproducing pianos of all kinds, Mr. Saul is well known for his rebuilding work and for his research in the field.*

*"My interests in the reproducing piano have dominated nearly all of my spare time over the past several years. I've become involved with these instruments' technical, historical, and musical aspects – the whole spectrum. Needless to say, the reproducing piano has become a central influence on the way of life within the Saul household," he noted in a recent letter to the editor.*

The Angelus
REPRODUCING GRAND—
HALLET and DAVIS—CONWAY and MERRILL PIANOS

AMPICO

IMMORTAL MASTERS of the PAST and PRESENT
have had their superb compositions recorded by the world's greatest pianists through the instrumentality of the
AUTO DE LUXE
WELTE-MIGNON

SCHULZ
REPRODUCING GRANDS
Aria Divina or Welte-Mignon (Licensee) Actions

The APOLLO
TRADE MARK REGISTERED
Reproducing PIANO

The HUPFELD DEA PIANO:
Playing automatically recorded rolls of most famous Pianists.

The SOLO CAROLA
INNER-PLAYER
the Most Marvelous Musical Invention of the Century

THE WELTE BUILT
WELTE-MIGNON
REPERFORMING PIANO*
(Original)

THE WORLD'S FOREMOST PIANISTS
Record Their Playing Exclusively For
THE DUO-ART
Reproducing Piano

Welte-Mignon
(Licensee)
THE MASTER'S FINGERS ON YOUR PIANO

# UNDERSTANDING THE AMPICO

*by David L. Saul*

## Introduction to the Ampico

The reproducing system which came to be known as the Ampico was developed independently as this century's first decade was drawing to a close. By 1913 the American Piano Company had adopted the system, naming it the Stoddard-Ampico in honor of its inventor, Charles F. Stoddard. The name Ampico-Artigraphic was also used for a time, but the designation that endured after a few years was simply the Ampico.

The Ampico quickly established itself as a major competitor in its field. After its introduction in Knabe and Haines Bros. pianos the mechanism soon found its way into the American Piano Company's full line. Chickering, Marshall & Wendell, and Franklin pianos were brought into the Ampico family as were subsequently the J&C Fischer and the Ampico-Symphonique. The renowned Mason & Hamlin made its appearance after that firm's business interests were acquired in 1924. An instrument of extraordinary reputation, the Mason & Hamlin brought an extra dimension of prestige to the Ampico line. In due course yet other brands appeared; a few examples of Steck, Weber, and Steinway Ampicos are extant, dating from the years following the Aeolian-American merger in 1932.

The Ampico was enthusiastically received abroad as mechanisms were exported for use in leading foreign pianos. British makes included Broadwood, Challen, Chappell, Marshall & Rose, Collard & Collard, Rogers, and Hopkinson. Germany's Grotrian-Steinweg and Austria's Bösendorfer were available with the Ampico, as were also Canada's Willis and Australia's Beale.

Ampico's offering of sizes and styles was certainly no less diversified than the competition's. Models in a variety of period furniture styles were routinely listed in dealers' catalogues, and even more elaborate instruments were built to order for special customers. Selected piano cases were shipped to Italy for hand carving, a job sometimes requiring upward of two years to complete and resulting in a "one of a kind" instrument.

In terms of size the Ampico set a record of sorts with the tiny spinet style Baby Ampico of the late 1930's. Reflecting a trend toward smaller pianos, this most diminutive of reproducing pianos stood in contrast to the stately concert grand Ampico marking the opposite extreme of size. While the latter was not a regular production item, it could at one time be ordered through any Ampico dealer.

# AMPICO

## Types of Ampico Mechanisms

Over the years the Ampico appeared in many interesting variations, including a foot-pumped model called the Marque-Ampico. At one time the Marque-Ampico was offered in several makes of pianos, but production was eventually discontinued as electrically powered reproducers proved to be much more popular.

The last of all reproducing pianos to appear in regular production was the spinet style Ampico mentioned earlier. Introduced in 1938, this petite model was offered in Fischer, Marshall & Wendell, and Steck pianos. It is interesting to note that in many (if not all) instances, these different brands of pianos are absolutely identical to each other in this spinet style, the only difference being the piano name decal!

The spinet model is frequently called the Baby Ampico, although that name was originally applied to a small studio upright introduced around 1927. Standing only about four feet high, instruments of the studio upright style have their spoolboxes accessible from the top. Without sliding doors in the customary location there is little in the way of visual evidence to suggest the reproducing character of these small and attractive pianos. In addition to the models mentioned earlier, the studio upright appears in Chickering pianos as well as the English Hopkinson.

While the Ampico mechanism underwent some rather significant changes during its production lifetime, the basic method of expression control prevailed with only minor changes. In each of its various forms the Ampico expression system combines a scale of intensity steps or degrees with a crescendo scheme. While gradual changes in loudness are produced by a crescendo device, intensity steps can be activated to provide accents or sudden dynamic changes. The crescendo is operable at either of two speeds under the control of appropriate expression coding. The intensity steps, totaling seven in number, can be selected rapidly in any sequence. Step and crescendo effects are merged together, or in their combined effect, summed. Accents and contrasting dynamic effects can thus be relegated to one part of the system specially designed for such purposes while another part accommodates changes of a more gradual nature. The complete Ampico mechanism contains two expression units which operate separately and independently (with one notable exception) to govern bass and treble sections of the piano keyboard. The exception is found in later Ampicos which utilize a single crescendo mechanism common to both bass and treble. The Model B and spinet style Baby Ampicos fall into this category. The Model B Ampico also contains certain features to extend and supplement the basic expression scheme which has been described.

There are three distinct models of the Ampico mechanism. The earliest of these, identified with the Stoddard-Ampico and the Ampico-Artigraphic instruments, was superseded around 1920 by the Model A. The latter predominated until the Model B was introduced in 1929. The highly sophisticated Model B mechanism appears only in grand pianos, although its forerunners were installed in both uprights and grands. The few upright Ampicos built in 1929 and in later years continued to utilize Model A expression components.

## The Early Ampico

The Stoddard-Ampico / Artigraphic model can be identified by a modifying power lever labeled LOUD-SOFT-NORMAL. Most Ampicos of this vintage are also equipped with two knobs which move in slots as the roll plays. The knobs are part of a unique repeating device which can replay any desired portion of a musical selection automatically. These instruments are commonly fitted with pneumatic stacks manufactured by the Auto Pneumatic Action Company — the same firm that built the competing Welte Licensee mechanism.

The expression devices are similar in many ways to those of the more familiar Model A, although the earlier design was more complicated.

Grand installations always utilize a drawer under the piano keyboard to house spoolbox and controls — a precedent followed without exception in all subsequent Ampico grands as well. Technical details of this model are covered in the 1919 Ampico "Inspector's Instruction Book," which in its reprinted edition also contains the 1920 supplement applicable to the Model A.

## The Model A Ampico

The Model A Ampico, produced and marketed throughout the reproducing piano's peak years of popularity, was built in far greater numbers than either of its relatives. This model can be identified by a modifying switch labeled SUBDUED-MEDIUM-BRILLIANT. In a grand this switch will be found in the drawer, situated rearmost in a row of four switches directly to the left of the spoolbox. In the upright a corresponding set of switches is located in the spoolbox, the modifying switch being located directly above the other three on the left-hand side.

Introduction of the Model A coincided approximately with the American Piano Company's acquisition of the Amphion Company of Syracuse, New York, a firm specializing in high quality player actions and already manufacturer of the Artecho reproducing mechanism. Design of the Model A Ampico was strongly influenced by Amphion's production tooling and technology. Valves, pneumatic stacks, and other components were adapted or borrowed from existing Amphion designs. The removable valve block was an Amphion development. Patented in 1912, this valve unit became a standard Ampico fixture with the advent of the Model A. While basic features of Stoddard's original expression system were retained, the design was improved and simplified. The scheme for manual control of dynamics via finger operated expression buttons was redesigned with greatly reduced complexity. Step intensity units were changed from double valve to single valve operation, and many detailed mechanical improvements were incorporated. During the course of the Model A's production, technical improvements continued to appear; valves, pneumatic stacks, and other components underwent significant changes in later years.

Service publications applicable to the Model A are the Ampico 1923 "Inspectors' Reference Book" and the aforementioned 1920 supplement to the 1919 edition.

### The Model B Ampico

The Model B was publicly introduced as the New Ampico, and the choice of words couldn't have been more descriptive. The New Ampico's mechanism incorporated a veritable multitude of innovations. The most outwardly conspicuous of these is a large spoolbox permitting the use of special "jumbo" rolls that play up to 30 minutes. The relatively large take-up spool gives the Model B Ampico drawer a distinctive appearance. A further clue to identification is the tempo control which uses a rotating dial-like pointer with a semi-circular scale; earlier Ampico models have a sliding tempo indicator and linear scale. The Model B Ampico is comparatively rare today, its production having been severely curtailed by the economic events of 1929 and the 1930's.

From an engineering viewpoint the Model B mechanism represents a complete departure from earlier technology. Every component of the Model B was designed to meet the reproducing piano's special requirements. Use of ordinary player hardware at any point in the system had been ruled out from the beginning. The expression system is not only quicker acting and more accurate than the old, but it is less complicated mechanically. Mechanical simplicity is, in fact, a keynote feature of the entire system — a remarkable achievement (and a testimonial to the ingenuity of the inventor, Dr. Clarence Hickman) in view of the Model B's many new features and high level of technical sophistication.

The 1929 "Ampico Service Manual" is devoted exclusively to the Model B and contains an excellent technical description of the system. "Re-Enacting the Artist," a book by Larry Givens (originally written as a chapter to this Encyclopedia, but then issued in book form by the Vestal Press when Mr. Givens' material exceeded the requirements of the present volume) gives an in-depth view of the Ampico and its development, with emphasis on Dr. Hickman's development of the Model B.

The same research program that produced the Model B also led to modernization of roll production. As new technology replaced the old, the method of making new Ampico recordings was completely revised. After the Model B's design had been finalized, changes were incorporated into Ampico rolls to take full advantage of the Model B's potential. Although expression coding was revised in certain ways, a most ingenious scheme was devised whereby the new so-called Ampico B rolls would play satisfactorily on the earlier Ampico models as well. With compatibility thus assured, the new type rolls appeared on dealers' shelves around 1927 — a date well in advance of the earliest production of pianos containing the Model B system.

The Model B operates best, as might reasonably be expected, with B rolls designed especially for it. Earlier Ampico rolls can be played with some success, although a minimal loss of expression cannot be avoided. This loss stems chiefly from the Model B's use of a single crescendo mechanism which cannot respond to separately varying bass and treble crescendo coding. Rolls of the B type, in contrast to the earlier Ampico rolls, contain identical crescendo coding for bass and treble.

As the depression years ensued, a novel device called the Ampichron was introduced as an optional accessory for the Model B. The Ampichron (Ampichron derives from AMPIco + TeleCHRON) incorporates an electrically driven clockwork mechanism which enables the Ampico to mark the time of day musically. A special roll was made for use with the Ampichron, providing chime effects and a series of hourly musical selections throughout the day and evening. Use is by no means limited to the special roll; the timing unit can be set to repeat any desired musical selection on a regularly timed basis. The Ampichron can also operate similarly to the modern clock radio, with the Ampico sounding forth after a predetermined time setting is reached.

In view of its late introduction and optional nature, it is not surprising that the Ampichron is quite rare. Should an Ampichron-equipped instrument be encountered, it can be readily identified upon inspection of the Model B drawer. The panel to the left of the spoolbox will contain a rectangular brass plate surrounded by a metal frame. The plate contains three small circular dials and engraved instructions for operating the Ampichron.

"Spanish Ampico Grand," Style 14GE. "Antique walnut richly carved with highlights in antique gold; appliques of chased metal over velvet. Hand wrought Spanish iron work. 5'3¾" long."

**March 22, 1914, advertisement in the New York Times features the introduction of the Stoddard-Ampico. (Courtesy of Richard Howe)**

**Right and below are shown the title page and several other portions of Ampico's hardbound 1925 catalogue. The list at the bottom of the page gives pianists who had recorded for the Ampico (or for Hupfeld) up to that date.**

**A number of artists' performances were licensed from Ludwig Hupfeld A.G. of Leipzig, Germany. Most of these Ampico transcriptions appeared earlier on Hupfeld Dea and/or Triphonola reproducing piano rolls. Note that a number of the same artists recorded for Welte as well (see Welte reproducing piano section of this book).**

**Over the years artists would often change their recording contracts. Several artists' performances are available on Ampico, Duo-Art, Hupfeld (Dea and Triphonola), and Welte (original and Licensee) rolls! As information published in the AMICA "Bulletin" has noted, the same masters were used for Ampico, Duo-Art, and Welte (Licensee) rolls later — in the 1930's.**

*A CATALOGUE OF MUSIC FOR*

The

AMPICO

A LIST
OF THE RECORDINGS OF PIANISTS WHOSE ART
IS THUS PRESERVED FOR PRESENT DAY
MUSIC LOVERS AND FOR POSTERITY

*TOGETHER WITH SHORT BIOGRAPHIES
OF MANY OF THE COMPOSERS AND ARTISTS
AND NOTES ON THE MUSIC*

AC

THE AMPICO CORPORATION
*NEW YORK : MCMXXV*

*ADDITIONAL RECORDINGS MADE IN EUROPE*

THE CATALOGUE IS AUGMENTED BY A COLLECTION OF RECORDINGS MADE IN EUROPE AT THE LABORATORIES OF LUDWIG HUPFELD, WHICH ARE AVAILABLE FOR AMPICO OWNERS THROUGH SPECIAL ARRANGEMENT WITH THE LUDWIG HUPFELD COMPANY

*The recordings listed in this collection include the playing of the following artists:*

| | |
|---|---|
| EUGEN D'ALBERT | OSSIP GABRILOWITSCH |
| WILHELM BACHAUS | EDVARD GRIEG |
| HAROLD BAUER | JOSEF HOFMANN |
| FERRUCCIO BUSONI | PIETRO MASCAGNI |
| TERESA CARREÑO | CAMILLE SAINT-SAËNS |
| ALFRED CORTOT | WASSILY SAPELLNIKOFF |
| ARTHUR FRIEDHEIM | XAVER SCHARWENKA |

ALEXANDER SCRIABINE

*CONTENTS*


Frontispiece: Frederic Chopin . . . . . . . . Facing Title
Introduction: The Appreciation of Music . . . . . . . Page 11

Part I—Artists' List: Recordings listed under the names of artists who have played them . . . . . . . . 13-198

Adler, Clarence . . . 13-15
d'Albert, Eugen . . . 201
d'Alexandrowska, Luba . 15-16
Allen, Frances Potter . 16
Arden and Fairchild . . 17
Arden and Lambert . . 16
Ariani, Adriano . . . 16
Augiéras, Pierre . . . 17
Ayres, Cecile . . . . 17

Bachaus, Wilhelm . . 202
Ball, Ernest R. . . . 17
Barber, Lyell . . . . 17
Barth, Hans . . . 17-18
Bauer, Harold . . 203-204
Beebe, Florence . . . 18
Bergé, William E. . . . 19
Berliner, Dorothy . . . 19
Bert, Corrine de . . 19-20
Bodanzky, Artur . . . 21
Bond, Carrie Jacobs . . 20
Borchard, Adolphe . . 22-23
Boshko, Victoria . . . 23
Bowman, Otto H. . . 23-24
Brailowsky, Alexander . 25
Braun, Robert . . . . 24
Brinkman, Florence . . 24
Brockway, Howard . . 26-40
Brownell, Elspeth . . . 24
Browning, Mortimer . . 24
Buell, Dai . . . . . 42
Buhlig, Richard . . . 41-42
Burg, Clarence . . . 42
Busoni, Ferruccio . 205-206

Cady, Harriet . . . . 45
Campbell, David . . . 45
Carreño, Teresa . . 43 and 207
Carroll, Adam . . . . 44
Chaloff, Julius . . . 45-46
Chapman, Walter . . . 46
Chemet, Reneé . . . . 46
Chenoweth, Wilbur . . 46
Chiapusso, Jan . . . 47-48
Church, Marjorie . . . 48
Clair and Pollock . . . 48
Confrey, Zez . . . . 49
Cooper, Charles . . . 50-51
Copeland, George . . 52-54
Cortot, Alfred . . . 208
Cutchin, Esther Marvin . 48

Davies, Reuben . . . . 54
Davis, Leonard . . . . 54
Decker, Walter . . . . 54
Delcamp, J. Milton . . 55-57
Desmond, Helen . . . . 57
Dietrich-Hollingshead, Ursula 57
Dillon, Fannie . . . . 57
Dilworth, George . . . 57-58
Dixon, Frederic . . . . 58
Dohnányi, Erno . . . 59-60

Donahue, Lester . . . 58
Duke, John . . . . 62-63
Dumesnil, Maurice . . 61-62

Ecker, James . . . . 63
Edgar, Helen Louise . . 63
Eisler, Paul . . . . 63
Elizondo, Artemesia . . 63-64
Ellis, Melville . . . . 64
Erle, Francis . . . . 64
Eustis, Rosamund . . . 64

Fairchild, Edgar . . . 64-67
Farrar, Geraldine . . . 68
Fink, E. A. . . . . 69
Fox, Felix . . . . . 69
Frances, Annette . . . 69
Friedberg, Carl . . . 69
Friedheim, Arthur . . . 209

Gabrilowitsch, Ossip . . 210
Gallico, Paolo . . . . 69
Gerdts, Felix . . . 69-72
Gilbert, Harry M. . . . 75
Giovanni, Irene di . . . 72
Glass, Julia . . . . . 76
Godowsky, Leopold . . 73-75
Goode, Blanche . . . . 76
Goodson, Katharine . . 76
Gordon, Phillip . . . 77-78
Grange, Ina . . . . . 76
Grieg, Edvard . . . . 211
Grofé, Ferdie . . . . 79
Gruen, Rudolph . . . . 80
Grunn, Homer . . . . 80
Gunn, Alexander . . . 80

Hageman, Richard . . . 81
Hambourg, Mark . . . 82
Hanke, Hans . . . . 83
Hansen, L. H. . . . . 80
Harrison, Mary E. . . . 84
Hejtmanek, Bodzka . . 83
Henneman, Gertrude . . 84
Henrion, Theodore . . 84-85
Henrion and Brockway . 85
Herbert, Victor . . . 86-87
Hill, Alta . . . . . 85
Hillsberg, Ignace . . . 85
Himmelreich, Ferdinand . 85
Hochman, Arthur . . . 87
Hofmann, Josef . . . 212
Hoschke, Frederick Albert . 87
Howard, John Tasker . . 88
Hyde, Herbert E. . . . 88

Ilgenfritz, McNair . . . 88
d'Indy, Vincent . . . 89-90

Jacobi, Victor . . . . 90
Joiner, Joseph . . . . 90
Jones, Elizabeth Gay . . 90

Kendall, Edwin . . . . 90
Kerekjarto, Duci de . . 91
Koven, Reginald de . . 100
Klemen, Bertha . . . . 91
Kmita, Andrei . . . 91-99
Kreisler, Fritz . . . 101-103
Kroeger, Ernest R. . . 103
Kuhler, Mary Fromeyer . 103

La Croix, Aurora . . 103-104
La Farge, Jean . . . . 104
La Forge, Frank . . . 104
Lambert, Alexander . . 104
Lambert, Joseph . . . 104
Lambert and Kmita . . 104
Lamson, Carl . . . 105-106
Landow, Max . . . . 107
Lane, Eastwood . . . 106
Lane, Victor . . . 106-107
Lange, Henry . . . . 108
Laros, Earle . . . . 109
Lavarro, Enrico . . . 109
Lecuona, Ernesto . . 109-110
Lederer, Harry . . . . 110
Lefévre, Henry . . . . 110
Leginska, Ethel . . 111-112
Leopold, Ralph . . . . 112
Levitzki, Misha . . 113-116
Lhévinne, Josef . . 117-118
Liszniewska, Marguerite Melville . 112
Loesser, Arthur . . 118-119
Lopez, Vincent . . . . 120
Loth, Leslie . . . . 119

MacDermid, James G. . 121
MacFadyen, Alexander . 121
Maier, Guy . . . . 121-122
Maier and Pattison . . 122
Manecoles, Emelio . . 123
Marvin, John . . . . 123
Mascagni, Pietro . . . 213
Mason, Louise . . . . 123
Mayer, Estella . . . . 123
McManus, George . . . 123
McNabb, George . . . 123
Melamet, Mrs. D. S. . . 125
Mérö, Yolanda . . . . 128
Mirovitch, Alfred . . 124-125
Moiseiwitsch, Benno . 126-128
Morrey, Grace Hamilton . 128
Morris, Edward . . . . 128
Münz, Mieczyslaw . . 129-130

Nash, Frances . . . 131-132
Navas, Raphael . . . . 132
Ney, Ely . . . . . 132-133
Noe, J. Thurston . . . 136
Nyiregyhazi, Erwin . . 134-136

Original Piano Trio . . 136
Ornstein, Leo . . . 137-140


CONTENTS—*Continued*


Pascal, Julian . . . 140
Pattison, Lee . . . 140
Pelletier and Loesser . 140-142
Pelletier, Wilfred . 142-143
Piastro, Mishel . . . 143
Pierson, Maude . . . 144
Pollock, Muriel . . . 144
Présent, Rata . . . 144
Proctor, George . . . 144
Pyle, Wynne . . . 145

Rachmaninoff, Sergei . 146-149
Randegger, Giuseppe . 145
Reichenthal, Ralph . . 150
Reisenberg, Nadia . . 145
Reyes, Juan . . . 151
Rice Gitz . . . . 151
Rivers, Claire . . . 145
Robinson, Carol . . . 153
Rosenthal, Adele . . 153
Rosenthal, Moriz . . 152
Ross, Gertrude . . . 153
Rubinstein, Arthur . 154-155
Russell, Alexander . . 153
Rybner, Cornelius . 155-156

Saint-Saëns, Camille . . 214
Samaroff, Olga . . 157-158
Sapellnikoff, Wassily . 215
Scharwenka, Xaver . . 216
Schmitz, E. Robert . 159-160

Schmitz, Fred A. . . . 158
Schnabel, Artur . . 161-163
Schnabel-Tollefsen, Augusta 163
Schnitzer, Germaine . 164-165
Scionti, Silvio . . . . 158
Scriabine, Alexander . . 217
Sébestyén, George . . . 160
Seligman, Isiah . . . . 160
Shipman, Harry . . . . 163
Shipman and Fairchild . 163
Silber, Sidney . . . . 166
Simon, Morris . . . . 167
Sklarevski, Alexander . . 167
Smith, George . . . . 167
Smith, Harold . . . . 167
Souvaine, Henry . . 168-169
Spaeth, Sigmund . . . 167
Steeb, Olga . . . 169-170
Sterling, Al . . . 170-171
Sterling and Arden . . 171
Stojowski, Sigismund . . 172
Strauss, Richard . . 173-174
Sullivan, Dan . . . . 171
Suskind, Milton . . 175-180
Suskind and Loesser . 180-182
Sutherland, Alice . . . 174
Swart, Stuart . . . . 174
Szumowska, Antoinette . 183

Thompson, Ann . . . . 183
Tillotson, Frederic . . . 184

Tovar, José Conrado . . 184
Tovey, Henry D. . . . 183
Truxell, Earl . . . . 184
Tucker, Mercedes O'Leary . 184
Turpin, H. P. . . . . 184

Utz, Lilian . . . . . 184

Van den Berg, Bram . . 185
Van Katwijk, Paul . . . 184
Van Vollenhoven, Hanna . 184
Volavy, Marguerite . 186-191
Volavy and Brockway . 191-192

Ward-Stephens . . . . 192
Wehrmann-Schaffner, Eugenie 192
Wendling, Pete . . . . 193
Whittaker, James . . . 193
Wille, Stewart . . . . 193
Winogradoff, Eleanor . . 193
Winston, Elizabeth . . . 194
Winternitz, Otto . . . 194
Wiswell, Jean . . . . 194
Wittgenstein, Victor . 194-195

Yon, Pietro . . . . . 195

Zadora, Michael . . . . 195
Zardo, Redento . . . . 197
Zeisler, Fanny Bloomfield 196-197
Zucca, Mana . . . 197-198
Zygman, Flora . . . . 198

82 THE PURCHASER'S GUIDE TO THE MUSIC INDUSTRIES, 1926

THE AMPICO IN THE MUSIC ROOM OF VINCENT ASTOR, ESQ.

# The Complete Leadership of the AMPICO

THE supremacy of the Ampico in the field of Reproducing Pianos is incontrovertible at every point from which such instruments are intelligently judged. ~ The Ampico can reproduce all the effects possible to any reproducing piano — and in addition, certain other effects essential to a perfect reproduction which are impossible to other instruments. The means for reproducing these effects are protected by United States patents issued exclusively to the Ampico, ~ Not only does the roster of Ampico artists show a greater number recording for it than for any other piano, but it shows absolute leadership in that it has the greatest number of the world's ranking pianists recording for it exclusively; the greatest number of distinguished composers recording their own works; and of gifted, temperamental pianists playing the lighter classics; and the most imposing list of artists specializing in popular music and music for dancing.

The Ampico is found exclusively in fine pianos—of long built and carefully guarded reputation for quality — including three of the four great pianos in general use on the American concert stage.

*THERE IS BUT ONE GENUINE AMPICO*
obtainable in the following Pianos:

KNABE · MASON & HAMLIN · CHICKERING
J. & C FISCHER MARSHALL & WENDELL HAINES BROS.
*and for Canadian Distribution also in the* WILLIS

THE AMPICO CORPORATION - - New York

**This 1926 Ampico features a favorite advertising theme of the period: an illustration of The Instrument in the home of a famous person. Just about anybody who was anybody, from the Vatican to the vaudeville stage, lent his name to reproducing piano advertising of the 1920's.**

# AMPICO

Right: Description of the Ampico in the 1926 issue of "The Purchaser's Guide to the Music Industries." Note that mention is made that the term "re-enacted" was copyrighted by the American Piano Company.

**AMPICO.**—A supreme development of the so-called "reproducing piano" (manufactured by the Ampico Corporation, a division of the American Piano Company, New York). A new invention which marks a distinct advance in the art of producing music by scientific means. The Ampico embodies the result of many years of experimentation by its inventor, Charles Fuller Stoddard. It is not a player in the ordinary sense, but a highly developed and sensitized musical instrument which has brought the utmost scientific accuracy to the recording and re-enacting of the actual performance on the piano of the world's greatest pianists. It siezes and records imperishably every phase of expression in their playing and renders this again in all it artistic fullness. The first formal presentation of the Ampico was made at a public recital at the Hotel Biltmore in New York City, October 8, 1916. At this recital Leopold Godowsky played two numbers, each of which was *re-enacted (*Copyright, 1922, A. P. Co.) on the Ampico by means of a record roll previously made by the artist. The recording duplicated Godowsky's touch, tone color and phrasing so exactly as to be indistinguishable from the performance of the artist himself. Similar demonstrations, in which some of the greatest living pianists have participated, have been held in practically every important musical center in the country. The Ampico has appeared with unqualified success as soloist with the great symphony orchestras of the country, the recorded playing of the artist being substituted for that of the living pianist, and on February 3, 1920, there was given in Carnegie Hall, New York, a remarkable concert, at which five of the world's greatest pianists, Godowsky, Levitzki, Moiseiwitsch, Ornstein and Rubinstein, appeared in joint recital, in which their playing was heard in direct comparison with its repetition by the Ampico. This most exacting test resulted in a complete triumph for the Ampico. The Ampico is especially remarkable for its ability to give tone coloring effects. When an Ampico recording is taken, it shows not only what notes were struck, but also how long each string vibrated. Each note perforation in an Ampico roll represents the length of time that that string vibrated when the artist made the recording. In other words, the "singing tone" of each note is controlled individually by its perforation. The Ampico may also be used as a player. Remarkably sensitive controls are provided by which the operator may impart his own interpretation to the piece. The Ampico is a pneumatic mechanism, which may be operated either by foot pumping or electric motor power. The results obtained by either foot or motor-propelled models are identical. No part of the Ampico mechanism is in direct contact with the strings, sounding board and key or pedal action of the piano. Neither the tone nor the action of the instrument is in the slightest degree impaired for hand playing. Another exclusive feature of the Ampico is the automatic repeat device. This device may be set so that the composition in its entirety will be automatically repeated as often as desired. This feature is particularly valuable for dancing and for the student pianist. The Ampico may be had in the following makes of pianos: The Knabe, Chickering, Mason & Hamlin, Haines Bros., Marshall & Wendell, Franklin, J. & C. Fischer, also in the following famous English makes: John Broadwood & Sons, Chappell, Collard & Collard, Marshall & Rose, and Rogers pianos, and for the Canadian distribution also in the Willis. It is installed in both grand and upright styles, and in either case the mechanism is entirely concealed within the instrument. The system of installation of the Ampico absolutely avoids any distortion of the case or alteration of the action of the piano, so that it remains unimpaired and unchanged for playing by hand. The Ampico is also obtainable in a foot propelled model which is known as the *Marque Ampico*. It was installed in the Armstrong, Brewster, Franklin and Foster pianos, to which refer.

Below: An Ampico advertising description of "The Affair at the Biltmore." Note that the trade journal description at the right notes that Godowsky "played two numbers," and the advertisement below places the number at four: "Immediately after the conclusion of four of the selections Mr. Godowsky played. . ."

*From The New York Globe, Oct. 11, 1916.*

**GOLOWSKY VERSUS GODOW KY'S RECORD**

Once upon a time the great musician held that music could not exist where the artist himself did not actually produce the notes, and the player piano and phonograph called forth his silent scorn. So, also, not so long before that, the painter called the photograph humbug and the work of the devil, sir!

The affair at the Biltmore held last Sunday would have been a scandal five years ago. For fancy, that great pianist Leopold Godowsky actually permitted a music roll record of his renditions to be heard on the Ampico immediately after he personally had performed them. And the audience compared notes!

Indeed, as remarkable as the experiment itself is the extraordi y success achieved by the almost human instrument.

## *The Affair at the Biltmore*

ON Sunday Afternoon, October 8th, the Music Room of the Biltmore held a distinguished audience of musicians, critics, and musical connoisseurs, who had assembled to hear Leopold Godowsky play—and to marvel at the perfect reproduction of his playing on the Knabe-Ampico.

Immediately after the conclusion of four of the selections Mr. Godowsky played, the Knabe-Ampico reproduced the same numbers from records he had made for it. So perfect was the reproduction—so marvelous the fidelity of the replica to the performance of Mr. Godowsky, that the audience was first amazed—then moved to the most enthusiastic applause.

The introduction by Mr. Victor Wittgenst in, one of the brilliant younger pianists, had prepared the audience for a result that had hardly b en dreamed possible by any piano of the player type, as well as the willingness of Mr. Godowsky o lend his art to the proving of the Ampico. Yet the perfection of the performance astounded every hearer. Here, indeed, was musical perfection—perfection that stood the *acid test* as no other instrument had ever dared apply it.

In operating the Knabe-Ampico no pump ng or personal effort is required, and, in addition to reproducing the playing of the world's greatest pianists, it may be played by hand as the ordinary piano, or with any standard 88-note roll, as the player. The Ampico ranges in prices from the Stoddard-Ampico at $750 to the Knabe-Am ico Grand at $1,800.

*You are cordially invited to attend a demonstration of the Knabe-Ampico in the Ampico Studios.*

# A LIST OF THE WORLD'S MOST PROMINENT PIANISTS WHO HAVE APPEARED IN THE LAST TWENTY-FIVE YEARS WITH AN ANALYSIS OF THEIR RECORDING WORK WITH REFERENCE TO ITS AVAILABILITY FOR THE AMPICO AND OTHER REPRODUCING PIANOS

**An Official List of the World's most prominent Pianists who Have Appeared in the last 25 Years.**

d'Albert, Eugen
Bachaus, Wilhelm
Bauer, Harold
Borchard, Adolphe
Brailowsky, Alexander
Buhlig, Richard
Busoni, Ferruccio
Carreño, Teresa
Chiapusso, Jan
Copeland, George
Cortot, Alfred
Cottlaw, Augusta
Dohnányi, Ernst von
Dumesnil, Maurice
Friedberg, Carl
Friedheim, Arthur
Friedman, Ignaz
Gabrilowitsch, Ossip
Ganz, Rudolph
Gieseking, Walter
Godowsky, Leopold
Goldsand, Robert
Goodson, Katharine
Grainger, Percy
Grieg, Edvard
Grunfeld, Alfred
Hambourg, M
Hess, Myra
Hofmann, Josef
Hutcheson, Ernest
d'Indy, Vincent
Jonas, Alberto
Lamond, Frederic
Landowska, Wanda
Leginska, Ethel
Lerner, Tina
Levitzki, Mischa
Lhévinne, Josef
Mero, Yolanda
Mirovitch, Alfred
Moiseiwitsch, Benno
Münz, Mieczyslaw
Ney, Elly
Novaes, Guiomar
Nyiregyhazi, Erwin
Orloff, Nicolas
Ornstein, Leo
de Pachmann, Vladimir
Paderewski, Ignaz J.
Pauer, Max
Powell, John
Pugno, Raoul
Rachmaninoff, Sergei
Reisenauer, Alfred
Rosenthal, Moriz
Rubinstein, Arthur
Saint-Saëns, Camille
Samaroff, Olga
Sapelnikoff, Wassily
Sauer, Emil
Scharwenka, Xaver
Schelling, Ernest
Schmitz, E. Robert
Schnabel, Artur
Schnitzer, Germaine
Scott, Cyril
Scriabine, Alexander
Siloti, Alexander
Strauss, Richard
Tansman, Alexandre
Zadora, Michael
Zeisler, Fanny Bloomfield

**61 of them or 84.7% may be heard on the AMPICO**

d'Albert
Bachaus
Bauer
Bloomfield Zeisler
Borchard
Brailowsky
Buhlig
Busoni
Carreño
Chiapusso
Copeland
Cortot
Dohnányi
Dumesnil
Friedberg
Friedheim
Friedman
Gabrilowitsch
Ganz
Gieseking
Godowsky
Goldsand
Goodson
Grieg
Grunfeld
Hambourg
Hofmann
d'Indy
Lamond
Landowska
Leginska
Lerner
Levitzki
Lhévinne
Mero
Mirovitch
Moiseiwitsch
Münz
Ney
Nyiregyhazi
Orloff
Ornstein
Pauer
Pugno
Rachmaninoff
Reisenauer
Rosenthal
Rubinstein
Saint-Saëns
Samaroff
Sapelnikoff
Sauer
Scharwenka
Schmitz
Schnabel
Schnitzer
Scott
Scriabine
Strauss
Tansman
Zadora

**41 of them or 56.9% may be heard on the DUO ART.**

d'Albert
Bachaus
Bauer
Busoni
Carreño
Copeland
Cortot
Cottlaw
Dumesnil
Friedberg
Friedheim
Friedman
Gabrilowitsch
Ganz
Godowsky
Goodson
Grainger
Hambourg
Hess
Hofmann
Hutcheson
Jonas
Lamond
Landowska
Leginska
Lerner
Mero
Ney
Novaes
de Pachmann
Paderewski
Powell
Rubinstein
Saint-Saëns
Sauer
Scharwenka
Schelling
Schmitz
Scott
Siloti
Zadora

**34 of them, 47.2% may be heard on the WELTE MIGNON**

d'Albert
Bloomfield Zeisler
Buhlig
Busoni
Carreño
Dohnányi
Friedberg
Friedheim
Gabrilowitsch
Ganz
Gieseking
Grieg
Hambourg
Hofmann
Lamond
Landowska
Lhévinne
Mero
Ney
Novaes
de Pachmann
Paderewski
Pauer
Saint-Saëns
Samaroff
Sapelnikoff
Scharwenka
Schelling
Schnabel
Schnitzer
Scott
Scriabine
Strauss
Zadora

**17 of them may be heard on all three instruments AMPICO, DUO ART WELTE MIGNON**

d'Albert
Busoni
Carreño
*Friedberg
*Friedheim
*Gabrilowitsch
*Ganz
Hambourg
*Hofmann
*Lamond
*Landowska
*Mero
Ney
Saint-Saëns
Scharwenka
*Scott
Zadora

*These artists who may be heard also on the AMPICO and WELTE MIGNON are listed by the DUO ART as exclusive with them.

**13 of them may be heard on the AMPICO and DUO ART but not on the WELTE MIGNON**

*Bachaus
*Bauer
Copeland
*Cortot
Dumesnil
*Friedman
Godowsky
*Goodson
*Leginska
Lerner
*Rubinstein
*Sauer
Schmitz

*These artists who may be heard also on the AMPICO are listed by the DUO ART as exclusive with them.

**13 of them may be heard on the AMPICO and WELTE MIGNON but not on the DUO ART**

Bloomfield Zeisler
Buhlig
Dohnányi
Gieseking
Grieg
Lhévinne
Pauer
Samaroff
Sapelnikoff
Schnabel
Schnitzer
Scriabine
Strauss

**4 only may be heard on the DUO ART and WELTE MIGNON but not on the AMPICO**

*Novaes
de Pachmann
*Paderewski
*Schelling

*These artists who may be heard on the WELTE MIGNON are listed by the DUO ART as exclusive with them.

**15 may be heard only on the AMPICO, never having recorded their playing for any other reproducing piano, and are exclusively AMPICO artists.**

Borchard
Brailowsky
Chiapusso
Goldsand
d'Indy
Levitzki
Mirovitch
Moiseiwitsch
Münz
Nyiregyhazi
Orloff
Ornstein
Rachmaninoff
Rosenthal
Tansman

**7 may be heard only on the DUO ART, never having recorded their playing for any other reproducing piano and are exclusively DUO ART artists.**

Cottlaw
Grainger
Hess
Hutcheson
Jonas
Powell
Siloti

**None may be heard only on the WELTE MIGNON.**

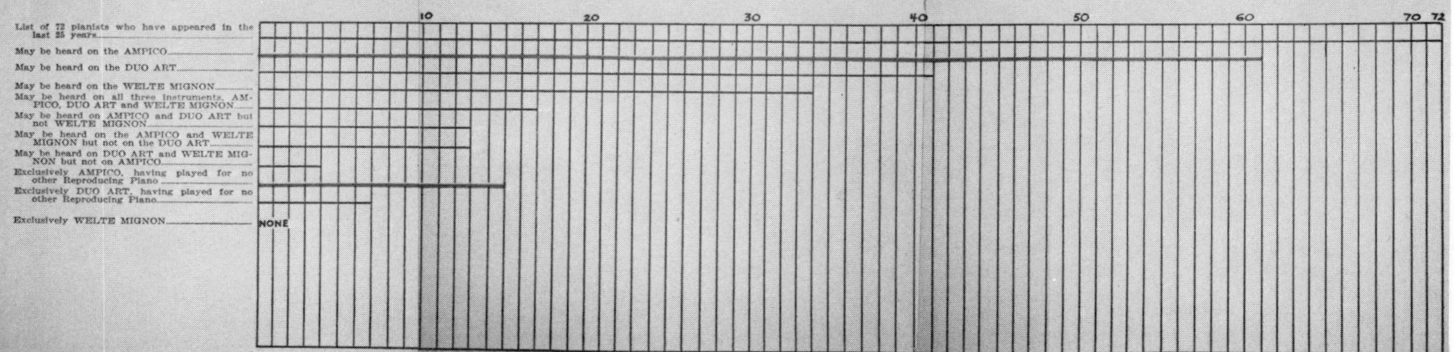


This "list of the world's most prominent pianists who have appeared in the last twenty-five years with an analysis of their recording work with reference to its availability for the Ampico and other reproducing pianos" is rather misleading. Undoubtedly a list of "the world's most prominent pianists" would contain different names if prepared by Welte or Duo-Art advertising copy writers! The list given above appears to be directed against Duo-Art in particular. Duo-Art was Ampico's chief competition at the time. In 1932 the Ampico and Duo-Art parent companies were merged to form the Aeolian American Corporation, and presumably such comparisons were no longer needed!

# A List Of The Artists Of January 1st, 1928 Who May Be Heard On The Ampico

*New names are constantly being added to the list of Ampico artists so that any published list is complete only on the date of publication. This list of January 1st, 1928 shows a total of 335 who may be heard on the Ampico.*

Abbott, Calvin
Adler, Clarence
d'Albert, Eugen
d'Alexandrowska, Luba
Allen, Frances Potter
Altschuler, Modest (*Conductor*)
Arden, Victor
Ariani, Adriano
Augiéras, Pierre
Axt, William
Ayres, Cecile
Bachaus, Wilhelm
Ball, Ernest R.
Barber, Lyell
Baranoff, Sascha
Barth, Hans
Bauer, Harold
Beebe, Florence
Bellin, Jacob H.
Bergé, William E.
Berliner, Dorothy
Bert, Corrine de
Bianculani, Luigi
Bier, Allan
Billings, Earl
Bloomfield Zeisler, Fanny
Bodanzky, Artur (*Conductor*)
Bond, Carrie Jacobs
Borchard, Adolphe
Boshko, Victoria
Bowman, Otto H.
Brachocki, Alexander
Brailowsky, Alexander
Braun, Robert
Brinkman, Florence
Brockway, Howard
Brownell, Elspeth
Browning, Mortimer
Buerger, Julius
Buhlig, Richard
Burg, Clarence
Busoni, Ferruccio
Cadman, Charles Wakefield
Cady, Harriet
Campbell, David
Carreño, Teresa
Chaloff, Julius
Chapman, Walter
Chemet, Reneé
Chenoweth, Wilbur
Chiapusso, Jan
Church, Marjorie
Clair, Herbert
Coffer, Mathilde
Colber, E. Fred
Cone-Baldwin, Carolyn
Conover, Agnes
Cooper, Charles
Copeland, George
Copland, Aaron
Cortot, Alfred
Cutchin, Esther Marvin
Dai Buell
Davies, Reuben
Davis, Leonard
Decker, Walter
Desmond, Helen
Dietrich-Hollingshead, Ursula
Dillon, Fannie
Dilworth, George
Dixon, Frederic
Doguereau, Paul
Dohnányi, Ernst von
Donahue, Lester
Duke, John
Dumesnil, Maurice
Duryea, Oscar
Echániz, Jose
Ecker, James
Edgar, Helen Louise
Eisler, Paul
Elizondo, Artemesia
Ellis, Melville
Erle, Francis
Eustis, Rosamund
Farrar, Geraldine
Fauré, Gabriel
Fink, E. A.
Fox, Felix
Frances, Annette
Friedberg, Carl
Friedheim, Arthur
Friedman, Ignaz
Friml, Rudolf
Gabrilowitsch, Ossip
Gallico, Paolo
Ganz, Rudolph
Garrison, Iliff
Gerdts, Felix
Gieseking, Walter
Gilbert, Harry M.
Giovanni, Irene di
Glass, Julia
Godowsky, Leopold
Golde, Walter
Goldsand, Robert
Goode, Blanche
Goodson, Katharine
Gordon, Phillip
Grange, Ina
Grey, Frank H.
Grieg, Edvard
Gruen, Rudolph
Grunn, Homer
Gunn, Alexander
Hageman, Richard
Hambourg, Mark
Hanke, Hans
Hansen, L. H.
Harrack, Charles de
Harris, Tomford
Harrison, Mary E.
Henneman, Alexander
Hejtmanek, Bozka
Henneman, Gertrude
Henrion, Theodore
Herbert, Victor
Hill, Alta
Hilsberg, Ignace
Himmelreich, Ferdinand
Hochman, Arthur
Hofmann, Josef
Horst, Louis
Hoschke, Frederick Albert
Howard, John Tasker
Huntley, Gertrude
Hyde, Herbert E.
Ilgenfritz, McNair
d'Indy, Vincent
Jacobi, Victor
Janssen, Werner
Joiner, Joseph
Jolas, Jacques
Jones, Elizabeth Gay
Kazounoff, Bernece
Kendall, Edwin
Kerekjarto, Duci de
Kerr, George
Koven, Reginald de
Klemen, Bertha
Kmita, Andrei
Kosloff, Alexis
Kreiselman, Gertrude
Kreisler, Fritz
Kroeger, Ernest R.
Kuhler, Mary Fromeyer
La Croix, Aurora
La Farge, Jean
La Forge, Frank
Lambert, Alexander
Lambert, Joseph
Lamson, Carl
Lamond, Frederic
Landow, Max
Landowska, Wanda
Lane, Eastwood
Lane, Victor
Laros, Earle
Lavarro, Enrico
Lecuona, Ernesto
Lederer, Henry
Lefévre, Henri
Leginska, Ethel
Leopold, Ralph
Leschetizky, Marie Gabrielle
Levitzki, Mischa
Lhévinne, Josef
Liszniewska, Marguerite Melville
Loesser, Arthur
Loth, Leslie
Macbride, Winifred
MacDermid, James G.
MacFadyen, Alexander
McManus, George
MacNabb, George
Maier, Guy
Mana Zucca
Manecolas, Emelio
Marvin, John
Mascagni, Pietro
Mason, Louise
Mayer, Estella
Melamet, Mrs. D. S.
Merola, Gaetano
Méro, Yolanda
Miessner, W. Otto
Mirovitch, Alfred
Moiseiwitsch, Benno
Morano, Loretto
Morrey, Grace Hamilton
Morris, Edward
Münz, Mieczyslaw
Nash, Frances
Navas, Raphael
Nearing, Homer
Ney, Elly
Noe, J. Thurston
Norfleet, Helen
Nyiregyhazi, Erwin
Orloff, Nicolas
Ornstein, Leo
Pascal, Julian
Pattison, Lee
Pauer, Max
Pelletier, Wilfrid
Perkins, Ray
Perry, Gray
Peters, Jessie
Piastro, Mishel
Pierson, Maude
Pollock, Muriel
Present, Rata
Proctor, George
Pugno, Raoul
Putz, Egon
Pyle, Wynne
Rachmaninoff, Sergei
Randegger, Giuseppe
Reinecke, Carl
Reisenauer, Alfred
Reisenberg, Nadia
Reyes, Juan
Rice-Gitz
Rickenbach, Paul
Rivers, Claire
Roberts, Lee S.
Robinson, Carol
Rosenthal, Adele
Rosenthal, Moriz
Ross, Gertrude
Ross, Stuart
Rubinstein, Arthur
Russell, Alexander
Rybner, Cornelius
Saint-Saëns, Camille
Samaroff, Olga
Samuels, Homer
Sapellnikoff, Wassily
Sauber, William
Sauer, Emil
Savino, Domenico
Scharwenka, Xaver
Schmitz, E. Robert
Schmitz, Fred A.
Schnabel, Artur
Schnabel-Tollefsen, Augusta
Schnitzer, Germaine
Scionti, Silvio
Scott, Cyril
Scriabine, Alexander
Sébestyén, George
Seligman, Isiah
Shackley, George
Sheridan, Frank
Shipman, Harry
Silber, Sidney
Simon, Morris
Sklarevski, Alexander
Smith, George
Smith, Harold
Souvaine, Henry
Sowerby, Leo
Spaeth, Sigmund
Sprague, Louis W.
Steeb, Olga
Steinfeldt, John M.
Sterling, Al
Stern, Lucie
Stojowski, Sigismund
Strauss, Lawrence
Strauss, Richard
Sturkow Ryder
Sullivan, Dan
Suskind, Milton
Sutherland, Alice
Swart, Stuart
Szumowska, Antoinette
Thompson, Ann
Tillotson, Frederic
Tolces, Toska
Tompkins, "Chick"
Tovar, José Conrado
Tovey, Donald F.
Tovey, Henry D.
Truxell, Earl
Tucker, Mercedes O'Leary
Turpin, H. P.
Utz, Lillian
Van den Berg, Brahm
Van Katwijk, Paul
Velázquez, José
Vertchamp, Joyce Albert
Volavy, Marguerite
Voorhees, Don
Ward-Stephens
Wayburn, Ned
Wehrmann-Schaffner, Eugenie
Wendling, Pete
Whittaker, James
Wille, Stewart
Williams, Guy Bevier
Winogradoff, Eleanor
Winston, Elizabeth
Winternitz, Felix
Winternitz, Otto
Wiswell, Jean
Wittgenstein, Victor
Yon, Pietro
Young, Victor
Zadora, Michael
Zardo, Eric
Zygman, Flora

## Supremacy In Popular Artists

Ampico supremacy in its artists playing popular music is evident in the lists of brilliant exponents of the art of interpreting music for dancing, and the current musical comedies and operettas.

No other reproducing piano can offer anything comparable with this list, all of whom are now recording exclusively for the Ampico, and many of them have never recorded their playing except for the Ampico. They are names of pianists and composers of international reputation, widely known and acclaimed through their appearances in stage productions of the highest class.

Vincent Lopez
Zez Confrey
Frank Banta
Vincent Youmans
Roy Bargy
Lee Sims
Adam Carroll
Ferdie Grofe
Edgar Fairchild
Ralph Rainger
J. Milton Delcamp
Frank Black
Richard Rodgers
Henry Lange
Ralph Reichenthal

**The following is a list of styles in which the Ampico was available (circa early 1929):**

**Upright Ampico Styles:**

**Marshall & Wendell – Style 5GE – Mahogany finish 4'2"**

**Ampico Grand Styles:**

**J&C Fischer – Style 14GE – Mahogany or Walnut 5'3"**
**Marshall & Wendell – Style GE – Mahogany 5'**
**Marshall & Wendell – Style GE Louis XVI Mahogany 5'**
**Marshall & Wendell – Style GE Wm.& Mary Mahogany 5'**
**Marshall & Wendell – Style GE Florentine – Walnut 5'**
**Chickering – Style 350 – Mahogany 5'4"**
**Chickering – Style 351 – Walnut 5'4"**
**Chickering – Style 375 Sheraton – Mahogany 5'4"**
**Chickering – Style 376 Florentine – Walnut 5'4"**
**Knabe – Style 53GE – Mahogany or Walnut 5'3"**
**Knabe – Style 53GE Louis XV – Walnut 5'3"**
**Knabe – Style 53GE Louis XVI – Walnut 5'3"**
**Knabe – Style 58GE – Mahogany or Walnut 5'8"**
**Knabe – Style 58GE Louis XV – Walnut 5'8"**
**Mason & Hamlin – Style RA – Mahogany 5'8"**
**Mason & Hamlin – Style RA Colonial – Mahogany 5'8"**
**Mason & Hamlin – Style RA Florentine – Walnut 5'8"**
**Mason & Hamlin – Style RA Louis XV – Walnut 5'8"**
**Mason & Hamlin – Style RA Louis XVI – Walnut 5'8"**
**Mason & Hamlin – Style RA Sheraton – Mahogany 5'8"**

**In addition to the above list we mention Mason & Hamlin styles RAA (6'1"), RBB (6'11"), and RCC (8'11") which were built only on special order. A few RAA and RBB model Mason & Hamlin pianos were built later with the Model B mechanism, but there is no record of similarly equipped Style RCC instruments having been produced.**

# AMPICO

## AND THE GREAT PIANISTS OF THE LAST QUARTER CENTURY

THE absurd claims that are being made concerning the so-called "exclusive" services of recording pianists make especially interesting this frank analysis of a very interesting situation.

In the strict sense of the word no artist can be termed "exclusive" if his playing may be heard through the medium of more than one reproducing piano. There is a group of artists who are genuinely "exclusively" Ampico in that they have never recorded their playing for any other reproducing piano, being unwilling to admit that any other does justice to their art. In the list of Ampico artists there are fifteen of these. It is brilliant with the names of Rosenthal, Rachmaninoff, Brailowsky, Levitzki, Mirovitch, Moiseiwitsch, Münz, Ornstein, Orloff, and others, all of whom are in the first rank of living pianists. From the list herewith of seventy-two ranking pianists no other so-called reproducing piano can show more than seven literally "exclusive" artists, with hardly a single name to rank with those who thus record exclusively for the Ampico.

**Above and right: "Ampico and the Great Pianists of the Last Quarter Century." The listing of the pianists appears on page 282.**

Most of the pianists of the older generation have recorded their playing for several companies, and, while they may be at present under an exclusive contract to play for one instrument only, this does not give exclusiveness, in the real sense of the word.

The Ampico Corporation, and other makers of reproducing instruments, have at present contracts with a large number of pianists who have previously recorded for other instruments. Such artists are referred to by the Ampico Corporation as *now* exclusively Ampico to make it clear that there is no claim or implication that they may be heard only on the Ampico. The chart on the inside of these pages makes the whole situation easy of visualization. Viewed from every angle the list of Ampico artists stands without a real rival. In the last analysis its proudest distinction is that select circle of genius represented by those who have insisted that the Ampico alone is worthy of perpetuating their art. Such giants can be heard on an actual piano only when playing in person or through their Ampico recordings.

Is not this a true exclusiveness in the best and only real sense of the word?

The list of pianists used in this analysis may be regarded as official for it has been made with the valuable assistance of several of the leading music critics of New York and Boston.

AMPICO

Chickering Stoddard-Ampico upright reproducing piano. This instrument originally sold for $1675 in 1919. The top panels and bottom panels have been removed to facilitate a view of the interior.

View of the bottom part of the Chickering Ampico described to the left. (William Singleton Collection).

Appreciated by a relatively few persons as recently as 1960, reproducing pianos are now being appreciated by thousands of collectors and other enthusiasts who have learned that they are not musical curiosities but are instruments capable of really outstanding serious performances. Collector groups such as the Automatic Musical Instrument Collectors' Association (AMICA), the Musical Box Society International, and, in Britain, the Player Piano Group, have done much to further research and interest into these instruments in recent years.

Above: Wm. Knabe grand piano with Style B Ampico mechanism. (Singleton Collection).

Right: The underside of another Knabe grand piano incorporating a Style B Ampico action. As the network of tubing, dozens of connections, and other features show, these are rather complex mechanisms. However, with patience, understanding, and care reproducing pianos can be restored to their original musical excellence. Refer to David Saul's general comments on rebuilding for more on this subject.

THE AMPICO is probably the most remarkable invention in connection with music since the invention of the piano itself. It is impossible to convey adequately the true significance and the marvel of the performance of the AMPICO to one who has not heard it.

It re-enacts the playing of the pianists who have recorded for it so minutely and with such extraordinary perfection that it is impossible to distinguish it from the actual performance of the living pianist.

On many occasions the AMPICO has been subjected to the test of being heard publicly in the same concert with the artists themselves, repeating, immediately after the performance by the living pianist, the same piece from a recording previously made at the AMPICO Studios in New York.

The opinions of the critics writing of these occasions are probably the best evidence which can be presented of what the AMPICO does. In several of the larger cities of our country, Leopold Godowsky, Mischa Levitzki, George Copeland, Arthur Rubinstein, Leo Ornstein and Benno Moiseiwitsch have appeared in these joint recitals with the AMPICO.

The critic of the Musical Courier, reviewing one of these concerts writes:

"To those who heard this instrument for the first time, it was a revelation." In emphasizing the extent to which the AMPICO reflected the individual style of each pianist, this journal continues: "Those who are not strangers to the work of these pianists are aware of the fact that each of them has a distinct mode of musical expression. Nevertheless, the reproductions of their characteristics were amazingly faithful—Copeland's celebrated command of touch and tone, Levitzki's clarity and musicianly phrasing, Ornstein's coloring and ability to project the mood of his music, Rubinstein's incisive rhythms and general brilliant qualities as a virtuoso in the traditional style—*the Ampico reflected them all with human understanding.* Always there was fidelity, even to the most subtle nuance, and charming spontaneity."

Philip Hale, critic of the Boston Herald, is well known to musicians as one of the most discriminating judges of musical interpretation. His interest in this triumphant demonstration of the unique qualities of the AMPICO evidenced itself in a long review in which, amongst other things, he said:

"The AMPICO piano made remarkable reproductions of the characteristic interpretations of these pianists. At times the pianist would stop playing; the AMPICO would go on as if he were not idle. Then the pianist would again take up the wondrous tale. In some instances the performance by the AMPICO of the whole composition was identical with the original; in other instances the *Ampico surpassed what had gone before, and thus did justice to the pianist when he had fallen below his own standard.* Especially noteworthy were the many charming nuances. Not for a moment was there any suggestion of rigid, inflexible, purely mechanical mimicry. *The playing was as free, elastic, spontaneous as though a gifted mortal were the performer.*"

Mr. H. T. Parker, critic of the Boston Transcript, observes at the conclusion of an extended appreciation: "It is customary to call this recording, this reproduction, the mechanical process of a material age; but to the pianist at least, there is a very personal element, while the listener needs only a little imagination to make it uncanny."

The AMPICO not only faithfully renders the letter of the virtuoso's playing, but catches his spirit. It brings into the home the playing of the greatest pianists in the world, playing the great classic masterpieces, the finest artistry of temperamental artists who contribute the lighter classics, operatic selections, old songs, and masters of syncopation whose playing of current popular ragtime, musical comedy and music for dancing, is all of the highest order.

In a word, the AMPICO provides music of all kinds ideally played. Special literature regarding the AMPICO will be furnished upon request.

AMPICO

STYLE 52

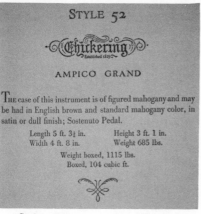

Chickering
Established 1823

AMPICO GRAND

THE case of this instrument is of figured mahogany and may be had in English brown and standard mahogany color, in satin or dull finish; Sostenuto Pedal.

Length 5 ft. 3½ in. Height 3 ft. 1 in.
Width 4 ft. 8 in. Weight 685 lbs.
Weight boxed, 1115 lbs.
Boxed, 104 cubic ft.

**Style 52, a popular Chickering Ampico A model.**

STYLE 58

Chickering
Established 1823

AMPICO GRAND

THE case of this instrument is in figured mahogany and may be had in English brown and standard mahogany color in satin or dull finish; sostenuto pedal.

Length 5 ft. 8 in. Height 3 ft. 3 in.
Width 4 ft. 11¾ in. Weight 800 lbs.

Weight boxed, 1250 lbs.
Boxed, 104 cubic ft.

STYLE 65

Chickering
Established 1823

AMPICO GRAND

THE case of this instrument is in figured mahogany and may be had in English brown and standard mahogany color in satin or dull finish; sostenuto pedal.

Length 6 ft. 5 in. Height 3 ft. 3 in.
Width 4 ft. 10 in. Weight 956 lbs.

Weight boxed, 1406 lbs.
Boxed, 104 cubic ft.

**Type A Ampico grand pianos made by Chickering — as illustrated in a catalogue of the 1920's. Picturing the instruments in elegant surroundings was a popular way to illustrate reproducing pianos of all makes during this era. (Catalogue and other information courtesy of William Singleton).**

STYLE 52 FLORENTINE

Chickering
Established 1823

AMPICO GRAND

THERE is an extraordinary charm in this beautiful piano. The restraint of the best of the style known as "Renaissance" is brought to its designing. Its case of rich walnut, the ornamentation treated in dull gold and colors in the Florentine manner, gives it a highly decorative value.

Length 5 ft. 3½ in. Height 3 ft. 1 in.
Width 4 ft. 8 in. Weight 685 lbs.

Weight Boxed, 1115 lbs.
Boxed, 104 cubic ft.

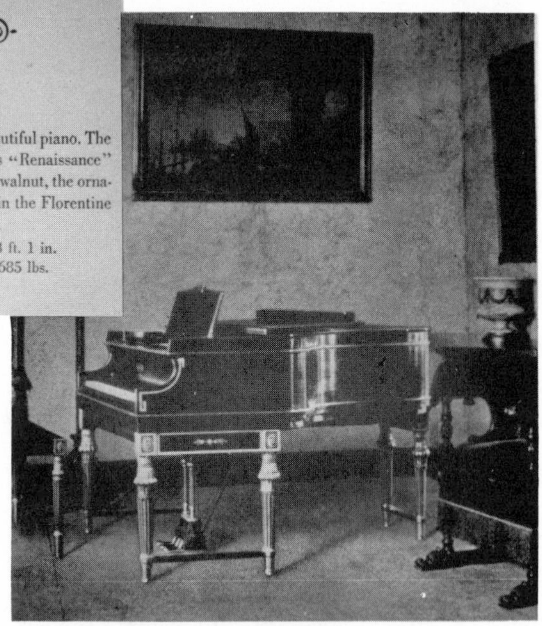

**Louis XV Case**

THE case of this instrument is of figured mahogany, and may be had in standard mahogany and English brown color either in satin or dull finish; Sostenuto Pedal; duet bench to match.

*Also obtainable without the Ampico as Style J.*

| STYLE 58 LF | STYLE J |
|---|---|
| Length 5 ft. 8 in. | Length 5 ft. 8 in. |
| Width 4 ft. 11¾ in. | Width 4 ft. 11¾ in. |
| Height 3 ft. 3 in. | Height 3 ft. 3 in. |
| Weight 800 lbs. | Weight 645 lbs. |
| Weight, boxed, 1250 lbs. | Weight, boxed, 950 lbs. |
| Boxed, 104 cubic ft. | Boxed, 86 cubic ft. |

$1875. straight grand
3975. ampico

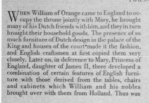

## William and Mary
1689—1702

When William of Orange came to England to occupy the throne jointly with Mary, he brought many of his Dutch friends with him, and they in turn brought their household goods. The presence of so much furniture of Dutch design in the palace of the King and houses of the court made it the fashion, and English craftsmen at first copied them very closely. Later on, in deference to Mary, Princess of England, daughter of James II, there developed a combination of certain features of English furniture with those derived from the tables, chairs and cabinets which William and his nobles brought over with them from Holland. Thus was the style known as "William and Mary" created. It has a substantial simplicity, together with a pleasing intimate quality that gives it an extraordinary personality and seems peculiarly the furniture of the home. The domestic, home-loving nature of William and Mary, their honesty of purpose and fine integrity, their affection for each other, all seem to be reflected in the wholesome, sterling qualities of the style that bears their name. It is one particularly adapted to the case of a grand piano, and it has been most successfully applied in this beautiful little instrument. In combination with furniture of other periods it seems at its best.

## Louis XVI
1774—1793

Toward the close of the reign of Louis XV, French society, weary of the domination of the King's mistresses, the intrigues and extravagances of court life, looked forward to the impending death of the King and the accession of his grandson and the beautiful Marie Antoinette, daughter of Maria Theresa of Austria.

Already her influence was felt at court. She abhorred the pomp and ceremony of official functions; she preferred the small house given to her husband as a residence pending his accession, and loved to busy herself in her garden and dairy.

When her husband came to the throne as Louis XVI, architecture became more simple, scrolls and curves gave way to straight lines, classic columns and pilasters reappeared in architecture and interior decoration. Instead of irregular shaped panels and super-abundant ornamentation, we find rectangular panels formed by simple mouldings.

The great master-craftsmen, quick to sense the change in popular taste, set themselves to the creating of a style which will ever remain one of the most beautiful in all the history of art and decoration.

The piano shown here is of the simpler type of Louis XVI, one which combines perfectly with other periods, giving artistic touch to the room containing it.

## Style 52 WM

Chickering
Established 1823

### WILLIAM and MARY AMPICO GRAND

The case of this instrument is of plain mahogany, obtainable in English brown color in satin or dull finish; Sostenuto Pedal; duet bench with music compartment to match.

*Also obtainable without the Ampico as style FWM*

| Style 52 WM | Style FWM |
|---|---|
| Length 5 ft. 3½ in. | Length 5 ft. 3½ in. |
| Width 4 ft. 8 in. | Width 4 ft. 8 in. |
| Height 3 ft. 1 in. | Height 3 ft. 1 in. |
| Weight 685 lbs. | Weight 520 lbs. |
| Weight, boxed, 1115 lbs. | Weight, boxed, 855 lbs. |
| Boxed, 104 cubic ft. | Boxed, 86 cubic ft. |

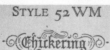

**Various Chickering Ampico grands, Style A, are shown here.**

## Style 52 LS

Chickering
Established 1823

### LOUIS XVI AMPICO GRAND

The case of this instrument is of figured mahogany and may be had in English brown color, in satin or dull finish; Sostenuto Pedal; duet bench with music compartment to match.

*Also obtainable without the Ampico as style GLS*

| Style 52 LS | Style GLS |
|---|---|
| Length 5 ft. 3½ in. | Length 5 ft. 3½ in. |
| Width 4 ft. 8 in. | Width 4 ft. 8 in. |
| Height 3 ft. 1 in. | Height 3 ft. 1 in. |
| Weight 685 lbs. | Weight 520 lbs. |
| Weight, boxed, 1115 lbs. | Weight, boxed, 855 lbs. |
| Boxed, 104 cubic ft | Boxed, 86 cubic ft. |

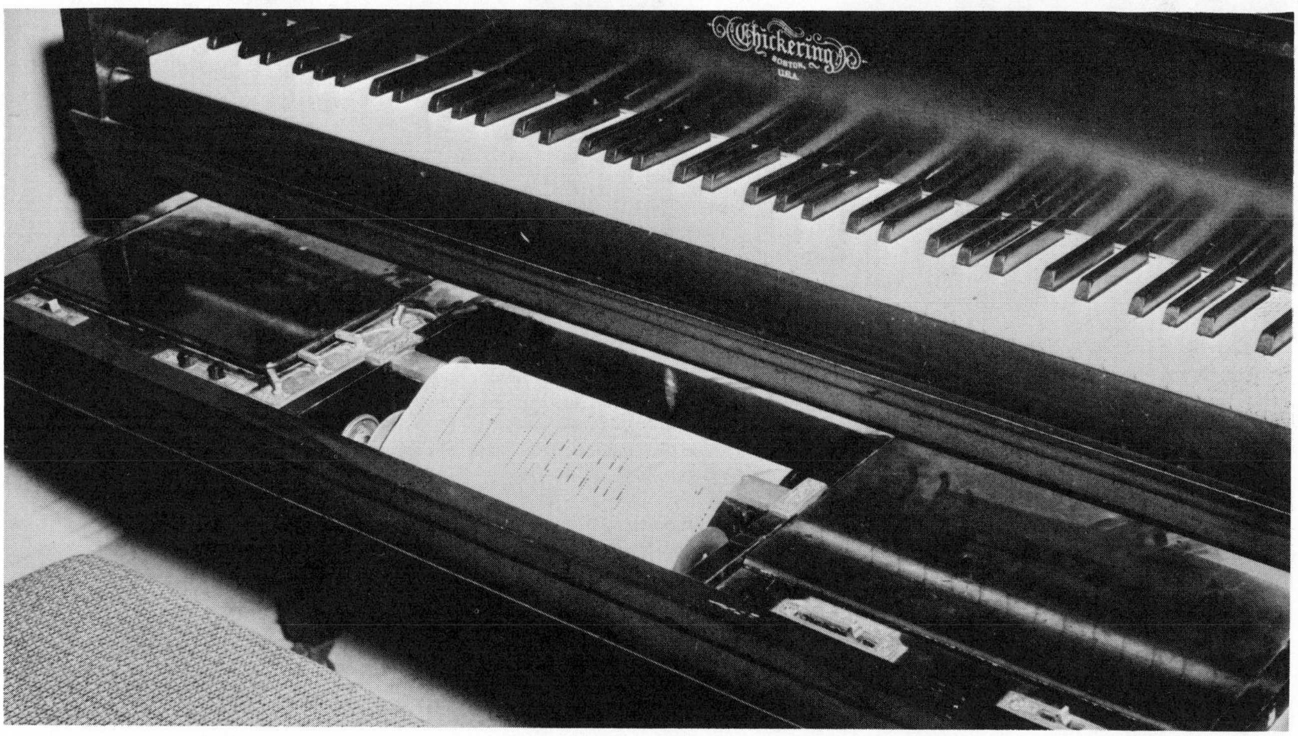

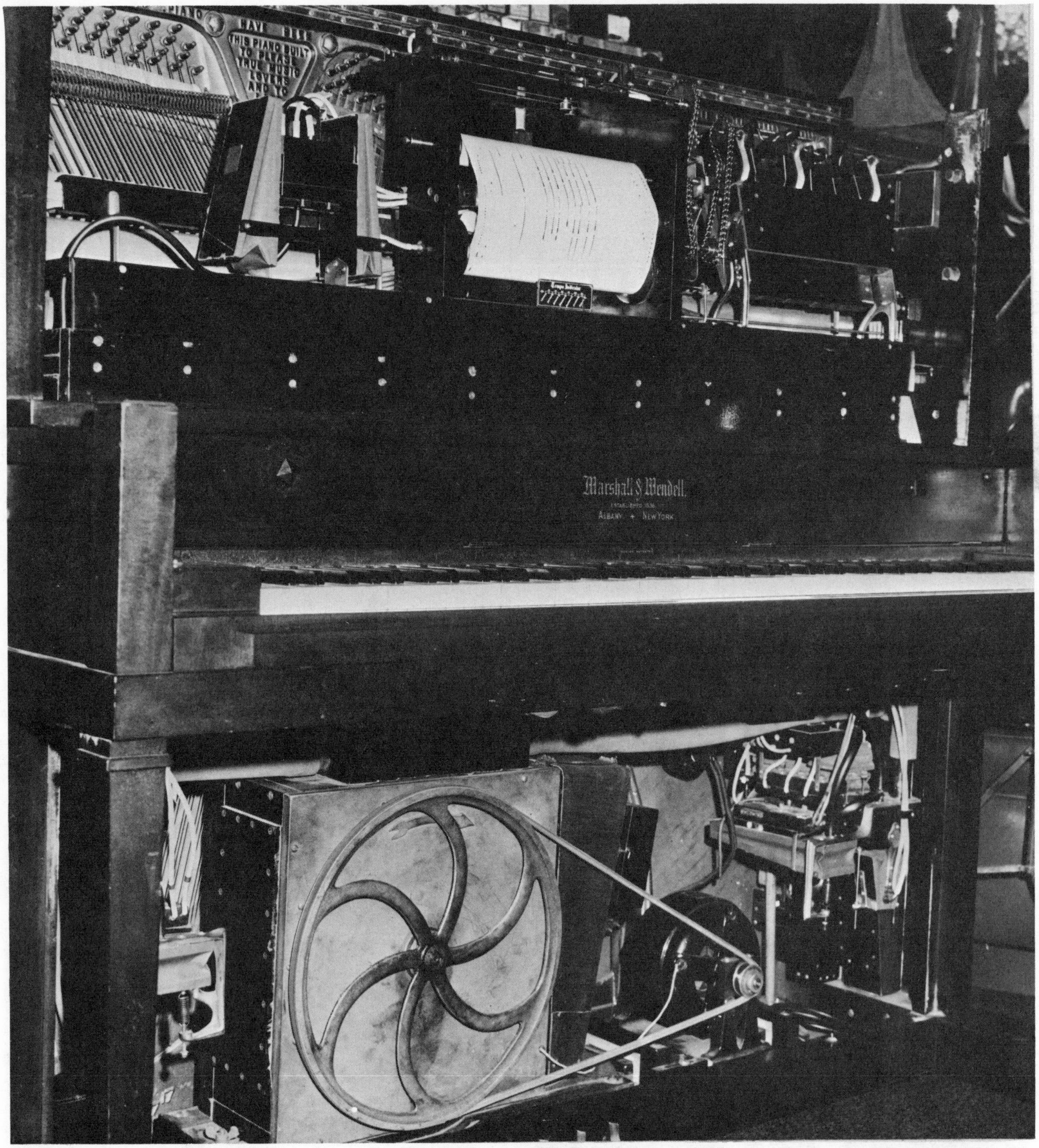

Among upright Ampico reproducing pianos, probably more Marshall & Wendell instruments were made than were those of any other make. On the piano itself the quality of the instrument was made known to the purchaser by the exposition awards (see left) reproduced in gold decals on the underside of the lid, by the "This piano built to please true music lovers and to last a life time" notation cast into the piano plate, and by other prominently displayed assurances of quality.

Exposition awards were a popular advertising gimmick during the late 19th and early 20th century. In return for entering an exhibition (and paying to do so) the manufacturer was assured of a "gold medal" or similar commendation. Of course gold medals would have been expensive to produce and would have reduced exhibition profits, so at least in one instance (the Louisiana Purchase Exposition of 1903) the "gold medals" were actually of cheap bronze – however each had the wording "GOLD MEDAL" on it!

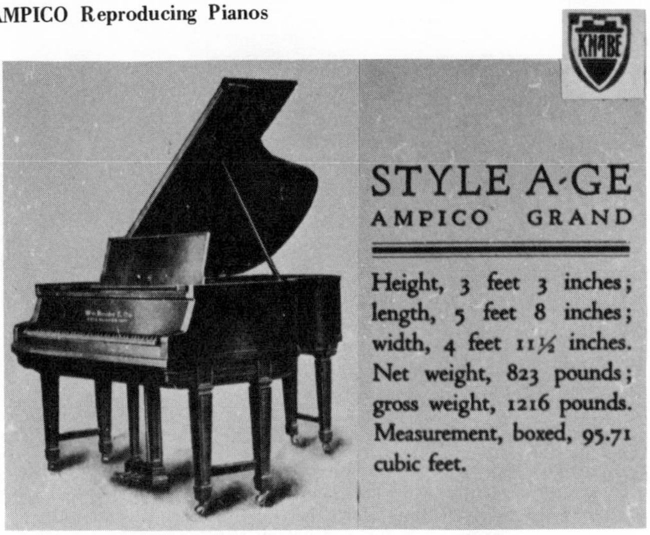

STYLE A-GE
AMPICO GRAND
Height, 3 feet 3 inches; length, 5 feet 8 inches; width, 4 feet 11½ inches. Net weight, 823 pounds; gross weight, 1216 pounds. Measurement, boxed, 95.71 cubic feet.


Knabe Style A Ampico grand known as Style A-GE. Among Ampico pianos Knabe was second only to Mason & Hamlin in price. In addition to standard models (such as those shown on this page), special art design cases could be obtained on special order.

STYLE K-GE
AMPICO UPRIGHT
Height, 4 feet 8¾ inches; depth, 2 feet 5 inches; width, 5 feet 4¼ inches. Net weight, 911 pounds; gross weight, 1187 pounds. Measurement, boxed, 89.11 cubic feet.


Knabe A Ampico upright, Style K-GE.

STYLE J-GE
AMPICO UPRIGHT
Height, 4 feet 4¼ inches; depth, 2 feet 4¾ inches; width, 5 feet 1 inch. Net weight, 779 pounds; gross weight, 1055 pounds. Measurement, boxed, 86.14 cubic feet.


Knabe A Ampico upright, Style J-GE.

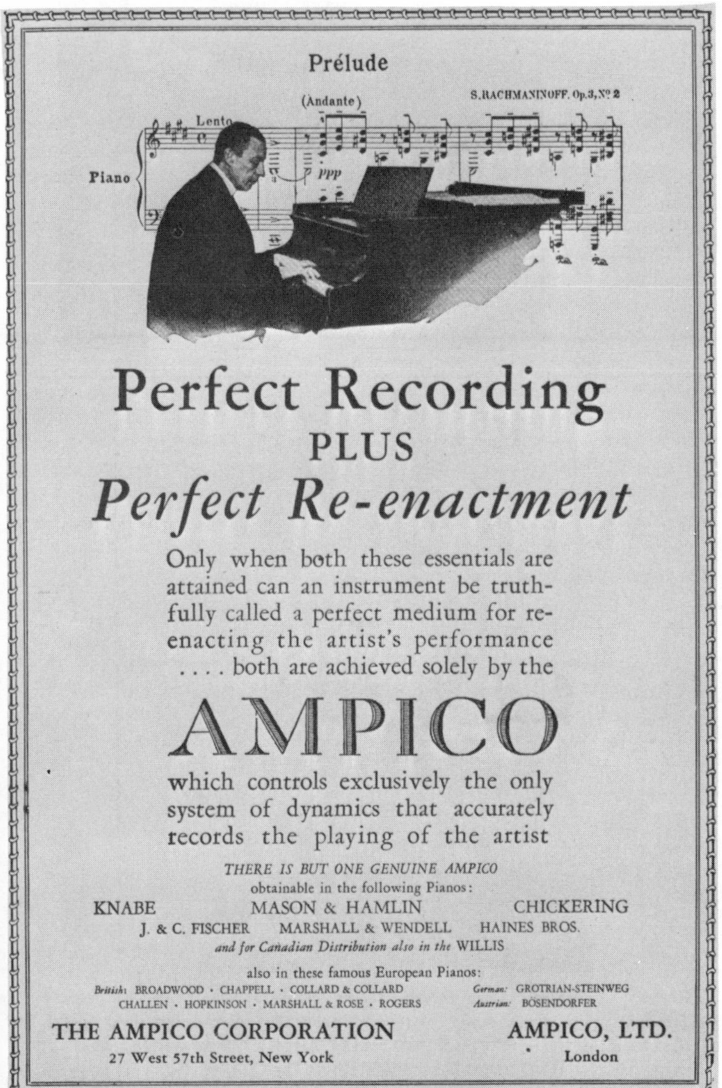


Ampico advertisement (from "Player Piano Treasury").

Knabe Ampico reproducing grand piano, A type, in an ornate case.

Left: Ampico's last marketing effort was a spinet model as shown (from "Player Piano Treasury"). While this 1938 advertisement features a Knabe (or Fischer, if you look at the piano fallboard), the identical instrument was available with Steck and possibly other decals. Irrespective of the name on the instrument, all were identical – just the name was different!

Above and below: Views of a "Steck" Ampico spinet. To cram so many mechanisms into such a small space almost required a shoehorn! Note that the roll loads into the top of the piano. (David Saul photos)

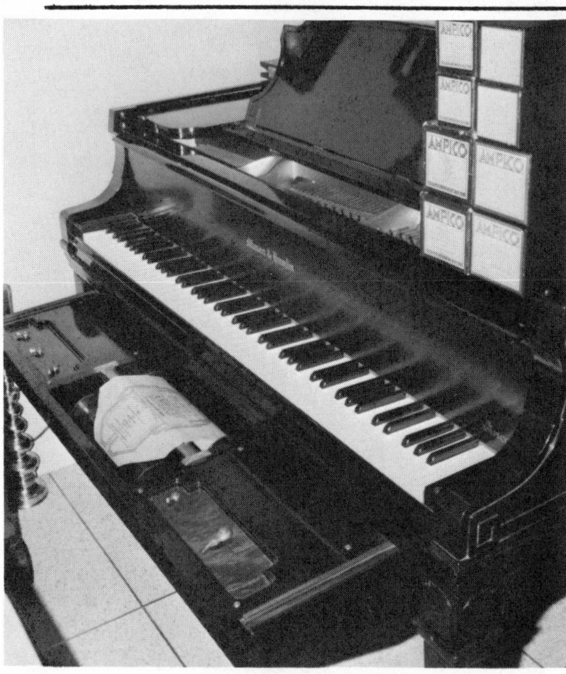

5'8" Mason & Hamlin Ampico B, serial No. RA42532, in the collection of Ivan and Joan Shapiro. Some 250 Mason & Hamlin Ampico B's were made, the "top of the line" in the Ampico series.

Chickering 9' grand piano incorporating an Ampico A mechanism, circa 1926. Ivan Shapiro, the owner, notes: "There are several features about the piano that lead me to believe it was made for travelling concert use. There are moving skids along the bass side. There are three legs instead of six (most concert hall instruments have three; home model reproducing pianos usually have six). The piano is equipped with interchangeable A.C. and D.C. motors, presumably for adapting to changing types of electricity on a tour."

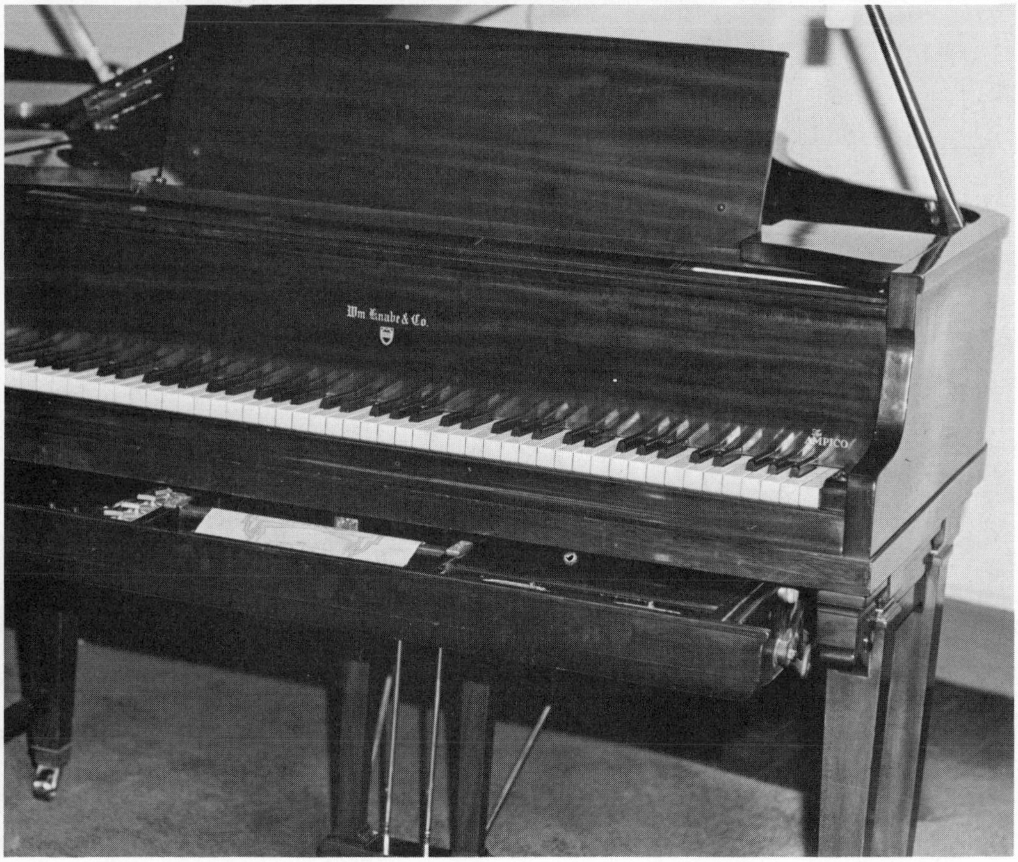


Above: Ampico B mechanism in a Knabe grand piano. Note the rich grain of the wood, a hallmark of many Knabe grands.

Left: Ampico A mechanism in a 5'4" Knabe grand piano made in 1928. Note that the mechanism controls are of the sliding type in the A Ampico and are of the dial type in the style B (as shown at the top of this page). (Ellsworth Johnson photos).

Today collectors can order quality recuts of original Ampico, Duo-Art, and other rolls from various sources. A new industry of piano rebuilding and roll recutting was born in the 1960's and continues today.

Left: Steinway & Sons Model B Ampico. This instrument, owned by Mr. Donald Carter of Vestal, New York, is a regular Steinway Style S built in 1937 (Serial No. 288461), according to a letter from Henry Z. Steinway, president of Steinway & Sons. The Ampico mechanism was installed later at the East Rochester, N.Y., factory after the instrument was sold to its original owner. (Harvey Roehl photo).

Below: Another unusual Steinway Ampico B. This instrument, originally a conventional Steinway grand piano, was converted by the Aeolian - American Company in 1942 to the Ampico configuration. The drawer is shown extended from the front of the piano – in the position used to insert and remove rolls, to adjust the tempo, and to otherwise operate the Ampico. (William Singleton photo of the instrument owned by Mr. and Mrs. Bernard F. Hallenberg).

## UNDERSTANDING THE ARTECHO

*by David L. Saul*

Note: The Artecho system was also called the Apollo and the Celco.

The Artecho system enjoyed a comparatively short lifespan in the reproducing piano market. It faded into obscurity in the mid-1920's, barely a decade after its introduction. Artecho's business interests were originally controlled by the Melville Clark Piano Company of DeKalb, Illinois, although the Artecho mechanism itself was built by the Amphion Company — the same firm which for many years produced Ampico mechanisms as an American Piano Company subsidiary. The Melville Clark firm offered the Artecho in its line of Apollo pianos. The same system was also offered as the Celco, and with that designation was installed in Emerson, Lindeman, and A.B. Chase pianos.

In September, 1919, the Apollo Piano Company, a firm jointly owned by the Rudolph Wurlitzer Company and by the Amphion Piano Player Company, acquired the Melville Clark Piano Company. Wurlitzer, using the Apollo name instead of Artecho, then installed the Amphion-produced mechanism in its own line of pianos. The Wurlitzer Apollo Reproducing Piano was marketed for several years, but never achieved widespread popularity.

Rolls were produced by the QRS Company (which, incidentally, was formerly owned by Melville Clark). In 1921 a fairly elaborate catalogue of QRS Artecho rolls was published. Many Artecho rolls were adapted from Welte-Mignon performances under terms of a special agreement with that firm, and Ampico recordings were the basis of some of the later issues.

Legal Note: By an agreement dated January 30, 1920, Welte agreed "upon demand of Wurlitzer to furnish to Wurlitzer one proper master record of each music roll in its piano catalogue (except the rolls recorded by 36 selected pianists excluded from the agreement), for use by Wurlitzer as masters in making music rolls herefrom, and Wurlitzer shall pay Welte for each such master roll the sum of $10. Wurlitzer agrees that it will not use marginal perforations which would permit the rolls manufactured by it to be used on other instruments made by Welte, the Auto Pneumatic Action Co. [Welte Licensee], or Amphion [Ampico]." The agreement further stated that Wurlitzer "expressly promises and agrees that it will not use the name 'Welte' or 'Welte Mignon' in any manner, on any mechanisms, or on any music rolls, except that the music rolls and labels on the boxes of music rolls made from Welte masters may bear a legend as follows: 'Played by (name of artist) for M. Welte & Sons, Inc. or M. Welte & Söhne' (as the case may be) — always followed by the word 'Licensed.'" A somewhat similar agreement was made in 1921 with Q.R.S.

In the instances in which Artecho rolls were made from Ampico, Welte, or Q.R.S. masters the expression coding had to be revised, of course, to match the technical features of the Artecho system. Some of the Artecho rolls made from Q.R.S. masters are simply ordinary Q.R.S. rolls (intended for the foot-pumped home player piano) with expression perforations added.

Rolls of the Artecho type were issued with a specially styled Apollo label after Wurlitzer began using the system. On occasion the Apollo labels were even glued over already-present Artecho labels! "Apollo" was a popular name, and other rolls using it appeared from time to time. Those of a reproducing nature and associated with the Artecho system have the word Apollo in white letters against a dark blue background at the top of the label.

Drawers are utilized in all grand piano installations of the Artecho family. A distinctive feature for identification purposes is the so-called Modulator Lever found in the drawer (or in the upright's spoolbox) whose operating positions are labelled NORMAL and SOFT. Many examples have elegantly crafted and artistically detailed drawer hardware. The silver-like lustre of metalwork in such installations highlights the appearance of wood panels handsomely finished to match the piano in which the drawer is installed.

Some caution must be exercised in identifying pianos bearing the Apollo name as that particular designation was used in connection with many types of instruments over the years, ranging in variety from ordinary foot-pumped players to expression pianos of the Recordo and Welte families. Some late Wurlitzer-built pianos bear the Apollo name but have other mechanisms. Apollo pianos with Welte (Licensee) actions are known. As noted, the Apollo nomenclature is confusing in regard to rolls and the pianos themselves. Check carefully any Apollo offered to be sure you are obtaining what you are seeking.

In its technology the Artecho bears a striking resemblance to the Ampico, a situation which is not surprising in view of the fact that both systems were manufactured by the same firm. Pneumatic stacks, detachable valve blocks, and many other components are virtually identical in the two systems and many parts are fully interchangeable. The Artecho expression system, however, is quite different in design from its contemporary Ampico counterpart. In spite of mechanical differences, the mechanism responds to expression coding patterned closely after the Ampico scheme.

Artecho, like Ampico, employs a combination of intensity steps and crescendo operation, and the explanation found under the Ampico section of this book is applicable with only minor changes. The intensity step scheme is virtually identical to Ampico's except for locations of corresponding types of expression ports on the respective tracker bars. The reason for this is explained by a May 3, 1921, agreement between Amphion and Wurlitzer: "The arrangement of the holes in the tracker bar and the holes in the music roll to be used by the said second party (Wurlitzer) for cooperating with said devices to give expression in playing shall be differently arranged from the standard of such holes as now used by said first party (Amphion) and the American Piano Company for its Ampico action and shall be incapable of operating with the rolls made to said (Ampico) standards."

Artecho's method of crescendo operation is unique, however. The Artecho system uses a single-speed crescendo device which operates rather quickly. When slower crescendo operation is called for, the unit can be activated by a series of short impulses to produce the effect of a more gradual crescendo. The piano keyboard is divided into two sections with separate expression units independently controlling the bass and treble dynamics.

An interesting feature of the Artecho system is the so-called pianissimo device. Providing an extra intensity step below "normal" for extremely soft playing, this feature was later adopted in principle for use in the Model B Ampico.

## UNDERSTANDING THE ARTRIO-ANGELUS

*by David L. Saul*

The Artrio-Angelus, usually just called the "Angelus" in original sales literature, was a product of the Wilcox & White Company of Meriden, Connecticut, a firm well known for its many pioneering developments in the field of roll operated instruments. Introduced in 1915, the Artrio-Angelus reproducing system was offered in Wilcox & White pianos as well as in other selected piano brands, among which were the products of Mehlin & Son.

Financial difficulties overtook Wilcox & White in the aftermath of World War I. By 1921 the firm was bankrupt. The plant was sold to Conway Industries in 1922. Conway already controlled several firms at the time, foremost among which were the Hallet & Davis Piano Company and the Simplex Player Action Company. Following the change in ownership all facilities in Meriden were shut down with the exception of the Angelus recording laboratory.

Simplex took over Artrio-Angelus production, redesigning the mechanism to incorporate many of its own player action components. Although many mechanical features were radically changed, the basic principles of operation were retained; the Simplex-produced mechanism responds to the same rolls as the earlier Wilcox & White type. The redesigned system was offered in Hallet & Davis, Merrill, and Conway pianos. The "Artrio" was dropped in later years and, as noted earlier, the system was known as the Angelus.

Grand pianos containing the Wilcox & White mechanism had their spoolboxes situated above the keyboard in a fashion similar to the Duo-Art. The redesigned Simplex mechanism, however, was housed in a drawer. In the latter type of installation the drawer contains not only the spoolbox, but the entire pneumatic stack and expression mechanism as well. "The entire playing unit is in the drawer, which is readily removable from the piano — no folding rubber tubes" noted an Angelus advertisement. Piano keys are activated via a set of "roller wires," arranged so as to permit the instrument to be played with the drawer in any position.

Installations were by no means limited to grand pianos. Both early and late types of mechanism were installed in uprights as well. Although the Angelus' popularity never reached the level enjoyed by members of the "big three" — Ampico, Duo-Art, and Welte — production continued through the 1920's until the close of the decade.

Recordings for the Angelus were made in a specially equipped laboratory in Meriden. In spite of the Angelus' minority status in the reproducer field, a rather impressive library of recordings was offered. Many top artists recorded for the system. Included were Harold Bauer, Ossip Gabrilowitsch, and Leopold Godowsky. In the field of lighter music the names of George Gershwin, Felix Arndt, and Eubie Blake are found among the listed artists.

Many musical selections were recorded exclusively for the Angelus. In this category is found what must be the longest work ever issued on piano rolls — Godowsky's performance of his own "Triakontameron" in a thirty roll set! Although most Angelus rolls were recorded specifically for that system, some selections were adapted from Duo-Art performances. A few catalogue entries are also identified as originating from "foreign recordings." Angelus recording activities continued at Meriden until 1926, at which time all roll production facilities were sold to the QRS Company. QRS continued to make new recordings until about 1930.

The expression coding scheme used in Angelus rolls follows closely along the lines of the Duo-Art coding method, although there are some significant differences. The collector who is thoroughly familiar with Duo-Art operation will encounter little difficulty in understanding the Angelus. The so-called "melodant" perforations in Angelus rolls are similar in nature and physical appearance to Duo-Art's theme perforations (i.e., "snakebites") and are similarly used for accenting purposes. The Angelus' solo and accompaniment playing powers correspond in principle to Duo-Art's theme and accompaniment, respectively. In contrast to Duo-Art's method of operation, however, the Angelus' solo and accompaniment regulators are not independent but, rather, are connected in tandem. The Angelus coding scheme employs five tracks for solo expression and three for accompaniment. Accompaniment playing power is double-regulated by virtue of the tandem configuration and thus is controlled by all eight tracks of expression coding. When solo (theme) is activated, the accompaniment regulator is simply bypassed, and solo notes are governed in their dynamic power by five tracks of expression coding. The keyboard is divided into two sections to permit application of solo power independently to either bass or treble while the other section remains under accompaniment control. While the Angelus' philosophy of dynamic control parallels Duo-Art's in certain respects, the expression mechanisms of the two instruments are engineered in totally different ways.

Technical information for both Wilcox & White and Simplex versions of the Angelus can be found in the respective service manuals, both of which are available in reprint form.

----------

Note: Do not confuse with the similarly-named "Angelus" player piano.

Left: An advertisement for the Angelus player piano. "If you prefer [to the music of a regular Angelus player piano] the actual performance of such great masters as Godowsky, Bauer, Yolande Merö, Herma Menth, and Gabrilowitsch to your own interpretations then your want is filled by the Artrio Angelus Reproducing Piano — the electrically-operated Angelus achievement that is the admiration of the music world."

Note: A general history of Wilcox & White, written by Alan R. Pier, appeared in Vol. XVI, No. 2 of the Musical Box Society "Bulletin" (1969). Refer also to the organette and player reed organ section of this book. Information concerning Wilcox & White player organs is given.

## UNDERSTANDING THE DUO-ART
*by David L. Saul*

The Aeolian Corporation's Duo-Art Pianola was formally introduced in 1913. This instrument, later re-named the Duo-Art Reproducing Piano, won widespread acceptance and popularity, maintaining an enviable marketing position as long as reproducing pianos were built and sold.

The firm that conceived and built the Duo-Art was large and dynamic. The New York based company's many-faceted activities extended far beyond national borders, permitting business operations on a worldwide scale. With showrooms in London, Paris, Madrid, and Melbourne, Duo-Arts were distributed on an international scale. Recording studios were established in London and New York, and rolls were manufactured at both locations.

The Duo-Art was featured in Steinway pianos in addition to Aeolian's own makes, which carried the well-known names of Weber, Steck, Wheelock, Stroud, and Aeolian. Sizes ranged upward from baby grands and compact studio uprights, with the largest of Steinway and Weber concert grand Duo-Arts measuring over nine feet in length. Case styles ranged from conservatively simple to exceedingly ornate, with custom art cases available in period furniture styles to match any decor. The very ornate instruments frequently required special orders to be placed months in advance and were extremely expensive. As a result, most Duo-Arts built and sold were conservative in terms of style and appearance.

Duo-Arts are quite easy to identify, with the names "Aeolian" and "Duo-Art" usually displayed quite conspicuously. If the name is not found for some reason, a glance at the tracker bar will reveal two sets of vertically elongated holes or ports (with four holes per set) located at opposite ends of the tracker bar. These special openings have the appearance of slots and are situated above the level of the other holes. These rather conspicuous ports are used for reading the Duo-Art's special form of dynamic coding.

Duo-Art grands have their spoolboxes built into the piano case above the keys. Exceptions are a very few late Duo-Arts which are equipped with drawers. The nearly universal case style with built-in spoolbox necessitated an extension of the overall piano length of approximately six inches.

Some Duo-Arts of very early manufacture have electrically powered vacuum pumps situated in separate cabinets, the early pumps being too large to conceal within piano cases. Duo-Art was not alone in this practice; in fact, Welte Mignon established the precedent. This configuration, expensive to build and not very practical from a logistics viewpoint, was terminated after more compact pumps became available.

A few foot-pumped Duo-Arts were made in both upright and grand styles. Some of these contained only half of the Duo-Art expression system, with remaining musical expression hopefully supplied through the artistry of the owner's feet. Most Duo-Arts are electrically powered and contain the complete and fully automatic expression system.

The Duo-Art differs in principle from most other reproducers in its employment of separate expression controls for theme and accompaniment use. Some notes, such as those of a melody, seem to predominate musically, being played louder as a general rule. For expression control purposes it is convenient to designate such notes as theme notes. Afforded less emphasis are certain other notes which fall into the accompaniment category. The Duo-Art's expression regulators simultaneously provide two playing powers or levels; one louder and the other more subdued. These are for theme and accompaniment use. Both levels are automatically variable as established by appropriate expression coding in the music roll, following the time-varying dynamic patterns of an artist's recorded keyboard performance. A scale of 16 steps or degrees ranging from very soft to moderately loud is used for accompaniment playing. A separate scale (which is regulated to a slightly louder level; e.g., when the theme bellows are collapsed 4/16" the accompaniment bellows will have to collapse 5/16" to play at exactly the same level) provides 16 additional steps for theme use.

The Duo-Art's accompaniment dynamics normally control the loudness of all playing except at those instants of time when theme notes occur in the music. Whenever theme notes occur, a rapid switching feature "overrides" the accompaniment and applies theme power, thus boosting loudness and producing the required accents. The theme mechanism is extremely fast in operation and is activated by pairs of tiny holes (sometimes called "snakebites" because of their similarity in appearance) which apply theme power at the instant of passing over a special port in the tracker bar. Theme power can be applied independently to bass or treble sections via theme ports at either end of the tracker bar.

Historically, the Duo-Art theme mechanism is an extension of Aeolian's Themodist principle which was invented by J.W. Crooks in 1900. The Themodist in its basic form is limited to two fixed, or in some cases manually variable, power levels. The Themodist employs "snakebite" perforations to accent selected notes, but utilizes no other automatic expression coding. The more sophisticated Duo-Art reproducing mechanism makes theme and accompaniment automatically variable to reconstruct the dynamics of recorded musical performances. Duo-Arts are generally equipped to play Themodist and ordinary player rolls as well as the special reproducing rolls made for exclusive Duo-Art use. However, only the Duo-Art rolls activate the reproducing mechanism.

Until very near the end of production, the Duo-Art mechanism retained substantially its original form and design. Certain improvements were incorporated with the passing of time, but the basic design of the expression system was not altered. As a consequence, all Duo-Art rolls are fully compatible with all Duo-Art pianos. Thus Aeolian's products are characterized by a greater degree of uniformity than was achieved by either of its two main rivals, Ampico and Welte.

On July 31, 1932, a public announcement was made of an impending merger, and within a few weeks the Aeolian Corporation was united with the American Piano Company (builder of the hitherto competing Ampico). Both types of reproducing pianos continued to be built by the newly-formed Aeolian American corporation, although production was severely curtailed as the country's economy was tragically impaired by the great depression.

Engineering efforts continued, although on a limited scale, and by about 1935 a totally redesigned Duo-Art mechanism had been introduced for use in grand pianos. The new system featured a drawer rather than a built-in spoolbox of the sort used for so many years previously. The new Duo-Art drawer was actually an adaptation of the Model B Ampico drawer; the two types being virtually identical aside from the tracker bars. The Duo-Art expression system was also redesigned to incorporate a unit now known among collectors as a "fan-type" expression box. The name derives from the fan-like appearance of the redesigned accordion pneumatics. The so-called accordion pneumatics are a distinctive feature of the Duo-Art expression system. The redesigned Duo-Art system also featured a pneumatic stack generously employing aluminum in its construction. The late introduction of these drawer-equipped Duo-Arts resulted in very few of these being built, with the result that they are quite rare today.

After about 1930 custom Duo-Art installations became available which featured a rather elaborate roll playing facility located some distance away from the piano. The Concertola unit, housed in its own furniture-styled cabinet, was actually an automatic roll changer that could provide an extended musical program of an hour or more. The precisely and beautifully crafted Concertola incorporates a "ferris wheel" arrangement, and its mechanism superficially resembles the automatic changers made by Hupfeld, Philipps, and Wurlitzer for coin operated pianos and orchestrions. The Concertola accommodates ten Duo-Art rolls. These can be played in sequence or can be selected individually by means of a small remote control tablet equipped with pushbuttons. An ingenious mechanism even sets the tempo correctly for each roll (specially-coded tempo perforations are cut into the roll leader for this purpose).

The full line of Concertola products also included a unit for playing special "long recordings" (which were never produced in quantity) and also Concertola units for use with Aeolian pipe organs.

Many variations exist among Duo-Arts regarding their internal arrangements of components, routing of tubing, and even the mechanical design of valves and pneumatic stacks.

For example, some of the earliest instruments contained double-valve pneumatic stacks; i.e., using two valves per note, rather than the single-valve arrangement found in the vast majority of Duo-Arts. Some of the later grand models had their tracker bar tubing routed around the piano action rather than through slots between the keys, thereby simplifying the task of servicing piano actions. Some of the later English Duo-Art grands had pneumatic stacks built into the upper part of the piano directly behind the spoolbox, rather than attached underneath as in most Duo-Art instruments. In spite of these and other differences, however, uniformity of basic design is very much in evidence in all Duo-Arts.

The reader will find the 1927 service manual, available in reprint form, to be useful for its detailed technical description of the Duo-Art mechanism.

———————

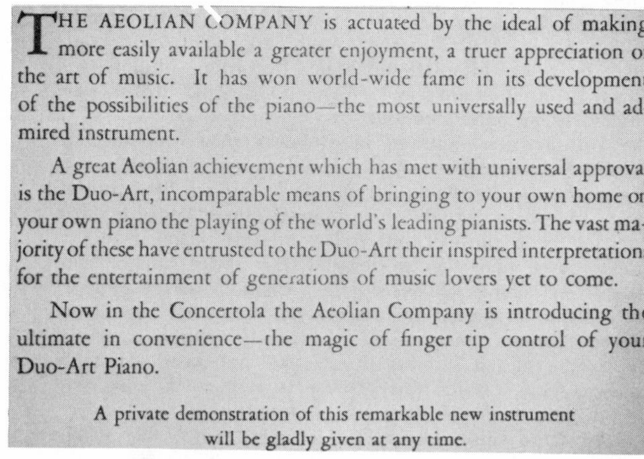

THE AEOLIAN COMPANY is actuated by the ideal of making more easily available a greater enjoyment, a truer appreciation of the art of music. It has won world-wide fame in its development of the possibilities of the piano—the most universally used and admired instrument.
A great Aeolian achievement which has met with universal approval is the Duo-Art, incomparable means of bringing to your own home on your own piano the playing of the world's leading pianists. The vast majority of these have entrusted to the Duo-Art their inspired interpretations for the entertainment of generations of music lovers yet to come.
Now in the Concertola the Aeolian Company is introducing the ultimate in convenience—the magic of finger tip control of your Duo-Art Piano.
A private demonstration of this remarkable new instrument will be gladly given at any time.

GEORGE STECK
STYLE NY
The rich two-tone effect and the overlay panels of figured veneers on the legs lift this case out of the conventional type of grand.
LENGTH 5 ft. 1½ in.
MAHOGANY AND WALNUT


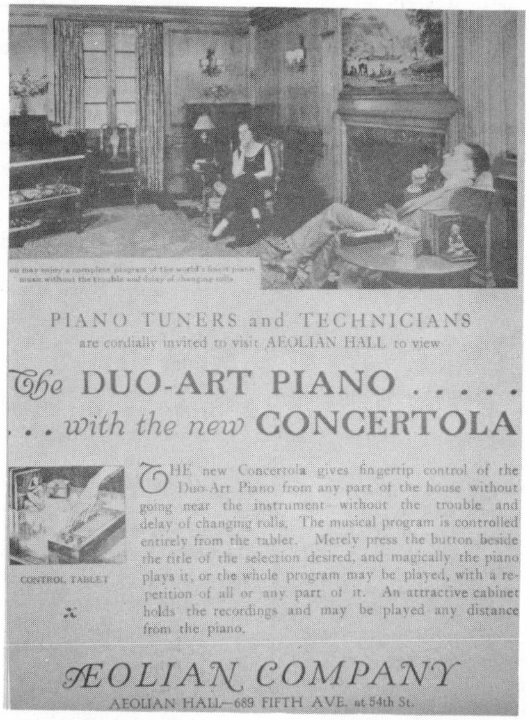

STEINWAY
STYLE XY
The unfailing merit of simplicity of design is here combined with true artistic relation of graceful curves and proper proportions.
LENGTH 5 ft. 7 in.
MAHOGANY AND WALNUT


The Duo-Art Concertola (circa 1930)

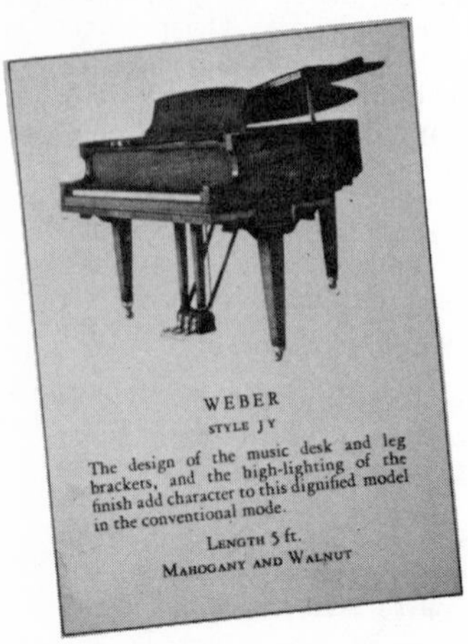

WEBER
STYLE JY
The design of the music desk and leg brackets, and the high-lighting of the finish add character to this dignified model in the conventional mode.
LENGTH 5 ft.
MAHOGANY AND WALNUT

WEBER
STYLE JBY LOUIS XVI
Unusually effective is this model with its three-legged truss, finely tapered and fluted legs, and beautiful woods in contrasting tones.
LENGTH 5 ft.
MAHOGANY AND WALNUT

WEBER
STYLE JDY SPANISH
The quaint simplicity of Old Spain is apparent in this case, with its wrought iron braces, carved geometric patterns, and desk of figured wood in contrast to the walnut of the case.
LENGTH 5 ft.
WALNUT ONLY

WEBER
STYLE JAY LOUIS XV
The exquisite harmony of line associated with this period has been effectively emphasized by the high-light finishes. The carving and proportions are particularly graceful.
LENGTH 5 ft.
MAHOGANY AND WALNUT

THE world of music at your fingertips—this is literally the privilege of the owner of the Duo-Art Piano with the new Concertola. Simply touching a button beside the title of the music you choose, magically makes the piano play the selection, or you may enjoy the entire program without interruption, with a repetition of any selection or the complete program as the whim of the moment dictates. All this may be done without moving from your chair, without going near your piano. With only the tablet near you, you may control your program of Paderewski, Bauer, Hofmann, the lighter classics, the latest musical comedies, lively dance tunes, any favorite selection. And yet should you or any guest wish to play the piano between numbers, its action will be found perfect, for every Duo-Art Piano primarily is designed for hand playing

THE playing of the world's greatest pianists is available in your own home through the perfect reproduction of the Duo-Art. Hearing these renditions is the same as hearing the artist as he plays in public. Every shading of tonal quality, every nuance of melodic beauty is faithfully reproduced.

Now, through the Duo-Art Piano with the new Concertola, those who entertain with music are given the ultimate convenience of fingertip control of selected music for their own pleasure, and of carefully chosen programs or selections for their guests. Varying a musical program being played on a piano perhaps in another room is a matter of simply touching a button. Those who would enjoy the advantages of this ultra-convenient mode of entertaining should attend a demonstration of the Duo-Art Piano with the new Concertola.

# THE DUO-ART PIANO WITH THE NEW Concertola

**Developed in the late 1920's, the Concertola mechanism was offered for sale for use with the Duo-Art reproducing piano and, in an expanded (wider roll) version, with the Duo-Art pipe organ. Although single-roll Concertola units were made, in its most popular form the unit consisted of a 10-roll automatic changer in a cabinet separate from the piano. Operation was by means of a push-button panel. As the tempo of rolls varies, rolls for use on the Concertola must be encoded on the leader with special perforations which operate a series of bellows. These bellows, collapsing either singly or several at a time, serve to move the tempo control to the desired position.**

**The Concertola offered the advantage of playing the rolls more smoothly. In a regular reproducing piano the vacuum in the tracker bar varies with the intensity or dynamic level of the passages being played. Sometimes during a forte passage the increased vacuum will cause the paper to temporarily slow down in its travel. The Concertola mechanism applies consistent vacuum at all times, regardless of the expression on the roll, and obviates this problem.**

**The Concertola was introduced too late to achieve significant sales. Had it been introduced in the early 1920's, doubtlessly it would have been extremely popular.**

Above: A Mason & Hamlin Duo-Art reproducing piano. The purchaser of this instrument had it made to her order in the early 1930's. Visiting an Aeolian American Corporation showroom, she was impressed with the repertoire of classical music available on Duo-Art rolls. A professional musician herself, the lady preferred, in her words, the "cello-like tone" of the Mason & Hamlin to the tone of any other piano. Told that the Duo-Art mechanism was available in the Steinway, Weber, and other pianos, but not the Mason & Hamlin, she said "Can you make a Mason & Hamlin Duo-Art for me?" Two years and thousands of dollars later, this Mason & Hamlin Duo-Art, equipped with the Concertola roll system, was ready!

Left and bottom left: Two varieties of the Single Concertola, a unit which plays one roll at a time. Only a few of these were made.

Below: Push-button panel for operating the 10-roll Concertola. It is not known how many of these were made. Serial numbers on existing 10-roll units seen by the author are in the 200 and 300 series, so perhaps several hundred were sold. This seems unlikely, however, in view of the precipitate decline of Duo-Art sales after 1927 and in view of the high cost of the Concertola.

THE SINGLE CONCERTOLA

THIS form of the Concertola in both cabinet and end-table models provides for the use of single Duo-Art Recordings—either from the regular Duo-Art Library; or the new "Program Rolls". These rolls play from 15 to 20 minutes and offer many new possibilities for Duo-Art programs—such as selections of the latest dance music playing as long as an orchestra piece, combinations of carefully chosen salon music as a soft accompaniment to dinner, tea or bridge, and elaborate piano works never before available on one roll.

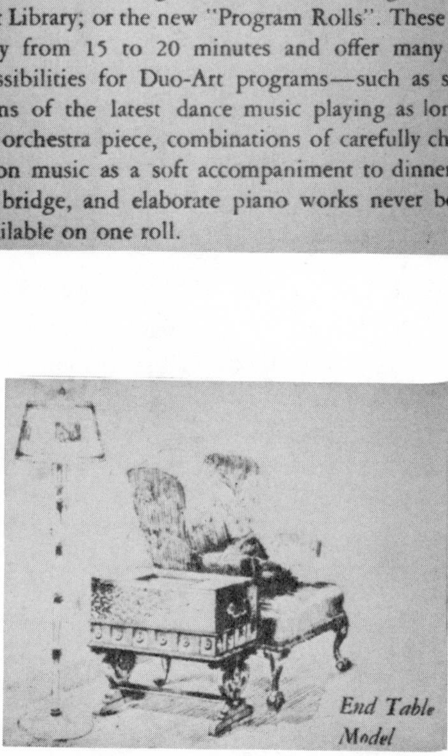


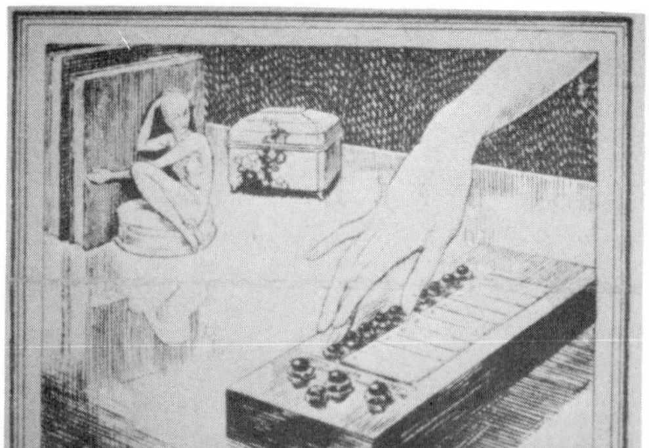

FINGERTIP CONTROL

The program is controlled entirely from this tablet which may be moved about in any convenient position or additional tablets placed in any room in the house.

A handsome cabinet holds the recordings which the Duo-Art plays. It may be in the same room or in some other part of the house.

THE AEOLIAN COMPANY
ORIGINATORS AND SOLE MANUFACTURERS OF THE PIANOLA, TAKE UNUSUAL PLEASURE IN PRESENTING A NEW AND WONDERFUL DEVELOPMENT OF THAT INSTRUMENT

THE DUO-ART PIANOLA

WHEN The Pianola, the first successful instrument of its type, was given to the public fifteen years ago, the hitherto inaccessible Art of Music was literally thrown open to the world.

The Pianola made the pianoforte available to everyone. It conferred on all the inestimable privilege of musical self-expression with music's noblest instrument.

Many and notable have been The Pianola developments during intervening years. Every forward step in what has now become a great world-industry, has originated in this famous instrument. Today, The Pianola offers to every music-lover, trained or otherwise, the ideal means for playing the pianoforte.

THE NEW PRINCIPLE IN THE DUO-ART PIANOLA

In The Duo-Art Pianola is added a new and an extraordinary element of interest to that which The Pianola already possessed. Not only can it be played by hand, or music-roll, but

IT WILL PLAY ITSELF, WITH PERFECT ART

Through the medium of a new, electric-pneumatic action and specially prepared music-rolls, The Duo-Art Pianola will reproduce the actual performances of eminent pianists, with all the charm and individuality of the original rendition. Every slightest variation of tempo, every subtle tone-shade, every nuance, every elusive rubato is portrayed with a fidelity that is amazing and has never before been even approached.

The Duo-Art Pianola is undoubtedly the greatest achievement in the history of the piano industry. It has aroused the utmost enthusiasm in all to whom it has already been shown. The Aeolian Company is desirous that every present owner of a Pianola or a Player-piano of other make, as well as the public in general, shall have an opportunity to see and hear this great invention. It has therefore arranged for

INFORMAL DEMONSTRATIONS

Every afternoon, at Three o'clock, The Duo-Art Pianola will be played in the Steinway Salons at Aeolian Hall.

In addition, private demonstrations will be given at any hour during the business day to all who call. These demonstrations are free and attendance will entail no obligation of any kind.

The Price of The Steinway Duo-Art Pianola is $1500. Convenient terms involving a moderate initial payment and subsequent monthly payments may be arranged. Liberal allowances will be made on Pianolas, player-pianos of other make and regular pianos in exchange for The Duo-Art Pianola.

THE AEOLIAN COMPANY, AEOLIAN HALL, N. Y.

**Left: March 1, 1914, advertisement in the New York Times features the introduction of the Duo-Art: "Through the medium of a new, electric-pneumatic action and specially prepared music rolls, the Duo-Art Pianola will reproduce the actual performances of eminent pianists, with all the charm and individuality of the original rendition . . ." (Courtesy of Richard Howe)**

**Steinway Duo-Art piano in a carved Spanish-style case; from the collection of the editor. A similar instrument is owned by the University of Illinois.**

*Robert Armbruster*

ROBERT ARMBRUSTER was born in Philadelphia in 1896, and received his musical training in that city, studying for several years with the late Constantin Sternberg who honored Mr. Armbruster by dedicating to him his last book of essays. He began to play the piano in early childhood, won local renown as a prodigy, and made his first appearance as soloist with the Philadelphia Orchestra while yet a mere lad. He served in the Naval Reserve in the World War, and was chosen thereafter as the pianist to appear at the White House in Washington on the occasion of a big diplomatic dinner, receiving therefor a gold medal bearing the President's Coat-of-Arms. A pianist of great technical proficiency, musicianly understanding and sincerity, and gifted with poetic insight, Mr. Armbruster records his playing for the Duo-Art Piano exclusively.

**Robert Armbruster, who recorded hundreds of rolls for Duo-Art, as he appeared in the 1927 Duo-Art catalogue. In the 1970's Robert Armbruster became an active member of the Automatic Musical Instrument Collectors Association (AMICA) and was a featured performer at several meetings.**

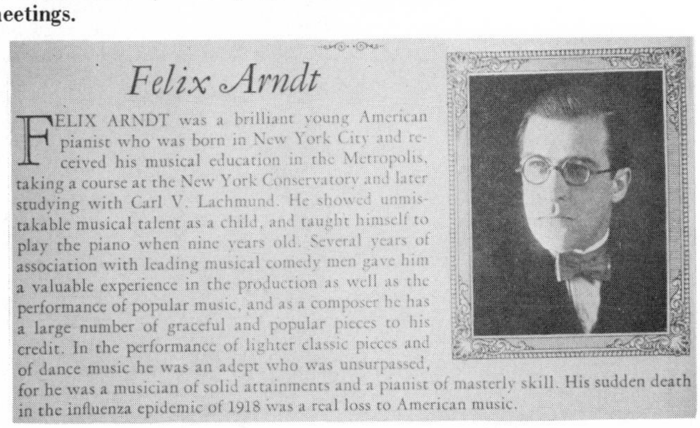

*Felix Arndt*

FELIX ARNDT was a brilliant young American pianist who was born in New York City and received his musical education in the Metropolis, taking a course at the New York Conservatory and later studying with Carl V. Lachmund. He showed unmistakable musical talent as a child, and taught himself to play the piano when nine years old. Several years of association with leading musical comedy men gave him a valuable experience in the production as well as the performance of popular music, and as a composer he has a large number of graceful and popular pieces to his credit. In the performance of lighter classic pieces and of dance music he was an adept who was unsurpassed, for he was a musician of solid attainments and a pianist of masterly skill. His sudden death in the influenza epidemic of 1918 was a real loss to American music.

## NEW YORK RETAIL PRICES

NET CASH

### AUTOMATIC INSTRUMENTS

| *Name* | *Style* | *Size* | *Wood* | *Price* |
|---|---|---|---|---|
| Aeolian Pianola | 559-T | 4′—6⅞″ | Mah. Satin Finish | **$595** |
| Aeolian Pianola | 543-T | 4′—6½″ | Mahogany | **595** |
| Aeolian Pianola (Metro-Them.) | 551-P | 4′—6½″ | Mahogany | **650** |

### FOOT-OPERATED DUO-ART PIANOS

| | | | | |
|---|---|---|---|---|
| Stroud | 600-P | 4′—6¾″ | Mahogany | **695** |
| Wheelock | 142-P | 4′—6¾″ | Mahogany | **795** |

### ELECTRIC DUO-ART PIANOS

| | | | | |
|---|---|---|---|---|
| Stroud | 593-P | 4′—6¾″ | Mahogany | **995** |
| Wheelock | 141 | 4′—6¾″ | Mahogany | **1150** |
| Steck | 322 | 4′—5 ″ | Mahogany | **1350** |
| Weber | 59 | 4′—5 ″ | Mahogany | **1600** |

### GRAND DUO-ART PIANOS

| | | | | |
|---|---|---|---|---|
| Aeolian | RR | 5′—2½″ | Mahogany | **1850** |
| Steck | HR | 5′—6 ″ | Mahogany | **2085** |
| Weber | WR | 5′—8 ″ | Mahogany | **2500** |
| Weber | FR | 5′—11½″ | Mahogany | **3000** |
| Steinway | XR | 6′—1¾″ | Mahogany | **3875** |
| Steinway | OR | 6′—5 ″ | Mahogany | **4275** |
| Steinway | AR | 6′—11¼″ | Mahogany | **4675** |

The above prices do not include cost of freight and handling when instruments are sold outside of New York City.

THE AEOLIAN COMPANY

New York — Feb. 1, 1924

# DUO-ART

**Right: Description of the Duo-Art from the 1920 edition of "The Purchaser's Guide to the Music Industries."**

**Below: Duo-Art roll catalogues of the 1920's were lavish productions and featured a story about each artist and his featured selections. The Gershwin description is typical. It is interesting to note (not mentioned in the description) that George Gershwin first became interested in music by listening to a coin operated nickelodeon piano.**

**DUO-ART PIANOLA PIANO, THE.**—The Duo-Art Pianola Piano is the reproducing piano manufactured by The Æolian Company, New York. This remarkable instrument was introduced to the public during the fall of 1913 and is the latest and greatest contribution by The Æolian Company to the automatic piano art. The Duo-Art (that is, representing two arts—the art of the performer and the art of the interpreting pianist) embodies three instruments in one: pianoforte, player-piano and reproducing piano. This instrument represents years of development by the Æolian corps of experts and inventors in continuation of earlier important inventions of the same company, including the Metrostyle and Themodist. The Metrostyle, a very remarkable invention, won the respect and indorsement of all the great composers and artists for the Pianola, the trade-name by which The Æolian Company's player-pianos are designated. The Themodist, another exclusive Æolian invention, enabled the Pianola automatically to voice the theme in the music roll so as to sound over the accompaniment. The Duo-Art Pianola Piano has been enthusiastically indorsed by leading artists and musicians of this country and Europe, and many of the great pianists such as Paderewski, Hofmann, Bauer, Ganz, Grainger, etc., have contracted to record exclusively for this reproducing piano. The Duo-Art has appeared as soloist with many of the leading orchestras of the country, having played a complete concerto in Æolian Hall, New York, accompanied by the New York Symphony Orchestra, conducted by Walter Damrosch. Also at Philadelphia with the Philadelphia Symphony Orchestra, conducted by Leopold Stokowsky; with the Chicago Symphony Orchestra, conducted by Eric DeLamarter, with the San Francisco Symphony Orchestra, Alfred Hertz conducting; with the Detroit Symphony Orchestra, Ossip Gabrilowitsch, conductor; with the Cleveland Orchestra, Nikolai Sokoloff, conductor; with the Cincinnati Symphony Orchestra, Eugene Ysaye, conductor; with the New York Philharmonic Orchestra, Josef Stransky and Rudolph Ganz, conductors. This last concert was one of the regular series given by the orchestra, the Duo-Art having had the unique distinction of being substituted in place of the living artist. The remarkable patented mechanism of the Duo-Art reproduces not only the notes, tempo, phrasing and attack, but also every tone gradation precisely as originally played and recorded by the artist, including all the dynamics of his rendition with the innumerable gradations from pianissimo to sforzando, all crescendos and diminuendos, whether of abrupt or extended length; also all pedal effects of the artist in the use of the sostenuto and soft pedals; also all other expression effects so true to the individuality of the respective artists who recorded the original Duo-Art rolls that their style and identity is unmistakably to be recognized in their performance by the Duo-Art Pianola. In short, the Duo Art music rolls embodied in the Duo-Art Pianola Piano reproduce the individual manner and musical personality of the recording artists in a truly remarkable manner. The artist's original master record is made automatically as he plays on a specially devised recording Duo-Art piano, the artist playing the composition by hand on this piano in the characteristic manner which he desires to record, and the automatic mechanism recording in the form of perforations in a moving sheet not only all of the notes but all of the artist's expression effects, including tempo, rhythm, dynamics and pedaling, exactly as played. As soon as the artist has finished his performance, the perforated music roll recording his rendition is immediately available for insertion in the Duo-Art piano to reproduce the original performance. In this way the leading artists have permanently recorded for all time their characteristic piano interpretations, and these are available for the enjoyment of all users of the Duo-Art piano in a rapidly growing catalogue which already includes over eight hundred Duo-Art rolls.

## *George Gershwin*

GEORGE GERSHWIN, who records his piano playing exclusively for the Duo-Art, was born in Brooklyn, N. Y., on September 26, 1898. When he was thirteen years old his mother bought a piano and decided that young George must learn to play it. A new and hitherto undreamed of world was opened to him. He learned rapidly and well, the best of his early teachers being Charles Hambitzer, who gave him his first lessons in harmony and his first real reverence for music, but who died before his pupil had gone very far. Later he studied harmony with Eduard Kilenyi, and after that took some work in composition with Rubin Goldmark, for early in his piano lessons he had begun to dabble at writing. When sixteen he went to work as a "song plugger" for a music publisher, often playing piano all day for vaudeville acts and far into the night at cafés. This led to his engagement to play for the chorus rehearsals of various musical shows. Meanwhile he kept trying his hand at composition, until, in 1918, with "I Was So Young and You Were So Beautiful," he found himself launched as the author of a popular song hit. Since that successful start his work has shown a steady advance.

### *Duo-Art Records by George Gershwin*

RHAPSODY IN BLUE, Part II: Andantino and Finale *George Gershwin* 68787 1.75

BEYOND question George Gershwin's "Rhapsody in Blue" is the most imposing and the most important composition thus far achieved by anybody in the jazz idiom. Its title is particularly appropriate, for it is freely rhapsodic in form and it makes plentiful and effective use of the contrasting discords which the jazz artists call "blue notes." It is really a Concerto in Fantasia form for Piano and Jazz Orchestra (the first of the kind ever written). It was commissioned by Paul Whiteman, and had its first performance at Mr. Whiteman's now historic concert, in Aeolian Hall, New York, on February 12, 1924, with the composer at the piano.

Everybody who takes any interest at all in American music will want to hear this Rhapsody. It is a remarkable work, from every point of view. It has a throbbing, pulsating vitality, and a glamour of great popular appeal. It discloses a genuine melodic gift—novel, individualistic and fine; an astonishing skill in handling the new harmonies produced by American jazz bands; a still more noteworthy ability in the invention and manipulation of striking rhythms; and a happy facility in the arrangement of form.

It has been said that delicacy, even dreaminess, is a quality that Gershwin alone brings into jazz music. Something of this phase of his talent is shown in the impressively beautiful theme of the *Andantino*, beginning the Second Part of the Rhapsody incorporated in the present Duo-Art Record of the composer's own brilliant and masterly performance. And this finely expressive theme itself demonstrates his command of melodic ideas quite as convincingly as the Finale shows his ability to pile up a powerful and thrilling climax.

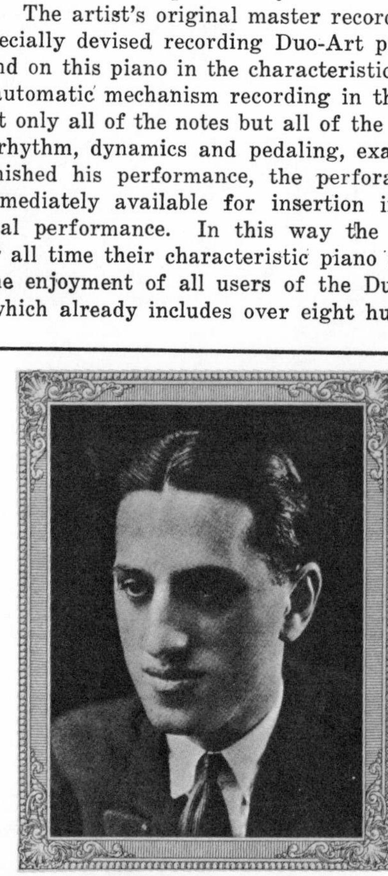

The Steinway Italian Duo-Art

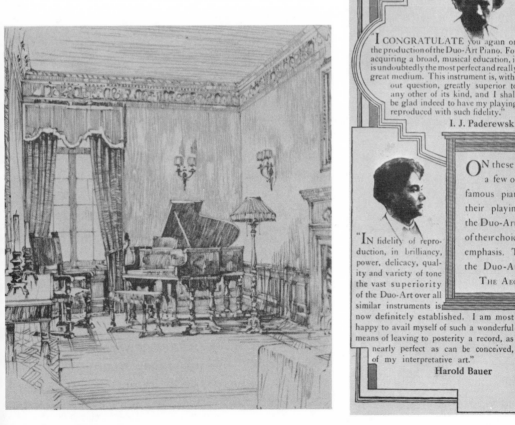

Duo-Art advertising of the 1920's. Above is a roll bulletin of May, 1927. The line drawings at the left side of this page are from "The New Aeolian Hall," a book issued in 1927. The artists noted below recorded their playing "almost exclusively," not completely exclusively — as they are, in some instances, to be found on Welte, Artrio Angelus, and other types of rolls!

THE WORLD'S FOREMOST PIANISTS
Record Their Playing Exclusively For
THE DUO-ART
Reproducing Piano
"I CONGRATULATE you again on the production of the Duo-Art Piano. For acquiring a broad, musical education, it is undoubtedly the most perfect and really great medium. This instrument is, without question, greatly superior to any other of its kind, and I shall be glad indeed to have my playing reproduced with such fidelity."
I. J. Paderewski
"My Duo-Art rolls correctly reproduce my phrasing, accent, pedaling, and are endowed with my personality. They are my actual interpretation with all that implies. One thing is certain; in the reproduction of my playing, the Duo-Art is so far superior to any other instrument of its kind there can be no real basis for comparison."
Josef Hofmann
On these pages are pictured a few of the world's most famous pianists who record their playing exclusively for the Duo-Art. The significance of their choice does not require emphasis. The supremacy of the Duo-Art is world-wide.
The Aeolian Company
"In fidelity of reproduction, in brilliancy, power, delicacy, quality and variety of tone the vast superiority of the Duo-Art over all similar instruments is now definitely established. I am most happy to avail myself of such a wonderful means of leaving to posterity a record, as nearly perfect as can be conceived, of my interpretative art."
Harold Bauer
"I CONSIDER the Duo-Art Piano a most important and valuable means for musical development. The pianists' interpretations are works of creative art, as truly as are the writings of the composer. The Duo-Art Piano by bringing the fruits of the pianists' creative genius before countless people is destined to fill a high mission in the musical life of the future."
Ossip Gabrilowitsch

Right: Weber Duo-Art in Louis XVI case as illustrated in "The New Aeolian Hall," a 1927 book issued to commemorate the opening of Aeolian's lavish headquarters.

Below: An original bill of sale for a Steinway Duo-Art reproducing grand piano (Style XR) contracted for in late 1927 and paid for in early 1929, following delivery of the instrument. Despite the expensive cost of the Duo-Art in a Steinway case, thousands were sold in the 1920's. Steinway was the premier piano in which the Duo-Art was usually installed, but the author did learn of a New York lady who was diffident about the Steinway tone and had a Duo-Art Concertola (roll changer) mechanism installed in conjunction with a Mason & Hamlin piano in the early 1930's, at which time the Aeolian Company and the American Piano Co. were one and the same. (Original bill of sale courtesy Ellsworth Johnson).

THE WEBER LOUIS XVI DUO-ART

Form 156B

**Purchase Agreement**

Account No. 2055

December 19 1927

To The Aeolian Company:

Please enter, subject to your approval and acceptance, my order for the following goods to be delivered as soon as possible.

One Steinway Grand Duo-Art & Bench

Style X.R. Modern Finish Wal No. 259714

for which I agree to pay the sum of

PURCHASE PRICE $7000.00 Seven thousand dollars DOLLARS

as the purchase price which is payable as follows, namely:

ALLOWANCE is to be allowed for second hand

all right, title and interest to which goods the Purchaser hereby grants and transfers to the Company, and warrants the title thereto,

OTHER ALLOWANCE $ DOLLARS

A Duo-art Grand Piano is to be loaned until the above instrument is completed by Aeolian Co

DEPOSIT $ 1000 DOLLARS

and the balance 10 days after delivery of the goods.

For any extension of time agreed to by the Company for the payment of the amount first above mentioned, or any part thereof, I agree to pay interest at the rate of six per cent (6%) per annum on any unpaid balance from the date of delivery of said goods until the same is paid in full.

It is agreed that title to the said goods shall not pass and the same shall remain the property of the Aeolian Company until the said purchase price and any interest due thereon is paid in full.

In the presence of George H. Schaffer

Purchaser's business address 189 Montague St

Bklyn. N.Y.

Purchaser [signature]

Home Address 1783 Fifth Ave. N.Y.

Accepted
THE AEOLIAN COMPANY
By [signature]

BILL OF SALE
WE HEREBY GRANT AND TRANSFER TO THE WITHIN PURCHASER ALL RIGHT, TITLE AND INTEREST IN THE GOODS PURCHASED FROM US HEREUNDER, AND WARRANT THE TITLE THERETO.
The Aeolian Company
4/13/29 By

DUO-ART

THE Duo-Art Pianola is the highest modern development of the pianoforte.

It is primarily a piano of conventional type—a Steinway, Weber, Steck or Stroud, with all the fine tonal qualities that distinguish these well-known instruments. The action and keyboard for hand playing are identical with other pianos of the same make.

IT is a player-piano of truly remarkable capacity, providing the Pianolist with easy and complete control of every phase of musical expression possible upon the pianoforte. It is an instrument of such broad artistic possibilities that it will interest not only the layman but also the experienced musician who will find in it the enjoyment of a limitless repertory.

AS a reproducing piano—as an instrument for re-creating the interpretations of the great artists of the pianoforte, it is truly revolutionary in its attainments. Guided by the wonderful Duo-Art records, the Duo-Art Pianola actually repeats in every shading of tone and tempo the pianist's original performance.

AEOLIAN representatives in every principal city of the United States are prepared to demonstrate this wonderful new instrument. We invite you to write for address of representative nearest you and an interesting Booklet of the Duo-Art. Please address Department E 11.

▾ ▾ ▾

*Steinway Duo-Art Pianola*
*Other models are the Steck, Stroud and famous Weber. Moderate prices.*

**Above: The innards of a Weber upright Duo-Art reproducing piano. The mechanism works on the same principles as the Duo-Art grand pianos but is mechanically laid out quite differently. The 6-section pump in the bottom of the case operates slowly and is very quiet.**

**Left: Description of the Duo-Art from an Aeolian advertisement. The "Pianola" designation was later dropped from the Duo-Art nomenclature.**

**The following listing reflects some of the sizes and styles of Duo-Arts available in the mid-1920's:**

**Among upright models the following were popular: Stroud Style 593-P which measures 4'7" high; Wheelock Style 141 4'7"; Steck Style 322 4'5"; and Weber Style 59 4'5".**

**Among the grand piano styles were the following: Aeolian Style RR which measures 5'2" in length; Steck HR 5'6"; Weber Style WR 5'8" and Style FR 5'11"; Steinway Style XR 6'2", OR 6'5", and AR 6'11".**

**Above: The new Aeolian Hall at 5th Avenue and 54th Street as it appeared in a 1927 sketch. Owned by an investor, the building was leased to Aeolian for a beginning rent of $150,000 per annum.**

Right: Two prominent personalities of the 1920's, "Roxy" and "Babe" Ruth, enjoyed their Duo-Art pianos.

"ROXY" and his DUO-ART PIANO

DUO-ART PIANO in the home of "BABE" RUTH

BOTH through his radio programs and through his palatial theater, S. L. Rothafel ("Roxy") has become an American institution. His bright, clever, varied and delightful programs are full of human interest and understanding, and seem to have the unusual quality of pleasing everybody. In making up those remarkable programs "Roxy's" chief assistant and greatest inspiration is the Duo-Art Piano. This instrument—a Steinway Duo-Art Grand Piano in a Spanish Period Design—occupies the place of honor in his office-studio, together with a very extensive collection of Duo-Art Music Rolls of the world's best music. Besides many hundreds of standard piano works, this collection includes also the wonderful Duo-Art Accompaniment Rolls, so that he has immediately accessible a most artistic interpretation of just the music he wishes to hear. "Roxy" is of course an ardent music lover—and an enthusiastic "booster" for the Duo-Art.

In another field of activity George Herman ("Babe") Ruth is also an American institution. And the "Babe" also is a great music lover. Many of the happiest hours he spends in his new home in New York City are spent with the Duo-Art Piano, which was his wedding gift to his bride. It is a Weber Duo-Art Grand, in William and Mary Period style, walnut finish. Mrs. Ruth chose the Weber particularly because of its beautiful tone.

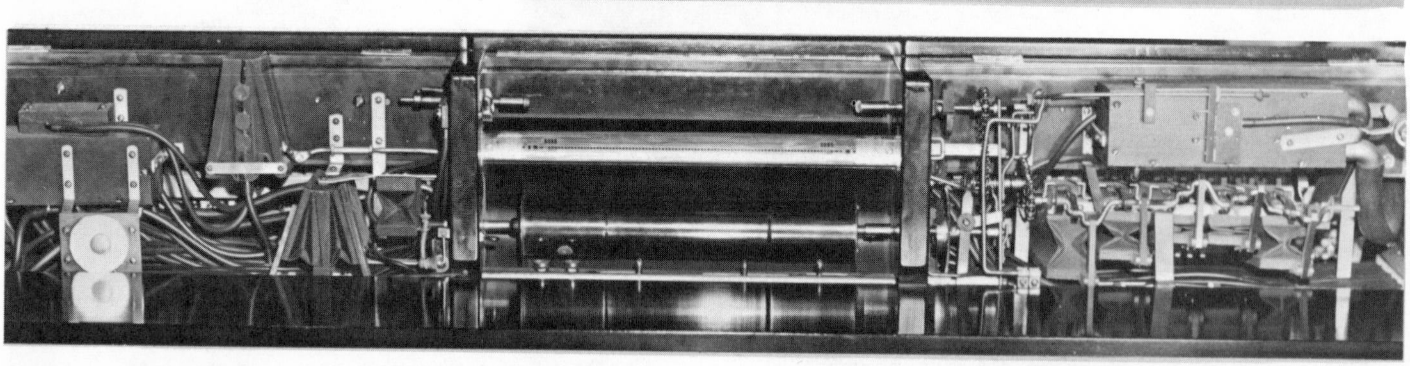

This spoolbox, from a Stroud Duo-Art 5'4" piano made in 1932, is one of the later models. All of the controls are in the spoolbox (rather than under the usual hinged key slip). This model was redesigned to the extent that no tubing passed through the piano action key frame – making it possible to easily remove the piano action for regulation. All tubing from the tracker bar fans to the extreme bass and treble sides of the casework where it goes through easily-detached junction blocks. Note also the absence of conventional Duo-Art tracker "ears." This model has a single hole in each end of the tracker bar for tracking purposes, similar to the 4-hole Welte tracker system except that the Duo-Art system requires no valves... the holes being bleeds as the tracker ears were. (Courtesy Ellsworth Johnson).

Four photographs of a fine Weber Duo-Art grand piano restored for Mr. and Mrs. John Watson by William Singleton of St. Louis.

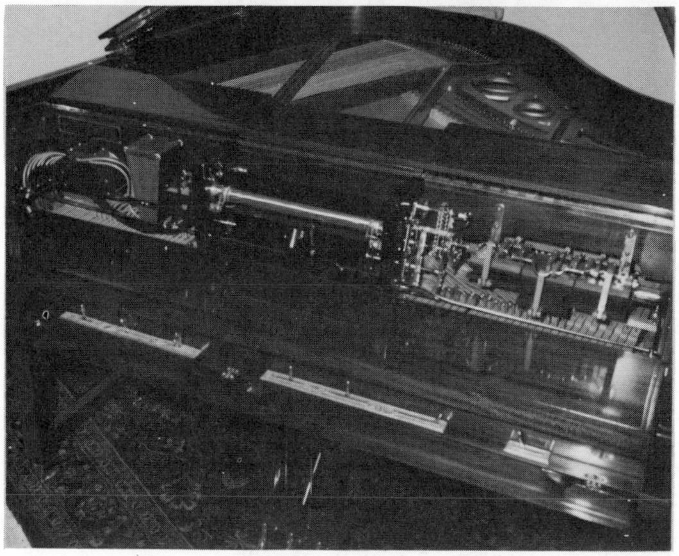

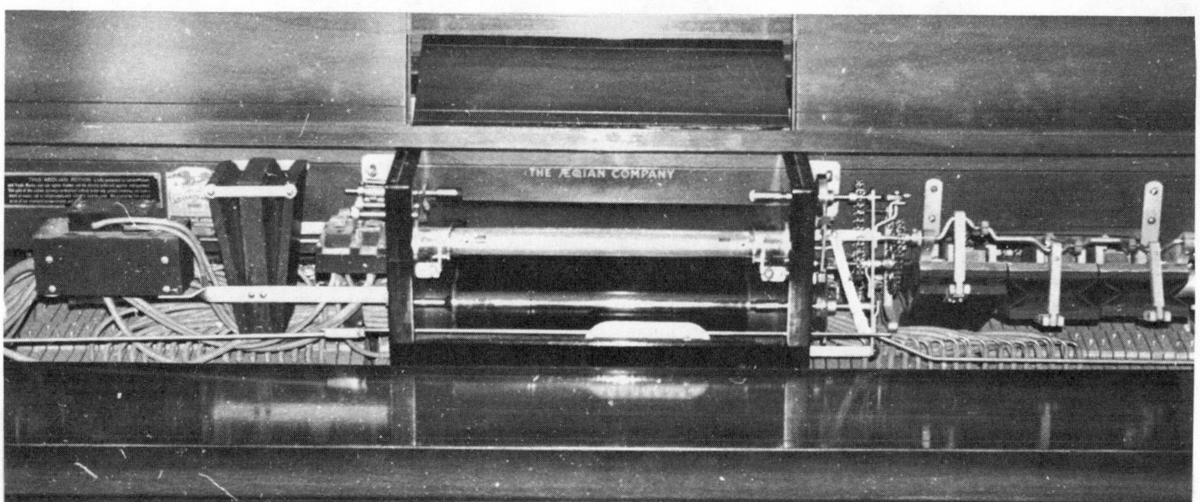


Spoolbox from a Duo-Art grand of the 1920's. Note that the tubing from the tracker bar goes between the keys in the keybed. Later models (see illustration on another page) were built differently.

Above: A beautiful example of a 1926 Steinway Duo-Art model OR reproducing grand piano of Louis XVI style. The overall length of the instrument is 6'5". The piano entertains those who visit the Ellsworth Johnson home in Spokane, Washington.

Right: A Weber Duo-Art grand of the 1920's. Weber Duo-Art pianos were once very popular. In September, 1918 the following Duo-Art pianos were being produced. Uprights: Stroud Style 592-P \$975; Steck Style 320-P \$1375; Weber Style 58-P \$1600; Steinway Style S \$1800. Grands: Steck Style MM \$2300; Weber Style FF \$2500; Steinway Style X \$2800; Steinway Style O \$2950.

Steinway Duo-Art 6'5" grand piano in Louis XVI case. Formerly owned by Mr. Jules Pierlow of St. Louis, the piano is now in the collection of Mr. J.B. Nethercutt. The instrument is in a bright red case with a multitude of hand painted Chinese village and landscape scenes. (William Singleton photo).

## —AudioGraphic Music Rolls—



In 1927 the Aeolian Company introduced AudioGraphic music rolls — Duo-Art (and regular 88-note as well) rolls with a story, musical analysis, biographical data, and other information printed on them. Thus the AudioGraphic roll not only recorded the music, it recorded the history of the composition as well.

To select the pieces to be presented on AudioGraphic rolls, special committees of prominent musicians and musical authors and educators were established in America, England, France, Germany, Spain, Belgium, and Argentina. These committees met regularly and gave their recommendations and endorsements for coming selections.

The advertising for the AudioGraphic rolls was elaborate: "The Elgar Variations, termed 'Enigma' by the composer, have long possessed the compelling element of mystery. Who were the actual persons (represented only by initials on the published score) at whom these musical compositions were directed? No one has ever known or will know the identity of all these until he reads Sir Edward Elgar's own confession in AudioGraphic Music, in which he also tells the charming story of how he came to write this famous work." Certain Wagner compositions were made with annotations by Richard Wagner's son, Siegfried, who gives "in AudioGraphic Music an authentic and intimate version — the first ever given the world — of the origin and meaning of his renowned father's works." Who could better explain Ravel's compositions than Ravel himself? Likewise, Paderewski provided data for the annotation of his own compositions played by himself. Most AudioGraphic advertising was in this vein.

AudioGraphic rolls were informally divided into several categories including Biographical Rolls (with detailed biographies at the beginning of each roll), Analytical Rolls (with explanations of the musical score printed throughout the roll; this necessitated stopping the roll at intervals to read the text), Running Comment Rolls (with marginal notes throughout the roll; brief notes that can be read as the roll plays), Annotated Rolls (with a veritable "music appreciation course" on the roll — a combination of history, music, etc.), and Children's Rolls. In addition, for the player piano (regular 88-note; not Duo-Art reproducing) a series of History of Music Rolls was produced. These latter rolls were used with a supplementary handbook, "The Listener's History of Music."

AudioGraphic Music Rolls were introduced as the Aeolian Company's fortunes were waning and as the reproducing piano was ending its greatest period of popularity. Had they been introduced a decade earlier, in 1917 instead of 1927, they undoubtedly would have been a great success. While AudioGraphic Music Rolls were moderately successful, the quantities sold were small compared to earlier Duo-Art roll issues.

An 'AudioGraphic' Roll being submitted for the approval of The British Committee.

Present: Sir Alex. C. Mackenzie, K.C.V.O., D.Mus., LL.D., D.C.L. (in the Chair); Sir Hugh P. Allen, C.V.O., M.A., D.Mus.; Sir Henry J. Wood, D.Mus., F.R.A.M., F.R.C.M.; J. B. McEwen, M.A., D.Mus., F.R.A.M.; Prof. J. C. Bridge, M.A., D.Mus.; J. Airman Forsyth (Secretary).

'AudioGraphic' Music

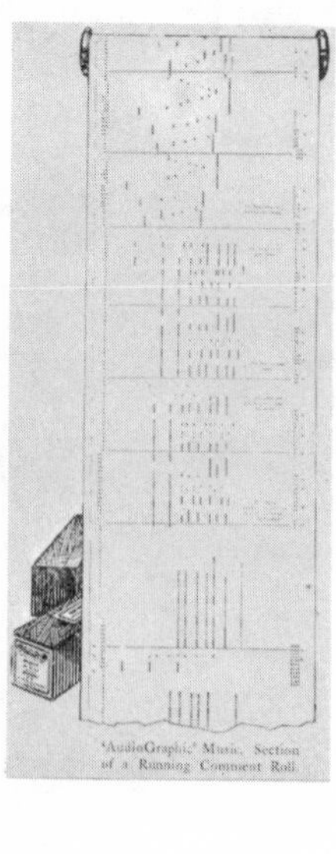

'AudioGraphic' Music. Section of a Running Comment Roll.

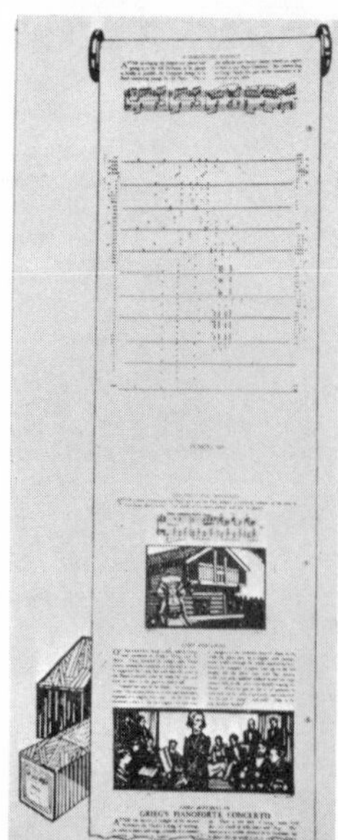

'AudioGraphic' Music. Section of an 'Analytical' Roll.

'AudioGraphic' Music. Section of a 'Biographical' Roll.

Above left: a "Running Comment Roll." Above center: an "Analytical Roll." Above right: a "Biographical Roll." The idea of incorporating a "story" as part of a music roll was not new; earlier player piano rolls (certain minstrel rolls, for example) incorporated the same basic idea.

## THE AEOLIAN COMPANY

*The following history of the Aeolian Company was written in 1937 by or for William Alfring, and is presented here through the courtesy of Douglas Hickling, who acquired the information from Mr. Alfring's son. The Aeolian Company traces its beginning to 1878 (some accounts say 1876) when the Mechanical Orguinette Company was founded. The following account is of interest as it gives information concerning the financial history of Aeolian; information that did not find its way into Aeolian catalogues of the period. For more information concerning the Aeolian Company and its predecessors, please refer to the organette section of this book. Aeolian organettes, player reed organs, and player pipe organs are discussed in detail there.*

*Note: Some minor editing has been done to the following account. For instance, the line which read in part "the Mechanical Orguinette Company which manufactured reed organs" was corrected to "the Mechanical Orguinette Company which sold reed organs," as the firm sold instruments made by others.*

The Aeolian Company was organized in 1887 as an outgrowth of the Mechanical Orguinette Company [founded in 1878] which sold reed organs operated by a perforated music roll.

In recording the history of the Aeolian Company, its growth and earning record, it must be borne in mind that the preponderance of the Company's sales, and practically all of its profits, resulted from the sale of automatically-operated musical instruments, starting with the Mechanical Orguinette, continuing with the Aeolian Organ (player reed organ), and then the Aeolian Orchestrelle (a larger player reed organ), and then followed by the Pianola piano-player, and then through further development, the Duo-Art reproducing piano. The annual sales of the Company expanded to upwards of $11,000,000 in the years immediately following the World War, and as late as 1926 over 85% of its business was in reproducing pianos, player pianos, and other roll-operated instruments.

The falling off in sales and profits began several years before the depression of 1929, when the sales of player pianos and reproducing pianos were adversely affected by radios and combination phonographs, and, as a result, interest in player instruments dwindled.

The player piano reached its peak in 1923 when 192,000 were manufactured in the United States; instruments with a total sales value in excess of $59,000,000. This dropped to 88,000 by 1927 (total sales value: about $28,000,000), and by 1931 it had decreased further to just 2200 instruments with a sales value of only $650,000. Today there are probably fewer than 250 player pianos manufactured in the United States by the entire industry.

The Aeolian Company is probably best known as the pioneer mass-marketer of the push-up piano player. The Pianola, a push-up or cabinet-style player, was pushed up to the keyboard of a straight piano (the term used in the trade to designate a piano playable only by hand), and by means of a roll furnished the performer the opportunity to play the piano.

As a development of the Pianola, the Pianola Piano came into existence. It was the same mechanism placed inside of a piano instead of on the outside. With the development of this type of instrument the Aeolian Company made its original effort to acquire ownership and manufacturing rights to pianos of known reputation and musical merit. The Weber piano was first acquired, and later the George Steck was added. For a time an effort was made to market these instruments as straight pianos, as well as instruments into which the Pianola mechanism was incorporated.

As public acceptance in the purchase of a piano is influenced as much almost on proper exploitation of piano names as on musical merit, a real effort was made to exploit the Weber piano name. Paderewski was brought to this country. Aeolian financed a tour which featured Paderewski playing the Weber exclusively. Largely as a result of the success of this exploitation and the threat to Steinway prestige, an agreement was entered into with Steinway & Sons in 1909. The substance of the agreement was that Aeolian would withdraw from the active exploitation of straight pianos, particularly the Weber, and would be granted the exclusive right by Steinway to incorporate the Pianola into the Steinway instruments. Steinway & Sons further agreed not to enter the player piano business. A further condition of this agreement provided that the Aeolian Company was to buy and pay for a minimum of 600 new Steinway pianos per year for the installation of the Pianola.

This contract with Steinway & Sons proved to be a valuable asset to the Aeolian Company, as it had no difficulty from the time of making the contract until 1927, when the player business began to fall off, in disposing of the required annual number of Steinway Pianolas (which at one time commanded a price as high as $4000 for the smallest size). This agreement further cemented the relationship of Aeolian with its dealer organization throughout the United States, because of the value to the dealer in handling the Steinway Pianola in conjunction with the Steinway straight piano. The Aeolian-Steinway dealers often constituted the strongest and most progressive dealers in the larger cities.

Through the strength of this representation it was possible for the Aeolian Company to secure a small amount of straight piano business in addition to its player piano business, although, as stated before, the amount was a small percentage of the total piano business of the Company — as late as 1926 being less than 15% of the total.

During the years up to 1927 the Company had consistent growth. In 1916, in order to diversify its activities, it entered into a large scale production of phonographs and records. While the sales of these flourished for a time, phonographs later proved unprofitable, and in 1925 the Company retired entirely from that field.

Other efforts were made from time to time to diversify its activities, by the manufacturing of speed boats and aeroplane parts for example, but none of these efforts resulted in any profit to Aeolian.

Starting in 1928, following the general falling off in the player piano business, the Company experienced a decided shrinkage in its sales volume which, with the overhead connected with its retailing and other selling activities and its factories, resulted in losses to the firm. This condition was worsened by the further reduction of business caused by the general economic recession which began in 1929 . . .

In addition to its pianos, the Aeolian Company also manufactured pipe organs. These, like its player pianos, were automatically-operated with a perforated paper music roll. Practically its entire output of pipe organs were what is known as residence organs — that is, pipe organs sold for installations in large private homes, and not pipe organs for institutional organizations, churches, and auditoriums, which are made for hand-playing by an organist and not for use with a music roll. The Company's pipe organ business likewise began to fall off after the general business depression, until today the total pipe organ sales to residences in the United States is less than $40,000. At one time Aeolian alone had residence pipe organ sales in excess of $1,000,000 per year.

The sales results and profits of the Company have been unsatisfactory since 1927. However, in reviewing the results, they must be considered in the light of the problems which confronted the Company. Viewed in this light, much has been accomplished.

In 1928, faced with a declining business, the Company was confronted with many problems: It had bank loans amounting to $2,150,000. It operated four major factories, all of which were operating unprofitably. The lease on Aeolian Hall (5th Avenue and 54th St., New York City), in view of the diminishing volume of business, carried an excessive rent. The Steinway contract was burdensome; these pianos were beginning to accumulate in excess of current requirements, which, due to the sales decline, were considerably less than the contracted 600 pianos per year, which cost the Company approximately $600,000. The Pipe Organ Department was running at a serious loss, both from the manufacturing and from the selling standpoints. The accounts due the Aeolian Company from the Aeolian Company, Ltd., of England, were not being reduced, and the indications were that more money would have to be provided from America in order to successfully carry on that business.

Starting in 1928, drastic economies were effected in the operation of the business. During the two fiscal years ending June 30, 1931, operating expenses and charges were reduced approximately $1,400,000, and from that date until the formation of the Aeolian American Corporation in August, 1932 a further reduction of about $400,000 was achieved.

As it became increasingly evident that the piano industry was more and more dependent on the sale of straight pianos, one of the problems of the Company was to strengthen its position in this field. An opportunity presented itself when the American Piano Company went into receivership in 1929, and the Mason & Hamlin Company, which was owned by American, was acquired in 1930 by Aeolian. The Mason & Hamlin inventory, together with the debentures of the American Piano Company acquired at that time, were purchased by the Aeolian Company on a basis which returned a profit to Aeolian. In addition, the valuable Mason & Hamlin piano was added to the Aeolian line. Even with this activity, it became necessary for Aeolian to consolidate its manufacturing in two instead of four plants. By the end of 1931 even the two factories were lacking sufficient business to avoid overhead losses. These factory losses for the five year and two month period from July 1, 1928, to August 31, 1932, notwithstanding the most rigid economy of operation, amounted to more than $1,300,000.

In August, 1932 a combination was formed with the American Piano Corporation, which was also operating its factory at a loss. American, however, was not dependent on the sale of reproducing and player pianos to the extent that Aeolian was, and had a broad dealer representation in the Knabe, Chickering, and other well-known instruments which American made.

As a result of this combination, the Aeolian American Corporation was formed to manufacture and market the products of both companies. Each company (American and Aeolian) contributed all of its piano trade names, patents, and scales, one factory, $500,000 in inventory, and $100,000 in cash. Each firm received for the same a half interest in the Aeolian American Corporation. The Aeolian American Corporation has been outstandingly successful. During its operation, beginning in August, 1932 and continuing to the close of its last fiscal year on April 30, 1936, a period of three and three-quarters years, its sales have amounted to more than $5,500,000, with a net profit in excess of $350,000 – of which $275,000 has been declared as dividends and about $85,000 added to the surplus account. The Aeolian American Corporation has no debts, except current obligations, and enjoys the best dealer representation to be had in this country. For the eight months ending December 31, 1936, both sales and profits exceed any previous similar period, and it would appear that its profits this year [in 1937, the year in which this article was written – Ed.] will exceed $200,000.

As a further evidence of the necessity of the drastic reorganization that was effected in forming the Aeolian American Corporation, it is interesting to note that of 105 piano manufacturers in business in 1928-1929, fewer than 50 are still in business, and 5 of these manufacturers are doing approximately 61% of the business being done.

The Aeolian American Corporation has enjoyed a high percentage of all the business done in the United States and, as far as it is possible to determine, has made about as much profit in the sale of pianos as have all the other companies combined.

In 1932 the Aeolian Skinner Organ Company was formed by the Aeolian Company and the Skinner Organ Company. As previously stated, the Aeolian Company's pipe organ business consisted almost wholly of pipe organs sold for use in homes, and since 1929 that business has almost ceased.

The Skinner Organ Company was the leading manufacturer of church and auditorium organs, although it also produced residence organs. On the basis of contributions of assets to the Aeolian Skinner Organ Company, the Skinner Organ Company received 60% of the stock of the new company, and the Aeolian Company received 40%. In payment for this 40% interest Aeolian contributed pipe organ assets consisting of raw material, machinery, and a small amount of work in process. Contributed also was the music roll inventory; the master rolls and an extensive group of rolls for sale. $50,000 cash given by Aeolian completed the deal. The assets contributed, aside from the cash, would have had practically no ordinary realizable value. Even though the Aeolian Skinner Organ Company has been operated most economically, and has had the combined sales appeal of both the parent companies, it has not so far been able to operate at a profit, due to the fact that up to this writing [1937] there has been but little upturn in the demand for pipe organs of all kinds. The Aeolian Skinner Organ Company, however, is in a strong financial position, having current assets on December 31, 1935 – the date of its last annual statement – of $517,000, of which $390,000 is in cash and accounts receivable; and liabilities of only $26,000.

The total output of pipe organs in the United States during the year 1935 was only a little over 10% of the normal pipe organ business done in the United States each year in the pre-1929 era.

In 1924 the Aeolian Building on West 42nd Street was sold, and in 1925 negotiations were started for a 63-year net lease on a new building to be created by an investor, who acquired a site at 5th Avenue and 54th Street and erected a building, the specifications of which were approved by the Aeolian Company. The annual rental payable to the landlord under the lease was agreed to be a fixed percentage on an agreed valuation for the land and a fixed percentage on the amount invested in the building.

It was, however, further agreed that regardless of the annual rent payable to the landlord as determined by these percentages, the rent would in no event exceed $150,000 a year for the first ten years, and that whatever it fell short in the first ten years would be added to the next 53 years of the lease. On the completion of the building and the final determination of the rental payable to the landlord, it resulted in $150,000 annually for the first ten years and $260,000 annually for the next 53 years of the lease. This annual rental is, of course, in addition to taxes, which have amounted to about $70,000 annually, insurance, and other carrying charges of the property – all of which Aeolian was to assume.

In 1929, in order to reduce the rent burden to the Company, part of the space on the first floor and several floors in the building were sub-leased to Elizabeth Arden for a term of 15 years at $100,000 per year gross. It was later necessary to modify this lease to $80,000 a year, but even with the return from this sub-letting the rent burden to the Company was excessive, and were it to run beyond the 10-year period, when the annual rent would be increased to $260,000, it would have been sufficient to wreck the Company.

After prolonged negotiations a modified agreement was made with the landlord, whereby the annual rent payable by the Company to the landlord was reduced to $96,000 a year from December 1, 1932, to January 31, 1937, which would complete the first ten years, and on the latter date the lease becomes cancelled.

The Steinway contract, which, as previously pointed out, was a distinct asset to the Company during the time that the reproducing pianos and other player pianos flourished, became a liability in 1928, and provided for payments beyond the Company's resources. The agreement with Steinway provided that Steinway pianos purchased by the Company could only be sold as reproducing pianos, and while the Company was obligated to take them, it could not dispose of them as straight pianos. By 1928 the Company's inventory of Steinway pianos was increasing beyond its requirements, and the Company was faced with the obligation to take 600 more each year. This entailed a cost, including the reproducing actions, of an annual average cost of $600,000. [Ed. note: This would put the Aeolian Company's cost at about $1,000 for each Steinway Duo-Art.]

By 1933 the Company had accumulated an excess inventory of Steinway pianos of which a large portion, amounting to over $225,000, was in the same condition as received from Steinway & Sons, the Company having done nothing toward the placing of reproducing player actions in these pianos because of the drastic falling off in business. Furthermore, the Company's liability under the contract with Steinway entailed an obligation to purchase Steinway pianos, to the expiration of the contract in 1934, amounting to more than $1,700,000. After prolonged negotiations the contract was terminated, with friendship and good will continuing between both companies.

In 1928 Aeolian had owing to it from the Aeolian Company, Ltd. of England $1,800,000 which it was unable to collect. The English Company was suffering from very much the same conditions as the Company here. It operated a large plant in Hayes, Middlesex, which was running at a loss, and the volume of business in England was being reduced steadily.

The American officials of the Aeolian Company, in order to liquidate some of the assets of the English Company, so that payment could be made on its debt, were compelled to take even more drastic action there than in America. This resulted in the entire shutdown of the English factory. A contract was made with a competitive manufacturer to make their pianos for them under the Aeolian specifications. As a result of the liquidation of these English assets, the English Company was able to pay the American Company $675,000 in the three years from 1931 to 1933 . . .

Now [in 1937] the piano industry is slowly but surely returning to a more normal basis. The Company has maintained its commanding position in the industry and will benefit to a larger extent than any of its competitiors by the increased demand for pianos which is taking place. There is reason to view the future with confidence and optimism.

———————

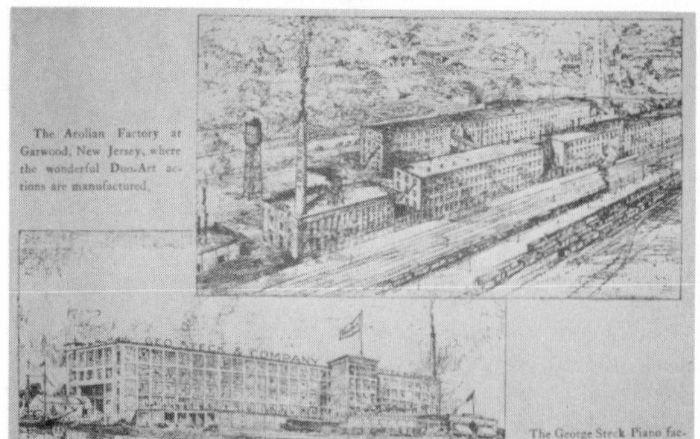

The Aeolian Factory at Garwood, New Jersey, where the wonderful Duo-Art actions are manufactured.

The George Steck Piano factory at Neponset, Mass., one of the Great Plants of the Aeolian Company.

Mr. and Mrs. I. J. Paderewski listening to one of Mr. Paderewski's Duo-Art recordings

## HUPFELD REPRODUCING PIANOS
*by Claes O. Friberg*

The year 1904 is very important in the history of reproducing pianos. Every collector probably knows that this was the year when Welte introduced the Welte-Mignon in Europe, but another interesting thing happened in the same year: the firm of Ludwig Hupfeld A.G. put on the market the Phonoliszt electric reproducing piano. The term "reproducing piano" actually was not used at that time, and it is true that the Phonoliszt piano did not have the same reproducing capabilities that the Welte-Mignon had, so the right term today would be "semi-reproducing piano."

The forerunner of the Phonoliszt was the foot-operated Phonola piano that appeared on the market just after the turn of the century. It played 73 notes on the piano from the lower F to the upper F. The Phonoliszt tracker bar had 77 holes of which 5 holes were used for expression purposes, so the lower F-sharp was omitted from the scale. The pneumatic stack was not divided into bass and treble, and the expression system had three steps: forte, mezzo-forte, and piano. These steps could be reached slowly or rapidly. When the system is in zero position the two expression bellows (MF-bellows and crescendo-bellows) are both open and this makes the instrument play piano.

The five expression holes of the Phonoliszt system are: (1) sustaining pedal, (2) piano (with crescendo bellows operating rapidly), (3) mezzo-forte (operating MF bellows rapidly), (4) crescendo (operating both crescendo and MF bellows slowly), and (5) bass hammer rail.

The Phonoliszt piano was manufactured up to 1930, but during the 1920's its primary production was in connection with the famed violin player, the Hupfeld Phonoliszt-Violina. That instrument could play the Phonoliszt system as described above both in connection with the violin and in solo performances.

The Hupfeld firm knew that the Phonoliszt was not on the same level as the Welte-Mignon, so in the following year, 1905, a first class reproducing piano was developed under the name of DEA (usually written in all capital letters in the Hupfeld literature). This system was installed in upright pianos and grands of first class quality such as Rönisch, Blüthner, and Grotrian-Steinweg. The DEA was the only Hupfeld reproducing system that also appeared in vorsetzer (i.e., push-up automatic player) form.

Many important pianists and composers were invited to record their music for the DEA – for example, D'Albert, Busoni, Cortot, Godowsky, Grieg, Landowska, Mascagni, Saint-Saëns, Planté, Reger, Scharwenka, Scriàbine, and many others. The testimonials of the pianists are full of admiration for the DEA. Of course, Hupfeld asked the artists to give these testimonials for use in advertising [as did Hupfeld's competitors for their own respective makes of reproducing pianos and recording artists], but one cannot help but think that the DEA artists were impressed with the DEA system and the reproduction of their own performances on it. Alfred Grünfeld wrote, for example: "And the DEA plays! The DEA has the hands, the power, the distinction, the soul, and the mood of the artists who record their music on this wonder. There is a second D'Albert, a second Busoni, and a second me. Everyone who listens to one of my rolls on the DEA listens to me!"

The DEA uses wide rolls measuring approximately 16" across and has a 106-hole tracker bar. 85 holes are used for the piano ranging from A to A, and the remaining holes are for expression and control functions.

The DEA reproducing system is a rather complicated device, but when properly adjusted it will play as well as any properly adjusted Welte-Mignon, Ampico, or Duo-Art – and, as is the case with the other systems as well, there are enthusiasts who believe that the DEA is superior.

The DEA pneumatic stack is divided into bass and treble, and each section has six firm steps. In the expression box there is one slide on each side. The position of the slides determines how much air will be allowed to pass into each side of the stack. When the roll has ended the playing, the left slide is moved entirely to the left, and the right slide is moved to the right. This is the zero position and results in the lowest vacuum level in the stack. When a roll begins to play, the holes in the tracker bar determine to which of the firm steps the slide should go. The more to the left the right slide goes, and the more to the right the left slide goes, the louder the treble or bass will play. The slide can travel from any of the firm or fixed steps to any other step desired. There are two holes in the tracker bar which decide the speed of the slides. When neither hole appears the slides travel slowly. Hupfeld claimed that it was better to have four fixed steps between bass and treble (by comparison, the Welte-Mignon has only one fixed step), and certainly this is indeed an advance as it would be more advantageous to have more levels on the roll than just mezzo-forte.

The pedaling system of the DEA is interesting. It works from the on-off system, but both functions work from the same place on the roll by means of a multiplexing system. Two holes are placed in the same lateral position on the tracker bar, with one hole above the other. When pedal on is needed a small oblong performation appears on the paper and when passing over the two holes 4 simple pneumatic functions will happen: (1) the upper hole is opened, (2) the lower hole is open (both holes are open now), (3) the upper hole is then closed, and, as the hole in the roll passes, (4) the lower tracker bar hole is then closed. On this fourth function the dampers will be activated.

The off function necessitates four other functions on the same two holes, but this time a round performation appears so that: (1) the upper hole is opened, (2) then the upper hole is closed, (3) the lower hole is opened, and as the short perforation completes its travel over the tracker bar, (4) the lower hole is closed. In spite of this rather complicated and ingenious device, a quick pedaling is not impossible – although it must be admitted that the sustaining pedal cannot work as quickly from on to off and vice-versa as on other reproducing systems.

The purpose of the DEA was to compete in quality with the Welte-Mignon. The Welte-Mignon became dominant in Europe. The DEA system, while possessing many excellent features, never gained anything near the popularity of the Welte-Mignon. One of the reasons was that Welte was known as the "inventor" of the reproducing piano, and to many persons the name of Welte meant reproducing pianos. Hupfeld was better known in connection with its large series of orchestrions and its foot-operated home player pianos – in which fields it dominated the European market. Also the DEA was more expensive. DEA production was discontinued just before the First World War. The last instruments made were vorsetzers.

After the war Hupfeld announced its third (and last) reproducing piano: the Triphonola. The DEA, as noted, was very expensive due to its elaborate mechanisms and construction. In order to be more competitive, Hupfeld decided that the Duo- and Tri-Phonola pianos should be of the 88-note type with the ordinary standard 88-note paper width. The tracker bar had ten holes for the expression system. Combinations of certain holes would, as on most other types of Hupfeld instruments with multiplexing, mean reroll or motor-off. This saved space on the tracker bar and provided more holes for other functions. The Triphonola (or Tri-Phonola, it was spelled in two forms) plays all 88 piano notes. The piano stack is a standard 88-note stack of the type used in other Hupfeld products including electric Animatic pianos, in the home-type 88-note players, and in certain later orchestrions. This standardization resulted in economies of production. The Duophonola and Triphonola instruments are identical, except that the Triphonola has foot pedals for foot-operation in addition to the electric motor. In the following description the term Triphonola will adequately cover the Duophonola as well.

**DEA.** MAËSTROPLAYER DEA, MAËSTROPLAYER-PIANO DEA and MAËSTROPLAYER-GRAND-PIANO-DEA.

Contrary to the Phonola which requires personal activity, the Dea instruments are operated by means of electric power and therefore are selfplaying. They reproduce the playingof more than 100 most famous artists of the world in a perfect and natural manner.

Years ago the Hupfeld Co. had succeeded in constructing a piano with automatic tone shading, however further developments have brought these instruments to the highest Standard so that now they are unexcelled and are regarded by artists as the best ever created in this particular line.

The tone volume embraces seven octaves and the interpretation of the various pieces is so deceiving that artists at once recognize their own playing or that of their fellow artists which is manifested by many flattering testimonials.

The Maëstroplayer Piano Dea was also the first reproduction piano equipped with a key-board, which allows hand playing at any time and which is indispensable for tuning of the piano. Also for Dea pianos and Grands leading instruments are used as Blüthner, Grotrian-Steinweg and Rönisch.

The pneumatic stack is divided into bass and treble, and further into accompaniment and theme. The tracker bar provides for theme perforations in the same location as the Duo-Art. There is one pneumatic system for accompaniment and one for theme. Each system has two bellows that can move from open to closed position and vice-versa either slowly or rapidly. One of the bellows is the expression from PP to MF, and the other is the expression from MF to FF. The zero position of the system is mezzo-forte, i.e., one bellows (PP - MF) closed and the other (MF - FF) open. This is unlike most other systems which have PP as the zero position.

As mentioned, the tracker bar has 88 holes for playing the piano notes and 10 holes for expression. The tracker bar layout from left to right is: (1) hammer rail, (2) accompaniment MF - PP, (3) theme MF - FF, (4) sustaining pedal, (5) bass theme perforation, (6 to 93) piano notes, (94) treble theme perforation, (95) fast operation of accompaniment bellows, (96) MF - PP theme, (97) fast operation of theme bellows and, (98) accompaniment MF - FF. A combination of 1 and 95 is reroll; a combination of holes 1 and 97 serves for motor-off.

When the system plays accompaniment the vacuum will be the same in both sides of the pneumatic stack, but the vacuum in the theme system will only influence the side of the stack for which the theme perforation appears. The other side will still (if the theme hole is not open) be operated from the vacuum in the accompaniment system. The Triphonola was the first Hupfeld piano with a tracking device. There were various systems such as feelers, two holes on each side of the tracker bar, etc.

In spite of the efforts Hupfeld made to market reproducing pianos on a large scale, it seems that they never succeeded. Today the rarest Hupfeld system is the DEA. In many cases the mechanism was taken out of fine DEA pianos in the 1930's, and the extremely wide rolls were thrown away as they were difficult to store easily.

The Phonoliszt is also a rare instrument. It is found also in the Phonoliszt - Violina combination, as noted earlier. The Triphonola appears more frequently, but the roll libraries are seldom anything but popular tunes from the 'twenties. Good classical rolls for the Triphonola obviously were never marketed in quantity. The DEA instruments, on the contrary, are mostly found with fine collections of classical rolls. This indicates that Hupfeld directed the DEA instruments to the customer with a classical preference, and directed the Triphonola to the buyer who preferred light entertainment.

Today the DEA and Triphonola are much-desired collectors' items. The owner of a DEA reproducing piano can rest assured that he has one of the very best instruments ever produced in this field. This comment refers not only to the ingenious reproducing system, but to the fantastic quality of the Hupfeld craftsmanship that went into these instruments.

Hupfeld's best sellers were orchestrions and foot-operated home player pianos. They so dominated the latter field that approximately 75% of the player pianos found in Germany today are of Hupfeld manufacture.

The Hupfeld family was proud of the DEA when it arrived on the market. Mr. Ludwig Hupfeld was photographed together with most of the pianists in the recording studio. He took a deep personal interest in the DEA and its abilities.

It is interesting to note that two Hupfeld instruments were used in Ludwig Hupfeld's personal mansion: a Phonoliszt - Violina and a foot-operated 88-note home player piano — one of the most intricate Hupfeld instruments and one of the simplest ones!

Raoul Pugno records for the Hupfeld Dea reproducing piano.

Recording for the Hupfeld Dea: scenes at the Hupfeld music salon in Leipzig. Photographs taken during the 1907-1909 period. (Courtesy of Günther Hupfeld)

—Hans and Marie Hermanns—

Alfred Grünfeld records for the Dea. The lady seated near the keyboard is Mrs. Ludwig Hupfeld.

—Leopold Godowsky—

—Arthur Friedheim—

—Gabriel Fauré—

—Carl Reinecke—

—Emil Sauer—

—Xaver Scharwenka—

—Max Schillings—

HUPFELD

—Max Pauer—

Engelbert Humperdinck records for the Hupfeld Dea.

—Theodor Szántó—

—Joaquin Valverde—

—Lucien Würmser—

—Eugen D'Albert—

—Wilhelm Backhaus—

—Ferrucio Busoni—

—Alfred Cortot—

—Pietro Mascagni—

—Dr. Max Reger—

# THE HUPFELD PLAYER-PIANO.

THE firm of **Hupfeld** was originally established in 1892 for the purpose of manufacturing on a large scale all kinds of mechanical musical instruments. At that time mechanical music was mainly produced by instruments of the musical box type. The tinkling sound resulting from the turning of a handle was looked upon as the utmost that could be hoped for in the way of producing music, unless one were prepared to spend years in learning and practising the Piano, Violin, etc.

For some years, however, attempts had been made to use Rolls of perforated paper for the purpose of playing the organ. Mr. Hupfeld had carried these experiments a step further. He was convinced of the possibility of playing the Piano by means of a perforated roll, and as a result of his experiments a Piano Player in Cabinet form was evolved, that is to say, a machine in no way forming part of the Piano, but an entirely separate entity placed in front of the keyboard.

This was very quickly perfected and numerous patents were obtained. For some years the factory was almost entirely engaged in the production of these Piano players. It was not until the early years of the present century that a successful method was found of embodying the player mechanism inside the Piano. Numerous technical difficulties stood in the way, but by 1904/5 these were overcome and the present day Player Pianoforte came into being.

The first **Hupfeld Player Pianos** were of the 73 note type only, that is to say, large sections of the Piano in the extreme bass and the extreme treble were not operated by the Player mechanism at all.

About 1908 the full compass player, playing the whole of the 88 notes of the Piano was perfected, and this is the type now in general use all the world over. Numerous special devices for emphasising the melody notes, working the loud pedal, etc., were added, to which further reference will be made later.

The **Hupfeld Player** acquired an enormous reputation on the Continent of Europe, where in fact for many years it was practically without competition. So busy indeed was the manufacturer kept by his continental orders that little or no effort was made to develop the English market.

In 1910, however, a few Blüthner Pianos were sent to London which were fitted with the **Hupfeld Player,** and these at once roused considerable interest amongst connoisseurs. The ease with which they could be operated, the responsiveness to the touch of the operator, the superlatively high standard of workmanship, were something of a revelation to the English Piano dealers. With little or no advertising the **Hupfeld Player** was proclaimed as a product of the very highest class. It may almost be said to have won its reputation "overnight."

Ever since that time there has been a steady demand for the **Hupfeld** productions, particularly, it should be added, amongst those who may be described as Player Piano enthusiasts. Improvements are of course constantly being effected, the firm of **Hupfeld** possessing in fact not less than 250 patents.

Among other features it is interesting to note that in its present form the use of wood and rubber has been almost entirely eliminated, and the action is now mainly a metal product.

The great bulk of the Player actions produced by the factory in the past has been of the well-known type operated by pedals. In recent years however, additional types operated by the ordinary electric light current of domestic use, having for their object the reproduction of the performances of the great Pianists, have been introduced. As a result it is now possible to buy the **Hupfeld Player** in three different forms:

1. The ordinary foot-blown Player referred to above, which is known as the **Solophonola;**
2. The player reproducing the original performance of a Pianist and operated solely by the electric current, known as the **Duophonola,** and
3. The player which can, at the option of the owner, be operated either by pedals like the Solophonola, or used in the same way as the Duophonola. This is the famous **Triphonola.**

Inasmuch as all these instruments can, of course, be used by hand as ordinary pianos, it will be seen at once that every conceivable requirement is provided for.

Those who want to play themselves, giving vent to their own musical feeling, that is to say, those who wish to enjoy all the sensuous delights of playing the Piano with the facility of a brilliant Pianist, will naturally turn their attention to the Solophonola. The purchaser who, although a lover of music, is doubtful of his own ability to give an adequate performance of the works of the Great Masters, will tend to be interested in the Duophonola, while the Triphonola caters for both types of buyers.

It is largely a matter of taste. We must confess that we ourselves favour either the Solophonola or the Triphonola, because of the possibility of using them oneself. **To play the Piano** is the ambition of most people; both the Solophonola and the Triphonola enable them to do so, while the Duophonola, although to a great extent controllable by levers, is mainly intended to relegate the owner to the position of listener.

In the following pages will be found a description of the varying types.

# THE SOLOPHONOLA.

It has been explained above that this is a Player which is operated by pedals only, that is to say, without the human element the instrument is dumb. We emphasise this because we want to bring it home to the reader that in this player it is the human element, with its varying moods and emotions, that predominates. With the Solophonola you play the Piano yourself every bit as much as you would were you playing by hand, and this is so because the makers have solved the problem of making the action respond to the lightest touch of the operator. The pedals are so sensitive that with the slightest extra pressure a forte or fortissimo effect can be obtained, while only the very minimum of effort is required to obtain the pianissimo and more delicate shades of tone. Another point is the feeling of "touch" which the operator enjoys through the pedals. Every nuance of expression is attainable. He can stroke out the tone of the Piano as does the most soulful pianist one can imagine. In short, the Solophonola turns the untrained music-lover into a magician who can charm not only himself but also his hearers. With little or no practice every vestige of mechanical effect is eliminated.

It must not be supposed that the pedals are the only means provided for obtaining musical expression. The auxiliary "gadgets" of the Solophonola are unique in their efficiency and above all in their simplicity. There is, for example, the SOLODANT, which enables the performer to emphasise the melody notes. Easily worked (its use can be learned in a minute or two), this device in itself makes the Solophonola stand out pre-eminent amongst Piano players. Then there is the lever for graduating the accompaniment. With this the melody or theme of a composition can be emphasised while the accompaniment can be made to rise or fall to the will of the performer. There is, too, a device for **automatically** operating the **"loud" or sustaining Pedal,** and also for making the so-called "soft Pedal" come into action when necessary without any effort on the part of the performer. You can by means of the TRANSPOSER play any composition in NINE different keys. The advantage of this in accompanying Songs need not be

RÖNISCH-HUPFELD

Solophonola

GRAND PLAYER-PIANO

Length, 6 ft. 2 ins. Full Scale (88 Notes). Rosewood Case.

Special Features:—Patent Metal Action, Turbine Wind Motor, Solodant, Graduated Expression Control, Transposer, Antennæ Tracking Device, Automatic Pedal Drop.

RÖNISH-HUPFELD

Triphonola

Similar in appearance to above, is a Pedal-Electric Reproducing Piano, which may be operated either electrically or by means of the pedals.

enlarged upon—it is obvious. A TRACKING DEVICE to keep the Music Roll in position is of vital importance. In the Solophonola the tracking device does its work silently and efficiently.

It only remains to add that the Solophonola is the very last word in high-class workmanship. Remove the front panel of a **Hupfeld Player Piano** and you will experience the same glow of pleasure that you enjoy when you open up the bonnet of the tip-top motor car. Its conglomeration of highly finished metal parts proclaim it at once a "proper engineering job." Every note is a single unit interchangeable with any other note. One of these units can be removed and re-inserted in a few seconds if desired. Accessibility has been considered in the construction. The prospective owner need not be alarmed at the prospect of having to make continual adjustments; he need never touch the action. Should, however, any small adjustment be found advisable by the Piano tuner, for example, this accessibility constitutes a great advantage. What might take hours in the old-fashioned wooden Player can be done in a few minutes on a **Hupfeld.** All parts are made of a non-corrosive metal, which ensures not only durability but also enables the whole mechanism to withstand the most adverse climatic conditions.

To sum up, the **Hupfeld Solophonola** is, without doubt, the very finest example of Player Piano construction in existence, and can be thoroughly commended to the discriminating purchaser.

# The DUOPHONOLA and the TRIPHONOLA.

We now come to the more recent developments in the Player world, the so-called Reproducing Pianos. We have mentioned above that the **Hupfeld Duophonola and Triphonola,** with the aid of the ordinary electric light current, can reproduce the performance of the great Pianists. This result is of course only attained by using a special type of Music Roll on which the performance in question is faithfully recorded. Before going into further details concerning the Player action, it may be as well to give a short explanation of the method by which this record is obtained.

Instead of taking the score, the manufacturer engages a pianist of recognised ability and distinction, who is capable of performing a composition in a way to satisfy even the most punctilious critic. The artist is informed that it is desired to obtain a reproduction of say, a Nocturne of Chopin. He seats himself at the piano, and performs his nocturne precisely as he would do were he performing at a concert in the presence of a critical audience. He gives rein to his emotions and plays the composition as he feels that it should be played. He introduces into his playing all the rallentando, accelerando, rituendo effects, and nuances which go to make up an artistic as compared with a mere mechanical performance.

The making of the actual record is a perfectly simple matter. Every note of the piano is connected by an electric wire to a corresponding row of pencils which are superimposed on a strip of paper revolving on a drum. Every time the artist strikes a note, the corresponding pencil is brought into contact with the paper. So long as the artist keeps his finger on the note, the pencil produces a line on the paper. Immediately he releases the note the pencil leaves the paper and the line is brought to an end. It will thus be seen that if the pianist strikes a chord with even the slightest arpeggio effect, this is immediately reproduced on the pencil record. When he plays a scale each note is reproduced just that length of time during which the artist holds his finger on that particular note. If he makes a pause on any one note, so is this shown on the record by the extra length of pencil line resulting from this pause. Should he accelerate a certain passage, so will this be recorded by the shortening of the pencil lines. When he has finished the composition, the strip of paper with the pencil lines is taken from the drum of the reproduction instrument, and wherever the pencil lines are visible the paper is perforated. From this "Master Roll," rolls to an unlimited number can be manufactured.

The touch or dynamic force is recorded by means of a separated pneumatic contrivance which records the force with which each note is struck by the Pianist. This record is then combined with the record of the tempo explained above, by the addition of extra side perforations at the margin of the Roll. These are generally called the expression perforations.*

It is not proposed to give a long description of the technical working of these expression holes. It is sufficient here to explain that they control the touch of the Player action in precisely the same way as the human operator does through the pedals of the Solophonola. From the lightest shades of pianissimo to the heaviest fortissimo the original touch of the Pianist is recorded.

We can now visualise a performance by the Duophonola or the Triphonola. Imagine, for example, we want to hear the Ballade in G minor played by Busoni. The Roll is inserted, the button is pressed and immediately a veritable miracle is performed. The opening phrase of this monumental work swells out with all the majesty and force that the Great Master, Busoni, could give to it. We hear his interpretation of one of the world's masterpieces. On the Duophonola or the Triphonola you can actually hear Grieg play one of his own compositions. In short, The **Hupfeld Reproducing Piano** brings the world's greatest composers and performers into your own home. In lighter vein you can have Jazz and dance music. And what better accompaniment to dancing in the home than that of a full-toned Piano? Remember, it is the instrument itself you hear, not a mere distorted reproduction. Press the button, the music you want is there. At the end of the piece, the Roll, without your moving a finger, will re-roll itself automatically, ready for another performance. Such is the Reproducing Piano!

* In this connection it is interesting to note that with many if not all Reproducing Players except the Hupfeld, there are no additional expression perforations on the margin of the Roll. The holes at the end of the scale, that is the extreme bass and treble, are used for expression purposes, with the result that the notes at both ends are dumb. The Duophonola (and of course, the Triphonola) plays every note on the score and the original record need never be faked as is the case with other Players.

Do not, however, imagine that you have no control whatever over the Reproducing Pianoforte. The Tempo can be set to suit your liking and if you wish you can put in your own expression, when using an ordinary roll, by means of the Expression levers and buttons provided. Full instructions how to do this are given in our Brochure—"How to play the **Hupfeld,**" which gives in simple language the little help that is needed to enable you to obtain the utmost satisfaction from all three types of Players—Solophonola, Duophonola, and Triphonola. Thus the Duophonola need not be entirely automatic, although, of course, as already explained, it is primarily constructed for those who want to listen rather than perform.

So-called, because it can be used in three ways, electrically, by pedalling, or by hand, the **Triphonola** is the culminating point in automatic Piano playing. It can be used with pedals like the Solophonola, by those who wish to perform themselves, or it can be used as a reproducing Player as described above.

With the **Triphonola** all tastes are catered for, and this, too, at a very small extra cost as compared with the Duophonola. We would recommend the purchase of a Triphonola in preference to a Duophonola for many reasons. One does not always want to be only a listener. Remember that, sooner or later, the owner or one of his friends will want "to have a shot at it" himself. Electric light currents have been known to fail; with the Triphonola you always have the pedals as an alternative. **You can use the same** Rolls for either purpose, so do not be alarmed at the prospect of having to keep a double stock on hand. But, above all, we repeat, remember that **if you want to do so you can play the Triphonola yourself.** Think well of this before you are tempted to buy a Player without pedals. The real joy of a Player Piano lies in the fact that you can play it yourself, whereas with the wireless or the Gramophone you can only listen. Therefore, say we, buy a Player Piano!

HUPFELD
Hupfeld-Phonoliszt m. 10 Rollen-Magazin und elektrischer Fernschaltung

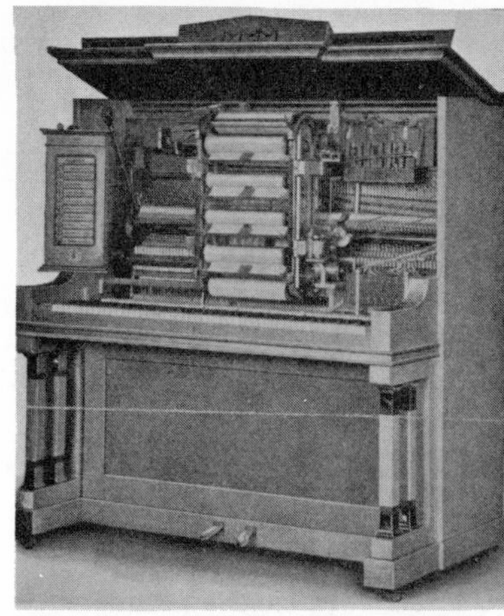

Hupfeld Phonoliszt piano with 10-station roll changer. By means of a wallbox with an index pointer any one of the ten rolls can be selected by the patron. This system, shown here on a Phonoliszt, was also available on orchestrions and Phonoliszt-Violinas, according to the Hupfeld literature.

Phonoliszt pianos were sold both for home and commercial use. Most apparently were used in business establishments; relatively few were sold to private residences.

Hupfeld-Phonoliszt
mit Künstler-Notenrollen, die das Original-spiel von 140 ersten Künstlern wiedergeben
Das erste Kunstspiel-Klavier


Hupfeld Phonoliszt piano made for commercial use. Operation was via a remote wallbox. A number of different Phonoliszt case designs, most plainer in design than this one, were introduced over the years.

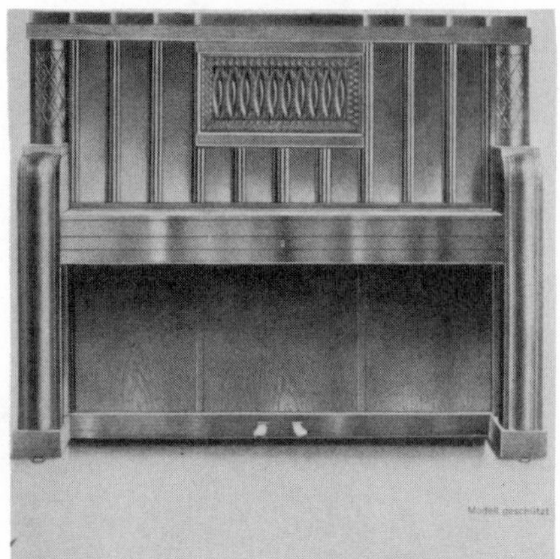

MEISTERSPIEL-PIANO DEA

MEISTERSPIEL-PIANO DEA

MEISTERSPIEL-FLÜGEL DEA IIIA
zur selbsttätigen Wiedergabe des Künstlerspiels mittels pneumatisch-elektrischer Kraft ohne persönliche Einwirkung :: Der höchste Punkt in der Entwicklung des Klavierspielinstrumentenbaues :: Länge 2,15 m Klaviatur jederzeit benutzbar

MEISTERSPIEL-DEA

HUPFELD DEA: Several varieties of the Hupfeld Dea reproducing piano. The two upper illustrations are of upright keyboard models. The lower left is of a Rönisch grand piano with a built-in Dea mechanism. At the lower right is a Dea vorsetzer push-up piano player. Dea pianos were superbly built of finely-crafted materials and with excellent workmanship.

The Philipps Duca

The Duca, Philipps' entry into the reproducing piano field, was produced from about 1908 to the late 1920's (and was advertised through the 1930-1931 period). Many different styles were made, including vorsetzer, cabinet, upright, and grand models. One type of Duca grand piano utilized a 3-roll automatic changer compactly built into the space between the center of the keyboard and the music rack.

Over 2,000 different Duca roll titles were produced. A Duca catalogue of the early 1920's listed rolls by the following pianists: Ugo Afferni, Eugen d'Albert, Conrad Ansorge, Germaine Arnaud, Fr. Bäcker-Gröndahl, Felix Baer, Pitt Bittong, Fritz von Bose, Marte Braun, James Brown, Ferrucio Busoni, Teresa Carreño, Maria Carreras, Maria Theresia Conzen, Alfred Cortot, Augusta Cottlow, Francois de la Croix, Norah Drewett, Kurt Drücker, Paul Eggert, A. Emch, Lonny Epstein, Leo Eysoldt, Ida Feinmann, Alban Förster, Anton Förster, Hans Förster, Fr. Franz, Carl Friedberg, Arthur Friedheim, Ignaz Friedman, Ossip Gabrilowitsch, Rio Gebhardt, Berthe Marx-Goldschmidt, Paul Goldschmidt, Alfred Grünfeld, Heinz Hanitsch, Irene Hendorf, Willy M. Jinkertz, Else Kallmeyer, Marie Kaufmann, Fr. W. Keitel, A. Knoof, Erich Wolfgang Korngold, James Kwast, Frieda Kwast-Hodapp, Frederic Lamond, Louise Löhr, Fritz Malata, Moritz Mayer-Mahr, Marc Meytschik, Helene Moillet-Gobat, Jose Vianna da Motta, Theodor Müller-Reuter, Otto Neitzel, Marie Oppenheimer, Ellen Pairan, Edmund Parlow, Max von Pauer, August Philipps, Oswald Philipps, Hans Pfitzner, Alexander Pohl, Raoul Pugno, Wynne Pyle, Ella Rafelson, Willy Rehberg, Walter Rehberg, Bruno Hinze-Reinhold, Alice Ripper, Eduard Risler, Julius Röntgen, Anatol v. Roessel, Camille Saint-Saëns, Wera Schapira, Xaver Scharwenka, August Schmid-Lindner, Adolf Schmitt, Arthur Schnabel, Germaine Schnitzer, B. Schröder, Richard Singer, Paula Stebel, Johann Strauss, Adolf Tandler, Frieda Thury, Ernst Toch, Josef Treis, Gaspard de Vienne, Elfriede Vogel, Josef Weiss, S. Wilberg, Lucien Würmser, Johann Wysmann, and Michael v. Zadora.

August and Oswald Philipps were the "& Sons" of J.D. Philipps & Sons. Most rolls were numbered in rotation (beginning with No. 1, "Cupid's Garden" played by Hans Förster). Dance rolls were numbered in the 5,000 series; rolls for vocal accompaniment, in the 6,000 series; rolls for violin accompaniment, in the 7000 series; rolls for cello accompaniment, in the 7,500 series; rolls for "trios, quartettes, et al accompaniment" in the 7,550 series. Only a few of the last three roll types were issued.

Philipps employees at the Bockenheim factory, as shown in a photograph taken during the 50th anniversary celebration in 1927.

1930 advertisement featuring the Duca reproducing piano and other Philipps instruments including theatre and residence pipe organs.

The foot-pumped Ducanola was available in upright and grand piano and vorsetzer styles.

1910 advertisement for various Philipps products including the "latest novelties," the Duca Vorsetzer and a cabinet-style (keyboard-less) Duca reproducing piano.

## UNDERSTANDING THE RECORDO

*by David L. Saul*

The name "Recordo," which originally designated a roll manufacturing concern and its products, has come to be applied colloquially to a class of expression coded rolls and to the instruments which play them — both of which have been produced in many variations and by a number of different manufacturers over the years.

Instruments which play Recordo-type rolls utilize a simple and straightforward method of dynamic control and are customarily termed "expression pianos" rather than reproducing pianos. The expression piano's relatively uncomplicated mechanical system provides a substantial amount of dynamic control without laying claim to the amount of precision found in more sophisticated reproducing instruments.

The central aspect of Recordo's business operation was roll making, not piano building. The resulting situation was favorable to the adoption of standardized expression coding. As a consequence, the Recordo system provides the only example of an expression scheme which could be used universally throughout the industry. Many piano makers adopted the Recordo system, frequently offering expression models to supplement their lines of conventional players. Each firm had to provide its own mechanical components, with the result that mechanisms responding to Recordo rolls took on approximately as many different forms as there were player action manufacturers at the time! Wurlitzer, Welte, and the American Piano Co., each of whom had their own reproducing systems, also made Recordos in small quantities!

In spite of its many variations, the expression piano is easy to identify by virtue of the unique appearance of its tracker bar. At either end of the tracker bar's usual line of ordinary-sized holes will be found five rather conspicuous expression ports. These special openings, totaling ten in number, are elongated so as to have the appearance of slots. The Duo-Art also has slotted holes of similar size, but only four on each end of the tracker bar.

Rolls with Recordo-type coding first appeared in the late 'teens and were produced by the Imperial Music Roll Company of Chicago, Illinois. The name originally used was "Imperial Automatic Electric." The Recordo designation did not appear until around 1920 or so at which time the Recordo Player Roll Company was formed as an Imperial subsidiary. Recordo's business interests were subsequently acquired by the QRS Company, and that firm continued production of rolls under the QRS Recordo label. In due course other roll companies were licensed to make rolls with Recordo-type expression coding, and in some cases the QRS Company produced expression rolls bearing special names and labels. An example of this is the QRS-produced Aria Divina Reproducing Roll.

Listed alphabetically, the more popular makes of rolls with Recordo-type coding, the so-called "expression rolls," are the following: Aria Divina Reproducing Roll, Imperial Automatic Electric, International for Expression Pianos, MelOdee Expression Roll, Pianostyle for Expression Pianos, QRS Recordo, Recordo, Rose Valley Recording Roll, U.S. Auto-Art, Vocalstyle Home Recital Series, Vocalstyle Reproducing, and Vocalstyle Reproduco.

Although expression rolls were standardized to a large extent, complete uniformity was not achieved. At least three variant types of expression coding are found among rolls of the Recordo family. Accordingly, the rolls are not strictly interchangeable on all expression pianos. This fact has not been widely known or appreciated in past years, and the resulting confusion has had a damaging effect on the artistic reputation of expression pianos. Unfortunately, the differences are not always easily discernible upon casual inspection; neither were these differences widely publicized by the manufacturing community at the time. The rationale for each type of expression coding will clarify itself somewhat as the subject of dynamic control is discussed.

The Recordo system of expression employs a scale of fixed intensity steps or degrees. Division between bass and treble sections of the keyboard is found only in a soft pedal action of sorts, which may be applied independently to bass or treble. In all other respects dynamic control is commonly applied. A single regulating mechanism applies varying degrees of vacuum to the entire pneumatic stack under control of the music roll's expression coding.

In its most prevalent form, the expression piano utilizes a scale of five regulated degrees of vacuum. Four special ports are provided on the tracker bar to operate the system's single regulating mechanism. (The remaining six ports operate pedals or other auxiliary devices.) With all four ports covered, the lowest playing power predominates. The four ports, when opened individually to atmosphere, produce four successively higher-valued degrees of vacuum to complete the five-step scale. Should more than one port be opened simultaneously, the highest-valued one to be opened overrides the others and produces its own characteristic degree of loudness; the higher the vacuum level, the louder the playing.

As originally conceived and produced, the Recordo (erstwhile Imperial Automatic Electric) system did not operate in precisely this way. The four expression ports were opened in various combinations during the course of playing to produce many more than five steps. Mechanisms designed to play rolls of this sort did not respond in the override fashion described earlier but, instead, responded uniquely to certain combinations of opened ports. Four expression ports permit a maximum of sixteen different coding combinations. In the early system twelve from among the possible sixteen were actually employed, producing a scale composed of twelve intensity steps.

The twelve-step intensity scale, after being used for a time, was supplanted by the five-step scheme. This change occurred after the original Recordo firm had been absorbed by the QRS Company. Five-step coding prevailed throughout the most active years of the Recordo system's employment, and a substantial majority of expression pianos are equipped to play rolls so coded.

Complicating matters still further, another change was made in 1926. At that time a sixteen-step intensity scale was introduced. QRS Recordo rolls incorporated the change in new recordings produced after that date, and sixteen-step coding also appears in the QRS-produced Aria Divina Reproducing Roll. The change resulted in a new crop of Recordo-type mechanisms, contributing still further to the already existing plethora of mechanical designs. Making a positive determination of which type of mechanism is installed in a given piano is not an easy task and generally requires the services of a qualified technical expert. The type of coding in a particular roll of the Recordo family can frequently be inferred from the roll's brand and identification number after the collector has gained sufficient experience in such matters.

M. Schulz Co. of Chicago advertised the Aria Divina in the 1920's. Schulz, one of America's leading piano makers, also installed Welte (Licensee) reproducing actions in some of its instruments. For more information about Schulz, see "The Western Electric 'Selectra' — An Idea Lingers On" in the Western Electric Piano Co. section of this book.

## UNDERSTANDING THE WELTE MIGNON

*by David L. Saul*

### Introduction

The distinction of being first belongs to the Welte Mignon. As a new century was dawning, that which might be regarded as the quintessence of the pianistic art submitted for the first time to the portraiture of the reproducing piano roll. The Welte Mignon, or the "Welte Artistic Player Piano" as it was first called in America, gave utterance to the reproducing roll's patterns and established a precedent that was to mark the beginning of a new era in mechanical music.

These developments took place around the turn of the 20th century in the laboratories of M. Welte and Sons of Freiburg, Germany. Already a leader in the automatic musical instrument field, Welte could boast of a record of achievements that included many significant innovations, notably in the design and construction of large orchestrions.

The Welte Mignon ("Mignon," or "small" was in reference to the size of the new instrument – it was indeed small in contrast to the firm's huge orchestrions!) reproducing piano made its debut in the form of a cabinet-style upright piano built without keyboard and played solely by the agency of music rolls. A typical example appeared not unlike a fine piece of furniture, with a carved facade concealing from view the instrument's innermost nature and purpose. Examples of this "keyboardless" style are not unknown (but are quite rare, however) among other reproducers: the curious cabinet-style Chickering Ampico is an example of another make; however, only Welte built them in significant numbers. In due course Welte's offerings were expanded to include reproducing pianos constructed along more conventional lines.

Another form in which the Welte Mignon made an early appearance was the Vorsetzer. The name derives from a German word meaning "setting or placing in front" and translates into English only in the most awkward fashion.

In basic terms the Vorsetzer can be described as a mechanical push-up piano player of the reproducing type. The mechanism was installed in a furniture-styled cabinet with a row of mechanical fingers at keyboard height. Levers were provided at the bottom to operate sustaining and soft pedals. When the Vorsetzer was carefully positioned before a piano, felt-covered fingers assumed the artistic role traditionally reserved for human hands.

The practical attributes (one could use the piano for hand playing, if desired) of built-in reproducing systems outweighed those factors favoring the Vorsetzer, and with the passing of time a greater number of Welte Mignon instruments took the more familiar built-in (or "einbau" in German, for "in built") form.

The cabinet-style upright Welte Mignon was made only in small numbers during the 1920's as the buying public sought pianos which could be played in the usual way. Vorsetzers, however, continued to enjoy a limited popularity with buyers who wished to retain the family's prized piano but who also wanted to hear artists' rolls. Vorsetzers continued to be built and sold until the end of Welte production, although accounting for a relatively small fraction of sales.

Earlier pianos with built-in mechanisms were not always entirely self-contained. The ungainly vacuum pumps of the day would not fit into the cases of certain grand piano styles and thus were housed in separate cabinets matching the piano's style and wood finish. The ancillary cabinets stood little more than knee high. The arrangement came to be known as "cow and calf" for reasons of appearance. The bovine epithet is misleading in that it conveys no hint of the excellent quality and craftsmanship which characterize these fine instruments.

The Welte reproducing system was often described in advertisements by the term "floating crescendo." This is aptly fitting since the Welte expression device operates in a continuously variable manner throughout its entire loudness range. Only one fixed step, MF (mezzo-forte), is employed.

In simplified terms, loudness of playing is changed either slowly or very quickly by activating one of two types of valve assemblies called "crescendo" and "sforzando" (frequently anglicized to "forzando") respectively. This is accomplished automatically as the music roll's expression coding passes over the tracker bar. Another ingenious device, the mezzo-forte unit, provides a sort of reference point and prevents accumulation of dynamic errors that might otherwise become noticeable. The dynamics of a recorded performance can be replicated during playback by activating these features at appropriate times, either separately or in combination. Two identical and completely independent expression devices separately control the bass and treble sections of the keyboard. Expression valves are of the lock-and-cancel type, utilizing short perforations to turn expression functions on or off at the correct instant.

Three distinct versions of the Welte reproducing system were manufactured under the auspices of the parent firm, and the total count increases to four when the American-built "Licensee" is added to the list. All types share the same basic operating principles, but they differ substantially in mechanical design and with respect to the types of rolls which can be played. Music roll standardization was the rule in the case of American Welte Mignon products, but two additional roll types were made for European use.

### The Welte Licensee

Welte Mignons most frequently encountered in the United States of America are of the Licensee type, containing mechanisms made by New York's Auto Pneumatic Action Company. That firm, at one time one of America's largest manufacturers of player piano actions, built its own version of the Welte Mignon system under a licensing agreement authorizing the use of Welte patents. The Licensee's full name is the Auto Deluxe Welte Mignon Reproducing Piano. In popular use it was often noted as the "Welte (Licensee)" with the "Licensee" part in parentheses.

The Licensee mechanism was the result of a complete redesigning of the Welte system. Its components bear little noticeable resemblance to other Welte hardware.

Although the Welte original and Licensee mechanisms differ from each other in appearance, their basic principles are the same. The Licensee plays the same types of rolls as the American-made (rather than made in Germany) "Original Welte-Built Welte Mignon," which retained major engineering features of the German instruments. With certain advertising claims and counterclaims to the contrary, there is little in the way of evidence to suggest that Auto Pneumatic's re-engineering might have given rise to significant differences in artistic character. Much of the rationale for redesigning was undoubtedly rooted in more practical matters of production engineering – working out a design well suited to large scale production within the capabilities of Auto Pneumatic's factory machines and tooling.

Grand models of the Licensee are equipped with drawers containing their respective spoolboxes and related components. This practice contrasts with that which prevails in all other Welte Mignon grands which, with a few exceptions to be noted, have their spoolboxes situated above the keys. The Welte Licensee is identifiable by virtue of three switches mounted inside the spoolbox. These switches, found in both uprights and grands, are functionally designated as LOUD PEDAL, REPLAY, and TRANSFORMING LEVER.

The Auto Pneumatic firm did not build pianos. Its role was that of a supplier to piano builders throughout the industry. As the Licensee mechanism was offered the various manufacturers, the list of Licensee-equipped piano brands grew to include well over a hundred names.

The following, by no means a complete list, is a representative cross section of piano brands using the Licensee mechanism: Baldwin, Kranich & Bach, Hardman, Mehlin & Sons, Sohmer, Ivers & Pond, Hazelton, Stieff, Kurtzmann, Acoustigrande, Schulz, Christman, Bush & Lane (in the late 1920's an automatic changer device was offered by this firm), Conover, Kimball, Packard, Premier, and Francis Bacon. The reader seeking detailed technical information on the Licensee will find the original service manual or a reprint thereof to be quite useful.

### The Original Welte

The Original Welte-Built Welte Mignon, or simply the Original Welte (as it is more commonly known), was manufactured in the United States under the auspices of the parent German firm. Reproducing pianos of this type were marketed in the post World War I era in competition not only with other brands of reproducers, but also in competition with the Licensee instruments. Many advertisements of the day more or less conspicuously reflected this aspect of competition with comments as "the Welte-Built Welte Mignon is Supreme," and from the opposite camp, "This modernized Welte Mignon is licensed under the original Welte patents." The rivalry was apparently no more than skin deep, as some of the pneumatic stacks installed by the Original Welte firm were purchased from the builders of the Licensee.

The expression devices and many other parts of Original Welte instruments resemble their European counterparts in mechanical design. The spoolboxes and tracker bars, however, are scaled to American standards (as opposed to the metric system prevalent in continental Europe). American-made Welte rolls (one variety of which is called the DeLuxe Reproducing Roll) can be played on either the Licensee or Original Welte instruments. Apparently influenced by European practice of running rolls at a common speed, the Original Welte firm's rolls are marked at tempo 80 - 90.

Original Welte grand pianos have their spoolboxes situated above the keys in all but a very few early examples which are equipped with drawers. The Original Welte (U.S.A.-built) mechanisms were installed in upright and small to medium-size grand pianos as well as Vorsetzers. Original Welte pianos bear no identification other than Welte Mignon. These instruments, for the most part, appear to have been built in this country by the Estey Piano Co. (of Indiana; no connection with the Estey Organ Co. of Brattleboro, Vermont).

An interesting mechanical feature of Original Welte pianos is the high-speed blower type of vacuum pump found in such instruments. Other Welte Mignons are generally equipped with pumps having some arrangement of large bellows connected to a crankshaft. A brief technical description of this type of instrument appears in William Braid White's book, "Piano Playing Mechanisms."

### The "Red Welte"

The first Welte Mignons built in Germany played a larger type of roll frequently (but not always) issued on red paper. As a result, collectors and historians often refer to these as "Red Welte" or "Red Paper Welte" instruments.

The earliest Welte reproducing pianos sold in the United States also played the larger type of roll, whose paper measures about 12 7/8" wide. Although the physical size and spacing of holes is different, the tracker scale (i.e., the arrangement and order of note and expression tubing connections) is similar to that of the American-made Welte instruments with one minor exception. The large European rolls contain special coding, not found on domestic rolls, to activate a vacuum pump power boost (via a motor speedup) during loud passages. In contrast to the American practice of using speeds or tempos which varied from one roll to another, the Welte firm used a single speed common to all of the large rolls. As a result, there are no tempo indications printed on the leaders of Red Welte rolls.

Mechanisms using the large roll were installed in grand pianos, upright models with and without keyboards, and Vorsetzers. European Welte Mignon instruments are most easily identified by their conspicuously large tracker bars and spoolboxes, and by German language labeling of controls and switches (exceptions: instruments sold in England and America, imported from Welte in Freiburg during the pre World War I era, had English inscriptions).

Beautifully crafted gears and mechanical hardware attest to the superb workmanship and quality that went into these instruments. Some excellent Red Welte examples are found in German-built Steinway pianos built in Steinway's Hamburg factory. Many of Europe's own finest pianos accommodated the red paper rolls, including the Bechstein, Blüthner, Ibach, Feurich, and Seiler. The Welte firm also produced its own brand of piano (which bore the firm's own name).

The Welte Artistic Player built in America prior to World War I was virtually identical to the European style insofar as the reproducing mechanism was concerned. The American instruments are most easily distinguished from their European counterparts by English-system measurements for parts (not metric) and, in some cases, by an American brand name of piano (such as Krakauer and Mason & Hamlin).

Examples of such American-made pianos of pre World War I vintage are owned by several collectors in this country. These instruments play the large, red paper rolls.

### The "Green Welte"

The Green Paper Welte Mignon, or "Green Welte" as collectors know it, is so-called because of the predominating color of its music rolls. The Green Welte represents a later development after the international adoption of American roll size standards — 11¼" paper width and nine holes per inch across the tracker bar. (Note: This "international adoption" was not quite complete; several European manufacturers continued to use metric-based scales.) Although the physical size of the green rolls is the same as their American counterparts, the expression coding is substantially different. Welte engineers developed a method of operating the existing expression devices with simplified coding and implemented a new tracker scale based on the revised principle. Green Welte coding differs from the conventional Welte Mignon scheme in its use of an extended perforation passing over a single hole in the tracker bar to accommodate each function requiring alternate use of two tracker bar holes in the regular roll. The lock-and-cancel scheme is not used in the Green Welte system.

The modified coding leaves more space on the rolls for playing notes, with the result that the Green Welte is the only full-fledged reproducing system that plays all of the piano's 88 keys. All other systems delete a token number of keys from the seldom used extremes of the keyboard in order to allow sufficient room for expression coding in the roll margins. Conventional Welte Mignon instruments play 80 notes. The green rolls run at a single, common speed as do the larger red rolls. The speeds are not the same; the green rolls run somewhat slower.

The Green Welte mechanism was installed in the same brands of pianos as the Red Welte. The Green Welte was never marketed in America. Those seen here today have been imported by Welte enthusiasts in recent years.

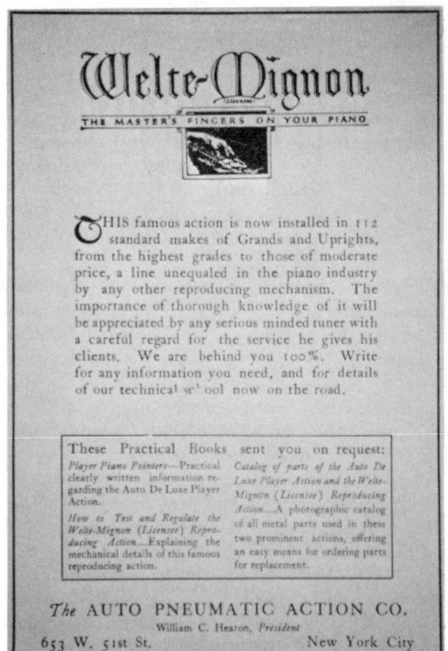


**An Auto Pneumatic Action Co. advertisement in a 1927 issue of "The Tuners Journal" notes that "This famous action is now installed in 112 standard makes of grands and uprights, from the highest grades to those of moderate price, a line unequalled in the piano industry by any other reproducing mechanism." Later advertisements were to note that over 115 different piano brands utilized this action.**

WELTE

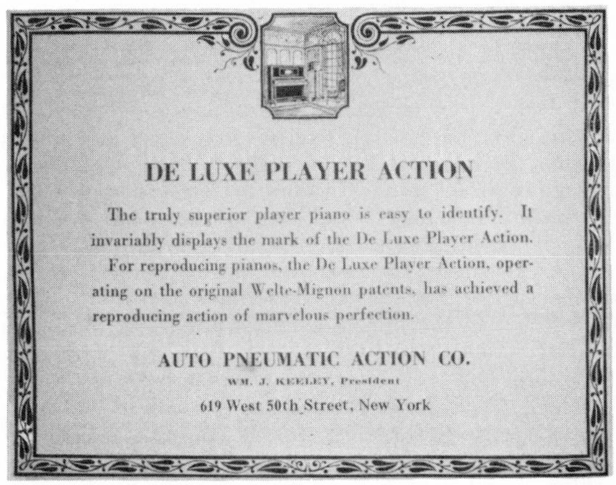


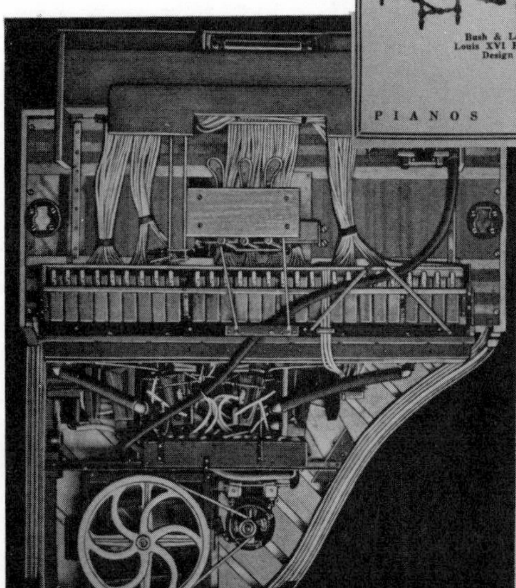

**Welte-Bockisch Patents**
**Acknowledged Fundamental**

(From the Musical Courier Extra; September 17, 1921)

The following statement has been sent out to the trade regarding the settlement of the controversy over the basic validity of the Welte-Bockisch patents in the manufacture of reproducing piano mechanisms:

The Welte Mignon Corporation, New York, is the owner of the Welte-Bockisch basic patents, acknowledged as the fundamental patents governing reproducing player pianos.

The suit of the Welte Mignon Corporation against the Aeolian Company for alleged infringement in its Duo-Art construction of the Welte-Bockisch patent has been finally settled out of court. The Aeolian Company has taken out a license under this patent, as have previously the Auto Pneumatic Action Company, the Amphion Player Piano Company, and the American Piano Company, maker of the Ampico reproducing piano.

The fact that the Aeolian Company, after long and careful consideration, has taken a license under this Welte - Bockisch patent and has agreed to pay royalties in common with the other manufacturers mentioned above and thus has recognized and acknowledged the validity of the patent, places beyond question the claim of the Welte Mignon Corporation as to the fundamental nature of the reproducing piano patent. . ."

Editor's Note: The makers of the Ampico and Duo-Art paid a royalty of $2.50 per reproducing piano for the use of the Welte patent. It must be noted that the Welte mechanisms were not copied — just the fundamental patented concept of using variations in the vacuum level to produce variations in piano expression. — Q.D.B.

## The Multi-Reproducer

Made by the National Piano Manufacturing Company (also known as the National Automatic Music Company) of Grand Rapids, Michigan, the Multi-Reproducer attachment plays Welte (Licensee) rolls and is housed in a furniture cabinet. A "ferris wheel" or magazine type of roll changer holds eight rolls, any desired one of which may be selected at will by pushing an appropriate button to the left of the roll unit. When each roll is put on its spool, a small dial must be turned by hand to the correct tempo setting.

The roll is "read" pneumatically in the regular manner. A series of pneumatics with electrical contacts convert the vacuum impulses to electric coding. The piano, which may be located at any desired distance from the roll changer cabinet, has a corresponding unit which then re-converts the electrical coding to vacuum impulses (which then travel to the pneumatic stack of the piano and operate it in the usual manner).

Although called the "Multi-Reproducer" by National (the maker), the Bush and Lane Piano Company billed the unit as the "Multi-Control" when it was advertised for use in conjunction with their pianos.

Marjorie Barkley McClure, novelist from Fairlawn, Ohio, purchased one of these and wrote of it (as quoted in "The Music Trade Review," issue of January 2, 1926):

"At this very moment my piano is concluding a program of eight rolls that arrived from your department a few hours ago, and I am swept so high upon the towering waves of sheer sound beauty that I must express to you — somebody — my delight in this instrument.

"When I look back to last June and remember the day I heard of the Bush & Lane Welte Mignon (Licensee) reproducing piano with Multi-Control — quietly, without heralding of trumpets or superlative adjectives — I do not wonder that, at the time, I thought my informant must be mistaken. It did not seem possible that this idea could be incorporated in the wood and metal of an instrument, made in my own Michigan, and I not know it.

"I had wanted a reproducing piano for so long! I had looked and inquired but always I knew that in my exceedingly busy life I would be annoyed by the need to manipulate the rolls. When my mood is for music I want to forget myself in it, forget the mechanism and have it go on and on while I dream or think, read or write, unconscious of the machinery that controls the action. To have to rise after each roll and exchange it for another would be, for me, a blemish on the joy of it. So I had waited, letting the hunger go unappeased and then, that June day I heard through the Bush & Lane Company of the Multi-Control.

"It was not long after it was installed in our living room that I went to Neahtawanta, Michigan, for a brief holiday. I heard at once that Dorothy Miller Duckwitz was there in her summer studio and that she was reading my novel, 'High Fires,' and wanted to meet me..." (And so on, you get the idea — Ed.) It seems (so Miss McClure's letter continued) that Mme. Duckwitz had earlier recorded for Welte and that her in-person playing was indistinguishable from that on the music rolls, etc. etc.

Although Bush & Lane advertised that it had "many models" of the Multi-Control Welte (Licensee) grand pianos for sale, apparently few sales materialized — for such units are very rare today. The same National Piano Manufacturing Company also made "National" coin pianos with 8-roll changers. Unlike the Multi-Control units, the National coin pianos were made in large quantities.

1926 advertisement (top right of page) for the Multi-Reproducer. Above and left: Views of a Multi-Reproducer in the J.B. Nethercutt Collection.

## INTRODUCTION OF THE WELTE-MIGNON

*The Welte reproducing piano, at first called the Mignon and later the Welte Mignon (in the early years without hyphen; later usually hyphenated as Welte-Mignon), was perfected in 1904. The author's conversations with Richard C. Simonton (who was a personal friend of Edwin Welte and Karl Bockisch in the 1940's and who spent several months in Freiburg in the company of these two gentlemen), perusals of contemporary German music trade publications (most notably "Zeitschrift für Instrumentenbau"), and interviews with persons once connected with the Welte firm have produced hitherto unpublished information concerning the introduction of this instrument; information that is absent from later "official" published histories of the Welte-Mignon as presented in Welte catalogues.*

*Karl Bockisch, son of a family of Alsace vintners, spent his childhood in Anaheim, California – a community founded by German immigrant farmers. Success eluded the Bockisch family in California, so Karl and his parents returned to Germany. Bockisch married Edwin Welte's sister, thereby gaining a foothold in the Welte firm.*

*Bockisch quickly demonstrated his business and technical abilities. By the early 1900's most of Welte's business decisions were his. Sometime around the turn of the century Bockisch conceived the idea of what was to later become the Welte-Mignon reproducing piano. Together with Edwin Welte, Bockisch worked on the reproducing concept. By 1904 a successful instrument was produced. Most of the inventive ideas were Bockisch's, but credit was officially given to Karl Bockisch and Edwin Welte on an equal basis.*

*What should the instrument be named? Edwin Welte proposed that it be called the Welte Mignon. Karl Bockisch, long resentful that his name was virtually unknown to the public, objected vigorously – and a heated argument resulted between the two men. This resentment, incidentally, was to last for several decades. Later (in the 1930's) Bockisch acquired control of the Welte firm.*

*The Welte-Bockisch argument produced a stalemate in 1904. As a compromise the instrument was offered simply as the Mignon – without the Welte prefix.*

*Hugo Popper, majority stockholder of Popper & Co. of Leipzig, was one of Karl Bockisch's closest personal friends. It was Hugo Popper who furnished encouragement to Bockisch during the development of the Welte reproducing piano, and it was Hugo Popper who made possible the recording contracts with prominent pianists of the day. Popper's business relationship with Welte during the c.1905 period included a contract which gave Popper & Co. the exclusive right to sell Welte orchestrions and other instruments in Germany and in several other countries. Although no details of the arrangement survive today, it is apparent that Welte produced certain orchestrion components (including cabinets) for Popper. As a result many orchestrion case designs which were sold by Welte (particularly in the 1908-1914 years) as part of the Welte Brisgovia series were earlier sold by Popper under various Popper & Co. trade names. Refer to the Popper & Co. section of this book for additional details of the Popper-Welte relationship.*

*An early pictorial news announcement concerning the Mignon was published in the March 11, 1905 issue of "Zeitschrift für Instrumentenbau." In the March 21 issue of the same magazine a detailed description of the Mignon's exhibition (together with Welte-made orchestrions sold by Popper) at a Leipzig trade fair was published.*

*During the 1905-1910 period the close relationship between Popper and Welte continued. Hugo Popper controlled most Mignon sales within Germany, although Welte did some limited advertising under its own name. In addition, Popper had a financial interest in Welte's American operations. Referring to the sale of Welte orchestrions in America, Hugo Popper observed that "America is one of our best markets, and we sell many orchestrions there." Such instruments bore the Welte name; Popper & Co. instruments were never sold under the Popper name in the United States. Following Hugo Popper's death in 1910 the Popper-Welte agreement was modified or cancelled. Later Popper advertisements feature the Stella reproducing piano and omit the Mignon; and Welte advertised and sold its own instruments on a large scale in Germany.*

*The 1905 Mignon announcement (translated by Claes O. Friberg) follows:*

**"ARTISTS RECORDING IN THE MUSIC SALON OF POPPER & CO. IN LEIPZIG:**

**"Outside in the streets the rumble of traffic goes on, while up in the magnificently furnished parlors of Popper & Co. in Reichsstrasse an attentive audience is gathered to hear a concert performed by the noted Berlin professor, Xaver Scharwenka – and also to witness the recording of his performance, complete with all nuances and fine points, so that it can be reproduced in exact detail for coming generations of listeners.**

**"Business associates and close friends of Popper form a close circle around the Feurich concert grand piano, an instrument with a rich and resonant tonal quality. Except for a cable of wires leading from the piano to a recording device that stands nearby there is nothing to betray that in this grand piano and in the recording equipment there are wonderful components – devices which work together in an unbelievable and secret way.**

**"The maestro [Scharwenka] places his chair in the correct position before the keyboard and plays a few trial chords and runs. Inspired, he gives a signal to Karl Bockisch (the son-in-law of the elder Mr. Welte of Freiburg) who now starts the apparatus. The most wonderful harmonies come forth from the magnificent piano as the hands of the artist glide over the keyboard. Scharwenka plays one of his own compositions first: a selection based on inspirations from his youth. He then goes on to play well-known works of other composers, giving us an evening of musical entertainment that we will never forget.**

**"During the performance the recording is made, but nothing is divulged to the audience about that process. There is just the distinguished Mr. Bockisch, the intelligent artist and the chief inventor of the device, sitting there by his mysterious equipment. A paper roll slowly passes through the recording instrument. To gaze upon this device one would never suspect that it is recording the artist's performance for the future. After the recording is made, the grand piano and the recording device are both locked and sealed so as to keep the inner workings in strict confidence.**

**"The master compositions are now ready to be perforated. Then they will be thoroughly tested. Finally they will be commercially available as part of the repertoire of the wonderful 'Mignon' instrument made by M. Welte & Sons in Freiburg. The distribution of the 'Mignon' as well as of the Welte orchestrions is handled solely through the firm of Popper & Co.**

**"We have reproduced a picture for our readers of the 'Mignon' instrument and also one of the recording session of about two weeks ago that took place in the Popper music salon. The piano virtuoso Moritz Grünfeld is shown with the royal piano manufacturer (his firm makes pianos for royalty) Hermann Feurich of Leipzig."**

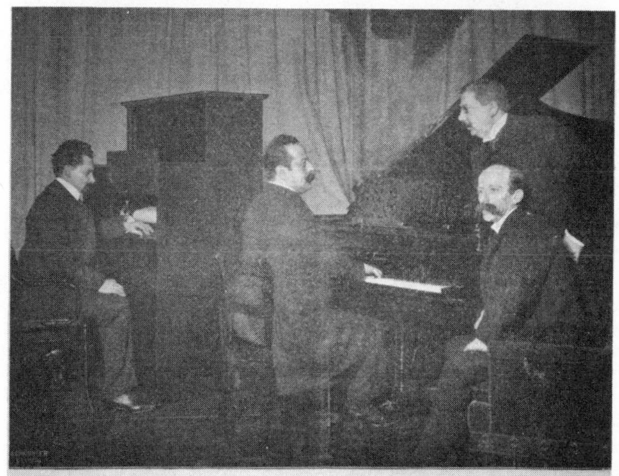

Karl Bockisch (Welte & Söhne) Moritz Grünfeld. Hermann Feurich. Hugo Popper.

Aufnahme für den Wiedergabe-Apparat „Mignon" im Musiksalon von Popper & Co.

„Mignon."

## A PERSONAL EXPERIENCE WITH WELTE

by Richard C. Simonton

*The following article, printed with the permission of the author, first appeared in FM & Fine Arts Magazine. Mr. Simonton visited Freiburg several times during the 1940's and 1950's and obtained much information concerning the Welte operations in Europe and America, many details of which would have been otherwise lost to history. Later, Mr. Simonton and Walter S. Heebner, a former vice president of Capitol Records, released a series of Welte reproducing piano performances recorded on stereo discs, the "Welte Legacy of Piano Treasures."*

### How It All Began

It all started in 1832. Michael Welte, the grandfather of my friend Edwin Welte, had completed his apprenticeship to a Black Forest clockmaker who specialized in making musical clocks, each with a set of small wooden pipes which played short tunes.

Michael Welte was exceptionally adept in the making of the musical portion of the clocks. After he completed his apprenticeship and entered business on his own, he found that his patrons bought his clocks more for their musical qualities than their timekeeping abilities. He therefore dropped the clock mechanism and devoted his time to perfecting and enlarging the musical instrument, which evolved into the later famous Welte self-playing organs and pianos.

Michael Welte

The climax of Michael Welte's early career came in 1848 when, after three tireless years, he successfully demonstrated the original orchestrion — a self-playing organ which was really a gigantic version of the mechanism formerly contained in the clocks. This orchestrion had many sets of pipes and played complicated musical compositions in harmony. It was actuated by pinned cylinders — huge rollers with pins placed around the circumference. When the cylinders were slowly revolved, the pins operated levers which opened valves which allowed the passage of air into the pipes. In that way musical compositions were played. Though pinned cylinder orchestrions were very large, very expensive, limited in repertoire, and of a limited market, the Welte firm built this type of instrument exclusively until 1885.

### Paper Roll Orchestrions

In 1885 Berthold Welte, one of Michael Welte's sons, decided to produce the firm's products with mechanisms which used perforated paper rolls, rather than the cumbersome cylinders. When a hole occurred in the paper it actuated a pneumatic mechanism by allowing the atmosphere to enter through the hole and displace a vacuum. This paper roll system, later adopted as the standard by makers all over the world, was first used on large scale instruments by Welte in 1887.

### Beginning of the Welte Mignon

By 1895 the Welte firm developed a successful paper roll operated player piano, one of the first such devices to be made on a commercial basis. This early player piano was entirely mechanical. The paper was punched out by hand by using a piece of printed sheet music as a guide. In the terms of the trade it was a "designed roll." There was no attempt at expression other than maximum or minimum loudness. What the pianos lacked in subtlety of dynamics they compensated for in volume. But the Weltes were true artists; they were convinced that the public would buy better reproduction if it could be perfected.

So, in the early 1900's Edwin Welte, grandson of Michael, and his associate, Karl Bockisch, developed a machine known as a "Vorsetzer." This complex device had felt-covered "fingers," one for each piano key. It was placed in front of a piano's keyboard (the name "Vorsetzer" means "sitter in front of" in German), the same position occupied by the pianist. When a roll was put on its tracker bar it actuated the mechanism within the Vorsetzer in such a way that these "fingers" came down and depressed the keys with the same dynamics and in the same order as in the original artist's performance. The mechanism also faithfully reproduced the artist's use of piano pedals. By this method a performance could actually be played back from the master roll, much as we do with our modern tape recorders today.

Every precaution was taken to get conditions as nearly equal as possible to the original performance. The wooden fingers of the Vorsetzer were made the same length as a man's fingers from the pivot of his wrist to the tips, so that the same power of touch would produce the same dynamic strength on the piano as the artist when he struck the keys during the making of the master rolls.

At this point all of the mechanical steps had been perfected for the creation of an artists' library of recorded music to accompany the instruments, trademarked the "Welte Mignon," which the Weltes sold. These gentlemen launched a program of recording the finest keyboard artists of the day. A valuable library of artists' rolls would be a supplement and an aid to the selling of Vorsetzers and other Welte Mignon styles (cabinet, upright, and grand pianos incorporating the same mechanism within), reasoned Welte.

Considerable praise is due these men for their vision in selecting artists. At this time composers such as Granados and Debussy were struggling young musicians and had not yet come into their own, but their artistry was recognized by the Weltes. They contracted with them for their services. It is because of this foresight that the actual performances of these artists are preserved today.

### Recording the Artists

It was always Karl Bockisch's job to handle the talent, many of whom were very temperamental. They had quite a time with Debussy, an egomaniac who once stood up and said "There have only been produced so far in the world two great musicians, Beethoven and me." Oddly enough he made these Welte recordings at an early age before he achieved his fame! Karl Bockisch, however, knew talent when he heard it.

Paderewski was every bit as difficult. He was living in Switzerland at the time. He would not answer a letter. Finally the Weltes received a note from a servant stating that if they would present themselves at his villa, the "master" would talk to them. So Bockisch and Welte went to Switzerland, hats in hand. After being kept waiting a number of hours, a white haired figure in a velvet robe descended the staircase in a grand manner. Fortunately, negotiating with Paderewski was considerably easier than getting to see him initially.

In sharp contrast to Debussy and Paderewski, Ravel was very quiet, very tractable, and very easy to get along with. He came, performed at a recording session and that was that. Josef Hofmann, whom they recorded in 1913, was also one of their favorites. They were quite fond of him as an individual.

Edwin Welte and Karl Bockisch were idealists. As a matter of fact, some of the rolls which cost them the most to produce earned them the least amount of money.

They did, however, have a number of "best sellers." Olga Samaroff was one. Olga Samaroff, whose real name was Hickenlooper, was from Galveston, Texas. She was Leopold Stokowski's first wife. She was a young girl when the Welte firm recorded her, and they adored her. She subsequently became a great teacher in New York City. Many of the fine pianists of later years were once Samaroff's students.

Gustav Mahler did four recordings for Welte, for which he was paid a substantial price — but they didn't sell ten copies of each in the early years. At the time he was not accepted, but Welte and Bockisch were men of vision and knew that in time Mahler would achieve fame.

Frank Marshall did a lot of work for Welte. When Albañiz came to record he brought Marshall with him, claiming that Marshall played his works better than he did. Grieg was another composer who felt that others could do a better job with his music. Grieg would personally do only three tunes. He laughed and said, "Other people play my music better than I do."

### The Welte Business

The years from 1905 to the late 1920's were golden years for the Welte musical empire. The home of any self-respecting American or

European millionaire wasn't really complete without a reproducing piano. Most of these instruments were either made by Welte or were licensed under Welte patents. Virtually every crowned head of state in the world possessed a Welte instrument.

The stock market crash of 1929 and the subsequent worldwide depression ended the days of lavish spending. The inevitable happened; the Welte empire began to crumble.

### My Own Interest In Welte

My own interest in Welte actually started when I was a small boy. The local millionaire in our city was a meat packer who had made a

Typical residential installation of a Welte Philharmonic Organ.

fortune during World War I by canning horsemeat with a picture of a prize steer on the can! In order to make the town conscious of his wealth, he imported a very expensive Welte pipe organ, and had it equipped with a Welte roll-playing mechanism. I can't remember the circumstances leading up to my invitation to his home, but nevertheless I was there and heard the magnificent instrument. I was so intrigued with it that I never forgot the experience. I must have been ten or eleven years old, and at that point I vowed someday I too would own an instrument that would be capable of playing the Welte rolls.

Well, it took me many years to achieve this. . . and by the time I was in a position to have a pipe organ in my home, Welte rolls were no longer being manufactured, and none was available. So, my first contact with the Welte firm was in search of Welte rolls for my pipe organ. As soon as hostilities ended after World War II, I sent a letter to the last known address of the firm in Freiburg, Germany. I eagerly awaited the developments.

After some months I received a despondent reply from Edwin Welte who told me that the factory was destroyed and that there were no rolls available, but that he had in his possession, in his home, about sixteen organ rolls which he would be glad to send me in exchange for food. They were literally starving and would be most happy to convert these rolls into some form that they could eat. I was equally happy to send them food for the rolls. In due course the rolls were shipped, and I received them. However, I was so touched by their plight that I continued to send food, and from that humble beginning a warm friendship developed.

After many months Edwin Welte told me of the work done in gathering together the vast library, of the playing of famous pianists, and he impressed upon me the great value of the unique master roll library which was wrapped in mothballs and put away. Both he and Karl Bockisch were elderly men, there were no heirs to the business, the plant was totally destroyed, and it looked as if future generations would be forever denied the privilege of hearing the great artists they had recorded.

Few people on this side of the Atlantic knew that these master rolls existed. In fact, the era of the reproducing piano had been largely forgotten.

Edwin Welte sent me some old literature which contained photographs of the artists and copies of their signed testimonials to the fact that the artists themselves had actually recorded and commented on the faithful reproduction of the Welte instruments. It presented a very imposing roster of famous artists and composers and showed promises of being musically important. I realized immediately that these recordings had commercial possibilities. However, I first needed the answer to one major question: Was the artistry, even after having been recorded on these specially-prepared master rolls, worthy of the men who performed, or was it lacking in subtlety and reminiscent of the old parlor player piano?

Proving this point was not simple. The only conclusive means was to be able to hear the actual reproduction of some of the masters and let experts decide. The only place I knew of where they could be heard was in Germany, and then only under very difficult conditions.

### The Welte Rolls Play Again

There followed a furious exchange of letters across the Atlantic. In searching for a solution the fact came to light that the local radio broadcasting station in Freiburg had a Magnetophon, or the original prewar German magnetic tape recorder which was later copied very widely by American manufacturers. But there was no recording tape available in all of Germany. The answer was to air mail some tape from here and pray that it would fit. The Magnetophon, however, was in the

Above: Steinway upright and grand pianos with Welte reproducing mechanisms.

Left: Some of Welte's medallic awards.

broadcasting station as a permanent fixture and the piano with its associated reproducing apparatus was in Edwin Welte's home. This impasse was solved by suggesting that a telephone line be used to connect the two, and not meeting with any apparent opposition from the French occupation officials, it was done on a temporary basis.

Soon all arrangements were completed and, after many exasperating delays, the day set for the demonstration recording arrived. Fourteen selections were reproduced on the Welte apparatus, sent over the telephone line to the Magnetophon in the station and recorded in a form which could be sent to the United States to serve as a listening test to evaluate the musical performance. All that remained was to get the tapes from the station to my hands.

The next day Edwin Welte called on the French Commandant to ask for the tapes so he could send them to his American friend who was eagerly awaiting them. He was told that the French government had officially seized the tapes, and that they never intended that he should have them, much less send them to America – of all places.

Of great assistance at this time was a young Ukrainian displaced person who had been a German prisoner of war. After his capture on the Russian front he was sent to Freiburg to teach languages at the Freiburg University. Mr. Welte had met him there where both had been assigned duties by Hitler's government. Since the war this young man had been employed at the radio station. The French officer evidently was not aware that he and Edwin Welte had been good friends. The young Ukrainian was the first to tell Mr. Welte that the French officer was not going to release the recorded tapes as they appeared to have value and the officer hoped to sell them.

One night the tapes in a wrapped package were left on the officer's desk, and at closing time our friend hid himself in a closet so as to be inside after the French civilian supervisors had locked the door behind them.

With only the dim moonlight filtering in, he opened the package on the commandant's desk, carefully preserving the cord and paper. With some other rolls of magnetic tape I had sent by regular mail, he set about recording duplicates. There was only time to copy five of the selections as his friend, a fellow displaced person, was waiting to take the 2:40 a.m. train back to Frankfurt and had agreed to take the package into the American Zone and airmail it to me.

He worked up to the last minute, and then magnetically spoiled the recordings on the originals so they couldn't be used, and then he carefully repacked them so as to make it appear as if it had happened in transit. With the tape wrapped in a rag hidden under his shirt, he climbed over the transom, kept out of sight by staying in the back alleys until he got where his friend was waiting, and together they went to the railway station. In a dark section along the way they transferred the package to the other man's clothing. There were always occupation officials at the stations to open all baggage and examine travel documents. It wouldn't do to have the tape in evidence, as too many questions would be asked. As it was, the tape got to Frankfurt, in the U.S. Zone, without further incident. It was soon across the Atlantic and in my hands.

Almost without pausing I had the tapes reproduced and conventional acetate records made from them. The instant I heard the first reproduction I realized that the artistry was excellent, even though the multiple re-recording had introduced some pitch variation and distortion. This didn't matter as it meant that the master rolls were good, and I could go back to them and, with proper recording apparatus, get good records. These would be as good as the actual playing of the great composers and artists themselves.

### The Trip to Freiburg

The next step was to plan a trip to Europe and to seek permission to enter the occupied zones. My wife and I arranged for the care of our two small children, and on September 28th we sailed on the Queen Elizabeth.

Our first sight of Freiburg was one which we shall never forget. The vista of a demolished city is one which an American cannot conceive of unless he has seen it first hand. The first thing we saw from the railroad station was the twisted wreckage of the once-awesome Welte facotry. While our bags were being taken through customs and subjected to inspection by French officials I strolled over to the edge of the platform and saw the many buildings which had once been the stronghold of the Welte empire, virtually a dynasty in the music history of the world.

All that remained were heaps of brick, twisted steel, and shells of buildings that could never be used again.

In the latter part of World War II when the Allies bombed Freiburg (Freiburg was not a strategic target; it was a university town that was bombed in retaliation for an earlier German raid on the English university town of Coventry), the Welte factory and 65% of the city was reduced to nothing but useless piles of smoking rubble. One of the machines for playing the Welte master rolls was destroyed in the factory, but, fortunately, the other had been dismantled and stored in a safe place. There was only one man alive who knew how it was constructed and how it should be operated. This man was Karl Bockisch who, at this time, was in his 70's. Because of the proximity of the Welte factory to the railroad station, a prime target, the priceless master rolls had been transferred to a parsonage in the Black Forest and had been hidden in a barn. There they remained until October, 1948, when we came to Germany.

Once we were set up and recording we worked tirelessly many hours a day. Often we would do a recording as many as five or six times because something had interrupted us or because a noise had ruined the sound. One time the distraction might be an airplane, another time the crackling of the wood fire in the little stove in a corner of the room. Of course, all of the beautiful homes like Edwin Welte's had central heating, but during the postwar hardship there was no coal available. They were allowed a few cords of wood to last all winter. To use the

WELTE-VORSETZER

Note: Mustel & Cie., the Paris piano and organ firm, manufactured "Maestro" reproducing pianos under the Welte Mignon patents. The Maestro reproducing pianos used regular red Welte Mignon rolls.

Left to right: Karl Bockisch (with his elbow on the orginal recording machine connected to the piano), d'Albert (recording a composition), and Edwin Welte. Note the housing for the mercury trough that is under the piano keyboard.

small supply sparingly Welte and others set up little stoves in one or two selected rooms and fashioned makeshift chimneys. We had to keep the stoves going because it was the only way we could keep the piano in tune. Sometimes in the middle of a recording the power would suddenly fail for a few seconds, or else the frequency would shift and change the speed of our machine. Often we did a recording over and over until we were assured that it was as near to perfection as possible.

A cousin of one of the Welte neighbors was a German civilian employee in the French Sureté office. This lad had heard rumors that we were being watched. It seems that the French knew we were there (we made no attempt to hide our presence), and had realized that we were doing something which might have value to them. They planned to detain us when we were ready to start for the border into France. They had every right to seize our recordings under the laws of an occupied land.

Naturally it distressed us to know that we were being watched and that these hard-earned recordings might be taken from us when we crossed the border back into France. While we had originally allowed five days – Monday through Friday – for completing our recording task, we realized that we must speed things up in order to throw the French off the track. We worked every day from nine in the morning until two or three the following morning in an attempt to hurry things along. After we finished our session for the night there would be no streetcars at that late hour, so we had to walk nearly three miles from one side of Freiburg to the other. As a result of our long hours, we completed our work one day earlier than we had planned.

We did not want to go through French customs again, but wanted to ship the clothing and personal effects through France to be picked up by our ship when it stopped at Cherbourg, after sailing from Southampton. It was possible to ship the equipment in bond and not have to pass French customs again. Consequently, we fooled the French officials by not going back into France but by taking our recordings in an old German suitcase, with a minimum amount of personal effects, and going north instead into the American zone.

There were no boundaries or control points within the three western zones in Germany. A person could travel freely without knowing where the actual zone boundary was. We boarded the train one Sunday afternoon from the temporary shed which was the Freiburg station. Because of the scenic beauty of the Freiburg area there were many visitors for the weekend from larger cities. Thus it was possible to carry aboard our personal luggage as well as the old valise without being noticed. Soon the train chugged off. Before very long we were seeing signs in English. At last we were in the American Zone – and were on our way home with the knowledge that we had a part in the preservation of some of the world's greatest music!

## HOW IS IT POSSIBLE?
### –The Welte Technique Explained–
by Ben M. Hall

*Note: Mr. Hall, a former Time Magazine staff member, former editor of Show Magazine, and author of "The Best Remaining Seats" (a history of the golden age of the movie theatre), died in 1970. The following description, used with the permission of Mr. Richard C. Simonton, was used in a booklet which accompanied the "Welte Legacy of Piano Treasures" record album.*

A most remarkable reproducing instrument was a device invented by the German geniuses, Edwin Welte and Karl Bockisch- circa 1900! The Welte firm produced the first reproducing system for pianos, a system which was as different from the then-current player piano mechanism (capable only of playing back the notes of the music as perforated on the roll, with none of its expression or shading) as today's stereo recordings are different from Edison cylinders. Welte gave reproduced piano music a soul.

The Welte recording and reproducing system was a marvel of sheer mechanics. In its way it seems more remarkable than the electronic wonders of today, and somehow it seems to stand as a sort of monument to mechanical genius at the peak of its cog-wheeled, cammed and levered pneumatic glory. It made its debut in 1904. Briefly, here is how the Welte worked its magic:

The recording unit, connected to a Feurich grand piano in the Welte music hall, contained a roll of specially-aged, thin paper, marked off into 100 parallel lines. Poised over each line was a little wheel of extremely soft rubber, with pointed edges. Each wheel was in contact with an ink supply, and in this much of the process it resembled a small offset printing press. Under the keyboard of the recording piano was a trough filled with mercury; attached to the underside of each key was a slim rod of carbon. As the key was depressed, the rod dipped into the mercury and an electrical contact was established between it and an electromagnet connected to the corresponding inked roller in the recording machine. The harder the artist hit the key of the piano, the

WELTE

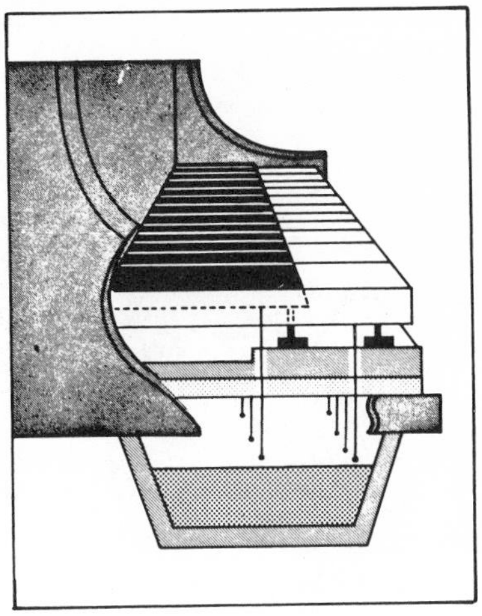

Keyboard and mercury trough.

deeper the carbon rod would plunge into the mercury, and the stronger the current between the rod and the electromagnet would be. The harder the inked rubber wheel was pressed against the moving paper roll, the wider the mark it printed on the paper. The pianist's pedaling and speed of attack was captured in the same way.

After a selection had been finished, the paper roll was removed from the recording machine and run through a chemical bath to fix the colloidal graphite ink which had been printed on it by the rollers. The ink was electrically conductive, and when the roll was ready to play back, it was put into a master reproducing Welte Mignon piano which "read" the markings in much the same manner that the magnetic ink on bank checks is "read" by automated banking equipment today.

Shortly after recording a selection the artist returned to the Welte music hall and found a Welte Vorsetzer "seated" at the same piano where he had been playing. But nobody laughed when the Vorsetzer sat down at the piano. The results were astonishing! When the instrument was turned on the Vorsetzer re-created the pianist's own performance – with every pause, every shade of expression, every thundering chord! The master roll was then laboriously hand punched to translate the ink markings into perforations on paper rolls which would have the same results when played on a Welte Mignon reproducing piano in a music lover's home.

Feurich grand piano incorporating the Welte-Mignon reproducing system.

—Eugene d'Albert—

—Vladimir Horowitz—

—Raoul Pugno—

—Fannie Bloomfield Zeisler—

Nocturne fis-dur
Opus 15 Nr. 2

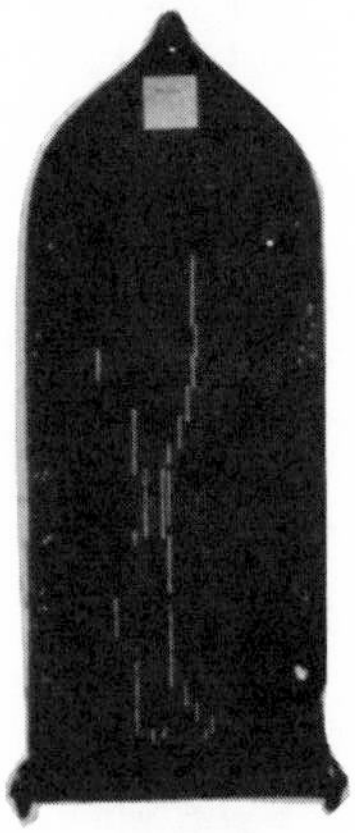

Pugno

Saint-Saëns

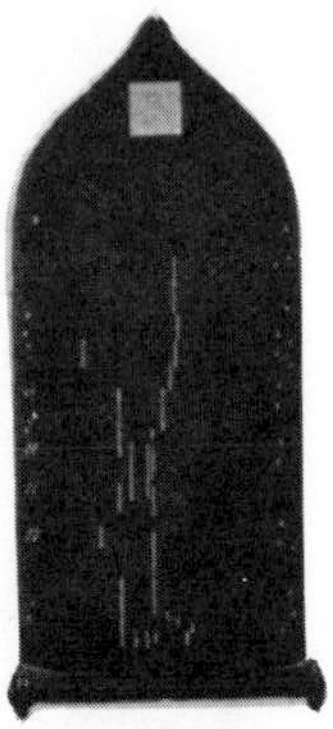

Busoni

Scharwenka

—Wilhelm Stenhammer—

—Yolanda Merö—

—A. Scriàbine—

—Frieda Kwast-Hodapp—

**Welte photographed pianists who recorded for the firm. These pictures were often used in Welte's advertising and were usually accompanied by a glowing testimonial to the Welte system. On this and on several other pages we show some of these photographs, mostly taken at the Freiburg factory.**

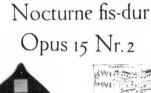

**Above center is a graphic representation of different artists' interpretations of the same selections. Pugno, Saint-Saëns, Busoni, and Scharwenka play the same Chopin composition.**

**Today Welte and other reproducing piano rolls are prized as "living records" by musical historians and collectors. The in-person performances of pianists of years past can "come to life" again. What a shame it is that today's artists cannot be similarly immortalized for future generations to enjoy.**

—Walter Gieseking—

—Annette Essipoff—

—Wilhelm Backhaus—

—Wilhelm Kienzl—

—Frank Marshall—

—Maria Avani Carreras—

## SOME TESTIMONIALS:

**Arthur Nikisch** writes:

I consider the reproduction-apparatus "Welte-Mignon" as an epochmaking invention. The reproduction of the pieces played by an artist on the apparatus, is in every respect (whether it concerns the technique or the musical and poetical element) such a wonderfully natural one, that it is difficult to believe that the artist himself is not present and performing personally. The value of the invention consists therefore, not only in its eminent instructive influence on the learner, but it is also especially valuable for those who wish to hear at any time a distinguished artist and to have an hour of perfect artistic enjoyment.

**Eugen d'Albert** writes:

How astonishing and deeply affecting it is to hear one's own playing, recorded years before. réndered with the utmost perfection by the Welte-Mignon.

The reputation which the Welte-Mignon pianos enjoy, of being the best instruments of the kind, rests on the unshakable foundation of this faithful reproduction of individual play; and it is a source of pleasure and artistic satisfaction to me to have confided to the Welte-Mignon to-day an extensive and varied programme which will transmit my art to posterity.

**Wilhelm Backhaus** writes:

Mignon is to me one of the wonders of the world. I do not know what new words of praise one could invent for the instrument which enables the collecting of all pianistic greatness in one's salon, to have these artists, always in best of form, play to one's heart's content. Happy he who can provide himself with this joy in his own home.

**Walter Gieseking** writes:

The reproduction of my piano-playing on the "Welte-Mignon" is by far the most finished and faithful that I have ever heard and exceeds greatly my highest expectations; I am full of sincerest unstinted admiration

—Zecchi—

—Emil von Sauer—

—S. Liapounow—

—Ignace Jan Paderewski—

—Rudolph Ganz—

—Joseph Lhevinne—

—Edwin Fischer—

—Emil Paur—

—Felix Mottl—

—Dirk Schäfer—

—A. Glazounow—

—R. Leoncavallo—

—Arthur Nikisch—

—Josef Hofmann—

—Frederic Lamond—

—Ferruccio Busoni—

### Some Welte Artists

Eugen d'Albert
Konrad Ansorge
Wilhelm Backhaus
Tosta Di Benici
F. Bloomfield-Zeisler
Alfred Blumen
Fritz v. Bose
Frederigo Bufalletti
Richard Buhlig
Richard Burmeister
Ferruccio Busoni
Teresa Carreño
Aurelia Cionca
Paul de Conne
Fannie Davies
Claude Debussy
L Diémer
E. von Dohnanyi
Michael Douloff
Felix Dreyschock
Wladimir Drosdoff
Sandra Droucker
v. Edelsberg
Myrtle Elvyn
Annette Essipoff
Gabriel Fauré
Edwin Fischer
Carl Friedberg
Arthur Friedheim
Herbert Fryer
Ossip Gabrilowitsch
Rudolph Ganz
Walter Gieseking
A. Glazounow
A Goldenweiser
Irene Eneri Gorainoff
Arthur de Greef
Edward Grieg
Alfred Grünfeld
Mark Hambourg
Paula Hegner
Alfred Höhn
Josef Hofmann
Nelly Hofmann
E. Humperdinck
G. Igumnoff
Ella Jonas
L. Kaschperowa
Charlton Keith
Wilhelm Kienzl
Marceline Kimontt
Hedwig Kirsch
Clotilde Kleeberg
Emma Koch
A. Koretschenko
Télémaque Lambrino
Frédérie Lamond
Wanda Landowska
Sándor László
R. Leoncavallo
Theodor Leschetitzky
Joseph Lhévinne
S. Liapounow
Gustav Mahler
Vera Margolies
Frank Marshall
B. Marx-Goldschmid
Vera Maurina
Yolanda Merö
Nikolaus Medtner
E. Meyer-Helmund
M. Meytschik
Ida Michaelsohn
Comt. H. Morsztyn
Vianna da Motta
Felix Mottl
Otto Neitzel
Elly Ney
Arthur Nikisch
Vladimir v. Pachmann
Ignace J. Paderewski
Max Pauer
Emil Paur
Gertrud Pepperkorn
Egon Petri
Raoul Pugno
Frieda Quast-Hodapp
Ella Rafaelsohn
Max Reger
Carl Reinecke
Alfred Reisenauer
Alice Ripper
Anatol von Rössel
Romanowsky
Cornelius Rübner
Camille Saint-Saëns
Olga Samaroff
Thomas San Galli
Wassili Sapellnikoff
Emil Sauer
Dirk Schäfer
Xaver Scharwenka
Ernst Schelling
Max Schillings
Arthur Schnabel
Germaine Schnitzer
D. Schorr
Georg Schumann
Cyril Scott
A. Scriàbine
Martha Siebold
Emil Sjoegren
Joseph Slivinski
Bernh. Stavenhagen
Paula Stebel
Wilh. Steenhammer
Emma Stember
Richard Strauß
Colin Taylor
Vera Timanoff
L. Uzielli
Max Vogrich
Septimus Webbe
Felix Weingartner
Josef Weiß
Hans Weitzig
Karl Wendling
Isabella Wengerowa
Lucien Wurmser
Michael von Zadora
Heinrich Zöllner
Georg Zscherneck

**The list of Welte artists was a long one. Published rosters changed as new pianists became popular and old ones forgotten. Spelling in Welte catalogues was anything but consistent, as names in some cases were anglicized for the American and English markets. Josef and Joseph were used interchangeably; Quast-Hodapp or Kwast-Hodapp were used as were Leschetitzky or Leschetizky, Essipoff or Essipow, etc.**

—E. von Dohnanyi—

—Olga Samaroff—

—Theodor Leschetitzky—

—von Koczalsky—

**The Welte Vorsetzer as shown in various homes in America and Europe. By using this device one could retain a favorite piano and still hear artists' music.**

**The Welte Mignon cabinet piano as shown in different locations in America and Europe.**

Upright Steinway Welte

## TYPES OF WELTE MIGNON PIANOS

At the Freiburg plant Welte mechanisms were built in the pianos of several different manufacturers, the most popular of which were Blüthner, Feurich, Ibach, and Steinway. In addition, many pianos were simply marked with the Welte name.

Upright models were available in two main formats: a piano of normal appearance with the mechanisms built within (this was the usual way), or a tall upright piano with the pumps and expression mechanisms located at the top of the case (as illustrated at the center, left).

Grand pianos, for the most part, had the tracker bar at the top front of the case (certain rare models, including some grands built in America, had the roll mechanism located vertically in the front). As illustrated below, some models had the vacuum pump located in a separate cabinet which could be stored behind the piano or in another room.

Pianos with built-in mechanisms were called "Einbau Weltes" in Europe (from einbau = built within) to distinguish them from the Vorsetzer or push-up models.

As most piano cabinets were similar in appearance, we illustrate just a few on this page. In addition to standard models, special case designs could be ordered at additional expense. Some of these custom cases were masterpieces of art and decoration.

—Welte Recording Pianos—

Two types of pianos, Feurich and Steinway, were used in Welte's Freiburg salon to make musical recordings. The piano frame of each instrument had many artists' autographs on it.

—Dr. Richard Strauss records for Welte—

Berdux Welte grand.

Feurich Welte grand.

Ibach Welte grand.

Steinway Welte grand.

---

Blüthner Welte

Feurich Welte

Ibach Welte

Seiler Welte

Blüthner Welte grand

Made in smaller quantities than the electric models were foot-pumped Welte pianos of various makes. Most buyers preferred the automatic operation offered by electric instruments, but some preferred the personal expression interpretation made possible by pumping the instrument by foot. Other foot-pumped instruments were intended for homes without electric service. Typical case designs are illustrated here.

Feurich Welte grand

Ibach Welte grand

WELTE

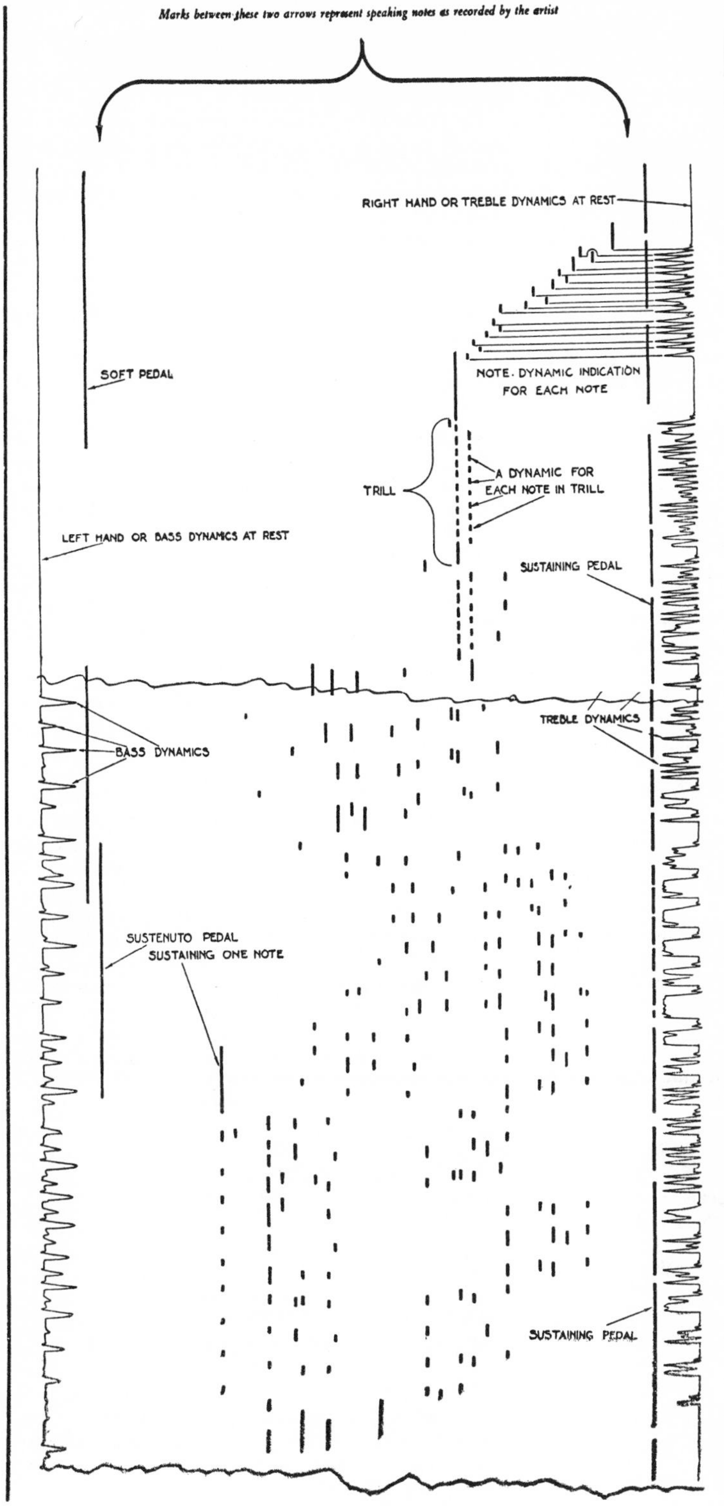


This photograph of a section from an original recording of Chopin's Etude in F Major shows how every detail of the artist's playing is graphically recorded while he plays. ¶With this absolutely authentic "tone picture" as a guide, the making of records for Welte Mignon (Licensee) Reproducing Pianos is free from every vestige of guesswork. Nothing is added or substracted that the artist does not himself put into his music, so that the record is not a mere approximation, but an exact reproduction of his playing. ¶What may be called the "film of the music camera" receives impressions of every detail of both his fingering and pedaling. ¶The exact position of every note played is fixed by faint vertical lines corresponding in number to the keys on the piano. The staggered lines on the extreme right and left are the means by which the mechanism, like the delicate needle of the seismograph that records the slightest tremor of the earth, graphically indicates exactly the degree of pressure with which the artist struck the keys, thus faithfully recording the finest shading of his interpretation.

An explanation of the Welte recording system — as given in a Welte catalogue.

## IN THEIR OWN WORDS...
### —Edwin and Carl Welte—

*The following paragraphs are excerpted from two of Edwin Welte's many letters to Richard C. Simonton. Written in the English language, the letters give an interesting insight into the later years of the Welte firm and some of the postwar problems.*

*In a separate letter, Carl Welte, who read of the Richard Simonton Welte roll recording project in a New York Times article, writes of the Welte history in general. Carl Welte, now deceased, was a resident of America for most of his life.*

Edwin Welte writes (April 6, 1948)
Dear Mr. Simonton!

We were very happy when we received yesterday your kind letter. You must have had a fine time on your trip to Mexico in your beautiful car. My first long trip in a car was with an American friend in his large Lozier. We were invited by Mr. Frank Seaman, of the Seaman advertising offices in New York. That was in 1912. We had tire troubles at least every 100 miles. In the next year I bought my first car, a Benz.

While I was never a politician, I was always interested in history and culture, so it is hard for me to keep away from writing and talking about it. Stalin will decide what can be done in Germany. As long as there is no peace I would advise not to invest any money of importance in the organ business in Germany. Such things should only be thought about at the present. I will keep my eyes open for you.

While it is hard to ship music rolls from Germany, I am now trying to get rolls from the owners of several Welte movie theatre organs in Switzerland. These organs were delivered with music roll mechanisms in the consoles. The rolls were used when the organist took an intermission. The organs are not used anymore, I am told.

There is no doubt either that you will have a Steinway-Welte for your new home. I now have a list of Steinway-Welte owners. Everywhere Stalin is in the way. Before we buy and pay it must be safe to get the piano on board a ship and not let it fall into the hands of Stalin.

One or two Germans in New York are the successors to Gittins and now own all of the master rolls we once sent to New York. I would like to buy or borrow some of these rolls for a short time to make hand-cut copies. I need some of these rolls for Mignon customers.

It would be splendid if you could come to Freiburg this summer and we could talk over everything personally. However, I don't believe it will be possible this year. Stalin doesn't allow it yet. He will fool around a little time longer, until it will not be possible anymore for a country with some self-respect left to stand his insults any longer. The Hitler story will repeat itself.

I thank you very much for giving me your opinion about the Lichtton-Orgel (an electronic organ operated by photocells).

In 1905 my uncle, Emil Welte, who successfully managed our branch in New York since 1865, came to Freiburg and explained that he did not want to have anything to do with the selling of the Welte Mignon in America. He declared that no competition against such firms like the Aeolian Company was possible. I went myself to New York and started the Welte Artistic Player Company on Fifth Avenue, in 1906. Aeolian tried to bluff me. I turned around and made them pay me a royalty for every (Duo-Art) reproducing piano they sold! World War I resulted in my losing everything there.

Sincerely,
Edwin Welte

Edwin Welte writes (April 13, 1948)
Dear Mr. Simonton!

We are now preparing to make the recordings by connecting our microphone by telephone line to the radio station...

I intend to record in the following succession: As a pianist, first came Paderewski, who was later the President of Poland. After him came in fame, so far as United States customers were concerned, Josef Hofmann. Then came Bloomfield-Zeisler, who visited us several times here in Freiburg.

Pianists who made repeated tours in America included: Busoni, Carreño, Reisenauer, Max Pauer, Joseph Lhevinne — who is now living in New York, he and his family are very nice people, Lamond — who died a few weeks ago, Gabrilowitsch — now conductor of the Philharmonic Orchestra in Chicago or Philadelphia?, he was the husband of Olga Samaroff, now she is music critic of prominent papers — a charming lady and a splendid pianist.

As composers who played I wish to mention Prof. Eugene d'Albert, Claude Debussy — great modern composer and a good pianist, Glazounow — Russian composer and pianist, Granados — Spanish composer and pianist, Leoncavallo — Spanish composer, Prof. Max Reger — prominent German composer and good pianist. Also Camille Saint-Saëns — prominent French composer and pianist; Scriàbine — Russian composer and pianist; Richard Strauss, very prominent German composer.

Prominent conductors of great orchestras in the U.S. were Gabrilowitsch, Mahler (Philharmonic Society), and Emil Paur (Metropolitan).

Mr. Burnam in the U.S. is well informed about the artists. It would be well to get in touch with him. He is very loyal to me and is a poor old fellow now. He will tell you of the German who owns the Welte Mignon business in the U.S.A. They received from Freiburg a master copy of all rolls up to 1914.

Sincerely yours,
Edwin Welte

Carl Welte writes to Richard Simonton from his home in Norwichtown, Conn., on April 29, 1950
Dear Mr. Simonton:

Your name first came to my attention in a New York Times article of March 26th and also in a Time Magazine article of April 3rd.

I was particularly impressed to learn that you visited Freiburg and called upon my cousin Edwin Welte and his brother-in-law, Karl Bockisch. Having visited there myself seven times since 1901, I am taking the liberty of writing to you in the hope of sharing some reminiscences.

The old firm was known as M. Welte & Soehne, G.m.b.H. (Limited) and was located on Lehener Strasse between Clara and Wensinger Strassen. Edwin sent me a picture of the factory showing the walls which were all that remained of it after the air raids of November 24, 1944.

My uncle, Berthold Welte (Edwin's father), Uncle Michael, Jr., and Emil Welte (my father) were brothers, sons of the founder, Michael Welte, Sr., who was born in Vöhrenbach, Black Forest, in 1807 and died in Freiburg in 1880.

The old firm was founded in 1832 by Michael Welte and later he admitted his three sons. In 1901, the grandsons, Edwin and Carl, were admitted into the firm plus Karl Bockisch, who had married Edwin's sister. Karl Bockisch was born in 1878, Edwin 1876, and Carl, 1872, so I am the oldest survivor of the firm. The Preferred Shares or assets of the German firm were divided amongst the older Weltes and the surplus after the 5% for the Preferred Shares was paid out was divided as follows: 3/12 to Karl Bockisch, 4/12 to Edwin Welte, and 5/12 to Carl M. Welte.

Whenever I visited Freiburg, my visits lasted several months at a time. I enjoyed the hospitality of the Weltes, among them my father's married sisters. The surrounding countryside is very beautiful. What do you think of the grandeur of the scenery around Freiburg and the cheerful inhabitants of the town?

I was in Freiburg in 1901 when Edwin was working on the device, later known as the Welte Mignon, which reproduced the exact interpretation of the pianist when his playing was recorded. Edwin brought the first Welte Mignon to New York City in 1904 where it was exhibited in our New York studio and, later in the same year, at the St.Louis World's Fair.

My father, Emil Welte, came to the United States in 1865 and opened a store on East 14th Street, New York City, opposite Steinway Hall. The American branch was known as M. Welte & Sons, Inc. Later a studio was opened at 557 Fifth Avenue. This showroom was continued until World War I when the assets of the firm were taken over by the Alien Property Custodian. The holdings of Mr. Edwin Welte and Mr. Karl Bockisch were sold at public auction — my father and I having retired earlier from the business. Some prominent people took over the American branch. Later, the American firm went out of business. The same thing happened to the main house in Freiburg which went bankrupt in 1933.

The Welte factory was completely destroyed by the American flyers in two devastating air raids on Freiburg in November, 1944, when 75% of the old city of Freiburg was destroyed. Mr. Bockisch did repair a part of the buildings and is continuing in the trade of repairing organs and pianos.

My cousin Edwin is working on a new model Lichttonorgel, as he calls it. His first successful model was destroyed by air raids while on exhibit in Leipzig. I believe a better title for his new style organ would be the Photo-Cell Organ. Perhaps he explained the new organ to you. According to the reports I read after it was exhibited at the Philharmonic in Berlin in 1938, it must be a marvelous instrument, far superior to any electronic organ yet produced since it actually reproduces the photographed tones (from discs) of the finest organs in Europe. I hope you did get the opportunity to hear it so I can get your valuable point of view.

Sincerely,
Carl M. Welte

Steinway grand piano with Welte-Mignon reproducing system. The top cover has been folded back on its hinges to permit a view of the roll mechanism and the vacuum motor. (Claes O. Friberg Collection; Nordisk Pressfoto by Knud Henrichsen)

## THE END OF AN EMPIRE . . .

Overall view of the Welte factories at the height of their glory c.1912-1914. At the left is the Welte mansion, complete with an apartment for visiting pianists. The corner building in the center foreground is Welte's original Freiburg plant. Many additions were built over the years. All of this was destroyed in an Allied bombing raid during World War II (in reprisal for the German raid on Coventry, England — a town which, like Freiburg, was best known for its long-established university).

Edwin Welte, as photographed by Richard C. Simonton during a walk in the Black Forest.

The once-elegant Welte mansion.

The large factory building in the center of the Welte complex.

The main entry to the Welte display and recording salon.

## THE OTHER REPRODUCING AND EXPRESSION SYSTEMS

*by David L. Saul*

Pianos with automatic expression of one kind or another appeared in abundance over the years. Many, if not most, of those listed here faded into obscurity after a relatively short time.

### The Telektra and Tel-Electric

The Tel-Electric Company's system played rolls made from thin sheets of brass rather than the paper used by other makers. Made in two main styles, the Tel-Electric (which sold for $350 for the basic model) and the Telektra ($450), the units were attachments designed to be installed on just about any type of existing upright or grand piano. A bank of electromagnets was mounted under the keyboard. Each magnet was connected to a corresponding key by a wire. The rolls were housed in a console unit which could be located at any distance away and which was connected to the bank of magnets by a thick cable.

Dynamic control was accomplished via an electrical switching arrangement. Under control of expression coding, different voltages were applied to electromagnets to control the various notes' striking forces.

A Telektra advertisement quoted in "Player Piano Treasury" notes: "The Telektra consists of two parts, the player itself or transmitter (the console unit) and a small box containing a bank of electromagnets that is attached to the underside of the piano keyboard, each one of these magnets operating a single key. This small and attractive box containing the bank of electromagnets, the only part directly attached to the piano, is connected with the transmitter by a small cable which may be of any desired length. The current from the transmitter vitalizes these magnets and the keys are depressed — depressed with a soft, velvet-like touch or with thunderous force according to the strength of the electric impulse which the person playing has under his absolute control.

"The Telektra uses practically indestructible music rolls cut in a metal ribbon thinner than paper. They cannot shrink or swell. Damp weather has no effect on them. The expression cut into these rolls is as indicated by the composer, to be used or not as you may elect.

"The Telektra may be attached to your own piano regardless of its make, age, or style in a few hours' time in your own home. While electricity is the motive power of the Telektra, electric current is not necessary in the home. Batteries are furnished.

"Without any assistance on your part the wonderful Telektra will play your piano with perfect musical expression while you and your guests are gathered around the dinner table. You may turn to the transmitter at any time and by a mere turn of the wrist vary the interpretation to suit either your guests or your own particular musical fancies. Regardless of where in the house your piano may be situated, this distinctive Telektra feature enables you to easily and comfortably enjoy the luxury of the most artistic piano playing."

### The Solo Carola

The Cable Company's Solo Carola incorporated a novel mechanical scheme in which each piano hammer's striking distance was individually variable. Notes occurring simultaneously anywhere on the keyboard could be struck with varying degrees of force within the available dynamic range. These instruments are characterized by the unusual design of their tracker bars, which contain so-called "solo slots" over each playing note.

A Solo Carola advertisement noted: "There is one Solo Slot over each note. Each slot is connected with a small bellows which independently controls the position of each piano hammer. You will notice that the roll perforations register exactly with these solo slots before the ordinary striking openings (underneath the solo slots) are reached. Thus each piano hammer is automatically set in any desired position before the note is struck.

"The Solo Carola faithfully reproduces the playing of famous pianists with all their individualities of touch, accent, nuance, and rhythm. . ."

The Solo Carola, which could play regular 88-note player piano rolls in addition to the special Solo Carola rolls, was sold only in limited quantities. This type of piano is very rare today.

### Other Systems; Comments and Credits

Many coin-operated instruments were equipped with dynamic control systems. Expression pianos such as the Seeburg Style X and the Wurlitzer Autograph Piano, to mention just two of many, were sold in modest numbers. Some of the larger orchestrions, particularly those of European origin, featured sophisticated dynamic control capabilities. The "Friburgia" orchestrions by Welte featured piano arrangements adapted from the Welte Mignon artists' recordings. The Hupfeld Pan Orchestra also used artists' arrangements for the piano part of the performance, as did the Philipps Paganini. These instruments were designed to play serious musical performances capable of pleasing critical audiences.

A number of types of reproducing pianos appeared in foreign countries. The Hupfeld Dea made a very early appearance, following almost immediately the introduction of the Welte Mignon. The Dea was made in a wide variety of upright, grand, and Vorsetzer formats. A special model featured a reproducing piano in combination with Hupfeld's Violina violin-player. Known as the Dea-Violina, it was sold only for a year or two and was supplanted by the Phonoliszt-Violina which featured violins in combination with the Phonoliszt system (a fairly sophisticated system which might be properly termed as "semi-reproducing"). Other Hupfeld types with varying degrees of expression and reproducing capabilities included the Duophonola and Triphonola (these used the same reproducing system, a major system not unlike the Dea in concept but using a narrower roll), and the Clavitist. Hupfeld reproducing and expression pianos were manufactured by the thousands and achieved wide popularity in Europe, South America, and elsewhere. In America they were sold by Ernst Böcker of New York City. Hupfeld reproducing pianos were extremely well engineered and built.

The Popper & Company "Stella" instruments were made for home and for public use. Those made for commercial purposes were of the coin-in-the-slot type and were controlled by nearby wallboxes.

J.D. Philipps & Sons of Frankfurt-am-Main, Germany, produced many instruments in the "Duca" series. Featuring artists' rolls recorded by prominent performers of the day, the Duca instruments were available in upright, grand, and Vorsetzer styles. First introduced about 1908, Duca reproducing pianos were made in large quantities until about 1928. As did Hupfeld, Philipps equipped some models (rare today) of its reproducing pianos, including grand styles, with automatic roll changing devices. Duca rolls were made in two main widths — the standard width for use on the Duca pianos and a special extra-wide style for use in playing piano solos on the large Paganini orchestrions. (Paganini orchestrions regularly used special Paganini rolls; however, for solo piano performances the aforementioned Duca rolls, designated as "PD" rolls, could be used.)

Throughout the history of player piano advertising, many regular (i.e., non-expression or non-reproducing) instruments were advertised as being able to play "just like a human pianist," or something in a likewise vein. The "individual interpretation" of an advertised instrument was to be added by the person foot-pumping the piano and was not already cut into the music roll, as many sales descriptions would have had the readers believe. Such regular 88-note and related players are covered in another section of this book and are not to be confused with the reproducing and expression instruments discussed here.

Detailed historical and technical information, music rolls, catalogues, advertisements, and other collectors' desiderata are understandably scarce in America for systems not among those of the "big three" — Ampico, Duo-Art, and Welte. One should never assume arbitrarily, however, that lesser known brands are lacking in merit. Business and competitive conditions frequently favored certain brands to the exclusion of others perhaps equally deserving in terms of quality and artistic character. The collector who aspires to own a truly unusual reproducing piano may find this situation to his liking. Armed with spirit and determination, such an individual may very well find himself conquering "new territory" in the collecting field, thus contributing still further to the growing body of knowledge already accumulated through the efforts of many dedicated members of the collecting community.

In closing, this writer wishes to extend a special note of thanks to the many persons, mostly members of the Automatic Musical Instrument Collectors' Association (AMICA), who generously contributed background information for the material presented here. Particularly deserving in this regard are Jim Elfers, Ken Caswell, Bob and Ginny Billings, and Ed Hayden.

# A Musical Miracle

## The SOLO CAROLA INNER-PLAYER

### the Most Marvelous Musical Invention of the Century

THE perfect Player-Piano has been produced. In fact it was produced two years ago, but it has never been our policy to experiment at the expense of the public. And so for many months this instrument has been tested in every conceivable way.

Over one hundred and seventy-five thousand dollars and eight years of ceaseless labor have been spent in perfecting it.

With this announcement all other so-called "solo devices" become obsolete—or nearly so.

In playing the SOLO CAROLA you cease to be conscious of the feeling that the music is being *ground out*. For this instrument is the *only* one that has complete solo control. You experience then, the thrill and pleasure of playing a composition pianistically—perfectly.

## The Principle of the Solo Carola

Like many great inventions, the mechanism of the SOLO CAROLA is simple.

If you place your foot upon the so-called "soft pedal" of a piano and then strike downward upon a key, you cause a hammer to fly forward about an inch, striking a string and sounding a note.

If you next take your foot off the "soft pedal" and strike a second key, the resulting tone will be much louder than the first. Because when you released the pedal the hammer dropped backward to nearly double its former distance from the string. When you again struck the key, the hammer (traveling about two inches this time) struck the wire with greater force, causing a louder tone.

The principle of the SOLO CAROLA is a development of this simple theory.

A piano has eighty-eight hammers. When not in the act of striking a note, all eighty-eight hammers lie at an equal distance from the strings against a bar which is called a "rest rail." In the ordinary piano and player-piano this "rest rail" may be moved to either of two fixed distances from the strings.

In the SOLO CAROLA the mechanism corresponding to the "rest rail" is movable. When you wish to play softly you merely pump softly and the hammers automatically and instantly move up close to the strings. When you wish to play louder you pump slightly faster and the hammers strike from greater and greater distances the faster you pump.

It is simple—it is automatic—it requires no levers to operate.

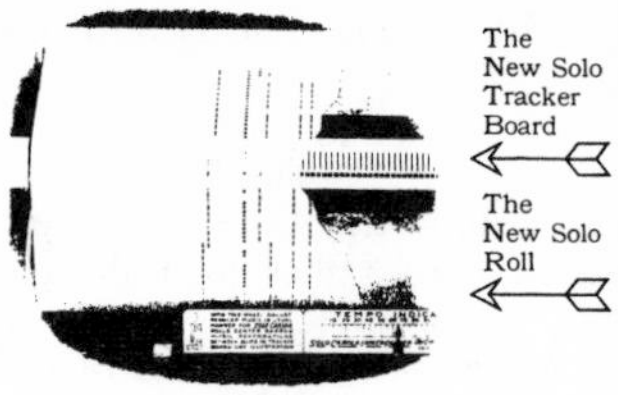


And now the invention that's most important of all. Notice the long vertical openings in the tracker-board, shown in the accompanying illustration. They are called Solo slots. There is one over each note. Each slot is connected with a small bellows which independently controls the position of each individual piano hammer. You will notice that the roll perforations register exactly with these solo slots before the ordinary striking openings (shown underneath the solo slots) are reached. Thus each piano hammer is automatically set in any desired position before the note is struck. Thus you see, in how simple a manner this player produces an infinite variety of solo effects never before approached on any other player-piano.

## Individual Features

The SOLO CAROLA is the *only* player-piano ever made on which you can strike any of the eighty-eight solo or accompaniment notes either independently or simultaneously with varying degrees of power.

The SOLO CAROLA is the *only* player-piano that eliminates completely the mechanical effect in reproducing music.

The SOLO CAROLA is the *only* player so constructed as to be able to play *every* composition ever written for the piano without mutilation or rearrangement just as it was written and just as great artists play it. The SOLO CAROLA will play any standard 88-note player roll made.

The SOLO CAROLA faithfully reproduces the playing of famous pianists with all their individualities of touch, accent, nuance and rhythm.

In *every* respect the SOLO CAROLA is the most wonderful player-piano that has ever been made. We simply can't help being enthusiastic about it—nor can you when you own one.

## Musicians Endorse the Solo Carola

Eminent pianists agree that the performance of the SOLO CAROLA is thoroughly musical and supremely artistic.

Some of the most celebrated pianists now living make records for the SOLO CAROLA exclusively because it is the *only* player-piano which reproduces accurately just what they play—just as they play it.

The SOLO CAROLA will astonish and delight you.

With it you may play the softest, dreamiest waltz or the most thunderous crash of martial music in a way heretofore absolutely impossible with a player-piano.

You have only to see, to hear and to play it yourself to be convinced that the *perfect* player-piano has at last been produced.

**Tear Off and Mail this Coupon NOW!**

THE CABLE COMPANY,
Wabash and Jackson, Chicago.

*Gentlemen*: You may send me catalog and complete details of your new *SOLO CAROLA INNER-PLAYER*, together with the name of the warerooms nearest me at which I may personally inspect one.

Name ______

Address ______

World's Greatest Manufacturers of Pianos and Inner-Player Pianos

**The Cable Company**

Wabash and Jackson
Chicago

# The CAROLA Solo Inner-Player

Why one *piano* is better than another is often a matter of opinion. You may prefer a certain piano and your neighbor another without either of you knowing just why.

But why the CAROLA Solo Inner-Player is better than all other player-pianos is a matter of exact, indisputable science.

For the CAROLA Solo Inner-Player is the *only* player-piano in the world that can strike solo and accompaniment notes simultaneously or independently throughout the entire length of the keyboard and with any degree of power desired.

In other words, despite advertised claims, the CAROLA Solo Inner-Player is the *only* player in the world that can actually reproduce the playing of great musicians.

Reprints of the analysis made by *Scientific American* of solo mechanisms mailed on request.

**THE CABLE COMPANY · Chicago**

Makers of *Conover, Cable, Kingsbury and Wellington Pianos, Carola Solo Inner-Players, Euphona Inner-Players and Euphona Home Electrics*

**Advertisements for the Solo Carola, circa 1916. (From "Player Piano Treasury").**

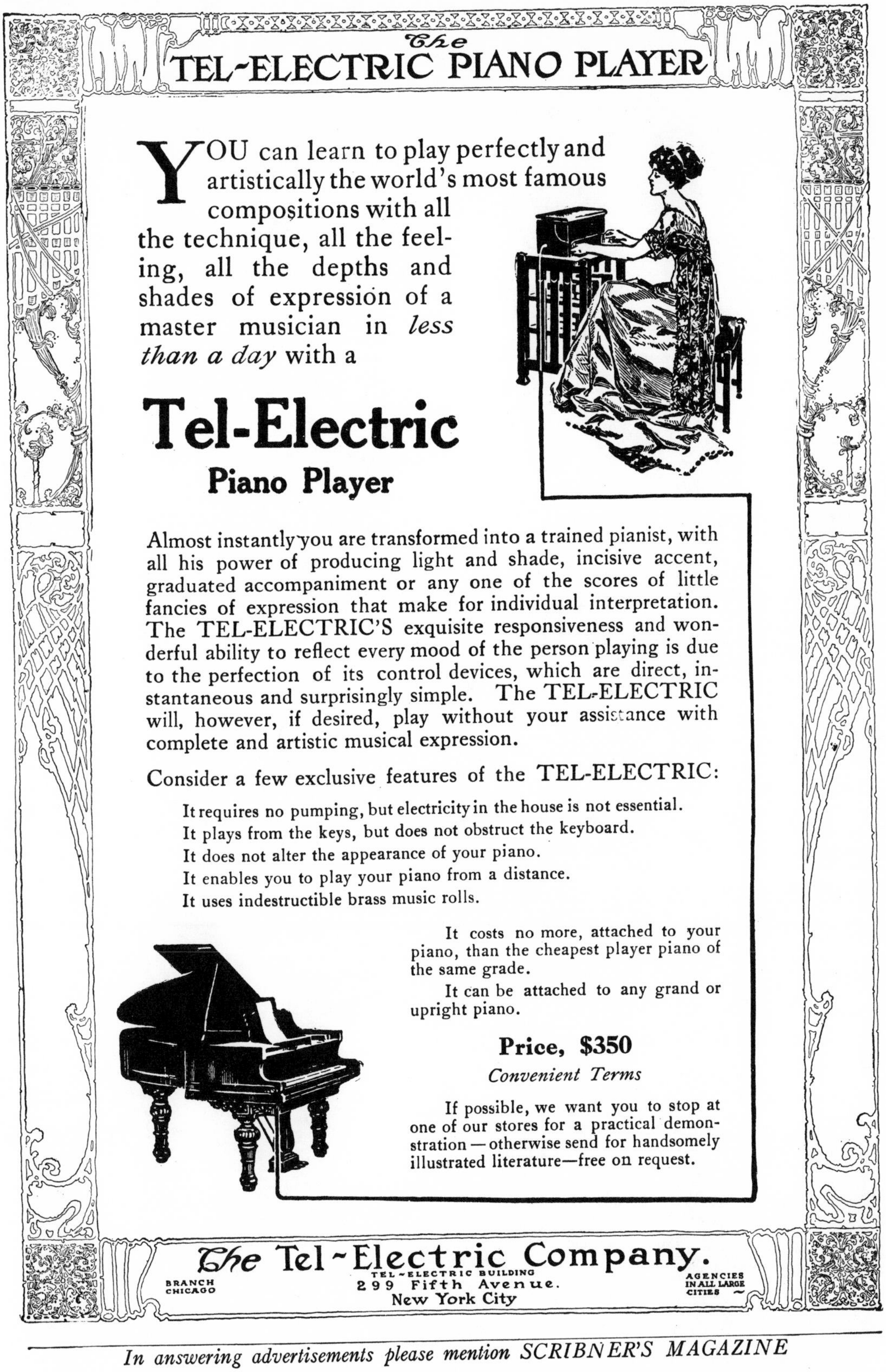

The
TEL-ELECTRIC PIANO PLAYER
YOU can learn to play perfectly and artistically the world's most famous compositions with all the technique, all the feeling, all the depths and shades of expression of a master musician in *less than a day* with a
Tel-Electric
Piano Player
Almost instantly you are transformed into a trained pianist, with all his power of producing light and shade, incisive accent, graduated accompaniment or any one of the scores of little fancies of expression that make for individual interpretation. The TEL-ELECTRIC'S exquisite responsiveness and wonderful ability to reflect every mood of the person playing is due to the perfection of its control devices, which are direct, instantaneous and surprisingly simple. The TEL-ELECTRIC will, however, if desired, play without your assistance with complete and artistic musical expression.
Consider a few exclusive features of the TEL-ELECTRIC:
It requires no pumping, but electricity in the house is not essential.
It plays from the keys, but does not obstruct the keyboard.
It does not alter the appearance of your piano.
It enables you to play your piano from a distance.
It uses indestructible brass music rolls.
It costs no more, attached to your piano, than the cheapest player piano of the same grade.
It can be attached to any grand or upright piano.
Price, $350
Convenient Terms
If possible, we want you to stop at one of our stores for a practical demonstration — otherwise send for handsomely illustrated literature—free on request.
The Tel-Electric Company.
BRANCH CHICAGO
TEL-ELECTRIC BUILDING
299 Fifth Avenue.
New York City
AGENCIES IN ALL LARGE CITIES
In answering advertisements please mention SCRIBNER'S MAGAZINE


1911 advertisement for the Tel-Electric. The Tel-Electric and its companion instrument, the Telektra, were very successful. Thousands were sold. A Tel-Electric roll catalogue of the 'teens noted that rolls were grouped in the following numerical series: classical music, numbered from 1 to 4999; sacred, 5000 to 5999; operatic, 6000 to 7999; songs and ballads, 8000 to 9999; Negro songs, 10,000 to 11,999; marches and two-steps, 12,000 to 12,999; dance music, 13,000 to 13,999; national war songs, 14,000 to 14,999; accompaniment, 15,000 to 15,999; college songs, etc., 16,000 to 17,999; transcriptions and variations, 18,000 to 18,999; in a lighter vein 19,000 to 19,999; and "duets – either primo or secondo part to be played by the Tel-Electric player, and the other part to be played by hand," 25,000 to 25,999. Not all numbers in each serial range were actually used, although the catalogue does contain thousands of different selections.

(Note that the above grand piano picture is printed in reverse; the lid opens the wrong way!)

# COIN-OPERATED PIANOS
## —and—
## ORCHESTRIONS

**Orchestrions**
**Violin Players**
**Mechanical Pianos**
**Mechanical Zithers**
**Theatre Photoplayers**
**and related instruments**

**Roll Manufacturing**

# ORCHESTRIONS, COIN-OPERATED PIANOS, PHOTOPLAYERS
## barrel pianos, violin players, and related instruments

### ORCHESTRIONS

#### Introduction

Among collectors of automatic musical instruments orchestrions have always occupied a place of fascination. This is due in part to the musical ability of these mechanical wonders and in part to the very idea of what they are: imitators of a human orchestra. Indeed, some of the more sophisticated orchestrions – some of those produced in Germany during the 20th century being examples – are to a human orchestra in apparent sound production what an Ampico, Duo-Art, or Welte reproducing piano is to a human pianist. Of course, not all or even most orchestrions are fully orchestral in the sense that a human orchestra is, but such instruments are a lot of fun anyway. Hearing "If I Could Be With You One Hour Tonight" played on a snappy and well-regulated Seeburg KT Special or listening to "Turkey in the Straw" on a perky Coinola orchestrion is a musical experience that no collector should miss.

On a larger scale the classic orchestrions made by Hupfeld, Weber, Welte, Popper, Philipps and other German manufacturers can produce creditable performances of entire symphonies, often with such magnificent presence of sound and overwhelming majesty that the listener tingles with excitement, admiration, and awe at the performance!

#### What is an Orchestrion?

What exactly is an orchestrion? The term defies precise definition. For practical purposes most collectors today consider an orchestrion to be a pneumatically-operated instrument which contains a piano plus a number of other orchestral effects such as drums, a xylophone, a rank of pipes, or similar additions. Technically, these are known as piano orchestrions.

19th century orchestrions, for the most part, are based around a softly-voiced pipe organ, rather than a piano. The drums, xylophone, and other orchestral effects provide accompaniment to the music of organ pipes.

Other types of orchestrions are mechanically, rather than pneumatically, operated. Barrel pianos with xylophone, drums, and other effects added are sometimes characterized as orchestrions. Likewise, disc-operated pianos with orchestral effects are sometimes referred to as orchestrions. (Disc-operated orchestrions are discussed in the disc music box section of this book; refer to listings under Lochmann, Polyphon, Regina, and Symphonion.)

Lewis Carroll in "The Hunting of the Snark" said, "Whatever I tell you three times is true." Perhaps following this advice many early manufacturers thought that calling any type of instrument an "orchestrion" would make it one! Hence, we have such diverse items as a small-hand cranked mechanical dulcimer being called a Piano Orchestrion and certain small paper roll organettes, the Orchestrion Harmonette for example, being given the same designation!

#### Early Orchestrions

Orchestrions, or automatic orchestras, have a beginning early in history. The dividing line between organs and orchestrions of the early days is not sharply defined. In "The Story of the Organ," C.F. Abdy Williams describes what must be one of the earliest uses of the "orchestrion" term:

"In 1789 the Abbê Vogler, at that time chapel-master to the king of Sweden, exhibited at Amsterdam an organ on a new principle, the invention of which had occupied him for many years. It had the power of crescendo and diminuendo, by means of swell shutters, and although its size was so small that it could easily be carried from place to place, it had four keyboards of more than five octaves, and a pedal clavier of 39 notes. He gave it the name of 'orchestrion,' and after exhibiting it at Amsterdam, brought it to London in 1790, where he was engaged to build an organ for the Pantheon on his new system . . ."

Dr. Alexander Buchner, in his book "Mechanical Musical Instruments," describes several other early orchestrions, including the "mechanical orchestra" constructed during the 1789-1801 years by J.G. Strasser, a clockmaker of Petersburg. This instrument, which contained a large number of pipes, played works by Haydn, Mozart, and Eberl in unabridged form.

Shortly after the year 1800, Johann Nepomucene Maelzel (1772-1838) produced the Panharmonicon. No less a musical personage than Ludwig van Beethoven helped with its musical program. In fact, Beethoven's "Wellington's Victory" was written expressly for this orchestrion. The Panharmonicon was destroyed in World War II, and the author has not encountered a precise description of it. However, extant photographs show the instrument contained several hundred pipes plus a goodly quotient of drums and other percussion effects.

Leonhard Maelzel, Johann's younger brother by eleven years, built the Orpheusharmonicon, an instrument which was admired by Beethoven, Salieri, Hummel, and other composers when the instrument was exhibited in 1814. In 1828 Leonhard Maelzel presented a concert featuring the Orpheusharmonicon, Panharmonicon, and several other instruments. Held in the Regional Estates Hall in Vienna, the program concluded with "all of the instruments playing together in a characteristic arrangement of sound effects."

The Componium, built by Dietrich Nicholas Winkel (inventor of the metronome; although the invention was wrongly credited to Maelzel in later years), was completed in 1821. Designated as a "composing machine," the Componium is described by Buchner as follows: "The Componium consists of two main parts, an orchestrion and the special mechanism which does the composing. It was originally equipped with seven cylinders, but only three have been preserved, pinned with works by Mozart, I. Moscheles, and L. Spohr . . . The Componium must first be 'fed' the theme, and then when a lever is pressed the machine begins to compose. The bars are interchanged by lengthwise gearing of the cylinders, and thus create endless variations. Mahillon [curator of the Brussels Conservatoire, the present home of the Componium] calculated that the Componium could play 14,513,461,557,741,527,824 variations; if each lasted five minutes that meant 138 trillion years before all the possible combinations had been exhausted."

Buchner also describes other early orchestrions, including an instrument exhibited in Leipzig in 1829 by C. Heinrich and J. Bauer ("with flute registers, fisharmonica, 15 horns, 15 trumpets, 2 kettle drums, Turkish cymbals, and a large drum"); instruments made by J.H. Heller of Berne, Switzerland ("the larger of the two instruments he exhibited at the Vienna World Exhibition in 1873 had 40 registers and 633 notes with 12 cylinders"); orchestrions built by J. Deutschmann of Vienna ("replaced 24 players"); and instruments built by Mamert Hock in Saarlouis, by Karrer & Co. in Teufelthal, by Mermod (of music box fame) of St. Croix, by James and John Blessing in Prague, by F. Blazek and V. Hrubes of the same city, and by Gebr. Riemer in Chrastava. Buchner further notes that a large orchestrion, designated as the Psycho, was built in the United States in 1874 by J.A. Clarke and Neville Maskelyne.

In Germany, the Blessing family at Unterkirnach, Michael Welte in Vöhrenbach (he later moved to Freiburg), Daniel Imhof, also of Vöhrenbach, and the Kaufmanns in Dresden were all prominent in the orchestrion-building business in the years before 1860. It is interesting to note that Blessing, Kaufmann, and Welte each claimed to have coined the "orchestrion" term!

Orchestrions of the early 19th century were operated by a pinned cylinder. From a mechanical viewpoint they differed little in concept from a cylinder-operated music box. Each note in the orchestrion's musical program was represented by a corresponding pin in the cylinder or barrel. In an instance in which a note had to be sustained – a continuous tattoo on the snare drum or the holding of a note on a pipe, for example – this was accomplished by an extended pin which resembled a staple. This held the note for as long as the length of the pin surface.

The early barrel-operated orchestrions were entirely mechanical, as opposed to the pneumatic system used in later years. In the early instruments all of the mechanisms were directly connected. If a note on a pipe was to be sounded, the pin on the cylinder would physically engage a lever mechanism which would mechanically open a valve or pallet. Similarly, lever mechanisms would actuate escapements for such effects as the snare drum, kettle drum, cymbals, etc.

The basic music of the early orchestrions was provided by ranks of pipes. In fact, "mechanical pipe organ" would be a better descriptive term for these instruments. When one sees a photograph of a mid-19th century orchestrion containing hundreds of pipes one imagines a tremendous, even overwhelming, tonal power. However, in actuality this was not the case. These instruments were voiced softly for the most part and were designed for use in residences. As noted in the Welte orchestrion section of this book, Michael Welte's 1100-pipe orchestrion of the 1850 era was probably no louder than a 100-pipe Welte piano orchestrion of the early 1900's. The former instrument was probably voiced on about one to one and one-half inches of wind pressure; the latter on six to eight inches – thus nearly equating the volume of the two.

Unlike later instruments, the early orchestrions were almost universally without pianos. The power to operate the instruments was obtained from a large weight which, in most instances, weighed hundreds of pounds. The weight was cranked by hand up to a height of five to ten feet above the floor. As it ran down it imparted energy to the orchestrion by means of an escapement.

Visually the early barrel-operated orchestrions are very similar. They are usually found in tall cabinets measuring eight to ten feet or more in height. The cabinets are usually glassed in on the front and sides. More often than not, the cylinders are visible in a horizontal position across the front at the convenient (for changing cylinders) waist or chest height. Some large orchestrions were built with two barrels which operated alternately. The pipes of early instruments were usually arranged in a radiating "sunburst" fashion. This display format gives a classical beauty to the few such instruments which survive today.

Following the pioneering efforts of various makers, a large orchestrion-building industry developed. This activity was headquartered in the southern part of Germany, particularly in the Schwarzwald (Black Forest) area, where such makers as Heizmann, Welte, Imhof & Mukle, and Blessing held forth. The business was what has been termed a "cottage industry." Often such instruments, even the largest sizes, would be made from components made by dozens of artisans who worked in their homes. The "factory" would be used to assemble the orchestrion parts, not to make them. A recent newpaper article about Vöhrenbach, once a center for orchestrion building, noted: "Have you ever wondered why so many homes in Vöhrenbach have such large living rooms? The reason is that many years ago the assembly of large orchestrions was done in these residences . . ."

In later years, some cylinder-operated orchestrions were made with pneumatic actions. The cylinder pins opened tiny pallet valves which, in turn, actuated a pneumatic mechanism which operated the pipes and other effects.

From Germany the orchestrions were shipped to all parts of the world. In England the orchestrions of Imhof & Mukle and M. Welte & Söhne were especially popular. In America, Welte instruments achieved great popularity, and hundreds were sold – mostly to members of the social register.

## Paper-Roll-Operated Orchestrions

The use of a cylinder in an orchestrion had its limitations. First of all, the cylinder was of a fixed diameter and turned at a fixed speed. A tune usually either had to be chopped down considerably (although some large instruments could play one selection by using several revolutions of the cylinder) or else expanded with irrelevant trills and countermelodies in order to make it fit the precise circumference of the cylinder. Thus a simple air such as "The Last Rose of Summer" might be embellished to ridiculously repetitive length while "The William Tell Overture" might emerge as a mere fragment of the original composition.

Cost was another factor. The cylinders were expensive to produce. It was not uncommon for large cylinders to cost several hundred dollars apiece – and that was in the time when a dollar was worth a dollar! The weight of the cylinders, especially those of very large orchestrions, posed another problem. Even with a muscled helper it was no easy task for the owner to change one. Another important factor was that cylinders did not lend themselves to mass production. The making of each cylinder was the result of many, many hours, even days, of painstaking craftsmanship. It was natural that the pinned-cylinder system would be abandoned once a good substitute was found.

Although suggestions and perhaps experiments were made earlier (refer to Professor Merritt Gally's paper roll system for operating orchestrions and changing up to ten pipe registers that was publicized in an 1879 article, "The Autophone" [reprinted in the organette section of this book]), the paper roll was not generally used on orchestrions until the early 1890's. Welte started using paper rolls for certain of its instruments in 1887. About five years later, Imhof & Mukle followed with its "music leaf" system; a sturdy manila paper roll actuated spring-loaded brass keys which, in turn, controlled a pneumatic system. Imhof & Mukle also produced a series of orchestrions which used rolls made of perforated thin brass! By the year 1900, the advantages of paper rolls were realized by nearly every orchestrion manufacturer. Although cylinder-operated orchestrions were made until World War I, the market was small after the turn of the century. It is interesting to note that an analogous situation occurred in the music box field. The invention of the disc-type music box and its popularization made the mass production of music box discs feasible. Hundreds of discs could be punched out in the time it took to make just one cylinder. The cylinder music box industry virtually disappeared when disc-type boxes achieved popularity with the public.

The paper roll system offered many advantages for orchestrion use. It did not operate the mechanisms mechanically but, rather, used an intermediate pneumatic system of bellows and valves. This permitted an amplification of force. A tiny hole in the music roll could, with equal facility, operate an immense bass drum beater or sound a pipe scarcely the size of your little finger.

The perforated paper roll could be made in almost any length. A short tune could be programmed on ten to twenty feet of paper. A symphony might use one to two hundred feet.

Rolls were also adaptable to mass production. Once a master roll was prepared, hundreds or thousands of identical copies could be punched out automatically at the rate of a dozen or more at a time.

The result was that once the roll system was firmly established new orchestrion rolls were available for just a few dollars each. A comprehensive library of music could be stored in the space of a small bookshelf, and even a child could change the rolls easily.

By the year 1900 the German makers controlled the orchestrion business. Welte, Imhof & Mukle, and Hupfeld established salons and sales outlets in London, New York, Paris, and other large cities. Sales progressed at such a rate that the factories could hardly keep pace, despite expansion and re-expansion. Leipzig, Germany, the center of the disc-type music box industry, became prominent in the piano orchestrion business. Hupfeld, Lösche, Popper, and several other firms were located there. Earlier firms such as Welte and Imhof & Mukle converted their operations to the manufacture of roll-operated piano orchestrions and became financial monoliths with worldwide operations.

———————

## Orchestrions in America — The Beginning

At the turn of the twentieth century orchestrions were virtually unknown in public places in America. To be sure, such personages as Adolph Sutro, Claus Spreckels, P.T. Barnum, Jay Gould, and Henry Frick owned orchestrions during the 1880-1900 years, but these were strictly for enjoyment in their private pleasure palaces.

In 1902, Farny Wurlitzer (one of the three sons of Rudolph Wurlitzer, founder of the Rudolph Wurlitzer Co.) attended the Leipzig Trade Fair and was absolutely astounded by the magnificent display of orchestrions shown by Ludwig Hupfeld. Mr. Wurlitzer, despite his association with one of the largest musical retailing firms in the United States, had never seen such instruments before!

Farny Wurlitzer correctly guessed that these orchestrions would be wonderful things to sell in America. He endeavored to set up a business connection with Hupfeld, but that firm's terms (full cash payment in advance) were too onerous, so a more lenient arrangement was made with another orchestrion maker, J.D. Philipps & Sons of Frankfurt-am-Main, Germany. Under the terms of this agreement the large Philipps orchestrions (which were sold in Europe under the Philipps Pianella, and later, the Philipps Paganini names) were sold in America as the Wurlitzer Mandolin PianOrchestra, the Concert PianOrchestra, and the Paganini. As Wurlitzer was quite concerned with concealing the Philipps origin of these orchestrions no public mention was made of the connection with the German firm. In fact, Wurlitzer went a step further and liberally stamped "Manufactured by the Rudolph Wurlitzer Company" on them in many places.

During the 1890's and the beginning years of the twentieth century the public's interest in automatic musical instruments of all kinds was fanned from a spark into a flame. In the field of music boxes this was the period of mass marketing by Polyphon, Regina, Symphonion, and others. Pneumatically-operated reed organs, piano players, and other instruments for home use were flamboyantly advertised and, as a result, these sold by the tens of thousands.

In the field of orchestrions this era provided the seed for what was to become their golden age. As noted earlier, the only types of orchestrions available in America in the 1890's were those imported from Germany, and these were mostly enjoyed in private homes. In an occasional public place a mechanical musical instrument could be found. Barrel pianos made by one of the eastern United States craftsmen or, more likely, imported from France, Italy, or Germany, were used in moderate numbers. Some orchestrions made by Welte and other German firms were used in public places, but their number was small.

## The Early Coin Piano and Orchestrion Market in America

In 1898 the firm of Roth & Engelhardt of St. Johnsville, New York, introduced a small cabinet-style 44-note piano under the Peerless trademark. This piano was operated by a paper roll and featured a vacuum pump, a pneumatic stack, and most of the other ingredients that were to be standard for the next several decades. This small Peerless is considered to be America's first coin-operated pneumatic "nickelodeon" piano (although it is not the first pneumatic coin-operated American instrument; that distinction belongs to the Encore Banjo).

In 1897 the Rudolph Wurlitzer Company, pleased with the enthusiastic reception given to the coin-operated Regina music boxes handled by the firm, commissioned Eugene DeKleist of North Tonawanda, New York, to build a coin-operated piano. In 1899 the Tonophone, a hybrid instrument which featured a pneumatic system which was actuated by a pinned wooden cylinder, made its appearance. The Tonophone was immediately successful. Wurlitzer sold thousands over the next several years. The Rudolph Wurlitzer Company later purchased the DeKleist interests and, on January 1, 1909, took over the entire operation in that upstate New York city.

About 1901 DeKleist made a 44-note piano to compete with the Peerless. Sold by Wurlitzer as the Pianino, this compact nickel-in-the-slot music maker achieved instant success.

By 1910 the industry had grown a hundredfold. There were several dozen different makers of coin pianos and orchestrions, each marketing pianos under different names. Very few of these firms were manufacturers in the strictest sense of the term. Most were assemblers. They purchased their pianos from one source and from other suppliers acquired the motors, tracker bars, coin mechanisms, and even music rolls.

About this time it was realized that coin-operated pianos in themselves were not sufficient to insure a good sales volume or give the impression of having, as they say in merchandising today, a "full product line." Hence, a wide variety of orchestrions was produced.

Chicago became a center for the industry. The Operators Piano Company, the J.P. Seeburg Piano Company, the Marquette Piano Company, and several other manufacturers were located there. In other parts of the United States the Automatic Musical Company (later to become the Link Piano and Organ Co.), the North Tonawanda Musical Instrument Works, the Berry-Wood Piano Player Company, and others were busy making instruments.

Some of these orchestrions were fairly simple in construction and format and consisted of a basic upright keyboard-type piano to which were added perhaps one rank of pipes or a xylophone and a drum or two. Other orchestrions were crammed with orchestral effects. The Cremona Orchestral J, the "top of the line" instrument of the Marquette Piano Company, contained in an upright case a piano, mandolin attachment, bass drum, snare drum, tympani effect, cymbal, triangle, xylophone, and two ranks of pipes. The most expensive Berry-Wood orchestrion, the Style A.O.W., had somewhat similar specifications except for some variations such as two beaters on the snare drum and a set of orchestra bells.

The most ornate keyboard orchestrion ever made in the United States was produced by the J.P. Seeburg Piano Company. The Style H Solo Orchestrion contained a whole bandbox full of instruments within its art-glass and statue-fronted ornate case. "Masked Marvel – equal to a seven man orchestra," said Seeburg proudly!

The large orchestrions were much more elaborate than basic keyboard pianos and, consequently, cost more to produce. Their retail prices were much higher than were those of simple nickel-in-the-slot pianos. In 1914 a typical coin piano sold for an average of about $500 to $700. At the same time some of the larger and more elaborate orchestrions readily brought $1500 to $2500 or more.

### Orchestrions in the 1920's

The coming of Prohibition in 1920 killed off the market for most large orchestrions. In fact, it played havoc with coin-operated instruments in general. Most firms went out of business or cut back production at that time. A few others fell victim to the 1921 business depression. By 1925 there were only a few makers left.

In the years from 1900 to 1920 the Rudolph Wurlitzer Company was America's leading seller of coin pianos and orchestrions. It produced and/or sold a wide variety of models including the tiny Pianino, the larger Automatic Player Piano, the Solo Violin Piano, the Mandolin Quartette and Sextette, the distinctive-appearing Automatic Harp, and others. About 1250 PianOrchestra and Paganini orchestrions were sold at prices mostly in the $2000 to $10,000 range. About 100 of these were equipped with cases built in Wurlitzer's North Tonawanda factory; the others were imported from Philipps.

However, when the 1920's arrived the Rudolph Wurlitzer Company had another preoccupation: the theatre pipe organ. By this time Wurlitzer was the leading builder of pipe organs for theatre use. These organs, called Wurlitzer Hope-Jones Unit Orchestras, retailed mostly in the $10,000 to $30,000 range each. Hundreds of these organs were sold each year during the halcyon mid-1920's. This tremendous volume caused the coin piano and orchestrion department to be relegated to a position of secondary importance. As a result, the Rudolph Wurlitzer Company was only a minor factor in the coin piano and orchestrion business after the early 1920's.

A sampling of the orchestrion trade in America in 1925 would have revealed that two makers had the lion's share of the business. Way out in front was the J.P. Seeburg Piano Company. Close behind was a secretly-owned Seeburg subsidiary, the Western Electric Piano Company. Behind these two leaders were several other makers, notably the Nelson-Wiggen Piano Company and the Operators Piano Company.

Orchestrions of the mid-1920's were different from the earlier styles. The most popular type was the small compact keyboardless style – of which the Seeburg KT and KT Special are examples. These instruments were much smaller than the earlier keyboard-style orchestrions and were more suited for use in cabarets and speakeasies, the private, smoky, and intimate unofficial watering places of the Prohibition era. Indeed, this cabaret use sparked a small revival of the industry for a short time in the 1920's, so that in 1924 and 1925 the music trade papers were full of comments about "good times" in the business.

However, the days of orchestrions and coin-operated pianos were numbered during the 1920's. The radio, despite the fact that most were played for patrons free, became the star attraction of many public places. In 1927 talking pictures became a commercial reality. This, combined with the popularity of the radio, increased the demand for music as sung by famous personalities. The coin-operated phonograph, which entered service in the 1890's and which co-existed with the coin-operated piano for years, forged ahead. As if this was not enough, the Depression provided the finishing touch. By 1932 the business was, for all practical purposes, dead. The few companies that were still in existence at the time owed their lives to diversification into other fields. Wurlitzer and Seeburg became the two leading makers of juke boxes or, as the makers preferred to call them, "automatic phonographs." Link didn't survive in the music business, but the principal, Ed Link, went on to make his name famous in the field of aviation trainers. Most other firms simply vanished.

----------

### Orchestrions – The Worldwide View

The pattern of orchestrion popularity which characterized the market in the United States was true of Europe also, except that the European market, unaffected by Prohibition, was much more active in the 1920's.

The European makers, particularly the Germans, had a head start. Orchestrion building was a large industry in Germany even before the American industry was born. As discussed earlier, the firms of Blessing, Imhof & Mukle, Welte, and others enjoyed an immense market during the 19th century.

The 1900 to 1910 years were ones of great innovation in Germany. A real competition in orchestrion size and musical ability was started among the different makers. The result was that thousands of what we call "classic orchestrions" today were produced. Some of these produced really lifelike music of an almost unbelievable realism. The Hupfeld Pan Orchestra and the Weber Maesto, for instance, were expressly created to play serious music in a realistic manner. These were sold by means of enthusiastic testimonials garnered from dozens of Europe's leading musicians and orchestra conductors.

Of all the manufacturers of automatic musical instruments in the world, the firm of Ludwig Hupfeld was the largest. Hupfeld covered the spectrum of automatic instruments from reproducing pianos to orchestrions, from violin-players to theatre organs. The two main lines of Hupfeld orchestrions were designated the Helios and Pan. Helios instruments were offered in five basic degrees of instrumentation ranging from the Helios I to the Helios V. The latter instrument measured nearly twenty feet wide, contained about 1500 pipes, and had 49 control registers! As such, it was the largest orchestrion ever made on a production-line basis by any firm. It is interesting to note that Helios instruments could be ordered from the factory in any one of three degrees of voicing or loudness: (1) very soft for residential use, (2) medium for use in restaurants and hotels, and (3) loud for use in skating rinks and open-air pavilions.

The Hupfeld Pan, introduced after 1910, was Hupfeld's finest effort. A 124-hole tracker bar provided several solo scales, provision for very sophisticated piano expression and effects, and for just about every automatic device deemed desirable to emulate a human orchestra. The great cost of the Hupfeld Pan instruments (most cost from about $10,000 to $20,000) precluded widespread popularity, but they were sufficiently popular that over 1,000 different Pan music rolls were cut.

In the 1920's, Hupfeld introduced two new types of orchestrions. The Symphony Jazz was usually equipped with saxophone and lotus flute pipes, percussion effects, and bells and was intended to play music in the jazz idiom. "Jazz" became a popular word for inclusion in orchestrion names, and other makers produced instruments with somewhat similar titles. One of the most interesting orchestrions of all time was produced by Hupfeld in the late 1930's. Designated as the Violina Orchestra, the instrument featured three real violins accompanied by a piano, pipes, and percussion effects.

M. Welte & Söhne of Freiburg, Germany, made few orchestrions after 1914. Although the firm remained in business until the 1940's, most efforts in the 'teens and 'twenties were concentrated on making the Welte-Mignon reproducing piano and the Welte Philharmonic Organ. Welte established an American factory at Poughkeepsie, New York, and assembled orchestrions, reproducing pianos, and other instruments there in the years before World War I.

Popper & Company and Paul Lösche, both of which were located in Leipzig, produced a large and illustrious series of orchestrions from the turn of the century through the 1920's. Many large Popper orchestrions have a warm, rich tonal quality; surviving examples are pleasant to hear today. J.D. Philipps of Frankfurt-am-Main, the firm that provided Wurlitzer with the Wurlitzer-trademarked PianOrchestra and Paganini orchestrions, continued in business until the late 1920's. By 1927, the 50th anniversary of the firm, the marketplace demand was for small and compact orchestrions and not for the large classic models. A Philipps catalogue of that year features many compact Philipps Jazzband models, several varieties of photoplayers, and a line of Duca reproducing pianos.

In Waldkirch, Germany, Gebr. Weber (Weber Brothers) produced nearly 3000 instruments from 1880 to 1930. In the late 1920's the Weber pneumatic systems were redesigned. Most orchestrions of other makers were designed by persons who had little or nothing to do with arranging the music rolls used on the instruments. Utilizing the genius of Gustav Bruder, a first-class musician and a person thoroughly familiar with pneumatic mechanisms, Weber produced a series of what can best be called "reproducing orchestrions." The musical realism and presence of these late-generation Weber orchestrions was unexcelled. It took up to three weeks for Gustav Bruder to make a single music roll as a great deal of time was necessary to incorporate elaborate expression effects for each instrument. High initial cost precluded a widespread sale of the late Weber Solea, Maesto, and Elite orchestrions, just as high cost earlier restricted the market for Hupfeld's sophisticated Pan series.

The "big five" European orchestrion makers – Hupfeld, Philipps, Popper, Weber, and Welte – actively distributed their products in North and South America. Importation of automatic musical instruments from Germany ended for all practical purposes with the advent of World War I. After the war ended, only a few German instruments, mostly smaller pianos and musical novelty items, were sold in the Americas.

---

## COIN-OPERATED PIANOS AND RELATED INSTRUMENTS

### Mechanical Pianos (Barrel-Operated Pianos, etc.)

Mechanically-played stringed instruments have a long history. In his book, "Player Piano," Arthur W.J.G. Ord-Hume relates that Samuel Bidermann was making spinet pianos that could be played either by a pinned barrel or by hand in the early 17th century. Marin Mersenne's 1636 writing is quoted by Ord-Hume: "One can still recall in our time the invention of drums or barrels employed to play several pieces of music on spinets without the use of the hand, for the Germans are so ingenious that they make them play more than fifty different pieces by means of several springs which, when set in motion, activate several figures which leap and move to the rhythm of songs without any need to touch the instrument after having wound it up." An even earlier instrument was listed as a "virgynal" (Note: a virginal is a small harpsichord-like instrument which is usually placed on one's lap while being played) and was catalogued in 1547 with the collection of musical instruments left by King Henry VIII: "An instrumente that goethe with a whele without playinge uppon, of woode vernisshed yellowe and painted blewe with vi round plates of siluer [silver] pounced with antike garnisshed with an edge of copper and guilte."

Throughout the 18th century mechanical pianos (the term "mechanical" is often used today to distinguish the early cylinder-operated instruments; the term "pneumatic" refers to those which use a paper roll; the term "automatic" refers to both types) were made in Europe and were sold for use in homes, although some were used in public places. Many were of the cabinet-style or keyboardless type. A typical instrument was described in 1892 by Paul de Wit in the catalogue of his collection: "Music cabinet in rococo from the middle of the 18th century, with a clock which starts the music cylinder on each hour. At the same time, little wooden hammers strike the strings, whose sound is also reinforced by a bell-accompaniment in the octave. A very interesting specimen." Production of such instruments was not done in large factories but was accomplished, for the most part, by individual craftsmen who built each one by hand.

During the 19th century, barrel-piano making became a factory business. London became one center of manufacturing, and such firms as Clementi, Collard & Co.; Flight & Robson; and T.C. Bates & Son enjoyed an active business in the early decades. Paris was another center, and several dozen makers, mostly individuals working in small shops, produced a variety of instruments.

Barrel pianos became very popular after 1850. From then until 1900, many pianoforte builders and orchestrion builders produced barrel pianos as well. Imhof & Mukle manufactured many different varieties, including some in ornately hand-carved cabinets. Gavioli & Cie., famous Paris organ builders, made many barrel pianos, most of which were equipped for coin operation and were used in public places. Ludwig Hupfeld and J.D. Philipps, both of whom later achieved renown in the piano orchestrion field, produced barrel-operated pianos in the 1880-1900 period. Most instruments, however, were made by individual craftsmen. London, Paris, Brussels, Antwerp, and several Italian cities all had many different artisans in the field.

In America, barrel pianos were manufactured by a number of firms in eastern cities, particularly New York City, Philadelphia, and Baltimore. In addition, large numbers of instruments were imported into America from European sources. Most barrel pianos in America were used commercially, either as street pianos or in taverns and other public locations.

Although barrel pianos were made throughout the 1920's in Belgium, the industry in other countries diminished in the 1900-1905 years when pneumatically-operated pianos became popular, and ended with the advent of World War I in 1914.

Barrel-operated pianos were made in thousands of variations. There were few standard models; and each one was apt to differ in some way from the last. Many, particularly those built in France, Belgium, and Italy, were housed in very ornate cases, often with gilt engraved designs and with frosted and bevelled glass panels. A typical barrel piano played from 6 to 10 tunes. Some, particularly those used in streets, were operated by continuous hand winding. Most used in public places were spring-wound. Toward the end of the 19th century, electric motors and water motors were provided with some models.

Many different types of piano actions were used. Most were simple and were actuated by a pin in the barrel which, when it came into contact with a lever arm attached to the piano hammer, caused the hammer to lift and then fall back against the string, the speed of travel being accelerated by a small spring. Other barrel pianos featured reiterating actions. A staple-like bridge pin in the barrel would cause a special mechanical action to sustain a given note by repeatedly striking the same hammer against the strings. Still other instruments (Wurlitzer's Tonophone, made by DeKleist and first sold in 1899, is an example) utilized a pinned barrel to actuate a pneumatic system.

Often other instruments were added to barrel pianos. Drums were a popular accessory, as were sets of xylophone bars and bells. Some barrel pianos incorporated pipes (usually just one or two ranks) and were designated as orchestrions. Frati and Hupfeld built many of these.

Many other types of mechanically-operated pianos were built, especially in the 1880-1910 years. Disc-operated pianos, designated as orchestrions and containing drums, bells, and other effects, were sold by Lochmann, Polyphon, Regina, and Symphonion. Mechanical pianos (without a pneumatic system) which used rewind-type or endless rolls made of heavy manila paper or cardboard were made by many different firms, including the above-mentioned disc-piano makers. Ludwig Hupfeld made thousands of these instruments and was probably the leading producer of this type. Folding cardboard music books were used by several French and German makers. Some instruments even used music books made of hinged aluminum sheets!

In addition to the full-sized or nearly-full-sized mechanical pianos, many related smaller instruments were made. Some of these were of dulcimer or zither size. The Chordephon disc-operated mechanical zither and the Triola roll-operated zither are examples. The Piano Melodico and the impressively-named Piano Orchestrion, small book-operated stringed instruments, were extremely popular in the 1880's and 1890's and were sold by the tens of thousands. Most of these smaller-sized mechanical "pianos" were used in homes, not in commercial locations.

———————

## Pneumatically-Operated Pianos – The American Market

As noted earlier, the first pneumatically-operated American-made piano to be made in commercial quantities was a 44-note instrument introduced in 1898 by Roth & Engelhardt of St. Johnsville, New York. This started a trend, and within a few years there were many different types of 44-note pianos on the market. In a colorful way, Harvey Roehl described these early instruments in "Player Piano Treasury:" "A type of automatic piano found early in the history [of coin-operated pianos] was the 44-note cabinet style. Just what logic dictates this particular number of notes is not clear, unless it just happens that since 44 is half of 88, which is the normal piano scale, some genius figured that perhaps half a piano is better than none at all. Examples of machines using this scale are the Mills Automatic Pianova (also sold as the Electrova and Pianova), the Wurlitzer Pianino, certain models of the Peerless line, the North Tonawanda Musical Instrument Works Pianolin, and others . . . Undoubtedly the standardization of roll manufacture which was agreed on at the great Buffalo, New York, convention in 1908 did much to forestall further development of the 44-note piano as a type, because no standardization was ever carried out for this scale. Each 44-note piano used rolls which would fit it, and no other make. A great disadvantage of any scale of less than 88 notes is that most music is composed with the assumption that all these notes will be available when the music is played, so that when these are scored for use with a machine having a lesser number, the arranger is often obliged to all but mutilate the work to make it fit . . ."

The Regal and the Electrolin were two other popular 44-note piano makes. The three best-selling 44-note pianos were the aforementioned Pianolin, Pianino, and 44-note Peerless. Specimens of 44-note pianos surviving today are usually of one of these three types.

In the early days of the home piano player market the 65-note roll was the most popular size. Spaced at 6 holes to the inch on the tracker bar, this roll included enough of the piano scale that most musical compositions could be played without having to sacrifice any of the musical score. The 65-note home player roll format was adapted for coin piano use by adding holes for limited expression and control use and for the operation of up to two extra instruments, one instrument of which was usually a mandolin attachment. Designated as type "A" and made in 10-tune length (usually) and of 11 1/4" width, this roll became standard with many manufacturers. By 1910 most coin-operated pianos used the "A" roll. A list of piano makes which used the 10-tune "A" roll comprises several dozen names. The leading ones were Cremona, Seeburg, and Coinola and, in later years, Western Electric and Nelson-Wiggen. In America today the A-roll coin piano is the most common type of instrument found in collections of old-time "nickelodeon" instruments. Rolls for this type of instrument, both old rolls and ones recut in modern times, are plentiful and inexpensive. Virtually any melody that was popular in America from 1900 to 1935 can be found on "A" rolls.

While most A-roll instruments consisted of a piano with a mandolin attachment, many featured an extra instrument as well. In the earlier years a rank of violin or flute pipes was a popular addition. In the 1920's the extra cost of providing a wind-pressure system to operate the pipes proved to be too much, and for competitive reasons the xylophone (which could use the same vacuum system utilized by the piano) became the most-used extra instrument. In America A-roll pianos, even ones with a rank of pipes or a xylophone, were not designated as orchestrions. That distinction was usually reserved for instruments with drum and trap effects.

Many manufacturers produced coin pianos which used special rolls. Type "A" rolls of 10-tune length generally sold for about $3.50 per roll, an amount equivalent to 35c per tune. By making an instrument take a special type of roll, a manufacturer could have a captive market for his rolls and could charge more. This was an important reason why

Wurlitzer used distinctive rolls (not interchangeable with rolls used by other manufacturers) on its instruments. Wurlitzer 65-Note Automatic Player Piano rolls, the musical equivalent to the industry's "A" rolls, sold for from 40c to 80c per tune over the years. Link, Berry-Wood, and Peerless (Engelhardt) also used distinctive rolls, as did several other leading manufacturers.

The most active period in the American market for coin-operated pianos was in the years immediately preceding World War I. The demand for music in public places was seemingly insatiable, and coin piano makers could sell whatever they built. A Wurlitzer catalogue of that era noted that coin-operated instruments were ideal for use in amusement parks, billiard halls, beer gardens, bowling alleys, excursion boats, cafes, confectioneries, cigar stores, clubs, dance halls, drug stores, department stores, groceries, hotels, lodges, lunch rooms, news stands, post card studios, railroad depots, and restaurants. While grocery stores and post card studios represented a trivial market, one of the best markets for coin pianos was one that Wurlitzer neglected to mention: houses of ill repute, or "sporting houses," as they were called. Talks with old-timers in the piano trade reveal that such places were the best customers, especially for the more expensive instruments. Business was so good that cash on the barrelhead for a brand-new Seeburg, Link, or Wurlitzer piano was no problem at all. Some instruments in plush "houses" were equipped with 25c or 50c slots – while instruments with 5c slots in more mundane locations were not played as often! As Harvey Roehl wrote in "Player Piano Treasury," "what better device for stimulating a fast turnover of trade than a coin piano in the parlor with a roll of fast, snappy two-minute tunes!"

Following the adoption of Prohibition in 1920, most taverns closed their doors, at least officially. A new market for coin-operated pianos developed with the thousands of intimate speakeasies that sprang up. The large keyboard-type pianos of earlier years fell from favor, and new, compact cabinet-style instruments became the best sellers. Most pianos sold in America during the 1920's were the products of Seeburg, Western Electric, and Nelson-Wiggen, were of the cabinet format, and used 10-tune "A" rolls. It is interesting to note that in Europe small cabinet-type coin pianos never became popular. Most instruments sold during the 1920's in Europe were of keyboard styles.

By 1928, only a few coin pianos were being made each year in the United States. Deliveries made by the few companies then still in business were made from inventories unsold from earlier times.

The market for coin-operated pianos and orchestrions in America can be summed up as follows:

Pre-1900: Barrel-operated pianos and orchestrions, mostly imported from Europe, were popular.

1900-1905: 44-note pianos were the best-sellers.

1905-1910: Keyboard-style instruments, many of which used type "A" rolls, began their popularity. 44-note pianos, while still popular, were diminishing in importance.

1910-1915: Larger instruments became popular. Seeburg, Wurlitzer, Operators, Marquette, Peerless and others found ready markets for their expensive keyboard-style orchestrions. Piano orchestrions imported from Welte, Hupfeld, Imhof & Mukle, and Philipps sold well. 1910-1915 were the best years of the coin piano and orchestrion market. More new companies were established, more advertising in trade papers was placed, and more of the large and expensive instruments were sold during these five years than at any other time.

1915-1920: World War I cut off importation of European instruments. American coin piano makers found business was slower. Competition increased and prices fell. Peerless, Berry-Wood, and several other firms had financial difficulties.

1920-1925: Following a slow start and a depressed outlook because of Prohibition, business picked up sharply. Cabinet-style instruments became most popular. 1924 and 1925 are record years for the sale of cabinet instruments by Seeburg, Western Electric, and Nelson-Wiggen.

1925-1930: Business was good in 1925. In 1926 sales of coin-operated instruments fell sharply. By 1930 the popularity of the radio, talking pictures, and phonographs plus the worldwide economic depression ended the coin piano industry.

---

## Pneumatically-Operated Pianos – The European Market

The European market for coin-operated pianos was dominated by Ludwig Hupfeld of Leipzig, Germany. The Hupfeld firm secured an early patent position in pneumatic instruments. This, plus aggressive merchandising methods, gave Hupfeld what probably amounted to 50% or more of the market. What remained was divided up among several dozen other manufacturers.

During the late 1890's and early 1900's Hupfeld, Dienst, Kuhl & Klatt, Popper, Lösche, and Philipps produced thousands of keyboard-type coin pianos, many of which contained a mandolin and an extra instrument such as a rank of violin or flute pipes. Imhof & Mukle and Welte, although very active in the market for large orchestrions, produced very few keyboard-style instruments in the smaller sizes. Unlike their American counterparts, the German makers did not adopt a standard roll, even for smaller instruments. The American type "A" roll has no European counterpart. The 44-note piano, an American favorite during the 1900-1905 years, was not made in Europe, although a number of limited-scale pianos were constructed – a 36-note Hupfeld instrument, for instance.

The German market reached its height during the five years from 1909 to 1914. The pages of "Zeitschrift für Instrumentenbau," the leading German trade magazine of this time, make fascinating reading. Hardly a month went by without each of the leading makers announcing a new model. As happened in America, dozens of smaller firms entered the coin piano business. Most made only a few models, usually of the piano-with-mandolin or the piano-with-mandolin-and-xylophone format. Hupfeld supplied pneumatic actions for many such companies.

The German coin piano business enjoyed an active export market. Until World War I ended exports in 1914, most leading German firms had sales outlets in other European countries. Belgium and Holland were especially active, and tens of thousands of instruments were sold there. England, France, Spain, and other countries provided additional markets. South America represented another sales opportunity. Dienst, Hupfeld, and Philipps, to mention just three firms, issued catalogues in Spanish specifically for South American distribution, particularly in Argentina.

From 1914 to the early 1920's the business slowed considerably. Hupfeld, the leading piano maker, converted most of its factory capacity to producing war materiel. Many others did the same.

In the 1920's the activity increased again. Especially in demand were keyboard-style pianos. Large orchestrions were produced only in small numbers. The market for keyboard instruments was exceptionally good, and thousands were sold, mainly by Hupfeld, Popper, and Philipps – although Weber and Lösche remained quite active. Certain countries that represented active markets before World War I – England, Argentina, France, and the United States, for example – bought few German instruments in the 1920's. The main demand was from Germany itself and from Belgium and Holland, with Belgium being the best export customer.

The end of the coin piano market in Germany followed lines similar to those in the United States, but the German market extended for a year or two longer. The business declined sharply after the 1925-1926 years. By the end of 1932 the leading German coin piano makers were either out of business or had entered other fields.

Coin-operated pianos were manufactured by several European firms outside of Germany, but production was limited. In Belgium, Pierre Eich made several different models, most of which contained pipes or harmonium reeds. Several other Belgian firms, Bursens and DeRoy (Symphonia) are examples, purchased German instruments and modified them for the Belgian market by adding accordions, drums and traps, and other effects. Decap, the well-known Antwerp maker of dance hall organs, produced a small number of coin-operated pianos as well.

In France, Gavioli and Limonaire, both prominent firms in the fairground organ business, produced coin-operated pianos, but most of these were of the barrel-operated or book-operated types.

In Austria, Hofmann & Czerny, trading as the Continental Musikwerke, produced many different roll- and barrel-operated instruments.

## THEATRE PHOTOPLAYERS

What is a photoplayer? Basically, a photoplayer is an orchestrion or automatic orchestra specifically designed for theatre use to accompany and to provide sound effects for silent movies. To this end, photoplayers have a special format: their profile is usually wide and low – for use in the orchestra pit just below the movie screen. Unlike a coin-operated orchestrion, the photoplayer is equipped with pedals, buttons, and other controls to enable the operator to supplement the automatic operation by adding extra effects as desired.

Production of photoplayers became an important business in the 1910-1912 years. While production of some firms continued into the late 1920's, the height of the market was in the 'teens – especially from about 1915 to 1920. In America thousands of photoplayers of various makes were sold during this time. In Europe the market, while not as large or varied as in the United States, was still quite active.

In their simplest form photoplayers consisted of a piano with a few extra effects added. An example is the Wurlitzer Style D Duplex Orchestra. This consisted of a keyboard piano with mandolin and two ranks of pipes: violin and flute. Music was provided automatically by means of paper rolls, the same as used on certain Wurlitzer orchestrions. Wurlitzer noted that the Style D was ideal for a theatre of 150 seats and that "this is an ideal instrument for a very small house where drums might be too loud . . . Has violin and flute pipes, yet takes up no more space than a good sized upright piano . . . It is an instrument built by us particularly for professional work – built to stand the wear and tear that instruments get in public places."

Similarly, the American Photo Player Company offered the Fotopiano, a junior version of its elaborate Fotoplayer (trademark) instruments.

However, when we think of photoplayers today we usually think of a large instrument with a center piano or console unit and with two large side chests, each of which contains pipes, drums, and other effects. It was in this format that most photoplayers were made. The center or console section contains an upright piano with one (usually) or two keyboards. It contains the roll mechanism or, often, two roll mechanisms. The operator selected one or two rolls with music appropriate to the movie being shown. Seated at the instrument he then operates the sound effects (such as the fire gong, telephone bell, locomotive whistle, bird call, etc.) as the roll plays the music. Should a change of music be desired he can switch from one roll to another or use a fast-forward or reverse control to go to another spot on the same roll. The end result is that a single operator can give a musical performance worthy of a small orchestra.

In this book we list photoplayers in the individual sections pertaining to the firms which made them; firms which, with few exceptions, also made orchestrions and other automatically-played instruments. Such firms include: American Photo Player Company (produced the Fotoplayer series of instruments); Berry-Wood Piano Player Co. (advertised in 1913 that it would soon be adding photoplayers to its line of coin pianos); Ludwig Hupfeld (made many varieties of theatre instruments including the Kino-Pan, Theatre Violina, etc.); Link Piano and Organ Co. (makers of several varieties of theatre instruments); Marquette Piano Co. (produced Cremona photoplayers in several styles); Mills Novelty Company (produced Mills Melody Violins for theatre use); Nelson-Wiggen Piano Co. (made the Selector Duplex Organ); North Tonawanda Musical Instrument Works (produced several types of the Ideal Moving Picture Orchestra); Operators Piano Co. (its Reproduco piano - pipe organ was a best seller); Peerless Piano Player Co. (made the Photo Orchestra); J.D. Philipps & Sons (produced some photoplayers which used Paganini orchestrion rolls); Piano Player Manufacturing Co. (advertised the Symphony Automatic Orchestra which used Welte-built equipment); J.P. Seeburg Piano Co. (made many varieties of photoplayers); M. Welte & Sons (made several types of photoplayers; sold the Multitone series of instruments); Rudolph Wurlitzer Co. (made many different photoplayers; production figures are given in the Wurlitzer photoplayer section of this book).

How many photoplayers were made? The exact figure will never be known. In 1921 there were 17,824 theatres devoted exclusively to the showing of moving pictures, according to a film industry yearbook of that date. If we estimate that 1,000 of these theatres in 1921 had pipe organs (Wurlitzer, the largest maker of theatre pipe organs, had completed just over 500 instruments by the end of that year), this leaves nearly 17,000 theatres as potential candidates for a photoplayer. Most theatres, possibly half of that total, provided music simply by having a full-time pianist play by hand during the shows. Possibly a few hundred others had more elaborate music provided by a small group of musicians or an orchestra.

Subtract further an amount to account for some theatres having no music at all (Vachel Lindsay, the poet, was a prolific writer about the film industry during its early years. A favorite Lindsay complaint was that theatres without music usually were filled with the sounds of loud talking by the audience), and you have a possibility of several thousand theatres that might have employed photoplayers. It is the author's estimate that about 8,000 to 10,000 photoplayers were made in America and Europe during the 1910-1928 years. Best sellers were the Reproduco (made by Operators Piano Company), American Photo Player Company instruments, and those made by Seeburg and Wurlitzer.

In 1916 Wurlitzer advertised that "every day more than two

million people listen to Wurlitzer music!" By 1928 the popularity of sound movies virtually ended the market for photoplayers and theatre organs. The photoplayer business was dead by 1930.

Photoplayers, once plentiful, are rare today. What happened to them all? Fires, floods, termites, the scrap heap – each consumed many. When collecting old-time orchestrions, photoplayers, and related instruments became popular in the 1950's most such instruments were nowhere to be found. Only a few dozen photoplayers survive today.

---

## OTHER TYPES OF INSTRUMENTS

In addition to coin pianos, orchestrions, and photoplayers, several other types of automatic instruments found use in public places during the late 19th and early 20th centuries. Among these are:

VIOLIN PLAYERS: The challenge of playing the violin by mechanical means has appealed to many persons over the years. Professor Wauters, who was employed by the Automatic Musical Company of Binghamton, New York, made several models of the Royal Violista, a pneumatically-operated automatic violin, in the 1908-1910 years. First announced in 1907, the Royal Violista was said at that time to have been "the culmination of seven years of continuous labor and experiment." Hegeler & Ehlers, a German firm, marketed a piano with a violin attachment in 1908. The instrument, given the name of Geigenpiano ("violin piano" in German), was evidently produced in small numbers. J.W. Whitlock of Rising Sun, Indiana, experimented in the early 20th century with an automatically-played cello which employed 15 rosined discs which played on as many strings. The project was abandoned, however, before the prototype model was completed. E. Dienst of Leipzig and J.D. Philipps & Sons of Frankfurt-am-Main each experimented with violin players. The Dienst barrel-operated violin player was produced in modest numbers.

In the 1920's two French inventors, Emile d'Aubry and Gabriel Boreau, devised the Violonista, a violin player which utilized a mechanical bow and which was activated by a pneumatic mechanism.

In the late 1920's Popper & Co. introduced the Violinovo, a roll-operated violin player. Although the instrument was featured in music industry trade advertisements for several years, few instruments were sold.

Of the many attempts to make a violin-playing device, only two ever achieved commercial success. The Virtuosa, an automatic violin-player invented by H.K. Sandell and made by the Mills Novelty Company in the early 20th century, was made in limited numbers. In 1909, the Pianova-Virtuosa, later called the Violano-Virtuoso, was exhibited at the Alaska-Yukon-Pacific Exposition. This instrument featured a violin on which four strings were played by revolving rosined celluloid discs. Accompaniment was provided by a 44-note piano. The Violano-Virtuoso was electrically (rather than pneumatically) operated. The instrument was a great success, and Mills sold over 4,000 Violano-Virtuosos in the 'teens and 'twenties. Capitalizing on its success with the Violano-Virtuoso, Mills produced the Viol-Xylophone (violin and xylophone combination), the String Quartette (several automatically-played violins and a cello), and the Viol-Cello (violin and cello combination), but none of these other instruments was ever commercially successful.

Ludwig Hupfeld produced the Violina, a device containing three real violins. On each violin one string was played (giving a total of three playing strings in all) by a rotating horsehair bow. The Violina was produced in combination with the Clavitist (a basic coin-operated piano), the Phonoliszt (an expression piano), and the Dea (a reproducing piano). Shortly after 1910 the Phonoliszt-Violina became the standard model, and the others were dropped. Although production figures are not known, it has been estimated that perhaps 10,000 Phonoliszt-Violina instruments were made from then until 1930. 600 Phonoliszt-Violinas were sold in the city of Antwerp, Belgium, alone! In the late 1920's another variation of the Violina, the Violina Orchestra, was produced. This instrument consisted of three violins (playing one string each) in combination with a piano and other effects. The Violina and its many forms are discussed in the Hupfeld section of this book.

BANJO PLAYERS: The only such instrument ever made in quantity was the Encore Automatic Banjo. The fascinating business history of the Auto Manufacturing Company, one of two firms which made Encore Banjos, is given in detail elsewhere in this book. The Banjorchestra, an Encore Banjo in combination with a piano and other effects, was sold in the 'teens by Peerless and by Connorized.

AUTOMATIC HARP: The Automatic Harp, produced by the J.W. Whitlock Company of Rising Sun, Indiana, was sold by the Rudolph Wurlitzer Co. It was popular during the 1905-1915 decade.

SELF-PLAYING XYLOPHONE: Actually a misnomer, the Self-Playing Xylophone consisted of a series of automatically-played orchestra bells (made of metal). It was made by the Automatic Musical Company of Binghamton, New York.

AUTOMATIC CHRYSOGLOTT: A self-playing chrysoglott (metal bars with resonators, played by felt-tipped piano-like hammers), the Resotone Grand, was sold by the Resotone Grand Company of New York City. Evidently a large market was envisioned as the firm produced several dozen different multi-tune music rolls for the instrument, but few Resotone Grands were ever sold.

---

## FEATURES OF COIN PIANOS, ORCHESTRIONS AND RELATED INSTRUMENTS

### Construction of Cases and Cabinets

Woods Used: By far the most popular wood finish used for coin-operated pianos, orchestrions, and photoplayers was oak. American-made instruments used quartered oak with a prominent grain pattern; European-made instruments used straight-sawed oak. To a much lesser extent, walnut and mahogany were used.

Surface Finishes: Most instruments were finished in the natural wood color. White, green, or brown fillers rubbed into the grain of light or dark-stained or black-painted oak produced a beautiful finish. This technique was employed by Wurlitzer, Hupfeld, and several others. White-painted and gold-trimmed orchestrions were occasionally made by Welte, Imhof & Mukle, Philipps, Hupfeld, and Wurlitzer. Certain Pianolin instruments made by the North Tonawanda Musical Instrument Works and certain Cremona orchestrions made by the Marquette Piano Company, to cite just two examples, were also made in this finish. Seeburg instruments of the early years have a dark finish made by rubbing black filler into the open grain of the oak surface. Many cabinet-style Seeburg instruments of the 'twenties have a whitish finish, somewhat like limed oak in appearance.

Ornamentation: American-made keyboard-type instruments made during the 1900-1910 years usually had beveled clear glass panels; instruments made after that date usually had art glass panels. European-made keyboard-type instruments usually had beveled mirrored panels or cloth-backed panels with brass or other decorative grillwork; art glass was rarely used. Large keyboardless orchestrions of the cylinder-operated type (e.g., those by Welte, Imhof & Mukle, et al) usually were made with clear glass windows on the front and each side; sometimes cloth panels were used. Large keyboardless piano orchestrions of later years were decorated with art glass panels, beveled mirrors, grillwork, and other embellishments. Lamps made of art glass were used on many American instruments, particularly those of the 1910-1920 decade. European instruments used brass lamps with beaded glass fringes. The rotating "wonder light" was a popular addition to certain Wurlitzer instruments and to many different types of European orchestrions. Motion-picture effects were available on most types of orchestrions built during the 1900-1920 years. These effects consisted of a painted scene (on glass or parchment sandwiched between clear glass) on the back of which were projected silhouettes of zeppelins, trains, volcano eruptions, aeroplanes, and other moving things.

## Extra Instruments Used

The mandolin attachment was a basic feature of many coin pianos. In its simplest form this attachment consisted of a cloth or leather strip on which metal studs were affixed. When called for by the music roll, the mandolin strip or bar would drop between the piano hammers and the piano strings. A metallic mandolin-like tone resulted. Many varieties of mandolin attachments were made, including the Nelson-Wiggen "banjo attachment" which used hardwood blocks instead of metal studs, the Coinola (also used by others) system which used a series of wood pegs, and an early Seeburg system which used a series of brass strips which rested against the piano strings (below the hammer striking point) and which vibrated against the strings after they were struck. A special type of mandolin attachment, the so-called "harp effect," was used on certain large Wurlitzer, Philipps, and Hupfeld orchestrions. This device consisted of a separate belt-driven reiterating set of wooden hammers which struck the piano strings above the regular piano hammers. A similar device was used for the mandolin portion of the Wurlitzer Mandolin Quartette and Sextette.

Pipes used in keyboard-type pianos and orchestrions were usually of the violin or flute type. These pipes, technically called "flue pipes," generate sound by the action of air against the pipe mouth. Unlike reed pipes (which generate their tone by the vibrating action of a free or a beating reed), flue-type pipes require a minimum of tuning and adjusting. The raspy sound of violin pipes could, with proper tuning and with appropriate arrangement of the notes in the music roll, imitate the sound of a violin in a creditable manner. Certain pianos with violin pipes were thus designated as "violin pianos."

Larger instruments, particularly keyboardless orchestrions, used other varieties of pipes in addition to flute and violin. Larger-scale string-family pipes representing the effects of viola and violoncello were popular. Smaller-scale flutes representing piccolos, and larger-scale flutes or bourdons were also popular. Reed-type pipes used in large orchestrions and photoplayers included clarinets (the most popular), oboe horn (or jazz trumpet), and, in certain early instruments, brass trumpets and trombones.

The volume of a given rank of pipes is dependent upon two factors: (1) the wind pressure used, and (2) the voicing or tonal character. Hupfeld, for one, offered orchestrions with three types of voicing: soft, medium, and loud. Presumably the wind pressures varied in each instrument also. Most 19th century orchestrions used about 1 to 3 inches of pressure in the pipe chests. Piano orchestrions of the 20th century used, for the most part, 6 to 8 inches.

Only rarely did a coin piano, orchestrion, or photoplayer manufacturer build his own pianos. These were usually ordered from a piano factory. In America the Haddorff Piano Company, the Seybold Piano Company, and several others supplied most of the pianos used by coin piano makers. Only a few firms (Wurlitzer, for example) made their own. In Europe the same practice was followed. Rönisch, Lipp, Irmler, Schwander, and other pianos were used. Some factories installed cheaper pianos in their less expensive models and high-quality pianos (Lipp and Feurich, for example) in their higher-priced instruments. Contrary to popular opinion, pianos used in coin-operated instruments were often of much higher average quality than were typical instruments sold for home use. They had to be durably built in order to stand the heavy use they sustained!

Orchestra bells, usually of the metal-bar type (but occasionally of the tubular type or of the saucer bell type), were a popular addition. In America they were used by Wurlitzer, Nelson-Wiggen, Marquette, Operators, and several other makers. In Europe nearly all coin-operated piano makers used them. Xylophone bars (made of wood) were likewise used. Often a manufacturer would use one type and not the other. For instance, Wurlitzer instruments often included bells; rarely a xylophone. For Seeburg instruments the opposite was true.

Drum and trap effects used in coin pianos, orchestrions, and photoplayers were varied. Basic orchestrions usually were equipped with a bass drum and a snare drum. Sometimes a tympani or kettle-drum effect would be achieved by installing two extra single-stroke beaters or one extra reiterating beater on the bass drum. A cymbal and triangle were two other popular additions. Used less often were such percussion effects as a tenor drum (a small-size drum without snares), wood block, castanets, tambourine, tubular chimes, tom-tom, and crash cymbal. Photoplayers, especially very large ones, incorporated many different and unusual sound effects including bird whistle, fire gong, crockery smash, locomotive whistle, pistol shot, and other imaginative items.

## Expression Capabilities

Most smaller types of coin pianos used the piano soft pedal and sustaining pedal for expression effects. Most American-made keyboard-type orchestrions had no additional expression capability except for a loud-soft control on the drums. The intensity of the pipes is not regulatable.

Swell shutters were used in a few types of American-made keyboard instruments (certain Wurlitzer and Coinola instruments are examples). Swell shutters, or louvers, were used in nearly all photoplayers and in many types of European orchestrions, large and small. The volume of the pipes was controlled by the shutter opening: in the closed position the pipes played softly; open, they played loudly. Some instruments provided for the shutters to be partially open in any one of several degrees.

Certain types of pianos provided additional expression by varying the vacuum level used in the piano pneumatic stack. The Seeburg Style X and the Wurlitzer Autograph Piano are two examples of such instruments sold in America. In Europe many different expression-type pianos were used in commercial locations. The Popper Stella, the Hupfeld Phonoliszt, and the Philipps Duca are examples. Certain types of large orchestrions incorporated expression pianos. These orchestrions were capable of very sophisticated musical effects.

## Other Aspects

Coin Operation: Most American-made coin pianos and orchestrions were equipped with coin slots. In addition, it was a usual practice to install wallboxes at different locations around a restaurant, tavern, etc. For this purpose Seeburg, Mills, Wurlitzer, and other makers furnished wallboxes, usually for about $5 to $10 each. In Europe it was the practice to use wallboxes on all instruments, large and small. Only rarely were pianos and orchestrions equipped with coin slots. In America and in Europe owners of very large orchestrions would often have special program cards printed. A patron could thereby request a particular tune, and the waiter or restaurant attendant would play it for him. Sometimes a varying price schedule was charged, depending upon the length of the tune. A short selection might cost 5c; a long one, 10c or 20c. A few Hupfeld instruments were equipped with remote-selecting wallboxes which enabled the patron to select from a distance the tune desired. Usually the owner of the instrument would install a push button behind the bar or counter. During slow times he would furnish music "on the house." Wurlitzer recommended that PianOrchestra owners do this between busy periods. Most American-made pianos were equipped with an accumulator device whereby 10, 15, or 20 coins could be deposited at one time, and then an equivalent number of tunes would play. Most European-made instruments were not equipped with accumulators and would register just one coin at a time.

Solo Arrangements: Certain types of coin piano and orchestrion rolls feature solo arrangments. Such arrangements have the xylophone, orchestra bells, pipes, or other extra instruments scored separately in the music roll. As such scoring is usually done in the upper two octaves or so of the piano note scale, the piano is muffled or disengaged in that section when the solo part plays. (Otherwise the piano and the solo instrument would play the same notes at the same time, and the solo effect would be lost.) Instruments which play solo arrangements are considered to be particularly desirable by collectors today.

Sales and Distribution: Most manufacturers sold their instruments through music dealers. Such dealers would often handle several different lines of instruments at the same time. The sales through such outlets varied. Extremes are provided by such examples as a Canton, Pennsylvania, music store which sold just one automatic instrument (a Wurlitzer Pianino sold in 1916), and Duwaer & Naessens, an Amsterdam, Holland, outlet for Hupfeld, Welte, and others, a firm which sold approximately 6,000 Hupfeld coin-operated instruments over the years. The discount policy of the manufacturers varied. In America, Wurlitzer might typically charge $1500 wholesale and $2100 retail for a given instrument; Seeburg, $900 to $1200 wholesale for an instrument with the same retail value. As might be expected, Seeburg achieved more sales through independent dealers. Wurlitzer had its own company-owned outlets in many leading cities. Most dealers offered time payment plans whereby a customer could pay 10% to 25% down and then pay for the balance over a period of time with receipts from its cash box. Many sales were made directly to route operators by the manufacturers. An active operator might maintain a route of 100 to 300 instruments. Link, Seeburg, Western Electric, and the Operators Piano Company were particularly active in this field. Sometimes manufacturers would put their own instruments out on location. Various Wurlitzer agencies did this, as did the Auto Manufacturing Company (maker of the Encore Banjo), National (of Grand Rapids, Michigan), and several others.

Collecting Coin-Operated Pianos Today: Coin-operated pianos and orchestrions are popular collectors' items today. Examples of most different types, particularly of the smaller sizes, survive today – although none is really common. In America the two most plentiful (but not necessarily the least expensive) such instruments today are the Seeburg Style L cabinet A-roll piano and the Mills Violano-Virtuoso (of the single-violin type). Certain other instruments, many varieties of large Hupfeld, Philipps, Weber, and Welte orchestrions, for example, are unknown today. All types of coin pianos and orchestrions are enthusiastically collected. Part of their appeal, if not most of it, is their lively and entertaining music. But part is also the romance attached to such instruments – the thought of the "good old days" and all the enjoyment the instruments once provided.

Mechanical Zither „Arpanetta“ with interchangeable music sheets.
Cítara mecánica „Arpanetta“ con hojas de música para cambiar.

—"Arpanetta" Mechanical Zither—

The Arpanetta, a mechanical zither marketed around the turn of the 20th century, used folding cardboard music books. Apparently only a few Arpanettas were ever sold.

A somewhat similar instrument, the Volks Klavier (not illustrated), used a heavy paper strip and was popular in Germany around the turn of the 20th century.

The Triola mechanical zither was made by the thousands from the late 'teens through the 1920's. Using a 25-note paper roll the Triola is played by turning a crank at the lower right of the instrument. Only the treble notes are played automatically. The bass notes are played by watching for the numbers 1 through 6 printed on the roll and strumming the desired group of bass strings when the numbers appear.

The Triola patents were issued to Paul Riessner in 1919.

## CHORDEPHON MECHANICAL ZITHER

—Chordephon Musikwerke; Leipzig—

Introduced in the early 1890's, the first Chordephons were hand-cranked. Spring-wound models appeared in 1896 and coin-operated models shortly thereafter. Produced by the Chordephon Fabrik von Musikwerken (Claus & Co.), Chordephon mechanical zithers were sold by sales agents all over the world. H. Peters & Co. and Ludwig Hupfeld, both of Leipzig, were the main wholesale distributors.

Chordephons were made in several sizes. The most popular was the 44-note system which used 36 cm. diameter discs. Although instruments were sold for several years thereafter, the main years of Chordephon popularity were from 1895 to 1910. Toward the end of that period Chordephon sales declined, mostly from a waning interest in disc-type "music boxes," but also due to competition from Lochmann, Polyphon, and others who made mechanical instruments with a zither-like sound.

Later (c.1912) advertisements for the Chordephon appear under the name of Weissbach & Co., the firm which also manufactured the Komet series of disc-type music boxes. The factory was located at Georgstrasse 8, Leipzig-Gohlis.

Today, Chordephons are regarded as very desirable instruments by collectors. Properly tuned and regulated the Chordephon plays with a brilliant ringing zither-like sound.

---

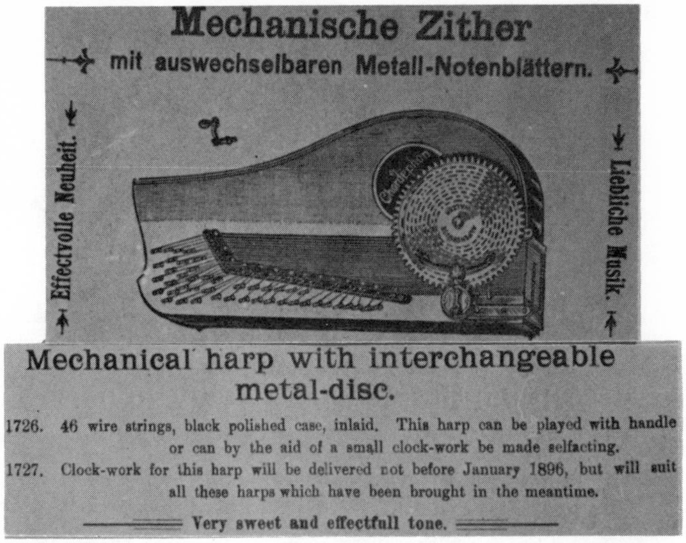


Early Chordephon advertisement from 1895 catalogue. Hand-cranked, but the notice is given that clockwork (spring-wound) models will be available in 1896.

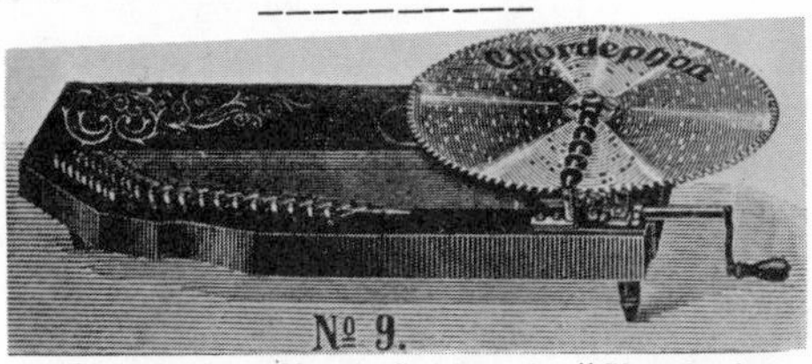


Chordephon No. 9. Sold as the "Chordephon Bijou." 30-note size. Hand cranked. Measures 50 cm. wide by 22 cm. deep by 11 cm. high. Sold for 48 German marks in 1904. Discs measured 28.5 cm. in diameter and cost 1.40 marks each.

Chordephon No. 10. 44-note size. "Plays for six minutes" using the clockwork mechanism (shown separately above the instrument; the clockwork fit under the instrument when in use). Sold for 76.50 marks in 1900.

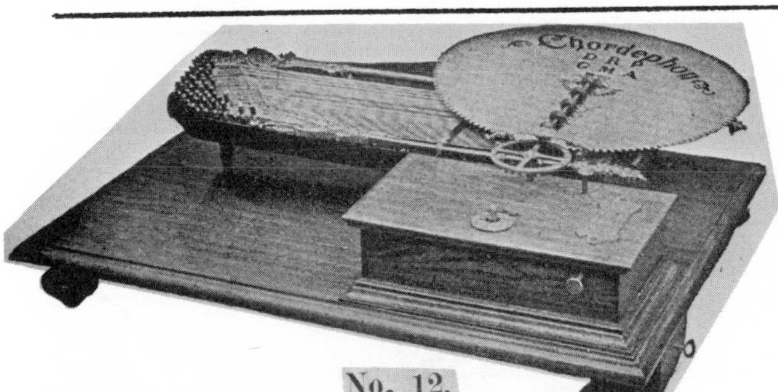


Chordephon Nos. 11, 12, 12-A. In 1900 this model was designated as No.11 if operated by an on-off lever; 12-A if coin-operated. In 1904 the designation was changed to No. 12 (coin-operated) and No. 11 was discontinued. "Plays for ten minutes." 44 notes. No. 11 cost 183 marks in 1900; 12-A, 198.75 marks. No. 12 cost 265 marks in 1904. Extra 36 cm. diameter tune discs cost 2.80 marks each.

Chordephon No. 15. "Hand-Cranked Chordephon." 44-note size. Measures 65x25x12½ cm. Sold for 45 marks in 1900.

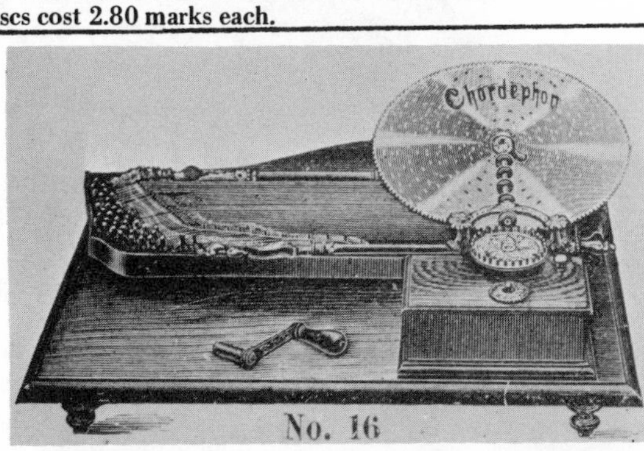


Chordephon No. 16. The "Salon Chordephon." 44-note size. "Plays for six minutes." Measures 66x48x19 cm. Spring-wound. Sold for 144 marks in 1900; 192 marks in 1904.

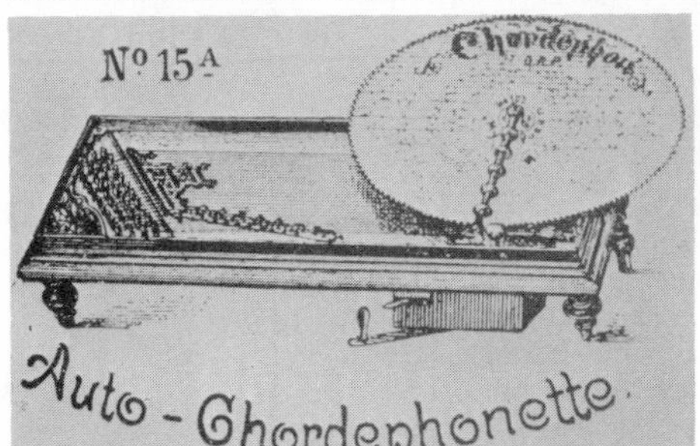


Chordephon No. 15-A. "Auto-Chordephonette." Clockwork version of No. 15. Sold for 90 marks in 1904.

Chordephon No. 17. 44-note size. Vertical format. Coin-operated. 116x60x22 cm. in size. Sold for 241.50 marks in 1900; 322 marks in 1905. Extra discs of the standard 44-note, 36 cm. diameter size sold for 2.25 marks in 1900; 2.80 marks in 1905.

Chordephon No. 18. 44-notes. 148x71x44 cm. "Plays 24 minutes." Sold for 434 marks in 1905.

Chordephon No. 19. 44-note size. Coin-operated (as are all of the vertical models shown here). 130x60x24 cm. size. "Plays for ten minutes on one winding." Sold for 276 marks in 1900; 368 marks in 1904.

Chordephon Nos. 21 and 21s. (21: top part only; 21s: with bottom stand.) "Plays for 24 minutes." Measurements of 21s: 240x84x58 cm. 44-note size. No. 21 sold for 405 marks in 1900; 21s for 502.50 marks.

Chordephon No. 20. 44-note size. 148x72x46 cm. "Plays for 24 minutes."

Coin-operated table model (mechanism built into top drawer) Chordephon. 1909 advertisement. The advertisement notes the availability of "Concert Zithers, Zither Quartettes, and Christmas articles."

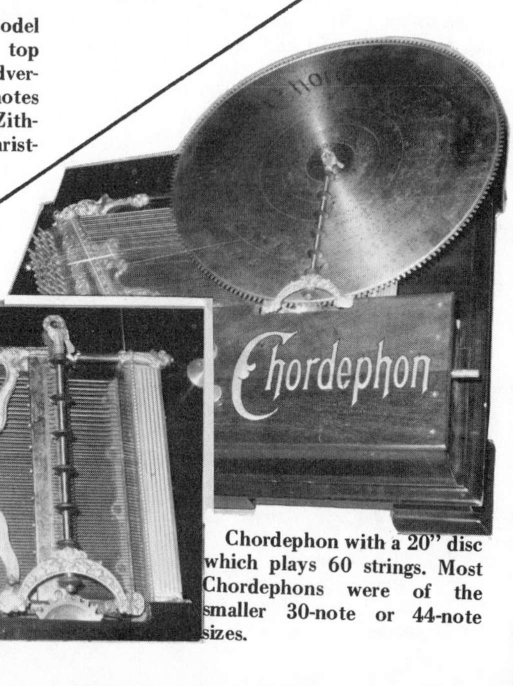


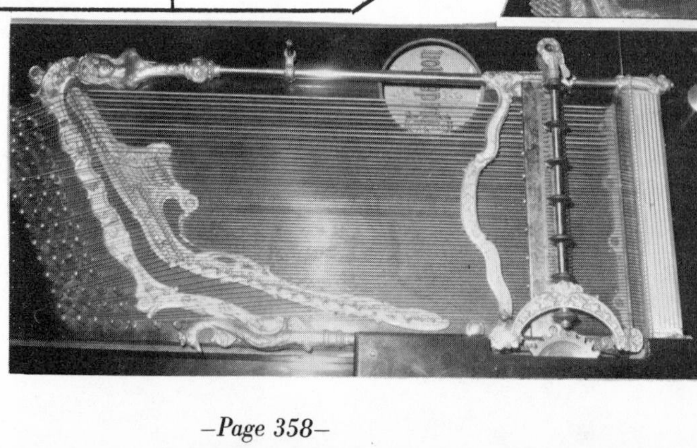

Chordephon with a 20" disc which plays 60 strings. Most Chordephons were of the smaller 30-note or 44-note sizes.

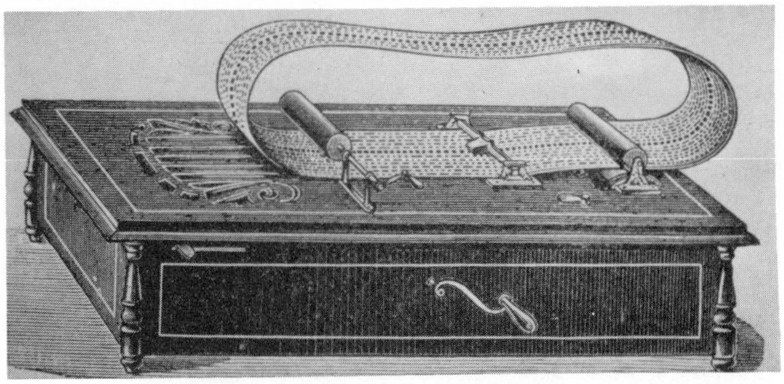

Orpheus Mechanical Zither. Two main models, each of 24-note size. No. 18 with long legs on the case is shown above. This instrument sold for 116 German marks in 1904. No. 17 is of similar design but has short legs. The instruments measure 89 cm. long by 45 cm. wide.

The Orpheus used 33 cm. diameter 24-note Ariston (hand-cranked reed organ or organette) discs.

The Melodette, or Automatic Piano,
The most marvellous mechanical invention of the age. It will play any tune that ever was written, in a melodious and pleasing manner. Difficult and simple music produced in a masterly style, and it can be played by a child as well as by a grown person, and will furnish music for social gatherings of any description, playing hour after hour, without any knowledge of music being required in the operation. The most wonderful of all musical inventions; a machine which in a purely mechanical manner produces any kind of music, Waltzes, Polkas, Marches, &c., &c., without any practice or knowledge of music whatever; in this respect far superior to any music-box, even though it costs many times as much, for there is no limit whatever to the number of tunes it will play. This instrument is on a somewhat similar principle to the wonderful Phonograph, the perforations in a flexible strip producing the effect. It has just been perfected (the accompanying cut showing it in its improved form), and is having the largest sale ever obtained by a musical instrument in the country. It has solid metal cases in imitation of green bronze; the notes or bars (the music producers) are metal, on same principle as a tuning-fork, which produce clear and most melodious notes, and never get out of tune; the bars are struck by strikers, the same as the wires are in a piano, only they work automatically instead of by the fingers. The strip of prepared paper in which the tune is stamped or perforated, is about 10 inches wide, and as it passes through the rollers and over the keys the strikers spring through the perforations in the paper and strike the right note; this is all done automatically, without any assistance from the operator (except turning the rollers), and the tune is played perfectly. It would be one of the most appropriate presents to make anyone, especially where there is no other musical instrument. Its execution is admirable, and its capacity or capability almost unlimited. It is selling faster than any musical instrument ever invented. The music is fine, and everybody delighted. The regular retail price of the Melodette is only $5, including a selection of popular tunes. Address, The Massachusetts Organ Co., 57 Washington Street Boston, Mass., U. S. A., Sole Manufacturers. SPECIAL OFFER—Agents Wanted—We wish a good Agent in every town, and big money can be made selling these instruments. We will send a sample instrument to any one wishing to act as our agent, for $3.25, Boxed Free, including music price lists, etc., and will give territory. Order at once. $50 a week easily made. We have 1000 testimonials.


The Melodette or Automatic Piano was sold in the 1880's and 1890's by the Massachusetts Organ Company of Boston. The Massachusetts Organ Co., a master of ballyhoo advertising, describes the instrument in terms similar to that used for the many organettes sold at the same time by the firm.

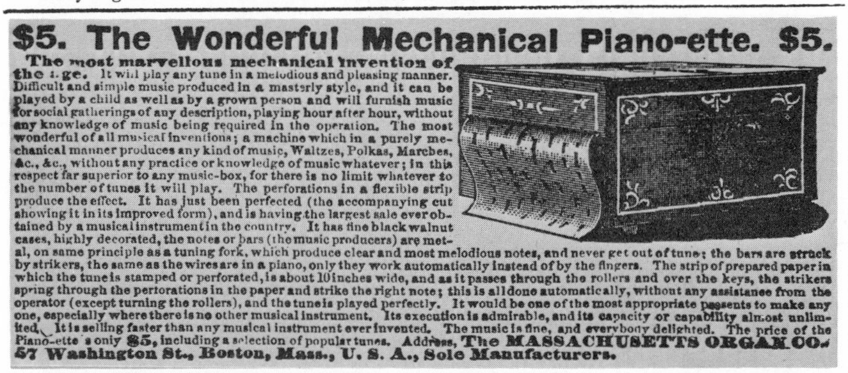

$5. The Wonderful Mechanical Piano-ette. $5.
The most marvellous mechanical invention of the age. It will play any tune in a melodious and pleasing manner. Difficult and simple music produced in a masterly style, and it can be played by a child as well as by a grown person and will furnish music for social gatherings of any description, playing hour after hour, without any knowledge of music being required in the operation. The most wonderful of all musical inventions; a machine which in a purely mechanical manner produces any kind of music, Waltzes, Polkas, Marches, &c., &c., without any practice or knowledge of music whatever; in this respect far superior to any music-box, for there is no limit whatever to the number of tunes it will play. The perforations in a flexible strip produce the effect. It has just been perfected (the accompanying cut showing it in its improved form), and is having the largest sale ever obtained by a musical instrument in the country. It has fine black walnut cases, highly decorated, the notes or bars (the music producers) are metal, on same principle as a tuning fork, which produce clear and most melodious notes, and never get out of tune; the bars are struck by strikers, the same as the wires are in a piano, only they work automatically instead of by the fingers. The strip of prepared paper in which the tune is stamped or perforated, is about 10 inches wide, and as it passes through the rollers and over the keys, the strikers spring through the perforations in the paper and strike the right note; this is all done automatically, without any assistance from the operator (except turning the rollers), and the tune is played perfectly. It would be one of the most appropriate presents to make any one, especially where there is no other musical instrument. Its execution is admirable, and its capacity or capability almost unlimited. It is selling faster than any musical instrument ever invented. The music is fine, and everybody delighted. The price of the Piano-ette is only $5, including a selection of popular tunes. Address, The MASSACHUSETTS ORGAN CO. 57 Washington St., Boston, Mass., U. S. A., Sole Manufacturers.


The Mechanical Piano-ette plays tuned metal bars and was marketed with the similar Melodette by the Massachusetts Organ Co. Despite the claim that "It is selling faster than any musical instrument ever invented" (the same claim, illogically, was made at the same time for the Melodette!), few Piano-ettes were ever sold.

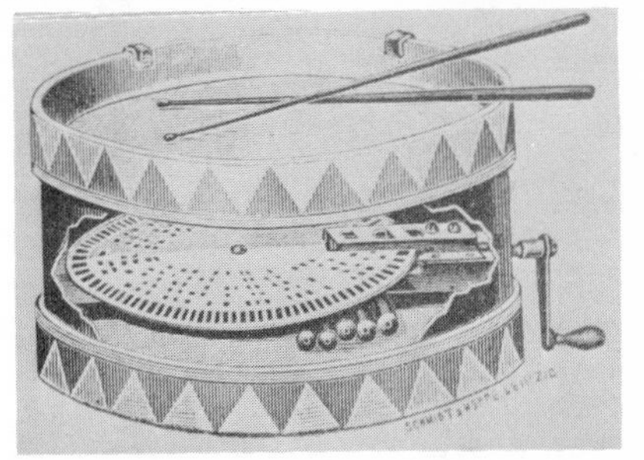

"Mechanical Drum," a disc-operated snare drum. Sold as a children's toy in 1905. "Plays infantry marches, cavalry marches, retreats," etc. according to the original catalogue.

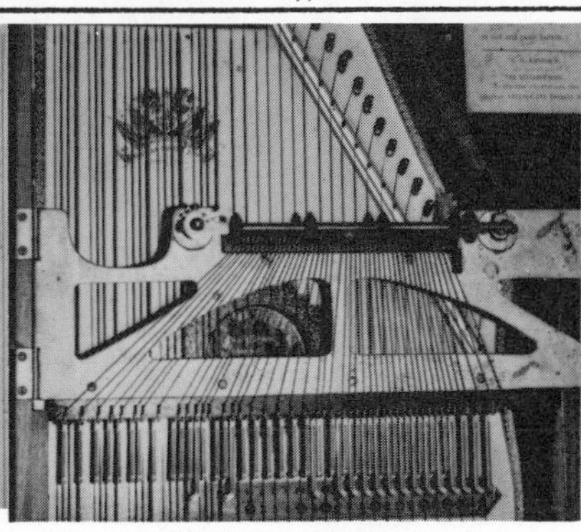

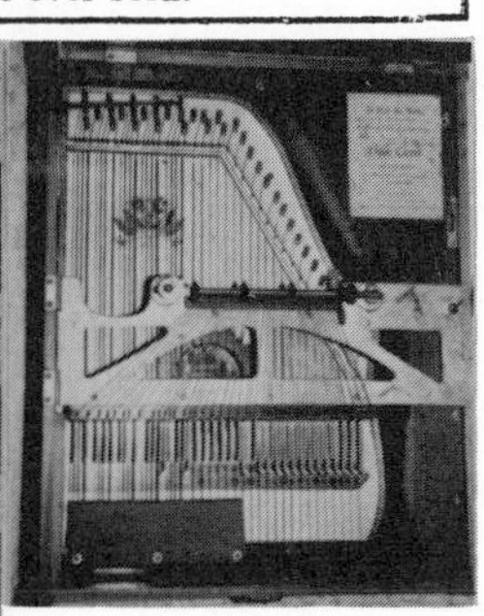

Guitarophone No. 2½.

—Guitarophone—

The Guitarophone, a mechanical zither, was made in several forms in the 1890's and later years. Illustrated here is a model labeled "Menzenhauer Guitar-Zither No. 2½. Patented May 29, 1894. Menzenhauer by Oscar Schmidt. American Guitar Zither." and the notation "U.S. Guitar Zither Co., Oscar Schmidt . . ." The device was patented in the U.S. under Nos. 147,341 and 147,342.

The Guitarophone, a device of German origin, was sold in America by the U.S. Guitar Zither Co. of 36-50 Ferry Street, Jersey City, N.J., a firm of which Henry Langfelder (who also worked with F.G. Otto & Co., makers of the Capital Cuff Box) was a principal. Langfelder returned to his native Germany in the late 1890's and headed Menzenhauer & Schmidt, a firm which acquired the Kalliope Musikwerke in 1919. Menzenhauer & Schmidt made many different forms of mechanical zithers, including models which used paper strips.

The instrument shown here is from the Amos Fowler Collection. It was distributed by a sales agent who labeled the box: "A.O. Krieger; New England Agent; The Guitarophone; 272 Hyde Park Avenue; Hyde Park, Massachusetts." The instrument measures 9½" high (lid closed) by 18" wide by 21½" deep. The Guitarophone is spring-wound and uses a 14½" disc with projections on the underside. The projections actuate tiny hammers which strike the strings. The instrument is coin operated via a 1c slot.

Hand-cranked pianos operated by folding cardboard music books were sold by the tens of thousands during the late 19th and early 20th centuries. Made mainly in Germany and Italy these instruments provided music by the action of a cardboard sheet as it passed over a spring-loaded key frame. Ratchet or sprocket driven music books were used in some models, but most used a system of rubber-covered pinch rollers to pull the music books through the key frame.

The book-operated pianos of this type usually have a ringing mandolin-like sound made possible by a reiterating piano hammer action.

The above instrument is shown with the key frame in the open position. (Lewis Graham photograph)

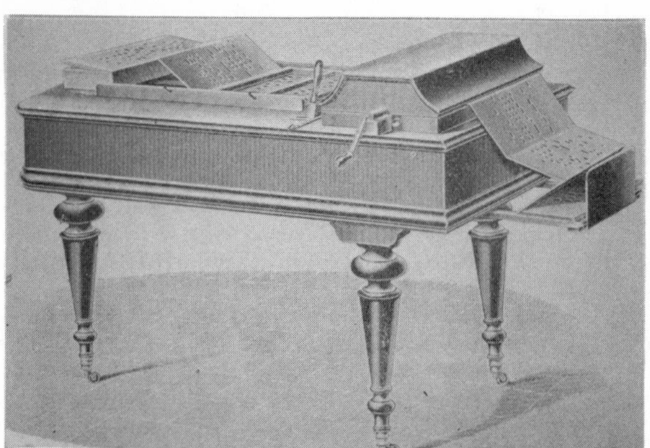

"Orchestra Piano" of 6-octave, 73-note range. Uses 46.3 cm.-wide music books. Sold for 800 German marks in 1904. "Classic repertoire of about 1000 music selections: operas, dances, marches, symphonies, fantasies, serenades, etc."

Advertisement for "Melody Pianos" made by G. Racca of Bologne, Italy. "10,000 instruments sold. 4 different models of 4 and 6 octaves." (from "Player Piano" by Arthur W.J.G. Ord-Hume)

"Piano Orchestrion" Model 2S (30-note in black finish); 2N (30-note in walnut); 3S (49-note in black finish). Available with drums and with coin operation at extra cost.

"Piano Orchestrion" Model 1S (in black finish); 1N (walnut). Cost 710 and 720 German marks in 1904.

"Piano Orchestrion" 30-note style. No. 4 (with hot air motor); No. 4E (with electric motor)

"Piano Orchestrion" Instruments

Operated by folding cardboard music books, these instruments, designated by such names as "Piano Orchestrion," "Piano Melodico," etc., were designed for home or public use ("It is sufficient for entertaining a party of 200 persons in a ballroom."). Most models were hand cranked, however some hot air motor models and some spring-wound (rare) models were produced. Coin slot models were made for use in cafes and other commercial locations. These instruments were exceedingly popular from about 1890 to 1910 and were sold by the tens of thousands, mainly in Europe and America.

"Piano Melodico." 30-note (54 strings) style. No.1 (black finish with gold engraving); No.1a (with mandolin effect and expression); No.3 (in deluxe case); No.3a (deluxe case; mandolin effect and expression). Cost from 160 to 268 marks in 1904. Deluxe case (with music shelf) shown above.

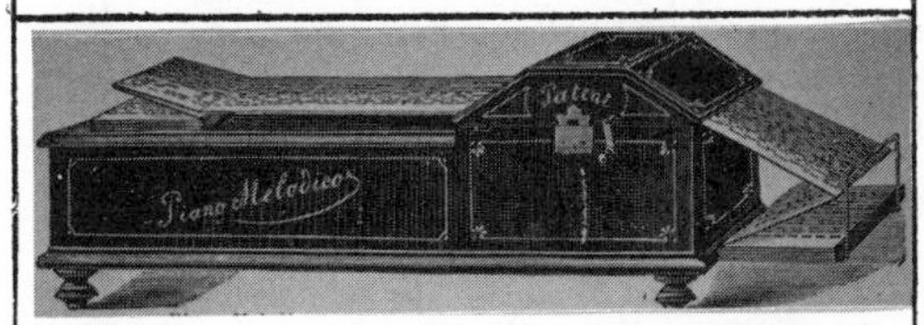


"Piano Melodico" – regular style No. 1 and 1a.

"Concerto No. 201." 89 steel strings. "Played with handle; automatic piano and forte regulator. Mandolin attachment. Elegant ebony cabinet." (circa 1895)

"Piano Melodico Orchestrion No. 19." 30 notes; 54 steel strings. Illustration from 1895 catalogue.

Left: Hupfeld's hand-cranked push-up piano playing apparatus as shown at the left used an Ariston-type disc and had a 36-note range. In 1900 this device sold for 90 marks (hand-cranked model) or 100 marks (spring-wound model). Discs were 1.50 marks apiece. Designated as "Hupfeld's Pianoplaying Apparatus No. 10" this appliance was sold worldwide.

The "Antiphonel," patented by Alexander DeBain, a Frenchman, in 1846, uses rectangular wood "planchettes" as its music source. Each planchette is studded with pins. Arthur W.J.G. Ord-Hume quotes the description of this instrument as it appeared in the catalogue of the Great Exhibition of 1851: "The projections [of the key frame] are pressed down to perform the music by a piece of hard wood, studded with pins, which is forced over the surface. The piece is held down by a bar placed over it, and the pressure regulated by springs. Having placed [the planchette] on the Antiphonel, it is passed over the key frame by turning a handle, and as the pins on the [planchette] come into contact with the Antiphonel keys, the notes are struck, which are loud or soft as required. The [planchettes] may be from 4" to 24" long. 8" will contain as much as is written on a page of music paper. Any number of pieces may be used for compositions of greater length. . ."

Another version of the Antiphonel consisted of a portable device which could be placed on the keyboard of a piano or organ and operated in the manner described above.

(Lewis Graham photograph)

Hupfeld's Pianospiel-Apparat No. 20–21
zum Vorstellen. 61 Tasten spielend.


Hupfeld's "vorsetzer"-type piano player. 61 notes. Made in rewind (as shown) and endless roll styles. Sold in large numbers from about 1895 to 1905.

Hupfeld's patented piano-playing mechanism had a 61-key range. In America a similar device was sold as the "Pianotist." In 1900 Hupfeld advertised that "about 4000 of these instruments and over 1,000,000 meters of music have been sold."

Hupfeld's piano player powered by a water motor attached to a pipe line. In the 1890-1905 years when home electric power was in its infancy Hupfeld and other makers offered water motors, hot air engines, battery sets, and large spring motors as power sources.

Piano of the street piano type with a cardboard roll music system instead of the usual pinned cylinder. Made in 43 and 53 note sizes. Illustration from an 1895 catalogue.

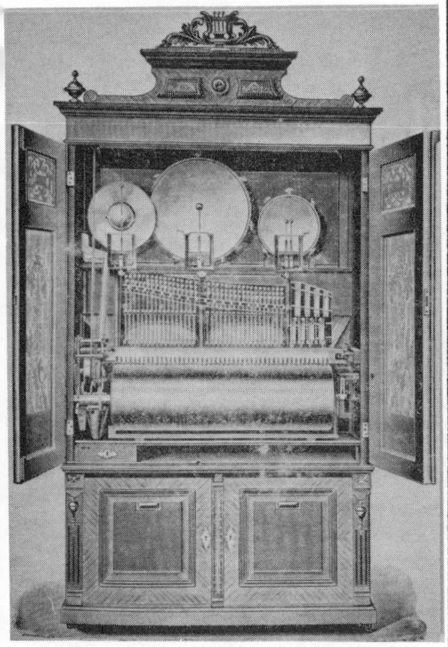

"Orpheus No. II Piano Orchestrion," a barrel-operated piano with eight orchestra bells and with percussion effects. "Ideal for dance music in large locations." This instrument sold in Germany for 1560 marks in 1904. Extra cylinders of eight tunes each cost 150 marks.

Similar instruments were made in France, Belgium, Italy, America, and other countries. This general type of instrument achieved its height of popularity from about 1880 to 1905, although production extended much earlier and much later.

The "Excelsior Piano Orchestrion," a 51-note piano with eight bells and two drums, used an 8-tune cylinder which measured 11¼" in diameter. Power was provided by turning a flywheel at the left rear of the instrument. The line engraving shown above appeared in several European musical merchandise catalogues from 1895 to 1905.

Such instruments were made in hundreds of different case and style variations. Those shown on this page are typical.

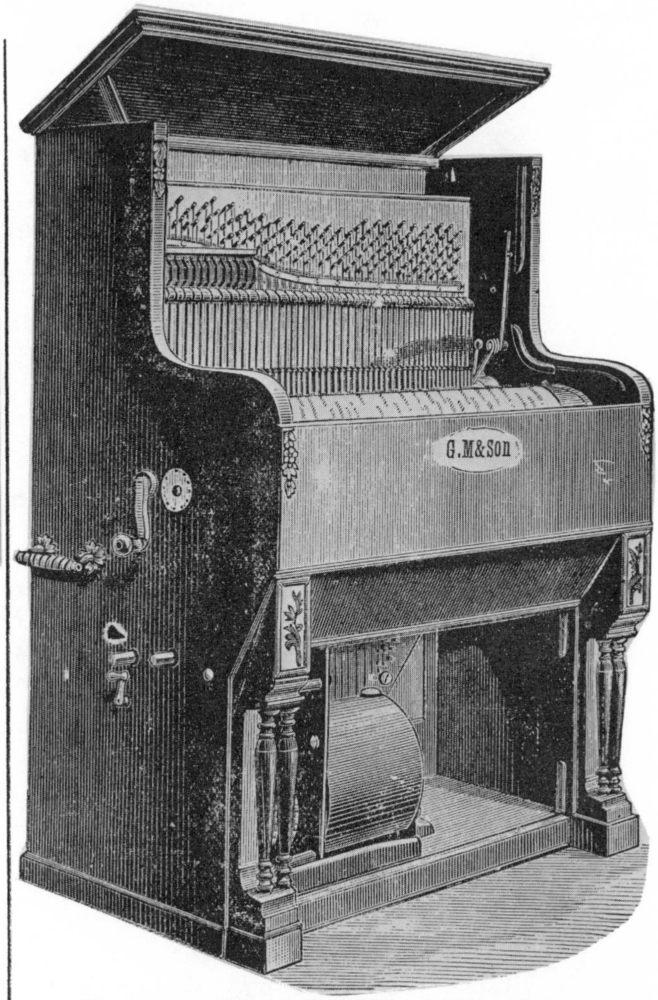


Barrel-operated piano sold by Molinari & Son of New York City (see Molinari organ section of this book).

## Grand piano orchestrion No. 143.

Played by handle or driven by motor. 61 notes, best pianoforte wire strings, full iron frame large barrel playing 8 large tunes; 8 sets of bells, bass drum, patented wire drum, timpani, self-acting dampers. Solid oak case 76 × 56 × 29 inches.

**No. 144.** The same but with 71 notes and 11 sets of bells. Most powerful effective tone.

Left: "Grand Piano Orchestrion," a 61-note hand-cranked barrel piano as illustrated in an 1895 catalogue of Peters & Co. of Leipzig, Germany.

—Cylinder or Barrel-Operated Pianos—

These instruments are commonly called "street pianos" by collectors today. In their basic form these instruments consist of a barrel-operated keyboardless piano which is operated by turning a hand crank. Often extra effects were added: a set of bells, one or two drums, or a xylophone. Smaller models were mounted on 2-wheeled carts and played in city streets. At one time street pianos were a common sight in many large U.S. cities. In Europe such instruments were especially popular in Italy, Spain, and England.

Larger instruments (such as the one shown at the upper left of this page) were made for stationary use in dance halls, restaurants, and similar locations. Many of these, particularly those made in Belgium, France, and Italy, had very ornate fronts with frosted beveled glass panels, ornate carvings and inlay, and other decorations. Some were made in imitation of other instrument designs. Van Roy, a Belgian maker, produced several barrel pianos which had the external appearance of miniature Hupfeld Helios Ic/31 orchestrions. Others were made to appear like fairground organs (Gavioli made several models of these as did Limonaire).

Although some of the larger firms, Gavioli for instance, made barrel-operated pianos, the industry was primarily composed of dozens if not hundreds of small factories with from one to a half dozen employees. Such instruments were made in virtually every country in Europe. In America barrel-operated piano factories were mainly active in the larger eastern cities, particularly New York and Baltimore.

For detailed information about barrel-operated pianos the reader may refer to the book "Player Piano" by Arthur W.J.G. Ord-Hume; published by George Allen & Unwin, Ltd., London.

Early (c.1840) barrel-operated keyboard piano manufactured by Theodore C. Bates and Son of 6 Ludgate Hill, London. The Bates firm, maker of barrel organs and pianos, established a reputation for high quality instruments. In his book, "Player Piano," Arthur W.J.G. Ord-Hume notes that the Bates enterprise was situated at several different addresses in London over the years and was at 6 Ludgate Hill sometime in the 1833-1847 years. (Photograph by Lewis Graham; instrument presently in Bellm's Cars & Music of Yesterday Museum, Sarasota, Florida)

No. 43.
Mechanisches Cymbal-Pianette,
auch mit der Hand spielbar.
Grösste Neuheit. 44 Tasten. Grösste Neuheit
Grösse: 120 × 82 × 52. Netto-Gewicht ca. 100 kg.
Dieses Cymbal-Pianette ist ein neues, in Form eines Pianos ausgeführtes Saiten-Instrument, welches den nämlichen Ton erzeugt wie vorstehendes Cymbal No. 40. Dasselbe kann sowohl mechanisch als auch mit der Hand gespielt werden.

**Mechanical Cymbal-Pianette**

Made by J.M. Grob & Co. (predecessor of Ludwig Hupfeld A.G.; see Hupfeld section of this book), the Mechanical Cymbal-Pianette could be played mechanically or by hand. The compass was 44 notes.

**Gloria Concerto Orchestrion**

This piano orchestrion, sold by Hupfeld in 1900, used folding cardboard music books to play a 49-note scale (87 actual piano strings). Contains piano, bass and snare drums, cymbal, and triangle. Three mechanical figures.

Concerto No. 11

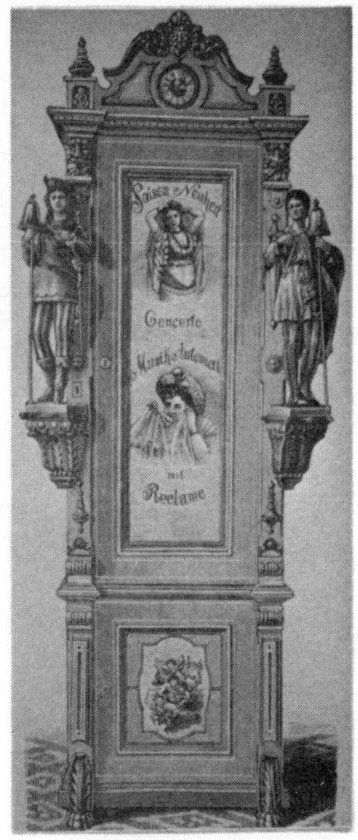

Concerto No. 12

**Concerto Orchestrion**

The above two styles were sold by Hupfeld in 1900. Instrumentation consists of piano strings, 15 bells, drum, and triangle. The music is in cardboard book form. Available were models powered by a hot air motor, spring clockwork mechanism, or electric motor.

Style 11 but without drum, bells, and triangle was known as Style 6. Style 12 but without statues and clock was known as Style 13. Models powered by a hot air motor were given the suffix M (as 11M); with electric motor, E; with spring mechanism ("Federwerk" in German), F.

Small hand-cranked mechanical pianos (often called "mechanical dulcimers" today) of the type illustrated above were made in large numbers during the 19th century. Such instruments were once popular in the streets of London and other cities. For this purpose they were outfitted with a carrying strap.

**Barrel Pianos**

The three barrel pianos shown above were among many models sold by Ludwig Hupfeld around the turn of the 20th century. The model at the upper left was designated as the "Piano Orchestrion No. 44" and contained 51 notes, 8 bells, and percussion effects. "Musical effect of ten musicians" noted the catalogue description. Sold for about 800 marks. The instrument centered above was designated as the "Excelsior Orchestrion No. 44" and contained the same instrumentation as Piano Orchestrion No. 44.

The instrument at the upper right was designated as the "Excelsior Piano Orchestrion." Available with or without coin slot and with electric motor or hot air motor operation.

## EARLY AUTOMATIC PIANOS

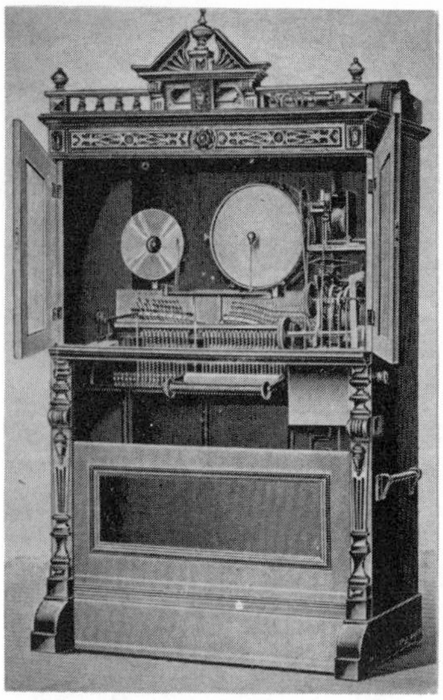

Left: "Piano Mandolin Orchestrion," an early (1904) instrument built both in barrel-operated and roll-operated (as illustrated) formats. Used a short (about 40' long) heavy paper roll. The mechanisms have many mechanical linkages as on barrel-operated pianos.

"Model K Pneumatic Orchestra Piano." Uses endless cardboard music books. Contains piano, orchestra bells, violin and flute pipes, bass and snare drums, and cymbal. Sold by J.M. Bon & Co. of Leipzig in 1904 (all instruments on this page are from the 1904 Bon catalogue).

"Model J-14 Pneumatic Orchestra Piano." With piano, bells, pipes (violin, flute, cello, and non-functional trumpets), bass and snare drums, and cymbal. Uses music books.

## SÄCHSISCHE ORCHESTER-MUSIKWERKE

—Leipzig-Wurzen, Germany—

This firm produced a series of colorful mechanical pianos. Those shown below were advertised c.1900-1905. Music was played via a system of hinged aluminum sheets as illustrated.

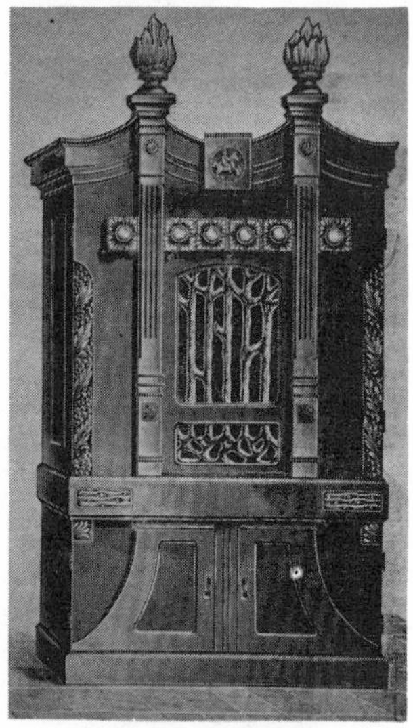

—Quintett, Model B—

—Trio, Model B—

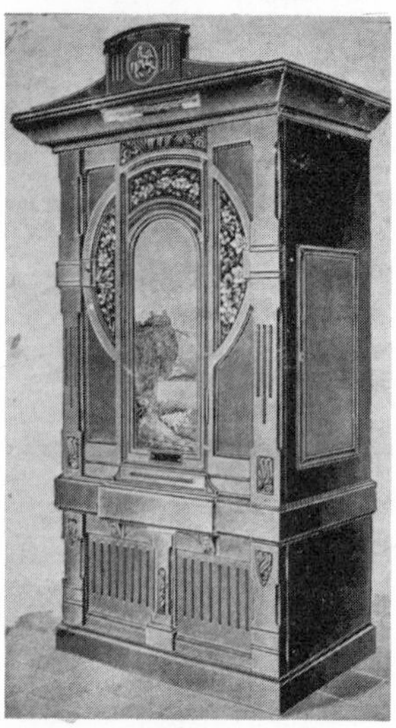

—Trio, Model W—

—Trio, Model M—

### —String Orchestras: Trio and Quintett—

Operated by music books made of hinged aluminum sheets, these instruments provided "string music for concert and dancing purposes."

Instrumentation of the Trio consists of a 76-key music system which plays violin, flute, "piano effect," bass and snare drums, cymbal, triangle and castanets. The Trio was made in several models including B, BE (with electric lighting effects), M, W (with lighting effects), and WO (same as W but without lighting effects).

Instrumentation of the Quintett consists of a 112-key music system which operates pipes (violin, flute, cello, clarinet), "piano effect," bass and snare drums, cymbal, triangle and castanets. Dimensions of the Model B Quintett: 2.9 meters high by 1.5 meters wide by 0.8 meters deep. Made with or without electric light effects on the front.

Cases of the Trio and Quintett were available in walnut, mahogany, or oak.

At the right are two views of the Model B Trio showing the interior.

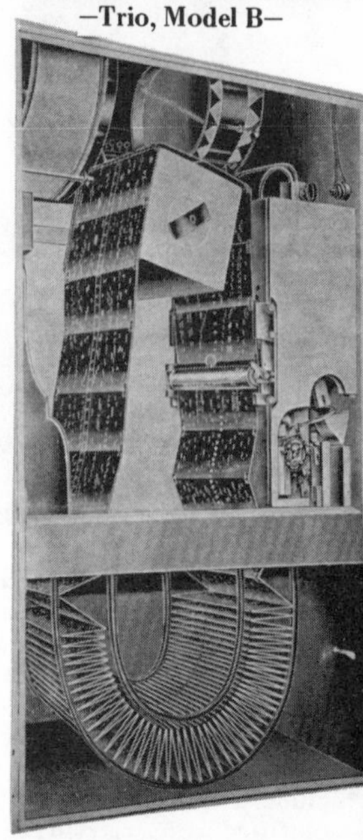

# The American Photo Player Co.

**AMERICAN PHOTO PLAYER COMPANY**
**—The "Fotoplayer"—**

*This capsule history of the American Photoplayer Company has been adapted from an article by Mr. Tom B'hend which appeared in the May, 1965, issue of "The Console." It is with Mr. B'hend's permission that we use his writing.*

PHOTOPLAYER! The very word creates a flashback to the early part of the century — to the time Bill Hart was bringing order to the screen's wild and wooly west, and Pearl White was left hanging onto a small bush on the edge of a precipitous cliff so that movie patrons would be sure to return "next week" to see her become entangled in some other hair-raising escapade!

The mechanical music makers, or "photoplayers" — there were several makes on the market, such as Cremona, Seeburg, Wurlitzer, et al — arrived at the time motion pictures were in their infancy. The photoplayers served well the uses to which they were put. During their most popular period, the 1914-1916 years, almost every city in the nation had one or more theatres.

Very small theatres, houses with fewer than 200 seats, were apt to have had just a simple upright piano or player piano in the orchestra pit. Very large theatres with many hundreds of seats, or thousands, were candidates for large built-in Wurlitzer, Robert Morton, or other types of theatre pipe organs. It was the middle range — the theatre with 200 to 700 or so seats — that provided the home for the photoplayer.

In the Rialto, Bijou, Capitol, Dreamland, Lyric, and other theatres in countless thousands of towns all across America the photoplayer brought tears to the audience one moment and laughter the next.

Although there were variations, the basic photoplayer consisted of three main parts: a center or "console" unit which was a modified upright piano type of device with one or sometimes two keyboards, one or two roll mechanisms, and appropriate pedals, buttons, and other controls for operating the novelty effects.

To the left of the console was a large side chest and to the right, another equally large chest or cabinet. These chests were filled with all sorts of interesting things — including ranks of pipes, organ reeds, drums, cymbals, gongs, bells, whistles, and other gadgets.

To operate the photoplayer the person seated at the console would put two (usually) rolls on the player unit. The "Fotoplayer" units made by the American Photo Player Company used regular 88-note home player piano rolls. The rolls provided the music. It was up to the operator to turn on and off the various ranks of pipes and to operate the sound effects devices as they were needed.

As the action progressed on the flickering screen he would switch from one roll to another to keep with the dramatic mood — and, as called for, he would actuate the horses' hooves, auto horn, bird whistle, or whatever.

At intermission time, rolls of standard or old-time favorite tunes would be put on the instrument to play automatically — as the operator would leave for a few minutes of well-deserved rest.

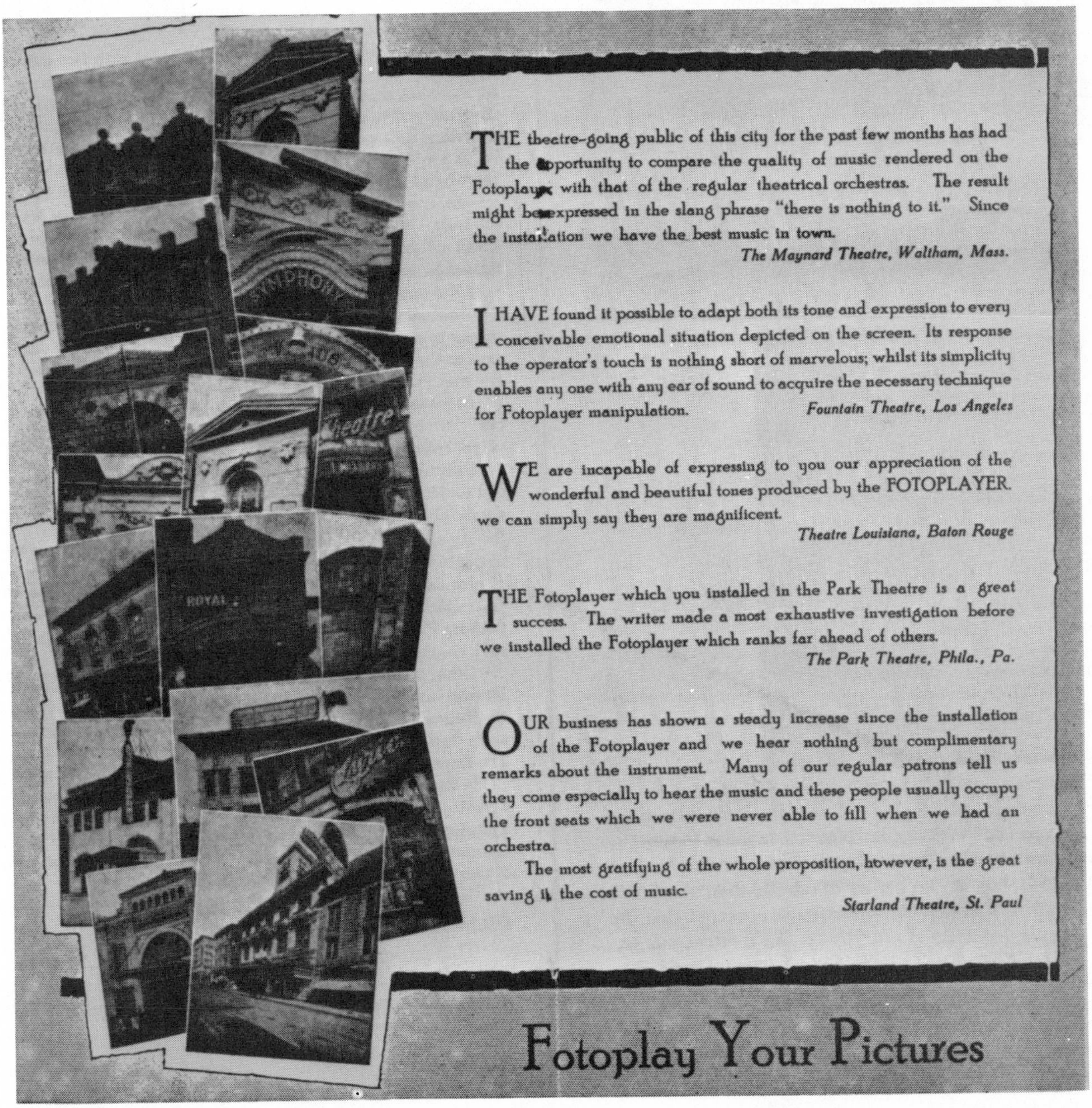

ROYAL
THE theatre-going public of this city for the past few months has had the opportunity to compare the quality of music rendered on the Fotoplayer with that of the regular theatrical orchestras. The result might be expressed in the slang phrase "there is nothing to it." Since the installation we have the best music in town.
The Maynard Theatre, Waltham, Mass.
I HAVE found it possible to adapt both its tone and expression to every conceivable emotional situation depicted on the screen. Its response to the operator's touch is nothing short of marvelous; whilst its simplicity enables any one with any ear of sound to acquire the necessary technique for Fotoplayer manipulation.
Fountain Theatre, Los Angeles
WE are incapable of expressing to you our appreciation of the wonderful and beautiful tones produced by the FOTOPLAYER. we can simply say they are magnificent.
Theatre Louisiana, Baton Rouge
THE Fotoplayer which you installed in the Park Theatre is a great success. The writer made a most exhaustive investigation before we installed the Fotoplayer which ranks far ahead of others.
The Park Theatre, Phila., Pa.
OUR business has shown a steady increase since the installation of the Fotoplayer and we hear nothing but complimentary remarks about the instrument. Many of our regular patrons tell us they come especially to hear the music and these people usually occupy the front seats which we were never able to fill when we had an orchestra.
The most gratifying of the whole proposition, however, is the great saving in the cost of music.
Starland Theatre, St. Paul
Fotoplay Your Pictures

*Chicago's Lyon & Healy Co., a Fotoplayer agent in that city, maintained a school for operators of that instrument. Classes were given regularly. In this picture can be seen three different units, including a Style 45 in the left foreground.*

Considering the thousands of photoplayers which once entertained movie-going America, it is rather surprising that so few are to be found today – although many stories have been told about how these instruments were veritable workhorses, playing no less than four hours per day and in most cases about 12 to 14!

As an indication of the hard use these instruments originally received, we quote a letter received from an American Photo Player Company customer who wrote in 1917:

"After investigating all makes of instruments we have decided to place with you an order for a Fotoplayer to be installed in our Lyric Theatre which is in the Loop District of Chicago.

"We purchased this instrument from you for two reasons: first – we consider it to be the best instrument of its kind manufactured; and, second – we are satisfied that it is the most durable make. The Lyric Theatre, in which this instrument is to be installed, is one of the few theatres in the United States which remain open 24 hours a day throughout the year, and this instrument will be played by two operators and will have very hard use.

"We want the music for the Lyric Theatre to be as up-to-date as possible and the Fotoplayer, in our estimation, is the ideal instrument for picture work."

It is not surprising that with such hard usage many of these instruments were simply junked when their usefulness had ended.

Apart from their main use in theatres, a few were sold to cabarets and funeral homes. Today, one might fortunately locate a forgotten instrument hidden away in a barn, in a basement somewhere, or boarded up under the new wide screen of a theatre – but, for the most part, photoplayers have passed on to oblivion. . . and are remembered only as a part of the nostalgic recollection of Saturday at the movies in the "good old days."

In later years the subject of our story, the American Photo Player Company, became part of the Robert Morton Pipe Organ Co. We are concerned here with the American Photo Player Company and its very popular product, the "Fotoplayer."

The invention of the "Fotoplayer," this firm's trademarked name for its theatre photoplayer, coincided with the growth years of the motion picture. In fact, it was the apparent need for a greater volume of sound than could be provided by a single piano and special sound effects that probably prompted the development of photoplayers in general.

Rinky-tink player pianos, even concert grands in some instances, provided the background for honey-haired heroines, vile villains, and handsome heros when movies were first shown in converted store buildings. A good pianist could really enhance the film action. A poor pianist merely added to the noise provided by the ceiling fans in the summer or the steam radiators in the winter.

While these sounds were better than no music at all, the piano left much to be desired – especially if one happened to be seated in the rear rows. In many instances the early nickelodeon theatres ("nickel" for the 5c admission charge; "odeon" is the Greek word for "theatre") were former stores which had been hastily converted to the showing of motion pictures. At best, the smaller theatres enabled the piano sound to reach to the back rows; but in larger theatres of this type, called "shooting galleries" by the trade, the sounds emanating from an upright piano became enfeebled and died before reaching the ears of patrons seated at the back of the house.

Another drawback was the lack of expression or effective tonal shading. Always an important adjunct of motion picture presentation, it was gradually realized that the background music could exert tremendous influence over an audience. In the earliest days pianists had to play with the strength of Hercules or Samson to get the horses through the pass or sound a grand crash finale.

Something was definitely needed. Almost anything that could produce a better and louder sound would have been welcome. A full-fledged human symphony orchestra would, of course, have been ideal – but this would have posed an insurmountable financial problem. At 5c or even 15c per ticket admissions could not have even approached the covering of expenses.

During this time, out on the Pacific coast – in the town of Berkeley, California – two brothers were toying with the musical answer to the small theatre's problem. They were busy inventing something that would create a marked change in the exhibition of motion pictures.

And these two Californians weren't the only ones with the same idea – several other companies were building similar contrivances full of whistles, reeds, klaxon horns, cymbals, triangles, traps, percussions, etc. – all compactly housed in chests designed to fit in the orchestra pit right under the movie screen.

The precise moment when the first photoplayer came into existence is now lost to history, but once the first one sounded off in a movie house, the race was on to flood all movie houses with the roll-operated devices.

Seeburg, Wurlitzer, Bartola, Cremona, and other brands entered the selling spree. Among these and other makes the Fotoplayer became one of the best sellers.

The Fotoplayer, the musical answer to the movieman's dilemma, was the brainchild of the Van Valkenburg brothers of Berkeley. It was pushed into prominence by a dynamic piano salesman, Harold J.

Werner, who saw in the Fotoplayer a tremendous potential for nationwide theatre music.

Werner, a successful salesman in the Nevada area for the Eilers Music Co. of San Francisco, returned to Oakland, California, and was told of the Van Valkenburg invention by Mr. Fred Ricksecker who, from time to time, had sold instruments for Eilers, but who was at that time engaged in promoting some theatre advertising stunts. Ricksecker had met the Van Valkenburgs and their associate, Guy Jacobus, who were trying to make and sell Fotoplayers.

Ricksecker and Werner formed a sales organization to handle distribution of the instruments. There was an understanding that if the manufacturing arm of the business could not keep up with the sales demand, then the sales organization would take over control of the factory also. This event was not long in coming. Rapid acceptance of the Fotoplayer resulted in a flood of orders, and the agreement providing for the taking over of the factory was put into effect.

Ricksecker sold his interest in the firm back to Werner and became a southern representative for the firm.

The new combined manufacturing and selling firm was advantageous to both groups. The unified organization became the American Photo Player Company. Werner then provided additional financing and the resources and the manufacturing capacity were dramatically increased.

So great was the demand for Fotoplayers that it was easy to find distributors in large cities throughout the nation. The music house of Lyon & Healy in Chicago not only stocked various models but conducted a photoplayer school to instruct students in the art of playing the machines. Further east, Wanamaker's Department Store held the franchise.

As a marvel of easy operation, the Fotoplayers could be handled by any person whether he was musically skilled or not. All he had to do was put the appropriate music rolls on the player unit and pull the cords for the various sound effects.

Veteran organ repairman Henry Pope once recalled that a well versed operator could play the rolls and work the traps in a manner that would make the Fotoplayer sound as if it were hiding an orchestra!

It is believed that 1925 was the last year in which the Fotoplayers were made, but sales continued (using instruments in inventory) through at least 1927, and advertisements appeared in trade papers as late as 1928. By the latter year the silent movie was nearly obsolete — and "talkies" were the latest thing.

The Fotoplayers were versatile inasmuch as they could utilize any of the thousands of different titles available for the standard 88-note home player piano — the type of roll the Fotoplayer used.

The Filmusic Company of Hollywood, California, produced "Picturolls" — special sound effects and background "mood" music for Fotoplayers and their contemporaries. More often than not, however, the Fotoplayer operator would go to his local music store and buy regular 88-note Q.R.S., U.S. Music Co., MelOdee, etc. rolls of the latest hit tunes. It was sometimes the practice to put the date on the roll box or roll leader each time the roll was played. This prevented the same roll from being played over and over too often and assured a fresh program of music.

### Business Details

At the inception of the American Photo Player Company Werner was elected president, Guy Jacobus was named secretary and treasurer, and Mervyn Samuels became vice president. The Van Valkenburg brothers, inventors of the Fotoplayer, did not enter into the management of the firm.

Shortly after the company opened for business the management was expanded to include Louis Abrams and R.P. Matthews as officers. Matthews was placed in charge of sales in the New York area. He prepared most of the Fotoplayer advertising which appeared in various trade papers and magazines. He later served in a similar capacity with the Robert Morton Company.

At one time during the 'teens, president Werner negotiated a contract with a local piano manufacturing company in Cincinnati, Ohio. This agreement provided that American Photo Player would distribute these other pianos in its various sales offices throughout the country. In conjunction with the arrangement, the American Photo Player Company opened an office in Cincinnati. This relationship was short-lived, however, and the office was soon closed.

*A large Fotoplayer holds forth in a theatre pit of years ago. Note the cabinet of rolls at the right.*

From time to time arrangements of one sort or another were entered into. The Wicks Organ Company of Highland, Illinois, built Fotoplayers on contract as a supplemental supplier for a short time. The San Francisco sales branch of the American Photo Player Company became a representative for the J.P. Seeburg Piano Company and sold a small quantity of Seeburg coin-operated instruments while the arrangement lasted.

While music rolled forth in theatres from a seemingly endless supply of Fotoplayers, all was not well with the business end. Late in 1922 serious financial difficulties were encountered. An article in the September 8, 1923, issue of "Music Trades" noted, "The Photo Player Company was formed following a conference of stockholders and creditors for the purpose of devising the best plan for conserving the assets of the American Photo Player Company."

The new concern was incorporated with a capital stock of $600,000. The board of directors consisted of Fred E. Ouer, assistant cashier of the Anglo & London – Paris National Bank; C.B. Lastreto, president of the foreign trade firm of Lastreto & Co.; Frederic R. Sherman, vice president of Sherman, Clay & Co., musical instrument retailers; L.P. Grunbaum, formerly connected with the American Photo Player Company; George F. Detrick, president of the Sacramento Northern Railroad Company; Louis H. Brownstone, a leading San Francisco attorney; and Benjamin Platt, a Los Angeles music dealer.

All advertising was carried on under the American Photo Player Company name until the year 1925 when the name of the Robert Morton Organ Company (which at the time was operating the company) was used. In that year the Berkeley factory was closed down, and all operations were consolidated under the roof of the Robert Morton Organ Company in Van Nuys, California.

### About Fotoplayers

Fotoplayers produced in the 'teens came in many varieties, often custom made to suit a particular location. Sizes ranged from the simple "Fotopiano" – a twin-roll player piano – to very large Fotoplayers which were nearly 20 feet wide. By the late 'teens the models were standardized.

A circa 1920 price list indicates the regular Fotoplayer models of that period and their prices: Style 15, $2,875.00; Style 20, $3,650.00; Style 25, $4,675.00; Style 35, $6,000.00; Style 40, $6,600.00; Style 45, $8,700.00; and Style 50, $10,750.00.

Judging from the financial difficulties the firm encountered, these prices – while certainly expensive enough in their day – were still not high enough to produce a profit. Considering the sheer amount of instrumentation of the Fotoplayers, they probably could not be made today for three or four times the prices of years ago.

A catalogue of the Fotoplayer styles noted:

"The moving picture industry has established the value of adequate musical accompaniment for the successful presentation and popular reception of photoplays.

The FOTOPLAYER is the first instrument manufactured for the purpose of describing motion pictures with appropriate music. It contains a piano, reed organ, and organ pipes for orchestral effects.

The FOTOPLAYER substitutes an orchestra in the power and range of the musical expression and the double tracker device enables the entire instrument to be controlled by one operator – permitting an accurate musical interpretation of screen action.

The FOTOPLAYER may be played manually or by rolls, and the double tracker control provides an instant change to fit the mood of the silent drama.

The FOTOPLAYER installation is an artistic and economic success.

### Fotoplayers Today

Fotoplayers were exceedingly well built throughout. In fact, one could say that they were "overbuilt" in that much of the care taken for interior woodwork finishing, easy modular construction for convenient repairs, etc. was not necessary from a sales viewpoint. However, this quality pays dividends today – and Fotoplayers of all kinds are highly desired by collectors.

---

The American
Photo Player Company

General Offices and Showrooms:

NEW YORK — 62 West 45th St.
CHICAGO, ILL. — 64 E. Jackson Blvd.

SAN FRANCISCO, CAL.
109 Golden Gate Ave.

This picture taken a half century ago shows a Fotoplayer in the orchestra pit of a theatre.

Taken in the 1920's, this picture shows a craftsman leaning over the front of the piano and connecting tubing to the master chest behind it.

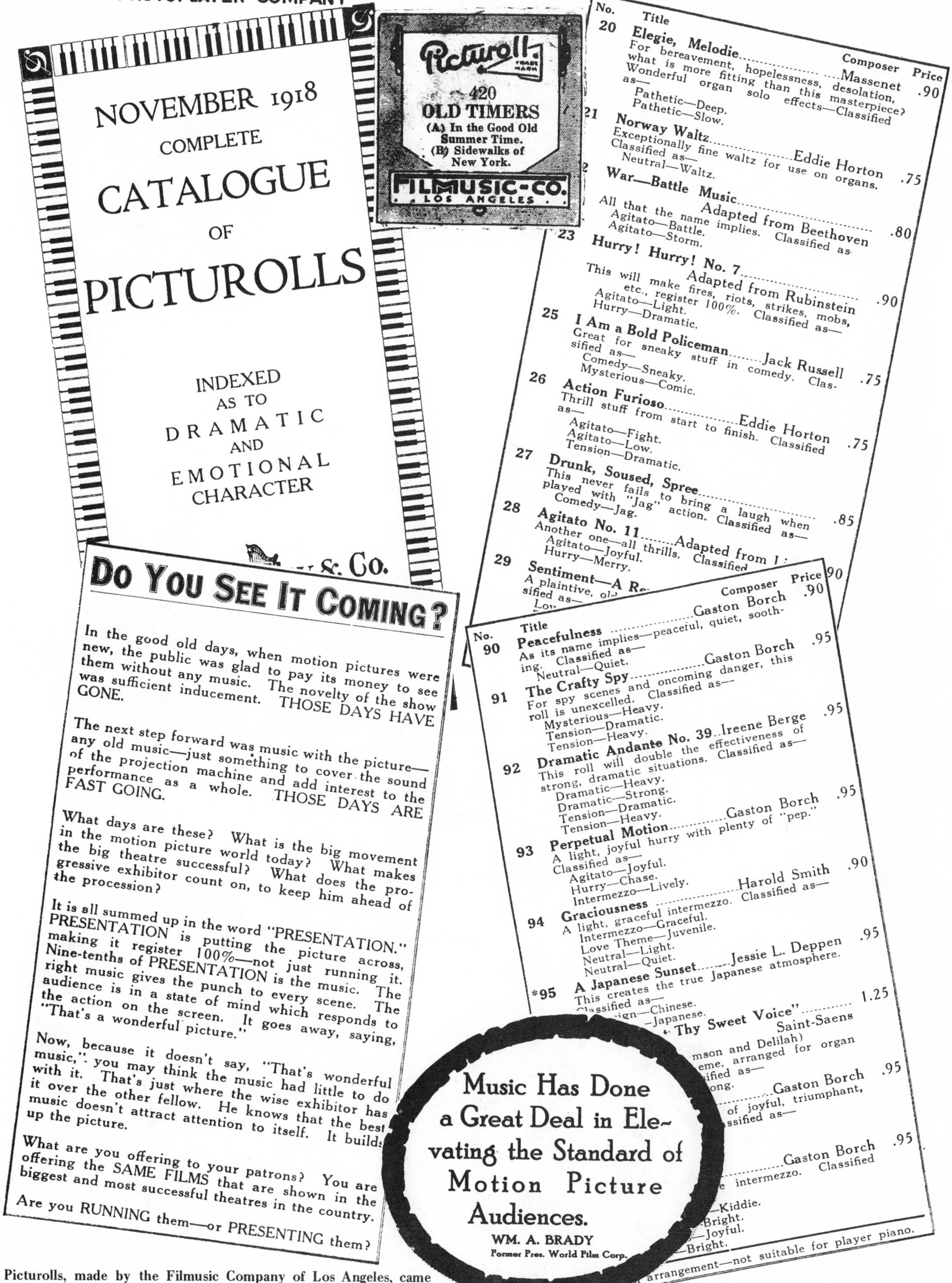

NOVEMBER 1918
COMPLETE
CATALOGUE
OF
PICTUROLLS
INDEXED
AS TO
DRAMATIC
AND
EMOTIONAL
CHARACTER
& Co.
Picturoll
TRADE MARK
420
OLD TIMERS
(A) In the Good Old Summer Time.
(B) Sidewalks of New York.
FILMUSIC-CO.
LOS ANGELES
No. Title Composer Price
20 Elegie, Melodie.....Massenet .90
For bereavement, hopelessness, desolation, what is more fitting than this masterpiece? Wonderful organ solo effects—Classified as—
Pathetic—Deep.
Pathetic—Slow.
21 Norway Waltz.....Eddie Horton .75
Exceptionally fine waltz for use on organs. Classified as—
Neutral—Waltz.
2 War—Battle Music.....Adapted from Beethoven .80
All that the name implies. Classified as
Agitato—Battle.
Agitato—Storm.
23 Hurry! Hurry! No. 7.....Adapted from Rubinstein .90
This will make fires, riots, strikes, mobs, etc., register 100%. Classified as—
Agitato—Light.
Hurry—Dramatic.
25 I Am a Bold Policeman.....Jack Russell .75
Great for sneaky stuff in comedy. Classified as—
Comedy—Sneaky.
Mysterious—Comic.
26 Action Furioso.....Eddie Horton .75
Thrill stuff from start to finish. Classified as—
Agitato—Fight.
Agitato—Low.
Tension—Dramatic.
27 Drunk, Soused, Spree.....85
This never fails to bring a laugh when played with "Jag" action. Classified as—
Comedy—Jag.
28 Agitato No. 11.....Adapted from L
Another one—all thrills. Classified
Agitato—Joyful.
Hurry—Merry.
29 Sentiment—A R
A plaintive, ol
sified as—
Lov
DO YOU SEE IT COMING?
In the good old days, when motion pictures were new, the public was glad to pay its money to see them without any music. The novelty of the show was sufficient inducement. THOSE DAYS HAVE GONE.
The next step forward was music with the picture—any old music—just something to cover the sound of the projection machine and add interest to the performance as a whole. THOSE DAYS ARE FAST GOING.
What days are these? What is the big movement in the motion picture world today? What makes the big theatre successful? What does the progressive exhibitor count on, to keep him ahead of the procession?
It is all summed up in the word "PRESENTATION." PRESENTATION is putting the picture across, making it register 100%—not just running it. Nine-tenths of PRESENTATION is the music. The right music gives the punch to every scene. The audience is in a state of mind which responds to the action on the screen. It goes away, saying, "That's a wonderful picture."
Now, because it doesn't say, "That's wonderful music," you may think the music had little to do with it. That's just where the wise exhibitor has it over the other fellow. He knows that the best music doesn't attract attention to itself. It builds up the picture.
What are you offering to your patrons? You are offering the SAME FILMS that are shown in the biggest and most successful theatres in the country.
Are you RUNNING them—or PRESENTING them?
No. Title Composer Price
90 Peacefulness.....Gaston Borch .90
As its name implies—peaceful, quiet, soothing. Classified as—
Neutral—Quiet.
91 The Crafty Spy.....Gaston Borch .95
For spy scenes and oncoming danger, this roll is unexcelled. Classified as—
Mysterious—Heavy.
Tension—Dramatic.
Tension—Heavy.
92 Dramatic Andante No. 39..Ireene Berge .95
This roll will double the effectiveness of strong, dramatic situations. Classified as—
Dramatic—Heavy.
Dramatic—Strong.
Tension—Dramatic.
Tension—Heavy.
93 Perpetual Motion.....Gaston Borch .95
A light, joyful hurry with plenty of "pep." Classified as—
Agitato—Joyful.
Hurry—Chase.
Intermezzo—Lively.
94 Graciousness.....Harold Smith .90
A light, graceful intermezzo. Classified as—
Intermezzo—Graceful.
Love Theme—Juvenile.
Neutral—Light.
Neutral—Quiet.
*95 A Japanese Sunset.....Jessie L. Deppen .95
This creates the true Japanese atmosphere.
Classified as—
—Chinese.
—Japanese.
Thy Sweet Voice".....1.25
Saint-Saens
mson and Delilah)
eme, arranged for organ
ified as—
ong.
Gaston Borch .95
of joyful, triumphant,
ssified as—
Gaston Borch .95
intermezzo. Classified
—Kiddie.
—Bright.
—Joyful.
—Bright.
arrangement—not suitable for player piano.
Music Has Done a Great Deal in Elevating the Standard of Motion Picture Audiences.
WM. A. BRADY
Former Pres. World Film Corp.


Picturolls, made by the Filmusic Company of Los Angeles, came ready for just about every imaginable screen sequence – as this montage of catalogue pages shows.

# VARIOUS STAGES OF FOTOPLAYER SETUP

FIRST: Place bass and treble case the proper distance apart, which can be ascertained by measuring between the lugs that hold the master chest to side cases. See that they are perfectly square, using a string, as shown, to line up.

SECOND: Place MASTER CHEST as shown, being careful not to disturb the leather packing on the universal joints. Never rely on the universal joints to take up the unevenness of the cases. They should be absolutely square.

FOURTH: Tighten screws on universal joints on end of wind trunk. Do not force these screws. They must enter squarely and easily. You will also note that the vacuum supply has been connected. Supply pipes may now be connected and the entire instrument tested out from master chest.

FIFTH: Move piano into place.

THIRD: Screw universal joint to MASTER CHEST

SIXTH: Connect piano to MASTER CHEST

SEVENTH: Place trap pulls.

**Scenes from the helpful booklet "Installation, Care, and Operation of the Fotoplayer" — issued with each Fotoplayer instrument sold. In the forepart of the book four admonitions were given: (1) Do not experiment. (2) Keep your instrument oiled and graphited. (3) Keep the instrument clean. (4) Keep it in tune.**

Above: Left side chest from the Style 25 Fotoplayer in the collection of Harvey and Marion Roehl of Vestal, N.Y. Lower photo: Right side chest of the same instrument.

Early Style 40.

Very early Fotoplayer styles: These models from the early 'teens were made in limited quantities. The standard styles were the 20, 25, 35, 40, 45, and 50 shown on the bottom of this page and on the pages to follow. Note the ornate top gallery on the center instrument and on the piano part of the bottom unit. Fotoplayer sidechests have an oak latticework in front of thin cloth panels, usually of a light brown or golden color. Behind the panels are swell shutters. To permit views of the interior the Fotoplayer catalogue illustations of most models are with the latticework and swell shutters removed.

THE FOTOPLAYER is a marvel of technical construction producing the most beautiful organ, piano and orchestral effects.

The FOTOPLAYER music is human and a real satisfaction to critical taste and an enjoyment to the little ones.

The FOTOPLAYER may be used for vaudeville purposes. The entire instrument can be played manually—the pedal attachment permitting the pianist to play the drums and cymbals.

The FOTOPLAYER is designed to withstand the wear of continuous use. Permanent construction is made possible by superior workmanship, material and finish.

Perfect tonal qualities produce a human and artistic performance.

The double tracker device, permitting the operation by roll, is an economic advantage.

Hundreds of satisfied exhibitors pay eloquent tribute to the merits of the FOTOPLAYER.

A style to "fit your pit."

Write for further features.

The Pantomimic Drama Has Helped Music Just As Music Has Helped the Pantomine.

JOHN PHILIP SOUSA

## FOTOPLAYER STYLE 20

THE Style 20 FOTOPLAYER is a marvel of up-to-date technical construction, designed and built expressly to meet all the needs of motion picture houses of smaller seating capacity.

### SPECIFICATIONS FOR FOTOPLAYER—Style No. 20

Length, 10 ft. Width, 3 ft. 1½ in. Height, 5 ft.
Piano extends 8 inches

High Grade Player Piano—Double Tracker Device

Tremolo
Piano Muffler

Pipes for Orchestral Effects:
Violin, Cello, Flute

TRAPS AND EFFECTS AS FOLLOWS:

Bass Drum
Pistol Shot
Cymbal
Tom-Tom
Thunder or Tympani
Snare Drum
Door Bell
Telephone Bell

Fire Gong
Tambourine
Castanets
Klaxon
Chinese Crash Cymbal
Steamboat Whistle or
Locomotive Whistle
Wind Siren
Cathedral Chime

The FOTOPLAYER is constructed of the finest hard woods throughout and the workmanship is the best.

Style No.20 – the smallest Fotoplayer style with an attached side chest. A piano (without side chest) unit, the "Fotopiano," was produced but is not illustrated here.

THE AMERICAN PHOTOPLAYER COMPANY

## FOTOPLAYER STYLE 25

THE FOTOPLAYER is a beautiful product of fine material and workmanship and is built to withstand the gruelling tests of a motion picture theater.

**SPECIFICATIONS FOR FOTOPLAYER—Style No. 25**

Length 14 ft. 4 in. Width 2 ft. 4 in. Height 5 ft.
Piano extends 14 inches.
High Grade Player Piano with double tracker device.
Piano muffler—Tremolo.

PIPES FOR ORCHESTRAL EFFECTS:

Violin Flute Violoncello
Set of Orchestral Bells (31)

TRAPS AND SOUND EFFECTS:

| | |
|---|---|
| Bass Drum | Steamboat Whistle or |
| Cymbal | Locomotive Whistle |
| Snare Drum | Castanets |
| Chinese Crash Cymbal | Pistol Crack |
| Tom-Tom (Chinese) | Sleigh Bells |
| Tympani or Thunder | Klaxon |
| Wind Siren | Bird Whistle |
| Tambourine | Cathedral Chime |
| Door Bell or | |
| Telephone Bell | |

Finished Stickley Oak, Swell Shutters, Suitable Bench, Lighting Fixtures over double tracker. Combination Blower Plant equipped with motor of sufficient capacity.

## FOTOPLAYER STYLE 35

THE FOTOPLAYER is easily handled by one operator, rendering at all times music that harmonizes with the picture. It is a musical instrument, producing magnificent orchestral and organ tones, and in every respect up-to-date as an example of technical instrumental construction.

**SPECIFICATIONS FOR FOTOPLAYER—Style No. 35**

Length 14 ft., 7½in. Width, 3 ft. 1¾in. Height, 5 ft.
Piano extends 8 inches.
High Grade Player Piano—Double Tracker Device
Pressure Reed Organ, 7 Stops:

| TREBLE | | BASS | |
|---|---|---|---|
| Oboe | 4' | Diapason | 8' |
| Diapason | 8' | Echo | 8' |
| Principal | 8' | | |
| Cornet | 8' | Clarionet | 16' |

| | |
|---|---|
| Tremolo. Piano Muffler | Door Bell or |
| Pipes for Orchestral Effects: | Telephone Bell |
| Violin, Flute, Violoncello | Fire Gong |
| Reed Organ and Pipes 65-Note Range. | Bird Whistle |
| Traps and Effects as follows: | Tambourine |
| Set of Orchestra Bells (31) | Castanets |
| Bass Drum | Horses' Hoofs |
| Pistol Shot | Klaxon |
| Cymbal | Sleigh Bells |
| Tom-Tom | Chinese Crash Cymbal |
| Thunder or Tympani | Steamboat Whistle or |
| Snare Drum | Locomotive Whistle |
| | Wind Siren |
| | Chinese Wood Drum |
| | Triangle |

Total number of Reeds in this Instrument, 195. Total number of Pipes, 103, ranging in pitch from 4' to 16'. Quarter-sawed Oak Case, Stickley Oak finish, Swell Shutters, Suitable Bench. Equipped with Light and Fixtures over Double Tracker, Combination Blower Plant equipped with Motor of sufficient capacity. Case design subject to change.

**Above: Style 35 Fotoplayer. Catalogue illustration showing the unit with the side chest fronts on. The piano units of most Fotoplayers were made by the Kohler & Campbell Company. The Standard Pneumatic Action Co. furnished the player roll mechanism. Identical mechanisms were used on the "Y" styles of Wurlitzer photoplayers (see Wurlitzer section of this book).**

**Left: Style 25 Fotoplayer. This was probably the single most popular Fotoplayer model. The sale price was a not-inexpensive $4675.00 about 1920. All Fotoplayers seen by the author have been in light golden oak wood of the "Stickley Oak finish" described in the Fotoplayer catalogue.**

---

THE moving picture industry has established the value of adequate musical accompaniment for the successful presentation and popular reception of Photoplays.

The FOTOPLAYER is the first instrument manufactured for the purpose of describing motion pictures with appropriate music.

It contains a piano, reed organ and organ pipe for orchestral effects.

The FOTOPLAYER substitutes an orchestra in the power and range of musical expression and the double tracker device enables the entire instrument to be controlled by one operator—permitting an accurate musical interpretation of screen action.

The FOTOPLAYER may be played manually or by roll, and the double tracker control provides an instant change to fit the mood of the silent drama.

FOTOPLAYER installation is an artistic and economic success.

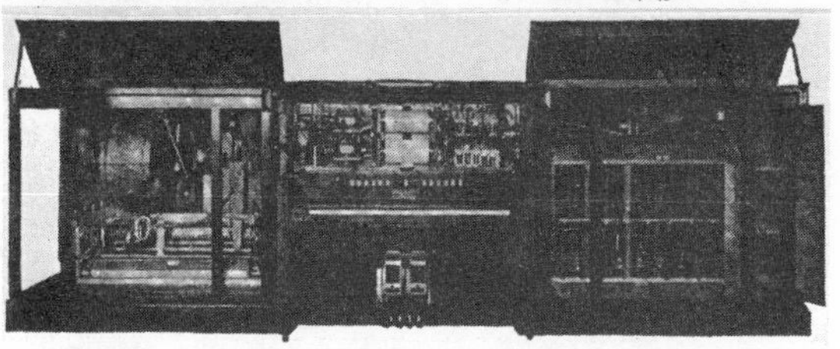

# FOTOPLAYER STYLE 40

## SPECIFICATIONS FOR FOTOPLAYER—Style No. 40

Length, 16 ft. 6 in. Width, 3 ft. 7 in. Height 5 ft.
Piano extends 8 inches.
High Grade Player Piano—Double Tracker Device

Pressure Reed Organ, 6 Stops

| | | |
|---|---|---|
| TREBLE | Oboe | 4′ |
| | Diapason | 8′ |
| | Principal | 8′ |
| BASS | Diapason | 8′ |
| | Echo | 8′ |
| | Clarionet | 16′ |

Tremolo
Piano Muffler

Pipes for Orchestral Effects:
Vox Mystica, Flute, Cornet, Violoncello
Reed Organ and Pipes
65-Note Range.

TRAPS AND EFFECTS AS FOLLOWS:

Set of Orchestra Bells (31)
Bass Drum
Pistol Shot
Cymbal
Tom-Tom
Thunder or Tympani
Snare Drum
Door Bell or
Telephone Bell
Fire Gong
Cathedral Chime
Tambourine
Castanets
Horses' Hoofs
Klaxon
Sleigh Bells
Chinese Crash Cymbal
Steamboat Whistle or
Locomotive Whistle
Wind Siren
Triangle
Chinese Wood Drum
Bird Whistle

Total number of Reeds in this Instrument, 195.
Total number of pipes, 141, ranging in pitch from 4′ to 16′.
Quarter-sawed Oak Case, Stickley Oak finish, suitable Bench.
Equipped with Light and Fixture over Double Tracker,
Combination Blower Plant, equipped with Motor
of sufficient capacity. Case design subject
to change.

**Style 40. Sold for $6600.00 about 1920. Illustration with the side panels and swell shutters removed to show the interior.**

# FOTOPLAYER STYLE 45

Length, 17 ft. 4 in. Width, 3 ft. 9 in. Height, 5 ft.
Piano extends 8 inches.
High Grade Player Piano — Double Track Device.

Pressure Reed Organ, 3 Stops:
Diapason, 8′ Principal, 8′ Clarionet, 16′
Tremolo
Piano Muffler

PIPES FOR ORCHESTRAL EFFECTS:

| TREBLE | BASS |
|---|---|
| Vox Mystica | Viol d'Orchestra |
| Cornet or Quintadena | Violoncello |
| Flute | Dulciana or Quintaton |
| Flute d'Amour | Reed Organ and Pipes |
| Viol d'Orchestra | 65-Note Range |

TRAPS AND EFFECTS AS FOLLOWS:

Set of Orchestra Bells (31)
Xylophone
Bass Drum
Pistol Shots, Double
Cymbal
Tom-Tom
Thunder
Snare Drum
Door Bell or
Telephone Bell
Bird Whistle
Chinese Wood Drum
Triangle
Fire Gong
Cathedral Chime
Tambourine
Castanets
Horses' Hoofs (Improved)
Klaxon
Sleigh Bells
Chinese Crash Cymbal
Steamboat Whistle or
Locomotive Whistle
Wind Siren
Locomotive Exhaust
Automobile Exhaust

Blower Plant equipped with motor of sufficient capacity.
Quarter-sawed Oak Case, beautifully finished.
Equipped with Electric Light over Double Tracker.
Suitable Bench. Case Design subject to change.
Total number of Reeds in this Instrument, 195; total number of pipes, 244, ranging in pitch from 4′ to 16′.

**Style 45. Surviving photos of theatre installations show that the Style 45 was a very popular model. One can be seen in the Lyon & Healy music school illustration in the introduction to this section, and another can be seen on a page following this one.**

The Constructive Policy of Musical Interpretation for the Film Should Go Hand in Hand with the Future Prosperity of the Motion Picture Industry.
J. STUART BLACKTON
V. P. Greater Vitagraph Co.

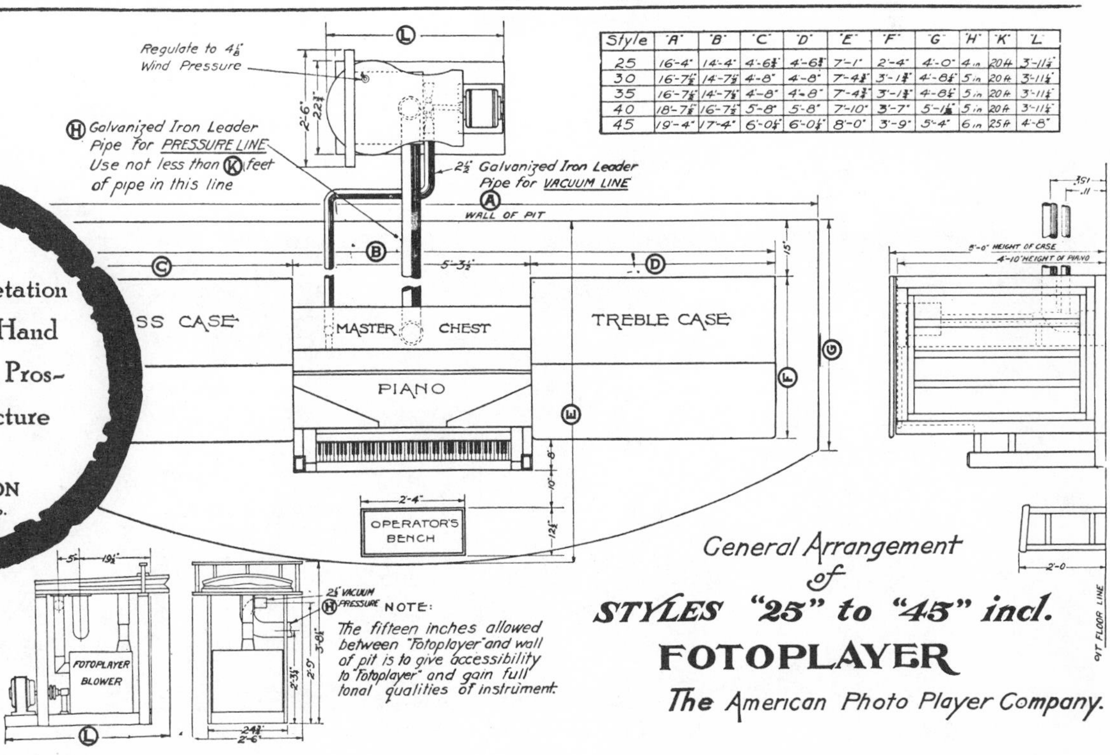

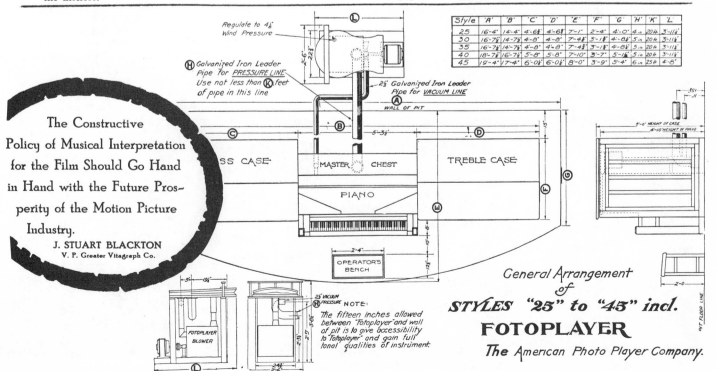

| Style | "A" | "B" | "C" | "D" | "E" | "F" | "G" | "H" | "K" | "L" |
|---|---|---|---|---|---|---|---|---|---|---|
| 25 | 16'-4" | 14'-4" | 4'-6¾" | 4'-6¾" | 7'-1" | 2'-4" | 4'-0" | 4 in | 20 ft | 3'-11¼" |
| 30 | 16'-7½" | 14'-7½" | 4'-8" | 4'-8" | 7'-4¾" | 3'-1¾" | 4'-8¼" | 5 in | 20 ft | 3'-11¼" |
| 35 | 16'-7½" | 14'-7½" | 4'-8" | 4'-8" | 7'-4¾" | 3'-1¾" | 4'-8¼" | 5 in | 20 ft | 3'-11¼" |
| 40 | 18'-7½" | 16'-7½" | 5'-8" | 5'-8" | 7'-10" | 3'-7" | 5'-1¼" | 5 in | 20 ft | 3'-11¼" |
| 45 | 19'-4" | 17'-4" | 6'-0¼" | 6'-0¼" | 8'-0" | 3'-9" | 5'-4" | 6 in | 25 ft | 4'-8" |

General Arrangement of STYLES "25" to "45" incl. FOTOPLAYER
The American Photo Player Company.

The "Fotoplayer" TRADE MARK REGISTERED

# FOTOPLAYER STYLE 50

BERKELEY, CALIFORNIA, FACTORY

Style 50. This immense Fotoplayer was the largest of the regular piano console styles. The original sale price about 1920 was $10,750.00. Containing 412 pipes, 195 reeds, and just about every sound effect ever devised, the Style 50 was better endowed than were many large theatre pipe organs. Note that the catalogue description mentions "improved" horses' hoofs. What were "unimproved" ones like?

Below is an installation diagram for the Style 50. Fotoplayer instruments operated on four and one-eighth inches of wind pressure. Wurlitzer, Seeburg, and most other types of photoplayers operated on five to six inches of wind pressure. Blower units for most manufacturers in the field were supplied either by the Kinetic Engineering Company of Philadelphia, Penna., or the Spencer Turbine Company of Hartford, Conn. The latter firm can still supply units nearly identical to the originals.

## SPECIFICATIONS FOR FOTOPLAYER — Style No. 50

Length, 21 ft. Width, 5 ft. Height, 5 ft. 2 in.
Piano extends 8 inches.

High Grade Player Piano
Double Tracker Device
Pressure Reed Organ, 6 stops

TREBLE:

Oboe . . . 4'
Diapason . . 8'
Principal . . 8'

BASS:

Diapason . . 8'
Echo . . . 8'
Clarionet . . 16'

Tremolo. Piano Muffler
Pipes for Orchestral effects:
Treble Swell Organ:
Vox Mystics, Flute, Gemshorn
Cornet, Melodia,
Flute d'Armour,
Viol d'Orchestre.
Bass Swell Organ:
Violoncello, Diaphone,
Flute d'Amour.
Great Swell Organ:
Open Diapason.
Reed Organ and Pipes
65-Note Range.

Traps and effects as follows:
Set of Orchestra Bells (31)
Pistol Shots or Gattling Gun
Bass Drum. Xylophone
Telegraph Key
Crackling Flames or
Breaking Brush
Cymbal. Tom-Tom
Thunder or Tympani
Snare Drum with Jazz Effect
Door Bell or
Telephone Bell
Fire Gong
5 Cathedral Chimes
Waves Bird Whistle
Wind. Cow Bell
Triangle. Tambourine
Castanets. Horse's Hoofs
Auto Horn. (Improved)
Sleigh Bells. Siren
Chinese Cymbal
Steamboat Whistle or
Locomotive Whistle
Automobile Exhaust
Locomotive Exhaust
Chinese Wood Drum

Quarter-sawed Oak Case, Stickley Finish, Independently operated Swell Shutters for both treble and bass. Suitable Bench. Electric Lights over Double Tracker. Special Blower Plant. Case Design subject to change.

Total number of Reeds in this Instrument, 195.

Total number of Pipes, 412, ranging in pitch from 4' to 16'.

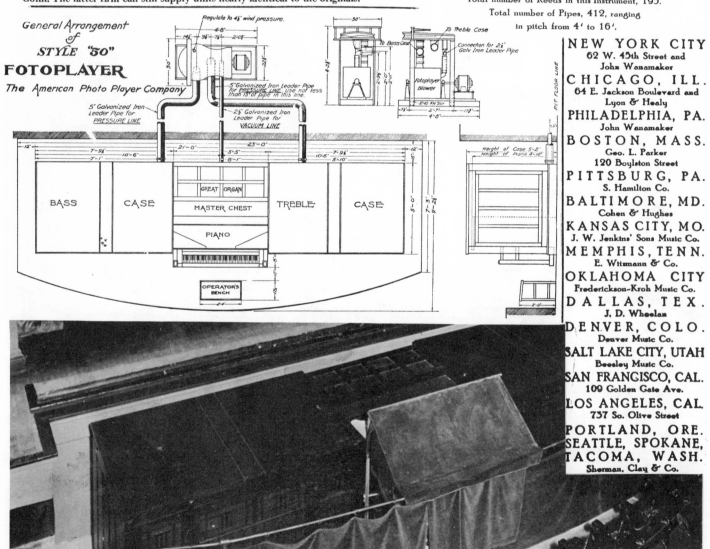

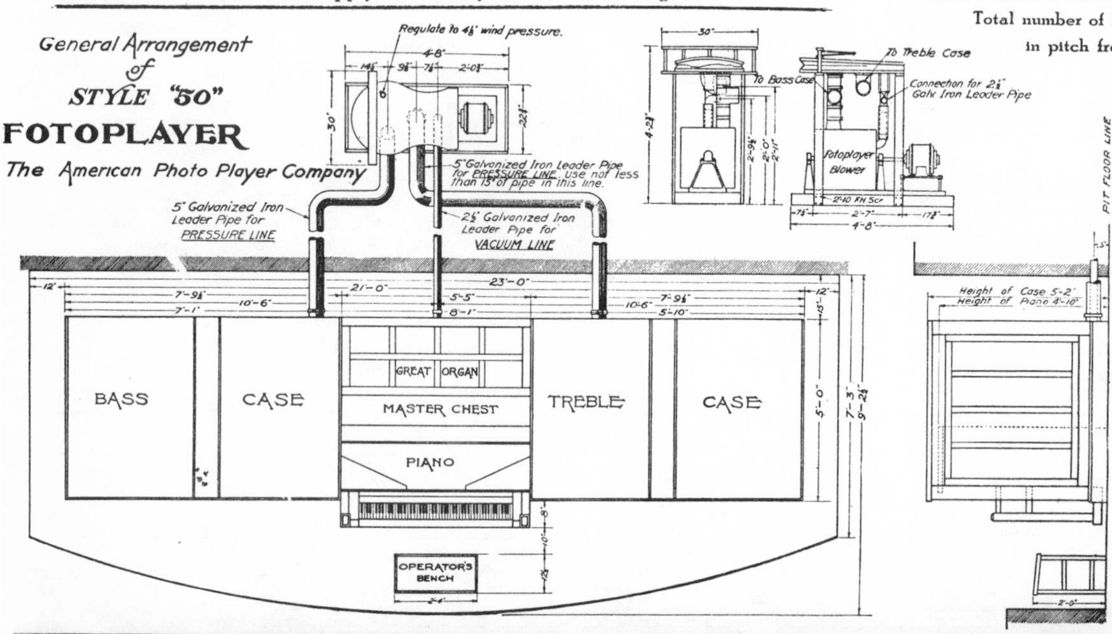


NEW YORK CITY
62 W. 45th Street and John Wanamaker
CHICAGO, ILL.
64 E. Jackson Boulevard and Lyon & Healy
PHILADELPHIA, PA.
John Wanamaker
BOSTON, MASS.
Geo. L. Parker
120 Boylston Street
PITTSBURG, PA.
S. Hamilton Co.
BALTIMORE, MD.
Cohen & Hughes
KANSAS CITY, MO.
J. W. Jenkins' Sons Music Co.
MEMPHIS, TENN.
E. Witzmann & Co.
OKLAHOMA CITY
Frederickson-Kroh Music Co.
DALLAS, TEX.
J. D. Wheelan
DENVER, COLO.
Denver Music Co.
SALT LAKE CITY, UTAH
Beesley Music Co.
SAN FRANCISCO, CAL.
109 Golden Gate Ave.
LOS ANGELES, CAL.
737 So. Olive Street
PORTLAND, ORE.
SEATTLE, SPOKANE,
TACOMA, WASH.
Sherman, Clay & Co.

Style 50 Fotoplayer, with a canvas shield for the operator, in a theatre pit.

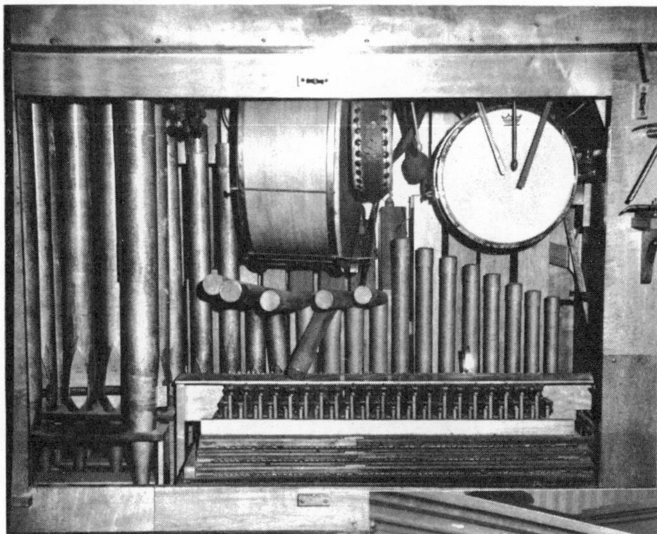

ANATOMY OF A FOTOPLAYER: This beautiful Style 45 from the Lipe Collection is shown before restoration. Directly above is the piano console with two 88-note roll mechanisms. The rope pulls operate the various percussion effects. The upper left of the three connected pictures shows the left side chest; the center, the overall unit; and the lower, the right side chest. Fotoplayers are exceedingly well built — they are among the finest of the old-time automatic instruments in this respect. "They had to be," one collector has observed, "or they would have fallen apart from all the use they had."

This Style 39 Fotoplayer is one of several organ-type (without a piano in the console) instruments made. Larger yet were the Robert Morton theatre organs made during the 1920's. Some of these latter models were called "Wonder Mortons."

In addition to theatre models, Fotoplayer models were made for use in private homes. A number of installations, particular in California, were made on special order. The pipes and percussion were usually housed in a wall behind latticework.

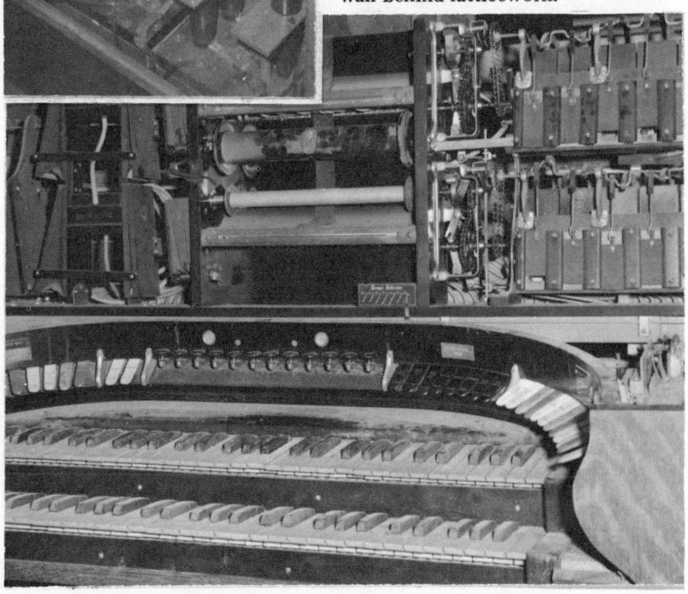

The "Fotoplayer"
TRADE MARK
REGISTERED

The Voice of the Screen

"Style 60 DeLuxe"

"Style 50"

The center unit shown at left was used to "create" both the Style 50 and 60 shown here. The side chests of the Style 60 were merely an artist's conception! The ornate top gallery, a detail of which is shown directly above, is likewise a fabrication — as you can see. "American Orchestra" was the designation used on certain instruments before "Fotoplayer" became standard.

---

View of the loading dock of the Berkeley plant. A small yard engine may be seen at the extreme left.

Above: Checking out a newly-made "Fotoplayer." It is one of the standard styles. Can you identify it from the descriptions on other pages?

Right: View of an immense Style 50, the largest regularly-made "Fotoplayer." This same illustration, but with the side chest lids removed, was used as the catalogue picture for this model. The front wooden latticework has been removed to show a view of the interior.

An early factory of the American Photo Player Company. "Berkeley factory" is the caption on the back of this early photograph.

Later factory in Berkeley, California.

Factory in Van Nuys, California.

"Fotoplayers" at Berkeley. As the left-hand illustration shows, the instruments being built at this particular time incorporated pianos made by Jacob Doll & Sons (of New York City; the Doll firm built Electrova instruments, among others). Other "Fotoplayers" used pianos by Winter & Co. or by Kohler & Campbell.

"Now, look busy girls!" This may have been what the photographer said before snapping this "posed" scene. No rubber tracker bar tubing ever went in the spot to the right of the tracker bars, as the girls would have you believe!

"Fotoplayer" units in ranch-style cases (with protruding top posts) being manufactured in the Berkeley plant.

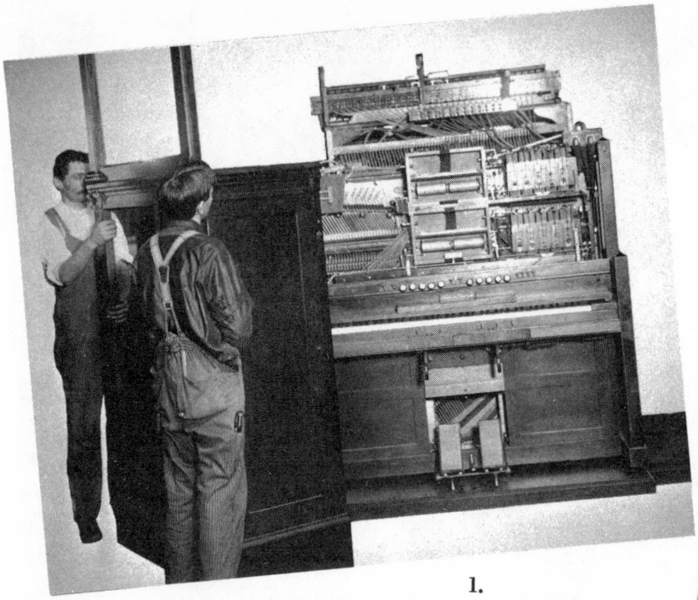

1.

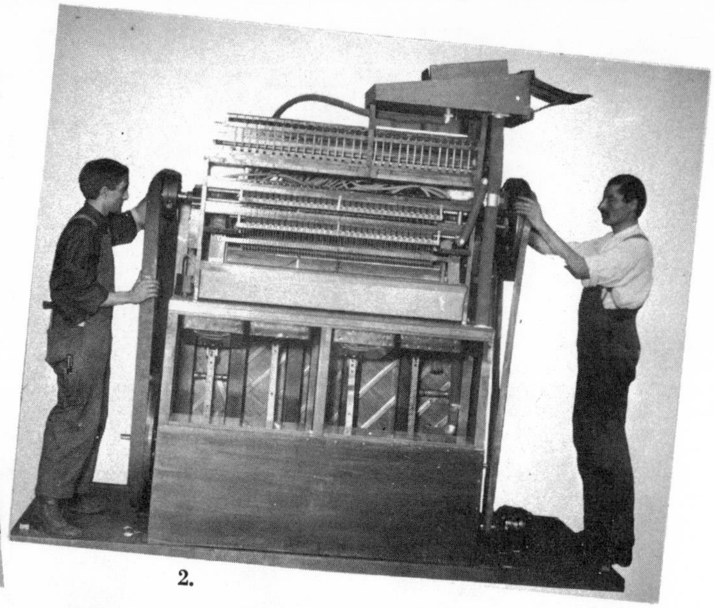

2.

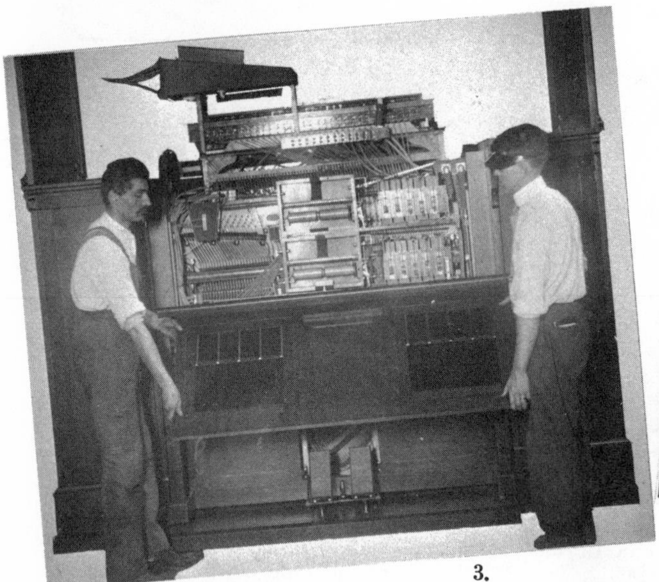

3.

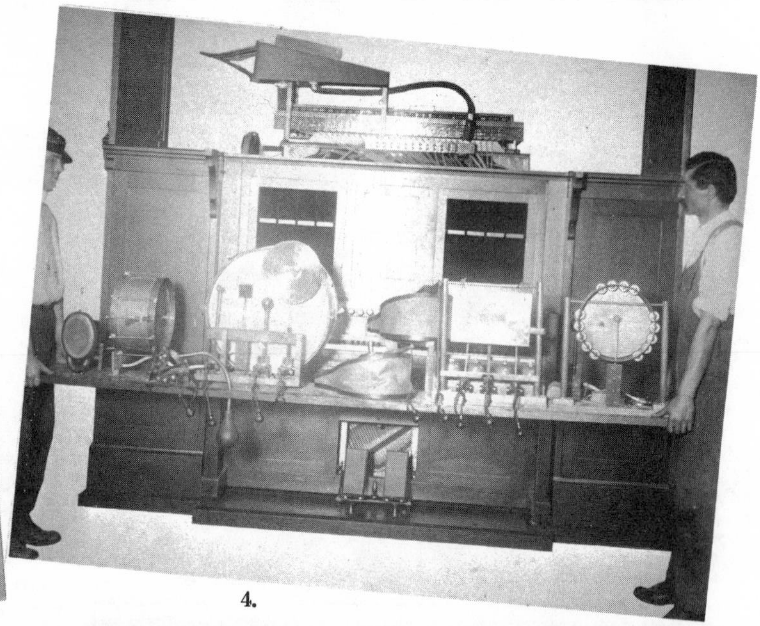

4.

### —An Unusual "Fotoplayer"—

These early pictures show a "Fotoplayer" orchestra being assembled. Such instruments were intended not for pit use in theatres, but for locations in which the tall height of the instrument was not a handicap.

Picture 1: The basic piano unit, with chests mounted above it, is in place on the floor of the orchestra. Picture 2: Rear view of instrument showing the large reduction pulleys for the pumps (which are in the bottom of the unit). Picture 3: The two side panels are in place; the front piano panel is about to be put in place. Picture 4: The "toy counter" or sound effects department is about to be lifted into place. Picture 5: The cover of the orchestra is attached.

Apparently, large scale production of such units was contemplated as the photographs have been retouched (to remove the background) and have been prepared for catalogue use. Very few were actually made.

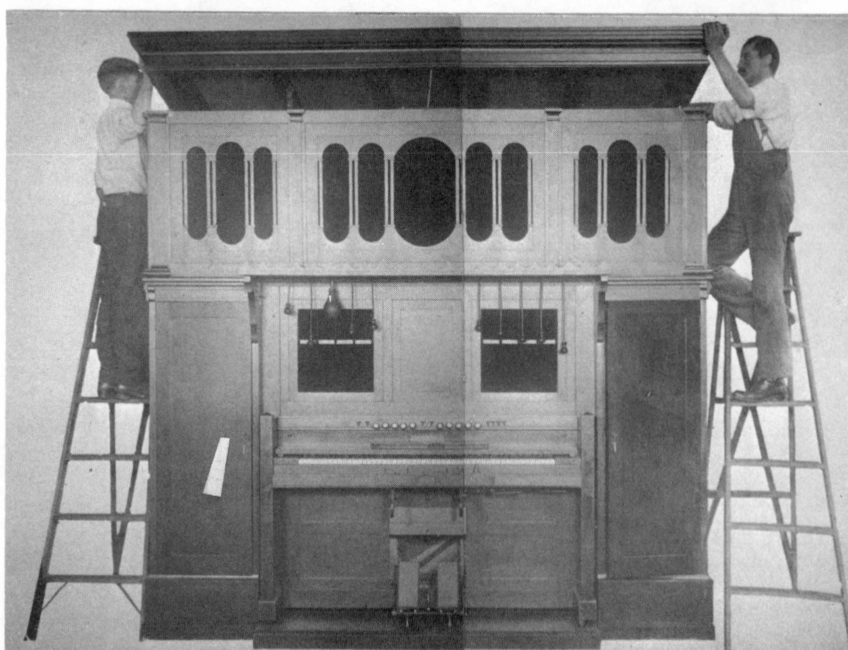

5.

"Fotoplayer" News Notes

From December 9, 1912 newspaper article: "According to an announcement made today by B.R. Van Valkenburg, general manager of the American Photo Player Co., whose plant at Addison and Bonar Streets was destroyed by fire Sunday at a loss of approximately $60,000, work will commence soon on a new $22,000 building to be erected on the same site... The new structure will be three stories high and will be of brick. It will occupy a space of 85x100 feet, as compared with 85x90 occupied by the destroyed plant. Work is to begin at once on a new $12,000 American orchestra for the Berkeley theatre, whose $10,000 machine was destroyed in Sunday's fire. The player will represent an orchestra of 20 pieces and a chromatic set of aluminum chimes will be added . . ."

From c.1913 undated article: "The first carload of machines manufactured in Berkeley by the American Photo Player Co. will be shipped today. The first machine finished in Berkeley has been sold to the Regents Theatre of Oakland, of which Mayor Mott is one of the owners. The machine, in addition to a piano, contains a pipe organ and all the instruments of a six-piece orchestra.

The company is composed entirely of local men, the principal owners of the stock being P.G. Jacobus, B.R. Van Valkenburg, and H.A. Van Valkenburg. The latest type of machine produced is called the "double tracker" photoplayer. The double action allows the motion picture operator to change instantly from one form of music to another, according to whether the situation shown on the screen be serious or comic."

Special Note:

Much of the illustrative material concerning the American Photoplayer Company, particularly the factory scenes, unusual styles, and related items, are from a picture scrapbook loaned to the author by Mr. Richard Schlaich of San Francisco, California.

Above: A large and impressive orchestrion-like photoplayer. Too tall for theatre pit use, this and similar instruments may have been intended for cabarets, dance halls, and other such locations. The above example has "Winter & Co." on the piano fallboard, indicating that the piano part of the instrument is of that brand. At the above center is lettered "Oakland, Calif." — the very early home of the American Photo Player Company.

Left: One of the smaller "Fotoplayer" styles, this instrument incorporates ranks of clarionet, flute, and violin pipes, according to the lettering on the console tabs. The swell shutter arrangement at the bottom is not unlike that later used on the Reproduco (made by the Operators Piano Co.).

American Piano Player Co.
MANUFACTURERS
LOUISVILLE, KY.

AMERICAN PIANO PLAYER COMPANY
—Louisville, Kentucky—

### A Typical Study

The history of automatic musical instruments is dotted with small firms, many of which stayed in business for only a year or two — or, sometimes, not even that long. The names of these companies are all but forgotten today and their instruments, never made in large quantities (and, in some instances, never made at all!) are rare or are non-existent.

The various music industry publications, ever-eager to help a potential advertiser and to promote the trade generally, were apparently glad to publish whatever news releases were sent in. While these same publications are a very valuable source of information today (countless hours have been spent by the author poring through files of them!), the information must, in many instances, be taken with a grain of salt. A bit of puffery such as XYZ Piano Co. "is in the highest commercial standing" was often followed an issue or two later by the same firm's obituary.

The history of the American Piano Player Company is typical. We might mention that the term "Piano Player" (rather than, as one might expect, "Player Piano") appears often in the early days as part of a company name. The Berry-Wood Piano Player Company and the Peerless Piano Player Company are the best-known examples. A "piano player" was any device which caused a piano to play automatically. So, if one built such devices one was in the "piano player" business. An examination of the only American Piano Player Co. instrument known to the author reveals that many of the mechanisms are by Wurlitzer. As one of the advertisements mentioned a "multiple music roll system up to 30 tunes" (a description that would fit the standard Wurlitzer Automatic Roll Changer which used six 5-tune rolls), it may be that the American Piano Player Company never did make anything and did nothing more than sell Wurlitzer instruments under a different name or, perhaps, install Wurlitzer mechanisms in ordinary upright pianos. With this information in mind, read the following:

### Genesis

In 1909 the American Piano Player Company, with a capital stock of $25,000.00, purchased a 100,000 square-foot factory from the American Tobacco Company. Located at 828-840 South 26th Street in Louisville, Kentucky, the factory was situated on three acres of ground.

In an article in the March 24, 1910, issue the trade paper "The Presto" gave a report of the budding new business:

"The factory is well-equipped with modern engines and boilers and up-to-date piano making machinery; in fact it has every facility which brains and money can bring together for the making of players... The company is now in good shape and much at home in the new plant from which it is shipping its product with the regularity that their quality insures. George S. Williams, the inventor of the American player and superintendent of the factory, was very busy on the day that "The Presto" called. He has been hustling just that way ever since the factory was removed to Louisville. The further personnel of this company includes some men of large wealth, like J.B. Wathen, its president, than whom no man stands higher in the estimation of Louisville people..."

In its advertising the American Piano Player Company noted that its product was "universally conceded to be the most practical and reliable player that can be fitted inside the case of any piano... Our coin-operated piano is a money-getter. Novel expression devices, one piece magazine coin slot, automatic time lock on keyboard, money change making device, multiple music roll system up to 30 tunes..."

1910 was a period of tremendous expansion in the coin-operated piano business. Coin pianos were relatively new to the American scene, and almost any company entering the field had no trouble carving out a respectable chunk of the market. Indeed, many of the firms which were later to become giants — Seeburg, Operators Piano Co., Marquette, et al — were rapidly growing at this very time.

### Exodus

Something went wrong somewhere for the American Piano Player Company. An article in the December 8, 1910, issue of "The Presto" had the following to report (evidently the writer forgot about the article which the same publication had carried on the preceding March 24th — the earlier article which applauded the wealth of the company and the quality of its product!): "AMERICAN PIANO PLAYER COMPANY FAILS — LOUISVILLE INDUSTRY IN HANDS OF RECEIVER... The American Piano Player Company of Louisville, Ky., is in the hands of a receiver. According to the attorney for the failed concern the difficulties of his clients were brought about because the corporation had issued so much promotion stock in the beginning for patents and a mechanical device that they found they were unable to continue business and pay all of their creditors in full. The patents were not perfected, the players gave only ordinary satisfaction, and it required an enormous sum to keep them in repair. Besides this, the corporation never did have enough money to start with, and has been hard pressed for funds since the very beginning... On December 1, 1910, the American Piano Player Company was duly adjudicated bankrupt..."

During the era from about 1900 to 1935 similar stories were repeated dozens of times.

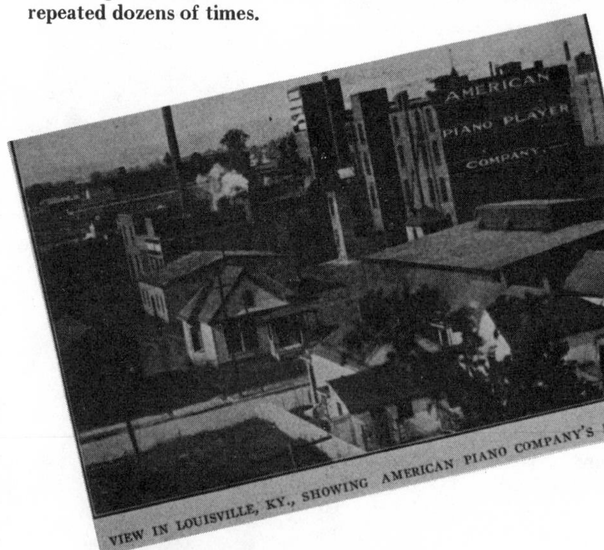
AMERICAN
PIANO PLAYER
COMPANY
VIEW IN LOUISVILLE, KY., SHOWING AMERICAN PIANO COMPANY'S PLANT.

PLAYERS THAT PLAY
HAVE YOU SEEN
THE NEW
American Piano-Player?
It is now made in Louisville, Kentucky, and is universally conceded to be the most practical and reliable Player that can be fitted inside the case of any Piano.
For home use the American Player gives the operator control of the expression without the bother of pedaling.
Our Coin Operated Player is a money-getter. Novel expression devices, one-piece magazine coin slot, automatic time-lock on key-board, money change making device, multiple music roll system up to 30 tunes.
We have an attractive proposition to offer Piano Manufacturers.
THE AMERICAN PIANO-PLAYER CO., Louisville, Kentucky

THIS LOUISVILLE INSTRUMENT IN BIG DEMAND

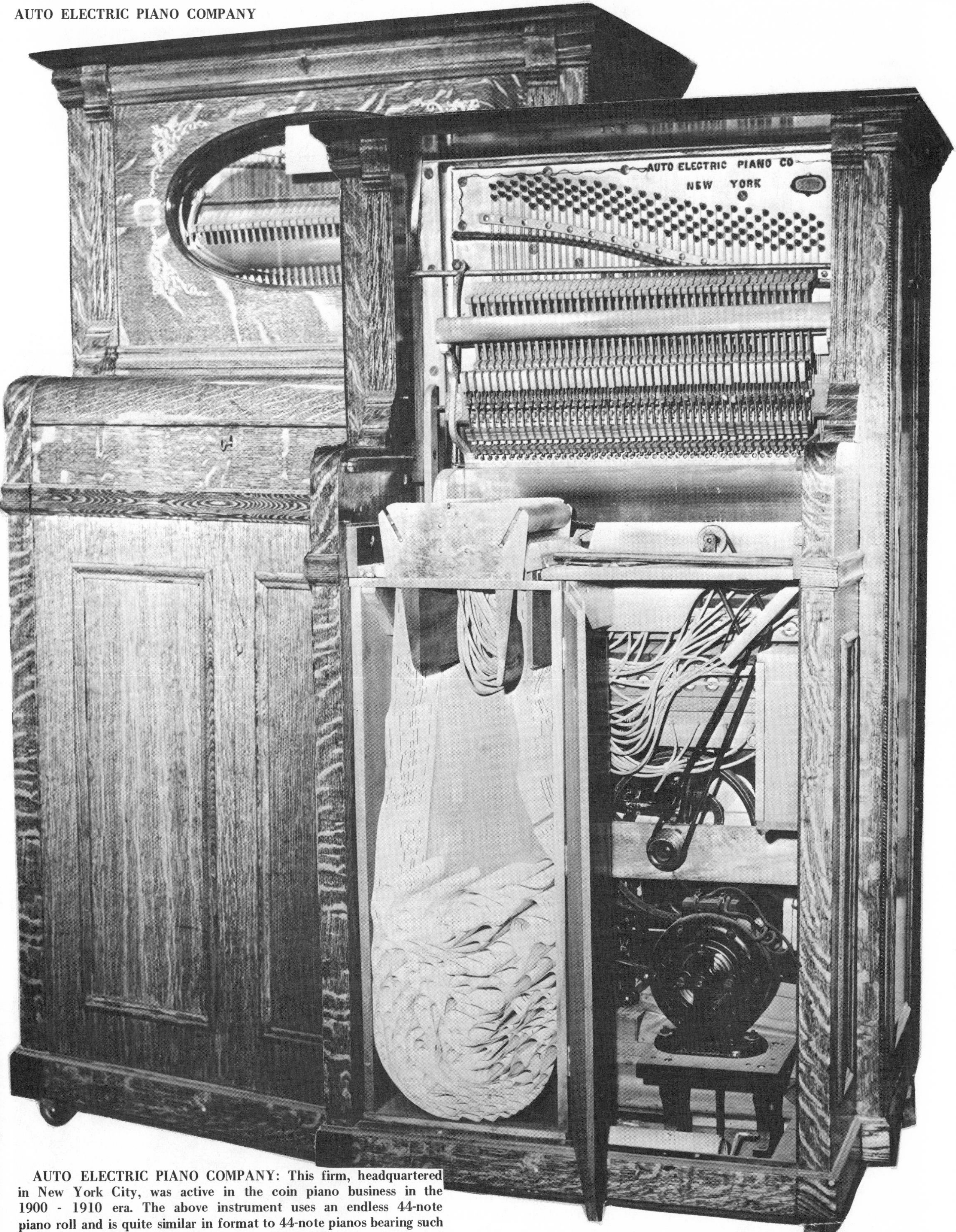


AUTO ELECTRIC PIANO COMPANY: This firm, headquartered in New York City, was active in the coin piano business in the 1900 - 1910 era. The above instrument uses an endless 44-note piano roll and is quite similar in format to 44-note pianos bearing such other contemporary names as Peerless, North Tonawanda Musical Instrument Works, and Regal. (Roy Haning and Neal White photograph)

## AUTOMATIC ORCHESTRA COMPANY
—(sales agents) Detroit, Michigan—

John A. Marquette of Detroit, Michigan, was a sales agent and operator of coin pianos and orchestrions during the 'teens and early 'twenties.

Business was conducted by the Marquette Musical Company, also known as the Automatic Orchestra Company. The trademark "Marcola" was used on some of the instruments. Although Marquette reconditioned and sold used coin pianos of many American makes and was one of the early sales agents for Nelson Wiggen, his most curious product was the Marcola orchestrion shown on this page.

Evidently at least two of these were made, for two are known to exist today. The instrument was made by taking a keyboardless cabinet-style piano manufactured circa 1910 by the Automatic Musical Company of Binghamton, New York, forerunner of the Link Piano and Organ Co. The chassis of the original instrument was stripped of its doors (which were indeed there originally as evidenced by the hinge marks) and top and then was placed intact inside of a larger cabinet! The cabinet, of impressive style with two large art glass panels at the top front and a transfer musical design on the large bottom panel, was of quartered oak. Two hanging lamps, not shown in our picture, were at each top side.

To conceal the Binghamton origin of the instrument, an "Orchestra Company, Detroit Michigan" cast overlay was made. This, when fitted to the piano plate, caused the instrument to read: Automatic Orchestra Company, Detroit Michigan" — as we illustrate. The orchestrion was equipped with four new coin slots, of the same exterior design as used on Berry - Wood pianos, in order not to miss a single nickel!

The two Marcola orchestrions known each use regular Link RX endless rolls.

Chronology of Marquette

Mr. Roger Gregg has furnished the following chronology of John A. Marquette's activities, as taken from Detroit city directories:

1908: John A. Marquette, salesman. 1098 Champlain.

1909 to 1914: Marquette Musical Co., John A. Marquette, general manager. Electric pianos and coin-operated machines of all descriptions. 168 Helen Avenue.

1915: Same, but 794 Woodward.

1916: Same, but 3998 Woodward Ave. Also selling phonographs.

1917: John A. Marquette, proprietor of Marquette's Cafe, 1 to 3 Palmer Blvd.

1918, 1919: J.A. Marquette Musical Co. & Cafe. Home: 147 Moss Ave. H.P.

1920, 1921: J.A. Marquette Real Estate & Insurance. Marquette Music Co. (Harry E. DeSchryver, manager). 163-165 Arizona Ave.

John A. Marquette is not mentioned after 1922. DeSchryver is mentioned until 1931 as a seller of coin-operated games, phonographs, and electric pianos.

Above: Piano plate with "Orchestra Company..." overlay in place.
Below: The true identity is revealed by removing the plate.

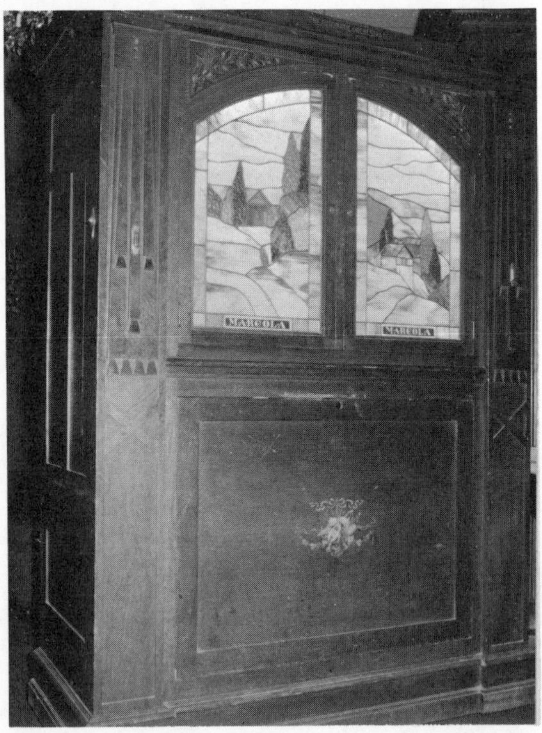


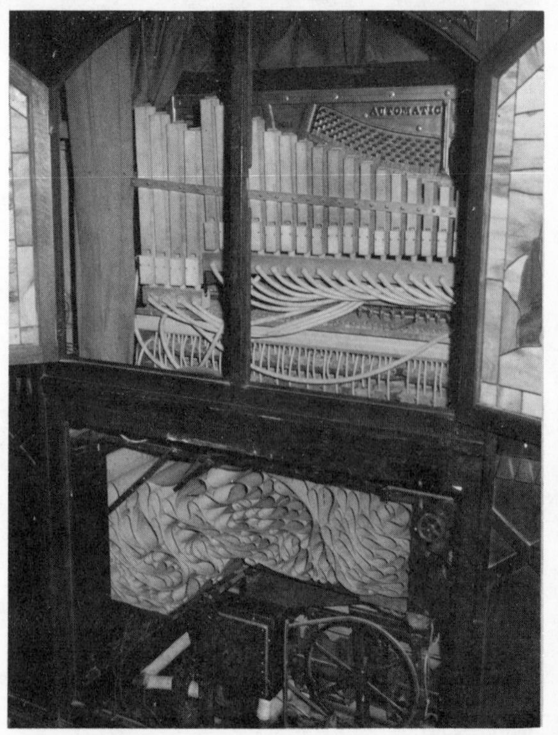


Views of a Marcola orchestrion sold by the Automatic Orchestra Company of Detroit, Michigan. At the top of the instrument, on the outside and above the art glass, is the notation: "Manufactured by the Automatic Orchestra Co.," and "manufactured" it indeed was! (H.E. van der Boom and Rice Berkshire collections)

## M. BARBIERI

In 1925 and 1926 M. Barbieri's "Electro-Musical Inventions" were sold through the firm of Ditta Strumenti Musicali BOTTALI of Milan, Italy. Sales were by means of catalogues and by exhibits at fairs, the Fashion Fair of Milan (1925) and the International Exposition at Turin.

By means of the Barbieri system rolls could be recorded from a piano or organ keyboard. Rolls were cut directly on a device called the Autoperforator. Immediately following the recording, the rolls could be played back by means of the Automusicograph — a roll player which could be attached to a piano or organ.

Of sophisticated concept, the Barbieri recording system in its most deluxe form employed two keyboards, each connected to the same Autoperforator, so that intricate solo and solo-with-accompaniment performances were possible. The organ recording device had buttons to push for recording three levels of expression, nine organ registers, and control perforations — such as tremolo and general cancel.

The Barbieri system exhibited at the Fashion Fair employed two organ cabinets (called "Orchestrals") and a piano. The manufacturer, Soc. Anon. Brevetti Barbieri Milano, used the trademark "Sabbaem" on its products.

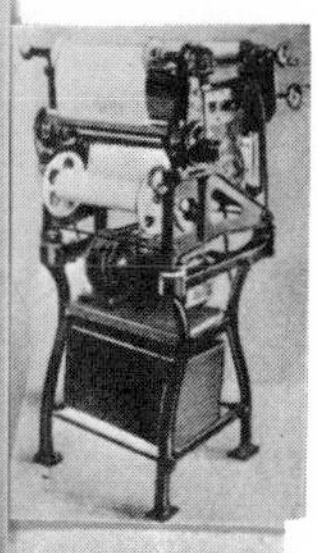

## HEGELER & EHLERS

The piano factory of Hegeler & Ehlers, located in Oldenburg i. Gr., Germany, marketed a piano with violin attachment in 1908. The piano, pneumatically operated, used a 72-note paper roll. The two highest octaves were mechanically coupled (by means of long rods as shown in the lower right illustration on this page) to a real violin which was mounted on top of the piano pin block at the upper right. The violin itself was played by means of an endless belt which came into contact with one or more strings. Small fingers connected to the rods leading up from the piano action depressed to stop the string at the desired intervals and to produce the correct note.

Although little is known of the Hegeler & Ehlers "Geigenpiano" (Violinpiano), the device probably proved impractical, especially in comparison to the easier-to-maintain violin pipes, a small rank of which would have served the same tonal purpose. It is curious that the case design is such that the patron using the Geigenpiano would not have been aware of the unusual violin mechanism within.

## BERRY-WOOD PIANO PLAYER COMPANY

**Headquartered in Kansas City, Missouri, the Berry-Wood Piano Player Company was a major force in the American coin piano industry prior to World War I.**

**In 1907 Berry-Wood introduced the "Auto Electric Piano Player," an electric coin operated piano with the roll mechanism attached to the back of the piano behind the sounding board. This rear location provided ample room for the large bin which stored the loops of the endless paper roll. The Auto Electric Piano Player (the term "Piano Player" – rather than the now more familiar "Player Piano" – was used as in the early days such mechanical devices were thought of as attachments for playing the piano; later, especially after about 1910, the self-contained units became popularly known as player pianos) was a great commercial success. Berry-Wood testimonials of the 1907 era cite orders for carload lots.**

**In 1911 the first Berry-Wood orchestrions, designated as "Auto-Orchestras," were introduced. In 1912 the largest Berry-Wood orchestrion ever made, the Style A.O.W., made its debut.**

**Capitalizing on the growing market for coin operated pianos and on the expansion of its own business, Berry-Wood opened branches in San Francisco and New York City. The San Francisco branch was especially active and sold a great quantity of instruments. Several years later the tide of Berry-Wood's fortunes turned. The firm went out of business before 1920.**

**Many of the Berry-Wood pianos were offered in two different styles: with the continuous or endless roll mechanism which used a large closed loop of paper (the Link Piano Co. was famous for this type of roll also) and with the regular rewind type of roll. The endless rolls were made earlier and, as the market preference for the rewind type of roll emerged, the rewind type mechanism was offered as an option. The "R" in a Berry-Wood catalogue designation meant "rewind." For instance, the Style A.O.H. Auto-Orchestra described as "A.O.H." used the endless type of roll. With the rewind type of mechanism the same style was designated "A.O.H.R."**

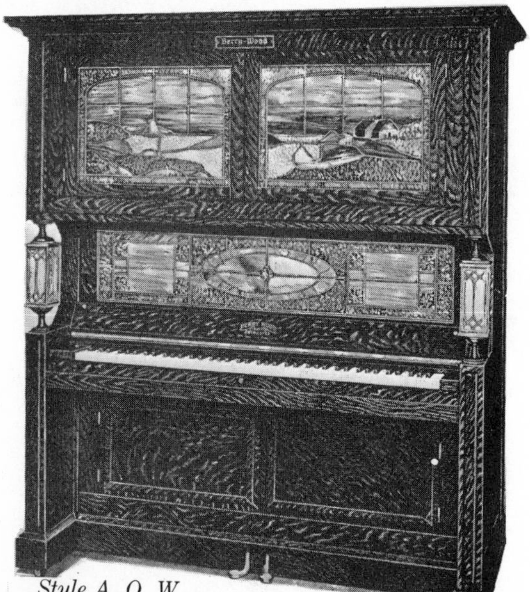


*Style A. O. W.*
*In Rewind Music Only*

CONTAINS Celebrated Berry-Wood Rewind Player. Case six feet high, ordinary width. Mission Design and Finish. Beautiful Art Glass Panels and Lamps. Has Thirty-four wood Flute Pipes, Thirty-four Violin Pipes, Coupler giving Ninety-two Pipe Tones. Twenty-five Steel Bells, Twenty-five Bar Xylophone, Kettle Drum, Castinets, Crash Cymbal, Triangle, Bass and Snare Drum, Cymbal, Device for drumming on rim; also Tambourine and Mandolin. Equivalent to a ten piece orchestra.

**Style A.O.W. – the largest Berry-Wood orchestrion. Introduced in 1912 it was mainly sold in the 1912-1914 years. The "device for drumming on the rim" (of the snare drum) is an unusual feature.**

**All Berry-Wood instruments were of the keyboard style and were based on upright pianos. No cabinet type (keyboardless) instruments were made, to our knowledge.**

**As Berry-Wood went out of business early in the coin piano field's history the Berry-Wood instruments were considered obsolete by the mid-1920's and many were junked at that time. According to one brochure, by 1925 there was only one supplier of Berry-Wood rolls still in business – and that supplier was lamenting the lack of interest in his rolls and was threatening to discontinue cutting them unless more business was forthcoming.**

**In 1913 Berry-Wood announced that it would soon add photoplayers to its line of products. In the absence of any extant catalogue illustrations, news releases, etc. picturing or describing these photoplayers we must surmise that either none was made or else that very few were made. None is known to exist today.**

**Berry-Wood coin pianos and orchestrions are fairly scarce today. Several different types of Berry-Wood rolls were produced to use on the instruments. The rolls are not interchangeable with instruments of other makes.**

**Berry-Wood instruments are well made and are very attractive. With the exception of certain early models which have clear beveled glass front windows (with "Berry-Wood" etched on the glass) most Berry-Wood pianos and orchestrions are ornamented with beautiful opalescent art glass panels which are illuminated from behind as the instrument plays.**

**Interior of an endless-roll piano.**

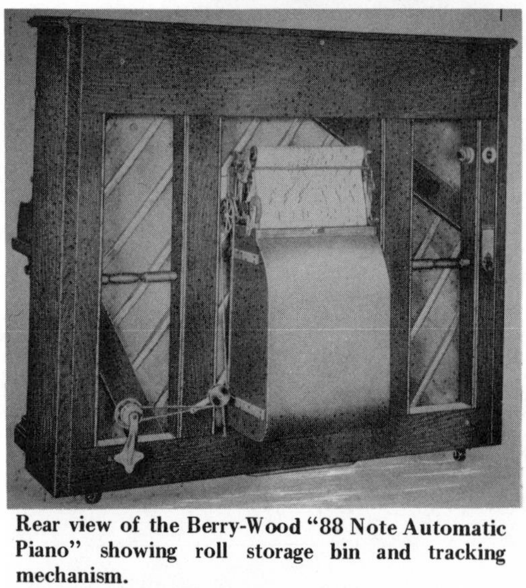

**Rear view of the Berry-Wood "88 Note Automatic Piano" showing roll storage bin and tracking mechanism.**

**Coin slot device on the Berry-Wood "88 note" piano.**

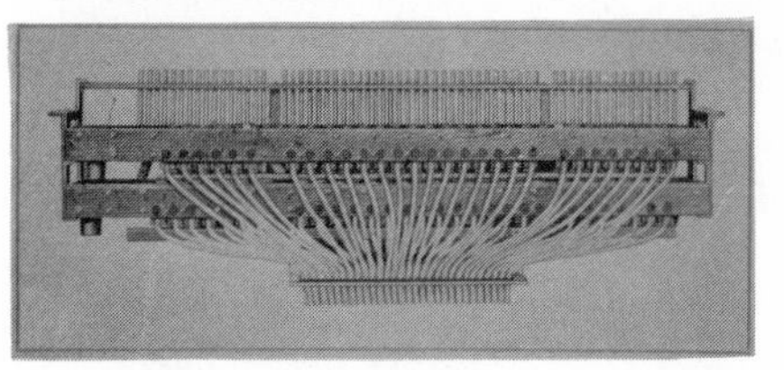

**Pneumatic stack from a Berry-Wood piano. The upright wooden rods at the top actuate the piano hammers.**

**4-part vacuum pump from a Berry-Wood piano.**

Left: Style A.O.S. Auto Orchestra orchestrion. "88-note" piano plus a rank of either flute or violin pipes, bass drum, snare drum, cymbal, and triangle. As "A.O.S." it uses 5 tune endless rolls. In the rewind style (A.O.S.R.) it uses 8-tune rolls.

Right: Style 15. "88-note" piano scale using expression rolls. Available 3 ways: (1) as a piano alone; (2) with violin pipes; (3) with flute pipes. Rewind type rolls with 4 to 8 selections per roll.

Above: The Berry-Wood "Auto Electric Piano Player." This instrument was made in two basic roll types: the so-called "65-note" which actually played 62 piano notes and the "88-note" which played 84 piano notes. These instruments used the endless type of roll. "This mechanism is placed at the back of the piano where it is easily accessible when a change of music is desired and where it does not mar the beauty of the piano inasmuch as it is impractical and impossible to put it inside the ordinary size piano case." Variations in the piano case design occur. Some have oval rather than rectangular glass panels. Pianos of this type were the backbone of Berry-Wood's business in 1907 and 1908.

Styles C, L, and C-B. Style C plays the piano ("88 notes") with endless rolls. Style L is the same, but with rewind rolls. Style C-B uses endless rolls and has 25 steel orchestra bells in addition to the piano.

Style E. Uses "88-note" rewind rolls of 8 to 10 tunes per roll. 4'10" high, 5'5" wide, 2'2½" deep. "The classic design of this case makes it particularly effective in rooms having artistic surroundings." - noted the Berry-Wood catalogue.

*Style F.*

*In Rewind Music Only*

CONTAINS Celebrated Berry-Wood Eighty-eight Note Player Action, Thirty-seven wood Flute or Violin Pipes. All mechanism contained in a rich Teak-wood finished case, Beautiful Swell front center Art Glass Panel, Two Oval Side Panels of Harp Design, Double Veneered Case, Full Iron Plate, 7⅓ Octaves. Full Extension Automatic Music Desk, Three Strung Unisons; imported German Wire, Full Copper Wound Bass Strings, Built-up Pin Blocks of Rock Maple Double Repeating Action, Billings Brass Flanges, Best Ivory Keys, Fourteen Pound Hammers. *Magazine Slot*

*In ordering state whether Flute or Violin Pipes are wanted*

Style A.O.H. (or A.O.H.R. with rewind rolls) orchestrion. "88-note" piano player action, 37 wood violin pipes, 37 wood flute pipes, bass drum, snare drum, cymbal, and triangle. "Equal to a six piece orchestra."

## BLESSING
—Unterkirnach, Germany—

The Blessing family's prominence in the manufacture of automatic musical instruments spanned several generations and extended from the 1790's to the 1920's. Although factory production of instruments ceased in the 1920's, repair work and custom work was carried on through the 1960's.

Martin Blessing (1774-1847) sold clocks and other devices in Russia from 1791 to 1805 (and later from 1809 to 1814). In 1805 he returned to his native country, Germany, and began the production of portable hand-cranked barrel organs and organ clocks. A partnership was formed with brother Karl Blessing (1769-1820).

Following Karl's death in 1820, the School of Martin Blessing was established. Many Black Forest orchestrion and organ clock makers (Michael Welte was prominent among them) served their apprenticeship here. Joseph Blessing was manager of the training center.

In 1829 the Blessing works made a mammoth 164-key instrument which had fifteen pipe registers. This was sold to a customer in London for the astonishing sum of 150,000 marks.

The Blessing factory was continued by Jacob Blessing (1799-1879), by Wolfgang Blessing, and by other members of the family until the main facilities closed in the 1920's. Custom work and repair work was continued after that date. An example of the later instruments is the "Robot Band" constructed during the 1950's on special order for Lewis Graham of New York. Featuring an earlier Philipps & Söhne electric piano (originally made circa 1925) the Robot Band includes an automaton piano player figure, a drummer, and an accordion player.

Blessing instruments made during the 19th century included portable hand-cranked organs in many varieties, organ clocks including many with automaton figures, and barrel-operated orchestrions. Emphasis was placed on orchestrions, and in the early years Martin Blessing advertised himself as an "orchestrion'builder" — the same designation used later by Jacob and Johann Blessing.

Blessing orchestrions stylistically resembled contemporary instruments made by other Black Forest firms — Welte, Heizmann, Imhof & Mukle, Bruder, et al. Blessing barrel-operated orchestrions were built until the early 20th century. During the 19th century Blessing instruments were exhibited at expositions and fairs in London, Paris, and other cities and were awarded many medals. Blessing also sold many orchestrions to Russia, particularly Petrograd (Leningrad) and Moscow.

During the decade before World War I the factory of Wolfgang Blessing produced a series of orchestrions operated by paper rolls. Some of these were quite large and featured motion picture effects, "wonder lights," and other scenic devices on the front. Although catalogues were prepared in several languages, apparently the distribution of these instruments was limited. Such Blessing orchestrions have all but disappeared today.

About 1910-1914 Blessing sold many examples of the "Beethophon Reproducing Piano," an instrument which featured hand-played rolls. Production was limited, however, in comparison to the Welte-Mignon, Hupfeld Dea, and other leading makes, and Blessing never became an important factor in the reproducing piano field.

In the 1920's a series of Jazz Band Orchestrions was popular. Made in both barrel-operated and roll-operated styles, the Jazz Band Orchestrions were given such designations as "Polyvox," "Jazzy," and "Little Jazz Band Orchestra." The roll-operated models used a 6-holes-to-the-inch 11¼" wide roll — the same general specification as used for the then-popular American "A" roll, although the tracker scales of the Blessing rolls were arranged differently. Many of these Blessing instruments of the 1920's were sold in France and Germany.

In Unterkirnach, deep in Germany's Black Forest, the factory building of Blessing still stands today.

----------

Above: Xylophone Piano, Model I. Piano with xylophone.

Right: Case design for the "Export I," an orchestrion with: piano, one register of violin and cello pipes, one register of gedeckt pipes, xylophone, and drum and trap effects. 3 meters high. The same catalogue illustration was also used for "Export II," an orchestrion which measured just 2.7 meters high and contained piano, xylophone, mandolin, and drum and trap effects. Popular circa 1912.

Left: "Carmen," keyboardless orchestrion from about 1912. Contains piano, mandolin, two ranks of pipes, xylophone, bells, and drum and trap effects. Crescendo shutters in the top of the case provide expression. With motion picture scene on the front.

(Credit note: Most illustrations courtesy of Farny Wurlitzer and Alain Vian.)

Above: "Jazy" (or "Jazzy"), a barrel-operated "incomparable little jazz band orchestra." Contains piano, bass drum, tenor drum, cymbal, and wood block. Popular during the 1920's.

Above: "Matador" orchestrion. With piano, mandolin, harmonium, 8 ranks of pipes, xylophone, bells, and drum and trap work. 4.1 meters high by 3.5 meters wide by 1.1 meters deep. Motion picture effects on front.

Left: "Orchestrion in Burgform" (orchestrion in castle form). "House of the Magicians." Instrumentation the same as the "Carmen" orchestrion. With a "wonder light," automaton figures, motion picture effects, and other gadgetry this orchestrion is one of the most unusual-appearing instruments of its kind. 3.2 meters high by 2 meters wide by 1.2 meters deep. Made circa 1912.

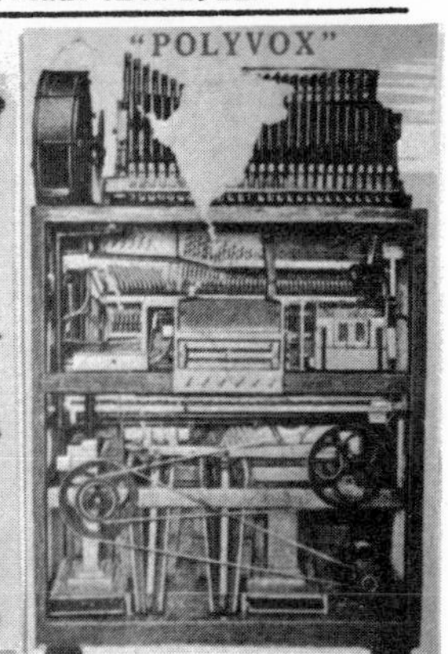


Above: Polyvox Model A. With 51-note piano, 27-note xylophone, 27-note mandolin, 27 flute pipes, bass drum, tenor drum, cymbal, tambourine, castanets, and triangle. 2.7 meters high by 1.65 meters wide by 0.8 meters deep. Usually made in a mahogany or oak case with brass trim ornaments. Popular during the 1920's. Roll-operated.

Above: General case design for Polyvox models B, C, D. Upper right: Interior of Model B. Right: Interior of Model C. Instrumentation: B: 51-note piano, 27-note mandolin, 15-note xylophone, plus drum and trap effects. C: 51-note piano, 27-note mandolin, plus drum and trap effects. D: 51-note piano, 27-note mandolin. Measurements of all instruments: 2.3 meters high by 1.5 meters wide by 0.75 meters deep.

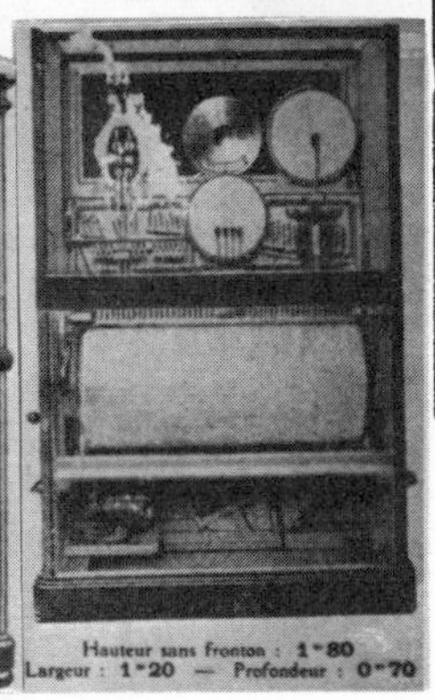


Above: "Bijou Jazz Band Orchestra," a barrel-operated orchestrion with piano and drum and trap effects.

Right: "Jazbandor — Grand Orchestra Jazz Band." Barrel-operated piano with 8 tubular chimes and drum and trap effects. 2.3 meters high by 1.36 meters wide by 0.71 meters deep.

## CHICAGO ELECTRIC PIANOS
### –Smith, Barnes & Strohber Co.–

"Chicago Electric" brand pianos were manufactured by the Smith, Barnes, & Strohber Company which, at one time, maintained manufacturing facilities in North Milwaukee, Wisconsin, and had sales offices at 1875 Clybourn Avenue, Chicago. Later the firm was a division of the Continental Piano Company.

Certain Chicago Electric piano cases are similar in some details to certain Coinola (made by the Operators Piano Co. of Chicago) cases – indicating that both firms may have ordered cabinet parts from a common supplier.

Evidently the output of Chicago Electric instruments was limited for these are quite rare today. To our knowledge, all Chicago Electric coin pianos use regular type "A" rolls.

It is possible that these instruments were made on a contractual basis by the Operators Piano Company – however, this is just speculation. It is certain, however, that the Smith, Barnes and Strohber Company never entered the coin piano field in a serious way. Rather, it appears that a few different styles were made in order to explore the market – as was done by quite a few other producers of regular upright and grand pianos.

---

Chicago Electric coin pianos. In addition the author has seen a cabinet piano with mandolin and xylophone similar to the Style K but with extended front posts running from the top to the bottom of the case. Pianos identical to the one pictured at the bottom of this page – with "NEW SCALE" on the piano plate – were used in certain Multitone instruments (see Operators Piano Co. and Welte sections of this book).

*The* CHICAGO ELECTRIC MODEL K

*The* CHICAGO ELECTRIC MODEL EL-2

WHEREVER there is a happy crowd —there is music. That's a tip. Wherever there is happy music—there is a crowd. That's a tip for the owners of public gathering places.

It is music that puts the life in any amusement establishment. Restaurants, ice cream parlors, theatres, parks, gardens or pavilions.

Here is music that pays its own way—pays a profit, too.

You can have it tomorrow.

We are offering you the Chicago Electric Piano—coin operated—that furnishes music of the quality that pleases. The real quality of piano playing that people like. Especially popular with young people.

This has been accomplished by making the piano good—building it after the plan of a successful player piano. This is a modern electric piano of the highest order, constructed to serve without difficulty.

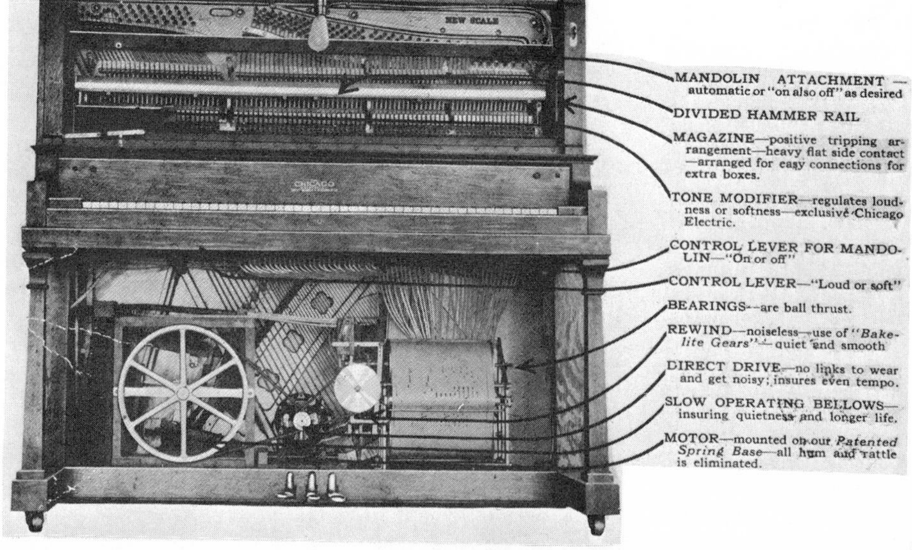

## E. DIENST

Founded in 1871, the firm of E. Dienst & Co. of Leipzig-Göhlis, Germany, produced a line of barrel-operated pianos and orchestrions until the late 1890's and then produced a series of pneumatic instruments during the early 1900's. Dienst maintained two sales outlets in America (New York City and Chicago), one of the few German piano makers to do so. Dienst instruments were sold under a variety of names including "Mezon" and "Pneuma." ("Pneuma" was also used by the firm of Kuhl & Klatt of Berlin). The pneumatic mechanisms of the roll-operated Dienst instruments were licensed under the Ludwig Hupfeld patents. Dienst keyboard pianos bear a close resemblance to contemporary instruments of Hupfeld, Heilbrunn, Kuhl & Klatt, and other German makers of the early 1900's.

A circa 1904 catalogue was multi-lingual (German, French, English, Spanish, Italian, and Russian captions) and noted that "Instruments are cross-strung with the best repeating mechanism; with ivory keys and ornate top gallery. Illustrations and prices for any desired [custom made] style and design supplied on application. The pianos can be played by hand in the ordinary way. The right to make deviations in details of design is reserved. The latest novelty is the self-acting pneumatic mandolin [attachment]. Pleasant and clear tones. Very effective. The mandolin can be stopped at will."

Certain illustrations were used in both Dienst and Kuhl & Klatt catalogues; some of the keyboard piano illustrations shown here can be used to identify Kuhl & Klatt instruments as well!

----------

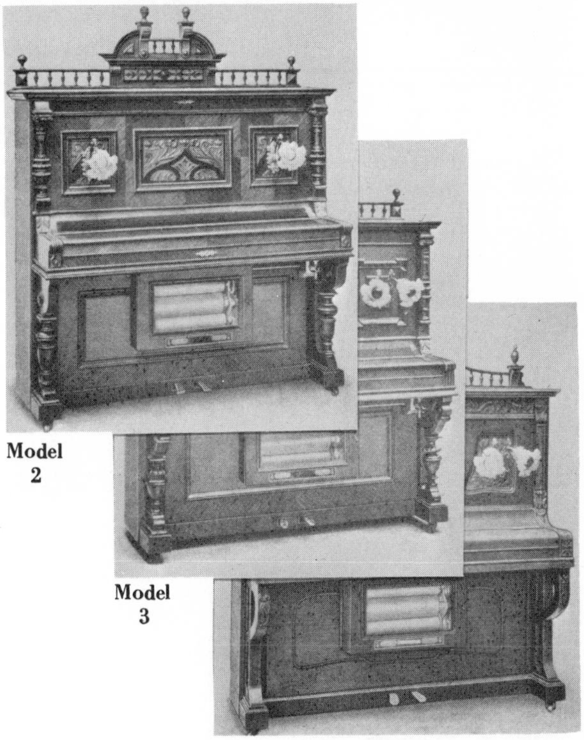

Model 2

Model 3

Model 3-B

Model 1

Model 1-B

Model 4

Model 6

Model 8

Piano with "wonder light" attachment.

Special lighting effects were available for Dienst instruments. At the upper left is an apparatus with "effective and changing illuminated painted panes representing a battlefield. Each cannon shock is represented by a burst of flame." At the upper right is the naval equivalent: "Effective and changing scene representing a naval battle. Each cannon shock is represented by a burst of flame."

Modell 3: ca. 144 cm hoch, schwarz oder nussbaum blank.
Modell 4: ca. 130 cm h., jungdeutsch, matt nussbaum Ahorn-Füllungen.
Modell 2: ca. 138 cm hoch, schwarz oder nussbaum blank.

Dienst instruments from a 1904 catalogue. Models 2, 4, and 3 shown at the left and the "Special Model for Austria and Hungary" shown at the above left were also used to illustrate Kuhl & Klatt catalogues. The instrument at the upper right is a typical Dienst piano orchestrion of the keyboardless style. Dienst maintained sales outlets in Cairo, Chicago, Christiana, Hamburg, Lyon, New York City, Paris, and Vienna. A branch wholly-owned by Dienst was located in Brussels, Belgium. The main works were located at Eisenacherstrasse 39/40 in Gŏhlis, a district of Leipzig, Germany.

Hupfeld's patented piano-player apparatus as used in certain Dienst, Kuhl & Klatt, and other German-built instruments of the early 1900's.

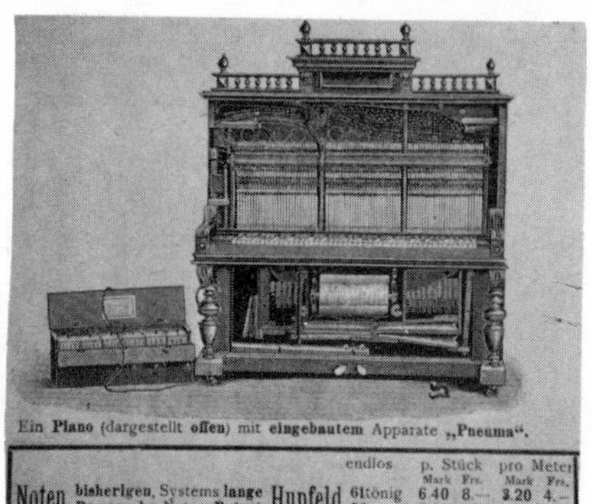

Ein Piano (dargestellt offen) mit eingebautem Apparate „Pneuma".

| | | endlos | p. Stück Mark | p. Stück Frs. | pro Meter Mark | pro Meter Frs. |
|---|---|---|---|---|---|---|
| Noten | bisherigen Systems lange Pressspahn-Noten, Patent Hupfeld | 61tönig | 6.40 | 8.– | 3.20 | 4.– |
| | | 76 „ | 7.60 | 9.50 | 3.80 | 4.75 |

Grand piano equipped with the Hupfeld apparatus (installed by Dienst).

# DIENST

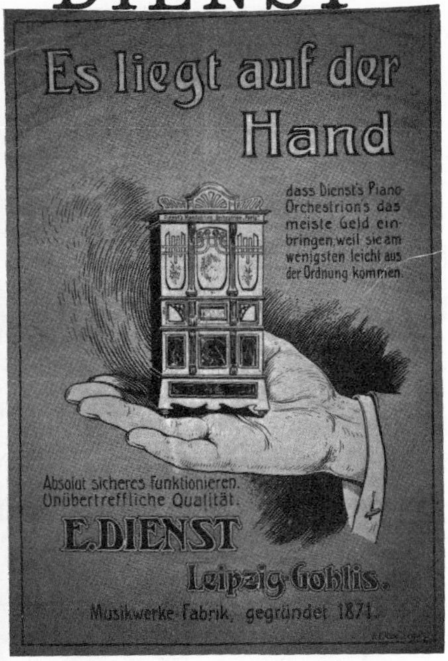

Above and left are illustrations from Dienst advertisements of the 1908-1910 period. Dienst produced many interesting engravings showing orchestrions in use (as in the guest house scene at the upper left), glorifying the instruments (showing the instruments circling the earth, surrounded with resplendent sun rays, etc.), and showing the orchestrions in obscure locations (the Chilean Andes, the Sahara Desert, etc.).

August Eduard Dienst, founder of the firm, is shown to the right. In 1871 he founded the firm which bore his name. He was a pioneer manufacturer in what was later to become the world's busiest city in the automatic musical instrument trade. Dienst advertisements of the 1900's often carried the tag line "first Leipzig accordion and automatic musical instrument factory" ("Erste Leipziger Accordion und Musikwerke-Fabrik"). Non-automatic products of the Dienst enterprise included accordions sold under the "International" name and furniture marketed under the "Kosmos" label. August Eduard Dienst died in 1912 at the age of 69 years.

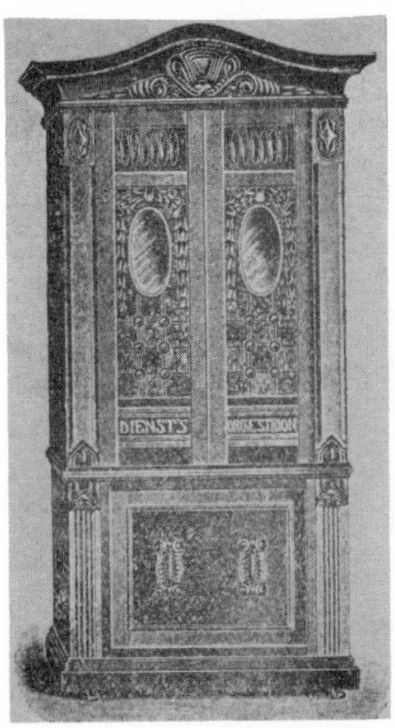

Dienst orchestrions of the 1900-1910 decade.

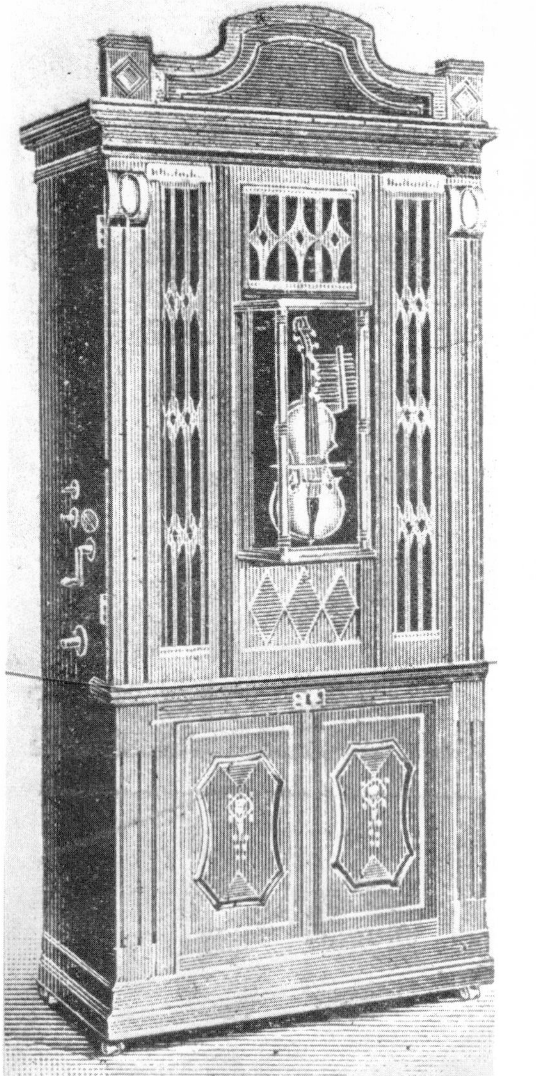

Dienst's Self-Playing Violin

Dienst's Self-Playing Violin (in German as originally advertised, Dienst's Selbstspielende Geige) was first produced in 1910. In 1911 and 1912 these were sold in modest numbers, probably to the extent of several dozen instruments in all.

Dienst's Self-Playing Violin was barrel-operated and was powered by hand-winding a weight-drive mechanism. The tunes were programmed on pinned wooden barrels. The instrument was billed as being "without pipes; with real violin." The price, including two barrels, was 2200 Marks.

Dienst Orchestrions
on the High Seas

Dienst orchestrions entertained sailors aboard the battleship Dresden (shown above). To the right is a large orchestrion which entertained passengers aboard the ill-fated Lusitania. Dienst orchestrions were used aboard a number of German and English passenger ships on the North Atlantic route. An advertisement of 1908 noted that special Dienst construction for changing climatic conditions made the firm's orchestrions especially suitable for maritime use.

Zampa

Perla Orchestrion

Three barrel-operated Dienst instruments offered by Dienst in 1910.

Capella Orchestrion

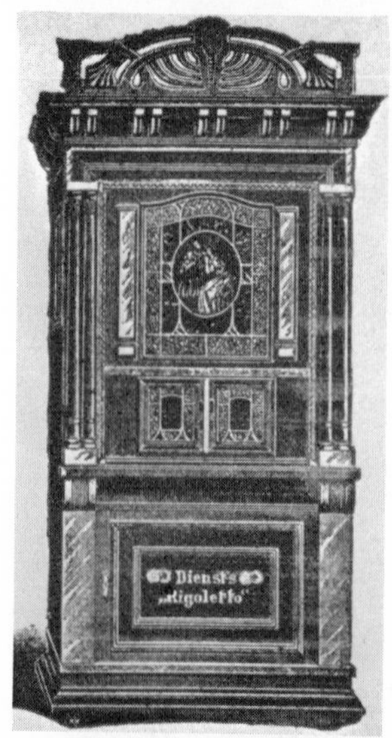

Rigoletto Orchestrion

## PIERRE EICH
—Ghent, Belgium—

During the early 20th century the firm of Pierre Eich of Ghent ("Gand" in the Flemish language), Belgium produced a variety of automatic musical instruments. Most Eich products were distributed within Belgium itself, so the instruments were little known on a worldwide scale. The Eich firm produced instruments until 1939, the year the factory closed. Thus the company was one of the last makers of electric pianos in the world.

Following the 1939 closure most of the remaining Pierre Eich instruments, rolls, and other accessories were acquired by the Van Hyfte Piano Co. of Ghent. Certain records and catalogues were acquired by Mr. A. Baude. The editor is indebted to these sources for much of the information given here.

The three most popular Eich instruments were the Super Violin (a piano with mandolin attachment and violin pipes), the Solophone (a piano with from three to six ranks of pipes, depending upon the model), and the Piano-Jazz (a piano with accordion and [in some models] drum and trap effects). These were made in a wide variety of case styles throughout the 1920's and 1930's. The pianos were purchased from Schwander (J. Herrburger) and other piano factories. Pierre Eich added the instrumentation.

During the 1920's and 1930's several models of the Accordeon [sic] Jazz, a roll-operated instrument containing loudly-voiced accordion reeds and, sometimes, drum and trap effects, were made. The Accordeon Jazz contained no piano, although some models were built in cases which resembled an upright keyboard piano. Other models were built in compact cabinets which measured about 4' high.

In the early 20th century Pierre Eich manufactured many book-operated fairground organs. Most of these had ornate facades and were sold for use with carnivals and other shows.

In 1939 Pierre Eich designed a number of keyboard-style pianos and orchestrions with very modernistic facades — designs resembling Mortier and Decap dance hall organs of the period. However, the coming of World War II and the closing of the Eich factory precluded any further development of these interesting designs.

The Pierre Eich factory still stands in Ghent today.

Pierre Eich Solophone in an especially ornate carved oak case. Ranks of pipes in the top of the case represent flute, clarinet, saxophone, violin, viola, and cello. (James Prendergast Collection)

Right: Pierre Eich Solophone in a modernistic case of the 1930's. The mahogany cabinet is ornamented with art glass, lamp sconces, and beveled mirrors.

Instrumentation of the Solophone varied from one example to another. The one illustrated here contains violin-type pipes primarily.

Oscar Grymonprez stands between a Pierre Eich Piano-Jazz (sometimes called an Accordeon [sic] Orchestra) and a Solophone. Made in Belgium, Pierre Eich instruments were mainly distributed in that country.

Pierre Eich Super Violin: The Pierre Eich Super Violin (or "Super Violon" as it was originally designated in the Flemish language) consists of a keyboard piano, mandolin attachment, and a rank of thirty well-made and carefully-voiced violin pipes. The violin solo part of the piano scale is arranged so that the piano can be silent during the playing of the violin pipes, or the violin pipes can play one series of notes while the bass part of the piano plays an entirely different series of notes as accompaniment. Expression is provided by a swell shutter in the top of the instrument.

The Super Violin, made in large numbers during the 1920's and 1930's, was one of the most popular of the Pierre Eich instruments. Several case design variations are shown here. Those shown above and to the left are late styles from the 1930's. Those at the immediate and upper right are from the 1920's. Note that the instrument to the immediate right has the roll located below the keyboard.

Above: Pierre Eich Accordeon Jazz from the 1920's. Contains accordion reeds, saxophone pipes, and other effects.

Left: A Pierre Eich book-operated fairground organ. The Eich firm made many different models of fairground organs during the early 20th century.

## ELECTROVA COIN-OPERATED PIANOS

### –Jacob Doll & Sons–

From about 1905 to 1920 the firm of Jacob Doll & Sons of New York City marketed a line of coin-operated pianos under the "Electrova" label.

An early trade directory notes:

"ELECTROVA CO., – Manufactures the "Electrova" coin-operated piano. Has a large equipped plant at 117-124 Cypress Avenue, New York. The Electrova Co. was one of the first to enter the field of the coin-operated piano and has built up a large trade on the merit of reliability of its up-to-date instruments which possess every modern device and many patents devoted entirely to the manufacture of this instrument. It is being handled by many of the representative dealers, who have had a large sale with it all over the country. It is manufactured in both the coin-operated electric 44-note (cabinet) and 88-note keyboard players. Concern in highest financial and commercial standing."

It is evident that many Electrova instruments were made by other manufacturers. For instance, Electrova decals appear on certain instruments (such as Style F) made by the Peerless Piano Player Company of St. Johnsville, New York, and instruments (44-note cabinet players) made by the Pianova Company of New York City. Since writing the "Guidebook of Automatic Musical Instruments" (the predecessor to the present volume) the author has examined a Weser Brothers "Nickel Player" (trademark) piano which has an identical case to the Electrova Style 66 – indicating some type of relationship between the two firms. The "Nickel Player" is illustrated in the Weser section of this volume.

Style "66"—Art Style. Expression Player

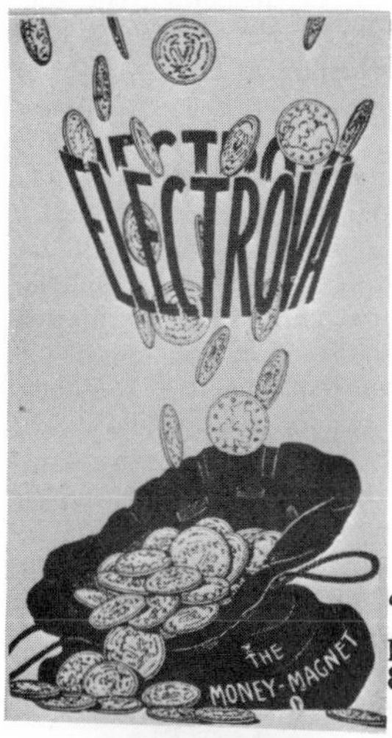

Style 65

Style 65 A

Styles 65 and 65-A are the same except that the "A" stands for "Art" – and the latter has art glass panels. Both types made with either 10-tune 88-note rolls or 5-tune 65-note rolls.

Style 66 was made with 65-note and 88-note rolls (the buyer's choice) also. Also made with one rank of pipes, either flute or violin. Some models had hanging lamps at each end of the front panel, rather than post lamps as illustrated.

In other words, the above basic Electrova cases were made with a wide variety of interiors!

A May 13, 1912, Electrova price list quoted the following wholesale figures with an additional 5% discount for paying within 30 days:

| | |
|---|---|
| Style 65 w/65-note | $300 |
| Style 65 w/88-note | 325 |
| Style 65-A w/88-note | 340 |
| Style 66 w/88-note | 375 |
| Style 44 | 200 |

The above quotation represented a discount from the retail price and was made to the Warren Piano Co. of Evansville, Indiana. (Address: 627 Main St.)

–Style 44–

Height: 66 inches;
Width: 36 inches;
Depth: 24 inches.

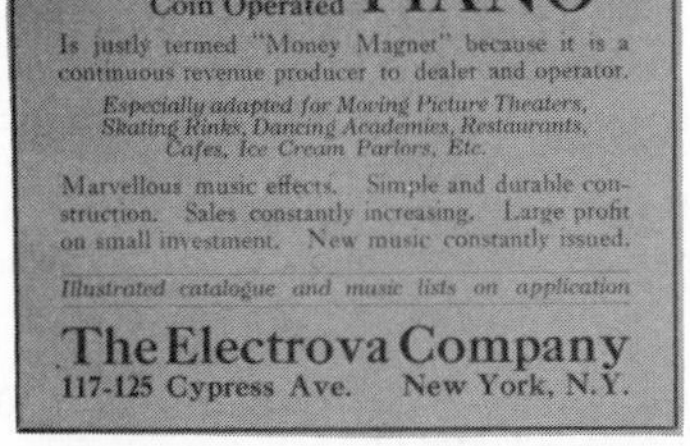


ELECTROVA CO., THE.—Manufactures the "Electrova" coin-operated piano. Has a large equipped plant at 117-124 Cypress avenue, New York. The Electrova Co. was one of the first to enter the field of the coin-operated piano and has built up a large trade on the merit of reliability of its up-to-date instruments, which possess every modern device and many patents devoted entirely to the manufacture of this instrument. It is being handled by many of the representative dealers, who have had a large sale with it all over the country. It is manufactured in both the coin-operated electric 44-note and 88-note keyboard players. Concern in highest financial and commercial standing.

Electrova "puff" from a music trade directory in the 'teens.

## THE ENCORE AUTOMATIC BANJO
### —The Auto-Manufacturing Co.—
### —The American Automusic Co.—

### Introduction

The Encore Automatic Banjo is today one of the most interesting automatic musical instruments which have survived from years ago. The concept of a real banjo automatically operated by tiny mechanical "fingers" and playing in a very realistic manner is a fascinating one. However, until the publication of this section the history of the Encore was unknown.

A few years ago the author of this Encyclopedia received a telephone call from Mr. Christian Verbeke, bookseller. "Would we be interested in a carton of old papers, invoices, ledgers, and sales brochures relating to a type of banjo which played automatically?," asked Mr. Verbeke. "I certainly would!," was my quick reply. Within a few minutes a price was agreed upon. Several days later the material arrived at my home.

The next day or two was spent unravelling the details of what was a series of hopes and failures, a dream that never quite managed to come true. The voluminous letter file, excerpted in the "Ordeal by Letter" section which follows, tells the story vividly. Also, it gives an insight into how an automatic musical instrument business was operated in the years when coin operated devices were just beginning to become popular.

The Encore Automatic Banjo was first conceived by Charles B. Kendall of Boston, Massachusetts. By spending $20,000 to $30,000 (accounts differ) for a long string of patent rights, some of which related only obliquely to automatic instruments, he secured a strong patent hold on the concept of playing a stringed instrument by mechanical means.

By 1896 a firm to make and distribute the Encore was incorporated. By 1897 the Encore was a reality — and instruments were being used in public places.

Two main companies were formed to handle the Encore. One was the American Automusic Company which was located in New York City. Owned in large part by the O'Connor family (owners also of the Connorized Music Company), the American Automusic Company owned or controlled several other subsidiary Banjo distributors in the United States. The "territory" of the American Automusic Company evidently included all of the United States except the states of Maine, New Hampshire, Vermont, and Massachusetts. Those four states were the exclusive right of the New England firm first known as the New England Automatic Banjo Company and the Eastern Specialty Company and, later, in reorganized form as the Auto-Manufacturing Company.

An "official history" of the company, and a quite distorted one as far as financial success and potential are concerned, was written on June 9, 1903 by Charles B. Kendall. This "history," distributed in the form of a prospectus to several securities agents and private investors, is valuable for the details of how the Encore was first developed (including an electromagnetic version — an instrument unknown until its mention in this prospectus was found).

### "THE ENCORE AUTOMATIC BANJO"
### by C.B. Kendall (1903)

"I present to you some facts and figures concerning the business that I have been closely allied with for the past seven years.

"The Automatic Banjo is broadly covered by U.S. Letters Patent that make it an absolute monopoly upon all stringed instruments whereby the tone of a string is changed by automatically changing its length; and the perforated music sheets that are used upon said patented instruments; viz., of the type of the banjo, mandolin, guitar, violin, etc. There have been issued over thirty patents so far and assigned to the company, and there are important improvements on hand that can be patented which will give the invention a new term of seventeen years, whenever it is thought wise to file application therefor.

"Our patents cover the electro-magnetic, pneumatic, and mechanical methods of operation.

"The first automatic banjo was constructed upon the electro-magnetic system, but the magnets then used were of the telegraphic type, too jerky and noisy to be practicable. Furthermore, the only electric current then available was taken from the street lighting lines at 110 volts which causes so much sparking upon the perforated paper music as to sometimes burn them up and endanger the premises. At that time storage or primary batteries were out of the question.

"The next model was made upon the pneumatic system, and was satisfactory. A company was formed and the business begun in New York in 1897. A system of agencies was established in various parts of the United States, giving to an agent the exclusive right in his territory, upon his buying a fifteen year lease of a certain number of automatic banjos at from $300 to $500 each, spot cash. No instruments have ever been sold. The music was leased in the same way, at $3 per roll (5 tunes each).

"The pneumatic system did not continue as satisfactory as was expected, on account of its complications and the many troubles arising therefrom, and the limited area of territory that could be occupied, even in the large cities, because of the unavoidable necessity of using the street light electric current for a motive power. The result has been universal dissatisfaction and complaint among the agents, and a very small amount of business. For lack of capital no special effort has been made for nearly two years by the Company to develop business or to improve the instrument, but the nickel-in-the-slot banjos now being operated in Greater New York upon the percentage plan, and which are in their fifth year of service, receiving but indifferent attention and not much new music, earned in 1902, $11,481.82 after deducting commissions and charges of proprietors of the places where they were installed. The earnings thus far in 1903 maintain the average receipts of 1902, showing the permanency of the profits.

"The new Magnetic Piano Player requires an electric current of 6 volts and 2½ amperes to operate it. It has 65 magnets for the keys and two large ones for the pedals. The banjo requires only 46 small magnets; nothing to correspond with the large pedal magnets, and therefore could not use over 4 volts and 1 ampere as compared with 110v. and .85 amperes required to operate the present pneumatic banjo.

The advantages to be gained in adopting the electro-magnetic system are many and valuable, such as the use of primary and storage batteries, thus permitting the location of the banjo everywhere; reducing the cost of construction at least 25%; the cost of maintenance to not more than one-third the requirements of the present system; the elimination of 90% of all the troubles that cannot be avoided in the pneumatic system, as well as affording opportunities for introducing more tunes and many points of expression that are impossible in the present instrument. In the matter of maintenance of the banjo operated upon the electro-magnetic system, I have no doubt that 20% of the receipts will cover labor, repairs, and music, after the master piece (stencil) is prepared.

"As the present managers of our Company are disinclined to do any experimenting or investing new capital to extend the business, I have arranged to sell out my interest in all other departments of the Company's business and buy the banjo assets entire, believing that an enormous and exceedingly profitable business can be built up in the immediate future. The universal testimony has been that we had the greatest money earner in the world when the pneumatic troubles were eliminated. Of the assets enumerated in the enclosed schedule, the 32 patents cost over $30,000; and the 1800 music stencils over $27,000; the 128 banjos now being operated in Greater New York over $25,000; and the balance about $6,000 — total $88,000.

"Our invention has never been contested and we are acknowledged to have, by our seven years' continuous service, an unassailable position, by 'public acquiescence.' Furthermore, the automatic banjo is the only slot machine that has never had to reduce its original coin, a nickel; all others now use one cent.

"I desire to take over the Banjo business; obtain additional capital and reorganize it, being firmly convinced that every dollar put into it will pay 100% per annum profit, if conducted on an extensive scale.

"Please consider the information concerning the electro-magnetic system confidential, and, if the enterprise that I have so imperfectly outlined is of interest to you, I should be pleased for an interview for further consideration. I do not wish to sell my interests, but desire to associate them as a minority with some party or parties who will organize a new Company; take up the enterprise properly and develop it.

"Yours very truly,
(signed) C.B. Kendall."

Author's note: The above "prospectus" and the figures that follow this paragraph are "padded." The New York City part of the banjo business was available to Kendall for $10,000, not "over $25,000" as stated; in earlier balance sheets the patents were said to have cost "about $20,000," not "over $30,000" as stated in the prospectus, and so on. Also padding the situation is that the 1800 music stencils valued at $27,000 were acquired as part of the $10,000 deal for the New York City business!

Throughout the records of the American Automusic Company and those of the Auto-Manufacturing Company the firms accuse each other of treachery and accuse many of their customers, agents, and others with whom business was done, of insincere transactions. It appears from the material quoted here that Mr. C.B. Kendall, mastermind of the various Banjo companies, was quite an expert at this sort of thing himself!

Below, we continue with Mr. Kendall's prospectus:

"Inventory of Assets Available for Reorganization"

"Our 32 U.S. Letters Patent cover in the broadest sense all types of automatic stringed musical instruments, and perforated music sheets wherein the tone of a string is changed by automatically changing its length. The original cost of this group of patents was over $30,000.

| | |
|---|---|
| Thirty two patents | $30,000.00 |
| Stock, etc. on hand | 6,000.00 |
| 1800 (about) Banjo Music Stencils @$15 | 27,000.00 |
| 128 Banjos operating in Greater New York | 25,000.00 |
| TOTAL: | $88,000.00 |

"The net receipts of Automatic Banjos operated in Greater New York during 1902 and up to June 1, 1903 are as follows:

"1902: January $1283.25; February $783.33; March $964.22; April $862.76; May $1018.46; June $918.74; July $830.29; August $993.42; September $908.78; October $1011.98; November $949.80; December $956.79. Average number of Banjos operated during the year: 139 1/3 instruments. Average receipts per Banjo per week: $1.59.

"1903: January $1162.36; February $882.23; March $943.72; April $888.73; May $1009.08. Average number of Banjos operated during five months: 128 instruments. Average receipts per Banjo per week: $1.76."

Mr. Kendall then further continued with a lengthy evaluation of the potential of the Banjo. This study noted that the ideal number of Banjos in use would be one per every 3000 inhabitants of a city – and for the top 90 cities containing a total of 18 million inhabitants, this would mean a potential of some 6000 Banjos.

Of significance is the statement that "This number can be made and installed in one year from the completion of the machinery, tools, etc. at a cost not to exceed $65 per instrument, including all factory expenses, freight, cost of installation, superintendent's salary, etc."

Other interesting figures are the estimate that one man could supervise the maintenance of 180 Banjos and that another man could collect from the same number each week. Normal maintenance and repairs would amount to 14c worth of supplies per Banjo per week. Over a three year period the 6000 Banjos would bring in a net profit, after expenses, totaling $1,864,200.00!

The American Automusic Company

The main manufacturer and sales agent for the Encore was the American Automusic Company of New York City. Offices were maintained at 53 Broadway; a factory at 227 Bleecker St. This firm apparently licensed or partially owned several other Encore distributors, mainly in eastern states.

The American Automusic Company was owned nearly entirely by W. Scott O'Connor of the Connorized Music Company, manufacturer of music rolls for push-up piano players. An inventory dated March 21, 1903 reveals that all of the Encore patents were owned by this firm, as were such other items as: 128 Encores located in Greater New York, plus one "in the process of manufacture at the Bleecker St. factory," plus one more at the 53 Broadway office; 5 experimental Encore Banjos; 78 electric motors; 7 new mahogany cabinets; 25 new oak cabinets; and many parts.

All of the music rolls for the various Encore distributors were made by American Automusic. Several hundred tunes were prepared for the Banjo. These were listed alphabetically in the roll catalogues prepared by the firm. The usual practice was to combine five tunes into a "made program." Such programs could be assembled to suit a client's preference, or the customer could select from any one of several hundred 5-tune rolls carried as standard stock. Music roll production was erratic, anything but in step with new and popular tunes, and there was much complaining about it from the various Banjo distributors.

A four-page leaflet, "The King of Slot Machines," was issued to promote the Encore. Various features of the Banjo were listed, including:

"The method of 'stopping' and 'picking' the strings follows faithfully the manual method, but, not being subject to the physical limitations of the latter is, from a technical standpoint, much more thorough and comprehensive, and by thus broadening the range of execution renders it feasible to reproduce musical combinations and orchestrations that are impossible of accomplishment by the manual expert... The precision and monotony which stamp all other automatic musical instruments as 'mechanical' are eliminated, leaving only a varied brilliancy of tone and execution that renders it impossible to detect mechanical operation by other than visual proof. From the fact that each picker can strike its string six hundred strokes per minute, the long sought for 'sustained note' on a musical stringed instrument is practically accomplished, making it possible to introduce and combine mandolin effects whenever required in the rendition of a selection.

"The Company is offering 'The Encore,' a nickel-in-the-slot automatic banjo for operation in public places after the well established method of the coin controlled devices already in use. These instruments are furnished with a music roll containing five popular selections, one of which is rendered by the insertion of a nickel in the slot provided for that purpose. The music sheets are made in the form of an endless belt, traveling through a system of rollers, and will thus repeat as often as desired without handling and by the simple insertion of the coin. The instrument is operated directly from any incandescent electric lighting circuit, and consumes about the same amount of power as an ordinary 16-candle incandescent lamp. The average time for the rendition of a tune is about a minute and a half, and, therefore, the earning capacity of the instrument is about two dollars for each hour of actual work.

"By making daily changes of music in each instrument installed, by the interchange of rolls in use, and by the infusion of new music, a sufficiently varied program is provided to sustain the interest and custom of the public.

"By special arrangement with all of the music publishers in the United States, the Company is provided with advance copies of all new music, which is immediately turned over to their corps of experts to be transcribed for use in the Automatic Banjo. Their catalogue, which now comprises upwards of 2,000 numbers is, therefore, kept thoroughly up to date, and the patrons of the Banjo are ensured the opportunity of enjoying the very latest musical selections."

The same brochure, reprinted on another page of the present Encyclopedia, gives "10 Reasons Why the Automatic Banjo is the King of Slot Machines." One reason, No. 5, is "Because it is not a music box..." This was probably in reference to the immensely successful coin operated Regina music boxes of the same era.

In 1903 the American Automusic Company, in which Mr. O'Connor's interest alone amounted to an original investment of $38,690.00, was offered to Charles B. Kendall, the man who had set up the business and sold it the patents and other things to begin with, for $15,000 and then for $10,000. Whether or not a sale was consummated is not known, but apparently some type of arrangement was made whereby Kendall took over at least part of the enterprise (after an effort to delude other investors into thinking he had some $88,000.00 invested in it, as noted in earlier paragraphs). In later years The Connorized Music Company and the Peerless Piano Player Company offered for sale the "Banjorchestra," an orchestrion which contained an Encore Banjo apparatus (presumably made up from used parts on hand) in combination with a piano and trap effects.

### The Auto-Manufacturing Company

The Auto-Manufacturing Company, successor to the New England Automatic Banjo Company and the Eastern Specialty Company, was founded in 1901 by a reorganization of the earlier firms. The "Ordeal by Letter" story in this Encyclopedia, a comedy of errors as related by selections from the firm's correspondence, tells how the company had high hopes to begin with. Inquiries from many prospective purchasers were fended off with abrupt letters stating that Banjos were not for sale but were available only for lease (with the lessee receiving a stingy 20% of the proceeds). Other inquiries were warded off with a sort of fool's pride — the company was "too busy" to do anything except tend to the Banjos it had on location in the Boston area and to dream of large deals, including distribution overseas. As the end neared in 1903, an effort was made to sell some Banjos, but by then it was too late. Without even a single employee to assist him, Charles B. Kendall continued the business until about 1906.

The 1905 and 1906 files of the company are full of threatened lawsuits (including a suit filed by the Commissioner of Corporations who stated that, despite many notices, the required annual reports of the Auto-Manufacturing Co. had not been filed for two years earlier). What happened after 1906 is not related in the files. Diminishing receipts and diminishing interest in the Banjo, an instrument which was a novelty when first installed but which then grew wearisome quickly, combined to make the Encore obsolete. By 1916 used Banjos were being sold for as little as $25 each.

### The Encore Banjo — Additional Data

The total number of Encore Banjos is not recorded. Apparently about 350 to 400 were made by the Auto-Manufacturing Company and its forebears, the New England Automatic Banjo Company and the Eastern Specialty Company.

Far more were made by the American Automusic Company in New York. Serial numbers such as 3,593, 3,654, and others in the 3500 to 3700 range indicate that perhaps several thousand may have been made there; but there is a good possibility that the numbering system was not continuous and that far fewer were actually made. Unlike the Auto-Manufacturing Company, the American Automusic Company did sell its instruments. Several dozen sales agents, primarily music stores and operators of arcade devices, offered the Encore for sale at prices mostly in the $350 to $500 range.

According to Mr. Kendall's prospectus as quoted earlier, certain early Encores were made with electromagnetic systems. Evidently these were either limited production models or experimental models; few, if any, found use "on location." Experimentation was continual. A foot-pumped model was constructed for home use, but it never was marketed. The idea of electromagnetic operation continued to the very end of Encore production, but such instruments were purely experimental. Production-line models were all of pneumatic construction with pumps and bellows.

Several different variations of the Encore are known today. Two main types of roll systems are known — early models which load via the back door and later styles which load from the front. Later models have heavier duty picker mechanisms than do the early styles. The cabinets of the early styles are slightly more ornate and have curved-top rather than straight-top doors at the bottom.

The roll mechanism employed was evidently a standard type sold by an outside supplier. Identical mechanisms (but with different tracker bars) are found on certain early Peerless pianos and on the Resotone Grand automatic chrysoglott.

Cases were mainly in quartered oak, although the American Automusic Company inventory reveals that some mahogany cases were prepared.

### The Encore as a Collectors' Item Today

The unique appearance of the Encore and its catchy sound make it a favorite with collectors today. The device really does a creditable job of banjo playing, provided, of course, that it is properly restored and properly tuned and regulated. As all four strings can be played at once, elaborate music arrangements are possible and are, indeed, found on certain rolls.

The pneumatic system is well constructed and durable. Much of the service trouble experienced years ago must have been due to the very nature of the banjo instrument itself: the banjo head, made of animal membrane, was highly susceptible to changes in humidity. Dampness would produce a slackness in the head, the pressure of the strings on the wooden bridge would push the head inward, and the pickers would miss entirely or imperfectly make contact with the strings. Conversely, a dry period in the weather would tighten the head more than it should have been, and the strings would be too close to the pickers — with the result that the pickers would snag. Today the collector can replace the membrane head with a weatherproof plastic head (made opaque and with the appearance of the original) to obviate this problem.

The banjo itself (we are referring now to the regular hand-played instruments) is often called the traditional American instrument. Whereas most other types of instruments, stringed and otherwise, were developed elsewhere, the banjo is considered native. The Encore Automatic Banjo, which first appeared in public places as early as 1897, was probably the first coin operated American-made pneumatic instrument. So, here is a truly Americanized instrument!

Once plentiful, the Encore is rare today. Mr. Kendall's Encore fortune, ever eluding his grasp in the early 1900's, would be assured today if he were living and could sell his instruments to collectors!

American "Automusic" Co.

53 BROADWAY, NEW YORK.

Classification of Music

... AND ...

LIST OF PROGRAMS TO DATE JAN. 1, 1900.

MARCHES AND TWO STEPS.

For Cake Walks, etc., see Coon Selections, page 8.

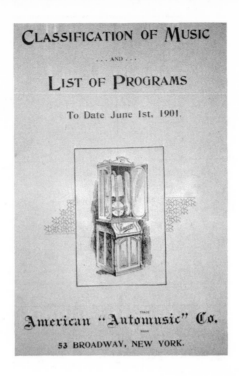

| | | | |
|---|---|---|---|
| Anniversary. | *Rosey* | Beau Ideal. | *Sousa* |
| Ambassador. | *Witt* | Belle Chicago. | *Sousa* |
| Apollo. | *Holst* | Battle Ship. | *Sutton* |
| Amberside. | *Lansing* | Bon Ton Souvenir. | *Reinhard* |
| Alumni. | *Van Baar* | Belle of New York. | *Clark* |
| American Girl. | *St. Wenchen* | Bridal Day. | *Heinzman* |
| Arabian Nights. | *Sachs* | Black America. | *Zickel* |
| America forever. | *Paull* | Bostonia. | *Lansing* |
| Admiral Dewey's. | *Smith* | Boston Letter Carriers. | *De Witt* |
| Admiral Schley's. | *Lapin* | Band in the Park. | *Connolly* |
| At the Charity Ball. | *Clappe* | Boston Tea Party. | *Pryor* |
| But one Vienna. | *Schrammel* | Cecil Two-step. | *Megone* |
| Bridesmaids. | *Gebert* | Corporal's Guard. | *Grover* |
| Bankers. | *Jones* | City Guard. | *Babb* |
| Bocaccio. | *Von Suppe* | Cotillion. | *Mac Gregor* |
| Boulanger. | *De Sormes* | Commander-in Chief. | *Witt* |
| Belle of the Season. | *Bratton* | Corinne Grand March. | *Kremer* |
| Bride Elect. | *Sousa* | Cannibal King. | *Drafuss* |
| Ben Hur. | *Paull* | Charlatan. | *Sousa* |
| Bohemia. | *Grover* | Chautauqua. | *Garing* |
| Belle of Columbia. | *Brooks* | Chinatown. | *Rosey* |
| Bridal. | *Wagner* | Charge of the Rough Riders | *Casey* |
| Blue and Gray at Santiago. | *Lamb* | Colored Regiment. | *Grover* |

1

CLASSIFICATION OF MUSIC

... AND ...

LIST OF PROGRAMS

To Date June 1st, 1901.

American "Automusic" Co.

53 BROADWAY, NEW YORK.

NEW

CLASSIFICATION OF MUSIC

... AND ...

LIST OF PROGRAMS

APRIL 1ST, 1903

American "Automusic" Co.

53 BROADWAY, NEW YORK

**—American Automusic Co.—**

**Above: All Encore music apparently was made in New York by the American Automusic Company (later the Connorized Roll Co.). Above are shown title pages to some early music lists. Music was a great problem, as the accompanying "Ordeal by Letter" feature shows.**

**Left: "Where they were" in the New York City area circa 1905. Original typewritten list from the American Automusic Co. records. Perhaps some survive today.**

**Below: 1902 records showing 1902 deliveries of 93 new Banjos and 28 used ones and 1200 music rolls; 1903 deliveries of 7 new Banjos and 7 used ones and 406 rolls (1903 figures as of May 27th of that year).**

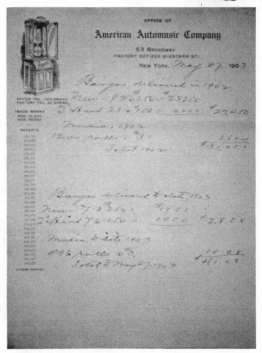

| | |
|---|---|
| St.I.Ferry,St.George, | Darcy,8th.Ave.&43rd.st. |
| " " " Foot B'way. | Daly, 11th.Ave.&42nd.st. |
| Oscar Frost,Broad&Front St. | Lane&Delancy,6th.ave.&30th.st. |
| J.Foubrig,3ParkRow. | H.Hawers,111th.st.&3rd.Ave. |
| Mercer&Gleason,106ParkRow | J. Miller, 117th.St.&3rd.Ave. |
| Boassells,Madison&catherine St. | Marquitz,107-108th.st.&3rd.Ave. |
| Lane&Walensi 21 Bowery. | Williams, Lenox Ave.&111th.St. |
| " " " 157 1/2 Bowery. | Clark,111th.St.&8th.Ave. |
| " " " 197 Bowery | Higgins, 115th.St.&8th.Ave |
| " " " 273 " | Bornheim, 124th.St.&LenoxAve. |
| " " " 299 " | Cadwalder, 73 West 125th. St. |
| J. Kulbe,109 E.9th St. | Barbey, 136th.St.&8th Ave. |
| Gaffney,3rd Ave &9th St. | Wild, 146-147sts.&Amstr.Ave. |
| Penn.Hotel,3rd Ave.&10th.St. | Roberts, 12th.Ave.&130th.St. |
| Lenz,3rd.Ave.&12th St. | Ft.Lee Ferry, Edgewater, N. J. |
| Putnam House,4th.Ave.&26th.St. | McCarty, 37th.St.&B'way |
| Redner,Lex.Ave.&42nd.St. | Duehme, 79th.St.&ColumbusAve. |
| Ledwith,45th.St.&3rd Ave | Eller, 68-69st.&185 AmsterdamAve. |
| Bogner,58th St.&3rd Ave. | Thoefel, 67th.St.&B'way. |
| Ebling, " " " " " | Morris, 54th.St.&8th.Ave. |
| Sullivan, 329 E.59th St. | Clancy&Hennessey,54th.St.&8th.Ave. |
| Reilly,59th.st.&1st.Ave. | Devaney Bros. 51st.&8th.Ave. |
| FirstAveHotel,1st.Ave.near 60th St. | Clancy&Hennessey,48thSt.&8th.Ave. |
| Kull,61st.&1st.Ave. | Galliger, 46th.St.&B'way. |
| Muller,63rd.St.&2nd.Ave. | Fitzgerald, 50th.St.&7th.Ave. |
| Mallon,65th.St.&1st.Ave. | Roeber, 54-55th.St.&6th.Ave. |
| Miller,66th.St.&3rd.Ave. | McSherry, 34th.bet.1st.Ave.&river |
| Woyistek,73rd.St.&1st Ave. | 34th.St.Ferry, this side. |
| Rousar,1438,1st.Ave.near 76th.St. | " " " Long Island Side. |
| Butts,79th.St.&2nd.Ave. | Rice, 30th.St.bet.6th.Ave.&B'way. |
| Ahearn, " " " " | Weber&Fields, 29th.St.&B'way. |
| Weidt,1565 Ave. A.cor.83rd.St. | Eden Musee, 23rd. St. |
| Langhorst,2nd.Ave.bet.89&90th.st. | Bettuer, 116 University Place & 13th |
| Mabouis,92nd.St.&3rd.Ave. | Donlin, Bleecker& Barrow, |
| Conklin,132 E.125th st. | Aumann, South 4th. Bedford Ave. |
| Sam Leoy,126th.st.&3rd.Ave. | Hatton, Grand St. Union Ave. |
| Bredes,3rd.Ave.near 129th st. | Skelly, Graham Ave. Meserole. |
| Ellier&Heines, 3rd.Ave.&138th.st. | Hussenbuttel, B'way. &FlushingAve. |
| Greite,138th St.&ParkAve. | Sinden cafe, B'way.Sinden st. |
| The Wigwam, 142nd.St.&3rd.Ave. | 1565 B'way. (Edwards) |
| Haight,151st.&Morris Ave. | Roberts, 1596 B'way. |
| Mayer,152nd.st.&3rd.Ave. | Vogels, B'way. &Cooper Sts. |
| Haught, 156th.St.&3rd.Ave. | Durr, B'way. & Hewes St. |
| McLoughlin,158th.St.&3rd Ave. | Fishers, Harrison Ave. &Lynch St. |
| Zimmer&Smith, 161st.&Courtland Ave. | Suhr, 2465 Atlantic Ave. Vesta. |
| Helms, Bleecker&Downing Sts. | Van Sise, Fulton& Vesta |
| CommercialHotel,Varick&Houston Sts. | Rademacher, 55 Ralph |
| Kelley,Hudson&10th.St. | Roth, Fulton St. &Bedford Ave. |
| Kelley,Hudsonbet/10th.&B'way. | Lynch, Fulton St.Franklin St. |
| Konow&Hughes,West&Perry,sts. | Marcy Ave. &Fulton St. (Sheriff) |
| Reher,#425 West&11th.st. | 16 Fulton St. |
| Fromkers, West&12th.st. | Fockes, 140 Fulton St. |
| Donnelly,Bethune&Hudson | Coffey, Washington&High St. |
| Fryangle, 14th.&9th.Ave. | McLaughlin, Washington near Tillary |
| Dowds, 14th.&9th.Ave. | Graves, Myrtle Ave. Jay. |
| Cross Hotel,8th.Ave.near 14th.st. | Kussel, Jay & Willoughby St. |
| McKays, 8th Ave.near 16th.st. | Smithsonism, Smith near Fulton. |
| Meagher,10th.ave.near 23rd.st. | Nolans, Livingston & Hoyt, |
| Glahns, " " " 24th. " | Nolans, 42 Smith St. (475) |
| Arlington Hotel, 8th.ave &30th.st. | Eihler, Smith & Atlantic Ave. |
| Cosgrove,6th.Ave.&36th.St. | Long Island R.R.Station. |
| Lane Bros. " " " 39th st. | Flatbush Ave. |
| Reiss, " " 39&40th.st. | |
| Swartze&Arps, B'way.&41st. | |
| Mercer&Rentel, 8th Ave.&39th st. | |

OFFICE OF

American Automusic Company

53 BROADWAY

FACTORY 227-229 BLEECKER ST.

NEW YORK, May 27 1903

OFFICE TEL. 1370 BROAD
FACTORY TEL. 20 SPRING

TRADE MARKS

PATENTS

OTHERS PENDING

Banjos delivered in 1902
New - 93 @ $250 = $23250
2d Hand 28 @ $150 = 4200 $27,450
Music 1902
1200 rolls @ $3 = 3,600
Total 1902 $31,050

Banjos delivered to date 1903
New - 7 @ $250 = $1750
2d Hand 7 @ 150 = 1050 $2800
Music to date 1903
406 rolls @ $3, 1208
Total to May 27 1903 $4108

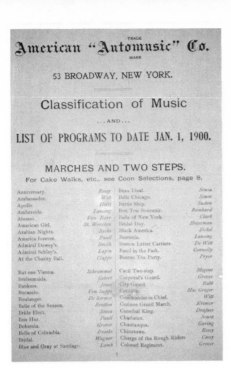

Different types of Encore crests. Top: That used on most Auto-Manufacturing Co. instruments and possibly some American Automusic Co. ones as well. Middle: Crest used by the American Automusic Co. of New Jersey (owned by the New York firm) lists many of the Encore patents. Bottom: Small plaque on the front of an early Encore Banjo.

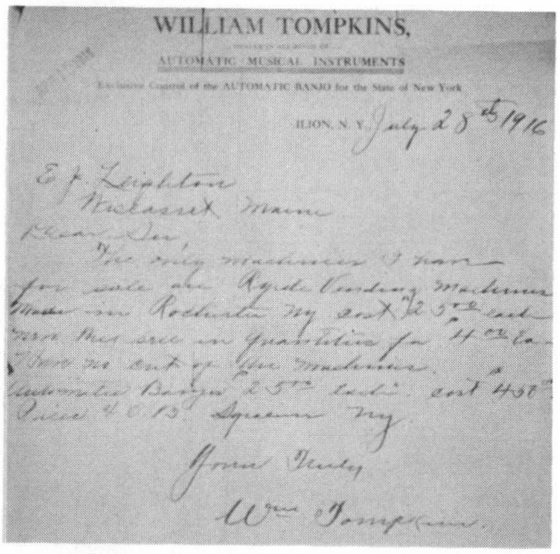

WILLIAM TOMPKINS,

AUTOMATIC MUSICAL INSTRUMENTS

Exclusive Control of the AUTOMATIC BANJO for the State of New York

ILION, N. Y. July 28th 1916

E. J. Leighton

Wiscasset Maine

Dear Sir,

The only machines I have for sale are Ryde Vending Machines made in Rochester Ny cost $25.00 each ... in quantities for $4.00 ea. ... Automatic Banjos $25.00 each cost $430 ... Syracuse Ny

Yours Truly

Wm Tompkins

William Tompkins of Ilion, N.Y., offers Encore Banjos for $25.00 each in 1916. Fame is fleeting — and the Encore's day in the sun was just a memory by this time.

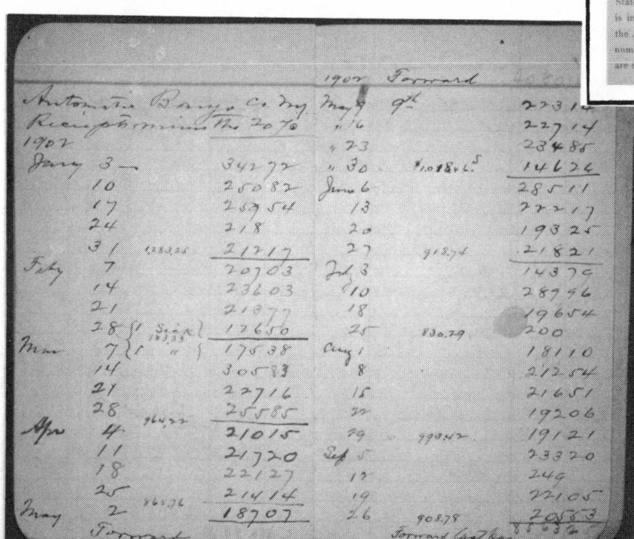

Automatic Banjo Co. Ny Receipts ... 1902

| 1902 | | | | 1902 | Forward | |
|---|---|---|---|---|---|---|
| Jany | 3 | | 342 72 | May 9 | 9th | 223 14 |
| | 10 | | 250 82 | 16 | | 227 14 |
| | 17 | | 259 54 | 23 | | 234 85 |
| | 24 | | 218 | 30 | $1,018.6 | 146 26 |
| | 31 | 1,283.25 | 217 17 | June 6 | | 285 11 |
| Feby | 7 | | 207 03 | 13 | | 222 17 |
| | 14 | | 236 03 | 20 | | 193 25 |
| | 21 | | 218 77 | 27 | 918.74 | 218 21 |
| | 28 | | 176 50 | July 3 | | 143 79 |
| Mar | 7 | | 175 38 | 10 | | 287 56 |
| | 14 | | 305 83 | 18 | | 196 54 |
| | 21 | | 227 16 | 25 | 830.79 | 200 |
| | 28 | 964.22 | 255 85 | Aug 1 | | 181 10 |
| Apr | 4 | | 210 15 | 8 | | 212 54 |
| | 11 | | 217 20 | 15 | | 216 51 |
| | 18 | | 221 27 | 22 | | 192 06 |
| | 25 | 862.76 | 214 14 | 29 | 998.42 | 191 21 |
| May | 2 | | 187 07 | Sept 5 | | 233 20 |
| | | | | 12 | | 249 |
| | | | | 19 | | 221 05 |
| | | | | 26 | 903.78 | 205 53 |

Forward ... Forward last page

American Automusic Co. account book showing New York City receipts averaging just over $200 per week in 1902.

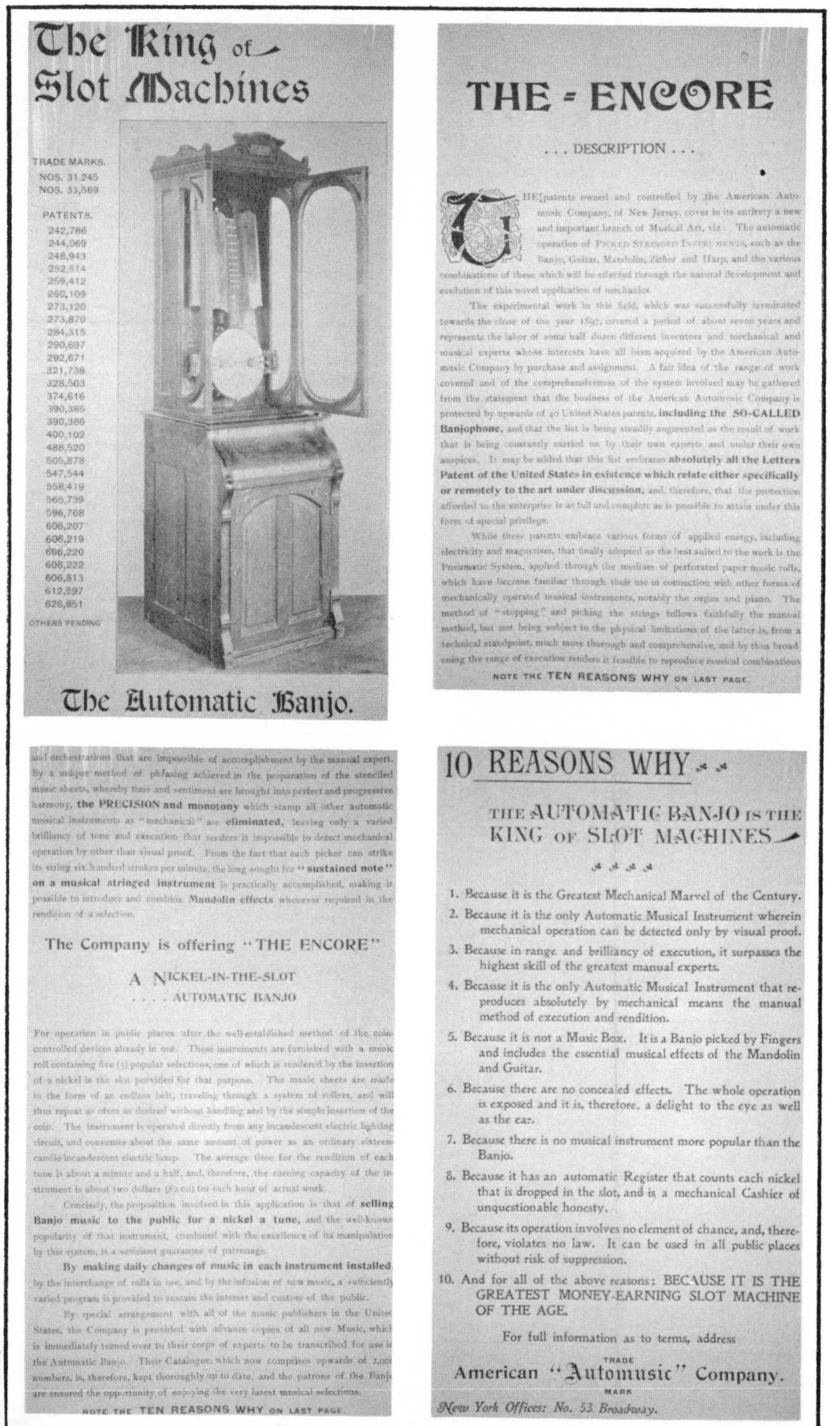

# The King of Slot Machines

TRADE MARKS.
NOS. 31,245
NOS. 33,569

PATENTS.
242,786
244,069
248,943
252,614
259,412
260,109
273,120
273,870
284,315
290,697
292,671
321,738
328,503
374,616
390,385
390,386
400,102
488,520
505,878
547,544
558,419
565,739
596,768
606,207
606,219
606,220
606,222
606,813
612,597
626,851
OTHERS PENDING

The Automatic Banjo.

# THE - ENCORE

. . . DESCRIPTION . . .

THE patents owned and controlled by the American Automusic Company, of New Jersey, cover in its entirety a new and important branch of Musical Art, viz.: The automatic operation of PICKED STRINGED INSTRUMENTS, such as the Banjo, Guitar, Mandolin, Zither and Harp, and the various combinations of these which will be effected through the natural development and evolution of this novel application of mechanics.

The experimental work in this field, which was successfully terminated towards the close of the year 1897, covered a period of about seven years and represents the labor of some half dozen different inventors and mechanical and musical experts whose interests have all been acquired by the American Automusic Company by purchase and assignment. A fair idea of the range of work covered and of the comprehensiveness of the system involved may be gathered from the statement that the business of the American Automusic Company is protected by upwards of 40 United States patents, **including the SO-CALLED Banjophone,** and that the list is being steadily augmented as the result of work that is being constantly carried on by their own experts and under their own auspices. It may be added that this list embraces **absolutely all the Letters Patent of the United States in existence which relate either specifically or remotely to the art under discussion,** and, therefore, that the protection afforded to the enterprise is as full and complete as is possible to attain under this form of special privilege.

While these patents embrace various forms of applied energy, including electricity and magnetism, that finally adopted as the best suited to the work is the Pneumatic System, applied through the medium of perforated paper music rolls, which have become familiar through their use in connection with other forms of mechanically operated musical instruments, notably the organ and piano. The method of "stopping" and picking the strings follows faithfully the manual method, but not being subject to the physical limitations of the latter is, from a technical standpoint, much more thorough and comprehensive, and by thus broadening the range of execution renders it feasible to reproduce musical combinations

NOTE THE TEN REASONS WHY ON LAST PAGE.

and orchestrations that are impossible of accomplishment by the manual expert. By a unique method of phrasing achieved in the preparation of the stenciled music sheets, whereby time and sentiment are brought into perfect and progressive harmony, **the PRECISION and monotony** which stamp all other automatic musical instruments as "mechanical" are **eliminated,** leaving only a varied brilliancy of tone and execution that renders it impossible to detect mechanical operation by other than visual proof. From the fact that each picker can strike its string six hundred strokes per minute, the long sought for **"sustained note" on a musical stringed instrument** is practically accomplished, making it possible to introduce and combine **Mandolin effects** whenever required in the rendition of a selection.

The Company is offering "THE ENCORE"

A NICKEL-IN-THE-SLOT
. . . . AUTOMATIC BANJO

For operation in public places after the well-established method of the coin-controlled devices already in use. These instruments are furnished with a music roll containing five (5) popular selections, one of which is rendered by the insertion of a nickel in the slot provided for that purpose. The music sheets are made in the form of an endless belt, traveling through a system of rollers, and will thus repeat as often as desired without handling and by the simple insertion of the coin. The instrument is operated directly from any incandescent electric lighting circuit, and consumes about the same amount of power as an ordinary sixteen-candle incandescent electric lamp. The average time for the rendition of each tune is about a minute and a half, and, therefore, the earning capacity of the instrument is about two dollars ($2.00) for each hour of actual work.

Concisely, the proposition involved in this application is that of **selling Banjo music to the public for a nickel a tune,** and the well-known popularity of that instrument, combined with the excellence of its manipulation by this system, is a sufficient guarantee of patronage.

**By making daily changes of music in each instrument installed,** by the interchange of rolls in use, and by the infusion of new music, a sufficiently varied program is provided to sustain the interest and custom of the public.

By special arrangement with all of the music publishers in the United States, the Company is provided with advance copies of all new Music, which is immediately turned over to their corps of experts to be transcribed for use in the Automatic Banjo. Their Catalogue, which now comprises upwards of 2,000 numbers, is, therefore, kept thoroughly up to date, and the patrons of the Banjo are ensured the opportunity of enjoying the very latest musical selections.

NOTE THE TEN REASONS WHY ON LAST PAGE.

# 10 REASONS WHY

THE AUTOMATIC BANJO IS THE KING OF SLOT MACHINES

1. Because it is the Greatest Mechanical Marvel of the Century.
2. Because it is the only Automatic Musical Instrument wherein mechanical operation can be detected only by visual proof.
3. Because in range and brilliancy of execution, it surpasses the highest skill of the greatest manual experts.
4. Because it is the only Automatic Musical Instrument that reproduces absolutely by mechanical means the manual method of execution and rendition.
5. Because it is not a Music Box. It is a Banjo picked by Fingers and includes the essential musical effects of the Mandolin and Guitar.
6. Because there are no concealed effects. The whole operation is exposed and it is, therefore, a delight to the eye as well as the ear.
7. Because there is no musical instrument more popular than the Banjo.
8. Because it has an automatic Register that counts each nickel that is dropped in the slot, and is a mechanical Cashier of unquestionable honesty.
9. Because its operation involves no element of chance, and, therefore, violates no law. It can be used in all public places without risk of suppression.
10. And for all of the above reasons: BECAUSE IT IS THE GREATEST MONEY-EARNING SLOT MACHINE OF THE AGE.

For full information as to terms, address

American "TRADE Automusic MARK" Company.

New York Offices: No. 53 Broadway.

Above: American Automusic Co. leaflet describing the Encore. Note that one of the "10 Reasons Why" is that the Encore "is not a music box!"

FOR SALE ON EASY TERMS
BY THE
AUTOMATIC
. MUSICAL .
. COMPANY .
51 CHENANGO ST., BINGHAMTON, N. Y.



Left: The Automatic Musical Co. of Binghamton, N.Y. was one of many Encore sales agents. The firm later developed into the Link Piano and Organ Co.

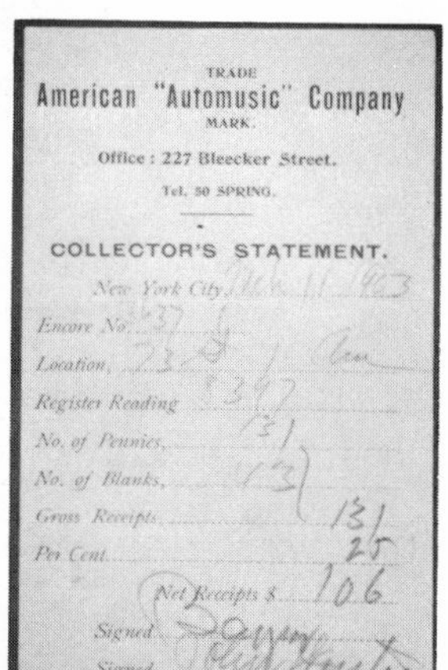

TRADE
American "Automusic" Company
MARK.

Office: 227 Bleecker Street.

Tel. 30 SPRING.

COLLECTOR'S STATEMENT.

New York City, Mch 11 1903

Encore No. 337

Location, 23 ...

Register Reading 8397

No. of Pennies, 131

No. of Blanks, 43

Gross Receipts 131

Per Cent. 25

Net Receipts $ 106

Signed ...

Signed ...

Right: A routeman's statement shows that an Encore equipped with a 1c slot took in 131 one-cent pieces which, after a 25% commission to the establishment owner, netted the firm $1.06. Also 43 "slugs" were taken in!

Auto-Manufacturing Co. stock certificate.

F. R. PENDLETON, PRESIDENT. STATEMENT. C. B. KENDALL, TREASURER.

BOSTON, ______ 190

Auto-Manufacturing Co.,

FACTORY: 34-42 OSBORNE STREET, CAMBRIDGEPORT.
OFFICES: 17 MILK STREET, BOSTON.
TELEPHONES. 694 CAMBRIDGE. 4740 MAIN.

IN ACCOUNT WITH June 30 1903

| | | |
|---|---|---|
| Banjos in Maine | 29 | |
| " " ASIK | 3 | |
| " " Brockton | 3 | |
| " " Boston | 6 | |
| Clair | 1 | |
| CBK Chicago | 2 | |
| Worcester & Fitchburg | 2 | 46 |
| Banjos in factory in process | | 51 |
| N.E. " " " " | | 32 |
| | | 129 |
| N.E. in Fall River | | 2 |
| Hampshire in Store | | 1 |
| [illegible] | | 1 |
| | | 133 |

A 1903 inventory shows 133 Banjos in stock.

# THE RECORD OF THE Encore

PROPRIETORS:

AUTO-MANUFACTURING CO.

17 Milk Street, Boston.

| | |
|---|---|
| One in St. Louis, Mo., one year ..... | $1,985.00 |
| One in Boston, Mass., one month ... | 171.20 |
| One in Altoona, Pa., one week ...... | 80.00 |
| One in Johnstown, Pa., one week ... | 60.00 |
| One in Harrisburg, Pa., one day .... | 19.65 |

Extract from a report of the Swiss member of the **Jury of Award of Class 17**, at the **Paris Exposition of 1900.**

"Mr. C. B. Kendall of Boston, U. S. A., exhibited his Automatic Banjo, one of the most interesting automatic instruments of the day. A banjo (mandolin with four strings) placed vertically in an elegant case, is operated by pickers, imitating the action of the fingers. These pickers are operated by little pneumatics, and are made to vibrate the strings at the rate of 600 times per minute. The long note, if a long note is desired, by pressing the strings on the instrument, is thus practically executed, which renders possible the production of orchestral combinations, almost surpassing in power and delicacy of expression, the playing of the hand.

"From a mechanical point of view, the effect of returning the pickers to their places without touching the strings, is worthy of great note.

"The music is notated on perforated paper sheets, these operated by means of compressed air, on the buttons which press the strings to hold the note at will on the neck of the banjo."

Cover of Encore promotional brochure.

Banjos now running, June, 1st. 1906.

| | | | |
|---|---|---|---|
| Adams, Mass, | Greylock House, | Encore | 310 |
| Pittsfield, Mass, | 162 North St, | " | 305 |
| Holyoke, " | ,Yoerg's, Appleton, St. | " | 304 |
| Holyoke, " | ,Nugent Hotel, | " | 300 |
| Holyoke, " | ,Cor. Appleton & Race St. | " | 303 |
| Holyoke, " | ,Clutterbuck Barber Shop, | " | 224 |
| Holyoke, " | ,35 Dwight St. | " | 229 |
| Springfield, " | ,Hotel Gilmore, | " | 238 |
| Springfield, " | ,183 Main, St. | " | 243 |
| Springfield, " | ,City, Hotel, | " | 317 |
| Springfield, " | ,U. S. Hotel, | " | 242 |
| Worcester, " | ,Carberry School St. | " | 259 |
| Worcester, " | ,31 Pearl St. | " | 269 |
| Webster, " | ,H. Dupre, | " | 227 |
| Southbridge, " | ,N. J. Gervais, | " | 255 |
| Newton, " | ,257 Washington, St. | " | 299 |
| Boston, " | ,Dowd Bros. Howard St. | " | 253 |
| Boston, " | ,868 Washington, St. | " | 256 |
| Boston, " | ,Hayes Coffee House, Wash. St. | " | 315 |
| Athol, " | ,Commercial House. | " | 291 |
| Quincy, " | ,Hotel Greenleaf, | " | 312 |
| Quincy, " | ,Harlow, Drug Store, | " | 226 |
| Atlantic, " | ,Haniford, Drug Co., | " | 271 |
| Winchester, " | ,Young & Brown, | " | 292 |
| Somerville, " | ,Cor. Broadway & Franklin St. | " | |
| Arlington Hts, " | ,Waiting Room, | " | 251 |
| Stoneham, " | ,C.O. Currier, | " | 284 |
| Stoneham, " | ,277 Main, St. | " | 249 |
| Attleboro, " | ,Beatty & Bowen, | " | 319 |
| Attleboro, " | ,Beatty & Bowen, | " | 231 |
| Attleboro, " | ,G. I. Simpson, | " | 307 |
| Attleboro, " | ,P. J. Crosby, | " | 285 |
| Salem, Ma " | ,Colonial Drug, | " | 308 |
| Lynn, " | ,37 Central Sq. | " | 290 |
| Lynn, " | ,Hyman's Lunch, | " | 320 |
| Dover, N.H., | ,Curtis Lunch, | " | 281 |
| Saco, Me. | ,Gannon's, | " | 274 |
| Portland, " | ,Jefferson Bowling Alley, | " | 252 |
| Chisholms Mills, Me. | ,Union Club, | " | 236 |
| Brunswick, Me. | ,Morton Bon Bon Co., | " | 293 |
| Gardner, " | ,King Barber Shop, | " | 234 |
| Augusta, " | ,F. L. Hopkins, | " | 276 |
| Augusta, " | ,John Cormier, | " | 221 |
| Augusta, " | ,Goodrich, | " | 282 |
| Skowhegan, " | ,Merwin's, Cigar Store, | " | 268 |
| Lewiston, " | ,Dairy, Lunch, | " | 301 |
| Lewiston, " | ,314 Lisbon St. | " | 260 |
| Lewiston, " | ,Lincoln & Chestnut Sts. | " | 244 |
| Fitchburg, Mass. | ,Waiting Room, | " | 273 |
| READING, " | ,Lunch, Room, | " | 321 |
| Athol, " | ,City Hotel, | " | 248 |

Banjos not running June, 1st. 1906.

| | | | |
|---|---|---|---|
| North Adams, Mass. | ,Welch, State St. | Encore | 311 |
| Holyoke, " | ,400 High St. | " | 220 |
| Webster, " | ,A. C. Parent, | " | 264 |
| Milford, " | ,P. J. Donahue, | " | 302 |
| South Fram. " | ,American Express Office, | " | 270 |
| No. Attleboro, " | ,Express Office, | " | 283 |
| Malden, " | ,Bowling Alley, Pleasant St. | " | |
| Peabody, " | ,Express Office, | " | 294 |
| Lowell, " | ,J. H. Tebbitts, | " | 278 |
| Boston, " | ,Bergen, 65 Beach St, | " | 241 |
| Boston, " | ,Mo Gee, Court St. | " | 266 |
| Boston, " | ,25 Green, St, | " | 287 |
| Quincy, " | ,Hotel Hancock, | " | 296 |
| Sanford, Me. | ,G.G. Brown, | " | 286 |
| Portland, " | ,Bracy, Fore St. | " | 230 |
| Portland, " | ,Middle St. | " | |
| Lewiston, " | ,Barber Shop, Lisbon St. | " | 309 |
| Augusta, " | ,Hotel North, | " | 279 |
| Augusta, " | ,Drummond, 71 Green St, | " | 247 |
| Bar Harbor, " | ,Woodbine Club or Joy's Cafe. | " | 275 |
| So. Brewer, " | ,F.W. Burnett, | " | 240 |
| Millbury, Mass. | ,Fourtellotte, House, | " | 233 |
| Boston, or Quincy, " | ,International Storage Bat. Co., | " | 277 |
| Fitchburg, Mass, | ,Whalom Park Cafe. | " | 314 |
| Fitchburg, " | ,Whalon Park, | " | 246 |
| Springfield, " | ,Baab, New Gilmore, | " | 238 |
| Worcester, " | ,Commonwealth, Hotel, | " | 2[illegible]4 |

Here's where they were — now see if you can find one! They're probably all gone now, but here is where they were on June 1, 1906 when the bankrupt Auto-Manufacturing Co. was looking for someone to buy it.

GENTLEMEN:—I wish to say that I am satisfied in every respect with the Encores. **I am selling off all my other slot machines** and giving my whole time and energy to the Banjo. **They give me very little trouble even in the sea air,** where I expected to find some. Yours truly,

RICHMOND COUNTY AUTOMUSIC CO.,

NEW BRIGHTON, N. Y. GEO. BALSDON, MGR.

EDEN MUSEE AMERICAIN CO.,

55 West 23d Street.

GENTLEMEN:—When we placed your Automatic Banjo in our Winter Garden, it was with the idea of filling in the gap when the orchestra was not playing. **It has fully come up to our expectations** and to judge by the remarks made by visitors, we are more than satisfied with the experiment. The tunes played on it are up-to-date, **and the music fills our large hall.** Yours truly,

NEW YORK. RICHARD G. HOLLAMAN.

Encore testimonials printed by the Auto-Manufacturing Company.

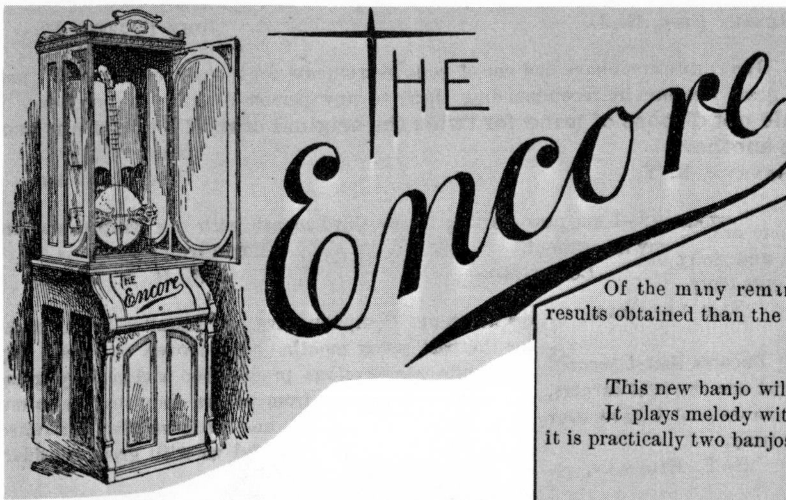


# PRESS NOTICES.

MUSICAL TRADE.

Of the many remarkable novelties of the age, none is more astonishing in the results obtained than the new Automatic Banjo.

MUSICAL GAZETTE, BOSTON.

This new banjo will execute as much as two players can.

It plays melody with harmony and in addition accompaniment, so that in effect it is practically two banjos playing.

THE PHONOSCOPE.

The Automatic Banjo is one of the latest and most ingenious mechanical musical instruments, as it does all that human fingers can do to produce tuneful melody. Thus the most difficult music can be played automatically with the same effect, both in tune and harmony, as if performed by a professional.

NEW YORK HERALD.

KOSTER & BIALS:—The Encore, an Automatic Banjo, was one of the novelties of the programme. It scored a "hit."

NEW YORK TIMES.

A novelty that pleased last night was an Automatic Banjo.

DAILY MERCURY.

The Encore is indeed a marvelous Automatic Banjo, and is the latest mechanical achievement.

EVENING TRAVELLER, BOSTON.

I notice one of the latest inventions to catch the nickel is an Automatic Banjo. This machine is certainly a corker, and a great money maker, too.

CHICAGO CHRONICLE.

This nickel-in-the-slot will call forth the soul-stirring melodies. Returns expected to exceed the yield of the Klondike region.

NEW YORK JOURNAL.

Millions in the Banjo.

**Press Notices from a promotional brochure issued by the Auto-Manufacturing Company. Compare the ebullience of these notices with the actual facts as delineated in the "Ordeal by Letter" feature in this section!**

GENTLEMEN:—The Encore arrived just one week ago, and has earned net $32.40. I will be in New York Friday, and arrange to buy two or three more.

Yours,

SHAMOKIN, PA. J. C. MOYER, of DANVILLE, PA.

GENTLEMEN:—**For the six months** that I have had the **Encore it has never been out of order**, which is something extraordinary for a slot machine. My machine in Johnstown has **netted me as high as $50.00 in one week.** It is not only a money earner but has also increased my business. Yours truly,

HOTEL WINDSOR, ALTOONA, PA. JOHN KEYES.

GENTLEMEN:—After six months' trial, it gives us great pleasure to be able to advise you that our investment in the "Encore" is as great a success financially, as is the instrument mechanically. We are thoroughly satisfied with the results.

Yours truly,

13 NIAGARA ST., BUFFALO, N. Y. BUFFALO AUTOMUSIC COMPANY.

GENTLEMEN:—Your Banjos are all working finely. Have given entire satisfaction. I am having no trouble of any kind. Yours truly,

25 ARTHUR ST., BINGHAMTON, N. Y. F. H. BROWN.

GENTLEMEN:—I cannot say enough in its favor. Everything has been perfectly satisfactory to me. I consider it a wonderful machine. Yours very truly,

CENTRAL VALLEY, N. Y. C. B. BARKER.

**Testimonials of Encore Automatic Banjo users. From the same publication as the above.**

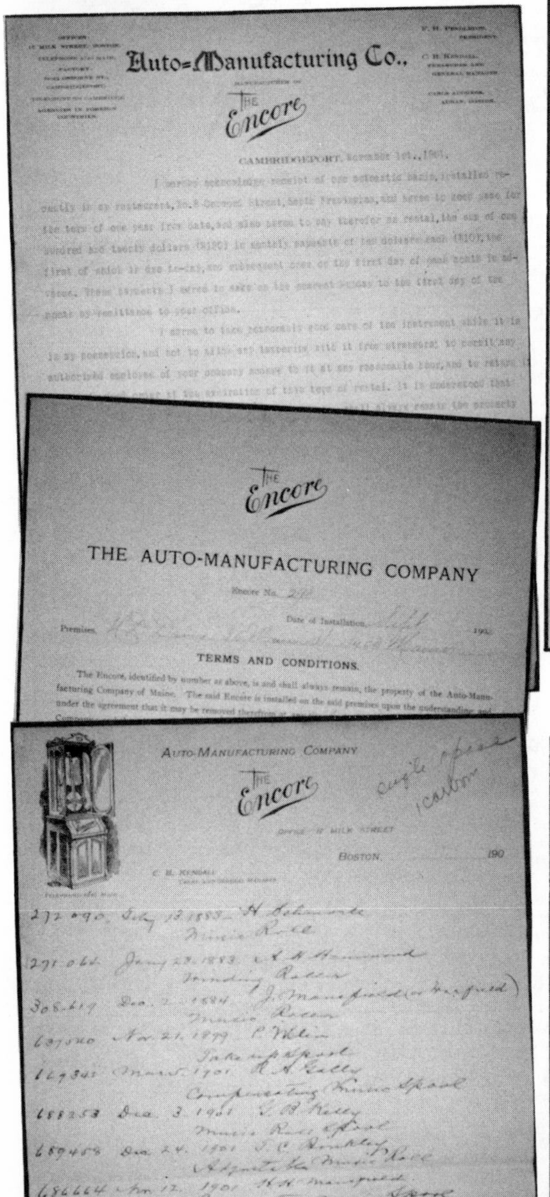
Auto-Manufacturing Co.

The Encore

THE
Encore
THE AUTO-MANUFACTURING COMPANY

TERMS AND CONDITIONS.

AUTO-MANUFACTURING COMPANY

THE
Encore

BOSTON. 190

**Various Auto-Manufacturing Co. letterheads.**

Following are selections from the letter files of the Auto-Manufacturing Company. This firm, newly reorganized with the assets of the old New England Automatic Banjo Company and the Eastern Specialty Company, began business with optimism in 1901. New capital provided by Davis & Soule, investors from Waterville, Maine, was intended to provide the means to reap a treasure of cents and nickels from countless Encore Automatic Banjos on location.

What actually happened is related in the letters to follow. . .

*Cast of Characters:*

*Charles B. Kendall: Treasurer of the Auto-Manufacturing Company, Mr. Kendall was the "father of the Encore Banjo" and was instrumental in developing it and setting up distributorships. The Auto-Manufacturing Company, a re-organization of two earlier Banjo firms, was set up under his direction and guidance.*

*F.R. Pendleton: President of the firm, a minority shareholder (one $10 share!). He did his best to supervise the day to day operations of the company.*

*C.W. Davis: Of the firm of Davis and Soule of Waterville, Maine. An outside investor who was prompted to invest in the firm on the basis of the glowing reports of the Banjo's potential as furnished by Mr. Kendall.*

*The American Automusic Company: The New York City firm which controlled most of the Encore business in the U.S., except for the few states allotted to the Auto-Manufacturing Co. This firm was sole supplier of paper rolls for the Encore.*

March 4, 1901
New England Telephone & Telegraph Co.

Will you kindly hasten the installation of the telephone that we ordered from you on the 2nd. We are very much in need of it, and should be greatly obliged if you would install it this week if possible.

Auto Manufacturing Co.
C.B. Kendall, Treasurer

March 4, 1901
Mr. E.S. Votey
The Aeolian Company
New York

I write to inquire when I can have an interview with you concerning the matter we talked of the last time we met. The Encore Banjo shown at the Paris Exposition and other sample instruments are in this office, which we opened this morning for public use. I should much prefer that you come here and should also be pleased if Mr. Tremaine were coming to Boston soon that I might show him our Encore for household use. If neither of you is coming to Boston within a few days, I will try to call upon you in New York.

Auto Manufacturing Co.
C.B. Kendall

Mr. Henry Waterman
441 Tremont Building
Boston

We are now occupying the rooms at 17 Milk Street, formerly rented by you, and have found that one of the safes is locked, and as we have not the combination, we are unable to open it. If you can give us the numbers of the same, we shall be glad to call on you for that purpose.

Auto Manufacturing Co.
F.R. Pendleton, President

A.F. Unkel
Richmond, Va.

We enclose a preliminary prospectus of the condition and prospects of this company. Five thousand shares are offered at $5 per share, which, according to the estimates in the prospectus, will earn 80% per annum. The 550 Encore Banjos mentioned are those on hand and in process of construction. We believe that several thousand more can be sold that will yield 50% profit, if sold outright, or 100% profit per year if rented.

We enclose a form of application for the purchase of shares, if you should decide to invest.

Auto Manufacturing Co.
F.R. Pendleton, President

(Note: Many other stock prospectus letters were sent out during the second and third weeks of March)

The Pittsburgh Press
Pittsburgh, Pa.

Thank you for your letter in response to your noticing our recent ad in the Boston Herald. In reply we say that it is not easy to convince us, after the experience we have had, that advertising - even in the best of papers - gives satisfactory results. However, as you seem to have confidence in your own paper in this regard we make you this proposition: You can insert this ad for one week, and if the result brings us any business we will pay you twice the price you ask.

Auto Manufacturing Co.
C.B. Kendall

The Aeolian Company
New York

Your reply per my letter to Mr. Votey is at hand, and the contents carefully noted. In reply, we will say that it is perfectly natural that you should be timid about the probable popularity of the Automatic Banjo after having such a close association with the Aeolian (Orchestrelle) and the Pianola, and that you should come to the conclusion that the public taste favors those styles of instruments principally. We believe, however, that notwithstanding the inferior tone and character of the banjo [Editor's note: !] in comparison with your instruments, that there is a vast popular demand for the banjo and banjo music . . .

On another point, could you quote us a price to furnish music rolls for our banjos, including the laying out and cutting of the stencils, if we arrange the music for your guidance?

C.B. Kendall
Auto Manufacturing Co.

March 19, 1901
H. LeGrand, Esq.
Philadelphia

Thank you for your letter concerning supplying us with spring motors for our Banjos (for use in locations without electricity). Experimentation in this direction has already cost us thousands of dollars, and without satisfactory results.

If you have a type of motor that will operate the Automatic Banjo, and you stand ready to guarantee it, you may send it to us for testing - and we will either pay for it or return it. The price of $60 each would be a serious objection to our adopting it, but even that excessive price would not be absolutely fatal if we were sure of a requisite benefit from its use...

C.B. Kendall
Auto Manufacturing Co.

General Electric Co.
Boston

Send us the details on your alternating current motors as per our letter. It may mean a contract for 500 for you.

If you will call at our office I shall be pleased to have you see and hear the Encore Banjo for household use which was exhibited at the Paris Exposition of 1900. It is a new instrument for household use, and we think it will prove to be very popular. This will be an entirely new field - and a larger one, we think, than the slot instruments for the commercial market.

C.B. Kendall
Auto Manufacturing Co.

Messrs. Davis & Soule
Waterville, Maine

I have received your $900 and have opened a bank account. I deposited with your check another check recently received for repairs - our "first blood" - in the amount of $14.

Of course, the first money will vanish rapidly, with the greatest demand on your $5000 guarantee coming at the beginning. Soon 50 Banjos will be finished and installed - and revenue will begin coming in.

You may rest assured that all of us connected with the company will do our level best to show that the Automatic Banjo business has plenty of vitality, and personally I feel more confident of success than I have for three years...

C.B. Kendall

R.L. Stanton
Providence, R.I.

I enclose for your inspection a tentative agreement of the type we shall make with our rental customers. As you see, we have the right to remove the Banjo at any time, and the customer has the right to order it removed within 24 hours notice. They pay the actual cost of installing, and receive as their profit 20% of all that the Banjo takes in (the customer gets 20% - we get 80%).

C.B. Kendall
Auto Manufacturing Co.

April 22, 1901
Messrs. Cotton & Haley
Boston

We enclose $180 in part payment of our bill to Mr. C.E. Smart. As we have said, we will send you the balance in a few days - and I hope this will be satisfactory.

Auto Manufacturing Co.
F.R. Pendleton, President

April 23, 1901
Puritan Trust Co.
Boston

We herewith respectfully apply for a four months loan of $10,000... By the end of 4 months from now our assets will yield an income of not less than $2500 per month, and there is no question of our depositing from earnings alone at least $1000 per month from the day we begin operations: Monday, April 29th.

Auto Manufacturing Co.

April 23, 1901
American Automusic Co.
New York

You will see by our letterhead that a new company has been formed here and has taken in all the rights of the New England Automatic Banjo Co. and the Eastern Specialty Co. and C.B. Kendall, covering the manufacture (Editor's note: This is an important point: Encores were manufactured both in New England and in New York) and use of Encores in the states of Maine, New Hampshire, Vermont, and Massachusetts. We are now completing the 160 Encores which are in the factory at 746 Main St., Cambridgeport, Mass., and shall proceed to install them for service as soon as possible.

The question of music becomes an important one, and so we can formulate our orders, we wish to inquire if you will take a $500 cash order of not less than 5 copies of each roll, giving us the option of making our own combinations of tunes for each roll, and charging us 50c per tune for all that we may order of the total of not less than $500. We do not wish any tunes to be over 1¼ minute in length and as near to one minute each as the phrasing of the music will permit...

Will you let us have one copy of all the music you have cut and arranged for the Encore, so we can make a selection for our own repertoire? Will you permit us to return the rolls we do not wish to retain?

C.B. Kendall
Auto Manufacturing Co.

April 25, 1901
American Automusic Co.
New York

In regard to the machines which have strayed away from their proper territory under license to the New England Automatic Banjo Co., your president, Mr. O'Connor, once suggested in regard to the Encore that turned up in Bridgeport or New Haven, that there would be no trouble if we paid the cost of returning the instruments to their proper location.

Now, as another Encore has gotten out of its proper territory and has gone to St. Louis, it appears that we may have more of the same trouble. We would like to have such machines replevined wherever they may be found, but we may have some difficulty about giving necessary bonds in different localities around the U.S. If it is agreeable to you, we will pay $25 to you whenever we are notified that one of our machines has strayed from its proper locality - and you can then take care of the bonds.

We have not received the picker friction strings and screws, nor the fibre cams with the rubber cushions, nor the up to date catalogues of music for which we wrote some time ago.

C.B. Kendall
Auto Manufacturing Co.

W.A. Barry
Waterville, Maine

We note by your letter that the pickers of your Banjo do not operate properly. Something must be wrong with your electrical connections. The faulty working of the pickers is due to a too low vacuum pressure or too little air drawing through the valves. This may be caused by improper tracking of the music roll or by too slow speed on the main shaft. The shaft should make about 180 rpm to maintain the proper vacuum so that the bellows reservoir is up tight. If you do not find the fault in your instrument please let us know and once and we will endeavor to help you.

F.R. Pendleton
Auto Manufacturing Co.

May 4, 1901
American Automusic Co.
New York

We received yesterday a case of music. We have partially gone over the tunes, but so far do not find any of recent issue. If not too much trouble, could you at least send us an invoice of the shipment or a list of what the box contains. If the latest music is not in this lot, can you forward same soon? Also, please ship the parts ordered some time ago.

F.R. Pendleton
Auto Manufacturing Co.

May 6, 1901
American Automusic Co.
New York

After a complete examination of the box of music received from you we find only 7 tunes in the lot are numbered from 135 up. As the later numbers since No. 135 are the ones we are most anxious to get, will you please send one copy of each roll from 135 up?

F.R. Pendleton
Auto Manufacturing Co.

(The following is typical of many letters sent at this time)

May 16, 1901
Mr. O.H. Crone
18 Hanover St.
Boston

We are now prepared to install promptly our "Improved Automatic Banjo," in the city of Boston, and appreciating the desirable location of your place of business and also the class of patronage you cater to, we feel that it would prove mutally profitable to place one upon your premises on a commission basis.

Whatever objectionable features we have had to contend with in the past have been overcome and remedied; thus justifying us in our conclusion that the greatest mechanical marvel of the century will please you as well as your patrons, and prove an attraction beyond comparison with any other similar device.

The instrument will be kept in perfect condition, and the music the very latest of popular successes, changed frequently enough to suit the most fastidious.

If you are favorably disposed and desire to give the Banjo a trial, we will, with pleasure, have our representative call and arrange with you.

Auto Manufacturing Co.
C.B. Kendall

May 17, 1901
Mr. Edmond Willcox
Boston

We desire to have you call on us for discussion of obtaining further capital in the development of our business. We think we can offer exceptional opportunities for those who are seeking a legitimate and profitable enterprise.

Auto Manufacturing Co.
C.B. Kendall

May 17, 1901
Mr. Henry Soule

I depended upon getting a check for $700 today as I had planned accordingly. I do not know how soon I will receive this from you, but if it is possible for you to mail the check tomorrow morning it will be a very great help to me. If you will wire me as to the probability of receiving it tomorrow, I will be greatly obliged to you. If I cannot receive the check tomorrow, please let me know if I can depend on it for Monday. I dislike to disturb you, but think you will understand the situation.

Auto Manufacturing Co.
C.B. Kendall

May 16, 1901
American Automusic Co.
New York

(Telegram:) SEND FULL LINE ENCORE BANJO TESTIMONIALS AND PRESS NOTICES TODAY IMPORTANT.

May 20, 1901
American Automusic Co.
New York

We sent you a telegram asking for testimonials and hope they can be forwarded by today's mail... We are trying to push matters as regards to the expansion of our business and wish to strengthen our position...

Can you give us a list of 12 or 15 records of star earnings of the Banjos in various parts of the country, such as "One Encore in St. Louis – receipts for first year $1985.00." This listing will be valuable to us for presenting Banjos in their most attractive form.

We have now located 8 Banjos on a percentage basis, but probably ½ of them will have to be moved for lack of satisfactory patronage...

Auto Manufacturing Co.

May 21, 1901
Mr. C.G. Hume
Shawmut, Maine

I write that we are now prepared to do business with the Encore Banjo with you as was discussed earlier. The question of introducing the Banjo to the state of Maine is now under consideration, and I am writing to you first about it.

You will note that we have greatly improved this instrument and have been able to remedy the defects of the past. If you are agreeable, we believe we can make you a beneficial proposal.

I enclose a circular which we are sending out in the state of Massachusetts, also a copy of a personal letter we address to some well known person in each town in the state. I also send you a copy of testimonials that are now typewritten, and will be printed later, which give you an idea of the reputation the Encore has under good business conditions.

Auto Manufacturing Co.
C.B. Kendall

May 22, 1901
American Mutoscope and Biograph Co.
New York

Will you kindly furnish us with the names of good parties to make an estimate upon iron cases for our Automatic Banjos? We have noticed the tastely and elegant designs of your Mutoscope cases, and are considering the matter of substituting iron for our oak cabinets.

C.B. Kendall
Auto Manufacturing Co.

May 28, 1901
American Automusic Co.
New York

Thank you for your letter regarding the "tramp" Banjo of ours in St. Louis. We have failed to discover where our Banjo No. 98 was last located. The last party using it here in Boston said it was removed by the New England representative in June, 1898. We know nothing of its whereabouts after that.

We will, however, do everything in our power to help recover this strayed instrument from St. Louis and hope to be successful in locating the culprits who have surreptitiously removed it.

We enclose with this a catalogue of 20 rolls of music numbered from 201 to 220 inclusive, and have made them up as we wish to use them here. Please cut them and forward them to us as early as possible. In our new instruments the paper is to run upward and forward as one faces the music paper - which is the opposite direction from formerly.

There are to be 5 copies each of 20 rolls, total 100 rolls, at @$2.50, equals $250.00 which please charge to our account.

C.B. Kendall
Auto Manufacturing Co.

May 31, 1901
W.A. Barry
Waterville, Maine

We have sent you via American Express two rolls of music. We apologize for the delay, but the rush of business at this time has kept us all very busy.

F.R. Pendleton
Auto Manufacturing Co.

May 31, 1901
American Automusic Co.
New York

Please forward to us at your earliest convenience the roll numbers that were absent from your earlier shipment.

We have inspected the quantity of music you sent over earlier, using a system of having three different people listen to the different tunes and each marking them according to the grade they deemed them worthy.

Auto Manufacturing Co.

June 3, 1901
British Mutoscope & Biograph Co.
London, England

Thank you for your letter. I have written to the American Automusic Co. in New York and have asked them, as a favor to me, to fill your order at the earliest possible date.

Permit me to say to you confidentially, that I expect ere long, to be able to duplicate any rolls you may have, if you continue to have difficulty in procuring music from New York.

Concerning our instruments here, we now get efficient and uninterrupted service from them and have been able to collect, without difficulty, from $7 to $10 per week each.

C.B. Kendall
Auto Manufacturing Co.

June 6, 1901
J.A. Holt
Brockton, Mass.

I was in Brockton yesterday and installed the Encore in the drug store at 200 Main St. Another one, at the Waiting Room, 85 Center St., is all ready to run with the exception of being connected to the electric wires which cannot be done until permission is obtained from the electric company. We left a package at 200 Summer St. for you - it has music rolls so you can change music on the Banjos in your area. There are now 3 machines in Brockton. The 3rd one at McGuire's is ready to run as soon as it is connected. The other two are running. On the 17th of June, when the Park opens, we shall probably have one more there.

I wish you success in your business.

F.R. Pendleton
Auto Manufacturing Co.

June 11, 1901
American Automusic Co.
New York

We are very much disappointed at not receiving any music recently. We are especially anxious to get some more as we have several instruments that are waiting to go to different locations as soon as music is received.

C.B. Kendall
Auto Manufacturing Co.

June 18, 1901
Iola Cafe
Brockton, Mass.

We have been notified that your machine does not get enough patronage with a nickel slot, so we inform you that we think the Encore will pay better with a penny slot.

Our business has been so pressing, here in Boston, and we have been putting out so many machines, that we are all out of penny slots at this time. However, we expect to get more soon, and will make the changeover for you.

F.R. Pendleton
Auto Manufacturing Co.

June 19, 1901
W.J. Maguire [sic]
Brockton, Mass.

We understand from our Mr. Holt that our Automatic Banjo in your store is not running. We have had some conversation with the people in Providence who own your electric wires and they have promised to see you soon about it. As they have not yet done so, we think you are justified in making a connection on their wires and paying according to the number of tunes played on the machine - the actual price of the current used.

It is hurting the machine to have it sitting there idle as people are liable to get the idea that it is out of order and will not work.

F.R. Pendleton
Auto Manufacturing Co.

June 21, 1901
American Automusic Co.
New York

We are utterly at a loss to understand why we have not yet received any of the music that we have ordered - and why no attention has been paid to the receipt of several of our recent letters...

C.B. Kendall
Auto Manufacturing Co.

June 22, 1901
F.U. Foss Novelty Co.
Lynn, Mass.

Your letter has been referred to us. We put out the Encore Banjo on lease; we have no instruments for sale. We have not entered Lynn, and if you are in a position to contract for a stated number of these instruments, we should be pleased to confer with you concerning the matter.

C.B. Kendall
Auto Manufacturing Co.

June 22, 1901
James Kirkland
Durban, Natal
South Africa

We have learned that you are located in business in Durban and that possibly you may be in a position to take up our line of business in connection with your own.

We have a "nickel in the slot" Automatic Banjo, known here as the "Encore." Its performances are almost beyond belief, and it has proved a very great success. We have a great variety of music and can accommodate customers with whatever they desire.

We are convinced that a lot of money can be earned in South Africa with this instrument, and whoever takes the matter up will secure a very valuable concession.

C.B. Kendall
Auto Manufacturing Co.

June 24, 1901
American Automusic Co.
New York

We acknowledge with thanks the receipt of 20 rolls of music on our first order of 125 rolls. We find that this music has no numbers on it. It is necessary that the numbers should be on our rolls, just as it is with your own music. Also, we find no programs or tune cards with this lot. We would like to have this corrected in the future.

We find that several rolls have bad blotches of black grease and assume that this will be remedied in the future.

We thank you for the little music we have received, and trust that more of our order will be forthcoming at once.

C.B. Kendall
Auto Manufacturing Co.

June 26, 1901
C.G. Hume
Salem Willows, Mass.

We understood you to say over a month ago that you would inform us about sending you one or two Encores. Unless we hear from you at once, we will assume that you have dropped the matter.

Auto Manufacturing Co.

June 26, 1901
A.M. Doane
Salem Willows, Mass.

We have been waiting to hear from you about the Encore you said you wanted to have installed in your place. We want you to inform us whether or not you want a Banjo.

Auto Manufacturing Co.

June 28, 1901
Warren Hunt
Old Orchard, Maine

Would it be of any use to make an attempt to put in some of our improved Automatic Banjos in Old Orchard, after the unhappy experience of yours of two years ago? We have overcome the former difficulties and should like to know how you feel about the matter.

Auto Manufacturing Co.

July 1, 1901
American Automusic Co.
New York

We received 20 programme cards for the 20 rolls of music that you sent us and were surprised to find them typewritten. These were not what we sent for. We can typewrite them here, if that is all that is to be done. We expected to receive your regular printed programmes, the same that you furnish with your own music.

C.B. Kendall
Auto Manufacturing Co.

July 1, 1901
Messrs. Daniels & Co.
Wall Street
New York

I wish to make an application for a loan of $7500. upon equipment we have here, including about 160 Automatic Banjos...

At present the demand is greater than the supply, and the earnings upon those instruments that are already in service average better than $100 per year each.

Auto Manufacturing Co.

July 8, 1901
J.A. Holt, Agent
Brockton, Mass.

We have not heard anything about new locations for Banjos in Brockton. I think that the city might hold one or two more. Can you not locate the two which are now sitting at the express station, in good paying places? You and I will both make much money thereby. We should hate to have these instruments returned to Boston.

F.R. Pendleton
Auto Manufacturing Co.

July 8, 1901
Castle Billiard Hall
Boston

Please deliver to us the Encore as it has been sitting in your store unconnected since May 16th. It is advisable for us to remove the instrument elsewhere so it can earn some money.

Auto Manufacturing Co.

July 11, 1901
Dominion Atlantic Railway Co.
Kentville, Nova Scotia

We are aggressively introducing as a novel attraction to passengers upon public steamships, etc., as well as stationary locations in cities, the Encore, an automatic banjo operated as a nickel in the slot device. These are unusually attractive and give entire satisfaction wherever introduced.

We propose to introduce these instruments on your line of steamers operating between Boston and Yarmouth, etc. We will pay you 20% of the receipts.

We can confidently assure you that these instruments will not only furnish a high standard of entertainment to your passengers on the steamers, but also that receipts will unquestionably be an important revenue to your company.

C.B. Kendall
Auto Manufacturing Co.

July 19, 1901
Relay House
Nahant, Mass.

We have received your letter and are very sorry to note that your machine is out of order once more. It seems that it is always the case that things go wrongly when one most wishes them to go rightly. We will send a man to you tonight...

Auto Manufacturing Co.

July 19, 1901
Boston Elevated Railway Co.
Boston

In reply to your inquiry concerning one of our past workmen, Mr. Roy H. Frick, please be advised that we always found him to be a most satisfactory employee.. We would be most pleased if he obtains a good position with you. The reason he left us was on account of scarcity of work, and we laid him off together with others.

F.R. Pendleton
Auto Manufacturing Co.

July 19, 1901
American Automusic Co.
New York

We are very much put out at not receiving the music from you which we ordered a long while ago, and we are at a loss to know why you have not sent it... It is now time for us to have a new supply, or our business will suffer seriously.

F.R. Pendleton
Auto Manufacturing Co.

July 23, 1901
American Automusic Co.
New York

Our being supplied with the latest music is for your own interest as much as it is for ours. At present wherever our instruments are installed the cry of "chestnuts" is everywhere heard. They say, "Oh, why don't you give us something new?" and they name over a multitude of recent musical productions that are heard on all other automatic musical instruments but ours, and ask why we don't produce some of them...

We have also been aware that novices are at work on your cutting machines because of some of the imperfections in music rolls received from you lately... The frequency of deficiencies seems to be increasing.

As we have written to you many times before, we are suffering for music. Our business is curtailed, our prospects not encouraging, and our customers and stockholders are murmuring, and we cannot offer a satisfactory explanation...

If you can send just a part of our order it will help to remove the dissatisfaction which is rapidly growing at this end of the line.

C.B. Kendall
Auto Manufacturing Co.

July 27, 1901
Mr. C.W. Davis
Waterville, Maine

I intend to soon send you a detailed statement of the total receipts of every Encore we have put into service since we were organized, but I have been busy and only have time before the mail goes out to give you a few figures:

One Encore took in $26.83 the first month and $32.54 the second. Another took in $10.35 the first week. The smallest receipts for a machine were $4.22 in one month. This Encore was moved and is now earning at the rate of $19.75 per month.

The first Encore was installed on May 3, 1901. We now have 35 in service, including one installed today.

C.B. Kendall

July 29, 1901
Mr. C.W. Davis
Waterville, Maine

I give herewith corrected figures on the Banjos. 34 instead of 35 instruments are out. Total days in service for all instruments: 951. Total receipts: $454.47. Average receipts per instrument: $13.36. Average receipts per instrument per day: 47¾ cents.

We have one man out sick, and I am too busy to write extensively, but the above figures speak more eloquently than I can.

C.B. Kendall

July 29, 1901
G.G. Orton
Ashland, Mass.

We received your card about connecting the Banjo, and inform you that we shall probably not get around to it until Wednesday. We are sorry to have delayed the matter so long, but our man has had more work than he can do, and all our other men are equally busy. Please accept our apologies.

F.R. Pendleton
Auto Manufacturing Co.

July 29, 1901
Twigg & Johnson
West Medford, Mass.

We had fully intended to ship long before this the Automatic Banjo which was ordered on July 12, but through an extreme rush of business we have been unable to do so. We trust that we shall be able to send your order sometime this week.

F.R. Pendleton
Auto Manufacturing Co.

July 31, 1901
D. Holland
Revere Beach, Mass.

We fully expected that our collections at the beach would be sufficiently large to warrant the expense of maintaining the instrument at your place of business. But, we have been disappointed. In view of the fact that collections are so small, we have concluded to remove all of our instruments from Revere Beach.

F.R. Pendleton
Auto Manufacturing Co.

(Editor's note: The same letter was sent to three other customers in Revere Beach)

August 1, 1901
W.Hunt & Co.
Malden, Mass.

We understand you would like to have an Encore installed at your drug store in Malden. If we can place several other machines in Malden within the next week or two we will let you have one too. At present we do not care to put just one in Malden as the expense would be too great.

You would receive 20% commission - our regular terms. We shall not be able to give you the 25% commission you suggest, and if you can consider the Encore only on that basis, then no further words are necessary. We have made the price of 20% and cannot deviate from it in the slightest degree. All of our other customers are satisfied with this.

F.R. Pendleton
Auto Manufacturing Co.

August 3, 1901
Mr. C.W. Davis
Waterville, Maine

I desire to inform you that the 26 machines we are now running in the city of Boston had receipts last week of $65.77. You will see that it nets us over $2.50 per week per machine.

You can easily see that more machines mean more money, and I can say that our present expenses will practically operate 100 machines - so we are anxious to get 100 machines out as soon as possible.

C.B. Kendall

August 9, 1901
Relay House
Nahant, Mass.

We have decided to remove the Encore Banjo from your hotel tomorrow, as we feel that it is not giving you satisfaction - and we don't want to keep it there when it is such a put-out to you. We are very sorry indeed that the machine has behaved in such a manner, and regret the trouble. We have tried our best, but it seems that the instrument will not run in your location without constant watching. Perhaps it is the dampness, for they give no trouble in Boston...

F.R. Pendleton
Auto Manufacturing Co.

August 12, 1901
Charles Nadeau
Eastport, Maine

In reply to your letter, we say that the Encore Banjo is never sold. Our only terms are a lease or rental. We have leased some for $400 for a 15-year lease, which is practically equivalent to a sale, and if you care very much to get one I might let you have one on these terms.

However, we are putting no Banjos in Maine at present. If we should later make arrangements in your state, we will open negotiations with you. Just at present it seems impossible to do business with you.

F.R. Pendleton
Auto Manufacturing Co.

August 14, 1901
American Automusic Co.
New York

We received from you yesterday via American Express 30 rolls of music, and were very much put out to find them in as bad, if not a worse condition than those received from you formerly...

We also do not appreciate your substituting tunes. One instance of this occurrence is in roll No. 210 in which you substituted "Goodbye, Dolly Gray," for "Old Log Cabin in the Lane," and also "Hunky Dory" instead of "Limber Libby." However, in this instance this may be an improvement, so we will keep it as it is, but in the future please do not do it without notifying us.

Another roll, No. 206, has been changed by substituting "Patty O'Carrol's Jigs" for "Paddy Handley's Goose." This former tune is absolutely of no use whatsoever as there is no character or music to it, while the latter tune has considerable merit...

F.R. Pendleton
Auto Manufacturing Co.

Editor's note: On or about August 13, 1901 a fire damaged the factory and damaged $12,257.09 worth of merchandise and tools. Part was covered by insurance.

August 17, 1901
B.J. Lehan
Reading, Mass.

There will be some delay in sending the Encore to you as we have had a fire in our factory that will set us back ten days or two weeks in our orders.

F.R. Pendleton
Auto Manufacturing Co.

August 22, 1901
A.L. Austin
Burlington, Vermont

Thank you for your letter about a used machine you purchased from O.S. Dodds. We can make you no figure on purchasing same as we don't know what condition it is in, nor anything about it whatsoever. We think, however, that it is one of the old style machines, which are now out of date, and which would be of very little value to us. We do not care to make you any offer on it.

F.R. Pendleton
Auto Manufacturing Co.

August 31, 1901
American Automusic Co.
New York, N.Y.

It may be possible for us to lease some of your instruments in different parts of the U.S. outside of our own territory, under some new plans we have in mind. Will you give to us the same prices and terms given to your other selling agents?

If you will do this, we will make an effort to help you get rid of some of your instruments.

C.B. Kendall
Auto Manufacturing Co.

September 4, 1901
Temple Electric Light Co.
Temple, Texas

In reply to your letter we inform you that our Banjos are put into service on the 15 year lease plan, and at the end of that time, for $1, the lessee takes full title. The price is $350 cash, f.o.b. Boston or New York, including 5 rolls of music of 5 tunes per roll.

C.B. Kendall
Auto Manufacturing Co.

September 11, 1901
Davis & Drake
Boston

In reply to your letter of the 10th, we will say that we will attend to the removal of the Banjo as soon as we can spare a man to do it. We regret that you want it taken out for all others have found that it does help their business and would be sorry to have them removed.

F.R. Pendleton
Auto Manufacturing Co.

September 17, 1901
American Automusic Co.
New York

It is very essential for the life of our business that we should have some up to date music. The general complaint is that we are very much behind. All the other automatic musical instruments have everything that is up to date played by them - and, of course, our customers expect the same...

The calls for new music have become so urgent that we attribute our diminishing receipts, which we announce with regret, to that cause and that alone.

Auto Manufacturing Co.

September 17, 1901
C.W. Davis
Waterville, Maine

We have had presented to us a 10 day sight draft for $295.05 by American Express Co. in Paris for storage, etc. against machines that are there and which have not been returned to this country. So, I suppose there will be no avoiding the payment of this draft on the 27th. I hope, therefore, that you will be successful in your effort to find somebody to induce capital into our company.

C.B. Kendall

September 20, 1901
Griffith Colt
61 Via Torino
Palazzo Soncinio
Milano, Italy

Thank you for your letter about the Encore. I accept your personal guarantee of payment of the money within 90 days of the arrival of the machine at Genoa. I will personally prepare and inspect a machine for you - and will select music which I think will be most likely to be acceptable to you and your people there.

I believe you will have no difficulty in establishing a fine reputation for the instrument, as the music as it is played on it, although it is not an orchestra, or an Aeolian, or an opera company, will prove to be a very interesting novelty even to the high class music lovers of Italy.

We are also hoping to produce what we call the "Household Banjo," that is, one without a slot and one that can be played either with electricity or with a foot treadle like an organ or pianola. I mention this to give you an idea of the possibilities of the future.

C.B. Kendall
Auto Manufacturing Co.

September 25, 1901
C.W. Davis
Waterville, Maine

Mr. Kendall is away for the day, and it occurs to me to write and ask for money for the payroll, which I understand you told Mr. Kendall you would provide and which he wrote you would amount to $129. As we make up our payroll on Friday, I thought it best in the absence of Mr. Kendall to write to you in time for you to send the check on Thursday.

F.R. Pendleton

September 26, 1901
To Whom It May Concern:

This letter is written in recommendation of Mr. Day who has just left our employ. We were forced to let him go on account of scarcity of work and our being obliged to reduce expenses. We have the best of feelings toward him and wish him success...

F.R. Pendleton
Auto Manufacturing Co.

September 30, 1901
C.W. Smith
Medford, Mass.

In regard to the Automatic Banjo which we were to send you we must again apologize for not having sent it, and will say that we have not yet caught up with our orders. There are many applications prior to yours which we have not yet filled, and it will take us some one or two weeks to get them all taken care of.

F.R. Pendleton
Auto Manufacturing Co.

Editor's note: The above letter is similar to several others sent out at that time.

October 3, 1901
Messrs. Davis & Soule
Waterville, Maine

We acknowledge receipt of $150. The writer believes that from the indications here in Boston that business is looking better than ever before, and that we are now on the brink of success.

F.R. Pendleton

October 5, 1901
Mr. C.W. Davis
Waterville, Maine

One thing I overlooked entirely earlier, and have a great deal of delicacy in bringing it up now, for reasons that are obvious - the earnings of the machines for two weeks, which does take care of the payroll for this week, would not, of course, furnish enough to pay our office and factory rent.

I assume that these advances that you have been making will soon be very quickly returned to you. The earnings for the past few weeks show a trifle over $2 per machine. We are getting ready to put out more machines. Business is certainly looking well.

Could you forward to Mr. Pendleton a check for $100?

C.B. Kendall

October 8, 1901
J.R. McGurn
Westboro, Mass.

Thank you for your inquiry. We cannot discuss business with you at present for we are so busy here in Boston and vicinity that we are unable to supply the demand, and cannot extend our business until we get caught up on our orders...

F.R. Pendleton
Auto Manufacturing Co.

October 10, 1901
C.W. Davis
Waterville, Maine

One thing I must mention is the necessity for a check to meet our payroll on Saturday...

C.B. Kendall

October 11, 1901
Frank Brooks, Jr.
Mystic, Conn.

In reply to your letter we will say that we should be very glad to do business with you in some way, either by establishing an agency or by renting you machines. We will say, however, that we cannot do anything just at present as our business in Boston is so pressing that we are unable to supply the demand, and we cannot do any business outside for some time to come. We will place your letter on file...

F.R. Pendleton
Auto Manufacturing Co.

October 12, 1901
C.W. Davis
Waterville, Maine

I write to give you the result of the week's collections on 30 machines, which is $66.53 net. These are city machines. The outside machines will average even better, but our collections are very irregular on them.

We did not hear from you this morning as we hoped, and assumed that you did not reach home in time to send us a draft for this week's payroll; and, believing this to be the case, we drew on you at sight today for $125.

You can also imagine that we have some small bills and items that have to be attended to in addition to the payroll... I hope to be able to visit you in Waterville and will travel there so as to arrive early Monday.

C.B. Kendall

October 12, 1901
John A. West
South Framingham, Mass.

In reply to your letter, we will say that we shall be unable to fill your order at present, as our business in Boston is so pressing that we cannot supply the demand here...

We will keep your letter on file...

F.R. Pendleton
Auto Manufacturing Co.

October 14, 1901
Mr. C.B. Kendall
(who is in Maine on a trip)

I have been told that some Banjos are being sold in Lewiston, Maine for their taxes, which amount to about $17 or $18, and he tells me that one was actually bought for $18. There are 5 machines now in Lewiston, and it does seem to me that it would be advisable to get them back here even if the taxes have to be paid, for they surely are worth something to us, and more than that, I do not wish them to be scattered promiscuously in their present disorderly condition, and at that price, it will hurt our own business. I write to you now that you may stop over at Lewiston on your way back, if you see fit, and talk with the tax collector.

F.R. Pendleton

October 18, 1901
Davis & Soule
Waterville, Maine

(Telegram) DRAFT HUNDRED TWENTY FIVE DOLLARS UNPAID. IMPORTANT. ANOTHER PAYROLL TOMORROW. AUTO MANUFACTURING CO.

October 18, 1901
Xavier Lambert
Norwich, Conn.

We note you are coming to Boston Tuesday morning... We shall be glad to talk with you but fear that the conversation will be barren of results, as we are not prepared to talk at all on any business outside of Boston and vicinity at present...

F.R. Pendleton
Auto Manufacturing Co.

October 22, 1901
Messrs. Davis & Soule
Waterville, Maine

We are sorry to have to report that one concern to whom we owed

$175.00 put an attachment on us this morning. We would like to suggest that you send us $175...

We are expecting to have some gentlemen at the factory in a few days from whom we expect to receive some capital for our business.

We managed to get out three new machines yesterday, and hope to get one or two more out this week. Our Mr. Kendall is talking with Mr. Boyd, a potential investor, who may provide $10,000.00.

F.R. Pendleton

October 23, 1901
Messrs. Davis & Soule
Waterville, Maine

I had an interview with Mr. Surbridge today which was exceedingly brief and without favorable result. He was very gruff and short and said he was not selling stocks on commissions, he already had a lot of corporations of his own, etc. etc. I tried my best to give him a few moments of talk, but he peremptorily declined for lack of time.

I also saw Mr. Soden who said he had no money to invest at present.

I have an an appointment with Mr. Phillips and Mr. Boyd to go to the factory tomorrow morning. Mr. Phillips said he would not have any money immediately, but expected to have some within a week or two. Mr. Boyd thinks favorably in our direction...

C.B. Kendall

October 26, 1901
Messrs. Soule & Davis
Waterville, Maine

I learned yesterday that you were very busy in the midst of your annual meeting, and assumed therefore that that was the reason we had not heard from you during the week. Of course you will understand without any further explanation that we are in desperate straits here, and that I have had to resort to an act that I very much dislike to do, namely, to draw a sight draft on you to cover our needs. The amount is $175.

I have managed to get together enough to take care of the payroll today, but I do not feel justified in trying to go any further with the load that I am now carrying, without definite assurance of more money. I have therefore laid off a good deal of our help for next week...

We shall have to suspend putting out any instruments for the time being. I shall endeavor to press Mr. Boyd and Mr. Phillips to make their investment in our company some time next week, which, if they do, will be of considerable help.

It seems as though we must come into some money before long. The showing is good and there is a splendid opportunity for a great business, and I shall do my best to corral it.

C.B. Kendall

November 5, 1901
Mr. B.J. Lehan
Reading, Mass.

In regard to your want for an Automatic Banjo, we are apparently just as far from sending the instrument as ever, for we still have considerable unattended to business here in the city which promises good returns for little expenditure.

We no longer want to have out of town machines on a commission basis, as some collections are poor. We will rent one for $15 per month. If more than this is not made on the price out of the earnings, a gain will be made by you on the customers it brings in.

F.R. Pendleton
Auto Manufacturing Co.

November 6, 1901
International Trust Co.
Boston

This is to certify that at our recent meeting of directors Mr. F.R. Pendleton was elected as treasurer of the company to fill the vacancy left by the resignation of C.B. Kendall.

F.R. Pendleton
Auto Manufacturing Co.

November 8, 1901
Thomas Keller
Port Huron, Mich.

We are not just now in a position to quote you prices or terms of any kind on the Automatic Banjo. We are confining ourselves to our Boston business and this is all we shall be able to take care of for some time...

F.R. Pendleton
Auto Manufacturing Co.

November 8, 1901
Frank Brooks, Jr.
Mystic, Conn.

In reply to your letter of the 2nd, we would say to you again as we did before, we are not in a position to do anything with you now, but may be in the future. Our business is such locally that we cannot properly look after it, and we must decline all applications until we get better caught up with all the orders we have in at the present time.

F.R. Pendleton
Auto Manufacturing Co.

November 13, 1901
Mr. Hammond, Gen. Mgr.
Boston Transcript

In regard to our recent matter in which you agreed to let our company break its lease on the first day of January rather than the first day of March, we should like to have a letter from you confirming this. If possible, we would even like to leave the premises sooner...

F.R. Pendleton
Auto Manufacturing Co.

J.A. West
South Framingham, Mass.

Our man will be to see you tomorrow afternoon. This will give him time to work on the instrument. We are glad that the sacred roll which we sent you proved satisfactory. We are not sure, however, that we can get another one ready by Sunday, as sacred tunes seem to be very scarce - so if we do not get another, you will have to use the one you have for your Sunday concert.

F.R. Pendleton
Auto Manufacturing Co.

November 14, 1901
Wadsworth, Howland & Co.
Boston

We understand that you have telephoned stating that our check given to you recently has been refused payment. We assure you most emphatically that there never was a time when the writer drew a check on any bank where there were not funds to meet it. There have most certainly been funds in our bank to take care of all the outstanding checks, and there always will be.

F.R. Pendleton

November 16, 1901
Mr. J.H. McGurn
Westboro, Mass.

We are aware that our agent advised you that you would be getting a banjo in 10 days or two weeks, but we did not promise it to you. It is always impossible for us to promise anyone an instrument due to our great rush of business.

We shall be glad to send you an Encore as soon as we can find the time to do so, but we are so busy now that we cannot say just when we will get around to you. We trust you will be able to wait for a short time longer.

F.R. Pendleton
Auto Manufacturing Co.

November 21, 1901
Mr.W.E. Lyon, Collection Agent
Boston

You will remember that in the past we have given you small items for collection. We now have an item we would like to get settled and wish your services in the matter. We enclose an itemized bill for the amount, and give you the man's address.

This bill was incurred by Mr. Babcock's having thrown a cut glass bowl through the front of our machine while in the store of Mr. M.C. Page, 124 Broad St. He is liable for the amount and has promised payment, but has not done so... We hope you can collect this account and send us your check for $8 soon.

F.R. Pendleton
Auto Manufacturing Co.

November 26, 1901
American Automusic Co.
New York

Please let me make one more appeal for up to date music. We are suffering extremely for the want of it. Our collections which hitherto have been very good show a decrease, and we can see very plainly that our business will be much hurt if we do not have some new music very soon.

It would seem that if the American Automusic Co. cannot supply us that we should be justified in obtaining music from other sources. We request that you send us something new at the earliest possible moment.

F.R. Pendleton
Auto Manufacturing Co.

December 2, 1901
Allen & Endicott Bldg. Co.
Cambridgeport, Mass.

We are today removing from our offices here to our factory in Cambridgeport and will locate our offices and factory together in the future.

Auto Manufacturing Co.

November 11, 1901
W.A. Dalton
Massabesic, N.H.

In regard to the Automatic Banjo, we can let you have one on the following terms which are our invariable rule for all rental instruments: $25 for 1 month, $60 for 3 months, $90 for 6 months - payable in advance.

We are not seeking out of town trade at the moment as we have not yet filled all of our Boston orders. However, if you want an instrument at the above terms we can let you have one.

F.R. Pendleton
Auto Manufacturing Co.

December 23, 1901
Nelson Haynes
S. Framingham, Mass.

In regard to your order for 5 Encore Banjos, please accept our apology for the delay in writing. We can give you five machines as soon as we get motors to go with them. The reason we have none in stock is that we do not expect to use any more here in Boston (the currents here being about to change to direct).

We will say that although we had no doubt that your references would be good, we were surprised to see how good they were. All spoke of you in the highest terms...

F.R. Pendleton
Auto Manufacturing Co.

January 13, 1902
Mr. F.W. Cantwell
Fall River, Mass.

Would you like to rent one of our Banjos again? For coin in the slot use we are now making a special rental price of $72 for six months or $12 per month.

F.R. Pendleton
Auto Manufacturing Co.

January 13, 1902
C.S. Hudson
Provincetown, Mass.

Are you ready to open negotiations for one of our Automatic Banjos as you mentioned two or three months ago. We are now catering more and more to an out of town trade and are placing machines rapidly for 6 month rental terms.

There are as yet no Banjos on Cape Cod, so it would be to your advantage to place one in your store.

F.R. Pendleton
Auto Manufacturing Co.

January 25, 1902
C.H. Foster
Worcester, Mass.

If you are in need of music as an attraction for your place of business, let us call your attention to our Automatic Banjos. We are now renting them at greatly reduced prices and are putting out machines of the latest improved type. These instruments are being used here in Boston for Gypsy camps and other amusement resorts, and give better satisfaction than any other kind of music. We shall be pleased to do business with you.

F.R. Pendleton
Auto Manufacturing Co.

February 3, 1902
Mills Novelty Co.
Chicago, Illinois

Will you kindly forward to us illustrations and prices of the different peanut vending machines which you carry? We would like the list prices, and also your prices to us. Although they are a little out of our line, we would like to buy some if there is enough in it to pay us for the trouble.

F.R. Pendleton
Auto Manufacturing Co.

(Note: The following is typical of several letters sent out at this time)

February 5, 1902
Boehm's Cafe
North Lawrence, Mass.

We would respectfully call your attention to our Automatic Banjos, one of which we think would be an attraction as a musical instrument and a slot machine in your place of business... A number of Boston restaurants are using them, as they find it increases their trade, besides proving a good investment as a money earner. We are sure that your patrons would be much pleased with it, and if you decide to rent a Banjo, you will not regret it.

We can furnish an instrument for $15 per month on a six month contract. If this is interesting, write to us at once as we have only a limited number of Banjos left and we are rapidly renting these.

F.R. Pendleton
Auto Manufacturing Co.

February 8, 1902
Nelson Haynes
S. Framingham, Mass.

We cannot understand why you have not paid the balance due on the rental of the Banjos... We have sent several statements, but have not heard from you.

We have lived up to our agreements. We hope to hear from you soon.

F.R. Pendleton
Auto Manufacturing Co.

February 15, 1902
Nelson Haynes
S. Framingham, Mass.

We acknowledge receipt of $20 on account toward your bill. We enclose a statement showing the balance due...

If you should wish to purchase the 5 machines which you now have, we can make you a good deal for spot cash, if you can raise the money. We are willing to do this in order to get a little money to turn over for other things.

F.R. Pendleton
Auto Manufacturing Co.

February 28, 1902
Dennison Mfg. Co.
Cambridgeport, Mass.

In regard to your occupying part of our factory, about which we have spoken, we will say that we will allow you that portion of our floor near the elevator, as designated, for $20 per month.

F.R. Pendleton
Auto Manufacturing Co.

March 8, 1902
Robson's General Store
Mattapan, Mass.

We understand that you want to purchase an Automatic Banjo. We do not sell them, but make a 15 year lease carrying ownership at the end, which amounts to the same thing. Our price is $400, but at this time we are in a position to make a very liberal reduction, and if you want a machine at all, we cannot fail to please you.

F.R. Pendleton
Auto Manufacturing Co.

(Note: About this time C.B. Kendall, who formerly was treasurer but later resigned, was appointed president of the firm. Correspondence is addressed to him at the Grand Hotel, New York City - his new residence)

Mr. C.B. Kendall
Grand Hotel, New York

I am sending you two certificates of condition to be filed with the Massachusetts Commissioner of Corporations...

You will notice that the profit and loss account is very large. The amount of money received from machines is very small compared to the large amounts spent in expense... We have thus made a loss of nearly $27,000.00 in the year.

Perhaps it will not be necessary for you to swear to these certificates,

as that can be done here, which perhaps will be sufficient. So, if you will sign and return them I will be grateful...
F.R. Pendleton
Auto Manufacturing Co.

March 25, 1902
Nelson Haynes
S. Framingham, Mass.
We enclose statements herewith showing $100 due to us right now. We must urgently request that you settle this account at once. We are in VERY GREAT NEED of funds just now, and this account will help us.
F.R. Pendleton
Auto Manufacturing Co.

April 9, 1902
A.I. Mitchell
East Milton, Mass.
In regard to your patent on automatic mandolins, we would say that we have it already covered in our claims on automatic musical instruments. Should we manufacture an automatic mandolin, it would be much less expensive and more convenient to do it under our own patents. It is unlikely, therefore, that we could ever use your invention. It is therefore idle for us to take it up further.
F.R. Pendleton
Auto Manufacturing Co.

April 29, 1902
John H. Perrigo
Milo, Maine
We understand that you wish to handle Automatic Banjos in your territory. We are not just ready to talk about business in the state of Maine, but would like to hear from you concerning how many machines you can handle and the basis on which you can work.
F.R. Pendleton
Auto Manufacturing Co.

(Note: The following letter is typical of several written during this period)

May 2, 1902
M.J. Murray
Boston
We understand that you wish to reduce your Banjo rental and don't want to continue paying $12 per month for it. We are much surprised at this attitude on your part as you were represented as being a man who always lives up to a contract without manifesting any disposition to "squeal" as it is called.
Now, Mr. Murray, we don't want to get the better of you nor force you to pay for something you don't want, but we wish to be reasonable, and ask you to be the same. We believe that if the Banjo in your store had earned $30 or $40 per month you would not have offered any extra to us. You went into it with your eyes open, and now you want us to stand your loss. This is not fair, any more than it would be for you to ask your landlord to lower your rent if business went slack.
We believe you to be a fair man, and think you should do your part.
F.R. Pendleton
Auto Manufacturing Co.

July 12, 1902
Burns & Co.
Bennington, Vermont
Replying to your letter, our rental price is just $15 per month. When you consider that one of our machines will earn in Vermont, a new field, no less than $3.00 per day, and probably a great deal more, you will see that you are making a very good investment. If the machine won't earn as much as $3 per day, then you haven't a good location, and we wouldn't want to rent you one at all - for it would hurt our present good record.
F.R. Pendleton
Auto Manufacturing Co.

July 12, 1902
F.V. Clifford
Laconia, New Hampshire
Thank you for your letter. We will do business with you at a $15 per month rental, payable in advance, on a 6 month contract.
Inasmuch as New Hampshire has not yet been worked, there is no doubt a splendid field there, and Banjos should earn from $3.00 to $10.00 per day, as they do in other areas. We shall be glad to hear from you further.
F.R. Pendleton
Auto Manufacturing Co.

July 16, 1902
Messrs. Davis & Soule
Waterville, Maine
For some days it has been my intention to have a long talk with you concerning the affairs of the Auto Manufacturing Co.... There are many things which I wish to say which do not seem to go down easily on paper, and yet I realize that even were I in Waterville, it would not be easy to find an uninterrupted hour with you.
Just at this time the income of the company is much less than heretofore, as our Boston rental machines, which were all leased in January, have now run out their contracts and have been removed... Then, too, many commission machines have had to be removed as gas is taking the place of electricity, and other customers have gotten tired of the Banjo. This simply goes to show that Boston is a poor field for our work. Locations must be gotten elsewhere.
This is hard to do as one of my men has left, and I cannot afford to hire him back. I am now left with one man, and he can spare no time to hunt locations. We are greatly hampered by lack of money, and consequently we are living from hand to mouth. Our splendid factory is not being used, except for storage. We have no up to date music, nor any money to buy any with. There are many other unpleasant features which are naturally connected with a poverty stricken company.
I believe that much business can be done in the upper half of New England, and if this company were properly financed, I do not see why a good business on a large scale might not be conducted...
I think that considering the Banjo is perfected, and that it is well liked everywhere, it especially would pay phenomenally in untried locations and much money can be made.
It would seem a shame to let this company drop, when everything is so well in line, and the prospects quite bright.
I will not ask for more money. I am ashamed to, and I will not put myself in a position of one who is draining Davis & Soule. I mean to do the very best with what I have, and I shall fight to the last gasp. We are now very very poor, and it seems impossible to pull out without reinforcements, for we are holding on by our nails, and it is risky to try for a fresh hold for fear of losing that which we now have. Yet, if we can only get one finger over a few new locations, perhaps we can get a good hand grasp. About my trip to Maine, please let me know your wishes in the matter. I think new business would result from such a trip.
I enclose a bill of $50 from the American Express Co. The company is teasing rather hard for this amount. Please advise me on it.
F.R. Pendleton
Auto Manufacturing Co.

August 13, 1902
F.V. Clifford
Laconia, N.H.
Replying to your letter of the 10th, we will say that we appreciate the position you are in, and in order that you will feel that we wish to do our utmost to help you out after having contracted for a machine which proves less remunerative than you expected. We will give you a reduced rate, if you order a second Banjo. You can have a second one for $10 per month, and a third for $8.
F.R. Pendleton
Auto Manufacturing Co.

August 25, 1902
C.W. Davis
Davis & Soule
Waterville, Maine
I find it is necessary to have more funds for the business here, and suggest $200. We have six machines now in Portland, Maine, and are trying Bath and Lewiston, and later shall go further north.
I have concluded from my experience in Massachusetts with Revere Beach and Nahant that cities pay better. Portland Island and cape resorts are too foggy and damp.
F.R. Pendleton
Auto Manufacturing Co.

August 25, 1902
Frederick A. Currier
Chairman, License Commissioners
Fitchburg, Mass.
We have been referred to you as the authority on the subject of allowing our Automatic Banjos in the liquor stores in your city. We

understand that there is a feeling against music in barrooms, and that your board has decided against it. We will say that the subject has been discussed in several precincts here in Boston, and that the police commissioners, each in his own district, have allowed the Banjos to remain. So far as we can learn there has been no disorder caused by them, and is it our belief that there is less where the machines are placed. The Banjo does not play loudly enough to attract men from the street into the saloon, but simply interests them while there, and the novelty and entertainment furnished often distracts from a fight.

Hoping that we can be allowed to install our machines in Fitchburg, we remain,

Yours respectfully,
Auto Manufacturing Co.

August 29, 1902
C.W. Davis
Davis & Soule
Waterville, Maine

Your check for $200 arrived yesterday. Thank you. We are working fast to get new locations established. Mr. Day goes to Bath (Maine) tonight, and takes a machine with him. We have two more locations in Saco and Biddeford. He also goes to other cities in Maine, and I shall try myself to go to Bangor the following week. We also expect to get two or three more orders from the same man in Bath, and two more in Laconia, New Hampshire. So the prospect is good.

F.R. Pendleton
Auto Manufacturing Co.

October 7, 1902
C.W. Davis
Davis & Soule
Waterville, Maine

I recently returned from New York City. I obtained no satisfaction whatever from the American Automusic Company, except some things which I picked up by the way. I saw Mr. Andrews, the manager, Mr. Conrou, the superintendent at the factory, and finally after several calls, Mr. O'Connor, the president. They all tried to make me believe that they were perfectly satisfied with their New York business, that it was a permanent thing, etc., and Mr. O'Connor took the extreme of this ground, making me the ridiculous proposition to sell out the patents and territory, retaining New York machines and business (which he wouldn't sell at any price) for $25,000.00. You can see how ridiculous this is, for we would be getting practically nothing, as a good part of the country is irrevocably let out to other agents, and they would have to be bought up.

So, I gave up all hope of getting anything there, and hunted up Mr. Kendall on 42nd St. He has an office there. I had a long interview with him, and we went over the whole Automusic deal thoroughly. I learned that Mr. Kendall has an option to buy out the whole business, New York and everything, for $10,000.00. I told him of our ideas, and he said he would help where he could. He wanted the Auto Manufacturing Co. to get the Automusic Company, as was the original intention. He wanted Davis & Soule to get out so he could get hold of the business himself sometime as he believes there is yet money in it.

Now, I have learned enough to show me that we cannot do any business at all with Automusic without Mr. Kendall's cooperation as he has certain holds on them that nobody else has. Moreover, I believe that he will help us in any way he can. But it seems that it would be fearfully complicated as no one can understand their books, several experts having given up the job, and that the directors have done many illegal acts in times past, and two lawsuits are now pending, and in many ways the entire thing would be difficult to unravel.

Our earnings from machines in Maine are falling off considerably, and we are going behind again.

You asked me what I should do with this if it were mine. I really think it is a forlorn hope. I can see nothing ahead but disappointment piled on disappointment. Of course, I believe there is a possibility of turning it around - to our advantage, but it is exceedingly dangerous to trade in white elephants, especially when they are sick, for they might die before you can dispose of them.

F.R. Pendleton
Auto Manufacturing Co.

October 8, 1902
J.C. Humphreys
Bath, Maine

We are sorry you cannot use the machine for a longer time. However, as you do not want it, we will remove it and place it elsewhere...

F.R. Pendleton
Auto Manufacturing Co.

December 18, 1902
G.N. Varney
Manchester, N.H.

We are glad to hear that you are interested in being one of our agents.

As for earnings, we expect our Banjos to take from $6 to $15 per week... Our satisfactory machines in Maine are taking in $7 or $8 per week, and those which take in less are on the list to be changed to other locations. Some will keep up an average of $6 or $8 right along, while the majority will start at $12 or $15 and drop in a month or so to $2 or $3. It is thus obvious that the machines must be moved frequently....

F.R. Pendleton
Auto Manufacturing Co.

March 12, 1903
M.E. Wilkinson
Groveton, N.H.

Replying to your letter, it is necessary for you to attach your Banjo to the electric wires, as it will not run otherwise. We note that you have current only at night, but this should not deter you as in such cases the evening trade generally makes up for the loss during the day.

We really think a Banjo would do well running just evenings and beg to suggest that if you do not take one now at the special $150 price offered, you will probably never have another chance. This would be much better than renting one for six months, for even if the Banjo took in just $1 per evening, it would pay for itself in six months at the $150 price.

F.R. Pendleton
Auto Manufacturing Co.

March 13, 1903
Callahan & Co.
Lynn, Mass.

We understand that you want one or more Automatic Banjos. Right now you can get one at a price which has never been approached before. Although we are still selling (or, rather, leasing for fifteen years) our new Banjos for $400 each, we are closing out our stock of used ones, and offer you one at $150. These are perfect in every respect and are practically the same as new instruments. Some of our customers prefer them to our new machines. If you want one, secure one before it is too late.

F.R. Pendleton
Auto Manufacturing Co.

April 7, 1903
Frank LePage
Lewiston, Maine

In regard to the Banjo about which you wrote some time ago, we have had no reply to our answer. We conclude that you do not want a Banjo at this time. We will say, however, that we have just taken a nice used one in on trade and will refit and put it into good condition and will make a special price of $125 on this one only. Perhaps this will interest you. If so, please advise us at once.

F.R. Pendleton
Auto Manufacturing Co.

April 23, 1903
American Automusic Co.
New York

In the music received from you yesterday we found one tune in very bad condition. "In the Good Old Summertime" in roll No. 185 was made of very poor paper, with hard fibrous pieces all through it. Near the end of the piece, the music had been patched, and a botchier job I never saw. It was done with mucilage, lapped for about two inches, the edges were flopping, and the whole thing was stiff as cardboard...

F.R. Pendleton
Auto Manufacturing Co.

June 2, 1903
M.E. Wilkinson
Groveton, N.H.

I will say that I am very sorry that the Banjo is not paying as well as you expected. I regret that you will have to lose money, but if I were to take it back, we would lose money too. However, if you will keep it for two more months at $12 per month, then I will take it off your hands and ship it to Maine...

F.R. Pendleton
Auto Manufacturing Co.

June 2, 1903
L.E. Day
Bangor, Maine

On your trip for us through Maine this time, don't bother about the Bar Harbor stop.

I sold a used Banjo for $100 today as I feel confident that the party can sell quite a few of the older machines at a net of $100 each to us. I have made up my mind to put them all at this price instead of $150 if they hang much longer, and the poorer ones at $75. Anyway, we will do this when we need the money.

F.R. Pendleton
Auto Manufacturing Co.

July 9, 1903
E.W. Cantwell
Fall River, Mass.

Thank you for your offer to put an Encore Banjo in your store on commission. I cannot do this, but will make you a special price of $80 cash for one instrument or two for $100, as they are already stored in Fall River.

F.R. Pendleton
Auto Manufacturing Co.

July 21, 1903
Ford Motor Company
Detroit, Michigan

We are in receipt of your letter and the blank form, which we have filled out and return herewith. We should like to handle your machines, for we think they are good ones so far as can be judged from your descriptive matter. It seems to be the best of its kind, for we have also catalogues of many other makes.

In regard to terms of the agency, we cannot make them for we are in ignorance of the subject. We have never handled automobiles, nor in fact, any other article other than our own output. Our intention is to handle about three kinds of automobiles, of different styles and prices, so that no one of them will directly compete with any other, but that we shall be able to suit almost any prospective purchaser. We also want to handle the best machine in each class.

It seems to us that we are well fitted for an agency, for many reasons. We are manufacturers of Automatic Banjo slot machines, and have done business with this article in Europe for about six years. The market is not so good there for the banjo as it was, and we are now working the slot machine in New England, where this company is well, and is favorably known. On account of our name, Auto Manufacturing Co., we frequently receive letters and telephone calls asking about what kinds of automobiles we handle...

Our office and plant is just off Massachusetts Avenue in Cambridge, just outside of Boston, on the main thoroughfare, and right opposite the famous Charles River Park. We are surrounded by the best of roads and have ample room in our factory, and the best of facilities for demonstrating machines. Our mechanics are the best in the business, and are accustomed to dealing with delicate and intricate machinery. We could almost build a car here.

We hope to hear from you soon.

F.R. Pendleton
Auto Manufacturing Co.

August 11, 1903
Haynes-Apperson Co.
Kokomo, Indiana

We are writing to you with a view of opening negotiations toward our handling your New England agency. We are just taking on agencies for automobiles in addition to our regular business, and it seems to us that your automobile would make a good addition...

We are well located, just outside of Boston, and close to the wealthy Back Bay district. We are well and favorably known through all of New England, the upper part of which is already quite well covered by our agents. We think an arrangement with you will be to our mutual advantage.

F.R. Pendleton
Auto Manufacturing Co.

August 20, 1903
C.W. Davis
Davis & Soule
Waterville, Maine

I will come to see you tomorrow. I will bring a plan that has been brewing in my mind for many months. It seems that our Banjo slot machine business, if combined with other coin operated instruments, could not fail to produce good results. The Banjo is a good thing, and a very good thing, but we are so handicapped and our work is very hard. Combine the Banjo with other types of instruments on our routes, then it should pay. Just now we are distressed.

I start my trip with practically not a dollar, depending on the machines to pay my way. But, what I care for principally is Mr. Day, whom we owe sixty dollars. I shall call Mr. Soule's attention to this and hope something can be done.

F.R. Pendleton
Auto Manufacturing Co.

August 20, 1903
Mr. Soule:

Will you please pardon me for calling your attention to a matter which I consider pressing? The company owes Mr. Day $60, and as he is going on a little pleasure trip to New York tomorrow, taking in our Worcester and Fitchburg machines on his way, he really needs the money. I practically promised him as well as I could that I would get some from you to send him; otherwise he probably could not afford to go. I may not get a chance to mention this to you tomorrow, so hope you will be able to send a check to New York yourself. L.E. Day, Hotel Winsonia, 44th St. I don't ask for myself, Mr. Soule, and yet I am about as bad off, for I start on the Maine trip Monday with only about $2 in my pocket, or whatever I can collect from the Stoneham machine tomorrow. But, I shall feel satisfied if you will look after Day. The rent due August has not been paid, and there may be trouble there, too.

F.R. Pendleton
Auto Manufacturing Co.

—THE END—

Editor's note: For the most part we have addressed and signed the letters as they were done originally. Some letters were simply signed "Auto Manufacturing Co.," for instance. Others were signed by the firm name and the name of Kendall or Pendleton. Also, the letter copies are not all dated, but as they are in chronological sequence there is no difficulty in following the "story."

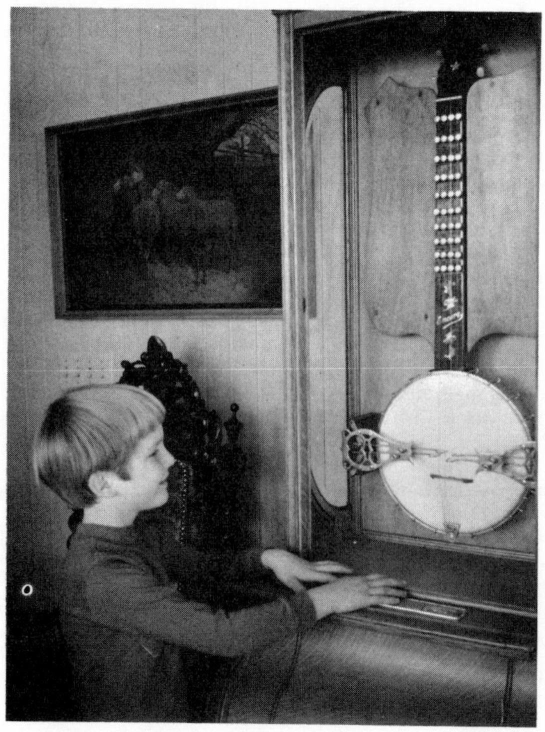

**Lee Bowers, the author's son, watches and listens to an Encore Banjo as it plays "Old Folks at Home."**

Above: View of the most-usually-seen type of Encore Banjo (compare the location of the roll mechanism and the design of the picker apparatus with the one pictured on the Anatomy of the Encore Automatic Banjo page). The pickers on the above instrument are larger and the roll mechanism is more conveniently located. This particular instrument, from the Jerry Cohen Collection, was probably made in New York City by the American Automusic Company.

Right: View of the lower front panel of a late style Encore now in the J.B. Nethercutt Collection. The inset panels are rectangular, in contrast to the curved-top panels of the earlier styles.

The fretboard has ten leather-covered buttons on each of the four strings. These buttons depress when a string is picked, causing the desired note to sound.

View of the back side of the fretboard showing rubber tubing leading to the pneumatics which operate the buttons on the strings.

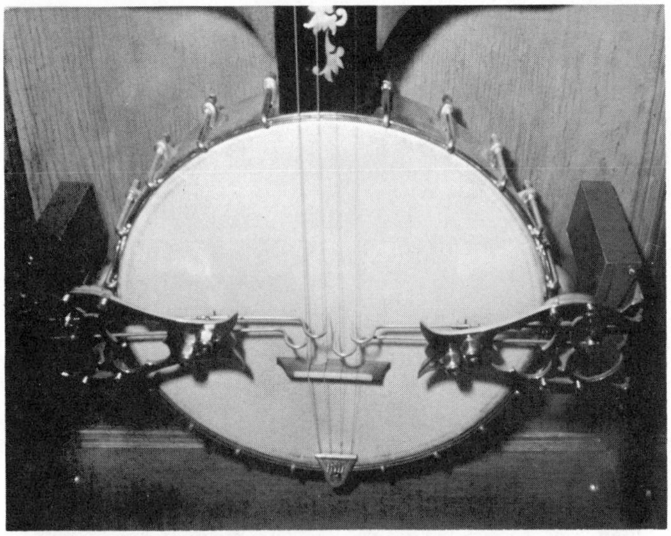

The four banjo strings are picked by metal hooks which travel in an ellipsoidal path – picking the string when the pneumatic collapses and lifting clear of the string as the pneumatic opens on the return stroke.

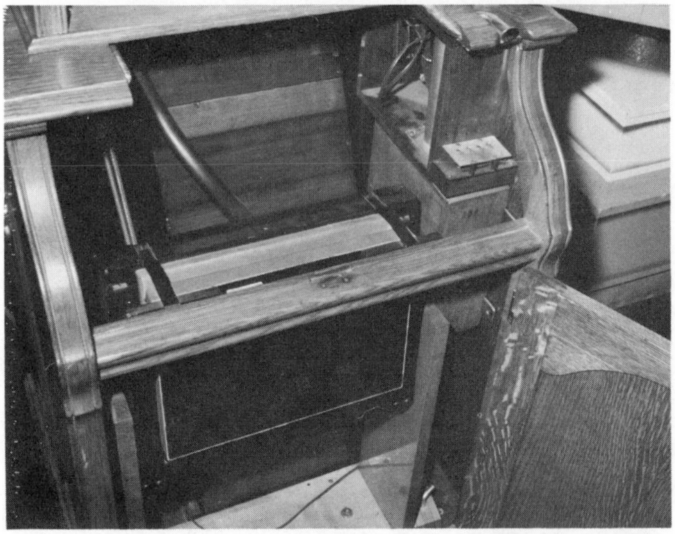

The vacuum reservoir near the front of the case. The model illustrated is of the scarcer type with the roll accessible only from the back side. Most have the roll mechanism located in the front (see other page in this section).

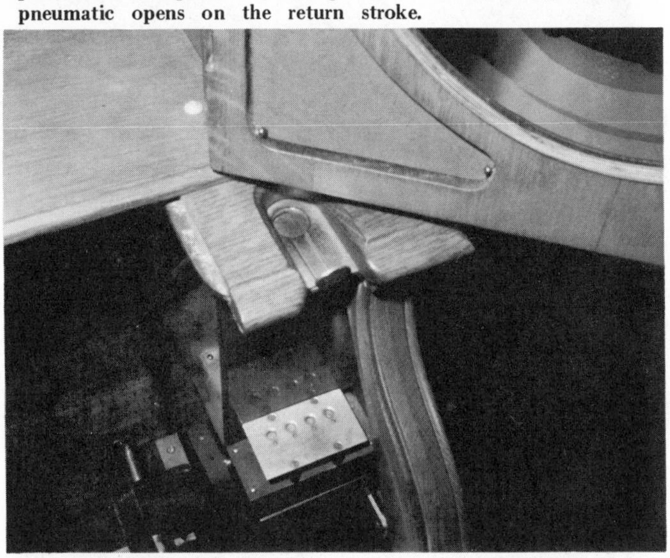

The coin slot of the Encore is of the push-pull type and has a counter which registers up to 9999 and which keeps a tally of the nickels (or, rarely, cents) deposited. Few other contemporary musical instruments had such a device.

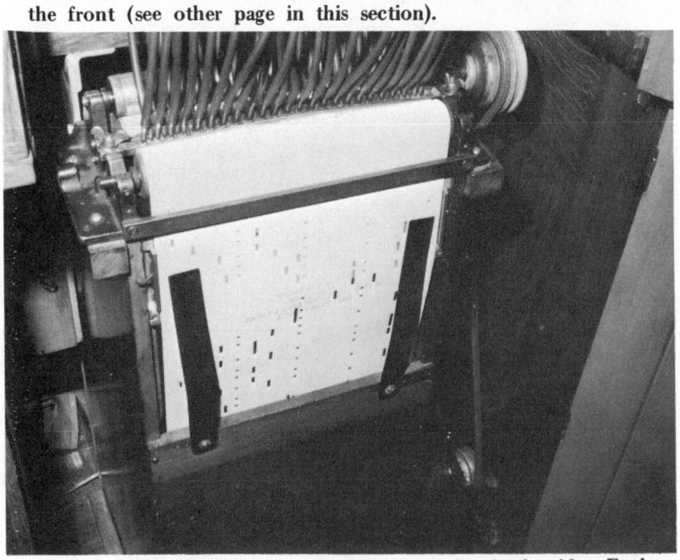

The roll mechanism as viewed from the back side. Each musical note requires two holes in the roll – one for actuating the picker and one for the fret button. The holes are D-shaped (rounded at one end) on most Encore rolls.

## ETZOLD & POPITZ
**—Leipzig, Germany—**

The firm of Etzold & Popitz acted as sales agent for Polyphon, Saxon Orchestrion Manufactory, and other manufacturers. In 1909 the firm produced (or sold; the distinction is not clear) an instrument described as an "Electric Piano WITH VIOLIN." Barrel-operated (mostly) and pneumatic orchestrions were sold under the Eldorado name; certain other pneumatic instruments under the Serenata label. Representative examples are shown here.

This large Eldorado orchestrion, featured in a Leipzig music industry fair in 1910, is housed in a case quite similar to that used for J.D. Philipps' Model 15 Pianella (see small illustration to the left).

Etzold & Popitz advertisement showing two barrel-operated instruments, the Eldorado Piano I (left) and the Eldorado Orchestrion XXIII (right).

1903 advertisement featuring a wide variety of products including the Polygraph, a typewriter made by the Polyphon Musikwerke.

Eldorado No.IX

Eldorado No.X

Eldorado No.XI

Above left to right: Eldorado weight-driven orchestrions. IX, piano with percussion effects; X, piano with xylophone, mandolin, flute and violin pipes; XI, instrumentation same as X, but with cello pipes in addition. Each instrument also featured percussion effects. These were sold in 1907-1908.

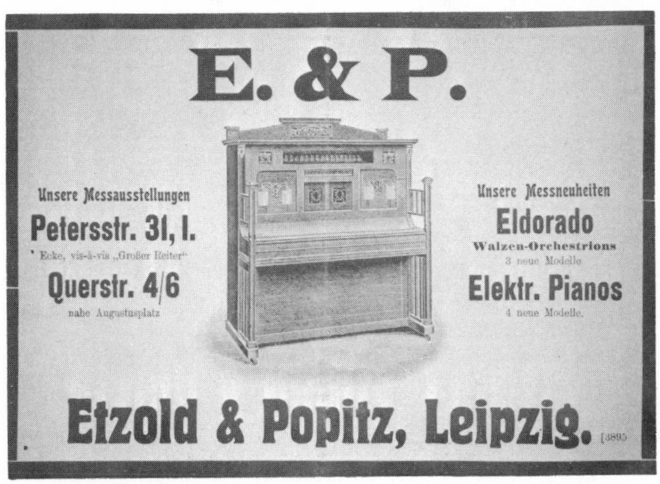


1909 advertisement illustrating an automatic piano with xylophone. The advertisement notes that at a forthcoming trade show three new barrel-operated Eldorado orchestrions and four new electric [roll-operated] pianos will be shown.

## FRATI & COMPANY
(Pianos and Orchestrions)

Frati & Co. of Berlin, a firm prominent in the manufacture of fairground organs and hand-cranked smaller organs (see other Frati section of this book), entered the piano field in the late 19th century.

The first instruments made were barrel-operated pianos, usually of eight tunes. Some of these were directly hand-cranked on a continuous basis when playing; others were spring wound. Many of these were shipped to the United States and sold to amusement park outfitters.

Later, pneumatic pianos were introduced. A type made for the home featured a crank at the right side. This crank operated a bellows system and a stiff manila paper roll at the same time. Notes were sustained by a reiterating mechanism which produced a ringing tone.

Around the turn of the century the "Fratinola" name was applied to pneumatic pianos. The first pianos and orchestrions (usually with one or two ranks of pipes plus percussion effects) had the roll located in its own special glass-fronted compartment placed below the keyboard. Later, when the roll box was concealed within the case above the keyboard Frati made much advertising value of the fact that "the roll is inserted ABOVE THE KEYBOARD, which greatly facilities attending to it."

By 1910 the Fratinola line encompassed over a dozen styles and case variations, all basically keyboard pianos — the larger models of which had pipes and percussion effects added. Those with percussion were known as Fratinola Orchestras. A violin-imitating instrument which achieved a violin tone through the medium of pipes was designated as the Fratinola - Sarasate. Sarasate, the famous violinist, was living at the time and may have endorsed this instrument.

Larger orchestrions, classic orchestrions as they would be called today, were keyboardless and were given the "Fratihymnia" name. These ranged in size from Fratihymnia No. 1, a piano with limited effects, to the huge and impressive No. 7 which imitated a military band. Many case styles were produced in the Fratihymnia series. Most were made in the 1910-1914 era, although some were produced as late as 1923-1925 (and sold by Philipps; see below).

In 1923, J.D. Philipps & Sons, a piano and orchestrion maker located in Frankfurt am Main, acquired the Frati firm. The "Fratinola" instruments were continued, although the cases were changed to resemble closely those of contemporary Philipps pianos. By 1925 the Fratinola line was the same as Philipps' own Pianella series; the only difference being that some instruments emerging from the Philipps factory were given "Fratinola" labels and others were given "Pianella" labels. Production of such Fratinola instruments was discontinued about 1927. Early (pre-1924 or 1925) Frati instruments use their own Frati rolls in several different styles; later Fratinola pianos use Philipps "PM" rolls.

Although Frati produced over two dozen different piano and orchestrion styles, the firm was not a major factor in the coin piano and orchestrion business. In a field that was overshadowed by Ludwig Hupfeld and, to a lesser extent, was the domain of Philipps, Popper, Weber, and Welte, the Frati company played a minor role. -

The Frati organization was wracked by internal difficulties (see Claes O. Friberg's "The Portable Hand-Cranked Barrel Organ" section of this book). When Frati's empire, based mostly on organs, was coming to a close the coin piano was in its ascendancy — and the two never quite meshed.

----------

**Frati & Co., Berlin,**

Early
Frati Instruments

Left: "Orchestra Piano with chimes, snare drum, bass drum, cymbals, and violin pipes; 66 keys, 8 tunes; highly elegant model especially fitted for dancing saloons, concert halls, restaurants, casinos, etc. Powerful music of most striking effect. Style No. 2. Price without violin pipes: 1100 marks; with pipes, 1200 marks. Each additional 8-tune barrel, 160 marks."

Right: "Hand and Handle Piano. Model No. 1. Piano, with one 8-tune barrel 950 marks; same, but with violin pipes 1100 marks. Each extra barrel: 75 marks." Four advantages were given in the catalogue: (1) A note can be held for any length of time; (2) Elastic touch of the piano hammers, like hand playing; (3) Little strain on piano parts, due to low friction; (4) Correct reproduction of the music.

—Early Fratinola Orchestra—

This early roll-operated Fratinola orchestrion, called the "Fratinola Orchestra," dates from about 1900 - 1905. The roll is located behind a glass window in its own compartment below the keyboard — a location also used in early Hupfeld, Kuhl & Klatt, and other contemporary German coin pianos. At this time Frati's main production of pianos was of the barrel-operated type. Roll-operated pianos were relatively new at this time and did not completely obsolete the earlier barrel type until about 1910.

Fratinola
No.1
No.3

Fratinola
No.4

Fratinola No. 2

Fratinola
No. 5

Fratinola
No. 6

Fratinola
Xylophon
No. 7

Fratinola
Xylophon
No. 8

Fratinola - Sarasate
No. 12; No. 13

Fratinola Xylophon No. 8b

Fratinola
Symphonica
No. 10

Fratinola
Orchestra
No. 11

Fratinola
Xylophon
No. 9

Fratinola No. 9
(late style)

Fratinola No. 1; No. 3. No. 1: an electric piano. No. 3: the same as No. 1 but with "zither accompaniment." Also available with extra lighting effects. No. 1 cost 2300 marks new; No. 3, 2500 marks.

Fratinola No. 2: Same as No. 1, but with motion picture effect built into a top gallery extension. 2800 marks.

Fratinola No. 4: Electric piano with post lamps or illuminated bronze figures at the ends of the keyboard. Zither (mandolin) attachment optional. 2500 marks; +200 marks additional for zither.

Fratinola No. 5: Electric piano (with mandolin for 200 marks extra). Different case style than preceding. 2500 marks.

Fratinola No. 6: Electric piano with motion picture scene (zeppelin and railway) in the top gallery. Zither attachment optional. 2800 marks.

Fratinola Xylophon No. 7: Electric piano with mandolin attachment and xylophone. 2900 marks.

Fratinola Xylophon No. 8 and 8b: Piano, mandolin, and xylophone. 3100 marks.

Fratinola Xylophon No. 9: Piano, mandolin, xylophone. Xylophone mounted horizontally (preceding models had vertically-mounted xylophones). 3400 marks.

Fratinola Symphonica No. 10: Piano with violin pipes. 3300 marks. Same, but with motion picture effect on front: 3700 marks.

Fratinola Orchestra No. 11: Piano, violin pipes, kettle drum, bass drum, triangle, chimes. "A perfect substitute for a string band." 4000 marks. Same, but with motion picture effects on front: 4250 marks.

Fratinola - Sarasate No. 12; No. 13: Piano with violin pipes. "This instrument represents a truly marvelous achievement which, with regard to the modern art of manufacture, has attained the highest degree of perfection. The cleverly imitated bowing of the violin produces a fascinating noble tone which, in connection with the harmonious accompaniment of the piano, gives such a soul-inspiring rendering of the music that it hardly seems possible that this can be a mechanical rendering." No. 12, with mirrored front: 4300 marks. Same, but with motion picture effects on front: 4700 marks. No. 13 in Flemish case: 4600 marks.

—Fratinola Instruments—

Made from the 'teens through the late 1920's, the Fratinola instruments were the basic Frati line of coin-operated pianos and pianos with one or several instruments added. The instruments on this page are from a circa 1912 catalogue.

The Fratinola - Sarasate, named after famed violinist Pablo Sarasate, imitated the violin by the medium of pipes. The original catalogue description notes that the music is quite expressive.

After the mid-1920's Fratinola instruments were made under the auspices of J.D. Philipps & Sons. Fratinola pianos of this era bear a close resemblance to those marketed under Philipps' own "Pianella" trademark (see Philipps section of this book). The late-model Fratinola No. 9 shown here is an example. Other late Fratinola instruments use Philipps "PM" rolls and are simply Philipps Pianella instruments with "Fratinola" labels, there being no other difference whatever.

Fratinola
Symphonica No. XIV
Expression piano with xylophone and mandolin effect. With expression and tremolo. "Elegant model, ideal for the best restaurants and cafes."

Fratihymnia
No. 1; No. 2

No. 2

The model at left was designated as No. 1 and No. 2; the above model is a No. 2 in a special case.

No. 5

Fratihymnia
No. 2; No. 3
The style shown at left was designated as No. 2 and No. 3, depending upon the instrumentation.

Fratihymnia
No. 4, No. 5
The style with distinctive spiral columns was designated as No. 4 and No. 5, the designation depending upon the interior contents.

–Fratihymnia No. 4; No. 5–
The above style was known as No. 4 or No. 5, the designation depending upon the instruments in the interior.

FRATIHYMNIA ORCHESTRIONS

The Fratihymnia designation was dependent upon the instrumentation. The same number was often assigned to different exterior designs, as the illustrations on this page show.

Fratihymnia No. 1: Piano, flute pipes, violin pipes, bass and snare drum with expression, cymbal, and triangle. "The ideal substitute for a modern orchestra." Original cost: 3900 marks.

Fratihymnia No. 2: Piano; pipes representing violin, viola, flute, cello; harp effect; kettle drum; bass and snare drums; castanets; chimes; triangle. Also available in special "Alpine" case: "The style of a house in the mountain district – with a pretty landscape scene in the center of the facade which is animated with a turning windmill and waterfall. If desired, multicolored chirping birds can also be furnished at extra cost." Various No. 2 models cost 4600, 4800, or 5200 marks.

Fratihymnia No. 3: Piano; pipes representing violin, viola, flute, bassoon, cello, clarinet, harp effect, xylophone, cymbals, kettle drum; bass and snare drums; tambourine; triangle; castanets; and chimes. "Besides the regular instruments, the new effect of the cymbals is very striking which, in conjunction with that of the xylophone, imparts a particular shade of tone color to the roaring volume of sound and the very precise playing with expression – affording the listener a real treat." 6200 marks.

Fratihymnia No. 4: Piano; pipes giving effect of violin, flute, clarinet, oboe, fagott, cello, piccolo, string bass; harp effect; cymbals; xylophone; orchestra bells; kettle drum; bass and snare drums; tambourine; triangle; castanets. 8600 marks in case as shown at lower left; 9600 marks in "deluxe" case with spiral columns.

Fratihymnia Nos. 5, 6, and 7: see following page for instrumentation. Original costs were: No. 5 in case as shown at left: 11,000 marks, in case with spiral columns 12,500 marks, in case shown on following page 13,800 marks. No. 6: 14,200 marks. No. 7: 15,400 marks.

Extras: Nos. 1 and 2 could be equipped with xylophone for 400 marks extra; any Fratihymnia could be equipped with "church bells" for 500 marks extra.

—Fratihymnia No. 6—

Made in several case styles — including that at the immediate left and that at the lower left (the same case as Fratihymnia No. 7).

"This instrument represents a symphony orchestra and contains, besides a very large piano with expression, pipes representing violin, viola, cello, flute, clarinet, oboe, cornet, and piccolo. In addition there is a harp effect and a xylophone. The percussion operates either loudly or softly and includes snare drum, bass drum, cymbals, castanets, triangle, chimes, etc.

"Each single artistic instrument resembles that in an orchestra. Together the tones are combined in fascinating harmony."

Case variations were made upon request. Motion picture effects, statuary, or other decorations could be obtained in place of the beveled mirrors shown at the left. Only a few of the large Fratihymnia orchestrions were ever made, but those few are of great artistic beauty, as those illustrated on this page indicate.

—Fratihymnia No. 7—

Fratihymnia No. 7, shown below as illustrated in a circa 1914 catalogue, is one of the largest Frati orchestrions ever made. The No. 7 apparently has loud voicing and "contains all the instruments of a complete military band." Note that "If desired, the front spaces or squares can be filled with animated pictures or with any other desired equipment. . ."

—Fratihymnia No. 6—

Case same as No. 7, but with violin, cello, flute, oboe, and other symphony orchestra-type instruments, instead of military band instruments. With concert (softer) voicing.

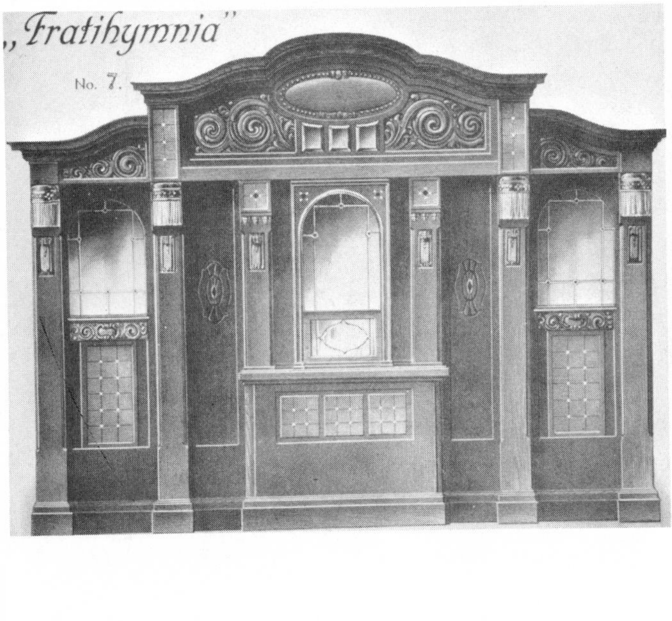

—Fratihymnia No. 5a—

Fratihymnia No. 5 was made in several case styles. That designated "5a" is shown above. Instrumentation includes: piano, pipes representing violin, flute, clarinet, oboe, double bass, and English horn; harmonium, harp, cymbals, xylophone, snare drum, kettle drum, bass drum, triangle, castanets, tambourine, and chimes. "If desired, the music of this instrument can also be supplemented by the imitation of the ringing of church bells, at no extra charge."

During the 'teens and 1920's a number of Seeburg instruments were made with the Harwood name on the piano fallboard. These instruments were otherwise identical to regular Seeburg models and were simply examples of "private label" manufacturing done by one firm for another.

The Harwood orchestrion shown in the accompanying illustration is particularly interesting. It was obtained many years ago by Mr. A. Valente who acquired it from the J.P. Seeburg Piano Company files. The Harwood is in a wooden cabinet identical (except for the art glass) to the Peerless Wisteria orchestrion (see Peerless section of this book). A similar instrument was sold as the Seeburg Style J. Containing a piano, two ranks of pipes, and (in some specimens) limited trap effects, the Style J used the type "H" orchestrion roll.

Inasmuch as Seeburg and Peerless, two non-related (to our knowledge) firms, each used the same basic case, the possibility is strong that both Seeburg and Peerless ordered their piano cases from a common supplier — a practice once common in the industry.

## K. HEILBRUNN SÖHNE

The firm of K. Heilbrunn Söhne produced a line of coin operated electric pianos during the late 1890's and early 20th century. The illustrations we show here are from Heilbrunn catalogues of 1902 and 1906 and depict electric pianos similar to those contemporaneously sold by Dienst, Hupfeld, and other German makers. Except for minor differences in trim and casework most models are like each other.

The 1906 catalogue noted: "Our instruments are of agreeable, large, and full tone, cross-strung, trichord, with complete iron frame, ivory keys, and have perfect repetition. All parts are made of the best material. They are therefore especially adapted for use in connection with a piano-player. The touch or quality of the instrument is not disturbed by the mechanical apparatus, and our pianos can always be played by hand. The piano-player is combined with the piano in such a technical and artistic fashion that the solidity and usefulness of the instrument can be guaranteed for many years."

Sold under the trade name "Virtuos," Heilbrunn instruments were made for both home and commercial use. Commercial (electrically-operated) instruments are shown here. For home use the firm made upright and grand pianos and player pianos.

Above: Cover of Heilbrunn Price List No. 3, circa 1902.

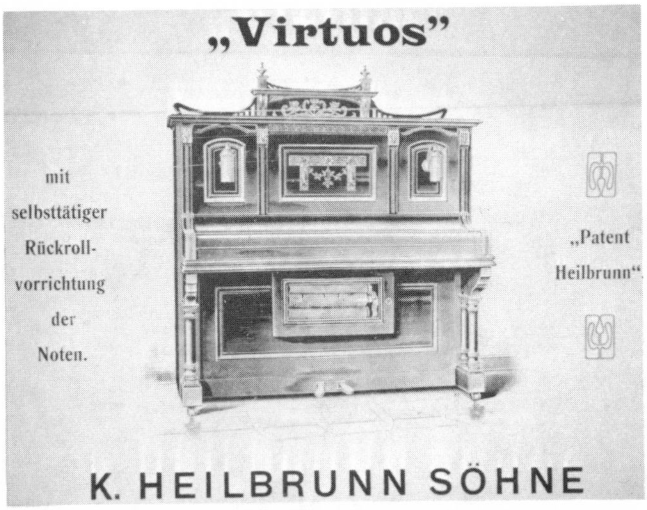


Model P

Model A

Model B

Model C

Model E

Model D

Model G

Model F

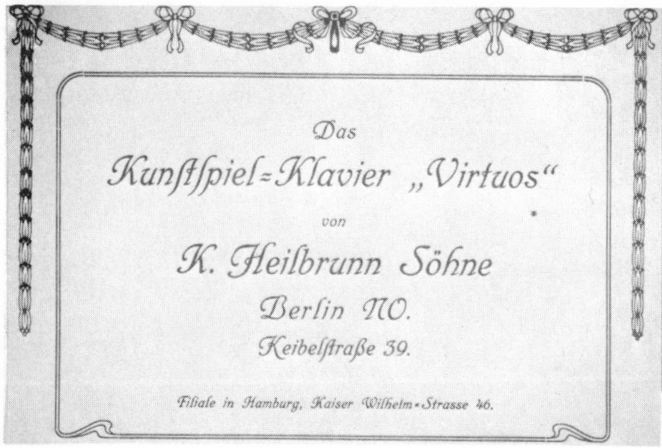

**Model C**

**Model H**

**The instruments on this page are mostly from the 1906 Heilbrunn catalogue. There is little difference between these and the earlier-shown 1902 models. Note that Model K on this page is the same as Model C shown earlier.**

**Model L**

**Model N**

**Model J**

**Model K**

**Model M**

**Model O**

**Model Q (Renaissance style)**

**Model R**

**Heilbrunn pianos for the home.**

**Model T**

During the late 19th century Sigmund Heizmann manufactured several different styles of barrel operated organs and orchestrions. An 1874 account of the commercial activities of Vöhrenbach, Germany, names Heizmann and the competing firm of Imhof & Mukle as the two main makers of automatic musical instruments in that Black Forest town.

The example illustrated is on exhibit at the "Music Boxes to Street Organs" Museum in Utrecht, Holland, and is shown courtesy of that institution.

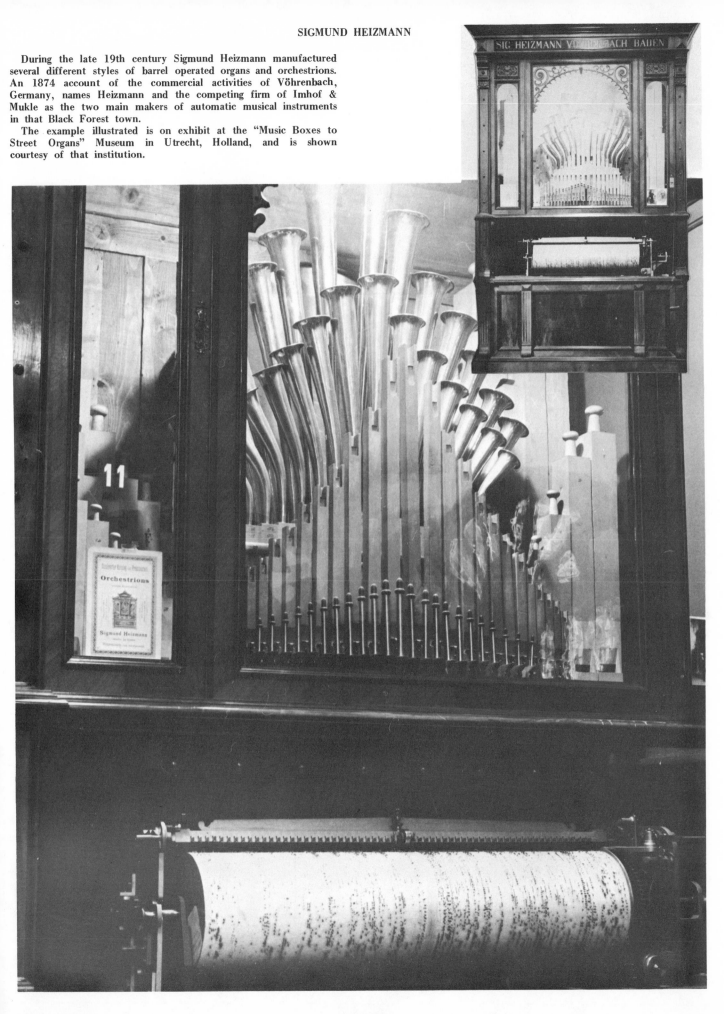

## HOFMANN & CZERNY
### –Continental Musikwerke–

The large piano and musical instrument factory of Hofmann & Czerny A.G., of Vienna, Austria, entered the field of theatre photoplayers and theatre pianos about 1910. The firm employed about 500 persons at the time and produced about 5,000 instruments yearly, primarily regular (non-player) upright and grand pianos. The title page of its catalogue proudly proclaimed, "The largest and most important factory of Austria - Hungary."

Several varieties of "Kinophon" (brand name) photoplayers were produced. While not roll operated (and thus not "automatic" musical instruments), they do bear a close resemblance to theatre photoplayers produced in America.

Automatic musical instruments produced by Hofmann & Czerny include several varieties of keyboard pianos and a series of barrel-operated harmoniums. For example, Model XXX was described as "Auto-Harmonium with cylinder. Vacuum system with knee swell. 1 cylinder playing 6 pieces. This instrument may be played by hand, but by turning a crank it may also be used as an automatic harmonium. . ."

----------

Modell XIII und XIIIa

Modell XXII, XXIII, XXIV

The Piano-Violin is the darling family-instrument of the future. An excellent concert-pianino of 7¼ octavos here is united to a magnificent imitation of violin-play. By means of ingenuously devised swelling arrangements, the player has the possibility to obtain the most charming effects, from a dreaming pianissimo up to the vigourously marked sound of the fiddle-stick. The piano may be played alone or with violin-accompanyment. On demand, this instrument also is furnished, besides the violin, with an Italian mandolina and with a natural flute.

Height ab. 2·46 yards, breadth ab. 1·70 yards. Net ab. 770 lbs., gross ab. 1100 lbs

Model XXX.

Auto-Harmonium with cylinder, 1 play. Sucking air system with knee-swell.

1 cylinder playing 6 pieces. This instrument may be played by hand, but by turning a crank, it may also be used as an automatic Harmonium. Appropriated for all aims.
1 play: 4 octavos, 8' diapason.
Height about 1·21 yards. Breadth about 0·88 yards.
Net about 122 lbs., Gross about 200 lbs.

Model XXXI.

Auto-Harmonium with 2 plays, with cylinder. Sucking-air system with knee-swell.

This instrument may be played by hand, but also used as an automatic instrument making an artistic effect.

Adapted for all means. 1 cylinder, playing 6 pieces. 2 pieces, 5 octavos, 8 registers, 8' diapason, 4' flutes, 8' melodia, 4' viola, 8' dolce, 8' echo, bass-forte, soprano-forte.
Height about 1·30 yards, Breadth about 1·22 yards.
Net about 190 lbs., Gross about 333 lbs.

This giant-kinophone is a work of art of a special kind. One player alone governs the same and becomes a true wonder, as, with his two hands alone, he is able to let us hear a complete symphonia-orchestra and, besides, according to our wishes, the song of the birds, the sound of the bells, wind, storm, thunder, shots of rifles, the clashing of the whip, the "houppe" of the autos, the telephone-bell, a forge in the forest and the voice of the cuckoo. This mecanism contains the following instruments: an excellent piano with cross stringa and iron frame, a magnificent italian mandolina, a harmonium with 4 plays, 5 octaves, 16' bourdon, 8' melodia, 8' wind-harp, 4' flute in the far, besides this, trumpets, flutes, piccolo, imitation of a violon, bassoon, a set of bells, large and small drum an cinelles, 10 plays, 2 manuals, 27 registers, knee-swells and manual-couple. Blowing of the bellows be electricity.

Breadth of the 3 instruments about 6·05 yards, height about 1·65 yards.

Net weight about 2600 lbs, gross weight about 3500 lbs.

Modell XV

Modell XII, XIIa, XI und XIV

## HOFMANN & CZERNY (continued)
### —Continental Musikwerke—

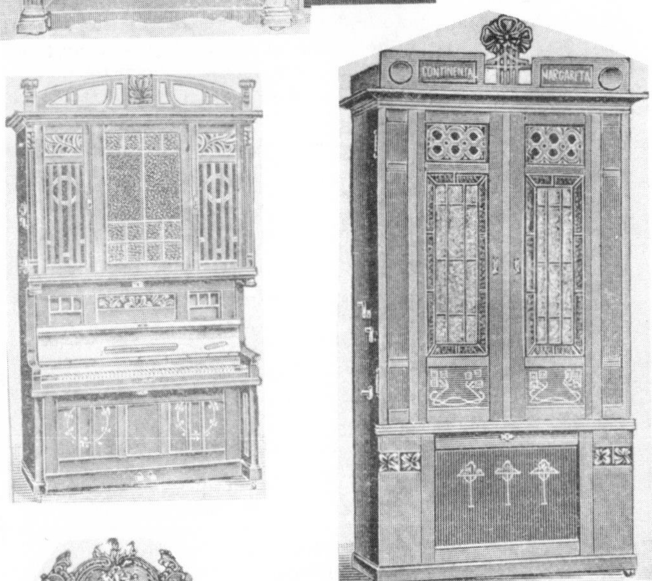

Above are some Continental instruments of the 1900-1910 decade, including the Continental Orchestrion (upper left) and Margareta Orchestrion (lower right). To the left is a book-operated organ offered in 1911.

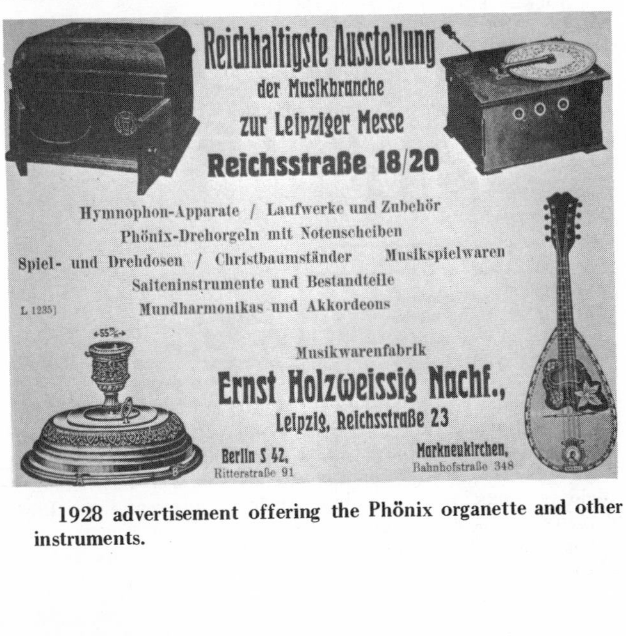


1928 advertisement offering the Phönix organette and other instruments.

## ERNST HOLZWEISSIG
### —Leipzig, Germany—

During the 1890-1930 period Ernst Holzweissig Nachf. was one of Leipzig's most active instrument makers and agents. Products included automatic pianos and orchestrions, phonographs, and related items. The Hymnophon phonograph was the firm's most popular product during the early years.

The beautiful Holzweissig trademark.

Bravo Orchestrion.

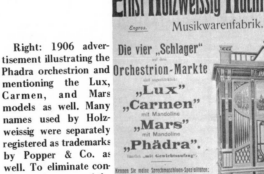

Right: 1906 advertisement illustrating the Phadra orchestrion and mentioning the Lux, Carmen, and Mars models as well. Many names used by Holzweissig were separately registered as trademarks by Popper & Co. as well. To eliminate confusion, the name of the seller was often added to the description — as "Holzweissig's Phadra," "Popper's Triumph," etc.

1904 advertisement illustrating the Musica Orchestrion and mentioning the Aida, Carmen, Bravo, Triumph, Rheingold, and Preciosa models.

# LUDWIG HUPFELD A.G.
## —A History—

*by Q. David Bowers and Claes O. Friberg*

### Scope of the Hupfeld Firm

Ludwig Hupfeld A.G. (Ludwig Hupfeld, Inc.) was the largest manufacturer of automatic musical instruments the world has ever known. In an era when such prominent firms as the Regina Music Box Company and the Rudolph Wurlitzer Company employed hundreds, Hupfeld employed thousands!

Hupfeld's interests touched virtually every branch of automatic instruments from the 1890's to the 1930's. Disc music boxes (via an ownership interest in Symphonion), organettes, home player pianos, expression pianos, reproducing pianos, orchestrions, violin players, theatre photoplayers, and theatre pipe organs were all made by the Hupfeld domain.

"The Glorious Era of Hupfeld" could well be the subject for a book by itself, so fascinating and diversified were the firm's products. On the following pages and in the reproducing piano section of this book we illustrate and describe them.

### The Early Years

In Leipzig-Eutritzsch an art shop was founded in 1880 (some Hupfeld catalogues say 1872) under the name of J.M. Grob & Company. Grob and his two partners, A.O. Schultze and A.V. Niemczik, began dealing in mechanical musical instruments in the summer of 1882. From that point onward the firm grew steadily. In 1883 the firm began manufacturing its own instruments. In 1884 the first patents were obtained.

Among the first patents was one for an autoharp. This small zither-like instrument was able to play standard accompaniment chords when certain bars were depressed. In its first form the autoharp was not a mechanical instrument but was played by hand. Later styles were modified for mechanical playing by discs or paper rolls.

In 1888 J.M. Grob & Co. devised a practical mandolin effect for a barrel piano. This system gave a fine staccato striking of the string as long as the corresponding keys were moved by pins or bridges on the wooden cylinder.

In 1886 a player for pianos and organs was perfected. This attachment could be affixed to a regular piano or organ and was operated by a perforated tune sheet. Another ingenious early device was a system devised for a 36-note player action. This unit allowed the piano hammer to fall back immediately from the string after it made contact, regardless of whether or not the pneumatic action was returned to its normal or "off" position. Grob player mechanisms were licensed to other firms.

J.M. Grob & Co. took over the distributorship for a number of musical instrument manufacturers in the Leipzig area. Among those was the celebrated firm of Ehrlich, maker of the Ariston hand-cranked reed organ or organette. In 1886 Grob acquired the sole agency for Ariston instruments. Later the system was modified for use in a disc-operated push-up piano and organ player.

### Ludwig Hupfeld

1892 was a turning point for J.M. Grob & Co. Ludwig Hupfeld took over the firm this year and continued the production of instruments in the Grob factory in Leipzig-Eutritzsch. The name was changed to Hupfeld Musikwerke, although the Grob & Co. designation was used in advertising until about 1900.

The firm continued its agency for other manufacturers. The firm became the largest distributor of Symphonion music boxes. Later Hupfeld acquired an ownership interest in Symphonion. Other music boxes such as Kalliope, Fortuna, and the Chordephon zither were sold in large numbers.

Hupfeld began experimenting with pneumatic instruments. These efforts were soon rewarded by a number of successful designs. Push-up players and pianos with roll systems under the keyboard were produced. Many of these roll systems were sold to other piano makers who used them in their own instruments.

In 1899 Hupfeld moved to a newly-built factory at Apelstrasse No. 4 in Leipzig-Eutritzsch. The firm grew steadily and the factory was enlarged several times. In 1904 the production reached such dimensions that more working capital was necessary. The firm was incorporated under the name of Ludwig Hupfeld A.G.

Soon even the new factory was too small, so they commenced building another facility in 1909. By 1911 this new factory, which cost two million gold marks, was ready in Böhlitz-Ehrenberg, near Leipzig. After the dedication in the summer of 1911 the factory became Hupfeld's new home. Today pianos are still being built in the same structure.

The new building measured 275 meters long and had a tower 63 meters high. At the top were a water tank and several storerooms. The complete factory building measured 100,000 square meters (about a million square feet) and contained several separate production areas, kitchens and dining rooms, washrooms, closets, and elaborate social facilities. By 1912 some 1200 workmen were employed there. Within a few years the number had risen to about 2000. In addition, many more workers were employed at the various Hupfeld branch factories and outlets.

During World War I much of Hupfeld's production was transferred to weapons for the army, but some musical instruments were made as well. In 1917 Hupfeld acquired the Rönisch piano factory in Dresden, Germany — a firm which for the preceding two decades had delivered most of its production to Hupfeld. Also in 1917 the A.H. Grunert piano factory in Erzgebirge was taken over. Grunert had been a supplier of middle-grade pianos to Hupfeld.

In 1925 financial crises overtook many firms. During the next several years many, if not most, companies in the automatic musical instrument business were dissolved or combined with other firms. In 1926 Hupfeld merged with Gebr. Zimmermann, and the name was changed to Leipziger Pianoforte & Phonolafabriken, Hupfeld-Gebrüder Zimmermann A.G. During the preceding decade Hupfeld had opened several branch factories. Following the merger with Zimmermann most of these branches were closed so that only the large factory at Böhlitz-Ehrenberg and two branch factories were still at work.

E. BÖCKER

THE ONLY HOUSE WITH THE COMPLETE LINE OF AUTOMATIC INSTRUMENTS

WAREHOUSE AND SHOWROOMS: 231-233 Tenth Avenue
STUDIO: 26 West 38th Street, New York City

The ORIGINAL PIANO-ORCHESTRAS:
Rival the best Human Orchestras in sweetness of tone and expression.

The Great PHONOLISZT-VIOLINA:
Natural and with soul-playing automatic Violin, called "World's Eighth Wonder."

The HUPFELD DEA PIANO:
Playing automatically recorded rolls of most famous Pianists.

The HUPFELD SOLOPHONOLA PIANO:
The height of perfection in Player-Pianos without any rival.

The PHONOLISZT AND UNIVERSAL PIANO:
Refined automatic Piano with recorded rolls.

The HELIOS ORCHESTRIONS:
With their wonderful instrumentation.

The PAN-ORCHESTRIONS:
Automatic Roll Device, holding from ten to twenty rolls with a possibility of playing 140 different selections without changing.

The BÖCKER ECHO PIANO ORCHESTRA:
The only unsurpassed Orchestra with Echo; Greatest attraction.

The ORIGINAL AND WONDERFUL VIOLANO: (Name Copyrighted.)
The original instrument imitating the Violin through pipes.

The latest creation is the Phonoliszt-Violina with
TWO CIRCULAR BOWS AND SIX VIOLINS
Possessing a magnificent fullness of tone like a small Orchestra.

All the above wonderful automatic instruments, with which no other similar instruments can be compared, are controlled in the United States ONLY by

E. BÖCKER
Warehouse and Showrooms:
231-233 Tenth Avenue
Studio: 26 West 38th Street,
NEW YORK CITY

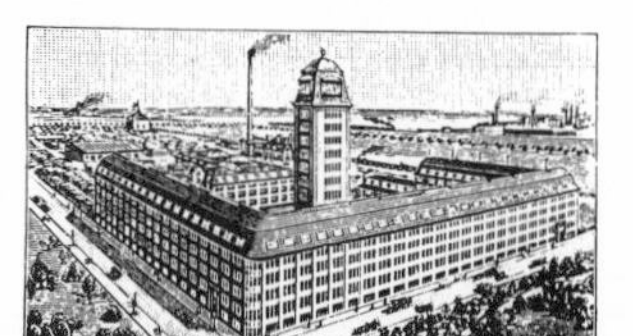

One of the Factories Behind Our Goods

1913 Advertisement of E. Böcker, one of Hupfeld's American distributors. In the above listing the Phonoliszt Violina, Dea, Solophonola, Universal, Phonoliszt, Helios, and Pan instruments are Hupfeld products. The others were made by different firms. Böcker sold many pianos and orchestrions for use in lavish New York City mansions, on Hudson River steamboats, in private clubs, and other locations.

The production of pneumatic instruments was finally stopped about 1930, although the production of music rolls continued until at least 1933-1934. After 1930 Hupfeld made such diverse items as radios, record players, furniture, billiard tables, and gambling machines. In 1936 the factory was again directed to the production of war materiel, and during the 1940-1945 era only such military items were made.

After World War II ended, Germany was divided into two parts. Leipzig was located in the zone that came under Russian control. The new land of the DDR (East Germany) was founded.

During the war some parts of the Hupfeld factory, including the tower, suffered bomb damage. The tower was repaired, but some other damaged sections of the factory were demolished. The building of pianos (not automatic) began anew in the remaining sections.

In 1946 the name of the firm was changed to VEB Leipziger Pianofabrik and later to VEB Deutsche Piano Union ("VEB" means "company owned by the people"). Under talented management the company has now grown to be one of the largest piano factories in the world. The Hupfeld and Rönisch names are still used on certain of its products.

During the war and after the war all of the remaining things pertaining to automatic instruments were destroyed. The glorious past of Hupfeld in the automatic musical instrument business was all but forgotten. A July 25, 1968, letter from VEB Deutsche Piano Union was written to Q. David Bowers and noted that "We are the successors to the former Hupfeld and Zimmermann Companies. We are very sorry to inform you that we are not in possession of any catalogues or printed matter relating to Hupfeld orchestrions, player pianos, etc. Besides, we have no music rolls, components, etc. anymore owing to the fact that the manufacture of the said Hupfeld instruments stopped such a long time ago. We now make only normal pianos and grand pianos – in large quantities. We are now a nationalized organization. One member of the Hupfeld family [Günther Hupfeld – Ed.] is still active with it. The manufacture of Hupfeld player pianos, etc. began just about the beginning of the century and continued until about 1930."

The recipient of that letter was pleased, but saddened at the same time, a few months later when another historical inquiry from another person who wrote to the Hupfeld factory was simply referred to him in America. Hupfeld had forgotten its past and apparently wanted no part of it. Although the firm can now look forward to a brilliant future in the production of regular musical instruments, it is a pity that such wonderful instruments as the Dea, Helios, Pan, Phonoliszt-Violina, and other Hupfeld creations that once caused a sensation in all parts of the civilized world are now just dim memories. Sic transit gloria!

## Some Types of Hupfeld Instruments

On the following pages and in the reproducing piano section of this book we describe the various Hupfeld automatic musical instruments in detail. First, however, here are some introductory comments:

Hupfeld Player Pianos: The Hupfeld player piano was given the "Phonola" trademark and was first made with special Hupfeld 73-note rolls. After 1908 when the 88-note system was standardized Hupfeld built Phonolas with the 88-note mechanism as well. These pianos incorporated the theme perforations first used by the Aeolian Company. The name "Solodant" was given to these instruments. Countless thousands were sold.

At the beginning of the 20th century there were some disagreements between the Aeolian Company and Hupfeld. Aeolian claimed that Hupfeld had stolen the name of Pianola in 1902 and had simply translated it into German to derive the "Phonola" trademark. Hupfeld was sued by Aeolian. Aeolian lost, and the Phonola name was vindicated.

The Aeolian Company, successful in its marketing endeavors in many different countries of the world, seems to have met with failure in the German market. In 1920 Hupfeld took over the Aeolian-owned Steck piano factory in Gotha, Germany, and commenced production of a Hupfeld-Gotha player piano which incorporated the Phonola mechanism in a Steck case.

The Universal: The Universal was a simple orchestrion with piano, mandolin, and a 10-note section of bells or xylophone bars. Housed in deluxe cases, certain models were given the name of Concert Universal. Certain still larger instruments with 30-note xylophones were designated as Concert Universal Grand and Concert Clavitist Universal models. Some of these latter instruments could play Clavitist and Phonoliszt piano rolls as well as orchestrated rolls. Another Universal type with drums was designated as the Universal Orchestra.

The Helios Orchestrion: The Helios Orchestrion was manufactured in many different case designs and interior configurations. Using special Helios rolls these instruments could play a wonderful range of effects. In terms of the quantities originally produced, the Helios models were the most popular classic orchestrions of the early 20th century.

The Pan Orchestra: The Pan Orchestra featured a 124-hole tracker bar (spaced 9-to-the-inch) which enabled it to combine various instruments and registers in many, many ways. This was the most sophisticated and expensive instrument ever built by Hupfeld. In fact, with the exception of the limited-production Weber Elite, the Hupfeld Pan Orchestra was the most sophisticated and expensive instrument ever built by anyone. The Pan Orchestras were made in several standard styles including models O, I, II, III, and IV, and in a photoplayer format known as the Kino-Pan. The Pan Orchestra was a marvelous combination of technology and music. It is a shame that more weren't made!

Animatic Orchestrions: During the 1920's a number of Animatic orchestrion styles were made. These were inexpensive instruments which contained a piano, mandolin, and sometimes a 10-note xylophone. Separate cabinets with drums could be added. A number of keyboard-style instruments of the Animatic type were also built with

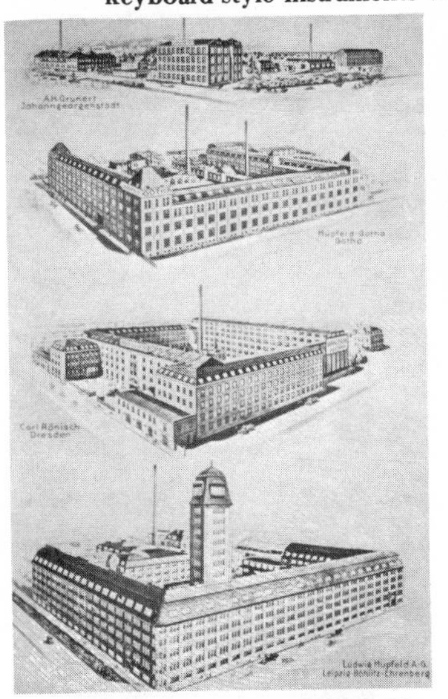

Above: Four of the Hupfeld factories of the 1920's: the A.H. Grunert piano factory in Johanngeorgenstadt, the Hupfeld-Gotha (formerly Aeolian) factory in Gotha, the Carl Rönisch piano factory in Dresden, and the main Hupfeld works in Bohlitz-Ehrenberg.

"Maestro-Phonoliszt Model T" piano in keyboardless cabinet.

All-purpose Hupfeld keyboard orchestrion case used for certain Helios, Clavitist, and other models.

the drums and other effects in the case. The Animatic Jazz Piano was one of the popular models. Later, the Symphony Jazz Orchestra (or "Sinfonie Jazz" – as Hupfeld called it) was made. This featured a piano with drums, bells (with resonators), a rank of saxophone pipes and a rank of lotus flute pipes. The Symphony Jazz produced music in the modern idiom – and was the latest thing in the 1920's.

Hupfeld Violin Players: Hupfeld produced the world's most successful violin player, the Violina. Early Violinas were made with a violin only (without piano). The first production-line instrument was the Phonoliszt-Violina which was introduced in 1907 and first offered for sale in 1908. The Phonoliszt-Violina was a combination of the Phonoliszt semi-reproducing piano with a 3-violin Violina mechanism.

In 1908 and 1909 Dea-Violina instruments (a combination of the Dea reproducing piano with Violina mechanisms containing 3 [later, 4] violins) were produced. The Dea-Violina, priced at 12,000 Marks, was a featured attraction at the Crystal Palace in Leipzig in June, 1909. Large volume production of the Dea-Violina was envisioned, but the complex mechanisms of the instrument necessitated extensive maintenance – and the Dea-Violina was discontinued. The Clavitist-Violina, a combination of the Clavitist piano and the Violina mechanism, was produced for a short time also.

After 1910 the Phonoliszt-Violina became the featured Hupfeld violin player. This instrument was made in many forms. Style B was by far the most popular, but styles A, C, and the Theatre-Violina achieved excellent sales. A Phonoliszt-Violina with six violins was mentioned in the musical instrument industry trade papers.

The Violina Orchestra, a Hupfeld orchestrion incorporating three violins with a piano and accompanying pipe and percussion effects, was produced in the late 1920's to the extent of about twenty instruments.

In addition to Phonoliszt-Violina instruments with real violins, several varieties of Phonoliszt-Violinas with violin pipes were produced.

Hupfeld Reproducing Pianos: The Dea (often spelled in all capital letters: DEA) used very wide rolls and was developed in 1905. Hupfeld could not effectively compete with Welte, the dominant maker of reproducing pianos at that time. Although the Dea was as good as the Welte-Mignon (or perhaps even better from a technical viewpoint) it was made only in limited numbers – mostly in Rönisch upright and grand pianos and in vorsetzer or push-up models. Dea production was discontinued after World War I.

About 1920 the Duophonola and Triphonola appeared. These instruments used the same basic system, but each was of different construction. The Duophonola and Triphonola each sold very well.

Other Hupfeld Products: Hupfeld was a marketing as well as a manufacturing organization, and for this reason the Hupfeld name is sometimes found on non-Hupfeld-built instruments, particularly small instruments of the circa 1900 period. In the 1920's Hupfeld built a number of theatre pipe organs. About the only major instrument field in which Hupfeld was not active was fairground organs.

### Hupfeld Instruments Today

Examples of most major Hupfeld instrument types survive in collections today. Hupfeld instruments were built in a quality manner and were capable of playing serious music. A properly restored and carefully regulated, and here the emphasis is on "properly" and "carefully," Hupfeld instrument can be a wonderful experience to hear.

(Credit note: Q. David Bowers and Claes O. Friberg thank Günther Hupfeld, son of Ludwig Hupfeld, for providing much information that would have been otherwise lost to history.)

Of the many Hupfeld branches, the firm of Duwaer & Naessens of Amsterdam and 's Gravenhage (The Hague), Holland, was one of the most active. The pictures show the Electric Orchestrion Department on the first floor and the Electric Piano Department on the third floor of the Amsterdam building. Thousands of Hupfeld instruments, including a large number of the Phonoliszt Violina, Helios, and Pan models, were sold by the firm.

(Illustrations courtesy of E. Jan Schoondergang)

ONS GEBOUW TE AMSTERDAM
STADHOUDERSKADE 19-20

HUPFELD
DIRECTIE
DUWAER NAESSENS
AMSTERDAM UTRECHT 'sGRAVENHAGE

## EARLY HUPFELD INSTRUMENTS

From 1872 to about 1900 most Hupfeld instruments were smaller - at least in comparison to the firm's later products. A wide variety of mechanical piano playing devices, mechanical dulcimers, and similar devices were made. Early Hupfeld roll operated instruments used a key frame to "read" the holes punched in a heavy manila paper roll — much on the order of Imhof & Mukle instruments.

On this page are shown a representative variety of these instruments. There were many different variations in case designs as many different brands of pianos were used in connection with the piano players. These instruments were sold until about 1905 - 1908 when the thin paper roll type of instrument made the earlier styles obsolete.

In addition to the instruments actually manufactured by Hupfeld, many music boxes, reed organs, and other devices made by others were sold under the Hupfeld label.

Most of the Hupfeld instruments shown on this page were usually sold with an ebony finish, often with gold striping or lettering. In an age in which electricity was more of a novelty than a commonplace installation most instruments were operated by hand. For those who wanted truly automatic operation Hupfeld sold a series of water motors, hot air motors, and battery operated electric motors for use with the various instruments.

Push up player for the piano or organ. Style 10. Hand cranked. Cardboard disc music.

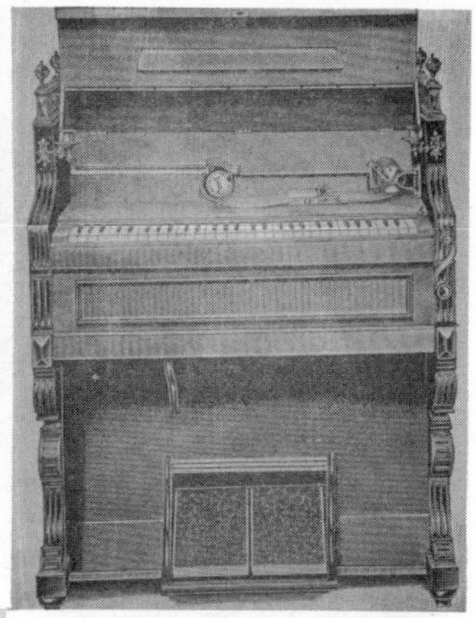

Mechanical Harmonium Style 8. The roll playing mechanism is above the keyboard.

Style 21 61-note push up type piano player.

Piano Playing Attachment No. 30 - could be fitted to uprights or grands.

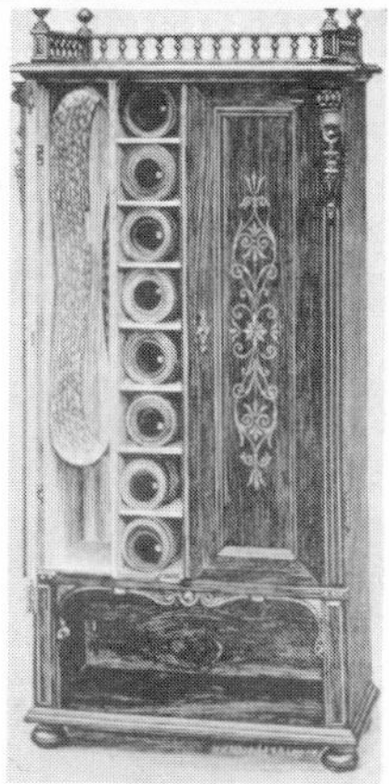

Cabinet for the storage of music rolls.

Style 161 "Aeolion" Flute Orchestrion. With 100 pipes. About 8' high.

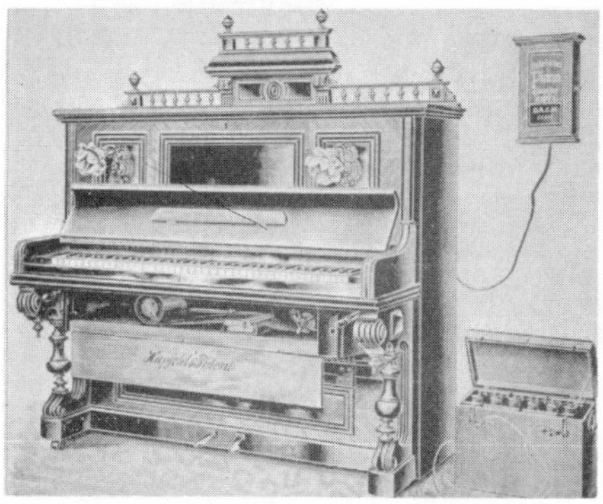

Style 71 Electric Piano. Mechanism is fitted below the keyboard.

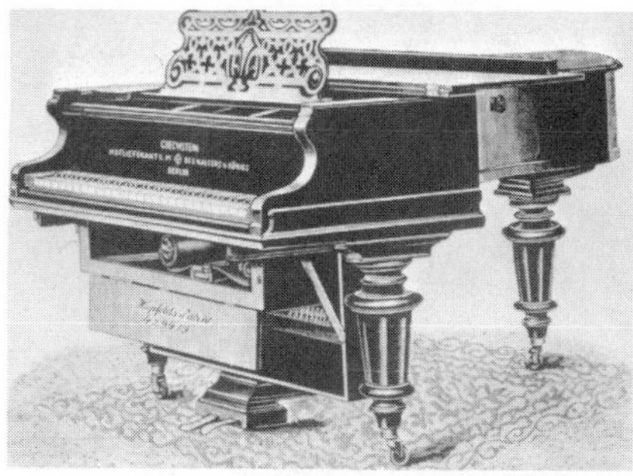

Style 30 F - Grand piano player.

Model I Gothic. Electric orchestrion. 5 registers. 200 pipes. Bass drum, snare drum, triangle, cymbal.

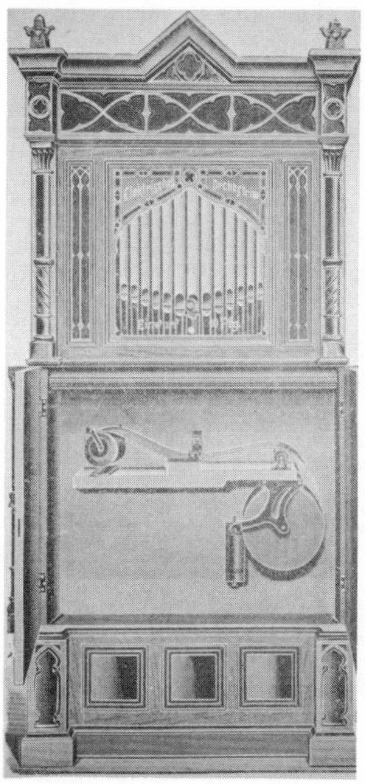

Interior view of Model I showing the heavy manila paper roll.

Model V. With 5 registers and about 200 pipes. Offered in 3 voices: for rooms, hotels, or dance halls.

Model X. Models I, V, X, and XI were available with either: (1) 3 registers, 125 pipes, or (2) 5 registers, 200 pipes.

Model XI. About 9½' high. Uses music roll about 200' long.

Universal Style A electric piano with decorative gallery on top. Although the large Helios orchestrions may be more romantic and interesting today, the largest part of Hupfeld's production, in terms of the number of instruments produced, went to the smaller instruments such as the Universal, Animatic, Clavitist, Phonoliszt, etc. styles.

Above 3 instruments, left to right: Concert Universal No. 30; Universal AI; Concert Universal No. 2.

Universal Pianos

The Universal pianos were the basic type of Hupfeld "nickelodeon." Models were available in a variety of case styles and with a variety of interior specifications. The most popular were: (1) Universal Mandolin piano with piano and mandolin. (2) Universal piano with 10-note xylophone and with mandolin. (3) Universal with 10-note set of orchestra bells and with mandolin. (4) Universal with 30-note xylophone and with mandolin. (5) Universal with 30-note set of orchestra bells and with mandolin.

A Hupfeld Music Roll Roster

This listing, while not complete, still gives an idea of the immense variety of Hupfeld rolls made over the years: Phonola, Triphonola, Animatic, Symphony Jazz, Clavitist, Universal, Clavimonium, Pepita, Dea, Helios (in several varieties), Pan, Clavitist-Violina, Dea-Violina, Phonoliszt-Violina, and Violina Orchestra. Perforators were kept busy turning out more than 5 million rolls per year!

Animatic Clavitist with orchestra cabinet.

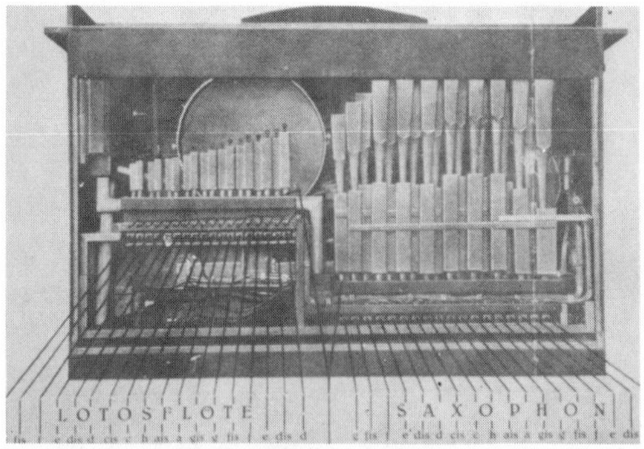


Upper back of a Symphony Jazz orchestrion. A rank of lotus flutes is to the left; a rank of saxophone pipes to the right. The Symphony Jazz (called "Sinfonie Jazz" by Hupfeld) was popular in the 1920's.

Animatic Clavitist xylophone piano.

Animatic Clavitist and Symphony Jazz
Pianos and Orchestrions

88-note Animatic music rolls provide piano music with basic expression. Serial numbers run from 50,000 to about 60,200. Sometime before 1920 the basic Animatic roll layout was modified to provide controls for drums and traps. Later, certain Animatic rolls were designated as "Special" rolls with an "S" prefix. Others were designated as "Symphony Jazz" rolls and had an "SJ" prefix. The tracker bar layouts of these were slightly different. However, with a switching device on the instrument the different rolls could be accommodated. During the "jazz" era of the 1920's most of the smaller Hupfeld instruments used these rolls. Although the instruments were often smaller, they had more percussion effects than did the Helios styles and thus required a different roll.

Concert Clavitist piano at a seaside resort.

Phonoliszt electric piano in the Rheingold Restaurant.

Excelsior Phonoliszt in a military academy recreation room.

### Phonoliszt and Clavitist Pianos

The Phonoliszt and Clavitist were two popular styles for home as well as public use. Phonoliszt rolls reproduced the playing of famous pianists such as d'Albert, Busoni, Hofmann, Grünfeld, Grieg, Carreño, Scharwenka, et al. The expression of the Clavitist was more limited. Thousands of different roll titles were cut for each style of instrument; some rolls with expression and others without.

CLAVIMONIUM – a piano and reed organ combination for use in theatres. Uses Clavitist rolls. A lever can be set in any of 3 positions: piano music only, piano and organ, or organ only. 4'7" high. 660 pounds weight.

The purchaser of a Hupfeld piano could customize it by adding an optional gallery. Some of the larger galleries had moving picture and lighting effects. Note that the instrument at the above right is a Clavimonium with a tall lighted gallery added. These thin facades would add to the height of a regular piano and give it an impressive appearance.

## HUPFELD PHONOLISZT-VIOLINA

### Automatic Violin with Piano

In the field of automatic musical instruments there were two commercially successful violin players. Both incorporated violin(s) with an automatic piano. In Chicago, Illinois, the Mills Novelty Company produced the electromagnetically operated Violano-Virtuoso which featured either one or two violins (depending upon the model) in combination with a 44-note piano. In Leipzig, Germany, Hupfeld produced the pneumatically operated Phonoliszt-Violina, an instrument combining three violins with a keyboard expression piano. Thousands of each type were produced.

Hupfeld began experimenting with a violin player shortly after 1900. Like other instrument makers Hupfeld realized the novelty of an automatic violin and the large potential market for it. An early Hupfeld attempt mated an electric piano with a single violin on which three strings were played. This idea proved unfeasible. The instrument was then revised to incorporate a Phonoliszt expression piano in combination with three violins, each of which had one playing string (and three non-playing strings for "show").

The New York City distributor described the Phonoliszt-Violina in a leaflet entitled, "Phonoliszt-Violina — The Eighth Wonder of the World." The description gives an idea of how the instrument operates:

"The self-playing Violina is provided with real violins operated by a horsehair bow and means the solution of a problem that has been vainly sought for centuries.

"It can be easily understood what difficulties had to be overcome from a technical point of view to solve this problem, as contrary to the piano, where the production of tones is based on the already provided keyboard in connection with inside mechanism, on the violin some way or method had to be found to produce the tone.

"The violins are placed inside of a rotating horsehair bow with 1350 horsehairs, with which they are brought in touch during the playing. The bow, same as with hand playing, comes in contact with the violin under different grades of pressure to produce the tone graduation either soft or loud or any shading required for artistic violin playing. Also, all other effects and finesses in playing are provided for, such as staccato, legato, glissando, vibrato, as naturally as by hand playing, and where the sordino effect is necessary it certainly will surprise you, as it works without any noise as by human hand.

"Violin virtuosos and great band leaders after hearing the Phonoliszt-Violina have been astounded at the faultless technique and marvelous interpretation.

"The most admirable quality of the Phonoliszt-Violina is its soul, thus the most important factor in violin playing has been accomplished to give soul to this only self-playing violin.

"The Phonoliszt-Violina consists of three violins and the self-playing Phonoliszt Autograph Player which accompanies the violin in the most artistic manner. Imagine hearing a Josef Hofmann, Arthur Friedheim, Ferruccio Busoni, Harold Bauer, Wilhelm Backhaus, or Eugene d'Albert playing the piano as a solo instrument or accompanying a Zimbalist, Kubelik, or Sarasate. For this is the Phonoliszt-Violina.

Model B Hupfeld Phonoliszt-Violina. In the top section one string on each of three violins is played by a rotating circular horsehair bow. Accompaniment is provided by a Phonoliszt expression piano using artists' roll arrangements. In the above illustration the decorative grill is removed to show the violins. The Model B was by far the best selling Phonoliszt-Violina model. Thousands were made.

Model B Phonoliszt-Violina. There were many case variations in position and style of the lamps, decoration of the wood panels, size of the cabinet itself, etc. This illustration is from a 1912 catalogue.

The Hupfeld Phonoliszt-Violina found a ready market with restaurant owners as the public was intrigued by the interesting and melodious instrument. In such locations they were usually operated via wallboxes.

"One can readily repeat the words of one great well known man who, after he had heard the instrument, said: 'It beggars description.'

"The Phonoliszt-Violina repertoire has been compiled on the same principle as for other instruments, so that all the different tastes are duly considered. Not only are there folksongs, marches, waltzes, and the latest hits in light opera, but also violin concert pieces and even duets. This repertoire is constantly growing by new and selected additional pieces."

The Phonoliszt-Violina was first produced (on a production-line basis) in 1907 and was first marketed in 1908. Advertising for the Phonoliszt-Violina reached its zenith in the 1910-1914 years. During this time many prominent violinists heartily endorsed the Hupfeld violin player. The April 5, 1912, testimonial by noted violinist Efrem Zimbalist was typical: "Certainly the Phonoliszt-Violina is the eighth wonder and marvel of our time." Hupfeld returned the compliment by calling Zimbalist "the world's greatest violinist" in advertisements which featured his laudatory comment.

The most popular Phonoliszt-Violina was the Model B. This was essentially a Phonoliszt expression piano with a case extension on top. At the upper center front a curved-front section held the three violins and their playing apparatus. The violins were enclosed by latticed doors which folded outward to display the mechanisms. The pianos were often of Rönisch make. Most Style B instruments were of mahogany, but walnut, oak, and possibly other woods were occasionally used.

The Style A contained the same apparatus as the Style B but had a more traditional case style resembling Hupfeld keyboard orchestrions of the era. The Style C had modernistic lines and was a later introduction.

A few Phonoliszt-Violina instruments with six violins and two rotating horsehair bows were made. In 1913 (actually the advertisement was prepared in 1912) E. Böcker, the New York distributor for Hupfeld, announced: "The latest creation is the Phonoliszt-Violina with two circular bows and six violins." Apparently production was quite limited.

In the 1920's emphasis was placed on the Phonoliszt-Violina as a theatre instrument for providing background music for films. Many of the standard Model B instruments were used for this purpose simply by installing them in theatres and letting them play uninterruptedly throughout the performance. A special "Theatre Violina" was also produced. This was made in two parts — a keyboard piano and a side cabinet containing three violins — to make the profile low for use under the screen in the orchestra pit. Many, if not all, of these were equipped with multiple roll mechanisms so that two or more rolls of varied musical character could be stored on the instrument.

In addition to the Phonoliszt-Violinas containing real violins several different models were developed with violin pipes. These used regular Hupfeld Phonoliszt-Violina rolls.

Hupfeld conducted many experiments with different types of violin-playing mechanisms. Ludwig Hupfeld, Robert Frömsdorf, Johann and Ludwig Bajde (original inventors of the Violina concept; later owners of the Klaviolinfabrik Bajde & Co. in Schischka, near Laibach, Austria-Hungary — producers of the Klaviolin, a foot-pedal and keyboard-operated mechanical violin; the firm went bankrupt in 1913), Gustav Karl Hennig and Ernst Hennig were granted many patents on the subject throughout the 'teens.

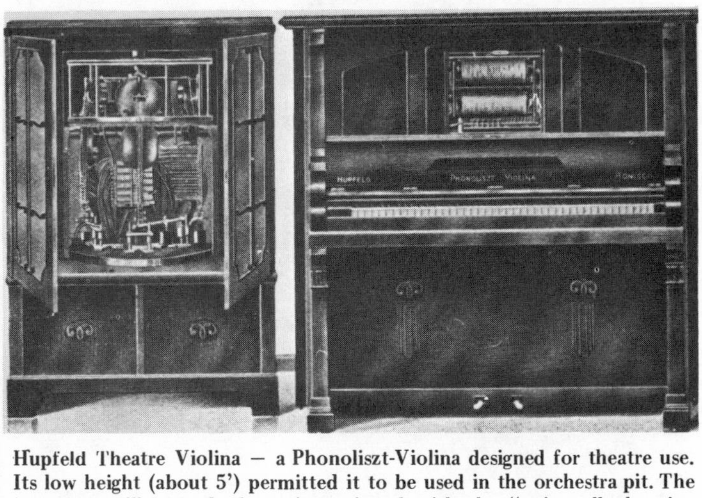

Hupfeld Theatre Violina — a Phonoliszt-Violina designed for theatre use. Its low height (about 5') permitted it to be used in the orchestra pit. The instrument illustrated above is equipped with the "twin roll changing mechanism" - a device that stores two rolls and allows them to be changed quickly.

Hupfeld Model C Phonoliszt Violina. The Model C was a latecomer to the series. Most were sold in the 1920's. The case is of modern design.

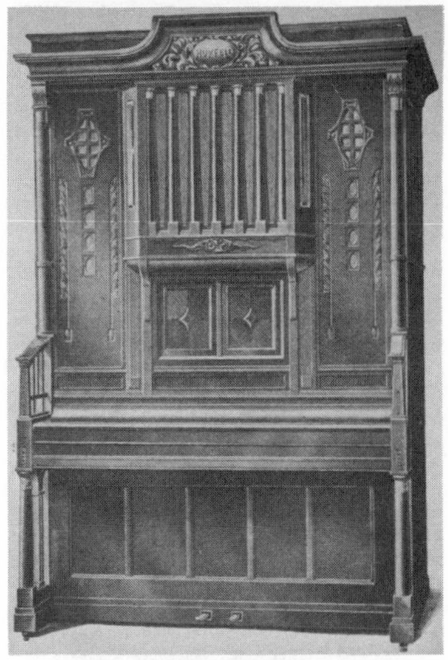

Model A Phonoliszt-Violina. During the years from about 1908 to 1914 the A and B models were standard. Later the Style A was discontinued in favor of the B and the new Model C.

Model C - interior view. In the bottom is the compound vacuum pump. The roll mechanism is in the center. At the top are the three violins and the bowing mechanisms.

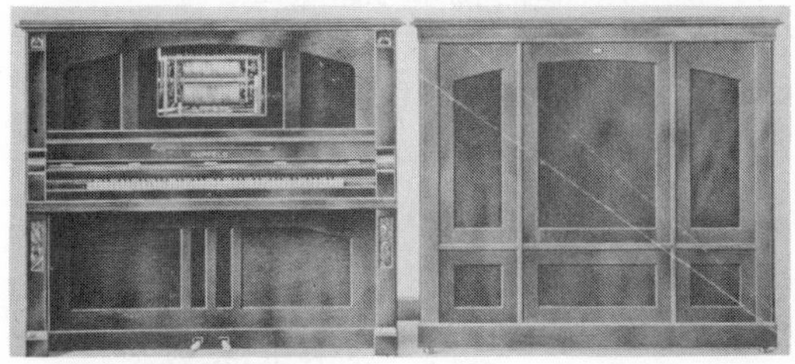

Theatre Violina with violin pipes. Equipped with the twin roll changing mechanism. The violin sound was produced by violin-toned wooden pipes housed in the right side cabinet.

## A PLAYER-VIOLIN

THE FACT that a mechanical violin player has been devised, together with a description of the principle on which it works, has been announced already in these columns. We are now able to give a more detailed account of the instrument, together with illustrations of it, from an article contributed by A. Troller to *La Nature* (Paris, June 8). Every one, says Mr. Troller, knows the mechanical piano, whose latest form reproduces faithfully even the interpretation of a talented artist. Its performances are surely worthy of being called wonderful. But what word, asks our writer, shall we find for this new instrument, which associates the violin and the piano?

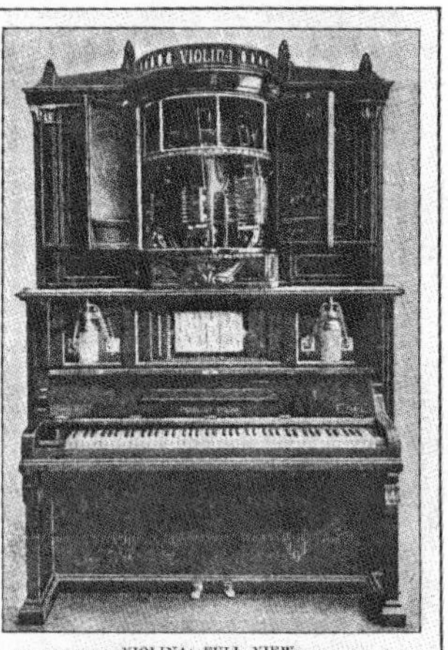

VIOLINA: FULL VIEW.

The violin, if we are to believe those who play it, is the most difficult of musical instruments—that which requires from the player the finest ear, the most skilful manipulation, and the greatest musical sensibility. How can it be that these qualities may be obtained from a mechanism—no matter how complex and ingenious? Mr. Troller answers:

"The results given by the 'Violina,' which is the instrument's name, are really surprizing; an ample and varied tone, perfect modulation, without leaps or shocks, and all the accustomed effects of the violin.

"We are not prepared to say that to hear the 'Violina' is the same as to listen to a virtuoso; the emotions that it evokes are not, and can not be, so deep; but they are still of a high artistic quality, and it is to be hoped that the mechanical violin may rid us forthwith of all our mediocre performers.

"The mechanical piano, as is well known, depends essentially on the following arrangement—a roll of paper, properly perforated, turns before the openings of a series of tubes, connected with a reservoir of slightly comprest air. The air that is allowed to pass through the perforations in the paper enters the tubes, which conduct it to what are practically so many little comprest-air motors, actuating the hammers of the piano. . . . . . .

"In the 'Violina' the mechanical principle is the same—pneumatic control of all the movable organs, regulated by means of a roll of perforated paper. But there can be no question . . . of causing the strings of the violin to vibrate by means of an ordinary bow. The solution found by the inventors of the 'Violina' is of remarkable originality; it constitutes the essential

THE THREE VIOLINS AND THE ROTATING BOW.

novelty of the instrument. The bow of the 'Violina' is formed, as our figure shows, of numerous fibers stretched on a movable horizontal circle. As it would be difficult to act simultaneously on the four strings of a single violin, it was decided to use a group of three violins, each having only one active string.

"The circular bow turns, and its speed, sometimes retarded, sometimes accelerated, is controlled by one of the little comprest-air motors of which we have spoken. Ordinary violins, whose stems are hinged on pivots, are prest against the turning bow, and the pressure of contact corresponds to the intensity of the sound that is to be obtained. Movable fingers, actuated also by pneumatic means, depress the string at the desired moment, so as to give the tone its proper pitch. . . . . . .

"How are the perforated rolls prepared that control the movements of the three violins? They are executed with minute care by workmen who are at the same time musicians of the first rank. Here must be noted a sensible inferiority of the 'Violina' to the latest model of automatic piano. The latter may reproduce the performance of a master, the perforation being done automatically by the playing of the artist. It is not the same with the 'Violina.' It would hardly be possible for a violinist in manipulating his bow to actuate a perforating mechanism and so prepare rolls adapted to the instrument.

"However this may be, the automatic piano and violin combined offer us a most agreeable duet and an infinitely varied repertory. The instrument reflects the greatest credit on the mechanical skill of its inventors, five Austrians whose names deserve to be recorded here—Messrs. Bajde, Karl and Ernst Henning, Froensdorf, and Hupfeld."—*Translation made for* THE LITERARY DIGEST.

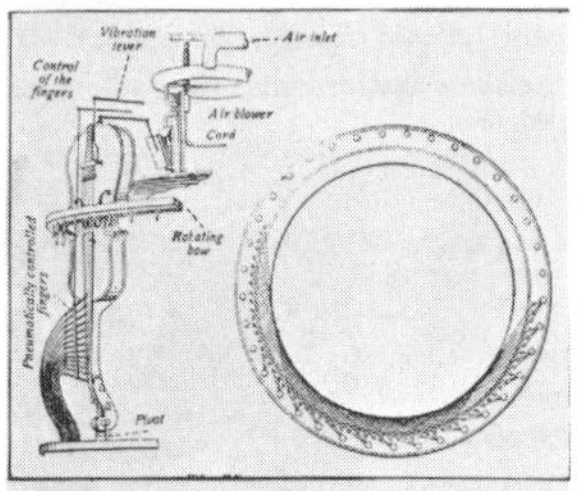


THE VIOLIN AND ITS PNEUMATIC CONTROL.

**Description of the Phonoliszt-Violina from a 1912 issue of the "Literary Digest." "Froensdorf" (in the last paragraph) should be "Frömsdorf;" "Henning" should be "Hennig."**

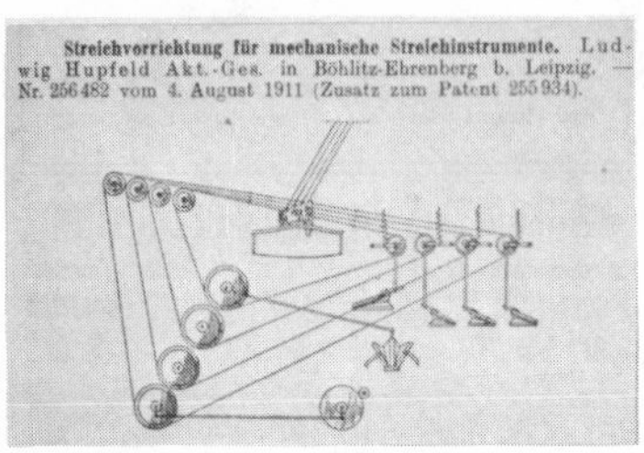


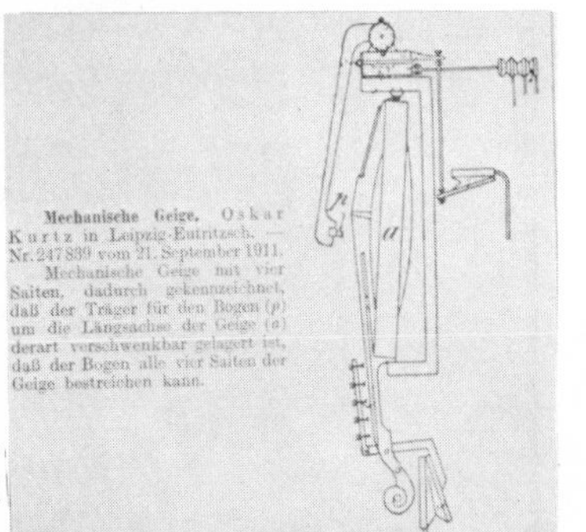


**A few of the many violin player patents issued to Hupfeld, Bajde, and others during the 1905-1915 years.**

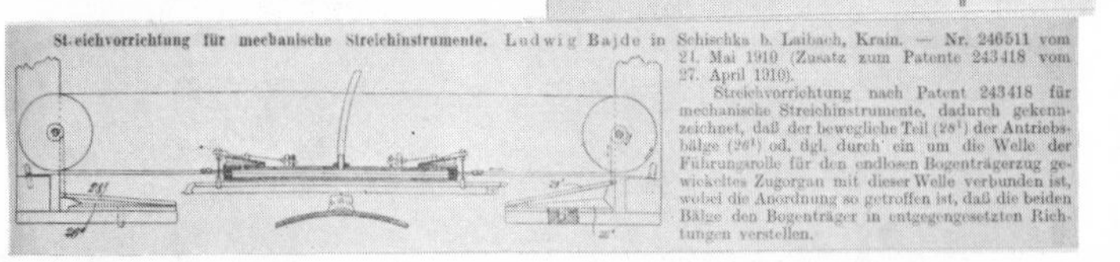


**A Chronology of the Violina**

**(See illustrations in right-hand column.) After much experimentation the Phonoliszt-Violina was first offered for sale in 1908. At first it was called the Violina-Phonoliszt. Featured at several trade shows, the instrument was an instant success. At the June, 1909 music exhibit at Leipzig's Crystal Palace a new product, the Dea-Violina, was introduced. Soon afterward Hupfeld marketed three varieties of the Violina — combinations with the Dea, Clavitist, and Phonoliszt pianos. By 1910 (see 1910 advertisement directly to the right) the Dea-Violina and Clavitist-Violina were discontinued, and Hupfeld's efforts were concentrated on the Phonoliszt-Violina.**

**1908: Introduction of the Phonoliszt-Violina.**

**1909: Introduction of the Dea-Violina.**

**1909: Offering of the Dea-, Clavitist-, and Phonoliszt-Violina.**

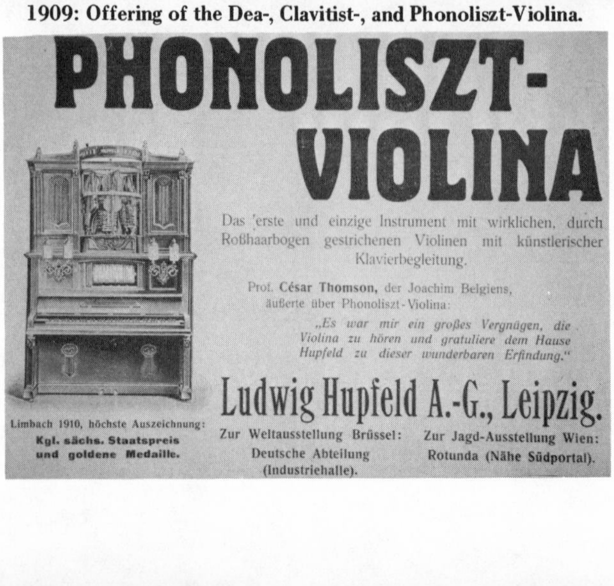

## PHONOLISZT-VIOLINA ROLLS

To catalogue the Phonoliszt-Violina rolls in an organized manner Hupfeld divided music into several categories and assigned distinctive numbers to each.

"Romantic Music" was the 31,000 serial number category. Examples are: "Where Roses Bloom" (31,009); "Evening Song" (31,014); and "On the Sea" (31,016).

"Parlor Music" comprised the 33,000 series. Examples: "Love's Dream After the Ball" (33,001); "Dream of a Dairy Girl in the Alps" - violin duet (33,002); "Sing Me to Sleep" (33,029).

Automatic rolls (with special leader for use on the automatic roll changer) were assigned to the 35,000 series. These rolls were of varied character and usually had several tunes per roll.

"Opera and Light Opera Music" filled the 36,000 series. Examples: "Tales of Hoffmann" (36,001); "Cavalleria Rusticana" (36,013); and "Selections from Orpheus in the Underworld" (36,031).

"Popular Music and Dances" occupied the 37,000 series. Examples: "Old Folks at Home" (37,017a); "Dixie" (37,017b); "Red Wing" (37,086); "Alexander's Ragtime Band" (37,105).

"Classic and Modern Music" comprised the 38,000 series. Examples: "Humoresque" (38,010); "Tschaikowsky's Concerto for Violin, Op.35" (38,046).

"Dances and Marches" were in the 39,000 series. Examples: "Soldiers in the Park" (39,001); "Thousand and One Nights Waltz" (39,017).

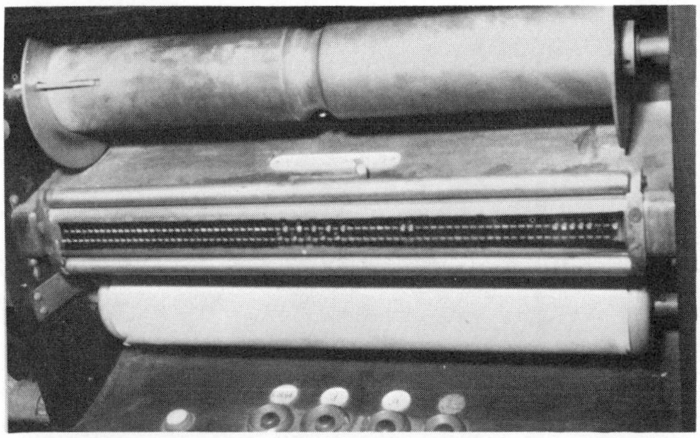

Tracker bar of the Phonoliszt-Violina. By means of a switching mechanism it can play two types of rolls: (1) Phonoliszt-Violina rolls using the top set of tracker bar holes, and (2) Phonoliszt artists' rolls using the bottom set.

View of the violin mechanism. Note the "fingers" which stop the strings at the desired lengths.

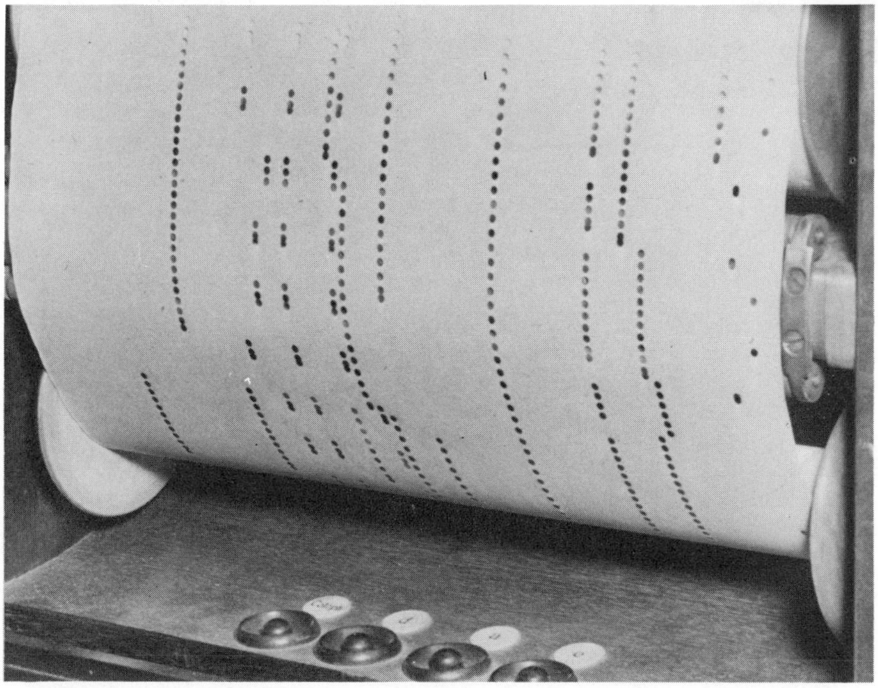

A Phonoliszt-Violina roll (with combined piano and violin music) on the tracker bar. The buttons below are used to tune the violins.

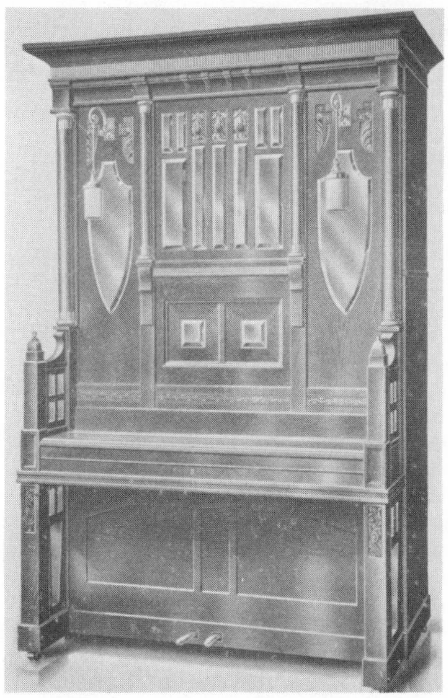

Phonoliszt Violin Pipe Piano. The violin sound is produced by pipes. As with the regular Phonoliszt-Violina models this instrument uses either Phonoliszt (piano only) or Phonoliszt-Violina (piano and violin) rolls.

Left: Model II; Above: Model I.

Model B Phonoliszt-Violina with duplex roll mechanism. (Claes O. Friberg photo)

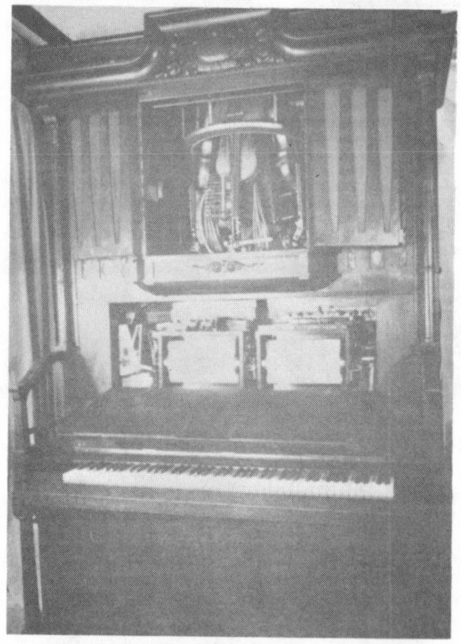

Model A Phonoliszt-Violina with duplex roll mechanism. (Netherlands Film Museum photo)

Hupfeld Phonoliszt-Violina Model B with "double roll changing mechanism." This illustration shows the ingenious device which holds two rolls. Either Phonoliszt rolls or Phonoliszt-Violina rolls (or one of each) can be put on the instrument. The roll mechanism "senses" the type of roll and shifts the tracker bar appropriately to play the desired type of roll. Made originally for use in a theatre, the roll mechanism also has a "fast forward" feature to permit any part of the roll to be selected quickly for playing. This device was known as a "Kipp mechanism." (Collection of the author)

## HUPFELD VIOLINA ORCHESTRA

In 1926 Hupfeld introduced the Violina Orchestra. Two main designs were produced: Model I (without keyboard; in a case somewhat similar to a Hupfeld Pan Orchestra I) and Model II (with keyboard; in a case resembling a Model B Phonoliszt-Violina with attached side chests).

The Violina Orchestra contained a piano, the Violina mechanism with three violins, harmonium, flute and clarinet pipes, and drum and trap effects. Four different types of rolls could be used on the instrument: (1) Special Violina Orchestra rolls which played all of the effects; (2) Phonoliszt-Violina rolls (of special 9-to-the-inch spacing; not the regular Phonoliszt-Violina rolls) which played the piano and violins; (3) Hupfeld Animatic-T rolls which played the piano with expression effects; and (4) Regular 88-note home player piano rolls which played the piano only. To properly utilize the instrument's potential it was necessary to use the special Violina Orchestra rolls.

Mr. Herbert Becke (son of the former general director of Gebr. Zimmermann) and Günther Hupfeld have estimated that about twenty Violina Orchestras were made. The instruments were exhibited at various trade fairs from 1927 to 1929 and attracted favorable comments from newspaper reporters and trade journal editors.

Hupfeld orchestrion exhibit of the early 1900's. The instruments shown are those mainly sold during the 1900-1910 years. Most orchestrions made during this time used paper rolls, but a number of barrel-operated instruments (the Atlantic and Continental models were most popular) were also made.

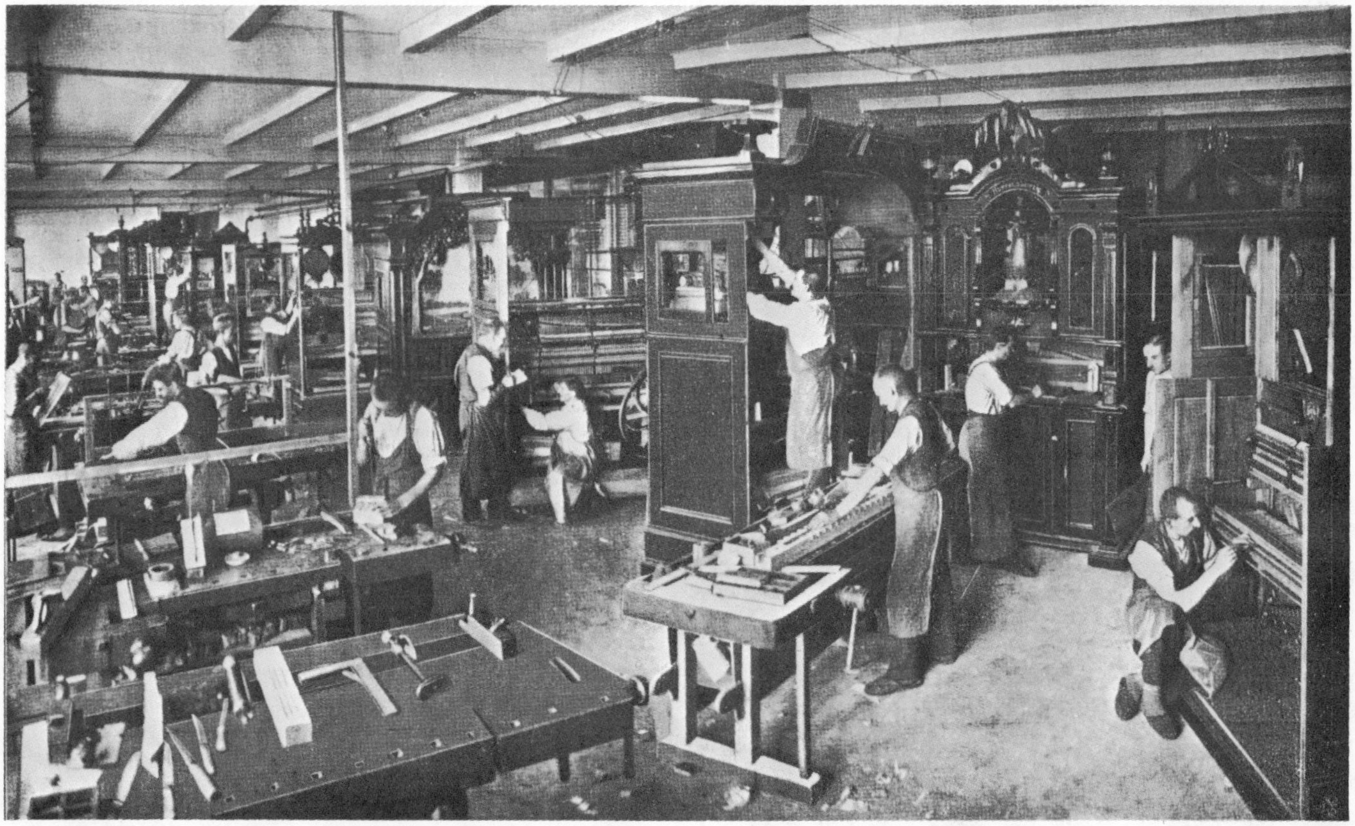

A Hupfeld factory scene during the early 1900's. About a dozen large orchestrions are shown in various stages of assembly. At this time the factory was located at No. 4 Apelstrasse in Leipzig-Eutritzsch. On the factory premises several showrooms were maintained. There Hupfeld-made instruments were displayed as were other instruments for which Hupfeld was a distributor — Symphonion music boxes and Ariston organettes, for example.

1903 Hupfeld orchestrion advertisement.

## HUPFELD HELIOS ORCHESTRIONS

Of all large orchestrions ever made the Helios models were the most popular. Although no production figures are available we would estimate that the number of the larger keyboardless styles manufactured was well into the thousands. Unfortunately, of that number only a small quantity remain today. Some of the most beautiful Helios orchestrions are known to us only by catalogue illustrations. No specimens have survived the inexorable march of time.

The Helios models were the backbone of the Hupfeld orchestrion business. First made shortly after the turn of the 20th century, Helios styles were produced well into the late 1920's and possibly even in the 1930's. Helios rolls were cut at the Hupfeld factory as late as 1933.

Models in the Helios series ranged from the compact Helios Orchestra Piano and other keyboard models with instrumentation ranging from a basic piano with mandolin and xylophone to the immense and wonderful Helios V — an almost unbelievable orchestrion that contained nearly 1500 pipes and represented an orchestra of 100 to 120 musicians!

*Hupfeld Helios I/22 orchestrion in a restaurant.*

Hupfeld Helios orchestrions were arranged into five basic "Classes," as the factory called them. Each class, beginning with Class I, had an increasing amount of instrumentation. Several different varieties of Helios rolls were made as larger instruments had more register combinations. The basic type of Helios roll was used on Class I and II (and some III) instruments. Larger instruments used different rolls.

To give a general idea of the Helios orchestrions and their history and musical ability we reprint (with editing for brevity's sake) excerpts from the Hupfeld "Helios Art Orchestrion" catalogue issued about 1912:

### Helios Orchestrions — General Information

In the following description of the equipment and the musical nature of the Helios Orchestrions the Hupfeld firm has been guided by material information as the performance of the Helios Orchestrions is already known by many.

*Dance music provided by a Helios II/25 orchestrion.*

*Skating to a Helios Ia/20 orchestrion.*

Only data of a factual nature have been used as we want to tell the reader as much as possible. Our description of the Helios instruments is not an exhaustive one as we do not want to reveal our factory secrets of manufacture and construction. (Editor's note: this secrecy was common in the industry. Hupfeld was especially reluctant to share information as it was the largest firm in the world in the field and had many unique ideas) We are, however, willing to permit serious buyers to look into the interior of the instruments and to furnish any further explanation that may be desired.

All Hupfeld orchestrions are equipped with the wind motor device. By this method we can regulate the tempo of the music independent of current fluctuations. This is of great importance for dance orchestrions since it insures an exact and absolutely accurate playing of the music.

With the register controls (which operate automatically, if desired, from the music roll) the volume of the Hupfeld orchestrion can be set to play from 1/3 to full strength so as to adapt to your particular needs. The Hupfeld orchestrions, even the larger models, can be made to play so softly that they are suitable for small rooms. Such instruments are particularly suited for use in movie theatres as well.

Hupfeld cabinets reveal a massive type of construction and the finest execution. They are the result of a free competition of artists thoroughly experienced in this field. The initial expensively-produced prototype designs are tested, consultations are held, necessary changes are made — resulting in an ideal combination. That we have succeeded in choosing a happy medium between the artistic requirements and public demands is proven by the Helios models shown in our catalogues — they are at the very height of public taste.

In the model designation, the first number is for the class, the second is for its case design. Hence, Helios I/22 means a Class I instrument specification installed in case design No. 22. So far as space requirements permit, the works for different classes can be installed in cabinets of other models. Thus the works of a Helios Class II can be installed in the cabinet of a Class III model, and vice versa.

All Hupfeld Helios orchestrions can be had with motion picture or changing light effects on special order. Special requests as to wood types and custom cabinets are gladly taken under advisement and proposals to suit your decorating needs by first-rate architects are supplied without obligation.

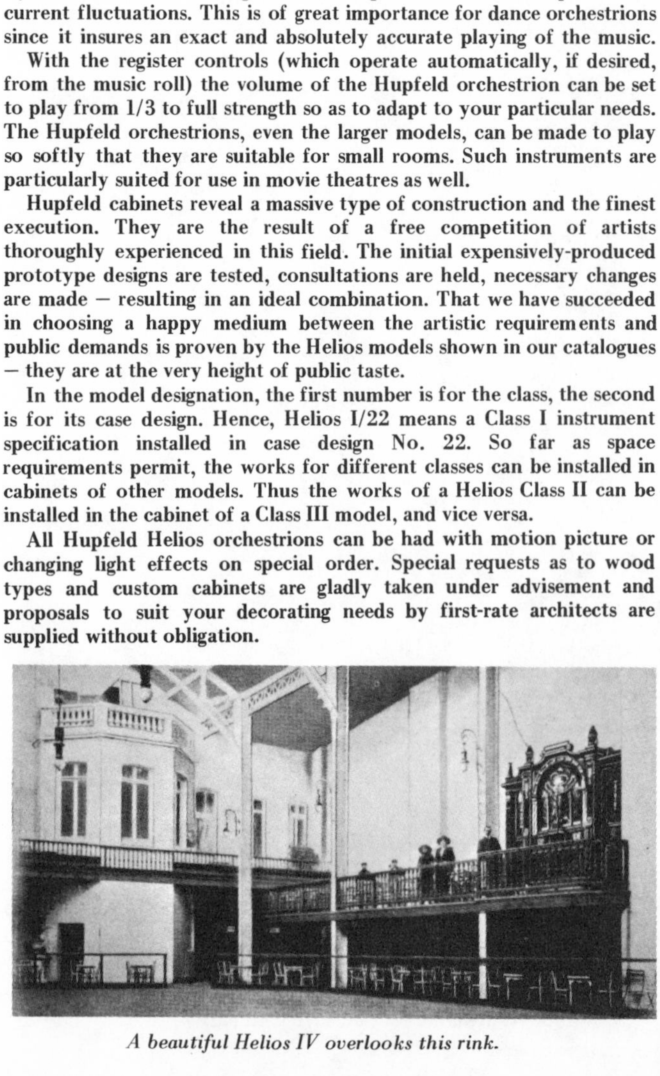

*A beautiful Helios IV overlooks this rink.*

*A banquet with a Helios IV in the background.*

By means of a register panel provided in each orchestrion the individual registers, percussion instruments, etc. can be switched off.

The Helios Orchestrion can be operated by a push button contact or by wallboxes with slots to accommodate any coin. Unless otherwise specified, we use slots for ten cent pieces.

Let us know if your Helios is to be used for concerts, dances, or both. According to your wish and need we can voice the instruments to soft, medium, or loud specifications.

If desired for coin operation, long rolls — overtures for example — can be provided with extra stops so that two or three coins must be inserted in order to hear the entire selection. Other rolls are shorter and contain from one to six individual selections with a stop at the end of each tune. After the last piece has been played the roll rewinds automatically. The Helios Pepita has its own roll - usually of ten tune length.

The Hupfeld firm is the largest in the world. The music roll repertoire is distinguished by its extent and artistry. A large staff of musical experts under the direction of a conductor is constantly at work with new arrangements. New tunes receive special consideration, so the owner of a Hupfeld orchestrion is constantly offered the latest hit songs. The music paper is sturdy and has a rag content. Hupfeld rolls are so moderate in price that a large repertoire can be acquired without great cost. The Hupfeld factory has always developed its musical repertoire artistically as well as numerically. The buyer of an orchestrion should put the greatest importance on this point for he knows exactly how great a role sufficient variety in music and offering of the latest compositions plays in actual practice. He who has observed with what interest his guests ask for new pieces and how these are preferred will admit that the profitability of a music instrument is considerably increased by the ability to satisfy the public's wishes at the right time.

Ten Commandments for Innkeepers and Movie Owners

1. There is no more ideal means of entertaining a crowd than with music. Young and old, rich and poor succumb to its magic. Music is the soul of your business.

2. You can dispense with everything else more readily than with music. Make up your mind about music in a hurry before your neighbor gets ahead of you.

*Ballroom music courtesy of a Helios I/34.*

3. Think well whether you should offer live music or an automatically playing instrument. If you compare the lowest fees of musicians for a year with the cost of buying the most expensive Hupfeld instrument, you will choose the latter.

4. A Hupfeld instrument is the best and most reliable employee. It works day and night for you, never plays incorrectly, and everything that it earns belongs to you. Its only salary is a little electricity.

5. Consider seriously what is fitting for your place of business and your guests. The Hupfeld firm has been supplying cafes, restaurants, hotels, dance halls, movies, etc. for years and has something to offer you too. It can satisfy every taste. Just describe your room and express your wishes!

6. If you get an instrument that is superior to others, success is yours. Some of your colleagues have even named their businesses after our instruments - such as: "Cafe Violina," "Violina Theatre," "Phonoliszt Restaurant," and "The Hupfeld Room." A sign saying "HERE THERE IS A HUPFELD INSTRUMENT" will draw crowds.

7. Don't condemn the self playing instruments if you have heard a poor one once. There are good and bad musicians too. The Hupfeld instruments remove all criticism by artistic playing, faultless functioning, and indestructible sturdiness.

8. Never let your choice be determined by a cheaper price. Instead, rely on the quality of the instrument. Consider that no one is giving away anything and that the best is the cheapest in the long run.

9. Don't forget that the public demands variety in music. The Hupfeld instruments have the greatest music repertoire and constantly offer the newest hits, dances, marches, and concert pieces.

10. Think of the fact that every day many Hupfeld instruments are playing in all parts of the world for the satisfaction of everyone. Their fame is well founded! The high opinion of experts, artists, and purchasers proves it. You can have complete confidence in the Hupfeld factory and its representatives. The large factory makes possible first class instruments at moderate prices.

If you follow these words of advice, you will be protected from harm and will also increase your profits by increasing your trade. You will regret that you didn't order a Hupfeld instrument sooner!

So ended the Hupfeld catalogue description... From the collector's viewpoint today the Helios orchestrions are very popular. They are well made and can be restored without undue difficulty. The larger instruments are built on a modular basis which permits individual components - orchestra bells, the xylophone assembly, etc. - to be removed easily without the necessity of dismantling the entire works. As Hupfeld's catalogue noted years ago, the musical arrangements are quite good. Of particular interest are the solo arrangements which can be occasionally found. Solo rolls take a particular instrument such as a xylophone and base an entire arrangement around it with the other instruments providing accompaniment.

The outstanding visual appearance of the Helios orchestrions combined with their musical ability have made these great attractions in the collections that are fortunate to own them. To see and hear a Hupfeld Helios orchestrion resplendent with its beautifully ornate case is to truly recapture in person the golden era of automatic orchestras.

*A beautiful Hupfeld Helios I/31 orchestrion (left side of photo) is a highlight of the magnificent private collection of Mr. Jerry Cohen.*

## PEPITA AND HELIOS MANDOLINA
### Hupfeld Orchestrions

Pepita and Helios Mandolina orchestrions were the smallest cabinet style (keyboardless) Hupfeld orchestrions. Pepita orchestrions took a special roll, usually of 10-tune length.

Helios Pepita Specifications: Model I: Violin pipes with piano accompaniment and triangle. Model II: Violin pipes with piano accompaniment, triangle, bass and tenor drums, Chinese cymbal. Model III: Piano with expression, harp effect, triangle, bass and tenor drums, Chinese cymbal. Model IV: Piano with expression, harp effect, xylophone, triangle, bass and snare drums, Chinese cymbal. Model V: Piano with expression, harp effect, violin pipes, bells, castanets, triangle, bass drum, snare drum, Chinese cymbal. Model VI: Piano with expression, harp effect, violin pipes, xylophone, bells, castanets, triangle, bass and snare drums, Chinese cymbal.

Helios Mandolina Specifications: Overstrung piano with expression. Mandolin effect. Orchestra bells, bass drum, tenor drum, and Chinese cymbal. Optional xylophone. The mandolin effect predominates tonally, providing an interesting and pleasing sound.

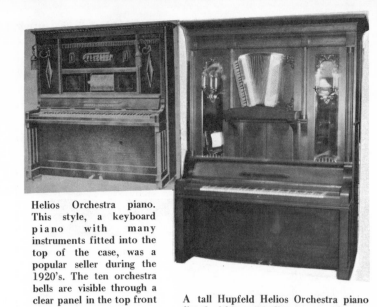

Helios Orchestra piano. This style, a keyboard piano with many instruments fitted into the top of the case, was a popular seller during the 1920's. The ten orchestra bells are visible through a clear panel in the top front of the case.

A tall Hupfeld Helios Orchestra piano fitted with an accordion.

Pepita I and II/44

Xylophone Mandolina

Helios Mandolina I/48

Pepita III and IV

Pepita III and IV/45

Pepita V and VI

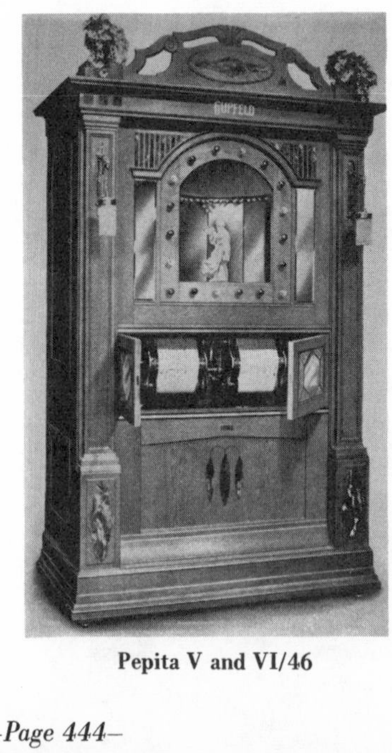

Pepita V and VI/46

Pepita V and VI/47

Helios Ia/20 orchestrion.

Helios I/22 orchestrion.

Helios Ib/29 orchestrion.

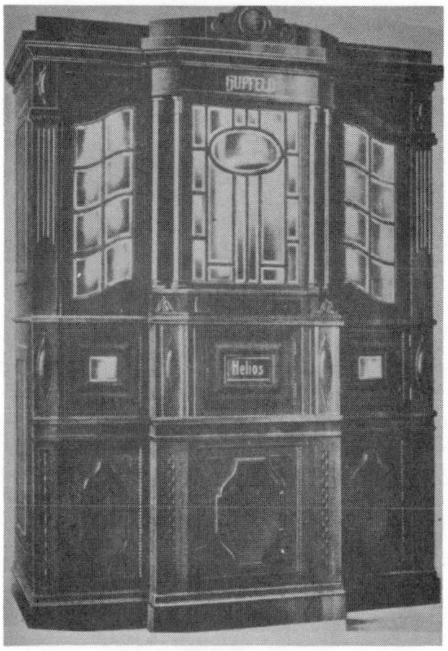


Helios Ib/29 orchestrion.

Helios I/30 orchestrion.

Helios I/30 orchestrion.

Helios I/34 orchestrion.

Helios Ib/37 orchestrion.

Helios Ic/40 orchestrion. This style has a very large case and could probably use Class II works on special order (see text).

Helios I/31 orchestrion.

**Tracker Bar Layout — Hupfeld Helios I**
**Numbered left to right**

This layout was taken from a Hupfeld Helios Ic orchestrion. The Helios roll is 11 5/8" wide and is spaced approximately 7 holes per inch.

1. Clarinet or oboe pipes on
2. Crash cymbal
3. Bass drum
4. Cello and violin pipes on
5. Snare drum, first beater
6. Xylophone and flute on
7. Snare drum, second beater
8. Note B (bells only)
9. C (bells only)
10. C sharp (bells only)
11. D (bells only)
12. D sharp (bells only)
13. Note E
14. F sharp
15. G sharp
16. A
17. A sharp
18. B
19. C
20. C sharp
21. D
22. D sharp
23. E
24. F
25. F sharp
26. G
27. G sharp
28. A
29. A sharp
30. B
31. C
32. C sharp
33. D
34. D sharp
35. Sustaining pedal on
36. Note E
37. Cancel all registers
38. Note F
39. Piano soft (low vacuum)
40. F sharp
41. Piano off
42. Note G
43. Coin trip (shutoff)
44. to 69 inclusive. Notes in order from G sharp to A
70. E (bells only)
71. F sharp (bells only)
72. G (bells only)
73. G sharp (bells only)
74. A (bells only)
75. Mandolin on
76. Aeoline or viola pipes on
77. Flute pipes on

Notes: The bells play from a special solo section in two parts on the roll: holes 8 to 12 and 70 to 74 inclusive. This means that the pipes and piano can play notes different from those of the bells at the same time — permitting solo effects. The bells are "on" all the time and play when the bell holes in the tracker bar are uncovered. The roll is multiplexed to a certain extent, which permits the roll to be relatively narrow but have many register controls, etc. Holes 39 and 43, when operating together, are "rewind" - separately they have other functions as noted in the tracker layout. Holes 4, 76, and 77 each have three openings, one above the other, in the tracker bar. In the Hupfeld Ic orchestrion at hand we observed that hole no. 4 operates the "violin pipes on" when a short perforation crosses the 3 vertical holes. When a long perforation crosses the holes so that two of the three holes are uncovered at the same time then both violin and cello ranks turn on. Hole no. 76 turns on the viola rank with a short perforation and both the viola and aeoline ranks with a long one. Hole no. 77 evidently can be similarly multiplexed, but the instrument examined was not connected in this way.

Another Helios layout, this one recently provided to us by Günther Hupfeld, differs in that the playing notes are marked differently: Hole 8, A; 9, A sharp; 10, B; 11, C; 12, C sharp; 13, D; 14, E; 15, F sharp; 16, G; 17, G sharp; 18, A; 19, A sharp; 20, C sharp; 21, C; 22, C sharp; 23, D; 24, D sharp; 25, E; 26, F; 27, G sharp; 28, G; 29, G sharp; 30, A; 31, A sharp; 32, B; 33, C; 34, C sharp; 36, D; 38, D sharp; 40, E; 42, F; 44 to 69 inclusive, notes in order from F sharp to G; 70, D; 71, E; 72, F; 73, F sharp; and 74, G.

Larger Hupfeld Helios styles used differently laid-out rolls in order to accommodate the additional effects.

**Helios Class I Orchestrions**
**———Instrumentation———**

**Standard instrumentation: Overstrung piano with mandolin effect, registers of pipes for the voices of violin and violoncello, orchestra bells, bass drum, Chinese cymbal, snare drum, and expression effects. Xylophone on special order.**

**Class Ib instrumentation: As preceding, but with flute pipes in addition.**

**Class Ic instrumentation: As preceding, but with clarinet reed pipes and large bass pipes in addition.**

**Note: Some Helios models have the standard curtain type of mandolin attachment. Others have a "harp effect" type with vibrating wooden hammers that strike above the regular piano hammers. The Wurlitzer Mandolin Quartette (see Wurlitzer section of this book) is based upon a similar mechanism.**

Helios I/32 orchestrion.

Hupfeld Helios Rolls

The Hupfeld Helios roll catalogues list hundreds of different melodies comprising just about every imaginable type of music from ragtime to popular to deep classical. The numbering system runs from No. 1 to at least No. 2345. (Our catalogue has No. 2345 released in November, 1933, as its last entry - but there may have been later ones) The abbreviation "Hs." for "Helios" appears on many of the roll labels.

Large bass reed pipe from a very large Helios model!

INTERIOR view of a Helios Ib/29. What Hupfeld wouldn't do years ago, we'll do for you now! Hupfeld rarely published interior views as this would be giving away "trade secrets." At the left are three rows of pipes. These are all of the violin family and provide the sounds of violin (shortest rank), viola, and violoncello. In the lower center and partly visible are the metal orchestra bells. To the right is the tenor or snare drum. Above it is the large bass drum. A very small part of the xylophone beater action is seen just below the bass drum. At the upper center of the photograph the left side of the Chinese cymbal is visible. In the top of the case, and not showing in the illustration, is a large set of swell or crescendo shutters for volume control.

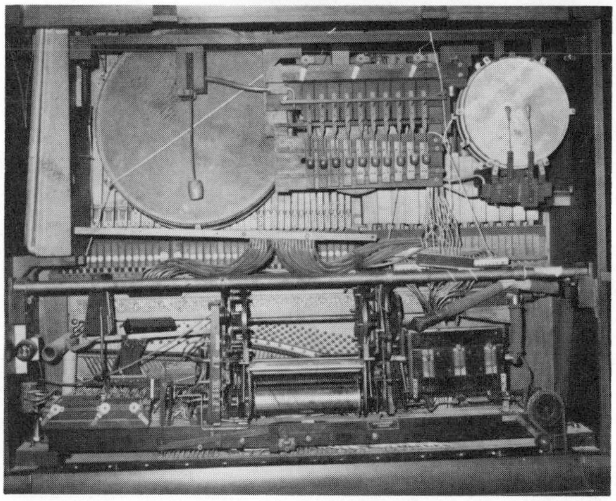

INTERIOR view of a keyboard style Helios Orchestra Piano. At the lower center is the single roll mechanism (without a roll on it). To the right is the vacuum "wind motor" which provides a variable speed roll drive. At the upper left is the bass drum, in the center the set of ten orchestra bells, and at the right the tenor drum with two beaters. Behind the traps are several ranks of pipes. The Chinese cymbal is concealed behind the orchestra bells. Hupfeld keyboard orchestrions are well built and are constructed on a modular basis. The turning of a few nuts will easily release sections of the instrument, thus permitting them to be worked on.

Hupfeld Helios orchestra bells.

Specifications of
Helios Class II Orchestrions

The buyers of Helios orchestrions of all styles, I through V, were offered several options of tonal character. An instrument could be voiced softly for use in a home or small room, medium volume for dancing, or loud volume for use in skating rinks. This was done by adjusting the wind pressure and voicing the pipes appropriately before the instrument left the factory.

The Helios II instruments were available in regular or "concert" specifications. Each had the same instruments, but the concert type had extra expression controls on the piano.

Helios II basic instrumentation: Overstrung piano with automatic pedal and expression effects, mandolin effect, pipe registers for: aeoline, violin, flute, piccolo, clarinet, viola, cello, bass cello (concert instruments) or bass flute (regular instruments), orchestra bells, trapwork including bass drum, Chinese cymbal, and snare drum. The trap work can play with expression effects. Xylophone optional.

The Helios II instruments use regular Helios rolls of the type used for classes I, II, and III. (IV and V required special rolls to play all of the effects, although the I, II, and III rolls would play on them).

——————————

**Helios II/36 — Called the "Rococo" model by Hupfeld.**

**Helios I/31 in a dance hall.**

**Dancing to a Helios II/24.**

**Restaurant music by a Helios II/26 orchestrion.**

Helios II/24 orchestrion. A departure from the traditional styling, the II/24 has a modern appearance.

Helios II/25. Standing 10'6" high the II/25 was large, beautiful, and musical!

Helios II/25. This general case style, first used on the II/25 Helios orchestrions as shown above and also above left, was one of the most beautiful used by Hupfeld. It was also one of the most popular, and many II/25's were made. The same basic case style was used for the center portion of certain larger Hupfeld orchestrions such as the Helios IV and, in the Pan Orchestra series, the Super Pan and Excelsior Pan.

Helios II/26 orchestrion.

Helios II/26 orchestrion.

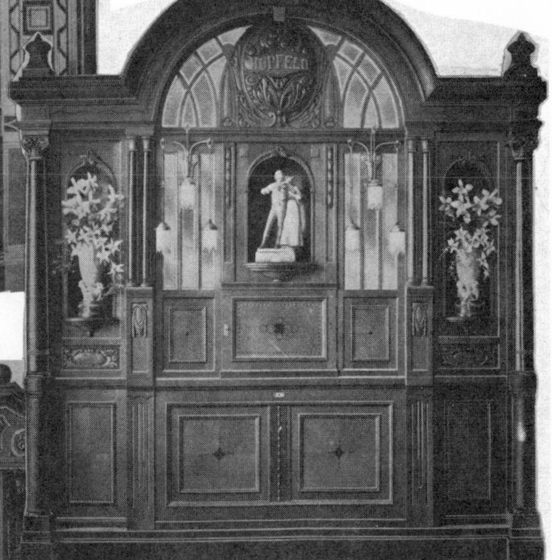

Helios II/33 orchestrion. Measurements of this instrument are: 10'10" high, 10'5" wide, and 5' deep. The Hupfeld catalogues noted that case designs were subject to change and that special designs were available to the buyer who wished a "custom" instrument. For this reason very few of the larger styles were identical from instrument to instrument. There were usually minor differences in the placement of decorative lamps, substitution of art glass for mirrors and vice versa, etc.

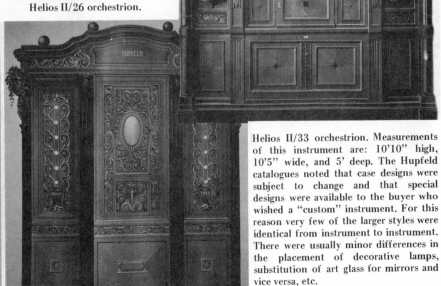

Helios II/35 orchestrion.

Helios II/41 orchestrion.

Helios III/19 orchestrion.

This large and elegant restaurant features a Helios III/19 for its musical entertainment. In such locations the music was often provided free by the management. In other instances coin wallboxes were used.

Helios III/19 orchestrion. Catalogue description: An orchestrion of great effect with regard to its music and appearance. Helios III develops a magnificent fullness of tone, quite sufficient for the largest halls. By the use of the swell shutters and by the loud and soft expression on the piano and trapwork, the rendering of every type of composition is possible. Powerful fortissimo alternates with the most delicate pianissimo. The massive case is built of oak, elegantly shaded in silver gray color.

# Testimonials of Artists about the Hupfeld Helios-Orchestrions

**Paul Prill**, conductor by royal appointment, Munich:

Your Helios-Orchestrions are remarkable for their fine appearance as well as for their delightful and rhythmical music. The delicate pianissimo, the perfect tone shading, the powerful fortissimo and the rhythm of the beating instruments all combine to produce a performance charming to the ear even of a connoisseur. When Orchestrions are mentioned, your Helios instruments ought always to be given the first place.

*Berlin*, January 21th, 1908. (signed) **Paul Prill.**

**Oscar Straus**, the famous composer of the operetta "Waltz dream":

The Helios-Orchestrions are strikingly effective, not only on account of the full tone-character, accentuation and rhythm, but also by reason of their magnificent stylish and highly-finished exterior. The music of these instruments has reached such a high artistic degree, and the repertoire is so voluminous, that anybody, even an expert musician will be satisfied. The Helios-Orchestrions can hardly be equalled, much less surpassed.

*Vienna*, Decembre 28th, 1907. (signed) **Oscar Straus.**

**Johann Strauss**, the well-known composer and conductor of orchestra says:

I was greatly delighted by the music of your Helios-Orchestrions. Being myself a musician I was eager to hear what the sounding effect would be, and I must confess that nothing is missing from the music whether it be euphony, fulness of tone, rhythm, or accentuation with either the smallest or the largest of the Helios-Orchestrions. The beating instruments pleased me particularly, as they play with perfect exactness, pointing the accentuation just as though played by an expert musician. Altogether I consider the Helios-Orchestrions to be of first-class quality an quite unsurpassable.

*Leipzig*, Decembre 13th, 1907. (signed) **Johann Strauss.**

Helios III/27 orchestrion. "As much a pleasure to the ear as the exterior is to the eye."

Helios III/28 orchestrion. "Caused a sensation at the 1910 World's Fair."

Helios III/38 orchestrion. With richly matched wood paneling.

Helios III/42 orchestrion - with rich paneling, lighting, and moving effects.

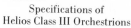

Helios III/42 orchestrion — a case design from the mid-1920's. Helios models kept in production for a long time were changed in case design over the years.

Specifications of
Helios Class III Orchestrions

Regular specifications: Cross strung piano with separate expression controls for bass and treble sections. Mandolin effect. Pipe registers for: violin, aeoline, flute, piccolo, clarinet, oboe, horn, bassoon, viola, cello, double bass, and bass violin. Orchestra bells. Percussion consisting of bass drum, Chinese cymbal, and tenor drum - each with expression. Xylophone optional. Provides finely modulated music of powerful fullness of tone corresponding to a full orchestra. Suited for recitals even in the largest halls.

Concert specifications: Piano as preceding. Mandolin effect. Pipe registers: violin, horn, flute, piccolo, clarinet, trumpets, cello, bass horn, principal, double bass, bass viol, and trombone. Orchestra bells. Percussion as preceding. Xylophone optional. Tonal character corresponds to a wind orchestra. Especially suited for dance and concert music in halls.

Helios IV orchestrion.

Helios V orchestrion.

Specifications of Helios IV

Piano with expression effects. Pipes representing: violin, tenor violin, violoncello, concert flute, piccolo, flute, clarionet, gamba, aeoline, saxophone, oboe, bugle, Vienna flute, bass, bass viol, cello, bassoon, trumpet, and double bass. Harp effect. Xylophone, orchestra bells, castanets, chimes, triangle, kettle drum, cymbals, bass drum, tenor drum, several bird whistles, and other effects. Dimensions about: 10'7" high (with the top decorations, 12'4"); width 13'2"; depth 4'6".

Specifications of Helios V

The largest regular production orchestrion ever made. About 1500 pipes are controlled by 49 registers via a multiplexed roll. Hupfeld noted: "The 49 registers consist of 7 for bass, 9 for accompaniment, 22 for melody, 11 for solo. Represents 100 to 120 performers. The effects of the music are stupendous, reproducing all the charms of an orchestra, full of harmonies and tone shadings..." About 14'9" high, 19'9" wide, 8'2" deep.

HUPFELD

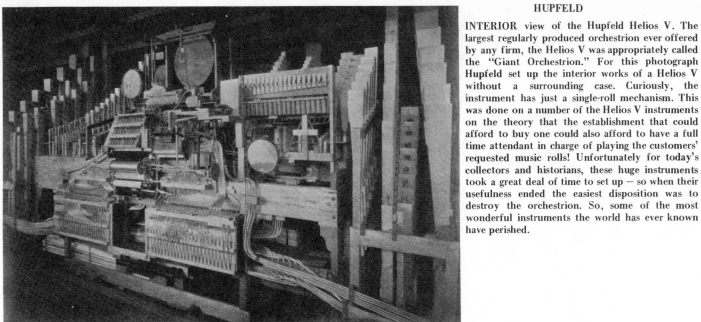

INTERIOR view of the Hupfeld Helios V. The largest regularly produced orchestrion ever offered by any firm, the Helios V was appropriately called the "Giant Orchestrion." For this photograph Hupfeld set up the interior works of a Helios V without a surrounding case. Curiously, the instrument has just a single-roll mechanism. This was done on a number of the Helios V instruments on the theory that the establishment that could afford to buy one could also afford to have a full time attendant in charge of playing the customers' requested music rolls! Unfortunately for today's collectors and historians, these huge instruments took a great deal of time to set up — so when their usefulness ended the easiest disposition was to destroy the orchestrion. So, some of the most wonderful instruments the world has ever known have perished.

# Testimonials of Artists about the Hupfeld Helios-Orchestrions.

**Edmund Eysler**, the composer of the operetta "Brother Straubinger":

I have taken much interest in your Helios-Orchestrions and as I have only to do with living orchestras I was so much more astonished at the really perfect performances of your orchestrions which are worked by air and electricity I do not know what to admire most, the excellent mandoline, the accentuation of the music, or the splendid beating instruments. Each instrument seems to possess its true quality of tone, and in the whole performance one recognises the axact and rhythmical playing of a good orchestra.

*Vienna*, November 23th, 1907. (signed) **Edmund Eysler.**

**Leo Fall**, the composer of the operettas "The Merry Countryman" and "The Dollar Princess":

Probably in no other branch of work has such great progress been made as in the technical science of musical instrument building. The difference between the usual old orchestrions and the modern Helios-Orchestrions of Hupfeld is as day and night, for the music in rendered with perfect tone-graduation and is arranged with excellent taste. Concert pieces as well as Dance and Military music are perfectly played by the various Helios models and their artistic value and handsome appearance fully justify my calling them instruments of the highest class. They fully replace an orchestra

*Vienna*, December 4th, 1907. (signed) **Leo Fall.**

**Alfred Grünfeld**, the celebrated composer and pianist of Vienna writes:

When I listened today to your Helios-Orchestrions I could not help but calling "Bravo, well done". The music produced by your instruments is a real treat even for the professional musician.

*Leipzig*, January 11th, 1909. (signed) **Alfred Grünfeld.**

**Rudolf Nelson**, the well-known Cabaret star writes:

Great progress is to be observed in all branches, particularly in orchestrion building, and your Helios-Orchestrions are the embodiment of progress and perfection. They are distinguished by the really astonishing effects obtained by the extremely skilful choice and arrangement of the different instruments. These include even a mandoline, xylophone, harp, bells &c. and by these means the purpose of obtaining a richly-coloured musical sketch is achieved with the greatest success.

*Berlin*, January 11th, 1908. (signed) **Rudolf Nelson.**

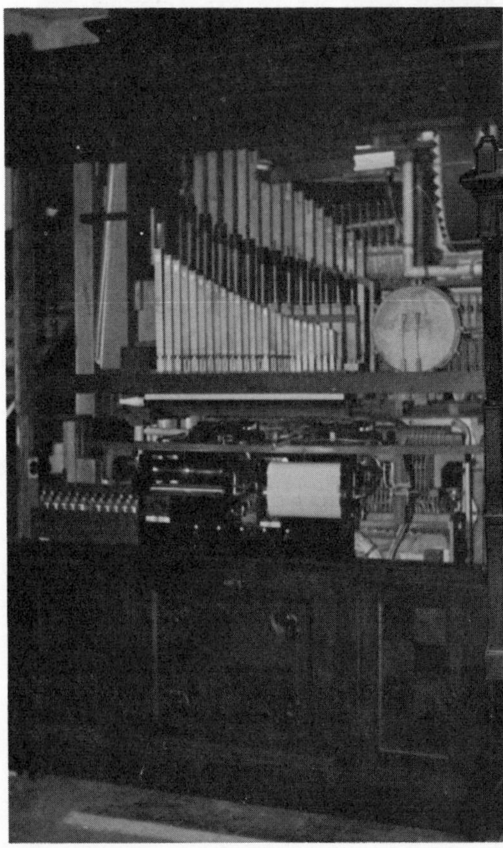

INTERIOR view of a Hupfeld Helios I/31 orchestrion. This one is equipped with the duplex roll mechanism. The exterior of the instrument is shown directly above.

—Hupfeld at the 1910 Brussels World's Fair—

During the 1890's and early 20th century the various German orchestrion manufacturers would exhibit their products several times a year at trade shows held in Leipzig. Occasionally the firms would exhibit abroad, but such foreign shows usually included just a few representative instruments, usually those of smaller sizes. The 1910 World's Fair held in Brussels, Belgium was an exception. It was held at the height of the German orchestrion industry. The German firms spared no expense to install lavish exhibits complete with large orchestrion models.

At the 1910 event Ludwig Hupfeld had several salons. Above is shown the main concert salon which featured Phonola player pianos (shown at the left side of the photograph), a Phonoliszt-Violina (center right), and several varieties of the Dea reproducing piano (to the right). Concerts were given at regular intervals.

To the left is shown part of the Hupfeld orchestrion exhibit. Against the back wall is a magnificent Helios IV, an orchestrion first introduced in 1908. Another large orchestrion, a Helios III/28 (not shown here), was also a featured attraction. Later, the design of the III/28 was revised to incorporate a scene of the exterior of the 1910 Brussels World's Fair exhibit hall.

CLAVITIST-ORCHESTER

Left: Hupfeld Clavitist Orchestra. Known as the "War-time Model" (Kriegs-Modell), this instrument was produced during World War I. Models included: Clavitist Orchestra I, with piano only (sold for 1400 Mk.); II, with piano and harp-effect (reiterating piano hammer attachment), 1550 Mk.; and III, with piano, harp-effect, and 10-note xylophone or orchestra bell set, 1775 Mk. Case measurements: 1.90 meters high, 1.24 meters wide, 0.55 meters deep. Introduced in 1914. Available with or without the Hupfeld automatic roll changer.

Right: Sinfonie Jazz Orchester (Symphony Jazz Orchestra) Model 19. Popular in the 1920's, the Model 19 incorporated a piano, saxophone and lotus flute pipes, bells, and percussion effects. Rolls, mainly numbered from 50,000 to 61,000, were of the Animatic type. Those specifically designated for the Sinfonie Jazz had SJ prefixes to the roll numbers. Most SJ rolls were arranged to emphasize the lotus flute rank, a series of tremulated flute pipes which, when played solo and one note at a time, produced a haunting melody with a catchy rising and falling in pitch effect.

Animatic-Clavitist Modell 19
Sinfonie-Jazz-Orchester

## HUPFELD PAN ORCHESTRAS

Hupfeld regarded the Concert Pan Orchestras (they were usually referred to as "orchestras" rather than "orchestrions" in Hupfeld's literature) as their finest accomplishment. Even today, when technical marvels have become commonplace, one cannot help but admire the mechanisms of these wonderfully intricate instruments.

Using an extensively multiplexed 124-note roll, the Pan had the capability of playing several different orchestral voices, each one playing different notes, at the same time! This was accomplished by the use of several different musical scales which did not overlap. The piano of the Pan was of the reproducing type and could re-enact artists' performances.

Here is what Hupfeld said about the Pan:

"The Concert Pan Orchestras have a pneumatic action of highest quality. The cabinets of each model are chosen by using artistic considerations, as are the orchestral voices within the case.

"The music of the Pan Orchestras lets you discover that these are neither organs nor orchestrions. Rather, they form a special class which can only be compared with a live orchestra.

"The musical parts of the Pan are entirely independent from each other. At any time a given voice or rank of pipes or particular instrument can be brought out tonally above the others. The Pan comprises all degrees of tonal power from the hushed piano to the thundering fortissimo. The drum and trapwork is recorded from a man's hand and imitates it exactly as it ranges from tender gracefulness to strong and tense rhythm.

"The connoisseur of music has at his call the wonderful strains from Tristan, Parsifal, an entire symphony, a violin concert with the accompaniment of an orchestra, or, yes, even a duet. Solo performances on the cello, flute, xylophone, organ, and other instruments are possible as are trios and chorales.

"Max Bruch, Hubert Cuypers, Julius Prüwer, Richard Strauss and other masters of music have participated in the actual recording or directing of Pan music rolls and have given their art to them so that the full orchestral performance as played by the Pan leaves no desire unsatisfied. The noble and rich modulation, the artistic instrumentation, the charming harmony and blending of the tones, the piquant rhythm, and the realistic delivery give fully the illusion of an orchestra of live performers.

"All Pan Orchestra models include a reproducing piano. This is available exclusively in the Pan instruments and makes possible the reproduction of actual performances from over 200 of the foremost pianists of the world.

"The music produced is in keeping with the elegant exteriors of the Pan Concert Orchestras which, in all styles and models, can suit the best rooms. Also, we frequently install Pan instruments without cases. These are secluded in a niche or separate room and play into a room through lattice work...

"Because of its outstanding musical performances the Pan is very popular. Pan Orchestras are found in castles, manor houses, villas, spas, restaurants, theatres, drawing rooms, and on finely appointed boats. All over the world the Pan has come to be appreciated and valued as a work of art..."

Even the least expensive Pan Orchestras cost several thousand dollars, and some of the large ones cost $10,000.00 to $15,000.00 or more. This necessarily limited the market for the Pan to those who could afford these sums. Most of the Pan instruments have long since been destroyed. It was with sadness that the author purchased a duplex Pan tracker bar unit a few years ago. The magnificent orchestrion of which it had been a part had been destroyed years earlier and, for some reason, only the tracker mechanism had been saved.

The Pan was Hupfeld's best foot forward, its finest achievement. If such an instrument never before existed but were produced for the first time today it would cause a sensation. It is easy to appreciate what an effect the Pan had on its listeners years ago.

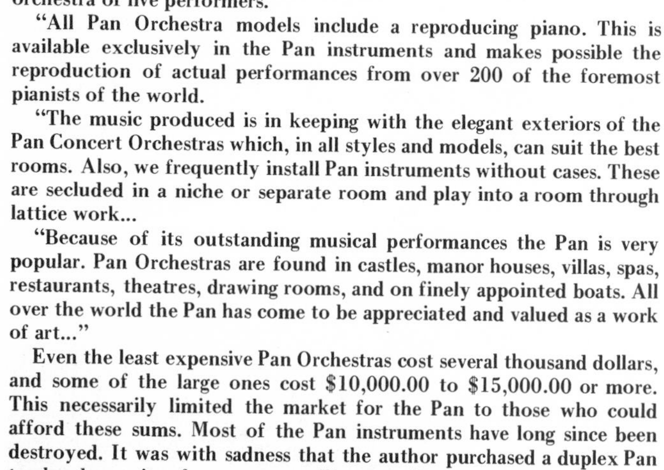

The perforation of music rolls at the Hupfeld factory.

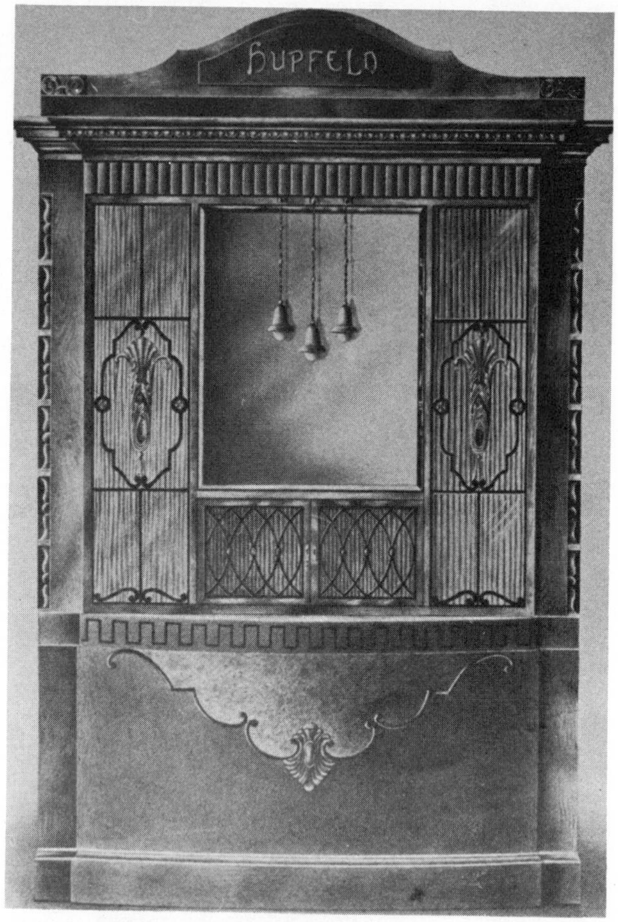


Concert Pan Orchestra – Model I

Left: An attractive specimen of the Model I Pan Orchestra. An accordion has been attached to the front. These additions were often made by Hupfeld dealers at the request of customers. This Pan measures about 10' high. It is equipped with the 10-roll automatic changer. Formerly located in San Francisco, the orchestrion is now a part of the Freiheit Collection in Ohio.

This photograph, taken in the 1930's shows either a Hupfeld Pan or a Hupfeld Violina Orchestra (the case is a Violina Orchestra case) which has had an accordion added.

Concert Pan Orchestra – Model O

Concert Pan Orchestra – Model II

Concert Pan Orchestra – Model III

Concert Pan Orchestra – Model IV

**Model 1-A Kino-Pan. Measures about 10' wide by 6' high by 3½' deep. Cost $3500 in 1925. Uses duplex roll mechanism. Model 3, a somewhat similar-appearing model, uses the double roll changer (2 changers x 10 rolls each). Both instruments may be operated by remote control from the projection booth.**

An unidentified Hupfeld orchestrion from the 1930's. The modernistic case design is typical of orchestrions of all makers during the very late 1920's and early 1930's.

### Pan Orchestra Rolls

Over 1,000 different selections were produced for the Hupfeld Pan. These ranged from popular numbers to classical pieces and just about every type of music in between. Some of the longer classical pieces were actually programmed on sets of three to five rolls per set – making a truly wonderful and complete performance possible.

Pan rolls are of 124-hole width and are mainly in the 90,000 series, although a few dozen were produced in the 91,000 range. Pan rolls were cut from about 1912 to the mid 1930's, so nearly all major pieces of music written during this period - and many earlier selections as well - are available as part of the Pan repertoire.

Hupfeld Theatre Organ. During the 1920's and 1930's Hupfeld produced several styles of theatre organs of the unit orchestra type. The console of one is shown above.

Hupfeld Excelsior Pan Orchestra: This instrument took two years to build. Completed in 1926, it was delivered to the Postzegel Hotel in 's Hertogenbosch, Holland. In that location it remained until it was acquired by Eugene DeRoy in 1966. Unlike many orchestrions the Excelsior Pan had been carefully cared for from the time it was newly installed until Mr. DeRoy removed it in 1966. The instrument could be operated in either of two ways: by a wallbox or by a pushbutton operated by the hotel owner. The Excelsior Pan Orchestra is now in the J.B. Nethercutt Collection.

INTERIOR view of the upper part of a Style I Pan Orchestra showing just a very few of the many effects of the instrument. At the lower left are ranks of violin and viola pipes. The light colored rectangle above them is the front of the reed harmonium section. To the right are the clarinets. Not visible in the picture are the orchestra bells, xylophone, drum and trap effects, and other instruments. The Pan has solo expression chambers within the main case. Combined with the expression of the main top shutters this gives an exceptionally wide range of volume control. By means of this any desired instrument can be brought out above the others for solo passages.

—The Hupfeld Super Pan Orchestra—

Designated as the "Super Pan" by Hupfeld, this magnificent instrument was built circa 1922 in the same case used for the Helios IV. The instrument is equipped with a double automatic roll changing device which permits twenty rolls to be stored on the instrument at one time. The rolls play alternately: a roll on the left side changer, then a roll on the right side changer, and then back to the left. Interior instrumentation of the Super Pan consists of many ranks of pipes, percussion effects (such as xylophone, bells, etc., drums and traps), and a piano with expression mechanisms. The Super Pan, probably the largest regular style in the Pan Orchestra series, is capable of a virtually unlimited range of musical ability and can represent anything from a concert pianist playing solo to a full symphony orchestra. The instrument, used in Holland from the 1920's through the early 1960's, was originally sold by Duwaer & Naessens, the Hupfeld outlet in that country. Found by Eugene DeRoy, the Super Pan Orchestra is presently in the collection of Q. David Bowers.

———————————

Pan Roll Mechanisms

Three main types of roll mechanisms were used on the various Hupfeld Pan instruments. Most orchestrions were equipped with the 10-roll automatic changer, although a few were equipped with a duplex (two single rolls side by side) mechanism. Theatre Pan Orchestras were usually equipped with the double automatic changer - two 10-roll changers side by side.

## Hupfeld Roll Mechanisms

Hupfeld instruments were available with a number of different roll mechanisms. The following is the original catalogue description of some of the more popular types:

Helios Orchestrions are available with a duplex roll mechanism (two single roll mechanisms side-by-side) operated by remote control. The patented duplex system has been a favorite for dance halls. It guarantees uninterrupted dance music which may, of course, be stopped and restarted by you any time. Here is how the duplex system works:

(Duplex System) In the instrument is a switching device consisting of three buttons. When button no. 1 is depressed the current is turned on and one of the two rolls begins to play. The roll plays automatically until the end is reached and then it rewinds automatically without any action by the operator. If one presses again button no. 1 the second roll plays, and it likewise rewinds at the end. If one wants to change the music during the playing at any place he presses buttons 2 and 1 simultaneously. The first roll, whose play was interrupted, rewinds and the second roll at the same time starts to play. If one pushes button no. 3 the roll that is playing stops. It will play again as soon as button no. 1 is pressed. This device has been created for pauses in the music — for example, to provide an opportunity to collect dance money from the patrons. From this description it should be clear to you that no interruption of the music takes place unless you, the manager, want it. If desired, remote control can be used to provide switching from any place distant from the instrument.

(Duplex System, continued) For movie theatres a Helios orchestrion with the duplex system and remote control offers great advantages. The switching can be done by the projectionist. In the movies you can change from lively to slow music without any pause. Two lamps placed on the control switchboard - one red and the other green - indicate by turning on and off which of the two rolls is playing so that any error is averted.

(Duplex System, continued) For restaurants the duplex mechanism on Hupfeld orchestrions has proved to be very practical. The host can control the switching. If you use rolls with three to six selections per roll this will give up to twelve pieces - which guarantees the guests the desired variety.

Hupfeld orchestrions with the ten roll automatic changer: This permits your choice of a desired selection by simply adjusting a pointer on a remotely located wallbox or control panel. It is unique — no other manufacturer has it. The adage "time is money" has always been significant for the restaurant industry. There it is clear that the player piano industry has endeavored for a long time to simplify the operation of the machine by means of a device that would eliminate constant changing of the rolls. Former roll changer systems permit the changing of rolls only in an established sequence. The music lover had to be content with whatever piece was next in line. Hupfeld has remedied this problem. The patron can now have his favorite tune without consulting the proprietor. The 10-roll automatic changer is the really perfect roll changing device.

(Automatic Roll Changer) A little wallbox, which can be installed at any desired distance, is connected by cable with the instrument. This box can be equipped for coin operation or it can be operated by a push button. It has a program listing the numbers from one to ten. We now choose our favorite from the ten pieces and put the indicator dial on the number desired. Now we insert a coin or push the button and the roll desired is automatically selected from the magazine of ten and played. This process is completely noiseless. During the play the indicator remains on the number selected and at the end of the piece moves automatically to the next number. The next piece will play when contact is again made unless we put the pointer at another selection. By the pointer's position we always know what piece is playing.

(Automatic Roll Changer, continued) The Hupfeld ten roll system makes two types of use possible: (1) One inserts 10 rolls with 10 different pieces of music and can then select the piece(s) to be played as described above. (2) One puts in 10 automatic rolls of 3 to 6 selections per roll - up to 60 pieces altogether - and then plays them in order without the use of the tune selector.

(Double Automatic Roll Changer) Among all the inventions in the field of motion pictures, the double automatic roll changer for two times 6 or 10 rolls is one of the most important. The double roll changer is a device that is simple to operate and which imparts to Hupfeld orchestrions an importance that goes far beyond the limits of a musical instrument. A Hupfeld orchestrion with double automatic roll changer and remote control has come into the motion picture industry as a new and reliable member and takes the place of a theatre orchestra...

(Double Automatic Roll Changer, continued) In this device two magazines or revolving mechanisms containing 6 or 10 rolls each are placed side by side. A cable with a switchboard at the end leads from the instrument to the control area. The movie manager can then set up a program. The 12 or 20 rolls necessary are chosen to conform to the character of the film being shown. These rolls are put into the changers in the correct sequence. We must take care that the two changers alternate — that is, when the changer at the right begins with the first roll then the changer on the left follows with its first roll. Then the first changer plays its second roll and the second changer likewise plays its second roll, etc. The double changer offers uninterrupted music for a duration of two to three hours or more without repeating even one piece of the repertoire! In the event that for a certain scene a slower melody must suddenly follow a gayer melody, then through simple switching the playing roll can be stopped and rewound while, at the same time without pause in the music, the corresponding roll on the other changer can be brought into play.

(Other Mechanisms) Automatic roll changers are made in 3, 6 and 10 roll capacities for installation in orchestrions. A 2-roll "twin" mechanism is made for theatre instruments as is the Citoplex, a snap-in, snap-out roll holder which permits quick changes. And then, of course, there is the single roll tracker bar which is standard.

*The Hupfeld Citoplex mechanism made easy work of quickly changing single rolls. An attendant was required.*

*Hupfeld duplex roll system (without roll on right side).*

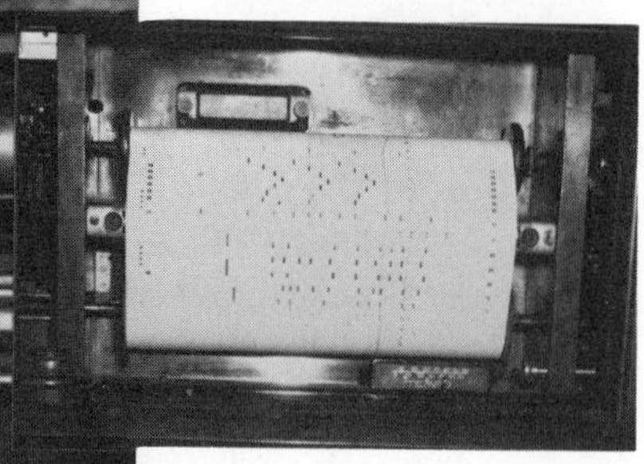

*Standard Hupfeld single roll mechanism (from a Hupfeld Dea in the British Piano Museum).*

## HUPFELD

Right: Hupfeld wallbox for an instrument equipped with the 10-roll changer. The pointer device at the bottom (patented June 28, 1912) indicates the number of the tune being played. Another variation of Hupfeld wallbox permitted the restaurant patron to actually select the tune desired. This latter wallbox type was used in combination with a changer device similar to that shown at the left.

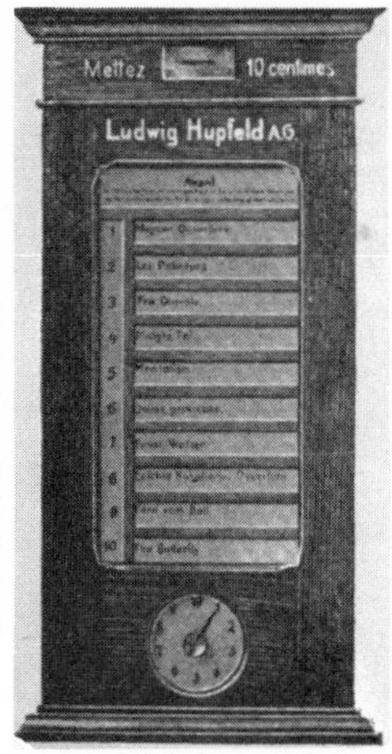

Left: This old photograph from the files of the former New York City Hupfeld distributor shows the fabulous 10-roll automatic changer. Here's how it selects: To the left of the main changer mechanism is a slotted metal drum firmly attached to the center shaft of the changer. There are ten slots, each in a different lateral position, and ten metal "fingers" poised above the drum. When a desired tune is selected the appropriate metal finger presses against the surface of the drum as the entire changer mechanism and the drum rotate. When the desired opening is beneath the finger the finger plunges into the hole and stops the drum from rotating further. At that point the desired roll is in the playing position.

Above left: View of a six-roll Hupfeld changer from a keyboard Helios orchestrion. Above right: Hupfeld catalogue illustration of a 6-roll changer loaded with rolls and with a roll in the playing position. Most changers were either of the 6 or 10 roll capacity.

Standard Hupfeld single tune wallbox.

The wonderful Hupfeld Double Automatic Roll Changer. This device was made in 6-roll and 10-roll sizes. A very long program without repetition could be performed on an instrument with this device.

1911 illustrations of the new Hupfeld factory in Böhlitz-Ehrenberg, near Leipzig. The factory stands today and is used for the production of regular (non-player) upright and grand pianos.

Glorification of the Helios: This 1925 advertisement depicts a Helios II/25 orchestrion on a display pedestal. This particular case design was one of Hupfeld's most popular and most attractive. In addition to the II/25, the design was incorporated as the central unit of the Helios IV (with lesser instrumentation known also as the II/43 and III/43), the Excelsior Pan Orchestra, and the Super Pan Orchestra.

In August, 1926 Ludwig Hupfeld A.G. merged with Gebr. Zimmermann, an established piano manufacturer of excellent reputation. The new industrial empire was known formally as the Leipziger Pianoforte u. Phonolafabriken Hupfeld - Gebr. Zimmermann A.G. By 1926, sales for self-playing instruments had diminished sharply. Most instruments made by the newly combined firm were of regular upright and grand piano styles.

1930 Hupfeld advertisement featuring a wide array of products including phonographs, billiard tables, radios (note the radio-tube Hupfeld trademark above right), sound apparatus for motion pictures, and pipe organs. All of these were noted as being "new." Earlier products still carried in stock included: "Artistically-playing instruments, Phonola and Tri-Phonola; Electric artistically-playing pianos and orchestras [orchestrions]; and Animatic artists' rolls."

February, 1932: One of the last Hupfeld advertisements for automatic musical instruments. According to Günther Hupfeld (son of Ludwig Hupfeld) and the present management of the VEB Union Piano Co. (successors to Hupfeld), production of new instruments stopped about 1930. The "New item: Sinfonie Jazz with self-playing tango-accordion" listed above is undoubtedly a previously-made instrument which was newly equipped with the accordion feature.

Yesteryear at Hupfeld: The King of Saxony, Friedrich August (shown at the far left), visited the Hupfeld factory on January 30, 1912. Hupfeld instruments enjoyed the patronage and interest of royalty from many lands including the Emperor of Russia, the King of Denmark, the King of Portugal, and "a great number of other royalties" – noted a 1910 Hupfeld catalogue. (Illustration courtesy of Mr. Günther Hupfeld, son of Ludwig Hupfeld).

Today at the Hupfeld firm: Many of the original structures are still intact. The VEB Deutsch Piano Union, state-owned successors to the Hupfeld enterprises, continues the manufacture of pianos, although not automatic ones. The Hupfeld name is still used as a trademark for several different types of keyboard pianos for the home. These are marketed worldwide by Demusa, the East German musical instrument export agency. At the left is the Hupfeld factory as it appeared in the summer of 1971. Above is shown the political slogan, "Der Leninismus Der Marxismus unserer Epoche!," as affixed to one of the factory walls.

## A TEMPLE OF SOUND

*A 1911 visit to the showrooms of Ludwig Hupfeld A.G. (Translated by Claes O. Friberg).*

Immortality! What heavenly promise – and mankind's strongest desire. A message heard by everyone; but many lack faith. And yet the human soul strives to escape the horror of vanishment.

Mankind has ceased to delay the decay of mortal remains by mummification or other means of preservation and has by and by abandoned the idea of metempsychosis as well. In life and death alike, one is now prepared to do without the "snake that is gnawing at our heart," wishes to have one's human remains destroyed by the blaze of fire and turned into ashes, no longer dreading the thought of a dreamless and eternal sleep. And yet, having to depart from this life fills the human heart with deep and fearful anxiety. How bitterly difficult it is to let death bereave us of our dear ones, and how painful it is to suffer the passing away of great creative artists, witnessing their oblivion and being grieved by the silencing of their direct manifestations.

Since early days art has indeed enabled yearning mankind to memorialize the outward appearance of a venerated or beloved dead, but no memory nor any description could carry beyond the grave the voice of a beloved family member, or the magic of an inspiring orator, or the song of a celebrated singer, or the gifted artist's playing. In our day inventive human spirit sought to remedy this privation by way of ingenious mechanisms, and indeed some success has been achieved. The phonograph has brought to us for thirty years now the voices of the living and also the voices of those who have died since. The phonograph holds faded memories, and the cinematograph reflects personalities and events from anywhere and any time by the medium of motion pictures.

These all have been recently superseded by mechanically-playing instruments. True to every note and touch, these instruments resound the musical recitals of all prominent artists of our time, and also of those who have since passed away. In manufacturing these astounding devices of sound perpetuation the art has progressed recently from keyboard instruments to the field of stringed instruments, the latter being far more difficult to cope with mechanically.

Two years ago, during the second Exhibition of the Music Trade at the Crystal Palace in Leipzig, the world-famous Leipzig manufacturers of piano instruments, the Ludwig Hupfeld Corporation, along with their Dea Masterplay-Pianos, rendering the playing of outstanding virtuosi to perfection, exhibited the Dea-Violina. This instrument became the subject of amazement and admiration – as the first instrument to combine the automatic playing of a violin by the stroke of horsehair bows with the accompaniment of an automatically-played reproducing piano.

The Dea-Violina contained four violins, played by a horsehair-covered steel bow, and cost 12,000 gold marks. Since that time the Violina mechanism has been improved considerably. The new instrument, known as the Phonoliszt-Violina, is available for only 8,400 marks.

In order to get acquainted with this new Phonoliszt-Violina I recently visited the Hupfeld Music Palace on Petersstrasse in Leipzig. Impressive hallways, filled with giant coffin- and tomb-like Solodant Phonolas and Dea reproducing pianos containing sound to be resurrected, lead to a staircase, surrounded by huge flower urns and then, over carpeted steps, upstairs. The upper floors' halls, with their walls decorated in subdued colors, embellished here and there by bronzed wreaths, remind one of an ancient temple. At the far end of one of these rooms, filled with rows of chairs in concert hall fashion, a dais carries various pianos and, in front of these, various Hupfeld vorsetzer-type piano players.

My friendly guide, the manager of the music department of the Ludwig Hupfeld Corporation, a gentleman named Riemann, inserted parchment rolls and by slightly touching a handle produced the playing of d'Albert, Busoni, Friedheim, and other great artists. It was indeed their own playing that I heard. I was terrified by those strange parchment rolls that contained, so to speak, such a spellbinding part of each artist's personality. Mr. Riemann, who dealt with them so carelessly, suddenly seemed to be a kind of omnipotent being who, by means of some fiendish power, had taken from the artists' their reflections and shadows – and thereby, an immortal piece of their souls. And yet I had to admit that the preservation of musical performances had actually brought us something wonderful: the rescue of something personal, something mortal, from the abyss of vanishment. No longer valid is Friedrich v. Schiller's lamentation:

*Here magic dies with the artist*
*And, as the sound lingers in the ear,*
*The moment's quick inspirations disappear,*
*And no lasting work guards its glory.*

But even so, my companion inspired me with awe, and it was with a certain anxiety that I accepted his suggestion to leave this temple of sound and its great piano players. Only reluctantly did I follow Riemann into another room.

Once more we were surrounded by this strange dusk. When my eyes again became accustomed to the half-light I noticed, along the wall of the new room, a baldachin-like ornament. Just as I was about to ask whose throne this was, enthralling and melancholic violin strains sounded from beneath the baldachin – *Solveig's Song*, by Grieg, filled with fervor and soul. I became possessed by the idea that a spirit was held by wicked powers in the piano under the baldachin. Scarcely had this song, so reminiscent of life, come to an end, when I saw my enigmatic guide approach the baldachin again. There was a short rattle, and then a passionate mazurka was played with a sensuous violin-vibrato. My heart quickened and I was gripped by a keen desire to look at the spirit of the violin, who played so magically well and whom I suspected had devilish ties. Eager to fight, I rushed toward the baldachin . . . ! Then, however, Mr. Riemann approached me and, smilingly, he asked me in his quiet and businesslike way whether he might now proceed to demonstrate and explain the strange mechanism of the Phonoliszt-Violina.

My hallucinations disappeared and I saw my so unjustly suspected guide open the doors over or, rather, built into, the piano under the baldachin. Then, by touching a lever, he started the rotation of a circular steel bow, the inside of which was lined with strong horsehair strands. The bow, its speed depending on the degree of strength of stroke required, rotated around three almost vertically-attached violins. Either one or the other of the violins turned its strings toward the bow, thus producing the tone commanded by one of the air-operated fingers placed over the finger boards. The lower half of the instrument consists of a piano-playing apparatus which renders perfectly the playing of master pianists in accompaniment to the violins. The Phonoliszt-Violina, driven by an electric motor, works with perfection and renders a superb imitation of all modulations and of all the violinist's strokes – the staccato and legato, the glissando and tremolo, the finest vibrato and sordino sound as well.

This outstanding technical achievement of the human mind is truly amazing. As it is more difficult to play the strings than it is to master the keys of a piano, the creation of the Phonoliszt-Violina must have been much more difficult than the invention of artistically-played pianos. Considering the quality, the sound, and the distinguished design of the Phonoliszt-Violina, which, along with its other qualities, can be operated easily by a non-professional, it is well understandable that this instrument, despite its yet-high sales price, has found many enthusiastic customers. But, alas, words are not enough to give a true impression of this marvel. Those interested ought to listen to the Phonoliszt-Violina for themselves. Opportunity is provided by concerts held frequently at the Hupfeld Temple of Sound on Petersstrasse, and admission is free of charge.

---

*The preceding article, written by journalist A. Smolian in 1911, is interesting for its almost poetic descriptions of Hupfeld instruments. The description of the introduction of the violin players is not correct. The Phonoliszt-Violina was introduced prior to the Dea-Violina. When the Dea-Violina, for which great success was expected, proved to be unfeasible from a marketing viewpoint, the Phonoliszt-Violina became the only Hupfeld violin player made after about 1910.*

*To the right is a view of the Hupfeld Music House on Petersstrasse in Leipzig. This illustration was used in Hupfeld advertisements of the early 1920's.*

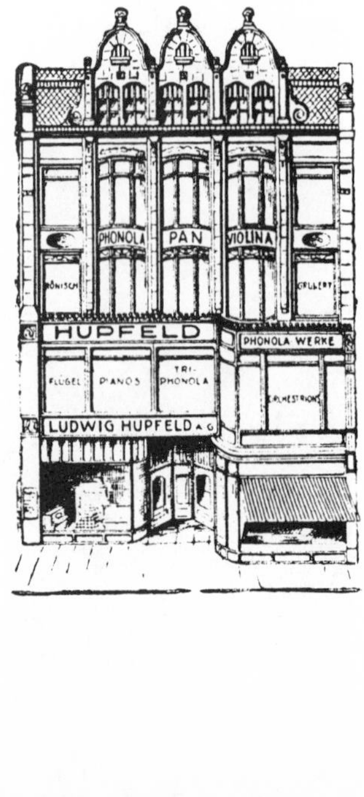

## IMHOF & MUKLE

### History of the Firm

Daniel Imhof, a Black Forest maker of flute-playing clocks and other instruments, founded his business in 1848 (one account says 1845). In 1874 the Imhof & Mukle firm was established in Vöhrenbach, Germany. A "company history" notes:

"The mechanical musical instrument industry in the Black Forest has in the course of time passed through many phases. Up to the end of the last century, it formed a branch of the clockmaking industry, and old illustrations show that at that time regular clocks and musical clocks were turned out of the same workshops.

"In time these two industries progressed until finally they constituted separate branches and separated, or, more exactly, the musical instrument making became a separate industry.

"The Black Forest has produced a number of very famous artists, or orchestrion manufacturers, as they called themselves as this art developed. Besides the workers employed in the factories, quite a number were employed in their homes; more especially the inserting of brass pins and staples in the rolls (Editor's Note: the reference is to wooden cylinders) formed a lucrative employment for many, particularly women.

"Many of these numerous orchestrion factories have ceased to exist. Outside competition grew up, and only a few found it possible to keep pace with the times. Amongst the foremost of those who were able to keep up with the running is to be found our firm. We are indebted for the founding of our company to the mechanical-works maker Daniel Imhof, who served his apprenticeship with a Neukirch clockmaker. As was the case with so many intelligent inhabitants of the Black Forest, the Revolution of 1848 brought about a great change. His having taken an active part in the political struggles of this troubled and turbulent year necessitated his leaving home and country.

"He proceeded to London, and in the same house in which our branch office (Imhof & Mukle, 110 New Oxford Street, London W.C.) is to be found today, he carried on the sale of automatic musical instruments which he imported from the Black Forest.

"In the year 1874 he returned to his native land and founded with his partner, Mukle, under the name of Imhof & Mukle, an orchestrion factory in Vöhrenbach. The factory expanded and soon ranked amongst the most prominent Black Forest factories in this field.

"At that time the cylinder-operated orchestrion was generally acknowledged to be the most perfect form of this instrument. In this class our instruments occupied a prominent and important position. However, we continually endeavored to improve our products. Our entirely unrivalled Music Leaf System (Editor's Note: this refers to the Imhof music roll made of very heavy manila paper and operated with a key frame rather than by a tracker bar), which is protected by patents, may be mentioned as a very important invention.

"Through the epoch-making Music Leaf System, our business made enormous strides and our factory was brought up to the position which it occupies at the present day. Ceaseless activity has enabled us continually to extend our business, and today we are reckoned as one of the first houses in this field. Our plant is splendidly fitted out both mechanically and technically, and we have at our disposal a large staff of experienced workers.

"Our instruments are first class, and are distinguishable by their full tone and perfect manner of playing, and at same time, by their architectural beauty and the tastefulness of their external designs. We would especially emphasize that our instruments are made only from first class material and may be reckoned amongst the most durable which are put on the market."

### Early Imhof & Mukle Instruments

As the above history indicates, the early Imhof & Mukle instruments were operated by a pinned cylinder. From 1848 until about 1900 the firm made a wide variety of flute-playing clocks (called "organ clocks" by collectors today), a number of different styles of barrel pianos, including some with long overtures and in ornate cases — for residential use, and orchestrions and organs of various types. Most of the automatic organs were small cabinet-style instruments with attractive veneer and fittings. Voiced on low pressure, they played soft and melodious music — usually operatic overtures.

Motive power for the larger barrel-operated Imhof & Mukle instruments was furnished in the early days by heavy weights which were cranked up and which then dropped slowly as the instrument played. In the 1900 - 1905 years, buyers had a choice of weight-driven or electric instruments. Shortly thereafter, weight-driven instruments were discontinued.

The pre-1900 Imhof & Mukle orchestrions resembled in a family way the contemporary instruments of Welte, Heizmann, Philipps, and other German orchestrion builders. Generally, the instruments were quite tall, usually between 9 and 12 feet, and had clear glass on the front and on each side. The pinned cylinder was usually visible behind glass, as were the pipes, drums, and other effects. Most, if not all, of these early orchestrions contained no piano.

The pipes were arranged in the "sunburst" fashion, radiating from the center of the pipe cluster or rank. This, of course, called for a symmetrical arrangement of pipes rather than a purely chromatic arrangement in ascending or descending order, such as was used in later years when the pipes were hidden from view.

In 1862 Imhof & Mukle exhibited a large orchestrion at the International Exhibition. Duplicates of this instrument were offered for sale in the Euterpeon Rooms at 547 Oxford St. in London. An advertisement is descriptive:

"Self-acting instruments have been constructed for centuries past, but have always borne the impression of the general knowledge of mechanism and music of the time being. Instead of simple actions, the most complicated and awkward designs were used and, therefore, would have better been termed motionless, rather than self-acting instruments; but self-acting instruments are as sure to act as perfectly as other machines, if properly constructed on scientific principles, which is proved by the great successes we have achieved in our instruments, and particularly in our Orchestrion and all our instruments of later years, which are more durable than any pianoforte or church organ, even in tropical climates, which we can prove by testimonials.

"The Orchestrion constructed for the International Exhibition of 1862 contains the most perfect scale to produce varieties of tone and orchestral effects. It is capable of giving expression to the music played, with greater ease and precision, than any other instrument ever made. All the music is arranged by Messrs. I.& M. themselves; the quantity of machinery used is less than one half the amount used in other instruments of even smaller size; and instead of winding up in five or six places, as in other large self-acting instruments, this has only two windings, both on the same side of the instrument — and it winds so easily that even a child can work it, which is another important success; nevertheless, there is an abundant supply of wind. The pipes are so placed that the whole can be tuned from the sides, without removing a single pipe, and are not liable to get out of tune, as they all have free speaking room.

"The barrels can be conveniently removed in or out from the front, which is an important saving of additional space required for instruments of other makers. The barrels are marked on a separate machine, independent of the Orchestrion, and these barrels can be used in all other instruments of the same size. An additional tempo regulator is attached to the main machinery, which obtains the 'rallentando' and 'accellerando' so necessary in music, and removes all the mechanical stiffness.

"Should the framework stand uneven, the key frames are so connected that they will follow in their proper places and thus insure proper playing at all times. This supersedes the old mistaken principle of building all in a supposed perpetual way. There are no levers attached to the bellows, because such levers are always liable to cause clicking and noise, and also require continual oiling. The mechanism of the Orchestrion will be found to work without the slightest noise, and is warranted to remain so."

### 20th Century Imhof & Mukle Instruments

Sometime around the turn of the century Imhof & Mukle introduced what it referred to as its "Music Leaf System." Basically the system consisted of a long roll of music made of tough manila paper (one early advertisement depicts two fellows engaging in a tug-of-war at each end of an unyielding roll!) wound on a wooden spool. The titles of the tunes on the roll or, in some instances, just the character of the music (such as "popular marches") were lettered in black on the spool end. The music roll played very slowly, so a greater amount of music could be programmed per foot than was the case with regular rolls on thin paper. This slow playing and compact arranging was a necessity: the Imhof & Mukle rolls sometimes play for about a half hour — and the quantity of manila paper needed to do this at regular speed would not have fit on the rolls.

Most automatic pianos and orchestrions which use paper rolls "read" the rolls by passing them over a tracker bar. This bar consists of a row of neatly aligned holes through which a vacuum (usually) is introduced. A hole in the paper when passing over an appropriate hole in the tracker bar will cause a flexible pouch to move, which in turn activates an operation which collapses a bellows, causing a piano hammer to strike the strings, a beater to strike the drum head, or whatever.

While some later Imhof & Mukle instruments used the standard tracker bar system with thin paper rolls, most used a key frame system similar to that used in European fairground and dance organs. Instead of music books (as the organs used), however, the Imhof & Mukle instruments utilized very heavy manila paper rolls; rolls which were tough enough to withstand the constant pressure of the spring-loaded brass keys in the key frame.

These heavy manila rolls were expensive. In 1908 typical Imhof & Mukle rolls sold for $22 to $28 – several times the cost of competitors' paper rolls. After about the World War I period a number of Imhof & Mukle instruments were made with tracker bars and thin paper roll systems.

The Imhof & Mukle empire flowered in the early 20th century. Many Imhof instruments were sold through the London branch, and many others were sent to other parts of the world. A wide variety of orchestrions and pianos was produced. These ranged from keyboard pianos with orchestral effects – the "Corrector" and "Commandant" are examples – to large orchestrions such as the "Tribute," "Lohengrin," and the mighty "Valkyrie" and "Admiral."

Imhof spared no efforts to make the cases as attractive as possible. Ample use of wood carvings, motion picture scenes, revolving "wonder lights," and, in later years, art glass, made the orchestrions as eye-catching as any the competition offered.

Imhof orchestrions were, for the most part, rather softly voiced. A real effort was made to make these instruments popular in private homes, on board yachts, and in similar locations – an effort which was rewarded by the sale of hundreds of orchestrions to such buyers. M. Welte & Sons, an orchestrion manufacturer, was the main competition in this area.

The market for the larger instruments which formed the greater part of the Imhof & Mukle business dwindled sharply after World War I. Imhof's competitors – Welte, Philipps, Hupfeld, et al – diversified and concentrated production on reproducing pianos, home players, coin-operated pianos in smaller cases, and other instruments which made up the post-World War I market. Imhof continued with the production of orchestrions and, as a result, virtually ceased business by the late 1920's, although some operations were continued through the early 1930's.

The former Imhof & Mukle factory still stands in Vöhrenbach. Part is used for a garage and part as apartment-type living quarters. When visited by the author in 1971 no visible signs of the early Imhof business remained – except for an ornately designed door with a musical motif.

The London branch, which was always an active sales outlet, went through a series of transformations. In another form the company survives in England today. Trading as "Imhof's," the firm is a leading retailer of television sets, phonographs, and other appliances.

The E. Boecker Organ and Orchestrion Co.

During the early years of the 20th century, hundreds of Imhof & Mukle orchestrions were imported into the United States and sold by the E. Boecker Organ and Orchestrion Company. Later named the Original Orchestrion and Piano Co., the firm had several New York City addresses over the years, including 229 to 233 10th Avenue, 26 West 38th Street, 14 to 16 West 17th Street, and 1923 Fulton Street (Brooklyn). The same firm also sold Weber and Hupfeld orchestrions and organs made by Ruth and Bruder.

Boecker's (also spelled Böcker) customers were many and included the Hudson River Day Line steamers which plied the river from New York to Albany, many nickelodeon theatres (who set up orchestrions and played them continuously throughout the screen performance), and a number of private clubs and mansions. New York's Jockey Club boasted a large built-in Imhof & Mukle orchestrion, possibly the largest ever sold in this country.

Boecker advertised: "The celebrated Imhof & Mukle Orchestras perform automatically by means of perforated rolls made of the heaviest obtainable manila paper. They are not mechanical in sound, but play with expression, an artistic touch, and a fullness and sweetness of tone not found in other automatic musical instruments. We carry eighteen different styles in stock at all times. We also design and furnish orchestras to conform with decorations in private residences and high class restaurants." Further on the subject of custom-made orchestrions, Böcker noted: "Orchestrions are built to fit any space, no matter how small or large, after designs made by us or furnished by the customer. Orchestrions have an exquisite and sweet tone with a volume that can be regulated as desired. Time of building is eight to twelve weeks. Designs and estimates furnished on application."

One of the most fascinating orchestrions ever built by any maker is the Lord 3, an instrument which is actually two-in-one. In addition to the main orchestrion there was a smaller unit, an "echo" orchestrion connected by wires to the main instrument. The echo orchestrion played its own solos! Boecker extensively advertised and featured the Lord 3 and evidently sold at least several of them. In 1913 a Boecker advertisement featured the Lord 3 as the "Echo Piano Orchestra – the only orchestra with echo; greatest attraction." The reader may refer to a following page for a description of this interesting orchestrion.

As was the standard modus operandi of orchestrion importers (e.g., Wurlitzer who imported from Philipps), Boecker nowhere mentioned Imhof & Mukle to his buyers. For all the buyer knew, these immense orchestrions were being manufactured in Manhattan! A typical news release, this one from the July 6, 1907, issue of "The Music Trades," is indicative:

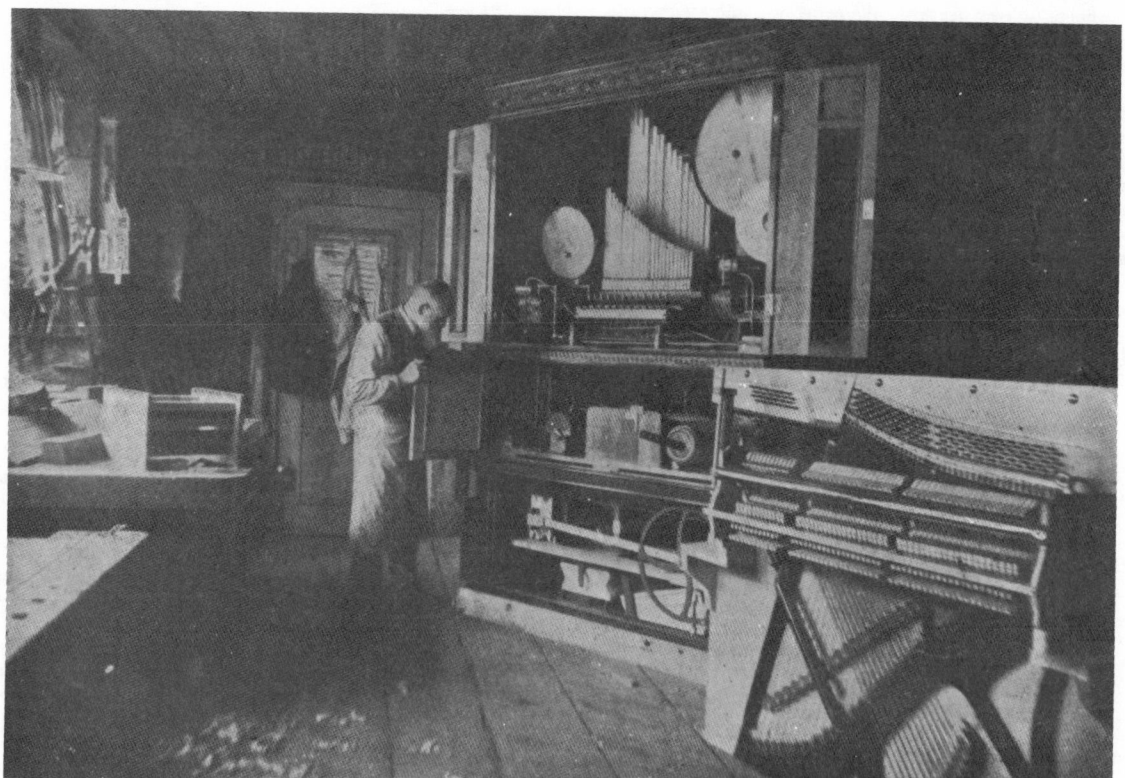

An Imhof & Mukle orchestrion under construction at the Vöhrenbach factory, circa 1910. (Illustration courtesy Carl Jung)

"THE BOECKER ORCHESTRION LUCRETIA – The Latest Style Placed on the Market by the E. Boecker Organ and Orchestrion Co.: The E. Boecker Organ and Orchestrion Co. of 229 Tenth Avenue, New York, has just placed on the market the handsome orchestrion shown in the accompanying illustration, which is designated by the manufacturers as the Lucretia. Remarkable tonal effects are produced with this instrument, and the case design is very attractive. Mr. Schilling, of the company, stated that recently a well-known orchestra leader listened for more than an hour to the playing of this orchestrion, and stated that the rendition was in every way a marvelous one. The manufacturers state in their catalogue that 'this instrument plays solos on the xylophone in a manner that will actually surpass the playing of the best artist in the world! It has a full, strong sound, contains first-class overstrung upright piano, violin, viola, and violoncello pipes, mandolin and harp, chimes, snare drum, bass drum, kettle drum, cymbal, and xylophone. The solos on the xylophone are wonderful to hear."

On June 28, 1914, the assassination of the Austrian Archduke Francis Ferdinand at Sarajevo touched off the fuse that ignited World War I. Within months imports of orchestrions from Germany ceased – and the importing firms such as the Rudolph Wurlitzer Co. and M. Welte & Sons had their source of supply severed. So would have E. Boecker – except that financial difficulties beset the firm in early 1914, and on June 11th, 1914, just slightly more than two weeks before Sarajevo, the following announcement appeared: "On Thursday, June 11th, 1914, we shall sell at public auction the entire stock imported by E. Boecker of 231-33 Tenth Avenue, New York City, consisting of Piano Orchestras, manufactured by Imhof & Mukle, which rival human orchestras in sweetness of tone and expression... All instruments must be sold, and easy terms will be accepted, subject to previous arrangements. Over 2,000 music rolls for different instruments will also be sold. Contracts can be made with experienced men for the taking care of the instruments."

Exactly what happened to all of the Imhof, Hupfeld, Weber, and other instruments in the Boecker stock is not precisely clear. It is known that a half dozen Hupfeld Phonoliszt Violina violin-playing machines, several large Imhof orchestrions, and a few other instruments found their way into the Mangels Museum at Coney Island. In the 1950's these were sold to Horn's Cars of Yesterday (now Bellm's Cars and Music of Yesterday) in Sarasota, Florida. Some of these have been retained for restoration by the museum; others have been dispersed to various other collections. The repair business of the Boecker firm went to the late George Messig of Brooklyn, New York – who informed the author in 1964 that "I still have quite a few parts from the Boecker stock – including some pipe chests from some of the huge Imhof & Mukle orchestrions."

What happened to Ernst Boecker? He headed west. Followed by several boxcars full of Imhof & Mukle orchestrions, he moved to Huntington Park, California, and settled there. During the 1920's many of these instruments were operated by him or by his successors in various locations in the Los Angeles area. About 1950 what remained of the Boecker hoard was sold to the Pacific Piano Company of North Hollywood. Since that time the orchestrions, all of which needed restoration due to their age and use, have found new homes. Several from this hoard have passed through the author's hands.

### Imhof & Mukle Miscellany

The fund of knowledge concerning Imhof & Mukle instruments is not complete, and the author would welcome correspondence with anyone with information concerning models not depicted here.

Rolls for the orchestrions were of several different types. Catalogues indicate that the same roll was used for the following styles: Reclame, Badenia, Patriarch, Herold, Tribut, Corso, and Galant. Several hundred different rolls were available, including a number of xylophone solo rolls. Most of the repertoire was standard fare (an extensive selection of operas, symphonies, marches, and traditional songs), but a number of now-forgotten but then-important tunes were available. Samples: "The Yiddish Rag," "I've Been Out with Charlie Brown," "I Do Like to be Beside the Seaside," and the not-quite-forgotten melody, "The Teddy Bears' Picnic."

Another catalogue indicates that the following instruments used the same roll: Lucia, Tell, Lohengrin, Venus, Lucretia, and Valkyrie (Walküre). While most of the titles were of overtures (e.g., William Tell, Mignon, Zampa, Martha, Light Cavalry, Semiramide, Tannhauser, and Oberon), waltzes (e.g., Estudiantina, Blue Danube), some others caught the author's eye when reading over the list of hundreds of rolls: "Pass Dat Possum," "The Longest Way Round is the Sweetest Way Home," and "My Name Is Morgan, But It Ain't J.P.!"

Imhof & Mukle roll-operated orchestrions were offered in walnut and oak woods. Most were constructed of the latter. Surviving specimens indicate that many, if not most, sold by Boecker in the United States were painted white with gold trim.

Imhof & Mukle rolls were made in the United States by Boecker (who actively solicited this business by suggesting that customers send him lists of their favorite tunes), in Belgium by Eugene DeRoy's Symphonia Piano Roll Co., in England by the Imhof outlet there or by an agent of that outlet, and by the Imhof firm itself in Vöhrenbach.

When reading a "stop list" of Imhof & Mukle, the reader is reminded that what appears to be, for instance, many ranks of pipes such as "violin, viola, and cello," may actually represent one rank of pipes – in this case, a rank of violin pipes extending from the treble ("violin") range down into the bass ("cello") range. The ambiguous description of pipes was practiced by nearly all orchestrion makers. The same practice is followed in the pipe organ industry. Dozens of different tabs or knobs on the console may, in actuality, represent just a dozen or so ranks of pipes. Thus a large rank of flute pipes may be described as providing piccolo, flute, bass, sub-bass, and other effects.

A solicitation made by Ernst Boecker about 1913, a letter describing the Admiral Orchestrion, comes close to indicating what is in that instrument – and shows the different effects controlled by registers:

Mammoth All-Chromatic Wonder Piano-Orchestra
–Admiral–

Electro-pneumatic action. Admiral No. II is especially adapted for large concerts and ballrooms and takes the place of a full orchestra. It renders any kind of musical selection.

Tonal Dispositions

Cross-stringed inverted grand piano
(for forte, fortissimo, and piano effects)
Mandolin and harp effects
Contra-bass register
Bass open register
Octave bass register (tin metal pipes)
Tenor bassoon or bass saxophone register
Bass bassoon register
Violin register (controls 3 ranks)
Vienna flute register
Double flute (doppelflute) register
Piccolo and octave flute register
Cello register especially for solos
Saxophone register especially for solos
Bassoon register for solos
(in expression box for triple-tonguing effects)
Xylophone register especially for solos
(as NO living artist can play!)
Chimes (steel bars) register especially for solos
Chinese cymbal
Bass drum
Kettle drum (tympani)
Military snare drum
Reroll (automatic)

The same name (Tell and Dinorah are examples) was often used for instruments in cases of greatly differing appearances. In most, but not all, instances the interior specifications were the same.

An expense voucher, now in the Boecker papers in the author's possession, shows that work was done for a customer who paid the following: railroad fare $2.20; supper 75c; carfare 20c; 3 hours of work on Thursday $4.50; railroad fare $2.20; taxi fare 75c. Another customer, a Mr. Ehlers, was charged $96 for 6 rolls, $3.50 for a day's meals, 60c each for 74 new small bellows, and 15 hours worth of labor for $22.50.

Today Imhof & Mukle orchestrions are fairly rare. Most which survive can trace their origin to the Boecker stock or to sales from the London showroom. Few have been located outside of England and the United States. When properly and carefully restored an Imhof & Mukle orchestrion is a very fine musical instrument. The tone is soft and sweet, not at all loud, and may be said to play with "an artistic touch and a fullness and sweetness of tone" – as the advertisements of long ago stated.

———————

## IMHOF & MUKLE

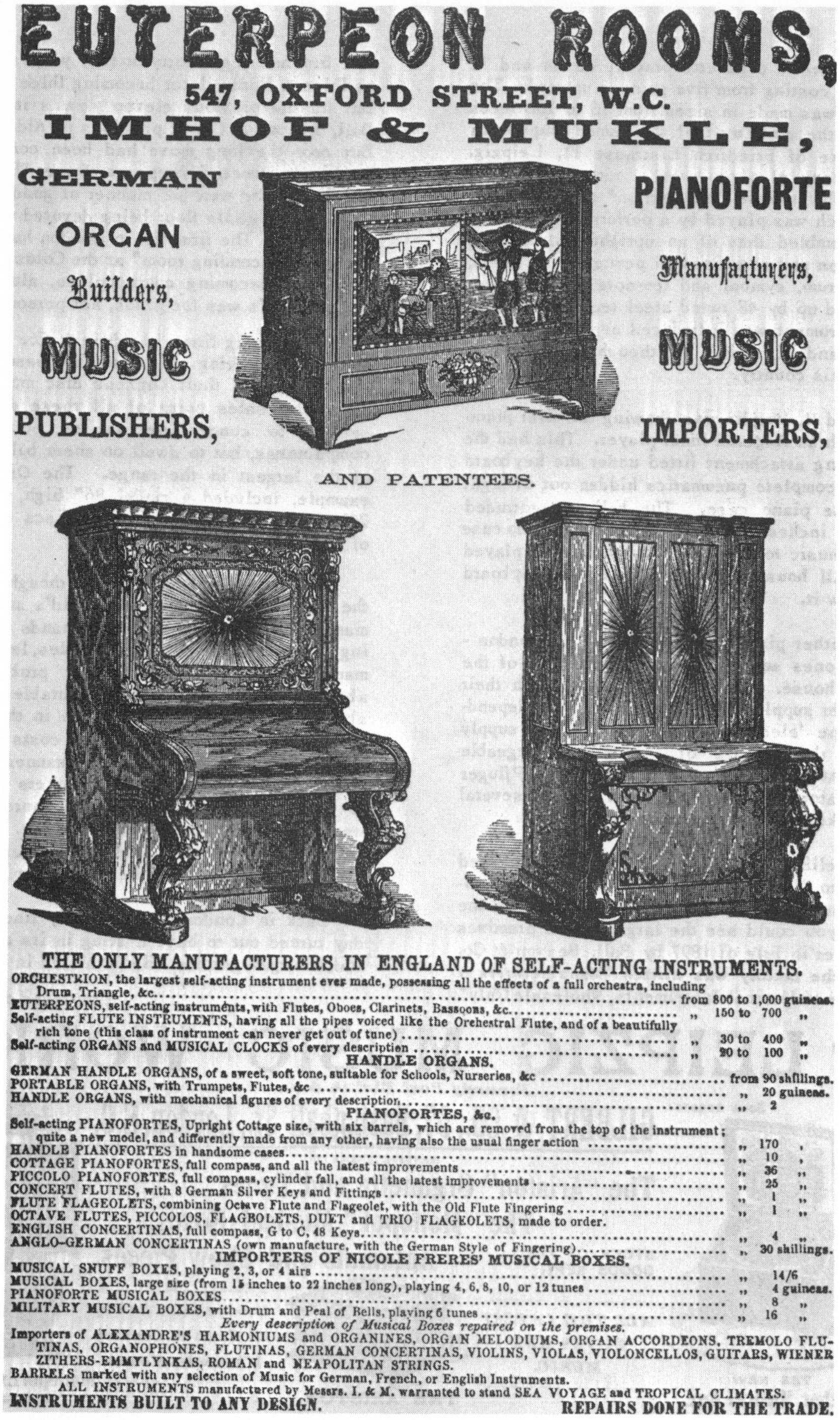
EUTERPEON ROOMS,
547, OXFORD STREET, W.C.
IMHOF & MUKLE,
GERMAN
ORGAN
Builders,
MUSIC
PUBLISHERS,
PIANOFORTE
Manufacturers,
MUSIC
IMPORTERS,
AND PATENTEES.
THE ONLY MANUFACTURERS IN ENGLAND OF SELF-ACTING INSTRUMENTS.
ORCHESTRION, the largest self-acting instrument ever made, possessing all the effects of a full orchestra, including Drum, Triangle, &c. ........ from 800 to 1,000 guineas.
EUTERPEONS, self-acting instruments, with Flutes, Oboes, Clarinets, Bassoons, &c. ........ " 150 to 700 "
Self-acting FLUTE INSTRUMENTS, having all the pipes voiced like the Orchestral Flute, and of a beautifully rich tone (this class of instrument can never get out of tune) ........ " 30 to 400 "
Self-acting ORGANS and MUSICAL CLOCKS of every description ........ " 20 to 100 "
HANDLE ORGANS.
GERMAN HANDLE ORGANS, of a sweet, soft tone, suitable for Schools, Nurseries, &c ........ from 90 shillings.
PORTABLE ORGANS, with Trumpets, Flutes, &c ........ " 20 guineas.
HANDLE ORGANS, with mechanical figures of every description ........ " 2
PIANOFORTES, &c.
Self-acting PIANOFORTES, Upright Cottage size, with six barrels, which are removed from the top of the instrument; quite a new model, and differently made from any other, having also the usual finger action ........ " 170 ,
HANDLE PIANOFORTES in handsome cases ........ " 10 ,
COTTAGE PIANOFORTES, full compass, and all the latest improvements ........ " 36 "
PICCOLO PIANOFORTES, full compass, cylinder fall, and all the latest improvements ........ " 25 "
CONCERT FLUTES, with 8 German Silver Keys and Fittings ........ " 1 "
FLUTE FLAGEOLETS, combining Octave Flute and Flageolet, with the Old Flute Fingering ........ " 1 "
OCTAVE FLUTES, PICCOLOS, FLAGEOLETS, DUET and TRIO FLAGEOLETS, made to order.
ENGLISH CONCERTINAS, full compass, G to C, 48 Keys ........ " 4 "
ANGLO-GERMAN CONCERTINAS (own manufacture, with the German Style of Fingering) ........ " 30 shillings.
IMPORTERS OF NICOLE FRERES' MUSICAL BOXES.
MUSICAL SNUFF BOXES, playing 2, 3, or 4 airs ........ " 14/6
MUSICAL BOXES, large size (from 15 inches to 22 inches long), playing 4, 6, 8, 10, or 12 tunes ........ " 4 guineas.
PIANOFORTE MUSICAL BOXES ........ " 8 "
MILITARY MUSICAL BOXES, with Drum and Peal of Bells, playing 6 tunes ........ " 16 "
Every description of Musical Boxes repaired on the premises.
Importers of ALEXANDRE'S HARMONIUMS and ORGANINES, ORGAN MELODIUMS, ORGAN ACCORDEONS, TREMOLO FLUTINAS, ORGANOPHONES, FLUTINAS, GERMAN CONCERTINAS, VIOLINS, VIOLAS, VIOLONCELLOS, GUITARS, WIENER ZITHERS-EMMYLYNKAS, ROMAN and NEAPOLITAN STRINGS.
BARRELS marked with any selection of Music for German, French, or English Instruments.
ALL INSTRUMENTS manufactured by Messrs. I. & M. warranted to stand SEA VOYAGE and TROPICAL CLIMATES.
INSTRUMENTS BUILT TO ANY DESIGN.
REPAIRS DONE FOR THE TRADE.

IMHOF & MUKLE

Imhof & Mukle barrel orchestrion.

Above: Late 19th century advertisement for Imhof & Mukle's London showrooms. Among the items offered are orchestrions (from 800 to 1000 guineas [1 guinea = about $5 U.S. funds at the time]), euterpeons ("self-acting instruments with flutes, oboes, clarinets, bassoons, etc."), and many other types of pianos, organs, and related instruments. Note that cylinder music boxes by Nicole Frères are offered also.

—————————

Nomenclature note: Certain Imhof & Mukle orchestrion specifications are not consistent with pipe terminology. "Violin bass" and "bourdon," two entirely different types of pipes (bourdons are bass flutes), are used synonymously in certain listings – the description of the Admiral orchestrion of the 1920's, for example.

Two early Imhof & Mukle orchestrions of the barrel type.

LEOPOLD MUKLE.
ORCHESTRIONS
For Yachts and Steamship Saloons.
Worked by compressed air, entirely without weights.
Factory, Furtwangen, Baden, superintended by Joseph Mukle.
All particulars may be obtained from
92, Albany St., Regent's Pk.
LONDON, N.W.
ORCHESTRION

Leopold Mukle established his own London showrooms in the 1890's and offered instruments made in Furtwangen, Germany. The model shown above features an anemometer-type compressed air drive. Leopold was formerly with I.&M.'s London store.

The Imhof & Mukle factory in Vöhrenbach, Germany. This photograph, taken about 1910, shows firemen climbing ladders to the roof. Perhaps this was a practice exercise, for several building inhabitants are peering unconcernedly from the windows.

This building still stands in Vöhrenbach today and, save for the IMHOF & MUKLE lettering, is just about the same as it was when this picture was taken.

Above: Large built-in orchestrion installation made in Vöhrenbach and installed in the Jockey Club in New York City. The above illustration is furnished from a large watercolor drawing, an original prospectus for the instrument, currently owned by Albert Imhof.

Right: A 19th century Imhof & Mukle orchestrion powered by an external engine. This orchestrion is of the barrel-operated type.

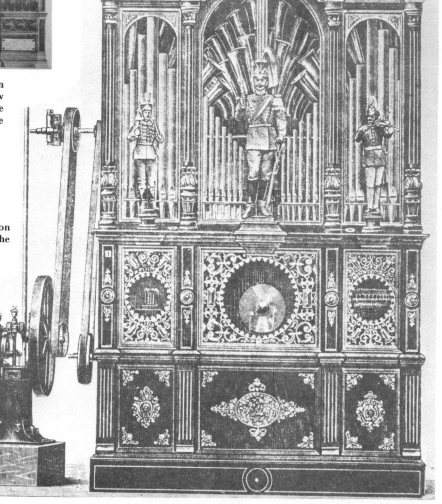

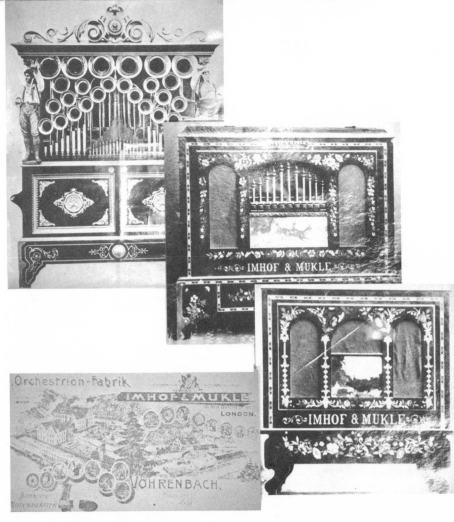

Imhof & Mukle manufactured portable hand-cranked barrel organs (two instruments shown at lower right), small military band organs (such as the one with brass trumpets shown at the right), and larger pavilion and concert band organs — such as the ornate instrument shown at the top of this page.

Although Imhof & Mukle manufactured a limited number of loudly-voiced organs, the main interest of the firm was orchestrion making. Note the "Orchestrion-Fabrik" (orchestrion factory) designation on the company's letterhead as shown at the bottom of this page.

Daniel Imhof, founder of the orchestrion firm. Daniel I was the grandfather of Albert Imhof (who provided much of the information given in this section).

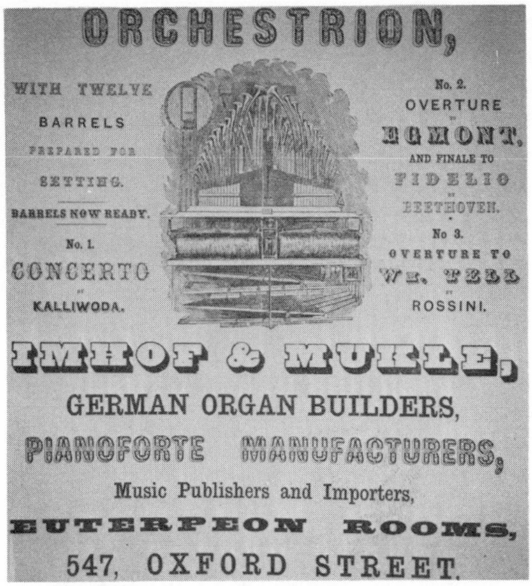


This Imhof & Mukle poster of the 1860's illustrates a barrel organ, a typical Imhof product of the time. From the London showroom hundreds of instruments ranging from barrel pianos to huge organs and orchestrions were sold. A favorite of the gentry, many of these were installed in country halls and mansions.

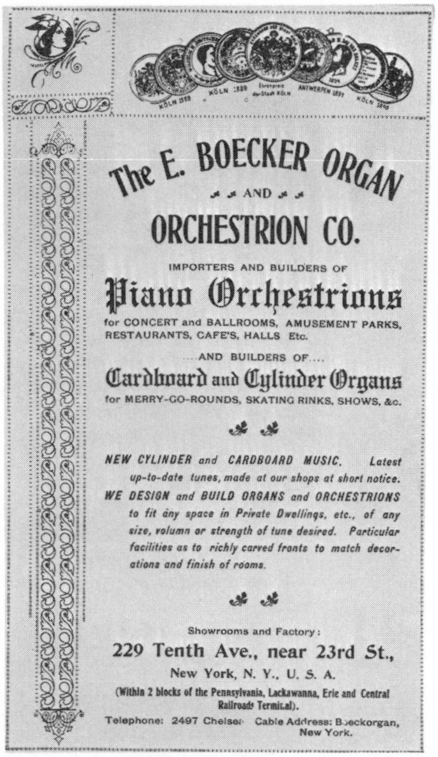

—Cornet Orchestrion—

Boecker noted: This instrument represents a string and brass band. It contains a piano, violin pipes, cornets (in view), chimes, snare drum, bass drum, and cymbal. Books of music of any length desired are priced from $20 up. The mechanisms are enclosed in a finely ebonized and elegantly gilded ornamental case.

---

(No.1)
—Corrector 3—

(No.2)
—Commandant 1—

(No.3)
—Lord 1—

(No.4)
—Reclame—

(No.5)
—Tribute—

(No.6)
—Herold—

(No.7)
—Zanetta—

Note: Imhof was particularly fond of certain names, "Dinorah" being a prime example, and used the same designation for several different instruments over a period of years.

(No.8)
—Badenia 1—

—Imhof & Mukle Orchestrions—

(No.1): Corrector 3, piano with mandolin and xylophone; (No.2): Commandant 1, "The Commandant 1 reproduces the playing of a violin with piano accompaniment." With mandolin attachment; (No.3): Lord 1, with piano, mandolin, xylophone, violin pipes, orchestra bells, bass drum, and cymbal. Plays violin solos. 275 cm. high; (No.4): Reclame, with piano, orchestra bells, bass and snare drums, cymbals. 258 cm. high; (No.5): Tribute, with piano, violin and cornet pipes, xylophone, orchestra bells, bass and snare drums, cymbal. 282 cm. high; (No.6): Herold, with piano, violin pipes, orchestra bells, bass and snare drums, cymbal. 273 cm. high. Made in several case designs, the most popular of which is shown here; (No.7): Zanetta, with piano, violin and flute pipes including bass ranges, orchestra bells, bass and snare drums, tympani effect, and cymbal. 300 cm. high; (8): This Imhof & Mukle orchestrion features an interesting broken arch top to its case and a motion picture effect of a siren-girl on a fountain rock; (9): An Imhof & Mukle orchestrion with a colorful art glass front. The interior contains a piano, violin pipes, xylophone, drums, and other effects.

(No.9)

—Corrector 2—
Piano, mandolin, and xylophone. The xylophone bars are arranged symmetrically (with the longest near the center) and are visible at the top.

—Corrector 4—
Piano, mandolin, and xylophone. The xylophone is mounted horizontally and is visible at the top.

—Corrector 5—
A basic keyboard "nickelodeon" piano; one of the smallest instruments in the Imhof line. Note the large double front doors to permit access to the roll system.

—Corrector 1—
Piano, mandolin, and xylophone (mounted vertically at the top). The large roll door permits easy changing of rolls. Fortunately for posterity, most Imhof instruments were not of the keyboard styles but were large classic orchestrions! Early Imhof advertising reveals that keyboard styles such as the Corrector and Commandant series were not "pushed." The emphasis was on the larger and more expensive models without keyboards.

The best proof of the durability of the Music Rolls!

"The best proof of the durability of the music rolls!" — so reads the caption of this Imhof & Mukle advertisement. Made on heavy manila paper stock the rolls were indeed strong.

Commandant 2 — Measuring about 7½' high, this Imhof orchestrion contains piano, mandolin, pipes, and drum and trap effects. The spiral columns and the lavish use of beveled mirrors make this a very elegant model.

—Dinorah—

—Venus—

—Patriarch—
(or Hercules)

—Badenia—

Dinorah: "This instrument contains a first class overstrung upright piano, violin and flute and clarinet pipes, bass and snare drums, cymbal, and orchestra bells. Height: 9'9", width 6'6", depth 3'3". $2150. Music rolls: $22.50 each."

Venus: "A very large orchestrion for concert and ballrooms. It contains a first class grand piano, double violins in an expression chamber, violin, viola, and cello pipes, flute and piccolo pipes, bassoons and trumpets, orchestra bells, snare drum, bass drum, and cymbal. The instrument plays with a surprising volume of tone, rising from the finest pianissimo to the grandest fortissimo, producing surprising variations. Equal to an orchestra of 24 pieces. Height: 11'10", width: 8'9", depth: 3'5". $3150. Music rolls: $26 each."

"Rolls have from 3 to 7 pieces in each roll, depending upon the length of each piece, and will play one or all pieces without interruption, if desired. Rerolls automatically after playing last piece, so instrument will play any number of hours without repetition."

Patriarch (or Hercules, as it was called later): "In the Patriarch is found a first class piano, mandolin, violin pipes (in a case with swell shutters), flutes, xylophone, orchestra bells, bass and snare drums, and Chinese cymbal. Featured are xylophone solos. The instrument has rolls that are about 90 meters long so that a complete program can be presented without interruption. Height: 271 cm.; width: 190 cm.; depth: 108 cm." The front depicts a motion picture effect of an Alpine scene with rushing waterfall.

Badenia: "An electric orchestrion of such extraordinary construction that it is especially recommended for concert and dance halls. The music is very harmonious and has artistic expression. The Badenia contains a choice piano, violin pipes (in an expression cabinet), violin and cello pipes, orchestra bells, bass and snare drums, and a Chinese cymbal. The scene on the front features a choice of a fountain, a waterfall, or a volcano in eruption — as the buyer chooses. Height: 275 cm.; width 170 cm.; depth 105 cm. The design and voicing of the instrument may be modified as desired."

This beautiful Imhof & Mukle orchestrion, now on display at Bellm's Cars and Music of Yesterday Museum in Sarasota, Florida, has a wonder light and three motion picture scenes! Instrumentation consists of piano, xylophone, bells, and percussion effects.

This Imhof orchestrion features a piano, a rank of violin pipes, and various percussion effects.

—Corso— The Corso features a moving scene with a large Niagara-like waterfall. Popular about 1908.

—Lucia—

Above and right: two designs of the Lucia orchestrion. Note the beautiful art glass design which features a sailing ship.

The Boecker description of the type at the right is as follows: This instrument contains a first class upright piano, a set of very soft double violin pipes in an expression chamber, other violin and cello pipes, orchestra bells, bass and snare drums, tympani, and cymbals. Produces by registers no less than 8 different effects. The instrument plays with mandolin accompaniment, the most difficult operas or, if desired, any new and up-to-date music, in such an artistic way as to surpass anything ever heard before. 10'7" high, 5'11" wide, 3'3" deep. $1800. Rolls: $20 each. Especially adapted for high class restaurants, halls, concert rooms, dining rooms — in fact, everywhere where high class music equal to an orchestra of about 15 musicians is desired. The program of music is unlimited.

View of some of the symmetrically-arranged pipes in an early Imhof & Mukle orchestrion presently on view at the British Piano Museum (High Street; Brentford, Middlesex). This instrument uses a manila paper roll. Most barrel-operated early Imhof orchestrions had the pipes arranged symmetrically; later roll-operated ones had pipes in chromatic order. The British Piano Museum instrument is a transitional orchestrion with symmetrical pipes but with roll operation. Imhof & Mukle orchestrions were once very popular in England, and many were sold from the Oxford Street showroom in London. As of this writing the British Piano Museum has two examples of these melodious instruments.

—Lucia—

Roll mechanism from the Imhof & Mukle orchestrion in the British Piano Museum. The rolls are long (nearly 100 meters in length in some instances) and play slowly — permitting a lengthy musical program. The rolls are "read" by a key frame, much in the manner of a standard folding cardboard book organ. Each roll is on a wooden spool which slides in and out at the left. The roll shown is marked "Medley with American Airs."

—Lohengrin— One of at least two case designs of this instrument. With piano, violin and cello pipes, orchestra bells, bass and snare drums, and cymbal. 290 cm. high by 166 cm. wide by 90 cm. deep. The front is a beautiful art glass scene as shown above.

Orchestrion for Private Residences. Boecker noted: The above is one of our specially designed orchestrions for a private residence on upper 5th Ave.

—Venus—

With piano, mandolin, xylophone, several ranks of violin and flute pipes, orchestra bells, bass and tenor drums, tympani, and cymbal. 320 cm. high by 270 cm. wide by 134 cm. deep. "The xylophone plays solos in imitation of a master xylophonist." A popular model, the Venus was made in several case style variations. The attractive cabinet features an electrified statue in a mirrored niche, lamps at the upper left and right corners of the case, and a rotating wonder light.

—Dinorah—

With piano, pipes representing violin, flute, piccolo, cello, and clarinet, bass and tenor drums, cymbal, and orchestra bells. 300 cm. high by 200 cm. wide by 100 cm. deep. In attractive cabinet with cloth-backed ornate wooden latticework. One of at least three Dinorah case style variations.

—Lucretia—

Piano, pipes representing violin, viola, and violoncello, an attachment for mandolin effect, orchestra bells, snare drum (tenor drum), bass drum, cymbal, tympani, and xylophone. 9'9" high, 7' wide, 37" deep. Sold for $2950 in 1907. Music rolls were $26 each.

—Lohengrin—

Piano, mandolin, xylophone, drums and traps, and ranks of pipes for violin (in expression chamber), flute (in expression chamber), cello, fagott, and saxophone. About 10'9" high.

—Tell—

Violin-Solo Mandolin Piano Orchestrion. With piano, mandolin, pipes for violin, cello, and flute, orchestra bells, bass and snare drums, and cymbal. The violin pipes are housed in a special expression chamber. When the violin pipes play the piano may be dampened to near silence, permitting violin solos.

—Admiral I—

RIGHT: Admiral orchestrion, Style I. One of the largest Imhof styles made. 385 cm. high, 355 cm. wide, and 155 cm. deep. Weight: 3600 pounds. With piano, mandolin, contra bass, bass, octave bass, tenor bassoon, 2 ranks of violins, flute, piccolo, cello, and other effects. The Admiral orchestrions used a roll measuring about 11¾" wide with 84 keys.

—Tell—

Piano, pipes for violin, viola, cello, flute, piccolo, bassoon, trumpet, and baritone; orchestra bells, bass and snare drums, tympani effect, cymbal. 11'4" high, 8'9" wide, 5' deep.

—Trumpeter of Sackingen—

Piano, violin and flute pipes, plus a rank of trumpet pipes. "The figure of the trumpeter is life size, elegantly costumed, and raises and lowers his arm and plays the most difficult trumpet solos beautifully." 9' high, 6'10" wide, 3'3" deep.

VALKYRIE ORCHESTRION

—Valkyrie—

The Valkyrie (or "Walküre" – in German) model was billed as "The Grandest Instrument Ever Produced." Two different case designs are shown above and left. The original Boecker catalogue description for the type at left read: 12'10" high, 10'10" wide, 5'6" deep. Suitable for very large public or private ballrooms and concert rooms. Case in any wood or finish; art nouveau style. The instrument is the most wonderful anywhere in the world. It plays the most difficult operas and other music in a way that far surpasses an orchestra of 40 musicians! It plays with a force, a precision, a brilliancy of execution and with a full tone beginning with the softest and sweetest pianissimo and swelling to the grandest fortissimo. The music is exquisitely sweet and the orchestrion is such a success that it cannot be described: it must be heard. Valkyrie contains a piano, 50 violin pipes, 18 double violins, 25 stopped violins, 22 double viola, 19 violoncellos, 12 violin bass, 38 double piccolos, 43 Vienna flutes, 22 flutes, 12 double bass, 18 clarinets, 18 trumpets, and 18 baritones. In addition there are suitable drum and trap effects. The entire system is operated with seven automatic registers producing surprising variations. This is a winner as crowds will flock for miles to hear the concerts given by this orchestrion. Rolls have from 3 to 7 pieces. Music rolls: $28.00 each.

The Lord series of orchestrions, Styles 1, 2, and 3, all featured violin music. The 1 and 2 orchestrions were self-contained; the Lord 3 is unique with its Distant Echo cabinet.

—Lord 3 Orchestrion with Echo—

The Lord 3 orchestrion is unique in the annals of automatic musical instruments. It has an echo instrument — a smaller companion orchestrion located at a distance from the main instrument! Echo chambers are a standard feature of pipe organs, especially church organs, but this counterpart in an orchestrion is the only such instance known. The original catalogue description is given below. A number of these were produced, and several were sold in the United States by Boecker. Some had pleated curtains in place of the two long side mirrors in the echo instrument. The use of an electric, rather than a pneumatic, connection is rare also. The "violin string mechanism with vibrating arrangement" probably refers to a rank of violin pipes with a tremolo attachment.

Dimensions of main instrument: 330 cm. high by 235 cm wide by 130 cm deep. Echo orchestrion: 280 cm. high by 195 cm. wide by 90 cm. deep.

Unrivalled! A Great sensation!

## Lord 3

**Piano-Orchestrion with Distant Echo and Distant Violin-Solo.**

• • •

Unique of its kind and a novelty of the first grade!

The operation of the two instruments is carried out by means of electricity and the distant echo and at the same time the distant violin solo can be displaced any desired distance from the main work. The main work can also be employed alone, so that it can be used as Piano Orchestrion. But the instrument can also be so arranged that the two mechanisms play together and thus a larger orchestra is reproduced.

In order to obtain the main effect of the accessory mechanism, namely the distant echo, **the main works work so that, for example in a piece being played, when the main instrument is cut off, the accessory mechanism (echo mechanism) reproduces the echo.** The registering of the accessory instrument is regulated from the main work. After the repetition by the distant echo, the accessory instrument is disengaged and the main instrument again plays.

With the distant violin solo is in this way a brillant and more effective result obtained in that in the accessory instrument a very realistic violin is arranged. In order to bring the distant violin solo into operation, the mechanism is so arranged that the piano accompaniment is performed on the main instrument whilst the accessory instrument is producing the violin solo. The effect is very deceiving. You can imagine that you are actually listening to a veritable violin.

By means of most artistic arrangement of the notes a great variation is obtainable with these two instruments. Distant echo and distant violin solo can be played in the same piece or the main instrument can be operated alone for a time and then the two instruments together or the main instrument can be played and in the distance the violinist accompanies.

The **Main instrument of the Lord 3** is composed as follows:

First class overstrung Piano, Mandoline, Double Violins (entirely enclosed in a crescendo box), Muted Violins, Flutes, Set of Bells, Big and little Drum, Real Chinese Cymbal.

**The Piano is provided with Forte and Piano Pedal and an extra pedal for Violin Solos.**

The **Distant Echo and Distant Violin Solo instrument** comprise the following:

Viola-Dulciana with Bourdon, Violin string mechanism with vibrating arrangement.

The whole is enclosed in a crescendo box and provided with Forte and Piano.

—Admiral II—

Billed as the "Mammoth All-Chromatic Wonder Piano-Orchestra," the Admiral II was the largest and most instrument-filled orchestrion in the Imhof line. Measurements are approximately 11'10" high by 14' wide by 5' deep. A specimen in the author's collection differs somewhat in the panel decorations from the one illustrated at the right, indicating that at least two case style variations were made. The 11¾" wide 84-key Imhof roll is arranged to play solos on the violin, cello, saxophone, bassoon, xylophone, and bells. A complete stoplist, under the title of "Tonal Dispositions," appears in the introduction to this Imhof section.

Existing records reveal that immense Imhof & Mukle orchestrions, including the Admiral II, were once in regular use in America, particularly in the New York City area and on the West Coast. As these spectacular instruments once caused a great deal of attention — indeed, they were the featured attractions of the places that owned them — some photographs must have been taken of the orchestrions in their original locations. The author would be pleased to correspond with anyone with such illustrations, either of Imhof or of any other kinds of instruments. Such "on location" pictures help to re-create the flavor of the era in which they were used.

—Galant—

—Corso (or Commandant)—

—Badenia 2—

Galant: (or "Gallant"). 285 cm. high by 245 cm. wide by 120 cm. deep. Piano, mandolin, violin and flute pipes, xylophone, bells, drums and traps. Rolls arranged for xylophone solo specialities. Note that the top gallery is similar to that used on the Tribute orchestrion also.

Corso or Commandant: Known variously as the Corso or the Commandant (both of which names were also used for other Imhof orchestrions — thus adding to the confusion!), this model measures 305 cm. high by 195 cm. wide by 113 cm. deep. It was advertised as "imitates perfectly the violin." A number of these were once sold in America.

Badenia 2: The Badenia 2 piano orchestrion featured xylophone and bell solo arrangements. Measurements are: 270 cm. high by 172 cm. wide by 107 cm. deep. As were other Imhof orchestrions, the Badenia 2 was made in several case style variations, including one with a wonder light on top and with side cabinets.

Dinorah: One of several Imhof instruments which bore this name over a period of years. The specimen illustrated at the right measures 275 cm. high by 162 cm. wide by 104 cm. deep. Instrumentation consists of piano, mandolin, violin pipes, xylophone, bells, and drum and trap effects. At each side of the case are two mechanical figures which appear to play the mandolin and guitar and move their heads and eyes. At the center is a motion picture effect.

—Dinorah—

**IMHOF & MUKLE**
**Instruments of the 1920's**
**(roll-operated)**

—Corrector 2—
Electric piano. "This instrument is first class and can be recommended. The music is artistically arranged."

—Corrector 3—
Electric piano with mandolin and xylophone. "The xylophone performs the most difficult solos. The mandolin only plays in suitable passages."

—Corrector 5—
Electric piano with mandolin and xylophone. Case design variation of Corrector 3.

—Corrector 6—
Electric piano. Case design variation of Corrector 2.

—Commandant 2—
Violin piano. "The Commandant reproduces the music of a real violin [via violin pipes — Ed.] with piano accompaniment. Absolutely accurate reproduction of the violin tones; solos can be played in an artistic and imposing manner."

—Tribut—
"Xylophone Mandolin Piano Orchestrion. This unrivalled instrument comprises: first class piano, violin pipes, xylophone, set of bells, drums and traps. The crescendo effect gives the instrument a fine gradation of tone." 2.8 meters high by 1.65 meters wide by 1.05 meters deep.

**Imhof & Mukle**
**Paper-roll-operated**
**instruments**

On this page are shown the instruments offered for sale in the very last Imhof & Mukle catalogue, an offering of eight different models made during the 1920's. Unlike their predecessors, these instruments are played with thin paper rolls and have standard vacuum-type piano tracker bars.

The change from heavy manila paper rolls to thin paper rolls began about 1915. For a number of years instruments of both types were made. By the early 1920's the thin paper rolls became standard.

Most Imhof & Mukle instruments known today are of the earlier type. Thin paper roll instruments are very rare.

Note that the names such as "Corrector," "Commandant," "Tribut," etc. are the same as used for different instruments in earlier years.

—Dinorah—
"Orchestrion for Violin Solos." Contains: piano, mandolin, double violin [pipe] rank, solo violin register, clarinet pipes, flutes, cello bass pipes, bells, drums and traps. 3 meters high by 2.05 meters wide by 1.05 meters deep.

—Admiral—
"Mandolin Piano Orchestrion for Concerts." Built for concert and dance hall purposes. Contains: piano, mandolin, cello bass pipes, cello pipes, violin solo register, double violin rank (bourdon pipes), tin-octave (piccolo), clarinet pipes, flutes, bells, drums and traps. With large swell or expression shutter in the top of the case.

Height: 3.4 meters. Width: 3.25 meters. Depth: 1.45 meters.

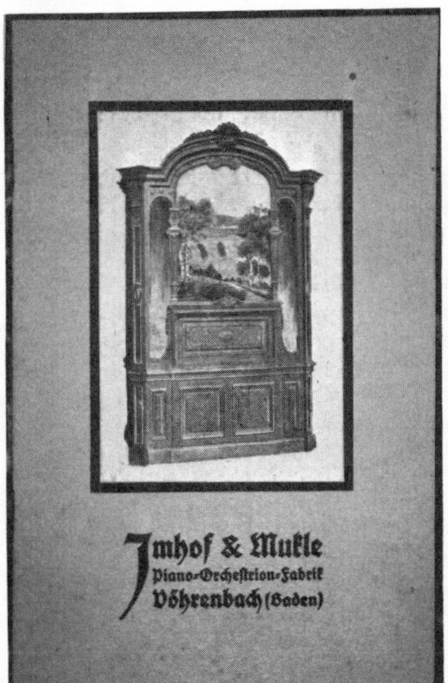


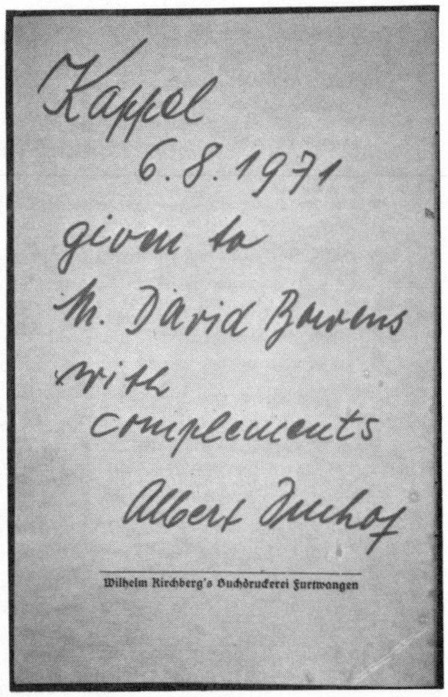


Cover and inscribed flyleaf of c.1910 Imhof & Mukle orchestrion catalogue given by Albert Imhof to Q. David Bowers on August 6, 1971.

## —A Visit with Albert Imhof—

During the course of gathering material for this book the editor made many trips to Germany, particularly to the Schwarzwald or Black Forest area, the location of Vöhrenbach, Freiburg, Waldkirch, and other communities active in the field of organ and orchestrion building years ago.

One trip, taken with the author's family and Claes O. Friberg in July and August of 1971, was particularly fruitful as it resulted in meeting with Albert Imhof, former co-owner of Imhof & Mukle.

After spending the evening of August 5th as house guests of Willy Rombach, Vöhrenbach industrialist and nephew of Albert Imhof, we journeyed for an hour or so to Kappel, a quaint Black Forest village. There we met Albert Imhof who resides in a large home there with his wife.

Albert Imhof was unaware of the worldwide resurgence of interest in the history of automatic musical instruments. During the past ten or twenty years he had written to the Italian government to inquire concerning the whereabouts of an Imhof & Mukle orchestrion sold to a palace in that country years ago, to several other former customers of the firm, and to several persons in England who had been associated with Imhof & Mukle in the early days. With one or two exceptions these letters received no replies.

Thus it was with curiosity at first, and then with enthusiasm, that we were greeted on the morning of August 6th. The next several hours were spent poring through a large scrapbook, old Imhof & Mukle catalogues (one of which was presented to the author), and other data — and talking of the days of many years ago.

Much of the information was already known as the editor had previously acquired the pictorial archives of Ernst Boecker, New York City distributor for Imhof. This was fortuitous as we had many unanswered questions which resulted from earlier study of Imhof data. We asked Albert Imhof about some of the things that were puzzling us:

Question: Have you had contact with other collectors or historians in the automatic musical instrument field? Are you aware of the great interest today in the products of the former Imhof & Mukle firm and of old-time instruments in general?

Albert Imhof: No, I was not aware that such a great interest existed. There has been some interest in the local papers and some stories about Black Forest clockmakers and organ builders have appeared from time to time. Also there have been some articles about the Welte Mignon piano made in Freiburg. Here is a Decca record made in England of an Imhof orchestrion. This orchestrion was sold in 1879 to the Tower Ballroom in Blackpool, England, and is still playing there, although it has been repaired in modern times and has been converted to play another type of roll.

Question: Do you recall the Ernst Boecker firm?

Albert Imhof: Yes, they sold a lot of instruments in America for us. However, when they went bankrupt in 1914 they owed us a great deal of money, and the situation was a severe blow to our finances here at the factory in Germany. Incidentally, one of the most famous of all Imhof & Mukle orchestrions was the huge instrument that we made especially for the Jockey Club in New York City.

Question: Who were your other distributors?

Albert Imhof: Our largest outlet was the Imhof & Mukle branch in London. This was managed by Geoffrey Imhof for many years. This firm, which still trades today under the name of Imhof's, sold our organs, orchestrions, and other instruments. I spent quite a bit of time there myself, as did other members of my family. The London branch was a general musical showroom and sold phonographs, music boxes, and other musical merchandise in addition to instruments of our own manufacture. We sold many Imhof & Mukle orchestrions and organs to large residences and country homes in England. They were very popular. Another very active agent was P.J. Beckx of Tegelen, Holland. The last orchestrion that Imhof & Mukle made, a huge roll-operated instrument with many pipes and orchestral effects, was shipped to Beckx in Holland. I wonder if it still exists. Imhof & Mukle orchestrions were very popular in Holland as the people there really enjoyed the music of the instruments. Other Imhof & Mukle orchestrions were sold around the world by agents in leading cities.

Question: Do you know of any large orchestrions, Imhof & Mukle or otherwise, that survive in their original locations in Europe today?

Albert Imhof: Near Waldkirch there is a Weber orchestrion with moving figures. It is in a hotel in Bleibach, although I heard that it was sold to another hotel in a nearby town recently. In Holland there is a large Hupfeld orchestrion in 's Hertogenbosch, or at least there used to be several years ago. [Editor's note: the Weber orchestrion is the one located at the Guesthouse of the Sun and is pictured in the Weber section of this book; the Hupfeld in Holland was a Pan Orchestra and was acquired several years ago by the late Eugene DeRoy — the instrument is now in America.] There aren't any orchestrions in use in any of the Black Forest towns anymore. There is a museum of clocks and some musical instruments at Triberg, as you probably know.

Question: Did you visit the factories of Weber, Bruder, and others in Waldkirch or Welte in Freiburg? [All of which are located comparatively close to Vöhrenbach — Ed.]:

Albert Imhof: No, these firms were competitors so I never went there. All of the factories kept to themselves as the business was very competitive at the time. I know nothing about Weber, for instance, or what they did.

Question: Welte, for instance, used some of the Waldkirch firms as a source for pipes and components. It was usual to order supplies from outside firms, sometimes even from competitors. Did Imhof & Mukle do this?

Albert Imhof: We made nearly all of our components right in Vöhrenbach. We did buy wooden pipes from the firm of Schoenstein in Villingen and we bought metal pipes from another supplier — whose name I don't recall. We purchased high grade pianos from Irmler in Leipzig and Lipp in Stuttgart. These were used in our piano orchestrions. The other parts were made by us.

Question: Many of the Imhof & Mukle cases are quite artistic. Who designed them? Did you make your own cases or did you buy them elsewhere?

Albert Imhof: No one in particular designed the orchestrion cases; we all played a part. There were no formal designs, we just built them. The cases were made in our own factory. The lumber mill that supplied our seasoned wood still stands in Vöhrenbach.

Question: Who arranged the music for the rolls? How many of the thick manila paper rolls could you cut at once? When did you start making thin paper roll instruments?

Albert Imhof: There were many different music arrangers in the early years. Later, I was one of two arrangers who made orchestrion rolls. The thick manila paper rolls were produced two at a time on the perforator. When the thin paper rolls were introduced these new rolls were made five at a time. The new style of paper rolls came into being about 1915.

Question: The very late Admiral orchestrion, the type that used thin paper rolls, looks quite a bit like the Popper & Company "Gladiator" orchestrion of the 1920's. Was there any connection between your firm and Popper?

Albert Imhof: No, there was no connection at all. I am not familar with the Popper "Gladiator" orchestrion. However, I do know that one of our very large orchestrions was sold to replace a large Popper orchestrion owned by a restaurant in The Hague, Holland. When we installed the Imhof & Mukle orchestrion they gave me a postcard of the Popper orchestrion which they used formerly. [Ed. note: The postcard depicts a Popper & Co. "Goliath" orchestrion in a special case built with a facade similar to a large dance hall organ — a most unusual design for a Popper instrument!]

Question: Do you have any records of the quantities made of the different Imhof & Mukle orchestrions? How many, for instance, were made of the Valkyrie, Lord 3 with Echo, and the huge Admiral II instruments?

Albert Imhof: No such records are in existence. I can tell you, however, that the Valkyrie [Walküre] was one of our most popular models among the large orchestrions. Only five or six were ever made of the Lord 3 with Echo and only about 6 or 7 of the Admiral II orchestrions were produced. When we completed an orchestrion it was a great event. We would assemble the instrument in the street outside of the factory doors. There it would be photographed. In fact, most of our catalogue pictures were taken in this way. Then the townspeople would gather around and hear a concert played on the orchestrion before it was dismantled and shipped away. We were very proud of these orchestrions and they played beautiful music.

Following our question and answer session we looked through Mr. Imhof's collection of memorabilia. The illustrations of the thin paper roll instruments of the 1920's shown here were borrowed from Mr. Imhof, as were several of the other illustrations. Since our visit we have received a number of newspaper clippings from Mr. Imhof. From various Black Forest papers, these stories indicate that the rich musical history of the area — a tradition of making musical clocks, barrel organs, orchestrions, fairground organs, and other instruments — is appreciated by the local citizens. However, it is lamented that fewer such instruments remain in the Black Forest than in other places!

—————————

Right: This photograph, taken in the Imhof & Mukle factory in the late 1920's, shows the very last Imhof orchestrion to be shipped. Sent to Beckx in Holland, the instrument was installed in a large restaurant in that country.

Note that the instrument uses a thin paper roll of the type used on most Imhof & Mukle instruments after about 1915.

Lower right: An early price list of Imhof & Mukle orchestrions offers eleven different styles. These instruments are of the type with the pipes arranged symmetrically behind a clear glass front, instruments similar in appearance to those made by Welte, Bruder, and others during the late 19th century.

Imhof & Mukle's period of activity extended from the firm's founding in 1874 to the late 1920's, a span of over a half century. During that time Imhof & Mukle products achieved a worldwide fame.

—Ramona—
Popular in the early 1920's was the Ramona, a keyboard instrument which was described as "a violin and piano combination; uses 88-note artist-played rolls." Many of these were sold in Belgium, Holland, and Germany.

Claes O. Friberg (left), Albert Imhof, Mary Bowers, Q. David Bowers, and in the foreground, Wynn Bowers, on the steps of the Albert Imhof home during a visit there on August 6, 1971.

Credit note: The editor is indebted to Mr. Albert Imhof, former co-owner of Imhof & Mukle, Mr. Willy Rombach, and Herr Wolf (Burgermeister of Vöhrenbach, Germany) for making available historical information, illustrations, and other data that might have been otherwise lost to history.

The firm of Imhof & Mukle and its history is a matter of civil pride in Vöhrenbach. In today's fast-paced world the events of yesteryear are all too quickly forgotten. Not so with Vöhrenbach. The town, essentially unchanged in appearance since the Imhof & Mukle days, is aware of its history and is proud of it.

Imhof & Mukle Orchestrions — Circa 1895

An Imhof & Mukle price list offered instruments which used perforated rolls made from thin brass sheets. "These instruments are much better as you can keep a dozen pieces of music in the space formerly occupied by just one barrel. Also, these metal music rolls are more durable than manila paper rolls because brass is not subject to temperature changes or tearing." Albert Imhof told the author that "the brass music rolls were not successful because they were too heavy [in comparison to the manila rolls]."

No. 1: 85 pipes; 2.8 meters high; 1.56 meters wide; 0.8 meters deep; Price: 2000 Mk.

No. 2: 159 pipes; 3 meters high; 2.28 meters wide; 0.87 meters deep; Price: 3500 Mk.

No. 3: 190 pipes; 2.77 meters high; 1.66 meters wide; 0.75 meters deep; Price: 3000 Mk.

No. 4: 240 pipes; 3.07 meters high; 1.93 meters wide; 0.96 meters deep; Price: 3700 Mk.

No. 5: 270 pipes; 3.2 meters high; 1.95 meters wide; 1.0 meters deep; Price: 4500 Mk.

No. 6: 360 pipes; 3.4 meters high; 2.25 meters wide; 1.4 meters deep; Price: 5500 Mk.

No. 7: 396 pipes; 3.72 meters high; 2.71 meters wide; 1.42 meters deep; Price: 6400 Mk.

No. 8: 420 pipes; 4.7 meters high; 2.8 meters wide; 1.3 meters deep; Price: 7500 Mk.

No. 9: 489 pipes; 4 meters high; 3.2 meters wide; 1.5 meters deep; Price: 11,500 Mk.

No. 10: 537 pipes; 4.7 meters high; 4 meters wide; 1.6 meters deep; Price: 14,000 Mk.

No. 11: 597 pipes; 5.3 meters high; 5 meters wide; 1.9 meters deep; Price: 18,000 Mk.

## KAUFMANN

—Dresden, Germany—

Members of the Kaufmann family were pioneers in the automatic instrument field. By the 1840-1850 period, the Kaufmanns had devised a wide range of automatic instruments. These were exhibited in Denmark, Germany, England, Russia, Sweden, and other countries and drew crowds at each stop.

In his book, "Mechanical Musical Instruments," Dr. Alexander Buchner relates that the firm was founded by Johann Gottfried Kaufmann (1752-1818), who established a small factory in Dresden. His automatic musical instruments, mainly of the organ clock and barrel organ types, attracted the attention of Napoleon, who sent an order for a flute-playing clock. Johann Gottfried's son Frederick (1785-1866) received an education in music and instrument building. Frederick joined his father, and together they produced a mechanical trumpeter (c.1810) and the "Belloneum," a barrel-operated organ which played reed pipes.

From 1810 to 1812 the Kaufmanns went on tour throughout Germany and met many prominent composers, authors, and statesmen. Following his father's death in 1818, Frederick continued the business and constructed many different types of instruments, some for exhibition and others for sale.

In 1837 Frederick went on a tour to Denmark, Sweden, and Russia. In 1838 he began work on a new series of instruments, including improved versions of the "Symphonion" and "Chordaulodion." The latter instrument was barrel operated and contained a "piano, flutes, clarinets, clappers, and kettle drum, and performed even very difficult music with exact gradations of tone." The "Chordaulodion" description is interesting as it notes that the instrument contained a piano. Most orchestrions of this era were built with pipes and percussion only (and without a piano). Note also that the "Chordaulodion" played with expression. How the expression of this instrument of the 1830's compared with later and more sophisticated instruments is not known.

From 1842 to 1844 Frederick Kaufmann, accompanied by his son Frederick Theodore Kaufmann (1823-1872), went on another tour. On the return journey from Copenhagen, Denmark, to Germany their ship was wrecked in a storm, and all of the prized instruments were lost. The Kaufmanns, their lives spared, returned to Dresden and began work on new versions of their automatic instruments. In 1851, after five years of work, a large orchestrion was finished. In 1854, the instruments of the Kaufmann family were exhibited in Munich. Following that display, the Acoustic Cabinet, a musical showroom and exhibit, was established in Dresden. This display continued for a number of years thereafter.

In 1851, on one of their many tours, the Kaufmann instruments were exhibited in London, in Buckingham Palace, for Queen Victoria, Prince Albert, and other members of the royal family. The July 5, 1851, issue of "The Illustrated London News" presented this account:

"On Saturday the 21st, at St. Martin's Hall, there was a private exhibition of the following new instruments — the 'Orchestrion,' the 'Chordaulodion,' the 'Symphonion,' and the 'Trumpet Automaton' — all of which were self-acting. There was also exhibited the 'Harmonichord,' which is played upon like the organ, with manuals and pedals.

"Herr Kaufmann and his son, the inventors of the above instruments, are from Dresden, and for many years have been unremittingly occupied in perfecting their novel conceptions. Our artists have illustrated the 'Orchestrion;' it is most picturesque in appearance, and most complete in its action, of the five instruments. It will be seen from the engraving that it is a combination of the brass and wood instruments; for every one of those metallic and wooden tubes has an eloquent speaking voice. The front of the lower portion of the case being opened, one discovers the percussion instruments, the kettle and military drums, and the triangle. The 'Orchestrion' was invented by Herr Kaufmann, Junior. It was five years before he had completed this marvelous mechanical contrivance, as a substitute for a full military orchestra — the tones of flutes, flageolets, clarionets, cornets, bugles, trumpets, bassoons, horns, oboes, trombones, drums, etc., being most successfully imitated.

"There can be no mistake — all the instruments depicted in our illustration actually emit sound, and are by no means decorative. How the maker has so ingeniously contrived that the cylinders move with such mathematical exactitude, and that the supply of wind (of course, varying for each tube) should be so precisely regulated, is scarcely to be conceived even by the thoroughly initiated in matters of mechanics and acoustics. For instance, it is almost miraculous to hear the slight and shade of this invisible instrumentation, to mark the just gradations of crescendo, diminuendo, and sforzando, besides the usual fortes and pianos. We have never heard anything so perfectly astounding as the finale of the 'Don Giovanni:' shutting one's eyes, it seemed as if the famed vocal and orchestral forces of Costa were exclaiming at one time, with portentous effect, 'Trema!' In the dance music, the three different times going on in the finale were observed with unerring precision, the mechanical agents doing what the living artists will rarely accomplish — keep together. Nothing could be finer than the 'Coronation March' from Meyerbeer's 'Prophete.' Godfrey's Coldstream Band must look to their playing, for the 'Orchestrion' is a formidable rival . . .

"Furstenau's variations on themes from 'Il Flauto Magico,' of Mozart, on the 'Symphonion,' was another triumph of mechanical skill, containing flutes, piccolo, clarionets, cymbals, and drums, with pianoforte [sic] accompaniment: the precision with which the chromatic scale, ascending and descending is attained, would dismay a Richardson or a Remusat. The 'Chordaulodion' comprises flute and string play.

"The 'Trumpet Automaton' is a figure not unlike Mario in the 'Puritani,' with the instrument at its mouth. It was invented many years ago by Herr Kaufmann, and won the admiration of Karl Maria Von Weber. What is most remarkable and inconceivable in this extraordinary piece of mechanism is that it produces double sounds of equal strength and purity, and flourishes in octaves, tierces, quints, etc., are heard. Perhaps this acoustic curiosity may supply some key to Vivier's wondrous horn effects, certain notes accompanying particular chords. If this discovery should be established, that one instrument can do the same with equal perfection as two instruments, it may lead to something, as natural intonation may surely effect what a piece of machinery can do.

"We have not as yet referred specially to the execution of each instrument, but the greatest marvel was when the 'Harmonichord' [an upright piano played by the rubbing of rosined discs against the piano strings — it was hand played, not mechanical — Ed.], played by Herr Kaufmann, and the four mechanical instruments, all were heard at one time in a fantasia on our national melodies. This is truly a miracle, for sometimes one instrument is heard as a solo, and the other relieves it at the exact stand; then two go together, and finally all the works are in movement, keeping exact time, and each one having its special duty to perform. The triumph of mechanical ingenuity can no further go, and the visit of Herr Kaufmann and his son to this country will no doubt be patronized largely. Their difficulties must have been enormous; first, in the just investigation of sound; and, secondly, in its application by mechanical means. To construct such instruments without models, for they are quite original, the maker must be a musician, a mechanic, a mathematician, and a philosopher.

"The first public performance was on Tuesday, the 24th, the instruments having been [privately] exhibited on the 11th at Buckingham Palace before her Majesty [Queen Victoria], Prince Albert, and the royal family. On their way to this country, Herr Kaufmann and son gave concerts, with the greatest success, at Leipzig and Hamburg . . ."

Notes: The "Automaton Trumpeter" survives today in the Deutsches Museum in Munich. Kaufmann barrel-operated pianos, organs, and automata of other types have, for the most part, disappeared. Today's collectors, who are often asked the question "Do you ever play all of your instruments at the same time?," should take note of the 1851 concert in which this was done with apparent success!

The Kaufmann performance at Buckingham Palace, 1851.

# LINK PIANO COMPANY, INC.

MANUFACTURERS OF *Automatic Musical Instruments* *Pianos and Organs*

183-185 WATER ST.

532 REPUBLIC BLDG.
CHICAGO

BINGHAMTON, N.Y.

LINK PIANO COMPANY, INC.
(Automatic Musical Company)

The Link Piano Company was a continuation of the Automatic Musical Company which was founded in Binghamton, New York, around 1900. The owners of Automatic, two brothers named Harris, produced several varieties of coin pianos. Most, if not all, were of the keyboard type and featured a piano with mandolin attachment or a piano, mandolin, and one extra instrument – usually a rank of flute pipes. One of their best known early products, a piano with mandolin instrument with a beveled clear glass front, was sold under different trade names by Caille Brothers (a Detroit firm that primarily made and sold gambling equipment) and by Lyon & Healy.

The Harris brothers were interested in experimenting and research and, in the course of this work, produced some interesting instruments. Successful on a limited scale was the "Self-Playing Xylophone," an instrument that played not the xylophone (by definition, a xylophone has wood bars, from the root "xylo" which means "wood") but a set of metal glockenspiel bars. Unsuccessful were at least two different types of automatic violin players, each known as a "Royal Violista," produced by Professor Wauters at the Automatic Musical Co. plant circa 1908 - 1910.

During the early years the Automatic Musical Company purchased the pianos for its instruments from the Schaff Piano Company of Huntington, Indiana. Around 1910 Automatic was on the verge of bankruptcy. A committee of creditors appointed Edwin A. Link, who was with Schaff Piano Co., to come to Binghamton to save the firm. Mr. Link saw possibilities with the future of the Automatic Musical Company and cancelled his affiliation with Schaff and took over the ownership and control of the New York firm. Manufacturing in Binghamton began once again in February, 1913. In 1916 the Link Piano Company was incorporated. During the early 1920's the Link Piano Company employed up to 125 workers (the figure of 60 workers is specifically given for the year 1924) to turn out about 300 coin operated pianos and a dozen or so theatre pipe organs each year.

Link's interest in theatre music led to the production of the Link theatre organs, sold as "C. Sharpe Minor Unit Organs," and to several different types of automatically operated pit instruments. Most of the Link theatre instruments were distributed within a few hundred miles of Link's upstate New York factory, but some went farther to Michigan, Illinois, and other states.

Mr. Ed Link (right) shows a 2-E piano to the author during a visit to the Link home in 1965.

Mr. Link plays a selection on a Link theatre organ installed in a special building on the grounds of his home.

The Link coin pianos were mainly of the keyboard types in the early years. After the discontinuation of the relationship with Schaff, the basic pianos were purchased from the Haddorff Piano Co. of Rockford, Illinois. To the basic piano the various pneumatic components, extra instruments, and other features were added at the Link factory.

Most keyboard style Link pianos featured a piano with mandolin or a piano, mandolin and a set of flute pipes. During the interregnum period when the Automatic Musical Company was being changed to the Link Piano Company a number of instruments were made with "Automatic Musical Co." cast into the piano plate and with "Link" on the fallboard decal. Later, the xylophone became the most popular extra instrument

A Link 2-E coin piano with mandolin and xylophone - a favorite Link model in the "good old days" and a favorite with collectors today!

The clear glass front of the 2-E permits a clear view of the marimbaphone or xylophone as it plays.

in the Link pianos. During the 1920's most Link pianos featured a xylophone (called a "marimbaphone" by Link) with a repeating or reiterating action. The shift from pipes to xylophones was partly an economic consideration and prevailed throughout the automatic musical instrument industry. The pipes required a pressure system in addition to the regular vacuum system, but the xylophone could operate on the same vacuum system as regularly used for the piano.

In keeping with changing public tastes and the desire for smaller instruments Link's production during the late 'teens and the 1920's was mainly of the cabinet type of instrument.

Mr. Ed Link, son of Edwin A. Link, told us that about 80% of the Link pianos and orchestrions were originally sold to route operators rather than to individual proprietors of business establishments. The operators liked the Link instruments as they were particularly easy to service. Any faulty pneumatic on the pneumatic stack could be taken off simply by removing two screws. Another pneumatic could then be slipped into its place in a matter of minutes.

Without exception the Link (and also the earlier Automatic Musical Co.) instruments utilized the endless roll system. The "roll" of music was one long continuous loop. This system was the standard in the coin piano industry in the early 1898 - 1905 years, but, with the exception of Link, the other makers had dropped it in favor of the easier-to-change rewind type of roll. However, as Link's instruments were mostly cared for by experienced route operators, the endless roll was no objection. In fact, the operators considered it to be an asset as the music would play continuously without a pause for rewinding. To the novice the endless Link roll appears to be hopelessly snarled, but in practice the loops remain untangled and the system works very well. It is interesting to note that the same basic idea is used today for the storage of continuous magnetic tapes and films.

Link music rolls come in three basic types: "RX" rolls are used on basic coin pianos with mandolin or with mandolin and one extra instrument. "A" rolls (not to be confused with the regular 10-tune rewind type of "A" roll used by other makers) have special perforations and are used on Link orchestrions.

Most "RX" and "A" rolls produced during the late 'teens and the '20's were of fifteen tune length. Certain earlier rolls have different lengths; some have but a single tune.

For the Link pipe organ a special Style "C" roll was produced. Many of the Link theatre organs and all of the Link pit organs were equipped with roll players. Most of these players accommodated four rolls, each in a separate compartment with each having its own tracker bar. By pushing buttons from the projection booth or elsewhere the rolls could be switched quickly from one to another, a feature which enabled the music to change mood in keeping with the theme of the picture.

Today collectors consider Link rolls to be among the best to listen to. The arrangements are snappy and are full of life. As with any type of roll there are, of course, exceptions, but with Link rolls the percentage of popularity is high. Some of the xylophone arrangements in particular are excellent.

Arranging of the Link rolls was done primarily by Ray Deyo (who continued making rolls under the "Deo" (sic) label after Link went out of business in the late 1920's) and Bill Sabin. Deyo, not a musician himself, arranged most of the coin piano and orchestrion rolls by laying them out on a drafting board. Sabin, who was formerly first clarinetist with Sousa's band, arranged most of the pipe organ rolls. Three perforating machines were used in the factory. Each could turn out from ten to fifteen rolls at a time. Each 15-tune length roll took about two hours to cut.

Unlike the Link organs, the Link pianos and orchestrions were widely distributed throughout America. Following the closing of the Link factory Edwin A. Link personally tended a route of dozens of Link instruments in California during the late 1920's. Probably the largest Link customer was the Lockwood Piano Company of Rhode Island. This firm had 300 Link instruments!

Today most comprehensive collections contain at least one Link instrument. Fortunately, enough survive that any collector willing to pay the current price can usually locate a nice instrument.

This model was called the "Reliable."

Automatic Musical Co. early coin piano with mandolin. The bin to the lower right of the keyboard held the endless roll. This particular model was exceedingly popular and was sold by other firms (such as Mills Novelty Co., Caille Brothers, the Regina Music Box Co., and Lyon & Healy) as well as by the firm that made it. The bin slides out for changing the rolls.

Motor and 3-part vacuum pump for the Automatic Musical Co. coin piano.

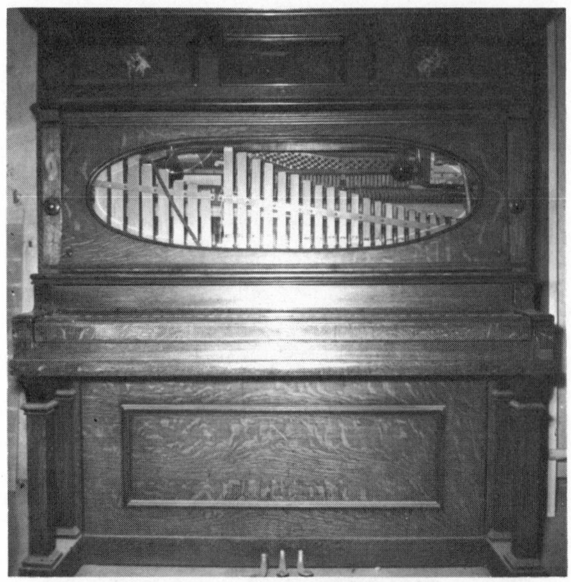

This early Automatic Musical Co. coin piano has a mandolin and a rank of flute pipes and is equivalent to the later Link Style C. The roll is housed in the top part of the case. A beveled clear glass panel gives a nice view of the interior "in action."

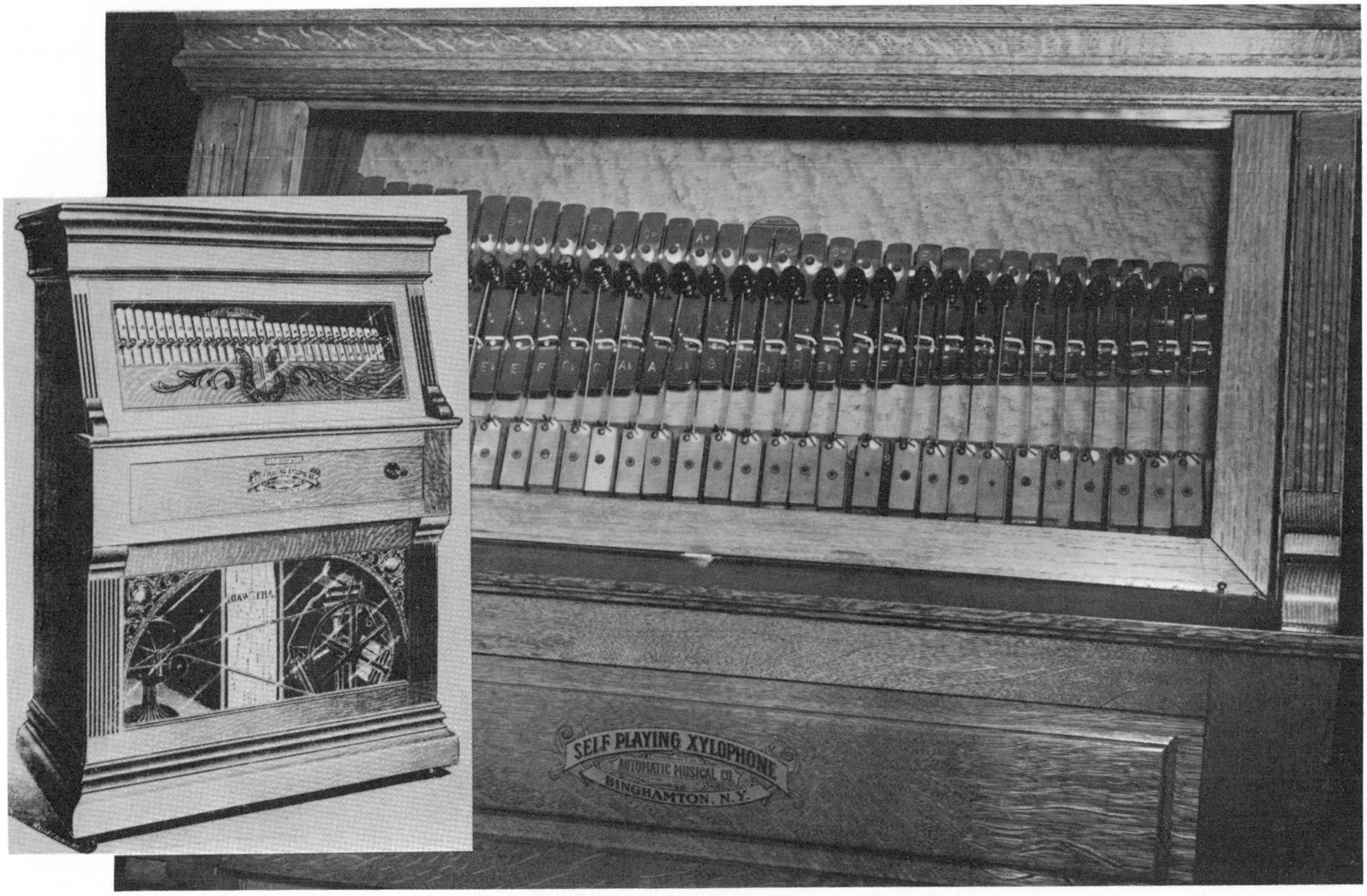


Automatic Musical Co. "Self Playing Xylophone". Plays solo melodies on metal bars.

Interior view of a Link Style C piano with mandolin and flute pipes. Note endless roll at the top.

General case design for Style 2 cabinet Link coin pianos (but usually with clear glass).

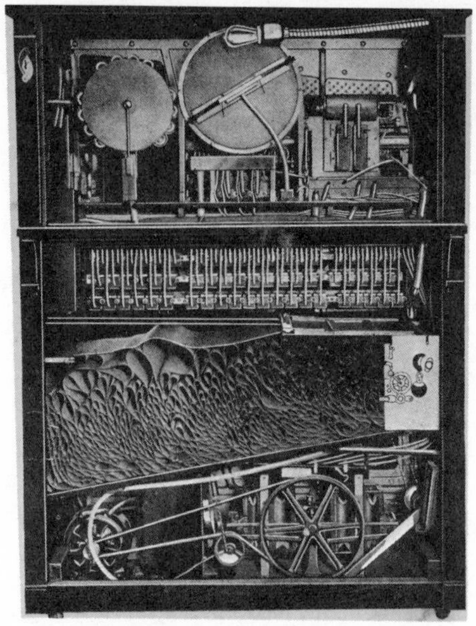

Link 2-B cabinet orchestrion.

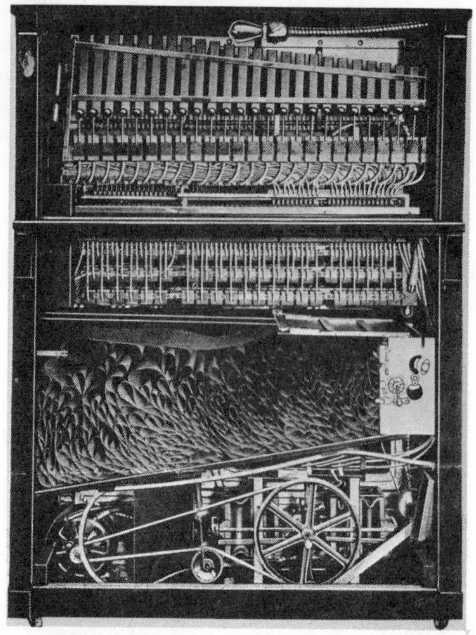

Link 2-E piano with xylophone.

Specifications of Link 2-B and 2-E

Style 2-B: Cabinet style orchestrion with piano, mandolin, snare drum, triangle, tom-tom, tambourine, and wood block. Also Style 2-BE with xylophone in addition to the other instruments.

Style 2-E: Cabinet piano with mandolin and xylophone or "marimbaphone." This was the best selling Link coin piano during the 1920's. It used the Link "RX" roll. Although some 2-E's have art glass, most were made with clear glass as owners wanted customers to have a view of the interior. The xylophone is of the repeating or re-iterating type.

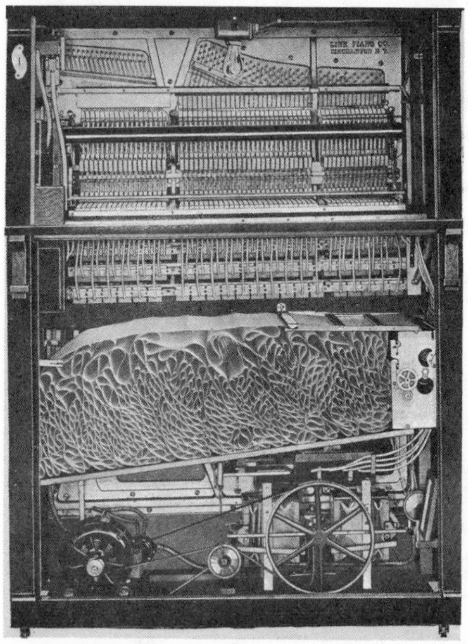

Link Style 2 coin piano with mandolin.

Tracker Bar Layouts
for Link RX and A Rolls

Tracker bar holes in order from left (toward back of piano) to right.

Link RX Layout

1. Soft expression off
2. Soft expression on
3. Marimba on
4. Sustaining pedal
5. Lowest playing note
65. Highest playing note
66. Coin trip (shutoff)
67. Marimba on (as No. 3)
68. Mandolin on
69. Mandolin & marimba off
70. Blank

Link A Layout

1. Soft expression off
2. Soft expression on
3. Blank
4. Sustaining pedal
5. Tambourine
6. Left snare drum beater
7. Center snare drum beater
8. Right snare drum beater
9. Triangle
10. Tom-tom
11. Right wood block beater
12. Left wood block beater
13. Violin pipes on
14. Violin & flute pipes off
15. Flute pipes on
16. Bass drum (or triangle)
17. Lowest playing note
65. Highest playing note
66. Coin trip (shutoff)
67. Mandolin on
68. Mandolin off
69. Blank
70. Blank

"The Link Case DeLuxe" - a two tone walnut case available for keyboard instruments.

Outside View
Style A, AX, B, C, D, E

Height, 6 ft. 4 in.; width, 5 ft. 6 in.; depth, 2 ft. 8 in.
Case design subject to change.
Art Glass Front, (design subject to change.)
Case, Oak, Mission Finish, or Two Tone Walnut.

Case as used with Link styles A, AX, B, C, D, and E. These were made by the Haddorff Piano Co. of Rockford, Illinois, and shipped empty to Link, who then added the pneumatic components.

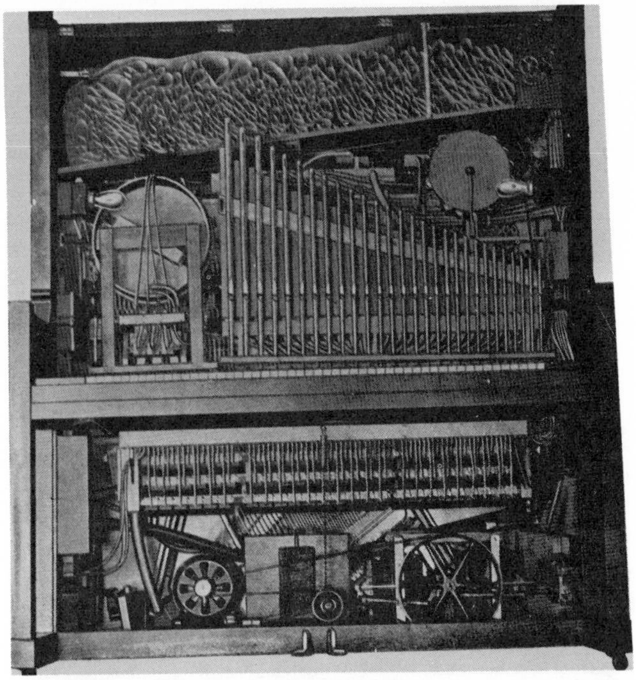

Link Style A orchestrion. Keyboard type with piano, mandolin bar, violin pipes, flute pipes, snare drum, triangle, tom-tom, tambourine, and wood block. The violin pipes are of metal, the flutes of wood. Only a few of these large orchestrions were made.

Link Style AX orchestrion. Keyboard piano with mandolin attachment, marimbaphone (xylophone), snare drum, triangle, tom-tom, tambourine, and wood block. Link orchestrions such as this one used the special Link "A" roll which was usually of 15-tune length.

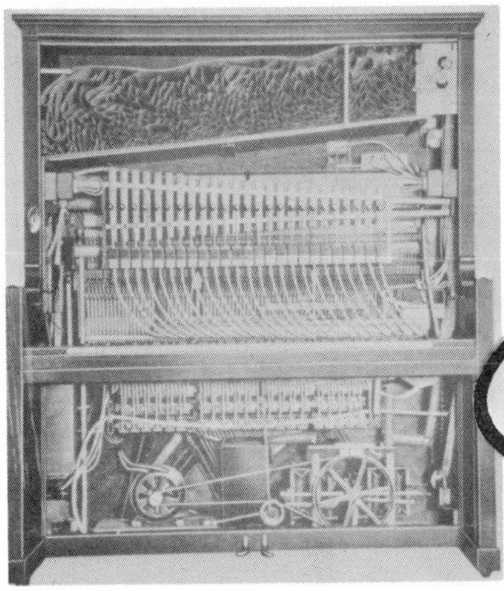

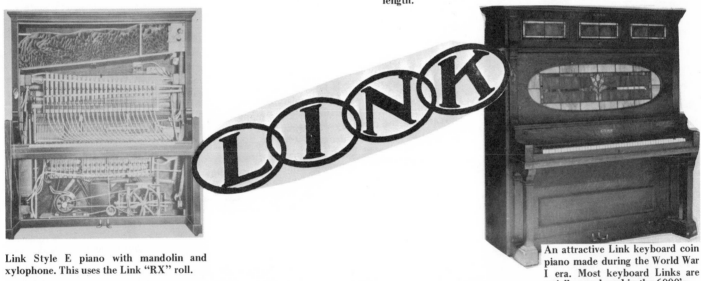

Link Style E piano with mandolin and xylophone. This uses the Link "RX" roll.

An attractive Link keyboard coin piano made during the World War I era. Most keyboard Links are serially numbered in the 6000's.

"Link your Theatre to Success" proclaims this advertisement. Link made a series of photoplayers for use in orchestra pits. Music could be switched from any one of 4 rolls to any other by means of remote control buttons. These were popular during the 1920's.

Console of a Link theatre pipe organ. At the top is a roll mechanism for playing rewind type rolls — so organ rolls of other makers could be used on the Link instrument.

Above and below: Link Style R – piano, mandolin, violin or flute pipes.

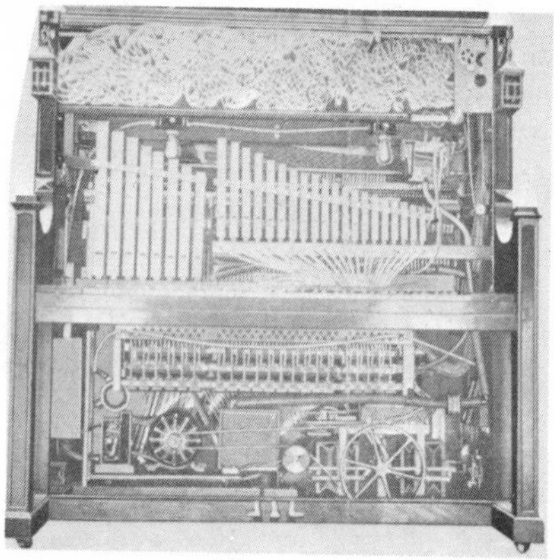

*On the afternoon of November 6, 1965, Harvey Roehl, Murray Clark, and the author interviewed Edwin A. Link at his Binghamton, New York home. Mr. Link has done what few men have accomplished: he has achieved outstanding success in several fields. The Link name is as well known in aviation (Link trainers) and oceanography today as it was in the field of pianos and organs years ago. In Mr. Link's own words he tells some aspects of "the good old days." (Transcript of original tape recording done by Mr. Art Reblitz)*

Q. David Bowers: Most of the Link pianos had plain glass. Why did you make so few with art glass?

Edwin A. Link: It was a case of the customers' desire. Of course, the pianos were made in three main types – just a plain piano, a piano with xylophone or pipes, and the drum combination. The model A sold for $1750. About 80% or more of all the pianos were sold to operators who put them on location on a commission basis. Some operators would run as many as 200 or 300 pianos. Later, when the pianos went out they operated phonographs, and still later, pinball machines, and so forth.

Harvey Roehl: You once developed a phonograph, didn't you?

Link: The Autovox, a coin selective machine. The first patent I ever had was the design for this.

Roehl: Did it have a pneumatic mechanism?

Link: No, it was purely mechanical. It had two stacks of five records each on two spindles. The spindles divided in the middle; you could raise the spindles and slip the records in, and then select any one of the ten by push button.

Roehl: Was this successful?

Link: Quite successful; we made quite a few of them. Unfortunately, this was done just before the 1929 crash came along. When the crash came along the Link Piano Company went out of existence and I went out looking for a job!

Roehl: What happened between the time that the piano and organ business went phooey in 1929 and the time that you started being successful with the trainers?

Link: Well, I started the trainers in 1926, so I was working on a trainer before the piano factory folded up. The first trainers were built there; that's why they have so many piano and organ parts in them. When the piano and organ factory folded in 1929 I was working on trainers in my spare time, after hours and on Saturdays and Sundays. When it folded there was no more business. Meantime I had learned to fly and I had a commercial license, so I had to go out and earn my living by flying. I guess it was a good thing for me that the factory did fold because I did better with trainers than I ever would have with pianos!

Roehl: One night when I was a kid I remember hearing an airplane. I opened the window and looked out and saw an airplane which must have been flying about 200 feet up, with a "Spaulding Bread" sign on the bottom.

Link: That was me, probably in 1930. I had a piano roll mechanism in the plane and I would punch out the rolls for different messages. The holes would light the proper lights for "Spaulding Bread," "Enna Jettick Shoes," and others. I put a venturi tube in the slipstream of the airplane and that created the vacuum. It was a player piano in the air!

Roehl: Was this any great commercial success?

Link: For three or four years I did pretty well with it. I owned the plane and made the sign mechanism. I later put one on a big Tri-motor Ford. I had three of them in all. Another thing I did to attract attention was to make a 10-note pipe organ. I had a big wind-driven air compressor under the Ford's wing and the organ was played by rolls! The pipes had to be loud or nobody could hear it.

Murray Clark: The MP Junior (motion picture "photoplayer") was just a straight piano with a four-roll mechanism. What was the Motion Picture Senior? Was that a combination organ and piano?

Link: No, it was either an organ or a piano. I don't think they had both.

Bowers: What's this organ in this picture (referring to an unnamed pipe organ with a horseshoe console and a Link roll mechanism near the top center), with the roll mechanism on top?

Link: We used to put a single roll mechanism on instruments so they could play other types of rolls.

Roehl: Did you have many acquaintances among the other piano manufacturers like Cremona and Seeburg?

Link: I didn't very much. My father did, but I mostly worked in the factory.

Roehl: Is it true that the Link Company never made a piano, but bought them from the Haddorff Piano Company?

Link: That's right. What they call the "cases" were made up there; just the back of the piano and the case. All of the actions were installed here.

Bowers: You mentioned when you visited (referring to an earlier Ed Link visit to the Bowers home) that you made an experimental instrument for skating rinks. Could you tell us more about that?

Link: It was actually one of those calliopes. We attached a Link roll playing mechanism to it so that it would make a lot of noise for skating rinks.

Bowers: Did you make the calliopes?

Link: No. We made the player mechanisms and then sold the calliopes with the Link system in them.

Clark: Was all of the Link roll arranging done by Mr. Sabin?

Link: No. There were two men that did most of the work. Bill Sabin did most of the organ roll work. He was first clarinetist in Sousa's band. The piano rolls were mostly made by Ray Deyo, who died only a few years ago.

Clark: I heard that one or the other couldn't play the piano. Is that true?

Link: Neither one of them could really play the piano. Sabin was a clarinetist and could play the piano a little bit, but Deyo could hardly play at all. They both arranged the rolls on the drawing board. We also had some hand-played rolls, and every one had to be edited.

Clark: Did Deyo and Sabin work the entire span from around 1910 to 1929 producing the music?

Link: They were really the chief two. There was somebody else who used to work there part time but I don't know who it was. We had some people come in to record but Deyo and Sabin did all of the editing afterwards.

Clark: These Link piano rolls are musically above average for music that was cut on the drawing board.

Link: We used to think so, and our customers thought so at the time.

Clark: Do you recollect where the paper was manufactured?

Link: No, I don't. It was made specially for the rolls. Some paper would absorb moisture and become wider; then it wouldn't match up with the tracker bar. Our paper was specially made and treated, and it came in by the carload.

Roehl: Can you give us any information about the production and perforation of rolls?

Link: We had three perforating machines and they perforated either ten or fifteen rolls at one time, I'm not sure which. They'd run through an entire roll in about two hours. The masters were on regular thick cardboard. After the company closed down they disposed of all of that and burned it up.

Clark: How did your father come into buying the Automatic Musical Company?

Link: My grandfather's business was making Schaff Brothers pianos in Huntington, Indiana. They made the cases which the Automatic Musical Company bought. When the factory went bankrupt in 1910 my father took it over to try to get his money out of it. He did better with the player pianos than he did with the straight hand-played pianos, so he sold the factory out there and started building here. The Automatic Musical Company was located on Water Street, the same place as the Link Company. As a matter of fact, IBM started in that building. That was originally the Bundy Time Recorder building.

Bowers: Do you know anything about early Automatic Musical Company products such as a violin-playing machine?

Link: I don't know much about what the Automatic Musical Company made.

Roehl: I heard a man from the Fowler Piano Company say that they bought a whole lot of pianos for $5 each (when the Link factory closed) and just ripped the mechanisms out and sold them as straight pianos.

Link: The whole thing was just given away. All the rolls were taken out – rooms full of them – and just burned up.

Roehl: When the thing was a going concern, was the money in the pianos or in the rolls? Or did you have to carry the rolls at a loss in order to sell the pianos?

Link: As far as I know, neither one of them was run at a loss. It was always fairly profitable.

Clark: My brother spoke with your sister two years ago, and she told him that after the Link Piano Company failed in 1929 your father, mother, and sister went to the West Coast. She indicated that much of the income on which they lived was derived from nickels from a circuit of pianos which your father owned or maintained. Is this true?

Link: My father had to go to the West Coast because of his health. He couldn't stand the winters here. I think he then acquired some pianos which he operated.

Clark: Then, did your father understand the pianos as well as you did?

Link: He didn't design them; that's the interesting part. George Thayer ran the plant and was connected with the designing.

Clark: What would you assume might have been the grand total of Link piano production from 1910 to 1929?

Link: About six per week. One a day – they worked on Saturdays. We had a good business right up to the crash. One of the troubles was that so many pianos were being sold on time and the customers couldn't pay. That's when I went out as a full time aviator.

Clark: Did you have a number of women working in the valve and pneumatic department?

Link: Yes. There's one woman still alive who worked up there. I found her name in one of the organ chests when I was working on it. (Ed Link was working on the restoration of a Link pipe organ – the instrument that was eventually presented to the Roberson Memorial Center in Binghamton, N.Y. – Ed.) She had written "Covered by Jessie Wilmot, 1926." I don't know of anybody else who is alive who worked on them.

Clark: Would one woman be able to cover enough pneumatics to meet your supply?

Link: There must have been thirty or forty doing this. We had about one hundred people altogether in the plant, or even maybe one hundred and twenty five. I used to come in from my summer vacations when I was a kid and work in the plant. Cover pneumatics and do all sorts of other things. I went through the whole business.

Roehl: Somebody told me that the wood for the pneumatics was soaked in hot shellac. Does that sound right?

Link: No, but they were soaked in hot glue.

Bowers: Did you ever take machines of other manufacturers in on trade?

Link: If they did, I don't know it. I didn't spend much time in the business end at the time.

Clark: Did you ever buy a competitor's product and bring it in and dismantle it to get ideas?

Link: I never remember it. We we always felt that we were ahead of the competitors. I suppose that everybody thought that, but I think we were.

Clark: Well, we collectors can compare various machines, and they all have their weak spots. Any machine which uses the unit valve system has to have the pneumatic stack nearly destroyed in order to restore it!

Link: That was the idea – we sold new unit pneumatics! The piano which played real hard would wear out in a certain range, but the rest of the pneumatics were not really bad. Instead of having to throw away the whole pneumatic action you could replace the bad pneumatics. This is why the operators liked Link pianos. They could come in with a couple dozen pneumatics, screw them in and never even take the piano out.

Clark: How can Link pianos be dated? We can't tell by the serial numbers.

Link: If you'll take out the pump and look at the bottom, the date when the piano was made is usually written in there. Usually the fellow who assembled the piano wrote the date and time in. It was the assemblers' own idea.

Clark: Do you remember a dealer named Lockwood?

Link: I remember him very well. He had 300 Link pianos; he was the biggest Link operator.

Roehl: I met Lockwood a few years ago and he was full of stories. He told me about selling them in the good old days. He went to one place and worked all day to sell a Link piano to a tavern owner. The barkeeper finally convinced the owner that he should buy it, so Lockwood said, "Well, now, what cycle electricity do you have?" The guy said "Electricity? We have no electricity here." And he looked around, and sure enough, the place was all lit up with gas lights. No sale! He told me about another time that he went down and sold one to a house of ill repute. The madam called him back about a week later, and was mad because the piano wouldn't run. He went down to see what the trouble was and found it wouldn't operate properly because it was so plugged with money that the coin chute was all jammed up!

Link: When old pianos came back for rebuilding, they were always good for $5 or $10 underneath the keys! We used to put half dollar slots on some pianos. That was a lot of money then. Quarter slots were quite common. So they weren't all NICKELodeons!

Bowers: What kind of places put a half dollar slot on a piano?

Link: There were some real ritzy spots.

Clark: Did you have busy periods and slack periods in the year?

Link: I don't remember any slack periods. Business was pretty steady. We didn't have any pickup help at all.

Bowers: Mr. (Farny) Wurlitzer told me that Prohibition in January, 1920 was a severe blow to their business. Was it to Link too?

Link: For a while, yes. Then it picked up again when the speakeasies became popular.

Roehl: I've been told that the Boston Candy Kitchen in Binghamton had a Double Mills. Did they also have a Wurlitzer orchestrion?

Link: A lot of these places had a piano for a few years and then they'd get tired of it and get a new one because their customers liked something different. I think they did have a Double Mills. They had a Link down there at one time and they had a great big Wurlitzer (Style 12 Mandolin PianOrchestra – Ed.) at another time.

## ORIGINAL-MUSIKWERKE PAUL LOCHMANN GmbH

—Leipzig, Germany—

From about 1907 to World War I, Paul Lochmann produced a series of Original Walzen Orchestrions (Original Barrel Orchestrions). Unlike the disc-operated instruments made by Lochmann, Original barrel instruments did not have quotation marks around the Original [as "Original"] term.

Walzen-Pianino No. 60

Original-Orchester-Klavier No. 50

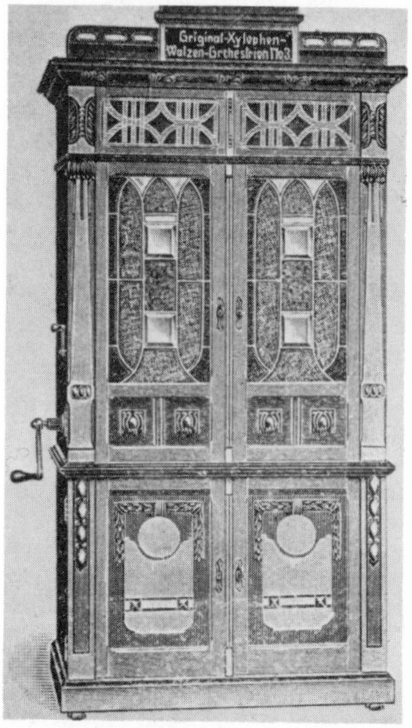

Original-Xylophon-Walzen-Orchestrion No.3

Original Walzen-Orchestrion No.1

On this page are shown barrel pianos and orchestrions made by Lochmann. Lochmann's greatest fame, however, came from his work with Symphonion and, later, with his Lochmann "Original" disc music boxes and disc-operated pianos. The reader may refer to the disc music box section of this book for more information on these other Lochmann products.

Walzen-Piano Nr. 9 mit Mandoline.

Walzen-Piano No. 9

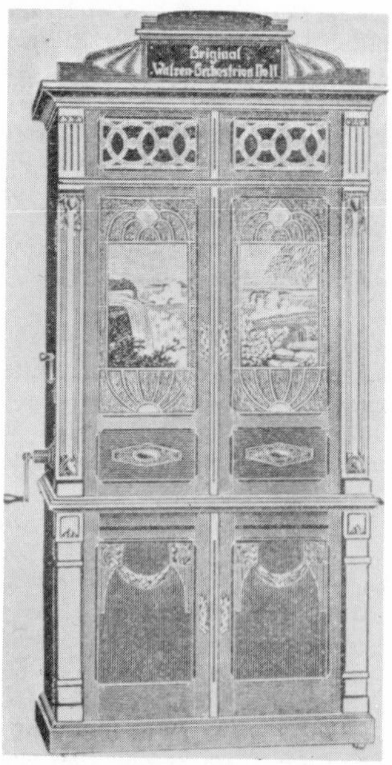

Original Walzen-Orchestrion No.11

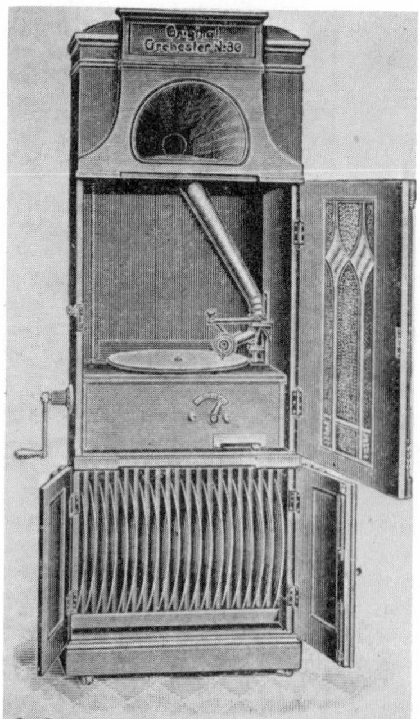

Orchester Nr. 30 für 50 cm Pathé-Platten.

Lochmann Miscellany

The Original Musikwerke produced a number of coin-operated phonographs, including Original Orchester No. 30 (left) and No. 40 (right), which used 50 cm. Pathé records. Many different arcade games were also manufactured. A shooting gallery with moving figures is shown above.

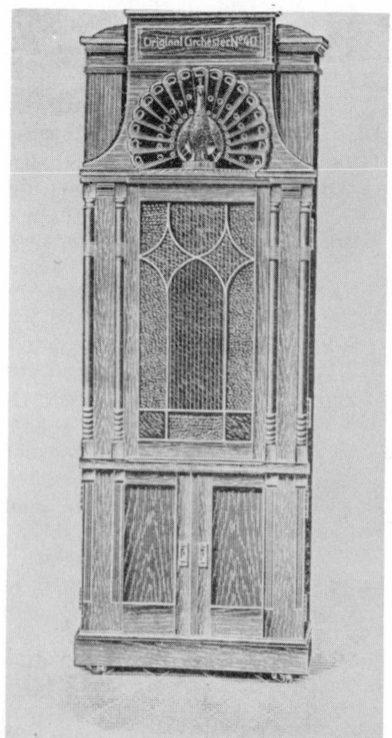

Orchester Nr. 40 für 50 cm Pathé-Platten.

## PAUL LÖSCHE
### –Pianos and Orchestrions–

During the early 20th century the firm of Paul Lösche, known as the Leipzig Orchestrion Works, produced a wide variety of pianos and orchestrions from factories in Mockau and Gohlis, near Leipzig, Germany. Showrooms and concert salons featuring Lösche products were maintained in the German cities of Berlin, Leipzig, and Essen.

Lösche was a major firm in the German orchestrion market. However, unlike Welte, Philipps, Hupfeld, and Weber, who marketed their products all over the world, Lösche confined its efforts mainly to Germany, Belgium, and England.

Lösche engaged in contract manufacturing; the making of orchestrions which were then sold to other firms which marketed them under private labels. For this reason and also because of the limited distribution of Lösche products they are not well-known to collectors and historians today. This present Encyclopedia listing is the first such delineation of Lösche instruments to appear in a modern publication.

Peter Yepetto of Manchester, England, sold a number of Lösche orchestrions under his own name in the 1910 - 1914 years (mainly). In 1904 J.M. Bon, musical retailer with outlets in Brussels, Belgium, Hamburg, Germany, and Copenhagen, Denmark, in addition to main offices in Leipzig, offered several models of Lösche instruments for sale. Not identified as Lösche products, they were offered as "Titania Orchestrions."

Certain Lösche instruments bear marked resemblance to those of Popper, Hupfeld, and Philipps, indicating that all of these firms may have ordered cabinet parts from common suppliers.

The most popular Lösche instrument was the "Flute and Violin Solo Piano," an orchestrion which was sold by the hundreds from the 'teens until the mid-1920's. Like other Lösche instruments it uses a perforated paper roll with widely-spaced perforations.

The firm was founded on October 2, 1902, and continued in business until about 1930. In later years the featured products included several varieties of the "Jazz Band Piano," the "88-Note Reproducing Piano," and the "Reproducta."

"Losche electric art-playing pianos; orchestrions, pianos" reads the above — a metal plaque originally affixed to a Lösche wallbox.

Lösche "concert hall" showroom in Berlin. In stylish surroundings the various Lösche instruments were displayed.

Lösche showroom in Leipzig. Note the push-up piano player in the foreground. A tall keyboard violin piano is at the right.

–Model B Art-Playing Piano–

–Model D Art-Playing Piano–

Using hand-played rolls recorded by prominent pianists the Art-Playing Pianos, of which two are shown above, featured a "high quality piano constructed with special mechanisms which permit every nuance of playing, from pianissimo to fortissimo."

–Mandolin-Piano–

–Xylophon-Mandolin-Piano–

With the self-explanatory names of "Mandolin - Piano" and "Xylophon - Mandolin - Piano," these two Losche instruments filled the need for a coin-operated (via a nearby wallbox) piano of small size. The catalogue noted that "Light effects of all sorts, if demanded [were available]" and that case style variations could be produced on special order. These illustrations are from a Lösche catalogue of the early 1920's.

—Violin Solo Piano—

With piano, mandolin, violin pipes (and sometimes also with flute pipes), and xylophone. 99" high by 63" wide by 30" deep. "Suitable for coffee houses, restaurants, and private drawing rooms" noted the catalogue.

—Flute and Violin Solo Piano—

The most popular Lösche instrument, this was made in several variations. Most have violin and flute pipes for solo arrangements with the accompaniment of piano and mandolin. Some have a rank of clarinet pipes in addition; still others have a xylophone added. 250 cm high by 160 cm wide by 90 cm deep. Usually in straight-sawed light oak cases; occasionally seen in mahogany.

LÖSCHE

—DeLuxe Xylophone-Mandolin-Piano— Model L

With piano, mandolin, xylophone, bass drum, snare drum, and cymbal. 266 cm high by 163 cm wide by 90 cm deep. A motion picture effect scene ornaments the top part of the case. Note the lavish use of beveled mirrors!

—Model 2— ("Titania I")

—Model 2—

—Model 3—

—Model 1— ("Titania II")

Model 2 (also sold as the "Titania I") orchestrion; two case style variations shown above. "Concert orchestrion, also suitable for dance purposes. The instrument produces sonorous, but agreeable and sweet, music and is therefore much in favor." Contains piano, 46 pipes representing flute, violin, and viola, orchestra bells, and drum and trap effects. 9'4½" high by 5' wide by 2'8" deep. Model 3: Similar to foregoing but with set of 14 orchestra bells displayed in the form of a bell lyre on the front. Model 1 (also sold as the "Titania II"): "With illuminated side panels, fine metal statue, and charming lighting effects. Wonderful and strong music replacing the best concert or dance orchestra." Piano, 120 pipes (for effects of violin, viola, cello, and flute), mandolin, 18-note set of orchestra bells, and drum and trap effects. Also available with clarinet pipes. 9'8½" high by 6' wide by 2'10" deep. "About 200 different music selections" available on rolls for this instrument, noted the catalogue. According to the late Eugene DeRoy, Model 1 was one of the most popular of the early Lösche orchestrions. The large Lösche instruments illustrated here were popular during the first decade of the 20th century.

–Model 4–

–Model 1-M–
(later, Model 12)

–Model 3-M–

–Model 2-M–

–Lösche Orchestrions–

Model 4: Piano, mandolin attachment, drums and traps. 9'2½" high. Model 1-M: Piano, mandolin, 180 pipes, drum and trap effects. 9'8½" high. "Most elegant orchestrion, light green oak with brass decorations, waterfall (or statue, if desired), splendid light effects of wonderful illumination. "Changing reflector" ("Wonder light") at top. Later offered as "Model 12" with the dimensions given as 10' high (we remind readers that the dimensions in this catalogue are from the original listings; experience has shown that they are just approximate; this is a good example!). Model 3-M: Piano, mandolin, violin and flute pipes, xylophone, drums and traps. "Available in green-finished oak, or any other color desired." 9'8" high. Model 2-M: Made in several styles, see another page for another case style and for specifications (which are also applicable to the one illustrated on this page). Model 1-A: Piano, 150 pipes (for effects of violin, viola, cello, flute, clarinet, and baritone), bass drum, snare drum, cymbals, castanets, and orchestra bells. A mandolin attachment is fitted to the piano. Available in oak or walnut (rare) woods. 9'6½" high. "Any tune desired may be arranged to your order on a music roll for this instrument." Model 1-K: Piano, 150 pipes, mandolin attachment, drums and traps. Made in light green oak cabinet with choice of moving scene (as illustrated) or statue. A popular model, 1-K was made from about 1904 until the early 'twenties. 9'8½" high. Model 8: Piano, mandolin, xylophone, violin and flute pipes, drums and traps. About 9' high. With colorful automatic waterfall scene in the center.

–Model 1-A–

–Model 1-K–

–Model 8–

## Model 2 M.

Latest Novelty.

### Suitable for coffee-houses, restaurants and drawing-rooms.

Most elegant piano-orchestrion with automatic modulation from the finest piano to the strongest forte:

sweet and agreeable music.

Parisian orchestra: first-class overstrung piano, clarinets, violins and flutes, mandoline, xylophone and percussion instruments. Modern case in light green oak or any other colour, with art stained glass and brass decorations.

**Music-sheets rolling back automatically.**

Height: 3 yards, 2½ inches — Width: 1 yard, 2 feet, 4 inches
Depth: 2 feet, 9½ inches Weight about: 9 cwt.

## Model 6.

Very elegant orchestrion, in oak of every demanded colour, with artistically painted panels and fine brass decorations. It contains: overstrung piano, mandoline, excellent xylophon and percussion instruments (large and small drum, Chinese cymbals). The instrument produces a sweet and agreeable music, therefore it is suitable as concert-orchestrion or for dancing purposes.

Light effects of all sorts, if demanded.

**Music-sheets rolling back automatically. Extensive repertoire.**

Heigth: 2 yards, 2 feet, 2 inches – Width: 1 yard, 1 foot, 9 inches
Depth: 2 feet, 9½ inches — Weight about 6½ cwt.

## Orchestrion Model 5.

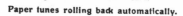

Highly elegant and fashionable case in oak of any desired colour, furnished with fine vitrifications of various colours, on desire with light effects. The instrument contains: first-class overstrung piano, mandolin, xylophone, complete set of percussion instruments, consisting of big and small drum and chinese cymbal, further excellently intoned violin-flutes.

Very suitable for concert and dancing purposes.

**Paper tunes rolling back automatically.**

Heigth: 2 yards, 2 feet, 11 inches — Width: 1 yard, 2 feet Depth: 1 yard
Approximate weight abt 7 cwt.

## Orchestrion Model 20.

### High class dancing and concert-orchestrion.

Elegant casing in oak of any desired colour, with brass mountings, artistic vitrifications and electric incandescent lamps in various colours. In the centre inset mirror splendidly illuminated, with figure or light effect. The work contains: first rate overstrung piano, mandolin, violins, violin-flutes, viennese flutes, piccolo flutes, cello, tuba, basses, besides complete set of percussion instruments, tambourine and xylophone.

Owing to this rich equipment the orchestrion is a perfect substitute of a large and excellent music band.

**Paper tunes rolling back automatically.**

Height: 3 yards, 1 feet, 6 inches — Width: 3 yards, 8 inches
Depth: 1 yard, 10 inches — Approximate weight: 15½ cwt.

## Orchestrion Model 40.

### Grandios Orchestrion for concert and dancing.

This instrument in an imposing, architectonic perfect and beautiful case in oak of any desired colour, provided with artistically luminous effects and finest facetted mirrors, performs, owing to its richness in instruments a sublime, varying music, fullsounding and sonour, replacing therefore fully a musical band.

The instruments contains: a cross stringed piano, the following pipe registers: violins, violinflutes, Viennese flutes, piccolos, cello, tuba, trumpets, trombones, besides kettle-drum and drum, chinese cymbal, tambourine, xylophone, mandolin and tinkling cymbal-harps.

**Automatic change of tunes. Great selection of tunes.**

Height: 3 yards, 2 feet, 5 inches — Width: 3 yards, 1 foot, 7 inches
Depth: 1 yard 1 foot — Approximate weight: 20 cwt.

Jazz Band Piano (1928)

LÖSCHE

–Model 30–

A popular model in the 'teens, the Model 30 has the following instrumentation: Piano, mandolin, pipes (for violin, piccolo, flute, trumpet), xylophone, and drum and trap effects. A "wonder light" is built into the top gallery. 305 cm. high by 330 cm. wide by 110 cm. deep.

–Model 2-K–

With piano, mandolin, pipes (violin, flute, clarinet), xylophone, drums and traps. 282 cm. high by 162 cm. wide by 96 cm. deep. At the center is a statue of a young lady. To each side are colorful scenes of full-rigged sailing ships on the high seas. At the top is a "wonder light."

–Model 9–

Note that this is basically similar to a 2-K with side wings added. 282 (or 272, catalogues differ) cm. high by 300 cm. wide by 96 cm. deep. An animated waterfall scene is at the center. Statues are in each of the two side wing niches.

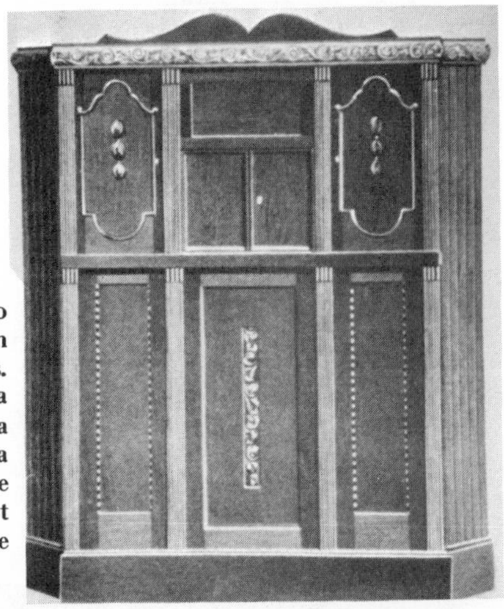

–Model 4–

Right: Model 4 "Salon Piano Orchestrion." A modern instrument from the 1920's. Just 175 cm. high. Contains a "piano and modern orchestra apparatus which, thanks to a special mechanism, offers the most decent and finest harmonious music" reads the catalogue.

**Model 50.**

**Splendid Orchestrion for concert and dancing.**

This instrument in an imposing, architectonic perfect and beautiful case in oak of any desired colour, provided with artistically luminous effects and finest facetted mirrors, performs, owing to its richness in instruments a sublime, varying music, fullsounding and sonour, replacing therefore fully a musical band.

The instruments contains: a cross stringed piano, the follo wing pipe registers: violins, violinflutes, Viennese flutes, piccolos, cello, tuba, trumpets, trombones, besides kettle-drum and drum, chinese cymbal, tambourine, xylophone, mandolin and tinkling cymbal-harps.

**Automatic change of tunes. Great selection of tunes.**

Height: 3 yards, 2 feet, 5 inches — Breadth: 3 yards, 1 foot, 7 inches — Depth: 1 yard, 1 foot — Weight: 22 cwt. pounds about.

Model 50, the largest Lösche orchestrion. Compare to the case of the Hupfeld Helios IV (see Hupfeld section of this Encyclopedia) and you will note that the structural portions (but not the inset decorative panels) are of the same basic conception. Several Model 50's were made.

–Selecta–

Concert orchestrion from the 1920's. With piano, mandolin, pipes (violin, flute, cello, clarinet, fagott), xylophone, bells, drums and traps. 305 cm. high. "Specially adapted for the finest concerts or other amusement music."

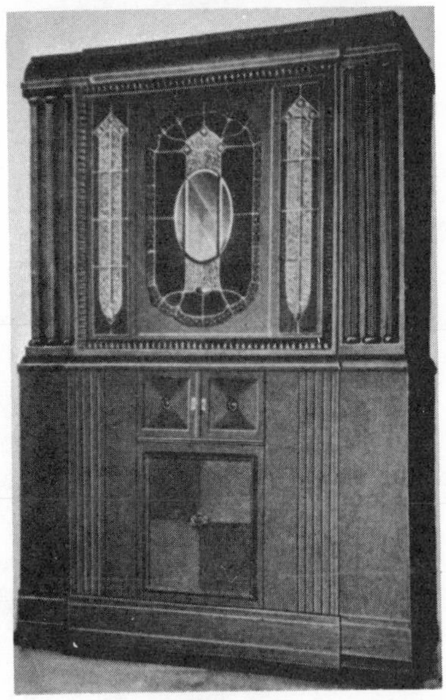

–Model 1-A–

Piano, mandolin, pipes (violin, flute, cello, clarinet), xylophone, drums and traps. 9' high. From the 1920 period. Note that an earlier Lösche instrument of different format was also called 1-A (see other page).

## LYON & HEALY
### "Empress Electric"

From about 1905 to 1925 the well-known musical supply house of Lyon & Healy in Chicago marketed a line of coin operated pianos and orchestrions. These were manufactured by others and sold under Lyon & Healy brand names such as Empress Electric and Majestic.

The Pianette, a 39-note piano operated by a metal disc, was made by F.G. Otto & Sons in New Jersey and was sold by Lyon & Healy. The Majestic, Junior, a 44-note cabinet piano similar to contemporary Electrova, Regal, etc. models, was sold in modest numbers.

### "Empress Electric" Instruments

During the 'teens Lyon & Healy sold nearly a dozen different styles of electric coin-operated pianos under the Empress Electric name. Most of these instruments are identical interior-wise to Coinola instruments made by the Operators Piano Company of Chicago and were made by the Operators firm. The case styles, however, are distinctively different from the Coinola models and, as such, the Empress instruments are treated as a separate series in this book. The pianos, too, are different and in many instances bear Lyon & Healy brand names such as Washburn (usually) or Leland on the piano plate. Generally, Empress instruments use the same types of rolls as used on contemporary Coinola pianos — A rolls for smaller pianos with mandolin and up to one extra instrument; O rolls for instruments with percussion and for instruments with solo xylophone, bells, or pipes.

Empress instruments were mainly sold in the midwest. They are fairly scarce today.

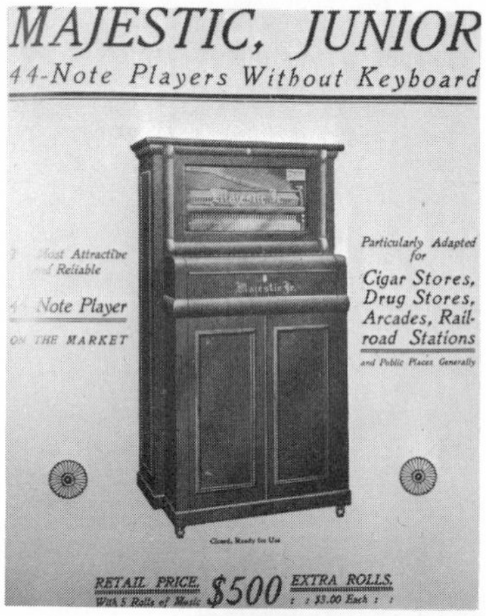


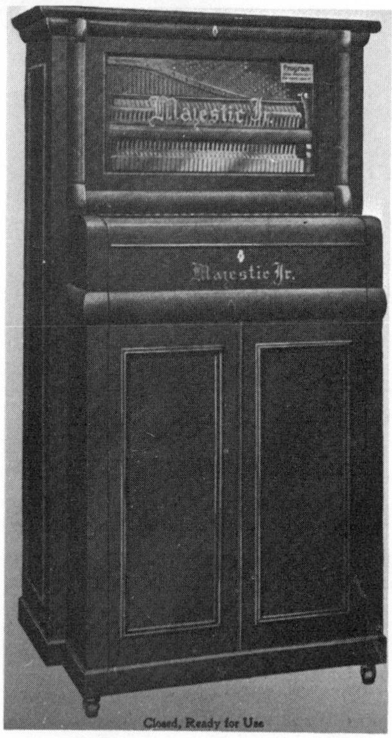


The Majestic, Junior, a 44-note cabinet piano of the early 1900's. Using an endless roll, it is quite similar to Electrova, Regal, and other 44-note instruments of the era.

OUR PIANETTE...A 39-NOTE PLAYER, OPERATED BY SPRING MOTOR
Hundreds of Cigar Stores, Cafes, Drug Stores and Public Places of Every Character are looking for Money Making Pianos, Operated by Spring Motors
NO ELECTRIC CURRENT IS NEEDED TO OPERATE THIS PIANO.
Dealers, whose territory includes towns where they have no electric current, or where there is only a
day current, should avail themselves of the opportunity offered in the sale of the Pianette. All cities and
towns where they have electric current are using electrically operated players in tremendous quantities. The
opportunity is now at hand for supplying small towns; a small investment in one of these instruments will
net magnificent returns to its owner. The first man in each town to take advantage of this offer is going to
get the big money.
List of tunes will be cheerfully furnished upon application. All of the latest, up-to-date music is made
for the Pianette; waltzes, two-steps, songs, sacred selections and popular music is arranged and can
be obtained at a very nominal cost.
THE PIANETTE is an automatically adjusted self-playing piano, operated by a long-running spring
motor contained in a metal barrel, and all of the mechanism is enclosed in a dust-proof box. The action is
of metal, making it impervious to dampness, and plays thirty-nine notes; has a double row of hammers with
dampers, permitting full expression to the rendition of each tune. The soundboard and frame are of the
regular piano type and is 75 inches high, 33 inches wide, 17 inches deep, weighs 420 pounds.
The instrument can be changed to play once or twice for each nickel deposited, or, if desirable for
home use, can be operated by a lever attachment. This instrument will play twenty-five minutes on one
winding, which makes it suitable for dancing. Each tune being on a steel disc, similar to that used in a
music box, makes the music indestructible and therefore economical. Tunes are changed by shifting the
tune disc and the entire construction of the instrument is so simple that it cannot easily get out of order.
The case design is very similar to that of our Majestic, Jr., and taking everything into consideration, is
a most compact, neat and attractive little Piano.
We supply these instruments in either Oak or Mahogany finish and will be glad to give full particulars
as to terms and prices on request.

The Pianette, a disc-operated piano manufactured by F.G. Otto & Sons in New Jersey — and sold by Lyon & Healy (and others as well).

The Majestic, an endless roll piano made in Binghamton, N.Y. by the Automatic Musical Co. (which later became the Link Piano & Organ Co.). This model, sold by Automatic as the "Reliable" style, was sold under many other names as well — by Caille Bros. of Detroit, by Lyon & Healy, and by several other firms.

# SOLO EXPRESSION TWIN TRACKER EMPRESS

This Nelson-Wiggen cabinet piano in the collection of Al Svoboda bears a Washburn (Lyon & Healy trade name) piano plate. It is possible that Lyon & Healy sold Nelson-Wiggen instruments in the 1920's. The above instrument is the only such instrument thus far called to our attention.

Solo Expression Twin Tracker Empress: In February, 1923, some 20,000 promotional leaflets describing the Solo Expression Twin Tracker Empress were printed. Using a double-width paper roll, the instrument could play without pause — in a manner identical to that of the Nelson-Wiggen Selector Duplex Organ (see Nelson-Wiggen section of this book). The sales literature noted:

"The unique features... will commend themselves to all who have any acquaintance whatsoever with piano construction. Twin Tracker: The two trackers are end to end... Double Width Roll: The roll plays in both directions, forward and reverse, one tracker for the downward and the other for the upward movement. This means no waste of time or energy for rewinding, no rolls torn from high speed rewinding. Nine Degrees of Expression: Seven degrees of expression are considered the extent obtainable in hand playing. The Solo Expression Empress has nine degrees of intensity."

The description went on to note that "The Empress Piano (as is every part of the mechanism) is the product of our own factory — built with the same discriminating care with which we build pianos for the home."

From a technical viewpoint the Solo Expression Twin Tracker Empress offered a "Steel Wind Chest — of square steel tubing that will last forever," a "Unit Valve Action — of which each valve and pneumatic is a single and easily removable unit," and other easy to service features.

The Mandolin Piano

Empress Electric
Pianos
LYON & HEALY
CHICAGO

Bottom board removed to display effects

The Drum Piano

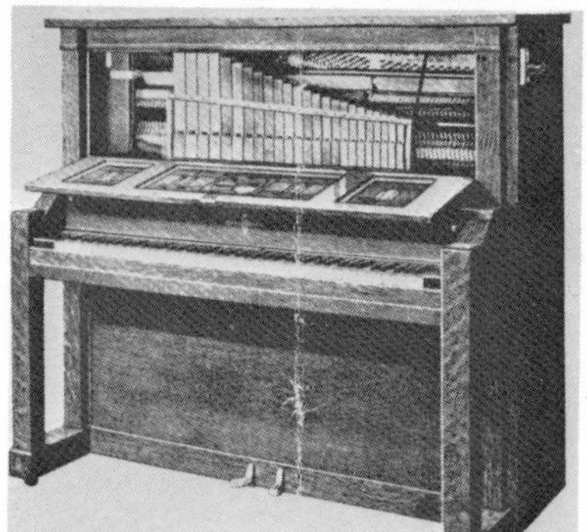

Front panel open to display pipes

The Flute Pipe Piano

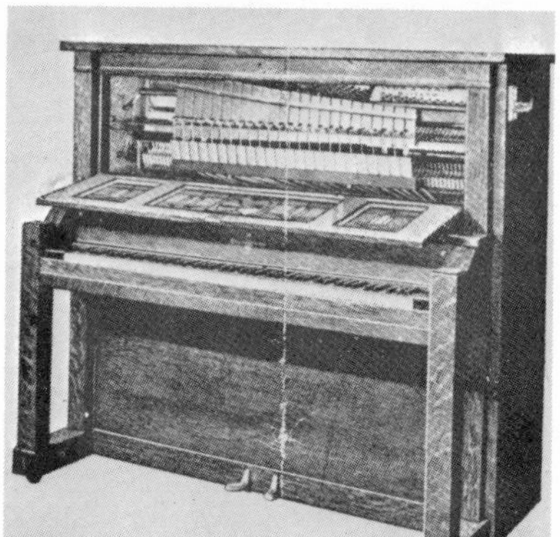

Front panel open to display bells

The Bell Piano

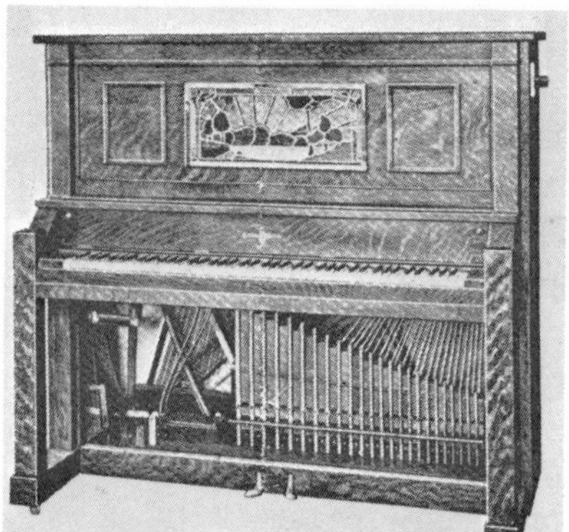

Bottom board removed to display effects

Combination of Flute and Violin Pipes

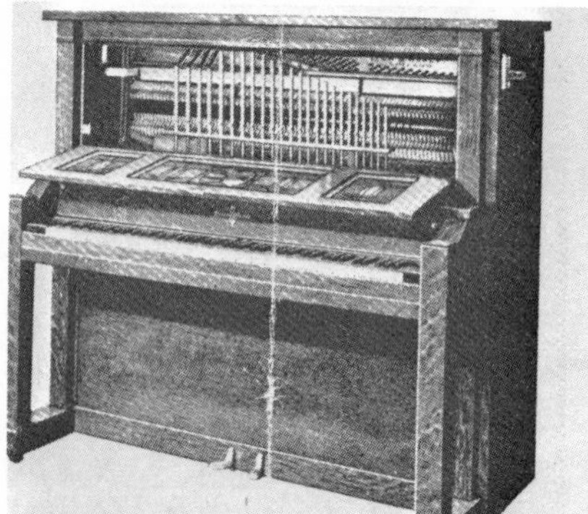

Front panel open to display pipes

The Violin Pipe Piano

Empress Electric (Coinola) instruments: The styles shown on this page are combinations of Lyon & Healy piano cases (usually of the Washburn make) with Coinola interiors. Case designs varied, and in addition to those shown here, a number of instruments were made with the same case design as the Solo Expression Twin Tracker Empress shown on another page.

The Mandolin Piano uses a regular 10-tune A roll; most other styles use Coinola type "O" rolls, although some piano, mandolin, and one extra instrument (a rank of pipes, a xylophone, or a set of bells) models used the A roll. A comparison of the Empress Electric models with Coinola instruments (see the Operators Piano Co. section of this book) will show the relationship. The Empress Style Y, for instance, is identical so far as the interior is concerned with the Coinola Style X orchestrion.

The Little Empress Electric Cabinet Player was made by Operators and was produced in several different styles ranging from a simple "vorsetzer" type apparatus to more intricate devices with all of the orchestral effects of the Coinola X orchestrion except, of course, the piano itself.

The search for information concerning automatic instruments of the past is often a trail crossed with red herrings. Several years ago the author inquired at the main offices of Lyon & Healy in Chicago. In response to an inquiry concerning sales literature and other information about Empress Electric coin pianos an official of the firm said, "Sure, I remember coin pianos and orchestrions. They were once all around Chicago. But Lyon & Healy never had anything to do with that type of business. We never bought or sold or became involved. Our business was with instruments for private homes — grand pianos, phonographs, and so on. You must be thinking of Seeburg. Perhaps they can help you!"

Bottom board removed to display effects

Piano with Complete Orchestral Effects

Mission Oak Finish

*Empress, Style Y*

*Contains piano, bass drum, snare drum and tympani with loud and soft stroke, cymbal, triangle, Indian block, orchestra bells and mandolin attachment.*

The Little Empress Electric Cabinet Player

*Fits any piano and makes an Electric out of it*

It is only a new application of the same reliable mechanism which has distinguished all of the Lyon & Healy Empress Electric Pianos.

Installation consists of motor, pump and steel roll frame with rewind bellows. Cabinet, complete, rests on key blocks, directly over the keys of piano (see cut) with two braces extending over top of piano, to hold it securely in position.

Plays ten-piece rolls, in 88-note range, on rewind system, and each pneumatic has an individual finger resting on each key; coin slot, 1-20 nickels.

Retains its regulation and requires no attention.

Finished in mission oak or mahogany.

# THE MARQUETTE PIANO COMPANY

MANUFACTURERS

Cremona Automatic Musical Instruments
Theatre Orchestra-Organs

2421-2439 Wallace Street

CHICAGO, U.S.A.

**The Cremona** Three in One—Electric Piano, Player-Piano and Regular Piano. Easily Convertible at Will.

**The Cremona** A Magnet for Crowds
A Magnet for Nickels

## MARQUETTE PIANO COMPANY

From 1905 to about 1920 the Marquette Piano Company of Chicago manufactured a variety of different coin pianos, orchestrions, and photoplayers under the "Cremona" trademark.

Beginning as a manufacturer of piano actions and components Marquette entered the coin piano field in 1905, thus establishing itself as one of the first American firms in the industry. Initial production was mainly keyboard style coin pianos which used the standard ten-tune "A" roll. This type of instrument, of which the Style 3 is the best known example, had clear glass panels on the front. Each panel was highlighted by a transfer design of a golden singing canary.

Following the lead of J.P. Seeburg (who worked for Marquette c.1905 - 1907 before starting his own business) Marquette instruments were ornamented with beautiful opalescent art glass panels beginning around 1910. After the "A" roll keyboard pianos proved successful several varieties of Cremona orchestrions were manufactured. The best known of these were the Orchestral K and the Orchestral J, large keyboard style instruments. In addition a few cabinet style (keyboardless) orchestrions were produced.

To get its share of the theatre photoplayer market several different varieties of Cremona instruments called "Theatre Orchestras" were produced. The Solo Style O and the Solo Style M3 seem to have been the most popular, but, like other photoplayers of other makes, Cremona Theatre Orchestras of all kinds are exceedingly rare today.

A number of Cremona coin operated instruments were built with the Cremona Tune Selecting Device — an apparatus which permitted the patron to select the tune desired rather than to just play whatever tune happened to come up next on the roll. Instruments with the Tune Selecting Device use the special type "M" rolls which have special

*Upper front section of Orchestral J orchestrion showing beautiful art glass (Frank Adams Collection)*

perforations to control this ingenious device. Although the tune selector was well made and certainly did its job excellently, the attachment was never popular — possibly because of added cost or possibly because the average patron was not accustomed to using such a device.

In the early 1920's some Cremona-labeled instruments were built with Seeburg components in the interior as a result of an interrelationship in later years between the flourishing J.P. Seeburg Piano Co. and the faltering Marquette Piano Co. Cremona instruments were mainly marketed in the period from 1905 to 1920, however.

Cremona instruments are remarkable for their quality. In his book, "Player Piano Treasury," Harvey Roehl observes: "Most connoisseurs of the mechanical piano consider the Cremona to be just about the Rolls-Royce of the field..." From a marketing viewpoint Cremona instruments were "overbuilt." The interiors were usually lined with beautiful bird's eye maple and the interior chest and striker actions were made of mahogany, an attention to quality that could not have been appreciated by the Cremona patron in the "good old days" as these features were hidden from view. However, the collector today does appreciate what the Marquette firm did years ago.

In addition to the Cremona instruments Marquette also manufactured coin pianos on a contract basis for other manufacturers. An instrument virtually identical to the Style 3 Cremona was made for the Regina Music Box Co. and bore the latter firm's markings. Likewise, there is evidence that certain instruments sold by the Piano Player Manufacturing Co. of Cincinnati, Ohio, and Covington, Kentucky, under the "Rhapsodist" label were made by Marquette.

Three main types of rolls are used on the various Cremona instruments.

Basic coin pianos with mandolin attachments or with one extra instrument (such as a rank of violin or flute pipes) use the standard 10-tune "A" roll — the roll that was the standard of the coin piano industry.

Orchestrions such as the Orchestral J and K and certain cabinet-style orchestrions use the 10-tune orchestrated "M" roll which has perforations for drums and traps, extra instruments, and controls. In addition, Cremona instruments that use the Tune Selecting Device (including basic pianos with mandolin attachment equipped with this selector) use the "M" roll.

The Cremona Theatre Orchestras such as the Solo styles O and M3 use a 134-note "S" roll which provides the capability for operating the many effects of these elaborate photoplayers. For added versatility some of the photoplayers use regular 88-note home player piano rolls in addition to the "S" rolls.

As might be expected, most Cremona pianos known today are of the basic keyboard "A" roll styles. The larger orchestrions and photoplayers are quite rare. The cases of Cremona orchestrions are unusually beautiful. In keeping with the Marquette attention to detail, the art glass is often more finely wrought and more intricate than that found on other piano types.

**MARQUETTE (Cremona)**

**Style A – Art (Early case)**

**Style A – Art (Later case)**

**Style A – Art**
**Another case design of the Style A – Art.**

**Style 4**
**Note similarity to Style 5 on another page.**

## CREMONA "A" ROLL PIANOS

**This instruments use the standard 65-note "A" roll. Illustrations cover about the 1908 - 1920 period, during which period case designs changed but the designations remained constant. (See several varieties of Style A – Art, for instance.)**

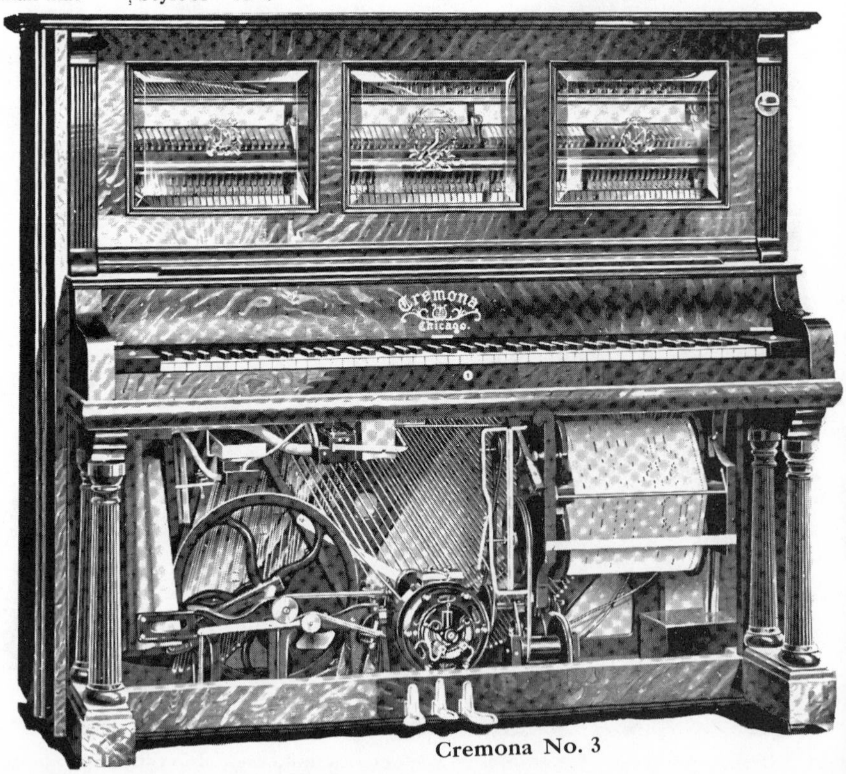


Cremona No. 3

**Above: Style C –Art. Piano with mandolin. (Also sold as "Rhapsodist, Style B" by the Piano Player Mfg. Co.)**

**Right: Style 3 Cremona, open view showing interior. (Also sold as a "Reginapiano" by the Regina Music Box Co.)**

**MARQUETTE (Cremona)**

Cremona — Style 2

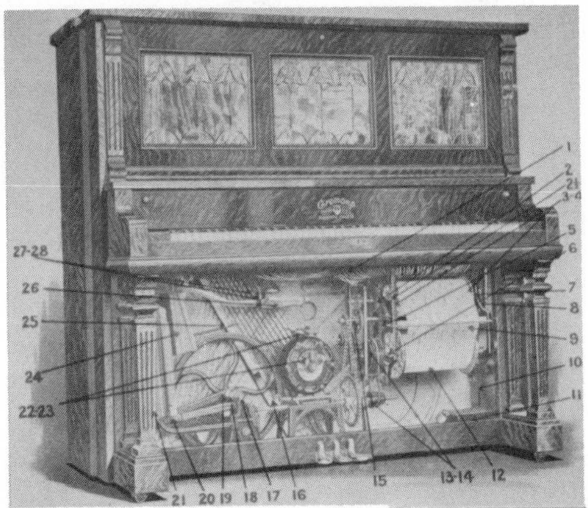


**Another Cremona "A" roll piano. This illustration is from an instruction sheet printed in Spanish explaining the Cremona features.**

## THE Cremona ELECTRIC PIANO
(COIN OPERATED)

**Style 5**
**Quite similar to Style 4. Offered in mahogany and walnut woods.**

THE Cremona Electric Piano is the most widely imitated instrument of its kind in the world today. Makers of other electric pianos, when confronted with the necessity of adding new features in order to compete with any degree of success with the Cremona, invariably turn to it for inspiration and guidance.

Among the original features introduced by the Cremona, which are rapidly becoming universal, are the following:

The Cremona was the first instrument playing from ten to twenty tunes from a single roll, and plays today twice as many pieces from one roll as the ordinary electric piano.

The Cremona perfected the magazine coin slot, and was the first electric piano to use it with success. This practical attachment permits of the insertion of from one to twenty nickels at the same time, and playing the entire roll consecutively, or any number of tunes singly, at the will of the operator.

THE Cremona was the first electric piano to use special, individual music rolls in addition to the regular style in common use. This unique device makes it possible to play the most intricate and beautiful music exactly as performed by skilled artists.

The Cremona has an entirely original and exclusive mandolin attachment—the first and only one of its kind—operated with a simple, practical action, which by merely pressing or releasing a convenient push button, may be made to play mandolin continuously, ad libitum, or regular, as desired.

The Cremona was the first instrument that contained the entire mechanism in a single case without marring its artistic appearance or obstructing free access to any part at any time.

The Cremona was the first electric piano made in all particulars exactly like a regular hand piano, without suggesting its three-fold character to the observer.

### Cremona Characteristics

THE Cremona affords added attraction to homes, clubs, bar-rooms, dance-halls, ice-cream parlors, motion picture theatres and other places of amusement—in fact, is positively essential to their greatest success and highest earning power.

The Cremona is not only inexpensive in its first cost, but may be bought on terms by which it earns a net profit above monthly payments and cost of operation and repairs.

A practical demonstration of the simple and reliable operation of the Cremona is the fact that, while it takes four men and a boy to keep fifty ordinary players in order, one man and a boy can easily take care of sixty Cremonas with less trouble, fewer complaints and better satisfaction.

In the larger cities, where automatic player-pianos are subjected to continuous rough usage, the Cremona is preferred above all others, and outsells all ordinary electric pianos by two to one. This fact is in itself indisputable evidence of the superior qualities of the Cremona, as this class of users puts them to the severest tests and finds them absolutely reliable and trustworthy.

We invite comparison of the Cremona price with those of all other electric pianos. It will be found that the Cremona is the least expensive of all instruments of equal grade.

**Above are some of the claims made for the Cremona piano. Sometimes very early Cremona instruments are found with "Seeburg" labels. J.P. Seeburg sold Cremona pianos before he manufactured his own.**

---

**CREMONA STYLE G PIANO**
**—With violin or flute pipes—**

**Style G: Although most known examples of the Style G have flute pipes (in most Cremona catalogues this style is designated as "Style G – Flute"), the description at the right shows that at least some were made with violin pipes.**

**Another variety of the Style G (represented in the Gilkerson Collection) has a shorter case than those illustrated here and has stopped flutes instead of the usual open ones.**

**The Style G was one of the more popular Cremona makes. Ruggedly built and handsome, a number of these are represented in collections today.**

*Style G, Flute (or Violin)*

One of the most popular instruments of the Cremona line. Piano can be played manually or with roll; the roll is orchestrated and will select its own instrumentation, or the instrumentation may be selected manually. For cafes, buffets, dance halls and large candy stores this model is particularly fitted.

**CASE**—Specially designed colonial case of quarter cut oak. Will stand hard service. Regularly furnished in mission finish; mahogany if desired. Three beautiful art glass panels of geometric design in top frame. Fitted with two handsome brass trimmed art lamps. Both panel and lamps illuminated when piano is playing. Full Empire top.

**CONSTRUCTION**—Piano is full 7⅓ octaves. Decorated bronzed plate. New improved overstrung scale, International pitch. Imported music wire. Three strings in unison. Double copper wound bass. New type double repeating action with Billings patent brass flanges. Ivory keys. Imported felt hammers.

**INSTRUMENTATION**—Piano, Mandolin and Flute Pipes (or Violin Pipes if preferred). The Pipes and the Mandolin may be played either singly or together with piano accompaniment, as desired.

**FEATURES**—

**Modulant**—The latest improved automatic expression device; varies the tonal expression from very loud to very soft without impairing the perfect rendering of the music.

**Tempulator**—A new device by which the time of the music when played automatically can be varied to suit the nature of the piece, or to secure the fine time variation required for the modern dances.

**Distant Control**—When desired can be equipped for operation from a distance, either by push button or wall boxes.

**Magazine Slot**—For coin operation. Instrument is furnished with or without as desired. Slide to take nickel or other coin, as ordered. From one to twenty coins can be registered at a time. Our coin slide eliminates defective and odd size coins and steel slugs.

**Multiple Tune Music Rolls**—Plays standard music rolls of ten, fifteen or twenty pieces.

**Coin Boxes**—Iron Coin Boxes with substantial locks are used.

**Motor**—Special type quiet running piano motor—voltage and current as desired.

**DIMENSIONS**—Height 67½ inches; Width 64 inches; Depth 28½ inches.

**WEIGHT**—Boxed for shipment 1,190 pounds.

THE MARQUETTE PIANO CO. CHICAGO

Cremona Orchestral K — "Orchestral" was Marquette's term for "orchestrion," and it was often used generically in advertising — such as "our latest orchestral is. . ." The above illustration shows the upper part of a fine Orchestral K in the private collection of Jerry Cohen. With its beveled clear glass and art glass front, its arches with colorful lamps in the niches, and its pretty oak case the Orchestral K is an instrument of rare beauty. It uses type "M" rolls.

## Cremona — Orchestral K

A late development in the Cremona Orchestral is the Style K. Altogether a wonderful instrument full of remarkable musical results. Built especially for high class trade desiring a superior instrument.

**CASE** — A new and original Grecian design, made of the finest quarter sawed oak. Regularly furnished in mission oak; other finishes to order. Beautiful art glass panels in top frame. Two brass trimmed art lamps. Design subject to change without notice.

**CONSTRUCTION** — Piano is full $7\frac{1}{3}$ octaves. New improved overstrung scale. Three string unisons, double copper wound bass. New type repeating action with patent brass flanges. Ivory keys. Imported felt hammers.

**INSTRUMENTATION** — Three sets of pipes for effects of flute, piccolo and violin, piano, mandolin, triangle, tambourine and castanets.

**FEATURES** —

**Modulant** — The latest improved automatic expression device; varies the tonal expression from very loud to very soft without impairing the perfect rendering of the music.

**Expression Shutters** — Automatically controlled.

**Distant Control** — When desired can be equipped for operation from a distance, either by push button or wall boxes.

**Piano Mute** — Operated by knob on side of piano.

**Tempulator** — A new device by which the time of the music when played automatically can be varied to suit the nature of the piece or to secure the fine time variation required for the modern dances.

**Magazine Slot** — For coin operation. Instrument is furnished with or without slot as desired. Slide to take nickel or other coin, as ordered. From one to twenty coins can be registered at a time. Our coin slide eliminates defective and odd size coins and steel slugs.

**Multiple Tune Music Rolls** — Plays 88-note specially orchestrated music rolls.

**Coin Boxes** — Iron Coin Boxes with substantial locks are used.

**Motor** — Special type quiet running piano motor — voltage and current as desired.

**DIMENSIONS** — Height $67\frac{1}{2}$ inches; Depth $30\frac{1}{2}$ inches; Width 64 inches.

**WEIGHT** — Boxed for shipment about 1,295 pounds.

THE MARQUETTE PIANO CO. CHICAGO

## Cremona — Orchestral, Style J

A perfectly balanced orchestra; self-contained in a single instrument, occupying the same floor space as a piano. Especially adapted for use in cafes, candy kitchens, dance halls and similar locations of the best sort. For dancing purposes this instrument is furnished with an encore device.

**CASE**—Finest grade carefully selected quarter sawed white oak. Mission finish. Illuminated colored colonial art glass panels in artistic and harmonious designs.

**CONSTRUCTION**—Piano is full 7⅓ octaves. Decorated bronzed plate. New improved overstrung scale—International pitch. Three stringed unisons. Double copper wound bass. New type double repeating action with patent brass flanges. Ivory keys. Imported felt hammers.

**INSTRUMENTATION**—Piano, Mandolin, Flute Pipes, Violin Pipes, Bass and Snare Drums, Cymbal, Triangle, Xylophone, (choice of unatone if desired) and tympani.

**FEATURES**—

**Modulant**—The latest improved automatic expression device; varies the tonal expression from very loud to very soft without impairing the perfect rendering of the music.

**Tempulator**—A new device by which the time of the music when played automatically can be varied to suit the nature of the piece to secure the fine time variation required for the modern dances.

**Distant Control**—When desired can be equipped for operation from a distance, either by push button or wall boxes.

**Magazine Slot**—For coin operation. Instrument is furnished with or without as desired. Slide to take nickel, dime, quarter or other coin, as ordered. From one to twenty coins can be registered at a time. Our coin slide eliminates defective and odd size coins and steel slugs.

**Multiple Tune Music Rolls**—Plays special 88-note orchestrated music rolls of ten, fifteen or twenty pieces.

**Bellows**—Cremona Slow Speed Bellows. New-born calfskin lining. Stationary centerboard. Phosphor bronze bearings.

**Coin Boxes**—Iron Coin Boxes with substantial locks are used.

**Motor**—Special type quiet running piano motor—voltage and current as desired.

**DIMENSIONS**—Height 80 inches; Width 65 inches; Depth 29 inches.

*Style J, Orchestral*

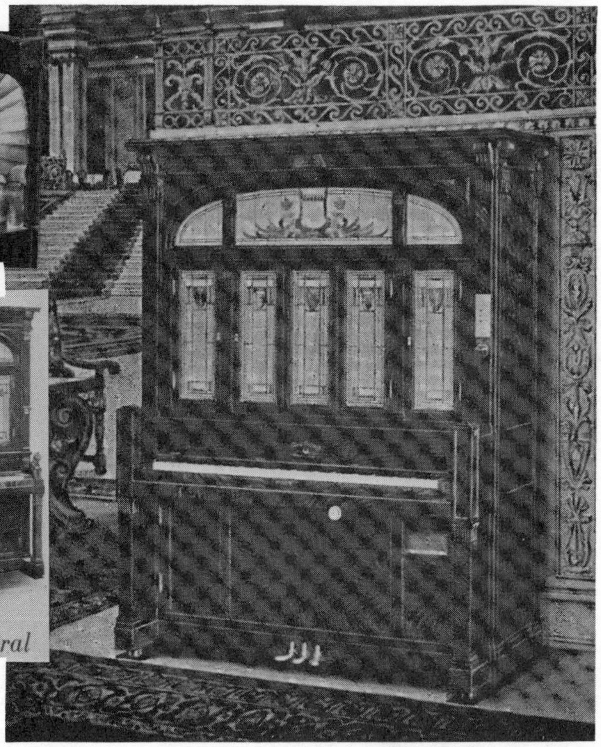

**Original Cremona catalogue material relating to the Orchestral J – the largest orchestrion produced by Marquette. It uses the solo "M" roll (as do the Orchestral K and also instruments with the tune selector). There are two main case styles – with gilded lions at the end of the keyboard and with posts. Art glass variations include the standard model with clear beveled glass and art glass combined, and a scarcer type with bright opalescent blue in place of the clear glass.**

---

**The Cremona Tune Selecting Device is unusual in its effective "foolproof" mechanism by which "no manipulation of the indicator whatever can make the instrument miss playing the desired selection." Orchestrated type "M" rolls have special perforations at the edges which actuate the Tune Selecting Device. Styles 20 and 30, while not utilizing all of the orchestration on the roll, use this "M" roll (as do regular orchestrions J and K – without tune selectors). The "M" roll was truly multi-purpose!**

**Tune selectors were made by other firms. Refer to the Seeburg Style Z Selective Roll Piano, the National, the Hupfeld remote-control selecting mechanism, and the Western Electric Selectra for other examples.**

Cremona

STYLE 20—Tune Selecting

### CREMONA TUNE SELECTOR

Especially adapted for coin operation. Piano can be played by hand or automatically, as desired. Music roll is placed above, being very easy of access. Any tune can be selected and p layed at will.

SPECIFICATIONS

**CASE**—Best selected quarter sawed oak case. Regularly furnished in mission oak finish; other finishes as desired. Illuminated art and plate glass panels with coppered bars. Design subject to change.

**CONSTRUCTION**—Piano is full 7⅓ octaves. Decorated bronzed plate. New improved overstrung scale—international pitch. Imported music wire. Three strings in unison. Double copper wound bass. New type double repeating action with patent brass flanges. Ivory keys. Imported felt hammers.

**FEATURES.**

**Tune Selecting Device**—Plays selectively or in rotation as desired. Automatic or manual speed control.

**Transmission**—Beltless shaft drive. Noiseless—dependable.

**Mandolin Attachment** which may be cut in or out manually or automatically or may be set for continuous playing.

**Modulant**—The latest improved automatic expression device; varies the tonal expression from very loud to very soft without impairing the perfect rendering of the music.

**Distant Control**—When desired can be equipped for operation from a distance, either by push button or wall boxes.

**Magazine Slot**—For coin operation. Instrument is furnished with or without as desired. Slide to take nickel, dime, quarter or other coin, as ordered. From one to twenty coins can be registered at a time. Our coin slide eliminates defective and odd size coins and steel slugs.

**Multiple Tune Music Rolls**—Plays special 88 note orchestrated music rolls of ten and fifteen pieces.

**Coin Boxes**—Iron Coin Boxes with substantial locks are used.

**Motors**—Special type quiet running piano motors—voltage and current as desired.

**DIMEMSIONS**—Height 57 inches; Width 64 inches; Depth 18½ inches.

**WEIGHT**—Boxed for shipment 1,000 lbs.

*Style 30*

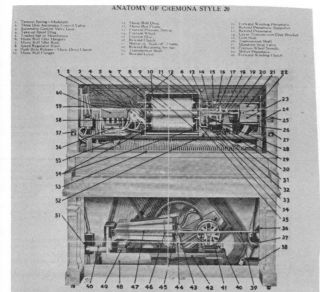

ANATOMY OF CREMONA STYLE 20

1. Tension Spring—Modulant
2. Three Disc Automatic Control Valve
3. Automatic Control Valve Gear
4. Take-up Spool Drag
5. Tracker-bar or Mouthpiece
6. Music Roll Idler Hangers
7. Music Roll Idler Rods
8. Speed Regulator Knob
9. Push Slide Release—Music Drive Clutch
10. Music Roll Flanges
11. Music Roll Drag
12. Music Box Frame
13. Friction Pressure Spring
14. Friction Wheel
15. Friction Disc
16. Rewind Clutch
17. Shifter or "kick-off" Frame
18. Rewind Retaining Springs
19. Transmission Shaft
20. Rewind Lever
21. Forward Winding Pneumatic
22. Rewind Pneumatic Supporter
23. Rewind Pneumatic
24. Upper Transmission Gear Bracket
25. Coin Slide
26. Transmission Shaft
27. Mandolin Stop Valve
28. Friction Wheel Spindle
29. Shifter Pneumatic
30. Forward Winding Clutch

31. Shifter Pull Rod
32. Music Drive Worm
33. Shifter Lever
34. Music Drive Clutch
35. Automatic Speed Regulator Gear
36. Lower Gear Bracket
37. Junction Box
38. Iron Money Box (Magazine switch box above not shown)
39. Lower Transmission Shaft
40. Motor Adjusting Knob
41. Motor
42. Equalizer Board
43. Crank Shaft Transmission Gears
44. Crank Shaft Bracket
45. Bellows Links
46. Exhauster Boards Connection Spring
47. Exhauster Bellows
48. Equalizer
49. Safety Valve
50. Tension Regulator for Equalizer
51. Main Pneumatic Action Cut-off Valve
52. Trip for Action Cut-off Valve
53. Regulating Strip—Pneumatic Action
54. Take-up Spool Flanges
55. Ratchet Pneumatic for Automatic Control Valve
56. Automatic Control Valve Cut Out
57. Modulant Control Valve
58. Automatic Control Valve Ratchet Lever
59. Modulant
60. Distributing Valve Box

### *Relating to the Tune Selecting Device*

The Cremona tune-selector, **fully protected by Letters Patent,** is the only perfect tune-selecting instrument. It does not require additional expense for separate music rolls, as it uses a **single multiple piece 88 note roll, same as used on standard Cremona instruments.**

**The method of operation** is very simple: one merely inserts the coin and turns the indicator to the number of the piece desired. The **mechanism automatically selects its piece** by winding or rewinding at a high rate of speed, always in the proper direction until the number at which the indicator is set is reached when it slows down to the proper speed and begins to play.

In case the indicator is changed, even while the machine is winding forward or re-winding, the machine will either reverse or continue in the same direction, as the change may require, until the number last indicated is reached and **by no manipulation of the indicator whatever can the instrument be made to miss or play its own selection.**

When it is desired to have the instrument play the selections in **rotation**—as does the ordinary automatic instrument—the indicator is simply set on the letter "R" at either side of the dial. If a distant slot box is used it will always play in rotation when coins are inserted—no matter how the indicator is set, but will play selectively again as soon as the piano slot is used.

Another strong feature of this device is the **combination automatic and manual control speed regulator.** The automatic speed regulator controls the speed automatically and is the only one in use which insures **absolute uniform tempo** for every piece on the roll. This result is effected without bringing parts in contact with the music roll. This method of control has been found objectionable on many speed regulators, due to the tearing of the paper, which objection is eliminated with this device.

The instrument is **beltless,** being equipped throughout with **direct noiseless gear, shaft transmission,** and is absolutely reliable, extremely simple in principle and constructed of the highest grade of material and workmanship.

THE MARQUETTE PIANO COMPANY
CHICAGO, U. S. A.

**This cabinet orchestrion in the Al Svoboda Collection features the Tune Selecting Device (the mechanisms of which can be seen through the clear glass at the upper right). In the bottom part of the cabinet are two ranks of pipes – violin and flute.**

Upper part of the instrument — showing two ranks of pipes, the xylophone, bass and snare drums, cymbal, and other features. The large art glass front panel has been removed for photography. (See it on the first page of the Marquette section.)

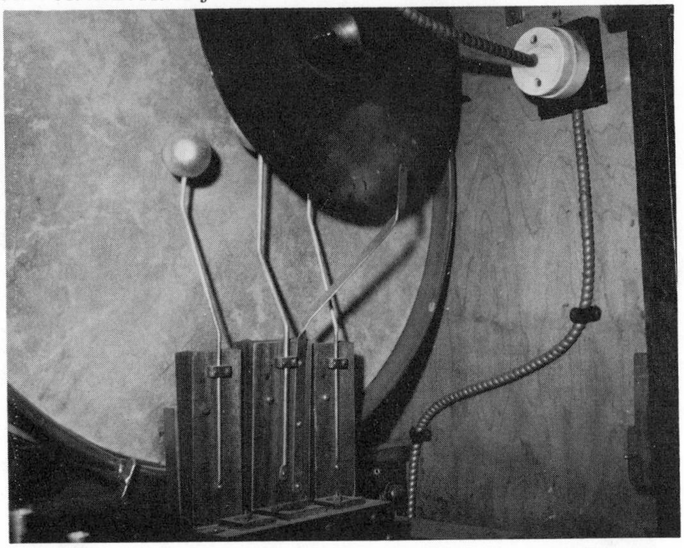

Bass drum and cymbal. The center beater is the "bass drum" striker. The two side beaters are the "tympani" or "kettle drum" strikers — as arranged on the music roll.

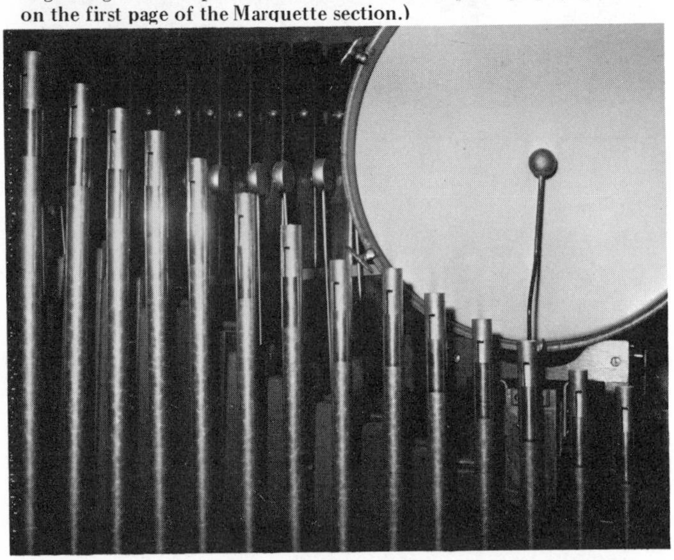

The snare drum repeats or reiterates with a sustained roll effect as long as the snare drum hole is open on the tracker bar. At the upper left can be seen some of the rosewood xylophone bars.

There are two ranks of pipes in the Orchestral J — a rank of flutes and a rank of violins. The latter pipes are of metal in this instrument, although they are usually of wood in instruments of this type.

Vacuum pump and reservoir in the left bottom of the case. Note the adjustable spring which regulates tension on the reservoir and, hence, the level of vacuum.

Orchestral J roll mechanism — an "overengineered" device that could have been built with many fewer parts as, indeed, Seeburg, Coinola, and others of the period did.

# Cremona Theatre Orchestra

## SOLO STYLE O

This two-manual theatre orchestra as will be noted by the specifications includes an unusually wide "instrumentation." With sufficient volume for the largest moving picture theatres, its tones and expression are so perfectly controlled as to adapt it for use in the smaller houses if desired.

A particular feature of this style is the beautiful Solo effects of violin, piccolo, flute, bass, saxophone, 'cello, xylophone, vox humana, etc., obtainable with harmonious and perfectly balanced accompaniments. The Solo orchestrated roll controls automatically the arranging and rearranging of the instrumentation and of the tone shutters, giving the perfect expression and technique of the master artist and plays on indefinitely until stopped.

When equipped with the single music roll system, it plays automatically either the specially orchestrated 134-note Solo music roll or standard 88-note player music, the change from one to the other being made at will. With the duplex music roll system, the rolls are located side by side as shown in the illustration, change from one to the other being made instantaneously by the pressure of a single button.

The sforzando pedal fills a much desired requirement of the performer as it enables him to bring the full organ into instant use and as quickly back to its former combination.

The console or central unit is of the height of an ordinary piano, giving the musician an uninterrupted view of the screen or stage.

### INSTRUMENTATION

**Console**

Mandolin
Piano

**Organ, Orchestral—Swell Cabinet**

Violin.
Stopped Flute.
Saxophone (or 'Cello).
Vox Humana—Bass.
Vox Humana—Treble.
Stopped Diapason (or Bass).
Organ Swell.

**Drum—Swell Cabinet**

Snare Drum.
Bass Drum.
Tympani.
Cymbal.
Castanets.
Tambourine.
Tom Tom.
Triangle.
Cathedral Chimes.
Xylophone.

### WIND PRESSURES

Blast 6 inches.
Suction 25 inches.

**Auxiliary Stops**

Super-Coupler.
Sub-Coupler.
Sforzando.
Tremolo.
Modulant.
Soft Pedal.
Piano Bass.
Piano Treble.
Piano to Organ.

### TRAP EFFECTS

Auto Horn.
Door Bell.
Horse Trot.
Cow Bell.
Bird Call.
Fire Gong.
Train Whistle.
Wind Siren.
Steamboat Whistle.
Church Bell.
Crash Cymbal.
Train Bell.
Clog.
Chimes.
Tom Tom.
Sleigh Bells.

**Description of the Solo Style O Cremona photoplayer. The third paragraph at the left is in error – the model shown is not the duplex mechanism, but is the single (using the 134-note "S" roll) tracker bar style. Any Cremona photoplayer could be ordered with either single or duplex system.**

Cremona—Theatre Orchestra, Solo Style M3

**Cremona Solo Style M3 Photoplayer – This was one of the more popular Cremona photoplayer styles. The instrument illustrated above is shown with a duplex mechanism using two 134-note rolls. Cremona photoplayers were available with the following roll systems: (1) Single tracker bar using 88-note home player piano rolls; (2) Duplex tracker bars using 88-note rolls and 134-note "S" rolls; (3) Duplex mechanisms using two "S" rolls; (4) Single tracker bar using "S" rolls. Although we haven't seen or heard of one, it would be logical to assume that 88-note duplex mechanisms were available also.**

**Cremona photoplayers had their heyday in the 'teens. Evidently several hundred were sold. An instruction sheet gave details for caring for the instruments in various climes. For wet locations – the swamplands of Arkansas and Louisiana, for instance – a light bulb in each side chest chased the dampness away. In desert locations pans of water had an opposite effect.**

**Cremona Solo Style M Photoplayer. The model illustrated above is equipped with two 134-note "S" rolls. Centered between the two rolls are two program cards listing the ten tunes on each roll. By means of a switching device the operator could play one roll or the other, alternating as often as he wished. Rewind and "fast forward" controls permitted any desired tune to be selected in a matter of seconds.**

**As could other makes of photoplayers, the Cremona instruments could be operated remotely (from the projection booth) by a push-button panel. This panel controlled the switching from one roll to the other and could turn the instrument on and off. It could not operate any of the sound effects normally controlled from the foot pedals. However, with an "S" roll in place most of the interior instruments could be turned on and off automatically – and the absence of a fire gong or steamboat whistle wouldn't be missed.**

## The Cremona Tune Selector

*by Art Reblitz*

Many automatic musical instruments have their music program in a set, predetermined order. A customer desiring to hear a certain song on a non-selective instrument often has to play through several others first. Manufacturers of mechanical musical instruments were always aware of this disadvantage, and even by the 19th century they had developed clever mechanisms to overcome it.

Barrel organs and pianos, disc and cylinder music boxes, and cylinder phonographs were all marketed with manually operated tune selecting devices. These older mechanical musical instruments used two distinct types of mechanisms. One type brought separate tune sheets into contact with the note-playing levers, just as a modern coin operated phonograph picks out separate records and feeds them to a single tone arm. Early examples of this type include the Regina, Polyphon, and Symphonion disc changing music boxes, and Regina and other selective cylinder phonographs. The other type of selective mechanism involved programming two or more tunes on the same memory unit (barrel, cylinder, disc, etc.) and then shifting it around to bring different areas programmed with different music into contact with the note-playing mechanism. Examples of this type are barrel pianos and organs, and cylinder music boxes, which shift the cylinder sideways to bring new rows of pins into alignment with the key frame, comb teeth, etc. An unusual type of disc box, the Sirion, was made to operate on this principle, shifting the disc sideways one track to play the star wheels with alternate rows of projections. The New Century disc-shifting box operates similarly.

The former method of tune selection was easily adaptable to roll-played instruments since it is not much harder to pick a music roll out of a magazine than it is a disc or a cylinder. In this type the piano has a single tracker bar and a mechanism for bringing different rolls to it. Magazine or revolver type roll changers were made by Wurlitzer, Philipps, National, Hupfeld, Aeolian, and others for a wide variety of instruments including theatre photoplayers, orchestrions, and even reproducing pianos and organs!

The second method of selecting songs, by shifting a cylinder or disc sideways to bring different areas of its surface into contact with the note-actuating mechanisms, was harder to adapt to roll-operated instruments. In a cylinder or disc-operated machine each song had to be of the same length, a length determined by the circumference of the cylinder or disc. With music rolls, however, it was impractical to perforate parallel songs, but it was easy to make multi-tune rolls by adding one melody after the other. This provided the instruments with music of great length, but it introduced problems in designing a selector mechanism which could tell when one song ended and the next began. The mechanisms used to solve these problems were some of the most ingenious devices ever used in pneumatic roll-played instruments. One such device was the Marquette Piano Company's tune selector used on certain Cremona pianos. Here is how the Marquette mechanism works:

Cremona tune-selecting machines all used type M rolls which have the following control perforations at the margins of each roll:

A. "Counter" – appears in the middle of each song.

C. "Play" – at the beginning of the roll.

D. "Play" – after hole C and before each song.

1. "Shut-off" – at the beginning of the roll, after hole C; also after each song except No. 10.

E. "Fast Forward / Rewind" – before each song and simultaneous with hole D; also after song 10, before H.

F. "Rewind" – after song 10.

H. "Shut-off" – after song 10 only.

Holes C, 1, and F are the same, respectively, as the play, shut-off, and rewind holes on other types of coin piano rolls. When the knob on the tune selector is turned to position "R" ("Rotation"), these holes in the roll make the piano operate as if it had no selector.

The tune selector barrel has two main sections, both of which are channeled. Tubing from holes D and E is connected to one section, and tubing from the play, rewind, and fast-forward pneumatics is connected to the other section.

The front section of the selector barrel is turned in steps by the knob on the front of the cabinet. It has positions 1 through 10 and R (Rotation). The rear section of the selector barrel is turned by the roll. It is normally locked into position, but whenever hole A comes up, a pneumatic releases the lock, and the barrel is allowed to turn one step in the direction the roll is moving. This counter has eleven positions. When a roll is first put on the machine, the counter is in position 1. As each song plays, the counter is moved one notch, so position 2 is before song 2, 10 is before song 10, and 11 is after song 10.

The knob may be positioned in various relations to the counter: knob in "R" or rotation position; knob at the same number as the counter; knob at any number higher than the counter; knob at any number lower than the counter.

Condition One: (knob at "R," counter in any position): holes D and E are blocked; machine responds only to non-selective perforations C, 1, F, H. The counter continues to work from hole A, so the counter barrel remains in step with the roll.

Condition Two: (knob at the same number as the counter): channels in the counter barrel connect hole D with the play pneumatic; machine shifts to play.

Condition Three: (knob at any number higher than the counter): channels connect hole E with the fast-forward pneumatic. When a coin is inserted, the machine shifts to fast forward and continues to do so until the counter catches up with the knob. At that time the channels are restored to Condition Two, and the roll shifts to play.

Condition Four: (knob at any number lower than the counter): channels in the barrel connect hole E with the rewind pneumatic. When a coin is inserted, the machine shifts to rewind and rewinds until the barrel counts down to the same number at which the knob is set. This restores the channels to Condition Two, and the machine shifts to play.

In simpler terms, the roll automatically follows the counter to wherever the knob is set and then plays that song. This is made possible and foolproof only by having three separate slots in the roll (A, D, and E) to operate the selector.

If the knob is left at a certain song, the Cremona will repeat that song as often as a coin is deposited. It is assumed that the customer who deposits money in the piano will either set the knob for the desired song or turn it to "R". However, if the selector always worked like this, patrons using a remotely located wallbox would always get the same tune unless the knob were set at "R". For this reason, tubes D and E go through a cut-out block which is normally open. When a coin is dropped in a wallbox, a magnet in the piano opens a channel to a valve which blocks the two selector tubes and makes the piano play in rotation regardless of where the knob is set. When the piano shuts off, it reconnects the tubes so the selector will work when the next coin is dropped into the piano itself.

Everything is now accounted for except hole H, the shut-off after song 10. Regular (non-selective) M roll pianos rewind the roll after 10 and then shut off. If the knob on a selector is set at 10, however, the piano will rewind after 10, get to the beginning of 10, shift back to "play" and repeat the song over and over for one nickel. For this reason, the first shut-off hole (before song 1) is taped off. The machine shuts off after 10, and another nickel is required to rewind the roll and play the first song, either with the selector or on rotation. A non-selective machine does not have the shut-off tubed to hole H, so that hole is ignored.

If this lengthy description makes the selector sound terribly complicated, study the accompanying photographs and you will see how neat and compact it really is. This selector is foolproof as long as no one reaches inside the cabinet and manually pushes the counter barrel out of phase with the roll, and the roll has no rips or tears on the left side (which will activate the counter more than once per song). The machine may be given a workout by turning the knob back and forth without letting it play a song, but it will always end up at the last number at which the knob is set.

---Art Reblitz

(Note: The foregoing appeared earlier in the Musical Box Society "Bulletin" and is used with permission of that Society.)

The Cremona tune selector — view from the front. Installed on certain early Cremona instruments, the tune selector is controlled by perforations in a special type "M" roll.

View from the top of the left side of the Cremona tune selector mechanism. (Photographs on this page by Art Reblitz)

CABLE ADDRESS "COIN"
CODES: WESTERN UNION UNIVERSAL EDITION
A.B.C. 5TH EDITION-LIEBERS STANDARD

TELEPHONES
CAPITOL 2110 TO 2115

MILLS NOVELTY COMPANY

WORLD'S LARGEST MANUFACTURERS OF ALL KINDS OF

COIN OPERATED MACHINES

4100-4118 FULLERTON AVENUE

CHICAGO

## THE MILLS NOVELTY COMPANY
—Chicago, Illinois—

### Early Mills Musical Instruments

Today the Mills Novelty Company is remembered mainly for the Violano - Virtuoso, an ingenious automatically-played violin with piano accompaniment that was one of the most popular coin operated instruments ever made in America. However, the Violano was just one, albeit the most important, of a number of interesting products sold during the 20th century by Mills.

During the thirty years from 1900 to 1930 the Mills Novelty Company of Chicago marketed a wide variety of automatic musical instruments. Though primarily a manufacturer of gambling machines and, to a lesser extent, arcade machines, the Mills Novelty Company found early that music had great appeal. From the early days of the 20th century until the mid-1930's virtually every catalogue of the Mills line contained automatic musical instruments of one type or another.

*Above: The Mills owl trademark appeared on most gambling machines and some musical instruments as well.*

*Left: The Automatic Pianova was manufactured by the Pianova Co. of New York and sold by Mills.*

In the very early days of the company (circa 1900 - 1905) most, if not all, instruments offered were manufactured by others and simply sold under the Mills label. During this time Mills sold a 44-note arcade piano and billed it as the "Mills Automatic Pianova." Actually, this instrument was probably made by the Pianova Company of New York City and was sold through various distributors, including Mills, who marketed it under various other names. (The Electrova Company sold the identical instrument as the "Electrova Style 44.") The Regina Sublima Piano, manufactured by the Regina Music Box Company of Rahway, N.J., was another product sold by Mills. As was the case with the Pianova, the Regina Sublima was sold by others also. For instance, Wurlitzer offered it as the "Wurlitzer Tremolo Piano." During this time the Mills Novelty Company supplied completely equipped arcades to various customers. The automatic piano was an important part of any arcade — and for this reason, among others, automatic pianos were sold as part of the Mills line.

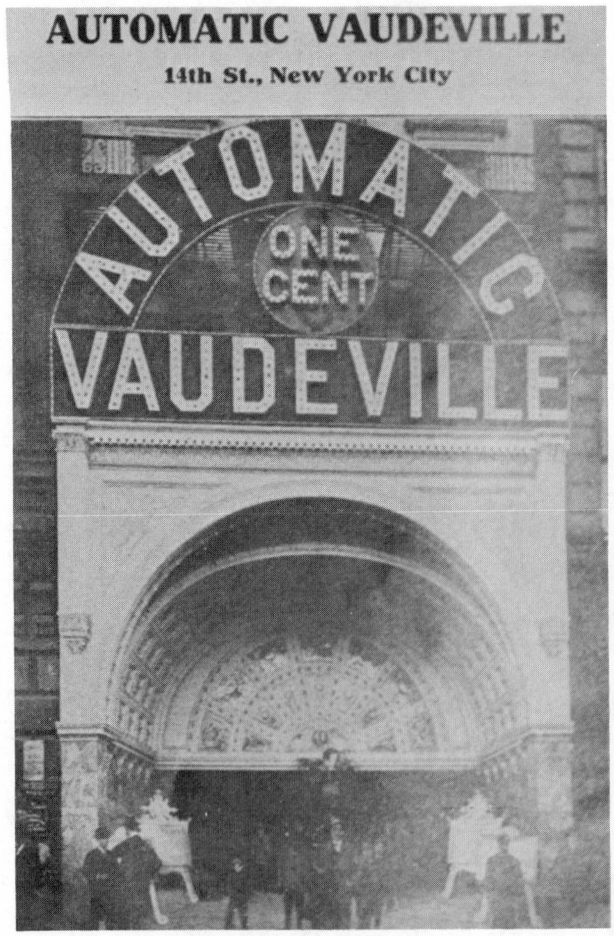

*Above and left: Arcade machines were a Mills specialty. For $2000 to $4000 one could buy a completely stocked amusement parlor. Today early Mills arcade devices such as the Illustrated Song Machines lined up in a row at the left are highly desired by collectors.*

*Above: Mills Duplex Musical slot machine. Left: Mills Musical Dewey. This device, named after the hero of Manila, was the most popular of the dozens of different Mills slot machines made.*

### Musical Slot Machines

While not strictly musical instruments per se, the Mills Novelty Company sold a wide variety of musical gambling machines. Mills slot machines such as the "20th Century," the "Dewey," the "Duplex," the "Owl," etc. were offered with built-in music boxes as an extra feature. These large cabinet-style floor-standing console gambling machines were operated by a crank in the front. After a coin was deposited in the slot of the player's choice, the lever was depressed, and a large reel on the front turned rapidly. At the same time the lever was depressed to actuate the reel it also wound the music box and started it playing. The music boxes used as part of these gambling machines were, for the most part, cheap European boxes with short cylinders and of indifferent musical quality. (Note: At least two different Mills slot machines utilized Regina disc movements, but these were made only in limited quantities.)

Interestingly enough, the purpose of the musical gambling machine was not primarily to entertain or to spiritually uplift the person who was playing the device; rather, the musical feature was intended to circumvent laws regarding slot machines. To quote from a Mills catalogue of the 1909 era: "The musical attachment is very large and renders the machine permissible in many places where a plain machine could not be operated." The same evasive tactic was employed years later by manufacturers of "Profit Sharing Player Pianos." The theory was that the player of a gambling machine who deposited a coin received fair value for his money, irrespective of whether he won or lost the game of chance, because during the process the instrument delivered a tune.

Evidently these early Mills slot machines with music boxes were sold by the thousands. How curious it is that a legal quirk made the nation's largest manufacturer of slot machines one of the largest distributors of cylinder music boxes as well!

### The Automatic Virtuosa (Violin Player)

In 1904 a young man named Henry K. Sandell joined the Mills firm. Although he was just twenty seven at the time, young Sandell had already distinguished himself as an inventor and had patented a number of devices in the electrical and mechanical fields. One of Sandell's first projects at the Mills Novelty Company was the perfection of an automatic violin-playing machine. The result, first marketed in 1905 or 1906, was offered as the "Automatic Virtuosa." Like other contemporary Mills instruments it was housed in a quartered oak cabinet with cast iron feet and with a large sign on the top.

The violin-playing part of the instrument contained a real violin complete with four strings and tuning pegs. The violin was sturdily mounted with clamps at each end. The bowing action of a human artist was simulated by a series of four rosined celluloid discs which revolved and played the strings, either one, two, three, or all four at once.

The counterpart of human fingering of the strings was provided by a bank of electromagnetically controlled mechanical "fingers" which stopped each string at predetermined intervals called for by the holes in a roll. The entire device was operated by a perforated paper music roll which was "read" by a series of wire brushes reading through the roll onto a common contact roller. The first rolls produced were usually one tune in length. Although the primary market for the Automatic Virtuosa was in arcades, the early Mills publicity concerning it endeavored to give it much wider appeal. An advertisement of the time noted:

"Arcades, parks, and pleasure resorts will find the Mills Virtuosa the most novel and attractive automatic machine introduced since the beginning of coin-controlled machines, and for this reason it will be well patronized and will pay for itself in a very short time.

"Every hotel, cafe, and refreshment parlor should have the Mills Virtuosa because it will royally entertain customers with the latest music with no expense to the house, and besides it will yield a large and steady income. It takes the place of an orchestra and makes money for you instead of causing you to spend it for salaries (for musicians).

"Drug and cigar stores, dry goods houses, and, in fact, almost any kind of store can draw additional trade by having the Mills Virtuosa... Operators will find the Mills Virtuosa the most interesting machine they have ever handled because it is easily placed in good locations and becuase of the large amount of money it will take in... Vaudeville theatres will find the Automatic Virtuosa a star act as a musical novelty... For the home the Automatic Virtuosa will furnish a most refined music, rendering not only the popular airs, but the most difficult and exquisite music at any time simply by pressing a button. For the entertainment of the family and friends it is simply unequalled..."

Apparently the Automatic Virtuosa achieved only modest success. The number produced is not known — but it could not have been very large as the Automatic Virtuosa is an extreme rarity today.

### The English Tour of the Virtuosa

In the spring of 1908 an Automatic Virtuosa was shipped to England and was exhibited at the well-known Waring Department Store in London. The Mills advertisements notwithstanding, it was recognized that the violin alone offered a rather thin musical program. To give it a

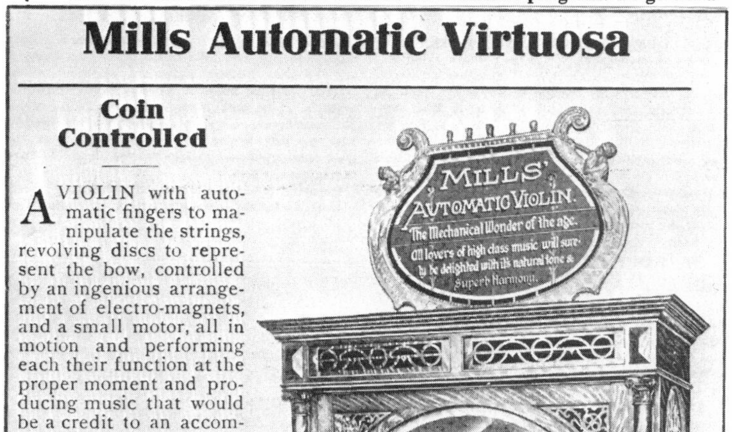

Mills Automatic Virtuosa
Coin Controlled
A VIOLIN with automatic fingers to manipulate the strings, revolving discs to represent the bow, controlled by an ingenious arrangement of electro-magnets, and a small motor, all in motion and performing each their function at the proper moment and producing music that would be a credit to an accomplished musician—a violin turned into a thing of life—an automaton working with the precision of human hands controlled by brain, muscle and nerve.
The average coin-controlled musical machine is usually sadly out of tune, and its loud, harsh-sounding notes grate upon the ear of those musically inclined the least, not to mention the effect upon the trained ear of the accomplished musician. These serious objections have been carefully studied from a scientific standpoint, with the result that all of them have been eliminated. The resulting music is of a nature to be most pleasing to the ear; not too loud to be annoying in a public place, but soft and sweet, with volume enough to be heard from a reasonable distance. (For further particulars, address "Violin Dept").
Size, 5 feet 11 inches high; 3 feet wide; 21 inches deep.
Shipping weight, 420 lbs.
Boxed for foreign shipment: Dimensions, 76x41x26 inches. Weight, 520 pounds.
MILLS' AUTOMATIC VIOLIN.
The Mechanical Wonder of the age.
All lovers of high class music will surely be delighted with its natural tone & Superb Harmony.


*Mills Automatic Virtuosa: This early instrument, housed in an ornate quartered oak and metal-trimmed cabinet, featured an automatically played violin. It was the forerunner of the famed Violano - Virtuoso.*

greater appeal the Automatic Virtuosa was played in accompaniment with a human pianist who sat nearby and played a piano at the appropriate time.

The Automatic Virtuosa created a sensation in London. Following its department store appearance, it made a circuit comprising most leading British towns. It played to packed houses wherever it was shown. Virtually every newspaper in Great Britain devoted extensive coverage to it. The Birmingham Gazette reported on March 13, 1908: "Everything that a fine violinist could do, the machine did, and did perfectly. It executed trills and shakes, picked the strings, or played sliding notes just as the composition demanded, and throughout there was no sound or sign of mechanical origin save only the slight buzzing of the motor, a difficulty which should easily be overcome."

The Liverpool Journal of Commerce reported on March 31, 1908: "A private performance was given at the Empire Theatre yesterday in connection with the Mills Automatic Violin which is to render a number of selections each evening this week at the Lime Street House. The new invention is a distinct novelty, and the manner in which some really difficult operatic excerpts were played at yesterday's performance aroused the wonder as it contributed to the delight of the hearers. By means of an electrical mechanism the necessary manipulation both of fingers and bow are produced with the greatest facility, whilst even expression is so well counterfeited as to deceive all but the expert."

Another newspaper reported that at an appearance at the Southampton Hippodrome the Automatic Virtuosa received "enthusiastic and unstinting applause." In another account, the Bath Weekly Chronicle (issue of May 16, 1908) referred to the machine as a "10,000 pound sterling automatically operated fiddle."

Among those who heard of the Automatic Virtuosa during its London tour was His Majesty, King Edward VII (Edward ascended to the throne following Queen Victoria's death in 1901). The king asked that the Automatic Virtuosa be brought to Windsor Castle and played for him. Concerning this command performance, the Mills Novelty Company noted:

"Naturally, we decided to make the performance one which should delight His Majesty and show the instrument to its fullest advantage. To make sure that the violin and its accompaniment should harmonize perfectly, we had a skilled pianist rehearse the accompaniment time and time again on a piano placed in our studio... It was all exceedingly satisfactory, but we concluded that to be complete the instrument must have its own self-playing piano, making outside talent unnecessary. Thus originated the idea of combining the two instruments, and Mr. Sandell immediately set to work, making his designs for the remarkable piano..."

On the eve of the royal performance, the King of Denmark, father of Queen Alexandra, died. All festivities came to an immediate end, and King Edward's royal request was withdrawn. Mills noted that the final outcome was a disappointment but went on to say that "the promised event had served a useful purpose in suggesting a self-playing piano."

### The U.S. Patent Office Takes an Interest

All of this publicity in England had an interesting result. Newspaper clippings were sent to the United States and ultimately reached the United States Patent Office in Washington, D.C. The Patent Office officials knew only that the Automatic Virtuosa was of United States origin but did not know who made it. Accordingly, they cabled the United States Consul in London to investigate the situation and report further. At this time, in the early part of 1909, the Patent Office was busy preparing an exhibit for the Alaska Yukon Pacific Exposition which was to be held later that year in Seattle, Washington. The government exhibit was to consist of outstanding American inventions.

Three Patent Office representatives visited the Mills factory in Chicago. They learned of the Automatic Virtuosa and saw the beginning attempts to incorporate a self-playing piano as part of the design. A contemporary Chicago newspaper account entitled "Wonderful Violin Player" noted that: "Mr. H.C. Armstrong of the U.S. Patent Office is in Chicago arranging for the government Patent Office exhibit at the Alaska - Yukon exposition, to be held at Seattle this year.

"Mr. Armstrong was authorized by the government to select from among the millions of registered patents such ones as in his mature judgment represented the most meritorious ideas of the last decade. The conditions imposed were that the ideas chosen must illustrate not only industrial progress, but should also typify the greatest strides made by the industrial arts and sciences for the benefit of mankind. This list, as finally determined upon, is as follows: The steam turbine principle of power transmission; the modern system of light generation and distribution; the Ives Kromskop and the Ives Calorimeter, each of which further the art of color photography; the Telepost, a system of telegraphical importance; the International harvesting machinery for modern farming, which will be shown in a panoramic manner; the Mills Pianova - Virtuosa, an electrical violin player with automatic piano accompaniment.

"Mr. Armstrong is enthusiastic in his encomiums for the two Chicago items in the above list, which are the last two named. Himself a lover of music, he names the automatic violin as the most wonderful of the list. Said he, "Consider the intricacy of the subject and imagine the mass of technical details to be overcome to enable an automatic violin device to reproduce the compositions of Chopin, Brahms, Liszt, Beethoven, Mascagni, and all the world's master musicians with tonal certainty and precise technique. It is a marvelous instrument."

### The Violano-Virtuoso

The above newspaper account is remarkable for its description of the Virtuosa, with the newly added piano, as the "Pianova-Virtuosa." Nowhere else in contemporary literature have we found it referred to with the "Pianova" designation. Evidently the name was changed shortly thereafter.

When the Patent Office exhibit opened at the Seattle Exposition, the Mills entry was billed as the Violano - Virtuoso, and the instrument was known by that name from then on. The piano was built in as the rear portion of the instrument. For servicing, the piano action and harp swing out from the back on a separate caster. A contemporary catalogue illustration shows that the piano was of the usual type (with bass notes at the left end and treble notes at the right end) and was apparently manufactured by the Pianova Company of New York City. Probably because Pianova furnished the piano the instrument was first tentatively designated as the "Pianova - Virtuosa." The same piano

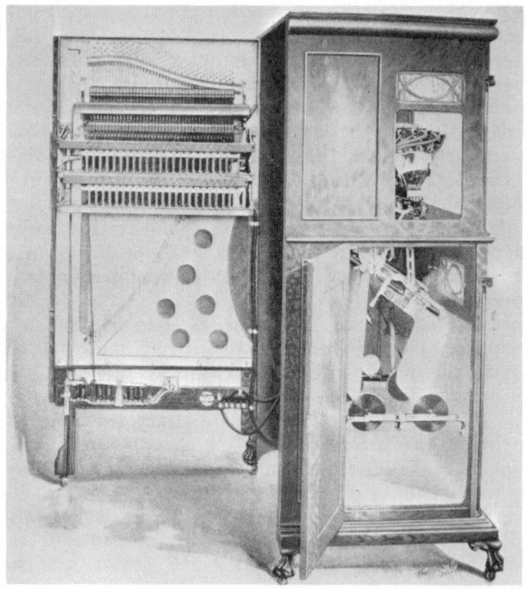

*Following the English tour of the Automatic Virtuosa, it was decided to incorporate a piano into the instrument — thus creating a piano and violin combination. The first type of piano used was of the regular style with the bass notes at the left and the treble notes at the right. Like later styles, the piano formed the back door of the device — a convenience which permitted easy access and servicing. Soon after the introduction of this model the instrument was redesigned. Later instruments have symmetrical pianos with the longer strings in the middle.*

*This style, the first design of the Violano - Virtuoso, was short-lived and was possibly sold only to the extent of a few dozen, if indeed that many, instruments.*

plate used in this early Mills instrument was also used in the Engelhardt Banjorchestra (an automatic banjo band), the Pianova 44-note piano, and several other brands of instruments.

Although the Violano - Virtuoso, complete with violin and piano, was shown at the 1909 Alaska Yukon Pacific Exposition, it was not ready for the general market at that time. Probably considerable time was necessary to set up production line facilities and to iron out the inevitable "bugs" which must have accompanied its introduction. On June 1, 1911, the following announcement was released:

"The Violano - Virtuoso is introduced at this time to the music trade and to music lovers generally, somewhat earlier than the management had intended. Since the AYPE at Seattle in 1909, the instrument has been the subject of constant study, and many improvements have been made, for it has been and is the policy of the management not to offer the Violano - Virtuoso to the public until both the violin and piano attachment have been made as nearly perfect as possible.

"The opportunity presented by the Piano Trade Exhibition, however, for the demonstration of the Violano - Virtuoso is one that we cannot neglect, particularly as we have been urged to avail ourselves of it by a vast number of music lovers who have heard the instrument in the past two years. We have, therefore, taken space at the exhibition and shall be glad to go into the fullest detail of explanation and demonstration of the Violano - Virtuoso."

The same announcement asked for "a possible further indulgence of a few weeks in the matter of delivery to purchasers."

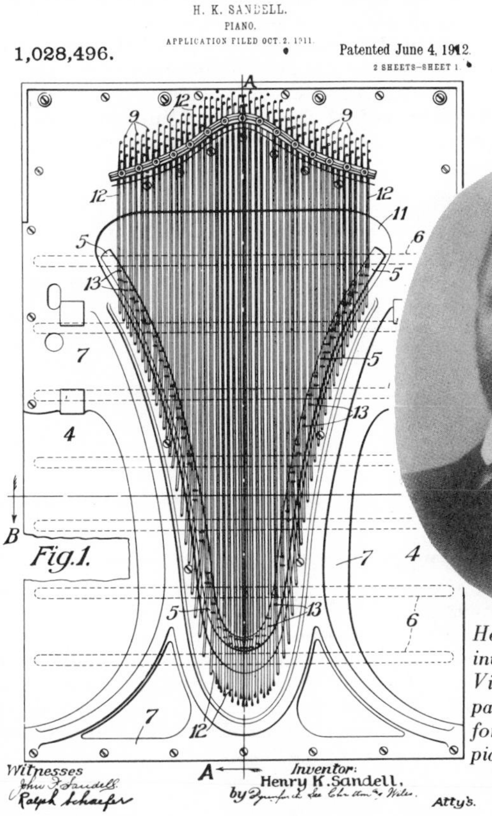

*Henry K. Sandell, inventor of the Violano, and the patent drawing for the unusual piano.*

On June 4, 1912, Henry K. Sandell patented an invention (the application had been filed on October 2, 1911) for a seemingly new type of piano with the bass strings in the center and with the treble strings arranged symmetrically on each side. This arrangement distributed the stress more evenly on the piano plate and prevented the instrument from going out of tune as quickly as would normally be the case. As the instrument was played by means of electromagnets, the order in which the strings appeared on the piano harp was of no particular consequence as long as the electromagnets were hooked up in the correct sequence. To the hearer there is no difference in tone.

The idea of a symmetrical piano, although it was successfully awarded the 1912 patent, was evidently copied from earlier ideas – including possibly the symmetrical piano used by Polyphon and Regina for the large "Concerto" disc-operated orchestrion (which was introduced in the United States in 1903 and which featured a symmetrical piano) or the Lochmann "Original" Concert-Piano.

Considering the 1912 patent date for the Mills symmetrical piano and considering that no piano-type Violanos had been released to the public as of the June 1, 1911, announcement, the instruments with the non-symmetrical pianos (the ones made by Pianova) must have been

## VIOLANO-VIRTUOSO

**Self-Playing Violin With Piano Accompaniment**

PAGES of description could not do justice to this truly magnificent instrument which the U. S. Government has signally honored and designated as one of the *greatest scientific inventions* of the age.

The Violano-Virtuoso *combines in itself two of the world's most beautiful instruments—the violin and piano.* Either may at will be played alone. Together their tones blend in sweetest harmony giving practically all the effects of a splendid stringed orchestra.

Musicians rave over its music, which is indeed rendered with the wonderful inflection, technique and dramatic force of the greatest Maestros.

### The World's Greatest Musical Attraction

No composition is too difficult for the Violano-Virtuoso. Classical, operatic, and popular music are all equally well played. There is no disagreeable suggestion of the mechanical. Every note is clear, full and true. The faults common to other automatic players are all successfully eliminated. It is without doubt the *musical masterpiece of the day.*

The Violano-Virtuoso may best be defined as a violin with piano accompaniment. The violin is played by a finger-like arrangement of electro magnets operated by a small motor. These violins are built specially for us by our own expert violin makers from the most carefully selected woods. With proper usage they should increase in value with each succeeding year.

The case of the instrument is artistically designed in the graceful classical style now so highly favored and comes in your choice of several rare woods. The ordinary electric lighting current supplies the necessary motive power and by simply touching a button the instrument may be started and stopped at will.

The music rolls used in the Violano-Virtuoso rewind automatically and are made of very tough specially prepared paper, the edges being mechanically trimmed as they are perforated insuring accuracy and perfect harmony.

For hotel and restaurant men, theatrical managers, proprietors of arcades, skating rinks, etc., the Violano-Virtuoso fills a long existing need. The novelty and almost human playing of the instrument attracts widespread attention. Furthermore it most satisfactorily takes the place of an expensive orchestra at a great saving in cost. The exquisite quality of its music finds favor with the most fastidious patrons. The Violano-Virtuoso proves therefore a most profitable investment. Full particulars and a beautiful illustrated art catalogue will be sent free to anyone on request.

*The intriguing Mills Viol-Cello was produced only in small numbers.*

released in late 1911 and early 1912. They are of sufficient rarity today that the author has never seen one; each of the dozens of Violano - Virtuosos examined has had the later symmetrical piano format.

### Other "Viol-" Instruments

In late 1912, or possibly in 1913, the Violano - Virtuoso had achieved an early measure of sales success. So enthralled was Mills with the success of the Violano-Virtuoso that it issued a lavishly illustrated catalogue, "The Electrical Mastery of Music," which offered in addition to the Violano - Virtuoso, two other instruments: the Viol-Cello and the Viol-Xylophone. The former instrument was essentially a Violano - Virtuoso with a cello rather than a piano for accompaniment. The second had a xylophone rather than a piano. It is not known whether either of these two novelties was ever produced on a commercial basis.

Mr. Oswald Wurdeman, formerly a Mills distributor, informed the author some years ago that the Viol-Cello was not a success as Mills could not find a way to "finger" the cello strings properly. However, at least one Viol-Cello was made, and perhaps the instrument even saw limited production. We have heard that one was used years ago in the Hippodrome in Los Angeles and that another held forth in a hotel lobby in Opelika, Alabama.

Apparently some difficulties of one sort or another attended the introduction of the Viol-Xylophone also. The Mills catalogue illustration of this instrument is but an artist's retouching of a stock photograph of the curved-case "commercial" model of the Violano - Virtuoso. So, perhaps the Viol-Xylophone was just an idea and never a reality.

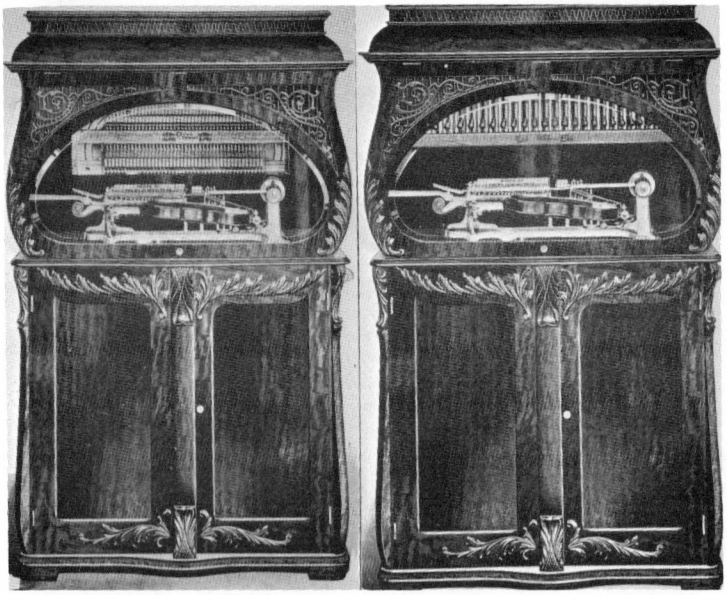

*The same, only different! The standard Mills catalogue illustration for its "Commercial" model Violano is shown at the above left. To create the Viol-Xylophone an artist simply did some artwork on the upper part — to show what appear to be xylophone bars. Note that both cabinets are otherwise identical.*

In later years Mills devised another instrument based on the Violano - Virtuoso. Called the Mills String Quartette, the instrument was an ingenious arrangement of three violins (similar to those used in the Violano - Virtuoso) and a cello! The illustration we've seen was from a Mills catalogue, and close examination leads us to believe that it wasn't an artist's conception and that at least one String Quartette was actually made.

It has been said that the saddest words of tongue or pen are "It might have been." Considering the popularity of the Violano - Virtuoso with collectors today, it would have been nice if the other Mills instruments — the Viol-Cello, the spectral Viol-Xylophone, and the String Quartette — had been made in reasonable quantities also. Alas, this was not the case.

## Mills Advertising

The Mills people were masters of advertising technique. In the book "Put Another Nickel In," I quoted what I consider to be one of the most interesting items of Mills advertising ever produced concerning the violin player — the statement that the violins used in the machine actually INCREASE IN VALUE after they are purchased. To quote the Mills catalogue:

"When we first began building the Virtuoso we bought violins from the greatest violin makers, at an average cost of $300.00 apiece, but even these were not good enough — so we set about making better ones ourselves. . . These violins are of the famous Stradivarius model, having a beautiful, rich, soft tone. . . Every Violano - Virtuoso therefore not only has a 'trained' (by playing it at the factory before installing it in the machine) violin, but also one that continues to improve until, after a year or more of use, the violin which at first was worth only $300.00 may well be valued at $1000.00."

That the Violano was a boon to mankind and could improve the ambience of any place or occasion was amply suggested by Mills who recommended the following locations for its use (we quote excerpts from the Mills catalogue):

FOR THE HOME — At first it was our intention to present the Violano - Virtuoso to the musical profession for use in public recitals, concerts, operas, etc.; but on account of the widespread demand among well-to-do music lovers for such an instrument we have decided to supply this need first. To the hostess the Violano - Virtuoso gives a delightful, unfailing source of entertainment for her guests. She can arrange a musical program suitable for any occasion and know that it will please the most critical of the company. How could an evening or a dinner party be made more enjoyable than by the works of the master composers, or by the latest opera selections, rendered with all the skill of the most noted concert artists? The Violano - Virtuoso is always ready to give you a greater variety of selections than any musician can offer. . .

THE CHILDREN'S PARTY — "The reason that boys and girls leave home," once said a keen observer, "is that so few homes are made interesting for young people. The natural craving for amusement very often overcomes personal attachments." If you have sought for means to make your home attractive and have failed to solve the problem, why not get a Violano - Virtuoso? With it you can provide a source of constant interest and entertainment. You can buy a piano or a violin, but consider that it will be years before a child can play either of them

*A "Home" model Violano - Virtuoso entertains convivial diners.*

well, and then only if practice has been a daily duty constantly performed. Why should you spend money for music lessons, and why should the satisfaction of enjoying the best playing of the best compositions be deferred when you can have a Violano - Virtuoso now? If you, as a child, had to sacrifice the advantages given by the Violano - Virtuoso, see that your children have them.

*The Hotel Lobby*

THE HOTEL LOBBY – The traveling salesman, the occasional diner, and the resident guest all will welcome the instrument which relieves so completely the usual monotony of hotel life and which drives away the "loneliness of the crowd." Where heretofore it has been necessary to employ an orchestra of several pieces and often to endure only an imperfect program, it is now possible to bring the most famous violinists to play in the dining room, the parlor, or the lobby.

*At the Club*

AT THE CLUB – When a man goes to his club he wants to get away from the little worrying things which are inseparable from business. He wants amusement, something which will rest his brain and let him forget the grind and the hustle. Suppose that the directors could employ a company of the most accomplished musicians who would constantly be on hand ready to play the best selections whenever called for. Would it not arouse the interest and enthusiasm of every member? Why then should not a Violano - Virtuoso be made a part of the club equipment?

*At the Restaurant*

AT THE RESTAURANT – The manager of a famous restaurant once said "We have the best chef money can get, we have an unsurpassed variety of food, competent service, and a richly decorated dining room; and yet, if we did not supply entertainment for our patrons our business would fall off to half of what it now is." Orchestras can be hired, but they will work only at certain hours; they do not always play well enough to please very critical people, and they make an expense which is a large item on the wrong side of the yearly statement. Why not take the cost of orchestra help and use it to decorate the room, to add rare dishes to the menu, or to improve the service? A Violano - Virtuoso will "let the musicians out" and will soon be paid for by the saving.

*A Dream of a Dance*

A DREAM OF A DANCE – Think of gliding through the steps of a Strauss waltz played as only masters can play it, and with all the beauty that the composer himself would put into it if he were present. Waltz, two-step, schottische, barn dance, or the classic minuet are all played with perfect harmony by the magic touch of the instrument which is always ready, which never becomes fatigued, and which is never subject to "moods." The dancing academy will find in the Violano - Virtuoso, not only the best instrument for use in teaching the various steps, but one which will give a much more distinctive character to the music than the piano and violin as played by the usual assistants.

*On the Ocean Liner*

ON THE OCEAN LINER – With all the games and amusements provided by the great steamship companies for their passengers, there is nothing which can fill the place of music, nothing which can make the time pass so agreeably in fair weather or in foul. The Violano - Virtuoso will be the next innovation in steamship equipment. The boat which carries one of these instruments can give daily musical programs of such high character that only praise can result.

FOR THE RAILROAD TRAIN – Performers cannot be considered, a player piano is too bulky, a talking machine is too crude; but now, there is the Violano - Virtuoso which will occupy no more space than one of the large easy chairs, and which will completely satisfy the universal demand for music.

*Sacred Concert*

SACRED CONCERT – One of the perplexing problems of the church today is to obtain attendance. Empty pews where even the most scholarly preachers preside give evidence of the need of something which will add to the interest offered by good sermons. But you will notice that the churches which provide the best music are the ones which as a rule are more nearly filled. Here then is the solution of the matter. Make the church more attractive by giving the public the opportunity to hear musical programs such as are seldom offered except by highly paid artists – and this can be done through the medium of the Violano - Virtuoso.

FOR THE MERCHANT – Announcements of Violano - Virtuoso concerts to be given in the store on certain days are sure to bring

**hundreds of people who ordinarily would not come and many of whom will buy before they leave. In fact, so popular can such events be made that admittance by ticket may be required to prevent overcrowding. (QDB editorial comment: !!!)**

A Teacher of Teachers
He who wishes to master the violin as the great performers have mastered it can call to his aid at any moment the world's music masters, with all their personality faithfully reproduced.
Or, should he desire a skilled piano accompanist, he has but to push a lever that stills the violin and permits the piano to play alone.

**A TEACHER OF TEACHERS — He who wishes to master the violin as the great performers have mastered it can call to his aid at any moment the world's music masters, with all their personality faithfully reproduced. Or, should he desire a skilled piano accompanist, he has but to push a lever that stills the violin and permits the piano to play alone. For teachers, for accompanists, for advanced performers on either piano or violin, the Violano - Virtuoso is an ever-present, ever-willing aid.**

**Testimonials played a prominent part in advertising for the Violano. Various state governors, prominent musicians, city officials, and others had their comments concerning the Mills Violano reproduced in the sales literature. Some comments were quite plausible, but others almost seemed to have been written by a Mills publicity agent. For instance, a Mr. Zahner of Chicago reported that "Your instrument surpassed any and all cafe music that I have ever heard. My opinion was soon confirmed when a musical friend of prominence came in while a favorite selection was being rendered and immediately inquired, 'When did you put in that swell orchestra?' "**

**Another Mills correspondent, a Mr. Chatkin, noted: "It far eclipses** anything that I have ever seen in all my experience, and I even prefer it **to a big orchestra on account of the masterly way in which it plays the most difficult pieces and even pieces which most orchestras would not attempt. . ."**

**William Jennings Bryan, silver-tongued orator of the Platte and perennial presidential candidate, was happy to say that he "just had the pleasure of hearing your Automatic Violin and Piano. It was certainly a surprise to me, as it must be to all who have not before heard it. The tones could hardly be more perfect, and the execution is admirable. . ."**

George M. Cohan, march composer extraordinaire, heartily endorsed **the musical wonder: "The Automatic Violin is a wonderful invention and I heartily feel that it will prove a great success. The first time I heard it playing my song 'The Grand Old Flag' I rushed to make the acquaintance of so fine a soloist and discovered this marvelous piece of machinery . . ."**

**If more entertaining advertising was ever produced by any manufacturer of automatic musical instruments, we've yet to learn of it — although Wurlitzer came in a close second. Wurlitzer's Paganini Violin Piano was just the thing to "carry the most critical audience by storm" — and so on.**

Violano Data

**In the years from 1912 to the time when production was discontinued, around 1930, the Violano - Virtuoso was offered in a number of different case styles. As is true of many products which achieve market success, the quality of the casework declined as the instrument became more popular. At the same time the retail price more than doubled.**

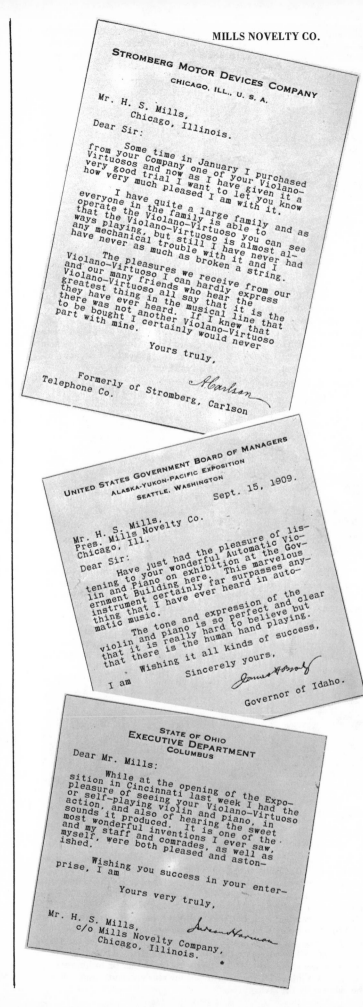

STROMBERG MOTOR DEVICES COMPANY
CHICAGO, ILL., U. S. A.

Mr. H. S. Mills,
Chicago, Illinois.

Dear Sir:

Some time in January I purchased from your Company one of your Violano-Virtuosos and now as I have given it a very good trial I want to let you know how very much pleased I am with it.

I have quite a large family and as everyone in the family is able to operate the Violano-Virtuoso you can see that the Violano-Virtuoso is almost always playing, but still I have never had any mechanical trouble with it and I have never as much as broken a string.

The pleasures we receive from our Violano-Virtuoso I can hardly express and our many friends who hear the Violano-Virtuoso all say that it is the greatest thing in the musical line that they have ever heard. If I knew that there was not another Violano-Virtuoso to be bought I certainly would never part with mine.

Yours truly,

A. Carlson

Formerly of Stromberg, Carlson Telephone Co.

UNITED STATES GOVERNMENT BOARD OF MANAGERS
ALASKA-YUKON-PACIFIC EXPOSITION
SEATTLE, WASHINGTON

Sept. 15, 1909.

Mr. H. S. Mills,
Pres. Mills Novelty Co.
Chicago, Ill.

Dear Sir:

Have just had the pleasure of listening to your wonderful Automatic Violin and Piano on exhibition at the Government Building here. This marvelous instrument certainly far surpasses anything that I have ever heard in automatic music.

The tone and expression of the violin and piano is so perfect and clear that it is really hard to believe but that there is the human hand playing.

Wishing it all kinds of success,

I am Sincerely yours,

James H. Brady

Governor of Idaho.

STATE OF OHIO
EXECUTIVE DEPARTMENT
COLUMBUS

Dear Mr. Mills:

While at the opening of the Exposition in Cincinnati last week I had the pleasure of seeing your Violano-Virtuoso or self-playing violin and piano, in action, and also of hearing the sweet sounds it produced. It is one of the most wonderful inventions I ever saw, and my staff and comrades, as well as myself, were both pleased and astonished.

Wishing you success in your enterprise, I am

Yours very truly,

Judson Harmon

Mr. H. S. Mills,
c/o Mills Novelty Company,
Chicago, Illinois.

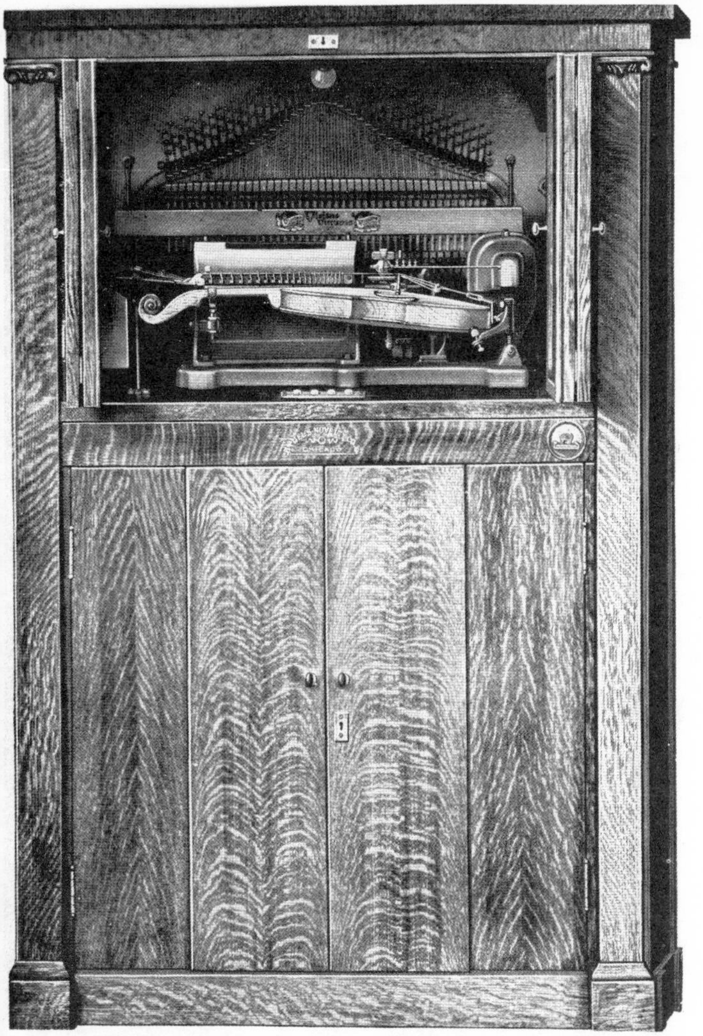

*Although this section of the book shows many Violano case designs, the one which represents most of the production (as evidenced by numbers known today) is that shown above. Known as the "Single Mills" by collectors, the instrument features a violin and piano in a rectangular case. Most were of mahogany. The above catalogue illustration shows one in quartered oak wood.*

We find that the early instruments are masterpieces of furniture design; some of them may actually be called elegant. The "Home Model" of the 1913 era featured two large fluted Corinthian columns on each side with two additional fluted pilasters on the front doors. The "Automatic" or "Commercial" model of the same period featured bevelled glass, elaborate scrollwork, and curved sides.

A few years later the cases were simplified to a more austere rectangular appearance. In addition to the regular single-violin models a new variety, the DeLuxe Model, was featured. This instrument contained two violins but was otherwise identical to the single-violin models. A circa 1925 catalogue lists three basic Violano - Virtuoso styles: two of the styles are of the single-violin type, known as the Grand (sometimes called the Baby Grand) and the Concert Grand models, and the other is the double-violin, or DeLuxe model.

In addition to modifying the case design, the interiors were changed also. Later instruments used a larger roll of five tunes — usually laid out with two fox trots, then a waltz in the middle, and then two more fox trots. Classical and operatic selections, including long-playing numbers, were listed in the Mills catalogues, but, as the majority of rolls were produced for nickel-in-the-slot use in public places, most rolls were of popular tunes. Over the years the roll mechanism was redesigned and relocated, most of the other interior parts were rearranged, and many mechanical improvements were made (although some worthwhile features such as the "glissando" feature and the tiny pincers for plucking the strings for staccato effects were deleted in later models). The early system of tuning pegs was replaced by a set of four weights (or eight weights on the model with two violins) which exerted a constant tension on each string, thereby keeping it in tune for a longer period of time. The finger magnets were redesigned to be just a fraction of their former size and were housed under an aluminum cover which bore a seemingly interminable list of patent numbers on it.

You will recall that the Patent Office picked the violin player as being one of the more interesting items invented in the decade that preceded the 1909 Alaska Yukon Pacific Exposition. Well, that "decade" lasted a lifetime so far as Mills was concerned. When the last Violano was taken out through the Mills factory doors in the 1930's it carried a plaque which read: "Violano - Virtuoso; Designated by the U.S. government as one of the eight greatest inventions of the decade." Thousands of Violanos before it also carried this proud notice.

The number of Automatic Virtuosas and Violano - Virtuoso machines produced is not known. It cannot be ascertained by serial numbers alone, as serial numbers were evidently issued in overlapping sequence. That is, certain later instruments bear lower serial numbers than do certain earlier instruments. It is our opinion, however, that approximately 4500 were produced. Of this number, several hundred survive today. With the exception of a few dozen instruments, all are of the single-violin model.

Production of the Violano-Virtuoso probably ended about 1930. A 1931 Mills catalogue features the instrument, but it may have been just a listing of earlier-made instruments still in stock. Rolls for the Violano - Virtuoso were cut by Mills as late as 1935, and possibly even later. Years later, in 1970, the Mills Novelty Company name was resurrected for use by lawyer and Violano enthusiast Don Barr of Santa Monica, California, who devised a clever perforator for the recutting of earlier Violano rolls.

From the standpoint of today's collector, the Violano - Virtuoso is one of the most interesting automatic instruments. It is because of this interest that we have taken the space here to give an in-depth story of the Violano and its development. The instruments are sufficiently plentiful today that any collector seriously desiring to own one and able to afford the market price can acquire one within a reasonable length of time. The public interest factor of the Violano is just as great today as it was fifty years ago. Show an uninitiated newspaper reporter a fine collection of automatic instruments complete with many extreme rarities, and he will inevitably single out the Violano - Virtuoso as the one instrument around which to build a feature story.

The Violano - Virtuoso was one of the few American-made mechanical musical instruments which was distributed on a worldwide scale. These machines were shipped to virtually every part of the globe. England was a particularly receptive area for the Violano, and hundreds were sold there. Perhaps Mills recognized the potential of the English market following the 1908 tour of the Automatic Virtuosa.

Today it is a practice in the jukebox industry to take machines which are five to ten years old and to rehabilitate them, update them in some respects, and to export them to overseas points. This is not a new idea, and Mills did the same thing in the 1920's. It took Violano - Virtuoso instruments which had served a useful life in the United States and reconditioned them, sometimes changing certain components to reflect advances in technology made since the instrument was built. The updated and rebuilt Violano was then shipped to England, Holland, or to some other foreign point where it saw yet another period of use.

### The Mills Melody Violins

In order to round out the picture, a few other Mills automatic musical instruments must be mentioned. To capitalize on the theatre photoplayer market the Mills Melody Violins were produced. In its simplest form this instrument consisted of a Violano - Virtuoso with a

*In Virginia City, a prime Montana tourist attraction, this two-violin Mills Violano - Virtuoso plays for dining room guests. Virginia City features many old-time musical instruments of various kinds.*

"The Violano is not only paying us an average of $160.00 per month, but has increased our business more than 25%, all of which we want to thank the Mills Novelty Company for inducing us to install this instrument. We have been very particular in checking the reaction of our customers and find that we have new faces and are making many new friends each day."

Fern Cafe, Oklahoma.

*The Mills Violano - Virtuoso was just what the doctor ordered for the Fern Cafe located somewhere in Oklahoma.*

keyboard built on the front of the case. The keyboard was mounted on a sliding fixture and could be concealed within the main case when not needed for hand playing.

A more elaborate model contained a side chest with three more violins in it. According to the catalogue description of this interesting hand-played instrument, it was then "possible to play any number of violins — from one to a hundred — from a keyboard in the way in which pianos or organs are ordinarily played." For several years we have heard rumors that one of these instruments was installed in a leading Chicago department store years ago, but we have not been able to find any photographic proof of this.

A byproduct of the Melody Violins idea was an automatic violin and playing mechanism designed as an attachment to be used with a theatre pipe organ. By means of an appropriate stop on the console the violin could be played from the organ keyboard. The violin and attendant mechanisms were housed in the pipe chambers.

For adapting a regular Violano - Virtuoso for theatre use an interesting accessory, the Four Feeder, was introduced. Never made in quantity, and perhaps only made on an experimental basis (our information is based solely upon a catalogue illustration), this device consisted of four regular Violano roll mechanisms mounted in a special cabinet. By means of remote pushbuttons the music could be switched from one roll to another. The gadget was similar in concept to a four-roll music roll feeder sold by the Link Piano and Organ Company as the "M.P. Jr." for use with Link theatre pipe organs.

### The Mills Magnetic Expression Piano

The Mills Magnetic Expression piano, sold in the 1920's, was essentially an expanded version of the piano part of a Violano - Virtuoso. It consisted of a 65-note piano (whereas the Violano - Virtuoso contained a 44-note piano) housed by itself in a case with three glass panels on the front. As was the case with the Violano, the Mills Magnetic Expression Piano was electrically operated via solenoids. An interesting variety of the Mills Magnetic Expression Piano had a diorama of racing horses in the front and was known as the Mills Race Horse Piano. Both the Race Horse and the regular model are occasionally seen in collections today. Both types use a special Mills Electric Piano roll. Although rolls were not made in quantity, what rolls there are in existence today are quite listenable and expressive.

### The Violano Orchestra

Sometime during the 1920's the Violano Orchestra, a cabinet which could be attached to the Violano - Virtuoso, was introduced. This attachment permitted the Violano to play the bass drum, snare drum, tom-tom, wood block, and cymbal in accompaniment to the regular piano and violin music. The Violano Orchestra attachment required special wiring and used a special Violano Orchestra roll, many of which had green rather than white (the color of regular Violano labels) program labels.

The Violano Orchestra was made only in limited quantities. The rolls, also quite scarce, are excellently arranged with a catchy rhythm. It is unfortunate that Mills did not go into the orchestrion business, for its entry would undoubtedly have been excellent.

Mills almost did go into the orchestrion field. An entry, the Mills Piano Orchestra, was made in the mid-1920's. Essentially a Mills Magnetic Expression Piano with the various trap instruments of the Violano Orchestra added (and all built into a large single case), the unit was never marketed in quantity. The author knows of no surviving Mills Piano Orchestras today, although the fact that old-time Mills dealer Oswald Wurdeman once saw and heard one at a Chicago trade show indicates that at least one must have been produced. The Violano Orchestra attachment connected to a Violano - Virtuoso contains the essential features of the Piano Orchestra (plus a violin as well) and probably gives a fair conception of how the ephemeral Piano Orchestra must have sounded.

### Trouble in Paradise

The Mills financial empire flourished during the decades through the 1930's. The business was built mainly upon the manufacture of arcade devices and gambling machines, with musical instruments purely as incidental items (although the 4500 or so violin players at average costs of $1200 to $3000 each must have brought in nearly $10 million over the 1905 - 1930 period).

All three of these categories — gambling equipment, arcade machines, and automatic instruments — declined in profitability as laws (for gambling equipment) tightened and public tastes changed during the 1930's and 1940's.

Mills, once a very prosperous firm (it even maintained a yacht, the Minoco, for entertaining customers!), sought to bolster its declining fortunes by diversifying into a number of other areas. A Mills electric coin phonograph or jukebox placed only as an also-ran in a field in which Seeburg and Wurlitzer came in with flying colors. The Mills Pan-O-Ram, a machine which played sound movie shorts (an instrument which was promoted heavily by a son of President Franklin Roosevelt, by the way), was a modest success during the late 1930's and early 1940's — but nothing like the earlier success of slot and arcade machines.

Still later the Mills Novelty Company changed its name to Mills Industries, Incorporated, and manufactured such items as automatic ice cream freezers. The firm went out of business in the 1950's.

HOME OF MILLS NOVELTY CO., 4100 Fullerton Ave., Chicago, Ill., U. S. A.


*The Mills factory at 4100 Fullerton Avenue as it was shown in the 1931 Mills catalogue.*

*Art Reblitz, musical historian and arranger of new music rolls, is shown in front of 4100 Fullerton in this 1966 photograph taken by the author.*

The author, on a journey which led to the locations of most old-time musical instrument factories in America and Europe, visited the former Mills building at 4100 Fullerton Avenue in Chicago a few years ago. An hour or two was spent in the building which at that time was occupied by a decal manufacturing company and a rug making concern. It was my hope to find a scrap of original literature or, better yet, an "old-timer" with some recollections of past days of glory. Alas, no such mementos or persons were found. In fact, a gentleman with whom I spoke knew no more about the Mills Novelty Company than the fact that, for some unknown past reason, MILLS NOVELTY COMPANY was emblazoned on an old smokestack at the rear of the building.

MILLS AUTOMATIC VIRTUOSA

The Mills Automatic Virtuosa, first sold around 1905 or 1906, was made in the two different styles shown above. The one at the right is the later of the two and appeared in a 1907 Mills catalogue. The Hervey Hotel in Mobile, Alabama, reported on March 22, 1907: "We have in our Tappe Room one of your automatic violins. . . It has been much admired by our patrons."

H. K. SANDELL.
ELECTRIC SELF PLAYING VIOLIN.
APPLICATION FILED JAN. 3, 1911.

1,028,495. Patented June 4, 1912.
6 SHEETS—SHEET 2.

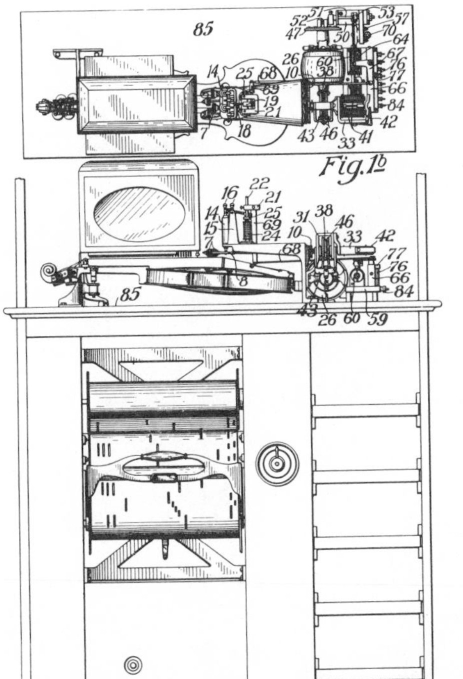


This "Home Model" Violano - Virtuoso, illustrated in a 1912 catalogue, uses a special music roll and has several features not found in later models, including a central oiling system, pincer-like string pickers (in addition to the usual bows) for special effects, etc. Patent drawings are shown above. A specimen in the Barr Collection was originally in the home of company president Herbert S. Mills. Later "Home Model" Violanos have clear glass front doors (instead of solid wood doors) and use the standard Violano roll.

Above is shown the first case design for the Violano - Virtuoso incorporating a piano in addition to the violin. This type was also called the Pianova - Virtuosa for a short time in 1909. Following the production of a pilot model in 1909 (for the Patent Office show mentioned in the text) the Violano underwent further development. Initial marketing began in 1911. Shortly thereafter this style was discontinued and a new type (with a symmetrical piano) was introduced.

Violano-Virtuoso

Commercial Model Violano: Made for a number of years in the 'teens the Commercial Model was coin operated and featured a curved case. In the earliest models (see above) the back of the piano was curved to the case contour.

Commercial Model Violano: Later model with rectangular piano case section behind. Don Barr, Violano historian, believes some of these cases were originally ordered for making Automatic Virtuosas and later had the piano part added on.

The early "Home Model" Violano-Virtuoso in the Don Barr Collection. This instrument was once in the home of Herbert Mills. (Photograph by Dan Adams)

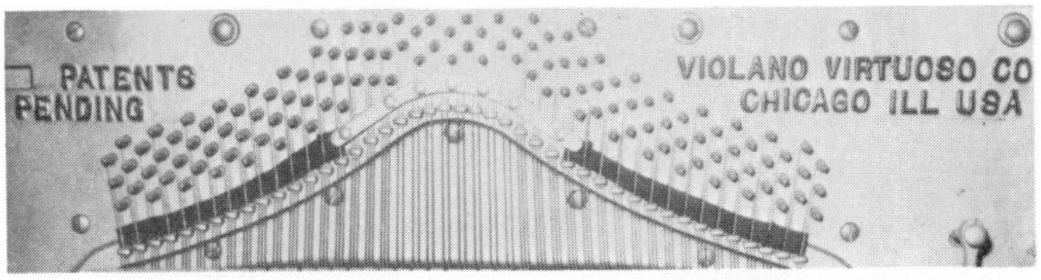

Piano Plate Peculiarities: Above are three types of piano plate castings: (1) Early type from Commercial Model, serial no.116, with "Patents Pending." (2) Slightly later type from serial no.196, a Home Model, with "Patent Allowed." Both of the first two have "Violano Virtuoso Co." Mills initially set up a separate company to sell the Violano - Virtuoso, perhaps because of the somewhat "uncultured" reputation of its main business (slot machines), but soon dropped the idea. (3) Usual style of piano plate with "Pat. June 4, 1912" as seen on Violano serial no.2270. This last style is that used on all but the very early models.

This restaurant, gaily decorated with banners for the holidays, has a Violano against the left wall.

Restaurants were the largest single customer for the Violano Virtuoso. A sign in the above picture offers lunch for 20c!

This progressive hotel provided its patrons with Mills music.

Taken at the Mills factory about 1915 this illustration shows Commercial Model instruments and regular models being assembled.

# Lower Cabinet of Violano

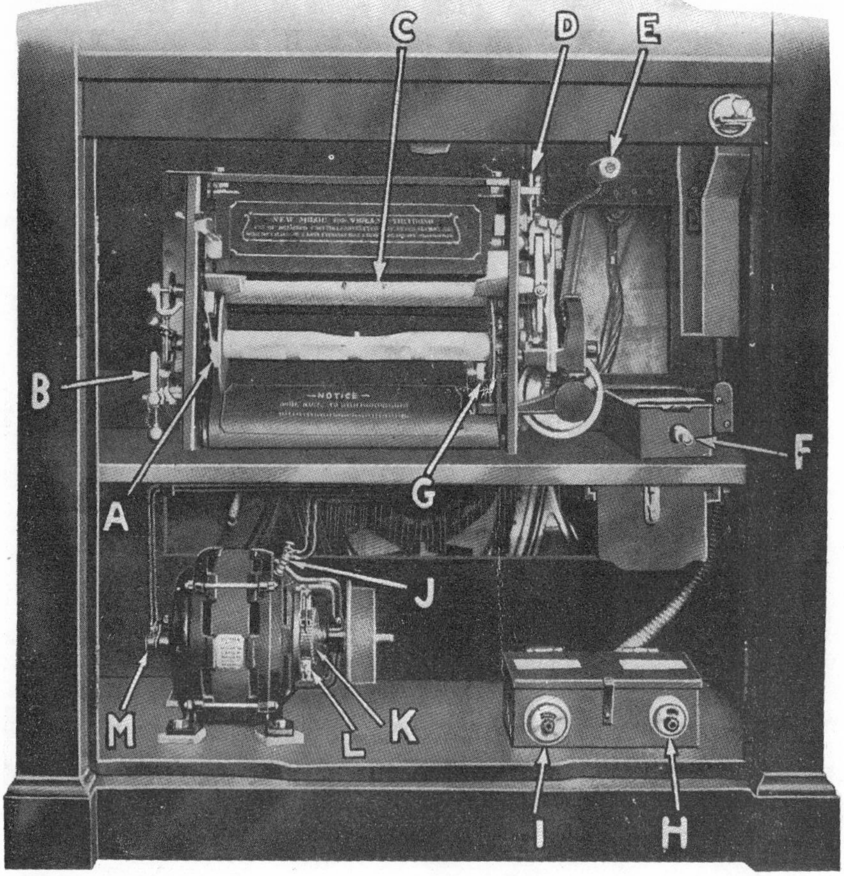


A—Lower Spool Brake.
B—Governor.
C—Contact Roller.
D—Feeder Trip Lever.
E—Staccato Coil.
F—Reverse Switch.
G—Reverse Switch.
H—Feeder Switch.
I—Piano and Violin Switch.
J—Direct Current Connecting Posts.
K—Converter Commutator.
L—Direct Current Brushes (Converter).
M—Alternating Current Connecting Posts and Brushes.

*Drawing No. 1*

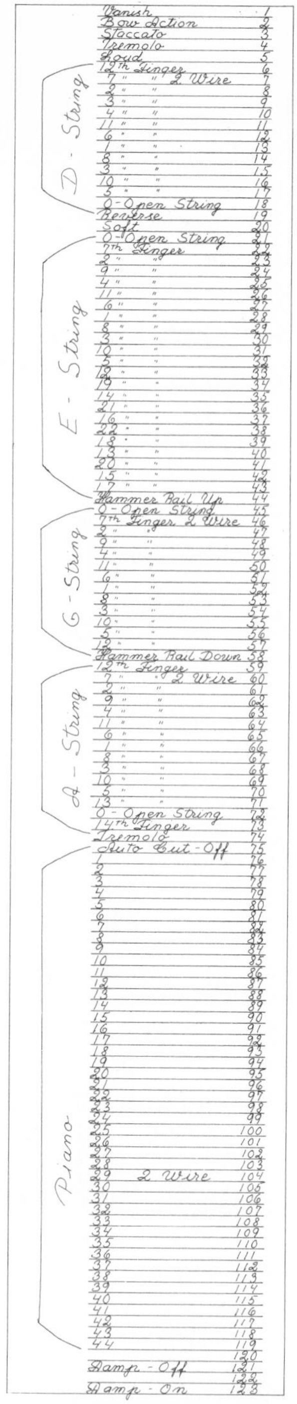

| Group | Function | Position |
|---|---|---|
| | Vanish | 1 |
| | Bow Action | 2 |
| | Staccato | 3 |
| | Tremolo | 4 |
| | Loud | 5 |
| D - String | 12th Finger | 6 |
| | 7 " " 2 Wire | 7 |
| | 2 " " | 8 |
| | 3 " " | 9 |
| | 4 " " | 10 |
| | 11 " " | 11 |
| | 6 " " | 12 |
| | 1 " " | 13 |
| | 8 " " | 14 |
| | 3 " " | 15 |
| | 10 " " | 16 |
| | 5 " " | 17 |
| | 0-Open String | 18 |
| | Reverse | 19 |
| | Soft | 20 |
| E - String | 0-Open String | 21 |
| | 7th Finger | 22 |
| | 2 " " | 23 |
| | 9 " " | 24 |
| | 4 " " | 25 |
| | 11 " " | 26 |
| | 6 " " | 27 |
| | 1 " " | 28 |
| | 8 " " | 29 |
| | 3 " " | 30 |
| | 10 " " | 31 |
| | 5 " " | 32 |
| | 12 " " | 33 |
| | 19 " " | 34 |
| | 14 " " | 35 |
| | 21 " " | 36 |
| | 16 " " | 37 |
| | 22 " " | 38 |
| | 18 " " | 39 |
| | 13 " " | 40 |
| | 20 " " | 41 |
| | 15 " " | 42 |
| | 17 " " | 43 |
| | Hammer Rail Up | 44 |
| G - String | 0-Open String | 45 |
| | 7th Finger 2 Wire | 46 |
| | 2 " " | 47 |
| | 9 " " | 48 |
| | 4 " " | 49 |
| | 11 " " | 50 |
| | 6 " " | 51 |
| | 1 " " | 52 |
| | 8 " " | 53 |
| | 3 " " | 54 |
| | 10 " " | 55 |
| | 5 " " | 56 |
| | 12 " " | 57 |
| | Hammer Rail Down | 58 |
| A - String | 12th Finger | 59 |
| | 7 " " 2 Wire | 60 |
| | 2 " " | 61 |
| | 9 " " | 62 |
| | 4 " " | 63 |
| | 11 " " | 64 |
| | 6 " " | 65 |
| | 1 " " | 66 |
| | 8 " " | 67 |
| | 3 " " | 68 |
| | 10 " " | 69 |
| | 5 " " | 70 |
| | 13 " " | 71 |
| | 0-Open String | 72 |
| | 14th Finger | 73 |
| | Tremolo | 74 |
| | Auto Cut-Off | 75 |
| Piano | 1 | 76 |
| | 2 | 77 |
| | 3 | 78 |
| | 4 | 79 |
| | 5 | 80 |
| | 6 | 81 |
| | 7 | 82 |
| | 8 | 83 |
| | 9 | 84 |
| | 10 | 85 |
| | 11 | 86 |
| | 12 | 87 |
| | 13 | 88 |
| | 14 | 89 |
| | 15 | 90 |
| | 16 | 91 |
| | 17 | 92 |
| | 18 | 93 |
| | 19 | 94 |
| | 20 | 95 |
| | 21 | 96 |
| | 22 | 97 |
| | 23 | 98 |
| | 24 | 99 |
| | 25 | 100 |
| | 26 | 101 |
| | 27 | 102 |
| | 28 | 103 |
| | 29 2 Wire | 104 |
| | 30 | 105 |
| | 31 | 106 |
| | 32 | 107 |
| | 33 | 108 |
| | 34 | 109 |
| | 35 | 110 |
| | 36 | 111 |
| | 37 | 112 |
| | 38 | 113 |
| | 39 | 114 |
| | 40 | 115 |
| | 41 | 116 |
| | 42 | 117 |
| | 43 | 118 |
| | 44 | 119 |
| | | 120 |
| | Damp - Off | 121 |
| | | 122 |
| | Damp - On | 123 |

## HOW TO INSERT ROLL IN INSTRUMENT

Take hold of music roll with pin to left, insert right hand side of roll into feeder first, then push left hand side in as far as it will go. After roll is in, see that it revolves easily by spinning it around several times. This will show that each end is seated properly, then take end of music roll and pass it back under contact roller "C" and back and under lower spool and hook on pin. (See Drawing No. 1, Page 5.)

When inserting the music roll into the feeder after you have put the roll in place, spin it around two or three times with the hand before putting the paper behind the contact roller and hooking it on to the lower spool. The reason for this is sometimes the roll will not be placed all the way into the machine and might cause the paper to tear, but by spinning it this cannot happen, because it will not spin unless it is placed in correctly.

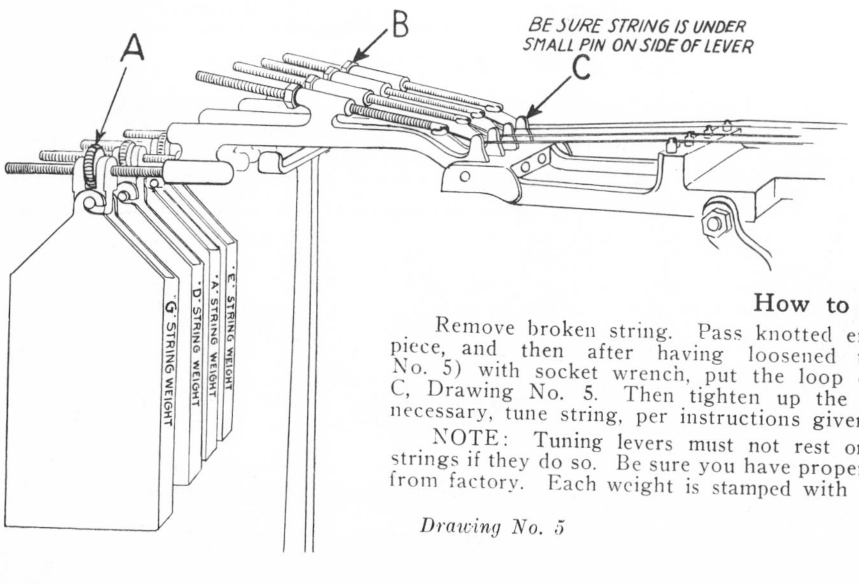


**VIOLANO INSTRUCTIONS: "How to" details from a Mills service manual of the 1920's. At the above right is the Mills equivalent of a tracker bar layout; a listing in order of the 123 positions on the Mills roll.**

**Incidental Note: In 1926 a "Violano Speaker System" – a microphone placed in the Violano and speakers placed throughout a restaurant or other location – was made available using Kellogg brand sound equipment.**

## How to Replace String

Remove broken string. Pass knotted end of new string through proper hole in metal tail piece, and then after having loosened the weight lever by turning nut "B" (Drawing No. 5) with socket wrench, put the loop end of string over the hook and under little pin C, Drawing No. 5. Then tighten up the weight lever again until it hangs horizontal. If necessary, tune string, per instructions given on page 8.

NOTE: Tuning levers must not rest on bracket as they will not keep proper tension on strings if they do so. Be sure you have proper strings in proper place. Each String comes marked from factory. Each weight is stamped with the proper letter, as G, D, A, E.

*Drawing No. 5*

## Coin Operating Device

When you install your Violano Virtuoso we recommend that you use our special coin operating device which may be connected with the Violano by the insertion of two small screws. This device, when connected, permits the instrument to play upon the deposit of a coin. Price of this device is $2.50.

## Push Button

If you do not want this coin operating device, your Violano comes equipped with a push button, by means of which you can start and stop the instrument. This push button can be placed any place in your store where it will be convenient to you.

## Wall Boxes

We also supply wall boxes. These are coin operating boxes that can be placed on the wall in different places in your store and make it convenient for customers to operate the instrument. When wall boxes are used with the instrument it is not necessary to have our special coin operating device mentioned above.

## Prices on Supplies

| | |
|---|---|
| Music Cabinet | $150, Cash |
| Violano Music Rolls | $5 each, Cash |
| Wall Boxes | $10 each, Cash |
| Piano Music Rolls | $4 each, Cash |

*All orders must be filled out on Mills Novelty Co. Order Blanks and all checks must be made payable to Mills Novelty Co.*

**Price list of supplies from a 1926 Mills catalogue. Wallboxes were quite popular and many locations used them.**

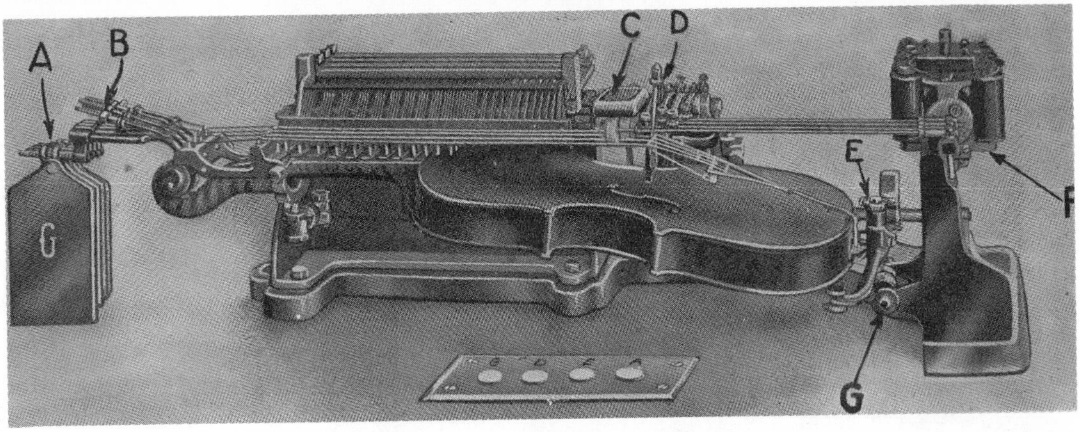


## HOW TO TUNE VIOLIN

The self-tuning device on the Mills Violano will keep the Violin in perfect tune. The weights are so sensitively balanced as to take up all expansion or contractions of the Strings and thus keep it at the proper tension all the time. We furnish the proper strings, which are stretched, calipered and tied, so when put on the Violin they should be in tune. If for any reason this is not the case, they can be tuned by turning Set Screw "A." (Drawing No. 4.) Turning this screw to left, or away from you, will increase weight on string and bring string to a higher pitch. Turning it to right, or towards you, will decrease weight and bring string to a lower pitch.

Tuning levers should be kept at a horizontal position. This can be obtained by adjusting Nut No. B. (Drawing No. 4.) This nut does not affect the tuning of the violin.

In order to tune Violin, first reverse feeder by pulling out Reverse Switch so as to separate feeder brushes from contact roller, and shut feeder Switch "H" off. (See Drawing No. 1.) This will allow the bows to revolve without music playing. Also pull forward trip lever D. (Drawing No. 1.)

By pressing button marked "A" on tuning device in front of violin (Drawing No. 4) "A" on piano is struck with open "A" string on violin. When they both sound in unison the "A" string is in tune with the piano. You can raise or lower pitch of strings by turning screw No. "A" as instructed above.

By pressing button "E" the "E" on the "A" string is given, and also open "E" string. The open "E" string must sound in unison with the "E" on "A" string. If not, raise or lower "E" string by turning the screw No. "A."

Pressing button "D" gives open "A" string and also the "A" on "D" string. The "D" string must sound in unison with the open "A" string. If not, raise or lower "D" string by turning screw No. "A."

By pressing the "G" button open "D" is given and also "D" on "G" string. The "G" string must sound in unison with the open "D" string. If not, raise or lower "G" string by turning screw No. "A."

If tuning button stays down and plays continuously, unscrew plate and lift out and see if spring contacts are causing small pin on bottom of tuning button to stick down—if so, bend out springs slightly. If one note plays continuously when roll is being played this is probably the cause.

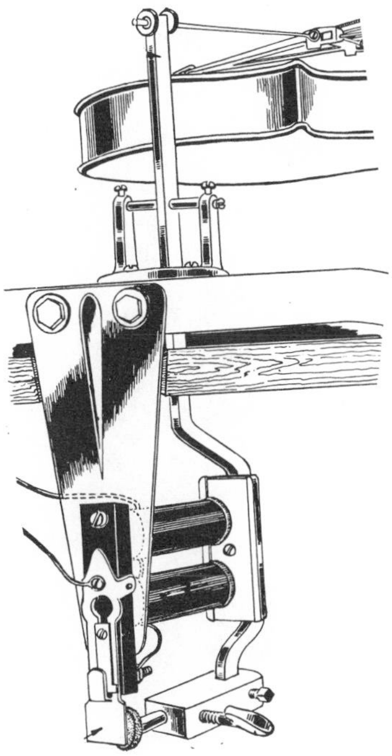

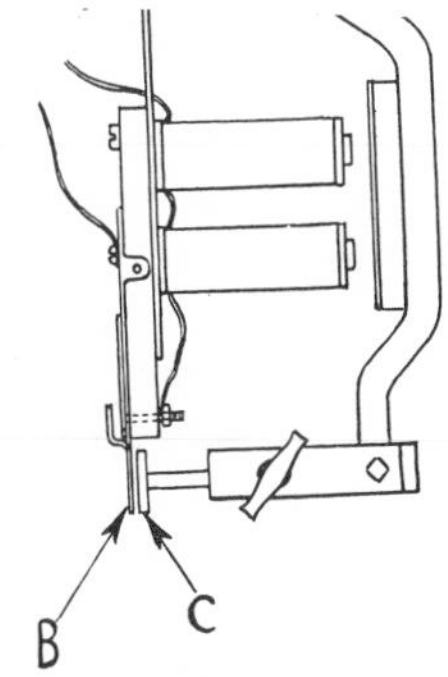


**The tremolo produces a vibrato effect by shaking the violin bridge. Oscillation is accomplished by a make-and-break contact as shown at B-C above. Early Violanos lack the automatic tremolo and use instead a tremolo hole scored in the music roll.**

### Grand Model Violano-Virtuoso

One Violin; 44 Note Piano.
*Price*—$2,000.
*Terms:* $300 cash with order, balance of $1,700 in 25 equal installments of $68 each (with interest) due each month after receipt of instrument.
*Specifications:* Shipping weight—1100 lbs. Dimensions—5 ft. 4 in. high; 3 ft. 7 in. wide; 2 ft. 7 in. deep.
*Finishes:* Red Mahogany, Brown Mahogany, Oak (dull or polished).

### Concert Grand Model Violano-Virtuoso

One Violin; 44 Note Piano.
*Price*—$2,500.
*Terms:* $375.00 cash with order, balance of $2,125 in 25 equal installments of $85 each (with interest) due each month after receipt of instrument.
*Specifications:* Shipping weight—1250 lbs. Dimensions—5 ft. 5 in. high; 4 ft. 1 in. wide; 2 ft. 9 in. deep.
*Finishes:* Red Mahogany, Brown Mahogany, Oak (dull or polished).

**The Grand Model and the Concert Grand sold for $2000 and $2500 each in 1925. For some reason, special terms of 25% down and the balance in six equal monthly instalments were given just to theatres. Others received more lenient terms, as the fine print above shows. Most instruments were of mahogany wood. Thousands of tunes were available on Violano rolls, usually of 5 tunes each. Each tune plays for several minutes; longer than the usual 2 minutes of most other coin operated instruments (such as Seeburg, Wurlitzer, etc. pianos).**

## MILLS VIOL-XYLOPHONE AND VIOL-CELLO

## MILLS NOVELTY CO.

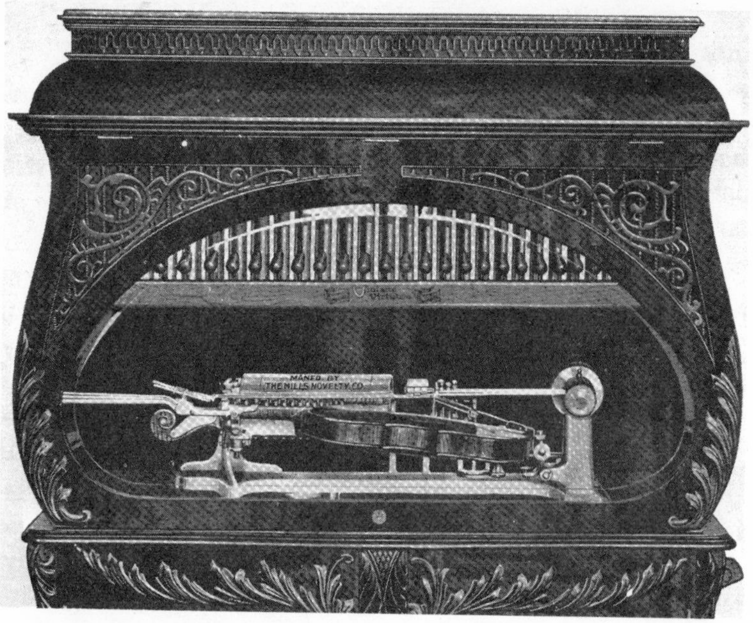


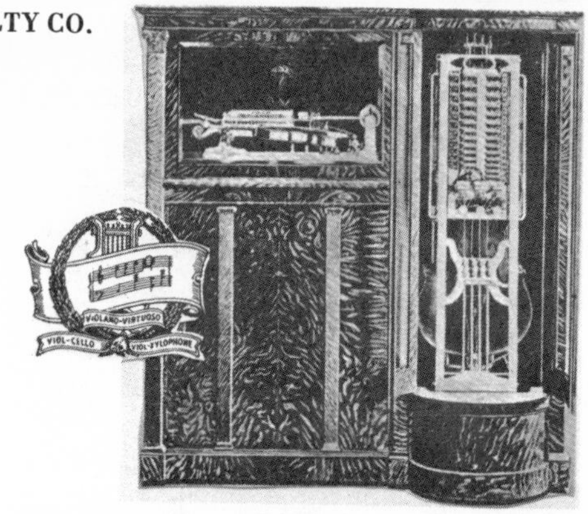


Above: Mills Viol-Cello. The left part contains a violin with mechanisms similar to those in the Violano - Virtuoso. Accompanying the violin is a large cello mounted in the upright cabinet to the right. See text of accompanying article for more information on this and on the Viol-Xylophone.

Left: Mills Viol-Xylophone. A Mills artist created the Viol-Xylophone by retouching a stock photograph of a Violano - Virtuoso. It is doubtful that a xylophone would have provided better accompaniment than the usual piano would; and perhaps for this musical reason the Viol-Xylophone was never commercially made.

---

## DELUXE VIOLANO-VIRTUOSO (with two violins)

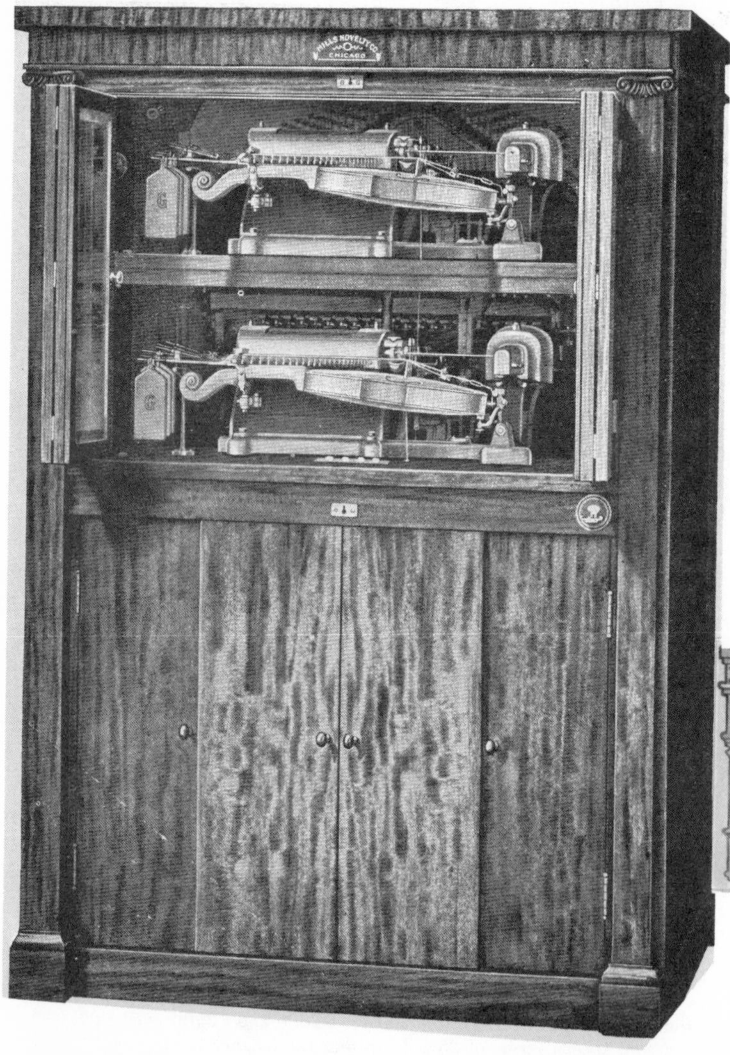


DeLuxe Violano-Virtuoso: Called the "Double Mills" by collectors today, the DeLuxe model was sold to the extent of several hundred instruments, mostly during the 1920's. It uses the same roll as does the single model.

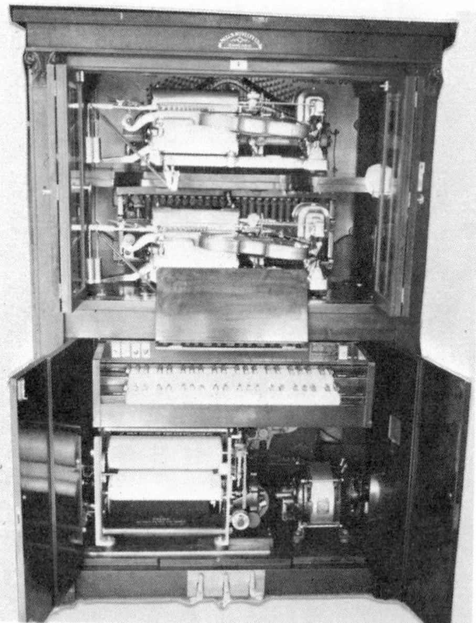

Overall view of the keyboard Violano showing the foot pedals (two of which control the violin bow speed). See enlarged illustration of this on another page.

Violano Virtuoso
SELF-PLAYING
VIOLIN AND PIANO

### De Luxe Model Violano-Virtuoso

An Automatic Electric Piano of 44 Notes and Two Violins.

*Price*—$3,000.

*Terms:*—$450 cash with order, balance of $2,550 in 25 equal installments of $102 each (with interest) due each month after receipt of instrument.

*Specifications:* Shipping weight—1350 lbs.

Dimensions—5 ft. 9 in. high; 4 ft. 1 in. wide; 2 ft. 10¾ in. deep.

*Finishes:* Red Mahogany, Brown Mahogany, Oak (dull or polished).

Above: This unusual DeLuxe Violano - Virtuoso was made for shipboard use where it could be hand played to entertain passengers. Evidently made in the 1920's, it has a number of unusual features. The tension is maintained not by weight arms (as it usually is), but is provided by a series of springs and variable solenoids. A similar system was used on the pipe organ chamber violin made for use with theatre organs (see text of accompanying article) and was patented in 1926. The keyboard is sliding and can be pushed into the case and concealed by the bottom doors when not in use. (Ed Zelinsky Collection; photograph by Mel Locher)

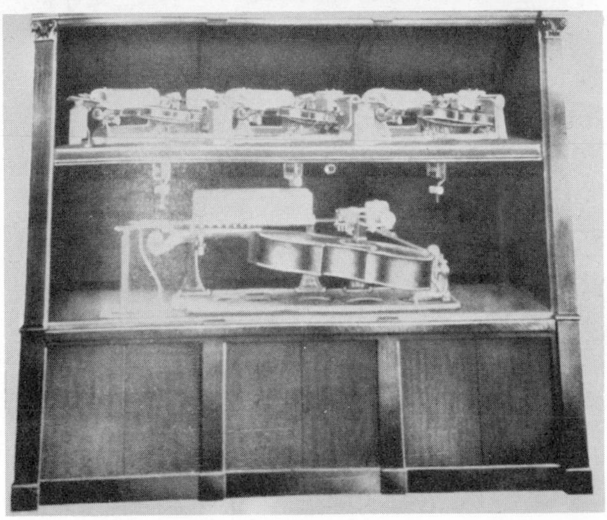

Right: The Mills String Quartette featured a cello (on the bottom shelf) and three violins, the latter mounted at an angle on the top shelf. It is possible that several of these were made for a photo of the Mills factory shows a number of cellos being made in the violin workshop. The text mentions that Mills Viol-Cellos were once seen in the Hippodrome in Los Angeles and in a hotel lobby in Opelika, Alabama. The descriptions of these instruments were ambiguous, and it is possible that one or both may have been a String Quartette.

View of the two violins, one above the other, in the DeLuxe (or "Double Mills") Violano - Virtuoso. The violins are in clear view – which undoubtedly produced more coins in the slot in the "good old days."

Partially visible behind the upper violin is the upper part of the symmetrical Violano piano. Some very early models had a clear glass panel separating the piano from the violin.

Left side of the lower violin. Seen at the extreme left are the tuning weights which exert constant tension on the strings. To the right are the tiny mechanical "fingers" which stop the strings at desired intervals.

Right side of the lower violin. The four rods extending from the bow motor are each equipped with a celluloid bowing disc. Above is a rosin cake holder. Four tuning buttons are in the foreground.

The top part of the Orchestra cabinet shows the tom-tom, wood block, and bass drum (which is lighted from within). The instrument uses Violano Orchestra rolls or, by means of a switching device, regular Violano rolls. (The latter for piano and violin only.)

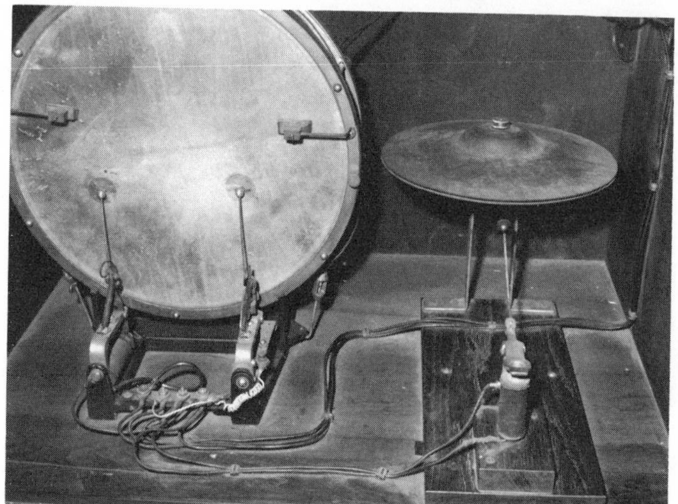

The lower part of the Orchestra cabinet has a snare drum (with two beaters – one for single tap and one for roll) and cymbals. The Orchestra attachment was sold for both single and double Violano models.

Roll mechanism of the Violano. Tiny wire brushes touch the metal contact roller through holes in the roll – and cause the proper notes to be actuated.

The symmetrical piano of the Violano. Two rows of magnets operate the piano hammers. The symmetrical design distributes the stress on the piano plate evenly.

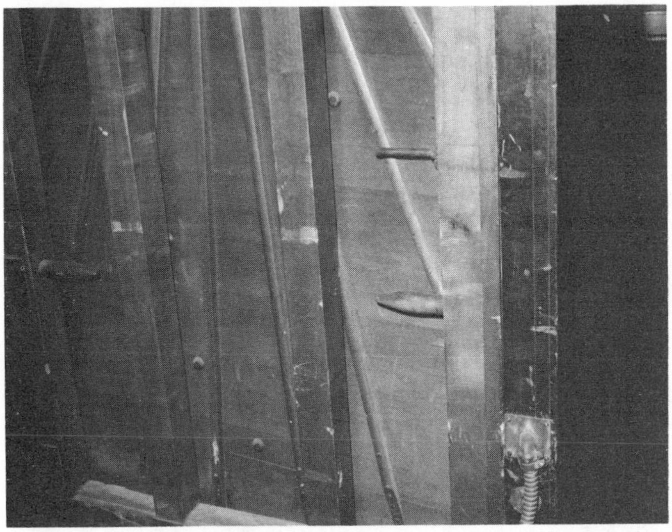

Back view of the Violano showing the ribbed spruce sounding board of the piano. At the right is the top of the shielded metal electrical cable which leads to the Violano Orchestra cabinet.

Piano in the swung-out position. The piano is actually the back door of the instrument – a feature that makes servicing and access to the interior very convenient. The piano is on its own caster and opens and closes easily.

Rear view of the bow motor. This operates at various speeds depending upon the musical passage being played. To the right are the magnets which, by means of bellcranks, bring the bows into contact with the strings.

These large bundles of wires lead from the electrical brushes to the piano solenoids and other controls. Fortunately for collectors, the Violano wiring was originally of excellent quality and seldom has to be replaced today.

Mills Melody Violins: From a double keyboard any number of violins could be played — "from one to one hundred," according to the catalogue. Originally intended for use in theatres, auditoriums, large stores, and similar places needing background music, the Melody Violins were made only in small numbers.

Four Feeder: This cabinet contains four regular Violano - Virtuoso roll mechanisms electrically connected so that the music from any one of them can be selected at will by pushing a button in a remote location. Designed for accompanying films, the unit had little use — probably because the Violano - Virtuoso is not loud enough to fill a theatre with music.

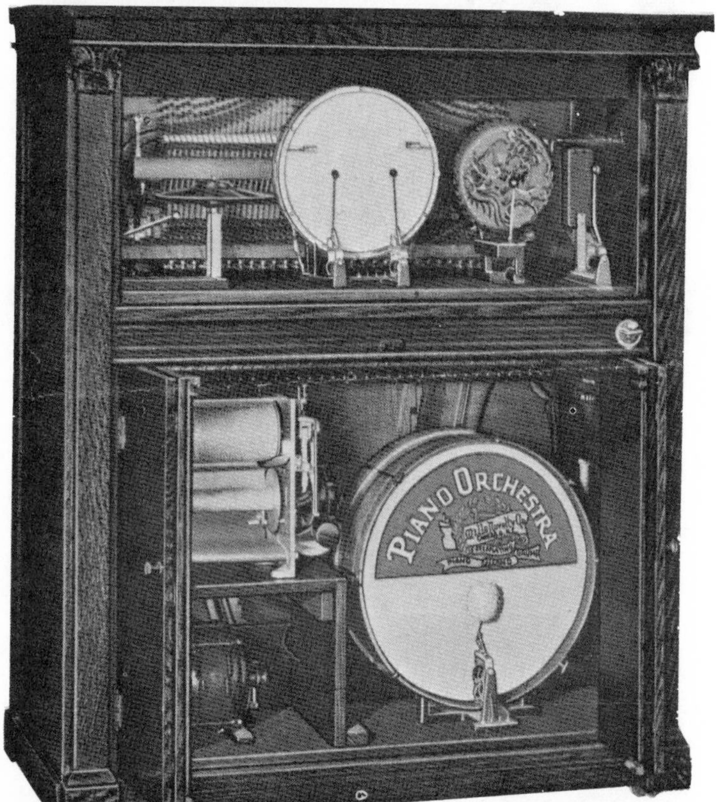

# Mills Piano Orchestra

Piano and Drums in single cabinet.

A combination of Magnetic Expression Piano and Violano Drums.

Ten dance selections on every music roll.

Restaurants, etc., where there is dancing. Sure to be popular with the public.

Price is exceptionally low for this piano orchestra.

Earnings reported $50.00 to $100.00 a month.

Mills Piano Orchestra: This orchestrion is built around a Mills Magnetic Expression Piano (65 notes; symmetrical arrangement to piano strings). Although little is known about the Piano Orchestra today, evidently at least some were commercially sold as the above description notes that "Earnings reported $50 to $100 a month." As is the case with other music makers made by Mills, the Piano Orchestra is completely electromagnetic. Nearly all coin pianos, orchestrions, violin players, and other large mechanical instruments made by others were pneumatically operated.

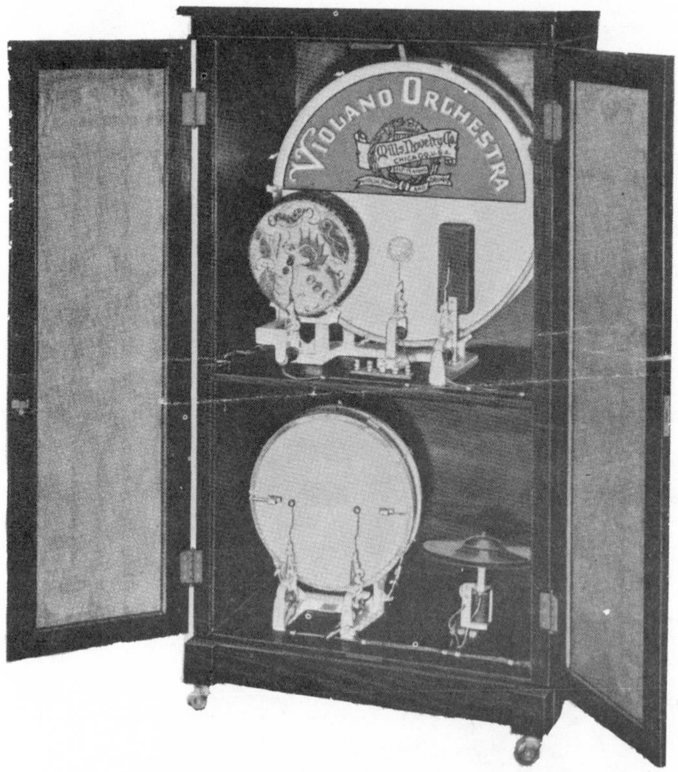

# Complete Orchestra For Dancing

These drums, combined with either DeLuxe or Grand Model Violano, make a complete dance orchestra.

With DeLuxe Violano—makes six piece complete orchestra; two first Violins, two second Violins, Piano and Drums, including Base Drum, Snare Drum, Chinese Tom-Tom, Wood Clapper and Cymbals.

With Grand Model Violano—makes four piece complete orchestra; first violin, second violin, Piano and Drums as above described.

Drums and Violano played from single music roll. Brings you latest dance music—new dance rolls obtainable every month.

Complete orchestra twenty-four hours a day. Ideal for any place where there is dancing.

Attracts young people. Increases business. Big extra cash profits—owners reporting intake of $75.00 to $200.00 per month.

Drums can be attached to any Violano carrying a serial No. above 1200.

Mail the post card for additional information.

Violano Orchestra: Combined with a two-violin Violano the Violano Orchestra cabinet makes a "six piece complete orchestra" with two first violins, two second violins, piano and drums, including bass drum, snare drum, Chinese tom-tom, wood block, and cymbals. The instrument uses a special Violano Orchestra roll, usually of 5-tune length, and usually with a green label. Instruments originally equipped with the Violano Orchestra carried the suffix "X" after the serial number — such as 2178X in the author's collection.

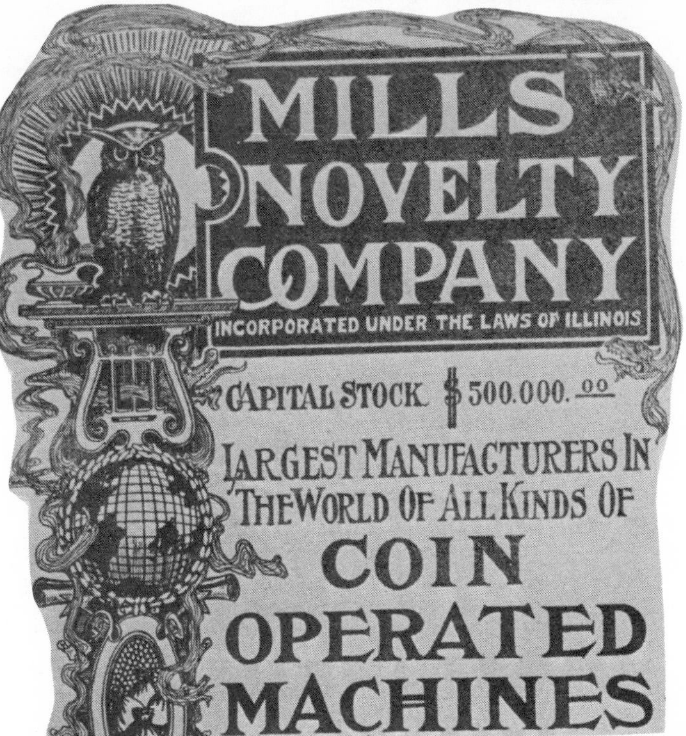

MILLS MAGNETIC EXPRESSION PIANO

Magnetic Expression Piano

65 Notes.

*Price*—$800.

*Terms:* $150 cash with order, balance of $650 in 13 equal installments of $50 each (with interest) due each month after receipt of instrument.

*Specifications:* Shipping weight—1100 lbs. Dimensions—5ft. 5 in. high; 4 ft. 7½ in. wide; 2ft. 2¼ in. deep.

*Finishes:* Red Mahogany, Brown Mahogany, Oak (dull or polished).

Mills Magnetic Expression Piano. Sold in the 1920's and early 1930's, this unit is a solenoid operated 65-note piano with the same piano string layout as used on the 44-note Violano (see above illustration).

---

## *Race Horse Piano*

Thrilling and Amusing—Big Money Maker

### *How It Operates*

Six numbered horses line up at the minature judges stand and start off around the race track (as shown in the illustration). They disappear around the bend in the track only to appear a few seconds later dashing down the home stretch. It's thrilling—fascinating—keeps the crowd on their toes with excitement. They can't wait for the next race. They deposit nickel after nickel while the same piece is being played. A few seconds completes a race so the crowds can have ten or fifteen races while one piece of music is being played. Every time a nickel is deposited the horses start on another race so this instrument may take in 50c or 75c while a single selection of music is being rendered.

Friendly groups stand around trying to guess the winner each time. If their favorite doesn't win the first time, they are anxiluos for another race. They want to guess the winner, and they play it again and again. They not only drop nickel after nickel into the instrument, but also liberally settle their arguments with drinks, cigars, and other merchandise.

### *How Profits Are Divided*

The Race Horse Piano is usually purchased by the dealer, but can be installed by operator on a commission basis, the dealer receiving from 25% to 40% of gross receipts for the use of his location.

*Average Monthly Earnings $150.00 to $300.00*

MILLS NOVELTY CO. CHICAGO, U.S.A.

The Race Horse Piano is an interesting variety of the Magnetic Expression Piano and uses the same roll. The horses, mounted on continuous belts, move from left to right across the front of the case. "Put Nickel in Slot for a Program of Pleasing Selections; Listen to Music of Masters Electrically Reproduced" reads the brightly colored front panel.

(1)

SHIPPING WEIGHT 73 LBS.
Mills Oracle Letter Writter
This is Cupid's new Post Office. A penny will get a letter for you, whether married or single. There are four compartments, each filled with different letters. It is automatic and the latest winner out.


(2)

SHIPPING WEIGHT 600 LBS.
16 WAY
Mills 20th Century Twins
Mills 20th Century Twins is the greatest twin machine ever built. It is made up of any coin combination of Nickel, Quarter, Half Dollar or Dollar Machines. It is two machines in one. Write for a special circular of this one.


(3)

(4)

(5)

(6)

(7)

(8)

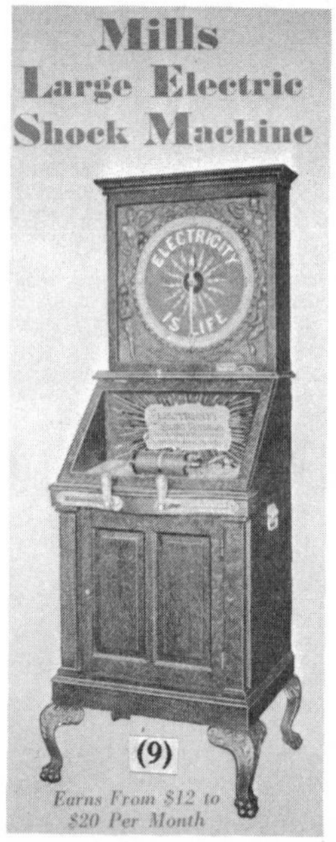

Mills
Large Electric
Shock Machine
ELECTRICITY
IS LIFE
Earns From $12 to
$20 Per Month


(9)

(10)

### –MILLS ARCADE MACHINES–

On this page are shown just a few of the hundreds of different arcade and gambling machines made by Mills from the 1890's until the late 1930's. They are, in order: (1) Fortune telling madam; (2) Oracle Letter Writer which produces a pre-printed love letter upon receipt of a cent or nickel; (3) 20th Century Twins – double slot machines like this saved on tax stamps – one tax stamp for what was, in essence, two devices; (4) Cover of 1929 catalogue; (5) World Horoscope dispenses fortune cards; (6) Automatic Phonograph made in cylinder and disc styles; (7) Auto Stereoscope; (8) Illustrated Song Machine made in cylinder and disc styles; (9) Electric Shock Machine – "Patrons can see what they can stand."; (10) Mills Roulette; (11) Cupid's Post Office – "There's a letter in the mail for you."; (12) Mills Electric Phonograph, circa 1931, with dynamic speakers; (13) Embossing Machine.

The Mills arcade and gambling machines have a rich history – and their story would make an interesting book in itself!

(11)

(12)

SHIPPING WEIGHT 205 LBS.
Mills
Embossing Machine
Your choice of six different Emblems. This is the greatest money maker ever made. Write for full description.


(13)

NATIONAL AUTOMATIC MUSIC COMPANY
NATIONAL PIANO MFG. CO.
—Grand Rapids, Michigan—

The National Automatic Music Company, later known as the National Piano Manufacturing Company (no connection with other similarly-named firms in St. Johnsville, N.Y. and in New York City), was located in Grand Rapids, Michigan.

This firm was mainly active in the 1920's. The main product was a coin piano, resembling a keyboard piano in appearance but not having a keyboard, which was equipped with an 8-roll automatic changer. Each roll was of one-tune length. Selection of the desired tune was made by dropping a coin through any one of eight numbered coin slots which corresponded to the tune program. Later, in 1926, a related device, the Multi Reproducer, a remote cabinet which stored eight Welte (Licensee) piano rolls and which was connected by cable to a Bush & Lane reproducing piano, was sold.

National pianos were made in two main formats: The first, and most popular, was the type shown on this page. The second resembled the first in general appearance but had a diorama of racing dogs or horses built into the top section.

National pianos were made with the route operator in mind. Many bore the notation: "Property of the National Automatic Music Co.," implying that the firm may have leased rather than sold the instruments. MUSIC CHANGED WEEKLY is lettered in gold on the glass front of many of the instruments that survive today, indicating that a new program was once a regular feature.

Distribution of the National appears to have been spotty. The most popular single area by far was California. To a lesser extent National pianos were used in New York, New Jersey, and in a few other states. Rolls for the National were made by National itself in Grand Rapids and also by the Clark Orchestra Roll Co. of DeKalb, Illinois.

The National has many unusual features. These are illustrated and described below.

1.

5.

6.

3.

2.

7.

4.

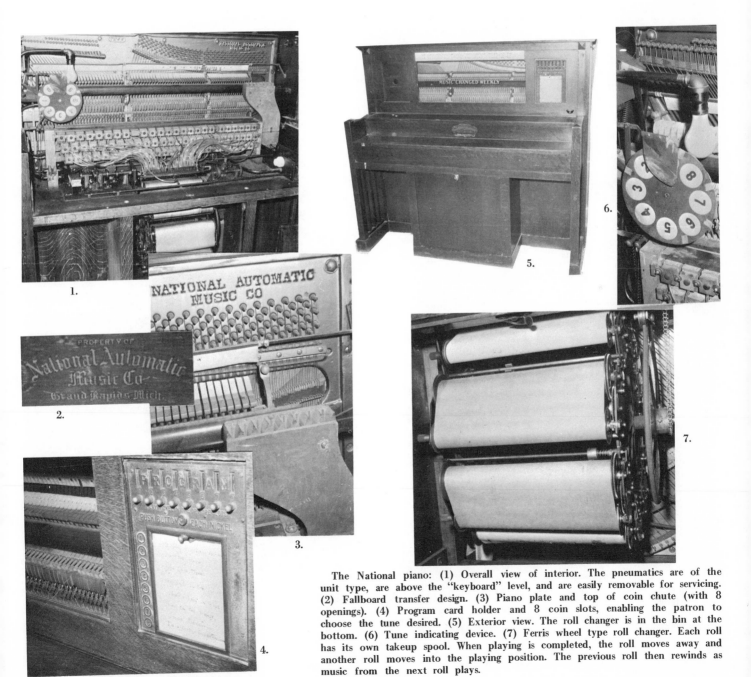

The National piano: (1) Overall view of interior. The pneumatics are of the unit type, are above the "keyboard" level, and are easily removable for servicing. (2) Fallboard transfer design. (3) Piano plate and top of coin chute (with 8 openings). (4) Program card holder and 8 coin slots, enabling the patron to choose the tune desired. (5) Exterior view. The roll changer is in the bin at the bottom. (6) Tune indicating device. (7) Ferris wheel type roll changer. Each roll has its own takeup spool. When playing is completed, the roll moves away and another roll moves into the playing position. The previous roll then rewinds as music from the next roll plays.

The Nelson-Wiggen Piano Company was a latecomer to the coin-operated piano business. Its activity was mainly confined to the decade 1920-1930 during which it produced a dozen or so different types of automatic musical instruments. Most were of the cabinet (keyboardless) style.

As did Link and several other manufacturers, Nelson-Wiggen purchased many of its pianos from the Haddorff Piano Company of Rockford, Illinois. Nelson-Wiggen, in fact, may have been headquartered in Rockford for a short period of time for the Rockford address appears in certain advertisements of the firm. To the basic Haddorff piano and case Nelson-Wiggen added the various controls, pneumatic components, xylophone, etc. as the instrument required.

Unlike most other coin piano makers of the 1920's, Nelson-Wiggen produced most of its cabinet pianos and orchestrions with clear glass fronts. Art glass was used only on a small number of instruments. Nelson-Wiggen wanted its instruments to appear as fine pieces of furniture suitable for sophisticated settings. Many of the orchestrions with fine walnut cases and with neatly hung curtains behind the clear glass achieve this image nicely.

In later years Nelson-Wiggen produced some so-called "profit sharing pianos" which contained a slot machine apparatus in the top portion. Certain of these were made with the "Gray Piano Co." label. Other Nelson-Wiggen instruments contained arcade skill devices made by the A.B.T. Company. These instruments are exceedingly rare today.

For most of its business tenure Nelson-Wiggen was headquartered at 1731-1735 Belmont Avenue in Chicago. The building still stands today.

Collectors consider Nelson-Wiggen coin pianos and orchestrions to be among the best quality instruments ever made and, accordingly, they are in strong demand and bring a premium.

Nelson-Wiggen instruments with piano, mandolin, and up to one extra instrument (usually a xylophone) use the standard 10-tune "A" coin piano rolls, although a few were originally equipped, for some reason, to use "4X" or "G" orchestrion rolls. Orchestrions with drums and traps use the standard "4X" or "G" rolls ("4X" and "G" rolls have the same tracker bar layout; the "4X" rolls are arranged for xylophone and the "G" rolls, with long perforations in the treble, are arranged for pipes). The Nelson-Wiggen Style 8, an unusual orchestrion containing piano, mandolin, xylophone, and orchestra bells, comes in either "A" or "4X" roll format.

The Nelson-Wiggen Selector Duplex Organ was made mainly for use in funeral parlors. It uses a special Selector Duplex roll of ten tunes. The roll is of double width and plays the first five tunes from one side of the roll while the roll goes slowly forward, and then it plays the second five tunes from the other side of the roll as it goes slowly in reverse. This permits uninterrupted music. The Selector Duplex organ is beautifully made, and when non-funereal music is played on it, sounds sprightly, cheerful, and melodious!

Most Nelson-Wiggen instruments have walnut cases. The standard quartered oak veneer used by the rest of the industry was used only rarely in products of this firm.

The Casino-X, a small cabinet-type "A" roll piano of the mid-1920's. Measurements are 55" high by 39½" wide by 23½" deep. "The distinctive 4-way pump is standard on the Casino-X as on our larger instruments. This insures the proper playing of the instrument as it provides an ample supply of air (vacuum) at all times. Bellows capacity should always be sufficient to take care of the small leaks that sometimes develop. The player stack incorporated in this small instrument has the latest features, being constructed on the individual unit system."

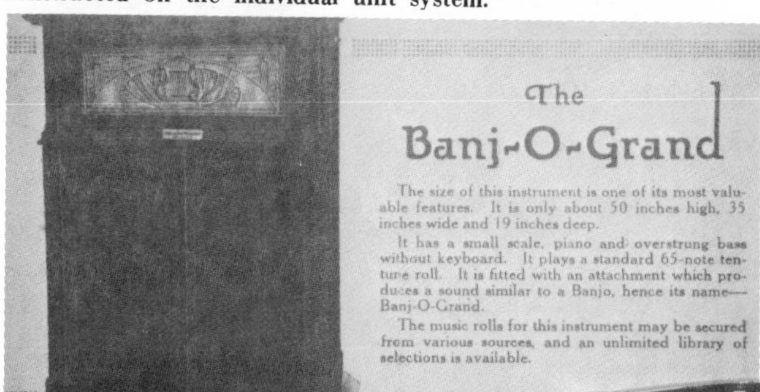

The
Banj-O-Grand
The size of this instrument is one of its most valuable features. It is only about 50 inches high, 35 inches wide and 19 inches deep.
It has a small scale, piano and overstrung bass without keyboard. It plays a standard 65-note ten-tune roll. It is fitted with an attachment which produces a sound similar to a Banjo, hence its name—Banj-O-Grand.
The music rolls for this instrument may be secured from various sources, and an unlimited library of selections is available.

The Banj-O-Grand. "A" roll cabinet piano with mandolin bar. The mandolin bar is made of small leather-covered blocks of wood, one for each note, suspended from a small curtain. When these blocks are hit by the piano hammers, and the blocks in turn hit the piano strings, a catchy "banjo" tone is the result. The Banj-O-Grand and Casino-X pianos were also made with built-in slot machines, race horse dioramas, and other gambling devices on special order.

Top: Style 2: The "Pian-O-Grand," a piano with mandolin and one rank of pipes — either violin or flute, as the buyer preferred.

Style 3: "Pian-O-Grand." Piano with mandolin and orchestra bells (rarely) or xylophone — of the "folded" type. The Style 2 and 3 use regular 10-tune "A" rolls.

STYLE 4X
Walnut, Mahogany, Mission Oak, Silver Grey Oak

Style 4X: Piano, mandolin, and limited trap effects. Uses type "4X" or "G" rolls of ten tunes each. One of the most popular styles, the 4X was made in large quantities beginning in the early 1920's.

Interior View

**Style 5 Orchestra**
*With Violin and Xylophone*

Style 5 Orchestra: Piano, mandolin, bass drum, snare drum, xylophone, metal violin pipes, and trap effects. A very rare type of orchestrion, apparently only a few were made. Uses "4X" or "G" rolls. Of all the orchestrions made by Seeburg, Western Electric, Nelson-Wiggen, et al, which use G rolls, the Style 5 was the only one to have both xylophone and pipes.

# Style 5-X

*Contains piano, banjo attachment, set of Marimbas, snare drum and triangle. Plays a standard orchestrated ten-tune roll.*

Style 5X Orchestra: Piano, mandolin (called "banjo attachment" in the original sales brochure), xylophone, snare drum, and triangle. Uses 10-tune "4X" or "G" orchestrion rolls. Made in walnut (usually), mahogany, and oak woods. 68" high by 46" wide by 27" deep; weight: about 800 pounds. As were most Nelson-Wiggen cabinet orchestrions the 5X instruments were usually fitted with cloth curtains behind clear glass panels. However, the catalogue noted that this style could be supplied with art glass on special order. Nelson-Wiggen aspired to the "upper class" segment of the coin piano market. Cloth curtains were intended to lend an air of dignity to the case, as was the use of walnut – a fine furniture wood. A 1925 advertisement noted: "Case designs are particularly high class. One of our big features is soft music – any automatic can play loud; ours play soft. Real music." Surviving specimens today indicate that the 5X was one of the most popular Nelson-Wiggen orchestrion styles.

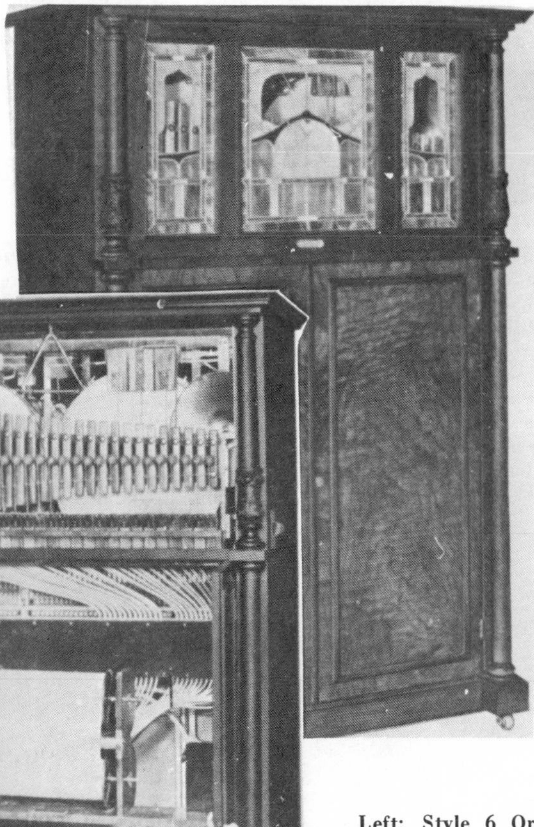

Left: Style 6 Orchestra. Piano, mandolin attachment, xylophone, bass drum, snare drum, cymbal, triangle, tympani effect, castanets, and wood block. 68" high by 46" wide by 27" deep. Uses standard 10-tune "4X" or "G" rolls. As the dimensions indicate, this orchestrion was made in the same basic case as the above 5X; only the instrumentation is different, being more extensive in the Style 6. Only a few Style 6 instruments were made with art glass (as pictured); most had clear glass fronts with curtains behind the glass. Style 6 was a popular model, and quite a few were made. It was designed to compete with the Seeburg KT Special and the Western Electric orchestrion of comparable instrumentation.

Get More Money with this combination Orchestra Piano and A. B. T. Target
Simple in construction, marvelous in its money-making possibilities, refined and tuneful music. Nothing like it on the market.
Operators will be interested in this combination instrument because its earnings are greater than any straight automatic piano or target. Successful operators are buying these instruments in large quantities.
Receipts from automatic pianos, while sure and certain, can be increased with the Target attachment because people like to shoot. The Target will keep the piano alive and continually producing more money. It is strictly legitimate, manufactured by us to enable the operator to be assured of a better income.
STYLE "6T"
Furnished in Walnut finish. Actual size of instrument. Height, 68 inches; width, 46 inches; depth, 27 inches.
Contains piano with banjo attachment, xylophone, bass drum, snare drum, cymbal, triangle, tympany, castanets and Indian block. Plays a ten-tune orchestrated roll.
Weight, boxed for shipment 800 lbs.
Let them "shoot" at this for a Tune
One tune for hitting the Red, two for hitting the White, and four tunes for hitting the Blue. Gun loads with 5c coin. Orchestra or Piano may be played in regular way, by inserting coin in slot, in addition to Target skill. Uses standard roll. Simple, complete mechanism, built with the famous A. B. T. Target, in connection with the NELSON-WIGGEN "BETTER AUTOMATIC" PIANO.

**Above: Style 6T Orchestra. Basically a Style 6 Orchestra with a shooting gallery attachment, this orchestrion was designed for those with a gambling instinct. A marksman could win four tunes instead of the usual single tune for a nickel! On the other hand he might end up with silence! Comparable games of skill were fitted into other Nelson-Wiggen orchestrions during the late 1920's in a last-ditch attempt to shore up sagging sales of instruments that were fading in popularity with the public. The "strictly legitimate" aspect of the Style 6T, as noted in the above sales presentation, was only the opinion of the seller. In practice such games of chance were highly illegal in many locations.**

**Above: Style 8. Piano, mandolin attachment, xylophone, and orchestra bells. 55" high by 39½" wide by 24" deep. Made in walnut (usually), mahogany, and oak. Colorful green and red art glass at the top. Made in two styles, each with a different note scale on the xylophone and bells. One type used 10-tune "A" rolls and changed from xylophone to bells alternately by means of a switcher valve. A rarer type used "G" rolls and employed the two pipe registers (violin and flute) of the "G" roll to operate the xylophone and bells.**

**Above: Style 7. Sold as: "The Nelson-Wiggen Full Orchestra Keyboard Piano, Style 7. Contains the following instruments: piano of seven and one-third octaves, xylophone, banjo attachment (mandolin), bass drum, snare drum, tympani, cymbal, triangle, castanets, and Indian block. The Style 7 renders the widest range of orchestral effects with a perfection that gives the greatest satisfaction. . . The shrewd investor looking for a steady flow of profits from his instruments will not overlook this wonderful instrument." Despite the enthusiasm of the maker the Style 7 was not one of Nelson-Wiggen's better sellers, and only a few were made. It is interesting to note that the Style 2, 3, and 7 keyboard pianos are built into small upright pianos of a type regularly used for home players –**

Side View, showing removable organ cabinet.

**Selector Duplex Organ. Nelson-Wiggen's answer to the Reproduco, the Selector Duplex had the same instrumentation: piano, stopped diapason, flute, and quintadena pipes. Measurements are: 5'3" wide by 4'8" high by 2'6" deep (plus a 1'1" cabinet for the diapason pipes). "Player Piano Treasury" notes: "The outstanding feature of this particular model was the duplex characteristic of the music rolls. The music was cut in such a manner that when the roll went forward the organ would play from one set of holes, and then play from the other side of the roll and from another set of holes as the roll was rewinding." This permitted continuous music. Although advertised for theatres, lodges, etc. most were used in mortuaries – and most music rolls surviving for this instrument today are of the sacred type of music.**

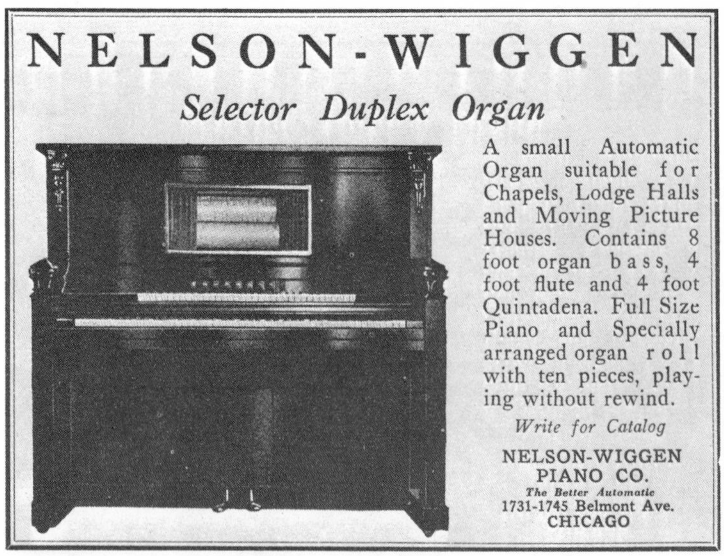

Overall interior view. The general layout is similar to contemporary Western Electric and Seeburg instruments. Most Nelson-Wiggen instruments are of walnut, a wood used only sparingly by other makers.

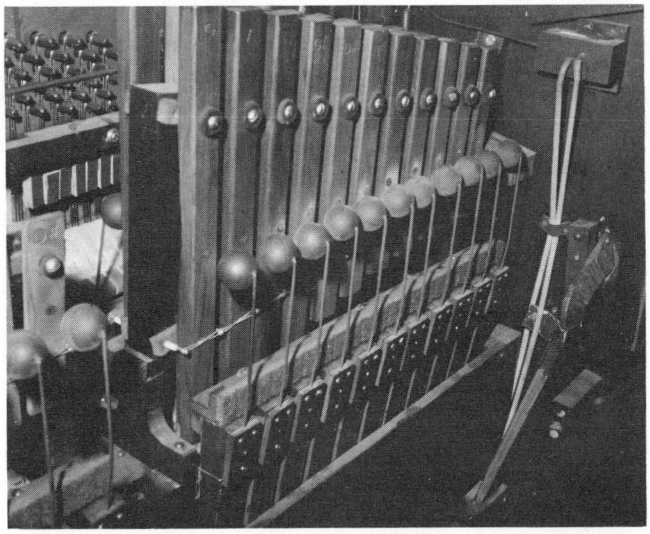

Liberty brand xylophone (made by the Kohler-Liebich Co.) is of the "folded" type – half of the bars are on the front side and half on the back. Certain other Style 8's used Deagan xylophones of slightly larger scale.

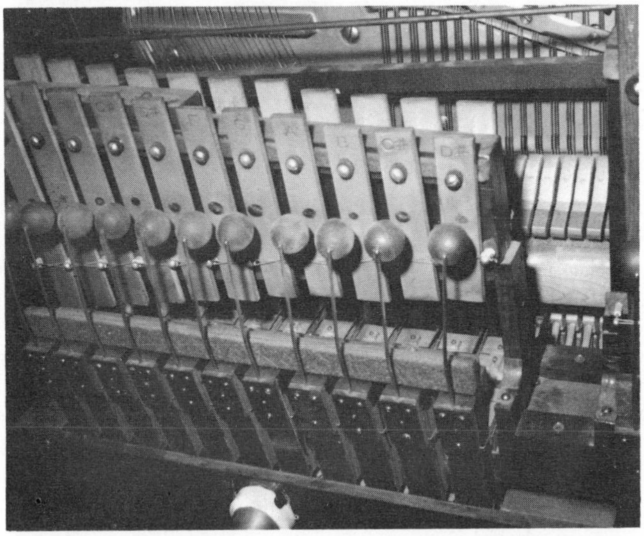

Set of 22 orchestra bells at the upper left. It also is of the folded type. The xylophone and bell bars play alternately by means of a switching valve.

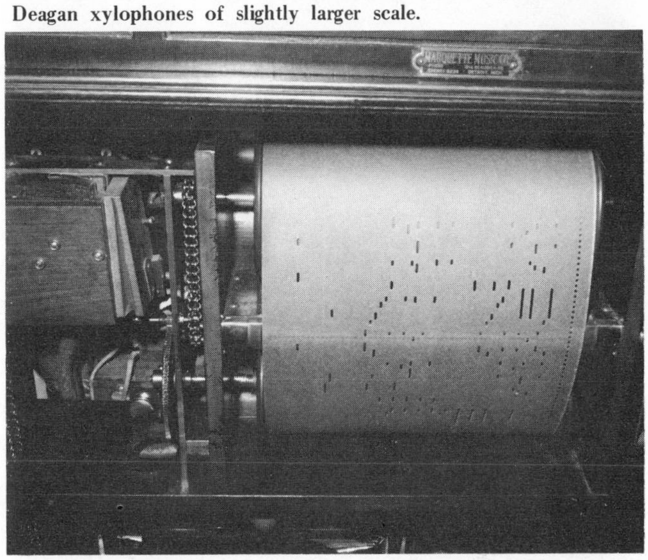

Roll mechanism using type "A" rolls (some other Style 8's used G or 4X rolls). The forward-to-rewind shifting mechanism is to the left.

The pump is of the four-part "box" variety. Pumps of somewhat similar design were used in Coinola and Seeburg pianos of the mid-1920's.

Accumulating mechanism for registering nickels as they are dropped in the slot. Each nickel moves the ratchet wheel one notch forward; each tune played moves it back a notch.

The Nelson-Wiggen building as photographed by the author in 1965. Located on Chicago's Belmont Avenue, the building has seen many different tenants since Nelson-Wiggen days. "I don't know what you are talking about," was the reply to the author's "Do you know anything about a piano company that was once located here?" The right part of the building, as illustrated in the advertisement below, either was never built or was destroyed since the 1920's. During the preparation of this book and the earlier volume, "A Guidebook of Automatic Musical Instruments," the author endeavored to visit as many original factory sites of American and European instrument builders as possible. 1731 Belmont Avenue was one of the best-preserved!

View of some of the percussion effects in a Nelson-Wiggen Style 6 orchestrion. These interesting components are mounted in the top of the case, in full view behind the clear glass panel. (Sam Gordon Collection)

Where the
" *Better Automatic* "
is made

## NEUE LEIPZIGER MUSIKWERKE
## A. BUFF-HEDINGER

The Neue Leipziger Musikwerke A. Buff-Hedinger was the successor to the Leipzig Musikwerke (which was formerly Paul Ehrlich & Cie.). Buff-Hedinger expanded the Ehrlich line (which consisted of many varieties of organettes including the best-selling Ariston and music boxes including Monopol) to include several varieties of orchestrions and coin pianos. Those shown here are from the 1905-1910 period. Trade names used include Primavolta, Toccaphon, and Buff-Hedinger's Piano-Orchestrion.

Buff-Hedinger's Piano Orchestrion

Buff-Hedingers Piano-Orchestrion.

Primavolta.

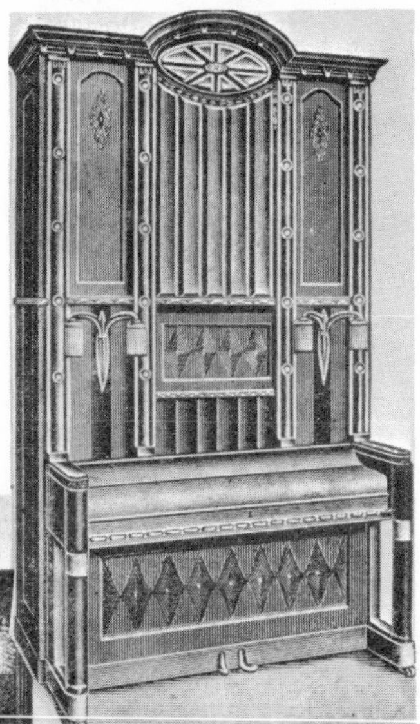

Primavolta Trio (piano w/violin and flute pipes).

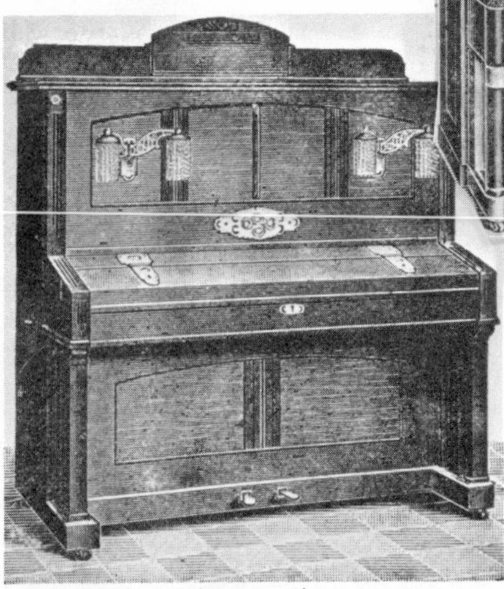

Kunstspiel-Klavier „Primavolta".

Kunstspielklavier „Toccaphon" mit Xylophon u. Mandoline.

## SAXON ORCHESTRION MANUFACTORY
### (Sächsischen Orchestrionfabrik F.O. Glass)
### —Klingenthal, Germany—

The Sächsischen Orchestrionfabrik (not to be confused with the similarly-named Sächsische Orchester-Musikwerke of Leipzig) produced a series of barrel-operated and roll-operated pianos and orchestrions from the late 1880's until World War I. Those shown here date from the 1905-1912 period. Trade names used include Eldorado and Valsonora. Emphasis was on barrel-operated instruments, and more of these were made than were roll-operated types. Distribution was through sales agents in Leipzig and elsewhere.

Valsonora O.

Valsonora OO.

Barrel orchestrion c.1905.

Above: two Valsonora models. Each contained a 24-note piano, an 8-note mandolin, 8 xylophone bars, triangle, tenor drum, and cymbal. A bass drum was available for 60 Marks extra. Valsonora 0 measured 228x100x63 cm. and sold for 1125 Mk. Model 00 measured 225x95x60 cm. and sold for 1150 Mk. Barrels contained 6 tunes each and measured 48 cm. long by 25 cm. in diameter.

Paul Ehrlich.

Paul Ehrlich (March 21, 1849 - January 17, 1925) was a man of many talents in the musical instrument field.

Buff Hedingers Xylophon-Klavier „Toccaphon".

## NIAGARA MUSICAL INSTRUMENT COMPANY
—North Tonawanda, N.Y.—

### Niagara Coin Pianos

During the 1910 era the Niagara Musical Instrument Company (also known as the Niagara Musical Instrument Manufacturing Co.) produced several different varieties of coin pianos and orchestrions in addition to the band organs which were the main product of the firm (see Niagara band organ section of this book).

A 1911 price list offered the following:

| | |
|---|---|
| En-Symphonie Without keyboard | $1400 |
| En-Symphonie With keyboard | 2200 |
| Clariphone | 1800 |
| Pianagara, 44 notes | 500 |
| Violophone, 56 notes | 850 |
| Oratorio, 88 notes | 1200 |

Niagara spelling was erratic, and the same instrument was called a Violiphone in one piece of literature and a Violophone in another; a Pianagara once and then a Pianiagara.

The En-Symphonie, essentially a pipe organ which played from regular 65-note home player piano rolls, was sold to the extent of several dozen specimens, mostly without keyboard. The Violiphone combined a piano, mandolin, and violin and flute pipes in a cabinet. Music was provided via a standard 10-tune "A" roll. "We have concentrated in the Violiphone seven years of experience, devoted to building automatic instruments exclusively, making it mechanically the best instrument of its kind that has ever been produced; in the simplicity of its working parts, as well as in the character of the music and the almost human expression with which it plays." As did other Niagara instruments, the Violiphone featured something called "Direct Attacque" which resulted in "mechanical simplicity."

Certain Niagara instruments were sold under the "Peerless" trademark (refer to the Peerless Piano Player Co. section of this book), indicating a possible connection between the Niagara and Peerless firms.

Niagara went out of business shortly before World War I. The firm was never a major factor in the coin piano business and, consequently, its instruments are rare today.

———————

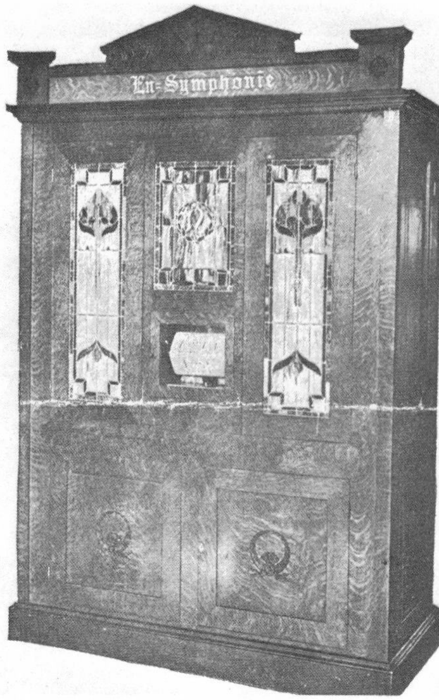


**Niagara Musical Instrument Mfg. Co.**
NORTH TONAWANDA, N. Y.

The keyboardless En-Symphonie. Niagara factory records (incomplete) reveal that Carlin & Schoen of Pittsburgh ordered one instrument on 3/22/1911; C.E. Gable of Sharon, Pa., sold 3 En-Symphonies in March, 1911; Greenwood & Sons of Youngstown, Ohio, sold 3 En-Symphonies in the same month; E. Krenter (spelling unclear) of Sheboygan, Wisc., ordered one instrument on 4/1/1911; on 4/15/1911 an En-Symphonie was sold to the Brice Moving Picture Show of Homestead, Conn.; and in May, 1911, one En-Symphonie was shipped to Jesse Walton of 1115 S. Hope St., Los Angeles. Where are they all now?

Niagara cabinet-style "A" roll piano with mandolin. Note the Peerless plaque directly below the coin slot on the right side of the instrument. The Niagara is a ruggedly built instrument and was made to withstand hard use. Niagara coin pianos of all types are very rare today.

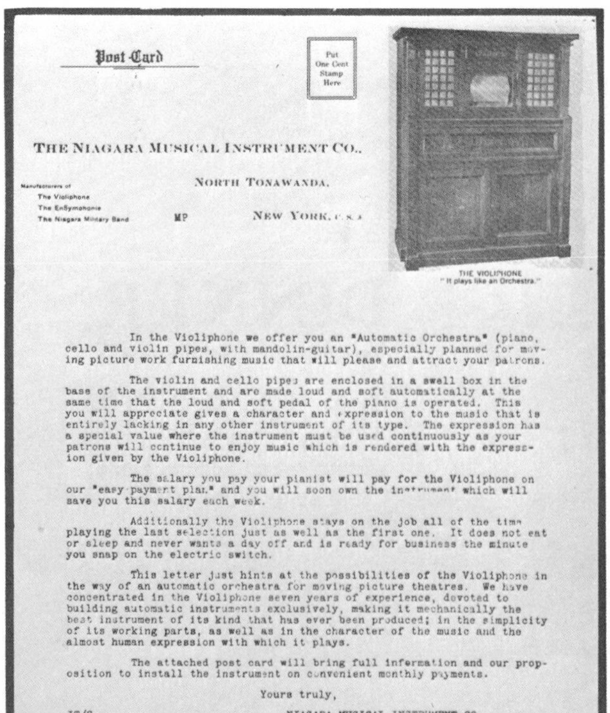

Post Card

Put One Cent Stamp Here

THE NIAGARA MUSICAL INSTRUMENT CO.,
NORTH TONAWANDA,
NEW YORK, U.S.A.

Manufacturers of
The Violiphone
The EnSymphonie
The Niagara Military Band

MP

THE VIOLIPHONE
"It plays like an Orchestra."

In the Violiphone we offer you an "Automatic Orchestra" (piano, cello and violin pipes, with mandolin-guitar), especially planned for moving picture work furnishing music that will please and attract your patrons.

The violin and cello pipes are enclosed in a swell box in the base of the instrument and are made loud and soft automatically at the same time that the loud and soft pedal of the piano is operated. This you will appreciate gives a character and expression to the music that is entirely lacking in any other instrument of its type. The expression has a special value where the instrument must be used continuously as your patrons will continue to enjoy music which is rendered with the express-ion given by the Violiphone.

The salary you pay your pianist will pay for the Violiphone on our "easy payment plan" and you will soon own the instrument which will save you this salary each week.

Additionally the Violiphone stays on the job all of the time playing the last selection just as well as the first one. It does not eat or sleep and never wants a day off and is ready for business the minute you snap on the electric switch.

This letter just hints at the possibilities of the Violiphone in the way of an automatic orchestra for moving picture theatres. We have concentrated in the Violiphone seven years of experience, devoted to building automatic instruments exclusively, making it mechanically the best instrument of its kind that has ever been produced; in the simplicity of its working parts, as well as in the character of the music and the almost human expression with which it plays.

The attached post card will bring full information and our proposition to install the instrument on convenient monthly payments.

Yours truly,

JT/S NIAGARA MUSICAL INSTRUMENT CO.

The Mechanical Simplicity of the DIRECT ATTACQUE in all Niagara Instruments represents an experience of years in making automatic instruments exclusively.

Above: Sales literature for the Violiphone.

## NORTH TONAWANDA MUSICAL INSTRUMENT WORKS
(also Rand Company, Inc.)
(also Capitol Piano and Organ Co.)

### The Early Years

The North Tonawanda Musical Instrument Works was founded circa 1906 by a group of employees who left the nearby Eugene DeKleist factory. From then until about 1929 the North Tonawanda, New York, firm produced an interesting variety of coin pianos, orchestrions, photoplayers, and band organs.

The best known North Tonawanda instrument today is the Pianolin, a 44-note cabinet piano accompanied by violin and flute pipes. These were originally sold by the many hundreds, if not by the thousands. "This instrument is designed and gotten up to fill a much needed want in the picture arcade and moving picture show business and also to furnish orchestra music in cafes, restaurants, ice cream parlors, dance halls and places of every description where people congregate for recreation, also railroad stations, waiting rooms, department stores, saloons, and tonsorial parlors" read an all-encompassing early advertisement.

The late Joseph Bacigalupi, son of Peter Bacigalupi and a partner in the firm of Peter Bacigalupi & Sons, furnished the author with that company's files from the 1905 - 1925 era. Over a period of years Bacigalupi handled North Tonawanda, Cremona (made by Marquette), and several other makes of instruments. "The fastest selling pianos we ever handled were Pianolins," he said. "When they first came out around 1906 or 1907 there was a demand for coin pianos of any kind. We bought as many Pianolins as the factory would sell us, and still we couldn't keep them in stock."

During the early years the main products were the Pianolin and a large series of skating rink organs (see the band organ section of this book). Later, the firm produced the Sextrola, an expanded version of the Pianolin with a set of bells added and in a larger case, a series of keyboard pianos, and several large and ornate orchestrions — the Orchestrina in at least two case variations and the Mando-Orchestra. These latter instruments were sold only in small numbers. In 1922 a part of the factory was cleaned out and several unused Mando-Orchestra cabinets were given to employees.

### The Endless Roll System

Most keyboardless North Tonawanda instruments from the Pianolin through the Mando-Orchestra use an endless roll. This system was used during the 1900 - 1910 period by many different manufacturers, but one by one they converted to the more convenient (it could be changed faster and took up less room in the instrument) rewind roll system. There were a few holdouts with the endless system, and North Tonawanda was one of them (although in the 1920's it, too, changed to the rewind system). The demise of the endless roll system was hastened in part by such advertisements as the Wurlitzer cartoon showing the owner of an endless roll type of instrument becoming hopelessly entangled in the paper rolls, much as in the tentacles of an octopus!

To counter this and similar opposition North Tonawanda advertised: "The music, perforated paper rolls, is in the form of endless rolls. This system has been adopted after careful and severe test with respect to steadiness of time to music and preservation of paper. It is a well known fact and is admitted that the tempo of spooled music varies, caused by the speed of the paper being increased as the diameter of the roll increases, consequently changing the tempo of the music, and can only be regulated and adjusted by hand to get anything like satisfactory results; also that in rewinding the paper is damaged, is rolled over on edges, and will move from side to side of the flanges, thereby closing tracker bar holes — resulting in sluggish notes or often no notes at all. The endless roll system is the only practical one for automatic played instruments and is being adopted by the leading manufacturers of this line of instruments."

Author's note: The tempo increase of rewind music was often compensated for by "stretching" out the notes toward the end of the roll — so the above situation is not apropos to all rewind-type rolls.

### The Capitol Piano and Organ Company

About 1920 The Capitol Piano and Organ Company was set up as a 51% owned subsidiary of the North Tonawanda Musical Instrument Works. The leading figures in the new offspring, William Getz and Samuel Kissberg, aggressively marketed the firm's products (something that had been done rather inconsistently and certainly not aggressively during the preceding decade). This resulted in many sales for Capitol, particularly of the keyboard type pianos. These keyboard pianos used

# It is Just Like a REAL Jazz Orchestra

This 1922 Capitol Jazz Concert Orchestra will

**Crowd Your Place** **Increase Your Business** **Double Your Profits**

SOMETHING ENTIRELY NEW!

**Attention**

YOU want more business. This Jazz Orchestra will get you more business. People passing your doors will stop to listen to the sweet music and will drop in—spend their money and come again and again with their friends, which means—Big Crowds—Big Business—Big Profits.

Don't Delay — Every day you are without this trade winner, you are Losing Business.

This Capitol Jazz Orchestra is a 1921 Invention—entirely different from the old style electric pianos and organs you have seen in the past. This is a Real Musical Instrument that plays with Human Expression that the people want and enjoy.

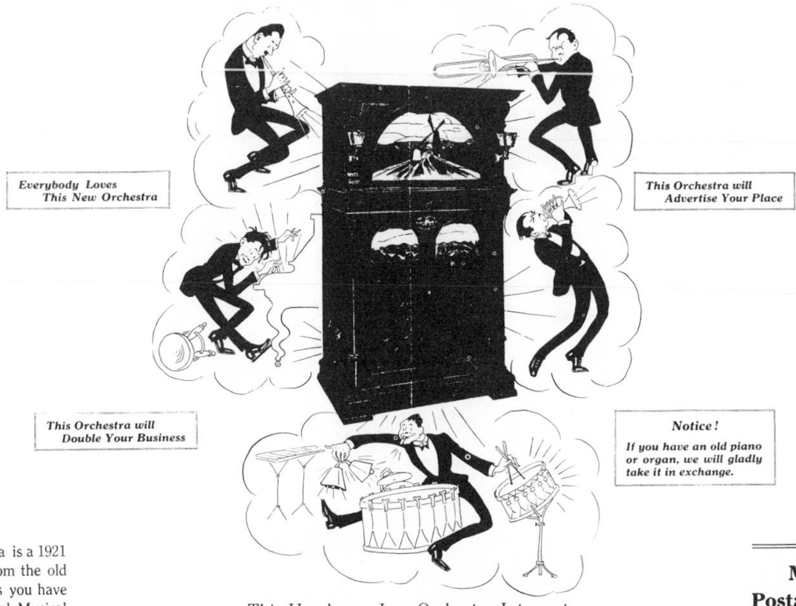

Everybody Loves This New Orchestra
This Orchestra will Advertise Your Place
This Orchestra will Double Your Business
Notice!
If you have an old piano or organ, we will gladly take it in exchange.


This Handsome Jazz Orchestra Interprets
Classical and Operatic Music with the Same Human Effect

**It Pays for Itself**

IN order to introduce this new Orchestra we will install it in your place at practically no expense.

Your customers will go wild about it and never stop dropping nickels into it to hear it play and in that way it will pay for itself.

If you cannot call, mail today the enclosed post card and we will tell you how you can get this wonderful business getter so that it costs you practically nothing.

**Mail back the enclosed Postal and we will send you full Information FREE.**

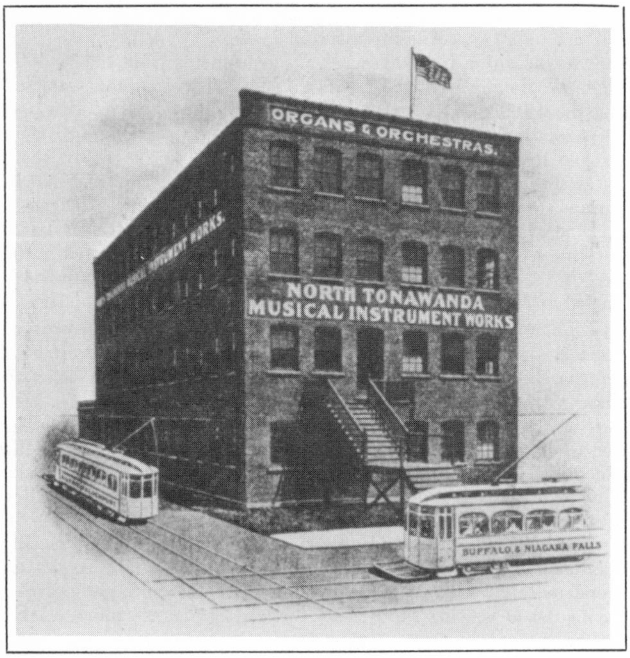


The North Tonawanda Musical Instrument Works as shown in a catalogue from the 1910 period.

The roll mechanism on a rewind-type North Tonawanda coin piano.

special 14-tune type "L" rolls and, later, regular 10-tune type "A" rolls bought from the Clark Orchestra Roll Co. of DeKalb, Illinois.

Capitol sought to upgrade the image and romantic appeal of the then-outdated Pianolin and renamed it the "Midget Orchestra." The Sextrola, never a popular machine, became the "Bluebird Orchestra." The "Mando-Orchestra" was given the up-to-date title of "Capitol Jazz Concert Orchestra," and so on. The main problem was that Messrs. Getz and Kissberg came too late. By 1920 the golden years of the coin piano and orchestrion business were over.

Almost all types of North Tonawanda Musical Instrument Works instruments can be found with Capitol Piano and Organ Company labels. As the two companies are really one we include them both together in this section.

### Fox Music Co.; Electrotone

North Tonawanda did a lot of contract manufacturing for other companies. Factory records show that Midget Orchestras and keyboard pianos were delivered to the Fox Music Company of Kansas City, Missouri, as late as 1929. The Electrotone Automusic Company also sold North Tonawanda products under another name.

The usual practice was to put just the center part of the North Tonawanda decal on the instrument, the part that read "MUSICAL INSTRUMENT WORKS." The buyer could then put "ELECTROTONE" or whatever he pleased above it! Examples are illustrated on the pages to follow.

### North Tonawanda Photoplayers

As did most other firms in the field, North Tonawanda manufactured a line of photoplayers. These same instruments were later sold by Capitol in the 1920's.

A December 31, 1914, letter from North Tonawanda to Peter Bacigalupi & Sons of San Francisco, tells the merits of the Style G (same as the later Capitol Style F) photoplayer:

"The perfect balancing of the instrumentation and the especially arranged music places the Ideal Moving Picture Orchestra in advance of any other instrument of its kind on the market today.

"The tremolo, the slurring of the violins, together with the exquisite shading of expression in the instrument is marvelous, the traps being played exactly as a trap drummer would play them.

"There are buttons directly before the operator to control the effects and get what he desires, whether it be a church organ, string quartette, country fiddler, drum corps, or whatever – all with piano accompaniment, steam whistle, doorbell, and various other imitations of different noises.

"The music roll is directly in front of the operator (this was a rewind roll and this advertisement was written later than the above-quoted endless roll ad – Ed.) and can be controlled so that any of the selections may be played at will.

"Good music cannot possibly be gotten out of an instrument of this kind by using ordinary 88-note piano music, for the simple reason that no provision is made in that kind of music for anything but piano (Ed. note: this is a slur directed toward Fotoplayers and Wurlitzer "Y" series instruments, both types of which were far more successful than North Tonawanda photoplayers ever were!) therefore in order to obtain the very best musical effects, it is imperative that the music should be specially arranged for an automatic orchestra of this type. . .

"Now, friend, these instruments are both new and far above the ordinary ones you have heard about in the past and have music that cannot be equalled by any of our competitors. The reason why we have

## RAND COMPANY, INC.

MUSICAL INSTRUMENT DIVISION

MANUFACTURERS OF

PLAYER PIANOS
REPRODUCING PIANOS
AUTOMATIC PIANOS
THEATRE ORCHESTRAS
BAND ORGANS
PIPE ORGANS

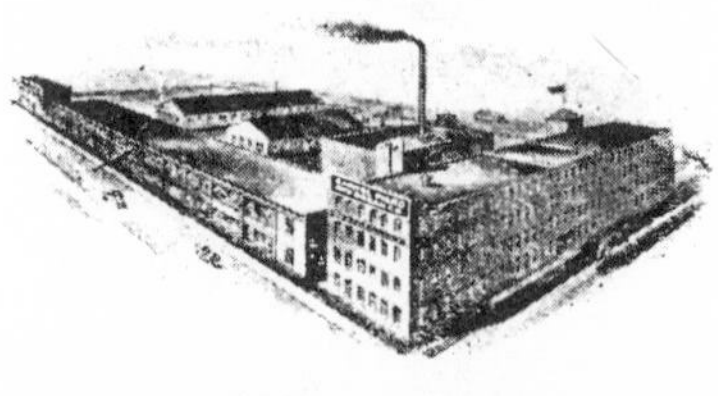

OWNERS

NORTH TONAWANDA MUSICAL INSTRUMENT WORKS

SALES OFFICES IN ALL PRINCIPAL CITIES

MAIN OFFICE AND FACTORY

NORTH TONAWANDA, N. Y.

Paul Eakins is shown with a North Tonawanda Sextrola when the instrument was on exhibit in St. Louis' Gay Nineties Melody Museum in the late 1960's.

North Tonawanda Midget Orchestra.

better musical results is that we really have the greatest experts in this line in this country, nearly all of them having had many years experience in the oldest factory in America (Ed. note: this refers to Eugene DeKleist's nearby plant), and some of them having been at the heads of the oldest and best European factories.

"We solicit your investigation and hope that you will be interested to the extent of either calling at the factory or ordering one of them at an early date for a tryout. . ."

Despite this pleading letter few photoplayer orders ever came over the doorstep.

The Rand Company, Inc.
An Interview with Benjamin G. Rand

Shortly before 1920 the North Tonawanda Musical Instrument Works was taken over by the Rand Company, Inc. (which is now a part of the Remington Rand organization). In February, 1966, the author and Harvey Roehl prepared a list of questions and submitted them to Benjamin G. Rand, a former officer of the Rand Company. From his retirement home in Florida Mr. Rand furnished some previously unpublished information in response to our inquiries:

"Your letter of February 3rd was a surprise to me as I have given very little thought to the musical part of my life experience in the manufacturing field. Let me make it clear that the manufacture of musical instruments was never more than an incidental stepchild in the thought and planning of the real developers of the Rand Company or Remington Rand.

"That just 'came along' when Rand bought the capital stock of the North Tonawanda Musical Instrument Works. Our first contact with that corporation was printing labels for the boxes of perforated music rolls that they made for their instruments. It developed that they could and would make wood and metal parts of our index card and record devices for offices. This association led to the above mentioned purchase when their business deflated greatly when the United States entered World War I in 1917. Their management failed to profit in war work when we needed more facilities — so we thus secured a good four-story plant and a good piece of vacant ground.

"After a few years the group of North Tonawanda Musical Instrument Works former shareholders formed the Artizan Company, which never really got off the ground. The men in that company were John Birnie, F. Morganti, Henry Tussing, and W.F. Schultz.

"In answer to your other questions:

"The Rand Company took over the North Tonawanda Musical Instrument Works about 1918 and continued making musical instruments until 1925 (Editor's note: Existing North Tonawanda photo files in our possession show that shipments were made until 1929, although perhaps these instruments were manufactured earlier). The Artizan Company was started when World War I ended.

(In reply to a query concerning the notice on the Rand letterhead that the firm made reproducing pianos, theatre orchestras, and pipe organs): "We made no pipe organs, either church organs or theatre organs, during the Rand Company's operation.

"The manufacture of the Pianolin, a 44-note piano introduced shortly before 1910, was continued by the Rand Company.

(In reply to our question: What was the relationship with the Capitol Piano and Organ Co.?): "The Capitol Piano and Organ Company was incorporated with the Rand Company 51% owner and with William Getz and Sam Kissberg 49% owners. They were Wurlitzer salesmen in New York City who came to us unsolicited, and we formed Capitol as a selling effort in New York City. They sold a good number of coin operated pianos and collected weekly.

(In reply to other questions): "We only made a very few Sextrolas. I cannot recall the Mando-Orchestra or the Orchestrina. The competing Niagara Musical Instrument Company was formed by people with little or no experience in the field. In my opinion this is why they were never a major factor in the industry. During our ownership no band organs were made, although we repaired some. We continued to make music rolls for band organs of previous manufacture."

PIANOLIN

(No.1)

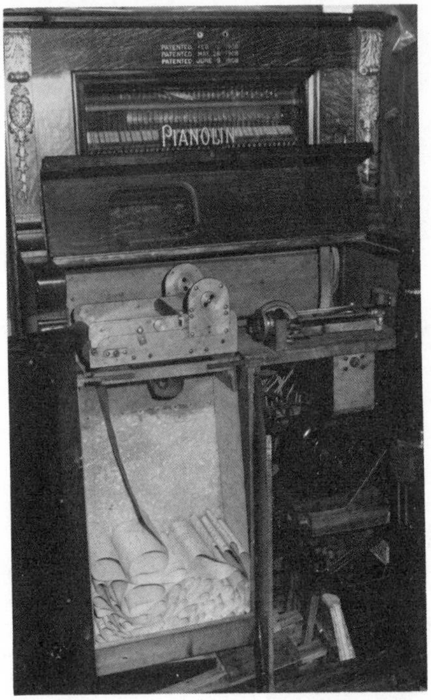


(No.2)

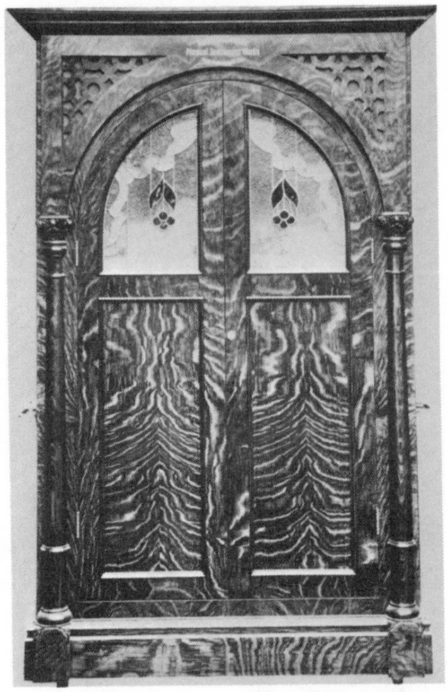

(No.3)

(No.4)

(No.5)

**–PIANOLIN–**

**Instrumentation consists of a 44-note piano with the accompaniment of violin and flute pipes (which play all the time; they are not controlled by registers). One of the earliest North Tonawanda instruments, and certainly the most successful in terms of the quantities made.**

**(No.1) Standard Pianolin design with clear glass panel at top; (No.2) Interior of the Pianolin – from the Roehl Collection; (No.3) "Midget Orchestra," new name for the Pianolin sold by Capitol. (No.4) Pianolin Style A with art glass panel; (No.5) Pianolin Style B, with straight-front case and with two art glass panels; (No.6) Pianolin A in white enamel case decorated with paintings.**

**Nearly all Pianolins sold were of the type as illustrated by our No.1 above. Very few straight-front or art glass models were made.**

(No.6)

---

**Sextrola**

**Sextrola "A" 52 Notes**

## Sextrola "B"

A 52-Note Orchestrion

THE "Sextrola" is recognized by musicians and the trade to be a superior instrument for medium-sized picture theatres, dance halls, restaurants, cafés, ice cream parlors, etc.

The case is an arts-and-crafts design; built of first quality oak, satin finish, and with three fine, colored art-glass panels which are lighted up, when the music is started, by dropping a coin in the slot.

There is a knob on the outside of the case with which the pipes are shut off, and another one to soften the piano; also an almost invisible push button to drop coins through the slot when the music is not wanted during prohibitive hours. Tempo regulator inside of case to govern time of music.

The music is in the form of endless paper rolls (twelve selections to the roll), one of which is included in the price of the instrument and is passed through our patented steel tracker box which does not permit it to get out of track; therefore, no trouble is ever encountered with this perfect system.

The tracker bar is divided by a wire screen which catches all of the dust and dirt; thus preventing the clogging of the valves. Workmanship and material fully guaranteed.

***Dimensions:—***

Height, 6 ft. 6½ in.; length, 4 ft. 2 in.; depth, 2 ft. 6 in.

***Instrumentation:—***

Piano, 44 notes, with loud and soft pedal and with mandolin attachment; 44 cremona-toned pipes; representing first violin, second violin, viola and "cello"; set of orchestra bells. Swell box in rear to add expression to music.

**Sextrola: The Sextrola, made in models A and B (Style B was also sold as the "Capitol Bluebird Orchestra"), combined the features of the Pianolin with a set of orchestra bells – all housed in a large and ornate case. Uses special Sextrola roll.**

Sextrola "B"—52 Notes

12 Selections

## Automatic Keyboard Piano Style "L"

*Dimensions:*
Height, 4 ft. 5½ in.; length, 5 ft. 5½ ins.; width, 2 ft. 5½ in.

*Instrumentation:*
Piano, seven and one-third octaves, with mandolin attachment, loud and soft pedal.

Set of very fine violin or flute pipes.

Clever automatic expression device.

**Style L keyboard piano. Made first using a special 14-tune "L" roll, and later using the standard 10-tune "A" roll. The "clever automatic expression device" is a single swell shutter in the back of the case.**

**Top left: Keyboard "A" roll piano with a rank of violin or flute pipes; similar to Style L but with the roll visible through clear glass; Above left: Midget Orchestra (do not confuse with Pianolin, also called by this name) made in 1928 for the Fox Music Co. of Kansas City, Mo. Above right: Enlargement of Midget Orchestra photo detail showing Fox Music Co. label. A number of different North Tonawanda instruments were sold by Fox under the Fox name.**
**Interior views of an "A" roll Style L piano of the 1920's.**

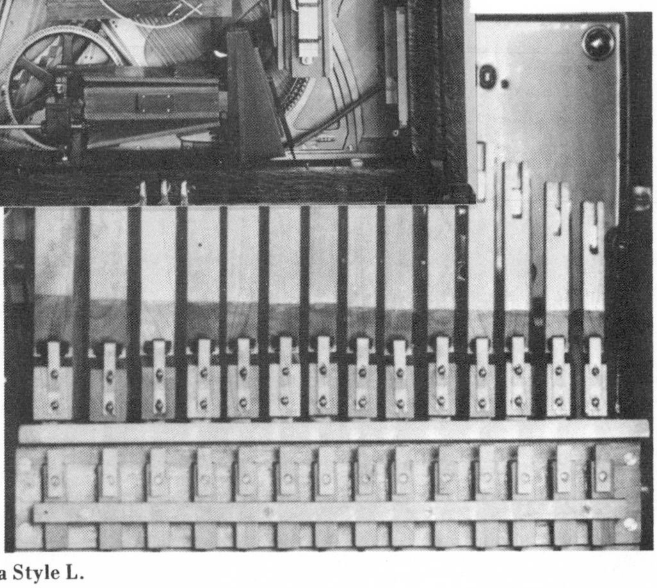

**Interior views of a Style L.**

**Previously unpublished photograph from an employee of the North Tonawanda Musical Instrument Works shows this coin-in-the-slot piano with what appears to be pedals for foot pumping (note rectangular panel at the bottom of the case). Photograph dated 1929. Similar instruments, but without the art glass or coin slot, were sold as "Premier" brand home player pianos. Can a reader offer an explanation?**

ORCHESTRINA

## ORCHESTRINA and MANDO-ORCHESTRA

The Orchestrina: Made in at least two different case styles, as shown at the left side of this page, the Orchestrina is one of the largest orchestrions ever made in America. Measurements are 9'6" high by 6'4" wide by 3'8" deep.

The catalogue description notes: "The case is made of quartered oak, of fine figure and piano finish. Two beveled panels or art glass panels are in front. Lamps inside the case are illuminated when the music is started. It is suitable for any occasion or location as it plays dance music, latest ragtime or popular selections, as well as classic overtures, and is very successfully used in moving picture theatres, dancing academies, hotel lobbies and dining rooms, restaurants, cafes, summer resort pavilions, and in private residences.

"Using a 87-note roll, the instrumentation consists of 191 sounding notes representing an orchestra of twelve men. Piano, two first violins and two second violins (pipes), viola, cello, string bass, first and second clarionets, trap drums with loud and soft stroke, cymbal, castanets, and 13 orchestra bells."

The instrument uses a special Orchestrina roll of the rewind type. The Orchestrina was made only in very small quantities; probably fewer than two dozen instruments.

The case design shown at the lower left was also sold as the "Capitol Symphony Orchestra."

The Mando-Orchestra: The original catalogue description of the Mando-Orchestra, sold also as the "Capitol Jazz Concert Orchestra," appears at the right. Of particular interest is the 25-note mandolin. This was a mechanical device which was identical in concept to the Wurlitzer Mandolin Quartette.

Orchestrina

## Mando-Orchestra—87 Notes

THIS instrument is considered a marvel by musicians; on account of its splendidly-balanced orchestration, the fine shading of expression in its music and its great carrying power. Moving picture theatres, dance halls, dining rooms, cafés, restaurants and all other places where orchestra music is needed demand an instrument of this kind.

The case is made of the best quality of quartered oak with piano finish, and with an elaborate, colored art-glass panel in the top part depicting a scene in Holland; while the two art-glass panels in the lower part show a western landscape; both of which are displayed to great advantage by electric lights inside the instrument when playing; the two outside art-glass lamps being lighted at the same time.

The stops are controlled by the perforated paper music, so that violin and cello solos are beautifully rendered.

Operated by an electric motor which, with two ten-piece rolls of music, is included in the price.

*Dimensions:*—

Height, 9 ft.; length, 5 ft.; depth, 3 ft. 4 in.

*Instrumentation:*—

80 cremona-toned pipes; representing one first violin, one second violin, one viola, "cello" and stringed bass; 44-note piano, with loud and soft pedal; 25-note mandolin, playing first and second parts; set drummers' traps, consisting of bass and snare drums with loud and soft stroke; cymbal, crash cymbal, Chinese wood drum, castanets, tom-tom and set of orchestra bells with resonators.

THEATRE ORGANS
ELECTRIC PIANOS
*and* ORCHESTRAS

THE CAPITOL

"Music is the Life of the Nation"

PIANO *and* ORGAN CO.

Showrooms: 331 West 34th St., New York

COIN-OPERATED
PIANOS *and* ORCHESTRAS
MILITARY BAND ORGANS

Very large North Tonawanda photoplayer with two keyboards. Previously unpublished design, style unknown, from the factory records.

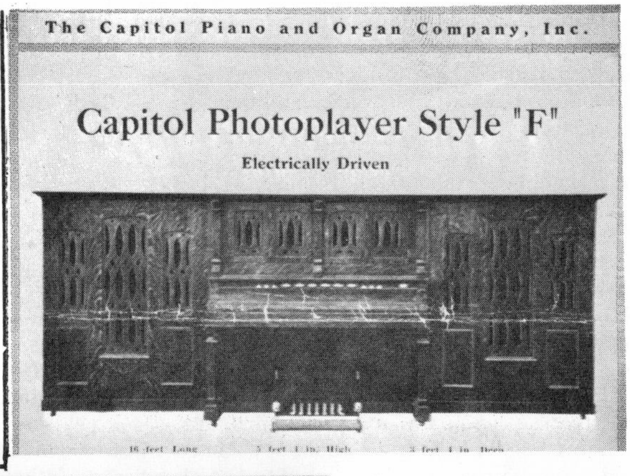


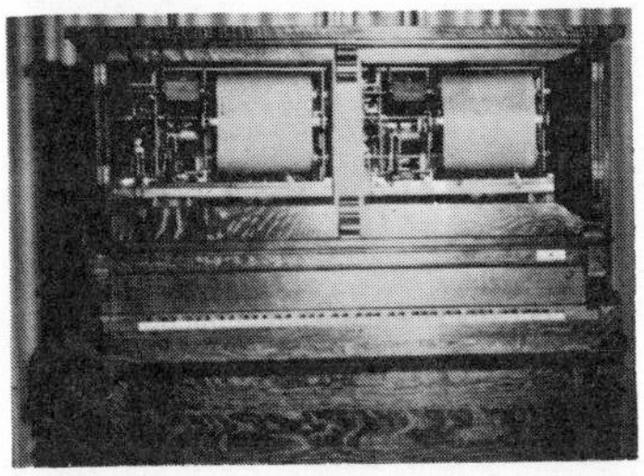

Electrotone duplex "A" roll piano made by North Tonawanda. Found in an abandoned theatre by collector Leslie Hagwood. An illustration of the Electrotone decal on this instrument appears to the right.

Decals used on various North Tonawanda instruments.

Capitol Style F photoplayer (also sold as North Tonawanda Style G). Introduced in 1914. Minor case variation shown at the left.

A NEW SENSATION
The Capitol Solo Violin-Cello Piano
"It takes the place of Human Musicians."
Plays the
Piano
Violin
Viola
Cello
Bass Violin
A thoroughly dignified and refined musical instrument only suitable for the finest places where good music is required and appreciated.
5 feet 5 in. Long 5 feet 4 in. High 3 feet 3½ in. Deep


Various North Tonawanda photoplayers from the 1920's. Actually, you're not seeing three pianos; you're seeing the same one three times! The two at the left are identical; the one at the right (Style H) is the same piano used in the other illustrations, but with a side chest pushed up to the right side. A comparison of the wood grain will confirm this. The same technique was used to make "different" varieties of North Tonawanda Musical Instrument Works band organs (see band organ section of this book).

THE Capitol style "H" Photoplayer is a very high grade orchestral instrument, reproducing music such as is ordinarily only available from an orchestra. The instrumentation represents a full 88-note high grade piano with pipes reproducing first and second violins, viola, 'cello, bass viol, first and second flutes, piccolo, bass and snare drums, cymbal with loud and soft strokes, bird whistle, tympanni, tom tom, chinese wood drum, castanets, baby cry, locomotive whistle, steamboat whistle, telephone and door bells, and automobile horn.

This wonderful instrument will delight your patrons because it gives all the satisfaction of the real orchestra, yet never strikes a harsh note when automatically operated. It gives a perfect reproduction of the full orchestra with the natural tremolo and slurring of the violins; the pathetic strains of the 'cello; the clear, sweet tones of the flute. With our double spooled music system containing twenty separate pieces to the roll, or manually played, every possible scene in a photoplay may be easily followed.

This instrument is designed and built by expert craftsmen and master musicians, all within our own plant, and is superior in tone and finish to any instrument of equal price. Each instrument is fully guaranteed to please. It will require little or no attention and may be played electrically from the ordinary electric light socket.

## OPERATORS' PIANO COMPANY

The Operators' Piano Company of Chicago was a leading force in the mechanical musical field from about 1904 to the mid-1930's. This firm produced a wide variety of coin operated pianos and orchestrions which were sold under the "Coinola" name. These instruments ranged from compact cabinet style instruments to the large CO and SO orchestrions.

In the early years Coinola produced keyboard style instruments about the size of an upright piano but usually slightly deeper in order to accommodate the interior mechanisms. The basic nickelodeon pianos with mandolin attachments use regular 10-tune "A" rolls.

Coinola orchestrions use a special style "O" roll. The musical arrangements on these rolls are particularly well done, making Coinola orchestrions great favorites with collectors today. The "O" roll music has a special solo section for the set of bells, xylophone, a rank of pipes, or other solo instrument. By subduing the piano notes the solo instrument carries the melody at intervals throughout a particular tune.

The best known Coinola orchestrion is the Style X. Originally billed as "the most popular orchestrion that has ever been made," the X features a set of bells or a xylophone as the solo instrument with drums and other percussion effects in addition. These extra instruments are fitted into the bottom of the piano.

*The innards of a Coinola Style CO orchestrion of the 1920's.*

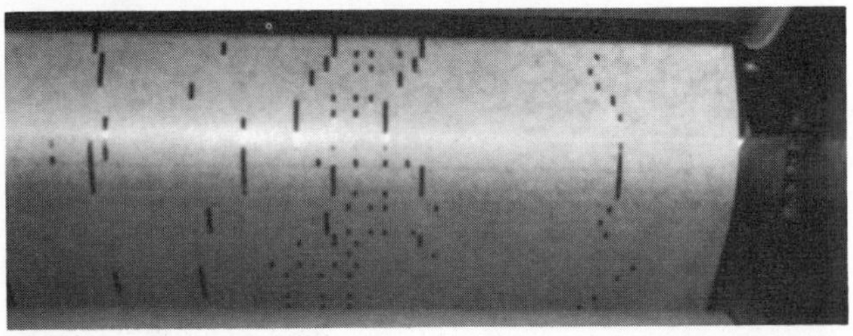

*The solo "O" orchestrion roll as it passes over the tracker bar of a Coinola orchestrion. At the far right are separately scored solo perforations.*

In 1917 Coinola introduced its line of Midget Orchestrions — keyboardless cabinet style instruments in a variety of forms ranging from basic "A" roll instruments with piano and mandolin to "full orchestra" orchestrions with piano, mandolin, xylophone (the featured solo instrument), bass drum, snare drum, and other percussion effects. Production of these was continued through the late 1920's.

In addition to making Coinola instruments the Operators' Piano Company did a large contract manufacturing business for other retailers. For Welte it produced the "Multitone" series of keyboard pianos and orchestrions. For Lyon & Healy, leading musical merchandisers in Chicago, the "Empress Electric" line of coin pianos and orchestrions was made. The Empress instrument series was quite extensive and comprised over a dozen different models. For most Empress instruments the Operators' Piano Company supplied just the interior components. The pianos themselves were provided by Lyon & Healy and were of such trade names as "Washburn" (mainly) and "Leland."

The Rockola Profit Sharing Player Piano (an "A" roll cabinet piano with a slot machine mechanism in the top part of the case) and the "Victor Coin" and "Victor" pianos were likewise equipped with

*Coinola Style X orchestrion. The Operators' Piano Company billed this as "the most popular orchestrion ever made." The Style X is all percussion (no pipes). Models were made with the buyer's choice of a wooden xylophone or a metal set of orchestra bells. The xylophone or bells played the solo part. Style O rolls are excellently arranged - and it is hard to beat a Coinola X when it comes to toe-tapping rhythm!*

**PRICE LIST**

**Effective January 1st. 1925**

**Subject to Revision**

| | |
|---|---|
| Cupid | $ 700 |
| Midget—Style A | 775 |
| Midget Orchestrion V (Violin) | 875 |
| " " F (Flute) | 875 |
| " " X (Xylophone) | 875 |
| " " K (Violin and Flute) | 1,050 |
| " " O (see catalogue Page 9) | 1,250 |
| Style C Regular | 1,000 |
| " C Xylophone | 1,200 |
| " C Flute | 1,200 |
| " C-2 | 1,375 |
| " C Reproducing | 1,075 |
| " C-K | 1,275 |
| " X | 1,575 |
| " CO | 2,200 |
| " SO | 2,300 |

**The Operators Piano Company, Inc.**

L. M. Severson, President

Manufacturers of

**AUTOMATIC MUSICAL INSTRUMENTS**

Electric Pianos, Orchestrions, Theatre and Mortuary Organs

**CHICAGO**

mechanisms provided by the Operators' Piano Company on a contract basis.

For the theatre trade (and, to a much lesser extent, the mortuary trade) the Operators' Piano Company produced the Reproduco series of piano pipe organs. Most styles contained three ranks of pipes and used "OS" (for "Organ Series") or "NOS" (for "New Organ Series") rolls interchangeably. The OS and NOS music is arranged in a particularly cheerful and sprightly manner, making the Reproduco instruments very popular with collectors today. Certain larger styles of the Reproduco had an attached side cabinet, and some used a special "Unified Reproduco" roll of greater width. These Unified Reproducos were pneumatically connected so as to "unify" (to permit assigned stops or ranks to be drawn at specific tonal lengths and to permit ranks to be switched from one keyboard [or to the pedalboard] to the other) the instrument using the basic idea of the theatre organ. Most of the Unified Reproducos contained pipes only and had no piano. Reproducos, especially the smaller and more compact ones, achieved wide popularity. Hundreds, if not thousands, were sold.

The largest Coinola orchestrions ever made, the Style CO and the Style SO, were introduced in March, 1920. The CO was a keyboard orchestrion with the extra instruments (xylophone as the solo instrument plus drums and traps) housed in a case extension on top. The CO was fronted with an attractive wingspread eagle design done in opalescent art glass. The SO contained a crash cymbal and a rank of violin pipes in addition to the instruments of the CO and was housed in a keyboardless cabinet. Although no exact figures are known to us we have estimated by working with statistical probability using the serial numbers of the several SO orchestrions we have seen that about 40 may have been made. Probably 75 to 100 CO orchestrions were sold. These two orchestrions, high on the "most wanted" lists of collectors today, were introduced for sale at a time in which the popularity of large orchestrions was fading in favor of the more compact cabinet styles (which found a more ready use in speakeasies, etc. of the early Prohibition years) — so sales were poor at the time. What collector wouldn't like to "shop" from the original Coinola price schedule of 1925 that listed Midget orchestrions at $875 to $1250 each, the X at $1575, and the CO and SO at $2200 and $2300 respectively!

The Operators' Piano Company had as subsidiaries the Capitol Roll & Record Co. and the Columbia Music Roll Company. As a general rule the arrangements featured on these rolls are outstanding. The great "listenability" of the music rolls that fit on them accounts to a large extent for the popularity of Coinola orchestrions and Reproduco piano/pipe organs today.

OPERATORS PIANO CO.

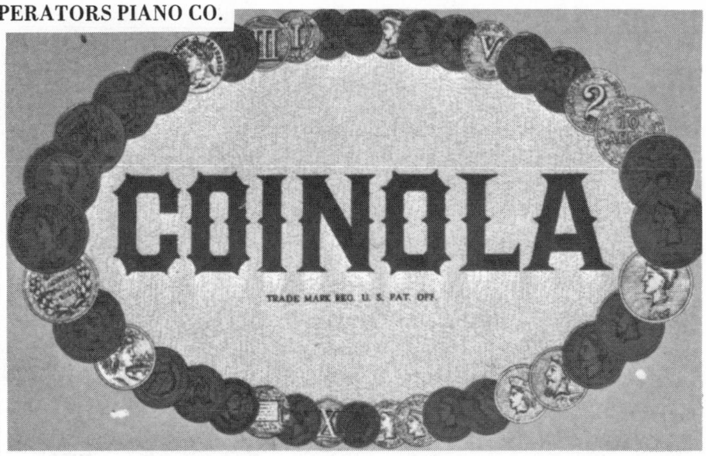


Above: The Coinola trademark was an oval of forty overlapping coins and medals.

Right: Rockola Profit Sharing Player Piano. This instrument was manufactured by the Operators Piano Company and sold to Rockola. The latter firm, a manufacturer of automatic phonographs today but primarily an operator of vending and weighing machines in the 1920's, outfitted the pianos with slot machine attachments. Several dozen were made by Rockola. Other similar profit sharing player pianos were distributed by Gray, Evans, and others.

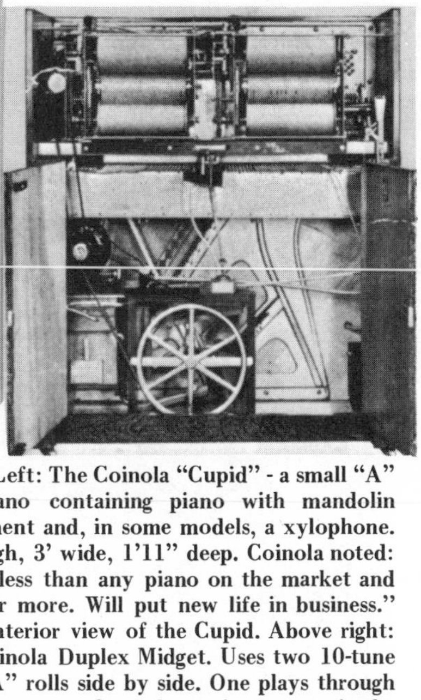

Upper Left: The Coinola "Cupid" - a small "A" roll piano containing piano with mandolin attachment and, in some models, a xylophone. 4'7" high, 3' wide, 1'11" deep. Coinola noted: "Costs less than any piano on the market and gives far more. Will put new life in business." Left: Interior view of the Cupid. Above right: The Coinola Duplex Midget. Uses two 10-tune type "A" rolls side by side. One plays through tune-by-tune to the end as coins are put in the slot. When the end of the 10th tune is reached, then the other roll starts playing from the first tune as the previously played roll is rewinding. This piano, a limited production model, offered a 20-tune program (rather than the usual 10) and also no pause for rewinding. Normal pianos are silent as the roll rewinds.

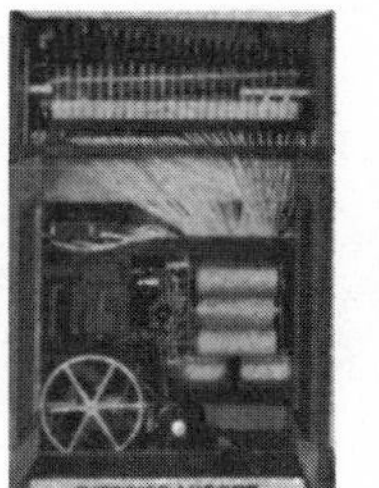

INTERIOR MIDGET
ORCHESTRION STYLE X

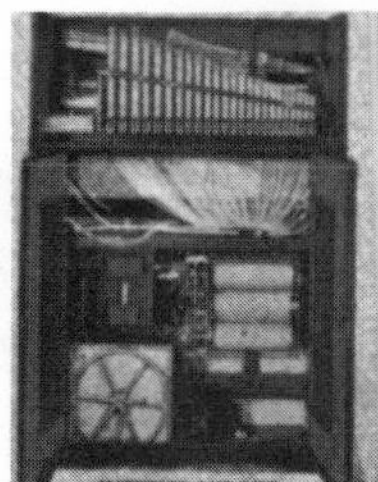

INTERIOR MIDGET

EXTERIOR COINOLA MIDGET

Coinola Midget Orchestrion has proven to be the most successful keyless instrument ever manufactured. It is equipped with the same "trouble proof" rewind mechanism and twenty coin magazines as the keyboard styles, and is a large "money getter." A handsome case design—quartersawed oak veneered in rich mission finish. Beautiful art glass panel as show on cut.

Midget A plays piano and mandolin using regular 65 standardized music.
Midget Orchestrion X plays piano, mandolin and two octaves of solo Xylophones with vibrating pneumatics, using solo O music roll.
Midget Orchestrion F. plays piano, mandolin and two octaves of rich mellow solo flute pipes, using solo O music roll.
Midget Orchestrion V. plays piano, mandolin and two octaves of solo violin pipes, using solo O music roll.
Midget Orchestrion K. plays piano, mandolin and two octaves of solo flute and violin pipes, using solo O music roll.

The Coinola Midget Orchestrion was introduced in 1917 and became a best seller. It uses the style "O" orchestrion roll. They were made in several different styles with the letter designation pertaining to the solo instrument. Thus Midget Orchestrion V featured a piano and mandolin with violin pipes playing solo; F with flute pipes as solo; X with xylophone or orchestra bells as solo. The Style K had both violin and flute pipes. The Style O Midget Orchestrion had a xylophone (usually) or bells (rarely) plus drums and traps and was thus somewhat similar in specifications to the Style X orchestrion. Behind the cloth grillwork in the bottom of the case were two sliding wooden shutters which could be put in any desired position to regulate the volume of the orchestrion to match the room in which it was situated. Coinola Midget Orchestrions are favorites of collectors today.

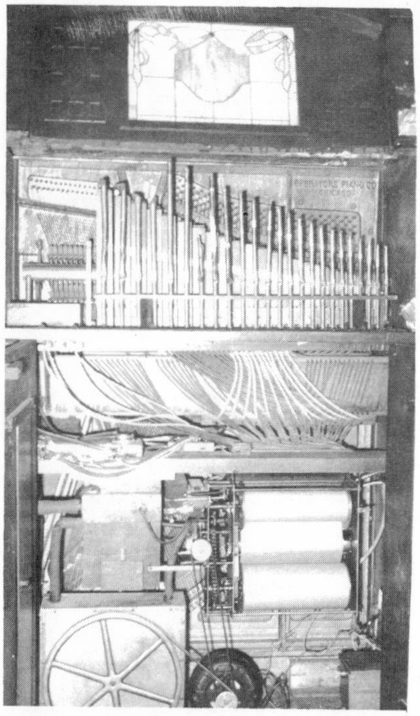

Above: Coinola Midget Orchestrion, Style K, in the DeBence Collection. This instrument has wooden flute and metal violin pipes playing the solo part. The metal violin pipes are essentially the same as the "salicional" pipes available today from organ supply firms. Fortunately for collectors, most needed parts for any mechanical piano or orchestrion restoration are available cheaply today.

Right: Exterior of a beautiful Midget Orchestrion from the Lewis Graham Collection. This instrument, in quartered oak, was originally distributed by W.H. Aton, a Coinola dealer in Mason City, Iowa. Note the tilted coin slot - a feature of many Coinola and Empress Electric instruments.

View of yet another surviving specimen of the Midget Orchestrion, Style K. The upper front panel is hinged to the top lid and lifts up and out of the way to permit servicing the interior. Because of their long length the three bass pipes in the metal violin rank are mitered so as to fit in the case.

Upper right section of the piano plate on a Midget Orchestrion. The Haddorff Piano Co. of Rockford, Illinois made many pianos for Operators in the 1920's. Some of the piano plates had no identification at all, but most had THE OPERATORS PIANO CO. as shown.

Style "J" regular—instrumentation piano and mandolin—65 standardized music.

Style "J" Reproducing instrumentation, piano and mandolin—88 note C Expression music.

Interior same as style "C" Reproducing Piano, page 4.

Style "JX" instrumentation, piano, mandolin, and two octaves Xylophone with vibrating pneumatics, using solo O music roll.

Interior same as CX, page 3.

Style "JF" instrumentation, piano, mandolin, and two octaves of solo flute pipes, using solo O music roll.

Interior same as CF, page 3.

Style "JK" instrumentation, piano, mandolin, two octaves of solo flute pipes and two octaves of violin pipes, using solo O music roll.

Interior same as CK, page 4.

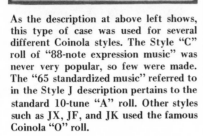

EXTERIOR COINOLA
STYLE'S J REG—J REPRODUCING J X—J F J K

As the description at above left shows, this type of case was used for several different Coinola styles. The Style "C" roll of "88-note expression music" was never very popular, so few were made. The "65 standardized music" referred to in the Style J description pertains to the standard 10-tune "A" roll. Other styles such as JX, JF, and JK used the famous Coinola "O" roll.

INTERIOR MECHANISM STYLE S J. REG.—C REG. (65 NOTE TYPE.)

INTERIOR STYLE C 2.

INTERIOR STYLE C K.

Style "C2" case is massive oak veneered Mission finish case with beautiful art glass panels. Instrumentation orchestrion, piano, mandolin, two octaves solo flute pipes, snare drum, bass drum and cymbal, using solo O music roll.

Style "CK" has same case, instrumentation—piano, mandolin and two octaves of solo violin pipes and solo flute pipes, using solo O music roll.

Style "C" Reproducing Piano has same case—instrumentation, piano and mandolin. This is a Reproducing Expression Piano, using Expression C 88 music roll.

EXTERIOR STYLE C 2—C K AND C REPRODUCING PIANO

INTERIOR STYLE C—REPRODUCING PIANO

This case design was used for styles C2, CK, and C. The C2 was an orchestrion and contained a rank of wooden flute pipes (mounted in an inverted position under the keybed of the piano) plus drum and trap effects. A related type of orchestrion was made using tuned organ reeds (24 notes) instead of flute pipes. The CK featured two ranks of pipes - 24 wooden flutes and 24 metal violins - in the bottom of the piano. As did the C2, the CK used the Coinola "O" orchestrion roll. The Style C "reproducing piano" was really an expression piano (not a full reproducing piano) that used the special "C" roll.

STYLE C Case is a rich massive art design case of figured oak veneer in rich Mission finish.

STYLE C Regular instrumentation, piano and mandolin, using standardized 65 note music roll.

STYLE CX—Instrumentation piano, mandolin and two octaves of Xylophones with vibrating pneumatics, playing solo O Music roll.

STYLE CF—Instrumentation, piano, mandolin, two octaves of solo flute pipes, playing solo O music roll.

EXTERIOR STYLE C REG. C X AND C F

INTERIOR STYLE C F.

Style C case. Several different types of Coinola instruments used this case. Style C comprised a piano with mandolin attachment and used a regular "A" roll. CX had piano, mandolin, and xylophone (or bells) and used the solo "O" orchestrion roll. Style CF featured piano, mandolin, and a rank of flute pipes (24 pipes tuned from A sharp to A) and coinciding with the upper 24 notes on the piano). Coinolas of this case design are especially handsome and rugged looking. The finish is usually of quartered oak.

INTERIOR STYLE C X

ORCHESTRION CABINET. INTERIOR.

Coinola push-up orchestrion cabinet. Used an "O" roll and contained all components of the Style X - except the piano. For use, the cabinet was placed in front of a piano keyboard which it played with tiny mechanical "fingers."

The Midget Auto Organ made its debut in 1918. It contained a piano, mandolin attachment, and two ranks of fairly large size (for a coin piano) organ pipes. Despite the optimistic proclamation by Louis M. Severson, the company president, that "The demand developing for the Style O Midget indicates that it will prove one of our biggest sellers," few were made or sold. Style "O" rolls are cut for a 24-note solo pipe section, not a 49-note section (such as the Midget Auto Organ had), so perhaps the music was less than ideal on it. OS or NOS rolls, such as used on the Reproduco, would have been better suited. Virtually all piano makers regularly announced new models with great fanfare proclaiming that many orders have already been booked. But, in the long run, most makers settled down with a dozen or so standard models. But, from a historical viewpoint these short-lived models are very interesting.

**MIDGET AUTO ORGAN A BIG SELLER**

**New Style O Instrument Is Latest Addition to Line of Operators Piano Co.**

CHICAGO, ILL., July 10.—The latest addition to the line of the Operators' Piano Co. is the Style O Midget auto organ. This instrument was first exhibited at the National Music Show and there attracted much attention because of its great musical merit and the beauty of its design and finish. The instruments are now ready for shipment and many orders have been booked, the company announces. The Style O Midget is a high-class automatic orchestra consisting of solo flute, stop diapason, mandolin and piano. It has a forty-nine note solo instrumentation of solo flute and stop diapason organ pipes and is constructed either with or without the coin-operating device. It is an ideal instrument for the home as well as being especially adapted for high-class confectioneries, hotels, restaurants, drug stores, theaters, or other high-class entertainment. It is equipped with the famous Coinola trouble-proof mechanism which is an outstanding feature of all the Operators Co.'s line.

Style O Midget Auto Organ, Which Instrument Is Rapidly Gaining in Popularity, Evidenced by the Increasing Demand from All Over the Country

It has all the features of the high-grade pipe organ of the smaller type and while its tone volume is large enough for all purposes the musical merit of the instrument is very pronounced. It appeals especially to those who care for soft, refined music. The rolls used in Style O are specially cut for it and include the best in operatic as well as popular music.

"The demand developing for the Style O Midget," said Louis M. Severson, president of the company, "indicates that it will prove one of our biggest sellers. Those who have seen it praise it unstintedly and many orders have been booked. Without doubt it is the highest class coin-operated instrument ever manufactured."

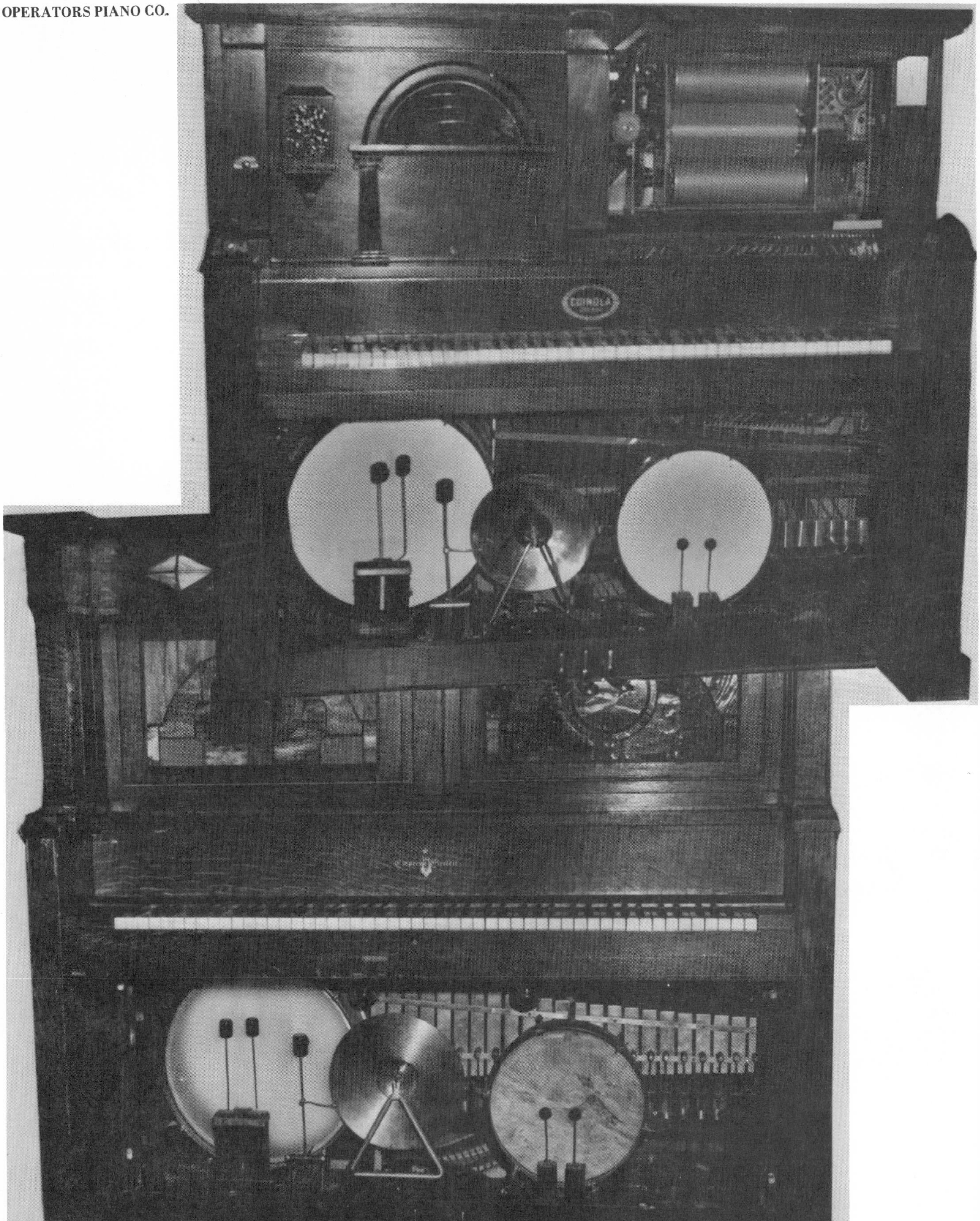


Above: Coinola Style X in the Jerry Cohen Collection. This instrument has a xylophone, bass drum (with tympani beaters), cymbal, triangle, snare drum, wood block (hidden behind the snare drum), and the usual piano and mandolin.

Lower: Empress Electric Style Y orchestrion. Distributed by Lyon & Healy, this contains the Coinola X mechanisms in a different style of case. This particular specimen has the metal orchestra bells.

Exterior view of the Coinola Style CO orchestrion (as depicted in an early salesman's catalogue). This large and handsome orchestrion contains an impressive array of instruments and uses the popular solo "O" orchestrion roll. Unfortunately only a few CO orchestrions are extant today.

Outside view of the Coinola SO orchestrion. The largest orchestrion in the Coinola line, the SO is keyboardless, contains many different instruments, and uses the solo "O" roll. Serial numbers are in the 300,000 series. Apparently fewer than fifty of the SO model were manufactured.

A similarly-styled but slightly smaller cabinet was used to house a rare variety of Reproduco organ; a coin-operated instrument with pipes (but with no piano), which used the OS and NOS rolls. Instead of the center art glass panel, the Reproduco featured a set of display pipes.

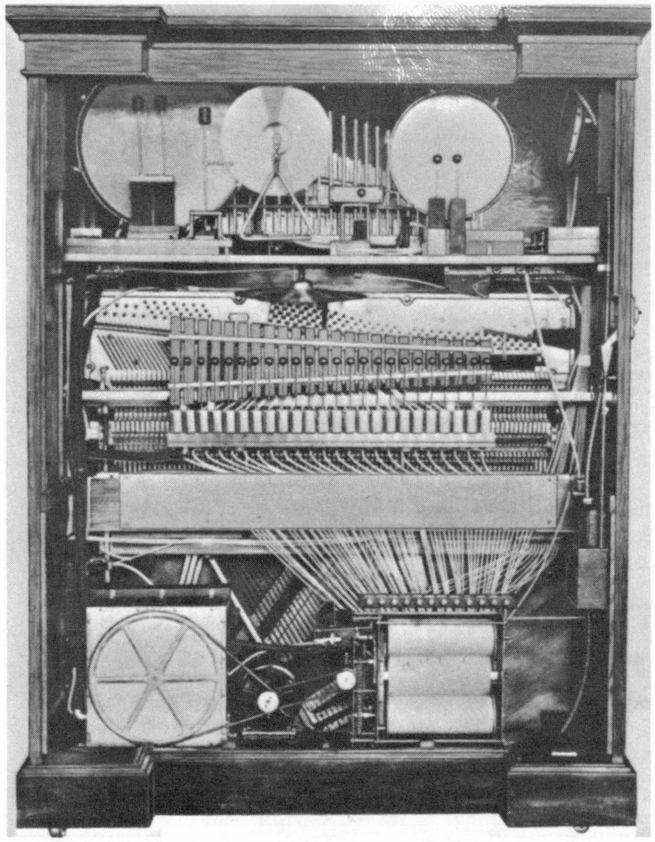

Interior view of the Coinola SO orchestrion.

REPRODUCO
Reg. U. S. Pat. Office

Pipe Organs

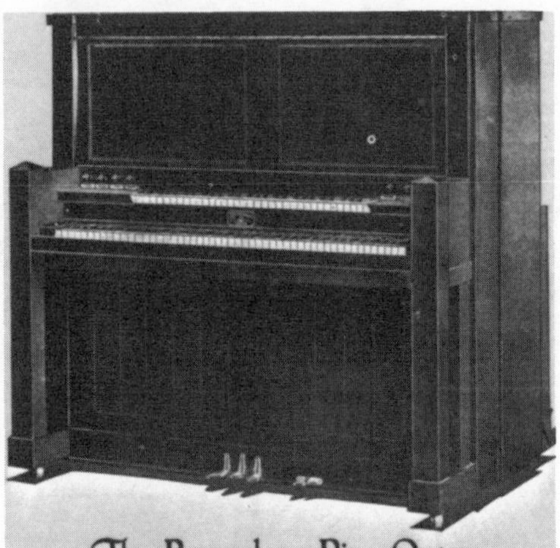

The Reproduco Pipe Organ

The Reproduco piano/pipe organ was an outstanding success. Well over 1,000 were sold, mostly to theatres in the 1920's. These instruments use style "OS" or "NOS" rolls interchangeably. The lilting and "catchy" sound of the Reproduco has made it popular with collectors today.

## TRACKER BAR

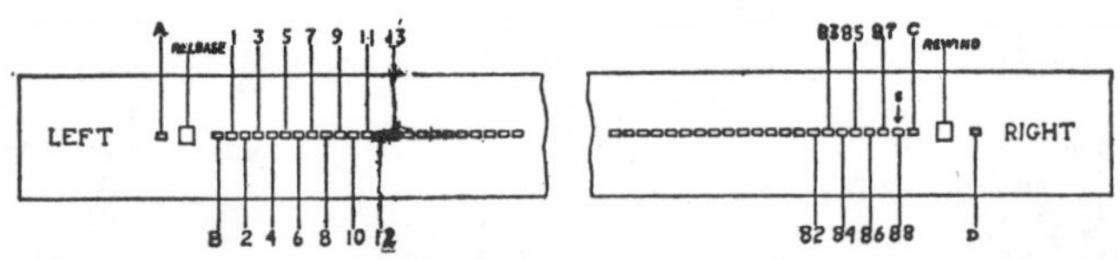


**Super Reproduco Figure 5**

A Vox on and off for flute
B Viola on and off for quint
C Xylo on
D Vox - Viola - Xylo off
1 Piano hammer rail soft
2 Piano sustain
3 Organ swell off
4 Organ swell on
5 Piano muffler off
6 Diapason on
7 Flute on
8 Flute off
9 Diapason off
10 Piano muffler on
11 Treble split rail on
12 Treble split rail off
13 First playing piano note A natural
82 Last playing piano note F sharp
83 Quint off
84 Quint on
85 Tremolo
86 Mandolin
88 Stop

**Super Junior Reproduco Fig. 5**

B Viola on and off for quint
D Viola off
1 Piano hammer rail soft
2 Piano sustain
3 Organ swell off
4 Organ swell on
5 Piano muffler off
6 Diapason on
7 Flute on
8 Flute off
9 Diapason off
10 Piano muffler on
11 Treble split rail on
12 Treble split rail off
13 First playing piano note A natural
82 Last playing piano note F sharp
83 Quint off
84 Quint on
85 Tremolo
86 Mandolin
88 Stop

**Reproduco Organ Figure 5**

1 Piano hammer rail soft
2 Piano sustain
3 Organ swell off
4 Organ swell on
5 Piano muffler off
6 Diapason on
7 Flute on
8 Flute off
9 Diapason off
10 Piano muffler on
11 Treble split rail on
12 Treble split rail off
13 First playing piano note A natural
82 Last playing piano note F sharp
83 Quint off
84 Quint on
85 Tremolo
86 Mandolin
88 Stop

Tracker bar layouts for three types of Reproduco organs. The Super Reproduco, the Super Junior Reproduco, and the Reproduco all use "OS" or "NOS" rolls. The larger models have extra effects controlled by tracker bar holes A, B, C, and D.

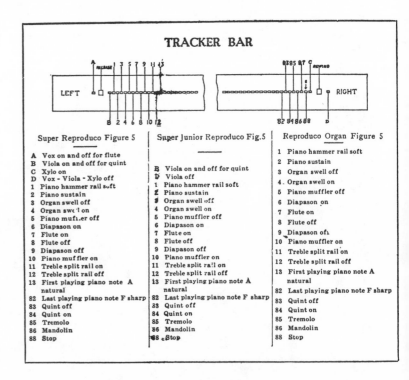

Interior view of a standard Reproduco. Above are the twin roll mechanisms which permit continuous playing of the music (one roll plays as the other rewinds). For playing by hand the instrument has two keyboards — the upper for playing the pipes and the lower for playing the piano. Controls to the left and right of the upper keyboard permit manual selection of ranks (when the instrument is played by hand; otherwise the rolls operate the controls automatically). Below the keyboard are the quintadena (bright metal pipes in foreground) and flute (wooden) pipes.

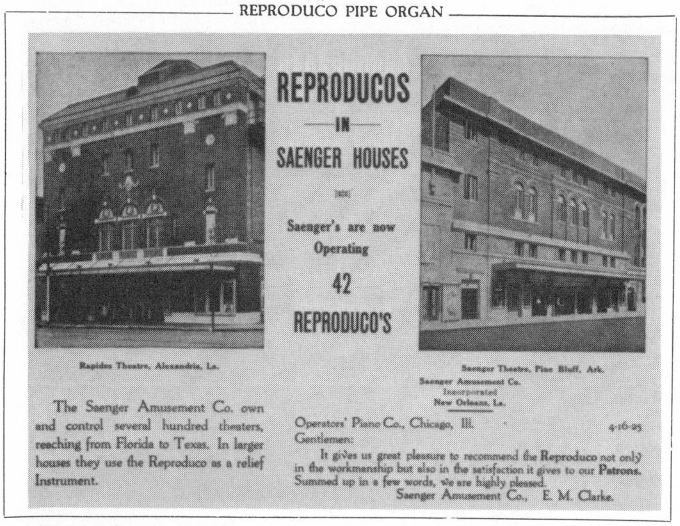


This early advertisement attests to the popularity of the Reproduco for theatre use.

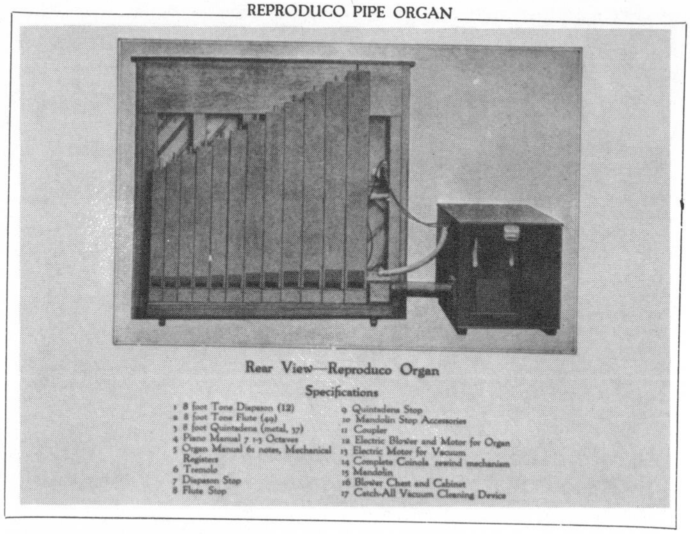


This rear view of a standard Reproduco shows twelve 8-foot-tone diapason pipes mounted behind the piano sounding board. To the right is the blower and vacuum unit.

Intended for theatre use, the Super Junior Reproduco has four ranks of pipes (instead of the usual 3 found in regular models). The pipes are inside of and behind the side cabinet. The console unit contains a single roll mechanism, the piano, and some of the controls. The regular Reproduco organ seems to have been the workhorse model of the line and more elaborate models such as the Super Junior Reproduco (pictured at the left) were made only in very limited numbers.

The Reproduco's Competition

Virtually identical in interior specifications to the Reproduco were the Seeburg Celesta and MO organs, the Nelson-Wiggen Selector Duplex organ, and the Wurlitzer Organette. Unlike the Reproduco (which found its main use in theatres) the other makes were sold primarily to funeral parlors. The popularity of the Reproduco today is explained in part by the lively theatre-type music found on the "OS" and "NOS" rolls made for it.

Above: The Super Reproduco. This large instrument contains a xylophone in addition to several ranks of pipes. Like the Super Junior Reproduco it was made only in small numbers. The symmetrically arranged pipes on the front of the side cabinet are decorative and not functional. The above instrument, pictured from a salesman's catalogue, is made of quartered oak. Most Reproduco organs were made of walnut.

The Unified Reproduco pictured above uses a special roll of the same name. Intended mainly for mortuary use the instrument does not have a piano. The chimes in the side cabinet provide an additional musical effect.

The twin-manual Unified Reproduco is of the "horseshoe" style – a configuration made popular years earlier by noted organ innovator Robert Hope-Jones.

This below-the-keyboard view of the Unified Reproduco shows some of the pipes and some of the seemingly endless footage of rubber tubing needed to operate the unification system. Unification permitted the shifting of ranks from one manual to another for added versatility.

These felt-lined swell shutters are in the upper portion of the console. The Unified Reproduco is capable of elaborate expression effects.

REPRODUCO PIPE ORGAN

# Satisfied Reproduco Owners

Partial List of Theatres

Palace, Waycross, Ga.
Strand, Jesup, Ga.
Amusus Theatre, Lincolnton, Ga.
Rivoli Theatre, Rome, Ga.
Colonial, Vidalia, Ga.
Rivoli, LaGrange, Ga.
A. H. McCarty, Barnesville, Ga.
W. P. Riggins, Jesup, Ga.
Lindale Auditorium, Lindale, Ga.
J. E. Simpson, Milien, Ga.
Rex, Hopkinsville, Ky.
Liberty Franklin, Ky.
Dreamland, Guthrie, Ky.
Palace, Bowling Green, Ky.
Orpheum, Fulton, Ky.
Bleach, Owensboro, Ky
Dreamland, Bowling Green, Ky.
Houston, Houston, Miss.
City, Philadelphia, Miss.
New Theatre, Emory, Miss.
Liberty, Malden, Mo.
Roth's West Asheville, N. C.
Eagle Theatre, Asheville, N. C.
Royal, Wilmington, N. C.
Ideal, Gastonia, N. C.
Capital, Asheboro, N. C.
Broadway, Reidsville, N. C.
Princess, Henderson, N. C.
Lyric, Rocky Mount, N. C.
Princess, Shelby, N. C.
American, High Point, N. C.
Victory, Wilmington, N. C.
Cameo, Rockmont, N. C.
Broadway, Mt. Airy, N. C.
Taylor, Edenton, N. C
Richard, Ahoskie, N. C.
Iris Belmont, N. C.
Osborn, Hillsboro, N. C.
Princess, Fayetteville, N. C.
C. I. Gresham, Mooresville, N. C.
Sunset Amus Co., Charlotte, N. C.
Charlotte, Charlotte, N. C.
Broadway, Columbia, S. C.
Palace, Charleston, S. C.
Lincoln, Charleston, S. C
Dreamland, Chester, S. C.
Albert Sottile, Charleston, S. C.
S. G. Rogers, Marion, S. C.
Strand, Nashville, Tenn.
Rialto, Nashville, Tenn.
Rialto, Nashville, Tenn.
Tony Sudekum, Nashville, Tenn.
Hillsboro, Nashville, Tenn.
Cameo, Memphis, Tenn.
American, Memphis, Tenn.
Princess, Memphis, Tenn.

Concord Theatre, Concord, Tenn.
Booth's, Sweetwater, Tenn.
Booth's, Greenville, Tenn.
Lillian, Martin, Tenn.
Sudekum's, Harriman, Tenn.
Tom Young's, Dyersburg, Tenn.
Strand, Tallahoma, Tenn.
Howard, Lebanon, Tenn.
Rivola, Winchester, Tenn.
Princess, Columbia, Tenn.
Lillian, Clarksville, Tenn.
Majestic, Clarksville, Tenn.
Dixie, Paris, Tenn
Dorodele, Copperhill, Tenn.
Dixie, Russellville, Tenn.
Strand, Morristown, Tenn.
Franklin, Franklin, Tenn
Gem, Jackson, Tenn.
Cameo, Etowah, Tenn.
J. P. Sharp, Humboldt, Tenn.
Oldhams McMinnville, Tenn.
Princess, Murfreesboro, Tenn.
Dixie, Lewisburg, Tenn.
Princess, Morristown, Tenn
Best, Pulaski, Tenn.
Victory, Richmond, Va.
Jake Wel's, Richmond, Va.
J. D Wineland, Picher, Okla.
World-In-Motion Theatre
Kansas City, Mo.
Strand Theatre, Hays, Kans.
Mainstreet Theatre, Lexington, Mo.
Wallis Bros. & Johnson, Russell, Kans.
Nusho Theatre, Wetumka, Okla
New Grand Theatre, Pittsburg, Kans.
Royal Theatre, Hoisington, Kans.
Rainbow Theatre, Sulphur, Okla.
Consolidated Amus. Co., Ardmore, Okla.
Mrs. W. T. Brooks, Broken Arrow, Okla.
Empress Theatre, Osawatomie, Kans.
Summit St. Theatre, Kansas City, Mo.
Sam Fillson Opera Co.,
Scott City, Kans.
A. R. Powell, Guthrie, Okla.
Liggett Theatre, Madison, Kans.
Regent Theatre, Kansas City, Mo.
Empress Theatre, Paola, Kans.
Beatrice Amusement Co.,
No. Platte, Nebr.
Rivoli Theatre, St. Joseph, Mo.
Cantwell Theatre, Marceline, Mo.
Anton S'epka, Okemah, Okla.
W. A. Weaver, Hartshorne, Okla.
Hickory Theatre, St. Joseph, Mo.
Cozy Theatre, Wagoner, Okla.
Rialto Theatre, Hobart, Okla.

Loula P. & Wesley Williams,
Tulsa, Okla.
Cosmo Theatre Co., Winner, S. Dak.
Liberty Theatre, Columbus, Kans.
C. E. Allison, Rush Springs, Okla.
Jackson Theatre, Pawhuska, Okla.
Art Theatre, Tulsa, Okla.
Kemp & Hughes, Heavener, Okla.
J. A. Scott, Chandler, Okla.
State Theatre, Elk Point, S. Dak.
Liberty Theatre, Watonga, Okla.
A. J. Kremer, Stanton, Nebr.
Dunkin Theatre, Cushing, Okla.
S. B. Callahan, Broken Bow, Okla
D. V. Terry & L. N. Sewell,
Woodward, Okla.
Lancaster, Wilbern & Spears,
Duncan, Okla.
Sultana Theatre, Williams, Ariz.
Alice T. Hamly, Clinton, Okla.
Centro-American Theatre,
Kansas City, Mo.
A. H. Records, Hebron, Nebr.
Lyric Theatre, Tulsa, Okla.
Majestic Theatre, Oakland, Nebr.
E. E. Sprague, Goodland, Nebr.
Mrs. M. R. Johnson, Tulsa, Okla.
Walmur Amus. Co., Bristow, Okla.
Orpheum Theatre, Joplin, Mo.
Strand Theatre, Tulsa, Okla.
C. B. Kelley, Wakeeney, Kans.
Cozy Theatre, Tulsa, Okla.
Cozy Theatre, Hollis Okla.
Strand Theatre, Muskogee, Okla.
H. G. Stettmund, Jr., Chandler, Okla.
Wichita Theatre, Wichita, Kans.
H. B. Duering, Garnett, Kans.
Cozy Theatre, Winfied, Kans.
Sequoyah Theatre, Tahlequah, Okla.
45th St. Theatre, Kansas City, Mo.
Cozy Theatre, Pratt, Kans.
Bays Theatre, Blackwell, Okla.
Gilbert Theatre, Beatrice, Nebr.
Beatrice Amus. Co., Holton, Kans.
Sun Theatre, York, Nebr.
C. W. Hermes, Ellinwood, Kans.
Yale Theatre, Henryetta, Okla.
Francis Theatre Braman, Okla.
R. D. Howell Holdenville, Okla.
Fox & Maricle, Grandfield, Okla.
Gust Mestdagh, Kansas City, Mo.
Dixie Theatre, Mt Park, Okla.
Grand Theatre, Collinsville, Okla.
Empire Theatre, Altus, Okla.
L. C Largen, Creighton, Nebr.
Crystal Theatre, Scribner, Nebr.

Elite Theatre, Greenleaf, Kans.
C. G. Miller, Atkinson, Nebr.
Kemp & Hughes, DeQueen, Ark.
Oklahoma Theatre, Norman, Okla.
Walmur Amus. Co., Cushing, Okla.
Acme Theatre, Winslow, Ariz.
Geo. Marlow, Atoka, Okla.
R. Lewis Barton, Stroud, Okla.
Palace Theatre, Syracuse, Nebr.
Community Theatre, David City, Nebr.
Tackett Theatre, Coffeyville, Kans.
Strand Theatre, Lincoln, Nebr.
R. V. Mayes, Erick, Okla.
Geo. Herber, Apache, Okla.
Favorite Theatre, Schuyler, Nebr.
H. F. Kennedy, Broken Bow, Nebr.
Crystal Theatre, Wayne, Nebr.
Weeks Theatre, Dexter, Mo
F. B. Pickrell, Pawhuska, Okla.
Rialto, Birmingham, Ala.
Norwood, Birmingham, Ala.
Famous, Birmingham, Ala.
Princess, Birmingham, Ala.
N. Birmingham, Ala.
West End Family, Birmingham, Ala.
Camco, Birmingham, Ala.
Five Points, Birmingham, Ala.
Wescon Co., Birmingham, Ala.
Princess, Birmingham, Ala.
Capitol, Birmingham Ala.
Frolic, Birmingham, Ala.
Dixie, Birmingham, Ala.
Dixie, Birmingham, Ala
Wheeler, Montgomery, Ala.
The Leak Co., Montgomery Ala.
Cricket, Collinsville, Ala.
Tiger Theatre, Auburn, Ala.
Jaffe's Ensley, Ala.
Belle, Gadsden, Ala.
Lee, Eufaula, Ala.
Rose, Tuskegee, Ala.
Star, Tuscaloosa, Ala.
Diamond, Tuscaloosa, Ala.
Jaffe's Bessemer, Alabama
King's, Tuscaloosa, Alabama
Palace, Molton, Alabama.
Princess, Booneville, Ala.
Wadesonia, Caleria, Ala.
Lightman's, Camden, Ala.
Palace, Piedmont, Ala.
W. D. Patrick, Florala, Ala.
Princess, Florence, Ala.
Lyric, Sheffield, Ala.
Strand, Tuscumbia, Ala.
Gary, Fairfield, Ala.
Franklin, Ensley, Ala.

Peerless

TELEPHONE, MADISON SQ. 8292

# PEERLESS PIANO PLAYER CO.

F. ENGELHARDT & SONS, PROPS.

WESTERN UNION TELEGRAPH CODE USED ADDRESS "PIANOPLAY" NEW YORK.

MAKERS OF Peerless AND Harmonist AUTOMATIC AND PLAYER PIANOS

FACTORIES - ST. JOHNSVILLE N.Y.

NEW YORK: 14-16 EAST 33RD STREET (NEAR FIFTH AVENUE)

CHICAGO: 339 SO WABASH AVENUE TELEPHONE HARRISON 7413

HIGHEST AWARDS - GOLD MEDALS BUFFALO 1901 ST. LOUIS 1904 PORTLAND 1906 JAMESTOWN 1907 SEATTLE 1909

General Offices:

## PEERLESS PIANO PLAYER COMPANY

(Roth & Engelhardt)
(Engelhardt Piano Co.)
(National Music Roll Co.)
(National Piano Player Co.)
(National Electric Piano Co.)

### Introduction

From about 1890 to the late 1920's the various firms enumerated above produced a wide variety of automatic musical instruments, a line ranging from push-up piano players (the staple product of the 1890's and the source of the Peerless Piano Player Co. name) to coin pianos, orchestrions, and theatre photoplayers.

Most of the electrically-operated pianos and orchestrions made over the years were sold under the Peerless trademark, and it is the Peerless name that is well known to collectors and historians today.

The "St. Johnsville (New York) News" of January 4, 1893, printed a feature article on the then-budding firm of Roth & Engelhardt. We excerpt it:

"Roth & Engelhardt: Messrs. Roth & Engelhardt have in the space of three short years built a business in pianoforte actions, the success of which is almost beyond comprehension. Mr. Roth was for many years with Alfred Dolge, and Mr. Engelhardt became, in the course of time, the head of the action department of Steinway & Sons, in which, as in every other department of that firm's factories, only the best class of work is allowed to pass.

"The gentlemen, who are the subject of these remarks, getting their heads together, decided that the manufacture of piano actions offered a remunerative field for an enterprising firm. They accordingly commenced the business and rented a small factory in New York City. They soon found customers for their products, but realizing that manufacturing in New York City was attended by extremely heavy expenses, they looked about for a more suitable site for a factory to accommodate the growing business.

"Finally the selection was made of St. Johnsville. The village was glad to get such an industry within its limits and did many things to aid the firm in making its final choice. The town possessed many facilities for the furtherance of such a business, and one important feature was that it is some 200 miles nearer Chicago and western points than any other city containing piano action factories. This meant a saving of freight to the consumers, many of whom were located in the Chicago area.

"Here they found a small brick building which soon was too small. Additional room was required before two years' time had elapsed; a new brick building 122x30 has been added to the main factory, and it has now been decided to still further enlarge the plant by another building 150x50, the foundation of which is now under way. A new boiler house 40x40 will be built and a larger boiler and engine will be installed to operate the extensive plant.

"The firm is composed of two enterprising and energetic young men, both masters of their business. Mr. Roth remains in New York City where the firm has an office at 2293 Third Avenue. From this location the entire business part of the firm's operations is conducted. In St. Johnsville, Mr. Engelhardt looks after the practical part of the business continually and superintends all operations personally. Thorough with these gentlemen means thorough, and explains the splendid success of their business. If this firm has taken such gigantic strides in three years, who can predict were they will be in ten years or less time?"

By the mid-1890's the firm had on the market several models of push-up piano players, some of which contained banks of organ reeds. A 1903 advertisement for the Roth & Engelhardt Piano Player noted that the unit "combines high efficiency, great durability, and simplicity of execution." It was further noted that the unit "is the smallest player made: height 33 inches, depth 15 inches, width 43 inches. Net weight: 187 pounds."

### Coin Pianos and Orchestrions

In 1898 the Style D, a keyboard style electric coin piano with the endless-type roll located behind the piano sounding board, was introduced. This established Peerless products as the first American-made coin pianos (antedating the 1899 Wurlitzer Tonophone by one year). Shortly thereafter, the Peerless Style 44, a cabinet piano of 44 notes, made its debut. This latter instrument incorporated many of the same mechanisms found in the contemporary Encore Automatic Banjo (the roll mechanism and a number of case trim parts, for example). Inasmuch as Peerless later sold the Banjorchestra, an automatic banjo band which contained an Encore Banjo, there may have been some business connection between the two firms.

In the 1900 - 1910 decade the Peerless products proliferated to the point at which over a dozen different models were offered for sale. These were halcyon years for the coin piano business and Peerless, with its early start, together with the Rudolph Wurlitzer Company had the lion's share of the market.

An article in the April 14, 1910 issue of "The Presto," a music trade publication, gives an interesting view of the Peerless activities at that time:

"The Great Industry at St. Johnsville, New York — Modern Activities of a Pioneer House in Producing Goods That Are Sold Throughout the Countries of the World:

"A visit to the great plant, or group of factories, of F. Engelhardt & Sons, at St. Johnsville, N.Y., is a lesson, a pleasure and a duty for the trade paper man. It is well to visit the Engelhardt factories, for there are not many establishments of this kind in the country. It adds to the keenness of interest in this modern factory — producing a variety of products in and related to musical instruments — when a contrast is made of its present up-to-the-minute productivity with the time it was a plodding pioneer along an unbeaten path.

"The Engelhardt grounds, some two or three acres in extent, extend a thousand feet or more along the New York Central Railroad, while just beyond are the Mohawk River and the West Shore Railroad; so that the company has a super-abundance of transportation. The grounds are occupied by seven buildings, used for the different lines of the company's manufacture.

"Chief among these industries are their piano action, key, keyboard, ivory and ivory polishing departments; their player factory, their music cutting factory, their milling department, etc. — seven factories in all.

"The Main Building: One of these seven factories is their latest building achievement, the big main building erected a year or so ago, and dedicated by a notable banquet within its walls. As factories go, it is a magnificent and imposing structure. In it the Peerless and the Harmonist instruments are made.

"The line of business at the Engelhardt plant comes more particularly into the limelight in connection with automatic pianos and player pianos than in its other lines, although all departments play a prominent part in the trade.

"Such instruments as the Peerless and the Harmonist are more widely advertised than other products, making this branch truly a great business.

"The Peerless electric pneumatic piano is manufactured in all its forms, and is an instrument especially adapted for public places, moving picture theatres, summer pavilions, and other assemblies where such music is required. The Harmonist is a close second to their Peerless.

"The Peerless: The Peerless has had a very wide range of sale, which is constantly increasing. There is a large export trade to the South American countries, to Australia, and to the musical instrument importing nations of the earth generally.

"These instruments were widely introduced when twelve of the sixteen battleships that went around the world for Uncle Sam were fitted out for that memorable cruise with Peerless players.

"A great many people in the several foreign ports who went aboard on festal occasions, etc., heard them, and at other places some of these players were taken to halls or houses on the land to contribute their melodies to the festivities of the day or night. Thus they played a very important part in the entertaining.

"To Roth & Engelhardt, and the succeeding firm, F. Engelhardt & Sons, credit is due for the development of the electric piano from the more or less crude instrument it was some years ago to its present fineness.

"Constant improvement and radical departures in invention by the firm have aided in bringing this class of instruments into their present worldwide recognition as musical instruments.

"As has been said, the Peerless is a pioneer in its line, but the Engelhardt firm was first also in the cutting of music rolls, a department which has been in operation since 1899. Their music roll cutting is their own industry, and they are introducing novelties and specialties in the rolls they cut. For instance their roll known as the RR is a 20-piece roll, and their latest DXM roll is for special use.

"Putting it briefly, as A.D. Engelhardt says, 'You see, we never stand still.' His statement is like an axiom, for the firm is constantly studying out new work, meeting changing demands and varying requirements.

"This is seen in their music roll building where the investment in master pieces for new rolls is said to be about $50,000. And the house is going on constantly making new instruments in modern styles and in beautiful case designs.

"The method of operating the Peerless is simple. An electric motor placed within the piano does the work. It is wired complete, and the piano is supplied with cord and plug, ready to attach to the socket of any incandescent lamp.

"The Peerless pianos are used in Cuba, South America, Australia, Africa, on the Gold Coast, in the furthest confines of Alaska and the Klondike, and in many more of the uttermost corners of the earth."

### Peerless in the 'Teen Years

Peerless products reached their high water mark in the 1912 - 1914 years. Over a dozen different electric coin pianos and orchestrions were offered to prospective buyers. The top of the line Style O or DeLuxe Orchestrion found a ready sale, as did the smaller but even more highly ornamented (with colorful art glass) Wisteria and Arcadian models. News releases of the era spoke glowingly of the Photo Orchestra, a theatre photoplayer which used the type "O" Peerless orchestrion roll.

All was roses for the firm when Alfred Dolge, historian of the piano business in America and a close personal friend and business associate of the Engelhardts (Dolge's factory, in nearby Dolgeville, N.Y., provided many raw materials and accessories for the Peerless products) wrote in 1913:

"Among the pioneer makers of coin-operated electrical self-playing pianos, F. Engelhardt & Sons have earned a reputation for their products. With the laudable ambition to out-do one another in creating something new, or to improve the old, the members of this firm have introduced perhaps more novelties in their particular line than any other house. Starting with the simple automatic player having one music roll, they are now building fourteen different models, among them being the Peerless Orchestrion with an entire keyboard of 88 notes equipped with a rewind music drawer mechanism holding perforated rolls containing fifteen selections. The instrument is furthermore provided with thirty-two wood pipes to produce either violin or flute effects, bass and snare drums, cymbal and triangle, tympani and crash cymbal effects, sets of castanets and solo mandolin. All of these orchestra effects are produced automatically and correctly directly from the perforated music roll, true to the composer's interpretation.

"The factories of the concern, located at St. Johnsville, N.Y., are of the most modern construction, and are in charge of Walter L. Engelhardt, while Alfred D. Engelhardt attends to the business end of the enterprise, under the guidance of their father.

"At the great expositions at Buffalo, 1901, St. Louis, 1904, Portland, 1906, Jamestown, 1907, and Seattle, 1909, their player pianos and orchestrions received invariably the highest award for excellence."

Perhaps the most interesting Engelhardt product of the 1910 - 1920 era was the Banjorchestra, an automatic banjo-band orchestrion. Also advertised and sold by the Connorized Music Company of New York City, the Banjorchestra was billed as "an automatic banjo supported by tambourine, triangle, bass and kettle drums and castanets, accompanied by an automatic piano. It is operated by an electric motor... Its case design is highly artistic. It is finished in mahogany and the banjo and traps may be seen through a large plate glass in the upper door. It is equipped with an automatic rerolling device, automatic expression devices for the piano, and an automatic muffler for the banjo... The Banjorchestra is a highly artistic automatic instrument which may be used in place of the banjo orchestra, which has become popular in dancing salons, owing to its adaptability to the dance music of the day..."

Banjorchestras were made in at least two main case styles: the plate-glass-fronted model described above and a differently designed cabinet with an art glass front.

The coin piano business suffered a depression in the late 'teens. This, coupled with the advent of Prohibition in 1920, forced many manufacturers and distributors in the automatic musical instrument business into receivership or bankruptcy. These events plus some unfortunate ventures into stock market speculation ended the Engelhardt empire.

### The 'Twenties

Just what happened during the reorganization of F. Engelhardt & Sons is not clear. Several different firms emerged. The National Electric Piano Company seems to have taken over the general line of Peerless coin operated instruments. Several new styles, notably keyboard-type orchestrions with the various pipes and percussion effects fitted into a case not much larger than a normal player piano, were introduced and sold with some success during the 1920's. Specimens seen by the author have borne both "National" and "Peerless" trademarks together. (Note: These "National" pianos have no connection with the Grand Rapids, Michigan, firm with a somewhat similar name.)

The National Electric Piano Company produced in limited quantities a small cabinet-style orchestrion which used the Coinola type "O" orchestrion roll, a confusing situation as one of the most popular Peerless rolls of the time was also known as an "O" roll and was of entirely different size and scale!

The National Music Roll Company was active during the 1920's and evidently was a subsidiary of the National Electric Piano Company. The firm noted that it could supply "Peerless rolls for Peerless automatic pianos and orchestrions and for ALL STYLES of Electric 65-note rewind pianos." In addition, such brands as "Master Record" and "Auto Inscribed (Temporized)" 88-note rolls were produced for the home player piano market.

Some type of arrangement between National and the Operators Piano Company (makers of Coinola products) must have been in effect. National sold rolls produced by Capitol and Columbia (subsidiaries of Operators) and labeled them simply by pasting a National program listing over the previously-affixed Capitol or Columbia label. Such rolls are occasionally seen in collections today, indicating that quite a few must have been sold originally.

National apparently never standardized the name it used in advertising or on its pianos. "National Electric Piano Company" was used most often, but "National Piano Player Company" was also used, as was the old "Peerless Piano Player Company" name.

The Engelhardt Piano Company appears to have conducted a separate but closely related business. A letter furnished to the author by Arthur List, Jr. was obtained by Mr. List when he acquired an Engelhardt piano from its original owner. The letter, bearing the late date of April 1, 1929, bears the letterhead "ENGELHARDT PIANO COMPANY; Manufacturers of Automatic Musical Instruments — Bell Pianos, Flute Pianos, Xylophone Pianos, Coin Operated Pianos, Reproducing Player Pianos, Orchestrions, Banjorchestras, Player Pianos, and Midget Orchestrions." The letter, which is about tightening up chests and components, notes that "Evidently the piano has dried out and by tightening up the pneumatic action as suggested above, your troubles will be eliminated," and is signed by A.B. Engelhardt.

Engelhardt marketed pianos in the 1920's under the "Engelhardt" label. Some of these instruments bore "Peerless" plaques also — the same nameplates that were concurrently used by the National Electric Piano Company. Certain Engelhardt and National literature was identical, except for the manufacturer's name, and both firms sold the same instrument models!

Complicating matters still further is an entry in the 1928 edition of "Fox's Music Trade Directory" which notes that the Engelhardt firm is "entirely owned by the Welte Co., Inc." The notation reads: "Engelhardt Piano Company: Office and factory — St. Johnsville, N.Y. Established 1916. Name of piano owned or controlled — Engelhardt... A co-partnership. Now entirely owned by Welte Co., Inc. to which refer."

Separate notations in the same Fox Directory list the National Electric Piano Company ("National Electric Piano Co. Offices and factories — St. Johnsville, N.Y. Manufacture electric coin-operated pianos and orchestrions") and the National Music Roll Co. ("National Music Roll Co. Offices and factory — 26 William Street, St. Johnsville, N.Y. Rolls for coin-operated pianos. Also regular player rolls. Frederick J. Kornburst, president and owner.").

Instruments extant today reveal that the Engelhardt - Peerless - National group must have had connections with many other makers and sellers in the piano trade. An early connection with the Encore Banjo is suggested by the similarity of Peerless and Encore components and by the fact that the Connorized Music Co., an owner of the Encore interests (see Encore section of this book), was a sales agent for the Banjorchestra. Certain coin pianos manufactured by Niagara and by Electrova (Jacob Doll & Sons) are known with "Peerless" nameplates on them.

### General Comments

Most early Peerless instruments were of the endless-roll type. Many of these had the roll mechanisms mounted behind the sounding board of the piano, a location which permitted easy servicing but which had the disadvantage that the piano had to be kept some distance away from the wall. One of the first Peerless orchestrion types consisted of a Peerless electric piano (with endless roll system) on the top of which were mounted an exposed bass drum, snare drum, and cymbal. Later models were more conventional and had the drums and traps enclosed within the case.

Later Peerless instruments used rolls of the standard or "rewind" type. Until the 1920's when several models were made which used regular 65-note "A" rolls and Coinola "O" rolls, Peerless and related instruments used their own distinct roll types perforated in the St. Johnsville, New York, factories. Often these rolls were marked with the type of instrument on which they were to be used: RR, DX, Trio, Elite, and DeLuxe, as examples. Rolls were interchangeable among several different Peerless styles, in some instances. For example, the Peerless type "O" or "DeLuxe" roll, a wide roll not to be confused with the similarly-named Coinola roll, fit on the Arcadian, Wisteria, DeLuxe Orchestrion (also known as the "M" or "O" Orchestrion), and on the Photo Orchestra photoplayer. This particular roll was also known as a "20,000 Series" roll, and rolls of this type bore numbers in this range. Similarly, other Peerless rolls were known as the "10,000 Series," "50,000 Series," and so on. Standardization of company names, model designations, roll type designations, and similar consistencies were unknown at Peerless, a fact which is oft-times confusing to the collector today.

An interesting example of Peerless inconsistency, if indeed another example is needed, is an orchestrion once owned by the author. On the front fallboard was the lettering "Peerless Piano Player Company," and on the piano plate inside, the transposed "Peerless Player Piano Company" designation!

In 1965 the author and Larry Givens spent an interesting afternoon in St. Johnsville. Scarcely a soul remembered what was once the town's main industry — and the Engelhardt buildings which once hummed with the activities of roll cutting and orchestrion building served a somewhat ignominious use (from a collector's viewpoint) as the main factory of the Little Falls Felt Shoe Company. In nearby Dolgeville, the former factories of Alfred Dolge stood in gleaming white stone, ostensibly not much different than they must have appeared in the first decade of the 20th century. The shipping docks were loaded not with felt piano hammers destined for shipment to Engelhardt down the way, but with Daniel Green brand slippers currently produced there.

"Peerless," a strange name now in St. Johnsville, is quite familiar to collectors. Peerless instruments are particularly admired for their rugged and usually vividly-patterned quartered oak cases ornamented with some of the most colorful and decorative art glass ever used in American coin pianos (see below for an example).

Peerless Style 44: 44-note cabinet piano which uses an endless roll. The design (with scalloped beveled glass panel) shown at the top of the page was the most popular. (Most photographs on this page courtesy of Mr. Carlo Polidori; St. Johnsville, N.Y.)

Style D Peerless: Coin operated piano with the roll mechanism located behind the piano sounding board. At the top of the page is a rear view of a Style D. Operation is via a coin box attached to a shelf mounted on the side of the piano. Below: Gary Sage is shown with the Style D Peerless in his collection (Lyle Martin photo). The tubing goes downward from the pneumatic stack, through an aperture in the base of the piano, to the tracker bar and roll mechanism at the rear. Early Berry-Wood coin pianos are of similar concept.

FACTORIES OF F. ENGELHARDT & SONS, ST. JOHNSVILLE, N. Y.

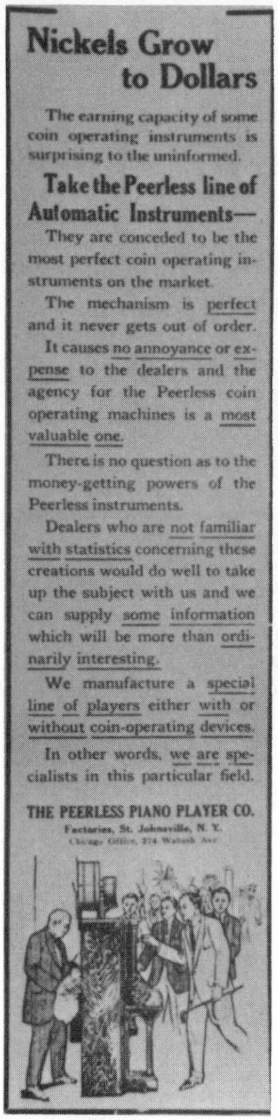
Nickels Grow to Dollars

The earning capacity of some coin operating instruments is surprising to the uninformed.

**Take the Peerless line of Automatic Instruments—**

They are conceded to be the most perfect coin operating instruments on the market.

The mechanism is perfect and it never gets out of order.

It causes no annoyance or expense to the dealers and the agency for the Peerless coin operating machines is a most valuable one.

There is no question as to the money-getting powers of the Peerless instruments.

Dealers who are not familiar with statistics concerning these creations would do well to take up the subject with us and we can supply some information which will be more than ordinarily interesting.

We manufacture a special line of players either with or without coin-operating devices.

In other words, we are specialists in this particular field.

THE PEERLESS PIANO PLAYER CO.
Factories, St. Johnsville, N. Y.
Chicago Office, 274 Wabash Ave.

**"Mr. Moneybags" reaps the profits from an early Peerless orchestrion — as per the advertisement at the left. In the first edition of this book we theorized that such an orchestrion with exposed drums might only be an artist's conception. Subsequently, H.B. McClaran furnished us with a photograph of a surviving instrument now in his collection (see above illustration).**

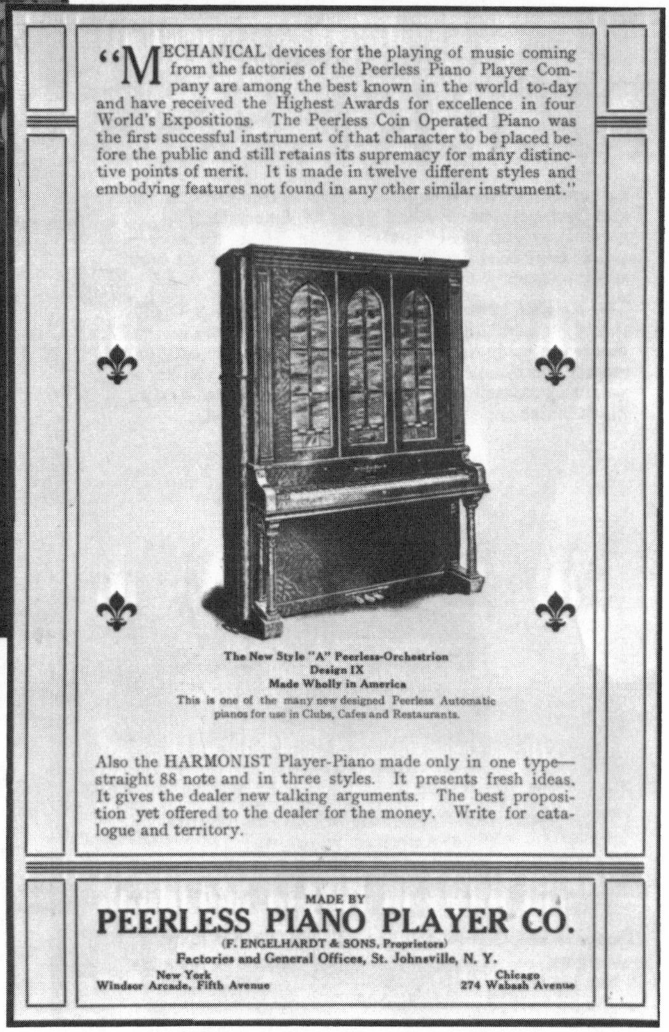
"MECHANICAL devices for the playing of music coming from the factories of the Peerless Piano Player Company are among the best known in the world to-day and have received the Highest Awards for excellence in four World's Expositions. The Peerless Coin Operated Piano was the first successful instrument of that character to be placed before the public and still retains its supremacy for many distinctive points of merit. It is made in twelve different styles and embodying features not found in any other similar instrument."

The New Style "A" Peerless-Orchestrion
Design IX
Made Wholly in America
This is one of the many new designed Peerless Automatic pianos for use in Clubs, Cafes and Restaurants.

Also the HARMONIST Player-Piano made only in one type—straight 88 note and in three styles. It presents fresh ideas. It gives the dealer new talking arguments. The best proposition yet offered to the dealer for the money. Write for catalogue and territory.

MADE BY
PEERLESS PIANO PLAYER CO.
(F. ENGELHARDT & SONS, Proprietors)
Factories and General Offices, St. Johnsville, N. Y.
New York — Windsor Arcade, Fifth Avenue
Chicago — 274 Wabash Avenue

**Peerless Style A Orchestrion (circa 1911)**

*Peerless*

DID you ever hear of the London tailor who noticed that when a street piano came under his window and played "God Save the Queen" the machines of his operators slowed down to keep time with the music?

It took him just about a minute to size up the situation.

He hired a man by the day to play good, rollicking, *swift* tunes, with the result that the work of his shoproom trebled itself. This was a natural, though unconscious, result, an instinctive compliance with the demand of the musical tempo.

Does your enterprise need a stimulant?

Give it some *Peerless* tonic and watch it brace up. The *Peerless* is a business booster of the Big Bull Moose variety. It will change the entire atmosphere of your establishment and put backbone into the most spineless employee. It will give *you* an optimistic viewpoint that by natural attraction will induce patronage.

The *Peerless* will advertise you. It never gets tired, doesn't belong to the union, works overtime without extra pay, never gets sulky or dopey, has no bad habits, and is always "fit" and ready for business.

The *Peerless* stimulates the appetite, increases the thirst, lightens the feet and the spirits, and loosens the strings of the pocketbook.

It's a coin-coaxer, a money-wheedler, a nickel-winner.

It's the *big thing* for which you have been looking.

Do your requirements call for a single piano or an orchestra?

The *Peerless* supplies either—in fact, two, three, four or five instruments in one.

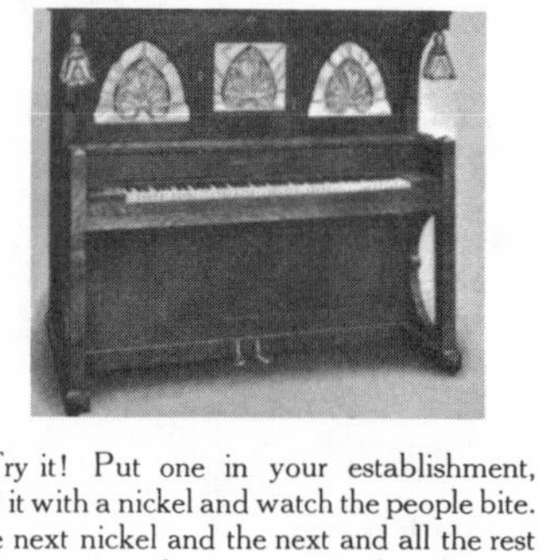

Try it! Put one in your establishment, bait it with a nickel and watch the people bite. The next nickel and the next and all the rest will come out of your customers' pockets.

Make it easy for them—have the slot connections where they can't help but see them. The suggestion is all that's needed.

Tell us what you need, and we will recommend the right instrument.

Mail communications will have our immediate attention.

THE PEERLESS PIANO PLAYER CO.
F. ENGELHARDT & SONS, Proprietors
ST. JOHNSVILLE, N. Y.
NEW YORK — CHICAGO

MODEL "WISTERIA"
Plays 88 notes. Equipped with set of Pipes (either Violin or Flute), Castanets, Triangle.
For full description see Bulletin No. 7.


**Above: Peerless Wisteria orchestrion, one of the most popular models of the 'teens and early 1920's. Containing piano, violin or flute pipes, castanets, and triangle, the instrument uses type "O" Peerless 20,000 Series rolls. The Wisteria cabinet is identical, save for the art glass design, to the case used for certain Harwood and Seeburg orchestrions — indicating that these various firms may have obtained their cabinets from a common supplier.**

**Left: An early Peerless advertisement.**

Peerless piano with mandolin. This is a model from the 1910 era with the roll mechanism in the upper part of the instrument. Note that Engelhardt is misspelled "Englehardt" on the piano plate.

Peerless instruments were mainly distributed in the northeastern part of the United States and in the Pacific Coast states. Agencies were set up with leading piano dealers in metropolitan areas.

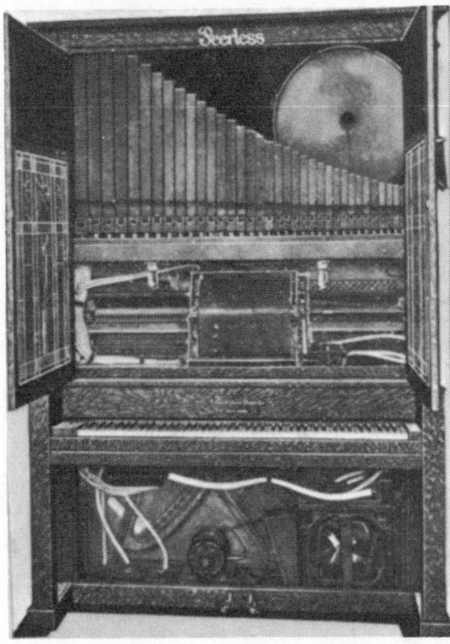


Peerless DeLuxe Orchestrion: The largest regular orchestrion in the Peerless line. Known also as the Style O (with coin slot) and the Style M (with remote control push button operation for theatre use). Several variations were made, including a model with the pipes arranged in a pyramidal or symmetrical design.

In the late 1950's Arthur Sanders of the Musical Museum at Deansboro, N.Y., purchased the remaining parts and components from the Peerless factories. Included was a large wooden crate containing about two dozen sheets of art glass for the DeLuxe Orchestrion.

ORCHESTRION
Style "O"
Model De Luxe

| Height | Width | Depth |
|---|---|---|
| 7 feet 7 inches | 5 feet 3 inches | 34 inches |

Containing the well-known pneumatic player action playing the *entire key-board* of piano—88 notes. Equipped with re-wind music drawer mechanism holding perforated rolls containing fifteen (15) selections. Rolls can be changed instantly. After last selection has been played, it stops, re-winds automatically, and begins with first piece.

Contains magazine coin slot mechanism holding upward from one to twenty coins.

Full Piano—88 notes, seventy-two wood pipes producing effects of violin, flute and cello. Bass and snare drums, cymbal and triangle. Tympani and crash cymbal effects. Set of castanets. Solo mandolin. All orchestral effects are produced automatically and correctly direct from the perforated roll and true to the composer's interpretation.

Fumed oak, wax finish. Brass trimmed throughout. Art glass panels with gold torches bearing flaming globes. Electric lamps illuminate interior of instrument when playing.

Using rolls containing fifteen (15) selections, which re-roll automatically after last selection has been played, although any piece can be repeated by means of pneumatic push buttons provided, which will re-roll the piece to any desired part and another button will start it playing again. A feature not found on any similar instrument.

Music rolls for all instruments made in our own factories from original masters.

Rolls available for the Model De Luxe Orchestrion are listed in the 20,000 series.

PEERLESS ORCHESTRION
Model Arcadian

*Measurements*

| HEIGHT | WIDTH | DEPTH |
|---|---|---|
| 6 feet | 5 feet 4 inches | 34 inches |

*Mechanism* Containing the well-known *Peerless* pneumatic player action playing the *entire key-board* of piano—88 notes. Equipped with re-wind music drawer mechanism holding perforated rolls containing fifteen (15) selections. Rolls can be changed instantly. After last selection has been played, it stops, re-winds automatically, and begins with first piece.

Contains magazine coin slot mechanism, holding upward from one to twenty coins.

*Orchestration* Full Piano—88 notes. Set of wood pipes, thirty-two in number (either violin or flute, optional with the purchaser). Bass and snare drums, cymbal and triangle. Tympani and crash cymbal effects. Set of castenets. Solo mandolin. All orchestral effects are produced automatically and correctly direct from the perforated roll and true to the composer's interpretation.

*Case* Fumed Oak or Circassian Walnut. Brass trimmed throughout. Art glass panels (Arcadian scene) with upright standards bearing artistic lamps. Electric lights illuminate interior of instrument when playing.

*Music* Using rolls containing fifteen (15) selections, which re-roll automatically after last selection has been played, although any piece can be repeated by means of pneumatic push buttons provided, which will re-roll the piece to any desired part and another button will start it playing again. A feature not found on any similar instrument.

Music rolls for all Peerless instruments made in our own factories from original masters.

Rolls available for the Model Arcadian Orchestrion are listed in the 20,000 series. See supplementary Music Bulletins.

Left: Peerless Arcadian Orchestrion. Made in several different case design variations, the most popular of which is shown at the left. The Arcadian was popular in the 1912-1914 era. This instrument uses the type "O" Peerless roll as also used on the DeLuxe and Wisteria orchestrions.

Peerless Arcadian orchestrion of an unusual case style. (Jerry Doring Collection)

This beautiful Peerless orchestrion in the Roy Arrington collection features the metal violin pipes arranged in a symmetrical design. Although symmetrical pipe arrangements are common in organs and in early large orchestrions (such as Welte), their use in keyboard type piano orchestrions is rare. The orchestrion illustrated has the roll mechanism located behind the piano sounding board. The tubing leading to the tracker bar may be seen at the bottom of the instrument. (Dan Adams photograph)

**ENGELHARDT PIANO COMPANY**

EXPRESSION PLAYER PIANOS OR HOME ELECTRICS, PLAYER PIANOS, COIN OPERATED PIANOS, PIPE PIANOS, ORCHESTRIONS, BANJO ORCHESTRAS AND PHONOGRAPHS

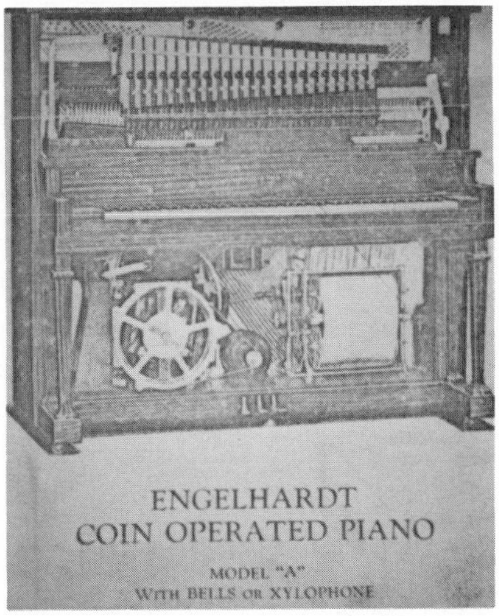

| Height | Width | Depth |
|---|---|---|
| 4 feet 8 inches | 5 feet 4 inches | 2 feet 4¾ inches |

The pneumatic or player action is built in upper part of Piano, above key-board and directly behind fall-board. We have adopted the principle of individual units for each pneumatic or note mechanism in the Piano, each one an exact duplicate of the other, interchangeable, and each unit complete in itself screwed to the front channel board with two screws. All working parts are built within the piano case, permitting piano to stand flush against the wall. All parts standardized and therefore easily interchangeable.

Equipped with magazine slot device holding upward from one to twenty-four coins. Additional boxes or pay stations can be obtained from us which can be connected to piano. Slot is especially designed to return slugs, and pennies will not operate Instrument.

Original design supplied in Oak or Mahogany. Brass trimmed thruout. Special Art Glass Panels. Electric Lamps illuminate interior of Instrument when playing.

Supplied with solo mandolin device, operating direct from perforations in music roll. Music drawer is below keyboard and back of lower panel and direct connected with pumping apparatus by shaft, thus eliminating belting.

Using rolls containing twenty selections or less—this being optional with the owner. The music re-rolls automatically after last selections have been played and stops, and is then ready to start off again. Expression is operated direct from music drawer by special control automatic to obtain best possible effects far superior to any similar instrument.

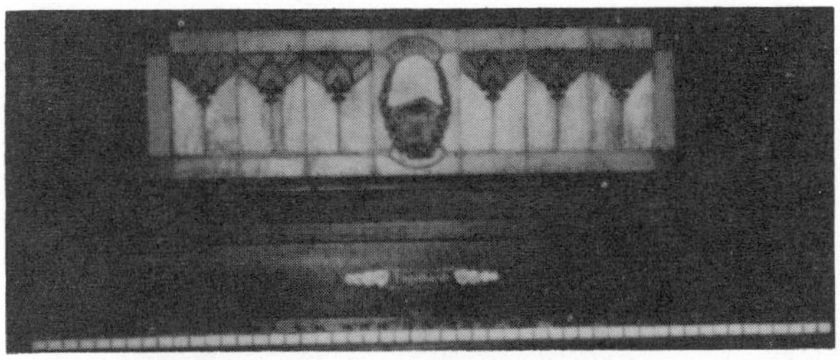

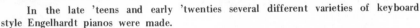

In the late 'teens and early 'twenties several different varieties of keyboard style Engelhardt pianos were made.

---

**Engelhardt Coin Operated Piano Orchestrion**

MODEL "F"

| | Height | Width | Depth |
|---|---|---|---|
| Measurements | 5 feet 9½ inches | 3 feet 4 inches | 2 feet 6 inches |

**Case** Original design supplied in Dull Finish Mahogany. Combination Clear and Art Glass Panel, making an exceedingly attractive effect. Art Glass Panel subject to change without notice. Electric Lamps illuminate interior of instrument when playing.

**Slot** Equipped with magazine slot device holding upward from one to twenty-four coins. Additional boxes or pay stations can be obtained from us which can be connected to instrument. Slot is especially designed to return slugs, and pennies will not operate instrument.

**Music** Using rolls containing ten selections. The music re-rolls automatically after last selection has been played and stops, and is then ready to start off again. Expression and traps are operated direct from music drawer by special control tubes to obtain best possible effects.

**[illegible]** Piano, Mandolin, Snare Drum, Bass Drum Effect, Cymbals, Flute Pipes. Equipped with device whereby any instrument may be shut off at will.

Model "F" (1) as Piano and Mandolin.
Model "F" (2) as Piano, Mandolin, Bells or Xylophone.
Model "F" (3) as Piano, Mandolin and Flute Pipes.

Model F Engelhardt: The Model F was one of the most popular Peerless types. It was available with various contents ranging from a simple piano with mandolin attachment to a compact orchestrion. The above description of the Model F is from the listing as it originally appeared in Bulletin No. 5 of the Engelhardt Piano Company (supplied to us courtesy of Mr. Carl Barker).

The same basic cabinet was also used to house the Engelhardt Banjorchestra. In addition, a number of Electrova coin pianos and orchestrions (sold by Jacob Doll & Sons) were contained in identical cabinets.

The Style F was available with an art glass front (as illustrated), with a beveled-edge clear glass panel front, or with a solid wood front.

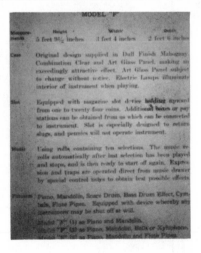

# The Best Time Is NOW

THERE are more prospects at this season NOW than at any other time of the year for

## Engelhardt Coin-Operated Instruments

Engelhardt Models B, C and D

Coin-Operated Pianos

Coin-Operated Pipe Pianos

Coin-Operated Piano Orchestrion

Engelhardt Banjorchestras with or without slot

Automatic Reproducing Pianos for the Home

NEW STYLES ARE READY

*Made by*

## ENGELHARDT Piano Company

St. Johnsville, New York

Theatres, Confectioners, Ice Cream Parlors and other public resorts reap a harvest of nickels this time of the year from coin-operated instruments, and a little sales talk backed up by our catalog will convince many a one, and make many a sale in the next few weeks. There is a market for Engelhardts in every town.

**Above: Case design for models B, C, and D (designation according to interior components). Note also the reference to "Automatic Reproducing Pianos for the Home." Few of these were ever made.**

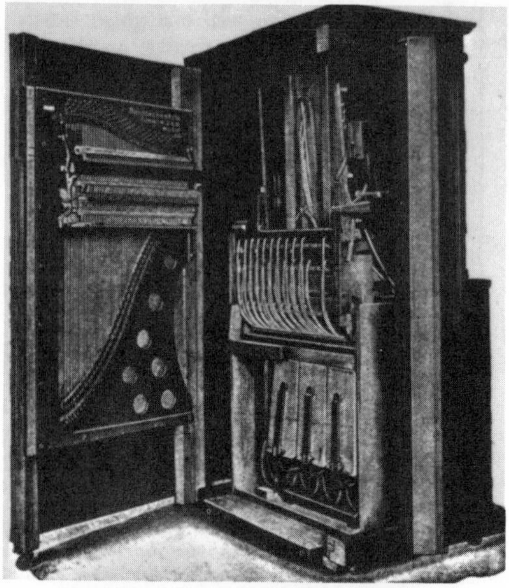

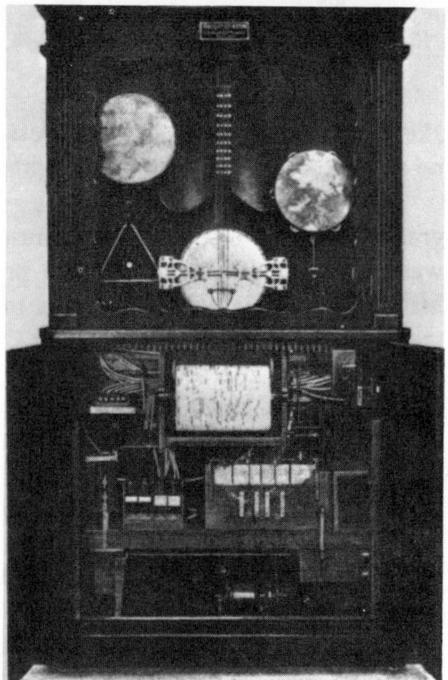

SPECIFICATIONS

ENGELHARDT BANJORCHESTRA

| Measurements | Height | Width | Depth |
|---|---|---|---|
| | 5 feet $9\frac{1}{2}$ inches | 3 feet 4 inches | 2 feet 6 inches |

**Mechanism** We have adopted the principle of individual units for each pneumatic or note mechanism in the Piano, each one an exact duplicate of the other, interchangeable, and each unit complete in itself screwed to the front channel board with two screws. All working parts are built within the case, permitting instrument to stand flush against the wall. All parts standardized and therefore easily interchangeable.

**Slot** Equipped with magazine slot device holding upward from one to twenty-four coins. Additional boxes or pay stations can be obtained from us which can be connected to instrument. Slot is especially designed to return slugs, and pennies will not operate instrument.

**Case** Original design supplied in Mahogany. Brass trimmed thruout. Plain or special Art Glass Panels. Subject to change without notice. Electric Lamps illuminate interior of instrument when playing.

**Features** Piano, Automatic Banjo, Chinese Drum, Tambourine, Triangle, Snare Drum, and Bass Drum Effect, operated direct from perforations in music roll. Music Drawer directly behind lower doors, easily accessible, and direct connected with pumping apparatus by shaft, thus eliminating belting.

**Music** Using rolls containing ten selections. The music rerolls automatically after last selection has been played and stops, and is then ready to start off again. Expression and traps are operated direct from music drawer by special control notes to obtain best possible effects.

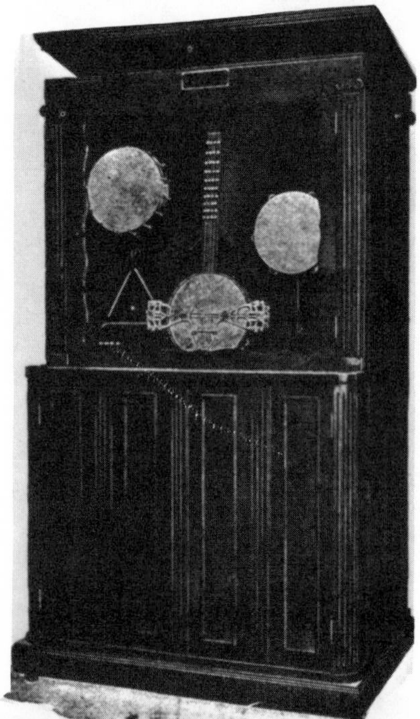

**The Engelhardt Banjorchestra was made in two main styles: the model shown at the top of the page (this style was also sold by the Connorized Music Co. of New York City) and the type in the Style F cabinet shown directly above. The 44-note piano in the Banjorchestra was made by the Pianova Co. of New York and is identical to that used in early models of the Mills Violano Virtuoso.**

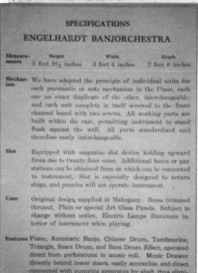

ART CABARET
New National Type

COLONIAL ELITE TYPE

## —National "Peerless" Pianos—

The National Electric Piano Company sold nearly a dozen different models of coin pianos during the 1920's. Those described on this page were the most popular.

Art Cabaret pianos: Although the art glass designs varied somewhat, most pianos of this designation resembled the model illustrated at the upper left of this page. The catalogue illustration bears the "Peerless Piano Player Co." name on the piano fallboard, although most were made with the National name. Art Cabaret pianos were made in four main styles: Style A — with piano and mandolin. Style B — with piano, mandolin, and violin or flute pipes. Style C — with piano, mandolin, bass and snare drums, cymbal, and triangle. This model was known as the "Semi-Orchestrion." Style D — with piano, mandolin, bass and snare drums, cymbal, triangle, and violin or flute pipes. The Style D was known as the "Theatre Orchestrion." The catalogue illustration at the lower left (furnished to us by Paul Eakins) notes that Styles A, B, C, and D sold for $950, $1100, $1250, and $1350 respectively. The interior illustration is an artist's conception. Note that all of the violin pipes are inaccurately shown as being of the same length!

Colonial Elite pianos (usually referred to simply as "Elite"): Instruments of the Elite designation had cases more ornately styled than the Art Cabaret type. Elite instruments had more elaborate art glass and two hanging lamps. The interiors of Elite styles E, F, G, and H were the same as Art Cabaret styles A, B, C, and D in that order. Original selling prices were: E $1000, F $1150, G $1325, and H $1400.

| Measurements | Height | Width | Depth |
|---|---|---|---|
| | 4 ft. 8 in. | 5 ft. 4 in. | 2 ft. 5½ in. |

**Mechanism** The Pneumatic or Player Action is built in the upper part of piano an[d] above the keyboard and directly behind the fall board, making it pos[-]sible to easily adjust each Power Pneumatic independently, the same a[s] in all our best types. The instrument is built so it can stand flus[h] against the wall.

**Slot** Equipped with our new simplified magazine slot device holding upwar[d] from one to twenty-four coins. Additional boxes or pay stations can b[e] obtained from us to operate from any room or part of the building, per[-]mitting the instrument to be controlled from any point.

**Case** Original design in dark wax finished or fumed oak, brass trimmed, wit[h] special art glass panels in artistic coloring, beautifully illuminated whe[n] the instrument is playing.

**Features** Supplied with our Solo Mandolin Device, operating direct from perfora[-]tions in the music roll. Equipped with our latest Rewind Music Drawer Mechanism holding perforated rolls containing 10 selections, or more i[f] desired, placed in front of instrument directly behind the art glass panels, making it easily accessible, and enabling the rolls to be change[d] instantly. Instrument furnished complete with electric motor for any style of current. This instrument can be played by hand the same as any ordinary piano.

**Made in Four Styles**
ART CABARET, Style A—Playing Piano and Mandolin.
ART CABARET, Style B—Playing Piano, Mandolin and Pipes, either Flute or Violin.
ART CABARET, Style C—Playing Piano, Mandolin, Bass and Snare Drums, Cymbals and Triangle (Semi-Orchestrion).
ART CABARET, Style D—Playing Piano, Mandolin, Bass and Snare Drums, Cymbals, Triangle and Pipes—Flute or Violin (Theatre Orches[-]trion).

**Music** Uses rolls containing ten to twenty selections which reroll automatically after last selection has been played, although any piece can be repeated by means of push buttons provided, and which will reroll the piece to any desired part, and another button will start it playing again, a fea[-]ture not found on any similar instrument. Music for ALL PEERLESS and NATIONAL instruments made in our OWN FACTORIES from ORIGINAL masters. Rolls available for our new ART CABARET ar[e] listed in our Monthly Bulletins of new music in the 10,000 series.

| Measurements | Height | Width | Depth |
|---|---|---|---|
| | 4 ft. 8 in. | 5 ft. 4 in. | 2 ft. 5½ in. |

**Mechanism** The Pneumatic or Player Action is built in the upper part of piano and above the keyboard and directly behind the fall board, making it pos[-]sible to easily adjust each Power Pneumatic independently, the same as in all our best types. The instrument is built so it can stand flush against the wall.

**Slot** Equipped with our new simplified magazine slot device holding upward from one to twenty-four coins. Additional boxes or pay stations can be obtained from us to operate from any room or part of the building, per[-]mitting the instrument to be controlled from any point.

**Case** Original design in dark wax finished or fumed oak, brass trimmed, with special colonial art glass panels and hanging lamps. Electric lamps in the interior together with the colonial hanging lamps illuminate the in[-]strument when playing, bringing out in a striking manner the design and beautiful coloring of the art glass.

**Features** Supplied with our Solo Mandolin Device, operating direct from perfora[-]tions in the music roll. Equipped with our latest Rewind Music Drawer Mechanism holding perforated rolls containing 10 selections, or more if desired, placed in front of instrument directly behind the art glass panels, making it easily accessible, and enabling the rolls to be changed instantly. This instrument plays the full keyboard of 88 notes and has a great volume of tone, which is easily regulated by our subduing device so it can be brought down to play very softly or set to develop a greater volume as may be desired. Instrument furnished complete with electric motor for any style of current. This instrument can be played by hand the same as any ordinary piano.

**Made in Four Styles**
COLONIAL ELITE, Style E—Playing Piano and Mandolin, full key[-]board of 88 Notes.
COLONIAL ELITE, Style F—Playing Piano, Mandolin and Pipes—Flute or Violin.
COLONIAL ELITE, Style G—Playing Piano, Mandolin, Bass and Snare Drums, Cymbals and Triangle (Semi-Orchestrion).
COLONIAL ELITE, Style H—Playing Piano, Mandolin, Bass and Snare Drums, Cymbals, Triangle and Pipes—Flute or Violin (Theatre Orches[-]trion).

**Music** Uses rolls containing ten to twenty selections which reroll automatically after last selection has been played, although any piece can be repeated by means of push buttons provided, and which will reroll the piece to any desired part, and another button will start it playing again, a fea[-]ture not found on any similar instrument. Music for ALL PEERLESS and NATIONAL instruments made in our OWN FACTORIES from ORIGINAL masters. Rolls available for our NEW COLONIAL ELITE are listed in our Monthly Bulletins of new music in the 30,000 series.

Durable — Artistic — Simple

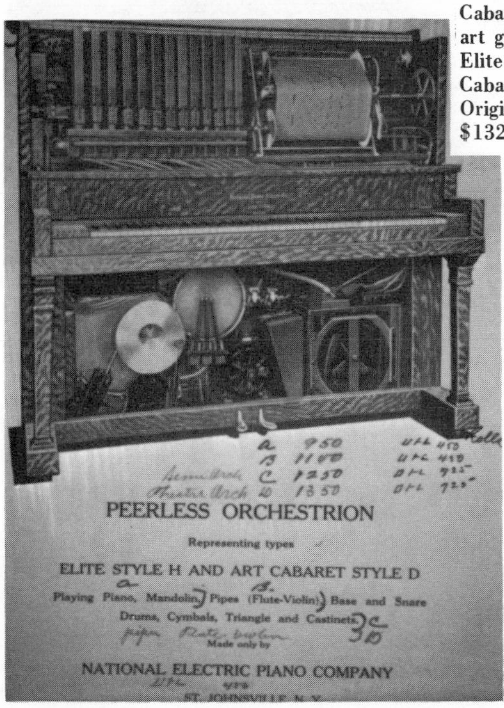

PEERLESS All-Hit Music Rolls — NATIONAL Electric Pianos

**KINDLY REMEMBER**

NATIONAL Coin Operated Pianos Have These PEERLESS Features

In changing your Music Rolls you simply remove the Art Glass front panel, when the ENTIRE MECHANISM is BEFORE you; easily controlled by SPECIAL push buttons provided for your convenience.

All the inconvenience of changing Music Rolls and adjusting mechanism from the floor underneath the keyboard is thereby avoided.

NATIONAL instruments have the fine singing qualities of the best pianos whether played by hand or electricity.

You have the benefit of our THIRTY-TWO YEARS EXPERIENCE in all the branches of Piano-Making and the cutting of ELECTRIC Piano Rolls.

We own and operate the largest electric music cutting equipment and make OUR OWN MASTER RECORDS from which we cut the WELL KNOWN PEERLESS MUSIC ROLLS for ALL MAKES of ELECTRIC Pianos, including PEERLESS instruments of ALL STYLES. Address all correspondence

NATIONAL ELECTRIC PIANO CO.
ST. JOHNSVILLE, N. Y.

NATIONAL Electric Pianos — PEERLESS All-Hit Music Rolls

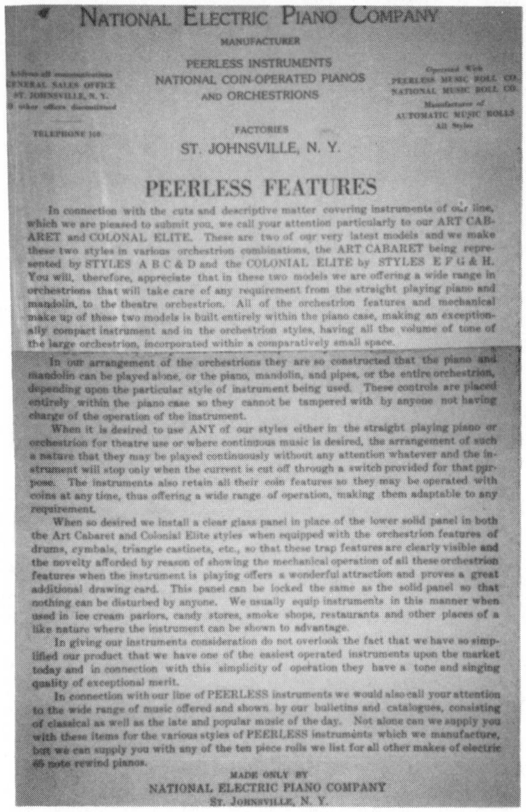

NATIONAL ELECTRIC PIANO COMPANY

MANUFACTURER

PEERLESS INSTRUMENTS
NATIONAL COIN-OPERATED PIANOS
AND ORCHESTRIONS

Address all communications GENERAL SALES OFFICE ST. JOHNSVILLE, N. Y. All other offices discontinued

Operated With PEERLESS MUSIC ROLL CO. NATIONAL MUSIC ROLL CO. Manufacturers of AUTOMATIC MUSIC ROLLS All Styles

FACTORIES
ST. JOHNSVILLE, N. Y.

**PEERLESS FEATURES**

In connection with the cuts and descriptive matter covering instruments of our line, which we are pleased to submit you, we call your attention particularly to our ART CABARET and COLONAL ELITE. These are two of our very latest models and we make these two styles in various orchestrion combinations, the ART CABARET being represented by STYLES A B C & D and the COLONIAL ELITE by STYLES E F G & H. You will, therefore, appreciate that in these two models we are offering a wide range in orchestrions that will take care of any requirement from the straight playing piano and mandolin, to the theatre orchestrion. All of the orchestrion features and mechanical make up of these two models is built entirely within the piano case, making an exceptionally compact instrument and in the orchestrion styles, having all the volume of tone of the large orchestrion, incorporated within a comparatively small space.

In our arrangement of the orchestrions they are so constructed that the piano and mandolin can be played alone, or the piano, mandolin, and pipes, or the entire orchestrion, depending upon the particular style of instrument being used. These controls are placed entirely within the piano case so they cannot be tampered with by anyone not having charge of the operation of the instrument.

When it is desired to use ANY of our styles either in the straight playing piano or orchestrion for theatre use or where continuous music is desired, the arrangement of such a nature that they may be played continuously without any attention whatever and the instrument will stop only when the current is cut off through a switch provided for that purpose. The instruments also retain all their coin features so they may be operated with coins at any time, thus offering a wide range of operation, making them adaptable to any requirement.

When so desired we install a clear glass panel in place of the lower solid panel in both the Art Cabaret and Colonial Elite styles when equipped with the orchestrion features of drums, cymbals, triangle castinets, etc., so that these trap features are clearly visible and the novelty afforded by reason of showing the mechanical operation of all these orchestrion features when the instrument is playing offers a wonderful attraction and proves a great additional drawing card. This panel can be locked the same as the solid panel so that nothing can be disturbed by anyone. We usually equip instruments in this manner when used in ice cream parlors, candy stores, smoke shops, restaurants and other places of a like nature where the instrument can be shown to advantage.

In giving our instruments consideration do not overlook the fact that we have so simplified our product that we have one of the easiest operated instruments upon the market today and in connection with this simplicity of operation they have a tone and singing quality of exceptional merit.

In connection with our line of PEERLESS instruments we would also call your attention to the wide range of music offered and shown by our bulletins and catalogues, consisting of classical as well as the late and popular music of the day. Not alone can we supply you with these items for the various styles of PEERLESS instruments which we manufacture, but we can supply you with any of the ten piece rolls we list for all other makes of electric 65 note rewind pianos.

MADE ONLY BY
NATIONAL ELECTRIC PIANO COMPANY
ST. JOHNSVILLE, N. Y.

Odds and ends from Peerless advertisements of the 1920's. The pointing finger shown below is pointing to the coin slot on a fine Peerless Wisteria orchestrion owned by Tom Sprague.

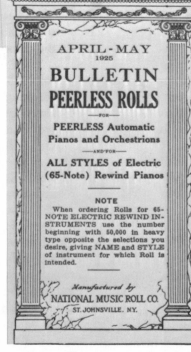


Above: From the letterhead of the National Music Roll Co., a National Electric Piano Co. subsidiary. Right: Cover of the April - May, 1925 Bulletin for Peerless rolls.

The Peerless factories, now the headquarters of the Little Falls Felt Shoe Co., as they appeared during the author's visit in 1965.

## J.D. PHILIPPS & SONS
### —Frankfurt, Germany—

### The Early Years

Johann Daniel Philipps began in the automatic musical instrument business at the age of 23 when he built a barrel orchestrion for the Germania, a hotel and dance hall in Frankfurt-am-Main, Germany. In 1877 the firm of Philipps and Ketterer was started. In the early years a branch factory was maintained in Vöhrenbach. The Ketterer relationship lasted nine years. In 1886 the Frankfurt Orchestrion and Piano Instrument Factory — J.D. Philipps was formed. In 1911 the name was shortened to the Frankfurt Music Factory — J.D. Philipps & Sons A.G. Headquarters were in Bockenheim, a district of Frankfurt. A trademark, "Philag" (a contraction of Philipps A.G.), was used in later years.

During the 1880's and 1890's the firm's principal products were barrel operated pianos and orchestrions. These early orchestrions were built on standard lines and resembled the products of Welte and other contemporary builders. Weight-driven, the instruments had large bellows in the bottom of the case and symmetrically arranged pipes, usually displayed behind clear glass windows, in the upper part. Some of these were from ten to twelve feet in height. The music was programmed on a pinned wooden barrel of one to eight tunes in length. Barrel orchestrions were listed in Philipps catalogues as late as 1909 (and perhaps even later), but by this time they were technically obsolete.

In 1896 Philipps produced its first paper-roll-operated instruments. By the 1900-1902 years several varieties of orchestrions were being marketed. The Pianella name was assigned to these in 1903.

### Orchestrions of the 1900 - 1910 Decade

The Pianella series of orchestrions, produced mainly in the first decade of the twentieth century, contained several dozen different styles ranging from small upright pianos with mandolin attachment to huge concert instruments over twelve feet in height and containing close to 400 pipes.

The Pianella instruments were given colorful, often fanciful, names such as Ideal, Harmonia, Silvia, Iris, and Caecilia.

The rolls used on the Pianella pianos and orchestrions are of several types:

"PM" rolls — This is the basic Philipps orchestrion roll. An abbreviation of "Pianella Mandoline," the PM roll is used on most types of Philipps keyboard pianos with mandolin; with mandolin, xylophone, and other instruments; and on the large classic keyboardless orchestrions with from one to six ranks of pipes (in general; there were exceptions to this). The PM roll is identical to the Wurlitzer Mandolin PianOrchestra roll.

"PMX" rolls — The same basic size (23cm. width) as PM rolls, but not for orchestrion use (there are no drum or trap perforations). Special solo section for the xylophone.

"PE" rolls — Special rolls with piano, mandolin, and xylophone. Used on smaller keyboard pianos. Neither the PE nor PMX rolls were used for more than a few years.

"Style 17 PianOrchestra" rolls — For use on certain early Philipps instruments Wurlitzer made "Style 17 PianOrchestra" rolls. These rolls feature a special 13-note solo section for the orchestra bells. The original Philipps designation for this roll type is not known.

"PC" rolls — Orchestrated rolls for use on very large Pianella orchestrions; generally those with 7 or more ranks of pipes. Identical to Wurlitzer's Concert PianOrchestra rolls. PC is an abbreviation for Pianella Caecilia (or Cecilia — after the goddess of music), the type of orchestrion on which this roll was first used.

"Pianella Orchestra" rolls — A special extensively orchestrated roll for use on the Pianella Orchestra orchestrion.

Note: Of the above rolls, the PM rolls were used on perhaps 90% of the orchestrions made by Philipps during this decade, and the PC rolls went to perhaps 5% or so. The PMX, PE, and other rolls are listed here for historical purposes — they played no significant role in Philipps' sales.

Like Hupfeld, Popper, and other orchestrions of this era, the Philipps Pianella instruments were richly decorated with beveled mirrors, "motion picture effect" scenes with moving zeppelins, steamboats, and other devices, with "wonder lights" (called "marvel lamps" by Philipps, a revolving wonder light could be ordered as an option on just about any style of Philipps orchestrion; the cost was $24 extra), and with other ornate embellishments. Perhaps the ultimate in visual wonderment was the "Castle" model which had, among other things, a tower clock, several scenes including one with an erupting volcano, two wonder lights, artificial plants and flowers, and dozens of twinkling lights!

Philipps was proud of two main Pianella features: the small width of the music rolls (the holes were spaced more closely together than on competitive types of rolls) and the "revolver mechanism," an automatic roll changer.

### Music Roll Advantages

In the preface to its 1909 catalogue Philipps had the following to say about its music roll system and other Pianella features:

"What distinguishes our excellent Piano Orchestrions from all other makes is not their elegant tasteful exterior or the unrivalled arrangement of their instrumentation or the patented revolver mechanism, but especially the small music rolls which are employed for all our instruments.

"Being about 23cm wide, which means only about half the normal size employed by other makes, our small music rolls include nevertheless the largest scale of notes. As dampness very easily makes the paper swell, thereby putting the instrument out of order, it is clear that this inconvenience increases in proportion to the size of the rolls.

"The result is, that while large rolls will easily get out of order from being kept in some damp place, our small ones would certainly resist in any case, because their very small size prevents them from swelling to such an extent as to affect the working in any way.

"This capital invention is also patented so that it can only be used on our own instruments. For instruments that we export to different countries this system is of the very highest importance, as it assures them a faultless action in any climate.

"Thanks to the principle of employing the best material regardless of cost, adapting to our instruments the very latest in improvements, we have been able to make Pianellas popular not only in our country but also to export them to all parts of the world.

"Our Pianella Piano Orchestrions can be attached to any wire of the electric light installed in your house. When ordering please indicate the kind and force of the electric current. . ."

### The Revolver Mechanism

Although Hupfeld, Popper, and several other firms used automatic roll changers in later years, the first commercially successful one appears to be the "Revolver System" devised by Philipps in 1903 - 1904 and patented in Germany in 1905. This system employs three, five, six (the most-often used number), or ten rolls mounted in a magazine around a common spindle – in a manner not unlike a Ferris wheel. When one roll is finished playing, the changer moves ahead one position and plays the next roll in order.

The "Revolver Mechanism" has stood the test of time. Even today collectors agree that this roll changer is one of the best ever devised. Made of machined steel parts, and very accurately aligned, the mechanism can go through countless cycles without giving trouble.

Of the Revolver device Philipps said (in the 1909 catalogue):

"The Revolver System for the Automatic Change of Music Rolls – By means of this most clever invention 6 paper rolls can be inserted at a time in our instrument, just like the cartridges of a revolver, and will change automatically.

"Supposing that on each roll there are 4 pieces, the orchestrion would then play 24 different pieces, beginning at the end all over again without any help or attention at all.

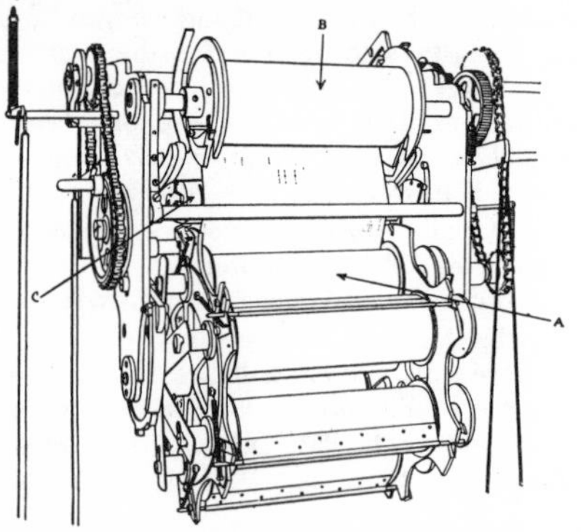


"How delightful to listen to a whole concert without being obliged to frequently change the rolls – and how nice to be able to prepare beforehand the program which you would like your friends to hear.

"And, if the orchestrion is in a hotel or ballroom how very convenient it is for the manager to change the tunes for dances automatically – thus saving a lot of time and trouble and keeping the instrument from being touched by unskilled hands.

"If the operation is not by coin, each piece may be started separately by simply pressing a button which, if desired, can be placed anywhere in the room or house.

"The rolls can be taken out and changed any time, singly or together. This remarkable invention can be used only on our instruments."

The roll changer was available on most Philipps instruments at an extra cost of $75.00 (for instruments sold in the U.S. by Wurlitzer, the extra cost was $200.00). The mechanism was made in capacities of 3, 5, 6, and 10 rolls. Later, some 12-roll instruments were made (in this instance the rolls were not all around a center spindle; a linked-together belt of rolls extended below the main revolver mechanism).

### The Wurlitzer Relationship

In 1902 Farny and Howard Wurlitzer, representing the Rudolph Wurlitzer Company of Cincinnati, Ohio, U.S.A., visited the Leipzig Trade Fair. At the exhibits there they saw large orchestrions made by Hupfeld. Desiring to make arrangements for the importation of these instruments into America, the Wurlitzer brothers negotiated with the Hupfeld representatives. No agreement was reached, and Hupfeld referred Wurlitzer to J.D. Philipps & Sons.

After due discussion it was agreed that Wurlitzer would have exclusive representation rights to Philipps instruments in the United States. In 1903 the first order, a group of four Pianella orchestrions, arrived at the Wurlitzer premises. From then until World War I, Wurlitzer imported over one thousand Philipps instruments. In addition, many Philipps components such as roll mechanisms, xylophones, and other devices were imported for use in certain orchestrions (Mandolin PianOrchestra style nos. 12, 15, 16, 18, 28-B and early photoplayers) made in Wurlitzer's North Tonawanda, N.Y., factory.

Orchestrions using the PM rolls were sold as Wurlitzer Mandolin PianOrchestras; instruments using PC rolls were sold as Wurlitzer Concert PianOrchestras. A number of Philipps Paganini instruments were imported from 1911 to 1914 as were a lesser number of Philipps Duca reproducing pianos.

Illustration from a Wurlitzer catalogue. Note "Pianella Ideal" on the top crest. Wurlitzer forgot to retouch the photograph!

As all Wurlitzer Mandolin PianOrchestras except styles 12, 15, 16, 18, and 28-B and as all Concert PianOrchestras and Paganinis were imported from Philipps (although Wurlitzer made no mention of the Philipps origin of these instruments in its advertising or promotion), the reader is urged to refer to the Wurlitzer section of this book for additional information and illustrations concerning many of the larger Philipps styles.

### Philipps - Wurlitzer Cross References

As noted, Philipps gave its instruments names such as Silvia, Iris, etc. Wurlitzer designated its instruments with numbers, such as Style 32 Concert PianOrchestra. Here is a cross reference giving the Philipps names and the Wurlitzer numbers (in instances in which the information is known):

| Philipps Name | Wurlitzer Style No. |
|---|---|
| Pianella Brillant | Style 27-B Mandolin PianOrchestra |
| Pianella Special | Style 17 PianOrchestra |
| Pianella Victoria Xylophone | Style 28-A Mandolin PianOrchestra |
| Pianella Ideal | Style 19 Mandolin PianOrchestra |
| Pianella Ideal (later) | Style 39 Mandolin PianOrchestra |
| Pianella Harmonia | Style 20 Mandolin PianOrchestra |
| Pianella Monopol | Style 30 Mandolin PianOrchestra |
| Pianella Monopol Xylophone | Style 30-A Mandolin PianOrchestra |
| Pianella Silvia Xylophone | Style 34 Mandolin PianOrchestra |
| Pianella Silvana Xylophone | Style 33 Mandolin PianOrchestra |
| Pianella Caecilia | Style 32 Concert PianOrchestra |
| Pianella Special B | Style 38-B Mandolin PianOrchestra |
| Pianella Monopol | Style 30-B Mandolin PianOrchestra |
| Pianella Celesta | Style 40 Mandolin PianOrchestra |
| Pianella Mandolino | Style 29-C Mandolin PianOrchestra |
| Pianella Orchestra (later) | Style 43 Concert PianOrchestra |

### Quantities of Pianellas Manufactured

From a study of serial numbers we would estimate that between 2000 and 4000 large Pianellas were made from about 1902 to 1914. Of this number about 1000 were sold in the United States by Wurlitzer.

Other Philipps trading areas included England and continental Europe. Of the European countries, the largest markets were in Germany, Belgium, and Holland – in that order. In addition to those made by Philipps, rolls for these instruments were cut by Wurlitzer (U.S.A.), Symphonia (Antwerp, Belgium), L. Fluess (Antwerp), and Euterpe (Amsterdam, Holland).

Orchestrion and piano assembling room in the Philipps factory.

Producing grand pianos, some of which incorporated Duca reproducing systems.

Assembling pumps and reservoirs at the Philipps factory.

Pneumatic stack and pipe chest department.

Philipps cut rolls on the premises for its various instruments.

### Instruments of the 1910 - 1920 Decade

By 1910 Philipps introduced two major additions to its line of instruments. The Duca, a reproducing mechanism, re-enacted the playing of famous pianists. Ducas were made in a wide variety of styles including upright coin-operated models for public places and upright and grand pianos for the home. In the 1920's Duca production hit its stride and eclipsed greatly the manufacturing of orchestrions. In the several years following its introduction the Duca sold well and garnered dozens of testimonials from leading musicians of the day.

The crowning jewel in Philipps' crown was the Paganini. Introduced in 1910, the Paganini in its basic form featured violin solos (by means of violin pipes) with piano accompaniment. Larger instruments, the Paganini Orchestrions, were patterned after the earlier PC-roll instruments (the manufacture of PC instruments, the ones Wurlitzer called "Concert PianOrchestras" in the U.S., was discontinued a short while later). Generally speaking, Paganini Orchestrions had fewer pipes than PC instruments, but had more expression effects. The piano part of the Paganini was based on the Duca reproducing system.

### The Paganini

Philipps advertised that the Paganini was the summation of what orchestrion builders had long tried to achieve. The following is from Philipps' catalogue (excerpted for brevity):

"Orchestrion construction is the supplanting of manual playing with mechanical devices. The first instruments constructed did not satisfy critics, but patience and industriousness finally led to perfection. Ideas succeeded ideas, new inventions superseded obsolete systems, and the mechanisms experienced a radical change. Even when the pinned cylinder was replaced by the more convenient music roll the ethics of music were sometimes forgotten and the instruments often left much to be desired.

"The era of dissonant and noisy instruments was really just a transitory period leading up to the present — a time which was achieved with labor and diligence. The orchestrion now stands high in excellence and artistic merit.

"Great demands were made on orchestrions — their task being to exemplify complete orchestration, and although at the present, the best instruments meet all requirements in this respect, the spirit of invention accepts no restrictions. It has always set for itself higher ideals, the same being successively achieved.

"For instance, the violin, possessing the noblest and most melodious qualities as a solo instrument, has hitherto been beyond the range of possibility for mechanical, artistic reproduction. But this, the most soul-inspiring of all instruments, which, in the hand of the master, laughs and weeps, ought and must be successfully included in the repertoire of the pneumatic instrument. Many attempts were made to obtain this end (Ed. comment: including attempts by Philipps who patented a real-violin player in 1910, but found it wouldn't work well in actual use), but very few met with any degree of success. The equipment with real violins suffers from the disadvantage that real violins remain in tune only a short time.

"Having obtained such success with our Duca Reproducing Piano we attempted to try a combination which should represent performance on a real violin. We considered this instrument from a truly artistic viewpoint and spared no pains to obtain a corresponding musical performance which, with the aid of a first class staff of artists, we eventually succeeded in accomplishing in a most satisfactory manner.

"These instruments we have named after the greatest and most fascinating of violinists, Paganini. This is a very important event in the history of pneumatic instruments.

"The difficulties have been overcome, the real violins were abandoned on account of their sensitiveness and the need to keep tuning them, and the problem was solved in another way: our Paganini instruments not only give a representation of violin playing (by means of pipes — Ed.), but even perform the finest nuances, the slightest vibrato, and a crescendo and diminuendo full of soul, and a perfection of artistic beauty. We place the Paganini on the market with the awareness that we are offering an instrument of a very high class order."

### Paganini Data

At the outset Philipps called the models with piano and pipes "Paganini Violin Pianos" and called orchestrated models (with drums and other percussion effects) "Paganini Orchestrions." Later, all instruments were called "Paganini Orchestrions." From time to time variations occur such as (in a 1927 catalogue) "Paganini Reproducing Orchestrion."

The Paganini uses a 130-note roll with solo perforations for the pipes and piano. This extended solo scale makes elaborate musical performances possible. As was the case with Pianella instruments, Paganinis could be ordered with the Revolver Mechanism.

Paganini instruments were sold in the United States by Wurlitzer.

J.D. Philipps (left) and his two sons (above).

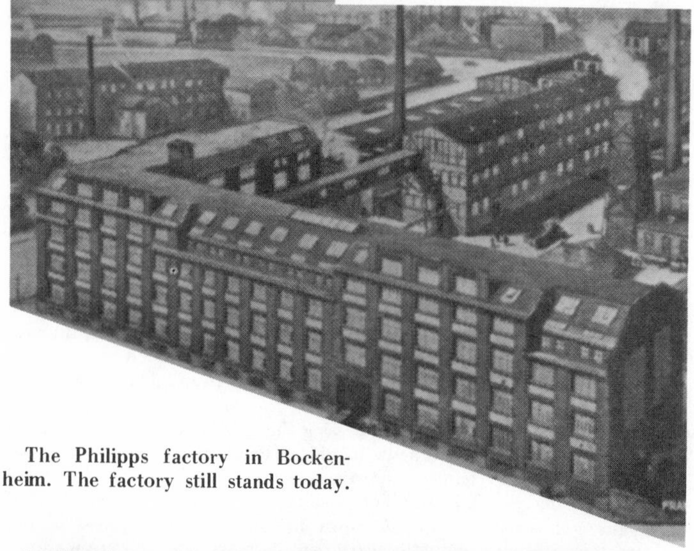

The Philipps factory in Bockenheim. The factory still stands today.

Philipps factory scene (circa 1927).

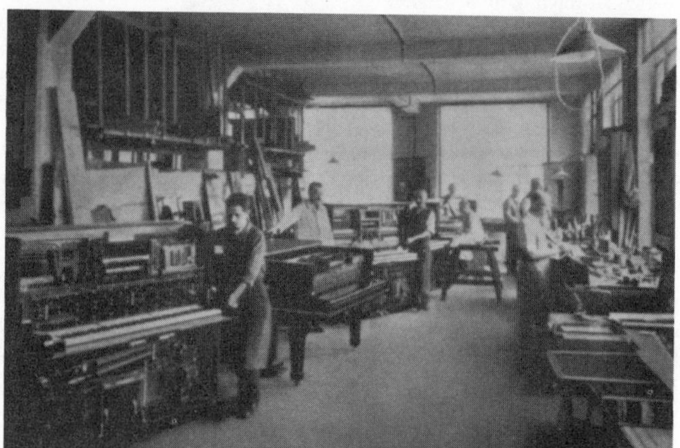

Assembling upright pianos with player mechanisms.

### Instruments of the 1920-1930 Decade

By 1920 large classic orchestrions were passe. Production of the huge Pianella instruments came to an end. The only Pianellas made in large quantities were the keyboard styles with mandolin and xylophone.

The jazz era came with the 1920's, and Philipps was eager to become a part of it. Using the convenient PM rolls a new series of modern-appearing jazz band instruments was marketed. Philipps' enthusiasm for these instruments was carried over in the title (the exclamation point is Philipps', not ours): "Philipps SUPER JAZZBAND ORCHESTRA!"

Paganinis were made throughout the 1920's, but not in the quantities of the preceding decade. A 1928 Philipps price list loaned together with other information to us by Christopher Ross notes that four different styles of Paganini Orchestrions (Nos. 3, 4, 5, and 14) were being sold in that year, as were two styles of Paganini Violin Pianos (Nos. 1 and 3), and two different styles of theatre photoplayers (Nos. 10k and 5k) using Paganini rolls.

Coin-operated Duca pianos continued to sell well. (Commercial use of reproducing pianos was quite successful in Europe but notably unsuccessful in the United States.)

### Big Business

In 1923 Philipps acquired the venerable firm of Frati & Co. of Berlin. Frati was a leading maker of fairground organs in the late 19th century. At the time of the acquisition the leading Frati products were electric pianos and orchestrions (the latter known as "Fratinola" and "Fratihymnia" styles). Fratinola and Fratihymnia designs were modified to use PM rolls. By 1925 Frati and Philipps instruments were the same; some had Philipps labels and some were sold with Frati insignia.

On January 1, 1925 the firm of Wilhelm Arnold, A.G. (founded in 1830), of Aschaffenburg, Germany, was added to the rapidly expanding Philipps holdings. The Arnold factory was one of Germany's leading makers of good quality upright and grand pianos and was about as large as the Philipps firm itself. The leading Arnold trademark was "Bülow," a piano named after Hans von Bülow, leading German pianist of the late 19th century.

By 1927 Philipps had five factories — two in the original location in Bockenheim, a suburb of Frankfurt-am-Main; the former Frati factory in Berlin; and two large former Arnold factories in Aschaffenburg.

By 1929 Philipps was virtually out of business. Public places found the radio to be more popular than coin operated orchestrions. On the home front the economic situation was shaky and demand for pianos of all kinds plummeted. The Frankfurt and Berlin factories were shuttered and production was centered in Aschaffenburg. The former Philipps catalogues, some of which were works of art, were replaced by a pocket-size forlorn listing of just 14 instruments, most of which were small keyboard-type pianos using PM rolls. Sales dwindled. For a while radios and radio cabinets were made and some furniture was manufactured. Then came the end.

### Requiem for Philipps

Today Philipps instruments, especially the orchestrions in the PM, PC, and Paganini roll series, are avidly sought by collectors. As Philipps was responsible for the large and elegant Mandolin and Concert PianoOrchestras, among the most spectacular instruments ever to grace the public places in our country, this German firm has a warm spot in the hearts of American collectors.

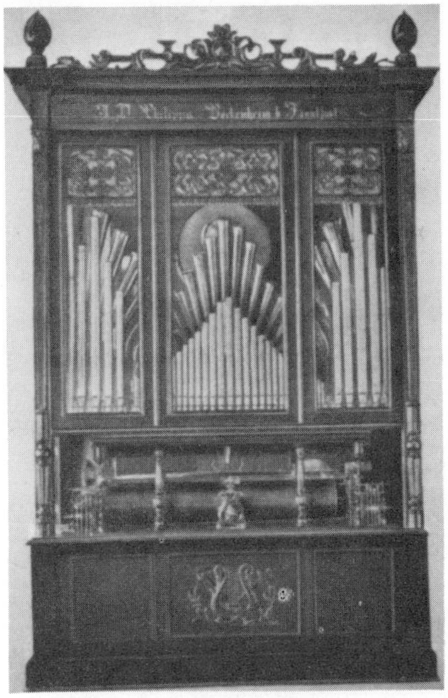

Large barrel-operated Philipps orchestrion from the 1880's.

## —PHILIPPS BARREL-OPERATED ORCHESTRIONS—

From the inception of the Philipps business until paper roll instruments became popular in the early 1900's barrel or cylinder orchestrions comprised most of the firm's production.

At the left is shown a tall orchestrion in the classic style with symmetrically arranged pipes, including some in a sunburst pattern. Similar appearing instruments were made by Welte, Imhof & Mukle, and other German orchestrion builders of the late 19th century. No attempt at distinctive case designs or pipe arrangements was made, so often it is difficult to attribute such an instrument to its maker unless it is labeled. Complicating the identification is the fact that many early orchestrion makers ordered the mechanical parts (such as the cylinder drive gears and pump mechanisms) from common suppliers.

Philipps cylinder-operated orchestrions are quite rare today.

At the right is a cylinder orchestrion from the early 20th century. Called "Pianetta" orchestrions, these were made in seven different styles — with letter designations from Pianetta A to Pianetta G. Sale prices ranged from $400 to $600 each. Extra cylinders cost about $30 to $40 apiece. Each cylinder had eight tunes programmed on it.

Pianetta orchestrions were listed in the 1909 Philipps catalogue and were probably sold until about 1911 - 1913.

Pianetta case design for styles A and B. Instrumentation of Style A: piano, mandolin, 13 bells, drums, and wood block. Style B is the same plus a xylophone.

## —SCENES AT THE PHILIPPS FACTORY — MARCH, 1890—

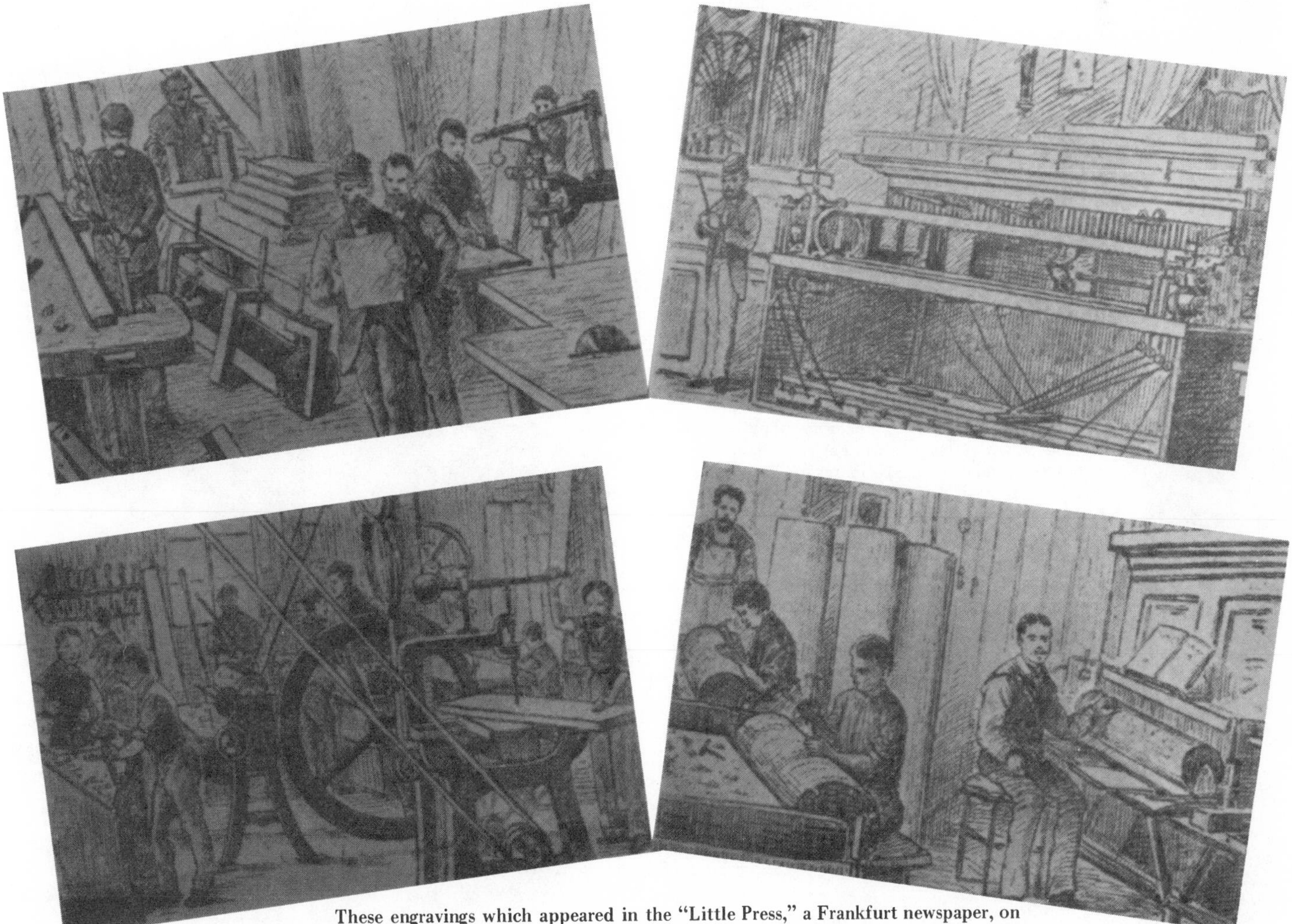

These engravings which appeared in the "Little Press," a Frankfurt newspaper, on March 14, 1890, show activity at the Philipps factory. At the upper right is the bottom section of a large orchestrion; at the lower right cylinders are being pinned. (Information courtesy Heinz Kuhn)

Pianella piano Style PC 7 (for "Pianella Corona" 7). Piano, mandolin, xylophone. Uses PM roll. One of the most popular Pianella piano styles.

# PHILIPPS PIANELLA

PIANELLA PIANOS

(No.1)

(No.2)

(No.3)

(No.4)

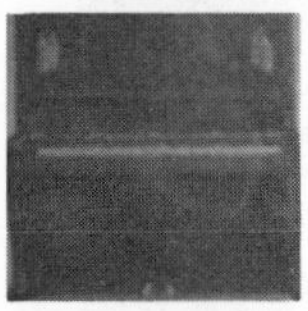

(No.5)

(No.6)

(No.7)

## –PHILIPPS PIANELLA PIANOS–

We illustrate some of the more popular styles of the Pianella piano. Each uses the PM roll. Most were available with a roll changer for $75 extra. For $90 to $125 extra a gallery with a lighted waterfall, windmill, or other scene could be added to any model.

Our numbers and the Philipps styles to which they refer are: (No.1) Style PC 3, piano with mandolin; (No.2) Style PF 1, piano with mandolin; (No.3) Style PC 3 equipped with roll changer; (No.4) view of single roll mechanism in Pianella piano; (No.5) Style PA 12 uses special Pianella "Artists' rolls" sold as PA and PCA rolls; (No.6) Style PC 13, piano, mandolin, xylophone. Xylophone is lighted when playing; (No.7) Hans von Bülow name on metal piano plate of Pianella made in Aschaffenburg in the late 1920's; (No.8) Style PF 2, piano, mandolin, xylophone; (No.9) Style PC 19, piano, mandolin, xylophone (lighted when playing); (No.10) Pianella with glass window in front to permit viewing of the roll as it plays; (No.11) Style PC 6, piano, mandolin, xylophone in ornate case. Illustrated instrument is equipped with automatic roll changer, although most of this style were not. Note that the case has a built out extension on front to house the device.

PM rolls were made by Philipps from the early 1900's to about 1930. Most rolls are of four tune length. In later years large quantities of PM rolls were made by Symphonia (Eugene DeRoy).

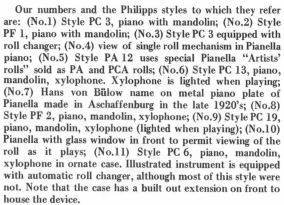

(No.8)

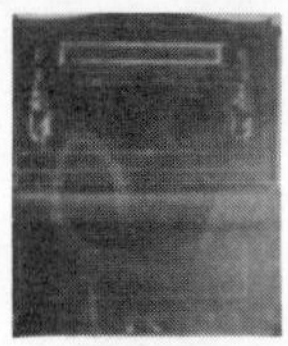

(No.9)

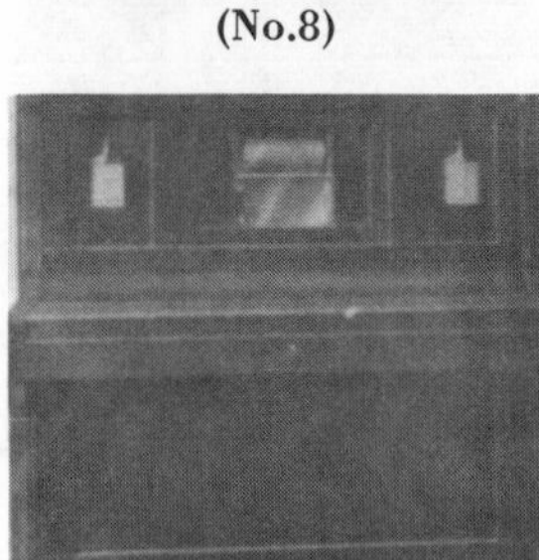

(No.10)

(No.11)

Introduction of the Pianella

On April 17, 1903, Philipps registered the Pianella trademark. In August, 1903 "What Is Pianella?" teaser advertisements appeared. Soon the answer was given: according to Philipps the Pianella term referred to the best self-playing instruments made. Note that the above right advertisement mentions Cincinnati and Chicago, the locations of the Rudolph Wurlitzer Co., Philipps' U.S. sales agent.

The first Philipps paper-roll-operated instrument, an orchestrion, appeared in 1896. A roll-operated piano was introduced in 1898. After mid-1903 the Pianella name was given to most roll-operated coin pianos and orchestrions made by the firm.

Left: The Philipps exhibit at the 1910 Brussels World's Fair — one of the most prominent events in the history of orchestrions. Occurring at the height of the orchestrion business, the Brussels event attracted spectacular displays from many different German manufacturers.

The instrument awarded the Grand Prize is a Style 9 Paganini Orchestrion (refer to the Wurlitzer section of this book for information on the Style 9 and other Paganini instruments). Also shown in the picture are several keyboard-style Pianella pianos and orchestrions.

Philipps
Pianella-Orchestrion im Piedmont-Hotel Atlanta, Ga.
Bei Präsident Taft's Empfang zu dem großen „Possum-Dinner" im Piedmont, Atlanta's Zwei Millionen Dollar Palast-Hotel stand der Präsident direkt vor
Philipps Pianella-Orchestrion.
Frankfurter Musikwerke-Fabrik J. D. Philipps & Söhne Akt.-Ges., Frankfurt a. Main


President Taft Appreciates the Pianella

In 1912 Philipps proudly featured President William Howard Taft (U.S. president 1909-1913) in several of its advertisements and in its orchestrion catalogue. "At President Taft's 'Possum Dinner' reception at Atlanta's palatial two-million-dollar Piedmont Hotel the President is shown in front of a PHILIPPS PIANELLA ORCHESTRION" notes the the caption to the picture. President Taft was pleased with the instrument and found that it played "just like a symphony orchestra." Philipps carefully retouched the photograph so that the crest on the instrument read "J.D. Philipps & Söhne." Actually the instrument was sold by Wurlitzer (Philipps' U.S. agent) and must have borne the "PianOrchestra" name.

Glorifying the Orchestrion: Depicting The Product on a pedestal was a favorite way to advertise orchestrions. This Philipps Pianella illustration appeared in 1913.

"The most important novelty of 1905 — pneumatic instruments with automatically-changing rolls!" proclaims this Philipps advertisement which introduced the Philipps Revolver System. The Philipps automatic roll changer gained immediate acceptance and soon became a popular addition to Philipps instruments of all kinds, from 3-roll changers built into grand pianos to 10- and 12-roll changers built into large orchestrions.

For theatre use many varieties of electric pianos and orchestrions were made. The Duplex Piano shown above featured two rolls mounted side-by-side. A 1912 advertisement offered: "Artistically-playing instruments — The Duplex Piano and the Paganini Duplex Violin Orchestrion for the moving-picture theatre — with operation by remotely-located controls. Operates automatically! Instruments can also be equipped with Duplex Revolver Mechanisms!" The Duplex Revolver Mechanisms featured two 6-roll (although other specifications could be ordered) changers mounted side-by-side. This provided a 12-roll program capacity with continuous playing; as one roll rewound, a roll on the other changer would play.

(No.1) Pianella Corona

(No.2) Pianella Corona DeLuxe No.10

(No.3) Pianella Corona C.D.E.

(No.4) Pianella Celesta

(No.5) Pianella Mandolino Xylophone

(No.6) Pianella Corona f.

(No.7) Pianella Brillant

**—PHILIPPS PIANELLA PIANOS AND ORCHESTRIONS—**

(No.1) Piano with mandolin and violin pipes; (2) Piano, mandolin, xylophone. Also available with drums and with one rank of pipes; (3) Piano, mandolin, violin pipes, xylophone; (4) Pianella Celesta with piano, mandolin, violin and flute pipes, drum and trap effects. (5) Orchestrion with piano, mandolin, violin and flute pipes, percussion effects. Note the similarity of this case style to several others listed in the Wurlitzer Mandolin PianOrchestra section of this book; (6) Pianella Corona "f" — Piano, mandolin, xylophone. Top part is a facade for displaying lighting effects; (7) "Brillant" orchestrion with piano, mandolin, bells, percussion effects (but no pipes). Sold for $600 new; (8) Pianella Special "B" — Variation of a very popular Philipps style (sold also as Wurlitzer Style 38-B Mandolin PianOrchestra). Piano, mandolin pipes, percussion effects. One of the more compact Pianella classic orchestrions; height is about 8'.

Pianella orchestrions sold by Philipps were usually finished in the natural wood color. Those brought to the United States by Wurlitzer were sold in a wide variety of finishes including driftwood (brown with green filler in the oak wood pores), silver fox (black with white filler), and others.

(No.8) Pianella Special B

Pianella Victoria

Orchestrion with piano, mandolin, violin and flute pipes, and percussion effects. Recommended for restaurants, hotels, and cafes. Sold for $750 new in 1909. "Motion picture effects and statue available at extra price."

Pianella Mandolino

Orchestrion with piano, mandolin, violin and flute pipes, bells, and percussion effects. Sold for $1050.00 new in 1909. Approximately 10' in height. The automatic roll changer (holding six rolls) is visible through a clear glass panel in the front.

Pianella Special

Piano, mandolin, violin pipes, orchestra bells (13-note set), and percussion effects. About 9' high. The bells are mounted in bell lyre form vertically on the front. A pneumatic mechanism and strikers are directly behind it. Pianella orchestrions with exposed bells were especially popular during the 1900 - 1910 decade. Later they were discontinued.

Pianella "Peacock"

With piano, mandolin, xylophone, pipes, and percussion effects. The lighting effects on this are spectacular and consist of a center scene, a peacock with an illuminated revolving tail, two wonder lights, and fifteen mirrored lights! Compare to Wurlitzer Style 47 Mandolin PianOrchestra. Made with PM or PC roll system.

Pianella Mandola

Piano, mandolin, violin pipes, xylophone, and percussion. Uses PC rolls (why it does so is not clear as most PC instruments have 7 or more ranks of pipes. With Alpine scene and waterfall in the center. About 9½' high.

Pianella Caecilia

Large concert orchestrion with many effects (see Wurlitzer Style 32 Concert PianOrchestra specification list which is identical). Uses PC rolls. With front decorated with parade cymbalstern. Sold for $2000 new in Germany in 1909. Roll changer was $75 extra. Illuminated moving scene available at extra cost.

# Philipps

PHILIPPS

Model 17
Philipps Pianella

Above: The Pianella Orchestra was the ultimate Philipps orchestrion listed in its 1909 catalogue. This elegant instrument measures 12' high. It sold for $3000.00 in that year. Instrumentation is comparable to the Wurlitzer Style 43 Concert PianOrchestra (see Wurlitzer section of this book). The Pianella Orchestra evidently used a special roll. In the same catalogue PM rolls sold for $6 each and PC rolls for $7. This orchestrion used a special roll, designation unspecified, which sold for $7.50.

Model 3
Philipps Pianella

Model 9
Philipps Pianella

Model 7
Philipps Pianella

Model 15
Philipps Pianella

Model 16
Philipps Pianella

Model 5
Philipps Pianella

The Philipps factory at the corner of Philipp Reis Strasse and Ohmstrasse as photographed by the author in 1966. It was the author's aim to visit as many American and European instrument factories and factory sites as possible. A surprising number of original buildings still stand, but with just a few exceptions there is no indication any longer of their former musical use.

By the mid-1920's Philipps had five factories. However, the one in Bockenheim (as illustrated to the left and above) was the central location. It was here that the illustrious PM, PC, Paganini, and other pianos and orchestrions were mostly made. The Palm Garden, a deluxe hotel in which the agreement between Wurlitzer and Philipps was made in 1902, still stands in all its glory a few miles from the Philipps factory.

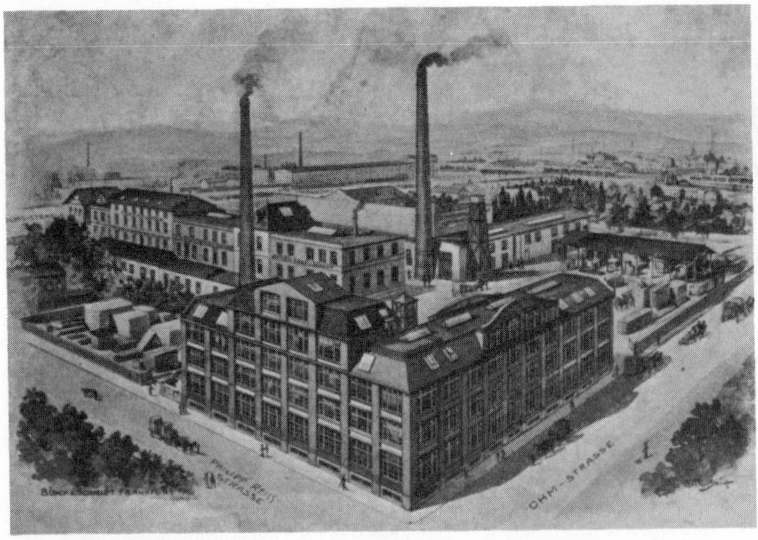


The Philipps factory in Bockenheim, a suburb of Frankfurt, as shown in a 1912 catalogue.

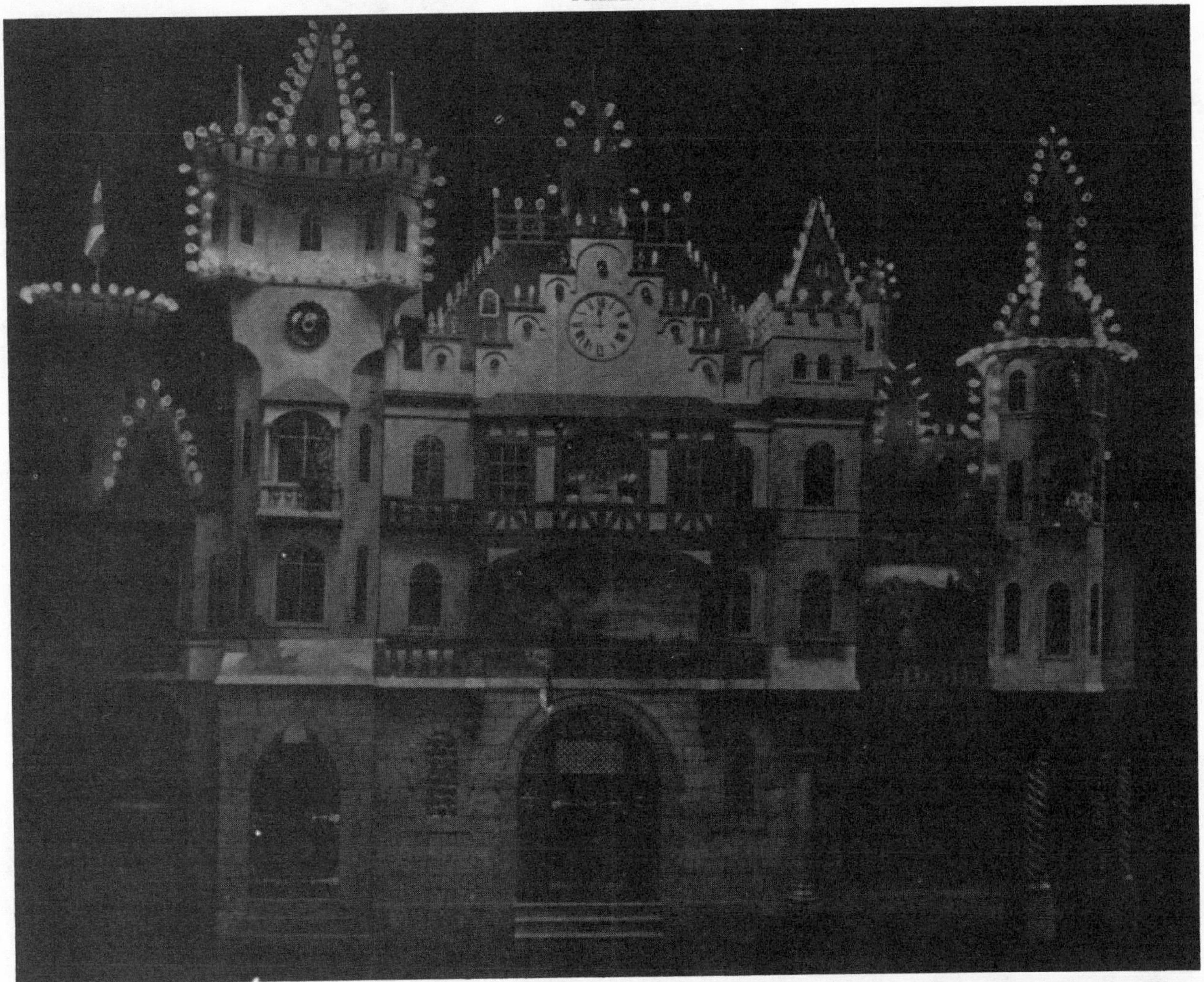

Pianella "Castle"

Resembling something from Coney Island or perhaps the Arabian Nights, the Pianella Castle is the largest (in terms of architectural size) orchestrion ever built by Philipps. The instrument is mostly composed of a decorative facade. Effects include two wonder lights, a clock (which reads 14 minutes to 12), windowed balconies, artificial flora, two motion picture scenes, one with an erupting volcano and the other with an Alpine waterfall, dozens of light bulbs, and doubtless some other effects and gadgets which aren't apparent in the above illustration! Dimensions are: 19½' high by 23' wide by 6' deep. Uses PC rolls. "Concert and dance orchestrion particularly effective for very large restaurants."

It is not known how many of these monoliths were made. Perhaps there was only this one — as illustrated in a Philipps poster of 1910.

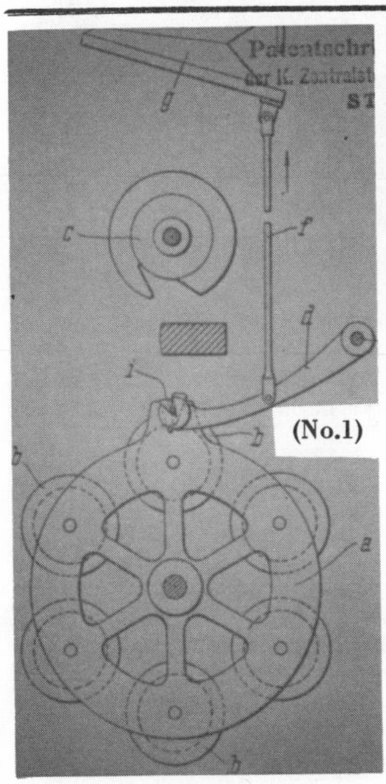

(No.1)

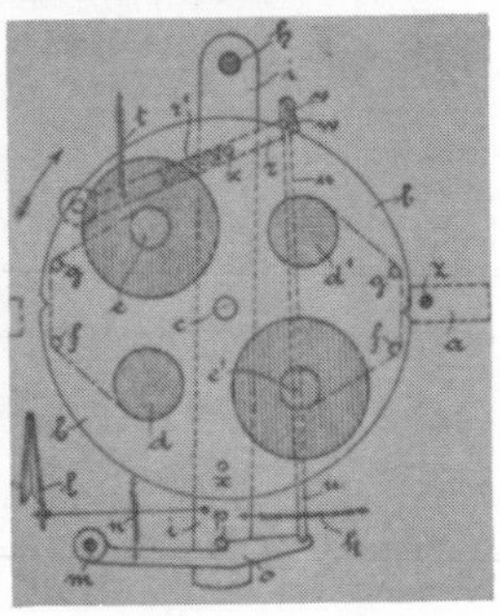

(No.2)

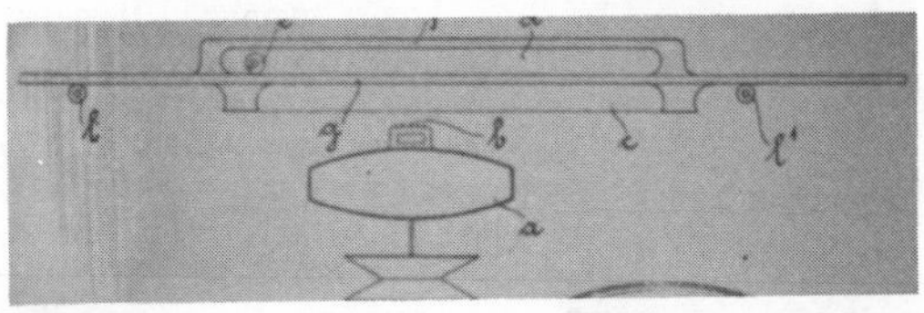

(No.3)

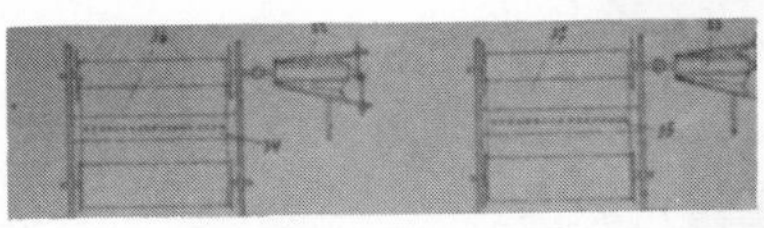

(No.4)

(No.5)

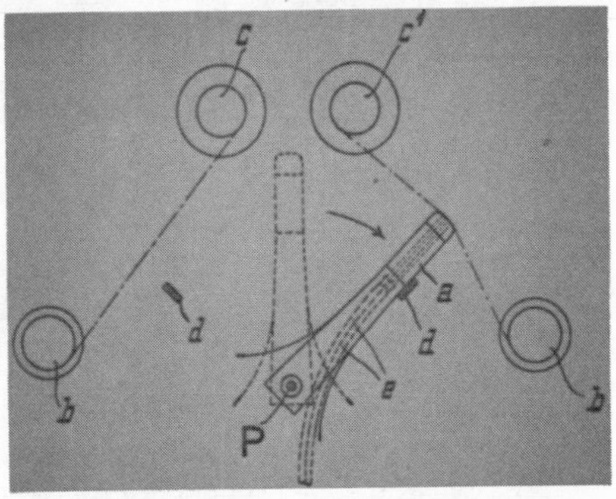

—Interesting Philipps Patents—

(1) Basic patent for the automatic roll changer. The lifting arm D takes the wire rod across the front of a roll and brings it up over the tracker bar (shaded rectangle) to be engaged by C, the take-up spool. (2) Design for a two-roll changer for use in movie theatres; the unit could be spun quickly to switch in mid-roll from one tune to another. (3) Unsuccessful violin-bowing mechanism patented in 1910. (4) Duplex side-by-side roll mechanism (with switching from one roll to another done by solenoids). (5) Interesting pivoting tracker bar device which could be switched from one roll to another for fast changes in music. Made for use in theatre instruments.

(No.1)

(No.2)

(No.3)

(No.4)

## —PHILIPPS JAZZBAND ORCHESTRIONS—

(No.1) Philipps Jazzband Piano; case for styles I (piano, mandolin, jazz drums and traps), II (the same plus violin pipes), and III (the same as II plus flex-a-tone). Also Ia, IIa, and IIIa with saxophone pipes added to each style. Note that Philipps is misspelled "Phillipps" in the picture. (No.2) Jazzband Orchestra! With 6-roll changer. Piano, pipes (violin, clarinet, trumpet, saxophone, lotus flute, flute), mandolin, and jazz drums and traps. About 9' high. (No.3) Jazzband Piano Style IVa. Piano, mandolin, saxophone pipes, and jazz drums and traps. (No.4) Alternate case style for Jazzband Piano Styles III and IIIa (see above for specifications). All of these Jazzband Pianos and Orchestrions use PM rolls with "special jazz arrangements."

## —Philipps Instruments with Accordions—

For use mainly in Belgium Philipps instruments were modified and accordions were added. The late Eugene DeRoy informed the author that he once had a very thriving business with these. Some were ordered in special cases from the Philipps factory, but usually these accordion models were made by taking existing instruments, often used ones, and altering the cases. Pipes, if the instrument had them, were usually removed and the accordion was tubed in to play as called for by the pipe registers. Pianos made by Popper & Co., Kuhl & Klatt, and others were similarly converted.

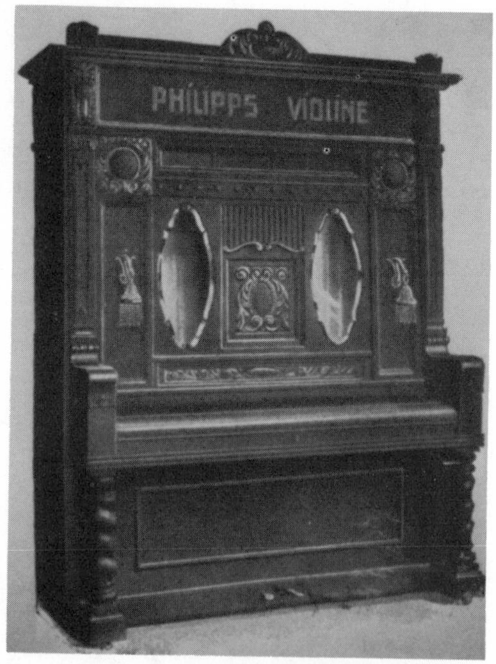


Philipps Style PC 10. Piano, mandolin, xylophone, violin pipes, drum and trap effects. Also made in the same case were instruments in varying combinations of the above, such as piano, xylophone, and percussion (no pipes). A very popular style during the 1920's.

The tracker bar of a Philipps PM instrument can be removed quickly for cleaning. It snaps in or out in a few seconds' time.

Philipps Violin Orchestra

Style PF 10. This compact orchestrion is just five feet tall. Contains piano, mandolin, and 30 violin pipes. Uses regular PM rolls. Made by Philipps in the late 1920's, the Violin Orchestra was sold only in small numbers.

## PHILIPPS DUCA REPRODUCING PIANOS
(for use in public places)

(No.1)

(No.2)

(No.3)

(No.4)

(No.5)

—Philipps Duca Pianos—

We illustrate a few of the many case designs, most of similar appearance, of the Duca reproducing piano — upright models for coin box use in public places. Styles are: (No.1) Style P.D.Ph.; (No.2) Style P.D.6; (No.3) Style P.D.2; (No.4) Interior view of a representative Duca piano; (No.5) Style P.D.5. Each style was available with or without the automatic roll changer. To accommodate the changer, cases were made 4" higher in instruments with this device. The Duca instruments were made in large quantities in the 1920's.

## PHILIPPS DUOLA PIANO

The Philipps Duola was made in the 1920's. It uses an 88-note piano roll and is played by means of coin wallboxes at different locations. (European instruments rarely were equipped with coin slots; nearly all used remote wallboxes.) The Duola case is virtually identical to Pianella piano Style PF 1. In practice, cases were interchanged between various Duola, Duca, and small PM styles.

## PHILIPPS PAGANINI PIANOS AND ORCHESTRIONS

Left: "Paganini Monster Orchestrion, Style 12." And, a monster it is! Measuring 12' high, this instrument has instrumentation similar to that listed for the Style 10 Wurlitzer Paganini Orchestra (see Wurlitzer section). "Represents a string orchestra of 40 to 50 musicians."

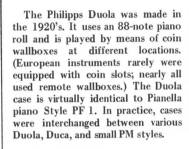

Style 13

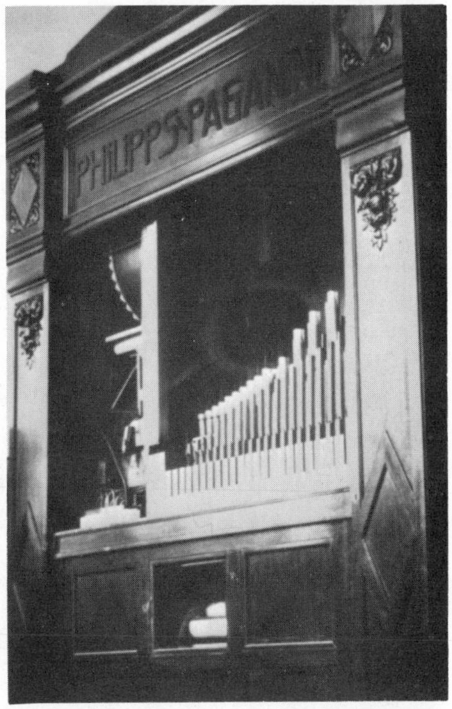

PHILIPPS
PIANELLA PAGANINI-ORCHESTRION
MODEL No 1

WITH REVOLVING MECHANISM

Elegant oak-case with beautiful carving and glass decorations. The centre front panel is filled with a valuable tapestry, and facetted mirror decorations are interspersed. Violin-playing is reproduced in a most perfect manner, with suitable pianoforte accompaniment. An instrument worthy of all praise, equally applicable for private rooms as for Cafés and first-class restaurants.

| | |
|---|---|
| Height | 8 ft. 4 in. |
| Breadth | 6 „ 4 „ |
| Depth | 2 „ 8 „ |
| Net weight | 1430 lbs. |

Music-rolls bear the mark P. P.
Selections according to our Paganini Lists.

The listener is most agreeably surprised by the marvellous performances on our Paganini-Orchestrions, the same meeting the highest requirements of musical connoisseurs.

Above center: Style 13 Paganini Orchestrion from a Philipps catalogue of 1913.

Above right: Paganini Style 14 Orchestrion presently on display at the "Music Boxes to Street Organs" Museum in Utrecht, Holland. Formerly used in Belgium; sold to the museum by Eugene DeRoy about 1960. Has 10-roll automatic changer.

Left: Model 1 Philipps Paganini Orchestrion. Somewhat differently proportioned (wider in relation to its height) than the Wurlitzer Style 1 illustrated in the Wurlitzer section of this book. Contains a Duca piano and one rank of pipes.

Note: Special Paganini Duca rolls were made with piano-only (no pipes) arrangements. These were simply Duca roll arrangements cut on a wide paper Paganini roll.

Pianella Style C. No.8 – Piano, mandolin, and xylophone. Uses PM rolls. "Superior modern get-up; oak with facetted mirror front and electric lighting." This and other Philipps instruments on this page are from a catalogue issued by Cesar Costers, Belgian agent for Philipps in the 1920's. Earlier, Costers was an agent for Imhof & Mukle.

Pianella Style C. No. 7 – Piano, mandolin, and xylophone. Uses PM rolls. The motion picture effect of a zeppelin flying over a wintry landscape was also used on an earlier Pianella keyboardless orchestrion sold by Wurlitzer.

PHILIPPS

Paganini Violin Piano, Style 4 DeLuxe – Piano and many ranks of violin pipes. Uses Paganini rolls or Duca rolls (on special spools). The most ornate of the keyboard Paganini styles.

Pianella Style C. No.9 – Uses PM rolls. "Splendid modern case in dark brown oak with facetted mirrors and brilliant electric double lamps on the console." Piano, mandolin, and xylophone. Note that case is built out at the front to accommodate the automatic roll changer.

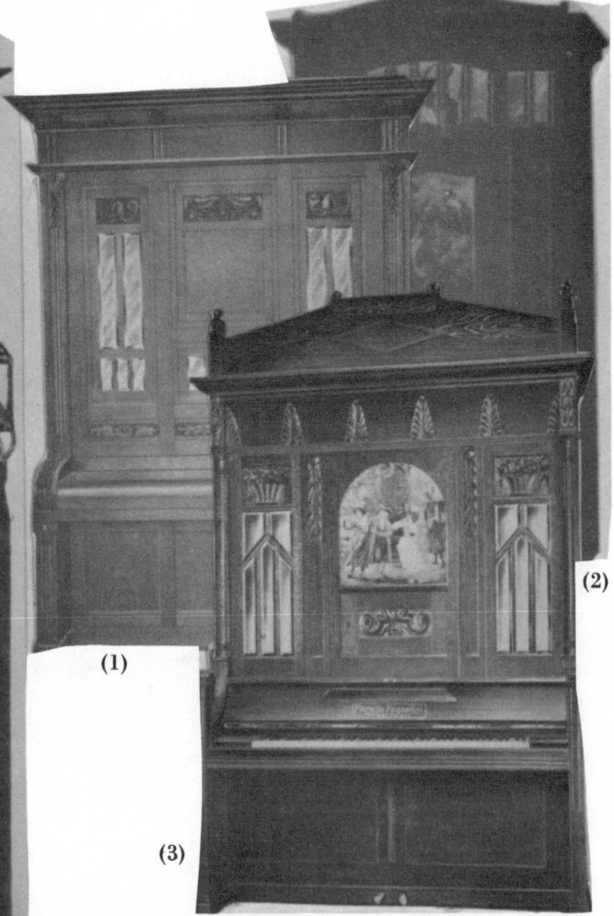


(1) Paganini Violin Piano, Style 1. With keyboard. (2) Pianella Style 51. Keyboardless. About 9' high. Piano, mandolin, violin pipes, drum and trap effects. Uses special PE rolls. (3) Paganini Violin Piano, Style 2. With keyboard. The Styles 1, 2, 3, and 4 keyboard Paganini instruments were made until the late 1920's. Their ornate and elegant appearance combined with the soft and pleasant music produced, made these quite popular. Style 3 with keyboard is illustrated on another page.

 PHILIPPS

Paganini Style 3 — This beautiful Paganini in mahogany wood is owned by Christopher Ross of Victoria, British Columbia. In 1928 his grandfather, R.P. Butchart (founder of Butchart Gardens — one of Canada's prime tourist spots today), visited Germany to select an instrument appropriate for his home. At the Philipps showroom he saw and liked the Style 3 Paganini and ordered one made in a special case with solid wood panels instead of beveled mirrors on the front. Shipping and delivery arrangements were made through the Willis Piano Co. of Victoria. Philipps noted on the order: "Time of delivery to be 2 or 2½ months after date of order. The facetted mirrors will be replaced by wood panels. There will be best workmanship and solid construction to get full satisfaction, hoping to be favored with your further orders."

The illustration is with the upper and lower panels removed in order to show the interior mechanisms. Below is an original Philipps catalogue view of a Style 3.

## PHILIPPS

Philipps Duplex Paganini Violin Orchestra: Model 10 (above left) and 10a (above right). Sold for use in motion picture theatres, the Duplex Paganini Violin Orchestra was produced in two main styles, each of which measured 1.72 meters high by 1.78 meters wide by 1.07 meters deep. Model 10 used two single-roll mechanisms side-by-side; Model 10a, two 6-roll automatic changers (for a total capacity of 12 music rolls) arranged side-by-side.

A Style 3 Paganini Lives Today: Years ago this lovely Style 3 Paganini furnished music to the patrons of a restaurant. Today it is a prized possession in the private collection of Dr. and Mrs. George Coade, California collectors and musical instrument enthusiasts. Situated in the living room of the Coade residence, the instrument has been featured in concerts for the Musical Box Society, the Automatic Musical Instrument Collectors Association, and other groups.

Equipped with a 5-roll automatic changer, the Paganini can play for about an hour without repeating a selection. Most Paganini rolls are of four-tune length. The repertoire of this instrument is varied and ranges from classics such as "The William Tell Overture" and the opera "Martha," to such modern favorites as "Bye Bye Blackbird."

In the left picture Dr. Coade and his three daughters, Caroline, Nancy, and Sarah, watch a Paganini roll unwind on the floor.

## A TALKING ORCHESTRION!

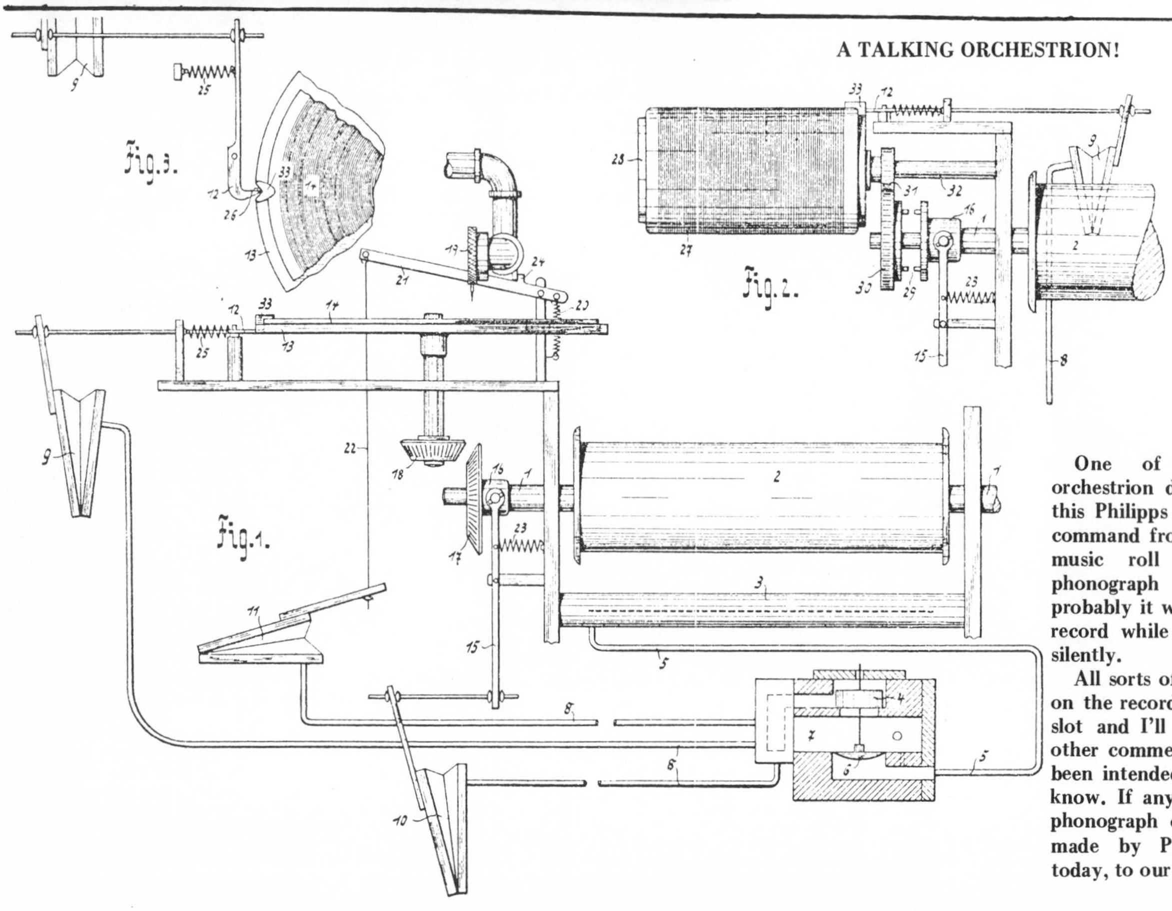

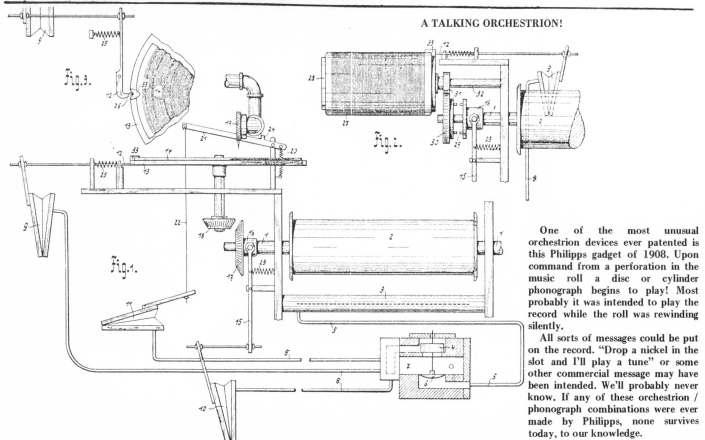

One of the most unusual orchestrion devices ever patented is this Philipps gadget of 1908. Upon command from a perforation in the music roll a disc or cylinder phonograph begins to play! Most probably it was intended to play the record while the roll was rewinding silently.

All sorts of messages could be put on the record. "Drop a nickel in the slot and I'll play a tune" or some other commercial message may have been intended. We'll probably never know. If any of these orchestrion / phonograph combinations were ever made by Philipps, none survives today, to our knowledge.

(No.1)

(No.2)

(No.3)

—Orchestrion Art—

Visual effects were a popular addition to the orchestrions of years ago. In this respect Philipps instruments were outstanding. On this page we illustrate some interesting scenes and other effects from Philipps instruments. All effects are from orchestrions pictured in this book in the Wurlitzer PianOrchestra and Philipps orchestrion sections. Can you identify them?

(No.1) Scene of Mt. Vesuvius from Wurlitzer 30-B Mandolin PianOrchestra; (No.2) Tapestry scene from Wurlitzer Style 32 Concert PianOrchestra; (No.3) Harp-playing goddess from the front panel of the Philipps Pianella Orchestra; (No.4) Wonder light (Philipps called them "Marvel lamps") from a Wurlitzer Style 47 Mandolin PianOrchestra; (No.5) Proud peacock with brilliant tail from a Style 47; (No.6) Also from the Style 47 is this scene of a zeppelin racing a riverboat. Both are mounted on endless cords and are operated by pulleys. (No.7) Wintry snowscape with zeppelin — from Style 28-B Mandolin PianOrchestra sold by Wurlitzer; (No.8) Ancient fountain scene from Style 38-B Wurlitzer Mandolin PianOrchestra.

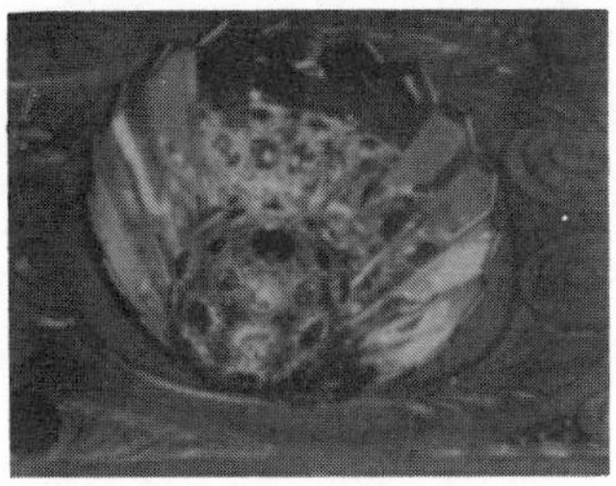

(No.4)

(No.5)

(No.6)

(No.7)

(No.8)

Rhapsodist brand instruments were manufactured (or at least sold by) the Piano Player Manufacturing Company which gave its address at the "foot of Scott Street" in Covington, Kentucky, just across the Ohio River from Cincinnati. In other advertisements the firm listed its name in transposed fashion as the Player Piano Manufacturing Company, and in still other listings the address was given as Cincinnati rather than Covington. Confusing? The confusion is compounded by the fact that there is little in the way of concrete information available about the Piano Player Manufacturing Company.

Rhapsodist coin pianos are similar in many respects to contemporary (circa 1910) Cremona models. One model, the Rhapsodist Style B, is identical (save for a few minor art glass details — see the Cremona section of this Encyclopedia for comparison) to a Cremona piano. It is possible that the Piano Player Manufacturing Company made none of its own instruments but just sold those of others. The notice in a catalogue, "If interested, write at once as the demand is heavy and it may take some little time to fill your order," may indicate that the instruments were obtained elsewhere and then sold under the Rhapsodist label.

The Symphony Automatic Orchestra advertised for theatre use by the firm consists of two Welte Brisgovia Style B-1 orchestrions flanking a theatre stage with a drawn-in artist's conception of a piano in the orchestra pit.

In the absence of information to the contrary we assume that the Piano Player Manufacturing Company did very little manufacturing, and that the name might better have been the "Piano Player Selling Company." Actually, little selling was done either. The one Rhapsodist piano known to the author is indeed a Cremona. The rarity of Rhapsodist instruments indicate that the firm lasted only a short time. The author would welcome correspondence from anyone with more information to offer.

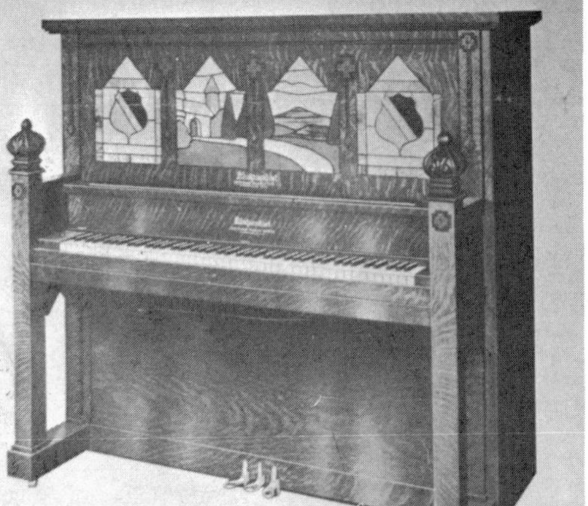

STYLE B

**Coin-operated Electric Piano**

with Mandolin Attachment

STYLE B

**Description**

The only difference between styles A. and B. is the case and art panels. The case is handsome mission and the art panels very pleasing to the eye. This is a very popular style.

Double veneered, mission oak case, illuminated art glass panels, seven and one-third octaves, overstrung full copper wound bass, three unisons throughout. Full iron frame. Brass flange action, German felt hammers. Finest grade ivory keys, polished ebony sharps.

This instrument is equipped with Automatic Mandolin Attachment Improved magazine slot that plays one to twenty nickles. And our patented re-wind machine that practically eliminates all Automatic troubles.

Motor is of the highest grade and furnished either in A. C. or Direct Current. Can be furnished with ten cent slot if so desired, without extra charge.

**Reed Violin Attachment.**

Above Piano is also equipped with our Patented Automatic Reed Violin Attachment, giving Violin effect, if so desired. Prices upon request.

Style B Rhapsodist: Identical (save for a few art glass design details) to the Cremona "Style C — Art" coin piano, this Rhapsodist instrument was probably manufactured by the Marquette Piano Company of Chicago.

# *Rhapsodist Orchestra*

**A perfect Orchestra, to be operated by Perforated Roll or by hand. A very desirable Instrument for Moving Picture Theaters and other places of Amusement.**

**Orchestration**

Full 88 Note Piano, 37 Violin Pipes that are a perfect imitation of the Violin, 25 bar Professional Rosewood Xylophone, Solo Mandolin, Base Drum, Snare Drum, Crash Cymbal and Triangle. Small levers on the right side of keyboard enables you to cut out any of the instruments that you do not wish.

The entire combination of above Orchestra can be played by hand, or Automatically with Perforated Roll.

**Description**

Double veneered, mission oak case, three illuminated art glass panels, two illuminated art lamps, seven and one-third octaves, overstrung full copper wound bass, three unisons throughout. Full iron frame. Brass flange action, German left hammers. Finest grade ivory keys, polished ebony sharps.

This instrument is equipped with Automatic Mandolin Attachment.

Our patented Re-wind Machine makes it an automatic wonder. Supplied with either A. C. or D. C. Motor. When playing, automatically the current is turned off and on with an electric switch, we can however supply it with Magazine Slot Attachment, if so desired, without extra charge.

Rhapsodist Orchestra: This large keyboard orchestrion features a piano, 37 violin pipes, a 25-note xylophone, mandolin attachment, bass drum, snare drum, cymbal, and triangle. The description notes that the instrumental effects may be played by hand (in addition to the regular roll operation), if desired.

STYLE A

Right: Rhapsodist Style A coin piano with mandolin attachment. The description of the Style B (see left) applies also to the Style A, except for the case design. Like the Style B, the Style A appears to be a Cremona instrument.

# THE "SYMPHONY" AUTOMATIC ORCHESTRA

MADE IN ANY SIZE DESIRED.

PLAYED BY HAND OR AUTOMATICALLY WITH PERFORATED ROLL.

**Especially designed for MOVING PICTURE HOUSES, THEATERS, and other Places of Amusement.**

Correspondence Solicited.

Above: The above illustration is an artist's conception of the "Symphony" Automatic Orchestra. The instruments at each side of the stage are Welte Brisgovia Style B-1 orchestrions (see Welte section of this book for more information). It is unknown whether any of these "Symphony" installations were ever made. The catalogue description notes that the "Symphony" orchestras were available in price ranges from $1500 to $20,000. Perhaps it was intended to use a pair of large Welte Concert Orchestrions in the higher priced combinations. Inasmuch as the Rudolph Wurlitzer Company owned 48% of Welte's American interests and the Piano Player Manufacturing Company was selling Welte instruments in America this would seem to imply some type of connection between Wurlitzer and the Piano Player Manufacturing Co., but such a connection, if it ever existed, cannot be verified today.

Left: Violin Rhapsodist was the name of this keyboard piano with violin pipes, xylophone, and mandolin attachment. "Full 88-note piano, 37 violin pipes of the highest quality that perfectly imitate the violin soloist, 25-bar professional rosewood xylophone, and solo mandolin effect. Three small levers on the side of the keyboard enable you to shut off any one of the effects that you do not wish to play" noted the original catalogue.

## PIANOTIST COMPANY
### (Adek Mfg. Co.)

In the 1900 - 1905 era the Pianotist Company, successor to the Adek Manufacturing Company, produced several different models of automatic pianos. "Automatic Piano Co." and "Automaton Piano Co." were among the several other names used by the firm.

The Pianotist was a roll-operated piano which transmitted power to the piano hammers by means of a rotating power roller similar to that used in certain electric typewriters today. A 1903 advertisement noted that the Pianotist Piano Player "operates by foot treadle, electricity, or water motor."

The "Nicklin" Nickel-in-the-Slot piano player, a commercial version of the Pianotist, could be adapted to any upright piano. A 1903 advertisement noted that the Nicklin was the "simplest, most compact, durable and positive acting coin device on the market. Slugs will not operate it. Our customers' receipts range from $12 to $100 weekly." Although the same advertisement noted that "The 'Nicklin' Piano Player is fully protected by Letters Patent of the U.S.A. and others pending; it is manufactured and controlled solely by us," similar instruments were made by others. The leading maker of this general type of instrument was Ludwig Hupfeld of Leipzig, Germany, a firm which made and sold similar instruments beginning in the 1890's.

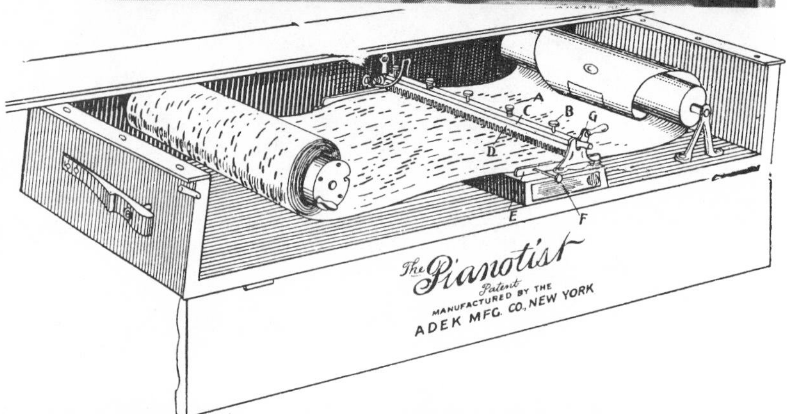

## POPPER & COMPANY
### —Leipzig, Germany—

From the 1890's until shortly after 1930, Popper was one of the world's leading automatic musical instrument firms.

The Popper line of instruments was extensive. In the early days around the turn of the century the instruments were barrel operated. A number of different piano and orchestrion styles were offered. Some of these — the Aida, Danubia, Tonika, and Othello are examples — were offered as late as 1913 - 1914. To distinguish them from the roll-operated "piano orchestrions," catalogues of Popper, Hupfeld, and other firms designated barrel ("Walze" in German) orchestrions as Walzen orchestrions.

Roll operated instruments were made for use in the home, in churches, in restaurants and other locations. The Eroica and Mystikon instruments shown on a following page are typical of those made for the playing of serious or sacred music.

Far more of Popper's instruments went to places of public entertainment. By 1909 Popper advertised that it had "a full line of instruments for public places, including cinema theatres and roller skating rinks."

Smaller Popper instruments included the Stella reproducing pianos for home and (mainly) commercial use, a series of Violin Pianos which imitated the playing of a violin through the medium of pipes, and the very extensive "Welt Piano" series of coin pianos. In the "Welt" series are many different keyboard styles, most of which are decorated with hanging lamps and beveled glass panels. A "design your own" piano section of the Popper catalogue (Hupfeld offered a similar service) enabled the prospective purchaser to pick out a basic upright piano and then add on the top a decorative scene of his choosing, a mirrored panel, a statue or two, or another decorative feature, topping everything by a crest or a railinged gallery.

In response to the jazz era of the 1920's Popper introduced a series of Jazzband Orchestrions. The modernistic cabinet designs of these were in contrast to the ornate painted scene and beveled glass instruments of the preceding decade. Some of these Jazzband Orchestrions had a Swanee Whistle, a type of sliding flute, displayed on the front.

The most spectacular of all Popper instruments were the huge piano orchestrions of the 1900-1920 era. These classic keyboardless instruments ranged from the popular Salon Orchestra, Luna, and similar styles to the immense Gladiator and Goliath. Some of these were made by M. Welte & Sons in Freiburg and were marketed by Popper. Others were made by the Popper firm in its own factory.

These large Popper orchestrions are interesting for some of their unusual effects. The Matador used two different types of music rolls, a violin solo with piano accompaniment roll on one tracker bar and an orchestrion roll on another. The colorful Clarabella featured a mechanical lad who blew real soap bubbles from the front of the instrument to the audience, an early-day version of "champagne music!" The Con Amore orchestrion displayed tiny mechanical birds which fluttered and tweeted while the music roll rewound — so the patrons would not lose attention during this normally-silent period.

In a more mechanical vein, the Popper "Triplex" and 10-roll changer units are interesting. These units feature instant snap-in, snap-out cartridge loading of a new musical program.

At one time Popper & Co. orchestrions were very popular in the Americas. A large export business was conducted by the firm. Many Popper catalogues were multi-lingual and contained descriptions in German, French, English, and Spanish.

The late Eugene DeRoy, an old-timer in the orchestrion business (from the 1920's onward) and a friend of the author since our meeting in 1963, was very fond of Popper orchestrions. One of them, a Gladiator Symphony Orchestrion, played a part in a World War II spy story:

Mr. DeRoy was engaged in the repair and upkeep of band and dance organs, orchestrions, and other automatic instruments. His Antwerp, Belgium, business also made new music rolls for Popper, Hupfeld, Philipps, Weber, and other instruments. Shortly after the German occupation of Belgium he received a notice to report for work in a German aircraft factory. Immediately he "disappeared" and joined the underground forces engaged in gathering intelligence and supplying it to the Allies. To facilitate this work he took an assumed name and traveled from place to place as an itinerant organ repairman.

It might seem strange that such a non-military craft would be allowed by the Germans, but this was due to a partial "hands-off" situation so far as disturbing the musical arts was concerned. As a side note we might mention that when the Welte piano factory in Freiburg, Germany, was converted to the production of gunsights and other war materiel, the production of Welte reproducing piano rolls was allowed to continue in a section of the building!

As a travelling repairman DeRoy kept track of railroad train arrivals and departures. For the Allies it was far better to bomb a railroad station when a train was there loading or unloading, so this information was quite valuable.

At a German military base the troops had commandeered a large Popper Gladiator Symphony Orchestrion for use in a club there. The only trouble was that it wouldn't work. DeRoy, under his alias, was sent for. In Mr. DeRoy's words: "The repair job was a simple one and it could have been done in a few days. However, I liked the surroundings there and it was a good place to get wartime information, so I dragged the job out to take six months. The Germans never knew the difference!"

So much for orchestrion intrigue stories!

On the following pages we illustrate some of the more popular Popper models. Note that Popper followed what we think is the excellent practice of giving names — Gladiator, Oberon, Luna, Iduna, Roland, etc. — to its larger instruments, rather than just catalogue numbers or letters.

Roll mechanism of a Popper & Co. keyboard orchestrion.

## HUGO POPPER

—a biography—

*Hugo Popper, co-founder of Popper & Co. and a leading figure in the Leipzig music industry, died on November 14, 1910. In its issue of November 21, Zeitschrift für Instrumentenbau carried a biography of Hugo Popper as part of his obituary notice. In the same issue Hugo Popper's close friend and business associate, Karl Bockisch (of M. Welte & Sons), wrote: "On the 14th of this month the first chairman of the Society of German Music Manufacturers (Der Verein Deutscher Musikwerkefabrikanten), Mr. Hugo Popper of Leipzig, died. The Society had in him a true and honest member for many years and has lost a valued associate who for a number of years also was a member of its board of directors. The Society had in Hugo Popper a member with distinguished characteristics from both personal and commercial viewpoints, a member who steadily worked in a self-sacrificing and in an unselfish way for the best interests of the Society. His memory will be preserved with honor . . ."*

*The Popper biography/obituary in the same issue was written by Paul Daehne. Translated from the German text by Claes O. Friberg and edited for brevity, it is given herewith:*

Hugo Popper

The history of man is often a happy one — and many wonderful things happen. On the other hand, tragic events occur from time to time. Such a tragic event is the recent death in Leipzig of Hugo Popper. He was brave and fought for his life, but an insidious disease overcame him.

Everyone who knew Hugo Popper regrets the loss of this great and generous man. Through his nature, his talents, and his tireless energy he was an example of a man who used his life fruitfully. Here was a person who would never take advantage of others for his own purposes; he would do what was right for his friends and acquaintances. Here was a great man in his field, that of music.

Hugo Popper had ambitious plans for the future. That he will never fulfill these is something we all regret. At the moment there is no one other person who can take his place to carry on his heritage. The poet realizes the dilemma when he queries: "What are the hopes and the plans that the human being — the transient human being — is building?"

Hugo Louis Popper was born to the family of an Austrian military officer. His home was with the song-loving Bohemians (of whom Smetana and Dvorak have written). At the time when Anton Dvorak was active in Prague's golden era, Hugo Popper was born — on April 21, 1857 in the shadow of the distant Hradschins. As a growing boy, Popper's mind was filled with artistic thoughts and ambitions. He loved the Slavic tunes — their improvisations filled with the splashing of Bohemian mountain streams, secret melancholy, and the enthusiasm of that impassioned race. But his first love was the rhythmic and precisely-played march music of the military band — a special love which would later mean a great deal to him.

Hugo Popper was designated for a military life. It was soon realized that the mind of this young man was far too quick and far too energetic and active to be put into the limits of military thinking. He dreamed of other fields that would be more meaningful to him. One fine day our young soldier took off his military uniform and donned the suit of a businessman.

The world provides endless opportunities for the brave. Conscious of this, Hugo Popper began his ambitious career. His heart was full of initiative and enthusiasm. He looked to the Balkan countries where the culture and surroundings were favorable. In a short time success was his.

It is now [1910] twenty years since this active man amassed a large sum of money. Financially secure, Hugo Popper then had an idea which was to bring him even more success and prosperity. Seeking further intellectual enrichment and a furthering of his business, Popper went from Prague to Leipzig — the central location for industrial exhibitions and the focal point for learned artists and scholars. In Leipzig art and science combined to furnish the inspiration for many successful business enterprises. Leipzig was indeed the right place for Hugo Popper! His energy, his fantastic intelligence, and his character soon made him welcome in the highest places.

In 1891 Popper met another active man, Hugo Spangenberg, who became his business partner. (Spangenberg has since died.) At the time of its founding the firm of Popper & Co. specialized in the export of merchandise to the Oriental countries. An important turn of events was brought about by the great progress in manufacturing mechanical musical instruments in Leipzig during the early 1890's. Popper became aware of the great activity in the musical field and turned his efforts in this direction. In the year 1897 the firm was listed in Paul DeWit's "Adressbuch für Musikinstrumentenbranche."

Popper understood the events of the time and could see a bright future ahead. Such vision accounted for his success. Suddenly there was an enormous demand for Polyphons [disc-type music boxes]. The factory could hardly keep up with the demands of the marketplace. This was the golden age of the music box, and Popper's distributorship of Polyphons produced a great profit. At the beginning he worked together with the firms of H. Peters & Co. and Etzold & Popitz by handling much of their sales and advertising. Their businesses prospered with Popper's help. He secured the agency for the musical products of Racca [mechanical piano manufacturer of Bologna] and sold Racca instruments at such a fast rate that the factory could not keep pace with all of his orders!

Inside Hugo Popper a fire was burning. With each success the flame burned still brighter. Now that his business was in excellent order the artistic spirit moved and stimulated him. At this time he met with Karl Bockisch and Edwin Welte of the famous firm of M. Welte & Sons of Freiburg. These three men agreed to work together on a certain project. They envisioned a wonderful thing: a self-contained reproducing piano which would record and then play again all of the compositions of the great masters; an instrument which could record and reproduce the temperament and characteristics of the world's foremost pianists. Truly this was an admirable idea, but it was very hard to see how this would be carried out in actual practice. If such a device could be made it would mean that the playing of artists — something which would normally vanish into the air — would be preserved so as to be available to the most distant people in future centuries.

This is not the place to tell about all of the possibilities that such an invention would mean. Why describe an instrument that now can speak for itself? The inventors achieved a wonderful cultural success through the creation of the incomparable 'Mignon' instrument — truly a work of magic — which reproduced the musical geniuses for all generations to enjoy. The technical part of the 'Mignon' was the work of Bockisch and Welte in Freiburg.

Now there arose another problem which could only be solved in a very delicate way: how would the most prominent musicians and musical masters receive the 'Welte-Mignon?' The inventors' minds had done something wonderful. Good! Wouldn't the prominent composers and the famous pianists be distrustful of a competitor? Would they look with interest on the 'Mignon' or would they turn away from it so that it would be unsuccessful and soon forgotten? Hugo Popper was a man of charm and courtesy. He was the right one to interest the artists in the new invention and to present the 'Mignon' from its most favorable viewpoint.

The greatest pianists followed Hugo Popper's invitation to come to Leipzig. They all heard and liked the 'Mignon' — and they became eager to give a part of their own performance to this instrument. In the recording salon of Popper & Co. in Leipzig many of the foremost pianists of the world met. Their recommendations, thoughts, and emotions about the 'Mignon' were all inscribed in a book which stands as a document of honor to the inventors.

In Hugo Popper's private gallery in his home there are many photographs of prominent 'Mignon' artists, each of whom has inscribed a personal sentiment. This is indeed a lofty collection: all of the great musical personalities are represented. Whom should we mention? They are all great! D'Albert, Busoni, Carreño, Dohnanyi, Annette Essipoff, Friedheim, Gabrilowitsch, the two Grünfelds, Hambourg, Humperdinck, Kienzl, Clotilde Kleeberg, Lamond, Leoncavallo, Mahler, Sofie Menter, Sarasate's friend Berte Marx, Neitzel, Elly Ney, Nikisch, Pachmann, Paderewski, Pugno, Reger, Reisenauer, Reinecke, Alice

Ripper, Saint-Saëns, Sapellnikoff, Sauer, Scharwenka, Schillings, Georg Schumann, Richard Strauss, Weingartner, and many others are represented!

An instrument that is closely related to the 'Mignon' and which serves the same purpose and which utilizes the same recording apparatus, but which has a different repertoire of artists' recordings, was built by Popper in his own factory. It is called the 'Stella' reproducing piano.

For his business Hugo Popper had the insight to acquire the most important technical patents and to employ people who could carry out his ideas. Popper was generous, never small-minded. He lived a joyful life in a grand style. He loved to see happy people around him. His vision and fairness produced many benefits for his employees. He valued his employees and associates highly and treated them with respect. In turn they were very loyal and followed his guidance.

When most men reach the plateau of success that was Popper's they would rest and say that they were satisfied. Not so with Hugo Popper. His ambition was to achieve even more. Besides working on numerous small inventions (not all of which were useful to his business) he spent a great deal of time thinking about orchestrions. He remembered his earlier days in Prague. He remembered all of the wonderful music and the sounds of the military orchestras, and he reproduced these sounds in some of the orchestrions he built – the Gladiator, for example. His earlier experiences in Vienna also helped to inspire these instruments. For their excellent playing of dances and waltzes Popper & Co. orchestrions are especially loved today. They have found many buyers – especially in America where the melodies from the old world are acknowledged and appreciated.

Hugo Popper's mind was filled with many ideas. Seeking to create something new and artistic, he built the 'Mystikon' and 'Eroica.' The first is a reproducing harmonium, and the second is a reproducing pipe organ. How we remember the wonderful times we have spent in Leipzig with Hugo Popper in his home, where we have completely forgotten about the world outside. He had a magnificent mansion furnished with elegant and artistic accessories, including a number of his own musical instruments. When going from one room to another you would see the golden ornaments, the statues, the flowers, and the wonderful paintings. Here in a completely noiseless room the genius of the instruments would play for us. Now we hear the flutes. Then suddenly comes the magnificent crescendo with the flaming brilliance of string voices! We are listening to the 'Mystikon!' We enjoy the sweet sound of the love song of Tristan and Isolde, Professor Bie's masterpiece. And then we hear the voices of the forest, the sweet singing of birds, and then Siegfried's horn sounding with joy, and then we dream the fantasy of the deep forest open before us – with sparkling shafts of sunlight, with bright flowers, with many wonderful things. What an inspiring experience!

And then we hear in this music room the rich choir voices of the 'Eroica' – fantastic, monumental, majestic! Far from the distractions of the ordinary concert hall we enjoyed these musical reveries provided by the instruments in Mr. Popper's personal collection. All of the instruments – veritable artists – seemed to perform for us and only for us. This seems impossible, but it was true. We heard their innermost feelings without which no real art would have been possible. We felt the vibrato of their very souls.

All of the Popper instruments, things of the highest creative order, fulfill a noble mission. For instance, in the far-away districts of the La Plata states it is difficult for churchgoers to obtain an organist. The 'Mystikon' reproduces for them the recordings of the world's foremost organ players. Overshadowed by towering palms 'Mystikon' instruments play in the Brazilian jungle!

By means of another invention Hugo Popper helped to create one's dreams. This instrument has a violin and mandolin with a piano accompaniment. The musical character is very delicate; the soul of the violin and mandolin have been reproduced perfectly. Everyone who has heard a melody played on this wonderful instrument considers it to be wonderful. The instrument, playing with soul and grace, resounds in our hearts. Close your eyes and you will see the high rocks of Sorrento, you will have an adventure on the Grand Canal of Venice, you will thrill to the serenades by Santa Maria della Salute. This was Popper's last achievement!

What Hugo Popper has done for the interests of the German musical industry will never be forgotten. Largely due to his efforts the industry has achieved its present high position. He was truly a leader in our field. Therefore he was also worthy of the presidency of the German committee for the International Industrial Exposition at Turin in 1911. As leader of the musical instrument division he did a large amount of work. But now someone else will have to complete it.

Shortly before the Michael's Fair in 1910 a heart and arterial disease struck this brave man. He who had given so much sunshine and happiness to others had to be hospitalized and later had to die. Hugo Popper departed the world with the knowledge that he had accomplished something great and that many people would thank him. He died with his brother-in-law Herman Möhle and his good friend Hermann Feurich at his side. His widow and six children kept him company until the very end.

Mr. Möhle and Mr. Bruno Kirsten, presently in the employ of the Popper firm, plan to continue the business in its finest traditions until Hugo Popper's eldest son is old enough to take over his father's enterprise.

At the funeral Mr. Karl Bockisch told of Hugo Popper and his accomplishments. Those who have been Hugo Popper's friends over the years will always remember this great man.

———————

Above: Two advertisements for Popper violin-playing instruments with real violins. The top advertisement notes that the Popper Welt-Piano Konzertist "with real violin" will be exhibited at the Leipzig Spring Fair in 1930. The lower advertisement dates from 1931 and features the Violinovo violin-player. The Violinovo was extensively advertised in 1930 and 1931.

Above: Popper Triumph orchestrion in modern case. Popper assigned names (rather than just model numbers) to its larger orchestrions. Instrument names included Titania, Trompeter, Extra, Helvetia, Viola, Arion, Verdi, Perfect, Artist, Mimosa, Regina, and others – many of which are shown on these pages. In 1904 Popper advertised that over forty different orchestrion models were available from the firm! In addition to instruments made in its own factory the Popper firm sold many Welte orchestrions. The Welte orchestrions were incorporated into the Popper catalogues and were given distinctive Popper names (which differed from Welte's designations for the same instruments).

Certain Popper names, Triumph for instance, were used over a long span of years and were applied to several different types of instruments. Early Popper Triumph orchestrions were barrel-operated; later styles were pneumatically-operated and were modern in design (as shown above).

# Popper & Co.

## BARREL-OPERATED PIANOS AND ORCHESTRIONS

Mandolin (Barrel) Piano

Phadra II

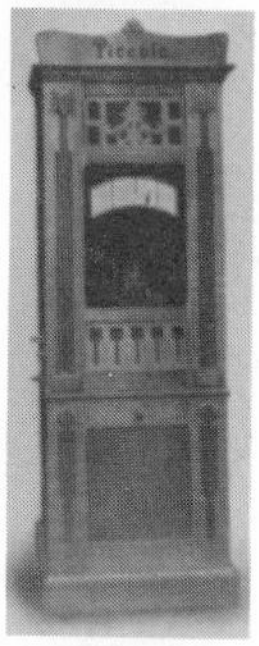

Piccolo

Aida Luxus No.2

Danubia

Aurora

Tonika

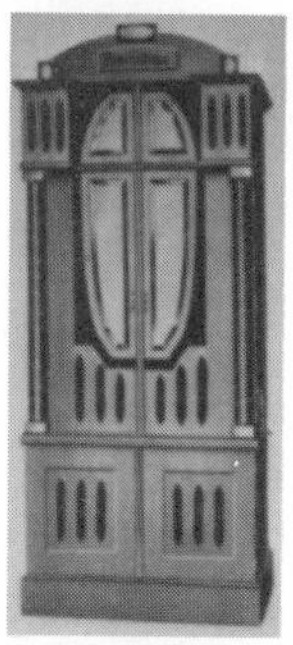

Bravissimo

Othello

Lola

Triumph

Popper Barrel Pianos and Orchestrions: Barrel-operated instruments as described in the September 1, 1913, Popper catalogue. Prices charged (in German marks – to obtain approximate dollar equivalent at the time divide by four; hence 1600 Mk = $400) for each style were: Mandolin Walz (barrel) Piano 1930 Mk.; Phadra II 1640 Mk. with bass drum or 1600 Mk. without this feature; Piccolo 680 Mk.; Aida Luxus No.2 2350 Mk.; Danubia 1760 Mk.; Aurora 1450 Mk.; Tonika 860 Mk.; Bravissimo 1600 Mk.; Othello 1250 Mk.; Lola 1350 Mk.; Triumph 1560 Mk. Extra barrels, usually of six tunes per barrel, ranged in price from 50 marks for the Piccolo to 165 marks for the Aida Luxus (which means "DeLuxe") No.2. Each instrument was furnished with two barrels as part of the purchase price.

Popper Othello Orchestrion: The original catalogue description follows: "Mechanical piano orchestrion with mandolin and xylophone. Othello is delivered in a tasteful case with painted glass panels and contains 31 piano keys, 18 of which operate also the mandolin, 10 xylophone keys, drum, cymbals, and triangle. Othello is delivered with two barrels, playing 6 different tunes. The tune can easily be changed by turning a handle. The second barrel can be stored in the lower part of the case. By special arrangement every tune may be played 1 to 5 times after insertion of one coin. Very moderate price! Othello offers a beautiful, strong, and varied musical output on account of the instrumentation it contains." (J.B. Nethercutt Collection; Lewis Graham photo)

# Popper & Co.

(No.1)

(No.2)

(No.3)

(No.4)

(No.5)

Note: The numbers on this page are OUR numbers (not Popper's) and are for the use of readers who may want to refer to them. Most were unnumbered by Popper.

(No.6)

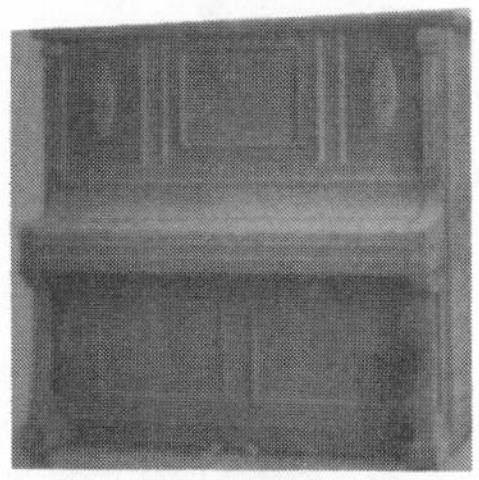
(No.7)

(No.8)

**POPPER REPRODUCING PIANOS**

Shown here are eight different case styles of the "Stella" reproducing piano made by Popper. Most were designed for use in public locations where they were operated by coin wallboxes. "The music selections are artists' recordings captured accurately by an apparatus of the greatest technical perfection and rendered on the Stella reproducing piano in an exact manner with all of the finenesses and characteristic qualities."

**POPPER VIOLIN PIANOS**

(No.9)

(No.10)

(No.11)

(No.12)

(No.15)

(No.13)

Popper Violin Pianos: Instrumentation of these tall and attractive keyboard instruments is described as follows (from the original catalogue): "Best natural imitation of violin playing. A better class instrument. Violin solos are accompanied by the piano, allowing even the most difficult violin concertos to be performed with technical perfection. A mandolin attachment produces a most agreeable variation in the musical combination." The catalogue also noted (exclamation points courtesy of the Popper copy writer): "Requires tuning rarely! Artistically arranged music!"

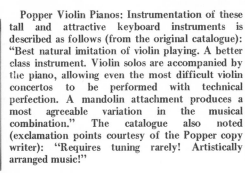

(No.14)

RECORD PIANO: An under-the-keyboard attachment and interior mechanisms which "require but little space and provide excellent music. Excellent expression." The unit could be ordered built into a piano case (as illustrated to the left) made by Popper, or the mechanisms could be attached separately to another piano.

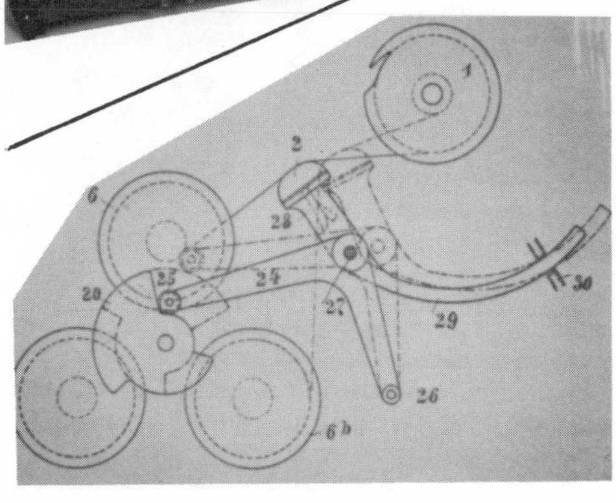


Popper "Triplex" Roll System: Patented on March 7, 1911 (see patent drawing at left) the Triplex unit holds three music rolls and plays them one after the other. For a fast change of program the entire Triplex mechanism can be easily removed and replaced with another Triplex unit with three different rolls on it. The Triplex was an optional "extra" on most Popper instruments and cost about $75 additional. The No.15 Violin Piano at the upper right is equipped with a Triplex unit. In actuality, few Triplex units were ever sold.

Above: "Eroica" reproducing organ designed for church use. Plays artists' rolls and sets the registers automatically. Illustration circa 1909.

Right: "Mystikon," a large roll operated harmonium (reed organ) which was also primarily intended for use in churches and similar places. Used hand played rolls (recorded by performing artists).

# Popper & Co.

## POPPER "WELT" PIANOS

(No.1)

(No.2)

(No.3)

(No.4)

(No.5)

(No.6)

(No.7)

(No.8)

(No.9)

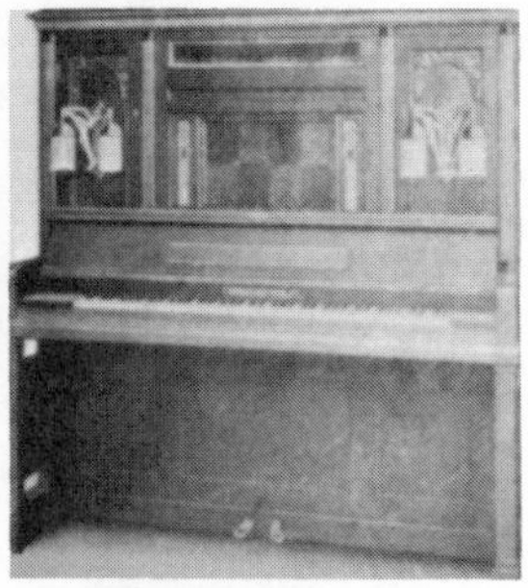

(No.10)

Popper "Welt" Pianos: "Welt," which means "world" in German, was the name given to a series of keyboard pianos and orchestrions. Those illustrated in this section of this page, our numbers 1 to 10 inclusive, are with piano and mandolin or with piano, mandolin, and xylophone. As instrumentation was never tied to rigid standards, some were made on special order with drums and other percussion effects. Most were coin operated by means of remotely-located wallboxes. German pianos (all makes) rarely had built-in coin slots.

(No.11)

(No.12)

Larger "Welt" Pianos: The three in this section are instrumented with piano, mandolin effect, xylophone, and, in the top section, one or two drums, a cymbal, and a triangle. The scenes are illuminated from behind and show moving effects such as fountains and waterfalls.

(No.13)

(No.14)

(No.15)

No.14, the DeLuxe Superba model, and No.15, the Salon Superba, were built with what the late Eugene DeRoy described as: "A separate unit with zither or mandolin strings played by a special attachment. This device was in the top part of the case. After they had been on the market for a time, the service problems became so great that later models of these omitted the gadget."

In addition each of the Superba pianos had a horizontally mounted xylophone that was visible through a rectangular beveled glass window above the roll door.

(No.16)

Left: Poppers "Welt Piano Style O" – Orchestrion with piano, mandolin, one rank of pipes, xylophone, drums and traps. Automatic "motion picture effect" scenery.

Right: "Phonoradio" – One of the last Popper & Co. products, the Phonoradio was intended to combine the appeal of the piano with that of the radio. At the time of the introduction of the Phonoradio in the 1920's the radio was giving serious competition to coin pianos in public places. The two-for-one Phonoradio offered the listener a choice. The piano part of the one illustrated at the right had a mandolin attachment. Phonoradios were also made with orchestrion interiors.

(No.17)

(No.18)

(No.19)

Two more Superba styles (see description above). The xylophone in these instruments can play solo effects as it operates from its own set of perforations on the Superba roll. Embellished with large beveled mirror panels, two statues, and four electric lamps with glass bead fringes, these Superba pianos are beautiful as well as melodious.

(No.20)

(No.21)

(No.22)

(No.23)

These Popper coin pianos of the 1920's have modern-appearing cases. Note that No.20 is made by adding a top case extension to No.21 – the bottom parts are identical. No.20 has a painted panel with three musicians and the lettering "The Happy Jazzband." The case extensions on top of the instruments contain drum and trap effects. Some were made with one or two ranks of pipes in addition. Note the virtual identity of No.22 with No.17, the Phonoradio. No.22 was originally catalogued as: "Welt Piano with jazz band percussion effects in top extension."

# Popper & Co.

## CLASSIC PIANO ORCHESTRIONS

(No.1) Bianca

(No.2) Bianca

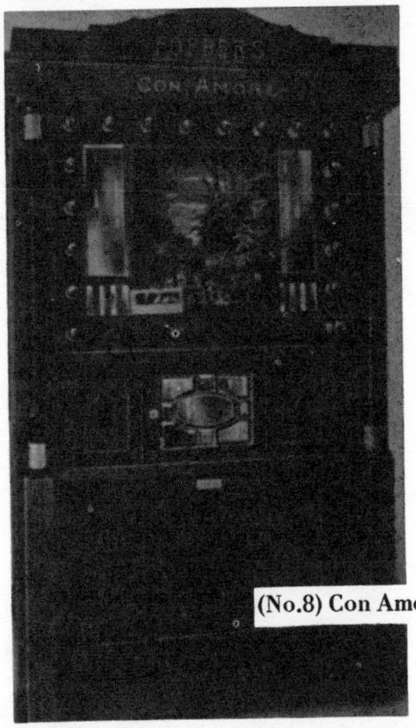

(No.8) Con Amore

(No.9) Matador

(No.3) Ohio

(No.4) Oberon

(No.5) Violin Piano

(No.6)Puck

(No.7) Carmina

## POPPER ORCHESTRIONS (Mostly 1912 - 1920)

(No.1) (No.2) Bianca model. With piano, mandolin, xylophone, bells, drums, triangle, cymbal. Recommended for "dance and concert purposes." Two case designs shown.

(No.3) Jazzband Orchestrion "Ohio." From the 1920's. About 10' high; weight 2300 pounds. Contains piano, imitation banjo (a 1920's description of what was earlier a mandolin attachment), violin, violoncello, saxophone, flex-a-tone, and complete set of jazz drums and traps.

(No.4) Oberon. Called a "Xylophone - Orchestrion." With piano, mandolin, xylophone, bells, violin and cello pipes, bass and snare drums, cymbal, and triangle.

(No.5) Violin Piano with Mandolin. Keyboardless style. Piano, mandolin, violin pipes.

(No.6) Puck. Contains piano with vibrating hammers.

(No.7) Carmina. Piano, mandolin, bells, drums, triangle, cymbal. Xylophone optional.

(No.8) Con Amore. With piano, mandolin, several ranks of pipes, drums, and traps. "Amidst a southern landscape well represented by plastic palms, beautiful birds with charming movements of their heads and beaks are twittering during the rerolling of the music rolls."

(No.9) Matador. With two tracker bars using two different types of rolls (Ed. note: a very unusual situation in the annals of orchestrions) — one for piano and violin solos and the other for full orchestrion effects. With optional remote control unit for operation from the projectionist's booth in movie theatres.

(No.10) Diva. Piano, mandolin, bells, several ranks of pipes, drums, triangle, cymbal. With extra loud voicing for use in skating rinks and dance halls.

(No.11) Clarabella. Piano, mandolin, xylophone, bells, drums, triangle, cymbal. On some models a figure of a boy mechanically blows soap bubbles on the front!

(No.12) Extra. Piano, mandolin, violin pipes. Uses "Stella" reproducing rolls.

(No.13) Iduna. Piano, mandolin, several ranks of pipes, xylophone, bells, drums, triangle, cymbal. "A first class concert orchestra suitable also for dancing."

(No.14) Luna. Piano, mandolin, xylophone, bells, several pipe ranks, drums, triangle, cymbal. "A most remarkable concert orchestrion."

(No.15) Rex 1920. One of the first "modern" case designs. Piano, mandolin, xylophone, violin and cello pipes, bells, drums, and traps. Orchestration the same as the Salon Orchestra No.1. "1920" is part of the instrument name — it was sold as the "Rex 1920."

Note: With the exception of the Ohio and the Rex 1920, these instruments are from Popper's catalogues of 1912 and 1913. The tiny Puck is similar in sound to the Wurlitzer Mandolin Quartette.

The arrangements on Popper & Co. orchestrion rolls are excellent, for the most part, and collectors today consider Popper instruments to be among the finest orchestrions ever produced.

(No.10) Diva

(No.11) Clarabella

(No.12) Extra

(No.13) Iduna

(No.14) Luna

(No.15) Rex 1920

1905 exhibit of Popper & Co. orchestrions held by agent Carl Schmitt in Hagen, Germany. The large orchestrions are, left to right: Puck in deluxe case, Aurora, Vindobona (mostly concealed behind the entry post), Con Amore (in Moorish case), Luna (the large white instrument), and Ben Akiba. Certain of these were made by M. Welte & Sons and were marketed by Popper — thus accounting for the resemblance between these and certain Welte Brisgovia orchestrions (mainly sold c.1908-1914).

1907 Popper & Company advertisement featuring the Arcophon ("the first 'string piano' with hand playing"), the Animochord ("the first real string orchestrion" — with violin, viola, and cello and with the accompaniment of a Feurich piano), and the Mignon reproducing piano. The Mignon reproducing piano was offered by special arrangement with M. Welte & Söhne of Freiburg.

Two Popper orchestrion models offered in 1902: the Tonika (top illustration) and the Stella.

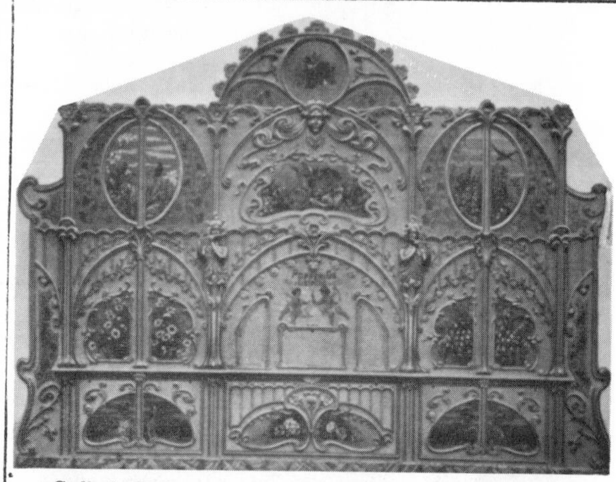

Goliath Orchestrion: In 1910 Popper & Co. introduced the Goliath orchestrion as shown above. With a dance-organ-style facade measuring 6.50 meters wide by 4.55 meters deep, the instrument was made to compete with dance organs in Belgium and Holland. "It plays like an orchestra of 60 performers" noted the original advertisement. The instrument depicted above was sold to the Mille Colonnes Restaurant in The Hague, Holland.

1906 advertisement offering: "New — Gigantic Concert Orchestrion for 30,000 Marks — New!"

# Popper & Co.

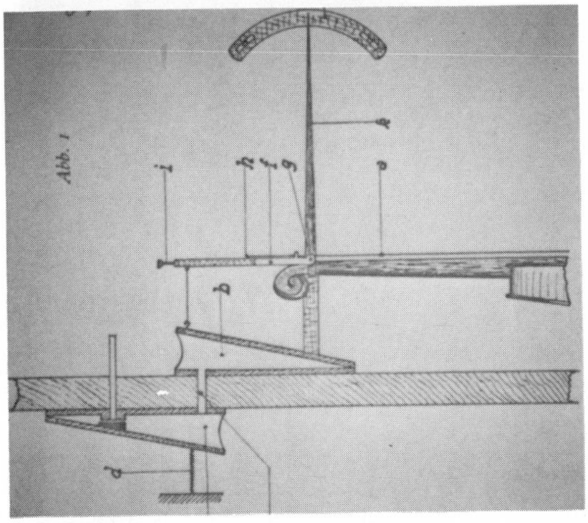


Left: 1930 Popper patent drawing for a device for varying the tension on a violin string. A violin-playing instrument, the Violinovo, was heavily advertised by Popper around this time. However, few instruments were actually sold — for the market for automatic instruments was in its final stage.

The author's search of U.S., German, and other patent office records revealed that literally dozens of different applications were made for violin-playing devices. The only two commercially successful violin players (thousands of each were sold) were the Mills Violano-Virtuoso and the Hupfeld Phonoliszt-Violina.

Popper Salon Orchestra No. 3. Contains the same instrumentation as Salon Orchestra No. 1. "No.3 is furnished with the patented Popper's ten-roll arrangement for the rapid change of music rolls. By pressing a button or inserting a coin all music pieces of the ten rolls of the magazine can be played one after another. The music pieces on each roll are visible from the outside behind a pane of glass. Any desired music roll may be played at will by means of a selector device. The magazine may be changed easily. The complete magazine of 10 rolls may be removed from the instrument and replaced with another one containing ten more rolls."

This device, patented in Germany (No.278554) on August 30, 1913, is one of the most ingenious and practical roll handling devices ever produced for an automatic musical instrument. $200 was the extra charge to install this mechanism on a Popper orchestrion. For some reason — and it probably wasn't the cost, for the extra-cost Wurlitzer and Philipps roll changers sold very well — only a few of these ingenious Popper 10-roll units were produced.

**ANATOMY OF A SALON ORCHESTRA No.1** — Manufactured from about 1912 until well into the 1920's, this was one of the most popular Popper orchestrion models ever made. Instrumentation consists of a piano, mandolin, xylophone, bells, bass and snare drums, cymbal, and triangle. An extended rank of pipes is arranged in a double row and represents violin and cello. Some units (such as the one illustrated at the right — from the Nethercutt Collection) have a harmonium as well.

In the top of the case are louvered swell shutters for expression effects. The front is a "motion picture effect" scene which is backlighted and shows two waxing and waning torches in the marble patio of an ancient Roman villa. The Salon Orchestra No.1 measures 9'6" high by 6' wide by 3'3" deep. (Photograph, as are several others in this book, by Harold Woodworth of the Whittier, Cal., Daily News.)

# Popper & Co.

Roland

This very large orchestrion is one of the latest made by Popper & Co. Dating from the late 1920's the instrument reflects the modern case designs used on smaller models of the period.

Measuring about eleven feet high, the orchestrion is immense by any standard. The featured solo instrument is the Swanee Whistle mounted in a niche on the front. Above this device a series of recessed panels constantly changes colors (the light changes are actuated by a belt-driven switch tripping unit located within the case). Other instrumentation includes piano, mandolin, ranks of pipes including a large rank of saxophones, and drum and trap effects.

The market for large orchestrions of all kinds was very limited in Europe and America during the 1920's, and only small numbers were sold in comparison to the sales figures of the preceding decade. Those made in Europe often had a "jazz" theme either in the instrumentation (for instance, the saxophone is the most prominent pipe rank in the above orchestrion) or in the name of the machine (such as "Jazzband Orchestrion").

By the late 1920's large orchestrions were noncompetitive. Costing thousands of dollars and requiring a large room in order to be used effectively they were overwhelmed by the competition of radios (which cost a few hundred dollars at most) and, during the early 1930's, of coin operated disc phonographs.

(Above instrument from the J.B. Nethercutt Collection)

Protos

The Roland (above) and Protos (left) are keyboard orchestrions from the 1920's. The modernistic styling is probably due to the Bauhaus architectural influence of that period. Some of the Philipps Jazzband Pianos are quite similar in appearance (although without the Swanee Whistle).

The Swanee Whistle (trademarked name) or, as it was described in the sales literature, the lotus flute, is prominently mounted in full view on the front of each of these models.

Inside the Popper Roland Orchestrion: These illustrations are from the Roland pictured at the upper left of this page. To the left is a closeup view of the Swanee Whistle. A sliding stopper, connected by the rod extending from the bottom of the flute, moves up and down and varies the pitch. Above is seen the upper inside portion of the Roland, showing a rank of violin pipes, drums, and other effects.

How the Swanee Whistle works: At the upper right the heart of the system can be seen. A series of pneumatics, one for each playing note, is connected to the upper range of the piano notes. Each pneumatic has a different spacing and is connected to a common bar by a small cord. When several pneumatics collapse at once, the bar is pulled down the distance of the widest-spaced pneumatic in the series. Spacing increases in size from the lowest to the highest note, so the highest note is the one that determines how far the bar will be pulled down. By means of a connecting cord, power assisted by being wrapped around a continually rotating capstan, the rod in the Swanee Whistle is pushed up an appropriate distance — and sounds the desired note. Thus the Swanee Whistle solo follows the highest note throughout a musical passage.

# Popper & Co.

## LARGE PIANO ORCHESTRIONS

(No.1) DeLuxe Salon Orchestra

(No.2) Gladiator No.2

(No.3) Gladiator No.1

(No.4) Simson

(No.5) Salon Orchestra No.2

(No.6) Simson

(No.1) DeLuxe Salon Orchestra. Piano, mandolin, xylophone, bells, pipes representing flute, violin, and clarinet in ranges from bass to treble, drums, and trap effects.

(No.2) Gladiator No. 2. The Gladiator was made in several case styles, three of which are shown on this page. Instrumentation is similar for all.

(No.3) Gladiator No.1. Piano, mandolin, bells, several ranks of pipes, extensive drum and trap effects. Xylophone available at extra cost. "A first class concert orchestrion suitable also for dance halls." This is a style of the early 1920's.

(Nos. 4 and 6) Simson. Piano, mandolin, bells, pipes representing flute, violin, and clarinet, xylophone (at extra charge), drums, and traps.

(No.5) Salon Orchestra No. 2. Called a "Drawing Room Orchestrion" by Popper in its English catalogues. With piano, xylophone, bells, several pipe ranks, drums, triangle, and cymbal. Salon Orchestras were especially recommended for drawing rooms and clubs. They had a very warm and mellow sound.

Note: The reader interested in classic orchestrions of this period will find a comparison of Popper cases to Hupfeld and Philipps (also Wurlitzer, who sold Philipps) cabinets to be interesting. For instance, No.6 on this page is almost the twin of a Wurlitzer Mandolin PianOrchestra Style 33 (which was made by Philipps).

These huge Popper orchestrions, once made by the hundreds, are exceedingly rare today.

(No.7) Gladiator

(No.7) Gladiator Symphony Orchestrion. Piano, mandolin, xylophone, bells, piccolo flute, violin pipes, muted strings, violin solo, clarinet, flute, violoncello, viola, horn, bass flute, trombone, bass violin, bass, snare drum, kettle drum, cymbals, and triangle. 11'4" high, 14'2" wide, 4'8" deep. Four of these were sold in Belgium in the late 1920's, one of which was later owned by the author.

(No.8) Goliath

(No.8) Goliath. With lighted beacon beckoning like the Alexandria Lighthouse of ancient times, the Goliath was one of the largest orchestrions ever made anywhere. Standing 13' high and about as wide, and weighing 6200 pounds, the instrument contained just about every effect ever put in a piano orchestrion. Some of the stopped bass pipes and bass trumpets in this and in the Gladiator Symphony Orchestrion are from six to eight feet in length. It is not known how many Goliaths were made. Eugene DeRoy, who was familiar with most aspects of the orchestrion business in Europe from about 1920 onward, never saw one of this style.

# REGINA MUSIC BOX COMPANY

—Rahway, New Jersey—

Note: This section covers the coin-operated pianos sold by the Regina Music Box Company. For Regina disc-type music boxes see the Regina music box section of this book.

## Introduction

The Regina Music Box Company, America's dominant firm in the disc music box field, began selling coin-operated pianos shortly after 1900. These pianos are in three main categories:

(1) The Regina Concerto, a disc-operated piano which uses 32" diameter tune sheets, is covered in the Regina music box section of this book.

(2) A number of paper roll operated pianos were purchased from American firms and were sold under the Reginapiano and Regina Piano Player names.

(3) The Regina Sublima, made in several forms, was Regina's leading entry in the coin piano field.

Shortly after 1900, Regina sensed that the disc music box business was waning. Coin-operated Regina disc boxes were immensely popular during the late 1890's, but after about 1905 the demand fell sharply. More popular were the 44-note coin pianos made by Peerless, Wurlitzer, and other firms and the then-new keyboard pianos made by the same firms. To gain a foothold in this market Regina purchased coin pianos from Polyphon, Marquette, Peerless, and possibly a few other firms — and marketed them under the Regina name.

Regina based its greatest piano selling efforts on the Sublima Piano, an instrument which was mechanically operated (instead of pneumatically) and which used a very heavy manila paper roll. By 1912 the Sublima was unable to compete effectively with the wide variety of thin paper roll instruments being sold by Seeburg, Wurlitzer, and other firms. Had Regina developed a series of paper roll pianos and orchestrions the firm undoubtedly would have shared in the fantastic market for such instruments before and during the World War I years. Regina didn't do so, and although Sublima Pianos were shipped from the factory as late as 1921, Regina was an insignificant force in the market after about 1910.

## The Regina Sublima Piano & Mandolin Orchestra

The Regina Sublima Piano (not to be confused with certain Regina disc boxes which also used the "Sublima" name) is a mechanical piano. Most were equipped with a large and powerful spring motor which had to be wound by hand after several tunes were played. Some were equipped with electric motors.

The five-tune roll, usually made of green-colored very heavy manila paper (to withstand the force of the metal fingers which "read" the holes) is pressed against the metal keys of the mechanical action by a slotted wooden roller. When one of the metal keys enters a hole in the roll it actuates the mechanism for a piano hammer. The hammer then reiterates or continually vibrates against its piano strings while the key remains in the note hole in the roll. The music produced is somewhat like a mandolin.

The mechanisms vary from model to model. Some have a single-stroke piano action (the hammer strikes the string once for each time a hole appears in the roll) combined with a reiterating action that can be turned on or off by a lever on the right side of the instrument. Most Sublimas are equipped with loud-soft levers.

Early models of the Sublima were imported from the Polyphon Musikwerke of Leipzig, Germany. Included among the imported styles was one model which measures about 8' high and which has a rotating drum at the top on which are affixed advertising cards or scenes. Sublima Pianos of Polyphon origin were made of walnut or oak. When the Sublima's success became apparent, Regina imported only the piano plate (and strings) and the mechanical piano action from Polyphon and manufactured the cabinets in its Rahway factory. All Regina Sublimas seen by the author have German-made pianos (identifiable by German notations on the scale — such as the German "Dis" instead of the American "D sharp").

Manufacture of Sublima Pianos with American-made cabinets evidently commenced after November, 1904, for all specimens seen have 7-digit serial numbers, the Regina system employed after that date. Shipment of these instruments began in 1906 and reached its peak in the 1907 - 1912 years, although previously-made Sublimas were shipped until 1921.

Most models were sold as the "Regina Sublima Piano." Some were sold as the "Sublima Piano, Jr." Many of those with the reiterating mechanism controlled by an on-off lever were sold as the "Regina Sublima Piano & Mandolin Orchestra" — a name that must have sounded quite impressive to the original buyers! The Rudolph Wurlitzer Company sold some Sublimas under the "Wurlitzer Tremolo Piano" name.

An advertisement for the Sublima noted: "SOME DEALERS WOULD BE SURPRISED if they knew about the profits that other dealers are making with Reginas. Take for instance the Regina Coin Operated Instruments. They are sleepless and tireless in their earning capacity, and dealers who have handled them do not hesitate to praise their money-getting qualities in the most enthusiastic terms.

"A REGINA product which is just now attracting wide attention is the Sublima Piano, Jr. The illustration will give a fair idea of its external appearance, but the instrument must be heard and examined to appreciate all of its merits. The Sublima, Jr. is built along new and original lines, and we have in its manufacture attained a degree of perfection in the way of EXPRESSION which is not duplicated in any other mechanical instrument on the market. It plays upon PIANO STRINGS by means of a large roll of heavy and very durable paper, the power being furnished either by spring motor or electric motor as desired. It will pay you to at once investigate the merits of this instrument, which is the latest Regina product, as territory is being rapidly assigned for its sale."

The Sublima was made in several different models and case styles. They are listed below. The serial numbers are, as noted previously, in the 7-digit series. For instance, serial number 3010001 on an instrument would mean that the instrument is a Style 301 Sublima and the particular instrument was number 0001 among those made.

STYLE 301 REGINA SUBLIMA PIANO: Serially numbered from 3010001 to 3011192, but with many numbers omitted in the sequence. About 100 made. Shipped from the factory from 1906 to 1918, but mainly in the earlier years. No. 3010019 was shipped on January 14, 1907, to the Polyphon Musikwerke in Leipzig, Germany, perhaps so that Polyphon could compare one of the Regina-cased instruments with those of its own manufacture.

STYLE 302 REGINA SUBLIMA PIANO: Serially numbered from 3020001 to 3021804, but with many numbers omitted. About 150 made. Shipped from the factory during the 1906 - 1918 years, but mostly 1906 to 1910.

STYLE 303 REGINA SUBLIMA PIANO: Serially numbered from 3030001 to 3031322. About 1250 made totally. Shipped from 1906 to 1921, but mostly in the earlier years. The last one, No. 3031322, was shipped on May 3, 1921, to John H. May of Graphite, New York. Style 303 was the second most popular Sublima model.

STYLE 304 REGINA SUBLIMA PIANO: Serially numbered from 3040003 to 3041880. About 1770 made, making Style 304 the most popular of all Sublima instruments. Style 304 was usually sold as the "Regina Sublima Piano & Mandolin Orchestra." Shipments were made from 1906 to 1921, but mostly in the earlier years.

Note: The total of approximately 3270 Regina-cased Sublimas made, not taking into consideration earlier models imported in their entirety from Polyphon, makes the Sublima one of the most successful early American coin pianos ever made. Some entries in Regina ledgers note in handwritten script that certain models were "Sent out with Library Card" — the meaning of which is not known to the author.

## The Reginapianos

The Regina factory records list several types of instruments which are referred to as Regina Outside Piano Players, Regina Interior Piano Players, and Reginapianos. Some of these were intended for home use. Others were used commercially.

The records mention specifically that four pianos of the "Peerless" trademark (made by the Peerless Piano Player Co. of St. Johnsville, N.Y.) were sold in 1910. Examination of an extant Reginapiano reveals that it is a standard Cremona Style 3 made by the Marquette Piano Company of Chicago, Illinois.

The Regina records are inconclusive as to which pianos were intended for commercial use and which were used in homes. The factory ledgers have a "Key Numbers — Cash Box and Doors" column. In certain listings the designation "R" is given; in other listings a specific number is given. It may be the case that "R" instruments were made for "residence" use and had no cash box, while the pianos for which cash box key numbers are given were the coin-operated ones. The author would welcome correspondence from anyone having old advertisements or other information pertaining to these instruments.

REGINA PIANO PLAYER, STYLE A. Serially numbered from 101 to 544 inclusive. About 500 instruments sold from 1905 to 1910. The ledgers note that numbers 101 to 125 inclusive are "**Regina Outside**

Piano Players." These instruments are probably push-up piano players, possibly of the foot-pumped variety. Probably made only for residential use. The factory records further note: "Reginapianos [note that the terminology is changed to "Reginapiano" from "Piano Player" – although the Style A nomenclature is retained] – Interior Players from 126 Up." As shipments of these were made to private individuals, piano retail houses, and to furniture stores, and as these have the "R" designation in the "Key Numbers" column, we theorize that these were all for residential use. Interesting note: The ledger records that No. 184 was shipped to "Ingersoll – San Francisco – Sample destroyed in earthquake."

REGINAPIANO, STYLE B. About 85 of these were sold from 1906 to 1910 inclusive. These instruments were evidently made on contract by another piano firm as Regina did not assign Regina serial numbers to them. Rather, the serial numbers marked on the pianos as received, and neither continuous nor in numerical order, are given. To aid in the identification of any specimens which may come to light today, we mention that most serial numbers are in the 22,000 to 35,000 range, although a few are higher or lower. Evidently these were also intended for home use.

REGINAPIANO, STYLE C. Little is known about this style. Two specimens, numbers 496 and 497 (Regina serial numbers), were sold in 1908.

REGINAPIANO, STYLE D. About 90 of these were sold from 1906 to 1910. Regina did not assign serial numbers to these. Rather, the serial numbers marked on the pianos as received, and neither continuous nor in numerical order, are given. Most serial numbers are in the 77,000 to 84,000 range. Some have Regina-assigned numbers (491, 535, 536, and 538) and are the identical instruments (shipped to the same buyers on the same dates) as also listed under Style A. The notation "Transferred in A" appears after each listing, so evidently there was some confusion.

REGINAPIANO, STYLE E. Two sold in 1908, serial numbers (Regina) of 499 and 500. Marked "Transferred in A" in the ledger, so apparently there was little difference between the Style E and the A.

REGINAPIANO, STYLE "PEERLESS." Four instruments sold in 1910. Two Peerless serial numbers are given, nos. 1497 and 39,129. Purchased from Peerless, as noted in the introductory text. Probably coin operated.

REGINAPIANO, STYLE J. About 75 sold from 1908 to 1912. Regina did not assign serial numbers to these, but used the original manufacturer's numbers. Serials are in the 87,000 to 119,000 series. Probably a coin-operated model made by the Marquette Piano Company of Chicago, Illinois. This conjecture is supported by numerous sales to route operators such as the Schmidt Automatic Piano Co. (Milwaukee) and the Alps Amusement Company (St. Louis), and the assigning of cash box keys to the instruments. It is possible that these instruments were shipped directly from Marquette to the buyers, for the following states (none of which is close to Rahway, New Jersey) represent all but one of the buyers' addresses: Colorado, Montana, Wisconsin, South Dakota, Iowa, Indiana, Missouri, Illinois, Wyoming, and Texas. The solitary exception is an error in the factory records: No. 3041203 was shipped on August 11, 1911 to Max Chilinsky of Mammoth Junction, New Jersey. Sensing that 3041203 seemed to be a Sublima serial number (a 7-digit number with a Style 304 prefix) the author turned to the Style 304 section and found that this instrument was indeed a Style 304, and not a Style J at all. Furthermore, the correct destination was written in as "Mamoth Junction" [sic] and then corrected to what really was the right location: Monmouth Junction. So, a multiplicity of errors occurred with this single listing! Mammoth, Mamoth, or Monmouth; Style J or Style 304? Such questions often confronted the author in searching through the records and are why such notations as "about 85 were made" are used, rather than a precise figure (unless, of course, a precise figure is indicated by the records – and the records seem unequivocal).

Commentary

The early model of the Style A "Outside Piano Player" was called "Model 936" for a short time. Two Style A instruments, numbers 111 and 115, were first given the Model 936 appellation and then transferred to the Style A ledger.

The Marquette-made (Cremona Style 3) Reginapiano Style J consisted of a keyboard piano with mandolin attachment and used type "A" 10-tune coin piano rolls.

**SUBLIMA PIANO, JR.**

Regina advertisement illustration for the Regina Sublima Piano, Jr., the case design usually designated as Style 303. The lettering "Regina Sublima Piano" is on the front.

THE REGINA CO.

Main office and factory, RAHWAY, N. J.

Broadway and 17th Street, NEW YORK — 259 Wabash Ave., CHICAGO

Manufacturers of REGINA MUSIC BOXES, REGINAPIANOS, REGINAPHONES, REGINA CHIME CLOCKS — Distributors of VICTOR TALKING MACHINES and EDISON PHONOGRAPHS

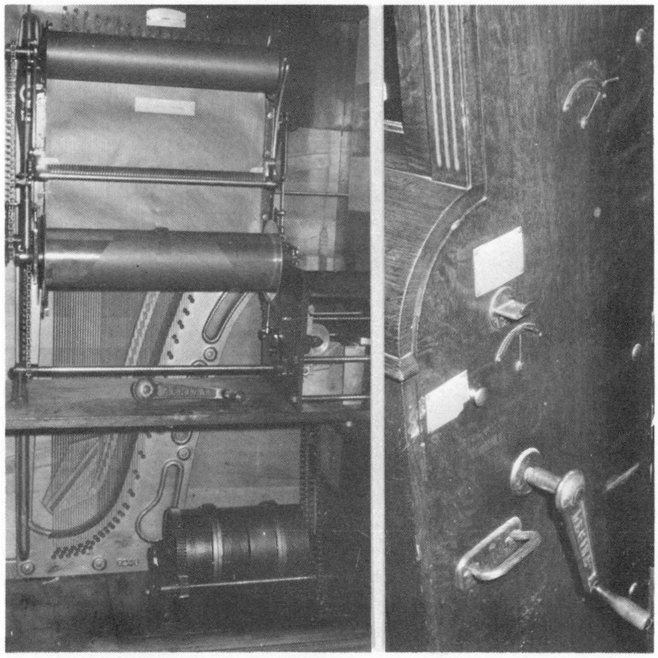

Above: Details of a spring-wound Style 303 Regina Sublima Piano. Winding the large double spring barrels requires quite a bit of energy and requires one or two minutes of time. Although Regina numbering was not always consistent, generally the Sublimas with rectangular front panels were designated as Style 303's. Those with oval panels were sold as Style 304's.

Right: Style 303 Regina Sublima Piano with electric motor drive. Some Style 303's (and 304's) were equipped with motors at the factory. Many others were converted to electrical operation later.

Views of a Style 304 Regina Sublima Piano & Mandolin Orchestra. These came in several different case design variations including models with round columns on the front (as shown above) and other models with grooved flat pilasters (similar to the Style 303).

The "Mandolin Orchestrion" card at the right lists five tunes: "My Clarabella, Waltz," "Underneath the Stars," "Babes in the Woods," "Hula Hula," and "Garden of Roses."

Most Style 304 instruments, but not all, were in cases with oval panels and windows and had the Sublima Piano & Mandolin Orchestra designation.

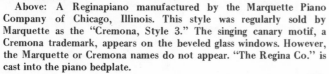

Above: A Reginapiano manufactured by the Marquette Piano Company of Chicago, Illinois. This style was regularly sold by Marquette as the "Cremona, Style 3." The singing canary motif, a Cremona trademark, appears on the beveled glass windows. However, the Marquette or Cremona names do not appear. "The Regina Co." is cast into the piano bedplate.

Above: The pump and roll drive unit of the Regina. Left: Singing canary motif on center beveled glass panel. Below: "The REGINA Co. is boldly cast into the piano plate.

RESOTONE GRAND

Made by the Resotone Grand Company of New York City, the Resotone Grand dates from the early 20th century. It uses an endless-type roll and incorporates a roll mechanism and certain related features similar to those used on the Encore Banjo and certain Peerless 44-note pianos of the 1898-1903 era.

The music is provided by a series of felt-tipped piano hammers which strike metal bars. Each bar is equipped with a rectangular resonator. The result is a soft, warm, and lingering tone that is quite pleasant to hear.

The Resotone Grand, technically a self-playing chrysoglott, was originally made for home use. The coin slot appears to be an early (c.1910) feature that was added after the instrument was made. The pneumatic action consists of a series of easily-disassembled metal unit valves, an ingeniously-devised and quite advanced concept for the era. The Resotone Grand is well made of high quality components. Evidently a large production was contemplated. This never materialized, and, as a result, the Resotone Grand is of great rarity today.

# J. P. SEEBURG PIANO COMPANY

MANUFACTURERS

## SEEBURG PIPE ORGANS AND SELF-PLAYING ORCHESTRAS

### J.P. SEEBURG PIANO COMPANY

The J.P. Seeburg Piano Company of Chicago was one of the top names in the automatic piano and orchestrion business in America. In the 1920's it was THE leader and had the lion's share of the business (in the earlier 1900 - 1920 years Wurlitzer was dominant).

Beginning about 1907 this firm entered the market with a series of coin-operated 65-note pianos which used the type "A" roll. Some of these very early Seeburg instruments were made by the Marquette Piano Company, for which firm J.P. Seeburg was a sales outlet, but soon this affiliation was dropped and the Seeburg company was on its own.

*Circa 1911 Seeburg factory scene showing "Style C – Art" pianos being made.*

Within a few years the large and ornate Style G and Style H orchestrions were added to the Seeburg line. These and other early Seeburg instruments were distinguished by their rich and colorful art glass fronts. Mr. N. Marshall Seeburg, son of J.P. Seeburg, informed the author that Seeburg pioneered the use of decorative art glass in coin piano cases in America.

The "Music Trade Review," issue of October 26, 1912, did a feature story on the then-young Seeburg firm. We reprint it herewith as it provides a contemporary view of this illustrious company:

"The J.P. Seeburg Piano Company"

THE J.P. SEEBURG PIANO CO., Makers of Coin-Operated Pianos.

"Dealers the country over are rapidly awakening to the fact that opportunity for increased business and enhanced profits is to be found in coin controlled instruments.

*America's Best Seller! – The small Seeburg "L," called at first the "Cabinet" piano and, later, the "Lilliputian," was made by the thousands. More Seeburg L's were made than were any other single type of coin piano in America. Today these perky little instruments are popular with collectors.*

"While a few retail piano houses here and there have in the past made a success in this line, they have been as a rule larger concerns who have been able to conduct a separate department of their business in charge of specially trained experts.

"Within the past few years, however, there has been such a remarkable development in these instruments as to eliminate any objections or prejudice that may exist against them so far as the regular piano trade is concerned.

"In the first place, the coin controlled piano has been perfected to such an extent mechanically as to no longer need the constant attention of men especially versed in the construction as was formerly the case. No tuner who has had any experience with player pianos will have any difficulty in meeting the requirements necessary in properly caring for a coin controlled instrument.

"Last, but by no means least, the introduction of really artistic cases has aided in opening up avenues for the installation of such instruments in places which were formerly closed to them and has proved the finishing touch, so far as the piano trade is concerned, as with this last development instruments are now available which the piano dealer need not hesitate to place in his wareroom for fear of detracting by their appearance from his regular stock of instruments.

"J.P. Seeburg, president of the J.P. Seeburg Piano Company, of Chicago, has won an important position in the coin controlled electric piano field and especially as a consistent and successful exponent of their adaptability for handling by the regular piano trade.

*This Seeburg showroom of the pre-World War I era shows several photoplayers, coin pianos, and orchestrions on display. (From "Put Another Nickel In.")*

"Not only for his creation of 'art cases' as applied to coin controlled pianos is he entitled to much credit, but the character of the Seeburg instruments throughout and the innovations of a practical character which are being continually embodied in them, together with the policy of constant improvement in the smallest detail, wherever possible, stamp their maker as a progressive of the highest type.

"Glancing back over the career of Mr. Seeburg leads one to believe that he has been all his life training definitely, albeit unconsciously perhaps, for the particular branch of the musical instrument business in which he is engaged. A practical piano maker, versed in all branches of the actual construction of pianos, factory superintendent, piano action manufacturer, manufacturer of player actions and large dealer in electric coin controlled pianos — these are the successive steps which preceded the foundation of his present business, which has made wonderful strides in a comparatively short period of time. Surely a man of such training and knowledge might be expected to do large things and to produce an instrument well balanced in every part. Such a man would naturally demand that the piano itself be a good instrument,

*Seeburg moved every few years as business grew. The above Erie Avenue location was pictured in a 1913 catalogue.*

*Part of the old Seeburg factory at 1500 Dayton St. in Chicago. From this location thousands of coin pianos were shipped in the 1920's.*

*This private club entertained its patrons with Seeburg G orchestrion music in 1912. The colorful Style G was one of the most popular Seeburg instruments.*

capable of bearing the excessive strain imposed upon it, that the actions be the best obtainable for the purpose, that his pneumatic mechanism be constructed upon scientific and practical lines, that no part of the instrument be slighted at the expense of any other, while his knowledge both of the regular piano trade and of the coin controlled business would naturally suggest innovations and improvements, adapting it to a wider field of usefulness and new channels of distribution.

"Adjoining the manual training high school which Justus P. Seeburg attended when a boy in his native town of Gothenburg, Sweden, stood the Malinjos piano factory, where the young man spent considerable time outside of school hours, and made up his mind that when he learned a trade it should be that of piano making. After he had finished school he came to this country, and on his arrival in Chicago sought employment in a piano factory.

"He was speedily put through the different departments of the factory as his mechanical aptitude and interest in his work became manifest, and soon was known as an expert action finisher and regulator. After six years spent with another factory in this capacity he went with one of the largest concerns in the west in charge of the construction of one of their makes of instruments.

"In 1895 he went to Rockford, Illinois, and became one of the organizers of the Kurtz-Seeburg Action Co. After a couple of years he sold his interest in the business, and returning to Chicago, became interested in a new company engaging in the manufacture of pneumatic player actions and player pianos. (This was the Marquette Piano Co., maker of "Cremona" instruments — Ed.) When this company later brought out an electric coin operated piano, Mr. Seeburg was quick to see the opportunity before this type of instrument. He then withdrew and organized the J.P. Seeburg Piano Co., marketing the coin operated output of the (Marquette) company. The business developed so rapidly that he soon decided to engage in the manufacture of electric coin operated pianos. His associates in the J.P. Seeburg Piano Co. enthusiastically supported him in his move and factory quarters were secured on Clybourn Avenue. In a few months the Seeburg electric coin operated piano made its appearance.

"Besides doing an immense local retail business, Mr. Seeburg soon commenced reaching after the wholesale trade, going after the regular piano trade as well as route operators. Many dealers quick to realize the value of a Seeburg agency, have built up a most profitable business with these instruments, displaying the handsome art styles in their

OSBORN PIANO PLAYER CO.

Minneapolis, Minn., December 24, 1913.

J. P. Seeburg Piano Company,
Chicago, Illinois.

Gentlemen:—

We are mailing you flash-light photos of the Shubert Theatre, St. Paul, showing auditorium and pit where we have placed one of your Style G Orchestrions. This theatre is playing stock this season, and using the "G" in place of an orchestra with the best of satisfaction. It has been in over three months and we have not had a single call to it. In fact we have had so little trouble with your complete line that we feel that you have the best there is on the market. Of the seventy or more instruments we have had from you the past year, not one has failed to work when connected to the electric current.

Thanking you for many favors and wishing you success, we are
Yours very truly,
A. D. Osborn.

warerooms and in their windows, side by side with regular pianos of famous makes.

"The company is now shipping the Seeburg pianos to all parts of the country, and has important business connections on both the Atlantic and Pacific coasts. Successive additions to the factory quarters on Clybourn Avenue being insufficient to keep up with the demand for the company's product, they moved the past month to the new modern manufacturing building at 415-421 South Sangamon Street, near Van Buren, where they have double the space formerly occupied by them, and with the addition of much new machinery will double their output.

"A late addition to the line is the Seeburg violin piano, style E. In this unique and beautiful instrument a variety of musical effects can be secured by the simple manipulation of a handy button. Either a straight piano solo, combination violin (pipe) and piano effects, combination mandolin and piano, or combined violin, mandolin, and piano can be obtained at will. Like all of the Seeburg innovations it has met with instant demand."

Seeburg in the 'Teens

The 1910 - 1920 decade was a good one for the coin piano business in America. During the earlier part of this era coin pianos were catching on with the public, and just about anyone who put an electric motor and coin slot in a piano found a ready sale with it. In such an atmosphere Seeburg, with its line of several different piano styles and with its growing system of distributors, had just about all the business it could handle.

By the middle of the decade Seeburg moved again – this time to factory quarters at 413-419 West Erie Street in Chicago. A large line of theatre photoplayers was introduced. Called "Pipe Organ Orchestras," these instruments generally had a center or "console" unit flanked by two side chests. The side cabinets contained pipes, drums, and sound effects. Over a dozen different styles of theatre photoplayers were

*Surrounded by leather covered chairs and linen topped tables this Seeburg H played music in a hotel dining room years ago.*

produced. These used regular Seeburg orchestrion rolls, either Style G or Style H (usually), as originally made for Seeburg orchestrions with the same name.

Seeburg photoplayers were immensely successful, and it is probable that over 1,000 were sold – mainly at prices in the $3,000 to $5,000 range.

Sensing a demand for such a product, the J.P. Seeburg Piano Company introduced a small keyboardless piano. Originally called simply the "Cabinet" model, the designation was soon changed to the "Lilliputian" or, more familiarly, the "Style L." This particular instrument went on to be the most popular type of coin piano ever produced in America. Thousands were originally made and, of that number, hundreds still survive today.

Sensing also a demand for large theatre pipe organs the Seeburg firm formed a company to produce "Seeburg - Smith" theatre organs. Several dozen installations were made and some sales literature was printed. However, the organ division was soon sold as Seeburg found that its sales and service abilities were in the line of smaller instruments.

Throughout the 'teens Seeburg experimented with many different types of instruments. Some, such as the Phono-Grand (a combination expression piano and phonograph introduced in 1917), achieved a modest sales success. Others, the P-G-A (a coin piano built in the phonograph-like Phono-Grand case) for example, were dropped quickly from the line when sufficient sales or demand failed to materialize.

| Style | Retail | Wholesale |
|---|---|---|
| A | 650.00 | 300.00 |
| B | 750.00 | 325.00 |
| C | 850.00 | 350.00 |
| E | 950.00 | 400.00 |
| F | 1050.00 | 425.00 |
| G | 1500.00 | 650.00 |
| H | 2500.00 | 850.00 |
| J | 1800.00 | 700.00 |
| K | 650.00 | 275.00 |
| L | 1350.00 | 550.00 |
| M | 2850.00 | 1250.00 |
| O | | |
| P | 950.00 | 475.00 |
| Q | 1250.00 | 625.00 |
| R | 4000.00 | 2000.00 |
| S | 1950.00 | 975.00 |
| Cab. | 350.00 | 150.00 |

*1918 price list of Seeburg instruments. Note the generous markup from wholesale to retail! The Style L noted here is the orchestrion; the later Style L "Lilliputian" appears on this list as "Cab." M, P, Q, R, and S are photoplayers. Note the incredible markup on a Style H orchestrion. It's too bad our parents or grandparents didn't buy a half dozen and save them for us!*

The outstanding success of the J.P. Seeburg Piano Company was due in part, of course, to the durability, attractive appearance, and general excellence of the Seeburg instruments. But the business ability of the firm must be given a generous share of the credit also.

Unlike many other firms, Seeburg standardized its parts as much as possible. The roll mechanism which went into the small Seeburg Style L cabinet piano contained many of the same parts as the mechanism which went into the large Style H Solo Orchestrion. This simplified servicing the instruments, training technicians, and keeping parts inventories.

Seeburg did not have company-owned sales outlets but, rather, relied upon piano dealers in various cities. These dealers were given a wholesale discount which was extremely generous and which, no doubt, was a prime reason why dozens of different dealers promoted the Seeburg line for all it was worth.

As examples of this discount schedule we note that the popular Style G orchestrion retailed for $1500.00 (in 1918) but cost the dealer just $650.00 – a profit to the dealer of $850.00! The small Style L piano netted the dealer a profit of $200 when he sold it for the $350 list price! By way of comparison we note that another manufacturer of orchestrions had a popular model which listed for $2100.00 retail – with a $1700.00 wholesale price. It is no wonder that Seeburg instruments were so popular with piano dealers!

In addition, the Seeburg Piano Company generated quite a few inquiries itself – and passed them along to local dealers. Seeburg thus helped the dealer to sell Seeburg instruments. A letter loaned to us by Mr. Don MacDonald, Jr. serves to illustrate how Seeburg worked hand-in-glove with its outlets. We don't know whether or not a sale was ever made, but certainly Seeburg put forth quite a bit of effort on behalf of its dealer, the Sanders-Dreyer Piano Company of St. Louis, Missouri:

"To the Sanders-Dreyer Piano Co.

Gentlemen:

J.J. Reilly of the Princess Theatre, Alton, Illinois, has been dickering with us for a 'Celesta DeLuxe Player Pipe Organ.' I saw him yesterday and was talking with him on the telephone today...

"It might be well for you to make a trip to Alton and see Mr. Reilly. You no doubt know that your wholesale price on the 'Celesta' is $1085 and we have quoted him a price of $2250. I am enclosing a cut (illustration) of this instrument for fear that you have none at hand so if you care to go to Alton and see this man it is barely possible that you can get him interested...

–J.P. Seeburg Piano Company"

In the 'teens were introduced the popular Style K and KT cabinet pianos. These, through a process of evolution, became the familar "Seeburg Eagle" instruments – one of the mainstays of the Seeburg line. The Style K featured a piano and mandolin in combination with an extra instrument – either a xylophone (usually) or a rank of violin or flute pipes. The Style KT was essentially a Style K in a slightly larger case and with a tambourine, triangle, and castanets added.

*This drug store soda fountain dispenses chocolate malted milk shakes to the accompaniment of Seeburg piano music. Taken in the "good old days" this photograph appeared in the 1913 Seeburg catalogue.*

### Seeburg in the 'Twenties

By the early 1920's Seeburg was the dominant firm in the coin piano business in America. The widespread adoption of Prohibition had closed the market for large instruments such as the Style G and H orchestrions (which were kept in stock but which were made only in exceedingly small quantities after 1920) and had opened up a new market for cabaret type instruments — cabinet style pianos such as the Style L and the popular K and KT.

During the 1920's Seeburg concentrated on cabinet instruments. A novelty was provided by the Seeburg "Grayhound," a cabinet piano with a diorama of eight racing dogs. The KT Special, a cabinet orchestrion introduced in 1925, was immediately successful.

From a large complex of buildings at the corner of Blackhawk and Dayton streets in Chicago Seeburg produced several thousand pianos per year — probably about 15,000 from 1920 to 1927.

When doing research for "Put Another Nickel In," we obtained from Mr. N. Marshall Seeburg an interesting revelation. In Mr. Seeburg's own words: "One interesting sidelight is the fact that we (the J.P. Seeburg Piano Co.) bought and owned the Western Electric Piano Company. It was necessitated by our desire to stimulate more competition among the Seeburg dealers who had exclusive territories and really needed competition. That is why none of our officers appeared on the [Western Electric] board in order to cover up the ownership."

It seems probable that in the 1920's Seeburg acquired what was left of the business of the Marquette Piano Company ("Cremona" instruments), the firm with which J.P. Seeburg had first worked in the coin piano trade years earlier.

By 1927 Seeburg's coin piano business had slowed to a trickle. The factory was converted for the production of coin operated phonographs (the early models of which were housed in cabinet piano cases and which used vacuum pumps and pneumatic mechanisms for part of their operation). Again, Seeburg showed its market awareness and dexterity by leaving the coin piano business at the right time. As such it was one of just a handful of coin piano makers to stay in business — although in an entirely different product line.

**SEEBURG**

MARCH 1, 1924

| | |
|---|---|
| Style A - - - - | $1150 |
| Style B - - - - | 1175 |
| Style E - - - - | 1400 |
| Style EX - - - | 1400 |
| Style G - - - - | 2350 |
| Style H - - - - | 3150 |
| Style K - - - - | 1150 |
| Style KX - - - | 1150 |
| Style KT - - - | 1175 |
| Style L - - - - | 850 |
| Style X (Reproducing) | 1500 |

*Prices Include Free Installation With Five Coin Slot Boxes*

| | |
|---|---|
| Style L - - - - | $ 850 |
| Style A - - - - | 1150 |
| Style B - - - - | 1175 |
| Style E - - - - | 1350 |
| Style EX - - - | 1350 |
| Style E Special - - | 1650 |
| Style G - - - - | 2250 |
| Style H - - - - | 3000 |
| Style K - - - - | 1150 |
| Style KX - - - | 1150 |
| Style KT - - - | 1175 |
| Style KT Special - | 1500 |
| Style X (EXPRESSION REPRODUCING) | 1400 |

*Above left and directly above: Seeburg price lists. The one directly above is circa 1926. Note that some prices have been lowered from the 1924 levels.*

*Gentlemen: I have used your SEEBURG Player Organ in the Crystal Theatre for about ten years, and find your instrument very serviceable. I can honestly recommend it as the best of its kind, for the amount invested.*

Yours sincerely, Harry M. Drye,
SAVOY THEATRE, Minneapolis, Minn.

*Gentlemen: We are using three SEEBURG Pianos and one SEEBURG Organ. Your SEEBURG Organ has been in operation for the last eleven years, an average of about six to eleven hours a day. We find them the best electrical instrument on the market.*

Yours truly, Tony H. Nellesen,
CAPITOL & CREIGHTON THEATRES,
Fort Wayne, Ind.

**Seeburg Automatic Instruments**

— SOLD TO —

THEATRES
LODGES
CONFECTIONERS
RESTAURANTS
CABARETS
DANCE HALLS
RINKS
CAFES

FORT SIDE INN

Whitemarsh, Mont. Co., Pa., November 21, 1913.

Mr. Julius Wellner, Philadelphia, Pa.

My Dear Mr. Wellner:—

The Seeburg Orchestrion, Style "H" which you sold me for my Dining Room, is certainly giving great satisfaction. All the former instruments that I had gave me a great deal of trouble, but I must say that during the five months' time which I had this instrument, it has been playing continuously without any trouble whatever. My patrons are delighted with it, and I am sure it is a very good investment for me. I will be very glad to recommend this instrument to all my friends. I think I have a sale for one of these instruments; if you will call at my place of business sometime in the near future, we will talk this matter over. I am,

Yours very truly,
William P. Green, Prop.

SIMPLICITY · RELIABILITY · ENDURANCE · SEEBURG

Gentlemen:—

It gives me great pleasure to inform you that the orchestrion which I purchased from you last November has proven a great success, and that my business has increased 25 per cent, which I attribute wholly to the Seeburg orchestrion style "G."

I cannot express too highly my approval of the musical qualities of the Seeburg orchestrion, as well as the way the instrument has been running without getting out of order, considering that in the past eleven months there has gone through this instrument over thirty thousand (30,000) nickels.

The receipts from the orchestrion has far surpassed my expectations. I now own this instrument, with only the expense to me of the initial payment down.

It gives me great pleasure to recommend your instrument to anybody, whether interested or not, and I certainly shall be a booster for you whenever an opportunity presents itself.

Wishing you success, and hoping to install one of your new style "H" solo-orchestrion in the near future, I beg to remain,

Very truly yours,
Frank Wasikowski.

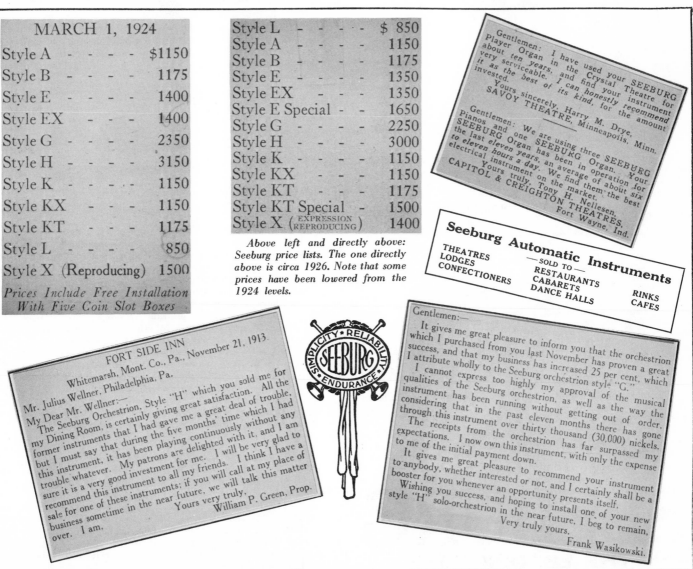

ROLLS FOR SEEBURG INSTRUMENTS

*Cover from a Seeburg roll bulletin of the late 1920's. Seeburg owned the Automatic Music Roll Co.*

The following types of rolls were used on Seeburg automatic instruments:

**For All Standard 65-Note Rewind Coin Operated Pianos Also SEEBURG Styles A, B, C, E, F, K, PGA and L**

A-1364 SPECIAL XYLOPHONE ARRANGEMENT
1. Under the Moon, Fox Trot.
2. Who-oo? You-oo! That's Who, Fox Trot.
3. She's Got "It," Fox Trot.
4. I've Lived All My Life Just For You, Waltz.
5. Who's That Pretty Baby? Fox Trot.
6. My Sweet Yvette, Fox Trot.
7. Baby Your Mother, Fox Trot.
8. Things That Remind Me Of You, Waltz.
9. Someday You'll Say "O. K." Fox Trot.
10. She Don't Wanna! Fox Trot.

"A" rolls: This type of roll contained provision for the piano, mandolin attachment, one extra instrument (usually a xylophone or rank of pipes), and limited piano expression effects. This was the basic Seeburg piano roll and was used on most types of coin pianos without drums or trap effects; instruments such as styles A, B, C, E, F, K, L (Cabinet), Grayhound, and P-G-A.

**For SEEBURG Styles G, KT, KT Special, E Special, Orchestrions, and Styles P, Q, and W Motion Picture Players. Also adapted for Western Electric Style A and G Orchestrions**

G-907 NATURAL MELODY HITS
1. Highways Are Happy Ways, Fox Trot.
2. A Night In June, Fox Trot.
3. Roam On My Little Gypsy Sweetheart, Fox Trot.
4. Good News, Fox Trot.
5. Miss Annabelle Lee, Fox Trot.
6. Baby Feet Go Pitter Patter, Fox Trot.
7. The Calinda, Fox Trot.
8. Someday You'll Say "O. K.!" Fox Trot.
9. Oh! Ya! Ya! Fox Trot.
10. Who's That Pretty Baby! Fox Trot.

"G" rolls: Used on small and medium size instruments with drum and/or trap effects. Styles of instruments using G rolls include: KT, KT Special, E Special, G, and smaller sizes of Seeburg photoplayers. The "G" roll has the same width (11¼") and the same hole spacing (6 holes to the inch) as the "A" roll, but has extra perforations for drum and trap effects and other controls. The "G" roll is identical in arrangement to the type "4X" roll used on other orchestrions made by Nelson-Wiggen and Western Electric.

# SEEBURG
## THE LEADING LINE

**For SEEBURG Orchestrions Styles J and H, New Styles W and M, S, and R, and Pipe Organ-Orchestra, and Celesta DeLuxe Pipe Organ**
**Organ: Order these also for your Organs. They are popular.**
**NOTE: These rolls will play all Orchestrion effects, except Organ, on Styles M, S & R.**

H-1132 NATURAL MELODY HITS
1. Highways Are Happy Ways, Fox Trot.
2. A Night In June, Fox Trot.
3. Roam On My Little Gypsy Sweetheart, Fox Trot.
4. Good News, Fox Trot.
5. Miss Annabelle Lee, Fox Trot.
6. Baby Feet Go Pitter Patter, Fox Trot.
7. The Calinda, Fox Trot.
8. Someday You'll Say "O. K.!" Fox Trot.
9. Oh! Ya! Ya! Fox Trot.
10. Who's That Pretty Baby? Fox Trot

"H" rolls: Used on the large J and H orchestrions; also on most types of large Seeburg "Pipe Organ Orchestra" photoplayers.

**For SEEBURG Celesta De Luxe Pipe Organ and Styles S, M, R, T, V and A De Luxe, Pipe Organ Orchestras**

**HAND PLAYED ORGAN ROLLS**

MSR-1134 ORGAN LIGHT COMEDY
1. Call Of the Sylphs ................ Frascard
2. Moonlight Dreams .................... Spry
3. Dancing Marionette .................. Gahm
4. Before the Footlights .............. Manney
5. The Dansant ....................... Moquin

"MSR" rolls: Same basic format as the type H rolls, but usually without orchestration (provision for drums and traps). Feature pipe organ arrangements; intended for use on large Seeburg photoplayers and on the later piano - pipe organ instruments such as the "M.O." and the "Celesta DeLuxe."

**For SEEBURG Style X, Xpression Pianos. These rolls will not play on any other Seeburg instrument excepting the Style X, also adapted for Apollo X**

XP-420 SIX ROUNDS OF HITS
1. Under the Moon, Fox Trot.
2. Who-oo? You-oo! That's Who! Fox Trot.
3. After I've Called You Sweetheart, Waltz.
4. Roam On My Little Gypsy Sweetheart, Fox Trot.
5. Someday You'll Say "O. K." Fox Trot.
6. The Calinda, Fox Trot.

"XP" rolls: 11¼" wide 9-holes-to-the-inch rolls with semi-reproducing expression effects used on the Style X keyboard coin-operated expression piano and on the Phono-Grand combination piano and phonograph. The "XP" layout is the same as certain Apollo (made by Melville Clark Piano Co.) roll specifications.

The above are the main types of Seeburg rolls. In addition "HO" and "MO" rolls (the initials probably represent "Home Organ" and "Mortuary Organ") were made for self-contained pipe organs; a piano - pipe organ instrument introduced in 1927 was advertised as using "TR" rolls, but we've never seen an actual roll of this type; the Style Z Selective Roll Piano played a 6-tune "special cut 65-note electric rewind roll" (according to the original catalogue description), but we've never seen one; regular 88-note home player piano rolls could be used on certain types of Seeburg instruments including the Style X and Phono-Grand and on certain Seeburg photoplayers equipped with an 88-note roll frame (in addition to a G or H roll frame).

*The Automatic Music Roll Co. sold rolls cut for it by the Clark Orchestra Roll Co. of DeKalb, Illinois. Very early Seeburg rolls were of three types designated as S, SS, and SSS. About 1914 or 1915 these designations were changed to A, G, and H respectively.*

*"A" rolls which fit on many types of Seeburg pianos (and those of other makers, too) were sold under Automatic Music Roll Co., Clark, Lind, Capitol, Columbia (same as Capitol), U.S. Music Roll Co., Marquette, and a few other names. "G" rolls were sold by Automatic, Clark, Capitol, and Columbia. "H" rolls were sold by Automatic and Clark.*

SEEBURG Keyboard Pianos with Mandolin Attachment (Styles A and B).

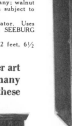

Style B

## STYLE "A"—"The Sturdy Performer"

**Piano with mandolin attachment.**

UNIQUE and attractive. Notable for its simplicity of construction and absolute reliability. New and original scale of seven and one-third octaves, over-strung copper bass, three unison throughout.

Double veneered hardwood, finished in oak or mahogany; walnut at slight extra cost. Art glass panel, design subject to change without notice.

Equipped with automatic loud and soft control; tempo regulator. Uses Style "A", 65-note, ten-selection music roll with the famous SEEBURG automatic rewind system.

Height: 4 feet, 9½ inches; Width: 5 feet, 3 inches; Depth: 2 feet, 6½ inches. Weight, boxed for shipment: 900 lbs.

## STYLE "B"—"The Artistic Automatic"

**Piano with mandolin attachment.**

HANDSOME and serviceable. Its appearance is a distinct factor in coaxing its operation. New and original scale of seven and one-third octaves, over-strung copper bass, three unison throughout.

Double veneered hardwood case. Finished in oak or mahogany; walnut at slight extra cost. Full art glass panel in top frame, design subject to change without notice.

Equipped with automatic loud and soft control; tempo regulator. Uses Style "A", 65-note, ten-selection music roll with the famous SEEBURG automatic rewind system.

Height: 4 feet, 9½ inches; width: 5 feet, 3 inches; Depth, 2 feet, 6½ inches. Weight, boxed for shipment: 900 lbs.

Style B

**Styles A and B: These two styles are the same mechanically. The Style B cases have fancier art glass and trim and were originally sold for $25 to $100 more than the A styles. Many, many different Style B variations were made; a few of the more interesting ones are shown on these pages.**

Style A

Style A

Style B

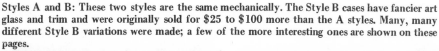

1—Shut-off button.
2—Tracker bar.
3—Thumb screw for lining up paper.
4—Magazine.
5—Money box.
6—Music Roll.
7—Thumb screw for lining tracker.
8—Tension spring for music rolls.
9—Shifter.
10—Motor.
11—Friction Drive Wheel with rubber belt.
12—Friction spring.
13—Pitman rod.
14—Pumps.
15—Reservoir.
16—Valve to cut off player action when rewinding.
17—Valve for soft pedal.
18—Valve for sustaining pedal.
19—Pedalpneumatics.

**The above illustration shows the roll system, pump, reservoir, and other lower components of a typical A or B Seeburg piano. Seeburg instruments were built ruggedly and could take a lot of wear and tear with a minimum of servicing. They were probably the most durable American coin piano in this regard.**

## SEEBURG Keyboard Pianos with Mandolin Attachment

Style C – Art
Popular in the early 'teens

Above: A view of the elaborate art glass scene from a Style C – Art piano. The scene is rich with green foliage, blue water, azure sky, and other chromatic features. This basic case was made with art glass lamps on the front posts in the early days; later the lamps were omitted. The same case, but built slightly deeper, was also used for the Style E Violin.

Art glass scenery on a Style B

The Land of the Midnight Sun is the motif of this Style B.

## SEEBURG Pianos with Mandolin and One Rank of Pipes (Styles E and F)

STYLE E VIOLIN
MADE WITH FLUTE OR VIOLIN PIPES

Interior Style F

STYLE E
INSTRUMENTATION:
PIANO, VIOLIN AND MANDOLIN, OR PIANO, FLUTE AND MANDOLIN

New and original scale of seven and one-third octaves, overstrung bass, and three unisons throughout. Double casters. The top frame contains an elaborate art glass panel in center with fancy wood panels at sides, and burnished brass art lamps hanging at each side. Double veneered hardwood case finished in mission oak. Contains one set of 25 violin, or flute pipes, giving actual effects. Equipped with automatic mandolin, and pipe attachments, loud and soft lever, and tempo regulator on outside below key-bed. Any instrument can be shut off at will. Magazine slot registering 1 to 20 coins. Music roll "S" contains from 10 to 20 selections on Seeburg rewind system. Art glass design subject to change without notice. When ordering specify whether violin or flute pipes are desired. Height—4 feet 9 inches. Width—2 feet 5 inches. Length—5 feet 6 inches. Weight boxed for shipment, about 1,000 pounds.

Early Style B pianos offered the buyer a piano with mandolin attachment and the choice of either violin pipes or flute pipes. The Style F (pictured below and right) differs in that its case is higher. Style E sold for $950.00 in 1918.

Exterior Style F

STYLE F
Case Design Patented
INSTRUMENTATION:
PIANO, VIOLIN AND MANDOLIN, OR PIANO, FLUTE AND MANDOLIN

Massive appearing artistically designed case, 6 inches higher than an ordinary piano, but no larger in the length or width. Featuring a row of small art glass panels at top and elaborate coppered art glass illuminated panels and colonial art lamps hanging at sides. Double veneered hardwood case finished in mission oak. Equipped with automatic mandolin and pipe attachments, loud and soft lever, and tempo regulator on outside below key-bed. Any instrument can be shut off at will. Magazine slot registering 1 to 20 coins. Music roll "S" contains from 10 to 20 selections on Seeburg rewind system. Art glass design subject to change without notice. When ordering specify whether violin or flute pipes are desired. Height—5 feet 5 inches. Width—2 feet 4 inches. Length—5 feet 4 inches. Weight boxed for shipment about 1050 pounds.

A Style F provides music for a soda parlor circa 1912.

**SEEBURG Pianos with Mandolin and Xylophone (Style E)**

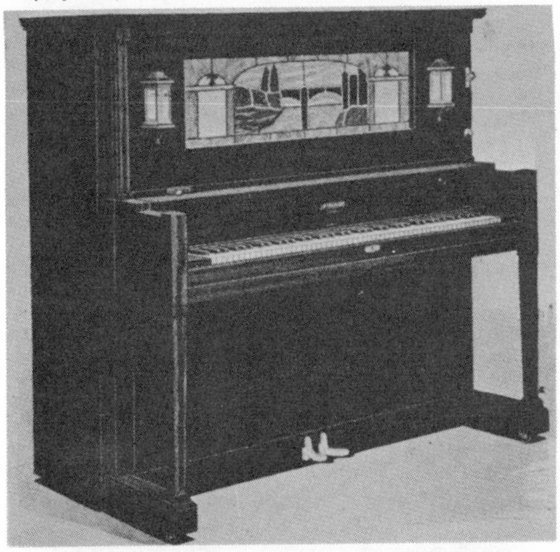

STYLE "E"—"The Automatic Master"

**Piano, xylophone, and mandolin attachment.**

A MODEL in refinement of case design. New and original scale of seven and one-third octaves, over-strung copper bass, three unison throughout.

Double veneered hardwood case, finished in oak or mahogany; walnut at slight extra cost. Elaborate art glass panel with burnished brass art lamps at each side in top frame, design subject to change without notice.

Equipped with automatic loud and soft control; tempo regulator. Uses Style "A", 65-note, ten-selection music roll with famous SEEBURG automatic rewind system.

Height: 4 feet, 9½ inches; Width: 5 feet, 3 inches; Depth: 2 feet, 6½ inches. Weight, boxed for shipment: 900 lbs.

The Style E of the 1920's featured a xylophone as the added instrument. During the late 'teens this particular case design (with two coach lamps; an art glass scene with a wooded landscape, sometimes with clear glass "sky" to permit a view of the interior) could be purchased with pipes (violin or flute) or with xylophone. Some catalogues list the Style E with pipes as the "Style E" and the Style E with xylophone as "Style EX."

Left: Noted ragtime pianist Max Morath admires a Seeburg E in the Roehl Collection.

Below: Xylophone from a Style E.

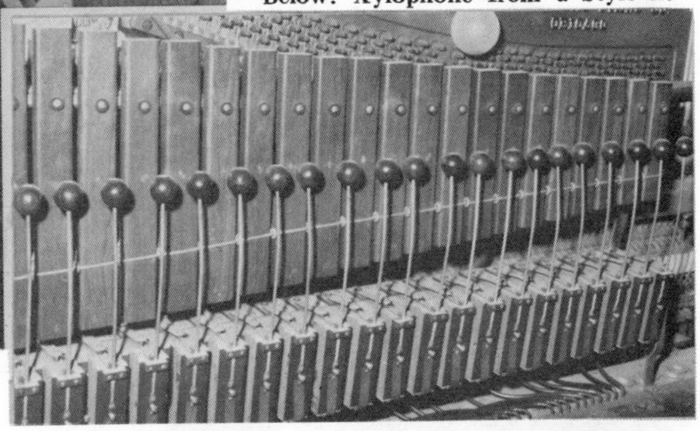

---

**SEEBURG (Style L or "Cabinet" Piano)**

Style "L"—Smallest Electric Piano made. Also has Mandolin Attachment. Uses Standard 65-Note Music Roll. Dimensions—Height: 51½"; Width: 36½"; Depth: 23½"

**Late Style L**

**Early Seeburg L with full length front doors.**

**Early Style L**

**Seeburg Style L: In the early years this style was known as the "Cabinet" model. Later, the designation was changed to the "Style L" or "Lilliputian." Today collectors fondly know the Style L as the "Seeburg Junior."**

**There are several variations of the Style L. Most are in quartered oak wood, but a few are in mahogany. Earlier models have two full length front doors extending from top to bottom. Later styles have four doors; two at the top in front of the roll mechanism and two bottom doors. Early models have a reciprocating pump mounted on the right side wall of the bottom of the case (see illustration to the right). Later models have a box-type 4-part pump hidden behind a large pulley (see illustration center above). The art glass is more or less standard. The only variation is that some have a clear glass "sky" portion in the scene to permit a view of the music roll as it plays.**

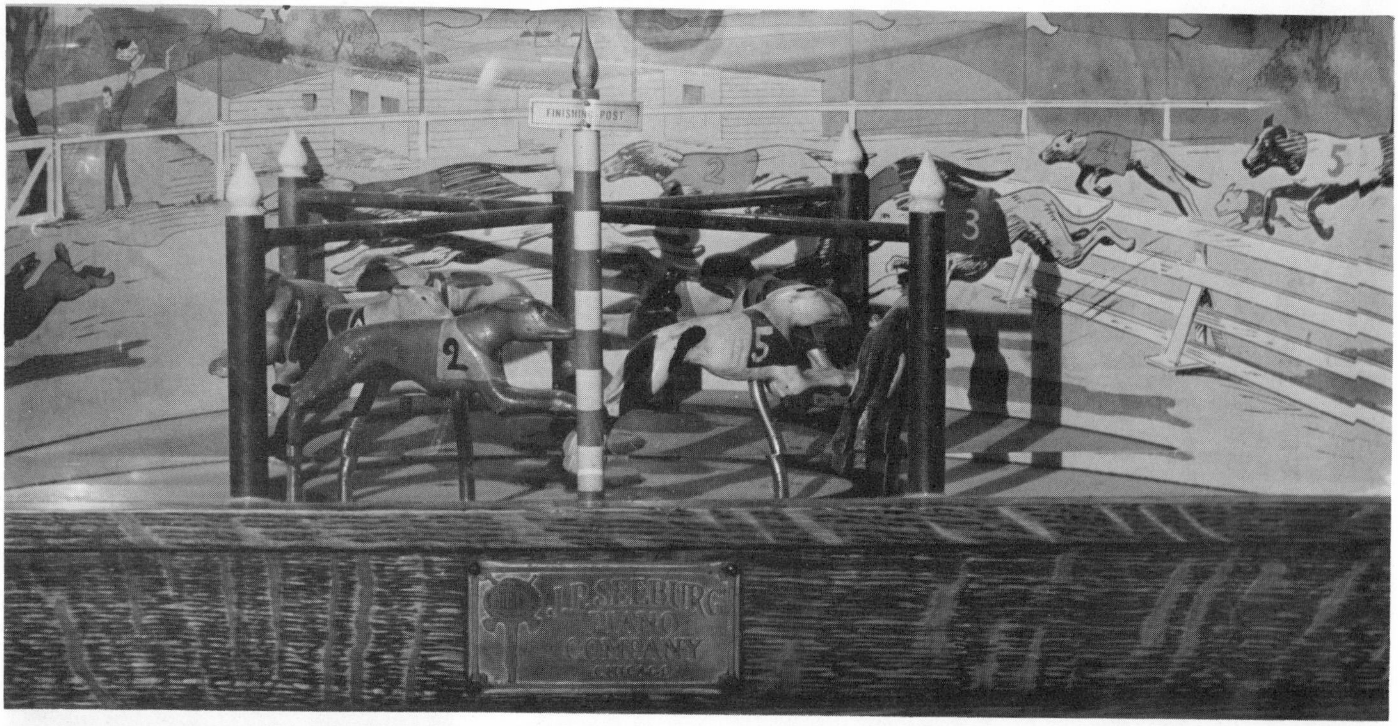

**SEEBURG GRAYHOUND RACE PIANO**

"Grayhound"—Automatic Piano combined with 8-dog race. A wonderful novelty. Dimensions—Height: 51½"; Width: 36½"; Depth: 26½"

Seeburg Grayhound: (Or "Greyhound" – both spellings were used). This interesting and lively coin piano is basically the same as a Seeburg L but is in a slightly larger case. When a nickel is dropped in the slot a pack of dogs whirl madly around a center post. Within less than a minute the dogs slow to a stop. The one whose nose is closest to the finishing post is the winner. Such a piano was a great attraction for taverns. The losing bettor was a candidate to drop the next nickel into the piano or, more likely, to buy the next set of drinks! These were made until the very late 1920's. A specimen in the Coade Collection has a completely modernized and redesigned pneumatic stack with all of the pneumatics scarcely the width of a finger and all arranged in a single row (rather than stacked in a deck as per usual); the pneumatics are built as an integral unit with built-in valves.

**SEEBURG P-G-A COIN PIANO**

Seeburg P-G-A. (or just PGA, without hyphenation – it was described both ways). The P-G-A was evidently a measure whereby cases ordered for the Seeburg Phono-Grand (see description on a following page) were utilized to make coin-in-the-slot pianos once it was realized that the Phono-Grand was not going to be a good seller. An art glass panel and coin slot were added to the outside; "A" roll mechanisms were put on the inside – and the result was the P-G-A. The P-G-A means "Phono-Grand, A-roll". Evidently only a very few P-G-A pianos were ever made.

**SEEBURG STYLE Z**

Style Z – Selective Roll Piano. Little is known concerning the Style Z, except that it was short-lived and few were sold. It used a six-tune roll (probably a special "A" roll) and had a tune selecting device. The catalogue description read: "The newest Seeburg invention. Height 4'10", width 5'3", depth 2'6". Plays a special cut 65-note electric rewind roll. The big feature of this marvelous instrument is that the person dropping the coin can select the particular number they wish to hear played. Program of music printed in plain view in special slot arrangement on piano; selection is made by simply turning indicator opposite name of piece desired. Ornamental slot arrangement showing music program and full directions for selecting the number to be played."

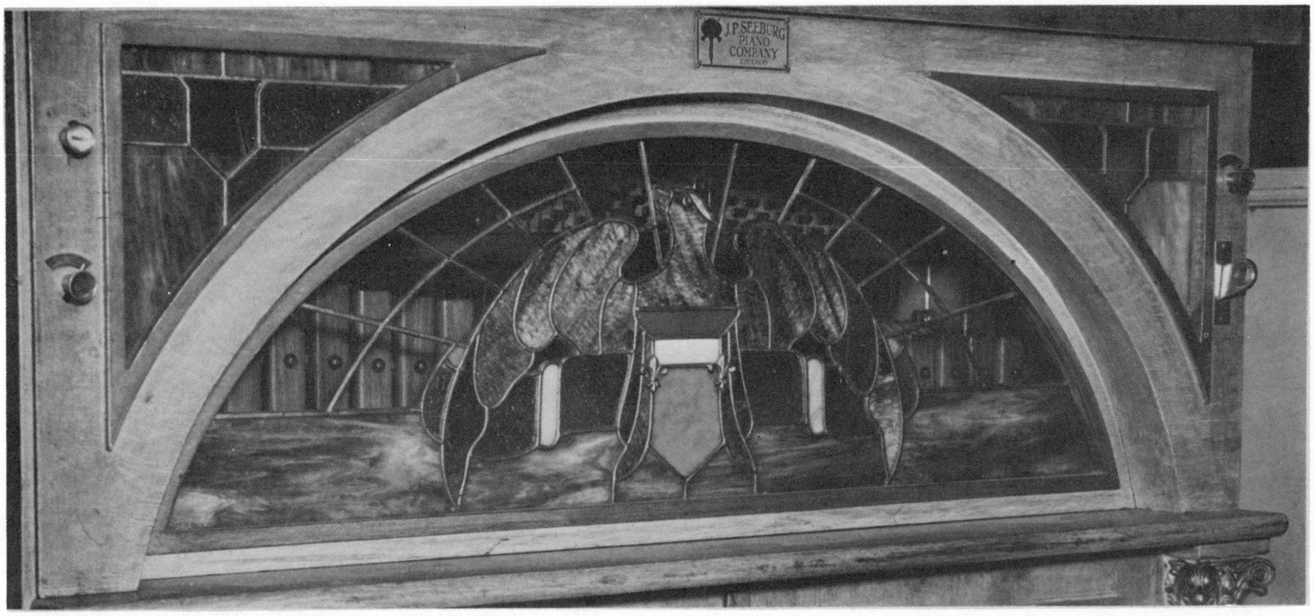


**Styles K and KT: These instruments were second only to the Seeburg L in popularity and total numbers manufactured. Basically, the Style K is a cabinet piano with mandolin and an extra instrument — a rank of violin pipes, a rank of flute pipes, or a xylophone. Early models were with pipes; late ones with xylophone. The K uses a standard type "A" coin piano roll. The KT is the same as a K, but in a slightly deeper case, and with the addition of castanets, triangle, tambourine, and (rarely) snare drum. The KT uses the type "G" or "4X" roll which is scored to accommodate the extra percussion effects. Early models featured art glass with a scene of two dancing girls (other variations occur, but most were with the dancers). Later models were standardized with the spread eagle design. These latter instruments are called "Seeburg Eagles" by collectors today. The K and KT instruments were very popular, and thousands were sold from the mid-teens to the late 1920's. Quite a few, mostly of the xylophone K and KT type, survive today. When pipe models and xylophone models were being made concurrently for a few years the models with violin or flute pipes were known as "Style K" and those with xylophone, as "Style KX." Just before the KT Special was introduced some eagle-design cabinet orchestrions were made with KT Special components.**

STYLE K—"Midget Orchestrion"

Case Design Patented

Beautiful case design of a size made especially for corners and small places where a larger instrument could not be used. Containing a 58 note piano without keyboard. A set of 25 pipes either violin, or flute, also mandolin attachment. Equipped with loud and soft lever, and automatic mandolin and pipe attachments. Any instrument can be shut off at will. Magazine slot registering 1 to 20 coins, using regular Seeburg electric piano music roll "S" containing from 10 to 20 selections on Seeburg rewind system. Art glass design subject to change without notice. When ordering specify whether violin or flute pipes are desired. Height—5 feet 2 inches. Width—1 foot 8 inches. Length—3 feet 10½ inches. Double veneered hardwood case finished in mission oak. Weight boxed for shipment, about 700 pounds.

STYLE KT

This is the same as the style "K" with the added attractiveness of the castenets, triangle and tambourine.

**Early K and KT with pipes.**

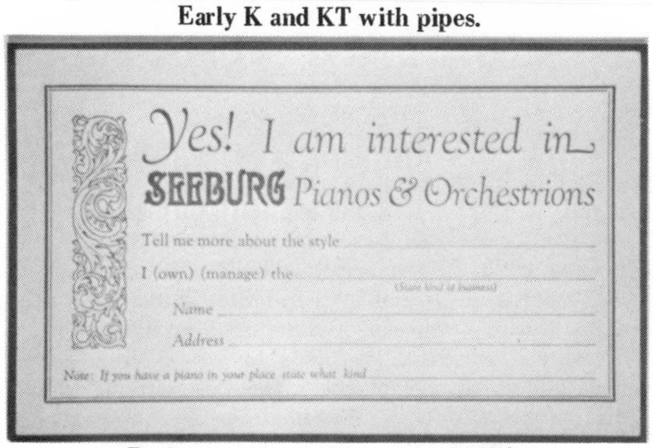

*Yes! I am interested in*
**SEEBURG** *Pianos & Orchestrions*

Tell me more about the style ____________
I (own) (manage) the ____________
(State kind of business)
Name ____________
Address ____________

Note: If you have a piano in your place state what kind ____________

**Business reply card from the 1920's.**

**Late Style K and KT with xylophone.**

STYLE "K"—"Midget Orchestrion"

Case design patented

**Piano, mandolin and xylophone.**

FANCY and effective. Beautiful case design; 61-note scale of exceptional tone quality.

Double veneered hardwood case, finished in silver grey, gold trimmings, or regular mission oak. Attractive art glass, electrically illuminated from within. (Design subject to change without notice.)

Automatic loud and soft control; mandolin and xylophone "off and on" controls. Uses Style "A", 65-note, ten-selection music roll with famous SEEBURG automatic rewind system.

Height: 5 feet, 2 inches: Width: 4 feet; Depth: 1 foot, 10½ inches. Weight, boxed for shipment: 800 lbs.

STYLE "KT"

Same as the Style "K" with the added attractiveness of castanets, triangle, and tambourine. Uses Style "G", 65-note, ten-selection music roll.

J. P. SEEBURG PIANO CO. MANUFACTURERS, CHICAGO

SIMPLICITY · RELIABILITY · ENDURANCE · SEEBURG

Interior of a late Style K with xylophone. This style could be ordered two ways: with single stroke or repeating xylophone beaters.

Interior view of an early Style K with violin pipes. The upper front panel, which was removed when this picture was taken, is of the dancing girl type. The K and KT instruments with pipes were costlier to make as they required a pressure system to operate the pipes, in addition to the regular vacuum system for the piano, mandolin, and controls. The K and KT with xylophone could use the same vacuum system and required no pressure system at all and, hence, were more economical to produce.

Interior of late Style KT with xylophone. Note the castanets, triangle, and tambourine near the top of the case.

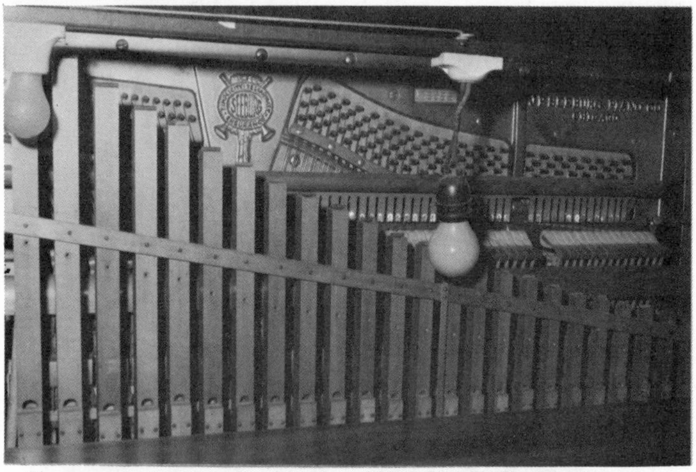

Upper part of a Style K with pipes (this particular K with pipes has an eagle front). The pipes are of the harmonic flute variety with tiny holes drilled at the nodal points (midway up the pipe).

Interior view of a Style KT with violin pipes (front has the eagle glass). These late eagle machines with pipes are very rare and are highly desired today.

Style "C"—Piano; Xylophone, Mandolin. Uses Standard 65-Note Music Roll. Dimensions—Height: 56½"; Width: 40"; Depth: 26".

Style C – The "Xylophonian." 54-note piano with xylophone and mandolin. (Do not confuse with earlier Style C – Art, a keyboard piano with mandolin). Introduced circa 1925. Center art glass is of a "theatre curtain" motif and is quite similar to the sides of the art glass used in the KT Special. Catalogue description follows: "A winner. Designed especially to provide in a small case the added novelty of the xylophone without cramping the tone chamber . . . Finished in silver gray highlighted in gold; or in dark oak. Ornamental art glass of special design subject to change."

SEEBURG

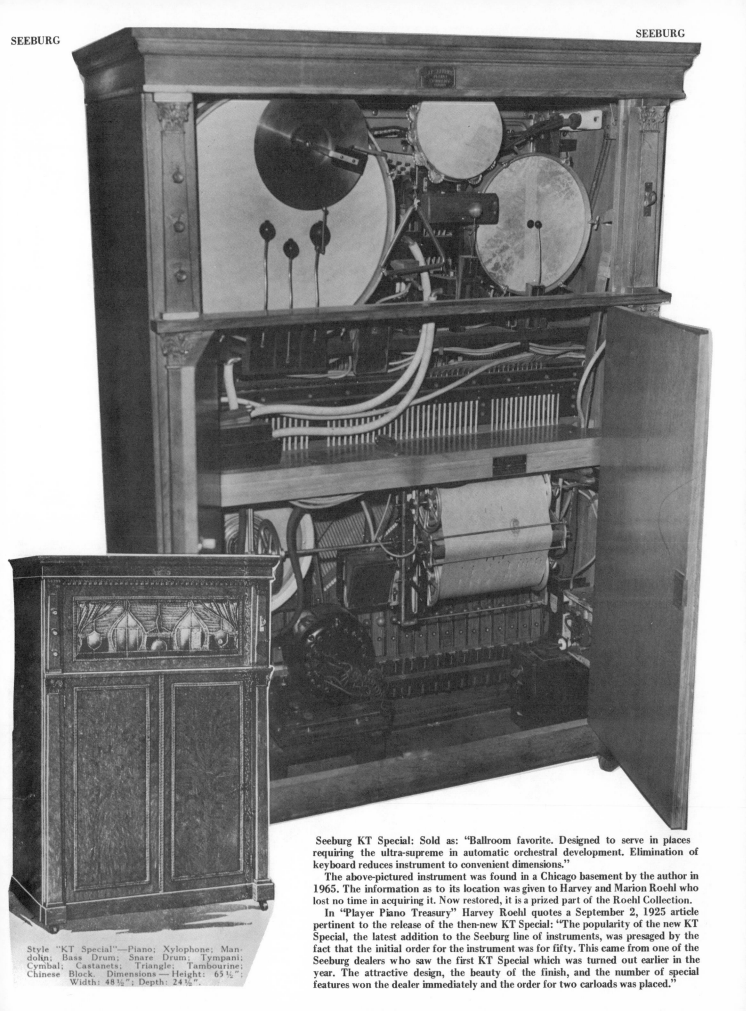

Style "KT Special"—Piano; Xylophone; Mandolin; Bass Drum; Snare Drum; Tympani; Cymbal; Castanets; Triangle; Tambourine; Chinese Block. Dimensions — Height: 65½"; Width: 48½"; Depth: 24½".

**Seeburg KT Special: Sold as: "Ballroom favorite. Designed to serve in places requiring the ultra-supreme in automatic orchestral development. Elimination of keyboard reduces instrument to convenient dimensions."**

**The above-pictured instrument was found in a Chicago basement by the author in 1965. The information as to its location was given to Harvey and Marion Roehl who lost no time in acquiring it. Now restored, it is a prized part of the Roehl Collection.**

**In "Player Piano Treasury" Harvey Roehl quotes a September 2, 1925 article pertinent to the release of the then-new KT Special: "The popularity of the new KT Special, the latest addition to the Seeburg line of instruments, was presaged by the fact that the initial order for the instrument was for fifty. This came from one of the Seeburg dealers who saw the first KT Special which was turned out earlier in the year. The attractive design, the beauty of the finish, and the number of special features won the dealer immediately and the order for two carloads was placed."**

Overall interior view of the E Special. This instrument, introduced in the 1920's, was produced only in small quantities. Far more popular during this era were the keyboardless or cabinet style orchestrions.

At the upper left inside of the E Special is the tambourine. The E Special uses a "G" (or "4X" – the two are the same) roll. As the E Special (and KT Special) has more instruments than a G roll can accommodate, a switching device permits one hole to operate two instruments.

STYLE "E SPECIAL"—"The All-Purpose Orchestrion"

**Piano, mandolin attachment, xylophone, bass drum, snare drum, tympani, cymbal, triangle, castanets, tambourine, Chinese block.**

DESIGNED to serve a dual purpose—that of an automatic orchestrion, and thru the convenience of the keyboard, piano can be manually played whenever desirable.

Double veneered hardwood case, finished in mission oak, or dull mahogany. Service doors in upper panel set with ornamental art glass; burnished brass art lamps at each side; design subject to change without notice. Program holder back of glass.

Equipped with loud and soft control; tempo regulator; special shut-off device for all orchestration instruments. Uses Style "G", 65-note, ten-selection music roll, with famous SEEBURG automatic rewind system.

Height: 4 feet, 9½ inches; Width: 5 feet, 3 inches; Depth: 2 feet, 9 inches. Weight, boxed for shipment: 1100 lbs.

Upper right of the E Special – showing the snare drum, wood block, and triangle. By means of a switching device the wood block and triangle play alternately from the same tracker bar hole.

Below the keyboard is the xylophone. It is of the reiterating or repeating type and will sustain a note (by rapidly vibrating a beater) when a tracker bar hole is uncovered. The instrumentation of the E Special is identical to that of the KT Special.

Lower right of the E Special – showing the bass drum and cymbal (which operate from a single beater). In addition the bass drum has two smaller beaters for tympani or kettle drum effect.

## SEEBURG STYLE X EXPRESSION PIANO

STYLE "X"—"Expression"

**Straight piano, reproducing expression, almost human in accompiishment.**

MASTERFULLY exact. Designed for locations demanding a reproducing instrument—real artistic interpretation. Also constructed for home use when so desired.

Handsome in construction, finished in either oak, dull or bright mahogany, or choice walnut, all double veneered.

Improved scale of seven and one-third octaves, over-strung copper bass, three unison throughout with full metal plate and bushed tuning pins. Selected ivory keys.

Special tempo regulator with graded scale; tracker-bar adjuster; separate "on and off" control located in front of roll chamber; rewind control. Uses specially arranged Style "XP" 4 to 6 selection reproducing roll. Also accommodates all standard 88-note rolls.

Height: 4 feet, 9½ inches; Width: 5 feet, 3 inches; Depth: 2 feet, 6½ inches. Weight, when boxed for shipment: 900 lbs.

**Made in either oak or mahogany wood the Style X uses either special Seeburg "XP" expression rolls or regular 88-note home player piano rolls. In addition, certain types of Apollo rolls (the Wurlitzer expression piano system) can be used on it. The relatively high price ($1500 in 1924) plus the fact that "locations demanding a reproducing instrument" were few and far between resulted in slow sales for this model. Wurlitzer had a similar experience with its Autograph Reproducing Piano – a similar type of instrument. The original catalogue description at the left notes that these were also made for home use.**

## SEEBURG PHONO-GRAND

**Proudly displaying a new Phono-Grand in the far corner, this Chicago living room of 1917 was intended to be the ultimate in sophistication. The description at the right notes that "prominent architects are figuring on the Phono-Grand as a part of the furnishing of apartment houses."**

### A Combination
#### —Unique and Charming

THE two most popular musical instruments the world has ever known are the piano and the phonograph. No home seems complete unless it contains one or both of the instruments. The limitations of the piano have not been in the piano itself, but in the ability of our people to use it.

Player pianos, operated either in person or by electric motor, have increased the enjoyment of piano music, but the cost of purchasing both a reproducing piano and a satisfactory phonograph has made a rather heavy expenditure.

Through the desire to have the music of both of these instruments available to every home, American ingenuity has brought forth an instrument which completely satisfies this need.

This new instrument has been named The Phono-Grand. It is a combination of the piano and the phonograph in an ideal form. The case is but slightly larger than that of a full-size phonograph—of the same appearance, dainty and graceful of design.

Both instruments are electrically operated, separate motors being used for each.

The Piano plays all standard 88-note Player-Piano rolls. It is especially adapted to the Q. R. S. Expression Rolls, with which it reproduces naturally and beautifully the playing of the master pianists.

The Phonograph is of the latest type and plays all phonographic records. Its tone quality is unusually full and clear.

The Phono-Grand measures 55" in height. It is 34" wide and 21" deep.

The phonograph, as you see, is in the upper part of the case. It is operated by a small and absolutely noiseless electric motor, which is placed just below the turntable. The entire phonograph can be lifted out when it is necessary to tune the Piano.

There are receptacles on either side for holding phonograph records and music rolls.

Below, in front, is the simple mechanism which controls the operation and expression of the player-piano.

**The Phono-Grand was introduced in 1917 and sold in limited numbers until the early 1920's. Containing the same essential mechanisms as the Style X (see top of page) the instrument can use "XP", Apollo, or regular 88-note player piano rolls.**

**Cases were made in mahogany (usually) or in quartered oak. The roll is conveniently located at a height which permits changing from one's favorite armchair. This was a gentleman's piano.**

October 6, 1917 — THE MUSIC TRADES

# SEEBURG COMBINES PIANO WITH PHONOGRAPH

### Announces the Phono-Grand Instrument that Plays Rolls and Records and that Occupies No More Space than Large Phonograph

CHICAGO, ILL., Oct. 3.—The J. P. Seeburg Piano Co. has added to its line an instrument differing widely from anything on the market. It is known as the Phono-Grand, and its name expresses, in effect, what it is—a combination phonograph and grand piano. It is a small instrument with a big tone and its beauty, originality and reasonable price are making it very attractive to dealers. The first Phono-Grand was placed on display in the warerooms of the company, tenth floor of the Republic Building, last week. But even before it was in shape for display, the company had many orders for Phono-Grands on their books. These were received from dealers who had simply been told about the instrument.

The Phono-Grand is in size little bigger than the ordinary phonograph. It is a little over 4 ft. high, 31 in. deep and 35 in. in width. The designs are very striking, and special attention is being given to the beauty of the veneers used in its finish. One's first impression of it is that it is an elaborately designed phonograph. One lifts the cover and places the records in place just as in the case of the regulation talking-machine. There are several original features about the phonograph's construction, and it is equipped to play any make of record. The electric motor, specially built, is absolutely noiseless. Then the tone of the phonograph is exceptionally large and clear, which is due to the unique construction of the tone chamber and something else. The "something else" is the sounding-board of the grand piano part of the instrument. This swells and broadens the tone, giving it a surprising volume. Right under the tone chamber of the phonograph is the player mechanism and on either side are receptacles for phonograph records and music rolls. There is space for dozens of records and for nine large music rolls. The piano plays regular eighty-eight-note rolls. It is operated electrically, and by means of the various automatic expression devices interprets the numbers with much artistry. The expression devices and other features are covered by patents. The piano has a special scale, and this and the arrangement of the instrument give it a tonal volume equal to that of many grand pianos.

The Phono-Grand is designed for use in the home and is especially adapted for use in apartments where space must be considered. It takes up no more space than a large phonograph, is designed with a view to making it a beautiful piece of furniture, and gives the owner all the variety of phonograph and piano music. The company began working on the Phono-Grand a long time ago, and before deciding to put it on the market it was submitted to every possible test. Improvement after improvement was made before it satisfied J. P. Seeburg, head of the company, and the experts who for months gave all their time to it.

"The demand for an instrument that would fit comfortably into the small apartment of to-day started us on the track of the Phono-Grand," said J. P. Seeburg to The Music Trades representative. "We are convinced that we are at last able to fully meet this demand and this belief is shared by all who have seen the instrument. It gives the family all that any phonograph can give them and a player-piano that plays any music just as the composer desired to have it interpreted. In homes where dancing is one of the pastimes—and it is in the great majority of homes—the Phono-Grand will give them phonograph music or grand piano music, just as they desire. It will even give them both, for the task of synchronizing the talking-machine and piano has been solved. And all this is furnished at about the price an ordinary upright piano costs. We have a great variety of cases coming through, and we plan to build Phono-Grands to harmonize with the finishing of music rooms. In fact, at the present time

The New Seeburg Phono-Grand

prominent architects are figuring on the Phono-Grand as a part of the furnishing of apartment houses. A number of designs have already been made, and we expect soon to announce the first of the apartments which will offer its tenants free phonograph and piano music. These designs provide for a very attractive piece of furniture to take the place of the regulation false fireplace or ponderous bookcase one finds in the apartment living-room. The Phono-Grand stands between two cases, harmonizing with it in design. These cases can be used for books, for music, for phonograph records or music rolls. With this arrangement the ordinary music cabinet—which in some cases is larger than the Phono-Grand—can be dispensed with. In other words, instead of a large piano or player-piano a large phonograph, a large music cabinet and a large and usually unattractive bookcase, the purposes of all these are served by an attractive wall adornment that will not take up as much space as an ordinary upright piano.

"Dealers who have seen the Phono-Grand are enthusiastic over it, and we are getting orders from all of these, while some who have only been told about it have been so impressed that they placed good advance orders.

"The mechanism of the instrument is trouble-proof, practically, and the full Seeburg guarantee covers the Phono-Grand. Its reasonable price places it within the reach of the great majority of buyers, and this is an item that appeals strongly to dealers. We have already had numerous requests for exclusive agencies, and dealers predict a tremendous demand, not only because of the musical merit of the instrument, but because of its originality. It is something new, something different, something with original talking points, and so the dealers want it."

A number of Phono-Grands are now coming through and the company will have a limited supply ready for the holiday trade.

Seeburg Style L Automatic Orchestra. Uses "G" rolls and contains the same instrumentation, except one rank of pipes instead of two, as the Seeburg G orchestrion.

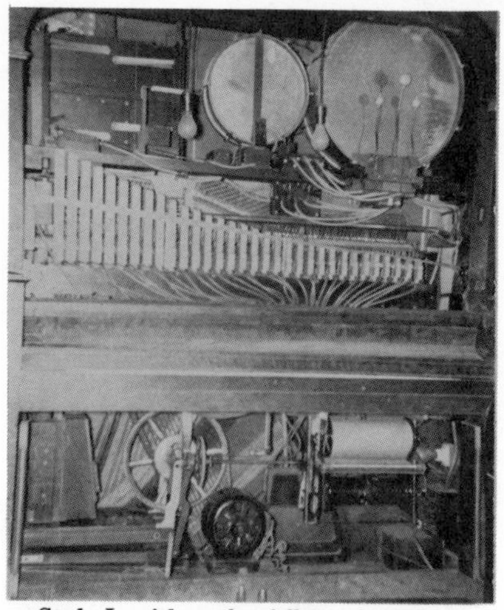

Above: Seeburg Style L with rank of flute pipes. Left: Seeburg Style L with rank of violin pipes. The Style L orchestrion was produced only in limited numbers and is quite rare today. Do not confuse this Style L designation with the omnipresent tiny Style L cabinet piano. (Svoboda and Klavestad Collections)

# STYLE G—Art Style
## ORCHESTRION

STYLE "G"—"Art Style Orchestrion
Piano, two sets of wood pipes (violin and flute), mandolin attachment, bass drum, snare drum, tympani, cymbal and triangle.
EXCEPTIONAL volume. A wonderful exrmple of the remarkable accomplishment in automatic music. New and original scale of seven and one-third octaves, over-strung copper bass, three unison throughout. Ornamental full iron plate, imported tuning pins and music wire; highest grade imported wool hammers; best grade ivory keys and ebony sharps. Electrically illuminated from within.
Double veneered hardwood case, finished in durable mission oak.
Equipped with automatic "loud and soft" control; tempo regulator; shut-off device for orchestrion effects. Uses Style "G", 65-note, ten-selection music roll with famous SEEBURG automatic rewind system.
Height: 6 feet, 7½ inches; Width, 5 feet, 10½ inches; Depth: 2 feet, 4½ inches. Weight, boxed for shipment: 1300 lbs.
J. P. SEEBURG PIANO CO.
MANUFACTURERS, CHICAGO
SIMPLICITY · RELIABILITY · ENDURANCE
SEEBURG


Above: Catalogue description of the Seeburg Style G orchestrion. Called the "Art Style," this is one of the most attractive of all American orchestrions. Many different music rolls featuring excellent arrangements were made for the Style G. Today collectors consider the Style G to be a prime addition to any exhibit of automatic musical instruments.

Seeburg G Orchestrion: While 95% or more of the Style G orchestrions made were of the style with torches pictured at the left, there were some other colorful and interesting varieties. At the right is a type with sailing ships and boy musicians (Givens Collection); just below is the earliest style of G with hanging lamps, mirrored outer panels and with two inner panels with tropical birds. Two hanging lamps are above the mirrors. Some of these have one rank of metal and one rank of wood (instead of two ranks of wood) pipes; at the lower right is a colorful style with an escutcheon and sailing ship design (Ex. A.C. Raney Collection; now in the Benson Collection).

Seeburg Style G orchestrion from the author's collection. For years this was a featured attraction in Valente's Nickelodeon Tavern in Chicago. I have always had a soft spot in my heart for the Seeburg G. The very first orchestrion I ever heard anywhere was a similar instrument in the Roehl Collection. On my first visit there in 1960 I heard the tune "Japansy." Since then that tune has always brought back memories whenever I've heard it again (on a G roll recut by Flemington, N.J., collector Ed Freyer).

Early Seeburg G's (and other Seeburg orchestrions) had "Upright Grand" on the fallboard decal. Slightly later ones had "Orchestrion" in straight letters (as in the catalogue illustration at the left). Still later ones had "ORCHESTRION" in gracefully flowing letters – as shown above. Most Seeburg G's were equipped with nickel slots; a few had dime slots; fewer still had quarter slots.

## SEEBURG STYLE J ORCHESTRION

STYLE J—"Soio-Orchestrion"

Case Design Patented

INSTRUMENTATION WITHOUT DRUMS:

New and original scale piano of seven and one-third octaves and three unisons throughout, with mandolin attachment, 68 pipes giving effects of violin, piccolo, flute, obo and clarinet, triangle, castanetes, and xylophone. The rolls used on this instrument are hand arranged and play wonderful solo effects. Equipped with tempo regulator on outside below key-bed. Any instrument can be shut off at will. Magazine slot registering 1 to 20 coins. Music roll "SSS" contains 10 selections on Seeburg rewind system. Art glass design subject to change without notice. Height—6 feet ½ inch. Width—2 feet 7½ inches. Length—5 feet 7½ inches. Double veneered hardwood case finished in circassian walnut. Weight boxed for shipment, about 1200 pounds.

**Style J Orchestrion: This orchestrion was made in several designs: the usual type as illustrated at the right (note that the description mentions "SSS" rolls – the early name for "H" rolls), the rare type as illustrated above, and also in a case virtually identical (except for the art glass treatment – the Seeburg has sailing ships; the Peerless has a spectral goddess in flowing robes) to that of the Peerless "Wisteria" orchestrion. Oak (mostly), walnut, and mahogany were the wood finishes available. The design at right is of stunning beauty. The art glass panels in the front posts are lighted from within.**

---

## SEEBURG STYLE H ORCHESTRION

STYLE "H"—"Solo Orchestrion"

**Piano; xylophone; 68 pipes, giving violin, piccolo, flute, and clarinet effects; mandolin attachment; bass drum; snare drum; tympani; cymbal; triangle, and castanets.**

"MASKED MARVEL." Equal to seven man orchestra. Equipped with patented soft drum control, enabling instrument to render wonderful solo effects.

Double veneered hardwood case finished in mission oak (silver grey finish by special order); adorned with two hand carved wood Caryatids, representing "Strength and Beauty," typical of this combination of excellence in case design.

Tempo regulator; automatic loud and soft controls; uses special Style "H", 88-note, ten-selection music roll with famous SEEBURG automatic rewind system.

Height: 7 feet, 3 inches; Width, 6 feet, 4 inches; Depth, 2 feet, 10½ inches. Weight, boxed for shipment: 1800 lbs.

**Seeburg Style H Orchestrion: If someone were to award a prize for the most ornate keyboard orchestrion design ever produced in America, chances are that the Style H would win it uncontested. With its two statues (named Strength and Beauty – a closeup of "Beauty" is shown at the right), its four large and colorful art glass panels, its three hanging art glass lamps, and the overall elegance of the case, the H is awesome and impressive.**

**Above and left: Unusual art glass design of the Seeburg H; with escutcheons at the center and nautical scenes below.**

# STYLE H

### SOLO—ORCHESTRION

**The H was a popular model, especially in the 1911 - 1920 years (although this style was made as late as 1926), and hundreds were sold. Nearly all were of the standard art glass design as pictured at the above left. Most were made in quartered oak wood; a few were produced in mahogany.**

**The H roll features a separate solo section. The treble piano notes can be shut off, permitting the violin or flute pipes to play solo melodies.**

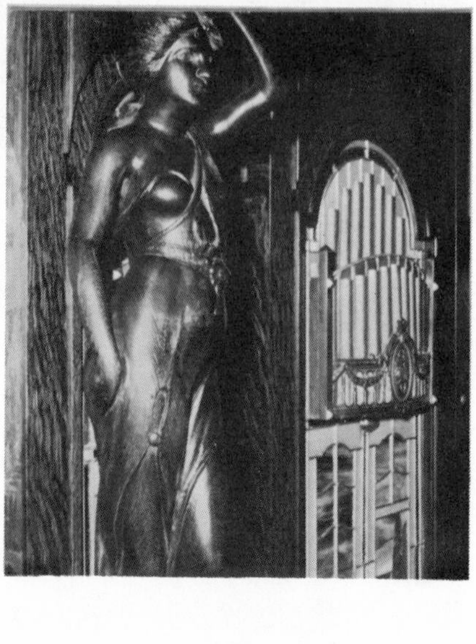

**Above:** Upper interior view of a Seeburg H orchestrion. Now a part of the Givens Collection, this instrument saw years of service in a Toronto, Canada, restaurant. It is a late instrument and was one of the very few H's made in the 1920's. At the very top can be seen the snare drum (left) and bass drum. The latter has three beaters; the two small side ones are for the tympani effect. Between the two drums are the black castanets. The two ranks of pipes, harmonic flutes in the foreground and, behind them, the violins, rise from right to left. In the foreground is the xylophone.

**Left:** This ice cream parlor of 1912 went all the way and invested in a Seeburg H.

# SEEBURG

**Style "M. O." Reproducing Pipe Organ**

CONSTANTLY on the alert for new sources of prospects, we are now developing an entirely new market for SEEBURG Reproducing Pipe Organs. Special co-operative methods of advertising are being used. Those dealers who already have secured the franchise for this instrument will be the first to profit in this new field.

**These instruments use "MSR" rolls.**

**The Style "MO," "Celesta," and "Celesta DeLuxe" organs were made with one or two keyboards and were primarily intended for the mortuary trade (although a few saw church use and fewer still were used in theatres). The above instrument is from the Murray Clark Collection.**

**With its somewhat Gothic case this Seeburg organ, now in the Givens Collection, was once just the ideal instrument to set the somber mood necessary for solemn services. Unlike the other Seeburg mortuary organs shown on this page, the above instrument has no piano. The instrumentation consists of many ranks of pipes. Special "HO" and "MO" rolls can be played on it. For a comparative instrument see the Unified Reproduco Organ made by the Operators Piano Co. (see Operators Piano Co. section of this book).**

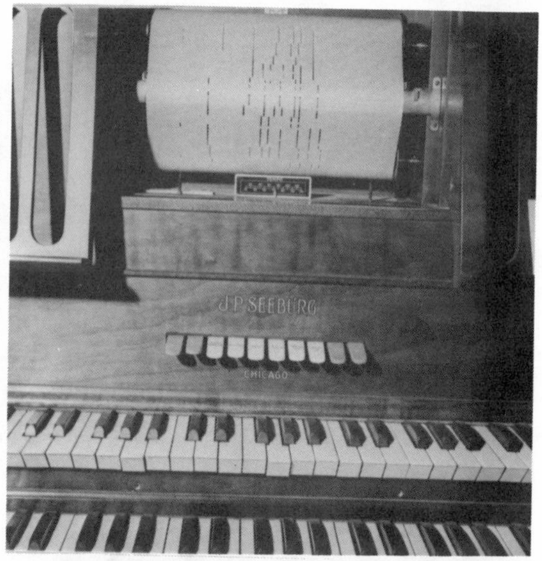
J.P. SEEBURG
CHICAGO

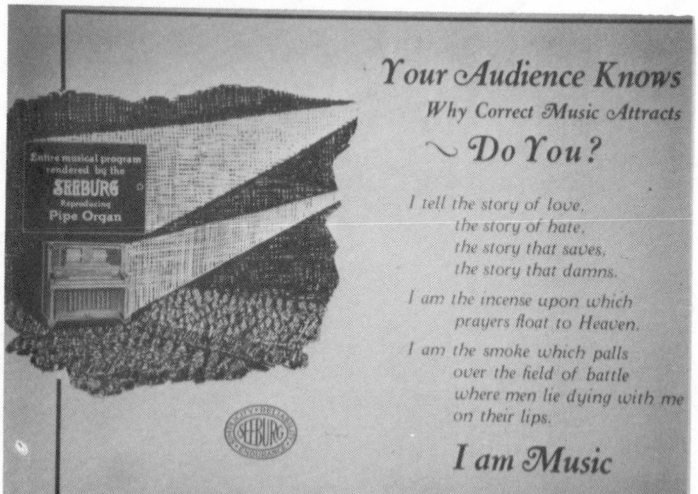
Your Audience Knows
Why Correct Music Attracts
Do You?
Entire musical program rendered by the
SEEBURG
Reproducing
Pipe Organ
I tell the story of love,
the story of hate,
the story that saves,
the story that damns.
I am the incense upon which
prayers float to Heaven.
I am the smoke which palls
over the field of battle
where men lie dying with me
on their lips.
SEEBURG
I am Music

**SEEBURG**
**Twin-Roll**
**Reproducing**
**Pipe Organ**

**Style TR: Seeburg Reproducing Pipe Organ. Introduced in 1927 as silent movies came to an end, the Style TR was in the wrong place at the wrong time (or, perhaps, the right place at the wrong time). In any event, the instrument — billed as the latest thing for the musical accompaniment of silent films — met with a near-zero sales reception. It is important historically as being probably the last type of automatic roll-operated instrument introduced by Seeburg in the early years.**

**The TR used: "Hand played organ rolls of the TR type. Full and complete selection. Dramatic, ballads, light dramatic, plaintive, marches, incidental, and interpretive."**

**Instrumentation: 88-note piano; 24 8-foot stopped diapason pipes, 61 flutes, 37 quintadena pipes.**

**For automatic operation from the projection booth a "Play Your Complete Musical Program with One Finger!" feature provided an 8-button remote control panel which permitted turning the organ on and off, selecting either the right or left side roll, rewinding either the left or right roll, and advancing in "fast forward" either the right or left roll.**

# The Soul of The Film

# SEEBURG Pipe-Organ Orchestra

*"Wondrous range of orchestration makes the SEEBURG reputation"*

*"Without the trouble to arrange the SEEBURG makes an instant change"*

**Smaller Seeburg photoplayers: The three instruments pictured at the top of this page use the type "G" orchestrion roll.**

**Style P photoplayer.**

**Style Q photoplayer.**

**Style W photoplayer: Unlike the P and Q photoplayers, the Style W has two ranks of pipes: violin and flute. It uses the type G orchestrion roll and must have sounded like a Style G orchestrion. Other instrumentation: bass drum, snare drum, cymbal, triangle, tympani effect, wind siren, bird whistle, tambourine, fire gong, mandolin, and xylophone. The pipes are provided with a tremolo (vibrato) effect. Sold for $1500 wholesale; $3500 retail. The high "retail" prices of the photoplayers permitted Seeburg to offer generous time-payment terms to theatre owners!**

**SEEBURG PHOTOPLAYERS**
**(Using H and MSR rolls)**

# Seeburg Photo Player

**Style W: Later model which uses H and MSR rolls (Do not confuse with smaller Style W at upper right of this page).**

**INSTRUMENTATION, "S"**

| | |
|---|---|
| Organ-Piano | Tympani Effect |
| Violin | Tom Tom Effect |
| Flute | Horse Trot |
| Bass 8' | Castanets |
| Tremolo | Fire Gong |
| Mandolin | Bird Whistle |
| Organ Swell | Door Bell |
| Bass Drum | Telephone Bell |
| Snare Drum | Triangle |
| Cymbal | Piano 88 Notes |

Cello

*An almost unlimited variety of effects may be obtained from key-board, such as: Cuckoo, Scotch Bag-pipe Effect, etc.*

Bass 16' Xylophone

**Style S photoplayer: Two illustrations, one of a single roll model and the other of a double roll (H roll on the bottom, 88-note piano roll on top) instrument. Actually, any Seeburg photoplayer could be ordered with two roll mechanisms if desired. The instrumentation list at the left has been amended (at the factory) by writing in "cello, bass 16', and xylophone" in addition to the printed items.**

"Seeburg Motion-Picture-Player"
Style "M"
FOR MOTION PICTURE THEATRES
A COMBINATION
ORCHESTRION AND PIPE ORGAN
INSTRUMENTATION:

A seven and one-third octave piano, with mandolin attachment, 104 pipes representing violin, flute, piccolo 2 feet—melodia 8 feet—echo 8 feet—clarinet 8 feet—bass 8 feet—in fact full organ range with swell and tremolo; bass drum, snare drum, kettle drum effect, cymbal, triangle, tympani, tom tom, xylophone, crash cymbal, castanets, fire gong, steamboat whistle, locomotive whistle, locomotive bell, cow bell, thunder effect, wind siren, bird call, baby cry, telephone and door bell, horse trot and automobile horn. Separate 61 note organ key-board. Equipped with the Seeburg solo effect features and hand arranged rolls "SSS" containing 10 selections. Height—5 feet 3 inches. Width—3 feet 3 inches. Length—12 feet 3 inches. Double veneered hardwood case, finished in mission oak. Weight boxed for shipment about 2000 pounds.

**Judging from testimonial letters printed by Seeburg, the Style M must have been one of the best selling models.**

# Seeburg Pipe-Organ Orchestra

## Seeburg Pipe-Organ Orchestra, Style "R"

Equipped with an orchestrated music roll which is specially arranged to bring out the manifold tone combinations of the instrument—covering the organ, piano and orchestral tones, including a magnificent set of **twenty chimes,** also drums, etc., which makes the instrument superior to a human orchestra. The Seeburg **SOLO** music rolls are hand interpreted (hand played) so that they actually reproduce the playing of world-famous pianists and organists. The Seeburg Shutter (swell) for tone and expression control is a vastly superior device compared with the usual "swell." It reduces the tone to a mere murmur or pianissimo and increases it to an immense fortissimo and the varying degrees of expression between these extremes.

**Built with one or two rolls.** Double veneered hardwood case finished in dull mission oak. Equipped with the Seeburg **SOLO**-effect features and hand arranged rolls containing three to ten selections. Height 5 feet 3 inches. Width 3 feet 9 inches. Length 13 feet 4 inches. Weight boxed for shipment about 2500 pounds.

**INSTRUMENTATION, "R"**

| | |
|---|---|
| Organ-Piano | Octave Coupler |
| Violin | Crescendo Pedal |
| Flute | Castanets |
| Bass Melodia 8' | Tambourine |
| 'Cello | Mandolin |
| Vox Humana 8' | Tom Tom Effect |
| Xylophone | Telephone Bell |
| Cathedral Chimes 20 notes | Door Bell |
| | Fire Gong |
| Tremolo | Horse Trot |
| Bass Drum | Tympani Effect |
| Snare Drum | Steamboat Whistle |
| Cymbal | Bird Whistle |
| Crash Cymbal | Baby Cry |
| Triangle | Wind Siren |
| Organ Swell | Thunder Effect |
| Piano 88 Notes | |

ODEON THEATRE, SAVANNAH, GA.

*"SEEBURG music full of life — instant change from drum to fife"*

PENN THEATRE, PITTSBURGH, PA.

**Above: Penn Theatre – home of a Style R purchased in August, 1915.**

We take pleasure in stating that both the style "R" Pipe Organ installed in our Odeon Theatre, as well as the Style "S" installed in our Folly Theatre, have given us complete satisfaction in every way.

We were at first quite dubious about making the switch from orchestra to Seeburg Player, however the two Seeburg instruments have so far exceeded our expectations that we would not think of going back to the old regime.

Very truly yours,

ODEON & FOLLY THEATRES.

## World Famous Artists Make Master Records for Seeburg Music Rolls

THE pianist's composition is recorded by means of electric wires connected with the recorder placed behind the piano. When you consider that the celebrated artists who make these records are paid hundreds of dollars for recording a single composition, and that the Seeburg music rolls are reproduced from such records, you will then get an adequate idea as to the artistic results which can be obtained from the Seeburg Pipe Organs, and Self-Playing Orchestras in connection with which these artists' music rolls are used. The result is similar to listening to a phonograph record by Kreisler, the great violinist, or Caruso, the wonderful tenor.

**Illustration of a Style R high on the balcony in a dance hall.**

# Seeburg Pipe-Organ Orchestra

The Music Master of Every Situation

**INSTRUMENTATION, "T"**

| | |
|---|---|
| Organ-Piano | Octave Coupler |
| Violin | Castanets |
| Flute | Tom Tom Effect |
| Bass 8' | Fire Gong |
| 'Cello | Steamboat Whistle |
| Xylophone | Thunder Effect |
| Tremolo | Wind Siren |
| Organ Swell | Baby Cry |
| Piano 88 Notes | Bird Whistle |
| Bass Drum | { Telephone Bell |
| Snare Drum | { Door Bell |
| Cymbal | Horse Trot |
| Crash Cymbal | Triangle |
| Tympani Effect | |

*An almost unlimited variety of effects may be obtained from key-board, such as: Cuckoo, Scotch Bag-pipe Effect, etc.*

**Style T: This particular style was always equipped with the double roll system. The upper roll is an 88-note home player piano roll; the lower can be either an H or an MSR roll. The "MSR" designation came from this roll's initial use on photoplayer styles M, S, and R.**

*"SEEBURG value quickly seen as music changes with the screen"*

## Exclusive Advantages Found in the Seeburg Pipe-Organ Orchestras

THE Self-Playing feature lends itself to such an artistic tone production as was never believed possible until brought out in Seeburg solo instruments.

The Seeburg music rolls are actual records of the playing of world famous musicians. The artists who make these rolls receive hundreds of dollars for the making of a single record, which attests to the artistic excellence of the reproduction of their playing by means of the Seeburg rolls.

The patented Seeburg **cut-out** buttons make it possible to play any selection with whatever tone combinations one wishes to get. In other words, while the music roll is so cut that it selects its own instrumentation, the same roll can be made to play combinations of organ, violin and flute, etc., or these combinations can be cutout and others played. In this way a given selection can be played with any instrumentation desired.

Another valuable feature; when the instrument is playing by the roll, any selection on the roll can be chosen when wanted; for instance, if No. 5 which is playing happens to be a lively piece and the picture changes from a lively to a sentimental scene, the roll can be run forward or back to a selection which will exactly fit the picture.

**A Seeburg Makes the Pictures Talk**

*Good Music Plus Dramatic Effects*

*Vaudeville Music*

**Style V. Instrumentation is the same as Style PO (see below) plus xylophone and mandolin. In actuality, Seeburg specifications often varied considerably from those listed in the photoplayer catalogues.**

**INSTRUMENTATION, "PO"**

| | |
|---|---|
| Organ-Piano | Castanets |
| Violin | Triangle |
| Flute | Tom Tom Effect |
| 'Cello | Bird Whistle |
| Bass Melodia 8' | Wind Siren |
| Vox Humana 8' | { Telephone Bell |
| Tremolo | { Door Bell |
| Bass Drum | Fire Gong |
| Snare Drum | Horse Trot |
| Cymbal | Tympani Effect |
| Octave Coupler | Organ Swell |
| Crescendo Pedal | Tambourine |
| Piano 88 Notes | |

*An almost unlimited variety of effects may be obtained from key-board, such as: Cuckoo, Scotch Bag-pipe Effect, etc.*

**Style PO: Without a roll mechanism, Style PO was made for hand playing only.**

SIMPLICITY • RELIABILITY • ENDURANCE — SEEBURG

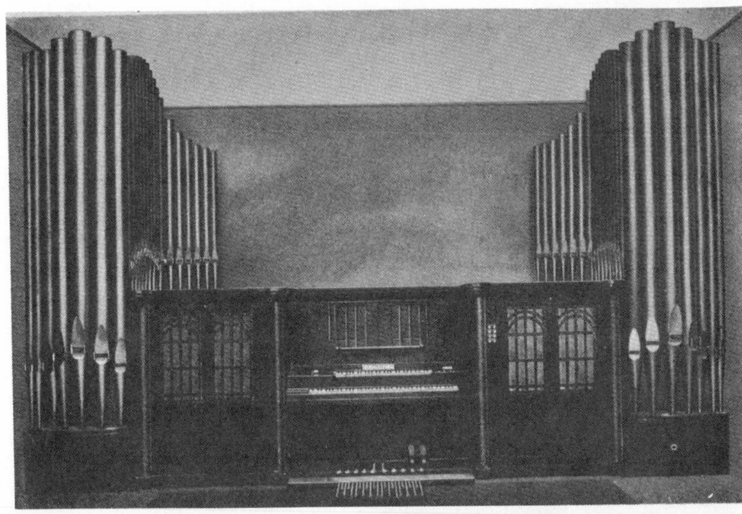

**Style A DeLuxe: The A DeLuxe is essentially a Style R with a rank of external 16' pedal bourdon pipes added. (Note: the impressive side pipes in the above illustration are decoration only and are not the 16' bourdon pipes referred to!). The 20-note chimes of this and other Seeburg photoplayer models are not orchestra bells but are tubular hanging chimes. The external 16' bourdon pipes have electromagnetic actions.**

---

**Seeburg was very successful in the photoplayer market and ranked with Wurlitzer and the American Photoplayer Company as a leading factor in the field. The period of greatest activity was from about 1914 to 1920.**

**"A" DE LUXE**
**FULL ORGAN REPRESENTING THE FOLLOWING INSTRUMENTS**

| | |
|---|---|
| Organ-Piano | Piano 88 Notes |
| Open Diapason 8' | Chimes 20 notes |
| Stopped Diapason 8' | 'Cello |
| Bassoon and Oboe 8' | Octave Coupler |
| Vox Humana 8' | Crescendo Pedal |
| Violin | Bass Drum |
| Xylophone | Snare Drum |
| Organ Swell | Electro-pneumatic action |

**PEDAL ORGAN**

Pedal Bourdon 16' — Manual to pedal couplers

**SOUND EFFECTS**

Cymbal, Crash Cymbal, Triangle, Castanets, Tambourine, Bird Whistle, Baby Cry, Wind Siren, Thunder Effect, TomTom Effect, Steamboat Whistle, Horse Trot, Tympani Effect, Telephone Bell, Door Bell

*An almost unlimited variety of effects may be obtained from key-board, such as: Cuckoo, Scotch Bag-pipe Effect, etc.*

*SEEBURG Players do not fail—*
*SEEBURG music don't get stale"*

**Seeburg's unidentified poet laureate wrote the above doggerel and other verse which was sprinkled through its Pipe Organ Orchestra catalogue.**

## STANDARD PIANO PLAYER
—Oregon, Illinois—

Made in the town of Oregon, Illinois, the Standard Piano Player instruments were made in several different varieties. Most were of the endless roll type with the roll mechanism located behind the piano sounding board.

Standard pianos with mandolin attachment or with mandolin and one extra instrument (usually a rank of pipes) used 10-tune "A" rolls, but of a special endless or continuous loop format specially made by the Clark Orchestra Roll Co. 5-tune "A" rolls were made also.

In addition, at least one Standard instrument had percussion effects and used an endless-type "G" or "4X" roll.

Little is known about the Standard instruments. The author would welcome correspondence from anyone with original Standard catalogues or other literature.

Note: Do not confuse the Standard Piano Player instruments made in Oregon, Illinois, with the much more common "Standard" brand home pianos and player pianos made during the 'teens and 'twenties by Hardman, Peck & Co. of New York City.

Many endless-roll Standard Piano Players were converted to regular rewind-type rolls in later years, thus accounting for Seeburg, Cremona, etc. roll mechanisms occasionally seen in Standard coin pianos today.

—————————

Above: A Standard piano somewhat similar to the Sprague instrument (see left), but with art glass in the front panel. All of the Standard pianos shown here use endless rolls.

Above: View of an early endless-roll Standard coin piano. The beveled clear glass panel permits a view of the interior. (Tom Sprague collection)

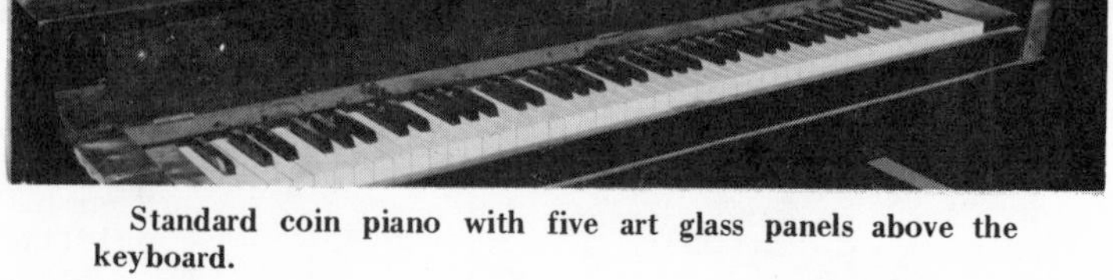

Standard coin piano with five art glass panels above the keyboard.

## SYMPHONIA PIANO ROLL CO
## EUGENE DE ROY
### —A recollection—

*During the 1960's the late Eugene DeRoy was of great assistance to the author in the search for information concerning automatic instruments, locating original factories and factory sites, and in providing first-hand information from the automatic musical instrument era. The following narrative, which takes the form of the author's personal recollections of Mr. DeRoy, gives some interesting aspects of the business in years past.*

It was in 1963 or 1964, I recall, that I received a thin blue paper airmail envelope with an Antwerp, Belgium postmark. Upon opening the missive I noted a rubber-stamped "SYMPHONIA" heading above the message.

The contents of the letter were fascinating. During 1962 and 1963 I spent quite a bit of time writing to and visiting various persons in Europe in an effort to track down a few orchestrions made years earlier by Hupfeld, Philipps, Popper, and other firms. I wrote to collectors, museums, and to just about any other name I could find that might possibly have a scrap of information about these nostalgic music-makers. At the time there was little collector interest in large orchestrions in Europe. The situation was mainly due to lack of specimens to collect. At the same time, I might mention, there was an intense interest in military band organs — called fair organs there — an interest which continues unabated today. During a visit to Germany about this time I was amazed to learn from an organ dealer that he had just sold an instrument to a collector in England for the sum of $29,000.00. To be sure, the organ was a very large and impressive one.

During my quest for orchestrions and orchestrion information (I sought original catalogues and literature just as avidly as the instruments themselves) letter after letter was answered with, "Sorry, I don't have any Hupfeld orchestrions, nor do I know of anyone who does . . ." — or something in a similar vein.

The Symphonia letter was different. The writer, Eugene DeRoy, not only said that he knew of a number of surviving orchestrions, but he went on to say that he once made music rolls for virtually every different orchestrion type. He then proceeded to list new music rolls he currently had in stock for the Hupfeld Helios, Hupfeld Pan, the Weber orchestrions of various types, and others — instruments which by that time, after much futile searching, seemed to me to be almost legendary and unobtainable.

An exchange of correspondence followed. My first purchase from Mr. DeRoy was a Pianella Style C piano — a small keyboard instrument with a xylophone mounted horizontally at the top. In describing the Pianella Mr. DeRoy sent a photocopy of an old catalogue illustration. From this clue I found that he had a wonderful selection of old-time historical material.

Next from Mr. DeRoy came a beautiful Hupfeld Helios II/25 orchestrion with a duplex roll mechanism. This impressive instrument measured 10'6" high and was from the era of elegant orchestrions — the years just after the turn of the 20th century. I lost no time buying the Helios for the quoted four-figure sum. As might be logically expected, on my next European trip (I went there frequently on business) I planned to stop in Belgium to visit Mr. DeRoy personally.

His rendezvous instructions, relayed to me in advance in a letter, went something like this: "I shall meet you at the airport. From there we shall go to my daughter's home which is not far away. I shall then show you your Hupfeld as she lives with her." I will never forget Mr. DeRoy's charming trait of imparting human "him" and "her" names to his orchestrion descriptions!

After viewing the Helios II/25 which was languishing in a rather dirty and disassembled state in a cramped garage we drove to Mr. DeRoy's combined home and workshop in Borgerhout, a district of Antwerp. There I met Mrs. DeRoy, his charming wife.

Years earlier Symphonia had been a factory type of operation which was located at different times in several parts of Antwerp. Now the Symphonia Company was a small over the counter shop which did its main business in selling piano parts such as new felt hammers, strings, piano hardware, and the like.

In Mr. and Mrs. DeRoy I found a veritable gold mine of information pertaining to my favorite hobby subject: the "good old days" when coin operated pianos, orchestrions, reproducing pianos, music boxes, and other self-playing instruments reigned supreme on the musical scene.

Mr. DeRoy (I never called him by his first name) entered the field of automatic musical instruments in the early 1920's. His father-in-law was a barrel organ maker, and from him Mr. DeRoy learned the trade. At this time barrel-operated instruments of all kinds were losing favor to the newer and more conveniently operated paper roll types. Paper

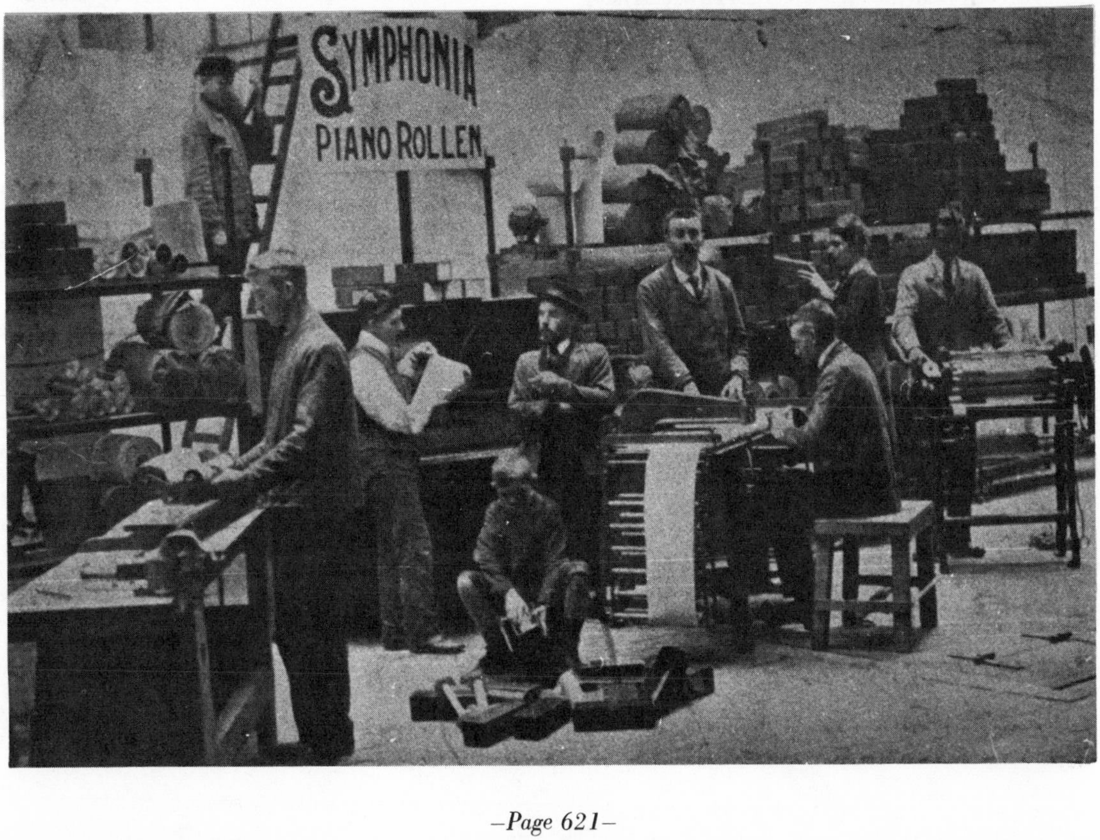

music rolls were cheap and could be made quickly as new popular tunes captured the fancy of the public. To capitalize on this market the Symphonia Piano Roll Company was born.

It was soon learned that there was a very large market for rolls to go on the many types of coin pianos and orchestrions made in Germany by Philipps, Hupfeld, Weber, Popper, Welte, and a host of others. The manufacturers of the orchestrions viewed the production of music rolls as a necessary bother to help sell the instruments. Mr. DeRoy viewed the production of music rolls as a profitable and worthwhile business in itself.

By coming on the market with new tunes faster than the orchestrion makers could, and by charging less for the rolls, Symphonia soon had a thriving business. It was all the firm could do to keep up with the flood of orders that kept pouring in from all over Europe and, to a lesser extent, from other parts of the world. I remember Mr. DeRoy mentioning that he had several customers in Canada for Hupfeld rolls and that one of them, a Newfoundland gentleman, had ordered as recently as the late 1950's.

At first the orchestrion makers resented this incursion into their private music roll making preserve. Soon they learned that the availability of inexpensive and really up-to-date Symphonia rolls for their instruments sharply increased the sale of their orchestrions – and the attitude changed from one of hostility to one of cooperation. They began furnishing Symphonia with new tracker scales and layouts as new types of instruments were introduced.

One maker, Imhof & Mukle of Vöhrenbach, Germany, refused to go along with Mr. DeRoy's business. In answer to a request for a tracker bar layout scale for each of the Imhof instruments Mr. DeRoy was told that the making of Imhof rolls would not be possible and that, furthermore, they would not release any of the "top secret" scale information to him. To this Mr. DeRoy replied, "All I have to do is see one of your instruments and in less than an hour I can figure out for myself all of the information I need." Which he did!

During this time Ludwig Hupfeld of Leipzig, Germany, was the world's largest maker of automatic musical instruments. From their factory came a stream of mechanical marvels ranging from home player pianos to reproducing pianos, from small coin pianos to gigantic Helios and Pan orchestrions.

Mr. DeRoy was on semi-amiable terms with Hupfeld as he made all sorts of music rolls to fit that firm's instruments – a situation they weren't exactly delighted with, but one which they tolerated in view of the ever-increasing Hupfeld sales in Mr. DeRoy's home country of Belgium. Mr. DeRoy was a perceptive and intelligent man. It was with a twinkle in his eyes that he told me, "I wrote to Hupfeld and asked if I could visit their factory in order to familiarize myself with the instruments so as to do a better job with the music rolls. When I went there I found that it was a wonderful operation – and I spent quite a bit of time 'stealing with my eyes.' They viewed the making of orchestrions as a super-secret process. The person who explained the making of music rolls to me did it with equal awe and reverence. What he did not know was that I not only understood all about making rolls, I knew all about the inner parts of even the most complicated Hupfeld instruments as well. While they thought I was having a good time as a vacationing tourist in their plant I was actually learning much information that enabled me to make the Symphonia Company more efficient."

The automatic musical instrument business in the 1920's was, as might be expected, highly competitive – so Hupfeld's attitude was not surprising, nor was Imhof's earlier refusal. In later years after each of these firms ceased making instruments and rolls they turned over their customer lists to Symphonia – a move that was profitable for Mr. DeRoy and that was good customer relations for the factories, or what was left of them.

As I was very interested in the history of automatic musical instruments I asked Mr. DeRoy every question I could think of during our first visit. In subsequent years I visited Mr. DeRoy several other times, and each time there were many more questions. Sometimes the answer to one question would make me think of two more questions to ask!

Mr. DeRoy personally liked the violin players best of all. He admired the Hupfeld Phonoliszt-Violina immensely and recalled that at one time there were six hundred (!) of these instruments located in the city of Antwerp alone. I was amazed to hear such a staggering figure and asked if Brussels and other Belgian cities had similar quantities. "No, because the Hupfeld distribution was irregular," he said. "While there were six hundred sold in Antwerp, none at all were sold in Brussels. Of course, there may have been a few Phonoliszt-Violinas there as the instruments were often resold on a second-hand basis."

He related that he had written to all of his former customers for Symphonia-made Phonoliszt-Violina rolls in an effort to locate a surviving instrument to keep as a memento for himself. At that time, in 1963 or 1964, he thought of the good times of years earlier and decided that a Hupfeld violin-player would be the ideal item to bring back these memories. His searching efforts were in vain. Seemingly all of the six hundred Phonoliszt-Violinas had vanished into thin air. It was with pleasure a year or so later that I found an owner of one of these instruments and gave Mr. DeRoy the information. He happily tracked it down and made a deal to buy it. Over the years Mr. DeRoy had heard of the Mills Violano-Virtuoso violin-player made in Chicago, Illinois, but had never seen or heard one. After reading about it in my book, "Put Another Nickel In," he decided he should own one! I obtained one of these and shipped it to him in Belgium.

When I first met Mr. DeRoy I had visions of locating vast quantities of orchestrions in Europe. Mr. DeRoy's mailing list contained thousands of names, and among these people and places there must be at least a few hundred who still had instruments – or so I reasoned. While I was able to locate several fine classic orchestrions through Mr. DeRoy, most of the time the search led to a blank wall. "Sorry, but our place was flooded in 1935," or, "We burned the Weber orchestrion in 1939," or, "It was destroyed during the war" were typical answers to inquiries.

Mr. and Mrs. DeRoy traveled with me thousands of miles through Europe in quest for instruments. I planned these excursions to include a number of the original factory buildings in which the instruments were made years ago.

The Philipps factory, home of the famed Wurlitzer Mandolin PianOrchestra and Concert PianOrchestra orchestrions sold in America, still stands at the corner of Philipp Reis Strasse and Ohmstrasse in Bockenheim, a suburb of Frankfurt-am-Main, Germany.

At one time or another we visited the factories or factory sites of Weber, Pierre Eich, Welte, Mortier, and several others. Unhappily, none contained any material remains of their former musical glory – although an occasional faded sign could be seen.

The surviving orchestrions that Mr. DeRoy had kept in the back of his mind over the years were tracked down by him within a year or two of our first meeting. When he learned that I was interested in the subject he started an intense letter-writing campaign to find what he could. No one had approached him on the subject before I did, and he was at first surprised, and then very pleased, that someone cared about saving and rebuilding the few instruments that managed to survive the ravages of the years.

I gave him the names and addresses of other collectors in America and in England, a step which soon led to a lively commerce for him. I kept hoping that he would write to me someday with news of finding a Philipps Paganini orchestrion, a large Concert Welte, or perhaps a Hupfeld Helios V, but, alas, these instruments never materialized.

I kept track of surviving large Philipps orchestrions and came to the conclusion that most of them that are known today were rescued from locations here in the United States where they were sold years ago by Wurlitzer. Apparently the attrition rate for large orchestrions in Europe was even higher than it was in America!

Of the orchestrions that Mr. DeRoy found, the one that impressed me most was the Hupfeld Excelsior Pan Orchestra. Over the years Hupfeld made many types of automatic instruments. Around 1912 the Hupfeld Pan Orchestra was introduced. This marvelous piece of

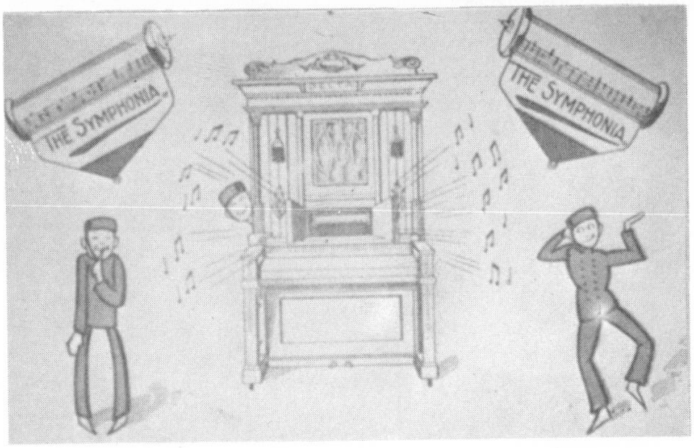


"Delta" brand pianos sold by Mr. DeRoy in the 1920's.

technology had a 124-hole wide tracker bar that gave the orchestrion the capability of playing five or more musical sections all at once – all "solo" if you please! Of course, this is an oversimplification – but, suffice it to say, if a prize is ever given for mechanical gadgetry and sophistication it will be awarded to the Hupfeld Pan.

"I can take you to see the largest orchestrion I know of," Mr. DeRoy said during one of my visits. "It has been in the family of the present owner for a long time, so it is not for sale – but it is worth traveling to see anyway."

The trip from the Symphonia shop to see the Pan took several hours. Leaving Antwerp we motored to the Holland border. The attendant at the crossing waved us through as Mr. DeRoy showed his national identity card and said a few words in Flemish. Through the towns of Breda, Tilburg, and the picturesque Dutch countryside we drove until we came to 's Hertogenbosch, a medium-size city. Mr. DeRoy was not sure of the exact location of the point in the city we wanted to reach, so he stopped several times to ask directions to the Postzegel Hotel.

The Postzegel (which means "postage stamp" in Dutch – the man who built it was a stamp hobbyist) was located on a small side street. I entered the restaurant part of the hotel, half expecting to find a run-down place that had seen better years long ago. Instead I was pleasantly surprised to see a cheerful, well-kept, and spotlessly clean dining room highlighted with warm oak paneling and colorful glass.

At the back of the dining room, and framed by a low but wide doorway – reposing in all its glory and looking as if it had been put there only yesterday – was the Hupfeld orchestrion! It was simply immense. It was beautiful!

A surprise came when the owner offered to play it for us. In the United States and in Europe I have come across perhaps a dozen orchestrions still in their original locations, but few played, and fewer yet played well. The Pan turned in a very creditable performance considering that it hadn't been rebuilt in the nearly forty years since it was made. I peered through the glass door at the center front and saw that it had the famed Hupfeld automatic roll changer, a device which I had wistfully looked at in Hupfeld catalogue illustrations but had never seen in operation.

As any collector would do, I asked (via Mr. DeRoy who spoke the Dutch language) if we could see the inside of the instrument. The answer was no. So, after listening to it for a few more tunes we went on our way, thankful that we at least had the opportunity to hear it and see it, if only the outside of the case.

During this time I traveled to Europe frequently. My main business interest was rare coins. My main destination was usually London to attend auction sales there. I once estimated that I have spent more time in London than in any other city in the world, including cities in the U.S.A. During these coin-hunting forays I would usually find a day or two to fly to Belgium and visit Mr. DeRoy (and also with Leonard Grymonprez, a collector - dealer - enthusiast who lived there). On several of these visits we made it a point to drive to Holland again to see the Hupfeld Pan. Later we were able to see the inside and, still later, to purchase it. At the time of purchase, an event that was arranged by Mr. DeRoy, he said that when it was set up and playing in America he would like to come to see and hear it. I looked forward to the day.

The Black Forest area of Germany has many musical memories. This was the birthplace of the larger types of band organs and orchestrions, not to mention the famed Welte Mignon reproducing piano. In Freiburg the firm of M. Welte & Söhne held forth from 1872 until the factory was demolished in an Allied air raid in 1944. In the hills above Freiburg is the hamlet of Vöhrenbach, home of Imhof & Mukle, the orchestrion builders. The Imhof building still stands. From the collector's view it serves a somewhat ignominious purpose today: it is an auto repair garage.

About twelve kilometers from Freiburg via a winding road lies Waldkirch. This town, complete with the ruins of an ancient castle overlooking it from a nearby hillside, looks little different today than it must have looked several decades ago when it was the locale of several of the world's most prominent automatic instrument makers.

Alas, the firms of Bruder and Ruth, two of the most famous band organ builders, have perished. The Weber Brothers' orchestrion factory no longer hums with the activity of building Solea, Maesto, Elite, and other fine instruments.

It was fun to spend time in Waldkirch with Mr. DeRoy. He was partial to Weber orchestrions and was pleased to see that the factory of the Weber Brothers still stood. During my visits with Mr. DeRoy, "WEBER ORCHESTRION," lettering now (1972) gone, was boldly emblazoned on the side of the ex-factory.

One by one Mr. DeRoy checked out the names on his mailing list – about 6000 names in all! Most names were sent postcards. Most were quickly returned by the post office with the French, Dutch, German, Belgian, or other equivalents of "Addressee Unknown," or "No Longer in Business." But a few did respond, and these were followed up by Mr. DeRoy with an in-person visit. On one trip to the Black Forest we stopped to check on two instruments. Although they were not large nor extremely valuable, it was interesting to see them in their original locations. In the town of Bleibach a small hotel named "Gasthaus Sonne" (Guesthouse of the Sun) was still using a Weber orchestrion. It was a very early one that used folding cardboard music. The establishment was so proud of this musical relic that it sold a picture postcard featuring the instrument.

In another nearby town, Zell, I saw an even earlier barrel-operated Weber orchestrion with dancing figures at the top. I recall one of the instruments we saw that day was priced to us for something like $7000 and the other wasn't for sale. Perhaps one or both have new homes with collectors by now.

Mr. DeRoy was very kind to me, and I learned a lot from him. Because of him much information that might have been otherwise lost to history forever made its way into the first edition of this book and into the present volume.

Mr. DeRoy remembered and loved the instruments from years gone by. As he had access to no restored instruments it was many years ago that he last heard the different types of large orchestrions play. He would have enjoyed visiting America – as he intended to do. He would have enjoyed our people and the private and public musical instrument collections here.

Mr. DeRoy will never visit America. In the summer of 1969 we received word from his daughter, Mrs. Jeff Baets, that Mr. DeRoy had succumbed to illness. He will be fondly remembered by many. The musical scene today is more pleasant for his having passed our way.

Eugene DeRoy at his arranging table. "Way Down Yonder In New Orleans" is being laid out for an orchestrion roll.

## SYMPHONION COIN PIANOS AND ORCHESTRIONS
(Symphonionfabrik A.G.; Leipzig)

Symphonion, one of the world's leading manufacturers of disc-type music boxes, entered the coin piano and orchestrion field in the early 1900's. By 1907 the firm was producing over a dozen different models. Mechanical types were designated as String Orchestras; pneumatic types as Piano-Orchestras, Mandolin-Orchestras, and Xylophone-Orchestras. The trademark "Symphoniola" was used on some pneumatic instruments, especially those produced during the 1900-1914 years. Refer to the Symphonion music box section of this book for detailed information on the history of the Symphonion firm.

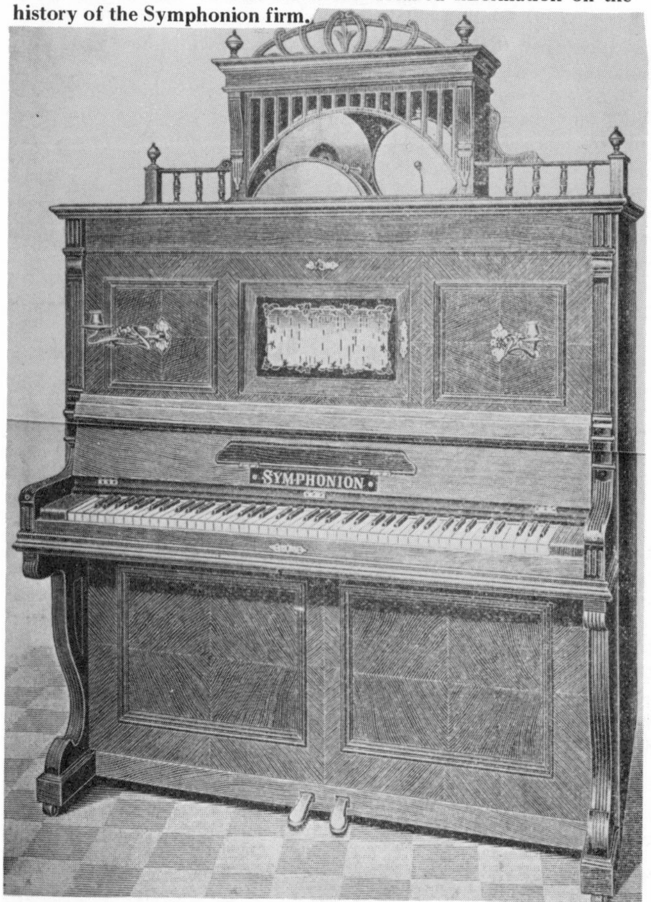


Piano Orchestra No. 80 (c.1904)

Mandolinen-Orchester No70

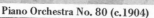

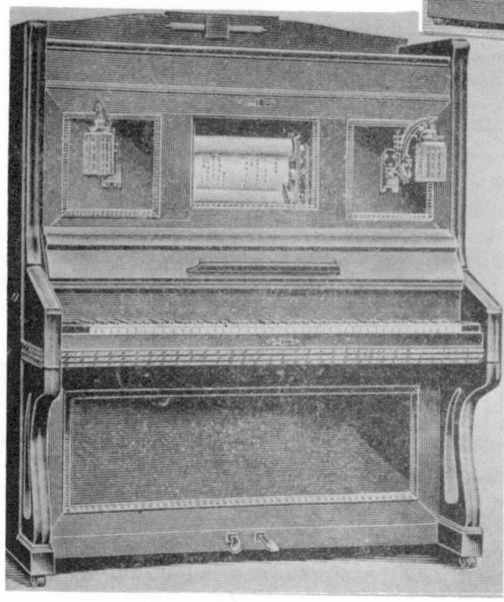

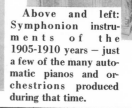

Above and left: Symphonion instruments of the 1905-1910 years — just a few of the many automatic pianos and orchestrions produced during that time.

Symphonion String Orchestras. The above two instruments were produced c.1906-1907 and were available in two forms: operated by metal discs or by heavy paper rolls. The instrument shown at the right, String Orchestra No. 1N, was produced c.1907-1910 and used a heavy paper roll. The action was mechanical, not pneumatic. Polyphon made many similar instruments (refer to Polyphon music box section of this book).

## GEBRUDER WEBER (Weber Brothers)

In the late generation products of Gebr. Weber the art of sophisticated orchestrion building and music arranging achieved its zenith. The largest surviving Weber style, the "Maesto" orchestrion, exhibits an almost unbelievable musical dexterity. Research indicates that the Weber "Elite," of which none is known today (alas!), was even more remarkable.

*The Weber orchestrion factory as it appeared in September, 1966 when this photograph was taken. The notation "WEBER ORCHESTRION" is still visible on the end of the building. From this edifice came some of the finest automatic musical instruments the world has ever known.*

The firm of Gebr. Weber, last headquartered at 3 Bismarckstrasse in Waldkirch, Germany, was founded in 1880. During the early years production was mainly composed of cylinder or barrel operated pianos and orchestrions. Many of these had mechanical figures on a display stage at the top of the instrument.

Around the turn of the century Weber changed from the cylinder type of instrument to the pneumatic type. The music was programmed on folding cardboard music books, similar to those used in organs. The folding book period of Weber's history was short lived, and soon Weber pianos and orchestrions were operated by perforated paper music rolls.

While many manufacturers in Europe and America concentrated on the quantity produced, it is fair to say that Weber's main concern was the musical quality. Among the earliest Weber paper roll instruments were the Weber Violanos. These contained a piano and a large rank of violin pipes. The violin part of the music was arranged to play solo, thus providing a remarkable realism. The New York City distributor recommended these as being concert type instruments "Very attractive and appropriate for music rooms, giving a rich softness in appearance."

*Weber's Violano - Style One. Concert piano with violin pipes. Said to have been popular in New York City's Fifth Avenue mansions!*

Weber pianos and orchestrions come in many forms. Performing violin solos to the accompaniment of an expression piano are the Violano and the later Unika. Xylophone solos with piano are played by the Grandezza - the best-selling Weber instrument of the 1920's. Other Weber pianos and orchestrions feature combinations of several different instruments.

According to Gustav Bruder, who was responsible for many of the best Weber music rolls, Weber from 1926 to 1930 endeavored to produce several orchestrions of true concert quality. Today, the best known of these are the Solea and the Maesto. Each of these features a special solo chamber for clarinet pipes plus a complement of other pipes, percussion instruments, etc. in combination with a concert-quality piano (usually a Feurich). About this time the Weber Elite, an instrument which had been in the Weber line since about 1912, was completely redesigned. The Elite featured five or six solo chambers, each with its own expression controls. Unfortunately for posterity, the three or four Elites originally made have seemingly all perished. What a shame! Fortunately, several Solea and Maesto orchestrions are still with us.

*The Weber Maesto - a sophisticated orchestrion produced during the late 1920's.*

A number of points of difference in Weber music roll arrangements may be noted. In most types of other orchestrion rolls the various instrumental components are brought in and out of play at regular intervals. Hence the xylophone may be turned on, remain on for a passage or two, and then shut off. Many other types of rolls play the melody once through and then repeat it once or twice again exactly as it was played the first time, until the required tune length is reached. Not so with Weber rolls. The Weber control registers constantly change. The xylophone may be brought into play for just a single note or for just a few notes and then remain silent until it sounds again to accent a passage or to play a realistic solo. An almost subliminal bass drum roll heightens crescendos in the larger Weber orchestrions. Many other sophisticated features combine to achieve an almost human performance. Upon hearing the "12th Street Rag" on the Weber Maesto one knowledgeable collector said that it was "virtually indistinguishable from the Paul Whiteman phonograph record of the same tune."

Elaborate expression controls contribute to the realistic music of the Weber instruments. As an example, the rank of clarinet pipes in the larger orchestrions is housed in its own expression chamber inside the main cabinet. Not only is the clarinet volume regulated by the main crescendo or swell shutters on the top of the instrument, it is further given expression by its own set of swell shutters which can open or close instantly or with a measured slowness, as the perforations in the roll dictate. These shutters have the remarkable ability of being able to be set in any position (just not "open" or "closed") from closed through fully open and any intermediate degree in between. It is difficult to describe the "Weber sound" in words, but an hour's time spent listening will demonstrate why the Weber is nearly the universal favorite of old timers once in the automatic musical trade.

**Many of the early Weber instruments feature colorful moving picture scenes on the front. Later ones are richly ornamented by brass lamps and fittings and with beveled glass mirrors.**

**From 1880 to about 1930 Weber produced about 3,000 instruments. We estimate that production was on the order of 100 instruments per year during the 1920's.**

**Weber Unika. Piano with mandolin attachment and one rank of violin pipes (arranged to play solo). Recommended for "cafes, restaurants, and grand dance halls." One of Weber's most popular models.**

**Weber Grandezza. Piano, mandolin, and xylophone. Xylophone seen through clear glass panel. Xylophone arranged as solo on the music roll. A very popular model.**

**Above: Weber Brabo orchestrion as seen on exhibit at the British Piano Museum in London. Piano with mandolin, violin pipes, and xylophone. Equipped with elaborate and very effective expression mechanisms. To play violin or xylophone solos the upper part of the piano is shut off - so that the solo instruments can be heard alone. Accompaniment is provided by the piano bass. Mainly manufactured during the 1920's when Weber had a good share of the market for concert type instruments capable of playing serious music very realistically.**

**Far left: Front glass panel of a Weber Salon Piano with Violin. The fountain has a "motion picture effect" - by means of a mechanical lighting apparatus behind the painted glass scene the fountain appears to cascade. This photograph was taken of an instrument that saw service for years in a Kansas City hotel.**

**Near left: Weber Violano - Style Two. Piano with violin pipes. The Weber Violano instruments use a special wide Violano roll with solo perforations for the violin section. The extensive expression mechanisms produce very realistic violin effects. This particular Style Two instrument measures 9'2" high, 5'9" wide, and 3' deep - impressive specifications for an upright keyboard piano! The catalogue noted "Special cases built to order."**

**Weber Salon Piano with Violin. Original Weber catalogue illustration. These were popular circa 1910 - 1914.**

**Weber orchestrion with animated figures - as shown at the Guesthouse of the Sun, Bleibach, Germany. This is a very early Weber instrument and dates from the late 19th or early 20th century.**

WEBER

Weber's Violano - Style 3. A fair number of the Styles 1, 2, and 3 were sold in the New York City area prior to World War I.

Weber Solea orchestrion in deluxe case (c.1910-1914). Many carvings, curved beveled mirrors, and a mechanical scene combine to make a beautiful instrument. During this period Weber made several custom designs.

Weber Solea - Case design variation. A scene of an alpine castle dominates the center.

Weber Euterpe orchestrion. Popular before World War I.

Weber Styria - one of the most popular Weber styles. This case design was popular during the 1920's. The Styria contains piano, mandolin, violin pipes, flute pipes, castanets, xylophone, drums, and traps. Some were made with side cabinets for roll storage.

An early case design of the Styria. As was true of most Weber orchestrions, the Styria was available in many stylings. This is the largest Weber keyboard orchestrion.

Weber Solea - Case style No. 2. Also available with side cabinets for roll storage.

Weber Isola – An early orchestrion model.

Upper left: Weber Otero orchestrion. Above, right: Weber Venezia (piano, mandolin, drums, traps). Uses Erato roll.

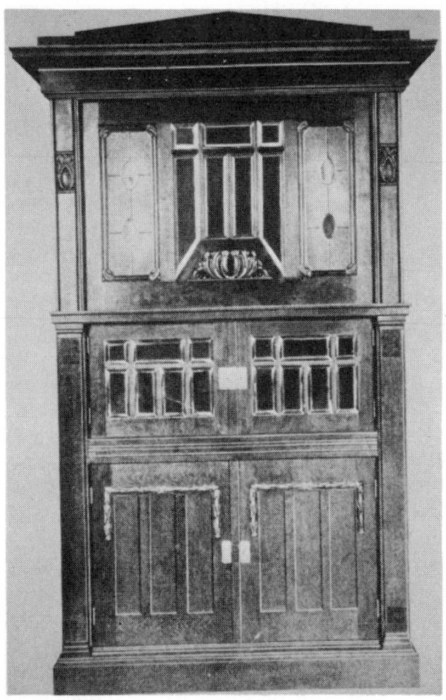

Above Left: Weber Erato orchestrion with piano, mandolin, and xylophone. An early instrument. Above right: Weber Erato - another case design. Near right: Another Weber Erato variation. Far right: Weber Graziella orchestrion with piano, violin and flute pipes, drums, and traps.

WEBER

Above: A Weber Otero orchestrion made in the late 1920's. Shown with the upper rectangular panel removed, permitting a view of the interior. This type of instrument contains a piano of excellent quality (usually made by Feurich), a rank of violin pipes, a rank of flute pipes, a mandolin attachment, castanets, drums, and traps. At each side are cabinets for the storage of rolls. Generally, most Weber instruments - keyboard or cabinet types - were available with or without roll storage cabinets as desired by the buyer. The elaborate beveled mirrors on the two front doors (in front of the roll mechanism) are a typical Weber feature. The tasteful use of mirrors and brass trim gives most Weber instruments an appearance of rich elegance. In many case design variations the Otero was produced from about 1910 to 1930.

Weber Solea orchestrion - case design variation. Note the side cabinets for roll storage and the waterfall scene.

Standard Otero design of the 1920's. In this period the use of motion picture effects gave way to cloth grilles or mirrored panels. This was a very popular instrument during the '20s, and dozens were sold.

Weber Otero with beautiful mechanical scene in the center.

Weber Otero Earlier case with motion picture effects.

Weber's Elite Orchestra. The largest Weber orchestrion. At the time this book was prepared the author knew of no surviving specimens. In correspondence Mr. Gustav Bruder (of the famed Bruder family of organ builders) mentioned that some of this style were made and shipped to Russia in 1914 - but their whereabouts are now unknown. Perhaps one of our readers can track one down someday! It would be quite a find!

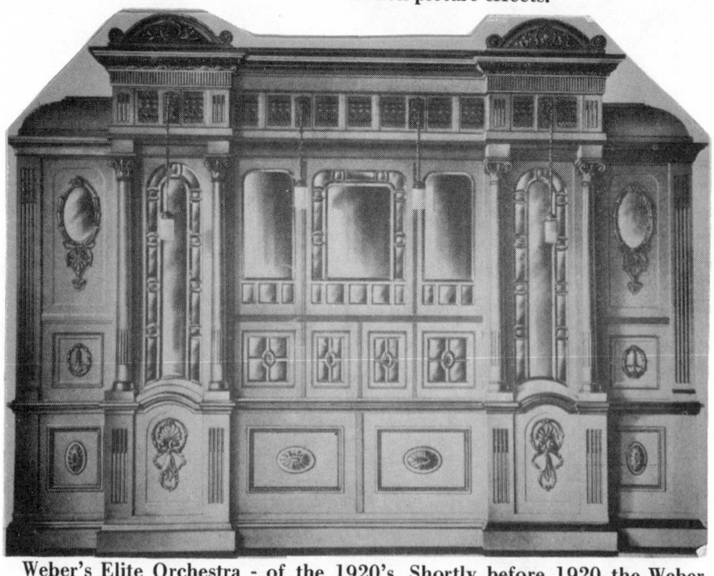

Weber's Elite Orchestra - of the 1920's. Shortly before 1920 the Weber Elite was mechanically redesigned. Evidently just three were made. In a letter to the author Gustav Bruder noted: "Since 1919 only three Weber Elite orchestrions were built. Early in the 1920's a single Elite was built. It played in the old manner, but with improved mechanisms. In 1927 and 1928 two more were built, each with very sophisticated improvements. Their marvelous mechanisms gave them unlimited expression effects and register combinations... These late Elites not only had swell shutters over the main orchestrion case but also had on the inside five or six more expression chambers, each with its own swell mechanism to increase or decrease the appropriate solo voice as called for. These instruments were made for use in the largest rooms..." In advertising the Elite Weber said that it represented an orchestra of fifty musicians. Case measurements of the Elite (1920's style) are: 12 feet high, 16'3" wide, and 5' deep.

Note: For more information about Weber Maesto music rolls, most of which were arranged by Gustav Bruder, refer to the Bruder organ section of this book. Some early experiences of Gustav Bruder are recounted.

Weber's Maesto orchestrion - the largest surviving style of Weber orchestrion. Produced and sold in the 1920's the Maesto was described by Weber thusly: Unequalled concert orchestra, dance and jazz band. An incomparable electro-pneumatic artistic orchestrion comprising a piano of the first order (by Feurich), violin, violoncello, flutes, clarinet, trumpets, saxophone, lotus flute, jazz trumpets, complete xylophone, and assorted percussion instruments including bass drum, castanets, snare drum, tambourine, triangle, cymbal, and wood block."

The Weber Solea and Maesto orchestrions use the same type of roll interchangeably. The Soleas produced during the 1920's closely resemble the Maesto orchestrions in sound and musical capability. There are some differences in the internal mechanisms and the Maesto has several additional effects.

A rich musical repertoire was made for the Solea and Maesto. Classical favorites such as the Poet and Peasant Overture, William Tell Overture, Orpheus in Hades, Madame Butterfly, and Bizet's Pearl Fishers are available on single rolls and play from ten to fifteen minutes or so. Other rolls are of a popular nature and (usually) have four tunes on each. Such selections as Charmaine, 12th Street Rag, My Blue Heaven, Silver Threads Among the Gold, Piccolo Pete, Swanee, Indian Love Call, and Tico Tico are thrilling to hear on the Maesto today - just as they must have been decades ago!

Weber's Maesto orchestrion - a view with the front panels removed. At the top left may be seen the crash cymbal, a small part of the bass drum, the snare drum, and some of the xylophone beaters. At the upper right some of the pipes are seen. The trumpets and jazz trumpets are the ones with the conical metal horns. In front of them are the flute pipes (not visible) and, in the front row, the violin pipes. The clarinet pipes are housed in a special solo expression chamber behind the trumpet pipes. The roll mechanism is at the lower center. In the bottom of the case are the pumps and reservoirs for vacuum and wind pressure. As is the case with other very large orchestrions, the Maesto is built on a modular basis. Most components can be easily removed separately without having to dismantle the entire instrument. This means that such an instrument can be rebuilt one section at a time. Most large orchestrions of various makes are very well made of quality parts. In their day they were the "top of the line" - as, of course, they are today with collectors.

## WEBER

—G.J. Gérard—

During the 1920's the main foreign outlet for Gebr. Weber instruments was the G.J. Gérard agency in Brussels. Although Gérard handled products of other manufacturers as well, emphasis was on Weber pianos and orchestrions. Gérard was a Weber stockholder. The ties were further strengthened by the marriage of Otto Weber to a Gérard daughter.

The illustrations on this page are from a Gérard catalogue issued in the 1920's.

Above: A sorry plight: a cafe without music. Below: A cafe with a Gérard piano — what a difference!

Front of the main Gérard showroom at Rue des Fabriques 1a, Brussels, Belgium. In this location dozens of different instruments were on display for prospective customers. A workshop was maintained for the repair of electric pianos and orchestrions.

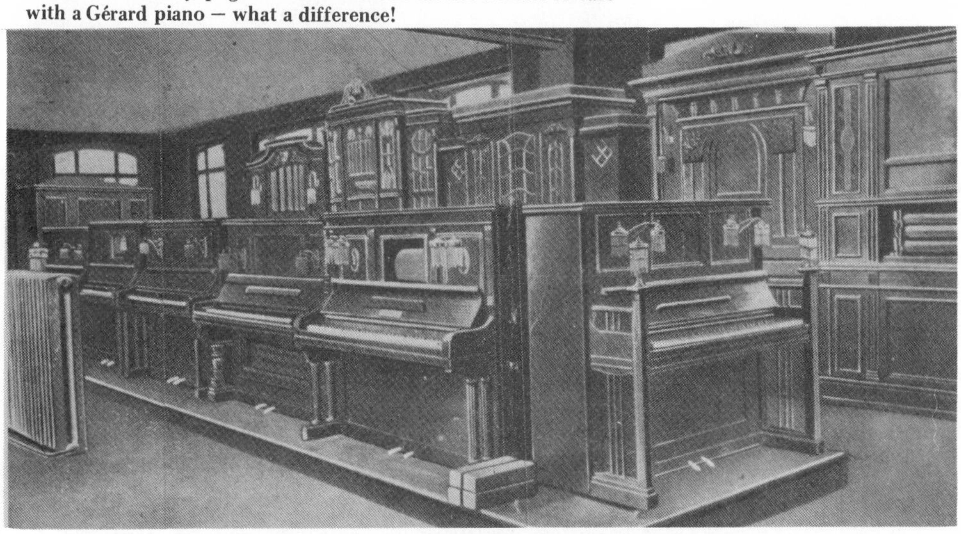

General display salon at Rue des Fabriques 1a.

Branch salesroom at Boulevard Maurice Lemonnier 189, Brussels. On display were regular pianos, player pianos, electric pianos, and orchestrions.

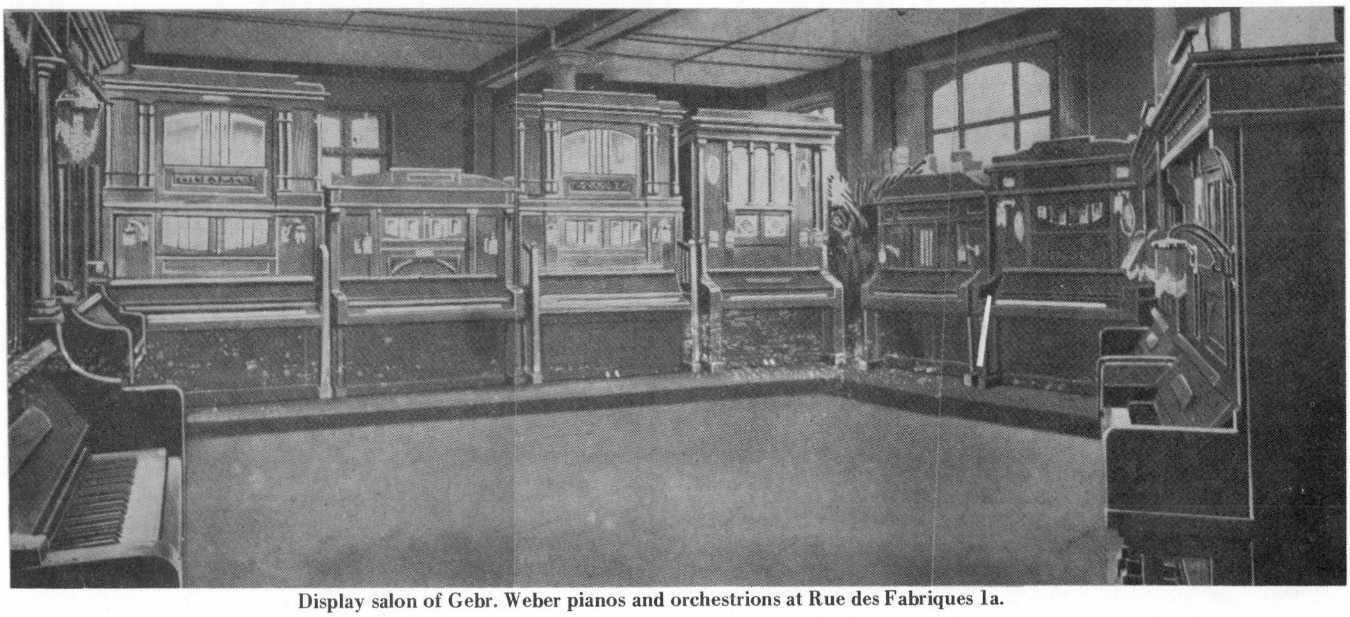

Display salon of Gebr. Weber pianos and orchestrions at Rue des Fabriques 1a.

# M. WELTE & SONS

## Scope of the Welte Business

The name "Welte" was affixed to many different types of automatic musical instruments in the one hundred and twenty years from about 1832 to 1950. The first Welte products, made by Michael Welte, founder of the firm, were tall clocks with a rank of organ pipes. The final Welte product, made by Edwin Welte, a grandson of Michael, was the Lichttonorgel — an electronic organ that was made in prototype form in the late 1930's and 1940's.

In the intervening years the Welte musical dynasty covered the far reaches of the earth. First Welte orchestrions, and then the Welte Mignon reproducing pianos, received the highest acclaim from musicians, royal personages, and the general public.

While orchestrions and reproducing pianos were the most widely sold Welte automatic instruments, the firm also offered home player pianos, residential pipe organs, theatre organs, military band organs, and other related instruments. To the Welte factory and showroom in Freiburg, Germany, and to its New York salon came "the world's most prominent musicians" and, equally important, the buyers such as "members of the Upper 400" — as one Welte advertisement boldly stated.

In this section of the book we discuss and illustrate Welte orchestrions. In separate sections we treat the Philharmonic Organs and the famed Welte-Mignon reproducing piano. As the history of all Welte instruments is closely intertwined, the reader is urged to refer to these other sections also. And, on two pages of the fairground organ section of this book we illustrate the "Concert Orchestra Organs" which played a minor role in Welte's history.

# WELTE ORCHESTRIONS

## The Beginning of the Welte Business

In 1827 Michael Welte, then twenty years of age, was apprenticed to Joseph Blessing, a maker of musical clocks, "musical cabinets" (self-contained organs for home use), and other automatic musical instruments. For five years Welte worked at the Blessing workshop in Unterkirnach, a town in the southern part of Germany's Black Forest.

From Blessing the young worker learned how to make musical clocks, every piece of which had to be crafted by hand. Mass production techniques were unknown at the time and the shop tools were of the most basic hand types.

In his spare time he experimented with different musical mechanisms and, at a school in a nearby town, studied music theory. Thus he laid the groundwork for opening his own business.

In 1832 Michael Welte left Blessing and started his own shop in Vöhrenbach, a small Black Forest town that was his birthplace in 1807. Vöhrenbach, like several other towns in the area, had several other musical instrument makers. Of these, the firm of Imhof & Mukle achieved prominence in later years.

According to a later Welte catalogue, Michael Welte soon achieved a reputation for his accurate work and startling innovations in the musical clock field. "Orders poured in from all over Europe. Although he employed no salesmen, the excellence of his wares proved to be their most effective advertisement." The Welte business prospered and had to be enlarged almost from year to year.

From the beginning Michael Welte realized the value of tastefully designed cases. The inner workings, of course, had to be acceptable, but it was the cabinet that made the difference between an expensively priced elegant instrument and an inexpensive plain one. Welte chose the former route and, according to the Welte catalogue, "Welte musical clocks came to be marks of the homes of the cultured."

The main attraction of Welte's clocks was the pipe organ section — a pinned cylinder organ with from one to three small ranks of stopped flute pipes. Young Welte read of the compositions that Haydn and Mozart wrote especially for flute playing clocks — and dreamed of what the immortal musicians could have done with an even larger musical apparatus.

## The First Welte Orchestrion

In 1849 (or 1848 — accounts differ) Michael Welte exhibited for the first time an immense automatic pipe organ on which he had worked for the preceding three years. "The public nicknamed the instrument 'orchestrion' because it successfully imitated a many-voiced orchestra of artists in Karlsruhe. It was a marvel of mechanical skill, containing eleven hundred pipes, which were actuated by thousands of small pins set on drums. These represented musical melodies and harmonies, which might be said to be 'written' upon three large wooden cylinders which rotated with a precision such as had been supposed unattainable before.

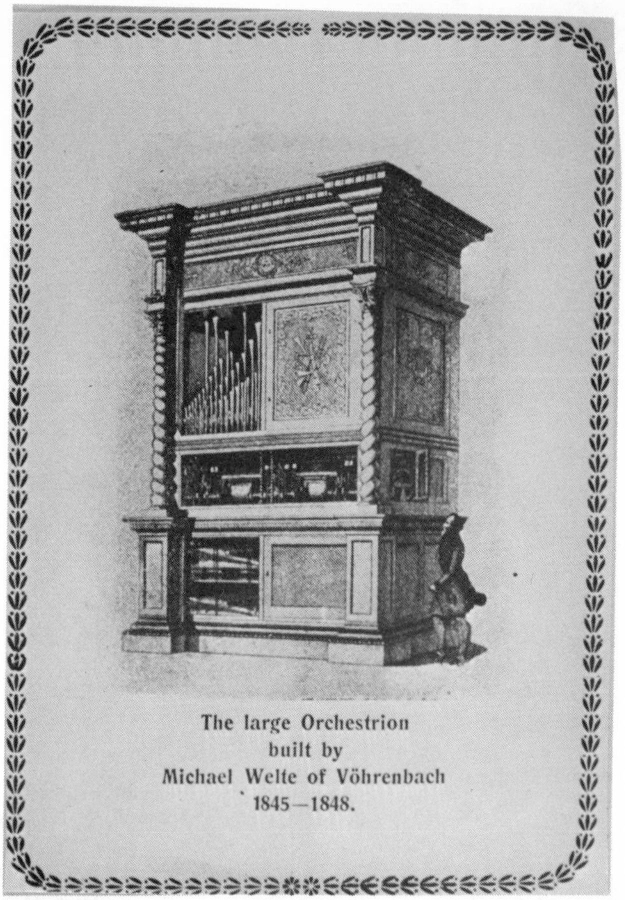

The large Orchestrion
built by
Michael Welte of Vöhrenbach
1845—1848.

"The fame of the new invention drew people from near and far. The Grand Duke of Baden himself came to hear and see it, and then, proud of this achievement of his country's industry, presented the inventor with an album (Editor's note: The album was a prized possession of the Welte family for years; in 1944 it was severely charred when the Freiburg factory burned) in which he wrote the following tribute:

"I share with all those who are enjoying your instrument in their admiration of your work, while, furthermore, I am particularly gratified at having an opportunity, my dear Mr. Welte, to express to you my satisfaction that it was a citizen of Baden whose artistic instinct and perseverance succeeded in accomplishing something so exquisite and wonderful. — Leopold, Grand Duke of Baden; April 30, 1849.

"Vincent Lachner, the famous composer, also came to hear the new orchestrion, which in the meantime had won the highest award at an exhibition in Karlsruhe — a gold medal, and wrote: 'It is not nearly a mechanical performance, without life or soul, that reaches the ear of the hearer; no, he fancies that he is listening to the work of living human forces, conscious of their artistic aim.'

"The fame of the orchestrion had in the meantime traveled through all of Europe. From Frankfurt-am-Main, where the Bundestag, the representative body of most of the German states, held its sessions, the request came to exhibit the new invention before it was delivered to its purchaser. The request was complied with, and princes, savants, famous statesmen, and dignitaries wrote their appreciation in the album of the Grand Duke of Baden.

"Other equally perfect instruments followed this first one, and wherever they were shown during the great industrial and world expositions, in London 1862, Paris 1867, Philadelphia 1876, Munich 1885, Vienna 1892, Chicago 1893, Paris 1900, St. Louis 1904, Seattle 1909, and in many other fairs, the instruments received without exception the highest award."

## The Business Grows

In 1865 the oldest son of the founder, Emil Welte, came to America and established a Welte showroom in New York City. Exhibited there were several large orchestrions and a consignment of flute-playing clocks (which Welte continued to manufacture, although in small numbers). Prominently displayed were the testimonials of European royalty.

"Success was instantaneous" in the New York office — an early Welte catalogue noted. A huge orchestrion, said to be the "world's largest," was sold to the Atlantic Garden, an entertainment hall in the same city. The "Wild West" proved to be a good area for sales, too. To the mining camps high in the Rocky Mountains went several

Welte orchestrion with two barrels. Circa 1890.

orchestrions, including some really large ones. The sale of one instrument invariably caused a local sensation when it was first exhibited — and resulted in the sale of others. By word of mouth and by using the praising letters received from happy customers, Welte orchestrions sold almost as fast as they could be imported.

Within the next several decades the Welte orchestrion customer list expanded to include most ruling heads of Europe, several different Indian maharajahs, steamships of several transatlantic lines, and many members of the Social Register. Names such as Vanderbilt, Whitney, Sutro (of Comstock Lode fame), P.T. Barnum (proprietor of the American Museum and the "greatest show on earth"), the Mellon family of Pittsburgh, famed opera star Adelina Patti, and dozens of others were used in Welte advertisements, often with accompanying testimonials stating that life in the castle or mansion would be dreary without the lilting strains of the Welte Cottage or Concert Orchestrion.

A Welte barrel-operated orchestrion of the 1880's.

The barrel and related mechanisms of a large Welte orchestrion.

### Types of Welte Orchestrions

From 1849 until about 1890, Welte orchestrions were of the pinned cylinder type. The appearance and operation of these was virtually the same as the orchestrions made by Imhof & Mukle, Philipps, and other craftsmen of the late 19th century.

The bottom part of the orchestrion contained several large bellows which provided the needed wind pressure to blow the pipes. At about waist-level, a convenience for changing the music program, a large pinned cylinder (or sometimes two cylinders — in large models) was located. Programmed on the barrel was one very long selection or several shorter ones. Each note or percussion action was represented by an individual pin. For sustained notes a bridged pin with a staple-like appearance was used. The barrel was shifted continually to the side (or sometimes all at once — as in a standard cylinder music box) by a spirally-cut screw feeding gear. A program might take as many as seven, eight, or nine revolutions of the barrel to complete. Such a program could last ten to twenty minutes on a barrel of large diameter.

Barrels were expensive. It was not unusual for several hundred dollars to be charged for a single barrel with one overture on it! Barrels were heavy and care, not to mention strength, was needed to change them properly. As the barrels were of fixed diameter and turned at an unvarying speed, the length of the musical selection had to be cut or else expanded to fit the space available. It was these disadvantages that the later music rolls overcame.

Above the barrel was the main pipe chest. By means of levers which were connected to wires or rods leading to the pipe pallets the pins in the barrel could actuate the desired notes. On the pipe chest were arranged the wooden and metal pipes, often several hundred in number. Unlike later instruments, these early orchestrions were voiced on low pressure — usually 1½" to 3" (most later orchestrion used about 6" of pressure), and more pipes were needed to achieve the desired volume. It is quite probable that the tonal volume of Michael Welte's first 1100-pipe orchestrion was no greater than the later roll-operated Brisgovia orchestrions with fewer than 100 pipes!

The pipes were of two main types: In the forefront of the orchestrion, and usually arranged in a radiating "sunburst" configuration, were bright yellow brass reed pipes — trumpets and trombones. Also in the front, but usually mounted vertically, were gray metal flue pipes with violin-family or flute voicing. Behind the metal pipes were arranged large wooden bass pipes which provided the foundation tone of the instrument. Drums, cymbals, and other percussion devices were often mounted near the top of the instrument and in the center, so as to maintain the symmetry of the pipe arrangement.

Welte's pinned cylinder orchestrions contained no piano, nor did the similar orchestrions of other manufacturers, with just a few exceptions.

Motive power was provided by a heavy weight — often of 500 to 1000 pounds in size — which was lifted to the top of the orchestrion (the weight was hidden in the back and went up and down in its own wooden-cased chute) by winding a large crank handle. As the weight dropped it turned gears and cranks to operate the bellows and to turn the barrel. A large Welte barrel orchestrion in the Larry Givens Collection, an instrument acquired originally by the Mellon family in 1874, has separate hand-wound motors for the snare and bass drums. Before playing a selection, one must not forget to wind the drums or they won't operate!

The cases of Welte and other barrel orchestrions were rectangular in shape. On the front, and often on the two sides as well, were large panels of clear glass which permitted a view of the radiating pipes and the cylinder. A top "gingerbread" railing or gallery was often added for extra ornateness.

Early Welte barrel orchestrions were very large. Several standard models were made in heights from fifteen to twenty feet! Even "small" instruments of this type were eight to twelve feet high.

### Paper Roll Orchestrions

Over the years Welte advertised that the firm was first with paper roll operated pneumatic instruments. A typical claim follows:

"Paper Music Rolls. In 1887, a new Welte patent surprised the world: this invention, the use of paper music rolls in connection with a pneumatic action, revolutionized the trade, as it did away with the expensive and bulky wooden music cylinders. . . Protected by patents in all countries, and for years absolutely without any competition, the financial success of the new idea, which is now imitated in every piano player, organ, and orchestrion all over the world, was splendid."

While Welte may have been the first to apply paper rolls to large orchestrions, it certainly was not the first to use paper music rolls in connection with a pneumatic action.

In his book "Re-Enacting the Artist," Larry Givens notes: "Before the middle of the 19th century several inventors were working on a new method of actuating instruments by means of perforated sheets of cardboard or paper. In 1842, one Claude-Felix Seytre of Lyons, France, was granted what appears to be the pioneer patent in the field of music rolls. Though Seytre's sheets were driven by sprocket holes along the edges and were made of flexible cardboard of a thickness much greater than regular music roll paper, there can be little doubt that he deserves credit as the first man to conceive (or at least to describe and patent) the basic idea for a flexible music sheet. In 1848, a patent was issued to Alexander Bain of Great Britain which clearly describes and illustrates a perforated music roll of regular thickness. . ."

Though more evidence is hardly needed, we might mention the "Orchestrone" series of paper roll reed organs which were made by the Munroe Organ Reed Co. (of Worcester, Mass.) and sold by the thousands from about 1879 onward. These organs used a tracker bar over which a paper roll passed. An opening in the roll then actuated an intervening valve (a pneumatic action) which then admitted air to the reed, causing it to sound.

We mention the above in order to set the historical record straight. From the perspective of decades later we are in a position to take a worldwide view of musical instruments and musical instrument patents of many different innovators. Many "new" ideas weren't really new; many money-earning patents could have been successfully contested by licensees (we are speaking now of the entire field of automatic instrument patents; not just of Welte) had they known then what we know now. But, finding out such things is the purpose of historical research.

The introduction of the paper roll system to Welte orchestrions revolutionized the industry. The pinned cylinder was replaced by a fragile, yet durable enough for its intended purpose, music roll which could be produced not on a one-at-a-time basis, but by the thousands by means of automatic duplicating devices (roll perforators). The cost of a roll was not $100 to $300, or even $50, but just a few dollars. The musical performance could be arranged on the music roll as the composer intended and could be five minutes in length or twenty minutes, or any other time up to the practical limit of the quantity of paper that could be wound on the roll.

Previous purchasers of barrel-operated Welte orchestrions were given the opportunity to have their instruments converted to the new paper roll pneumatic system at no extra charge (as Welte correctly envisioned that a rich market for music rolls would develop). About 90% of the owners of the older machines took advantage of this opportunity.

From about 1890 until about 1914 the well known Cottage and Concert Orchestrions were produced. The Cottage instruments were the smaller models in the line. Made in standard styles 0, 1, 2, and 3 these ranged in size from the Style 0 which was 8'2" high and which cost $1200.00 in 1907, to the Style 3 which was 8'11" high and cost $1800.00. Each had several ranks of pipes and drum and trap effects. After about 1910 the smaller Cottage styles were renamed "Concert" orchestrions and were given more modern-appearing cases.

The regular Concert Orchestrions were those numbered from Style 4 through Style 10. To please the buyer who might find the proffered Style 10, which measured 14'5" high by 16'8" wide and which cost $12,000.00 in 1912, too small Welte thoughtfully noted "Larger orchestrions built to order."

Cottage and Concert Orchestrions of the 1890 - 1914 years resembled their earlier barrel organ ancestors in appearance. The cases were tall, usually fronted with clear glass, had the pipes arranged symmetrically, and had about the same interior components with the exception, of course, of the music system which in these styles was of the paper roll type.

Early Cottage and Concert instruments were weight driven. By about 1900 most mansions and other potential Welte orchestrion locations were serviced by electricity, so operation was by electric motor. Until as late as 1906 the motor was priced separately from the main instrument, in the event that the prospective buyer couldn't use it.

Like their early counterparts, the Cottage and Concert Orchestrions had no piano. All were made in Welte's Freiburg, Germany, factory. Toward the end of production these instruments were offered in America with "an American-made piano, available at extra cost."

Among the Cottage and Concert Orchestrions are to be found some of the most beautiful Welte instruments ever made. These instruments were immensely popular, and evidently they were sold by the thousands. Fortunately, Welte felt that the word of a satisfied user was worth two words by an advertising copy writer, so whenever possible it illustrated its catalogues with photographs of Welte orchestrions in all types of diverse locations and sprinkled the pages with testimonials. These pictures survive today and tell us of the circumstances in which the instruments were used.

Orchestrions were a great attraction, and customers were ever-willing to write enthusiastic letters about them — such as this letter from a Philadelphia ice cream parlor owner who used one in his business, said so, and then went on to praise the orchestrion's suitability for home use also:

Right: Duplex roll mechanism as used on certain styles of Welte orchestrions during the 1908-1914 period (mainly).

2320 North Front St.
Philadelphia, Penna.
Dear Messrs. Welte:

I have had one of your Orchestrions for the past eighteen months and from my experience in that time, I have no hesitancy in recommending them to anyone contemplating purchasing. During this time it has been in my Ice Cream Parlor, where it has been an object of astonishment and delight to the crowds who daily come to see it, as well for its magnificent appearance as for the beautiful music it furnishes. For the home an Orchestrion is the very acme of taste and elegance, fully equalling in tone and general execution any first class orchestra. The increase in the volume of my business, which I attribute to its presence in the Parlor, has been sufficient to pay for itself ten times over.

Yours truly,
George Heppe

Brusendorff & Co., owners of a Boston restaurant, reported concerning their No.6 Concert model: "Nothing but the highest compliments we receive daily from musical critics as well as from the public in general." The Coeur D'Alene Company of Spokane, Washington, also had a Style 6 which "increased our business over 25%, at the same time it has brought to our place a better class of people, in fact, the very best in the city." Edward E. Barney, president of the Virginia Navigation Company, reported that his ships, the Pocahontas and the Ariel, each benefited from having Welte orchestrions aboard. In New York City one Charles H. Albers gave what was perhaps the ultimate praise: he called his place of business the Albers' Orchestrion Hall! Mr. Albers was evidently a man about the world as he wrote, "Having seen all kinds of mechanical musical instruments in the old world as well as the new, I can only say that the Welte Orchestrion possesses superior possibilities in the perfect rendering of all classes of music. The tones are beautiful and the expression and execution simple and marvelous."

Of the many famed personages who owned large Welte orchestrions none was more appreciated by Welte than Madame Adelina Patti, world renowned opera singer. In her rambling stone castle, Craig-y-nos, in the Swansea Valley of South Wales the diva entertained celebrities from all over the world.

Among her very favorite possessions was a large Welte orchestrion. Shortly after the magnificent instrument arrived Mme. Patti wrote to Welte:

"On my return from South America I was surprised and much gratified to find the orchestrion I ordered last February already finished, set up in perfect working order. Having listened attentively to the various airs it performs, I must frankly admit that it exceeds my expectations, both to the artistical rendering of the music and the extreme ease of its operation."

Another letter to Welte noted: "I have much pleasure in saying how greatly I appreciate the marvelous Orchestrion you made for me, which has been the admiration of all the royal personages and celebrities who have listened to this perfection of mechanism and melody under my roof."

In 1892 The Strand Magazine printed an illustrated interview with Mme. Patti and a tour of Craig-y-nos. The reporter wrote: "A huge orchestrion, brought over from Geneva, and which plays every conceivable air, from Clairette's song in "La Fille de Madame Angot" to the Pilgrims' March in "Tannhauser," is always played when a game of billiards is commenced, and whilst Mme. Patti handles her cue, or watches her opponent's game, she sings half-unconsciously the while to the tunes given by her favorite instrument."

In several different Welte orchestrion catalogues of the 1890 - 1910 era the Patti instrument was featured on the first page.

For the wealthy purchaser Welte recommended the larger Concert instruments, Style 7 through Style 10 which, in Welte's words, "Contain all the orchestral effects presented in Style 6, but increased in the number of pipes as to their relative difference in size, representing a much larger and more efficient orchestra, and are especially adapted to private residences, hotels, restaurants, halls, and in fact everywhere that high class music is desired."

Many of the larger Concert Orchestrions were sold without cases. In such instances the purchaser built them into a wall recess or had his own custom cabinet made. William P. Snyder, Esq. of Sewickley, Pennsylvania, paid $11,559.85 for "One large pneumatic orchestrion, No.10 size, built according to drawings and specifications (without case) including 12 rolls of music."

### Welte in Freiburg and Poughkeepsie

"The success of the Welte business in both hemispheres made a further enlargement of the home factory necessary, and as Vöhrenbach was too far from the main road of traffic for the steadily growing trade of the house, the entire Welte establishment was transferred to Freiburg in 1872," reported a Welte catalogue.

Freiburg, a quaint university town nestled in the verdant hills of the Black Forest, was the only sizable city in the area. The relatively large population provided a good work force for the new factory. Located directly across the tracks from the railroad station the new establishment had convenient shipping facilities for the dispatching of orchestrions to all parts of the world.

The Freiburg factory, initially a modest two-story stone structure, was expanded tenfold over the years until an impressive complex of buildings represented the cornerstone of the Welte empire. A music salon featured in beautifully furnished surroundings examples of the Cottage and Concert Orchestrions, the Welte Mignon piano, and, later, a large Philharmonic Organ. The walls were hung with framed letters from prominent patrons and with medallic awards received at expositions.

Here were located the recording devices for the making of Welte Mignon reproducing piano rolls and Philharmonic Organ rolls. A special suite in the nearby gabled 3-story Welte mansion was set aside for the "visitor of the week," as Edwin Welte put it.

Welte prospered with the inflationary times of the 1920's. The most expensive items in the Welte line at that time, the Philharmonic Organs, were bought by the hundreds for installation in homes, movie theatres, aboard ocean liners, and for many other uses. Welte Mignon reproducing pianos were even more popular and were sold by the thousands. By the mid-1920's the large orchestrions were a thing of the past, but the sales of instruments on hand from previous years continued until about 1930.

The great Depression of the 1930's brought the demise of virtually every automatic musical instrument maker in Europe and America. The checks for $3500 for a Welte Mignon in a Steinway or Feurich piano, $12,000 for a Concert Orchestrion, or $20,000 for a Philharmonic Organ were no longer being written. Sales plummeted. In 1933 Welte was bankrupt.

Reorganization followed and the Bockisch family gained control of the enterprise. Karl Bockisch and Edwin Welte, inventors of the Welte

Above: Wall box for a Welte orchestrion.
Left: Welte's Poughkeepsie plant.

Mignon, manufactured pipe organs for church and auditorium use during the 1930's. During World War II the Welte factory was commandeered for use in manufacturing gunsights, although a special section containing music roll perforation equipment remained in operation (and made Welte Mignon rolls). In November, 1944, American B-17 bombers leveled most of Freiburg and the Welte factory with it. (For more on this subject, the reader is urged to refer to the Welte Mignon section of this book and the personal experiences of Richard C. Simonton in Freiburg during the late 1940's.)

Despite the large factory facilities, Welte farmed out much of its work. High in the hills of the Black Forest a craftsman with a metalworking lathe made mechanisms for the roll systems, in the neighboring town of Waldkirch the organ-making factories supplied many of the wooden and metal pipes used in Welte orchestrions, and dozens of other small and large shops throughout the Black Forest made parts and pieces on a contractual basis. Such suppliers often tended their farms and fields during the summer. In the winter when the snow lay several feet deep and travel was impossible the farmers earned an income by making parts for Welte. With the first spring thaws a trip into nearby Freiburg would result in a handsome payment for the winter's work.

Following the arrival of Emil Welte in America in 1865 the business in the United States grew rapidly. When the Welte Mignon reproducing piano, perfected in 1904 and marketed beginning in 1905, was ready to be sold, in Welte's words, "It was an artistic and financial success. In order to introduce the new instrument into America a company was formed here in 1906 by the inventors and owners of the patents, the grandsons of Michael Welte, among themselves. A building was leased on Fifth Avenue for exhibition purposes. Concerts were given, and the Welte Studio, within a few months, became the Mecca of all music students and lovers.

"Since then, as in Europe, we have been unable to fill the rapidly growing demand, and the building of a factory here in America has become an absolute necessity, not only for the Welte Mignon, but for our large line of orchestrions and organs... The factory is now completed and is located at Poughkeepsie, New York..." (Editor's Note: the factory building still stands there; home of a razor blade manufacturer.)

In the Poughkeepsie factory Welte Mignon pianos of all types — uprights, grands, and the Vorsetzer models — were made or fitted into pianos of other manufacturers. Welte Philharmonic organs were made in

Pipes in a large Welte Brisgovia orchestrion owned by Robert Johnson.

their entirety. Large orchestrions were assembled there; the cases were made, coin mechanisms were fitted, and pianos were installed. The pipework and pneumatic systems were imported from the main factory in Freiburg. Orchestrions shipped from the New York factory included Cottage and Concert models, certain Brisgovia styles, and a number of residential orchestrions based upon the specifications of the Concert models but mostly in solid wood (without clear glass panels) cases and with the pipes arranged in normal order (in ascending order of size from treble to bass, rather than the symmetrical configuration).

By an agreement dated February 12, 1914, the Rudolph Wurlitzer Co. acquired 48% of the American Welte firm, M. Welte & Sons, Incorporated. (Wurlitzer acquired 2400 common shares representing 48% of the common stock of the firm. The price paid was $30 per share. In addition $66,500.00 worth of preferred stock was acquired at the par value of $100/share.) According to the original agreement, Wurlitzer was "desirous of interesting itself in and managing the business of said M. Welte & Sons, Inc."

The operations of the American branch continued until World War I brought about the seizure of a substantial portion (1762 common

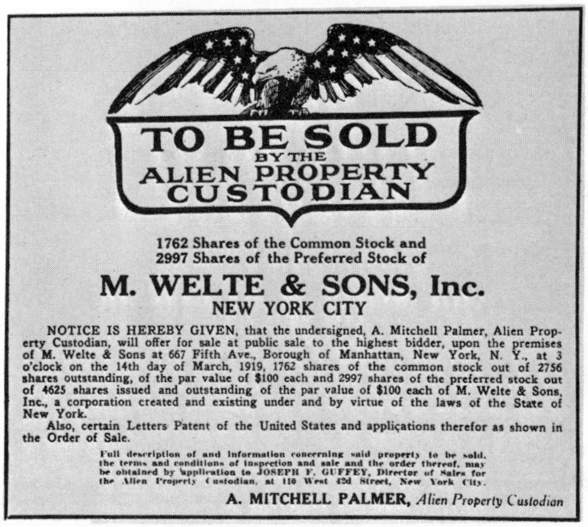

TO BE SOLD
BY THE
ALIEN PROPERTY
CUSTODIAN

1762 Shares of the Common Stock and
2997 Shares of the Preferred Stock of

M. WELTE & SONS, Inc.
NEW YORK CITY

NOTICE IS HEREBY GIVEN, that the undersigned, A. Mitchell Palmer, Alien Property Custodian, will offer for sale at public sale to the highest bidder, upon the premises of M. Welte & Sons at 667 Fifth Ave., Borough of Manhattan, New York, N. Y., at 3 o'clock on the 14th day of March, 1919, 1762 shares of the common stock out of 2756 shares outstanding, of the par value of $100 each and 2997 shares of the preferred stock out of 4625 shares issued and outstanding of the par value of $100 each of M. Welte & Sons, Inc., a corporation created and existing under and by virtue of the laws of the State of New York.

Also, certain Letters Patent of the United States and applications therefor as shown in the Order of Sale.

Full description of and information concerning said property to be sold, the terms and conditions of inspection and sale and the order thereof, may be obtained by application to JOSEPH F. GUFFEY, Director of Sales for the Alien Property Custodian, at 110 West 42d Street, New York City.

A. MITCHELL PALMER, *Alien Property Custodian*

shares; 2997 preferred shares) of the M. Welte & Sons, Inc. stock still in the hands of the Welte family. On March 14, 1919, the Alien Property Custodian sold this part of the Welte interest at public sale. A group headed by George W. Gittins assumed control of the corporation at that time.

The Alien Property Custodian confiscation and resale of the Welte interest was viewed dimly by the Welte family, as would be logically expected. In postwar years the relationship between the Freiburg firm and the New York one changed from one of cooperation and mutual promotion of instruments to one of just tolerance. Although several licensing agreements were made between the two branches in later years, the advertising, product development, and other business went in different directions.

The Poughkeepsie factory was closed. A trade journal of the 1920's noted: "Welte Mignon Corporation; President: George W. Gittins; secretary: Robert H. Gittins; treasurer: H.W. Wilson. Has extensive and well-equipped factories in the Borough of Bronx, New York City, where a very large and modern plant is devoted to the manufacture of Welte-Built Welte Mignon reproducing grand and period grand pianos, Welte reproducing pipe organs for residences, clubs, lodges, theatre, and concert work, and to the manufacture of artists' recorded music rolls. Studios, salesrooms, and offices at 665 Fifth Avenue, perhaps the most beautifully appointed studios devoted to music in the City of New York." In addition to the Bronx factory, another factory, mostly devoted to making pipe organs, was opened in Sound Beach, New York.

It took a while for the new business to gain momentum again. A letter of July 14, 1920, addressed to Peter Bacigalupi, San Francisco music sales agent, notes: "We have your letter in which you tell us that you would be pleased to receive literature on our instruments. We haven't anything very attractive to send you at this time but we are enclosing herein a small catalogue which we are using temporarily. We could not make you any quotations, however, for various reasons. The first is that we haven't any goods manufactured today to offer to the trade at this time..." On August 1, 1927 the firm went through another reorganization and emerged as the Welte Company, Inc. Offices were at 695 Fifth Avenue and factories in New York City at 297 East 133rd St. and 112-114 Lincoln Avenue. The new officers were: W.E. Fletcher, president; R.T. Lytle, vice-president; W.J. Webster, treasurer; and H.B. Walmsley, secretary. Annual factory "capacity" (an often-used term in the piano trade — it had little relation to actual sales) was 5,000 grand pianos and 50 pipe organs.

A few years later the reproducing piano business came to an end. What remained of the Welte Philharmonic Organ business was transferred to W.W. Kimball Company of Chicago.

Welte orchestrion sales came to an end in America shortly before 1920. When the Poughkeepsie factory was vacated a number of completed and partially completed orchestrions, including some very large ones, were sold at bargain prices for scrap and parts.

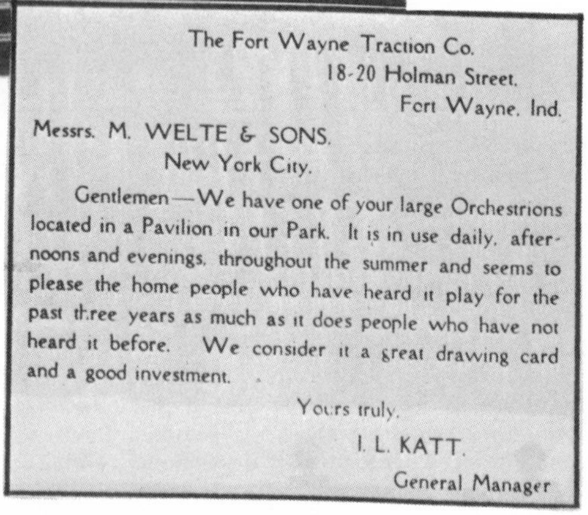

The Fort Wayne Traction Co.
18-20 Holman Street,
Fort Wayne, Ind.

Messrs. M. WELTE & SONS,
New York City.

Gentlemen—We have one of your large Orchestrions located in a Pavilion in our Park. It is in use daily, afternoons and evenings, throughout the summer and seems to please the home people who have heard it play for the past three years as much as it does people who have not heard it before. We consider it a great drawing card and a good investment.

Yours truly,
I. L. KATT.
General Manager

### The Brass Band Orchestrions

Sometime in the 1905 - 1910 period a new series of instruments known as Brass Band Orchestrions was launched. With very loud voicing of the pipes (although softer voicing was available on special order) these instruments were sold as "Roller Skating Rink Orchestrions — replacing a full brass band; specially built for rinks, dance halls, and other amusement places." Built with a symmetrical arrangement of pipes and on the same general order as the Concert Orchestrions of the same period, the Brass Band orchestrions used Concert, Brisgovia, or Philharmonic I and II rolls interchangeably.

Models in the Brass Band series were the Donar, an orchestrion measuring 9'4" high which was sold as "Replacing a military band orchestra of about 12 men," the Wallhall, a larger orchestrion representing a 20 to 25 piece band, and the largest in the series, the Wotan, which replaced a "complete brass band of about 30 to 35 men."

Quite a few Brass Band Orchestrions were sold in America. They found use on merry go rounds, in skating rinks, and similar locations. Some Brass Band Orchestrions were voiced on lower pressure to sound more like the Concert Orchestrions and were sold for use in ballrooms and pavilions.

### Welte Piano Orchestrions

About 1907 Welte added a series of piano orchestrions to its line. Unlike the Cottage and Concert Orchestrions of the same period, the piano orchestrions had a piano as the main instrument — in the same manner as did contemporary piano orchestrions of Hupfeld, Philipps, et al.

These orchestrions were given the name of "Brisgovia," after the ancient name of Breisgau, the section of Germany in which Freiburg was located. These orchestrions were assembled in both the Freiburg and the Poughkeepsie factories as we noted earlier. Introduced on the market about 1908 the Brisgovia instruments were offered as follows:

"Piano Orchestrions — representing an orchestra in accompaniment with a piano — BRISGOVIA — Elegant modern cases with artistic stained glass panels, bronze ornaments, and wonderful electric light effects. Automatic rewinding of the music rolls. Nickel-in-the-slot attachment if desired. The piano is made in America and is of the most perfect tone quality and durability."

Brisgovia C

A large catalogue offering several hundred different Brisgovia rolls (which were also suitable for use on Welte Concert and Brass Band orchestrions and on smaller Philharmonic Organs) was given to each purchaser of an instrument. The rolls available covered a wide range and included overtures such as "Zampa," "Orpheus in Hades," "William Tell," and other favorites; several dozen different operas including "Madame Butterfly," "Tannhauser," and "Lohengrin" (the latter was available in a 4-roll set); symphonies by Beethoven, Brahms, Dvorak, and others; and a wide variety of popular tunes. "Please ask for a special list of popular American songs" a page in the catalogue noted.

Brisgovia piano orchestrions were made in a number of case design variations of the basic styles A, B, C, and D. In addition, a small keyboard orchestrion, Style E was offered.

A separate series of piano orchestrions, the Friburgia (named after Freiburg) and the Divina, was offered. Containing piano, xylophone, and percussion instruments, these used music rolls made from hand-played masters with the percussion effects added.

A Friburgia advertisement stated: "The Friburgia reproduces the personal interpretation and human touch of the pianist. The most wonderful result has been accomplished by the use of paper music rolls recorded from the playing of pianists, in cooperation with an expression device that regulates the modulation of tone and balances the melody and accompaniment to the finest shade."

This expression was accomplished by means of a divided pneumatic stack which permitted the bass and treble sections of the piano to play at different intensities independent of each other.

Sometime before World War I, M. Welte & Sons made an arrangement with the Operators Piano Company of Chicago. Certain "Coinola" coin pianos were purchased and resold as the Welte "Ideal" and "Multitone" instruments. Intended for use as theatre photoplayers, the Multitone orchestrions had foot pedals to operate such effects as a doorbell, auto horn, lion roar, and locomotive whistle. These Coinola instruments in disguise used regular Coinola rolls: type "O" orchestrion rolls for the Multitone and type "C" 88-note expression rolls for the Ideal.

—AN EARLY WELTE—

Photographs showing the radiant "sunburst" pipe arrangement (above) of a cylinder operated Welte orchestrion now in the Larry Givens Collection. At the left is shown a portion of one of the cylinders.

This instrument was originally purchased about 1874 and was installed on the staircase landing of the palatial Mellon home in Pittsburgh, Pennsylvania. Larry Givens, who has done considerable research on the subject, advises us that many large mansions in that area — those owned by the Snyder, Frick, Mellon, and other families — once had Welte orchestrions. On June 15, 1905 "one large pneumatic orchestrion, No.10 size, without case" was sold to William P. Snyder, Esq. of Sewickley, Pa., for $11,559.85.

Many large orchestrions were made without cases so they could be fit into room walls behind grillwork or louvered shutters — much in the manner of a pipe organ installation.

WELTE

—Style 0—

"Miniature Orchestrion," as Welte designated this type. 8' high. Cost $1050 in 1905.

—Style 1—
Cottage Orchestrion
Cost $1200 in 1907. 8'2" high, 4'10" wide, 2'10" deep. Pipes, snare drum, triangle. Mainly for residential use.

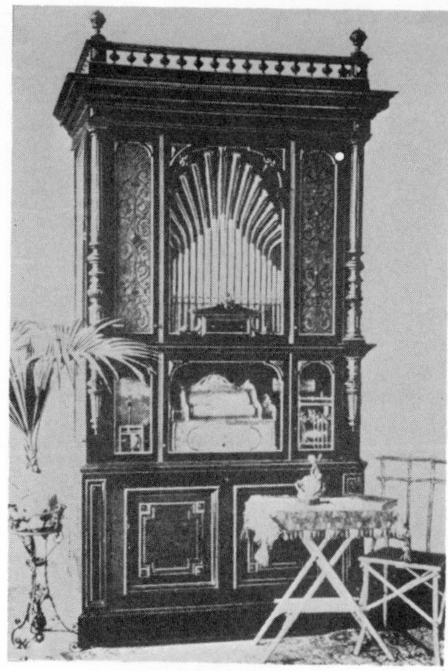

—Style 2—
Cottage Orchestrion
8'11" high, 5'6" wide, 2'10" deep. Pipes, drums, triangle, cymbal. Cost $1500.00 in 1907.

—Style 3—
Cottage Orchestrion
8'11" high, 6' wide, 3'4" deep. Cost $1800.00 in 1907. For use in public and residential locations.

—Style 5—
Concert Orchestrion
10'9" high, 7'3" wide, 3'10" deep. Cost $2800.00 in 1907.

Style 6 Concert Orchestrion
11' high, 7'9" wide, 4'3" deep. Cost $3500 in 1907.

Styles 7 and 8
Concert Orchestrions
Style 7: 11' high by 8'3" wide by 4'7" deep. Cost $4300. Style 8 (illustrated): 12'10" high, 10'1" wide, 4'10" deep. Cost $5500.

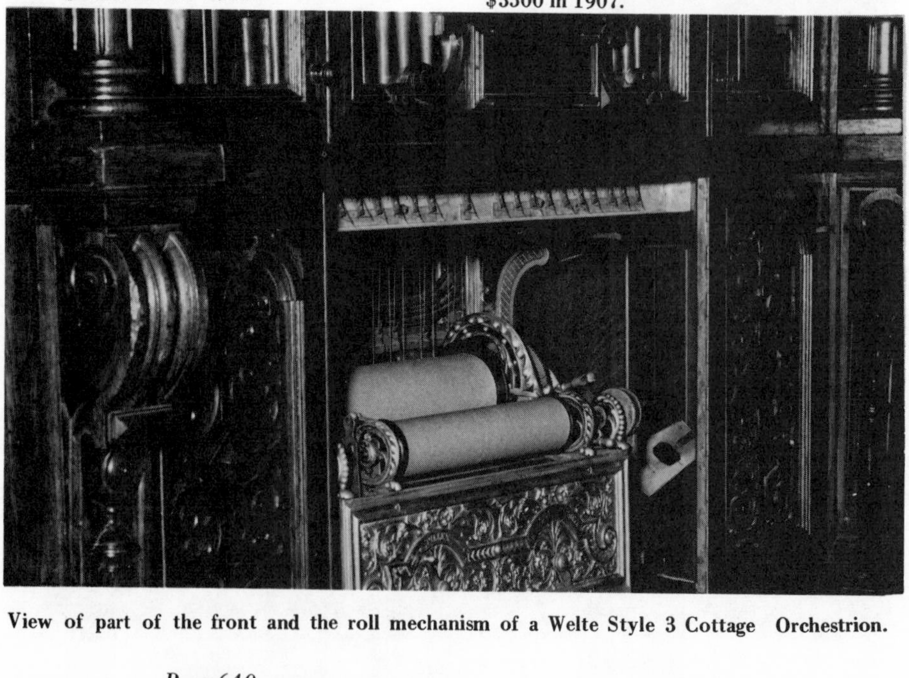

View of part of the front and the roll mechanism of a Welte Style 3 Cottage Orchestrion.

Welte orchestrion in Zaharakos' Soda Parlor in Columbus, Indiana. As of this writing (1971) the instrument is still in its original location!

A Welte orchestrion furnishes music for this fine restaurant.

Owned by Mr. Alex Jordan of Madison, Wisconsin, this pinned cylinder Welte dates from the 1870-1880 decade.

Owned by a Savannah, Georgia, brewery in the 1880's this gigantic Welte appears to be nearly twenty feet high! Like so many others of its kind, the whereabouts of this magnificent instrument are unknown today. (Photograph courtesy of Lewis Graham)

Note the Welte orchestrion in the background of this tavern. Photograph from the early 1900's.

FREDERICK W. VANDERBILT ESQ.
New Port, R. I.

**New York City.**

After more than two years thorough use of the Orchestrion you constructed especially for the „Niagara" I think you will be pleased to hear that it has given perfect satisfaction both at sea and in harbor. I feel that the Yacht would not now be complete without it.

**Howard Gould, Esq.**

H. R. H. PRINCE GEORGE OF GREECE
Canea.

H. H. THE MAHARAJAH OF KARPURTHALA
East India.

H. H. PRINCE BURHANEDDIN EFFENDI
Constantinople.

VENDOME HOTEL
Chicago, Jllinois.

WILLIAM PENN ESQ.
Taverham Hall
Norwich, England.

H. C. FRICK ESQ.
Pittsburgh, Pa.

**Tampa, Flor.**

The Orchestrion, I have in my house is very easily kept in order and ready at all times, with proper attention, to furnish entertainment for myself, family and guests. I am pleased to recommend their work to any persons desiring to provide themselves with an instrument in music that will be a source of most excellent entertainment.

**H. B. Plant, Esq.**
Tampa - Bay - Hotel.

## *No. 4*
# Concert-Orchestrion

**Contains all the striking devices.**

Height 10 ft. 2 inches. -- Width 7 ft. — Depth 3 ft. 10 inches.

| | |
|---|---|
| Price, including 12 music rolls . . . | $ 2400. |
| Extra music rolls, each . . . . . . | $ 10. |

FRANK J. GOULD ESQ.
Private riding ring
New York City.

WILLIAM K. VANDERBILT ESQ.
New York City.

CHAS T. YERKES ESQ.
Chicago Jll.

H. H. MAHARAJAH OF PATIALA
East India.

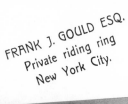

Styles 9 and 10 Concert Orchestrions—

Style 9 Concert Orchestrion (illustrated above) measures 13'1" high by 11'1" wide by 5'3" deep. The selling price was $7000.00 in 1908 and $8000 in 1914. Style 10 (not shown) came in many custom-made case designs and sold for $10,000 in 1908 and $12,000 in 1914. Measurements were: 14'5" high by 16'8" wide by 9'9" deep. The Adelina Patti orchestrion illustrated on another page in this section was a Style 10. For those who wanted even more immense instruments Welte thoughtfully noted that "Larger orchestrions are built to order."

On this page: A Welte orchestrion in the home was a supreme status symbol in America from about 1870 to 1910. Welte catalogues of the period are filled with glowing praise from society personages — some of whom (Pittsburgh industrialist William P. Snyder, for example) had several orchestrions: one "at home," one at sea on a yacht, and a third at a summer residence at Newport, Rhode Island, or a similar spa. On this page are shown some of Welte's residential installations.

**Craig-y-nos Castle.**

I have much pleasure in saying how greatly I appreciate the marvelous Orchestrion you made for me, which has been the admiration of all the royal personages and celebrities who have listened to this perfection of mechanism and melody under my roof.

**Adelina Patti-Nicolini.**

Adelina Patti, world-famous opera star of the late 19th century, lived in Craig-y-nos Castle, a palace complete with its own theatre, indoor garden, music room, and, in the billiard room, a huge Welte orchestrion. Many, if not most, kings and queens and other castle-dwellers in Europe had Welte orchestrions, so it was only fitting that Mme. Patti should have one also.

Welte was particularly proud of this installation and featured it in many catalogues and brochures. What happened to the instrument? The story is an all-too-familiar one. Shortly before 1920 it was moved to a summer camp in Douglas, Isle of Man. A gentleman who used to care for the instrument wrote the author: "It met with a series of accidents. First it was flooded. Then it caught fire. Finally it was broken up and burned for firewood."

–PHOTOGRAPHIC FILM-FLAM–

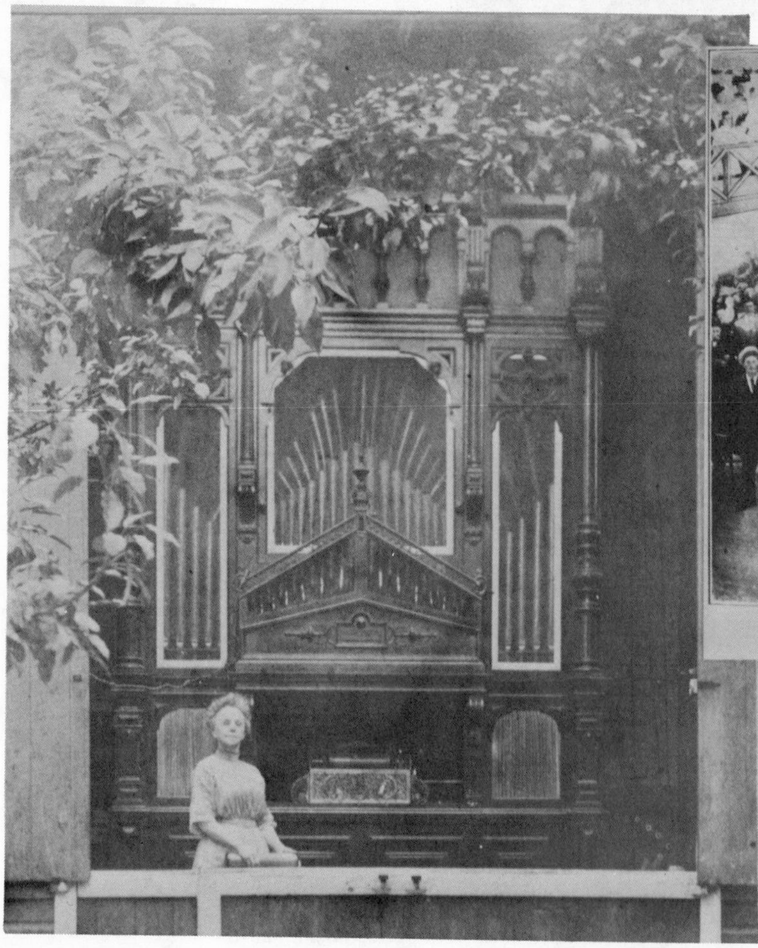

At Robison's Park, Fort Wayne, Ind.

Above is a Welte catalogue illustration of an orchestrion "on location." Featured in one of the author's earlier publications, it drew the attention of Terry Borne. Mr. Borne furnished the photo at left which is how the Welte really appeared. The above photo is a fake – rather obvious upon second glance – made by putting together several photos of groups of people and a drawing of a Welte. Notice how the back part of the crowd has been airbrushed out. Similar photographic "compositions" grace several different Welte catalogues.

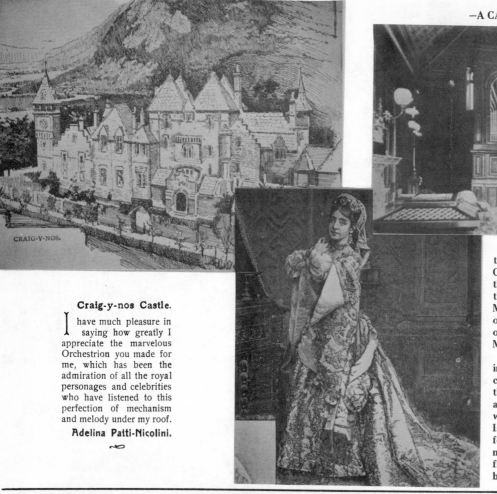

The Atlantic Garden, a mammoth New York City beer and pleasure hall, had as its featured attraction a Welte orchestrion — actually, two Welte orchestrions. . .

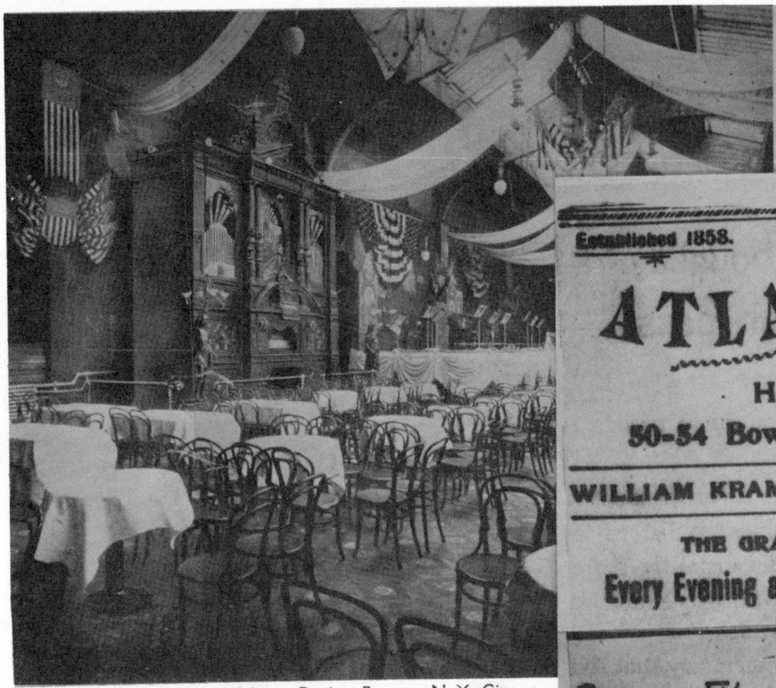

William Kramer's Sons' Atlantic Garden, Bowery, N. Y. City
Largest Orchestrion ever built, taking the grand prize at the Chicago World's Fair

The Atlantic Garden's first orchestrion, the gigantic white instrument pictured below, was the first large Welte orchestrion ever sold in America. Imported by Emil Welte in 1865 it was sold to this famous New York pleasure spot. For many years it was billed as "The World's Largest Orchestrion." Thousands came to see and hear it.

In 1893 Welte exhibited a gigantic orchestrion at the World's Columbian Exposition in Chicago. Following its appearance there, it was sold to the Atlantic Garden — where it replaced the earlier Welte instrument. The later Welte is shown in the photograph above. To the right is a broadside or poster (furnished to the author by Mr. Milt Larsen of Hollywood's "Magic Castle") advertising the Welte: "Mammoth Pneumatic Orchestrion — plays daily from 10 A.M. to 7 P.M."

What happened to this glorious orchestrion? About 1907 the Atlantic Garden, orchestrion and all, burned to the ground.

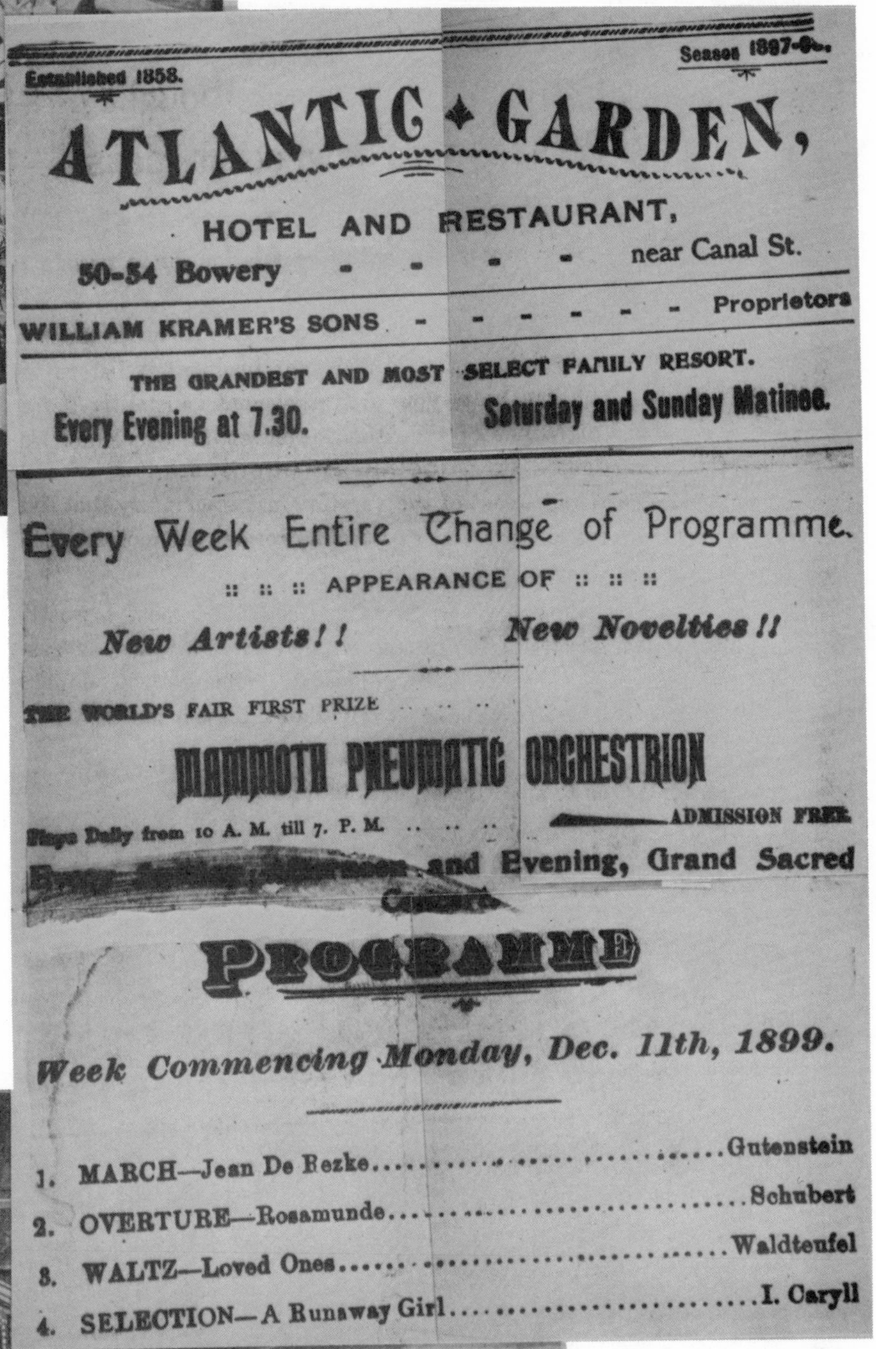

Established 1858. Season 1897-9

ATLANTIC GARDEN,

HOTEL AND RESTAURANT,

50-54 Bowery - - - - near Canal St.

WILLIAM KRAMER'S SONS - - - - - - Proprietors

THE GRANDEST AND MOST SELECT FAMILY RESORT.

Every Evening at 7.30. Saturday and Sunday Matinee.

Every Week Entire Change of Programme.

:: :: :: APPEARANCE OF :: :: ::

*New Artists!!* *New Novelties!!*

THE WORLD'S FAIR FIRST PRIZE .. .. ..

MAMMOTH PNEUMATIC ORCHESTRION

Plays Daily from 10 A. M. till 7. P. M. .. .. .. ADMISSION FREE

and Evening, Grand Sacred Concerts

PROGRAMME

*Week Commencing Monday, Dec. 11th, 1899.*

1. MARCH—Jean De Rezke .......... Gutenstein
2. OVERTURE—Rosamunde .......... Schubert
3. WALTZ—Loved Ones .......... Waldteufel
4. SELECTION—A Runaway Girl .......... I. Caryll

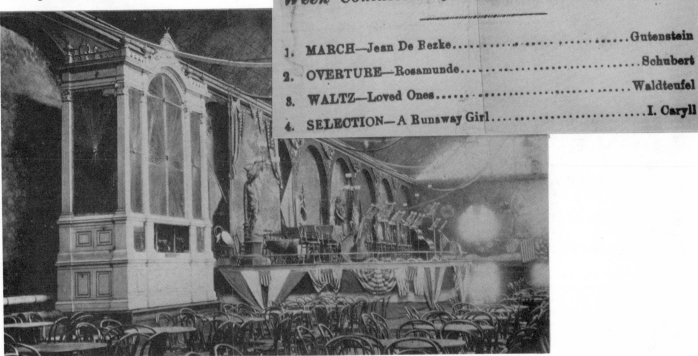

Style 1
Concert Orchestrion
Later style from the 'teens. 8'9" high by 4'7" wide by 2'10" deep. Several ranks of pipes, small drum, triangle.

—Style 2—
Concert Orchestrion
Later style from the 1914 era. 9'7" high, 5'8" wide, 2'11" deep. Several ranks of pipes, bass and snare drums, cymbals and triangle. "Equal to an orchestra of about seven pieces."

—Style 3—
Concert Orchestrion
From the 1914 era. 9'8" high, 6'7" wide, 3' deep. 1st and 2nd violin pipes, bass violin, flute, trombone, clarinet, oboe and piccolo, tenor drum, bass drum, cymbals, triangle. Motion picture scene on front.

—Style 4—
Concert Orchestrion
From the 1914 era. 10'4" high, 7' wide, 4' deep. Ranks of pipes plus drum and trap effects. "This instrument allows us to reproduce the compositions of our greatest masters with accuracy and finest orchestral effects, representing about twelve pieces."

BRISGOVIA A — Piano orchestrion with one rank of violin pipes, bass and snare drums, cymbals, triangle, xylophone, and piano. Two different case variations shown above. 7'9" high by 5'8" wide by 2'7" deep. From the 1910 - 1914 period.

BRISGOVIA A-1 — Piano orchestrion with two ranks of pipes, xylophone, drums, and traps. 8'8" high by 6'4" wide by 3' deep. A popular style from the pre-World War I years. Below are scenes of a Brisgovia A-1 in a movie theatre and in a soda fountain.

BRISGOVIA B-1 — Orchestrion with piano, several ranks of pipes, xylophone, drums and traps. 9'11" high, 7'4" wide, 3'8" deep. Automatic scene with zeppelin on front. A very popular style from the 1912 - 1914 period.

BRISGOVIA C — 11' high by 7'6" wide by 4' deep. A very popular style. Piano orchestrion with several ranks of pipes, drums, and traps. Above instrument is equipped with the Double Tracker Board holding two rolls.

## WELTE

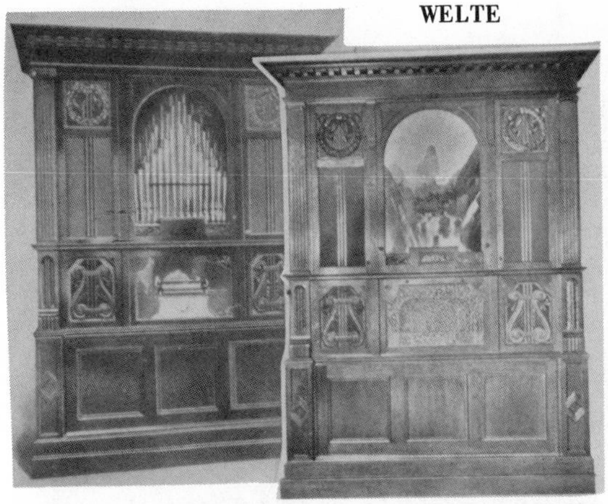

## Brass Band Orchestrion
### WALLHALL

Replacing a military band of about fourteen pieces.

**Specifications**

| | |
|---|---|
| 1st and 2d Cornet | Oboe |
| 1st and 2d Clarinet | Flute with Xylophone |
| Trumpet | Snare Drum |
| Alto | Bass Drum (imitation Kettle Drum) |
| Trombone | Cymbals and Triangle |
| Contra Bass | |
| Bourdon | |
| Piccolo | |

**Dimensions**

Height, 10 ft. 6 in. Width, 8 ft. 8 in.
Depth, 4 ft. 7 in.

Case is of Renaissance design of solid, dark oak. The upper middle panel is a hand-painted picture representing a mythological scene of "Hope"; when illuminated depicts a temple on a high eminence throwing a strong searchlight. An iridescent rainbow appears and a rocky falls shows rushing waters. These effects are obtained by means of electric light devices behind the picture.

**WALLHALL – Brass Band Orchestrion. Sold mainly in the 1910 - 1915 era, the Wallhall carried a price tag of $3500.00. The original catalogue description is given above.**

### Piano Orchestrions

| | |
|---|---|
| Brisgovia A | $1250 |
| " A1 | 1650 |
| " B | 2200 |
| " B1 | 2800 |
| " C | 3600 |
| " C Luxus | 3900 |
| " D | 5200 |

### Orchestrions

| | |
|---|---|
| No. 1 | $1350 |
| " 2 | 1700 |
| " 3 | 2100 |
| " 4 | 2800 |
| " 5 | 3400 |

### Orchestrions (Cont'd)

| | |
|---|---|
| No. 6 | $4000 |
| " 7 | 4800 |
| " 8 | 6200 |
| " 9 | 8000 |
| " 10 | 12,000 |
| Donar | $2400 |
| Walhall | 3500 |
| Wotan | 5000 |
| Friburgia | $1200 |
| Divina | 1050 |
| Ideal 88-note Player | $750 |
| Multitone No. 1 | 850 |
| Multitone No. 2 | 950 |

These prices include an electric motor and twelve rolls of music.

**Welte's 1912 price list issued in America.**

**DONAR – Brass Band Orchestrion. Smallest ("only" 9'4" high!) instrument in the Brass Band series. Sold for $2400 in 1912. "Replaces a military band orchestra of about 12 men."**

**Above left: Welte Style C Brisgovia Piano Orchestrion, one of several case design variations. Note the resemblance of style between this and the Wurlitzer Style 31 Concert PianOrchestra shown in the Wurlitzer section of this book.**

**Above right: Style C DeLuxe Brisgovia Piano Orchestrion. This style with a mirrored front was made about 1913.**

**Early styles of Welte orchestrions, the Cottage and Concert styles, were made without pianos (except that on request American customers could have an American-made piano installed at extra cost). The Brisgovia series of orchestrions, popular mainly in the 1910 - 1915 years, were based around a piano as the main instrument. Unlike the earlier instruments which found their main use in private residences and in very large public halls, the Brisgovia orchestrions were used mostly in smaller business establishments. Hundreds of Welte orchestrions of various types were once in use throughout America.**

**FRIBURGIA – Piano Orchestrion. Piano, xylophone, drums, and traps. "This most wonderful result has been accomplished by the use of paper music rolls recorded from the playing of pianists, in co-operation with an expression device that regulates the unlimited modulation of tone – and the melody and accompaniment is balanced to the finest shade."**

**"Friburgia" is in honor of Freiburg, the German town in the Black Forest where these were built.**

**Friburgia orchestrions were popular in America from about 1912 to 1915. Original photographs show that they were especially popular in restaurants.**

## Brass Band Orchestrion WOTAN

Replacing a military band of about twenty pieces.

### Specifications

| | |
|---|---|
| 1st and 2d Cornet | Bourdon |
| 1st and 2d Clarinet | Piccolo |
| Trumpet | Oboe |
| Alto | Flute with Xylophone |
| Trombone | Snare Drum |
| French Horn | Bass Drum (imitation Kettle Drum) |
| Baritone | Cymbals and Triangle |
| Bass | |
| Contra Bass | |
| Saxophone | |

### Dimensions

Height, 12 ft. 9 in. Width, 9 ft. 3 in. Depth, 4 ft. 10 in.

Case of dark gray-green oak with three illuminated glass scenes, the middle representing the fire scene from the Walküre picturing Siegfried and Brunnehilde. On each side panel are scenes from Switzerland, showing waterfalls. By means of special mechanism the water appears to be rushing continuously.

**—THE WELTE WOTAN—**

**The Wotan was one of the most popular Brass Band Orchestrion styles. The most expensive instrument in that series, it sold for $5000.00 in 1912. Two different case styles (one with painted scene; one with clear glass) are shown at the left.**

**Above: A Welte puzzle! Strewn in seeming disarray (but actually all marked and in order) over the floor are all of the parts to a Welte Wotan orchestrion! When acquired the huge instrument was in a long-ago-shuttered ballroom. The main entrance was removed to make room for the wall of a bowling alley. The result was that the instrument had to be disassembled piece-by-piece and carried through an opening about eighteen inches wide! All of this was done in good order. At the right the same instrument is shown during its resurrection. Later the case was assembled around it.**

Brisgovia Orchestrions were made mainly from about 1910 to 1914. "Brisgovia" is the ancient name for "Breisgau," the section of Germany in which Welte was located.

BRISGOVIA B — Piano orchestrion with three ranks of pipes, xylophone, drums, and traps. 9'8" high, 6'8" wide, 3'2" deep. On the front is a motion picture scene with an erupting volcano. As the pictures here show, this was a very popular orchestrion in America.

Welte, Brisgovia O. (letter O, not numeral 0). Circa 1912.

BRISGOVIA A-1 — Piano Orchestrion. Case variation of this popular style. 8'8" high, 6'4" wide, 3' deep. Circa 1912.

BRISGOVIA D — Piano orchestrion. With pipes representing violin, flute, cello, viola, trumpet, piccolo, clarinet, French horn, trombone, oboe, bassoon, bourdon, and contra bass. Also with drum and trap effects. 11'10" high; 9'8" wide; 4'11" deep. Two case design variations are shown here. This was the largest regular orchestrion in the Brisgovia series. Popular circa 1910 - 1914.

BRISGOVIA C — Piano orchestrion. 11' high by 7'6" wide by 4' deep. Popular circa 1912 - 1914. Lemp's Cafe & Wine Co. of Denver, Colo. wrote a testimonial: "It gives us much pleasure to testify to the most wonderful musical qualities of my instrument, Brisgovia C, also to its durability. It has given satisfaction in every detail. My patrons are pleased equally as well as we are. We have noted a considerable increase in our business which shows that this investment will be a profitable one."

Contemporary photographs show that Welte orchestrions were very popular in the mountain state of Colorado.

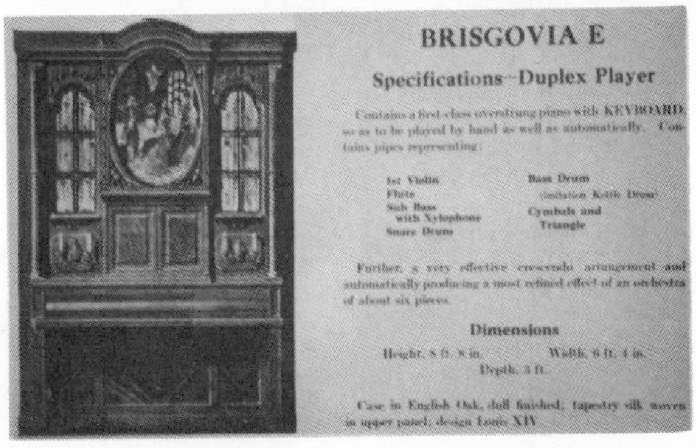

BRISGOVIA E

Specifications—Duplex Player

Contains a first-class overstrung piano with KEYBOARD, so as to be played by hand as well as automatically. Contains pipes representing:

| | |
|---|---|
| 1st Violin | Bass Drum |
| Flute | (imitation Kettle Drum) |
| Sub Bass with Xylophone | Cymbals and Triangle |
| Snare Drum | |

Further, a very effective crescendo arrangement and automatically producing a most refined effect of an orchestra of about six pieces.

Dimensions

Height, 8 ft. 8 in. Width, 6 ft. 4 in. Depth, 3 ft.

Case in English Oak, dull finished; tapestry silk woven in upper panel; design Louis XIV.

**New York, City.**

The Orchestrion purchased of your firm in 1894 has given entire satisfaction and after six years of continual playing, the instrument is in perfect condition, during which time no expense aside from cleaning and tuning has accrued. We are delighted with the instrument and take pleasure in recommending same to lovers of good music. I am with regards

**F. A. Fowler, Esq.**

**Washington D. C.**

I take great pleasure in recommending your Orchestrions. The one in our ladies hall has given so much satisfaction that my only regret is, I did not get one much larger. Every evening between seven and nine o'clock the ladies hall is filled with our guests, who over and over again express their delight at its perfect rendition of the most difficult music. I shall be glad to be of any use to you in regards to it.

**T. F. Roessle**

Prop. The Arlington House.

Gold Medal Karlsruhe 1849.
Silver Medal Donaueschingen 1849.
Gold Medal Villingen 1858.
Gold Medal Karlsruhe 1861.
Only Prize Medal for Orchestrions London 1862.
Prize Silver Medal Paris 1867.
Prize Medal Santiago, Chili, 1875.
Gold Medal Karlsruhe 1877.
Gold Medal and Diploma of Honor, Calcutta, India, 1884.
Gold Medal Antwerp 1885.
Only Gold Medal Freiburg i. B. 1887.
Gold Medal and Diploma of Honor, Munich 1888.
Diploma of Honor, Music Exposition Vienna 1892.
Medal and Diploma, World's Columbia Exposit., 1893.
1 st. Medal and Diploma, Industrial Exposition, Strassburg 1895.
Gold Medal and Diploma of Honor, Baden-Baden 1896.
Gold Medal Paris 1890.
Gold Medal Lille 1902.

**Welte orchestrions were sold all over the world. Hundreds were sold in the United States. Atlantic coast resorts, Rocky Mountain towns, San Francisco taverns, Newport summer "cottages" – these and 101 other places were homes for these ornate Welte instruments.**

(1)

(2)

## —AMUSEMENT PARK ORCHESTRIONS—

**Welte did a land office business selling large orchestrions to amusement parks all across America. On this page are the following photographs: (1) Welte Wotan Brass Band Orchestrion featured in concerts in a large outdoor park; (2) Welte Wotan situated on its own island in another amusement park. It was kept constantly playing to furnish a carnival mood. (3) Welte (left background) furnishes music for a carousel; (4) Music a la Welte in the Nicolett Roller Skating Rink, Minneapolis, Minn.; (5) More Welte merry go round music; (6) Huge Welte orchestrion on a balcony in the pavilion of the Detroit & Windsor Ferry Company's park on Bois Blanc Island; (7) The Rivers of Venice, an amusement attraction, lures customers with Welte music.**

(3)

(4)

(5)

(6)

(7)

This large and impressive Welte orchestrion was formerly in the Packard (of automobile fame) home in Michigan. The instrument was made in Welte's Poughkeepsie, New York, factory in the 1912-1914 period and sold for a reported $20,000 new. Via a duplex mechanism it plays "100 P.O." (100-note Piano Orchestrion) rolls. The orchestrion contains a large-scale piano, hundreds of pipes (including brass trumpet and brass trombone), a xylophone, and other features. The case is in the Louis XVI style and is of striped mahogany and is American-made, as noted. The piano is American-made also. The orchestrion chassis and pneumatic system were made in Welte's Freiburg plant.

Some of the pipework and other effects in the large Welte piano orchestrion once owned by the Packard family.

## "THE MULTITONE"

MOTION PICTURE AND
CABARET MIDGET ORCHESTRA

*OPERATED BY A SINGLE MUSICIAN OR WITH MUSIC ROLL AUTOMATICALLY*

THERE has been such a demand of late for a Piano with Mandolin and various DRUM TRAPS suitable for Moving Picture and Cabaret use that we have added three new styles to meet these requirements. In these Instruments the Piano and ALL THE EFFECTS can be PLAYED BY HAND, or played AUTOMATICALLY by means of paper music rolls.

A great number of the Picture Houses throughout the United States use only Piano Player and Drummer, and these musicians are only able to play about one-third of the time the show is on. With our instrumen it is possible to have music all the time. Any ordinary Piano Player can play it, with the drums and all the effects, and follow the pictures equally as well and in as satisfactory a manner as a ten or fifteen-piece Orchestra. It does not require an Expert Organist to play this Instrument, as with most of the other so-called Photo Players or Picture Show Instruments. It is impossible for a Piano Player to play continuously for hours, so that with the music rolls it can be played Automatically part of the Show, and the Piano Player play for the balance of the Show, THUS GIVING A VARIETY OF CONTINUOUS MUSIC THROUGHOUT THE ENTIRE PROGRAM.

M. WELTE & SONS
273 FIFTH AVENUE, NEW YORK

## ADDED ATTACHMENTS

For Styles ONE and TWO

"MULTITONE"

BY means of an Auxiliary KEYBOARD and FOOTBOARD, placed adjacent to the Piano, additional attachments can be played by the Piano Player. The Auxiliary keyboard can be turned aside and the Piano played as it ordinarily would be. The Piano can be played alone, or each of the other Instruments can be played alone, or in combination, as desired.

*ATTACHED KEYBOARD PLAYS:*

ORCHESTRA BELLS
PARSIFAL BELLS
XYLOPHONE
CATHEDRAL CHIMES

*ATTACHED FOOTBOARD PLAYS:*

DOOR BELL
TELEPHONE BELL
FIRE GONG
LOCOMOTIVE BELL
TAMBOURINE

CASTANETS
HORSES' HOOFS
AUTO HORN
SLEIGH BELLS
CHINESE CYMBAL
STEAMBOAT WHISTLE

LOCOMOTIVE WHISTLE
WIND SIREN
BABY CRY
CANARY BIRD
LION ROAR

CASE: The case is as fine an example of the artist's design and master cabinet-maker's art as can be found. It is carved with the most original designs with rich decorations of gold and beautiful French art glass panels.
DIMENSIONS: Height—5 feet. Width—5 feet 4 inches. Depth—2 feet 6 inches.

## "MULTITONE"

Style TWO

CONTAINS *a strictly high-grade Piano built to withstand constant, regular usage.* Equipped with rewind music mechanism, with rolls containing either 5, 10, 15 or 20 tunes which re-roll automatically after last selection has been played, although any piece can be repeated by means of pneumatic push buttons provided, which will re-roll the piece to any desired part and another button will start it playing again. A feature not found in any similar instrument. Roll can be changed instantly. Coin 20-point contact magazine slot playing from 1 to 20 times, included, when requested.

ORCHESTRATION: Contains Piano playing Automatically full 88 notes, Automatic Mandolin Attachment, Bass Drum, Kettle Drum, Snare Drum, Triangle, Cymbal, and full scale Xylophone with tremolo effect. Piano and all these Attachments play Automatically and can also be played by the Piano Player as shown by the accompanying picture in which can be seen buttons and pedals for their operation.

**Above and right: Descriptions of the Welte Multitone Style One, Two, and A instruments made for the firm by the Operators Piano Co. of Chicago. Style Two is the same as a Coinola X, but with foot pedals added.**

**Above: Welte "Theatre Piano" with duplex mechanisms for uninterrupted music during movie scenarios. Various styles were made. The above one is in a Feurich piano case.**

## "MULTITONE"

Style ONE

CONTAINS *a strictly high-grade Piano built to withstand constant, regular usage.* Equipped with rewind music mechanism holding rolls containing either 5, 10, 15 or 20 tunes, which re-roll automatically after last selection has been played, although any piece can be repeated by means of pneumatic push buttons provided, which will re-roll the piece to any desired part and another button will start it playing again. A feature not found on any similar instrument. Rolls can be changed instantly. Coin 20-point contact magazine slot playing from 1 to 20 tunes, included, when requested.

ORCHESTRATION: Contains full 88-note Piano which plays Automatically the full 88 notes, and also plays Automatically the Mandolin Attachments, Bass Drum, Snare Drum, Triangle and Cymbal. The Piano, Mandolin Attachment, Drums and other effects can also be played by the Piano Player, as shown by the accompanying picture, in which can be seen pedals for their operation.

**Funny Coincidence: Compare the above encircled description with that at the upper right. Actually, Welte (sellers of the Multitone) and Peerless were related, so the coincidence is explained. (Similarity first noted and called to the attention of the author by Art Reblitz)**

**A TANGLED WEB: M. Welte and Sons had its fingers in many pies. Involvements with other firms in America were almost too numerous to count. Here are some of them: By secret agreement, Welte's American interests were 48% owned by the Rudolph Wurlitzer Co. Welte sold under its own name band organs made by Bruder and Ruth, some keyboard orchestrions made by the Operators Piano Co., and, in the very early days, some instruments made by Philipps. An interlocking arrangement was made with the Peerless interests in St.Johnsville, N.Y., culminating in complete ownership of the firm (see excerpt at the bottom of this page — "Engelhardt Piano Co."). The Piano Player Mfg. Co. of Cincinnati, Ohio, and Covington, Ky., sold Welte orchestrions under the "Symphony Automatic Orchestra" name. In the reproducing piano field, Welte obtained patent license payments of $2.50 per instrument made of Duo-Art, Ampico, and several other types of instruments. Over 100 different brands of pianos purchased the later Welte Mignon (Licensee) piano actions made by the Auto Pneumatic Action Co. (which paid a royalty to Welte). The list of cross-licensing and other agreements is a long one.**

*Music* Using rolls containing fifteen (15) selections, which re-roll automatically after last selection has been played, although any piece can be repeated by means of pneumatic push buttons provided, which will re-roll the piece to any desired part and another button will start it playing again. A feature not found on any similar instrument.

Music rolls for all Peerless instruments made in our own factories from original masters.

Rolls available for the Model Arcadian Orchestrion are listed in the 20,000 series. See supplementary Music Bulletins.

**Funny Coincidence Dept: Compare the encircled part of the description (for a Peerless orchestrion) with that for the Multitone at the left of this page. Perhaps the last line should read: "A feature not found on any similar instrument — except other instruments!!!"**

**ENGELHARDT PIANO COMPANY.**

Office and Factory—St. Johnsville, N. Y. Established—1916. Name of Piano Owned or Controlled—Engelhardt. Types of Instruments Manufactured— Engelhardt coin-operated Pianos, Bell Pianos, Xylophone Pianos, Orchestrions, Banjo-orchestras, Flute Pianos, Violin Pianos, Reproducing Player-Pianos, Player-Pianos, Midget Orchestrions, Midget Bell Pianos, Midget Flute Pianos, Midget Violin Pianos, Midget Xylophone Pianos. A co-partnership. Now entirely owned by Welte Co., Inc., to which refer.

## WESER BROTHERS

Founded in 1879 by John A. Weser, the firm made a large variety of upright and grand regular pianos and player pianos, some of the latter bearing the "Marveola" trademark.

Of interest to automatic musical instrument historians is the "Nickel Player," a coin-operated electric piano housed in a case identical to the Electrova Style 66 (see Jacob Doll & Sons section of this book).

A 1913 description of an electric version of the Marveola may have referred to this instrument: "The 'Marveola' can be played by electricity... Its special, unique features include the ability to play with proper expression and tempo any standard 65-note or 88-note player piano roll, with much expression and musical feeling. It has an automatic rerolling feature of great value and the patented 'Virtuoso' accenting device..."

The Nickel Player indeed does have an unusual accenting device — a rotating cam wheel which introduces loud or soft expression into the music from time to time at random (not in any way coordinated with the music roll!) moments.

Pneumatic coin trip system of the Weser.

Interior view.

## ERNST WILDBREDT

In the 1910 - 1914 era Ernst Wildbredt of Grosse Frankfurter Strasse 44, Berlin, advertised a series of "pneumatic artistic-playing pianos" and noted that "violin pianos are a specialty."

Their Model I, illustrated on this page, was described as a "Flute and Violin Piano — The instrument is provided with the finest faceted mirrors, brass fittings, richly carved woodwork, and contains a first class overstrung piano as well as splendidly toned concert flutes and violin pipes, performing alternately in an artistic manner, especially solos with piano accompaniment. In addition, the piano is equipped with mandolin and xylophone... The instrument produces very fine and artistic music of a kind suitable for coffee houses, restaurants, and private drawing rooms. Height: 99 inches; width 63 inches; depth 30 inches."

Wildbredt, a small firm with a limited output, was one of many dozens of small companies which flourished during the golden years of the automatic piano business.

Western Electric Piano Company

TELEPHONE
MOHAWK 3420

832-850 BLACKHAWK STREET

CHICAGO

Manufacturers of
Coin Operated
Electric Pianos

SELECTRAPHONE
Amplified-Automatic
Phonograph

## WESTERN ELECTRIC PIANO COMPANY

Secretly owned by the J.P. Seeburg Piano Co. (see Seeburg section of this Encyclopedia) the Western Electric Piano Company was purchased shortly after it was founded by Seeburg's "desire to stimulate more competition among the Seeburg dealers who had exclusive territories and really needed competition." (In the words of N. Marshall Seeburg in a communication to the author.)

From about 1924 until the late 'twenties (although the company remained a legal entity until bankruptcy proceedings in 1933) Western Electric produced a line of coin operated pianos and orchestrions, mostly of the cabinet type. To avoid easy detection by the public and those in the trade, the easily-visible portions of the Western Electric instruments – the cases, the pumps, roll mechanisms, etc. – were different from Seeburg products. However, the serial numbers of the pianos (mostly in the late 150,000 and in the 160,000 series) are concurrent with contemporary Seeburg pianos of the 1920's and many of the interior parts, the pneumatic stacks of certain pianos for instance, are the same.

Western Electric pianos were durably built and enjoyed a good reputation with dealers and routemen who operated them in various locations. In the Minneapolis area Oswald Wurdeman had 350 of them out "on location" earning money!

In "Player Piano Treasury" Harvey Roehl reprints a trade-paper news item about Western Electric. Dated June 12, 1926, the article gives an idea of the success of the firm at that time:

"Busy Times at Western Electric Piano Co."

"Full Production Going on with Overtime Work to Catch Up on Rush of Orders... At the plant of the Western Electric Piano Co., makers of 'The Finest' line of automatic pianos and orchestrions, 429 West Superior Street, there is much activity at present carrying out plans for the removal of the company to the much larger quarters at 900-912 Blackhawk Street... The new plant will give the company more than double its present floor space and will be one of the most modern of its kind in the country. 'While our growth has been rapid,' said B.C. Waters, secretary and general manager of the company, 'it has been expected by us. We knew when we started in business that we had a product of highest quality and we also felt that we had exclusive features that could not but find popularity with the dealer and the ultimate purchaser. The success which has come to us proves that we did not overestimate matters. Every month since our inception has shown a gain over its predecessor and the present year has been exceptionally busy. Our line has been taken on by dealers in all parts of the country and months ago we realized that our quarters were inadequate.

"'In spite of the fact that we have been running at capacity and working overtime, we have been way behind in orders for months. We expect in our new location to soon catch up on business and to be in a position to take care of orders promptly.

"One of the features that has made The Finest line talked about is the 'Selectra.' This is a device by which the operator of an instrument can select at will any tune on the ordinary ten-tune roll. Instead of taking the numbers in rotation, he can make his choice, touch a button, and the tune he wants is played sooner.

"Many other novelties have been introduced, and in the near future the company will make some important announcements along this line. All are designed to create more interest in the automatic instrument on the part of the public, and that they will do so is the testimony of dealers who have been 'let in' on some of the new ideas.

"The new ideas are worked out by the officers of the company. A.F. Larson, president, is one of the best known manufacturers of automatics in the country. He has devoted his life to this work and in addition to knowing every detail of the business has an inventive turn that is remarkable. R.I. Wilcox, vice-president, is also widely known for his inventive genius, and Mr. Waters, although he is devoted especially to the selling of instruments, is a practical man of wide experience and is the father of many ideas embodied in the product."

Note: 900 Blackhawk St. was the side entrance to the J.P. Seeburg factory! Waters and Larson, officers of the Western Electric firm, were earlier the officers of the Marquette Piano Company, makers of the Cremona line of instruments.

### Types of Western Electric Instruments

Most Western Electric pianos made used standard 10-tune "A" rolls and were built into cabinets. Only a very few instruments were made with keyboards. A few orchestrions (which used "G" or "4X" rolls) were made, but the number must have been exceedingly limited as few are known today.

Of special interest is the "Selectra" tune-selecting device. At the upper left side of the instrument a calibrated dial was placed. A nearby program card listed the ten tunes and gave the dial setting for each tune (the dial setting for each tune varied from roll to roll and had to be computed for each new roll put on the instrument). The patron could point the indicator at the right spot on the dial, drop a nickel in the slot, and the roll would go into rewind or fast-forward until the beginning of the desired tune was found – and then it would play. To operate the Selectra device special slots had to be cut into the rolls at the tune divisions. This was usually done (a razor blade and some patience were required!) by the route operator, although some rolls could be ordered pre-cut from the Clark Orchestra Roll Co.

Nearly all Western Electric pianos were built into quartered oak cabinets, usually finished a natural brown color. The art glass was usually interspersed with some beveled clear glass sections to permit a view of the roll and some of the interior parts. The art glass designs were generally plainer than those of Seeburg. "The Finest" was the trade name given to the line of Western Electric pianos.

One of the most interesting Western Electric products was the "Derby," an A-roll piano which featured a diorama of race horses. When a nickel was dropped in the slot the horses would race around and around, and then stop. Each time a new nickel was deposited the horses would start up again. To increase the influx of nickels, many of the Derby pianos had the accumulating mechanism blocked off – so that if additional nickels were deposited during the playing of a tune, the horses would re-race, but no credit was given for additional tunes once the one playing ended.

During the late 1920's the "Selectraphone," a coin-operated phonograph similar to the contemporary Seeburg "Audiophone," was introduced. These were made into the early 1930's.

Note: Western Electric could never make up its mind exactly where on Blackhawk Street it was located – not that it made any difference anyway. Various advertisements and letterheads have such street numbers as 832, 850, 900, 910, and 912!

### Western Electric Pianos Today

Today collectors regard Western Electric instruments as being among the most desirable American-made nickelodeon pianos. Like similar Seeburg instruments, they are ruggedly built and have lots of reserve vacuum capacity – so that minor leaks, or perhaps an amateurish rebuilding job, will not be noticed! The Selectra mechanisms must have been a nuisance to their owners (but not so to collectors today who find them to be fascinating!) and many were ripped out or otherwise disconnected.

Western Electric "Derby" (Collection of Mr. and Mrs. Jerry Cohen)

MAKE 1925 BUSIER
You can do this with
The Finest
AUTOMATIC
ELECTRIC
PIANOS
and
Orchestrions
Selectra Model "S"
This Great Line Has Many Exclusive Features Including the Wonderful
SELECTRA
Which Enables You to Select Tunes at Will from the 10-Tune Standard Music Rolls
The Finest
Is Highest Quality and Sells at a Sensible Price
Get the Agency and make sure of a busy 1925.
Selectra Model "B"
Mascot Model "C"
WESTERN ELECTRIC
PIANO CO.
429 West Superior St.
CHICAGO


1925 advertisement featuring several different styles. Actually, few keyboard styles were made; most were of the cabinet format.

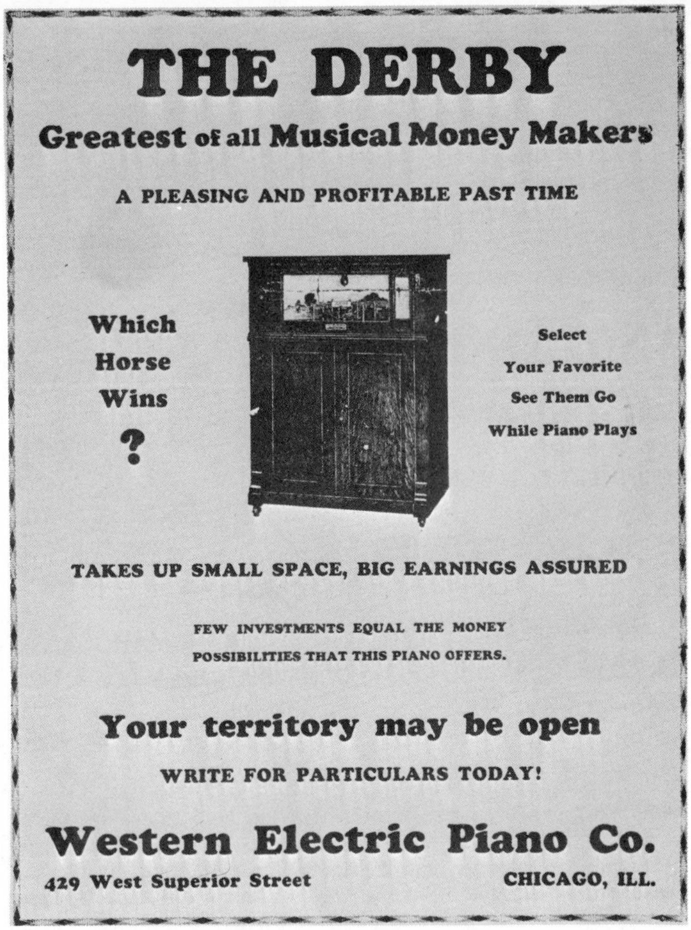

THE DERBY
Greatest of all Musical Money Makers
A PLEASING AND PROFITABLE PAST TIME
Which
Horse
Wins
?
Select
Your Favorite
See Them Go
While Piano Plays
TAKES UP SMALL SPACE, BIG EARNINGS ASSURED
FEW INVESTMENTS EQUAL THE MONEY
POSSIBILITIES THAT THIS PIANO OFFERS.
Your territory may be open
WRITE FOR PARTICULARS TODAY!
Western Electric Piano Co.
429 West Superior Street
CHICAGO, ILL.


Western Electric "Derby" — Drop a nickel in the slot and the horses go spinning 'round and around, and where they'll stop nobody knows! A great item for spirited conversation and wagering in a tavern years ago, the Derby is a favorite with collectors today. The Seeburg "Greyhound" is similar in concept.

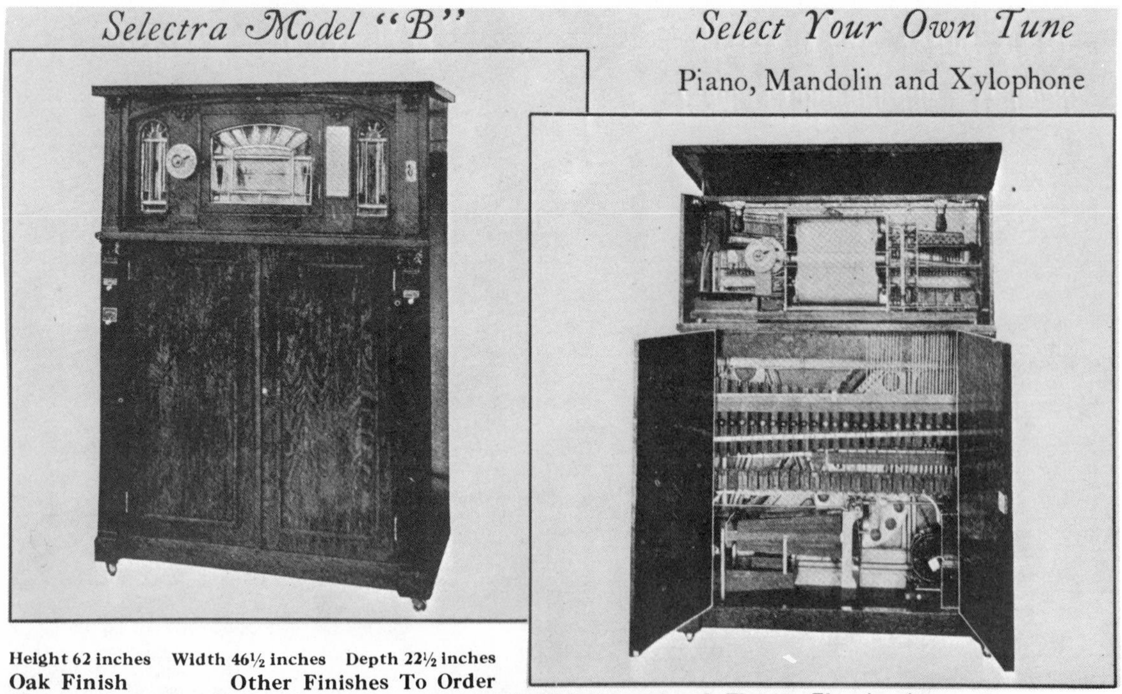

Selectra Model "B"
Select Your Own Tune
Piano, Mandolin and Xylophone
Height 62 inches Width 46½ inches Depth 22½ inches
Oak Finish Other Finishes To Order


The Model B was the most popular Selectra-equipped Western Electric piano. Note the indicator dial to the left of the center glass panel. Without the Selectra feature a similar model was known as the Style X.

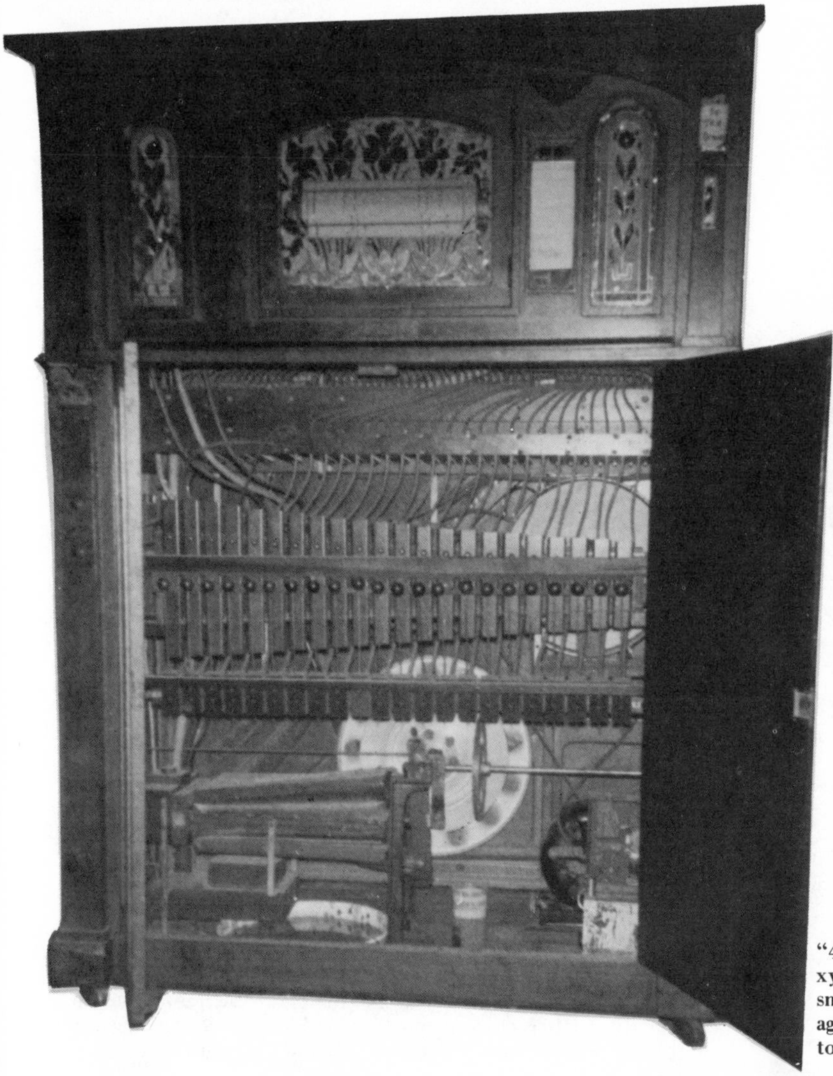

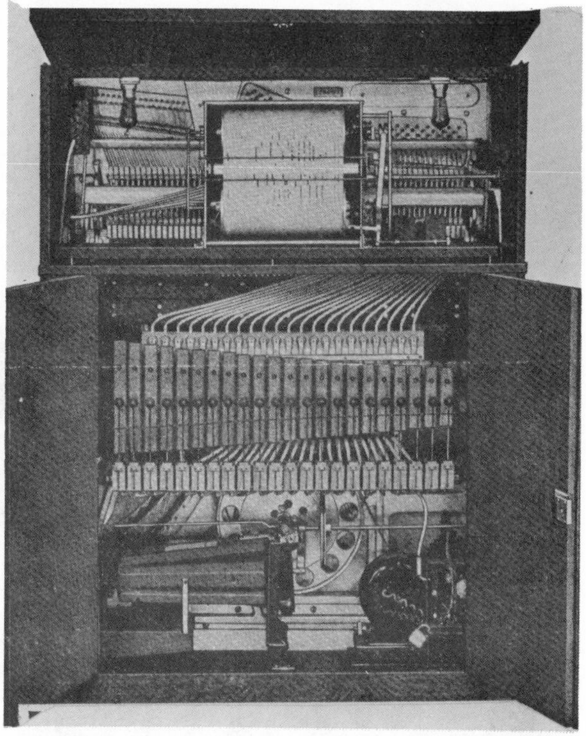

ABOVE: Western Electric Style X: Piano, mandolin attachment, and xylophone. Cabinet styling similar to the Selectra B. The same large cabinet style was also used for a piano/mandolin instrument — with lots of empty space left over!

LEFT: Western Electric orchestrion. Using a "G" or "4X" roll the instrument plays piano, mandolin, xylophone and limited percussion effects. (Photo snapped "on location" in an Illinois tavern a few years ago by David Junchen. Note pan of water near pump to keep up the humidity!)

A Large Western Electric Orchestrion

Western Electric's counterpart to the Seeburg KT Special was the style pictured above (with non-original bottom doors). Containing piano, mandolin, xylophone, bass drum, snare drum, tympani, wood block, and other effects the instrument uses "4X" or "G" orchestrion rolls. Apparently very few such instruments were originally made as they are very rare today.

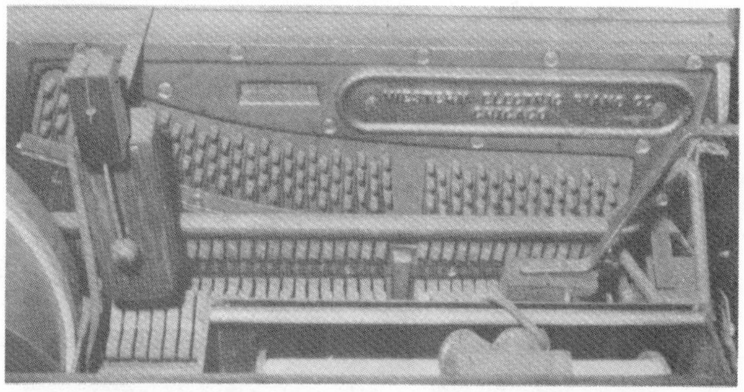

View of the wood block, triangle, and part of the piano.

The bass drum and cymbal are to the left of the roll frame.

The Treasures of Another Era . . .

**Treasured by one era and forgotten by the next: A group of Western Electric and Seeburg coin pianos, nearly two dozen in all, was found in mouldering sadness in a damp barn in Georgia by Wyatte Pittman. Sadly, hundreds of other Western Electric pianos met similar fates over the years. When the Age of Coin Piano Appreciation came in the late 1940's many of these fine instruments were gone forever. If only the owners had heeded the motto of the present-day Fair Organ Preservation Society: Whilst looking to the future, do not forget the glories of the past.**

**The Western Electric "Selectra"**
**—An idea lingers on—**

*Acting upon the suggestion of Harvey Roehl, I wrote to Mr. Otto Schulz, president of Chicago's American Automatic Typewriter Co., makers of the "Auto-typist." The Auto-typist is pneumatically operated and has a selector mechanism (for pre-programmed paragraphs to be typed) based upon the "Selectra" device used in Western Electric coin pianos. As Mr. Schulz's letter has some interesting comments concerning the end of the coin piano field and shows how an old-time idea finds application today, we reprint portions of it herewith:*

My grandfather organized the M. Schulz Co. in 1869 and we manufactured reed organs and, later, pianos. He died in 1899 and my father succeeded him. Starting about 1900 we made players, first buying the actions from Simplex and other people. From 1907 on we made all of our own actions including, later, electric reproducing actions for grand pianos. We never entered the coin operated field. The first year I was in the business, 1923, we built 11,000 pianos of which 8500 were players. The business held up through 1926, but in 1927 fell by 50% due to the wide acceptance of the radio with built-in dynamic speakers. Grigsby-Grunow's Majestic swept the music industry and by the end of 1928 we were practically out of the player piano business and our sales had fallen by 80%. My dad died in '29 and the family decided to liquidate the business. In 1932 I heard of this company (the American Automatic Typewriter Co.) as another application of the type of thing we had been doing and on which we could use at least part of our employees and facilities. It was a small business and in financial straits, but we took it over and slowly built it up.

Montgomery Ward was a neighbor of ours and I tried to sell our automatic typewriter to their treasurer. They were hand typing some of their collection letters, the ones in which they made a threat or demand. The others were mimeographed. He had 10 forms he was using, including his "attorney" letters. He wanted an automatic typewriter that would select any one of these letters while the girl was putting in the stationery and typing the heading. "If we can turn a dial and get the letter we want, the way we dial radio stations, we'll be interested."

In those days the coin pianos were as obsolete as player pianos were. The new saloons that had just opened were equipped with radios. Coin operated phonographs were starting to come back. Finally, in South Chicago near the mills, I found a Western Electric coin piano with the Selectra mechanism. It looked like the most practical solution to our typewriter letter-selecting problem, so I bought it and tore out the Selectra mechanism – and we built our first selector Auto-typist. Montgomery Ward ended up buying 28 of them!

When I found that Seeburg owned the Western Electric Piano Company I called Noel Seeburg and had lunch with him. He was also a neighbor and I knew him well. He explained Western was in bankruptcy and there was to be an auction in a couple of months. He said we should wait and buy the patents – and he would give me the Selectra patent which had been issued in 1927 (although pianos with this device had been made for several years earlier – Ed.). At the sale the patents were knocked down for $10.

The only bid of any size at all was from a lawyer for the Western Electric Company who wanted to buy the name, and did. It seemed the Western Electric Piano Company was older than the Western Electric Co., an American Telephone and Telegraph Co. subsidiary. I formally bought the Selectra patent from Noel Seeburg and paid him $1. You could buy a lot of things for one dollar in 1933. Noel's Seeburg Co. was in 77-B at the time, one step above bankruptcy, and he wanted me to make his cabinets – for he was sure that coin operated phonographs would come back in a big way. He said he might need 200 a day! I went to my bank to ask if I could get a loan to finance the business, and the very astute banker wanted to know if I was crazy and gave me a flat NO. Within a year Seeburg was doing a business of a million dollars a month and netting a very substantial profit.

Justus Seeburg, Noel's father, was an extremely clever inventor. Before we built our own player actions we bought some from him. In the coin field he did a lot of their designing. Fortunately he lived to see the comeback of the company and Noel's success in building it into a profitable business again.

Note: In a more modern vein, I am enclosing some literature on our automatic typewriters and on test equipment we build for office machine manufacturers. We also built pneumatic programmers for Expo '70 that controlled automatic displays in many of the buildings. Our "player piano" is accepted because it is reliable, easy to repair, and long-lived.

Yours very truly,
———Otto Schulz

# THE RUDOLPH WURLITZER CO.

MANUFACTURERS, IMPORTERS, WHOLESALE AND RETAIL DEALERS IN

## EVERYTHING MUSICAL

### THE RUDOLPH WURLITZER COMPANY
—North Tonawanda, N.Y.—

#### The Early Years

The Rudolph Wurlitzer Company had its inception in 1856 when Rudolph Wurlitzer, a German immigrant, took his capital of $700 and began selling musical instruments, primarily woodwinds, in Cincinnati, Ohio. For the first few years sales were mainly of instruments imported from Germany. During the Civil War manufacturing of drums and percussion instruments began. In 1865 a branch store was established in Chicago. About 1870 the partnership of Wurlitzer and Brother was formed. In 1890 the Rudolph Wurlitzer Company was incorporated.

During these years Wurlitzer's main business was the sale of regular (hand-played) instruments of various kinds. A few imported music boxes and hand-cranked organs were stocked, but these formed a minor part of the total sales.

#### The Relationship with Regina

In the 1890's Wurlitzer secured a distributorship for Regina music boxes. This was during the great growth period for disc boxes, and the Regina instruments sold very well. In time Wurlitzer became the largest single Regina sales outlet.

In 1896 Wurlitzer suggested to Regina that some of its music boxes be equipped with coin slots for operation in public places. The idea was adopted. Regina coin-operated boxes became an instant success. This furnished a valuable insight into the fantastic potential for coin operated musical instruments — a field that was later to become the mainstay of the Wurlitzer operations.

#### Early Coin Pianos

In 1897 Eugene DeKleist, a barrel organ maker from North Tonawanda, New York, visited the Wurlitzer offices in Cincinnati. DeKleist was encouraged to develop a coin operated piano. In 1899 the Tonophone made its appearance. This electrical piano played ten tunes from a pinned wooden barrel. The initial order was for 200 Tonophones at $200 apiece. These found an instant reception with the public. More Tonophones were ordered from DeKleist and then more Tonophones again. During the next several years an estimated one to two thousand were sold to an enthusiastic market of tavern owners, hotels, and similar attractions.

Shortly after 1900 the Pianino, a small keyboardless paper roll operated coin piano, made its debut. Following that were the Mandolin Quartette, Mandolin Sextette, and the Automatic Player Pianos (trade name) of 88-note and 65-note specifications.

All of this business from Wurlitzer made Eugene DeKleist a wealthy man. Less and less attention was paid to running the factory and more time was given to leading the good life. DeKleist moved his office away from the factory and visited the manufacturing facilities only two or three times a year! A decline in quality and resultant customer

*Early automatic instrument featuring tubular chimes — made by DeKleist and sold by Wurlitzer circa 1904.*

complaints were inevitable. Faced with a worsening situation Wurlitzer gave DeKleist an ultimatum: sell out to us or we'll take our business away and set up facilities to manufacture band organs (another item that Wurlitzer bought from DeKleist in quantity) and coin pianos elsewhere. In January, 1909, Wurlitzer assumed control. From that time onward the Wurlitzer factories in North Tonawanda accounted for nearly all of the coin operated instruments sold by that firm, plus an extensive line of other types of instruments as well.

#### The 65-Note Automatic Player Piano

First introduced to the public in 1908 the 65-Note Automatic Player Piano soon replaced the earlier coin operated 88-Note Automatic Player Piano and became the mainstay of the Wurlitzer coin piano business.

The 65-Note piano was embellished by adding a rank of pipes, either violin or flute, thus creating the "Violin Piano — Style A." Then came other models with both violin and flute pipes plus drum and trap effects as well — the Style C orchestrions.

The Wurlitzer Automatic Roll Changer, a device which holds six 5-tune rolls and changes them in sequence automatically, was incorporated into 65-Note Automatic Player Pianos of all types as an optional feature available for $100 to $200 extra cost. Models equipped with the changer had an "X" suffix. Thus a Style A with a roll changer was known as a "Style AX."

Production of 65-Note instruments of various kinds was continued through the late 1920's. Some of the instruments were sold as late as 1934 and rolls were cut by the factory until about 1935.

Wurlitzer Automatic Player Piano rolls (as 65-note rolls were later called — the "65-Note" designation was dropped in later years) were also used on several different types of Wurlitzer theatre photoplayers. With the possible exception of the style "A" roll (used by Seeburg, Cremona, and several other manufacturers) the Wurlitzer Automatic Player Piano roll was made in larger quantities and with a wider selection of tunes than any other type of coin piano roll in America. A Wurlitzer roll catalogue issued about 1923 listed two thousand (!) different tunes that were carried in stock at that time! Of course quantity doesn't necessarily equate with quality — and many of the musical arrangements were, as we would say today, just so-so.

#### The PianOrchestras and the Paganini

In 1902 Howard and Farny Wurlitzer (two of the three sons of Rudolph Wurlitzer) visited the annual Leipzig Trade Fair in Germany.

*This 1906 view of the Cincinnati showroom shows seven very large orchestrions (six PianOrchestras and one Welte orchestrion, the latter possibly taken in on trade), three band organs, and two automatic pianos. The orchestrion at the center rear (behind the keyboard piano) is a Style 17 PianOrchestra. You can find a description of it on another page.*

On display there were several different types of very large orchestrions — a type of instrument which the two Wurlitzers had never seen before. They were very impressed with the size and musical qualities of these awesome machines and thought that the Wurlitzer firm would do well to distribute them in America.

The firm of Ludwig Hupfeld dominated the exhibits. Wurlitzer approached Hupfeld and proffered an agreement whereby Wurlitzer would have the exclusive right to sell Hupfeld instruments in the United States (they would be sold under the Wurlitzer label). It was also proposed that Farny Wurlitzer spend several months working in the Hupfeld factory to gain familiarity with the orchestrions and their construction. Negotiations were stalemated on this latter point as Hupfeld feared Wurlitzer would use the knowledge to set up competing facilities in America. Not easily discouraged, the Wurlitzer sons turned their search elsewhere — and learned of J.D. Philipps & Söhne, a small manufacturer of orchestrions in Frankfurt. The Philipps line was not as extensive as Hupfeld's, but the quality was satisfactory. They agreed to the Wurlitzer business proposal. Subsequently Farny Wurlitzer spent six months in the Philipps factory. The first order placed was for four Philipps "Pianella" orchestrions. These reached America in 1903 and were the first instruments to be sold under the Mandolin PianOrchestra name.

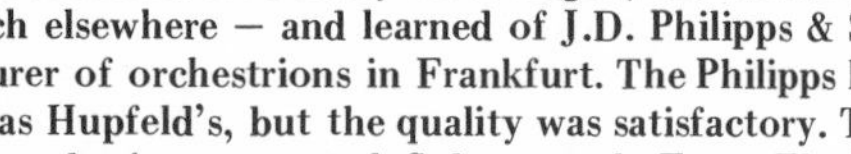

*The Style 10 Paganini Violin Orchestra had a list price of $10,000.00 and was Wurlitzer's most expensive orchestrion.*

From this time until about 1914 approximately 1,000 Philipps Pianella instruments were imported. The models with from one to six ranks of pipes (generally speaking) were known as Mandolin PianOrchestras and used the Philipps "PM" (for "Pianella Mandoline") or Wurlitzer Mandolin PianOrchestra rolls interchangeably. The larger models were called Concert PianOrchestras and used Wurlitzer rolls of the same name or Philipps "PC" (for "Pianella Caecilia") rolls. In the early days all rolls were imported from Philipps. Later Wurlitzer manufactured them in quantity in North Tonawanda. The Concert PianOrchestra rolls were also used on several different types of large Wurlitzer photoplayers (styles H, K, R, and U mainly) made in later years.

About 1910 Philipps introduced a new type of instrument, the Paganini. This orchestrion was made in over a dozen different models ranging from the basic instrument containing a reproducing piano (embodying the Philipps "Duca" system) plus one rank of violin pipes to very large Paganini Violin Orchestras with several ranks of pipes plus bells, xylophone, and percussion effects. The Paganini was intended to play serious and soulful piano and violin music. Wurlitzer advertised: "Put the Paganini in the place of the orchestra and your customers will never know but that they are listening to the finest violinist and pianist they ever heard... The Paganini is a thoroughly dignified, refined musical instrument of the highest grade suitable for the finest metropolitan hotels and cafes. It will not only make good under the most exacting conditions, but it is no exaggeration to say that it will carry the most critical audience by storm."

Although no precise figures are available it has been estimated that possibly one or two hundred of these were sold in America.

About 1913 Wurlitzer decided to manufacture PianOrchestras and Paganinis at North Tonawanda. In the case of the Paganini instruments the entire interior mechanisms were imported from Philipps and fitted into Wurlitzer-made cabinets. The Mandolin PianOrchestras were about half and half: the piano, drums, electrical systems, coin mechanisms, and cabinets were made in North Tonawanda; the other components (including just about all of the pneumatic system plus bells, roll changer, xylophone, etc.) were imported from Philipps. About 100 PianOrchestras of the Mandolin type were made in this manner.

### The Wurlitzer Harp

In 1905 Howard Wurlitzer visited a cafe near the main Wurlitzer offices in downtown Cincinnati. There he saw and heard an unusual instrument — a self-playing harp! Piqued by the machine he soon learned that it was made in nearby Rising Sun, Indiana, by J.W. Whitlock & Co. In short order an agreement was made whereby Wurlitzer would exclusively market these interesting instruments.

During the next decade approximately 1500 Harps were made, most of which were the squared-off Style A design. The rolls for the Harp were also made by Whitlock by using arrangements played on a specially contrived recording piano located in the loft of the Whitlock

*The graceful Style B Wurlitzer Automatic Harp shown in this 1966 photograph of the Carlsen Collection is a prize piece. Today Wurlitzer automatic instruments of all kinds are eagerly sought by collectors and museums who restore them to their musical abilities of yesteryear.*

factory. Each roll was of six-tune length.

The Wurlitzer Harp is a quiet instrument which has a tonal quality not unlike that of a guitar. It was in fact offered as "a most refined instrument for places where the piano cannot be used on account of its being too loud."

### Other Coin Pianos

The Autograph Piano introduced around 1915 featured piano music played with expression. From 1915 to 1926 some 85 Autograph Pianos were shipped from the factory. Designed for public places this instrument received a lacklustre reception, perhaps because tavern patrons preferred more snappy music than it provided. Likewise the Solo Violin Piano, a keyboard piano with the accompaniment of a rank of violin pipes mounted behind the piano sounding board, had indifferent sales results. 140 machines were shipped from 1919 to 1927.

In the early days before 1910 Wurlitzer purchased instruments from DeKleist (as noted earlier) and also from several other makers as well. The Regina Sublima Piano, a mechanical piano with a vibrating mandolinlike tone, was sold by Wurlitzer as the Wurlitzer Tremolo Piano. It is possible that certain Cremona coin pianos were also sold by Wurlitzer in limited numbers.

In addition to coin pianos Wurlitzer manufactured tens of thousands of regular upright and grand pianos for home use. In fact, after the early 'teen years coin pianos were only a small fraction of the total Wurlitzer factory output. Expression and reproducing pianos were made which incorporated the Recordo, Artecho, and Apollo systems. A number of pianos were made on contract for Welte (at one time Wurlitzer owned 48% of Welte's American interests) and were sent to Welte's Poughkeepsie, N.Y., factory.

### Theatre Photoplayers

Beginning about 1913 Wurlitzer entered the photoplayer market. The proliferation of nickelodeon theatres — storefront or other small theatres which showed silent films and charged 5c admission — brought with it a fantastic demand for accompanying music. Wurlitzer produced several different styles of theatre instruments. Ranging from a basic piano with two ranks of pipes to larger styles with two side chests, these photoplayers used Automatic Player Piano rolls or, on the very large models, Concert PianOrchestra rolls.

The most famous Wurlitzer theatre instruments were not automatic (i.e., roll-played) at all: the Wurlitzer Hope-Jones Unit Orchestras, the "mighty Wurlitzer" theatre organs, virtually dominated the organ industry and were sold to the extent of several thousand installations (at average prices mostly in the $10,000 to $30,000 range each) from about 1915 to the early 1930's.

### The Wurlitzer Business

By means of extensive advertising, colorful catalogues, and a large force of salesmen Wurlitzer dominated the coin piano and orchestrion field from about 1900 to 1920. By the latter year the production of the higher-priced theatre organs had become the mainstay of Wurlitzer's business, and development of coin operated instruments virtually ceased. Production during the 1920's was limited to case revisions and slight modifications of earlier types; nothing new was introduced. The thriving market for small cabinet-type coin pianos and orchestrions (a market that was served by Seeburg, Western Electric, Coinola, and others) was completely overlooked by Wurlitzer, unless one considers the relatively modest sales in the 1920's of the then-obsolete Pianino cabinet piano.

*These high society diners pictured on the front of a 1916 Wurlitzer catalogue are enjoying the music of a Style 30-A Mandolin PianOrchestra.*

During the preparation of an earlier book, "Put Another Nickel In," the author was given access to the Wurlitzer archives by Mr. Farny Wurlitzer, then chairman of the board of the firm. Farny was personally responsible for the introduction of the PianOrchestra and Paganini instruments into the Wurlitzer line, the manufacturing of automatic instruments of all kinds at North Tonawanda (he moved to North Tonawanda shortly after the acquisition of that facility in 1909, and supervised the operations there), and the entry of Wurlitzer into the theatre organ field (he first learned of Robert Hope-Jones in Elmira, N.Y., and was instrumental in the acquisition of the Hope-Jones organ business). Today we are indebted more than words can say to Farny Wurlitzer and his associate, Lou Rosa, for the wealth of production and pictorial data which appears on these pages and in "Put Another Nickel In."

*Mr. Farny Wurlitzer, former chairman of the board of the Wurlitzer Company, provided priceless assistance to the author (standing) during the preparation of this and other books about automatic instruments.*

*Display of Wurlitzer instruments (made by DeKleist) at the 1904 Louisiana Purchase Exposition in St. Louis. A variety of band organs and coin pianos is shown. Such displays were an important part of coin piano selling years ago. Early Wurlitzer machines proudly bore decals attesting to exposition awards. (Photo from "Put Another Nickel In.")*

**Wurlitzer Piano and Orchestrion Rolls**
**—for coin-operated instruments—**

A check list of different types of rolls used on Wurlitzer coin pianos, orchestrions, and photoplayers. Measurements are of the paper width only and do not include the spool ends. Rolls with asterisks (*) were made in two formats: with a wire rod across the end for use with the Wurlitzer Automatic Roll Changer or with a tab or hook for use with long-frame type instruments.

PIANINO* — 5½" paper width. Used on the Pianino, the Violin Pianino, the Violin-Flute Pianino, and the Bijou Orchestra (the Bijou Orchestras were equipped with roll changers). Earlier rolls usually of 6-tune length; later ones, 5. Some long-playing rolls of 10 or more tunes also made. Paper color (this applies to most other types of North Tonawanda-produced Wurlitzer rolls as well): earliest rolls red (a few purple); then white (some orange); then green (some slate-gray paper and some dark bluish-green as well).

MANDOLIN QUARTETTE — 7 5/16" paper width. Used on the Mandolin Quartette and Mandolin Sextette. Usually of 5-tune length.

65-NOTE PIANO* — Also called "Automatic Player Piano." 9 5/8" paper width. Used on the basic Wurlitzer 65-Note Player Piano and its larger variations such as A, AX, B, BX, C, CX, D, DX, LX, the "S" series, and other keyboard pianos and orchestrions. Also used on the Wurlitzer Caliola organ and several styles of Wurlitzer photoplayers including D, F, G, and O. Mostly of 5-tune or 10-tune length; also some of 15 and 20-tune length. Those for the roll changer usually of 5-tune length. Early rolls are scored to operate the piano, pipes, and necessary expression. Later rolls are more extensively orchestrated and include provision for bells and (rarely) xylophone.

88-NOTE PIANO — 10½" paper width. Used on the early electric Style A and Style B 88-Note Automatic Player Pianos. (Not to be confused with the 11¼" common foot-pumped home player piano roll.) Piano with limited expression effects. Usually seen on red paper.

HARP — 8½" paper width. Usually white paper. Usually 6 tunes per roll. Perforated at an 8-holes-per-inch scale by J.W. Whitlock & Co. Approximately 239 different rolls manufactured. Used on Style A and Style B Harps.

SOLO VIOLIN PIANO* — 12 1/16" paper width; wire rod end for roll changer. Piano with expression and violin pipes.

AUTOGRAPH PIANO* — 12 1/16" paper width; wire rod end for roll changer. Piano with expression effects. Made from hand-played master rolls.

MANDOLIN PIANORCHESTRA* — 8 7/8" paper width. Same as Philipps "PM" rolls. Used on Wurlitzer Mandolin PianOrchestra orchestrions. Extensive instrumentation. Usually of 5-tune length.

STYLE 17 PIANORCHESTRA — 8 7/8" paper width. Early roll with solo perforations for orchestra bells and with registers arranged differently than on the Mandolin PianOrchestra roll. Used on the Style 17 PianOrchestra.

CONCERT PIANORCHESTRA* — 8 7/8" paper width. Same as Philipps "PC" rolls. Used on Wurlitzer Concert PianOrchestra orchestrions and on very large styles of Wurlitzer photoplayers (such as styles L, H, K, R, and U). Usually of 5-tune length.

PAGANINI* — 13 9/16" paper width. Same as Philipps "PP" rolls (Philipps "PD" rolls which were of the same width and which feature "Duca" reproducing piano music only also were made for the Paganini). Usually of 4-tune length. Used on the Paganini pianos and orchestrions.

ORGANETTE — 8 7/8" paper width. Also known as "Style W Organ" rolls. Made for the Wurlitzer Organette piano / pipe organ instruments.

Notes: Other types of rolls were made for other Wurlitzer instruments outside the scope of this section. Pipe organ rolls included styles MO, Concert Organ, RJ (or 105-note), 130-note, 165-note (called "Reproducing Organ"). Band organ rolls were of several styles including the popular 125, 150, and 165 series and the rare 180. Certain very small Wurlitzer band organs used Pianino piano rolls! Terry Hathaway reports that certain Wurlitzer 65-Note Automatic Player Piano rolls were perforated in Cuba using Wurlitzer paper and Wurlitzer labels but on Cuban perforating equipment. As the tunes were of a popular nature perhaps an agreement was made whereby Wurlitzer's Cuban distributor made rolls for that market. Certain long playing 65-Note rolls were made by pasting two shorter rolls together end-to-end without regard to the roll tempo, necessitating use of the tempo-changing lever as these were being played (mostly on photoplayers). Rolls were offered for sale via catalogues of each type and also by monthly bulletins.

# THE TONOPHONE

WURLITZER

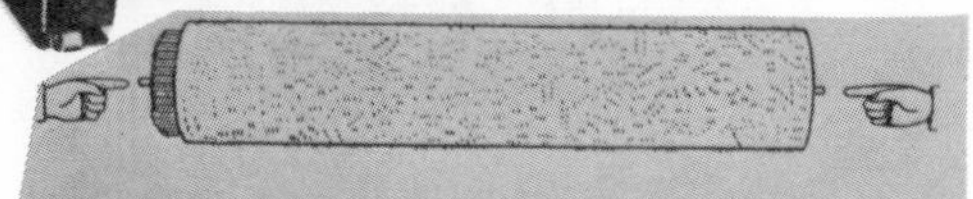

The "Tonophone" is the only Automatic Piano which has an almost indestructible cylinder with 10 tunes.

Style 1 and 2 (right):

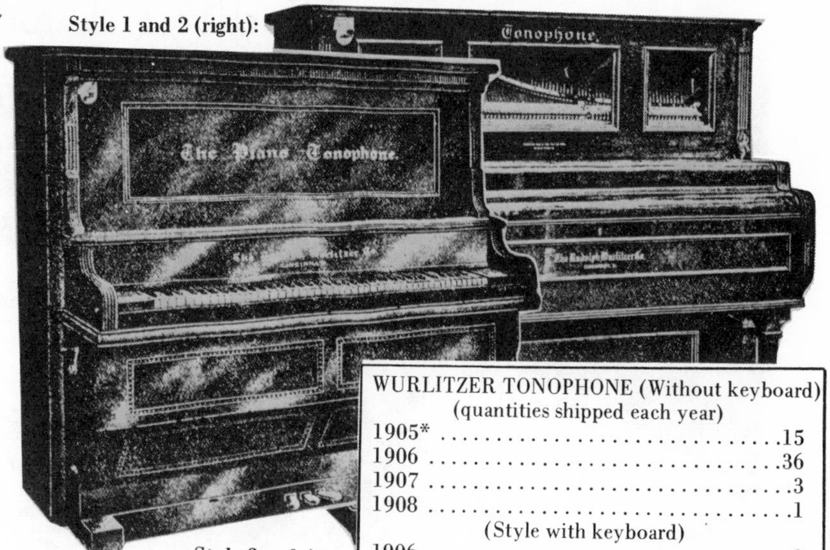

Style 3 and 4.

| WURLITZER TONOPHONE (Without keyboard) (quantities shipped each year) | |
|---|---|
| 1905* | 15 |
| 1906 | 36 |
| 1907 | 3 |
| 1908 | 1 |
| (Style with keyboard) | |
| 1906 | 3 |
| 1908 | 2 |

Notes: *Our figures show the tail-end of the Tonophone production only. An estimated 1000 to 2000 of these were made from 1899 to 1905. These were all made by DeKleist and sold by Wurlitzer. The first production run was 200 instruments.

**Tonophone: the first Wurlitzer coin piano. Used a 10-tune wooden cylinder. Three case styles are shown, including one with keyboard. Many Tonophones were later converted to 65-Note Automatic Player Piano rolls.**

## MANDOLIN QUARTETTE and MANDOLIN SEXTETTE

| MANDOLIN QUARTETTE (quantities shipped each year) | |
|---|---|
| 1906 | 52 |
| 1907 | 331 |
| 1908 | 101 |
| 1909 | 42 |
| 1910 | 38 |
| 1911 | 23 |
| 1912 | 1 |
| Total= | 588 |

Notes: First instrument shipped was No.10210 which left the factory on 2/4/1906. Some listings have the notation "with German mandolin attachment" indicating that the mechanisms may have been imported.

| MANDOLIN SEXTETTE (quantities shipped each year) | |
|---|---|
| 1908 | 4 |
| 1909 | 54 |
| 1910 | 64 |
| 1911 | 15 |
| Total= | 137 |

Notes: First instrument shipped was No.12291 which left the factory on 4/20/1908. First called "Mandolin Orchestrion" and then changed to "Mandolin Sextette."

Mandolin Quartette (later case design)

Mandolin Quartette (early case design)

Mandolin Sextette

**Mandolin Quartette (above and above right) and Mandolin Sextette (right). Introduced in 1906 the first Mandolin Quartette (above right — the type with oval windows) was billed as: "one of the most desirable musical instruments ever produced. It is a combination of mandolin effects accompanied by a piano. The music is much louder than that of any piano. . . and the trilling of the mandolin, together with the piano accompaniment, produces a charming musical effect that cannot fail to delight the most fastidious music lover." The mandolin section contains a ratchet-operated repeating mechanism identical to the "harp effect" found in certain Hupfeld and other German orchestrions. In fact, Wurlitzer imported many of the mandolin actions for this instrument from Germany. The musical sound is quite pleasing, and the Mandolin Quartette is a favorite with collectors today. Directly above is the later case style with rectangular windows. Instrumentation consists of a 34 note piano accompaniment section and a separately scaled 27-note mandolin section. The Mandolin Sextette uses the same roll as the Mandolin Quartette and has a rank of violin pipes in addition to the piano and mandolin. Measurements of the Mandolin Quartette are: 4'9" high by 4' wide by 1'11" deep.**

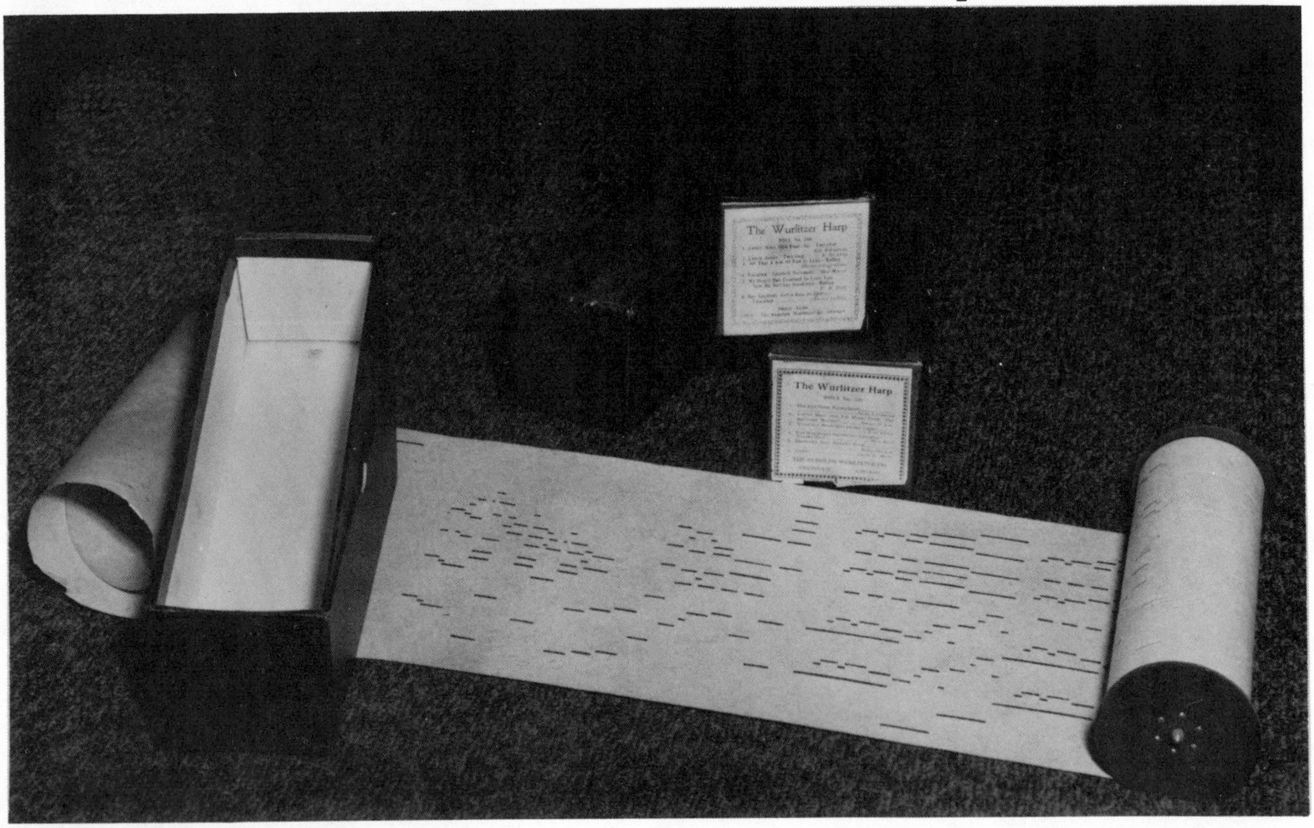

Wurlitzer Automatic Harp: After a year or so of experimentation J.W. Whitlock of Rising Sun, Indiana, patented the Automatic Harp in 1899. In 1905 an agreement was made whereby Wurlitzer bought 1000 instruments and distributed them on an exclusive basis. After the original order for 1000 harps was filled Wurlitzer ordered an additional thousand. Demand for the Harps waned and the total number produced of the second order was only about 500 machines. (This figure was provided to the author by the late Stewart Whitlock – who also made available the Whitlock archives and factory records).

Following the success of the Harp J.W. Whitlock experimented with a violin playing machine. A prototype which used fifteen rotating celluloid discs (a concept similar to that used on the Mills Violano Virtuoso) was partially completed. The project was dropped when the second Wurlitzer order for 1000 Harps was cancelled midway through its completion and both parties engaged in a lawsuit.

In later years the J.W. Whitlock Co. engaged in the manufacture of radios, race horse amusement machines, electric phonographs, and other items. Below is reproduced the Whitlock letterhead showing a Style B Automatic Harp.

J.W. Whitlock & Co.
Manufacturers & Inventors of
THE AUTOMATIC HARP
Rising Sun, Ind., U.S.A.

# THE WURLITZER HARP

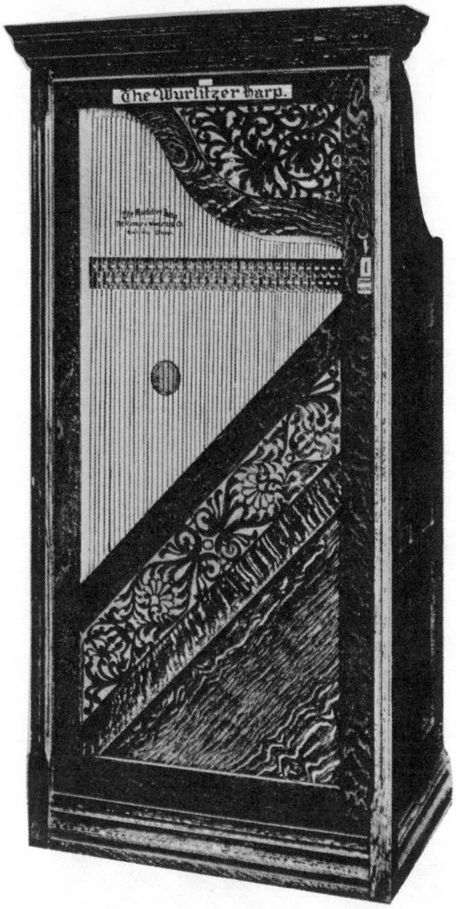

Above: Interior view of the Style B Automatic Harp. The inside chassis slips out of the case for ease in servicing.

Below: Style B Automatic Harp. The Style B was made in two subvarieties: with one circular hole in the top frame (as illustrated) and with five holes in the top frame. The Style B Harp is one of the most attractive automatic musical instruments ever made in America.

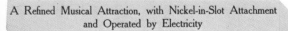

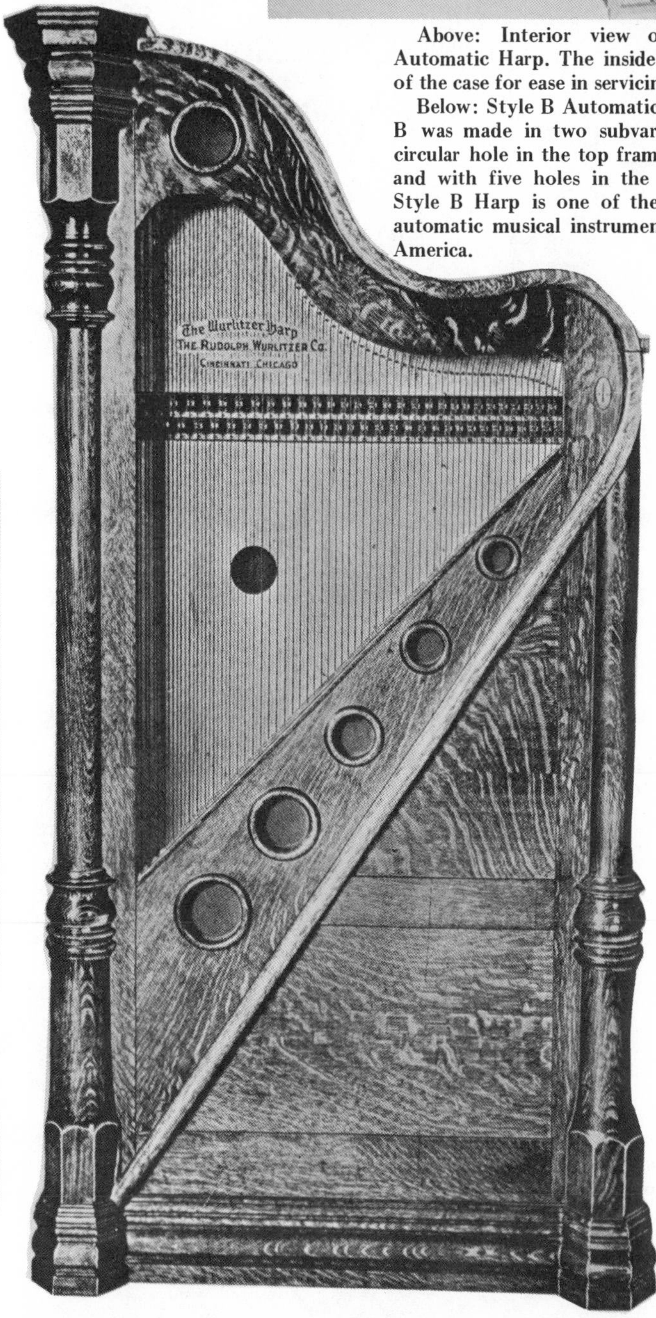


## A Refined Musical Attraction, with Nickel-in-Slot Attachment and Operated by Electricity

AFTER eight years constant labor and one year thorough test, the Wurlitzer Automatic Harp is now ready for the general market. This beautiful instrument is conceded by all to be the most wonderful as well as sweetest musical instrument ever produced. It is one of the latest additions to our automatic line, and as a refined musical attraction has no rival. The harp contains 60 strings in full view, being covered with plate glass, showing the operation of the almost human fingers as they pick them. It is operated by perforated paper rolls containing six tunes each.

The soft sweet music of the harp makes it especially desirable where a piano cannot be used, on account of its being too loud.

As a money maker, the "Wurlitzer Harp" has proven itself the king of them all.

### DESCRIPTION.

CASE: Handsome quarter-sawed oak with carved panels. HEIGHT: 6 feet 6 inches. WIDTH: 3 feet. DEPTH: 2 feet.

The perforated music rolls are only 8½ inches wide, contain six tunes each, and are automatically rewound in 30 seconds when the end of the roll is reached. A dial, with numbers from 1 to 6, always indicates the number of the tune that is being played. An electric light on the inside just above the strings, proves an attractive feature. A most important feature is the new coin detecting slot by which every coin dropped in the instrument can be seen; thus preventing the use of spurious coins and slugs to operate it.

**Price** . . . . . . . . . . . . . . . . **$750.00**
INCLUDING ONE ROLL OF MUSIC.

**Extra Rolls** . . . . . . . . . . . . **$7.50 each.**
LIST OF MUSIC ON REQUEST.

THE HARP IS FURNISHED WITH EITHER DIRECT OR ALTERNATING CURRENT MOTORS.

**When introduced the Style A Harp sold for $750. In later years the price was steadily lowered until it reached about half that figure.**

**Above: This view of the front of a Style B Automatic Harp shows the double row of tiny mechanical "fingers" which actually pluck the individual strings. At the time the Style B was introduced it sold for $600.00 (at the same time the Style A was listed for $100 less, or $500). When first distributed in Cincinnati, Ohio, in 1905 the Style A was an instant success. Within a matter of months nearly 200 stores and taverns in that city had instruments, and the Cincinnati Zoo had two of them! However, the novelty of the Harp waned quickly, and by the time that the Style B was introduced several years later the market had all but disappeared.**

**Right: The roll mechanism of a Style B Harp. On the second floor of the Whitlock factory the rolls for these instruments were made. The rolls were arranged by two women (one of them Mrs. J.W. Whitlock) who marked and edited pieces of sheet music and then played the tunes on a modified electric piano which was connected to a master roll perforator. The production perforator then made copies from the masters. From Stewart Whitlock, son of J.W., the author obtained the original sheet music, the factory records, the sales ledgers. A monograph covering all aspects of Automatic Harps is planned for release at a future date.**

**Wurlitzer Harp tracker bars were laid out in two ways: (1) with the treble notes on the left and the bass notes on the right (as shown above), and (2) with the bass on the left and the treble on the right. Rolls of the latter type sometimes had "New Harp" written in pencil on the roll leader.**

WURLITZER 88-NOTE PLAYER PIANO
(quantities shipped each year)

| | |
|---|---|
| 1906 | 65 |
| 1907 | 186 |
| 1908 | 88 |
| 1909* | 109 |
| 1910* | 90 |
| 1911* | 6 |
| Total= | 544 |

Notes: Beginning part way through 1909 figures are broken down into Style A (electric and with coin mechanism) and Style B (electric; without coin slot – for home use). Figures for 1909 on are: 1909 (unattributed 92; Style A 10; Style B 17 = 109 for year); 1910 (Style A 60; Style B 30); 1911 (Style A 3; Style B 3). Above quantities apply to early electric models only; vast quantities of foot-pumped 88-note players for home use were made by Wurlitzer until well into the late 1920's. Empirical evidence indicates that many of the 88-note Style A instruments were later converted at the factory to Style I or similar 65-note instruments and were given new identities (they were resold as new instruments and were even given new and later serial numbers – the earlier serial numbers were smoothed out and overstamped!).

**88-Note Player Piano: The Style B (upper right corner of page) is operated by a push button rather than a coin slot and is for use in the home. The Style A (other two illustrations) is coin operated for public use. Quite a few of these were originally made. Many of them were sent back to the factory in later years and were changed to use 65-Note Automatic Player Piano rolls. Like most other early Wurlitzer pianos the 88-Note instruments were mostly made in quartered oak wood. The rich grain plus the sculptured appearance make the Style A very attractive.**

# The Pianino *44-Note Electric Piano.*

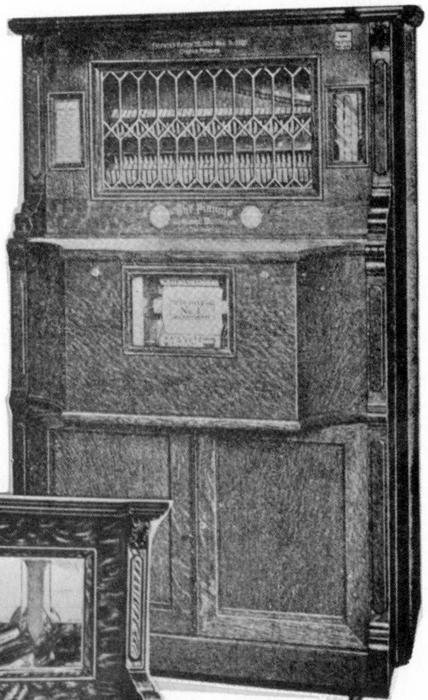

**The Pianino: Introduced shortly after 1900 the Pianino found a ready market in the booming demand for coin operated pianos of all kinds. Containing just 44 notes the Pianino competed with similar instruments made by Peerless, Electrova, Regal, North Tonawanda Musical Instrument Works, and others. Average specifications for Pianinos shown on this page are about: 5' high by 3'4" wide by 1'10" deep. Directly above is the earliest Pianino style; the top right illustration is of the most plentiful (speaking of numbers known today) Pianino style; at the direct right is a similar model but with art glass. These were made in limited numbers only. Produced for over 25 years the production run length of the Pianino is unmatched by any other American coin piano type.**

Wurlitzer Pianino
The standard 44-note Electric Piano with Mandolin attachment apd without keyboard. Equal in tone to that of any full scale Piano. This instrument is equipped with the long-tune roll frame playing a 6 or 12 tune roll; a feature that makes it remarkable.
Height, 4 ft. 5 in. Width, 2 ft. 10⅝ in. Depth, 2 ft. 7¾ in. Shipping weight, 500 lbs.


**The latest Pianino style (of the 1920's) had a flat front and art glass.**

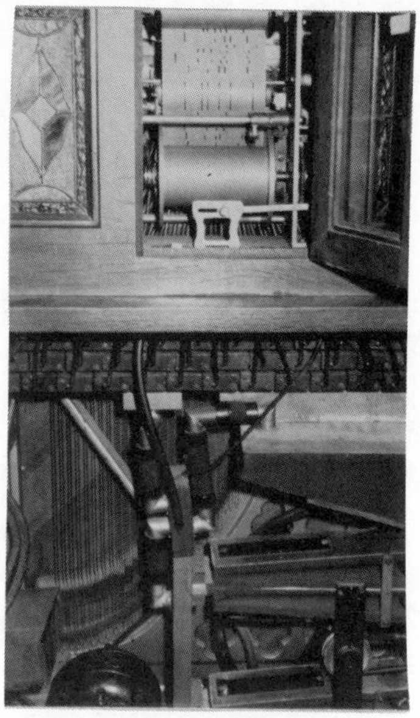

**Interior of flat front Pianino.**

WURLITZER PIANINO
(quantities shipped each year)

| | |
|---|---|
| 1905* | 87 |
| 1906 | 664 |
| 1907 | 686 |
| 1908 | 149 |
| 1909 | 90 |
| 1910 | 112 |
| 1911 | 117 |
| 1912* | 2 |
| 1913* | 6 |
| 1914 | 0 |
| 1915 | 1 |
| 1916 | 6 |
| 1917 | 14 |
| 1918 | 4 |
| 1919 | 2 |
| 1920 | 42 |
| 1921 | 22 |
| 1922 | 4 |
| 1923 | 30 |
| 1924 | 39 |
| 1925 | 34 |
| 1926 | 31 |
| 1927 | 18 |
| 1928 | 15 |
| Total*= | 2173 |

Notes: *Our figures commence with November 16, 1905. As the Pianino was an excellent seller in the several years preceding that date it would be reasonable to add an estimated 1000 to 2000 to the above figures, making the total number originally made about 3000 to 4000. No.10097 "Completes order for 500" according to the factory records. We presume that there were earlier orders also. No.10177 shipped 2/27/1908 was first of "New style" (possibly that without legs and with "bay window" front [earlier styles resembled miniature Tonophones in appearance]). No.10276 shipped 3/30/1906 was first with "New style action, new arrangement on rewind spool." No.12932 was first with "New style case" shipped 6/12/1909. Figures for 1912 and 1913 are incomplete and probably omit 100 to 200 instruments made those years. None was made at all in 1914. No.42020 shipped 6/7/21 noted as "New style Pianino" – probably first with straight front profile.

WURLITZER BIJOU ORCHESTRA
(quantities shipped each year)

| | |
|---|---|
| 1911 | 126 |
| 1912 | * |
| 1913 | 10 |
| 1914 | 14 |
| 1915 | 6 |
| Total= | 156 |

Notes: *Data incomplete; examples were probably produced in 1912. If we estimate 50 to 100 for that year we would have a total original population of 200 to 250 specimens. First Bijou Orchestra was No.15150 shipped on 2/17/1911. Most Bijou Orchestras were shipped to just two locations: Oklahoma City, Oklahoma, and Shreveport, Louisiana. In a 1965 conversation with the author, Mr. Farny Wurlitzer, then chairman of the board of the Wurlitzer Company, said "The Bijou Orchestra was one of our most popular instruments in the old days. We sold a lot of them to motion picture theatres." The Bijou Orchestra is a rare instrument today. In 1970 the author purchased three sets of Bijou Orchestra art glass from a seller who said that "the instruments were broken up for parts a few years ago." How sad!

VIOLIN AND VIOLIN-FLUTE PIANINOS
(quantities shipped each year)

| | |
|---|---|
| 1909* Violin | 1 |
| 1911 Violin | 11 |
| 1913 Violin | 117 |
| 1914 Violin | 9 |
| 1915 Violin | 16 |
| 1915 Violin-Flute | 1 |
| 1916 Violin | 32 |
| 1916 Violin-Flute | 32 |
| 1917 Violin | 19 |
| 1917 Violin-Flute | 6 |
| 1918 Violin | 4 |
| 1918 Violin-Flute | 12 |
| 1919 Violin | 63 |
| 1919 Violin-Flute | 3 |
| 1920 Violin | 101 |
| 1920 Violin-Flute | 10 |
| 1921 Violin | 39 |
| 1922 Violin | 17 |
| 1922 Violin-Flute | 1 |
| 1923 Violin | 30 |
| 1923 Violin-Flute | 10 |
| 1924 Violin | 5 |
| 1924 Violin-Flute | 28 |
| 1924 Flute* | 1 |
| 1925 Violin | 6 |
| 1925 Violin-Flute | 19 |
| 1926 Violin | 4 |
| 1926 Violin-Flute | 24 |
| 1927 Violin | 8 |
| 1927 Violin-Flute | 14 |
| 1928 Violin-Flute | 14 |
| Total*= | 677 |

Notes: No Pianinos with pipes are noted as such in the factory records from 1905 until 6/3/1909 when No.12755, the first with pipes, was shipped. However, extant early photographs suggest that some of the earlier Pianinos may have been equipped with violin pipes. If so, production figures would be included among the regular Pianino totals. We do not have the figures for 1912 and presume that an estimated several dozen instruments were made then – raising our total from a verified 677 to an approximate 700 or so. No.59666 shipped on 4/24/1924 was described as a "Violin Pianino (Flute)" – whatever that means! We presume that it was equipped with just one rank of pipes – those being flutes. In the late 1920's Violin-Flute Pianinos (and perhaps Violin Pianinos as well) were equipped with a xylophone as standard equipment.

Wurlitzer Violin Pianino
The regular Pianino (44 note Electric Piano with Mandolin attachment and without keyboard) combined with 21 Violin Pipes and 21 Flute Pipes.
The different case finishes are illustrated in natural colors on page 5.
Height, 4 ft. 8 in. Width, 3 ft. Depth, 1 ft. 9 in.

**Violin Pianino or Violin-Flute Pianino. Standard model (above) and two early styles (above right). About 700 of these were made over the years.**

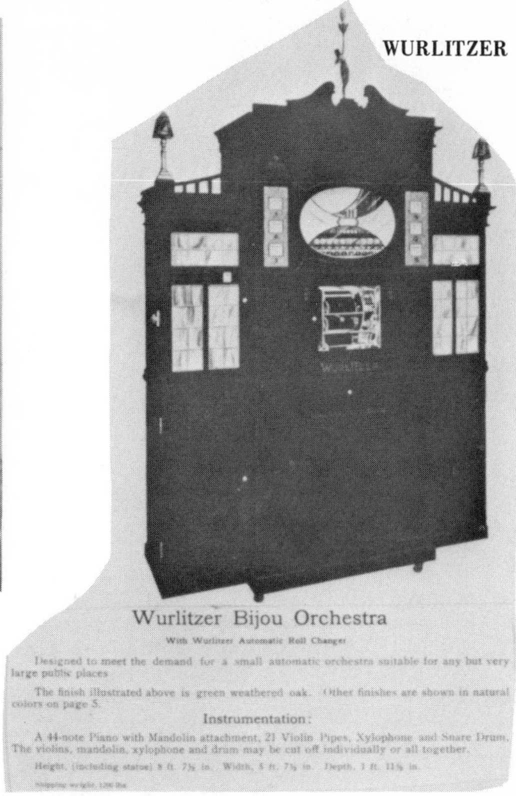

WURLITZER
Wurlitzer Bijou Orchestra
With Wurlitzer Automatic Roll Changer
Designed to meet the demand for a small automatic orchestra suitable for any but very large public places
The finish illustrated above is green weathered oak. Other finishes are shown in natural colors on page 5.
Instrumentation:
A 44-note Piano with Mandolin attachment, 21 Violin Pipes, Xylophone and Snare Drum. The violins, mandolin, xylophone and drum may be cut off individually or all together.


**Bijou Orchestra: Standing 8'7½" tall the Bijou Orchestra is an impressive orchestrion, especially in view of the fact that it uses the small Pianino roll! These were made in two main styles as shown above. The above left model has a "wonder light" and has two ranks of pipes: violin and flute. The model directly above (inside view) and above right has one rank of violin pipes. Bijou Orchestras are equipped with the Wurlitzer Automatic Roll Changer — a shortened version of the same device used in the 65-Note instruments.**

---

# WURLITZER
REG. U. S. PAT. OFF.
## AUTOMATIC PLAYER PIANO

WURLITZER STYLE I PIANO
—65-Note Automatic Player Piano—
(quantities shipped each year)

| | |
|---|---|
| 1907 | 2 |
| 1908 | 143 |
| 1909 | 217 |
| 1910 | 384 |
| 1911 | 288 |
| 1912* | 5 |
| 1913 | 407 |
| 1914 | 367 |
| 1915 | 292 |
| 1916 | 350 |
| 1917 | 463 |
| 1918 | 164 |
| 1919 | 194 |
| 1920 | 235 |
| 1921 | 41 |
| 1922 | 51 |
| 1923 | 51 |
| 1924 | 19 |
| 1925 | 11 |
| 1926 | 23 |
| 1927 | 7 |
| 1928 | 5 |
| 1930 | 1 |
| 1934 | 1 |
| Total*= | 3721 |

Notes: Figures for 1912 incomplete. If we add an estimated 300 more to this year we increase the overall total Style I's made to about 4000. First Wurlitzer 65-Note Automatic Player Piano was serial No. 10549 made in 1906 and shipped from the factory on April 19, 1907. Serial Nos. 26273, 30321, 33139, 40646, 42293, 80999, and 90310 were listed as "Style I Duplex" and had a double roll mechanism similar to that used in photoplayers. Such instruments were probably intended for theatre or cabaret use.

Interior of Wurlitzer 65-Note Player Piano

The mechanisms of the 88-Note Player Piano, Pianino, Mandolin Quartette and Mandolin Sextette, are practically the same.

*A—Slot approach.* *B—Magazine for coins.* *C—Action case.* *D—Music roll.* *E—Tracker bar.* *F—Take-up roll.* *G—Tempo Regulator.* *H—Music roll friction disc.* *J—Music roll friction pulley.* *L—Take-up roll friction disc.* *M—Take-up roll friction pulley.* *N—Mandolin attachment.* *O—Rewind device.* *P—Suction tube to action case.* *Q—Regulating valve.* *R—Feeder bellows.* *S—Pump sticks.* *T—Standard for shaft gear.* *U—Flexible shaft.* *W—Motor.* *X—Money drawer.*

**65-Note Pianos: On this page are just a few of the dozens of different case design variations made of 65-Note Automatic Player Pianos. Most were sold as "Style I". The "I-B" models were equipped with a 14-note set of orchestra bells. The piano shown at the top right of this section is the earliest case design as first shipped in 1907.**

WURLITZER STYLE I-B PIANO
(quantities shipped each year)

| | |
|---|---|
| 1922 | 4 |
| 1923 | 30 |
| 1924 | 5 |
| 1925 | 1 |
| 1926 | 1 |
| 1927 | 1 |
| Total= | 42 |

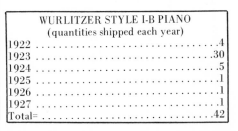

An interesting Egyptian case design (known as "Design No. 5") of the Style I piano. For years one of these was a prominent attraction in San Francisco's Cliff House collection until it burned with part of the instrument collection there in the early 1960's.

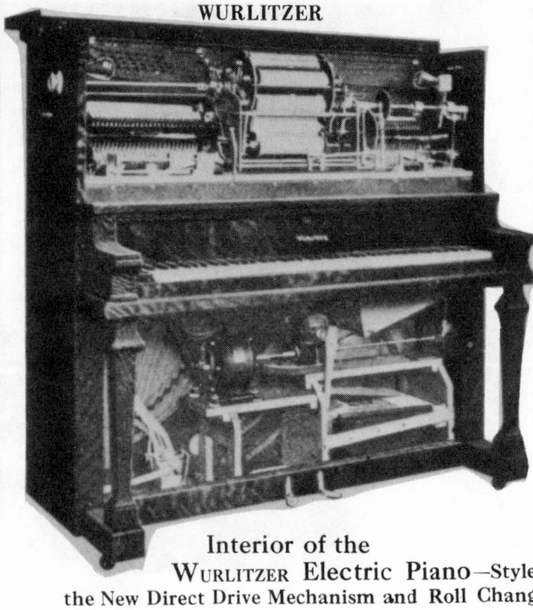

WURLITZER
Interior of the
WURLITZER Electric Piano—Style IX.
the New Direct Drive Mechanism and Roll Changer


Interior of the Style IX – showing the pumps below the keyboard and the Automatic Roll Changer above.

Style IX

Style IX – the most popular case design produced.

WURLITZER STYLE IX PIANO
(quantities shipped each year)

| | |
|---|---|
| 1910 | 2 |
| 1911 | 42 |
| 1912* | 2 |
| 1914 | 1 |
| 1915 | 20 |
| 1916 | 203 |
| 1917 | 411 |
| 1918 | 267 |
| 1919 | 178 |
| 1920 | 189 |
| 1921 | 108 |
| 1922 | 56 |
| 1923 | 88 |
| 1924 | 35 |
| 1925 | 25 |
| 1926 | 14 |
| 1927 | 17 |
| 1928 | 3 |
| 1930 | 1 |
| 1932 | 1 |
| Total*= | 1663 |

Notes: Figures for 1912 and 1913 incomplete. If we estimate another 50 or so Style IX instruments for those years we raise the total production to about 1725. It is quite possible that the figures for the Style I piano also include some of the Style IX due to forgetfulness in noting the "X" (meaning with automatic changer) part in the description. The first Wurlitzer automatic to be equipped with the automatic roll changer was IX piano serial No. 14373 shipped on September 24, 1910.

WURLITZER STYLE IX-B PIANO
(quantities shipped each year)

| | |
|---|---|
| 1922 | 30 |
| 1923 | 77 |
| 1924 | 26 |
| 1925 | 19 |
| 1926 | 9 |
| 1927 | 7 |
| 1928 | 2 |
| Total= | 170 |

Notes: Instrument also called "IBX" in factory records (probably a transpositional error by the record keeper). At least one was equipped with a snare drum and at least one other was equipped with a 30-note xylophone (same as used in the large Wurlitzer photoplayers).

Style I – "No.4, Special Design." Has three "wonder lights."

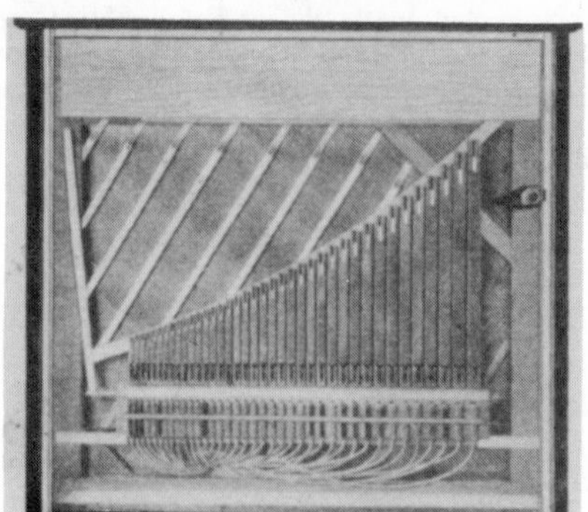

Rear view of Style A piano showing rank of violin pipes.

WURLITZER STYLE AX PIANO
—1 rank of pipes; roll changer—
(quantities shipped each year)

| | |
|---|---|
| 1911* | 64 |
| 1913 Style AX Flute | 1 |
| 1914 Style AX Flute | 14 |
| 1914 Style AX Violin | 6 |
| 1915 Style AX Flute | 3 |
| 1915 Style AX Violin | 4 |
| 1916 Style AX Flute | 19 |
| 1916 Style AX Violin | 6 |
| 1917 Style AX* | 2 |
| 1917 Style AX Flute | 17 |
| 1917 Style AX Violin | 15 |
| 1918 Style AX | 2 |
| 1918 Style AX Flute | 12 |
| 1918 Style AX Violin | 6 |
| 1919 Style AX | 3 |
| 1919 Style AX Flute | 20 |
| 1919 Style AX Violin | 11 |
| 1920 Style AX | 3 |
| 1920 Style AX Flute | 31 |
| 1920 Style AX Violin | 8 |
| 1921 Style AX Flute | 24 |
| 1921 Style AX Violin | 8 |
| 1922 Style AX Flute | 11 |
| 1922 Style AX Violin | 4 |
| 1923 Style AX | 1 |
| 1923 Style AX Flute | 9 |
| 1923 Style AX Violin | 1 |
| 1924 Style AX | 1 |
| 1924 Style AX Flute | 3 |
| 1925 Style AX | 2 |
| 1925 Style AX Flute | 1 |
| 1928 Style AX | 1 |
| Total*= | 314 |

Notes: Figures for 1912 not available. If we estimate that 50 were made, total increases to an estimated 365 or so. Some entries in later years were listed just as "AX" without mentioning style of pipes used. Most 1911 instruments were probably equipped with violin pipes.

WURLITZER AX-B PIANOS
(quantities shipped each year)

| | |
|---|---|
| 1923 (pipe style unknown) | 1 |
| 1923 AX-B Flute | 1 |
| 1925 (pipe style unknown) | 1 |
| Total= | 3 |

On the balcony above the main floor of this California restaurant is a Wurlitzer Style I piano. Eight boxes of rolls are on top of the piano. At each table along the wall is a coin slot wall box for playing the instrument. This photograph was one of several obtained from the files of the Leathurby Co. of San Francisco, a distributor for Wurlitzer instruments during the 'teens and for Seeburg pianos and orchestrions during the 'twenties. "On location" pictures of instruments are particularly interesting; and the author would welcome hearing from any readers having such photographs to share.

WURLITZER STYLE A PIANO
—65-Note w/1 rank of pipes—
(quantities shipped each year)

| | |
|---|---|
| 1908 | 4 |
| 1909 | 169 |
| 1910 | 380 |
| 1911 | 224 |
| 1912* | 2 |
| 1913 Style A Flute | 31 |
| 1913 Style A Violin | 7 |
| 1914 Style A Flute | 31 |
| 1914 Style A Violin | 9 |
| 1915 Style A Flute | 8 |
| 1915 Style A Violin | 3 |
| 1916 Style A Flute | 27 |
| 1916 Style A Violin | 6 |
| 1917 Style A Flute | 9 |
| 1917 Style A Violin | 2 |
| 1918 Style A Flute | 3 |
| 1918 Style A Violin | 1 |
| 1919 Style A Flute | 4 |
| 1920 Style A Flute | 14 |
| 1921 Style A Flute | 1 |
| 1922 Style A Violin | 2 |
| 1924 Style A Flute | 1 |
| 1925 Style A Flute | 3 |
| Total*= | 943 |

Notes: Figures for 1912 incomplete. If we estimate that 100 were made, figure for total is increased to about 1050. 1908 to 1912 instruments are not listed with the type of pipes contained; but most were probably with violin pipes. Serial No. 13679 was the first with "new style case."

Style A and AX: 65-Note Automatic Player Piano with one rank of pipes, violin or flute. At the above left is a late style of the AX as sold during the 1920's. Above right is an earlier model with lamps on the front corner posts. Most of the production of the Style A was of early instruments without art glass. As the accompanying chart shows, few were produced after 1912. Specifications (average): 4'10" high; 5'2" wide; 2'8" deep. Weight: 1200 pounds.

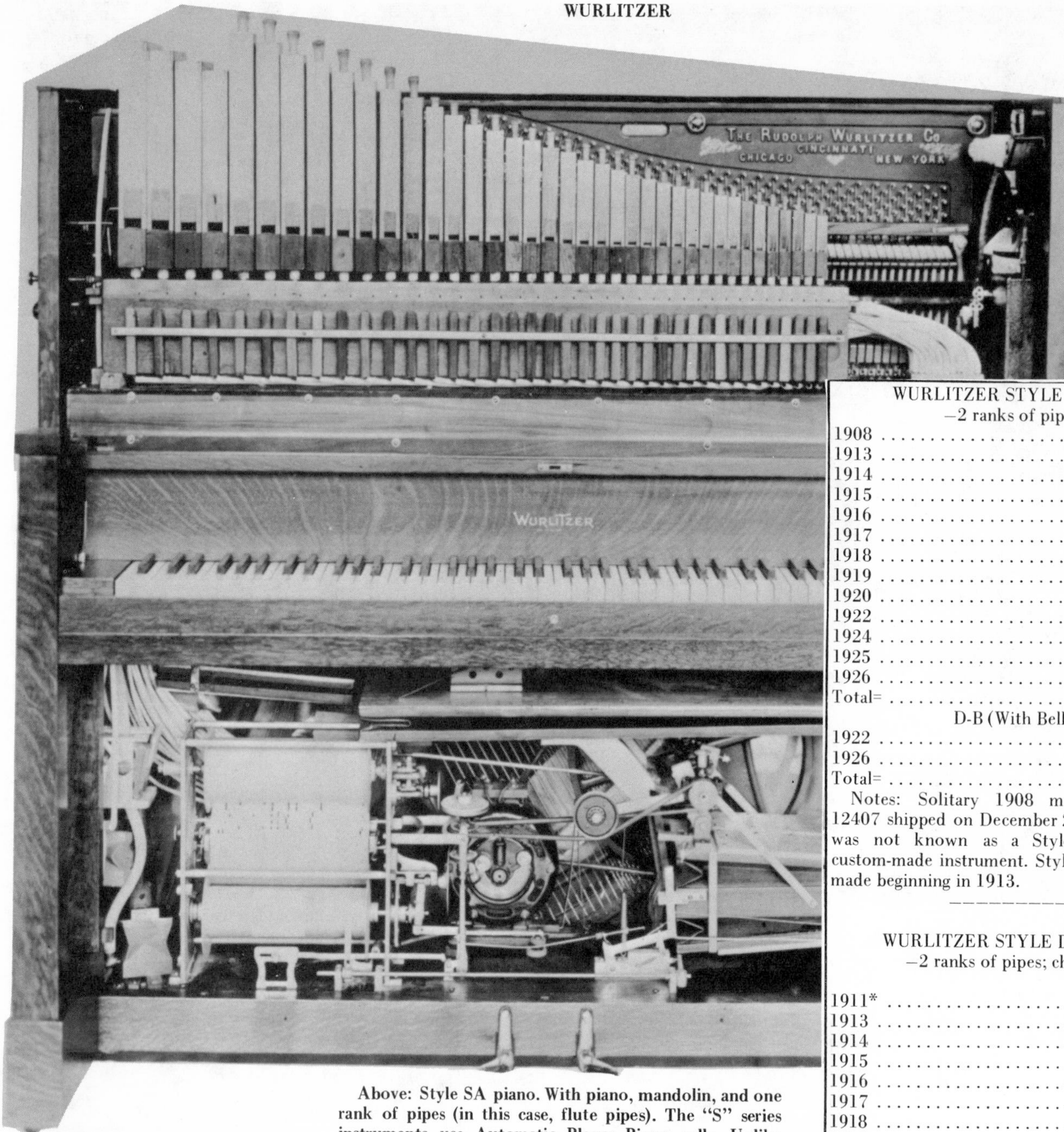

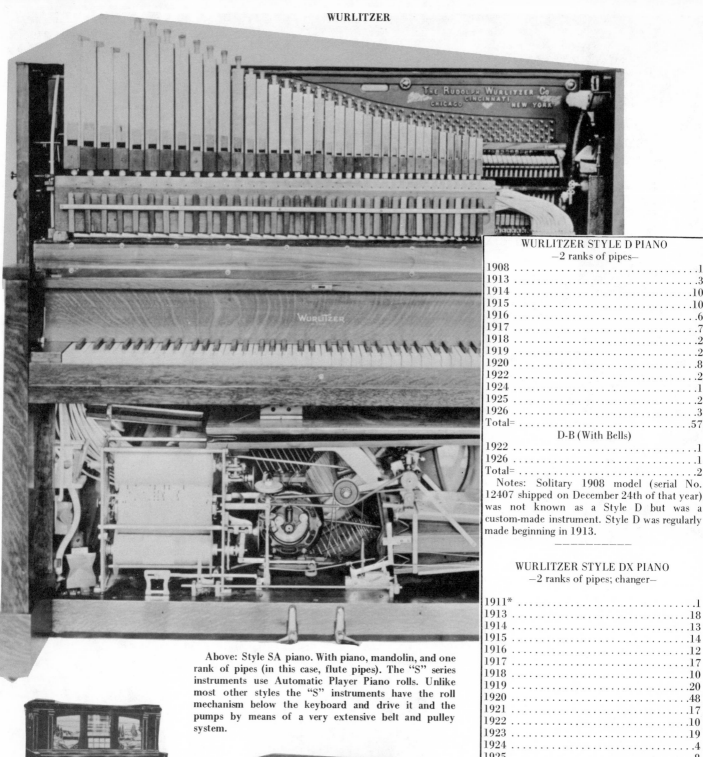

**Above: Style SA piano. With piano, mandolin, and one rank of pipes (in this case, flute pipes). The "S" series instruments use Automatic Player Piano rolls. Unlike most other styles the "S" instruments have the roll mechanism below the keyboard and drive it and the pumps by means of a very extensive belt and pulley system.**

Wurlitzer Violin-Flute Piano—Style DX

With Wurlitzer Automatic Roll Changer

A new style instrument that is far ahead of any now on the market.

It has all the exclusive Wurlitzer mechanical improvements, which make it practically trouble-proof, and for beauty of design and tonal quality it is unexcelled. The art glass designs vary somewhat.

The different musical sections can be cut off at will.

Instrumentation:

Piano with Mandolin attachment, 38 Violin Pipes (21 First Violin and 17 Viola), 38 Flute Pipes.

Height, 4 ft. 11 in. Width, 5 ft. 3 in. Depth, 3 ft. Shipping weight, 1250 lbs.

Wurlitzer Violin-Flute Piano—Style D

Same as above, except equipped with long tune frame instead of roll changer—playing 1, 5, 10, 15 and 20-tune roll.

**Style DX: Piano with mandolin and two ranks of pipes: violin and flute. Pipes are mounted behind the piano sounding board. At the left is an early model; above, one from the 1920's.**

WURLITZER STYLE D PIANO

—2 ranks of pipes—

| | |
|---|---|
| 1908 | 1 |
| 1913 | 3 |
| 1914 | 10 |
| 1915 | 10 |
| 1916 | 6 |
| 1917 | 7 |
| 1918 | 2 |
| 1919 | 2 |
| 1920 | 8 |
| 1922 | 2 |
| 1924 | 1 |
| 1925 | 2 |
| 1926 | 3 |
| Total= | 57 |

D-B (With Bells)

| | |
|---|---|
| 1922 | 1 |
| 1926 | 1 |
| Total= | 2 |

Notes: Solitary 1908 model (serial No. 12407 shipped on December 24th of that year) was not known as a Style D but was a custom-made instrument. Style D was regularly made beginning in 1913.

WURLITZER STYLE DX PIANO

—2 ranks of pipes; changer—

| | |
|---|---|
| 1911* | 1 |
| 1913 | 18 |
| 1914 | 13 |
| 1915 | 14 |
| 1916 | 12 |
| 1917 | 17 |
| 1918 | 10 |
| 1919 | 20 |
| 1920 | 48 |
| 1921 | 17 |
| 1922 | 10 |
| 1923 | 19 |
| 1924 | 4 |
| 1925 | 8 |
| 1926 | 6 |
| 1927 | 4 |
| 1928 | 2 |
| 1929 | 1 |
| 1930 | 1 |
| Total*= | 225 |

DX-B (With Bells)

| | |
|---|---|
| 1923 | 5 |
| 1924 | 3 |
| 1925 | 4 |
| 1927 | 4 |
| 1928 | 1 |
| Total= | 17 |

Notes: First Style DX was serial No. 16328 shipped on October 24, 1911. Total for 1912 not available. If we estimate 10 instruments, overall total for Style DX increases from 225 to 235.

## WURLITZER "S" SERIES PIANOS AND ORCHESTRIONS
(quantities shipped each year)

### STYLE S PIANO

| | |
|---|---|
| 1913 | 75 |
| 1914 | 78 |
| 1915 | 52 |
| 1916 | 203 |
| 1917 | 193 |
| 1918 | 68 |
| 1919 | 50 |
| 1920 | 98 |
| 1921 | 50 |
| 1922 | 36 |
| 1923 | 34 |
| 1924 | 26 |
| 1925 | 16 |
| 1926 | 18 |
| 1927 | 5 |
| 1928 | 4 |
| 1929 | 1 |
| Total= | 1007 |

### STYLE S-B PIANO (With Bells)

| | |
|---|---|
| 1922 | 11 |
| 1923 | 42 |
| 1924 | 9 |
| 1925 | 3 |
| 1926 | 2 |
| 1927 | 1 |
| Total= | 68 |

### STYLE SA PIANO
(one rank of pipes)

| | |
|---|---|
| 1913 Style SA Flute | 3 |
| 1914 Style SA Flute | 7 |
| 1914 Style SA Violin | 3 |
| 1915 Style SA Flute | 24 |
| 1915 Style SA Violin | 6 |
| 1916 Style SA* | 1 |
| 1916 Style SA Flute | 5 |
| 1916 Style SA Violin | 16 |
| 1917 Style SA | 1 |
| 1917 Style SA Flute | 5 |
| 1917 Style SA Violin | 18 |
| 1918 Style SA Flute | 6 |
| 1918 Style SA Violin | 5 |
| Total= | 100 |

Note: 1916 and 1917 instruments marked just "SA" did not have pipe style noted in the official records.

### STYLE SS ORCHESTRION

| | |
|---|---|
| 1914* | 5 |
| 1914 with violin pipes | 1 |
| 1915 | 1 |
| 1915 with flute pipes | 8 |
| 1915 with violin pipes | 4 |
| 1916 with flute pipes | 1 |
| 1916 with violin pipes | 1 |
| Total (*1914 incomplete)= | 21 |

### STYLE SF

| | |
|---|---|
| 1914 | 1 |
| 1915 | 3 |
| 1916 | 2 |
| 1917 | 4 |
| Total= | 10 |

### STYLE SC

| | |
|---|---|
| 1914 | 1 |
| 1915 | 12 |
| 1916 | 4 |
| 1917 | 3 |
| 1920 | 2 |
| Total= | 22 |

**Style S: With roll mechanism below keyboard. Above left is the first Style S as introduced in September, 1913. Above right is a late Style S from a 1925 catalogue.**

**Style SS — Wurlitzer Symphony Piano: Illustrated directly above and above right (interior view). Contains one rank of pipes, snare drum, bass drum, and triangle. A compact keyboard orchestrion which measures just 6'4½" high by 5'2" wide by 2'5" deep. Weight: 1350 pounds.**

**Style S Pianos in General: The "S" series of instruments made its debut in 1913. The chief distinction is that the "S" instruments have the 65-Note Automatic Player Piano roll mechanism below the keyboard. These instruments were made as "economy models" to compete with the lower priced instruments of others (in general Wurlitzer charged more for all of its instruments on a comparative basis than did Seeburg, Coinola, or others). They were not aggressively "pushed" but were kept on hand for competitive purposes. Very few "S" instruments are known today as they evidently had a shorter useful life than did the regular styles of Wurlitzer pianos and orchestrions.**

**Some of the "S" pianos of the 1920's had the same vacuum pump as did the tiny Wurlitzer Pianino, necessitating operating it at very high speed in order to obtain a sufficient vacuum.**

### DATING WURLITZER PIANOS

As our listing of Mandolin PianOrchestras by shipping dates indicates, the serial numbers don't have close relationship to the year the instrument left the factory. However, the following serial numbers give a general guide that may be useful.

| | |
|---|---|
| Serial 10,000 | Shipped 11/16/1905 |
| Serial 10,099 | Shipped 1/3/1906 |
| Serial 10,938 | Shipped 1/8/1907 |
| Serial 12,144 | Shipped 1/23/1908 |
| Serial 12,658 | Shipped 1/8/1909 |
| Serial 15,094 | Shipped 1/20/1911 |
| Serial 16,466 | Shipped 1/25/1912 |
| Serial 20,012 | Shipped 4/20/1913 |
| Serial 21,024 | Shipped 1/23/1914 |
| Serial 23,192 | Shipped 8/9/1915 |
| Serial 57,052 | Shipped 1/4/1924 |
| Serial 70,986 | Shipped 1/3/1925 |
| Serial 105,000 | Shipped Nov., 1927 |
| Serial 105,681 | Shipped 1/9/1928 |
| Serial 108,968 | Shipped 1/8/1929 |
| Serial 112,537 | Shipped 1/6/1930 |
| Serial 115,575 | Shipped 1/1/1931 |
| Serial 118,456 | Shipped 1/3/1932 |

Note: Numbers were often skipped and not used. The total numbers listed include mostly upright and grand pianos for home use — only a fraction are automatic musical instruments.

A.B. Peterson, proprietor of the Canyon Inn near Hayward, California, entertained his guests with this handsome Style CX orchestrion located in the dining room. This particular CX case design was the most popular of several CX styles made, judging from specimens surviving today.

This photograph is from the files of the Leathurby Co., distributors of Wurlitzer products in the San Francisco area years ago. Leathurby maintained a showroom of instruments and a special Roll Department with shelves full of Wurlitzer music. The San Francisco area was once very well populated with Wurlitzer coin pianos and orchestrions of all kinds from Pianinos to PianOrchestras.

Style C Orchestrion: Above are the two earliest styles of the Style C orchestrion or "Violin - Flute Piano" as it was initially designated. It was described thusly in the 1912 Wurlitzer catalogue: "We had long worked on the problem of an automatic musical instrument that would satisfactorily feature the delightful combination of piano, violin, and flute, and the success of the new Violin - Flute Piano is, therefore, doubly gratifying to us. This instrument combines a high-grade piano with special violin attachment and an up-to-date orchestrion. The instrumentation of the orchestrion section consists of 38 flute pipes, 21 violins and 17 violas, also a bass drum and orchestra snare drum. It plays from the same inexpensive perforated paper rolls used by the 65-Note Player Piano."

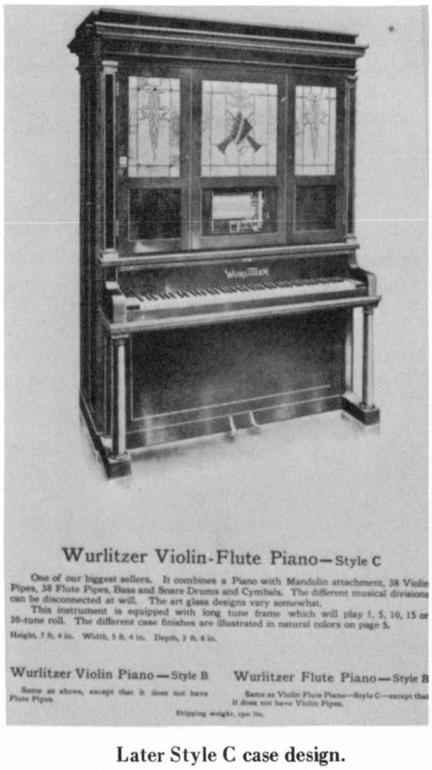

**Wurlitzer Violin-Flute Piano—Style C**

One of our biggest sellers. It combines a Piano with Mandolin attachment, 38 Violin Pipes, 38 Flute Pipes, Bass and Snare Drums and Cymbals. The different musical divisions can be disconnected at will. The art glass designs vary somewhat.

This instrument is equipped with long tune frame which will play 1, 5, 10, 15 or 20-tune roll. The different case finishes are illustrated in natural colors on page 5.

Height, 7 ft. 4 in. Width, 5 ft. 4 in. Depth, 2 ft. 8 in.

**Wurlitzer Violin Piano—Style B**

Same as above, except that it does not have Flute Pipes.

**Wurlitzer Flute Piano—Style B**

Same as Violin Flute Piano—Style C—except that it does not have Violin Pipes.

Shipping weight, [illegible]

Later Style C case design.

Style BX: Case design No. 9. One of many different case styles made. The "wonder light" attachment, popular with many different orchestrion makers in Europe (Philipps, Hupfeld, Imhof, Popper, et al), was a Wurlitzer exclusive in America. The device consists of a rotating jeweled ball with a light bulb in the center. The swirling colors are reflected in mirrored glass petals which surround the center unit. Wurlitzer recommended the wonder light as being "ideal for dancing."

WURLITZER STYLE B ORCHESTRION
With violin OR flute pipes
(quantities shipped each year)

| | |
|---|---|
| 1909* | 29 |
| 1910 | 113 |
| 1911 | 73 |
| 1913 Style B Flute | 45 |
| 1913 Style B Violin | 13 |
| 1914 Style B Flute | 44 |
| 1914 Style B Violin | 11 |
| 1915 Style B Flute | 6 |
| 1915 Style B Violin | 5 |
| 1916 Style B Flute | 6 |
| 1916 Style B Violin | 7 |
| 1917 Style B Flute | 4 |
| 1917 Style B Violin | 2 |
| 1918 Style B Violin | 1 |
| 1919 Style B Flute | 1 |
| 1919 Style B Violin | 1 |
| 1920 Style B Violin | 1 |
| 1920 Style B Violin | 1 |
| 1921 Style B Violin | 1 |
| Total*= | 363 |

Notes: Figures for 1912 not available. Estimated 50 to 75 instruments made in that year – a figure which if correct would raise the overall total to about 425 of this type. 1909 to 1911 years just noted in the records as "Style B" without reference to style of pipes used. From 1913 to 1921 a total of 42 Style B's with violins were made and 106 with flutes, indicating a customer preference for the latter pipe style.

A popular CX case.

A pretty BX orchestrion.

CX, Case Design No. 10

WURLITZER

Most popular CX style.

WURLITZER STYLE BX ORCHESTRION
With violin OR flute pipes
and automatic roll changer
(quantities shipped each year)

| | |
|---|---|
| 1911 | 36 |
| 1913 Style BX Flute | 11 |
| 1913 Style BX Violin | 11 |
| 1914 Style BX Flute | 18 |
| 1914 Style BX Violin | 36 |
| 1915 Style BX Flute | 23 |
| 1915 Style BX Violin | 18 |
| 1916 Style BX Flute | 17 |
| 1916 Style BX Violin | 35 |
| 1917 Style BX* | 3 |
| 1917 Style BX Flute | 46 |
| 1917 Style BX Violin | 45 |
| 1918 Style BX | 2 |
| 1918 Style BX Flute | 17 |
| 1918 Style BX Violin | 28 |
| 1919 Style BX | 3 |
| 1919 Style BX Flute | 39 |
| 1919 Style BX Violin | 28 |
| 1920 Style BX | 7 |
| 1920 Style BX Flute | 26 |
| 1920 Style BX Violin | 19 |
| 1921 Style BX | 1 |
| 1921 Style BX Flute* | 22 |
| 1921 Style BX Violin* | 7 |
| 1922 Style BX | 1 |
| 1922 Style BX Flute | 14 |
| 1922 Style BX-B Flute | 2 |
| 1922 Style BX Violin | 1 |
| 1922 Style BX-B Violin | 1 |
| 1923 Style BX Flute | 8 |
| 1924 Style BX-B* | 1 |
| 1924 Style BX Flute | 7 |
| 1924 Style BX Violin | 2 |
| Total*= | 547 |

Notes: Figures for 1912 not available; estimated 25 instruments which, if about correct, would raise the total number of BX orchestrions to about 575. 1911 just listed as "BX" without mention of the style of pipes employed. The same is true of the occasional later "BX" listings. BX-B refers to an instrument with orchestra bells and designated as BX-B in the records; although it is probably accurate to say that some others simply listed as BX also had bells. Note that the over 2-to-1 ratio of flute instruments to violin instruments of the Style B orchestrions is not true of BX as both types of pipes seem about equally popular. Beginning in late 1921 the BX instruments were built into the Turkish-style LX orchestrion cases. Later years are of this case design. 1921 figures break down as follows: BX Flute (11 early style cases; 11 LX-style cases); BX Violin (6 early style cases; 1 LX-style case).

**The above illustration from a Wurlitzer catalogue of 1916 shows a Style CX orchestrion on location in the dining room of Heingartner's Hotel in Brooklyn, N.Y.**

WURLITZER STYLE C ORCHESTRION
Violin AND flute pipes
(quantities shipped each year)

| | |
|---|---|
| 1909 | 40 |
| 1910 | 135 |
| 1911 | 74 |
| 1912* | 5 |
| 1913 | 34 |
| 1914 | 26 |
| 1915 | 7 |
| 1916 | 5 |
| 1919 | 1 |
| 1920 | 6 |
| 1921 | 1 |
| Total*= | 342 |

Notes: Figures for 1912 not complete. If we assume a total of 50 made, this would make approximate production figures for the Style C be close to 400. The factory records list the following serial Nos.: 12488, 12649, 12650, and 12651 under the term "Piano-Orch." We presume this means "Piano Orchestrion" (rather than the trademarked "PianOrchestra" – which was not being made at this time). If a reader has an instrument with one of the above serial numbers we can identify it correctly as a Style B, Style C, or whatever.

WURLITZER CX AND LX ORCHESTRIONS
With violin AND flute pipes
and automatic roll changer
(quantities shipped each year)

| | |
|---|---|
| 1911 CX | 85 |
| 1912* CX | 2 |
| 1913 CX | 69 |
| 1914 CX | 52 |
| 1915 CX | 33 |
| 1915 CX | 33 |
| 1916 CX | 38 |
| 1917 CX | 65 |
| 1918 CX | 42 |
| 1919 CX | 58 |
| 1920 CX | 75 |
| 1921 CX | 14 |
| 1922 CX | 1 |
| 1921 LX | 24 |
| 1922 LX | 49 |
| 1923 LX | 44 |
| 1924 LX | 32 |
| 1925 LX | 13 |
| 1926 LX | 4 |
| 1927 LX | 6 |
| 1930 LX | 2 |
| Total*CX= | 567 |
| Total LX= | 174 |
| Total* both CX and LX= | 741 |

**Style CX: Case design No. 12. During the 'teens Wurlitzer constantly changed the design of the B, BX, C, and CX cases. However, most shared common features: two upper front doors with long vertical panels of art glass, a rectangular art glass panel in the upper center, and a clear glass (framed with art glass) door in front of the roll mechanism. The particular model above features the roll changer. The knob at the left side of the case permits the patron to select which of the six rolls on the changer he wants to hear. This selection can only be done when the last of the 5 tunes on a roll has finished playing and the instrument has shut off.**

Notes: Figures for 1912 CX are incomplete. If we estimate a total production that year of 75 or so instruments then our CX total changes from 567 to about 650 and our overall total of CX and LX combined changes from 741 to about 825 or so. Some instruments were fitted with xylophones as an optional "extra." We have seen an early CX with a 30-note xylophone (the xylophone part was imported from Philipps of Frankfurt, Germany, and is identical to a PianOrchestra xylophone) and a late one with a Wurlitzer-made shorter-scale xylophone. At least one "LX" was made with the long-roll frame instead of the roll changer and should have been called "Style L" in the records. Some LX instruments surviving today have paper labels (on the left inside wall of the orchestrion) reading "CX" as the inspectors in the factory were used to calling a keyboard orchestrion with two ranks of pipes a "CX" and did not adjust to the "LX" designation quickly! Most CX instruments were in oak. Most LX orchestrions of 1921 to 1925 were oak; a few were mahogany. Most 1926 - 1930 instruments were walnut. The first LX was designated as a "New Style CX" (we list it under LX in our totals) in the catalogue, bore serial No. 42141, and was shipped to the Wurlitzer home office in Cincinnati, Ohio, on May 19, 1921. Among early variants of C and CX Wurlitzer orchestrions were models with a duplex side-by-side roll system (as in a photoplayer! – we don't know what the appearance would have been like as the case would have had to have been modified) and one (serial No. 15349 CX shipped on 2/19/1912) "without keyboard."

**Style LX: Introduced in mid 1921 the LX case design was the last in the Wurlitzer keyboard orchestrion series. The catalogue noted: "This instrument combines a piano with mandolin attachment, 38 violin pipes (21 first violin and 17 viola), 38 flute pipes, set of orchestra bells, bass and snare drums, and triangle. . . Height: 7'9"; width 5'4"; depth 2'5". Weight: 1500 pounds."**

WURLITZER STYLE EX PIANO
(quantities shipped each year)

| | |
|---|---|
| 1914 | 1 |
| 1915 | 7 |
| 1916 | 5 |
| 1917 | 13 |
| Total= | 26 |

**The Style EX featured a colorful peacock "wonder light" at the top. The first models produced were designated as "CX" so the above EX figures may be conservative (other EX's may be part of the CX figures given at the left of this page). Several of these were shipped to Montana and Idaho.**

The LX is surmounted by a brilliant "wonder light" which revolves as the instrument is playing. Sometimes called a "fascinator" by collectors, this electrical gadget is as much fun to watch today as it was years ago.

The extra instruments are in the top part of the case. At the front is the automatic roll changer which stores six 5-tune rolls, permitting a musical repertoire of 30 selections without repetition.

To the left is a portion of the snare drum; to the right, the bass drum. Between is a set of 14 orchestra bells. Above the bells are the bottoms of the xylophone strikers (only a few LX's had this feature).

A large bundle of tubing connects the instruments to the pneumatic stack. Because of all of the tubing, not to mention the roll changer and the interior instruments, tuning the piano in an LX is no easy task!

The pump system has two separate units: one for pressure (upper left) and one for vacuum (lower right). This system is somewhat redundant compared to the combination pumps of most other manufacturers.

The Wurlitzer Automatic Roll Changer was a staple feature of many Wurlitzer instruments. It was made under license from the firm of Verstraelen & Alter of New York City. Usually from $100 to $200 extra was charged for this device.

WURLITZER

**Wurlitzer Solo Violin Piano**

**Coin Operating Attachment**

The Solo Violin Piano combines practically a full eighty-eight-note piano with a scale of Violin Pipes, having a range of fifty-one notes. This combination provides for all the expression and accent necessary to play the best classical music.

This instrument is equipped with the Wurlitzer Patented Automatic Roll-Changer.

The music is arranged to play the Violin as solo, and the Piano as accompaniment.

Write for special catalog.

Height, 4 ft. 10½ in. Width, 5 ft. 1¼ in. Depth, 3¼ ft. Shipping weight, 1250 lbs.

12

WURLITZER

SOLO VIOLIN PIANO
(quantities shipped each year)

| | |
|---|---|
| 1919 | 36 |
| 1920 | 35 |
| 1921 | 39 |
| 1922 | 12 |
| 1923 | 6 |
| 1924 | 7 |
| 1925 | 3 |
| 1926 | 1 |
| 1927 | 1 |
| Total= | 140 |

Notes: Interesting details from the factory records... No.42182, a Solo Violin Piano shipped 5/23/1921 was later returned to the factory and converted to a Style AX coin piano (using another type of roll, the 65-note Automatic Player Piano roll) and then reshipped on 5/6/1927. No.105,162 was shipped on 12/31/1927 as part of a Unit Orchestra (Wurlitzer theatre organ) to Sydney, Australia. Many Solo Violin Pianos incorporated the Artecho reproducing system. At least one Solo Violin Piano was made with art glass panels rather than the usual violin-motif wood grille.

**Solo Violin Piano: The Solo Violin Piano was probably inspired by the Paganini Violin Piano. There are musical similarities between the two instruments and in the 1920's the same master rolls were often used to score rolls for each. The Solo Violin Piano was expensive (in 1920 it sold for $100 more – $2200 – than the more impressive appearing Style CX orchestrion) and played more softly than did the "nickelodeon" type of instruments. Demand was small and after the first three or four years few were sold. Today the soft and expressive music of the Solo Violin Piano makes one of these instruments a fine addition to any comprehensive collection.**

WURLITZER

**NET PRICE LIST OF**

**AUTOMATIC INSTRUMENTS**

EFFECTIVE MARCH 1, 1920.

This list cancels all former price lists.

| Style | Catalogue Page No. | Price |
|---|---|---|
| Pianino | 7 | $ 575.00 |
| Violin-Flute (Pianino) | 8 | 750.00 |
| S | 9 | 900.00 |
| I | 11 | 1100.00 |
| IX | 12 | 1200.00 |
| AX | 14 | 1500.00 |
| DX | 15 | 1700.00 |
| BX | 16 | 1900.00 |
| CX | 17 | 2100.00 |
| Solo Violin Piano | | 2100.00 |

**Price, F.O.B. Factory**

This 1920 price list shows the various coin pianos being sold at that time. Wurlitzer issued many different price lists, often revising prices several times per year. Changes were inevitably upward – inflation isn't new!

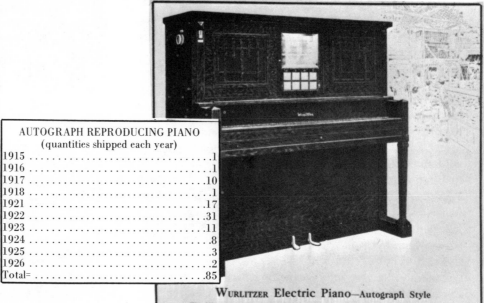

AUTOGRAPH REPRODUCING PIANO
(quantities shipped each year)

| | |
|---|---|
| 1915 | 1 |
| 1916 | 1 |
| 1917 | 10 |
| 1918 | 1 |
| 1921 | 17 |
| 1922 | 31 |
| 1923 | 11 |
| 1924 | 8 |
| 1925 | 3 |
| 1926 | 2 |
| Total= | 85 |

**Wurlitzer Electric Piano—Autograph Style**

The Wurlitzer Autograph Piano renders an absolutely true reproduction of the individual interpretations personally played by many of the world's renowned artists. The Autograph Piano is a distinct departure from any instrument ever manufactured for use in supplying musical entertainment in public places, especially designed to play the most difficult classical compositions COMPLETE. This Piano is to the PUBLIC PLACE of business, what the REPRODUCING PLAYER GRAND PIANO is to the PRIVATE HOME.

This instrument is equipped with the Wurlitzer Patented Automatic Roll-Changer.

Height, 4 ft. 9 in. Width, 5 ft. 1 in. Depth, 2 ft. 4¾ in. Shipping Weight, 1050 lbs.

**Autograph Piano: Featuring the recorded music of prominent pianists the Autograph Reproducing Piano was an appeal to the cultured listener who might care to part with a nickel. Public patrons preferred snappier tunes, so sales lagged. Seeburg had a similar experience with its Style X Expression Piano, a virtually identical type of instrument. The "mintage" of just 85 instruments makes this the shortest production of any major Wurlitzer type using its own distinctive roll.**

## MANDOLIN PIANORCHESTRA

During the 'teens Wurlitzer manufactured Mandolin PianOrchestra orchestrions at North Tonawanda, New York, using many interior components imported from J.D. Philipps (of Frankfurt, Germany). The Wurlitzer archives reveal that the following quantities were made: (listed in order of serial number, style, shipping date, and destination).

No.19641; Style 15; 6/9/1913 ............... New York City,N.Y.
No.19644; Style 12; 6/10/1913 ............... Pittsburgh, Pa.
No.19647; Style 15; 4/30/1913 ............... Oklahoma City, Okla.
No.19648; Style ?; 11/11/1913 ............... Dayton, Ohio
No.19649; Style 15; 7/14/1913 ............... New York City, N.Y.
No.19652; Style 16; 6/27/1913 ............... Minneapolis, Minn.
No.19653; Style 12; 7/25/1913 ............... Dayton, Ohio
No.19654; Style 12; 5/26/1914 ............... Trinidad, Colo.
No.19660; Style 12; 9/25/1916 ............... Cincinnati, Ohio
No.19661; Style 12; 6/23/1913 ............... Galveston, Texas
No.19699; Style 12; 9/23/1913 ............... New York City, N.Y.
No.19971; Style 15; 10/25/1913 ............... New York City, N.Y.
No.19972; Style 12; 1/26/1915 ............... Helena, Arkansas
No.19974; Style 15; 3/5/1914 ............... San Francisco, Calif.
No.19982; Style 12; 12/30/1914 ............... Shreveport, La.
No.20012; Style 12; 4/20/1913 ............... Cincinnati, Ohio
No.20031; Style 16; 11/29/1913 ............... San Francisco, Calif.
No.20032; Style 12; 5/23/1913 ............... Rochester, New York
No.20033; Style 12; 11/28/1913 ............... New York City, N.Y.
No.20035; Style 18; 5/16/1913 ............... Trinidad, Colorado
No.20037; Style 12; 12/30/1913 ............... Shreveport, La.
No.20038; Style 15; 11/8/1913 ............... Jacksonville, Fla.
No.20040; Style 12; 11/29/1913 ............... San Francisco, Calif.
No.20041; Style 16; 3/7/1913 ............... Milwaukee, Wisconsin
No.20966; Style 12; 1/26/1915 ............... Helena, Arkansas
No.20967; Style 12; 12/30/1913 ............... New York City, N.Y.
No.20968; Style 12; 3/7/1914 ............... Milwaukee, Wisconsin
No.20969; Style 12; 12/24/1913 ............... New York City, N.Y.
No.20970; Style 12; 5/4/1914 ............... Rochester, New York
No.20971; Style 15; 12/26/1913 ............... Fort Smith, Arkansas
No.20973; Style 12; 3/10/1914 ............... New York City, N.Y.
No.20974; Style 12; 2/17/1914 ............... New York City, N.Y.
No.20975; Style 28-B; 7/23/1913 ............... Cincinnati, Ohio
No.20976; Style 15; 5/11/1914 ............... Chicago, Illinois
No.21010; Style 12; 1/25/1914 ............... St. Louis, Missouri
No.21029; Style 12; 12/20/1913 ............... Shreveport, La.
No.21030; Style 12; 12/30/1913 ............... Shreveport, La.
No.21031; Style 12; 9/29/1916 ............... Milwaukee, Wisconsin
No.21032; Style 12; 3/9/1914 ............... Albany, N.Y.
No.21033; Style 12; 11/21/1913 ............... Rochester, New York
No.21034; Style 12; 1/23/1914 ............... Springfield, Ohio
No.21035; Style 16; 5/11/1914 ............... Chicago, Illinois
No.21036; Style 12; 3/17/1914 ............... Columbus, Ohio
No.21037; Style 12; 4/15/1914 ............... Detroit, Michigan
No.21038; Style 12; 5/27/1914 ............... Chicago, Illinois
No.21039; Style 12; 1/25/1914 ............... Helena, Arkansas
No.21040; Style 12; 12/30/1913 ............... Shreveport, La.
No.22137; Style 12; 9/27/1915 ............... Galveston, Texas
No.22138; Style 12; 5/1/1914 ............... New York City, N.Y.
No.22139; Style 12; 1/25/1914 ............... Helena, Arkansas
No.22140; Style 12; 3/9/1914 ............... Rockville, Conn.
No.22141; Style 12; 7/17/1914 ............... St. Louis, Missouri
No.22142; Style 16; 5/1/1914 ............... Alexandria, La.
No.22143; Style 12; 3/13/1914 ............... New York City, N.Y.
No.22144; Style 12; 2/16/1914 ............... New York City, N.Y.
No.22145; Style 12; 2/26/1914 ............... Clason Point, N.Y.
No.23189; Style 15; 7/28/1915 ............... St. Louis, Missouri
No.23191; Style 15; 8/5/1915 ............... New York City, N.Y.
No.23192; Style 12; 8/9/1915 ............... Syracuse, N.Y.
No.23194; Style 12; 5/12/1915 ............... New York City, N.Y.
No.23195; Style 15; 11/6/1915 ............... Stamford, Conn.
No.23196; Style 16; 10/1/1915 ............... New York City, N.Y.
No.23197; Style 12; 9/27/1915 ............... Galveston, Texas
No.23198; Style 28-B; 7/23/1915 ............... Cincinnati, Ohio
No.23199; Style 15; 9/27/1915 ............... Galveston, Texas
No.23200; Style 15; 10/4/1915 ............... New York City, N.Y.
No.23201; Style 18; 8/7/1915 ............... New York City, N.Y.
No.23202; Style 28-B; 7/23/1915 ............... Cincinnati, Ohio
No.23203; Style 12; 6/17/1915 ............... Kemmerer, Wyoming
No.23204; Style 12; 9/27/1915 ............... Galveston, Texas
No.23205; Style 16; 10/13/1915 ............... Tampa, Florida
No.23955; Style 12; 10/6/1915 ............... Atlanta, Georgia

(continued on next page)

**Style 12 Mandolin PianOrchestra: Containing 37 violin and violoncello pipes, piano, mandolin, bass drum, snare drum, and cymbal, the Style 12 (made in two case design variations — see lower right for other style) was the most popular type made at the Wurlitzer factory in North Tonawanda. Examination of surviving examples reveals that the interior mechanisms were made for the most part by Philipps and the exterior cases were made by Wurlitzer. The author's interest in large classic orchestrions began when a Style 12 similar to the above was seen in the collection of the late Otto Carlsen of Monrovia, California. The combination of the peacock "wonder light," the impressive size of the instrument, and its volume of ragtime music combined to kindle a desire to learn as much as possible about these instruments — a project which eventually led to the preparation of this Encyclopedia.**

Wurlitzer PianOrchestra—Style 12
With Wurlitzer Automatic Roll Changer

Instrumentation:

Piano — Orchestration of 37 Violin and Violoncello Pipes
Chimes — Bass and Tenor Drums, Cymbals and Mandolin Attachment.

Height, 8 ft. 6 in. Width, 5 ft. 6 in. Depth, 3 ft. Shipping weight, 1500 lbs.

**Style 12 Mandolin PianOrchestra: Unfortunately, the factory records do not distinguish between this case style and the other Style 12 illustrated above. Evidently a number of each were produced. All PianOrchestras made in North Tonawanda used the roll changer; either of 6-roll or 12-roll size. These changers are beautifully made of machined steel and were imported from Philipps. Once properly adjusted the PianOrchestra roll changers are virtually trouble free and can operate through thousands of tunes without requiring the least bit of attention.**

**Wurlitzer Mandolin PianOrchestras (made in North Tonawanda, N.Y.)**

**Style 15 Mandolin PianOrchestra: Two minor case design variations are illustrated above; one with a statue on the front and lamps with beaded shades on top, and the other without statue and with art glass lamps. Both types were made in North Tonawanda during the 'teens. Contains: piano, 13 orchestra bells, xylophone (30-note), 37 violin and violoncello pipes, bass drum (with tympani effect), snare drum, triangle, tambourine, and castanets. 8'3" high, 5'9" wide, 3'2" deep. Weight: 1500 pounds.**

Wurlitzer Mandolin PianOrchestra—Style 16

With Wurlitzer Automatic Roll Changer

The art glass designs vary somewhat.

Instrumentation:

| | |
|---|---|
| Piano | Orchestration of 42 Violin and Violoncello Pipes |
| Chimes | Bass, Snare and Kettle Drums |
| Xylophone | Triangle Tambourine Castanets |

Height over all, 8 ft. 8 in. Height without Globes, 7 ft. 10 in. Width, 5 ft. 10½ in. Depth, 2 ft. 11 in. Shipping weight, 1600 lbs.

**Style 16 PianOrchestra: According to several sources one of these ornate instruments held forth for many years on an Atlantic City pier. The specimen shown above left with the doors open and bottom panel removed is from the Klavestad Collection. Earlier it was a featured attraction in a Minneapolis restaurant which featured an oriental decor and had live canaries flitting about the dining room!**

**Style 18 Mandolin PianOrchestra: Made in North Tonawanda during the 'teens. The case bears a family resemblance to the Style 12. These tall and impressive classic orchestrions are among the most elegant automatic musical instruments made in America. It's a shame that 999 PianOrchestras weren't made instead of just 99 — for PianOrchestras of all kinds are exceedingly rare today. Brilliant art glass, a sparkling "wonder light," snappy ragtime music at the drop of a nickel — what more could be asked of a piece of Americana? These are exciting instruments!**

WURLITZER PianOrchestra—Style 18

Instrumentation:

| | | | |
|---|---|---|---|
| 30 Violin Pipes | Bells | Cymbal | Triangle |
| 30 Flute Pipes | Xylophone | Kettle Drum | Tambourine |
| 24 Violoncello Pipes | Bass Drum | Snare Drum | Castanets |
| Piano | | | Mandolin attachment |

2 Automatic Stops for Pipes

Height over all, 9 ft. 3⅜ in. Width, 5 ft 6⅝ in. Depth, 3 ft. 5¼ in. Shipping weight 1600 lbs.

No.24098; Style 12; 11/26/1915 .................. Tampa, Florida
No.24099; Style 15; 11/17/1915 .............. Jamaica, New York
No.24100; Style 16; 11/24/1915 ............... Jacksonville, Fla.
No.24101; Style 18; 11/12/1915 ................. Shreveport, La.
No.24103; Style 15; 12/13/1915 ............ New York City, N.Y.
No.24104; Style 12; 11/18/1915 ................ Chicago, Illinois
No.24295; Style 15; 12/27/1915 ................. Alexandria, La.
No.24296; Style 12; 9/26/1915 ................ Philadelphia, Pa.
No.24298; Style 12; 12/15/1915 ............. Rock Springs, Wyo.
No.24299; Style 12; 7/15/1916 ............. New York City, N.Y.
No.24300; Style 12; 5/19/1916 ............. New York City, N.Y.
No.24301; Style 18; 9/14/1916 ............... Detroit, Michigan
No.24302; Style 12; 12/11/1916 ............... Cincinnati, Ohio
No.24303; Style 15; 6/29/1916 ................... Peoria, Illinois
No.24304; Style 12; 7/8/1916 ................ Bridgeport, Conn.
No.24363; Style 12; 9/30/1916 ................. Cleveland, Ohio
No.24364; Style 12; 12/15/1916 ............ New York City, N.Y.
No.24365; Style 15; 9/25/1916 .................. Hamilton, Ohio
No.24366; Style 12; 12/8/1916 ................. Chicago, Illinois
No.24367; Style 12; 12/11/1916 .............. St. Louis, Missouri
No.24368; Style 12; 12/15/1916 ............ New York City, N.Y.
No.24369; Style 15; 8/13/1916 ................. Chicago, Illinois
No.27157; Style 18; 5/16/1917 ............. New York City, N.Y.
No.27166; Style 12; 5/10/1917 .............. St. Louis, Missouri
No.27167; Style 18; 4/25/1917 ............... Conshohocken, Pa.
No.27168; Style 12; 1/26/1917 ................... Dayton, Ohio
No.28564; Style 18; 7/10/1917 ............. New York City, N.Y.
Total PianOrchestras = .................................. 99

Notes: The 99 PianOrchestras are as follows: Style 12 (61 made); Style 15 (19 made); Style 16 (8 made); Style 18 (7 made); Style 28-B (3 made); and one style number not known as it was omitted in the shipping list.

Interesting questions raised by the above list include: Why were the style 28-B instruments shipped only to Cincinnati? All PianOrchestras shipped to the small town of Helena, Arkansas, were on one purchase order (order No. 14376) and may have all been shipped in one year, although the records indicate shipping in January, 1913 and January, 1914. Similarly, instruments Nos. 19982 (shipped 12/30/1914) and 21040 (12/30/1913) are both on purchase order No. 14377, indicating that they both may have been really shipped on the same year; most probably they were. Similar indications of dating errors appear throughout the Wurlitzer shipping records.

Of the 99 PianOrchestras in the above list only four specimens (two Style 12's, a Style 15, and a Style 16) are known by the author to survive today. (Other Mandolin and PianOrchestras survive in addition to those four; the others were imported in their entireties from Philipps.)

The amount of fascinating (at least to the author!) minutiae to be gleaned from original factory records is tremendous — but in the interest of readability and brevity we must condense the data. However, the foregoing Wurlitzer listing gives the reader an idea of the type of raw data we have to work with.

Twelve-roll changer in the Style 15 Mandolin PianOrchestra owned by the author. The instrument was located for years in a New York City ice cream parlor. Found by Mrs. Ruth Bornand, it was sold to Messrs. Haning and White of Troy, Ohio. From there it went into the Carlsen Collection and was subsequently acquired from that source. The 12-roll changer permits a program of 60 tunes (about two hours' worth of music) without repetition.

Six-roll changer in the Style 30-A Mandolin PianOrchestra in the Coade Collection. This finely machined mechanism is a work of art – at least to the eyes of an orchestrion connoisseur!

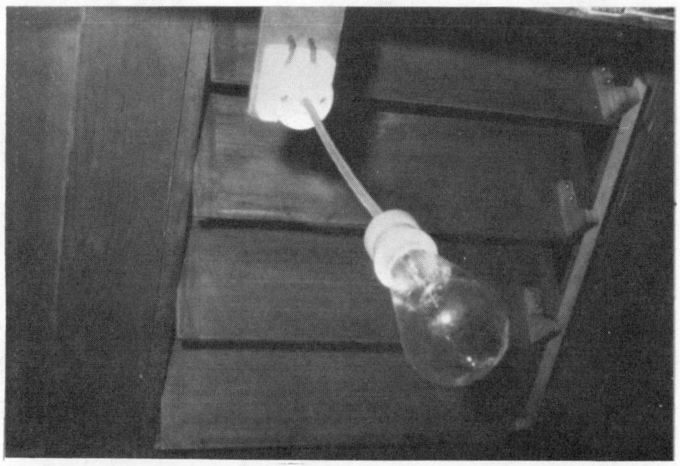

Louvered swell shutters in the top of the 30-A provide expression and volume variations. This particular 30-A was formerly located in Auburn and Skaneateles Junction, New York.

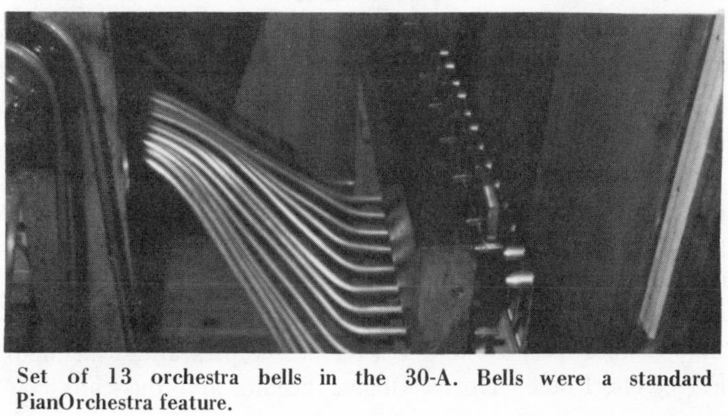

Set of 13 orchestra bells in the 30-A. Bells were a standard PianOrchestra feature.

Style 17 PianOrchestra: Three case design variations are shown above. One of the earliest models the Style 17 used its own special roll which featured solo arrangements for the orchestra bells or glockenspiel. It is possible that certain other very early PianOrchestras used the Style 17 roll as well.

Above: Late Style 18 Mandolin PianOrchestra (imported from Philipps). Left: An early Style 18 likewise imported. A North Tonawanda Style 18 is shown on another page.

## WURLITZER MANDOLIN PIANORCHESTRA
### ...Tracker bar layout.
*(Philipps Pianella Mandoline scale)*

1. Clarinet pipes on.
2. Clarionet pipes on.
3. Coin trip.
4. Snare drum.
5. Sustaining pedal off.
6. Register cancel.
7. Kettle drum.
8. Kettle drum.
9. Triangle.
10. Bells on.
11. (Hole not used).
12. Mandolin bar on.
13. Sustaining pedal on.
14. to 27. Playing notes on the piano, beginning with C and going in order to C sharp.
28. Rewind.
29. Continuation of notes beginning with D and going chromatically to B (hole No.50)
51. (Not used)
52. to 76. Continuation of notes in order beginning with C and ending with C.
77. Swell shutters open.
78. Swell shutters closed.
79. Violoncello pipes on.
80. Violin (gamba) pipes on.
81. Flute pipes on.
82. Piano soft pedal off.
83. Drum expression loud
84. Tambourine.
85. Bass drum and cymbal.
86. Castanets
87. Piccolo pipes on.
88. Xylophone on.

**Notes on the Mandolin PianOrchestra scale:** Pipe ranks with 49 notes begin at hole no. 26 and continue to the end of the playing notes. 42-note ranks begin at hole 34, 30-note ranks at hole 46 and the bells (13-note set) at hole no. 64 - and all go to the end of the musical scale.

# The PianOrchestra
*"King of Automatic Musical Instruments."*

THE PIANORCHESTRA is, without question, the most wonderful self-playing musical instrument ever built. It is a combination of all the different instruments used in a full symphony orchestra, assembled in a single magnificent case, and arranged to play in solo and concert work, exactly the same as a human orchestra.

It is next to impossible to convey an idea of the PianOrchestra's magnificence with printer's ink. The many handsome styles must be seen and heard to obtain a fair conception of their appearance and musical possibilities. However, a faint idea of their musical possibilities may be had from the following list of instruments they contain: Piano; Bass, Tenor and Kettle Drums; Triangle, Cymbals, Xylophones, Chimes, Castanets, Tambourine, First and Second Violin Pipes, Viola and 'Cello Pipes, Double Bass Pipes, Flutes and Clarionets, Mandolins, Saxophones, Trombones, Flageolets, French Horns, Oboes, Piccolos and Bassoons.

Left: Wurlitzer advertisement for the PianOrchestra. These were recommended for hotels, larger cafes, beer gardens, dancing pavilions, steamships, bowling alleys (!), penny arcades, ice cream parlors, five cent theatres, and amusement resorts.

Wurlitzer Mandolin PianOrchestras
(made by Philipps)

The PianOrchestra STYLE 19 **Price, $1,800** Including Four Rolls of Music

SOLD FOR CASH OR ON EASY PAYMENT PLAN

OAK CASE

Size { 9 ft. 5 in. high. 5 ft. 4 in. wide. 2 ft. 8 in. deep.

Piano, 62 notes, overstrung bass, with automatic loud and soft pedal.
Orchestrion, 67 pipes, producing violin, violoncello and piccolo.
Chimes, 13 bars.
Bass drum, tenor drum, cymbals.

Style 19 Mandolin PianOrchestra. Early case design (Philipps made).

The PianOrchestra STYLE 20 **Price, $2,250** Including Four Rolls of Music

SOLD FOR CASH OR ON EASY PAYMENT PLAN

DESCRIPTION

RARELY has the woodcarver's art produced better results than presented in the embellishment of this case. Divided in six panels, the surface is ornamented with a handsome display of designs in arabesque and scroll work, distributed in a manner to blend to an artistic whole. In the upper left and right panels are the medallions of Beethoven and Mozart, two of the greatest masters in the domain of music, and the mention of whose names thrills the hearts of millions of enthusiasts. In the palatial abode of wealth this magnificent work would harmonize with the most luxurious surroundings.

The mechanical arrangements are in keeping with the elegance of the exterior. Reclining in indolent repose, what can be more fascinating than to feast the eye on the rich carvings, while from the interior are conjured forth the rich, vibrating tones of the instruments, which commingly dissolve into enchanting melody and, filling the soul with rapturous delight?

OAK CASE

Size { 9 ft. 10 in. high. 6 ft. 2 in. wide. 3 ft. 2 in. deep.

Piano, 62 notes.
Orchestrion, 92 pipes, producing violin, viola piccolo, violoncello.
Chimes, 13 bars.
Bass drum, tenor drum, cymbals.

Style 20 Mandolin PianOrchestra. Early case design (Philipps made).

Style 20. Price, $2,600, Including 6 Rolls of Music and One Slot Box (3 Automatic Figures.)
Style 20A. Same, with Plain Panels Instead of Automatic Figures, $2,300.

Style 20 and 20-A Mandolin PianOrchestra. This was a popular style circa 1903 - 1907 and was imported from Philipps. Quite a few were sold, mainly in the eastern United States.

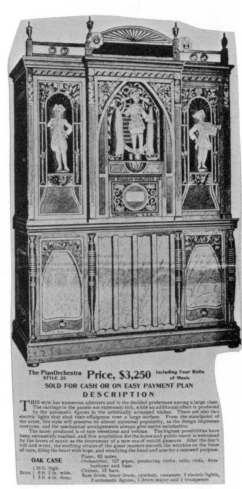

Style 21: An early model with an extending keyboard, an exception to the keyboardless rule. (Philipps made).

Style 27-B Mandolin PianOrchestra. Contains piano, xylophone, bells, drums (no pipes). 9'1" high; 4'11" wide; 2'6" deep.

PianOrchestra, Style 22 **Price, $3,500** Including Four Rolls of Music

SOLD FOR CASH OR ON THE EASY PAYMENT PLAN

DESCRIPTION

THE skill of the mechanic and the talent of the artist were happily united in producing this splendid work—the acme of human ingenuity and conception. In every detail the most pains-taking care is visible, and as a result the exacting demands of the fastidious have been considered, and the voice of the carping critic has been silenced. Towering ten feet aloft and of nine feet seven inches width, this majestic masterpiece charms at every point. The exterior is lavishly decorated with carving and glass arrangements, but throughout a pleasing simplicity, as dictated by a fine taste, has been preserved. At the sides there are two projecting wings, which are carved in keeping with the general design. At the top of the three upper panels orchestra chimes are displayed, which accompany the music. The superstructure consists of a semi-circle adornment, embellished at the top by a carved harp. In the center of the former there revolves an electric light enclosed in a bulb, which is studded with glass of various colors, and which is reflected from the mirrored background, producing an effect of dazzling, oriental splendor.

The musical arrangements are also of the highest order, and no labor has been spared to produce an execution that equals the best performances of the orchestra. To such an extent has this succeeded that the most trained ear discovers nothing to censure, the concerts affording the hearers endless delight.

OAK CASE

Size { 10 ft. 6 in. high. 9 ft. 7 in. wide. 3 ft. 7 in. deep.

Piano, 62 notes.
Orchestrion, 165 pipes, producing violin, clarionet, flute, piccolo, violoncello and saxophone.
Chimes, 13 bars.
Bass drum, tenor drum, cymbals, castanets, one revolving electric light producing wonderful electrical effect.

Style 22. One of the larger early styles. Several were sold circa 1903 - 1908.

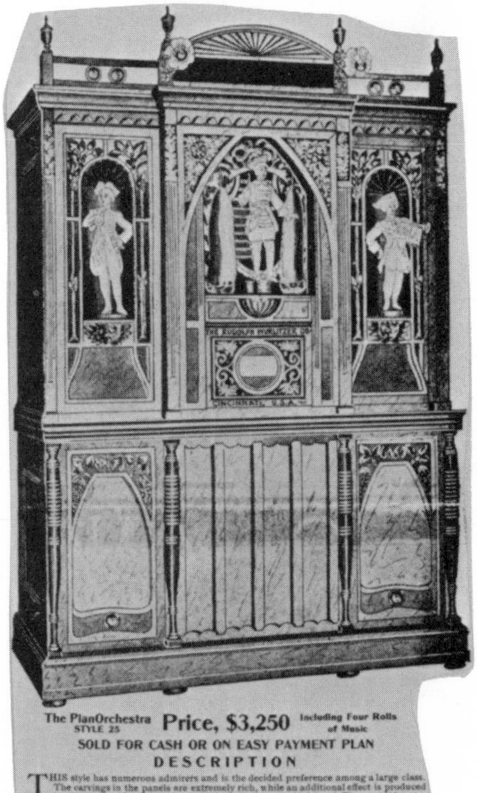

The PianOrchestra STYLE 25 **Price, $3,250** Including Four Rolls of Music

SOLD FOR CASH OR ON EASY PAYMENT PLAN

DESCRIPTION

THIS style has numerous admirers and is the decided preference among a large class. The carvings in the panels are extremely rich, while an additional effect is produced by the automatic figures in the artistically arranged niches. There are also two electric lights that shed their effulgence over a large surface. From the standpoint of the artist, this style will preserve its almost universal popularity, as the design impresses everyone, and the mechanical arrangements always give entire satisfaction.

The music produced is of rare sweetness and volume. The highest possibilities have been successfully reached, and this acquisition for the home and public resort is welcomed by the lovers of music as the forerunner of a new era of untold pleasure. After the day's toil and worry, the soothing strains of the great masters smooth the wrinkles on the brow of care, filling the heart with hope, and steadying the hand and arm for a renewed purpose.

OAK CASE

Size { 10 ft. high. 6 ft. 2 in. wide. 3 ft. 4 in. deep.

Piano, 62 notes.
Orchestrion, 127 pipes, producing violin, cello, viola, flute baritone and bass.
Chimes, 13 bars.
Bass drum, tenor drum, cymbals, castanets, 2 electric lights, 3 automatic figures, 1 drum major and 2 trumpeters

Style 25. Another early Mandolin PianOrchestra style imported from Philipps.

Wurlitzer Mandolin PianOrchestra—Style 28
With Wurlitzer Automatic Roll Changer
Instrumentation:
Piano with Mandolin attachment
37 Violins — Bass Drum and Cymbals
18 Violoncellos — Snare Drum

Style 28 (or 28-A with the addition of a xylophone). Three different case styles. All made by Philipps. See Philipps section of this book for other orchestrions of this genre.

Wurlitzer Mandolin PianOrchestra
—Style 28 B With Automatic Roll Changer

Instrumentation:
Piano with Mandolin attachment
37 Violins — Bass Drum and Cymbals
18 Violoncellos — Snare Drum
Height, 9 ft. 2 in. Depth, 2 ft. 8 in. Width, 6 ft. 4 in. Shipping weight, 1600 lbs.

Style 28-B. The above Mandolin PianOrchestra style is from Philipps and sports a colorful scene on the front. Factory records indicate that three Style 28-B PianOrchestras were made in North Tonawanda, but the case design of these must have differed from the above (none with mechanical scenes was ever made in this country; U.S. ones had art glass fronts). A 28-B similar to the above was found in disrepair in a Pennsylvania dance pavilion by Larry Givens in the late 1950's. It is now part of the Walker Collection.

Wurlitzer Mandolin PianOrchestra—Style 29 C
With Wurlitzer Automatic Roll Changer
The finish illustrated is brown oak. Other finishes are shown in natural colors on page 5.
Instrumentation:
Piano with Mandolin attachment
30 Violins — 30 Violas — 12 Piccolos — Kettle Drum and Cymbals
24 Violoncellos — 18 Flutes — Chimes — Bass and Snare Drums
Xylophone — Tambourine
Height, 10 ft. Width, 6 ft. 8 in. Depth, 3 ft. 4 in. Shipping weight, 2200 lbs.

Style 29-C Mandolin PianOrchestra — three distinctly different case style variations. The catalogue noted (of the style at the left above): "On each side are a couple of tasty Corinthian columns, and the center space is given over to one of our brilliant oil paintings, arranged for the novel and eye catching motion picture effect. The scene depicted is that of a forest stream winding its way through the meadows, and plunging over an idyllic waterfall. When the instrument plays, the interior lights and special mechanism convert the scene into a vivid motion picture of the most absorbing interest." In the 1950's one of these was found hidden behind a plastered-over wall in the old Banner Theatre in Los Angeles. It is now the property of Mr. Walter Knott of Knott's Berry Farm in Buena Park, California.

Wurlitzer Mandolin PianOrchestras
(made by Philipps)

Style 30 Mandolin PianOrchestra.

Height, 10 ft. 1 in. Width, 6 ft. 6 in.


WURLITZER

Style 30-A. Contains piano, mandolin, 30 piccolos, 30 violins, 19 violas, 37 flutes, 30 violoncellos, xylophone, bass and snare drums, tympani effect, cymbal, orchestra bells, triangle, castanets and tambourine. "One of the most popular PianOrchestra styles," according to Mr. Farny Wurlitzer. Most had rippled glass; the above model with art glass is unusual.

Mandolin PianOrchestra —Style 30 B

Height, 10 ft. 8 in. Width, 6 ft. 5 in. Depth, 3 ft. 10 in.

The lurid glow of fire and lava issuing from the mountain top and the brilliant coloring of the cloud of smoke overhanging the mountain top make a life-picture that rivets the attention from first to last.

The painting is bordered by an attractive urn-shaped frame having bas relief figures of cherubs at the upper corners, and French bevel plate mirrors on either side.

Below the painting a plate glass door admits a view of the wonderful Music Roll Changing Device in operation.

There are also a number of handsomely carved bas relief figures on the front of the instrument, and the entire front is, as the description indicates, brilliantly illuminated when playng. So much for the decorative end of this elegant instrument.

Musically considered, it is even better than it looks. It combines all the possibilities of both the Mandolin and Xylophone styles of PianOrchestra, and the musical effects it produces are far superior to anything within the range of any but the foremost human orchestras found in the largest metropolitan centers.

The 121 wood and metal music pipes are so evenly distributed and perfectly balanced that their response to the action of the marvelous automatic stops can only be compared to the intelligent action of the best orchestra players, working under a skilled director.

INSTRUMENTATION:

*A High Grade Piano, with Mandolin Attachment.*

| | | |
|---|---|---|
| *37 Violins.* | *20 Saxophones.* | *Triangle.* |
| *12 Violoncellos.* | *22 Violas.* | *Castanets.* |
| *15 Piccolos.* | *Xylophone, 30 Bars.* | *Bass and Snare Drums.* |
| *15 Flutes.* | *Chimes, 13 Bars.* | *Kettle Drum and Cymbals.* |
| | *Tambourine.* | |

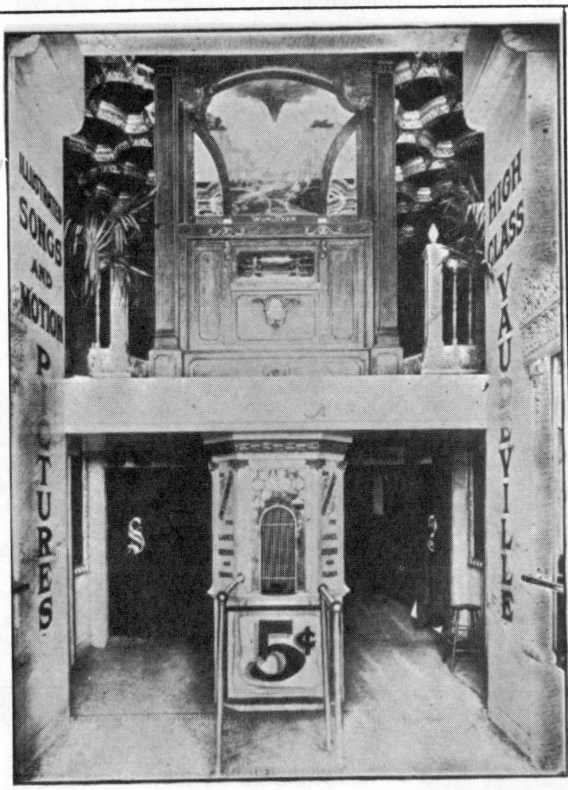


Style 30-B Mandolin PianOrchestra. The above illustration shows one of these in use in the "good old days" drawing patrons into the Silver Palace, a nickelodeon theatre in San Francisco. A good many PianOrchestras went into theatres. Some were used as drawing cards in the front lobby or near the ticket window. Others were simply allowed to play nonstop during the film presentation.

## The Wurlitzer PianOrchestra provides just the entertainment that everyone likes

There is as much difference in the quality of its music and the "music" of a majority of automatic musical instruments as between a human orchestra and a hurdy-gurdy. The Wurlitzer PianOrchestra is so nearly a "Human" Orchestra as to defy detection.

There is nothing of the mechanical in its playing. Seated in another room, and not knowing of the existence of this instrument, you would never question but that it is a real flesh and blood organization of ten trained musicians.

Wurlitzer Mandolin PianOrchestra—Style 33 A

With Wurlitzer Automatic Roll Changer

Instrumentation:

Piano with Mandolin attachment

| | | | |
|---|---|---|---|
| 49 Violins | 30 Piccolos | Chimes | Kettle Drum and Cymbals |
| 30 Violoncellos | Xylophone | Bass and Snare Drums | Triangle and Tambourine |
| | | | Castanets |

Height, 10 ft. 6 in. Width, 6 ft. 6 in. Depth, 3 ft. 10 in.

Shipping weight, 2600 lbs.

Wurlitzer Mandolin PianOrchestras
(made by Philipps)

Mandolin PianOrchestra
—Style 34
XYLOPHONE
PIANORCHESTRA
WURLITZER
Height, 10 ft. 10 in. Width, 9 ft. 6 in. Depth, 4 ft. 3 in.
PRICE—Including Automatic Roll Changing Device, 6 Rolls of Music and 1 Slot Box. .$3,500.00
This style may also be had without Roll Changing Device. Price........... 3,300.00


Style 34 Mandolin PianOrchestra. "The finest regular style of the Mandolin PianOrchestra built. It is a magnificent musical instrument, fit, both from an architectural and a musical standpoint, to grace the finest public resort in the land."

Style 38 Mandolin PianOrchestra. Contains: piano, mandolin, 25 violins, 10 violas, 7 violoncellos, xylophone, bass and snare drums. "One of our recent and most notable triumphs in producing a PianOrchestra of the highest grade of excellence at moderate cost ($1850.00). The case design is chaste and elegant. . . The music cannot possibly be equalled by any but the most skilled human orchestras." — original catalogue description.

Style 34-A. Contains piano, mandolin, 49 violins, 19 violoncellos, 30 violas, 30 flutes, 30 clarinets, 30 piccolos, xylophone, bells, drums, and percussion effects. 10'10" high, 9'9" wide, 4'3" deep. 3000 pounds weight. This and the Style 34 are the most extensively instrumented of the Mandolin PianOrchestras.

## One thing is certain—
## you want more business!

### A Wurlitzer PianOrchestra will get you more business

Wurlitzer PianOrchestras are right now getting *more* business for 762 other men in your same line almost everywhere the sun shines. (Testimonials by the basketful.) What a PianOrchestra has done for others it will do for you. *The Wurlitzer PianOrchestra* will give you entertainment of cabaret variety—at practically no cost.

The public drops the coins that play the music, thereby putting the instrument upon a basis that is self-paying.

You have heard the beautiful music of a 10-piece orchestra and have seen couples dance the fox trot, one step and hesitation, and you wished perhaps, that *you* could afford to employ a 10-piece orchestra and make your place just as attractive.

We can place a *PianOrchestra* in your establishment—give you practically the same volume and quality of music as a 10-piece orchestra, and you can add these entertainment features or dances and draw just as big crowds.

The Wurlitzer PianOrchestra is equipped with the wonderful

AUTOMATIC ROLL CHANGER

that makes it possible for it to play as many as thirty different selections without change or attention — classical, operatic, dances, songs, and all the national airs. A musical program of from one and a half hours' to three hours' duration, can be arranged without attention.

Every feature of this Automatic Roll Changer is patented by the Rudolph Wurlitzer Company, and cannot be found in any other instrument.

Mandolin PianOrchestra, style unknown, sold in the United States circa 1912. Illustration from the Wurlitzer archives.

WURLITZER PianOrchestra

Made by J.D. Philipps & Söhne of Frankfurt-am-Main, Germany, about 1912-1914 this magnificent orchestrion was sold in Europe as the Philipps Model 11 and in America as the Wurlitzer Style 34A Mandolin PianOrchestra. This instrument, which entertained the patrons of a restaurant for many years, is in the Terry Hathaway Collection today. (Dan Adams photograph)

Wurlitzer Mandolin PianOrchestras (made by Philipps)

**Wurlitzer Mandolin PianOrchestra**

With Wurlitzer Automatic Roll Changer

The art glass designs vary somewhat.

**Instrumentation:**

Piano with Mandolin attachment

| | | |
|---|---|---|
| 25 Violins | 10 Violas | Bass Drum and Cymbals |
| 7 Violoncellos | Xylophone | Snare Drum |

Height, 8 ft. 6½ in. Width, 4 ft. 10 in. Depth, 2 ft. 6 in. Shipping weight, 1500 lbs.

Style 39 Mandolin PianOrchestra. Piano, mandolin, 30 violins, 12 violoncellos, xylophone, drums, and trap effects.

Style 40 Mandolin PianOrchestra. Piano, mandolin, 42 violins, 12 violas, 30 violoncellos, xylophone, drums, and percussion effects.

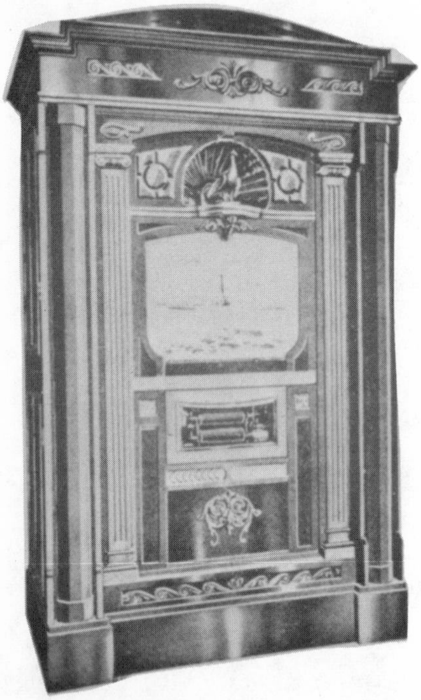

Style 40-A. Contains: piano, mandolin attachment, 30 violin pipes, 12 violoncello pipes, xylophone, chimes, bass drum, snare drum, tympani effect, tambourine, and cymbal. 9' high, 4'3" wide, 3'4" deep. Weight: 2000 pounds. Case similar to the Style 40 (see upper right of this page) but with peacock "wonder light" at the upper center above a lighthouse and sea scene.

PianOrchestras in the Wurlitzer Section: The PianOrchestras illustrated in the Wurlitzer section are those definitely known to have been imported from Philipps (or made in the U.S). As our selection for this section is based on styles actually pictured in the Wurlitzer archives it may be incomplete. Other Philipps styles (see Philipps section of this book) may well have been imported and sold as PianOrchestras also. In fact, this is very probable.

Style 47 Mandolin PianOrchestra.

Mandolin PianOrchestra sold in the U.S. circa 1912. Style unknown. (From the Wurlitzer archives).

## PIANORCHESTRAS

| Style | Catalogue Page No. | Price |
|---|---|---|
| 12 | 23 | $ 2200.00 |
| 18 | 24 | 2950.00 |
| 29C | 25 | 3500.00 |
| 33 | 26 | 4050.00 |
| 30A | 27 | 3800.00 |
| 47 | 28 | 4050 00 |
| 34A | 29 | 5250.00 |
| 32A | 30 | 5750.00 |
| 3 Paganini | 33 | 4250.00 |
| 2 " | | 3700.00 |
| 1 " | | 3500.00 |

May 15, 1920 Wurlitzer price list showing instruments in stock.

# Concert PianOrchestra

## Wurlitzer Concert PianOrchestra—Style 72 A

With Wurlitzer Automatic Roll Changer

Instrumentation:

| | | | |
|---|---|---|---|
| Piano | 30 Flutes | 10 Bassoons | Chimes |
| 70 Violins | 30 Piccolos | 10 Bass Violins | Bass and Snare Drums |
| 30 Violoncellos | 30 Clarinets | 16 French Horns | Kettle Drum and Cymbals |
| 18 Violas | 20 Oboes | 10 Trumpets | Tambourines |
| 26 Saxophones | 14 Bass Clarinets | Xylophone | Triangle |

Tremolo and Castanets

Height, 12 ft. Width, 7 ft. 4 in. Depth, 4 ft. 3½ in. Shipping weight, 4000 lbs.

## Concert PianOrchestra—Style 43

Height, 11 ft. 9 in. Width, 7 ft. 10½ in. Depth, 5 ft. 7½ in.

PRICE—Including Automatic Roll Changing Device, 6 Rolls of Music and 1 Slot Box...$7,500.00

This style may also be had without Roll Changing Device. Price........... 7,300.00

INSTRUMENTATION:

*A High Grade Piano.*

| | | |
|---|---|---|
| *30 Violins.* | *30 Saxophones.* | *26 Brass Trombones.* |
| *30 Violas.* | *30 Clarionets.* | *Xylophone, 30 Bars.* |
| *30 Violoncellos.* | *30 Oboes.* | *Chimes, 13 Bars.* |
| *26 Bass Violins.* | *26 French Horns.* | *Bass and Snare Drums.* |
| *30 Flutes.* | *26 Flageolets.* | *Kettle Drum and Cymbals.* |
| *30 Piccolos.* | *26 Bassoons.* | *Triangle, Tambourine and Castanets.* |

Also a *Tremolent* for producing the tremolo effect in the music and an *automatic swell* to produce shading and expression.

## Wurlitzer Concert PianOrchestra—Style 31

With Wurlitzer Automatic Roll Changer

Instrumentation:

| | | | |
|---|---|---|---|
| Piano | 26 Saxophones | 26 Bass Violins | Triangle |
| 56 Violins | 30 Oboes | Bass and Snare Drums | Tambourine |
| 30 Violoncellos | 30 Flutes | Kettle Drum and Cymbals | Castanets |
| 30 Violas | 30 Piccolos | Chimes | |

Height, 10 ft. 6 in. Width, 6 ft. 10 in. Depth, 3 ft. 11 in.

→

WURLITZER

## Wurlitzer Concert PianOrchestra—Style 31 A

With Wurlitzer Automatic Roll Changer

Instrumentation:

| | | | |
|---|---|---|---|
| Piano | 30 Flutes | 26 Bass Violins | Triangle |
| 56 Violins | 30 Oboes | Chimes | Tambourine |
| 30 Violoncellos | 30 Piccolos | Bass and Snare Drums | Castanets |
| 30 Violas | 26 Saxophones | Kettle Drum and Cymbals | |

Height, 10 ft. 6 in. Width, 6 ft. 10 in. Depth, 3 ft. 11 in. Shipping weight, 3500 lbs.

## Wurlitzer Concert PianOrchestra—Style 68 C

With Wurlitzer Automatic Roll Changer

Instrumentation:

| | | | |
|---|---|---|---|
| Piano | 30 Flutes | 12 Bassoons | Xylophone |
| 65 Violins | 30 Piccolos | 20 Bass Clarinets | Chimes |
| 26 Violoncellos | 30 Clarinets | 10 Bass Violins | Bass and Snare Drums |
| 15 Violas | 24 Oboes | 26 French Horns | Kettle Drum and Cymbals |
| 26 Saxophones | Triangle | Tambourines | Tremolo and Castanets |

Height, 10 ft. Width, 10 ft. 9 in. Depth, 4 ft. 4 in. Shipping weight, 4200 lbs.

## WURLITZER CONCERT PIANORCHESTRA

### ...Tracker bar layout.

*(Philipps Pianella Caecilia Scale)*

1. Bass violin pipes on.
2. French horn (gedeckt) pipes on.
3. Saxophone pipes on.
4. Snare drum.
5. Sustaining pedal off.
6. Register cancel.
7. Kettle drum.
8. Kettle drum.
9. Triangle.
10. Bells on.
11. (Hole not used)
12. Crash cymbal.
13. Sustaining pedal on.
14. Quintadena pipes on.
15. Violin-gamba and gamba bass pipes on.
16. Oboe or clarionet pipes on.
17. Piccolo pipes on.
18. Tremolo on.

19. to 27. Playing notes on the piano beginning with F and going in order to C sharp.

28. Rewind.
29. Continuation of notes beginning with D and going chromatically to B (hole No.50)

51. Coin trip.

52. to 76. Continuation of notes in order beginning with C and ending with C.

77. Swell shutters open.
78. Swell shutters closed.
79. Violoncello pipes on.
80. Second violin pipes on.
81. Flute pipes on.
82. Piano soft pedal off.
83. Drum expression loud.
84. Tambourine.
85. Bass drum and cymbal.
86. Castanets.
87. Piano on.
88. Xylophone on.

**Notes on the Concert PianOrchestra scale:** The scale of the pipes on the bass pipe chest extends from hole 19 and includes all of the musical notes through no. 45. The notes on the treble pipe chest run from hole no. 46 and include all of the musical notes through hole no. 76. The xylophone range is 46-76 also. The range of the bells is from hole 64 to hole 76.

WURLITZER

# Concert PianOrchestra

WURLITZER

## Instrumentation:

Piano
56 Violins
30 Violoncellos
30 Violas
26 Saxophones
30 Flutes
30 Piccolos
30 Clarinets
30 Oboes
26 French Horns
26 Bass Violins
Chimes
Bass and Snare Drums
Triangle
Tambourine
Castanets
Tremolo
Kettle Drum
Cymbals

**Style 32 Concert PianOrchestra: The three smaller pictures on this page are of instruments designated as Style 32 Concert PianOrchestra. The larger one was designated Style 32-A. These use the Concert PianOrchestra roll which has more register controls than does the Mandolin PianOrchestra roll. In tracking down Concert PianOrchestras in the United States the author learned of one (similar to that pictured at lower right) that was used for years in a Wisconsin theatre and then taken out about 1931 or 1932; one that was sold in the Los Angeles area in the 1920's and which is now at Disneyland (instrument now modified, but originally similar to that pictured at the upper right of this page); and a Style 32-A that entertained patrons of the Silver Palace Hotel (now demolished – Ed.) in Leadville, Colorado. Probably 50 to 100 were sold originally in the United States.**

Concert PianOrchestra

# Wurlitzer Paganini Violin Piano

This San Francisco theatre, shown in a circa 1914 picture from the files of the Leathurby Co., has its music provided by a Style 3 Paganini. In the days just before photoplayers became popular it was often the practice to put an orchestrion in a theatre and let it play continuously throughout the performance. The music was not keyed to the action on the screen (the later photoplayers did this), but in the early days of the nickelodeon theatre this did not matter much. The orchestrion music set a convivial mood that entertained moviegoers and kept them coming back for more — and this was what was important!

Paganini Violin Piano—Style 1

With Wurlitzer Automatic Roll Changer

Represents a Piano in combination with a Violin.

Height, 8 ft. 8½ in. Width, 6 ft. 6 in. Depth, 3 ft. 3 in. Shipping weight, 1400 lbs.

Paganini Violin Piano—Style 2

With Wurlitzer Automatic Roll Changer

Represents a Piano in combination with 2 Violins.

Height, 9 ft. 4¼ in. Width, 6 ft. 6 in. Depth, 3 ft. 5½ in. Shipping weight, 1500 lbs.

Paganini Solo Violin Piano—Style 3

With Wurlitzer Automatic Roll Changer

Represents 2 Violins with Organ and Piano accompaniment.

Height, 8 ft. Width, 6 ft. 3 in. Depth, 3 ft. 1 in. Shipping weight, 1800 lbs.

**Various Wurlitzer Paganini styles.**

# Paganini Violin Piano

Style 1 Paganini. Reproducing piano and one rank of violin pipes.

Style 2 Paganini. Reproducing piano and two ranks of pipes.

Style 3 Paganini. Reproducing piano, two ranks of pipes, and harmonium (reed organ).

Above: The Paganini illustrated above is, in our opinion, one of the most beautiful orchestrions ever made. The Wurlitzer archives picture one of these with "San Francisco" etched on the clear glass in front of the roll changer door and note that it was sold by Kohler and Chase, musical instrument dealers in that city. What happened to this elegant masterpiece is not known. Sic transit gloria — fame is fleeting — and it's inconceivable to think that such works of musical art were once destroyed, as countless orchestrions were.

Above and right: Two models of the Paganini Violin Orchestra. The Style 10 (right) contained a reproducing piano, violin pipes, flageolets, clarionets, piccolos, cello pipes, cornet pipes, xylophone, orchestra bells, bass drum, snare drum, cymbal, tympani effect, castanets, and harmonium (organ reeds). The measurements are: 11'4" high; 8'10" wide; 6' deep. Weight: 4200 pounds. This was the most expensive Wurlitzer orchestrion style and sold for $10,000. At least 3 of these were sold by Wurlitzer in the U.S.

**Paganini Violin Orchestra—Style 10**

## Paganini Violin Piano

This instrument is the latest Wurlitzer triumph and the very highest type of refined musical instrument.

The work of the Paganini Violin Piano will be best appreciated by musical persons who understand and appreciate good music. This instrument reproduces the actual playing of a piano and violin by artists of the highest rank, the violin leading and the piano playing the accompaniment.

The Paganini will play everything in music from the popular hits to the big classical numbers with a correctness of technic and musical shading that will positively amaze the listener.

Take a position in another room or turn your back on this new musical wonder and you will find it impossible to say that you are not listening to the best work of a finished pianist and violinist, thoroughly accustomed to playing together in concert.

The Paganini has been tried out in the very finest places and in every case it has caused a sensation, so *different* is it in every respect.

A visitor in a fine cafe or hotel restaurant of today notices that the music comes drifting in, so to speak, not loud, but in soft, delicate strains that can be plainly heard and enjoyed by those who wish to stop their conversation to listen, while it is so soft as not to interfere with low conversation by those who wish to talk.

The Orchestra usually is hidden in such places, and as said above, the music seems to *drift* in.

That is the exact niche the Paganini fills. It really seems made to order for just such refined places. Put the Paganini in the place of the hidden orchestra and your diners will never know but that they are listening to the finest violinist and pianist they ever heard. When they discover that the artist musicians are entirely automatic, their interest deepens. The charm of the music grows and grows with repeated hearings.

In a word, the Paganini Violin Piano is a thoroughly dignified, refined musical instrument of the highest grade, suitable for the finest metropolitan hotels and cafes. It will not only make good under the most exacting conditions, but it is no exaggeration to say that it will *carry the most critical audience by storm.*

**Paganini orchestrion; Philipps Style 6.**

**Paganini orchestrion; Philipps Style 8.**

**Paganini orchestrion: Philipps Style 9. 12'6" high; 10'8" wide; 5'10" deep. 3630 pounds. In white case with gold trimmings. A work of art!**

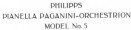

PHILIPPS
PIANELLA PAGANINI-ORCHESTRION
MODEL No. 5

WITH REVOLVING MECHANISM

Very elegant, dark-brown, oak case with inlaid panels of a lighter colour on each side. Facetted mirror in centre panel with a cornucopia of artificial flowers, and to the right and left flowers in bronze relief. The numerous carvings and beautiful columns supporting the top are also worthy of mention. The specification and musical equipment is the same as model No. 6, securing a perfect musical representation.

| | |
|---|---|
| Height | 11 ft. — in. |
| Breadth | 7 „ 6 „ |
| Depth | 4 „ — „ |
| Net weight | 1848 lbs. |

Music-rolls bear the mark P. P.
Selections according to our Paganini Lists.

We are confident of our Paganini Violin Orchestrions obtaining unbounded admiration.

PHILIPPS
PIANELLA PAGANINI-ORCHESTRION
MODEL No. 6

WITH REVOLVING MECHANISM

The most fastidious taste in respect to appearance as well as musical capabilities is catered for in the construction of this model. Elegant mahogany case fitted with columns, the intervening panels being decorated with real bronzes in the empire style. Mirrored panels run parallel with the side columns, a valuable tapestry occupying the centre. The specification is arranged for select chamber-music consisting of a first-class piano, harmonium, violins with flageolet tones, flutes, clarionets and percussion instruments: the equipment therefore gives a most effective and natural representation of a full symphony-orchestra.

| | |
|---|---|
| Height | 11 ft. 2 in. |
| Breadth | 7 „ 8 „ |
| Depth | 4 „ — „ |
| Net weight | 1804 lbs. |

**Wurlitzer Organette or Style W Orchestra: This piano / pipe organ combination found use in theatres and mortuaries where it played background music.**

WURLITZER ORGANETTE
(STYLE W ORCHESTRA)

(quantities shipped each year)

| | |
|---|---|
| 1924 | 4 |
| 1925 | 8 |
| 1926 | 103 |
| 1927 | 109 |
| 1928 | 23 |
| 1930 | 2 |
| Total*= | 249 |

Notes: Introduced as the "Style W Orchestra" – later changed to the "Organette." Nearly all were in walnut wood. In addition to the above figures and totals there were 2 "Style Z Organettes" shipped in 1927 and 16 in 1928; 1 "Style L Organette" shipped in 1928 (the serial was No.106,186 – if a reader has it now, let us know how it differs!); 2 "Style YW Organettes" (these presumably used regular 88-note home player rolls as Wurlitzer added a "Y" to signify this in the nomenclature for various styles) shipped in 1927; and Wurlitzer "Mortuary Organettes" shipped as follows: 1928 (12), 1929 (7), 1930 (1), 1931 (1), and 1933 (1). These additional styles numbering 43 instruments altogether raise the overall Organette total from 249 to 292 instruments.

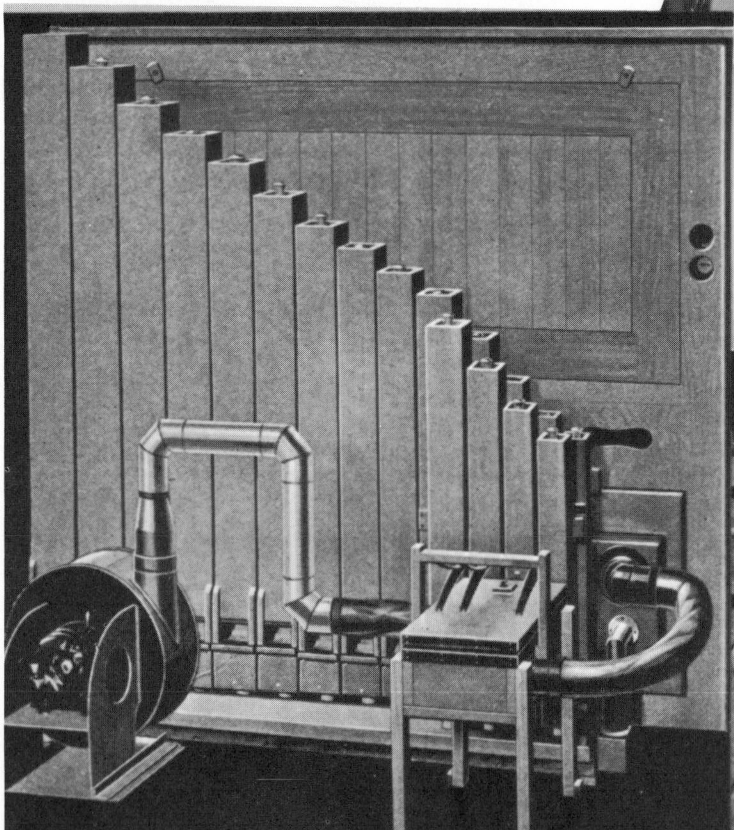

**Above: Rear view of the Organette showing the bass pipes and, in front of them, the swell shutters for the enclosed quintadena and flute pipe section. A Spencer "Orgoblo" provided wind pressure.**

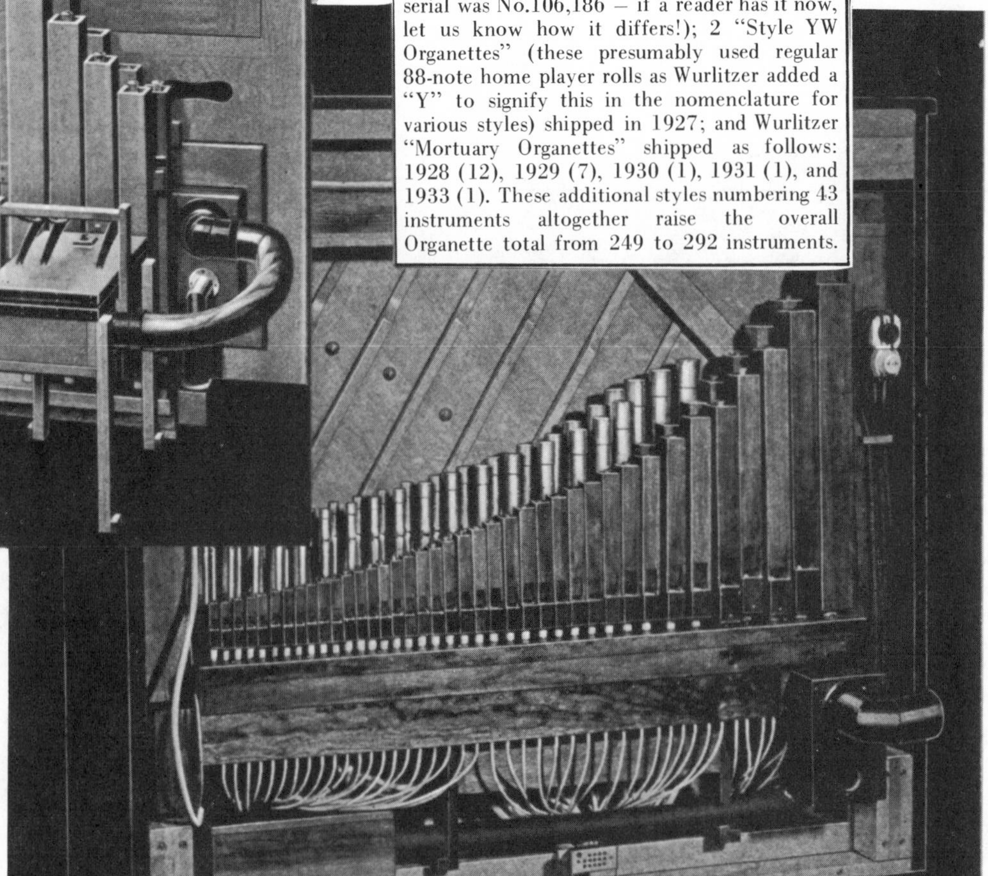

**Right: Interior view of the quintadena and flute pipe section. Located just behind the piano sounding board these ranks were covered with a set of louvered shutters for expression control.**

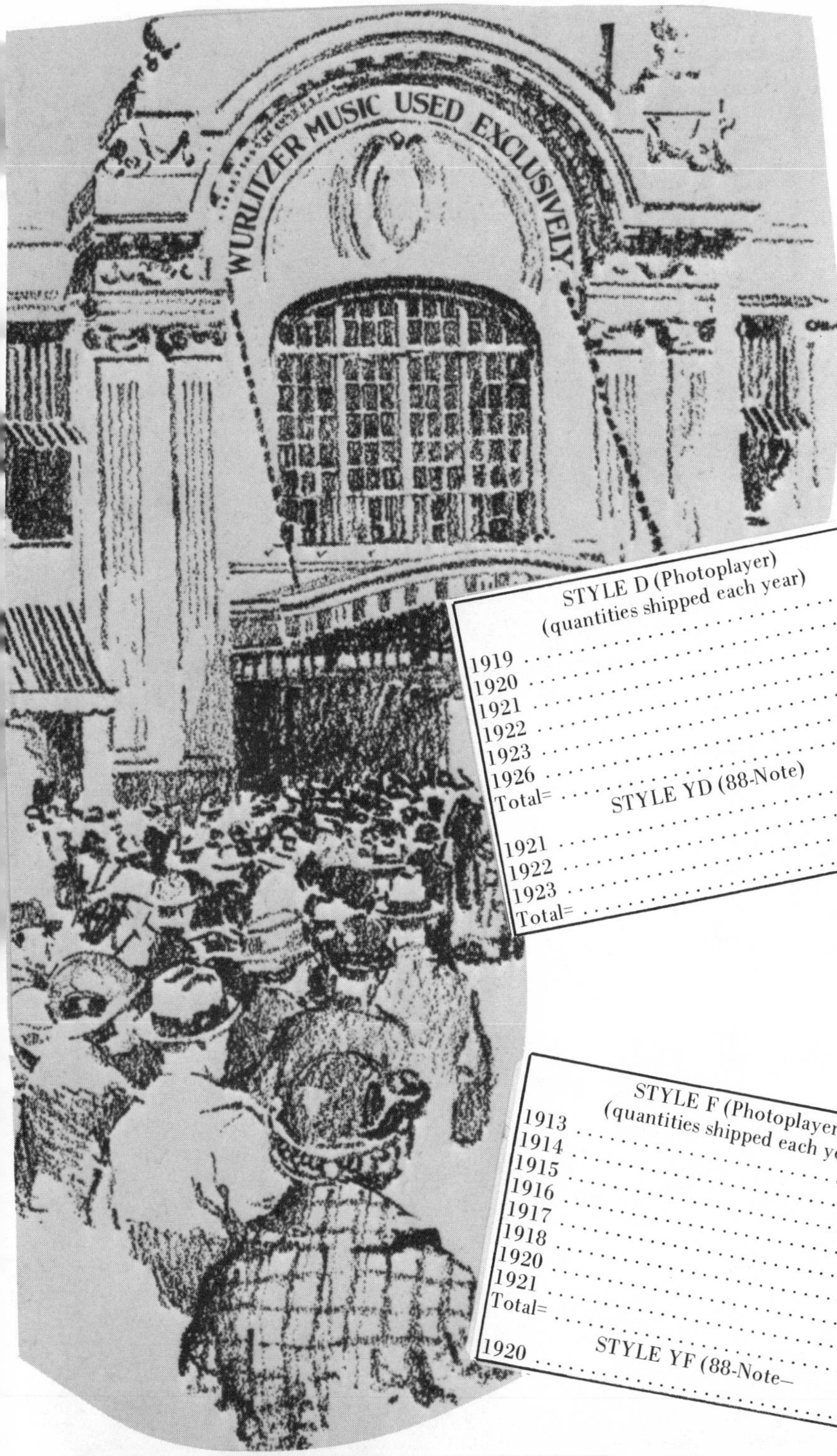


# WURLITZER

MUSIC - *for* THEATRES

## One-Man Orchestras :: *for* Theatres *of* :: Seating Capacities *of* 250 to 750 or more

STYLE D (Photoplayer)
(quantities shipped each year)

| | |
|---|---|
| 1919 | 13 |
| 1920 | 17 |
| 1921 | 10 |
| 1922 | 5 |
| 1923 | 10 |
| 1926 | 1 |
| Total= | 56 |

STYLE YD (88-Note)

| | |
|---|---|
| 1921 | 2 |
| 1922 | 1 |
| 1923 | 1 |
| Total= | 4 |

Style D Duplex: The smallest Wurlitzer theatre photoplayer, the Style D Duplex Orchestra was advertised as being suitable "for a theatre of 150 seats. . . This is the ideal instrument for a very small house where drums might be too loud." Instrumentation consists of a piano and two ranks of pipes: violin and flute. The duplex roll mechanism uses two long playing Automatic Player Piano rolls. The Style YD is the same as the Style D except that it uses two regular 88-note home player piano rolls instead of the Automatic Player Piano rolls. Only 56 of the Style D and 4 of the YD were made. During the formative years of the theatre business there was lots of money available, and it's our guess that the Wurlitzer salesman tried to interest the prospective purchaser in a more expensive model.

STYLE F (Photoplayer)
(quantities shipped each year)

| | |
|---|---|
| 1913 | 54 |
| 1914 | 30 |
| 1915 | 26 |
| 1916 | 14 |
| 1917 | 13 |
| 1918 | 10 |
| 1920 | 3 |
| 1921 | 2 |
| Total= | 156 |

STYLE YF (88-Note–

| | |
|---|---|
| 1920 | 1 |

Style F: Above are two case designs of the Style F photoplayer. The one on the right is embellished with art glass panels. The side cabinet contains: bass drum, snare drum, triangle, cymbal, and effects for horse trot, tambourine, tom-tom, fire gong, and telephone bell. A circa 1915 catalogue offered the Style F for $950.00.

The Canyon Inn near Hayward, California, was a good Wurlitzer customer. It had two instruments, a CX orchestrion and a Style F photoplayer. The above photograph was taken about 1916 and shows the photoplayer ensconced in a corner of the dining room. The Wurlitzer Company sold most of its photoplayers (which it called "One Man Orchestras") for use in theatres. However, extant photographs and advertisements show that quite a few were used in cabarets, night clubs, restaurants, and similar locales where the instrument was usually operated by a pianist or organist — much in the way an electronic organ is used for nightclub entertainment today.

Sometimes for restaurant use the photoplayer would be displayed on a balcony and operated by remote control by coin boxes or, during slow periods, by the owner who could start it by pushing a button.

Today collectors consider photoplayers of all kinds to be very desirable. They are an ideal party instrument — and everyone can have fun pushing pedals and buttons!

Measurements of the piano part of the Style F are: 4'10" high by 5'2" wide by 2'9" deep. The Drum cabinet is 3'1" high by 2'9" wide by 2'10" deep. The total shipping weight is 1250 pounds.

Roll mechanism of a Style F photoplayer (Tom Sprague Collection).

**Style G: Contains piano, mandolin, violin pipes, flute pipes, drums, and sound effects. Overall width is 9'8" including piano and side chest. Height is 4'10" and depth is 2'9". Weight: 1600 pounds. Uses the Wurlitzer Automatic Player Piano roll.**

| STYLE G (Photoplayer) (quantities shipped each year) | |
|---|---|
| 1913 | 172 |
| 1913 GX* | 4 |
| 1914 | 220 |
| 1914 GX | 2 |
| 1915 | 119 |
| 1915 G-L Duplex | 1 |
| 1916 | 18 |
| 1916 G-L Duplex | 1 |
| 1917 | 24 |
| 1918 | 21 |
| 1919 | 42 |
| 1920 | 47 |
| 1921 | 17 |
| 1922 | 8 |
| 1923 | 6 |
| 1924 | 3 |
| 1925 | 1 |
| 1926 | 2 |
| Total= | 708 |

Notes: Style GX was equipped with the automatic roll changer and was probably intended for restaurant or cabaret use rather than theatre use. It is not known how the 1915 and 1916 G-L Duplex models differ from the regular G models if indeed they do.

WURLITZER

—NET PRICE LIST—

of

Wurlitzer Motion Picture Theatre Orchestras

EFFECTIVE MARCH 1, 1920

This List Cancels all former Price List.

| Style | Price |
|---|---|
| "D" Duplex Roll......... | $ 1750.00 |
| "G" Duplex Roll .... | 2100.00 |
| "O" Duplex Roll ..... | 2500.00 |
| "U" Duplex Roll ..... | 4000.00 |
| "K" Duplex Roll ..... | 5850.00 |

F. O. B. Factory

WURLITZER

The following are the prices for the

| Style | Price |
|---|---|
| Y O ............... | $ 2700.00 |
| Y U ............... | 4000.00 |
| Y K ............... | 5850.00 |

Equipped with the 88 Note Duplex Roll System.

F. O. B. Factory

*The Rudolph Wurlitzer Co.*

New York Cincinnati Chicago

| STYLE O (Photoplayer) | |
|---|---|
| 1915 | 82 |
| 1916 | 78 |
| 1916 Style O-L* | 1 |
| 1917 | 36 |
| 1918 | 34 |
| 1919 | 49 |
| 1920 | 91 |
| 1921 | 52 |
| 1922 | 19 |
| 1923 | 15 |
| 1924 | 7 |
| 1925 | 7 |
| 1926 | 2 |
| 1927 | 1 |
| Total= | 474 |

| STYLE YO (88-Note) | |
|---|---|
| 1915 | 5 |
| 1916 | 32 |
| 1917 | 15 |
| 1918 | 16 |
| 1919 | 14 |
| 1920 | 10 |
| 1922 | 1 |
| 1923 | 6 |
| 1924 | 1 |
| Total= | 100 |

Notes: Description of Style O-L not available. Most YO photoplayers shipped to San Francisco.

**Style O: More Style O Wurlitzers survive today than do any other single Wurlitzer theatre model. Instrumentation includes: piano, mandolin, violin and flute pipes (including bass pipes), plus drums and effects for castanets, horse trot, tom-tom, fire gong, door bell, kettle drum, and bird whistle. Made in several different cabinet styles which differ mainly by the ornamental latticework on the side chests.**

Style YO: Most models of Wurlitzer photoplayers were available with 88-note home player piano roll mechanisms. Such instruments bore the prefix "Y". The above Style YO uses the 88-note roll and has the same instrumentation as the Style O photoplayer. The Standard Pneumatic Action Company built the roll mechanism part of the various Y models.

An early model of the Style O.

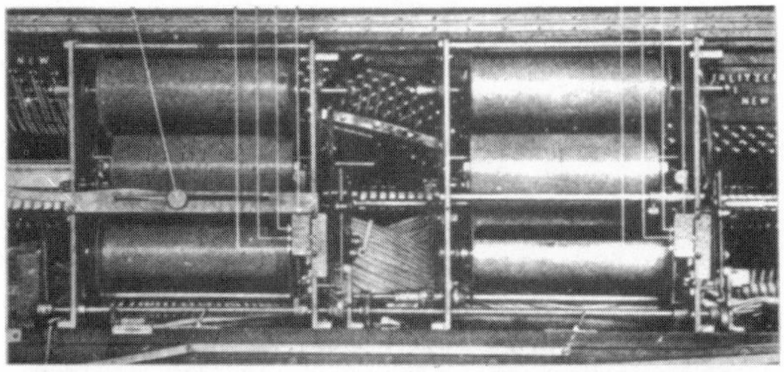

View of the duplex roll mechanism of a Wurlitzer Style O photoplayer. With march music on one roll and slow or sentimental music on the other the photoplayer operator could accompany most action on the silver screen.

This Style O photoplayer has particularly ornate curlicues as decorations on the front of the side cabinets. Swell shutters on each cabinet permit volume variations.

MISCELLANEOUS PHOTOPLAYERS

Several one-of-a-kind notations appear in the factory records: Style YN (one made in 1918); Style Z (one made in 1916); Style YC (one made in 1920); Style Y Duplex (listed in 1923 – probably should have read "YO" or some other designation as Y was just the prefix); Style N (two made in 1915). In addition several foot-pumped home player pianos equipped with duplex 88-note mechanisms were made over the years. These were called "Duplex 88-Note Pianos" and were sold to theatres.

| STYLE V (Photoplayer) | |
|---|---|
| 1916 | 8 |
| 1922 | 8 |
| 1923 | 31 |
| 1924 | 1 |
| Total= | 48 |

Left: The Style V photoplayer (not illustrated) was made only in limited quantities.

The right side chest of a Style YO photoplayer. The ranks of violin and flute pipes are in several rows.

Left side chest and center piano unit of a Style YO photoplayer. This was found in a Chino, California, theatre where it had resided since 1920.

| STYLE R (Photoplayer) | |
|---|---|
| 1913 | 2 |
| 1914 | 54 |
| 1915 | 8 |
| Total= | 64 |

Style R: The massive-appearing single side chest of the Style R is crammed with organ pipes and various percussion effects. This impressive instrument uses the Concert PianOrchestra roll. These rolls were originally used on the large Concert PianOrchestra orchestrions. Their extensive instrumentation and register controls made them ideal for large photoplayers as well. The hundreds of photoplayers that used Concert PianOrchestra rolls made an active market for this type of roll in the 1920's, by which time the earlier orchestrions were passing from the scene. Most late Concert PianOrchestra rolls are thusly of the "mood music" type.

| STYLE U (Photoplayer) (quantities shipped each year) | |
|---|---|
| 1915 | 64 |
| 1916 | 19 |
| 1917 | 15 |
| 1918 | 10 |
| 1919 | 23 |
| 1920 | 21 |
| 1921 | 12 |
| 1922 | 3 |
| 1923 | 1 |
| 1924 | 1 |
| 1925 | 1 |
| 1927 | 1 |
| Total= | 171 |
| STYLE YU (88-Note) | |
| 1916 | 1 |
| 1917 | 2 |
| 1918 | 2 |
| 1919 | 8 |
| 1920 | 14 |
| 1921 | 3 |
| 1923 | 3 |
| 1924 | 7 |
| Total= | 40 |

Above: Style U photoplayer; two case design variations. This style was also called "Style CU" and "CU Duplex." These use Concert PianOrchestra rolls and have two full ranks of pipes covering violin, cello (the bass part of the violin rank), flute, and bass (the bass section of the flute pipes), plus a complement of drums and sound effects. The author once owned one of these from a Pennsylvania theatre via Larry Givens and once found another in extreme disrepair under a stage in a Miamisburg, Ohio, movie house.

| WURLITZER STYLE L (Photoplayer) | |
|---|---|
| 1913 | 7 |
| 1914 | 3 |
| 1915 | 3 |
| 1916 | 1 |
| Total= | 14 |

Note: As this instrument has an electropneumatic action it is more properly a theatre organ than a photoplayer; however we list it as it uses the same Concert PianOrchestra rolls as used on the large photoplayer styles H, K, R, and U.

WURLITZER
REG. U.S. PAT. OFF.

Left: The large Style L has an electropneumatic action and is more properly a theatre organ than a photoplayer. However, as it uses Concert PianOrchestra rolls we include it in this section. The sale price was $7500.00 in 1915. The large side cabinet is 11' high by 10' wide by 5' deep! The shipping weight of both units is 9000 pounds.

## Wurlitzer Pipe Organ-Orchestra Styles H and K

PRICE, STYLE H Single Roll System, $3,500 — PRICE, STYLE K — Single Roll System, $4,500
PRICE, STYLE H Duplex Roll System, $3,850 — PRICE, STYLE K — Duplex Roll System, $4,850

Styles H and K: The catalogue noted: "This style can be played by a pianist or with the paper music roll. It was the first instrument put on the market that fully met the requirements of the motion picture theatre. . . The effects are simply marvelous and the instrument must be heard to be fully appreciated." Uses Concert PianOrchestra rolls. 5'2" high, 15'4" wide, 3'3" deep.

# PIPE ORGAN ORCHESTRA STYLE "K"

## SUITABLE FOR HOUSE WITH SEATING CAPACITY FROM 500 TO 700

**Above: Styles H and K. This beautiful photoplayer has a wealth of interesting instruments inside! The factory specifications are: piano, violin pipes, cornet pipes, oboe pipes, cello pipes, doppelflutes treble and bass, bass drum, snare drum, kettle drum or tympani effect, cymbal, orchestra bells, triangle, cow bell, tambourine, steamboat whistle, horse trot, auto horn, cathedral chimes, and door bell. The preceding are in the Style H. The Style K has the same instrumentation plus a set of vox humana pipes and a xylophone. $1000.00 extra was charged for the K. About 1915 the H sold for $3500 and the K, $4500.00. The next year the prices were $3850 and $4850 respectively.**

**Wurlitzer photoplayers which use Concert PianOrchestra rolls are exceedingly rare today. Probably most of them were later replaced by Wurlitzer theatre organs as the movie house owners realized the fantastic effect that music had on enjoyment of the film and, more important, attendance figures.**

**Of the Style K a 1924 catalogue noted: "The orchestral quality is particularly adapted for photoplays and not only gives realism to the picture, but it enhances the beauty as well for it interprets the proper spirit and action. The magnitude of organ tones is marvelous, and in variety and beauty of tone color it excels any pit instrument ever produced. The player can reveal the same sensitive feeling of an artist playing upon a violin, or he can cause the instrument to burst forth into the most thunderous storm effects."**

| STYLE K (Photoplayer) (quantities shipped each year) | |
|---|---|
| 1913 | 42 |
| 1914 | 67 |
| 1915 | 43 |
| 1916 | 40 |
| 1916 Style K-L* | 2 |
| 1917 | 12 |
| 1918 | 14 |
| 1919 | 32 |
| 1920 | 21 |
| 1921 | 10 |
| 1922 | 5 |
| 1923 | 2 |
| 1924 | 4 |
| 1927 | 1 |
| Total= | 295 |

| STYLE YK (88-Note) | |
|---|---|
| 1915 | 1 |
| 1916 | 2 |
| 1917 | 1 |
| 1918 | 3 |
| 1919 | 6 |
| 1920 | 11 |
| 1921 | 2 |
| 1923 | 3 |
| 1924 | 1 |
| Total= | 30 |

Notes: Specific description of "Style K-L" of 1916 and how (or if) it differed from the regular Style K is unknown. Style K bearing serial number 25350 was built in 1916 and not shipped from the Wurlitzer factory in North Tonawanda until 1927! Perhaps it was used for testing rolls. Most of the "Y" (with 88-note duplex roll mechanisms) of all kinds such as YD, YF, YK, YO, etc. were originally shipped to San Francisco. We presume that as this city was the main selling center for American Photoplayer Co. "Fotoplayer" instruments (which used 88-note rolls also) this created a demand for instruments using this roll type – and Wurlitzer distributors in the San Francisco area kept competitive by offering Y-series Wurlitzer photoplayers.

**Styles H and K: case design variation with ornamental pipes.**

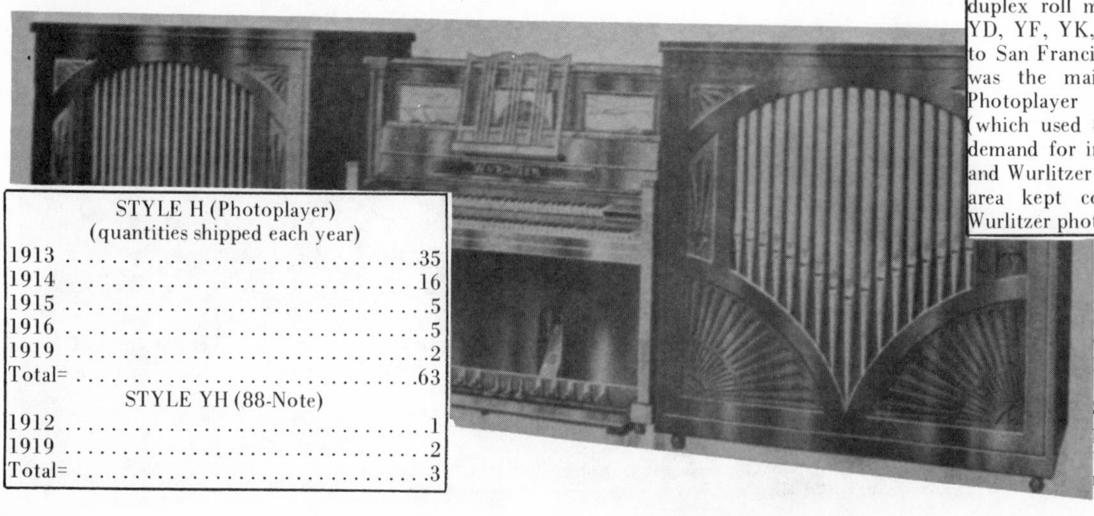

**Styles H and K: case design variation with ornamental pipes on the side chest fronts and art glass in the top of the piano unit.**

| STYLE H (Photoplayer) (quantities shipped each year) | |
|---|---|
| 1913 | 35 |
| 1914 | 16 |
| 1915 | 5 |
| 1916 | 5 |
| 1919 | 2 |
| Total= | 63 |

| STYLE YH (88-Note) | |
|---|---|
| 1912 | 1 |
| 1919 | 2 |
| Total= | 3 |

**So great was the Wurlitzer photoplayer business that at one time in 1916 the factory was six months behind in filling orders!**

## AMERICAN-MADE COIN-OPERATED PIANOS
### —Miscellaneous Manufacturers—

From about 1900 to 1925 many different American piano manufacturers and sellers issued coin-operated pianos. The major makers are listed individually in this book. Some of the others, lesser-known entries in the coin piano field, are listed below.

Most of these instruments consist of an upright piano with mandolin attachment. A few models have an extra instrument, a xylophone or a rank of pipes, added. Most were made to use the standard 10-tune type "A" coin piano roll. The instruments were often made by adding pump and roll systems (such as the "kit" sold by the Monarch Tool and Manufacturing Company of Cincinnati, Ohio) to upright home-style pianos. The addition of a panel of clear glass or art glass, a coin slot, and a few other accessories made a coin-operated "nickelodeon."

Names of Miscellaneous American Coin Pianos:

American; Anderson; Ariston; Armstrong (sold "A" roll instruments; also sold Wurlitzer keyboard coin pianos which used 65-note Wurlitzer Automatic Player Piano Rolls); Auto Electric and Autoelectra ("A" roll pianos and 44-note pianos); Billings; Caille (sold pianos of other makers, including early Automatic Musical Co. [pre-Link] instruments); Carleton (Price & Teeple); Colonial; Concertrola; Cote; Decker Brothers; Eberhardt; Electra; Evans; Haines; Heller; Howard; Ideal; Jewett; William A. Johnson; Kibby; King; Kreiter; Lehr; Monarch; National; Netzow; Originators; Presburg; Price & Teeple (Carleton); Reed; Reichard; Schaeffer; Schleicher & Sons; Schultz; Seltzer (of Pittsburgh; most are Coinola pianos bearing the Seltzer name); Starr; Thayer; Victor Coin; Waltham ("A" roll pianos, including several models with extra instruments such as violin or flute pipe ranks); Watson; Wilson; and others.

The Pianotainer, a cabinet style coin piano sold by the Fox Music Company of Kansas City, Missouri, in the 1920's. Fox sold instruments made for the firm on contract by the North Tonawanda Musical Instrument Works (see that section of this book) and others.

The Pianotainer uses standard 10-tune "A" rolls.

### —Electric Emporium Orchestra—

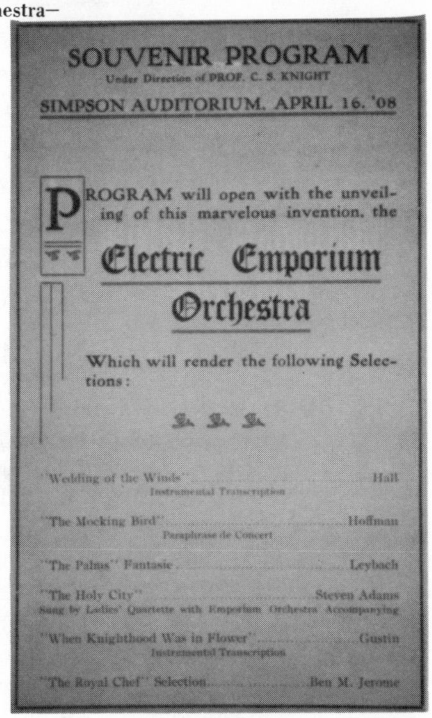

SOUVENIR PROGRAM

Under Direction of PROF. C. S. KNIGHT

SIMPSON AUDITORIUM, APRIL 16, '08

PROGRAM will open with the unveiling of this marvelous invention, the

Electric Emporium Orchestra

Which will render the following Selections:

"Wedding of the Winds" .......... Hall
Instrumental Transcription

"The Mocking Bird" .......... Hoffman
Paraphrase de Concert

"The Palms" Fantasie .......... Leybach

"The Holy City" .......... Steven Adams
Sung by Ladies' Quartette with Emporium Orchestra Accompanying

"When Knighthood Was in Flower" .......... Gustin
Instrumental Transcription

"The Royal Chef" Selection .......... Ben M. Jerome

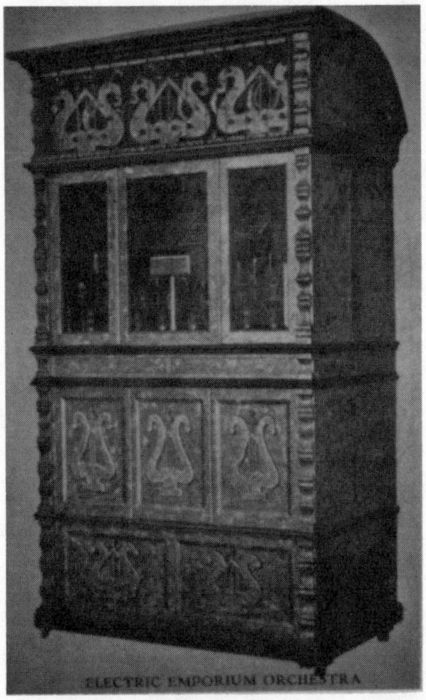


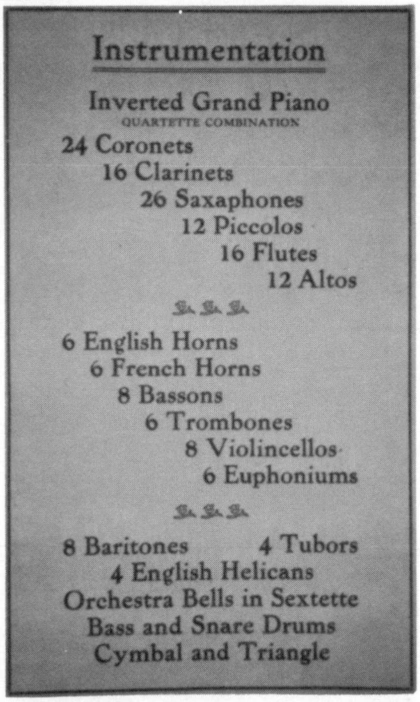

Instrumentation

Inverted Grand Piano
QUARTETTE COMBINATION
24 Coronets
16 Clarinets
26 Saxaphones
12 Piccolos
16 Flutes
12 Altos

6 English Horns
6 French Horns
8 Bassons
6 Trombones
8 Violincellos
6 Euphoniums

8 Baritones 4 Tubors
4 English Helicans
Orchestra Bells in Sextette
Bass and Snare Drums
Cymbal and Triangle

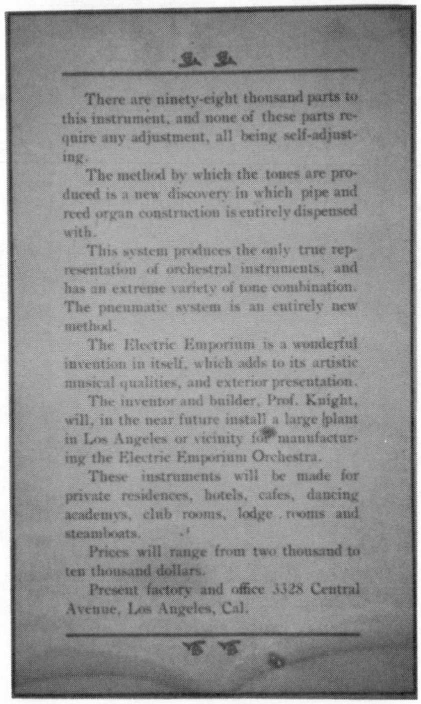

There are ninety-eight thousand parts to this instrument, and none of these parts require any adjustment, all being self-adjusting.

The method by which the tones are produced is a new discovery in which pipe and reed organ construction is entirely dispensed with.

This system produces the only true representation of orchestral instruments, and has an extreme variety of tone combination. The pneumatic system is an entirely new method.

The Electric Emporium is a wonderful invention in itself, which adds to its artistic musical qualities, and exterior presentation.

The inventor and builder, Prof. Knight, will, in the near future install a large plant in Los Angeles or vicinity for manufacturing the Electric Emporium Orchestra.

These instruments will be made for private residences, hotels, cafes, dancing academys, club rooms, lodge rooms and steamboats.

Prices will range from two thousand to ten thousand dollars.

Present factory and office 3328 Central Avenue, Los Angeles, Cal.

The Electric Emporium Orchestra, introduced in 1908 by Prof. C.S. Knight of Los Angeles, California, was billed as "the only true representation of orchestral instruments . . ." Grandiose plans were laid: "The inventor and builder, Prof. Knight, will in the near future install a large plant in Los Angeles or vicinity for manufacturing the Electric Emporium Orchestra. These instruments will be made for private residences, hotels, cafes, dancing academies, club rooms, lodge rooms, and steamboats. Prices will range from two thousand to ten thousand dollars."

Through the courtesy of David Bright and David Robinson, the author has examined the surviving prototype of the Electric Emporium Orchestra. The "Inverted Grand Piano, Quartette Combination" (mentioned in the advertisement at the upper right) is an ordinary upright piano probably made by Schaff in Indiana. The instrument uses regular 65-note home player piano rolls to which registers and controls have been added near the outer edges. The "new discovery in which pipe and reed organ construction is entirely disposed with" consists a series of metal pipe resonators similar to trumpet horns. Beneath each resonator is a sound chamber into which speak several reeds, each with a different tonal quality. As several reeds share the same horn, an economy of sorts is effected. Prof. Knight was evidently unaware of the basic principles of organ pipe construction. The reed cavity is designed so that only a small percentage of the reed sound will actually enter the resonator; the rest is lost in destructive interference.

Although the above Cote advertisement mentions "Coin operated players" the firm made very few such instruments.

Ricca & Son of New York City produced many different instruments under the "Regal" trademark.

The Regal 44-note cabinet piano competed with such products as the Pianova, Electrova, and Pianolin during the first decade of the 20th century. Regal 44-note pianos were mainly sold in the northeastern United States. They used an endless roll, as did their contemporaries.

The "Tammany Non-Pneumatic Player Piano" as shown above was advertised in 1910. The firm also made several varieties of console-style organettes (paper roll operated reed organs of small size) with coin slots for commercial use.

Price & Teeple's Style X is shown above. The instrument uses a regular 10-tune "A" roll. Several varieties of "Carleton" (trademark) instruments were made.

Right: Two varieties of Profit-Sharing Player Pianos. Such instruments, made by Nelson-Wiggen and by the Operators Piano Company, were sold in limited numbers in the late 1920's. Both of these advertisements (which bear remarkably similar text) appeared about 1928.

Dr. David Rockola advised the editor that fifty cabinet-style "A" roll pianos were purchased from the Operators Piano Company. Rock-Ola added the gambling mechanisms and sold the instruments under the "Rock-Ola Profit-Sharing Player Piano" name.

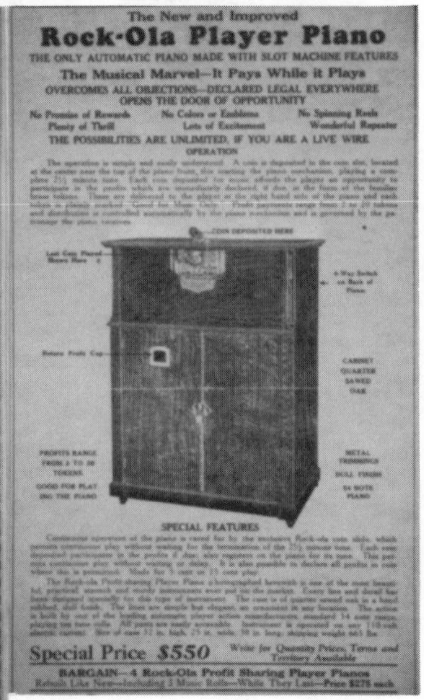

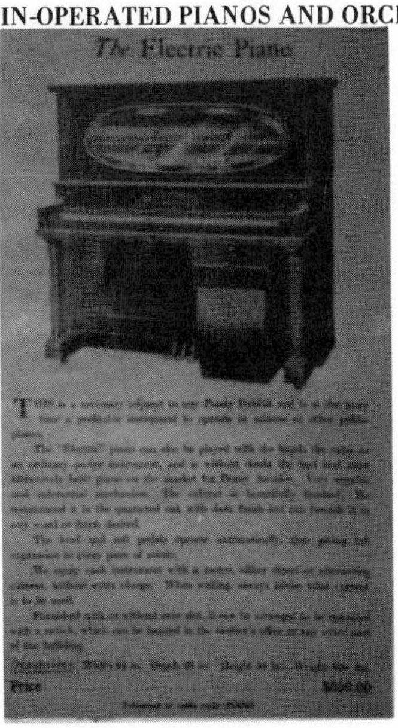


Caille Brothers (Detroit) advertisement for the Caille Electric Piano, an instrument made by the Automatic Musical Company (predecessor of Link) of Binghamton, New York. Caille, a manufacturer of slot machines, offered the piano as "a necessary adjunct to any Penny Exhibit [arcade] and is at the same time a profitable instrument to operate in saloons or other public places."

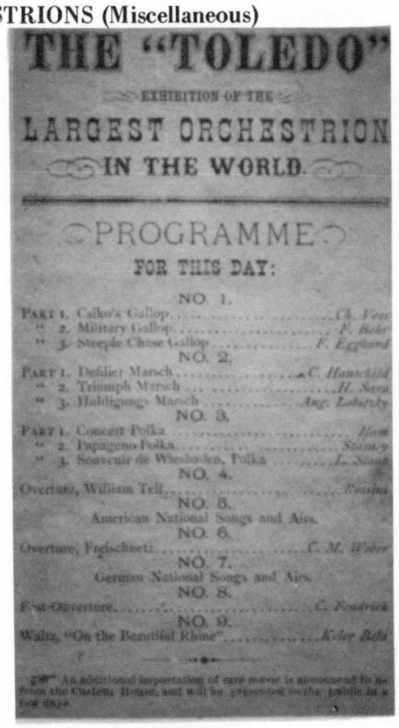

THE "TOLEDO"

EXHIBITION OF THE

LARGEST ORCHESTRION

IN THE WORLD.

PROGRAMME

FOR THIS DAY:

NO. 1.

NO. 2.

NO. 3.

NO. 4.

Overture, William Tell, ...

NO. 5.

American National Songs and Airs.

NO. 6.

NO. 7.

German National Songs and Airs.

NO. 8.

NO. 9.

Waltz, "On the Beautiful Rhine" ...

The "Toledo," an orchestrion made in the Black Forest section of Germany, was billed as the "largest orchestrion in the world" in this announcement of the early 1870's. The instrument, originally built as a caseless model but later furnished with a case made in Chicago, measured 32 feet high! Do any photographs of this mammoth orchestrion exist today?

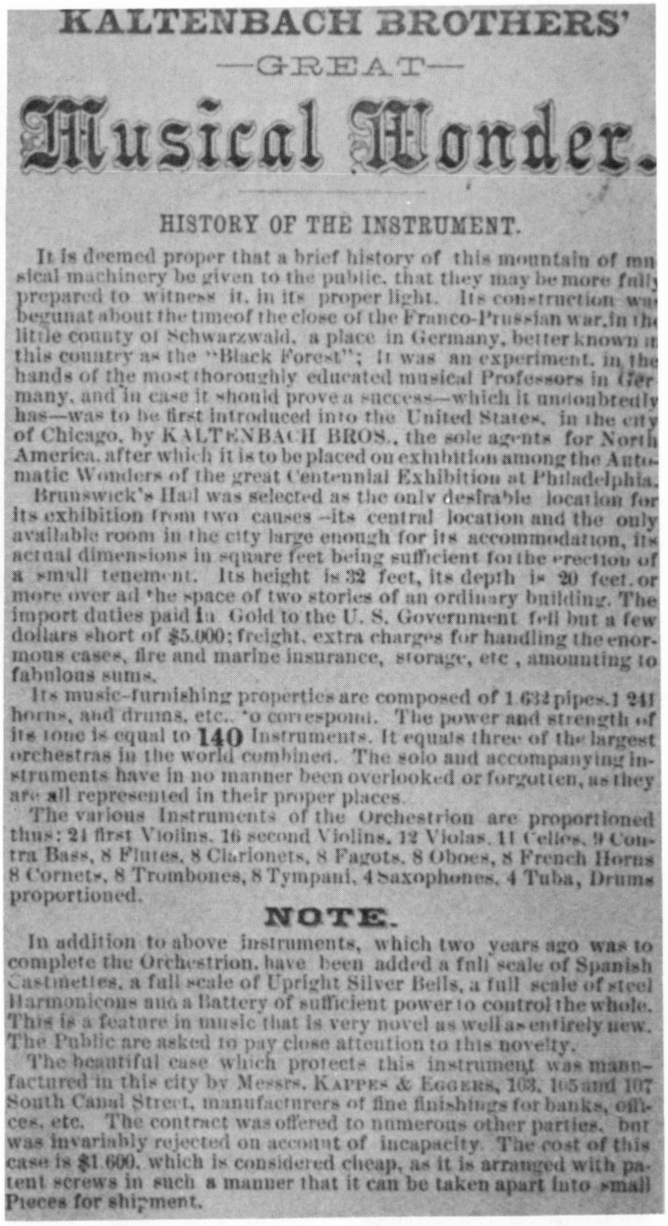

KALTENBACH BROTHERS'

—GREAT—

Musical Wonder.

HISTORY OF THE INSTRUMENT.

It is deemed proper that a brief history of this mountain of musical machinery be given to the public, that they may be more fully prepared to witness it, in its proper light. Its construction was begunat about the timeof the close of the Franco-Prussian war, in the little county of Schwarzwald, a place in Germany, better known in this country as the "Black Forest"; it was an experiment, in the hands of the most thoroughly educated musical Professors in Germany, and in case it should prove a success—which it undoubtedly has—was to be first introduced into the United States, in the city of Chicago, by KALTENBACH BROS., the sole agents for North America, after which it is to be placed on exhibition among the Automatic Wonders of the great Centennial Exhibition at Philadelphia.

Brunswick's Hall was selected as the only desirable location for its exhibition from two causes—its central location and the only available room in the city large enough for its accommodation, its actual dimensions in square feet being sufficient for the erection of a small tenement. Its height is 32 feet, its depth is 20 feet, or more over all the space of two stories of an ordinary building. The import duties paid in Gold to the U. S. Government fell but a few dollars short of $5.000; freight, extra charges for handling the enormous cases, fire and marine insurance, storage, etc., amounting to fabulous sums.

Its music-furnishing properties are composed of 1.632 pipes, 1 241 horns, and drums, etc., to correspond. The power and strength of its tone is equal to **140** Instruments. It equals three of the largest orchestras in the world combined. The solo and accompanying instruments have in no manner been overlooked or forgotten, as they are all represented in their proper places.

The various Instruments of the Orchestrion are proportioned thus: 24 first Violins, 16 second Violins, 12 Violas, 11 Celles, 9 Contra Bass, 8 Flutes, 8 Clarionets, 8 Fagots, 8 Oboes, 8 French Horns 8 Cornets, 8 Trombones, 8 Tympani, 4 Saxophones, 4 Tuba, Drums proportioned.

NOTE.

In addition to above instruments, which two years ago was to complete the Orchestrion, have been added a full scale of Spanish Castinettes, a full scale of Upright Silver Bells, a full scale of steel Harmonicons and a Battery of sufficient power to control the whole. This is a feature in music that is very novel as well as entirely new. The Public are asked to pay close attention to this novelty.

The beautiful case which protects this instrument was manufactured in this city by Messrs. KAPPES & EGGERS, 103, 105 and 107 South Canal Street, manufacturers of fine finishings for banks, offices, etc. The contract was offered to numerous other parties, but was invariably rejected on account of incapacity. The cost of this case is $1.600, which is considered cheap, as it is arranged with patent screws in such a manner that it can be taken apart into small Pieces for shipment.

versammeln sich zur Zeit der
Messe in Leipzig, Petersstr. 41,
I. Etage rechts in der Exposition
der
Ersten Prager Musikwerke- und
Orchestrionfabrik
Diego Fuchs, Prag
Leistungsfähigste Bezugsquelle für
Wiederverkäufer.

The ACKOTIST Piano
(Coin and Plain Electrically Operated.)
AN ABSOLUTELY PERFECT INSTRUMENT.
SOME GOOD TERRITORY STILL OPEN.
AcKotist Player-Piano Co.,
Office and Factory, FALL RIVER, MASS.

A FULL LINE of WINNERS
THE "ACKOLIN" COIN-OPERATED PIANO 65-NOTE ENDLESS ROLL
THE "ELECTROLIN" 44-NOTE COIN-OPERATED PIANO
THE "ACKOTIST" ELECTRIC PIANO
"ACKERMAN" PLAYER PIANO and Perforated Music Rolls
PRICES RIGHT DISCOUNTS LARGE
AcKerman Player Piano Co.
E. D. ACKERMAN, Pres't.
48 West 27th Street - - - New York


Ackerman Player Piano Company, the Pianotist Co. (see another page of this book), and the Ackotist Company were all one and the same.

H. Peters & Co., Leipzig
Unser Messmusterlager befindet sich auch zur Ostervormesse nur Theaterplatz 1, II.
Alleinverkauf: Wiener Continental-Orchestrions
Alleinverkauf: Klingsor-Sprechapparate u. Automaten ohne Trichter
Hapeco: Elektrische Pianos
Kunstspiel-Pianos.
Pneumatische Orchestrions
Petrophon: Sprechapparate und Starkton-Automaten.
Schallplatten: Zonophon, Homokord, Kalliope und Polyphon.
Ganz hervorragende Pianos in billigen und mittleren Preislagen.
Kalliope-, Original-, Polyphon- und Symphonion-Fabrikate.


H. Peters & Co. of Leipzig was one of that city's leading musical instrument distributors during the 1890-1914 period. The 1909 advertisement shown above mentions that electric pianos, orchestrions with xylophone and mandolin, artistic-playing (expression) pianos, music boxes, phonographs, and other musical products are available.

Orchester-Pianos
mit Mandoline u.
Xylophon.
Erstklassiges Fabrikat.
Schübbe & Co.,
Berlin N., Bergstraße 34
Älteste Spezialfabrik für Orchester-Pianos.

W. A. JOHNSON PIANO CO.
PIANOS AND PLAYER-PIANOS
Office and Factory, Champaign, Ill.

The Waltham Piano Company made several different models of coin pianos which used "A" rolls.

**Pyrophon-Musikwerke**
**Ernst Berger, Leipzig 25,** Tauchaerstrasse 9, Nähe Krystallpalast.

Neue Modelle
in
**Elektrisch-pneumatischen Pianos**
**Orchestrion**
mit neuartigen, plastischen Lichteffekten.
**Sprechapparate**
im Ton und Eleganz ohne Konkurrenz.
**Unterhaltungs-Automaten,**
fortwährend zugkräftige Neuheiten.
Liefere sämtliche existierende Automaten.
Ständiges Musterlager. Kataloge gratis.

---

**Orchester-Piano**
Gesetzlich geschützt!
**Der neue Verkaufsschlager für Gastwirte, Kaffees, Tanzdielen usw.**
Ein **einziger** Musiker kann viele Instrumente bedienen! Wesentlich ist der besonders billige Preis! Interessenten werden um den Besuch in **Berlin** gebeten.
**RUDOLPH VIERLING, Pianofabrik,**
Berlin SO 36, Kottbuser Straße 5 Fernsprecher: Moritzplatz 7041

---

**Piano-Orchester**
**„International" mit Walzen**
moderne neue Werke mit herrlicher Musik.
**F. Machinek & Söhne**
Fabrik der Piano-Orchester „International"
**Wien XVII/3,** Ortliebgasse 5.
[3902

---

**Piano-Orchestrionfabrik**
**J. & A. Gössl, Wien VI/2**
Gumpendorferferstrasse 81.
**Walzen-Orchestrions**
mit Gewichtsaufzug, mit Mandoline und Xylophon.

---

*Patent.* [474
*Pneumatisch.*
*Papiernoten.*
**Das Beste und Vollendetste**
Apollo-Violinflöten-Piano-Orchestrions. Apollo-Violinflöten-Orchestrions.
Apollo-Piano-Orchester.
**Apollo-Musikwerke** Max Espenhain & Co.,
Leipzig-Gohlis,
Dorotheenstrasse 27.
Contor und Musterzimmer in Leipzig, Nicolaistr. 2, II.

---

**Sprechmaschinen**
eigener Fabrikation.
Staunend billige Preise.
Verlangen Sie unbedingt erst meinen Katalog, ehe Sie anderweit bestellen.
**Probesendung bereitwilligst.**
**Schallplatten-**
Großvertrieb, daher billigste Händlerpreise.

**Elektr. Pianos und Orchestrions**
neuester Konstruktion, nur erstkl. Fabrikate. Großvertrieb, daher Originalfabrikpreise. Billigst für Händler. Verlangen Sie Kataloge bzw. Spezialofferte. [8314
**„Hermes"-Musikwerke Arno Bauer,** Chemnitz i. Sa.

---

**Grösste Piano-Orchestrion-Fabrik Österreich-Ungarns**
**Gustav Stingl,**
**Wien X,** Randhartingergasse 7.
**Spezial-Erzeugung** von **Piano-Orchestrions** mit Walzen, Gewicht- und Federaufzug. Erstklassige Fabrikate, exakte, künstlerisch arrangierte Musik, reiche Tonfülle. Garantie für solideste Ausführung.
— **Letzte Neuheit:** —
**Piano-Orchestrion mit Mandoline.**
D. R. G. M. Nr. 233033,
österr. Patent Nr. 17103 und 18191.
Mäßige Preise, franko verzollt ab österreichische Grenzstation.
Illustrierte Preisliste gratis und franko. [5318

---

***Robert Günther***
*Berlin C. 17 Lange Str. 65*

*Flügel- u. Piano-Fabrik*
*Kunstspiel-Pianos*
*Elektrische Pianos*

---

**Georg Heinrich & Co.**
**BERLIN NO,**
Elisabethstraße 61. [10155
**Fabrik mechan. und pneumat. Musikwerke.**
**- Piano -**
mit Mandoline, Xylophon und Geigenbegleitung (imit.).

---

Elektrisches Kunstspiel-Piano
**„Chitarrone"**
mit Zitherspiel-Vorrichtung
wird auch als Handspielpiano mit Zithervorrichtung geliefert.

Zitherkonzert-Automat
**„Celestino"**
(ersetzt 4 Zitherspieler).

**Orchestrion „Bellisore" und „Annalies"**
sind hervorragende Neuheiten.
Man verlange Offerte.

Sämtliche Neuheiten sind eigene Modelle und patentamtlich geschützt.

**A. Lüneburg-Musikwerke**
**Altona-Ottensen**
Rothestraße 61.
**Filiale: Hamburg,** Michaelisstraße 10, I.
Gegründet 1888.
Vielfach mit nur ersten Preisen prämiiert.
Fabrikation. Engros. Export.

Musterausstellung zur Leipziger Messe:
**Hotel „Fürstenhof"**
**Leipzig,** Löhrsplatz 4. [7330
Ferner werde ich zur Messe verschiedene unentbehrliche Neuheiten für Automatenhändler ausstellen.

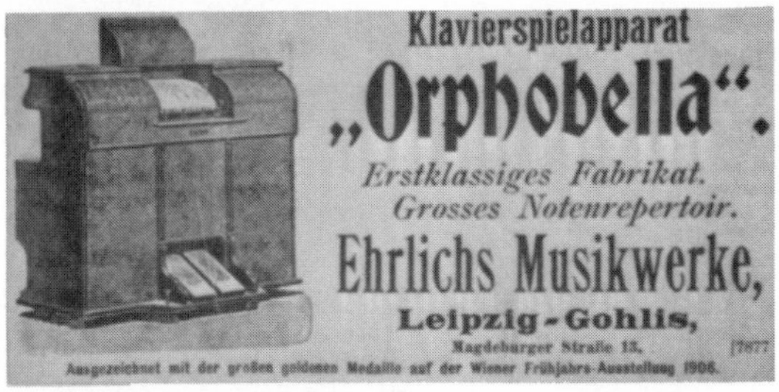


Ehrlichs Musikwerke (full name: Ehrlichs Musikwerke Emil Ehrlich) advertised in 1904 that it manufactured "a line of piano-players (one of which, the Orphobella, is shown above), orchestrions, hand-cranked organs, and disc-type music boxes." Instruments were usually marked "Ehrlich."

Instruments made by the Berliner Orchestrionfabrik Franz Hanke & Co., circa 1906-1908. The Philharmonia model is shown at the left. Other trade names used included Roland, Berolina, and Victoria. The firm's factory was located at Chausseestrasse 88, Berlin N. 39.

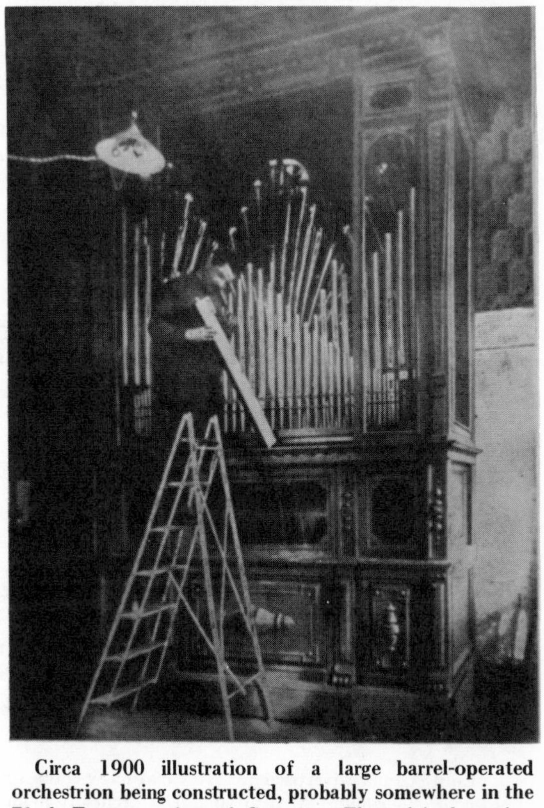

Circa 1900 illustration of a large barrel-operated orchestrion being constructed, probably somewhere in the Black Forest section of Germany. The original caption read: "Large orchestrion of the old-style construction. All flute, violin, trumpet, and trombone voices are produced by metal pipes." (Illustration furnished by Carl Jung)

**Cocchi, Bacigalupo & Graffigna**

The Soleil ("Sun") series of orchestrions produced by Cocchi, Bacigalupo & Graffigna included Soleil I (piano, bells, violin pipes, drum and trap effects), Soleil II (piano, violin and viola pipes, bells, drum and trap effects [clarinets or trumpets available at extra cost]), and Soleil III (illustrated above) which contains: piano; violin, viola, cello, contrabass, clarinet, flute, and piccolo pipes; bells, drums, and other percussion effects. 2.4 meters high by 2.3 meters wide by 1.05 meters deep. Sold for 7200 Marks in 1904. Soleil orchestrions used perforated paper rolls. The Pianophon, a push-up piano player, was also marketed by the firm in the early 1900's. The principal products, however, were portable hand-cranked barrel organs.

Emil Asmus advertised in 1904 that he was the successor to Cocchi, Bacigalupo & Graffigna. The orchestrion illustrated is one of the Soleil series.

—Sirene Orchestrion—

Sold in 1904 by the J.M. Bon Co. of Leipzig, Germany, the Sirene was offered as an "Electropneumatic concert and dance orchestrion." Paper roll operated, the instrument contained a 42-note piano section and a 22-note section for violin, viola, cello, and flute. Additional effects included a glockenspiel, drums, and percussion effects. Sold for 2400 marks in 1904.

**KUHL & KLATT**

In the 1900-1910 years the firm of Kuhl & Klatt of Berlin offered a series of electric pianos, most of which were sold under the "Pneuma" trademark, similar to contemporary instruments sold by Dienst, Hupfeld, and others. The original Kuhl & Klatt pneumatic systems were made under Hupfeld patents; later the firm developed its own systems.

During the 1920's many Kuhl & Klatt instruments were imported into Belgium and were converted to jazzband orchestrions. These were sold under the "K.K. Accordeon" name by Eugene DeRoy and others. Three different K.K. Accordeons are shown on this page. During the same era a number of Kuhl & Klatt accordion reed instruments (reeds only; no piano) were also made.

PUMP and REWIND
THE MONARCH TOOL & Mfg' CO., Cincinnati, Ohio


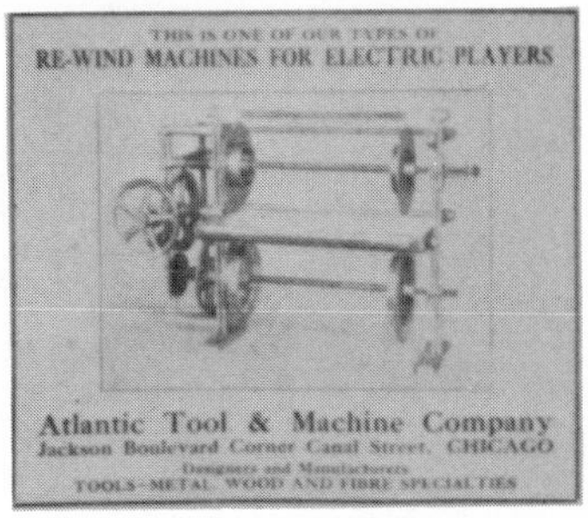

—Accessories for Automatic Instruments—

Few coin piano and orchestrion builders constructed their own parts. Usually such components as pipes, roll mechanisms, drum and trap effects, and other hardware, not to overlook the pianos themselves, were purchased from suppliers. The function of the coin piano maker was to assemble these parts and (usually) build the pneumatic actions and controls.

The Monarch Tool & Mfg. Co. of Cincinnati, Ohio, was a leading supplier to American builders. The firm made tracker bars, pumps, roll frames, etc. for a wide variety of firms including at one time or another Seeburg, Wurlitzer, Operators Piano Company, and dozens of other companies. Many different piano makers made a modest entry into the coin piano field by adding Monarch mechanisms to regular home pianos. The editor visited Monarch in 1966 and talked with Mr. M.A. Hall, the son of the founder and the present owner of the firm. In addition to making piano components Monarch made wall boxes for Seeburg, Welte, Wurlitzer, Mills, Cremona, and others. Monarch moved from Cincinnati to Covington, Ky., in 1928 and has operated in Covington ever since.

The Atlantic Tool & Machine Co. supplied roll mechanisms to Seeburg and certain other Chicago makers. The firms of J.C. Deagan and the Kohler-Liebich Co. supplied perhaps 90% of the orchestrion xylophone and bell units used by Chicago manufacturers during the 'teens and 1920's. Two firms, the Kinetic Engineering Co. and the Spencer Turbine Co. (ad not shown), supplied nearly all of the blowers made for photoplayers made by Wurlitzer, American Photo Player Co., and others. Wilson supplied drums and traps to Seeburg, Mills, and others. Gottfried made pipes for Operators Piano Co. and other Chicago firms.

In Germany many different firms supplied roll mechanisms, organ pipes, case ornaments, and other accessories to coin piano and orchestrion builders. The advertisements of two of these firms, Ernst Gehlhar and Jac. Wiedel, are shown on this page.

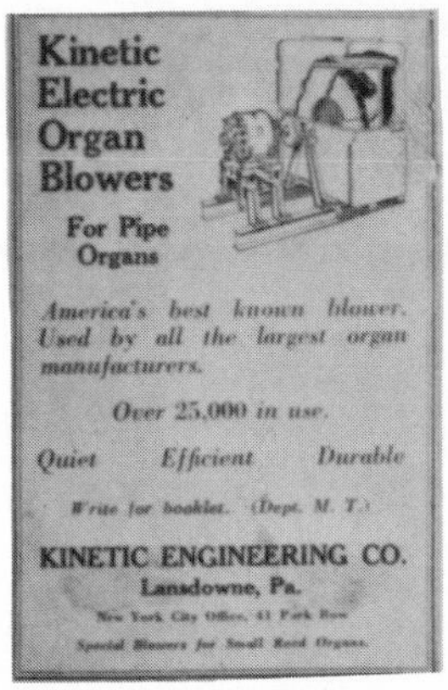

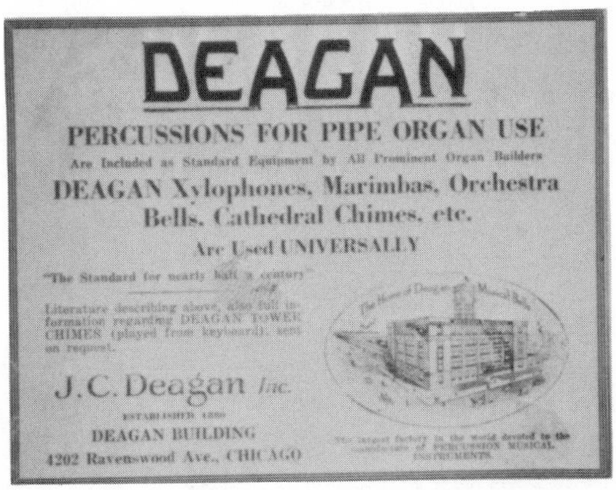


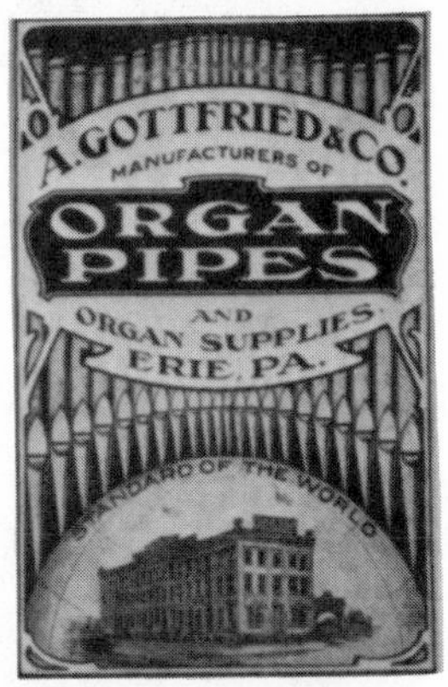

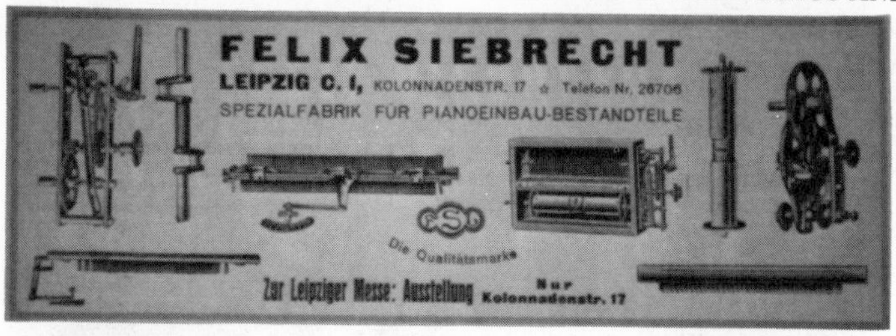

## Suppliers of Components

Shown on this page are advertisements (from the 1900-1915 period) of some of the many firms which supplied components to makers of music boxes, electric pianos, orchestrions, and other automatic instruments:

Felix Siebrecht (hardware including tracker bars, roll frames and transmissions, crankshafts, drive gears, etc.), Alfred Lamy (music box springs, gear trains and barrel-shifting mechanisms for orchestrions, etc. — a prime supplier to Black Forest manufacturers), Vincenz and Ferdinand Demetz (artistic figures and electric lighting effects for orchestrions and organs), W. Adolf Beck (music roll paper), Heinrich Marx (electric lamps for pianos and orchestrions), Gustav Schönstein (wallboxes, organ pipes [his main business], and related components for orchestrions, etc.), Leistner & Co. (piano wire, machines and tools for the piano industry), Carl Haberstroh (leather), R. Moog (artistic statues for orchestrions), Union (bells), Schramberger Uhrfedernfabrik (metal springs for clocks, music boxes, phonographs, etc.), and J. Koepfer & Söhne (spring motors, gear trains, governor assemblies, etc. for mechanical instruments — a main supplier to Black Forest orchestrion builders).

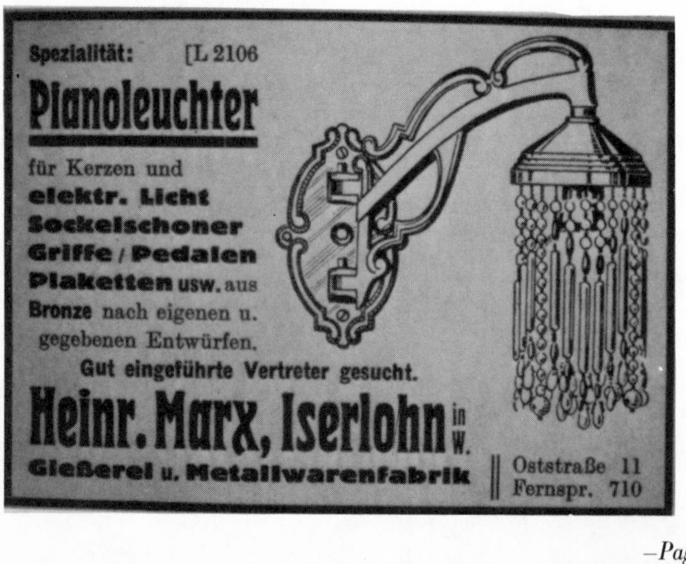

## WALLBOXES
### —for Coin Pianos and Orchestrions—

Wallboxes were a profitable investment for the instrument owner. They made it easier for patrons to play the coin piano or orchestrion. Typically, such boxes were placed at tables or along the wall of the dance floor. A coin dropped in the wallbox made contact with a switch. This in turn operated a solenoid in the instrument. In America the leading maker of these was the Monarch Tool & Mfg. Co. Monarch made the crank-type wallboxes shown here as well as the others used by Seeburg, Wurlitzer, Marquette, and Mills. Most wallboxes originally sold for about $7.50 to $15.00. In Europe most wallboxes were made of wood and had an advertisement or program card on the front.

**The Monarch Tool & Mfg. Co.**

MANUFACTURERS OF

"MONARCH" DISTANCE WALL BOXES FOR NICKELS, DIMES AND QUARTERS. PIANO PLAYER HARDWARE. REWIND MACHINES FOR ELECTRIC PIANOS. MAGAZINE SLOT BOXES. COIN SLIDES. COIN CHUTES. BENT BRASS TUBES AND SOLDERED ELBOWS. T'S ANDY'S METAL SPECIALTIES OF EVERY DESCRIPTION

120-22-24 OPERA PLACE CINCINNATI, OHIO

Seeburg: (1) Early crank-type. (2) Type in the form of a Seeburg coin piano, with front legs. (3) Later piano-type with solid lower front.

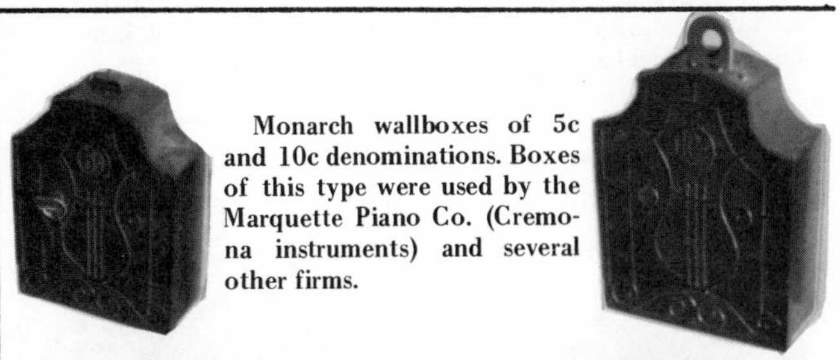

Monarch wallboxes of 5c and 10c denominations. Boxes of this type were used by the Marquette Piano Co. (Cremona instruments) and several other firms.

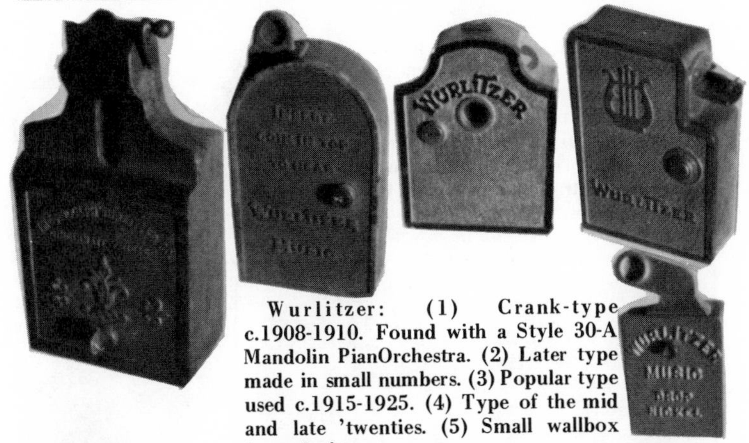


Wurlitzer: (1) Crank-type c.1908-1910. Found with a Style 30-A Mandolin PianOrchestra. (2) Later type made in small numbers. (3) Popular type used c.1915-1925. (4) Type of the mid and late 'twenties. (5) Small wallbox from the 'teens.

Wallbox sold by Operators Piano Co. in the 'teens. Used with Coinola pianos.

Mills wallbox for the Violano-Virtuoso.

Hoeffler Mfg. Co., an active agent for Seeburg, Wurlitzer, and others.

Small wallboxes used by Leathurby and Bacigalupi, two of San Francisco's most active firms in the coin piano and orchestrion field.

Link wallbox with space for program card. Made to Link's order by a Binghamton, N.Y., foundry.

Wallboxes for "The 20th Century" (left) and "The Daisy Piano Player." The Daisy, patented Sept. 21, 1909, by J.B. Obermeier of Milwaukee, was a piano-playing device which could be attached to any upright piano, according to information contained in the patent.

Lösche wallbox used to operate coin pianos and orchestrions.

Unusual German wallbox: The number of coins to be deposited, from 1 to 5, is indicated by a numeral in the circular hole on the front. A balance-arm device is adjustable. For 1-coin operation the weight is close to the fulcrum; for 5-coin, the maximum distance away. When the requisite coins fill the pan, the balance tips and contact is made.

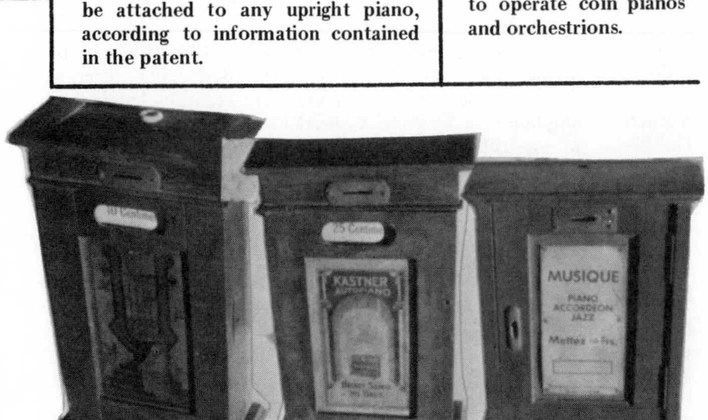


Coin piano and orchestrion wallboxes: (1) Hofmann & Czerny (Continental Musikwerke, Vienna). (2) Kästner Autopiano (with "It brings the sun into your house" inscription). (3) Pierre Eich (Ghent, Belgium).

## TOKENS AND MEDALS
### pertaining to
### Automatic Musical Instruments

From about 1860 to 1935 many tokens and medals pertaining to automatic musical instruments were issued. Most of these were used to pay winnings in slot machines, on the theory that a "Good for 5c in the Piano" token was legal (whereas a regular nickel wouldn't be — for that would be paying out money, which was illegal in many places). Most tokens of this type were issued by distributors and agents, rather than by the slot machine manufacturers themselves. Other tokens were used to advertise an attraction: the great Welte orchestrion owned by the Atlantic Garden, for example. Still others (the Ludwig token shown here is an example) were given out as advertisements by music stores. The tokens shown here pertain specifically to musical instruments. (Illustrated pieces are from the author's collection)

This English-penny-size brass token was undoubtedly used around the turn of the 20th century to operate a large disc-type music box. Issued by the Liverpool (England) Musical Box Depot.

"F.U. Foss Novelty Co., Manufacturers and Operators of Coin Operating Machines, Lynn, Massachusetts" is the inscription on this "Good for One Tune" token of the 1910 era. Note: In the Encore Banjo section of this book we reprint a June 22, 1901, letter from the Auto Manufacturing Co. to F.U. Foss.

Typical tokens issued by agents, taverns, etc. A tavern of the 1900-1920 period would typically contain a slot machine or other amusement device that paid out these "Good for Music Only" or "Good for 5c Drink or in the Piano" tokens, for paying out money would be illegal. But who was to know if the friendly bartender would exchange these tokens for coins!

"Grand Concert Every Night — Admission Free / Atlantic Garden, 50 Bowery, New York, 1863" reads this token. Although they bear the date 1863, these tokens were used for several decades after that time. The Atlantic Garden, owned by William Kramer's Sons, featured a mammoth Welte orchestrion. This vast beer garden (illustrated in the Welte orchestrion section of this book) burned down in 1907.

"Good for 10c Trade — Drop in Orchestrian" beckons the inscription on this 10-cent-size token issued by San Francisco's Cliff House in the 1900-1906 period. This famous seaside resort used many different coin-operated pianos and orchestrions over the years, including two Wurlitzer Tonophones, a Wurlitzer Concert PianOrchestra, and others. The owner in the 1890's, Adolph Sutro (who made his fortune in Nevada's Comstock Lode), had a Welte orchestrion in his palatial home which overlooked the Cliff House.

Two different die varieties of a coin-piano token issued by the National Piano Manufacturing Company. To compare the two, note the height of the F in MFG and the size of the stars on each. The GOOD FOR 1 PIECE OF MUSIC letters are taller and thinner in the right-hand piece.

Token issued for use in the Caille Puck, a slot machine with a Swiss cylinder music box movement. Owners of the Puck were doubly safe from the law: the slot machine was a "musical instrument," not a gambling device, and should a patron happen to win, he would receive tokens instead of money!

This bronze token, issued by Ludwig & Co. and distributed by music stores, mentions the award given at the 1901 Pan-American Exposition (held in Buffalo, N.Y.; this is the event at which President McKinley was assassinated) to "The Claviola Piano Player" and other instruments.

"W.S." was probably a tavern owner. His "Good for One Tune" token features the same design on both sides.

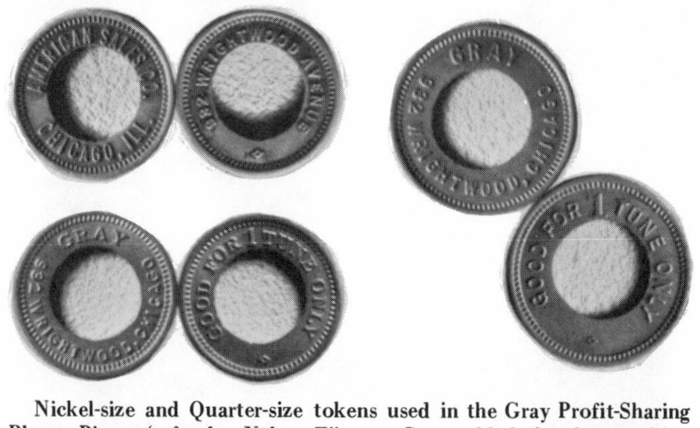

Nickel-size and Quarter-size tokens used in the Gray Profit-Sharing Player Piano (mfg. by Nelson-Wiggen; Gray added the slot machine mechanisms to it) and other gambling devices of the late 1920's.

Dime-size token bearing an inscription on one side only: "Western Automatic Music Co."

"Good for One Tune or 5c in Trade / Write for Catalogue" — a token issued for use in slot machines made by the Watling Manufacturing Company of Chicago.

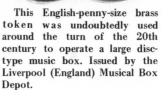

**They Were Proud of Their Instruments . . .**

Years ago, restaurants, hotels, and other locations often gave a musical program to each visitor. This program would list the available tunes on the orchestrion or other instrument. Three typical programs are shown here.

"Programme of the Celebrated ORCHESTRION — Electro-Pneumatic Artistic — SOLEA" proudly proclaims this program issued in the 'twenties by the Cafe Fribourgeois. The instrument, a Weber Solea in a custom-designed case, was installed in 1914.

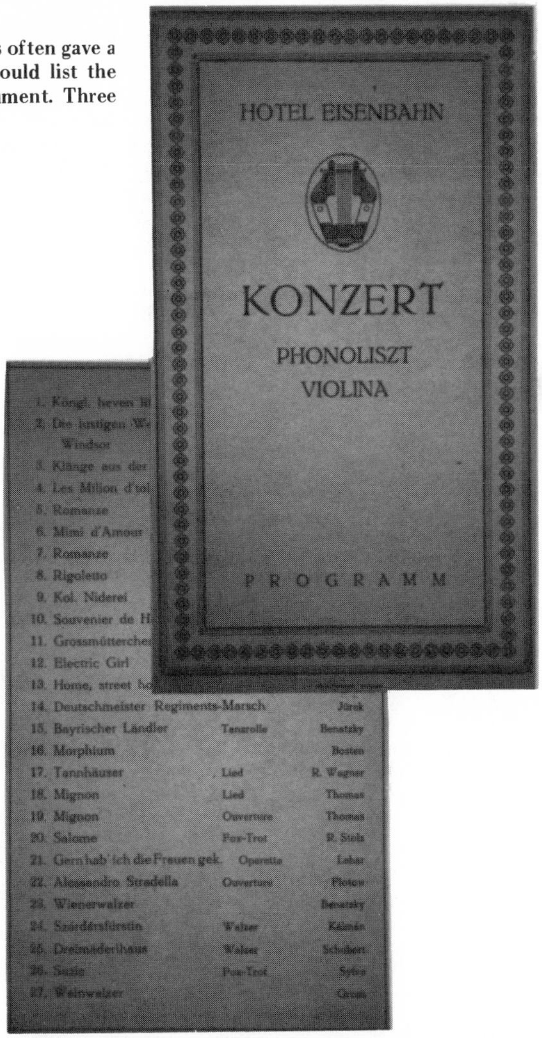


1. Königl. heven hi
2. Die lustigen W
Windsor
3. Klänge aus der
4. Les Milion d'tol
5. Romanze
6. Mimi d'Amour
7. Romanze
8. Rigoletto
9. Kol. Niderei
10. Souvenier de H
11. Grossmütterche
12. Electric Girl
13. Home, street ho
14. Deutschmeister Regiments-Marsch — Jurek
15. Bayrischer Ländler — Tanzrolle — Benatzky
16. Morphium — Bosten
17. Tannhäuser — Lied — R. Wagner
18. Mignon — Lied — Thomas
19. Mignon — Ouverture — Thomas
20. Salome — Fox-Trot — R. Stolz
21. Gern hab' ich die Frauen gek. — Operette — Lehar
22. Alessandro Stradella — Ouverture — Flotow
23. Wienerwalzer — Benatzky
24. Szardasfürstin — Walzer — Kálmán
25. Dreimäderlhaus — Walzer — Schubert
26. Suzie — Fox-Trot — Sylva
27. Weinwalzer — Gross

"CONCERT — Phonoliszt-Violina" program issued by the Hotel Eisenbahn of Sursee, Switzerland. The instrument, a Style B, was a great attraction.

—Hupfeld Pan Scale—

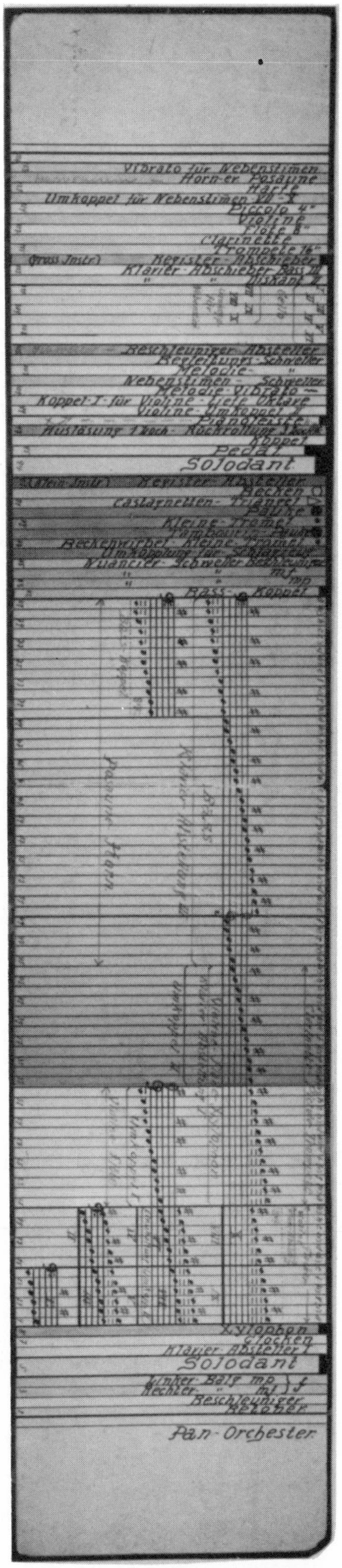


Original Hupfeld Pan Orchestra tracker bar scale or layout used in the 1920's by Ludwig Hupfeld A.G. (Author's collection; gift from Günther Hupfeld)

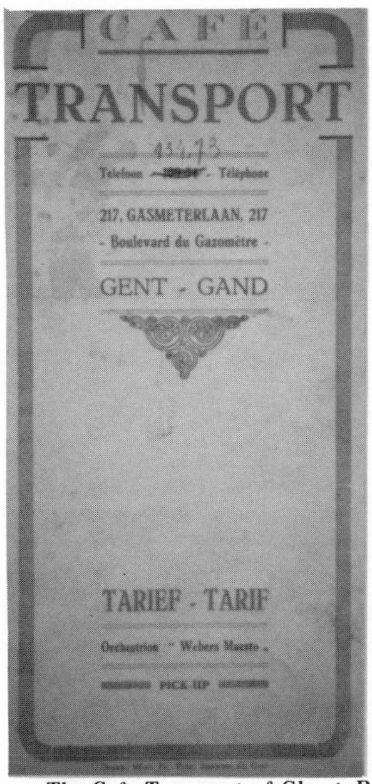


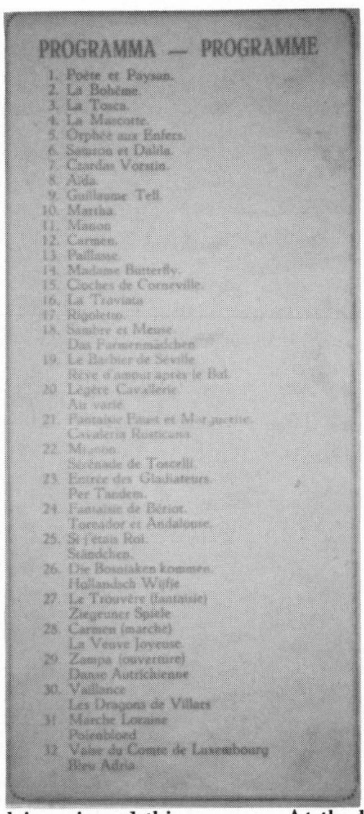

PROGRAMMA — PROGRAMME

1. Poète et Paysan.
2. La Bohème.
3. La Tosca.
4. La Mascotte.
5. Orphée aux Enfers.
6. Samson et Dalila.
7. Czardas Vorstin.
8. Aïda.
9. Guillaume Tell.
10. Martha.
11. Manon.
12. Carmen.
13. Paillasse.
14. Madame Butterfly.
15. Cloches de Corneville.
16. La Traviata.
17. Rigoletto.
18. Sambre et Meuse.
Das Farmermädchen
19. Le Barbier de Séville.
Rêve d'amour après le Bal.
20. Légère Cavalerie.
Air varié.
21. Fantaisie Faust et Marguerite.
Cavaleria Rusticana.
22. Mignon.
Sérénade de Toselli.
23. Entrée des Gladiateurs.
Per Tandem.
24. Fantaisie de Bériot.
Toreador et Andalouse.
25. Si j'étais Roi.
Ständchen.
26. Die Bosniaken kommen.
Hollandsch Wijfje
27. Le Trouvère (fantaisie)
Ziegeuner Spiele
28. Carmen (marche)
La Veuve Joyeuse.
29. Zampa (ouverture)
Danse Autrichienne
30. Vaillance
Les Dragons de Villars
31. Marche Lorraine
Poirebloed
32. Valse du Comte de Luxembourg
Bleu Adria

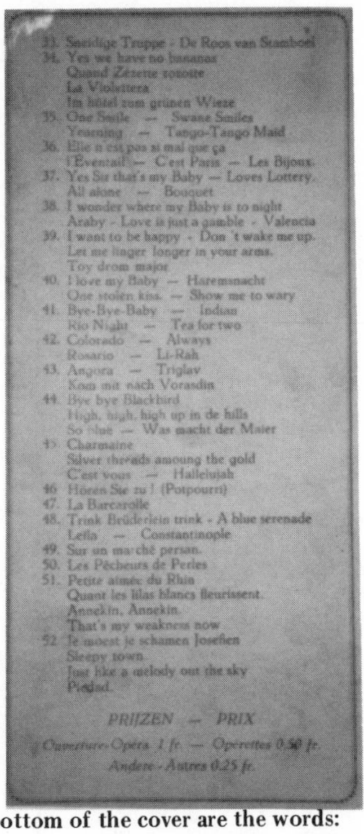

33. Smidige Truppe - De Roos van Stamboel
34. Yes we have no bananas
Quand Zézette zozote
La Violettera
Im hôtel zum grünen Wieze
35. One Smile — Swane Smiles
Yearning — Tango-Tango Maid
36. Elle n'est pas si mal que ça
l'Eventail — C'est Paris — Les Bijoux.
37. Yes Sir that's my Baby — Loves Lottery.
All alone — Bouquet
38. I wonder where my Baby is to night
Araby - Love is just a gamble - Valencia
39. I want to be happy - Don 't wake me up.
Let me linger longer in your arms.
Toy drum major
40. I love my Baby — Haremsnacht
One stolen kiss. — Show me to wary
41. Bye-Bye-Baby — Indian
Rio Night — Tea for two
42. Colorado — Always
Rosario — Li-Rah
43. Angora — Triglav
Kom mit nach Varasdin
44. Bye bye Blackbird
High, high, high up in de hills
So blue — Was macht der Maier
45. Charmaine
Silver threads amoung the gold
C'est vous — Halleluiah
46. Hören Sie zu ! (Potpourri)
47. La Barcarolle
48. Trink Brüderlein trink - A blue serenade
Leila — Constantinople
49. Sur un marché persan.
50. Les Pêcheurs de Perles
51. Petite aimée du Rhin
Quant les lilas blancs fleurissent.
Annekin, Annekin.
That's my weakness now
52. Ik moest je schamen Josefien
Sleepy town.
Just like a melody out the sky
Piedad.

PRIJZEN — PRIX

Ouverture-Opéra 1 fr. — Operettes 0.50 fr.
Andere - Autres 0.25 fr.

The Cafe Transport of Ghent, Belgium, issued this program. At the bottom of the cover are the words: Orchestrion — "Weber's Maesto." Cost of music was: an overture or opera, 1 franc; an operetta, 0.50 franc; single selections, 0.25 franc each. The request and the appropriate payment was given to an attendant. Your request would then be played. The Maesto, presently in the author's dining room, entertains a new generation of diners!

# MUSIC ROLLS AND THEIR MAKERS

*by David L. Junchen*

## The Beginnings

With the exception of music boxes, nearly all mechanical music makers extant today operate via the medium of a perforated piece of paper. Music boxes have their musical teeth plucked by pins which protrude from the surface of either a cylinder or a disc of metal. Before the late 1880's virtually all self-playing automatic musical instruments, including types (such as pianos and orchestrions) later operated by paper rolls, operated by means of cylinders.

Welte claimed to be the first to use a perforated roll for a pneumatically operated instrument, although this claim is discounted today as several other roll operated instruments are known to have existed before the Welte 1887 introduction. Exact details of the early history of the perforated paper roll will perhaps never be certain, but it is safe to say that Welte was certainly a pioneer in the popularization of rolls for use in larger self-playing instruments. In fact, Welte was so convinced of the superiority of the roll over the pinned cylinder that the firm offered to convert its previously sold cylinder instruments to play paper rolls, at no charge to the customer.

## Rolls vs. Cylinders

It is not hard to see why the pinned cylinder was abandoned after the introduction of the paper roll. Among the points of superiority of rolls over cylinders are these:

(1) The cost differential was enormous. Cylinders might cost up to several hundred dollars each, while multi-tune rolls containing equivalent music might cost only several dollars apiece. To cite an example, a cylinder for the Wurlitzer Tonophone, having ten songs pinned on it, cost $40. A typical five-tune Wurlitzer Automatic Player Piano roll might cost $4 or so – or just one tenth as much!

(2) The amount of information that could be put on a cylinder was quite limited, due to the finite surface area available for pinning. A compromise had to be reached between the length of playing time and the number of notes that could be played. If you wanted a long playing time, the number of available playing notes would be small; or if you wanted a large number of playing notes, the playing time would be limited. Rolls had no practical limitations of playing time or number of playing notes.

(3) The smaller physical size of a roll as compared to a cylinder enabled machines using rolls to be built more compactly.

(4) Changing rolls was easier than changing cylinders, in both time and strength required. A large orchestrion cylinder might weigh sixty pounds or more and be perhaps five feet long and one foot in diameter. The advantages of the roll, several of which could be carried in one hand, were obvious.

Following Welte's lead, most mechanical musical instrument manufacturers began equipping their instruments to play via the roll system. Some gave the customer a choice of either cylinders or rolls on each model; band organs sold during the early 20th century by Wurlitzer and the North Tonawanda Musical Instrument Works are examples. This practice was soon abandoned, however, and by 1910 cylinders were mainly a thing of the past.

The wide scale adoption of rolls was not without problems, however. When a new instrument was introduced by a manufacturer, a new roll scale was usually devised for it. This meant that rolls were made especially to fit each machine and, for the most part, were not interchangeable. This practice soon got out of hand, especially with regard to rolls for home player pianos. At one time there were at least five different scales of rolls being sold for home player pianos in the United States, with the result that one player manufacturer, Melville Clark, actually offered a piano that would play all five types of rolls!

This chaotic condition was ended by the 1908 convention of music manufacturers in Buffalo, New York, where standardization of scales was adopted, at least insofar as home player pianos were concerned. The major coin operated instrument manufacturers, such as Seeburg, Marquette (Cremona), Wurlitzer, and Operators (Coinola), still used rolls which, for the most part, would operate only their own instruments. They did standardize somewhat within their own companies to the extent that one type of roll would operate several different models of machines.

## Roll Scales

The scale of a roll is a definition of how the information contained in the roll is laid out on the paper. Four factors define the roll scale:

(1) The width of the paper. Examples of wide variation in this regard are the tiny 2 5/8" wide rolls used on the Mascotte hand-cranked reed organ and the huge (21 1/16" wide) rolls used to operate the Austin Premier Quadruplex pipe organ player and the 21 1/4" wide rolls used on the early (circa 1877) Needham Musical Cabinet.

(2) The total number of holes available transversely across the paper.

(3) The spacing between the holes, generally given in terms of holes per inch (in the United States). Home player piano rolls, for example, are spaced nine holes per inch of width. Nearly all rolls maintain the same hole spacing for the entire width of the paper. Interesting exceptions are the rare Resotone Grand and certain Cecilian pianos which use rolls with the perforations at the edges spaced more widely than those at the center!

(4) The function of each hole position. Although most holes are used for playing notes, in an orchestrion (for example) many other holes are used for non-tonal percussions such as drums, to turn various registers or pipe ranks on and off, to control expression devices, and for auxiliary functions such as initiating the rewind of the roll.

It is not my intent in this discussion to give an exhaustive account of every type of roll ever made, nor will I list many roll scales, as most scales are already documented in other literature. I do believe, however, that by listing and discussing several of the most widely used American orchestrion scales the reader will gain a good insight into the design and workings of all scales.

The preference of one type of music over another and the like for one type of roll over another is often a matter of personal opinion. In this discussion I give my opinions which may differ from the opinions of others. After all, enjoying music is an art, not a science!

## The "G" Roll Scale

Many American orchestrions are operated by one of two types of rolls, style "G" and the Wurlitzer 65-Note Automatic Player Piano rolls. Both of these rolls are multi-purpose rolls; that is, they are used to operate more than just one model of machine. To help understand how this is possible, let us first examine the G scale. This scale was devised by the J.P. Seeburg Piano Company and was originally designated as the "SS" scale until it was changed to "G" around 1920.

The G roll, like many rolls for American roll operated instruments, is 11 1/4" wide. It has 65 transverse hole positions, spaced six per inch. Forty eight of these are used for playing notes; the remaining 17 are used for percussion and controls, as follows (from left to right across the tracker bar):

1. Piano soft pedal
2. Piano sustaining pedal

3-26. Chromatic scale, G sharp to G, beginning with piano note No.24

27. Flute pipes on
28. Rewind
29. Flute pipes off
30. Snare drum
31. Drum expression off (loud)
32. Drum expression on (soft)
33. Shut off (sometimes called "coin trip")
34. Tympani
35. Bass drum and cymbal
36. Tympani
37. Violin pipes off
38. Reverse
39. Violin pipes on

40-63. Continuation of chromatic scale, G sharp to G

64. Mandolin on
65. Triangle

Now we'll begin a discussion of the G scale. The chromatic scale of 48 playing notes is divided in half, being interrupted in the middle of the roll by a number of control perforations. The reason for splitting the scale this way is unknown today. With the exception of G and H rolls, virtually every other American roll has its chromatic scale running continuously and undivided. Seeburg J and H orchestrions, which use the H roll, have a pipe solo section of 34 notes, and the H chromatic scale is divided on the roll such that the upper section is 34 notes. Seeburg G orchestrions, however, have a pipe compass of 32 notes, which fails to explain the division into two groups of 24 notes each. Perhaps Seeburg wanted to complicate the scale purposely to make copying by competing manufacturers more difficult, a trick employed by Gebr. Weber (whose orchestrion music arrangements were superb and were envied by others in the business). One would think, however, that if complication were the aim of Seeburg, the firm could have made the scale more complex than by merely dividing the chromatic scale.

No doubt many readers are wondering why a Seeburg G orchestrion can make so much lively and listenable music, inasmuch as with only 48 playing notes it's only slightly better than half a piano! Little 44-note pianos such as the Pianolin, the Pianino, and certain Peerless instruments don't make nearly as much music. The Seeburg secret is that the lowest octave of the note scale is actually connected to two octaves on the piano, the unison notes 24-36, plus the octave below, 12-23. This sneaky way of getting a full bass compass, however, has an unfortunate consequence. The lower octave of piano notes is always coupled to the upper octave and cannot be turned off by the roll (as it can be on Weber Maesto orchestrion rolls, for instance). Some if not most chords which are played in the note range 24-36 sound muddy when played in the 12-23 range, where they are also played by the automatic octave coupler in the piano.

To illustrate this problem, suppose an arrangement calls for the chord illustrated which is a full and resonant chord in the note range 24-36:

If a G rolls plays these three notes, the orchestrion will actually play:

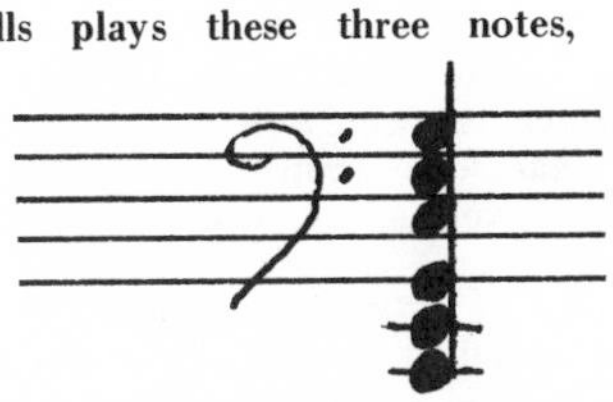

because of the automatic octave coupling in the piano. If you play this example on a piano you will immediately hear unmusical results. Faced with this dilemma, G roll arrangers had a choice of two courses of action. First, they could make arrangements such that chords would never be played which, when affected by the octave coupler, would sound discordant. The second choice would be to make the arrangements in the normal way, with no regard for the fact that the piano's octave coupling would cause many discordances. To the arrangers' credit, they chose a middle of the road course of action between the two extremes. It is amazing that the results were as good as they were, considering the musical odds that the arrangers were working against.

The organ pipes of the Seeburg G orchestrion are comprised of a rank of violin pipes and a rank of flute pipes, each of 32-note compass or range. These pipes play from the upper 32 notes of the 48-note chromatic scale, in unison with the piano notes. Actually, the violin pipes play in unison with the piano and the corresponding flute pipes play one octave higher in pitch. The pipes are controlled by two sets of "lock and cancel" holes. One hole turns the rank on and a second hole turns the rank off.

The piano's mandolin attachment is controlled in a different way. It has only one control hole and is turned on only as long as a continuous roll perforation passes over its tracker bar hole. Actually, the perforation is not continuous; it is a series of closely spaced holes called a "chain perforation." This chaining is done to give strength to the roll, since a long continuous perforation would be the equivalent of severing the paper lengthwise!

Just why the G scale uses one control scheme for the pipes and another for the mandolin, I don't know. A much more economical use of holes would have been to make the pipe and drum expression controls of the chain perforation type, thus saving three holes, which could then have been used effectively for more playing notes. Alternatively, all controls could have been of the lock and cancel type, with one "on" hole for each function, but only one "off" hole which would serve as a general cancel for all the functions. This latter method was used by a number of German orchestrion builders and in the United States by several of the reproducing piano manufacturers.

The percussion controls of the G roll are fairly straightforward. The bass drum and cymbal, tympani, and triangle holes are single stroke; that is, the instrument is struck once for each hole in the roll passing over its respective tracker bar hole. By the way, "tympani" is a fancy way of saying "soft beaters on the bass drum." The snare drum is a reiterating or continuous rolling instrument. That is, the orchestrion will sound a continuous snare drum roll for as long as a snare drum perforation appears in the roll. For a snare drum tap or single beat, the hole in the roll must be very short so that the reiterating mechanism striking the drum, which is similar in operation to a vibrating door bell striker, will be able to complete only one stroke, hence sounding a tap instead of a snare drum roll.

Herein lies a problem, however. If the snare drum beater mechanism is adjusted to give a realistic roll, it will be too fast to react to single taps which may be called for and will play two or three taps instead. Conversely, if the beater is slowed down to the point at which it will respond properly to single taps called for by the roll, the snare roll will then be too slow and will sound more like a rapid series of taps than like a continuous drum roll. This problem was overcome on the "O" rolls (used on Coinola orchestrions, to which refer) by providing two holes for the snare drum, controlling two separate beaters, one for single tap and one for a continuous roll.

Three holes on the G roll are used for controlling the movement of the roll itself. The rewind hole causes the roll to rewind at the end, and when it gets back to the beginning the reverse hole (sometimes called "rewind to play") shifts the gears and starts the roll in forward motion again. The shut off hole shuts the machine off at the end of each song on a multi-tune roll, so the machine plays only one song for each coin deposited.

The G scale was devised for the first Seeburg model with percussion, the Style G orchestrion. The next models with percussion, the styles H and J, used a new scale of roll, the H roll. The next Seeburg orchestrion, the Style L Automatic Orchestra, also used G rolls. The L Automatic Orchestra was similar to the G but was in a differently designed case and had only one rank of pipes. Other orchestrion styles were later introduced by Seeburg, the styles KT (made with one rank of pipes or, in later years, with xylophone), KT Special, and E Special, for example. Rather than devise new roll scales for these machines, Seeburg engineered them to operate from the existing G scale. They accomplished this in a musically questionable way, as will be seen.

The Style KT is a keyboardless cabinet orchestrion with the following instrumentation (as found on a typical circa 1925 model): piano, mandolin, xylophone, castanets, tambourine, and triangle. A check of the G scale will reveal that it has no provisions for three of these instruments: the xylophone, castanets, and tambourine. These three instruments are controlled thusly: the xylophone is controlled by the flute holes and the castanets and tambourine operate simultaneously(!) from the snare drum hole. In my opinion, this is one of the most illogical orchestrion instrumentations I have ever encountered!

The KT Special has the instrumentation of the KT but with the addition of snare drum, cymbal, wood block, bass drum, and two tympani beaters. The snare drum, cymbal, bass drum, and tympani play from their properly appointed G scale holes, and the tambourine is connected to operate simultaneously with one of the tympani beaters! This leaves the castanets and wood block which operate via a multiplexing system – a rare feature in American orchestrions.

Multiplexing means that a hole ordinarily having one function may have a completely different function, depending on other conditions in the roll at that time. In the KT Special the multiplexed hole is No.35 which ordinarily controls the bass drum and cymbal. It is changed to control the castanets and wood block whenever the piano soft pedal (hole No.1) is also used. The E Special is identical in instrumentation to the KT Special but is housed in a case with a keyboard (instead of a cabinet, as the KT Special) – and operates in the same manner.

The G scale was used for orchestrions of several other manufacturers: Nelson-Wiggen, Western Electric, and on a few models made by Standard (of Oregon, Illinois).

Nelson-Wiggen called the rolls used for their orchestrions "4X" rolls, since the first model in the Nelson-Wiggen line of percussion orchestrions was the Style 4X. The scale of 4X rolls is the same as for G rolls, but the arrangements differ slightly. The Nelson-Wiggen instruments use single stroke xylophones, whereas Seeburg instruments were built both ways — with either single stroke or reiterating xylophones. When 4X rolls call for the xylophone, the arrangements suddenly "come alive" with extra notes running all over the place — to take full advantage of the single stroke xylophone. This is unnecessary on instruments with reiterating xylophones and which use G rolls.

Although G and 4X rolls are identical in scale, the best musical results are obtained when machines with pipes or with reiterating xylophones play G rolls, and when instruments with single stroke xylophones play 4X rolls. The reason is that pipes react better when playing the relatively sustained arrangements of G rolls instead of the relatively choppy arrangements of 4X rolls. Likewise, single stroke xylophones sound rather "empty" playing G rolls (as they hit just once — at the beginning of the long sustained perforation), but are quite lively playing 4X rolls.

### The Wurlitzer 65-Note Automatic Player Piano Scale

As mentioned earlier, two leading popular types of American orchestrion rolls are the G and the Wurlitzer 65-Note Automatic Player Piano rolls, which I will abbreviate as "APP." Although Wurlitzer produced a wide variety of different scales of rolls for its various instruments, the vast majority of surviving Wurlitzer machines use the APP roll. This roll is 9 5/8" wide and has 75 hole positions of the unusual spacing of about 8 1/8 holes per inch. Their functions are as follows:

1. Shut off
2. Piano soft pedal and mandolin on
3. Piano soft pedal and mandolin off
4. Piano sustaining pedal on
5. Piano sustaining pedal off
6. Snare drum

7-71. Chromatic scale A to C sharp (piano notes 13 to 77)

72. Flute pipes on, violin pipes off
73. Flute pipes off, violin pipes on
74. Bass drum and triangle
75. Rewind

Note that there is no "reverse" or "rewind to play" hole for reversing gears when the roll has completed rewinding. Instead, Wurlitzer used a mechanical device in the take up spool to detect when the roll had completed its reverse motion.

The 65-note playing scale is the same as that of 65-note home player pianos — the standard American piano scale before the nearly universal adoption of the 88-note home player piano scale. No bass octave coupling is necessary with the APP scale, unlike the situation with the previously discussed G roll. In fact, more music can be put in the APP chromatic scale than in the majority of other orchestrion scales. I'm speaking now in terms of the arrangement of the musical notes. In terms of controlling the auxiliary instrumentation, however, the APP roll is a real "Rube Goldberg" situation! To wit:

(1) Only two holes are available for percussion instruments, one for snare drum and one for bass drum and triangle. Have you ever heard either a dance band or a symphony orchestra play the bass drum and triangle together?

(2) The piano soft pedal and the mandolin cannot be operated independently. You must have both or neither. This removes an important expression capability for to soften the piano you must also turn on the mandolin attachment.

(3) The pipe control mechanism was another innovation in the same vein. You can play either the flute pipes or the violin pipes, but not both. Nor can you play the piano alone, without pipes.

Wurlitzer enthusiasts, please don't get the idea that I'm condemning your favorite instruments! I enjoy listening to Wurlitzer APP instruments as much as anyone. They are certainly among the most "honky-tonk" sounding of all machines. I just want to illustrate the excellent musical potential (because of the large note scale) that was built into these instruments but which was never used because of the illogical control system. Some Wurlitzer enthusiasts have modified the controls on their orchestrions to permit more musical versatility. In my opinion this is one modification that is justified.

After the adoption of the APP roll as the Wurlitzer standard, Wurlitzer saw the desirability of adding a set of orchestra bells to its orchestrions. Unfortunately, the APP roll made no provision for control of any additional instruments, so the Wurlitzer engineers put their heads together and did some productive thinking of the type they should have done when the roll was first devised! They produced a multiplexing scheme for the on-off control of the bells, which works as follows: holes 4 and 5, operated simultaneously, turn the bells on, and the simultaneous operation of holes 2 and 3 turns them off. In the mid-1920's Wurlitzer offered an xylophone as an optional extra in the Style LX orchestrion. To turn the xylophone on, more multiplexing was used — namely holes 72 and 73 together. To turn the xylophone off holes 2 and 3 were used together — the same holes as used for the bells.

### Rolls with Solo Sections — O and H Rolls

In the orchestrion rolls so far discussed, the pipes, xylophone, and bells share the same playing holes as the upper notes in the piano, and it is not possible to play these extra instruments independently without playing the corresponding piano notes as well.

Several companies devised schemes to circumvent this difficulty, the two most popular American ones being Seeburg and Operators Piano Company (Coinola) with their instruments which used H and O rolls respectively. These two scales possess a remarkable similarity to each other (they both use identical chromatic scales, for example) so it seems apparent that ideas for one of the scales was "borrowed" from the originator of the other. Both scales were introduced about 1910.

Both of these rolls make provision for playing the extra instruments independently of the piano — or in "solo" arrangements. The solo instruments share the upper range of the piano's chromatic scale, as in regular orchestrion rolls, but provision is made for turning the piano off in this range so the instruments can play in solo, with the lower piano notes as accompaniment.

For a considerable length of time many collectors and historians have been under certain delusions concerning O and H rolls. It is my opinion that most of these notions are the result of an incomplete understanding of all of the facts — and for the benefit of the 99+% of collectors whose collections don't house both types of instruments using these two types of rolls, I present the facts so that some proper conclusions can be drawn. The two most popular, yet as we shall see, not quite correct, notions are:

(1) O rolls can make twice as much music as any other kind of American orchestrion roll.

(2) H instruments look impressive but are incapable of playing as much music as many smaller types of machines.

To help unravel the facts, I will list the scales of both types of rolls for comparison.

H Scale — paper 15 1/4" wide, spacing 6 holes per inch:

1. Piano soft pedal
2. Piano sustaining pedal

3-34. Chromatic scale E to B (piano notes 20-51)

35. Flute pipes off
36. Flute pipes on
37. Rewind
38. Violin pipes off
39. Violin pipes on
40. Piano off in solo section
41. Piano on in solo section
42. Reverse
43. Xylophone off
44. Shut off
45. Xylophone on
46. Castanets
47. Drum expression off (loud)
48. Drum expression on (soft)
49. Snare drum
50. Bass drum and cymbal
51. Tympani
52. Tympani

53-86. Solo section, C to A (piano notes 52-85)

87. Mandolin
88. Triangle

O Scale — paper 11 1/4" wide, spacing 9 holes per inch:

0. Reverse
1. Tympani
2. Bass drum and cymbal
3. Tympani
4. Wood block

5. Snare drum tap
6. Snare drum roll
7. Triangle
8. Piano sustaining pedal
9. Piano soft pedal off
10. Piano soft pedal on
11. Mandolin off
12. Mandolin on
13. Pipes on
14. Xylophone or bells on
15. Drum expression on (soft)
16. Drum expression off (loud)
17. Xylophone or bells off
18. Shut off
19. Pipes off
20-61. Chromatic scale E to A (piano notes 20-61)
62-85. Solo section, A sharp to A (piano notes 62-85)
86. Tambourine
87. Crescendo (raises vacuum level in entire instrument)
88. Crash cymbal
89. Rewind

Now let's list the points of superiority of each scale for purposes of comparison. First, for the O scale:

(1) It has better control of the snare drum by providing separate tap and roll beaters instead of just one roll beater as on the H.

(2) Two extra percussion instruments are provided for; the wood block and the crash cymbal.

(3) Slightly more expression is possible through the crescendo device. The H has inherent expression possibilities which do not appear on the tracker scale (and which I shall discuss later) which tend to offset the advantages of the O's amplifier, however.

Here are the H scale advantages:

(1) Three extra instrument controls are provided in the H scale, as opposed to only two in the O scale. Even in the Coinola SO orchestrion, which has two ranks of pipes, both ranks turn on and off simultaneously from the same control holes.

(2) The solo section in the H, of 34 notes, is much larger than the 24-note solo section of the O roll.

(3) The piano can be turned on or off in the solo section, as desired. In machines using O rolls the piano is automatically muted whenever the solo instrument is turned on, so no separate control is available for it.

(4) H instruments can play any number of notes simultaneously in the solo section, but O machines, due to physical limitations in the machines themselves, can play only one or two notes at a time and still achieve good results.

(5) By virtue of the large scale of the H solo section, it has an inherent expressive capability in that the solo melody can be played softly by only one note, or gradually louder by two, three, or four, or more notes playing simultaneously.

My intention here is to present the facts. Given the advantages of the O scale vs. the advantages of the H scale, as listed in the preceding paragraphs, it is easy to see that the O and H scales are at least equal in the musical possibilities of each. Why, then, do myths persist, namely that O rolls are superior to all other American-made orchestrion rolls and that H rolls are inferior to O rolls?

I believe a rational basis for this can be found, based upon knowledge of collector psychology. As a roll arranger (I have arranged melodies in recent years for both O and H rolls and have asked collectors which styles of arrangements they like best) I have noted that collectors have a mania for percussion effects. The more the merrier! Since the O roll does have the most sophisticated percussion controls of all American rolls, it would be easy to get carried away on this point alone, without taking the other factors into consideration. Another reason is that people tend to like the familiar and to shun the unfamiliar. Inasmuch as there are several times more machines extant which play O rolls rather than H rolls, collectors are understandably less familiar with H instruments.

Another subtle, but important, factor is the arrangements on the available rolls. O rolls had good arrangements throughout their period of introduction. It wasn't until the mid and late 1920's, however, that the arrangers of H rolls began to take full advantage of all the instrumentation available to them. Unfortunately, of the small number of surviving original H rolls, only a small percentage are these rolls of later vintage. So not only do people hear O rolls more than H rolls, but for a given H roll they are more likely than not going to hear a roll which may not use the H orchestrion to its fullest advantage.

### Special Purpose Rolls

The rolls discussed thus far have been multi-purpose rolls; that is, they play a number of different models of machines. By far the greater number of rolls, by type, are special purpose rolls; that is, rolls that are designed for only one particular instrument. The musical advantages of special purpose rolls are obvious. The arranger of a multi-purpose roll is always hampered because he must compromise the arrangement to play several varieties of machines, all with different instrumentation. The arranger of a special purpose roll, however, is at liberty to take full advantage of the musical abilities of the exact instrument for which he is arranging.

Why not, then, aren't all rolls special purpose? The reasons are, of course, economic. Just imagine, for example. what would happen if each new automobile model required a different fuel. The cost of all the various fuels would be tremendous, not to mention the difficulty of obtaining the particular fuel you would need anywhere you might want it. The same analogy can be carried over to mechanical musical instruments. It just wasn't economical for the manufacturer or for the purchaser to have a different type of roll for each instrument.

### Types of Paper Used for Rolls

Over the years dozens of kinds of paper have been used for music rolls. The paper used has been of widely differing quality — with the result that some rolls are well preserved today, several decades after their manufacture, while other rolls are so fragile as to be playable only with extreme care.

A list of music roll paper requirements may be of interest:

(1) The paper must be strong so that the flanges of the roll spool won't tear its edges and so it won't tear after being perforated.

(2) The paper must be thin in order to keep the diameter of the finished roll reasonable.

(3) The paper must be capable of being perforated cleanly — without shedding undue lint and fibers.

(4) The paper must be smooth in order to pass over the tracker bar with minimum friction.

(5) The paper must stay flat without warping or buckling.

(6) The paper must have good ageing characteristics.

(7) The paper must be fairly resistant (no paper is completely resistant) to changes in humidity which cause it to shrink or expand.

(8) A final note: One might think that cost would be a major factor, but it isn't. Interestingly enough, the paper is one of the least of all the costs involved in the production of a roll. The costs of perforator running time, labeling, spooling, and boxing are all more significant than the cost of the paper.

Of all the types of paper used years ago, one seems to be superior to the rest: a paraffin impregnated or "dry waxed" paper used by several orchestrion roll manufacturers. Wurlitzer's variety usually had a green color, while the rolls of other makers often were gray in tint. Other kinds of paper may have been strong when they were manufactured fifty years ago, but most have become brittle in varying degrees today. Among the poorest paper used was that on which Capitol 88-note home player piano rolls were perforated. It was virtually newsprint paper! This is particularly distressing as these rolls have some of the finest musical scoring to be found on 88-note rolls. Fortunately for collectors today, many of the early rolls of various types are being recut on better quality paper — so that another generation of enthusiasts can enjoy them again.

Today the dry waxed paper is still the favorite with roll makers. Some synthetic paper substitutes have been tried. Several, notably mylar and a nylon-impregnated paper, have been found quite satisfactory. However, these have the disadvantage of being quite costly in comparison to dry waxed paper.

Our discussion of roll papers concludes with mentioning several other substances used for rolls. The Telektra and Tel-Electric players used thin brass sheeting in which the appropriate holes were punched. Imhof & Mukle used a heavy and almost indestructible manila paper several times thicker than the .004" (approximately) thick paper used for most piano rolls. Certain large band organs and dance organs used folding cardboard music. Strictly speaking, the latter is not a "roll," because the thick cardboard folds into a flat stack or book, rather than being wound onto a spool.

## Arranging of Music Rolls

Arranging is the process whereby a musical score is devised and transcribed into the perforations on a music roll. The first thing the arranger does is to work out the musical arrangement that will sound best on the particular instrument for which he is making the roll. In the case of orchestrions, he must keep in mind the limitations of the instrument (such as an abbreviated chromatic scale), the scale of the pipes, whether the xylophone is single stroke or reiterating, the size of the solo section (if any), and so on. His work is like that of an orchestral arranger (who must likewise know the instrumentation of his orchestra and the ranges and capabilities of the individual instruments).

Once the musical arrangement has been made, it must be translated into terms of holes on a music roll. This process requires much less skill than making the musical arrangement as it is merely a mechanical translating process from one "language" to another. This translation can be carried out by a person following a simple set of rules, as least as far as the less musically sophisticated arrangements are concerned. This translating process can be accomplished in several ways:

(1) By having a person manually cut holes in a blank roll corresponding to the notes on the score of the arrangement.

(2) In the case of a simple piano arrangement, by having a person play the arrangement into a recording piano which automatically punches holes in a roll corresponding to the notes played.

(3) By a combination of each of these methods.

The simplest process is the second one, that of having a pianist record an arrangement via a recording piano. In some instances the recording piano doesn't actually punch a piano roll, but draws pencil lines corresponding to the location of the holes. These lines can then be punched out manually by an operator using a simple hand punch. I've used the word "piano" here in relation to recording, but organ rolls were recorded in the same way by using a recording machine connected to a pipe organ.

In general, if the song to be hand played on a recording piano were anything other than a dance number in strict tempo, the resulting recording would be reproduced for sale exactly as it was played. In the case of dance music requiring strict tempo, however, the hand played roll is used only as an intermediate guide. The roll manufacturers of years ago wanted metronomic precision for dance music; a precision greater than the artists were capable of playing. Therefore, the notes of the hand-played roll were transferred by hand to another roll in which the accuracy of the beats could be maintained. In this transferring process much editing frequently occurred as well. This altered the original performance somewhat, but maintained its general flavor. The American Piano Company developed a machine which would automatically compensate for the artist's tempo inaccuracies. Many of the Ampico reproducing piano rolls were thus "tempo corrected."

Another "recording" method is that used by celebrated piano roll arranger J. Lawrence Cook. His piano is connected to a perforating machine. The recording piano is different from the usual in that it is equipped with extra devices which hold notes above that which could be controlled with just ten fingers. Mr. Cook works in very slow motion, a few notes or chords at a time, and his finished product is a master roll which can be used directly on a mass-production perforator. In reality, Mr. Cook does not actually "play" the recording piano, but uses it as an aid to get the perforations onto the master roll.

Earlier I stated that the first step in arranging is to make the actual arrangement and then transcribe it to a roll in terms of perforations. Some arrangers are able to do both these operations simultaneously. To explain how this is possible, you must first understand that a good musician is able to "hear" in his mind the notes on a score by merely looking at them, without actually having them played by an instrument. A good roll arranger can look at the perforations on a music roll and "hear" them in the same way. Therefore, he will be able to write his musical thoughts directly in terms of roll perforations, rather than having to go through the medium of musical staff notation first.

## Tempo Compensation

Although my discussion of roll arranging is a general one (a detailed treatise on the subject would fill a large volume!), the problem of tempo compensation is worthy of brief attention.

In most roll-operated instruments the roll is propelled through the instrument by being pulled through by a revolving take-up spool. As the paper builds up on the take-up spool, the outside diameter of the paper and spool increases, with the result that the paper is gradually pulled faster and faster through the instrument. If no compensation were put in the roll, the music would play faster and faster as the roll neared its end. The compensation required is adjusted for by spacing the perforations at the end of the roll further apart than at the beginning, so that even though the paper travels faster at the end, the tempo of the music remains reasonably correct.

In most roll perforators the paper is pulled through by a series of rubber "fingers" which grip the paper and tug it through the perforator in discrete steps of about 1/16" at a time. By changing the ratchet wheel on this paper feed mechanism, the steps can be lengthened toward the end of the roll, thus accomplishing the desired tempo compensation. On many ten-tune orchestrion rolls a common practice was at adjust the tempo compensation three or four steps throughout the roll length.

Some types of roll drives required no tempo compensation in the rolls. The best known of these drives is the style which pulls the paper over the tracker bar by gripping the music roll between a capstan and a pinch roller — much in the manner of a tape recorder. Many so-called "endless" types of rolls, such as those made by Link, the North Tonawanda Musical Instrument Works, Berry-Wood (early types only), and others, used this system as did certain rewind-type instruments made by Gebr. Weber and Imhof & Mukle.

The second type, used notably by Mills Novelty Company and Wurlitzer (on very early instruments only), featured an ordinary take-up spool which was fitted with a little roller which detected the diameter of the roll as it built up. This roller was directly (Wurlitzer) or indirectly (Mills) connected to the roll drive so that the speed of the take-up spool decreased as its diameter increased — thus causing the paper to travel at a uniform speed from beginning to end.

## Important American Roll Manufacturers of Yesteryear

In this section I discuss the major American manufacturers of rolls for non-home use. Reproducing piano rolls are covered in another section of this book, and 88-note home player piano rolls are adequately covered in "Player Piano Treasury," by Harvey Roehl, so duplication of that material would be redundant here. Also, I will not cover the many manufacturers of rolls for specialized instruments which were not produced in quantity or which survive only in limited numbers today (such as the Encore Banjo, Niagara instruments, etc.).

## Automatic Music Roll Company

Located in the Seeburg factory in Chicago, the Automatic Music Roll Company was a Seeburg subsidiary which sold rolls used by Seeburg instruments and, in the case of A and G rolls, used by instruments of other manufacturers as well.

Automatic was formed circa 1920 when the QRS Company ceased the manufacture of Seeburg rolls. Automatic did no perforating. It had the rolls cut on a contractual basis by the Clark Orchestra Roll Company. Clark did all of the arranging and perforating. As a result, the musical arrangements on rolls issued by both Clark and Automatic were the same in many instances.

Clark 4X rolls were identical to Automatic G rolls except that when the xylophone is called for in 4X rolls the music is arranged for single stroke beating. In the late 1920's, just before Automatic went out of business, the extra expense of arranging Automatic G rolls was eliminated, with the result that late Automatic G rolls are identical to 4X rolls.

A list of rolls sold by Automatic includes:

A rolls: The industry standard 65-note roll used in coin pianos without percussion instruments. Although collectors today commonly refer to this type of roll as an "A" roll, Automatic was the only company which actually gave it the "A" designation. Other manufacturers used a generic description such as "Standardized 65-note rewind electric piano roll," or something in a similar vein.

"SR" rolls: ASR, GSR, HSR — the A, G, or H refers to the type of roll and the SR stands for "Special Request." These rolls were made for individual customers and were not regular issues.

BH rolls: A large roll (15 1/4" wide; spacing of 9 holes to the inch) used by certain Seeburg - Smith theatre pipe organs.

G rolls: 65-note orchestrated roll used on Seeburg orchestrion styles G, KT, KT Special, E Special, etc. and on certain of the smaller Seeburg theatre photoplayers.

H rolls: Large (15 1/4" wide; spacing of 6 holes to the inch) roll used on Seeburg H and J orchestrions and by most of the larger Seeburg theatre photoplayers.

HO rolls: 11 1/4" wide, 9 holes to the inch roll used in self-contained Seeburg pipe organs used for home and mortuary use.

MO rolls: A roll used in certain Seeburg mortuary organs. Name similar to the Wurlitzer MO rolls used in Wurlitzer mortuary organs; however, the two rolls feature different scales.

MSR rolls: Somewhat similar in scale to H rolls, but featuring organ arrangements (rather than piano-oriented orchestrion arrangements as found on H rolls) and usually (but not always) without percussion effects. Used interchangeably with H rolls on certain large Seeburg photoplayers.

RO rolls: Identical to HO rolls mentioned previously.

TR rolls: Used in a piano-pipe organ instrument introduced in the late 1920's; the Twin-Tracker theatre instrument.

XP rolls: Used in Seeburg styles X and Phono Grand, and also in early Melville Clark Apollo home pianos.

Z rolls: A "special cut 65-note roll" (according to the Seeburg catalogue) used in Style Z Selective Roll pianos.

Of the above rolls, the A is the most plentiful style, followed by the G and then the H, MSR, and XP. The other styles are quite rare.

Among the last Automatic rolls I have information about are roll numbers A-1505 (featuring such tunes as "Makin' Whoopee," "Me and the Man in the Moon," "Carolina Moon," and "Suzianna," among others) and G-007 and H-1221. These latter two rolls each have the same ten tunes, including "Wedding Bells," "A Precious Little Thing Called Love," and "A Room With a View." The songs on A-1505 were copyrighted in 1928, as were the songs on G-997 and H-1221, with the exception of two 1929 songs on the G and H rolls — which gives an idea of the time when Automatic went out of business.

### Capitol Roll and Record Company

Located at 721 North Kedzie Avenue, Chicago, in the Operators Piano Company building, the Capitol Roll and Record Company was a subsidiary of Operators, the builder of the justly famed Coinola and Reproduco instruments.

Before 1924 the Columbia Music Roll Company (22 South Peoria St., Chicago) was the maker of rolls for instruments made by Operators. In 1924 the name was changed to Capitol and the address was changed to Kedzie Avenue, as noted.

Capitol made A, C, and O rolls for Coinola and Empress instruments, and OS, NOS, and large "Unified Reproduco" rolls for Reproduco instruments. They also made 88-note rolls for home players under the labels of Columbia (circa 1920-1924), American, Capitol, Cecile, Challenge, Stark, Sterling, Supertone (made for Sears & Roebuck), and Synchronized. Capitol also made G rolls (for some reason unknown to me; it would seem that this would mainly benefit Seeburg, a competitor).

Most of the musical arrangements for Capitol rolls were obtained from the hand playing of Chicago pianists and theatre organists, including James Blythe, Clarence Johnson, John Honnert, Irma Glen, Eddie Hanson, and Pearl White — to name just a few of the dozens of artists who recorded for Capitol at one time or another. Their performances were first done on a recording piano. The arrangements then were edited extensively before they were issued on music rolls. The resulting rolls usually were about 50% performer and 50% editor so far as musical stylistic traits were concerned, but this editing was in excellent musical taste. The final product was the "Capitol sound" which collectors so enthusiastically admire today.

After an editor made an 88-note arrangement from an artist's hand played recording, an arranger in the orchestrion roll department would take this arrangement and use it as a basis for laying out the song on A, C, G, and O rolls. He would have to alter it to accommodate the shorter note scales of the orchestrion rolls. He would also add slots to control the drums and other effects. In some cases the orchestrion roll arranger would modulate to a different key for the second chorus, particularly in the case of A rolls, whereas the 88-note, G, and O arrangements were usually left in their original key.

Exceptions to the hand played rolls were certain ethnic (Polish, Spanish, etc.) rolls, many of which were completely arranged by hand on a drawing board — without an artist's recording for guidance.

Most of the 88-note arrangements stemmed from hand-played recordings, although certain marches and other types of songs were done drafting board style.

As did other roll makers, Capitol sometimes invented pseudonyms for certain artists — so that one pianist might appear under several different names.

Capitol went out of business around 1934. In the final period of operation the firm used QRS arrangements as the basis for orchestrion rolls, apparently in a final attempt at economy. One of the final ten-tune roll lineups is found on 2446 (A) and G-511: "The House is Haunted," "Cocktails for Two," "Little Man, You've Had a Busy Day," "Waitin' at the Gate for Katy," "True," "Carioca," "I'll String Along with You," "Why Do I Dream Those Dreams," "Love Thy Neighbor," and "All I Do is Dream of You."

Roll No. 2447 (an A roll) features: "Love in Bloom," "Lost in a Fog," "Rain," "Stars Fell on Alabama," "Two Cigarettes in the Dark," "I Saw Stars," "Out in the Cold Again," "Boo Hoo, I'm Crying for You," "Sweetie Pie," and "In the Chapel in the Moonlight."

Capitol rolls are collectors' favorites today. These rolls, scarce in original form, are available today in the medium of recuts — so that enthusiasts everywhere can enjoy once again the toe-tapping Coinola and Reproduco music that delighted patrons of public places in the 'twenties.

### Clark Orchestra Roll Company

Clark, the dominant American concern in the manufacture of orchestrion rolls in the 1920's, was started in 1920 in DeKalb, Illinois, by Ernest G. Clark, who was at that time in charge of the coin-operated roll division of the QRS Company. Ernest Clark was a brother of Melville Clark, who had originally founded the QRS Company. Clark was in business until the early 1940's. Sometime after this the perforating equipment was purchased by Roesler - Hunholz in Milwaukee, Wisconsin, but for some reason that firm never took delivery and the mechanisms were eventually scrapped, as were the master rolls.

In addition to making rolls on contract for other concerns, Clark sold many rolls under its own label. Clark roll types known today include styles A, M (for certain Cremona instruments), O (for certain Coinola and Empress instruments), XP, 4X, and rolls for the Nelson-Wiggen Selector Duplex Organ and for the National (made in Grand Rapids, Michigan) coin piano equipped with a roll changer.

The musical arrangements of Clark rolls originated from two main sources: 88-note QRS arrangements and the hand arranging of persons on the Clark staff. In the 1920 to 1924 years about half the songs on Clark rolls originated from each source respectively. After about 1924 QRS arrangements were used exclusively for the basis of piano orchestrion rolls. Marion Wright did most of the organ roll arranging at the Clark factory.

The non-QRS arrangements in the early 1920's were mostly the work of P.M. Keast, a talented musician. He could imitate the style of any of the QRS artists (such as Kortlander, Arden, Wendling, et al) or he could come up with fantastic musical ideas of his own. Mr. Keast produced some particularly excellent arrangements in the 1921 - 1922 years.

Much information about the Clark and Capitol organizations was obtained in a 1970 interview with Mr. Keast. Excerpts from this interview are reproduced elsewhere in this book.

After 1929 Clark discontinued the production of O and M rolls. National rolls were discontinued in the mid-1930's. In the later years of Clark operation only A and 4X rolls were made. Among the last Clark rolls were these:

4X-415 which featured "Shake Down the Stars," "Alice Blue Gown," "The Singing Hills," "Cecilia," "South of the Border," "A Lover's Lullaby," "Leanin' on the Ole Top Rail," "Woodpecker Song," "You'd Be Surprised," and "Fools Rush In."

1522 (A) which was titled "Yuletide Parade" and which featured "Barnum and Bailey Favorite," "Snow King," "Bombasto," "Wake Up America," "Washington Post," "Santa Claus is Coming to Town," "Silent Night," "Little Town of Bethlehem," "Bells of St. Mary's," "Hark! The Herald Angels Sing," "Adeste Fideles," "God Bless America," and "Jingle Bells and Auld Lang Syne."

### Columbia Music Roll Company

Located at 22 South Peoria Street in Chicago, Columbia started bsuiness around 1920 to supply rolls for Operators Piano Company instruments when the QRS coin operated roll division was acquired by Ernest G. Clark. Before this time QRS had been making the A and O rolls used in Coinola instruments.

In its first year of operation, Columbia used some QRS arrangements for its orchestrion rolls, but later it used all its own material. In 1924 the Columbia Music Roll Company became the Capitol Roll and Record Company. See the preceding information about Capitol for the further history of this company.

### Cremona

Cremona rolls were sold for use on instruments manufactured by the Marquette Piano Company of Chicago. The rolls were manufactured by QRS (in the pre-1920 years) and Clark (in the 1920's) and included roll types A, M, and S. See the Cremona instrument section of this book for further information on this firm.

### Filmusic

The Filmusic Company of Los Angeles, California, issued 88-note rolls under the "Filmusic Picturoll" and "Pop" labels. These rolls were scored especially for use on American Photo Player Co. "Fotoplayer" instruments and other photoplayers which used 88-note rolls. Perhaps the most famous artist to record for Filmusic was theatre organist Jesse Crawford. Another Filmusic artist was Vern Elliott (who, in the late 1950's, helped organize Aeolian Music Rolls, Inc., makers of new 88-note home player piano rolls).

### Lind

Lind was a sales organization which pasted its own labels on Clark rolls and sold them as Lind rolls.

### Link Piano Company

Link rolls were made by the Link Piano Company of Binghamton, N.Y., solely for their own instruments. Link made several types of rolls, the most important being types A, C, and RX. Each of these rolls is 12" wide and contains 70 perforations, spaced six to the inch. Link A rolls were made for use on Link orchestrions (with percussion effects). RX rolls were made for piano instruments with mandolin and, in some instances, an extra effect such as a marimbaphone (xylophone) or a rank of flute or violin pipes. C rolls featured organ arrangements and were used mainly on Link theatre instruments.

The arrangements for Link rolls were done by two men, G. Raymond Deyo and William D. Sabin. Deyo started working for the Automatic Musical Company, the forerunner of the Link Piano Company, in 1905 at the age of seventeen. Later, Deyo arranged most of the RX and A rolls. Sabin primarily arranged the C rolls.

After the Link Piano Company ceased the manufacture of rolls, Ray Deyo assumed the customer list, supplies on hand, and other effects and began to make RX rolls for what remained of the market for them. The diameter of the holes in the "Deo" brand ("Deyo" was shortened to "Deo" for use in the Deo Roll Company name) rolls is larger than that in the earlier Link-made rolls, so it is possible that Mr. Deyo modified the original Link perforator or made a new one.

Link-made RX rolls are generally of 15-tune length and have serial numbers in the 15,000 series. A few 10-tune Link rolls with serial numbers in the 10,000 series are known to collectors today.

Deo rolls generally use QRS arrangements, notwithstanding the fact that Ray Deyo certainly could have made the master rolls using his own arrangements. By the mid-1930's the Deo Roll Company's business had dwindled to the vanishing point. Around 1934 the perforator was scrapped and the remaining rolls were used as firewood.

### Mills Novelty Company

Mills manufactured two main types of rolls for use on its instruments: Violano Virtuoso rolls for the violin player of the same name and rolls for use on the Magnetic Expression Piano.

Most Mills rolls were hand played on a recording device which punched a master roll as the artists performed. To record a Violano Virtuoso roll two musicians were necessary, one at a piano keyboard and one at a keyboard which controlled the violin. Some very early Mills rolls appear to have been entirely hand arranged (on a drawing board). These very early rolls are not numbered and have a different tracker layout from the later rolls. These rolls had special perforations for devices such as string pluckers, intermediate fingers, an oiling piston, and a bow-reversing mechanism — features not found on later Violano instruments.

The first standard Violano Virtuoso rolls, offered in a 1912 catalogue, were available in either single selections or multiple tune rolls. The first single numbered roll was No.100, "I've Loved Her Ever Since She Was A Baby." The playing time was three minutes. The roll sold for $1.25. The first multiple tune roll appears to have been No.1A. This roll sold for $5 and featured these three 3-minute tunes: "Where The River Shannon Flows," "The Honolulu Rag," and "Silver Threads Among the Gold."

In later years multiple rolls were the standard and single selections were made only in limited numbers. The usual Violano Virtuoso roll of the 1920's was apt to contain five songs — two fox trots, a waltz in the middle, and two more fox trots. Of course, there were a number of specialty rolls such as ethnic rolls, classical rolls, all-waltz rolls, violin solo rolls, and, rarely, piano solo rolls. There were also special rolls (with drum and other percussion effects scored) made for the Violano Orchestra.

An example of a very late Violano Virtuoso roll is No.3119 which features the usual five tunes, two of which are "It Isn't Fair" and "I Looked At Your Picture."

### QRS Company

Unquestionably the dominant concern in the music roll business was QRS, a firm which is still very much in business today. Begun shortly after 1900 by Melville Clark, the QRS Company saw the rise and fall of the player piano empire in the 1920's, the consequent lack of interest in the 1930's and 1940's, and the renaissance of the player piano beginning in the mid-1950's. In its busiest year, 1926, QRS sold almost 10,000,000 rolls! The low point in sales was 1952, a year in which just 200,000 rolls were marketed. In the early 1970's QRS roll sales averaged about 500,000 rolls per year.

Our discussion here is mainly concerned with QRS rolls produced for use on automatic instruments (as contrasted with 88-note home players). Before 1920, QRS made rolls for Seeburg in styles S, SS, and SSS (these designations were later changed to the familiar roll letters A, G, and H respectively). For Operators Piano Company many type O orchestrion rolls were made. These O rolls had no manufacturer listed on the label, and the Seeburg rolls were marked with the "Seeburg" name. I have never seen any orchestrion rolls bearing a QRS label, but this does not mean that none exists, for information from the early years is incomplete today.

The QRS orchestrion roll operation was acquired in 1920 by Ernest G. Clark, who was then its manager. This department was relocated and became the Clark Orchestra Roll Company. Many of the basic piano arrangements used for Clark orchestrion rolls were obtained directly from QRS home player rolls. When QRS was making orchestrion rolls before 1920, however, virtually all of the arrangements were different from the QRS home player rolls of that era. I'm not sure why this was done, unless QRS believed that superior quality resulted from the tailoring of a roll to the scale of the particular instrument it was being arranged for. Or, perhaps the feasibility of adapting the home rolls for orchestrion use simply hadn't occurred to QRS.

### United States Music Company

This Chicago firm was active in the orchestrion roll business from its beginnings shortly after the turn of the century. During the mid-teens the company discontinued its orchestrion rolls and concentrated on the home player roll market. The firm was acquired by QRS in 1926.

The United States Music Company made several varieties of orchestrion rolls, including what were later known as O, A, and Link RX. The Link RX rolls made by the U.S. Music Company are rare today. A specimen owned by Ed Freyer bears the notation, "Manufactured for Automatic Musical Company."

I have encountered several U.S. Music Co. rolls which are identical to regular 65-note A rolls, with the exception of hole positions 1 and 2. These holes, normally used for piano soft and for the sustaining pedal, appear to be perforated for a bass and snare drum.

### Rudolph Wurlitzer Company

Wurlitzer manufactured a tremendous quantity of rolls, all of which were used on its own instruments. The list of Wurlitzer roll types manufactured over the years includes:

Autograph Reproducing Piano rolls: for the Autograph Piano, an expression piano (see the Wurlitzer section of this book for detailed information on this and the other Wurlitzer models mentioned here).

Caliola rolls: for the Caliola, Wurlitzer's entry into the calliope market. Caliola rolls are of the same scale and layout as 65-note Automatic Player Piano rolls, but have arrangements especially suited for pipes.

Concert PianOrchestra rolls: for the Wurlitzer Concert PianOrchestra orchestrions and for larger Wurlitzer photoplayers. The scale was first devised by J.D. Philipps (of Frankfurt am

Main, Germany) and was known as the "PC" (for "Pianella Caecilia") roll.

Automatic Harp rolls: for the Wurlitzer Automatic Harp, styles A and B. Manufactured by the J.W. Whitlock Company (of Rising Sun, Indiana) for Wurlitzer. About 250 different Harp rolls were made. Production continued until the mid-'teens. The rolls were arranged by two women, one of whom was a member of the Whitlock family, and were recorded by playing an upright piano which had special sensing devices attached to it. Unlike the harp-type arrangements that might be expected, the rolls feature piano arrangements. The library of Harp master rolls, all of the original sheet music used to score the Harp rolls, and the factory ledgers and records were acquired by Q. David Bowers some years ago.

Mandolin PianOrchestra rolls: used on the Wurlitzer Mandolin PianOrchestra orchestrions. Identical in scale to the Philipps "PM" rolls made by J.D. Philipps of Frankfurt am Main, Germany. The scale was devised by Philipps and later adopted by Wurlitzer.

Mandolin Quartette rolls: used on the Mandolin Quartette and Mandolin Sextette.

Military Band Organ rolls: were made in four main series, designated as styles 125, 150, 165, and 180, plus specialized early rolls for such instruments as the "Mammoth" and "Monster" organs.

MO rolls: used by certain Wurlitzer self-contained mortuary organs made mostly in the late 1920's. 11 1/4" wide, spacing of nine holes to the inch.

Organette (or Style W Theatre Orchestra) rolls: Used by the Wurlitzer Organette.

Paganini Violin Piano rolls: used by the various Paganini expression orchestrions. Scale first devised by J.D. Philipps of Frankfurt am Main, Germany, and designated as the style "PP" (for Philipps Paganini) roll.

Pianino rolls: used by the Pianino, the Violin - Flute Pianino, the Bijou Orchestra, and related instruments.

Rolla Artis rolls: expression piano rolls, mainly intended for home use.

Solo Violin Piano rolls: for the Solo Violin Piano.

Theatre Organ rolls: made in a number of different sizes and styles over the years, including types with 97, 105, 130, and 165 hole width.

88-Note Player Piano rolls: for the early electric piano of the same name.

65-Note Automatic Player Piano rolls: the roll used on most standard Wurlitzer keyboard "nickelodeon" pianos and orchestrions. It is probably safe to say that during the production of Automatic Player Piano rolls (which began about 1908 and which, as of this writing in 1971, is still being continued by Mr. T.R. Tussing, who purchased some of the Wurlitzer roll making equipment in the 1930's) more different songs found their way onto rolls of this type than on any other orchestrion roll style.

The earliest Wurlitzer 65-Note Automatic Player Piano roll may have been the one designated as No.1 and having these tunes: "Florida Rag," "Whistle – Intermezzo," "Waving Palms," "Ragtime Nightmare," and "Bachelor Maids." However, Wurlitzer followed the practice (during early years only) of re-using earlier catalogue numbers once a particular roll fell from favor. Hence, another roll, also designated as "No.1", is known with entirely different tunes!

From the first 65-Note Wurlitzer roll, or "APP" roll as I call it earlier in this section, to the mid-1920's the rolls were arranged at the North Tonawanda factory. Beginning in the 1920's, QRS masters were used and Wurlitzer added the appropriate controls, percussion, and other extra effects.

### Things to Come; Acknowledgments

The idea of making new music rolls is similar to the idea of owning a press to print money! Actually, the manufacturing of a perforator and the consequent use of it is a lot of hard work, and of the many who have started in this field, only a few have achieved success. However, hope springs eternal – and I am sure that coming years will see many more successful perforators being built, including many which will incorporate solid-state devices and other modern technology.

Automatic musical instruments are being appreciated for what they are: ingenious devices capable of turning out serious (or frivolous and light – as the occasion and taste dictate) music capable of providing pleasure and enjoyment. The key to the enjoyment of any instrument is the music available for it. From basic nickelodeon instruments such as Seeburg A roll pianos to wonderfully complex orchestrions such as the Hupfeld Pan and Weber Maesto newly arranged music as well as recut music from older times will come. A new era of enjoyment is in the offing as interest in roll making increases by leaps and bounds.

In closing, I make special acknowledgment to Art Reblitz and Alan Lightcap for supplying me with certain information for this article; information I couldn't have obtained elsewhere.

———David L. Junchen

## RECOLLECTIONS OF P.M. KEAST
### Edited by Art Reblitz

*During 1969 and 1970, Art Reblitz, music roll arranger and historian, conducted an extensive correspondence with Mr. P.M. Keast of Elmhurst, Illinois.*

*Mr. Keast's recollections, edited somewhat but essentially unaltered so as to preserve the flavor of his thoughts, are of interest as they provide an insight into the roll manufacturing business in the Chicago area and the personalities involved.*

### P.M. Keast, an Autobiography

Excerpts from a letter dated December 8, 1970, from P.M. Keast, then owner of the Keast School of Music in Elmhurst, Illinois, to Art Reblitz:

"Here is a chronological summation of my roll making connections and activities over the period 1917 to 1930:

"I joined the QRS roll division of the Melville Clark Piano Company at DeKalb, Illinois (my home town) in the fall of 1917 working in the arranging department.

"Two types of rolls were produced – the QRS rolls for player pianos and rolls for coin operated mechanical musical instruments, the latter chiefly for the J.P. Seeburg Piano Company and the Operators Piano Company.

"My initial assignment was with style O rolls for Coinola orchestrions (made by Operators). I arranged and edited the music for the scale of these rolls and composed drum, violin pipe, flute pipe, etc. parts and located operating slots for them. Later I worked with the arranging and editorial staff on piano rolls. This work afforded me an opportunity to study the styles of Arden, Kortlander, Wendling, Confrey, and Roberts – the backbone of the artist pianists whom I was able to duplicate by hand (reasonably well, I like to believe).

"About 1920 Melville Clark died and Tom Pletcher acquired control of the QRS Company and moved it to Chicago. I went along but maintained my home in DeKalb. When Ernest G. Clark (brother of Melville) acquired the mechanical roll department in 1921 and moved it back to DeKalb I went with him to be in charge of the arranging department of the Clark Orchestra Roll Company.

"Clark continued to make all of Seeburg's rolls, but Operators Piano Company developed a roll department of its own under the direction of Mr. R.V. Rodocker, formerly head of the coin operated mechanical division of QRS. It was called the Capitol Roll and Record Company and was located at 721 North Kedzie Avenue in Chicago. This outfit made rolls under the Columbia and Capitol labels. In addition, 88-note home player rolls were made for Sears & Roebuck.

"In the spring of 1924 I left the Clark Orchestra Roll Company and joined my old friend Rodocker at Capitol where I remained until the Depression caught up with the company in the spring of 1930. Since then I have pioneered in the instrumental music field in the public schools of Chicagoland and have retired since 1954. The Keast School of Music is my retirement interest.

"So much for my personal activities.

"Regarding your question concerning the conversion of 88-note piano rolls into the 65-note scale for mechanical instruments, it is difficult to draw a word picture of the procedures. Some were entirely rearranged on what was called 'master paper,' a fairly stiff but pliable paper, by hand from the music – marches and waltzes for instance, or from the hand played roll itself, keeping in mind the limitations of the automatic instrument such as power, the 65-note scale, etc.

"We also used a duplicating machine for some rolls, particularly those not in strict rhythm, such as 'Nola' by Felix Arndt. This method required rearranging and editing to meet the special needs of the instruments.

"We never, to my recollection, used a keyboard to record 'O' roll parts.

"We used an arranging board at QRS and Clark. Capitol used a different but equally effective method.

"On page 163 of Harvey Roehl's excellent book, 'Player Piano Treasury,' Clark's 'Coin Slot' describes the process of punching masters quite correctly. Phil Oberg was the operator while I was with Clark and Art Norberg preceded him at QRS. Both were very fine workmen.

"The arranger (or recording machine) indicated the desired note by drawing lines on the master paper. The unit of measurement was 'one punch.' The master puncher located a punch at each end of the line and a slot was then cut between the two punches (as indicated by dotted lines). This slot thus became a note.

"A two sided rhythm scale was used to determine the placement of the notes rhythmically and we used two scales – 3/4 and 4/4 on one side and 2/4 and 6/8 on the other. Forward movement of the master paper was controlled by a ratchet cog wheel device. Final editing and correction of mistakes followed the 'puncher' and 'cutters' and the master was then OK for use in cutting the rolls.

"I had two pianos and an arranging board in my work room, and I enjoyed every minute of it.

"With regard to names and addresses, I am sorry to say that I have been out of touch with former associates for many years and can be of small help here, I'm afraid. The best I can do is give you the names of those whom I can recall.

"Legend: P.R. = Piano Rolls. A. = Automatic (coin operated). O. = Organ music.

"QRS at DeKalb, 1917: Fred Phillips (arranger P.R.); Roy Lauer (arranger P.R.); Zignor Swanson (arranger P.R.); P.M. Keast (arranger P.R. and A.); Mike Kommers (arranger A. and O.); R.V. Rodocker (arranger A. and O.; superintendent); Art Norberg (master puncher); Violet Glass (master cutter); Myrtle Beyer (master cutter); Art Boesenberg (production manager – boxing).

"Clark Orchestra Roll Co. at DeKalb, 1921 - 1924: Ernest G. Clark (owner and manager); P.M. Keast (arranger A.; chief); P.H. Keast (my brother) (arranger A.); Harry Hamilton (arranger A.; drummer; drum parts); Marion Wright (arranger O.); Phil Oberg (master puncher); Violet Glass (master cutter); Myrtle Beyer (master cutter).

"Capitol Roll and Record Co. at Chicago, Illinois, 1924 - 1930: R.V. Rodocker (arranger P.R., A., O.; head of department); P.M. Keast (arranger P.R., A.); H. Gullman (arranger P.R. and A.; died in 1925); plus one more person, whose name I don't recall, who did a little bit of everything.

"All of the hand played rolls were recorded in the studio in Chicago under the direction of Lee S. Roberts and Max Kortlander. Max was the real work horse. Rarely did any of the recording artists visit DeKalb, so we didn't know them personally. However we all greatly admired and appreciated their talent and skill. Some rolls were recorded under a nom de plume arrangement, such as Scott and Watters who were really Roberts and Kortlander. (Ed. note: Watters was a name later used also by J. Lawrence Cook.) Poetic license, I guess!

"Mr. Reblitz, I sincerely hope I have been able to throw a little light on what might very well be called a 'lost art.' This brief look 'behind the scenes,' as it were, has been a real pleasure, I assure you, and I appreciate your interest in my former work.

"The mystery of piano roll making was indeed just that for me in 1917, but it was so fascinating that the time seems only yesterday and it is all so clear to me that I feel I could take up tomorrow right where I left off over forty years ago.

"Very few of us of the old regime are left, I'm afraid, and the old techniques have been replaced by more modern ones which is as it should be. My view is a nostalgic one, of course, but I feel that society suffered a great loss when the player piano and the coin operated mechanical instrument passed out of our lives."

–––Sincerely,
P.M. Keast

January, 1932 65-note (type "A") coin-piano roll catalogue issued by Capitol.

Catalogue No. 2, issued by the United States Music Co. in January, 1910, offered rolls for $1.50 each, or $1.25 in lots of a dozen or more. Offered were these rolls: In the 70,000 series, rolls for Peerless Style M and Style 44; in the 75,000 series, rolls for Standard, Imperial, and Favorite (65-note type); in the 80,000 series, rolls for Reliable, Majestic, Automatic, Binghamton, Hamilton, and Thayer (65 note; most of these were the Automatic Musical Company's "Reliable" piano sold under different names); 85,000 series, rolls for Peerless 65-Note Style D; 90,000 series, rolls for Ackolin, Electrova, Ackerman, and Edison (65-note coin pianos); 95,000 series, rolls for Pianova, AutoElectra (or AutoElectrola), Regal, Imperial, Majestic Jr., Electrova, and Electrolin (all 44-note cabinet-style pianos). Rolls were of 5-tune length and were endless.

The United States Music Company billed itself as the "largest makers of electric piano music in the world" at the time.

September-October, 1935 Clark Orchestra Roll Co. "Bulletin." The latest-dated Clark offering seen by the author is an August 25, 1942, letter which notes: "We have quit the roll business and have only one or two rolls left out of a good-sized assortment – from the stock on hand when paper seemed to be more valuable, as such, than in roll form, when junking it for defense purposes . . ."

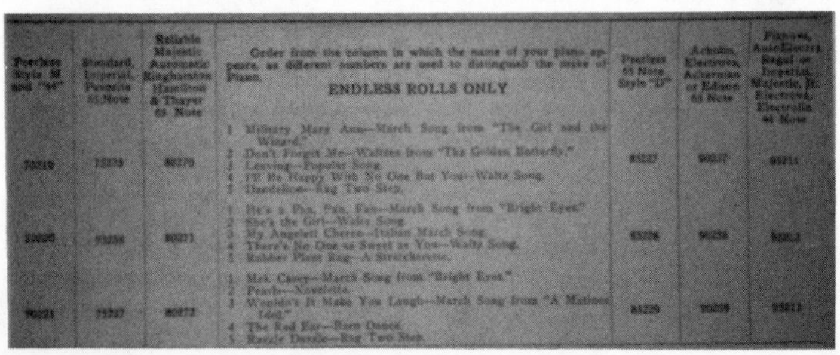

The Clark Orchestra Roll Co.
Tells Its Own Story...

We reproduce selected features that once appeared in "The Coin Slot," house publication of the Clark Orchestra Roll Co., and in a series of brochures. They give an insight into some of the "behind the scenes" activity at this roll making firm. (Information courtesy of Mr. A. Valente and the Vestal Press)

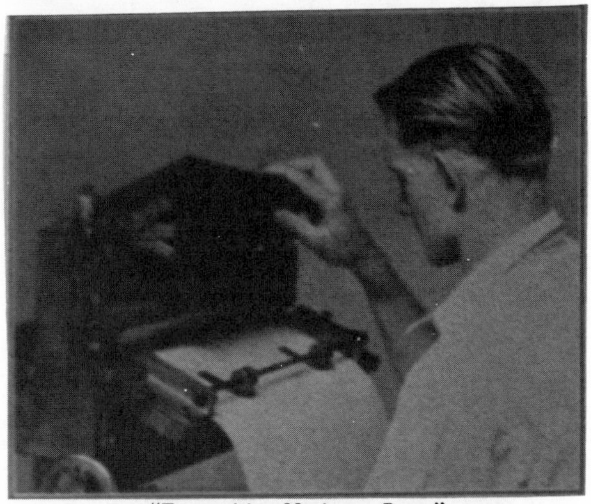

"Typewriting Music on Paper"

"You may never have heard of typewriting music on paper but isn't that just what Mr. Oberg appears to be doing? The punch machine he operates resembles a typewriter with its banks of keys and levers, and the notes are perforated in the master record in much the same way that characters are typed on your letterhead in a typewriter.

"When the master record comes from the recording piano it is simply a roll of paper with a lot of pencil lines. Not even Paderewski could produce music from such a sheet. But under the expert hand of Mr. Oberg the master record is perforated correctly and with mathematical precision and it then becomes a real music sheet capable of producing music when played on the test piano. Clark Orchestra Rolls can hardly help being the most accurate and perfect electric piano rolls made."

"11,000,000 Feet of Music"

"The fact that his department turned out over 11,000,000 feet of music last year doesn't seem to be worrying Mr. Larson as he guides a score of sheets of music paper through this continuously moving perforating machine.

"As the master sheet passes over the tracker bar before his eyes, where he can watch its operation, punches are biting into a moving pile of sheets of paper on the table below, reproducing every note from the master above. Specially treated paper is used in order to eliminate shrinking and swelling resulting from changes in humidity and temperature.

"One of the greatest enemies of perfect player operation is lint and dust. If cheap and carelessly made electric rolls are used on your piano, bits of paper and lint are sucked into the tracker bar holes, eventually clogging them. By cutting Clark Orchestra Rolls UPSIDE DOWN, the feather edge produced as the punches pierce the paper is formed on the side of the paper which is NOT in contact with the tracker bar of the piano.

"Every step in the manufacture of Clark Orchestra Rolls is hedged about with safeguards which guarantee perfect performance of the completed roll."

"Miss Harmes – The Trouble Shooter"

"The cost of making Clark Orchestra Rolls could be greatly reduced if they were taken as they come from the perforating machines and made ready for shipment, but Miss Harmes believes that things done by halves are but one-fifth begun.

"This young lady carefully compares the finished cutting with an original which is kept on file. If any extra notes are discovered or omissions noted, corrections are made with her small hand punch, before the cutting is allowed to proceed to the next operation.

"Fortunately, Miss Harmes' services are not needed continually but her watchful eye is a guarantee of the accuracy of Clark Orchestra Rolls. Note: Quantity production methods do not include this step in manufacture because of its cost."

"Getting the Jazz on Paper While It's Hot"

"Getting the jazz on paper while it's hot is part of the work of Mr. Wright in the making of Clark Orchestra Rolls. As snapped here, he is playing 'Smilin' Through' for use on one of the standard 65-note electric piano rolls.

"As his fingers strike the keys of the recording piano, the notes are automatically transcribed on a moving master record in the form of short and long lines which later become perforations under the sharp punch of the master machine. Nine other compositions must be recorded to compose, with the piece he is playing, a ten-tune roll.

"In addition to the recording of compositions, a conference of the musicians of the arranging department is held each month to select the best of the new music and to determine the most desirable grouping of numbers into rolls. The ability of the musicians to pick the best music and to inject into the records the snap and pep of the dance orchestra determines the quality of the finished roll and the amount of money it will earn when used on a coin piano.

"Judging by the number of voluntary commendations received from users of these famous rolls, there is a 'something' in Clark Orchestra Rolls that tickles the public palate."

**"Meet Mr. Keast, Our Editor"**

**"Did you ever meet a music roll editor? If not, shake hands with Mr. Keast, the editor of Clark Orchestra Rolls.**

**"Here he is at work eliminating the 'bum' notes made by the recording pianist — perhaps Mr. Wright — and censoring the style and the arrangement. No matter how skillful the recording pianist may be, errors are likely to creep into his playing and unless they are caught and corrected before the master is completed, they will produce glaring inaccuracies in the finished roll.**

**"Mr. Keast's wide experience as a dance orchestra leader gives him a real appreciation of dance rhythm and melody and enables him to secure perfect tempo and harmony in every Clark Orchestra Roll. That is why the public is willing to spend more money to listen to them."**

THE COIN SLOT

Vol. 1 December, 1925 No. 7

Devoted to increasing profits from electric pianos. Published monthly by Clark Orchestra Roll Company, DeKalb, Illinois, and distributed exclusively to dealers.


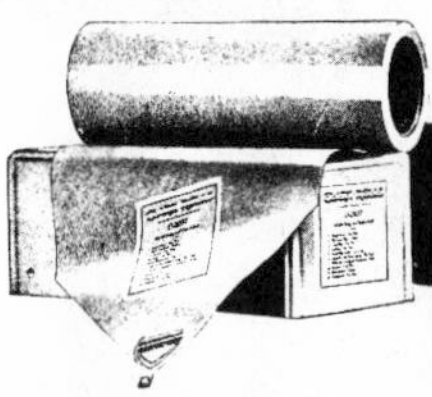

Coinola and Empress orchestrions, as well as all orchestrion combinations are served by this style "O" CLARK ORCHESTRA ROLL.

### ALMOST ONE PIANO A DAY IS JUSTER'S RECORD

Twenty automatic pianos in thirty days is the record made by Mr. Juster of Green Bay, Wisconsin, who is successfully selling Western Electric coin pianos throughout the northwest.

The secret of Mr. Juster's success is hard work and a good piano. The record he is making can be equalled by any other energetic dealer who has faith in himself and realizes the size of the automatic field.

"There isn't any other article in the world," declared Mr. Juster to a Coin-Slot representative, "that will pay for itself like the automatic player. An auto is an expense. So is any other merchandise you can name. But an automatic piano will actually pay its own way in a short time."

He asked especially that no names be mentioned in reporting the interview but it is a matter of record that some of his piano buyers have earned as high as $250.00 in a month while the payments may run only $50.00. But no matter what the piano earns, he pointed out, the purchaser will always have the monthly payments materially reduced thru the earnings of the instrument.

Asked what one thing was most important in the sale of automatics, Mr. Juster replied that new music was the main requirement and he so arranges his sale prices as to cover a year's service in tunings and repairs, with a change of music EACH WEEK.

Mr. Juster has touched upon two points eternally emphasized by the Clark Orchestra Roll Company: the fact that automatics are EASY to sell because they pay their way and the importance of late rolls. Music dealers who have never sold automatic pianos have yet to experience the thrill of a sale devoid of the resistance encountered in selling a player piano which is simply an outright expense with no means of returning the investment except in enjoyment.

When music dealers generally come to realize that automatics are a valuable and money-making line to sell, the few dealers who already know that fact will find it harder sailing. Perhaps the initiated few would prefer to "let the ignorant ones sleep on", as one dealer expressed himself.

---

We wonder where the music publishers find names for all of their compositions. There must be some alliance with the person or persons who name Pullman cars. Perhaps it would be possible to combine their efforts and use the same names on both cars and music.

---

Black Romeo: "Did you get those flowers I sent you, honey?"
Black Flapper: "Nothin' else but."
Black Romeo: "Did you like those flowers I sent you, honey?"
Black Flapper: "Nothing else but, Romeo."
Black Romeo: "Did you wear the flowers, honey?"
Black Flapper: "Nothin' else but."
Black Romeo: "Is that so, honey, what did you pin 'em on?"

---

It's a lucky thing for the few music dealers who know the money which can be made with automatics that the rest of the trade isn't wise. There are rumors of a Society For The Supression Of Knowledge Of The Money To Be Made With Automatics. Applications are now being received by the secretary, Earl G. Alden.

---

Buy a new roll of music every week.

### AS A TYPIST, MR. OBERG POUNDS A TERRIFIC KEY

Punch! Punch! Punch! The song of the shirt has nothing on the music made by Phil Oberg as he typewrites the latest jazz or heart-throb ballads onto the slowly moving master with this ingenious punching machine.

Phil didn't undergo a course in pugilism before taking up his work with the Clark Orchestra Roll Company. Although he is known as a master puncher—his work is musical and not fistic. Long years of experience in this important task have given him the knack of anticipating the right punch to deliver a "knock-out" when the music is finally played on the automatic piano.

Before Mr. Oberg receives the master for punching, it leaves the recording machine as a roll of paper with a lot of short and long pencil lines spattered on, apparently without regard to order or purpose. The uninitiated would say a youngster had been permitted too free a use of the lead pencil but to Mr. Oberg's experienced eye every line means a certain note on the piano and it is possible to read the melody from the master just as the musician plays from the printed score.

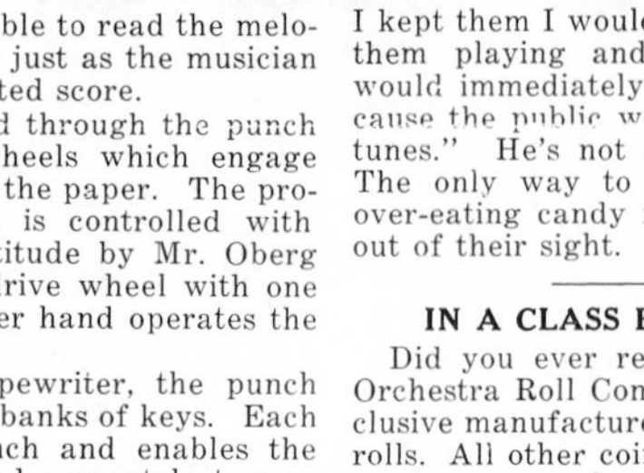

The master is fed through the punch machine by cog wheels which engage holes in the edge of the paper. The progress of the sheet is controlled with mathematical exactitude by Mr. Oberg who operates the drive wheel with one hand while the other hand operates the punches.

Not unlike a typewriter, the punch machine consists of banks of keys. Each key controls a punch and enables the operator quickly and accurately to perforate the proper note.

Odd as it may seem, Mr. Oberg punches only the beginning and end of the long notes and observers are tempted to point out his oversight. But there is a reason for the omission. It is far quicker and just as effective to connect the first and last perforations of each note by the cut of a sharp knife. And this is just what is done by girls who complete Mr. Oberg's work on the punch machine. And when the master finally leaves the perforating department it is an actual music roll although hardly adaptable to the ordinary player piano because of its greater width. It is, however, tested and played on special pianos which enables the editor to catch mistakes and to check harmonies.

But how does the master make the finished roll, you ask? How can hundreds of rolls be produced from the one master?

Wait. Next month's Coin Slot will reveal the wonderful process by which the masters are duplicated.

---

An automatic piano that is not producing for its owner is nothing more than a piece of furniture. Why not pass a law compelling all automatics to go to work?

---

Said an automatic piano owner the other day, "I burn up all my old music rolls after they've served a month. If I kept them I would be tempted to keep them playing and I know that that would immediately stop the income because the public won't play to hear old tunes." He's not so far wrong either. The only way to keep children from over-eating candy is to keep the candy out of their sight.

### IN A CLASS BY OURSELVES

Did you ever realize that the Clark Orchestra Roll Company is the only exclusive manufacturer of automatic music rolls. All other coin-operated music roll producers are also manufacturers of automatic pianos or players. Perhaps that explains the superiority of Clark Orchestrat Rolls over music produced by firms with divided interests. With us music rolls are our sole interest, not a means for selling more pianos.

CLARK ORCHESTRA ROLLS
are the popular rolls for electric pianos.
Snappy, melodious musical arrangement; programs selected to suit public taste; careful construction; and a long margin on sales, make them a profitable line for you to sell.
65-NOTE REWIND ROLL
A ten-tune roll for all standard rewind electric pianos. Unbreakable fibre containers and substantial cardboard cores are features in keeping with the high musical quality of the roll. Supplied on either 3-inch or 3 1-2 inch cores.
"STANDARD" ENDLESS
This five-tune endless roll plays the "Standard" coin-operated players. It is made for both styles A and G.
"O" 88-NOTE ORCHESTRATED ROLL
Ten pieces. The original 88-note orchestrated roll for Coinola and Empress Orchestrions. Especially arranged to produce effective traps accompaniment.

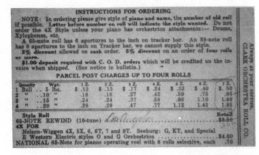

An advertising brochure of the 1920's illustrated these three types of Clark rolls. The accompanying text was: "WHAT FEET TELL— What happens to YOUR feet when you listen to a lively tune? Righto! You can't keep them from beating a staccato rat-tat-tat on the floor. The livelier the music the harder they work. The feet then are a sure gauge of the quality of a tune. And that is where Clark Orchestra Rolls surpass the ordinary electric piano music. Because they DO set feet a-going and keep them active, you may be sure that they meet with public approval. And there's no need pointing out that if a roll is LIKED, it brings in the nickels! Three of the most popular styles of Clark Orchestra Rolls are illustrated on the inside of this folder. Look them over carefully, then write for catalogues."

## Clark Orchestra Rolls

Are Made for the Following Automatic Instruments

**65-Note Rewind Coin Operated Electric Pianos**
**Also Calliopes and Calliaphones**

**Using 3½ Inch Core**

Capitol
Chicago Electric
Cremona Styles, 1, 2, 3, G, A-Art, B-Art, C-Art.
Eberhardt
Empress 65-note
Engelhardt
Eusymphonic
Gordon-Howard Calliope
Harwood
Heller
Howard
Jewett
Lehr
Marquette
Midget Orchestra
Monarch
Violophone
Western Electric A, C. F-J, X, Derby
American
Carleton
Casino
Casino X
Coinola A and C and Cupid
Colonial
Cote
Nelson-Wiggen Style 1 Banj-O-Grand Style 2 Banjo X Style 3 Styles 4 and 8
Originators
National 20R
Nat'l. Calliope Corp.
New-Tone Air Calliope
Presburg
Price & Teeple
Regina
Reichard
Schaeffer
Seeburg A, B, C, E, F, K, L. & P. G A.
Starr
Tangley Calliaphone
Victor
Western Electric Styles A, C, X, J.

**Using 3 inch Cores**

Anderson
Ariston
Armstrong
Autoelectrola
Billings
Concertrola
Decker Bros.
Electratone
Evans
Haines
Ideal
Wm. A Johnson
Kibby
King
Kreiter
Netzow
Reed
Rhapsodist
Schultz
Standard F and GR
Waltham
Watson
Wilson

Music for these Instruments is always in stock and your orders will be promptly filled.

Rolls for Credit Must be returned within 5 days from receipt of order.

See other pages for styles 4x, 5x, 5, 6, 6T, 7, G, KT, KT Special, P, Q, W,—Also Seeburg XP Rolls.

**INSTRUCTIONS FOR ORDERING**

NOTE: In ordering please give style of piano and name, the number of old roll if possible. Letter before number on roll will indicate the style wanted. Do not order the 4X Style unless your piano has orchestrion attachments:— Drums, Xylophones, etc.

A 65-note roll has 6 apertures to the inch on tracker bar. An 88-note roll has 9 apertures to the inch on Tracker bar, we cannot supply this style.

2% discount allowed on cash order. 5% discount on an order of four rolls or more.

$1.00 deposit required with C. O. D. orders which will be credited on the invoice when shipped. (See notice in bulletin.)

**PARCEL POST CHARGES UP TO FOUR ROLLS**

| Quantity | Wgt. | 1 Z. | 2 Z. | 3 Z. | 4 Z. | 5 Z. | 6 Z. | 7 Z. |
|---|---|---|---|---|---|---|---|---|
| 1 Roll | .. 5 lbs. | $ .13 | $ .13 | $ .17 | $ .24 | $ .33 | $ .40 | $ .50 |
| 2 " | ..10 " | .18 | .18 | .27 | .42 | .59 | .75 | .95 |
| 3 " | ..15 " | .24 | .24 | .37 | .59 | .86 | 1.10 | 1.40 |
| 4 " | ..20 " | .29 | .29 | .47 | .77 | 1.12 | 1.45 | 1.85 |

| Style Roll | Retail |
|---|---|
| 65-NOTE REWIND (10-tune) | $3.00 |
| 4X FOR Nelson-Wiggen 4X, 5X, 6, 6T, 7 and 8T. Seeburg: G, KT, and Special E Western Electric styles O and G Orchestrion | $4.60 |
| NATIONAL 65-Note for pianos operating reel with 8 rolls selective, each | .70 |

Always at your service.
CLARK ORCHESTRA ROLL CO.

BULLETIN
CLARK ORCHESTRA ROLLS
September-1925
ELECTRIC PIANO MUSIC

# CLARK ORCHESTRA ROLL COMPANY

MANUFACTURERS OF

CLARK ORCHESTRA ROLLS

**HAND-PLAYED MUSIC FOR REPRODUCING ORGANS, AUTOMATIC PIANOS AND ORCHESTRIONS.**

*Roll-Makers For 40 Years*

**DE KALB, ILLINOIS**

LEABARJAN MANUFACTURING Co.
—Hamilton, Ohio—

*The following history of the Leabarjan Manufacturing Company, maker of the Leabarjan Music Roll Perforator, was provided by David L. Junchen in a letter to the author/editor of this book. Mr. Junchen tells of a May 6, 1969, conversation with Leo F. Bartels, formerly a principal of the Leabarjan firm:*

I have just concluded a very pleasant conversation with the last owner of the Leabarjan Company, Leo F. Bartels. The company was incorporated October 10, 1911, with a capital of $100,000. John C. LEAse was the inventor of the perforator, and Carl BARtels joined the firm also. Mr. JANzen was the financial backer. Hence "LEABARJAN." Carl Bartels was the company president, his son Leo was secretary, and Franz Janzen was vice president and treasurer.

In later years Carl and Franz abandoned their interest in the company. Its operation was continued by Leo until he sold the company in 1928 to some men who wanted to use it for a machine show. He credited the demise of the company to the rising popularity of the phonograph. The building, at 521 Hanover Street in Hamilton, has been razed, and another structure now stands there. None of the original investors in Leabarjan ever received even a single cent in dividends!

Although Leabarjan ceased business in 1928, inquiries are still being received by the firm! Most of these letters, forwarded to Mr. Bartels by the Post Office, are from collectors and others who want to locate Leabarjan perforators.

Mr. Bartels estimates the total production of perforators was under 1,000. The most popular model, the No. 5, sold for about $75. A number of production perforators (which made up to 16 copies from a master roll) were sold. Several dozen of these larger models, all electrically-driven (except for one hand-cranked model!), were made.

One of the company's founders, Franz Janzen, saw the perforator as a valuable educational device, and to a certain extent it was — but, of course, this was a very limited market. The greatest market for the perforator, and particularly for the production perforators (which sold for around $500), was to composers who wanted to plug their own songs when the major roll companies wouldn't! Mr. Bartels said that a considerable foreign market existed, particularly in South America. He said that no really large-scale production perforators (such as the 64-roll unit used by Q-R-S) were made. Bartels mentioned that famed roll-arranger J. Lawrence Cook got his start by perforating on a Leabarjan!

———David L. Junchen

# LEABARJAN

## The Leabarjan Perforator in the Schools

The above illustration shows one of the Leabarjan Perforators, Style 5, being used for educational purposes in a public school room. The music teacher is demonstrating the use of the machine to a group of students.

The Leabarjan Perforator affords a very interesting and successful method of teaching the time values of notes and rests, the position of notes on the staff, the piano key-board, different scales, and all the fundamental principles of music. The science of music is a separate and fundamental subject, the problems of which should be mastered, if possible, before the instrument of expression is chosen. This is possible where the student learns to make a perforated music roll—with the Leabarjan Perforator genuine music study will be a pleasure and the student will be anxious to accomplish a greater task each day.

The Leabarjan Perforator will give the music student a tangible record of his knowledge of music; a record that will not only be a book of notes that he has written or from which he has played or studied, but a roll of perforated music that will immediately reveal the accuracy of his musical understanding.

## Q-R-S MUSIC ROLLS, INC.
### —a history—

*The following history was written by Brian Williams and appears here through the courtesy of Ramsi P. Tick, owner of Q-R-S. Note: "QRS" has used several different forms of punctuation over the years, including QRS, Q.R.S., and Q-R-S, the latter form being the one currently used in company correspondence.*

Q-R-S Music Rolls was established in 1900 as a subsidiary of the Melville Clark Piano Company. We are the oldest and largest manufacturer of player piano rolls in the world today.

The meaning of the three Q-R-S initials has been lost with the passage of time. The best explanation we can discover is the motto "Quality, Real Service" or "Quality Roll Service" – as printed in some of our old catalogues.

Q-R-S grew to become the largest roll manufacturer in the world during the early 1920's. During the 'twenties and early 'thirties, Q-R-S purchased many other small roll companies and was involved several times with the government concerning antitrust violations.

Q-R-S became the Q-R-S DeVry Corporation during the mid-1920's and branched out into many other home entertainment areas. Motion-picture cameras and projectors, phonographs and Q-R-S-label records, and Q-R-S Redtop Radio Tubes were among other products sold by Q-R-S. Q-R-S Neon Signs, once affiliated with our firm, exists today as a separate company in California.

During the 1920's, Q-R-S sold as many as ten million rolls per year and maintained factories in Chicago, New York, San Francisco, Toronto, Sydney (Australia), and Utrecht (Holland).

Max Kortlander was a leading recording artist for Q.R.S. during the 1920's and was in charge of the recording department. While with Q-R-S he published several songs, one of which, "Tell Me," became a hit.

Also employed by Q-R-S during this era was J. Lawrence Cook, the company's featured artist specializing in hot rags and Dixieland songs.

When the Depression hit the piano roll industry, roll sales dropped to five million per year. Q-R-S DeVry went through bankruptcy. Max Kortlander purchased the roll division of the corporation and named it Imperial Industrial Corporation. J. Lawrence Cook was the only recording artist retained by the new company.

With the exception of the Aeolian American Corporation, which continued to manufacture rolls (including Ampico and Duo-Art reproducing piano rolls) until the late 1930's, Q-R-S was the only piano roll maker to continue operations after the Depression. Roll sales continued to decline during the 1930's. An upturn came during World War II. Sales went up to about one million per year. In postwar years, roll sales declined to a low point of under 200,000 rolls annually.

During the 1950's, people began to rediscover the player piano. With this renewed interest in the field, Aeolian marketed a new spinet-type player piano called the Hardman Duo. Presently, Aeolian is marketing several models of player pianos. In 1968 about 3,500 were sold. At the present time (1971) several other firms are in the player business. Total production is estimated at several thousand instruments per year. Currently Q-R-S manufactures just under a half-million rolls annually.

In the early 1960's, Aeolian re-entered the roll business. The Aeolian factory is located in Oregon, Illinois. J. Lawrence Cook has arranged many of the rolls.

In the mid-1960's, Larry Givens and John Gourley formed Givens-Gourley, Inc. The firm produced Melodee (brand) rolls during the late 1960's. Presently, Larry Givens, a Givens-Gourley co-owner, produces new and recut rolls (including reproducing piano rolls) for collectors. The original Ampico perforators are used in the Givens facilities in Wexford, Pennsylvania.

When Max Kortlander died in 1961, the Imperial Industrial Corporation was purchased by Ramsi P. Tick. The corporate name was changed to Q.R.S. Music Rolls, Inc. The facilities were moved to Buffalo, New York, in August, 1966. Today, Q-R-S employs six part-time arrangers and adds two new songs to its catalogue every week. The number of active titles in the Q-R-S catalogue is maintained at a level between 2500 and 3000, in order to facilitate production and inventory control. Older songs are removed from the catalogue as their popularity decreases, but the masters are retained so that they can be returned to the active catalogue at any time.

The production of piano rolls has changed very little since the 1920's. The equipment used by Q-R-S today is the same used then.

To make a player piano roll, the recording artist first arranges the song to utilize the many extra features available on a piano roll. Then the artist plays the song on a recording piano which punches the notes he plays into a cardboard master roll. The recording piano is equipped with two rows of stops which allow the artist to hold down extra notes and create a four-hand arrangement with only two hands. The piano operates at a very slow speed and may be stopped at will. Thus it requires between 6 and 8 hours to punch the first master roll.

After the master roll is made on the recording piano, it is edited to correct any errors. Wrong notes are removed by covering them with Scotch Tape. Missing notes are added by cutting with a razor blade. The master roll is then used on a production perforator which can produce 64 copies of the master roll in ten minutes.

The title and tempo of the roll are stamped on each copy by hand. The point is cut on the end of the roll with a double-blade paper cutter. The end tab or hook is pasted onto the point by hand. Words are stenciled onto each roll. Then the rolls are spooled and boxed. The rolls are now ready to provide toe-tapping music from yesteryear – or the latest hit tunes.

Victor Arden

VICTOR RECORD and Q.R.S. PLAYER ROLL ARTIST

Max Kortlander.

MANAGER RECORDING DEPARTMENT of Q.R.S. MUSIC CO.

Q·R·S
TRADE MARK REG.
PLAYER ROLLS
are Better

Lee S. Roberts,

VICE-PRESIDENT, Q.R.S. MUSIC CO. and WORLD'S LEADING AUTHORITY on PLAYER ROLLS.

# ACME NEWARK MACHINE WORKS, INC.

DESIGNERS AND BUILDERS OF SPECIAL MACHINERY AND TOOLS

115-117 MONROE STREET

NEWARK, N. J.
U. S. A.

The Acme Combination Master Roll and Music Roll Perforator is an ideal automatic machine for producing five hundred to one thousand music rolls per day. It is practical for either a large or small music roll manufacturer. Machine is furnished complete with steel paper rack holding sixteen rolls. Packed in two cases for export. Gross weight about 1800 pounds. Net weight 1400 pounds. Occupies a floor space of ten by three feet.

PLATE 8

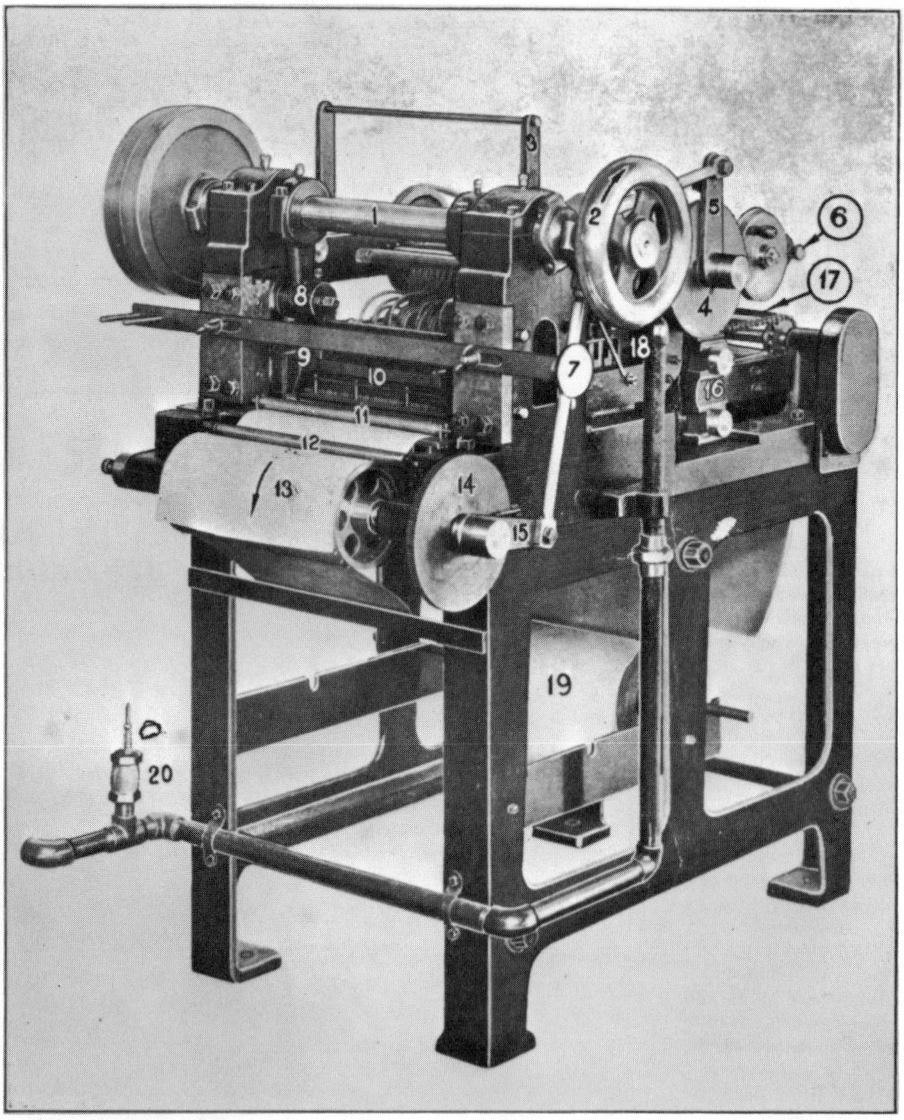


1 MAIN SHAFT.
2. HAND WHEEL.
3. MASTER ROLL HOLDER.
4. MASTER DRUM RATCHET.
5. RATCHET ARM AND PAWL.
6. GEAR FOR REWINDING MASTER ROLL.
7. BELT SHIFTER.
8. ECCENTRIC WRIST PINS.
9. PAPER TRIMMING KNIVES.
10. PUNCHES AND SELECTOR HOLDER.
11. TENSION ROLL FOR MASTER PAPER.
12. ECCENTRIC ROLL FOR ADJUSTING MASTER PAPER.
13. LOWER MASTER DRUM.
14. FEED RATCHET FOR LOWER MASTER DRUM.
15. RATCHET ARM AND PAWL.
16. PAPER FEED BEARING BRACKETS.
17. PAPER FEED MECHANISM.
18. AIR VALVE TO PNEUMATICS
19. BLANK MASTER ROLL PAPER.
20. AIR ESCAPEMENT VALVE.

**Music roll perforating was once a large business in the United States. Devices sold for music roll cutting ranged from small perforators designed to cut one roll at a time to large production-line machines such as the Acme device shown above. According to the above description it could cut from five hundred to one thousand rolls per day. From twelve to eighteen rolls were usually cut at once.**

Music Rolls of Modern Times . . .

These photographs, taken in the 1960's, show that the process of music-roll-making has changed very little over the years.

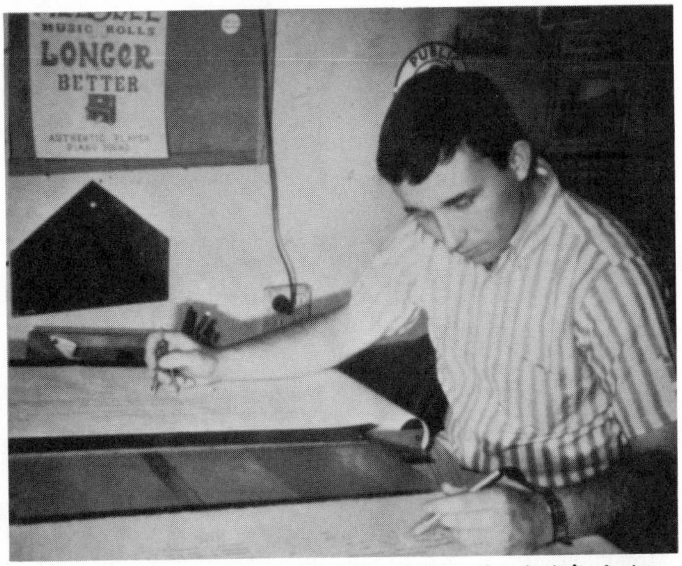


After the master roll is recorded directly from the pianist's playing a production master is copied from it. The production master roll is the roll from which hundreds of thousands of copies are made on high-production perforating machinery. The master roll is several times longer than the original roll, for purposes of accuracy and speed of perforation. This 1967 photograph shows John Gourley checking a production master against the original roll. (Larry Givens photograph)

Ed Freyer of Flemington, N.J., uses a modified Acme perforator to produce recut type A, G, and Link rolls for collectors. (Vestal Press photograph)

A partial view of the twin perforator used by Givens-Gourley, Inc. in the 1960's. Thirty rolls are perforated at once; fifteen thicknesses of paper on each side. The production master roll (left) and the right-hand perforator unit are shown here. The left-hand perforator is not visible. (Larry Givens photograph)

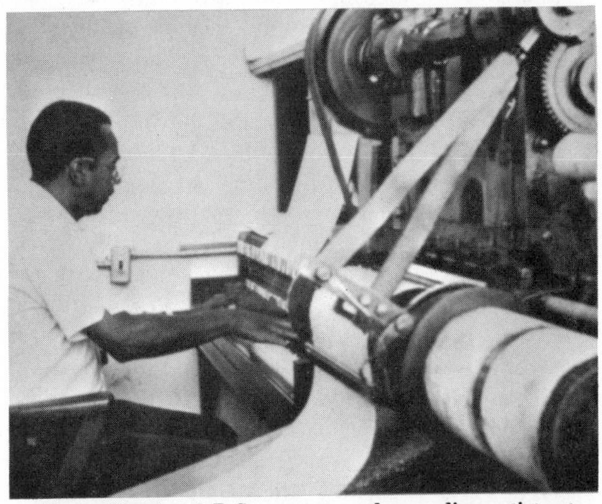

Rudy Martin, Q-R-S arranger and recording artist, at the recording piano. Note two rows of "stops" above the keyboard. These hold down extra notes. The master roll is in the foreground. (Q-R-S Music Rolls, Inc. photograph)

Left: Gary Graley stencils words on a piano roll at Q-R-S Music Roll Company's Buffalo, N.Y., factory. (Q-R-S photograph)

Right: Audrey Mazur winds new rolls onto plastic spools. (Q-R-S Music Rolls, Inc. photograph)

# HOW TO CARE FOR YOUR COLLECTION
## —and other comments—
*by Larry Givens*

Dictionaries habitually define "collector" in terms of "accumulator." The usual treatment of the word implies a certain haphazard assembling of a body of items for purposes of study, comparison, or exhibition. Thus, I cannot escape the conclusion that few lexicographers are collectors – because their definitions of the word omit what is to me the most important facet of collecting; *pleasure.*

Since most readers of the *Encyclopedia of Automatic Musical Instruments* will be collectors, or at least persons who are interested in collecting, hopefully I may assume a foreknowledge on the part of the reader of the pleasure which collecting may bring. It is difficult to describe, even to those who are familiar with it. And certainly the sphere of collecting illustrates the incredible diversity of human tastes. It is safe to remark that *nothing* is too unusual or bizarre to be collected. Matchbook covers, streetcar timetables, telegraph insulators, barbed wire, cigar bands, hearses, buttons, flatirons, hatpins, electric signs... the list could go on forever.

An advanced collector will sometimes force himself to incredible expense or inconvenience to acquire a piece which closes an important gap in his collection. Recently a close friend of mine, the owner of the most complete collection of steam locomotive builders' plates in the nation, told of a 1400-mile trip he made in search of an abandoned locomotive which he had seen in a photograph. On the slimmest threads of information, he succeeded in locating this locomotive, which miraculously still bore both of its builders' plates. The tale became grim as he related the story of his struggle to remove the plates, perched on a narrow walkway beside the engine's boiler, working for hours with hand drills and chisels in a blizzard of snow and freezing rain. Night came, and he was forced to work with a flashlight, holding it in his mouth while he relentlessly attacked the corroding hulk. A concert pianist by profession, his hands – his most valuable asset – became numb and raw. Finally, with a mighty lunge he tore the last rusted bolt from its mooring, staggered to his car with his precious cargo – and is now the possessor of two of the four known examples of this extremely rare type of locomotive plate!

This story, while unusual in the degree of effort expended by the collector, is typical of similar tales which could be told by collectors of mechanical musical instruments. Perhaps some enterprising film producer will, in the future, make a short screenplay of the story of a collector of coin pianos. It could be chaptered as follows:

THE SCENT; in which the collector overhears the dim and alcoholic recollections of an intoxicated barfly to the effect: "They had a big roller pianna with drums and violins and fancy glass in a speakeasy 'bout fifty mile north of here."

ON THE TRACK; in which the collector spends weeks of spare time in fruitless search of every likely spot "'bout fifty miles north."

FIRST SIGHT; in which the collector rubs a clear spot in the misty windowpane of a decaying building and catches a heart-stopping glimpse of an orchestrion sitting forlornly amid peeling wallpaper and heaps of rubbish.

STALKING THE PREY; in which the collector spends still more time attempting to locate the owner of the building and (hopefully) the owner of the instrument.

CLOSING IN; in which the collector is greeted at a creaking doorway by a senile rheumatic who croaks "Yes, we had a *tea room* there during Prohibition... But I'll have to talk to my brother Harry before I could sell the piano." (Harry has been dead for four years!)

THE KILL; in which the collector presses many green bills into the hand of the confused crone, persuades her to locate the key to the building, and dashes off to a local bar to try to find some form of animal life to help him load his dearly-bought acquisition.

VICTORY; in which the collector, glazed of eye and tremulous of hand, speeds out of town in his pickup truck, wearily trying to decide how much he can safely tell his wife he paid for the latest addition to The Collection.

Of course, collecting does not need to be this arduous! In the field of mechanical musical instruments, as in most other hobby fields, a number of dealers offer a wide variety of items in restored or unrestored condition for prospective purchasers. The beginning collector may be well-advised to make his first acquisitions from a reliable dealer until he has become sufficiently acquainted with the various facets of his field to be able to evaluate for himself the condition and price of prospective additions to his collection. Every veteran collector can tell tales of "getting burned" on unwise acquisitions; and, generally speaking, purchasing from a dealer of repute is the safest, albeit the least dramatic, way to avoid the pitfalls which may lie in the path of the beginning collector.

The beginner in the mechanical instrument field will be faced with important questions as he contemplates a purchase. He must ask himself: "Can I accommodate this instrument?" Obviously, a high-rise apartment dweller can hardly collect band organs – but he may be able to collect some of the less intrusive instruments quite comfortably.

The next questions might be: "Is it worth the price?" "Is the instrument's condition satisfactory, or will I have to spend additional time and money upgrading it?" "Are new music rolls available for it, or will I have to rely on locating old rolls?" "If the instrument needs service, can I do it myself?" These and other important aspects of prospective purchases must be considered carefully.

Perhaps the least "disruptive" type of mechanical instrument collecting would center about reproducing pianos and musical boxes. These instruments were originally intended to be *lived with,* in homes, in contrast to coin pianos, band organs, photoplayers, orchestrions, and most other instruments which generally require more space. Musical boxes can be placed about the house and provide much enjoyment when played at random moments; and a fine reproducing grand piano is an asset to any home from both the decorative and the musical standpoints.

## Housing the Collection

As previously stated, I believe that the prime *raison d'etre* of collecting, in any field, is the *pleasure* which the collector receives from his ownership of the objects he collects. Yet it is an unusual collector who makes his acquisitions without regard for their market value in case unforeseen necessity should force a sale.

Within recent years mechanical musical instruments have been rising in value at a rapid pace, and this has unquestionably helped to "bail out" the hapless collector who overpaid for what he bought five or ten years ago. In my opinion, the value of mechanical musical instruments will continue to rise in future years, as the fixed (or slightly dwindling) supply will have to satisfy an ever-increasing number of collectors who will have no choice but to pay the "going price" if they want to acquire pieces. Yet, as in every collecting field, it will be the rare and very desirable pieces – the large American and European classic orchestrions, the art-cased reproducing pianos, the large and intricate musical boxes, in short, the items that were "top of the line" decades ago when they were first sold – that will set the highest price records. From an investment viewpoint, the finer the instrument, the higher the price future owners will be willing to pay for it. Rarity and the prestige of owning them have combined to make such instruments the showpieces of any collection – and the items most easily sold for the best prices when a collection is dispersed.

As in any collecting field, the wise automatic musical instrument aficionado would do well to emphasize quality rather than quantity. Taking another field as an example, the collector of automobiles would be wiser to put his funds into one fine Duesenberg than a shed full of Chevrolets in "rough" condition!

As the collector of mechanical musical instruments struggles to fit his sixth piano into a space which can only accommodate five, his thoughts turn enviously toward the stamp collector or coin collector who can house his entire collection in one or two chests of drawers. "The space problem" is a term which needs no further definition to the instrument collector, or at least to those who have chosen to acquire the larger instruments. And, assuming that the space is found, the requirements for adequate maintenance and preservation of the instruments must then be considered. Temperature, obviously, must be controlled: extreme heat will destroy varnish and result in cracking of finishes, and extreme cold will permit moisture to accumulate with severe effects. Humidity should be kept as constant as possible to prevent seasonal swelling and shrinking of wood, with gradual loosening of glued joints, sticking or rattling of small wooden parts, and pressure or vacuum loss in pneumatic actions.

As far as possible, instruments should be kept away from sunlight to avoid rapid and irregular deterioration of their finishes. Ideally, instruments, as well as other objects of value, should be maintained at a temperature close to seventy degrees Fahrenheit, a humidity between forty and sixty percent (although many collectors in drier climates have found that twenty to forty percent is fine – the main thing to do is to keep the humidity constant once it is established, in order to prevent continual expansion and contraction of the wood), and in a location which is shielded from bright light most of the time. Few of us are able to give our instruments such perfect surroundings. However, possession of these instruments places, in a sense, an unwritten obligation upon their owners to provide storage conditions sufficiently favorable to their well-being that no deterioration of the instruments will occur.

Turning again to the automotive field for example, the hypothetical collector who purchases a fine classic 12-cylinder Packard and then "stores" it outdoors, fully exposed to the elements, is committing the same crime as the individual who disregards the leaking roof over his classic Weber orchestrion!

Instruments, particularly those of piano size and larger, should be moved (that is, relocated) as infrequently as possible. Regardless of how careful or how professional the moving personnel may be, in my opinion a certain amount of damage occurs each time a large instrument is relocated, and in many cases the damage is of an invisible nature. Pianos are extremely heavy objects, and if they are dropped even slightly, the shock effect to the wood fibers and glued joints is tremendous. Obviously, it does no harm to wheel a piano out from the wall for cleaning behind it – provided the casters are tightly screwed to the case, lubricated, and in good working order. But the relocation of large instruments by truck, with the concomitant loading and unloading, should be minimized. Sometimes damage can occur even when moving instruments out from the wall! I recall with particular horror an incident which occurred about ten years ago when I was rolling a large Link orchestrion forward. For some reason which I never did determine, the frame of the stained glass front was not fixed tightly to the case. As I swung one end of the instrument outward from the wall (with both hands occupied) I had the unforgettable experience of watching the glass front tilt forward in a lovely arc, then smash itself to bits on the concrete floor. Since that day I have become more cautious when moving instruments of any sort.

## Humidity as a Factor in Rebuilding

A moment ago we discussed ideal storage conditions for instruments. Now it might be beneficial to survey ideal *rebuilding* conditions, as related to pneumatic instruments.

I say "pneumatic instruments" because this class of instrument is the only one affected by climatic changes to any great extent. A small percentage of instrument collectors live in portions of the country which are relatively unaffected by winter cold; but by far the larger number of collectors must contend with the effects of artificial heat on their instruments. These effects can be largely mitigated through humidification of the area in which the instruments are kept. But desirable conditions in rebuilding shops are not the same as in storage areas!

When rebuilding pneumatic instrument mechanisms, it is advantageous to keep the shop area as dry as possible. In winter this is easily accomplished by the omission of artificial humidification; in summer, air conditioning is a great help in reducing atmospheric humidity. The aim is to *pull moisture out of the wood*, so that when the parts of the pneumatic systems are assembled, screws can be tightened firmly, gaskets can be compressed to their limit, and the systems can be made virtually airtight under dry conditions. Then, when the systems are replaced in their instruments and are operated under average humidity conditions, the wood will take on moisture, swell slightly, and become even *more* airtight!

The same modus operandi should be applied even when doing routine service work on instruments during the winter months, at which time the screws in the pneumatic units and other locations can profitably be tightened to eliminate leakage.

Care and Servicing of the Piano

Many mechanical musical instruments are constructed such that a piano constitutes the main, if not the entire, portion of the instruments' sound-producing capabilities. The pianos which were incorporated into these instruments were generally of high quality, particularly those which were intended for commercial use where the going was rough and the pianos had to take a constant beating. Frequently these pianos, when unearthed today, are still basically in good condition though they may have been denied any form of maintenance for years or even decades. Since mechanical pianos (except reproducing grands) are of the vertical type, I want to pass along a few hints on the improvement of vertical piano performance.

Most important of all – *eliminate lost motion.* The most deadly enemy of the vertical action is lost motion between jacks and hammer butts. Assuming that the piano action is not too badly worn, this lost motion under the butts can be removed quickly by simple adjustment of the capstan screws at the end of the piano keys. The adjustment should be made to a point at which there is no *free* motion of the whippen and jack – that is, the hammers should begin to travel toward the strings immediately upon the slightest depression of the keys. If necessary, the leather surfaces of the butts should be lubricated with powdered graphite at the points where the jacks strike them.

The screws which fasten together the various parts of the piano action are subject to shock and vibration, and tend to loosen quickly. All screws in the action assembly should be tightened periodically, especially those which anchor the hammer butts and the whippens to the main action rail. This takes half an hour for the average upright action, but it will pay dividends. Also, grasp each hammer head and test it for tightness on its shank: these seem to have a tendency to loosen on upright actions, particularly where mechanically operated. Needless to say, the other aspects of action maintenance should not be overlooked: hammers should be shaped to a rounded striking surface, letoff should be adjusted to 1/8" from the strings, and the backchecks should be adjusted with care. A word on this final point: the repetition of the action will be much improved if the backchecks are adjusted to catch the hammers *close* to the strings. Standard practice calls for the hammers to be checked approximately 5/8" from the strings, but in my experience 1/2" is a more suitable point for mechanical piano actions.

An elementary study of physics of bellows will quickly show that a pneumatic, on a constant suction, develops maximum closing force when it is in its wide-open position. Take full advantage of this fact by eliminating lost motion between the striker rods of the player stack and their corresponding impact pads on the piano action. If lost motion is present at this point, the most powerful and useful portion of the stroke of each pneumatic will be wasted – not to mention the resultant disagreeable noise from the sharp blow of the striker rods on the pads, and the rapid wear on the moving parts of the piano action due to their being struck rather than pushed.

Many elderly pianos can be given a surprising pickup in bass tone generation by twisting the bass strings two or three turns in the appropriate direction to tighten the wire wrapping around the core of each string. The whole set of bass strings can be twisted in little more than half an hour, and the results can be amazing. Slacken each string at its tuning pin, remove the loop from its hitch-pin, twist it (holding with pliers), re-install the loop on the hitch-pin, place the string through its appropriate stagger pins on the bridge, and re-tune it to normal pitch.

Speaking of tuning, this gives me the opportunity to lecture the reader on what is probably the most important facet of any mechanical musical instrument's ability to perform well. I speak, of course, of tuning. Most of us have heard the common remark of the layman; "I can't tell whether something is in tune or not" – and he may well be speaking absolute truth when he comments to this effect. However, what this same layman *could* distinguish is the quality of sound produced by a well-tuned instrument as contrasted with an identical instrument which is badly in need of tuning. Virtually any person's hearing is keen enough to discriminate in this manner, at least when comparing two instruments in quick succession. In my opinion, a feeble instrument which barely manages to operate, but which is in tune, is far easier to bear than the most vigorous and forceful instrument which is playing grossly out of tune.

I recall all too vividly an experience I had some years ago in a large city of the northeastern United States. I was paying a quick visit to a collector who had just completed restoration of a large and extremely rare American coin-operated orchestrion. He had done a superb job: the instrument was a splendid sight to view, and as he dropped a coin through the slot I eagerly watched the vacuum reservoir snap closed and the pressure reservoir fly open on the first spin of the pumps. "This will be something to remember," I thought to myself – and it surely was, although in a manner most grim. The orchestrion began producing the most petrifying racket I had ever heard. The rhythm of the music was discernible, but the composer himself would not have recognized whatever melody was playing. Mercifully, it was soon over, at which time I smiled wanly and made some inane remark to the effect, "That was really something."

A few questions about his restoration procedures brought forth the remark, "I meant to have the piano tuned while the machine was apart, but I got anxious to put it back together and begin listening to it." A quick comparison with one of the xylophone bars revealed that the average level of the piano was approximately two whole tones below the pitch of the xylophone and the pipes. At that point I suddenly recalled that I had several hundred miles of driving ahead of me and I was most regretful that I would be unable to remain longer to listen to the other instruments in this gentleman's collection.

The geometrical layout of the tone-generating portions of a piano is called the *scale* of the piano (not to be confused with the musical scales which can be practiced on the instrument). The scale designer is an extremely skilled individual, familiar with acoustics, stress relationships in metals and wood, musical requirements of the instrument, and all the other factors which must be considered in piano production. He determines the size of the sounding board, the placement of the bridges and ribs, the tension, length, and gauge of the strings, soundboard loading, and other things. He must try to hit the proverbial happy medium between a high-tension scale which will give his piano plenty of power but a harsh tonal quality, and a low-tension scale which will provide delicacy and sweetness of tone but at a reduced volume level. Once an effective scale has been created, it is a valuable asset of the piano maker. The scale designer of one of America's leading piano manufacturers told me a few years ago that the present scale of the concert grand piano made by his company has remained unchanged for nearly fifty years, because they have found no way to improve upon the tonal qualities of that scale.

Piano scales are designed to give optimum results at *concert pitch*, which today is standardized at 440 cycles per second for the fundamental frequency of A above middle C on the keyboard. The strings of a piano exert a force of approximately twenty-five tons on the iron plate of the instrument. Over a long time, this tension will cause the pitch of the piano to drop, due to the stretching of the string wire, changes in the soundboard crown, slight rotation of the tuning pins in the wrest block, and other factors. Often old pianos will be found which are a considerable distance beneath concert pitch but which have dropped evenly over the entire span of the keyboard, and are consequently not too badly "out of tune with themselves." In the case of orchestrions, photoplayers, and other instruments in which the piano must play in unison with fixed-pitch components such as a xylophone or pipes, the piano obviously must be maintained at concert pitch or the musical results will be disastrous. But a word of warning is in order: any piano which is permitted to play below concert pitch is not producing its full tonal capabilities. Even a slight reduction in pitch will cause changes which will reduce the efficiency of tone generation. For this reason it is imperative that pianos be *maintained at concert pitch*, at which point their full tonal potential can be realized.

The present concert pitch of A=440 cycles per second has been the standard in the United States since the early 'twenties. Earlier the pitch was at the A=435 standard, so a pre-1920 instrument must be tuned to the older standard in order to achieve the desired musical results.

When restoring mechanical musical instruments containing a piano, restringing and renewal of action parts should be considered carefully. In my experience, collectors are too prone to rush into an instrument and almost automatically tear out the old strings and hammers and action parts for replacement. Obviously, there are cases in which replacement is plainly called for: badly rusted strings or moth-devoured actions cannot produce good results. But in instruments which are still in reasonably good condition, see what can be done with the original parts before making any decisions about restringing or new actions.

Perhaps the best case in point is an instrument which represents one of the outstanding pieces in my own collection. In 1963 I had the good fortune to locate a Seeburg Style H orchestrion in Canada. I purchased it and brought it to my shop; and a few cursory taps on the keys indicated to me that the piano portion of the instrument would require extensive restoration. The tone was hollow and the volume weak; the bass section was the poorest I had ever heard. Faced with what I thought was major work on the instrument, I procrastinated: it sat untouched for months. Finally my ambition returned and I removed the various components of the orchestrion's upper compartment, thus exposing the piano. During the removal operation I noticed that the tubing from the piano playing stack to the upper chests controlling the pipes and xylophone had been transposed several steps downward, and I soon discovered why: the piano had gone more than two whole tones flat, and some unknown "craftsman" had attempted in a makeshift manner to keep the pipes and xylophone in step with the gradually flattening piano by relocating the tubing and thus effectively flattening the fixed-pitch components too! Probably this piano had never known a tuning since it left the Seeburg factory during the late 1920's. In an experimental humor, I decided to pull the piano up to concert pitch – an operation which must be performed carefully on instruments which are more than one-half tone low, or a cracked plate can result. As I tuned, my amazement grew. The piano, which had been about as musical as an empty washtub at its former pitch level, *came alive* as I raised it! The volume of sound increased severalfold; the tone quality became powerful and rich! I became particularly intrigued with the change in quality of the bass section, in which (recklessly risking string breakage) I pulled the strings upward through the entire distance during one blow of the hammers, thus hearing the complete transformation of quality without any interruption.

After completing the initial tuning, I did a quick regulation of the action, removing lost motion, shaping hammer heads, and fitting the player stack to the piano action carefully. I went over the tuning again, as the instrument had fallen nearly a quarter-tone as the result of having been pulled upward such a long distance all at once. This time the tuning held reasonably well, and I shall never forget the first experience of listening to many of the rolls I had acquired, until the wee hours of the morning, with only the piano portion of the instrument playing. Subsequently, of course, I tuned the instrument several more times, adjusted the action carefully, and twisted the bass strings, all of which served to increase the volume and quality of the piano tone still more. This Seeburg H orchestrion is one of my most prized pieces today, still playing on its original strings and action and certainly one of the most vigorous instruments of its type to be heard in this country.

If the owner of an instrument is not well acquainted with procedures of tuning and action regulation, it may be the safest course to employ a professional piano technician. It is rather a long job, at least in the case of the larger instruments, to remove the inner components in preparation for tuning the piano; and it would seem foolish to go through these procedures unless one could be sure that the tuning would hold for a reasonable length of time. Ultimately, of course, the owner of the instrument ought to learn how to maintain it, unless he has professional maintenance service. Learning how to tune aurally requires the investment of hundreds of hours of practice and experience. Many persons feel that an acceptable job can be produced with the various electronic tuning aids available through piano supply houses, and generally I would agree with this statement, providing that the person using the electronic device is completely familiar with it.

Tuning, of course, is only a fractional part of the maintenance of mechanical instruments which employ pianos. The pneumatic systems of these instruments, when properly restored, are usually quite trouble-free – but occasional attention is still required. Perhaps the simplest, and sometimes the most neglected, maintenance procedure is the periodic cleaning of the tracker bar. Many manufacturers of pneumatic instruments furnished a tracker bar cleaning pump with each instrument they sold, and this pump was not intended merely as an ornament! Music rolls, particularly new ones, shed a prodigious quantity of lint which can have a devastating effect on the performance of instruments. Frequent use of the tracker bar pump will keep the bleeds and tubing clear. In the absence of a tracker pump, a vacuum cleaner equipped with a long flat crevice nozzle can do an efficient job removing this lint.

### Lubrication; Care of Belts

Any mechanical device requires lubrication. Periodic attention with an oil can will benefit bearings, shafts, and gears throughout any mechanical instrument. In the case of a pneumatic instrument, the lubrication will probably be confined to the transmission assembly driving the music roll spools, the accompanying shafts or chains powering the transmission, the electric motor, and perhaps the rods and cranks driving the pump.

The emphasis should be placed on frequency of lubrication, rather than quantity: a little oil goes a long way, and there is no need to drench the instrument! Use medium-viscosity oil in spots where it will have to work itself into an inaccessible area (such as bearings carrying shafts) – and use heavier oil, or even light grease, at points which are exposed, such as gears. Felt packing in electric motors should be kept saturated with medium oil at all times.

Most electrically-operated instruments employ belts for the transmission of power from the motor to the various mechanisms. Rubber V-belts, flat leather, and round leather belts are the types most often used.

In the case of leather belts, it is imperative that proper tightness be maintained or slippage will unquestionably result. V-belts can be operated with more slack than leather belts, but in certain cases even these can slip somewhat. The safest course is to maintain adequate tightness (enough to take out slack, but not so much that damage to bearings will result) – then use dressing on the belts. This belt dressing is most convenient to use in liquid form, but occasionally it may be supplied in stick form which is also quite efficient. By applying a small quantity to the pulling surfaces of the belts while they are in motion, the dressing will spread evenly over the surfaces, providing positive purchase and eliminating slippage. After replacing belts, particularly leather ones, make a mental note to check them periodically for tightness, as new belts are liable to stretch slightly.

### Reproducing Grand Pianos

Of all mechanical musical instruments, the reproducing grand piano probably warrants the most careful maintenance. No other type of instrument is expected to produce music with the delicacy and expressive qualities of the reproducing piano. The demands made upon the instrument by the music rolls require that the piano itself, as well as the pneumatic mechanism, be maintained in top condition if the musical results are to be satisfactory.

My earlier remarks regarding tuning, action regulation, tracker bar cleaning, and lubrication apply to the reproducing grand piano just as to other classes of instruments. There are certain other additional factors, however, which must be considered in the grand. The regulation of the piano action is of the utmost importance throughout the dynamic spectrum, but particularly at pianissimo levels. The pianissimo performance of the piano will be improved if the letoff of the hammers is set slightly closer to the strings than the usual specification suggests. Most piano makers specify 1/8" as the letoff point, but 1/16" will provide a more velvety pianissimo without the frustration of missed notes. This smoothness of pianissimo is, of course, predicated upon the fact that the valve clearances in the pneumatic stack are adjusted to a maximum travel of 1/32". Excessive valve travel is *fatal* to soft playing. Another factor of prime importance in good pianissimo performance is the removal of all lost motion between the heads of the striker wires and their corresponding impact points on the lower surface of each piano key.

Earlier in this article I referred to the effect of seasonal variations in temperature and humidity on piano playing mechanisms. Reproducing pianos, with their requirements for precise adjustment of their pneumatic mechanisms, are particularly susceptible to these seasonal changes. It well befits any owner of a reproducing piano to learn how to make simple adjustments of the playing level of his piano, and these are generally not difficult even for the piano owner who is not mechanically inclined. A vacuum gauge and a test roll are always useful, but the adjustments can often be performed "by ear" with perfect results. Information and procedures for these operations can be found in other literature in the field, at least for the three types of reproducing pianos which were widely sold in this country – Ampico, Duo-Art, and Welte-Mignon.

To my knowledge, in no other type of mechanical musical instrument is the electric motor situated with the armature shaft in the vertical position, as found in reproducing grand pianos. This peculiar orientation of the motor throws the entire weight of the armature on the thrust washer at the pulley end of the armature windings. I have always been annoyed by the fact that these motors were not equipped with thrust *bearings* at this point; but apparently cost factors were as omnipresent to manufacturers of half a century ago as they are today. Most of the thrust washers which are found in reproducing piano motors are made of porous fiber which absorbed a quantity of the grease with which they were originally coated and thus provided a fairly satisfactory lubrication for a number of years of service. However, the original lubricant tended to become thicker with the passage of years, and this resulted in less efficient lubrication of the thrust washer's surfaces. This led to heating of the motor, which in turn only served to solidify the lubricant still faster. I have seen these motors barely able to start themselves, much less generate vacuum to play the piano, as a result of the sticky varnish-like remains of the original lubricant surrounding the thrust washer. It is imperative that these motors be taken apart for cleaning and lubrication every few years. The old grease should be wiped away and the thrust washer soaked in a solvent to remove as much grease as possible from its pores. It should then be re-lubricated using the best possible grade of grease (and I have found nothing which can surpass the molybdenum or lithium greases which have been developed for automotive use). While the motor is apart, the contacts and sliding parts of the starter switch should be cleaned and slightly lubricated where necessary.

### Care and Repair of Music Rolls

With the notable exception of musical boxes and other cylinder or disc-operated mechanisms, mechanical musical instruments are programmed from music sheets of perforated paper. Generally these are in the form of rolls, but even the folding cardboard "book" music is only a different form of the same basic perforated sheet, the origins of which date back to the early nineteenth century. Obviously, the owner of a mechanical instrument has to have music rolls with which to play it, and this fact has caused many a headache for collectors who are faced with increasing difficulty in locating original rolls in playable condition.

Sometimes original rolls which are in damaged condition can be acquired – or perhaps, by accident, good music rolls become damaged. At this point, the collector is faced with the necessity of repairing these rolls; and there are certain procedures which are wisely followed or additional damage may result when the rolls are played.

Music rolls can be repaired with tape, and it is of prime importance that the tape be of the permanent type which will not deteriorate with age. Ordinary pressure-sensitive mending tape is short-lived, and within the space of a few years it can turn music rolls into useless masses of gummy paper. Certain pressure-sensitive tapes are designed for book mending, and this variety is generally safe for music roll repair (Scotch No. 810 "Magic Mending" tape, not to be confused with ordinary "Scotch tape," is the most commonly found permanent tape).

In lieu of permanent pressure-sensitive tape, very satisfactory music roll repairs may be made with thin gummed "onionskin" tape, also made for book mending, which may be purchased at stationery supply stores. In the event one is hapless enough to acquire gummy rolls which have already been "repaired" with common pressure-sensitive tape, the tape can be removed by liberally soaking the back side of the paper with cigarette lighter fluid, which will soften the sticky portion of the tape enough to permit peeling it off and wiping away the remaining adhesive from the paper's surface.

Music rolls usually sustain their damage along their edges. Frequently only one edge of a roll will be torn or frayed, in which case the obvious repair procedure would be simply to apply tape along the damaged edge. However, this is a pitfall which an experienced roll-repairer will avoid! Application of tape to one edge of a roll will create an uneven buildup of the paper on its spools as it plays and rewinds on the instrument. The result may well be far greater damage to the roll than before! Also, the paper of the roll will acquire a permanent warp from the irregular stresses generated by the tight winding of the paper on its mended edge and its looseness on the opposite edge. When repairing music rolls, place the tape on *both* margins of the paper, to create an even buildup on the spools and equalize the tension on the paper as it passes over the tracker bar. Admittedly, this is twice as much trouble as taping only one edge; however, it will give excellent results, and it will serve the additional purpose of protecting the undamaged edge during future playing.

In the case of severely damaged rolls which are missing portions of paper, new sections may be set into the rolls quite successfully by tracing the outline of the missing sections onto new paper, cutting out the traced areas, and fitting them into the vacant spaces in the rolls. Tape the new section into the roll in such a manner that the edges of the new and old paper butt against each other (rather than overlap) to avoid uneven buildup of the roll on the spool as described in the preceding paragraph. Trim the marginal edge of the new paper *after* it has been taped into place, using a very sharp cutter and a straightedge.

In the event that music rolls require splicing, always arrange the splice such that it is diagonally oriented with respect to the roll margins. This will cause the splice to pass across the tracker bar during an interval of one or two seconds, rather than all at once – and the probability of air leaking under the paper will be reduced.

Many music rolls were manufactured in such a manner that their perforations contain "chain links" of paper which cross the perforations at intervals and provide lateral strength and resistance to sidewise buckling. Since these links must necessarily be quite small to avoid unwanted repetition of the notes being played, they are weak and are easily torn out. Their function is vital to music rolls with extended perforations (such as reproducing piano rolls), and in some cases they must be restored or the roll cannot be used at all. This can be accomplished by completely taping up the perforations, then re-punching the chain links with a sharp round punch of proper diameter (obtainable from suppliers of collectors' restoration materials). The tape will bridge the perforation and will provide chain links which may be considerably stronger than the originals. This same method may be used for strengthening music rolls by adding chain links to perforations which contained no links originally. In this case, the adhesive surface of the tape which is exposed through the perforation area should be rubbed with talcum powder to prevent unwanted adherence to the next layer of the music roll.

Although it may seem too patently obvious to warrant mention, I cannot forbear a brief reminder of the importance of proper alignment of music roll spools for long roll life. Virtually every type of roll-operated mechanical instrument contains some provision, either automatic or manual, for aligning the two roll spools with the tracker bar and with each other. Occasionally setscrews loosen, springs weaken, automatic tracking mechanisms malfunction, or some other cause will disturb the alignment of the entire spool box and tracker frame. Though this is admittedly an uncommon occurrence, it is good practice to glance at any music roll during the first few moments of its play, to catch any misalignment of the spools or the tracker bar.

### Whimsy

After twenty years of active collecting, I am reluctantly forced to conclude that the large segment of the population who are not collectors will never completely understand those of us who do collect. Through the years, thousands of persons have viewed my own collection of automatic musical instruments, and the great majority of these people have been intelligent, well-mannered guests who were genuinely interested in what they saw.

Inevitably, however, a small percentage of *infidels* have managed to get into the act. To these people the finest example of a rare and desirable instrument is a "crazy gadget" which is more an object of derision than something to be taken seriously. A typical dialogue might run along this line:

Infidel: "These things are all for sale, right?"

Collector: "No, these represent my personal collection and they are not for sale."

Infidel: "Well then, why do you have them? I mean, what *good* are they?"

Collector: "I have them because I *like* them. I'm interested in them historically as well as from the musical and mechanical standpoints."

Infidel: "You mean to tell me that you have these things just to keep for *yourself?*"

Collector: "That's right."

Infidel: "Gee, aren't they in good condition for being so old!"

Collector: "Most of these instruments have been painstakingly restored. They represent an expenditure of hundreds of hours of difficult work, and I can assure you that they were not in this present condition when I acquired them."

Infidel: "How much is all this stuff worth?"

Collector (grimly): "It's difficult to appraise these items because their values are changing, and I haven't attempted to add up their total w orth."

Infidel: "Do you ever turn all of them on at once?" (usually accompanied by uproarious laughter).

Collector (seething): "Get out. Out. Out. OUT!!!"

But, somehow we struggle through these wearisome incidents, which fortunately are outweighed by the many pleasures which result from our stimulating pursuit of mechanical instruments. Surely no one can deny that in terms of the expansion of historical awareness and appreciation, the cultivation of musical discernment, and the development of many excellent and long-standing personal friendships, collecting automatic musical instruments is a hobby which can be matched by few others.

# ORGANETTES
## —and—
# PLAYER REED ORGANS AND PIPE ORGANS

**Organettes**
**Player Reed Organs**
**Player Pipe Organs**
**and related instruments**

## ORGANETTES

### Introduction

The term "organette" refers to small hand-cranked instruments which produce music by wind pressure or vacuum acting on organ reeds. These range in size from small hand-held instruments (the Trumpetto is an example) with an 8-note scale to large instruments embracing a scale of many octaves; instruments which are in cabinets the size of a small upright piano. The dividing line between organettes and player reed organs is not a sharp one. Generally, larger keyboard-style instruments are referred to by the latter name, although the principles of operation are quite similar to those of the organette.

Organettes were generally made for indoor use. This differentiates them from certain varieties of hand-cranked barrel organs made by Gavioli, Limonaire, and others – loudly-voiced reed instruments intended for fairground use. In America the term "roller organ" has often been used to describe organettes. As the roller organ (operated by a pinned wooden cylinder) is just one of many different kinds of organettes, the organette term as used years ago in the music trade in America and as used today by collectors in Europe is preferable – and is used in the present text. The term "autophone" was used in the late 19th century to describe several different types of automatic musical instruments; organettes in particular. This term, occasionally encountered in early literature, was obsolete by 1890.

As a perusal of the following pages will indicate, the organette was called by many other names, some of which became trade or brand names, as well. Organina, organetta, orguinette, automatic organ, and auto organ were among such names.

As happened with the automobile, the airplane, and other products, the organette seems to have evolved from a combination of many ideas. Although numerous persons, John McTammany and Professor Merritt Gally in particular, claimed to be the inventor of the organette and related instruments, no one person was responsible.

An early organette-type of device is the Cartonium, constructed by J.A. Teste, an instrument maker of Nantes, France, in 1861, and presently preserved in the Museum of the Brussels Conservatoire. In his book, "Mechanical Musical Instruments," Dr. Alexander Buchner describes the Cartonium as "[similar in appearance to] a small harmonium without a keyboard and with forty-two free reeds arranged . . . in right-angled divisions of the air chamber. Each of these divisions has an opening to admit air to the chamber; the openings are covered by valves on the outer side. The air in the chamber is rarefied by two pumps and wedge-shaped bellows, worked by two pedals. When the valves are raised the reeds vibrate in the air sucked in; when they fall the reeds remain still. There is a device for perforating the cards attached to the instrument."

In the same book, Dr. Buchner further notes that "In this mechanism there were levers to control the valves vibrating free metal reeds. At the other end of these levers were jacks placed in a row the length of the box, and protruding slightly above the lid. In this position the jacks left all the valves open and all the reeds could vibrate at once. Above the jacks was a circular piece of metal with its edge almost touching the lid of the box; this sheet of metal had as many grooves as there were jacks, raised above the level of the lid to open the valves. If a piece of cardboard was passed between the metal sheet and the lid of the box, all the jacks were pressed down and closed the valves, rising only when there was a hole in the cardboard which allowed them to enter the groove again. All that was required to produce the sound of music was to pass through the Cartonium a strip of cardboard punched with holes according to a score. Smooth movement of the cardboard was ensured by rubber rollers turned by a crank; they held the entire breadth of the cardboard firm."

The foregoing, just one of several examples of early organette-type instruments, is described to counter the claims of John McTammany, who styled himself as "the inventor of the player piano" and as the inventor of the organette and player reed organ as well. McTammany, who did have many patents issued to him, mainly in the 1880's and 1890's, spent most of his later life trying in vain to prove his invention of these instruments. In a situation similar to that of the Selden Patents in the automobile industry, McTammany exacted licensing fees from several organette makers. Discredited by the music industry and ignored by Alfred Dolge in the latter's "Pianos and Their Makers" (published in two volumes in 1911 and 1913), McTammany published in 1915 "The Technical History of the Player," an attempt to vindicate McTammany's priority position. While present-day scholars and historians (e.g., Buchner, Givens, Ord-Hume, Roehl) do not consider McTammany to be the father of the pneumatic mechanism, sufficient McTammany-oriented data appears in early music industry annals that mention of the situation must be included here.

### Types of Organettes

Organettes were built in many forms. In America the preference was for roll-operated organettes of various types. In Germany, the other main area of organette manufacturing activity, the preference was for instruments operated by discs or heavy cardboard strips.

Leading types and a brief description of each follow:

Paper-as-a-valve type: In a typical organette of this type the organ reeds are located directly below the tracker bar openings. Vacuum (usually; however, pressure is sometimes used) is applied constantly to the reeds. When an opening occurs in the perforated paper music roll, air rushes through the large opening and directly causes the reed to sound. The first popular organette sold in quantity in America was the Trumpetto, an 8-note mouth-operated reed organ which used a rewind-type paper roll and operated on the paper-as-a-valve principle. H.B. Tremaine wrote that when he founded the Mechanical Orguinette Company in 1878 (Alfred Dolge cites an earlier date, 1876) the only popular organette-type instrument then in use was the Trumpetto. During the 1880's and 1890's the paper-as-a-valve instruments were made in many styles, usually as 14-key instruments using a paper strip or a rewind-type roll. The paper-as-a-valve system is simple. A vacuum supply, a set of reeds, and a method of passing a paper roll over the tracker bar are the essential features. Disadvantages include the need to use large tracker bar openings in order to admit a sufficient quantity of air to sound the reeds properly, a situation which limited the scale to about 14 to 20 notes on most instruments (exception: the huge E.P.

Needham Musical Cabinet which uses a 21 1/4" wide roll and has a larger scale) and which necessitated a larger music roll for a given number of playing notes. It is interesting to note that the Rolmonica (an organette sold as a "player harmonica" in 1928), one of the last organettes made for popular use, worked on essentially the same principle as one of the first, the Trumpetto.

Pneumatic action system: This system, embodying the same principles as used for the player piano and most other large pneumatic instruments, uses a tracker bar with small and closely-spaced holes. Each hole leads to a leather or rubber pouch which, when activated by the passage of air through a hole in the paper roll, causes a valve to act directly to admit air or vacuum to a reed or, in the case of instruments with secondary pneumatic actions, causes a valve to operate other mechanisms which, in turn, admit air or vacuum. The pneumatic action system was used by most organettes of the paper roll type after about 1885. The same principles were used in all but a few types of player reed organs. A very sophisticated and very early (1879) use of the pneumatic action system is described in a following section on "The Autophone," a reprint of a Scientific American article.

Key system: The music roll, a disc with projections on the underside, pinned roller, or cardboard strip operates a flap valve which covers the reed. When the metal or wire key is moved forward by a projection (or upward through a perforation in a sheet) the spring-loaded valve flap lifts and exposes the reed, thus causing the note to sound. In America the Gem, Concert, and Grand Roller Organs and certain early paper-strip-type organettes used this basic system. In Germany the key system was the most popular and was used on nearly all of the instruments made by Euphonika, Ehrlich, and Phönix, the three leading firms in the organette industry. Most German instruments use either a heavy strip or a disc made of cardboard or metal.

Some of the above principles were used in combination; a key-actuated pneumatic action system was used on certain Ehrlich instruments, for instance.

## The American Organette Industry

Massachusetts was the center of the organette industry in America. The premier firm in that state was the Munroe Organ Reed Company of Worcester. A history of this firm as printed in a Munroe catalogue notes that "The Munroe Organ Reed Company was organized January 1, 1869, with a capital of $13,300, and the manufacture of organ reeds commenced on Harmon Street, in the Wheeler Building, next east of the factory of the Taylor & Farley Organ Co. At first only half of one floor was occupied, their working force consisting of seven men. From the very first the Munroe Organ Reed was considered in most particulars the best in the market... The business increased, and in 1873 the capital stock was increased to $60,000, and in 1878 two-thirds of the entire building was secured for the rapidly increasing business.

"Even this increase in their accommodations was not sufficient, and arrangements were perfected with Stephen Salisbury to erect a factory on Union Street, directly south of the Loring & Blake Co.'s works. In December, 1879, the building was completed. The building is 135 feet long and about 54 feet wide and has five stories above the basement. Starting with a force of seven men, they have now on their payroll over two hundred workmen! In addition to the manufacture of reeds and organ materials, the company has recently added to their business the manufacture of Orguinettes, and has a standing contract with the Mechanical Orguinette Company, of New York, for the manufacture of their instruments, including all styles, which amount annually to over thirty-five thousand!"

By 1887 the output of the Munroe Organ Reed Company amounted to an advertised 50,000 instruments annually. The firm produced all of the early instruments for the Mechanical Orguinette Company (which changed its name to the Aeolian Organ and Music Company in the late 1880's) and instruments for dozens of other organette and player reed organ retailers as well. The Munroe Organ Reed Company name rarely appeared on its products; the seller's name was given. Munroe manufactured instruments under licensing arrangements with Professor Merritt Gally and John McTammany.

John McTammany, who earlier had two of his own factories in Worcester, was evidently employed by Munroe in the late 1880's, as per McTammany's statement that "Much has been said and written during the past few years about this and that concern having built up the automatic musical instrument business. But as a matter of fact, the Munroe Company [sic] of Worcester, Mass., turned out over 50,000 instruments a year, operating under a license from me [and Merritt Gally – Ed.], and to them and myself the country is indebted for the full development of the automatic musical industry up to that time – 1889. So that I had not only led in the invention of the player but in its manufacture also, and during the last two years of the existence of the Munroe Company I was general sales agent and controlled their entire output."

In 1892 the patents, supplies, and other assets of the Munroe Organ Reed Company were purchased by the Aeolian Organ and Music Company. Aeolian subsequently set up its own manufacturing facilities in Meriden, Connecticut, where it owned the Vocalion Organ Company. Celestina and Mandolina instruments were made in Meriden. The Wilcox & White Organ Company, also of Meriden, made some of these instruments also.

During the 1880's a thriving mail order organette business arose in America. The leading exponent in this field was the Massachusetts Organ Company in Boston. Paper roll instruments of the paper-as-a-valve type and of the pneumatic action type were sold by the thousands – 75,000 of the Gem Organetta alone, according to an advertisement. A typical ploy was to state, for instance, that the organette was worth $20 or equal to everyone else's $20 instrument. The price of The Instrument, however, wasn't $20 but was a super-bargain $10. Wait a minute! If you were an "agent" the price would be only $6. It was the task of the "agent" to show the instrument to friends and to "introduce" it to his area. Of course, all prospective buyers qualified as "agents" – and were entitled to the price which, in the case of the aforementioned Gem Organetta, was "less than the cost of manufacture."

The Massachusetts Organ Company was a master of ballyhoo. Examples abound in their advertisements of the day. Examples: (For a $10 Organina, a 16-note instrument) "Touch and expression of a superior organist are almost exactly reproduced, an effect which has never before been obtained in mechanical musical instruments... A more desirable instrument than a $100 French music box." Or, for the Mignonette Organina, likewise a 16-reed instrument: "It will fill any ordinary-sized hall and furnish acceptable music for any occasion which, by means of the swell, can be greatly varied in effect. For dances it is most admirable, and where otherwise musicians would have to be engaged, it will save its cost in one night." Many other sales agents made similar claims – which, if true, would have put every symphony orchestra in America out of business! The same sales techniques were used in England.

The American Automatic Organ Company, a firm connected with the Massachusetts Organ Company, helped broaden sales by ostensibly undercutting the latter firm's prices. About 1885 American billed itself as "the largest manufacturers of automatic mechanical musical instruments in the world, having been solely engaged in their manufacture for over five years." The firm offered the Gem Organetta for just $1.65 to whose who agreed to "distribute our circulars judiciously among friends." The Bates Organ Company, also of Boston, purchased organettes from several different manufacturers and offered them for sale, mainly in the $5 to $10 price range, in the 1880's and 1890's.

John McTammany's organettes, most of which were the 14-note paper-as-a-reed type, were distributed by McTammany himself, the Bates Organ Company, the Tournaphone Music Company (a Worcester, Massachusetts firm), the World Manufacturing Company, the Gately Manufacturing Company, and other agents (who sold other types of organettes [not just McTammany's] as well). The basic 14-note McTammany organette was also widely sold in Europe. The Tournaphone Music Company made a variety of paper-as-a-valve instruments, including large floor-standing or console models. John McTammany was evidently connected with this firm during the 1883-1885 period, if not for a longer time. Many Tournaphone products were sold by the Massachusetts Organ Company.

Any name that a selling agent desired would be stencilled on an organette. To cite but one example, the 14-note McTammany organette was sold as the Mechanical Orguinette, Mechanical Organette, Automatic Melodista, McTammany Orguinette, National American Organette, New Musical Orguinette, Victoria Organette, and Royal Orguinette.

In Meriden, Connecticut, the Wilcox & White Organ Company made several different varieties of organettes, some sold under the firm's own Symphonia label and others made with various stencilled names. The Wilcox & White instruments were well made. One model featured two banks of reeds with 20 reeds in each section.

Most types of paper roll organettes were provided with some type of expression mechanism, usually a simple hinged shutter which could be pushed down or lifted up to vary the volume. Many attachments, most of them useless so far as musical value is concerned, were offered. The Reed-Pipe Clariona offered "reed pipes" which were simply wooden channels above the reeds. Owners of these instruments found that it mattered little whether the reed pipe attachment was in place, so many of these which survive today lack this feature.

The Autophone Company of Ithaca, New York, owned by Henry B. Horton, produced the Autophone, a paper-strip organette, as early as 1878, as evidenced by a patent granted on it that year. Using a ratchet or a "click wheel" (as Horton called it) most Autophone models fed the paper strip through in a succession of stop-and-start steps, rather than in a continuous motion. Autophones were made in many forms, including table models and large foot-pedal-operated cabinet styles. In 1882 15,000 small-size and 3,000 large-size Autophones were manufactured by a work force of 45 persons.

The Autophone Company's main entries in the organette field were not Autophones, as successful as these were, but were the Gem, Concert, and Grand Roller Organs. Using a pinned wooden cylinder which directly actuated a hinged valve, these roller organs were a combination of simple and sturdy design with a rich tone. The Gem Roller Organ, the least expensive of the three instruments of this type, was produced in tremendous quantities (probably by the hundreds of thousands, if not over a million) and was the most popular brand of organette ever made in America. Such instruments were made at least up to 1914 (as evidenced by music trade directory listings).

The American market for organettes began in a small way in the 1870's, really flourished during the 1880's, was still quite active in the 1890's, and diminished during the early years of the 20th century. By 1900 such rival attractions as the home phonograph took the place of the organette as the premier instrument for inexpensive music in the home. The music box (disc type) offered competition also, but considering that the total production of the Regina Music Box Company (the leading American firm by far) was only about 100,000 instruments, a trivial figure in terms of organette production, and considering the much higher average cost of music boxes, the two types of instruments had little effect on the other's sales.

Production of organette-type instruments continued during the 20th century. As noted, the Autophone Company products were made at least until the beginning of World War I. In the 1920's and in modern times a number of novelty organettes have been sold. The Rolmonica, made by the Rolmonica Music Company and sold widely during the late 1920's and the 1930's, was built on the same basic principles as the Trumpetto of the 1870's. The QRS Play-a-Sax and Clarola of the same era operate in a somewhat similar manner. Chein & Co. of Burlington, New Jersey, has produced organettes in recent years.

## The European Organette Industry

The European organette industry was centered in Germany, although many instruments were made in England and France as well.

In Germany emphasis was placed on organettes operated by discs and sturdy perforated cardboard or metal strips.

The most successful of all German-made instruments was the Ariston, a disc-operated organette of 24 notes (usually). Introduced in the mid-1870's by Paul Ehrlich (who later was owner of the Leipziger Musikwerke), the Ariston was sold until the early 20th century. In 1890 an article about the instrument noted that "The Ariston, with its easily changed disc-shaped records, certainly is among the best and cheapest mechanical musical instruments. Well over 200,000 of these instruments and millions of records are already distributed throughout the globe, and therein lies the fascination that every nation rediscovers its national melodies on the Ariston. The Ariston record catalogue now includes nearly 4000 musical compositions. No nation of the world is disregarded — even Zulu-Kaffir music is obtainable!"

Ehrlich also made other types of organettes and was prominent in the field of disc music boxes.

Schmidt & Co. of Leipzig, known as the Phönix Musikwerke, manufactured a variety of organettes, most of which were operated by ringlike (with large open centers) metal discs. Small organettes using regular discs were made under such names as Piccolo, Diana, and Lucia. The Lucia was of 12-note scale and used a diminutive 12 cm. diameter (about 4 1/2") disc. On the other end of the scale was the Phoenix Orchestrion, a large upright coin-operated model which measured about 6' high.

The Phönix Musikwerke, like other manufacturers, produced a number of "stencil instruments" bearing the names of sales agents. However, most of the firm's products were marketed under the Ariosa, Intona, and Phönix labels.

The third leading German maker of organettes was the

Euphonika Musikwerke, also of Leipzig. Euphonika brands included Amorette, Atlas, Dolcine, Favorite, Harmonicon, Herophon, Iris, Libelle, Lucca, Lux, Mandolinata, and Manopan.

The Manopan, an organette which used a sturdy cardboard or metal strip, was the most popular of all Euphonika products. These were sold worldwide by the tens of thousands during the 1880's, 1890's, and early 1900's. As were most other large German organettes, Manopans were available in a number of variations – with soft or loud voicing, with single or double reeds, and in a variety of case woods. Strip-operated instruments related to the Manopan include the Dolcine, Erica, Kalophon, and the Kalliston series of instruments – organettes which use a metal strip which slips over the top of the instrument and is mounted vertically.

One of the most unusual of all organettes is the Herophon. In the Euphonika line, the Herophon was second in popularity only to the Manopan. Most Herophons use a square tune sheet which is fastened in a fixed position on the top of the instrument. To sound the notes the entire organ mechanism revolves beneath it!

The above German makers, the "big three" in the German organette industry, aggressively promoted the sale of their instruments all over the world. The Ariston and Herophon, to mention just two, were sold in large quantities in America. With the exception of very small models made as children's toys, the aforementioned German organettes were built very well. The rich and resonant tone plus, in many instances, tune selections numbering into thousands of choices, assured their sales success.

In England many organettes of the paper-as-a-valve type, most of which were made under licensing arrangements with John McTammany, were manufactured. These were marketed under a variety of names. Pneumatic-action paper roll Seraphones were sold by the tens of thousands also.

The Mignon, a pneumatic-action paper roll organ, was made in Germany. The Mignon was made in several different sizes; 22-notes was the most popular. The buyer could purchase the Mignon in two varieties – paper roll or paper strip. The Mignon was featured in many European musical merchandise catalogues during the late 19th and early 20th centuries. Jerome Thibouville-Lamy sold several varieties of strip-operated and book-operated organettes, some of which were made in that firm's factory in Grenelle, France.

Gavioli and Limonaire, the well known organ builders in Paris, produced many varieties of reed instruments, most of which were operated by pinned wooden cylinders or folding cardboard music books. Although there are exceptions (Gavioli's book-operated Organophone and Coelophone, for instance), most of the Limonaire and Gavioli instruments were of very loud voicing and were not intended for residential use. Such instruments are considered today to be a part of the fairground organ field.

### Other Instruments

Related to organettes are player accordions and concertinas. Many different varieties of pneumatically-operated (by perforated paper rolls) accordions were produced by the German firms of Seybold (in Strassburg-Meinau) and Hohner (in Trossingen). These were very popular, particularly in the jazz era of the 1920's, and were sold by the thousands. Player accordions were also made by Blessing of Unterkirnach, Germany. Several French manufacturers produced these instruments also.

Instruments with accordion reeds, Pierre Eich's Accordeon-Jazz for example, were made in Belgium. Accordions were also used as attachments to dance organs made by Decap, Mortier, and Bursens from the 1930's onward. These are discussed in another section of this book.

The Tanzbar, a roll-operated (by metal keys which push up against a strong paper roll) concertina, was made in Germany and sold throughout the world in the 1920's and 1930's. Two basic key sizes were made in dozens of different case styles. In America the Tanzbar was advertised heavily by Charles Pittle & Co. (New Bedford, Mass.) and other importers.

## PLAYER REED ORGANS

### Introduction

Player reed organs, most of which are of upright style with keyboard, developed from the organette. The first models appeared commercially in the late 1870's. Instruments produced in the 1878-1882 years include models by E.P. Needham, Merritt Gally, Taylor & Farley, and Taber. The last two were equipped with McTammany pneumatic actions.

Although some early player reed organs were made using the paper-as-a-valve system, the extremely limited scale made this impractical for serious musical purposes. Most player reed organs made in America used thin paper rolls and a pneumatic action system. In Germany barrel-operated and cardboard-strip-operated reed organs (usually called "harmoniums" in Europe) were popular. Several varieties of push-up (vorsetzer-style) organ players with cardboard disc or strip music systems were made in Germany also.

Player reed organs were extremely popular in America from about 1885 to 1910. By the latter year the player piano had captured the market for automatically-operated keyboard instruments used in the home.

### The American Player Reed Organ Industry

During the late 1870's and early 1880's several varieties of player reed organs appeared, as noted previously, but none was sold in quantity.

In 1883 the Aeolian Organ appeared. Writing in 1923, H.B. Tremaine (then president of the Aeolian Company) noted that "The earlier instruments were toys, pure and simple, and it was not until 1885 that the first instrument that could make a just claim to serious musical consideration was produced. This was called the Aeolian Organ [Ed. note: the 1885 date was in error by two years]. It was made with organ reeds and could be played either by means of an ordinary keyboard or a perforated music sheet. These were days when the industry was subjected to constant and varied vicissitudes. Musically and mechanically the Aeolian Organ was still in the early stages of its development, and the company producing it [Munroe Organ Reed Co. – Ed.] was beset with many difficulties. There were problems of manufacturing and selling that constantly taxed our small and inexperienced organization, and there was the handicap of insufficient capital that nearly wrecked us on more than one occasion.

"The music trade, as a whole, had little or no confidence in our instruments, and our wholesale business as a result was very small. Of our retail business in New York, perhaps an idea can be obtained from the fact that my father [W.B. Tremaine], at that time general manager of the company, told me that if we could sell one organ a week, he would consider it a very good business. During my first year with the company our retail sales amounted to $12,000. At the present time we consider we have had a poor *day* unless our retail sales exceed that amount."

The Aeolian Organ, of which Style 1050 was the basic model, was sold during the 1880's and 1890's. In 1892 the patents, supplies and parts, and other properties of the Munroe Organ Reed Company of Worcester, Massachusetts, were acquired.

In the 1890's business expanded to many times its former size. An improved player reed organ, Aeolian Organ Style 1500 which used a 46-note roll, was sold by the thousands. By the late 1890's the Aeolian Grand, a 58-note instrument, was the sales leader.

Around the turn of the 20th century the Grand was renamed the Aeolian Orchestrelle. "The Aeolian Orchestrelle is a home orchestra," one advertisement read. By means of beautiful and enticingly-written advertisements in popular magazines Aeolian succeeded in capturing probably 90% (Author's estimate) of the player reed organ market by 1905. What little remained of the market was split up among Wilcox & White, Estey, and a few other makers.

The Aeolian Orchestrelle, which used the 58-note Aeolian Grand music roll, was priced at from about $1000 to $2500 in 1903. Shortly after that time the Solo Orchestrelle, a large player reed organ which used 58-note rolls as well as 116-note Aeolian Pipe Organ rolls, made its appearance. Priced from about $2500 to $5000, the Solo Orchestrelle could play what Aeolian called "two-manual arrangements" which permitted elaborate countermelodies and a musical versatility not possible with the smaller 58-note rolls.

The Aeolian Pipe Organ, introduced around the turn of the 20th century, supplanted the sales of the Orchestrelle. By World War I, Aeolian player reed organ manufacturing was discontinued. Rolls for the Orchestrelle were produced in the 1920's, however.

In America, Aeolian player reed organs were manufactured in Worcester, Massachusetts, by the Munroe Organ Reed Company and later, in Meriden, Connecticut, by Aeolian's subsidiary, the Vocalion Organ Company. The Votey Organ Company, a firm which produced reed organs (including a small number of players), was merged into Aeolian.

The Munroe Organ Reed Company of Worcester, Massachusetts, America's leading producer of organettes during the 1880's and the source of Aeolian's instruments during that period, produced a series of Orchestrone organs. By 1885 several different models were being produced. Some models without keyboards are more properly a part of the organette series; larger with-keyboard styles, a part of the reed organ series. Some Munroe Organ Reed Co. player reed organs produced under the Gally patents featured expression controlled by perforations in the roll – a sophisticated feature found in few other reed organs regardless of size or cost. Other Munroe instruments used the simpler McTammany pneumatic action. Munroe Organ Reed Company instruments were what are known today in the piano trade as "stencil instruments." The name of the sales outlet, not Munroe's name, was stencilled on the instrument.

In 1892 the business of Munroe was acquired by the Aeolian Company, as noted previously.

In 1888 the Wilcox & White Organ Company of Meriden, Connecticut, introduced the Symphony player reed organ. From then until the early 1900's player reed organs were made in at least two roll sizes (the 10 1/4"-wide Symphony being the more popular). Wilcox & White's Symphony instruments were sold by the thousands. However, they were a distant second to Aeolian's sales in the player reed organ field.

Other American player reed organs: In 1897 the W.W. Kimball Company, Chicago piano and organ maker, introduced a player reed organ which it described as follows: "The latest improvement consists of a most ingenious pneumatic device which may be placed on either pipe or reed organs, rendering them self-playing without interfering with the regular use of the instrument by the organist. Anyone without musical knowledge can play the instrument and control its expression, variety, and power by the use of paper music rolls, the notes in which are perforated or cut by direct electrical connection with the keyboard of an instrument while being played by a skilled performer, thus reproducing in the perforated roll the interpretation of an artist." Few Kimball player reed organs were sold, however.

The Carpenter Organ Company marketed a player reed organ under the Auto-Organ name, the same term used earlier by the Autophone Company of Ithaca, N.Y., to describe certain of its organettes. The Farrand Company of Detroit marketed the Olympia Organ which was marked "Farrand & Votey" on the stop board. The Estey Organ Company (Brattleboro, Vt.), Loring & Blake (Worcester), E.P. Needham, Story & Clark (of Chicago; made the Orpheus player organ), Taber Organ Company (Worcester), and Taylor & Farley (Worcester) all produced player organs during the 1880-1910 period. Melville Clark, well known in the field of piano players and player pianos, sold several player reed organ models.

The number of obscure player reed organ trade names runs into the dozens. Many are stencil-type instruments made by Munroe and others. In the late 1890's and early 1900's many player reed organs were fitted with 65-note piano roll mechanisms to play standard player piano rolls.

Today the collector is most likely to encounter Aeolian organs of the 58-note roll type or, less frequently, Solo Orchestrelles, earlier Aeolian organs, and Wilcox & White Symphony organs. Other types are rarely seen.

## The European Player Reed Organ Industry

Around 1900 the Aeolian Company established a British subsidiary, the Orchestrelle Company, Ltd. With showrooms located at 225 Regent Street and outlets in nearly a dozen British cities, the Orchestrelle Company, Ltd. sold Orchestrelles and, later, Solo Orchestrelles which were assembled at an Aeolian facility in Hayes, Middlesex. Limited assembly (not production) facilities were also maintained in Paris by the Aeolian Company. In England and France the Orchestrelle was the most popular type of player reed organ sold. Orpheus, Olympia, and Symphony organs made in America were sold in England, as were several other makes, including instruments imported from France and Germany.

In Germany many different reed organ makers produced player models. Most of these were of the pinned cylinder or cardboard strip type. Several dozen different varieties were listed in German musical trade publications of the 1890-1914 era.

In Paris, Gavioli & Cie. produced many player reed organs for residential and church use. Most of these were built in upright cases similar to that of regular reed organs, but with a key frame for playing music books in the place normally occupied by the keyboard.

Wilhelm Spaethe of Gera, Reuss, Germany, produced player reed organs of the barrel-operated type and also of the paper roll type. Paper roll instruments were made in several different sizes and enjoyed excellent sales during the 1900-1910 period. During the same era Hofmann & Czerny of Vienna, Austria, produced several styles of barrel-operated and roll-operated instruments. The firm of Ludwig Hupfeld A.G. and its predecessor, J.M. Grob & Co., produced several dozen different types of player reed organs including disc-operated, cardboard-strip-operated, barrel-operated, and roll-operated styles. One of the roll-operated models, the Clavimonium, was popular during the 1920's as an accompaniment instrument for silent movies.

## PLAYER PIPE ORGANS

### Introduction

As discussed by Claes O. Friberg in his "Portable Hand-Cranked Barrel Organ" section of this book, automatically-played organs can be traced back for over a millenium. Most larger types of automatic organs built before the 19th century were one-of-a-kind instruments built for royalty and other patrons.

Player pipe organs, as discussed in this section of the book, are limited to softly-toned hand-cranked barrel organs made for residential or church use (loudly voiced instruments made for outdoor or fairground use are discussed elsewhere) and keyboard-type pipe organs, most of which were equipped with separate consoles or keydesks, made for home or theatre use and which were equipped for automatic operation. Orchestrions and theatre photoplayers, many of which are related to player organs, are also discussed in a separate section.

During the 19th century many barrel-operated keyboard-type player organs were built, especially in Europe. In "The Story of the Organ" C.F.A. Williams relates that in 1817 an immense organ was built by Flight and Robson of St. Martin's Lane, London, at a cost of ten thousand pounds sterling (nearly $50,000). The instrument, which was called the Apollonicon, could be played by six organists at once, and its six keyboards were so arranged that the players faced the audience. An observer noted in 1829 that it was the best organ he had heard in England, and related that the builders had used in it certain mechanisms previously unknown in the field. The Apollonicon was also provided with pinned barrels "which played overtures, quartets, and symphonies, the barrels changing the stops where necessary. Failing, however, to attract the public, it was taken down in 1840, and its materials were used for other organs."

Player organs have been made nearly continuously during the past several centuries. Production of most types, large and small, stopped in the early 1930's. However, automatically-played organs have been built in recent times, the Kimball player organ marketed in the mid-1960's and which used 88-note piano rolls and specially-arranged organ rolls being an example.

### Small Barrel Organs and Organ Clocks

Small hand-cranked barrel organs for home or church use were popular in Europe during the 18th and 19th centuries. The centers of production were England and France. In their book, "Church and Chamber Barrel Organs," Canon Noel Boston and Lyndesay G. Langwill describe about 125 different organ makers and agents who were active in Britain, mainly in the 1775-1850 years. In France, particularly in Paris and Mirecourt, the production of these instruments was a thriving industry. Other fine examples were made by builders in Austria, Czechoslovakia, Germany, and Russia.

Most British barrel organs were finely made, usually in highly finished cabinets which resembled fine pieces of furniture. Typically, such instruments contained from two to six ranks of pipes, the registration of which was controlled by a series of draw stops. Music was pinned on a wooden barrel, sometimes continuously in a spiral or helicoidal fashion but most often in a circular manner with from six to eight separate tunes. The British people, who enjoyed automatic music immensely but produced few instruments of their own (most were imported from Germany, France, or America), can be proud of these finely-crafted barrel organs.

In Austria and in Czechoslovakia many organ movements were incorporated into articles of household furniture – writing desks, small tables, sideboards, and similar pieces. Never mass-produced, such organs are rare today.

In the Black Forest section of Germany the organ clock industry thrived during the late 18th and early 19th centuries. Many builders who later gained fame with orchestrions and fairground organs – Blessing, Bruder, Imhof, and Welte are illustrious examples – began their trade by building hall clocks with organ movements, usually of small scale and of one to three ranks in size. Many had automaton figures which performed as the music played. Built for worldwide export, organ clocks intended for use in America would have such tunes as "Yankee Doodle," Stephen Foster melodies, and the like, those intended for use in the British Isles had barrels pinned with Scottish or English tunes, and so on. The organ clock business reached its peak in Germany in the 1800-1860 years.

### Player Pipe Organs

Many leading organ builders in America, England, France, and Germany incorporated roll players into certain of their instruments during the early 20th century. Many prospective purchasers of organs for their homes lacked the ability to play the organ, and the hiring of an organist was impractical. The advent of the self-playing residence organ opened up an entirely new field and resulted in millions of dollars' worth of such instruments being sold in the period from about 1900 to 1930.

American manufacturers who produced instruments for residential use include: Austin Organs, Inc. (makers of the Quadruplex system which used a tracker bar nearly two feet wide with about 240 holes in it!), Estey Organ Company (one of the earliest makers of instruments playing artists' rolls), George Kilgen & Son, W.W. Kimball Co., M.P. Möller, Inc. (makers of several styles of roll players, including one with six separate tonal sections, called the Möller Solo), Reuter Organ Co. (whose products included small self-contained player pipe organs), Ernest M. Skinner Co. (makers of "designed" highly orchestrated rolls; also of artists' rolls featuring famous organists), and the Wicks Organ Company.

The lion's share of the residential pipe organ market in America was captured by two firms: M. Welte & Sons and the Aeolian Company. The products of these companies are discussed and illustrated in detail on following pages.

Theatre pipe organs equipped with roll players were made by several firms. The Link Piano and Organ Company of Binghamton, New York, produced many instruments which played endless-type rolls housed in a separate cabinet. By means of remote control any one of four rolls could be selected instantly in order to provide fast changes in the character of the music. Link also made several instruments with rewind-type roll mechanisms incorporated into the organ console. The J.P. Seeburg Piano Company entered the theatre organ field by joining forces with the Smith-Geneva Organ Company to form the Seeburg-Smith Organ Company. A number of roll-playing instruments were made. Rolls were housed in separate cabinets made from cases of the type used for Seeburg cabinet-style coin pianos of the era, but without the art glass the pianos had. The Rudolph Wurlitzer Company, the premier force in the theatre organ field in America, produced between one and two hundred roll-played organs, some of which were for theatre use, but most of which were installed in residences.

In Europe roll players were installed by many builders of residence pipe organs. The theatre organ market was dominated by Welte. Some instruments were equipped to play Welte rolls of the Philharmonic series. Ludwig Hupfeld A.G. installed many theatre organs, some of which were roll-operated. Some of these used Pan Orchestra rolls as also used on a sophisticated Hupfeld orchestrion of the same name.

In addition to the previously-mentioned firms, many small organ builders incorporated mechanisms which used 65-note or 88-note piano rolls into their instruments. The Standard Pneumatic Action Company of New York built many 88-note player attachments for this purpose.

------------

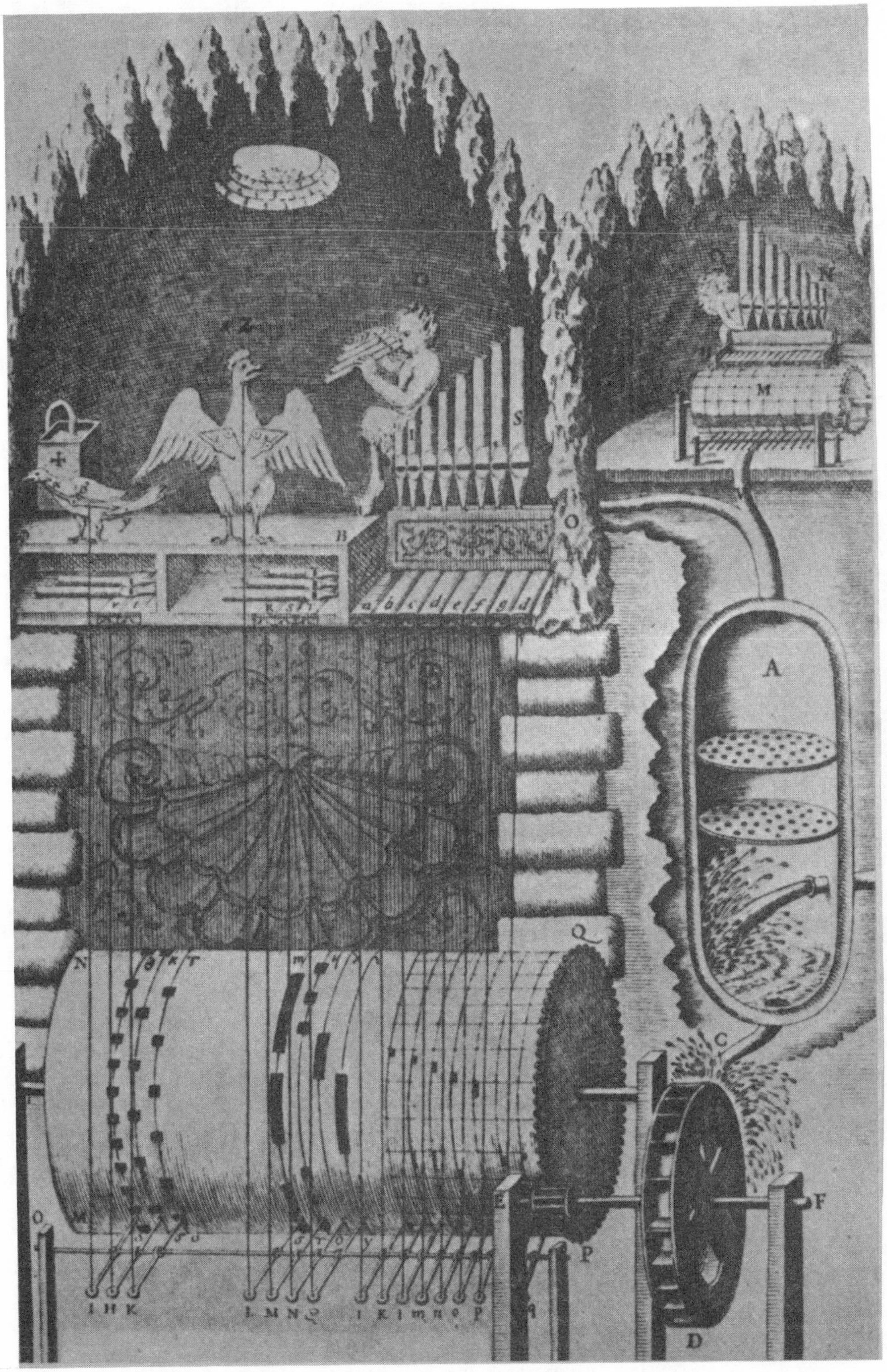

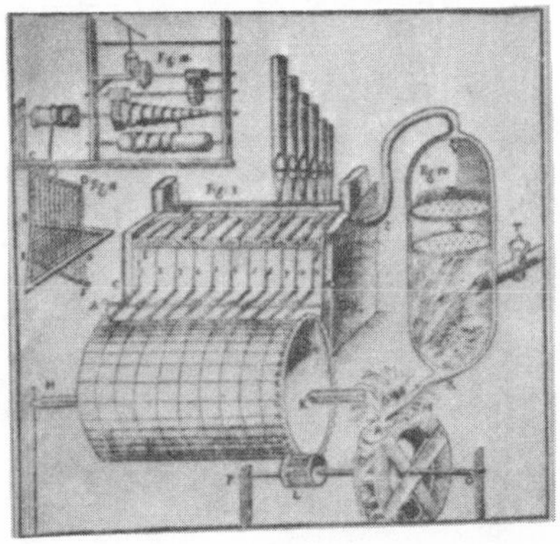

**—Organs of Antiquity—**

**Above: Mechanism of an automatic hydraulic (water-powered) organ as described by Athanasius Kircher, in "Musurgia Universalis," published in 1650, as translated by Henry George Farmer, in "The Organ of the Ancients," 1931: "For a hydraulic organ, three things are necessary: water, air, and a 'recording barrel.' First you construct a wind 'feeder' with diaphragms in the form of a sieve, and provided with two pipes — of which the larger will supply fresh water [taken from a mountain stream or other highly aerated source — Ed.]. Above the feeder will be a pipe which supplies wind to the windchest of the organ. Below the feeder will be the outlet pipe which escapes with great force and turns the driving wheel which powers the 'recording barrel.'**

**"The barrel, with its teeth arranged in musical order on the surface, will touch levers connected to the organ pipes. The levers will pull down the pallets or keys to which they are joined. This action will open valves, and thus the wind, forced violently into the windchest through the openings, will enter the organ pipes, and the desired harmony will finally be obtained.**

**"This automatic construction can be applied not only to organs but to stringed instruments."**

**Organ literature contains many references to automatically-played organs of ancient times. Most descriptions are theoretical (the above is an example) and do not refer to specific instruments actually constructed. Many are based upon impractical ideas or even impossible ones. Dr. Alexander Buchner's book, "Mechanical Musical Instruments," describes a number of these instruments.**

**Above: Hydraulic organ with mechanical figures as first described by Gaspar Schott in "Magiae Universalis Naturae et Artis (Part II, "Acustica")," 1657. (Illustration courtesy of Lewis Graham)**

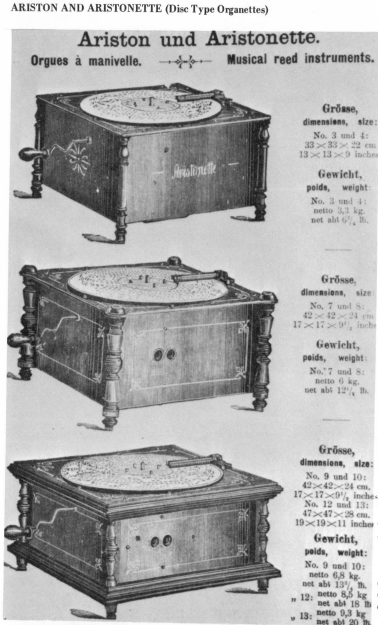

# Ariston und Aristonette.

**Orgues à manivelle. — Musical reed instruments.**

**Grösse,** dimensions, size:
No. 3 und 4:
33×33×22 cm
13×13×9 inches

**Gewicht,** poids, weight:
No. 3 und 4:
netto 3,3 kg.
net abt 6³/₄ lb.

**Grösse,** dimensions, size:
No. 7 und 8:
42×42×24 cm
17×17×9¹/₂ inches

**Gewicht,** poids, weight:
No. 7 und 8:
netto 6 kg.
net abt 12¹/₂ lb.

**Grösse,** dimensions, size:
No. 9 und 10:
42×42×24 cm.
17×17×9¹/₂ inches
No. 12 und 13:
47×47×28 cm.
19×19×11 inches

**Gewicht,** poids, weight:
No. 9 und 10:
netto 6,8 kg.
net abt 13³/₄ lb.
" 12: netto 8,5 kg / net abt 18 lb
" 13: netto 9,3 kg / net abt 20 lb.

## Ariston and Aristonette, musical reed instruments.

No. 3. 19 reeds, polished incised case, wooden motor wheels.
No. 4. 19 reeds, polished incised case, metal motor wheels.
No. 7. 24 reeds, polished incised case, wooden motor wheels.
No. 8. 24 reeds, polished incised case, metal motor wheels.
No. 9. 24 reeds, antique case polished, wooden motor wheels.
No. 10. 24 reeds, antique case polished, metal motor wheels.
No. 12. 24 harmonium reeds, fine polished large case, cold. lid, wooden motor wheels.
No. 13. 24 harmonium reeds, fine polished large case, cold. lid, metal motor wheels.

These instruments can also be had with **steel reeds** and with **tremolando.**
100 round card board tunes for No. 3 and 4 weight abt 10 lb.
100 " " " " " " 7—10 and 12 weight abt 13¹/₂ lb.

## PARTIAL LIST OF MUSIC FOR THE ARISTON.

PRICE, 50 CENTS FOR ANY TUNE.

1. Rule Britannia —
4 Long, Long Ago —
9 Military March — Richter
10 Wedding March — Mendelssohn
11 Weiner Wald-Waltz — Strauss
14 Loreley —
15 Last Rose of Summer — Martha — Flotow
17 German Hymn —
18 Juristenballe — Waltz — Strauss
23 Selection from Lucia
26 Farewell to the Forest — Mendelssohn
31 Austrian National Hymn —
33 God Save the Queen —
35 Italian National Song —
34 Mandolinata — Paladilhe
37 Blue Danube Waltz — Strauss
38 Frauenberg — Polka Mazurka —
39 Thou and Thou — Waltz — Strauss
48 Morning Papers — Waltz — Strauss
50 Watch on the Rhine —
53 Spanish National Dance —
61 Greeting to Leipzig — Waltz —
78 Miserere — Trovatore — Verdi
80 Victoria Polonaise —
82 Selection from Freischutz — Weber
84 Selection from Preciosa — Weber
88 May Song — Freischutz — Weber
90 Ah! So Fair — Martha — Flotow
94 El Sueno — Spanish Song —
95 Champagne Galop — Richter
96 High Life Quadrille — 6 PARTS —

101. Light Cavalry — Galop —
105 Polka —
109 On the Green Shore of the "Spree" — Bial
116 Minuet from "Don Juan" —
126 Wine, Women, and Song — Waltz — Strauss
130 Parade March — Richter
131 Home, Sweet Home —
133 The May Breeze —
141 Secret Love — Gavotte — Resch
143 Schottische — Richter
149 Chimes of Normandy — Waltz — Planquette
151 The Roses — Waltz — Metra
152 Les Faunes — Waltz —
154 March from Madam Angot
170 Tyrolienne from William Tell — Rossini
180 Far in the South — Spanish Song —
192 Faust Waltz — Gounod
205 Madam Angot — Waltz
206 Madam Angot — Polka
208 Tannhauser — March — Wagner
211 Hunting Song — Martha — Flotow
212 Selection from Zampa — Herold
238 Yankee Doodle —
250 I am the Little Postillion
270 Selection from Norma — Bellini
278 Robin Adair —
281 Selection from Ernani — Verdi
282 Selection from Lucretia Borgia — Donizetti
285 Fireman's Galop —
322 Blue Bells of Scotland —
334 Railroad Galop —

391. Weiner Blut — Waltz — Strauss
428 What will you do, Love? —
429 Silver Threads Among the Gold — Danks
430 In the Gloaming —
432 The Troubadour Song — Verdi
433 Bonne Bouche — Polka —
460 Mabel Waltz — Godfrey
461 Hilda Waltz — Godfrey
467 How Beautiful are Thine Eyes —
494 Carnival of Venice — Paganini
547 Never Before Waltz —
587 Roses from the South — Waltz — Strauss
734 "Oh, My Father," from Olivette — Audran
735 Cider Song — Chimes of Normandy — Planquette
745 Roses of the Alps —
748 Carmen Polka —
750 Colonel Polka —
801 Quadrille — 5 PARTS —
802 Waltz from Merry War — Strauss
805 Hymn — Sicily —
813 Schottische — Richter
914 Le Petit Bleu — Waltz —
915 Gillette de Narbonne — Waltz —
917 Polka —
918 Waltz from the Mascotte — Audran
919 The Good Time Waltz —
924 Spring Greeting Waltz — Richter
925 Fanny Rose — Polka Mazurka — Richter
935 Laura Waltz —
940 Tyrolienne National Song —

We are having published a large stock of American tunes, hymns, popular airs, etc.

Village Inn No.65

Orient No.89

Village Inn No. 65, a tableau of two beer drinkers and, above, three musicians, used a 24-note (33 cm.) Ariston metal disc to play 72 pipes (48 wood; 24 metal). A variation of this design, No. 61, featured a farmhouse with farmhands. Measurements: 306 cm. high by 125 cm. wide by 77 cm. deep. No. 65 sold for 1240 marks; 61a (without figures) 550 marks; 61b (72 pipes; same as No. 65) 1050 marks; 61c (deluxe model with 72 wooden pipes, 48 metal pipes including 31 trumpets, and percussion effects) 2750 marks.

Orient No. 89 featured two dancing girls plus two musician figures and used the standard 24-note Ariston reed mechanism played by a metal 33 cm. disc. Sold for 550 marks in 1905.

Ehrlich and others (e.g., Armin Sternberg & Bruder, maker of "Stellamont" instruments) used Ariston movements in combination with many different tableaux and coin-operated devices.

## ARISTON ORGANETTES

Introduced in 1876 by Paul Ehrlich of Leipzig, Germany, the Ariston quickly achieved success in the marketplace. In 1886 J.M. Grob & Co. (predecessor of Ludwig Hupfeld) acquired the sole agency for the distribution of the Ariston and other Ehrlich reed instruments.

From 1885 through the first decade of the 20th century Aristons were sold by the hundreds of thousands! In America they were handled by many music stores, department or dry goods stores, and mail order houses. In 1895 an American firm billed the Ariston as "the latest musical wonder" and noted that "the Ariston has 24-full size organ reeds. It plays operatic and dance music with a sparkle and brilliancy never before attained in an automatic organ. Exclamations of those hearing the Ariston: 'It sounds like several instruments;' 'Why, it is a full orchestra!;' 'A whole band!' Price $15, or with eleven discs, $20. Music sheets 50c each. We are having published a large stock of American tunes, hymns, popular airs, etc."

Ariston discs were usually made of an orange-colored cardboard, however metal-reinforced discs were available as were solid metal discs. The solid metal discs were recommended for use in coin-operated Ariston units (such as those shown at the upper right of this page). The 24-note 33 cm. Ariston disc was by far the most popular size. This disc was used also on the Orpheus automatic zither (see another page in this book for description of the Orpheus).

Ariston disc sizes: 29 cm. (used on the 19-note Aristonette); 33 cm. (used on most Ariston models; those of the 24-note size); 42.5 cm. (used on the Giant Ariston, a 36-note instrument).

Instruments not described to the left include: Aristonette No. 24 (vertical format; 45x35x25 cm.; 19 notes; sold for 35.50 marks in 1905); Ariston No. 22 (vertical format; 42x28x52 cm.; 24 notes; sold for 48 marks in 1905); No. 9-D (same as No. 9 but with double set [48] of reeds); Giant Ariston No. 14 (54x53x35 cm.; 36 notes; metal motor wheels; uses 42.5 cm. discs; sold for 109 marks in 1905); Giant Ariston No. 15 (same as No. 14 but in "plain cabinet"); Giant Ariston No. 23 (vertical format; 80x56x36 cm.; 36 notes; uses 42.5 cm. discs; sold for 116 marks in 1905).

**ORGANO ORGANETTE**

16 steel reeds. Uses 22.1 cm. metal discs. "Case in red or blue finish; with disc storage compartment." The above illustration appeared in 1914.

**LUCCA**
**LIBELLE**

Lucca (shown above): 14 notes. Black case measuring 19x19.5x14 cm. Uses 15.5 cm. discs (both metal and cardboard discs were available).

Libelle Style M: Case design similar to Lucca but slightly larger (22x22x14 cm.). Uses metal Lucca discs 15.5 cm. in diameter.

Manufactured by Euphonika (see below; also see below for another Libelle model).

**HELIKON ORGANETTES**

Manufactured by Paul Ehrlich (later, the Leipziger Musikwerke; still later, the Neue Leipziger Musikwerke A. Buff-Hedinger). Made in several styles.

Helikon No.1: 16 steel reeds. 24x23x15 polished black case. Uses 17 cm. cardboard discs.

Helikon No.1F: 16 steel reeds. 28.5x28.5x18.5 cm. polished black case. Uses 21.5 cm. metal discs.

Helikon No.1L: 16 steel reeds. 32x23x17.5 cm. case with carrying strap. Uses 17 cm. cardboard discs.

Helikon No.2: 16 steel reeds. 32x24x16 cm. case in cabinet form. Uses 17 cm. cardboard discs. (Illustration of front of No. 2 shown at right; illustration of the back of No. 2 is at lower right)

**EUPHONIKA MUSIKWERKE**
**Leipzig, Germany**

Founded in the 1890's, the Leipziger Musikwerke Euphonika was one of three leading organette makers in Leipzig. Together with Phönix and Ehrlich, Euphonika sold its products all over the world during the late 19th and early 20th centuries.

Euphonika brands included Amorette, Atlas, Dolcine, Favorite, Harmonicon, Herophon, Iris, Libelle, Lucca, Lux, Mandolinata, and Manopan. Many of these brands were different in name and case appearance only; the mechanisms were similar to each other and in some instances (Amorette, Atlas, and Mandolinata, for example) the discs were interchangeable with each other.

**LUX ORGANETTE**

16 steel reeds. 31x22x16 cm. polished black wood case. Uses 20 cm. metal discs. Sold for 18 marks in 1905.

**FAVORITE ORGANETTE**

(Not illustrated). Case similar to Lux but larger. 38x31x21 cm. Uses 26 cm. metal discs. Sold for 28.50 marks in 1905.

**IRIS ORGANETTES**

Iris I [sic; Roman numeral designation used]: 24 double (total 48) reeds. 43x47x33 cm. black polished case with gold decorations. Uses 32.5 cm. metal discs.

Iris II: 24 steel reeds. 42x42x26 cm. black case with gold decorations. Uses 32.5 cm. metal discs.

**LIBELLE ORGANETTE**

Libelle: 27 reeds. 38x33x21 cm. case with bright transfer decoration on top. Uses 26 cm. metal Favorite discs. Sold for 37 marks in 1905.

**EMPIRE ORGAN; MIDGET ORGAN**

Empire Organ: 16x16x9½" [sic]. 24 reeds. Midget Organ: 8x8x5½". 14 reeds. Made by A. Buff-Hedinger (successor to Ehrlich).

**HEROPHON AND HEROPHONETTE ORGANETTES**

Made by Euphonika, the Herophon series of instruments use square cardboard tune sheets, most of which had scalloped corners and metal-reinforced edges. The cardboard square remained fixed and the works of the organ mechanism revolved under it! The top of the instrument was usually decorated with a bright transfer design. A popular decal featured such musical luminaries as Offenbach, Beethoven, Wagner, Mozart, and Strauss. Herophonettes use 26 cm. square tune sheets; cardboard for Herophonette I and metal for Herophonette II. Herophones use either cardboard or metal (the user's option) squares measuring 33 cm. on a side. (Note: Some models used round discs; these are rare today.)

Herophonette I: 18 reeds. 39x39x30 cm. black case with gold engraving. Sold for 46.90 marks in 1905. Herophonette II: Same as No.I but with more powerful reeds. Sold for 50 marks in 1905.

Herophon O, I, II, and III: 24 reeds. Cases measure 48x48x30 cm. Higher-numbered models have stronger and louder reeds. Sold for 43 to 70 marks in 1905.

Herophon Excelsior IV: 24 reeds. 51x51x32 cm. case. Two models (different reeds) sold for 90 and 102 marks in 1905.

Herophons were extremely popular and thousands were sold. Most were of the regular Herophon (O to III) style.

## AMORETTE AND MANDOLINATA ORGANETTES

Amorette and Mandolinata organettes were made by the Euphonika Musikwerke in Leipzig. Both types of instruments used the same types of metal discs. Disc diameters of 22.5 cm. (for 16-note instruments), 26.5 cm. (18 notes), 30.5 cm. (24 notes), and 43 cm. (36 notes) were produced. A number of double reed models were made; these were designated by the suffix D. Case designs varied over the years (1890's and early 1900's) these were made. The designs shown on this page are typical. Amorette mechanisms were incorporated into a number of toys and novelties such as the Nativity scene, windmill, and wheelbarrow described here.

Euphonika, located at Petersstrasse 18 in Leipzig, made a number of other organettes, including such brands as Manopan, Herophon, Iris, and Lux.

Mandolinata organettes: No.1 35x26x20 cm. 16 notes. Uses 22.5 cm. Amorette discs. No.2 43x32x23 cm. 18 notes. Uses 26.5 cm. Amorette discs. No.3 44.5x37x23 cm. 24 notes. Uses 30.5 cm. Amorette discs. Instruments sold for 20, 30, and 40 German marks respectively in 1904.

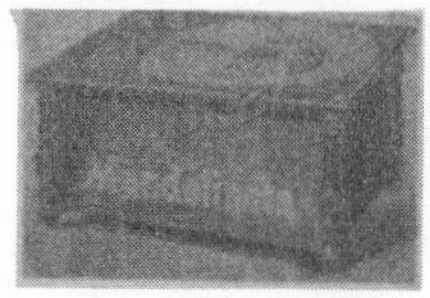

MANDOLINATA

Amorette No.16-M
28x21x17 cm. Black wood case. Uses 22.5 cm. discs.

Amorette No. 16-B
34x26x18 cm. Black case with corner columns. Uses 22.5 cm. discs. Sold for 16 marks in 1905.

Amorette No. 16-D
34x27x20 cm. Black case with latticework sound openings in top. Uses 22.5 cm. discs.

Amorette 16-A; 18-M
16-A: 34x25x18 cm. Uses 22.5 cm. discs. 18-M: 43x31x21 cm. Uses 26.5 cm. discs.

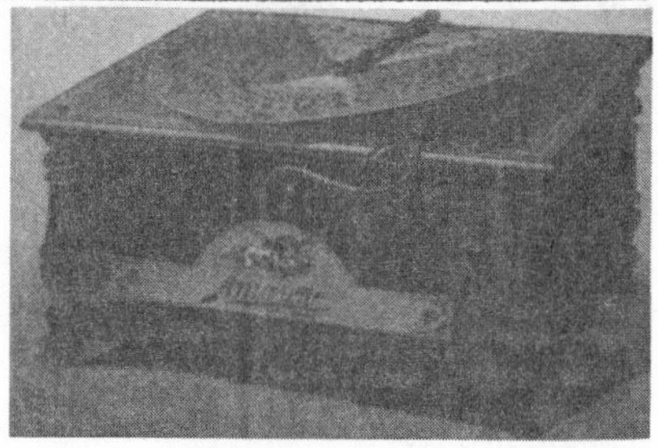

Amorette 16; 18; 18-D; 24; 24-D
Case with turned corner columns. No.16: 34x26x18 cm. Uses 22.5 cm. discs. No.18: 42x32x20 cm. Uses 26.5 cm. discs. No.18-D (double reed set) 44x35x22 cm. Uses 26.5 cm. discs. No.24: (24 reeds) 44.5x37x23 cm. Uses 30.5 cm. discs. No.24-D: (48 reeds) 47x37x26 cm. Uses 26.5 cm. discs. No. 24 was recommended as a "house instrument;" 24-D as a "dance instrument for restaurants and saloons."

Amorette No. 36
53x53x27 cm. "36 harmonium reeds and 8 double bass reeds." Black case with corner columns. Uses 43 cm. discs. Sold for 75 marks in 1905.

Amorette No. 36-D
53x53x29 cm. With double set of reeds (72 reeds). Uses 43 cm. discs. Instrument sold for 90 marks in 1905. Extra discs cost 2.40 marks each.

Amorette No. 48-TT
92x55x34 cm. Uses 43 cm. discs. 48 reeds plus drum and triangle.

# Amorette

Above: Amorette No. 16-Z. "English Cab" model. 93x47x65 cm. Uses 22.5 cm. discs. Sold for 40 marks in 1905.

No. 16-W
38x36x31 cm. Uses 22.5 cm. discs. Made with choice of mechanical figures including soldiers (German, Austrian, French, or English!), dancers, dancing bears, ballerinas, etc. The same options were available for No.16-F.

Amorette No. 24-Gl
45x39x35 cm. Uses 30.5 cm. discs. 48 reeds (double set of 24 reeds) plus 12 bells. Sold for 80 marks in 1905.

Amorette 18-S; 24-S
18-S: 54x36x23 cm. 36 reeds. Uses 26.5 cm. discs. 24-S: 61x39x28 cm. 48 reeds. Uses 30.5 cm. discs.

Amorette No. 16-F (above)
32x30x37 cm. Uses 22.5 cm. discs. In case with two dancing figures in niches on the front. Sold for 30 marks in 1905.

Above: Amorette No. 16-K. Child's wheelbarrow in oak. 98x29x27 cm. Uses 22.5 cm. discs. Sold for 18 marks in 1905.

Above: Amorette No. 16-WK. "Weihnachtskrippe" (Nativity scene) model. 26x21x31 cm. Uses 22.5 cm. discs.

Amorette No. 16-WM (see left)
38x30x44 cm. Uses 22.5 cm. discs. "Water Mill" model. With mechanical water wheel at the left side. Sold for 33 marks in 1905.

## MANOPAN ORGANETTES

Manufactured by the Euphonika Musikwerke, the Manopan was made in several different models — as enumerated below. Representative selling prices in 1904 were: Manopan O 42 Mk.; Manopan I 47.50 Mk.; Manopan II 65 Mk.; Manopan III 103 Mk., Manopan IV 132 Mk.; Manopan V 180 Mk. In the original German catalogue Manopans were given Roman numeral designations; in English descriptions (as below), Arabic numerals. Many case variations and reed complement variations were produced. For example, in 1904 there were three models of No.IV available: IV (w/harmonium reeds); IV-St. (w/steel reeds); and IV-N (in "Nussbaum" [German for walnut]). Tens of thousands of Manopans were made over a period of about 20-25 years.

### Manopan musical reeds instruments.

Black polished with gold linings. With Forte and Piano attachment.

| | | | | |
|---|---|---|---|---|
| No. 0, | Manopan | 24 | tongues | without Forte. |
| „ 1, | „ | 24 | „ | with Forte. |
| „ 1 B, | „ | 24 | „ | „ contra-bass. |
| „ 2, | „ | 24 | „ | double, (36) tongues. |
| „ 3, | „ | 39 | „ | Harmonium reeds. |
| „ 4, | „ | 39 | „ | „ „ |
| „ 5, | „ | 39 | „ | „ „ |
| „ 5St. | „ | 39 | „ | Excelsior-steel reeds. |

| | | | |
|---|---|---|---|
| No.0 | 50×29×27 cm. | 20×12×11 inch. | No. 0, netto 5 1/2 kg. net abt 12 lb |
| „ 1 | 52×29×27 „ | 26×12×11 „ | „ 1, „ 6 „ „ „ 13 „ |
| „ 1 B, | 52×29×27 „ | 26×12×11 „ | „ 1 B, „ 6 1/4 „ „ „ 14 „ |
| „ 2, | 52×34×29 „ | 26×14×12 „ | „ 2, „ 7 1/2 „ „ „ 16,5 „ |
| „ 3, | 66×38×34 „ | 26×15×14 „ | „ 3, „ 12 1/2 „ „ „ 28 „ |
| „ 4, | 74×40 1/2×36 „ | 30×16×14 „ | „ 4, „ 13 1/2 „ „ „ 31 „ |
| „ 5, | 84×40 1/2×47 „ | 34×16×19 „ | „ 5, „ 21 „ „ „ 46 „ |

Manopan case for Nos. 3 to 5 above; right: case for Nos.1 and 2..Nos. O to 2 used one style of music strip; 3 to 5 used a wider strip. Music strips were available in either cardboard or metal; most sold were of cardboard. A 1.3 meter (length) strip of cardboard for Nos. 3 to 5 cost 2.50 Mk.; a 2.6 meter strip, 5 Mk.

## Kalliston

Kalliston AGS

Kalliston-Pankalon BG DT

### KALLISTONETTE, KALLISTON, and KALLISTON-PANKALON ORGANETTES

Kallistonette CS: 24 steel reeds. 29x29x34 cm. case. Uses 11 cm.-wide strips measuring 120 cm. long. Sold for 30 Mk. in 1904; strips: 1.40 Mk.

Kalliston AS: 24 steel reeds. 31x31x37 cm. case. Sold for 45 Mk. Kalliston ADS: Same, but double reeds. Sold for 60 Mk. AS and ADS use 12.4 cm.-wide by 120 cm.-long zinc strips.

Kalliston AGS: 24 steel reeds plus bells. 31x31x47 cm. case. Sold for 59 Mk. Kalliston AGDS: Same, but double reeds. Sold for 78 Mk. Kalliston AGDO: 35x48x47 cm. case. Double reeds plus contrabass reeds; bells. Sold for 90 Mk. Use 12.4 cm.-wide by 120 cm.-long zinc strips (but of different arrangement from that used on Kallistons without percussion).

Kalliston Orchestrion (or Orchestrion Kalliston) AGDT: 24 double (48 total) reeds plus contrabass. Bells and drum. 35x48x57 cm. case. 12.4 cm.-wide by 120 cm.-long zinc strips (but of different arrangement than used on other styles). Tremolo attachment on some models.

Kalliston-Pankalon BG DT: 72 reeds; 3 contrabass; drum; bells. 42x53x62 cm. case. Uses special 17.5 cm.-wide by 120 cm.-long zinc strips. Sold for 124 Mk. in 1904.

**Drum-piccolo-manopan.**

16 steel reeds case black polished. The tunes are of durable long paper stripes.
Size: 14×8 1/2×13 inches.
Weight: net abt 5 lb.

### DRUM MANOPAN (or DRUM-PICCOLO-MANOPAN)

Made in several varieties: Nos. I and II with cases measuring 52x29x48 cm. With Manopan unit plus two drums, cymbal, and bells. Both use 86 or 172 cm. (length) cardboard strips. No. I sold for 72 Mk.; II (w/stronger reeds) for 84 Mk. in 1905. Nos. IV and V: Same instrumentation as preceding plus triangle. Case: 70x40x75 cm. Sold for 212 Mk. and 240 Mk. in 1904. Both use 130 or 260 cm. cardboard strips.

### ERICA ORGANETTE

16 steel reeds. Black case with gold engraving measures 30x21x21 cm. Uses 60 cm. (length) zinc tune strips. Sold for 17 Mk. in 1904. Extra tune strips cost 0.50 Mk. each.

### KALOPHON ORGANETTES

Kalophon E: 24 steel reeds. Black case. Sold for 35 Mk. in 1904.

Kalophon D: 24 double (total 48) reeds. Black case. Sold for 42 Mk. in 1904.

Cases of both measure 36x25x30 cm. Zinc strips measuring 120 cm. long sold for 1.40 marks each.

**Dolcine.**

16 steel reeds, case brown polished. The tunes are the same as used for No. 372 (above).
Size: 6 1/4×8×6 1/4 inches.
Weight net abt 4 1/2 lb.

### DOLCINE ORGANETTES

No.I: 16 steel reeds. No.II: 16 forte steel reeds. No.III 16 notes but some double reeds. Cases of I and II measure 16x20x16 cm. III measures 37x29x23 cm. Sold for 20, 22, and 45 Mk. respectively in 1904.

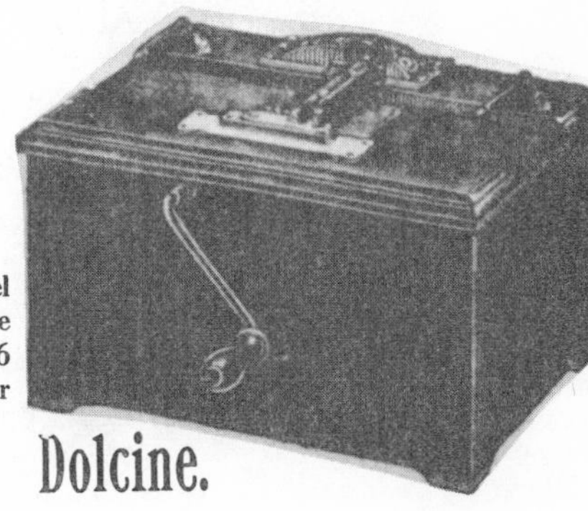

Dolcine.

MOTOR MANOPAN No.I: With gas or oil-fired hot air motor. 75 cm. wide by 75 cm. deep by 156 cm. high. Uses Manopan music strips arranged in folding book form. Manufactured by the Euphonika Musikwerke of Leipzig.

FLUTINA ORGAN No.0: 40x42x42 cm. 24 reeds. Uses Manopan music. Manufactured by the Euphonika Musikwerke.

FLUTINA ORGAN No.2: 40x42x36 cm. case. 24 double (total 48) reeds. Uses Manopan music.

## ORGANINA THIBOUVILLE.

**ORGANINA THIBOUVILLE**
Sold by Thibouville-Lamy, this instrument is provided with 24 reeds. 22 inches long by 13 inches wide by 12 inches high. "This small French organ, called after its inventor's name, Jerome Thibouville, surpasses in perfection all the instruments of its kind. By its quality of sound, sweet and melodious, the Organina Thibouville is far superior to the German productions of this class. . ." (Illustration courtesy of Arthur W.J.G. Ord-Hume)

**HENRY ORGAN**
95 cm. wide by 50 cm. deep by 190 cm. high. Made in several styles including hand-cranked (shown above) and hot air motor types. 39 reeds. Uses large-style Manopan music arranged in book form (as shown) or in a continuous loop.

## CŒLOPHONE ORCHESTRE.

**COELOPHONE ORCHESTRA**
Sold by Thibouville-Lamy. 37 reeds. 26 inches long by 14 inches wide by 17 inches high. "The Coelophone, invented by the celebrated Claude Gavioli [of Gavioli & Cie., Paris], improved and made at our Grenelle factory, is an instrument of a special nature on an entirely new system. . . The sound produced is powerful enough for 60 to 80 persons to dance to." Uses folding cardboard music books (as shown) or endless strips. (Illustration courtesy of Arthur W.J.G. Ord-Hume)

## SCHMIDT & Co.
### Phönix Musikwerke

Schmidt & Co., the Phönix (Phoenix) Musikwerke, of Leipzig, Germany, manufactured many different varieties of organettes. At the 1909 Easter Fair in Leipzig the firm exhibited examples of the Phönix, Ariosa, Intona, and Diana organettes, and featured the new "Phönix 42" – an instrument with 42 double (total of 84) steel organ reeds.

As did other makers, Schmidt & Co. made organettes under a wide variety of names, including some private labels for music wholesalers.

Among the smaller instruments made by the firm were the Piccolo and Diana, each of which used a small 14-note disc, and the Lucia, smallest of them all – an instrument which used a 12-note disc which measured only 12 cm. in diameter.

The larger Ariosa, Intona, and Sonora organettes used annular or ring-shaped discs made of zinc (or, rarely, of reinforced cardboard).

The various Schmidt & Co. instruments were sold worldwide.

### PICCOLO ORGANETTE (Disc Type)

Manufactured by Phönix. First marketed in 1903. Uses 14-note discs compatible with 16.5 cm. Diana discs but slightly thicker. Case measurements: 25x21x27 cm. Sold for 10 marks in 1904.

### LUCIA ORGANETTE (Disc Type)

Manufactured by the Phönix Musikwerke (Schmidt & Co.). One of the smallest disc-operated organettes, the Lucia has just 12 notes and uses a tiny 12 cm. diameter cardboard disc. Measurements are: 17x16x13 cm. The instrument cost 6.50 marks (about $1.50 U.S. funds) in 1904. Extra discs sold for 0.24 marks each.

### DIANA ORGANETTE (Disc Type)

Made by the Phönix Musikwerke, the Diana used 14-note discs measuring 16.5 cm. in diameter.

Above: Diana (black finish; 24x21x15 cm.); and Diana E (for "Erle" or alderwood; natural color with high gloss finish). Diana sold for 11 marks, Diana E for 12 marks, in 1904.

Right: Casket Model Diana as shown in a 1914 price list.

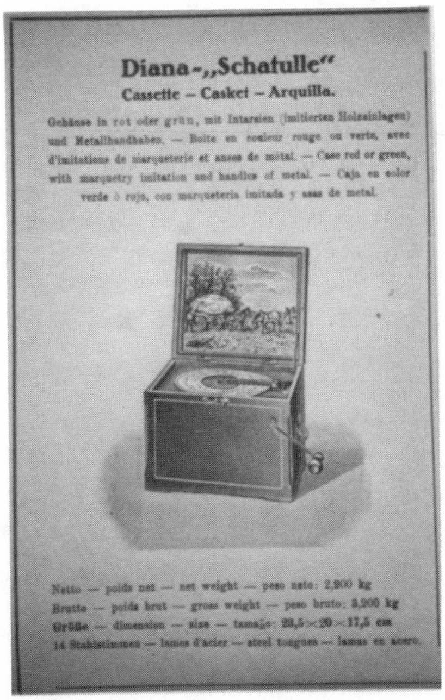


ARIOSA

Ariosa No. 1 and No. 2

No.1: 18 brass reeds. Sold for 24.50 marks in 1904. No.2: 18 steel reeds. Sold for 25.50 marks in 1904. Case measurements: 37x33.5x20 cm. Uses annular (ringform) zinc disc, the same type as used on the other Ariosa instruments shown here.

Ariosa No. 2-M

18 steel reeds. Case measurements: 40x34x22.5 cm. Music disc is situated differently and does not extend past the top edges of the instrument. The "M" in the nomenclature is from "mitte" or "middle" – the location of the disc. In polished black case. Sold for 28.50 marks in 1904.

Ariosa No. 3

18 double steel reeds (36 total reeds). Case measures: 38.5x33.5x25 cm. Polished black wood case. Sold for 35 marks in 1904. In a 1900 catalogue No. 3 is listed as having just 16 double reeds; this instrument sold for 26.25 marks.

Ariosa No. 3-M

18 double steel reeds (36 total reeds). Case measures 44.5x34.5x25 cm. Disc located in the middle of the instrument. Sold for 37 marks in 1904.

All Ariosa instruments shown here use the same type of annular disc. This disc is used also on the Sonora organette (see below).

### SONORA ORGANETTE (Disc Type)

The Sonora, a vertical-format version of the Ariosa, used regular annular Ariosa discs and was popular from about 1895 to 1905. The Sonora was made in two models: No. 35 with 18 steel reeds and No.35-N with 18 double steel reeds (for a total of 36 reeds). The case is of walnut and measures 33 cm. wide by 24 cm. deep by 51 cm. high. The No.35-N sold for 38 marks in 1904. Extra Ariosa/Sonora discs cost 1 mark each. Earlier, in 1900, the cost per disc was 0.78 marks.

## INTONA ORGANETTES (Disc Type)

Manufactured by the Phönix Musikwerke of Leipzig, Intona instruments were popular from about 1890 to 1915. Like the Ariosa, Sonora, and Phönix organettes made by the same firm, the Intona organettes use an annular disc.

**Intona No.0**
16 steel reeds. 32x25x29 cm. case. Uses standard 22 cm. diameter Intona annular (ringform) disc. Sold for 15.50 marks in 1904. Extra discs sold for 0.5 marks each.

**Intona No. 1**
16 steel reeds. 28x24x18 cm. case in black finish. Sold for 12 marks in 1900; 16 marks in 1904.

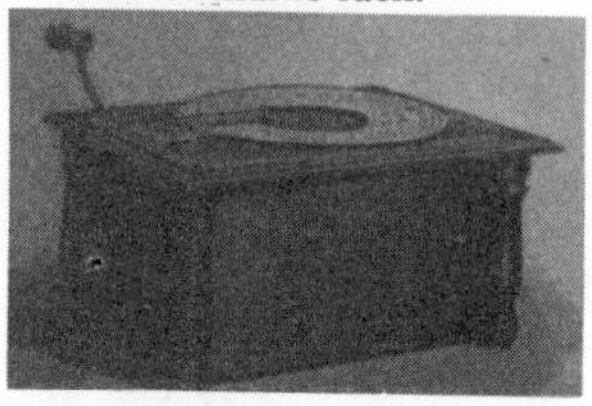

**Intona No. 2**
16 steel reeds. 34x26x19 cm. case in black finish. Sold for 12.40 marks in 1900; 16.50 marks in 1904.

**Intona No. 2-F**
The same as Intona No. 2, but with the case in rosewood or finished with a red or green surface. Sold for the same price as No. 2 in 1900 and 1904.

**Intona No. 3**
16 double (total of 32) steel reeds. 35x30x20 cm. case in polished black finish. Sold for 17.25 marks in 1900; 22 marks in 1904.

In H. Peters' 1895 catalogue the Intona and Ariosa were referred to as "Grand military Intona and Ariosa musical reed instruments."

**Casket Model Intona**
1914 catalogue description of an Intona built into a rectangular box with a hinged lid.

## STREET ORGAN

Left: Street organ (Strassenorgel) introduced in 1906 and sold for many years afterward. Uses harmonium reeds.

## PHÖNIX ORGANETTES (Disc Type)

Phönix (Phoenix) organettes were popular from about 1890 to 1915. Made in several different styles, most Phönix instruments used annular discs. Some larger styles used solid discs with the music arrangement around the periphery (see Phoenix Orchestrion on another page). Most large Phönix table and vertical models had a tremolo device.

**Phönix No. 34**
24 steel reeds (1900) or 27 including 3 contrabass reeds (1904). 47x35x25 cm. (1900) or 48x38x27 cm (1904) case. Sold for 28.15 marks in 1900; the 1904 model (slightly different, as noted) sold for 38 marks.

**Phönix No. 36**
The 1900 model had 24 reeds and measured 47x35x28 cm. The 1904 model had 27 reeds and measured 49x38x29 cm. Polished black case. Sold for 42 marks in 1900; 50 marks in 1904.

**(Left) Phönix No. 37**
1900 models: No.37 with 24 reeds; No.37b with 24 double (total 48) reeds. 58x44.5x30.5 cm. case. 1904 model: 24 double reeds (total 48) plus 3 contrabass reeds. 58x44.5x30 cm. case.

**(Right) Phönix No. 38**
1900 model: 78 reeds; with expression devices. 64.5x46x5x33 cm. case. 1904 model: 72 steel reeds plus 10 large contrabass reeds. 63x47x33 cm. case. Sold for 87 marks in 1900; 100 marks in 1904.

**-Phönix Discs-**
Nos. 34 through 37 use any of the following discs (the diameter lengthens the playing time; the width of the band remains constant): "A" (31 cm. diameter), "B" (33.6 cm.), or "C" (37 cm.). No. 38 uses a special "Type 38" disc measuring 51 cm. in diameter.

Not illustrated here: No. 35, a 24-note instrument with expression devices. Case measures 47x35x27 cm. Sold for 34.50 marks in 1900. No. 42, introduced in 1909, with 42 double (84 total) reeds. Used "Type 42" disc.

Left: Inner mechanisms of the Ariosa and Phönix.

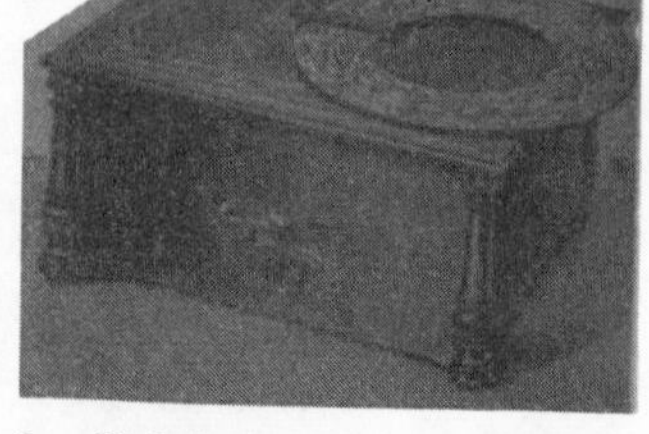

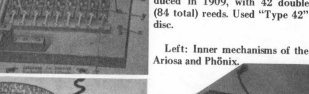

Left: 1895 catalogue illustration of a Phönix instrument. Right: 1900 illustration. Others are from the 1904 catalogue.

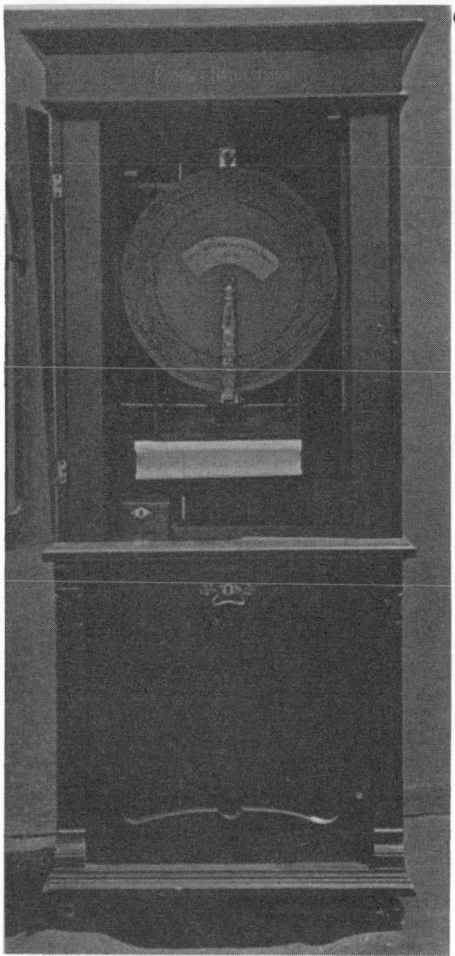

—Phoenix Orchestrion—

The Phoenix [sic] Orchestrion, made in a vertical format with a coin mechanism, uses a solid disc (but with the music arranged around the periphery as on the annular discs).

### BELLA ORGANETTE

Made by Phönix in Leipzig and sold c.1914, the Bella organette used a standard 14-note Diana disc. "Elegant dark polished cabinet; organ with interchangeable metal tune discs; may likewise be used as a toy piano. Equipped with 12 keys, 14 playing notes. 35x25.5x30 cm. Uses 16.5 cm. diameter Diana discs" noted a 1914 advertisement. Front and rear views are shown above.

Otero No. 12

Otero No. 14.

Otero No. 16

### OTERO ORGANETTES
(Made by Phönix)

Sold c.1914, Otero organettes were produced in at least three models. They were described as "Latest novelty. Otero crank organs with interchangeable pressboard tunes."

Otero No. 12: 20x19x13 cm. 12 reeds. Reddish-brown finished cabinet. 12 cm. diameter discs.

Otero No. 14: 26x24x18 cm. 14 reeds. Reddish-brown finished cabinet. 16 cm. diameter discs.

Otero No. 16: 33x31.5x20.5 cm. 16 reeds. Imitation rosewood cabinet. 22 cm. diameter discs.

### AMABILE ORGANETTES

Made during the early 20th century by Armin Liebmann (of Gera, Reuss, Germany), the Amabile appeared in several formats, including table models and large upright styles. The model shown above, an upright style with base cabinet, is equipped with organ reeds and has the accompaniment of two bells.

### ATLAS ORGANETTES

Manufactured by Euphonika in Leipzig. Sold mainly in America and England. Made in the same sizes as Amorette organettes. Most Atlas organettes are identical to Amorette organs except for the label.

### SONATINA MELODION

Made in 3 styles: No. 16 (16 reeds; 22.8 cm. discs; 37x29x22 cm.), No. 18 (18 reeds; 27.3 cm. discs; 43x32x22 cm.); No. 24 (24 reeds; 32.5 cm. discs; 46x40x27 cm.). All made in polished black cases. Sold for 18, 28, and 37 marks respectively in 1904. Also spelled as Sonatina Melodeon. "Melodion" is the spelling that appears on the instrument itself.

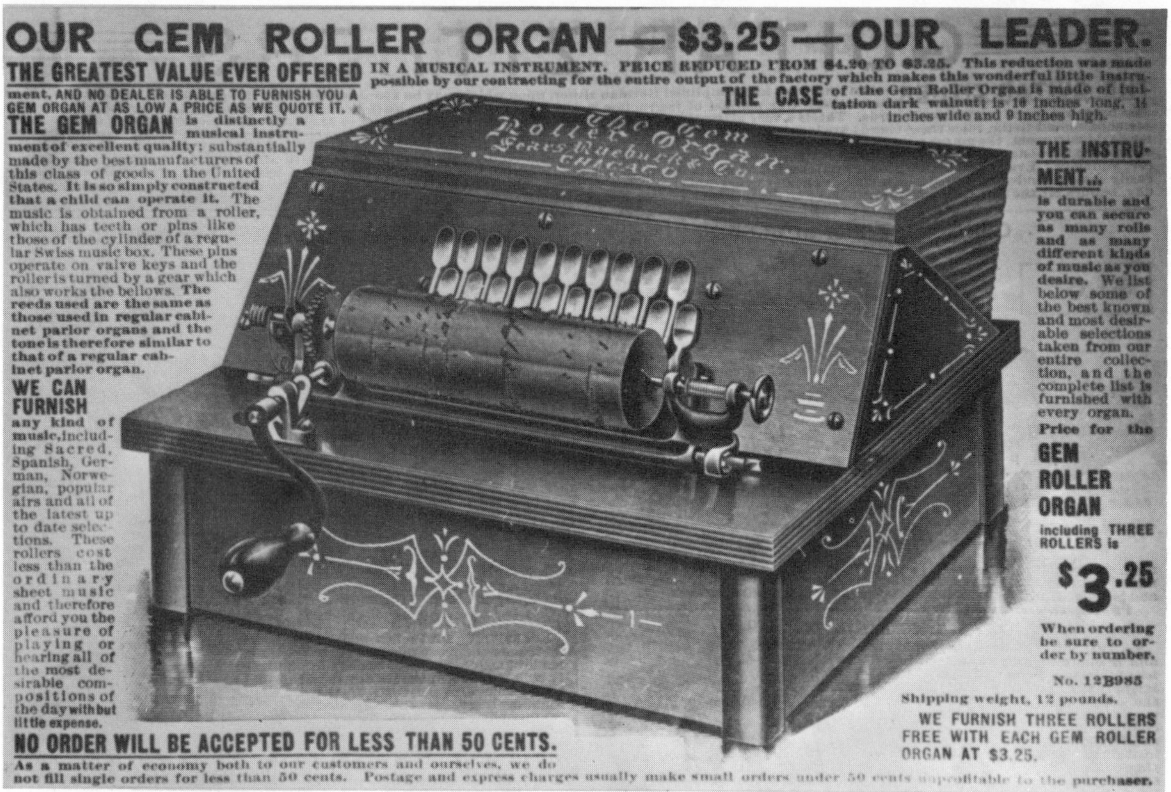


Left: Sears & Roebuck advertisement for the Gem Roller Organ. The statement "This [price reduction to $3.25] was made possible by our contracting for the entire output of the factory..." if true refers to an arrangement which lasted for only a short time. Gem Roller Organs and allied Autophone products were handled by hundreds of outlets, including most musical merchandisers, in America.

Wooden rollers for the Gem and Concert Roller Organs are interchangeable and measure 6 1/2" in length.

These 20-note instruments were originally known as "roller organs," a descriptive term that was later (and somewhat incorrectly) extended as a generic term for all types of small hand-cranked reed organs, roller organ styles and paper roll types.

Manufactured by the Autophone Company, owned by Henry B. Horton (who also owned the well-known Ithaca Calendar Clock Co.) of Ithaca, New York, the Gem Roller Organ and Concert Roller Organ each use a metal-pin-studded wooden cylinder on which a tune is arranged in helicoidal or spiral fashion. Turning a hand crank operates a vacuum (usually, although some pressure models were made) bellows and turns the wooden music "cob." When a pin in the roller comes into contact with the hinged end of one of the organ valves it causes the valve to lift, admitting air into the reed chamber and sounding the desired note.

Gem Roller Organs generally were made without the hinged glass front covers found on Concert models. Mechanically, both operate on the same principles, and both use the same size of "cob."

G.H.W. Bates & Co., one of the ballyhoo sales outlets for organettes, sold Gem Roller Organs in addition to many other styles.

—The Gem Roller Organ—
—The Concert Roller Organ—

Gem Roller Organ — scarce variety with a hinged glass front which mellows the sound of the music. (Arthur Sanders photograph)

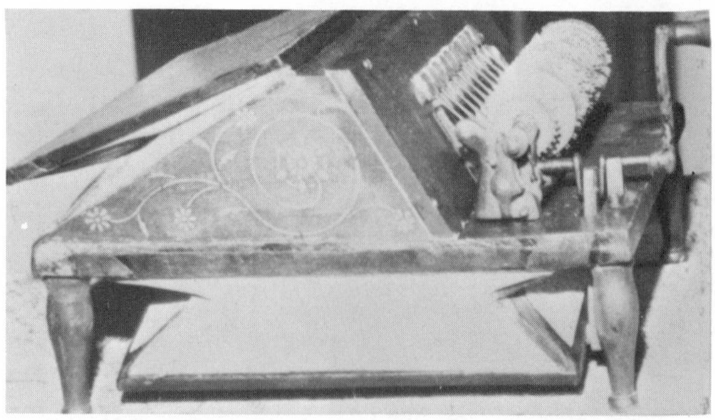

Gem Roller Organ. This early version uses pressure (rather than the usual vacuum) to operate the reeds. (Arthur Sanders photograph)

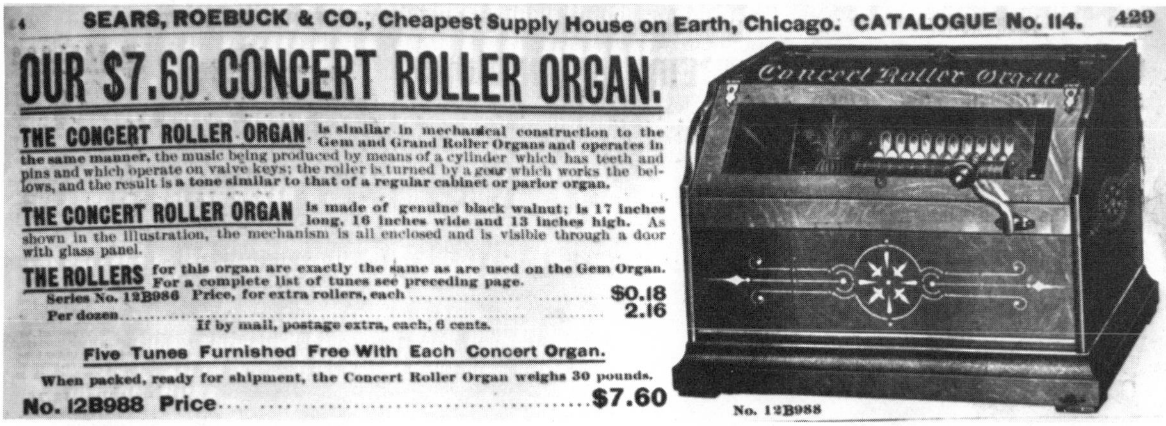

—Gem Roller Organ / Concert Roller Organ—

Above and to the left are two varieties of the Concert Roller Organ, an elegant (larger case; hinged front panel) version of the Gem Roller Organ. Note that the hand crank is at the left front side of one and at the right front side of the other.

Both Gem and Concert instruments were sold under many other "stencil" brand names by various outlets. Many Gems were sold under the "New American Musical Box" designation, and thousands of Concert instruments bore the "Chautauqua Roller Organ" label — to cite just two of the more popular names.

Although no figures are known today, it is probably accurate to say that hundreds of thousands (if not millions) of Gem and Concert instruments were produced. In one year in the 1880's some 14,000 roller organs and 200,000 wooden rollers were made! And, this was before the mass-merchandising efforts of Sears & Roebuck and others started!

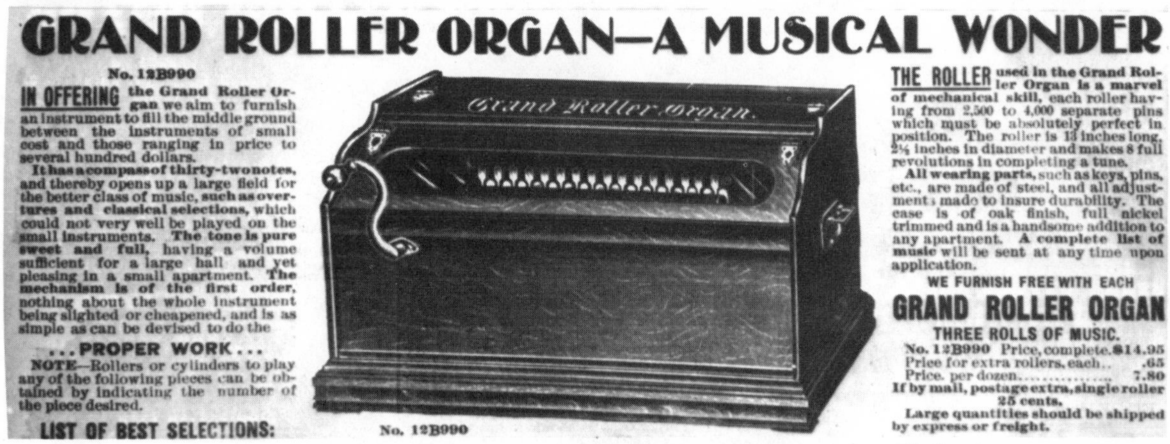


—Grand Roller Organ—

The Grand Roller Organ, the Autophone Company's top-of-the-line roller organ, is of 32-note scale and uses a 15" pinned wooden cylinder or "cob" (as these are called by collectors today). The number of Grand instruments sold was small in relation to the Gem and Concert models. As a result, Grand Roller Organs are fairly scarce today. Contributing to the original difference in production figures was the fact that many mail order houses (which competed on price alone; quality was of secondary importance) usually handled just the Gem, rarely the Concert, and almost never the Grand.

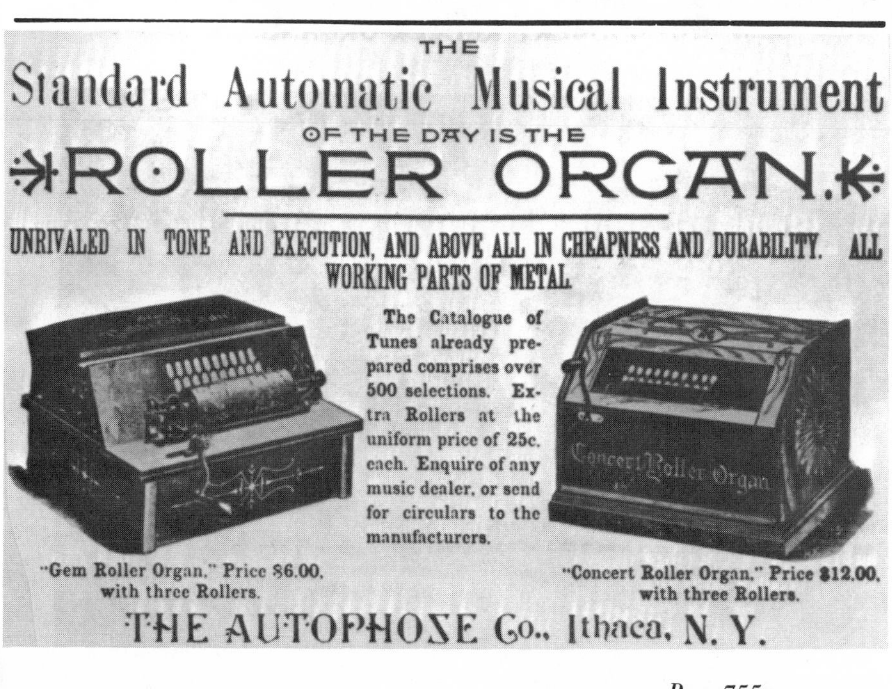


The Autophone Company devised a machine which pinned the wooden rollers automatically. With "each roller having from 2,500 to 4,000 separate pins which must be absolutely perfect in position" (as the above Sears advertisement notes) this automation of production was the key to the low price of these instruments.

Gem, Concert, and Grand Roller Organs were durably made of solid materials. Among contemporary organettes they were a musical success, both from the volume of sound produced and the arrangement and quality of the music. As such they are favorites with collectors today.

## —Autophone—

The Autophone (trademark) organette was made in several different forms by the Autophone Co. of Ithaca, New York. In 1882 15,000 small-size (table models) and 3,000 large-size (cabinet models) of the Autophone were made. Although other variations were made, the two main sizes of Autophones were the 22-key and 32-key models. Music strips are ratchet-fed and measure from about 5 to 7 inches in width, depending upon the model and the type of drive (edge-drive and center-drive instruments were made). Despite original manufacturing quantities of tens of thousands, Autophones are quite scarce today.

92 ITHACA AND ITS RESOURCES

(22 notes) selling for $5; the concert style, $12; concert style, with stand, (32 notes) $16, and the cabinet autophone, $35; and the company are also now manufacturing Prof. Cleaves' Patent Study Table, a most convenient and useful article for the student or writer. A working force of 45 people is employed, which number

Above: Some different Autophone models as depicted in "Ithaca and its Resources." (Courtesy of Larry Givens)

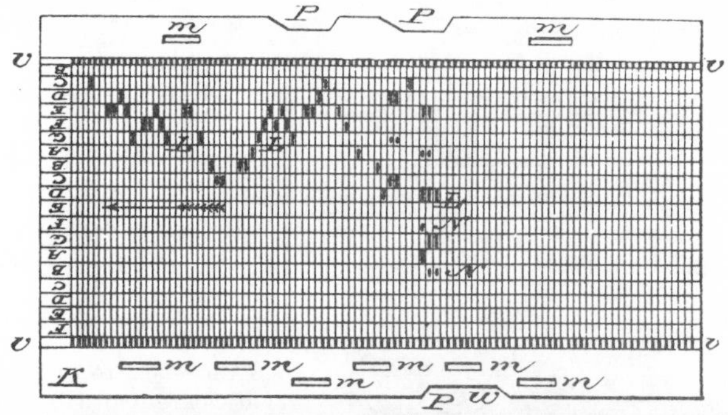


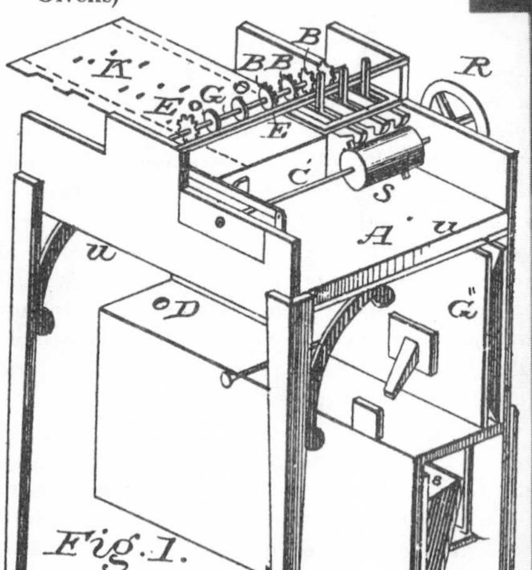


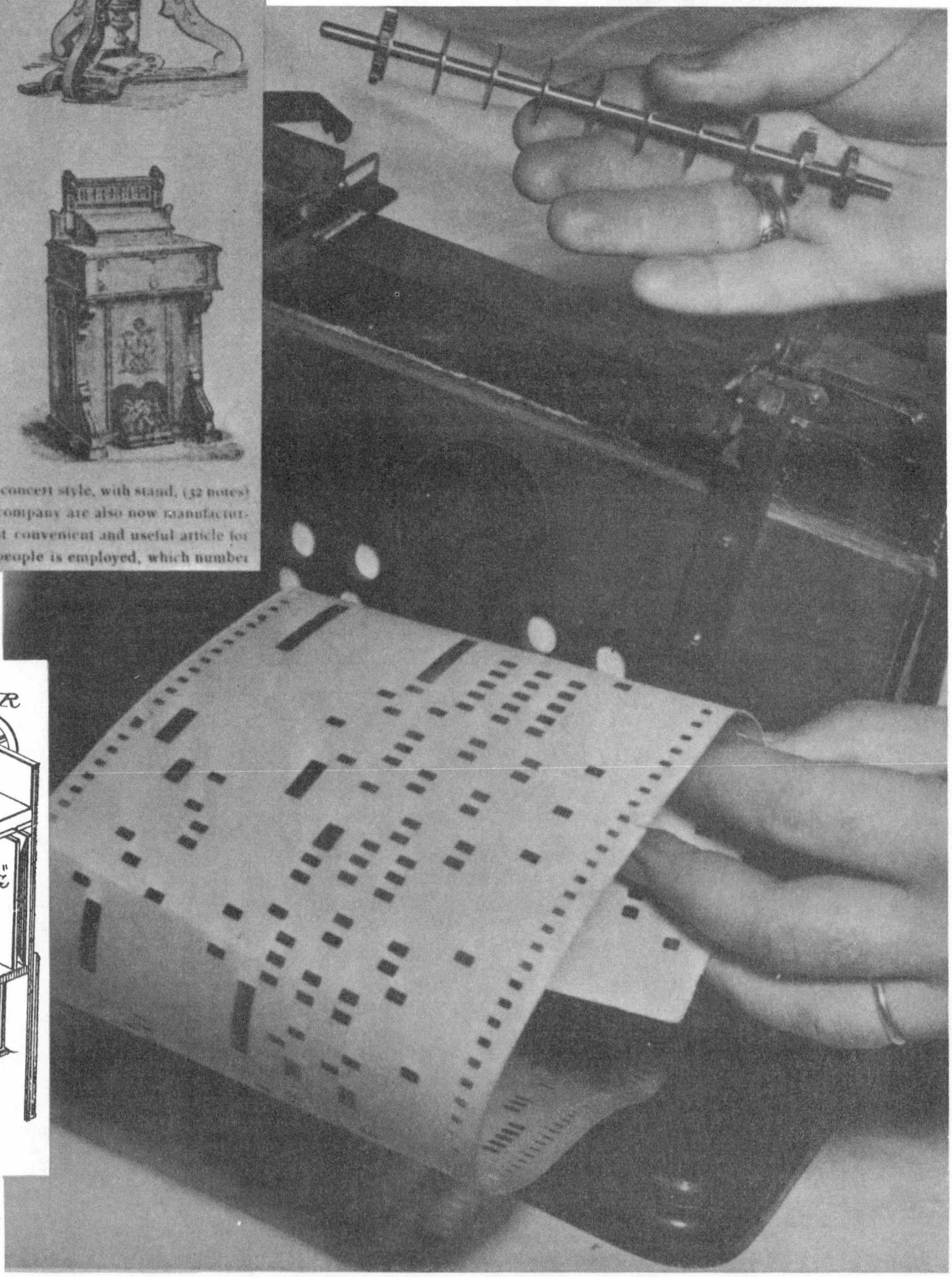

Above: Patent drawing for a large Autophone.

Right: The most popular Autophone model, a small hand-operated style.

## ORGANETTES (Merritt Gally's "Autophone")

### "AUTOPHONE"

*The following story, "The Autophone," is taken from the June 7, 1879, issue of Scientific American. While the article contains some inaccuracies (the autophone was hardly "the first successful invasion of the domain of music by automatic mechanism," nor was the music "prepared according to the rendering of the best artists" – as examples), the article is nontheless interesting as a contemporary view of a player reed organ (the same system was employed on Gally organettes also) of a design that was very sophisticated for its time. When this article appeared in 1879 player reed organs and organettes were just beginning to be marketed. By a decade later hundreds of thousands had been sold all over the world.*

The instrument illustrated by the accompanying engravings is the autophone [Ed. note: "autophone" is not capitalized in the original article – indicating its use as a generic term], for which letters patent have been issued in the United States and Europe to Professor Merritt Gally, of New York City. This instrument is claimed by the inventor to be both original in its conception and fundamental in its principle, and it is believed to be the first successful invasion of the domain of music by automatic mechanism.

The autophone is operated by a thin sheet of paper only 3 7/8" wide, punctured with small holes. The instrument is provided with any number of stops, and, if a reed or pipe instrument, with any number of sets of reeds or pipes. The invention is applicable to instruments of any quality, from the cheapest piano or cabinet organ to a grand church organ. The music sheet is prepared to represent not only the notes, but also the entire expression required to render the music in the most perfect and artistic manner.

The perforations in the sheet, which correspond with the stops, occupy such positions as to operate any stop, or number of stops for any passage, or note or part of a note, that will secure the best effect. It will be readily seen by a musician, says Professor Gally, that this is more than can be accomplished by the hands of the most expert performer. The hands being occupied in the fingering of the keys prevents the possibility of manipulating the stops when it would often be desirable to do so.

The mechanism, which is operated by the music sheet for the stops, is as sensitive and rapid in its action as that for the note keys, rendering it possible to produce an unlimited variety of "expression."

The accompanying illustration represents a cabinet organ to which the invention is applied. The woman represented at the organ is placing into its bearings the small spool containing the strip of perforated paper which is to produce the music. The mechanism by which this sheet operates is connected with the ordinary pedals of the instrument and therefore requires no skill except to operate the bellows. To give the reader an accurate idea of the dimensions of this sheet and the punctures, notes, stops, and "expression," we show the spool partially unwound in the accompanying illustration. This represents the entire range of notes, six stops, and the "expression" devices.

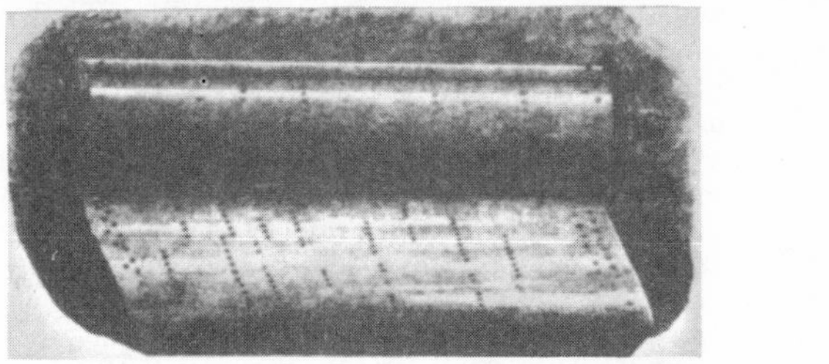

The size of the perforations, as will be seen, are exceedingly small, but sufficiently large for the perfect operation of the instrument. The mechanism is operated pneumatically, but these small openings in the sheet are not for the passage of air of the pipes or reeds of the instrument for producing the sound. The air passing through these small punctures simply trips sensitive devices that operate the valves which, in manual performing, are operated by the ordinary finger keys. The lines of punctures in the edges of the sheet represent the stops and "expression" devices. The air through these punctures operates the stops by means of a similar mechanism to that which opens the valves to the reeds or pipes.

Although the music with its "expression" is prepared according to the rendering of the best artists, the instrument is not limited to this or any set "expression" for the piece to be performed. For those without musical skill the "expression" prepared in the music sheet enables them to produce perfect music without requiring instruction or practice. [Ed. note: Examination of Gally instruments surviving today indicates that the "expression" referred to in this article is the varying of the volume of sound by means of one or two louvered swell shutters.]

The instrument, however, is not limited to the "expression" prepared in the music sheet, but affords to the accomplished musician the widest scope for the exercise of his personal taste and skill, the stops being absolutely under the control of the performer, so that he may vary the "expression" at pleasure. This is done with greater facility than by any ordinary arrangement of stops, being controlled by sensitive finger keys. Four of these finger keys are shown in the accompanying illustrations, and are located at each side of the receptacle [roll mechanism] of the punctured strip in connection with button strips. Otherwise than the fact that these button stops turn to the right and left to bring in or shut off the parts of the instrument which they represent, instead of being drawn and pushed, they operate in a manner similar to ordinary draw stops.

In our illustration one of the finger keys and its corresponding button stop is shown. Turning the button with the lettered portion toward the operator accomplishes the same result as drawing an ordinary stop, or turning the lettered portion at right angles, as shown in the engraving, accomplishes the same result as pushing in an ordinary stop.

The sheet or strip of music is marked at its head with the number of button stops which should be turned on before starting the mechanism. These stops, although turned on, are operative only when perforations in the edges of the sheet occur which indicate their action. Wherever these punctures do occur, even for a note or part of a note, or an entire passage, the effect of the stop is produced. Thus far it will be seen that the effect of the stops is limited to the set expression indicated by the punctures of the sheet. The variety which may be given in the expression to accord with the judgment or taste of the performer (which may differ from that in the music strip) is produced in the following manner: By the use of the finger keys the performer renders inoperative at will any of the stops represented in the sheet, and substitutes others at pleasure. The key is double-acting, arranged to be depressed at either end. Depressed at the right end (as depicted in our illustration) renders inoperative the stop that would otherwise come into action. Any stop that is turned off and not to come into action is thrown into action for the time desired by the pressure of the key at the left end. If the performer does not want to use any of the stops indicated in the music strip, all the button stops are turned off before commencing the piece, and by pressing on the different keys, each at the left-hand end, any variety of expression is given. These keys are very sensitive, requiring only a slight touch, but they perfectly and instantaneously control the stops of the instrument.

For example, a single note which for the best effect is to be begun softly, and would on an ordinary instrument be increased by the swell [shutters] only, is in this instrument increased not only by the swell, but by an accumulation of stops commencing, if necessary, with only a single stop, and ending, if desirable, with an accumulation of ten.

Although the time in which the music is written is, by the mechanical motion, strictly adhered to, nevertheless, to avoid mechanical appearance in the rendering of the music and to divest it of every feature that might be in the least objectionable, or that in any way might fail to realize the most perfect conception of the artist, the instrument is provided with an ingenious mechanical device, by means of which the tune may be instantly changed, accelerated, or retarded through any passage, note, or part of a note, or a "hold" made on a note, at the will of the performer, especially adapting the invention for rendering accompaniment for singing. The first key to the left of the receptacle for the sheet operates a mechanism for retarding the movement of the sheet for retarding the time of a passage, producing a "hold" or a perfect rest, which is not indicated in the arrangement punctured in the strip. The degree and duration of the retard is controlled by the degree of pressure applied to the key. A positive hold on the key produces a "hold" on the tone. A positive hold between the notes produces a "rest" the length of time the key is thus held.

[Editor's note: When automatic organs were first produced the makers placed great emphasis on the non-mechanical sound of the music. The ability of the instrument to perform with expression, as a human player would do, was given great consideration. To this end, organs were provided with swell shutters — usually not automatic; the Gally instrument described here is an exception — and instructions, usually printed on the roll, for changing stops or registers and varying the intensity of pedaling. Today collectors often overlook the fact that these early instruments, if played properly, can produce really brilliant musical performances. The original emphasis of the instruments' makers, the use of the organ to perform realistically, is largely forgotten today.]

To repeat a passage or part of a passage not arranged in the sheet to be repeated as ordinarily performed, and to enable the operator to repeat any part at will, once or successively, without limitation, the key just described, in connection with the draw-knob at the right of the receptacle, recalls for repetition any desired part of the music strip; the return being instantly made to prearranged limits, only so much of the strip being drawn as is desirable. The convenience of this device in singing, or in playing dance music, will be seen at once, as comparatively short strips answer the purpose as well or even better than very long ones, besides lessening their cost.

The instrument may be arranged for any number of octaves; the music strip, however, need not necessarily be increased beyond the width already mentioned.

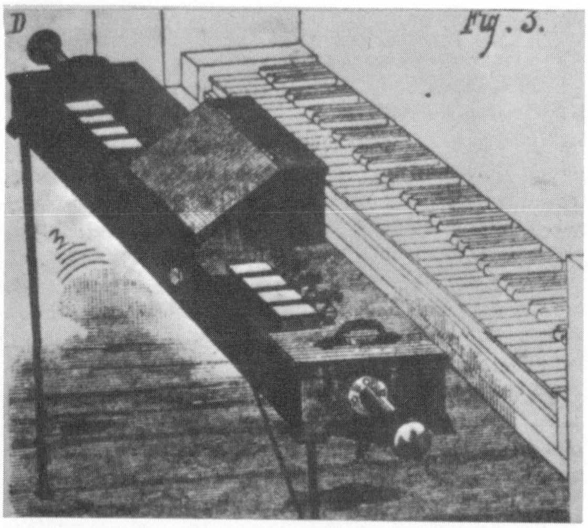


The autophone is not only adapted to organ music, but is equally well adapted to the piano. The "expression" produced upon the organ by the operation of the stops, in connection with the music sheet, is produced in a similar way upon the piano, the soft and loud pedals not only being acted upon by the music sheet, but the variety of touch required for the best effects is fully attained. This invention, as applied to the piano, as with the organ, is not limited to the set expression provided in the music sheet, but allows of great variety in the personal expression of the artist.

The autophone seems destined to prove invaluable in its application to orchestrions; the small, cheap music sheet accomplishing all, and even more, than the very expensive barrels of such instruments. The addition of variety in expression which this invention will impart to orchestrions, and which they have not heretofore possessed, will, it is claimed, increase their musical value.

The narrowness of the sheet, and the fact that it is not necessarily thick and cumbersone, but is light and cheap, are important qualifications. This music, we are informed, will be sold as cheaply as ordinary sheet music. It is made by machinery specially adapted to the purpose, and the perforations being so small, leaves it very strong and durable.

The autophone is adapted to instruments having a keyboard that may at pleasure be used for manual performing, as shown in the accompanying illustration, or it may form a part of an instrument not having finger keys, for use by those who are not musicians, and who do not desire the addition of the ordinary keyboard to the instrument. It is also made as an attachment to perform upon organs or pianos already in use, and may be readily placed upon or removed from the instrument.

The invention is represented in this form in the accompanying illustration in which the ordinary keyboard of an instrument is shown, the attachment being moved toward it to be placed ovcr the keys. If the instrument be a wind instrument, as an organ, the connecting rod, shown as attached to the foot pedals, is connected to the ordinary pedals of the organ, the pedals shown being used when the attachment is employed to perform upon a piano.

The attachment is fastened to the keyboard by padded binding screws. A line of strikers, corresponding with and striking upon the keys, are operated by mechanism similar to that already mentioned. Connections are also made from the attachments with the ordinary stops and "expression" devices of the instrument, and are operated by the punctures of the sheet or other finger stop keys, as heretofore explained. The rod supports are movable. In the form illustrated the attachment is light and portable, and may be easily carried by hand. When not desirable to have this portable a case is provided supported by casters.

Using the language of the inventor, the autophone is constructed on purely scientific principles, is as simple as it is wonderful, requires no adjustment, and is always ready for action. Its mechanism is so perfect and its operation so free, that it is not liable to get out of order, and, with ordinary care, will last for an indefinite period. It is, in all essential respects, unlike anything heretofore invented, either in structure, action, or musical results.

Professor Gally is better known to the public as the inventor and manufacturer of the Universal printing press. Further information regarding the autophone may be obtained by application to the inventor at his office, No.9 Spruce Street, New York City.

---

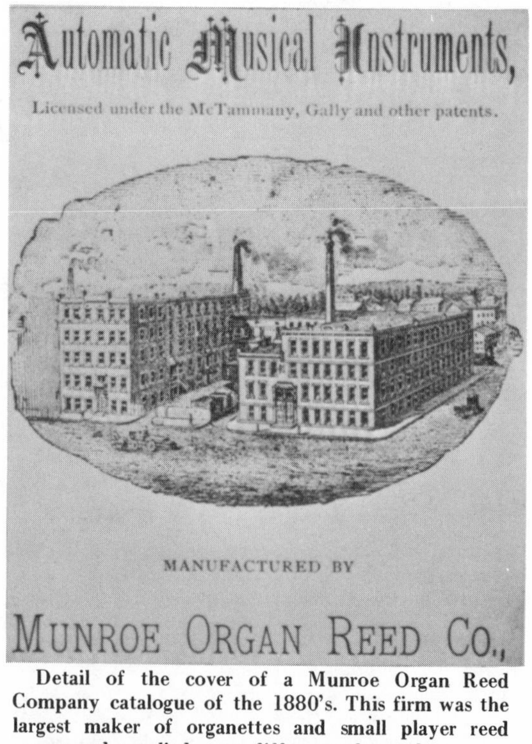


Detail of the cover of a Munroe Organ Reed Company catalogue of the 1880's. This firm was the largest maker of organettes and small player reed organs and supplied many different sales outlets.

The Jubal Orchestrone, illustrated on the opposite page, is the latest and best small musical instrument ever produced, possessing all the advantages and none of the defects of former instruments of this class. Its bellows capacity is greater, its reeds larger, and its tone more powerful than any instrument of its kind ever manufactured. While in quality of tone and means of expression it is equal to the best Cabinet Organ, though it does not cost one tenth as much. It has a simple pneumatic action not at all liable to get out of order, which consists of a circular diaphram pneumatic operated by gravity instead of springs as formerly, thus reducing the liability of getting out of order. In this instrument the paper does not act as a valve to the reeds, as in the old style, nor does it have fingers to get displaced in shipping or tear the paper in playing; on the contrary, the reeds are removed from the paper, therefore are protected and prevented from breaking and getting out of tune, as was the case with former instruments. So simple are they in principle that any one can take them apart and put them together. In construction it is strong, being made of solid black walnut, well put together, its panels handsomely carved and highly ornamented. The music sheets are less than three inches wide, while the spools on which the paper is wound do not occupy one fourth the space, yet hold twice the amount of music, which is warranted to last for years.

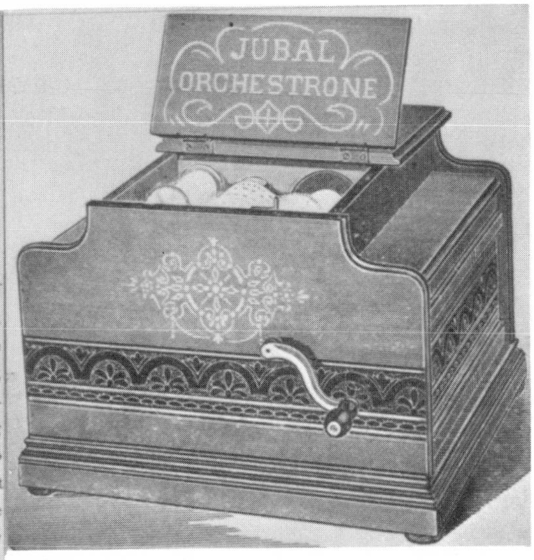


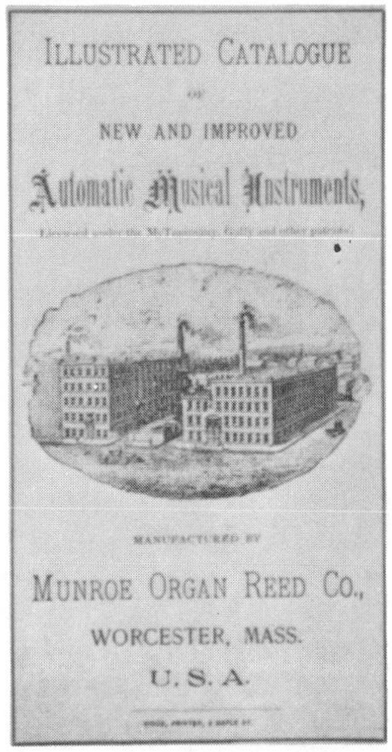


**Cover of Munroe Organ Reed Co. catalogue. Instruments made were "licensed under the McTammany, Gally, and other patents."**

**The Orchestrone: The Jubal Orchestrone, manufactured by the Munroe Organ Reed Company under the patents of Professor Merritt Gally, was quite advanced for its day. It featured a true pneumatic action in which the tracker bar openings were connected to pneumatic valve assemblies which, in turn, caused the reeds to sound.**

# DESCRIPTIVE PREFACE.

Automatic musical instruments which perform any tune, in any key, and in any kind of time and with perfect expression, and which any one can play, are no longer looked upon in the light of curiosities, since they may be found in thousands of homes throughout this country and Europe; but if additional evidence of their popularity were wanting, the simple fact that our manufacture alone having reached the enormous figures of 50,000 in one year would be sufficient. It will therefore be unnecessary for us to enter fully into the details of the principles working and construction of these instruments, (which are now as well known and common as the piano and organ,) but rather to point out the latest, numerous and important improvements and greatly reduced price which brings them within the reach of all.

The instruments illustrated in this catalogue are known as Orchestrones, and in many respects resemble the common Reed or Parlor Organ, using the same reeds, bellows, stops, swells and other devices, differing only in that they do not require any skill to operate them, so that any one, whether understanding music or not, can play any desired melody or harmony, sacred or secular, from the most plaintive dirge to the liveliest dance music, thus dispensing with years of study and the expenditure of thousands of dollars necessary to acquire the ability to perform on the ordinary organ; so that henceforth any man can be his own organist, any minister can lead his own choir, any teacher their school, while any member of a Pos Lodge or Encampment becomes at once by the assistance of the orchestrone fully qualified to lead his Order, playing in a perfect manner any composition authorized by the ritual, requiring nothing of the performer but to operate the bellows, furnishing either a finished solo performance, orchestral effect, or a rich accompaniment to the voice.

The music for these instruments consists of perforated paper, which is wound on small, light, and compact spools, (containing from one to six tunes,) which can be carried in the pocket without inconvenience or sent by mail to any part of the world at trifling cost, the price being much less than ordinary piano or organ composition, so that the range of music is absolutely unlimited, that the Orchestrone well represents organ and organist, music and musician, teacher and guide, and so is admirably adapted for Churches, Lodges, singing parties, dancing Academies and evening entertainments, and for any purpose for which an organist or teacher is employed. Special rolls of music made up to order.

**The Bijou Orchestrone, most popular of the Orchestrone table models, was made under the Gally patents. Like the Jubal Orchestrone, the Bijou Orchestrone had an indirect pneumatic action — rather than the customary system (used in most other paper roll organettes of the period) whereby the paper itself acted as a valve (when a hole in the paper exposes a tracker bar hole, air rushes into the hole and directly sounds a reed).**

**The "it only costs twenty five dollars" price (see description at the right) was simply too much money in a decade in which the Orchestrone's competition was priced at $5 to $10 or even less. As a result, production of the Bijou Orchestrone was quite limited in comparison with paper-as-a-valve organettes.**

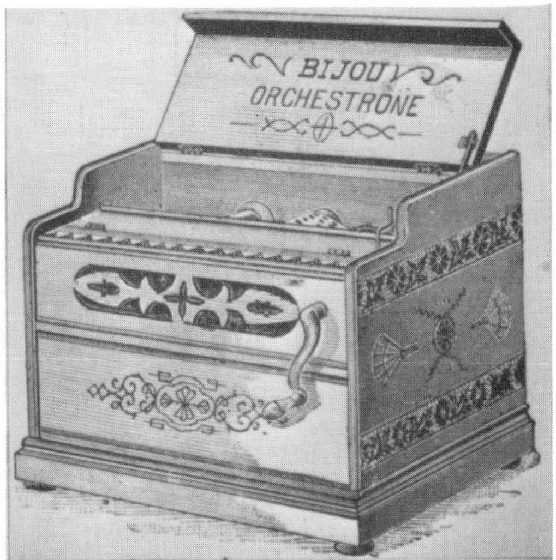


This instrument is larger, consequently is more powerful than the Jubal Orchestrone just described. It has a larger register or compass, consequently is capable of producing rich orchestral effects, and as it only costs twenty-five dollars, is within the reach of all. It has a fine, powerful tone, a rich, beautiful case, and is capable of producing the orchestral effects which have made our larger instruments so popular.

This instrument combines all the latest improvements upon which automatic musical instruments are now made, and is a marvel of simplicity and durability.

The development and success attained by automatic musical instruments, not only in this country, but in Europe, is largely owing to the skill, workmanship and superior facilities controlled by this Company, whose aim is only for the best and finest that can be made, regardless of cost. We invite the most critical examination of our different styles, both as to quality of tone and action, and also of material and manner of construction.

ORCHESTRONE,

Style 26 A.

It has been urged against instruments of this class that while they were marvels of perfection in every other respect, that they were still defective by reason of their want of expression; but in view of our latest development and wonderful improvements this objection can no longer be raised, and we take pleasure in calling the attention of our patrons to this new and wonderful feature of our latest instruments. On the opposite page is an illustration of what is called a floor instrument. It has double blow pedals, which are operated by the feet, like the common Parlor Organ; the music sheet is carried through the instrument by the aid of a small handle, in this way the performer can hold on any chord or retard at any point in the music without exhaust to air, as the pedals worked by the feet keep up a full supply. But the crowning triumph of this instrument is its automatic swell, which is operated by the perforations in the music sheet. The automatic swell is an ingenious contrivance not liable to get out of order, and consists of a common organ swell, to which is attached a small pneumatic bellows that is operated by air passing through the music sheet, which is arranged in such a manner as to open the swell spontaneously or gradually, or to open it entirely or partly, so that the expression assigned by the composer to any composition can be transferred to the perforated sheet and in the most satisfactory manner.

**Orchestrone Style 26-A (circa 1885).**

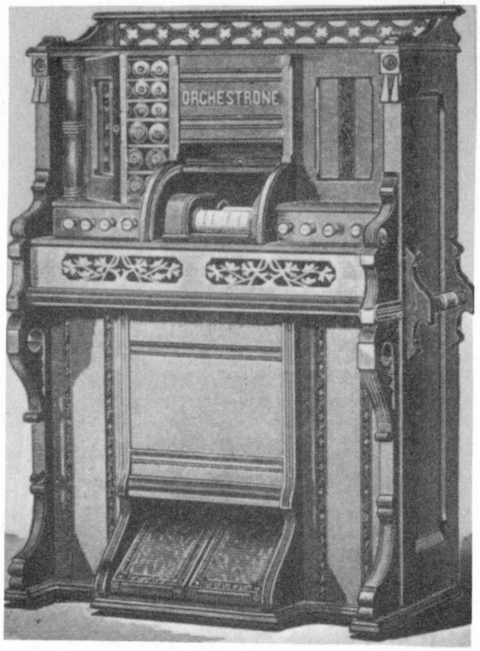


**Orchestrone Style 26-B (circa 1885)**

This instrument has the same compass as Style A and uses the same music, but possesses the following additional advantages, the most important of which is the wind motor or engine, which is a novel and ingenious device for operating the music sheet. This motor is governed by a stop, which is under the control of the performer and by which he is enabled to play in any tempo, fast or slow, by simply drawing out, or pushing in the metronome stop, and if desired may accompany the organ with violin, flute or cornet, the feet only being necessary to operate the Organ. The music sheet being carried through the instrument by the motor, which is operated by the bellows. This instrument has two full sets of reeds and sub-bass and is very brilliant and powerful, and is therefore more suitable for larger halls, churches, etc., than Style A.

ORGANETTE.

Length, 14 in. Width, 12 in. Height, 9 in. Weight, boxed, 16 lbs.
Price, with a selection of music, $8.00.

**Munroe Organ Reed Co. "Organette." (McTammany system)**

**Orchestrone case design used for Orchestrone 44-A and 44-C. Note the tiny hand-operated crank to the right of the music roll opening. The customary vacuum-operated roll drive motor is absent, and the music roll must be turned by hand. This is stated as an "advantage" in the description to the right: "For the convenience of teachers, and that the instrument may be entirely under the control of the operator, the [roll drive] motor is omitted in this style."**

**Most Style 44 Orchestrones used Professor Merritt Gally's system of pneumatic valves. Gally-licensed instruments were generally made with the roll facing sideways (as illustrated to the right). Other Style 44's were built with McTammany pneumatic actions and had the roll facing forward.**

We would particularly call attention of boards of Education, superintendents and school teachers, and all interested in the education of the youth to the advantages of Orchestrone Style 44 A, as a musical educator and valuable assistant to the school teacher, as by its use any teacher can give their pupils a most thorough musical training, and in primary schools especially is it desirable, as a relief from the monotony and irksome restraint so trying to children.

Any teacher, whether understanding music or not, by the aid of this instrument can open school with music in the morning while the children sing, and at intervals during the day an Opera, Overture, or some classic music of the great masters could be played, thus acquainting the children at an early age with compositions that under no other circumstances could they hear.

To this end we have arranged a complete set of vocal exercises for every grade, and by putting them in the instrument and allowing the pupils to accompany them with their voices, they will learn the difference in pitch of tones; they will also learn to recognize the different intervals as well as the melody and harmony, and as the instrument produces its own expression, they will soon be able to distinguish musical light and shade as well as time, in which this instrument surpasses any human performer. Furthermore, by watching the perforations in the sheet they will be enabled to distinguish the different length of notes as well as the different scales, all of which are furnished on spools for school use. For the convenience of teachers, and that the instrument may be entirely under the control of the operator, the motor is omitted in this style.

This instrument has the same scale, expression, devices and capacity as Style 44 A, including the music cabinets, and has in addition a high ornamental top, and is intended more for parlor use than Style 44 A. To parties who have voices to train but who have not the time or money to devote to that purpose, this instrument is invaluable, as by its aid and our specially arranged vocal exercises on rolls, he can without the aid of a teacher obtain a thorough course of training and voice development, such as can be obtained in no other way. The vocal exercise rolls furnished with these instruments are selected and arranged by the highest authority and are accompanied by all the instruction necessary. The music prepared for these instruments covers every grade and class, from the popular ballad to the massive symphony. Thus the lover of music, though not a player, has at his command the choicest musical gems, as without any technical knowledge whatever he can perform with a clearness and accuracy and a degree of execution which few performers can equal and none surpass. So that the musical student by the use of this instrument and the expenditure of a small amount for music can reproduce at his pleasure any or all the classic music ever written, as well as any work of the great masters. The same knowledge could not be obtained in any other way without the expenditure of thousands of dollars and much effort, if it could be obtained at all.

Taylor & Farley player organ

Taber player organ

(Munroe Organ Reed Co.)

Above left: Orchestrone Style 44-B. Uses the Professor Merritt Gally system of pneumatic valving. For a further description of this system please refer to the 1879 "Scientific American" article, "The Autophone," reprinted on another page.

Left: Orchestrone Style 44-E. Keyboard style with draw stops. Made with the McTammany pneumatic action.

John McTammany styled himself as "the inventor of the player piano," and, in 1915, published a book, "The Technical History of the Player," in which he attempted to discredit efforts of the Schmoele Brothers, Gally, and others. McTammany's tenuous claims were dismissed by most of the music industry although McTammany, as Selden did in the automobile industry, did succeed in obtaining via court action license payments from a number of manufacturers.

Above: Taylor & Farley (1881) and Taber (1880) organs with pneumatic actions (of the indirect type, in these instances) made with license payments to John McTammany.

—Trumpetto—
—Phonographic Cornet—

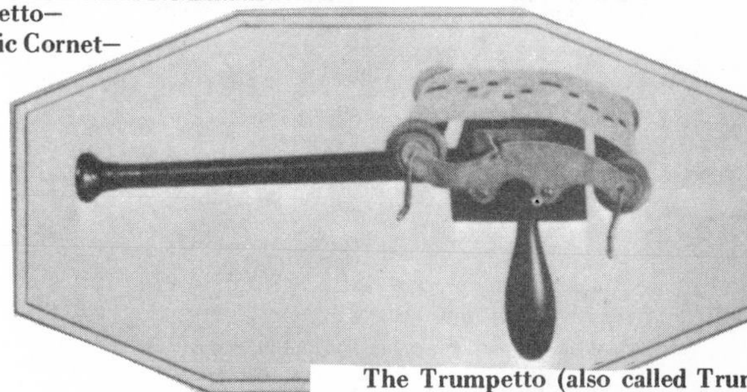

The Trumpetto (also called Trumpeto [by the Mechanical Orguinette Co.], the Phonographic Cornet, and other names devised by sales agents) was one of the first organettes to be marketed. By 1878 they were being sold by the thousands. Henry B. Tremaine, president of the Aeolian Co. during the late 1890's and the early 20th century, stated that this and a 14-note organette were the first products handled by that firm's predecessor, the Mechanical Orguinette Company, which was founded in 1878.

The Trumpetto is hand-cranked in the manner shown at the left. The scale is of just eight notes.

**PHONOGRAPHIC CORNET.**

**The Latest and Greatest Musical Wonder.**

The Phonographic Cornet is the latest invention in the musical line. The action of this instrument is almost marvellous. It plays the most complicated airs equal to a first-class Cornet solo. The picture represents the manner of playing: simply turning the little crank on the side produces most exquisite music. The music-producers are genuine first-class Organ Reeds, and the music itself is like that of a first-class Organ played on the high notes, with the flute stops out. *Any tune that ever was written can be instantly played on the Phonographic Cornet,* **without any instruction or knowledge of music whatever** *by the operator.* A little strip of paper in which the tune has been perforated, is placed in the instrument, and then simply turning the little handle brings out the tune in a clear and extremely melodious manner. Selections of choice music accompany each "cornet." Any child can play this instrument; the music is very pleasing; all the new tunes can be easily obtained, and no musical instrument in the world can provide more genuine entertainment, at home or in company, than the Phonographic Cornet. **Anyone** can play it, and produce the latest music in a manner that will surprise everyone. The instruments are all strongly and elegantly made of fancy woods, ebonized trimmings, and silvered bolts. They are packed in a neat case, with music strips, directions, &c., &c., and sent by express to any address for **$3**; *by registered mail, prepaid,* **$3.30.** Extra tunes, comprising all the latest popular music, are now ready.
Address **THE MASSACHUSETTS ORGAN CO., 43 Washington Street, Boston, Mass.**

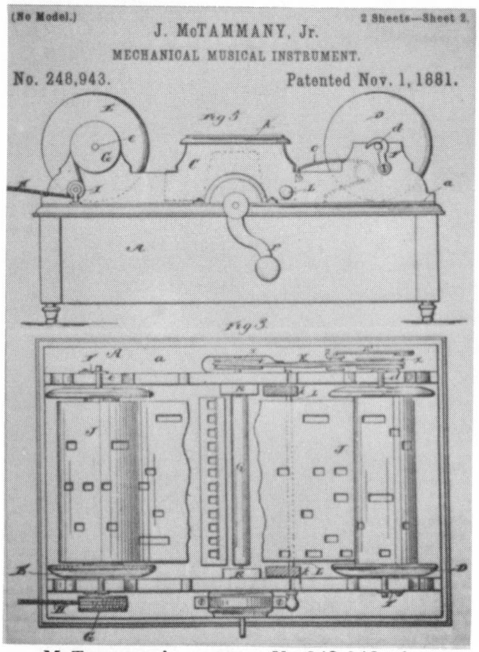


McTammany's patent No.248,943 for a pressure bar, rewind system, and other innovations. The instrument illustrated is a typical McTammany organette of the period. Many of somewhat similar style were sold by the Mechanical Orguinette Co.

McTammany's patent No.259,412 for a "movable set of organ pipes" (actually resonators and not pipes at all; these were used on the "Reed Pipe Clariona" sold in the 1880's), a music roll tightening belt (which passes over both spools as shown), and other ideas.

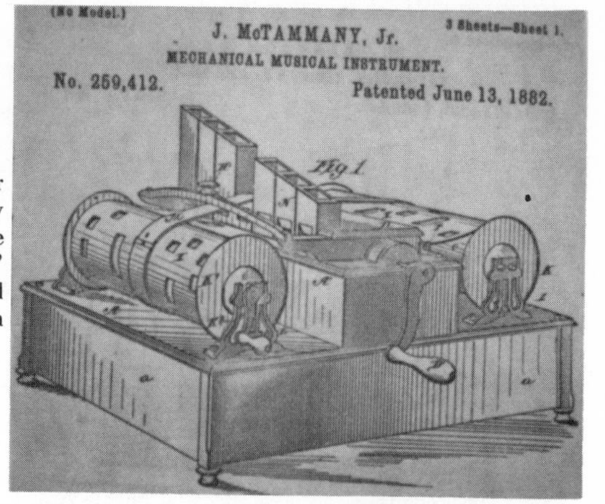


—McTammany Patents—

During the quarter century beginning in 1881, John McTammany patented over two dozen ideas pertaining to automatic instruments. For those wishing to delve into the subject, "The Technical History of the Player," by John McTammany may be consulted. On such grounds as "no model was submitted" (and thus, so reasons McTammany, the idea was invalid), "the idea was abandoned," etc. McTammany tried to establish himself as the inventor of the roll-operated (or strip-operated) musical instrument. It is interesting to note that McTammany overlooked submitting models for certain of his own patents, in fact for most of them, but this fact is conveniently omitted in his book.

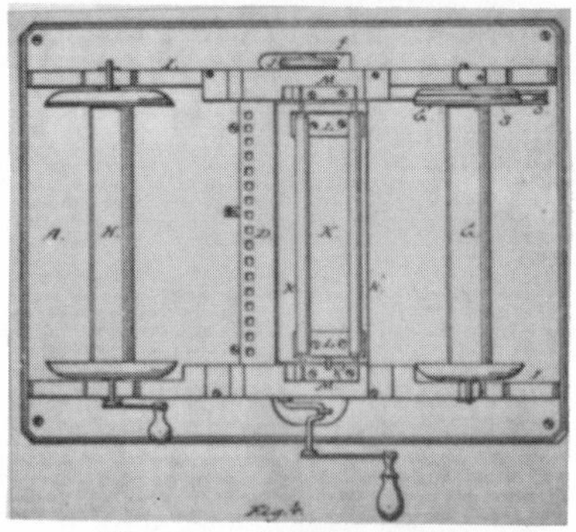

Top view of typical organette.

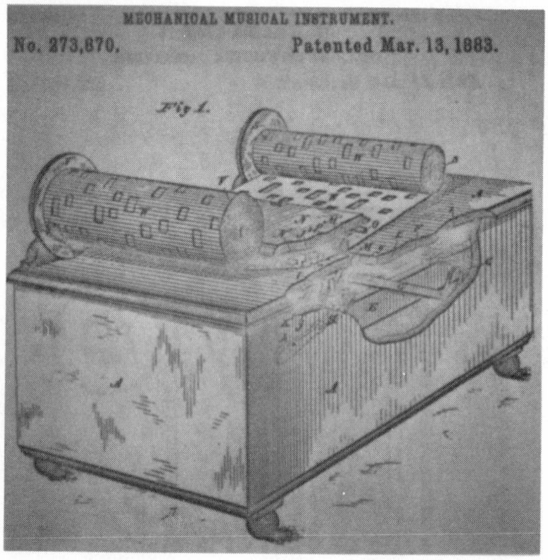


McTammany's patent No.273,870 for thirteen features pertaining to an organette operated by tiny metal keys which press against the music strip.

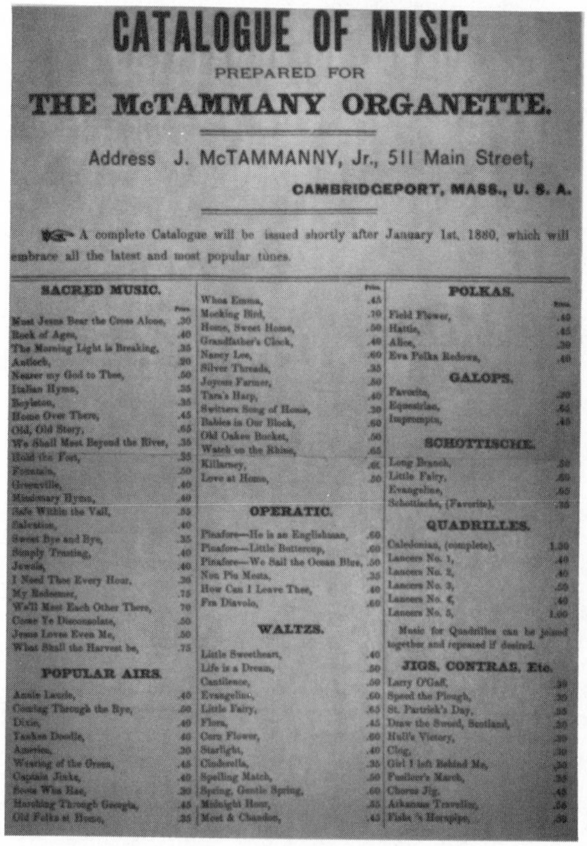

CATALOGUE OF MUSIC

PREPARED FOR

THE McTAMMANY ORGANETTE.

Address J. McTAMMANNY, Jr., 511 Main Street,

CAMBRIDGEPORT, MASS., U. S. A.

A complete Catalogue will be issued shortly after January 1st, 1880, which will embrace all the latest and most popular tunes.

SACRED MUSIC. (Price)

Must Jesus Bear the Cross Alone, .30
Rock of Ages, .40
The Morning Light is Breaking, .35
Antioch, .20
Nearer my God to Thee, .50
Italian Hymn, .35
Boylston, .35
Home Over There, .45
Old, Old Story, .65
We Shall Meet Beyond the River, .35
Hold the Fort, .35
Fountain, .50
Greenville, .40
Missionary Hymn, .40
Safe Within the Vail, .55
Salvation, .40
Sweet Bye and Bye, .35
Simply Trusting, .40
Jewels, .40
I Need Thee Every Hour, .30
My Redeemer, .75
We'll Meet Each Other There, .70
Come Ye Disconsolate, .50
Jesus Loves Even Me, .50
What Shall the Harvest be, .75

POPULAR AIRS.

Annie Laurie, .40
Coming Through the Rye, .50
Dixie, .40
Yankee Doodle, .40
America, .30
Wearing of the Green, .45
Captain Jinks, .40
Scots Wha Hae, .30
Marching Through Georgia, .45
Old Folks at Home, .35
Whoa Emma, .45
Mocking Bird, .70
Home, Sweet Home, .50
Grandfather's Clock, .40
Nancy Lee, .60
Silver Threads, .35
Joyous Farmer, .50
Tara's Harp, .40
Switzers Song of Home, .30
Babies in Our Block, .60
Old Oaken Bucket, .50
Watch on the Rhine, .65
Killarney, .46
Love at Home, .50

OPERATIC.

Pinafore—He is an Englishman, .60
Pinafore—Little Buttercup, .60
Pinafore—We Sail the Ocean Blue, .50
Non Piu Mesta, .35
How Can I Leave Thee, .40
Fra Diavolo, .60

WALTZS.

Little Sweetheart, .40
Life is a Dream, .50
Cantilence, .50
Evangeline, .60
Little Fairy, .65
Flora, .45
Corn Flower, .60
Starlight, .40
Cinderella, .35
Spelling Match, .50
Spring, Gentle Spring, .60
Midnight Hour, .55
Moet & Chandon, .45

POLKAS. (Price)

Field Flower, .40
Hattie, .45
Alice, .30
Eva Polka Redowa, .40

GALOPS.

Favorita, .30
Equestrian, .65
Impromptu, .45

SCHOTTISCHE.

Long Branch, .50
Little Fairy, .60
Evangeline, .60
Schottische, (Favorite), .35

QUADRILLES.

Caledonian, (complete), 1.50
Lancers No. 1, .40
Lancers No. 2, .40
Lancers No. 3, .55
Lancers No. 4, .40
Lancers No. 5, 1.00

Music for Quadrilles can be joined together and repeated if desired.

JIGS, CONTRAS, Etc.

Larry O'Gaff, .30
Speed the Plough, .30
St. Patrick's Day, .35
Draw the Sword, Scotland, .30
Hull's Victory, .30
Clog, .30
Girl I left Behind Me, .30
Fusileer's March, .35
Chorus Jig, .45
Arkansas Traveller, .56
Fisher's Hornpipe, .35

From the McTammany book: "Earliest roll catalogue, first printed 1877. Above is copy of 1879 reissue." Editor's note: Schmoele Brothers of Philadelphia, to cite one example, issued an earlier list (in 1876 for rewind-type paper music rolls used on the Electro-magnetic Orchestra exhibited at the Centennial Exhibition).

McTammany Organette Co. advertisement of 1883. Note that the instrument shown is of the same type depicted in patent 248,943 shown at the top of this page.

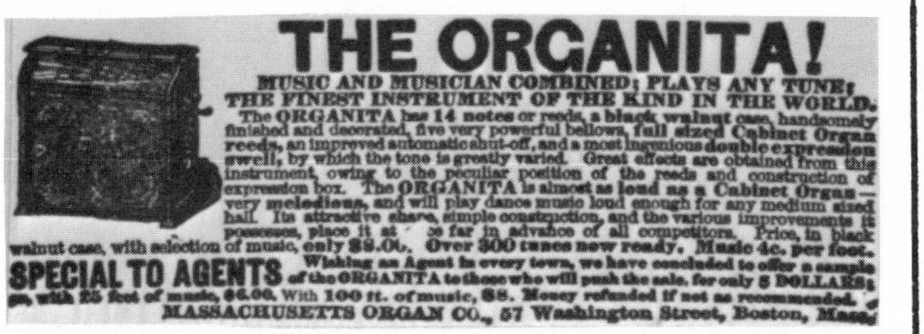

THE ORGANITA!
MUSIC AND MUSICIAN COMBINED; PLAYS ANY TUNE; THE FINEST INSTRUMENT OF THE KIND IN THE WORLD.
The ORGANITA has 14 notes or reeds, a black walnut case, handsomely finished and decorated, five very powerful bellows, full sized Cabinet Organ reeds, an improved automatic shut-off, and a most ingenious double expression swell, by which the tone is greatly varied. Great effects are obtained from this instrument, owing to the peculiar position of the reeds and construction of expression box. The ORGANITA is almost as loud as a Cabinet Organ—very melodious, and will play dance music loud enough for any medium sized hall. Its attractive shape, simple construction, and the various improvements it possesses, place it at once far in advance of all competitors. Price, in black walnut case, with selection of music, only $8.00. Over 300 tunes now ready. Music 4c. per foot.
SPECIAL TO AGENTS
Wishing an Agent in every town, we have concluded to offer a sample of the ORGANITA to those who will push the sale, for only 5 DOLLARS; with 25 feet of music, $6.00. With 100 ft. of music, $8. Money refunded if not as recommended.
MASSACHUSETTS ORGAN CO., 57 Washington Street, Boston, Mass.

A $10 Organ for $5.00
The Great Musical Wonder.
Plays 500 Tunes. Most charming musical instrument made. Plays Hymns, Songs, and Dance Music. Any one can play it. Our object is to introduce it at once, so as to sell thousands at the regular price, $10. To this end I will send one to any reader of this paper for $5. If you want the Best, send direct to Makers. We will please you. Just what you want to make home happy. Send $5.00 with this notice and we send Organ at once, all complete. Satisfaction, or money refunded. Address,
BATES ORGAN CO., 100 High Street, BOSTON, MASS.

PRICE 5 CENTS.
THE MASSACHUSETTS ORGAN CO.
Manufacturers and Dealers in
Organs, Mechanical Musical Instruments,
AND
MUSICAL MERCHANDISE.
Chesterfield, Chapel, Imperial Cabinet, and Royal Upright Organs.
ORGANINAS, ORGANITAS, TOY PIANOS, AND MECHANICAL PIANO-ETTES.
Mechanical or Automatic Musical Instruments a Specialty.
OFFICE AND SALESROOMS:
No. 57 Washington Street, Boston, Mass., U. S. A.
FACTORIES: CHELSEA, AND WORCESTER, MASS.
CHAS. H. SPAULDING, GENERAL MANAGER.


An assortment of ballyhoo-type organette advertisements from the 1880's and 1890's. Advertisements of the Massachusetts Organ Company, the American Automatic Organ Company (a thinly-disguised subsidiary of the previous firm), the World Manufacturing Company, and the Bates Organ Company are shown.

Such firms sold hundreds of thousands of instruments, if not millions. One advertisement noted (truly or otherwise) that over 75,000 Gem Organettas had been sold!

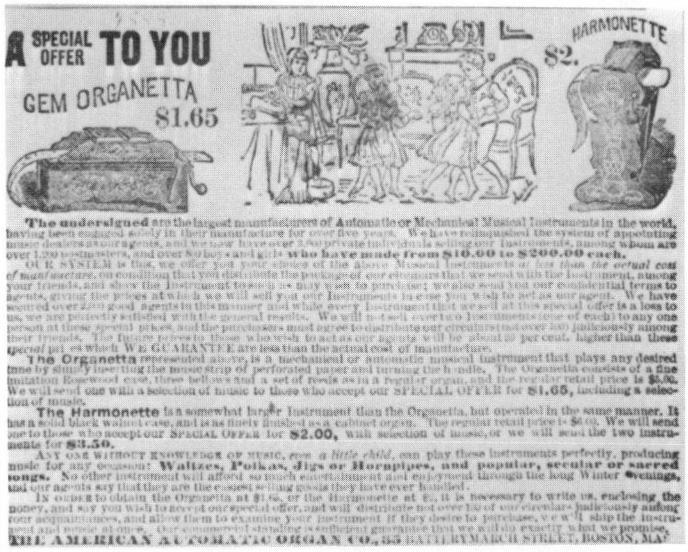

A SPECIAL OFFER TO YOU
GEM ORGANETTA
$1.65
HARMONETTE
$2.
The undersigned are the largest manufacturers of Automatic or Mechanical Musical Instruments in the world,
who have made from $10.00 to $200.00 each.
The Organetta
The Harmonette
SPECIAL OFFER for $2.00,
Waltzes, Polkas, Jigs or Hornpipes, and popular, secular or sacred songs.
THE AMERICAN AUTOMATIC ORGAN CO., 55 BATTERYMARCH STREET, BOSTON, MASS.

THE AUTOMATIC CABINET ORGAN.
For Parlor, Church, and Lodge Use.
This new and charming musical instrument fills a long expressed want for a powerful automatic instrument suitable for large rooms or Halls, and for Lodge or Church use. It uses perforated paper the same as other smaller instruments, but all the music comes on rolls or spools, making it very convenient to handle, and the closet in the lower part of the instrument will hold several extra rolls. The Instrument is 44 inches high, 19 inches wide, and 15 inches deep. It is made of black walnut, very highly finished and decorated in gilt. The scale of reeds in this Automatic Cabinet Organ has a compass of nearly 5 Octaves, and full justice can be done to elaborate musical composition. At the price it is a most desirable addition to any home and will repay in enjoyment tenfold the price. We box free and include a roll of music.
PRICE, ONLY $30.
MUSIC

THE AUREPHONE.
A New and Complete Mechanical Musical Instrument.
As shown by the picture, this instrument has the music upon rolls within its case, and as the music is played it is wound from one roll to the other; a most perfect and convenient arrangement. The tone is equal to a fine Cabinet Organ. The case is fine black walnut, handsomely decorated, and has a perfect Expression Swell, by means of which the quality of the music can be greatly varied to suit the musical taste of the performer. All the music for the AUREPHONE comes upon rolls or spools and each roll contains from 3 to 5 complete tunes. Being wound upon a spool it is very handy to take care of and is always in good order. After a roll is played through, simply lift the cover, when the same handle will wind the roll back on to the first spool in a quarter the time it took to play it; this is a great improvement. The price of the AUREPHONE, carefully boxed, with a roll of music, is only $10. This instrument is warranted to give perfect satisfaction.
The Tournaphone is a similar instrument to the Aurephone, but larger and with more notes or reeds. It is suitable for large Halls, Church, or Lodge use. The price of the TOURNAPHONE is $20, including a roll of music.
AUREPHONE


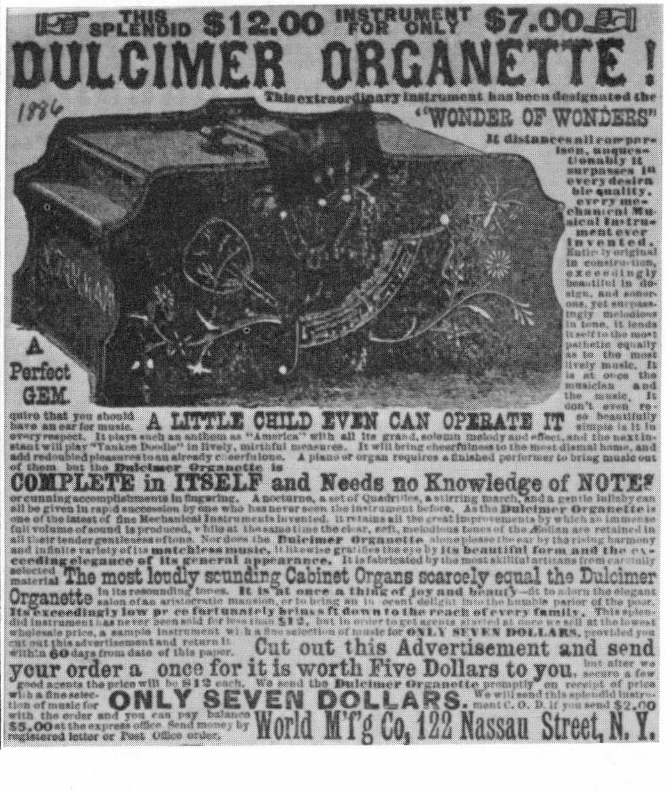

THIS SPLENDID $12.00 INSTRUMENT FOR ONLY $7.00
DULCIMER ORGANETTE!
1886
This extraordinary instrument has been designated the "WONDER OF WONDERS"
A Perfect GEM.
A LITTLE CHILD EVEN CAN OPERATE IT
COMPLETE in ITSELF and Needs no Knowledge of NOTES
The most loudly sounding Cabinet Organs scarcely equal the Dulcimer Organette
Cut out this Advertisement and send your order at once for it is worth Five Dollars to you.
ONLY SEVEN DOLLARS.
World M'f'g Co, 122 Nassau Street, N. Y.

THE ORGANINA.

MIGNONETTE STYLE.

IMPORTANT IMPROVEMENT.

Reference to the side engraving will show a small lever above the handle. Pressing this lever slightly CAUSES ALL THE FINGERS TO RAISE so that the music sheet can be inserted *without any hindrance*. This obviates any trouble that may hitherto have existed in inserting the music sheet, and *effectually prevents* the end of the music sheet from doubling up or becoming crumpled, greatly increasing the durability of the music.

THIS LEVER

Not only raises the fingers, but it also *closes all the valves* so that it is only necessary to press this lever to PREVENT THE DISAGREEABLE NOISE OF ALL THE NOTES SOUNDING AT ONCE at the end of the tune as they have heretofore done, and as they do in all other mechanical musical instruments.

THIS IMPROVEMENT will be included in all Organinas after this date, AT NO EXTRA EXPENSE.

To those having Organinas without this improvement, we would say that we will furnish it for 20 cents, postage paid, and any one can put it on, the only tool required being a gimlet.

It greatly enhances the value and salability of the Organina and places it another step in advance of all its competitors.

A wonderful triumph of mechanical skill, and the most perfect mechanical musical instrument in design, operation, and effect that has yet been produced.

RETAIL PRICE ONLY $10.

A mechanical musical instrument, with bellows, reeds, valves, swell, and automatic-finger action, using perforated paper strips to produce any desired tune; using the paper strips not as a series of valves, however, but as a pattern or stencil to operate the automatic fingers.

The true principle of a mechanical instrument is embodied in our system, namely: ***Automatic fingers which instantly open and shut, regularly constructed valves,*** GIVING PERFECT NOTES, with almost human manipulation and expression. ***Not paper as a valve,*** with its attendant imperfections and drawbacks. The automatic levers, which operate the valves in our instruments, act with a similar celerity and *touch* to the human finger, opening and closing the valves as in a cabinet organ, far different from other instruments using perforated paper as a valve, in which the note is gradually shut off, and consequently flattened as the paper passes along, requiring twice the force, twice the speed, and a greater length of paper than is necessary in our system, wherein the paper is not used to answer as valves, but as a pattern or stencil by which the automatic fingers are manipulated.

Mechanical Musical Instruments using perforated paper are not new to the trade in either this or foreign countries, but such instruments (hitherto using the paper as a valve) are, to say the least, extremely imperfect, and, while their sale has been certainly remarkable, there has been a constant demand for something with higher capabilities, having regularly constructed valves and capable of producing perfect music in expression, effect, and tone.

The Mignonette Style is 10½ inches high, 8¾ inches wide, and 8 inches deep; *weight*, when boxed, 10 lbs.; having SIXTEEN NOTES OR REEDS (*two more than any other similar-priced instrument*), and regular slide-valves; the music produced is very sweet and pleasing, suitable for any parlor or drawing-room, and will be preferred by many to larger and heavier styles. The case is black walnut, decorated in gilt, with nickel-silver trimmings, curved plate-glass panel (showing the action and operation of the automatic fingers, which is very interesting), *which exerts a wonderful effect upon the tone of the instrument by the reverberation of the tone upon the crystal plate.*

The mechanism throughout is first-class in construction, and very simple in design, easily taken apart, and not at all liable to get out of order.

The retail, or list-price, of the Organina (Mignonette Style) is **only $10,** a really wonderfully low price for so perfect an instrument. In ebonized cases and selected actions—**Price, $11.** In *solid* mahogany cases and extra selected actions—**Price, $12.**

The Organina is manufactured under the valuable patents granted O. H. Arno, Esq., by which means the *touch* and *expression* of a superior organist are almost exactly reproduced, an effect which has never before been obtained in mechanical musical instruments, and we believe it a better, more attractive, and more desirable instrument than a $100 French Music-Box, with its limited and monotonous arrangement of tunes. Our Organinas play *any tune*, which cost but a few cents apiece, and last for years.

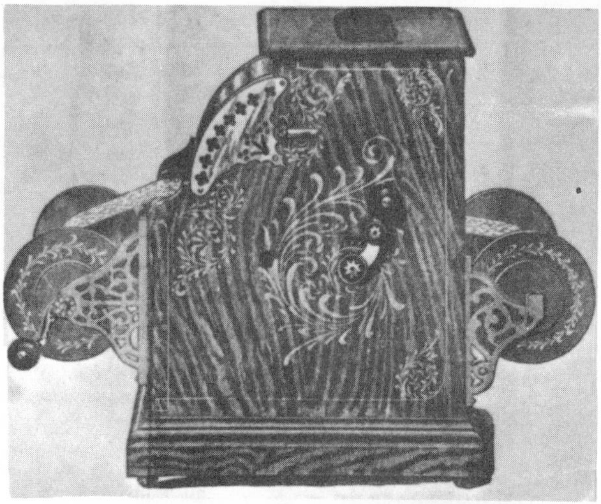

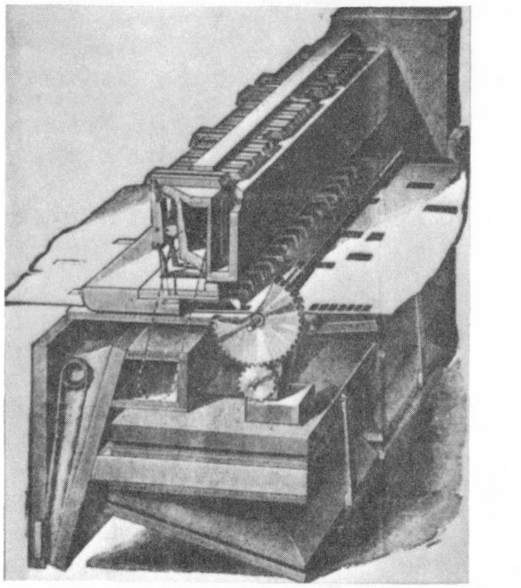

Massachusetts Organ Company advertisement for the Organina. The list of names of organettes sold by this firm is lengthy and includes the Organina, Organita, Imperial, Chesterfield, Royal Orguinette, Mechanical Orguinette, Orchestrion Harmonette, Organina Cabinet, Gem Organetta, Royal Organetta, Automatic Cabinet Organ, Aurephone, Tournaphone, Mechanical Organette, Mechanical Organetta, Organina Mignonette, and combinations of these names such as Royal Cabinet Orguinette, etc. The above advertisement notes "not paper as a valve" as a plus feature (it is mentioned in boldface type) while, at the very same time, an advertisement for the firm's Orchestrion Harmonette mentions as a prominent headline "Uses Paper As A Valve." (Author's comment: Hmm.)

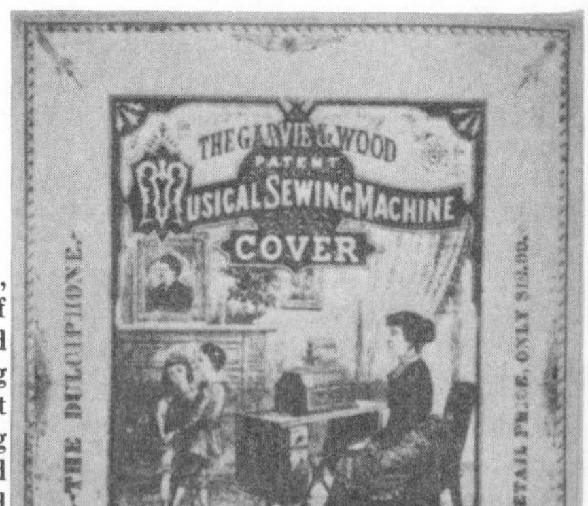

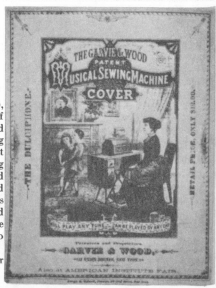

The Dulciphone or Automatic Organ, sold by agents such as Garvie & Wood (see illustration at right), the Royal Importing Company (see illustration above), and the Gately Manufacturing Company (of Boston), was designed to be used as a sewing machine attachment. Made by the Munroe Organ Reed Company in the 1880's, the Dulciphone was advertised as a "reed-pipe musical instrument possessing remarkable qualities and capable of being applied to any sewing machine. It is guaranteed to have at least four times the power and volume of tone of any other small automatic instrument, and has the carrying quality of a large pipe organ. . . This is the only small automatic instrument that will render slow or sacred music with a powerful and sustaining organ tone. It has quick and powerful utterance for dance music, and will carry with distinction throughout the extent of the largest dancing hall. . . Do not presuppose this instrument to be an Orguinette, as it is not. It is infinitely superior and very unlike anything of that kind or name. . . As we have no treadle or cabinet work to make (sewing machines having these) it will be readily understood why we can sell such a good instrument so cheap. Organ manufacturers, having to supply all these, must charge more without giving a better musical instrument. . ."

The Dulciphone was made in several different case style variations. (Illustrations courtesy of Arthur Sanders)

The Webber Singing Doll, sold by the Massachusetts Organ Company, appears to contain a small roller organ. "The singing attachment is concealed within the body. It is one of the most ingenious inventions of the age. It is a perfect musical instrument, finely made, not liable to get out of order and so arranged that a slight pressure causes the doll to sing one of the following tunes..." Made in three models: No.1, 22" high, $2.75; No.2, 24" high, $3.25; No.3, 26" high, $4.00. "The larger the doll, the larger the singing attachment..." 1883 advertisement.

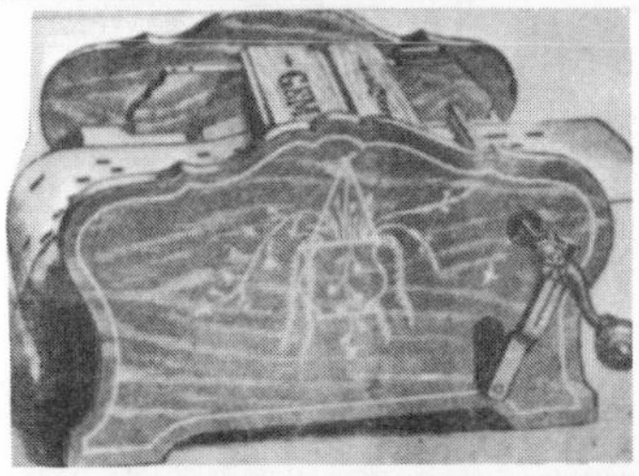

Above is shown the Gem Organetta, Style No. 1. To the right is Gem Organetta, Style No. 3. "The price of similar instruments has hitherto been $8, and the demand has constantly increased until now there are over 75,000 in use." The picture of the dancing children at the right was captioned: "A children's party; a little miss of eight years is playing a waltz, and her little friends are dancing; they are much better pleased than if Strauss himself were playing for them."

The Gem Organettas, styles 1 and 3 as shown, used an endless strip. A "roll attachment" permitting the use of rewind-type rolls cost $2 extra.

The Organina Cabinet. Billed as "the most complete mechanical musical instrument in the world." A close reading of the original text leads the reader to find that "most complete" apparently means "16 organ reeds." Case measurements: 20" long by 13" wide by 12" high. In a black or walnut case the Organina Cabinet sold for $20 in the 1880's.

Mechanical Orguinette or Royal Orguinette (also called the Organita). Sold for $9 "or $6 to those who will show it and take orders." "It is known the world over and has had the largest sale of any mechanical musical instrument."

Note: This Mechanical Orguinette bears no resemblance to the similarly-named instrument sold by the Mechanical Orguinette Co. during the 1880's. The latter instrument is of the type illustrated elsewhere in this book as the Munroe Organ Reed Co. "Organette."

Orchestrion Harmonette. 16 reeds. Sold for $8 "or $5 to anyone who will show it and take orders." J.P.D. Bilrick, apparently an "agent," gave the testimonial that "I have received the Harmonette and am greatly pleased with it. I have already orders for eight more."

## VICTORIA ORCHESTRIONETTE (Paper Strip Organette)

The most complete of all existing mechanical organs.

**No. 2.** 48 (24 double-) reeds, elegant black and gold case in cabinet form with a finished top piece.

The music-sheets are of three different lengths, playing complete set of waltzes or quadrilles operatic selections, ouvertures, hymnes, marches, polkas, latest comic songs etc.

VICTORIA ORCHESTRIONETTE
24 double (total 48) reeds. Case measures 16" wide by 13" deep by 24" high. Uses music strips. Made in Germany for the British market. 1895 illustration.

Mignon-Harmonieux Organ
Style IV (1904)

Mignon Organ
Style III (1904)

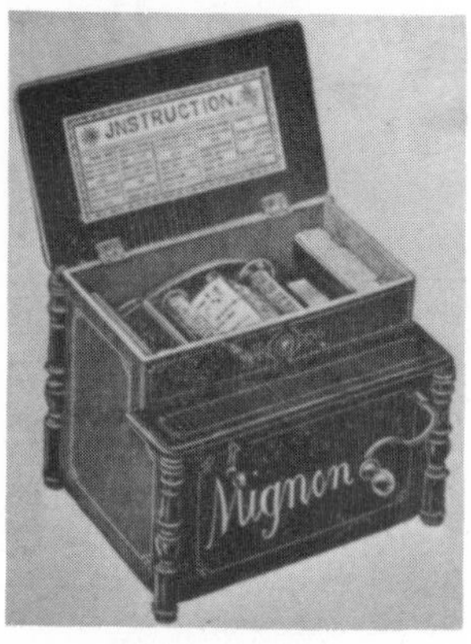


Mignon Organ
Styles I and II (1904)

Mignon Organ
Styles Ia and IIa (1904)

## MIGNON ORGAN (Paper Roll Organette)

Mignon Organ (1900 illustration)

Made by Bruno Geissler (and at least two other German firms over the years), the Mignon organettes were sold by the tens of thousands, mainly in Europe, by musical supply houses in Germany, France, England, and other countries. The Mignon was made in several different styles. Rewind-type and endless strip music systems were available.

Mignon Organs (literal translation: "small organs") were made in a variety of case styles in the 1890's and early 1900's.

—1895 Mignon Organ Models—

No.55N: 42x31x33 cm. case. 22 reeds. Black polished case with transfer decorations.

No.56N: 46x32x35 cm. case. 22 double (total 44) reeds. Black polished case with transfer decorations.

No.53: 67x49x48 cm. case. "40 reeds in three sets (total: 120 reeds) provide very rich and full organ tone. Large black polished and engraved case."

Note: All the preceding used rewind-type (spooled) music rolls.

—1900 Mignon Organ Models—

No.1: 35x46x34 cm. case. 22 reeds. Black polished case with transfer decorations. Sold for 35.50 German marks.

No.1½: Same, but endless music strip system.

No.2: 30x50x36 cm. case. 22 double (total 44) reeds. Black polished case with transfer decorations. Sold for 47.25 marks.

No.2½: Same, but endless music strip system.

Mignon-Harmonieux Organ ("small harmony organ")No.4: 67x49x48 cm. case. 40 notes, 120 reeds (in 3 sections). Sold for 142 marks. (Illustration same as No.IV shown at left).

Mignon-Harmonieux Organ No.4½: Same, but endless music strip system.

—1904 Mignon Organ Models—

No.Ia: 42x31x33 cm. 22 reeds. Black polished case with transfer decorations.

No.IIa: 46x40x33 cm. case. 22 double (total 48) reeds. Black polished case with transfer decorations.

No.I: 35x46x36 cm. case "in piano form" (with small front shelf). 22 reeds. Black polished case with transfer decorations.

No.II: 36x50x34 cm. case "in piano form." 22 double (total 44) reeds. Black polished case with transfer decorations.

No.III: 58x42x41 cm. case. 32 notes; 64 double reeds. Black polished case with gold engraving.

Mignon-Harmonieux Organ No.IV: 67x49x48 cm. case. 40 notes (120 reeds in 3 sections of 40 reeds each). Black polished case with gold engraving.

Notes: 1904 models available in either rewind-type or endless music roll form. Roman numerals were used in German catalogues; Arabic in French and English listings — so I and 1, II and 2, etc. can be used interchangeably. 1904 prices: I, Ia: 45 Mk.; II, IIa: 60 Mk.; III: 110 Mk.; IV: 180 Mk. Nos. I and II used one type of roll; III used another type; IV used still another.

Birthplace of an empire: The original Mechanical Orguinette Co. showroom at 831 Broadway, New York City. Then came larger quarters at 18 West 23rd St, then "more sumptuous quarters at 362 5th Avenue," and then two Aeolian Halls — not to mention a worldwide network of sales outlets.

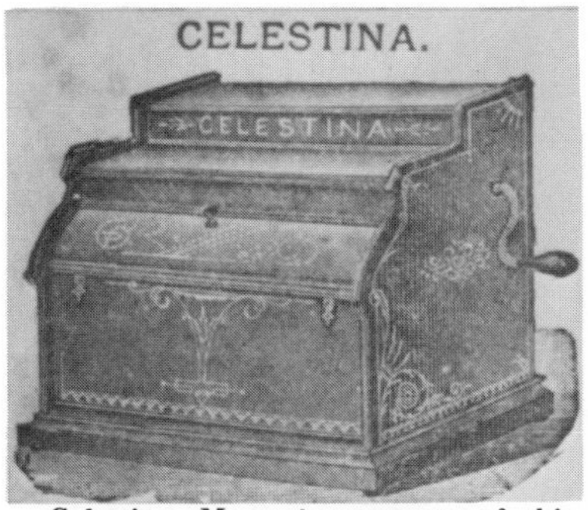

Celestina. Many instruments of this name and of similar appearance were made by Wilcox & White of Meriden, Connecticut. Other Celestinas of virtually identical appearance were made by the Munroe Organ Reed Co.

### Multinational Companies in the Automatic Musical Instrument Business

During the 19th and 20th centuries most firms in the automatic musical instrument business confined their trade to their home country. If their products were exported, sales were handled through agents in other lands.

Several firms were multinational, however, and established mostly-owned or wholly-owned subsidiaries or financed such businesses in other countries.

The Aeolian Company began in America in 1878. During the next half-century the firm established company-owned outlets in England, Germany (the Choralion Co.), Australia, and several other countries. M. Welte & Söhne, founded in Vöhrenbach, Germany, in the 19th century, established outlets in several different countries, including a factory and two salesrooms in America (Chicago and New York City). The Polyphon Musikwerke, of Leipzig, Germany, established (via financing and licensing/importing agreements) the Regina Music Box Co. in New Jersey. Imhof & Mukle, orchestrion builders of Vöhrenbach, Germany, opened a wholly-owned outlet in London. The outlet (in revised corporate form) is still in business today, several decades after the parent firm ceased operations.

Musical Boudoir Stand organette as sold by the Mechanical Orguinette Co.

Mandolina Organ — a model sold by the Mechanical Orguinette Co. in the 1880's. Probably made by the Munroe Organ Reed Company.

Mandolina organette (Munroe Organ Reed Co.)

Bijou Orchestrone. 17" wide by 14" deep by 12½" high. Uses 20-key 3 3/8" roll.

Seraphone. 17" wide by 12" deep by 11" high. Uses 20-key 3 1/2" wide roll. Shown with paper roll pulled out (not in playing position).

McTammany Organ. 15 1/2" wide by 12" deep by 6 1/2" high. Uses 14-key 7 3/4" wide roll. Roll can be in a long strip or in a continuous loop (as shown).

Harmonette. 10" wide by 11 1/2" deep by 11 1/4" high. Uses 17-key 5 1/4" wide roll.

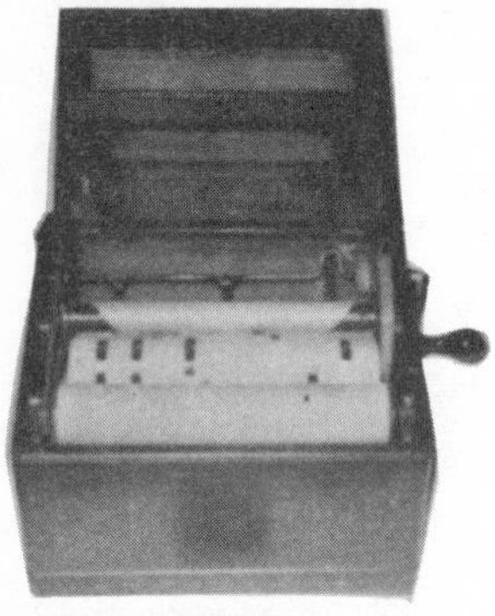

Aurephone. 12" wide by 9" deep by 8 3/4" high. Uses 17-key 9 1/2" wide roll. Expression shutter in top of lid (lid shown in the open position).

Autophone. 9 1/2" wide by 5" deep by 9 1/2" high. Uses a 22-key 5 3/8" wide music strip. Sprocket-driven ratchet feed; the roll moves forward in a succession of small steps, not in a continuous motion.

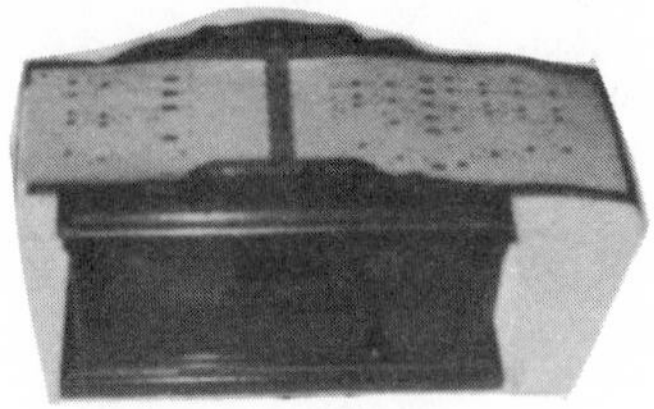

Auto-Organ. 9" wide by 13" deep by 6 1/2" high. Uses a 22-key music strip. Manufactured by the Autophone Co. of Ithaca, N.Y., in the 1880's.

Mandolina. 16" wide by 13 1/2" deep by 14" high. Uses a 20-key 5 1/2" wide music roll.

Euphonia. 10 1/4" wide by 7 1/2" deep by 7 1/2" high. Uses a 16-key 5 3/4" wide music roll.

Reed-Pipe Clariona. Two views. Measures 11" wide by 10" deep by 13" high. Uses a 14-key 8" wide roll. The "reed pipe" device is a resonator chamber which is placed over the top of the music roll. The device has little effect on the quality of the music. The top of the "reed pipe" section can be opened and closed for expression effects.

("Doc" Abrams Collection)

ORGANETTES (Paper Roll Type)

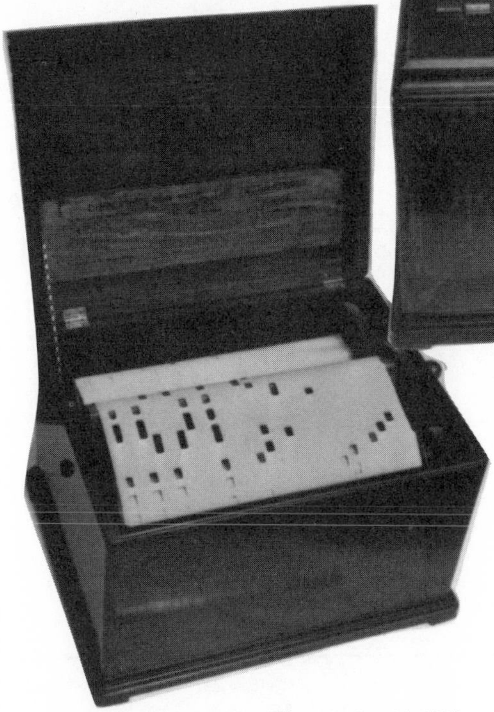

Tournaphone. 18 1/2" wide by 14 1/2" deep by 12" high. Uses a 25-key 13 1/4" wide roll. An expression shutter is in the lid. Note that the roll feeds from the top of one roll, over the reed openings, and winds on the bottom of the take up spool — an unusual way.

Celestina. 15" wide by 13" deep by 13 1/2" high. Uses a 20-note 5 1/2" wide roll. One of the most popular of all paper roll organettes, the Celestina was sold by the thousands.

Musette. 14 1/4" wide by 11 1/2" deep by 12 1/4" high. Uses a 16-key 3 1/2" wide roll.

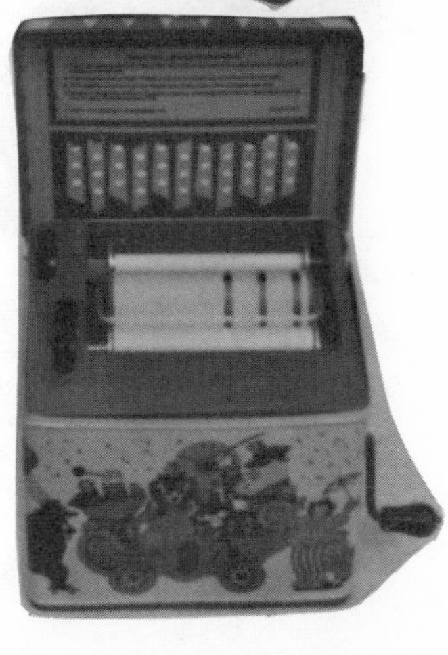

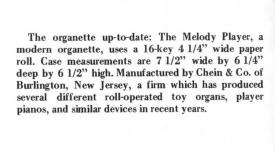

The organette up-to-date: The Melody Player, a modern organette, uses a 16-key 4 1/4" wide paper roll. Case measurements are 7 1/2" wide by 6 1/4" deep by 6 1/2" high. Manufactured by Chein & Co. of Burlington, New Jersey, a firm which has produced several different roll-operated toy organs, player pianos, and similar devices in recent years.

("Doc" Abrams Collection)

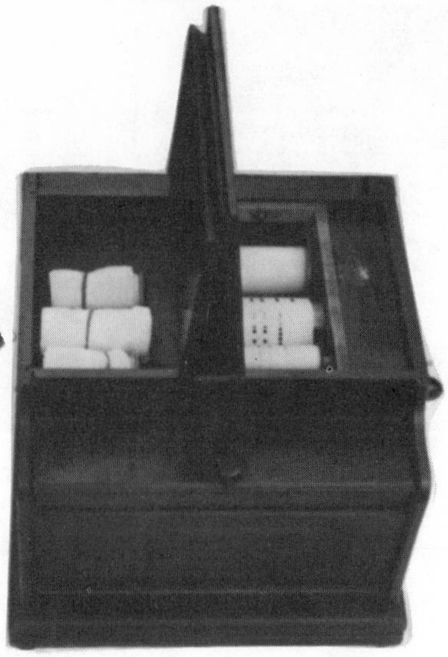

Mascotte. This instrument uses a tiny 2 1/2" wide paper roll of 14 keys, one of the smallest rolls ever used on a pneumatic musical instrument. The two top panels (shown in the open position at right) provide a means for expression.

Grandphone. 12" wide by 14 1/2" deep by 9 1/2" high. Uses a 14-key 3 3/4" wide roll.

Symphonia. Style with drive and rewind cranks located at the front of the case. 17 1/8" wide by 13 3/4" deep by 13 3/4" high. Uses a 20-key 5 1/8" roll. Manufactured by the Wilcox & White Organ Co. of Meriden, Connecticut.

Symphonia. Style with drive and rewind cranks located at the right side of the case. 18" wide by 14 3/4" deep by 13 3/4" high. Uses a 20-key 5 1/8" wide roll.

("Doc" Abrams Collection)

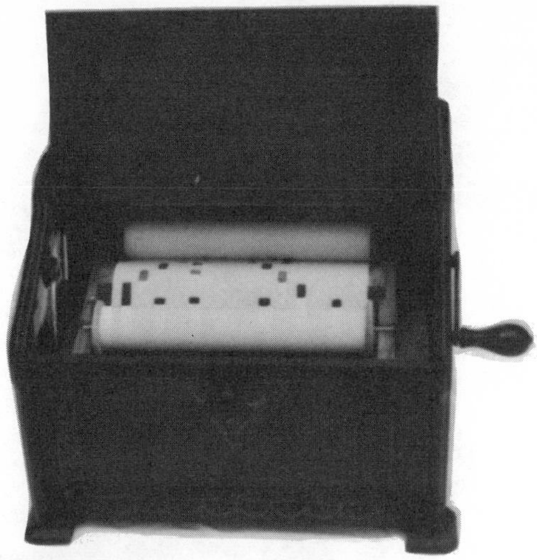

Musical Casket No. 2. 12 1/2" wide by 10 1/2" deep by 9 1/4" high. Uses a 14-key 7 3/4" wide roll.

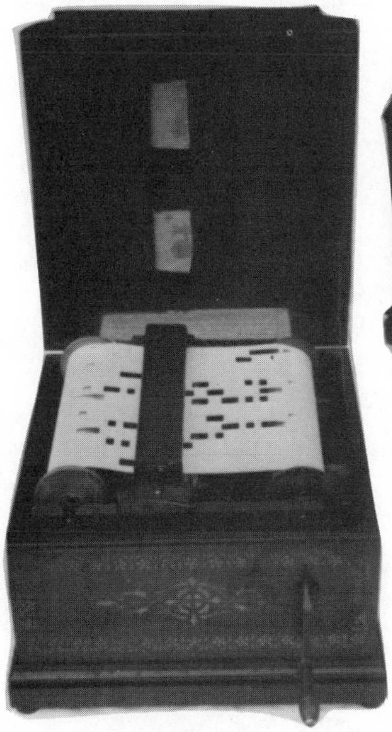

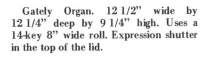

Gately Organ. 12 1/2" wide by 12 1/4" deep by 9 1/4" high. Uses a 14-key 8" wide roll. Expression shutter in the top of the lid.

Automatic Melodista. 11" wide by 9" deep by 8 1/2" high. Uses a 14-key 7 3/4" wide paper strip or continuous loop.

Organina. 9" wide by 8 1/4" deep by 11" high. Uses a 16-key 8 1/4" wide paper strip or loop. Expression panel in top of case. Bears the American Automatic Organ Co. name – a distributor of this organ.

("Doc" Abrams Collection)

ORGANETTES (Paper Roll Type)

Autophone. Unusual model with center pull ratchet feed (most Autophones use ratchet-driven sprockets which engage holes along the edge). 14 1/2" wide by 10 1/2" deep by 11 1/2" high. Uses 32-key 7 1/8" paper strip. Powered by a lever (visible at the right in the photograph).

Royal Upright Organette. 12 1/4" wide by 8 1/2" deep by 10 3/4" high. Uses a 14-key 7 3/4" wide paper strip or continuous loop. Expression is provided by two hinged panels in the top of the instrument.

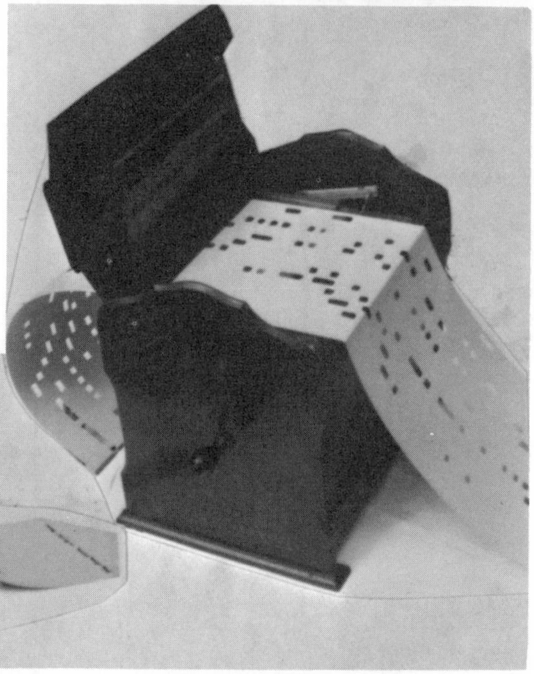

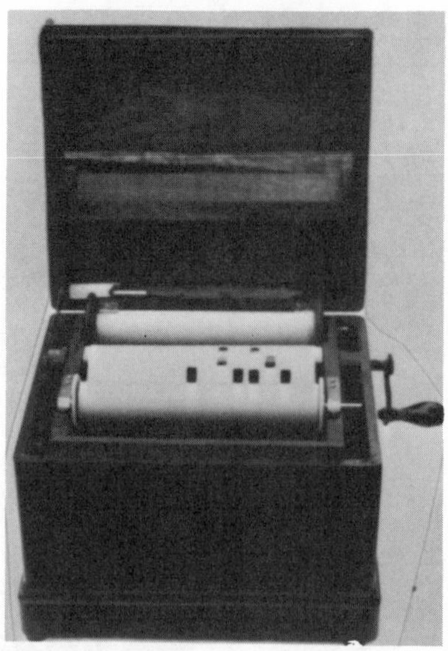

Melodia. 12" wide by 10 1/4" deep by 10 3/4" high. Uses a 14-note 7 3/4" wide paper roll.

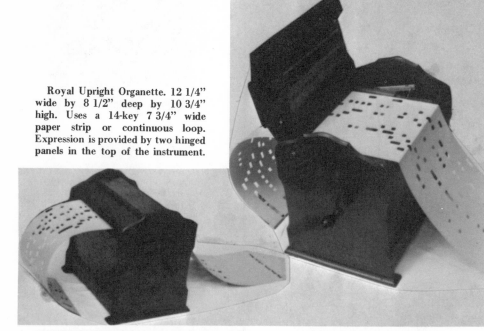

Wilcox & White organette; unusual model with two reed banks with 20 reeds in each section. 21" wide by 19" deep by 18" high. Uses a 20-key 5 1/2" roll. Three push buttons in the top provide control for treble, alto, and bass. A sophisticated organette that was made in limited numbers.

("Doc" Abrams Collection)

Musical Organette. (McTammany design). 13" wide by 11" deep by 7 1/2" high. Uses a 14-key 7 3/4" wide music strip or loop. Two views: the far left illustration shows the instrument with the top section in place; the immediate left view shows the instrument with the top part removed. Note the large rubber-covered drive roller.

Organita. 11 1/2" wide by 8" deep by 11 1/2" high. Uses a 14-key 7 3/4" paper strip or continuous loop. On this and other continuous loop instruments the organ is supported at the sides so that there is a slot opening between the bottom of the organ and the top of the surface on which it rests, to permit the passage of the music loop.

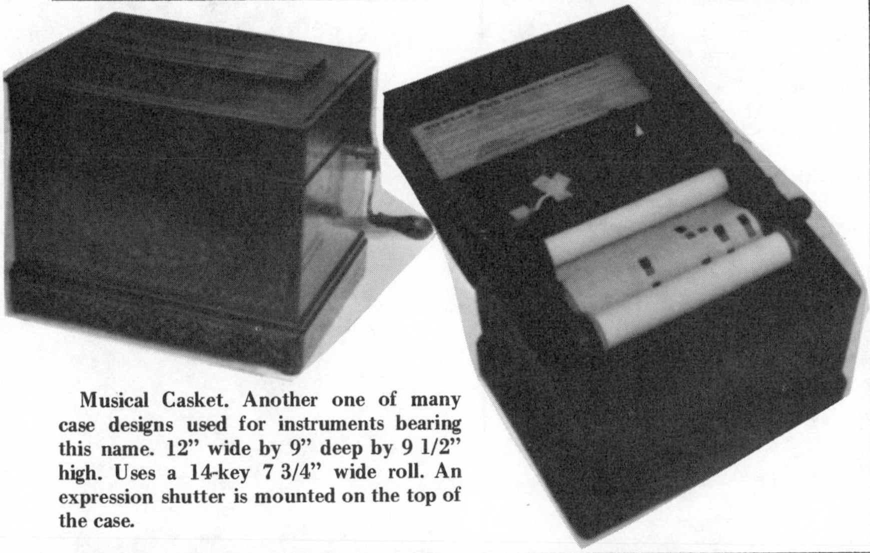

Musical Casket. Another one of many case designs used for instruments bearing this name. 12" wide by 9" deep by 9 1/2" high. Uses a 14-key 7 3/4" wide roll. An expression shutter is mounted on the top of the case.

National American Orguinette. 14" wide by 12" deep by 7" high. Uses a 14-key 7 3/4" wide paper strip or continuous loop. Mostly sold in England (despite the name!).

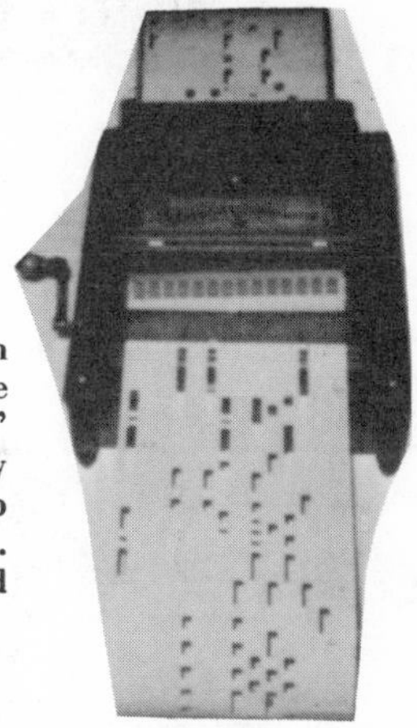

Musical Organette. (McTammany design). A large and early instrument which uses a 14-key 7 3/4" wide roll.

("Doc" Abrams Collection)

Ballyhoo in England too! Advertisement for the Orchestral Organette, a 28 reed ("the range of music is practically unlimited") instrument.

Most reed organ manufacturers in Germany produced automatic instruments also. Two roll-operated models (circa 1909) are shown here. Other types were made using cardboard strips, pinned wooden cylinders, and other systems.

Above left: The Seraphine. Sold in Germany in the 1890's, this instrument was made in several models: No. 1 (18 notes); Excelsior Seraphine No. 2 (18 double [total 36] notes). Above right: Seraphine Cabinet. 18 notes. Music was available in two forms: continuous strips (as shown) and in book form.

Log Cabin Organ, a rather crudely built paper roll organette. Case measures 27x27x13" in size. (Stephen M. Leonard photograph)

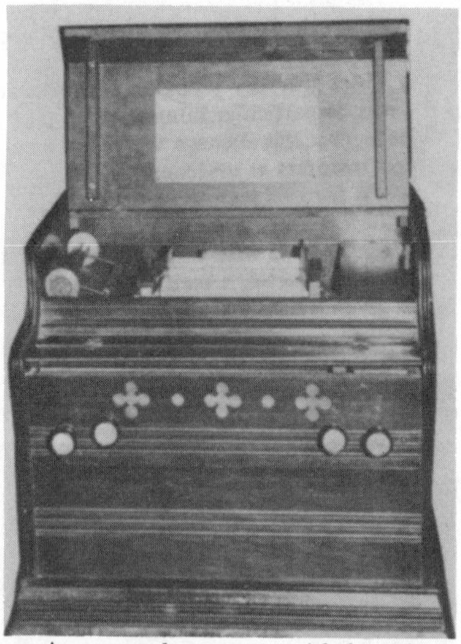

An unusual organette with four draw stops. (This and the Orchestral Organette advertisement shown at the top of this page are from the Musical Box Society of Great Britain publication, "The Music Box," – courtesy of Arthur W.J.G. Ord-Hume)

Celestina-type paper roll organette, the "Pneumatic Organ" sold by J.R. Holcomb & Co. of Cleveland, Ohio. Boyle Brothers, Morgenstern & Lockwood, and other agents sold similar instruments under their own names.

# SELF-PLAYING ACCORDIONS, CONCERTINAS, HARMONICAS

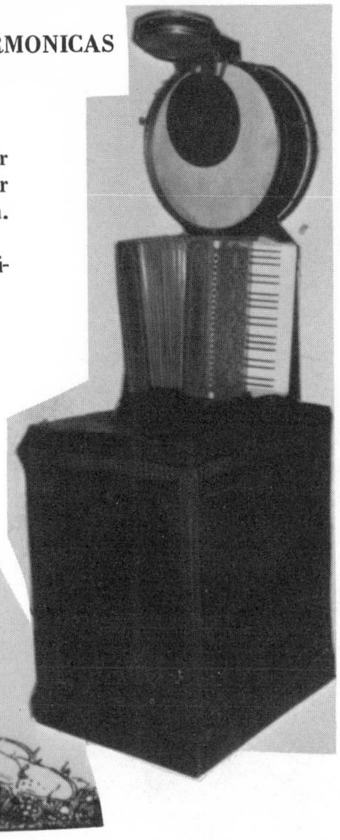

Right: Seybold "Electric Organa" accordion player with drums and traps. Uses a 70-note 8"-wide paper roll. Measures 2'3" wide by 2'9" deep by 7'9" high. (Steve Kukich Collection).

Below: Hohner foot-pumped Organa player accordion (from an advertisement of the 1930's).

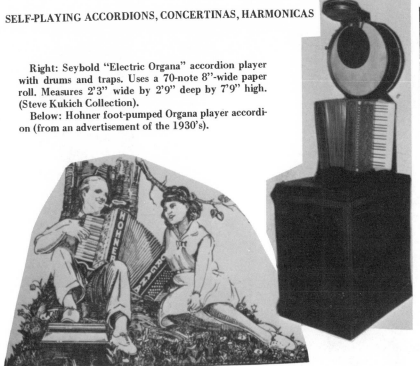

## —AUTOMATIC ACCORDIONS—

Seybold; Hohner

During the 1920's and 1930's the German firms of Seybold and Matth. Hohner produced a large number of accordion-players. Roll-operated, these came in many formats. Hohner's "Magic Organa" was made with accordion only and also with percussion effects added. Power was provided by an electric motor which drove a vacuum pump. Hohner also made several varieties of foot-pumped roll-operated accordions. The foot pedal / vacuum pump unit was compact and was designed to be operated unobtrusively. A long vacuum tube could be connected from the separate foot pump to the accordion (which had the appearance of a regular hand-played instrument) by running the tube up the operator's pantleg, through the shirt, and out through the shirtsleeve, at which point it connected to the accordion. Thus if the operator's feet were concealed from view (a small cloth-covered table with a money dish was ideal) the listener would think that the accordion was being hand played. Matth. Hohner, actively in business today in Trossingen, West Germany, has been the world's leading builder of harmonicas and similar devices for many decades. Automatic instruments were but a small part of its activity.

Seybold manufactured a series of accordion players, some of which were quite similar to Hohner products. A Seybold "Electric Organa" jazz band is shown above. Other Seybold instruments incorporated a cabinet-style (keyboardless) piano and had an accordion and percussion effects mounted on top. Still others used accordion reeds within a cabinet.

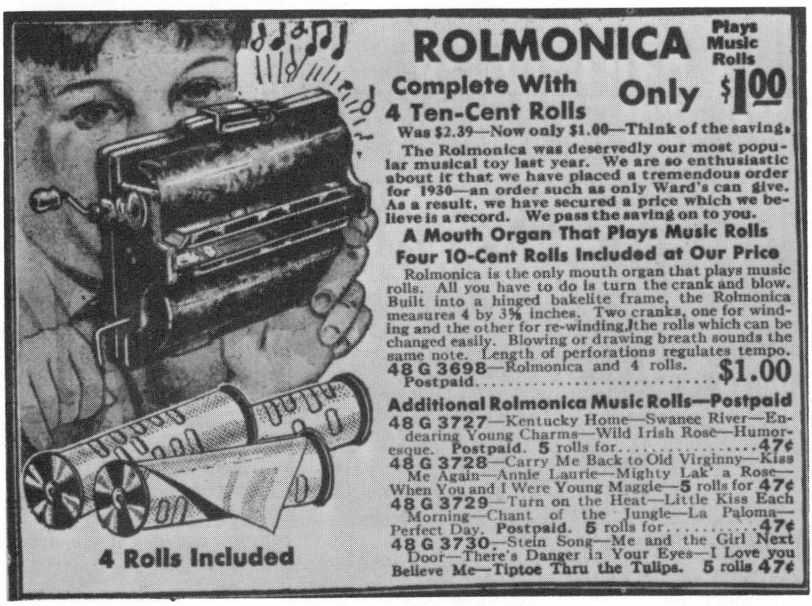


## —TANZBAR CONCERTINAS—

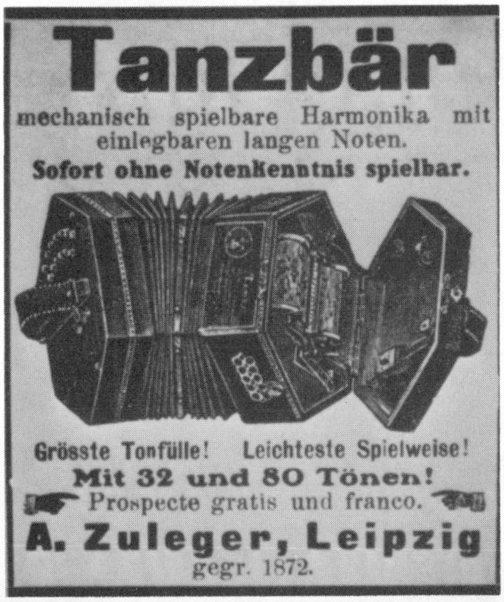

TANZBAR

Made by A. Zuleger of Leipzig, Germany and sold worldwide from shortly after 1900 to the 1930's, the Tanzbär (literally "Dancing Bear" – "Tanz" is the German word for dance; "Bär," the word for bear) player concertina was made in many different styles over the years. Power is provided by opening and closing the concertina (good chest muscles are required!). The roll is advanced by a ratchet drive which is operated by continually depressing and releasing a lever at one end of the instrument. When the tune ends, the roll is rewound by turning a small crank. Several varieties of organettes which use Tanzbär rolls were made in plain rectangular cases. Some were made in the 1930-1950 years.

## —ROLMONICA—

Introduced in 1928 by the Rolmonica Music Company of Baltimore, Maryland, the instrument was patented on November 2, 1925 and June 5, 1928. Sold as "The only harmonica that plays with a music roll the same as a player piano" and as "A player piano in your pocket," the Rolmonica uses a small paper roll.

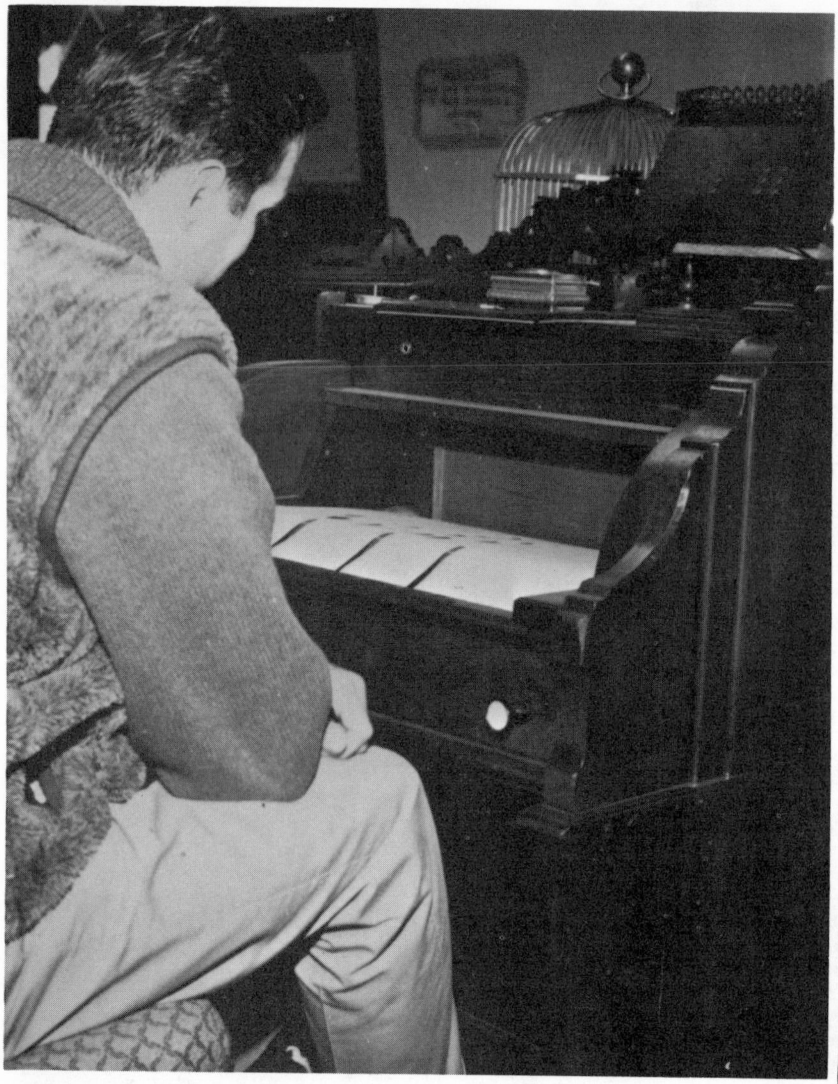

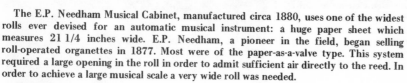

The E.P. Needham Musical Cabinet, manufactured circa 1880, uses one of the widest rolls ever devised for an automatic musical instrument: a huge paper sheet which measures 21 1/4 inches wide. E.P. Needham, a pioneer in the field, began selling roll-operated organettes in 1877. Most were of the paper-as-a-valve type. This system required a large opening in the roll in order to admit sufficient air directly to the reed. In order to achieve a large musical scale a very wide roll was needed.

Credits: Most of the illustrations in the organette section of this book are from original sales literature provided by Claes O. Friberg, Larry Givens, and Lloyd Kelley. "Doc" Abrams and Arthur Sanders provided additional valuable assistance.

Mechanical Harmonium sold by Ludwig Hupfeld in the 1890's. The instrument uses a heavy cardboard music sheet.

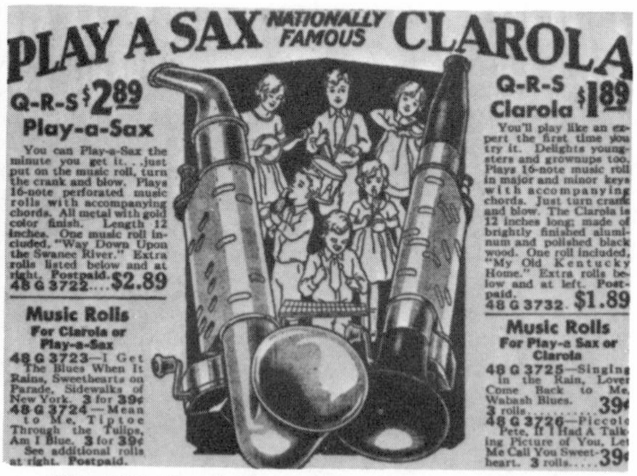


The QRS Play-A-Sax, sold in the early 1930's, uses a 16-note paper roll. When an opening in the roll uncovers a reed hole in the instrument the appropriate note plays. The QRS Clarola was of identical concept but differed in the appearance of the instrument.

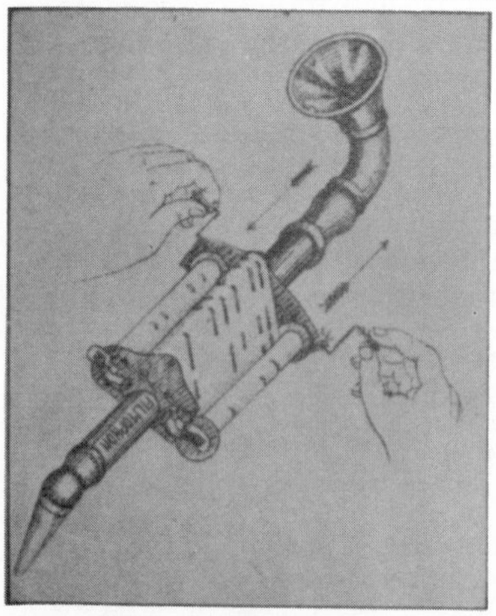

Left: J.C. Seydel's Filmophon (also called the Filmosaxophon). A somewhat similar instrument, the Filmo-Clarinette, was sold at the same time (in the 1930's). Note the similarity to the Play-A-Sax and the Clarola.

Above right: One of many Organista player organs made by Spaethe of Gera, Reuss, Germany. Wilhelm Spaethe and another firm, M. Hörügel (of Leipzig-Leutzsch), were Germany's leading makers of player harmoniums.

Bandoniphon: The Bandoniphon, a disc-operated concertina made in Germany, was popular c.1900-1910. It used an 18.5 cm. zinc disc and sold for 40 Mk. Extra discs cost 0.60 Mk. each. "Ideal for march and dance music" a 1903 description noted.

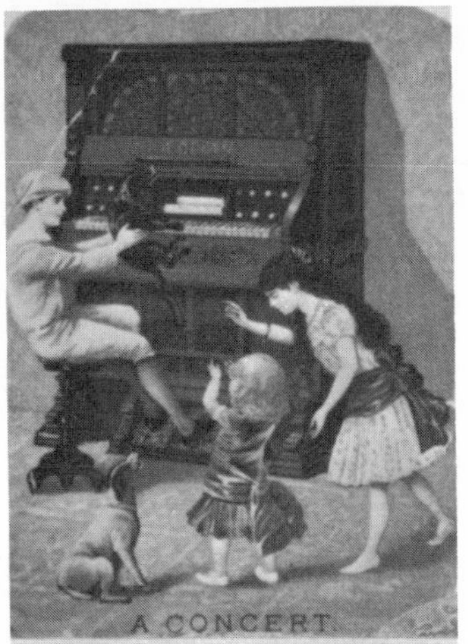

Aeolian Organ
—Style 1050—

The first Aeolian keyboard-type player reed organ to have mass sales, the Style 1050 was popular in the 1890's. At the left is a trading card from this era depicting "A Concert" — which, because of the roll, goes on interrupted despite all sorts of distractions! Note the name of the firm has been changed from the Mechanical Orguinette Co. to the Aeolian Organ & Music Company. The 831 Broadway address is the same.

Aeolian Organ
—Style 1500—

"This organ marked a definite forward step in the development of Aeolian instruments. Playing a 46-note roll, it was handsomely finished in beautiful case woods and polished like a piano." (From an Aeolian Co. history published by that firm in 1923)

—Aeolian Grand—

"This was the first Aeolian instrument to play the expanded 58-note roll. . ." noted an Aeolian Co. history. The Aeolian Grand 58-note rolls were later used on Aeolian Orchestrelle instruments as well. The illustration below shows a Grand. Note the zig-zag expression guide (to aid the operator in operating the knee swell) printed on the roll. The Aeolian name with the combined O-L was standard on most Aeolian instruments of the 1890's.

Aeolian
Orchestrelle
Style A

Illustration of the Style A Orchestrelle sold c.1900-1910. (Credit note: This and several other Aeolian illustrations are courtesy of W.J. Bassil, D.R. Berryman, and Arthur W.G.J. Ord-Hume)

**STOPS**

| BASS | TREBLE |
|---|---|
| Muted Strings | Muted Strings |
| Viola | Violin |
| Orchestral Flute | Orchestral Flute |
| Flute | Piccolo |
| Bass Clarionet | Clarionet |
| Trombone | Trumpet |

**PEDAL STOPS**

Contra Bass. Double Bass

**ACCESSORIES**

Tempo. Re-roll. Tremulant. Pneumatic to Manual.

**DIMENSIONS**

Height 4 ft. 11 in. Width 5 ft. 6 in. Depth 2 ft. 6 in.

STOPS

| BASS | TREBLE |
|---|---|
| Muted Strings | Muted Strings |
| Aeolian Harp | Aeolian Harp |
| Viola | Violin |
| French Horn | French Horn |
| Orchestral Flute | Orchestral Flute |
| Flute | Piccolo |
| Oboe | Oboe |
| Trombone | Trumpet |

PEDAL STOPS
Contra Bass. Double Bass

Model Francis the 1st

STOPS

| BASS | TREBLE |
|---|---|
| Muted Strings | Muted Strings |
| Viola | Aeolian Harp |
| Flute | Violin |
| Melodia | Piccolo |
| Trombone | Melodia |
| Tremulant | Trumpet |

PEDAL STOP
Contra Bass

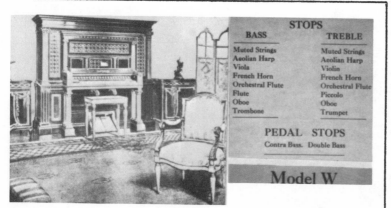

Model S

# Playing an Aeolian Orchestrelle

**No Musical Knowledge Necessary**

Style V. Price, $1500

LEADING AN orchestra is quite different from personally playing any musical instrument except

## *The Aeolian Orchestrelle*

The orchestral conductor experiences none of the wearying slavery of scales and exercises—and yet his temperamental control is just as pronounced. He throws himself into the spirit of the music in a far greater degree than does, for instance, the pianist, who is compelled to devote so large a proportion of his mental capacity to the mere sounding of the notes. This exacting technique is not necessary to the conductor of an orchestra. A wave of his baton introduces the different voices, swells or diminishes the tone or volume, produces the delicate pianissimo, the thunderous fortissimo.

The player of an Aeolian Orchestrelle can be likened to no one so much as to the conductor of an orchestra. The notes are sounded for him. He controls the registration of the tones, the shadings of tempo, the phrasing, the tone-coloring, all the orchestral effects are at the command of the owner of an Aeolian Orchestrelle. It can easily be learned by anybody and yet allows the greatest possible scope for study and improvement.

The Aeolian Orchestrelle is a home orchestra.

We would be glad to have you come and hear it play your favorite music—Wagner, Beethoven, Bach, Handel, Schubert, a delicious waltz, a stirring march, a bright two-step. The wonderful versatility of the Aeolian Orchestrelle makes it the most universally interesting musical instrument for the home.

We would be glad to have you come and try it yourself—you can learn to play it in ten minutes, master it in a month.

Aeolian, $75 to $750.
Aeolian Orchestrelle, $1,000 to $2,500.
Pianola, $250.
Call at any of the below addresses, or send for Catalogue M.

## THE AEOLIAN COMPANY

18 West Twenty-third Street, New York

500 Fulton Street, Brooklyn, N. Y. 124 East Fourth Street, Cincinnati, O.

Chicago, Lyon & Healy
Philadelphia, C. J. Heppe & Son
St. Louis, Bollman Bros. Co.
Boston, M. Steinert & Sons Co.
Baltimore, Wm. Knabe & Co.
Cleveland, B. Dreher's Sons Co.
Buffalo, H. Tracy Balcom
San Francisco, Kohler & Chase
Pittsburg, C. C. Mellor Co.
New Orleans, Ph. Werlein, Ltd.
Detroit, Grinnell Bros.
Portland, Ore., M. B. Wells
Washington, Wm. Knabe & Co.
Newark, Lauter Co.
Montreal, L. E. N. Pratte & Co.
Minneapolis, Metropolitan Music Co.

(Fleming & Carnrick Press, New York)

STOPS

| BASS | TREBLE |
|---|---|
| Muted Strings | Muted Strings |
| Aeolian Harp | Aeolian Harp |
| Viola | Violin |
| French Horn | French Horn |
| Orchestral Flute | Orchestral Flute |
| Flute | Piccolo |
| Oboe | Oboe |
| Trombone | Trumpet |

PEDAL STOPS
Contra Bass. Double Bass

Model W

**During the late 1890's and early 1900's the Aeolian Company placed many enticing advertisements in consumer magazines in America and Europe. The above advertisement is typical. Note that the Aeolian Organ (called "Aeolian" above and priced from $75 to $750) in various styles (from small cabinet styles to the Style 1500) is offered at the same time as the Orchestrelle. Later, other models were discontinued and advertisements and catalogues were devoted to Orchestrelles and large pipe organs only.**

STOPS

| BASS | TREBLE |
|---|---|
| Muted Strings | Muted Strings |
| Aeolian Harp | Aeolian Harp |
| Viola | Violin |
| French Horn | French Horn |
| Flute | Piccolo |
| Oboe | Oboe |
| Trombone | Trumpet |

PEDAL STOPS
Contra Bass. Double Bass.

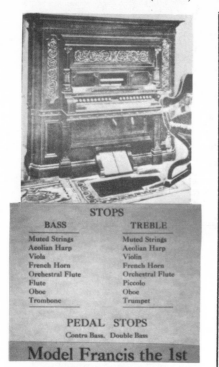

MODEL V

NAMES OF STOPS

| SWELL ORGAN | GREAT ORGAN |
|---|---|
| Oboe, 8 ft. | Open Diapason, 8 ft. |
| Clarionet, 8 ft. | Melodia, 8 ft. |
| French Horn, 8 ft. | Dulciana, 8 ft. |
| Salicional, 8 ft. | Flute d'Amour, 4 ft. |
| Stop'd Diapason, 8 ft. | Trumpet, 8 ft. |

| PEDAL | AEOLIAN ACCESSORIES |
|---|---|
| Bourdon, 16 ft. | Tempo Re-roll |

| ACCESSORIES | COMBINATION PEDALS |
|---|---|
| Swell to Great | Swell Piano |
| " " " Octaves | " Forte |
| Swell to Pedal | Great Piano |
| Great to Pedal | " Forte |
| Tremulant | Great to Pedal |
| Balanced Crescendo Pedal | Full Organ |
| " Swell " | |

—Style F Solo Orchestrelle—

The first Solo Orchestrelle placed on the market, the Style F was offered for sale at prices from $4000 to $5000. In England the model cost 1000 pounds sterling (about $4800). The Style F was made in at least two style variations as shown above. The top instrument (from the Larry Givens Collection) has non-functional pipes as a decoration between the front columns. The model shown below has wooden latticework backed by cloth. Some Style F instruments were installed with remote blowers. Most were foot-pumped, however. Several hundred Style F instruments were sold.

## The Aeolian Orchestrelle

STOPS

| BASS | TREBLE |
|---|---|
| Salicional | Salicional |
| Dolce | Dulcissimo |
| Muted Strings | Muted Strings |
| French Horn | Gemshorn |
| Flute d'Amour | Flute d'Amour |
| Melodia | Clarabella |
| Piccolo | Piccolo |
| Stopped Diapason | Doppel Flute |
| Clarionet | Clarionet |
| Bassoon | Oboe |
| Cornopean | Trumpet |

PEDAL STOPS

Contra Bass. Double Bass

ACCESSORIES

Tempo. Re-roll. Vox Humana. Pneumatic to Manual

DIMENSIONS

Height 8 ft. 4 in. Width 6 ft. 4 in. Depth 3 ft. 3 in.

PRICE £600 NETT

In Walnut, Mahogany, or Oak Case

Model Y

Model Y Aeolian Orchestrelle. Case style used for both 58-note and 116-note (Solo Orchestrelle) models. Mark Twain (nom de plume of Samuel Clemens) purchased a 58-note Style Y in 1904. It is presently on display at the Mark Twain Museum in Hannibal, Missouri. Clemens was very interested in the subject of organs and was one of the financial backers of Robert Hope-Jones when the Hope-Jones Organ Co. was located in Elmira, N.Y. (Later the firm was acquired by Wurlitzer and moved to North Tonawanda). Clemens lost heavily in this financial investment.

NAMES OF STOPS

MANUAL I.

| BASS | TREBLE |
|---|---|
| Muted Strings | Muted Strings |
| Æolian Harp | Æolian Harp |
| Melodia | Melodia |
| Bass Clarinet | Clarinet |
| Flute | Piccolo |

MANUAL II.

| BASS | TREBLE |
|---|---|
| Dolce Viola | Dolce Violin |
| Viola | Violin |
| French Horn | French Horn |
| Orchestral Flute | Orchestral Flute |
| Oboe | Oboe |
| Trombone | Trumpet |

PEDAL STOP

Contra Bass
Double Bass

ACCESSORIES

Vox Humana
Re-roll and Manual
Couplers { Grand, Normal, Reverse }
Right Expression Swell
Left Crescendo Swell

DIMENSIONS AND WEIGHT

Length, 8 ft. Height, 8 ft. Depth, 3 ft. 6 ins.
Net Weight, 1,370 pounds

Price £1,000 net

Above: "Two Manual and Pedal Orchestrelle" (the actual name by which this model was designated).

Solo Orchestrelles: Solo Orchestrelles, made in one-manual and two-manual styles, played what Aeolian called "Two Manual or Aeolian Pipe Organ Rolls." Later these were simply called "Aeolian Organ Rolls." By means of an ingenious double tracker bar arrangement the Solo Orchestrelles could play 58-note Aeolian Grand rolls (as used on most smaller Orchestrelle models) or the 116-note closely-spaced Aeolian Organ rolls. (Note: Aeolian Duo-Art Organ rolls, introduced several years later, are not compatible with the preceding.)

Most Aeolian Orchestrelle instruments (of all styles) were built in Meriden, Connecticut, by the Vocalion Organ Company (an Aeolian subsidiary) or in Hayes, Middlesex, England, by the Aeolian Company, Ltd. The English branch was originally called The Orchestrelle Co., Ltd. London salesrooms were maintained at 225 Regent Street.

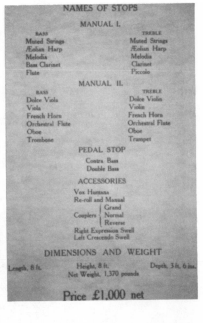

PLAYER REED ORGANS
(Aeolian)

Style XW Solo Orchestrelle. One of the smaller models in the Solo Orchestrelle line.

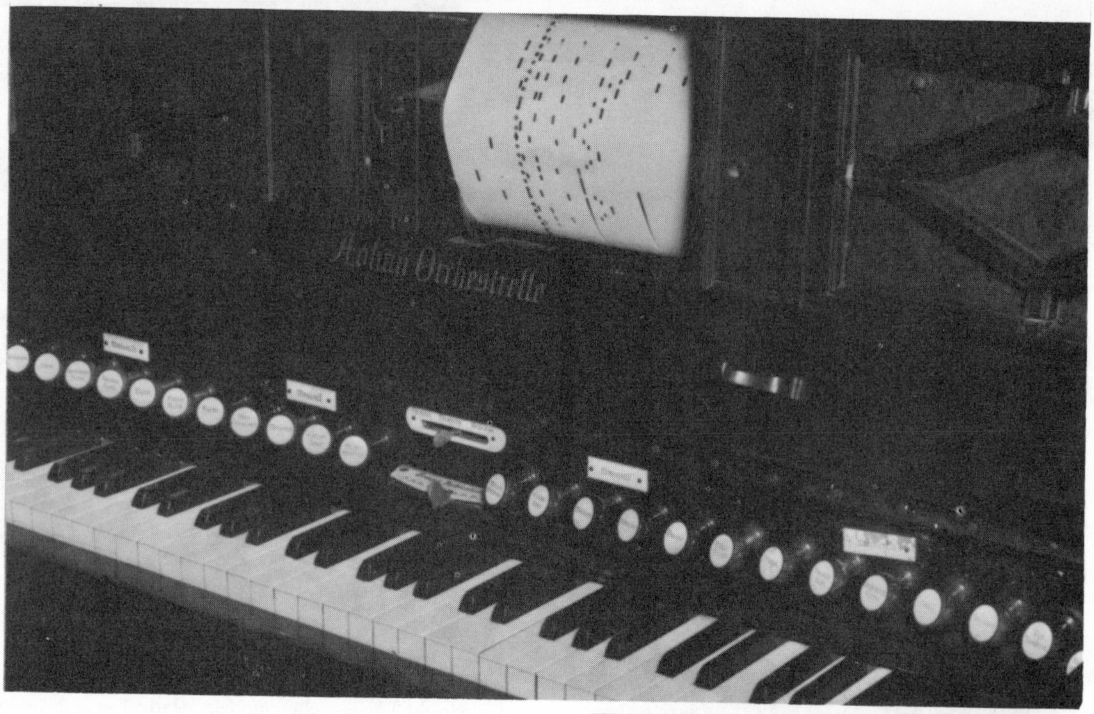


Details of a Style F Solo Orchestrelle. The lever under the roll has three positions: "Grand" (for playing 58-note rolls), "Normal" (for playing 116-note rolls), and "Reverse" (for interchanging certain functions of the lower and upper manuals, as frequently called for in the Solo rolls; analogous to the reverse coupler found on pipe organs). Aeolian Orchestrelles of various styles were available in a "dark shade of mahogany with a satin finish," in walnut, or in "any shade of oak." Surviving examples today indicate that mahogany was the most popular finish.

Solo Orchestrelle
—Style XY—

From near right to far right: 1. "Colonial Design." 2. "Mazarin Design." 3. "Louis XIV Design." All three models of the XY sold for $3250.00 when first introduced.

The same cases were also used for earlier models which played 58-note rolls only.

This Orchestrelle, a 58-note model built in the same basic case as the XY Solo Orchestrelle, was made about 1905. Minor trim details, particularly the ornamentation of the upper front panel, varied widely. There were also some style differences between American-made and English-made Orchestrelles. Some English models were produced with painted cases — a feature not seen (by the author) among American models.

To the right is the upper front section of the same Orchestrelle with the decorative front panel removed to show the many banks of organ reeds. Orchestrelles were made in pressure-operated and vacuum-operated styles. Pressure models have a glass door which slides over the roll compartment to make it airtight. Air under pressure is forced through the tracker bar openings when a hole appears in the music roll. Most large Orchestrelles, Solo and regular styles, are of the pressure type.

Symphony organ in an especially ornate case with gold-colored display pipes, carved friar statues, and other ornamentation. 6'6" high by 4'7" wide by 2'3" deep. Made in the 1890's.

## WILCOX & WHITE ORGAN COMPANY

—Meriden, Connecticut—

Founded in 1876 by Horace C. Wilcox, a Meriden silver-plate manufacturer, and Henry Kirk White, an organ builder from Brattleboro, Vermont, the firm manufactured many varieties of paper roll organettes and player reed organs. Some instruments were made on contract for the Mechanical Orguinette Co. (Aeolian Co. predecessor). Aeolian later acquired the Vocalion Organ Co. in the same city. The Wilcox & White Organ Co., which changed its name to the Wilcox & White Co. in 1897, worked closely with the Aeolian Co. in several areas.

Wilcox & White introduced the Symphony player reed organ in 1888. Many different case styles of the Symphony were made from 1888 through the first decade of the 20th century. Symphony organs have a vacuum action which sounds the reeds by means of a valve and pouch assembly. The Angelus Orchestral, a push-up piano player with organ reeds incorporated into the mechanism, was produced in at least three different styles.

The Symphony was a distant second to the Aeolian organs in terms of its share of the American market for keyboard-style player reed organs. An estimated several thousand Symphony instruments were produced.

(Credit note: Alan R. Pier, writing in the Christmas, 1969, issue of the Musical Box Society "Bulletin," and the Aeolian Company)

This Symphony instrument has exposed swell shutters on the front — an unusual feature. When the knee levers are operated, the shutters open and the reed banks can be seen.

Above: A Symphony organ as depicted in an early silent film. (From the Ripley collection of photographs) Below: The same style of Symphony as shown in an advertisement.

This Wilcox & White Symphony player reed organ is now an attraction in the musical hall of the Harvey and Marion Roehl home in Vestal, New York. The instrument was acquired in 1965 from the family in Oneonta, New York, who had purchased it new in 1895.

The various reed banks or registers are controlled manually by draw knobs. The volume is controlled by knee-operated swell levers. A tremolo effect — a revolving cardboard paddle placed above one of the reed bank openings — is controlled by a draw knob. As were most Symphony organs of the 1890's, the Roehl instrument is in a richly figured walnut case.

Mustel & Cie.

Founded in Paris in 1853 by Victor Mustel (1815-1890), Mustel & Cie. was continued after his death by his sons, Charles, Auguste, and Alphonse. The firm built harmoniums (reed organs) and pipe organs. During the 1890's and early 20th century self-playing organs were built using pinned cylinders and, later, perforated paper rolls.

As did many other firms, Mustel exhibited at expositions (including Paris 1855, London 1861, Paris 1878, Paris 1889, Chicago 1893, Paris 1893, Antwerp 1894, Amsterdam 1895, Brussels 1897, Paris 1900, London 1903, St. Louis 1904, Leige 1905, Milan 1906, and London 1908) and prominently displayed in its advertising the medals awarded to the firm.

The player reed organ shown above, the Concertal, was billed as "the most marvelous musical instrument in the world." Those interested could see it demonstrated at the Mustel showrooms in Paris at 46, Rue de Douai and in London at 80, Wigmore Street. A 1910 advertisement for the Concertal noted that the Grand Model of the Concertal offered "494 reeds which provide 10,000 symphonic combinations."

Schiedmayer

The Schiedmayer Pianofortefabrik of Stuttgart, Germany, produced a series of large player reed organs. The Scheola, as the instrument was named, was sold in several different styles.

Above left is Model Palestrina 5061, an instrument which measures 2.87 meters high by 1.70 meters wide by 0.83 meters deep.

Above right is Model Palestrina 5055, an instrument fronted with display pipes. Measurements are 2.75 meters high by 1.85 meters wide by 0.82 meters deep.

Both instruments are unusual in that they have two manuals. Two-manual player reed organs were made only by a few firms (Aeolian and Estey for example).

The Olympia, a player organ sold by the Farrand Co. of Detroit.

Story & Clark

Story & Clark of Chicago, Illinois, marketed the Orpheus player reed organ in the late 1890's. The London showroom (see the above advertisement) received its first Orpheus in 1898. Fourteen were sold during the first week, noted a story in an 1898 issue of "Musical Opinion."

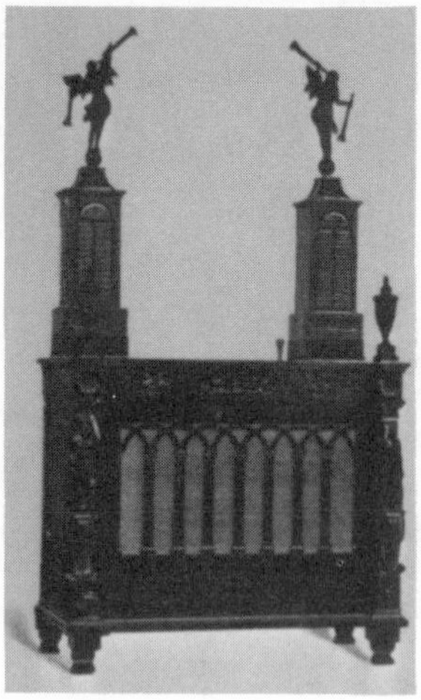

Left: "Small Flute-work in the style of the Empire, of the early 19th century. The instrument is contrived to play automatically, to which end a clockwork actuated by 5 weights is introduced. This clockwork moves a cylinder, which in turn makes the little pipes speak. Entire height, 120 cm.; breadth, 64 cm.; depth, 40 cm." — from the illustrated catalogue "Pearls from the Collection of Paul de Wit in Leipzig," published in May, 1892.

In the German language organs which play flute pipes are referred to as "Flötenwerke" — literally, "flute mechanisms." This nomenclature was applied to small orchestrions (if their instrumentation consisted mainly of flute pipes), small softly-voiced flute-playing instruments for home use (such as the one described above), and other residence organs with flute pipes.

Above: Dating from the mid-19th century, the above clock was probably made in Germany's Black Forest. The upper part of the clock displays a colorful oil painting of a Swiss lake and mountains. Above the scene is an animated stage containing five mechanical figures, each made in the form of a musician. The musical movement consists of a rank of flute pipes played from a pinned barrel.

Above: Rear view of the upper part of the clock. The organ pipes are arranged in pyramidal fashion.

Left: Front view of the upper section.

Below: Four automaton musician figures are mounted in front of the pipes.

Above and left: Flute-playing clock made by A. Mukle of Neukirch (in the Black Forest) during the early 19th century. The clock is housed in a richly figured cherry case. It is likely that the clock cabinet was made in America. It was often the practice to import the musical movement only, in order to save shipping costs and importation tariffs. Cases would be made in the importing country, in this instance the United States.

Left and right: A softly-voiced barrel organ manufactured c.1840 by Rolin Chomassin, organbuilder in Mirecourt, France. One of the four barrels is pinned on a spiral and provides an 8-minute rendition of the overture to the "Barber of Seville." The other barrels have ten tunes each. There are three ranks, each with twenty pewter pipes, and one group of three reed trumpets. (Collection of Dr. and Mrs. Howard Fitch)

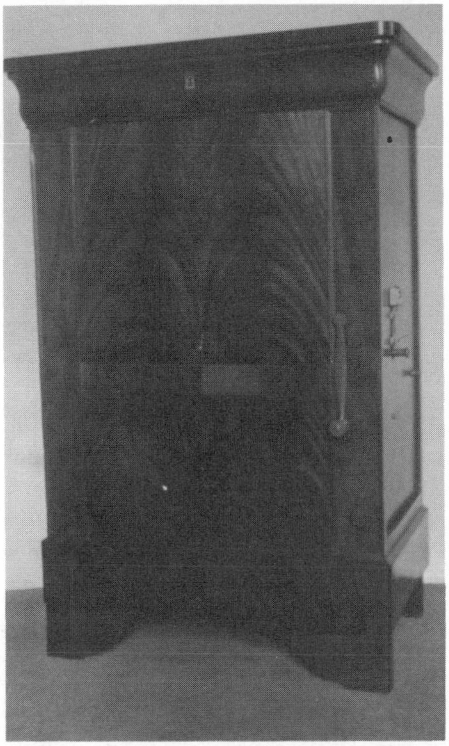

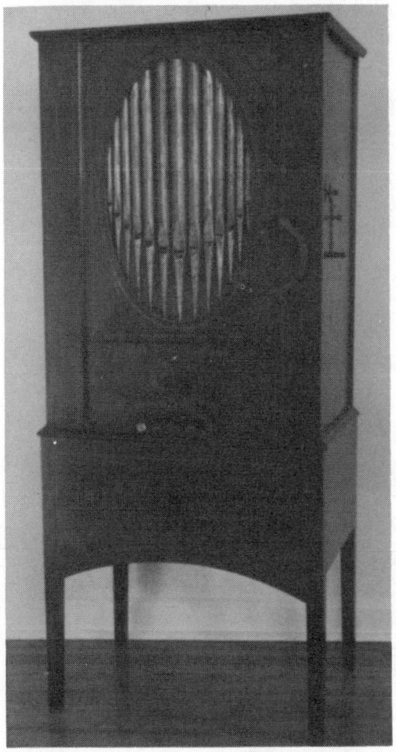

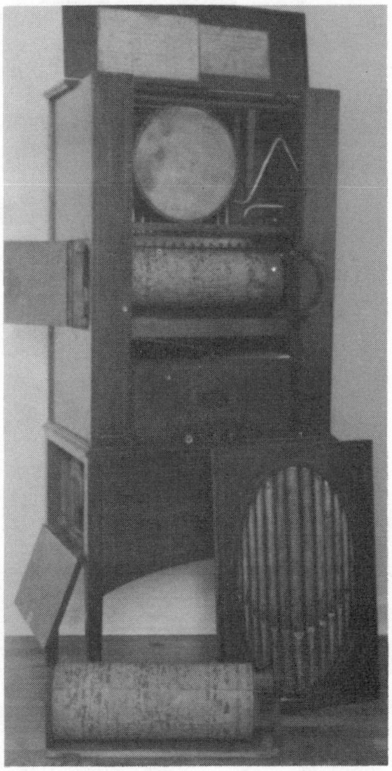

Parlor barrel organ manufactured c.1810 by George Astor & Co., 79 Cornhill, London. The instrumentation of this finely-crafted organ consists of three ranks of sixteen pipes each plus a drum and a triangle. As is true of other instruments of this period, the pipes on the front panel are for display only and are not operative.

George Astor was the brother of John Jacob Astor, who founded the Astor fortune in America. John Jacob served as agent in the United States for the musical instruments made by George.

The instrument depicted above has three barrels, each pinned with ten popular Scottish airs of the time. (Collection of Dr. and Mrs. Howard Fitch)

Many fine barrel organs for residential and church use were built in England, mainly during the period from 1775 to 1850. In their book, "Church and Chamber Barrel Organs," Canon Noel Boston and Lyndesay G. Langwill list about 125 makers and sales agents who handled these instruments during the 18th and 19th centuries.

**SMALL HAND-CRANKED PIPE ORGANS**

**(for residential use)**

**A beautiful barrel organ by James Davis of Chelsea, London. Made during the 1795-1815 period, this organ has eight barrels and measures 7'2" high by 2'10" wide by 2'2" deep. Different pipe registers are controlled by the draw stops on the front of the instrument. The pipes on the front are display, not functional. (Collection of Dan Adams)**

**This barrel organ dates from the mid-19th century and was probably made in England. It contains two ranks of pipes, one string-toned metal rank and one stopped wooden flute rank. Measurements are 2'6" high by 1'8" wide by 1' deep.**

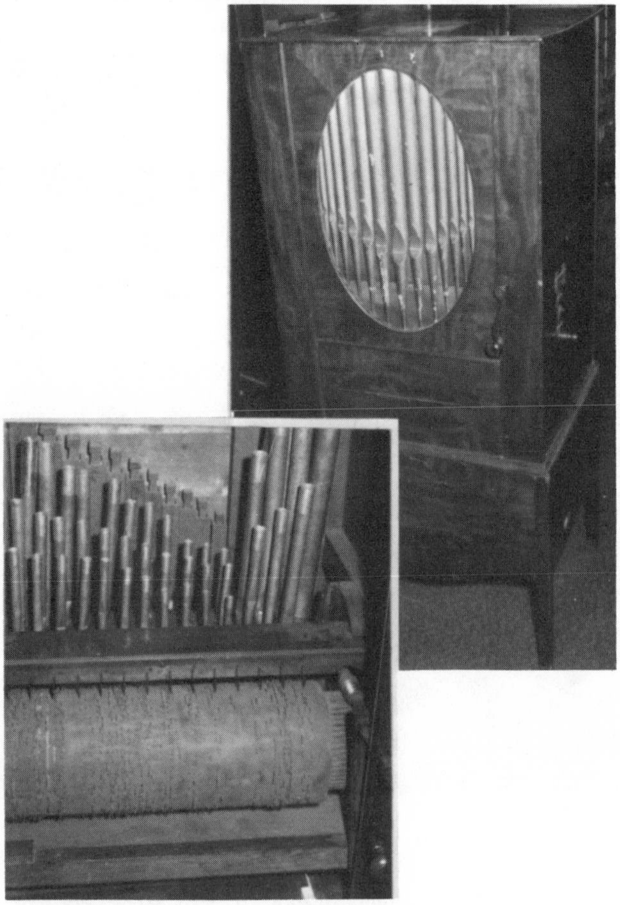

**Made in England, this instrument was sold on April 5, 1851, by the Pianoforte, Harp, and Music Warehouse, according to the original label on the inside of the instrument. Two barrels of ten tunes each play three ranks of metal string-toned pipes and one rank of stopped wooden flutes. Measurements are: 4'7" high by 2'1" wide by 1'9" deep.**

**Large self-contained Estey player pipe organ c.1912 as advertised by Estey's London outlet.**

**—Other Player Organs—**

**Refer to other sections of this book for information on player pipe organs made by firms which were primarily in the photoplayer, orchestrion, or electric piano business.**

**The Link Piano and Organ Co. (Binghamton, New York) manufactured a series of photoplayers and theatre organs. The Operators Piano Co. (Chicago) made the Reproduco in several forms, mostly in combination with a piano, but also as an organ-only instrument. The Nelson-Wiggen Piano Co. and the J.P. Seeburg Piano Co. (both of Chicago) made several varieties of roll-operated player organs combined with pianos. The American Photo Player Company produced many instruments which were, in effect, theatre pipe organs. The Rudolph Wurlitzer Company produced a large series of "One Man Orchestras," photoplayers for theatre use. These are discussed in detail in the Wurlitzer orchestrion section of this book.**

**Loudly-voiced player organs made for fairgrounds and skating rink use are described in a separate section of this book, as are dance hall organs.**

## THE ELECTROMAGNETIC ORCHESTRA
### (Electric Orchestra)

*The following story, excerpted from the Scientific American Supplement, 1876, describes the Electro-magnetic Orchestra (or Electric Orchestra) built by Schmoele Brothers of Philadelphia and exhibited at the 1876 Centennial Exhibition.*

*With certain features patented by Schmoele in 1873, the Electro-magnetic Orchestra is an interesting example of an early automatically-operated pipe organ.*

**The Musical Department of the Philadelphia Exhibition is very full and attractive, but the many curious and novel instruments contained therein seem hitherto to have escaped the attention of the hosts of voluminous descriptive writers who have done the rest of the show to the last dot. A correspondent of the Evening Post of this city, in a letter recently published by that paper, gives some interesting information of some instruments which are operated by electricity . . .**

**In the Horticultural Hall will be found a pipe organ with an electric action which, as it contains also drums, cymbals, etc., is styled an Electro-magnetic Orchestra [in another contemporary reference it is called an Electric Orchestra – Ed.] Externally it appears as an ordinary church organ, but without the ordinary keys, pedals, draw stops, etc. Nearby stands an ordinary four-legged table, beneath the top of which is found a keyboard, and underneath a coil of rope that contains insulated wires. This table may be moved a long distance from the organ and placed in any position with reference to it, and yet control all the speaking pipes, etc. But the most extraordinary point to be noticed is that the instrument itself plays whatever is required from notes. It reads automatically the music sheets that are placed upon it. It is readily perceived that if the musical characters were printed in metallic or conducting marks the electricity would distinguish between these and the non-conducting surface of the blank part of the paper. To save the necessity of setting up such costly type and going to press to obtain copies, the paper is simply perforated and a metallic plate placed underneath it.**

**This perforated paper is sold at prices varying from fifty cents to one dollar per yard, whether for fugues or symphonies, or dance music, national airs, etc. A copy of "Yankee Doodle" with metallic notes may be obtained in the hall for five cents. The music is placed on the organ rolled up, and is unrolled gradually as it passes under a row of charged feelers or "readers" whose function it is to distinguish between the notes, after which it is rolled up again.**

**The music itself is marked in the center of the paper, and on either side are the notes or perforations, as the case may be, that cause the requisite changes to be made in the stops, varying the power, quality, and combinations of tone to produce the desired effect at each particular instant. It should be observed that the mechanical effect of ordinary barrel organ music is not so readily perceived here, for the various modifications of speed, etc. that performers habitually make may be so readily imitated that anyone desiring the instrument to give some particular shade of expression to any one passage, or even a single note, may do so readily.**

**Staccato passages may be converted into legato by making the perforations a trifle larger and, vice versa, parts given to the flutes may be played by the clarinet or other instruments as desired, the drums may be made more or less vigorous in action, and the quickness of the strokes, obtained by a rapidly intermittent circuit breaker, may be increased or diminished. The force of wind may be controlled with equal ease. If, in the case of dance music, a variation in speed is required, it is simply necessary to touch the "fly" which is made to act as governor. All trills, shakes, and arpeggios are given with considerable clearness of definition.**

**The slightest mark or perforation will at the right moment of time send an electric current through the wire, as through a nerve, and will induce the corresponding magnet in the instrument instantly to give, like a muscle, the exact touch desired. The inventors assert that they are prepared to supply instruments of all sizes and in various styles, and give full priced lists with confidence. It is noteworthy that in the instrument exhibited the mechanism works noiselessly. No wind is lost in escaping puffs or power lost in friction.**

---

**Note: D. Appleton & Co.'s "Encyclopedia" (Vol. X) of 1885 describes the Schmoele instrument further (we quote in part): "One of the peculiarities of the Schmoele mechanism was the use of a music sheet of double width. The slots of the music, which would ordinarily occupy only one half of the entire width of the sheet, but would be very long and therefore liable to destruction [whatever that means – Ed.], were divided. Half the length of a slot was cut in half of the double sheet and the remainder in the other half. Two sets of electrical connections were used, one set beginning the notes and the other set completing them." Patent No. 145,532 (filed March 7, 1873; granted December 16 of the same year) describes the theory of the device and notes that it can be used to operate pianos as well as organs.**

## THE AEOLIAN PIPE ORGAN
## and
## AEOLIAN DUO-ART PIPE ORGAN

In 1896 the Aeolian Company, then active in the player reed organ field, acquired control of the Votey Organ Company, itself the successor to the Roosevelt pipe organ interests. Within a few years the Aeolian Pipe Organ made its appearance. In the 1905-1910 years, a time when Orchestrelles and Solo Orchestrelles (manufactured by a separate facility, the Vocalion Organ Co., a subsidiary located in Meriden, Conn.), sales of the Aeolian Pipe Organ progressed relatively slowly. In 1907 Aeolian advertised that "over two hundred Aeolian Pipe Organs have already been installed in homes throughout America and Europe." By 1910 the advertising was changed to read "over three hundred."

The Aeolian Pipe Organ is "not an expensive instrument," noted an advertisement that went on to say: "Contrary to widespread misconception — and even false report — the Aeolian Pipe Organ is not a high-priced instrument. From the point of view of durable satisfaction, of course, the best is always the cheapest. But also intrinsically, for the quality of its materials, workmanship, and artistic results, the price of the Aeolian Pipe Organ is fair and reasonable — and relatively low.

"Inasmuch as the Aeolian Pipe Organ is not a stock instrument, produced in quantity as are pianos and smaller instruments, but is designed and built only and wholly to order, and built specifically to suit the space and acoustic conditions of the room for which it is intended, the price is necessarily determined by the size and specific conditions of installation of each instrument."

The key to the above is the reader's interpretation of the phrases "not expensive" and "relatively low" — for the lowest-priced Aeolian Pipe Organ sold for $8,500.00! At prices ranging from this figure to over $30,000.00 the Aeolian Company didn't mind if sales were slow. By the end of the 1920's the total sales figure for the Aeolian Pipe Organ and its successor, the Aeolian Duo-Art Pipe Organ, crossed the 2000 mark, a heart-warming number.

In 1907 the Aeolian Pipe Organ was described as follows:

"At no time in the history of music has the organ received so much attention as at the present day, or won so much general appreciation on the part of all lovers of dignified and elevating music. That this appreciation is on the increase is evidenced by the continued demand for high-class instruments for private residences. . .

"Today the ideal organ for the home is a compound instrument, furnished on one hand with complete manual and pedal claviers, and all the requisite mechanical appliances for the use of the skilled organist; while, on the other hand it is provided with an absolutely perfect automatic, or self-playing, device commanding the entire musical resources of the instrument, and under easy control, by means of which musical compositions can be effectively rendered by those who are not skilled performers on the manuals, and who may have little or no knowledge of musical notation or of the meaning of the numerous signs associated therewith.

"This is provided for in the Aeolian Pipe Organ by the special construction of the Aeolian Solo System and by the use of its unique two-manual music rolls [usable also on the Solo Orchestrelle player reed organ — Ed.] which open up an entirely new world of organ effects — for they can, and do, render, without the slightest difficulty or uncertainty, complex musical compositions and transcriptions, utterly impossible of rendition by the organist who has only his two hands to command the manuals.

"Master arrangements of ancient and modern scores have been made for the Aeolian Pipe Organ by men representing the highest artistic standard in music, including: Felix Weingartner, Berlin; Felix Mottl, Munich; Arturo Vigna, Milan; Gustav F. Kogel, Frankfurt; Alfred Hertz, New York; Walter Damrosch, Victor Herbert, Wallace Goodrich, S. Archer Gibson, Samuel P. Warren, and others. In addition to these master arrangements, the most distinguished musicians are composing especially for the Aeolian Pipe Organ. Notable among these stands Camille Saint-Saëns, of Paris.

"To remove all difficulties from the way of the performer in producing the correct tonal effects, the Aeolian Company has devised a system of simple and easily-understood registration marks, whereby the performer is directed at each stage of the music as to which stops and combinations are required."

The Aeolian Pipe Organ was generally equipped to play 116-note Aeolian Pipe Organ (sometimes called just Aeolian Organ) rolls; however, some early instruments were made to use 58-note Aeolian Grand rolls and some other instruments (the organ in Aeolian Hall in London is an example) were made to use either 58 or 116-note rolls. The Aeolian Pipe Organ roll contained no registration or expression perforations, and such had to be supplied by the operator of the instrument.

In 1917 the Aeolian Duo-Art Pipe Organ made its debut. Using a very wide roll with closely-spaced perforations, the Duo-Art Organ was completely automatic and contained provision for the change of pipe registers and the operation of swell shutters.

"Today Aeolian Duo-Art Pipe Organs are to be found in many of the best known residences here and in Europe. It is no longer regarded as suitable only for the large mansion, but is being installed in numerous homes of modest size. The addition several years ago of the Duo-Art principle, by means of which the actual performances of leading pipe organists could be produced with absolute fidelity of detail, gave its acceptance additional stimulus. The pipe organ has been rightfully called 'The King of Instruments.' Only an orchestra can surpass it in richness and variety of effects. The Aeolian Duo-Art Pipe Organ is recognized as not only the first strictly residence pipe organ but as the leading example of its type," reported the Aeolian Company in 1927.

The list of Duo-Art organists featured Clarence Eddy, "the dean of American organists," and then continued with others in alphabetical order: Joseph Bonnet, Palmer Christian, Charles M. Courboin, Eric DeLamarter, Gaston M. Dethier, Clarence Dickinson, William Ripley Dorr, Marcel Dupre, Walter C. Gale, Archer Gibson, Harold Gleason, Chandler Goldthwaite, Wallace Goodrich, Charles Heinroth, Dion W. Kennedy, Edwin H. Lemare, Rollo F. Maitland, William H. Price, Alexander Russell, Charles A. Sheldon, Jr., Harry Rowe Shelley, Charles A. Stebbins, W.F. Steele, Uda Waldrop, and Pietro Yon.

Aeolian Duo-Art Pipe Organ roll players were made in a number of forms. Some were arranged to accommodate the earlier 116-note Aeolian Organ rolls as well. Roll mechanisms were available built into the organ console, housed in a separate cabinet, and, beginning in the late 1920's, in an automatic roll changer, the Concertola (a device also used in modified form for Duo-Art reproducing pianos), housed in a separate cabinet and operated by remotely located push buttons.

In the 1930's the pipe organ portion of the Aeolian firm was sold to the Skinner Organ Company of Boston, Massachusetts, itself a builder of roll-operated pipe organs earlier. In 1938 the Hammond Corporation marketed the Aeolian-Hammond electronic organ with a player mechanism built by Aeolian-Skinner. This instrument was not self-registering and used rolls, marked "Duo-Art," with a tracker bar spacing of 12 holes per inch. The Aeolian-Hammond organs were made to the extent of about 210 instruments in 1938.

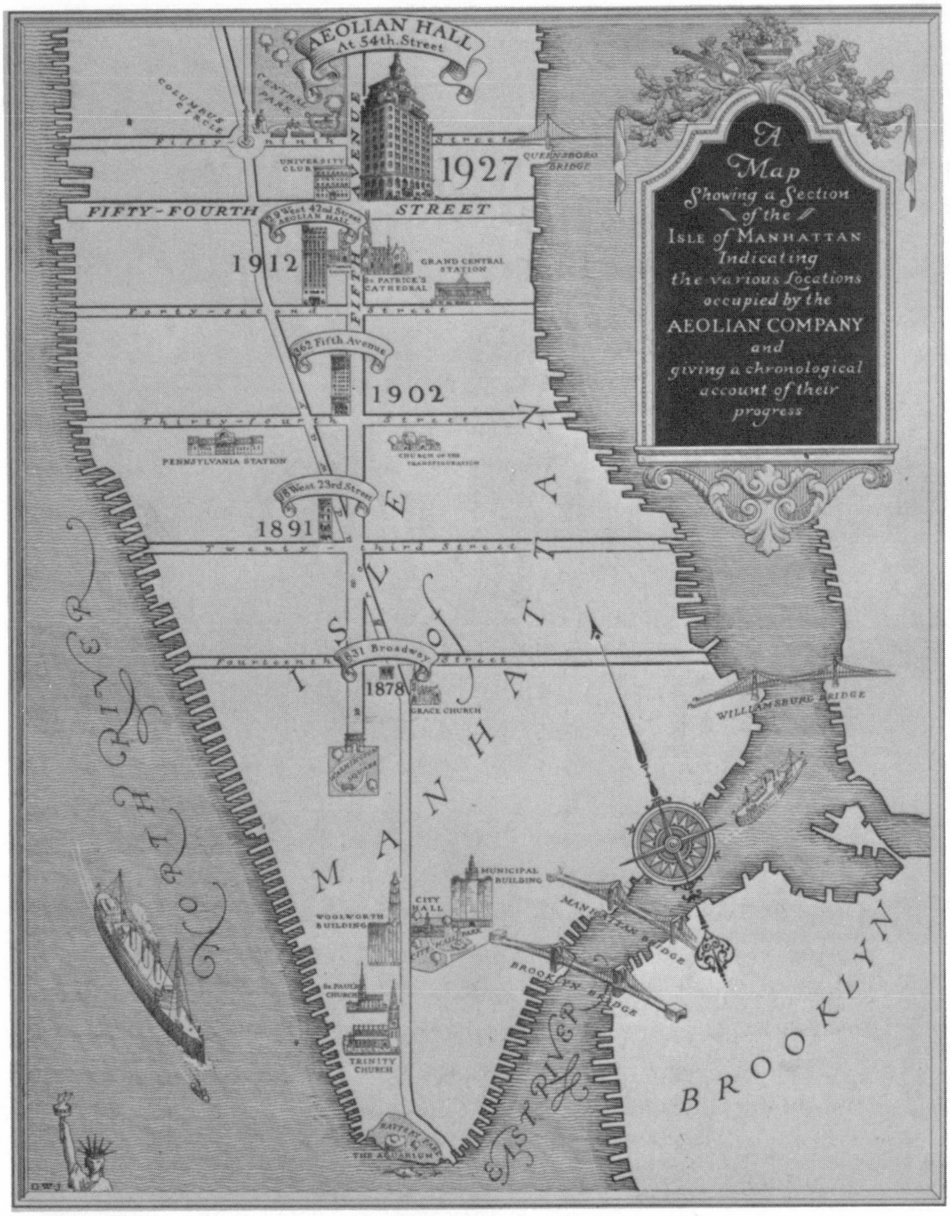

Duo-Art Organ Installation—Private House

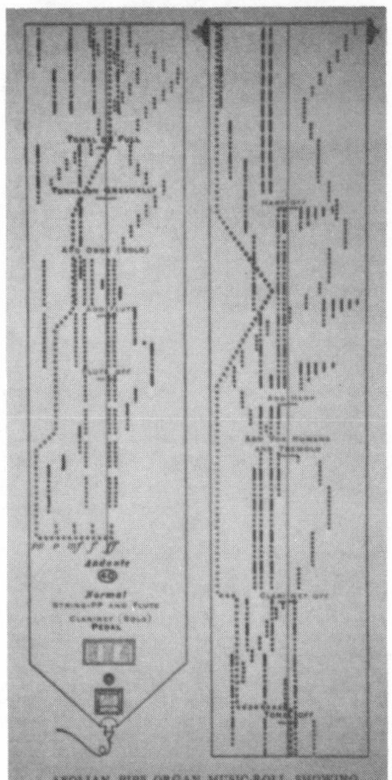
AEOLIAN PIPE ORGAN MUSIC-ROLL SHOWING TONE MARKINGS

Typical Aeolian Pipe Organ music roll with instructions for expression and register changes. From a 1910 catalogue.

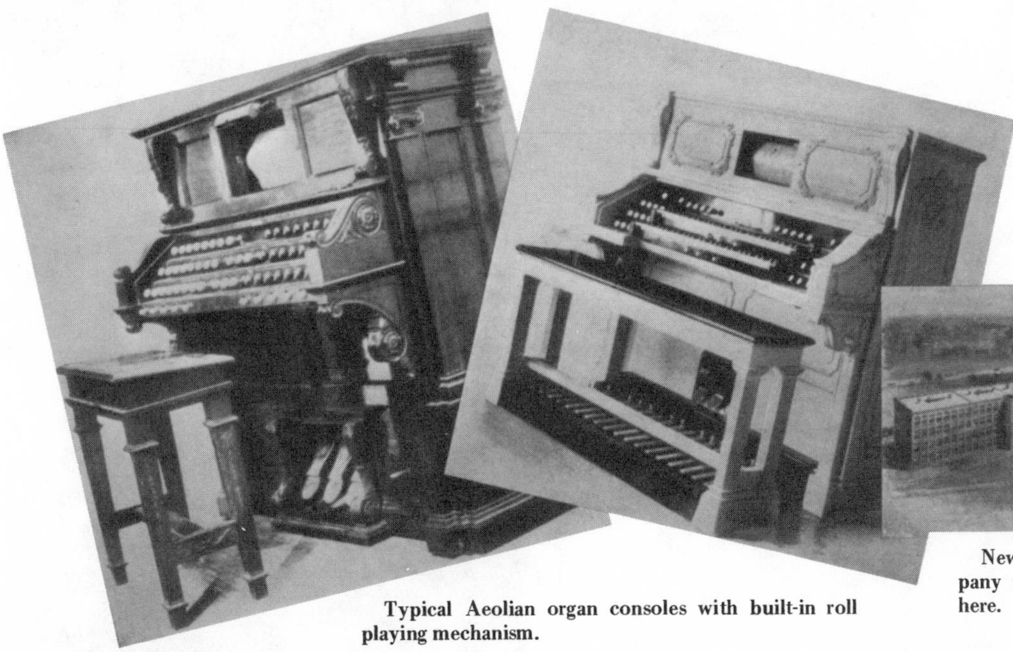

New Jersey factories of the Aeolian Company c.1914. Aeolian pipe organs were built here.

Typical Aeolian organ consoles with built-in roll playing mechanism.

**Some Aeolian Player Pipe Organ Installations**

(1)

(2)

(3)

(4)

(5)

(1) Aeolian Hall, London; (2) private home, Newport, R.I.; (3) private home, Lakewood, N.J.; (4) Aeolian Hall, Paris; (5) private home, Hamilton, Canada; (6) Charleton Towers, Malmesbury, England; (7) private home, New York City; (8) Aeolian Hall, New York City; (9) private home, Boston, Massachusetts; (10) manor in Saffron Walden, England.

(6)

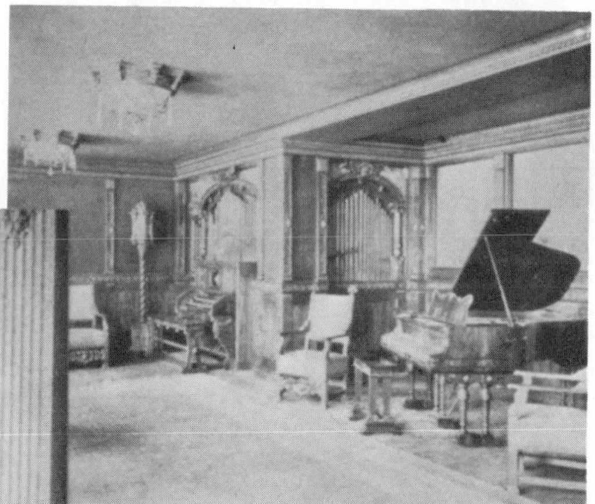

(8)

(7)

(9)

(10)

In 1938 the Hammond Corporation, well known manufacturer of electronic organs, introduced the Aeolian-Hammond Home Model B-A, the Aeolian-Hammond Player Organ.

Tonally and electrically the B-A is similar to the standard (not roll-operated) Model BC, an organ with one adjustable tremulant affecting both manuals and pedals equally, and an additional tone generator and appropriate switching for chorus effect. Floor dimensions are similar to BC (with pedal keyboard and bench – 48 3/8" wide by 49 1/2" deep), but with somewhat higher back section to accommodate the pneumatic section.

The player unit and pneumatic mechanisms were made by Aeolian-Skinner of Boston, Massachusetts, as were the several hundred different rolls produced for the Aeolian-Hammond.

The manual and pedal switches are played pneumatically from the roll. A box-type pump is located in the lower part of the cabinet. The rolls play the notes only. The various organ registers are changed by reading the appropriate instruction numbers as they appear on the roll throughout the music and changing the register keys manually. The register keyboards have black keys and white sharps and are located to the left of the two manuals (see illustration below). Expression is provided by watching the roll and and depressing the volume pedal accordingly. A tempo control is located to the right of the roll spoolbox.

Home Model B-A was produced from January through December 1938. The selling price was $2000. It is believed (from serial number observations) that about 210 instruments were produced during that time.

The Aeolian-Hammond Player Organ was advertised in a manner similar to that used to sell the Aeolian Orchestrelle thirty years earlier:

"Be Your Own Orchestra Leader. Today the interest in music for the home is gaining, not only as a cultural background but for relaxation and enjoyment. The technical directors of the Aeolian-Hammond companies have sensed this trend toward music. And they have designed an instrument, moderate in price, to bring to the discerning, one of the joys of life.

"If you are not a skilled musician the Aeolian-Hammond Musical Library of modern and classical music can furnish you with player rolls. "You may thrill your family, you may entertain your friends, or you may amuse yourself exploring the almost endless possibilities of the Aeolian-Hammond Player Organ. In it you have an exciting variety of musical notes and tone mixtures at your command. The lilt of the violin, the trill of the flute, the peal of the trumpet, or the resounding notes of the organ – each is ready to lend its particular charm to your own interpretation [the rolls were not self-registering, so this was played up as an "advantage" – Ed.] of the music. No longer need you depend on anyone else for your musical pleasure. For hospitality the Aeolian-Hammond gives you dance music; for appreciation and study – sonatas, symphonies, and operas. And in thoughtful moments you may play and ponder over the restful notes of the organ.

"See, hear and play this organ. And you will, without obligation, prove to yourself that you can be your own musical director, your own orchestra leader."

(Credit note: Information courtesy of Art Reblitz and Spencer Hagan [Director of Public Relations; Hammond Corporation])

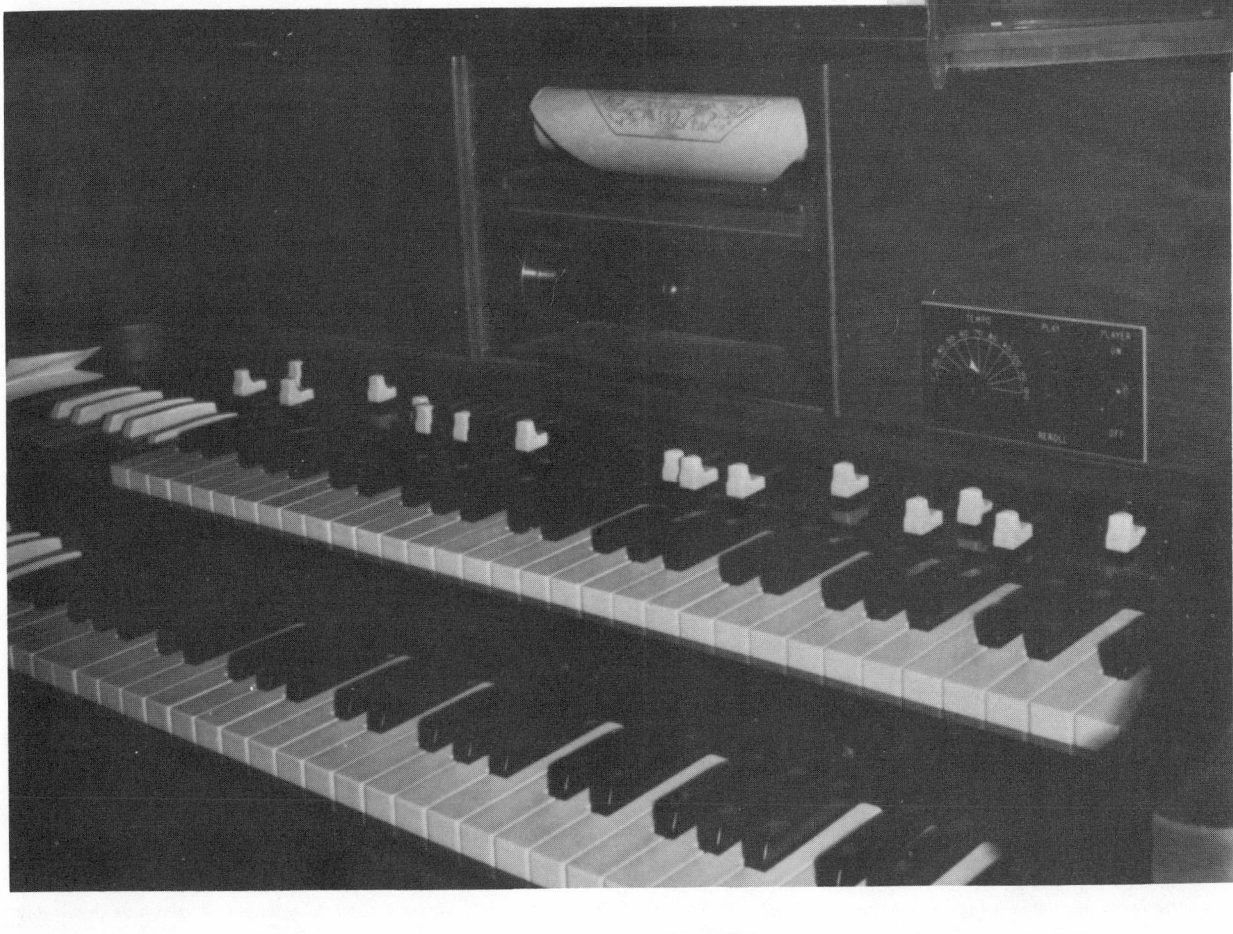

## THE WELTE PHILHARMONIC ORGAN

Introduced circa 1910, the Welte Philharmonic Organ was made in many different styles. "Smaller" organs were self-contained in ornate cases. Larger organs were usually built into a home or a music hall, in the manner of a standard pipe organ. (Note: Welte produced residence organs during the 1900-1910 decade also. These were usually called Salon Organs. These differed from the Philharmonic series.)

Dr. Max Reger performs on the Welte Philharmonic Organ.

Most Welte Philharmonic Organs of the smaller sizes – most self-contained instruments and smaller built-in installations – were designated Philharmonic I or Philharmonic II. Larger built-in models were mostly of Philharmonic III through Philharmonic VI size. Sizes I and II used the same type of roll; another type was used for the sizes from III to VI.

A Welte roll catalogue of the roll size suitable for III to VI sizes listed the following organists' performances: Samuel A. Baldwin, Jos. Bonnet, M. Enrico Bossi, F.J. Breitenbach, Joh. Diebold, M.J. Erb, William Faulkes, Eugene Gigout, Harry Goss Custard, Aug. Heim, Paul Hindermann, Thadda Hofmiller, C. Hofner, Alfred Hollins, Kohl, Edwin H. Lemare, J.J. Nater, Franz Philipp, Max Reger, Alfred Sittard, Herbert Walton, and W. Wolstenholme.

A roll catalogue issued by W.W. Kimball (see later notes) in the late 1930's includes such additional artists as: T. Tertius Noble, Charles Heinroth, J. Gautier, Lynnwood Farnam, O. Williams, H. Burkard, J.A. Beatty, A. Dubois, Hans Haass, O.M. Borrington, Leo Riggs, James P. Dunn, Hans Hauser, Sellars, and Clarence Eddy.

In addition the Philharmonic repertoire included some "designed rolls" (rolls laid out mechanically and not recorded by artists) and rolls transcribed from Welte orchestrion rolls.

Welte Philharmonic Organs were made in Freiburg, Germany, and in Welte's American factory at Poughkeepsie, New York. Those produced in Freiburg employed a tracker bar laid out on the metric scale; those in Poughkeepsie featured, for the most part, a tracker division laid out on the English scale. Rolls were made in both scales, so collectors today should verify rolls as to their compatibility (this can be done only by checking the rolls themselves; the boxes were not marked) before acquiring them.

Werner Bosch, formerly of the Welte factory in Freiburg, advised the author that "The last great orchestrions of Welte were built in the 1920's. The last Philharmonic organ with an automatic player attachment was built in 1936. Welte made large church organs and home organs until the war. The remainder of the enterprise was liquidated about the year 1950."

In the late 1940's Edwin Welte carried on extensive experimentation with an electronic organ which was known as the "Lichttonorgel," or "Light Tone Organ." The recorded sounds of famous European pipe organs were printed in the form of visible sound waves on clear discs.

Views of two Welte Philharmonic Organs: (1) Top: the instrument in the Jerry Doring Collection; (2) Below: an instrument found in an old New York mansion by Harvey and Marion Roehl; instrument now in the J.B. Nethercutt Collection.

The discs, one for each note in the organ, rotated and were scanned by a series of photocells, thereby producing a reproduction of the music. Although models were made and literature in the English, German, and French languages was prepared, the Lichttonorgel never reached the marketplace.

The Welte Philharmonic Organ was sold in large quantities – probably to the extent of several thousand instruments worldwide – mainly from about 1913 to 1929. At the Welte showroom at 273 Fifth Avenue, New York City, Welte Philharmonic Organ concerts were given regularly. After World War I the studios were relocated at 665 - 669 Fifth Avenue. A brochure of the 1920's noted:

"The various Welte activities are divided into several distinct departments: (1) The manufacturing and selling of the celebrated Welte Mignon (reproducing piano); (2) Building and installing the Welte Philharmonic Pipe Organ in private residences; (3) Manufacturing and selling pianos, player pianos, and grands; (4) The sale of Victor Victrolas and Victor Records in our Exclusive Victor Studios; (5) The sale of Pathé Phonographs and Pathé Records in an exclusive Pathé Store.

"The showrooms and studios where the retail business of this venerable house is conducted are located at 665, 667, and 669 Fifth Avenue, near 53rd St., New York, and are generally conceded to combine the art and sale of music to a higher degree than any other house in America.

"The one supreme musical instrument in the entire realm of music is the Welte Philharmonic Pipe Organ. This superlative instrument is built to order only, for studios, conservatories, and private residences, and is playable both by hand and by recorded music rolls which have been made by the world's greatest organists. The fact that this organ does

not require a skilled organist to play it and that the art of great organists like Lemare and Clarence Eddy is available upon it, precisely as if those great masters of the organ were seated at it, makes this the one incomparable and outstanding musical instrument deluxe of the age."

The large roll-operated pipe organs made by Welte, Aeolian (these first two firms were dominant in the field), Estey, Wurlitzer, Walcker, and others are the largest "automatic musical instruments" ever made. Although the scope of this book is mainly confined to self-contained instruments, the related large roll-playing organs are tied into the same history. For that reason we devote space to them in these pages.

The following descriptions are from a Welte booklet, "The Welte Philharmonic Organs," written about 1925. These paragraphs give a representation of how residence pipe organs were sold, how they were installed, and how they were enjoyed:

### The Welte Philharmonic Organ

The unparalleled success of the Welte Mignon reproducing piano with artists, as well as the public, inspired the firm to introduce the principle of reproducing artists' playing of the organ also, from which idea the Welte Philharmonic Organ has developed. As the Welte Mignon reproduces the playing of pianists, so this Welte Organ reproduces the playing of organists with amazing truth, not only as to mere technical perfection, but also in regard to the musical and artistic features. Many a friend and lover of the organ — the so-called Queen of Musical Instruments — is the possessor of one in his private house, but it fails to quite fulfill its high musical purpose for the simple reason that the artist who is to call it to life with perfect performance at any time is usually missing.

The owner of a Welte Philharmonic Pipe Organ, on the other hand, is able to enjoy in his own home, at any time he wishes, the most delightful works of organ literature in absolute perfection. Welte Artists' Rolls, recorded by the premier organists of the various cultured countries of the world, mediate to him this possibility by the automatic working of the keys, stops, swells, pedals, and couplers. The desire of some owners to influence the playing personally has also been considered. If he wishes to select the stops for a piece for himself, he may, by shifting a lever in the console of the Welte Organ, disconnect the automatic functioning of the stops, and select or change the stops, swells, couplers, etc. according to his own musical taste.

The manner of playing the Welte Philharmonic Organ is, therefore, threefold: (1) Regular playing by personal manipulation of the manuals and pedals, and all other accessories of a normal organ. (2) Absolutely automatic playing by means of Artists' Music Rolls. (3) Semi-automatic playing by working the keys by means of music rolls; but, by cutting off the automatic action of the stops, personally choosing and working the different accessories, according to the operator's own interpretation.

### Testimonials of Organists

As in the case of the Welte Mignon piano, the Welte Philharmonic Organ aroused the liveliest interest in the musical world; the most famous organists came to hear the instrument, and to record their own playing permanently on the music rolls. They expressed their joy at the successful working of the instrument in most enthusiastic terms.

Professor Dr. Max Reger, the famous composer, one of the first who heard and played for the Welte Philharmonic Organ, wrote in 1913: " I am delighted with the Welte Philharmonic Organ, and wish the greatest success to this fine instrument."

Professor Dr. Straube, the famous organist of St. Thomas' Church, one of the successors to J.S. Bach at Leipzig, wrote on August 14, 1921: "Posterity no wreaths for artists makes; but since the advent of the Welte Mignon piano and the Welte Philharmonic Organ, this word of Schiller's has lost its significance for musical reproducing artists. Later generations will become acquainted with the masters of our time in their own interpretations of their art. By its technique, time and mortality are overcome. Great moments of the spiritual life can be held fast forever."

### Music Roll Repertoire

Several thousand Artists' Rolls are available for the Welte Philharmonic Organ, offering a manifold selection for every taste. From the oldest stage of organ composition and organ works by: Sweelink (1562-1621), Samuel Scheidt (1587-1654), Buxtehude (1637-1707), and J.S. Bach (1685-1750) down to the modern works of: Prof.Dr. Max Reger, Cesar Franck, Ch. Widor, Edwin H. Lemare, William Faulkes, Alex. Guilmant, Th. Dubois, Prof. Enrico Rossi, organ literature is fully represented and is being added to constantly.

To round off the repertoire, parts of symphonies, oratorios, operas, and other concert music available for the organ, such as the symphonies and opera of Beethoven, valuable extracts from operas such as the Pilgrim Chorus from Tannhauser, the Prelude from Lohengrin, and the Spell of Good Friday from Parsifal, etc., have been recorded, and many other parts from old and new concert and stage works have been added and are reproduced with all the wonderful variety of tonal effects of a modern symphony orchestra. Thus the ownership of a Welte Philharmonic Organ makes it possible to have the best music in the most perfect rendering, with one's own choice of program, whenever desired.

Interesting comparisons between the works of one, or different, masters, within one or widespread epochs of musical creation, and likewise also the interpretations of one and the same work by various virtuosos in their individual rendering can be effected in any desired sequence. These possibilities, which have not existed hereto, promote the education and development of those with musical taste in a high degree, serving to keep those who lack time, leisure, and opportunity for visiting concerts and playing musical instruments artistically themselves, in touch with musical events.

### For the Cultured Home

The Welte Philharmonic Organ is a true ideal for people of means; an instrument which fulfills its purpose as well in the luxurious country mansion as in the city residence, and is able to satisfy to the fullest degree the manifold demands of the lover of music.

Not only from a musical point of view, but from a decorative one, will the organ gain by a suitable arrangement in the space available, and by architectural adjustment to the style prevailing in the surroundings, while adding distinction in point of ornament. It furnishes various motifs to the architect and decorator for the development of their ideas and abilities.

The busy man of affairs, jaded by the worries of the day, when at length he reaches home and settles himself in his peaceful music room, will feel a fresh world open before him as the strains of the Philharmonic Organ strike his ear. And in this, the chief intellectual pleasure he can treat himself to, he will not be alone; for he is able to extend his enjoyment to his circle of friends, revealing to them equally the glory of centuries past in the organ moods of Bach, Beethoven, Wagner, and others.

### Selecting and Installing the Organ

The first question for anyone desiring to possess a Welte Philharmonic Organ is that of available space. And here a distinction must be observed between the space for the installation of the organ pipes and accessories themselves, and the music room, hall, or salon in which the organ is to be heard. The size of the organ is not dependent upon the size of the latter; on the contrary, each organ is tone-regulated and voiced according to the size and acoustics of the room in which the organ is to be heard. In the music room, accordingly, we have only to care for the comfort of the listener. On the other hand, the actual size of the pipe organ will naturally depend upon the space available for the installation of the works (Author's note: And the ability to pay for it!), and in this respect a number of different solutions are possible.

The method most feasible and most popular is to set up the entire organ and mechanisms in a room adjoining the main music room. The sound and tone of the organ can then enter the music room through an opening in the wall, which may be artistically covered by an elegant wooden latticework, a "Gobelin" tapestry, or a scenic picture. The console will be in the music room, but the organ works, blower, etc. will be in a separate room.

The organ pipes can also be placed in a room below the music room; the tone entering it through an opening in the floor, hidden by an ornamental lattice, a bench, or a decorative cabinet.

The same arrangement can be adopted with an organ placed in a room above the music room; the sound entering through an ornamental fretwork in the music room ceiling.

Or, when large pipe organs are ordered, the space for the pipes may even occupy two floors or a small annex to the main building in which the music room is located.

Furthermore, the Philharmonic Organ may be built as a complete whole, like a large and self-contained piece of furniture, the case being adapted to the style of the music room. The motors and blowers, however, are usually placed outside the music room, in an adjoining room or in a cellar, to disguise the inevitable humming noise of the motor.

### Other Installation Details

The console should be placed in the music room, near the organ opening. If the distance between the organ and the console does not exceed thirty feet, the connection between the console and the works will be pneumatic. If the distance is greater, it will be electric.

After the prospective buyer studies the foregoing information, he should provide us, the manufacturer, with: (1) Plans of the house, in which the music room and the space available for the organ itself are marked; (2) Photographs of the music room, in order that we may submit decorative sketches for the organ case and console; (3) Particulars of the electric current available for the motive power.

The increasing distribution of the Welte instruments all over the world and the constant stream of appreciative tributes to our work from both artists and the public justify our hope that every purchaser of the Welte Philharmonic Organ will find his expectations fulfilled. The care bestowed upon the artistic perfection of the instruments and on the faultless execution of every part has made the achievements of Welte instruments possible and founded the now almost century-old reputation of the firm, whose ambition, today as ever, is to live up to its established high tradition of quality.

### Notes for Today's Collectors

So ends Welte's original description of the Philharmonic Organ. We give some notes concerning these instruments:

Most smaller Welte Philharmonic Organs had the motor and pumps built into the bottom of the cabinet (in contradiction to the above catalogue statement). The pumps in these instruments were of the bellows variety (those pumps located in remote chambers were of the centrifugal or turbine variety and were noisier) and operated very slowly, so as to be almost silent.

The American Welte organ business was taken over by Chicago's W.W. Kimball Company in the 1930's. During the 1930's some Welte installations, including some with an automatic 10-roll changing device, were made by Kimball — but the number was very small in comparison to the Welte instruments sold before the Depression.

The W.W. Kimball Co. may have cut rolls into the 1940's, as evidenced by this April 27, 1944 letter from Kimball to Mr. Richard C. Simonton:

"With respect to organ rolls, the situation is as follows:

"We have the complete set of masters which we secured from Welte originally, to which we ourselves have made some additions. It is from these masters we cut rolls which are sold and shipped to our customers and we have not carried a large stock of finished rolls because of a certain amount of deterioration which takes place in the paper while stored. This means that there is often some cutting expense involved

when rolls are ordered and that is one reason why our prices have not been marked down further. (Editor's Note: most rolls sold for $4 to $6 each, with an occasional roll at $10 to $12.50) Obviously there never has been and never will be sufficient annual demand for organ rolls such as will warrant a full-time roll department organization.

"However, we have discussed the situation, more particularly as it involves you, and here is what we are willing to do: If you order 25 rolls at a time, we will make a discount of 10%; 50 rolls, 15%; and 100 rolls, 20%. However, for the immediate future the deal will have to be contingent on our having already cut the rolls which you may order.

"We are about to make an inventory of the rolls which are available or almost ready for shipment and if you wish to wait until this is completed we will send you a copy of the list, or you can give us a list of those which you wish and we can simply check off those which are available.

"Will again search for a test roll and should we find one we will let you know more about it in the future."

Dr. Carl Straube plays the Welte Philharmonic Organ.

Vorsetzer-type Welte organ player.

A Welte Philharmonic Organ was an important part of many elegant homes built in the 1910 - 1930 era.

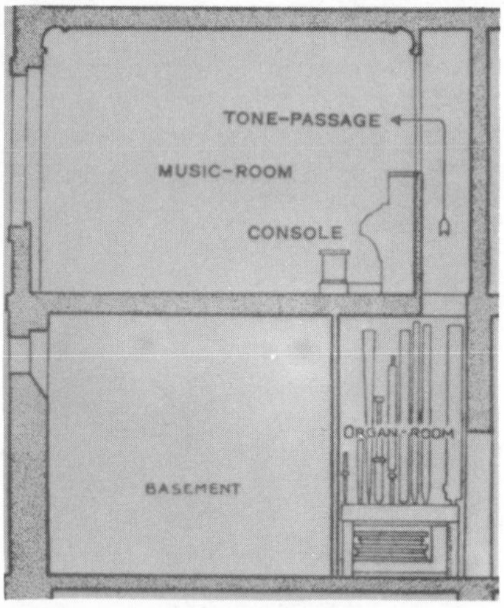


Above: How to install a Welte Philharmonic Organ. This illustration shows a basement installation with the sound carried to the music room via a special tone passage. Another popular method was to have grids in the floor directly above the chamber.

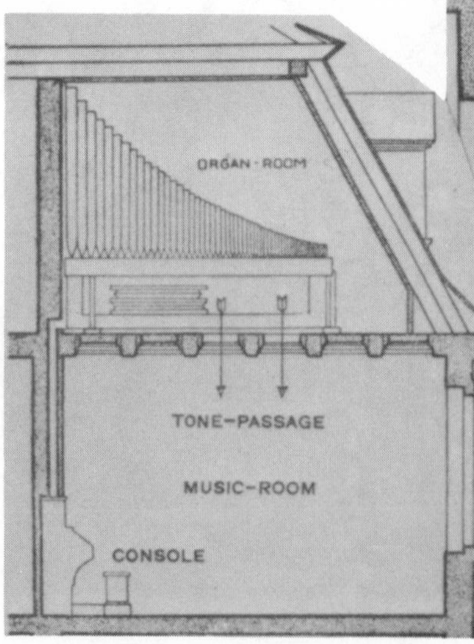


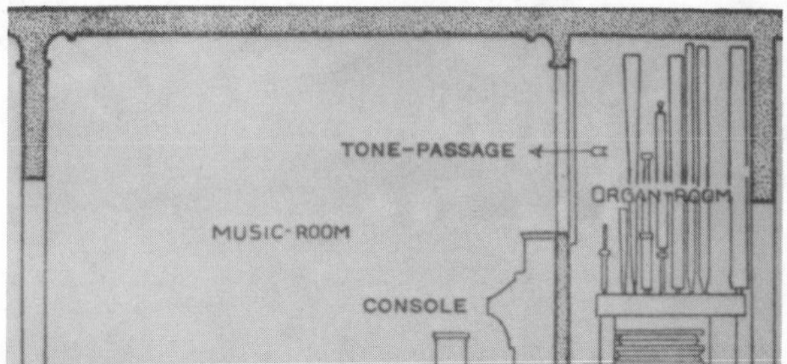

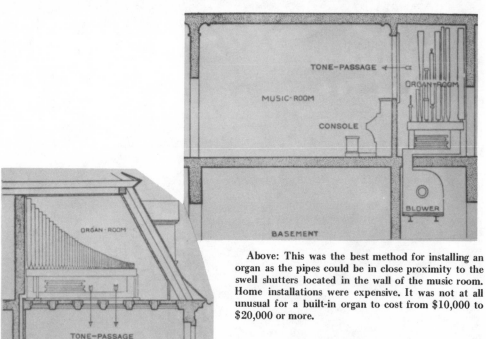

Above: This was the best method for installing an organ as the pipes could be in close proximity to the swell shutters located in the wall of the music room. Home installations were expensive. It was not at all unusual for a built-in organ to cost from $10,000 to $20,000 or more.

Left: If space could not be found elsewhere, as a last resort the organ pipes could be installed in the attic — as shown here. Welte was versatile — and if you could pay for the organ, Welte could find a way to install it!

Although this illustration was used in Philharmonic Organ advertising, the instrument pictured was made c.1904 and was of an earlier organ model.

This built-in organ faces a large living room.

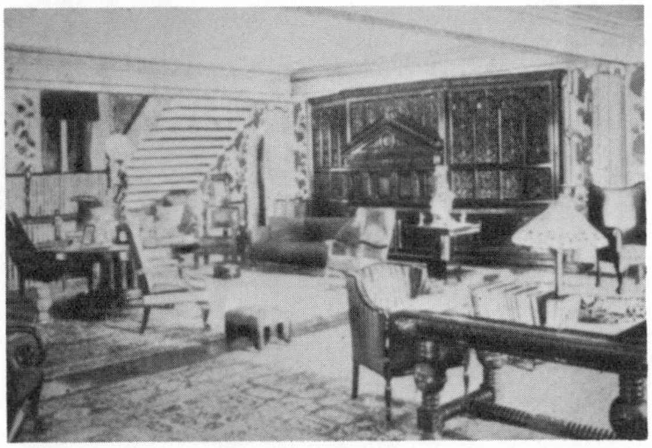

Library music: "Located in a fine library" noted the Welte catalogue description.

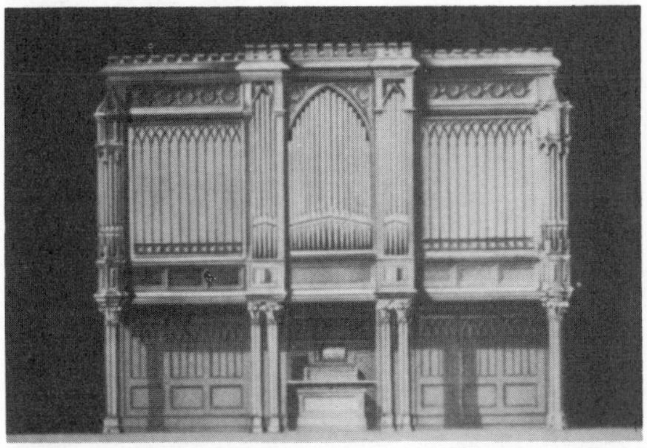

Music for the summer place: This large and ornate organ was part of a villa and was featured in several Welte catalogues.

Harrod's Department Store in London was the home of this large Welte Philharmonic Organ. The magnificent block-square store is still busy; the organ is, sadly, no longer there.

The above case design was a popular one – and dozens of this style were sold.

Featured in many advertisements of M. Welte & Sons (of N.Y.) was this Gothic Welte Philharmonic Organ.

Another one of the Welte Philharmonic Organs. This was a popular style about 1914.

Any self-respecting yachtsman should have a pipe organ on board! As the illustrations show, many elegant yachts had Welte Philharmonic Pipe Organs to entertain the guests. The illustration at left is of a Welte installation (note the roll mechanism is in what appears to be a "door") "aboard a large English steamship" – noted the catalogue. Welte Mignon pianos, Welte organs, and Welte orchestrions were standard equipment aboard ships of the North German Lloyd Line and aboard many English and American vessels as well.

## MORE WELTE PHILHARMONIC ORGAN INSTALLATIONS

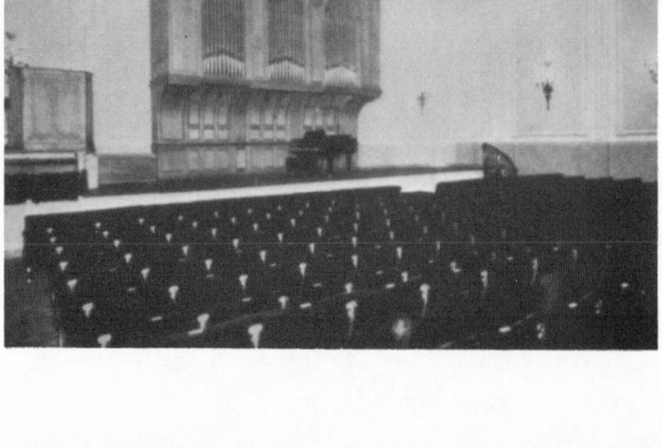

THE ESTEY RESIDENCE ORGAN

Do not dismiss the idea of a pipe organ in your home on the ground of cost, difficulty of installing, or the thought that maybe you would not care for organ music. Once really hear an Estey Pipe Organ and you will know that you like organ music, just as you like orchestra music. Once you want an organ, all the rest becomes easy—even the paying for it. A good organ can be bought for the price of a good motor car, and its addition becomes an architectural feature in your home. And you can play it yourself by means of the Estey Organist, a self-interpreting device.

### Estey Player Organs

Founded by Jacob Estey in 1846, the Estey Organ Co. (earlier, the J. Estey Co.) was located in Brattleboro, Vermont, from its founding until the factory stock was dispersed in the early 1960's. During the 19th century Estey was one of America's leading makers of reed organs, mostly non-player types. During the 20th century reed and pipe instruments were made, primarily for residence and church use. In 1912 Estey advertised that 400,000 instruments had been sold up to that date.

Estey player pipe organs were made in several styles. The rolls, marked "Estey Residence Organ," appeared to the extent of several hundred titles. Most Estey player organs were of the self-registering type and used artists' recorded rolls.

William E. Haskell, inventive genius of the firm, produced many innovations in the field of organ pipework, including a pipe-within-a-pipe (which made possible a pipe with short physical length but of long tonal length) which was used in the unique Estey Minuette Organ, a non-player pipe organ built in a case styled like a grand piano.

Estey was one of the few American organ builders with a worldwide business. Outlets were maintained in Europe, South America, and other locations.

### Wurlitzer Player Organs

In 1910 the Hope-Jones Organ Company of Elmira, New York, was purchased by the Rudolph Wurlitzer Company and moved to Wurlitzer's factory at North Tonawanda in the same state. Robert Hope-Jones, an Englishman, joined Wurlitzer and remained with the firm until, disillusioned with Wurlitzer's all-business and little-research policy, he committed suicide in 1914. During the 1890's and early 20th century Hope-Jones devised the theatre organ, or Unit Orchestra as he named it. Hope-Jones' research into pipe voicing and construction, organ unification, and acoustical principles of the organ was brilliantly conceived and makes informative reading today.

During the years from 1912 to 1939, but mainly in the 1920's, Wurlitzer built over 2200 Unit Orchestras, nearly all of which were installed in theatres. Only a few dozen were sold to homes, churches, and other non-theatre locations. The "Mighty Wurlitzer" reigned supreme in the theatre organ field and became world-famous.

The subject of the present text is automatically-played instruments, so despite the editor's general interest in Wurlitzer Unit Orchestras (a book on the subject is planned), the discussion here will be limited to roll players.

During the 1912-1939 period between 100 and 200 instruments were equipped with roll-playing devices. These were of the following types: 97-note or Concert Organ, 105-note or Style RJ, 130-note (only a few were made), and the largest, the 165-note Reproducing Organ style. Roll players were installed in several ways: built into the console (as shown above), into a separate roll cabinet (usual for the 165-note type), or mounted above the keyboard of an upright piano (if the Unit Orchestra was equipped with a piano; only a few were).

In addition to the preceding rolls, all of which were equipped for the automatic operation of stops and expression, some instruments were made with Standard Pneumatic Actions (trademark) and used regular 88-note player piano rolls. In the very early years (pre-1920) several types of duplex roll mechanisms were experimented with. One model had the playing notes on the first roll and the stops, expression, and controls on a second and much shorter roll.

Salonorgel mit Organola des Ing. Kettel in Düsseldorf.

E.F. Walcker & Cie.

E.F. Walcker & Cie. of Ludwigsburg, Germany, offered the Organola roll player attachment to its customers during the early 20th century. Hundreds of Walcker pipe organs, mostly produced for residence use, were so equipped. Above are shown a "salon organ with Organola" installed in Düsseldorf by Walcker in 1909, and an advertisement featuring the Organola "self-playing apparatus" which appeared in an issue of "Zeitschrift für Instrumentenbau" during the same year. E.F. Walcker is actively in the pipe organ and organ supply business today.

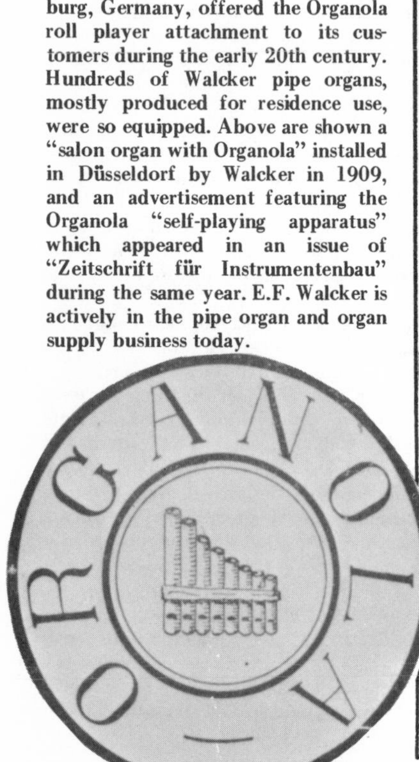


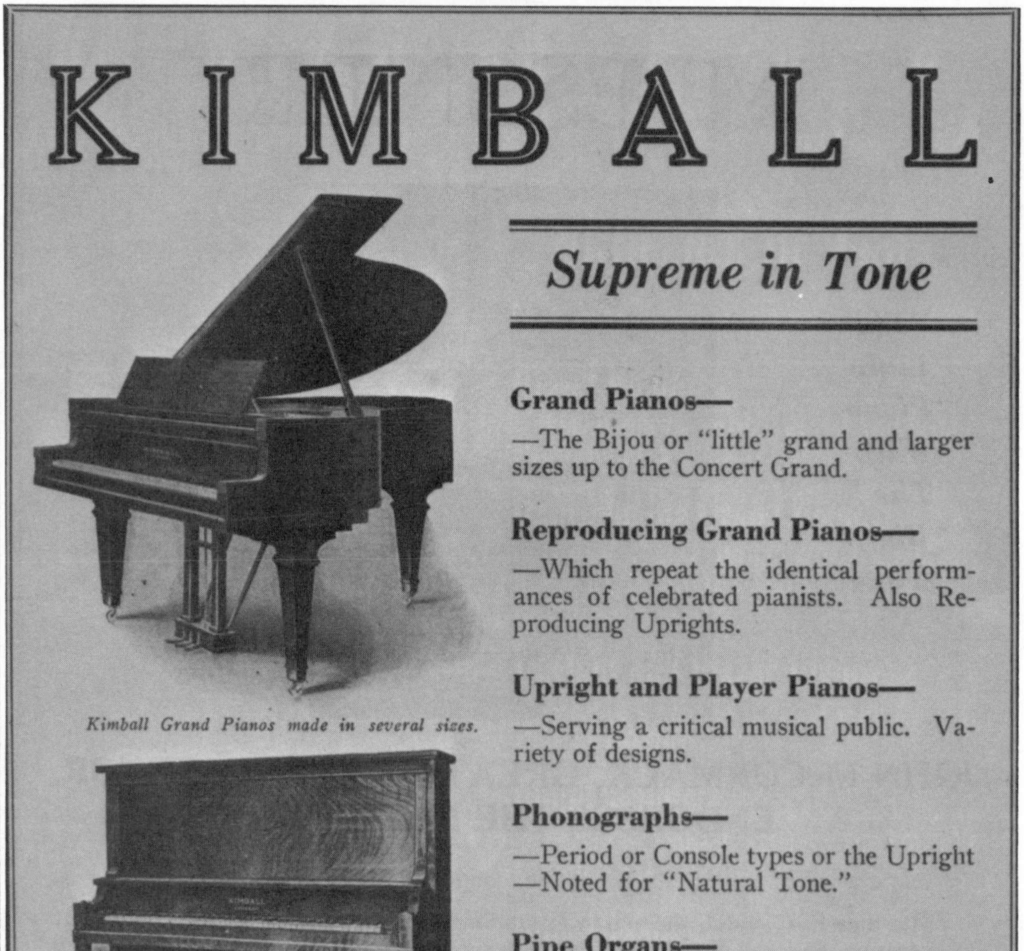

KIMBALL
Supreme in Tone
Kimball Grand Pianos made in several sizes.
Grand Pianos—
—The Bijou or "little" grand and larger sizes up to the Concert Grand.
Reproducing Grand Pianos—
—Which repeat the identical performances of celebrated pianists. Also Reproducing Uprights.
Upright and Player Pianos—
—Serving a critical musical public. Variety of designs.
Phonographs—
—Period or Console types or the Upright
—Noted for "Natural Tone."
Pipe Organs—
—For Church, Auditorium, Theatre, Residence—Praised for admirable blending of tone.
Music Rolls for All Player Pianos
Style 20
One of several Upright models.
KIMBALL instruments are known throughout the civilized world. The line is broadly comprehensive. Since 1857 a reliable name in the music industry.
Write for agency terms.
One type of Kimball Organ Keydesk
W. W. KIMBALL CO.
ESTABLISHED 1857
Manufacturers
Executive Offices: Kimball Bldg.
Chicago


Founded in 1857, the W.W. Kimball Co. manufactured organs from the earliest days until the 1930's or early 1940's. Concerning the roll-playing device, "The Piano and Organ Purchaser's Guide for 1913" noted: "Kimball pipe organs are now an established feature for lodges and private residences. They are especially so on account of the Kimball Soloist. This feature is a remarkable achievement in self-playing devices. Every imaginable combination of the grandest music is adapted to its possibilities. The catalogue of its library embraces practically the entire literature of music, from a Bach fugue to a Sousa march, a Beethoven sonata, or a Strauss waltz. The Soloist may be built in any organ and in no way interferes with the instrument manually."

Kimball produced player organs, although not in large quantities, during the 1920's. In his book, "Music for the Millions" (a history of Kimball), Van Allen Bradley wrote that "in 1932 the company bought the Welte-Tripp Organ Corp. of Sound Beach (a N.Y. suburb) along with its music roll libraries, recording devices, patents, good will, machinery, and right to manufacture. . . But it soon had a white elephant on its hands, for the coming of the depression had already combined with the phonograph to deal both the player piano and the player organ a death blow. Not a single player was made in the black year of 1932."

# FAIRGROUND ORGANS

**Calliopes**
**Dance Organs**
**Street Organs**
**Fairground Organs**
**Portable Hand-Cranked Barrel Organs**
**and related instruments**

# FAIRGROUND ORGANS, DANCE ORGANS, CALLIOPES
## —and related instruments—

### Introduction

Fairground organs comprise some of the most colorful automatic musical instruments ever made. These instruments, loudly-voiced so they could be heard above the surrounding din, provided music for merry-go-rounds, carnivals, circuses, amusement parks, skating rinks, and similar attractions. Typically, such an instrument contains several ranks of pipes, all voiced on high wind pressure (usually from eight to twelve inches of water-column pressure). In accompaniment to the pipes, limited percussion effects – usually a bass drum, snare drum, and cymbal – are used. Fairground organs were designed to play loudly – in order to be heard above the din of the carousel, dozens of skaters, or carnival rides and, equally important, to act as a Pied Piper to draw crowds from far and near.

Fairground organs, called "band organs" in the United States, have been used to entertain the public for over two centuries. Portable hand-cranked barrel organs, small versions of fairground organs, were known in the early 1700's, and perhaps even earlier. Before the 1890's most fairground organs were of the barrel organ type. The musical program, usually consisting of eight to ten tunes, was pinned on a wooden cylinder. Unlike barrel-operated orchestrions, most barrel organs did not advance automatically to the second tune once the first had been completed. Changing a tune involved disengaging a latch and moving the barrel slightly to one side or the other – in order to bring a new set of cylinder pins into play. If the show operator happened to be particularly busy the same tune would play on, and on, and on! In his book, "The Fairground Organ," Eric V. Cockayne relates that a showman once received a summons "for creating a nuisance by allowing his organ to play 'Won't You Come Home, Bill Bailey?' all day without stopping."

In the 1890's Gavioli introduced a new system which employed a key frame and folding cardboard music books. The Gavioli invention was soon adopted by most other organ makers, particularly by the builders of large instruments. Around the turn of the century, organs which used perforated paper music rolls were first sold. These achieved some usage, particularly among United States builders, on instruments of smaller sizes.

Unlike most other areas in the automatic musical instrument field, the business of building fairground organs never completely stopped. The largest and most magnificent instruments were built from about 1880 to 1914 (the beginning of World War I). Smaller instruments predominated in the 1920's. The Depression of the 1930's saw most organ firms go out of business, but the trade still lingered on. Today, a number of firms are busily building organs; instruments mostly of the portable hand-cranked barrel organ type (built by at least a half dozen makers). Some larger fairground organs are being built also. To be sure, the volume of business is just a shadow of what it used to be. Total production of all instruments during the 1960-1970 decade was less than it was for a typical single month around the turn of the twentieth century.

### Portable Hand-Cranked Barrel Organs

Made from the early 18th century (or possibly even earlier) to the present day, these instruments were especially popular from about 1830 to 1930. A following section, "The Portable Hand-Cranked Barrel Organ," written by Claes O. Friberg, describes these colorful instruments in detail.

### Fairground Organs

BARREL ORGANS: Barrel organs, operated by pinned wooden cylinders, were the main type made before 1900. In Europe the firms of Gavioli, Limonaire, Wellershaus, Bruder, and others produced these by the thousands. Most were turned by hand, a factor which limited their size. Some large styles were made, however. Turned by hand or by a water or steam engine, these instruments ranged in size up to over 100 keys. (The number of keys is equal to the number of control positions on the organ; the total number of playing notes plus controls for the percussion effects, registers, etc.) A few exceptionally large instruments in the 130- to 140-key sizes were also built. Certain types of barrel organs with brass trumpets and/or trombones were called "trumpet organs" by the original makers. Although the popularity of barrel organs (except small hand-cranked portable types) declined after 1900, such instruments were made as late as the 1930's. Compared to pneumatically-operated organs, barrel-operated organs offered the advantage of extreme ruggedness and durability. Such instruments could be played for long periods of time without any attention by the operator (although, as noted, an occasional change of music was recommended!).

BOOK ORGANS: Following Gavioli's introduction of the folding cardboard music book system in the early 1890's, most organ builders used this format. The folding cardboard music books played upon a key frame – a series of spring-loaded steel "fingers." When a hole occurred in the music book, a key would pop up. At the other end of the hinged key an orifice similar in function to a tracker bar hole would be uncovered. This in turn would actuate a pouch-and-valve system which would cause the appropriate pipe to speak. Other keys controlled the turning on or off of pipe registers, the operation of percussion effects (such as drums, xylophone, or bells), lighting effects, and other functions. The cardboard music book system offered several advantages: (1) Books could be made any desired length. Many different books could be glued together, on a continuous-loop system or in a large bin, to play a program of an hour or more without interruption or repetition. (2) Compared to cylinders (which might cost $100 or more each for a large instrument), books were inexpensive. (3) Books were easily stored and were easily shipped. A minimum of handling care was needed. Books were rugged. (4) The pneumatic system employed was faster-acting than the mechanical system used on barrel organs. More musical versatility, more sophisticated arrangements, and a wider range of instrumentation resulted. (5) Books (in comparison to paper rolls) were relatively unaffected by severe changes in humidity. The cardboard system tracked well (that is, the holes in the music passed over the corresponding keys in the key frame) and were not subject to tearing. With few exceptions, cardboard music was employed on large organs made from about 1900 to such instruments passed from the scene in the late 1920's and early 1930's. A variation, the so-called "keyless system," was used by certain builders. A music book was employed, but instead of the usual key frame with its spring-loaded "fingers," a regular tracker bar with round or square openings was utilized. The stiff cardboard books were held tightly against the tracker bar or "keyless frame" by a series of india-rubber pinch rollers.

PAPER ROLL ORGANS: Organs which used perforated paper rolls, rolls not unlike player piano rolls in general appearance, were built by several manufacturers. Introduced by Wurlitzer and several other makers shortly after 1900, it was soon learned that the paper roll system had many problems, especially if the organ was subjected to humidity extremes. The same type of organ which worked well indoors would fail when taken on the road as part of a carnival or circus. With an increase in the humidity, the paper expanded and started playing the wrong notes. Subjected to extreme dryness, the opposite would happen to the roll. Wurlitzer, the leading exponent of the paper roll system, solved this problem by developing an excellent-grade paraffin-coated paper. Even so, tracking was a problem in the larger instruments. Paper roll organs were made in two styles: (1) The most popular system, as used by Wurlitzer and several other primarily-American makers, used vacuum in the tracker bar to "read" the holes in the music roll. (2) Artizan in America, Gebr. Bruder in Europe, and several others used the pressure system. A slotted metal roller held the paper roll in place against the tracker bar. The blowing of air through a hole in the music roll would actuate the pneumatic valve system.

### Dutch Street Organs

The Dutch street organ, or "pierement" as it is called, differs in construction and in voicing from other organ types. These instruments, still actively used in Holland today, are described in the "Dutch Street Organ" section following.

### Calliopes

The calliope, a high-pressure instrument usually with brass pipes, was invented in America around the middle of the 19th century. Early models were operated by steam; hence the "steam calliope" term still in use today. During the period from about 1915 to 1935, the manufacturing of air calliopes, most of which were paper-roll-operated, was the speciality of several American firms. The Tangley Company of Muscatine, Iowa, had the lion's share of the calliope market, although National, Artizan, and a few others offered some competition.

Calliopes, their history and makers, are discussed in detail in a special section which follows.

### Dance Organs

Dance organs, some of which were made in gargantuan sizes and with unbelievably ornate facades, were made primarily in Belgium by the firm of Th. Mortier. Approximately 1400 dance organs were made by this firm during the first half of the twentieth century. Arthur Bursens, Gebr. Decap, Remond Duwyn, and others were also active in the market.

Decap is still active in the business today. Most modern instruments use electronic tone-generating systems instead of the traditional pipe ranks and have modern-appearing facades. The music produced hasn't lost its charm, and at last word Decap had a nice backlog of unfilled orders!

Unlike the other instruments discussed in this section, dance organs are softly voiced. The sound of many models is not unlike that of a theatre pipe organ.

### Collecting Aspects Today

Despite the fact that a Tangley calliope can be heard a quarter-mile away, a Bruder organ can play with sufficient volume to drown out the sound of a four-abreast carousel, and a Mortier dance hall organ can fill the most spacious ballroom with melodies, these instruments are avidly collected today – by enthusiasts who, for the most part, keep them in private homes.

The colorful appearance of the instruments, their music (which is nearly always arranged in a sprightly, never serious or solemn, manner), and the romance associated with the good times that they once created all contribute to the immense appeal they have today. Fortunately, the art of cutting cardboard music books was never lost – and many firms produce new books today. The idea of hearing "Lara's Theme," "Love is Blue," or some other relatively modern tune played on a fifty-year-old instrument is likewise appealing, and many enthusiasts have built large collections of music.

In England, the Fair Organ Preservation Society has pioneered this collecting interest. By the mid-1960's this group's membership exceeded that of any other organization devoted to old-time automatic instruments. Many of the pictures and much of the information used in the following section was obtained from Society members. In Holland, the Kring van Draaiorgelvrienden (circle of friends of the hand-cranked organ) has likewise contributed to the preservation of old-time instruments and their history.

Why are such instruments so popular? The answer is simple: they are a lot of fun! Could a better reason be found for collecting anything?

**This October, 1968 photograph shows Otto Bruder (left) talking to Giovanni Bacigalupo. At the time of his visit to Waldkirch, Mr. Bacigalupo said that over the years some 7,000 organs, mostly of the portable hand-cranked variety, had been made by the Bacigalupo family. In the background Curt Baum (left) talks with Gustav Bruder. (Photograph courtesy of Leonard Grymonprez)**

# THE PORTABLE HAND-CRANKED BARREL ORGAN

## —Its history and makers—

*by Claes O. Friberg*

### The Early History of Barrel Organs

The first reports of a barrel organ can be traced back more than a thousand years. An 1130 description tells that a certain Pabst Sylvester II from Reims, France, constructed and built a barrel system into an organ in the middle of the 10th century and thus created an early instrument of the barrel organ type. Even earlier references can be found, the "hydraulus" or water-organ invented by Ctesibius being an example, but precise descriptions of these early instruments are lacking.

About the year 1350 the pinned barrel system was used in connection with clock mechanisms in churches. In the 15th century this system was also used for a number of church organs. By the end of that century a number of fine instruments incorporated barrel systems for automatic playing.

In 1502 an incredible clockwork organ was fitted into Salzburg Castle in Austria. It contained more than 250 pipes and played every morning at four o'clock to awaken the townsmen for a day's work. Again it sounded when it was bedtime and time for closing the town gates.

Similar instruments were built in Germany, England, and other European countries. After 1600 a number of large barrel-operated pipe organs, some of which were really immense, were built for residential use in the music rooms of royalty and wealthy citizens. One such famous instrument was built in 1598 by Thomas Dallam of London. It contained a clockwork which indicated the positions of celestial bodies, a mechanical theatre, barrel-operated organ pipes, and a supplementary keyboard. Built to the instructions of Queen Elizabeth (1533-1603), it was presented to the Turkish sultan Mohammed III.

Common to all of the foregoing large organ mechanisms is their motive power: they were not hand-cranked but were mostly weight-driven or water-driven. It was not until about 1700 that the first portable hand-cranked barrel organs (in the sense that we know them today) made their appearance.

It is impossible to say who invented the very first hand-cranked portable organ. Like so many products of technology it seems to have "evolved," with many different craftsmen — organ builders, clockmakers, and musicians — each playing a part. Also making an early appearance were bird-organs or serinettes. These small hand-cranked organs were of limited scale (about ten pipes) and were intended to train birds to sing. Many of these serinettes were used simply for the enjoyment of their melodies.

The first descriptions and pictures of portable hand-cranked barrel organs were given in 1722 by Bonanni, who was in charge of a musical museum formed by Kircher (1601-1680) in Rome. The organ had 24 keys and the barrel was programmed with twelve tunes. It was described as an "organo portatile." It is not known whether the organ was obtained earlier by Kircher during his lifetime or whether the organ was added to the collection sometime between Kircher's death in 1680 and Bonanni's published description in 1722. The crank of the organ was on the right side end so that the organ grinder could play the instrument while he was walking. Later organs had a leg or stand that could be folded up, or were mounted on a pushcart.

Although first described in Italy, the portable hand-cranked barrel organ was probably first produced in Germany or Austria. Empress Maria Theresa (1717-1780) gave a barrel organ license to disabled soldiers. After the Napoleonic Wars ended many licenses were given out and the barrel organ became a common sight in the streets. Many of the German organ builders came from Italy however. Later names such as Frati, Bacigalupo, Chiappa, and Cocchi, to mention just a few, attest to this fact.

Portable organs of this type were rather expensive. In the middle of the 19th century a 24-key organ could cost the equivalent of about $1000 in terms of today's buying power. New organs built today cost from about $800 to $2000 depending upon the quality and scale. It is interesting to know that over the years barrel organs have kept pace nicely with monetary inflation!

### Construction and Musical Details

The portable hand-cranked barrel organ reached its ultimate form about 1830. The basic construction principles were never changed after that, and today the organs being built by such firms as Bacigalupo and Voigt are similar to models of the early 19th century. From 1912 onward paper roll organs were built by Bacigalupo. The barrel, keys, and rods were replaced by a tracker bar, a tracking device, and a series of pneumatics — but the rest of the instrument was similar to standard barrel-operated models.

All of the components of the barrel organ, except for the hand crank that is located on the right-hand side of the back of the instrument and except for the bass pipes that are glued to the bottom of the organ case, are located inside the case. The base on which the organ stands is screwed to the organ case and covers the bottom pipes on the sides. It can be removed easily when repair or tuning of the bottom pipes is necessary.

The hand crank turns a crankshaft which has two functions: (1) It turns the barrel around by means of two snail gears; one iron snail on the crankshaft meshes with a wooden snail gear mounted on the barrel; and (2) Two pump rods which push and pull four bellows up and down alternately to press air into a reservoir bellows. From the reservoir the air goes into the windchest.

Most organs of this type have from 8 to 12 tunes pinned on the barrel. The tune pins push the keys upward. A connecting rod is then pushed downward through a small hole in the windchest to open a valve. The valve then admits air through a channel leading to the base of an organ pipe. The desired pipe then plays.

The windchest is a complicated system of valves and channels. The largest of the portable organs have more than 100 pipes connected to the windchest and are arranged in register systems; up to four registers in some cases. Some elaborate models change one or two registers automatically, but these instruments are exceptions to the general rule.

Tunes are changed by lifting an "anchor" and moving the barrel slightly sidewise to another track so that all of the keys are in a slightly different position — ready to perform another tune. In his book, "The Fairground Organ," Eric V. Cockayne describes a Wright & Holmes barrel organ with an automatic tune-changing and repeating mechanism. This system was never used by builders on the European continent.

### Pinning a Barrel

Pinning a barrel is obviously a complicated job, but once the basic principles have been mastered a skilled music arranger can mark a 64-bar waltz tune in one hour. Some artisans do not even have to work out the organ arrangement in advance, but can work directly from the piano score or even from memory without the aid of sheet music.

The first step in barrel pinning is to glue paper on the barrel surface. Then the zero position — the place where all the tunes will start and end — must be marked. Some arrangers (the author for example) prefer to work with the barrel in the organ. Others use a pinning machine which holds the barrel. Some of these machines have a keyboard which can be adjusted to match the key positions on the organ. When a tune is pinned it must be laid out so that it will end just before the zero position, so that as many choruses as desired can be played after each other without interruption. Not all tunes have the same number of bars in the music. This problem is solved by a series of bar-wheels or gears which serve to spread the tune out over the entire barrel regardless of the number of bars it has. Thus a tune can be effectively "stretched to fit."

When a tune is pinned with the cylinder in the organ a large disc is placed on the center shaft of the barrel. The disc is divided into various numbers of bars and various different rhythms such as march (2/4, 4/4, or 6/8), waltz, tango, foxtrot, song, and so on.

The barrel is placed in the zero position. The arranger is then ready to begin. The key-pins are then pressed down on the barrel according to the musical score, thus marking the barrel with small pinpricks or holes. When a sustained note is needed the the beginning and end of the note are marked and a pencil line is drawn between the two points. Later a staple-like bridge will be fitted for the distance of the line. The 1/4 notes have normal pins with a smooth head, while 1/8 notes and staccato notes have sharp heads and are placed lower in the barrel. A staccato note is indicated by a small pencil mark beside the hole. Very short staccato notes are indicated by two pencil marks. There are many more rules that the arranger must observe. For instance, bridges must be ever so slightly shorter than the actual note value because the key-pin will take a brief moment of time to drop from the end of the bridge to its normal position and also because the pipe will sound for a fraction of a second after the key-pin reaches its rest position.

Bridges are made on a special device which can produce up to about fifty different lengths. According to Karl Bormann (in "Orgel und Spieluhrenbau") it took about three days to mark a barrel with 8 to 10 tunes (reference: Ignaz Bruder's notes). This seems to be a long time when we consider that in those early 19th century days a worker would stay on the job for more than 12 hours daily. However, if we add the time needed to put the pins and bridges then it would indeed take 35 to 40 hours, about the time mentioned. Also, Bormann says that first the melody was marked and then on the next turn of the barrel the countermelody and bass were added. Perhaps this system was used in some cases, but it would have been much more feasible to have marked the entire arrangement on one turn. Also, in this fashion the music would be arranged more precisely. As Bruder's arrangements were indeed excellent and precise it seems probable that he also arranged the entire score at once.

Most of the organ grinders hired the barrel organs from various companies. Usually a rental contract would provide for a specified number of new tunes to be pinned within the term of the contract, usually one year. Therefore, many organs had two barrels so that one barrel could be pinned with new tunes while the organ grinder was using the other. Not all tunes on a barrel were changed at once. Usually just two or three were changed at a time. This was done by removing the pins, gluing paper strips over the old holes and markings, and marking and pinning new tunes.

### A 1926 Survey of Barrel Organ Makers

In 1926 the following firms engaged in the manufacture (or at least advertised such) of portable hand-cranked barrel organs. Some were actually agents who had their name put on the organs. Allan Herschell Co. of North Tonawanda, New York, is an example.

#### GERMANY

Allstein: M.H. Howe, Kleebergstrasse 16

Berlin: Giovanni Bacigalupo, Schönhauser Allee 79 (firm founded 1891); Bacigalupo Söhne (owners: Giovanni Bacigalupo and Lino Gattorna), Schönhauser Allee 74a and 79; Eduard Hilger, Kastanienallee 34; A. Holl & Sohn, Alt-Landsberg-Süd; Albin Lenk, Frankfurter Allee 56 (founded 1875); Alfred Lenk, Schreinerstrasse 3 and Liebigstrasse 9

Bobischau, b. Mittelwalde, Schlesien: Franz Karger (founded 1882)

Borstendorf (Station Grünhainchen-Borstendorf, Sa.): Paul Schaarschmidt (founded 1899)

Düsseldorf: Gebr. Richter (owners: Eduard and Emil Richter), Schlosstrasse 65-67

Fürstenwalde a.d. Spree: A. Wittke, Wriezenerstrasse 1a

Halle a.S.: Giuseppe Rosasco, Trodel 2; Karl Stiller, Ludwigstrasse 15

Frankfurt Höchst a. Main: Heinrich Voigt, Königsteinerstrasse 103 (founded 1832)

Hannover: Adrian Fehrenbach, a.d. Christuskirche 10; Fritz Wrede (Hannover-Kleefeld), Scheidestrasse 20 (founded 1890)

Leipzig: Ernst Holzweissig Nachf. (owners: Georg and Ernst Simon), Reichstrasse 23

Magdeburg: Hermanne Bode, Grosse steinerne Tischstrasse 1; Raap & Sohn, Rote Krebsstrasse 37 (founded 1889)

Mülheim (Ruhr): Gebr. Wellershaus (owner: August Wellershaus), Hindenburgstrasse 32 (founded 1885)

Pirmasens: August Huber Jun., Hauptstrasse 71

Weimar: Franz Luther, Jacobskirchhof 12

Waldkirch i. Breisgau, Baden: Alfred Bruder, Kaiser Wilhelmstrasse; Gebr. Bruder (owners in 1926: Fritz Bruder and Franz Bruder), Goethestrasse 2; Wilhelm Bruder Söhne (owners: Franz Bruder II and Eugen M. Bruder), Langestrasse 5; A. Ruth & Sohn (owner: Adolf Ruth Jun.), Kastelbergstrasse (founded 1841)

#### AUSTRIA

Vienna: Franz Janisch (Joseph Janisch Nachf.) VII, Neubaugasse 47; Ferdinand Molzer & Sohn (owner: Ferdinand Molzer, Sr.) XIII/6 Reichgasse 42

#### CZECHOSLOVAKIA

Jung-Bunzlau (Mlada Boleslav, Böhmen): Franz Slabyhaud, Unterklostergasse 85 (founded 1860)

Kuttenberg (Kutna Hora, Böhmen): Adolf Bartunek, Tytgasse 496 (founded 1890)

Neuhaus (Jindrichuv, Böhmen): Josef Weber, Jungmannstrasse 27 (founded 1860)

Pilsen (Plzen): Josef Koudelka, Kolargasse

Prague: Johann Rubes, II Vysehradska Tr.; Johann Spicka, VI Hlavni Trida 28

Seestadt (Ervenice): Josef Loos (formerly Gebr. Loos), Brüxer Strasse 47 (founded 1847)

Uhersky Brod (Mähren): Blasius Zuja

Uherske Hradiste: Matth. Strmisko, Rybarnygasse (founded 1902)

#### BELGIUM

Antwerp: Emile de Vreese, Ballaerstraat 98; Vital Gosseye & Ed. Quateer, Duinstraat 62; Aime Koenigsberg Vve & Fils, Huybrechtstraat 32; C. Sammels, Lange Vlierstraat 25; Van der Mueren, Ballaerstraat 90

Ghent: J. Deprez, Quai de la Lys 38

Grammont: L. & Edmond Hooghuys, Rue de la Vigue 18 (founded 1880; successors to Louis Hooghuys)

Willebroeck: A. van Steenput Frères, Spoorwegstraat 25 (founded 1890)

#### FRANCE

Alfortville: Calembert, Rue de Vitry

Mirecourt: Poirot Frères, 5 Quai de Vieux

Nice: Nallino Frères, 36 Rue Bonaparte (founded 1872)

Paris: Ch. Marenghi, Avenue de Taillebourg 11e (founded 1902); Jerome Thibouville & Cie. (sales agents), 140 Rue St. Charles 15e

Valenciennes: Blanche-Petit & R. Goffart, 1 and 4 Avenue de Verdun (founded 1899)

#### ITALY

Airola: Giuseppe Abate

Bologna: Enrico Ogier, Viale Angelo Masini 20 (founded 1900)

Caltanisetta (Sicilien): D. Polizzi & Figli, Via degle Angeli

Casale Monferrato: Fratelli Venezia

Casalincontrada (Prov. Chieti): Michele D'Alessandro

Castrogiovanni: Donato Folisi

Cogollo del Cengio (Prov. Vicenza): Antenora Zordan, Via Umberto I.lo (founded 1848)

Como: Varesi & Pozzi, Via Carloni 5

Cuneo: Giuseppe Cavallo

Gambolo (Prov. Pavia): B. Bianchi

Giulianova (Prov. Teramo): Ferdinando D'Ascenzo, Via Colomia 16; Gerardo Janni, Via delle Giere 14

Milano (Mailand): Ditta Robbiati, Via Scaldasole 7; Ercole Rognoni, Via Conchetta 8

Napoli: Curci Fratelli, Via Roma 304/305; De Falco Fratelli, Via S. Sebastiano 40 (founded 1870); C. Fassone, Largo Tarsia 6; Bernardo Vivellino, Via Sapienza 11

Pavia: E.E. Mighavacca, Via S. Teorodoro 3 and Casa del Popolo 16e (founded 1888)

Novara: Antonio Montanini, Via S. Agabio (founded 1905); Ottina & Pellandi, Via Solferino 3 (founded 1884); Pietro Pombia, Corso Trieste 5; Pomella Fratelli, Corso Milano 10

Porto Maurizio: Maurizio Zuradelli, Via Giovanni Marsaglia 14

Ragusa Inferiore (Prov. Siracusa): M. Battaglia, Emanuele Largo Comizi 6; S. Borno, Via S. Francesco 38 (founded 1846); G. Giummarra, Via Orfanotrofio 65 (founded 1887)

Rieti (Prov. Roma): Giuseppe Boccanera; Doratore Tornitore

Treviglio (Prov. Bergamo): Ardenghi & Figli, Via Mazzini

Rome: A. Bianchetti & Figli, Via Cavour 206; Giuseppe Bonafede, Via Ricasoli 15; C. Bruttapasta, Via Montoro 15 and Via Flaminia 98; A. Marazzi, Via del Governo Vecchio 50; Fiore Mazza, Via Consolazione 112; Antonio Montese, Via Monserrato 9; Aless Scialanti, Via Cavour 175

Torino: Lino Miolis, Via Ornea 12; V. Restagno, Corso Vitt. Emanuele 90 and Via Romagnos 15; V. Vassalo, Via Michaele Angelo 1

#### UNITED STATES OF AMERICA

Detroit, Michigan: F.L. Flack, 16 Woodbridge Avenue East

Brooklyn, N.Y.: Molinari & Sons, 112 32nd Street

Coney Island, N.Y.: M.C. Illions & Sons, 2789 Ocean Parkway; W.F. Mangels Co.

North Tonawanda, N.Y.: Allan Herschell Co., Inc. (Spillman Engineering Corp.)

Philadelphia, Penna.: W.H. Dentzel, 3641 Germantown Avenue

#### HUNGARY

Bar-St.-Miklos: Drabek & Söhne, Nr.200

#### RUMANIA

Timisoara: Norbert Hromadka, IV Strada Vacarescu 29; Georg Huber, IV Strada Bratianu 16

### History of the Bacigalupo Family

We begin a brief history of a few of the more important makers of portable hand-cranked barrel organs:

The family of Bacigalupo no doubt was the leading manufacturer in this field. It all started when Giovanni Bacigalupo (1847-1914) went to London from his home town, Genoa, in 1867 and met Anselmo Frati. Frati maintained a small shop where he arranged and pinned music for barrel organs. Frati learned his trade earlier at the Gavioli works in Paris, and he now showed the young Bacigalupo how to arrange and pin.

After two years in London, Bacigalupo went to Germany and founded his own workshop for the purchase, sale, and repair of these organs. In the early days many instruments were shipped to Frati in London for barrel pinning. This cooperation between Bacigalupo in Germany and Frati in London continued for some time.

In 1870 Bacigalupo moved to Buchholzerstrasse No. 1 in Berlin and established his business at that address. One day Frati unexpectedly arrived from London. Frati disliked the English climate and came to Bacigalupo to discuss the formation of a new business in Berlin. Within a short time the firm of Frati & Co. was formed with Frati and Bacigalupo as co-owners.

The Frati business grew steadily, and in 1873 it became necessary to move to larger premises at Schönhauser Allee No. 73. Within a few years Frati's health began to decline. Later, in 1890, he decided to go back to Italy, the land of his birth, to seek a more favorable climate. This was to no avail; he was mentally ill and never recovered. In 1891 his interest in the Frati firm was bought out. Frati died shortly afterwards.

The firm was reorganized. Bacigalupo took the music arranger John Cocchi, and Graffigna, a businessman, into the firm as partners, and the firm of Cocchi, Bacigalupo & Graffigna was born. Soon over 100 workers were employed, making the firm Germany's largest in the portable organ field. This new era of prosperity soon came to an end. Cocchi was doing a poor job with the firm. When he went to San Francisco, California, in 1893 with six large organs the breakdown came. He sold all of the organs, spent the proceeds, and incurred an additional debt amounting to 20,000 gold marks! He was dismissed from the firm. In 1896 Cocchi formed a new firm with his father, Giuseppe Cocchi, at Lychenerstrasse 2/3 in Berlin.

Giovanni Bacigalupo had three sons and five daughters. The sons were: Louis Bacigalupo (1870-1957), Giuseppe Bacigalupo (1875-1922), and Giovanni Bacigalupo II who was born in 1889 and who is living today. Giovanni Bacigalupo II owns the firm of G. Bacigalupo.

In 1904 Graffigna died, and once again the firm was reorganized, this time under the name of Bacigalupo Söhne — owned by Giovanni Bacigalupo, Sr., and his three sons. In the following year the brothers parted. Louis went to the United States of America and founded his own firm there. Giuseppe started his firm under the name of G. Bacigalupo at Schönhauser Allee 79. Giovanni Bacigalupo II continued the firm of Bacigalupo Söhne with his father at Schönhauser Allee 74a.

In 1906 Louis Bacigalupo returned from California and went back to work with Bacigalupo Söhne. In 1907 he again went to America. He changed his surname to Bacigalupi and carried on an organ business until his death in 1957.

In 1922 Giuseppe died. The factory was continued by his son Giovanni until his death in 1933. In that year the business was taken over by a certain Luigi Bacigalupo who was entirely unrelated to the other Bacigalupo family until he married a daughter of Giuseppe (Giovanni's son). Giovanni Bacigalupo II did not want Giuseppe's old firm to continue to use the name of G. Bacigalupo when it was directed by Luigi who was not a "real" Bacigalupo, so Luigi was forced to change the name to L. Bacigalupo. The firm continued under this name until 1967 when Luigi died and the business came to an end.

In later years Giovanni Bacigalupo changed the name of his firm from Bacigalupo Söhne to G. Bacigalupo. This firm is still in business today at Schönhauser Allee 74a. This street is in East Berlin, and Giovanni Bacigalupo's firm is one of the very few private businesses in DDR (East Germany) today. A few new organs are produced each year, but mainly work consists of repair work done by the firm's three employees. Mr. Bacigalupo himself is in charge of music arranging for the barrels. He is one of the most gifted arrangers the portable organ field has ever known.

The Frati & Co. name was continued by setting up a semi-autonomous division after the reorganization and acquisition of control by the Cocchi, Bacigalupo & Graffigna interests. In the early 1900's the Frati division was sold to the Jacobi family and a Jacobi brother-in-law, Mr. Schmidthalz. Orchestrions, organs, and other instruments were made under the Frati name. The Russian Revolution cost Frati a loss of two million marks from its operations in that country. Financial difficulties set in, and J.D. Philipps & Sons, a Frati stockholder and the firm's major creditor, acquired the Frati operations in 1923.

### A. Ruth & Sohn

While the Bacigalupo firms were known for their fine portable barrel organs, the firm of A. Ruth & Sohn produced these and larger instruments as well. Andreas Ruth (born in 1813) founded this firm in Waldkirch in 1841 or 1842. Ruth learned the organ building trade from Ignaz Bruder (1780-1845) and had worked with Bruder's firm for several years before starting his own factory. The first Ruth products were small barrel organs and related instruments. The firm grew quickly, and soon large cylinder-operated organs with fully chromatic musical scales were built also.

In 1875 Andreas' son Adolf was put in charge of the factory. Later, in 1907, Adolf's son, Adolf, Jr. (1877-1938), continued the firm until 1938, with a 7-year interruption during World War I when he left to fight in the German army. After World War I the Ruth business was just a vestige of its former self and was mainly engaged in repairs of earlier instruments. For all practical purposes the manufacture of Ruth organs ceased just before World War I.

From 1900 to 1912 Ruth built a fine line of fairground organs. One of the smallest was Model 33 which had 52 keys. Styles 38 and 39 were the largest and had 96 keys. When the barrel became obsolete, Ruth used several music systems, including paper rolls and keyless cardboard (like that used by Wilhelm Bruder Söhne and Gebr. Bruder)

### Gebr. Wellershaus

The firm of Gebr. Wellershaus in Mülheim-Ruhr was founded by August Wellershaus (1861-1927) and Wilhelm Wellershaus (1867-1910). There were older organ traditions in the family. Wilhelm Wellershaus (1764-1821) founded in 1793 a firm for the repair of clocks. He was very interested in organs and experimented in the church pipe organ field.

Wilhelm's son Friedrich-Wilhelm (1796-1856) started his own business in 1832 and specialized in church organs and square grand pianos. Friedrich-Wilhelm's son Julius (1828-1911) followed his father's footsteps and entered the church organ field. Soon, small portable hand-cranked organs were built as were some very large cylinder organs, one model of which had 140 keys. Julius' sons August and Wilhelm founded the Gebr. Wellershaus firm.

Gebr. Wellershaus, although best known for barrel organs, built a large number of barrel-operated pianos and orchestrions as well. Many of these had animated figures on the fronts. All of these traditions were carried on later by August's two sons, August, Jr. (born 1897) and Emil (born 1900). The business came to an abrupt end in 1944 when a bomb completely destroyed the entire factory. This resulted in the loss of thousands of pipes, parts, components, and machines — and about fifty completed organs. It took several years to build up the factory again, but today it still is in business, mainly in the field of church organs and pianos, but some cardboard music books are still being cut for earlier instruments.

### Wrede

Fritz Wrede (1868-1944) was only 17 years old when he started in the organ business in Hannover-Kleefeld and began repairing and manufacturing small barrel organs with reeds. Later other instruments such as pan and trumpet organs of 24 to 36 keys were made.

In 1890 Wrede started the production of large cylinder-operated organs. From that time the firm grew rapidly. Around 1900 the book system was adopted for the larger fairground instruments. The production of the smaller hand-cranked barrel organs still continued, and the instruments of the firm earned an excellent reputation. Fritz Wrede worked very hard and did much of the work himself — from actually building the wooden pipes to the final tuning of the organs. He did not have many workers, but he was assisted by his wife, a son, and two daughters.

During World War I the organ building was discontinued and the small factory was used for the production of war materials. After the war ended Fritz Wrede started organ production again, and in the 1920's many organs were built. In 1933 the firm suffered severe financial problems, and the production was halted for some time. Fritz Wrede was not only a hard worker, he was a fighter as well. He started his business over again from the bottom. A small output of organs followed, but due to the fall in demand for these instruments, production never again reached pre-1933 levels.

In 1944 on March 28th the catastrophe happened: a heavy bomb attack on the town of Hannover completely destroyed the Wrede factory, and Fritz Wrede was killed in the ruins. His son and daughters decided that it would not be worthwhile to build up the factory again. Thus ended the history of Fritz Wrede's organ company.

### Chiappa

In London we find the organ company of Victor Chiappa. This firm was founded by Giuseppe Chiappa, an Italian, in 1864 when he came to London after having worked with Gavioli & Cie. in Paris. In 1867 he went to the United States of America, but he stayed there only until 1877 when he decided to return to London. He settled in London on Eyre Street Hill, a location where the works are still situated today under the management of Victor Chiappa.

Like most of the previously-mentioned companies, Chiappa started with the production of small hand-cranked barrel organs. Barrel-operated pianos were also made. In addition to selling instruments of its own make, the Chiappa firm was a sales outlet for Gavioli, Marenghi, Limonaire, Gebr. Bruder, and Wilhelm Bruder Söhne.

Giuseppe Chiappa had five sons, and two of them, Charles and Ludovico, carried on the business after Giuseppe's death. Ludovico was very musical and began arranging book music for organs in 1918. From this time onward the music was cut in London. Previously, music was imported from Gavioli and others.

Ludovico's son Victor continued the business after his father and through the difficult times of the 1930's. He still works today with four employees in the premises on Eyre Street Hill. The business consists of rebuilding and repairing organs and producing music books for the many fairground organs still in existence in England.

## The Bruder Family

One of the most important personalities in the barrel organ field was Ignaz Bruder, who was born in 1780 in Zell, Germany. He manufactured musical mechanisms (mainly for clocks) in Simonswald from 1806 to 1834, and from then on he built organs in Waldkirch – until his death in 1845. Ignaz was interested in learning a handicraft, but because his parents were poor people he had to learn the bricklayer's trade. He left home in 1797 and went to Mirecourt and Nancy (in France) where he first saw how barrel organs were made. He returned the following year with a small barrel organ which he copied and then donated to a blind beggar. In 1798 he settled in Simonswald where he worked as a bricklayer during the summers and repaired clocks during the winters. In 1804 he founded a company which made flute clocks. Beginning in 1806 these were fitted with moving figures. His first successful animated musical clock appeared in 1806 (a date which was later used by Wilhelm Bruder Söhne and also by Gebr. Bruder as their founding time). From 1806 onward the firm grew steadily.

Ignaz Bruder (January 31, 1780 - April 4, 1845) sired fifteen children, five of whom continued Ignaz Bruder's interest in building musical instruments. These were: Andreas Bruder (1807-1859), Xaver Bruder (1808-1888), Wilhelm Bruder II (1819-1882), Carl Bruder (who was born in 1823 and who later moved to Russia and built organs there), and Ignaz Bruder II (1825-1891).

Andreas and Xaver helped their father in his factory from 1829 until his death. In 1864 the four brothers (Andreas, Ignaz II, Xaver, and Wilhelm I) merged their interests and moved to a factory building in Goethestrasse in Waldkirch. Known as Gebrüder Bruder (Bruder Brothers), the firm was continued when the four brothers retired and turned the firm over to Ignaz II's son Fritz and Wilhelm I's son Franz. Ignaz II's remaining two sons formed Ignaz Bruder Söhne and the two remaining sons of Wilhelm I formed Wilhelm Bruder Söhne. All of these firms produced a large number of organs and orchestrions, with Gebr. Bruder having the largest volume of business.

## The Business Today

Today only the firm of Giovanni Bacigalupo builds barrel organs of the old type, and these are only built on special order. Such firms as Carl Frei, Jr., Wilhelm Tiedemann, Willy Vanselow, and others build roll-operated or book-operated small organs today, but due to the necessity of selling them for competitive prices they are of simpler design than their predecessors.

(Credit note: Information supplied by: Giovanni Bacigalupo; Douglas Heffer [photographs]; Mekanisk Musik Museum A/S; Jan L.M. Van Dinteren [and Kring van Draaiorgelvrienden] – Bruder genealogical information and general history)

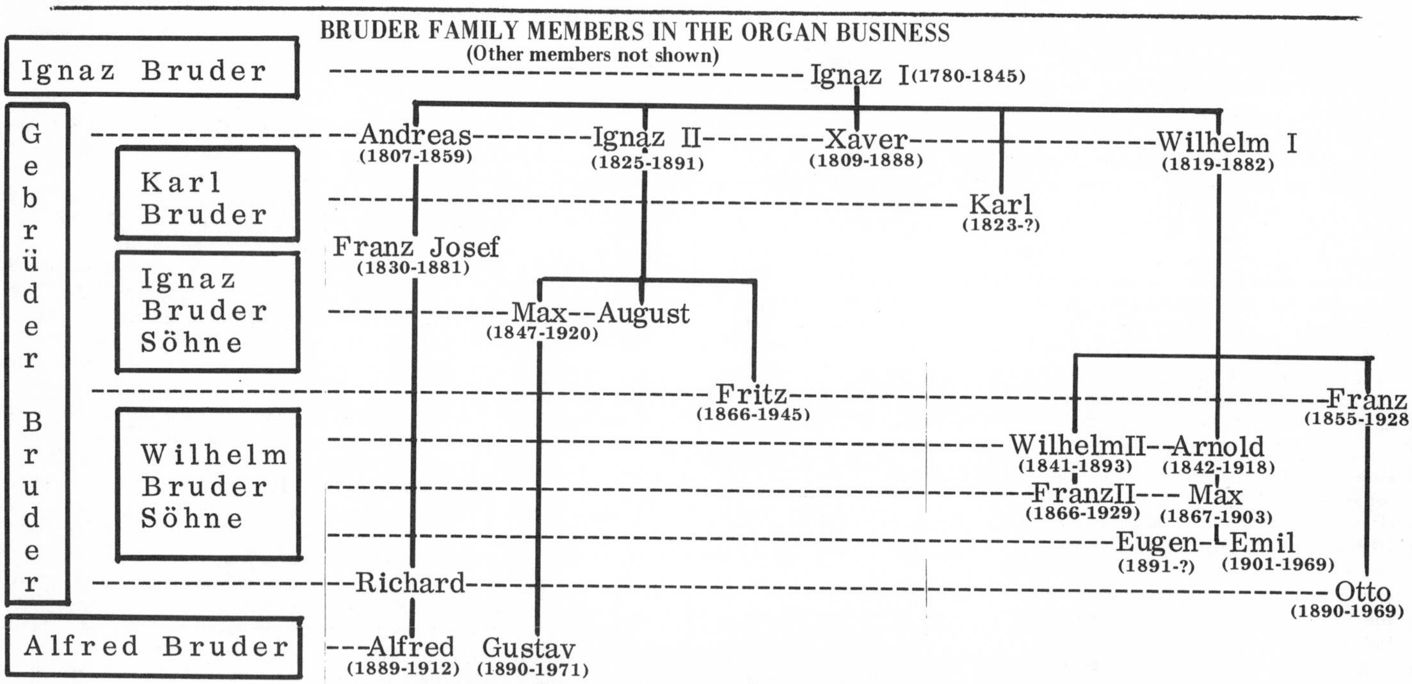


Above: "Bruder Family Members in the Organ Business" – a graphic representation of the Bruder heritage which began with Ignaz Bruder. Family members not engaged in the organ trade are not shown. The dates were obtained by Jan L.M. van Dinteren, whose sources of information included tombstones in the Waldkirch cemetery. Chart by Claes O. Friberg.

Right: Giovanni Bacigalupo plays one of his own compositions. (Photo taken in Berlin in 1965 by Douglas Heffer)

Left: Luigi Bacigalupo tries one of his own products. (Photograph taken by Douglas Heffer in front of Luigi Bacigalupo's workshop)

Below: An organ grinder from East Berlin photographed by Douglas Heffer in front of Luigi Bacigalupo's workshop. The instrument is a G. Bacigalupo hand-cranked barrel organ manufactured in the 1920's.

Above: Hand-cranked barrel organ by Cocchi, Bacigalupo & Graffigna.
Right: Organ by Bacigalupo Söhne.

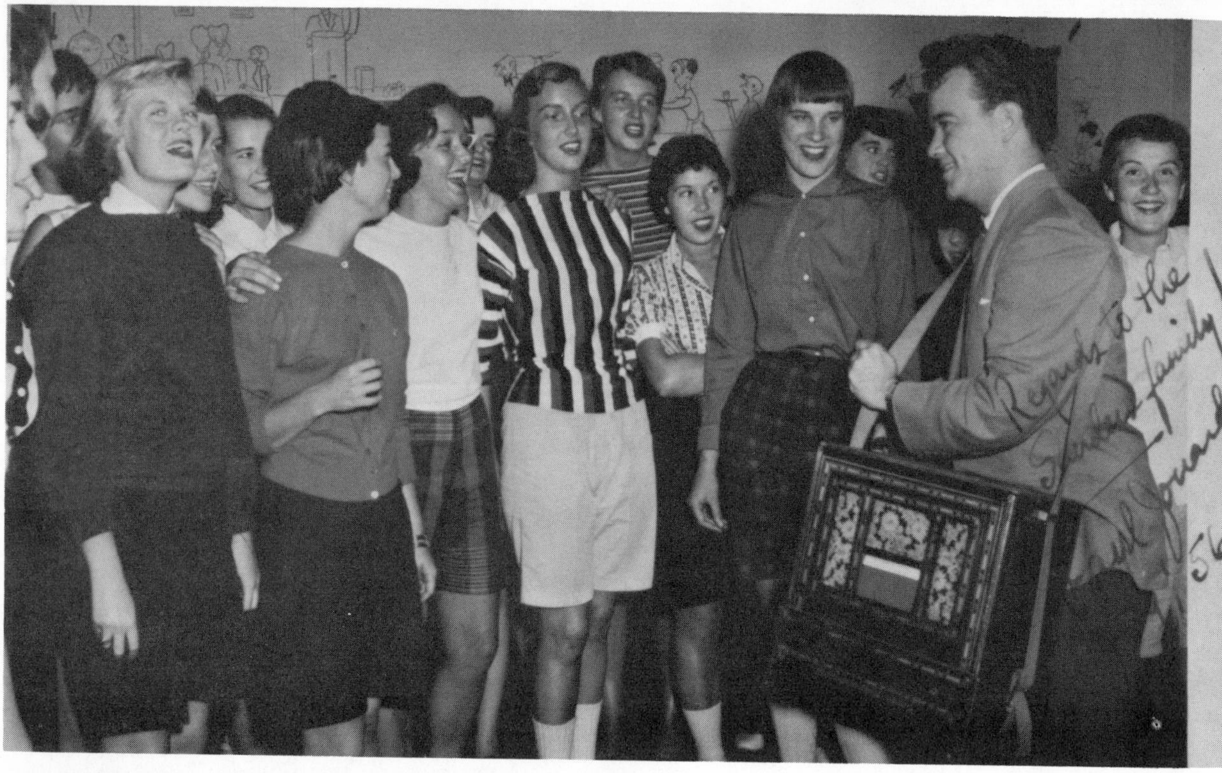

Above: Paul Jouard entertains a group of eager listeners with one of the Molinari hand-cranked barrel organs in his fine collection.

Below right: Other views of the Molinari organ in the Jouard Collection.

Left: Visitors examine small hand-cranked barrel organs at the Musical Museum in Deansboro, New York.

Above and left: Advertisements for Drehorgeln (hand-cranked barrel organs) printed in a German trade publication in the 1920's. The illustrations used are standard ones used by the magazine and do not represent specific instruments made by the Bruder or Bacigalupo firms.

Claes O. Friberg

Gebr. Riemer barrel organ in an ornate case. (Wallace McPeak photograph)

W.F. Holl (who died in the 1960's) with one of his new barrel organs.

Hand-cranked barrel organ made by Kamenik of Prague, Czechoslavakia.

Left: Organ made by Fritz Wrede of Hannover, Germany. Shown with front panel removed.

Right: Organ made by Rich. Töpfer of Berlin, Germany.

Above and left: Front and top/front views of a Bacigalupo Söhne 45-key trumpet organ. Note that the instrument is literally crammed with pipes – as are most hand-cranked barrel organs made years ago. Due to economic considerations, organs made by most craftsmen today are of simpler design with fewer pipes.

The Artizan Factories, Inc. were established in 1922 by a number of the original principals of the North Tonawanda Musical Instrument Works who left the latter firm after Rand obtained control. (See North Tonawanda Musical Instrument Works sections of this book for details)

The capital stock was $100,000.00 and the officers were: S.C. Woodruff, president; C. Maerten, treasurer; F. Morganti, vice president; and W.F. Schultz, secretary.

The firm produced a limited line of band organs. These were available with either endless roll systems or (usually) rewind-type rolls. Rewind-type rolls were offered in either a single roll or duplex format. The organs manufactured by this firm used compressed air (rather than the usual vacuum) to "read" the rolls as they passed over the tracker bar. This system was sound from a theoretical viewpoint as it eliminated clogging of the tracker bar, a problem in vacuum-actuated band organs.

In addition to building Artizan organs the firm undertook the repair of organs of other makes, often converting cylinder organs, cardboard book organs, and paper roll organs of other makes (especially of the North Tonawanda Musical Instrument Works) to use Artizan rolls.

In 1927 and 1928 the firm patented the Air-Calio, a calliope. These were sold in limited quantities. In addition, several different models of coin pianos, including some with pipes, were made. Sales of these were negligible and few are known today.

When Artizan entered the band organ business in 1922, Wurlitzer was not only dominant in the field, it was THE band organ business. The marketing abilities of Artizan were no match for Wurlitzer's, with the result that very few Artizan organs were ever made. It is ironic that most that were made were later converted by Wurlitzer to play Wurlitzer rolls!

When the author visited the factory site in 1967 the red brick building was still standing. The "high speed trolley line" that once ran by was a thing of the past and the organs and the dreams of the Artizan makers were long since gone.

### In Artizan's Own Words

The Artizan compressed air roll system was a valid one. Success was elusive for marketing reasons, not for mechanical reasons. The information below is from an Artizan instruction leaflet of the 1920's:

This company... is located at Erie Avenue and Division Street in North Tonawanda, New York, near to and adjacent to the High Speed Trolley line from Buffalo to Niagara Falls, and the trolley line from Buffalo to Lockport, Rochester, and the east. Each line stops in front of the plant. The factory, owned by us, is a brick building 40x130 feet, with 4 floors, is heated by steam and operated by electricity.

Our line of instruments covers military bands, electrically operated pianos, and automatically played orchestras from smallest to largest sizes.

Our military bands are the latest development in that line and are played by endless or spooled music rolls. We have patents pending on new improvements whereby the sensitive and troublesome suction system is dispensed with. By discarding the system and having only the compressed air system the number of working parts is reduced, the cost of maintenance is less, and troubles in keeping organs in good playing condition are reduced by over 50%.

Our reputation as organ builders, from 30 years experience, is well known. We use only the best of materials and skilled labor in the manufacture of our instruments and our instruments are as represented in every way.

A partial list of our improvements: (1) Elimination of the vacuum or suction system, the value of which cannot be estimated. (2) Cast malleable iron crankshaft, making breakage next to impossible. (3) Solid brass tracker bar, overcoming chance of leakage at joint and trouble cleaning tracker screen. (4) Unit blocks, taking valve action out of windchest. The unit blocks can be taken out, one at a time, by taking out two wood screws. There are no metal discs to corrode and destroy pouches. Pouches can be replaced, saving cost of blocks. (5) One train of gears on tracker frame system, eliminating any risk of not meshing as is the case when more than one train is used. (6) Positive gear drive from crankshaft to tracker frame, making slip impossible. (7) Cone friction drive for regulating time or tempo of music is so constructed that instant change of time is obtained by turning knob. (8) Construction of case whereby main bellows can be taken out of organ without knocking it down. (9) Cloth-covered rubber tubing used throughout organ, doing away with troublesome plain tubing and hard-to-repair lead tubing. (10) Direct connections from tracker bar to unit blocks, simplifying working parts and making location of trouble and repair work easier. (11) Waterproof glue used, making joints proof against sun, rain, and damp weather. We offer you instruments in which only the best of materials are used and with least possible parts, knowing one part is easier kept in order than two or more.

### Artizan Organs

The following Artizan organs are illustrated in this section:

Style A, 46 keys. Instrumentation of basses, wood trombones, wood trumpets, violin pipes, open and stopped pipes, 20" bass drum, 14" snare drum, and cymbal. In all 103 sounding instruments. 3 stops, one for trombones, one for trumpets, one for violins. 6'7½" high by 6'11" wide by 2'10" deep. Organs of the "A" group could be ordered with any one of these three roll systems: (1) duplex system using two 10-tune rolls; (2) single roll using an 18-tune roll; (3) endless roll system using endless rolls of 3 tunes per roll.

Style A-1. Instrumentation as Style A. Different case design.

Style A-2. Instrumentation as Style A. Also available with 14 bells for extra cost.

Style C, 52 (early catalogue notation, possibly a typographical error) keys, or 57 keys (probably). Instrumentation: basses, open, octave, and contra; wood trombones; wood trumpets; violin, open and stopped pipes in accompaniment and melody; 20" bass drum; 14" snare drum; cymbal. In all 136 sounding instruments. Three stops: one for trombones, one for trumpets, and one for violins. 7' high by 7'7½" wide by 2'10½" deep. Music roll system options the same as Style A. "The music is transposed and arranged by expert musicians with results surprising to band leaders and players."

Style C-1. 57 keys, the same as Style C but with different case design. Available optionally with 16 bells.

Style X-A, 46 keys. Instrumentation: basses, wood trumpets, 3 bassoons, violin pipes, flute pipes, bass drum, snare drum, cymbal. Also available without percussion effects. 4'1" high by 6' wide (with drums) or 3'6" wide (without drums) by 1'11" deep. Uses 10-piece spooled music rolls of the 46-key type. "Planned and designed for 'kiddie' and miniature rides of every description, and show platforms."

Style X-A-1. Instrumentation as Style X-A, but different case design. Available with or without drums.

Style X-A-2. Instrumentation as Style X-A, but different case design. Available with or without percussion.

### Artizan Organs Today

Few Artizan organs were made, and fewer yet survive. Most of those that do survive have been converted to play Wurlitzer type 125 or 150 organ rolls (but using the original Artizan mechanisms, except for the tracker bar system, and using the slotted roller over the roll to keep it pressed against the tracker openings) or have been converted to B.A.B. organ rolls.

———————

Note: The endless system of rolls, available on styles A and C but seldom ordered by customers, was a carryover of the endless system used earlier by the North Tonawanda Musical Instrument Works. In reply to a query from the author, Mr. Benjamin Rand told of the formation of Artizan: "After a few years [from the time that Rand took over] the group of North Tonawanda Musical Instrument Works former stockholders formed the Artizan Company, which never really got off the ground. The men in that company [at the beginning] were John Birnie, F. Morganti, Henry Tussing, and W.F. Schultz."

**ARTIZAN FACTORIES INC.**
MANUFACTURERS OF
AUTOMATIC AND MECHANICAL MUSICAL INSTRUMENTS
OFFICE FURNITURE AND FIXTURES
MILL AND MACHINE WORK

Style "A" Military Band—46 Keys

Style "A-1" Military Band—46 Keys

Style "A-2" Military Band—46 Keys

Style "C" Military Band—~~52~~ 57 Keys

Style "C-1" Military Band—~~52~~ 57 Keys

Style "X-A" Military Band—46 Keys

Style "X-A-1" Military Band - 46 Keys

Style "X-A-2" Military Band - 46 Keys

On this page are shown some of the Artizan organs made during the 1920's. As the accompanying text notes, these instruments divide themselves into three groups: the A, C, and X-A. Within each group there are different case designs to choose from. Style C was probably made only in the 57-key size. Original factory literature in the author's files shows the 52-key designation crossed out in ink and changed to 57 keys.

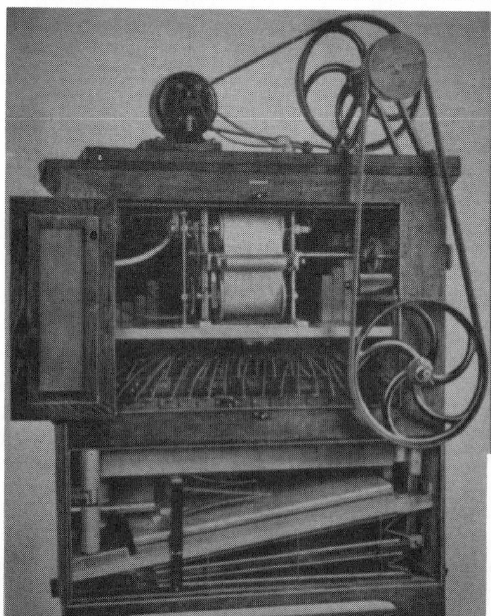

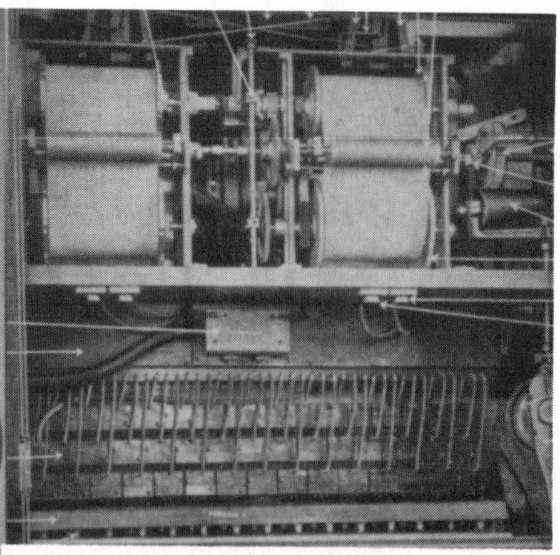

View of the back of two Artizan organs. The one on the left is of the single roll type; the one on the right, the duplex type. Note the slotted roller which holds the paper roll against the tracker bar, a feature necessitated by the compressed air reading system. In addition to rewind-type systems, some Artizans were built with endless roll systems.

**Importance of North Tonawanda**

North Tonawanda, New York, was the most important American center for the manufacture of military band organs. Eugene DeKleist pioneered the industry when he located there in the early 1890's at the behest of Armitage Herschell, amusement outfitters. From DeKleist's firm evolved the huge Wurlitzer works. Former DeKleist employees formed the Niagara and the North Tonawanda Musical Instrument Works companies. Principals of the latter firm then formed Artizan.

**THE BERNI ORGAN COMPANY**
**(importers and sales agents)**

FACTORY AND WAREROOMS:
219-221 WEST 19th ST., N. Y.

OFFICE AND SHOWROOMS:
216 WEST 20th ST., N. Y.

IN PRESENTING this catalogue, we take the pleasure and opportunity to thank our numerous patrons for their past favors and confidence placed in us—to those, however, who have never dealt with us, and consequently do not know our business methods, we desire to say that our reliability is vouched for by the hundreds of unsolicited testimonials we receive daily.

All our organs are constructed on the pneumatic system—thereby assuring the perfect regularity of their operation, rendering impossible the tearing of the cardboard music (such as unavoidably occurs with the paper-played spool system). Our mechanical action is so constructed that we have obtained the long desired results of prompt execution, viz.: "The direct attaque" and together with the incomparable harmony due to the perfect melody of every pipe used—and the aid of our famous registers—explains the superiority of our instruments and in the meantime justifies our success.

We have listed only those organs that have proven to be staple, most adapted to all outdoor amusements and which have given the best satisfaction to all expectations. The dimensions are made in accordance to the powerfulness and composition they represent, which is from 3 to 50 musicians.

We have added a line of organs specially constructed for travelling shows of all kinds, who heretofore have used bands, and the high reputation we have gained in this specialty is due to our straightforward guarantee and the production of an absolutely reliable instrument which will stand continuous transportation without losing its perfect orchestral harmony or get out of tune.

Our symphonic organs have replaced many bands in large amusement parks, a reliable tempo regulator is attached to all organs for skating rinks and dance halls, thus assuring the correct swing time that is essential to these amusements.

For Merry-Go-Rounds we have added the endless system of Cardboard music to our organs by means of which 10 to 15 selections can be played continuously without necessitating the slightest attendance.

THE BERNI ORGAN COMPANY.

**The Berni Organ Company was founded in New York City by Louis Berni, who came to America from Paris around 1900. A flamboyant showman, Berni's career is colorfully described in Frederick Fried's book, "A Pictorial History of the Carousel." Mr. Berni, it seems, liked nothing better than a hot controversy. His escapades with the "organ cartels" of Europe were many. During the 1920's Berni was an active Wurlitzer distributor. Later, Berni left America to spend the rest of his life living well in Europe.**

**The Berni Organ Company made no instruments of its own, but imported new and used organs from Gavioli, Ruth, Bruder, and others in France and Germany. Facilities were maintained, however, for the conversion of paper roll and cylinder organs to the cardboard music key frame system which used music books manufactured in Berni's own plant.**

**All sorts of organs were sold with the Berni imprint. The author, in fact, is the owner of a Wurlitzer 153 organ bearing "Berni Organ Company" as its only identification. A lively commerce in buying used organs in the U.S. and Europe and rebuilding them for resale resulted in hundreds of organs passing through the Berni premises. Frederick Fried estimates that Berni handled some 60% of the organs imported into America during the period of his firm's activity.**

BERNI

# "The Superb"---110 Key

**Representing a Symphony Orchestra of about 50 musicians.**
**The most perfect instrument ever built.**

## Instrumentation

| | |
|---|---|
| **Basses:** | 28 Stopped bottom pipes. |
| | 28 Open pipes. |
| | 14 Wooden reed pipes. |
| **Trombones:** | 14 Wooden reed pipes. |
| | 14 Brass reed trombones. |
| **Accompaniment:** | 30 Open pipes. |
| | 30 Stopped pipes. |
| | 15 Wooden reed pipes. |
| **Saxophones:** | 25 Open pipes. |
| **Barytones:** | 25 Wooden reed pipes. |
| **Trumpets:** | 25 Wooden reed pipes. |
| **Cornets:** | 25 Brass reed pipes. |
| | 21 Open pipes. |
| **Clarinets:** | 21 Stopped pipes. |
| | 42 Violin pipes. |
| | 21 Brass reed pipes. |
| **Violins:** | 150 Violin pipes. |
| **Piccolos:** | 150 Violin pipes. |
| | 25 Stopped pipes. |
| **Flutes:** | 25 Brass stopped pipes. |
| **Xylophones:** | 25 Steel. |
| | Total, 753 pipes. |

Price: $8,500, including 100 yards of music.

**American collectors owe a debt of gratitude to the late Mr. Berni for without him some of the most ornate instruments ever to touch American shores would still be in Europe or, for that matter, would never have been built!**

Magnificent carved front with life-size statues, the most elaborate facade ever made for an organ. The instrumentation the most complete; specially adapted for large amusement parks for concert purposes, dance halls, and skating rinks.

## DESCRIPTION

**Dimensions:** 30 feet long, 18 feet high, 5 feet wide.

## "The Reliance"---89 Key

**With bass and snare drums and cymbal set on detachable wings. The most perfect, powerful and melodious organ ever built; made to execute any selection or overture, accomplishing the exact effect of a Symphony Orchestra.**

| | |
|---|---|
| **Basses:** | 8 Bottom stopped pipes. |
| | 16 Open pipes. |
| | 8 Wooden reed pipes. |
| **Trombones:** | 8 Wooden reed trombones. |
| | 8 Brass trombones. |
| | 20 Open pipes. |
| **Saxophones:** | 20 Stopped pipes. |
| **Barytones:** | 20 Wooden reed pipes. |
| **Trumpets:** | 20 Wooden reed trumpets. |
| | 17 Brass reed pipes. |
| **Clarinets:** | 17 Open violin pipes. |
| | 17 Open pipes. |
| | 20 Open violin pipes. |
| **Accompaniment:** | 10 Stopped pipes. |
| | 10 Wooden reed pipes. |
| **Violins:** | 125 Violin pipes. |
| **Piccolos:** | 34 Open pipes. |
| **Flutes:** | 17 Brass stopped pipes. |
| **Xylophones:** | 17 Steel. |
| | Total, 412 pipes. |

**Four Pneumatic Registers**

Price: $4,500, including 100 yards of music.

**Above: "The Superb," indeed a superb 110-key instrument, probably nee Gavioli, was Berni's best foot forward. Several 110-key organs were originally sold in America. The specimen in the Dr. Robert Miller Collection (see Gavioli section of this book) was sold by Gavioli's own New York City office. Several others have been traced, with success for a while, and then with eventual failure. "That went up in smoke when the pier burned back in the 'thirties" was the fate of one 110-key organ; "It required so much repair after the 1938 hurricane that we just scrapped it," was the fate of another.**

**Left: "The Reliance," an ornate 89-key instrument which measures 22' wide by 18' high by 4' deep. Made by Ch. Marenghi of Paris.**

**Note: A doubtful "improvement" so far as collectors today are concerned was the register system which: "With one key we obtain the operation of 4 or 5 kinds of instrumental pipes [ranks] simultaneously – thereby necessitating less keys to the organs. . ."**

# Berni Organ Company

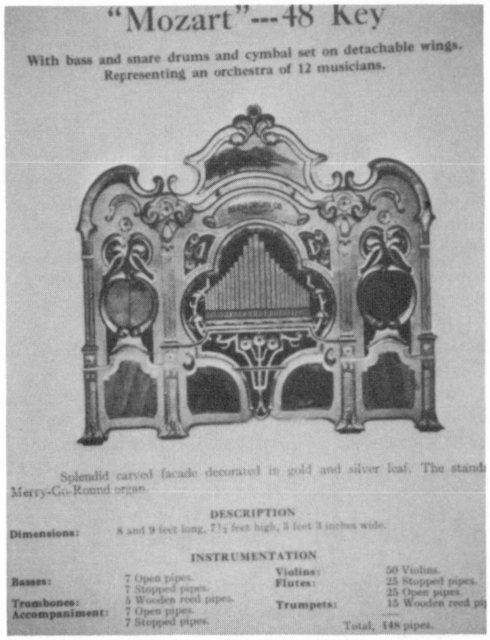

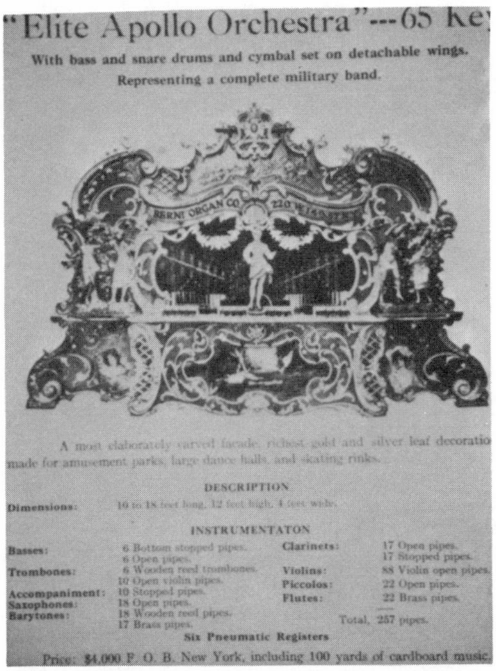


Berni Organs
(1913 - 1914)

To illustrate his catalogue Louis Berni used pictures from the literature of Gavioli, Bruder, and others. All original trademarks were replaced by the "Berni Organ Co." name and no indication was given of the instruments' true origin.

The pictures in the Berni catalogue were just "representative" of the instruments he sold, and actual instruments delivered were apt to differ considerably. Refer to the Gavioli section of this book and you will note that the "Elite Apollo Orchestra" (a name cribbed from Gebr. Bruder!) is illustrated by Gavioli's picture for its No. 717 organ of 89 keys.

Similarly, the 57-key "Berni Phone" shown on this page is of Gavioli origin (however, in this instance Berni concurs with Gavioli's key count of 57 and Gavioli's "25 musicians" estimate.)

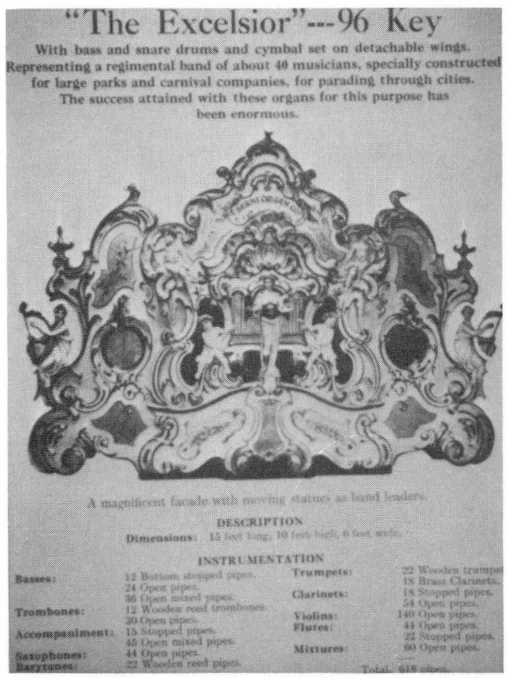

During the early years of the 20th century the E. Boecker Organ and Orchestrion Company, owned by Ernst Boecker (or Böcker) of New York City, imported a wide variety of automatic musical instruments from Europe. The firm's principal activity seems to have been the importation of piano-type instruments from Ludwig Hupfeld and Imhof & Mukle. Additional information concerning this aspect of Boecker's operations will be found in the Hupfeld and Imhof & Mukle sections of this book.

The Boecker enterprise continued in business until 1914. In that year the firm, then named the Original Orchestrion and Piano Company, went into bankruptcy.

Around 1908 Boecker issued an impressive catalogue which included descriptions of many styles of organs, primarily instruments imported from the Waldkirch, Germany, firms of Gebr. Bruder and Ruth & Sohn. Most organs were products of the latter firm. Illustrations from earlier Ruth catalogues were used in the Boecker presentation. It is interesting to note that at about the same time M. Welte & Sons, also of New York, issued a catalogue featuring some of the same Bruder and Ruth organs (See Welte band organ section of this book).

Boecker advertised that the firm was a "builder of cardboard and cylinder organs for merry-go-rounds, skating rinks, shows, etc. New cylinder and cardboard music — latest up-to-date tunes, made at our shops at short notice."

In another page of the firm's catalogue it was noted that: "We import and we build organs. We are importers of some of the very best European makes, and builders of any style organ that our customers may wish. We import and we build both cylinder and cardboard organs, after designs made by us or furnished by our customers. A special advantage is that at our factory we build organs and add as many pipes, etc., to the organ as our customers may wish, thus building organs that will play as strong as a band of 150 musicians if necessary.

"We wish to call particular attention to our new 'Perfection Organs' which we place for the first time this season on the market. These organs are built on an entirely new system and do away with the 'organ grinding sound' so often complained of. They play more on the line of a concert music, play very loud and sharp and are specially adapted to dance music, skating rinks, or merry-go-rounds.

"All our organs can be built any size our customers may wish. We are especially prepared to build organs for band wagons for street parades.

"We employ some of the best woodcarvers in our shops and build extra richly carved fronts when desired.

"Cylinders and paper music are made at our shops. We are prepared to make any music that our customers may wish to send in. All kinds of repairing, no matter what style of instrument, promptly executed."

The firm, while it never built organ chassis, did build some of its own facades. As suggestions, Boecker had an artist draw such models as 41 N and 54 B as shown in his catalogue. While the drawings are musically inaccurate (the display orchestra bells of model 54 B are all of the same size, for instance!), the sketches did furnish ideas for Boecker's customers. Other illustrations were simply taken from Bruder and Ruth catalogues. For instance, Boecker's 33 R to 36 R models are illustrated by Ruth's No. 36 A.

The Boecker instruments illustrated here are divided into several groups: Operated by pinned cylinders are several varieties of harmonipans (Boecker Nos. 1, 2, 3 M), hand-cranked "monkey organs" with pipes; claritons (Nos. 4 P to 8 P) with metal pipes and of powerful tone; "cornettinos" (9 P and 10 P) with exposed trumpets on the facade; military band organs (11 P to 19 R); and larger cylinder instruments designated as "concertinos," "concertos," and concert organs (20 P to 36 R).

Perforated cardboard organs, offered as having "pneumatic construction, new system, no teeth to come in contact with paper" (this apparently was similar to a form of the Bruder keyless system which used folding cardboard music books held tightly against the tracker bar by a series of rubberized rollers, or perhaps paper rolls were used — as Welte advertised for use on similar models), were assigned Boecker catalogue numbers 37 M through 41 N.

Catalogue numbers 50 B through 55 B were assigned to: "Perfection Organs — The dream of the organ manufacturer. The perfection of precision and exactness. Absolutely free from all troubles of the mechanism. The clear pneumatic suction action. There is nothing on the market that will compare with these organs in tune, arrangement of music, and correctness of playing. It is an organ built on an entirely new system and is the very perfection of the organ building art. It is perfection!"

Boecker's role as an organ importer was a minor one. However, he was important as the main United States importer of new Ruth & Söhn instruments. Several Ruth organs surviving today can trace their ancestry back to the Boecker enterprise.

THE E. BOECKER
ORGAN AND ORCHESTRION
COMPANY

1 M to 3 M.

4 P to 8 P.

# II CYLINDER ORGANS.

## a. HARMONIPANS.

| | | |
|---|---|---|
| No. 1 M. | HARMONIPAN, 33 keys, Cane flutes in view, Cylinder with 8 tunes | $ 115.00 |
| | Additional Cylinder | 35.00 |
| | Length 24½ in., Height 23 in. | |
| No. 2 M. | HARMONIPAN, 35 keys, Cane flutes in view, Cylinder with 9 tunes | 140.00 |
| | Additional Cylinder | 40.00 |
| | Length 24½ in., Height 23 in. | |
| No. 3 M. | HARMONIPAN, 44 keys, Cane flutes in view, Tremolo, Cylinder with 8 tunes | 155.00 |
| | Additional Cylinder | 50.00 |
| | Length 27 in., Height 26 in. | |

## b. CLARITONS.

Entirely new construction with nickel-plated Piccolos and brass Clarionets in view, elegant case.

| | | |
|---|---|---|
| No. 4 P. | CLARITON, Cylinder with 8 tunes | $ 120.00 |
| | Additional Cylinder | 30.00 |
| | Length 18½ in., Height 22 in. | |
| No. 5 P. | CLARITON, 33 keys, 10 brass Clarionets and 14 nickel-plated Piccolos in view, Cylinder with 8 tunes | 170.00 |
| | Additional Cylinder | 54.00 |
| | Length 21½ in., Height 23½ in. | |
| No. 6 P. | CLARITON, 44 keys, 13 brass Clarionets and 19 nickel-plated Piccolos in view, Cylinder with 8 tunes | 210.00 |
| | Additional Cylinder | 54.00 |
| | Length 28 in., Height 25½ in. | |
| No. 7 P. | CLARITON, 47 keys, 17 brass Clarionets and 19 Piccolos (double set) in view, three double Bass, chromatic scale, latest construction, special large Cylinder with 9 tunes and 80 bars | 265.00 |
| | Additional Cylinder | 73.50 |
| | Length 33 in., Height 37 in. | |
| No. 8 P. | CLARITON, 50 keys, 20 wood Clarionets, 18 Piccolos in view, three double Bass, Contra Bass, elegant Organ for Parks, loud but sweet music, special large Cylinder with 9 tunes, 80 bars | 315.00 |
| | Additional Cylinder | 77.50 |
| | Length 41½ in., Height 46½ in. | |

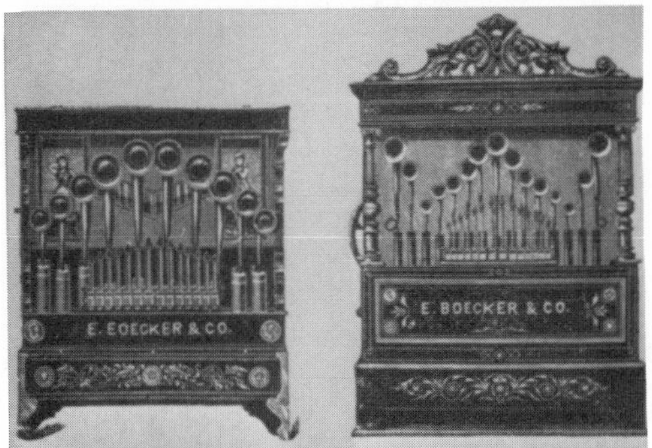


9 P. 10 P.

## c. CORNETTINO'S

For Side-Shows, Shooting Gallery's, Merry-go-rounds, etc.

| | | |
|---|---|---|
| No. 9 P. | CORNETTINO, 33 keys, 10 brass Cornets in view, Piccolos, Flutes, open and stopped Pipes, powerful deep Bass, very loud and attractive, Cylinder with 8 tunes | $ 175.00 |
| | Additional Cylinder | 48.00 |
| | Length 23 in., Height 28½ in. | |
| No. 10 P. | CORNETTINO, 38 keys, 12 brass Cornets in view, 14 Piccolos, Flutes, open and stopped Pipes, powerful deep Bass, splendid loud music, Cylinder with 9 tunes | 265.00 |
| | Additional Cylinder | 53.00 |
| | Length 30 in., Height 38 in. | |

Ernst Böcker

## d. MILITARY BAND ORGANS.

For Skating Rinks, Merry-go-rounds, Side Shows, Street Parades, etc. Exceedingly desirable instrument, where extra loud, far carrying tone of large volume is needed.

| | | |
|---|---|---|
| No. 11 P. | MILITARY BAND ORGAN, 43 keys, 15 brass Trumpets and 14 brass Piccolos in view, Flutes, violin Pipes, open and stopped Pipes, heavy Basses and Bombardons. Beautifully decorated. Cylinder with 10 tunes | $ 380.00 |
| | Additional Cylinder | 58.00 |
| | Length 42 in., Height 47 in. | |
| No. 12 R. | MILITARY BAND ORGAN, 57 keys, Trumpets, Bombardons, Clarionets and Piccolos in view, open and stopped Pipes, Bass and accompaniment Pipes, Cylinder 64 bars, 9 tunes | 675.00 |
| | Additional Cylinder | 73.00 |
| | Length 60 in., Height 67 in. | |
| No. 13 R. | MILITARY BAND ORGAN, same style as No. 12 R., 62 keys, Cylinder, 64 bars, 9 tunes | 725.00 |
| | Additional Cylinder | 77.00 |
| | Length 64 in., Height 67 in. | |
| No. 14 R. | MILITARY BAND ORGAN, same style as No. 13 R, with 2 automatic figures, playing bells, 66 keys, Cylinder, 64 bars, 9 tunes | 925.00 |
| | Additional Cylinder | 81.00 |
| | Length 67 in., Height 67 in. | |
| No. 15 R. | MILITARY BAND ORGAN, same style as No. 14 R, with 3 automatic figures (leader and 2 figures playing bells) 71 keys. Cylinder 64 bars, 10 tunes | 1125.00 |
| | Additional Cylinder | 86.00 |
| | Length 72 in., Height 69 in. | |

THE E. BOECKER ORGAN & ORCHESTRION CO.
22ᵈ 10th Ave., near 23rd St., NEW YORK, N. Y., U. S. A.

17 R to 19 R.

No. 16 R. MILITARY BAND ORGAN, same style as No. 15 R, with 3 automatic figures, 80 keys.
Cylinder 80 bars, 10 tunes ........ 1350.00
Additional Cylinder ........ 115.00
Length 79 in., Height 72 in

No. 17 R. MILITARY BAND ORGAN, same style as No. 16 R, with 5 automatic figures (one leader, 2 figures playing bells, 2 trumpeters), 90 keys.
Cylinder 80 bars, 10 tunes ........ $ 1675.00
Additional Cylinder ........ 127.00
Length 86 in., Height 75 in.

No. 18 R. MILITARY BAND ORGAN, same style as No. 17 R, with 7 automatic figures (one leader, 2 figures playing bells, 2 trumpeters and 2 dancing girls), 110 keys, Cylinder, 80 bars, 10 tunes 2400.00
Additional Cylinder ........ 152.00
Length 104 in., Height 83 in.

No. 19 R. MILITARY BAND ORGAN, 118 keys, open and stopped Pipes, bass and accompaniment Pipes, Violin Pipes, Flageolets, Piccolos, Clarionets with extra accompaniment Pipes, Trumpets, Bombardons, 9 automatic Figures (1 leader and 8 musicians), 6 revolving columes.
Cylinder 80 bars, 10 tunes ........ 3000.00
Additional Cylinder ........ 162.00
Length 111 in., Height 79 in.

On instruments No. 11 P to No. 19 R will be furnished snare and bass drums, and cymbal, either on top of organ or on the sides on brackets or in removable side partitions, if desired. Price from $75.00 up.

20 P.

*e. CONCERTINO'S AND CONCERTO'S.*

No. 20 P. CONCERTINO, 38 keys, 16 Piccolos in view, 12 Trumpets, Violin Pipes, open and stopped Pipes, sweet deep Basses, producing soft and yet powerful music. Cylinder 64 bars, 10 tunes ... $280.00
Additional Cylinder ........ 53.00
Length 41 in., Height 41 in.

No. 21 P. CONCERTINO, 43 keys, 14 Piccolos in view, 15 Trumpets, Violin Pipes, open and stopped Pipes, powerful Basses, Bombardons.
Cylinder 64 bars, 10 tunes ........ 320.00
Additional Cylinder ........ 58.00
Length 41 in., Height 46 in.

No. 22 R. CONCERTINO, 50 keys, Piccolos in view, 4 registers Pipes, Flageolets, pointed Pipes, Violin Pipes, open and closed pipes, Trumpets and Bombardons. Cylinder 54 bars, 10 tunes ........ 375.00
Additional Cylinder ........ 65.00
Length 55 in., Height 57 in.

23 R to 25 R.

THE E. BOECKER ORGAN AND ORCHESTRION CO.
22ᵈ 10th Ave., near 23rd St., NEW YORK, N. Y., U. S. A.

No. 23 R. CONCERTO, 57 keys, 5 registers pipes, Flageolets, Piccolos, pointed pipes, Violin pipes, open and stopped pipes, Trumpets and Bombardons. Very strong and full music, will defy any competition. Cylinder 64 bars, 9 tunes ........ 550.00
Additional Cylinder ........ 73.00
Length 61 in., Height 63 in.

No. 24 R. CONCERTO, 66 keys, 6 registers, Flageolets, Piccolos, pointed pipes, open and stopped pipes, Trumpets, Bombardons. Cylinder 64 bars, 9 tunes 700.00
Additional Cylinder ........ 81.00
Length 67 in., Height 66 in.

No. 25 R. CONCERTO, 76 keys, 6 registers, Flutes, Flageolets, Piccolos, pointed pipes, Violin pipes, open and stopped pipes, Trumpet with Flute accompaniment, Bass Trumpets, Bombardons.
Cylinder 80 bars, 9 tunes ........ 900.00
Additional Cylindar ........ 110.00
Length 74 in., Height 69 in.

No. 26 R. CONCERTO, style as No. 25 R, with 3 automatic figures (one leader) and 2 figures playing bells ........ 1100.00
Length 74 in., Height 69 in.

27 R to 29 R.

No. 27 R. CONCERTO, 96 keys, Flutes, Flageolets, Piccolos, pointed pipes, Violin pipes, Trumpets with Flute accompaniment, Bass Trumpets, Bombardons. Cylinder 80 bars, 9 tunes ........ $1400.00
Additional Cylinder ........ 135.00
Length 89 in., Height 77 in.

No. 28 R. CONCERTO, 116 keys, Flutes, Flageolets, Piccolos, pointed pipes, Violin pipes, open and stopped pipes, Trumpets with Flute accompaniment, Baritones, Bass Trumpets, Bombardons.
Cylinder 80 bars, 10 tunes ........ 1750.00
Additional Cylinder ........ 100.00
Length 110 in., Height 87 in.

No. 29 R. CONCERTO, 130 keys, Flutes, Flageolets, Piccolos, pointed pipes, Violin pipes, open and stopped pipes, double Basses, Trumpets with Flute accompaniment, Baritones, Bass Trumpets, Bombardons. Cylinder 96 bars, 10 tunes ........ 2150.00
Additional Cylinder ........ 197.00
Length 122 in., Height 91 in.

No 28 R. and 29 R will play the most difficult overtures and selections from operas.

33 R to 36 R.

## f. CONCERT ORGANS.

These instruments play forte and piano and are especially adapted for concert music, such as overtures, operas, etc.

No. 30 R. CONCET ORGAN, 58 keys, Bass and accompaniment pipes, Violin pipes, pointed pipes, Piccolos, Flageolets, Flutes, Trumpets, Bombardons, Automatic mixture pipes.
Cylinder 64 bars, 10 tunes ........ 650.00
Additional Cylinder ........ 73.00
Length 61 in., Height 63 in.

No. 31 R. CONCERT ORGAN, same style as No. 30 R, but enlarged scale, 66 keys. Cylinder 90 bars, 10 tunes 850.00
Additional Cylinder ........ 95.50
Length 77 in., Height 76 in.

No. 32 R. CONCERT ORGAN, same style as 31 R, but enlarged scale, contains 80 keys.
Cylinder 80 bars, 10 tunes ........ $1075.00
Additional Cylinder ........ 115.00
Length 79 in., Height 71 in.

No. 33 R. CONCERT ORGAN, 100 keys, Bass and accompaniment pipes, Violin pipes, pointed pipes, Piccolos, Trumpets with Flute accompaniment, Bass Trumpets, Bombardons, automatic register mixture Pipes, 3 automatic Figures (one leader and two figures playing bells).
Cylinder 80 bars, 10 tunes ........ 1750.00
Additional Cylinder ........ 140.00
Length 96 in., Height 79 in.

No. 34 R. CONCERT ORGAN, 114 keys, Bass and accompaniment pipes, Violin pipes, Cello pipes, Flageolets, pointed pipes, Piccolos, Pistons, Trumpets with flute accompaniment, Bass Trumpets, Baritones, Bombardons, two automatic registers mixture pipes, 11 Figures (one leader, 2 figures playing bells, 2 trumpeters, 2 dancing girls, 4 ornamental figures) and 2 revolving columns, Cylinder 80 bars, 10 tunes ..... 3000.00
Additional Cylinder ........ 157.50
Length 158 in., Height 89 in.

No. 35 R. CONCERT ORGAN, 128 keys, Bass and accompaniment pipes, Violin pipes, Cello pipes, Flageolets, pointed pipes, Piccolos, Pistons, Trumpets with Flute accompaniment, Bass Trumpets, Baritons, Bombardons, two automatic registers mixture pipes, 19 Figures (one leader, 2 trumpeters, 4 figures playing bells, 8 dancing girls, 4 ornamental figures) and 6 revolving columns, Snare and Bass drums and Cymbal. Cylinder 96 bars, 10 tunes ........ 4000.00
Additional Cylinder ........ 194.00
Length 184 in., Height 89 in.

No. 36 R. CONCERT ORGAN, 140 keys, Bass and accompaniment pipes, Violin pipes, Cello pipes, Flageolets, pointed pipes, Piccolos, Pistons, Trumpets with Flute accompaniment, Bass Trumpets, Baritons, Bombardons, two automatic registers mixture pipes, 25 figures (one leader, figures playing bells, trumpeters, violin players, dancing girls, ornamental figures), revolving columns, Snare drum, Bass drum, Kettle drum, Cymbal, Cylinder 96 bars, 10 tunes, wonderful attraction ........ 5250.00
Additional Cylinder ........ 211.00
Length 193 in., Height 93 in.

## III PERFORATED CARDBOARD ORGANS.

No. 37 M. ORCHESTRA ORGAN, 57 notes, contains Violin pipes, Flutes, pointed pipes, Flageolets, open and stopped pipes, Basses, Contrabasses, Trumpets, Bombardons, automatic register mixture pipes, Snare and Bass drums and Cymbal on removable side niches, elegant front in bright colors with artistic decorations.
Including 100 yards of music ........ $1100.00
Music sheets per yard ........ 75c
Length 64 in., Height 67 in.

No. 38 N. ORCHESTRA ORGAN, 60 notes, contains Violin pipes, Flutes, pointed pipes, Flageolets, heavy Basses, open and stopped pipes, Trumpets with accompaniment pipes, Trumpets with Flute accompaniment, Bombardons, automatic register, Snare and Bass drum and cymbal on removable side niches, with figure, richly decorated front. Including 100 yards of music 1200.00
Music sheets per yard ........ 80c
Length 111 in., Height 69 in.

No. 39 N. ORCHESTRA ORGAN, 70 notes, contains Violin pipes, Flutes, pointed pipes, Flageolets, heavy Bass, open and stopped pipes, mixture pipes, Trumpets with accompaniment pipes, Bombardons, automatic register, one Figure, Snare and Bass drum and cymbal on removable side niches, richly decorated front.
Including 100 yards of music ........ 1600.00
Music sheets per yard ........ 85c
Length 120 in., Height 69 in.

No. 40 N. ORCHESTRA ORGAN, 82 notes, chromatic scale, 4 registers open and stopped pipes, 3 registers Violin pipes, Cello pipes, Flutes, mixture pipes, Trumpets with accompaniment pipes, Basses, Contra Basses, Bombardons, automatic register, 3 automatic Figures, Snare and Bass drum and cymbal on removable side niches.
Including 100 yards of music ........ $2100.00
Music sheets per yard ........ 1.00
Length 126 in., Height 71 in.

40 N.

41 N.

No. 41 N. ORCHESTRA ORGAN, 94 notes, chromatic scale and full instrumentation, containing 4 registers, open and stopped pipes, 3 registers Violin pipes, Flutes, Violincello pipes, French horns, Trumpets and Clarionets with Flute accompaniment, Basses, Contra Basses, Bass Trumpets, Bombardons, Snare and Bass drum and Cymbal on removable side niches. This organ plays from the sweetest pianissimo swelling in volume to the grandest fortissimo.
Including 100 yards of music ........ 2950.00
Music sheets per yard ........ 1.25
Length 142 in., Height 79 in.

51 B.

## b. "PERFECTION" *ORGANS.*

**The dream of the Organ manufacturer. The perfection of precision and exactness. Absolutely free from all troubles of the mechanism. The clear pneumatic suction action.** There is nothing in the market, that will compare with these organs in tune, arrangement of music and correctness of playing. It is an organ built on an entirely new system and is the very perfection of the organ building art. It is **perfection !**

No. 50 B. PERFECTION ORGAN, 57 notes, containing open and stopped pipes, 3 registers Violin pipes, 4 registers Flageolets, Flutes, Violin, Piccolos and open Piccolo pipes, Trumpets with Flute accompaniment, Bass, Contra Basses, Quintatur, dulce Bombardons, automatic Piano and Forte register, Snare and Bass drum and Cymbal on removable side niches.
Including 100 yards of music ........ $1450.00
Music sheets per yard ........ 75c
Length 135 in., Height 82 in.

No. 51 B. PERFECTION ORGAN, same style as No. 50 B with richly carved front and one register more Violin pipes, including 100 yards of music 1550.00
Music sheets per yard ........ 75c
Length 135 in., Height 82 in.

No. 52 B. PERFECTION ORGAN, 76 notes, containing open and stopped pipes, 4 register Violin pipes, Cello pipes, Flageolets, Flutes, Violin Piccolos, Clarinets and Trumpets with Flute accompaniment, Basses, Contra Basses, Dulce Bombardons, mixture pipes, automatic register, Snare and Bass drum and Cymbal, 4 Figures (two with electric light), including 100 yards of music ... 2250.00
Music sheets per yard ........ 1.00

No. 53 B. PERFECTION ORGAN, 78 notes, same style as No. 52 B with automatic Xylophon register.
Including 100 yards of music ........ 2500.00
Music sheets per yard ........ 1.00

No. 54 B. PERFECTION ORGAN, 90 notes, containing open and stopped pipes, Violin pipes, Cello pipes, Flageolets, Flutes, Violin Piccolos, Trumpets and Baritons with Flute accompaniment, 12 chromatic Basses and Contra Basses, 12 chromatic Dulce Bombardons, **6 automatic registers,** Chimes and Xylophon, Snare and Bass drum, kettle drum, Cymbal. The first entirely chromatic organ ever built! This organ has effects never produced on organs before, having 6 automatic registers and playing from the sweetest pianissimo swelling in volume to the grandest fortissimo, equal to a band of 50 pieces.
Including 100 yards of music ........ 3000.00
Music sheets per yard ........ 1.25

No. 55 B. PERFECTION ORGAN, 100 notes, same style as No. 54 B with enlarged registers of Flutes and Violin pipes, open and stopped pipes, Cornets, Clarionets.
Price, depending on contents, carving and number of figures, etc. ......$3750.00 to 6500.00
Music sheets per yard ........ 1.40

52 B.

54 B.

53 B.

55 B.

# GEBRÜDER BRUDER
# IGNAZ BRUDER SOHNE
# WILHELM BRUDER SOHNE

The world's most famous organ building town was Waldkirch, located deep in Germany's Schwarzwald or Black Forest district. In this small town many different firms, including branches of Gavioli and Limonaire, manufactured hand-cranked organs, fairground organs, and related instruments and shipped them to all parts of the world.

Of all Waldkirch organ makers the foremost family was Bruder. In the 19th century the family members operated three firms: Gebrüder Bruder (Bruder Brothers), Ignaz Bruder Söhne (Ignaz Bruder's Sons), and Wilhelm Bruder Söhne (Wilhelm Bruder's Sons).

Ignaz Bruder (January 31, 1780 - April 4, 1845) sired fifteen children, five of whom (Andreas, Ignaz II, Xaver, Karl, and Wilhelm I) continued Ignaz Bruder's interest in building flute-playing clocks, small hand-cranked organs, and other musical devices.

Andreas and Xaver helped their father in his factory from 1829 until Ignaz I's death in 1845. In 1864 four of Ignaz I's sons (all but Karl) merged their interests and moved to a factory building in Goethestrasse in Waldkirch. Known as Gebrüder Bruder, the firm was continued in later years by certain sons of the original founders.

Two of Ignaz II's sons, Max and August, formed a separate firm, Ignaz Bruder Söhne. Two of Wilhelm I's sons, Wilhelm II and Arnold, formed still another firm, Wilhelm Bruder Söhne. All of the Bruder firms produced a large number of organs and orchestrions, with Gebr. Bruder having the largest volume of business.

The products of the three Bruder firms were quite similar over the years. Similar also were certain organs made in Waldkirch by Ruth & Sohn. Certain Ruth instruments employed facades identical to those used on Gebr. Bruder fairground organs.

In the early 19th century many flute-playing clocks, usually called "Spieluhren" or "Flötenuhren" (organ or flute-playing clocks) were made. Most contained between twenty and thirty pipes arranged in one or two ranks. Larger models had a more extensive musical scale, but only a few of these were made. Some clocks had trumpeters, automaton musicians, or other tiny moving figures.

From 1850 to 1900 the production of barrel-operated (and, later, roll-operated) orchestrions was a large industry in the Black Forest area. In the nearby town of Freiburg the firm of M. Welte & Sons became the world's leading maker of this type of instrument. In Vöhrenbach several makers produced barrel orchestrions. Other builders were located in Lenzkirch, Waldkirch, and other small communities. In Waldkirch the Bruders produced a wide variety of such instruments. In the 1890's Ignaz Bruder Söhne issued a listing of ten different cylinder organs and noted that the building of even larger instruments was a speciality of the firm.

While many large orchestrions were made by the Bruders, few of these survive today. Better known are the small hand-cranked organs which were made by the thousands for use on city streets, in carnivals, and in similar places where small but loudly-voiced musical instruments were needed to attract attention. The Bruder instruments, produced by all three Bruder firms, were sold all over the world.

From the late 19th century until the 1930's Wilhelm Bruder Söhne and Gebr. Bruder manufactured many different varieties of fairground organs. Early models were played by pinned wooden cylinders. Later organs used folding cardboard music books or music rolls.

Beautifully crafted with ornate facades and with powerfully yet sweetly voiced pipes the Bruder organs soon achieved worldwide fame. In America alone the Bruder instruments were imported by more agents than were the organs of any other European maker. Berni, Parker, Mangels, and Wurlitzer each imported Bruder instruments, in most instances concealing their original identity. Gebr. Bruder provided illustrations for its agents and even catalogues which provided a space for the agent's name and omitted any mention of Bruder.

A circa 1912 catalogue noted: "The organs and musical instruments described herein are first class. They are of strong and solid construction; only the best materials are used. The ornamentation of the cases is practical and artistic.

"The voicing and the musical effects are done with orchestral arrangement of the music books in mind. The [Bruder] instruments have gained a worldwide reputation as being the best in the domain of mechanical concert organs.

"The different models shown in this catalogue are in arrangement as well as in musical effects adapted to the purpose for which they are intended: merry-go-rounds, theatres, stage shows, concert or dancing music, or whatever.

"Special wishes of customers concerning the size or design of the instrument or the arrangement of the music are considered as far as possible.

"By a special method, the result of long years of experience, each instrument, if requested, can be constructed in a special manner to suit tropical climates; by this process the effects of tropical heat or humidity on musical instruments can be completely avoided. The execution of this Special Construction for Tropical Climates involves an additional 10% on the catalogue prices.

"The weights and sizes of the different instruments are only approximate as all improvements and innovations are at once adopted. As all our work is most carefully done we cannot guarantee delivery to an exact date.

"With regard to barrel organs, the music pieces can be supplied in accordance with the wishes of customers so far as it is possible, having regard for the different tonal scales of the instruments. In the case of instruments playable with folding cardboard music books, the music selections may be chosen from a list, but any other composition will be made without extra charge if it is suitable for the model. For music pieces not known in this country we ask our customers to send the sheet music, if possible arranged for orchestra, otherwise for piano.

"Repairs of all kinds are carefully done and are charged at the very lowest prices."

The Gebr. Bruder organ business closed in 1930. In later years customers of the former business were serviced by Otto Bruder, Gustav Bruder, and others who continued to make music rolls and books and to repair instruments.

Most 20th century large Bruder organs used folding cardboard music which played on keyless frames. These resembled an ordinary key frame in appearance but had a tracker bar instead of steel keys. The folding cardboard music books were firmly held in place by two rubber rollers and a slotted brass roller as they passed over the tracker bar.

Later, Gebr. Bruder manufactured a number of organs which used tracker bars and rewind-type perforated paper music rolls.

A number of Bruder organs, mostly Gebr. Bruder instruments, survive today. They are highly regarded as being among the best of their kind ever made.

(Information courtesy of Jan van Dinteren and Claes O. Friberg)

Note: For more information on the Bruder family refer to the "Portable Hand-Cranked Barrel Organ" pages by Claes O. Friberg.

—Similarity of Certain German Organ Facades—

The similarity of certain facades used by different German organ makers is accounted for by the common use of certain woodcarvers and suppliers. Ferdinand Demetz (see advertisement on page 710) carved facades and figures for Gebr. Wellershaus, Gebr. Richter, and for Gavioli, the French organ builder. Mariënfeld, the Hannover-Kleefeld sculptor, designed and carved the fronts for Fritz Wrede. Wrede's figures were made by Scheck (of Recklingen), the fronts were painted and gilded by Jäuslin, and percussion effects were obtained from Link (of Weissenfelds a.d. Saale). Joseph Dopp, famous Waldkirch sculptor, designed and produced fronts for Ruth, Gebr. Bruder, Wilhelm Bruder Söhne, and other Waldkirch firms — thus accounting for the similarity in appearance among certain of those firms' products. (Information courtesy of Jan L.M. van Dinteren)

## —Ignaz Bruder Söhne—

Ignaz Bruder Söhne manufactured a wide variety of organ clocks, hand-cranked organs, orchestrions, and church organs. Shown on this page are two orchestrions, one operated with a paper roll and the other with a pinned cylinder. The style on the left, designated as No. 1, was manufactured shortly after 1900. Note that the center plaque has been left blank — the illustration used was a "standard engraving" and could bear any name that the seller wished. The instrument shown at the right is barrel-operated and dates from the 1890's. At that time orchestrions were offered from 2,500 marks to 14,000 marks. Each was supplied with six cylinders of eight tunes per cylinder. Larger orchestrions priced up to 30,000 marks could be built on special order.

Ignaz Bruder Orchestrions: In the 1890's Ignaz Bruder Söhne offered the following orchestrion models:

| | |
|---|---|
| No.1 | 50 keys; 5 registers; 157 pipes; 2.8 meters high; Price: 2500 Mk. |
| No.1-A | 45 keys; variation of above; 1500 Mk. |
| No.1-B | 48 keys; variation of above; 2000 Mk. |
| No.2 | 60 keys; 6 registers; 200 pipes; 3.1 meters high; 3300 Mk. |
| No.3 | 65 keys; 7 registers; 216 pipes; 3.5 meters high; 4200 Mk. |
| No.4 | 74 keys; 8 registers; 261 pipes; 3.75 meters high; 5400 Mk. |
| No.5 | 79 keys; 11 registers; 309 pipes; 4.2 meters high; 7200 Mk. |
| No.6 | 85 keys; 332 pipes; 4.2 meters high; 8600 Mk. |
| No.7 | 96 keys; 12 registers; 433 pipes; 4.35 meters high; 11000 Mk. |
| No.8 | 110 keys; 14 registers; 542 pipes; 4.5 meters high; 14000 Mk. |

All of the preceding were equipped with drum and percussion effects. The number of registers for No. 6 was not given. Similar-appearing instruments were made by Imhof & Mukle, Welte, Heizmann, and others in nearby Schwarzwald (Black Forest) towns.

---

Gustav Bruder
(1890-1971)

## —Gustav Bruder—

Born in 1890, Gustav Bruder carried on the family tradition of music as soon as he was old enough to study the subject. In his own words (in a letter to Art Reblitz):

"I first came to the Gebr. Bruder organ factory as an apprentice in May 1908. I already had taken four years of school at the 6-year Waldkirch Realschule with good results. I attended the nearby Waldkirch Music School until I was 15 years old, obliged to acquire basic knowledge of music theory and piano playing. I later expanded this knowledge through diligent concert-going in nearby Freiburg and by playing in chamber music ensembles with good friends...

"During my apprenticeship in the organ factory of Gebr. Bruder (1908-1911) I was primarily engaged in practical organ building. However, I also often had the opportunity to help do voicing with the copartners of the firm who were responsible for tuning and voicing; and I also collected useful experience with this work. In actuality I learned the marking and arranging of cylinders and cardboard music for organs by listening when completed organs were regulated nearby and, in the process, when music arrangements were played through. I had to install my first self-marked barrel organ cylinder by myself. There were no music rolls for organs yet at the time [barrel and book organs were the types being made]. Music rolls were first introduced in the early 1920's by Gebr. Bruder. Of course, during my apprenticeship I occasionally had the chance to complete music arrangements for organs of various sizes.

"At the termination of my apprenticeship I first helped my old father with the production of barrel organs in his small factory for two years, and by the summer of 1913 I was first employed as a music-plotter and arranger by the Weber orchestrion factory..."

Gustav Bruder and a co-worker, Otto Kern, went on to arrange some of the most sophisticated arrangements ever produced for automatic musical instruments. These were used on Weber orchestrions of the 1920's. In the late 1920's when the Weber "Maesto" and "Elite" orchestrions were designed, Gustav Bruder played an important part.

An idea of Gustav Bruder's care and patience may be gained from his description of arranging a Maesto orchestrion roll: "In order to arrange and perfect a Maesto roll with four songs I spent an average of three weeks. When the notes were on paper, only half the work was done; then the entering of the complex register changes required an equal amount of time."

Wilhelm Bruder Söhne organ as pictured on the firm's letterhead of the 1920's.

Above: No. 76, small book-operated organ for use with small carousels, kiddie shows, etc. Cost 1400 marks circa 1930. Music books cost 1.6 marks per meter. 39 keys. 4 registers of pipes; bass drum, snare drum, cymbal.

No.77. Book-operated. Designated as the "Ersatz Walzenorgel" (Imitation Barrel Organ) model. 40 keys. 5 registers. Popular circa 1930. "With very loud, rich, and pleasing music" noted the catalogue.

Key frame, or, more correctly, "keyless frame," of a Wilhelm Bruder Söhne organ of the early 1930's. The instrument uses folding cardboard books which are pressed tightly against the tracker bar (with hole openings, not metal keys) by a slotted brass roller. Organs of Wilhelm Bruder Söhne and Gebr. Bruder were made in two main music systems: (1) the "keyless frame" cardboard system as shown above, and (2) the perforated paper roll system using rewind-type paper rolls.

Wilhelm Bruder Söhne organ somewhat similar in appearance to Wurlitzer's 146A, but with extra side panels. (Harry Beach Collection; Don MacDonald, Jr. photograph)

Above: The Wilhelm Bruder Söhne works as shown on the firm's letterhead. The ruins of the ancient castle on the hill still overlook the town today. Right: Wilhelm Bruder Söhne organ in the collection of Emil Baude.

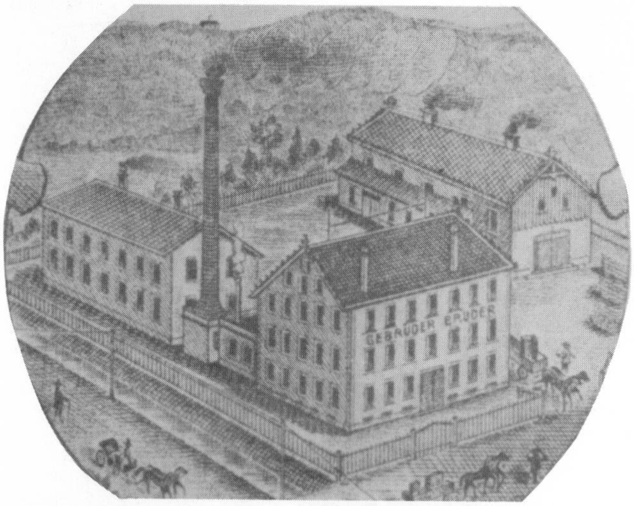

On this page are shown many varieties of Gebr. Bruder hand-cranked barrel organs. These were exported to all over the world.

To the left and right are two engravings picturing the Gebr. Bruder works in Waldkirch. The buildings are the same structures but they are arranged differently in the two illustrations! Such engravings are rarely accurate, as the editor has learned when visiting old factories in person. Usually the letterhead illustrations of various musical firms depicted grandiose factory complexes that were quite overstated.

## Flöten-Orgeln

mit angenehmer volltönender Flötenmusik.

Kasten mit Palisanderholz fournirt und auf allen vier Seiten eingelegt.

Nº 1. 2. 3. 4.

| No. | | Mark |
|---|---|---|
| 1 | **Uniflüte,** 24 Töne, 10 Stücke . eine weitere Walze<br>Grösse: 56 ctm. lang, 58 ctm. hoch, 33 ctm. tief.<br>Annäherndes Gewicht: 20 Kilo. | 290<br>48 |
| 2 | dto. 25 Töne, 10 Stücke eine weitere Walze<br>Grösse: 58 ctm. lang, 58 ctm. hoch, 33 ctm. tief.<br>Gewicht: 21 Kilo. | 312<br>50 |
| 3 | dto. 26 Töne, 10 Stücke (Contra-Bass) eine weitere Walze<br>Grösse: 62 ctm. lang, 60 ctm. hoch, 35 ctm. tief.<br>Gewicht: 23 Kilo. | 330<br>6 |
| 4 | dto. 30 Töne, 10 Stücke (Contra-Bass) eine weitere Walze<br>Grösse: 66 ctm. lang, 60 ctm. hoch, 35 ctm. tief. | 35<br>6 |

## Clarinettenorgeln.

Clariton.

Neue Konstruktion mit sichtbaren Messing-Clarinetten und Nickelpiccolos, sehr geschmackvolle Ausführung mit besonders starker volltönender Musik.

| No. | | Mark |
|---|---|---|
| 54 | 38 Töne, 12 sichtbare Messing-Clarinetten, 16 Nickel-Piccolo, Walze 64 Takt, 8 Stück<br>eine weitere Walze<br>Gewicht: 26 Kilo. | 48<br>8 |
| 55 | 47 Töne, 17 sichtbare Messing-Clarinetten, 19 Nickel-Piccolo, Basstöne 3fach, in den Tönen chromatisch, daher jedes Musikstück gut ausführbar. Walze 80 Takt<br>eine weitere Walze<br>No. 54 ist tragbar. | 65<br>10 |

Nº 54. 55.

## Orgeln mit Flöten und Trompeten

Kasten mit Palisanter fournirt und auf allen vier Seiten eingelegt

Nº 37. 38. 39.

| No. | | Mark |
|---|---|---|
| 37 | 38 Töne, Trompeten, Piccolos, 8 Stücke.<br>eine weitere Walze<br>Grösse:<br>Gewicht: | 39<br>72 |
| 38 | 40 Töne, Trompeten, Piccolos, grossen Bass, 8 Stücke<br>eine weitere Walze<br>Grösse:<br>Gewicht: | 42<br>78 |
| 39 | 42 Töne, Trompeten, Piccolos, grossen Bass, 8 Stücke<br>eine weitere Walze<br>Grösse:<br>Gewicht: | 44<br>84 |

## Harmoniflutes.

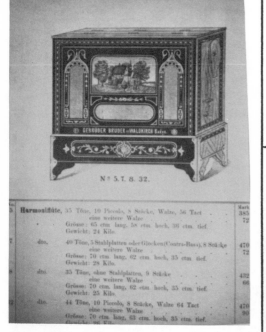

Nº 5. 7. 8. 32.

| No. | | Mark |
|---|---|---|
| 5 | **Harmoniflüte,** 35 Töne, 10 Piccolo, 8 Stücke, Walze, 56 Tact<br>eine weitere Walze<br>Grösse: 65 ctm. lang, 58 ctm. hoch, 36 ctm. tief.<br>Gewicht: 24 Kilo. | 385<br>72 |
| 7 | dto. 40 Töne, 5 Stahlplatten oder Glocken (Contra-Bass), 8 Stücke<br>eine weitere Walze<br>Grösse: 70 ctm. lang, 62 ctm. hoch, 35 ctm. tief.<br>Gewicht: 28 Kilo. | 470<br>72 |
| 8 | dto. 35 Töne, ohne Stahlplatten, 9 Stücke<br>eine weitere Walze<br>Grösse: 70 ctm. lang, 62 ctm. hoch, 35 ctm. tief.<br>Gewicht: 25 Kilo. | 432<br>66 |
| 2 | dto. 44 Töne, 10 Piccolo, 8 Stücke, Walze 64 Tact<br>eine weitere Walze<br>Grösse: 70 ctm. lang, 63 ctm. hoch, 35 ctm. tief. | 470<br>90 |

| No. | | Mark | Fres |
|---|---|---|---|
| 6 | **Harmonipan,** 44 Töne, 19 sichtbare Zauberflöten (Tremolo) 8 Stücke<br>eine weitere Walze<br>Grösse: 70 ctm. lang, 60 ctm. hoch, 33 ctm. tief.<br>Gewicht: 24 Kilo. | 385<br>72 | 480<br>90 |
| 29 | dto. 35 Töne, 17 sichtbare Zauberflöten, 9 Stücke<br>eine weitere Walze<br>Grösse: 59 ctm. hoch, 63 ctm. lang, 32 ctm. tief.<br>Gewicht: 22 Kilo. | 336<br>60 | 440<br>80 |
| 28 | dto. 33 Töne, 15 sichtbare Zauberflöten, 8 Stücke<br>eine weitere Walze<br>Grösse: 59 ctm. hoch, 63 ctm. lang, 32 ctm. tief.<br>Gewicht: 20 Kilo. | 264<br>54 | 330<br>72 |
| 27 | dto. 30 Töne, 13 sichtbare Zauberflöten, 8 Stücke<br>eine weitere Walze<br>Grösse: 58 ctm. lang, 59 ctm. hoch, 31 ctm. tief.<br>Gewicht: 18 Kilo. | 220<br>50 | 270<br>65 |
| 31 | **Flütepan,** 26 Töne, 19 sichtbare Zauberflöten, 10 Stücke (Tremolo)<br>eine weite Walze<br>Grösse: 62 ctm. lang, 60 ctm. hoch, 35 ctm. tief.<br>Gewicht: 23 Kilo. | 360<br>60 | 450<br>80 |

Die Zauberflöten obiger Instrumente können auf Wunsch der Besteller in Messing oder Schilfrohr angefertigt werden.

## Harmonipans.

Nº 6. 27. 28. 29. 31.

Nº 50. 51. 52.

## Orgeln mit Zauberflöten und Trompeten.

Kasten mit Palisander fournirt und auf allen vier Seiten eingelegt.

| No. | | Mark |
|---|---|---|
| 50 | 38 Töne, 10 Trompeten, 15 Zauberflöten, 8 Stücke | 420 |
| | eine weitere Walze | 72 |
| | Annäherndes Gewicht: | |
| 51 | 42 Töne, 10 Trompeten, 15 Zauberflöten, 2 Register-Pfeifen, 8 Stücke | 480 |
| | eine weitere Walze | 84 |
| | Annäherndes Gewicht: | |
| 52 | 45 Töne, 11 Trompeten, 17 Zauberflöten, 2 Register-Pfeifen, 8 Stücke | 510 |
| | eine weitere Walze | 90 |
| | Annäherndes Gewicht: | |

## Orgeln mit Trompeten
### für Schiesshallen und kleinere Caroussels.

Kasten von Nussbaumholz und blos vorn eingelegt.

| | Mark |
|---|---|
| 42 Töne, 10 Trompeten, 10 Piccolos, 4 Register, 9 Stücke | 492 |
| eine weitere Walze | 90 |
| Grösse: 64 ctm. hoch, 91 ctm. lang, 40 ctm. tief. | |
| 45 Töne, 10 Trompeten, 12 Piccolos, 4 Register, 9 Stücke | 576 |
| eine weitere Walze | 96 |
| Grösse: 74 ctm. hoch, 98 ctm. lang, 40 ctm. tief, | |
| 32 Töne, 10 Trompeten, 4 Register, 9 Stücke | 378 |
| eine weitere Walze | 64 |
| Grösse: 72 ctm. hoch, 73 ctm. lang, 38 ctm. tief, | |
| 48 Töne, 13 Trompeten, 5 Register, 10 Stücke | 600 |
| eine weitere Walze | 96 |
| Grösse: 95 ctm. hoch, 105 ctm. lang, 59 ctm. tief. | |

Nº 15 16 18 20

Nº 33.35.36.

## Salon-Concertinos,
### (Neueste Erfindung).

Speziell für Tanzmusik in Hôtels, Restaurants, kleinere Tanz- und Gesellschafts-Säle

| No. | | Mark |
|---|---|---|
| 33 | 38 Töne, Imitation v. Flöte, Violin, Violincello, Contra-Bass, 9 Stücke, Form Orgel | 60 |
| | eine weitere Walze | 9 |
| 35 | 48 Töne, Imitation von Flöte, Violin, Violincello, Contra-Bass, Form Piano | 84 |
| | eine weitere Walze | 11 |
| 36 | 60 Töne, Imitation von Flöte, Violin, Violincello, Contra-Bass, Form Orgel | 102 |
| | eine weitere Walze | 14 |

On this page are more barrel-operated hand-cranked Gebr. Bruder organs from the late 19th and early 20th centuries. Many Gebr. Bruder organs were sold through distributors — there were several in America, for instance — and are found today with names other than Bruder on them.

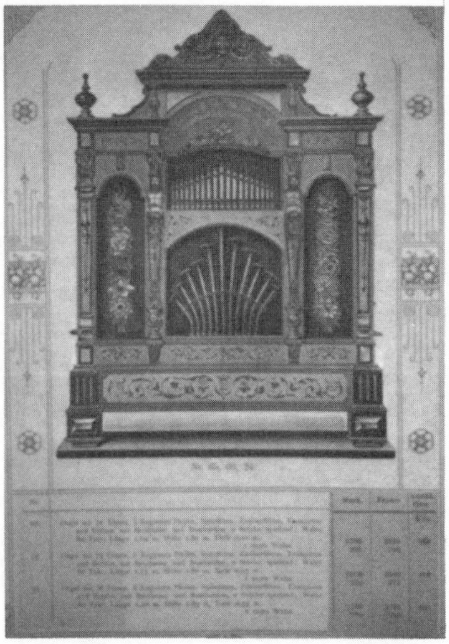

Gebr. Bruder hand-cranked barrel organs . . .

## BRUDER (Gebr. Bruder)

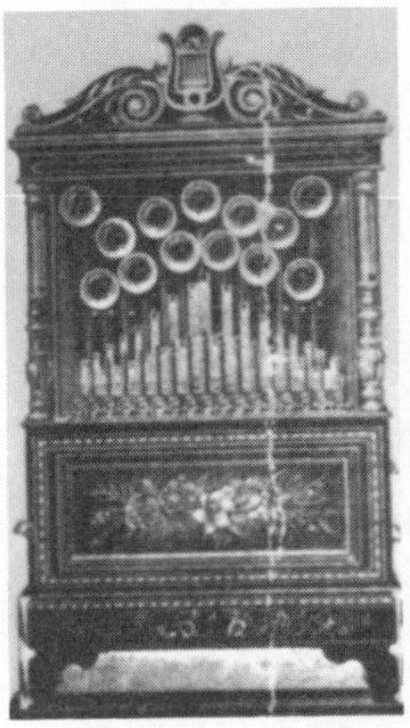

Above and right are four varieties of barrel-operated organs from the early 1900's. The same cases were used for several different models. The case at the immediate right was used for No. 61 (47 keys), 62 (50 keys), 26 (56 keys), 64 (63 keys), and 65 (70 keys).

Book-Operated Gebr. Bruder Organs:

"Universum." 42 keys. 244 cm. high; 235 cm. wide; 85 cm. deep. 157 pipes plus percussion effects.

"Symphony Orchestra Organ No. 100." 52 keys. "Musical effect of 8 musicians." Also No.100a with more pipes. Represents 12 musicians.

"Symphony Orchestra Organ No. 107." 52 keys. Represents 16 musicians. Also No. 106: "59 keys, same type as No.107 but with larger scale."

Left: "Great Symphony Orchestra Organ." No. 103 with 67 keys. "Musical effect of about 25 musicians." No. 104 with 80 keys. Represents 40 musicians. No. 105 with 94 keys. Represents 50 musicians.

Right: "Symphony Orchestra Organ – 'Sirene' " – Available in 59, 67, and 80-key models representing about 22, 30, and 40 musicians respectively. "Pompous facade, painted white and with bright gilt trim. 4 artistic figures. Instrumentation like a big orchestra with most wonderful tone effects."

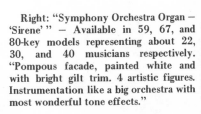

Left: "Symphony Orchestra Organ 'Terpsichore' " – Available in 67, 80, and 94-key models representing 34, 45, and 65 musicians. "Pompous facade, baroque style with artistic paintings, very rich gilding. Two dancing groups in sculpture plus three artistic paintings. Rich instrumentation; wonderful tonal shading. Suitable for shows as well as for large dancing and concert locations."

Right: "Elite Orchestra Apollo" (one of several Gebr. Bruder organs to bear this name). Made in 69, 80, and 106-key size. "These instruments unite all instruments of a modern orchestra . . . In order to increase the musical effect, this organ has automatic swell shutters. The front is white with gold and has 6 artistic statues. On the 106-key model three of the statues are life-size." The 106-key model sold for 25,600 marks in 1912.

Below: Gebr. Bruder price list of about 1912. The organs listed are operated by folding cardboard music books. Some were made later with paper roll systems.

# Price-list.

The prices standing under neath are calculated at barrel organs inclusive one barrel, at cardboard organs, inclusive 100 meters cardboards in a box.

## Barrel-Organs.

| | | |
|---|---|---|
| No. 61 | 47 keys ........ | Mk. 1600.— |
| | Extra barrel .. | „ 240.— |
| No. 62 | 50 keys ........ | „ 2000.— |
| | Extra barrel .. | „ 320.— |
| No. 26 | 56 keys ........ | „ 2400.— |
| | Extra barrel .. | „ 380.— |

## Big Barrel-Organs.

| | | |
|---|---|---|
| No. 64 | 63 keys ........ | Mk. 3200.— |
| | Extra barrel .. | „ 450.— |
| No. 65 | 70 keys ........ | „ 4000.— |
| | Extra barrel .. | „ 560.— |

## Concert-Barrel-Organs.

| | | |
|---|---|---|
| No. 66 | 52 keys ........ | Mk. 2600.— |
| | Extra barrel .. | „ 320.— |
| No. 67 | 56 keys ........ | „ 2900.— |
| | Extra barrel .. | „ 400.— |

## Big Concert-Barrel-Organs.

| | | |
|---|---|---|
| No. 68 | 64 keys ........ | Mk. 3550.— |
| | Extra barrel .. | „ 480.— |
| No. 69 | 72 keys ........ | „ 4500.— |
| | Extra barrel .. | „ 640.— |

## Concert-Barrel-Organs with Drums.

| | | |
|---|---|---|
| No. 70 | 58 keys ........ | Mk. 4000.— |
| | Extra barrel .. | „ 450.— |
| No. 71 | 65 keys ........ | „ 4800.— |
| | Extra barrel .. | „ 560.— |

## Symphony-Orchestra-Organs.

| | | |
|---|---|---|
| No. 100 | 52 keys ...... | Mk. 2250 — |
| | Cardboards p. m | „ 3.80 |
| No. 100 a | 52 keys ...... | „ 2900.— |
| | Cardboards p. m | „ 4.— |

## Symphony-Orchestra-Organs.

| | | |
|---|---|---|
| No. 107 | 52 keys ...... | Mk. 3400.— |
| | Cardboards p. m | „ 4.20 |
| No. 106 | 59 keys ...... | „ 4250.— |
| | Cardboards p. m | „ 4.80 |

## Big Symphony-Orchestra-Organs.

| | | |
|---|---|---|
| No. 103 | 67 keys ...... | Mk. 5300.— |
| | Cardboards p. m | „ 5.40 |
| No. 104 | 80 keys ...... | „ 7050.— |
| | Cardboards p. m | „ 6.— |
| No. 105 | 94 keys ...... | „ 9600.— |
| | Cardboards p. m | „ 8.— |

## Symphony-Orchestra-Organ "Sirene".

| | |
|---|---|
| 59 keys ................ | Mk. 5600.- |
| Cardboards per meter | „ 4.8 |
| 67 keys ................ | „ 6750.- |
| Cardboards per meter | „ 5.4 |
| 80 keys ................ | „ 8000.- |
| Cardboards per meter | „ 6.- |
| 80 keys with Xylophone | „ 8800.- |
| Cardboards per meter | „ 6.- |

## Symphony-Orchestra-Organ "Terpsichore".

| | |
|---|---|
| 67 keys ................ | Mk. 7000.- |
| Cardboards per meter | „ 5.4 |
| 80 keys ................ | „ 9600.- |
| Cardboards per meter | „ 6.- |
| 94 keys ................ | „ 14400.- |
| Cardboards per meter | „ 8.- |

## Elite-Orchestra "Apollo".

| | |
|---|---|
| 69 keys .............. | Mk. 16000.- |
| Cardboards per meter | „ 6.4 |
| 80 keys .............. | „ 20000.- |
| Cardboards per meter | „ 8.- |
| 106 keys .............. | „ 25600.- |
| Cardboards per meter | „ 9.6 |

## Elite-Orchestra "Apollo"

without mandoline, and a little les pompous frontside in white paintin and rich gilding, and with 3 statues.

| | |
|---|---|
| 65 keys ................ | Mk. 7200.- |
| Cardboards per meter | „ 5.7 |
| 69 keys ................ | „ 9000.- |
| Cardboards per meter | „ 6.4 |
| 80 keys ................ | „ 12000.- |
| Cardboards per meter | „ 8.- |

## Military-Symphony-Orchestra.

| | |
|---|---|
| 59 keys ................ | Mk. 4800.- |
| Cardboards per meter | „ 4.8 |

## Military-Symphony-Orchestra "Selection".

| | |
|---|---|
| 94 keys .............. | Mk. 28800.- |
| Cardboards per meter | „ 8.- |

Above: "Elite Orchestra Apollo." Made in 65, 69, and 80-key models representing 38, 40, and 56 musicians. Some of these were sold in the United States as Wurlitzer styles 165 and 166. "A less pompous [than the other "Elite Orchestra Apollo" shown at the top of this page] facade; painted white with rich gilding. 3 statues." Later models were without statues.

"Military Symphony Orchestra." 59 keys. "Musical effect of about 25 musicians. Extraordinarily strong military music. Instrumentation consists of trumpets, clarinets, etc., and, if desired, also brass trombones. Rich gilded facade in the oriental style."

Gebr. Bruder organ from the 1907 era. Several of this style were imported into the United States by Mangels, Berni, and others.

"Symphony Orchestra Organ — Sirene." This name was used for several different facade styles over the years. Many of the organs on this page resemble the products of Ruth, a firm also located in Waldkirch.

Above: "Symphony Orchestra Organ" — Circa 1905 model.

Above: "Great Symphony Orchestra Organ — Jubilaum." Popular circa 1905.

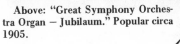

Right: "Orchestra Organ" — Facade used for No. 104 and No. 105 circa 1905.

Upper right: "Concert Barrel Organ" — Circa 1905. About this time barrel organs were being phased out in favor of book organs.

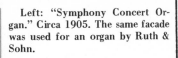

Left: "Symphony Concert Organ." Circa 1905. The same facade was used for an organ by Ruth & Sohn.

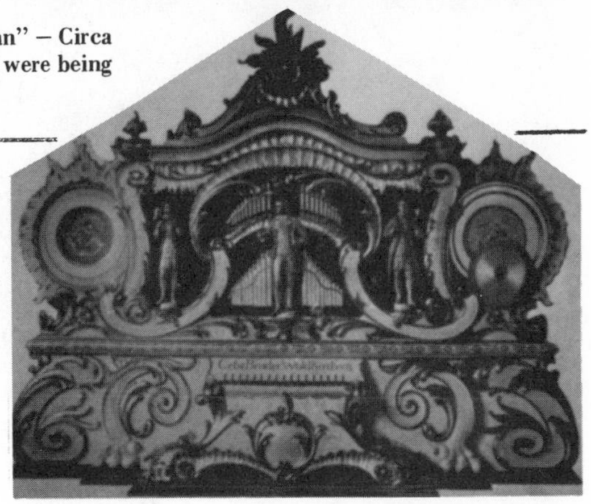

Right: "Orchestra Organ — Pompadour." Circa 1905. (Most illustrations on this page are courtesy of Carl Thomsen)

Left and below: Views of the "Military Symphony Orchestra 'Selection' " sold as an "Automatic instrument with 94 keys. Extraordinary effect. This instrument represents a complete military band of 15 men. These figures are dressed in real cloth coats and handle their instruments in the most natural manner with the music so that the people think they see a living band, the more so as the musicians move their heads and eyes. The organ is supplied with all of the orchestra instruments and plays from the very soft piano to the most powerful fortissimo the most difficult compositions. Baroque facade, painted white and gold, with rich sculptures and four statues. Musical effect of about 80 musicians."

---

Left: Large Gebr. Bruder organ installed as the facade of a moving picture show in Spain. Illustration from "Orgel und Spieluhrenbau" ("Organ and Automaton Clock Builders") by Karl Bormann, published by Sanssouci Verlag AG, of Zurich, Switzerland. This book traces the development of organ clocks and hand-cranked organs in the 19th century. Emphasis is on the products of Germany's Black Forest area and on the instruments of Ignaz Bruder in particular, although many other firms are discussed. Printed in the German language, the book is particularly valuable for its technical information: how the mechanisms operate, what ranks of pipes were used in the various instruments, etc.

## BURSENS ("ARBURO") ORGANS
—Antwerp, Belgium—

From a workshop and warehouse in Hoboken, a suburb of Antwerp, Belgium, Arthur Bursens and his partner, Frans de Groof, produced hundreds of dance organs, fairground organs, and what are known as "Dutch street organs."

In 1967 the author received a communication from Arthur Bursens stating that his warehouse full of organs was for sale. No time was lost in going to Belgium and, after due negotiations, the group of about three dozen instruments was acquired. These were subsequently brought to America and resold to collectors and businesses.

The Bursens family has been engaged in organ building for many decades. Joseph Bursens produced many fairground organs and dance hall organs with ornate carved fronts, many of which resemble the large Mortier organs shown elsewhere in this book.

In recent years Arthur Bursens has managed the firm. The best known Bursens products are the "Arburo" brand ("ARthur BURsens is the derivation of the trademark) dance organs. Made in literally dozens of different styles, most use a paper music roll, usually of four-tune length. These rolls have been made almost continuously for the past twenty or thirty years — with the result that such tunes as "The Yellow Rose of Texas," "Never on Sunday," and other modern melodies comprise much of a typical roll library. It is interesting to note that the hole spacing of the Arburo roll is the same as that used on large Popper & Co. orchestrions (the tracker layout, however, is different) as Bursens and Popper both ordered their roll mechanisms from the same supplier. Some Arburo organs, particularly the older ones, use folding cardboard music books of the 70 to 90 key range.

During his visit the author was surprised to learn that almost all Arburo components are made on the premises. Inquiring about a pile of rough-sawed lumber (with the bark still on it) we were told: "We'll make organ pipes from the wood after it has been seasoned."

### A Typical Arburo Organ

A typical roll-operated Bursens organ is about 7 to 8 feet high, as wide as that or slightly wider, and about 3 to 4 feet deep. The system is a combination of vacuum (to "read" the music roll and to operate certain controls and percussion effects) and pressure (for the pipes). The main chassis contains the pumps and, above them, the main chests on which ranks of string-family (violin, viola, and cello) and flute (flute and bass) pipes are mounted. Many instruments have jazz flutes, clarinets or other reeds, and other ranks in addition.

The percussion department usually contains a bass drum and snare drum (often with extra beaters for special effects), a tenor drum, tuned temple blocks, marraccas, cymbals, and other effects. A fine quality accordion ("I am very particular about the quality of accordions I use — and often have to pay $400 or so for each one," Mr. Bursens said) plays solo passages throughout a typical tune. The percussion effects are often mounted on the front of the instrument and detach from the main chassis for ease in moving.

A series of electric switches (actuated by perforations in the music sheet) provide changing lighting colors and intensities.

Arburo music rolls, for the most part, are excellently arranged and are enjoyable to hear. Rolls are cut today for these instruments by Arthur Prinsen of Brasschaat, Belgium (Mr. Prinsen is active in the arranging and cutting of all types of cardboard music and of several different types of paper organ and orchestrion rolls as well.)

### Dutch Street Organs

Like Gijs Perlee and several other organ builders of Holland and Belgium, Arthur Bursens has built many Dutch street organs. Many of these have been built up from raw materials. Others have utilized older organ parts, particularly facade sections and trim from ornate Mortier and other organs of an earlier era.

The tonal quality and appearance of Bursens pipework is far above average. This attention to quality has made Mr. Bursens a busy man. At last word from him he was a half year behind in filling new orders!

### Additional Comments

The Bursens organs we illustrate are typical of those made during the last thirty years. As noted earlier, most instruments differ in appearance from one another. There were no standard models produced in large quantities. As the original Bursens trading area was mainly in the small countries of Belgium and Holland, an effort was made to give each customer something different.

When we wrote the first edition of this book there wasn't much collector interest in modern Bursens, Decap, or Mortier dance organs. We noted at the time: "These instruments have been offered for sale in used condition on several occasions for prices varying from $1000 up to several thousand dollars, depending on the model and condition. Used Decap organs have fetched similar prices. . . These instruments of today may well be sought-after collectors' items in some distant day." Since that writing, the above-mentioned Bursens warehouse hoard has been dispersed, and dozens of other dance organs have been imported to America by various dealers and collectors.

Mrs. Kathy Weber listens to the catchy rhythm of an Arburo "Jazz Orchestra" organ made by Arthur Bursens. Like Decap dance organs of the 1950's and 1960's, the Arburo instruments are usually made with an accordion, drums, and other percussion effects — all arranged "on display" at the front of the instrument. The many ranks of pipework are concealed behind velvet curtains. While most modern Bursens organs have the roll system of music, some are equipped with key frames. Mr. Bursens is also active in the manufacturing of Dutch street organs. A 1968 issue of "The Key Frame," magazine of England's Fair Organ Preservation Society, noted that three out of four Dutch street organ contests held in recent years were won by Bursens instruments!

One of the dance organs, in this case a cardboard music system instrument, from the Bursens Warehouse Hoard receives a final checking before shipment. The decorative facade has been removed for servicing, thus revealing the innards of this large instrument. (Photograph by Leonard Nadel for Business Week Magazine; used courtesy of McGraw-Hill Publishing Company)

Vic Reina checks out the paper roll system of an Arburo dance organ made by Bursens. The two Bursens trademarks are "Ideal" (mostly cardboard music instruments) and "Arburo" (paper roll operated organs).

The author (left), Arthur Bursens (center foreground), and Terry Hathaway are shown in this 1967 photograph taken at the Bursens workshop and factory at 635 St. Bernardse Steenweg, Hoboken (a district of Antwerp), Belgium.

At the top of the page are shown some of the nearly three dozen Bursens organs acquired in the "Bursens Warehouse Hoard" purchase. No two Bursens organs are alike. All have differences, ranging from major to slight variations in detail.

The key frame of this organ plays a continuous loop of cardboard music. The music is fed from the left side, passes through the key frame, and is piled up on the right. This permits operation without an attendant.

Some of the pipework and percussion effects in the Bursens organ. The Bursens organs are beautifully made and have been acclaimed by collectors. Decap organs of somewhat similar construction are likewise popular.

Key frame with the slotted pressure roller lifted. The roller holds the music against a row of steel "fingers." When a hole appears in the music, the steel key is pushed through it – causing a note to sound.

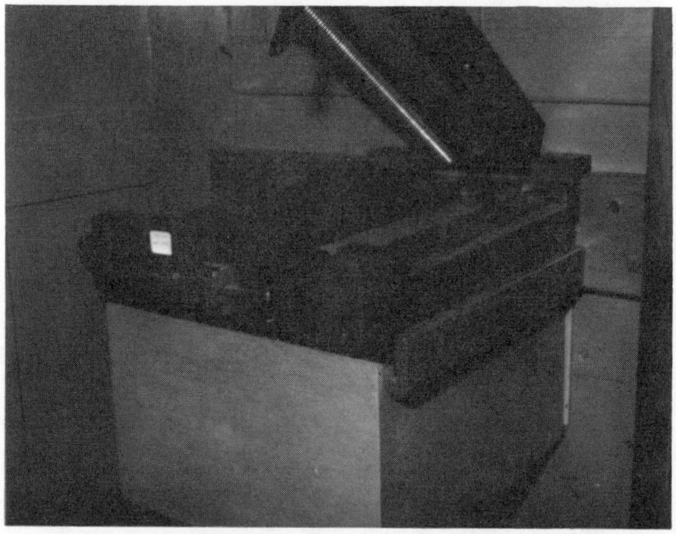

View from the right side of the key frame. Most European organs by Gavioli, Limonaire, Marenghi, Ruth, et al used the folding cardboard system. Only a few used paper rolls.

The jazz flute rank in the foreground has a tremulant and a mechanism which opens and closes a small hole in the back of the pipe, thus detuning it and causing a warbling sound. Jazz flutes are found in many types of Bursens, Mortier, and Decap organs.

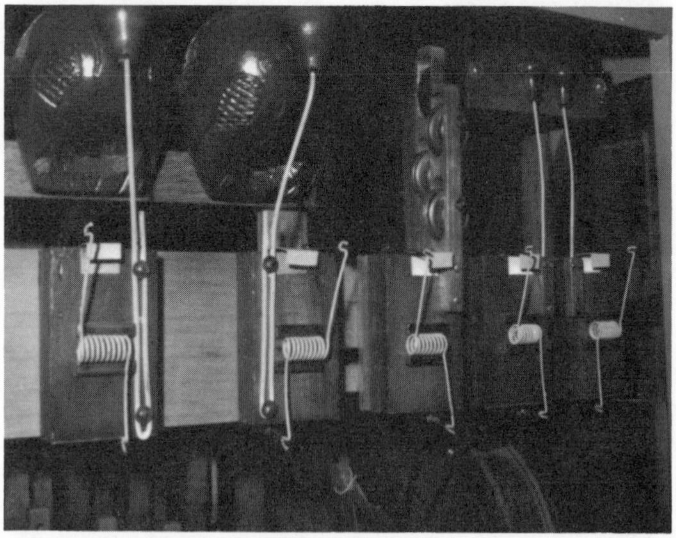

Part of the percussion department of the Bursens organ. At the upper left are Chinese temple blocks. To the right are tambourine jingles and a wood block with two beaters.

"Arburo" dance organ made by Arthur Bursens of Antwerp, Belgium. This impressive organ, one of the largest in the group of nearly three dozen Bursens instruments acquired by the author, is now a featured attraction at Bellm's Cars and Music of Yesterday Museum (see inset photo at right) in Sarasota, Florida.

The extensive pipework of the Arburo organ gives it a varied capability: depending upon the roll, the instrument can sound like a church organ or a military marching band! Built for use in a dance hall, the instrument has multicolored lights which flash on and off as the organ plays. All of the organs in the Bursens Warehouse Hoard were quickly sold to various collectors and museums, but in the process the author really got to know these instruments well! Some of the instruments were in new condition, having never been shipped from the factory before!

Calliopes are loudly-voiced instruments which produce music by admitting air under high pressure to stopped metal pipes. Calliopes were intended for outdoor use in circuses, parades, and similar situations.

The term "calliope" is from Calliope (originally "Kalliope" — "beautiful voice" in Greek), chief of the Muses in classical mythology. The word is pronounced in two different ways: "kally-ope" by circus people, and "kal-eye-o-pee" by everyone else! It has been written that one can tell if a person is from the circus by the way he pronounces this word!

The calliope, like the Encore Banjo, has the distinction of being an automatic musical instrument devised first in America, although it can be rightfully claimed that the calliope's ancestors are the barrel-operated organs which date back to ancient times.

An early steam-operated calliope was successfully manufactured by Joshua C. Stoddard, a Vermonter who settled in Worcester, Massachusetts, in 1845. An article, "Harmony in Steam," reprinted on a following page, notes that "[Stoddard's] first instrument consisted of 15 whistles, of graduated sizes, attached in a row to the top of a small steam boiler. A long cylinder with pins of different shapes driven in to it ran the length of the boiler. The pins were so arranged that when the cylinder revolved, they pressed the valves and blew the whistles in proper sequence . . . The first showing of the calliope — a keyboard version — took place on July 4, 1855, on Worcester Common . . . The instrument was a success and Stoddard patented the instrument in October of the same year."

Stoddard organized the American Steam Piano Company, a firm which produced a number of steam-operated calliope models of hand-played and automatic types. The firm supplied calliopes to riverboats, private yachts, and sent an instrument to London for exhibition in the Crystal Palace. A contemporary account relates that models were made with steam pressures ranging from five pounds per square inch to one hundred and fifty pounds. The latter instruments could be heard twelve miles away!

Although the previously-mentioned account relates that steam calliopes were used by the Pacha (sic) of Egypt and by a lighthouse on the bleak coast of Nova Scotia, most such instruments were used in the United States of America. Europeans considered the calliope to be an American type of instrument, and none of the European organ builders or other firms in the automatic musical instrument business made them.

While steam-operated calliopes are a romantic part of American folklore, few such instruments survive today. The circus calliope in its most familiar form is a device operated by compressed air. Calliopes were made by several American firms, mainly in the 1920-1935 years, although production of Tangley instruments continued to the Second World War.

### The Tangley Company

Founded in 1914 by Norman Baker, an enterpreneur who was involved in many different ventures over the years (including radio broadcasting, publishing, and patent medicine selling), the Tangley Company of Muscatine, Iowa, was the leading American maker of compressed-air-operated calliopes — called "air calliopes" for short.

A Tangley advertisement noted that "In 1914, Mr. Norman Baker invented and built the first Tangley Air Calliope, later perfecting the Calliaphone, which is the result of over twelve years of experimenting and experience. In the past twelve years we have seen many individuals enter the field as competitors, without experience in this line of instruments, and be forced to discontinue — which has caused many thousands of dollars of losses to their customers who cannot secure parts; these customers have often found their instruments to be inferior, with poor tone quality and volume. For over twelve years we have stood behind every Tangley instrument, and our product is now backed by a quarter of a million investment. We have built 98% of all air calliopes in use, and are exclusive builders of the Calliaphone."

Norman Baker also owned Radio Station KTNT, "the prettiest station in America" — as it was called. An advertisement beckoned listeners to "Hear this beautifully toned instrument [the Calliaphone] nightly from Station K-'TNT.' No other musical instrument broadcasts as beautifully as the Calliaphone, according to thousands of letters received from our listeners. We advertise our customers over the radio — thousands are curious to see this wonderful instrument, and the moment we mention you as using one, every radio listener in your territory will come to see it. Don't miss this big advertising stunt . . ."

Tangley made a number of different models, most of which were loudly-voiced and intended for outdoor use. Exceptions were Model ST-43 and ST-58 which were "low volume for inside use." The digits of the model designation indicate the number of pipes (or "whistles," as they were usually called by the various calliope builders) in the instrument. ST-43 has 43 pipes, for example.

The most popular Tangley model by far was the CA-43, a 43-pipe instrument which used 10-tune 65-note type "A" piano rolls. Coupling of the notes was necessary in order to use all of the holes on the roll. While the CA-43 and other roll-operated Tangley instruments could and did use regular "A" rolls, the best results were obtained from "A" rolls with special extended perforations, organ arrangements which permitted the pipes to sustain their tones longer than the piano-type arrangements. These special rolls were made with "Calliaphone" labels by the Clark Orchestra Roll Company of DeKalb, Illinois. CA-43 sold for various prices, mostly in the $1000 to $1200 range, over the years. Tangley advertised: "Model CA-43 [which plays automatically or by hand], outfit all painted, mounted — ready to go — ready to play — price [including car body] only $1895.00, less 5% for cash. If you have your own auto, complete Calliaphone equipment ready for mounting is only $1169.00, less 5% for cash. For manufacturers we can build special bodies shaped to resemble their product. Grennan Bakeries uses bodies resembling a large layer cake. Chase Candy Company's outfit resembles a package of their 'Domino Mints.' Dixie Cake Company's outfit resembles a large loaf of bread, and Butter Nut, Inc. has one shaped like a 5c gum package. They compel the attention of all."

During the 1920's the Tangley products were all sold under the Calliaphone name. The slogan, "The First New Tone in Forty Years," was often used. "New Tone" was the name used by the competing National Calliope Corporation, to which Tangley's slogan made an obvious reference.

The production figures for the various Tangley models are not known. However, as nearly all known Tangley instruments are of the CA-43 style, it is presumed that most were of this type. More CA-43 instruments survive than do those of all other makes and models of calliopes, including those made by other firms, combined.

### National Calliope Corporation

"New Tone Calliope" was the name given to the product of E.A. Harrington, who maintained a factory and showrooms at 706 Wyandotte Street, Kansas City, Missouri. New Tone instruments were made in two types; Model A which had 43 brass pipes, and Model B which had 53.

The Harrington business was later organized as the National Calliope Corporation. Production of the A and B models, both of which used regular 10-tune type "A" piano rolls, continued. Model B, the 53-note style, was the better seller of the two, and 90% or more of the National and Harrington instruments were of this specification.

National instruments were offered as: "A Crowning Achievement. National Air Calliopes are the last word in calliope engineering; they stand in a distinct class by themselves. They are the outgrowth of many years of tireless energy and scientific study by the highest type of calliope engineers. National Calliopes are constructed in our large factory, which is devoted exclusively to the manufacture of the world's finest air calliope, which instrument we are justly proud of. National Calliopes deliver satisfaction and represent 100 cents value for every dollar of the purchase price. National Calliopes will pay for themselves many times over. Shrewd national advertisers immediately realize the superiority of National Calliopes over machines of other manufacture. It has been a great source of pleasure to us to receive the hundreds of unsolicited letters and telegrams from our satisfied customers complimenting us on the superiority of the National Calliope. National Calliopes are sturdy in construction, simple in operation, and have a wonderfully pleasing tone and a splendid volume. You will make no mistake in purchasing one or more National Calliopes. They are the acme of perfection and are a machine you will be justly proud of."

It was further noted that the Eli Bridge Company, maker of the Eli Ferris Wheel, of Jacksonville, Illinois, sold "19 National Calliopes in 19 Months — The Eli Bridge Company has used other makes of calliopes during the past several years, but after a thorough investigation of the competitive machines, they promptly changed to National Calliopes, which they are using exclusively." Another slogan of the times was "Every day in every way the National Calliope family is growing larger and larger."

Styling itself [incorrectly — Ed.] as "the world's largest manufacturer of air calliopes," National noted that its instruments had the best tone, the loudest volume, and the best construction. Of the rolls it was said that "a splendid range of ten tune rolls is always available. The National Calliope automatically rewinds itself at the end of the roll, and starts all over again. Music rolls are rapidly and easily changed. Machine can be played by hand when desired by simply shutting off a lever on the front of the cabinet. A new music roll catalogue is published monthly and contains new and popular selections. Music rolls are decidedly low in price — and are $3.50 for single 10-tune rolls or just $3.00 each in quantities of twelve rolls or more."

National instruments were very well built and were of exceptionally pure tone (with few raspy harmonics). As such, they are highly desired by collectors today. However, in the 1920's National's popular 53-note model simply couldn't compete effectively with Tangley's simpler CA-43 instrument, so Tangley obtained the lion's share of the market.

Note: some National instruments were sold under the "Han-Dee" name.

Haney-Deem Manufacturing Company

In 1926 the Haney-Deem Manufacturing Company of 431 West 5th Street, Kansas City, Missouri, advertised a calliope: "Announcing! — The Han-Dee True Tone Calliope for rides, rinks, shows, fairs, boats, bands, and outside advertising.

"Once you hear the Han-Dee True Tone or self-played calliope you will be convinced of the difference. The Han-Dee Calliope placed near your rides will give them a new thrill and will increase your receipts."

Little is known about the Han-Dee instruments. The only instrument of that name seen by the author was a Model B National made by the National Calliope Corporation. Whether or not Haney-Deem Manufacturing Company made many (if any) of its own instruments is not known.

Artizan Factories, Inc.

The Artizan Factories, Inc., successors to the North Tonawanda Musical Instrument Works, patented the Air-Calio calliope in 1927 and 1928. Unlike other calliopes (Tangley, National, Wurlitzer) which use vacuum in the tracker bar to sense the perforations in the roll, the Air-Calio is all pressure-operated. A slotted roller holds the paper against the tracker bar to insure proper tracking. A description of the Air-Calio appears on a following page. The instrument uses a special roll. In addition, the Artizan Factories built at least one other model — a large calliope with instrumentation consisting of capped brass pipes (similar to those in the Air-Calio) plus loudly-voiced violin pipes and stopped bass pipes. The instrument, a band organ - calliope combination, could be played by rolls or from a keyboard located at the back of the instrument.

(For more information concerning the Artizan Factories, Inc. refer to the Artizan band organ pages of this book.)

Rudolph Wurlitzer Company

The Rudolph Wurlitzer Company of North Tonawanda, New York, produced the Caliola, a calliope which made its first appearance in 1928. From then through the 1930's 62 instruments were built. These instruments, described in detail in the Wurlitzer band organ section of this book, use Wurlitzer 65-Note Player Piano rolls with special Caliola (organ-type with extended perforations for sustaining notes) arrangements. Varieties of Caliolas include: (1) Without drums (usually) or with; (2) with wooden (usually) or brass pipes; (3) Without keyboard (usually) or with.

Had the Caliola been introduced in the early 1920's it would have undoubtedly captured a large share of the calliope market — considering Wurlitzer's aggressive merchandising methods. As it was, the Caliola appeared when the market for such instruments was waning.

The "forest" of brass pipes on an air calliope.

—Steam Calliopes—

Steam calliopes were popular on riverboats and as an accessory to other steam-operated devices during the 19th century. The American Steam Piano Company (see below) produced such instruments on a standardized basis; but most such instruments in use were made as one-of-a-kind units by boiler makers and steamfitters. Such musical instruments were a romantic part of life on the Mississippi River, and early accounts of steamboat travel often mention calliopes.

Two early accounts pertaining to steam calliopes are given below.

"THE CALLIOPE"

*Note: This account appeared in the "Illustrated London News," issue of December 3, 1859. Found by Lt. Col. Jackson Fritz, the article was reprinted in "The Music Box" – Vol. II, No. 6.*

A musical instrument known by the above name has been lately brought over from America by the inventor, Mr. Arthur S. Denny, and is now being exhibited for the first time in England in the transept of the Crystal Palace. It may be characterized as a steam organ, and consists of a framework of iron supporting two cylinders, upon which are arranged a series of brass tubes, answering to the open diapasons of an organ, but bearing a strong resemblance to the ordinary steam locomotive whistle. From a boiler situated beneath the flooring the steam is conveyed into the cylinders, and from them admitted to the pipes, which produce the notes, through double-balance valves, opened by levers in connection with wires acted upon by ordinary pianoforte keys, or by pegs on a set cylinder similar to that of a barrel organ.

The instrument at the Crystal Palace is the softest-toned ever made, and is played upon at a pressure of 5 pounds to the square inch – the maximum employed in the church organ being but five ounces . . . Instruments are constructed in which the force of steam may be increased to the extent of 150 pounds to the square inch, producing musical sounds thirty times as powerful as the present instrument. At this high pressure such an instrument is asserted to have been distinctly heard at a distance of twelve miles. The compass of sound is almost unlimited, from the soft tones of a musical box to a power sufficient to afford music to a whole city.

On account of the quantity of steam given off during the performance the instrument has not been hitherto available for indoor exhibition; but if, in place of steam, it be used with compressed air better music is produced with an equally powerful effect.

Various are the uses to which it is suggested that the power of the calliope be applied, amongst others as a means of conveying the orders of a general on the field of battle by signals to be heard by the whole army; it is also capable of being used as a substitute for chime bells, and in St. Louis and New Orleans it has often been employed in this manner. A lighthouse belonging to the English Government, and situated on the coast of Nova Scotia, is provided with a calliope for making signals. The Pacha of Egypt has one fixed on board his private steamer as a musical instrument; and in this way they are frequently used by others in the United States.

HARMONY IN STEAM

An expectant and excited group of passengers hurried aboard a train in Worcester, Mass. on the afternoon of July 4, 1856. The train was a holiday excursion bound for Fitchburg, Mass. The excitement was unusual even for a holiday because the trip was to feature a demonstration of the American Steam Piano Company's steam calliope. The huge instrument was mounted on wheels and attached to the rear of the train. Passengers settled in their seats and waited eagerly for the first notes. At 3 o'clock a young girl pressed down a key, releasing a jet of steam that gushed forth through a whistle and resounded off the distant hills. It was the first note of "Old Dan Tucker," and on its signal, the train began its journey. Throughout the journey the steam calliope rendered traditional favorites, its booming voice echoing through the New England countryside. Farmers and shop workers dropped their tools and came running to hear. It was a successful excursion, and marked the birth of an instrument that has thrilled and entertained Americans of all ages.

But perhaps the most thrilled of all was the calliope's inventor, Joshua C. Stoddard. His invention was a success and the girl who played the calliope on the trip was his 7-year-old daughter, Jennie. But in a short time his invention became the source of unhappiness to him. His parents were ashamed of the machine their son had built because they considered it useless and Worcester soon banned its playing within the city limits because of excessive noise. In later years, although calliopes could be found throughout the U.S., Stoddard did not earn any money from them.

Joshua C. Stoddard was born on his father's farm in Pawlet, Vt., on August 26, 1814. His father sent him to Pawlet Academy for formal schooling and trained him in farming at home. Joshua became interested in bees that his father raised on the farm, and soon became an enthusiastic beekeeper, a vocation that he worked at all his life.

It was while working on his father's farm that young Stoddard heard a train whistle for the first time. Every time he heard a train approach he would listen attentively for the whistle. He soon noticed that different whistles produced different tones. To the inquisitive youth this was fascinating, and later served as the basis for his idea for a steam calliope.

Young Stoddard lived with his parents until January 23, 1845, when he married Lucy Maria Hersey and moved to Worcester. The Stoddards lived in Worcester for 40 years and had 6 children; 5 boys and a girl. Stoddard made his money from an apiary while devoting his spare time to various inventions. His first successful invention was the calliope, which he completed a few years after his marriage. The first instrument consisted of 15 whistles, of graduated sizes, attached in a row to the top of a small steam boiler. A long cylinder with pins of different shapes driven into it ran the length of the boiler. The pins were so arranged that when the cylinder revolved, they pressed the valves and blew the whistles in proper sequence. The different shapes enabled the operator to play notes of varying length. Later, Stoddard replaced the cylinder with a keyboard. Wires running from the keys to the valves enabled the operator to play the instrument like a piano.

The first showing of the calliope—a keyboard version—took place on July 4, 1855 on Worcester Common. While Stoddard stoked the wood fire to maintain the pressure, his daughter Jennie played such tunes as "Yankee Doodle" and "Columbia, the Gem of the Ocean." The showing was a success, and Stoddard had his instrument patented in October of the same year.

Stoddard founded the American Steam Piano Company with financial backing from Worcester industrialists. Although the calliope enjoyed enthusiastic reception from the public, Stoddard was inept in handling the business. Soon, one of the company's financial backers, Henry A. Deny, began to take control from Stoddard. Within 5 years after the founding of the company, Stoddard was removed and Deny became president. Deny not only headed the company, but claimed the invention as his own.

Under Deny, the company prospered. Steam calliopes became popular on river steamships, in fairs, parades, amusemenf parks and circuses all over the country. Air-operated models are still found in circuses today, besides having become standard equipment on carousels.

After he had lost control of his company, Stoddard returned to farming and beekeeping. Still inventive, he patented a successful hay rake in 1870 and a fire-escape in 1884. In 1901 he invented a fruit-paring machine, but it was not successful. He died on April 4, 1902 in Springfield, Mass., bereft of reward—save the satisfaction of accomplishment from his idea of making harmony in steam.

ESSO OILWAYS FOR SEPTEMBER 1956

Above: An account of the calliope's invention (from "Esso Oilways;" reprinted in "Player Piano Treasury). Credit is given to Joshua C. Stoddard, a Vermonter who lived in Worcester, Massachusetts, for the first such instrument produced.

# YOU can earn $5,000 yearly

*Easy Work*

## Own a Profitable Outdoor Advertising Business

## $10.00 Per Hour for YOU!

**An opportunity for any energetic person who wishes to start a business of his own. You can earn $10.00 and more per hour by renting your CALLIAPHONE OUTFIT to Merchants, Theatres, Celebrations, Fairs, Shows, Rinks, Church Socials, Sales, Auctions, and numerous enterprises. The world is your field. You can travel from Coast to Coast, doing outdoor advertising in each city you visit. We can build any style outfit wanted.** Some use larger outfits with living quarters built in same.

The Calliaphone

PRONOUNCE IT "KA-LI-A-PHONE"

For truck mounting and advertising we recommend our Model CA-43 CALLIAPHONE (shown at the left) complete with direct connected engine-blower unit. The complete unit can be installed in just a few hours by any handy man. Full installation instructions furnished. Floor space only 40 inches wide, 50 inches deep. Calliaphone plays automatically or can be hand played by any ordinary pianist. One man operates and drives car. Plays continuously and rewinds automatically after playing ten tunes on roll. Big opportunity and big money.

## WHAT OTHERS HAVE DONE!

**Quite a number of men in the advertising game with Calliaphones are making small fortunes. Rube Wilkins, Manchester, Ind., writes: "I earned $6,000 in one season." Leslie Kelly, Kansas City, Mo., writes: "I now have two outfits working Kansas City and will soon want another."**

## YOU CAN DO!!

**Can be purchased for cash or on time with new low terms offered. Write, today, for catalog, prices and terms. We can furnish you with the Calliaphone for mounting in your truck, or can supply complete Automobile Calliaphone outfits. WRITE!**

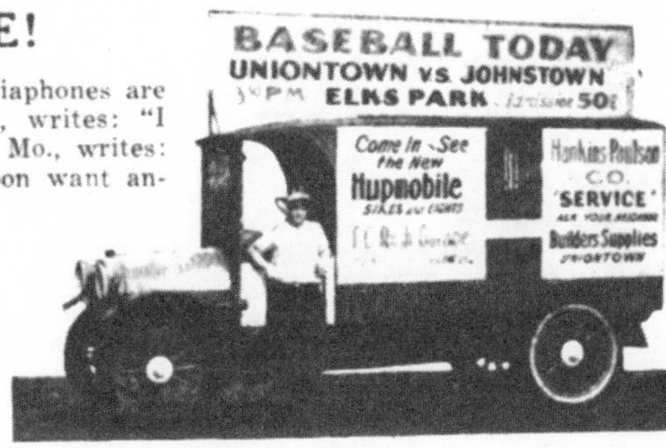


*EASY PAYMENT PLAN* *EARN WHILE YOU PAY*

**MUSCATINE TANGLEY CO. IOWA**

The above advertisement features the Calliaphone, manufactured by the Tangley Company of Muscatine, Iowa – the leading maker of air calliopes. Shown is Model CA-43, a 43-pipe instrument which plays automatically by means of 10-tune type "A" rolls. (Illustration from the October, 1931 issue of "TNT Magazine" – furnished by Donald G. Kemp)

### The Calliope in Advertising

During the 1920's the air calliope was extensively used for advertising. Mounted on the back of a truck or as part of a specially-constructed ornate wagon, such instruments attracted attention wherever they were heard. Above and left are two illustrations from a National Calliope Corporation brochure of the 1920's.

# A Model For Every Purpose

## Some Carry A Mile—Others Low As A Piano

### TONE

An Instrument with a Soul—combining a tonal development of wondrous sounds that are linked in golden chains of countless harmonies—entrancing—alluring.
Tones that fascinate; do not become monotonous; andpronounced *"The First New Tone in Forty Years"*.
Different from any tone in the world, since the "tom-tom."

### OPERATION

Plays automatically or by hand, has standard keyboard, 3½ octaves, 43 pipes, chromatic scale, (Model ST-58, has 58 pipes, about 4½ octaves). Uses standard 65-note music rolls, costing only $3.50 per roll of ten tunes. (Nearly 100 new rolls to select from each month). Simply move a lever to convert it from automatic to hand playing. Operates by electric motor, or engine, and plays continuousuly without attention. Has volume regulation that can be adjusted over a considerable range. The automatic music does not sound mechanical and many cannot distinguish it from hand played. For street advertising on automobile a small direct connected engine and plower is used. For low toned Theatre Models, a pipe organ blower is furnished. For rinks and rides, a 1 h. p. motor with rotary pressure blower is used.

### CONSTRUCTION

Built practically of metal throughout. Whistles of special brass alloy, a case of metal, finished in dark walnut. All pneumatics quickly detached, patented dust screen tracker bar, positive rewind brakes, separate "bleed" regulation, fewer control parts than other self-playing instruments. As fool and trouble proof as any instrument can be made. Guaranteed against defective workmanship or material. Action valves of brass—cannot rust. "Built to Stand the Hard Knocks." Fully guaranteed. Strongest built instrument on the market.

### MODELS

Model CA-43 is recommended for Rinks, Rides, Shows and Street Advertising. Plays automatically or by hand. Model CH-43 is hand played only, and used with Bands for Concert Work, or other uses that do not require an automatically-played instrument.
Model OH-43 is hand-played only, low volume like piano, and used with Orchestras, for Dance Halls, and Shows and especially traveling shows that use pianos. This model is smaller and lighter and used for any purpose where a piano is used.
Model ST-43 is used for Theatre Orchestra and Movies.
All above models have 43 pipes, 3½ octaves chromatic scale.
Model ST-58 is 4½ octave, 58 pipes, for Theatre Orchestra and Movies.

### SIZES AND WEIGHTS

Model CA-43 (Automatic) ........ Weight 335 lbs., Height 60 in., Width 32 in., Depth 24 in.
Model CH-43 (Hand played) ........ Weight 275 lbs., Height 60 in., Width 32 in., Depth 24 in.
Model OH-43 (Hand played) ........ Weight 160 lbs., Height 39 in., Width 32 in., Depth 24 in.
Model CA-53 (Automatic) ........ Weight 395 lbs., Height 65 in., Width 42 in., Depth 27 in.
Model ST-43 (Automatic) ........ Weight 335 lbs., Height 60 in., Width 32 in., Depth 24 in.
Model ST-58 (Automatic) ........ Weight 400 lbs., Height about 72 in., Width 42 in., Depth 30½ in.
Models CA-43 and CH-43 require 1 HP motors, and rotary pressure blowers. Blower is included with instrument. Model OH-43 includes combination motor-blower unit weighing only 20 lbs., and measures about 10 in. square. Price includes blower.
Model ST-43 and ST-58 operate with Pipe Organ blowers; low volume, for inside use.

### PRICES

Model OH-43 ........ $675.00
Model CH-43 ........ $675.00
Model CA-43 ........ $995.00
Model CA-53 ........ $1095.00
Model ST-43........ $1800.00, Includes Pipe Organ Blower.
Model ST-58........ $2250.00, Includes Pipe Organ Blower.
Electric Motor, 1 HP........ $65.00.
Direct Connected Engine........ $174.00. Engine outfit with 1500 watt generator, used for illuminating street advertising outfit and operating picture machine........ $450.00. 5% Discount for Cash. All prices F. O. B. Muscatine, Iowa. AIR CALLIOPES, hand or self-playing, $595.00 and up.

### Tangley Calliopes

Designated as the "Calliaphone," the Tangley air-operated calliope was made in several models, the most popular of which by far was Model CA-43. At one time Tangley advertised that "we have built 98% of all air calliopes in use . . ."

Tangley instruments use regular 10-tune type "A" coin piano rolls, some of which are especially arranged for calliope use (by having extended perforations to sustain the pipe notes) and are marked "Calliaphone." Such rolls were made by the Clark Orchestra Roll Co. of DeKalb, Illinois.

IT IS FEATURES SUCH AS THIS THAT OPEN WISE MEN'S EYES.

## *The New Tone Calliope*

WHEN BETTER CALLIOPES ARE BUILT HARRINGTON WILL BUILD THEM.

THIS INSTRUMENT BUILT TO STAND EVERY TEST.

NOT AN EXPERIMENT BUT A PROVEN SUCCESS

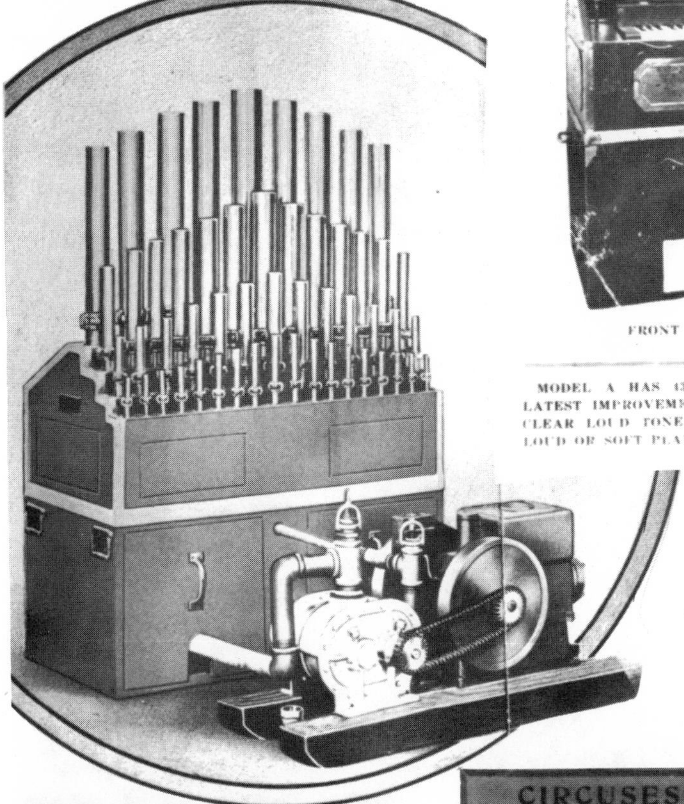

KEYBOARD WITH TOUCH LIKE THAT OF A PIANO—CAN BE PLAYED BY ANY PIANO PLAYER

FRONT VIEW MODEL A

MODEL A HAS 43 BRASS WHISTLES OF OUR LATEST IMPROVEMENT, STYLE AND MODEL FOR CLEAR LOUD TONE. REGULATING DEVICE FOR LOUD OR SOFT PLAYING.

CABINET CONSTRUCTED OF AUTOMOBILE STEEL TRIMMED IN ANGLE BRASS

BACK VIEW MODEL A

FLOOR SPACE 22x36 INCHES.
WEIGHT APPROXIMATELY 190 LBS.
BLOWER, 90 LBS.
MOTOR AND BLOWER OUTFIT, 280 LBS.

### "National" Calliopes

"National" brand air calliopes were made in two basic models, B (with 53 pipes — this was the most popular model by far) and A (with 43 pipes). These instruments appeared under several names, including "Harrington," "National," "New Tone," and "Han-Dee."

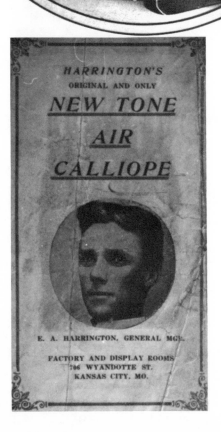

HARRINGTON'S
ORIGINAL AND ONLY
NEW TONE
AIR
CALLIOPE

E. A. HARRINGTON, GENERAL MGR.

FACTORY AND DISPLAY ROOMS
706 WYANDOTTE ST.
KANSAS CITY, MO.

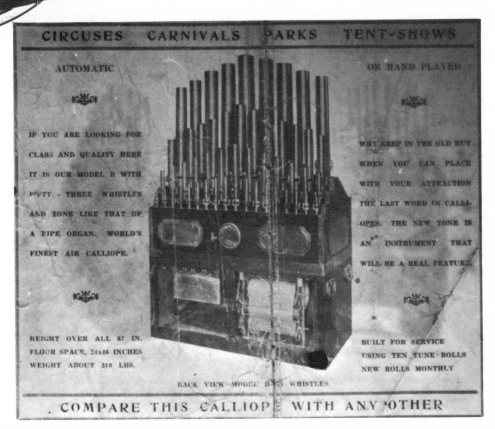

CIRCUSES CARNIVALS PARKS TENT-SHOWS

AUTOMATIC

IF YOU ARE LOOKING FOR CLASS AND QUALITY HERE IT IS OUR MODEL B WITH FIFTY - THREE WHISTLES AND TONE LIKE THAT OF A PIPE ORGAN. WORLD'S FINEST AIR CALLIOPE.

HEIGHT OVER ALL 67 IN.
FLOOR SPACE, 24x46 INCHES
WEIGHT ABOUT 310 LBS.

BACK VIEW MODEL B 53 WHISTLES

OR HAND PLAYED

WHY KEEP IN THE OLD RUT WHEN YOU CAN PLACE WITH YOUR ATTRACTION THE LAST WORD IN CALLIOPES. THE NEW TONE IS AN INSTRUMENT THAT WILL BE A REAL FEATURE.

BUILT FOR SERVICE
USING TEN TUNE ROLLS
NEW ROLLS MONTHLY

COMPARE THIS CALLIOPE WITH ANY OTHER

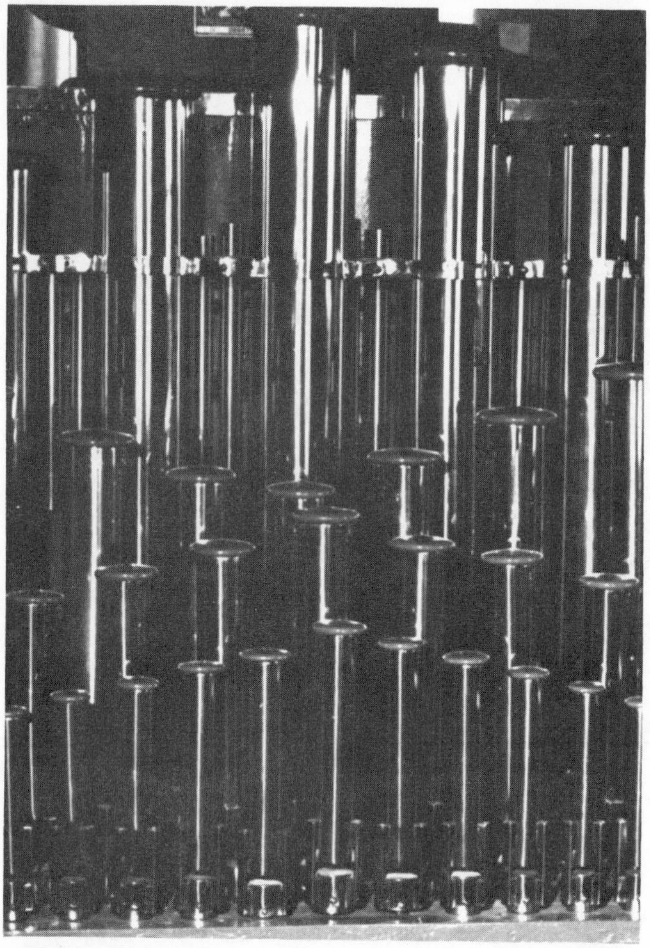

The Air-Calio, a calliope patented in 1927 and 1928 by the Artizan Factories, Inc. (North Tonawanda, New York), uses special rolls. This instrument was made only in small numbers. Above are shown some of the pipes in an Air-Calio in the Larry Givens Collection.

## A Big Musical Flash for the Midway

### —and It Speaks for Itself

The back view shown above gives an idea of the novel arrangement of the keyboard. When the instrument is played automatically this is pushed into place under the tracker frame shelf. We pride ourselves on having real organ touch on the keyboard. **FAST and SNAPPY**.

Key board is of three and three quarters octave register being C to A and by special arrangement all notes play.

The 29 tubular, vibrating stroke bells of pleasing tone can be cut on and off from the keyboard automatically, and are very effective for ballyhoo purposes. Being of great carrying power they practically double the volume of the instrument.

For truck advertising, the equipment shown, consisting of worm reducing gear drive and light weight, air cooled engine, driving the gear endless V belt, is ideal. The gasoline motor of prominent make starts with foot pedal starter, is quick starting, smooth and quiet running, electric governeur equipped and cannot be heard while the **AIR-CALIO** is playing. Being air cooled, there is no water slopping over, sizzling steam. No freeze ups in cold weather. Weight bare motor **40 lbs.** and with wooden stand and belt **85 lbs. Tried and proven a success under trying conditions.**

A ¼ hp. electric motor is interchangeable with gasoline motor on the same base. Heighth to center of shaft of motor and gasoline engine being the same.

With our own feeder system there are no outside air supply cases. Everything but the power outfit is in the instrument itself.

All parts are strong, rugged and made to stand the gaff. Easily tuned and all pipes readily separable for cleaning purposes. No stopped up, silent pipes had to clean. Easily serviced and tuned by the average tuner.

SIMPLE STURDY DEPENDABLE

GREAT VOLUME

FOURTEEN POINTS OF SUPERIORITY

# THE AIR-CALIO

## The New Calliope with an Extra Punch

1. **NO SUCTION USED**

   Suctionless system fully protected by patents Nos. 1,660,172 and 1,663,487. Operates entirely by compressed air. The air supply which blows the pipes operates the instrument.

2. **NO DUST SCREEN**

   No split tracker bar or dust screen because none needed. Dust is blown out thru tracker bar holes, instead of being sucked in.

3. **BELLS**

   Attractive toned tubular bells. Clear tone and of exceptional carrying power, with vibrating stroke. **Entirely air operated.** These are cut on and off in the music. It makes 'em listen.

4. **SPECIAL FEATURE**

   Special feature not found in any other instrument. Chests and valve mechanism built above pipe mouth level obviating flooding during rains.

5. **PIPES**

   Lower section of pipes detachable for cleaning purposes. Built to get greatest possible volume at minimum air pressures. Forty-six in number from 8 foot C to A.

6. **SMALL SIZE, LOW HEIGHTH**

   Dimensions. **Height four feet,** width 3 feet seven inches, depth three feet three inches. Easily mounted in any Ford or Chevrolet one half ton canopy top truck, with plenty of space to go between wheel housings. **WEIGHT 675 pounds.**

7. **ACCESSIBILITY**

   Every working part as easily accessible as your pocket.

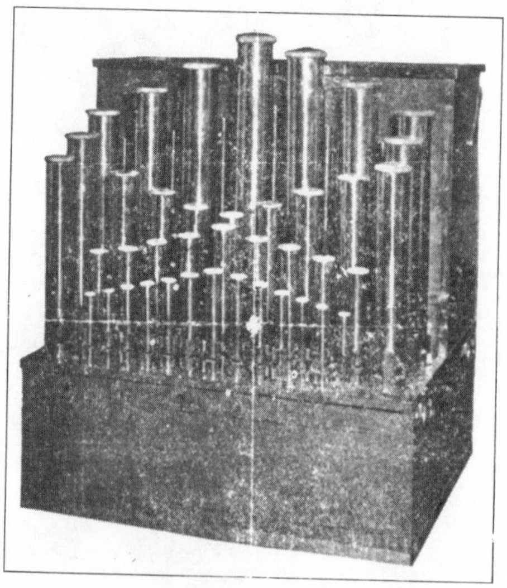

8. **EASY TUNING**

   Easiest tuning device ever conceived.

9. **MUSIC ROLLS**

   Music rolls specially arranged for the **AIR-CALIO—not for piano.**

10. **DRUMS**

    For rink purposes or where extra snap is wanted drums can be attached. This puts the time right for skating.

11. **AIR SUPPLY**

    Can be blown either by rotary blower, or preferably our own feeder system, as this does not deposit an oil film on working parts. Our system uses only ¼ h.p. Blower requires half horse motor.

12. **METAL CASE**

    Iron clad case beautifully finished in DUCO and all angles brass bound. Special 1½" x 2" angle around bottom for extra strength.

13. **MUSIC DRIVE**

    POSITIVE music roll drive. No air or suction motor used to pull music roll. Gear driven cone adjustable for tempo. NO drive chains or belts.

14. **MATERIAL**

    All material used in the AIR-CALIO is guaranteed to be of the highest grade obtainable.

## PARKS

The AIR-CALIO is entirely new and novel and with the bells added is an advertising attraction that gets more attention than any other musical instrument made.

Used to advertise your park and special attractions especially where crowds congregate, it will pull stronger than any form of advertising. Strictly portable, and can be used for your rink music as well.

Automatically, it plays from specially arranged low price rolls that are different, pleasing, full and well balanced musically.

**Patented June 1927 and February 1928**
**C. Maerten patentee**

The **AIR-CALIO** is the result of the comulative experience gained in 35 years of building of automatic organs.

**Manufactured by**
ARTIZAN FACTORIES, INC.
**Successors North Tonawanda Musical Instrument Works**

The incorporators of Artizan Factories, Inc., were also the original incorporators of the NORTH TONAWANDA MUSICAL INSTRUMENT WORKS.

## CARNIVALS

The best instrument of its kind on the market today, and it will stand the racket. Special voicing of pipes, pitched to play with the band, and lower bass tones than any caliope made, makes the instrument smooth, of pleasing tone and great volume, without being offensive.

It is flashy with its DUCO colors and brass bound angles, brass pipes and tubular bells. It is the only Caliope made playing bells with the pipes. Bells play from the keyboard and can be cut on and off with the pipes when played manually for platform ballyhoo.

The large pipes are well braced and solidly fastened to the metal covered case. Close the back doors and let it play in the rain. Won't hurt it a bit.

# John Cocchi, (Inh. Giuseppe Cocchi), Orgelfabrik

**Lychenerstr. 2/3, BERLIN N., Lychenerstr. 2/3.**

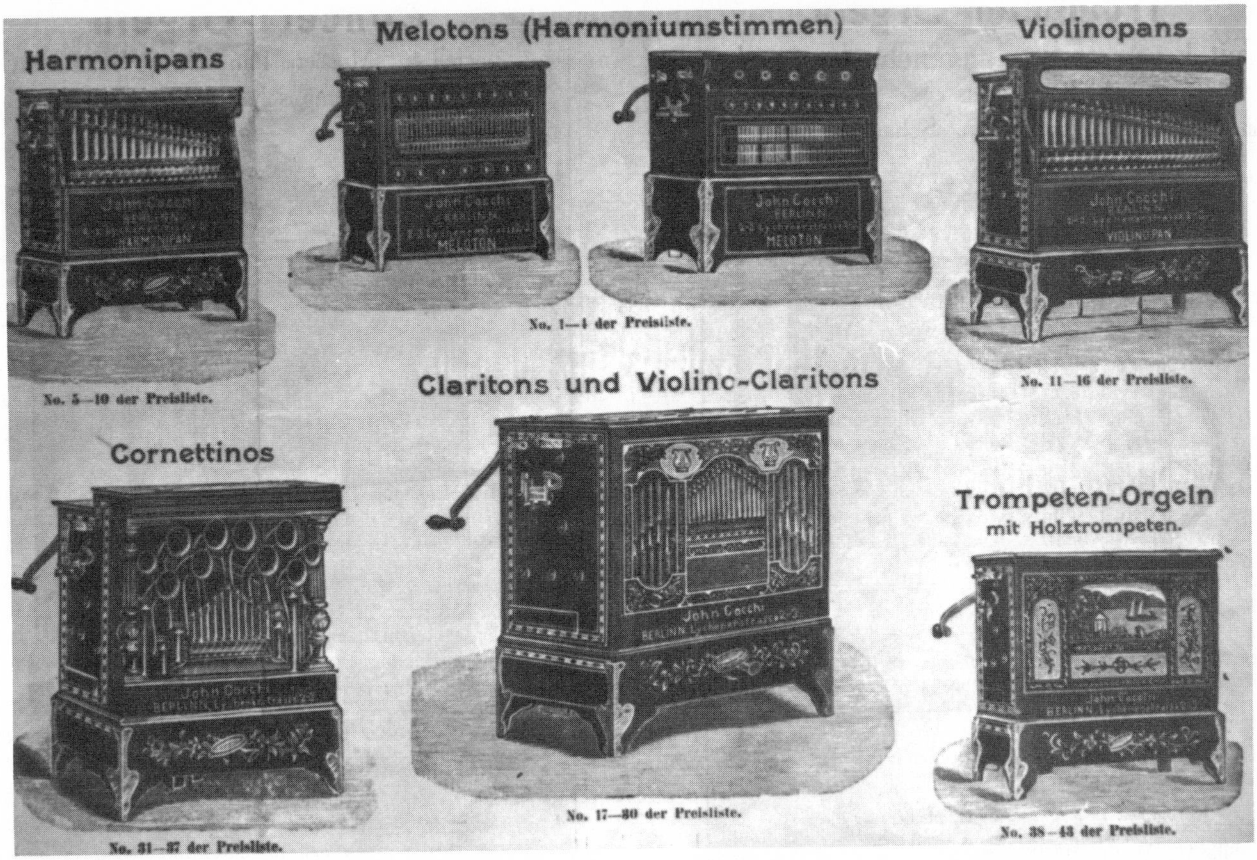

## JOHN COCCHI
—Berlin, Germany—

The organ factory of John Cocchi was founded by his father, Giuseppe, who manufactured a line of barrel-operated pianos and organs in the 1880's.

The John Cocchi instruments on this page, taken from Cocchi sales literature from about the year 1900, show that the principal instruments of the firm were small hand-cranked portable organs, or "monkey organs," as they are sometimes called by collectors today. The instruments were marketed under designations common in the trade at that time: the Meloton was an organ with harmonium reeds; the other organs used wooden or metal pipes and were designated with such names as Harmonipan, Violinopan, Cornettino, Clariton, and the descriptive term Trumpet Organ.

The firm of John Cocchi, Orgelfabrik was formed in 1896 when Cocchi separated from the firm of Cocchi, Bacigalupo, and Graffigna, makers of barrel pianos and organs of similar style to those later made by Cocchi.

Historian Arthur W.J.G. Ord-Hume reports that the firm of John Cocchi & Son was located in later years (until at least 1935) in London and specialized in the manufacture and repair of barrel pianos and organs.

Note: For more information concerning the Cocchi relationship with Bacigalupo refer to the text in Claes O. Friberg's "The Portable Hand-Cranked Barrel Organ" pages in this book.

## DECAP ORGANS
### —Gebr. Decap; Antwerp, Belgium—

Mention the term "dance organ" today and chances are that "Decap" will come to mind first. From a factory located in Antwerp, Belgium, the Decap Brothers turn out today an interesting series of large organs, often with electronic components, to fill what demand remains for this type of instrument in commercial locations. The modern Decap organs are mostly of futuristic design and have fibreboard or plywood fronts forming a showcase for such effects as accordion, drums, xylophone, and in some instances, automatically operated robot musicians! The music is still cut on folding cardboard books and played on a key frame, just as in older days. The music generation systems have changed. Instead of rank upon rank of pipes in the interior, most of the basic tones are provided by electronic organ mechanisms wired to speakers. Some models have real bass pipes to augment the electronic tones.

The new Decap organs are made up at the rate of about one per month (this production figure is as of 1971). Particularly elaborate models sell new for $10,000 to $12,000 or more.

The Decap Brothers' instruments are usually signed "Gebroeders Decap" when the instruments are destined for Flemish-speaking parts of Belgium and "Decap Frères" when intended for the French-speaking localities. "Gebroeders" and "Frères" mean "Brothers" in the respective languages. With some humor we recall once being offered an organ "made by Frères" — the seller noted. Upon responding quizzically I was told that Mr. Frères' first name was Decap, for the organ had "Decap Frères" on it very plainly!

During the 1920's and early 1930's Decap made a number of loudly-voiced fairground organs. These are very rare today as only a few were constructed originally.

During the same era several different styles of orchestrions (without piano, but with ornate orchestrion-like fronts, much in the same general format and concept as Mortier "orchestrions" of the same era). Most of these used perforated paper rolls, a departure from the usual folding cardboard standard. It is interesting to note that most of these Decap orchestrions had roll mechanisms identical to those used by Bursens (and also, by the way, Popper & Co. orchestrions!) and were obtained from a common supplier. As the tracker bar layout is of similar spacing to the Bursens, many collectors have converted Decap orchestrions (for which rolls are rare) to the Bursens or "Arburo" scale, for which rolls are readily available.

These Decap roll-operated orchestrions are generally of oak wood, have some art glass work at the front, have the roll accessible via a door at the center front, and are from about 8' to 10' high. Several styles of Decap electric pianos were made in the 1920's, but these were never produced in quantity as the firm concentrated on the organ type of instrument as its main product.

Decap dance organs known today are mostly of modernistic appearance. Ones made during the 1930's, 1940's, and 1950's are of pneumatic construction (this was before the time of the electronic organ use) and have many ranks of pipes, including some with interesting voicing — such as the popular jazz flute which produces a warbling or wavering sound. Some really immense Decap organs of 121-key specifications were made as regular production items. Although a few organs with slightly more keys were made by Decap and Mortier, the 121-key instruments were the "top of the line" as far as regular production line models were concerned. As such they are highly prized by collectors today. The dimensions of these instruments are awe-inspiring. It is not unusual for one to be over twenty feet wide and over twelve feet high!

Most Decap organs were of more modest specifications — with key ranges in the 60's, 70's, or 80's — and with dimensions of about eight to twelve feet wide and seven to nine feet high. The number of keys is usually computed by counting the number of slots in the roller which holds the cardboard music on the key frame. In some instances keys were left blank — so the number of keys is often slightly larger than the number of functional positions on the key frame.

When Mortier went out of business in the 1950's the firm's operations were taken over by Decap. As was the practice also of Bursens and Mortier, the Decap company made use where it could of used organ components. Many Decap organs known today are really old Mortier organs in disguise. They were acquired as trade-ins or bought as worn-out instruments, reconditioned thoroughly, provided with new and modern fronts (the old ornate fronts, sorry to relate, were chopped up and thrown away!) and then sold as "new" Decap organs. Especially in post-World War II years it was far more economical to make use of old organ pipes and chests than to make new ones.

Provided with some expertly-arranged music books a well-regulated Decap organ can be quite fascinating — both from a visual viewpoint (as the various effects such as accordion, cymbals, drums, etc. are in full view on most models) and a musical aspect. As such they are widely collected today.

Decap Orchestrions: Above and to the left are shown two typical Decap orchestrions. Operated by perforated paper rolls, these have tall facades similar to contemporary orchestrions of other manufacturers. Without piano, but with many ranks of pipes, these were intended for indoor use in cafes, restaurants, dance pavilions, and similar places. Typically Decap orchestrions are about 8' to 9' or so in height. (Most Decap illustrations courtesy of Leonard Grymonprez)

This large Decap organ displays three accordions as well as other jazz instruments on the front. The modernistic facade is typical of most Decap organs made since 1930.

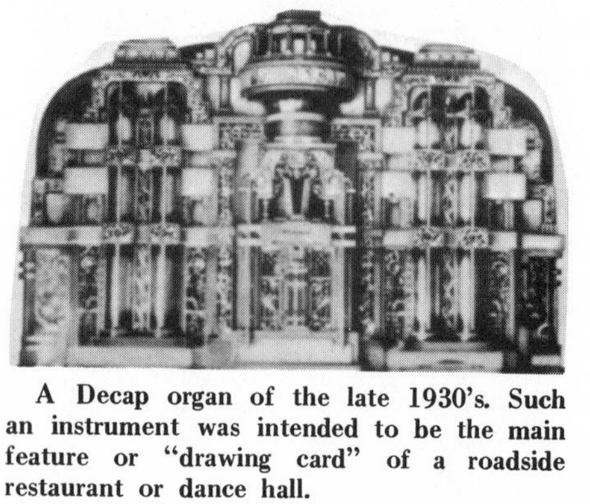

A Decap organ of the late 1930's. Such an instrument was intended to be the main feature or "drawing card" of a roadside restaurant or dance hall.

## TYPICAL DECAP DANCE ORGANS
**—Mechanical music modernized!—**

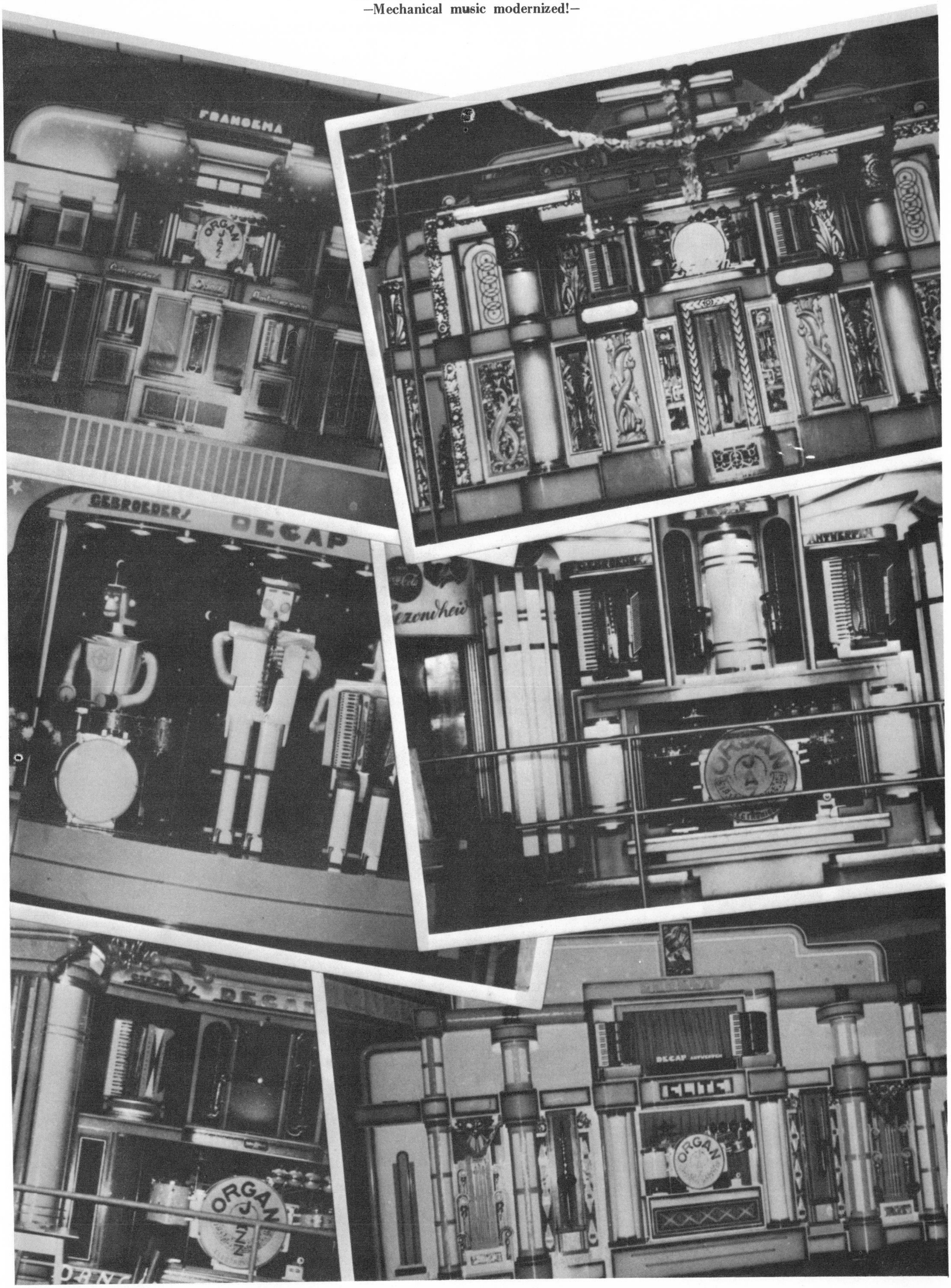

The Dutch street organ, or "Pierement" — the term that is given to this type of instrument in Holland — is an automatic pipe organ made for street use, the mechanism of which is activated by the turning of a wheel by hand; and the whole instrument is portable, usually mounted on a cart. Originally "pierement" referred to various types of organs. Today the term is mainly used by collectors to describe book-operated instruments. The "pierement" term appears to have originated shortly after 1900.

Much has been written about street organs and their place in Dutch life and culture. "From Music Boxes to Street Organs," by Romke deWaard, has done much to popularize the street organ with collectors. This book, the history of the pierement, traces the development of the instrument from the early days to modern times.

Romke deWaard attributes the beginnings of the street organ to three historical events: (1) The founding of a large street organ rental agency in Amsterdam, circa 1875, by the blind Leon Warnies of Belgium; (2) The construction of the first book-operated organs by Gavioli in 1892; and (3) The introduction of these book organs as street organs in the Netherlands by Warnies.

Leon Warnies died in 1902, just prior to the delivery of the first book organs to his rental agency.

The pierement or street organ is considered to be a typically Dutch instrument, notwithstanding the remarkable circumstance that, at least until about 1920, all street organs were foreign made. However, they were built with Holland as a destination. From the earliest days of the pierement onward, instruments were played in the streets of most larger Dutch cities, particularly Amsterdam, Rotterdam, and Groningen.

R. deWaard notes the tonal differences of the various organ types:

Fair organs, or band organs as they are called in America, have a much stronger and sharper sound [than have street organs] in which the upper registers are prominent. The accent in a fair organ is not on the heavy booming chords or pronounced rhythm, but is on the melody which emerges with a clear, brilliant sound. All of this is done by high-pressure violin pipes, augmented during the forte passages by mixtures. The countermelody is full and sonorous — in German organs, from the trumpets; in French and Belgian organs, from the baritones.

Dance organs are distinguished by the strongly accented rhythm of their music; the many short and powerful chords of the heavy and deep-sounding registers simply force the dancing couples to maintain the correct rhythm. Accompanying the pipes is a choice collection of percussion and novelty instruments. Dance organs are often of enormous size and have a great number of registers. Mortier, Decap, and Bursens were leading makers of these.

The street organ or pierement differs from dance and fair organs, especially in the lyrical and sensitive nature of the music and also its smaller size. While the dance and fair organs are powered by motors, the pierement is cranked by hand, which means that the bellows cannot be too large or too heavy. The number of registers and pipes are also more limited than in fair and dance organs. This is to make the street organs of manageable size for the renter to take to the streets. Particularly in Amsterdam there are high and steeply-inclined bridges that have to be negotiated.

Many early street organs were made by Gasparini and Gavioli. After 1910 Limonaire Frères became a leading builder for the Dutch market. Later, the Belgian firms of Bursens, DeVreese and, still later, Decap came into the picture.

The earlier cylinder-operated street organs were mostly of German manufacture, with Wellerhaus instruments being the best known. In later years the German instruments were replaced by book-operated organs mainly made in France and Belgium. A few German organs, particular those of Gebr. Bruder, were used in later years, but most were of French, Belgian, and, later, Dutch (e.g. Frei) make — as noted.

The Dutch formed sentimental attachments to their street organs and assigned colorful names to them. The deWaard book notes instruments with such names as Little Blue, Little White, Big Belly, Little Belly, Gold Top, Pointed Top, The Turk, The Arab, The Flower Girl, Blue Gasparini, Cry Baby, Diver, Cement Mill, and even Snot-Nose!

Pierements of the 'teens and early 'twenties were usually made with piccolo and clarinet pipes, but these were subsequently omitted from most street organ registers as these ranks went out of tune easily. More substantial pipes such as flutes and flute mixtures replaced them. Many street organs had three carved figures on the front. Often the figures were animated.

In 1921, Carl Frei, Sr. settled in Breda, Holland, and began to arrange music in a new, interesting, and artistic manner which changed the tonal character of the street organ. Frei constructed organs using a pipe complement slightly different from the earlier instruments, a new pipe arrangement which suited his music better. Other makers followed Frei's lead. From about 1920 to 1940 the street organ achieved its height of popularity.

After World War I the French-made organs (Gavioli, Gasparini, Limonaire) were imported in diminishing quantities. The French business was on the decline and some firms, Gavioli being the most important, were already defunct. The street organ building business was taken over by Bursens, Verbeeck, Decap, DeVreese, and several other makers. Their plants were located in Belgium, close to Holland's southern border. While many of these Belgian instruments were new, a good portion were made by modernizing older French (and, in a few cases, German) cylinder and book organs.

Most Belgian street organs made after about 1930 dispensed with the carved figures. Many of the earlier curlicues, pillars, and scrolls were reduced in size or eliminated. In their place painted panels, many with life-size figures, were mounted on the organ fronts.

After World War II only a few street organs were made, mostly in Belgium by Arthur Bursens. In Amsterdam, Gijs Perlee, well-known renter of street organs, fabricated a number of street organs, mainly with the use of parts from earlier instruments.

From about 1940 to the early 1950's street organs were largely forgotten. Restrictive legislation in some Dutch cities kept them from being used. The public seemingly didn't miss them. However, the underlying sentiment was still there — and in recent years the pierement has enjoyed a revival. They are to be heard again on Dutch streets. A collectors' association, Kring van Draaiorgelvrienden, publishes a bulletin, "Het Pierement," (The Pierement) devoted to the history and appreciation of these colorful instruments.

———————

Tonal Disposition of Street Organs:

Bass group of pipes: Large stopped pipes of 16' tonal length sometimes augmented with 8' speaking length pipes. Sometimes also augmented in forte passages with trombones.

Accompaniment group: Usually located in the rear of the organ case. Sometimes this rank consists only of a rank of open flutes; sometimes a rank of stopped flutes is added.

Melody registers: Consists mainly of violin pipes and a bourdon rank. Sometimes two, three, or even four ranks of violins are arranged in cascading or pyramidal fashion to augment each other. The bourdon consists of two rows of closed pipes, wider than the violins, arranged so that two pipes always speak for each note. The pipe in front is tuned several beats per second higher than the rear pipe. This produces a clear, undulating sound. The bourdon is used to achieve a lyrical, sweetly flowing, and sensitive quality. The violin register, usually placed in back of the double row of bourdons, gives a forceful and strong sound.

Harmony registers: The harmony section is ordinarily half an octave lower than the melody and ranges from 12 to 18 keys. In the Belgian-made instruments the harmony section consists of a celeste (a violin type of pipe but of larger scale) and a cello (twice the length of celeste) rank. Dutch-made Carl Frei instruments usually have an undamaris (literally, "waves of the sea") rank in the harmony section. The undamaris is a violin pipe which is twice the length of the pipes in the regular violin section.

Note: Refer to the individual sections on Bursens, Decap, Gavioli, et al in this book for more information about these firms.

———————

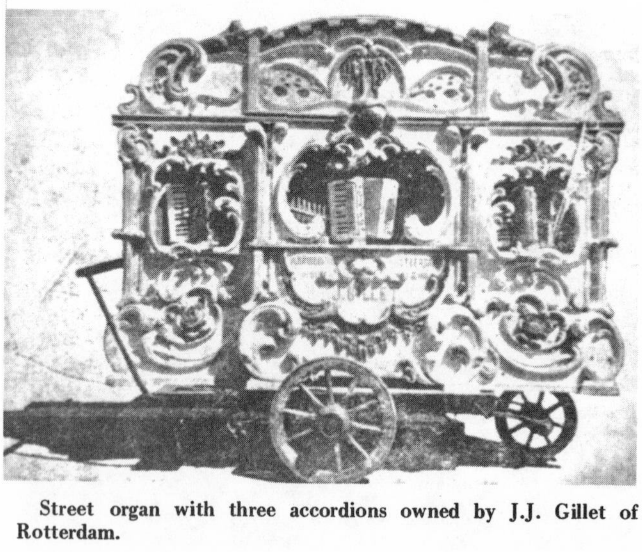

Street organ with three accordions owned by J.J. Gillet of Rotterdam.

# Music in Amsterdam

Whilst on holiday in the Netherlands, member Mr. W. Keating had the pleasure of visiting Mr. G. Perlee's Organ Works in Amsterdam, and was given a musical treat by way of a selection of tunes on the various organs which were in the works at that time. The instruments ranged from the small 23-key organs which The Perlee Family make for export to various countries (cases for which can be seen in Picture No. 1), to the large street organs which were in the works for repair or tuning. One of the organs shown in the first picture is one that was nearing completion after a complete rebuild. Picture 2 shows part of a proscenium in the course of being painted, whilst the third picture depicts the well known 64-key bursens street organ "Pipo" outside the organ works.

Picture No. 1

Picture No. 2

A visit to the Perlee works in Amsterdam. (Courtesy of the Fair Organ Preservation Society; the above appeared in the Society's publication, "The Key Frame.") The "orchestrion" at the left side of Picture No. 2 isn't a Hupfeld Helios Ic/31 orchestrion at all, even though it looks like one. It is a barrel-operated piano by Van Roy, who built the case as a small replica of the Hupfeld instrument.

## REMOND DUWYN

Remond Duwyn (or Duwijn, in the Flemish language) left the employ of Th. Mortier in Antwerp and founded his own organ building business in Wilrijk, Belgium. Instruments built by Duwyn were of the dance organ type.

The above-pictured instrument, photographed by the author in Tubize, Belgium, in its original restaurant location in 1966, is quite similar in appearance to certain of the "orchestrion" style organs made by Mortier. This Duwyn organ has a particularly sweet and mellow "warm" type of sound, a tonal characteristic said to be common to other Duwyn organs as well. (Instrument presently in the collection of Roy Haning and Neal White)

Duwyn was a limited-production builder whose output was probably on the order of just several instruments per year.

The dance organ type instruments produced in Belgium by Mortier, Decap, and Bursens and, in smaller numbers by Koenigsberg, Duwyn, and others, were never exported far beyond the borders of the country in which they were produced. In an era in which the automatic musical instruments of Hupfeld, Gavioli, Mermod Frères, and other European makers were enjoying a worldwide fame and reputation, the very concept of the dance organ and its tonal qualities was largely unknown to the music industry. Only since the 1950's has the musical value of these Belgian instruments been recognized — a time too late for worldwide sales, for the firms that made them, with the exceptions of Decap and Bursens, are gone forever, but in time for collectors and museums to preserve many of the remaining instruments in Belgium before they went the way of other automatic musical instruments whose original entertainment and commercial value had passed.

Frati & Co., located at Schönhauser Allee 73, Berlin (and other Berlin addresses over the years), was a leading maker of hand-cranked barrel organs during the 1880's, 1890's, and early 1900's. The firm was controlled by the Bacigalupo family of Berlin.

Small portable organs called Melotons contained organ reeds. The majority of instruments, the Harmonipans, Violinopans, Claritons, and Trumpet organs, contained organ pipes. These portable organs were Frati's forte, and more such instruments were made than of any other Frati product.

Medium-size barrel organs, hand-cranked but too large to be considered portable, were designated as Concertinos. Still larger organs were called Orchestrions, although they were not orchestrions in the usual sense of the word. Rather, they were large and ornate and loudly-voiced fairground organs.

Frati maintained an effective system of dozens of sales agents. In the United States, such firms as Pollmann, North Tonawanda Musical Instrument Works. Muzzio, and Molinari all imported Frati organs. Usually the Frati name was overlaid with a plaque bearing the name of the sales agent. In other instances the agent's name was put directly on the instrument, and there was no mention of the Frati firm. To help its agents Frati provided engravings (without the firm's name) for use in the agents' catalogues. This practice tended to make Frati anonymous to a degree. This bothered Frati not a bit for the company was at the top of the hand-cranked barrel organ industry during the late 19th century — and sales were what mattered the most.

Internal management problems plus the failure to change the Frati line from the barrel system (which for large organs was considered obsolete by 1910) to the cardboard system resulted in a decline of Frati's fortunes. A small entry into the coin piano and orchestrion market was made, and a number of beautiful Fratinola and Fratihymnia instruments made their appearance (see separate section of this book).

In 1923 the assets of Frati & Co. were acquired by J.D. Philipps & Sons of Frankfurt am Main.

FRATI & Co.

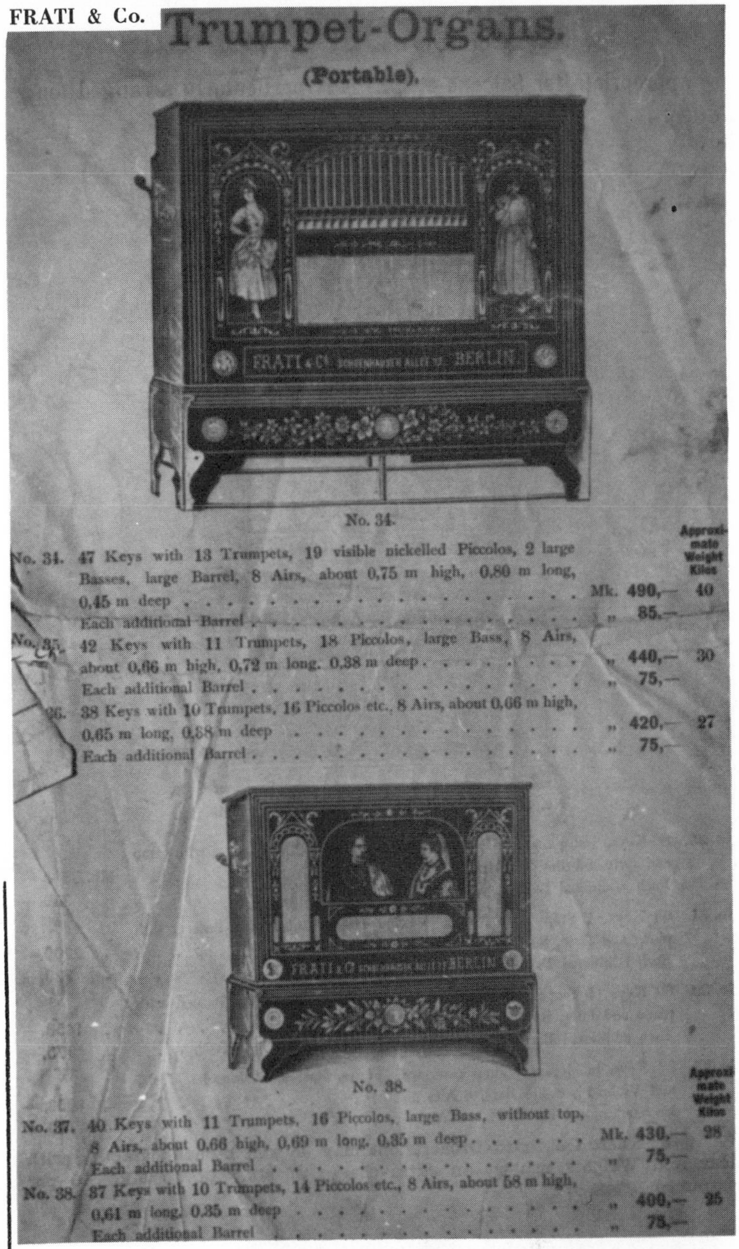

Trumpet-Organs.
(Portable).
FRATI & Co. BERLIN
No. 34.
Approximate Weight Kilos
No. 34. 47 Keys with 13 Trumpets, 19 visible nickelled Piccolos, 2 large Basses, large Barrel, 8 Airs, about 0,75 m high, 0,80 m long, 0,45 m deep . . . Mk. 490,— 40
Each additional Barrel . . . „ 85,—
42 Keys with 11 Trumpets, 18 Piccolos, large Bass, 8 Airs, about 0,66 m high, 0,72 m long. 0,38 m deep . . . „ 440,— 30
Each additional Barrel . . . „ 75,—
38 Keys with 10 Trumpets, 16 Piccolos etc., 8 Airs, about 0,66 m high, 0,65 m long, 0,58 m deep . . . „ 420,— 27
Each additional Barrel . . . „ 75,—
FRATI & Co. BERLIN
No. 38.
Approximate Weight Kilos
No. 37. 40 Keys with 11 Trumpets, 16 Piccolos, large Bass, without top, 8 Airs, about 0,66 high, 0,69 m long, 0,35 m deep . . . Mk. 430,— 28
Each additional Barrel . . . „ 75,—
No. 38. 37 Keys with 10 Trumpets, 14 Piccolos etc., 8 Airs, about 58 m high, 0,61 m long, 0,35 m deep . . . „ 400,— 25
Each additional Barrel . . . „ 75,—


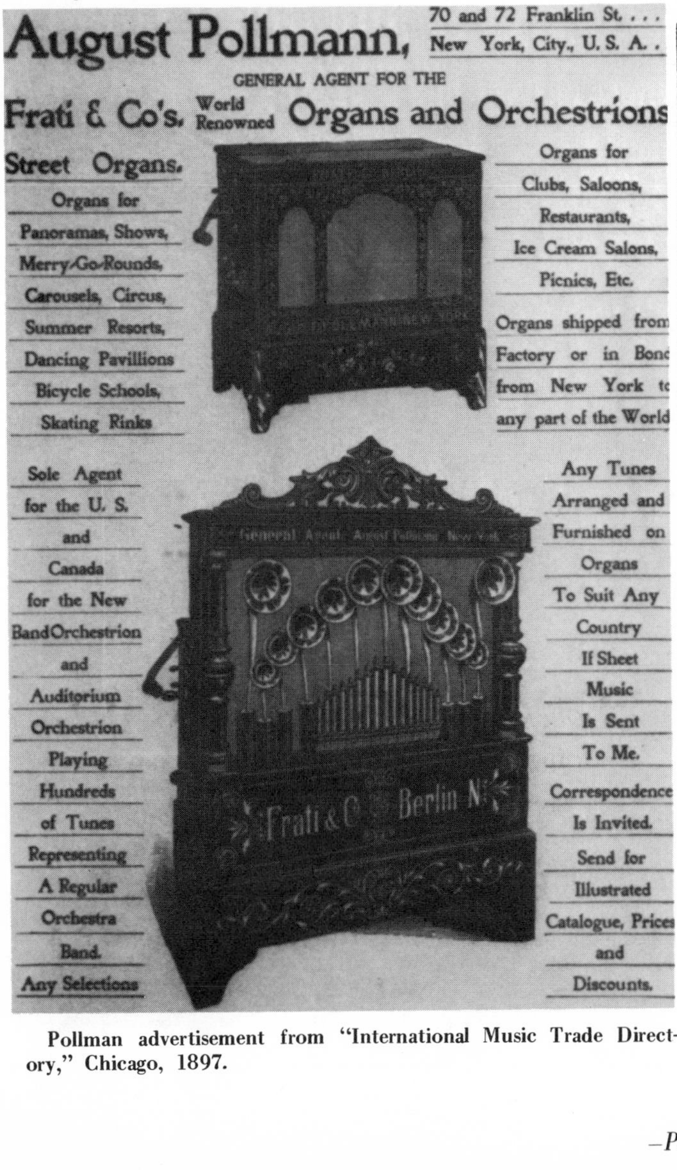


Pollman advertisement from "International Music Trade Directory," Chicago, 1897.

Right: A typical Concertino or hand-cranked organ made for carousels, panoramas, dance halls, and general entertainment use in the 1890's.

No. 21—24.

# Harmonipans.

## (Portable.)

**Visible cane-Flutes, soft agreeable Music not easily out of tune, hence especially recommendable.**

| | | | |
|---|---|---|---|
| No. 43. | 44 Keys, 19 visible cane Flutes, large Basses, Tremolo, 8 Airs, about 0,63 m high, 0,69 m long, 0,35 m deep | Mk. 440,— | 24 |
| | Each additionel Barrel | „ 75,— | |
| No. 44. | 40 Keys, 23 visible cane Flutes, Tremolo, large Barrel, 8 Airs, about 0,63 m high, 0,65 m long, 0,35 m deep | „ 400,— | 23 |
| | Each additional Barrel | „ 85,— | |
| No. 45. | 40 Keys, 24 visible cane Flutes, 1 Stop Pipes extra (**double Harmonipan**), Tremolo, large Barrel, 8 Airs, about 0,63 m high, 0,65 m long, 0,37 m deep | „ 460,— | 25 |
| | Each additional Barrel | „ 85,— | |
| No. 45a. | 40 Keys, 24 visible cane Flutes, 1 Stop Violin-Pipes, extra large Barrel, 8 Airs, about 0,70 m high, 0,65 m long, 0,37 m deep | „ 460,— | 25 |
| | Each additional Barrel | „ 85,— | |
| No. 46. | 33 Keys, 19 visible cane Flutes, 8 Airs (latest construction with Tremolo Mk. 10,— extra), about 0,60 m high, 0,64 m long, 0,35 m deep | „ 330,— | 21 |
| | Each additional Barrel | „ 75,— | |
| No. 47. | 33 Keys, 19 visible cane Flutes, 1 Stop Violin-Pipes extra, latest construction, 8 Airs, about 0,68 m high, 0,57 m long, 0,36 m deep | „ 380,— | 23 |
| | Each additional Barrel | „ 75,— | |
| No. 47a. | 35 Keys, 19 visible cane Flutes, 1 Stop Violin-Pipes extra, newest construction, 8 Airs, about 0,70 m high, 0,59 m long, 0,35 m deep | „ 400,— | 24 |
| | Each additional Barrel | „ 80,— | |
| No. 48. | 38 Keys, 19 visible cane Flutes and 5 visible Bells, Basses with Tremolo, 8 Airs, latest construction, about 0,61 m high, 0,64 m long, 0,36 m deep | „ 400,— | 26 |
| | Each additional Barrel | „ 75,— | |

**No. 45a, No. 47 and 47a are Violinopans.**

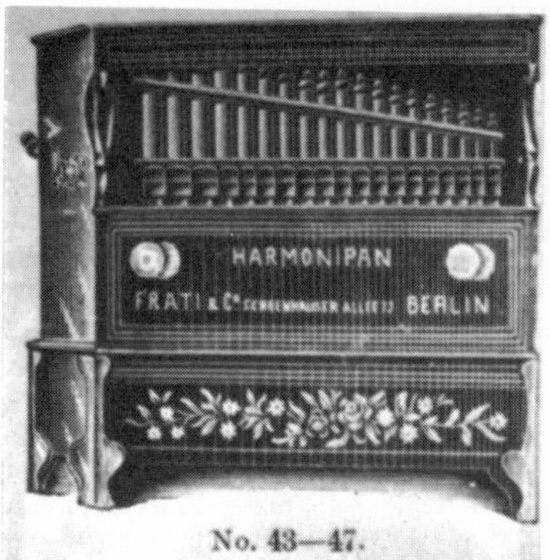

No. 43—47.

**Important note: For more information concerning the Frati firm, its internal problems, and its control by the Bacigalupo family, refer to Claes O. Friberg's "The Portable Hand-Cranked Barrel Organ" section of this book.**

# Claritons, System Frati.

## (Portable.)

**Latest Construction with visible nickelled Piccolos and visible brass Clarinets the latter varnished, so that they never get black.**

| | | | Weight Kilos |
|---|---|---|---|
| No. 49. | 50 Keys, 20 cane Clarinets, 18 visible Piccolos, Basses threefold, Contra-Basses, Barrel 80 Bars, 9 Airs, about 1,18 m high, 1,05 m long, 0,64 deep | Mk. 650,— | |
| | Each additional Barrel | „ 110,— | |
| No. 50. | Same Instrument with Drum | „ 750,— | |
| No. 51. | 47 Keys, 17 Clarinets and 19 visible double Piccolos, Basses threefold, chromatic, hence appropriate for Orchestra-Music, latest Construction, extra-large Barrel, 80 Bars, 9 Airs, about 0,95 m high, 0,84 m long, 0,53 m deep | „ 650,— | 45 |
| | Each additional Barrel | „ 100.— | |

**Nos. 49—51 especially recommendable for smaller Merry-go-rounds; not portable.**

| | | | |
|---|---|---|---|
| No. 52. | 46 Keys, 15 brass Clarinets and 21 visible nickelled double Piccolos, Basses threefold, large Barrel with 8 Airs, about 0,83 m high, 0,80 long, 0,43 deep | „ 550,— | 42 |
| | Each additional Barrel | „ 85,— | |
| No. 53. | 44 Keys, 13 brass Clarinets and 19 visible nickelled Piccolos, large Barrel, about 0,65 m high, 0,72 m long, 0,38 m deep | „ 490,— | 32 |
| | Each additional Barrel | „ 85,— | |
| No. 54. | 38 Keys, 12 brass Clarinets and 16 visible nickelled Piccolos, 8 Airs, about 0,62 m high, 0,64 m long, 0,39 deep | „ 430,— | 27 |
| | Each additional Barrel | „ 75,— | |
| No. 55. | Same Instrument with large Barrel | „ 450,— | 28 |
| | Each additional Barrel | „ 85,— | |
| No. 56. | 33 Keys, 10 brass Clarinets and 14 visible nickelled Piccolos, 8 Airs, about 0,60 m high, 0,55 m long, 0,37 m deep | „ 400,— | 23 |
| | Each additional Barrel | „ 75,— | |
| No. 57. | 35 Keys, 11 Clarinets, low Basses, large Barrel, 8 Airs, about 0,61 m high, 0,58 long, 0 37 m deep | „ 435,— | 25 |
| | Each additional Barrel | „ 80,— | |

Nos. 53—57.

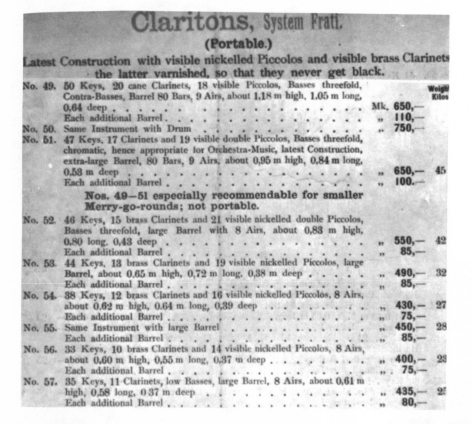

# Orchestrions.

No. 4. 108 Keys, largest Military Band Instrument, in Walnut Case with Inlayings, Revival-Style, with 26 visible brass Trumpets, among them 5 Trombones, 21 wooden Trumpets, 8 Bombardons, 17 visible brass Clarinets, Hautbois, Cornets, 38 visible nickelled Piccolos, Flutes, Basses, Contra-Basses, Drum, Bass-Drum and Cymbles, large Barrel, 9 Airs, without Motor . . . . . Mk. 6400,—
Each additional Barrel . . . . . . . . . . . . . . . . . . . „ 480,—

No. 5. 96 Keys, 22 brass Trumpets, 8 brass Trombones, Bombardons, wooden Trumpets, Hautbois, Clarinets, Flutes, Piccolos, Basses, Contra-Basses, Drum, 3 movable Figures, 12 stops, with piano and forte among them, 96 Bars, 9 Airs „ 5500,—
Each additional Barrel . . . . . . . . . . . . . . . . . . . „ 420,—

No. 6. 86 Keys, 19 brass Trumpets, 7 Trombones, Bombardons, wooden Trumpets, Cornets, Clarinets, Flutes, Piccolos, Basses, Contra-Basses, Drum, 3 movable Figures, 11 Stops with piano and forte among them, 80 Bars, 9 Airs . . „ 4500,—
Each additional Barrel . . . . . . . . . . . . . . . . . . . „ 370,—

No. 7. 80 Keys, 18 brass Trumpets, 6 Trombones, Bombardons, wooden Trumpets, 2 movable Figures, 11 Stops, 80 Bars, 9 Airs . . . . . . . . . „ 3600,—
Each additional Barrel . . . . . . . . . . . . . . . . . . . „ 340,—

No. 8. 72 Keys, 17 brass Trumpets, 5 Trombones, Bombardons, Cornets, Clarinets, Flutes, Piccolos, Basses, Contra-Basses, Drum, 2 movable Figures, 18 Stops, 80 Bars, 9 Airs . . . . . . . . . . . . . . . . . . . „ 2800,—
Each additional Barrel . . . . . . . . . . . . . . . . . . . „ 225,—

No. 4 about 2,35 m long, 3 m high, 1,27 m deep.

# Concertinos

(to be played by Handle)

**for Merry-go-rounds, Panoramas, Dancing-Saloons.**

No. 10. 60 Keys, 18 brass Trumpets, Trombones incl., Bombardons, Basses, Contra-Basses, cane Clarinets, Flutes, Piccolos, piano-forte Stop, 2 movable Figures, 8 Stops . . . . . . . . . . . . . . . . . . . Mk. 1700,—
Each additional Barrel . . . . . . . . . . . . . . . . . . . „ 160,—

No. 11. Same Instrument with Drum . . . . . . . . . . . . . „ 1800,—

No. 12. Same Instrument with Columns instead of Figures and without Drum . . „ 1500,—

No. 13. 53 Keys, 14 brass Trumpets, Trombones, Basses, Clarinets, Piccolos . . „ 1400,—
With Figures Mk. 150,— more.
Each additional Barrel . . . . . . . . . . . . . . . . . . . „ 135,—

No. 26—29.

No. 12 about 2 m high, 1,33 m long, 0,78 m deep.

No. 14—17.

No. 26. 58 Keys, Piccolos, 16 cane Clarinets, Flutes, wooden Trumpets, Cornets, Basses, Contra-Basses, Bombardons, Barrel 80 Bars, 9 Airs . . . . . . Mk. 1200,—
Each additional Barrel . . . . . . . . . . . . . . . . . . . „ 150,—

No. 27. 55 Keys, Piccolos, 16 cane Clarinets, wooden Trumpets, Flutes, Cornets, Basses, Contra-Basses, Bombardons, Barrel 80 Bars, 9 Airs . . . . . . „ 1100,—
Each additional Barrel . . . . . . . . . . . . . . . . . . . „ 135,—

No. 28. 53 Keys, nickelled Piccolos, 15 brass Clarinets, wooden Trumpets, Baritons, Bombardons, cane Cornets, Flutes, Basses, 80 Bars, 9 Airs, about 1 60 m high, 1,26 m long, 0,83 m deep . . . . . . . . . . . . . . „ 1030,—
Each additional Barrel . . . . . . . . . . . . . . . . . . . „ 125,—

No. 29. Same Instrument with Drum . . . . . . . . . . . . . „ 1130,—
Each additional Barrel . . . . . . . . . . . . . . . . . . . „ 135,—

In case other Coats of Arms should be wished for in the front-side of the instrument, please state them when ordering.

# Orchestrions

(to be played by Handle or Motor).

No. 1 about 3,50 m high, 3,15 m long, 1,65 m deep.

1. 116 Keys, largest Orchestra-Instrument, 24 brass Trumpets, 10 brass Bass-Trombones, Bombardons, wooden Trumpets, Hautbois, Clarinets, Cornets, Flutes, Piccolos, Basses, etc., 16 Stops with forte and piano, Bass Drum, Cymbles, Drum, 7 Figures striking Music-Instruments, Barrels 96 Bars, with 10 Airs, richest Model . . . . . . . . . . . . . . . . . . . . Mk. 9000,-
Each additional Barrel with 10 Airs . . . . . . . . . . . . . . . . " 540,-

The Frati instruments illustrated on these pages are all of the barrel-operated variety. Some very large models were motor-driven, but in the 1890's when electric power was more of a novelty than a widespread convenience, even these were usually hand-cranked by a seemingly tireless attendant.

In the United States, Frati organs were very popular during the 1880's and 1890's. Probably more of the Frati make were imported than any other. Various firms, mainly in the New York City area, provided up-to-date music by pinning new cylinders on their premises.

(Thanks to Carl Thomsen for many of the Frati illustrations used here)

## CARL FREI
—Waldkirch, Germany—

In Waldkirch im Breisgau, Germany, the firm of Carl Frei continues the business of building fairground organs today. Built on special order are loudly-voiced instruments of all sizes. A number of interesting models of the 1940's and 1950's are shown here.

The firm of Carl Frei has an illustrious history. Here it is, as written for this book by Carl Frei, Jr., and translated by Jan L.M. van Dinteren (an officer of Kring van Draaiorgelvrienden):

### History of the Carl Frei Firm

Carl Frei, Sr., was born on April 4, 1884, in Schiltach/Schwarzwald. He attended the music school in Waldkirch. At the age of 14 he wrote and arranged music for the Waldkirch Townmusic (Waldkircher Stadtmusik).

He served an apprenticeship in the organ factory of Wilhelm Bruder Söhne. In 1902 he moved to Paris and was hired as a music arranger and pipe voicer at the Gavioli works. Ludovico Gavioli admired Frei's work and wanted him to continue with his firm. However, when Gavioli opened a branch factory with Th. Mortier in Antwerp, Frei moved to Belgium and became the chief music arranger with Gavioli-Mortier. When Gavioli lost its financial arrangement with Mortier, Frei continued in the same position as arranger for the new firm of Th. Mortier S.A. Soon thereafter, Carl Frei opened his own factory in Antwerp. There he manufactured organs and also sold instruments imported from Ch. Marenghi of Paris. In 1914 Carl Frei had to close his factory because of the war.

In 1921 Frei founded a new organ factory in Breda, Holland. There he designed the special scales and pipe complements for Dutch street organs. The most popular models were in the 52-, 67-, 72-, and 90-key sizes. These instruments were especially constructed to withstand the damp climate of the Netherlands.

Carl Frei's innovations were very popular. Before long, they were copied by other street organ builders. His novel music arrangements on folding cardboard books were likewise imitated.

Street organs built using the Frei system required only a small amount of wind in comparison to instruments of other makes. They contained fewer reed pipes, which meant that the instrument did not have to be tuned very often. The new Frei organs were of a different tonal quality [sound color] and were widely admired. His best-known pipe registers were: bourdon-violin celeste, bifoon, tremolo, and undamaris. Undamaris and bifoon were especially desirable for use in organ arrangements of a softer nature. The 52- to 90-key organs used the key system. Later, larger instruments were built using a 112-keyless system. The 112-keyless instruments represented yet another innovation in size and in tonal quality.

The works in Breda continued until the advent of World War II forced their closing.

In 1946 Carl Frei, Sr., and his son, Carl, Jr., founded the Carl Frei & Sohn Orgelfabrik in Waldkirch. Here street organs and fairground organs were and continue to be built. Carl Frei, Sr., died on May 10, 1967, at the age of 83 years. He died without being ill. Since that time the business has been continued by Carl Frei, Jr.

—————————

112-keyless Carl Frei organ owned by Mr. G.T. Cushing. Although most organs have the name spelled as "Carl," some, especially those sold in Germany, have the "Karl Frei" spelling.

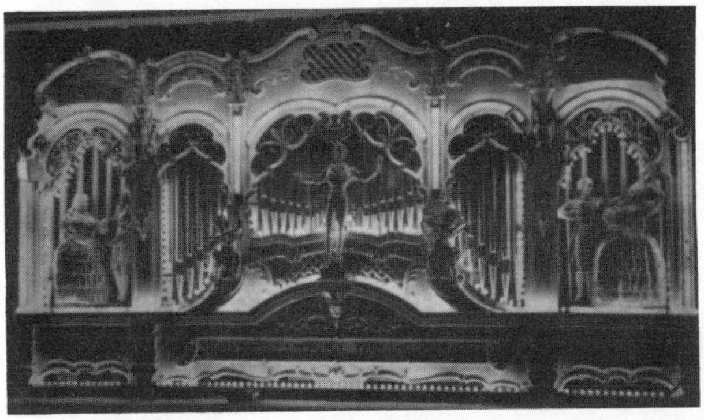

Model 89, No. 4 Carl Frei organ built in 1949. The facade is 6 meters long by 2.6 meters high. The instrument contains 374 pipes, 17 xylophone bars, and percussion effects.

112-keyless Carl Frei organ built in 1958. The instrument contains 537 pipes plus xylophone bars and drum and trap effects.

90-keyless Carl Frei organ built in 1949. Contains percussion effects, a 22-note xylophone, and the following pipes: 44 violins, 44 violin celeste pipes, 44 bourdon flutes, 66 master carillons, 18 trumpets, 18 cellos, 36 undamaris pipes, 36 biphone (bifoon) pipes, 36 accompaniment pipes, 24 basses, and 8 trombones.

Model No. 46 Frei organ built in 1953. Contains 327 pipes plus percussion effects. The facade measures 3 meters wide by 2.4 meters deep. The main case or chassis measures 1.8 meters wide by 2 meters high by 1 meter deep.

From the 'teens until the late 1920's, Gaudin & Cie., of Paris, France, manufactured a variety of organs, mostly of larger sizes, including those of 89, 98, and 112-key size. When Charles Marenghi died in 1919 the Gaudin brothers took over the Marenghi business and combined it with their own.

During the 'teen years Gaudin supplied loudly-voiced instruments to English showmen. Many of these had elaborate carvings and exposed brass trumpet pipes. Gaudin organs of the 1920's were mainly sold in Belgium (the main market for really large organs at that time) and were mostly softly voiced dance organs. Sales outlets were established in Lokeren and Antwerp, Belgium.

Gaudin organ with brass trumpets and loud fairground organ voicing. Used in England during the World War I era. Some types of Gaudin organs were very heavily carved. Some varieties had facades with medallions picturing famous musicians.

Gaudin fairground-type organ used on Farrar's gondola ride in the 'teens.

112-key Gaudin owned by the Helmond Organ Foundation operated by Tom Merkx and Hendrik Bocken. The instrument is a double-case type (with two of everything) and has nearly 1,200 pipes. It was built in 1924 and was originally sold to a dance hall in Wetteren, Belgium. (Colin Upchurch photograph; originally in "The Key Frame")

The firm of Gavioli & Co., headquartered in Paris, was the leading European maker of fairground organs during the 19th and early 20th centuries.

### Miss Gavioli's History

In his book, "From Music Boxes to Street Organs," Romke deWaard tells the history of Gavioli, as related by Miss Andree Gavioli in letters to Henri Bank.

The firm, with origins dating back to 1806 in Italy, was established in 1845 in Paris when Ludovic Gavioli I moved the family organ business there from Modena, Italy. Miss Andree Gavioli's remembrances are those of misfortunes: Ludovic Gavioli created an automatic musical instrument which portrayed King David playing a real harp. This automaton was given to a traveling fair concessionnaire who, despite solemn promises, never returned it. Another incident concerned a Russian to whom Ludovic consigned a mechanical instrument designated as a "Panharmonico." The instrument and sales agent disappeared. Another tale of woe concerned the Duke of Modena, Italy, who commissioned Ludovic Gavioli to build an orchestrion that would 'surpass all previous ones in sound and mechanisms.' This commission was duly carried out, and the Duke expressed his pleasure with the instrument... but never paid for it!

Miss Gavioli relates that another misfortune befell the firm when Ludovic entrusted his third son, Claude, with the management of the organ factory. An embezzling bookkeeper almost brought the firm to the brink of financial ruin, a plight that was averted at the last moment by enlisting the aid, in 1861, of a certain Yver whose qualifications did not include knowledge of organ building.

In 1863 Anselme Gavioli became manager of the company. During the war of 1870 the factory had to be moved temporarily to the Alsace region of France where, unfortunately, it was completely destroyed. After the war ended, the family moved back to Paris. Within a few years the business was operating successfully once again.

In 1901, Miss Gavioli relates, the firm suffered a stunning blow which was to handicap the firm from that time onward. The poor condition of the factory building foundations on the corner of Rue de Bercy and Quai de la Rapee necessitated almost complete reconstruction. The entire capital of the organization had to be invested in this unexpected project. Financial austerity measures were instituted, and the sales and organ building staffs were reduced. One of the firm's prized technicians, Charles Marenghi, left at this time and went together with a number of other ex-Gavioli people to found the Marenghi organ business.

Miss Gavioli continues with the story of a cartel that was to be founded by Gavioli, Gasparini, Marenghi, Limonaire, and other French organ builders. The purpose of this alliance was to standardize organ registers and key sizes so that such a wide array of instruments would not have to be built. This plan was evidently carried out, with Limonaire abstaining from the group, and increased profits resulted for a while.

The history ends when the managers of the firm, contrary to the wishes of Ludovic Gavioli II (who then represented the Gavioli family interests), directed the business away from organs into such other fields as vacuum cleaners. Ludovic II resigned. Shortly thereafter Gavioli & Cie. was liquidated.

### Historical Notes

Despite the misfortunes that befell the firm (and it seems that most firms in the business of making automatic instruments had misadventures in their business careers), Gavioli was a resounding success so far as the production of large quantities of instruments was concerned.

In a catalogue pubished by Gavioli's New York branch about 1905 the view is given of a worldwide prosperous firm of organ builders, which it apparently was at the time:

"The firm Gavioli, manufacturers of automatic musical instruments, was established in 1806, and through the last century carried on its business with ever increasing success.

"Following its great development and to better answer its purposes to meet the demand of further increasing business and, in consequence, the need of greater manufacturing facilities, the firm, a few years ago, was formed into a Limited Company (Société des Anciens Etablissements Gavioli & Cie.) with a capital equal to several millions of dollars.

"Its various establishments employ over 300 men. While the main house and manufacturing plant is in Paris, there are also two branches, one in New York City and another in Waldkirch (Baden, Germany), and, in addition, sales agencies in London, Manchester, Antwerp, Barcelona, Milan, etc.

"The instruments manufactured by this company are well known all over the world, and in every exhibition in which they have been entered, they have been awarded the highest prizes.

"They are adapted for every and all purposes where music is required, and are especially adapted for shows of all kinds, music halls, dance halls, open air pavilions, skating rinks, electric parks, and merry-go-rounds.

"The New York branch is located at 31 Bond Street, New York City, where there is always in stock a large assortment of the instruments described [in the Gavioli catalogue], and where, at any time, a practical demonstration of the various instruments will be given, and their workmanship, attachments, and simple running qualities fully explained by competent agents in charge.

"To those, in whose business it is necessary to employ musicians, no matter how few, a cordial invitation is extended to visit our New York branch, and hear and see the excellent work performed by these instruments and be convinced of the fact that the instruments will do the same, and even better and more satisfactory work than musicians. The saving in actual money, when compared to the wages of musicians, cannot be estimated.

"Music: A full stock of operatic, popular, and up-to-date cardboard music is always kept on hand. Orders for any particular or special pieces of music will be promptly supplied, as this branch has a complete cardboard marking and cutting department. One hundred yards of music will be given free with each instrument."

The New York outlet of Gavioli was short-lived, and it closed within a few years. The sale of Gavioli organs in the United States was then taken over by a number of general instrument importers. The North Tonawanda Musical Instrument Works is believed to have imported a number of Gavioli organs. Others were sold by C.W. Parker. The main sales agent appears to have been Louis Berni, who operated the Berni Organ Company. In 1912, 1913, 1914, and possibly some earlier years as well, Berni issued illustrated catalogues of impressive appearance. The illustrations were taken from the catalogues of Gavioli and of Bruder (Waldkirch, Germany), but no mention was made of their origin. "Berni Organ Company" was lettered on each picture.

When the importation of European instruments resumed after World War I, Gavioli was no longer in business.

The number of Gavioli organs sold in America is not known. The total was probably in the range of several hundred.

In England, Gavioli organs were the most important imported organ type. In "The Fairground Organ," historian Eric V. Cockayne relates that organs of this make were so popular that by the end of the 19th century the man who cared for a fairground organ was called a 'gaviman' regardless of the organ type!

Early organs imported into England were of the pinned cylinder type, usually with a facade of gleaming brass trumpets and trombones. These were hand-cranked, although occasionally they would be driven by a belt connected to a steam engine. The Biograph era, which lasted from the late 1890's until movie shows became indoor attractions around 1910, created a fantastic demand for fairground organs of all makes. Most of the demand was filled by Gavioli. At this time the largest standard size of the "Gavioliphone" (Gavioli's trade name) was the 110-key format. Eric Cockayne notes that these were first delivered in England in 1906 through Gavioli's London agent, Chiappa. By mid-1907 eight orders for the 110-key organs had been filled, and two additional orders were on hand. The instruments were advertised as having "been made with 110 keys so as to have a complete scale, making it absolutely unnecessary to have any larger size than this latest model, which is absolute perfection in tone and artistic design of the front. These organs are Messrs. Gavioli's masterpiece and result of six years of careful study."

The 110-key organs were subsequently sold in large numbers, perhaps to the extent of several dozen. There were no absolutely "standard models;" the facades were made to accommodate the wishes of the customer. Most 110-key instruments were equipped with doors for the entry and exit of the public. Some even had built-in ticket booths! This format, it should be noted, was not unique to Gavioli. Limonaire, Bruder, and Marenghi each made similarly huge instruments with doors and 25 to 40-foot wide fronts.

Shortly after the introduction of the 110-key Gavioli, a 112-key model was made. This was designated as a "keyless" model and used a paper roll instead of the customary key frame. The problems of making such a wide paper roll track properly under trying outdoor conditions of weather plus the long wait for music prompted most, if not all, of the six English customers for the 112-keyless instrument to convert their organs to key frame scales of lesser size. Gavioli made several other paper roll organs, but these also were not well received. The shrinking and expanding problem, which was solved in the U.S.A. by Wurlitzer using paraffined paper, is cited by historians as being a major factor in the decline of the Gavioli organs' popularity.

Unlike collectors today, the showmen of years ago were not concerned with keeping the organ mechanisms original. The main effort was directed toward keeping the organ operational with the least amount of expense and upkeep. To this end, many Gavioli organs, and instruments of other makers as well, were converted in England to standard scales. Eric V. Cockayne notes that "The first book organs to arrive in England were the 87-key Gaviolis and Limonaires. This scale underwent a number of modifications as the years went by and formed the basis of the 89- and 92-, 94- and 98-key scales which were eventually adopted as standard by many showmen when it became uneconomic to produce, or difficult to obtain, music of other sizes."

In the United States the B.A.B. Organ Company (operated in New York by Messrs. Borna, Antoniazzi, and Brugnolotti) converted many Gavioli and other organs to play B.A.B. paper rolls when cardboard music, which did not lend itself to mass-production techniques, became too expensive to produce. Other Gavioli organs in the United States were converted to play Wurlitzer music. The Wurlitzer factory archives record numerous alterations of this type.

The result was that just about any Gavioli organ still playing in England or in the United States by 1920 was not playing Gavioli music. These conversions of the Gavioli cardboard music scales to other cardboard scales or, in America, to paper rolls, plus the conversion of hundreds of earlier cylinder organs to these new scales, were expertly done, for the most part. In fact, were it not for a few ancient mounting holes visible here and there most conversions would be undetectable. Thus, most collectors prefer to keep their Gavioli organs in their converted state.

Two important inventions which were patented by Gavioli were the harmonic brake or "frein" — the adjustable metal plate used on the lower part of a wooden violin pipe to regulate the wind current and to make possible the adjustment of the tonal quality, and the system of cardboard music books. While both ideas may have been new to the field of fairground organs, they were not new to the field of music in general. The harmonic brake was invented earlier by one Charles Lemaire of Paris. The folding cardboard book was used by others long before Gavioli first used it in fairground organs in 1892. But, similar to Welte's constant advertisement of having invented the music roll in 1887, Gavioli's claim to have invented the harmonic brake and the cardboard music system was so ingrained into the minds of organ users (Lewis Carroll's "Whatever I tell you three times is true" comes to mind!) that even today many historians credit Gavioli with these innovations.

### Other Gavioli Products

While the firm of Gavioli is best remembered for its spectacular line of fairground organs, the company built thousands of other instruments as well. Small hand-cranked portable organs, or "monkey organs" as they are known today, were built by the thousands. These were made in various styles. Some had reeds such as those found in a harmonium, but voiced very loudly. Popular was a variety built in a case shaped like the outline of a violin. Small portable organs with pipes were made in many different styles from the mid-19th century until the firm ceased operations. Some of these had exposed brass trumpets, but most had the pipes concealed in the interior. Player harmoniums operated by pinned cylinders, a large line of barrel-operated coin-in-the-slot pianos, and even church organs (played by hand or by folding cardboard music books) were made. It is interesting to note that vacuum cleaners, items not normally associated with automatic instruments (except in cases of improvised use to augment an instrument's vacuum supply!), were the "diversification" into which Gavioli entered when the fairground organ business waned. It is coincidental that the famed Regina Music Box Company picked the same household product as being an ideal diversification when it ceased making instruments!

### Gavioli Instruments Today

Today Gavioli fairground organs are among the most prized of all the early organ types. Most that survive are of the folding cardboard type or those converted earlier from cylinders to cardboard. The availability of historical information about the firm, the ornate and elegant appearance of the organ facades, and the general undefinable "romance" that every old fairground organ has, all contribute to the popularity of Gavioli instruments today.

Extensive technical information concerning Gavioli instruments is available in the aforementioned "The Fairground Organ" book by Eric V. Cockayne. We are indebted to A. Colin Upchurch and to the Fair Organ Preservation Society for sharing their photographic files to provide pictures which, it is hoped, will serve to transfer some of the "glories of the past" to you as you gaze upon the instruments that delighted an earlier generation.

—————————

Military Concert Organ of 1882. The ornate case is decorated with carvings, grillwork, and eight candelabra. Gavioli was a pioneer in illumination of organ facades. Some organs made in the 1890's were equipped with gas lighting systems. The brass French horn tubing at the center is decorative and not functional. All of the playing pipes are concealed within the cabinet.

**GAVIOLI**
**—in 1882—**

The Gavioli catalogue of 1882 offered cylinder operated instruments in a variety of types, including "Military Concert" organs, pianos, hand-cranked portable organs, and harmoniums.

Above left: 25-key Uniflute, a portable hand-cranked organ which plays ten tunes. The above description notes that a 30-key (or "30 touches" in French) model was also available.

Above right: Cavalry Fanfare organ. The description mentions 12 trumpets, although only 11 are shown in the illustration. Similar types of instruments with exposed brass trumpets were made through the early 20th century.

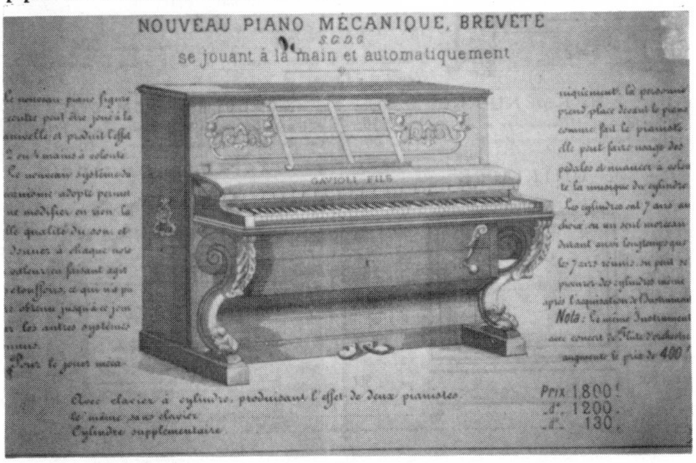


Gavioli cylinder-operated piano of 1882. Gavioli made many different types of cylinder pianos from the early years until about 1910. Most were of piano format like the one illustrated above, but others were built with carved organ-like facades. Usually provided with coin slot mechanisms, such instruments were widely used in cafes in France and other European countries.

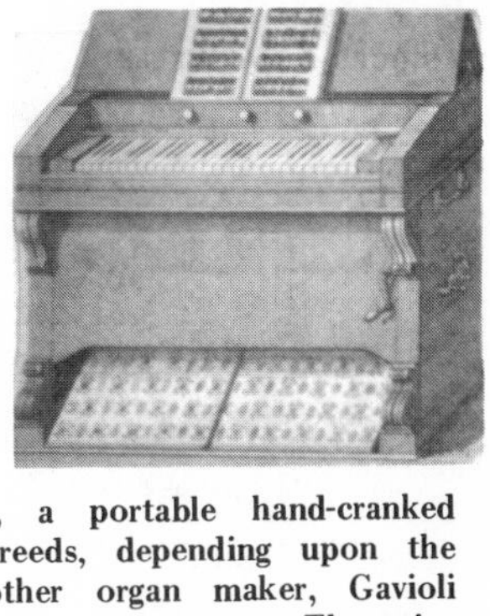

Above left: The Melodium, a portable hand-cranked organ with from 28 to 40 reeds, depending upon the model. More so than any other organ maker, Gavioli produced many models of such reed instruments. The price was approximately half that of an organ with pipes and the voicing was softer, so the Melodiums found a ready market.

Above right: Cylinder-operated harmonium of four octave scale. With three registers of reeds. Each cylinder is pinned with seven tunes. Also available in a 5-octave model of larger size. Such instruments were intended for indoor use in churches, meeting halls, and homes. In contrast with most other Gavioli products, the voicing was soft and mellow.

SOCIÉTÉ DES ANCIENS ÉTABLISSEMENTS

GAVIOLI & Co.

Offices: 175bis, Rue de Bercy
Works: 44, Quai de la Rapée
PARIS

ALL KINDS
OF
FULL BAND ORGANS & SLOT PIANOS
FOR
SHOWS, MERRY-GO-ROUNDS
DANCE HALLS, SKATING RINKS
ETC.

CARD BOARDS & CYLINDERS MADE TO ORDER

NEW YORK BRANCH
= 31, BOND STREET =
Telephone 5863 Spring

No.652
—35 Keys—
Represents an orchestra of 5 musicians.

No.618
—46 Keys—
With or without xylophone. Represents an orchestra of 10 musicians. 6' high.

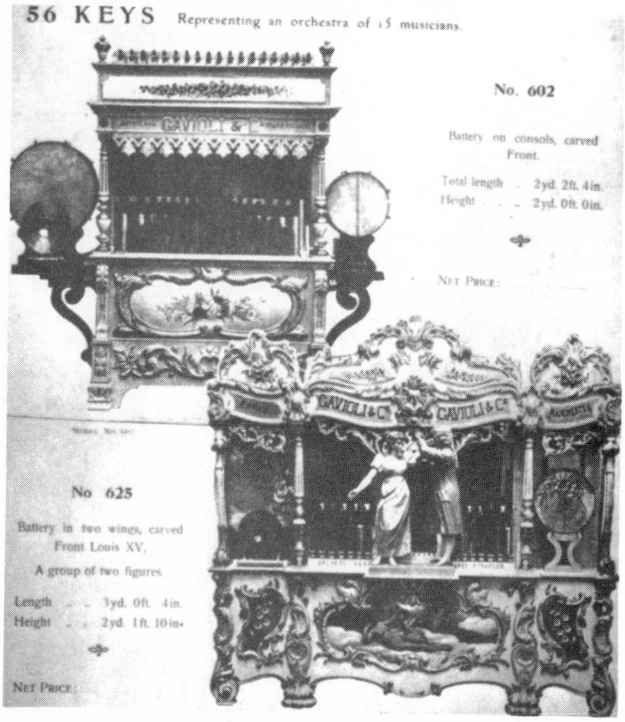

56 KEYS Representing an orchestra of 15 musicians.

No. 602

Battery on consols, carved Front.

Total length . . 2yd. 2ft. 4in.
Height . . . 2yd. 0ft. 0in.

NET PRICE:

No 625

Battery in two wings, carved Front Louis XV.

A group of two figures.

Length . . 3yd. 0ft. 4in.
Height . . 2yd. 1ft. 10in.

NET PRICE:

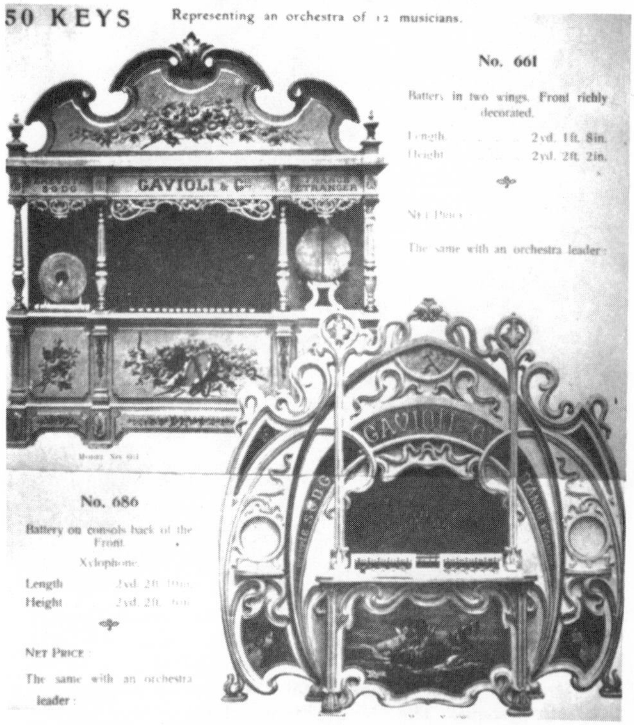

50 KEYS Representing an orchestra of 12 musicians.

No. 661

Battery in two wings. Front richly decorated.

Length . . . 2yd. 1ft. 8in.
Height . . . 2yd. 2ft. 2in.

NET PRICE:

The same with an orchestra leader:

No. 686

Battery on consols back of the Front.

Xylophone.

Length
Height

NET PRICE:

The same with an orchestra leader:

Styles 661 and 686. No. 661 was one of Gavioli's most popular models during the 1900 - 1910 era.

Left: No.673, 56 keys. Represents an orchestra of 15 musicians. 13' wide by 10'8" high.

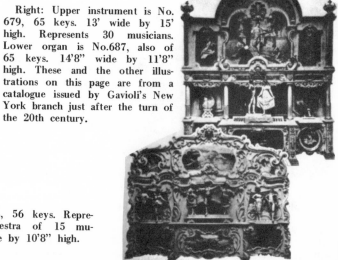

Right: Upper instrument is No. 679, 65 keys. 13' wide by 15' high. Represents 30 musicians. Lower organ is No.687, also of 65 keys. 14'8" wide by 11'8" high. These and the other illustrations on this page are from a catalogue issued by Gavioli's New York branch just after the turn of the 20th century.

# GAVIOLI

Left: No.648, a 57-key Gavioli organ of the 1905 era. Louis XV style ornate front. Xylophone. 3 carved figures. 12'6" wide by 10' high.

Above: No. 718, an 84-key Gavioli organ representing an orchestra of 40 musicians. Art nouveau front. Metal figures (instead of the usual wood). 18'6" wide by 13'4" high. This model was also sold by the North Tonawanda Musical Instrument Works (see North Tonawanda section of this book). The same interior but without the rich facade was available as Gavioli No. 430 and measured 12' wide by 8'4" high.

57-key Gavioli organ. Represents an orchestra of 25 musicians. 10' high. With 227 pipes comprising: 6 stopped and 6 open basses; 6 wood trombones; 102 open violin pipes and 17 stopped violins; 18 saxophones; 18 baritones; 18 piccolos; 18 brass flutes. With two automatic registers.

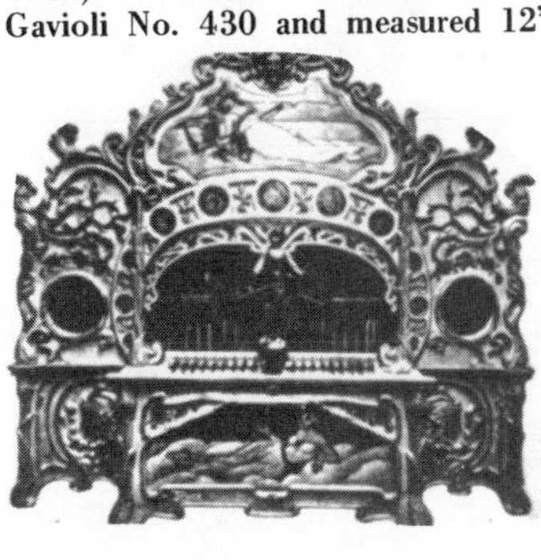

Above left: No. 650, 57 keys. Represents 25 musicians. 9' wide by 8'4" high. With orchestra leader figure on front.

Above right: No. 632, 65 keys. Represents 30 musicians. 20'8" wide by 13'4" high. With seven statues on the front.

Nos. 727, 660, 674, 685:

No. 727: 84 keys. Represents 40 musicians. Louis XV front. 8 metal figures on front. "Extra rich decoration." 20'4" wide by 14'2" high.

No. 660: 89 keys. Represents 50 musicians. Louis XV front. 7 figures. 18'8" wide by 13'4" high.

No. 674: 65 keys. Represents 30 musicians. "Front modern style." 7 figures in three groups. 21'8" wide by 15'10" high.

No. 685: 89 keys. Art nouveau front. Represents 50 musicians. 8 figures in 3 groups. 21'4" wide by 17'8" high.

Note: Facade measurements, while given to the nearest inch in the Gavioli catalogues, are apt to vary when actual instruments are measured. Also, as the same facade carvers were used in some instances by Gavioli, Marenghi, Bruder, and others the facades of certain models of these makes are quite similar.

–No. 727–

–No. 660–

–No. 674–

–No. 685–

Above: No. 717. 89 keys. Louis XV front with 5 metal figures and 100 electric lights. 17' wide by 11'4" high. Similar in styling to certain Bruder instruments.

Below: No. 640. 89 keys. Represents 50 musicians. Art nouveau facade. 7 figures in 3 groups. 16'2" wide by 12'8" high. Also available as No. 431 with simple painted front instead of the ornately carved style

Note: The above instrument, owned by Dutch showman Hubert Wolfs, burned in The Hague in 1948.

# GAVIOLI

No. 722. 50 keys. Represents an orchestra of 12 musicians. 14' wide by 11'8" high.

No. 432. 110 keys. Represents an orchestra of 120 musicians. "This model is made upon request: extra powerful for outdoor establishments, or symphonic for dance halls, skating rinks, music halls, etc." Available two ways: No. 432 with plain front; 17'6" wide by 12' high. No. 433 with front as illustrated. 31'8" wide by 16'8" high.

—110 Key Gavioli Organs—

The 110 key Gavioli organs were the largest regular Gavioli style (although a 112-key paper roll model was made but was not popular). The 110-key scale folding cardboard "book" organs were of the same basic interior specification as the earlier 102-key Gavioli barrel organs, but with eight automatic registers added.

Large and elaborate facades for the entrance and exit of the public were made for certain 110-key models. No. 336, illustrated below, measured over 38 feet wide. The musical part occupied the center section of the front. The wings were purely decorative and were made to act as the entire front of a theatre, tent show, or other attraction.

At the bottom of the page on the left is a 110-key organ used by Ball & Son in England, circa 1908. At the lower right is a 1907 110-key organ also used in England.

No. 434. 110 keys. "Front Louis XV, a model of style, artistic carving. Decorated doors for the entrance and the exit of the public. Electric lighting." 33'4" wide by 16'8" high.

No. 435
It represents a (real) orchestra of 120 musicians.


No. 435. 110 keys. Represents 120 musicians. "Front in highly decorated style, a swell organ above the main organ. Large doors for the entrance and the exit of the public. Electric lights with automatically changing colors." 38'4" wide by 18'4" high.

Left: The Bio-Tableau, an English traveling road show, attracted customers around the year 1900 with an older (circa 1870) Gavioli barrel organ. The organ was hand cranked. Note the rear wheels of a steam engine visible below the platform at the lower right.

Right: Rare 112-keyless (paper roll operated) Gavioli organ delivered to White's in 1908 and shown as part of White's traveling show. Note the ranks of bass pipes arranged in semicircular fashion at each side of the facade. The organ was later converted to play 98-key Marenghi music.

Below: Haggar's Royal Electric Bioscope, circa 1900. An 87-key Gavioli on the platform attracted patrons from far and wide. Power to operate the organ and the Bioscope show was provided by a steam engine located in its own housing at the right, across the stairs from the organ.

Above: Royal Wax-Work and Edison's Electric Animated Pictures — a traveling show in England around the turn of the century. The organ is a Gavioli with brass trumpets and dates from a decade or two earlier. Admission was a penny for children, twopence for adults.

Left: Murphy's Bioscope show featured a large 110-key Gavioli with facade equipped with entrance and exit doors.

# GAVIOLI

The "Glories of the Past" are brought to mind by these old photographs of Bioscope and ballyhoo shows from the turn of the century. Happiness, romance, gaiety, mirth, amusement, nostalgia, joy, wistfulness, and a dozen and one other emotions were created by these beautiful instruments of a long-lost era.

Even though these photographs are from another place and another time remote from today's electronic and atomic age one cannot help but share in the spirit of these old-time shows, just by looking at the pictures.

It is unfortunate that at least one Bioscope show wasn't preserved. What fun it would be to go to the show, attracted by hearing the Gavioli from blocks away, to enter the doors and view the promised marvels within!

Left: The Gavioli-Mortier organ presently on display at Utrecht's From Music Boxes to Street Organs Museum. Originally used in the town of Aalst, Belgium. An early instrument sold by Mortier (cf. Mortier section of this book for history of the Mortier-Gavioli relationship).

—112-Keyless Gavioli Organs—

The 112-keyless (roll operated) Gavioli organ was the last major model introduced by the Gavioli firm. Designed by Ludovic Gavioli II, these have a 25-note melody section. Six of the 112-keyless instruments were shipped to England following their introduction around 1906. Most of these organs were fitted with smaller scale Limonaire or Marenghi key frames, systems for which music was readily available in England. The cascading decks of violin pipes in the center section give the 112-keyless organs a distinctive appearance.

---

—110-Key Gavioli—

Left: A 110-key Gavioli organ displayed by Farrar & Tyler on the front of a travelling Bioscope show at the Wisbech Fair, March 1907. The dancing girls performed on the platform near the ticket booth and served as an added inducement for customers.

—89-key Gavioli/Marenghi—

Haggar's Electric Bioscope show, one of several owned by the Haggar firm, used an 89-key Gavioli with a Marenghi front. Note the hundreds of light bulbs on the facade, an impressive custom-made unit which also has doors at each side.

# GAVIOLI

J. Wingate & Son's Coliseum with 110-key Gavioli organ.

Cottrell's Coliseum with organ on stage. "Our Motto: to Instruct, Elevate, and Amuse."

Gregrafts Electric Bioscope. With steam engine on the right and an 89-key Gavioli on the left.

Cox Bros. Dragon gondolas. 112-keyless Gavioli working on 98-key frame. Photo taken in 1939.

Anderton's show with 87-key organ. Show front by Orton & Spooner. Organ is on the left stage; steam engine at the right.

Ornate gondola ride with early Gavioli barrel organ at the center.

(Photographs on this page courtesy of A. Colin Upchurch)

Symonds Grand Switchback Gondolas with 87-key Gavioli organ.

G. Green's Motors with gondola cars. 89-key Gavioli organ.

Tuby's Canadian Gondolas with 89-key Gavioli organ.

A Marenghi organ, shown because certain Gaviolis were sold with identical fronts. (See Marenghi section).

65-key Gavioli on Noah's Ark ride.

89-key Gavioli organ.

Clark's show with medium size Gavioli organ on the center stage.

Holland's Palace of Light with 89-key Gavioli organ.

89-key Gavioli with animated acrobatic figure at the center.

84-key cylinder-operated Gavioli organ. With 9 figures on front.

Scenic Railway with early Gavioli cylinder organ.

110-key Gavioli used as the front entrance to a Bioscope show, circa 1908.

GAVIOLI

—Gavioli Organs Live Today—

Pictured on this page are some of the Gavioli organs owned and cared for by members of the Fair Organ Preservation Society. These illustrations originally appeared in the Society's publication, "The Key Frame," and are used with permission.

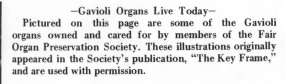

The 89-key "Grote Gavioli" or Great Gavioli owned by Mr. A.B. Mason.

Mr. Forrest's 65-key Gavioli organ.

89-key Gavioli organ owned by Mr. L.C. Byass.

Chester-Le-Street 98-key Gavioli organ with many cascading ranks of pipes. With cartouche reading "White Bros., Cardiff."

89-key Gavioli organ owned by Mr. P.S. Robinson. Shown mounted on a trailer, all ready for exhibition at a steam meet or a Fair Organ Preservation Society meeting.

89-key Gavioli organ owned by Arthur Mills. The facade is lettered "Music — Grand Gavioli Organ — Mirth."

110-key Gavioli organ owned by Dr. Robert Miller. For years this was an attraction at the skating rink at Euclid Beach, Cleveland, Ohio. It is one of the few surviving large Gavioli organs which saw original use in the United States.

89-key Gavioli owned by Mr. G. Flynn. The 89-key was particularly popular in England, accounting for a number of this size which survive today.

89-key Gavioli owned by Mr. A.E. Reed.

# ARMITAGE HERSCHELL
# HERSCHELL - SPILLMAN
# SPILLMAN ENGINEERING
# ALLAN HERSCHELL
## —Amusement Outfitters—

Founded in 1873 (or 1872, the firm's catalogues differ on this point) this North Tonawanda, New York, firm went through a succession of names, as the above title shows. From 1873 until it moved to Kansas in 1971, the Herschell enterprise was one of upstate New York's most colorful industries.

Although Herschell never manufactured any organs it was one of America's leading sellers of this type of instrument. So, like C.W. Parker, the firm merits inclusion in this catalogue if only for nostalgic and sentimental reasons to show how the band organs of yesteryear were used.

Every carousel just had to have a band organ. This was an inviolable rule. A merry-go-round without music would have been without spirit. Early carousels of the Armitage Herschell Company were called "Steam Riding Galleries," a term which continued in use until about 1910. Portable and with a canvas tent roof the Steam Riding Gallery was ideal for one-day stands. Patented couplings permitted it to be assembled or taken apart in a matter of just a few hours. Moving by railroad car the unit could literally play a different town each day. Motive power was provided by a steam engine located at a distance from the carousel and connected to it by a shaft. The organ was located at the center of the merry-go-round or, rarely, on the outside next to the steam engine and was driven by the same engine unit.

Early Armitage Herschell organs were European and were made by Frati & Co. and other makers. The instruments were of the pinned cylinder type and were usually small types with. brass trumpets on the front.

By 1909 the firm was known as the Herschell - Spillman Company. The catalogue of that year illustrated a wide variety of carousels, each equipped with a barrel organ. Some of the instruments were European, others were made in North Tonawanda. In addition to merry-go-rounds the firm offered the Razzle Dazzle, a circular swinging platform, a variety of backdrops for baseball-throwing games, several varieties of Ferris wheels, and even a line of automobile and marine gasoline engines.

Herschell - Spillman catalogues of the 'teens illustrate a variety of North Tonawanda Musical Instrument Works and Wurlitzer organs in use with carousels. Some of these are plainly marked with the organ makers' names, others have Herschell - Spillman markings. There was no consistency in this regard. Catalogues of the 1920's issued by Spillman Engineering and Allan Herschell make a point of showing the Wurlitzer (predominately) name boldly — even to the extent of painting it on the back side of an organ in one illustration, a location where not even promotion-minded Wurlitzer thought of putting its logotype! Wurlitzer was at this time the dominant factor in the American organ business, and doubtlessly this Wurlitzer advertising by Herschell was a way of reciprocating for referrals made by the organ firm.

For more information concerning the merry-go-round business in America the reader may refer to "A Pictorial History of the Carousel," by Frederick Fried.

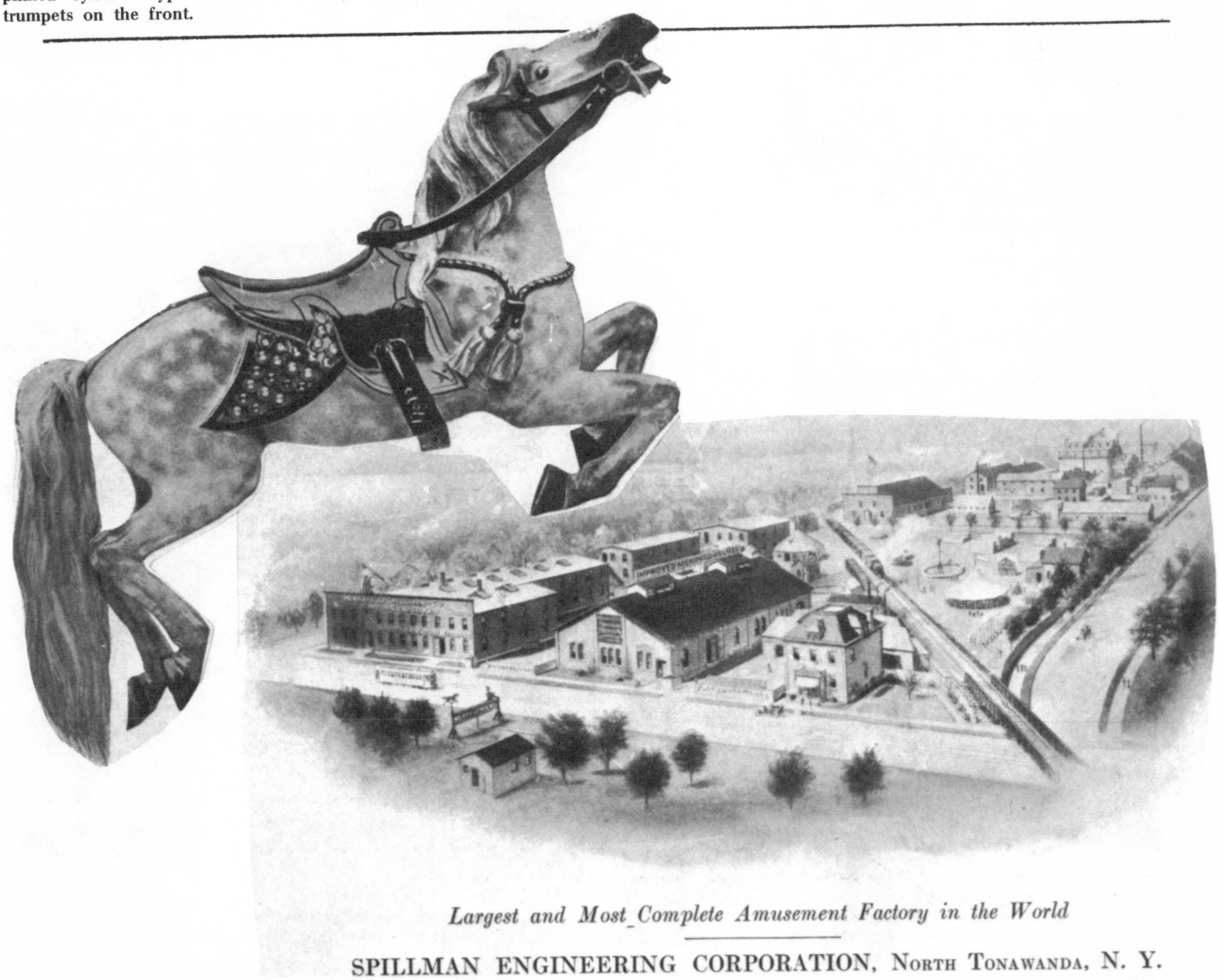

*Largest and Most Complete Amusement Factory in the World*

SPILLMAN ENGINEERING CORPORATION, North Tonawanda, N. Y.

Cover of "Catalogue F" – Herschell - Spillman Company, 1909.

Portrait of Allan Herschell, president of the Herschell - Spillman Company, pioneer operator and manufacturer of merry-go-rounds.

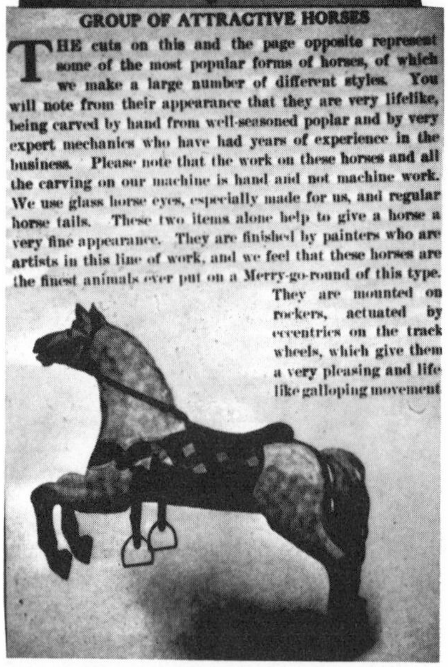

GROUP OF ATTRACTIVE HORSES

THE cuts on this and the page opposite represent some of the most popular forms of horses, of which we make a large number of different styles. You will note from their appearance that they are very lifelike, being carved by hand from well-seasoned poplar and by very expert mechanics who have had years of experience in the business. Please note that the work on these horses and all the carving on our machine is hand and not machine work. We use glass horse eyes, especially made for us, and regular horse tails. These two items alone help to give a horse a very fine appearance. They are finished by painters who are artists in this line of work, and we feel that these horses are the finest animals ever put on a Merry-go-round of this type. They are mounted on rockers, actuated by eccentrics on the track wheels, which give them a very pleasing and life like galloping movement

Right: High-jumping spirited horses from the 1909 catalogue. The firm carved its own horses, several at once, by using a copying or pantagraph lathe.

FACTORY NO. 2 OF THE HERSCHELL-SPILLMAN CO., NORTH TONAWANDA, N. Y.


—Herschell - Spillman Company—
(from the 1909 catalogue)

OUR NEW IMPROVED No. 1 STEAM RIDING GALLERY.
24 horses, 4 chariots. Seating capacity, 56 persons.

No. 2 OR THIRTY-SIX-HORSE RIDING GALLERY

Seating Capacity, 76 Adults.

We have designed for those desiring a machine of greater seating capacity what is known as our No. 2, or Thirty-six-Horse machine, with three horses abreast, the middle horse rocking in the opposite direction to the two outside ones.

This is built on the same general principle throughout as the No. 1 outfit with the exception that it is two feet larger (42 feet) in diameter, has 36 galloping horses instead of 24, and is, of course, built heavier to accomodate the additional load. It is equipped the same as the No. 1 outfit. It weighs about 19,000 lbs. and can be loaded in one railway box car.

Top illustration: "New Improved No. 1 Steam Riding Gallery" with 24 horses and 4 chariots. Seating capacity, 56 persons.

Below: Description of No. 2 Riding Gallery.

NEW PARK RIDING GALLERY. (Shown Without Tent.)
Seating capacity, 76 persons.

PARK RIDING GALLERY

THE illustration above shows our Gallery designed for Park and similar purposes. It has an outside diameter of 42 feet exclusive of tent, and carries 36 Galloping Horses, 4 large Chariots, and has a seating capacity of 76 adults.

This outfit is gotten up in a most elaborate style throughout, the center being composed of fourteen [illegible] carved and handsomely decorated with oil paintings. Forming a part of and corresponding in design [illegible] with this center is a large Military-Band Organ. It is one of the finest instruments ever used for [illegible], having 47 keys, including brass trombones, trumpets, piccolos, and clarionets, besides the bass and [illegible] and symbols.

The Park Riding Gallery. The band organ (enlarged view at top) is a Wurlitzer Style 150, made at the time by Eugene DeKleist of North Tonawanda, New York. The fourteen center panels match those on the organ facade.

Herschell - Spillman Company obtained its band organs from band organ makers in North Tonawanda, who at that time consisted of Eugene DeKleist and the North Tonawanda Musical Instrument Works. In later years Artizan organs were used also Sometimes the Herschell - Spillman name appeared on the organs; other times the name of the maker was used. The firm seems to have spread its business among the various organ makers, probably for reciprocal reasons as the organ companies often came into contact with potential buyers for amusement park equipment.

**NEW STYLE ELEGANT ORGAN**

ESPECIALLY DESIGNED FOR HERSCHELL-SPILLMAN CO.'S MERRY-GO-ROUNDS.

THIS Organ has 44 keys, four stops, and two barrels playing ten tunes each. It is a magnificent instrument, both as to volume and quality of tone, and is admired by all who listen to its splendid music. It is supplied at a moderate additional cost.

THE OCEAN WAVE

Is intended to be oper-
ated in parks or large
resorts.

CUT OF THE BEST FERRIS WHEEL ON THE MARKET

AS will be seen by the two cuts, the boiler and engine which we ordinarily use to drive these machines are of portable type, and the most convenient ever produced for this purpose. The boiler is 30 inches in diameter, 54 inches high, has 50 two-inch tubes, is stay-bolted around the fire-box, reinforced at the openings where steam pipes are attached, has a hand-hole that enables the crown sheet to be easily cleaned; also two hand-holes in the water legs.

The boiler is mounted upon good strong axles and springs, which, in turn, are supported by the latest and most approved wide-tired iron wheels; these are so constructed that there are no threads on the spokes at either end to work loose or strip, and they will hold firmly until the tire is practically worn out. The rear wheels are made especially strong to meet the extra weight placed upon them. The boilers are fitted with two injectors, safety valve, whistle, grates, blower, etc.

The engine is a fine, newly-designed, double engine, with two cylinders, two connecting rods, and a double-throw crank shaft. The front of the engine frame is left open, so that it is very easy to get at all the parts, which will result in its giving better service and lasting much longer, as it is convenient to keep it properly adjusted, cleaned, and oiled. The cylinders of the engine are supported by a strong cast-iron column at the back, and by two cold-rolled-steel columns in front, covered with brass jackets and fitted with nickeled nut covers. These columns, in turn, are secured to a strong, square, cast-iron base. The cast columns also carries the guides and receives the thrust of the cross-head. Integral with the base are the three crank-shaft bearings, which are lined with the best babbitt; the crank shaft is high-grade steel, and the cranks are set on the quarter; the connecting rods are crucible steel, having brasses in either end and the latest take-up wedges fitted to each box; the wedges are held in place by bolts with jam nuts; the cross-head shoe is brass, and has an adjustment so that the wear can easily be taken up, in fact, there is no part of the engine that is not adjustable.

Steam engines and boilers used to run portable merry-go-rounds.

**No. 18 MILITARY BAND ORGAN**

THE Organ regularly furnished is a No. 18 Military-Band Organ; it has 41 keys and is fitted with two barrels, each barrel containing eight up-to-date popular selections of music. The organ has a rich, powerful tone, and is supplied with trumpets, piccolos, and flageolets, and is a magnificent instrument. We also furnish cheaper or more expensive organs, in case the customer desires the same.

A Herschell - Spillman carousel on location in Durban, Natal (Africa).

## CAROUSELLES FOR PERMANENT LOCATION

### PARK CAROUSELLES

THE superb, imposing and brilliant appearance of Spillman Park Carouselles, has won them a lasting, world-wide reputation. The properly proportioned design of the machine, classes them as a feature attraction wherever located.

¶ The Carouselle illustrated on the opposite page, is one of the finest medium priced park machines in the country. It is 50 feet in diameter, built in 18 sections, with 3 rows of animals. This machine can be arranged to have the outside row stationary, of large size animals, or you can have 9 jumping figures and 9 stationary, or you can have them all jumping. The animals are Lion, Tiger, Ostrich, Stork, Giraffe, Charging Horse, Armored Horse, Deer, Goat, Zebra, Rooster, Frog, Dog, Cat. Inside rows, Horses trotting and galloping style.

¶ In addition to the animals, the outfit has two beautifully carved, stationary chariots. The arrangements and selections for animals, from our large stock, enables the customer to have a wide selection to fit his particular requirements.

¶ The Picture Panels around the center, enclosing the gears, are built in double sections, the upper portion tilting out. These Panels consist of a series of handsome scenic paintings, and the frame work is enriched by heavy carvings, mirrors and cut glass jewels. The massive outside cornice adds to the richness and striking appearance of the entire outfit.

¶ All rods are encased in polished brass, also the Horse Pipes. Machines may be wired for a profusive display of electric lights. Electric motor of sufficient H. P. to operate Carouselle, with starter, is supplied.

¶ We also build other styles of Park Carouselles, having 2, 3 or 4 horses in a row; 40, 44, 46 and 50 ft. in diameter. As most of these machines are built to special specifications, we invite the earnest attention of Park Managers. Our force of Engineers, Designers and Artists are prepared to, and have turned out some of the finest machines in the world.

¶ Prices quoted on request including motor, starter, tools and fixtures necessary to operate, also includes Organ Style 188 or 153, mailed on request.

## TWO-ABREAST CAROUSELLE

THIS handsome Carouselle is constructed along the same graceful lines as our three-abreast Carouselle as illustrated on page six. The same high class materials and improved locking devices enter into its construction.

¶ It is 40 feet in diameter with 24 large jumping horses and two stationary chariots. This machine has 14 sweeps same as our three-abreast Carouselle so as to give it a large seating capacity and a very imposing appearance. Therefore, it is not an ordinary two-abreast Carouselle, a makeshift or a cut down, but a Properly Designed Outfit. The cornice and inside picture panels are the same elaborately designed decorations as on our other machines. All rods are brass covered. The machine is wired for 210 electric lights. In fact, the limit of extra decorations is controlled by the selection of the purchaser.

¶ This machine also has inside drive with 10 H. P. gasoline engine. A 10 ounce khaki tent and 8 ounce sidewalls enclose and protect the outfit. New Telescopes doing away with the spiders and making the platforms clear. Horse pipes are bushed with red fiber to insure longer wear on telescopes, no iron and iron running together, making this device noiseless, no danger of grease, and when locked it will stay locked. Patent applied for. Quarter poles, ropes and tackle blocks supplied. Machine weighs only about 9½ tons.

¶ We call your attention to the design of our horses. You will notice the legs are carved in such positions that they can not be used as steps for mounting the animals. This eliminates the breakage by unruly persons and keeps your outfit looking in nice, first class shape.

¶ The price is moderate—within the reach of men of limited means and desirous of entering this profitable business.

¶ To any operator who intends traveling with one of these machines, he should minutely investigate every detail of the machine. Don't judge from appearance alone, look inside and find the real merits.

¶ This construction means to you: Safety, Strength, Simplicity, and Speed. And, moreover, it means a dependable machine to operate faithfully to give the best kind of service. Our machines control the amusement field.

¶ Price F. O. B. North Tonawanda, N. Y., including gasoline engine, organ, tent, tools and equipment to operate, are given in price list herewith.

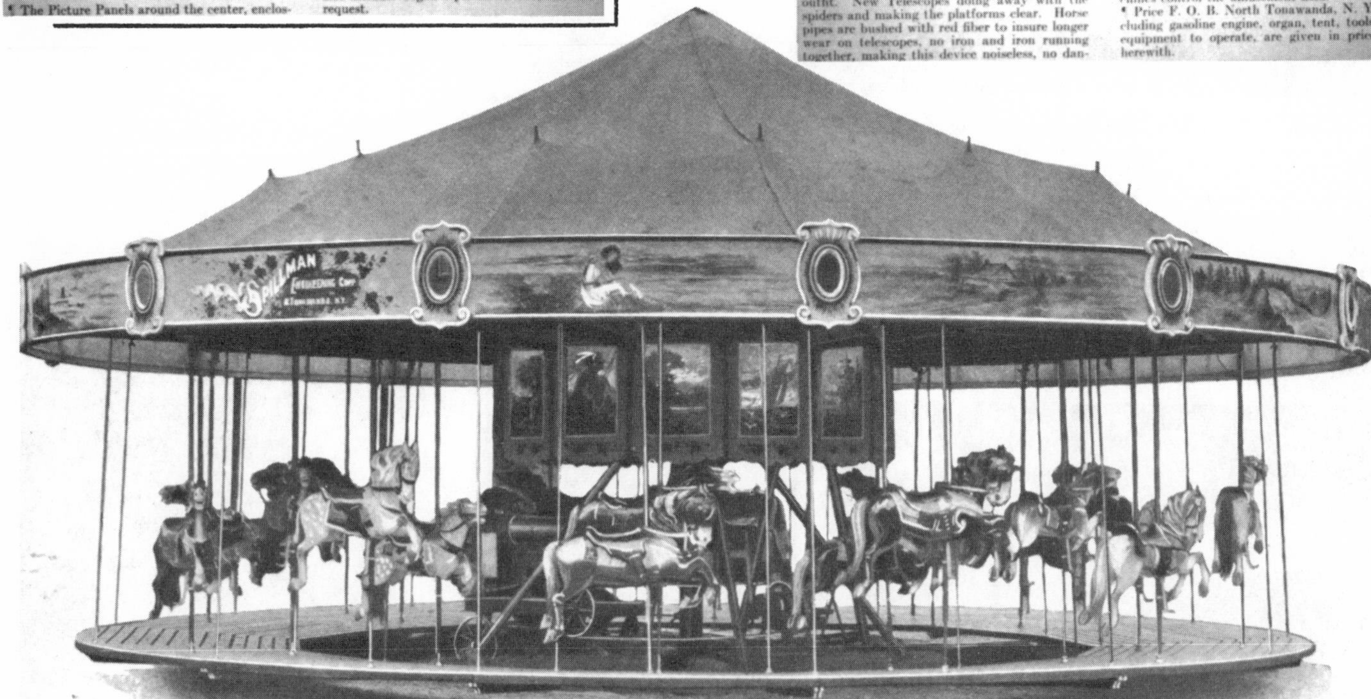


## THREE-ABREAST PORTABLE CAROUSELLES

THIS popular Jumping Horse Carouselle has been successfully operated from Coast to Coast with leading Carnival Companies, and in Parks, and requires no special introduction. IT is THE recognized money earner.

¶ It is designed especially for travelling, with interchangeable parts and assembles without bolts. Our new patented locking devices save so much time that it is really remarkable how quickly the machine can be erected. It has 36 jumping horses, 3 abreast, and 2 stationary chariots. The horses are large artistically carved animals, true to life, with an abundance of action—the finest horses on portable machines. The chariots are beautifully designed with heavy carvings. They are our acknowledged style that are taken quickly apart and packed in crate.

¶ The outside cornices at end of sweeps are a crowning feature, and works of art. The cornice is 24" wide, and is built of sheet metal, on wood frames, made of cypress so they will not rot out, and will last an indefinite time. This feature alone should be given your consideration for your own protection. You will not find this elsewhere. The Head Shields are of a new design, the frames of which are also made of cypress, and a Hand Carved Decoration on the outer edge, with a beautiful Carved Head for center. We also make a Head Shield with oval bevel-plated mirrors for center, making these decorations a work of art. ¶ New Telescopes, doing away with spiders, and making the platforms clear. (*Patent applied for.*)

¶ The picture panels at center consist of 14 large artistic oil paintings in enameled frames—which set off the machine nicely. All rods are covered with polished brass. Machines are wired for 210 lights on outside cornice and the inside picture panels.

¶ This outfit is the latest improved machine on the market, the quickest and easiest to set up and tear down. Every detail is carefully studied to make it more convenient to handle, and absolutely dependable without annoyance and expense of upkeep and repairs. Has inside drive with counter-shaft, clutch, brake and 10 H. P. gasoline engine, all ready to operate. Forty feet in diameter, and weighs only about 10 tons. A 10 ounce army khaki tent with 8 ounce sidewalls encloses the machine, and is the best made tent on the market for service and protection. Quarter poles, ropes and tackle blocks are supplied.

¶ Consider the superb attractiveness of this machine, together with the extreme quickness with which it may be erected. The only Real Road Carouselle on the road. The Prime Favorite of all carnival men, and playing with about 75% of the Carnivals. In parks it is equally successful—a long list of satisfied Park Managers to show for this.

¶ Prices. F. O. B. North Tonawanda, N. Y., including gasoline engine, organ, tent, tools and equipment to operate, are given in price list herewith.

**Illustrations from circa 1920 catalogue of the Spillman Engineering Co., successor to Herschell - Spillman. The catalogue, No. "C", offers merry-go-rounds equipped with Wurlitzer and North Tonawanda Instrument Works organs.**

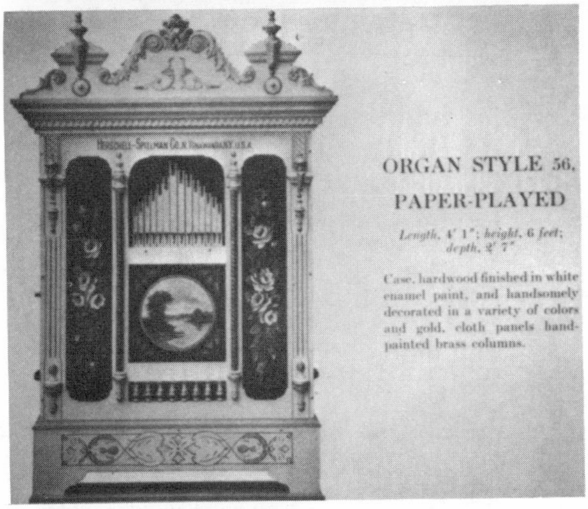

ORGAN STYLE 56,
PAPER-PLAYED
Length, 4' 1"; height, 6 feet; depth, 2' 7"
Case, hardwood finished in white enamel paint, and handsomely decorated in a variety of colors and gold, cloth panels hand-painted brass columns.

ARTIZAN FACTORIES INC
ORGAN STYLE A-2
46 Keys
Dimensions
Height 6' 5"
Width 7' 11½"
Depth 2' 10"

SPECIAL ORGAN,
STYLE 153
Length, 8' 8"; height, 7' 1"; depth, 3' 2"
With duplex, long roll tracker frames, latest mahogany or walnut shell drums with self-tightening tension rods. Oak veneered case natural finish, fancy white enamel front, hand carved scroll work in gold leaf and colors. Raised panels, decorated with landscapes and flower designs. Four rolls of music. Special prices quoted on request.
WURLITZER

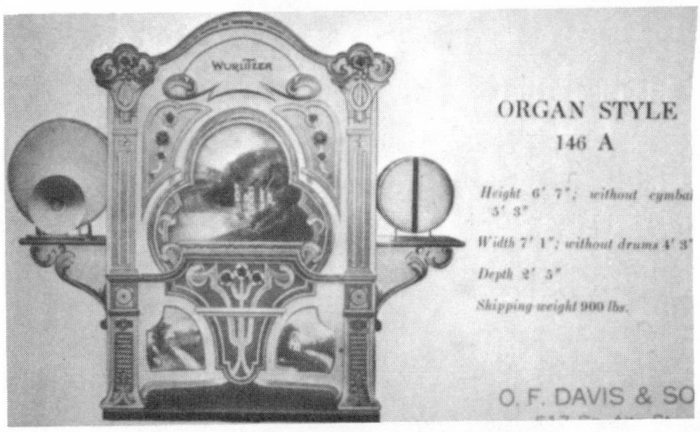

WURLITZER
ORGAN STYLE
146 A
Height 6' 7"; without cymbal 5' 3"
Width 7' 1"; without drums 4' 3"
Depth 2' 5"
Shipping weight 900 lbs.
O. F. DAVIS & SO


—Spillman Engineering Company—
—Allan Herschell Company—
(the 1920's)

On this page are illustrations from Spillman Engineering Company catalogues of c.1920 and 1923 and an Allan Herschell Co. (successor to Spillman) catalogue of 1925. The organs are types made by the North Tonawanda Musical Instrument Works (Spillman's Style 56), Artizan (Style A-2), and Wurlitzer Styles 146-A, 146-B, and 153. Style 153 was perhaps the most popular carousel organ ever made. More of these were sold for merry-go-round use than any other model.

At the top center is the Ticket Office ("Painted in any color wanted to suit purchaser. Price, $90") which Made It All Worthwhile.

(Original Wurlitzer et al descriptions of the organs are found in other sections of this book under the organ manufacturers' names)

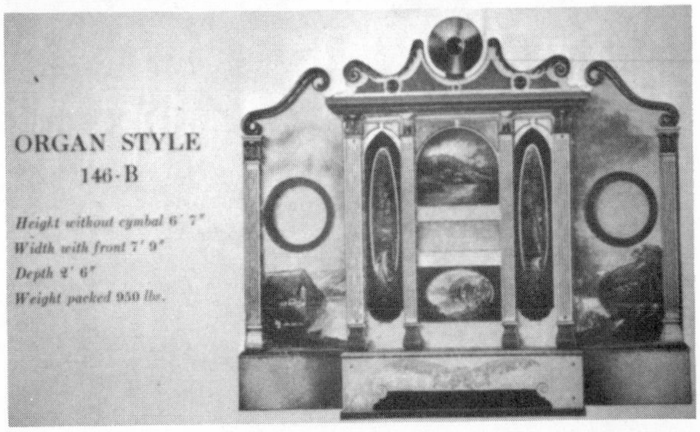

ORGAN STYLE
146-B
Height without cymbal 6' 7"
Width with front 7' 9"
Depth 2' 6"
Weight packed 950 lbs.

## LOUIS HOOGHUYS
### Grammont, Belgium

In 1880 Louis Hooghuys founded his business of manufacturing fairground organs. Later, the business was continued by his son, Charles Hooghuys, and still later and until fairly recent times by his grandson, R. Charles Hooghuys.

Most Belgian organ builders produced softly-voiced dance organs. Hooghuys was an exception. His instruments were very loudly voiced, were built as fairground organs, and were competitive with Gavioli, Marenghi, and other contemporary makes. In fact, the voicing of Hooghuys organs was generally louder than that of other fairground organ makers.

Hooghuys fair organs were built in many different sizes from small hand-cranked instruments of the portable type to huge organs with facades measuring twenty or more feet in width. One of these latter instruments is a featured attraction at the From Music Boxes to Street Organs Museum in Utrecht, Holland.

Certain large Hooghuys featured an unusual attachment: a mandolin/piano which played tuned piano strings. Few organs were equipped with these. Probably the hard fairground use that the organs received and the constantly changing humidity and temperature of such environments presented problems with keeping the piano strings in tune.

Hooghuys organs were built well and of good materials. The tone of extant Hooghuys organs is powerful and rich. As such the Hooghuys instruments are prized collectors' items today.

(Photographs courtesy of Emil Baude, Leonard Grymonprez, and the Fair Organ Preservation Society). Several different Hooghuys organs are shown on this page.

----------

**Aime KOENIGSBERG**
**—Antwerp, Belgium—**

**In the 1920's Aime Koenigsberg produced a series of dance hall organs, one particularly impressive example of which is illustrated on this page. Also, some instruments with louder voicing (for fairground use) were produced. The tonal disposition and general layout of Koenigsberg instruments is similar to that used by Th. Mortier of the same city.**

## LIMONAIRE FRÈRES
—Paris, France—

Founded in 1840, the firm of Limonaire Frères (Limonaire Brothers) advertised that it was the oldest firm in the organ business. Business was conducted from various addresses in Paris, the longest-used of which was 166 Avenue Daumesnil. Many Limonaire organs bore this street address as part of the gaily lettered decorations on their facades.

Around the turn of the 20th century Limonaire opened a branch in Waldkirch, Germany. Sales agents were maintained in Lyon and Mirecourt, France; Brussels, Belgium; Barcelona, Spain; Manchester, England; and Milan, Italy.

It was at a British salesroom of Limonaire organs that Eugene DeKleist, in 1892, met William Herschell, brother of Allan and George Herschell, amusement park equipment builders of North Tonawanda, New York. Sensing an opportunity for profit in America, Eugene DeKleist left the employ of Limonaire and, using his knowledge of the organ trade and with promised orders from Herschell in the offing, set up business in North Tonawanda in 1893. The North Tonawanda Barrel Organ Factory later became the manufacturing facility of the Rudolph Wurlitzer Company — the largest American maker of band organs. So, in a sense, Limonaire played a part in America's band organ heritage!

Early Limonaire organs were of the pinned cylinder type. From the late 1890's onward, most were of the folding cardboard or "book" system, although some paper roll or "keyless" models were made. Organs of the early 20th century ranged in size from 30-key models to 118 keys. 49-, 52-, and 60-key models were especially popular. Organs of this period were sold under the "Orchestrophone" trade name.

Particularly impressive were the large 100-key models with elaborate facades which included doors for the public to walk through! Some of these also incorporated a ticket booth and a barker's stand! Also impressive were certain "double case" models. These were of standard specifications but doubled — with two of everything. The intention was to obtain louder volume. Similar double case instruments were made by Gavioli, Ruth, and others.

In the 1920's Limonaire sold several different models of the "Jazzbandophone," an instrument with an organ interior but with jazz effects such as wood blocks, a klaxon, a Chinese gong, and other percussion instruments added. Despite advertising efforts the Limonaire instruments of the 1920's sold only in limited numbers. The peak years of the firm seem to have been from about 1900 to 1914 — when outdoor fairgrounds and traveling Bioscope shows were especially popular in Europe.

Limonaire instruments are highly desired by collectors today. The ornate facades, elaborate even on small organs, and the sweet tone of their pipes place them among the best of fairground organs.

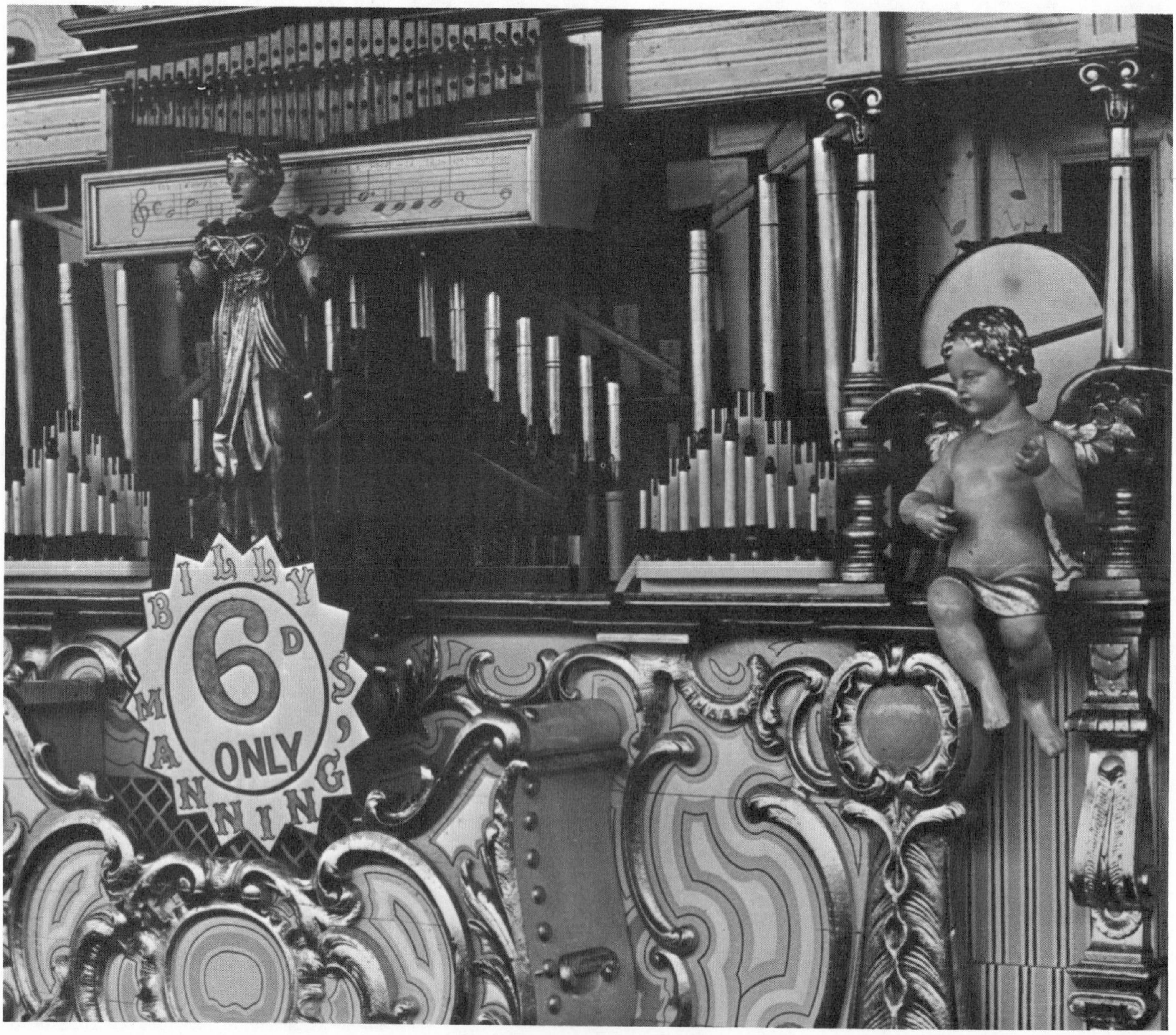

# ORCHESTROPHONES

N° 200.
*Orchestrophone* **30** *touches.*

N° 201.
*Orchestrophone* **35** *touches.*

N° 201 bis.
*Orchestrophone* **30** *touches.*

N° 216. — *Orchestrophone* **49** *touches. Art nouveau, avec piston cuivre*

N° 211. — *Orchestrophone* **49** *touches, avec batterie.*

N° 215. — *Orchestrophone* **49** *touches, Art nouveau.*

N° 214. — *Orchestrophone* **49** *touches, Art nouveau.*

N° 256. — *Orchestrophone* **49** *touches, ouvert.*

N° 255.
*Orchestrophone* **35** *touches, ouvert.*

N° 206.
*Orchestrophone* **43** *touches.*

On this and the next several pages are instruments from a Limonaire Frères catalogue of the 1905 era. Those marked "registres automatique" have automatic registers operated by perforations in the cardboard music. Non-automatic styles have registers that are set by hand before the performance begins.

Instruments of this period were sold under the "Orchestrophone" name. Later, in the 1920's, the "Jazzbandophone" organs were essentially the same as earlier ones pipe-wise, but were equipped with more modernistic facades and with jazz percussion effects.

The carvings on Limonaire organs are of high quality, and even small organs usually have ornate scrollwork.

N° 218. — *Orchestrophone* **49** *touches, grand modèle renforcé à doubles niches.*

## ORCHESTROPHONES

N° 217. — *Orchestrophone* **49** *touches, Art nouveau, renforcé.*

N° 225. — *Orchestrophone* **60** *touches, façade sculptée.*

N° 227bis. — *Orchestrophone* **60** *touches,* **3** *statuettes,* **2** *groupes de valseurs.*

N° 231. — *Orchestrophone* **87** *touches, genre art nouveau.*

N° 226. — *Orchestrophone* **60** *touches,* **3** *statuettes.*

# ORCHESTROPHONES

## AVEC REGISTRES AUTOMATIQUES

**reproduisant fidèlement la musique d'orchestre avec solo de violon, flûte, clarinette, basson, etc., ainsi que toutes les nuances de " forte " et de " piano ".**

N° 261. — *Orchestrophone* **38** *touches.*

*— Registres automatiques.*

## ORCHESTROPHONES

Nº 257bis. — Orchestrophone Registres automatiques.

52 touches.

Nº 262. — Orchestrophone 38 touches avec registres. — Façade sculptée

Nº 259. - Orchestrophone 52 touches, renforcé, façade riche

Nº 252. — Orchestrophone 57 touches, Registres automatiques.

Nº 276. — Orchestrophone 54 touches, sans batterie.

Nº 250. — Orchestrophone 67 touches, Registres automatiques.

N° 242. — Orchestrophone 89 touches, avec registres automatiques.

N° 243. — Orchestrophone 92 touches, avec registres automatiques.

N° 246. — Orchestrophone 100 touches, chromatique, deux portes, vingt-trois statuettes.

The two instruments at the bottom of this page are among the most ornate organs ever built. The mechanisms are all confined to the center section. The rest is simply a large false front or facade, including doors to admit the public to a Biograph show, magic performance, or other attraction. Such instruments were made in easily disassemblable sections as the shows that used them were constantly on tour. (Limonaire catalogue illustrations courtesy of Claes O. Friberg and Leonard Grymonprez)

N° 254. — Orchestrophone 100 touches, chromatique, deux portes, deux contrôles-caisses.

Limonaire Frères
—Jazzbandophone—

Left: Model No. 4; 84-keys.

Right: Model No. 2; 50 keys.

During the 1920's Limonaire Frères sold several varieties of the Jazzbandophone. Most were similar in appearance to traditional instruments; the Model No. 2 illustrated at the upper right is an example. Model No. 4 is starkly modernistic and resembles in a way the Decap dance hall organs produced in Belgium in the 1950's and 1960's.

Specifications of Model No. 4: Pipe ranks consisting of bass, contrabass, alto, contralto, violin, violoncello, piston, flute, and saxophone. A "celeste voicing effect" was used for some of the ranks. Other instrumentation includes: several drums, tambourine, bells, 4 castanets, 2 triangles, 2 cymbals, 2 wood blocks, a Chinese gong, and, mounted on the very top of the instrument, a klaxon or auto horn! The unit measures 3.85 meters wide by 2.65 meters high by 1 meter deep and weighs about 900 kilos.

Specifications of Model No. 2: Pipes consisting of bass, contrabass, alto, contralto, violin, violoncello, flute, hautbois, and effects of celeste and vox humana. Trapwork consists of bass and snare drums, cymbal, triangle, and wood block. Measurements, including the facade, are: 2.65 meters wide by 2.30 meters high by 1 meter deep. Weight = 400 kilos.

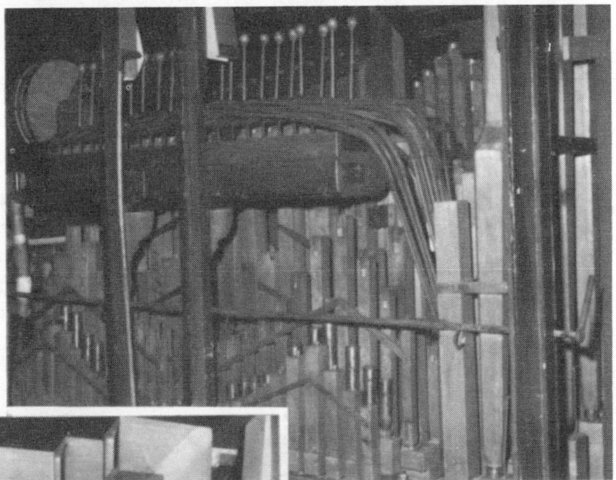

Views of a Jazzbandophone in the collection of Mr. and Mrs. Gordon Lipe. The front is of a cream color with gilt trim and painted scenes. The instrument was used in a large private home in France during the 1920's.

Like most other Limonaire products, the Jazzbandophone is constructed with high quality materials. Such instruments are highly sought by collectors today.

Waddington's Gondolas, a traveling ride which moved from town to town and participated in fairs and celebrations, was equipped with an 87-key Limonaire Frères organ. The instrument may be seen at the center front, just behind the ornate gondola.

Circa 1910 motor ride with the accompaniment of an 87-key Limonaire Frères fairground organ. The rides pictured on this page were used in England in the 1900 - 1914 era. Such hill-and-dale rides, used seldom in the United States, were very popular in Europe. The riding cars took many forms including gondolas, automobiles, railway coaches, carved animals, etc. And, no such ride was really complete without a fairground organ, the only musical instrument capable of being heard above all the noise of the ride mechanisms!

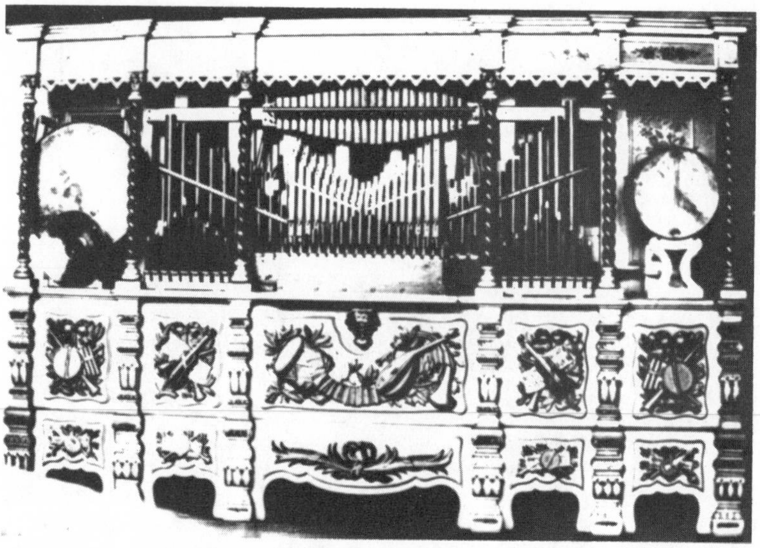

A 92-key Limonaire organ used in England circa 1910. This particular instrument has 33 wooden xylophone bars in place of the melody pistons usually found in this particular style. Many Limonaire organs were converted to play Gavioli or Marenghi music as music for these latter scales was standard in England.

The last word in modern fairground organs after the turn of the century was this 100-key Limonaire Frères Orchestrophone, shown on a promotional postcard issued by the Crafts family. The instrument had 13 registers, all automatic. The organ facade included large doors for the entry and exit of the public. A Bioscope show waited within!

—The Fair Organ Preservation Society—

The Fair Organ Preservation Society has generously made available for use in this book illustrations from the Society's publication, "The Key Frame." The F.O.P.S. motto, "Whilst looking to the future, let us not forget the glories of the past," might well serve as the credo for collectors of all types of automatic instruments. Certainly the over 1000 members of the Society enjoy all aspects of the fairground organs – their history, music, and preservation. Information concerning the group may be obtained by addressing: Hon. Secretary, Kenneth Redfern, Esq.; 3 Bentley Road, Denton; Manchester, England.

Credit Note: Most of the illustrations of Limonaire, Marenghi, and other fairground organs "on location" years ago were provided by A. Colin Upchurch of Sutton in Ashfield, Notts., England. Mr. Upchurch spent many hours sorting through his family's collection of some 3,000 old-time fairground pictures in order to find about 100 which clearly showed fairground organs. The photographs, made by Mr. Upchurch from the original promotional postcards, news clippings, and trade paper articles, show the colorful and romantic uses to which these magnificent instruments of yesteryear were put.

Pat Collins' motor ride. The firm of Savages, located in King's Lynn, England, was the manufacturer of this ride. Called the "moving top" type, rides such as this were sold from the 1890's onward, complete with a fairground organ, usually of Limonaire or Gavioli make. These organs were purchased in large quantities and were equipped with 87- or 89-key mechanisms so that standard music could be supplied by English music cutters.

Another Savages motor ride. The organ in the center, partially visible behind the 3-seat car, is an 87-key Limonaire.

Barnes' motor ride with an 87-key Limonaire organ equipped with protective glass panels. The ostensible reason for the glass panels was to protect the pipes and inner mechanisms from dust — and to act as a volume control when local residents complained too much!

# W. F. Mangels

## W.F. MANGELS CAROUSELL WORKS
(Amusement Outfitters)

The W.F. Mangels Carousell (sic) Works, located in Coney Island, New York, was established in 1880. Until well into the 20th century the firm was a leading supplier of merry-go-rounds, pleasure railways, arcade equipment, and related amusement devices.

For use with its carousels Mangels purchased organs from various sources including Frati, Bruder, and Wurlitzer (DeKleist). A circa 1907 catalogue noted: "Unlike some firms in our line, we do not claim that we build organs. . . but we are prepared to furnish the best organ that the European market affords; the Gebrüder Bruder organ has a reputation for beauty of design, splendid tone, and durability that stands unexcelled. We have in the past imported a number of these instruments to the greatest of satisfaction to our customers. These organs can be arranged to either play with cylinder or latest cardboard system. The larger instruments are capable of rendering the most wonderful music. A large repertoire, embracing all classical and standard music, may be selected from. Customers may also send in the printed notes of any composition and have the paper made up at standard prices."

Mangels carousel with Frati organ.

Mangels carousel with DeKleist organ.

Carousel with organ (artist's conception).

Mangels "Combination Galloping Horse Carousel" with organ in the center.

Bruder organ (Mangels' 1907 catalogue)

Bruder organ (Mangels' 1907 catalogue)

Bruder organ (Mangels' 1907 catalogue)

Bruder organ (Mangels' 1907 catalogue)

## CHARLES MARENGHI & Cie.

—Paris, France—

Charles Marenghi, a foreman at the Gavioli works in Paris, left Gavioli shortly after 1900. Taking a number of Gavioli workmen, including woodcarvers, with him, he established Ch. Marenghi & Cie. Within the space of just a few years Marenghi established his firm as a prominent factor in the fairground organ business. Under the name of "Ideal Orchestre," Marenghi organs were sold in key sizes of 60, 69, 87, 89, 92, 94, 98, 100, 102, and 104, and possibly several others. England, Belgium, France, and Germany furnished the main markets for Marenghi products.

When the Gavioli works closed, the unfinished organs, components, and other materials went to Limonaire and Marenghi, but mostly to the latter firm. As a result a number of Gavioli organs, including chassis of the 110-key size, were sold with Marenghi fronts. This, plus the fact that Marenghi employed wood carvers and facade designers who left the Gavioli works the same time that he did, resulted in a close similarity between Gavioli and Marenghi organ appearances — a situation which is often confusing today when old photographs are viewed.

A popular Marenghi scale was the 89-key specification. This was interchangeable with the 89-key Gavioli scale, except that certain registers were arranged differently.

As some of the accompanying photographs show, organs built with "show fronts" were equipped with spectacular lighting effects. In 1907 Marenghi applied for a British patent covering a system of changing multicolored lights, operated by coupling the lights to various ranks in the organ. In "The Fairground Organ," Eric V. Cockayne relates that certain "music books" containing nothing but light register changes were made, presumably to keep the show front interesting at times when music wasn't being played. In 1906 Marenghi applied for a British patent which covered the operation of several organ registers simultaneously from one single organ key. (Note: Louis Berni, an importer of Marenghi organs into the U.S.A., undoubtedly was referring to this when he advertised his "improved register system" — see Berni Organ Co. section of this book).

Charles Marenghi died in 1919. For several years thereafter his business was conducted by the Gaudin Brothers. Sales in the 1920's were mainly to customers in France and Belgium.

Beautiful Marenghi Ideal Orchestre organ, one of dozens of Marenghis sold in Belgium during the 'teens and 'twenties.

89-key Marenghi. (From "The Fairground Organ" by Eric V. Cockayne)

69-key Marenghi. (From "The Fairground Organ" by Eric V. Cockayne)

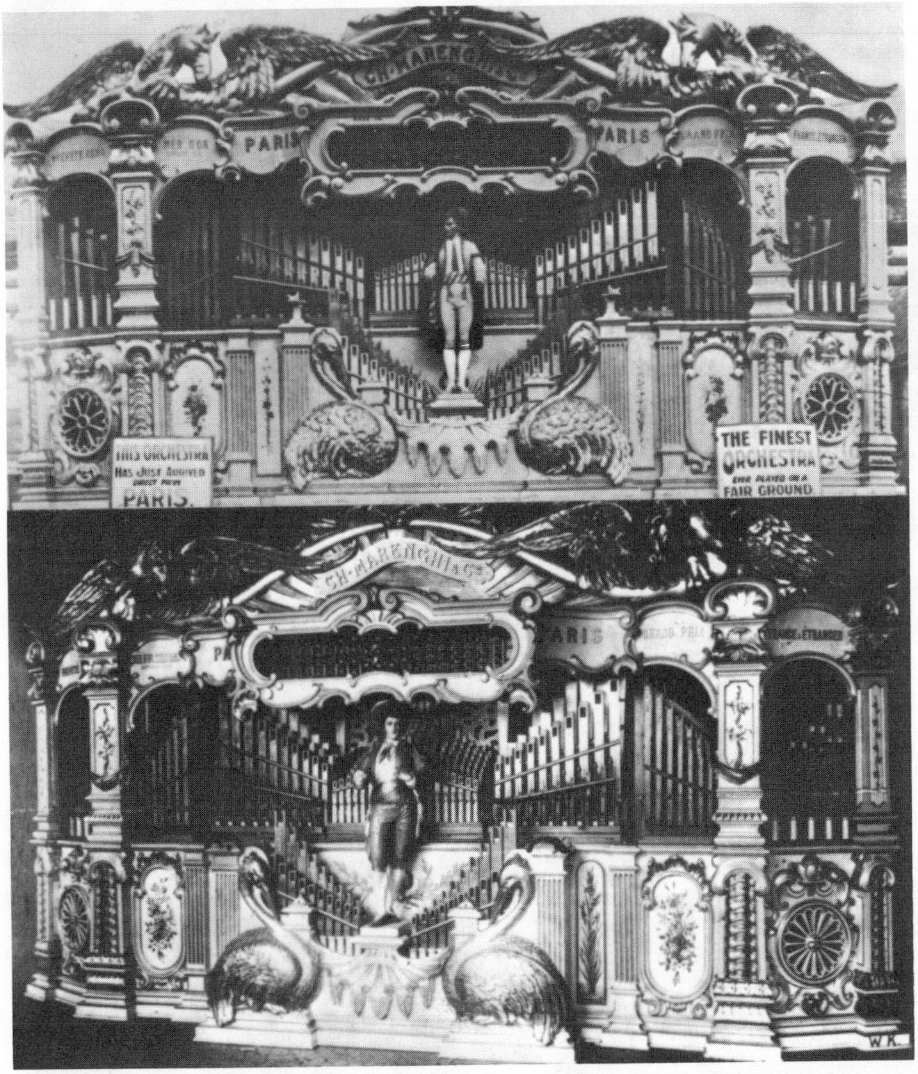


Top picture: Goldthorpe Marshall's 98-key Marenghi: "This orchestra has just arrived from Paris." "The finest orchestra ever played on a fairground." Bottom: Harniess Bros. 98-key Marenghi. This differs from the Marshall instrument only by some minor carving details.

92-key Marenghi organ in Wilson's Rodeo Switchback ride. Facade and some pipe arrangements were altered from former Bioscope show use.

The old-time Marenghi illustrations used here are, with just a few exceptions, from A. Colin Upchurch. The instruments are shown in use during the period from about 1905 to 1915. Identification of the key specifications is by Mr. Upchurch. Due to the confusing similarity between Gavioli and Marenghi appearances and due to the changing of the original scales by the organ owners, such attribution is tentative.

Right: A an early picture of the Royal Electric road show. The illustration dates from about 1910 and shows a large Marenghi organ on the left stage. The same model is shown in a factory photograph directly above. Note the seemingly countless electric lights dotting the facade. Marenghi was well known for spectacular multicolored lighting effects which changed as the different organ registers operated. At the right side of the picture on the right is a road locomotive made by Burrell. After the closing performance the Royal Electric troupe would pack its equipment into several cars, couple the units together, and haul them overland to the next destination. Road locomotives, common in England years ago, were not used to any extent in the United States.

President Kemp's "Theatre Unique" at the Nottingham Goose Fair, circa 1908. The instrument is a 104 double-case Marenghi with two of everything (except bass drums) that the normal 104-key size had. It is believed to be the most expensive Marenghi organ ever purchased by an English showman.

Left: President Kemp's "Palace of Light and Music" show. This picture dates from about 1908 and shows one of the first of several President Kemp shows to be equipped with a Marenghi organ. The instrument is of 92-key size. Hundreds of light bulbs adorned the facade and changed as the organ played.

Right: Anderton's 92-key Marenghi organ shown when it was first delivered to the yard of Orton & Spooner, amusement outfitters, circa 1907. Note the name "Anderton's" in lights and the hundreds of other bulbs on the facade. Lighting effects, derided by Marenghi's competitors when first introduced, were soon adopted by most of the organ building industry when it was learned that they greatly enhanced the drawing power of the instruments. Note also the free-standing statues. These could be ordered optionally from the Marenghi factory and were usually sold in sets of four.

Left: Marshall Hill's Scenic Railway shown circa 1910 with a new 98-key Marenghi organ. This particular organ is still in existence today.

Right: One of several traveling shows owned by the Collins family, the "Wonderland" had a beautiful facade with doors for entry and entrance at the sides, with three brilliantly lighted peacocks, at least a dozen statues, and hundreds and hundreds of light bulbs! The organ was a 104-key Marenghi with 17 registers.

Left: Marenghi organ used as the drawing card to attract viewers of a film about the "Heavyweight Championship of the World."

Right: 98-key Marenghi shown in winter quarters in England shortly after the instrument was delivered.

Left: Taylor's Bioscope Theatre, circa 1910. The facade is quite similar to the Collins show front shown on another page. 104-key organ size.

Right: 112-keyless Gavioli organ acquired in its incomplete state by Marenghi and finished with a Marenghi front. When Gavioli went into receivership, workmen from Limonaire and Marenghi finished certain organs then in process in the Gavioli works. Later, many unfinished organs went to Marenghi where they were sold as Ideal Orchestre organs with Marenghi facades.

Left: Relph & Pedley's show used an organ somewhat similar to that used by President Kemp's "Palace of Light and Music" – illustrated on another page. 92-keys.

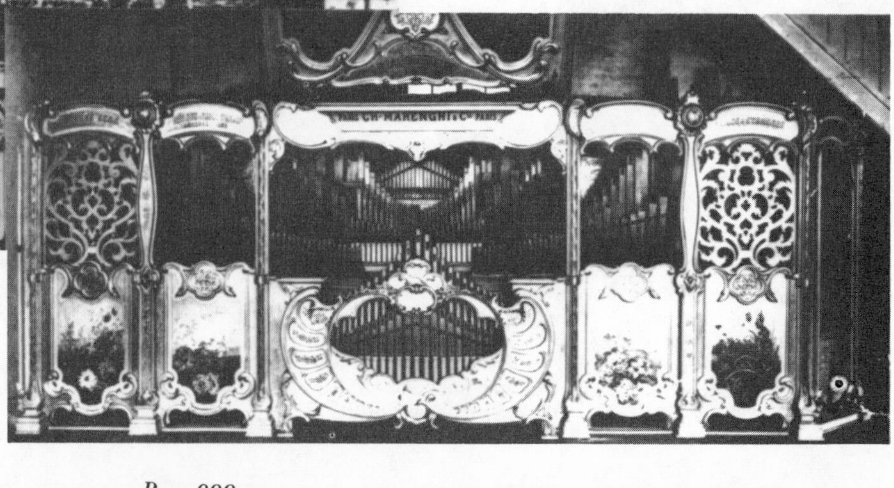

Right: 104-key Marenghi shown in the Verbeeck organ factory. The instrument is being converted from Bioscope use to a smaller facade size suitable for use on a scenic railway. This was a common practice, and most of the large Marenghi, Gavioli, and other organs from the Bioscope era were converted in this manner.

—Marenghi Organs—
1905 - 1915

Unlike most other fairground organ makers who had a wide line of instruments ranging from small 30 to 40-key instruments up to larger sizes, Marenghi concentrated on the larger sizes only. Instruments could be ordered with two types of voicing: loud for fairground use or soft for dance hall and indoor use. Many softly-voiced Marenghi organs were sold in Belgium where they competed with Th. Mortier in the dance organ business.

In the United States, Marenghi organs were imported by the Berni Organ Company of New York.

Technical information concerning Marenghi organs may be found in Eric V. Cockayne's "The Fairground Organ," published by David & Charles; Newton Abbot, England.

---

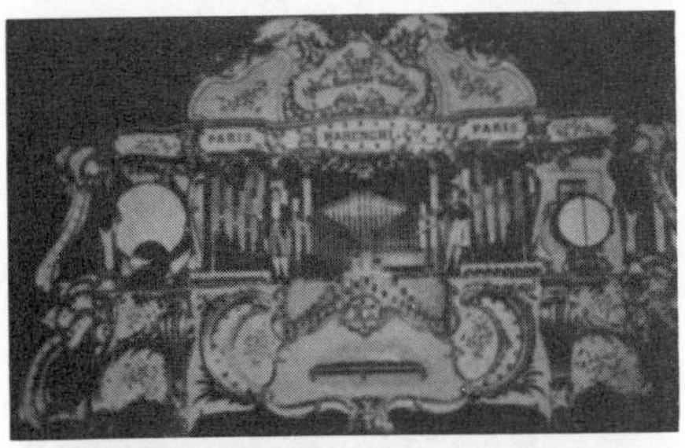

—Marenghi Organs—
Today

Owned by members of the Fair Organ Preservation Society, these organs provide Marenghi music for today's generation. Upper left: 89-key instrument owned by A. Middleton. "List and I Will Enchant Thine Ear" is lettered on the facade. Lower left: 89-key instrument with many visible ranks of pipes owned by H. Epton. Right: Immense 98-key Marenghi organ in the collection of G.T. Cushing. (Photographs from "The Key Frame" — courtesy of the Society)

## G. MOLINARI & SONS
—New York—

The firm of G. Molinari & Sons imported hand-cranked organs and barrel pianos from German and French makers to supplement instruments of their own manufacture. In the early 1890's, when duties for importing organs into the United States became restrictive, Molinari produced its own line of instruments.

In 1896 the firm advertised that "Our facilities for manufacturing are the most complete, as we have specially adapted machinery, invented and used only by us; our mechanics are the best that can be procured. Our well-stocked drying room of timber completely warrants our instruments to long durability... We are the oldest established house in the United States, as our organs were first put on the market in the year 1862, and now can be found in all parts of the United States. This is sufficient guarantee of the quality and reputation of our instruments." It was noted that "All our trumpets are made of wood, which stand climate better than metal. If brass trumpets are needed, we make them to order."

The Molinari business was most active in the 1880 - 1910 era. The instruments produced were of high quality and competed effectively with others made in America (by Eugene DeKleist of North Tonawanda, N.Y., for example) and with imported instruments.

At the 153 Elizabeth Street wareroom, operated by Joseph Molinari, a wide variety of musical instruments in addition to Molinari organs could be purchased.

---

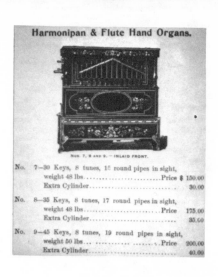

**Harmonipan & Flute Hand Organs.**

NOS. 7, 8 AND 9. — INLAID FRONT.

No. 7—30 Keys, 8 tunes, 15 round pipes in sight, weight 48 lbs ........ Price $ 150.00
Extra Cylinder ........ 30.00

No. 8—35 Keys, 8 tunes, 17 round pipes in sight, weight 48 lbs ........ Price 175.00
Extra Cylinder ........ 35.00

No. 9—45 Keys, 8 tunes, 19 round pipes in sight, weight 50 lbs ........ Price 200.00
Extra Cylinder ........ 40.00

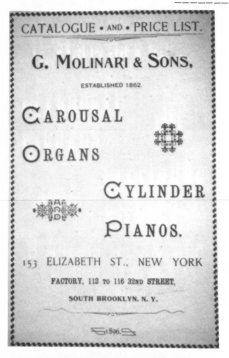

CATALOGUE • AND • PRICE LIST.

**G. MOLINARI & SONS,**

ESTABLISHED 1862.

CAROUSAL

ORGANS

CYLINDER

PIANOS.

153 ELIZABETH ST., NEW YORK

FACTORY, 112 TO 116 32ND STREET,

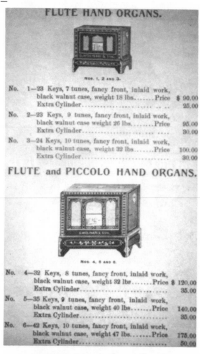

SOUTH BROOKLYN, N. Y.

1896.

**FLUTE HAND ORGANS.**

NOS. 1, 2 AND 3.

No. 1—23 Keys, 7 tunes, fancy front, inlaid work, black walnut case, weight 18 lbs........Price $ 90.00
Extra Cylinder ........ 25.00

No. 2—23 Keys, 9 tunes, fancy front, inlaid work, black walnut case weight 26 lbs........Price 95.00
Extra Cylinder ........ 30.00

No. 3—24 Keys, 10 tunes, fancy front, inlaid work, black walnut case, weight 32 lbs........Price 100.00
Extra Cylinder ........ 30.00

**FLUTE and PICCOLO HAND ORGANS.**

NOS. 4, 5 AND 6.

No. 4—32 Keys, 8 tunes, fancy front, inlaid work, black walnut case, weight 32 lbs........Price $ 120.00
Extra Cylinder ........ 35.00

No. 5—35 Keys, 9 tunes, fancy front, inlaid work, black walnut case, weight 40 lbs........Price 140.00
Extra Cylinder ........ 35.00

No. 6—42 Keys, 10 tunes, fancy front, inlaid work, black walnut case, weight 47 lbs........Price 175.00
Extra Cylinder ........ 50.00

**FLUTE & TRUMPET HAND ORGANS.**

NOS. 10, 11, 12 AND 13. — INLAID FRONT.

No. 10—32 Keys, 8 tunes, 10 Trumpets, weight 45 lbs. Price $ 150.00
Extra Cylinder ........ 40.00

No. 11—34 Keys, 8 tunes, 10 Trumpets, weight 47 lbs. Price 160.00
Extra Cylinder ........ 40.00

No. 12—37 Keys, 8 tunes, 12 Trumpets, weight 55 lbs. Price 175.00
Extra Cylinder ........ 45.00

No. 13—42 keys, 8 tunes, 12 Trumpets, weight 60 lbs. Price 200.00
Extra Cylinder ........ 50.00

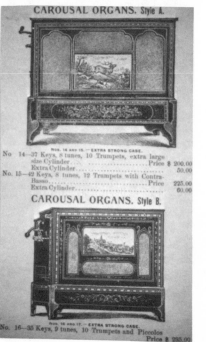

**CAROUSAL ORGANS. Style A.**

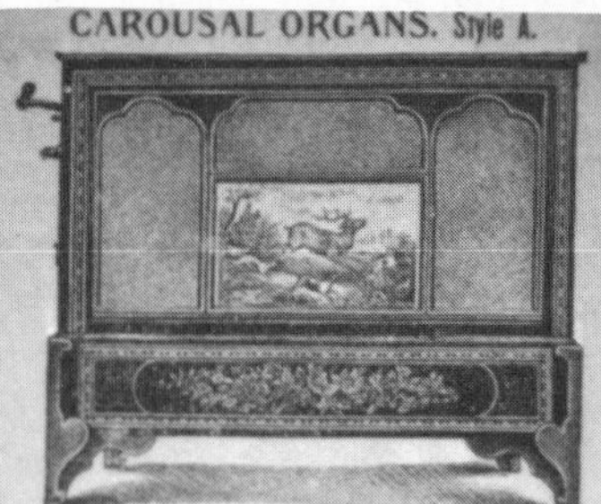

NOS. 14 AND 15. — EXTRA STRONG CASE.

No 14—37 Keys, 8 tunes, 10 Trumpets, extra large size Cylinder ........ Price $ 200.00
Extra Cylinder ........ 50.00

No. 15—42 Keys, 8 tunes, 12 Trumpets with Contra-Basso ........ Price 225.00
Extra Cylinder ........ 60.00

**CAROUSAL ORGANS. Style B.**

NOS. 16 AND 17. — EXTRA STRONG CASE.

No. 16—35 Keys, 9 tunes, 10 Trumpets and Piccolos Price $ 235.00

**CAROUSAL ORGANS. Style C.**
(LARGE SIZE).

NOS. 18, 19, 20 AND 21.

No. 18—35 Keys, 10 tunes, Trumpets, Piccolo in sight ........ Price $ 275.00
Extra Cylinder ........ 45.00

No. 19—35 Keys, 10 tunes, Trumpets, Contra-Basso and Piccolo in sight ........ Price 325.00
Extra Cylinder ........ 50.00

No. 20—50 Keys, 10 tunes, Trumpets and Piccolos in sight Contra-Bassos and 3 Bass Trumpets. Price 375.00
Extra Cylinder ........ 50.00

No. 21—58 Keys, 10 tunes, Trumpets and Piccolos in sight Contra-Bassos and Bass Trumpet. Price 450.00
Extra Cylinder ........ 60.00

**CAROUSAL ORGANS. Style D.**
(LARGE SIZE.)

NOS. 22 AND 23.

No. 22—60 Keys, 10 tunes, 15 Trumpets, Clarionets, Piccolos, Contra-Bassos, and Bass Trumpets Price 500.00
Extra Cylinder ........ 65.00

No. 23—68 Keys, 10 tunes, 17 Trumpets, Clarionets, Piccolos, Contra-Bassos, and Bass Trumpets Price 575.00
Extra Cylinder ........ 75.00

CAROUSAL ORGANS, Style F.
(LARGEST SIZE.)
No. 24—Brass Trumpets, Clarionets, Flute, Piccolos, Contra Bassos, Bass Trumpets, Drum, and Cymbols, with two wooden Figures elegantly carved, to play Triangles
Price $1500.00
Extra Cylinder 200.00

CAROUSAL ORGAN, Style E.
(LARGE SIZE.)
No. 24—9 tunes, Trumpets, Bass-Trumpets, Piccolos, Clarionets Flute, &c.


**The above barrel organ, operated by C. Feltman of Coney Island, N.Y., during the 1890's, was typical of a carousel instrument of this period. Instruments of somewhat similar appearance were made by others in the trade as well, Frati, Gavioli, Bruder, et al.**

Nos. 26, 27, 28 AND 29.
No. 26—40 Hammers, 10 tunes Price $ 165.00
With Panorama, Extra 10.00
Extra Cylinder 40.00
No. 27—42 Hammers, 10 tunes Price 170.00
With Panorama Extra 10.00
Extra Cylinder 40.00
No. 28—44 Hammers, 10 tunes Price 180.00
With Panorama, Extra 10.00
Extra Cylinder 50.00
No. 29—48 Hammers, 10 tunes Price 190.00
With Panorama, Extra 10.00
Extra Cylinder 50.00


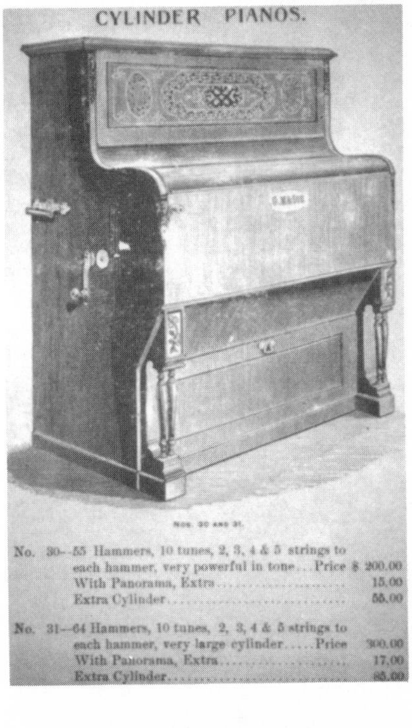

CYLINDER PIANOS.
No. 30—55 Hammers, 10 tunes, 2, 3, 4 & 5 strings to each hammer, very powerful in tone... Price $ 200.00
With Panorama, Extra 15.00
Extra Cylinder 55.00
No. 31—64 Hammers, 10 tunes, 2, 3, 4 & 5 strings to each hammer, very large cylinder.....Price 300.00
With Panorama, Extra 17.00
Extra Cylinder 85.00


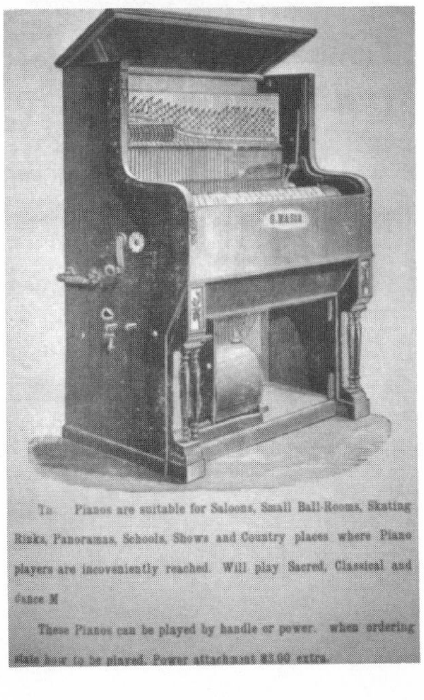

Pianos are suitable for Saloons, Small Ball-Rooms, Skating Rinks, Panoramas, Schools, Shows and Country places where Piano players are incoveniently reached. Will play Sacred, Classical and dance M
These Pianos can be played by handle or power. when ordering state how to be played. Power attachment $3.00 extra.

## Th. MORTIER, S.A.
### —Antwerp, Belgium—

### Introduction

From the Belgian factories of Theofiel Mortier came some of the most elegant organs the world has ever known. Some were in the form of temples; others resembled palaces. Even the simpler designs of the early years were triumphs of the woodcarver's art.

Unlike Bruder, Gavioli, Marenghi, and other organmakers, Mortier did not market its products on a worldwide basis. Most instruments were sold right in Belgium, the country of manufacture. A few found their way to Luxumbourg and the near provinces of France. Scarcely any went farther from home.

In recent years Mortier organs have attracted the attention of collectors and historians. Credit for a great deal of this Mortier renaissance goes to Leonard Grymonprez, organ builder and enthusiast of Ghent, Belgium. Mr. Grymonprez, whose family has been in the organ building business since the 19th century, furnished us with most of the illustrations for the Mortier section of this book.

We print below a history and an appreciation of the Mortier firm as written by Leonard Grymonprez:

### The Firm of Theofiel Mortier

A history of Mortier — makers of the best book-organs ever made!

Normally, if a factory has disappeared and, in this case, an organ factory, at least the buildings that housed it are still left. At the site of the Mortier factory in Antwerp everything is demolished — all of the buildings; everything. If you visit Waldkirch in Germany's Black Forest, the citizens there will proudly show you the buildings of Ignaz Bruder, Gebrüder Bruder, Gebr. Weber (number one in the world of orchestrions operating with paper rolls, in my personal opinion), and the buildings which housed the Waldkirch branch factories of Gavioli and Limonaire Frères. We in Belgium couldn't show anything to visitors in Antwerp concerning the renowned Mortier factory.

Mortier! — a name that still sounds to many ears as the Rolls Royce of the dance organs. Many diligent hands, good craftsmen, people with money, and good luck, were the basis of the start of Theofiel Mortier's enterprise in 1890.

First of all I have to tell you that Mr. Mortier wasn't an organ craftsman at all! Of course he loved organs very much, but the facts are that he was the owner of a great cafe, and an organ rental service, and — most important — had good public relations and was a first class businessman. For such a man the business was an open road before him.

One of the first persons who noticed these qualities in Theofiel Mortier was the father of the book-organ, Gavioli of Paris. And here we see how it all began.

In Mortier's cafe a fine Gavioli organ played almost constantly. At the same time Mortier kept on the lookout for a customer to buy it. When sold, Mortier ordered another one from Gavioli. This type of business prospered and within a couple of years it was necessary for him to build a workshop to repair organs.

In 1908 he had about ten men who were skilled in all types of organ repairs. Business became better and better for Mortier and also for Gavioli. In those days the instruments were mostly barrel or cylinder organs of 65 keys, but cardboard book organs were becoming increasingly more important as more and more customers found out about and asked for this type of instrument.

In the meantime Mortier's daughter went to Paris to learn about organs and how to arrange music for them. That was quite an undertaking for a woman in those days! For this favor Gavioli extracted a favor from Mortier: he was not to construct new organs.

Nevertheless, Mortier didn't concern himself with this condition, and his craftsmen started building a new organ to fill a customer's order. Gavioli didn't like this at all! Gavioli accused Mortier of making parts that were fully covered by Gavioli patents and brought him before a court of justice. At this point I have to say that many other organ makers used the Gavioli-patented systems without permission, but the reason Gavioli accused Mortier was probably mostly due to the fact that he didn't want to lose his most important sales outlet in Belgium.

The result of this famous and dramatic court case that lasted several years was that Mortier was obliged to purchase twelve new organs (without fronts; Mortier could make his own) each year from Gavioli & Cie. of Paris.

With his excellent business sense and clever mind Mortier devised an interesting scheme: he ordered so many new organs all at once from Gavioli that the Paris firm was not able to fill the order. Thus, according to the earlier terms of the court settlement, Gavioli lost all the rights of the sentence and Mortier was given a free hand in his own business.

By 1918 a new organ left the Mortier factory every two or three weeks. Business was so excellent that a customer desiring a new instrument would have to wait a year for it! By 1920 eighty good craftsmen worked there. People outside of the organ business became attracted to the magnificent instruments and to Mortier's business acumen and provided him with all of the financing he needed. It is no wonder that his firm emerged on top of all the others!

It was not only Mortier who built up the important factory and the name and the fame of the instruments. The team of craftsmen he had played a very important part. We shouldn't forget them for all the magnificent things they have done. Therefore, I will remind you of some of the more important:

Premier in importance were Guilliaume Bax and his two sons, Julius and Louis. Each of them was an artist in his craft. They were originally from France. Father Bax started in organ building as a young man, in a renowned church organ factory in Paris. His sons worked there also. This experience was a great benefit for them and also for Mr. Mortier. Some of the fine organ pipework invented by the senior Bax included: the baxophone (a saxophonelike pipe usually placed behind the wooden xylophone at the top part of large Mortier organs), the vibratone, and the nice jazz-flute.

The vibratone and jazz flute playing together in long passages give an effect not unlike that of a modern electronic organ, a Hammond, for instance. Bax also made several good improvements on other types of pipes and on many different organ parts.

Julius Bax was in charge of composing new music books for Mortier. Also, it was Julius who was responsible for bringing the low production levels of 1935 - 1936 back to a profitable business. He ordered from Chicago a new Hammond organ and information and instructions about it. In 1936 and 1937 Hammond was becoming very famous in the electronic organ industry. It was Julius' idea to incorporate a Hammond organ into the Mortier organ and have it operated automatically by the regular book-organ mechanism. It worked perfectly! Unhappily enough, people in those days were more interested in radios and phonographs than in book-organs. . .

The Bax family even constructed theatre organs for Mortier. They played these instruments themselves in the theatre on Sundays! One of those theatre organs is still operating today, but as a conversion to a church organ, in a suburb of Antwerp. When father Bax died this organ played the music at his funeral.

Famous were the Mortier organs for their very magnificent prosceniums (facades or fronts). A separate 10-man crew headed by

Paul Daelemans worked on the prosceniums exclusively. The art work was performed by August Souvenbrie.

In other sections, Josef van Loveren headed the pipemaking department and Josef van der Mueren supervised the music book manufacturing. If he were still alive he would tell you about the thousands of meters of books that were damaged by incorrect handling during a time early in the factory's history.

As music book composers in the factory we remember Frans Abel, Marcel Bartier, Bax, Carl Frei senior, J. Jilissen, H. Koninckx, Eugene Peersman, Urbain van Wichelen, and Pion (who was in earlier days the music composer for Gavioli in Paris). And, there was Mr. Mortier's daughter who had her own special music arranging section.

Apart from this group of Mortier specialists, we should mention some others. There was a lot of work for them in those days. Fasano, a cousin to the owner of the Fasano organ factory in Antwerp, emigrated later on to America (as did many other organ craftsmen). Duwyn, too, is worthy of mention. Duwyn left Mortier and started in Wilrijk, near Antwerp, a factory of his own. Several fine organs, some looking quite a bit like those of Mortier, left his factory. Even the Duwyn factory has disappeared now.

Well, then, there is a history of the Mortier house. I thought it would be a good thing to remember the factory and the people once again — all these great men who are no longer with us.

Mortier, a name, still sounds as clear as a bell in the hearts of many — but it is a sound of the past. I wonder why, and it does seem strange, how soon people forget some very nice creations. Magnificent instruments made for those same people. But maybe someday when we are tired of travel in outer space we will come back to them. . .

—So ends Leonard Grymonprez' narrative.

### Types of Mortier Organs

Mortier divided its productions into two types of instruments. Smaller instruments made for use in restaurants, cafes, etc. were known as orchestrions. Unlike other contemporary orchestrions, Mortier instruments did not have pianos. In fact, it would be more accurate to call them Mortier orchestrion-organs, for organs is what they were. Although they were smaller than the instruments that Mortier called organs, the orchestrions were hardly small in an absolute sense. Most were from eight to ten feet high; just as wide, and four to six feet deep. With the exception of a few that used perforated paper music rolls, the orchestrion - organs used folding cardboard music books. Most were of specifications from 68 to 84 keys, although a few were made in the 92-key size. Unlike the larger organs, the facades of some of the orchestrions were finished in natural wood (instead of painted) and had art glass panels. Usually the orchestrion - organs were made in two main sections: the back or chassis part contains all of the pipe work, the bellows, and all of the operating mechanisms; the front or proscenium part, often made in three or more detachable sections, was purely decorative.

As our illustrations on the following pages show, all of the Mortier orchestrion - organs were quite attractive. Some were spectacularly so.

The key frame mechanisms of the orchestrion - organs are usually at the left or right side of the chassis (unlike the larger organs in which the key frame is at the back). This permitted the instrument to be pushed tightly against a wall — a useful ability in an area with limited space.

It was the author's good fortune to become acquainted with Leonard Grymonprez and also with the late Eugene DeRoy in the early 1960's. At that time numerous Mortier orchestrions and organs were still in their original locations around Belgium. Since then they have become a popular export item to England, America, and other places — and the demand by collectors and enthusiasts has removed all but a few from where they once were. Although it was an unforgettable experience to go into a dance hall and see a splendid Mortier in its original location, it is probably best for posterity that collectors now own most of them. Now most are being cared for and are being restored to the condition they were in when first made in the 'teens, twenties, and thirties.

### Large "Classic" Mortier Organs

From about 1908 to 1930 Mortier built some of the most elegant automatic instruments ever to grace this earth. On the pages to follow many of them are illustrated. The originals of our photos are in many instances faded almost to the point of illegibility — but we thought that preserving this organ artistry of long ago was important enough for us to devote the space to it — and for you to bear with the lack of clarity evident in some of the pictures. The illustrations are courtesy of Leonard Grymonprez and represent archives from the Mortier factory and other pictures gathered over a period of many years. We number the pictures in order as they appear in the book. Readers of the earlier edition of this volume found the system useful when referring to the instruments, so we continue it here.

The classic early organs were made in a number of sizes with 84, 97, and 101 keys being among the most popular. Although a few paper roll operated organs were made, by far the majority were of the standard type with a folding cardboard music book system mounted at waist level at the rear of the instrument. An attendant operated the instrument by reaching for music books on a nearby shelf and feeding the leader into the key frame. Most later instruments were operated by electric motors but some early ones, including some really mammoth ones, were hand cranked!

Typically, a Mortier organ of the early or classic style measures about twenty to twenty five feet wide and fourteen to eighteen feet high. The facade, which is usually just a foot or two deep (some of the "temple" models are exceptions!), attaches to the chassis with brackets. The facade or proscenium is made in a dozen or so major sections, all put together with easily disassembled clamps. This was useful in the many instances in which these organs formed a part of a traveling show and were dismantled and reassembled every few days. Often a portable sectional wooden dance floor was set up in front of the organ and a canvas tent was erected over the entire project.

On many organs a chest of pipes is in a separate section near floor level at the front center of the organ. Another rank or two of pipes and often a xylophone as well are at the upper center at about the 8' level. These are visible through an opening in the facade. The xylophone and pipes are in a separate chest which is mounted on top of the main chassis.

The chassis itself is a separate wooden case (typical measurements: 6 or 7 feet high, 7 to 9 feet wide, 3 to 5 feet deep) with swell shutters in the front and sometimes in the top. The main chassis contains many ranks of pipes on a series of chests. Additional pipes are mounted horizontally under the chassis and sometimes still more pipes are affixed horizontally to the underside of the chassis top. The key frame, with a shelf extending to either side of it, is at the back of the instrument and is covered when not in use by a sliding door. Mounted on the floor of the chassis are the pressure pumps (all is pressure; there is no vacuum system) and reservoir.

To the sides of the chassis are extra case sections, often four side chests (two on each side of the chassis), but sometimes just two. These contain bass pipes, some of which usually can be seen through openings in the front carvings. The chests are connected by easily detachable mountings. It is possible for an experienced crew of several people to dismantle or erect one of these huge Mortier organs in less than an hour!

Although over 1000 of these classic organs were made, only a small percentage — perhaps one to two hundred — still survive today. Many were destroyed in accidents or misadventures, as the captions on the pictures to follow will tell. Still more were "modernized" by adding accordions, discarding major facade sections and replacing them with more up-to-date appearing panels, and otherwise altering their appearance and often their sound. Still others, and this includes quite a large number, were broken up and made into what we know as Dutch street organs. To do this the facades were discarded (although some of the trim and moldings were saved) as was much of the pipework. The pipes were revoiced. A new and much smaller front was made. The whole affair was mounted on a cart and, presto, we have a street organ. Books on the subject of Dutch street organs give due credit to Mortier in this regard.

Still other Mortier organs were used by the firm of Gebr. Decap to make modern dance organs. It was far more economical to use an existing Mortier chassis with all of its fine quality mechanisms than it was to build a new one — so dozens and dozens of classic Mortiers formed the basis for later modern Decap dance organs of different sizes.

### Later Mortier Instruments

Mortier continued in business until the early 1950's. Some very large organs, including some of over 120 keys in size (larger numbers of keys were needed to accommodate the accordion sections), were made from 1930 onward. Most of these had modern fronts which typify American and European architecture of the period (some call it "1933 World's Fair style"). The mechanisms and craftsmanship were excellent — and some really fine musical instruments were turned out during the early part of this 1930 - 1950 era. As noted in the Grymonprez description, some had electronic organs as part of the mechanisms.

According to Leonard Grymonprez, ownership of Mortier changed after the Second World War. Quality declined — and the instruments of that period were just a shadow of the earlier ones. Mortier lost its industry position and eventually went out of business. What was left of the situation was assumed by Gebr. Decap who, to this day, maintain an active dance organ business in Antwerp.

Mortier Orchestrions: (The style numbers for Mortier orchestrions are those assigned by the Mortier factory.) Above is the cover, "Orchestrions With Cardboard Music," from the original catalogue from which these Mortier orchestrion style numbers were obtained. Instrumentation of each consists of many ranks of pipes plus drum and trap effects.

–Style 30–
Mortier Orchestrion

–Style 37–
Mortier Orchestrion

–Style 34–
Mortier Orchestrion

–Style 33–
Mortier Orchestrion

–Style 29–
Mortier Orchestrion

–Style 31–
Mortier Orchestrion

–Style 32–
Mortier Orchestrion

–Style 36–
Mortier Orchestrion

–Style 27–
Mortier Orchestrion

–Style 28–
Mortier Orchestrion

–Style 41–
Mortier Orchestrion

–Style 26–
Mortier Orchestrion

Most of these are of oak wood in natural finish. Some have painted scenes on the front; others have stippled art glass (instead of the opalescent style used in the United States) or a statue or both. Styles 36 and 37 have painted facades with gilded trim. The Mortier "gilding" technique is still effective today: a silver base paint is overlaid with orange shellac. The result: a rich metallic gold color. Note the resemblance of 36 and 37 to some of the larger organ styles shown on following pages.

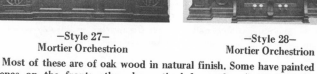

Above: Beautiful 84-key Mortier orchestrion (statue was not on it originally and was added when this picture was taken) somewhat similar to Style 39. If you like to compare the "architecture" (after all, some of these instruments are almost the size of buildings!) of various instruments, compare the above with a Hupfeld Helios IV orchestrion as shown in the Hupfeld section of this book. The resemblance is superficial (there was no connection between Mortier and Hupfeld), but it shows that "great minds think in the same channel" – or something. The interested reader can spot many other similarities throughout this book.

–Style 39–
Mortier Orchestrion

–Style 40–
Mortier Orchestrion

–Style 38–
Mortier Orchestrion

–Style 25–
Mortier Orchestrion

Above Right: Ornate Mortier orchestrion similar but not identical to Style 36 (Wallace McPeak and Jim Miller photo).

Directly Above: An unusual roll-operated Mortier orchestrion built into a rectangular cabinet about seven feet high. Only a few instruments using rolls were made. Most Mortier orchestrions used the standard folding cardboard music books. (Charles Barnes Collection)

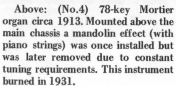

Mortier Organs – Early Classic Styles: The organs numbered from 1 through 40 on the following pages are mostly early styles from about 1910 to 1930. Important Note: the numbers are our own and bear no relation to Mortier style numbers. They are to aid dealers and collectors describing similar instruments.

Above: (No.4) 78-key Mortier organ circa 1913. Mounted above the main chassis a mandolin effect (with piano strings) was once installed but was later removed due to constant tuning requirements. This instrument burned in 1931.

(No.1) Original 76-keyless Mortier organ; one of the very few keyless styles made. A xylophone shows through the center aperture. Arranged in pyramidal fashion and situated near the bottom front directly before the swell shutters is a harmonic flute rank made of zinc. Left and right niches contain wooden violin and cello pipes.

Left: (No.5) Known as "The Emperor" this organ had a facade replete with eagles and dragons.

(No.2) Made circa 1909 - 1910 this instrument has a rank of metal harmonic flute pipes at the lower center. The organ fits just right in its original location – a dance hall. This was a popular style and a number were made.

(No.6) Originally a Gavioli, this organ was given a front by Mortier (see text). 91 keys. Parts of the facade exist today in Holland.

Above: (No.3) Keyless Mortier organ provided with a reed section mounted below the front harmonic flute pipes. This organ was once owned by Leonard Grymonprez' great-grandfather. Like other Mortier organs of this era the flat panels are decorated with colorful oil paintings.

Right: (No.7) Surmounted by a quadriga this elegant 84-key Mortier was originally built for the Victoria Palace dance hall in Ghent, Belgium. The quadriga and the life-size carved figures on the lower part of the organ are later additions but fit in nicely. Used from 1911 to 1936. Later sold to a travelling show. Sold by the Grymonprez firm in 1946.

(No.8) 90-key Mortier made on special order for the magnificent dance hall, The Emperor's Garden, in Antwerp, Belgium. Built around 1910-1911. Restored by Grymonprez in 1937. Later destroyed.

(No.9) This beautiful 90-key Mortier was made circa 1911 - 1912. It was destroyed in later years. Note the beautiful life-size trumpeter figures in each of the two side niches. Mortier statues were works of art. Often they were imported from famous woodcarvers in Italy.

(No.10) Mortier organ made circa 1912 - 1913 for the Brabo dance hall in Antwerp, Belgium. Later destroyed.

(No.11) Large Mortier organ of 90 or 91 keys built for an Antwerp dance hall about 1910. The front is a replica of the main entrance to the Brussels World's Fair of 1910! The organ is still extant but, sad to say, the front is not. The 1910 World's Fair was a showplace for automatic musical instruments. Hupfeld, Mortier, and most other notables of the industry had large displays there.

(No. 12) 90 or 91 key Mortier built around 1913 for the Black Cat dance hall in Antwerp. It sports two allegorical female figures and a team of horses. Later demolished.

(No.13) 81-key Mortier made around 1913 for a Brussels dance hall. Sold to a travelling troupe in the 1930's. Later destroyed. This was a popular design and several were made.

(No.14) 84-key Mortier built around 1926 for Mr. Cools, owner of a large dance hall at Erondegem, near Aalst. Nicknamed "The Turk," as the instrument's paintings were of Turkish people and places. Later destroyed.

(No.15) Large 86-key Mortier built around 1925 - 1926. Installed in a dance hall in Ostend, Belgium. Later destroyed, as were so many of these beautiful organs. Compare this organ to our No.31. This was a popular model.

(No.16) 92-key organ manufactured in 1928 for a dance hall in a Brussels suburb. Provided with a large bronze bell at the center near the top. Shown in the organ's original dance hall location.

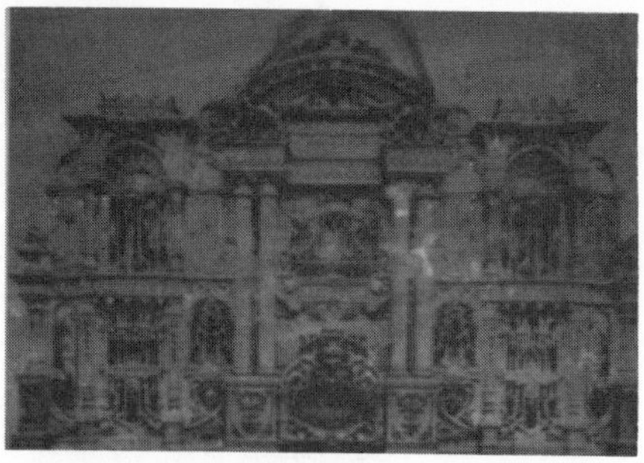

(No.17) Large 101-key Mortier built around 1923 - 1924. Now in the collection of Mr. C.E. Hine of Shaftesbury, England, but now without the original front. Illustration is from a very faded Mortier advertising card — as are many of the pictures used in this section.

(No.18) 92-key organ built in 1925 on special order for a luxurious dance hall near Brussels. The front is a replica of the Greek temple of Olympus! The world is only now recognizing these instruments for the art treasures they are.

(No.19) Mortier postcard picture of a 91-key organ manufactured circa 1926 for a dance hall in Wetteren, near Ghent, Belgium. Noted the railinged upper "balcony."

(No.20) 81-key organ built in 1913. Used in Ghent, Belgium.

(No.21) 101-key Mortier built in 1925 or 1926 for a dance hall in Jette, near Brussels. Nicknamed "the Six Columns," the organ was later destroyed.

(No.22) A very ornate early Mortier organ as shown on a bent, faded, and folded postcard. Note the family resemblance to this and the Style 36 orchestrion; also to the organs that we number 23 and 40 on these pages. (No. 23 is just to the right.)

(No.23) About 1400 dance organs and orchestrions were made over the years by Mortier. Of these, this one was the largest and most impressive of all! Measuring 36 feet wide, the instrument was built in 1926 for the owners of a dance hall in Roeselare, Belgium. The owners and patrons, accustomed to the loud music of Hooghuys and other types of fairground organs, were disappointed with the mellow dance organ tone. The instrument was then sold to the Thalia dance hall (as pictured above) in Blankenberge. The second owners made a fortune with the organ. On June 10, 1950, the Grymonprez firm acquired it without the front (which was destroyed). Later it was sold to a customer in Germany. The "Taj Mahal," No. 40 in this album of Mortier pictures, is of somewhat similar design. It, too, earned a fortune for its owners.

(No.24) 81-key chromatic organ built in 1913 for use in Tienen, Belgium. This organ is seemingly identical to No. 20, but as the pictures came from different sources the instruments may not be the same — just two of a popular model. At the right and below are details of some of the pipework of this beautiful organ.

(No.25) 81-key chromatic organ built in 1913.

(No.26) Organ in an unidentified Belgian location years ago.

(No.27) A large Mortier organ as shown on a faded postcard. "Orchestre Moderne" is lettered across the front. The attribution of this organ to Mortier is not certain, but is a good probability.

(No.28) 86-key Mortier organ built for a dance hall in Wetteren circa 1922 - 1923. From a Mortier postcard.

(No.29) 84-key Mortier organ built circa 1927 - 1928 and originally used in Ghent, Belgium. At one time the small country of Belgium had more organs per square mile than any province on earth!

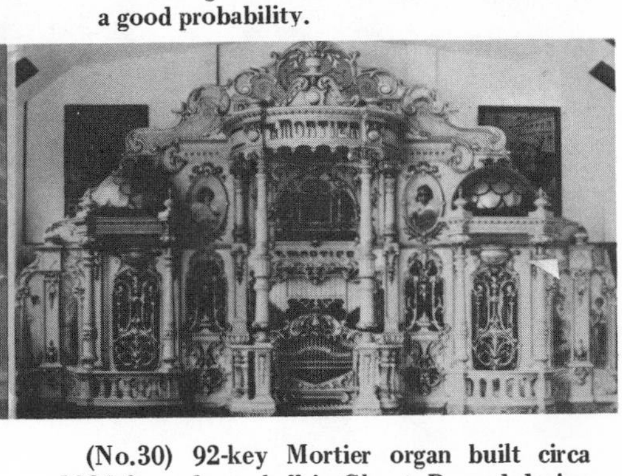


(No.30) 92-key Mortier organ built circa 1924 for a dance hall in Ghent. Burned during World War II. Shown in its original dance hall location.

(No.31) An organ similar to No.15, but with slightly different painted scenes. On location in France in 1968. (Alain Vian photo)

(No.32) 97-key special chromatic organ built in 1930 for a customer in Ghent. This was one of the last of the classic type organ fronts.

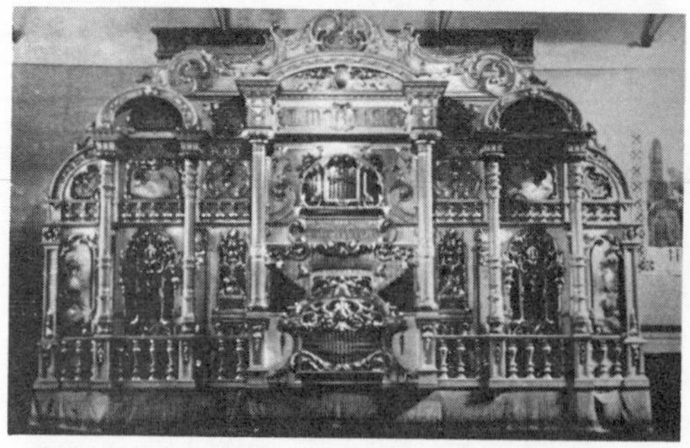

(No.33) A Mortier organ shown on a platform similar to that on which No.26 is mounted.

Rank of wooden trumpet pipes in a large Mortier organ. The wood pipes of various types in Mortier organs are all of good quality with good voicing.

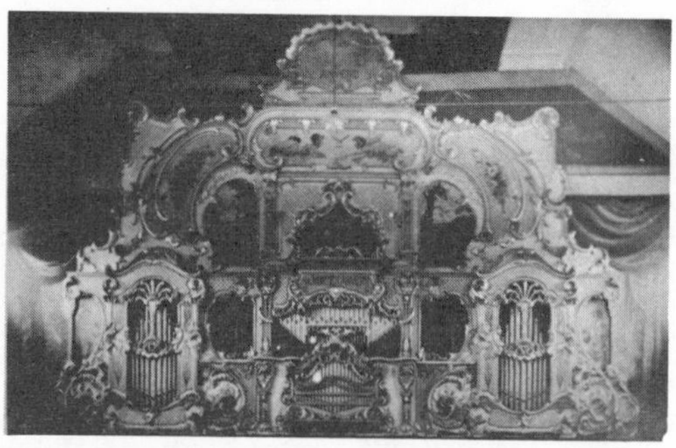

(No.34) 81-key Mortier organ built in 1913 for an establishment in Boom, Belgium.

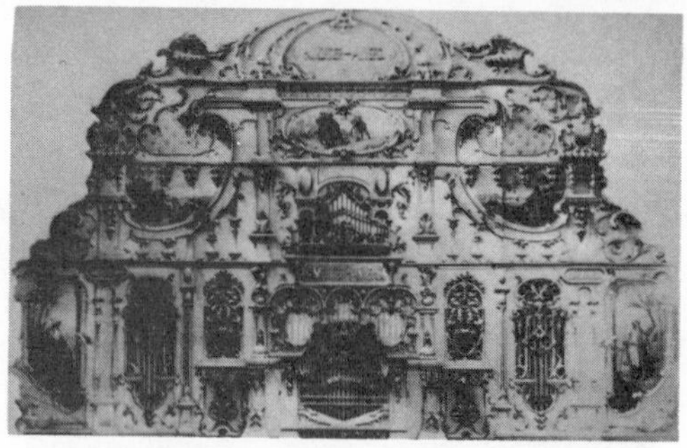

(No.35) 97-key chromatic organ, possibly built circa 1927. As noted, most of the Mortier pictures are from the Grymonprez files and were collected over a period of many years. We acknowledge Mr. Grymonprez' love for Weber orchestrions also — and appreciate the help he gave us with illustrations for the Weber section of this book.

(No. 36) 84-key Mortier organ built circa 1920 - 1921 for Boom, Belgium. The beautiful oil paintings on Mortier organs, the scenic panels, are done separately on a canvas backing. The canvas is then cut out to the required shape and glued to the organ facade. This canvas backing reduces chipping and renders the painting more or less immune to the many wood cracks that seem to be a natural feature of large organ fronts. Today the restorer can often make such paintings look just like new simply by cleaning them.

(No.37) This large 101-key Mortier organ is a transitional design between the curlicued styles of the 1920's and the modernistic format of the 1930's. Of fully chromatic design, the organ has a continuous range of playing notes from the lowest bass to the highest treble pipe. The pipework in the main chassis, some ranks of which are visible above, is arranged in cascading and pyramidal fashion. At the very front are the short jazz flutes. By means of a flexible pouch and an interrupted wind supply these seem to warble – and produce a sound that is much desired by collectors today.

For an excellent study of band organs and dance organs, including those of the Mortier firm, the reader is urged to secure a copy of "The Fairground Organ" by Eric V. Cockayne. The book is a technical treatise in laymen's terms and discusses the making and voicing of pipes, the construction of pipe chests, control units, the making of music books, the layout of music scales, and every other subject relevant to the study and collection of these instruments.

(No.38) This large and beautiful 97-key Mortier organ is a prized possession of Messrs. Roy Haning and Neal White of Troy, Ohio. The instrument is unusual in that, apart from the normal ageing, it is just like new. The paintings on the front, the gilding, and the other features couldn't have been much brighter when this organ left the Mortier factory decades ago!

Right: (No.39) Taken in January, 1966, this photograph shows Leonard Grymonprez (on the left) and his father, Oscar, standing in front of a 67-key organ made mostly of Mortier parts. Made for a present-day customer, the organ is much shorter than the tall Mortiers of old – simply because few people today have the sixteen to twenty foot high ceilings needed to house these instruments. Until collectors began appreciating Mortier and other Belgian instruments, something that happened in a big way beginning in the mid-1960's, the Grymonprez business was mainly the making of new dance organs from old ones. Now the firm also does a thriving business with collectors in England, America, and on the European continent.

"Taj Mahal"

(No.40) The "Taj Mahal," a huge and ornate 101-key Mortier organ. Terry Hathaway and the author (right) are dwarfed by the instrument — which measures about 26' wide by 20' by 15' deep. Above is a postcard picture issued by Mortier when the instrument was originally installed in 1924. Leonard Grymonprez describes the instrument: "This superior Mortier organ was delivered in 1924 to St. Jean's Palace, a dance hall in Antwerp, Belgium. The land on which St. Jean's Palace was located was needed for a new building project, and after court procedures the dance hall was razed. The Mortier was moved for a short time to the Agora dance hall in Ledeberg. The instrument was then sold and moved to Zelzate, a town located along the border between Belgium and Holland. It was installed in the Reseda dance hall located in the market square of Zelzate. The "Taj Mahal" Mortier brought its third owners great fame and wealth. The organ was operated until 1952. In the opinion of the Grymonprez family this particular Mortier is the largest and most finely-voiced organ in existence today. Together with an instrument (now destroyed) used in the Thalia dance hall in Ostend, the "Taj Mahal" is one of the two largest organs ever constructed by Mortier in the course of building about 1400 organs from the turn of the 20th century until shortly after 1950."

L. MORTIER

Large hand-carved figure on the "Taj Mahal." (Collection of Q. David Bowers)

## MORTIER ORGANS (Later Styles)

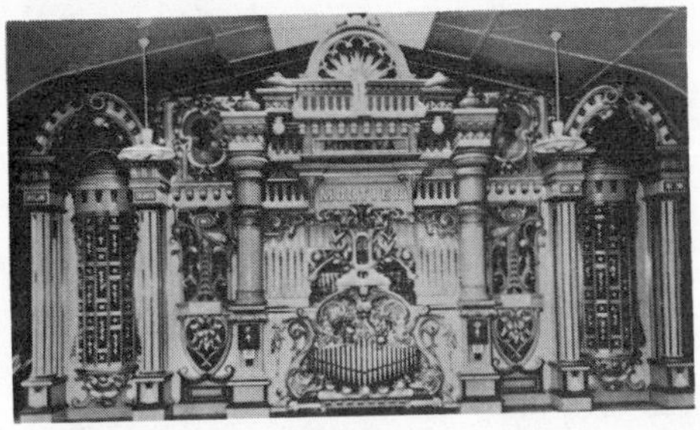

(No.41)

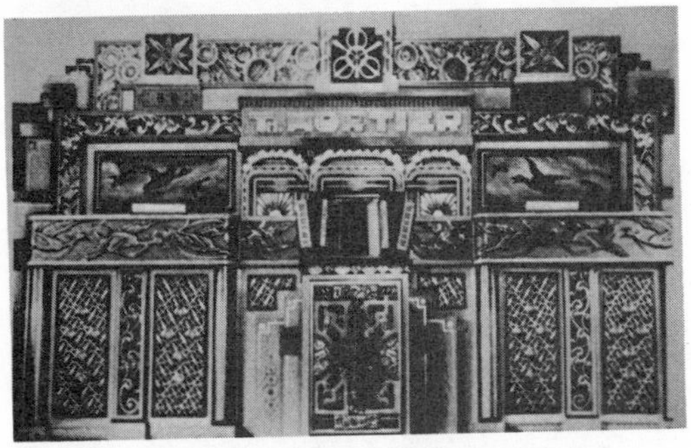

(No.43)

(No.46)

(No.48)

(No.42)

(No.44)

(No.45)

(No.47)

(No.49)

Nos. 41 to 49: Mortier organs of the 1930 - 1950 era. Information is known about the following numbers as illustrated above: (No.41) 92-key chromatic Mortier organ built in 1930. Named "Minerva." Note resemblance to No.45; (No.43) Postwar style with rectangular panels typical of the period; (No.44) This was one of the last dance organs to leave the factory in 1950. 112 keys with two accordions, two saxophones, and complete drums and traps. The organ was named after prince Boudewijn who later became king of Belgium; (No.45) Also named "Minerva" this organ, except for a slight rearrangement of the facade, is nearly identical to No.41; (No.46) 102-key Mortier organ built in 1938 - 1939 for use in Holland. Note the accordion, a standard feature on later instruments (accordions were later added to many earlier instruments as well). (No.48) 112-key Mortier organ built in 1938 - 1939 for use in Brussels.

These later Mortier instruments are mostly all chromatic. With modern percussion effects and with just about every extra instrument imaginable, they are very versatile musically. Those with accordions usually have the music arranged with the accordion as the solo instrument. For extra volume some late Mortiers have two or three accordions. Saxophones on these late instruments are simulated by the use of reed boxes; a real saxophone is mounted on the front for visual display and the valves are "operated" by pneumatics.

## MORTIER CAFE ORGANS
—Very late models—

(No.50)

(No.51)

(No.52)

(No.53)

Dating from the late 1940's and early 1950's, these Mortier cafe organs have starkly modernistic facades. As can be observed, the accordion is the featured solo instrument. The "pipework" in some of these is electronic, although often a real rank of bass pipes is used. Others contain complete wooden pipework as in the older and more traditional designs.

As of 1950 the only large automatic musical instruments being produced in quantity on a regular commercial basis were the modern cafe and dance organs being made by Mortier, Decap, and Bursens.

## JOHN MUZZIO & SON

—New York—

During the c.1910 period John Muzzio & Son of Park Row, New York, was an importer and manufacturer of organs. Unlike most importers, Muzzio illustrated the instruments with the makers' names on them, in many instances (such as the Frati & Co. organ near the center of this page). Other instruments were from Gavioli. Frati Harmonipans, Violinopans, and other hand-cranked portable organs were listed and identified as being "made by Frati."

Made in the Muzzio Organ Works, sometimes with the utilization of a Frati chassis, were a variety of Muzzio cylinder organs ornamented with scrollwork and side wings containing visible drums. An example is the organ at the lower right of this page which was described as: "No. 124. Muzzio organ. 43 keys, 9 tunes, your selections, with drums, visible piccolos, 4 movable figures - each with a different motion, fancy carved case... 6'4" high without top carving. $400."

(Illustrations courtesy Carl Thomsen)

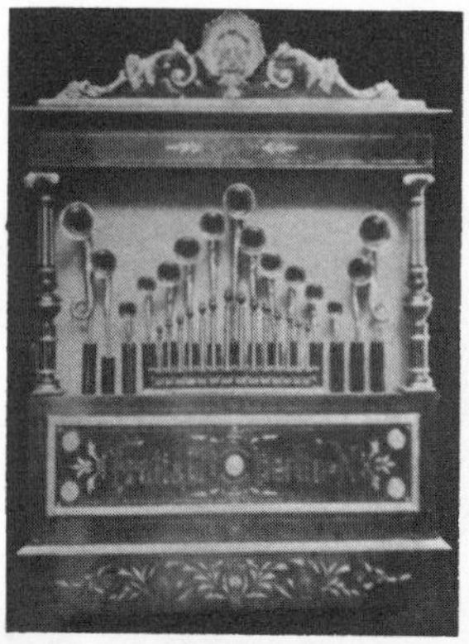

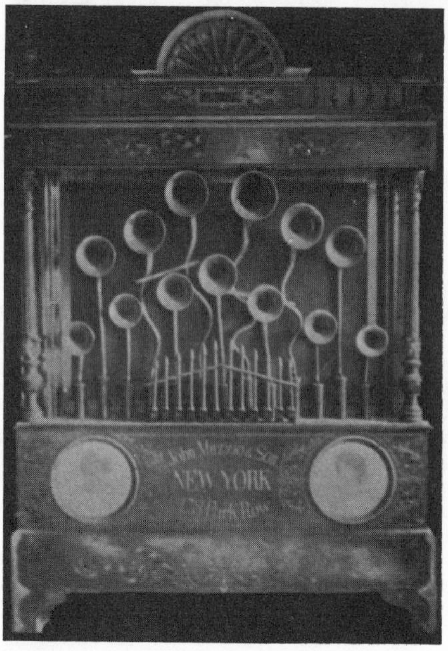


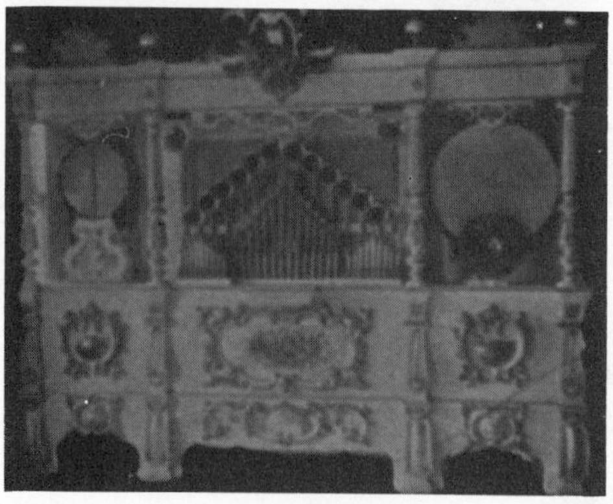

## NIAGARA MUSICAL INSTRUMENT COMPANY
### —North Tonawanda, N.Y.—

### Niagara Military Band Organs

From about 1905 until shortly before World War I, the Niagara Musical Instrument Company produced a variety of cylinder and paper roll operated military band organs. These closely resemble certain North Tonawanda Musical Instrument Works and certain Wurlitzer band organs of the same period.

To illustrate the different models in its catalogue, Niagara relied heavily on touch-up and composite work by its printer (who, by the way, also printed catalogues for the North Tonawanda Musical Instrument Works). Thus the illustration for the Style 180 is simply the illustration for Style 18, but with two drums and a cymbal painted on top.

Few Niagara military band organs survive in their original form today. Many, if not most, were converted to play Wurlitzer rolls (mostly Style 125 rolls) in later years and had the Wurlitzer name affixed to the front of the organ.

(Note: For information concerning Niagara coin pianos and orchestrions refer to the Niagara Coin Piano section of this book.)

———————

STYLE NO. 18

Operated by Pinned Cylinder,

41 Keys, 8 Selections.

STYLE NO. 180

Operated by Pinned Cylinder,

41 Keys, 8 Selections.

STYLE NO. 291.
Operated by Pinned Cylinder,
47 Keys, 8 Selections.

STYLE NO. 299.
Operated by Perforated Paper,
47 Notes, 18 Selections.

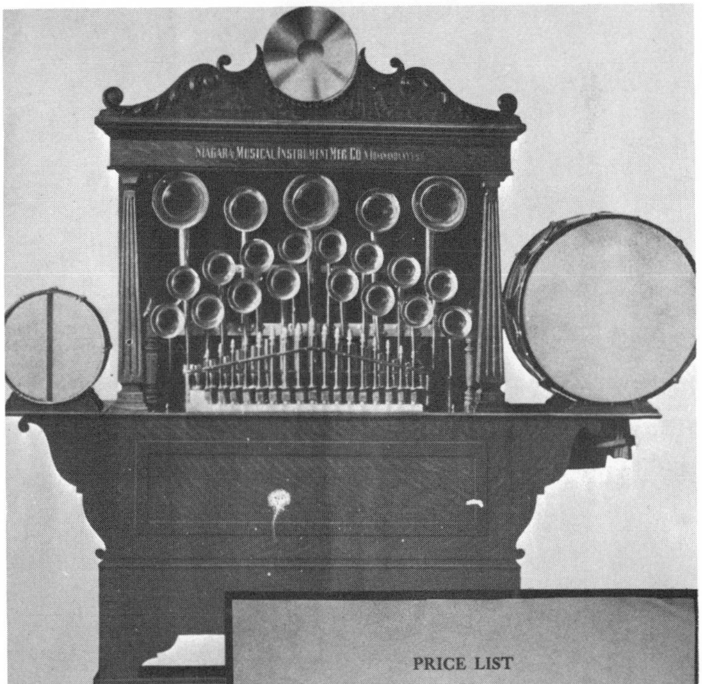


STYLE NO. 60.
Operated by Pinned Cylinder,
55 Keys, 9 Selections.

STYLE NO. 69.
Operated by Perforated Paper,
55 Notes, 18 Selections.

STYLE 290.

Operated by Pinned Cylinder,

47 Keys, 8 Selections.

STYLE 298.

Operated by Perforated Paper,

47 Notes, 18 Selections.

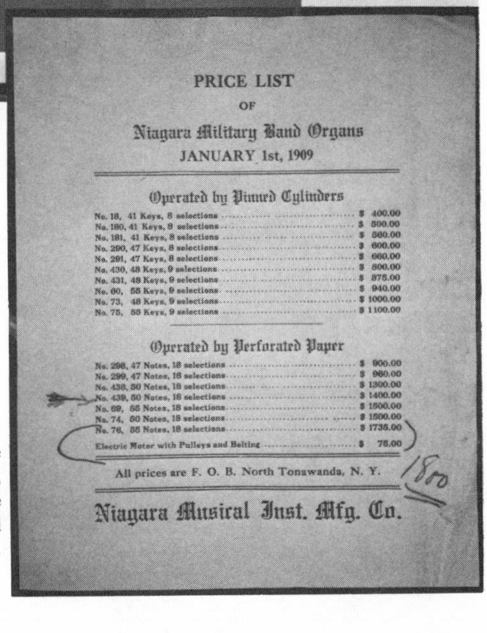

PRICE LIST
OF
Niagara Military Band Organs
JANUARY 1st, 1909

Operated by Pinned Cylinders

| | |
|---|---|
| No. 18, 41 Keys, 8 selections | $ 400.00 |
| No. 180, 41 Keys, 8 selections | $ 500.00 |
| No. 181, 41 Keys, 8 selections | $ 560.00 |
| No. 290, 47 Keys, 8 selections | $ 600.00 |
| No. 291, 47 Keys, 8 selections | $ 660.00 |
| No. 430, 48 Keys, 9 selections | $ 800.00 |
| No. 431, 48 Keys, 9 selections | $ 875.00 |
| No. 60, 55 Keys, 9 selections | $ 940.00 |
| No. 73, 48 Keys, 9 selections | $ 1000.00 |
| No. 75, 55 Keys, 9 selections | $ 1100.00 |

Operated by Perforated Paper

| | |
|---|---|
| No. 298, 47 Notes, 18 selections | $ 900.00 |
| No. 299, 47 Notes, 18 selections | $ 960.00 |
| No. 438, 50 Notes, 18 selections | $ 1300.00 |
| No. 439, 50 Notes, 18 selections | $ 1400.00 |
| No. 69, 55 Notes, 18 selections | $ 1500.00 |
| No. 74, 60 Notes, 18 selections | $ 1500.00 |
| No. 76, 55 Notes, 18 selections | $ 1735.00 |
| Electric Motor with Pulleys and Belting | $ 75.00 |

All prices are F. O. B. North Tonawanda, N. Y.

1800

Niagara Musical Inst. Mfg. Co.

Right: Niagara price list of January 1, 1909 showing the instruments offered at that time.

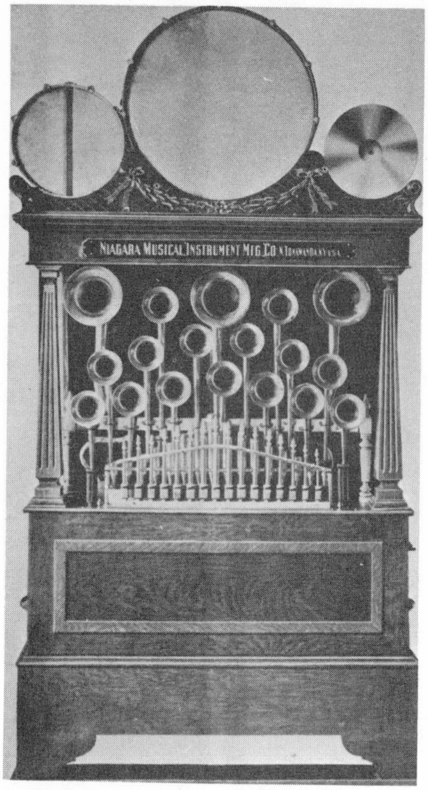

STYLE 430
Operated by Pinned Cylinder
48 Keys, 9 Selections.

STYLE 438
Operated by Perforated Paper
50 Notes, 18 Selections.

STYLE 431
Operated by Pinned Cylinder,
48 keys, 9 selections.

STYLE 439
Operated by Perforated Paper,
50 notes, 18 selections.

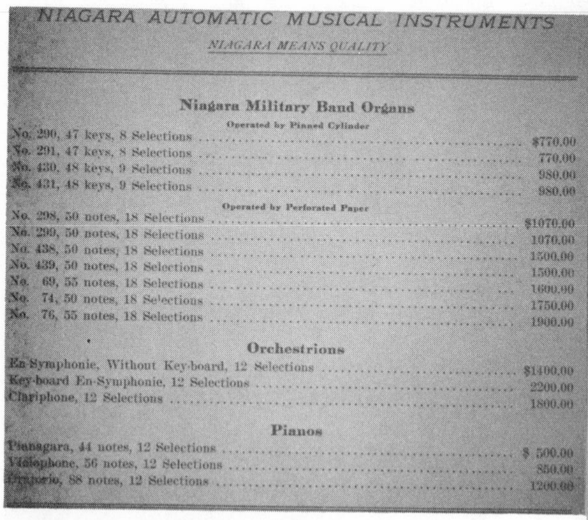

NIAGARA AUTOMATIC MUSICAL INSTRUMENTS

NIAGARA MEANS QUALITY

**Niagara Military Band Organs**

Operated by Pinned Cylinder

| | |
|---|---|
| No. 290, 47 keys, 8 Selections | $770.00 |
| No. 291, 47 keys, 8 Selections | 770.00 |
| No. 430, 48 keys, 9 Selections | 980.00 |
| No. 431, 48 keys, 9 Selections | 980.00 |

Operated by Perforated Paper

| | |
|---|---|
| No. 298, 50 notes, 18 Selections | $1070.00 |
| No. 299, 50 notes, 18 Selections | 1070.00 |
| No. 438, 50 notes, 18 Selections | 1500.00 |
| No. 439, 50 notes, 18 Selections | 1500.00 |
| No. 69, 55 notes, 18 Selections | 1600.00 |
| No. 74, 50 notes, 18 Selections | 1750.00 |
| No. 76, 55 notes, 18 Selections | 1900.00 |

**Orchestrions**

| | |
|---|---|
| En-Symphonie, Without Key-board, 12 Selections | $1400.00 |
| Key-board En-Symphonie, 12 Selections | 2200.00 |
| Clariphone, 12 Selections | 1800.00 |

**Pianos**

| | |
|---|---|
| Pianagara, 44 notes, 12 Selections | $ 500.00 |
| Violaphone, 56 notes, 12 Selections | 850.00 |
| [illegible], 88 notes, 12 Selections | 1200.00 |

The above 1911 price list offers various band organs (mostly roll-operated by this date, in contrast to the opposite situation as shown on the 1909 list on another page) for sale as well as several different varieties of orchestrions and pianos. Information about Niagara coin-operated instruments may be found elsewhere in this book.

STYLE 75
Operated by Pinned Cylinder,
55 keys, 9 selections.

STYLE 76
Operated by Perforated Paper,
55 notes, 18 selections.

Top of the Niagara line was the Style 75 (or 76) band organ. The Style 76 (paper roll operated) sold for $1735 in 1909. By 1911 the price had risen to $1900.

## NORTH TONAWANDA MUSICAL INSTRUMENT WORKS
### —Military Band Organs—

### Types of Organs Made

From about 1906 until the mid-'teens (Mr. Benjamin G. Rand, a later owner of the firm, stated that no organs were made after his group acquired the company in 1918) the North Tonawanda Musical Instrument Works made about two dozen different styles of band organs. Usually called "Automatic Military Bands" in the firm's catalogues, these were mainly used in skating rinks.

All North Tonawanda Musical Instrument Works organs use the endless roll system of music. For information concerning this roll system and concerning the history of the North Tonawanda firm the reader should refer to the North Tonawanda part of the coin piano and orchestrion section of this book.

Many North Tonawanda models are virtually identical in appearance to Niagara and Wurlitzer models. This, plus the fact that many North Tonawanda instruments were converted in later years to Wurlitzer music roll systems, sometimes makes identification of present-day instruments difficult.

A North Tonawanda catalogue of c.1913 noted: "During the past seven years we have so improved our Automatic Military Bands, by expert voicing of our pipes and by inventing new and ingenious mechanisms, so that today musicians and users acknowledge that we build the only real Automatic Bands in the country.

"Proprietors of skating rinks, ice rinks, park carousels, traveling carousels, merry go rounds, Ferris Wheels, circling waves, show platforms, etc. find that our instruments are perfect for their use; which accounts for the large number now being used for that purpose."

### Testimonials

To give some old-time flavor we reprint some North Tonawanda testimonials received from 1907 to 1910:

From Altman and Smeltzer, owners of the Eagle Skating Rink in Jeannette, Pa.: "We received our organ and set it up and everything was O.K. You told us that it was a DANDY, and so it is. It makes lots of good loud music and we have no more complaints now from our patrons about not hearing the music. . ."

From the Scranton Republican: "The new organ (Style 1100) at the Armory, with its tremendous power and its magnificent quality of tone, is one of the marvels of this city and should be heard by every musician in Scranton. I had the pleasure to hear some selections from the Opera of Martha played on this instrument with the most delicate shading, and at times tremendous brass band effect. The finale of the concert was the playing of Old Black Joe. Another composition was the Wedding of the Winds. The wonderful volume of tone in this instrument is just like a brass band of eighty pieces. . . I would advise our musicians and others to hear and see this wonderful instrument, and I am sure there will then be more people taking to the healthful exercise of skating."

From the Alexandra Pavilion & Rink, Hamilton, Canada: "We take great pleasure in stating that after having used the organ No. 1100 purchased from you we find it perfectly satisfactory in every way. It has done the work in better style than any band we ever had in the rink, and the crowds prefer it to the bands. We have had larger skating parties, and the popularity of the organ is evinced by the fact that we cannot now close our rink until 10:30 P.M. instead of 10 o'clock, the encores being so frequent that to carry out a programme of 12 numbers, it is necessary to run a half hour longer each evening. . . The Alexandra Rink is probably the finest rink on the continent, certainly the finest in Canada, and the mere fact that we installed your organ is evidence that we consider it good enough for our rink."

From E. Frank Vernon, professional skater: "It is a pleasure to work with an organ of your make, and wherever I find your instruments used, I find the rinks doing good business and the patrons speaking nicely of the music. For me, give me the North Tonawanda Musical Instrument Works make, first, last, and all the time."

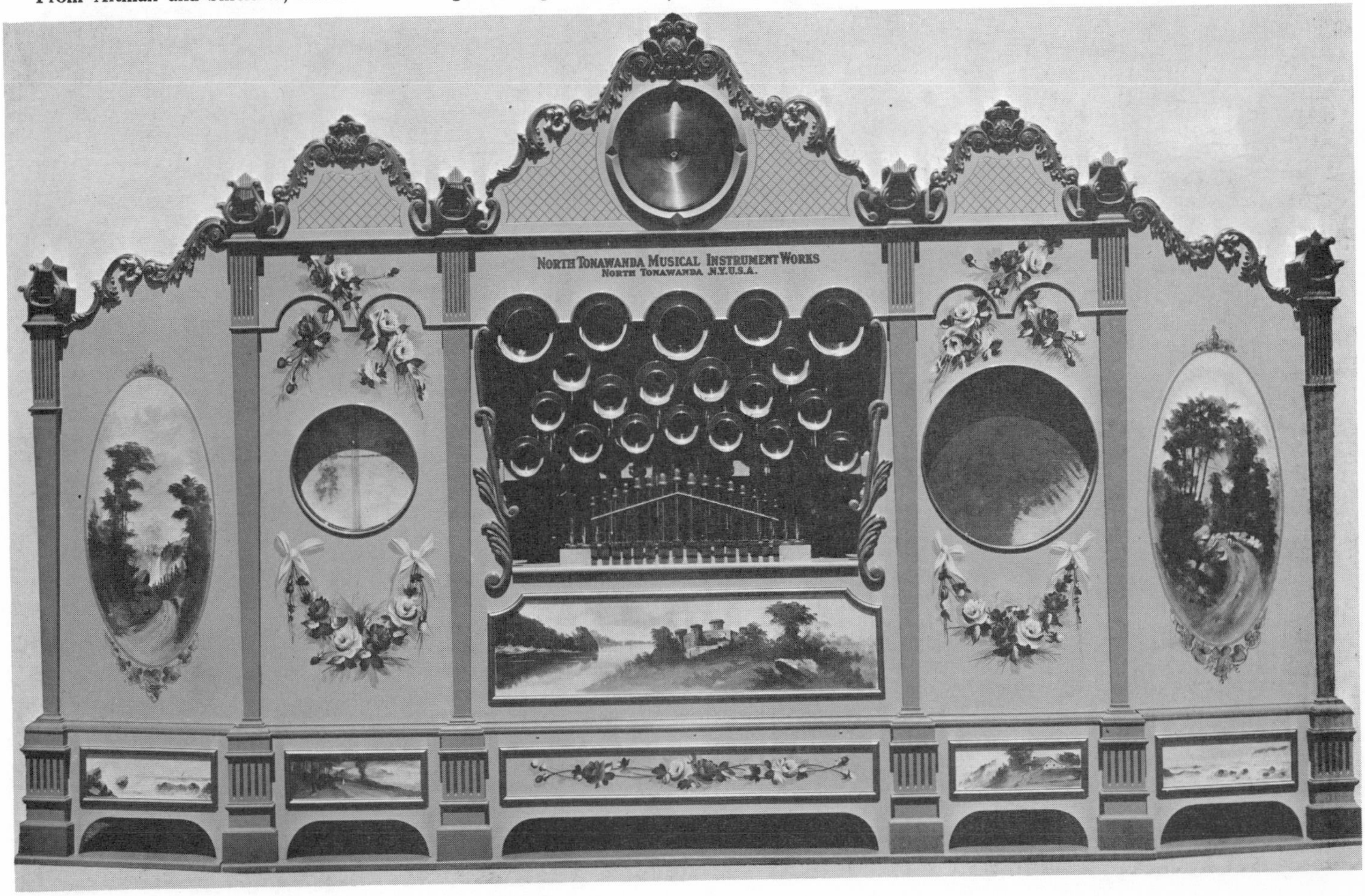

(No.1)
–Style 37; Style 137–

(No.2)
–Style 55; Style 155–

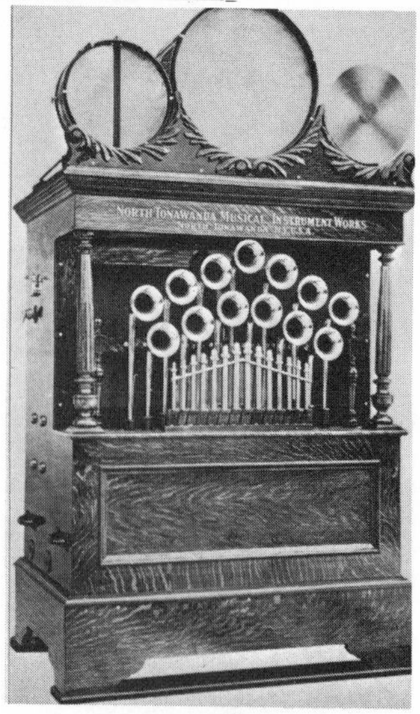

(No.3)
–Style 46; Style 146–

(No.4)
–Style 64; Style 164–

(No.5)
–Style 82; Style 182–

(No.6)
–Style 73; Style 173–

(No.7)
–Style 20 (and 19)–

**–North Tonawanda Band Organs–**

Nomenclature note: The first style given is for an organ with pinned cylinder operation; the second style has a prefix "1" and is the same design but with paper roll operation. Hence, Style 37 is cylinder operated; Style 137 has an identical appearance but is paper roll operated (by endless rolls).

(No.1) 44 keys; (No.2) 46 keys – Note that No. 1 and No.2 are the same case (compare wood grain) but with different top and sides; (No.3) 46 keys; (No.4) 46 keys; (No.5) 48 keys; (No.6) 48 keys – Note that Nos. 4, 5, and 6 are all the same case but with different tops and sides; (No.7) 36-key barrel organ, also known as Style 19 without the carved top or painted panels; (No.8) 52 keys.

The organs on this page were all loudly voiced and, with the exception of our No.7, were sold primarily for use in skating rinks. From the beginning of the North Tonawanda business in 1906 until manufacture of band organs was discontinued about ten years later, skating rinks accounted for about 90% of sales. In later years many of these instruments were converted to play Wurlitzer type 125 rewind rolls.

(No.8)
–Style 91; Style 191–

—Style 38; Style 138—
44-key organ with painted facade. 6'1" high. 14 violin pipes exposed on front and 72 pipes within. Three registers; one for violin, one for trombones, one for trumpets.

—Style 56; Style 156—
46-key organ. 6'2" high. Instrumentation same as Style 38 plus bass drum and snare drum.

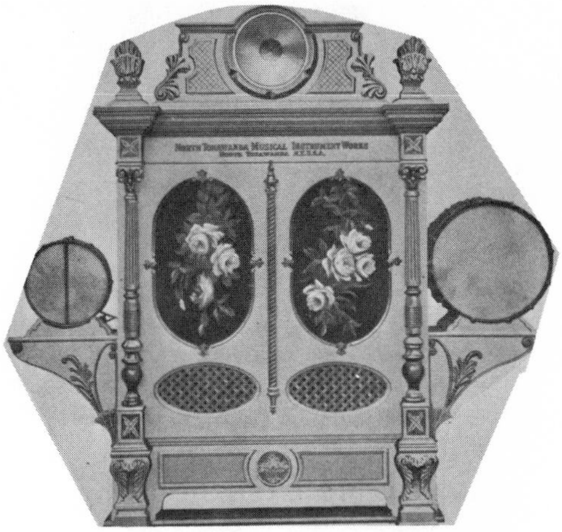

—Style 86; Style 186—
52-key organ. 7'1" high. Hardwood, finished in white enamel paint, handsomely decorated in a variety of colors.

—Style 159—
Late style of paper roll organ. 6'7" high. Decorated with Meyercord decals (the author acquired some extra ones with the factory records). Three registers; trumpets, trombones, violins.

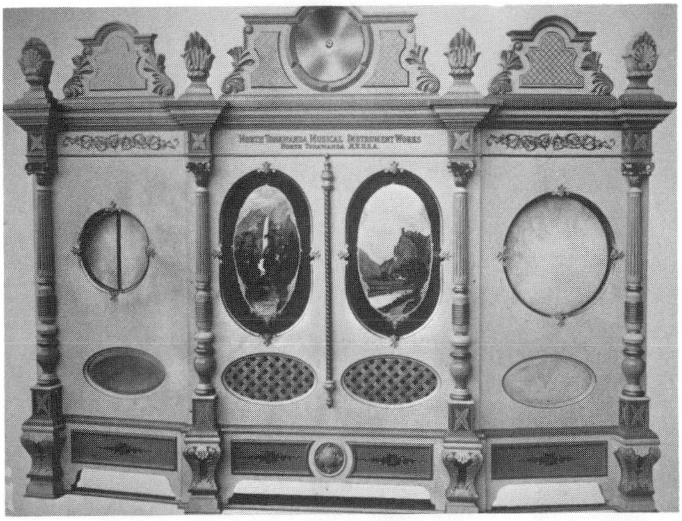

—Style 88; Style 188—
52-key organ. 8'7" wide, 7'1" high, 3'6" deep. 5 registers: trumpets, trombones, clarionettes, open bass, stopped bass. Finished in white enamel paint. Hand painted cloth panels in the center.

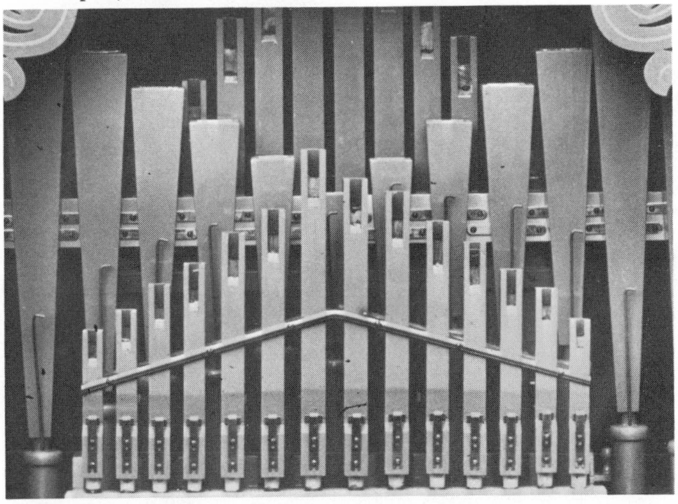

View of the front of Style 159 showing a rank of violin pipes in the foreground, a rank of wooden trumpet pipes behind them, and behind the trumpets a rank of octave violin (or viola) pipes.

Unidentified late style military band organ made in 1913 (from factory photographs).

–Style 58; Style 158–

(Also called Styles 57 and 157). 7'10" wide, 6'2" high, 2'7" deep. 3 registers: violins, trombones, trumpets. Drums are mounted on shelves behind the large side wings.

–Style 194–

"Available with duplex trackers, $100 extra." 13' wide, 7'9" high, 2'9" deep. 4 registers: piccolos, clarionets, trumpets, trombones. "The tone is round and powerful, the nearest imitation of a human band ever manufactured."

–Now and Then–

Then: The North Tonawanda Musical Instrument Works as it appeared in 1913.

Now: The same building as photographed by the author in 1965.

–Style 92; Style 192–

52-key organ. 8'9" wide by 7'9" high by 2'9" deep. 4 registers: piccolos, clarionettes, trumpets, trombones. This was a very popular early style for skating rinks. Attractively proportioned with ornate top gallery and applied wood carvings on the front.

–Style 184–

48-key organ. Paper roll operation. 10'1" wide, 7'4" high, 3'1" deep. 3 registers: violins, trumpets, trombones. One of the later styles.

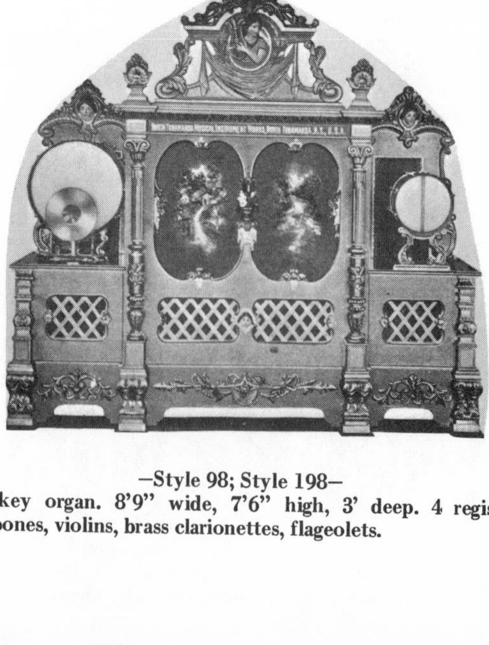

–Style 98; Style 198–

53-key organ. 8'9" wide, 7'6" high, 3' deep. 4 registers: trombones, violins, brass clarionettes, flageolets.

—Style 1100 with Motor Truck—

82-key organ mounted on a Mack truck chassis. "For circus and advertising purposes." "Top finished with scroll work among which may be placed hexagon signs which revolve, showing 6 signs, one every 30 seconds." Organ part measures 13'8" long by 6'9" deep.

—Style 100; Style 1100—

82-key organ. "The Militarograph" as named in the catalogue. 5 registers: trombones, trumpets, clarionettes, piccolos, violin pipes. 7'9" wide by 8'11" high by 3'6" deep. The largest regular style made by North Tonawanda Musical Instrument Works. Early testimonials reveal that this model was popular with very large rinks and auditoriums.

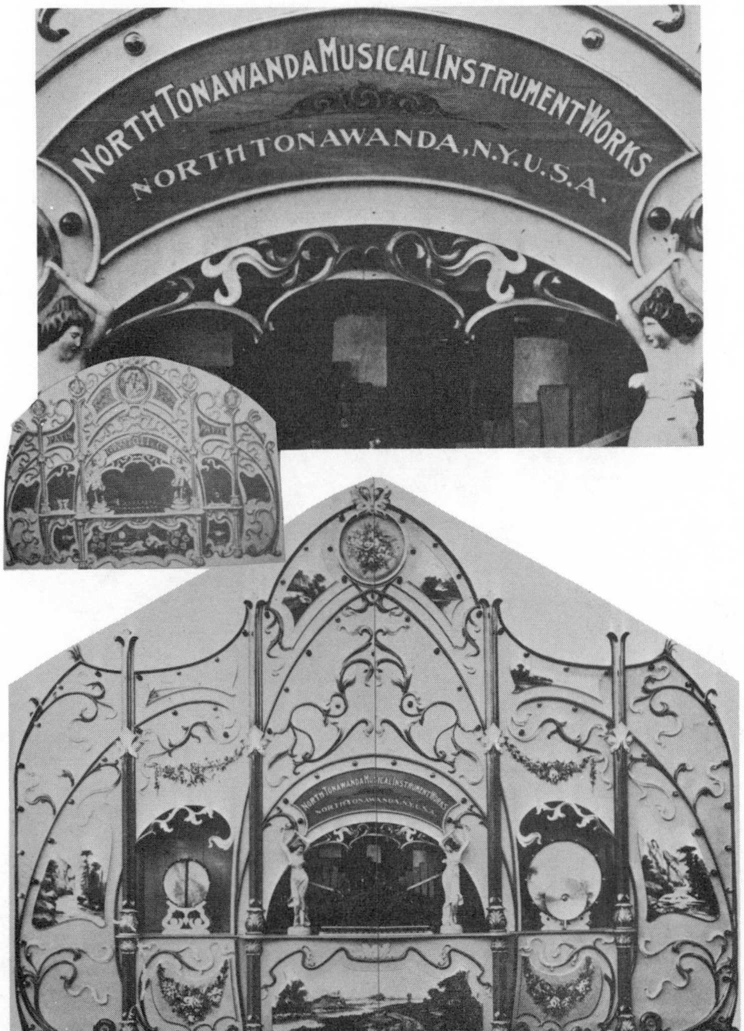

Unidentified organ from a 1913 factory photograph. It seems to be like a Style 55 (or 155) brass trumpet organ, but with a more ornate facade.

Gavioli! At least partly... The facade of this organ was imported from Gavioli & Cie of Paris (see small inset photo showing similar, but not identical, Gavioli instrument), and perhaps the interior was also (we haven't examined a specimen to determine this). 18'6" wide by 12'4" high. This is the only Gavioli / North Tonawanda organ of which we've seen an illustration. Were other Gaviolis imported?

## C.W. PARKER (Distributor)
### —Leavenworth, Kansas—

### Introduction

From the early 1900's until about 1930 the firm of C.W. Parker of Leavenworth, Kansas, distributed hundreds of barrel operated pianos and circus band organs. In the early years Parker imported instruments from Frati (of Berlin, Germany) and Gebr. Bruder (of Waldkirch, Germany). All makers' marks were removed and C.W. Parker's name was boldly emblazoned across the front.

In later years Parker sold organs made by the Rudolph Wurlitzer Company and calliopes made by Tangley. As Parker bought and sold used equipment as well, and as much of this was repainted and reconditioned before it was sold, the Parker name is likely to be found on almost any type of organ.

C.W. Parker was a colorful character. His story is well told in Frederick Fried's "Pictorial History of the Carousel."

Parker made and or sold all types of carnival and circus equipment. Most famous were his "Carry-Us-Alls," his trademark for carousels.

As an agent (and not a maker) of automatic musical instruments, Parker could have been well relegated to a footnote in this book. However, the author acquired a large file of Parker material, including many previously unpublished illustrations. We present some of the Parker photographs here — to capture the flavor of these nostalgic instruments and to show how they were used and how they were sold years ago. In a way, the part that band organs played in American life is just as important historically, and is certainly as interesting, as the case designs and other data comprising most of this volume. In this spirit we reprint an article which appeared in the Kansas City Star (December 29, 1912) and illustrate some of Parker's musical instruments.

### "A Ranch for Wooden Horses"

(Kansas City Star) "The Wooden Horse Ranch" they call it in Leavenworth. This is because so many wooden horses are made there. At this time two thousand wooden horses and some hundreds of wooden camels, bears, buffalo, and other animals are stored in the place, and thirty workmen are making more horses of wood as fast as they can.

These horses and other animals are shipped from Leavenworth to all parts of the world and the children from all nations ride them.

At a workbench in a corner an old German woodcarver is cutting the

*Above: An imported trumpet organ with three mechanical figures sold by C.W. Parker.*

*Right: Resplendent in this sunlit room is a new Bruder "Elite Orchestra Apollo" organ fresh from its packing crate. Or, is it a Wurlitzer 165? No, it isn't. Examination of the original photo by a magnifying glass reveals that it is a product of the famed Bruder family of Waldkirch, Germany. Parker imported many Bruder organs, including some really magnificent ones. All of these were sold as "made by Parker."*

*Military band organ sold by Parker. See Wurlitzer section for similar instruments.*

mane of a wooden horse with his chisel. He has already finished the uprearing head, with open mouth and distended nostrils.

"Where is that to go?" the visitor asks.

"To the Philippine Islands," is the answer.

And next summer, beneath the palms of Manila, thousands of Filipino boys and girls, with olive skins, will pay their pennies and climb astride the backs of these horses, and whirl away to the music of the mechanical organ which two other German workmen are finishing on another floor of the wooden horse factory, and while the horses gallop and the organ squeals in ragtime, and the little brown children scream delightedly, the waters of Manila Bay, beyond the Plaza, will be shimmering in the soft, tropical moonlight.

Horses Studded with Jewels

At another bench are another set of German carvers, and the horses they are making are studded with jewels – not with precious gems – but with rows of glass jewels, cut like diamonds, and ranging in size from as big as a silver dollar down to a dime, and red, blue, green, yellow, and white in color. The bridles and saddle trappings are lined with these imitation jewels set into the wood, and when the 48 horses on this "Carry Us All" whirl 'round and 'round in the light of the electric lamps, the galloping horses will be one brilliant rainbow sparkle, its glitter splendidly real to the eyes of the children of Boston.

For this collection of jeweled horses, more gaily caparisoned than the equine retinue of King Solomon himself, is being made to the order of a children's entertainer of Boston, and he is paying $8,500.00 for it.

Here is one of thirty horses, finished and ready to ship to Honolulu, for the joy of the Kanaka children. And another is going to Panama, and those wooden horses, all crimson and orange and gold, are to be ridden by the small señors and señoritas of that old seaport.

To Capetown, South Africa

Another, just beginning, is for Capetown, South Africa, and it will be shipped in time to be in operation there when next spring's snows melt from the top of Table Mountain.

This one, with the big wagon alongside, is for the boys and girls of Australia. Spread out upon the floor near it are the wooden carvings for a circus band wagon that is going along with the wooden horses.

Isn't it queer that a circus away off in Australia should send halfway around the world, to Leavenworth, Kansas, to have its carousel and band wagon made? The circus to which this is going travels overland and covers the whole of Australia in a season. The instructions sent by this circus owner of the Antipodes were that his band wagon was to be the most gorgeous thing of its kind ever made; the decorations on the sides were to be all hand carved and gilded with real gold, and there were to be plenty of mirrors in curves and ovals between the carvings.

And so the most expert wood carver in the shop was put to work on it, and the product of his skill is spread out on the floor, arranged just as it is to be on the sides of the circus band wagon, two carved Aphrodites, goddesses of love and beauty, rising from the sea, with trumpets to their lips, sounding a ballyhoo call to the Australian rubes to come and see, and around them a maze of gilded curliewurlies – gorgeous enough, surely, for the most exacting circus man.

Hundreds of Wooden Horses

And there you may stand, with the Missouri rolling just outside the back fence, and the Leavenworth trolley rattling past the front gate, and gaze down on that fantastic circus band wagon, and see visions, if your imagination is working well, of the curious eyes of children who will come out of the Australian bush to gaze at it. What queer faces, what strange scenes, its mirrored sides will reflect in the years before it is thrown into a junk pile in Sydney or Melbourne.

To the visitor who went through the factory last Friday it was all romance, these hundreds of wooden horses that were to entertain the children of the world, and he went with them to the isles of the tropic seas, and to the southernmost ends of the earth, and to the Canadian far north, and he saw the whirling carousel with its bobbing figures and heard the laughter of the world's children mingling with the strident music, and understood, for the language of laughter is the same for every clime – and he thought it was worth a man's while to be in a business of that kind – making fun for the children of the whole world.

Parker's Story

Parker used to have a peanut stand in Abilene and once, when a merry go round came to town he watched it gathering the children's nickels, and he bought one and started out. He was too good a business man to be satisfied with that and he began manufacturing the machines, and now he has the largest merry go round factory in the world, only he doesn't call them merry go rounds. He invented the name "carry-us-all," which is derived from the name of the old "carousel."

Parker makes all parts of his machines and organs in his factory in Leavenworth. And he owns three separate carnival companies that he transports on eighty-seven cars of his own, and last year this business alone brought him a profit of $46,000.00.

And all of this vast business is built upon the nickels of the world's children.

---

*From across the blue water came this attractive band organ. As did Wurlitzer when it imported instruments, the Parker firm sold such products as having been made in its own factory. Actually, Parker made no organs at all.*

*"The Old Plantation," a carnival attraction. One of many similar shows made and sold by Parker.*

*Above: Early Parker letterhead showing Abilene, Kansas, address.*
*Right: Some Parker grandeur.*
*Below: Photograph of the busy Parker factory.*

## BARGAINS OFFERED BY THE C. W. PARKER AMUSEMENT COMPANY

— ALL SUBJECT TO PRIOR SALE —

## YOU WILL NEVER FIND PRICES LIKE THESE AGAIN

1—Special Model 2 Abreast, with 24 horses; style 125 Organ; top and wall; ticket box; 6 cylinder gas engine. Ready to go for .......... **$800.00** cash

1—Parker open style seats; ticket box; gas engine drive; 35 ft. high; all reconditioned and painted. A bargain at .......... **$550.00** cash

1—Parker Baby Wheel, 14 ft. high; safety coaches; 24 capacity; motor drive; ticket box; reconditioned and ready to go, for .......... **$350.00** cash

1—Parker Safety Coach Wheel; Park model. Lessmotor .......... **$800.00** cash

1—24 Seat Chairoplane; motor drive; ready to work .......... **$350.00** cash

1—4 Abreast Parker Jumping Horse Carry Us All. Style 165 organ motor drive; complete ready to run, less top. A bargain .......... **$2000.00** cash

1—50 ft. Park Model Merry Go Round; out-side row of animals life size. Less top. Motor drive. Reconditioned. A beauty .......... **$2000.00** cash

1—Parker 35 ft. safety Coach Wheel; Q Model; Motor drive; 8 coaches; seating capacity, 32 adults. Ready to run .......... **$1500.00** cash

1—3 Abreast Parker, now operating in good location, and making money. Can leave machine there if desire, or move .......... **$1500.00** cash

1—Parker large Park Model Carry Us All. Now located in a prominent park on the West Coast. Operating and making money. Cost new $28,000.00. 85 capacity; 66 beautiful horses. Price .......... **$5000.00** cash

1—Parker built Crazy House; less banners and top .......... **$150.00** cash

1—German imported mechanical show. Cost new $5,000.00 .......... **$500.00** cash

1—Tangly Caliope, with blower; no motor .......... **$150.00** cash

1—Tangly Hand Player, with blower less motor .......... **$150.00** cash

1—Style 165 Organ; nice front .......... **$350.00** cash

1—Style 150 Organ; wooden pipes .......... **$250.00** cash

1—Style 125 Organ; Good .......... **$150.00** cash

25—Barrel Organs; no barrels furnished; as is .......... **$10.00** each

We have music, both rolls and cardboard; rolls **50¢** per tune; cardboard, **50¢** per yard, for all organs; also Tents, Banners and Curtains; also organ parts, such as pipes, all kinds and working parts, new and used. We are offering the above to make room for new production, and must clean it out at once; If you can use any of these items, call on us at once, as we don't expect them to remain on the market long.

— **All of the above is used but reconditioned** —

*Above: Truer words were never spoken! "You will never find prices like these again!" By today's standards a Tangley calliope at $150.00 (even without a blower!), a Style 150 organ "with wooden pipes" (This was probably not a Style 150, but another organ that used 150 rolls – the 150 has brass pipes across the front) at $250.00, a Style 165 at $350.00, and other values are fantastic bargains. As did other amusement device makers, Parker took in many instruments and rides on trade toward other models. To sell these trade-ins periodical clearance sales were held.*

*Left: Advertisement for a 1915 Parker wooden horse. To design these and other ornate frippery that was such an important part of circus gleam and glitter, Parker employed German workmen. Attracted by American pay scales many European artisans in this field came to the United States.*

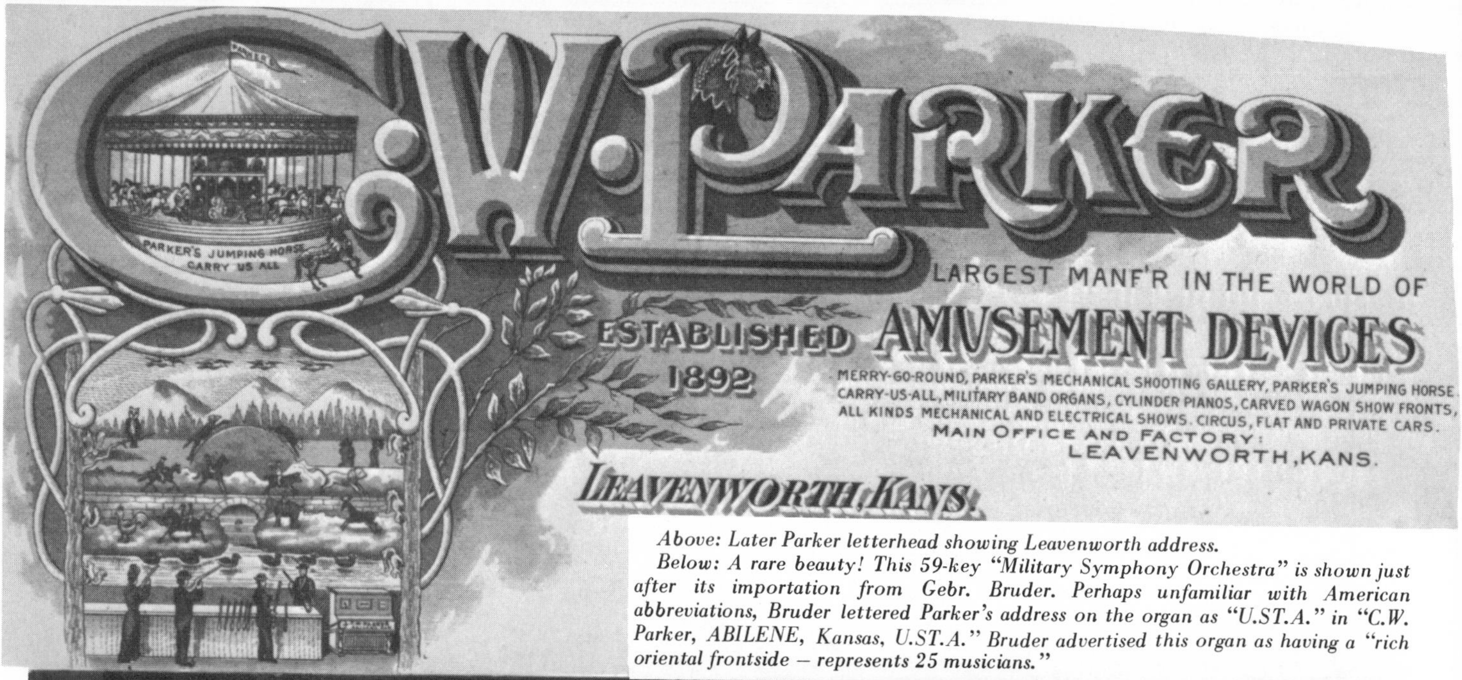


*Above: Later Parker letterhead showing Leavenworth address.*

*Below: A rare beauty! This 59-key "Military Symphony Orchestra" is shown just after its importation from Gebr. Bruder. Perhaps unfamiliar with American abbreviations, Bruder lettered Parker's address on the organ as "U.ST.A." in "C.W. Parker, ABILENE, Kansas, U.ST.A." Bruder advertised this organ as having a "rich oriental frontside – represents 25 musicians."*

Merry-go-rounds made with two, three and four-horses abreast, with rocking motion.

*On this page are clippings from a treasure trove of Parker literature and memorabilia. Directly above is a scenic railway with a band organ in the center. To the right is a Wurlitzer Style 147 organ with Parker markings. Below is what Parker captioned "Special 4-row Park Model machine operated in Alum Rock Park, San Jose, Cal. 44-ft. diameter at platform; 48-ft. at sweeps. A striking handsome machine operated in building." Note that the music is provided by a Tangley Calliaphone (calliope made in Muscatine, Iowa – see Tangley section of this book). The "Music by Calliaphone" lettering was on the original picture. The merry go round – oops, pardon! – "Carry Us All" – had a band organ as well. The rides were three for 25c.*

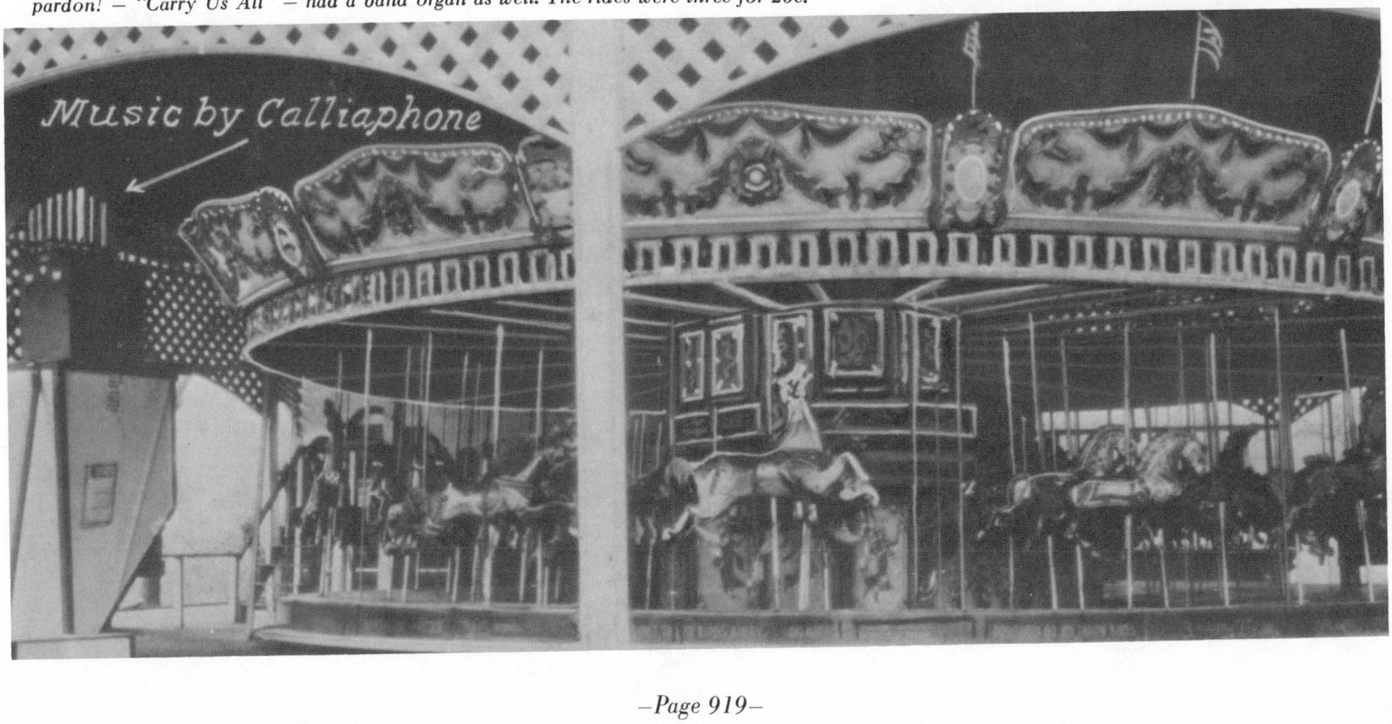

## A. RUTH & SOHN

—Waldkirch, Germany—

Born in 1813, Andreas Ruth learned the trade of organ clock making in Furtwangen after he completed his basic education. Following his apprenticeship he moved to nearby Waldkirch and worked with Xaver Bruder, one of the founders of Gebr. Bruder.

In 1841 (or 1842, accounts differ) Andreas Ruth established his own organ building firm in Waldkirch. From this evolved A. Ruth & Sohn (A. Ruth & Son), the name by which the firm was known until it ceased operations about 1940.

While Ruth made book organs of both key frame and keyless frame types during the 20th century, the establishment's main period of activity was in the 1870-1900 period during which it made dozens of different types of hand-cranked organs, all operated by pinned cylinders. Most of these were of the small "monkey organ" type.

Ruth exported instruments to all parts of the world. In America several agents sold Ruth organs, including the large fairground organs made during the 1900-1914 era. A number of these survive today.

The organs of Ruth & Sohn bear a close resemblance to those of Gebr. Bruder, as reference to the Bruder section of this book will show. The various Waldkirch organ builders shared the services of Joseph Dopp and other artisans and woodcarvers who produced virtually identical facades for their different employers.

Aug. Faller, lithographer and printer in Waldkirch, prepared catalogues for both firms during the late 19th century. Apparently it was much easier to use the same engraving, one time with "Ruth & Sohn — Waldkirch" and another time with "Gebr. Bruder — Waldkirch," than it was to make up separate engravings for each firm. The similarity of the organ cases and the common use of a single printing firm has made the identification of many models difficult for historians. Not making things easier is the fact that Gebr. Bruder, who continued in the organ repair business until about 1947 — long after Ruth was defunct, rebuilt many Ruth organs and put the Bruder name on them!

Tonally, large Bruder and Ruth organs differ from each other considerably. Bruder organs generally are louder and have a more fundamental tone (i.e., with fewer harmonics) due to the extensive use of flute and bourdon pipes. Ruth organs are generally more mellow and have more of a violin-type sound. The difference, hard to describe in print, is quite apparent when the organs are actually heard.

----------

Small carousel or fairground organs of the 1900 era. These were among the most popular of all Ruth instruments.

Cover of a Ruth catalogue of the 1900 era.

Andreas Ruth.

A. Ruth & Sohn Waldkirch.

19 — 20 und 21

Salon-Orgeln

für Museum- und Tanzsäle-Besitzer.

Der Prospekt vergoldet. — Sämmtliche mit Schwungräder.

| Nummer | Gewicht Kilo | Tiefe ctm. | Länge ctm. | Höhe ctm. | Ohne Schwungrad gehen 10 Mark ab. | Mark | Weitere Walze Mark |
|---|---|---|---|---|---|---|---|
| 19 | 220 | 70 | 128 | 155 | Orgel mit 56 Tönen, bestehend in Bass- und Begleitpfeifen, Geigenstimmen, Spitzflöten, Trompeten, Bombardon, Mixtur zum abstellen, 9 Stück spielend, Walze 64 Takt . . . . . . | 1200 | 150 |
| 20 | 220 | 72 | 110 | 160 | Orgel mit 59 Tönen, bestehend in Bass- und Begleitpfeifen, Clarinett mit Beistimmen, Spitz- und Zauberflöten, Trompeten, Bombardon, 8 Stück spielend, Walze 64 Takt . . . . . . | 1500 | 150 |
| 21 | 290 | 78 | 153 | 175 | Orgel mit 66 Tönen, bestehend in Bass- und Begleitpfeifen, Clarinett mit Beistimmen, Spitz- und Zauberflöten, Trompeten, Bombardon, 9 Stück spielend, Walze 64 Takt . . . . . . | 2000 | 200 |

"Salon Organs" — barrel organs of 56, 59, and 66 keys.

A. Ruth & Sohn, Orgelfabrik, Waldkirch, (Baden).

Concert-Orgeln

| Nummer | Gewicht Kilo | Tiefe cm | Länge cm | Höhe cm | Bei Angabe der Höhe ist der Aufsatz nicht mitgerechnet. | Mark | weitere Walze Mark |
|---|---|---|---|---|---|---|---|
| 20A | 230 | 76 | 132 | 155 | Orgel mit 56 Tönen, bestehend in Bass- und Begleitpfeifen, Geigenstimmen, Spitzflöten, Trompeten, Bombardon, Mixtur zum Abstellen, 9 Stück spielend, Walze 64 Takt . . . . . | 1300 | 160 |
| 21A | 300 | 80 | 149 | 165 | Orgel mit 64 Tönen, bestehend in Bass- und Begleitpfeifen, Geigenstimmen, Spitz-Flöten, Trompeten, Bombardon, Mixtur zum Abstellen, 9 Stück spielend, Walze 64 Takt . . . . . | 1600 | 190 |
| 22 | 385 | 86 | 176 | 171 | Orgel-Werk mit 72 Tönen, Bass- und Begleitpfeifen, Geigenstimmen, Spitz-Flöten, Trompeten, Bombardon, eine Mixtur zum Abstellen, 10 Stück spielend, Walze 80 Takt . . . . . | 1850 | 230 |
| 23 | 460 | 87 | 191 | 177 | Orgel-Werk mit 80 Tönen, Bass- und Begleitpfeifen, Geigenstimmen, Spitz-Flöten, Trompeten, Bombardon, eine Mixtur zum Abstellen, 10 Stück spielend, Walze 80 Takt . . . . . | 2350 | 300 |
| 24 | 530 | 190 | 214 | 183 | Orgel-Werk mit 90 Tönen, Bass- und Begleitpfeifen, Geigenstimmen, Spitz-Flöten, Trompeten, Basstrompeten, Bombardon, mit Mixtur zum Abstellen, 10 Stück spielend, Walze 80 Takt . . . . . | 3100 | 400 |

26, 27, 28, 29, 30, 31 ohne Säulen. 32, 33, 34.

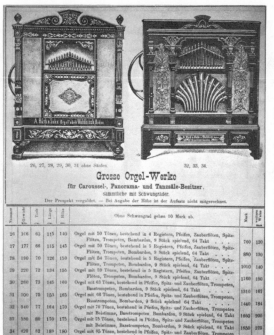

Grosse Orgel-Werke

für Caroussel-, Panorama- und Tanzsäle-Besitzer,

sämmtliche mit Schwungräder.

Der Prospekt vergoldet. — Bei Angabe der Höhe ist der Aufsatz nicht mitgerechnet.

| Nummer | Gewicht Kilo | Tiefe cm | Länge cm | Höhe cm | Ohne Schwungrad gehen 10 Mark ab. | Mark | weitere Walze Mark |
|---|---|---|---|---|---|---|---|
| 26 | 166 | 63 | 115 | 140 | Orgel mit 50 Tönen, bestehend in 4 Registern, Pfeifen, Zauberflöten, Spitz-Flöten, Trompeten, Bombardon, 9 Stück spielend, 64 Takt . . . | 760 | 120 |
| 27 | 177 | 66 | 115 | 145 | Orgel mit 50 Tönen, bestehend in 5 Registern, Pfeifen, Zauberflöten, Spitz-Flöten, Trompeten, Bombardon, 9 Stück spielend, 64 Takt . . . | 880 | 130 |
| 28 | 190 | 70 | 126 | 150 | Orgel mit 54 Tönen, bestehend in 5 Registern, Pfeifen, Zauberflöten, Spitz-Flöten, Trompeten, Bombardon, 9 Stück spielend, 64 Takt . . . | 1010 | 140 |
| 29 | 220 | 72 | 134 | 155 | Orgel mit 59 Tönen, bestehend in 5 Registern, Pfeifen, Zauberflöten, Spitz-Flöten, Trompeten, Bombardon, 9 Stück spielend, 64 Takt . . . | 1160 | 150 |
| 30 | 260 | 73 | 145 | 160 | Orgel mit 63 Tönen, bestehend in Pfeifen, Spitz- und Zauberflöten, Trompeten, Basstrompeten, Bombardon, 9 Stück spielend, 64 Takt . . . . | 1310 | 167 |
| 31 | 300 | 75 | 153 | 165 | Orgel mit 66 Tönen, bestehend in Pfeifen, Spitz- und Zauberflöten, Trompeten, Basstrompeten, Bombardon, 9 Stück spielend 64 Takt . . . . | 1440 | 184 |
| 32 | 340 | 77 | 164 | 170 | Orgel mit 70 Tönen, bestehend in Pfeifen, Spitz- und Zauberflöten, Trompeten mit Beistimme, Basstrompeten Bombardon, 9 Stück spielend, 64 Takt | 1660 | 200 |
| 33 | 380 | 80 | 170 | 175 | Orgel mit 75 Tönen, bestehend in Pfeifen, Spitz- und Zauberflöten, Trompeten mit Beistimme, Basstrompeten, Bombardon, 9 Stück spielend, 64 Takt | 1850 | 220 |
| 34 | 420 | 82 | 189 | 180 | Orgel mit 85 Tönen, bestehend in Pfeifen, Spitz- und Zauberflöten, Trompeten mit Beistimme, Basstrompeten, Bombardon, 9 Stück spielend, 64 Takt | 2260 | 300 |

Left and below: barrel organs from the 1900 era. Made for carousel use, these durable instruments were sold all over the world, particularly in America and Europe. Later similar case designs were employed for cardboard music book organs.

The illustrations used in Ruth catalogues were not identical to the instruments delivered. Standard illustrations were used over the years while the organs underwent modifications from time to time. Note, for example, that the organ pictured at the immediate left (the case design for models 32, 33, and 34) is the same as that used at the lower left of this page to illustrate Nr. 22, 23, 24, and 25.

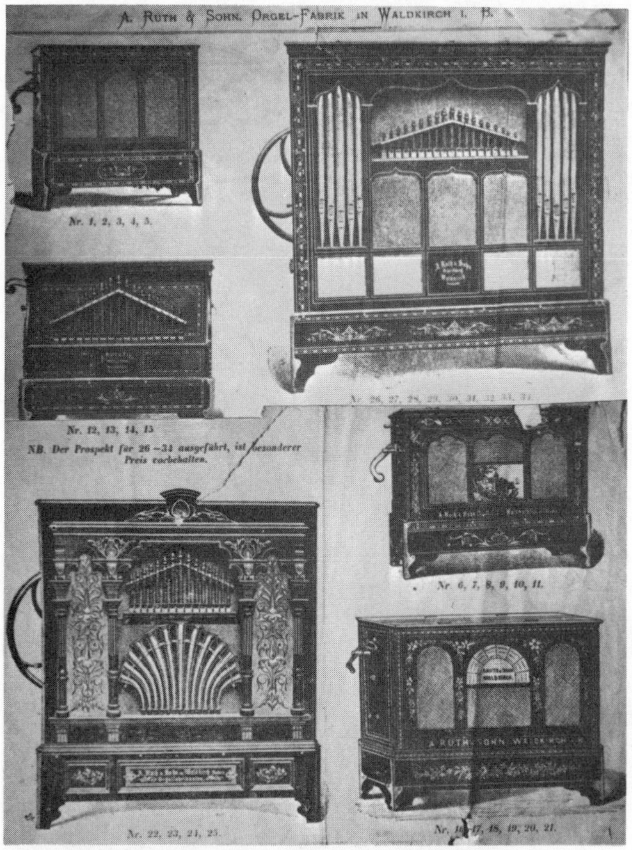


Left: A page from an A. Ruth & Sohn catalogue of the 1890's. Pictured are four case designs of hand-cranked organs and two larger organs, the latter for use with carousels and shows.

Hand-cranked organs were one of Ruth's most popular product lines. Thousands were sold during the late 19th and early 20th centuries. The production of these small organs was a sizable industry at one time. In Germany they were made by such firms as Bacigalupo, Biehler, the Bruder firms in Waldkirch, Cocchi, Frati, Haupt, Hesselmann, Hock, Holl, Kern, Lenk, Loos, Richter, Stiller, Töpfer, Voigt, Wellershaus, and Wrede — to mention the larger firms.

Grosse Concert-Orgel

für Panorama- und Museum-Besitzer.

Diese Orgel eignet sich in Folge ihrer Construction, forte und piano, vorzugsweise für Ouverturen, Quodlibets, überhaupt für Concertmusik.

Diese Orgel kann in einen gedeckten Eisenbahnwagen nicht verladen werden.

Der Prospekt vergoldet. — Mit Schwungrad.

| Nummer | Gewicht Kilo | Tiefe cm | Länge cm | Höhe cm | Bei Angabe der Höhe ist der Aufsatz nicht mitgerechnet. | Mark | weitere Walze Mark |
|---|---|---|---|---|---|---|---|
| 25 | 750 | 110 | 261 | 200 | Orgel-Werk mit 107 Tönen, Bass- und Begleitpfeifen, Geigenstimmen, Spitz- und Zauberflöten, Trompeten, Baridon, Bombardon, eine Mixtur zum Abstellen, 10 Stück spielend, Walze 80 Takt . . . . . . . . . | 4500 | 500 |

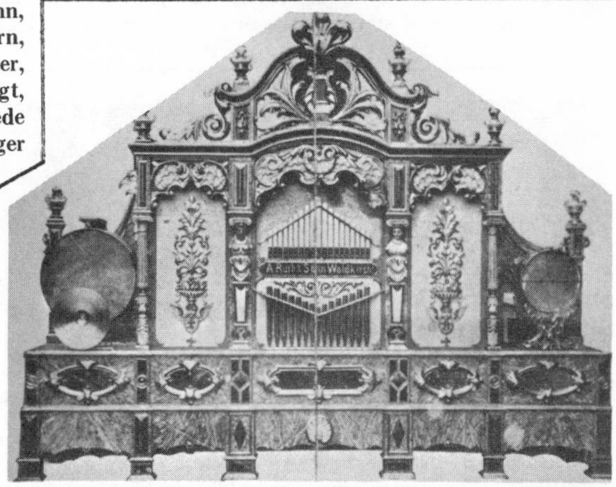


Orgel-Werke mit Notenblättern

mit schöner Fassade in schwarz und gold.

| Nummer | Länge cm | Höhe cm | Tiefe cm | | M | Pf |
|---|---|---|---|---|---|---|
| 35 | 145 | 168 | 76 | Carrousellorgel, immer forte spielend, mit 60 Clavis, die Instrumentierung wie No. 30 mit 50 Meter Noten vom Repertoir . . . . . . . . . . | 2000 | — |
| | | | | per Meter Noten vom Repertoir . . . . . . . . . . | 2 | 50 |
| | | | | und können solche nachgeschickt werden. | | |
| 36 | 185 | 177 | 95 | Concertorgel, forte und piano spielend, mit 76 Clavis, die Instrumentierung wie No. 23, grosser und kleiner Trommel mit Becken in Seitenflügeln zum abnehmen, mit 50 Meter Noten vom Repertoir . . . . . . . . . . | 3400 | — |
| | | | | per Meter Noten vom Repertoir . . . . . . . . . . | 3 | 50 |
| | | | | und können solche nachgeschickt werden. | | |
| 37 | 225 | 186 | 105 | Concertorgel, forte und piano spielend, mit 90 Clavis, die Instrumentierung wie No. 24, grosser und kleiner Trommel mit Becken in Seitenflügeln zum abnehmen, mit 50 Meter Noten vom Repertoir . . . . . . . . . . | 5000 | |
| | | | | per Meter Noten vom Repertoir . . . . . . . . . . | 4 | 50 |
| | | | | und können solche nachgeschickt werden. | | |

Der Preis der Musikstücke verdoppelt sich, wenn die Stücke nicht im Repertoir verzeichnet sind. Reichere bemalte Fassaden mit Figuren, drehbare Säulen etc. werden besonders berechnet.

Above: Style No. 35. Except for minor differences the same facade was used on a popular Bruder organ style (see Bruder section of this book).

Left: Descriptions in German of style nos. 35, 36, and 37 "Cardboard Book Organs with Elegant Facades of Black and Gold."

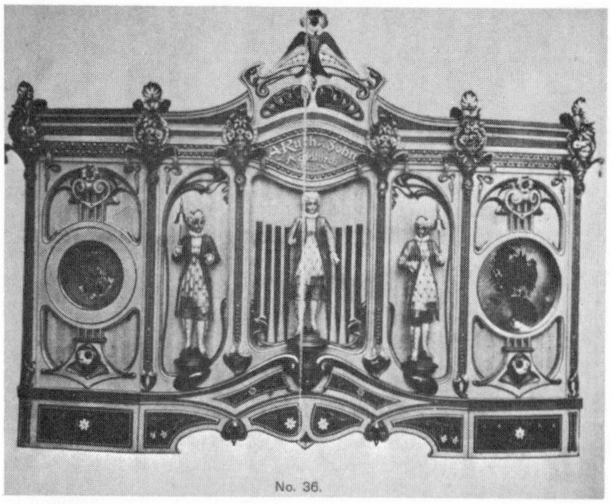


Above: Style No. 36 Ruth organ. 76 keys. Made in two styles: cardboard book operated and paper roll operated.

Above: Style No. 36-A. Manufactured circa 1905. Cardboard music system.

No. 38 Ruth organ. One of the larger Ruth styles. Refer to the E. Boecker and M. Welte (band organs) sections of this book for illustrations of styles similar or identical to certain Ruth models.

Organ owned by the Royal American Shows. A descriptive postcard issued by Hannau Color Productions notes "The organ has over 400 different pipes; over 6000 working parts and valves; countless pneumatics to play [the various effects]." The organ, which may have originally been a Gavioli, plays Ruth & Sohn music now. It was found, of all places, on a farm in Kansas! The organ was acquired by Royal American Shows in 1956 and was restored by Antonio Crescio.

A. Ruth & Sohn organ owned by Pavilion Amusement Park, Myrtle Beach, South Carolina, as depicted on a postcard issued by Plyler-Brandon Sales Co. "The organ was built for the World Exposition in Paris in 1900 . . . It measures 20' long, 11' high, and 7' deep and weighs about two tons. It is a 98-key instrument with about 400 pipes and eighteen carved figures. The instrument still operates with cardboard music composed about 1910 . . ."

## VERBEECK

### —Antwerp, Belgium—

The Verbeeck family, Pierre Verbeeck in Belgium and James Verbeeck in London, produced fairground organs during the early 20th century. Some of these were sold under the "Magic Orchestra" name. In the 1930's dance hall organs were added to the Verbeeck line. Some (the one illustrated at the lower right of this page is an example) bore the "Verbekson" trademark.

The Verbeeck business ended at the beginning of World War II. In recent years Johanne Verbeeck (son of Pierre) and his son John have renewed the family business by rebuilding older Mortier and other instruments. In addition, several new fairground organs of small size have been made.

In the 1920's many 87-, 89-, and 92-key organs were made. Many of these were compatible with Limonaire instrument scales. The 98-key Verbeeck, the size of most of the instruments shown on this page, was the most popular large model. The scale was compatible with the 98-key Marenghi layout.

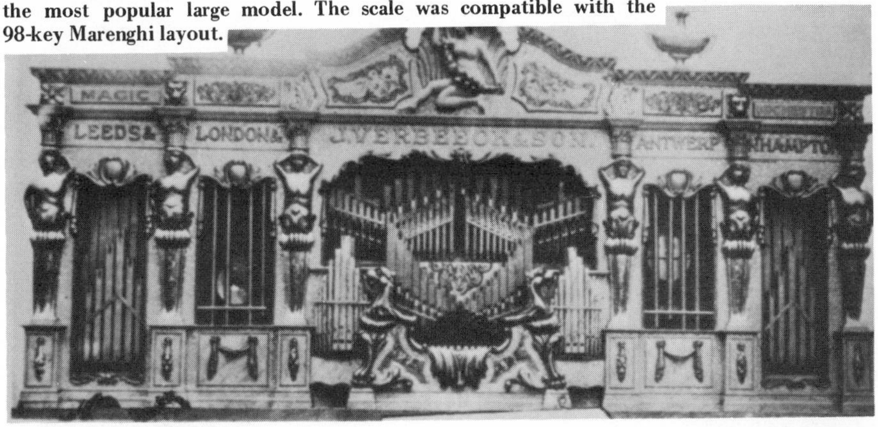

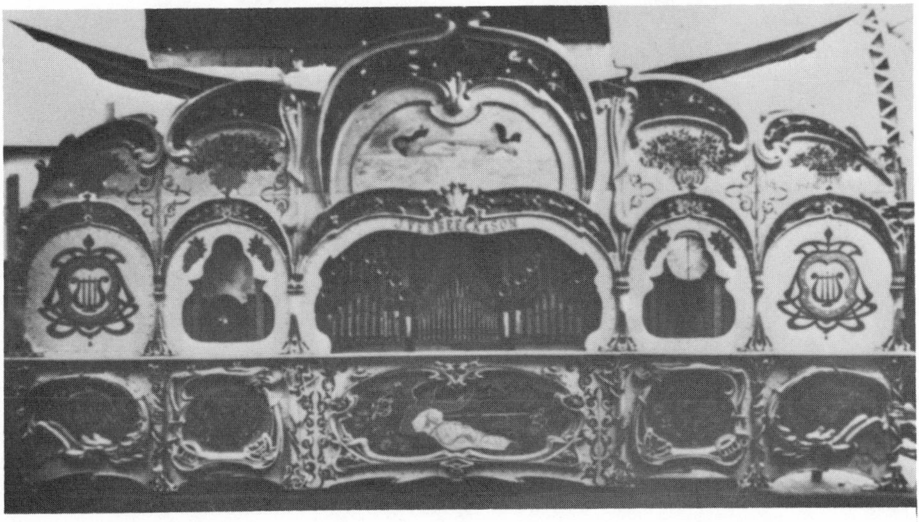

(Photographs by the Fair Organ Preservation Society; A. Lomas; Colin Upchurch)

GEBR. WELLERSHAUS
Saarn a/d Ruhr, Germany

The firm of Gebr. Wellerhaus in Saarn a/d Ruhr (later Mülheim-Ruhr, as Mülheim expanded to include the village of Saarn) was founded by August and Wilhelm Wellershaus. The firm was in business from the late 19th century until the factory was destroyed in a bomb attack in 1944. (Refer to Claes O. Friberg's "Portable Hand-Cranked Barrel Organs" section for more information.)

Wellershaus organs were widely distributed throughout Europe by means of sales agents. Most instruments of the late 19th century were enclosed in very ornate cases. Some of the larger instruments featured "wonder lights" and other electrical effects – style numbers 74-76 and 79 are examples.

During the early 20th century Wellershaus produced a series of cardboard book organs. These were mainly sold in Germany, Belgium, and Holland.

While not among the top several organ makers in terms of quantity production, Wellershaus did produce hundreds of instruments – most of which were distinguished by having heavily carved fronts.

(Information courtesy of Jan van Dinteren and Claes O. Friberg)

----------

Case design for nos. 25-27

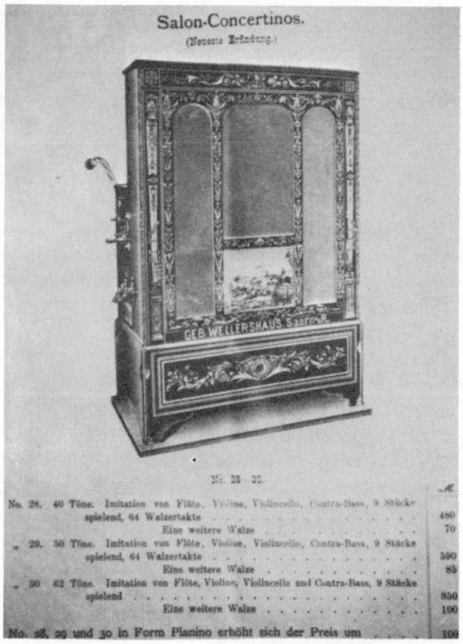

Case design for nos. 28-30

Case design for nos. 31-37

Case design for nos. 38-41

Case design for nos. 42-46

Case design for nos. 47-49

Case design for nos. 50-52

Case design for nos. 53-55

Case design for No. 56

Case design for No. 57

Case design for nos. 58-59

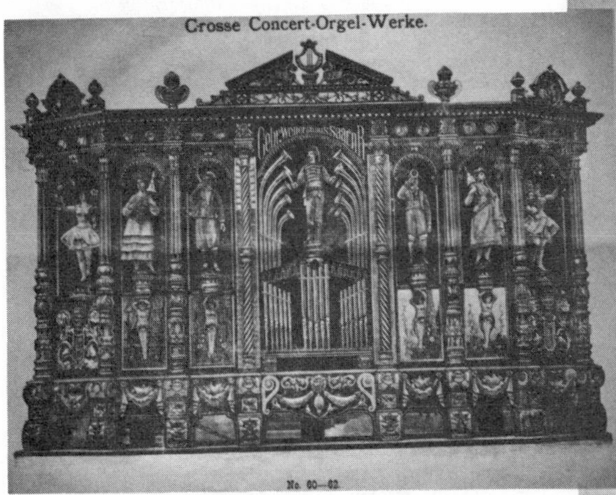


60-62. "Great Concert Organ"

Case design for nos. 63-64

Case design for nos. 66-70

Case design for nos. 74-76

Case design for nos. 77-78

Case design for nos. 80-82

Case design for nos. 83-84

Case design for nos. 87-89

Case design for nos. 85-86

Case design for No. 79

Above: 83-key Wellershaus book organ. (Altenburg Collection; F.O.P.S. photo)

Above: Wellershaus book organ (Wallace McPeak photo)

84-key Wellershaus organ in the G.T. Cushing Collection (A. Colin Upchurch /F.O.P.S. photo)

## M. WELTE & SONS
### —Military Band Organs—

About 1907 M. Welte & Sons of New York City issued a catalogue featuring "Concert Orchestra Organs." Surviving instruments indicate that these were actually made by Bruder and by Ruth of Waldkirch, Germany (which is located less than 10 miles from Welte's main factory site in Freiburg). Evidently Welte adapted its own paper roll system to these organs. Paper rolls bearing the Welte name were sold, and were possibly made, by Welte.

Welte's involvement in the field of band organs was short-lived. Very few organs were ever sold under the Welte name and a few years later the band organs were dropped from the extensive Welte line of automatic instruments.

The catalogue noted: The perforated music rolls which are about 120 to 150 feet long contain 1 to 5 pieces of music . . . Our stock in Freiburg and New York will always contain rolls of the latest pieces, ready for immediate supply. . . Automatically moving figures such as a conductor, musicians, etc. can be placed on the front of any organ at an extra charge of from $100 up per figure according to the size of same. . .

The organs were recommended as being suitable for dance halls, moving pictures, and merry go rounds.

**Organ A — Flute Organ**
44 flute pipes. 2'7½" high, 2'1½" wide, 1'2" deep. Cylinder organ with 9 tunes per barrel. Cost $275. Extra barrels cost $62 each.

**Organ C — Violin Organ**
Cylinder organ with 96 pipes. Cost $600. Cylinders @ $135. 4'7" high, 3'11" wide, 2'1½" deep.

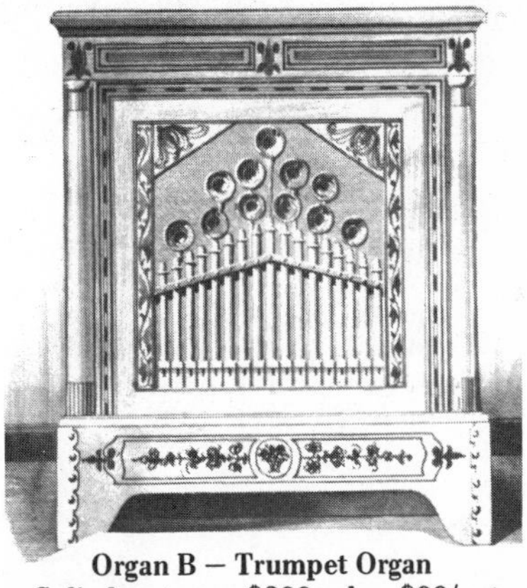

**Organ B — Trumpet Organ**
Cylinder type. $399 plus $99/extra cylinder. 78 pipes. 3'3½" high, 2'7½" wide, 1'2" deep.

**Organ D — Flageolet Organ**
Cylinder organ. $750 cost plus $110 per extra cylinder. 108 pipes.

**Concert Organ E**
Cylinder organ. $850 new; cylinders @$117. 158 pipes. 4'11" high, 4' wide, 2'4" deep.

**Concert Organ F**
Cylinder organ. $1200 cost plus $180 per extra cylinder. 232 pipes. 5'4" high.

**Concert Organ G**
Cylinder organ. 273 pipes. Cost $1700 new. Cylinders @$225. 5'6" high, 5' wide, 2'8" deep.

**Concert Organ II-A:** Roll operated. Cost $1275. Rolls @$5. 250 pipes. 5'5" high, 5'4" wide, 3'1" deep.

Concert Organ II-B. Same as II-A, but with different facade design. Trumpets concealed.

Concert Organ III: 312 pipes. $2200 cost. 5'8" high, 6' wide, 3'3" deep. Represents 20 musicians.

Note: Some of these dimensions must apply to the chassis (without facade), as otherwise the proportions are not correct. Refer to Concert Organ I for example.

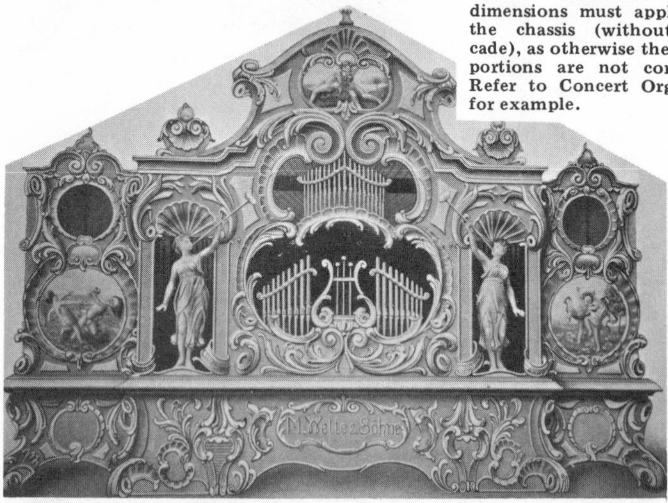

Concert Organ V: 386 pipes consisting of 54 bass flutes, 10 trombones, 122 mixed flutes, 54 violins, 54 harmonic flutes, 20 trumpets, 20 saxophones, 52 piccolos. Price with 18 music rolls was $4500. Extra rolls @$5. 10'6" high by 13' wide by 3'8" deep. "This instrument gives the effect of a full orchestra with all of its instrumental color, and is universally admired not only on account of its musical qualities but also for its artistic exterior."

WELTE

Concert Organ IV: 332 pipes. $3000 cost. 6'10" high, 7' wide, 3'5" deep. Rolls @$5.

Concert Organ I: 158 pipes. $980 cost. 4'10" high, 4'4" wide [sic], 2'6" deep. "In power equal to 10 to 12 musicians."

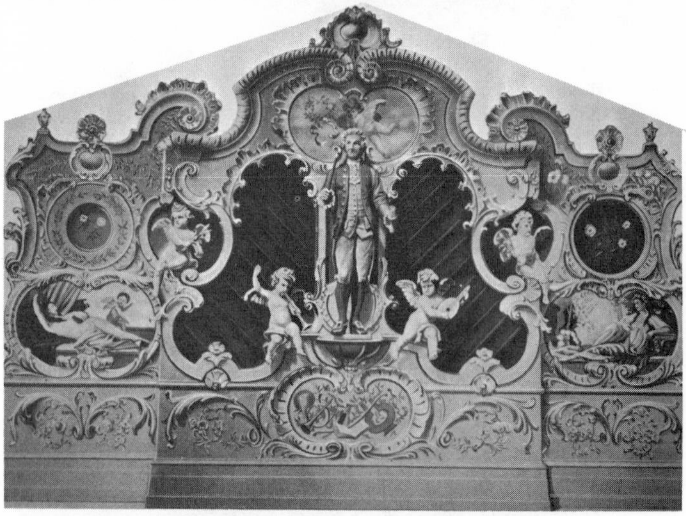

Concert Organ VI: 498 pipes including 96 flute bass, 24 trombones, 24 bassoons, 68 flutes, 68 violins, 34 piccolos, 34 clarionets, 50 trumpets, 25 oboes, 25 saxophones, 25 cornets, 25 chimes (bells). $6000, including 18 rolls. Extra rolls @$10. 9'10" high by 16'4" wide by 3'10" deep. "The most perfect imitation of an orchestra that can be imagined, reproducing all the various effects. The really marvelous rendering of orchestral compositions by this instrument is by means of paper rolls."

## WREDE

—Hannover-Kleefeld, Germany—

From 1890 until the early 1930's the firm of Fritz Wrede manufactured fairground organs. Those made from 1890 to about 1900 were of the barrel-operated variety. Later organs utilized the folding cardboard book system. In addition, Fritz Wrede manufactured many small hand-cranked portable barrel organs. The production of these smaller instruments was continued until the Wrede factory was demolished in an air raid on March 28, 1944.

(All photographs on this page are courtesy of Claes O. Friberg and depict instruments in the Oskar Lensch Collection)

## RICHTER

—Düsseldorf, Germany—

The firm of Gebr. Richter of Düsseldorf, Germany, manufactured many types of organs during the early 20th century. Although the firm made a number of small hand-cranked portable barrel organs, the firm is best known to collectors today for its larger fairground organs. Representative Richter fairground organs are shown below.

The firm's owners were Eduard and Emil Richter. The Gebr. Richter firm's height of activity was in the 1920-1930 decade.

## THE RUDOLPH WURLITZER COMPANY
—North Tonawanda, N.Y.—

In 1893 Eugene DeKleist (formerly VonKleist — he anglicized his name upon coming to America), a native of Düsseldorf, Germany, started the North Tonawanda Barrel Organ Works in North Tonawanda, N.Y. During the 1890's DeKleist manufactured barrel organs, barrel-operated pianos, automatic xylophones and chimes, and similar instruments — all mainly for the carousel and amusement park trade.

Beginning in 1897 DeKleist developed a relationship with the Rudolph Wurlitzer Company of Cincinnati, Ohio. Arrangements were made whereby DeKleist's factory (with the name now changed to the DeKleist Musical Instrument Manufacturing Company) sold all of its output to Wurlitzer who acted as the sole agent in the United States. In January, 1909, Wurlitzer acquired the DeKleist interests and began operating the factory under the Wurlitzer name (see coin piano and orchestrion section of this book for more information).

**North Tonawanda** EUG. DE KLEIST, Proprietor
**Barrel Organ Factory,**
**North Tonawanda, N. Y., U. S. A**
**Manufacturers of**
***Merry-go-Round Organs,***
***Military Band Organs,***
***Selt-Acting Orchestrions***
***And All Kinds of***
***Automatic Organs***
**For Private Houses, Libraries, Museums Pleasure Resorts Hotels, Etc.**
**Only Manufactory of the Kind in the United States.**
**Write for Catalogues. Inquiries Cheerfully Answerde**

### Early Pinned Cylinder Organs

Most of the band organs, usually referred to in Wurlitzer catalogues as "Military Band Organs," sold by Wurlitzer in the 1890's and the first few years of the 1900 - 1910 decade were operated by pinned cylinders. The 1905 - 1912 period was one of transition. During that time many models gave the buyer the option of either the cylinder or the paper roll type of operation. Shortly after 1912 the paper rolls became standard and the cylinder types were deleted from the Wurlitzer catalogue.

An early catalogue noted: "Pinned Cylinder Military Band Organs — for merry go rounds, ballyhoo, tent shows, excursion steamers, and all sorts of out-of-door amusement resorts. For years our pinned cylinder organs have been recognized as the best the world affords. Built in the largest, most complete factory in the world, of the best materials money can secure, by skilled mechanics with a lifetime experience in the business, they excel in tone, construction, mechanical simplicity, case design, arrangement of the music, and all the details necessary in a first class organ. The increasing demand for a first class pinned cylinder band organ has induced us to add several new styles with drums and cymbals."

Most of these early pinned cylinder organs were DeKleist-made, as noted. However, based on the examination of extant instruments, historians believe that Wurlitzer pinned cylinder instruments were also imported from one or two German makers as well, possibly Frati and Bruder. Wurlitzer did an active business with the conversion of barrel organs of all kinds to use Wurlitzer cylinders and, later, to use Wurlitzer paper music. Hence, there are many "hybrid" organs around with, for instance, Gavioli works and Wurlitzer music systems. These are not to be confused with the instruments originally sold by Wurlitzer — the type we list here.

Pinned cylinders had obvious limitations. Perhaps a bit harshly (in view of the fact that Wurlitzer had sold many pinned cylinder instruments just a few years earlier) Wurlitzer noted in its 1912 catalogue: "This important part of the equipment (a band organ) of a skating rink must be practical and perfectly adapted to the purpose, or it is worse than useless. We knew the old fashioned pinned cylinder organ, designed for merry go rounds (this is perhaps an escape clause in the condemnation — as these words were directed to skating rink owners — Ed.), could never be adapted to the purpose, because of the harshness of the music, the lack of means of regulating the tempo, the trouble and time necessary to change the music, the impossibility of putting a complete waltz or two-step on a cylinder (the music can not be any longer than the circumference of the cylinder), and the expense of new music. All of these defects, which made the pinned cylinder entirely out of the question for skating rinks, are entirely overcome in our paper roll band organ. . ."

Apropos of the above we might also mention that, at this time, Wurlitzer was actively encouraging pinned cylinder instrument owners to trade them in on the new paper roll organs or, failing that, to at least take advantage of the service which was thus advertised: "Remodel that Old Band Organ. During its long years of service that old organ has more than paid its way for you. Send it in when you can spare it, and we will give you an estimate on modernizing it. If you are interested, we will also make you a proposal to take it in trade towards the purchase of a later style instrument."

On the following pages we show many different styles of cylinder organs. If you like to observe minute details (many readers of our earlier editions did, and came up with some interesting observations, a number of which resulted in new information incorporated into the present volume) you will note that there is little difference between certain of the pinned cylinder organs and the later paper roll ones (Style 20-A, a cylinder organ, is in the same case as the later Style 150 paper roll organ, for instance). You will also note that the same photograph sometimes did double duty (as in the instance of the Style 140 picture which, when cropped of its drums and cymbal, became a Style 135 picture!). At the risk of digressing too far from our purpose here, we'll also mention that certain band organ illustrations must have been standard throughout the industry — for instance, some pictures that illustrate early Wurlitzer organs were also used to illustrate Molinari (a New York City organ firm) catalogues. To obtain a broader view of pinned cylinder organs and early paper roll organs the reader is urged to consult also the Niagara Musical Instrument Manufacturing Co. and the North Tonawanda Musical Instrument Works sections in this book. Both of these firms were located in the same city as Wurlitzer (North Tonawanda) and, in many instances, produced virtually identical products.

### Paper Roll Organs

In 1906 Wurlitzer noted in a catalogue that "We have only recently perfected the military band organ so as to use perforated paper rolls instead of the old-style pinned cylinders. The advantage of the paper rolls over the cylinders is so great that the results obtained produce an altogether different instrument. By the use of paper rolls we get a perfect repetition and can make the tunes of any desired length, both features impossible with the barrel organ.

"Aside from these most important improvements, the paper rolls are so much cheaper and convenient to change from one to another that

the owner can afford to have a variety of selections and change them frequently. Another important feature is the stop lever which is connected with the music-winding device and the suction bellows, by means of which the music may be stopped and started instantly without stopping the motive power.

"The music rolls are operated by our patented rewinding device as used on all our automatic instruments; by this device they are kept constantly wound on the spools, which keeps them in perfect shape on the tracker board. At the end of the last selection they automatically rewind, ready to repeat the program. . . The music rendered by these new style organs is very fine and effective, as is also the finish and general appearance of the cases, and there is nothing on the market that will so satisfactorily answer the purposes for which they are intended. . ."

The most important market for band organs during the pre-World War I years was the skating rink industry. Rinks were springing up by the thousands all across the United States and Canada. The brassy sound and the loud volume of the band organ made it ideally suited to rink use. We mention this as band organs are today more associated with circuses, merry go rounds, and the outdoor amusement industry. That market provided most of the sales in the 1920's, but far larger numbers of organs were sold to rinks in the 1900 - 1920 years.

The importance of the skating rink owner's patronage is pointed out by the fact that early catalogues were directed almost exclusively to skating emporiums:

From the 1912 catalogue: "Our perforated paper roll military band organs furnish better music to skate by than any musicians, and after the first cost of the organ, your music costs nothing, save the small expense of a few new music rolls occasionally. (Note: Wurlitzer music rolls were very, very expensive in comparison to the rolls of other makers — Ed.). These band organs are designed especially for the Rink Business, and must not be confused with promiscuous instruments [whatever they are! — Ed.] offered by manufacturers and music dealers who have nothing adapted to the purpose.

"The great demand for a practical band organ that will take the place of the musicians and save that enormous expense has led unscrupulous concerns to recommend all sorts of instruments for this business, with the result that many rink owners have been badly fooled.

"We were the pioneers in the building of band organs, and our perforated paper roll military band organs are the result of years of experience and conscientious effort to perfect an instrument that would perfectly do the work required in roller rinks. They have now been on the market five years, been throughly tested, and proved satisfactory in roller rinks in every state in the union, as well as in Canada.

"The rink owner buying one of these organs of suitable size for his rink, is placing himself in position to make money by saving the heaviest expense connected with the roller rink business; at the same time he makes himself independent of musicians, so that he can run his rink whenever he pleases and as long as he pleases."

From the introductory page to the 1921 catalogue: "Wurlitzer Military Bands produce the loud, lively, enjoyable music that everybody likes, and that cannot be drowned out by the noise of the skaters. . ."

The 1928 catalogue skips mention of skating rinks entirely and begins with: "Wurlitzer Military Band Organs produce lively, enjoyable music of such great volume that they are sure to attract crowds. . ."

### Early and Late Paper Roll Organs

Wurlitzer paper roll operated band organs can be divided into two general groups: early and late. While there was certainly overlapping of production of some early styles into later years (Style 125 organs were made until near the very end of the business), this grouping is valid for classifying the organs — and for understanding why most organs seen today are of the later type.

Early Paper Roll Organs: These were made mainly for skating rink use. Generally, they are in cases finished the natural wood color, usually light golden oak. As loudness was one of the prime considerations, most styles have brass horns. Drums and cymbals, when present on a particular style, are usually exposed on side shelves or on the top.

Later Paper Roll Organs: These were made for general purposes including skating rinks, but also for amusement parks, traveling shows, etc. Cases are painted overall and decorated with ornate vignettes and scenes. Only a few of the later styles have brass horns.

A chronology of certain models may be gained from those pictured in the following catalogues:

1906 catalogue: Pinned cylinder organs: No. 3534, No. 3535, No. 3536, No.3537 (same as 20-A), and the following paper roll organs: Styles 100, 105, 110, 120, 125, 130, 135, 140, 150, and the "Monster."

1912 catalogue: Pinned cylinder organs: Styles 18, 20, 20-A, 20-C, and 20-D; Paper roll organs: Styles 105 (early style with exposed brass trumpets), 125, 130, 135, 140, 150, 155 (the "Monster" model), and 160 (the "Mammoth" model).

1916 catalogue: Pinned cylinder organs (left over in stock from earlier production): Styles 17, 18, and 18-C; Paper roll organs: Styles 104, 125, 127, 147, 148, 150, 153, 163, 165, and 166.

1922 (approx.) catalogue: Paper roll organs: Styles 104, 125, 146 (early style; drums on shelves); 146-A (early style), 148, 153, 165, 168, and 166.

1925 (approx.) catalogue: Paper roll organs: Styles 103, 104, 105 (late style with painted case; no brass); 106, 125, 146-A (late style), 146-B (early style), 148, 153, 157, 165, and 180.

1928 catalogue: Paper roll organs: Styles 103, 105, 106, 125, 145-B, 146-A (late style), 146-B (late style), 148, 153, 157, 164, 165, 180, Caliola.

Note: the above data cannot be used as an infallible guide, for checking of production records vs. instruments surviving today indicates that old descriptions and illustrations were sometimes retained in new catalogues, even though such instruments were no longer being made (perhaps unsold or reconditioned ones were on hand for sale, however). It was the intent of the Wurlitzer catalogue to give the prospective purchaser an idea of what Wurlitzer products were available in general. Often a particular model was out of stock and the customer was encouraged to select an alternate model.

Today most instruments that survive are those made after 1920. While we have listed and illustrated many different models in order to give an overall view of the Wurlitzer production, the collector or enthusiast today will find the following models (all of the paper roll type; Wurlitzer cylinder organs are exceedingly rare) most prevalent today: Styles 103, 104 (late style; like 105 but without drums), 105 (late style), 125, 146-A (late style), 146-B (late style), 150, 153, and, quite a bit more elusive, the 157 and 165.

By the mid-1920's Wurlitzer had virtually no competition in the band organ business in America. As Wurlitzer kept up a steady output of new music rolls and as Wurlitzer parts were available, a long stream of earlier instruments made in the United States by North Tonawanda, Artizan, Niagara, and others, not to mention large numbers of imported Bruder, Gavioli, Ruth, Frati, and other organs, were converted to play Wurlitzer music.

The Bruder relationship: In the quaint Black Forest town of Waldkirch, the Bruder family engaged in the manufacture of band organs for several generations. Evidence suggests that there was a relationship between Bruder and Wurlitzer from about 1912 to 1920, interrupted only by World War I. From Bruder in Germany came components for a number of instruments and possibly some entire units. The same illustration used in the Bruder catalogue to illustrate the "Elite Orchestra-Organ Apollo" was used by Wurlitzer to illustrate its Style 165. Likewise, the Style 166 is identical to a larger Elite Apollo instrument. The facade of the Wurlitzer Style 146-A organ, the late style made in the twilight of the 1920's and the 1930's, is identical to the front of certain Bruder models. Even more significant is the fact that one of the surviving Wurlitzer 165 organs has Bruder valve chests and other components in it (but has a Wurlitzer-made roll frame). More information concerning the Wurlitzer - Bruder relationship would be welcomed as little is known now.

## WURLITZER MILITARY BAND ORGANS

**—Wurlitzer Archives Data—**

Beginning with organ No. 2960 (shipped early in 1916) and continuing through to the last organ that left the Wurlitzer factory (No. 4338, a Wurlitzer Style 165 shipped in 1939 to Ross Davis of Los Angeles) we have broken down the records into the different models produced. The dates covered are from late 1915 and early 1916 (there is some overlapping of years at the beginning) through to 1939. As the numbers were more or less continuous, our data covers some 1400 instruments.

### Dating Wurlitzer Organs

Numbers were assigned to Wurlitzer organs as they were shipped (a practice differing from that of pianos and orchestrions — numbers of the latter were assigned when production began; shipping may have been much later). With the exception of some overlapping of numbers at the end of 1923 and the beginning of 1924, the following chart will enable you to fix the date of issue of any Wurlitzer organ after 1916. We give the first instrument shipped during each year and the date of shipment:

| | | | |
|---|---|---|---|
| No.2960 | February 19, 1916 | No.4137 | January 15, 1929 |
| No.3043 | January 2, 1917 | No.4218 | January 8, 1930 |
| No.3125 | January 10, 1919 | No.4276 | January 5, 1931 |
| No.3219 | January 7, 1920 | No.4303 | May 3, 1932 |
| No.3332 | January 20, 1921 | No.4306 | April 27, 1933 |
| No.3407 | January 3, 1922 | No.4307 | July 3, 1934 |
| No.3500 | January 3, 1923 | No.4311 | February 27, 1935 |
| No.3617 | January 18, 1924 | No.4315 | March 4, 1936 |
| No.3737 | January 9, 1925 | No.4325 | February 26, 1937 |
| No.3811 | April 8, 1926 | No.4332 | January 31, 1938 |
| No.3911 | January 26, 1927 | No.4335 | April 20, 1939 |
| No.4021 | October 5, 1928 | | |

Notes: Only one instrument made in 1933, a Style 145 (serial nos. 4304 and 4305 were not used). Only one instrument made in 1933, a Caliola shipped on April 27th. In 1926 several organs were sometimes given the same number, so more were made this year than the difference between the beginning and ending serial numbers would indicate.

### Quantities of Band Organs Made

Below we list the quantities produced of each instrument, 1916 and later. Bear in mind that certain styles such as 105, 125, and 153, for example, were made in very large quantities prior to 1916, so our numbers are not representative of all that were totally made. Where our numbers are complete (in our opinion) we put an asterisk after the model number, as: "Style 180*". Production figures are given in parentheses after the year. It is possible that an instrument may have been on hand for many years and then shipped at a later date; for example, we doubt if the Style 16 cylinder organ shipped on 8/9/1915 was made even near that date.

For ease of use we list the following in order by model numbers. In instances of very large organs we give the shipping destination (where known) in the hope that perhaps one or two readers can put the information to use to track down one of the instruments!

**Style 16**

1915 (1 shipped)

**Style 17**

1915 (1); 1916 (1); 1919 (1)

**Style 18**

1916 (1)

**Style 18-A**

1916 (5)

**Style 18-B**

1915 (1); 1916 (1)

**Style 65**

1930 (1) — Note: this may have been intended to read "165."

**Style 103***

1923 (20); 1924 (15); 1925 (2); 1926 (13); 1927 (17); 1928 (7); 1929 (9); 1930 (4); 1931 (3); 1937 (1)

**Style 104**

1916 (3); 1919 (3); 1920 (5); 1921 (4); 1922 (6); 1923 (11); 1924 (19); 1925 (12); 1926 (6); 1927 (12); 1928 (8); 1929 (2); 1930 (1). Note: No.3643 shipped in 1924 was "Special, with drums."

**Style 105***

Late style; painted front. 1923 (1); 1925 (2); 1926 (24); 1927 (31); 1928 (27); 1929 (15); 1930 (16); 1931 (5); 1934 (1); 1935 (1); 1936 (3); 1937 (1) 1938 (1); 1939 (1)

**Style 106***

1926 (1); 1927 (6); 1928 (2); 1929 (2); 1930 (1)

**Style 125**

1915 (partial figure) 10; 1916 (28) — includes one "in 18-C case" and one "with Style 150 front"; 1917 (20); 1918 (5); 1919 (17); 1920 (22); 1921 (10); 1922 (11); 1923 (9); 1924 (14); 1925 (9); 1926 (12); 1927 (8); 1928 (22); 1929 (5); 1930 (6); 1934 (1)

**Style 126**

1916 (1); 1919 (1)

**Style 145***

1928 (1); 1929 (4); 1932 (1); 1935 (1)

**145-A***

1931 (1); 1938 (1)

**145-B***

1930 (2); 1935 (1); 1939 (1)

**Style 146**

1916 (13); 1917 (12); 1918 (3); 1919 (20); 1920 (33); 1921 (18); 1922 (18); 1923 (18); 1924 (14); 1925 (8); 1926 (4); 1927 (1); 1928 (1)

**Style 146-A**

1916 (7); 1917 (12); 1918 (3); 1919 (23); 1920 (29); 1921 (19); 1922 (28); 1923 (17); 1924 (22); 1925 (13); 1926 (5); 1927 (12); 1928 (4); 1929 (3); 1930 (3); 1934 (1); 1935 (1); 1936 (2)

**Style 146-B***

1922 (1); 1923 (2); 1924 (8); 1925 (8); 1926 (8); 1927 (4); 1928 (1); 1929 (6); 1930 (2)

**Style 147**

1916 (5); 1917 (1)

**Style 148**

1916 (1); 1917 (2); 1919 (2); 1921 (3); 1922 (3); 1923 (4); 1924 (8); 1925 (5); 1926 (6); 1927 (6); 1928 (3); 1929 (3); 1931 (1); 1936 (1)

**Style 150**

1915 (figure incomplete) 2; 1917 (2); 1918 (1); 1919 (3); Note: This was a very, very popular model, and large quantities were made prior to 1915.

**Style 151**

1921 (1)

**Style 153**

1916 (13); 1917 (11); 1918 (2); 1919 (21); 1920 (21); 1921 (17); 1922 (19); 1923 (13); 1924 (18); 1925 (11); 1926 (10); 1927 (8); 1928 (1); 1930 (3); 1936 (1)

**Style 157***

Shipping list by serial numbers: No.3414 2/10/1922 New York City; No.3440 4/21/1922 Washington, D.C.; No.3444 4/27/1922 New Bedford, Mass.; No.3454 5/16/1922 Toronto, Canada; No.3526 3/31/1923 Buffalo, N.Y.; No.3531 4/10/1923 Old Orchard, Maine; No.3536 4/16/1923 Reading, Pa.; No.3639 3/24/1924 Spillman Engineering Co., North Tonawanda, N.Y. (probably sold with a merry go round made by the Spillman firm); No.3654 4/14/1924 Old Orchard, Maine; No.3667 4/29/1924 Denver, Colo.; No.3679 5/13/1924 Coney Island, N.Y.; No.3766 4/30/1925 Spillman Engineering Co.; No.3827 3/26/1926 Spillman Engineering Co.; No.3833 4/24/1926 Asbury Park, N.J.; No.3860 6/19/1926 Spillman Engineering Co.; No.4058 4/27/1928 Spillman Engineering Co.; No.4109 8/17/1928 Lockport, N.Y.; No.4197 7/26/1929 Spillman Engineering Co.

Style 162

1915 (1)

Style 164

Shipping list (partial) covering units shipped after 1915: No.3062 3/29/1917 Whiting, Indiana; No.4172 5/17/1929 Sandusky, Ohio; No.4329 6/26/1937 New York City.

Style 165

Partial shipping list covering instruments shipped after mid-1915: No.2943 9/17/1915 to Sylvandell Amusement Co., Aurora, Ill. (see illustration of this installation on the Wurlitzer 165 page in this book). Organ repaired at the factory 12/19/1923 and shipped to Washington, Pa.; No.2992 4/28/1916 Rochester, N.Y.; No.3106 1/18/1918 Westview Park Company, Pittsburgh, Penna.; No.3124 12/30/1918 San Francisco, Cal.; No.3207 10/29/1916 New York City; No.3241 2/25/1920 Chicago, Illinois; No.3300 8/7/1920 New York City; No.3349 4/11/1921 Sea Breeze, N.Y.; No.3358 4/28/1921 Toronto, Canada; No.33786/25/1921 New York City; No.3437 shipped 4/20/1922 to St. Louis, rebuilt at the factory and reshipped 4/15/1925 to Cincinnati; No.3473 7/3/1922 New York City; No.3629 2/26/1924 Spillman Engineering Co., North Tonawanda, N.Y.; No.3763 4/29/1925 Spillman Engineering Co.; No.3779 shipped to Spillman on 5/29/1925, returned to the factory and reshipped on 4/12/1926 to Washington, D.C.; No.4292 5/29/1931 Rochester, N.Y.; No.4338 6/14/1939 to Ross Davis in Los Angeles – the last Wurlitzer automatic musical instrument to leave the factory!

Style 166

Partial shipping list covering last 3 instruments: No.2945 8/10/1915 Detroit, Michigan; No.3001 6/24/1916 to J. Diehl of Buffalo, N.Y.; No.3200 3/1/1918 to Denver, Colorado.

Style 168

Partial data: No.3329 shipped on 10/6/1920 to Dallas, Texas.

Style 180*

Shipping list: No.3439 4/21/1922 West Park, Colorado; No.3612 11/17/1923 Chicago, Illinois; No.3765 4/29/1925 Pacific Ocean Park, Long Beach, Calif. (destroyed by fire); No.4182 shipped on 6/19/1929 to Spillman Engineering, later repaired and reshipped 11/16/1936 to John L. Bell of Fort Wayne, Indiana; No.4275 11/27/1930 Waukegan, Illinois, rebuilt at the factory and converted to play Caliola rolls, reshipped 8/14/1935 to Harrisburg, Penna.

Caliola*

1928 (29); 1929 (21); 1930 (6); 1931 (4); 1933 (1); 1936 (1); First was No.4128 shipped 12/12/1928 to Chicago. Six instruments were made with brass pipes (Nos. 4169, 4170, 4185, 4190, 4198, and 4230). Others had all wooden pipes.

Types of Wurlitzer Band Organ Rolls

Early Wurlitzer instruments used several different types of rolls, the layouts and designations of which are not known to us now. The "Monster" and "Mammoth" organs used music rolls which contained from 1 to 3 selections and which sold for $10 per roll. The Style 125 roll had very early origins and may have been used on some of the smaller instruments of the 1905 - 1910 period.

By the 'teens the rolls were standardized into three main types: Style 125 rolls, Style 150 rolls, and Style 165 rolls.

A 1925 catalogue listed the following rolls available at that time and their prices:

Roll Price List

Style 125 Rolls
Four-piece rolls .................................. $5.25 each
Ten-piece (or length of 10 piece) rolls .................... 13.00
Style 150 Rolls
Used on styles No. 146, 146-A, 147, 148, 150, and 153.
Four-piece rolls .................................. 6.25
Ten-piece (or length of 10 piece) ........................ 15.00
Style 165 Rolls
Used on styles No. 163, 165, 166, and 168.
Five-piece (or 5-piece length) rolls ....................... 20.00
Ten-piece (or 10-piece length) rolls ...................... 30.00
Style 180 Rolls
Ten-piece (or 10-piece length) rolls ...................... 50.00

The catalogue noted: "Up to the minute music rolls for Wurlitzer organs are always obtainable. Popular music of the day, the tunes the crowd whistles and hums, are what you need for your musical program. Good lively popular music always brings the crowds – crowds bring the money. They stop, look, listen, and then ride. What a wonderful difference good music does make in the season's receipts!"

Wurlitzer Music Roll Paper
–a problem solved–

Regular music roll paper is unacceptable for most band organ applications, especially when an instrument is used outdoors. The ever changing humidity will shrink and expand the paper, resulting in great difficulties in making it track properly.

The worldwide solution to this problem was the music book. Used by Gavioli, Frati, Limonaire, and most other makers, the folding cardboard music book was so tough and durable that humidity had little effect on it. However, as nice as music books are, there is the problem of cost. Music books are made by hand one-at-a-time and, consequently, are expensive. Wurlitzer had a different solution.

Early Wurlitzer skating rink organs were used indoors. The red paper rolls used on them had some tracking problems, but they were not insuperable. Then came the outdoor amusement park business. Wurlitzer music rolls were a failure in those locations. There were two possibilities: (1) Make organs on the folding book system, or (2) Do something about the music roll paper.

Wurlitzer chose the latter. From an Erie, Penna., supplier a stock of paraffin coated paper was obtained. The result was a roll immune to the weather. Wurlitzer noted: "Our Weather Proof Music Rolls have revolutionized band organ construction... Cut on specially treated paper made especially for this use, these rolls are strong and durable and are made to stand long usage and temperature changes."

Fortunately, Wurlitzer used its paraffined paper for all other types of rolls (coin piano, orchestrion, theatre organ) as well. The paper has excellent ageing properties – and most Wurlitzer rolls from the late 'teens and 1920's play as well now as they did originally.

**WURLITZER BARREL ORGANS**

**Early organs imported from Germany or made by DeKleist.**

*Operated by pinned Cylinder.*

The Wurlitzer Automatic Bands are as supreme in their field as are the Automatic Orchestras. The difference between the two is about the same as that existing between an orchestra and a band. That is to say in the music of the Band Organs the brass instruments predominate, and therefore the music is louder.

There are two distinct types of Wurlitzer Band Organs, the pinned cylinder type, in which the music is arranged on large metal cylinders. This type is well adapted for merry-go-rounds, tent shows, excursion steamers and general bally-hoo work, where a great variety of tunes is not required.

For years our pinned cylinder Band Organs have been recognized as the best. They are built in the most complete factory in the world, by skilled mechanics with a lifetime experience in the business.

**No.3534 Pipe Hand Organ. "For tent shows of every description and general outdoor purposes." Sold with 3 cylinders of 9 tunes each. 31 keys, 4 registers. 10 trumpets; drum and bells. Case measures: 45½ inches high by 31½" wide by 20½" deep. The same illustration was used in a catalogue of Molinari (New York City organ maker and seller).**

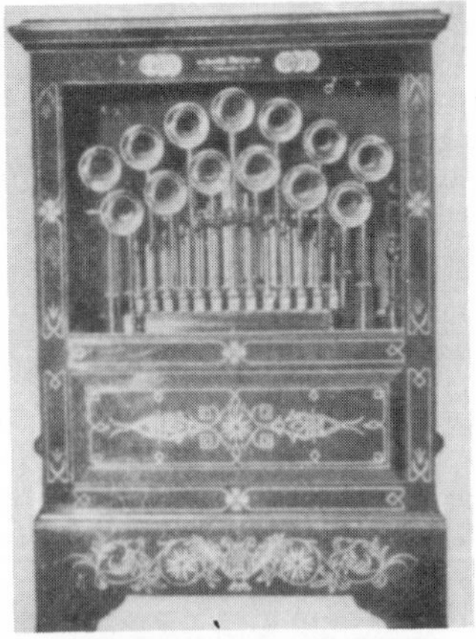

**Style 18 (also known as Style 3535). 41 key barrel organ. Outside visible: 13 brass trumpets, 13 brass piccolos, 13 wooden flageolets. Inside: 5 open basses, 13 open pipes, 6 stopped pipes. 11 accompaniment pipes. Bottom: 5 stopped basses, 7 stopped pipes, 10 accompaniment pipes. 1 hand register for controlling trumpets. 4'10½" high; 3'6" wide; 2'3½" deep. Sold new with 1 8-tune cylinder for $390. Extra cylinders of 3-tunes per cylinder @$56.**

**Military Band Organ.** (Barrel Type.)

Operated by Pinned Cylinders.

**Style 20 (also known as Style 3536). 46-key barrel organ. 5'7" high, 3'7" wide, 2'6½" deep. Outside visible: 3 trombones, 15 brass trumpets, 16 brass clarionets, 16 brass piccolos. Inside: 28 open pipes, 21 stopped pipes. Bottom: 28 stopped pipes. Three stops (registers operated by hand): 1 for clarionets, 1 for trumpets, 1 for trombones. Price including 8-tune cylinder $550; extra 3-tune cylinders were $65 each. Circa 1906.**

**Style 20-C. 48-key barrel organ. 8' high; 4'2½" wide; 2'6½" deep. $775 w/1 cylinder. Circa 1912.**

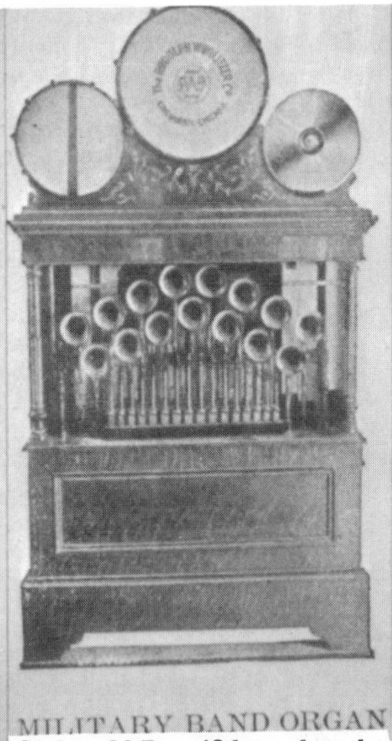


**Style 20-D. 48-key barrel organ. 7'6" high; 4'2½" wide; 2'6½" deep. Weight: 400 pounds. Circa 1912.**

*Style 18*

41 Keys—Music on Pin Cylinders.

Height 4 feet 10½ inches. Width 3 feet 6 inches. Depth 2 feet 3½ inches. Golden oak cases. Square back with hinged doors. Shipping weight 575 pounds.

Instrumentation

Outside, Visible—13 brass trumpets; 13 brass piccolos; 15 wooden flageolets.

Inside—5 wood trombones; 5 open basses; 13 open pipes; 6 stopped pipes; 11 pipes in accompaniment.

Bottom—5 stopped basses; 7 stopped pipes; 10 pipes in accompaniment; 1 stop for trumpets; 1 for trombones; 1 for flageolets; 1 for piccolos.

**Style 18 barrel organ.**

**Style 20-A (also known as Style 2537). 47-key barrel organ. Also sold as "Style 20-B, same as 20-A except that it has cymbal on top, bass drum in one wing and snare drum in the other. (20-A has no bass drum or cymbal). 7'2" high, 8'2" wide, 2'5" deep. This case was one of Wurlitzer's most popular and was later used to make the popular Style 150 paper roll organ. Instrumentation of 20-A: Outside visible: 3 trombones, 15 brass trumpets, 16 brass clarionets, 16 brass piccolos; inside: 28 open and 21 stopped pipes; bottom: 28 stopped pipes. 5 stops. Percussion: snare drum. Sold for $725 with 1 9-tune cylinder in 1912. Extra 9-tune cylinders were $65 each. Although the illustration is of a white case, most were in natural wood color.**

Style 16. 36-key barrel organ. Outside visible: 15 brass piccolos; inside: 15 wooden flageolets, 11 wooden trumpets, 11 open pipes, 15 violin pipes, 3 bass pipes, 7 accompaniment pipes; bottom: 3 basses, 7 stopped accompaniment pipes, 11 stopped pipes played with trumpets. 4 stops. Height: 3'5"; width 3'5"; depth 2'.

**Style 17**

41 Keys—Music on Pin Cylinders

Height 4 feet 1 inch. Width 3 feet 6 inches. Depth 2 feet 2 inches. Golden oak case. Shipping weight, 450 pounds.

Instrumentation

Outside, Visible—14 brass piccolos; 14 wood flageolets.

Inside—5 open basses; 5 stopped basses in octave; 14 violin pipes melody; 13 wood trumpets; 9 open pipes in accompaniment; 6 stopped pipes in accompaniment.

Bottom—5 stopped basses; 9 stopped accompaniment; 6 stopped melody.

Five Stops—1 for piccolos; 1 for flageolets; 1 for accompaniments; 1 for melody; 1 for trumpets.

**Price $600.00**

*Style 18C*

48 Keys—Music on Pin Cylinders

Height 6 feet 3 inches. Width 6 feet 10 inches. Depth 2 feet 6 inches. Golden oak case.

Square back with hinged doors. Carved top. Fluted columns in front. Shipping weight, 800 pounds.

Instrumentation

Outside, Visible—14 wooden flageolets; 13 brass trumpets; 14 brass piccolos.

Inside—5 wooden trombones; 5 open bass pipes; 10 open pipes in accompaniment; 14 open violin pipes.

Bottom—5 stopped bass pipes; 14 stopped pipes; 10 stopped pipes in accompaniment.

Four Stops, Outside—1 for piccolos; 1 for trumpets; 1 for flageolets; 1 for trombones; 1 stop inside for open pipes. Bass, snare drum and cymbal.

**Style 18-C**

---

*The* WURLITZER MILITARY BAND

**WURLITZER PAPER ROLL ORGANS**

This page begins the descriptions of the various Wurlitzer paper roll organs. The early skating rink organs are listed first; the later painted-front organs are listed toward the end.

Years ago thousands of Wurlitzer band organs were, as a catalogue put it, "successful from Coney Island, New York, to Venice-by-the-sea at Los Angeles, California."

For Skating Rinks
Carouselles
Fairs
*and*
Summer Resorts.

These instruments are designed by us especially for skating rink purposes. They are the result of many years experience and a thorough knowledge of the requirements of an instrument for this use. These instruments furnish better music to skate by than any musicians can. They play thousands of selections from paper

Above: The "Monster Military Band Organ," or, as it was more mundanely known as in later years, the "Style 155," is a 100-key instrument which measures 6'10½" high by 8'9" wide by 8'3" deep. This large almost-cubic box of brass and wooden pipes used a music roll and sold for $3250.00 in 1912. "This style is known as 'The Monster' and is designed to fill any but the very few extremely large rinks. In musical results it is equal to a band of from 12 to 15 pieces and will give perfect satisfaction in all rinks with floor space of from 10,000 to 20,000 square feet... The leaded glass panels which admit of a view of the numerous brass horns inside... may be removed, if desired, thus making the organ sound much louder."

On July 21, 1905, Mr. S. Burd, proprietor of the Massillon Skating Rink in Ohio (illustration above) wrote Wurlitzer and said: "My patrons like (The Monster) very much and many who do not skate come to hear the instrument. It is certainly a musical wonder. My rink, formerly an opera house, is 56x130 feet... and has a gallery that will seat 200 people. The cost of the rink was $31,000. I give this description so you can see that the rink and the organ correspond in beauty."

MONSTER MILITARY BAND ORGAN.
Style 155 (Paper Roll).
For Larger Skating Rinks.

"The Monster." See column at right for a description of this early paper roll instrument.

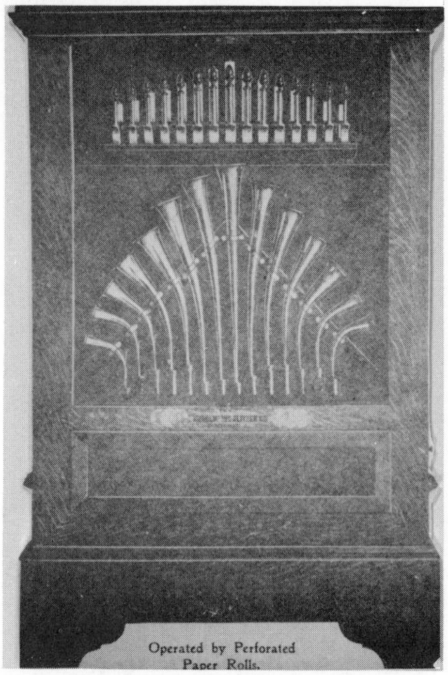


**(Style 120—38 Keys.)**

**DESCRIPTION OF INSTRUMENT.**

**OUTSIDE VISIBLE**—14 brass trumpets; 15 wooden flutes; 15 brass piccolos.

**INSIDE**—15 concert flutes; 14 open pipes with trumpets; 6 open pipes in accompaniment; 3 open pipes: 3 stopped pipes or three trombones in wood.

**BOTTOM**—3 stopped pipes with trumpets; 4 stops: 1 for piccolos, 1 for trumpets, 1 for open pipes with trumpets, 1 for concert flutes.

*The* WURLITZER MILITARY BAND

MILITARY BAND ORGAN. (Style 105—41 Keys

Case finished in Imitation Walnut or Rosewood with Engraved Scroll Work or can be had in Quartered White Oak if so desired.

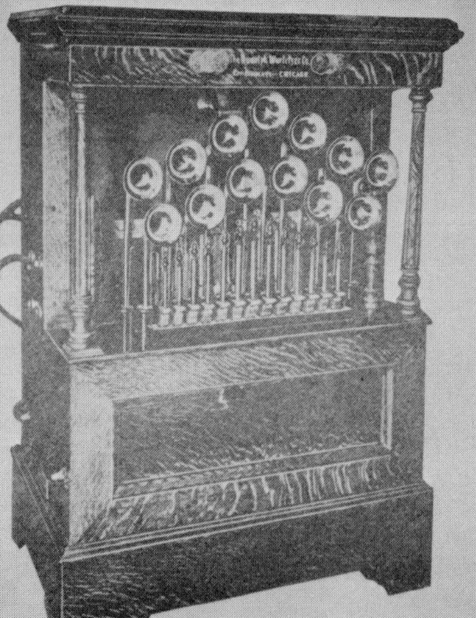

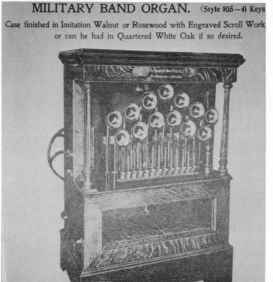

Operated by Perforated Paper Rolls.

DIMENSIONS—Width, 3 feet 6 inches; depth, 2 feet 3½ inches; height, 4 feet 10½ inches.

Style 105 is the same as Style 125 without the drums and will serve the same purposes where the drums are not desired.

*Style 104*

41 Keys—Music Played by Paper Music Rolls

Height 4 feet 1 inch. Width 3 feet 6 inches. Depth 2 feet 2 inches. Golden oak case. Shipping weight, 500 pounds.

Instrumentation

Outside, Visible—14 brass piccolos; 14 wooden flageolets.

Inside—5 open basses; 5 stopped basses in octave; 14 violin pipes melody; 13 wooden trumpets; 9 open pipes, in accompaniment; 6 stopped pipes in accompaniment.

Bottom—5 stopped basses; 9 stopped accompaniment; 6 stopped melody.

Five Stops—1 for piccolos; 1 for flageolets; 1 for accompaniment; 1 for melody; 1 for trumpets.

Price $550.00

**Early Style 104. This uses a Style 125 paper roll, as do probably most of the other organs on this page.**

DIMENSIONS—Width, 3 feet 7 inches; height, 5 feet 7 inches; depth, 2 feet 4 inches.

Style 120 is a powerful little instrument with a full rich volume of tone that makes a very satisfactory organ for the smaller skating rinks, dance halls, excursion boats, etc.

**PRICE - $675.00.**

This price includes six rolls of music, each roll containing three pieces.

**(Style 130—46 Keys.)**

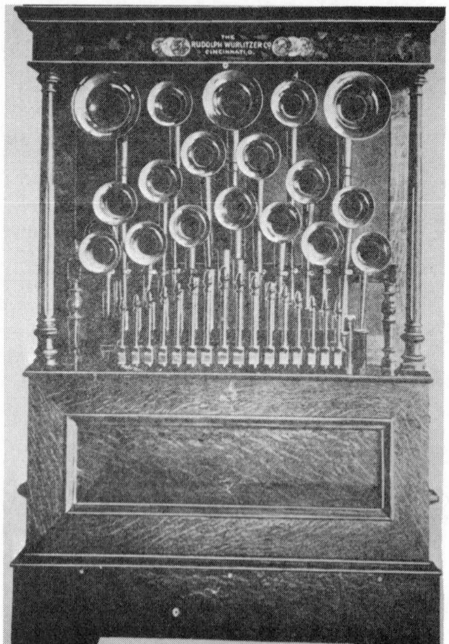

**OUTSIDE VISIBLE**—3 heavy trombones; 16 heavy clarionets; 16 heavy piccolos.

**INSIDE BOTTOM**—28 open pipes: 21 stopped pipes, 28 stopped pipes; 3 stops, 1 or clarionets, 1 for trumpets, 1 for trombones.

## *Style No. 125—Rink or Carouselle Organ*

*44 Keys*

PLAYED BY PAPER MUSIC ROLLS

Especially designed for small to medium size rinks.

**INSTRUMENTATION**

OUTSIDE, VISIBLE—13 Brass Trumpets; 13 Brass Piccolos; 13 Wooden Flageolets; 2 Drums; Cymbal.

INSIDE—5 Wooden Trombones; 5 Open Basses; 13 Open Pipes; 6 Stopped Pipes; 11 Pipes in Accompaniment.

BOTTOM—5 Stopped Basses; 7 Stopped Pipes; 10 Pipes in Accompaniment; 1 Stop for Trumpets; 1 Stop for Trombones; 1 Stop for Piccolos; 1 Stop for Flageolets. Bass Drum, Snare Drum and Cymbal.

**DIMENSIONS**

HEIGHT, 6 feet 3 inches. WIDTH, 6 feet 7 inches. DEPTH, 2 feet 3½ inches. SHIPPING WEIGHT, 800 lbs.

Style 100. 48-key paper roll organ. Sold for $575 in 1906. Case is similar in design to early barrel organs. Height: 4'2", width 4'1", depth 2'3".

Style 110. 44-key paper roll organ. 5'4" high; 4' wide; 2'3" deep. Sold for $650 in 1906. Possibly imported from Frati.

"Mammoth Military Band Organ" — or Style 160. 122 keys. 10'4" high, 10'6" wide, 4'6" deep. Sold for $5500 in 1912.

Right: Style 126. 44-note paper roll organ. 6'10" high, 7'6" wide, 2'8" deep. Outside visible: 14 violin pipes; inside: 5 wooden trombones, 13 wooden trumpets, 10 bass pipes, 27 acccompaniment pipes, 28 piccolo pipes, 14 flute pipes, 5 stopped bass for accompaniment, 9 other pipes for accompaniment, 14 stopped pipes (somewhat confused description is from an original catalogue). Uses Style 125 rolls.

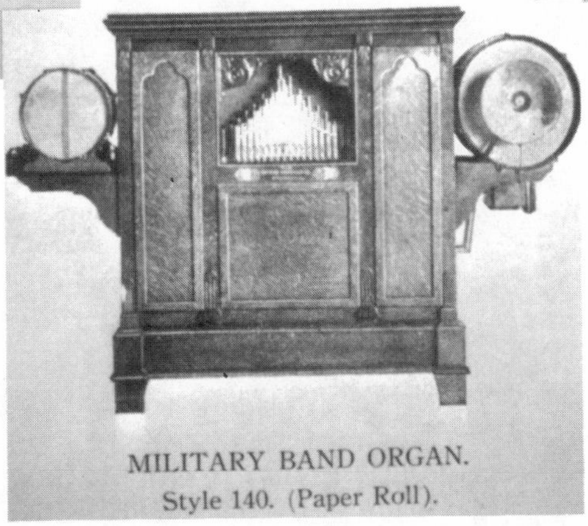


Style 140 (135, see left, is same specifications but without drums): 5'1½" high; 8'1" wide (Style 135 is 4'9" wide); 3'11" deep. Style 135 sold for $875.00 in 1912; Style 140 for $1050.00. Made for indoor skating rink use. Early organs such as this were commonly put right on the rink floor and were played for hours at a time. The early rink organs had single roll mechanisms (the duplex types were not introduced until later) and would play about 20 to 30 minutes per roll.

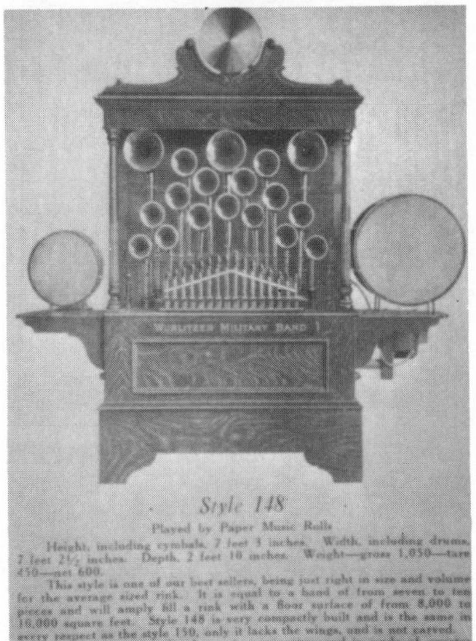


Style 148. Same as Style 130 but with drums and cymbal. One of these was shipped as late as 1936!

Style 135

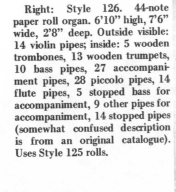

Original illustration of a Style 147 (upper right) and a 147 in use today (on a merry go round – Richard Lokemoen photo). Organ measures 6'10½" high; 7'3" wide; 2'4" deep.

Ornate wooden latticework is similar to that found on the Style A Automatic Harp (see Wurlitzer coin operated instrument section of this book). Sold for $700 in 1916.

*Style 127*

Dimensions

Height 6 feet 5 inches. Width, with wings, 8 feet 2½ inches. Depth 2 feet 5¼ inches. Weight packed for shipment, 1200 lbs. Requires ¼ H. P. motor to operate.

Instrumentation

Outside, Visible—13 brass trumpets; 13 brass piccolos; 13 wooden flageolets.

Inside—5 wooden trombones; 5 open basses; 13 open pipes; 6 stopped pipes, 11 pipes in accompaniment.

Bottom—5 stopped basses; 7 stopped pipes; 10 pipes in accompaniment; 1 stop for trumpets; 1 stop for trombones; 1 for piccolo; 1 for flageolets.

Price $1,000.00

**Style 127: Sold circa 1916 the Style 127 was a short-lived model. The interior mechanisms, specifications, and instrumentation are that of a regular Wurlitzer Style 125 organ – one of the most popular models. The ornate outside has a European flavor and was one of the earliest painted-front styles. At the time when a Style 125 sold for $775 the Style 127 was pegged at an even $1000.00. Few sales were forthcoming.**

*Style 150*

48 Keys—Played by Paper Music Roll

Height 7 feet 2 inches. Width 8 feet 2 inches. Depth 2 feet 5 inches. Shipping weight 1,230 pounds.

Instrumentation

Outside, Visible—3 heavy brass trombones; 15 brass trumpets; 18 brass clarionets; 16 brass piccolos.

Inside—27 open pipes, 22 stopped pipes.

Bottom—28 stopped pipes.

Bass and snare drums on sides, cymbals on top.

Stops—1 for clarionets; 1 for trumpets; 1 for trombones; 1 for open and 1 for stopped pipes.

Price $1,300.00

**Style 150: This was the second most popular Wurlitzer brass trumpet organ (Style 125 was first). Wurlitzer noted: This style is the most popular we build, owing to the fact that it exactly meets the requirements of the average size rink... It replaces from 7 to 10 human musicians and will amply fill a rink with a floor surface of 8,000 to 10,000 square feet. The cost of five musicians for evening sessions only will pay for this organ in a few weeks.**

**Long roll tracker frame (single roll mechanism). Used in early paper roll organs and many later ones, particularly smaller styles, also. At the front, just below the bottom spool, is seen the fast - slow tempo regulator by means of which the roll speed may be varied.**

**Duplex roll mechanism. "Enables you to keep the organ playing constantly without a moment's pause. Two long roll frames are used; so arranged that when one roll is rewinding or when one roll has reached its end, the other will start playing."**

*Style 163*

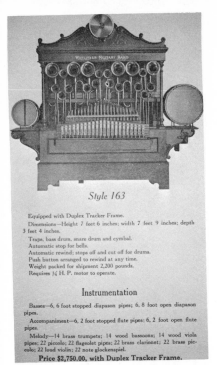

Equipped with Duplex Tracker Frame.
Dimensions—Height 7 feet 6 inches; width 7 feet 9 inches; depth 3 feet 4 inches.
Traps, bass drum, snare drum and cymbal.
Automatic stop for bells.
Automatic rewind; stops off and cut off for drums.
Push button arranged to rewind at any time.
Weight packed for shipment 2,200 pounds.
Requires ¾ H. P. motor to operate.

Instrumentation

Basses—6, 6 foot stopped diapason pipes; 6, 8 foot open diapason pipes.

Accompaniment—6, 2 foot stopped flute pipes; 6, 2 foot open flute pipes.

Melody—14 brass trumpets; 14 wood bassoons; 14 wood viola pipes; 22 piccolo; 22 flageolet pipes; 22 brass clarionet; 22 brass piccolo; 22 loud violin; 22 note glockenspiel.

**Price $2,750.00, with Duplex Tracker Frame.**

*Style No. 164—Band Organ*
*57 Keys*
FINISHED IN GOLDEN OAK

Equipped with drums on brackets on side of case easily detached. Drums can also be put on top of the organ if desired.

HEIGHT, when assembled, 8 feet 1 inch. WIDTH, when assembled, 11 feet. DEPTH, when assembled, 4 feet. WEIGHT, when packed, 3,000 lbs.

Duplex Tracker Frame.

8 Draw Stops for—Trombones, Trumpets, Clarionets, Piccolos, Cello, Flute and two Violins.

1 Automatic Stop for Glockenspiel.

INSTRUMENTATION

BASS—6 eight-foot Stopped Diapason Pipes; 6 four-foot Open Diapason Pipes, 6 Brass Trombone Pipes.

ACCOMPANIMENT

10 eight-foot Stopped Diapason Pipes; 10 four-foot Open Diapason Pipes; 10 four-foot Stopped Diapason Pipes; 20 two-foot Violin Diapason Pipes.

TRUMPETS—14 Brass Trumpets, 14 Wood Trumpets.

MELODY—22 Brass Clarionette; 22 Brass Piccolos; 22 four-foot Cello Pipes; 44 two-foot Violin Pipes; 22 four-foot Stopped Flutes; 22 two-foot Stopped Flutes; 22 Flagcolets; 22 Flutes, 22 Octave Violin, 22 Glockenspiel.

*Style No. 168*

Built in Oak veneered case, Dark Golden Oak finish.
Equipped with Style No. 165 Duplex Long Tune Tracker Frame.
Dimensions: Height, with Cymbal, 8 ft. 3 inches.
Height without Cymbal, 6 ft. 9 inches.
Width with drums, 11 ft. 0 inches.
Width without drums, 7 ft. 4 inches.
Depth, including crank, 4 ft. 2 inches.
Weight, packed for shipment, 2300 lbs.
Requires 1 H. P. motor to operate.

Instrumentation

| BASS | ACCOMPANIMENT |
|---|---|
| 6 Brass Trombones | 20 Stopped Pipes |
| 6 Open Wood Pipes | 20 Violin Pipes |
| 6 Stopped Wood Pipes | 10 Cello Pipes. |

Melody

| | |
|---|---|
| 22 Stopped Flutes | 22 Cello Pipes |
| 22 Stopped Flutes in Octave | 22 Violin Pipes in Octave |
| 22 Violin Pipes | 44 Flute Pipes |
| 22 Viola Pipes | 22 Brass Bassoon Pipes |
| 22 Flageolets | 22 Brass Piccolos |

22 Note Glockenspiel with automatic control.

Trumpets

| | |
|---|---|
| 14 Brass Trumpets | 14 Wood Trumpets |

Traps

Bass Drum, Snare Drum and Cymbal

Equipped with eight Draw Stops, by means of which volume of music can be cut down to any combination required, and organ used for small select skating or dancing parties, or full organ used for crowded floor. List of stops follows:

| | |
|---|---|
| 1 for Brass Trombones. | 1 for Wood Trumpets. |
| 1 for Brass Trumpets and Bassoons. | 1 for Stopped Pipes, Cello and Violins. |
| 1 for Cello and Flageolets. | 1 for Viola and Violins. |

**Look-alikes? These large brass trumpet organs all use the Style 165 music roll. The same photograph (although retouched) was used for No.164 and No.168. The only difference between Nos.164 and 168 is that the latter seems to have 22 more flute pipes; nonetheless the weight of the former is given as 3000 pounds and the latter (which is endowed with 22 more pipes) as 2300 pounds. Style 163 sold for $2750 in 1916. All of these three styles were designed primarily for skating rink use.**

---

## MOSTLY LATER WURLITZER STYLES (1920's and 1930's)

*Style No. 103—Military Band Organ*
*41 Keys*
PLAYED BY PAPER MUSIC ROLLS

Designed especially for Miniature Carousselles, Kiddie Swings and other children's amusements. Just the size organ for a Pit Show. An all-wood trumpet organ which holds its tone well and is not affected by sudden temperature changes. The organ is small, but very compact, and has exceptional volume for its size. It is easily transported when packed, and two men can easily carry the instrument about.

Built in an Oak Veneered Case, finished light Fumed Oak or Golden Oak. Paneled front handsomely decorated with landscapes or flower designs. A very attractive little organ.

Plays Style No. 125 long tune paper rolls, and contains all the late improvements we have incorporated in the larger organs.

INSTRUMENTATION

5 Wood Basses; 9 Wood Accompaniment Pipes; 14 Wood Violins; 14 Wood Flutes; 13 Wood Trumpets (on draw stop.)

DIMENSIONS

HEIGHT, 3 feet 6 inches. WIDTH, 3 feet 2 inches. DEPTH, 2 feet 1 inch (including crank-shaft extension). WEIGHT, NET, 235 lbs.; PACKED, 375 lbs.

**Style 103. This compact little organ was first introduced in 1923. Recommended as being "designed especially for miniature carousels, kiddie swings, and other amusements – just the size organ for a pit show," the 103 was ideal for traveling shows, due to its light weight.**

**Carousel miscellany: Wurlitzer never did decide how to spell "Carousel." The above description spells it "carouselle." At other times it is spelled "carousal," and, in the 1906 catalogue, as we spell it today, "carousel."**

**Below: Wurlitzer Style 105. Late style with painted facade and side wings. (See also earlier description of the No.105 brass trumpet organ – an instrument similar in number but not in specifications). First shipped in 1923, the late Style 105 was a popular instrument with traveling shows. The late Style 104 is identical to the 105 except that it does not have the bass drum, snare drum, and cymbal. All four organs described on the lower part of this page – Styles 103, 104, 105, and 106 – use the type 125 roll.**

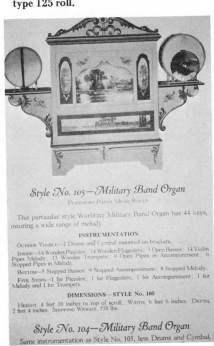

*Style No. 105—Military Band Organ*
PLAYED BY PAPER MUSIC ROLLS

This particular style Wurlitzer Military Band Organ has 44 keys, insuring a wide range of melody.

INSTRUMENTATION

OUTSIDE VISIBLE—2 Drums and Cymbal mounted on brackets.

INSIDE—14 Wooden Piccolos; 14 Wooden Flageolets; 5 Open Basses; 14 Violin Pipes Melody; 13 Wooden Trumpets; 9 Open Pipes in Accompaniment; 6 Stopped Pipes in Melody.

BOTTOM—5 Stopped Basses; 9 Stopped Accompaniment; 8 Stopped Melody.

FIVE STOPS—1 for Piccolos; 1 for Flageolets; 1 for Accompaniment; 1 for Melody and 1 for Trumpets.

DIMENSIONS—STYLE No. 105

HEIGHT, 4 feet 10 inches to top of scroll. WIDTH, 6 feet 6 inches. DEPTH, 2 feet 4 inches. SHIPPING WEIGHT, 550 lbs.

*Style No. 104—Military Band Organ*
Same instrumentation as Style No. 105, less Drums and Cymbal.

*Style No. 106—Military Band Organ*
PLAYED BY PAPER MUSIC ROLLS

This beautiful instrument is made with 44 keys. Built in Oak Veneered Case, fancy white enamel carved front, decorated with hand painted panels. Top Scroll hinged to top of organ.

INSTRUMENTATION

OUTSIDE, VISIBLE—2 Drums and Cymbal, with demountable Wings.

INSIDE—14 Wooden Piccolos; 14 Flageolets; 5 Open Basses; 14 Violin Pipes Melody; 13 Wooden Trumpets; 9 Open Pipes, in Accompaniment; 6 Stopped Pipes, in Melody.

BOTTOM—5 Stopped Basses; 9 Stopped Accompaniment; 8 Stopped Melody.

FIVE STOPS—1 for Piccolos; 1 for Flageolets; 1 for Accompaniment; 1 for Melody and 1 for Trumpets.

DIMENSIONS

HEIGHT, to top of Scroll, 5 feet 7 inches. HEIGHT, with Scroll down, 4 feet 4 inches. WIDTH, with Wings, 7 feet 3 inches. WIDTH, without Wings, 3 feet 7 inches. DEPTH, 2 feet 6 inches. WEIGHT, 600 lbs.

**Style 106. Introduced in 1906, only twelve of these were shipped from then until 1930! As a perusal of the specifications will indicate, Style 106 is essentially a Style 105 in a differently designed case. The center panels of these and the other organs shown here have scenes painted on a fine metal screen. Castles on the Rhine, South Sea isles, and similar exotic vistas were popular scenes.**

WURLITZER

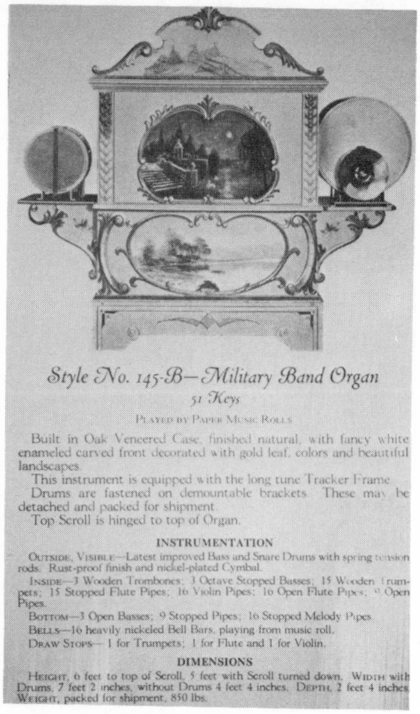

*Style No. 145-B—Military Band Organ*

*51 Keys*

PLAYED BY PAPER MUSIC ROLLS

Built in Oak Veneered Case, finished natural, with fancy white enameled carved front decorated with gold leaf, colors and beautiful landscapes.

This instrument is equipped with the long tune Tracker Frame.

Drums are fastened on demountable brackets. These may be detached and packed for shipment.

Top Scroll is hinged to top of Organ.

INSTRUMENTATION

OUTSIDE, VISIBLE—Latest improved Bass and Snare Drums with spring tension rods. Rust-proof finish and nickel-plated Cymbal.

INSIDE—3 Wooden Trombones; 3 Octave Stopped Basses; 15 Wooden Trumpets; 15 Stopped Flute Pipes; 16 Violin Pipes; 16 Open Flute Pipes; 9 Open Pipes.

BOTTOM—3 Open Basses; 9 Stopped Pipes; 16 Stopped Melody Pipes.

BELLS—16 heavily nickeled Bell Bars, playing from music roll.

DRAW STOPS—1 for Trumpets; 1 for Flute and 1 for Violin.

DIMENSIONS

HEIGHT, 6 feet to top of Scroll, 5 feet with Scroll turned down. WIDTH with Drums, 7 feet 2 inches, without Drums 4 feet 4 inches. DEPTH, 2 feet 4 inches. WEIGHT, packed for shipment, 850 lbs.

**Style 145 organs of all types (145, 145-A, and 145-B) were made in limited numbers beginning in 1928.**

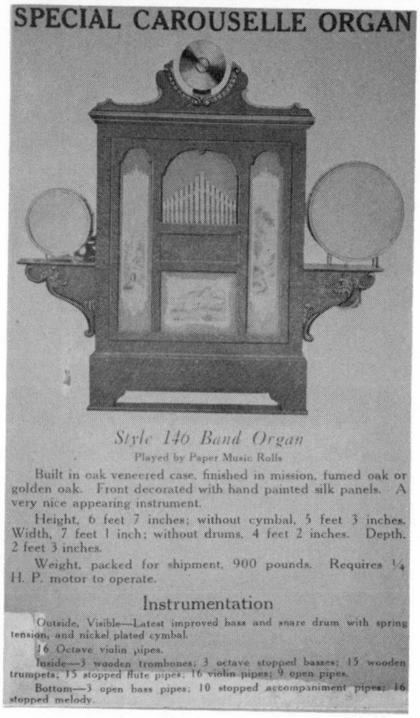

SPECIAL CAROUSELLE ORGAN

*Style 146 Band Organ*

Played by Paper Music Rolls

Built in oak veneered case, finished in mission, fumed oak or golden oak. Front decorated with hand painted silk panels. A very nice appearing instrument.

Height, 6 feet 7 inches; without cymbal, 5 feet 3 inches. Width, 7 feet 1 inch; without drums, 4 feet 2 inches. Depth, 2 feet 3 inches.

Weight, packed for shipment, 900 pounds. Requires 1/4 H. P. motor to operate.

Instrumentation

Outside, Visible—Latest improved bass and snare drum with spring tension, and nickel plated cymbal.

16 Octave violin pipes.

Inside—3 wooden trombones; 3 octave stopped basses; 15 wooden trumpets; 15 stopped flute pipes; 16 violin pipes; 9 open pipes.

Bottom—3 open bass pipes; 10 stopped accompaniment pipes; 16 stopped melody.

**Early Style 146 organ: These were made in the 'teens and early 'twenties.**

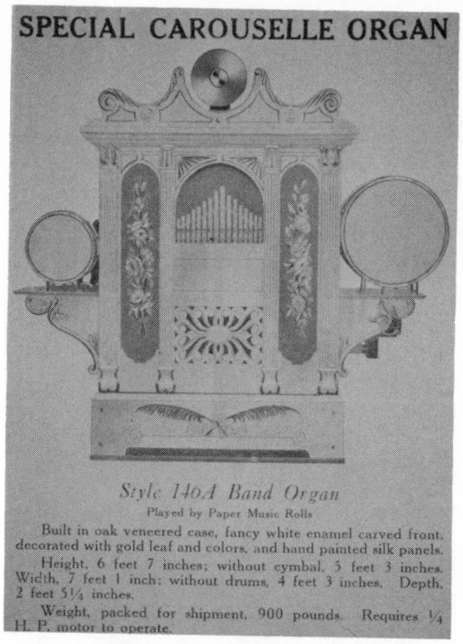

SPECIAL CAROUSELLE ORGAN

*Style 146A Band Organ*

Played by Paper Music Rolls

Built in oak veneered case, fancy white enamel carved front, decorated with gold leaf and colors, and hand painted silk panels.

Height, 6 feet 7 inches; without cymbal, 5 feet 3 inches. Width, 7 feet 1 inch; without drums, 4 feet 3 inches. Depth, 2 feet 5 1/4 inches.

Weight, packed for shipment, 900 pounds. Requires 1/4 H. P. motor to operate.

**Early Style 146-A organ. Sold as the "Special Carouselle Organ," the 146-A was produced during the 'teens and early 1920's. Organs such as this were usually mounted in the center part of a merry go round and were connected by a belt to the same motor that drove the merry go round shaft.**

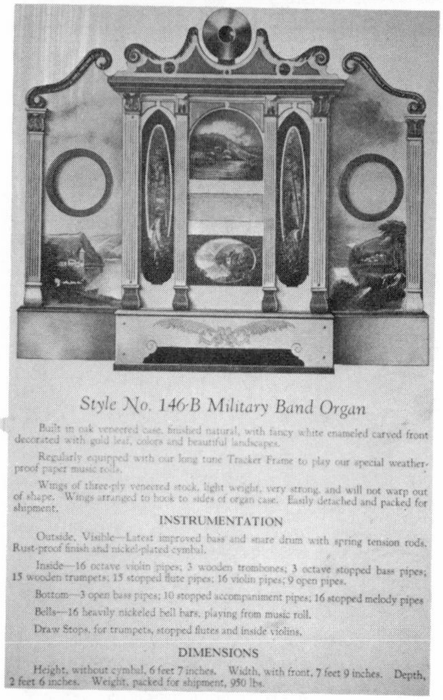

*Style No. 146-B Military Band Organ*

Built in oak veneered case, finished natural, with fancy white enameled carved front decorated with gold leaf, colors and beautiful landscapes.

Regularly equipped with our long tune Tracker Frame to play our special weatherproof paper music rolls.

Wings of three-ply veneered stock, light weight, very strong, and will not warp out of shape. Wings arranged to hook to sides of organ case. Easily detached and packed for shipment.

INSTRUMENTATION

Outside, Visible—Latest improved bass and snare drum with spring tension rods. Rust-proof finish and nickel-plated cymbal.

Inside—16 octave violin pipes; 3 wooden trombones; 3 octave stopped bass pipes; 15 wooden trumpets; 15 stopped flute pipes; 16 violin pipes; 9 open pipes.

Bottom—3 open bass pipes; 10 stopped accompaniment pipes; 16 stopped melody pipes

Bells—16 heavily nickeled bell bars, playing from music roll.

Draw Stops, for trumpets, stopped flutes and inside violins.

DIMENSIONS

Height, without cymbal, 6 feet 7 inches. Width, with front, 7 feet 9 inches. Depth, 2 feet 6 inches. Weight, packed for shipment, 950 lbs.

**Early Style 146-B organ.**

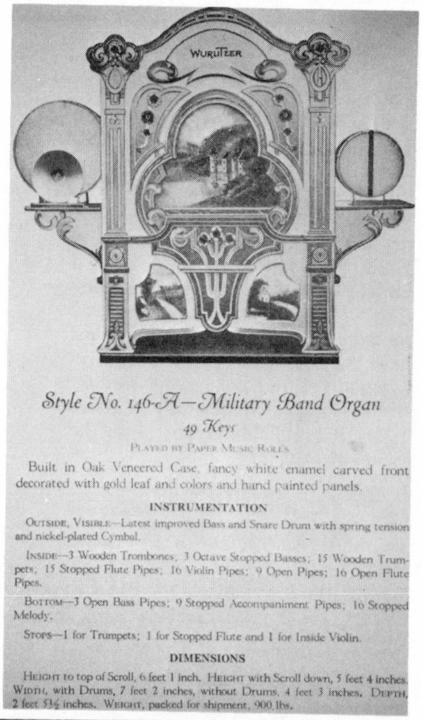



*Style No. 146-A—Military Band Organ*

*49 Keys*

PLAYED BY PAPER MUSIC ROLLS

Built in Oak Veneered Case, fancy white enamel carved front decorated with gold leaf and colors and hand painted panels.

INSTRUMENTATION

OUTSIDE, VISIBLE—Latest improved Bass and Snare Drum with spring tension and nickel-plated Cymbal.

INSIDE—3 Wooden Trombones; 3 Octave Stopped Basses; 15 Wooden Trumpets; 15 Stopped Flute Pipes; 16 Violin Pipes; 9 Open Pipes; 16 Open Flute Pipes.

BOTTOM—3 Open Bass Pipes; 9 Stopped Accompaniment Pipes; 16 Stopped Melody.

STOPS—1 for Trumpets; 1 for Stopped Flute and 1 for Inside Violin.

DIMENSIONS

HEIGHT to top of Scroll, 6 feet 1 inch. HEIGHT with Scroll down, 5 feet 4 inches. WIDTH, with Drums, 7 feet 2 inches, without Drums, 4 feet 3 inches. DEPTH, 2 feet 5 1/2 inches. WEIGHT, packed for shipment, 900 lbs.

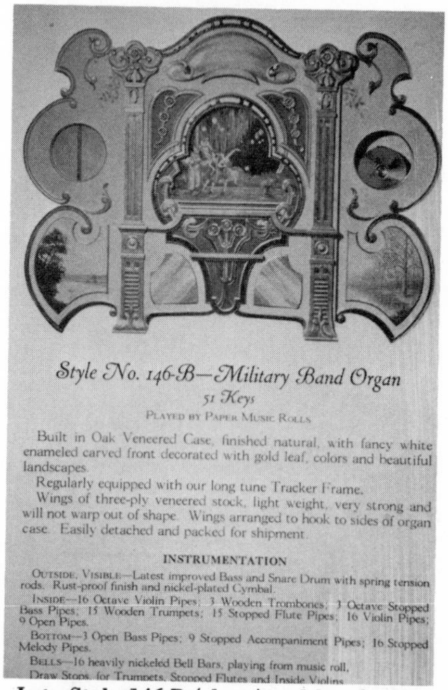

*Style No. 146-B—Military Band Organ*

*51 Keys*

PLAYED BY PAPER MUSIC ROLLS

Built in Oak Veneered Case, finished natural, with fancy white enameled carved front decorated with gold leaf, colors and beautiful landscapes.

Regularly equipped with our long tune Tracker Frame.

Wings of three-ply veneered stock, light weight, very strong and will not warp out of shape. Wings arranged to hook to sides of organ case. Easily detached and packed for shipment.

INSTRUMENTATION

OUTSIDE, VISIBLE—Latest improved Bass and Snare Drum with spring tension rods. Rust-proof finish and nickel-plated Cymbal.

INSIDE—16 Octave Violin Pipes; 3 Wooden Trombones; 3 Octave Stopped Bass Pipes; 15 Wooden Trumpets; 15 Stopped Flute Pipes; 16 Violin Pipes; 9 Open Pipes.

BOTTOM—3 Open Bass Pipes; 9 Stopped Accompaniment Pipes; 16 Stopped Melody Pipes.

BELLS—16 heavily nickeled Bell Bars, playing from music roll.

Draw Stops, for Trumpets, Stopped Flutes and Inside Violins.

**Late Style 146-B (above) and late Style 146-A (left).**

WURLITZER

**Wurlitzer Miniature Band Organ: That is the designation of the instrument pictured at the left, from a photograph supplied by Oswald Wurdeman. This particular instrument used regular 44-note Pianino coin piano rolls (see under "Pianino" in the Wurlitzer coin piano section of this book for more information). It is not known how many of these were made. The Wurlitzer Archives list that the following "Style 50 Kiddie Band Organ" instruments were made: 1931 (7 organs); 1934 (1); 1936 (1). Also listed are two "Tom Thumb Band Organ" instruments made in 1931.**

**Examination of one of these organs reveals that the instrumentation consists of but a single rank of pipes, one pipe for each note on the Pianino roll. The Miniature Band Organ is undoubtedly the smallest electric paper roll band organ ever made in the United States.**

# *Style No. 153—Duplex Orchestral Organ*
## *54 Keys*

**For Three-Abreast Carouselles and Open-Air Dance Pavilions**

With duplex long roll Tracker Frames, latest drums with self-tightening tension rods.

Oak Veneered Case; natural finish; fancy white enamel front; hand-carved scroll work in gold leaf and colors. Raised panels decorated with landscape and flowered designs.

### INSTRUMENTATION

BASSES—3 Wooden Trombones; 3 eight-foot Stopped Diapason Pipes; 3 four-foot Open Diapason Pipes; 3 two-foot Stopped Diapason Pipes.

ACCOMPANIMENT—9 Stopped Flute Pipes; 18 Violin Pipes.

MELODY—16 Stopped Flute; 16 Octave Violin; 15 Wooden Trumpets; 15 Cello Pipes; 32 Violin; 16 Open Flute; 15 Stopped Pipes; 16 Bell Bars.

TRAPS—Bass Drum; Snare Drum and Cymbal.

AUTOMATIC STOPS—1 for Octave Violin; 1 for Open Flute; 1 for Cello Pipes; 1 for Stopped Pipes; 1 for Bell Bars; 1 for Swell Shutters.

### DIMENSIONS

HEIGHT, with front, 7 feet 1 inch; without front, 5 feet 2 inches. WIDTH, with front, 8 feet 8 inches; without front, 4 feet 2½ inches. DEPTH, with front, 3 feet 8 inches; without front, 2 feet 7½ inches. WEIGHT, packed for shipment, 1,300 lbs.

**The Style 153 was produced for many years and is found today with many different styles of case painting. The basic design is after Gebr. Bruder of Waldkirch, Germany.**

**This photograph taken in the Wurlitzer factory shortly before 1920 shows several organs, including a Style 153 in the foreground, being tested prior to shipment. The 153 has numerous light sockets on the front. While some Wurlitzer instruments (such as the 157 pictured at the bottom of this page) were wired for lighting effects as standard equipment, it was mostly done as an "optional extra."**

**Style 157 Duplex Orchestral Organ. This large organ uses the type 165 roll. First shipped in 1922, Style 157 organs were produced until the late 1920's. The factory shipping list appears in the introduction to this section.**

# *No. 157—Duplex Orchestral Organ*
## *61 Keys*

**For Dance Pavilions, Carouselles and other Open-Air Amusements**

Built in Oak Veneered Case, natural finish.

Beautiful white enameled front, elaborately carved and decorated with gold leaf and colors. Panels and screen over swell shutters beautifully decorated with realistic landscapes. To further set off the organ, the decorative front is wired for thirty-four 16 C. P. lamps, with an additional red lamp in each drum. These lights are usually furnished in red, white and blue colors, and the organ makes a wonderful display at night.

**Equipped with Duplex Tracker Frame to Play same Rolls as Style 165 Organ**

### INSTRUMENTATION

BASS—6 Wood Trombones; 6 Stopped Diapason Pipes; 6 Stopped Octave Diapason Pipes.

ACCOMPANIMENTS—10 Stopped Flute Pipes; 10 Open Flute Pipes; 10 Open Piccolo Pipes.

MELODY—44 Violin Pipes; 22 Octave Violin Pipes; 22 Piccolo Pipes; 22 Open Flute Pipes; 22 Stopped Flute Pipes; 16 Bell Bars.

TRUMPETS—14 Wood Trumpets; 14 Wood Clarionets.

TRAPS—Bass Drum (automatic tension); Snare Drum; Cymbal.

AUTOMATIC STOPS—1 for Bells; 1 for Swell and Wood Trombones.

DRAW STOPS—1 for Wood Trombones; 1 for Wood Trumpets; 1 for Violins; 1 for Flutes; 1 for Piccolos.

### DIMENSIONS

HEIGHT, 8 feet 4½ inches. WIDTH, 12 feet 2 inches. DEPTH, 3 feet 10 inches. WEIGHT, packed for shipment, 1,900 lbs.

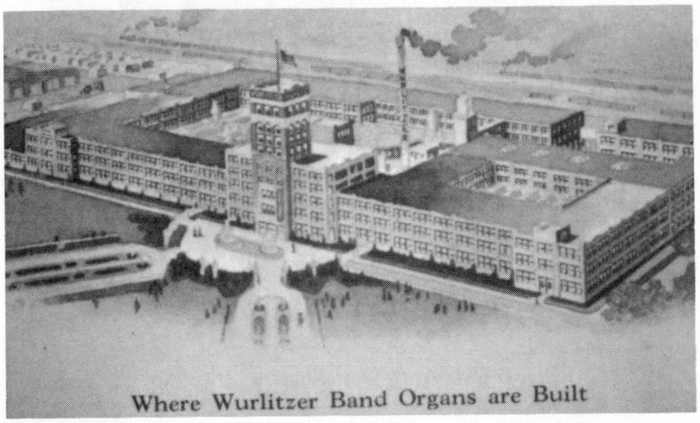


**View of the Wurlitzer factory after 1925 when the center tower and landscaped gardens were added (paid for by profits from the spectacular sales of Wurlitzer theatre organs at that time!).**

**Wurlitzer Style 165 Duplex Orchestral Organ**

Equipped with Duplex Tracker Frame.

Dimensions with front on Height 8 feet 5 inches; width 12 feet 8 inches; depth 4 feet 4 inches.

Dimensions without front Height 5 feet 10½ inches; width 6 feet 5 inches; depth 3 feet.

Weight Packed for shipment 3,000 pounds.

Automatic rewind; stops off and cut-off for drums.

Push button to rewind at any time.

## Instrumentation

Basses 6, 8-foot stopped pipes; 6, 8-foot open pipes; 6 wood trombones.

Accompaniment 10 stopped pipes; 10 open pipes.

Melody 14 wood trumpets; 14 wood bassoons; 14 wood viola pipes; 22 flute pipes; 22 piccolo pipes; 22 flageolet pipes; 22 open piccolos; 22 loud violin; 22 soft violin; 22 bells.

Traps Bass drum; cymbal; crash cymbal; triangle; snare drum; castanets.

Automatic swell shutters.

Automatic stops 1 for trombone; 1 for trumpets, 1 for bells, 1 for flute and piccolo; 1 for flageolet and open piccolo; 1 for loud violin; 1 for soft violin.

**The Style 165 is of 69-key specification. The 1928 catalogue noted that this type is ideal "for the largest type stationary carouselles, roller coasters, and other park installations. Used with great success in park dance pavilions." After 1920 the Style 165 reigned supreme as the largest generally available Wurlitzer organ (Style 180 was made only on special order). The early style pictured above has two large carved wooden figures on the front. Later models were simplified and these adornments were omitted.**

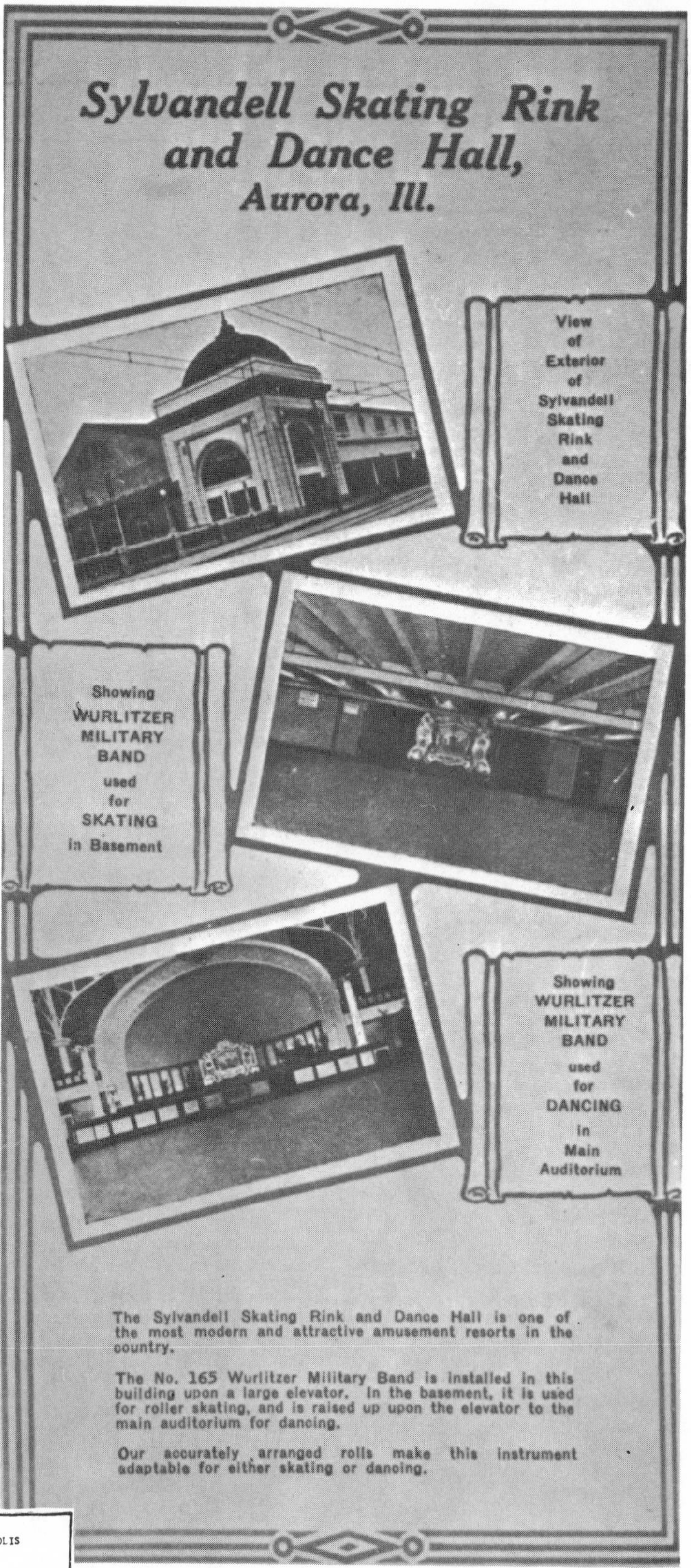

Sylvandell Skating Rink
and Dance Hall,
Aurora, Ill.
View of Exterior of Sylvandell Skating Rink and Dance Hall
Showing WURLITZER MILITARY BAND used for SKATING in Basement
Showing WURLITZER MILITARY BAND used for DANCING in Main Auditorium
The Sylvandell Skating Rink and Dance Hall is one of the most modern and attractive amusement resorts in the country.
The No. 165 Wurlitzer Military Band is installed in this building upon a large elevator. In the basement, it is used for roller skating, and is raised up upon the elevator to the main auditorium for dancing.
Our accurately arranged rolls make this instrument adaptable for either skating or dancing.


*Wurlitzer Band Organs are found Everywhere throughout the United States*

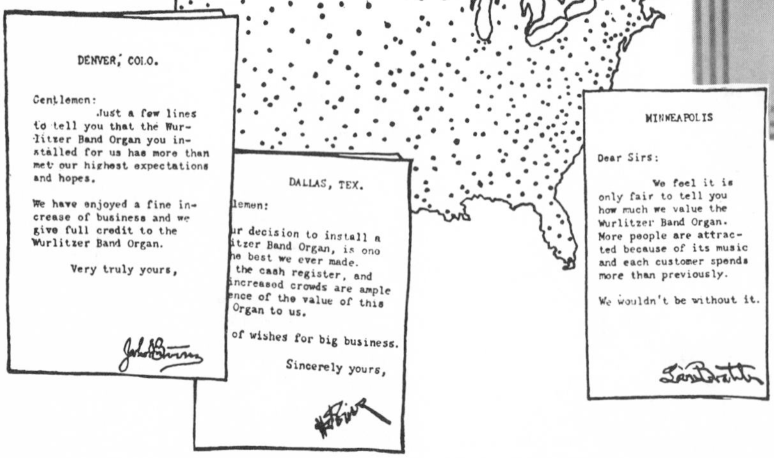


ence of the value of this

**Unlike coin pianos and orchestrions, theatre organs, and other Wurlitzer products of "the good old days," the band organs never fell from favor. Even through the 1930's and 1940's (before collectors started searching for automatic instruments intensely in the 1950's) these military band organs were actively used, bought, sold, and traded by carnival and circus people. This unwaning interest served to preserve a generous percentage of those Wurlitzer organs made since 1920.**

Style 166 Duplex Orchestral Organ

Band Organ Prices — Circa 1926. In the author's possession is a 1926 catalogue with many pencil notations as to organ prices at that time. The unknown former owner had taken the time to figure out the number of pipes in most instruments and the cost per pipe. This catalogue illustrates a Style 166 organ, although records indicate that none was shipped after 1918! 1926 prices were: Style 103, 55 pipes, $450 or about $8 per pipe; Style 104, 100 pipes, $700 or $7 per pipe; Style 105, 100 pipes, $850 or $8.50 per pipe; Style 106, 100 pipes, $950 or $9.50 per pipe; Style 125, 101 pipes, $1050 or $10½ per pipe; Style 146-A, 104 pipes, $1025 single or $1225 duplex, about $10 per pipe; Style 146-B, 106 pipes, $1150 and $1350, about $10 per pipe; Style 148, 127 pipes, $1250 or $1450, about $10 per pipe; Style 153, 154 pipes, $1900 or $12 per pipe; Style 157, 208 pipes, $2750 or $13 per pipe; Style 165, 212 pipes, $4250 or $20 per pipe; Style 166 $6500 (pipe figures not calculated); Style 180, 480 pipes, $8000 (pipe figures not given). Perhaps the former owner of the catalogue was a prospective buyer who wanted to get the "best value per pipe" and who was looking for an instrument priced less than the 166 or 180. We'll never know.

Style 166 Duplex Orchestral Organ. "Largest type duplex orchestral organ for installations where an organ more powerful than Style 165 is desired."

This beautiful and massive organ is the largest ever made to use the Style 165 roll. For years (before the 180 was introduced) this was the "top of the line" in the Wurlitzer organ series. In 1916 the Style 166 sold for $5500 (at the same time 165 sold for $3500; 163 for $2750; 153 for $1500; 150 for $1300; 148 for $1050; 147 for $700; 127 for $1000; 125 for $775; 104 for $550). It is probable that some of the Style 166 organs were imported from Gebr. Bruder of Waldkirch, Germany (who sold them under the name of "Elite Orchestra Organ — Apollo" in sizes of 65, 69, and 80 keys). Should one of our readers know of an extant Style 166 it is probable that it would be enlightening: if it was made in Germany then all of the hardware in the main chests would be with metric threads and specifications (the roll frames and certain other parts would have been made in the U.S. by Wurlitzer and would have non-metric dimensions). We made similar studies of PianOrchestras (see PianOrchestra section of this book) to determine that certain of these were made in the U.S. using some German parts. These determinations were later verified when the factory records showed that 99 PianOrchestras were made at North Tonawanda. It is probable that some of the Style 166 instruments were indeed made at North Tonawanda (see factory shipping list earlier in this section), but whether or not they had Bruder parts remains to be learned. We have seen a Style 165 with a mostly-Bruder interior.

Style 166 installed in Weinberg's Coliseum, Ice, and Roller Rink in Ann Arbor, Michigan.

## BROADWAY ROLLER RINK

1ST AVENUE AND BROADWAY, DENVER, COLORADO
*(Showing Installation of Style No. 166 Organ)*

Beautiful case similar to style No. 165 but somewhat larger. Elaborately decorated; hand-carved scroll work, finished in gold leaf, offset by light Venetian red and light green, against white enamel finish of case. Raised panels decorated with picturesque landscapes and flower designs.

Instrument equipped with Wurlitzer Duplex Tracker-frame.

Highest grade mahogany shell drums with improved self-tightening tension rods.

Automatic rewind; stops off and cut off for drums.

Push button arranged to rewind at any time.

Dimensions—Height 10 feet 4 inches. Width 17 feet 2 inches. Depth 4 feet 9 inches.

Weight packed ready for shipment, 3900 pounds.

Requires 1 H. P. motor to operate.

### Instrumentation

Basses—6, 8-foot stopped diapason pipes; 6, 8-foot open diapason pipes; 6 wood trombones; 6 brass trombones; 6, 4-foot open diapason pipes.

Accompaniment—10, 2-foot stopped flute pipes; 10, 2-foot open flute pipes; 10, 1-foot open flute pipes.

Melody—14 brass trumpets; 14 wood trumpets; 14 wood bassoons; 14 wood viola pipes; 22 flute pipes; 22 piccolo pipes; 22 flageolet pipes; 22 open piccolos; 22 loud violin; 22 soft violin; 22 prestant violin; 22 note glockenspiel; 22 uniphone bells.

Traps—Bass drum; cymbal; crash cymbal; triangle; snare drum; castanets; kettle drum.

Automatic swell shutters.

Automatic stops—1 for trombones; 1 for trumpets; 1 for bells; 1 for flute and piccolo; 1 for flageolet and open piccolo; 1 for uniphone bells; 1 for loud violin; 1 for soft violin; 1 for trombones and trumpets, brass; 1 for prestant violin; 1 for octave bass and accompaniment.

# *Style No. 180—Concert Band*

## *Style No. 180—Concert Band*

In introducing the Style 180 Organ, we have endeavored to produce an instrument that will give satisfactory results in the way of automatic band music for the largest skating rinks built.

The case design is similar to the cut shown above. The front is finished in white enamel, the hand-carved scroll-work decorated with colors and shaded bronzes. The raised panels beautifully decorated with landscapes or flower designs. The case is finished in light Golden Oak.

The instrument has the Duplex Tracker Frame, which is driven separately by a ¼ H.P. electric motor. This motor is operated by a remote control switch, so that the music can be cut off at any time without shutting off the power on the Blower line. This switch can be placed anywhere desired.

It is impossible to build Bellows strong enough to supply the wind for an instrument of this type. The suction and pressure is supplied by a specially constructed steel Blower, driven by a 3 H.P. electric motor which operates at 3,500 R.P.M.

**CASE DIMENSIONS**

HEIGHT, 7 feet 1 inch. LENGTH, 10 feet 7 inches. DEPTH, 4 feet 3½ inches.

**BASSES**

13—8-foot Stopped Diapason — 26—8-foot Open Diapason

**ACCOMPANIMENT**

26—2-foot Stopped Flutes — 26—2-foot Open Flutes

**TROMBONES**

18 Brass Trombones

**BARITONE**

18—4-foot Stopped Flutes — 18—4-foot Open Flutes

**MELODY**

30 Brass Clarionets — 30 Soft Violin Pipes
30 Violin Cello Pipes — 30 Stopped Diapason
60 Wood Violin Pipes — 30 Stopped Flutes

**FLUTES**

25 Flute Pipes — 25 Open Piccolos
25 Brass Piccolos — 25 Stopped Piccolos

**TRUMPETS**

25 Brass Trumpets

**BELLS**

30 Uniphone Bells, operating from music roll

**TRAPS**

1 Bass Drum, 12 inches x 30 inches — Cymbal
2 Snare Drums, 5 inches x 13 inches — Crash Cymbal
Chinese Block

Total number of pipes, 480
Playing notes, 88, with 36 additional notes controlled by couplers

Organ has 7 draw stops by means of which different combinations can be set to play, and the volume cut down and the tone of the organ softened, if desired.

**Wurlitzer Style 180 organ. Originally made to use special 180 rolls (at $50 each!), at least two of the five built were later converted (at the factory) to use Caliola rolls.**

**Wurlitzer Style 180 organ, serial No.4275, owned by the author for a short time during the late 1960's. This instrument uses Caliola rolls.**

# *The New Wurlitzer Caliola*

**For Amusement Parks, Rinks, Carouselles, Circus Riding Devices and Outdoor Advertising**

Just the instrument enterprising amusement interests have been looking forward to for years—something to attract the crowds—an entirely new musical instrument with a beautiful tone and remarkable volume. It plays from rolls or may be played by hand, creating beautiful musical effects. No class of amusement can afford to overlook this opportunity, as it is ideal for Circuses, Parks, Rinks, Riding Devices—in fact every amusement. As an outdoor advertising feature for Truck, Show Wagon or Ballyhoo Platform, there is no other instrument comparable to this New Wurlitzer Caliola.

**INSTRUMENTATION**

44-note Flute Pipes, either Wood or Brass. Equipped with or without Keyboard Plays ten-tune 65-note, Automatic Player Piano Roll. Operated by ¼ H. P. Electric motor or 1½ H. P. Gas Engine. Worm Drive Countershaft attached to case. Equipped with loud or soft volume control. Instrument can be furnished with Bass and Snare Drums at an additional charge.

**SPECIFICATIONS**

HEIGHT TO TOP OF SCROLL, 5 feet, 4 inches. HEIGHT WITHOUT SCROLL, 4 feet, 8 inches. WIDTH, 3 feet, 7½ inches. DEPTH, 2 feet, 10 inches. WEIGHT, 435 lbs., with countershaft and drive wheel.

FINISH—Red or Green Crackle Lacquer with carvings in Gold. Hand Painted Picture on Panel and Screens.

**Caliola: First shipped in 1928 the Caliola was Wurlitzer's answer to the calliopes being sold in large numbers by Tangley and National. The Caliola uses 65-Note Player Piano rolls with special Caliola (organ-type) arrangements. Varieties include: (1) Without drums (usually) or with; (2) with wooden (usually) or brass pipes; (3) Without keyboard (usually) or with. 62 Caliolas were built.**

# DICTIONARY
## —of—
# AUTOMATIC MUSICAL INSTRUMENT TERMS

# DICTIONARY
## —of—
# AUTOMATIC MUSICAL INSTRUMENT TERMS

*Introductory Notes*

*The terms are defined as per their usage today in the field of automatic musical instruments. Pipe definitions given are those used by collectors of orchestrions, fairground organs, etc. and differ in some instances from church organ nomenclature. Foreign-language terms, musical and non-musical, are given when such terms are regularly found in original literature or on the instruments themselves. Trade names are not listed (except as explanatory notes). Refer to the Index for trade names, manufacturers' names, etc.*

*The author thanks Claes O. Friberg, Larry Givens, Terry Hathaway, and Harvey Roehl for assistance with the following compilation.*

## A

**accompaniment.** 1. The part of a musical arrangement which accompanies or which is attendant upon the principal melody or theme. 2. (various automatic instruments) Extra instruments which accompany the featured instrument; e.g., a music box with drum and bells accompaniment; a piano with accompaniment of a rank of violin pipes.

**accordion.** [German = Accordeon]. Vacuum- or pressure-operated instrument which uses free metal reeds. Early models have buttons or valves for operation. 20th century models, sometimes called piano accordions, have piano-type keyboards for the right hand. Power is supplied by alternately pulling apart and pushing together the ends of the instrument. Roll-operated accordions with non-functional (but realistic-appearing) keyboards were made by Hohner, Seybold, et al. Accordions, powered by vacuum or pressure pumps, are found on dance organs (mainly).

**accordion bellows.** (or accordion pneumatics). A series of vacuum-operated (usually) bellows mounted atop each other. Variations in intensity levels (reproducing pianos), tempo settings (remotely-operated devices; e.g., the Concertola and certain Hupfeld theatre instruments), swell shutters (organs and orchestrions) can be achieved by collapsing the accordion bellows in sequence or by collapsing just one or several of the group. Often each individual bellows opens for a different distance or spacing. If, for instance, a series of bellows (e.g., in a Duo-Art) in an accordion bellows system can collapse 1/16," 1/8," 1/4," and 1/2," then any desired movement from 1/16" to 15/16" is possible by using one, two, three, or all four bellows.

**accumulator.** Stepping device used in an electric piano to tally the number of coins deposited in the slot.

**aeolian harp.** Ancient "automatic" musical instrument. Wind, directed by a funnel, blows on a series of stretched strings and produces a "singing" tone.

**aeoline.** String-toned pipes, usually made of wood and of 4' to 8' in length, used in certain large orchestrions (e.g., Hupfeld).

**aerophone.** An automatic instrument in which sound is produced by the vibration of air in a closed pipe. (cf. "Automatic Musical Instruments" by Dr. Alexander Buchner. Automatic instruments, called "automatophonic" by Dr. Buchner, are divided into three main categories: aerophones, chordophons, and idiophones. These terms are not in general use by automatic musical instrument historians today.)

**air motor.** Pressure- or vacuum-operated (usually) motor used to drive a music roll or (rarely) other devices such as pinned cylinders (for light-changing effects, bird whistles, etc.). Also called wind motor or vacuum motor (when vacuum-operated).

**Aladdin's lamp.** Rarely-used synonym for wonder light, or rotating jeweled light used to embellish orchestrions and organs (mainly c.1900-1920).

**android.** Mechanical figure, usually human in appearance; an automaton.

**arranged roll.** Music roll laid out or designed on a composing table, as opposed to a hand-played or directly-recorded roll. Also called a designed roll.

**arrangement.** 1. Translation of a musical composition for use on an automatic musical instrument. Some classical composers (e.g., Beethoven, Haydn) composed or arranged music specifically for automatic instruments. 2. A particular style of music layout on a roll, such as an organ arrangement for piano (with a series of successive holes which cause the piano hammers to repeat a note, thus "sustaining" it as in an organ), a solo arrangement, etc.

**art style.** Term used to describe cases or cabinets of pianos, orchestrions, etc. built in rococo, Louis XIV, XV, XVI, Renaissance, or other distinctive furniture styles. Such art-style instruments were usually sold for premium prices.

**artist's roll.** Usually used in the plural (artists' rolls; in German, Künstlerrollen) to describe rolls hand-played by prominent pianists. Such rolls incorporate expression effects and were used on reproducing pianos.

**autochange.** [mainly British usage]. Adjective used to describe an automatic disc-changing music box, such as an autochange Polyphon (or Polyphon autochanger).

**Automat** [German]. Coin-operated automatic musical instrument, especially a disc-type music box.

**automatic.** An automatic musical instrument; term used by certain manufacturers (e.g., Nelson-Wiggen Piano Co.) to describe coin pianos, orchestrions, and other instruments.

**automatic disc changer.** In a disc-type music box, a device which stores a quantity of discs (usually 10 or 12) and which plays them automatically, either in sequence or by manual selection. In its most common form (as used by most Polyphon, Regina, and Symphonion disc-changing instruments) the changer device stores the discs vertically in a holder resembling a toast rack. Each disc is lifted from the rack, played on the music comb assembly, and then returned to the rack. Also called disc-changer, disc-changing music box, automatic (as in original advertising: "Regina Automatic"), etc. Synonym: autochange box [mainly British usage].

**automatic musical instrument.** A musical instrument which plays a musical composition programmed on a pinned cylinder, disc, music roll, or other device, and which (usually) requires no musical knowledge on the part of the operator. A self-playing or mechanical musical instrument. The term "automatic" was originally used to describe all types of self-playing instruments. Although the term "mechanical" is often used synonymously today, "mechanical" was not generally used originally to describe instruments with sophisticated expression capabilities (e.g., certain large orchestrions, player pipe organs, reproducing pianos). Motive power for an automatic musical instrument may be provided by spring-wound clockwork, by an electric motor, by a weight-driven system, by foot-pumping, by turning a hand crank, or by other means.

**automatic roll changer.** Ferris-wheel type device (usually) which stores 2 to 12 perforated paper rolls and changes them automatically, usually in the sequence in which they are placed on the changer mechanism (or, if desired, a particular roll can be selected). Synonyms for automatic roll changers of this type: magazine system, revolver system. Several other variations occur, including a device made by Philipps which incorporates extra roll-holding sections (usually a total of 12) which hang below the basic revolver-type mechanism; and a 10-roll cartridge-type changer unit, called a "10-roll magazine" by Popper & Co., but constructed on different principles from those used in standard revolver- or magazine-type mechanisms. (Refer also to kipp mechanism for information about a 2-roll changer-type device.)

**automaton.** (Plural: automata). 1. A mechanically-operated doll or other small figure, usually resembling a person or (especially c.1880-1920) a monkey; an android. A mechanically-operated model; a sailing ship, an animal, a landscape with moving objects, etc. Automata are often provided with musical movements, usually of the

Typical **band organ** or **fairground organ** of the 1910 era. (Made by Gebr. Bruder of Waldkirch and sold worldwide.)

**Barrel orchestrions** of the 1900-1910 decade. The musical program is arranged on a pinned wooden **barrel.**

**Barrel organ** of the early 1900's. This loudly-voiced instrument, an organ intended for outdoor use, was made by John Cocchi of Berlin.

Barrel-operated harmonium, an instrument sometimes referred to as a meloton, of the 1900-1910 era. Many different types of barrel-operated instruments were made during the 19th and early 20th centuries.

**Bell box** made by Baker-Troll of Geneva. Note the ten **saucer bells** (refer to bell definition 1b).

cylinder type. 2. Any automatic musical instrument, especially a coin-operated one.

**automatophonic.** Adjective describing an automatic musical instrument. (Refer to "aerophone" definition earlier for explanation.)

**autophone.** 19th century term for a self-playing instrument, esp. a piano or organ. Later used as a trademark by the Autophone Co. of Ithaca, N.Y. (Autophone organette) and others.

## B

**band organ.** [mainly American usage]. Loudly-voiced self-contained organ designed for skating rink or outdoor use. Models with brass trumpets and trombones are called military band organs. Synonyms: fairground organ, fair organ, carousel organ.

**bandmaster.** Automaton figure in the form of a band leader or orchestra conductor. Used on the fronts of certain European fairground organs.

**banjo.** 1. Stringed instrument with the sound bridge mounted on a soundboard made of stretched skin. The Encore Banjo (circa 1900) is the only automatically-played banjo ever made commercially. 2. Banjo attachment: a damper made of parchment, paper, or thin metal. Used in a music box to provide a fanciful banjo-like tone. 3. A series of metal studs, wood strips, or similar material placed between the piano hammers and strings to produce a mandolin-like sound. Synonyms: harp, mandolin, zither effect.

**baritone.** 1. Organ pipe register sounding together two ranks: a rank of saxophone-type pipes and a rank of open flute pipes. 2. Large (4' to 8') softly-voiced reed pipe which produces a humming, nasal sound (also spelled as barytone).

**barrel.** Pinned cylinder, usually of wood, on which a musical composition is programmed for use in an organ, orchestrion, or piano. [Walze = barrel in German; hence Walzenorgel and Walzenorchestrion for barrel organ and barrel orchestrion.] 2. Housing for a coil spring, such as the spring barrel in a music box.

**barrel orchestrion.** An orchestrion with the musical arrangements on pinned barrels or cylinders, usually of wood. Popular during the 19th century. Manufactured mainly in the Black Forest area of Germany.

**barrel organ.** A loudly-voiced organ operated by a pinned wooden cylinder. Made for outdoor use.

**barrel piano.** Piano, usually without keyboard, operated by a pinned wooden cylinder. Those used in streets are called street pianos or hurdy-gurdies (the latter being an incorrect usage from a historical viewpoint).

**basement pump.** Remotely-located (usually in a basement or behind a partition) vacuum pump used to operate an automatic musical instrument, especially a reproducing piano. The basement pump term was originally used in connection with Duo-Art and Welte instruments.

**bass.** 1. The lower range of a musical scale (treble is the upper range). 2. General term (sometimes used in organ and orchestrion advertising) for pipes in the bass note range.

**bass drum.** Large (usually 14" diameter or more) drum, cylindrical in shape and with a head on each side. Found in many types of automatic instruments, especially fairground organs, dance organs, and orchestrions. Usually struck by a single large beater. Some have two additional smaller beaters which, when operated alternately, produce an imitation tympani or kettle drum effect (e.g., orchestrions made by Nelson-Wiggen and Seeburg). A few orchestrions have an additional small felt-padded striker which operates in a reiterating manner to produce a bass drum roll effect (e.g., large Weber orchestrions). The term "bass drum" is sometimes used to describe any drum (except a snare drum) or the larger of two small drums, even though the larger may really be a tenor drum. Such usage is found in descriptions of disc-operated pianos. (A small drum without snares is properly described as a tenor drum.)

**bass flute pipe.** Term sometimes used to describe the bourdon pipe, to which refer.

**bassoon pipe** (called orchestral bassoon in pipe organ literature). A reed pipe, imitative of the bassoon sound, sometimes found as the bass octave of a clarinet or oboe rank. Used in certain photoplayers and large orchestrions.

**baxophone.** Pipe rank, voiced somewhat like a saxophone, distinguished by having a large circular aperture at the center front of each pipe. Usually placed behind the xylophone on a dance organ. Invented by Guilliaume Bax of the factory of Th. Mortier in Antwerp, Belgium.

**beater.** Striking stick or metal rod used to sound a percussion instrument such as a drum, cymbal, bell, etc.

**Becken.** [German]. Cymbal.

**bedplate.** Metal plate or foundation, usually of brass (early instruments) or cast iron, used to support the music combs and attendant mechanisms of a disc-type or cylinder music box. Certain disc-type music boxes made c.1900-1910 (esp. by Regina) are designated as short bedplate boxes. The bedplates of these boxes, shorter than those found on earlier instruments, allow a greater percentage of the tonal vibrations to be transmitted to the music box case (as the bedplate is smaller, and less metal mass has to be set in vibration); hence a louder tone is produced. Certain early cylinder-type music boxes (esp. pre-1870 boxes of the overture type) have bedplates made of polished brass and are designated as brass bedplate boxes.

**bell(s).** 1. Usually used in the plural form to describe small percussion effects made of rigid metal and tuned to specific notes. The following types are found in automatic instruments: 1a. Bar bells, made of rectangular bars of metal (usually steel, rarely brass), and used as an accompaniment (or sometimes as a solo section) in a disc-type music box, orchestrion, fairground organ, and other large instruments. Usually arranged in a set of 12 to 24 (1 to 2 octaves). Also called orchestra bells or glockenspiel (in pipe organs). 1b. Saucer bells: cup-shaped (as in a telephone bell) bells, usually found in sets of 3 to 16 units, used (mainly) as an accompaniment in cylinder and disc music boxes of the late 19th century. Saucer bells have a higher harmonic content (more overtones) than bar-type bells and cannot be tuned easily to a specific note. Usually made of brass or steel. 1c. Tubular bells (or chimes): tuned steel (usually) or brass cylinder or pipe. Small tubular bells are found in certain disc-type music boxes (e.g., Lochmann "Original") and in disc-operated pianos. These are usually mounted horizontally, are arranged in a set of 12 or more, and are struck (usually by a small metal striker) at the center of the bell. Large tubular bells, usually called chimes, are hung vertically from cords and are struck near the top of the bell by a small hammer. Large tubular bells are found in hall clocks (usually of limited 4-note scale) and in photoplayers and pipe organs (usually a set of 12 or more). 2. Term used to describe the metal horn or resonator part of a reed pipe, usually a trumpet or trombone.

**bell box.** 1. Cylinder-type music box, usually of Swiss manufacture, usually containing from 3 to 16 tuned saucer bells in addition to the music comb(s). 2. Rare type of cylinder music box containing saucer bells only (without a music comb).

**bellows.** Two hinged boards or pallets, covered with airtight rubberized cloth or leather, which, when quickly collapsed by the introduction of vacuum or when quickly expanded by the introduction of air, cause a mechanism (such as a piano hammer, drum beater, etc.) to operate. Small bellows are usually called "pneumatics" [mainly American usage]. The bellows term also describes the leather-covered (usually) hinged sections of a vacuum or pressure supply pump used to operate an automatic instrument. (See accordion bellows for the description of another type.)

**bird box.** 1. Tiny bird automaton usually encased in a metal box. The box lid springs open, the tiny bird moves its wings and head, and a bird-whistle sound is provided by a bellows-operated flute within the box. 2. Cylinder music box with a tiny bird automaton built into the front of or otherwise attached to the music mechanism. The bird chirps as the music plays. Usually called "pièce à oiseau."

**Bird organ** of the disc-operated type. Illustration from a catalogue of 1903. This type is unusual; most bird organs use pinned wooden cylinders.

**Calliope** made in the 1920's by the National Calliope Corporation. Such instruments were once very popular, particularly in America.

CECILIAN
FARRAND ORGAN COMPANY
DETROIT, MICH.

Menzenhauer & Schmidt
„Favorite"

**Cabinet players**, or push-up piano players, of the early 1900's.

This Great Line Has Many Exclusive Features Including the Wonderful
SELECTRA
Which Enables You to Select Tunes at Will from the 10-Tune Standard Music Rolls
The Finest
Is Highest Quality and Sells at a Sensible Price
Get the Agency and make sure of a busy 1925.
WESTERN ELECTRIC PIANO CO.
429 West Superior St.
CHICAGO

**Cabinet style** coin pianos of the 1920's made by the Western Electric Piano Co. Of vertical format and without keyboard.

**bird organ.** Small hand-cranked organ containing a limited number (usually 7 to 14) of flute pipes. Originally used to teach canaries to sing. Later used (c.1880-1915) as a children's toy. Usually the music is arranged on a pinned wooden cylinder. Certain later novelty models use discs. Synonyms: canary organ, serinette.

**bird whistle.** Novelty effect used in certain orchestrions and photoplayers. Consists of a small metal flute pipe with the open end submersed in a liquid (usually a slowly-evaporating liquid such as glycerin [glycerol] or mineral oil). When the flute is blown a very realistic warbling bird call results. Tonal variations are obtained by varying the pressure or (usually) by intermittently blowing the pipe.

**bleed.** A restrictive orifice which allows air to be equalized (to return to its neutral position, so as to permit another operation to be performed) in tracker bar channels. (Note: if the bleeds become dust-clogged, the air equalizes slowly and the pneumatic actions will perform sluggishly; the importance of clean bleeds is often overlooked by collectors.)

**blower.** Circular fan, usually electrically-driven at high speed, which provides wind pressure (or a combination of wind and vacuum via two ports, one at the intake and one at the exhaust) for a large photoplayer or organ. Usually located at a distance and connected to the instrument by large-diameter tubing. Most used on U.S. instruments were made by the Kinetic Engineering Co. or the Spencer Turbine Co.

**book music.** Long strip of stiff cardboard folded zig-zag fashion into a compact pile or "book." Music is scored lengthwise on the book by rectangular (usually) perforations. Book music is usually played on a key frame (to which refer). [In French, books are called cartons.] Synonym: cardboard music.

**bourdon pipe.** Stopped-end flute pipe, usually of 4' to 8' in length, used to provide bass foundation tone in large orchestrions and organs. Sometimes called bass flute.

**box pump.** Pump made by arranging 3 or 4 (usually) bellows around a common central drive shaft. The bellows operate in sequence to provide an even vacuum or pressure supply. Usually called a rotary pump. Used in coin pianos, orchestrions, and reproducing pianos, esp. c.1910-1930.

**breveté.** [French]. Patented. Included here as the term is often found on the fronts of large organs, esp. Gavioli, Limonaire, and Mortier. Also sometimes appears as "Brevet SGDG" which means "patent without guarantee by the government" (sans garantie du gouvernement). Many people regard a patent as implying some type of official approval or guarantee of performance ("patent medicines" were sometimes regarded as having been tested and approved by the government, for instance), and the French were careful to make it clear that this was not the case.

**cabinet player.** Push-up piano player of the type popular c.1900.

**cabinet style.** Term used to describe an instrument, usually a piano or organ, of upright or vertical format and without keyboard.

**cafe organ.** Dance organ (to which refer).

**calliope.** Instrument with stopped flute-type metal (usually) pipes voiced on high pressure and intended for outdoor use. Barrel-operated or roll-operated (e.g., Tangley Calliaphone). Steam calliopes, made mainly during the 19th century, used steam to blow the pipes. Most 20th century calliopes are air-operated (via a pump or blower) and are properly called air calliopes. Calliopes were mainly used in America.

**cardboard music.** Book music (to which refer).

**carillon.** 1. Set of bells, usually of 3 to 4 octaves in range, played from a keyboard or by a pinned cylinder or other automatic device. Used mainly in clock and church towers. 2. Rank of small, thin, open metal pipes, usually brightly-voiced, mainly used in dance organs.

**carousel organ.** Fairground organ used on a carousel or merry-go-round. Synonyms: band organ, fairground organ, military band organ.

**cartel box.** Describes small or medium-size cylinder music boxes made during the late 19th century by Bremond, Mermod, Paillard, and others with factory-type assembly facilities (as opposed to the hand-crafted boxes made in the small workshops of earlier decades). [Term mainly used today by collectors in Europe.]

**castanets.** 1. Small cup-shaped clappers made of Bakelite, hardwood, or other substance. Sound is produced by striking the clappers against each other or against a mounting board. Used to accent rhythm in dance organs and orchestrions. 2. In cylinder music boxes, an effect made by metal strikers hitting a wood block or wood drum.

**cecilian.** Term used to describe home-type piano players and player pianos c.1900-1910. From Cecilian, a trademark used by Farrand and by Bush & Lane to designate instruments made by those firms.

**celeste.** 1. Tuning method in which two or more ranks of pipes (or two music combs), usually in the treble part of the scale, are purposely tuned slightly apart in pitch from each other. When the ranks are sounded together, the result is an undulating or beating sound which adds dimension and richness to the tone. 2. Any rank of pipes, usually of the flue type, which is tuned slightly different from and which is intended for use with (never for use solo) another rank. Often called vox celeste (celeste voice).

**cello.** 1. Stringed instrument of the violin family, but larger in scale and deeper in pitch. Properly, violoncello. Cello, originally written as 'cello, is a contraction. Automatically-played cellos were used in the Mills Viol-Cello and the Mills String Quartette. 2. String-toned pipe constructed in the manner of a violin pipe (usually with frein or harmonic brake), but of deeper tone than a violin pipe. Often (e.g., in Popper & Co. descriptions) a single rank of violin-type pipes is described as having violin (highest treble section), viola, violoncello, and cello (lowest bass section) pipes, although, as noted, violoncello and cello are synonymous from a strict usage viewpoint. 3. An effect made by causing tuned strings to vibrate by rubbing them with a rosined roller (cf. hurdy gurdy) or by activating them by using electromagnets.

**center drive.** Describes a common method for turning music box discs, esp. those of smaller (under 15") diameters. Fixed near the center spindle are one or more pegs which rotate with the center spindle and which engage corresponding holes near the center hole of the music disc, thus causing the disc to turn as the center spindle rotates. (Refer to edge-drive for another type of disc drive.)

**chain perforations.** Closely-spaced (separated by narrow paper "bridges") perforations in a music roll. Instead of a long open perforation, the chain perforation is used to give added strength to the paper and to minimize tearing. The bridges are very small and do not interrupt the flow of air in the tracker bar hole. The result is a continuously-sounding or sustained note.

**chime(s).** Usually used in plural form. Usually a type of tubular bell (see definition 1c under "bells" preceding). Term sometimes used (esp. in musical clocks) to describe small bar-type bells.

**chimney flute pipe.** Half-stopped flute pipe with a tubular "chimney" at the top. The jazz flute is a type of chimney flute. Synonym (in pipe organ terminology): rohrflute.

**Chinese block.** Wood block (to which refer).

**Chinese cymbal.** Crash cymbal (to which refer).

**chordophon.** General category of automatic musical instruments consisting of stringed instruments which are automatically hit by hammers, bowed, strummed, etc. Term used by historian Dr. Alexander Buchner (refer to definition of aerophone for more information). Term not generally used by collectors today. Note: Do not confuse with the Chordephon, a patented name for a variety of disc-played zither.

**Combs** on a cylinder music box. To the left is an **organ comb** used to actuate a small reed organ. To the right is a regular **music comb** consisting of tuned metal teeth.

**Cornettino** made by John Cocchi of Berlin, circa 1903. This type of portable hand-cranked barrel organ features cornet-type pipes on the front.

**Coin piano** in an especially ornate case, as shown in a faded photograph taken circa 1910 in the factory of J.D. Philipps & Sons (Frankfurt-am-Main, Germany).

**Coin piano** sold under the Empress Electric name by Lyon & Healy, Chicago musical instrument retailers. This interior view reveals some of the mechanisms, including the pump (left), the roll frame (right), and the coin chute (far right).

Player **concertinas** of the Tanzbär brand. Operation is by means of a perforated paper roll located at the right end of the instrument. Made in Germany, Tanzbärs were sold all over the world.

**chrysoglott.** Literally, "golden voice." A series of tuned metal bars which are struck by felt piano-like hammers. Behind each bar is a tubular resonator which gives a mellow, lingering tonal quality to the music. The Resotone Grand is an automatically-operated chrysoglott. Chrysoglotts are popular additions to large pipe organs.

**church organ.** Pipe organ (usually), voiced on low pressure, used in churches. Similar in tonal construction to a residence organ (as opposed to the theatre organ, a loudly-voiced instrument built to imitate an orchestra). Roll players were installed on church organs built by Aeolian, Welte, and others.

**Circassian walnut.** Walnut wood, usually with light mottling or veining, used for disc-type music box and coin piano cases, esp. c.1895-1925.

**clarinet pipe.** Softly-voiced mellow reed-type pipe, made with a cylindrical open resonator, used in orchestrions and photoplayers. Clarinet pipes of louder voicing are used in fairground organs.

**clarionet pipe.** 1. Brilliant-sounding reed pipe, usually with a brass resonator, used in fairground organs. 2. Term used (incorrectly) by certain orchestrion manufacturers (e.g. Wurlitzer and Philipps) to describe reed pipes of the clarinet and oboe horn types.

**clock.** Clocks or timepieces were popular attachments to music boxes, especially disc-type instruments. Musical clocks incorporating tuned chimes, organ pipes, music combs, and other devices, were made in many varieties.

**clockwork.** 1. Mechanism of a timepiece. 2. Spring-wound mechanism for powering a music box [mainly British usage].

**cob.** [Slang]. Pinned wooden cylinder, especially of small size such as that used on a Gem Roller Organ.

**coin chute.** On a coin piano the metal (usually) slide or chute leading from the coin slot to the coin-actuated starter switch and the coin box.

**coin-controlled.** Coin-operated (to which refer).

**coin detector.** Coin chute which stores the last several (usually 3 to 6) coins deposited and displays them behind a glass panel. In this way the use of a slug or counterfeit can be detected. Used in most types of slot machines (gambling devices) and in coin pianos made by DeKleist (early Wurlitzer), North Tonawanda Musical Instrument Works, and others.

**coin-freed.** Coin-operated [mainly British usage], esp. a device in which a coin actuates a mechanical linkage (which then actuates a music mechanism).

**coin-operated.** Describes an automatic musical instrument which plays when a coin is deposited in its coin slot or wallbox.

**coin piano.** Coin-operated piano, esp. an electric coin-operated piano. Synonym: nickelodeon [modern usage; refer to nickelodeon definition].

**comb.** 1. A series of tuned metal teeth arranged in a musical scale, a music comb. Used in disc-type and cylinder music boxes. 2. A series of levers, operated by a pinned cylinder or by star wheels, used to actuate other effects in a disc-type or cylinder-type box. (e.g., an organ comb actuates the reed organ accompaniment in a cylinder box; a bell comb, the bells in a music box.)

**compass.** Range of musical notes or playing scale. (e.g., the xylophone in a Philipps Pianella has a compass of 30 notes.)

**concertina.** Small accordion-like hand-held reed instrument operated in the manner of an accordion. Often of rectangular or hexagonal shape when viewed from an end. Automatically-operated concertinas include the Tanzbär (roll-operated) and the Bandoniphon (disc-operated).

**console.** 1. Key desk or keyboard unit of a pipe organ. Contains one or more keyboards (manuals), control stops, and other devices for operating the organ. 2. Center or piano section of a theatre photoplayer or pit organ.

**control lever(s).** Levers on the front of a player, expression, or reproducing piano which permit individual interpretation of a piano roll by the operator of the instrument. Expression effects such as pedaling can be operated in this manner. Used most often on player pianos, for expression and reproducing pianos have expression effects already provided in the roll (however, these effects can be overridden by control levers on some instruments). Term also applies to manually-set levers used to control functions such as reroll (in a player piano), tempo, etc.

**cor anglais pipe.** (English horn). A brilliantly-voiced reed pipe used in certain fairground organs and (in a larger-scale version) in theatre pipe organs.

**cornet pipe.** In fairground organs, a reed pipe similar in sound to but voiced slightly louder than a clarinet pipe.

**cornettino.** Late 19th century type of portable hand-cranked barrel organ featuring cornet-type pipes. Made by Gavioli, Limonaire, Cocchi, et al.

**coupled.** Describes two or more piano hammers or other sounding devices which are connected to play from the same hole in the music roll (or key in a key frame, etc.). In many coin pianos and orchestrions the bass piano notes are coupled for an additional octave (or more or less) to permit a better foundation of tone than would otherwise be possible from a 65-note music roll, for example.

**coupler.** Device, especially in a photoplayer or pipe organ, which permits the operator (or a music roll) to couple and uncouple at will additional sections of the instrument. Specific couplers are called bass couplers, sub-bass couplers, octave couplers, etc. in pipe organs.

**crash cymbal.** Large-size cymbal (to which refer), usually with a bent-over rim or lip and often (esp. in modern dance organs) studded with metal grommets to provide additional harmonics. Struck with great force by a wooden or felt-padded beater. Synonym: Chinese cymbal.

**crescendo.** The gradual increasing in loudness of the volume or intensity of music. Antonym: decrescendo: the gradual decreasing of volume or intensity of music.

**crescendo pedal.** On a photoplayer or organ, a pedal which, when depressed, will bring into play one-by-one all (or nearly all) of the ranks of the instrument. Synonym: sforzando pedal, (rarely) full-organ pedal.

**crescendo shutters.** Louvered swell shades or shutters which, when opened, increase the volume of music. Found on most types of large orchestrions, photoplayers, and organs. Synonyms: swell shutters, swell shades [American usage], expression shutters. Swell shutters is the term used most often by collectors today.

**cuff.** [Collector's term used today]. Descriptive of the sleeve-shaped truncated metal cone used on the Capital "cuff" boxes (made by F.G. Otto & Sons).

**cylinder.** 1. Barrel, usually of wood or metal, on which music is pinned. Examples: Metal wax- or cement-filled cylinders used in cylinder-type music boxes. Individual notes are represented by protruding metal pins. 2. Wooden cylinders used in barrel pianos, orchestrions, and organs. Individual notes are represented by protruding metal pins or staple-like bridges. 3. Wax or composition hollow sleeve used on early phonographs. The sound is recorded by grooves helically arranged on the cylinder. Usually of 2- or 4-minute playing length.

**cylinder music box.** Music box, usually containing one or more tuned metal music combs, having the music programmed on a pinned metal (usually of brass) cylinder. Popular during the 19th century. One of two main music box types (the other: the disc-type box).

**cymbal.** Plate-shaped metal disc, usually slightly concave, made of brass (stamped from a brass sheet, spun on a lathe, or wire-wound). Usually from 10" to 16" in diameter, although smaller cymbals are found on cylinder-type music boxes and on disc-operated pianos. Large cymbals are usually called crash cymbals or Chinese cymbals. Small- and medium-size cymbals are struck by wooden (usually) or metal beaters; large ones, by wood or by felt-padded beaters. A popular device for accenting the rhythm in a music box, orchestrion, or organ.

Piano-Orgel von Popper & Co. in Leipzig.

Modell 4.

**Display pipes.**

**Display pipes,** or non-functional pipes used for artistic purposes, add to the attractiveness of these organs. At the upper left is a piano-organ made in 1910 by Popper & Co.; upper right, a Model 4 Salon Organ made in 1911 by M. Welte & Söhne of Freiburg, Germany (similar instruments were also assembled in Welte's American factory); below, an immense player organ made by the Wirsching Organ Co. (of Salem, Ohio) in 1908 for the Maharajah of Mysore, India.

Orgel für den Palast des Maharajah von Mysore.
Erbaut von der Wirsching Organ Co. in Salem (Ohio).

**Electric lighting effects** galore are visible on the front of this ornate Philipps "Peacock" orchestrion. Two rotating "wonder lights," a peacock with a rotating illuminated tail, and other electric effects give the orchestrion a dazzling appearance. (Arthur Bronson collection)

**Disc music boxes** were extremely popular during the 1890's and early 1900's. These use interchangeable metal discs (a Mira disc made by Mermod Frères is shown above). At the left is artist Herb Mott's representation of a Regina disc-type music box in use in an ice cream parlor around the turn of the century. (Illustration courtesy of New Jersey Bell Telephone Co.)

**cymbal effect (or stop).** In some player reed organs a series of tuned saucer bells.

**Cymbalstern.** [German origin]. In cylinder music boxes a group of bells and jingles arranged on a small conical "tree." When shaken, a mellow cymbal-like sound results.

# D

**damper(s).** 1. In a cylinder music box a small piece of wire or bird feather (quill damper) which brushes against a tooth in a music comb and dampens or mutes its vibration before it is plucked again. 2. In a disc music box, a series of metal clips (set of dampers) which mute the vibration of the music comb teeth after they are plucked. 3. In a piano, a felt pad which mutes the string after it has been sounded. Controlled by the sustaining pedal; when the sustaining pedal is "on," the dampers are lifted and the notes are sustained. 4. Any device which mutes or dampens the sound of a percussion instrument. Dampers are used on bells, drums, and certain other effects in large orchestrions and organs.

**dance organ.** Self-contained player pipe organ, usually with an ornate facade, used in dance halls, cafes, and other locations, esp. in Belgium and Holland. Softly voiced (in comparison to fairground organs). Distinguished by the strongly accented rhythm of their music; the short and powerful chords of the heavy and deep-sounding registers maintain the dance rhythm. Usually of large size (8' to 20' or more in width) and fitted with a key frame system for playing cardboard music books. Later models (since c.1930) have novelty percussions, accordions, and other devices prominently displayed on the facades. Made by Bursens, Decap, Mortier, and others. Some modern (since c.1960) models use electronic tone generators instead of organ pipes. Synonym: cafe organ.

**declanche.** [French]. General cancel stop on an organ; turns all registers off.

**designed roll.** Music roll laid out or designed on a composing table, as opposed to a hand-played or directly-recorded roll. Also called an arranged roll.

**diapason.** Large-scale basic or foundation pipe rank in a residence or church organ. Not a solo rank, the diapason is used in combination with other ranks to provide a full and rich tone – the characteristic tone of an organ of this type.

**diaphone.** A basic or foundation (not solo) pipe invented by Robert Hope-Jones. The tone is generated by supplying wind to the pipe in intermittent bursts or puffs, the frequency of which determines the pitch of the pipe. Unlike most types of organ pipes, the volume can be varied (without altering the pitch) by increasing or decreasing the wind pressure. Used in most theatre organs and in certain early roll-operated Wurlitzer photoplayers (e.g., certain models of Wurlitzer's Style L). Synonym: thunder pedal [slang].

**disc.** Circular sheet of metal (for use on most types of disc music boxes), cardboard (for use on certain organette types), or composition cardboard-metal (for certain organettes) on which a musical program is arranged – by perforations or by projections extending from the underside. Almost always easily interchangeable, so that different tunes can be played on the same instrument. Also spelled as "disk." Synonyms [not in popular usage with collectors today]: record, tune sheet.

**disc music box.** (or disc-type music box). Music box on which a disc causes a music comb to be plucked by means of intervening star wheels (usually) or levers. One of two main music box types (the other: the cylinder-type box). Popular during the 1890's and early 1900's. Mfd. by Polyphon, Regina, Symphonion, and others.

**disc-operated piano** (or disc piano). Instrument in which piano strings, usually of short length (and more properly called a zither rather than a piano), are played by means of a metal disc. Mainly popular during the early 1900's. Mfd. by Lochmann, Polyphon, Symphonion, and others. An early type of disc-operated piano player of the push-up or vorsetzer type, was made by Hupfeld. This device is properly called a disc-operated piano player.

**disc-shifting music box.** Music box in which one tune is played during the first revolution of the disc, and then before the second revolution the disc spindle shifts laterally slightly and brings a new set of projections (and another tune) into play. Sirion and New Century disc-shifting boxes were made around the turn of the 20th century.

**display pipes.** On the front of an organ, non-functional pipes used for artistic reasons.

**doppel** [German]. Double. Doppelflute = a double-mouthed flute; Doppelmechanik = double mechanism.

**draaiorgel.** [Dutch]. Hand-cranked organ (usually of the barrel or cardboard music type).

**Drehorgel.** [German]. Hand-cranked barrel organ.

**driftwood finish.** Popular (c.1900-1925) brown oak finish made by filling the open wood grain with white or off-white finish. Used on coin pianos and orchestrions.

**drum and bells box.** Cylinder music box with the accompaniment of a drum and three or more saucer bells.

**dulcimer.** Small stringed instrument with strings stretched between two bridges and over a wooden sound board. Usually of small compass (about 2 octaves). Struck by small piano hammers. Mechanical dulcimers were made in several forms. Synonyms [in automatic musical instrument usage]: small barrel-operated piano, zither.

**duplex comb(s).** Two music box combs, both tuned to about the same pitch, and both played at the same time for an intended effect of extra volume. Usually mounted with one comb to each side of the same set of star wheels. Usually found in larger types of disc music boxes (usually 15" or more disc diameters). Duplex combs which are tuned in celeste (to which refer) fashion are called sublime harmonie combs. Such combs were used in cylinder- and disc-type boxes.

**duplex music box.** Music box containing two separate cylinders and two sets of music combs which play synchronously. Usually one cylinder mechanism is in front of the other.

**duplex roll mechanism.** Roll frame or spoolbox assembly in an electric piano, photoplayer, or orchestrion which accommodates two rolls, so that one roll can play while the other is rewinding. Mfd. by American Photo Player Co., Hupfeld, Marquette, Seeburg, Wurlitzer, et al. Also, duplex roll changer (two revolver mechanisms or automatic roll changers arranged side-by-side, with several rolls on each changer mechanism). Mfd. by Hupfeld and Philipps.

# E

**echo organ.** Separate pipe organ chamber placed at a distance from the regular pipe chamber(s). In automatic instruments the echo organ is used as part of the Imhof & Mukle Lord 3 orchestrions. Echo organs are commonly used with church and residence pipe organs.

**edge drive.** Type of drive used to power music box discs: 1. Gear type: the toothed edge of the metal disc meshes with a toothed drive gear (used on small movements, esp. Thorens). 2. Sprocket type: a toothed or knobbed sprocket wheel mounted underneath the disc near its outer rim engages with corresponding slots or circular holes near the outside edge of the disc (used on nearly all types of very large disc boxes).

**Einbau.** [German]. Built-in; describes a player piano or reproducing piano with the pneumatic mechanisms built into the piano case (as opposed to the vorsetzer type, to which refer).

**electric lighting effects.** Term used by coin piano and orchestrion manufacturers to denote moving-picture scenes, wonder lights, and other lighting effects available (usually at extra cost) with certain instruments.

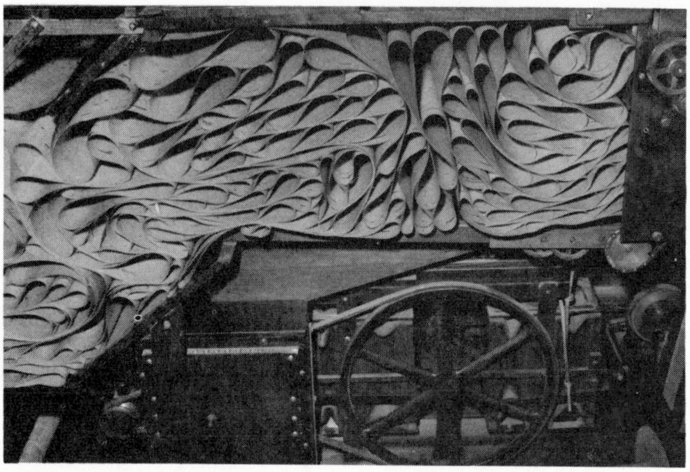

**Endless roll** systems of two pianos: at the upper left, an instrument made by the Automatic Musical Co.; directly above, a North Tonawanda Musical Instrument Works Pianolin.

Two **finials** decorate the top of this Regina music box; one finial on each side of the spooled railing.

Left: Ornate **facade** of a Philipps orchestrion, the "Castle" model, of the 1910 era.

Right: Ornate **facade** of a Gebr. Bruder fairground organ of the early 20th century.

**electric piano.** 1. Any electrically-operated piano (as opposed to a foot-pumped or hand-cranked piano). 2. Coin-operated piano, or coin piano. Term widely used by coin piano makers during the early 20th century. Synonym: nickelodeon [modern usage; refer to nickelodeon definition].

**end tab.** The end part of a piano roll, usually made of glue-backed cloth, to which an eyelet or hook is affixed for attaching the roll to the take-up spool.

**endless roll.** Roll type made by gluing the front and end of a roll together to form a continuous loop. As the roll passes over the tracker bar it is fed into a storage bin. Advantages: 1. The roll passes through the tracker bar at a constant speed, so no tempo compensation is needed from one part of the same roll to another part. 2. The mechanism is simpler as no rewind-to-play mechanisms are needed. Disadvantages: 1. Rolls take several minutes or more to change. 2. Rolls are easily damaged during the changing process. 3. A large amount of space is needed for the roll storage bin. Endless rolls were mainly popular c.1900-1910, although some manufacturers (e.g., Link, North Tonawanda Musical Instrument Works) used them in later years. Supplanted by the more popular rewind-type roll, to which refer.

**endless screw.** In a music box the spirally-cut worm gear used to drive the fan-fly or governor assembly.

**endstone.** In a music box governor assembly, the jeweled pivot which enables the governor fan to turn with a minimum of friction.

**English horn.** (cor anglais). A brilliantly-voiced reed pipe used in certain fairground organs and (in a larger-scale version sometimes called an English posthorn) in theatre pipe organs.

**equalizer.** Reservoir bellows for a vacuum or wind supply. Usually equipped with a pallet valve, the equalizer spills air or vacuum when the bellows moves beyond set limits – thus keeping the vacuum or wind supply regulated at a set level. The term is also sometimes applied to bellows without valves (such as a concussion bellows in a wind line) used to stabilize the vacuum or wind.

**escapement.** Any of several different types of mechanisms, usually incorporating a series of gears, which regulate the use of mechanical energy. (e.g., the escapement in a weight-driven orchestrion which converts the potential energy of the falling weight to drive the music barrel and the pumps).

**export packing.** Term referring to the shipping of a fairground organ, orchestrion, or other instrument in a metal-lined (and hence humidity-proof) wooden crate. Included here as the term is often found in early sales literature (e.g., Gebr. Bruder, Imhof & Mukle, Philipps, et al).

**expression.** The varying of the volume or intensity of music. This is done by operating the controls of an instrument (e.g., the pedals of a piano), by opening and closing swell or crescendo shutters, by varying the vacuum level in a piano (low vacuum = soft music; high vacuum = louder music), and by other means. An instrument is said to "have expression" if the musical performance can be varied in one of these ways. A music roll or music book may have expression cut in it to operate such controls automatically, or they may be operated by hand (e.g., as the expression shutter of an organette).

**expression piano.** An automatic piano, usually electrically-operated, which has the pedals automatically controlled and which has limited vacuum-level variations (e.g., the Recordo piano, the Seeburg Style X). Synonym: semi-reproducing piano.

**expression shutters.** crescendo shutters, to which refer.

**facade.** Front or proscenium, usually detachable. Term used mainly to describe the fronts of fairground and dance organs.

**fagott pipe.** Reed-type pipe used in certain large orchestrions. Similar to a bassoon in sound, but usually more softly voiced.

**fair organ; fairground organ.** Loudly-voiced self-contained organ designed for skating rink or outdoor use. Usually decorated with an ornate facade. Synonyms: band organ [mainly American usage], carousel organ, military band organ [describes an instrument with brass trumpets and trombones; mainly American usage].

**fan-fly.** Governor on a music box, orchestrion, or other instrument, usually weight-driven or spring-driven, which regulates the speed by means of air friction against the fanlike blades.

**feeder bellows.** Main bellows of a pump; supplies vacuum or wind pressure to an equalizer or reservoir.

**feeder motor.** Motor which drives a paper roll mechanism (term esp. used by Mills Novelty Co.).

**finial.** An ornament, a knob or other decoration affixed to an arch, gallery, or top crest of an automatic musical instrument, esp. a disc-type music box.

**flageolet pipe.** 1. In fairground organs a short cylindrical metal open flute often visibly displayed on the front of the instrument. 2. In orchestrions a short treble flute or a description of the highest one or two octaves of a flute rank.

**Flötenuhr.** [German]. Flute-playing clock or organ-playing clock, often of the long-case or "grandfather's clock" format.

**Flötenwerk.** [German]. Flute-playing automatic musical instrument, especially a medium- or large-size barrel-operated orchestrion comprised of several ranks of flute pipes. (Larger instruments with percussion effects and with other types of pipe ranks were called Orchesterwerke in early catalogues of Imhof & Mukle, Welte, et al.). [Term not in general use today.]

**flue pipes.** Pipes which produce their sound by the action of air against the edge of the pipe mouth in combination with the resonance of a column of air within an open or closed pipe. One of three basic families of pipes: (1) flue, as just described; (2) reed pipes, which produce sound by the vibrations of a free or beating reed; (3) diaphone pipes (rarely used), which produce sound by intermittent bursts of air introduced into the pipe. The flue pipe family encompasses many different popular types of pipes, including various flute and violin varieties. Flue-type pipes, unlike reed pipes, require a minimum of attention and care and will stay in tune for relatively long periods of time. For this reason flue pipes (usually violin and flute) were the main types used in smaller types of coin pianos and orchestrions.

**Flügel.** [German]. Grand piano (type with the strings arranged horizontally). German manufacturers classify pianos into three main types: (1) Flügel, or grand piano; (2) Klavier, or large upright piano; (2) Pianino, or small upright piano.

**flute pipe.** Type of flue pipe often used in orchestrions, photoplayers, organs, and other instruments. Usually made of wood, the flute produces a clear tone relatively free of harmonics. Flutes in the high treble range are called piccolos; those in the bass range are called bass flutes or bourdons. Varieties of flutes include open flutes, stopped flutes (a stopped flute is equal in pitch or tonal length to an open flute of twice the length – when all other dimensions are equal), and harmonic flutes (with a small hole at the nodal point in the center front of the pipe). Double-mouthed flutes are called doppelflutes. Flutes are the easiest to maintain of all common types of pipes. For this reason they found wide use in automatic instruments.

**flutina.** Term occasionally used to describe a small reed organ or harmonium section used as accompaniment in a cylinder music box.

**flywheel.** 1. A large, heavy wheel used to minimize the speed variation (due to varying loads) in an automatic musical instrument, particularly a large one. 2. The large iron wheel, equipped with a handle for hand-turning, found on the back of a dance organ, fairground organ, or street organ.

Above: Ellsworth Johnson changes the music roll on a fine Steinway Duo-Art reproducing **grand piano.**

Left: A **frein** or **harmonic brake** is at the mouth of each violin pipe in this Pierre Eich Solophone. (James Prendergast Collection)

**folded.** Term used to describe the halving of the length of an instrument by making it in two sections (as in folded xylophone or folded orchestra bells; esp. Nelson-Wiggen) or, in the case of organ pipes, by mitering the pipes so that the top half of the pipe is parallel and adjacent to the bottom half.

**forte.** Loud. (as opposed to piano, or soft). Forte is abbreviated as f. Fortissimo (very loud), as ff. Mezzoforte (moderately loud), as mf. Used in musical notation and in descriptions of instrument expression, esp. reproducing pianos.

**forte-piano box.** Type of cylinder music box with two music combs, one tuned loudly and the other tuned softly. Also called a piano-forte box. Mainly popular during the mid-19th century.

**forzando.** Variation of sforzando, to which refer.

**foundation tone.** Lowest musical tones in a pipe organ, fairground organ, large orchestrion, etc. A deep, rich bass tone provided by bourdon, violoncello, or other bass-range pipes. Used as accompaniment for other pipes or instruments, never as solo. These bass pipes are sometimes referred to as foundation pipes. Synonyms: bass section, bass registers, etc.

**frein.** [French origin; used universally]. Harmonic brake (to which refer) of a violin-type pipe.

**French horn.** Reed-type pipe imitative of a French horn. Slightly less brilliant than a trumpet. In fairground organs the French horn has a brass resonator similar in appearance to that of a trumpet. In pipe organs, the French horn has a capped gray metal conical horn.

**frères.** [French]. Brothers. As in Limonaire Frères, Mermod Frères, et al. Term listed here as it appears regularly in musical literature and is sometimes confused by the uninitiated. Interchangeable with Gebrüder (brothers in German). Bruder, the Waldkirch organ builder, gave the firm's name as Bruder Frères in its French-language catalogues and as Gebrüder Bruder in its German-language catalogues, for example.

**friction-wheel drive.** System used in certain electric pianos and orchestrions. Power is transferred from a flywheel to a drive shaft by means of a rubber-tired wheel which is affixed to the drive shaft and which rides on the lateral surface of the flywheel. Speed regulation is possible by moving the rubber-tired wheel closer to (for slower speed) or further from the center of the flywheel. (Used on Nelson-Wiggen and Seeburg instruments, for example.)

**full organ.** All ranks of an instrument (photoplayer or pipe organ) playing at once. (cf. crescendo pedal.)

**fumed oak.** Popular finish (c.1900-1925) for pianos, orchestrions, and pipe organs. Made by subjecting the unfinished oak to ammonia fumes, thus giving it a rich brown color.

**fusee drive.** Grooved conical pulley used in early clocks and cylinder music boxes. As the mainspring winds down the drive chain or cord winds on to the small end of the cone. The force thus remains fairly constant.

# G

**gallery.** Top crest or ornamentation, esp. a wide arch or a spooled railing, used on the top of a large upright automatic instrument (e.g., the gallery found on 27" Regina disc music boxes).

**gamba pipe.** Large (usually 4' or longer) string-toned flue pipe used in combination with other pipe ranks in a large orchestrion, photoplayer, or organ.

**gear train.** A series of interconnected gears in a clockwork or drive mechanism used to transmit motion or to change speed.

**Gebrüder.** [German.] Brothers. Usually abbreviated, as in Gebr. Weber (Weber Brothers), for example. (cf. frères.)

**gedeckt pipe.** Large (4' or longer) stopped flute, softly voiced, used in combination with other ranks (never solo) in large orchestrions, photoplayers, and pipe organs. Term often used synonymously with bourdon.

**Geigen.** [German]. Violin. Geigenpfeifen = violin pipes. Geigenpiano = violin piano (piano with violin pipes [usually]).

**glockenspiel.** Literally [in German] "bell playing." 1. Series of tuned bar-type bells (refer to bells, definition 1a). 2. In a theatre organ, bar-type bells played with a single-stroke action. (When the same bells are played with a reiterating or repeating action they are called orchestra bells.)

**golden oak.** Oak finished in a golden, natural color and coated with varnish. Sometimes called light golden oak. Term used to describe music box, coin piano, etc. finish c.1900-1925.

**governor.** Speed-control device in an automatic musical instrument. Many different types including: 1. Fan-fly type with rotating fan blades as used in cylinder- and disc-type music boxes and in certain barrel-operated automatic instruments. 2. Pneumatic type which regulates the speed of travel of a piano roll by varying the aperture which supplies vacuum to the vacuum motor. 3. Electrical type whereby rotating weights make and break contact (as used in the Mills Violano-Virtuoso, for example). 4. Electrical type whereby the current flow to a motor is controlled by a rheostat (system used in most European coin pianos and orchestrions). "Speed controller" would be a more appropriate name for certain non-self-adjusting "governors" such as type 4.

**grand format.** Term applied to certain very large cylinder music boxes made during the 1880's by Heller, Nicole, Lecoultre, and other Swiss makers.

**grand piano.** Piano with the strings lying in a horizontal plane. Usually supported by three legs (or by three pairs of legs on reproducing pianos). Sizes range from baby grand to concert grand. Flügel = grand piano in German. Upright pianos (with the strings arranged vertically) were sometimes described with such meaningless terms as "inverted grand" (cf. Electric Emporium Orchestra advertising), "cabinet grand" (many different makes of upright player pianos), and "upright grand" (cf. J.P. Seeburg advertising).

**grelotphone.** [French]. Series of tuned sleigh bells used on fairground organs (e.g., certain Marenghi instruments).

# H

**hand-cranked.** Operated by continuously turning a handle or crank. Examples: early barrel organs, most types of organettes, manivelle-type disc music boxes, Dutch street organs.

**hand-played roll.** Piano roll made by recording the actual performance of a human pianist. Hand-played rolls usually contain just the playing notes as recorded by the pianist. Expression, if present, is usually confined to pedaling. Hand-played rolls can usually be recognized by looking at the perforations. If the notes in a chord begin exactly at the same point and if the roll has a precisely-arranged appearance, then the roll is probably not a hand-played roll but is an arranged roll (or designed roll). Hand-played is a term originally applied to many different types of rolls, including regular 88-note home player piano rolls, coin piano rolls, etc. Synonym: hand-played arrangement. (Rolls which incorporate full expression and intensity effects are known as reproducing piano rolls or artists' rolls.)

**harmonic brake.** Metal strip, usually of brass and usually secured with two screws, placed at the mouth of a violin pipe to stabilize the tone and to enable it to speak more quickly. On large-scale violin-type pipes the harmonic brake is often made of a wooden roller. Synonyms: harmonic bridge, frein.

**harmonic flute pipe.** Pipe, usually wooden, used in orchestrions, photoplayers, and organs. The harmonic flute is open at the top and has a small hole at the nodal point (of the sound wave) about at the center

Left: Visible in this Mortier organ is a rank of **jazz flute pipes**, the pyramidal row of chimney flute pipes visible at the center of the picture.

The jazz era of the 1920's saw the production of several different **jazzband** orchestrions. A Model 9 Hupfeld Sinfonie Jazz (Symphony Jazz) orchestrion is shown above. Other jazzband orchestrions were made by J.D. Philipps & Söhne, Popper & Co., and Paul Lösche.

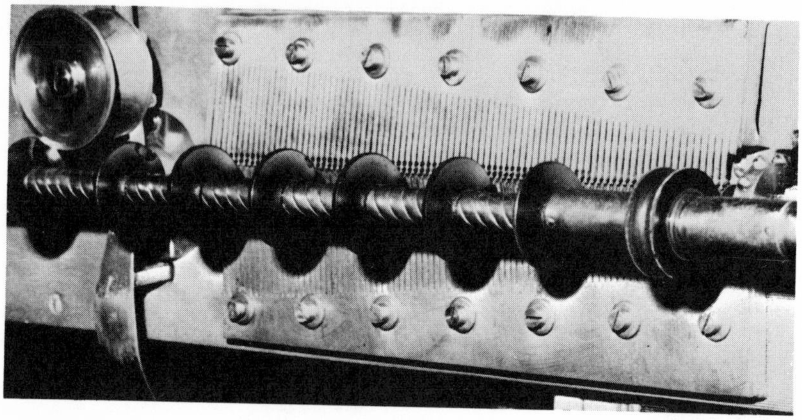

**Idler arm** of a Regina automatic disc-changing music box. The idler arm or pressure bar holds the disc against the star wheels as it plays.

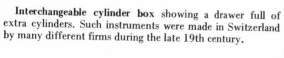

**Interchangeable cylinder box** showing a drawer full of extra cylinders. Such instruments were made in Switzerland by many different firms during the late 19th century.

of the front of the pipe. This hole permits the pipe to sound the second harmonic tone (rather than the fundamental or basic tone) with more prominence. The harmonic flute is equal in tonal length to a regular (non-harmonic) open flute of half its length. (Used in many types of instruments; most Seeburg coin pianos and orchestrions with flute pipes have harmonic-type flutes, for instance.)

**harmonium.** 1. Reed organ [the harmonium term is preferred to reed organ in Europe]. 2. One or more sets of organ reeds used as an accompaniment or even a solo instrument on certain photoplayers (most very large American Photo Player Co. instruments, for example), orchestrions (most Philipps Paganini instruments, for example), and other automatic instruments.

**harp.** 1. Instrument with 46 strings (usually) arranged vertically in a triangular frame. Played by plucking the strings. The Wurlitzer (Whitlock) Automatic Harp was popular during the early 20th century. 2. Metal plate or frame which bears the tension of the strings in a piano. Usually called a piano harp.

**harp attachment.** A popular attachment affixed to the combs of a music box or the strings of an upright piano. See banjo attachment for details. Synonyms: banjo, mandolin, zither attachment or effect.

**harp effect.** Specific term used by Philipps, Hupfeld, and other coin piano and orchestrion makers to designate a special piano action which mounts above the treble piano hammers (usually for about a two-octave range) in an automatic instrument. The hammers of the harp effect are made of hard wood or compressed felt, are actuated by a rotating splined shaft, and strike the strings in a reiterating manner – producing a realistic mandolin-like ringing sound. Popular c.1905-1925. The term was also used to describe a regular curtain-like mandolin attachment to a coin piano, so clarification is usually needed when the harp effect notation is encountered.

**harpe eolienne.** Cylinder music box type made by Bendon, Conchon, and certain other Swiss makers. With two combs, a long one with normally-tempered steel teeth, and a shorter one with harder and more brilliantly-toned teeth. A variation of the forte-piano box.

**height wheel.** In a disc-type music box, the small flat disc affixed to the center spindle to give the correct height to the center of the music box disc (so the surface of the disc will be even with the tops of the star wheels).

**helicoidal.** Descriptive of the arrangement of pins on a barrel-operated orchestrion; with the pins arranged in a continuous helix. The cylinder shifts continually to one side so that the pins are always aligned with the action keys. In this way a long selection (sometimes comprising from 6 to 12 revolutions of the barrel) can be played without interruption. Helicoidal music box: a cylinder music box with the cylinder pinned in a helicoidal manner (instead of the usual perpendicular-to-the-axis manner which requires the cylinder to be shifted in successive steps). Semi-helicoidal music box: a cylinder box with the pins arranged helically only at one point on the cylinder surface, so as to coincide with the cylinder during its regular shifting step (the cylinder shifts in successive steps in the manner of a regular box; during the brief moment of shifting, normally a time of silence, the music box continues to play as the pins are arranged on a diagonal in synchronization with the shifting apparatus). Allard of Geneva made many semi-helicoidal instruments.

**hidden drum and bell(s) box.** Cylinder box, usually mid-19th century, with bells and drum hidden beneath the bedplate.

**hurdy gurdy.** 1. Properly, a keyboard-type (usually) instrument in which the tuned piano strings are actuated by contact with a rotating rosin-covered wheel. Sometimes called the organistra or symphonia or [in French] the chifonie. Term also applied to lute-like stringed instruments whose strings are sounded by a rosined wheel. 2. [popular usage; incorrect by historical standards] Barrel-operated street piano. 3. [popular usage; incorrect by historical standards] Portable hand-cranked barrel organ, monkey organ.

## I

**idiophone.** Automatic musical instrument in which the notes are sounded by a resonant piece of metal, wood, or glass, divided into several categories (in Dr. Alexander Buchner's book, "Automatic Musical Instruments"): a. Instruments struck (chimes, etc.). b. instruments plucked (e.g., a music box comb). c. instruments activated by the movement of air (metal reeds in a harmonium, pipe organ, etc.). Refer to earlier notation under aerophone listing. Term not in general use today.

**idler arm.** On a disc-type music box the hinged (usually) bar on which several idler wheels are affixed. The idler wheels hold the disc in position as it plays. Synonym: pressure bar.

**inlay.** Designs made by setting pieces of colored wood, mother-of-pearl, polished metal, or other decorative substances into wood veneer, such as that on the lid of a music box. Synonym: marquetry (or marqueterie).

**inner-player.** Term used c.1900-1910 to describe a home player piano of the type with the pneumatic mechanisms built into the case (in contrast to the earlier push-up piano player type). Term not generally used by collectors today (inner-players are simply referred to as player pianos).

**intensity level.** Describes the degree of vacuum in a pneumatic action, esp. a reproducing piano action. A reproducing piano has many different intensity levels to vary the force with which the piano hammers strike the strings.

**interchangeable cylinder box.** Type of cylinder box in which cylinders may be interchanged by disengaging a cylinder, usually by using a lever device, from the arbor and putting another cylinder in its place. Additional cylinders are stored in a built-in drawer, cabinet, or storage case built for that purpose. Synonym: rechange box.

## J

**jazz flute pipe.** In dance organs, a chimney flute (or rohrflute) made in a special manner: with a special tremulant which consists of a pallet covering the outside opening of a small hole drilled in the back of the pipe, opposite the mouth. When a warbling effect is desired, the pallet opens and closes rapidly while the pipe is being sounded in the normal manner. The opening and closing of the hole temporarily detunes the pipe each time and produces the characteristic jazz flute sound. (See also vibratone, a related pipe.)

**jazz orchestra.** 1. Term used in the 1920's (e.g., by Capitol Piano and Organ Co.) to describe a piano orchestrion. 2. Term used by collectors today to describe a dance organ, esp. a small- or medium-size one.

**jazz trumpet pipe.** Brilliantly-voiced reed-type pipe used in certain large orchestrions (e.g., the Weber Maesto). Synonym: oboe horn [mainly in pipe organ usage].

**jazzband.** Term used to describe orchestrions during the jazz era of the 1920's. Used esp. by Hupfeld, Philipps, Popper, and other German orchestrion makers.

## K

**kettle drum.** In an automatic instrument (esp. a piano orchestrion) an effect obtained by alternately striking two small-size beaters on either side of a bass drum head. The term, which should be kettle drum effect as no separate drum is used, is found widely in orchestrion literature, e.g., Seeburg descriptions of nearly all of its large orchestrions and photoplayers. Synonym: tympani (properly, but not used as such, tympani effect).

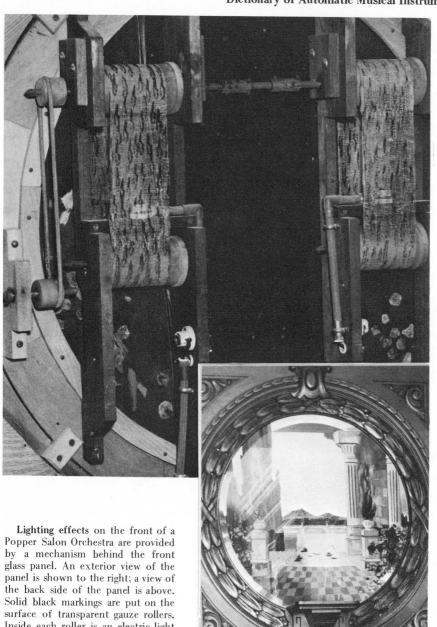

**Lighting effects** on the front of a Popper Salon Orchestra are provided by a mechanism behind the front glass panel. An exterior view of the panel is shown to the right; a view of the back side of the panel is above. Solid black markings are put on the surface of transparent gauze rollers. Inside each roller is an electric light bulb. As the gauze moves, the electric lights project light and dark areas on the back side of translucent paintings of flickering torches. The changing lights are visible from the front, and the torches appear to flicker and burn realistically.

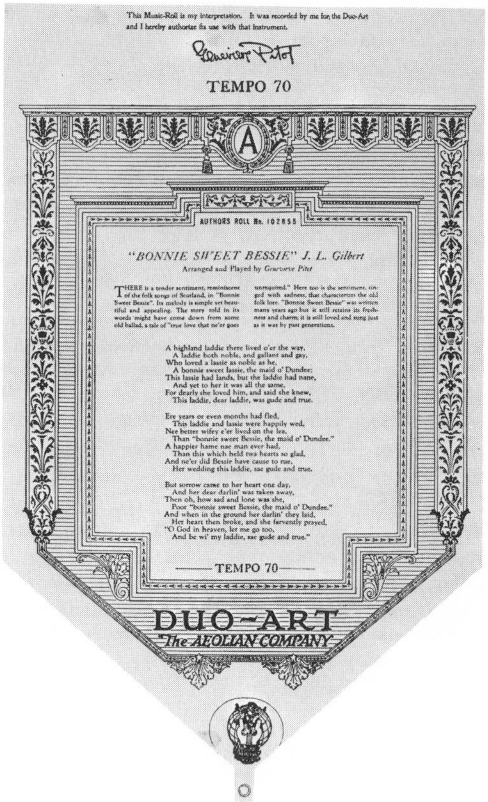


**Leader** on a Duo-Art "Author's Roll." The leaders of these rolls and of the later Audio-Graphic rolls are especially elaborate. Leaders of most types of other rolls give basic information such as the tune title(s) and the tempo.

**Magazine** device: a Hupfeld automatic roll changer which stores ten music rolls and plays them automatically in sequence or as per an automatic selecting device.

**key.** 1. Finger-operated control lever used to sound a note on a keyboard instrument such as a piano, organ, or accordion. 2. Musical pitch of an instrument or music arrangement (e.g., the key of C). 3. Actuating levers, usually made of brass, used to operate organ reeds (as in a cylinder music box with reed organ accompaniment), organ pipes (such as in a large barrel orchestrion), or a pneumatic system (as in the key frame of a fairground organ). 4. Key(s): the number of playing notes plus the number of control stops (for changing registers, stopping the instrument, rewinding the roll, etc.) on an automatic musical instrument, esp. a dance organ or fairground organ (such as a 98-key Marenghi organ, 101-key Mortier organ, etc.). 5. Detachable winding implement for tightening the mainspring on a clock, keywind music box, etc.

**key desk.** [Usually, but not always, written as two words]. Console (to which refer) of a pipe organ.

**key frame.** Device mainly used on fairground and dance organs, but used on many other types of instruments as well. Contains a series of spring-loaded steel (usually) levers. When one end of a lever pops up through a hole in a cardboard music book (to which refer), the other end of the lever or key opens an aperture which actuates a pneumatic action. The folding cardboard music book is pulled through the key frame by india-rubber pinch rollers. A durable system capable of withstanding rugged use and resistant to humidity changes. For these reasons most very large fairground and dance organs use the key frame system.

**keybed.** The foundation on which the keys of a piano or organ are placed in order to create the keyboard.

**keyboard.** A set of keys or levers, arranged in order of ascending pitch, which enables a piano or organ to be played by hand. Synonym [in pipe organ nomenclature]: manual.

**keyboardless.** Term used to descripe a piano or organ of upright or vertical format and without a keyboard. Synonym: cabinet style.

**keyless frame.** In a fairground or dance organ a music system which uses paper rolls or cardboard books and a regular tracker bar, rather than spring-loaded metal keys. Such instruments are sometimes called keyless (e.g., 112-keyless Carl Frei organ). [Term mainly used in Europe].

**key-wind box.** A cylinder music box, usually of the early or mid-19th century, in which the mainspring is wound by a detachable key (as opposed to lever-wind, to which refer).

**Kino.** [German]. Cinema or motion-picture theatre. Kino Orgel = theatre organ.

**kipp mechanism.** [German origin: kipp = tilting]. In an electric piano, photoplayer, or orchestrion, a device which stores two rolls between common end plates and which resembles a revolver or magazine mechanism. Usually used in theatres to accompany silent movies. One roll can be tilted or swung away from the tracker bar (without having to rewind the roll) so that the revolver-type mechanism can turn 180 degrees and bring the other roll into nearly-instant use. Each roll has its own take-up spool. Synonyms: tilting mechanism; Kippzwilling [German].

**Klavier.** [German]. Upright or vertical piano, usually of medium or large size (term never used to describe a grand piano; the latter is a Flügel in German). Small-size upright pianos are called Pianinos in German.

## L

**laminated comb.** 1. In a cylinder box a music comb arranged vertically and composed of individual teeth stacked on each other. Played by a vertically-mounted cylinder. Usually of very small musical scale and used in musical watches, musical seals, and similar items. 2. Term used (incorrectly, from a historical viewpoint) by collectors to describe a sectional comb, to which refer.

**leader.** (roll leader). The beginning or fore part of a music roll on which the end tab is affixed and on which the tune title(s), tempo, and other information is printed.

**lever-wind box.** Cylinder type music box, usually of the mid- or late 19th century, wound by a permanently-attached lever with a ratchet escapement. (Compare to key-wind.)

**light-changing gallery.** Optional attachment for a coin piano or orchestrion (esp. one of European manufacture) which contains a motion picture effect (to which refer).

**light(ing) effects.** Decorative electrical effects – blinking lights, wonder lights, motion-picture effects, and other illuminated devices – used on coin pianos, orchestrions, dance organs, and fairground organs. Intended to create attention and to attract the public.

**lock-and-cancel.** Descriptive of a control used to operate a pneumatic musical instrument. One short perforation locks the mechanism in the "on" position, in which position it remains until another perforation releases it to the "off" position. In this way an effect (a register, for example) can be "on" for a long period of time without having to use an extended (or chain-type) perforation.

**longue marche.** Cylinder music box equipped with multiple springs to provide an extended playing time after winding. [Term rarely used today by collectors.]

**lotus flute.** (In German, Lotos Flöte). Small-scale rank of stopped flute pipes, usually of limited musical range, used in orchestrions (e.g., Hupfeld Symphony Jazz and Pan Orchestra) and organs, mainly c.1910-1930. Usually equipped with a tremolo device which, together with music arranged to "slide" (i.e., glissando effect) from one note to the next, imparts a haunting, rising and falling tone to the music. Usually played as a solo effect using specially-arranged music rolls. (Compare to Swanee Whistle, to which refer.)

**loud pedal.** Sustaining pedal (to which refer) on a piano.

## M

**magazine.** 1. Device used to store 3 to 10 music rolls on a revolving mechanism. Rolls are changed automatically, usually in the sequence in which they are arranged on the magazine. Synonyms: automatic roll changer [American usage], revolver mechanism [European usage]. 2. Term sometimes used (esp. by Wurlitzer in the 1920's) to describe an accumulator, to which refer.

**mainspring.** Spirally-coiled or wound steel spring used to power a music box or other type of instrument.

**mandolin(e).** Mandolin [American usage] or mandoline [European usage]. 1. Mandolin(e) attachment for use on an automatic instrument (refer to banjo attachment, definition 2). Synonyms: banjo, harp, zither attachment or effect. 2. Device consisting of hard-tipped piano hammers which are operated by a splined shaft and which play in a reiterating manner (e.g., the mandolin part of the Wurlitzer Mandolin Quartette). Synonym: harp effect. 3. Type of music arrangement featuring reiterating piano notes, in a player piano roll caused by a series of closely-spaced perforations which cause a given piano note to strike repeatedly. Found on 88-note home player piano rolls and on coin piano rolls. Synonym: marimba arrangement, organ arrangement. 4. Type of music arrangement used on a mandolin(e) box (cylinder music box), to which refer.

**mandolin(e) box.** Cylinder music box with three or more teeth tuned to each note in its musical scale. Quickly-repeating mandolin-like sounds are produced by plucking adjacent notes in 1, 2, 3, etc. series (in a regularly-tuned music box a given note cannot repeat quickly for the tooth must be dampened before it is plucked again).

**manivelle.** Small musical instrument, esp. a small cylinder or disc-type music box, which is operated by continuously turning a hand crank (as opposed to spring-wound or clockwork models). [Term originally used in Europe; now used by collectors worldwide.]

**Mitered pipes** on the underside of a fairground organ. In order to fit large pipes into a restricted space the pipes have been mitered or cut.

**Oboe pipes** (bright metal rank with conical resonators) in a large Popper & Co. Gladiator orchestrion. Oboe pipes have a brilliant tone.

Typical **military band organ** of the early 20th century.

**manual.** Keyboard, esp. on a photoplayer or pipe organ.

**maracca** (or maraca). Hollow-gourd rattle containing small pebbles or seeds. Percussion effect used on dance organs.

**marimba.** 1. Xylophone (to which refer) with a resonator under each bar. 2. Marimba harp: large-scale marimba used in theatre organs. 3. Marimbaphone: term infrequently used to describe a regular xylophone (esp. by the Link Piano Co.). 4. Marimba arrangement: (refer to mandolin, definition 3). Synonyms: mandolin arrangement, organ arrangement.

**marquetry** (or marqueterie). Inlay, to which refer.

**master disc.** Large, heavy disc containing the original musical arrangement. Used in a music disc perforating machine to manufacture from 1 to 12 or more production discs. Regina made master discs by drilling holes at appropriate points in a heavy brass disc.

**master roll.** Roll, sometimes two or three times the length of a production music roll, used on a perforator to control the punches for making production rolls.

**mechanical musical instrument.** 1. General term used to describe all self-playing musical instruments (although certain types of pneumatic instruments with sophisticated expression capabilities – large orchestrions, reproducing pianos, and pipe organs, for example – were never originally designated as such). Synonym: automatic musical instrument, to which refer. 2. Self-playing musical instrument, especially one that is powered by a spring, is weight-driven, is hand-cranked, or is actuated by another form of clockwork (as opposed to electrically-driven instruments, most of which were originally designated as automatic rather than mechanical).

**melograph.** Keyboard device for transcribing hand-playing to musical notations suitable for use in pinning an organ barrel, etc.

**metallophon(e).** 1. Term sometimes used to describe vox humana pipes in a large orchestrion (term used by Hupfeld). 2. Synonym used for vibraton(e), to which refer.

**metronomic roll.** Piano roll arranged in strictly-followed tempo for dancing purposes.

**mezzo-forte.** Intensity or sound level of moderate loudness. In reproducing pianos, an intensity halfway between forte (loud) and piano (soft). Abbreviated as mf.

**mignon.** [French]. Small. Adjective used to describe any small object. Term mentioned here as "mignon" is sometimes construed as being an exclusive Welte trademark. Trademarked Mignon-named items include the Mignon organette, the Welte-Mignon (reproducing piano made by Welte; so-named as it was small in comparison to Welte's other products, large orchestrions), and to the Mignon reproducing piano (Welte system) sold by Popper & Co.

**military band organ.** [mainly American usage]. Fairground organ (to which refer) or band organ with exposed brass pipes on the front. Synonyms: skating rink organ, trumpet organ (mainly used to describe early barrel-operated models).

**mission finish; mission style.** Type of furniture styling used during the early 20th century. Characterized by heavy-appearing square lines, usually with slats and moldings. Usually of dark oak. Somewhat similar to ranch style (to which refer), but not necessarily with protruding posts, etc.

**mitered pipe.** Pipe which has been mitered or cut (giving it a "bent" appearance), usually at a 90-degree angle, so that it will fit into a short space. So long as the interior or speaking length of the pipe remains the same, the tone is unaffected by mitering. (Compare to folded, to which refer.)

**mixture.** In a pipe organ two or more pipe ranks of the same basic tonal family (but differing in harmonic development) which are sounded together by a single register. Usually used in the treble range to achieve a greater volume (to balance the more powerful bass).

**monkey organ.** Portable hand-cranked barrel organ, esp. one employed by an organ grinder and used in the streets.

**mortuary organ.** Paper-roll-operated piano - pipe organ unit (or sometimes an organ without piano) used to provide a musical background for mortuary services (e.g., Seeburg Style MO).

**motion-picture effect.** Lighting effect used on orchestrions and coin pianos. A series of silhouettes (of airships, vehicles, fish in a stream, etc.) are projected against the translucent back of a glass-fronted oil painting. The silhouettes are suspended from cords or are mounted on semi-transparent (made of a gauzelike material) belts and are moved across the scene by pulleys. Another type of motion-picture effect employs sequentially-lighted bulbs which provide realistic animation when used behind a translucent painted scene of a volcano, cascading fountain, etc. Popular c.1900-1920.

**movement.** Mechanism of an automatic musical instrument, esp. a small spring-wound disc or cylinder box. Musical movement.

**multiplexing.** The use of a single hole in a tracker bar (or key in a key frame, etc.) to perform multiple functions, usually in combination with other holes. Thus, for example, holes 1, 2, and 3 may have separate functions when used singly. 1 and 2 have yet another function when used at the same time; 1 and 3 have still another function; 2 and 3 have still another function. Used in certain types of reproducing pianos, large orchestrions, and other instruments to reduce the number of holes needed in the tracker bar (and, consequently, the width of the roll) to perform a given set of functions.

**music(al) box.** 1. Music box [mainly American usage; e.g., Regina Music Box Co.] or musical box [mainly British usage]. A cabinet, usually made of wood, which contains a disc-type or cylinder-type music box movement. 2. General term used by the public (but not by collectors) to describe any type of automatic musical instrument.

**music comb.** Series of tuned metal teeth arranged adjacent to each other and fastened to a common bedplate. Used to produce sound in a disc or cylinder music box. Made in many varieties. Also called musical comb.

**music leaf.** Music roll made of heavy manila paper (term esp. used by Imhof & Mukle).

**music roll.** Strip of thin paper (usually) on which music and control functions are arranged by a series of perforations. When played on a tracker bar the perforations cause a roll-operated instrument to perform. Two main music roll types: (1) rewind-type rolls (the most popular), to which refer; and (2) endless-type rolls, to which refer.

# N

**nickelodeon.** 1. An early theatre (mainly pre-1920) which charged 5c admission. Nickelodeon = nickel + odeon (the Greek word for theatre). Also called nickelodeon theatre. 2. Term used to describe a coin-operated piano, orchestrion, or similar instrument. [Strictly modern post-1940 usage; never used earlier in this context. Such instruments were called electric pianos, coin pianos, etc. Term generally used by collectors and the public in America today.]

# O

**oboe pipe.** Brightly-voiced reed pipe with conical metal resonator. Used as a solo rank in certain large orchestrions. Synonyms: jazz trumpet, oboe horn.

**octave.** 1. A musical interval of eight notes. Every note has double the number of vibrations of its corresponding note an octave lower and half the vibrations of its corresponding note an octave higher. 2. Term popularly used (but incorrect from a strict musical viewpoint) to describe thirteen equally-tuned half steps (the notes at each end

**Orchestra bells** in a coin piano of the 1915-1920 era (Empress Electric, sold by Lyon & Healy).

**Organettes**, small hand-cranked reed organs popular during the 1880-1900 years, were made in many different forms.

**Orchestrions** of the 20th century include these: At the left is a compact Seeburg Style KT, a cabinet orchestrion which was one of the most popular ever made. Thousands were sold during the 'teens and the 'twenties by the J.P. Seeburg Piano Company of Chicago, Illinois. Above is shown the mammoth Helios V orchestrion first introduced in 1909 by Ludwig Hupfeld of Leipzig, Germany. From the standpoint of instrumentation, the Helios V was the largest orchestrion ever produced on a regular production basis. To the right is a Seeburg Style H orchestrion, an instrument which probably holds the title of the most ornate keyboard-type instrument ever produced. The Seeburg H, the most expensive orchestrion in the J.P. Seeburg Piano Company's line, was produced from about 1910 to the late 1920's.

are counted; e.g., C to C), the twelve-toned equal temperament scale, into which the octave is divided on the piano and in most pipe ranks. Sometimes called the chromatic scale. In original catalogues (e.g., Operators Piano Co. description of Coinola percussions) and in popular usage today a "two octave" set of xylophone bars would mean a 24-note chromatic set, for instance. As noted, the 13-step terminology is often used – esp. in describing pipe ranks.

**octave coupler.** Refer to coupler definition earlier.

**orchestra.** Term used in the automatic musical instrument field to describe: 1. Any type of orchestrion. 2. A large orchestrion, especially one with sophisticated expression effects (e.g., the Hupfeld Pan was always referred to as the Pan Orchestra, never the Pan Orchestrion).

**orchestra bells.** Bar-type bells (refer to bells, definition 1a). 2. In a theatre organ, bar-type bells played with a reiterating or repeating action. (When the same bells are played with a single-stroke action they are called glockenspiel.)

**orchestra box.** Cylinder music box with added effects, usually saucer bells, a small drum, a wood block or wood drum, and, occasionally, a reed organ section or other accompaniment. Most were made in Switzerland. Mainly popular c.1880-1895.

**orchestra piano.** Keyboard-type orchestrion.

**orchestral.** Orchestrion (term mainly used by the Marquette Piano Co.).

**orchestrion.** Self-contained automatic musical instrument, esp. a large one, equipped with several different instruments in imitation of an orchestra. Usually contains some percussion effects (e.g., drums, cymbal, triangle, etc.). Main types include: 1. Barrel orchestrion: usually without piano; with many ranks of pipes and with percussion effects. Softly voiced. Made for indoor use. Popular during the 19th century. 2. Keyboard-type piano orchestrion: built around an upright piano; with one or more chromatically-scaled extra instruments (e.g., a rank of violin or flute pipes, a xylophone, a set of bells) and with percussion effects. Paper-roll operated. Popular during the early 20th century. 3. Large keyboardless piano orchestrion: contains a piano, several (usually) ranks of pipes, and many other effects, some of which are (usually) arranged to play solo melodies. Paper-roll operated. Popular during the early 20th century. 4. Small cabinet-style orchestrion: small cabinet, usually smaller than an upright piano, containing an abbreviated-scale piano, one or more chromatically-tuned extra instruments, and percussion effects. Popular during the 1920's, esp. in America (e.g., Seeburg KT, KT Special, etc.). Other uses of the orchestrion term (instruments which were designated as orchestrions by the original manufacturers, but which are considered to belong to other series): 5. Disc-operated piano of limited scale, sometimes with percussion effects (e.g., disc pianos made by Lochmann, Polyphon, and Symphonion). 6. Large disc-type music box, usually with 10 or 12 bells. 7. Mechanical (not pneumatic) piano of limited scale, plus percussion effects. Operated by a heavy manila paper roll (e.g., Regina Sublima and related Polyphon instruments). 8. Barrel piano with limited percussion effects. 9. Mechanical zither or dulcimer (e.g., the so-called "Piano Orchestrion," also sold as the Piano Melodico). 10. Paper-roll organette (e.g., Orchestrion Harmonette). Instruments listed from 5 through 10 are not considered to be orchestrions by collectors today. The term "orchestrion" was applied to many other non-orchestrion instruments over the years. Synonyms: automatic orchestra, orchestra, orchestra piano.

**organ.** Generally, an instrument on which music is played by means of tuned pipes or reeds. Among automatic musical instruments, the following main types are found: 1. Organette: small hand-cranked instrument which plays tuned reeds. 2. Player reed organ: large instrument, usually equipped with a keyboard, which plays tuned reeds. 3. Player pipe organ: large pipe organ, usually equipped with one or more keyboards or manuals, designed for providing music in a church, residence, or theatre. Usually not self-contained, but built in as part of a building. With paper-roll player built into the console or into a separate cabinet. 4. Portable hand-cranked barrel organ. 5. Fairground organ or band organ, with loudly-voiced pipes and ornate (usually) front. 6. Street organ or pierement: loudly-voiced instrument mainly used in the streets of Holland. 7. Dance organ: softly-voiced instrument, usually with ornate facade and of very large size, used in dance halls, esp. in Belgium and Holland. 8. Calliope: with a limited scale of flue-type pipes; played with extremely high air pressure. 9. Serinette: hand-cranked softly-voiced limited scale of flute pipes; used in the 18th and 19th centuries to teach birds to sing. 10. Any attachment consisting of one or more ranks of pipes or sets of reeds attached to another instrument. Examples: set of flute pipes in an organ clock, organ accompaniment in a cylinder music box, sets of reeds in a large photoplayer or organ. Orgel = organ in Dutch and German; orgue = organ in French.

**organ arrangement.** 1. On a piano roll, a type of music arrangement in which a series of closely-spaced holes causes a given note to reiterate – thus "sustaining" it. In the melody section grace notes often lead from one sustained note to another, giving a glissando effect. Synonyms: marimba arrangement, mandolin arrangement – these two types lacking the aforementioned glissando effect, however. 2. In an orchestrion or organ roll, an arrangement with continuous uninterrupted (except for the tiny bridges, if a chain perforation [to which refer] is used) perforations to sustain notes played by pipes. (Pipes playing a normal piano-type arrangement sound "choppy" due to the short duration of the notes.)

**organ attachment.** A set of reeds or one or more ranks used as an extra accompaniment or solo instrument in a large photoplayer or orchestrion. Synonyms: organ section, organ stop, etc.

**organ clock.** Hall clock containing from one to three limited-scale ranks of pipes (usually flutes).

**organ comb.** Series of actuating levers, similar to a music comb in appearance, which actuate the reed (or, rarely, pipe) organ accompaniment in a cylinder or disc music box.

**organette.** Small hand-cranked (usually) reed organ, without keyboard. Usually of very limited scale (14-20 reeds). Synonyms (used c.1880-1900; not used by collectors today except to describe specific instruments): organetta, organina, orguinette, and other terms intended to designate "little organ."

**overstrung.** In a piano the standard system of the late 19th century and later in which the bass strings are stretched across the lower portion of the treble strings in order to get the bass bridge location closer to the center of the soundboard (to improve tone generation), to conserve space, and to more evenly distribute tension on the metal piano plate. Such designations as "with seven-octave overstrung piano" are often found in original sales literature; however, in practice, non-overstrung (i.e., straight-strung) pianos were rarely used, so such descriptions were unnecessary. Synonym: cross-strung.

**overture box.** Cylinder music box, esp. a finely-made early (pre-1880) one, containing overtures or operatic selections, usually elaborately arranged on a large-diameter cylinder and played on a music comb with finely-spaced teeth.

# P

**pallet valve.** Small piece of wood, hinged at one end and faced with soft leather, used to cover an opening in a pipe chest, reservoir, or other pneumatic apparatus.

**paper roll organ.** Organette or small hand-cranked reed organ which uses a perforated paper roll or strip.

**Pauke.** [German]. Kettle drum or tympani.

**percussion.** (or percussion effect). Tonal effects produced by striking a device usually of fixed pitch or tonal character (as opposed to tunable piano strings, etc.). Two types: (1) Chromatic percussions with a series of units, each tuned to a corresponding note in a piano or organ scale. Examples: xylophone, orchestra bells. (2) Non-chromatic percussions such as a cymbal, bass drum, snare drum, tambourine, tenor drum, triangle, wood block, etc. In automatic instrument terminology, chromatic-type percussions are usually listed individually. Non-chromatic types are often described as "percussion" or "drum and trap effects." Example of a listing for a piano orchestrion: "Piano with xylophone and percussion effects."

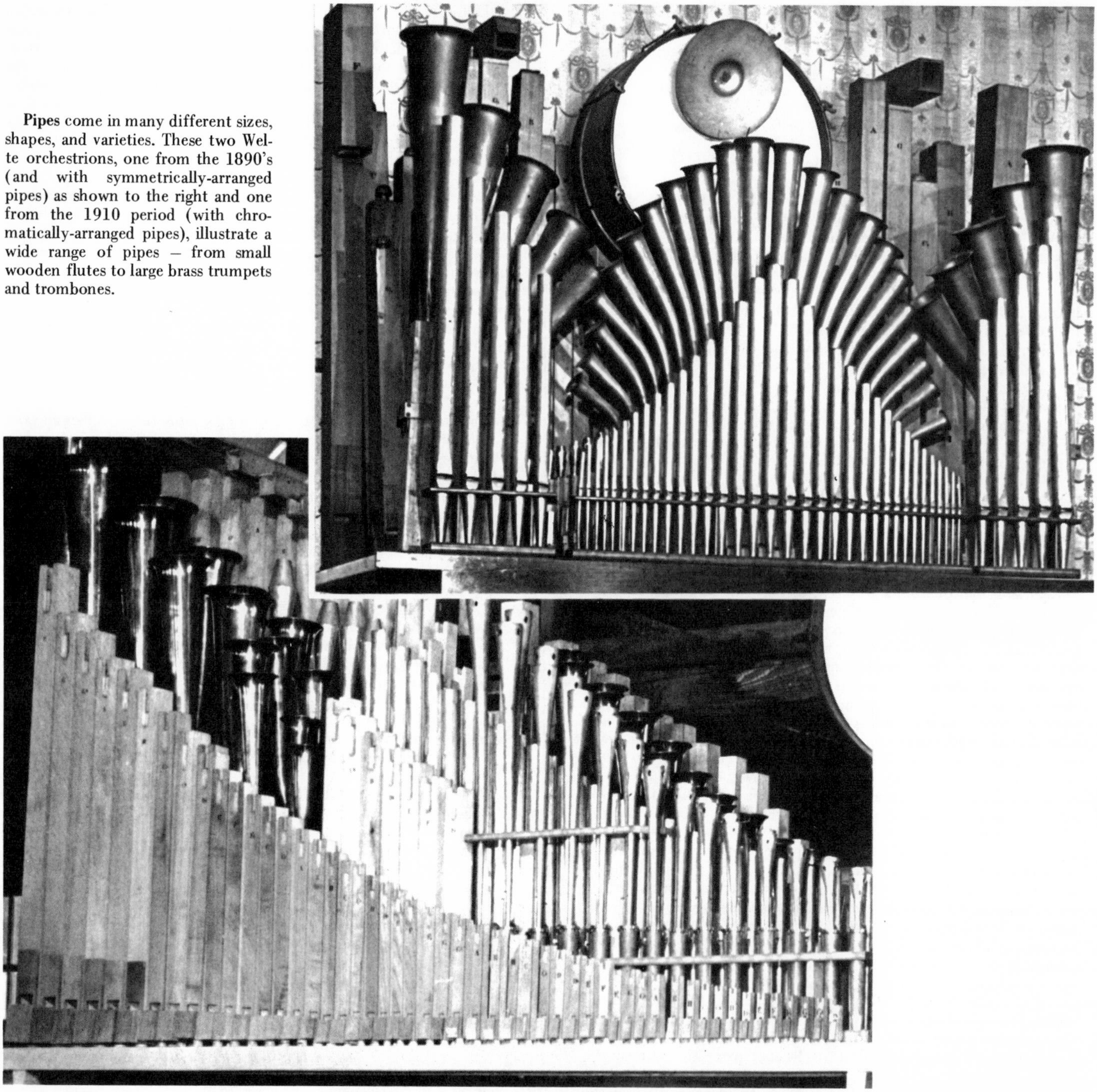

**Pipes** come in many different sizes, shapes, and varieties. These two Welte orchestrions, one from the 1890's (and with symmetrically-arranged pipes) as shown to the right and one from the 1910 period (with chromatically-arranged pipes), illustrate a wide range of pipes – from small wooden flutes to large brass trumpets and trombones.

**Photoplayers** under construction in the Rudolph Wurlitzer Co. factory in North Tonawanda, New York. During the 'teens and 'twenties Wurlitzer made thousands of these instruments for theatre use.

**perforation(s).** Holes in a music roll, music book, disc, etc. arranged in a manner to produce a musical performance when used on an automatic musical instrument. Perforator: machine which produces perforations, esp. in a music roll.

**phonograph.** An instrument which reproduces recorded sound waves by means of vertical or transverse grooves in a disc or cylinder. Used in combination with disc-type music boxes during the early 20th century (e.g., Miraphone and Reginaphone). Synonyms: gramophone, record player (disc-type only), talking machine (early usage), victrola (Victor Co. trademark, but generically used to describe disc-type instruments).

**photogram.** Term used (esp. by Welte) in the 1920's to describe the master recording of a pianist's performance.

**photoplayer.** Automatic musical instrument, usually consisting of a keyboard-type piano with one or two attached side chests which contain pipes, percussion instruments, and novelty sound effects. Usually with a single or duplex roll mechanism built into the piano case above the keyboard. Used to provide music and sound effects to accompany silent pictures. (Refer to photoplayers built by American Photo Player Co., Seeburg, Wurlitzer, et al.)

**Pianino.** [German]. Small upright piano. (In German, medium-size or large upright piano = Klavier; grand piano = Flügel.)

**pianista.** [French]. Piano-playing device; automatically-played piano (also used as a trademark name for specific instruments; e.g., Fourneaux's Pianista and the Thibouville Pianista).

**piano.** 1. Musical instrument with a manually-operated keyboard which actuates hammers (usually felt-covered) which strike tuned wire strings, usually of a range of several octaves or more, and which can be softened or sustained by means of foot-operated pedals. Automatically- played pianos were made in many forms, including barrel pianos, player pianos, reproducing pianos, orchestra pianos (orchestrions), etc. Some automatically-played pianos are keyboardless, the keyboard being unnecessary for automatic playing. 2. In musical notation, soft. Abbreviated as p. Also pianissimo (abbreviated pp.) or very softly (as opposed to the forte, or loud, notation).

**piano action.** The devices or connecting links between the keyboard and the strings of a piano; the devices which actuate the piano hammers.

**piano-forte box.** Forte-piano cylinder music box, to which refer.

**piano orchestrion.** Orchestrion which has a piano as the main instrument. The piano plays the basic musical theme and accompaniment; the additional instruments (such as one or more ranks of pipes, a xylophone, a set of bells, drums and traps, etc.) play intermittently.

**piano - pipe organ.** Name sometimes given to a piano with two or three (usually) ranks of pipes built into the same case (e.g., Reproduco, Nelson-Wiggen Selector Duplex Organ, Seeburg Style MO). Used in theatres and mortuaries in the 1915-1930 years.

**piano player.** An external (as opposed to built-in) device which pushes up to or otherwise attaches to a piano keyboard and plays the instrument by depressing the keys. Usually foot-pumped and operated by paper rolls. The forerunner of the player piano (which has built-in mechanisms). Popular c.1900. Synonyms: push-up piano player, vorsetzer (the latter term mainly used today to describe electrically-operated piano players with reproducing mechanisms).

**piano roll.** Perforated paper roll used to operate a piano player, player piano, expression piano, or reproducing piano.

**pianola.** Piano player or player piano. An Aeolian Co. trademark, the Pianola name was used in a generic sense in America and in Europe during the early 20th century. Most comprehensive German-English, French-English, etc. dictionaries give the term pianola to describe the player piano.

**piccolo.** 1. Pipe rank in orchestrions; similar in appearance to a wooden flute pipe and used in the top one or two treble octaves of the musical scale. 2. In orchestrions the name sometimes given to the upper range of a rank of flute pipes. (A rank of flutes is sometimes elaborately described as being a rank of "bourdon, flute, and piccolo" pipes, bourdon and piccolo referring to the lower and upper ranges.) 3. In fairground organs, a metal (usually) pipe, usually of polished brass, which is blown transversely (across the bottom of the pipe, rather than into the pipe) at high pressure. Usually with a wooden acorn-shaped plug at the top of the pipe. 4. In theatre pipe organs, a 2' stop of brightly-voiced wood or metal flute pipes. 5. An adjective meaning "small." A piccolo flute is a little flute, a piccolo drum is a little drum, etc. [Terminology rarely used by collectors today.] 6. A coin piano or orchestrion [slang, southern United States usage].

**pièce à oiseau.** [French origin]. Cylinder music box with a mechanical bird fitted into the front or top of the case.

**pierement.** Dutch street organ. [Term originally used only in Holland; now used by collectors worldwide.]

**pin.** In a music box cylinder or piano, organ, or orchestrion barrel a protruding piece of metal (usually straight, but sometimes staple-like in form – for sustained notes) which actuates a key, lever, or tooth which sounds the music or causes it to sound.

**pipe.** A tubular instrument which produces sound by the action of air against a reed or against the pipe mouth, in combination with the resonance of the air within the tube itself. Pipes are generally referred to as having a pitch or tonal length expressed in feet, such as 2', 4', etc. Pipes are usually either open at the top or closed. Generally, the tonal length of a closed pipe is twice that of a comparable open pipe (the same pitch sounded by a 2'-long closed pipe would take a 4'-long open pipe to produce). Pipes used in automatic instruments are of two main types: (1) flue pipes which produce their sound by the action of air against the edge of the pipe mouth in combination with a column of air; and (2) reed pipes which produce sound by the action of a vibrating reed (there are two types of reeds: free and beating); the reed sound is amplified by the upper part of the pipe which, on a reed pipe, is called a resonator or horn. A third type of pipe, the diaphone (to which refer), produces sound by intermittent bursts of air which are rapidly introduced into the base of the pipe under high pressure. Used in theatre organs and a few large photoplayers. Pipes are mounted on a pipe chest or windchest and are blown by air under pressure. Pipe pressure is measured in inches; the number of inches that a given pressure will force a column of water up an open glass tube. (Pressure for calliopes is sometimes measured in pounds per square inch – the amount of pressure that the air will exert against a one-inch square.) Wind pressures (measured in inches of water) commonly used in automatic instruments: Barrel orchestrions, 1 to 3 inches; piano orchestrions and photoplayers, 4 to 7 inches; fairground organs 8 to 12 inches. Pipes are tuned by adjusting the reed or by changing the tonal length of the pipe (by moving a tuning slide or stopper). Pipes are voiced to a specific wind pressure when they are built and cannot be interchanged with an instrument of significantly different pressure. Pipes are arranged in ranks and are controlled by registers or stops (see subsequent definitions of these terms). As our preceding definitions under the "piccolo" listing attest, pipe terminology varies widely from instrument to instrument. Automatic musical instrument manufacturers were often careless or imprecise with pipe descriptions (an egregious example: in PianOrchestra advertising, Wurlitzer called a bourdon [a bass flute of the flue-pipe family] a "French horn" [a brightly-voiced reed pipe]). Often fanciful names (e.g., "fanfare trumpet") were coined to describe basic ranks. Violin pipes and flute pipes are the two types most commonly found in automatic instruments; both of these types are of the flue-pipe family and require a minimum of tuning and maintenance. Reeds, which require tuning more often and which are more susceptible to clogging by dirt and dust, mainly are found in larger orchestrions. Reed pipes of trumpet and trombone voicing are a common addition to fairground organs, especially larger styles. When several ranks of similarly-tuned pipes are in the same instrument, care must be taken to separate the ranks sufficiently – otherwise the sound waves from two similarly-tuned pipes will cancel each other (the phenomenon known as destructive interference). Celeste tuning (to which refer) mitigates this problem. Certain ranks in large instruments are called foundation or fundamental pipes. These provide a rich bass sound which makes the treble pipes and solo pipes sound richer and fuller. Foundation pipes are never played alone, but are always used in combination with other ranks. Solo pipes are those with distinctive voicing which are used to play solo parts (or to carry the basic musical theme) while other

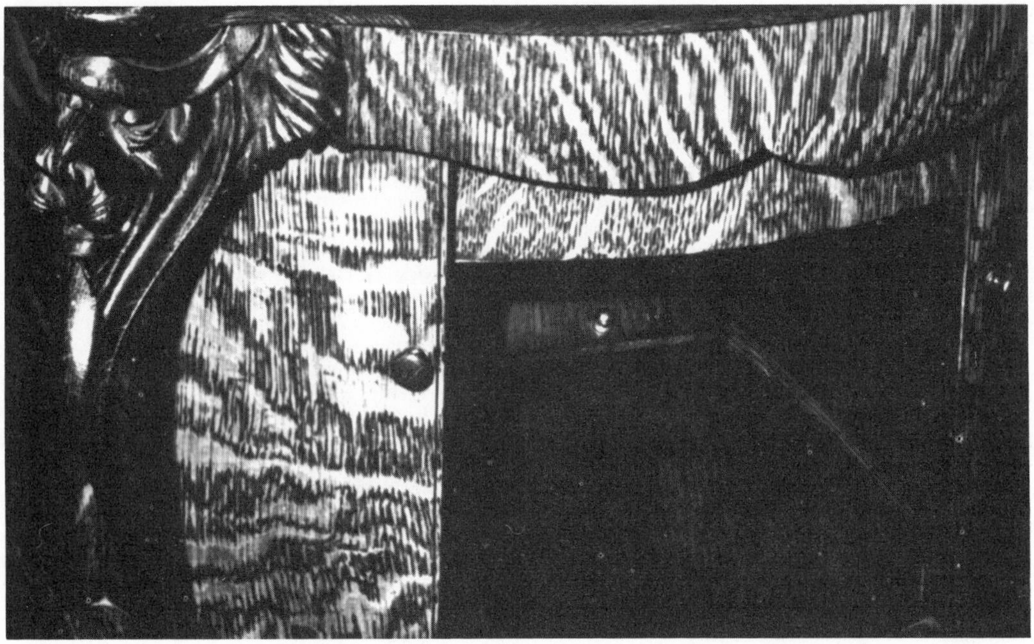

Left: This Style 240 Reginaphone displays the prominent grain characteristics of its **quartered oak** finish. Quartered oak was a popular American wood finish during the early 20th century.

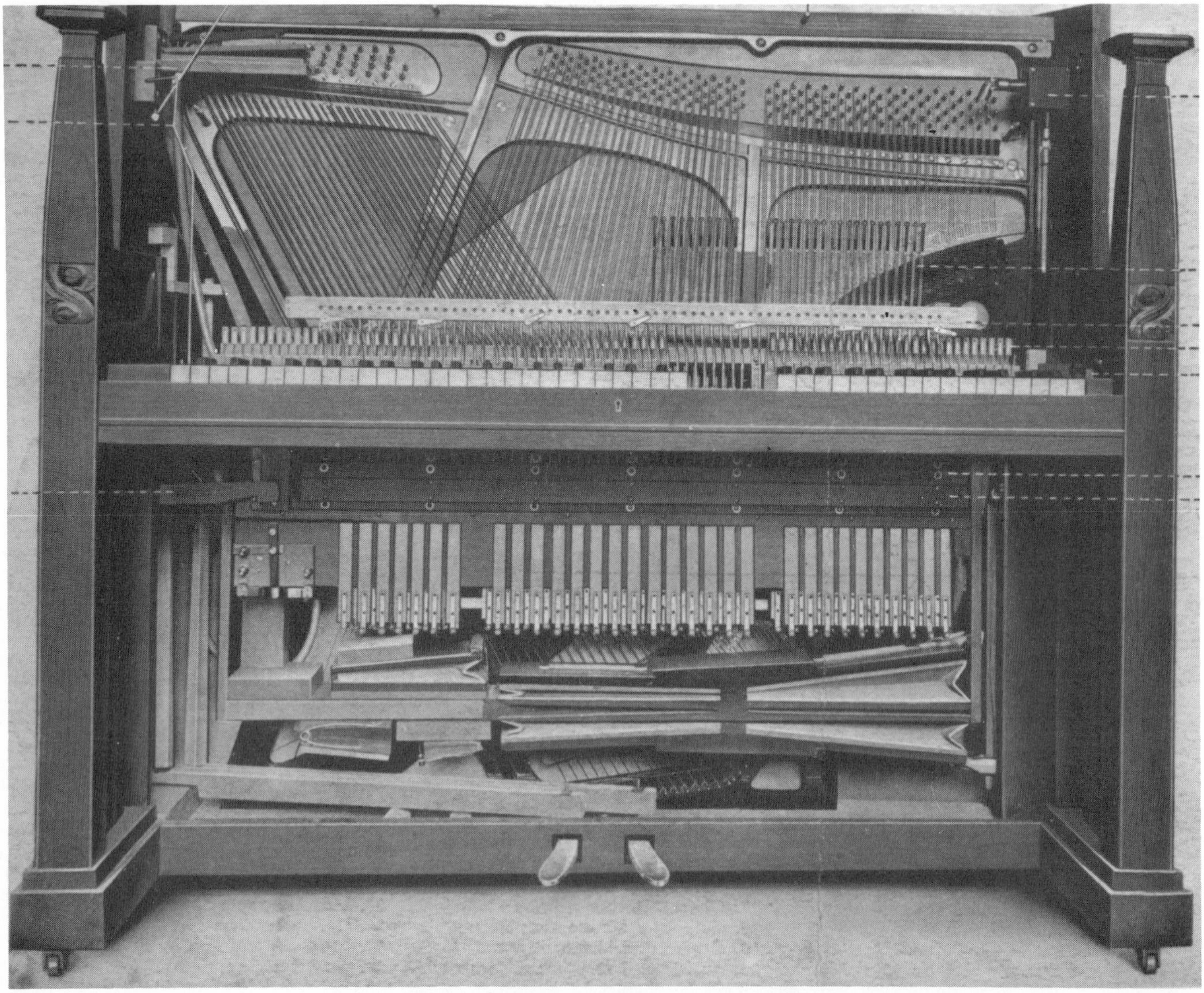

Part of the **pneumatic system** of a coin piano – the pumps, reservoirs, and pneumatic stack (the roll mechanisms and attendant devices are not shown).

ranks play accompaniment. Note: In Europe, pipe tonal specifications are often given in the English system (i.e., feet); except in England, wind pressures are measured in the metric system (i.e., centimeters).

**pipe chest.** Chest, usually made of wood, on which pipes are mounted. The interior is filled with air under pressure. Valves (usually of the pallet valve type) cause the pipes to speak. Synonym: windchest.

**pit organ.** Photoplayer, to which refer. So-called due to its placement in the orchestra pit of a theatre.

**planchette.** Wood strip containing pins or protruding studs arranged in the form of a musical composition (as used on DeBain's Antiphonel).

**platform movement.** Small musical movement used in certain 18th and 19th century watches and similar small items. Pins are arranged in musical sequence on the surface of a disc or platform. Separate steel teeth are arranged around the periphery so that the end of a given tooth will be activated when a pin in that position plucks it. Synonyms: turntable movement, carillons a musique [original French term used by Swiss makers of this type of movement].

**player.** 1. General term for an automatically-played instrument, esp. of the keyboard type. 2. Adjective describing an automatically-played instrument, esp. instruments for which manually-operated counterparts exist. Examples: player calliope, player piano, player organ, etc. 3. An attachment for operating an instrument automatically, used as a noun. Examples: piano player, roll player.

**player organ.** Player pipe organ, player reed organ. An organ which is automatically played by means of a paper roll or other system.

**player piano.** 1. Foot-pumped (usually) upright or grand piano with the pneumatic mechanisms built into the case (in contrast to the piano player, a device which contains the player mechanisms in a separate cabinet which is placed in front of the keyboard). Made for home use. Uses a roll of 65- (early), 73- (early European), or 88-note (universally used after 1908) size. Hundreds of different makes were produced during the early 20th century. Synonym: inner-player [early usage]. 2. Any type piano which uses a paper roll. 3. Any type of keyboard-style piano which uses a paper roll. [Usage by the general public. Collectors designate such specific instruments as coin-operated pianos, expression pianos, and reproducing pianos by their respective names and use the "player piano" term only as given in definition 1. here.]

**plectrum.** (plural: plectra). Device used to pluck a string (e.g., the wooden "finger" used to sound a note in the Wurlitzer Automatic Harp). Term sometimes also used to describe a device which plucks any tuned object (e.g., the star wheel which plucks a music tooth in a disc-type music box).

**plerodienique box.** Cylinder music box with the cylinder made in two parts, each of which shifts laterally outward from center during the tune changing process. Synonym: telescoping box (an early variant of the plerodienique).

**pluck.** To sound a tuned string, music box comb tooth, etc. by pulling it and releasing it quickly. The plucking device is called a plectrum.

**pneumatic.** 1. Adjective describing a musical instrument which is operated automatically by the action of wind pressure or vacuum (as opposed to mechanical, to which refer). 2. Small bellows, esp. one used in a pneumatic stack.

**pneumatic action.** The vacuum- or air-operated series of pouches, valves, and other devices used to sense the paper roll (or music book, paper strip, etc.) and cause an instrument to play automatically. Definition sometimes used to include auxiliary systems as well: pump, blower, reservoir, etc.

**pneumatic stack.** A series of air-actuated pouches, valves, and bellows, esp. in a piano or orchestrion, built as a coordinated unit and used to play a piano action automatically. (Definition does not include supporting mechanisms such as the pump, reservoir, tracker bar assembly, etc.)

**pneumatic system.** Complete system including tracker bar (or key frame or other sensing mechanism), pump, reservoir, pneumatic stack, windchest, etc. of an automatic musical instrument which utilizes wind pressure or vacuum to operate the player mechanisms.

**polytype box.** Cylinder music box, with multiple combs and a large number of teeth, which plays several different types of musical arrangements – sublime harmonie, mandoline, etc.

**portable hand-cranked barrel organ.** Loudly-voiced small organ operated by a pinned wooden cylinder. Made for outdoor use. Synonyms: monkey organ, hurdy gurdy [usage by collectors today; incorrect historically; refer to hurdy gurdy listing.]

**portative** (or portatile). Term, especially used in early days, to describe a portable hand-cranked barrel organ or other portable instrument.

**pouch.** In a pneumatic action a diaphragm which, when one face is acted upon by wind pressure or vacuum, causes a valve or key to operate. Synonym: puff [mainly European usage.]

**pressure bar.** In a disc-type music box, the bar (usually hinged at one end) which by means of idler wheels holds the disc against the star wheels in the playing position. Synonym: idler arm.

**prestant.** Short diapason-like pipe in a fairground organ. Plays with a bright string-like tone.

**program card.** List of tunes giving the program of a music box, coin piano, orchestrion, or other automatic musical instrument. Synonym: tune card.

**projection.** Term used to describe the protruding studs on the underside of a music box disc. Made by forming metal displaced by partially perforating the disc surface.

**proscenium.** [mainly European usage]. Facade or front, esp. of a fairground organ or dance organ.

**puff.** [European usage]. Pouch, either of the diaphragm type or the two-sided (pillow-shaped) type, used in a pneumatic instrument.

**pump.** 1. Bellows-operated device used to provide vacuum or wind pressure to operate an automatic musical instrument. Reciprocating-type pumps have 2, 3, 4 (or more in the case of very large instruments) sets of bellows which are mounted parallel to each other and which operate alternately. Rotary or box-type pumps have 3 or 4 bellows arranged equidistant from a central drive shaft; these bellows operate in sequence. Pumps were built into the cases of most instruments. (Compare to blower, a device which provides wind or vacuum by means of a high-speed fan.) 2. Tracker bar pump. Usually a hand-held device which produces vacuum by means of a piston in a cylinder. (Some automatic instruments, certain Link and Welte instruments for example, utilize a bellows-type pump attached to the instrument.) Used to clean lint and dirt from the tracker bar of an automatic instrument.

**push-up piano player.** A cabinet-style device which contains pneumatic mechanisms and which is pushed up to the piano keyboard in order to play the piano automatically. Usually foot-pumped. Synonyms: cabinet player, vorsetzer [the latter term is used by collectors today to designate electrically-operated push-up units with reproducing mechanisms, and is not generally used to designate foot-pumped models].

# Q

**quartered oak.** (or quarter-sawed oak). Popular American finish, usually applied as veneer, for music boxes, coin pianos, orchestrions, photoplayers, and certain other instruments during the 1900-1930 period. Obtained by cutting the wood so that the flat surfaces parallel the medullary rays of the wood (which extend outward from the center of the log). (Note: a careful restorer will always replace quartered oak veneer with like veneer; never with straight-sawed oak.)

**Reproducing pianos** were made in a wide variety of types, with Ampico, Duo-Art, and Welte-Mignon being the most popular. Other makes such as Dea, Triphonola, Duca, and Angelus each achieved modest sales. Above is a Hupfeld Dea recording session (with Planté, the famous pianist, at the keyboard).

*Arthur Rubinstein*

ARTHUR RUBINSTEIN is a Polish pianist of extraordinary talent, who studied under Joachim and Barth in Berlin and began concertizing in Europe when he was only twelve years old. He made his first visit to America in 1906, and displayed an amazing dexterity of finger and other technical acquirements remarkable in an adolescent. After thirteen years he returned to us as a finished artist and a musical interpreter of rare powers. He has been a great traveler and has concertized in all parts of the civilized world with brilliant success.

Mr. Rubinstein records his interpretations exclusively for the Duo-Art Piano.

*Duo-Art Records by Arthur Rubinstein*

**Reproducing piano** catalogues usually feature prominent pianists and their biographies. The Rubinstein description from a Duo-Art catalogue of 1927 is typical.

Interior Duplex Reproduco

Two **ranks of pipes** are visible below the keyboard in this Reproduco piano - pipe organ from the 1920's.

THE

WELTE-
PHILHARMONIC-
ORGAN

THE ORGAN FOR
THE CULTURED HOME

The playing of the world's greatest organists has been recorded: LEMARE, GOSS-CUSTARD, HOLLINS, WALTON, EDDY, REGER, STRAUBE, SITTARD, FISCHER, RAMIN, LANDMANN, MANIA, BONNET, DUPRÉ, BOSSI etc. Through selfplaying music-rolls the most beautiful examples of organ music, instrumental music, operas etc. can be reproduced on the Welte-Philharmonic-Organ, being rendered faithfully in all dynamic variation and personal musical feeling as expressed by the recording artist. Furnished with console (manual and pedals), the Welte-Philharmonic-Organ can also be played by hand.

**Reproducing pipe organs** typified by the Welte Philharmonic and the Aeolian Duo-Art, were popular additions to mansions during the 'teens and 'twenties.

**quatour.** Cylinder music box with four combs, each tuned differently.

**quintadena.** Stopped small metal flute, rich in harmonic content, used in certain automatic instruments, esp. piano - pipe organs (to which refer).

# R

**ranch style.** Popular early 20th century furniture style, usually utilizing oak, characterized by protruding beveled posts at the top and front corners. Used on many types of player pianos, on the Regina Style 81 Chime Clock, and on certain early American Photo Player Co. instruments.

**rank of pipes.** Single row of pipes, arranged in musical order and of the same type or tonal character. Examples: rank of violin pipes, rank of flageolets, etc. Sections of a single rank of pipes may be given individual names. For instance, a single rank of violin-type pipes may be called "violin, viola, and violoncello;" violin pertaining to the treble part, viola to the middle range, and violoncello to the bass. In orchestrion and organ nomenclature a listing of such terms does not necessarily correspond to the actual number of ranks in the instrument. Note: do not confuse with register. A register is a device for controlling one or more ranks of pipes, or even a portion of a single rank. A register may control several ranks of pipes (esp. in a pipe organ).

**rechange box.** Early and original name for the interchangeable cylinder music box.

**reciprocating pump.** Vacuum or pressure pump consisting of 2, 4 (or more) bellows placed parallel to each other and operated in sequence. (Compare box pump and rotary pump, which are different). Synonym: alligator pump [slang used by collectors].

**record.** 1. Phonograph disc. 2. Metal disc used on a music box [term not generally used today; originally used by Regina, et al.]. 3. Reproducing piano roll [term not generally used today; originally used by Welte and others; Ampico used the term "recording"].

**reed.** 1. Vibrating metal tongue which produces sound in a harmonium or reed organ. 2. Type of organ pipe: 2a. Free reed: a metal tongue which moves in and out of its aperture (called a shallot) freely as it vibrates. Used in reed organs and harmoniums, organettes, and in certain types of organ pipes, esp. those of soft and medium voicing. 2b. Beating reed: a carefully curved (according to principles of voicing) tongue covers the shallot opening (but is too large to enter it) and then springs back again as it vibrates. Mainly used for loudly-voiced pipes. 3. Music box comb tooth [term used by manufacturers c.1890-1910; not used by collectors today].

**reed pipe.** Pipe whose sound is actuated by a free reed or beating reed. One of two major types of pipes used in automatic instruments. (Refer to listings under "pipe" earlier.)

**register.** Control for operating one or more ranks of pipes in an organ or automatic instrument. Synonyms: stop, organ stop.

**regulator.** Spring-loaded bellows connected to the main vacuum or wind pressure supply in a pneumatic instrument. When fully open (in a pressure system) or closed (in a vacuum system) a pallet valve is actuated which opens the system briefly to the outside atmosphere and causes the the vacuum or pressure to return to its desired level. Another type of regulator utilizes the reservoir (to which refer) as a regulating device. Another type uses a spring loaded pallet valve affixed to a wind chest. When the pressure reaches a certain level the pallet opens. Most types of regulators, esp. those in larger instruments, are adjustable. Note: The term was also used to describe expression-regulating devices in certain instruments (e.g., Ampico).

**reiterating.** Constantly repeating. The repetition or repeated striking of a single note by means of a special mechanical or pneumatic action built for this purpose or by means of closely-spaced holes in a music roll. When an extended hole appears in the music roll (or when a staple-like bridge pin occurs in a pinned-cylinder instrument arrangement) the reiterating action will constantly repeat the note until the perforation has ended. In a key-actuated instrument, the reiteration action occurs when the key is lifted or depressed. (Compare to single-stroke.) Synonym: repeating.

**relay.** In a pneumatically-operated instrument a system of valves (sometimes called primary valves) between the tracker bar (or key frame, etc.) and the pipe registers or other effects. 2. In a large pipe organ, the separate apparatus for operating the unification (to which refer) system and controlling the operation of the various ranks and effects.

**repeating.** Reiterating, to which refer.

**reproducing.** Adjective used to identify an instrument which re-enacts a human artist's playing including expression characteristics (in addition to the musical notes).

**reproducing piano.** Automatically-played piano which, by means of special rolls, re-enacts a recording artist's performance, including different levels of intensity (independently controlled for bass and treble sections of the keyboard) in addition to the musical notes and pedal action. Distinguished from an expression (or semi-reproducing) piano by having multiple intensity levels. Rolls, called reproducing piano rolls or artists' rolls, are made from master rolls produced on a special recording piano which captures the nuances, idiosyncrasies of technique, and the attack of the performing pianist. The result is a very realistic performance when a reproducing piano is properly regulated. Reproducing pianos were made in upright, grand, and cabinet styles. Leading types produced c.1905-1930 were Ampico, Duo-Art, and Welte-Mignon. Certain large orchestrions (e.g., Hupfeld Pan, Philipps Paganini) incorporated reproducing-type mechanisms. Synonyms [used years ago in advertising; not used today]: artistic piano, re-enacting piano, master-playing piano, recording piano, reperforming piano. Note: In original advertising such terms as "artistic" and "uses artists' rolls" were used to describe regular (that is, non-reproducing) types of pneumatically-operated pianos – such as regular foot-pumped home player pianos.

**reproducing pipe organ.** Pipe organ which uses rolls recorded by organists and incorporating expression effects (e.g., Aeolian Duo-Art Organ, Welte Philharmonic Organ).

**reproducing reed organ** (or reproducing harmonium). Reed organ which uses rolls recorded by organists and incorporating expression effects (e.g., Popper's Mystikon).

**reroll.** When a rewind-type roll reaches the end of the playing notes, a special reroll (or rewind) perforation causes the roll frame to shift to the reroll position. The pneumatic mechanisms which actuate the playing notes are disengaged so no notes will be played when the roll is rewinding. Rerolling is done at high speed. When the leader of the roll reaches the tracker bar, a rewind-to-play hole in the tracker bar (or, in some instruments, a mechanical device fitted to the take-up spool) actuates a mechanism which shifts the roll frame from reroll to forward. The roll is then ready to play another performance. Rerolling is automatic on most electrically-operated instruments. Hand-cranked or foot-pumped instruments usually require that the roll mechanism be shifted manually to the reroll position. In French, reroll = retour; in German, zurück. Synonyms: rewind, reverse.

**reservoir.** Spring-loaded bellows for storing or for storing and regulating the wind supply from a pressure pump or the vacuum supply from a vacuum pump. Synonym: equalizer (if equipped with a regulator).

**residence organ.** Softly-voiced pipe organ made for residential use. Voicing somewhat similar to that of a church organ. (As opposed to the theatre organ which is voiced more loudly and which is intended to imitate an orchestra.)

**resonator.** 1. On a music box comb, the lead weights attached to the underside of teeth, particularly in the bass section, to cause them to vibrate more slowly and, hence, sound a lower note than would otherwise be the case. 2. On a reed-type organ pipe, the "pipe" part – the upper portion of the top which attaches above the reed part or boot. 3. On a chrysoglott, xylophone, or other chromatic percussion instrument a series of tubes, usually with closed ends, corresponding in length with the pitch of each segment of the percussion instrument and mounted below or behind the instrument. The resonators give the instrument a lingering, wavering sound which imparts a mellow, rich quality to the tone.

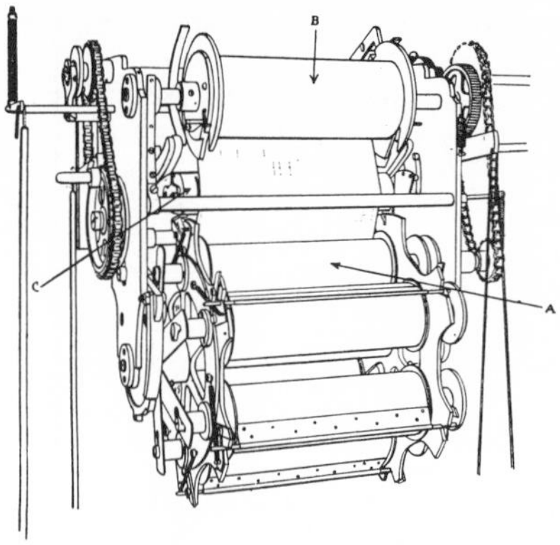

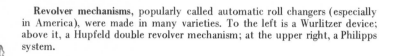

**Revolver mechanisms**, popularly called automatic roll changers (especially in America), were made in many varieties. To the left is a Wurlitzer device; above it, a Hupfeld double revolver mechanism; at the upper right, a Philipps system.

**Rookwood finish** as applied to a Style 67 Regina disc-type music box.

**Roll frames** of two instruments, a Bursens organ (above) and a Weber orchestrion (below).

**Saxophone** on the front of a Decap dance organ. (Svoboda Collection)

**revolver box.** Cylinder music box with three or more cylinders affixed to endplates which are mounted on a common shaft. The cylinders (each of which has several tunes on it) can be changed by rotating the entire assembly so that another cylinder is brought into the playing position adjacent to the music comb.

**revolver mechanism.** [mainly European usage]. Ferris-wheel type of device for storing three or more paper rolls and changing them automatically, usually in the sequence in which they are placed on the device. Produced by many manufacturers, including Aeolian, Hupfeld, Philipps, and Wurlitzer. Synonyms: automatic roll changer, magazine system.

**rewind.** Reroll, to which refer.

**rewind-type roll.** Standard and most-used type of paper roll (for piano, organ, orchestrion, etc.). Wound on a spool. The end tab of the roll is attached to a take-up spool which pulls the roll over the tracker bar as it plays. When the performance ends, the roll is rewound on the original spool. When rewinding is completed, the same performance can be heard again, or the roll can be exchanged with another. (Compare to endless-type roll, to which refer.)

**rohrflute pipe.** Chimney flute pipe, to which refer.

**roll.** 1. Perforated paper roll as used on a player piano, orchestrion, organ, etc. Can be of endless or rewind type (to which refer). 2. Sustained or reiterating striking action, particularly on a drum (as in snare drum roll).

**roll changer.** Ambiguous term referring to a roll mechanism which stores more than one roll. For specific definitions see duplex roll mechanism (two interconnected roll mechanisms mounted near each other on the same instrument), kipp mechanism, and automatic roll changer (also called revolver or magazine mechanism).

**roll frame.** The portion of a roll-operated instrument which contains the tracker bar, take-up spool, and mechanisms for shifting the roll spool and take up spool from rewind to play and vice-versa. Synonyms: roll case, spoolbox.

**roll player.** Refer to player, esp. definitions 2 and 3.

**roller organ.** 1. Organette which uses a small pinned wooden cylinder. 2. Any type of organette, including paper-roll operated models [American usage, informal; not really synonymous with many kinds of organettes.]

**rookwood finish.** Decorative finish applied to certain automatic instruments (esp. certain Regina music boxes of the c.1905 period). Separate scenes, usually in oil, are painted on different portions of the instrument. Portions not painted are finished a red mahogany color.

**rotary pump.** Box pump, to which refer.

# S

**safety check.** On a music box, a device which prevents damage to the music comb by locking the governor assembly (or the cylinder itself) if it suddenly speeds up or "runs away."

**saucer bells.** Refer to bells, definition 1b.

**saxophone.** 1. In an orchestrion or fair organ a reed-type pipe similar to a clarinet, but larger. 2. In an orchestrion, a reed-type pipe with a 4-sided inverted pyramidal wooden resonator, open at the large end. A popular addition to the jazzband-type orchestrions of the 1920's (e.g., certain Popper instruments, Hupfeld's Symphony Jazz Orchestra). 3. In a dance organ a visible but non-musical saxophone mounted on the facade. Behind the saxophone and concealed from view by a curtain is a rank of saxophone pipes. When a saxophone pipe is played, a corresponding key or valve on the saxophone is opened by means of a wire connected to a pneumatic. 4. In a dance organ a box containing saxophone-type reeds placed behind the bottom part of a non-musical but realistic-appearing saxophone. When a note is sounded, a corresponding valve is operated by a wire for visual effect. The sound seems to come from the open end of the saxophone if one is close to the instrument. Method 3, described previously, is more often used. 5. Name given to the bass part of a clarinet rank in an orchestrion (i.e., one rank of clarinet pipes may be described as "clarinet and saxophone").

**scale.** 1. Musical range of an instrument. Description or number of notes from the lowest playing bass note to the highest playing treble note. (This may differ from the actual number of piano notes.) For instance, a 65-note piano roll is played on a regular piano with an 88-note range, but the pneumatic part of the instrument would be described as having a "65-note scale." 2. The number of playing notes plus the number of holes necessary to perform register changes and other functions. Thus an instrument may be described as having, for instance, a 130-note scale. Synonym: key, definition 4 (to which refer). 3. Layout or diagram of the function of each note in a tracker bar, key in a key frame, etc.

**Schausteller Orgel.** [German]. Fairground organ. Literally, "showman's organ."

**Schlagwerk.** [German]. Percussion (non-chromatic) section of an automatic musical instrument, esp. of an orchestrion or organ.

**Schutz-marke.** [German]. Trademark. Included here as this notation is often found on music box discs, etc.

**sectional comb.** In a cylinder music box a comb made by affixing by screws groups of 1 to 5 teeth. A typical sectional comb has many such groups. Late 18th and early 19th centuries. (Sometimes incorrectly called a laminated comb, to which refer.)

**self-changer.** [Mainly European usage]. Automatic disc-changing music box.

**serinette.** Small hand-cranked and hand-held organ containing a limited number (usually 7 to 14) of flute pipes. Originally used to teach canaries to sing. Later used (c.1880-1915) as a children's toy. Usually the music is programmed on a pinned wooden cylinder. Certain later novelty models use discs. Synonyms: bird organ, canary organ.

**sforzando** (or forzando). 1. The sharp accenting of single notes or groups of notes. 2. In an organ or photoplayer a pedal which, when depressed, will bring into play one-by-one all (or nearly all) ranks of the instrument. Synonyms: crescendo pedal, full-organ pedal [the last is rarely used].

**short bedplate.** Refer to bedplate definition earlier.

**silver fox finish** (or silver oak finish or silver gray finish). Finish used on automatic instruments, esp. coin pianos and orchestrions, during the early 20th century. Open-grained oak (either quartered or straight-sawed) is stained black. The pores or open grains are then filled with a white pigment, and then the entire wood surface is varnished.

**single-stroke.** Type of pneumatic or mechanical action which causes a beater or hammer to strike just once when a note is sustained in the music arrangement. (Compare to reiterating, to which refer.)

**skating rink organ.** Band organ, usually with visible brass pipes, used to provide music in a skating rink. Synonyms: military band organ, trumpet organ (if cylinder-operated).

**sleigh bells.** Tuned sleigh bells, usually with one to six bells per note mounted to a board which is shaken, are found in certain fairground organs and in most theatre organs. Tuned sleigh bells = grelotphone in French.

**snail gear.** In a cylinder music box or barrel orchestrion the helically-cut gear or cam which shifts the cylinder laterally.

**snare drum.** Small two-headed (usually) drum with "snares" (tightly stretched pieces of gut or wires) which rattle against one drum head when the other drum head is struck. A popular addition to automatic instruments, esp. orchestrions, fair organs, and dance organs.

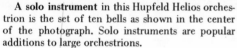

**A solo instrument** in this Hupfeld Helios orchestrion is the set of ten bells as shown in the center of the photograph. Solo instruments are popular additions to large orchestrions.

A famous American orchestrion, the Seeburg Style H, has **solo instruments** which play from an appropriate section on the music roll: a xylophone, violin pipes, and flute pipes. Only a few American orchestrions were ever built with the **solo instrument** feature.

Interior of a Hupfeld Sinfonie Jazz (Symphony Jazz) of the 1920's. Ranks of saxophone and lotus flute pipes are **solo instruments** and play special solo arrangements on the music roll.

Right: A **solo instrument** in this large Coinola orchestrion is the set of xylophone bars played from a special 24-note solo section in the type "O" orchestrion roll used by this (a Coinola SO) and other large Coinola and Empress Electric orchestrions.

**snuffbox.** Small pocket-size hinged box used (esp. in England) to carry snuff. Often fitted with a small cylinder music box movement. Popular during the 19th century.

**soft pedal.** In an upright piano a pedal which, when depressed, brings the piano hammers closer to the strings, thus causing them to strike more softly. In a grand piano the pedal shifts the keyboard laterally to cause a piano hammer to strike just 2 strings of a 3-string note, etc.

**sohn, söhne.** [German]. Sohn = son; söhne (sometimes spelled soehne) = sons. Included here as these terms are often a part of German firm names.

**solo arrangement.** Musical arrangement, esp. in an orchestrion roll, in which a solo instrument (to which refer) is featured.

**solo instrument.** In an orchestrion, organ, or other instrument, a chromatically-tuned (usually) extra instrument (such as a rank of pipes, set of xylophone bars or bells) which, on occasion, play the main theme or a solo part while the other sections of the instrument play accompaniment. Examples: A piano orchestrion, when playing a solo arrangement, has the treble part of the piano (which would normally play the theme of the music) disengaged. A solo instrument, a rank of violin pipes for instance, plays the theme or solo melody while the bass part of the piano plays accompaniment. When the solo has ended, the violin pipe register is turned off and the treble section of the piano is turned back on. Note: Piano orchestrions which play the treble piano notes and an extra instrument at the same time are not considered to be solo-type instruments. In a fairground organ, a brightly voiced rank of pipes may play a solo part while other pipes in lower octave ranges provide accompaniment.

**song roll.** Perforated paper roll with song words printed on it so the roll can be accompanied by singing, if desired. Synonym: word roll.

**sostenuto.** Pedal on a grand piano (usually the center of the three pedals) which selectively sustains notes or chords.

**sounding board** (or soundboard). A thin wooden board, usually made of spruce, to which the vibrations of piano strings, music box combs, or other sounding devices are transmitted, usually by means of a wooden bridge. The sounding board, usually found at the back of a vertical-style instrument or at the bottom of a horizontal-style instrument, amplifies the sound and gives it an additional timbre.

**spill valve.** Regulator valve which spills air (or admits air to a vacuum chamber) when pre-set limits are exceeded. (Refer to earlier regulator definition.)

**spoolbox.** The portion of a roll-operated instrument which contains the tracker bar, take-up spool, and related mechanisms. Synonym: roll frame, to which refer.

**stack.** Abbreviated term for pneumatic stack, to which refer.

**star wheel.** In a disc-type music box, an intervening star-shaped wheel which is struck by a projection on a disc and which, in turn, plucks a tooth in the music comb.

**steam organ.** 1. Archaic term for fairground organ or band organ. The term was derived from the organs' use with steam-driven carousels (occasionally steam power was also used to drive the crankshaft of the organ). 2. Archaic term for calliope.

**steam piano.** [19th century American usage]. Steam-operated calliope (e.g., products of the American Steam Piano Co.).

**stencil piano.** (or stencil organ). An instrument which bears a contrived name or trademark stenciled on the fallboard (or, in a piano, on the piano plate as well). The name of the actual manufacturer is not mentioned. A derisive term used by the music industry to indicate a cheap-quality instrument.

**stop.** 1. In a music box or other spring-wound instrument, a mechanical device (such as the patented Geneva Stop) which locks the winding shaft after a certain tension has been reached, thus preventing overwinding. Synonym: stopwork. 2. In an organ or other instrument with pipes: a register for controlling one or more ranks of pipes. In a pipe organ or reed organ manually-operated stops are located above the keyboard and are called draw-stops or draw-knobs.

**stoplist.** Listing or inventory of the stops on an organ console. The standard way of describing the musical specifications of an organ, esp. a large pipe organ.

**street organ.** Specially-constructed loudly-voiced organ designed for use on a handcart. Used mainly in Holland. Synonyms: Dutch street organ, pierement [the latter term is that used in Holland; the term is also used by collectors worldwide].

**street piano.** Hand-cranked barrel piano, usually mounted on a cart, used to play music in city streets, esp. during the 19th century.

**striker.** Beater or striking hammer, such as that used to sound a drum, xylophone, or other percussion-type instrument.

**sublime harmonie.** Widely-used comb arrangement in music boxes. Two nearly similar combs are tuned celeste (to which refer), thus giving an extra depth and richness to the tone. In cylinder music boxes, the sublime harmonie combs are often combined with one or more additional combs, and are given elaborate names such as sublime harmonie fortissimo, sublime harmonie octavo, etc., depending upon the tonal characteristic(s) of the extra comb(s).

**sustaining pedal.** In a piano a pedal which, when depressed, lifts the dampers (to which refer) from the piano strings, causing the vibrations to be sustained or continued until they fade naturally or until the sustaining pedal is released.

**Swanee Whistle.** Patented (in 1924) pneumatically-actuated slide whistle. The pitch rises and falls as the bottom slide or stopper is moved in and out. Sometimes called a lotus flute (although lotus flute refers also to a regular rank of pipes). Popular addition to jazzband-type orchestrions made in Europe in the 1920's.

**swell shutters.** (or swell shades). Crescendo shutters, to which refer.

T

**take-up spool.** In a roll-operated instrument, the powered cylinder to which the end tab of the roll is affixed. The take-up spool pulls the roll over the tracker bar.

**tambourine.** Wooden hoop with a drum-like head on one end. The hoop is inset with small metal discs or jingles which rattle when the instrument is shaken. A popular addition to orchestrions, photoplayers, etc.

**Tasten.** [German]. Keys on a piano or organ keyboard; metal keys in a fairground organ key frame.

**telescoping box.** Cylinder music box in which the cylinder expands outward from the center during the tune-changing process. Early variation of the plerodienique box.

**temple block(s).** Tuned gourd-like hollow blocks, usually with a horizontal slit at the end, used as percussion effects in certain dance organs.

**tempo regulator.** Manually-set device which regulates the speed of a music cylinder, disc, or paper roll. (Also, sometimes governor – to which refer.)

**tenor drum.** Small drum (usually under 12" in diameter) without snares. (Compare to bass drum.).

**theatre organ.** Pipe organ made for use to accompany silent films in a theatre. Loudly-voiced (usually with 15" and 25" pressure on certain pipe ranks). Contains pipes imitative of orchestra instruments. Contains tibia pipes as a main foundation rank. Unified control system (to which refer), and for this reason sometimes called a unit organ or a unit orchestra (the latter being a Wurlitzer trademark: Wurlitzer Hope-Jones Unit Orchestra). Usually with a horseshoe-shaped console with stop tabs arranged in semicircular rows.

Upper left: **Tune indicator** on a National electric piano (made in Grand Rapids, Michigan).

Above: **Tune selector,** a row of numbered slots, on a National coin-operated electric piano.

Left: Visible at the right side of the art glass panel on this Seeburg KT Special orchestrion is the number 4 on the **tune indicator** – which shows that tune 4 is now playing.

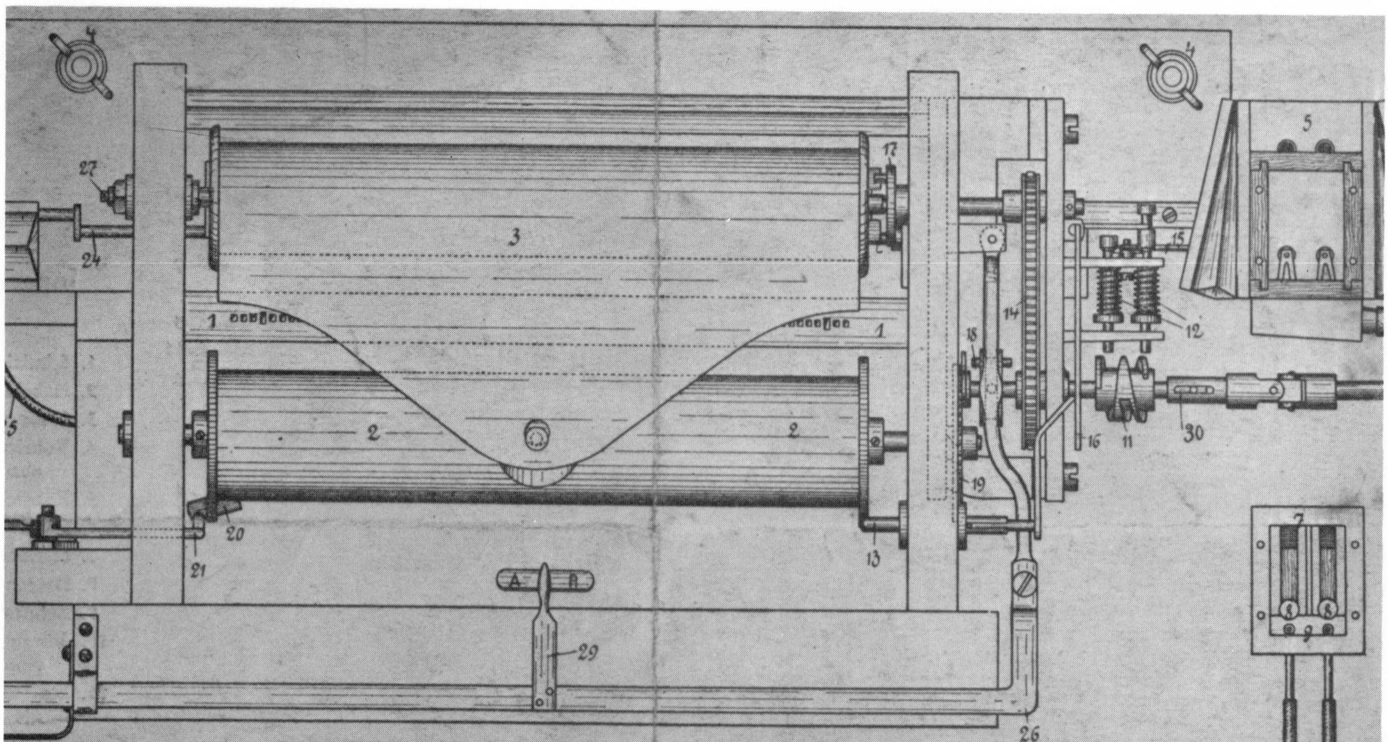

**Tracker bar** (partly covered by roll leader) and attendant assemblies on an electric piano.

**theme.** The subject part of a musical composition; the main melody (as opposed to the accompaniment).

**tibia pipe.** Large stopped bass flute pipe, usually with a leather-covered lip (to prevent the formation of upper harmonics and to assure a purer fundamental tone), used as a foundation rank in a theatre pipe organ. (Note: many other types of tibia pipes exist also.)

**tonal disposition.** Term occasionally used to describe or inventory the musical contents or specifications of a large instrument, esp. a fairground organ, dance organ, or orchestrion.

**tongue.** 1. Vibrating reed in a reed pipe or organ reed. 2. Term used, esp. by Regina, for music box tooth [not used by collectors today].

**Tonstufen.** [German]. Keys in an organ key frame.

**tooth.** 1. Tuned tine or projection, usually made of hardened steel, used to sound a note in a music comb. Synonyms [used years ago; not used by collectors today]: reed, tongue. 2. Projection in a gear (toothed drive wheel).

**touche.** [French]. Key on a piano or organ; key in an organ key frame.

**tracker action.** Early pipe organ system (not automatically-operated) in which the keys in the organ keyboard are directly connected to the pipe valves by means of thin wooden sticks.

**tracker bar.** In a roll-operated instrument the device containing a series of spaced openings through which air passes in order to actuate a pneumatic mechanism (or to directly sound a note, in the case of paper-as-a-valve organettes). Synonyms: tracker board [term rarely used], keyless frame [in fairground and dance organ terminology only].

**tracker bar layout.** (or tracker bar scale). Diagram or listing of the function of each hole in a tracker bar.

**tracking mechanism.** Device, esp. in a roll-operated piano or organ, which keeps the paper roll centered properly and aligned with the correct holes in the tracker bar. This is done by shifting the roll spool or the tracker bar laterally to correct any variance.

**transit box.** Term used to describe a simply-constructed case, usually of metal, containing a small cylinder music box movement. Considered by some to be temporary casing for shipping a musical movement from the maker to a sales agent (who would fit the movement in a more elaborate case).

**transposing device.** Device which enables the tracker bar, esp. of a piano, to shift laterally for up to several notes, so as to transpose the music arrangement to a higher or lower range for use in accompanying a singer. Not generally used in instruments with non-musical perforations (i.e., control perforations) in the tracker bar, for transposing the tracker bar would confuse the controls (exception: some very late Duo-Art reproducing pianos in which only the note-playing portion of the tracker bar shifts).

**treble.** The upper range of the musical scale (as opposed to bass).

**tremolo.** Rapidly repeated variation in the loudness of music. Achieved in several ways: 1. In certain pipe organs, by "shaking" the pressure supply. 2. In certain pipe organs and orchestrions, by beating repeatedly against the outside of a pressure reservoir (this also causes a slight variation in musical pitch). 3. In dance organs and certain fairground organs by: 3a. interrupting the wind supply and thus supplying air to the pipes in short puffs, or 3b. by arranging the music in an intermittent fashion so that a sustained pipe note sounds fully, then begins to die away, and then sounds fully again. 4. In certain orchestrions and organs by putting a butterfly valve in the main wind line. The valve opens and closes rapidly. 5. In reed organs, by placing a rotating paddle over the opening from a reed chest. Synonyms: tremulant, vibrato [popular usage, but incorrect technically; refer to vibrato definition].

**tremulant.** Tremolo, to which refer.

**triangle.** Round steel bar bent into a triangular shape. The ends are close but do not touch. Suspended from a cord and sounded with a metal striker. Widely used in automatic instruments.

**trombone pipe.** Brightly-voiced reed pipe, made of wood or of metal, used in fairground organs (mainly). Usually used as the bass part of a trumpet rank. Imitative of the trombone sound.

**Trommel.** [German]. Drum. Klein Trommel = tenor drum (small drum). Gross Trommel = bass drum (large drum).

**trumpet organ.** Barrel-operated (usually) fairground organ with trumpets, usually of brass and visible on the front.

**trumpet pipe.** In a fairground organ, a brilliantly-voiced reed pipe, made of wood or metal (usually brass), and imitative of a trumpet. Usually used with a bass accompaniment of trombones.

**tubing.** Thin bendable piping, usually made of lead composition (or, esp. in pianos, of rubber or rubber-type composition), used to connect the pneumatic portions of a large automatic instrument. Main wind trunks in very large instruments are often made of cardboard tubing, varnished or painted on the outside to assure airtightness.

**tubular bell(s).** Refer to bells, definition 1c.

**tune card.** Listing of tunes giving the musical program of a music box, coin piano, orchestrion, or other automatic instrument. Synonym: program card.

**tune indicator.** Pointer arm, numbered dial, or other device which indicates the number of a tune being played on a cylinder music box, coin piano, or other instrument.

**tune selector.** Device found on certain coin pianos and orchestrions (e.g., Cremona Tune Selecting Device, Western Electric Selectra, National coin pianos, etc.) which enables the patron to select a desired tune by turning a dial or knob or by dropping a coin in one of several numbered slots.

**tune sheet.** 1. Archaic term for music box disc (esp. used by Regina). 2. Seldom-used term for a music roll or perforated music strip.

**tune skipper.** Term used (esp. by Mermod) to describe a tune-selecting knob with pointer used on certain cylinder music boxes.

**tympani.** Kettle drum, to which refer. Sometimes spelled tympany.

**unda maris.** Literally, "waves of the sea." Pipe rank used in fairground, dance, and street organs. Usually tuned celeste (to which refer) and used in combination with another rank. With characteristic undulating sound.

**unification.** (or unified system). System used in most theatre organs and in some smaller instruments (such as certain mortuary organs with pipes only [without piano] made by Seeburg and Operators Piano Co.) whereby a large rank of pipes extending over many octaves from bass to treble can be drawn or used at any desired pitch. To be played from the same position on the keyboard (or tracker bar) a section of flute pipes, for instance, can be selected at 2' pitch (a treble section of the pipe rank), 4' pitch, or 8' pitch (the bass section). Or, by setting the 2', 4', and 8' stop tabs all at once, the same key will play three pipes – the same note at three different pitches. On multiple-keyboard organs a given rank may be switched from one keyboard to another.

**uniphone bells.** Bar-type bells, usually with a scooplike depression in the center, with a closed-end tubular resonator behind each bar. Used in certain fairground organs, in certain varieties of the Cremona Orchestral J orchestrion, and in a few other instruments.

**unit organ.** (or unit orchestra). Theatre pipe organ or other organ employing unification, to which refer.

**unit valve.** Easily-serviced type of pneumatic stack construction with individually-removable valve units.

De Luxe Model
Violano-Virtuoso
An Automatic Electric Piano of 44 Notes and Two Violins.
Price—$3,000.
Terms:—$450 cash with order, balance of $2,550 in 25 equal installments of $102 each (with interest) due each month after receipt of instrument.
Specifications: Shipping weight—1350 lbs.
Dimensions—5 ft. 9 in. high; 4 ft. 1 in. wide; 2 ft. 10¾ in. deep.
Finishes: Red Mahogany, Brown Mahogany, Oak (dull or polished).
Concert Grand Model
Violano-Virtuoso
One Violin: 44 Note Piano.
Price—$2,500.
Terms: $375.00 cash with order, balance of $2,125 in 25 equal installments of $85 each (with interest) due each month after receipt of instrument.
Specifications: Shipping weight—1250 lbs. Dimensions—5 ft. 5 in. high; 4 ft. 1 in. wide; 2 ft. 9 in. deep.
Finishes: Red Mahogany, Brown Mahogany, Oak (dull or polished).
See last page for Terms to Theaters.

**Violin** players were made in many different forms. To the left is shown the Royal Violista, a violin player made by Prof. Wauters of the Automatic Musical Co. (Binghamton, N.Y.). Above left are two models of the Violano-Virtuoso, an electromagnetically-operated violin player made by the Mills Novelty Company of Chicago. About 4,500 of these were produced. The Dienst Self-Playing Violin (upper right) was marketed in small numbers around 1910. The Hupfeld Phonoliszt-Violina (far upper right) was the world's most popular violin player; an estimated 10,000 or more were made. Below is a violin-playing device patented by Stems & Co. of Dresden in 1912. Stems, a manufacturer of pneumatic stacks and other components for automatically-played pianos, intended to offer the violin player as part of its line of builders' accessories.

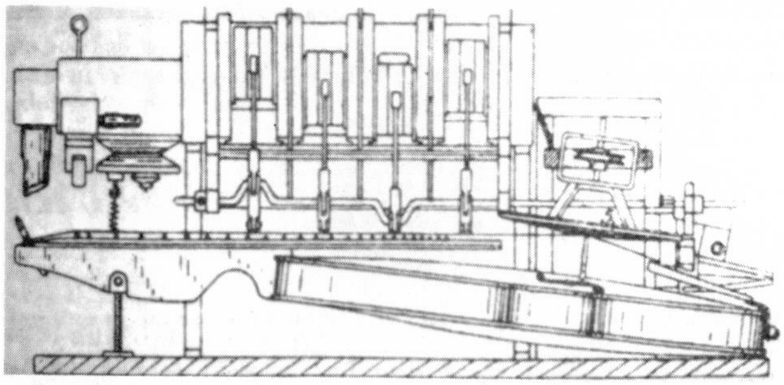

**Wallbox** made by Gustav Schönstein; one of dozens of different types of wallboxes made over the years. These devices, distributed throughout a business establishment, were an effective way to increase receipts from an electric piano, organ, or orchestrion.

One of the most popular automatic **zither** types was the Chordephon, an instrument made by Claus & Co. and later by the Musikwerke Chordephon & Komet, Weissbach & Co. Some Chordephon styles of the 1910-1914 era are shown here. Other automatic zithers include the Arpanetta, Guitarophone, Volks Klavier, and Triola — all of which are described on other pages of this book.

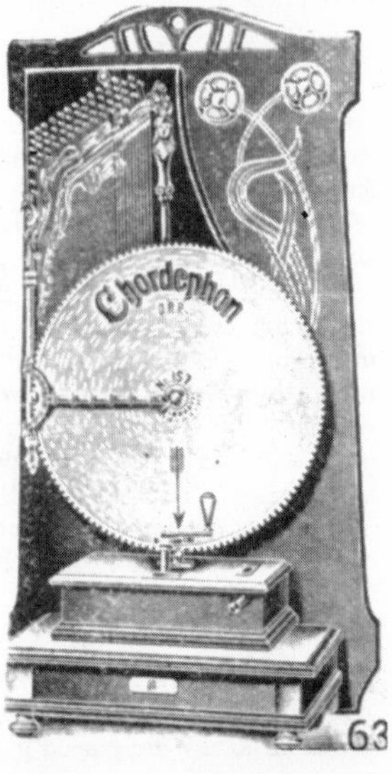

**upright piano.** Piano with the strings mounted vertically. (Compare to grand piano.)

**vacuum motor.** Air motor, to which refer.

**vacuum pump.** Pump, usually bellows-operated, which supplies vacuum to operate a pneumatic system.

**valve.** Device which controls the flow of air. Usually actuated by a pouch (diaphragm).

**valve chest.** Housing, usually made of one or more layers of wood, for the valves of a pneumatic action.

**vibrato.** A device which causes a rapid and repetitive change in pitch (e.g., a vibrato effect is achieved in the Mills Violano-Virtuoso by shaking the violin bridge). (Compare to tremolo.)

**vibraton(e).** Jazz flute pipe (to which refer) with a thin diaphragm of metal, plastic, or other substance mounted in a circular hole in the front of the pipe. When the pipe sounds, the diaphragm resonates and produces a buzzing kazoo-like sound. Synonym: metallophone [term used by Th. Mortier].

**viola pipe.** Pipe of the violin-pipe family, of low or middle-range pitch. Equipped with a harmonic brake (to which refer).

**violin.** 1. Treble-pitched 4-stringed instrument played with a rosined horsehair bow. The two commercially-successful automatically-played violins were the Hupfeld Phonoliszt-Violina and the Mills Violano-Virtuoso. 2. Flue type pipe, of raspy violin-like tonal quality, popularly used in coin pianos, orchestrions, and organs. The tonal quality is regulated by a distinctive-appearing harmonic brake (to which refer). Bass-voiced violin pipes are called cello or violoncello pipes, middle-range pipes are called violas, and treble range pipes are called violin pipes.

**violin piano.** Coin-operated piano with the addition of a rank of violin pipes. In some models the violin pipes can play solo arrangements.

**violoncello.** Violin-type instrument similar in format to a violin, but larger in size and lower in pitch. Synonym: cello.

**violoncello pipe.** Violin-type of pipe of low pitch (refer to violin, definition 2; and to cello). Synonym: cello.

**voicing.** 1. The process by which the tonal quality of a pipe is regulated (as opposed to tuning, which regulates the pitch). 2. Term used to describe the loudness, softness, or the harmonic or tonal character of a pipe. 3. The process by which the hardness of the felt piano hammer head is adjusted or regulated.

**voix celeste.** [French]. Reed organ accompaniment in a cylinder music box. Literally, "celestial voices."

**vorsetzer.** [German origin; term generally used by collectors today]. 1. An electrically-operated (usually) cabinet-style player containing a reproducing mechanism which uses reproducing piano rolls. The cabinet is equipped with felt-covered "fingers" and is pushed up to the keyboard of an upright or grand (usually) piano. The fingers and corresponding pedal mechanisms then automatically play the keyboard and pedals of the piano automatically. Vorsetzer = sitter-in-front-of in German. Vorsetzers with reproducing mechanisms were made with several different reproducing piano systems, including Hupfeld Dea and Welte-Mignon (but not Ampico or Duo-Art). [This definition, a vorsetzer with a reproducing mechanism, is the one generally used by collectors today.] 2. Any push-up piano player or device which is placed in front of a piano or organ keyboard to play it. Synonyms: cabinet player, piano player, push-up piano player.

**vox celeste.** String-toned pipe of undulating tonal quality, similar to an unda maris. Used in fairground organs.

**vox humana.** Pipe rank of the reed family, usually with a capped metal resonator. Literally, "human voice." Used in photoplayers and in several types of organs.

**wallbox.** Small box, connected to a coin piano or orchestrion by wires, with a coin slot. When a coin is deposited, an electrical contact is made which causes the instrument to play. An effective way of providing many coin slots throughout a business establishment, thus increasing the receipts of a single instrument. Note: European coin pianos were rarely equipped with built-in coin slots; a single wallbox was often attached to the outside of the case of such an instrument.

**Walze.** [German]. Barrel. Plural = Walzen. Walzenorgel = barrel organ. Walzen Orchestrion = barrel-operated orchestrion.

**water motor.** Water-driven turbine used mainly 1870-1905 (but used much earlier as well) to power automatic instruments in a time when electricity was not available in many areas.

**weight drive.** Power system used to operate organ clocks, early barrel orchestrions, and other instruments. A heavy weight (several hundred pounds or more in large instruments) is wound up to near the top of the instrument. As it falls it powers the instrument by means of an escapement.

**whistle.** 1. Pipe used in a calliope or bird whistle. 2. Term used to describe any type of pipe [informal; not generally used by collectors].

**wind motor.** Air motor, to which refer.

**wind pressure.** Pressure, usually measured in inches (or in centimeters) of water, of air used to operate pipes or pressure-operated pneumatic actions. (Refer to definition of "pipe" for further information.)

**windchest.** Pipe chest, to which refer.

**wonder light.** (or wonder lamp). Rotating jeweled ball, illuminated with a light bulb in the center, used as a decorative effect on certain coin pianos, orchestrions, and organs. Synonym: Aladdin's lamp [term rarely used].

**wood block.** 1. Hardwood block, usually hollow in the center or with a cavity, which is operated by striking with a wooden beater. A popular percussion effect in orchestrions and organs. 2. In a cylinder music box a hardwood block, usually hollow, struck by 5 to 8 metal beaters. Synonyms: castanets, wood drum.

**wood drum.** Wood block used in a cylinder music box (refer to wood block, definition 2). Synonyms: wood block, castanets.

**word roll.** Music roll with words printed on it, usually along the right-hand edge. Synonym: song roll.

**xylophone.** 1. Set of tuned wooden bars. From the Greek language: xylo = wood; phon = sound. (When equipped with resonators, a xylophone is called a marimba, to which refer). Synonym: marimbaphone [used by the Link Piano Co.; not general usage]. 2. Careless description of orchestra bells (which are of metal and thus, by definition of the word, cannot be a xylophone). [Term esp. used in Europe.]

**zither.** 1. Dulcimer-like stringed instrument. Mechanically-operated zithers include the Arpanetta, Chordephon, Guitarophone, and Triola. Strings are either plucked or struck with tiny hammers. (Note: in a non-automatic zither the strings are plucked by a plectrum.) 2. Banjo effect (refer to banjo definition 2). Synonyms: banjo, harp, mandolin attachment or effect.

Audsley, George Ashdown. *The Temple of Tone.* J. Fischer & Bro.; New York, N.Y., 1925.
Barnes, William H. *The Contemporary American Organ.* J. Fischer & Bro.; New York, N.Y., 1956.
Blesh, Rudi and Janis, Harriet. *They All Played Ragtime.* Grove Press; New York, N.Y., 1959.
Bormann, Karl. *Orgel- und Spieluhrenbau.* Sanssouci; Zurich, Switzerland, 1968.
Boston, Canon Noel and Langwill, Lyndesay G. *Church and Chamber Barrel-Organs.* Lyndesay G. Langwill; Edinburg, Scotland, 1967.
Bowers, Q. David. *A Guidebook of Automatic Musical Instruments, Vol. I and II.* The Vestal Press; Vestal, N.Y., 1967.
Bowers, Q. David. *Put Another Nickel In.* The Vestal Press; Vestal, N.Y., 1965
Bradley, Van Allen. *Music for the Millions.* Henry Regnery Co.; Chicago, Illinois, 1957.
Bragard, Roger and Delten, Ferdinand J. *Musical Instruments in Art and History.* Barrie and Rockliff; London, England, 1968.
Buchner, Dr. Alexander. *Mechanical Musical Instruments.* Batchworth Press; London, England, n.d. (c.1955).
Chapuis, A. *Histoire de la Boite a Musique.* Editions Scriptar; Lausanne, Switzerland, 1955.
Chapuis, A. and Droz, E. *Automata.* Editions du Griffon; Neuchatel, Switzerland, 1958.
Chew, V.K. *Talking Machines.* Her Majesty's Stationery Office; London, England, 1967.
Clark, John E.T. *Musical Boxes – A History and Appreciation.* George Allen & Unwin, Ltd.; London, England, 1961.
Cockayne, Eric V. *The Fairground Organ.* David & Charles; Newton Abbot, England, n.d. (c.1970).
deWaard, Romke. *From Music Boxes to Street Organs.* English language edition by The Vestal Press; Vestal, N.Y., 1962.
deWit, Paul. *Pearls from the Collection of Musical Instruments of Paul deWit in Leipzig (Saxony).* Paul deWit; Leipzig, Germany, 1892.
deWit, Paul. *Weltadressbuch der Musikinstrumenten Industrie.* Paul deWit; Leipzig (later, Breslau), Germany. Many different early 20th century issues.
Dolge, Alfred. *Pianos and Their Makers.* Covina, California, 1911 and 1913.
Farmer, Henry George. *The Organ of the Ancients.* William Reeves, Bookseller Ltd.; London, England, 1931.
Faust, Oliver C. *A Treatise on the Construction, Repairing, and Tuning of the Organ.* Tuners Supply Co.; Boston, Massachusetts, 1949.
Fried, Frederick. *A Pictorial History of the Carousel.* A.S. Barnes & Co.; New York, N.Y., 1964.
Givens, Larry. *Rebuilding the Player Piano.* The Vestal Press; Vestal, N.Y., 1963.
Givens, Larry. *Re-enacting the Artist.* The Vestal Press; Vestal, N.Y., 1970.
Hall, Ben M. *The Best Remaining Seats.* Bramhall House; New York, N.Y., 1961.
Helmholtz, Hermann. *The Sensations of Tone.* Reprint of 1885 edition by Dover Press; New York, N.Y., 1954.
Herzfeld, Von Friedrich. *Ullstein Musiklexikon.* Ullstein GmbH; Frankfurt-am-Main and Berlin, Germany, 1965.
Hoke, Helen and Hoke, John. *Music Boxes, Their Lore and Lure.* Hawthorn Books; New York, N.Y., 1957.
Holzhey, Gunther. *Flotenuhren aus dem Schwarzwald.* Berliner Union GmbH; Stuttgart, Germany, n.d. (c. 1960-1970).
Irwin, Stevens. *Dictionary of Pipe Organ Stops.* G. Schirmer, Inc.; New York, N.Y., 1962.
Junghanns, Herbert. *Der Piano- und Flugelbau.* Dr. Max Janecke, Bookseller; Leipzig, Germany, 1932.
Kircher, A. *Musurgia Universalis.* Rome, 1650.
Lewis, Walter & Thomas (organ builders). *Modern Organ Building.* William Reeves, Bookseller Ltd.; London, England, 1939.
Loesser, Arthur. *Men, Women, and Pianos.* Simon & Schuster; New York, N.Y., 1954.
Maingot, Eliane. *Les Automates.* Librairie Hachette; Paris, France, 1959.
Mangels, William F. *The Outdoor Amusement Industry.* Vantage Press; New York, N.Y. 1952.
Mattfeld, Julius. *Variety Music Cavalcade 1620-1969.* Prentice-Hall, Inc.; Englewood Cliffs, N.J., 1971.
McTammany, John. *The Technical History of the Player.* Musical Courier Co.; New York, N.Y., 1915. Reprinted by the Vestal Press; Vestal, N.Y., 1971.
Michel, N.E. *Michel's Organ Atlas.* Published by the author; Pico Rivera, California, 1969.
Michel, N.E. *Old Pianos* (and the successor volume, *Historical Pianos*). Published by the author; Pico Rivera, California, 1954, 1969.
Michel, N.E. *Michel's Piano Atlas.* Published by the author; Pico Rivera, California, various dates.
Mosoriak, R. *The Curious History of Music Boxes.* Lightner Publishing Corp.; Chicago, Illinois, 1943.
Ord-Hume, Arthur W.J.G. *Collecting Musical Boxes and How to Repair Them.* Crown Publishers; New York, N.Y., 1967.
Ord-Hume, Arthur W.J.G. *Player Piano.* A.S. Barnes & Co.; New York, N.Y., 1970.
Prasteau, Jean. *Les Automates.* Librairie Grund; Paris, France, 1968.
Read, Oliver and Welch, Walter L. *From Tin Foil to Stereo.* Howard W. Sams & Co.; Indianapolis, Indiana, 1959.
Roehl, Harvey. *The Player Piano, a Historical Scrapbook.* Century House; Watkins Glen, N.Y., 1958.
Roehl, Harvey. *Player Piano Treasury.* The Vestal Press; Vestal, N.Y., 1961.
Schonberg, Harold C. *The Great Pianists.* Simon & Schuster; New York, N.Y., 1963.
Schott, Gaspar. *Magiae Universalis Naturae et Artis; Part 2, Acustica.* 1657.
Sumner, William Leslie. *The Organ.* Philosophical Library; New York, N.Y., 1953.
Thompson, Oscar (editor). *The International Cyclopedia of Music and Musicians.* Dodd, Mead & Co.; New York, N.Y., 1964.
Van Atta, Harrison Louis. *The Piano and Player Piano.* Published by the author; Dayton, Ohio, 1914.
Webb, Graham. *The Cylinder Musical Box Handboook.* Faber & Faber; London, England, 1968.
Webb, Graham. *The Disc Musical Box Handbook.* Faber & Faber; London, England, 1971.
Whitworth, Reginald. *The Electric Organ.* Musical Opinion; London, England, 1940.
Wieffering, F. *Glorieuze Orgeldagen.* A. Oosthoek's Uitgeversmaatschappij N.V.; Utrecht, Holland, 1965.
Williams, C.F. Abdy. *The Story of the Organ.* Charles Scribner's Sons.; New York, N.Y., 1903.

---

Periodicals and Yearbooks

"The AMICA." News bulletin of the Automatic Musical Instrument Collectors Association.
"The Bulletin of the Musical Box Society International." Periodical of the Musical Box Society International.
"Bulletin of the National Association of Watch and Clock Collectors, Inc." Periodical of the National Association of Watch and Clock Collectors, Inc.
"The Coin Machine Journal."
"Deutsche Instrumentenbau Zeitung."
"Fox's Music Trade Directory of the United States."
"The Indicator."
"The Key Frame." Journal of the Fair Organ Preservation Society.
"Der Komet."
"The Music Box." Journal of the Musical Box Society of Great Britain.
"The Music Trade Review."
"The Music Trades."
"The Musical Courier."
"Musical Opinion"
"The Piano and Organ Purchaser's Guide."
"Het Pierement." Journal of the Kring van Draaiorgelvrienden.
"The Presto."
"Scientific American."
"The Tuners Journal."
"The World's Fair."
"Zeitschrift für Instrumentenbau."
"Zeitschrift für Musikwissenschaft."

Other Sources

Among other sources consulted during the preparation of this volume were: (1) patent records of France, Germany, Great Britain, and the United States; (2) sales catalogues, literature, prospectuses, record books and ledgers, roll catalogues, and other data from the various manufacturers of automatic musical instruments; (3) catalogues and books relating to various world's fairs and expositions at which automatic musical instruments were exhibited, from 1851 to 1933; (4) city directories; correspondence and personal visits with many persons (refer to "Those Who Helped" page in the fore part of this book).

## INDEX AND EASY-FINDING LIST

# INDEX AND EASY-FINDING LIST

## EXPLANATION OF THE INDEX
—and how to use it—

The Index and Easy-Finding List includes: trade names of instruments, manufacturers, names of persons connected with the field of automatic instruments, and general subjects. There are over 3,000 entries. For explanations and definitions concerning different types of instruments, components, technical information, etc. refer to the Dictionary of Automatic Musical Instrument Terms which begins on page 945.

Pianists, Organists: Certain persons are indexed as pianists or organists when their main references in this book pertain to these subjects, although these persons may have had other accomplishments as well (as composers, conductors, etc.).

Indexed are pages 15 to 944 inclusive. The Index does not cover the introduction or preface of the book, nor does it cover the Dictionary of Automatic Musical Instrument Terms (beginning on page 945).

Spelling Variations: (1) If the spelling of an instrument's or person's name was not consistent, entries appear in several places. Examples are the Niagara piano variously referred to as the Pianagara and the Pianiagara and the Hupfeld orchestrion referred to as the Sinfonie Jazz (in German-language catalogues) and as the Symphony Jazz (in English-language catalogues). (2) In surnames, the prefixes of de, von, and van all have the same meaning ("of"). The index follows the alphetization originally used by the person. Eugen d'Albert is listed under "A" and Eugene DeRoy is listed under "D", for instance. If spelling was inconsistent, then the prefix is not indexed. For example, dePachmann and vonPachmann spellings were both used to identify that pianist. We index the name under "P", not "D" or "V". (3) Names vary from language to language, as noted; indexing is by the most common usage as found in original catalogues, as imprinted on an instrument itself, etc. Examples of identity: xylophon and xylophone are interchangeable, as are Georg-George, Luxus-Deluxe, Wilhelm-William, Orchester-Orchestre-Orchestra, Geigen-Violin-Violon-Violine, Karl-Carl, Ludwig-Ludovico-Ludovic, music-musique-musik, Sons-Söhne-Soehne-Fils, Gebrüder-Frères-Brothers, etc. (4) Umlauted ö items are often interchangeable with oe: Böcker is correct spelling, as is Boecker, for instance. (5) Frères and Gebrüder (usually abbreviated as Gebr.) both are the same as Brothers. It was common practice to use Gebrüder before a surname (as Gebrüder Bruder, the Waldkirch organ builder) and Frères and Brothers after (as Bruder Brothers or Bruder Frères). For this reason Gebrüder items are indexed under the surname. For instance, refer to Bruder, Gebr. (under "B", not "G").

Descriptive Adjectives: Often instruments were given descriptive adjectives as part of their names in advertising: Grand, Concert, New, Deluxe, etc. If such designations were not usually a part of the product name or were used only occasionally, their use is considered adjectival and not a part of the name. If such designations were usually used (Concert PianOrchestra, DeLuxe Orchestrion, etc.) then they are indexed.

"&" is indexed as "and." Thus Adams & Smith would appear before Adams, Charles. The hyphen is disregarded and hyphenated words are indexed as two separate words (as original hyphenation was often irregular; Welte-Mignon vs. Welte Mignon, for example).

Genealogical designations such as I, II, and III do not necessarily refer to grandfather, father, and son but refer to oldest, next oldest, and youngest.

Parenthetical items are for explanatory and clarification purposes. Indexing is in order by names preceding the parentheses.

Multiple index entries are separated by commas except when semicolons are used to indicate an important multiple-entry section. For example, a listing such as: 53, 57, 78-85, 103; history and description of instruments 118, 120-125; 132, 145 means that the pages set off by semicolons (pp. 118, 120-125) are those pertaining to the history and description of instruments; the other entries are incidental references.

Credit notes which appear in parentheses () throughout the book are not indexed; refer to the "Those Who Helped" (page 4) section for a list of credits. Names of persons, including present-day collectors, authors, etc., included as part of the author's text are indexed. Listings of agents, pianists, trade names, etc. which appear in original advertisements are indexed, even though these names may not appear in the author's accompanying text.

——————————

### A


Abate, Giuseppe, 806
Abbott, Calvin (pianist), 283
Abel, Frans, 893
Abrahams, B.H. (cylinder and disc music boxes; B.H.A., Britannia, etc. trademarks), 19, 22, 26, 64, 66, 243, 249
Abrams, Louis, 369
A.B.T. Co. (amusement devices), 528, 530
Accordeon Jazz (Pierre Eich), 395, 396, 742
Accordeon Orchestra (Pierre Eich), 395
Ackerman, Edwin D., 582, 705, 722
Ackerman Player Piano Co., 705, 722
Ackolin (Ackerman piano), 722
Ackotist Player Piano Co., 705
Acme Newark Machine Works (Acme roll perforators), 728, 729
Acoustic Cabinet (Kaufmann display of automatic instruments), 480
Acoustigrande (pianos), 319
Adek Manufacturing Co., 582
Adler (disc music box made by J.H. Zimmermann), 100, 102, 103, 209, history and description 238-242, 249-251
Adler, Clarence (pianist), 279, 283
Admiral (Imhof & Mukle orchestrion), 464-466, 473, 476-478
Aeola (Symphonion music box), 222
Aeolian American Corp., refer to Aeolian Company
Aeolian Company (including its various company names over the years; from the Mechanical Orguinette Co. to the Aeolian American Corp.), 250, 255-258, 273, history and description of Duo-Art reproducing piano 295-310, financial history of Aeolian Co. 309-310, 321, 336, 405, 431, 504, 727, 740, 742-744, 761, 762, organettes 767, player reed organs 777-780, 781, pipe organs 788-790, Aeolian-Hammond organ 791, 793
Aeolian-Hammond (player electronic organ), 788, description of 791
Aeolian Music Rolls, Inc., 720, 721
Aeolian pipe organs, (refer also to Duo-Art pipe organ), 309, 742-744, 779, history and description of instruments 788-790, 793
Aeolian-Skinner Organ Co., 310, 788, 791
Aeolion Flute Orchestrion (Hupfeld), 433
Afferni, Ugo (pianist), 317
Aida (Holzweissig orchestrion), 429
Aida (Popper orchestrion), 583, 586
Air-Calio (Artizan calliope), 813, 839, 844
Albert, Eugen d' (pianist), 279, 282, 283, 308, 311, 314, 317, 326, 328, 329, 331, 336, 435, 436, 462, 584
Albert, Prince, 480
Albums, musical, 70, 72
Alexandra (Abrahams disc music box), 243
Alexandra (cylinder music box), 20, 63
Alexandrowska, Luba d' (pianist), 279, 283
Alfring, William, 309
Allard (cylinder music boxes), 19, 27, 29, 30, 41, 45
Allen, Frances Potter (pianist), 279, 283
Allen, Hugh, 308
Alps Amusement Co., 595
Altschuler, Modest, 283
Amabile (organette), 753
American (brand of music roll), 719, 725
American (brand of piano), 703
American Automatic Organ Co., 741, 763, 771
American Automatic Typewriter Co., 660
American Automusic Co., history and description of Encore Banjo 398-418
American Graphophone Co., 172, 182, 185, 186, 197, 202, 210
American Guitar Zither (mechanical zither), 359
American Music Box Co. (Monarch and Triumph music boxes), 104
American Mutoscope and Biograph Co., 407
American Orchestra (early American Photo Player Co. photoplayer), 378
American Photo Player Co. (later reorganized as the Photo Player Co.), 262, 352, history and description of instruments 367-381, 702, 709, 720
American Piano Co., 273, 276, history and description of the Ampico reproducing piano 277-292, 293, 302, merger with Aeolian 309-310, 318, 321, 718
American Piano Player Co. (of Louisville, Ky.), 382
American Sales Co., 712
American Steam Piano Co. (calliopes), 838, 840
Amorette (organette), 250, 251, 742, 747, description of 748, 753

Amphion Co., 277, 293, 321
Ampichron (attachment for the Ampico), 278
Ampico (reproducing piano), 273-276, history and description of 277-292, 293, 295, 319, 321, 654, 727, 734
Anderson (pianos), 703, 725
Anderton's (showmen), 867, 887
Angelus (player piano), 250
Angelus (reproducing piano), 294
Angelus Orchestral Piano Player, 258, 781
Animatic (Hupfeld pianos and orchestrions), 431-434, 440, 453, 460
Animochord (Popper orchestrion), 590
Annalies (Lüneburg piano), 706
Ansorge, Conrad (pianist), 317, 331
Antiphonel (early automatic piano), 362
Antoniazzi (principal of B.A.B. Organ Co.), 858
Apollo (orchestrions), 706
Apollo (pianos by Melville Clark and Rudolph Wurlitzer, some with expression or reproducing systems), 261, 293, 602, 611, 663, 719
Apollo Musikwerke (pianos and orchestrions), 706
Apollo Piano Co., 293
Apollonicon (early organ/orchestrion), 744
Arbuckle Brothers (agent), 210
Arburo (Bursens organs), history and description of 833-837, 846
Arcadian (Peerless orchestrion), 553, 554, description of 557, 558, 654
Arcophon (Popper), 590
Arden, Elizabeth, 310
Arden, Victor (pianist), 279, 283, 719, 721, 727
Ardenghi & Figli, 806
Aria Divina (expression piano), 318, 321
Ariani, Adriano (pianist), 279, 283
Arion (Popper orchestrion), 585
Ariosa (organette), 249, 741, description of 751, 752
Ariston (organette), 99, 129, 359, 430, 441, 533, 741, 742, history and description of 746
Ariston (pianos), 703, 725
Aristonette (organette), 746
Armbruster, Robert (pianist), 299
Armitage Herschell (amusement outfitter), 814, history and description of instruments, etc. 869-873
Armstrong (pianos), 281, 703, 725
Armstrong, H.C., 508
Arnaud, Germaine (pianist), 308
Arndt, Felix (pianist), 294, 299, 721
Arno, Oliver H. (inventor; associated with Massachusetts Organ Co. and other firms), 248, 764
Arnold, Robinson & Co. (agent), 124
Arnold, Wilhelm (piano manufacturer; later acquired by Philipps), 566
Arpanetta (mechanical zither), 356
Arrington, Roy, 558
Art Automaton (with Adler music box), 240
Art Cabaret (Peerless piano), 561, 562
Artecho (reproducing piano), 277, history and description of 293, 663
Arthur (Polyphon music box), 163
Artigraphic, refer to Ampico
Artist (Popper orchestrion), 585
Artizan Factories, Inc. (band organs, calliopes, etc.; successors to the North Tonawanda Musical Instrument Works), 537, 804, history and description of instruments 813-814, 839, 844, 871, 873
Artrio-Angelus (reproducing piano), 294
Ascenseur, L' (automaton), 74
Asmus, Emil (successor to Cocchi, Bacigalupo & Graffigna), 708
Astor, George & Co. (organs), 785
Astor, John Jacob, 785
Astor, Vincent, 280
Athelstane (Polyphon music box), 163
Atlantic (Hupfeld orchestrion), 438, 441
Atlantic Garden, 632, 645, 712
Atlantic Tool & Machine Co., 709
Atlas (organette), 742, 747, description of 753
Aton, W.H. (agent), 544
Aubry, Emile d', 353
AudioGraphic Music Rolls, 308
Audiophone (Seeburg phonograph), 656
Augiéras, Pierre (pianist), 279, 283
Aurephone (organette), 763, 764, 768
Aurora (Popper orchestrion), 586, 590
Austin Organs, Inc., 744
Austin Premier Quadruplex (pipe organ roll player), 714, 744
Auto-Chordephonette (mechanical zither), 357
Auto Deluxe Welte Mignon Reproducing Piano, refer to Welte Mignon
Auto Electric Piano Co., 383, 703, 722
Auto Electric Piano Player (Berry-Wood), 386, 387
Auto-Grand (Krell piano), 265
Auto-Harmonium (Hofmann & Czerny), 428
Auto Inscribed (music rolls), 553, 562
Auto-Manufacturing Co., 353, 355, history and description of Encore Banjo 398-418
Auto Orchestra (Berry-Wood), 386, 387
Auto-Organ (Autophone Co. organette), 768
Auto-Organ (Carpenter player reed organ), 743
Auto-Player (Krell piano), 265
Auto Pneumatic Action Co., 256, 277, 293, 319-321, 654
Auto Stereoscope (Mills arcade device), 526
Auto-typist, 660
AutoElectra (pianos), 703, 722
AutoElectrola (pianos), 722, 725
Autograph Piano (Wurlitzer), 339, 354, 611, history and description of 663-664 and 680, 720
Automata, 61, 62, 65, 69, 70, 73-85, 90, 91
Automatic Banjo Company of New Jersey, refer to Encore Banjo
Automatic Cabinet Organ (organette), 763, 764
Automatic Cashier & Discount Machine, 209
Automatic Harp (Whitlock/Wurlitzer), 348, 353, history and description of 662-664 and 666-668, 721, 938
Automatic Melodista (organette), 741, 771
Automatic Music Roll Co. (Seeburg subsidiary), 602, 718, 719
Automatic Musical Co. (predecessor of Link Piano Co.), 347, 353, 384, 402, 495, history and description of instruments 481-487, 703, 705, 720, 722
Automatic Musical Instrument Collectors Association (usually abbreviated as AMICA), 284, 299, 339, 578
Automatic Orchestra Co., 384
Automatic Organ (Dulciphone organette), 764
Automatic Piano (Melodette), 359
Automatic Pianova, refer to Pianova
Automatic Player Piano (Wurlitzer 65-note electric piano), 348, 351; history and description of 661, 663-665, 671-673, 675, 697, 699; 703, 714, 716, 720, 721, 839
Automatic Roll Changer (Wurlitzer), 661, 664, 671, 672, 679, 688
Automatic Vaudeville (arcade), 506
Automatic Virtuosa, refer to Virtuosa (Mills violin player)
Automaton Piano Co., 582
Automusicograph (Barbieri), 385
Autoperforator (Barbieri), 385
Autophone Co., 741 743, history and description of instruments 754-756, 768, 772
Autopiano (Kästner), 711
Autovox (Link phonograph), 486
Axt, William (pianist), 283
Ayres, Cecile (pianist), 279, 283

B

B.A.B. Organ Co. (band organs), 813, 858
Baby Ampico (reproducing piano), 277, 290
Bacigalupi, Joseph, 535
Bacigalupi, Louis (name changed from Bacigalupo, Louis), 807
Bacigalupi, Peter & Sons (agent), 535, 536, 637, 711
Bacigalupo, Giovanni I, 806, 807, 851
Bacigalupo, Giovanni II, 804-810
Bacigalupo, Giuseppe, 807
Bacigalupo, Louis, 807
Bacigalupo, Luigi, 807, 809
Bacigalupo Söhne, 806-809, 811, 812
Bäcker-Gröndahl, Fr. (pianist), 317
Backhaus, Wilhelm (pianist), 279, 282, 283, 308, 314, 329, 331, 436
Bacon, Francis (pianos), 319
Badenia (Imhof & Mukle orchestrion), 465, 469, 471, 476
Baer, Felix (pianist), 317
Baets, Els (Mrs. Jeff), 623
Bain, Alexander, 255, 635
Bajde, Johann (inventor), 437, 438
Bajde, Ludwig (inventor), 437, 438
Baker, Norman (owner, Tangley Co.), 838
Baker-Troll (music boxes), 19, 21, 31, 71

Balcom, H. Tracy (agent) 258, 778
Baldwin (pianos), 273
Baldwin, Samuel A. (agent), 792
Ball & Son (showmen), 863
Ball, Beavon & Co. (agent), 249, 250
Ball, Ernest R. (pianist), 279, 283
Band organs and related instruments (also called fairground organs, carousel organs, etc.), refer to general section 801-944
Bandoniphon (player concertina), 776
Banj-O-Grand (Nelson-Wiggen piano), 528, 725
Banjorchestra (orchestrion), 353, 400, 509, 553, 554, 559, description of 560
Banta, Frank (pianist), 283
Baranoff, Sascha (pianist), 283
Barber, Lyell (pianist), 279, 283
Barbieri, M., history and description of Automusicograph, Autoperforator, and other devices 385
Bargy, Roy (pianist), 283
Barnes (showman), 883
Barnum, P.T. (showman), 347, 634
Barr, Donald D., 513, 515, 516
Barrel organs, general description of 803; refer also to general section 801-944 for barrel organs and related instruments
Barrel organs, portable hand-cranked, history and description 805-812; refer also to individual firms such as Cocchi, Frati, Molinari, and others 801-944
Barrel pianos, general description of 349-350, 362, 891
Bartels, Carl, 726
Bartels, Leo F., 726
Barth, Hans (pianist), 279, 283
Bartier, Marcel, 893
Bartlett Music Co. (agent), 124
Bartola (theatre instruments made by Daniel Barton), 368
Bartunek, Adolf, 806
Bates, G.H.W. & Co. (organettes), 754
Bates Organ Co. (organettes), 741, 763
Bates, Theodore C. & Son, 349, 364
Battaglia, M., 806
Baud Frères (museum at L'Auberson, Switzerland), 68
Baude, Adolf, 395
Bauer, Arno, 706
Bauer, Harold (pianist), 279, 282, 283, 294, 300, 301, 308, 436
Bauer, J., 345
Baum, Curt, 804
Bax, Guilliaume (inventor of baxophone pipes), 892
Bax, Julius, 892, 893
Bax, Louis, 892
Beale (pianos), 277
Beatty, J.A. (organist), 792
Bechstein (pianos), 320
Beck, W. Adolf, 710
Becke, Herbert, 440
Beckx, P.J. (agent), 478, 479
Bedplate, description of bedplate in cylinder music box 18, 19
Beebe, Florence (pianist)
Beesley Music Co. (agent), 376
Beethophon Reproducing Piano (Blessing), 388
Beethoven, Ludwig v., 345
Behning (pianos), 267
Behr (piano player), 258
Bell (Polyphon music box), 163
Bell Piano (Lyon & Healy), 496
Bella (organette), 753
Bellin, Jacob H. (pianist), 283
Bellisore (Lüneburg orchestrion), 706
Bellm's Cars and Music Museum (Sarasota, Florida), 114, 465, 471, 837
Belloneum (Kaufmann), 480
Bells, cylinder music boxes with, description of 21, types of bell strikers 26
Bells, types used in disc music boxes 102, 105
Ben Akiba (Popper orchestrion), 590
Bender, Karl & Co. (agent), 249
Bendon, George & Co. (agent), 249
Berdux (pianos), 334
Bergé, William E. (pianist), 279, 283
Berger, Ernst, 706
Berliner, Dorothy (pianist), 279, 283
Berliner, Emile (phonographs), 172
Berliner Orchestrionfabrik Franz Hanke & Co., 707
Bernard, F.J., 104
Berni, Louis, 815, 816, 857, 885
Berni Organ Co. (band organs), 815-817, 823, 831, 857, 885, 889
Berni Phone (Berni organ trade name), 817
Berolina (Hanke orchestrion), 707
Berry-Wood Piano Player Co., 347, 348, 350-352, 382, 384, history and description of instruments 386-387, 718
Bert, Corrine de (pianist), 279, 283
Berthold, Julius & Co., 246, 251
Beutner & Co. (agent), 249
Beyer, Myrtle, 722
B'hend, Tom, 367
Bianca (Popper orchestrion), 589
Bianchetti, A. & Figli, 806
Bianchi, B., 806
Bianculani, Luigi (pianist), 283
Bidermann, Samuel, 349
Biehler (organs), 921
Bier, Allan (pianist), 283
Big Six (Mills slot machine), 92
Bijou Chordephon (mechanical zither), 357
Bijou Jazz Band Orchestrion (Blessing), 389
Bijou Orchestra (Wurlitzer), 664, 670, 671, 721
Bijou Orchestrone (organette), 759, 768
Billings (pianos), 703, 725
Billings, Bob and Ginny, 339
Billings, Earl (pianist), 283
Billon (music boxes), 250
Binghamton (pianos), 722
Bio-Tableau, 864
Biophonola (Hupfeld), 460
Birds, mechanical and/or musical, 77, 78, 90, 91
Birnie, John, 537, 813
Bittong, Pitt (pianist), 317
Black Cat (Caille slot machine), 94
Black, Frank (pianist), 283
Blake, Eubie (pianist), 294
Blanche-Petit & R. Goffart, 806
Blasius & Sons (agent), 124
Blazek, F., 346
Blessing (orchestrions, etc.), 346, 348, history and description of instruments 388-389, 742, 744
Blessing, Jacob, 388
Blessing, James, 346
Blessing, Johann, 388
Blessing, John, 346
Blessing, Joseph, 388, 632
Blessing, Karl, 388
Blessing, Martin, 388
Blessing, Wolfgang, 388
Bloomfield-Zeisler, Fanny, refer to Zeisler, Fanny Bloomfield
Bluebird Orchestra (North Tonawanda Musical Instrument Works), 536, description of 538
Blumen, Alfred (pianist), 331
Blüthner (pianos), 311, 312, 320, 334
Blyelle, Etienne, 127
Blythe, James, 719
Boccanera, Giuseppe, 806
Bocken, Hendrik, 856
Böcker, Ernst (also spelled as Boecker, Ernst), 339, 430, 437, 464, 465, 469, 472, 478, history and description of instruments 818-822
Bockisch, Karl, 321, 323-327, 336, 584, 585, 636
Bodanzky, Artur, 279, 283
Bode, Hermanne, 806
Boecker, Ernst, refer to Böcker, Ernst
Boesenberg, Art, 722
Bolex cameras, 36
Bollman Brothers Co. (agent), 778
Bon, J.M. & Co. (agent), 366, 489, 708
Bonafede, Giuseppe, 806
Bonanni (organs), 805
Bond, Carrie Jacobs (pianist), 279, 283
Bonnet, Joseph (organist), 788, 792
Book music, general description of, 803
Boom, Miguel (pioneer music box inventor), 99

Borchard, Adolphe (pianist), 279, 282, 283
Boreau, Gabriel (inventor), 353
Borland, J.E., 308
Bormann, Karl, 805, 806, 832
Borna (principal of B.A.B. Organ Co.), 858
Bornand, Adrian V., 40, 71
Bornand, Joseph, Sr., 35
Bornand Music Box Co., 35, 40
Bornand, Ruth, 40, 71, 121, 241, 683
Borne, Terry, 644
Borno, S., 806
Bortmann, G. (inventor), 102, 118
Bosch, Werner, 792
Bose, Fritz v. (pianist), 317, 331
Bösendorfer (pianos), 277, 289
Boshko, Victoria (pianist), 279, 283
Bossi, M. Enrico (organist), 792
Boston, Canon Noel, 744, 785
Bottali, Ditta Strumenti Musicali (Barbieri inventions), 385
Bowen (pianos), 321
Bowers, Lee, 416
Bowers, Mary, 479
Bowers, Q. David, 27, 162, 479, 481, 486, 487, 663, 721, 835, 902
Bowers, Wynn, 479
Bowman, Otto H. (pianist), 279, 283
Boyle Brothers (agent), 774
Brabo (Gebr. Weber orchestrion), 626
Brachhausen, Gustav(e), 99, 134, 144, 145, 170-172
Brachocki, Alexander (pianist), 283
Bradley, Van Allen, 800
Brailowsky, Alexander (pianist), 279, 282, 283
Brass Band Orchestrions (Welte), 638, 647, 648, 651
Braun, Marte (pianist), 317
Braun, Robert (pianist), 279, 283
Bravissimo (Popper orchestrion), 586
Bravo (Holzweissig orchestrion), 429
Breitenbach, F.J. (organist), 792
Bremond, B.A. (music boxes), 19, 27, 34, 49, 52, 72, 92
Brewster (pianos), 281
Briggs (pianos), 321
Bright, David, 703
Brillant (Philipps orchestrion; also known as Brilliant), 564, 570
Brinkman, Florence (pianist), 279, 283
Brisgovia (Welte orchestrions), 323, 580, 581, 590; history and description of instruments 637-638, 646-647, 649
Britannia (disc music box), 243, 249
British Mutoscope and Biograph Co., 407
British Piano Museum (Brentford, Middlesex, London), 472, 626
Broadwood, John, & Sons (pianos), 277, 281, 289
Brockway, Howard (pianist), 279, 283
Brown, James (pianist), 317
Brownell, Elspeth (pianist), 279, 283
Browning, Mortimer (pianist), 279, 283
Brownstone, Louis H., 370
Bruch, Max, 454
Bruder, Alfred, 806, 808
Bruder, Andreas, 808, 823
Bruder, Arnold, 808, 823
Bruder, August, 808, 823
Bruder, Emil, 808
Bruder, Eugen M., 806, 808
Bruder, Franz I, 808
Bruder, Franz II, 806, 808
Bruder, Franz Josef, 808
Bruder, Fritz, 806, 808
Bruder, Gebr., 464, 478, 623, 654, 803, 804, 806-808, 815, 817, 818, history and description of fairground organs and related instruments 823-832, 848, 857, 861, 884, 892, 914, 198, 920, 921, 927, 930, 931, 943
Bruder, Gustav, 349, 625, 628, 804, 808, 823, biography 824
Bruder, Ignaz I, 744 805, 806, 808, 823, 832, 892
Bruder, Ignaz II, 808, 823
Bruder, Ignaz Söhne, 808, history and description of orchestrions and organs 823-824
Bruder, Karl (Carl), 808, 823
Bruder, Max I, 808, 823
Bruder, Max II, 808
Bruder, Otto, 804, 808, 823
Bruder, Richard, 808
Bruder, Wilhelm I, 808, 823
Bruder, Wilhelm II, 808, 823
Bruder, Wilhelm Söhne, 806-808, 810, 817; history and description of organs and related instruments 823, 825; 855
Bruder, Xaver, 808, 823, 920
Brugnolotti (principal of B.A.B. Organ Co.), 828
Bruguier, Charles Abram, 90
Bruno & Son (agent), 210
Bruttapasta, C., 806
Bryan, Leon, 115
Bryan, William Jennings, 512
Buchner, Alexander, 17, 345, 346, 480, 739, 745
Buell, Dai (pianist), 279, 283
Buerger, Julius (pianist), 283
Bufalletti, Frederigo (pianist), 331
Buff-Hedinger, Adolf (successor to Paul Ehrlich's main enterprise), 533, 747, 774
Buhlig, Richard (pianist), 279, 282, 283, 331
Bülow (Arnold, later Philipps, piano named for Hans v.Bülow), 566, 568
Bundy Time Recorder Co., 487
Burg, Clarence (pianist), 279, 283
Burkard, H. (agent), 792
Burmeister, Richard (pianist), 331
Burndahl, Noël, 40
Bursens, Arthur (street organs; Arburo and Ideal dance organs), 352, 742, 804, history and description of instruments 833-837, 846, 848, 850, 905
Bursens, Joseph, 833
Bush & Lane (pianos), 268, 319, 321, 322, 527
Busoni, Ferruccio (pianist), 279, 282, 283, 311, 314, 317, 328, 331, 336, 435, 436, 462, 584
Butchart, R.P., 577
Byass, L.C., 868

C

Cabinet Piano (Seeburg Style L), 598, 600, 602, description of 605
Cable Co. (Atlanta, Ga. agent), 124
Cable Co. (pianos), 339, 340
Cadman, Charles Wakefield (pianist), 283
Cady, Harriet (pianist), 279, 283
Caecilia (Philipps orchestrion; also general designation for Philipps PC scale), 563, 564, 571, 662, 691, 721
Café Fribourgeois, 713
Café Transport, 713
Caille Brothers (manufacturers of gambling devices; agents for electric pianos), 24, description of musical slot machines 92-95, 481, 482, 495, 703, 705, 712
Calame, Paul, 63
Calembert (organs), 806
Caliola (Wurlitzer calliope), 664, 720, 839, 933, description of 944
Calliaphone (Tangley calliope), 725; history and description of 838, 841-842; 919
Calliope (disc music box; refer to Kalliope)
Calliopes, history and description of instruments, 838-844
Calvocoressi, M.D., 308
Camerer, E., Kuss & Co. (agent), 249
Campbell, David (pianist), 279, 283
Cann, John E., 170
Capella (Dienst orchestrion), 394
Capital ("cuff" music box made by F.G. Otto & Sons), 100-102, 106; history and description of instruments 134-141, 143
Capitol Piano and Organ Co. (sales outlet for North Tonawanda Musical Instrument Works), history and description of pianos and orchestrions 535-541; 725
Capitol Roll & Record Co. (Operators Piano Co. subsidiary), 543, 553, 602, 717, 719, 721, 722
Capt, Henri (sometimes spelled as Kapt, Henri; cylinder music boxes), 35, 47
Carleton (Price & Teeple pianos), 703, 704, 725
Carlin & Lennox (agent), 124
Carlin & Schoen (agent), 534
Carlsen, Otto, 663, 681, 683
Carmen (Blessing orchestrion), 388
Carmen (Holzweissig orchestrion), 429

Carmen (Polyphon music box), 163
Carmina (Popper orchestrion), 589
Carola, Solo, Inner-Player, refer to Solo Carola
Carpenter Organ Co., 743
Carreño, Teresa (pianist), 279, 282, 283, 308, 317, 331, 435, 584
Carreras, Maria Avani (pianist), 317, 329
Carroll, Adam (pianist), 279, 283
Carroll, Lewis (Snark quotation), 348, 858
Carry-Us-All (Parker carousel), 914-919
Carter, Donald, 292
Cartonium (by Teste), 739
Casino (Nelson-Wiggen piano), 528, 725
Castle (Philipps orchestrion), 563, 573
Caswell, Ken, 339
Cavallo, Giuseppe, 806
Cavalry Fanfare Organ (Gavioli), 859
Cecile (music rolls), 719
Cecilian (piano players and player pianos), 255, 268
Celco (reproducing piano), 293
Celesta (disc music box), 100, 246
Celesta (Philipps orchestrion), 564, 570
Celesta (Seeburg piano - pipe organ), 550, 600, 602, description of 616
Celeste (disc music box), 104
Celestina (organette), 740, 767, 769
Celestino (Lüneburg), 706
Chaillet, Octave Felicien, 171
Chairs, musical, 70
Chalets, musical, 70, 71
Challen (pianos), 277, 289
Challenge (music rolls), 719
Chaloff, Julius (pianist), 279, 283
Chaminade, Cécile Louise Stéphanie (pianist), 308
Chantavoine, Jean, 308
Chapel (Massachusetts Organ Co. organ), 763
Chapman, Walter (pianist), 279, 283
Chappell (pianos), 277, 281, 289
Chapuis, Alfred, 84, 87
Chase, A.B. Co. (pianos), 261, 293
Chautauqua Roller Organ, 755
Chein & Co., 741, 769
Chemet, Reneé (pianist), 279, 283
Chenoweth, Wilbur (pianist), 279, 283
Chesterfield (organ), 763, 764
Chevob & Cie., 104
Chiappa, Charles, 807
Chiappa, Giuseppe, 807
Chiappa Ltd. (pianos, organs, etc.), 249, 805, 807, 857
Chiappa, Ludovico, 807
Chiappa, Victor, 807
Chiapusso, Jan (pianist), 279, 282, 283
Chicago (Mills slot machine), 95
Chicago Electric (pianos), 390, 725
Chicago Symphony Orchestra, 300
Chickering (pianos), 261, 277, 280, 281, 283-287, 289, 290, 309, 319
Chime Clock (Regina), 103, 210, 211
Chitarrone (Lüneburg piano), 706
Chomassin, Rolin (organs), 785
Chordaulodion (Kaufmann), 480
Chordephon (mechanical zither), 350, history and description of instruments 357-358, 430
Christian, Palmer (organist), 788
Christman (pianos), 319
Christmas tree stands, musical, 70, 77, 100, 109, 130, 147, 216, 237, 246
Church, John Co. (agent), 210
Church, Marjorie (pianist), 279, 283
Cigarette cases, musical, 70
Cincinnati Symphony Orchestra, 300
Cionca, Aurelia (pianist), 331
Citoplex (Hupfeld roll-changing device), 458
Clair, Herbert (pianist), 283
Clarabella (Popper orchestrion), 583, 589
Clariphone (Niagara piano), 534, 908
Clark, Ernest G., 719-722
Clark, John E.T., 21, 22, 145, 172
Clark, Melville (and Melville Clark Piano Co.), 255, 261, 293, 602, 714, 719-721, 727, 743
Clark, Murray, 486, 487, 616
Clark Orchestra Roll Co., 527, 536, 602, 620, 656, 718-725, 838, 842
Clark's (showmen), 867
Clarke, J.A., 346
Clarola (organette), 741, 776
Claus & Co., 357
Clavimonium (Hupfeld), 435, 743
Claviola (Ludwig & Co.), 712
Clavitist (Hupfeld piano), 339, 353, 431, 432, 434, 435, 438, 453
Clavitist-Violina (Hupfeld violin player), 353, 432, 438
Cleaves' Patent Study Table, 756
Clementi, Collard & Co., 349
Cleopatra shadow box (automaton), 77
Cleveland Orchestra, 300
Cliff House (San Francisco tourist attraction), 61, 672, 712
Clocks, musical (the pages indicate clocks with musical movements; musical instruments with clock attachments, the Erato orchestrion for example, are numerous and are not indexed), 23, 24, 70, 86-89, 103, 120, 145, 149, 152, 163, 181, 210, 211, 214, 216, 219, 220, 224, 227, 229, 247, 784
Clown-Kapelle (automaton), 111
Cluett & Sons (agent), 258
Coade, Dr. and Mrs. George, 578, 606, 683
Coates, Albert, 308
Cocchi, Bacigalupo & Graffigna (organs and orchestrions), 708, 805, 807, 809, 845
Cocchi, Giuseppe, 807, 845
Cocchi, John, 807, history and description of instruments 845
Cockayne, Eric V., 803, 805, 857, 858, 885, 889, 901
Cocklin & Oyler (agent), 210
Coelophone (Gavioli), 742, 750
Coelophone Orchestra (Thibouville), 750
Coffer, Mathilde (pianist), 283
Cohan, George M. (composer), 512
Cohen & Hughes (agent), 210, 376
Cohen, Jerry, 417, 443, 500, 546
Coin-operated pianos, general description of, 349-352; refer to individual manufacturers throughout the book for specific types
Coinola (pianos and orchestrions made by the Operators Piano Co.), 210, 345, 350, 354, 390, 494, 496, history and description of instruments 542-548, 553, 554, 638, 654, 703, 711, 714-716, 719, 721, 725
Colber, E. Fred (pianist), 283
Collard & Collard (pianos), 277, 281, 289
Collins, Pat (showman), 883, 887
Colonial (pianos), 703, 725
Colonial Elite (Peerless orchestrion), 561, 562
Colonial Manufacturing Co., 210
Columbia (phonographs), 172 173, 179, 186, 192, 419
Columbia Music Roll Co. (Operators Piano Co. subsidiary), 543, 553, 602, 719, 721
Comb, musical, description of 17, illustration of typical comb 24, organ comb 29; types used in disc boxes 101, 102, 105; steps in manufacturing 175
Commandant (Imhof & Mukle orchestrion), 464, 469, 470, 476, 477
Componium (by Winkel), 345
Con Amore (Popper orchestrion), 583, 589, 590
Concert Barrel Organ (Bruder), 831
Concert Clavitist (Hupfeld piano), 431, 435
Concert Orchestra Organ (Welte band organ), 927, 928
Concert Orchestrion (Welte), 634-638, 640, 642, 643, 646
Concert Organ (Wurlitzer), 664, 799
Concert Pan Orchestra, refer to Pan Orchestra (Hupfeld)
Concert PianOrchestra (Philipps/Wurlitzer orchestrions), 347-349, 355, 563, 564, 566, 569, 571, 572, 579, 622; history and description of instruments 661-664, 690-692, 701-702; 712, 720
Concert Roller Organ, 740, 741, history and description of 754-755
Concert Universal (Hupfeld piano), 431, 434
Concertal (Mustel organ), 783
Concerto (mechanical dulcimer), 361
Concerto (Polyphon disc-operated piano), 116, 144, 145, 148, 158, 164, 168, 207, 208, 509
Concerto (Regina disc-operated piano with Polyphon mechanisms), 116, 145, 164, 171, 172, 201, 207, 208, 509, 594
Concerto Orchestrion (Hupfeld), 365
Concertola (Aeolian roll changer for the Duo-Art piano and organ), 295-298, 302, 788

Concertrola (pianos), 703, 725
Conchon (cylinder music boxes), 45
Concordia (clock), 247
Cone-Baldwin, Carolyn (pianist), 283
Confrey, Zez (pianist), 279, 283, 721
Connorized Music Co. 353, 398, 400, 401, 553, 554, 560
Conover (pianos), 319, 340
Conover, Agnes (pianist), 283
Continental (Hofmann & Czerny orchestrion), 429
Continental (Hupfeld orchestrion), 441
Continental Musikwerke (Hofmann & Czerny), 352, history and description of instruments 428-429, 705, 711
Continental Piano Co., 390
Continental Tobacco Co. (agent), 210
Conway (pianos), 294
Conway Industries, 294
Conzen, Maria Theresia (pianist), 317
Cook, J. Lawrence (roll-arranger), 718, 722, 726, 727
Cooper, Charles (pianist), 279, 283
Copeland, George (pianist), 279, 282, 283, 285
Copland, Aaron (pianist), 283
Cornet Orchestrion, 469
Corona (Philipps pianos and orchestrions), 568, 570
Corona (Regina's general name for music boxes equipped with the automatic changing device), 176, 178, 193, 194, 197, 202
Corona (Regina phonograph; usually designated as the Corona Talking Machine), 103, 171, 172, 212
Corrector (Imhof & Mukle), 464, 469, 470, 477
Corso (Imhof & Mukle orchestrion), 465, 471, 476
Cortot, Alfred (pianist), 279, 282, 283, 308, 311, 314, 317
Costers, Cesar (agent), 576
Cote (pianos), 703, 704, 725
Cottage Orchestrion (Welte), 634-638, 640
Cottlow, Augusta (pianist), 282, 317
Cottrell's Coliseum, 867
Courboin, Charles M. (organist), 788
Cox Brothers (showmen), 867
Coy, Hilaire Bornand, 71
Crawford, Jesse (organist), 720
Cremona (trademark for most coin-operated pianos and orchestrions made by the Marquette Piano Co.), 348, 350, 352, 367, 368, 486, history and description of instruments 497-505, 535, 580, 594-596, 599, 601, 656, 663, 709, 711, 714, 719, 720, 725
Crescio, Antonio, 922
Cricket (Mills slot machine), 92
Criterion (disc music box), 100, 101; history and description of 134, 136, 142, 143; 178, 246
Crooks, J.W., 295
Cuendet (cylinder music boxes), 31, 63
Cuendet, Emile L., 104
Cupid (Caille slot machine), 94
Cupid (Operators Piano Co. piano), 542, 543, 725
Cupid's Post Office (Mills arcade device), 526
Cushing, G.T., 855, 889, 926
Custard, Henry Goss (organist), 792
Cutchin, Esther Marvin (pianist), 279, 283
Cuypers, Hubert, 454
Cylinder, description of cylinder used in cylinder-type music box 17, 18
Cylinder music boxes, general description of instruments 15-96, history of 17-22

D

Daehne, Paul, 584
Daelemans, Paul, 893
Daisy Piano Player, 711
D'Alessandro, Michele, 806
Dallam, Thomas, 805
daMotta, Jose Vianna (pianist), 317, 331
Damrosch, Walter, 300, 788
Danubia (Popper orchestrion), 583, 586
Darre, Jean Marie, 308
D'Ascenzo, Ferdinando, 806
Davenport-Treacy Piano Co., 268
Davies, Fannie (pianist), 331
Davies, Reuben (pianist), 279, 283
Davis & Soule, 405-416
Davis, C.W., 405, 409-411, 414-416
Davis, James, 786
Davis, Leonard (pianist), 279, 283
Davis, Ross (showman), 933
Dawkins, Thomas & Co., 249
Daynes Music Co. (agent), 258
Dea (Hupfeld reproducing piano), 273, 279; history and description of instrument 311-314, 316; 339, 353, 430-432, 438, 453, 462
Dea-Violina (Hupfeld violin player), 339, 353, 432, 438, 462
Deagan, J.C. (tuned percussion effects), 531, 709
DeBain, Alexander, 362
DeBence, Jacob, 544
Debussy, Claude, 324, 331, 336, 340
Decap, Gebr. (dance organs, etc.), 352, 742, 804, 833, 836, history and description of instruments 846-847, 848, 850, 893, 905
Decker Brothers (pianos), 703, 725
Decker, Walter (pianist), 279, 283
deConne, Paul (pianist), 331
DeGreef, Arthur (pianist), 308, 331
deGroof, Frans, 833
DeKleist, Eugene (name anglicized from Von Kleist, Eugen), 347, 535, 537, 661, 664, 665, 814, 870, 871, 876, 884, 930, 934
de la Croix, Francois (pianist), 317
DeLamarter, Eric, 300, 788
Delcamp, J. Milton (pianist), 279, 283
Delta (pianos sold by Eugene DeRoy/Symphonia), 623
DeLuxe Orchestrion (Peerless), 553, 554, description of 557
Deluxe Player Action, 321
Deluxe Reproducing Roll, 320
Demetz, Ferdinand, 710, 823
Demetz, Vincenz, 710
Demusa, 461
Denny, Arthur S. (American Steam Piano Co.), 840
Denton, Cottier & Daniels (agent), 124
Dentzel, W.H. (amusement outfitter), 806
Denver Music Co. (agent), 258, 376
Deo Roll Co. (Ray Deyo), 482, 720
Deprez, J., 806
Derby (Western Electric piano), 92, description of 656-658, 725
DeRoy, Eugene (Symphonia music rolls, Delta pianos, etc.), 352, 456, 457, 465, 478, 490, 568, 574, 575, 583, 588, 593, biography 621-623, 708, 893
DeSchryver, Harry E., 384
Desmond, Helen (pianist), 279, 283
Dethier, Gaston M. (organist), 788
Detrick, George F., 370
Detroit Symphony Orchestra, 300
Deutsche Grammophon, 99, 103, 169
Deutsches Museum (Munich, Germany), 480
Deutschmann, J., 345
DeVreese, Emile, 806, 848
deWaard, Romke, 848, 857
Dewey (Caille slot machine), 93, 94
Dewey (Mills slot machine), 92-95, 507
deWit, Paul (publisher of Zeitschrift für Instrumentenbau and other publications), 349, 584, 784
Deyo, G. Raymond (music roll arranger; Deo Roll Co.), 482, 486, 487, 720
Diamond Jubilee (Polyphon music box), 163
Diana (organette), 741, description of 751
DeBenici, Tosta (pianist), 331
Dickinson, Clarence (organist), 788
Diebold, Joh. (organist), 792
Diémer, L. (pianist), 331
Dienst, E. (pianos and orchestrions), 351, 353, history and description of instruments 391-394
Dietrich-Hollingshead, Ursula (pianist), 279, 283
Dillon, Fannie (pianist), 279, 283
Dilworth, George (pianist), 279, 283
Dinorah (Imhof & Mukle orchestrion), 465, 469, 471, 473, 476, 477
Diorama (Kirsch & Co. disc music box), 104
Direct Attacque (Niagara), 534
Disc music boxes, history of 97-104, description of various types 97-251
Disc-operated pianos, 99, 100, description of 103-104; refer also to individual manufacturers, esp. Lochmann, Otto, Polyphon, Regina, and Symphonion

Ditson, J.E. & Co. (agent), 124
Ditson, Oliver Co. (agent), 124, 210
Diva (Popper orchestrion), 589
Divina (Welte orchestrion), 638, 647
Dixon, Frederic (pianist), 279, 283
Doguereau, Paul (pianist), 283
Dohnànyi, Erno (or Ernst) v. (pianist), 279, 282, 283, 331, 584
Dolcine (organette), 742, 747, description of 749
Dolge, Alfred, 552-554, 739
Doll, Jacob & Sons (many different pianos, including Electrova), 266, 321, 379, history and description of Electrova instruments 397, 554, 559, 655
Donahue, Lester (pianist), 279, 283
Donar (Welte Brass Band Orchestrion), 638, 647
Door knockers, musical, 70
Dopp, Joseph, 823, 920
Doring, Jerry, 225, 792
Dorr, William Ripley (organist), 788
Double Mills, refer to Violano-Virtuoso (Mills violin player)
Douloff, Michael (pianist), 331
Drabek & Söhne, 806
Drawing Room (Polyphon music box), 152
Drawing Room Orchestrion (Popper), 593
Dreher's, B., Sons Co. (agent), 258, 778
Dresden (German ship), 394
Drewett, Norah (pianist), 317
Dreyschock, Felix (pianist), 331
Drosdoff, Wladimir (pianist), 331
Droucker, Sandra (pianist), 331
Droz, Edmond, 84, 87
Drücker, Kurt (pianist), 317
Drum and bells, cylinder music boxes with, general description of 21
Drum Manopan (organette), 749
Drum Piano (Lyon & Healy), 496
Drum-Piccolo-Manopan (organette), 749
Dubois, A. (organist), 792
Duca (Philipps reproducing piano; mechanism also incorporated into the Paganini), 273, history and description of 317, 339, 349, 354, 564-566, further description of 575, 662, 664
Ducanola (Philipps), 317
Ducartist (Philipps), 317
Duckwitz, Dorothy Miller, 322
Ducommon-Girod, Frederick William (music boxes), 19, 35
Duke, John (pianist), 279, 283
Dulcimer Organette, 763
Dulciphone (organette), 764
Dumesnil, Maurice (pianist), 279, 282, 283
Duo-Art (late-generation Aeolian pipe organ), 295, 297, 779, history and description of 788-790
Duo-Art (reproducing piano made by the Aeolian Co.), 255, 273-275, 279, 282, 291, 294, history and description of 295-310, 312, 321, 336, 654, 727, 734
Duola (Philipps piano), 575
Duophonola (Hupfeld reproducing piano), 312, 315, 339, 432
Duplex (Mills slot machine), 95, 507
Duplex cylinder music box, 20, 42, 43
Duplex Orchestrion (Symphonion), 214, 234
Duplex Paganini Violin Orchestra (Philipps), 578
Duplex Piano (Philipps), 317, 569
Dupre, Marcel (organist), 788
Duryea, Oscar (pianist), 283
Dutch street organs, 833, 848, 849
Duwaer & Naessens (agent), 355, 432, 457
Duwijn, Remond (Flemish spelling of Duwyn, Remond), 850
Duwyn, Remond (dance organs), 804, history and description of instruments 850, 893
Dux (Polyphon automobile), 169
Dux (Polyphon piano), 168
Dyer, W.J. & Bro. (agent), 258

E

Eakins, Paul, 537
Eastern Specialty Co., 398, 400, 405, 406
Eberhardt (pianos), 703, 725
Echániz, Jose (pianist), 283
Echo Piano Orchestra, refer to Lord 3 Echo Orchestrion (Imhof & Mukle)
Eckardt (Christmas tree stands), 246; refer also to Gloriosa Christmas tree stands
Ecker, James (pianist), 279, 283
Eclipse (Caille slot machine), 93
Eddy, Clarence (organist), 788, 792, 793
Edelsberg, v. (pianist), 331
Edelweiss (disc music box), 247
Edgar, Helen Louise (pianist), 279, 283
Edison (electric pianos), 722
Edison, Thomas Alva, 171, 172
Edward VII, King of England, 508
Edwards & Roberts (cabinetmakers), 34
Eggert, Paul (pianist), 317
Ehrlich, Emil, 707
Ehrlich, Paul, 99, 102, 104, 129, 250, 533, 740, 741, 746, 747
Ehrlichs Musikwerke Emil Ehrlich, 707
Eich, Pierre (pianos, orchestrions, fairground organs, etc.), 352, history and description of instruments 395-396, 622, 711, 742
Eilers Music Co. (agent), 369
Einzig (Symphonion music box), 227
Eisler, Paul (pianist), 279, 283
Eldorado (orchestrions; sold by many agents), 419, 533
Electora (vacuum pump), 263
Electra (pianos), 703
Electratone (pianos), 725
Electric Emporium Orchestra, 703
Electric Orchestra (Schmoele), 787
Electric Orchestral Grand (Stella music box by Mermod Frères), 119
Electric Orchestrephone (Hupfeld), 249
Electric Organa (player accordion), 775
Electric Piano, refer to Magnetic Expression Piano (Mills Novelty Co.)
Electric Shock Machine (Mills arcade device), 526
Electric Symphonion (disc music box), 231
Electro-magnetic Orchestra (Schmoele), 762, history and description of 787
Electrolin (piano), 350, 705, 722
Electrotone Automusic Company (agent for North Tonawanda Musical Instrument Works et al), 536, 541
Electrova (pianos by Jacob Doll & Sons), 350, history and description of instruments 397, 494, 506, 554, 559, 655, 722
Elfers, James, 339
Eli Bridge Co. (amusement outfitters), 838
Elite (Peerless orchestrion), 554, 561
Elite (Gebr. Weber orchestrion), 349, 431, 623; history and description of 625, 628; 824
Elite Apollo Orchestra (Berni/Gavioli organ), 817
Elite Apollo Orchestra (Gebr. Bruder organ; also called Elite Orchestra-Organ Apollo), 830, 914, 931, 943
Elite Orchestra-Organ Apollo, refer to Elite Apollo Orchestra
Elizabeth, Queen of England, 805
Elizondo, Artemesia (pianist), 279, 283
Elliott, Vern, 720
Ellis, Melville (pianist), 279, 283
Elvyn, Myrtle (pianist), 331
Emch, A. (pianist), 317
Emerald (Polyphon music box), 163
Emerson (pianos), 293
Emmanuel, Maurice, 308
Emperor (Mortier organ), 896
Empire (Hupfeld piano player), 312
Empire Organ (organette), 533, 747
Empress (Mermod Frères Mira music box sold by Lyon & Healy), 51, 58, 125
Empress Electric (Lyon & Healy pianos and orchestrions), history and description of instruments 494-496, 542, 544, 546, 719, 725
Encore Banjo, 347, 353, 355, history and description of 398-418, 552, 554, 597, 838
Engelhardt, A.B., 553
Engelhardt, Alfred D., 553
Engelhardt, F. & Sons, refer to Peerless Piano Player Co.
Engelhardt Piano Co., refer to Peerless Piano Player Co.
Engelhardt, Walter L., 553
English Cab (Amorette organette), 748
EnSymphonie (Niagara orchestrion), 534, 908
Epstein, Lonny (pianist), 317
Epton, H., 889
Equitable Manufacturing Co., 196, 209

Erato (Gebr. Weber orchestrion), 627
Erb, M.J. (organist), 792
Erica (organette), 742, description of 749
Erika (F. Weber piano with endless roll), 707
Erle, Francis (pianist), 279, 283
Eroica (Popper organ), 583, 585, 587
Eroica (Symphonion 3-disc music box), 102, 214, 215, 225-227
Ersatz Walzenorgel (Bruder organ), 825
Espenhain, Max & Co., 706
Essipoff, Annette (pianist), 329, 331, 584
Estey, Jacob, 799
Estey Organ Co., 320, 743, 744, 787, 793, history and description of instruments 799
Estey Piano Co., 320
Etzold & Popitz, history and description of instruments 419, 584
Euclid Beach (Cleveland amusement park), 868
Eugene (Polyphon music box), 163
Euphona (pianos), 340
Euphonia (disc music box), 246
Euphonia (organette), 768
Euphonika Musikwerke, 249, 250, 740, 742; history and description of instruments 747-750, 753
Euphonion (disc music box), 145, 246
Eustis, Rosamund (pianist), 279, 283
Eusymphonic (pianos), 725
Euterpe (piano player), 257
Euterpe (music rolls), 564
Euterpe (Gebr. Weber orchestrion), 627
Euterpeon (Imhof & Mukle), 466
Evans, Edwin, 308
Evans, H.C. & Co. (amusement devices), 92, 543, 703, description of Profit Sharing Player Piano 704, 725
Excelsior (Berni organ), 817
Excelsior (Monopol music box), 250
Excelsior Pan Orchestra (Hupfeld), 449, 456, 460, 478, 622, 623
Excelsior Phonoliszt (Hupfeld semi-reproducing piano), 435, 438
Excelsior Piano Orchestrion, 363, 365
Excelsior Piccolo (Polyphon music box), 152
Excelsior Seraphine (organette), 774
Export (Blessing orchestrion), 388
Extra (Capital "cuff" music box by F.G. Otto & Sons), 135, 137-139
Extra (Popper orchestrion), 585, 589
Eysler, Edmund, 452
Eysoldt, Leo (pianist), 317

F

Fabriques Reunies, refer to Société Anonyme Fabriques Reunies
Fackler, Joseph, 249
Fair Organ Preservation Society, 660, 804, 858, 868, 882, 889
Fairchild, Edgar (pianist), 279, 283
Fairground organs and related instruments, history and description of 801-944
Fall, Leo, 452
Faller, Aug., 920
Farmer, Henry George, 745
Farnham, Lynnwood (organist), 792
Farrand & Votey, 743, 783
Farrand Organ Co., 255, 743, 783
Farrar & Tyler (showmen), 865, 866
Farrar, Geraldine (pianist), 279, 283
Fassone, C., 806
Faulkes, William (agent), 792
Fauré, Gabriel (pianist), 283, 313, 331
Favorite (organette), 742, 747
Favorite (pianos), 722
Fehrenbach, Adrian, 806
Feinmann, Ida (pianist), 317
Feltman, C. (showman), 891
Feurich (pianos), 320, 327, 334, 354, 590, 625, 629, 636
Feurich, Hermann, 323, 585
Fidelio Musikwerke, 65
Filmophon (organette), 776
Filmosaxophon (organette), 776
Filmusic Co. (music rolls), 369, 371, 720
Finest, The (Western Electric name for its line of pianos and orchestrions), 656, 658
Fink, E.A. (pianist), 279, 283
Finzer & Hamill (agent), 124
Fischer, Edwin (pianist), 330, 331
Fischer, J&C (pianos), 277, 280, 281, 283, 289, 290
Flack, F.L., 806
Fletcher, W.E., 637
Flight & Robson (organs), 349, 774
Florodora Tag Co. (agent), 210
Fluess, L. (music rolls), 564
Flute and Violin Solo Piano (Lösche), 489, 490
Flute Pipe Piano (Lyon & Healy), 496
Flutina Organ (organette), 750
Flynn, G., 868
Focht, James L., ruling on legality of antique slot machine 92
Folisi, Donato, 806
Footstools, musical, 70
Ford Motor Co., 416
Ford, Rita, 34
Forrest, Mr., 868
Förster, Alban (pianist), 317
Förster, Anton (pianist), 317
Förster, Hans (pianist), 317
Forsyth, J. Aikman, 308
Forte Piccolo (Mermod Frères cylinder music box), 22
Forte-piano cylinder music box, refer to piano-forte cylinder music box
Fortuna (J.H. Zimmermann disc music box), 100, 102, history and description of 238-242, 250, 251, 430
Foss, F.U. Novelty Co., 408, 712
Foster (pianos), 281
Fotopiano (American Photo Player Co.), 352, 370, 373
Fotoplayer (American Photo Player Co. photoplayer), 352, history and description of 367-381, 702, 720
Four Feeder (Mills Novelty Co. roll mechanism), 514, 524
Fourneaux (Pianista piano), 255
Fowler, Amos, 359
Fowler Piano Co. (agent), 487
Fowles, Ernest, 308
Fox (Caille slot machine), 94
Fox, Felix (pianist), 279, 283
Fox Music Co., 536, 539, 703
Frances, Annette (pianist), 279, 283
Frankfurter Musikwerke J.D. Philipps & Söhne, refer to J.D. Philipps & Söhne
Franklin (pianos), 277, 281
Franz, Fr. (pianist), 317
Fratelli, Curci, 806
Fratelli, De Falco, 806
Fratelli, Pomella, 806
Frati & Co. (pianos, orchestrions, and organs), 350, history and description of pianos and orchestrions 420-423, 566, 805-807, history and description of organs 851-853, 869, 884, 906, 914, 930, 931, 937
Frati, Anselmo, 806
Fratihymnia (Frati orchestrions), 420, 422, 423, 566, 807, 851
Fratinola (Frati pianos and orchestrions), 420-422, 566, 807, 851
Frederickson-Kroh Music Co. (agent), 376
Frei, Carl (Karl), Jr., 808, history and description of fairground organs and street organs 855
Frei, Carl (Karl), Sr., 848, history and description of fairground organs and street organs 855, 893
Freiheit, Harold, 454
French & Sons (pianos), 267
Freyer, Edward (music rolls), 613, 720, 729
Friberg, Claes O., 269, 311, 337, 430, 478, 479, "Portable Hand-Cranked Barrel Organs" article 805-812
Friburgia (Welte orchestrions), 339, 638, 647
Frick, Henry C., 347, 639, 642
Fried, Frederick, 815, 869, 914
Friedberg, Carl (pianist), 279, 282, 283, 317, 331
Friedheim, Arthur (pianist), 279, 282, 283, 313, 317, 331, 436, 462, 584
Friedman, Ignaz (pianist), 282, 283, 308, 317
Friedrich August (King of Saxony), 461
Friml, Rudolf (pianist), 283
Fritz, Jackson, 840
From Music Boxes to Street Organs Museum (Utrecht, Holland), 427, 575, 865, 874
Frömsdorf, Robert (inventor), 437, 438

Fryer, Herbert (pianist), 308, 331
Fuchs, Diego (organs and orchestrions), 705
Furber, J.B., 170

G

G. und H. Orchestrionfabrik (G. & H. Orchestrion Factory), 707
Gable, C.E. (agent), 534
Gabrilowitsch, Ossip (pianist), 279, 282, 283, 294, 300, 301, 308, 317, 331, 336, 584
Galant (or Gallant; Imhof & Mukle orchestrion), 465, 476
Gale, Walter C. (organist), 788
Gallico, Paolo (pianist), 279, 283
Gally, Merritt (organettes and player reed organs), 739, 740, 742, 743, 757-761
Gambling machines, musical, 24, 92-95, 507, 526, 704
Gambrinus (Symphonion music box), 103, 220
Ganne, Louis, 250
Ganter, Karl, 251
Ganz, Rudolph (pianist), 282, 283, 300, 308, 330, 331
Garrison, Iliff (pianist), 283
Garvie & Wood (agent), 764
Gasparini (fairground organs), 848, 857
Gast, Albert & Co., 257
Gately Manufacturing Co. (organettes), 741, 764, 771
Gattorna, Lino, 806
Gaudin & Cie. (fairground and dance organs), history and description of instruments 856, 885
Gautschi, H. & Son (agent), 210
Gavioli & Cie. (fairground organs, pianos, etc.), 349, 352, 363, 742, 743, 750, 803, 806, 807, 815-817, 823, 836, 848, 855, history and description of instruments 857-868, 876, 882, 885, 886, 888, 892, 893, 896, 906, 913, 922, 930, 931
Gavioli, Andree, 857
Gavioli, Anselme, 857
Gavioli, Claude, 750, 857
Gavioli, Claude & Fils, refer to Gavioli & Cie.
Gavioli, Ludovic(o), 855, 857
Gavioli, Ludovic II, 857, 866
Gavioliphone, refer to Gavioli & Cie.
Geater, Alfred (agent), 123, 251
Gebhardt, Rio (pianist), 317
Gehlhar, Ernst, 709
Geigenpiano (Hegeler & Ehlers violin player), 353, history and description of 385
Geisha (Polyphon music box), 163
Geissler, Bruno, 766
Gem Organetta (organette), 740, 741, 763-765
Gem Roller Organ, 740, 741, history and description of 754-755
Geneva (Polyphon music box), 163
Gérard, G.J. (agent), 631
Gerdts, Felix (pianist), 279, 283
Gerecke, William (agent), 251
Gershwin, George, 294, 300
Getz, William (principal of Capitol Piano & Organ Co.), 535-537
Giant Ariston (organette), 746
Gibson, L.T., 170
Gibson, S. Archer (organist), 788
Gieseking, Walter (pianist), 282, 283, 329, 331
Gigout, Eugene (organist), 792
Gilbert and Sullivan, 163
Gilbert, Harry M. (pianist), 279, 283
Gilford, Nancy, 308
Gillet, J.J., 848
Gimbel Brothers (agent), 210
Giovanni, Irene di (pianist), 279, 283
Gittins, George W., 336, 637
Gittins, Robert H., 637
Giummarra, G., 806
Givens-Gourley, Inc. (music rolls), 727, 729
Givens, Larry, 255, 278, 554, 614, 616, 634, 639, 686, 727, 729, 730, 739, 844
Gladiator (Popper orchestrion), 478, 583, 585, 593
Glass, F.O. (orchestrions), 533
Glass, Julia (pianist), 279, 283
Glass, Violet, 722
Glazounow, A. (pianist), 330, 331, 336
Gleason, Harold (organist), 788
Glen, Irma, 719
Gloria (Monopol music box), 131
Gloria (Société Anonyme Fabriques Reunies music box), 104, 250
Gloria Concerto Orchestrion (Hupfeld), 365
Godowsky, Leopold (pianist), 279, 281-283, 285, 294, 308, 311, 313
Goffart, R., 806
Gold Medal (Polyphon music box), 163
Golde, Walter (pianist), 283
Goldenweiser, A. (pianist), 331
Goldsand, Robert (pianist), 282, 283
Goldthwaite, Chandler (organist), 788
Goliath (Popper orchestrion), 478, 583, 590, 593
Goode, Blanche (pianist), 279, 283
Goodrich, Wallace (organist), 788
Goodson, Katharine (pianist), 279, 282, 283, 308
Goosens, Eugene (pianist), 308
Gorainoff, Irene Eneri (pianist), 331
Gordon (Polyphon music box), 163
Gordon-Howard Calliope, 725
Gordon Music Co. (agent), 141
Gordon, Phillip (pianist), 279, 283
Gorham (pianos), 321
Gosseye, Vital, 806
Gössl, J.&A., 706
Gotha (Hupfeld pianos), 431
Gottfried, A. & Co. (organ pipes), 709
Gould, Jay, 347
Gounod (clock), 247
Gourlay, Winter & Leeming (agent), 210
Gourley, John, 727, 729
Grace, Harvey, 308
Graffigna (principal of Cocchi, Bacigalupo & Graffigna), 807
Grafonola, refer to Columbia phonographs and to the American Graphophone Company.
Graham, Lewis, 75, 388, 544
Grainger, Percy (pianist), 282, 300, 308
Graley, Gary, 729
Granados, E., 324, 336
Grand (Aeolian reed organ), 743, 777
Grand Concert Organ (Bruder), 884
Grand Musical Hall Clock (Polyphon), 163
Grand Piano Orchestrion, 363
Grand Roller Organ, 740, 741, history and description of 754-755
Grandezza (Gebr. Weber xylophone piano), 625, 626
Grandphone (organette), 770
Grange, Ina (pianist), 279, 283
Graphophone, refer to American Graphophone Co.
Gray Piano Co., 92, 528, 543, 712
Grayhound (Seeburg piano), 92, 601, 602, description of 606
Graziella (Gebr. Weber orchestrion), 627
Great Symphony Orchestra Organ (Gebr. Bruder), 829, 830
Green, C. (showman), 867
Greenacre, Frank, 100, 243, 247
Greenwood & Sons (agent), 534
Gregg, Roger, 384
Gregraft's Electric Bioscope, 867
Greiner (music boxes), 19
Grew, Sydney, 308
Grey, Frank H. (pianist), 283
Greyhound, refer to Grayhound (Seeburg piano)
Grieg, Edvard, 279, 282, 283, 311, 324, 331, 435
Grigsby-Grunow, 660
Grinnell Brothers (agent), 197, 210, 258, 778
Grob, J.M. & Co. (predecessor of Ludwig Hupfeld AG), 365, 430, 743, 746
Grofé, Ferdie (pianist), 279, 283
Grosz, B. & Co., 237, 250
Grotrian-Steinweg (pianos), 277, 289, 311, 312
Gruen, Rudolph (pianist), 279, 283
Grünbaum, L.P., 370
Grünert, A.H. (piano maker; later a division of Hupfeld), 430, 431
Grünfeld, Alfred (pianist), 282, 311, 313, 317, 331, 435, 452, 584
Grünfeld, Moritz (pianist), 323, 584
Grunn, Homer (pianist), 279, 283
Grymonprez, Leonard, 623, 892, 893, 896, 900-902
Grymonprez, Oscar, 395, 896-898, 901
Guinness, Murtogh D., 20, 43

Guitarophone (mechanical zither), 108, 136, history and description of 359
Gulbransen (pianos), 261
Gullman, H., 722
Gunn, Alexander (pianist), 279, 283
Günther, Robert, 706

H

Haberstroh, Carl, 710
Haddorff Piano Co., 354, 481, 484, 486, 528, 544
Hadow, Henry, 308
Hageman, Richard (pianist), 279, 283
Haggar's Royal Electric Bioscope, 864, 866
Haines Brothers (pianos), 277, 280, 281, 289, 703, 725
Hale, Philip, 285
Hall, Ben M., 327
Hall, M.A., 709
Hallet & Davis Piano Co., 294
Hambourg, Mark (pianist), 279, 282, 283, 331, 584
Hamilton (pianos), 722
Hamilton (Polyphon music box), 163
Hamilton, Harry, 722
Hamilton, S. Co. (agent), 124
Hammond Corporation (electronic organs), 788, 791, 892
Han-Dee True Tone Calliope, 839, 843
Haney-Deem Manufacturing Co., 839
Haning, Roy, 683, 901
Hanitsch, Heinz (pianist), 317
Hanke, Franz (orchestrions, etc.), 707
Hanke, Hans (pianist), 279, 283
Hansen, L.H. (pianist), 279, 283
Hanson, Eddie, 719
Hardman (pianos), 319, 620, 727
Harmes, Miss, 723
Harmonette (organette), 763, 768
Harmonia (disc music box), 100, history and description of 107, 112
Harmonia (Philipps orchestrion), 563, 564
Harmonichord (Kaufmann), 480
Harmonicon (organette), 742, 747
Harmonist (Peerless), 522, 556
Harmonium-Polyphona, 168
Harniess Brothers (showmen), 885
Harp eolienne cylinder music box, 22
Harrack, Charles de (pianist), 283
Harrington, E.A. (calliopes), 838, 843
Harris, Tomford (pianist), 283
Harrison, Mary E. (pianist), 279, 283
Harrod's (London department store), 797
Hart, Bill, 367
Harty, Hamilton, 308
Harwood (pianos and orchestrions), history and description of 424, 556, 725
Haskell, William E., 799
Hasse, William F., 176, 177
Hathaway, Terry, 664, 689, 835, 902
Haupt (organs), 921
Hauser, Hans (organist), 792
Havelock (Polyphon music box), 163
Hayden, Ed, 339
Haydn (Symphonion music box), 223
Hayes Music Co. (agent), 124
Haynes-Apperson Co., 416
Haynes, John C. & Co. (agent), 210
Hays, Alex M. & Co. (agent), 39
Hazelton (pianos), 319
Heebner, Walter S., 324
Heeren Brothers & Co. (agent), 210
Heffer, Douglas, 809
Hegeler & Ehlers, 353, history and description of Geigenpiano (Violin Piano) violin player 385
Hegner, Paula (pianist), 331
Heilbrunn, K., Söhne, history and description of instruments 425-426
Heim, Aug. (organist), 792
Heinrich, C., 345
Heinrich, Georg (pianos), 706
Heinroth, Charles (organist), 788, 792
Heizmann, Sigmund, 346, history and description of orchestrions 427
Hejtmanek, Bodzka (pianist), 279
Helicoidal cylinder music box, 20
Helikon (organette), 747
Helios (Hupfeld orchestrions), 348, 363, 430-432, 434, 438, history and description of 442-452, 453, 457-460, 621, 622
Heller (pianos), 703, 725
Heller, J.H. (music boxes, orchestrions, etc.), 251, 345
Helvetia (disc music box), 247
Helvetia (Popper orchestrion), 585
Hendorf, Irene (pianist), 317
Henneman, Alexander (pianist), 283
Henneman, Gertrude (pianist), 279, 283
Hennig, Ernst (inventor), 437, 438
Hennig, Gustav Karl (inventor) 437, 438
Henrion, Theodore (pianist), 279, 283
Henry Organ (organette), 750
Henry VIII, King of England, 349
Heppe, C.J. & Son (agent), 177, 184, 210, 258, 778
Herbert, Victor, 279, 283, 788
Hercules (Imhof & Mukle orchestrion), 471
Hermann, Heinrich, 104
Hermanns, Hans and Marie (pianists), 313
Hermitage, S. & Sons (agent), 37
Herold (Imhof & Mukle orchestrion), 465, 469
Herophon (organette), 99, 742, history and description of 747, 748
Herophonette (organette), 747
Herrburger, J. (pianos), 395
Herschell, Allan Co. (amusement outfitters), 806, history and description of instruments, etc. 869-873
Herschell, George, 876
Herschell-Spillman Co. (amusement outfitters), 869-873
Herschell, William, 876
Hertz, Alfred, 300, 788
Hess, Myra (pianist), 282, 308
Hesselmann (organs), 921
Hexaphone (Regina phonograph), 172, 212
Hickling, Douglas, 309
Hickman, Clarence (developer of Model B Ampico), 278
Hilger, Eduard, 806
Hill, Alta (pianist), 279, 283
Hill, Marshall (showman), 887
Hillsberg, Ignace (pianist), 279, 283
Himmelreich, Ferdinand (pianist), 279, 283
Hindermann, Paul (organist), 792
Hine, C.E., 898
Hinze-Reinhold, Bruno (pianist), 317
Hirsch, Martin (agent), 237, 250
Hitler, Adolf, 326, 336
Hochman, Arthur (pianist), 279, 283
Hock, Mamert, 346
Hoeffler Manufacturing Co. (agent), 198, 210, 711
Hofberg, M., 774
Hofmann & Czerny (Continental Musikwerke), 352, history and description of instruments 428-429, 711, 743
Hofmann, Josef (pianist), 273, 279, 282, 283, 300, 301, 308, 324, 331, 336, 435, 436
Hofmann, Nelly (pianist), 331
Hofmiller, Thadda (organist), 792
Hofner, C. (organist), 792
Höhn, Alfred (pianist), 331
Hohner, Matth. (accordion players), 742, 775
Holborn (Polyphon music box), 163
Holcomb, J.R. & Co. (agent), 774
Holl, A. & Sohn, 806
Holl, W.F., 812
Holland's Palace of Light, 867
Hollins, Alfred (organist), 792
Holzweissig, Ernst, 251, history and description of instruments 429, 806
Home Organ (Seeburg), 602, 616
Honnert, John, 719
Hooghuys, Charles, 874
Hooghuys, Edmond, 806
Hooghuys, L. (the younger), 806
Hooghuys, Louis (the elder), 806, description of Hooghuys fairground organs 874
Hooghuys, R. Charles, 874

Hope-Jones, Robert (inventor), 551, 778, 799
Hope-Jones Unit Orchestra (unified theatre pipe organ made by Wurlitzer), 348, 663, 799
Hopkinson (pianos), 277, 289
Horn's Cars of Yesterday Museum (predecessor of Bellm's; Sarasota, Florida), 465
Horowitz, Vladimir (pianist), 328
Horst, Louis (pianist), 283
Horstmann, Henry, 207, 208
Horton, Henry B. (Autophone Co.; Ithaca Calendar Clock Co.), 741, 754
Hörügel, M. (organs), 776
Hoschke, Frederick Albert (pianist), 279, 283
Hospe, A. (agent), 124
Hotel Eisenbahn (Sursee, Switzerland), 713
Houck, O.K., Piano Co. (agent), 124, 210
House of the Magicians (Blessing orchestrion), 389
Howard (pianos), 703, 725
Howard, John Tasker (pianist), 279, 283
Howe, M.H., 806
Hromadka, Norbert, 806
Hrubes, V. (sometimes anglicized as Rubes), 346
Huber, August, Jr., 806
Huber, Georg, 806
Hudson River Day Line, 464
Humidors, musical, 70
Hummel, Johann Nepomuk (composer), 345
Humperdinck, Engelbert (pianist), 314, 331, 584
Hunter (pianos), 582
Huntley, Gertrude (pianist), 283
Hupfeld, Günther, 431, 440, 446, 460
Hupfeld, Ludwig (under various names including J.M. Grob & Co., Hupfeld Musikwerke, Ludwig Hupfeld AG, and Hupfeld - Gebr. Zimmermann), 132, 214, 249, 250, 256, 257, 261, 279, history and description of Phonoliszt (semi-reproducing piano) 311-316, 339, 345, 347-355, 357, 359, description of mechanical pianos 362, 363, 365, 391, 392, history and description of pianos, orchestrions, violin players, and theatre instruments 430-462, 464, 465, 489, 504, 564, 582, 583, 593, 621-623, 662, 665, 708, 713, 721, 743, 745, 776, 818
Hupfeld, Mrs. Ludwig, 313
Hutcheson, Ernest (pianist), 282
Hyde, Herbert E. (pianist), 279, 283
Hymnophon (phonograph), 429

I

Ibach (pianos), 320, 334
Ideal (Bursens dance organs), 833-837
Ideal (Mermod Frères cylinder music boxes), 30, 51, 53-56, 58, 60
Ideal (Operators/Welte pianos), 638, 647, 654, 703, 725
Ideal (Philipps orchestrion), 563, 564
Ideal Fidelio (automaton), 65
Ideal Moving Picture Orchestra (North Tonawanda Musical Instrument Works photoplayer), 352, 536
Ideal Orchestre (Marenghi organs), 885-889
Iduna (Popper orchestrion), 583, 589
Igumnoff, G. (pianist), 331
Ihlee & Horne (agent), 250
Ihlee & Sankey (agent), 250
Ilgenfritz, McNair (pianist), 279, 283
Illions, M.C. & Sons (amusement outfitter), 806
Illusions Automat (Fidelio), 65, 227
Illustrated Song Machine (Mills Novelty Co.), 526
Imhof, Albert, 467, 468, 477-479
Imhof & Mukle (pianos, orchestrions, and organs), 249-251, 346-349, 351, 353, 354, 427, history and description of instruments 463-479, 576, 622, 623, 632, 717, 718, 744, 767, 818
Imhof, Daniel, 346, 463, 468
Imhof, Geoffrey, 478
Imperator (Richter disc music boxes), 101, history and description of 244-245
Imperial (Abrahams disc music box), 243, 249
Imperial (pianos), 722
Imperial Automatic Electric (music rolls), 318
Imperial Cabinet (reed organ), 763, 764
Imperial Industrial Corp., 727
Imperial Music Roll Co., 318
Imperial Symphonion, refer to Symphonion Manufacturing Co.
Indy, Vincent d' (pianist), 279, 282, 283, 308
Infanta (Polyphon music box), 163
Ingleson, Isaac, 104
Inlay art in music boxes, 25
Interchangeable cylinder music boxes, description of 20, storage of cylinders 30
International (Dienst accordions), 393
International (Machinek orchestrion), 706
International (music rolls), 318
International Business Machines, 487
Intona (organette), 741, 751, description of 752
Iris (organette), 742, 747, 748
Iris (Philipps orchestrion), 563
Irmler (pianos), 354, 478
Isola (Gebr. Weber orchestrion), 627
Ithaca Calendar Clock Co., 754
Iturbi, Jose (pianist), 308
Ivers & Pond (pianos), 319

J

Jaccard, Ad., 121
Jaccard, Jules, 63
Jaccard, L.G., 20, 21
Jacobi (owner of Frati & Co.), 807
Jacobi, Victor (pianist), 279, 283
Jacobus, P. Guy, 369, 381
Jacot, A.D., 120
Jacot & Son (agent), 51, 58, 103, 104, 118, 120, 122, 124, 210
Jacot, Aristides H., 120
Jacot, Charles H., 58, 120
Jacot Music Box Co., refer to Jacot & Son
Janisch, Franz, 806
Janisch, Joseph Nachf., 806
Janni, Gerardo, 806
Janssen, Victor (pianist), 283
Janzen, Franz, 726
Jardines (organs), 251
Jäuslin (artist), 823
Jazbandor (Blessing orchestrion), 389
Jazy (also known as Jazzy; Blessing orchestrion), 388
Jazz Band Orchestrion (Blessing), 388
Jazz Band Piano (Lösche), 489, 492
Jazz Concert Orchestra (North Tonawanda Musical Instrument Works orchestrion), 535, 540
Jazzband (Philipps orchestrion), 349, 566, description of 574, 592
Jazzband Orchestrion (Popper), 583, 588, 592
Jazzbandophone (Limonaire Frères organ), 876, 877, 881, 882
Jazzy (also known as Jazy; Blessing orchestrion), 388
Jeanrenaud, Albert (inventor), 42
Jenkins, J.W. Sons Music House (agent), 210, 258, 376
Jewel boxes, musical, 70
Jewett (pianos), 703, 725
Jilissen, J., 893
Jinkertz, Willy M. (pianist), 317
Jockey Club (New York), 464, 467, 478
Johnson, Clarence, 719
Johnson, Eldridge R., 171
Johnson, Ellsworth, 306
Johnson, William A. (pianos), 703, 705, 725
Johnston, D.S. Co. (agent), 124
Joiner, Joseph (pianist), 279, 283
Jolas, Jacques (pianist), 283
Jonas, Alberto (pianist), 282
Jonas, Ella (pianist), 331
Jones, Art, 724
Jones, Elizabeth Gay (pianist), 279, 283
Jonson, G.C. Ashton, 308
Jordan, Alex, 641
Jordan Marsh & Co. (agent), 210
Jouard, Paul, 810
Jubal Orchestrone (organette), 759
Jubilaum (Gebr. Bruder organ), 831
Jubilee (Polyphon music box), 163
Judge (Caille slot machine), 94
Judge (Mills slot machine), 92, 94, 95
Juggler automaton (with Adler music box), 240

Junchen, David L., 659, 714, 726
Junghans (clocks), 103, 247
Junod, Alfred, 42, 63
Junod, André, 118
Junod-Turin, Arthur, 124

K

Kaim, F. & Sohn (agent), 783
Kalliope Musikwerke (disc music boxes), 99-103, 105, history and description of instruments 108-111, 136, 209, 247, 251, 359, 430
Kalliophon (combination music box and phonograph), 108
Kalliston (organette), 742, description of 749
Kalliston-Pankalon (organette), 749
Kallistonette (organette), 749
Kallmeyer, Else (pianist), 317
Kalophon (organette), 742, description of 749
Kaltenbach Brothers, 705
Kamenik (organs), 812
Kann, S. Sons & Co. (agent), 124
Kappes & Eggers, 705
Kapt, Henri, refer to Capt, Henri
Karger, Franz, 806
Karrer & Co. (music boxes, orchestrions, etc.), 251, 346
Kaschperowa, L. (pianist), 331
Kästner (pianos), 711
Kaufmann (orchestrions and other automatic instruments), 346, history and description of instruments 480
Kaufmann, Frederick, 480
Kaufmann, Frederick Theodore, 480
Kaufmann, Johann Gottfried, 480
Kaufmann, Marie (pianist), 317
Kazounoff, Bernece (pianist), 283
Keast, P.H., 722
Keast, P.M., 719, 721, 722, 724
Keating, W., 849
Keitel, Fr. W. (pianist), 317
Keith, Charlton (pianist), 331
Keller, Alfred (inventor), 102, 118, 124, 126
Kelley, Lloyd G., 170
Kellogg (electrical equipment), 518
Kemp, President (showman), 886, 887
Kendall, Charles B., 398-400, 405-413, 415
Kendall, Edwin (pianist), 279, 283
Kennedy, Dion W. (organist), 788
Kennedy, Patrick, 135
Kerekjarto, Duci de (pianist), 279, 283
Kern (organs), 921
Kern, Otto (music roll arranger), 824
Kerr, George (pianist), 283
Khartoum (Polyphon music box), 163
Kibby (pianos), 703, 725
Kiddie Band Organ (Wurlitzer), 940
Kienzl, Wilhelm (pianist), 329, 331, 584
Kilgen, George & Son (organs), 744
Kimball, W.W. & Co. (pianos and organs), 251, 319, 638, 743, 744, 794, history and description of player organs 800
Kimberly (pianos), 321
Kimontt, Marceline (pianist), 331
Kinetic Engineering Co., 376, 709
King (pianos), 703, 725
King's Universal Supply Co. (agent), 249
Kingsbury (pianos), 340
Kino-Pan (Hupfeld photoplayer), 352, 431, description of 455
Kinophon (Hofmann & Czerny photoplayer), 428
Kipp Brothers (agent), 198, 210
Kircher, Athanasius, 745, 805
Kirsch & Co., 104
Kirsch, Hedwig (pianist), 331
Kissberg, Samuel (principal of Capitol Piano & Organ Co.), 535-537
Kitchener (Polyphon music box), 163
Klavestad, Osborne, 682
Klaviolin (Bajde violin player), 437
Klaviolinfabrik Bajde & Co., 437
Kleberg (Polyphon music box), 163
Kleeberg, Clotilde (pianist), 331, 584
Klein, Henry (agent), 250, 251
Klemen, Bertha (pianist), 279, 283
Klingsor (phonograph), 705
Kmita, Andrei (pianist), 279, 283
Knabe, William & Co. (pianos), 258, 277, 279-281, 283, 284, 289-291, 309, 778
Knauth, A., 170
Knauth, Briesen, 134
Knauth, Nachod & Kühne (bankers), 99, 169, 170
Knight, C.S. (Electric Emporium Orchestra), 703
Knight-Campbell Music Co. (agent), 210
Knoof, A. (pianist), 317
Knott, Walter, 686
Koch, Emma (pianist), 331
Koczalsky, R. v. (pianist), 331
Koehler & Hinrichs (agent), 185, 207
Koenigsberg, Aime (dance organs), 806, 850, history and description of instruments 875
Koepfer, J. & Söhne, 710
Kogel, Gustav (organist), 788
Kohler & Campbell Co. (pianos), 374, 379
Kohler & Chase (agent), 124, 258, 694, 778
Kohler-Liebich Co. (tuned percussion instruments), 531, 709
Komet (disc music box), 100, history and description of instruments 112, 251, 357
Komet Victoria (disc music box), 112
Kommers, Mike, 722
Koninckx, H., 893
Konzertist (Popper piano), 585
Koretschenko, A. (pianist), 331
Kornburst, Frederick J., 554
Korner, Johannas J., 170
Korngold, Erich Wolfgang (pianist), 308, 317
Kortlander, Max, 719, 721, 722, 727
Kosloff, Alexis (pianist), 283
Kosmos (Dienst furniture), 393
Koudelka, Josef, 806
Koven, Reginald de (pianist), 279, 283
Krakauer (pianos), 320
Kramer, F.F. (agent), 124
Kranich & Bach (pianos), 319
Kranz-Smith Piano Co. (agent), 124
Kreiselman, Gertrude (pianist), 283
Kreisler, Fritz (pianist), 279, 283
Kreiter (pianos), 703, 724
Krell Piano Co., 124, 258, 265
Krenter, E., 534
Krieger, A.O. (agent), 359
Kring van Draaiorgelvrienden (Circle of Friends of the Mechanical Organ), 804, 848
Kroeger, Ernest R. (pianist), 279, 283
Kubelik, Jan (violinist), 436
Kuhl & Klatt (pianos), 251, 351, 391, 392, 574, 708
Kuhler, Mary Fromeyer (pianist), 279, 283
Kühne, P., 170
Kurtz, Oskar, 438
Kurtz-Seeburg Action Co., 599
Kurtzmann (pianos), 319
Kwast, James (pianist), 317
Kwast-Hodapp, Frieda (pianist), 317, 328, 331

L

Lachner, Vincent, 632
LaCroix, Aurora (pianist), 279, 283
LaFarge, Jean (pianist), 279, 283
LaForge, Frank (pianist), 279, 283
Lambert, Alexander (pianist), 279, 283
Lambert, Joseph (pianist), 279, 283
Lambrino, Télémaque (pianist), 331
Lamond, Frederic (pianist), 282, 283, 308, 317, 331, 336, 584
Lamps, musical, 70
Lamson, Carl (pianist), 279, 283
Lamy, Alfred, 710
Landow, Max (pianist), 279, 283
Landowska, Wanda (pianist), 282, 283, 308, 311, 331
Lane, Eastwood (pianist), 279, 283
Lane, Victor (pianist), 279, 283
Langdorff (music boxes), 250
Lange, Henry (pianist), 279, 283

Lange, Hermann (agent), 249
Langfelder, Henry, 108, 134, 136, 359
Langwill, Lyndesay G., 744, 785
Larkin Soap Co. (Regina customer), 180
Laros, Earle (pianist), 279, 283
Larson, A.F., 656
Lastreto, C.B., 370
László, Sándor (pianist), 331
Lateulere, Antoine (agent), 249
Lauberger & Gloss (pianos), 708
Lauer, Roy, 722
Lauter Co., 258, 778
Lavarro, Enrico (pianist), 279, 283
Leabarjan Manufacturing Co. (roll perforators), 726
Lease, John C., 726
Leathurby Co. (agent), 673, 676, 693, 711
Lecoultre (music boxes), 19
Lecoultre, David, 18, 23
Lecuona, Ernesto (pianist), 279, 283
Lederer, Harry (pianist), 279, 283
Lee, Markham, 308
Lefévre, Henry (pianist), 279, 283
Leginska, Ethel (pianist), 279, 282, 283, 308
Lehr (pianos), 703, 725
Leipziger Musikwerke, 129, 250, 533, 741, 747
Leipziger Musikwerke Euphonika, refer to Euphonika Musikwerke
Leipziger Musikwerke Phönix Schmidt & Co, refer to Phönix Musikwerke
Leipziger Orchestrionwerke, refer to Lösche, Paul
Leipziger Pianoforte & Phonolafabriken Hupfeld - Gebr. Zimmermann, refer to Hupfeld, Ludwig
Leistner & Co., 710
Leland (pianos), 494, 542
Lemaire, Charles, 858
Lemare, Edwin H. (organist), 788, 792, 793
Lenk, Albin, 806
Lenzkirch (clocks), 103, 145, 149, 181, 210, 214, 219, 220, 224, 227
Leoncavallo, R. (pianist), 330, 331, 336, 584
Leopold, Grand Duke of Baden, 632
Leopold, Ralph (pianist), 279, 283
L'Epee (music boxes), 19, 52, 67, 248
Lerner, Tina (pianist), 282
Leschetitzky, Theodor (pianist), 331
Leschetizky, Marie Gabrielle (pianist), 383
Levitzki, Mischa (pianist), 279, 281-283, 285
Lhévinne, Josef (pianist), 279, 282, 283, 330, 331, 336
Liapounow, S. (pianist), 330, 331
Libelle (organette), 742, 747
Libellion (Richter music box), 104, 244
Liberty (tuned percussion effects), 709
Lichtton-Orgel (Welte electronic organ), 336, 632, 792
Liebentanz & Richter, 707
Liebmann, Armin, 753
Lightcap, Alan, 721
Lilliputian (Seeburg piano), 598, 600, description of 605
Limonaire Frères (fairground organs, etc.), 352, 363, 643, 803, 807, 836, 857, 866, history and description of instruments 876-883, 885, 892, 923
Lind (music rolls), 602, 720
Lindeman & Sons (pianos), 293
Lindsay, Vachel, 352
Link & Son (pianos), 267
Link, Edwin A. (father), 481, 482, 487
Link, Edwin A. (son), 481, 482, 486, 487
Link (of Germany; supplier of percussion instruments), 823
Link Piano Co. (later known as the Link Piano and Organ Co.), 203, 265, 347, 351, 352, 355, 384, 402, 495, history and description of pianos, orchestrions, and theatre instruments 481-487, 514, 711, 718, 720, 729, 731, 744
Lipe, Gordon, 115, 377, 881
Lipp, Rich. & Sohn (pianos), 354, 478
Lisodis (Mermod Frères soap dispenser), 128
List, Arthur, Jr., 553
Liszniewska, Marguerite Melville (pianist), 279, 283
Litolff's, Henry, Edition of Brunswick, 250
Little Empress Electric Cabinet Player, 496
Little Falls Felt Shoe Co., 554, 562
Little Jazz Band Orchestra (Blessing), 388
Liverpool Musical Box Depot, 712
Lochmann "Original" (music boxes, disc-operated pianos, barrel pianos, etc.), 99, 100, 102, 103, 112, history and description of disc music boxes and disc-operated pianos 113-117, 214, 249-251, 350, 357, history and description of barrel pianos and orchestrions 488, 509
Lochmann, Paul, 18, 99, 113, 144, 213, 214, 251, 488
Lochmannscher Musikwerke, refer to Symphonion Musikwerke
Lockwood Piano Co. (agent), 482, 487
Loesser, Arthur (pianist), 279, 283
Log Cabin Organ (organette), 774
Lohengrin (Imhof & Mukle orchestrion), 464, 465, 472, 473
Löhr, Louise (pianist), 317
Lola (Popper orchestrion), 586
London (Polyphon music box), 163
Long-playing cylinder music box, 20
Longue marche music box, 20
Loos, Gebr., 806
Loos, Josef, 806
Lopez, Vincent (pianist), 279, 283
Lord (Imhof & Mukle orchestrion), 430, 469, 475
Lord 3 Echo Orchestrion (Imhof & Mukle), 430, 464, 475, 478
Loring & Blake Co. (organs), 740, 743
Lösche, Paul (pianos and orchestrions), 347, 349, 351, 352, history and description of instruments 489-493, 711
Loth, Leslie (pianist), 279, 283
Louis (Polyphon music box), 163
Lowe, Egerton, 308
Lucca (organette), 742, 747
Lucia (Imhof & Mukle orchestrion), 465, 472
Lucia (organette), 741, 751
Lucien (pianos), 321
Lucretia (Imhof & Mukle orchestrion), 465, 473
Ludden, Campbell, Smith & Co. (agent), 210
Ludwig & Co. (Ludwig & Wild; Germany), 247, 250
Ludwig & Co. (U.S.A.), 712
Ludwig & Wild, 247, 250
Luna (Popper orchestrion), 583, 589
Lüneburg, A. Musikwerke, 706
Lusitania (Dienst), 395
Luther, Franz, 806
Luther, J.D., 170
Lux (Holzweissig orchestrion), 429
Lux (organette), 742, 747, 748
Lyon & Healy, 124, 125, 136, 173, 210, 368, 369, 481, history and description of Empress Electric and other coin-operated pianos and orchestrions 494-496, 542, 778
Lyon, James, 308
Lyra (Symphonion music box), 221
Lytle, R.T., 637

M

Macbride, Winifred, (pianist), 283
MacDermid, James G. (pianist), 279, 283
MacDonald, Don, Jr., 600
MacFadyen, Alexander (pianist), 279, 283
Machinek, F. & Söhne (pianos, orchestrions, etc.), 706
Mack (trucks), 913
MacPherson, Stewart, 308
Maelzel, Johann Nepomucene, 345
Maelzel, Leonhard, 345
Maerten, C., 813, 844
Maesto (Gebr. Weber orchestrion), 348, 349, 623; description of 625, 629, 630; 713, 715, 721, 824
Maestro (reproducing piano manufactured by Mustel & Cie. under the Welte Mignon patents), 326
Maëstroplayer Dea, refer to Dea (Hupfeld reproducing piano)
Magic Orchestra (Verbeeck), 923
Magic Organa (player accordion), 775
Magnetic Expression Piano (Mills electromagnetic piano), 514, 524, description of 525, 720
Magnetic Piano Player, 398
Magnetophon (recording device), 325, 326
Mahillon, Victor, 345
Mahler, Gustav, 324, 331, 336, 584
Maier, Guy, 279, 283

Mail Cart (Monopol disc music box), 129
Main, W.F. Co., 180, 209
Maine, Basil, 308
Maitland, Rollo F. (organist), 788
Majestic (Lyon & Healy pianos), 494, 495, 722
Majestic (radio), 660
Malata, Fritz (pianist), 317
Mammoth All-Chromatic Wonder Piano-Orchestra, refer to Admiral (Imhof & Mukle orchestrion)
Mammoth Military Band Organ (Wurlitzer), 721, 931, 933, description of 937
Mando-Orchestra (North Tonawanda Musical Instrument Works orchestrion), 535, 537, description of 540
Mandola (Philipps orchestrion), 571
Mandolin(e) cylinder music box, description of 21
Mandolin Orchestra, refer to Regina Sublima Piano
Mandolin Orchestra (Symphonion), 624
Mandolin Piano (Lösche), 489
Mandolin Piano (Lyon & Healy), 496
Mandolin Piano (Popper), 586
Mandolin PianOrchestra (Philipps/Wurlitzer orchestrions), 347-349, 355, 487, 563, 564, 566, 570, 571, 579, 593, 622; history and description of 661, 662, 664, 681-690, 692; 711, 721, 943
Mandolin Quartette (Wurlitzer), 348, 354, 446; description of 661, 664, 665; 721
Mandolin Sextette (Wurlitzer), 348, 354; description of 661, 664, 665; 721
Mandolina (Hupfeld orchestrion), 444
Mandolina (organette), 740, 767, 768
Mandolina Organ, 767
Mandolinata (organette), 742, 747, 748
Mandolino (Philipps orchestrion), 564, 570, 571
Manecoles, Emelio (pianist), 279, 283
Mangels Museum, 465
Mangels, W.F. Co. (amusement outfitter), 806, 823, 831, history and description of instruments, etc. 884
Manopan (organette), 742, 747, 748, description of 749-750
Marazzi, A., 806
Marcola (pianos and orchestrions), 384
Marenghi, Ch. & Cie (fairground organs), 806, 807, 816, 838, 855-857, 861, 866, 867, 882, history and description of instruments 885-889, 923
Margareta (Hofmann & Czerny orchestrion), 429
Margolies, Vera (pianist), 331
Maria Theresa, 805
Mariënfeld (sculptor), 823
Marples, Robert, 251
Marque Ampico (reproducing piano), 277, 281
Marquette (Caille slot machine), 94
Marquette, John A. (Automatic Orchestra Co.), 384
Marquette Musical Co., 384
Marquette Piano Co. (Cremona coin pianos, orchestrions, and photoplayers), 348, 351-354, history and description of instruments 497-505, 535, 580, 594-596, 598, 599, 601, 602, 656, 711, 714, 720, 725
Mars (Holzweissig orchestrion), 429
Marshall & Rose (pianos), 277, 281, 289
Marshall & Wendell (pianos), 277, 280, 281, 283, 288, 289
Marshall, Frank (pianist), 324, 329, 331
Marshall, Goldthorpe (showman), 885
Marshall Piano Co. (division of J.P. Seeburg Piano Co.), 267
Martin, Rudy, 729
Marvel (Adler/Fortuna music box), 242
Marveola (Weser Brothers), 655
Marvin, John (pianist), 279, 283
Marx, Heinrich, 710
Marx-Goldschmidt, Berthe (pianist), 317, 331, 584
Mascagni, Pietro (pianist), 279, 283, 311, 314
Mascotte (organette), 714, 770
Maskelyne, Neville, 346
Maskelyne & Cook, 249
Mason, A.B., 868
Mason & Hamlin (pianos), 273, 277, 280, 281, 283, 289, 290, 298, 302, 309, 320
Mason, Louise (pianist), 279, 283
Massachusetts Organ Co. (organs and organettes), 248, 359, 740, 741, 761, 763-765
Master Record (music rolls), 553, 562
Matador (Blessing orchestrion), 389
Matador (Popper orchestrion), 583, 589
Matthews, R.P., 369
Maurina, Vera (pianist), 331
Mayer, Estella (pianist), 279, 283
Mayer-Mahr, Moritz (pianist), 317
Mazur, Audrey, 729
Mazza, Fiore, 806
McCarthy, Justin, 250
McClaran, H.B., 556
McClure, Marjorie Barkley (author), 322
McEwan, J.B., 308
McManus, George (pianist), 279, 283
McNabb, George (pianist), 279, 283
McTammany, John, 739-743, 758, 760-762, 768, 773
Mead, Lannon F., 172
Mechanical Cymbal, 359
Mechanical Cymbal-Pianette, 365
Mechanical Drum, 359
Mechanical Harmonium (Hupfeld), 776
Mechanical Organetta (organette), 764
Mechanical Organette, 741, 764
Mechanical Orguinette (organette; several different varieties made under this trade name), 308, 740, 741, 764, 765
Mechanical Orguinette Co., refer to Aeolian Co.
Mechanical Piano-ette, 359, 763
Medtner, Nikolaus (pianist), 331
Mehlin & Sons (pianos), 294, 319
Mekanisk Musik Museum (Copenhagen, Denmark), 115, 269
Melamet, Mrs. D.S. (pianist), 279, 283
Mellon family, 27, 634, 639
Mellor, C.C. Co. (agent), 210, 258, 778
MelOdee (music rolls made by Aeolian Co. subsidiary), 318, 369
Melodee (music rolls made by Givens-Gourley, Inc.), 727
Melodette, 359
Melodia (organette), 772
Melodium (Gavioli), 859
Melody Piano (mechanical dulcimer), 360
Melody Player (organette), 769
Melody Violins (Mills Novelty Co.), 352, 524
Menter, Sofie (pianist), 584
Menzenhauer & Schmidt (zithers; Kalliope Musikwerke), 108, 136, 359
Menzenhauer Guitar-Zither, 359
Merkx, Tom, 856
Mermod Frères (cylinder music boxes sold under Ideal, Peerless, and other names; disc music boxes sold under Mira, Stella, and other names), 18-20, 22, 29, 30, 35, description of cylinder music boxes 51-60, 66, 68, 71, 92, 99, 100-102, 104, 107, history and description of Mira, Stella, and related disc boxes 118-128, 210, 249, 251, 346
Mermod, Gustav(e) Alfred, 52
Mermod, Jaccard & King Co. (agent), 124
Mermod, Leon Marcel, 52
Mermod, Louis Philippe, 52
Mérö, Yolanda (pianist), 279, 282, 283, 328, 331
Merola, Gaetano (pianist), 283
Merrill (pianos), 294
Mersenne, Marin, 349
Messig, George, 465
Metall-Industrie Schönebeck (Polyhymnia disc boxes), 128
Meteor (Symphonion music box), 223
Metropolitan Advertising Co., 210
Metropolitan Music Co. (agent), 258, 778
Metrostyle (Aeolian Co.), 300
Meyer-Helmund, E. (pianist), 331
Meytschik, Marc (pianist), 317, 331
Mezon (Dienst pianos), 391
Michaelsohn, Ida (pianist), 331
Middleton, A., 889
Midget Auto Organ (Operators Piano Co.), 545
Midget Orchestra (two different basic coin piano types, one of the Pianolin style and the other using type A rolls, made by the North Tonawanda Musical Instrument Works), 536, 537, 538, 539, 725
Midget Orchestrion (Operators Piano Co.), 542-544
Midget Organ (organette), 747
Miessner, W. Otto (pianist), 283

Mighavacca, E.E., 806
Mignon (organette), 742, 766
Mignon (reproducing piano), refer to Welte Mignon
Mignon-Harmonieux (organette), 766
Mignonette Organina (organette), 740
Mikado (Polyphon music box), 163
Militarograph (North Tonawanda Musical Instrument Works band organ), 913
Military Symphony Orchestra (Gebr. Bruder organ), 830, 832, 918
Miller, Robert, 816, 868
Mills, Arthur, 868
Mills, Herbert S. (Mills Novelty Co.), 515, 516
Mills Industries, 514
Mills Novelty Co., history and description of musical slot machines 92-95, 350, 352, 353, 355, 413, 436, 482, history and description of the Violano-Virtuoso, electric pianos and orchestrions, arcade machines, and other devices 506-526, 709, 711, 718, 720
Mimosa (Popper orchestrion), 585
Minerva (Mortier organ), 905
Miniature Band Organ (Wurlitzer), 940
Miniature Orchestrion (Welte), 640
Minoco (Mills Novelty Co. yacht), 514
Minor, C. Sharpe Unit Organs (theatre organs named for organist C. Sharpe Minor; made by Link), 481
Minuette Organ (Estey Organ Co.), 799
Miolis, Lino, 806
Mira (Mermod Frères disc music box), 51, 58, 99-103, 106; history and description of 118, 120, 121, 123-125, 128
Miraphon(e) (combination Mira music box and phonograph), 58; history and description of 118, 120, 123, 128
Mirovitch, Alfred (pianist), 279, 282, 283
Mitchell, A.I., 414
Mitchell, Edward, 308
Mohammed III, 805
Möhle, Herman (Popper & Co.), 585
Moillet-Gobat, Helene (pianist), 317
Moisewitsch, Benno (pianist), 279, 281-283, 285
Mojon, Manger & Co. (music boxes), 249
Möldner & Skreta, 707
Molinari & Sons (pianos and organs), 363, 806, 810, 851, history and description of instruments 890-891, 930, 934
Molinari, Joseph, 890
Möller, M.P. (pipe organs), 744
Molzer, Ferdinand & Sohn, 806
Monarch (disc music box), 101, 104
Monarch (pianos), 703, 725
Monarch Tool & Manufacturing Co., 703, 709, 711
Monopol (disc music box), 99-105, history and description of 129-131, 214, 250, 533
Monopol (Philipps orchestrion), 564
Monster Military Band Organ (Wurlitzer), 721, 931, 933, description of 935
Montanini, Antonio, 806
Montese, Antonio, 806
Montgomery Ward (agent), 210, 660
Moog, R., 710
Morano, Loretto (pianist), 283
Morath, Max, 605
Morganti, F., 537, 813
Morgenstern & Lockwood (agent), 774
Morrey, Grace Hamilton (pianist), 279, 283
Morris, Edward (pianist), 279, 283
Mortier, Th. (dance organs), 622, 742, 804, 833, 836, 846, 848, 850, 855, 865, history and description of instruments 892-905, 923
Mortuary Organ (or Seeburg Style MO), 602, 616
Moses, Walter D. & Co. (agent), 258
Motion Picture Junior (Link MP Junior photoplayer), 486
Motion Picture Player (Seeburg photoplayer), 617
Moto-Playo Bench, 263
Motor Bus (Monopol disc music box), 129
Motor Car (Monopol disc music box), 129
Motor Manopan (organette), 750
Motor Player Corp., 263
Mottl, Felix, 330, 331, 788
Mozart (Berni band organ), 817
MP Junior (Link photoplayer), 486, 514
Mukle, A., 784
Mukle, Joseph, 250, 466
Mukle, Leopold, 250, 466
Muller, Alfred (agent), 249
Müller-Reuter, Theodor (pianist), 317
Multi-Control (National/Welte roll changer), 322
Multi-Reproducer (National/Welte roll changer), 322, 527
Multitone (Operators/Welte pianos and orchestrions), 352, 390, 542, 638, 647, description of 654
Munroe Organ Reed Co., 635, 740, 742, 743, 758-761, 764, 767
Münz, Mieczyslaw (pianist), 279, 282, 283
Murdoch, William (organist), 308
Murdoch's (agent), 251
Murphy, Gerald H. (agent), 250
Murphy's Bioscope, 864
Murray, Blanchard, Young & Co. (agent), 210
Murray, Spink & Co. (agent), 210
Musette (organette), 769
Museum of Music Collection, 75
Music Leaf System (Imhof & Mukle roll system), 463
Music rolls, the making of, 714-729
Musica (Holzweissig orchestrion), 429
Musical Boudoir Stand (organette), 767
Musical Box Society International 22, 284, 578
Musical Box Society of Great Britain, 22
Musical Cabinet (slot machine), 92
Musical Casket (organette), 771, 773
Musical China Closet (Regina), 103, 186
Musical Desk (Regina), 171, 197, 199
Musical Library Table (Regina), 103, 185, 190
Musical Museum (Deansboro, N.Y.), 810
Musical Organette, 773
Musical Salesman (Regina), 181, 183, 185
Musical Savings Bank (Regina), 180
Musical Savings Bank (Symphonion), 219
Musical Uno (slot machine; also known as Numero Uno), 92, 94, 209
Musician Clown Automat, 111
Mustel, Alphonse, 783
Mustel & Cie. (pianos and organs), 251, Maestro reproducing piano 326, history and description of the firm and Mustel player organs 783
Mustel, Auguste, 783
Mustel, Charles, 783
Mustel, Victor, 783
Muzzio, John & Son, 851, history and description of organs, etc. 906
Muzzio Organ Works, 906
Mystikon (Popper organ), 583, 585, 587

N

Nallino Frères, 806
Nash, Frances (pianist), 279, 283
Nater, J.J. (agent), 792
National American Organette, 741, 773
National Automatic Music Co. (of Grand Rapids, Michigan), 322, 355, 504, history and description of instruments 527, 703, 712, 719, 725
National Calliope Corporation, 725, 804; history and description of calliopes 838, 839, 842
National Electric Piano Co., refer to Peerless Piano Player Co.
National Music Roll Co. (Peerless subsidiary), 552-554, 562
National Novelty Co. (agent), 210
National Piano Manufacturing Co. (division of Jacob Doll; New York, N.Y.), 321
National Piano Manufacturing Co. (of Grand Rapids, Michigan), 322, 355, history and description of instruments 527, 703, 712, 719, 725
National Piano Player Co., refer to Peerless Piano Player Co.
Navas, Raphael (pianist), 279, 283
Nearing, Homer (pianist), 283
Needham, E.P., 714, 739, 740, 742, 743, 776
Needham Musical Cabinet, 714, 739, 740, 776
Neitzel, Otto (pianist), 317, 331, 584
Nelson, Rudolf, 452
Nelson-Wiggen Piano Co. (pianos, orchestrions, and organs), 92, 348, 350-352, 354, 384, 495, history and description of instruments 528-532, 602, 704, 712, 715, 716, 719, 725
Nethercutt, J.B., 307, 322, 417, 456, 792
Netzow (pianos), 703, 725

Neue Leipziger Musikwerke (Buff-Hedinger), history and description of instruments 533
New American Musical Box (organette), 755
New Century (Caille slot machine), 94
New Century (disc music boxes), 100-102, 105; history and description of 118, 124, 127; 504
New England Automatic Banjo Co., 398, 400, 405, 406
New Musical Orguinette, 741
New Polyphon Supply Co. Ltd. (agent), 127
New-Tone Calliope, 725, 838, 843
New York Philharmonic Orchestra, 300
New York Symphony Orchestra, 300
Newman, Ernest, 308
Ney, Elly (pianist), 279, 282, 283, 331, 584
Niagara Musical Instrument Co., history and description of pianos and orchestrions 534, 537, 554, 814, history and description of band organs 907-908
Nicholas II, Czar of Russia, 49
Nickel Player (Weser Brothers), 397, history and description of 655
Nicklin Nickel-in-the-Slot Piano Player, 582
Nicole (Polyphon music box), 163
Nicole Frères (music box manufacturers and agents), 19, 21, 25, 28, 31, 33, 39, 44, 49, 107, 145, 163, 210, 249-251, 466
Niemczik, A.V., 430
Nikisch, Arthur (pianist), 329, 331, 584
Nikisch, Mitja (pianist), 308
Noble, T. Tertius (organist), 792
Noe, J. Thurston (pianist), 279, 283
Norberg, Art, 722
Norfleet, Helen (pianist), 283
Norris & Hyde (pianos), 321
North Tonawanda Barrel Organ Factory (Eugene DeKleist), 876, 930
North Tonawanda Musical Instrument Works (and Capitol Piano & Organ Co.), 347, 350, 352, 353, history and description of pianos and orchestrions 535-541, 703, 714, 718, 813, 814, 844, 851, 857, 869, 871-873, 907, history and description of band organs 909-913, 931
Novaes, Guiomar (pianist), 282
Novello, Mark (pianist), 308
Numero Uno, refer to Musical Uno (slot machine)
Nyiregyhazi, Erwin (pianist), 279, 282, 283

O

Oberg, Phil, 722-724
Obermeier, J.B. (inventor), 711
Oberon (Popper orchestrion), 583, 589
O'Connor, W. Scott, 398, 399, 406, 415
Offenbach (clock), 247
Ogier, Enrico, 806
Ohio (Popper orchestrion), 589
Oliver (pianos), 267
Olympia (disc music boxes made by F.G. Otto & Sons), 100, 101; history and description of 134, 136, 143
Olympia (player reed organ), 743, description of 783
Olympia Music Box Co., 143
Olympia Musical Automaton Co., 136
On the Square (Mills slot machine), 95
One Man Orchestra (Wurlitzer photoplayers), 697-702
Opera glasses, musical, 70
Operators Piano Co. (Coinola pianos, Reproduco piano - pipe organs, etc.), 92, 347, 348, 351, 352, 354, 355, 390, 494, 496, history and description of instruments 542-551, 553, 638, 654, 704, 709, 711, 714, 716, 719-712
Oppenheimer, Marie (pianist), 317
Oracle Letter Writer (Mills arcade device), 526
Oratorio (Niagara piano), 534, 908
Orchestra cylinder music boxes, description of, 21
Orchestra Organ (Gebr. Bruder), 831
Orchestra Piano (mechanical dulcimer), 360
Orchestral (Barbieri), 385
Orchestral Grand (Stella disc music box by Mermod Frères), 119, 122
Orchestral J and K (Cremona orchestrions by Marquette Piano Co.), 348, 497, 498, 500-502
Orchestral Music Box (Roepke), 248
Orchestral Organette, 774
Orchestral Regina (disc music box), 201-203
Orchestrelle (Aeolian Co. player reed organ), 251, 255, 309, 405, 743, history and description of 777-780, 788, 791
Orchestrelle Co., Ltd. (agent), 250, 258, 743, 749
Orchestrina (North Tonawanda Musical Instrument Works orchestrion), 535, 537, description of 540
Orchestrion Harmonette (organette), 345, 764, 765
Orchestrion Kalliston (organette), 749
Orchestrions, general description of types 343-355; refer also to individual manufacturers throughout the book
Orchestrone (organettes and organs), 635, 743, 759, 760
Orchestrophone (Limonaire), history and description of instruments 876-883
Ord-Hume, Arthur W.J.G., 18, 22, 41, 53, 100, 104, 172, 213, 237, 242, 248, 249, 362-364, 739, 845
Organ clocks, 784
Organ combs in cylinder music boxes, 29
Organa (player accordion), 775
Organette (Munroe Organ Reed Co. organette), 760
Organette (Wurlitzer piano - pipe organ), 550, history and description of 664, 696, 721
Organettes, history and description of instruments and related player reed organs, 737-800
Organina (organette), 740, 763, 764, 771
Organina Cabinet (organette), 764, 765
Organina Mignonette (organette), 764
Organina Thibouville, 750
Organista (Spaethe), 776
Organita (organette), 763-765, 773
Organo (organette), 747
Organola (Walcker organ player), 800
Organophone (Gavioli), 742
Orgoblo (Spencer Turbine Co.), 696
Orguinette, refer to Mechanical Orguinette
Orient (Ariston automaton), 746
Original Dewey, refer to Dewey (Mills slot machine)
"Original" music boxes, pianos, etc., refer to Lochmann "Original"
Original Orchestrion and Piano Co., 464, 818
Original Piano Trio, 279
Original Welte (reproducing piano), refer to Welte Mignon
Originators (pianos), 703, 725
Orloff, Nicolas (or Nikolai) (pianist), 282, 283
Ornstein, Leo (pianist), 279- 281-283, 285
Orphenion (disc music boxes), 100, 101, history and description of 132-133
Orpheus (disc music boxes), 247, 250
Orpheus (mechanical zither), 359, 746
Orpheus (player organ), 251, 743, description of 783
Orpheus Piano Orchestrion, 363
Orpheusharmonicon (orchestrion), 345
Orphobella (Ehrlichs Musikwerke), 707
Orton & Spooner, 867
Osborn Piano Player Co. (agent), 599
Osborne (Polyphon music box), 163
Otero (Phönix organette), 753
Otero (Gebr. Weber orchestrion), 627, 628
Othello (Popper orchestrion), 583, 586
Ottina & Pellandi, 806
Otto, Albert, 134
Otto, Edmund, 134, 136
Otto, F.G. & Sons (Capital "cuff" music boxes, Criterion and Olympia disc boxes, Pianette, etc.), 53, 101, history and description of instruments 134-143, 171, 208, 359, 494
Otto, Frederick G., 134
Otto, Gustav, 134, 136, 140
Otto Manufacturing Co., 136
Ouer, Fred E., 370
Overture cylinder music box, description of, 28
Owen, Drs. Edith and Robert, 190
Owl (Mills slot machine), 92, 95, 507

P

Pachmann, Vladimir de (pianist), 282, 308, 331, 584
Pacific Piano Co., 465
Packard (automobiles), 652, 653
Packard (pianos), 319
Paderewski, Ignace Jan (pianist), 273, 282, 300, 301, 308-310, 324, 330, 331, 336, 584

Paganini (Philipps violin pianos and orchestrions; also distributed by Wurlitzer), 317, 339, 347-349, 352, 512; history and description of instruments 564-566, 569, 572, 575-578; 622; history and description of instruments sold by Wurlitzer 661, 662, 664, 680, 690, 693-695; 721
Paillard (music boxes), 19, 21, 27, 29-31, 36, 37, 43-46, 49, 52, 62, 66, 68, 71, 118, 247, 249, 251
Paillard, Alfred E., 136
Paillard, Amedee, 31
Paillard, C. & Co., 239
Paillard, Charles, 32
Paillard, M.J. & Co. (agent), 42, 136
Paillard, Vaucher Fils, 27
Pairan, Ellen (pianist), 317
Palestrina (Schiedmayer player organ), 783
Palm Garden (Frankfurt-am-Main), 572
Palmistry Fortune Teller (Mills arcade device), 526
Pan-O-Ram (Mills movie machine), 514
Pan Orchestra (Hupfeld orchestrion), 339, 348, 349, 430-432, 440, 449, history and description of 545-457, 478, 621-623, 713, 721, 745
Panharmonico (Gavioli), 857
Panharmonicon (orchestrion), 345
Panorama (Kalliope disc music box with racing horses), 108, 110
Parachute Safety Check (Jacot/Mermod device), 58, 59
Paris (Polyphon music box), 163
Park Riding Gallery, 870
Parker, C.W. (amusement outfitter), 823, 857, 869, history and description of instruments, etc. 914-919
Parker, George L. (agent), 376
Parker, H.T., 285
Parlow, Edmund (pianist), 317
Parr, Ellis, 99, 213
Pascal, Julian (pianist), 279, 283
Pasquale (pianos), 249
Pathé (phonographs), 118, 128, 488, 792
Patriarch (Imhof & Mukle orchestrion), 465, 471
Patti, Adelina, 634, 636, 643, 644
Pattison, Lee (pianist), 279, 283
Pauer, Max v. (pianist), 282, 283, 314, 317, 331, 336
Paur, Emil (pianist), 330, 331, 336
Pavilion Amusement Park, 922
Peacock (in German, Pfau; Philipps orchestrion), 571
Peerless (Mermod Frères cylinder music boxes), 51, 52, 56, 120
Peerless Piano Player Co. (pianos, orchestrions, and theatre instruments), 255, 347, 350-353, 382, 397, 400, 424, 509, 534, history and description of instruments 552-562, 594, 595, 597, 614, 654, 715, 722, 725
Peersman, Eugene, 893
Pelletier, Wilfred (pianist), 279, 283
Pendleton, F.R., 405-416
Pepita (Hupfeld orchestrion), 443, 444
Pepperkorn, Gertrud (pianist), 331
Perfect (Popper orchestrion), 585
Perfection Music Box Co., 243
Perfection Organ (E. Böcker), 818, 822
Perin-Shopard (agent), 39
Perkins, Ray (pianist), 283
Perla (Dienst orchestrion), 394
Perlee, Gijs (Dutch street organs), 833, 848, 849
Perrin, C.H. (pianist), 308
Perry, Gray (pianist), 283
Peters, H. & Co. (music boxes, pianos, etc.), 250, 357, 363, 584, 705
Peters, Jessie (pianist), 283
Petri, Egon (pianist), 331
Petrophon (H. Peters & Co.), 705
Pfitzner, Hans (pianist), 317
Pfluger Accumulatoren-Werke, 250
Phädra (Holzweissig orchestrion), 429
Phädra (Popper orchestrion), 586
Philadelphia Symphony Orchestra, 300
Philag (J.D. Philipps & Söhne trademark), 563
Philharmonia (Hanke orchestrion), 707
Philharmonic Organ (Welte), 325, 349, 636, 638, history and description of 792-798
Philipp, Franz, 792
Philipp, I., 308
Philipps & Ketterer, refer to J.D. Philipps & Söhne
Philipps, August, 317, 566
Philipps, J.D. & Söhne (J.D. Philipps and Sons), history and description of Duca reproducing piano 317, 339, 345, 347-349, 351-355, 388, 419-421, 489, 504, history and description of pianos, orchestrions, and theatre instruments (including Paganini and Pianella styles) 563-579, 583, 593, 621, 654, 662, 678, 681, 682, 684-692, 695, 720, 721, 807
Philipps, Oswald, 317, 566
Phillips, Fred, 722
Phoenix Orchestrion, 741, 752
Phoenix (organettes, etc.), refer to Phönix Musikwerke
Phönix Musikwerke (organettes, etc.), 244, 249, 251, 429, 740, 741, history and description of instruments 751-753
Phono-Grand (Seeburg piano/phonograph combination), 600, 602, 606, description of 611
Phonographic Cornet (organette), 761
Phonola (Hupfeld player piano; also known as Solophonola), 311, 312, 315, 430, 431, 438, 453, 460, 462
Phonolizst (Hupfeld semi-reproducing piano), 311, 312, 316, 339, 353, 354, 430-432, 435-440
Phonoliszt Violin Pipe Piano (Hupfeld), 439
Phonoliszt-Violina (Hupfeld violin player), 311, 312, 316, 339, 353, 430-432, history and description of 436-440, 453, 462, 465, 591, 622, 713
Phonoradio (Popper), 585, 588
Photo Orchestra (Peerless photoplayer), 352, 553, 554
Photo Player Co., refer to American Photo Player Co.
Photoplayers, general description of 352-353; also refer to individual manufacturers, especially American Photo Player Co., J.P. Seeburg Piano Co., and Rudolph Wurlitzer Co.
Pian-Auto (Krell piano), 265
Pian-O-Grand (Nelson-Wiggen piano), 528
Pianagara (also spelled as Pianiagara; Niagara piano), 534, 908
Pianella (Philipps orchestrions; also sold by Wurlitzer under the Mandolin PianOrchestra and Concert PianOrchestra trademarks, to which refer), 317, 347, 419-421, history and description of instruments 563-579, 621, 662, 684, 721, 807
Pianetta (Philipps orchestrions), 567
Pianette (disc-operated piano made by F.G. Otto & Sons), 134, 136, 208, description of 494
Pianiagara (also spelled as Pianagara; Niagara piano), 534
Pianino (Wurlitzer 44-note piano), 347, 348, 350, 355; history and description of 661, 663, 664, 669-671, 675; 715, 721, 940
Pianista (Fourneaux), 255
Piano-forte cylinder music box, description of 21
Piano-Jazz (Pierre Eich orchestrion), 395
Piano Mandolin Orchestrion, 366
Piano Melodico, 350, 359, 361
Piano Orchestra (Mills electromagnetic orchestrion), 514, description of 524
Piano Orchestra (Symphonion orchestrion), 624
Piano Orchestrion (barrel piano), 365
Piano Orchestrion (mechanical dulcimer), 345, 350, 361
Piano Player Manufacturing Co. (Rhapsodist, etc. pianos, orchestrions, and theatre instruments), 352, 498, history and description of instruments 580-581
Piano players, history and description of piano players and player pianos 253-270
Piano-ette (Mechanical Piano-ette), 359
Pianoforte, Harp, and Music Warehouse (agent), 786
Pianola (Aeolian player piano), 255, 257, 258, 299, 300, 309, 405, 431
Pianolin (North Tonawanda Musical Instrument Works), 350, 353, 535-537, description of 538, 539, 715
Pianophon (piano player), 708
PianOrchestra (Wurlitzer orchestrions), refer to Mandolin PianOrchestra and Concert PianOrchestra
Pianostyle (music rolls), 318
Pianotainer (Fox Music Co. piano), 703
Pianotist (piano player), 362, history and description of 582
Pianova Co. (pianos), 350, 397, 506, 508, 509, 560, 722
Pianova-Virtuosa (Mills violin player), 353, 508, 515
Piastro, Mishel (pianist), 279, 283
Piccolo (organette), 741, 751
Piccolo (Popper), 586
Pictures, mechanical and musical, 69, 77, 80, 85
Picturoll (music rolls), 369, 371, 720

Pièce à oiseau cylinder music box, description of 21
Pierement (Dutch street organ), 833, 848, 849
Pierlow, Jules, 307
Pierson, Maude (pianist), 279, 283
Pietschmann & Sohn, 246
Pion (music arranger), 893
Pipe Organ Orchestra (Seeburg photoplayers), 600, 602, history and description of 617-619
Pipe Organ Orchestra (Wurlitzer photoplayers), 701, 702
Pittle, Charles (agent), 742
Pittman, Wyatte, 660
Planté, Francis (pianist), 311
Platform music box movement, 23
Platt, Benjamin, 370
Play-a-Sax, 741, 776
Player Piano Group, 284
Player Piano Manufacturing Co., refer to Piano Player Manufacturing Co. 580, 581
Player pianos, history and description of 253-270
Player pipe organs, history, description, and general information 744, 745, 787-790, 792-800
Player reed organs, history and description of player reed organs, organettes, and related instruments 737-800
Plerodienique music box, description of 20, 42, 44
Pletcher, Tom, 721
Pleyel (pianos), 256
Pneuma (Dienst pianos), 391
Pneuma (Kuhl & Klatt pianos), 251, 391, 708
Pneumatic Orchestra Piano, 366
Pneumatic Organ (organette), 774
Pohl, Alexander (pianist), 317
Poirot Frères, 806
Polizzi, D. & Figli, 806
Pollmann, August (agent), 210, 851
Pollock, Muriel (pianist), 279, 283
Polydor (Polyphon trademark), 169
Polygraph (Polyphon typewriter), 169, 419
Polygraphon (Polyphon music box/phonograph combination), 144, 148, 158, 168
Polyhymnia (disc music boxes), 128
Polymnia (disc music boxes), 100, 104, 250
Polymobil (R.E. Olds automobile manufactured under license by Polyphon), 169
Polyphon & Regina Music Box Co. (agent), 210, 249
Polyphon Musikwerke (music boxes, pianos, etc.), 19, 99-104, 112-114, 116, 128, history and description of instruments 144-169, 170-172, 177, 181, 184, 201, 207-211, 214, 215, 220, 221, 225, 235, 237, 239, 246, 249-251, 347, 350, 357, 419, 504, 509, 584, 590, 594, 767
Polyphona (Polyphon pianos), 99, 144, 145, description of 168
Polytype cylinder music box, description of 21-22
Polyvox (Blessing orchestrion), 388, 389
Pombia, Pietro, 806
Pompadour (Gebr. Bruder organ), 831
Pop (music rolls), 720
Pope, Henry, 369
Popper & Co. (pianos, orchestrions, etc.), 145, 250, 323, 339, 345, 347, 349, 351, 354, 478, 489, 574, history and description of instruments 583-393, 621, 622, 833, 846
Popper, Hugo, 323, biography 584-585
Portable Box Organ (Symphonion music box), 217
Portable hand-cranked barrel organs, history and description of 805-812
Pouishnoff, Leff (pianist), 308
Powell, John (pianist), 282
Pratte, L.E.N. & Co. (agent), 258, 778
Praxinoscope (parlor entertainment device), 64
Preciosa (Holzweissig orchestrion), 429
Premier (Buff-Hedinger piano player), 533
Premier (North Tonawanda Musical Instrument Works piano), 539
Premier (pianos), 319
Premier Auto-Harmonium (Buff-Hedinger), 774
Presburg (pianos), 703, 725
Présent, Rata (pianist), 279, 283
Price & Teeple (Carleton, etc. pianos), 703, 704, 725
Price, William H. (organist), 788
Prill, Paul, 450
Primavolta (Buff-Hedinger piano), 533
Princess (Regina phonograph), 103, 171, 172, 212
Prinsen, Arthur (music arranger), 833
Proctor, George (pianist), 279, 283
Profit Sharing Player Piano (Evans, Gray, Rockola, etc. pianos with slot machines), 92, 507, 542, 543, 704, 712
Program cards (tune sheets) for cylinder music boxes, 27
Projections on music box discs, 106
Protos (Popper orchestrion), 592
Prüwer, Julius, 454
Psycho (orchestrion), 346
Puck (Caille slot machine), 24, 94, 712
Puck (Popper piano), 589
Pugno, Raoul (pianist), 282, 283, 313, 317, 328, 331, 584
Putz, Egon (pianist), 283
Pyle, Wynne (pianist), 279, 283, 317
Pyrophon Musikwerke, 706

Q

Q-R-S Music Rolls, Inc., 256, 293, 294, 318, 369, 719-722, 726, history of firm 727, 729, 742, 776
Quadruplex, refer to Austin Premier Quadruplex (organ player)
Quateer, Ed., 806
Quatour Expression Piccolo cylinder music box, 50
Quintette (Sächsische Orchester-Musikwerke), 366

R

Raap & Sohn, 806
Raby (Polyphon music box), 163
Racca, G. (mechanical dulcimers and pianos), 360, 584
Race Horse Piano (Mills electromagnetic piano), 92, 514, description of 525
Rachmaninoff, Sergei, 273, 279, 282, 283, 289
Radi-O-Player (player piano/radio combination), 263
Radiosonant (Hupfeld), 460
Rafelson, Ella (also spelled as Rafaelsohn) (pianist), 317, 331
Rainger, Ralph (pianist), 283
Ramona (Imhof & Mukle piano), 479
Rand, Benjamin C., 537, 813, 909
Rand Company, Inc., history and description of pianos and orchestrions 535-541
Randegger, Giuseppe (pianist), 279, 283
Ravel, Maurice, 308, 324
Razzle Dazzle (amusement device), 869
Reblitz, Arthur, 504, 514, 721, 722
Rechange music box, description of 20
Reclame (Imhof & Mukle orchestrion), 465, 469
Record Piano (Popper), 587
Recordo (expression piano), 293, history and description of 318, 663
Recordo Player Roll Co., 318
Recordon-Sulliger, Louis, 32
Redfern, Kenneth, 882
Reed (pianos), 703, 725
Reed, A.E., 868
Reed-Pipe Clariona (organette), 741, 762, 768
Regal Piano & Player Co. (pianos), 350, 494, 703, 722
Reger, Max, 311, 314, 331, 336, 584, 792, 793
Regina (Popper orchestrion), 585
Regina Company, refer to Regina Music Box Co.
Regina Music Box Co. (American subsidiary of Polyphon Musikwerke), 18, 19, 51, 53, 92, 99-104, 106, 134, 142, 145, 151, 153, 154, 164, 165, 169, history and description of music boxes, disc-operated pianos, and phonographs 170-212, 214, 215, 235, 251, 347, 350, 430, 482, 498, 504, 506, 507, 509, history and description of roll-operated pianos 594-596, 661, 725, 741, 767, 858
Reginaphone (Regina music box/phonograph combination), 58, 103; history and description of instruments 171, 172, 174, 176, 179, 182-184, 186, 190-192, 197-199, 202, 210, 212
Reginapiano (Regina pneumatic pianos), 99, 172, 498, history and description of 594-596, 725
Rehberg, Walter (pianist), 317
Rehberg, Willy (pianist), 317
Reichard (pianos), 703, 725
Reichenthal, Ralph (pianist), 279, 283
Reina, Vic, 834
Reinecke, Carl (pianist), 283, 313, 336, 584

Reisenauer, Alfred (pianist), 282, 283, 331, 336, 584
Reisenberg, Nadia (pianist), 279, 283
Reliable (Automatic Musical Co. piano; sold through many agents), 482, 495, 722
Reliance (Berni organ), 816
Relph & Pedley (showmen), 888
Reproducing Organ (Wurlitzer player pipe organ), 664, 799
Reproducing pianos, history and description of various types 271-342
Reproduco (Operators Piano Co. combination piano and pipe organ), 352, 381; history and description of 543, 545, 548-551; 719
Reproducta (Lösche), 489
Resotone Grand Co. (player chrysoglott), 353, 400, history and description of instrument 597
Restagno, V., 806
Reuge (music boxes), 19, 68, 91
Reuter Organ Co., 744
Revolver music box, description of 20, 31
Rex (Popper orchestrion), 589
Reyes, Juan (pianist), 279, 283
Rhapsodist (pianos and orchestrions sold by the Piano Player Manufacturing Co.), 498, history and description of instruments 580-581, 725
Rheingold (Holzweissig orchestrion), 429
Ricca & Son (pianos), 704
Rice, Gitz- (or Gitz-Rice) (pianist), 279, 283
Richter, Eduard, 806, 929
Richter, Emil, 806, 929
Richter, F.A. & Co., 244, 245
Richter, Gebr. (fairground organs, etc.), 806, 823, history and description of instruments 929
Rickenbach, Paul (pianist), 283
Ricksecker, Fred, 369
Riemer, Gebr., 346, 812
Riessner, Paul, 99, 144, 170, 172, 356
Riggin, Edward, 197
Rigoletto (Dienst orchestrion), 394
Ripper, Alice (pianist), 317, 331, 585
Risler, Eduard (pianist), 317
Rivenc, Ami (music boxes), 47, 250
Rivers, Claire (pianist), 279, 283
Robbiati, Ditta, 806
Robert Morton Organ Co. (theatre organs; acquired American Photo Player Co.), 367-370, 377
Roberts (Polyphon music box), 163
Roberts, Lee S. (pianist), 283, 721, 722, 727
Robinson, Carol (pianist), 279, 283
Robinson, David, 703
Robinson, P.S., 868
Robot Band (Blessing), 388
Rockola, 92, 542, description of Profit Sharing Player Piano 543 and 704
Rockola, David, 704
Rococo (Hupfeld Helios orchestrion), 448
Rococo (Symphonion music box), 220
Rodgers, Richard (pianist), 283
Rodocker, R.V., 721, 722
Roehl, Harvey and Marion, 255, 350, 351, 373, 486, 487, 498, 537, 605, 609, 656, 660, 718, 722, 739, 782, 792
Roepke, Carl Albert, 104, 248
Roesler-Hunholz, 719
Roessel, Anatol v. (also spelled as Rössel) (pianist), 317, 331
Rogers (pianos), 277, 281, 289
Rognoli, Ercole, 806
Rohlfing Sons Music Co. (agent), 124
Rola (Hupfeld billiards), 460
Roland (Hanke orchestrion), 707
Roland (Popper orchestrion), 583, 592
Rolla Artis (music rolls), 721
Roller organs, refer to organettes
Rolmonica Music Co., 740, 741, history and description of Rolmonica 775
Romanowsky (pianist), 331
Rombach, Willy, 478
Ronald, Henry, 308
Rönisch, Albert, 316
Rönisch, Carl (pianos; firm later acquired by Hupfeld), 311, 312, 315, 316, 354, 430, 431, 432, 437, 460
Rönisch, Hermann, 316
Röntgen, Julius (pianist), 317
Roosevelt (pipe organs), 788
Rosa, Lou, 663
Rosasco, Giuseppe, 806
Rose Valley Recording Roll (music rolls), 318
Rosenfield, L. (agent), 124
Rosenthal, Adele (pianist), 279, 283
Rosenthal, Moriz (pianist), 279, 282, 283
Ross, Christopher, 566, 577
Ross, Gertrude (pianist), 279, 283
Ross, Stuart (pianist), 283
Rossini (Polyphon orchestrion), 145, 165, 166
Roth & Engelhardt, refer to Peerless Piano Player Co.
Rothafel, S.L. "Roxy" (showman), 304
Roulette (Mills slot machine), 92, 526
Royal (Polyphon music box), 163
Royal American Shows, 922
Royal Electric Bioscope, 886
Royal Importing Co. (agent), 764
Royal Organetta (organette), 764
Royal Organette, 741
Royal Orguinette (organette), 764, 765
Royal Upright (organette), 763, 772
Royal Violista (Wauters/Automatic Musical Co. violin player), 353, 481
Royal Wax-Work, 864
Rubes, Johann (also spelled Hrubes), 806
Rubinstein, Artur (pianist), 279, 281, 283, 285, 308
Rübner, Cornelius (pianist), 331
Rückert, Bruno, 132
Russel, Alexander, 279, 283, 788
Ruth, A. & Sohn (fairground organs, etc.), 464, 623, 654, 806, 807, 815, 818, 823, 831, 836, 876, history and description of instruments 920-922, 927, 931
Ruth, Adolf, 807
Ruth, Adolf, Jr., 806, 807
Ruth, Andreas, 807, 920
Ruth, George Herman "Babe," 304
Rutt, R. Spurden (organs), 251
Rybner, Cornelius (pianist), 279, 283
Ryder, Hughes, 104, 134, 243
Rzebitschek (music box movements), 24

S

Sabbaem (Barbieri trademark), 385
Sabin, William D., 482, 486, 487, 720
Sächsische Drahtwaren-Fabrik Leistner & Co., 710
Sächsische Orchester-Musikwerke, history and description of instruments 366
Sächsischen Orchestrionfabrik F.O. Glass, history and description of instruments 533
Saenger Theatres, 550
Sage, Gary, 555
Saint-Saëns, Camille, 279, 282, 283, 311, 317, 328, 331, 336, 585, 788
Salieri, Antonio (composer), 345
Salisbury (Polyphon music box), 163
Salisbury, Stephen, 740
Salon Chordephon (mechanical zither), 357
Salon Orchestra (Popper orchestrion), 583, 591, 593
Salon Piano Orchestrion (Lösche), 493
Salon Piano with Violin (Gebr. Weber), 626
Samaroff, Olga (pianist), 279, 282, 283, 324, 331, 336
Sammels, C., 806
Samuel, Harold (pianist), 308
Samuels, Mervyn, 369
Sandell, Henry K. (inventor), 32, 353, 507, 509, 515
Sanders, Arthur, 136, 557
Sanders-Dreyer Piano Co. (agent), 600
Sandringham (Polyphon music box), 163
San Francisco Symphony Orchestra, 300
San Galli, Thomas (pianist), 331
Sapellnikoff, Wassily (pianist), 279, 282, 283, 331, 584
Sarasate (Frati piano), 421
Sarasate, Pablo (violinist), 421, 536, 585
Sauber, William (pianist), 283
Sauer, Emil v. (pianist), 282, 283, 308, 313, 330, 331, 585
Saul, David L., 273, 276, 293-295, 318, 319, 339

Savage, William, 249
Savages (amusement outfitters), 883
Savino, Domenico (pianist), 283
Savoyard (Polyphon music box), 149, 151
Saxon Orchestrion Manufactory (name used by the Sächsischen Orchestrionfabrik F.O. Glass in English-language advertising), history and description of instruments 533
Saxonia (disc music box), 244
Schaarschmidt, Paul, 806
Schaeffer (pianos), 703, 725
Schaff Brothers Co. (pianos), 267, 481, 487, 703
Schapira, Wera (pianist), 317
Scharrer, Irene (pianist), 308
Scharwenka, Xaver (pianist), 279, 282, 283, 311, 313, 317, 323, 328, 331, 585
Schaub, Adolph, 134
Schaub, Ferdinand, 136, 139
Scheck (sculptor), 823
Scheibe, Paul, 99, 214, 232
Schelling, Ernest (pianist), 282, 331
Scheola (Schiedmayer player organ), 783
Schiedmayer Pianoforte Fabrik, 783
Schiller, Friedrich v., 462
Schillings, Max (pianist), 313, 331, 585
Schlaich, Richard, 381
Schleicher & Sons (pianos), 703, 704
Schmid-Lindner, August (pianist), 317
Schmidt & Co. (of Leipzig), 244, 741, 751
Schmidt Automatic Piano Co. (agent), 595
Schmidt, Oscar, 359
Schmidthalz (of Frati & Co.), 807
Schmitt, Adolf (pianist), 317
Schmitt, Carl (agent), 590
Schmitz, E. Robert (pianist), 279, 282, 283
Schmitz, Fred A. (pianist), 279, 283
Schmoele Brothers (organ builders), 761, 762, 787
Schnabel, Arthur (pianist), 279, 282, 283, 317, 331
Schnabel-Tollefsen, Augusta (pianist), 279, 283
Schneider, Geo. Nachfolger (agent), 131
Schnitzer, Germaine (pianist), 279, 282, 283, 317, 331
Schönstein, Gustav, 478, 710
School of Martin Blessing, 388
Schorr, D. (pianist), 331
Schott, Gaspar, 745
Schramberger Uhrfedernfabrik, 710
Schrämli & Tschudin, 246, 251
Schröder, B. (pianist), 317
Schübbe & Co. (pianos and orchestrions), 251, 705
Schultz (pianos), 703, 725
Schultz, W.F., 537, 813
Schultze, A.O., 430
Schulz, M. Co. (pianos), 318, 319, 321, 660
Schulz, Otto, 660
Schumann, Georg (pianist), 331, 585
Schwander (pianos), 354, 395
Scialanti, Aless, 806
Scionti, Silvio (pianist), 279, 283
Scott, Cyril (pianist), 282, 283, 308, 331
Scott, H.A., 308
Scriàbine, Alexander (pianist), 279, 282, 283, 311, 328, 331, 336
Seals, musical, 86
Seaman, Frank, 336
Sears & Roebuck (agent), 143, 198, 210, 719, 721, 754, 755
Sébastyén, George (pianist), 279, 283
Seeburg, J.P. Piano Co. (pianos, orchestrions, photoplayers, etc.), 210, 339, 345, 347, 348, 350-355, 367, 368, 370, 376, 424, 486, 496-499, 556, history and description of instruments 598-619, 656, 660, 673, 680, 709, 711, 714, 715, 716, 718, 720, 721, 725, 733, 744
Seeburg, N. Marshall, 598, 601, 656, 660
Seeburg-Smith Organ Co., 600, 744
Seiler (pianos), 320, 334
Selden Patents, 739, 761
Selecta (Lösche orchestrion), 493
Selection (Gebr. Bruder organ), 832
Selective Roll Piano (Seeburg), 501, 602, description of 606, 719
Selector Duplex Organ (Nelson-Wiggen) 352, 495, 528, description of 530, 550, 719
Selectra (Western Electric pianos), 656, 658-660
Selectraphone (Western Electric phonograph), 656
Self-Playing Violin (Dienst violin player), 394, 481
Self-Playing Xylophone (Automatic Musical Co./Link automatically-played orchestra bells), 203, 353, description of 483
Seligman, Isiah (pianist), 279, 283
Seltzer (pianos and orchestrions), 703
Semi-helicoidal cylinder music box, description of 20, 21, 45
Semi-Orchestrion (Peerless), 561
Seraphine (organette), 774
Seraphone (organette), 742, 768
Serenadum (Berni organ), 817
Serenata (pianos), 419
Seth Thomas (clocks), 103, 184, 193, 210, 211
Severson, Louis M. (Operators Piano Co.), 542, 545
Sewing kits, musical, 70
Sextrola (North Tonawanda Musical Instrument Works orchestrion), 535-537, description of 538
Seybold (player accordions, etc.), 742, 775
Seybold Piano Co., 354
Seydel, J.C., 776
Seytre, Claude-Felix, 255, 634
Shackleton Collection, 35
Shackley, George (pianist), 283
Shäfer, Dirk (also spelled Schäfer) (pianist), 330, 331
Shapiro, Ivan and Joan, 290
Shaw, Geoffrey, 308
Sheldon, Charles A., Jr. (organist), 788
Shelley, Harry Rowe (organist), 788
Sheridan, Frank (pianist), 283
Sherman, Clay & Co. (agent), 210, 370, 376
Sherman, Frederick R., 370
Shipman, Harry (pianist), 279, 283
Shryock, Johnson Manufacturing Co., 210
Siebold, Martha (pianist), 331
Siebrecht, Felix, 710
Silber & Fleming, Ltd. (agent), 249
Silber, Sidney (pianist), 279, 283
Siloti, Alexander (pianist), 282, 308
Silvana Xylophon(e) (Philipps orchestrion), 564
Silvanigra (disc music boxes), 247
Silver Palace Hotel (Leadville, Colorado), 692
Silvia (Philipps orchestrion), 563, 564
Simon, Ernst, 806
Simon, Georg, 806
Simon, Morris (pianist), 279, 283
Simonton, Richard C., 323, 324, 336, 338, 794
Simplex (piano player), 258
Simplex Player Action Co., 294, 660
Sims, Lee (pianist), 283
Simson (Popper orchestrion), 592
Sinfonie Jazz, refer to Symphony Jazz (Hupfeld orchestrion)
Singer, Richard (pianist), 317
Singleton, William, 305
Sirene (Gebr. Bruder organ), 829-831
Sirene (orchestrion), 708
Sirion (disc-shifting music boxes), 100, 102, 106; history and description of 118, 124, 126, 127; 504
Sittard, Alfred (organist), 792
Six Columns (Mortier organ), 898
Sjogren, Emil (pianist), 331
Skinner, Ernest M. Co., refer to Skinner Organ Co.
Skinner Organ Co., 310, 744, 788
Sklarevski, Alexander (pianist), 279, 283
Slabyhaud, Franz, 806
Slivinski, Joseph (pianist), 331
Smith & Nixon Piano Co. (agent), 210
Smith, Barnes & Strohber Co. (Chicago Electric pianos), 390
Smith-Geneva Organ Co., 744
Smith, George (pianist), 279, 283
Smith, Harold (pianist), 279, 283
Smoking stands, musical, 70
Smolian, A., 462
Snyder, William P., 636, 639, 643
Société Anonyme Fabriques Reunies (music boxes), 104, 250

Société des Anciens Etablissements Gavioli & Cie., refer to Gavioli & Cie.
Sohmer (pianos), 319
Sokoloff, Nikolai, 300
Solea (Gebr. Weber orchestrion), 349, 623; history and description of 625, 627-629; 713
Soleil (Cocchi, Bacigalupo & Graffigna orchestrions), 708
Solo Carola (reproducing piano), 339, 340
Solo Expression Twin Tracker Empress (piano), 495, 496
Solo-Grand (Krell piano), 265
Solo Orchestrelle (Aeolian player reed organ), 743, description of 779-780, 788
Solo Violin-Cello Piano (North Tonawanda Musical Instrument Works), 541
Solo Violin Piano (Wurlitzer), 348, 663, 664, 680, 721
Solodant Phonola (Hupfeld piano), 431, 438, 462
Soloist (Kimball organ player), 800
Solophone (Pierre Eich), 395
Solophonola, refer to Phonola (Hupfeld piano)
Sonatina Melodion (organette), 753
Sonora (organette), 751
Soule, Henry, 407, 416
Southern California Music Co. (agent), 210
Souvaine, Henry (pianist), 279, 283
Sowerby, Leo (pianist), 283
Spaeth, Sigmund, 279, 283
Spaethe, Wilhelm (player organs, etc.), 743
Spangenberg, Hugo, 584
Special (Philipps orchestrion), 564, 570, 571
Special Carouselle Organ (Wurlitzer), 940
Spencer Turbine Co., 376, 696, 709
Spicka, Johann, 806
Spillman Engineering Corp. (amusement outfitters), 806, history and description of instruments, etc. 869-873, 932, 933
Sprague, Louis W. (pianist), 283
Sprague, Thomas, 562
Spreckels, Claus, 347
Springs, types used in cylinder music boxes 28, types used in disc music boxes 105
Stalin, Josef, 336
Standard (Hardman, Peck & Co. pianos), 620
Standard Piano Player (pianos), 620, 715, 722, 725
Standard Pneumatic Action Co., 256, 262, 263, 374, 700, 745, 799
Star (Caille slot machine), 94
Star Silver Depot (agent), 243
Stark (music rolls), 719
Starr Piano Co., 268, 703, 725
Stavenhagen, Bernh. (pianist), 331
Steam Riding Gallery (carousel), 869, 870
Stebbins, Charles A. (organist), 788
Stebel, Paula (pianist), 317, 331
Steck (pianos), 277, 290, 295, 296, 299, 303, 306, 309, 310, 431
Steeb, Olga (pianist), 279, 283
Steele, W.F. (organist), 788
Stefanie (orchestrion), 707
Steinert, M. & Sons (agent), 258, 778
Steinfeldt, John M. (pianist), 283
Steins, musical, 70
Steinway & Sons (pianos), 273, 276, 292, 299, 301-304, 306, 307, 309, 310, 325, 334, 336, 337, 552, 636
Steinway, Henry Z., 292
Stella (Mermod Frères disc music boxes), 51, 58, 99-103, 106, 107, 112; history and description of 118-125, 128; 249, 251
Stella (Popper orchestrion), 590
Stella (Popper reproducing piano), 323, 339, 354, 583, 584, description of 587
Stember, Emma (pianist), 331
Stenhammer, Wilhelm (pianist), 328, 331
Stereopticons, musical, 61, 70
Sterling (music rolls), 719
Sterling, Al (pianist), 279, 283
Stern, Lucie (pianist), 283
Sternberg, Armin & Bruder, 746
Stieff (pianos), 319
Stiller, Karl, 806
Stingl, Gustav, 706
Stodart (pianos), 321
Stoddard-Ampico (reproducing piano), 277, 279, 284
Stoddard, Charles F. (developed the Ampico), 277, 281
Stoddard, Joshua C., 838, 840
Stojowski, Sigismund (pianist), 279, 283
Stokowsky, Leopold, 300, 324
Story & Clark (pianos and organs), 251, 264, 743, 783
Stransky, Josef, 300
Strasser, J.G., 345
Straube, Carl, 793, 795
Straus, Oscar, 450
Strauss, Johann, 317, 450
Strauss, Lawrence (pianist), 283
Strauss, Richard, 279, 282, 283, 331, 334, 336, 454, 585
Street Organ (Phönix organette), 742
Street organs, refer to Dutch street organs
String Orchestra (Sächsische Orchester-Musikwerke orchestrion), 366
String Orchestra (Symphonion), 624
String Quartette (Mills Novelty Co. violins and viola player), 353, 510, 521
Strmisko, Matth., 806
Stroud (pianos), 295, 299, 303, 304, 306
Sturkow-Ryder (pianist), 283
Styria (Gebr. Weber orchestrion), 627
Sublima (Regina music boxes), 176, 178, 196-200
Sublima (Regina pianos), 145, 172, 506, history and description of 594-596, 663
Sublime harmonie cylinder music box, description of 22, patents 32
Sublime Harmonie Longue Marche (Paillard cylinder music box), 36
Sublime Harmonie Piccolo (Mermod Frères cylinder music box), 22
Sublime Harmonie Piccolo (Polyphon music box), 151
Sullivan, Dan (pianist), 279, 283
Sun Music Box Manufacturing Co., 246, 251
Super Jazzband Orchestra (Philipps), 566
Super Junior Reproduco (Operators Piano Co. piano - pipe organ), 548, 550
Super Pan Orchestra (Hupfeld orchestrion), 449, 457, 460
Super Reproduco (Operators Piano Co. piano - pipe organ), 548, 550
Super Violin (in Flemish, Super Violon; Pierre Eich), 395, 396
Superb (Berni organ), 816
Superba (Popper orchestrion), 588
Superfine (Capital "cuff" music box by F.G. Otto & Sons), 139
Supertone (music rolls), 719
Surprised Cook (automaton), 73
Suskind, Milton (pianist), 279, 283
Sutherland, Alicia (pianist), 279, 283
Sutro. Adolph, 347, 634, 712
Svoboda, Al, 495, 501
Swanee Whistle (patented automatic slide whistle), 583, 592
Swanson, Zignor, 722
Swart, Stuart (pianist), 279, 283
Symetrophon (Hupfeld), 460
Symonds Grand Switchback Gondolas, 867
Symphonia (Eugene DeRoy music rolls, pianos, etc.), 352, 465, 564, 568, history of 621-623
Symphonia (organette), 741, 770
Symphonica (Frati), 421, 422
Symphoniola (Symphonion pianos), 99, 624
Symphonion (Kaufmann), 480
Symphonion Co. (agent), 250
Symphonion Manufacturing Co. (of New Jersey; American branch of Symphonion Musikwerke; disc music boxes sold under Symphonion and Imperial Symphonion names), 53, 102, 142, 171; history and description of instruments 214, 215, 232, 235, 236
Symphonion Musikwerke (music boxes, pianos, orchestrions, etc.; Leipzig), 19, 32, 99-106, 114, 129, 144, 145, 148, 152, 170-172, 209, history and description of music boxes and disc-operated pianos 213-236, 237, 247, 250, 251, 347, 350, 430, 441, 504, history and description of roll-operated pianos and orchestrions 624
Symphony (Wilcox & White player reed organ), 251, 743, history and description of 781-782
Symphony Automatic Orchestra, 352, 580, 581, 654
Symphony Jazz (Sinfonie Jazz; Hupfeld orchestrion), 349, 432, 434, 453, 460
Symphony Orchestra (North Tonawanda Musical Instrument Works orchestrion), 540
Symphony Orchestra Organ (Gebr. Bruder organ), 829-831

Symphony Piano (Wurlitzer orchestrion), 675
Synchronized (music rolls), 719
Szántó, Theodor (pianist), 314
Szumowska, Antoinette (pianist), 279, 283

T

Taber Organ Co. (player reed organs), 742, 743, 761
Taft, President William Howard, 569
Taj Mahal (Mortier organ), 902-904
Tammany Concert Music Box, 704
Tammany Non-Pneumatic Player Piano, 704
Tammany Organet Co., 704
Tandler, Adolf (pianist), 317
Tangley Co. (Calliaphone calliopes), 725, 804; history and description of instruments 838, 839, 841, 842; 914, 917, 919
Tanzbär (player concertina), 742, history and description of 775
Tanzman, Alexandre (pianist), 282
Taylor & Farley Organ Co. (player reed organs), 740, 742, 743, 761
Taylor, Colin (pianist), 331
Taylor's Bioscope Theatre, 888
Tekstra, Bonnie, 91
Tel-Electric (piano player), 339, 341, 717
Telechron (clock), 278
Telektra (piano player), 339, 341, 717
Telescoping cylinder music box, description of 21, 44
Tell (Imhof & Mukle orchestrion), 465, 473
Terpsichore (Gebr. Bruder organ), 829, 830
Terry, R.R., 308
Teste, J.A., 739
Tetzner, Otto (Hupfeld director), 316, 461
Thaw, Evelyn Nesbit, 122
Thaw, Harry K., 122
Thayer (pianos), 703, 722
Thayer, George, 487
Theatre Orchestra (Cremona photoplayers made by Marquette Piano Co.), 497, 498, 503
Theatre Orchestrion (Peerless), 561
Theatre Violina (Hupfeld violin player), 352, 432, 437
Themodist (Aeolian expression system), 295, 300
Thibouville-Lamy, Jerome, 210, 249, 742, 750, 806
Thiebes Piano Co. (agent), 210
Thiebes, Stierlin Music Co. (agent), 190, 210
Thim, Johann, 707
Thomas, Frank W. (agent), 124
Thomas, Seth (clocks), 103, 184, 193, 210, 211
Thompson, Ann (pianist), 279, 283
Thompson, "Chick" (pianist), 283
Thorens, Hermann (music boxes), 19, 68, 99, 100, 103, 106, 247, 251
Thury, Frieda (pianist), 317
Tick, Ramsi P. (Q-R-S Music Rolls, Inc.), 727
Tiedemann, Wilhelm (organs), 808
Tiffany & Co. (agent), 210
Tillotson, Frederic (pianist), 279, 283
Timanoff, Vera (pianist), 331
Titania (Lösche orchestrion), 489, 490
Titania (Popper orchestrion), 585
Toccaphon (Buff-Hedinger piano), 533
Toch, Ernst (pianist), 317
Tolces, Toska (pianist), 283
Toledo (orchestrion), 705
Tom Thumb Band Organ (Wurlitzer), 940
Tompkins, William (agent), 402
Tonika (Popper orchestrion), 583, 586, 590
Tonophone (DeKleist/Wurlitzer piano), 347, 350, 352; history and description of 661, 665; 712, 714
Tooth spacing in cylinder music boxes, 29
Töpfer, Rich. (organs), 812
Tournaphone Music Co. (organettes), 741, 763, 764, 769
Tovar, José Conrado (pianist), 279, 283
Tovey, Donald F. (pianist), 283
Tovey, Henry D. (pianist), 279, 283
Treis, Josef (pianist), 317
Tremaine, H.B. (Aeolian Co.), 405, 739, 742, 761
Tremaine, W.B. (Aeolian Co.), 742
Tremolo Piano (Wurlitzer), 506, 594, 663
Tribut(e) (Imhof & Mukle orchestrion), 464, 465, 469, 477
Trio (Peerless), 554
Trio (Sächsische Orchester-Musikwerke orchestrion), 366
Triola (mechanical zither), 350, 356
Triphonola (Hupfeld reproducing piano), 279; history and description of 312, 315; 339, 432, 460
Triplex (Popper roll mechanism), 583, 587
Tritschler, John & Co. (agent), 249
Tritschler, Stephen F., 136
Triumph (Christmas tree stand), 237
Triumph (disc music boxes), 101, 104
Triumph (Holzweissig orchestrion), 429
Triumph (Popper orchestrion), 585, 586
Trivets, musical, 70
Trompeter (Popper orchestrion), 585
Trompeter of Sackingen (in English, Trumpeter; Imhof & Mukle orchestrion), 473
Troubadour (disc music boxes), 145, history and description of instruments 237, 250
Trumpet Automaton (Kaufmann), 480
Trumpetto (also sold as Trumpeto; organette), 739, 741, 761
Truxell, Earl (pianist), 279, 283
Tuby's Canadian Gondolas, 867
Tucker, Mercedes O'Leary (pianist), 279, 283
Tune Selecting Device (Marquette Piano Co. tune selector installed on Cremona instruments), 497, 498, 501, description of 504-505
Tune sheets (program cards) for cylinder music boxes, 27
Turk (Mortier organ), 897
Turntable (platform) movement, 23
Turpin, H.P. (pianist), 279, 283
Tussing, Henry, 537, 813
Tussing, T.R., 721
Twain, Mark, 779
20th Century (Mills slot machine), 92, 95, 507, 526
20th Century, wallbox for 711
Twin-Roll Reproducing Pipe Organ (Seeburg), 616, 719

U

Uhlig, Gustav, 78-80
Ullmann, Charles, 249
Ullmann, Jacques, 249
Underwood (pianos), 321
Unified Reproduco (pipe organ), refer to Reproduco
Uniflute (Gavioli), 859
Unika (Gebr. Weber piano), 625, 626
Unikon (music box), 248
Union GmbH, 710
Union Piano Co., refer to VEB Deutsch Piano Union (successors to Hupfeld)
United Piano Corp., 293
U.S. Auto-Art (music rolls), 318
U.S. Guitar Zither Co. (mechanical zithers), 359
U.S. Music Co. (music rolls), 369, 602, 720, 722
Universal (L'Universelle; cylinder music box), 20, 63
Universal (disc music boxes), 177, 184, 210
Universal (Hupfeld piano), 430, 431, 434
Universal Orchestra (Hupfeld orchestrion), 431
Universal Piano Co., 267
Universelle, L' (cylinder music box), 20, 63
Universum (Gebr. Bruder organ), 829
Uno, refer to Musical Uno (slot machine)
Upchurch, A. Colin, 858, 882, 886
Upright Concert Automaton (Adler/Fortuna music boxes), 240
Utz, Lillian (pianist), 279, 283
Uzielli, L. (pianist), 331

V

Valente, A., 424, 613
Valkyrie (Walküre; Imhof & Mukle orchestrion), 464, 465, 474, 478
Valsonora (Sächsischen Orchestrionfabrik F.O. Glass orchestrion), 533
Valverde, Joaquin (pianist), 314
Van den Berg, Bram (or Brahm) (pianist), 279, 283
Vanderbilt, William K. and Frederick W., 634, 642
Van der Mueren (organs), 806, 893
van Dinteren, Jan L.M., 808, 855
Van Hyfte Piano Co., 395
Van Katwijk, Paul (pianist), 279, 283
van Loveren, Josef, 893
Van Roy (barrel pianos), 363, 849

Vanselow, Willy, 808
van Steenput, A. Frères, 806
Van Valkenburg, B.R., 368, 369, 381
Van Valkenburg, H.A., 368, 369, 381
Van Vollenhaven, Hanna (pianist), 279
van Wichelen, Urbain, 893
Varesi & Pozzi, 806
Vassalo, V., 806
VEB Deutsch Piano Union (successors to Hupfeld), 431, 460, 461
VEB Leipziger Pianofabrik, 431
Velásquez, José (pianist), 283
Venezia (Gebr. Weber orchestrion), 627
Venezia, Fratelli, 806
Venus (Imhof & Mukle orchestrion), 465, 471, 473
Verbeeck (fairground and dance organs), 848, 888, history and description of 923
Verbeeck, James, 923
Verbeeck, Johanne, 923
Verbeeck, John, 923
Verbeeck, Pierre, 923
Verbeke, Christian, 398
Verbekson (Verbeeck organ trade name), 923
Verdi (Popper orchestrion), 585, 590
Verne, Adele (pianist), 308
Verstraelen & Alter, 679
Vertchamp, Joyce Albert (pianist), 283
Victolian (player reed organ), 251, description of 783
Victor (Bush & Lane piano), 268
Victor Coin (piano), 542, 703, 725
Victor Talking Machine Co., 171, 172, 792
Victoria (Abrahams cylinder music box), 66
Victoria (Hanke orchestrion), 707
Victoria (Komet disc music box), 112
Victoria Orchestrionette (organette), 741, 766
Victoria, Queen of England, 480
Victoria Xylophon(e) (Philipps orchestrion), 564, 571
Vienne, Gaspard de (pianist), 317
Vierling, Rudolph, 706
Vigna, Arturo (organist), 788
Village Inn (Ariston automaton), 746
Vindobona (Popper orchestrion), 590
Viol-Cello (Mills violin and cello player), 353, 509, 510, 520, 521
Viol-Xylophone (Mills violin and xylophone player), 353, 509, 510, 520
Viola (Popper orchestrion), 585
Violano (Gebr. Weber), 430, 625-627
Violano Orchestra (Mills violin player with percussion effects), 514, 522, 523, description of 524, 720
Violano Speaker System (Kellogg/Mills amplifier unit), 518
Violano-Virtuoso (Mills violin player), 353, 355, 436, 487, history and description of Violano-Virtuoso and related Mills instruments 506-525, 560, 591, 622, 711, 720
Violin-Flute Pianino (Wurlitzer), 664, 670, 721
Violin-Flute Piano (Wurlitzer), 674, 676
Violin Orchestra (Philipps orchestrion), 574
Violin Pianino (Wurlitzer), 664, 670
Violin Piano (Popper), 583, 587, 589
Violin Piano (Wurlitzer), 661
Violin Pipe Piano (Lyon & Healy), 496
Violin players, general description of 353; refer also to individual manufacturers, esp. Bajde (Klaviolin), Dienst (Self-Playing Violin), Hegeler & Ehlers (Geigenpiano), Hupfeld (Clavitist-Violina, Dea-Violina, Phonolizst-Violina, and others), Popper (Violinovo), and Mills Novelty Co. (Violano-Virtuoso)
Violin Rhapsodist (Piano Player Manufacturing Co.), 581
Violin Solo Piano (Lösche), 490
Violina (Hupfeld violin player developed by Bajde et al), refer to Clavitist-Violina, Dea-Violina, Phonoliszt-Violina, and Violina Orchestra
Violina Orchestra (Hupfeld orchestrion with Violina mechanism), 349, 353, 432, description of 440, 454
Violine (Philipps orchestrion), 575
Violinovo (Popper violin player), 353, 585, 591
Violiphone (Niagara), 534
Violista, refer to Royal Violista (Wauters violin player)
Violonista (violin player), 353
Violophone (Niagara), 534, 725, 908
Virginia City (restored Montana mining town), 513
Virginia Navigation Co., 636
Virtuos (Heilbrunn pianos), 425, 426
Virtuosa (Mills violin player), 353, 507, 508, 513, 515
Virtuoso (Weser Brothers), 655
Vivellino, Bernardo, 806
Vocalion Organ Co., 740, 743, 779, 781, 788
Vocalstyle (music rolls), 318
Vogel, Elfriede (pianist), 317
Vogler, Abbé, 345
Vogrich, Max (pianist), 331
Voigt, Alban (pianist), 249, 250
Voigt, Heinrich (organs), 805, 806
Volavy, Marguerite (pianist), 279, 283
Volks Klavier (mechanical zither), 356
Voorhees, Don (pianist), 283
Votey, E.S., 251, 405
Votey Organ Co., 743, 788

W

Waddington's Gondolas, 882
Wagner, Siegfried, 308
Walcker, E.F. & Cie. (organs), 793, description of player organs 800
Waldkircher Orchestrionfabrik Gebrüder Weber, refer to Weber, Gebr.
Waldrop, Uda (organist), 788
Wales & McCulloch (agent), 249
Walker, Melvin, 686
Walküre, refer to Valkyrie (Imhof & Mukle orchestrion)
Wallboxes for coin pianos and orchestrions, 355, 459, 519, 636, 709-711
Wallhall (Welte Brass Band orchestrion), 638, 647
Wallis & Son (agent), 249
Walmsley, H.B., 637
Waltham Piano Co., 703, 705, 725
Walton, Herbert (agent), 792
Walton, Jesse, 534
Wanamaker, John (agent), 124, 210, 369, 376
War, the senselessness of, 338
Ward-Stephens (pianist), 279, 283
Warnies, Leon, 848
Warren Piano Co. (agent), 397
Warren, Samuel P. (organist), 788
Washburn (pianos), 494, 496, 542
Watches, musical, 86, 87
Water Mill (Amorette organette), 748
Waterloo (Polyphon music box), 163
Waters, B.C., 656
Wathen, J.B., 382
Watkin, Will A. Music Co. (agent), 124
Watling Manufacturing Co. (amusement devices), 712
Watson (pianos), 703, 725
Watson, Mr. and Mrs. John, 305
Wauters, Prof., 353, 481
Wayburn, Ned (pianist), 283
Webb, Graham, 22, 24, 41, 66, 99, 104, 112, 114, 172
Webbe, Septimus (pianist), 331
Webber Singing Doll, 765
Weber (Aeolian Co. pianos), 277, 295, 296, 299, 302-304, 306, 309
Weber, F. (pianos), 707
Weber, Gebr. (orchestrions), 345, 348, 349, 351, 355, 464, 465, 478, 583, 621-623, history and description of instruments 625-631, 713, 715, 718, 721, 731, 824, 892
Weber, Josef (barrel organs), 806
Weber, Karl Maria v. (composer), 480
Weber, Kathy, 833
Weber, Otto, 631
Webster, W.J., 637
Wehrmann-Schaffner, Eugenie (pianist), 279, 283
Weihnachtskrippe (Amorette Nativity scene), 748
Weingartner, Felix, 331, 585, 788
Weiss, Josef (pianist), 317, 331
Weissbach & Co. (Chordephon mechanical zithers; Komet disc music boxes), 112, 357
Wellershaus, August, 806, 807, 924
Wellershaus, August II, 807
Wellershaus, August III, 807
Wellershaus, Emil, 807

Wellershaus, Friedrich-Wilhelm, 807
Wellershaus, Gebr. (fairground organs, etc.), 803, 807, 807, 823, 848, history and description of instruments 924-926
Wellershaus, Julius, 807
Wellershaus, Wilhelm I, 807
Wellershaus, Wilhelm II, 807, 924
Wellershaus, Wilhelm III, 807
Wellington (pianos), 340
Wellner, Julius, 210
Wells, M.B. Co. (agent), 258, 778
Wellsmore (pianos), 321
Welt Piano (Popper), 583, 585, 588
Welte Artistic Player Piano (early name used for Welte Mignon instruments sold in America), refer to Welte Mignon
Welte, Berthold, 324, 336
Welte, Carl M., 336
Welte, Edwin, 323-327, 336, 338, 584, 632, 636, 792
Welte, Emil, 336, 632, 637, 645
Welte (Licensee), refer to Welte Mignon
Welte, M. & Sons (including the Freiburg, Germany firm, M. Welte & Söhne; the American firm, M. Welte & Sons; and later firms, Welte Co., etc.; manufacturers of pianos, orchestrions, etc.), 42, 273, 279, 318, history and description of the Welte Mignon reproducing piano 319-338, 339, 345, 347-349, 351, 352, 354, 355, 464, 465, 478, 542, 554, 580, 581, 583, 584, 590, 622, 623, history and description of orchestrions 632-654, 662, 709, 712, 744, 745, 767, history and description of Philharmonic Organ 792-798, 818, 823, 858, history and description of fairground organs 927-928
Welte, Michael, 324, 336, 346, 388, 632, 634, 663
Welte, Michael, Jr., 336
Welte Mignon (Welte reproducing piano), 273-275, 282, 283, 295, 311, history and description of 319-338, 339, 349, 432, 478, 527, 584, 590, 623, 636, 637, 734, 793, 798
Welte-Tripp Organ Co., 800
Wendland, Paul, 99
Wendling, Karl (pianist), 331
Wendling, Pete (pianist), 279, 283, 719, 721
Wengerowa, Isabella (pianist), 331
Wentworth (pianos), 321
Werlein, Ph., Ltd. (agent), 778
Werner, Harold J., 368, 369
Werner Music House (agent), 124
Weser Brothers (pianos), 387, history and description of instruments 655
Weser, John A., 655
Western Automatic Music Co., 712
Western Electric Co. (division of A.T.&T.), 660
Western Electric Piano Co. (Seeburg subsidiary), 348, 350, 351, 355, 601, 602, history and description of instruments 656-660, 715, 724, 725
Weydig Piano Corp., 263
Whaley, Royce & Co. (agent), 210
Wheelan, J.D. (agent), 376
Wheelock (pianos), 295, 299, 303
Whight, George (agent), 250, 251, 783
White Brothers, 868
White, Henry Kirk, 781
White, Neal, 683, 901
White, Pearl (actress), 367
White, Pearl (keyboard artist), 719
White, Stanford, 122
White, William Braid, 320
Whiteman, Paul, 625
White's (showmen), 864
Whitlock, J.W. (Automatic Harp, etc.), 353, 662, 664, 666, 668, 721
Whitlock, Stewart, 668
Whitney & Currier Co. (agent), 258
Whittaker, James (pianist), 279, 283
Wicks Organ Co., 370, 744
Widor, Ch. M., 308
Wiedel, Jac., 709
Wilberg, S. (pianist), 317
Wilcox & White (pianos and organs), 251, 255, Artrio-Angelus reproducing piano 294, 740, 741, 743, 767, 770, 772, player reed organs 781-782
Wilcox, Horace C., 781
Wilcox, R.I., 656
Wildbredt, Ernst, 655
Wille, Stewart (pianist), 279, 283
Williams, Brian, 727
Williams, C.F. Abdy, 345, 744
Williams, George S., 382
Williams, Guy Bevier (pianist), 283
Williams, O. (organist), 792
Willis (pianos), 277, 280, 281, 289
Willis Piano Co. (agent), 577
Wilmot, Jessie, 487
Wilson (pianos), 703, 725
Wilson Brothers Manufacturing Co., 709
Wilson, H.W., 637
Wilson's Rodeo Switchback, 885
Wingate, J. & Sons Coliseum, 867
Winkel, Dietrich Nicholas, 345
Winn, Cyril, 308
Winogradoff, Eleanor (pianist), 279, 283
Winston, Elizabeth, 279, 283
Winter & Co. (pianos), 379, 381
Winternitz, Felix (pianist), 283
Winternitz, Otto (pianist), 279, 283
Wisteria (Peerless orchestrion), 424, 553, 554, description of 556, 557, 562, 614
Wiswell, Jean (pianist), 279, 283
Wittgenstein, Victor (pianist), 279, 281, 283
Wittke, A., 806
Witzmann & Co. (agent), 376
Wolff, A. (agent), 210
Wolfs, Hubert (showman), 862
Wolstenholme, W. (organist), 792
Wood, Henry J., 309
Woodruff, S.C., 813
World Horoscope (Mills arcade device), 526
World Manufacturing Co. (organettes), 741, 763
Wortham, H.E., 308
Wotan (Welte Brass Band Orchestrion), 638, 647, 648, 651
Wrede, Fritz (fairground organs, etc.), 806, 807, 812, 823, history and description of instruments 929
Wright & Holmes, 805
Wright, Marion, 719, 722, 724
Wulschner & Son (agent), 210
Wurdeman, Oswald, 510, 656, 940
Wurlitzer, Farny, 347, 487, 564, 661-663, 670, 687
Wurlitzer, Howard, 564, 661
Wurlitzer, Rudolph Co. (pianos, orchestrions, organs, etc.), 180, 186, 204, 210, 261, 293, 318, 339, 347-355, 367, 368, 374, 376, 382, 430, 446, 465, 487, 504, 506, 512, 535, 537, 552, 563-565, 569, 571, 572, 575, 576, 581, 593, 595, 598, 611, 637, history and description of coin pianos, orchestrions, and photoplayers 661-702, 703, 709, 711, 714, 716-718, 720, 721, 744, 873, history and description of theatre pipe organs 799, 803, 804, 813-815, 830, 839, 858, 869, 870, 872, 873, 876, 884, 907, 909, 911, 914, 915, 917, 919, history and description of band organs and related instruments 930-944
Würmser, Lucien (pianist), 314, 317, 331
Wysmann, Johann (pianist), 317

X

Xylophone Mandolin Piano (Lösche), 489, 490
Xylophone Orchestra (Symphonion), 624
Xylophonian (Seeburg piano), 608

Y

Yale Wonder Clock Co., 195, 209
Yepetto, Peter (agent), 489
Yerkes, Charles T., 642
Yon, Pietro, 279, 283, 788
Youmans, Vincent (pianist), 283
Young, Victor (pianist), 283
Ysaye, Eugene, 300

Z

Zadora, Michael v. (pianist), 279, 282, 283, 308, 317, 331
Zampa (Dienst orchestrion), 394
Zanetta (Imhof & Mukle orchestrion), 469

Zardo, Eric (pianist), 283
Zardo, Redento (pianist), 279
Zecchi, Carlo (pianist), 330
Zeisler, Fannie Bloomfield (pianist), 279, 282, 283, 328, 331, 336
Zimbalist, Efrem (violinist), 436, 437
Zimmermann, Gebr. (piano makers; merged with Hupfeld in 1926), 430, 431, 460
Zimmermann, Jules Heinrich (Adler and Fortuna disc boxes; musical retailer), 99, 102, 209, history and description of Adler and Fortuna instruments 238-242, 250, 251
Zither attachments, for cylinder music boxes 29, for disc music boxes 102
Zither Quartette, 358
Zithers, mechanical, general information 356-359
Zöllner, Heinrich (pianist), 331
Zonophon(e) (phonograph), 429
Zordan, Antenora, 806
Zscherneck, Georg (pianist), 331
Zucca, Mana (pianist), 279, 283
Zuja, Blasius, 806
Zuleger, A. (Tanzbär player concertina), 775
Zuradelli, Maurizio, 806
Zygman, Flora (pianist), 279, 283